The *Central Sinama–English Dictionary* presents the results of decades of intensive research on the Central Sinama language, a member of the Sama-Bajaw branch of Western Malayo-Polynesian. The Sama languages have many features that are of interest to typologists and theoretical linguists, and the *Dictionary* is a valuable contribution to the Sama literature, in addition to being an important practical resource for speakers of the language.

**Prof. Robert D. Van Valin, Jr.**
*University at Buffalo, The State University of New York, and*
*Heinrich Heine University Düsseldorf*

The Sinama–English dictionary is the kind of dictionary one always hopes for but rarely finds when searching for lexical, cultural, or grammatical information on lesser-researched speech communities. It is very rich, not only in the number of entries, but in that each entry contains very well chosen, highly idiomatic and culturally rich example sentences, in addition to notes on dialectal alternates as well as grammatical and cultural notes. Six decades of work in and with Sinama speech communities have gone into this dictionary, and the tremendous expertise resulting from a large team of contributors and researchers shows on every page. Definitely a major resource both for the speech community and the scientific community.

**Nikolaus P. Himmelmann**
*Universität zu Köln, Germany*

Tagna' pagkilāku ma si Bapa' Kemp Pallesen, ainu-inu aku bang angay dakayu' milikan pote' itu, ata'u to'ongan ah'lling Sinama maka alalom lagi' Sinamahanna min kasehe'an Sama. Bang tuwi' dakayu' a'a bilahi anayu pangaddatan bangsa saddī min bangsana, subay nianaran to'ongan bahasa sigām hasupaya tataima' maka anobsob ni pangatayan ya kab'nnalan kamaksuranna.

Tahatiku pa'in pipila waktu palabay ya kamaksuran kahāpan ma bangsa Sama, sinoho' aku e' si Bapa' Kemp anganad lexicography training and workshops supaya aniya' tabangna min bangsa Sama amajatu saga kabtangan Sinama bay na asal tasulatna ma labi t'llumpū' tahun bay katimbulna pat'nna' ma bangsa Sama, anganaran bahasa Sinama. Ya na itu kamaujuranna panimuk saga kabtangan bahasa Sinama, ya na *Central Sinama–English Dictionary*. Aheya to'ongan katabanganna Central Sinama diksyonari itu, mbal sadja ma saga bangsa saddī bilahi anganad maka angahati bissala Sama. Landu'to'ongan pagsarang-sukulan bangsa Sama, mbal na alopas pasal tasulat maka tasilang na h'llingna Sinama ma katilingkal dunya. Sambatan dakayu' papata Sama, "Bang alungay na bahasa, alungay na bangsa!"

**Omarjan I. Jahuran**
*Bangsa Sama Indigenous Peoples Mandatory Representative (IPMR),*
*South Ubian Municipality, Tawi-Tawi*

Napapanahon ang mga akda tulad ng diksiyonaryong ito. Idineklara ng UNESCO ang mga taong 2022 hanggang 2032 bilang Internasyonal na Dekada ng mga Katutubong Wika, na naglalayong maitaguyod ang kapakanan ng mga katutubong pamayanan at maaksyunan ang tuluyan na panganganib ng mga katutubong wika. Isa sa pangunahing adhikain ng Dekada ay ang pagpapatuloy ng mga adbokasiyang sumusuporta sa panunumbalik sigla ng mga katutubong wika.

Sa konteksto ng Pilipinas, mahalaga na maipatuloy ang mga nasimulan ng MTBMLE upang tunay na makamtan ng mga pamayanan ang isang edukasyon na makamasa at nagpapahalaga sa mga wikang kinagisnan. Kaya naman mahalaga ang ambag ng mga output ng language work tulad ng diksiyonaryo para makamit ng mga pamayanan ang Four Minima Requirements ng MTBMLE. Lalo na at ang disyunaryong ito ay produkto ng ilang dekadang pagkikipag-ugnayan sa pamayanang Sama. Isa itong mahalagang hakbangin para sa tunguhin na magamit ang wikang Sinama bilang wikang panturo sa loob ng mga paaralan.

*Louward Allen Zubiri*
*Mangyan Heritage Center, and*
*University of Hawaiʻi at Mānoa*

A well-constructed dictionary of another language reminds us that although language communities may differ in the outer circumstances of their culture, they still share many of the same emotions, ideas, and perspectives. This is as true for Central Sinama as for any other language, and is one of the reasons we need carefully researched and edited books like this, showcasing not just the words but also the everyday expressions which capture the vitality and complexity of its speakers and their lives. This dictionary is a great achievement. Whilst it may have been *lambang* ("hidden from view by an intervening item"), it is now available in plain sight, and shouldn't be missed!

*John Simpson*
*Formerly Chief Editor of the Oxford English Dictionary*

For me, the test of a great language description is that, when you've read it, you want to learn the language, and think it's actually within your grasp to do so. Its dictionary gives you so much detail about the people and their way of life that you feel you're beginning to know them, and makes you want to visit where they live. Ideally there are photographs to complement the verbal descriptions of the culture, extensive examples of everyday usage, and an illuminating introduction to the phonology and grammar, so that you can build up a picture of the character of the language, and get a sense of its unique expressive vision—another piece in the linguistic jigsaw of what it means to be human. This excellent dictionary ticks all these boxes.

*David Crystal*
*Honorary Professor of Linguistics, University of Bangor*
*Author of The Cambridge Encyclopedia of Language*

# Central Sinama–English Dictionary

# SIL International®
## Publications in Lingusitics
### 155

Publications in Linguistics is published by SIL International®. The series is a venue for works covering a broad range of topics in linguistics, especially the analytical treatment of minority languages from all parts of the world. While most volumes are authored by members of SIL, suitable works by others will also form part of the series.

## Series Editor
Susan McQuay

## Editorial Staff
Susan McQuay, Managing Editor
William Nies, Susan McQuay, Copy Editor
Eleanor McAlpine, Proofreader

## Production Staff
Priscilla Higby, Production Manager
Ian McQuay, Compositor
Barbara Alber, Graphic Designer

Cover photograph: A. Kemp Pallesen. Used by permission. A Sama Pagūng family.
Section 1.5 photographs taken by A. Kemp Pallesen. Used by permission.

# Central Sinama–English Dictionary

Compiled by A. Kemp Pallesen, Anne Carol Pallesen,
Lydia James, and Jeremiah Joy James

SIL International®

Dallas, Texas

© 2024 by SIL International®
Library of Congress Control Number: 2024934878
ISBN 978-1-55671-499-3 (pbk)
ISBN 978-1-55671-557-0 (hbk)
ISBN 978-1-55671-500-6 (ePub)
ISSN 1040-0850

Corrections may be sent to: info_philippines@sil.org

Copies of this and other publications of SIL International® may be obtained through distributors such as Amazon, Barnes & Noble, other worldwide distributors and, for select volumes, sil.org/resources/publications/:

SIL International Publications
7500 W. Camp Wisdom Road
Dallas, TX 75236-5629 USA

General inquiry: publications_intl@sil.org
Pending order inquiry: sales@sil.org
publications.sil.org

# Contents

# Maps

# Figures

# Tables

## FOREWORD

The Philippines, as an archipelago, has its distinct and rich culture -- a reflection of its diverse people and languages. Throughout the year, some languages evolve, and some deteriorate, making it crucial to document and publish linguistic materials.

The Sinama language has the potential to transcend in other regions given that its proud speakers are widely scattered around the Mindanao region, and in countries such as Indonesia and Malaysia.

The Department of Education (DepEd), as the lead government agency that formulates policies on basic education, believes in the knowledge vested in the child's native language. Through the implementation of the Mother Tongue-based Multilingual Education (MTB-MLE), learners receive instruction, teaching materials, and assessment in their respective regional or native language. This made learning comfortable for Kinder to Grade 3 learners, thus allowing them to know their identity more.

Through the MTB-MLE, materials that will contribute to the standardization and documentation of a language will surely help our teachers facilitate lessons using the learners' native language. May the publication of the Sinama-English dictionary pave the way for more materials advancing the study and language instruction in the country.

With the consistent call to produce more linguistic studies and resources, we are grateful to work along with individuals and institutions such as the Summer Institute of Linguistics (SIL) in developing programs and materials for language and education.

We offer our sincere appreciation to SIL for their continued work to develop widely accessible primers, workbooks, oral literature, dictionaries, and books that inspire educators, students, and every person who associates his identity to a language.

May this dictionary serve as an inspiration to the Filipinos, especially the Sama people, to continue celebrating the rich culture of the Pearl of the Orient.

**LEONOR MAGTOLIS BRIONES**
Secretary

# Foreword by Robert Blust[†]

The Sama-Bajaw languages of insular Southeast Asia are deserving of special attention for several reasons. First, like English, Spanish, French or other expansive colonial languages of the past 500 years, they are geographically displaced, a feature that sets them apart from nearly all other members of the Austronesian family. Second, they have an exceptionally heavy number of Malay loanwords. Third, they were traditionally spoken by people who lived on their boats, and who are variously characterized as "sea nomads," "sea gypsies," and the like.

What do I mean by "geographically displaced"? English is an example, as it is now the national language of a number of countries where it did not originate, while 500 years ago it was confined to England. The Samalan languages have a similar type of distribution on a far smaller scale within the island world of Southeast Asia. Sama-Bajaw dialects are spoken in several disconnected parts of the Philippines, including Inabaknon on Capul Island in the northern Bisayas, Mapun on a small island known variously as Mapun or Cagayan de Sulu, in the Sulu Sea north of Sabah, Yakan on Basilan Island immediately to the south of the Zamboanga peninsula of Mindanao, and in a number of dialects in the Sulu archipelago between the Philippines and Borneo. In Malaysia and Indonesia, Sama-Bajaw dialects are scattered over a wide area from western Sabah in northern Borneo, to Roti, Timor and other islands of the Lesser Sunda group, northern Sulawesi, and parts of the northern Moluccas as far east as Kayoa Island just west of Halmahera (for the most complete and accurate description of the distribution of Sama-Bajaw dialects/languages the reader is referred to Pallesen 1985:43–48).

The first question we must ask is why a single language, or group of very closely related languages, is scattered in small pockets over such a wide territory. The vast majority of languages originate in a particular location, and if their speakers migrate, it is through expansion into neighboring territory, not leapfrogging into distant locations. In the European context, languages like Polish or Serbian show the normal process of gradual expansion of an original language community into adjacent regions, while languages like English, Spanish, Portuguese, or French show a globally distributed leapfrogging pattern. We know from written records that the European colonial expansions were motivated primarily by trade (with religious conversion an ancillary factor), but we lack comparable records for the peoples of insular Southeast Asia. Nonetheless, based on what we do know about the global expansion of several European languages over the past half millennium, it is a reasonable guess that the scattered distribution of Sama-Bajaw languages is also a consequence of a past trading network that spanned the length and breadth of the Indo-Malaysian archipelago and reached northward into the southern and central Philippines.

This brings us to the second distinctive feature of Sama-Bajaw languages, namely their heavy borrowing from Malay. It is immediately clear that these are not Malayic languages, yet they have large numbers of Malay loanwords. Because of its key location along the Strait of Malacca between the Malay peninsula and Sumatra, Malay became an important trade language very soon after trade and cultural exchange began via the sea route between India and China, perhaps 2,000 years ago. By the time the first Dutch colonizers arrived in 1600, Malay could be used as a lingua franca in many coastal locations from Sumatra in the west to Papua in the east. As a result of this role (which favored its eventual adoption in slightly different forms as the national language of Indonesia, Malaysia, and Brunei, and its role as an official language in Singapore), Malay has been a source of loanwords in coastal languages of the Indo-Malaysian archipelago for centuries. What makes the presence of Malay loanwords in Sama-Bajaw languages different from this more general pattern is the sheer number of borrowings, and the specific character of some of them. As noted in Blust (2005:52), the Sama Bajaw languages have borrowed not only the usual types of words that many other languages in coastal Borneo and the Philippines have imported from Malay (e.g., binatang 'animal', harga 'price', kurang 'lacking, insufficient', lagi 'still, more', pérak 'silver', rugi 'loss in a business transaction', etc.), but have also acquired the eight-point system of terms for wind directions in the Malay sailing compass, suggesting that their traditional navigational skills were taught to them by Malay speakers. The only other language that has acquired this terminology from Malay is Malagasy (Adelaar 1989:9–11), and as pointed out by Blust (2005:45–47), exclusively shared lexical innovations suggest that both Malagasy and the Sama-Bajaw languages first evolved in the Barito river basin of southeast Kalimantan.

I need not go into every detail here, but the close historical connections of the Sama-Bajaw languages with a pre-European Malay-based pan-archipelagic trade network spanning the

Indo-Malaysian archipelago and the southern Philippines is further strengthened by the observation that Malay is the only other geographically displaced language in this part of the world. Indeed, the distribution of Malay dialects roughly parallels that of the Sama-Bajaw. The Malayic homeland almost certainly was southwest Borneo (Blust 2006), but by the time that Europeans arrived, Malay dialects were found in other parts of Borneo, most notably Brunei in the northwest, Banjarmasin in the southeast, and Kutai in the east, as well as Jakarta in western Java, Kupang at the western end of the island of Timor and Larantuka at the eastern end of the island of Flores in the Lesser Sunda islands, Ambon and Bacan in the central Moluccas (Collins 1996), and Manado in northern Sulawesi. Even on the island of Borneo, these Malay dialects are embedded in a network of Austronesian languages that are not closely related to them, indicating that their presence in these scattered locations is a product of secondary settlement. Once Islam reached insular Southeast Asia in the thirteenth century, it spread through the medium of Malay, accounting for the strong Islamic orientation of most if not all Sama-Bajaw communities, both in Indonesia-Malaysia and the Philippines.

This parallelism in the highly unusual geographical dispersal of both Malay and the Sama-Bajaw languages is a clear indication that the two groups were working together in managing a trade network that spanned much of insular Southeast Asia. The major products in this trade were cloves and nutmeg—spices that grew only in the Moluccan islands of eastern Indonesia, and that already were reaching Europe in Roman times. If we look again at the geographical distribution of Malay dialects, and of the Sama-Bajaw communities that roughly parallel them, we see evidence for a southern trade route from the Moluccas where the spices originate, through the Lesser Sundas to Java and Strait of Malacca, on to Sri Lanka, India, the Near East, and southern Europe, and a northern trade route to China through Manado in northern Sulawesi, Brunei in northwest Borneo, and the southern Philippines. There can be little doubt that this trade was initiated by Malays centuries before the Sama-Bajaw became involved, but once this land-based group from southeast Borneo was included, it appears likely that they dominated the northern trade route, leading to a greater involvement in the southern and central Philippines, while Malays in all likelihood dominated the southern route leading to India and beyond.

The reason for the traditional maritime lifestyle of the Sama-Bajaw now becomes obvious—trade requires the movement of goods over long distances and, in an island world, this means sailing which becomes so frequent that one abandons a land-based economy entirely and simply lives on one's boats. It is worth pointing out that other boat nomads, like the Moken/Moklen of the Mergui archipelago in peninsular Thailand and Burma, do not have a scattered distribution, and evidently adopted a maritime lifestyle as a type of refuge from conflict with other groups rather than as part of a long-distance trade network (White 1922).

The last part of the Sama-Bajaw story concerns the arrival of the Portuguese in the sixteenth century, and then the Dutch early in the seventeenth century in what is now Indonesia. Like Columbus, who mistakenly sailed west across the Atlantic instead of east around the southern tip of Africa in search of the "spice islands of the East," the first European explorers of insular Southeast Asia were motivated by a pursuit of wealth, and the spices of the Moluccas were worth their weight in gold in a European market hungry for exotic condiments. The competition was intense, both between the European powers who sought to control the spice trade, and the native peoples who had managed it in previous centuries. The Portuguese were pushed out by the Dutch, leaving scattered Portuguese enclaves in eastern Indonesia that no longer had any role in trade. More importantly for our story, under European colonial domination the spice trade was forcefully taken from the Malays and Sama-Bajaw speaking peoples, leaving them literally "unemployed." What do you do when you lose the source of not just your livelihood but your entire lifestyle? Like other maritime traders who were ousted from the riches they sought (e.g., the English in the Caribbean), they turned to piracy, and the Sama-Bajaw are still known in parts of Indonesia essentially as pirates.

Other Sama-Bajaw peoples, like the Jama Mapun on Mapun or Cagayan de Sulu Island and nearby areas (Casiño 1976), and the Yakan on Basilan Island (Behrens 2002), returned to a land-based economy, but some continued to live on houseboats anchored in specific locations and their livelihood was based on a fishing economy and local trade for necessities (such as rice) rather than long-distance trade for profit (Nimmo 1972). This is the last trace of a former lifestyle that was taken away from them by the rise of European colonialism during the past 500 years, yet like the languages of the usurping colonizers themselves, the distribution of the Sama-Bajaw languages reveals a past in which they were major players in the movement of goods that had a global impact.

For all of these reasons, we welcome this major dictionary of Central Sinama as a representative of this remarkable people.

## References

Adelaar, K. A. 1989. Malay influence on Malagasy: Linguistic and culture-historical implications. *Oceanic Linguistics* 28:1–46.

Behrens, Dietlinde. 2002. *Yakan-English dictionary*. LSP Special Monograph 40:2. Manila: Linguistic Society of the Philippines.

Blust, Robert. 2005. The linguistic macrohistory of the Philippines: Some speculations. In Hsiu-chuan Liao and Carl R. Galvez Rubino (eds.), *Current issues in Philippine linguistics and anthropology: Parangal kay Lawrence A. Reid*, 31–68. Manila: Linguistic Society of the Philippines and SIL Philippines.

Blust, Robert. 2006. Whence the Malays? In James T. Collins and Awang Sariyan (eds.), *Borneo and the homeland of the Malays: Four essays*, 64–88. Kuala Lumpur: Dewan Bahasa dan Pustaka.

Casiño, Eric. 1976. *The Jama Mapun: A changing Samal society in the southern Philippines*. Manila: Ateneo de Manila University Press.

Collins, James T. 1996. *Bibliografi dialek Melayu di Indonesia Timur*. Siri Monograf Bibliografi Sejarah Bahasa Melayu. Kuala Lumpur: Dewan Bahasa dan Pustaka.

Nimmo, H. Arlo. 1972. *The sea people of Sulu: A study of social change in the Philippines*. San Francisco, CA: Chandler Publishing.

Pallesen, A. Kemp. 1985. *Culture contact and language convergence*. Manila: Linguistic Society of the Philippines.

White, Walter G. 1922. *The sea gypsies of Malaya*. London: Seeley, Service.

# Preface

This dictionary has been many years in the making. The first step was taken in 1962, when I had the good fortune of being asked to investigate reports of a sea-going people in the remote Sulu Archipelago, with an emphasis on learning what languages they spoke. My basic tools were simple: (a) lists of English words chosen for their relevance to Southeast Asian cultures (Swadesh 200-word list and Reid 372-word list), and (b) some training in hearing and recording the words elicited. Over the next year, with a series of companions, I travelled the length of the Sulu Archipelago, from Zamboanga and Basilan in the north to Sitangkay in the southwest, recording a score of wordlists. We learned that Sinama (or Sama + place name) was the preferred name for the language. Welcomed and warned wherever we went, we worked through our wordlist and became alert to the "non-English" sounds. As we compared the lists and got an initial measure of their differences, it became clear that Central Sinama (my name for the language) was a distinct variety.

Beginning in 1963, my wife Anne and I with our first daughter (there were to be two more) were privileged to live in Siganggang Bay, just offshore from Lapak Island and looking across the channel to the town of Siasi (*M'ddas* in Sinama). This shallow bay, refreshed twice a day by incoming tides, was at that time home to a Sama Dilaut community of more than a thousand people living in their kin-based groups and practising the fishing techniques of their forebears. Their pole houses, some 100 of them, were organised along kinship lines into *tumpuk* (clusters of pole houses connected by walkways), each cared for by a headman. We lived as they did, in a pole house, with the rhythm of our days set by the tides, watched over by Ma'asiral, the headman of the *tumpuk* closest to our house. Though we began our life in Siganggang without a common language or purpose, and although our reason for living in their place was initially unclear to them, we were treated with unfailing dignity and courtesy. Our social blunders were tolerated. We began to feel accepted. My insatiable questions about their language, culture, values, and belief systems were answered with generosity, patience and an abundance of examples, even when, as often happened, we were slow to understand.

Our methodology was both simple and effective: to listen to the language all about us, noting what we guessed was the context, then recording the entries and examples on file cards, to be checked and discussed with native speakers. Some of our neighbors, men and women, proved to be gifted and enthusiastic teachers. We developed an orthography that has proved to be enduringly useful over the decades. We recorded thousands of Sinama phrases in real life situations, like the casual question from a passerby: *Pila bay pam'llinu saging ilū?* 'How much did you pay for those bananas?', and the follow-up to my answer, *Arōy! Halam ka bay amalos?* 'Good grief! Didn't you bargain?' It took us a while to realize that the exchange was not idle curiosity: we had become accepted as real people, and a foundation was being laid for this dictionary.

The conversations, stories, and explanations provided generously by people of various communities in the Siasi municipality in the years 1960–1980 have been the primary source of the entries recorded in this dictionary. Though all of these communities are oriented to the sea, there are significant cultural distinctions: those who have been settled for many generations in and around the Siasi and Tabawan Islands, and those who have more recently changed from a nomadic lifestyle to life in settled house groups. Though these groups and subgroups have their own distinctive and defining words, they have little difficulty understanding each other. This dictionary simply records subdialect forms without naming the subgroup in which they commonly occur.

The handwritten data on thousands of file cards were typed up on A4 sheets and bound into two volumes. Years later the data were entered in Toolbox (a data management and analysis tool for field linguists). Later still, in the early 2000s, the Toolbox data was transferred to FLEx (FieldWorks Language Explorer) so that it could, potentially, be made available online or in hardcopy.

Back to the family thread: growing social unrest in the southern Philippines made it advisable, in the early 1970s, for us as family to move to Zamboanga City (which by the way derives its name from the Sinama word *sambuwang* 'a mooring pole'). We took with us some of the Sama family who had been part of our lives for years, and who continued to take care of us and patiently answer my never-ending questions. My interest in the language, culture, and history of the Central Sama continued unabated, with the historical interaction between Sama and Tausug eventually becoming the topic of my doctoral dissertation (*Culture contact and language convergence*, University of California Berkeley 1977, published in 1985 as a Linguistic Society of the Philippines monograph).

In 1979, career changes and the educational needs of our three daughters took us back to New Zealand for the next twenty years. We kept in touch with Sama friends, made occasional visits, and had a growing sense of responsibility to do something useful with our field notes. I dreamed of making a dictionary of the data now in FLEx, making its resources available to all who are interested in this beautiful language: educators, researchers and, especially, to those for whom it is the mother tongue. The dream has now become a reality.

In 2004, the dictionary work that had hibernated for decades was resumed. Early definitions were revised and new ones added, together with examples that provided glimpses of Sama life as it was in the 1960s and 1970s. Of course, much had changed since then. Fishing stocks had been seriously depleted, and fishing techniques have had to adapt. The years of recovery after World War II had given way to new economic and political realities, but the Sinama language was flourishing. We decided, as a tribute to the lifeways and people of the past, to keep the words and illustrative examples recorded fifty to sixty years ago, but to continue adding to the database. The dictionary has continued to grow, not only in the number of its entries (currently 13,300), but in its relevance to modern Sama in their ever-changing world.

A dictionary of this caliber needs to be more than a collection of good definitions and examples. It should be supported as well by quality descriptions of the underlying grammar and phonology, which are not my forte, so it is with pleasure and pride that we introduce our colleagues and co-compilers Jeremiah and Lydia James. Their research into Sinama morphosyntax and discourse, together with their clear statements on grammar and phonology, have made a brilliant contribution to Sama-Bajaw studies in general and also to the needs of everyday users of the dictionary.

Cultures and languages continue to change, and so do dictionaries. Six decades since its first entries were made, this dictionary is still not final. It is our hope that its database will continue to develop, reflecting the ever-changing richness of the Sama people and their culture.

Kemp Pallesen

# A word from the co-compilers

We are in some ways leading a life parallel to Kemp and Anne's all those years ago: living in a context not our own, loving the Sama people, and enjoying the privilege of working with them on their beautiful language. To be sure, we are living in an apartment in Davao City, whereas Kemp and Anne lived in rural Sulu with their daughters, in a pole house over the water in a Sama community. And while the Sinama research project was already long-established by the time we joined the team, Kemp and Anne were the pioneers. Working from scratch, they designed the Sinama writing system, analyzed the grammar, and recorded thousands of words with their meanings and nuances. Standing on their shoulders has given us the best possible first decade of experience in this work.

The two of us first met at the Sama Dilaut community a mile from where we now live. We each spent a year of intensive language learning there, followed by further study as we pursued our Master's degrees. Our interests in Sinama syntax and discourse overlap and complement each other, leading to much discussion of linguistics in the home. We are supremely grateful to the Sama community members who have welcomed us into their lives, patiently taught us their language and culture, and corrected our mistakes with characteristic good humor. They have become dear friends to us and our young children.

It is a great honour for us, and a rare privilege, not only to benefit from the life and work of giants, but to collaborate with them closely on a project like this dictionary. Kemp and Anne have invited us to work extensively in the dictionary database itself: consolidating and harmonizing information to make it more accessible, and reworking definitions to reflect up-to-date morphosyntax and discourse theory. They have also trusted us to ask potentially provocative questions, such as "Does this language really have such a thing as adjectives?", and to do our best to find the answers (yes).

The Sinama dictionary is packed with information: not only words and definitions, but variant forms, usages, and grammatical information. Its entries are tied together by a dense web of cross-references that connect words with related meanings. The definitions and example sentences provide tantalizing glimpses into the geography, history, culture, lifeways, and beliefs of the Sama people in Sulu. In writing a User's Guide, we aimed to help the reader benefit from the dictionary's various features, and thereby to provide a key to unlock the riches it contains.

The two chapters that follow the dictionary provide brief descriptions of Sinama phonology, orthography, and grammar. These chapters have been purpose-written for this dictionary. They are not intended as an exhaustive grammar sketch, but rather explore in greater depth certain features of Sinama that are touched on briefly in the User's Guide. They are unavoidably more technical than the User's Guide, but our hope is that they will be accessible to interested non-linguists as well as to linguistic specialists.

The Sinama dictionary database, in its earlier stages, was an invaluable resource to us in our study and research. We are delighted that this product of Kemp and Anne's decades of patient work will now be available to all who are interested in the Sama people, their language, and culture. As you use this dictionary, may you enjoy some of the pleasure and wonder that we experienced in helping to prepare it. *Wassalam.*

Jeremiah and Lydia James

# Acknowledgements

Our years in the Philippines have been enriched by many remarkable people. We mention them by name and with love, beginning with Philippine Constabulary Sergeant **Balani Adjarani** who cared for us when we moved into our house in Siganggang Bay and insisted that visitors from ashore leave their firearms at the door; **Gerhard Rixhon** who was the first to encourage us to learn and write about Sama culture; **Rev. Sergio Diaz**, the CMA pastor and his wife who cared for our spiritual and physical wellbeing; **Mr Bantahon Tahir**, the Siganggang schoolmaster and landowner who kept an eye on us and intervened when necessary; **Nurustan Biral,** who worked in the Siasi Post Office and sent a message when we had mail, and who became a close friend; **Imam Matli'** who was the first imam we had ever met and who made a pastoral call when we first moved in; our warm-hearted neighbour **Bapa' Amisani**, a deep-water trap fisherman who loved us and trusted us to take his wife to Zamboanga for goiter surgery; **Panglima Ma'asiral** and his charming family, one of whom lived with us and fetched water from an inland water hole; **Luke Bahulluk**, a Sama Lipid Christian who went by dugout canoe to various Siasi communities to teach people to read (using the materials Anne had prepared); **Jadji Alamjani** and his wife **Halimaria** (familiar name **Bete'**), who had married across the social boundary between Sama Deya and Sama Dilaut, and who treated us as their kin, keeping us aware of dialect differences; **Ibnuhasi Maldani** (Bete's brother), who lived with us, accompanied us on many trips to Bukidnon for language workshops, and who continues to correspond with us in his old age; the various women who cared for us and to whom we owe much; Bete's niece **Nulmira Balbangsa** who lived with us and made it possible to get some work done; her widowed aunt **Ika'**, who became a best friend; **Lamda**, our near neighbor terminally ill with tuberculosis, whose elders not only allowed us to take her to Dr Sui Que to get the treatment that might (and did) save her life, but also exhorted their ritual ancestors to support what this Westerner was doing; **Humlani** (Lamda's brother), who would come in for a cup of coffee after fishing and stay for hours to answer our language questions; **Makapiga**, a young woman with a remarkable talent for explaining and illustrating Sinama words; **Pat and John Johnson,** who lived across the channel in a Sama Lipid community. **Bill Hall**, who was my partner on many extended language surveys; he and **Lee** worked with the Western Subanon language. **JoAnn Gault**, a much appreciated friend who has encouraged us with her insights into the semantics and grammar of a related language. A special tribute to our dictionary-making colleagues **Seymour and Lois Ashley** with their co-author **Irene Hassan** (for Tausug); **Charles and Janice Walton** (for Pangutaran Sama); **Dietlinde Behrens** (for Yakan); **Karen and Joe Allison**, followed by **Douglas and Phyllis Trick** (for Southern Sama); **Robin Forman**, followed by **Millard and Virginia Collins** (for Jama Mapun). **Meriam Bayo**, typesetter par excellence, who took the dictionary entries (on A4 sheets) and typed them faultlessly into the Toolbox program; **Scott Burton,** who transferred the Toolbox data into FieldWorks; the friends and colleagues, too many to name, who have encouraged and challenged us over the decades. Of great value to this project are **Mary Ruth Schroeder** (née **Biral**), a native speaker of Sinama and a fine translator; her husband **Luke,** who makes effective use of online media to enhance the appreciation of Sama culture and language; **Omarjan Jahuran**, from Tabawan, who is a valued guide to the wider Sama world. Also esteemed for their translation skills are **Johnson Bairali**, **Joefi Abdu**, **Dalmina Asiral**, and **Aida Jalmaani**. And last, though by no means least, **David Baines** of SIL's Dictionary and Lexicography Services, who with great patience and skill helped us survive the mysteries of FieldWorks.

**A word to readers, from the dictionary-making team:** We wish you satisfaction as you make use of this book. It is not just a list of words and meanings; it is also a tribute to an amazing people and a beautiful language. To those of you who speak Central Sinama as your mother tongue: please forgive us for meanings that aren't quite correct. *Ka'am atā asekot, ampunun pa'in kami bang aniya' kabtangan mareyom diksiyonari itu mbal abontol to'ongan. Halam tinu'ud! Mura-murahan, bang pa'in kam asalamat-baran.*

Wassalam! Min kami maglakibini.
Kemp and Anne Pallesen

# Part 1

# 1

# Introduction

## 1.1 Who are the Sama, and where do they live?

The sea peoples of insular Southeast Asia have long caught the attention of traders, travelers, and political powers from the Srivijaya kingdom in the first millennium to the researchers and missionaries of the nineteenth century, and, more recently, of anthropologists, linguists, educators, and democratic governments. Literary references and current usage have resulted in a confusing list of names for these peoples. They have been variously referred to as sea gypsies, sea nomads, pirates, Orang Laut,[1] Sama, or Bajaw.[2] These last two are endonyms.

Sama-Bajaw is the name coined (Pallesen 1985) for a discrete subgroup of Western Malayo-Polynesian.[3] Its historic homeland is the Sulu Archipelago, which separates the Mindanao Sea (Celebes) and Sulu Sea and extends from northeast Borneo (Sabah, Malaysia) to the Zamboanga Peninsula (at the southwestern corner of Mindanao Island). The three major high islands of this archipelago are Basilan in the northeast, Jolo in the center, and Tawi-Tawi in the southwest. Between these islands are numerous smaller high islands, atolls, and habitable shallows.

The Central Sinama language (ISO 639-3 sml), the language recorded and illustrated in this dictionary, is a member of the Sama-Bajaw subgroup. It is spoken by the Central Sama people, who have lived for many generations in the central part of the Sulu Archipelago, from the low islands of South Ubian in the southwest to the high island of Siasi, 50 km (31 miles) south of Jolo Island. Map 1 shows the locations of known Central Sama communities (shaded dark gray) in the Sulu region, the traditional range of Sama movement and activity.

Map 1. Sulu and adjacent coasts

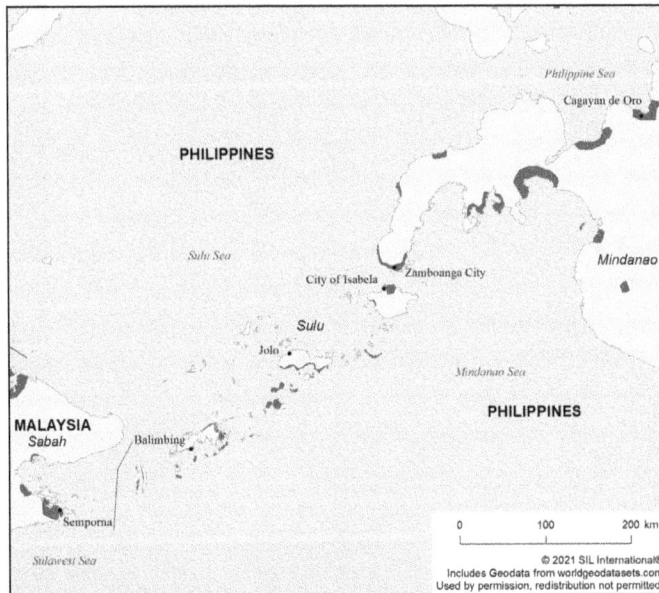

The Central Sama people comprise three subgroups, distinguished by lifestyle, social status, and minor differences in vocabulary.

---

1 Orang Laut, a Malay name meaning 'people of the sea', refers not only to the sea peoples of the Sulu and Celebes seas, but to sea-oriented people groups in general, including those of the Riau Province of Indonesia and the west coast of Thailand who speak languages only distantly related to Sinama.

2 Bajo is a name commonly used for Sama-Bajaw in Indonesia.

3 Western Malayo-Polynesian is a family of 500 or more languages spoken across the western Pacific from Taiwan to coastal Southeast Asia, and in the island nations of the Philippines, Malaysia, and Indonesia.

3

The first two groups are sea-oriented Sama who have no traditional links to a particular location. They are referred to collectively as Sama Dilaut ('ocean Sama'), or individually as:

a. Sama Paosol ('Sama who install house-posts') have been settled for generations in "saltwater" communities just offshore from a coastal town and with a reliable source of fresh water. They use the fishing strategies appropriate to the local situation, but are not emotionally bound to any specific place. If tensions become intolerable due to social pressures or an increase in the difficulties of making a living from fishing, entire kin groups may relocate to distant places, some as far as the Central Philippines or the Semporna coast of Eastern Sabah.

b. Sama Pagūng ('floating Sama') or Sama Palaʼu ('travelling Sama') live with their nuclear families on canoes or house-boats, and are sometimes seen throughout the Sulu Archipelago, along the coasts of Sibuguey Gulf to the north, on the east coast of Palawan, and on the coastal fringes of many Philippine towns and cities, as far east as Davao and as far north as Manila Bay: anywhere, in fact, that offers access to fresh water, onshore markets, and civil stability. Some of these nomadic Sama also maintain small houses on the fringe of a Sama Dilaut community.

The third group, Sama Deya ('land Sama'), have similar practical and emotional links to the resources and rhythms of the sea, but have been settled for many generations in the central region of the Sulu Archipelago, specifically the islands of the Siasi group to the north and Tabawan (South Ubian) to the southwest. They live on the coasts of these islands and harvest the resources of both sea and land. They are usually distinguished by the name of the island where they live. Though some still live in their ancestral homeland, many have relocated over the last fifty years, some northwards to Zamboanga and the Central Philippines, and some to the eastern coast of Sabah.

Map 2 shows the location of other Sama Dilaut communities.

Map 2. The Philippines and Malaysia (Sabah)

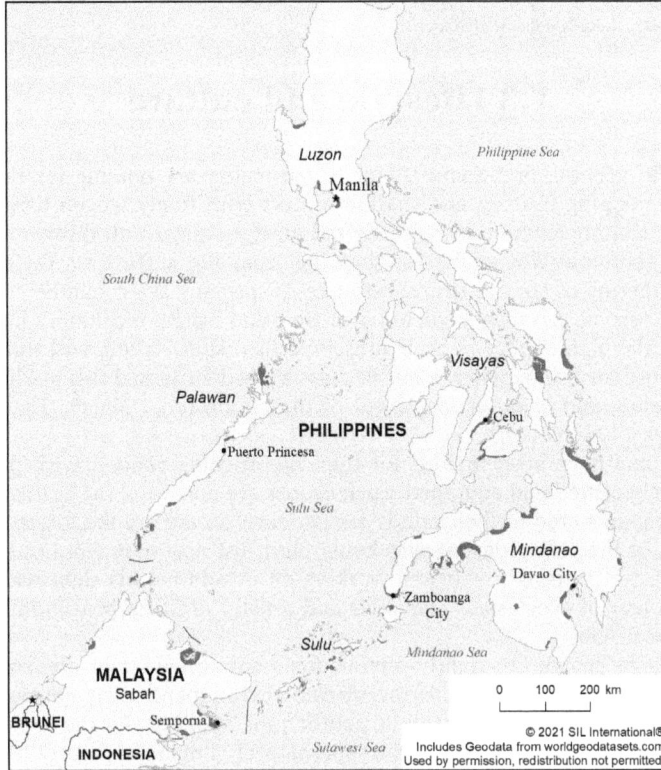

# 1.2 The number of Central Sinama speakers

There are several factors that make it difficult to determine how many people speak this language:

1. The mobility and wide distribution of its speakers, with at least one community in Indonesia (in the Konawe Regency of Southeast Sulawesi); several communities on the eastern Sabah coast of Malaysia; and many settlements in the Philippines, e.g., in the Sulu Archipelago, Zamboanga City, and Basilan Island and their nearby coasts; on the east coast of Palawan and on the fringe of scores of cities in the Visayas and southwest Luzon.

2. The diversity of names by which they are identified and counted (e.g., Sama, Samal, Pala'u, Bajaw, Moro, sea gypsies).[4]

3. Bilingualism in a language of higher social rank, such as Malay, Tausug, Cebuano, or Tagalog, which has in the past influenced responses to census questions.

4. Political pressure to declare oneself a member of an ethnic group other than Sama.

5. Incorrect or inadequately substantiated population figures in material published online.

These difficulties, however, have been significantly offset by documented accounts of cities on the eastern Sabah coast, and personal knowledge of Sama communities throughout Sulu and Tawi-Tawi; in coastal southwest Luzon and Manila Bay; and on the coastal outskirts of Cebu City and numerous cities on the Mindanao coast.

---

[4] Samal is an exonym for Sama Deya, used mainly by Tausug speakers; the name Bajaw is pejorative in the Philippine context, but acceptable in Malaysia or Indonesia.

Though a comprehensive census of Central Sinama speakers has not yet been undertaken, a reasonable estimate, based on a growing awareness of their presence in the central Philippines and coastal eastern Sabah, is at least 200,000.

## 1.3 Lifestyle and culture

The Central Sama in general, and Sama Dilaut in particular, are notable for the variety of their fishing techniques: trapping in deep and shallow waters with finely woven bamboo traps; fishing with hook and line; trolling for tuna using feathered lures; netting, both thrown and static; herding schooling fish into portable woven fences; spearing from the surface or diving for deep-water species; and the gathering of coastal strand resources (especially sea-cucumber, i.e., *bêche-de-mer*). Fishing stocks have become seriously depleted over time and fishing techniques have had to change. Perhaps because of the high quality of their preserved fish (split, salted, and sun-dried), *daing*, the inherited Sinama word for fish in general, has become a word for jerked fish in Philippine languages as far north as Ilocano, and in other languages of the region (e.g., Malay, Thai, and in minority languages of Southeast Kalimantan).

The Central Sama have been famous for their ocean-going canoes, with their planked sides and decks, elaborately carved and equipped. Such canoes are now rare; the craftsmen who built and carved them from a plan stored in their minds are no more. So too are the forests that provided the great logs. The last of the *pelang dapang* was being built just upstream from our house in the late 1960s. Lalli, the master craftsman who was working on it, told me his sight was failing; we were glad to help with a pair of eyeglasses. The skills and artistry of Sama boat-builders are now being redirected to smaller canoes.

The Central Sama people are rightly famous for many things: their amazing knowledge and exploitation of, and profound respect for, the marine environment; their navigational skills; their personal humility and dignity; their aversion to conflict; their concern for the well-being of strangers who come in peace; and their awareness of the supernatural in many aspects of life, notably in their relationship as kin groups with specific spirit ancestors (*pag'mbo'*).

Central Sama today are Muslim, though responsibility to these ancestors is still an important part of life in some families and communities. There is also a small Christian minority.

## 1.4 Central Sinama and its relationship with Proto Sama-Bajaw

Central Sinama is a daughter language of Proto Sama-Bajaw, a reconstructed member of the Western Malayo-Polynesian family of languages. The sister languages of Central Sinama are Bangingih,[5] Southern Sinama, Abaknon, Yakan, Mapun, Pangutaran, Sibuguey, Indonesian Bajaw, and West Coast Bajaw (Sabah).

It is evident that a Sama-Bajaw language has interacted historically with languages of the proposed Greater Barito group in South Kalimantan. However, it is far from clear that Proto Sama-Bajaw is itself a member of this group (contra Blust 2007). The data are better explained by the proposal that speakers of a Sama-Bajaw daughter language have at some historic time moved inland and interacted with speakers of one or more of the diverse Greater Barito languages. The interested reader may like to consult *Proto Sama-Bajaw and the Greater Barito proposal* (Pallesen, in draft) for further discussion of this historic link.

## 1.5 Photographs

This selection of photographs taken by Kemp Pallesen illustrates Sama life in Sulu in the 1960s and early 1970s, the context for the earliest stages of this dictionary project, and for the majority of its entries.

---

5 Bangingih (in the north of the Sulu Archipelago) and Southern Sinama are close relatives of Central Sinama. The three languages are sometimes referred to as Inner Sulu.

Figure 1. M'ddas (Siasi town) in the late 1960s. (See Preface)

Figure 2. Sama Dilaut village of Siganggang, Lapak Island across the channel from Siasi. (See Preface)

Figure 3. Pallesens' house on the deep water side of Siganggang. (See Preface)

Figure 4. Siganggang village, south end. (See Preface)

Figure 5. Bridal party arriving on three joined canoes. (See section 1.3)

Figure 6. Father and son retrieve *bubu* trap from deep water. (See section 1.3)

Figure 7. Rolls of woven fences (*ampas*) for trapping fish. (See section 1.3)

Figure 8. Sama mother spearing long-spined sea urchins (*tayum*). (See section 1.3)

Figure 9. Carved prow of a traditional pelang canoe. (See section 1.3)

# 2

## User's Guide

This chapter provides guidance on using the Central Sinama–English dictionary. Section 2.1 explains the meaning of the abbreviations. Section 2.2 explains how to look up a word. Section 2.3 describes the layout of dictionary entries. Section 2.4 explains the English–Sinama wordlist, and section 2.5 explains the use of the topical wordlists.

## 2.1 Abbreviations

| | | | |
|---|---|---|---|
| *abbrev.* | abbreviation | *interrog.* | interrogative |
| *adj.* | adjective | *intr.* | intransitive |
| *adv.* | adverb | *intrj.* | interjection |
| *adv. dem.* | adverbial demonstrative | *lit.* | literally |
| *adv. phrase* | adverbial phrase | *loc. n.* | locative noun |
| *advrs.* | adversative | *n.* | noun |
| *aff.* | affix | *neg.* | negator |
| *ant* | antonym | *num.* | numeral |
| *atr.* | atransitive | *prep.* | preposition |
| *C* | consonant | *pron.* | pronoun |
| *cf* | compare | *pt-wh* | part-whole |
| *clf.* | classifier | *ptl.* | particle |
| *conj.* | conjunction | *spec-gen* | specific-generic |
| *dem.* | demonstrative | *sp.* | species |
| *disc. mkr.* | discourse marker | *spp.* | several species |
| *ditr.* | ditransitive | *syn* | synonym |
| *fam.* | family | *tr.* | transitive |
| *fig.* | figurative | *v.* | verb |
| *e.g.* | 'for example' | *var.* | variant |
| *gen.* | genus | *voc. n.* | vocative noun |
| i.e. | 'that is' | | |

## 2.2 Finding a word

Section 2.2.1 describes the Sinama alphabet, with special attention to a few characters and symbols that might be unfamiliar to non-Sinama speakers. Section 2.2.2 explains how to remove prefixes, suffixes, and other affixes in order to find the meaning of the word the reader is looking for.

## 2.2.1 Alphabetical order

The entries of the Sinama–English dictionary are alphabetized by headword. The alphabetical order is:

ā a b k d ē e g h ī i j ' l m n ng ō o p r s t ū u w y

Three points require further explanation:

1. The letter *hamsa'* < ' > is used to represent both the glottal stop consonant /ʔ/ and the schwa vowel /ə/.

   a.  *Hamsa'* < ' > is alphabetized between <j> and <l>. For example, the word *ajatu* precedes the word *a'a*, which in turn precedes *alam*. The word *tikkup* precedes the word *t'kke*, which in turn precedes *toket*. (See section 4.2.1.1. The glottal stop /ʔ/, for a discussion of the use of < ' > to represent the glottal stop. See section 4.2.2. The vowels, for a description of the status of the schwa in Sinama.)

   b.  *Hamsa'* < ' > is not written word-initially. For example, the word *mbal* /əmbal/ begins with the letter <m>, not < ' >, and is alphabetized accordingly.

2. All letters in the Sinama alphabet have both long and short forms (section 4.3 Phoneme length), except for the consonants <h>, <ny>, and < ' >, and the central vowel < ' >. Long and short vowels are handled differently from long and short consonants.

   a.  Long vowels are indicated by a macron over the letter. Long vowels precede short vowels in alphabetical order: for instance, *kabā'* precedes *kaba'* and *ā'* precedes *a'a*.

   b.  Long consonants are written as a sequence of two identical consonants, and are alphabetized accordingly. For example, *baljanji'* precedes *ballabi-labi*, which in turn precedes *balmula*.

3. The two-letter combination <ng>, which represents the /ŋ/ sound at the end of the English word 'king', is alphabetized as if it were a single letter in the Sinama alphabet. It comes between <n> and <ō>. The combinations <ny> and <dj>, on the other hand, are *not* alphabetized as single letters, but rather as sequences of two letters. In other words, *nusa* comes before *nyata'* and *nyata'* comes before *ngā'*, because <ng> is a single letter that is alphabetized after <n>.

## 2.2.2 Words and affixes

The Sinama–English dictionary does not contain every possible Sinama word. New words can be created at any time by speakers of the language[1] by a process called derivation. This is where an affix (e.g., prefix, suffix, circumfix, or infix) is added to a word, creating (deriving) a word with a new meaning. For example, adding the prefix *pag-* and the suffix *-an* to *daing* 'fish', derives *pagdaingan* 'fish market'; adding the circumfix *ka-...-an* to the word *t'kka* 'to arrive', derives *kat'kkahan* 'destination'.

Other affixes are involved in a process called inflection, which signals a grammatical function such as passive voice or imperative mood (commands). For example, adding the inflectional suffix *-in* to the word *kose'* 'to wash' signals an imperative function, *kose'in* 'Wash [those]'. The dictionary does not list inflected words. Because the process of inflection is regular, an inflectional affix can be easily removed from a word and the meaning of the unaffixed word looked up.

This section provides guidance for dealing with affixed words. (For more information on the functions of affixes in Sinama grammar, please see chapter 5. For more information on finding derivatives and other complex forms in the dictionary, see section 5.2 Complex forms: Compounds, Derivatives, and Idioms.)

---

[1] Living languages are constantly changing, and Sinama is no exception. New words are added, old words are sometimes lost, and the meanings of words can change over time. Over the years, the dictionary database will expand due to the addition of new words to the language. Likewise, over time some of the entries will become dated, representing word meanings from a bygone era.

### 2.2.2.1 Prefixes aN-, paN-, and maN-

Several Sinama prefixes *aN-*, *paN-*, and *maN-*, end with an unspecified nasal consonant, represented by *N*. The form of this consonant varies according to the place of articulation of the following phoneme. In order to find a word that involves one of the inflectional prefixes. The non-Sama reader might have some difficulty with these prefixes because they disguise the first letter of the word they attach to. A reader who searches for a word like *amana'*, *panukay*, *mangalut*, or *magusaha*, for example, might need some guidance in removing the prefix and recovering the first "disguised" letter of the prefixed word.

The process of "disguising" is called nasal assimilation and it is described in more detail in section 4.7.1 Nasal assimilation and table 7. For now, here are some examples of the changes that take place when the prefix *aN-* attaches to a word:

  a.   When the word *pandi* 'bathe' is prefixed with *aN-*, the combination of N- + <p> becomes <m>: *aN-* + *pandi* → *amandi*.

  b.   When the word *kalang* 'sing' is prefixed with *aN-*, the combination of N- + <k> becomes <ng>: *aN-* + *kalang* → *angalang*.

  c.   When the word *indam* 'borrow' is prefixed with *aN-*, the combination of N- + <i> becomes <ngi>: *aN-* + *indam* → *angindam*.

Some sounds produce a more complex change. For instance,

  a.   When the word *mman* 'leak' is prefixed with *aN-*, the combination of N- + <mm> becomes <ng'mm>: *aN-* + *mman* → *ang'mman*.

  b.   When the word *humbu* 'emit smoke' is prefixed with *aN-*, the combination of N- + <h> becomes <ngah>: *aN-* + *humbu* → *angahumbu*.

  c.   When the word *dāg* 'climb up' is prefixed with *aN-*, the combination of N- + <d> becomes <ngand>: *aN-* + *dāg* → *angandāg*.

  d.   When the word *pagbuwa'* 'bearing fruit' is prefixed with *aN-*, the combination of N- + <pag-> becomes <mag->: *aN-* + *pagbuwa'* → *magbuwa'*.

For the purpose of finding a word in the dictionary, the reader must remove the prefix *aN-* (or *paN-*, or *maN-*) and recover the first letter of the prefixed word. Table 1 provides guidance for removing these prefixes.

Table 1. Guide to removing the prefixes *aN-*, *paN-*, and *maN-*

| First letters of affixed word | First letter(s) of unaffixed word | Example |
|---|---|---|
| <am> | <b> | am'lli → aN- + **b'lli** |
| | <p> | amikit → aN- + **pikit** |
| <an> | <s> | anoho' → aN- + **soho'** |
| | <t> | anahi' → aN- + **tahi'** |
| <anga> | <a> | angaksi → aN- + **aksi** |
| | <ka> | angalang → aN- + **kalang** |
| <angah> | <h> | angahumbu → aN- + **humbu** |
| <angal> | <l> | angalinig → aN- + **linig** |
| <angam> | <m> | angamanit → aN- + **manit** |
| <angan> | <n> | angananam → aN- + **nanam** |
| <angand> | <d> | angandāg → aN- + **dāg** |
| <anganj> | <j> | anganjaga → aN- + **jaga** |
| <angangg> | <g> | anganggawgaw → aN- + **gawgaw** |
| <ange> | <e> | angentom → aN- + **entom** |
| | <ke> | angeket → aN- + **keket** |
| <angi> | <i> | angindam → aN- + **indam** |
| | <ki> | angilā → aN- + **kilā** |
| <ang'> | consonant pair | ang'mbal → aN- + **mbal** |
| | <k'> | ang'llab → aN- + **k'llab** |
| <ango> | <o> | angolang → aN- + **olang** |
| | <ko> | angompol → aN- + **kompol** |
| <angu> | <u> | angulan → aN- + **ulan** |
| | <ku> | anguku' → aN- + **kuku'** |
| <angw> | <w> | angwakil → aN- + **wakil** |
| <mag> | <pag> | magbuwa' → aN- + **pagbuwa'** |

### 2.2.2.2 Prefixes *pag-* and *mag-*

The prefix *pag-* serves a variety of functions in Sinama grammar. Perhaps its most common function is to derive new words. The dictionary includes over a thousand of these derived *pag-* words. They are nearly all listed as subentries under the words from which they are derived. (The related inflectional affix *mag-* is a combination of the nasal prefix *aN-* and the prefix *pag-*, as described above and shown in table 1). So, for instance, **pagbuwa'** can be found listed as a subentry under **buwa'**. The prefix *pag-* must be removed to find the unaffixed word.

### 2.2.2.3 Other prefixes

Sinama prefixes other than *aN-* and *paN-* are easier to deal with. The prefixes *pa-*, *a-*, *paka-*, *maka-*, *paki-/piki-*, *maki-* and *miki-*, *ka-*, and *ta* must be removed to find the unaffixed word.

### 2.2.2.4 Prefix *Cau-*

The prefix *Cau-* indicates multiplicity, where 'C' represents any consonant that appears as the initial consonant of a stem. So for instance, *Cau-* + *palik* -> *paupalik* 'many thoroughly scattered', or *Cau-* + *kampung* -> *kaukampung* 'collective village-mates'. Finding the stem is not difficult. The reader simply removes the *Cau-* prefix.

### 2.2.2.5 Circumfix ka-...-an

The dictionary contains many words derived by the circumfix *ka-...-an*. It is one affix, made up of two parts. For example, *kab'ngkolan* (*ka-* + *b'ngkol* + *-an*) 'to have something stuck in one's throat'. These are mostly listed as subentries under the words from which they are derived. The unaffixed word can be found by removing *ka-* from the beginning of the word and - *an* from the end, so **kab'ngkolan** would be found as a subentry under **b'ngkol**.

### 2.2.2.6 Infixes -in- and -um-

The inflectional infixes - *-in-* and *-um-* are both inserted into a word immediately following the initial consonant. For example,

    a.   *-in-* + *bowa* → *binowa*

    b.   *-um-* + *l'ngngan* → *lum'ngngan*

When a word begins with a vowel, the infix becomes a prefix, attaching to the start of the word. In this case, - *in-* becomes *ni-*. For example,

    a.   *-in-* + *uban* → *niuban*

    b.   *-um-* + *abut* → *umabut*

To find the meaning of an infixed word like *binowa*, the reader needs to remove the infix and look up the unaffixed word **bowa**.

### 2.2.2.7 Suffixes -an, -un, and -in

Sinama has only three suffixes: *-an*, *-un*, and *-in*. Because they occur at the end of the word, they do not pose any difficulty. Suffixes can simply be removed to find the unaffixed word.

# 2.3 Dictionary entries guide

The Sinama–English dictionary contains two types of entries: (i) main entries, which may contain subentries; and (ii) cross-reference entries.[2]

## 2.3.1 Main entries

A main entry is composed of two sections: the headword section and the sense section. The headword section lists the word, phrase, or affix being defined, and provides grammatical and categorical information. The sense section gives the actual meaning of the headword, with related information.

Every main entry contains at least the following three components: a Sinama headword, its lexical class, and an English definition. A longer main entry could have as many as twelve different components. For instance, many entries have one or more Sinama example sentences with English translations. And some entries list variant forms, multiple senses and subsenses, subentries, and lexical relations. This section of the User's Guide is designed to help the reader navigate the various components of a main entry, in the hopes of maximizing the dictionary's usefulness and enjoyability.

---

2 This entire section on dictionary entries draws heavily on Berg (1991).

Figure 10 is a numbered guide to the twelve components a main entry can contain.

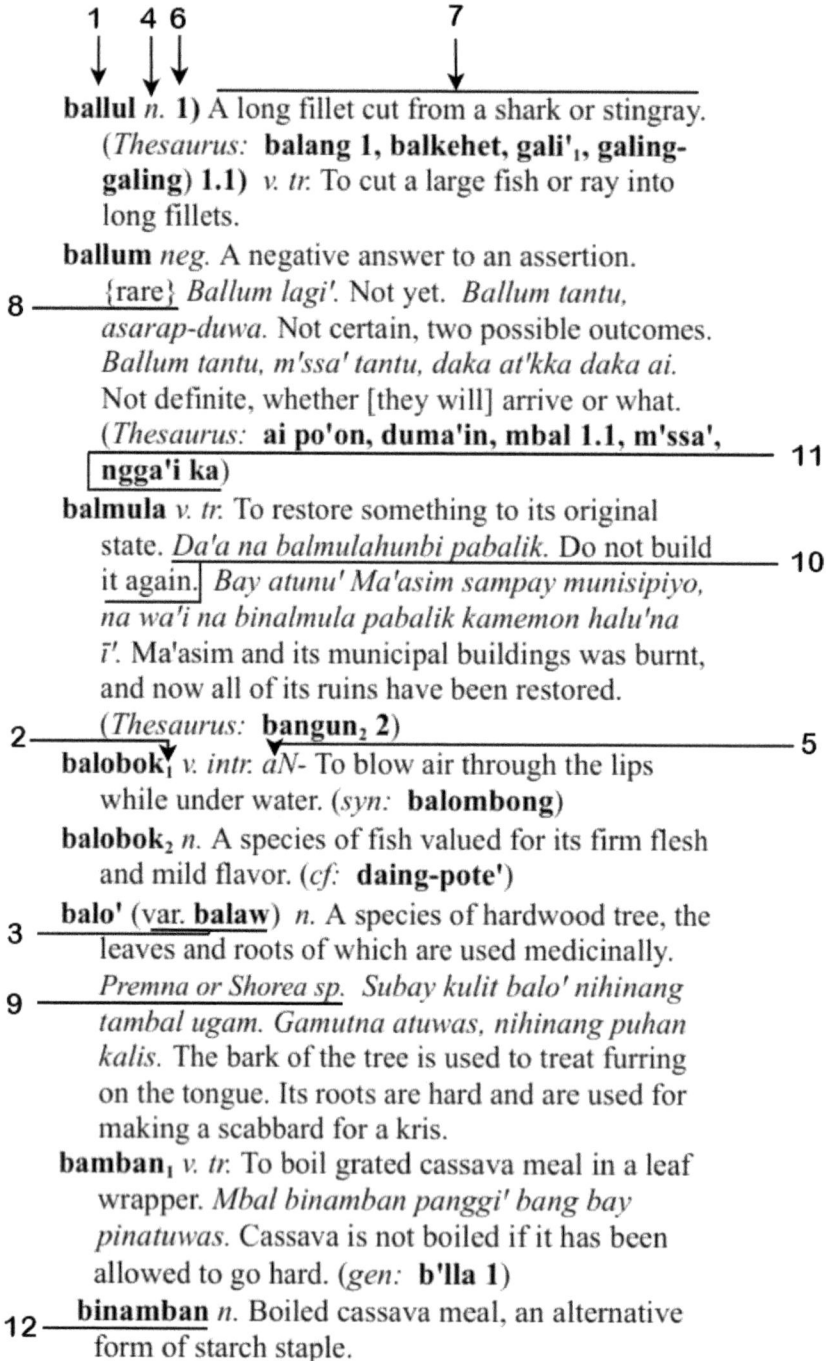

**1    4 6              7**

**ballul** *n.* **1)** A long fillet cut from a shark or stingray. (*Thesaurus:* **balang 1, balkehet, gali'₁, galing-galing**) **1.1)** *v. tr.* To cut a large fish or ray into long fillets.

**ballum** *neg.* A negative answer to an assertion. {rare} *Ballum lagi'.* Not yet. *Ballum tantu, asarap-duwa.* Not certain, two possible outcomes. *Ballum tantu, m'ssa' tantu, daka at'kka daka ai.* Not definite, whether [they will] arrive or what. (*Thesaurus:* **ai po'on, duma'in, mbal 1.1, m'ssa', ngga'i ka**)

**balmula** *v. tr.* To restore something to its original state. *Da'a na balmulahunbi pabalik.* Do not build it again. *Bay atunu' Ma'asim sampay munisipiyo, na wa'i na binalmula pabalik kamemon halu'na ī'.* Ma'asim and its municipal buildings was burnt, and now all of its ruins have been restored. (*Thesaurus:* **bangun₂ 2**)

**balobok₁** *v. intr.* *aN-* To blow air through the lips while under water. (*syn:* **balombong**)

**balobok₂** *n.* A species of fish valued for its firm flesh and mild flavor. (*cf:* **daing-pote'**)

**balo'** (var. **balaw**) *n.* A species of hardwood tree, the leaves and roots of which are used medicinally. *Premna or Shorea sp. Subay kulit balo' nihinang tambal ugam. Gamutna atuwas, nihinang puhan kalis.* The bark of the tree is used to treat furring on the tongue. Its roots are hard and are used for making a scabbard for a kris.

**bamban₁** *v. tr.* To boil grated cassava meal in a leaf wrapper. *Mbal binamban panggi' bang bay pinatuwas.* Cassava is not boiled if it has been allowed to go hard. (*gen:* **b'lla 1**)

**binamban** *n.* Boiled cassava meal, an alternative form of starch staple.

Figure 10. Numbered guide to main entries.

Legend: (1) Headword (2) Homonym number (3) Variant forms (4) Lexical class (5) Other grammatical information (6) Sense number (7) Definition (8) Usage (9) Scientific name (10) Example sentence and translation (11) Lexical relations (12) Subentries

### 2.3.1.1 Headword section (components 1–5 on the numbered guide)

The headword section may contain as many as five components:
- (1)  Headword
- (2)  Homonym number
- (3)  Variant forms
- (4)  Lexical class
- (5)  Other grammatical information

1.  **Headword**
    All dictionary entries begin with a headword: the word, phrase, or affix that is being defined. The dictionary is organized according to the alphabetical ordering of the headwords. Headwords are in bold font, to enable the reader to easily find the desired entry. Figure 10, label 1 shows the headword for **ballul**.

2.  **Homonym number**
    Homonym numbers are used to differentiate headwords that have the same spelling but different meanings. The homonym number is a subscript number on the headword. Figure 10, label 2 shows one pair of homonyms: **balobok$_1$** and **balobok$_2$**.

3.  **Variant forms**
    If a headword has variant forms, these are listed in parentheses immediately following the headword.[3] Types of variants include dialectal variants, free variants, spelling variants, and abbreviated forms (short variants).[4] Figure 10, label 3 shows the entry **balo'** with its variant **balaw** displayed immediately after the headword.

4.  **Lexical class (part of speech)**
    Lexical class refers to a word's grammatical category, such as noun, verb, adjective, pronoun, etc. (see section 5.1 Lexical classes). Lexical classes are also referred to as parts of speech. A headword's lexical class is displayed in abbreviated form (see 2.1 Abbreviations), and is in italic font. The lexical class is listed immediately after the headword, unless there are variant forms. If there are variant forms, the lexical class follows them. Figure 10, label 4 shows the lexical class *n* for the entry **ballul**.

    If a headword has multiple senses or subsenses, the position of the lexical class label(s) depends on whether the senses and subsenses all have the same lexical class. If they share a common lexical class, the class label follows the headword. But if they have different lexical classes, then each sense or subsense has a separate lexical class label which follows the sense number. In figure 10, for example, sense **1)** of **ballul** is labelled *n* and sense **1.1)** is labelled *v. tr.*

5.  **Other grammatical information**
    Entries for verbs and adjectives contain information on affixation and verb transitivity. This information immediately follows the lexical class label, and is printed in italic font. Figure 10, label 5 shows the *intr. aN-* label for **balobok$_1$** 1), indicating that **balobok$_1$** is an intransitive verb that takes the *aN-* prefix. If an adjective or verb is unaffixed it is marked *zero*. (For more on transitivity and affixation, see those sections in 5.1.1.2 'Verbs'). Table 2 gives examples of grammatical information labels for verbs.

---

3  Variant forms are also listed as headwords of cross-reference entries—see section 2.3.2 Cross-reference entries, especially figure 11.
4  The form of a word which is chosen as headword of the main entry is usually just the one first recorded by the compiler. It is not to be understood as more correct or standard; the variant forms are just as valid.

Table 2. Selected grammatical information labels

| | |
|---|---|
| *v. tr.* | Transitive verb (*aN-, Ø, -in-*) |
| *v. tr. -an* | Transitive verb (*aN-, Ø, -in-, -an*) |
| *v. tr. a-, ka-...-an, -an* | Transitive verb (*a-, ka-...-an, -in-, -an*) |
| *v. intr. pa-* | Intransitive verb (*pa-*) |

#### 2.3.1.2 Sense section (components 6–12 on the numbered guide)

The sense section gives the meaning of the headword, plus related information. This section can include up to seven components.

(6) Sense number
(7) Definition
(8) Usage
(9) Scientific name
(10) Example sentence and translation
(11) Lexical relations
(12) Subentries

6. Sense number

Whereas homonym numbers distinguish different headwords with the same spelling, sense numbers distinguish shades of meaning of a single headword. Sense numbers are presented as boldface numbers preceding each sense of a headword. Figure 10, label 6 shows the sense number 1) of **ballul**.

The dictionary also includes subsenses, represented by boldface subnumbers **1.1)**, **1.2)**, etc. For example, "**ballul 1)** *n* A long fillet cut from a shark or stingray" has a subsense, "**1.1)** *v. tr.* To cut a large fish or ray into long fillets." Besides distinguishing finer shades of meaning, often with differing lexical classes, subsenses are also used for pragmatic functions, e.g., discourse functions of conjunctions or aspectual uses of demonstratives.

7. Definition

The definition gives the meaning of the headword. Figure 10 label 7 shows the definition for sense **1)** of **ballul**: "A long fillet cut from a shark or stingray." Some definitions take the form of an equivalent English word or phrase, such as the definition for the negator **ai po'on**: "On the contrary; no way!" Other definitions describe the Sinama word in English terms, e.g., the definition for **bantilan**: "Posts used to raise a canoe above high tide level, for maintenance." Definitions may include descriptions of grammatical function as well as lexical meaning. For example, the entries for pronouns include English near-equivalents, information about person and number, and information about grammatical set. The definition for **kitam** reads: "We all; us all (first person plural, inclusive) [Set III]."

8. Usage

Some entries include a usage label indicating limitations on how the headword is used. These might be temporal limitations (e.g., archaic, obsolete, old-fashioned) or social limitations (e.g., euphemistic, vulgar, taboo). The usage label is displayed in curly brackets {...} immediately following the definition. The commonest usage label in the dictionary is {idiom}. Figure 10 label 8 gives an example of the usage label {rare} in the entry for **ballum**.

9. Scientific name

Many entries for names of animals and plants include Latin scientific names.[5] Scientific names

---

[5] Scientific names for these species have been gleaned from a wide variety of sources over the decades. These include: 1) A list of marine species from the Philippine Department of Fisheries; 2) Graduate student research

are displayed in italic font immediately following the definition. Figure 10 label 9 shows the scientific name for the word **balo'** (*Premna* or *Shorea* sp.).

10. Example sentence and translation

Many entries include one or more Sinama example sentences (in small italic font), with English free translations (in small regular font). The example sentences illustrate the headword in use. They are all composed by native speakers of Central Sinama, whether collected from conversation or composed for illustrative purposes. There is a wealth of cultural and linguistic material to be found in the example sentences—arguably one of the most valuable features of the Sinama–English dictionary. Figure 10 label 10 shows the example sentence and translation for **balmula**: "*Da'a na balmulahunbi pabalik.* Do not build it again."

11. Lexical relations

A main entry often includes one or more words whose meanings are related to the meaning of the headword. These words are listed in parentheses near the end of the sense section. If a headword has multiple senses, each sense might have a separate list of related words. Figure 10 label 11 shows related words for **ballum**.

Words can be related to the headword in a variety of ways, referred to as lexical relations. Table 3 gives a list of lexical relations found in the Sinama–English dictionary, with their abbreviations and descriptions, and examples of each.

---

into Sama fishing technologies; 3) Visual recognition by Sama neighbors of fish as displayed in pictorial resources (e.g., sharks of the world, commercial fish species, marine sports, etc.); 4) Dictionaries and wordlists compiled by SIL Philippines for a variety of languages; 5) I. H. Burkill's *Dictionary of the economic products of the Malay Peninsula*; 6) Douglas Yen's research (Bishop Museum, Hawaii) into the medicinal plants used by Sama healers.

Table 3. Lexical relations

| Lexical relation | Description | Example |
|---|---|---|
| Antonym (*ant*) | Links words with opposite meanings. | **bagay 1)** *n.* A friend. (*ant:* **banta 1**)<br>**banta** *n.* **1)** An enemy. (*ant:* **bagay 1**) |
| Compare (*cf*) | Compares or contrasts entries. | **bahaya alta'** *phrase* Addicted to getting rich. (*cf:* **beya' hawa**)<br>**beya' hawa** *phrase* Selfishly attached to something. (*cf:* **bahaya alta'**) |
| Part-whole (*pt-wh*) | Links one or more parts to a physical or conceptual whole. | **esok-mata** *n.* Sclera, the white of the eye. (*wh:* **mata**$_1$ **1**) |
| *Set* | Lists closed grammatical sets such as pronouns and demonstratives. | **akū** *pron.* I, me (first person singular) [Set I]. (*Set:* **iya, kā, kām, kamī, kitā**$_1$**, kitabi**$_1$**, kitām, sigā**$_1$**, sigām**$_1$) |
| Specific-generic (*spec-gen*) | Links specific types to a generic term. | **ansak** *n.* A basket woven from coconut leaflets. (*gen:* **baka'**$_2$)<br>**baka'**$_2$ *n.* A marketing basket woven of bamboo or rattan, has a rigid handle. (*spec:* **ansak, balatak, baluyut, basket, japang, kalanjangan, kampil, kanasto, salingkat, sugub, tampipi', tiklis**) |
| *Stages* | Lists words describing the stages of a process in order. | **botong** *n.* The mature unripe fruit of the coconut palm. (*Stages:* **kambung-kambung, botong-botong, bilu'uk, botong, gangkul, lahing, pangtusan**) |
| Synonym (*syn*) | Links words with exactly or nearly the same meaning. | **aksi** *v. intr. aN-* To sneeze. (*syn:* **pagba'anan**)<br>**pagba'anan** *v. intr. aN-* To sneeze. (*syn:* **aksi**) |
| *Thesaurus* | Groups words with an overlap in meaning. | **tagdok** *v. tr. -an* To kick something with the sole of the foot. (*Thesaurus:* **binti', sipa' 1, tindak 1**)<br>**binti'** *v. tr.* To kick an opponent's calf in a test of endurance. (*Thesaurus:* **sipa' 1, tagdok, tindak 1**) |

12.   Subentries

Subentries are the last element that may be included in the sense section of a main entry. Subentries list complex forms (i.e., compounds, derivatives, and idioms). A complex form is listed as a subentry under its first component. Subentry headwords are each listed on a new line, indented from the main margin, in small-type boldface. An example of a subentry in figure 10, label 12 is the compound form **binamban**, from **bamban**.

## 2.3.2 Cross-reference entries

Cross-reference entries are used for variant forms, abbreviated forms (short variants) and some complex forms. (Complex forms are described in sections 2.3.3 and 5.2.) On the page, cross-reference entries look similar to main entries, with the headword in bold font. But cross-reference entries generally provide very little information on their own—no lexical class, definition, or example sentences. Their purpose, rather, is to guide the reader to a relevant main entry. Cross-reference entries for variant and abbreviated forms merely point the reader to the entry for the relevant variant pair.

Figure 11 shows two cross-reference entries. The first, for **k'kkop**, is a variant form. The second, for **k'ddaw**, illustrates a slightly different situation. The existence of the Sinama word *pagk'ddaw-k'ddaw* could lead a non-native speaker to think that a word *k'ddaw* has been reduplicated and prefixed with *pag-*. But *k'ddaw* is not actually a word in Sinama. If a reader looks up *k'ddaw*, its cross-reference entry redirects the reader back to the main entry for *pagk'ddaw-k'ddaw*.

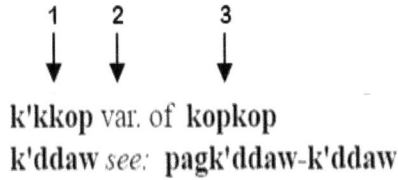

Figure 11. Numbered guide to cross-reference entries.

Legend: (1) Headword (2) Type of cross-reference (3) Cross-referenced entry

## 2.3.3 Complex forms (compound words, derivatives, and idioms)

Complex forms are words made up of more than one part. They include derivatives (made up of a word and an affix), compounds (made up of more than one word), and idioms (which have a literal and figurative meaning). Compound words and idioms do not appear as main entries or cross-reference entries. They are only listed as subentries. For example, in figure 10 the compound **binamban** is listed as a subentry under its first component part, **bamban₁**.

The most common types of derivatives are also only listed as subentries under the words from which they are derived. These include derivatives formed by the suffix *-an*; by reduplication; by the prefix *pag-*; and by the circumfix *ka-...-an*. Finding derivatives formed by the suffix *-an* or by reduplication is simple. For instance, the derivative **li'isan** is listed as a subentry under **li'is**; and the derivative **bid-bid** is listed as a subentry under **bid**. Finding derivatives formed by the prefix *pag-* or the circumfix *ka-...-an* requires a little more work. The reader must recognize these affixes and remove them to determine the unaffixed word. The derivative is then found listed as a subentry under the entry for the unaffixed word. For instance, **pagbono'** 'to fight each other' is listed as a subentry under **bono'** 'to hit or kill', and **kagoyakan** 'turbulence at sea' is listed as a subentry under **goyak** 'wave'.

Other derivatives, including those formed with the relatively common prefix *paN-* (e.g., *pangita'u* 'wisdom', from *ta'u* 'to know'), are listed as cross-reference entries. Cross-reference entries for derivatives look much like main entries: they contain grammatical information, definitions, and example sentences. But they also serve to point the reader from the derivative back to the word from which it is derived. The derivative can also be found listed as a subentry under that word, but the subentry does not include any example sentences.

# 2.4 English–Sinama wordlist guide

The English–Sinama wordlist follows the body of the dictionary. Each wordlist entry consists of an English word or phrase, followed by one or more Sinama words with similar meanings (homonym and sense numbers are provided where appropriate). Because the entries do not provide detailed definitions or grammatical information for the English words, the wordlist is not an English–Sinama dictionary in the full sense. Nevertheless, it is a valuable tool for the Sama student of English who is seeking a better understanding of some English word, and for the English-speaking student of Sinama who wishes to express some idea in that language.

# 2.5 Topical wordlists overview

Four topical wordlists follow the English–Sinama wordlist. These wordlists provide lists of words organized around different topics. These words can also be found in the body of the dictionary, but they are brought together in the wordlists as a way of highlighting aspects of Sama culture and the Sinama language that are of particular interest. Wordlist A: Marine species lists the Sinama names for over 700 species of marine animals and plants. It illustrates the profound depth and breadth of Sama knowledge of ocean life. Wordlist B: Sinama maritime vocabulary provides a selection of other words pertinent to the Sama ocean-based lifestyle, including words for tides, seasons, ocean conditions, weather, sailing and navigation, fishing strategies, and beliefs. Wordlist C: House construction lists parts of the house, building materials, and other words relating to house construction. Wordlist D: Classifiers lists noun classifiers, words used in counting specific types of objects (see section 5.1.2.5 Quantifiers).

# Part 2

# 3

# Dictionary

## 3.1 Central Sinama–English dictionary

# A a

**ā** *intrj.* **1)** 'I get it.' *Ā, buwattilu.* Ah, so it's like that. **2)** 'Hey, look.' *Ā, ngā'un.* Here, take it. **3)** 'You did, didn't you?' *Tuwan Sultan, bay sa ka amatanyag sara' panoho'an, ā?* Respected Sultan, you made a law widely known, did you not?

**a-₁ 1)** *aff.* Intransitive prefix: attaches to intransitive verbs, especially stative verbs; verbs whose single argument is undergoer-like; and verbs of arrival and departure. *Ahāp d'nda ka, rāng.* You are a fine-looking girl, dear. *Ap'ddi' kōkku, mbal kasandalan.* My head is aching, unbearable. **1.1)** *aff.* Transitive prefix: attaches to transitive verbs of cognition and emotion. *Alasa aku ma ka'a.* I love you.

**a-₂** *aff.* Adjective prefix: the most common affix found on Sinama adjectives. *Apunggul kayu inān ma deya T'lling, bay taluwa' baliyu.* The tree inland from T'lling Point has its top broken off, hit by the wind. *Bang ariki'-diki' nih'nnat tanganna bo' aheya alantik.* When small her hands are manipulated so that when they are big they will curve back [for dancing].

**āb** *v. tr.* To take bait, as a fish does. *Tininduk kita he' daing bo' wa'i niāb he' kalitan atawa kuhapo'.* A fish has taken our bait but a shark or a grouper has swallowed it whole. *Buwat anonda', ya bay panonda'an i' tinurul he' daing aheya, tininduk, niāb he' daing a'aslag.* Like when trolling, the trolling lure is followed by some large fish and struck at it, swallowed whole by a really big fish.

**aba-aba** *n.* A small bag for protective charms. (*gen:* **tambang₃ 1**)

**abakadol** *var. of* **abokado**

**abag** *adj.* *a-* Good, of quality. *A'abag pahāp angatubang daing itū.* The strings of fish facing this way are excellent. *Saging itu a'abag s'kkatanna. Kilāku ahāp bay bolehanna.* These bananas are fine in their separate hands. I reckon the full stalk must have been good. *A'abag pahāp daing itū.* These fish are excellent. (*cf:* **jatu 1**)

**abal** *n.* **1)** Rough waves where currents meet. *Ni goyak aheka, ni s'llog ala'at, ya hē' abal.* Into very rough seas, into adverse currents, that's *abal*. *Bang hal goyak angatubang, bang abal mbal.* If it is merely rough water it can be faced, if it is *abal* it cannot. *Taluwa' kami abal ma dilaut, hal kami magpagūng.* We ran into rough water out at sea, so we just floated. **1.1)** *v. intr.* *aN-* To make the noise of rough seas. *Angabal tahik, sōng t'bba.* The sea is roaring; it will soon be low tide. *Paligay bang a'llop pelangta, angabal, buwat saga batangan.* Especially when a canoe is overloaded, it makes a noise, like when its outrigger booms are involved. (*cf:* **la'ang 1, s'llog;** *Thesaurus:* **guyu 1, haus 1, sahabal**)

**abana** *see:* **duwa-abana**

**abang** *v. intr.* *pa-* To welcome people on arrival. *Sika'abang-abangan saga onde'-onde'.* The children are out en masse to welcome arrivals. (*Thesaurus:* **bāk₂, langgal₂ 2, pagsamban, sampang 1**)

**abas 1)** *n.* An itchy skin condition. *Abas itu akatol, amuwan l'kkang labi min buwa'-buwa' llaw.* Abas is itchy, and produces more serum than prickly heat does. *Abas itū ai-ai sali' m'ssang makanikita. Tagna' bay m'ssang, na magkatol. Abas is anything like a rash that happens to us. At first it is a rash, then it becomes itchy. (Thesaurus:* **buwa'-buwa' 1, kagutgut 1.1, katol 1.2, ugud**) **2)** *v. advrs.* *-in-* Suffering from skin rash. *Niabas iya. Abas itu akatol, amuwan l'kkang labi min buwa'-buwa' llaw.* She has an *abas* condition. *Abas* is itchy, and discharges more serum than prickly heat does.

**abat** *n.* **1)** A mild illness blamed on spirit beings. **1.1)** *v. advrs.* *ka-...-an* Indisposed or unwell due to some supernatural influence. *Subay kono' anulug gallang labu bo' mbal ka'abatan.* They say that one should wear a shell bracelet to prevent being affected by a spirit being.

**abay₁** *n.* **1)** A person or canoe in the same fishing group. *Ta'nda' pa'in tulis pelang, yuk kami, "Ina'an abayta."* When we saw the decorative lines of the canoe, we said, "That is our fleet-mate." **1.1)** *v. intr.* *pa-/aN-* To travel or work with another fishing vessel. *Gana dai' llaw angabay na kami ma si Di.* When daylight comes we will join with Di's fleet. *Pa'abay na daka sai* *ma kami*. Someone, goodness knows who, joined up with us. (*Thesaurus:* **beya'₂ 1**, **bunyug 1.2**, **dongan**, **sehe' 1.1**, **unung 1**)

**abayan** *n.* A fleet of fishing boats. *Sangka'abayan kami*. We are of one fleet.

**pagabay** *n.* **1)** A collective term for people fishing, traveling, or sitting together. **1.1)** *v. intr. aN-* To form a cooperative fishing project involving a number of canoes. *Magabay kita ni Tapa'an anonda'*. Let's go to Tapa'an as a fleet and fish by trolling.

**pangabay** *n.* A person in the same fleet or group; fleet-mate.

**abay₂** *n.* The period after a specific time event. *Maghinang abay min dai'-llaw sampay pas'ddop mata llaw*. They worked from the period after daybreak until the sun set.

**abay-kohap** *n.* Dusk; early evening. *Abay-kohap alempos na, magalib. Sali' halam aniya' llaw ta'nda', minsan keyat-keyatna. Abay-kohap* is dark already, evening prayer time. The sun is no longer seen, not even its light. (*Thesaurus:* **kohap 1**, **lekot-lendom**, **lempos**, **logob-logob**, **magrib 2**, **sū'-palita'an**)

**abay-subu** *n.* First light of day. (*Thesaurus:* **bukis₁**, **dai'-llaw**, **pagmanis-manis sobangan**, **pote' sobangan**, **subu₂ 1**)

**abbit** (var. **ablit**) *v. tr.* To mention or invite someone by name. *Bang magkawin na, subay tina'abbit kakampungan*. On the wedding, the relatives should be invited. *Bay bahā' kami abbitbi pi'itu supaya langpasanbi?* Did you invite us here in order to rob us?

**abbu** *n.* **1)** Pride in one's status. *A'a inān hal ama'nda'an abbuna*. That person is just making a show of his conceit. **1.1)** *adj. a-/-an* Proud of oneself; arrogant. *Ala'at bang a'a makalandu' abbuhan, bilang halam bagayna*. It is bad when a person is excessively proud, he often has no friends. *A'abbu si Anu, magl'lla-l'lla, magtanding dīna*. What's-his-name is conceited, pretending to be tough, looking at himself in a mirror. **1.2)** *v. tr. -an* To treat someone arrogantly. *Ka'a ya pangabbuhanku, sabab ilu ma ka'a bay arāk tunangku*. You are the target of my boasting, because you have the one I thought would be my sweetheart.

**pagabbu** *v. intr. aN-* **1)** To show off; to display boastfully. *Bang mamarahi pagabbuku, mbal aku kinabaya'an*. If my showing off is excessive, no one will desire me. **1.1)** *v. tr.* To draw attention to some real or pretended asset; to boast of an imaginary accomplishment. *Magabbu-abbu, sali' alanga atayna*. Showing off his status, kind of haughty. (*Thesaurus:* **pagbantug-bantug**, **pagheya-heya**, **pagmahatinggi**, **pagmalangkahi**, **pagpasanglit**, **pagtāp-tāp**)

**pagpa'abbu** *v. intr. aN-* To make a show of one's importance.

**pa'abbu** *n.* One who shows off; a braggart.

**pangangabbu** *n.* A boaster; a show-off.

**abila** *conj.* Under certain conditions; whenever. *Buwat a'a abakat, yukta, "Abila ilu mbal tambalannu, paheya ko' ilū."* Of a person who has a wound we say, "If you don't get that treated it will get worse." *Abila aku siniya-siya he' ina'-mma'ku, tantu aku tinaima' e' Tuhan*. If I were to be abandoned by my parents, God would surely accept me. *Abila na ka ni bohe', gana-gana ka magsumau'*. Whenever you go for water, you are bound to trip on something. *Yuk matto'a, "Abila onde' ilū saga tarugtul he' magbola ilū, dusanu sabab ka'a ya bay amowa iya pareyo'."* The parent said, "If that child happens to be hit by the ball players there, you'll be to blame because it was you who took him down onto the beach." (*Thesaurus:* **bang₁**, **bangsi'**, **basta**, **bo' na**, **gana**, **pagka**, **samantala'**, **talkala'**)

**abin** (var. **tabin**) *v. tr.* To keep essential things safe. *Hal busay tatabin maka panait*. Only the paddle and a bailer was saved. *Bay aku pakkom, wa'i na alungay kamemon. Yangkon ta'abinku busay maka peya'*. I capsized; everything was lost. All I secured was the paddle and a coconut shell. *Buwat kulaet itū angkan binowa ni ka'a pinahāp. Niabin he' sigā pagsū', sabab sōng t'ddo'*. Like this pressure lantern, the reason it is being brought to you is to have it mended. They want to be absolutely sure of having it for lamp-fishing because it will soon be calm. *Niabin palsuku'an min kariki'-diki'na*. Kept as a possession since he was small. (*Thesaurus:* **appula**, **habit**)

**abing** var. of **aging**

**abiyug** *v. tr.* To seduce or persuade to do what is wrong. *Abiyugun ba pi'ingga-pi'ingga kal'ngnganannu. Hatina, ameya' du sigām ma iya*. Make him go with you, regardless of where you are going. In other words, they go with him. *Illagin kar'ndahan magpangabiyug*. Be on guard against women who are in the habit of seduction. *Bang a'a ala'at kasuddahanna angabiyug pagkahina maghinang kala'atan*. A person of bad character persuades his fellow man to do bad things. (*Thesaurus:* **agpot 1**, **angin**, **egot-egot**, **logos 1**, **panhot**, **p'ggong**, **poleggaw**)

**abjan** *v. tr. -an* To retaliate to some hurt or harm. *Bang angastol a'a, da'a na abjanin bo' mbal paheya kalengogan*. If a man is angry, don't retaliate lest the disturbance gets worse.

**ablay** *v. intr. pa-* To lay an arm across someone's shoulder. *Pa'ablay ka ma bahaku*. Put your arm across my shoulder.

**pagablay** *v. intr. aN-* To put an arm across each other's shoulder, as people sitting or walking together. *Subay sigām magablay bang ma pal'ngnganan, tināw ta'bba*. They prefer to have their arms across each other's shoulders on a walk, afraid of being left behind.

**ablit** var. of **abbit**

**ablong** *n.* A large fish spear such as a harpoon. (*Thesaurus:* **pana' 1, sahapang 1, sangkil 1, saubang, s'llokan**)

**abokado** (var. **abakadol**) *n.* Avocado. *Persea americana.*

**abō'₁** var. of **bo'₁**

**abō'₂** var. of **bo'₂**

**abong** var. of **bōng**

**absen** *adj. zero* Absent from school or work. *Bay aku absen sabab aheka to'ongan sasaw maka kabimbanganku.* I was absent because I had so many troubles and responsibilities. (*cf:* **bukut₂, likut 1**)

**abu** *n.* 1) Ashes. *Maglampasu maka abu bo' alanu'.* Polish floors with ashes so they will be clean. *Peya' isihan abu maka kamanyan.* A coconut shell containing ashes and incense. (*Thesaurus:* **bale₅, buling**) 1.1) *v. intr. aN-* To turn to ash.

**abu-abu₁** *adj. zero* Gray or ashy color. *Kihampaw-bās abu-abu walna'na.* A sand-ray, grayish in color. (*gen:* **walna'**)

**abu-abu₂** *v. intr. aN-* To become unclear due to mist or darkness. *Angabu-ngabu na sali' būd, sali' angandom.* The mountains have become kind of indistinct, as though darkening with cloud. (*Thesaurus:* **ahud-ahud 1.1, buraw, hanaw-hanaw, pagba'ung-ba'ung**)

**abugaw** *n.* A lawyer; legal advocate. *Abugaw itu alanga min kapitan. Angahukum ma a'a mbal magsulut.* An *abugaw* is of higher rank than a barangay captain. He makes a judgment for people who don't reach an agreement. (*Thesaurus:* **huwis, po'on-sara', sara' 2**)

**abuggu'** (var. **habuggu'**) *v. tr. a-, ka-..-an, -an* To feel envious of. *Abuggu'an h'ndana, luba' bang maka'nda' a'a magbulawan.* His wife is jealous, especially when she sees someone wearing jewelry. (*Thesaurus:* **himuggu', iggil 1.1, imbū, jelus, jingki 1, lindi 1**)

**abuhan** var. of **sabba-abuhan**

**abunaw** *v. tr. -an* To take the blame; to accept responsibility. *Bang magsalla' bo' halam amayad, angabunaw aku.* When gambling with coins and someone doesn't pay, I guarantee payment. *Bang aniya' anunu bo' aku bay makaindam, aku ya atas. Magka'at pa'in bo' halam aniya' pangataskku ai-ai bay bowaku-i, mikiabunaw aku ni taga ai-ai. "Abunawin aku," yukku. "Bayaranku du bang aniya' tapihaku."* If you have something or other and I borrow it, I am liable. When it gets damaged and I have nothing to cover whatever I had gone off with, I ask someone with resources to be responsible. "Be responsible for me," I say. "I will pay when I am able to find something." *Bang aniya' ai-ai bay indamanku min ka'a, aku ya atas. Magka'at pa'in, bo' halam aniya' pangataskku ai-ai bay bowaku-i, mikiabunaw aku ni a'a taga ai-ai. "Abunawin aku," yukku.* If I have borrowed

anything from you, I am liable. When it gets damaged and I have nothing to replace what I had taken, I ask someone with resources to be responsible. "Be responsible for me," I say. (*Thesaurus:* **atas₂ 1, bahala'₁, kuwiraw, lawag-baran, siyal, tanggung₂**)

**abung** *v. intr. aN-* 1) To precede; go ahead of. *Angabung na pa'in iya bang an'bba.* She's always going ahead of the group when gathering strand food. 1.1) *v. tr.* To get ahead by overtaking.

**abut₁** *adj. zero* About to happen; imminent. *Pal'kkas kam, abut ulan, abut sangom.* Hurry up, it's about to rain, almost night.

**abut₂** *v. intr. pa-/-um-* 1) To reach a goal. *Mbal aku umabut. Tundugun aku man pelang.* I can't touch bottom. Ferry me by canoe. *Bang mbal maka'abut tambu' ilū, sugpatin maka lupis abō' umabut.* If that dipper won't reach, extend it with a piece of banana fiber so it does reach. *Ina'an na lansa sōng atulak bo' masi kita ma labayan. Subay kita pa'abut abō' makatumpang.* There's the launch about to leave, and we are still on the way. We must reach it to get a ride. *Pagabut kami ni Buli'-Lakit, na maī' na kami palayo-layo.* On reaching Rock Point, we anchored there for a while. (*cf:* **ā' 3**; *Thesaurus:* **kablit₂, sampay 2, t'kka₁ 1.1**) 1.1) *v. tr.* To get something by reaching. *Abutun, Oto'.* Reach it, Son. *Aku itū arai' na ta'abut.* As for me, my time has almost come.

**ka'abutan** *n.* What someone is able to reach or achieve. *Bang iya na ka'abut-abutan sigām, nihinang kubu' na.* If that's as much as they can manage, a temporary shack is built. *Pinende sīn bang maka'abut, mbal magtūy am'lli. Ni'nda' ya ka'abutanna.* Checks his money whether it will suffice, doesn't buy immediately. Sees how far it will go.

**pagabut** *v. intr. aN-* To meet up with each other; to come together in a fight. *Anangisan siyalina, halam sigām bay magabut.* Grieving for his younger brother [that] they had not caught up with each other. *Magga'ut maka sehe'ta magbono', arai'-arai' magabut na.* Friends pulling at each other, getting into a fight, about to make contact.

**pagabut umul** *v. intr. aN-* To last a lifetime. {idiom} *Magabut umul ko' tangkinu ilū.* That tank of yours will last forever.

**pangabut** *v. tr.* To find something by chance; to come across something.

**abut ma kara-kara** *v. advrs. ta-* Caught in the act; caught red-handed. *Ta'abut ka anangkaw ma kara-kara. Bang halam ta'abut ma kara-kara bo' hal tuhuma bay anangkaw, mbal b'nnal.* You were caught in the act of stealing. If you were not caught and it was just hearsay that you stole, then it is not proved true.

**abut-abut** *v. tr.* To persist at a task; keep doing. *Ina'an na lansa sōng atulak, bo' masi kita ma* *labayan. subay kita pa'abut-abut bo' makatumpang.* There is a launch about to leave, and we are still on the way. We'll need to keep hard in order to get aboard. *Sinahi'-sahi' iya bang maghinang, sali' niabut-abut.* Motivated by impatience when working, doing it persistently. *Bang aniya' angose' lai', sali' dai'-dai' iya, ma sabab aniya' bagayna ma luwasan, angabut-ngabut iya supaya aubus hinangna inān.* If someone is washing dishes, she sort of hurries because there's a friend outside. She works hard at it so her work gets done. *Sigām magtai'-anak bay niabut-abut e' saga sundalu, pinapatay.* The entire family was attacked persistently by the soldiers and killed.

**pagabut-abut** *v. intr. aN-* To occur persistently and repetitively. *Magabut-abut kasusahan deyom atay.* Their inner sorrows continue unabated. *Magabut-abut sadja pelang a'a am'ssi.* The canoes of men fishing just keep going and going. *Magabut-abut sigām magtimuk ma sakalibutna min subu-subu sampay ni kasangoman.* They kept gathering around him from early morning until night. (*Thesaurus:* **kara-kara**₁, **daran-daran** 1.1, **langkit** 1.1, **mumut**, **pagambat-ambat** 1, **pagkuwat**, **sigi-sigi** 1, **toldas**)

**aka** *var. of* **maka**₃

**akal** *n.* Residue in a liquid. *Asōban kami amangan akal lahing bang maglana' disi Ina'.* We love eating coconut residue when Mother and others make coconut oil. (*Thesaurus:* **angkas**₁ 1, **hali**₁ 1, **p'tti'**, **sapal**, **tai'-lahing**)

**akal-baran** *n.* Human remains; skeleton. (*Thesaurus:* **batang-tubu**, **pagdayaw** 1, **paltubu-tubuhan** 2, **tangkorak**)

**akal-bahal** *n.* Black coral. *Cirrhipathes spp. Gallang akal-bahal, aettom.* A coral bracelet, black.

**akasya** *n.* Monkeypod tree. *Albizia saman, subfam. Mimosoideae.*

**akay** *v. tr.* To contain; to fit into. *Mbal ta'akay buwas itū.* This rice won't fit in the container. *Ai-ai isita bo' ap'nno', yukta mbal ta'akay.* Whatever we are putting in and it is full, we say that it won't fit in. (*cf:* **isi**₁ 1.2)

**akkal** *n.* 1) Intellect; ability to think or reason. *Halam akkalan.* Having no sense. (*Thesaurus:* **pamikil**, **panahu'an**) 1.1) *v. tr. -an* To deceive or trick someone. *Bay aku ka'akkalan ma tinda, kulang pangahūg ma sīnku.* I was cheated at the store, short-changed. *Saupama buwat aku nsa' aniya' ap'ddi', amabā' aku ap'ddi' kōkku parahāl nsa'. Ya he' niōnan magakkal.* For example if I have no pain, I say I have a headache even though I don't. That is called deception. *Ka'a itū hal angakkal. Minsan aniya' ma ka'a, angamu' na pa'in ka ni kasehe'an.* You just deceive. Even though you already have some you keeping asking others for more. (*cf:* **lakbu'**₂; *Thesaurus:* **balidja**, **kaikit**₂ 1, **kidjib**, **kulli'** 1, **labba'**₁,

**lingu** 1.1, **parupang**, **puting** 1)

**akkal-akkal** *adv.* Pretending. *Ladjawta, hal sali' bin'lli akkal-akkal.* We make a low first bid, just pretending to buy.

**akkal-pikilan** *n.* Mental faculties; ability to reason. *Ala'an sipatta, halam aniya' akkal-pikilanta.* Our awareness has left us, we have no rational thought.

**barakkal** (*var.* **balakkal**) *n.* 1) A person of great intelligence and wisdom. (*cf:* **alim**₁) 2) Extraordinary wisdom.

**pangangakkal** *n.* Someone who is in the habit of cheating.

**akkul** *v. tr. -an* To persist; persevere. *Niakkulan na pa'in e'na bo' al'kkas akatis.* She worked at it persistently so it would be quickly completed. (*Thesaurus:* **dago'os**, **sugsig** 1, **tebot**, **tuyu'** 1)

**akkula** *var. of* **appula**

**akil-balig** *n.* Someone who is not fully mature. *Kulang panguntukanna, kulang pangannal, pasal akil-balig lagi'.* Lacking good sense, lacking thought, because still immature. (*cf:* **balig**)

**akon-akon** *n.* Resentment; grudge. *Nsa' akon-akon ma deyom atayku bang ka'a-i pasōd ni deyom luma'ku.* I don't have ill-feelings inside me when you come inside my house. *Kalu aniya' akon-akon tatau'nu ma deyom ataynu pasal kala'atan bay tahinangna ma ka'a.* You may have kept some resentment in your heart because of the harm he did you. *Buwat sali' bay aku pinah'llingan mbal ahāp he' si Bi inān, min duwa min t'llu. Sali' taga akon na aku ma iya.* Sort of like when Bi there said bad things to me, two or three times. It's as though I now have ill will towards him. (*cf:* **la'at atay**; *Thesaurus:* **agmol** 1, **buli'an**₂, **koto'-koto'**, **deyom-deyom atay**, **lagod-lagod**)

**aksi** *v. intr. aN-* To sneeze. (*syn:* **pagba'anan**)

**akū** *pron.* I; me (first person singular) [Set I]. (*cf:* =**ku**, **aku**₂; *Set:* **kā**, **kām**, **kamī**, **kitā** 1, **kitabi**₁, **kitām**, **iyā**, **sigā**₁, **sigām**₁)

**aku**₁ *v. ditr.* To take responsibility for. *Saupama atilaw kita d'nda, jari binangharan kita ₱300. Bang kita bilahi ma d'nda he', na angaku na kita. Bang kita mbal angaku, pasebog na kita.* Suppose we are inquiring about a girl, and the bride price asked is ₱300. If we like the girl then we accept the conditions. If not then we back out. *Niaku e'na pagpaiskul ba'anan siyalina.* He took the responsibility of supporting his various siblings' schooling. *Ipatan kami taluwa' palkala' bo' halam aniya' ai-ai sigām, na kami ya angaku, kami na anabang pila-pila.* Our live-in helper was hit with a situation and his people had nothing, so we were the ones to take on the responsibility, to help however much. *Akuhannu kami ma sukay, ma gastu, ma kamemon, apa kami tu'ud bowanu.* You take responsibility for us in regard to fares, supplies, everything, because it is you in fact who are taking us. (*Thesaurus:*

**pagnapaka, umbang**)

**aku₂** *pron.* I; me (first person singular) [Set III]. *Duma'in ka aku bay amaka'at lilusnu.* It wasn't me who wrecked your watch. (*cf:* = **ku, akū**; *Set:* **ka'a, ka'am, kami, kita, kitabi₂, kitam, iya, sigā₂, sigām₂**)

**akup** (var. **hakup**) *v. tr.* To scoop up with one's hands. *Bang aku amangan sinanglag subay niakup. Nda'un, akupta buwattē'.* When I eat pan-roasted cassava I like to scoop it up by hand. Look, we scoop it up like so.

**ād** *n.* 1) A fence; enclosure. (*Thesaurus:* **apis 1, buluyan, koral 1, kumbangan, kumbisan, likusan, sasak 1**) 1.1) *v. tr.* To enclose with a fence. *Aniya' isāb buwa' kayu nilibun, niād ko' da'a niā'.* Fruit trees are enclosed too, fenced so as not to be taken away. *A:* "*Pamagay kagingking itū?*" *B:* "*Pagādku luma'.*" A: "What is this cane for?" B: "For me to fence the house in with." *Magtūy alubu ād pangalikus da'ira.* The fence enclosing the city was quickly broken down.

    **āran** *n.* A fenced area. *Ād itū buwat kita mareyom āran itū.* The ād referred to here is like us being inside this enclosure.

**addat** *n.* 1) Custom; courtesy; manners. *Addat kami Sama.* Our Sama customs. *Ya addat kami maitu, mbal makajari bang siyali pinah'lla'an dahū min siyaka.* Our custom here is that it is not right for the younger sister to be married before the older. 1.1) *adj. a-* Polite; courteous. *Mahē' na sali' magbowa-bowa baranna pi'ingga-pi'ingga, sali' a'addat.* While he is there conducting himself all over the place, kind of courteous. *Subay ahanunut maka a'addat panambungbi.* Your response should be gentle and polite. (*Thesaurus:* **hatul₂, hongpot, pantun 1, papat 1, p'mpon 1, saldik, saltun 1**)

**addat-tabi'at** *n.* Courtesy shown in word and action. *Halam sigā an'ppu addat-tabi'at mma' sigā sabab napsuhan sigā ma pilak.* They have not followed the speech and behavior of their father because they are seduced by money. (*Thesaurus:* **apalal, kaul-pi'il, palangay**)

**pagaddat** *n.* 1) Courtesy; good manners; respect. *Halam aniya' pagaddatna a'a inān. Anaga'-naga' ma kamastalan.* That person has no manners. He calls teachers by their personal name. 1.1) *v. tr. -an* To treat with customary respect. *Buwat magaddat, pa'anduk ni a'a alanga.* As when showing respect, nodding the head to someone of higher status. *Bang matto'ata subay pinagaddatan.* Our elders should be respected. (*Thesaurus:* **pagmamay, pagmanja', palok 1, su'ap 1.1**)

**addun** *adj. a-* 1) Well-mixed, of food. *Bang a'addun, niā' nihinang bāng-bāng, ya panyam.* When it is mixed it is taken and made into cookies, those rice cakes. 1.1) *v. tr.* To mix ingredients. *Tagna' ilū, buwas tin'ppa ni linsungan. Puwas pa'in bay tin'ppa, niayak. Na akatis bay niayak ilū, niaddun*

*na. Sokal maka bohe' pagaddun iya.* At the start it is rice pounded in the mortar. After it has been pounded it is sifted. Then when it has been sifted it is mixed. Sugar and water are used for mixing with it. *Niaddun na tirigu maka ginisan ai-ai.* The flour and various ingredients are mixed.

    **addunan** *n.* Dough; batter.

    **pagaddun** *n.* Ingredients (cooking). *Sokal maka bohe' ya pagaddun tapung hē'.* Sugar and water are the ingredients for mixing with rice flour.

**adil** *adj. a-* Right-living; observing social and religious standards. *A'adil, mbal anganjahulaka', mbal a'abbu, mbal anangkaw, mbal magputing.* Right-living; he doesn't act treacherously, doesn't brag, steal, or tell lies. *A'adil iya, sali' mbal amangan pehē'-pehē'. Subay sali' apene' kinakanna.* He is scrupulous, like he won't eat just anything. He has to be selective with what he eats. (*cf:* **bontol 1, hāp 1.1**)

    **pagadil-adil** *v. intr. aN-* To pretend to be virtuous. *Magadil-adil dīna, parahāl umbul dakayu' pamomono'.* He pretends to be virtuous, but in reality he is a top-ranking killer.

**adjak-adjak** *v. tr.* To use a variety of things. *Niadjak-adjak e'na; ni'indalupahan.* He uses a variety of things; combining things of all sorts.

**adjal** *v. tr.* To prepare food for eating.

    **pa'adjal** *v. ditr.* To get someone to prepare food.

    **pama'adjalun** *n.* A person always busy preparing food.

**adji'** *v. tr.* 1) To study religious texts. *Angadji' Kura'an, angadji' madrasa.* Studying the Holy Koran, studying a religious curriculum. 2) To engage in study generally. (*Thesaurus:* **anad 1, istadi, ta'u₁ 1.2**)

    **pangadji'** *n.* A religious education, Islamic in particular.

**adjil** *see:* **ta'adjil**

**adjung** *n.* An archaic sailing vessel. *Pagkaut na, adjung si Datu' Am bay tinunu'.* Having gone out to sea, the adjung of Datu Am was burnt. "*Aku,*" *yuk sultan, "amowa ka'am min adjungku.*" "I," said the sultan, "will bring you on my adjung."

**adjung-adjung** *n.* 1) Upper plank of a canoe. *Subay kitabi magtapi' adjung-adjung.* We should attach an upper plank [to the canoe]. 1.1) *v. tr. -an* To install canoe planking. (*Thesaurus:* **tapi' 1.1**)

**adla** *adj. a-* Elusive; untamed; hard to catch. *A'adla itū sali' mbal pasaggaw, buwat du sapi'. Subay ma l'ppahan.* Adla is when something is not catchable, such as a cow. It should be in a free-range area. *A'adla isāb manuk. Bang sinaggaw alahi saga nireyom sagmot. Paleyang, mbal tasaggaw.* Chickens too are hard to catch. When they are being caught they escape into the scrub, flying up, unable to be caught. (*cf:* **emon**)

**admit** *v. tr.* To admit a patient to hospital.

    **pa'admit** *v. tr.* To have someone admitted to hospital.

**adōy** var. of **arōy**

**aes** *n.* Ice. (*cf:* **elo 1.1**)

**aes-aes** *v. intr. aN-* To be emitting vapor, as ice or boiling water. *Subay na angais-ngais bohe' bo' yampa nihūg buwas gandum, binugbug.* It should be close to boiling before the corn rice is dropped in to make gruel. *Tibu'uk pinagtebla' bo' yampa nihūg ni kaldero angaes-ngaes bohe'na.* Whole cassava crumbled away from the whole and dropped into a pot whose water is boiling.

**aeskrīm** *n.* Ice cream.

**ag-** var. of **mag-**

**agak** *adj. a-* 1) Careful not to damage. 1.1) *v. intr. pa-* To behave with special care because something is fragile. *Pa'agak du ka bang amissala, da'a ka abagas.* You should be careful when you speak, don't be harsh. 1.2) *v. tr.* To treat something carefully. *Agakun daing. Bang kita tininduk he' daing bo' anahut naelon, subay niagak.* Treat fish carefully. When a fish strikes [our hook] and the line is light, it should be treated with care. *Angagak-ngagak ka dīnu bang ka lum'ngngan.* Take care of yourself when you are walking about. *Bang kita tininduk he' daing bo' anahut naelon, subay niagak.* When a fish strikes [our hook] and the line is light, it should be treated with care.

  **agak-agak** *adv.* Gently; cautiously. *Amissala ka agak-agak bo' mbal abati' onde'.* Talk quietly so the baby doesn't wake up.

**agad₁** var. of **lagad**

**agad₂** *adj. zero* Game of two-up. *Agad itū bang kaba' maka ta'u pinagka'ob, basta samasunsang karuwa sīn.* Agad is when the opposite faces [of two coins] are placed together, the two faces being in opposition. (*Thesaurus:* **pagkabit, pagsalla' 1.1, pagtalang, sulang₂, tingka**)

**agal-agal** *n.* Edible seaweed. *Gracilaria.* (*Thesaurus:* **gamay, gulaman**)

**agama** *n.* Religion. *A: "Ai agamabi?" B: "Kami itū Muslim."* A: "What is your religion?" B: "We are Muslims." *Ya palkala' sigām hal pagjawaban pasal agama sigām.* Their controversy is simply a discussion about their religion.

  **pagagama** *v. intr. aN-* To practice one's religion. *Panubu' sigām ilū asal maga'agama.* Their descent group have always been devoutly religious people. (*cf:* **bogbog₁ 2**; *Thesaurus:* **isbat, pagma'aripat**)

**agap₁** *n.* Parrot (various species). (*spec:* **bukay, kangag, nyuli'**)

**agap₂** *v. tr.* To grope for something in the dark. *Bay angagap d'nda si Je.* J made advances to a girl [under darkness]. *Bay angagap d'nda si Anu.* What's-his-name made advances to a girl [under darkness]. (*Thesaurus:* **gagam, gindas, sadsad 1.1, sanaw, sassaw, tangkaw 1**)

**agasi** *n.* A mythical giant. *Na agasi itū ya anganggensang a'a inān.* Now this giant was what tore that man apart. *Pagp'ssi ya agasi itū, kasabitan ya anu i', ya pagal basi' i'.* When this giant was fishing, that whatsit, that metal cage, was snagged. (*Thesaurus:* **gansuwang, saitan-lagtaw**)

**agaw** *v. intr. pa-* 1) To push in ahead of other people. *Pa'agaw aku bang at'kka mma'ku, mbal aku aiya'.* I push in when my father arrives, I have no shame. 1.1) *v. tr.* To grab or seize something. *Niagaw d'nda duma'in ka h'ndana.* He seized a woman who wasn't his wife. *Si Nu agtūy angagaw sīnku.* Nu promptly grabbed my money. (*Thesaurus:* **lolog, longkop 1.1, longpos, pagkidnap 1.1, saggaw**)

  **agaw-buwa'** *v. intr. pa-* To outgrow an older sibling.

  **pagagaw** *v. intr. aN-* To contend strenuously for the same thing. *Aheka magagaw ati halam gandum tabuwanan kami. Ala'an kami apa aiya'.* Lots of people were grabbing from each other and we were not given any corn. We left because we were ashamed. *Angkan pinagagawan e' sigām saga hayop bay tataban sigām.* That is why they struggled over the cattle they had looted.

  **pagagaw-besod** *v. intr. aN-* To argue from opposing points of view. *Magagaw-besod, mbal sigā magkole'.* Arguing from different viewpoints, neither of them winning. (*Thesaurus:* **pagbagod, pagbengtod, pagdiskās, pagjawab 1.1, pagpayod 1.1, pagsalod, pagsu'al**)

  **pagagaw-bissala** *v. intr. aN-* To be involved in a war of words. *Maglugat, sali' magagaw-bissala pariyata'.* Arguing, waging an upward tug-of-words.

  **pagagaw-napas** *v. intr. aN-* To struggle for breath. {idiom} *Bay sigām ka'amu-amu'an e'na barakat minsan iya magagaw-napas.* He prayed a blessing over them even though he was struggling for breath.

**agaw-agaw** *v. intr. pa-* To be shading into another color. *Buwat gaddung pa'agaw-agaw ni biyaning.* It's like green that is almost yellow. (*Thesaurus:* **b'ttik 1, kolol 1, walna'**)

**agay** *voc. n.* Friend; pal. (*Thesaurus:* **bagay 1, beyang, bō, gge, panon**)

  **pagagay** *v. intr. aN-* To be in a close friendship relationship.

**agkā'** *intrj.* 'Ouch!' *Bang kita tatukul anak-tanganta magtūy kita akaōnan agkā'.* When we pound a finger, we immediately say ouch. *Kap'ddi'an aku, agkā'!* I am in pain, ouch! (*cf:* **pagdahing**; *Thesaurus:* **allā, anā, arī, arōy, aruhuy, asē, ayī, dā'₁, ē**)

**agdaw** *n.* Hardwood tree species, prized for its durable timber. *Vitex sp.* (*cf:* **amulawan, kayu-soha'**)

**aggal** (var. **gaggal**) *adj. a-* 1) Slow in response to stimulus or attraction. *Mbal iya a'aggal, magtūy patūy.* He doesn't hold back, he promptly goes straight for it. *Aggal-aggal daing aninduk, ngga'i* *ka patahunanna, tu'ud aglawanan mūpū.* The fish are somewhat slow to bite, it isn't the season for them; they are just waiting for the Pleiades to appear. *Minsan kinakan, yukta agaggal.* Even of food we say that is slow to get cooked. (*Thesaurus:* **kaku', hinay-hinay, lahan 1, lallay, pagene'-ene'**) **1.1)** *v. intr. aN-* To respond slowly to stimulus.

**agi** *see:* **kapagagi, pagagi, kuma'agi**

**agid** *see:* **pagagid**

**aging** (var. **abing**) *n.* **1)** An unintended co-occurrence. *Aging itū mbal kinata'uhan, sabu itū tinu'ud.* This word *aging* refers to something not known about [beforehand], *sabu* is deliberate. **1.1)** *v. intr. pa-* To interrupt without intending to. *Buwat kita palete, dangan man dampōng dangan man dampōng, pa'aging sali' lum'ngngan.* Like when we are crossing on a walkway, one from each end, sort of interrupting by walking. *Yuk dangan, "Amaindam ka tukul." Yuk isāb dangan, "Ōy, pa'aging ka. Itiya' isāb indamanku itū."* One says, "Let me borrow a hammer." The other says, "Hey, you're butting in. Here am I borrowing it too." *Pa'aging pasōd, ameya' ma a'a anambal.* Entering and getting in the way, along with people getting treatment. **1.2)** *v. tr. -an* To interrupt what another is doing. *Maghinang kita bo' aniya' pi'itu atawa angalingan, na mbal tatalusta bay hinangta. Niagingan kita he' bay angalingan.* We are doing something when someone comes by or calls out, then we cannot finish what we are doing. We are interrupted by the one calling out.

**pagaging** *v. intr. aN-* To interrupt each other's activity.

**agmol** *n.* **1)** Feeling of resentment. (*Thesaurus:* **akon-akon, buli'an₂, koto'-koto', deyom-deyom atay, lagod-lagod**) **1.1)** *v. tr. -an* To feel resentment towards someone. *Niagmolan, sali' mbal paluwas himumūngan, sali' magbogon-magbogon.* Held as a grudge, as when no word is uttered but hard feelings are being nursed.

**agmot-agmot** *n.* **1)** Resentment; an attitude of blame. **1.1)** *v. tr. -an* To hold someone responsible. *Saula na alungay bangka'na, aku ya niagmot-agmotan kono' bay ang'llo', parahāl tu'ud bay talaran.* Just because his canoe is missing, I am held responsible for having taken it, when in fact it just drifted away.

**agod** *v. tr.* To use a paddle as a lever or rudder when sailing across wind. *Subay min pabanogan bo' angagod. Saupama pelang maka banog, bo' bang aniya' baliyu mbal pa'agod bang ariki' busay.* We must be in a sailing vessel to *agod.* In a canoe with a sail, for example, when there is wind, it cannot be paddled across wind if the paddle is small. *Busay ya pagagod, bihing pelang ya pagagoran.* A paddle is the lever, the edge of the canoe is what you lever against. *Saupama pelang maka banog, bo' bang aniya' baliyu mbal*

*pa'agod bang ariki' busay.* A canoe under sail, for example, but unable to sail across wind if the paddle is small. (*Thesaurus:* **biluk 1.1, bintung 1, kabig, kauk, timpas**)

**pagagod** *n.* A pivot; fulcrum; rudder. *Busay ya pagagod, bihing pelang ya pagagoran.* A paddle is the rudder; the edge of the canoe is the fulcrum.

**agol** *n.* Mantle of certain shellfish. *Agol kima, ya palē inān, ya lapis kulitna. Aniya' isāb ma sirap.* The mantle of clams, the bit that slides, the film of its shell. Mussels have them too.

**agon** *adv.* Almost but not quite.

**agon-agon** *adv.* Nearly but not completely. *Bo' kasehe'anbi ilū tinugutan amole' amowa balanja' ma saga anak-h'ndabi, ya agon-agon patay otas.* Some of you will be allowed to go home to take supplies to your families who are about to die of hunger. *Pangisihan ndang, ya agon-agon abustak.* Worn-out containers, the ones ready to burst open. *Agon-agon aku alembo ma tahik.* I almost drowned in the sea. *Bang aku lum'ngngan bo' ap'ddi' kōkku, agon-agon aku lumigid.* When I am walking and I have a headache, I almost slip off the trail.

**sa'agon-agon** *conj.* About to; on the point of happening; as though done already.

**agon mbal** (var. **mbal agon**) *adv. phrase* Almost impossible. {idiom} *Bang kami atulak ni kapū'an dilaut, mbal agon ta'nda' Būd Siganggang itū.* When we leave for the islands out to sea, Siganggang Peak here is almost impossible to see. *Bang sakalina a'a inān maghinang mbal agon kasekotan.* When that fellow is absorbed in working he can slmodt impossible to approach. *Mbal na agon makaliyu d'nda man ina'na, subay lungbus mahal.* The girl can scarcely leave her mother, [therefore] the parents share of the bride-wealth should be fully paid. *Sagō' agon iya mbal makal'ngngan pagka mbal biyaksa.* But he was almost unable to walk because he was not accustomed to it. *Magtūy tak'bbal atayna, sali' alungay pangannalna, mbal agon makapam'nnal ma bay pangahaka ma iya.* He was immediately shocked, as though he had lost the power of thought, almost unable to believe what had been told him. (*Thesaurus:* **apit, arāk, himan-himan**)

**agpang** (var. **appang**) *n.* **1)** Defensive barrier. *Bang aniya' pat'nna' ai-ai bo' ma bihingan lamisahan, bo' halam aniya' agpangna, ahūg bang bay tajogjog.* If there are things placed on the side of the table, and it has no barrier, it will fall when shaken. (*Thesaurus:* **babag 2, lapad**) **1.1)** *v. tr. -an* To defend against movement or ball. *Bang magbasketbol na, agpangin pahāp kuntara ilu bo' mbal maka'agaw bola.* When playing basketball, block the opponent well so he cannot steal the ball.

**pagagpang** *v. tr.* To block or mark players of an opposing team. *Buwat magbalatin bang walu'* *puhu', mpat-mpat magagpang.* Like when playing a blocking game with eight people, four block the other four.

**agpot** *v. tr. -an* **1)** To coerce; to force to do. *Da'a na agpotin, ingga na baya'na ameya'.* Don't force him, he will go when wants. (*Thesaurus:* **abiyug, angin, egot-egot, logos 1, panhot, p'ggong, poleggaw**) **1.1)** *v. advrs. ka-...-an* To be caught in the act of doing something wrong. *Ka'agpotan, ta'abut anangkaw.* Caught in the act, come upon while stealing. (*cf:* **kara-kara₂**)

**agsāy** (var. **magsāy**) *adv.* Immediately; promptly. *Agsāy makasampig ni batu.* Struck a rock right away. *Agsāy amūng Lannang inān, yukna, "Subay na kam atulak bo' kam angutang sīn sabab ilu na kām at'kka baha'u."* The Chinese man there promptly spoke up, saying, "You have to be leaving [on a fishing expedition] for you to borrow money, because you have just recently arrived." *Magtūy binono' l'lla inān agsāy isāb amatay.* That man was immediately struck and immediately died. *Yuk si Ina', "Papole'un daing ilū, am'lli ka saddī." Agsāy iya am'lli daing baki'.* Mother said, "Put that fish back, buy something else." He promptly bought catfish. (*Thesaurus:* **dai'-dai'an, magtūy, sakadjap, saru'un-du'un, sigla' 1**)

**agtūy** var. of **magtūy**

**agung** *n.* **1)** Large brass gong. *Bang agung subay nilisag.* An *agung* should be struck with a rhythm. (*Thesaurus:* **buwa₁, kulintangan, gandang 1, titik 1**) **1.1)** *v. tr. -an* To accompany dancing with gong music. *Pa'agungun a'a ina'an, pas'lle'un.* Let that man play the gong, give him a turn. *Subay niagungan bo' ahāp kinale.* It should be accompanied by a rhythmic gong so it sounds good. *Bang d'nda magpangigal subay niagungan bo' ahāp kinale.* When women dance they should be accompanied by a rhythmic gong so it sounds good.

**aguwanta** *adj. zero* **1)** Able to do difficult work. *Aguwanta pahāp ka, bang hal hīs mint'dda!* You are certainly dominant, if it's only one win! **1.1)** *v. tr. -an* To manage difficult work. *Mbal tōp hinangku bang ngga'i ka katōpan ma aku, sabab ya buhatna palabi min kosogku. Mbal ka'aguwantahanku.* It is not appropriate for me to do something if it doesn't suit [my abilities], because its weight exceeds my strength. I cannot handle it. *A: "Sambutin mannilu, aguwantahin to'ongan." B: "Oy. Da'a patugutun. Aguwantahin min diyata' ilu."* A: "Take it as it comes down, control it completely." B: "Hey, don't let it come down. Control it from up there." *Mbal ka'aguwantahanku. Palabi buhatna min kosogku.* I cannot manage it. Its weight exceeds my strength. (*Thesaurus:* **anggap 1, anggop₂, bāng-bāng₁, bogbog₂, kole', gaga, tigayu'**)

**ahā** *intrj.* Interjection of surprise or fulfilment. *Ahā, sakali ta'abut Buli'-Lakit subay iya amowa pabīng.*

Well now, as soon as we got to Rock Point he must have us go back.

**Ahad** *n.* Sunday. (*cf:* **pitu'an**; *Thesaurus:* **Alba'a, Hammis, Isnin, Juma'at, Sabtu', Salasa**)

**aha'an** *n.* Emperor fish (of various kinds). *Lethrinus lentjan.* (*gen:* **kutambak**)

**ahat** *v. intr. pa-* **1)** To be somewhat able. **1.1)** *v. tr.* To do part of what is required. *A: "Maka'abut ka bahā' amat'nna' bubung ma diyata' luma' ilu?" B: "Ahatku bang mbal akosog baliyu."* A: "Can you reach as far as putting the roof ridge on top of the house there?" B: "I may do some of it if the wind isn't strong." *Akomay, mbal maka'ahatan dīna. Makalandu' abuhat bay bowana.* Feeble, unable to attempt it himself. What he carried was excessively heavy. (*Thesaurus:* **sulay₁ 1.1, tara'-tara'**)

**ahat-ahat** *v. intr. pa-* To develop bit by bit.

**ahāy** (var. **hahāy**) *intrj.* Sigh of fatigue or frustration. *Puwas ē' pahangad iya ni langit bo' anganapas paheya. Ahāy!* After that he looked up toward the sky and breathed a great sigh. Whew!

**ahil** *n.* Present times; the modern world. *Awal ni ahil.* From ancient times to the present. (*cf:* **awal₁, timpu 1**; *Thesaurus:* **tahun baha'u**)

**ahil-jāman** *n.* Modern times; nowadays. *Karupangan ya maumu nihinang he' saga kasubulan ma ahil jāman itū.* The foolish things that are so often done by teenage lads these days.

**ahin** var. of **hain**

**ahirat** (var. **hairat**) *n.* The afterworld (after death). *Bang kita amatay, bo' kita pinole'an na ni ahirat, tinilaw kita bang ai bay hinangta ma junna itū.* When we die and have been returned to the afterworld, we will be asked what we did here on earth. *Sidda landu' sigām ahalga' ma jantung kami min dunya sampay ahirat.* They are precious in our hearts from earth to heaven. *Minsan kita mbal pa'ddas maitu, amole' du ni ahirat.* Though we are not here permanently, we will go home to the afterworld.

**ahit** var. of **hait**

**aho'** *adv.* **1)** Yes. (*cf:* **mbal 1**) **1.1)** *v. intr. aN-* To assent to. *Hal angaho'.* [She] just says yes. **1.2)** *v. tr. -an* To give assent to something. *Angkan niaho'an e'na bay janji'na.* That's why he says yes to his previous promises.

**ahud-ahud** (var. **gahud-gahud₂**) *adj. -an* **1)** Seen faintly; barely visible. *Gahud-gahuran, atā ni'nda'.* Partly obscured, seen far off in the distance. **1.1)** *v. intr. aN-* To become hazy or cloudy. *Angahud-ngahud, sali' atā, buwat kita ak'tta-k'tta min Tiyanggi tudju ni Malusu', pariki'-pariki' pang'nda'ta Būd Tumantangis.* It is almost out of sight, as though far off, like when we set out for Malusu from Jolo. What we see of Mount Tumantangis gets less and less. *Ya ma tahik,* *bang saupama kita patuhun llaw itu, at'llak. Bang sangom angulan, ati kaut kita patuhun pabīng, angahud-ngahud deyom tahik. Hatina mbal at'llak, mbal angaut. Ma t'ngnga'.* In the sea, if for example we dive today, it's clear. If it rains overnight and we go out to sea and dive again, the sea is discolored. In other words it is not clear and not turbid. It is between the two. *Angahud-ngahud, buwat kita ak'tta min Tiyanggi tudju ni Malusu', pariki'-pariki' pang'nda'ta Būd Tumantangis.* It becames hard to see, like when we set out from Jolo for Maluso, our view of Mount Tumantangis gets smaller and smaller. (*Thesaurus:* **abu-abu₂, buraw, hanaw-hanaw, pagba'ung-ba'ung**)

**ahun₁** var. of **haun₁**

**ahun₂** var. of **haun₂**

**ai** *interrog.* What? *Ai kakannu?* What are you eating? (*Thesaurus:* **angay, buwattingga 1.1, magay, maingga, sai, sumiyan**)

**ai ba** *intrj.* What happens now? {idiom} *Ai ba, mangkinna sin'nsong, mangkinna paheya geret pelang inān.* Guess what, the more it was caulked, the bigger the hole in that canoe became.

**ai bang ai** *n. phrase* Whatever; this or that. {idiom}

**ai ka itū** *phrase* Guess what. {idiom} *Hayak-hayakan aku aholat pat'nna' ma lahat itū, halam aniya' lengogna. Ai ka itū, aniya' du pa'in.* I was disappointed in what I hoped from settling in this place, no troubles. But guess what, there is always something!

**ai lagi'** *phrase* What else? What next? {idiom} *Ai lagi', dorok gandum.* What else but corn rice.

**ai maka ai** *n. phrase* Whatever; anything. {idiom} *Halam ganta' bay ai maka ai, taggaha' hal palintuwad.* Though perhaps nothing whatsoever had happened, he suddenly fell prostrate.

**ai na ka** *conj.* Whatever; this or that. {idiom} *Bowa-bowahanna, ai na ka manusiya', ai na ka panyap.* The characteristic behavior of something, whether it's a person or equipment. *K'llut-k'llut bang at'ggol ma tahik, ai na ka tangan ai na ka tape'.* Wrinkled skin when in the sea for a long time, whether it is hands or feet. *Angangganding ni p'ttung na ka, ni tu'ung na ka.* Beating time on a section of bamboo or on a wooden box.

**ai po'on** *neg.* 'On the contrary; no way!' {idiom} *A: "Sai bay angahinang kappal pasōran ba'anan hayop?" B: "Nā si Nabi Musa." A: "Ai po'on, si Nabi Nū!"* A: "Who built the ship for all the animals to go in?" B: "The Prophet Moses." A: "Not so, it was the Prophet Noah!" (*Thesaurus:* **ballum, duma'in, mbal 1.1, m'ssa', ngga'i ka**)

**ai-ai** *n.* 1) Whatever; something or other. *Halam ganta' bay makani-ai-ai, taggaha' makabuwattitu.* It wasn't supposed that anything at all was going on, then this suddenly happened. *Bay kami katangakawan ai-ai.* We were robbed of various things. *Sinuwal ai-ai man deyo'ta. Suwal* refers to anything levered up from below us. 2) Things; possessions. *Aheka ai-aina.* He has many possessions.

**ai..ai** *phrase* This or that. {idiom} *Amene' ka, ai sinokalan, ai nilahingan.* Your choice, whether it should have sugar or grated coconut on it.

**pag-ai** *v. intr.* aN- To be in what kinship relationship with someone. *A: "Mag-ai kam?" B: "Magkaki kami min t'dda."* A: "What kin are you to each other?" B: "We are first cousins."

**Aid ul Pitri** *n. phrase* Holy day at the end of Ramadan. (*syn:* **Hailaya Puwasa₁**)

**ail** *v. tr.* -an To carry out ritual washing in preparation for prayer. *Bang magsambahayang subay magail dahū. Kinose'an na tangan sigā saga tape' sigā, talinga.* When praying, people should wash first. They wash their hands, their feet, ears too. (*Thesaurus:* **istinja', junub, peppet, puppu'**)

**pagail** *v. intr.* aN- To carry out ritual ablutions in preparation for prayer. *Bang magsambahayang subay magail dahū; kinose'an na tangan sigā, saga tape' sigā, talinga.* When people pray they should first carry out ablutions, washing their hands, feet, and ears.

**aisa** *n.* Evening prayer time. (*Thesaurus:* **asal, luhul₁, magrib 1, subu₂ 2**)

**ā'** (var. **hā'; nā'; ngā'**) 1) *v. tr.* To take or get something. *Ngā'un na, ma ka'a. Aniya' du ma aku.* Take it, it's for you. I have some too. 2) *v. tr.* -an To take something from a person (as a guarantee). *Ngā'in s'mmek sin a'a ya amiyarulan a'a liyu.* Take the garment of a man who goes guarantor for a stranger. 3) *v. tr.* To reach a goal or result. *Timbang wa'i atā min Manubal. Bang ahāp baliyu ta'ā' dang'llaw.* The open sea is far from Manubal. It can be reached in a day if the wind is favorable. (*cf:* **abut₂ 1**) 4) *v. advrs.* ka-...-an To be fined for an offense. *Bay kami ka'ā'an duwampū' pilak.* We were fined twenty pesos [lit. had twenty pesos taken from us].

**ā' h'nda** *v. tr.* To take a woman as wife. {idiom} *Si Mi, ya bay ngā'nu h'nda, sinokatan pahangdon bulawan.* Household goods of gold were the brideprice required for Mi whom you took to be your wife. *Damikiyanna saga anakna l'lla, bay ningā'an d'nda min bangsa saddi' pamah'nda sigām.* Likewise his sons, women were obtained for them from foreigners to be their wives.

**ā' la'at** *v. tr.* To take offense at. {idiom} *Hal aku amina'in, ati ngā'nu la'at.* I was only talking and you take offense.

**a'a** *n.* Person; human being. *Halam gi' aku a'a.* I was not yet a person [i.e. not yet born]. *Bang aniya' bahonos takalenu ma kariyata'an kayu inān sali' a'a magmahil, parugpak na kām.* Dad, there was someone in the market asking about you. *Bang aniya' bahonos takalenu sali' a'a magmahil, paragan kām!* When you hear rustling like the noise of people marching, run! *Buwat a'a alanga bo' areyo' lawang, subay iya pa'anduk bo' mbal sumantuk kōkna.* Like a tall man when the doorway is low, he should duck so he doesn't hit his head. (*Thesaurus:* **baran₂ 1, manusiya' 1, puhu' 1**)

**kapaga'a** *n.* Everything to do with one's status as a human being.

**pagka'a'a** *n.* Typical human behavior.

**a'a duwata** *n. phrase* Person in whom a duwata spirit is present. *Subay a'a duwata aningkō' apa iya ya pasōran jin.* It has to be a *duwata* medium who sits [on the ritual mat] because he is the one to be possessed by a djinn. *Binowa kita ni duwata bo' supaya kita pa'bba.* We are taken to a *duwata* person so that we will get well.

**a'a liyu** *n. phrase* Stranger; outsider; foreigner. *Pasagarinbi saga a'a liyu anakod buwa' kayu ma tana'bi.* Allow strangers to gather fruit from your property.

**a'a man deyo'** *n. phrase* Deep-sea spirit being. {idiom} *Ang'tting itū, sinōd he' a'a man deyo'.* This bloated state is the result of being entered by the being from the depths. (*cf:* **Ladja Sulayman**)

**a'a talus** *n. phrase* Person with prophetic gift of interpreting what is unknown. *A'a talus magtatali' uppi.* A seer who is an interpreter of dreams.

**alā** *var. of* **allā**

**alab-alab** *v. tr. -an* To be familiar with. *Lahat itu halam bay ka'alab-alaban e' matto'a kami.* This land was not well known by our forebears. (*Thesaurus:* **himangkan, ingat, pamapatahan, panghati, ta'u₁ 1**)

**alak** *n.* Alcoholic drinks. *Alak itū apa'it, sali' p'ddu daing ssana.* The *alak* referred to is bitter, it tastes like fish bile. (*Thesaurus:* **bil, binu, toba'**)

**alal 1)** *adj. a-* Taking a long time. *A'alal he'ta atulak.* We are taking a long time to leave. *A'alal ko' pagkamatay a'a itū.* The dying of this person is long drawn out. **2)** *v. advrs. -in-* To be suffering a delay. *Nialal ma kamatayna.* Delayed in his dying.

**alam₁** *n.* The earth; the physical world. *Ma alam dakayu' itū.* In this present world. (*Thesaurus:* **ayan, dunya, langit**)

**alam₂** *var. of* **halam₁**

**alam deyo'** *n. phrase* The environment beneath the sea. {idiom} *Alam diyata', mag'ntanan tana'. Alam deyo', saga magpam'ssi, ya mag'ntanan daing.* The world above is the sphere of those who work with soil. The world below is the sphere of those who use hook and line, who work with fish.

**alam diyata'** *n. phrase* The environment above sea level. {idiom}

**alam-pinole'** *n.* World to which all go home. *Alam pinole', ya na ahirat. Alam diyata', mag'ntanan tana'. Saga magpam'ssi, ang'ntanan daing. Ahirat,* that's the afterworld. The lands above are [the sphere of] those who are involved with land. The fishermen, they are involved with fish. *Alam pinole', ya na ahirat.* The world to which all return, that's *ahirat.* (*Thesaurus:* **sulga'**)

**alamat₁** *v. intr. aN-* To tell the future using divination. *Angalamat kita bo' supaya kata'uhanta kahāpan maka kala'atan. Bang ahāp, sinōng, bang ala'at nibbahan.* We use divination so we can know good times and bad times. If good then we proceed, if bad then we abandon [the plan]. *Bang llaw Juma'at subay angalamat dahū bo' yampa patūd. Bang ala'at e'ta ang'nda' putika'an subay da'a sinōngan l'ngngan.* When it is a Friday we should consult by divination first before setting sail. If what we see in the divination is bad, the journey should not be continued. *Llaw, sangom, makajari kita angalamat, basta duma'in ugtu-llaw atawa tonga'-bahangi.* Day or night, it's okay for us to use divination, so long as it's not [right on] noon or midnight. (*Thesaurus:* **kamot, limal, pag'nda'₂, putika'**)

**alamat₂** *n.* Respectful opening to a letter. *Alamat sulat itū deyo' min kami magtai'anak, angan-angan tudju ni ka'am.* This letter comes from our family, hopefully to you all.

**alambre** *n.* Wire netting; barbed wire. *Aniya' pilisu pap'ssut min ka'alambrehan.* A prisoner has slipped through the barbed wire enclosure.

**alang-alang** (var. **āng-āng**) *adv.* Hesitant.

**pagalang-alang** *v. intr. aN-* To be hesitant or undecided about some course of action. *Da'a ka magalang-alang. Bang b'llinu, dūlin na.* Don't be hesitant. If you are going to buy, then accept [the asking price]. *Apasu' kaldero bo' aniya' ngā'ku mareyom. Magāng-āng tanganku pako'ot apa ina'an apasu'.* The pot is hot and I have something to get out of it. My hand is hesitant about dipping in because it is hot.

**alas** *n.* Ace (of cards). *Lubakin doble alas.* Put down a pair of aces.

**alat-alat** *v. tr. -an* To decorate with paint.

**Alba'a** *n.* Wednesday. (*Thesaurus:* **Ahad, Hammis, Isnin, Juma'at, Sabtu', Salasa**)

**alkohol** *n.* **1)** Alcohol, as a lighting fuel or household solvent. *Karalletan alkohol, halam ni'nda' ai-ai pa'alung.* The alcohol caught fire, the things by the fire weren't noticed. **1.1)** *v. tr. -an* To fuel with alcohol. *Subay nialkoholan kulaet bo' akeyat.* The lantern needs to have alcohol put into it in order to give light.

**ali'an** *n.* A critical comment.

**pagali'an** *v. tr. -an* To voice criticism of someone. *Bang aniya' palabay, magali'anan kita ma a'a. Bang takale, ala'at, agbono' sadja. "Angay ka," yuk palabay i', "magali'an ma aku?"* When people are passing by, and we say something negative about some person. If it is heard, things are bad, leading inevitably to a fight. "Why," says the person passing by, "are you saying bad things about me?" *Buwat kami maka bitu'anunku, magali'an sigām atawa kami ya magali'an.* Like my divorced wife and me, they criticize me or we're the ones that criticize. *Pagpatay h'lla si Ab, magtūy iya magh'lla. Pinagali'anan iya e' kasehe'an, yuk-i, "Õy d'nda inān magtūy magh'lla."* When Ab's husband died, she immediately married. She was criticised by others, who said, "That woman, she got married right away."

**alim**₁ *n.* A person with supernormal knowledge and abilities; a seer. *A'a alim, minsan du mbal ata'u, sali' kinata'uhan he'na kamemon. Sali' atalus ba.* A seer, even though he hasn't known, sort of knows everything. He is like someone who sees the future. *Mbal kita makapah'lling ni alim, sali' halam aniya' pangita'uta. Sali' kamal kita.* We cannot speak to a seer, it is like we have no understanding of our own. It is as though we are deprived of speech. (*cf:* **barakkal 1**)

**alim**₂ *v. tr.* To take away someone's faculties; to make someone vanish. *Nila'anan pangannalta he' saitan, ya na nialim.* A demon took away our minds, that's what it means to be *alim*-ed. *Halam na mma'na onde'-onde' ilū, yuk suli-suli, bay kono' nialim ma dilaut.* That child no longer has a father, it is said that he was lost at sea [by a spirit]. *Nila'anan pangannalta he' saitan, ya na nialim. Sinaitan kita bang kita nialim.* A demon took away our minds, that's what it means to experience *alim*. We get done by some spirit being. (*cf:* **talap, t'kkob**)

**alimata** *v. tr. -an* To keep careful watch over someone. *Mbal ka'alimatahanta onde'-onde' bang ata'u magdeyo'-diyata'.* We can no longer keep a watch over children once they know how to climb up and down. (*Thesaurus:* **jaga 1.2, papag, peyan, tunggu' 1.1**)

**alimpunus** (*var.* **halimpunus**) *n.* Whirlwind over land. *Alimpunus itū min deyo', tabowa bagunbun pariyata'. Hunus sali' baliyu, bo' akosog du isāb.* A whirlwind is from below, with dust being carried up. A squall is like a wind, but it is strong too. *Tauwa' ka halimpunus!* You'll be struck by a whirlwind [said as a curse]! *Ameya' alimpunus itū ma badju, makah'bba' luma' isāb, sali' linug.* These whirlwinds come with wind, causing houses to collapse, like an earthquake. (*Thesaurus:* **boto'-boto'**₁, **buhawi'**₂ **1, kawas-kawas**)

**alis** *n.* Decorative black lines on skin.

**pagalis-alis** *v. tr. -an* To beautify a bride or groom with an artificial hair line and black marking. *Pinagalis-alisan bayhu' pangantin. Bang ngga'i ka pangantin mbal ka'alis-alisan.* Couples about to be married have their faces decorated with black paste [of soot]. If they are not a bridal couple they can't be decorated. (*Thesaurus:* **ari-ari 1, atal**)

**alistu** *adj. zero* **1)** Agile; dexterous. *Alistu aku magkalga.* I am quick at carrying goods. *Bang ka binowa magbola he' kasehe'annu, subay ka alistu ma laslaen ko' mbal kahūgan bola.* When you are brought in by your mates to play volleyball, if you are on the backline you must be agile so as not to be hit by a falling ball. (*Thesaurus:* **tangkis 1**) **1.1)** *v. intr. pa-* To be brisk or agile. *Pa'alistu ka bo' kita mbal taramuli.* Be agile so we are not left behind. **1.2)** *v. advrs. ka-...-an* To be outdone in speed and agility. *Mbal ka'alistuhan bang ero'.* A dog cannot be outdone in speed and agility.

**allā** (*var.* **alā**) *intrj.* Expression of dismay or surprise. *Allā, mbal aku am'lli bang buwattilu.* No way, I'm not buying if that's how it is. *Allā, magmahi si Delila ma si Samson, yukna, "Yukna in aku kalasahannu, saguwā' mbal aku pangandolannu."* Unexpectedly, Delilah complained to Samson, saying, "You said you loved me, but you don't trust me." *Alā! Ilu na llaw akeyat, pasilak na.* Hey, look! There is the sun shining and giving warmth. (*Thesaurus:* **agkā', allō, anā, arī, arōy, aruhuy, asē, ayī, dā'**₁, **ē**)

**Allah** *n.* God, the Supreme Being. (*cf:* **Tuhan**; *syn:* **Allahu Ta'ala 1**)

**Allahu Ta'ala** *n. phrase* **1)** God Most High. (*syn:* **Allah**) **2)** God's name.

**allō** (*var.* **alō**) *intrj.* Expression of surprise. *Pagpi' ni bohe' i', "Allō," yukna, "sahabbat."* Arriving at the water hole, he says, "Aha, friend." *Alō! Ilu na llaw akeyat, pasilak na.* Wow, there is the sun shining, giving out heat. *Allō, bang pasah'mpu ba'anan a'a, na mbal tagaga niatuhan.* Wow! When a group of people cooperate they cannot be fought against. *Alō, kami bay mahē' ma kubul, angobol-ngobol sundukna e' langaw.* Gross! When we were there at the grave, its marker was swarming with flies. (*Thesaurus:* **allā**)

**allō dayang** *intrj.* Expression of concern among women; 'Oh dear!' {idiom}

**almas** *n.* Weapons; firearms. *Almas itū sinapang, panimbak. Bang kalis, barung itū, pakokos.* An *almas* is a rifle, something for shooting. A kris or a cutlass is something worn as a hand weapon. *Almas isāb kalis, budjak, basta pangatu.* A kris and a spear are also *almas*, if used for fighting back. (*Thesaurus:* **hinanib 1, pakokos, pangatu, takos 1**)

**Almasi** *n.* The Messiah or Chosen One; Christ. (*cf:* **Isa Almasi**)

**Almasihin** *n.* A follower of Christ; a Christian. (*cf:* **Kristyan**; *Thesaurus:* **Isa Almasi**)

**almirul** (*var.* **amirul**) **1)** *n.* Laundry starch. *Bay na ginipitan panggi', sinaud bohe'na. Ubus ya bohe' i' pinato'ong mareyom undam. Binu'usan bohe'na, ya ta'bba ē', ya na halina tahinang amirul.* When the cassava has been squeezed, its liquid is caught. The liquid is then left to settle in a basin. Its water is tipped out and what is left is the *hali*, made into laundry starch. *Am'gga' kita bohe' panggi' nihinang hali pangamirul kakana'.* We squeeze out liquid from boiled cassava, which is made into hali for starching cloth. (*Thesaurus:* **kanji', sakkul**) 2) *v. tr.* To starch clothing. *Akatis bay angamirul, na nīllawan s'mmek ē'. Na bang atoho' na, pinilinsa na.* After starching, the clothes are put out in the sun. Then when dry they are ironed.

**alō** var. of **allō**

**alod₁** *adj.* a- Obstinate; inflexible. *A'alod, sali' ahunit.* Uncooperative, difficult [to deal with]. *A'alod kandaru itū, sali' ahunit.* This lock is stubborn, hard [to open]. (*Thesaurus:* **k'llas 1.1, gagga, tuwas 1**)

**alod₂** 1) *v. tr.* To straighten or shape a long item by wedging one end into a gap and applying force to the free end. *Bahangi-di'ilaw, bay angalod disi A batangan bangka'na.* The day before yesterday, A and others bent the [steel] outrigger booms of his canoe into shape. 1.1) *v. intr.* pa- To jam or wedge into a confined space. *Pa'alod na asal siput. Bay aku amahāp malkina si Babu' Pa.* The bolt was in fact jammed. I had been fixing an engine. *Aheka pelang ka, hāg ka, tunggul ka, mbal pasuhut pelangta. Pa'alod munda'na.* Whether it's a lot of canoes, or a house post, or a stump, the canoe won't come away. Its bow is wedged tight. 1.2) *v. tr.* -an To remove something by levering it out. *Yuk onde', "Angaloran aku tape'ku ma lantay."* The child said, "I'm levering my foot out from the floor slats." *Mbal pasuhut pelang, pa'alod munda'na. Subay nialod-aloran pinabontol.* The canoe won't come away, its bow is wedged tight, it should be levered out gently and kept straight. 2) *v. tr.* -an To secure one end of a long item to facilitate straightening. *Aniya' p'ttung taga bengkok, subay nialoran ma hāg bo' atilud.* A length of bamboo has a bend in it, it should be levered against a post to straighten.

**alom** *n.* 1) A bruise; hematoma. *Alom itū sali' ma llot ettom maka keyat.* A bruise shows between black and red. (*Thesaurus:* **lahod 1**) 1.1) *v. intr.* aN- To show dark under the skin. *Bang aniya' amah'llingan aku, angalom bayhu'ku, sali' ala'at s'mmuku.* When someone scolds me my face becomes dark red, and I look angry. *Angalom aku, sali' angal'ddom baranku, sali' ni'ila.* I am becoming red, as though my body is becoming dark, as though I have been birthmarked. 1.2) *v. tr.* -an To bruise by striking. *Bang aku bantungnu maka papan ma bukutku, nialoman aku. Mbal na paluwas laha'.* When you hit me in the back with a plank, I am bruised. The blood doesn't come out.

**alop₁** *v. tr.* To face someone. *Angalop aku ka'a.* I come into your presence. *Bay alopnu si Se di'ilaw.* You confronted Se yesterday. *Alopku taepan.* I face what is being typed. (*Thesaurus:* **anggop₁, arap, atubang 1, bayhu' 1.1, harap₁ 1.2**)

**alopan₁** *n.* Someone's physical presence; the area in front. (*cf:* **hadarat**; *Thesaurus:* **dahū'an 1, harapan₁, munda'an₁**)

**alopan₂** *n.* The genital area of a person's body. (*Thesaurus:* **kamama'u, harapan₂, munda'an₂**)

**pagalop** *v. tr.* To be face to face with each other; to be opposite. *Itiya' kita magalop. Ai gara'?* Here we are facing each other. What is there to discuss? *Binila' duwa bo' yampa pinapagalop bila'anna.* Divided into two and the divided pieces placed opposite each other. *Maginalopan kami.* We are looking at each other. (*cf:* **pagbilma'arup**; *Thesaurus:* **pagharap, pag'nda'₁, paglambung, pagtampal**)

**pagalopan** *n.* A face-to-face situation; a public context. *Da'a na aku paki'un ma pagalopan. Bang aku apaki' e'nu, magbono' kita.* Don't embarrass me in public. If you cause me embarassment we will fight.

**pagpatialop** *v. intr.* aN- To humble oneself in the presence of a superior. (*cf:* **pagpatihantak 1, pagsarahakan**)

**patialopun** *adj.* Very approachable.

**sama'alop** *adj.* To be face to face with someone.

**alop₂** 1) *n.* A feeling of tightness. *Nialop bayhu'ta. Aniya' alop llaw, aniya' alop api. Amigtal kuwitta.* Our faces feel tight. There is sun tightness, and a fire tightness. Our skin pulls taut. 2) *v. advrs.* -in- Feeling stretched or tight; taut. *Bang kita bay mag'llaw, binorakan maka buwas bo' ala'an alopta.* When we have been exposed to the sun, we apply rice paste to take away our feeling of tightness.

**alperel** (var. **alpiril**) *n.* Safety pin; brooch fastener. (*cf:* **kait 1**)

**alpiril** var. of **alperel**

**alta'** 1) *n.* Wealth; riches. *Ta'abut pinah'nda'an, yuk matto'a l'lla ya kinawin inān, "Kimmatin aku alta'ta. Kalu maka'abut dakayu' d'nda."* When the betrothal [stage] arrives, the elder of the man being married, says, "Give me an estimate of our resources. Maybe it will suffice for one woman." *Yuk matto'a l'lla ya kinawin inān, "Kimmatin aku alta'ta. Kalu maka'abut dakayu' d'nda."* The elder of the man being married says, "Give me an estimate of our resources. Maybe it will suffice for one woman." (*Thesaurus:* **kaniya', karaya 1, pagsauragal 1.1**) 1.1) *adj.* a-/-an Rich; affluent. *A'alta' a'a ina'an, hatina aheka alta'na.* That man is wealthy, in other words he has a lot of possessions. 1.2) *v. intr.* aN- To become wealthy. *Angusaha aku bo' aku angalta'.* I will work for a living so I get rich. 2) *v. advrs.* ka-...-an To have a financial penalty imposed. *Bang kita mbal bilahi pakawin, ka'alta'an kita.* If we are unwilling to get married [after agreeing], a fine is imposed on us.

**alta'-kalun** *n.* Natural resources (of land or sea). *Bang buwat a'a aheka usaha bo' hal sigām-sigām amangan iya. Halam magsarakka, halam saga magsarang-sukul. Bang asaki na bo' halam bay makapaghinang, ya na manukut sigā-i alta'-kalun.* Like people who have a good income but eat it all themselves. They don't give alms and don't offer thanks. When they get sick and haven't performed the ceremony, it is the natural resources demanding payment.

**pagalta'an** *v. intr. aN-* 1) To enjoy or experience wealth. 1.1) *v. tr.* To make someone wealthy. *Pinagalta'an kita he' Tuhan.* People are made wealthy by God.

**pangalta'** *n.* Wealth; riches.

**alti** *adj.* *-an* Beautiful; lovely. *Mbal manjari niōnan "Lingkatan pahāp l'lla inān" atawa "altihan l'lla." Subay "Ahāp l'lla."* It is not correct to say, "That man is so beautiful" or "so elegant". It should be "A fine man." *Altihan pahāp mandal ilū.* That kite there is really beautiful. (*Thesaurus:* **dorog₂ 1.1, hansam, hāp baran, himpit, jalang₁, lingkat 1.1, manis 1.1, polma 1.1**)

**pagalti-alti** *n.* 1) Adornments; decorations. 1.1) *v. intr. aN-* To draw attention to one's beauty. *Asidda aku magalti-alti bang aku ni M'ddas, sali' aku amahāp dīku.* I show myself off when I go to Siasi Town, as though I am making myself so fine. *Aebog aku ma ka'a, ka'a bay magalti'-alti' hē'. (D'nda ya aebog, abaya'an ka'a.)* I am attracted to you, you who have made yourself so handsome. (It's the girl who is attracted, wanting to have you.)

**aluk** *v. tr.* To console or comfort someone. *Bang kita angaluk, pinaruru' atawa pinagbinuwahan.* When we console [a child], it is breast-fed or has a lullaby sung to it. *Bang aniya' pamuwan mareyom sipuk maka'aluk atay-pasu'.* If something is given in secret it soothes angry feelings. *Mbal angaluk mma'ta-ina'ta bang kami niraplosan ma iskul.* Our parents don't comfort us when we get punished with a strap at school. (*Thesaurus:* **apu'-apu', dindang-dindang, sayudja' 1**)

**alud₁** *v. tr. -an* To shout at someone. *Aluranta, pahitanta saga.* We shout at [him], raise our voices.

**pagalud** *v. intr. aN-* To cry out loudly and persistently. *Bang iya ala'an min luma', aniya' hama'-hama' a'a. Bang sangom, makakale ka magalud, "Pareyom ka pi'itu."* When he leaves the house, there is a *hama'-hama'* spirit. At night you hear it shouting out, "Come in here." *Ap'ddi' kōk-atayku, mbal aku makal'ngngan, hal aku magalud.* My upper stomach hurts, I can't walk, I just cry out loud. (*Thesaurus:* **asang₂, kula'ak, galit, gasud, olang 1.1, pahit**)

**alud₂** *v. tr. -an* To weep loudly over a bereavement. *Bang amatay bapa'ku ka'aluran.* When my uncle

dies he will be wept loudly over. *Anangis na, angalud na, kabisahan. Asidda pangalud.* Crying quietly, crying out loud, suffering pain. Grieving so much. *Angaluran aku siyaliku. Anangis na, kabisahan. Asidda pangalud.* I am weeping loudly for my younger brother. Crying, hurting so much. Such weeping. *Bang aniya' amatay bo' magalud, akohot k'llongta.* When someone dies and people weep loudly, our throats are hoarse.

**alu'₁** *v. tr.* To threaten with physical harm. *Bang saupama aniya' onde'-onde' agbono', nialu' e' kasehe'anna bo' mbal isāb taluwa'.* For example, when a child is getting into a fight, he is threatened by his playmates but isn't actually hit. (*Thesaurus:* **dangka₁, hansom, sanggup**)

**pagalu'** *v. intr. aN-* To confront each other in a threatening way. *Magalu' onde'-onde' bang sōng magbono'.* Children threaten each other when they are about to get into a fight.

**alu'₂** *n.* 1) Dew. *Min gabun arai' alu', bang ngga'i ka min langit. Ya kata'uhanku min diyata'.* Dew is probably from clouds, if not from the sky. All I know is that it is from above. 1.1) *v. intr. pa-* To expose oneself to the night air. *Da'a ka pa'alu'. Sin'ppun ka.* Don't go out in the dew. You'll catch a cold.

**pa'alu'** *v. tr. -an* To expose someone to the night air by refusing him shelter. (*Thesaurus:* **inyaya, paulan, tanya₁**)

**alul** *n.* A raft. (*Thesaurus:* **balsa, plātbōt**)

**alum** *n.* A small tree, the leaves of which are used medicinally for pains and fever. *Melanolepis multiglandulosa.*

**aluminyum** *n.* Aluminum.

**alun** *see:* **panjang**

**alung** 1) *v. intr. pa-* To get close to a fire. *Da'a ka pa'alung ni lapohan bo' ka da'a atunu'.* Don't get close to the firebox lest you get burnt. *Karalletan alkohol, halam ni'nda' ai-ai pa'alung.* The alcohol caught fire, the things placed to warm by the fire weren't seen. (*Thesaurus:* **anok 1.1**) 2) *v. tr.* To gather where food is being served up. *Bang waktu pagkakan angalung na pa'in. Minsan halam bay sinagina, pasekot na pa'in.* He always turns up at mealtime. Even though not called, he keeps coming round. *Asidda pangalung onde'-onde' inān ni kaluma'an. Bang aku amangan bo' aniya' angalung makannak, ya pamakanku iya l'bbiku.* That child is in the habit of turning up at meals in the village. When I am eating and a kid comes close, what I give him are my leftovers. (*cf:* **aro' 1.1, donga'**)

**pa'alung** *v. tr.* To place something over the heat of a fire; to put something on to cook.

**amā** *n.* Anger; indignation; irritation.

**pagamā** *v. intr. aN-* 1) To display anger or irritation. *Pak'mmi' kitā, agamā halam pinakan.* We make a face, irritated at not being fed. *Hondongin pagamānu.* Stop your complaining.

**1.1)** *v. tr.* -an To display anger towards someone. *Mbal angasip saga a'a inān angkan bay pagamāhanku sigām.* Those people would not pay attention, which is why I scolded them. *Ai-ai pagamāhanta, ngga'i ka hal daginis. Ai-ai na pinagamāhan.* Anything we make a fuss about, not just one kind. Anything at all can be protested.

**amamali** (var. **mamali**) *n.* Spikenard, a species of thorny tree. *Aralia sp.*

**amamali-d'nda** *n.* Bandicoot berry. *Leea indica.*

**amanat** *n.* Awareness; information. *Taga amanat kita.* We are aware of something happening. *Pasampayun amanat itu ni kakampunganku ma Sabah.* Convey this information to my relatives in Sabah.

**amay-amay** *intrj.* 1) Be careful; be thoughtful; keep in mind. *Amay-amay, da'a ka anginum bīl.* Remember now, don't drink beer. (*Thesaurus:* **kamaya', ebot-ebot 1.1, hubaya-hubaya**) **1.1)** *v. tr.* -an To advise caution and diligence. *Ka'a ilū, sinoho' ka pehē'. Bay ka niamay-amayan he' si Mām.* You yourself were instructed to go there. Mam told you to be very careful about it. *Ya sadja pangamay-ngamayku ma ka'a, da'a bowahun anakku pehē'.* My only advice to you is this, do not take my child there.

**ambak** *n.* Frog.

**ambak-ambak** *n.* Piano accordion.

**ambahan** *see:* **pagambahan**

**ambal** *see:* **tai'-ambal**

**ambat** *adj.* a- 1) Quickly done. *Bang ka magsulat asidda ka a'ambat.* When you write you are very quick. *Isina a'ambat kinakan he' kuyya'.* Its contents were soon eaten up by monkeys. (*Thesaurus:* **amot-amot 1.1, dai'-dai' 1.2, sa'ut 1.1, saunu'**) **1.1)** *v. intr.* pa- To do completely. *Pa'ambat he'nu amangan.* Eat it all up. (*Thesaurus:* **anggap 1, lakap**) **1.2)** *v. tr.* To complete a complex task. *Buwat saupama aniya' kal'ngngananta, subay ambat-ambatta bo' al'kkas akatis, abō' kita makapuwas.* When for example we have things to be attended to, we should apply ourselves to the task so it is quickly completed and we are free to go. *Nianggapan itū, na sali' bay dakayu' bo' dakayu'. Pahilala'ku kamemon, buwat pelangku, pelang si Mu. Yukku, "Mbal na ta'anggapku amahalila', sali' mbal ta'ambatku." Anggap* is like when there has been one task after another. I was maintaining everything, like my canoe and Mu's canoe, and I said, "I cannot cope with the maintenance. It's as though I cannot get it all done."

**pagambat-ambat** *v. intr.* aN- 1) To do something repeatedly and persistently. *Magambat-ambat amusay. Amusay daran-daran.* Paddling without a break. Always paddling. *Sinahi'-sahi' bang amangan, minsan du ma tangan a'a. Yukta, "A'a itu kilāku sinahi'-sahi', halam bay makakakan*

*dapitu', sali' magambat-ambatan."* Impatient when eating, even while it is in someone's hand. Someone says, "I reckon this fellow is over-impatient, hasn't eaten for a week, going at it without a break." (*Thesaurus:* **langkit 1.1, mumut, pagabut-abut, toro-toro**) **1.1)** *v. tr.* To do something promptly.

**ambaw** *n.* Rat or mouse. (*cf:* **tikus**; *syn:* **babaw₁**)

**ambil-hati** *v. intr.* aN- To assume one is being talked about. *Buwat magistori kita, na bang aniya' akale ma kita, angambil-hati, yuk-i, "Patampalun pagsuli-sulibi ilū." Kabā'na iya inān sinuli-suli, bo' ngga'i ka.* Like we are chatting [swapping stories],"and someone listening to us gets the wrong idea. He says, "Be open with your talk." He thinks, mistakenly, that he is being discussed, but it isn't so. *Atagi sidda angambil-hati minsan bissara hām kapūsanna.* [She is] addicted to making wrong assumptions even when it's talk with no special purpose. (*Thesaurus:* **pagkamali', pagkasā' 1.1, pagsabali, ta'awil**)

**ambit₁** *v. tr.* To herd fish into shallow water. *Bang kita angambit subay bowata batu maka lubid. Pinatuntun batu pareyo', nihagul. Minsan k'llat pinabale-bale. Aniya' anipara, ati nihella' kaleya.* When we drive fish into a fenced area we need to take stones and cord. The stones are lowered and jigged up and down. Even ropes attached to stakes [may be used]. Some use goggles and the catch is hauled shorewards.

**ambitan** *n.* A fenced area. *Larung binowa palangi pang'ssol daing, ma bungsud birahan maka ma ambitan.* A scarer is carried when swimming to herd fish into a fish corral or fence area.

**pagambit₁** *v. intr.* aN- To make a living using the technique of herding fish into a fenced enclosure set up in shallow waters. *Buwat a'a magpangambit inān, bang aniya' daing tabowa patandan, bo' mareyom lekoman, na mbal makaluwas.* Like those people who catch fish by herding, when the fish are brought shorewards and are in the enclosure, they cannot go out. (*cf:* **pagampas**)

**ambit₂** *v. tr.* To hold hands. (*cf:* **tonda'₂**)

**pagambit₂** *v. intr.* aN- To hold each other's hand. *Saga pangantin bang bay kinawin magambit isāb.* Bridal couples after being married also hold hands. *Saga pangantin bang bay kinawin magambit isāb. Magambit lum'ngngnan.* Bridal couples after being married also hold hands. They walk along holding hands.

**amboway** *n.* A leguminous tree species. *Pongamia pinnata. Kayu ballak buwat luwa amboway. Aheka lalangga' ma amboway ma Siganggang.* The *ballak* tree looks like the *amboway*. There are many biting ants on the *amboway* tree at Siganggang.

**ambuhut** *v. tr.* -an To prepare pandanus for weaving. *Magpandan, agpandan d'nda llaw-*

*sangom angambuhut. Halam aniya' hinangna saddī min agambuhut.* Working with pandanus, women working and scraping pandanus night and day. They do nothing but scrape pandanus. (*Thesaurus:* **hait, salimi, tai' 1.1, tilas**₂)

**pagambuhut** *v. tr.* To earn an income by preparing pandanus leaves for weaving.

**ambul-dā'** *v. intr. aN-* To take offense at something heard or implied. *Da'a ka angambul-dā'.* Don't feel hurt. (*syn:* **mandā'-dā'**; *Thesaurus:* **anak-anak**₂, **kagit atay 1, la'at atay, tumpalak 1**)

**ambūng** *n.* Edible starch obtained from the sago palm. (*Thesaurus:* **lumbiya**)

**ambung** *n.* **1)** Large circular basket of woven cane. *Niranos nireyom ambung. Bang ngga'i ka mareyom ambung ap'kkal.* Packed into a basket. If it is not in a basket it comes apart. **2)** Small circular basket made from young coconut leaves. *Ambung nihinang min lokay masi patudjak, halam gi' abadbad, ya binowa e' onde-onde' analun, atawa an'bba.* *Ambung* type baskets are made from fresh coconut fronds still standing erect, not fully unfolded. They are the ones taken by children to get forest food or to gather sea food from the shallows. (*cf:* **baka'**₁)

**ambung-ambung**₁ *n.* A woven rattan container for a betel nut box.

**ambung-ambung**₂ *n.* **1)** A leaf awning of high quality. (*Thesaurus:* **kadjang, sapaw 1, sayap 1**) **1.1)** *v. tr.* To weave quality awning. *Duwa kadjang niambung-ambung, hatina kadjang pote' daun tigul.* Two woven awnings, white awnings of young nipa leaves.

**ambus** *v. tr.* To capture someone by means of ambush. *Sali' mundu ma T'lling, niabut he' sundalu minnē' maka minnitu. Niambus sigā.* Like the bandits at T'lling, reached by police from here and there. They were surrounded. (*Thesaurus:* **hapa' 1.2, holdap, ingu, sipi**₁ **1.1, tipu 1.1**)

**amin** *intrj.* **1)** Amen. **1.1)** *v. tr. -an* To bless an item by praying over it. *Lima mama'an ē' niaminan ma pagduwa'ahan. Jukup kapanyapanna.* Those five betel nut boxes were affirmed by amens at the prayer ceremony. Complete in all its contents.

**amirul** var. of **almirul**

**ammal**₁ *v. intr. aN-* To carry out religious duties diligently. *Bang sali' bulan puwasa, na angammal kita. Mbal kita amangan, subay ta'abut pas'ddopan llaw atawa dai' llaw lisag lima. Halam sali' aniya' hinangta.* When it is the month of fasting, we must carry out our religious duties. We do not eat until the setting of the sun or at dawn around five o'clock. We do virtually no work.

**ammal-ibarat** *n.* The religious commitment of a faithful believer. *Taga ammal-ibarat ko' ka'a ilū. Da'a ka magputing ma kasehe'an.* You have a religious commitment. Don't lie to others.

**pagammal** *v. intr. aN-* To be consistent in observing the precepts of Islam, particularly the month of fasting. (*Thesaurus:* **paglima-waktu, pagsanittiya, pagta'at**)

**pagammal-ibarat** *v. intr. aN-* To carry out diligently the precepts of Islam.

**ammal**₂ *v. tr. -an* To take care of anything of value. *Niammalan kita he' Tuhan, sali' nijagahan.* We are cared for by God, sort of watched over. *Ammalanta ai-ai ahalga'.* We cherish anything of value.

**amot-amot** *v. intr. pa-* **1)** To work quickly at a task. *Pa'amot-amot ka maghinang ilū bo' kita makal'ngngan.* Work fast there so we can go out for a walk. **1.1)** *v. tr.* To do something in a brief time. (*Thesaurus:* **ambat 1, dai'-dai' 1.2, sa'ut 1.1, saunu'**)

**ampa**₁ *conj.* And then; so that. *Bay sinaggaw e'na si Di ampa niusiba'an.* He seized Di and raped her. *Sa'angay subu halam aku bay makakakan. Yamboho' ampa makakakan na.* I haven't eaten since morning. Only just now able to eat. *Maglampasu' ka maka abu ampa alanu'.* Polish the floor with ash and then it will be clean. (*cf:* **ati**)

**ampa**₂ *see:* **pagampa-ampa**

**ampahan** *n.* Long-finned cavalla or kingfish. *Carangoides ciliarius.*

**ampal** *adj. a-* Hindered from moving freely. *Ya tundanan-i maka'ampal.* It's the things being towed that make it hard to progress. (*Thesaurus:* **pagang, sagang, sangsang, sapad, sulang**₁)

**ampan** *n.* Various flying insects such as locusts.

**ampan-dulu** *n.* Swarming locust; large grasshopper. (*Thesaurus:* **bilalang, tompang**; *syn:* **dulu**₁)

**ampang** *n.* Drying racks over the stern of a canoe. *Ayas-ayas man kīran, ampang-ampang man diyata' pansal.* The *ayas* drying racks are on the side, the *ampang* racks are over the stern. (*cf:* **ayas-ayas**)

**ampas** *n.* **1)** A moveable fish corral set in shallow marine banks. *Ampas itū taga logo. Bang kami angambit subay hal paldu.* The fence trap has a small trap at the end. When we drive fish, a cage should be enough to keep fish alive. (*cf:* **bungsud**) **1.1)** *v. advrs. ka-...-an* To be trapped by herded fish. *A: "Ka'ampasan bahā' pagal batu ina'an? Mbal pamakitāwan?" B: "Mbal kita pinakitāw e' saitan."* A: "Can that rock wall be used for trapping fish? Won't it be something scary?" B: "We won't be scared by spirits."

**pagampas** *v. intr. aN-* To make a living by catching fish using moveable fence traps set on shallow marine flats. (*cf:* **pagambit**₁)

**ampaw** *n.* Cakes of sugar-glazed popped rice. (*Thesaurus:* **biti'**₁, **bulitik**₂, **gagati'**)

**ampe** var. of **hampe**

**ampi'** var. of **hampi'**

**ampis** *v. intr. pa-* To stand together in one place. *Aheka a'a pa'ampīs.* There are a lot of people standing around. *Pa'ampis kam minnilu bo' mbal makal'ppa saga manuk. Bang aheka pa'ampīs mbal* *makalabay.* Just stand there so the chickens can't escape. If a lot of people are standing around they won't be able to pass. *Pa'ampis kam minnilu bo' mbal makal'ppa saga manuk.* Just stand there so the chickens can't escape.

**amp'llus** *n.* The sheath surrounding muscle tissue. *Amp'llus, ya mareyom baranta itū, patapil sadja ni atayta, pabutig.* The muscle tissue that is here in our bodies, simply providing support for our liver, and [sometimes] becoming enlarged. *Luku' inān taga amp'llus.* The pufferfish there, they have a sheath.

**ampogod 1)** *n.* Pimple. *Ampogod itu ahunit katambalan. Minsan ala'an pabīng du.* These pimples are hard to treat. Though they go away they recur. *Aniya' isāb ampogod ba'is, amaya'-maya'.* There are pimples too due to sexual desire, to wanting someone. (*Thesaurus:* **buwa'-buwa' 1.1, samuwa' 1.1**) **2)** *v. advrs.* -in- Afflicted with pimples. *Niampogod bayhu'na.* His face is pimply.

**ampud** var. of **angpud**

**ampu'** *see:* **pangampu'an**

**ampun₁** *v. tr.* To forgive someone. *A: "Ampunun pa'in aku bang aku bay makarusa." B: "Niampun kita he' Tuhan."* A: "Forgive me if I have committed an offense." B: "We are forgiven by God."

**ka'ampunan** *n.* Forgiveness; pardon; amnesty. *Angamu' sigām tabang maka ka'ampunan.* They plead for help and forgiveness.

**pagampun 1)** *v. intr.* aN- To forgive someone. **2)** *v. tr.* -an To forgive each other, often in a formal context. *Buwat kita magsagga' bo' sali' mbal magampun-ampunan, na bang sali' aniya' pamakaiya'nu, tabangkilnu aku.* Like us being in conflict but not forgiving each other, then if you have something to shame me with, you could remind me of it. *Bang saupama kita bay magbono' bo' magkahāp na, ya hē' niōnan magampun.* If for example we were fighting and then reconciled, that is called forgiving.

**pagpa'ampun** *v. intr.* aN- To seek forgiveness from someone. (*Thesaurus:* **deyo'₃ 2, pagkahāp, ū'ū**)

**pagpatiampun** *v. intr.* aN- To abase oneself when asking forgiveness.

**ampun₂** *voc. n.* Address to a person of high rank. (*cf:* **appa'**)

**ampun-ampun** *v. ditr.* To seek the help of God or a spirit being. *Bang bīlli saging bo' atahak, ni'isi ni lai' binowa ni mbo' niampun-ampunan.* When bananas, ripe ones, have been purchased, they are put on a plate and taken to the ancestor who is being asked for help. (*Thesaurus:* **amu'-amu'**)

**amu₁** *adj.* a- Appropriate; suitable. *Bang aku amuwanan ka'a subay a'amu, subay apatut.* When I give you something it should be appropriate, should be fitting. (*Thesaurus:* **matural, patut, tōp 1.1**)

**pagpa'amu** *v. intr.* aN- To speak plainly and truthfully.

**pa'amu** *v. tr.* To do something clearly or plainly, especially in regard to speech. (*cf:* **papatut**)

**amu₂** *v. intr.* maka- **1)** To please or satisfy. *Hinangun bang ai ya maka'amu ma ka'a, sabab ilu Tuhan taptap pagapi' ma ka'a.* Do whatever pleases you, because God is always there supporting you. **1.1)** *v. advrs.* ka-...-an Persuaded; satisfied with a result. *Ka'amuhan kita, bang saupama sinuli-sulihan kita; na yukta, "Ka'amuhan aku he' suli-sulinu ilu." Magtūy sali' kita kamattanan.* We are satisfied when, for example, we are spoken to and we say, "I am pleased with your speech." We are convinced right away. *Ka'amuhan Tuhan ma pangamu' si Sulayman ē'.* God was pleased with Sulayman's request. *Yukta, "Ka'amuhan aku he' suli-sulinu ilu."* We say, "I am pleased with what you say." (*Thesaurus:* **beya'₃ 1, bilīb, kompolme, dakayu'₂ 1, manghalapi, pagta'ayun, sulut 1, tayudtud, tuksu'**)

**pa'amu-amu** *v. tr.* To make something attractive. (*Thesaurus:* **mata-mata₁, pagpaelle'-elle', pagpa'nda'-pa'nda'**)

**amu'₁** *v. tr.* To ask for; to request. *Angamu'an iya sokal ina'na.* She is requesting sugar for her mother. *Angamu' aku tanud panahi'ku sanyawaku.* I will ask for some thread to sew my underpants. *Pa'amu'in ai-ai anaknu ni kami.* Let your children ask anything from us. *Bang ta'amu', tuwan sultan, soho'un lagi' pinapiha ma saga pagtatau'an sulat saga ka'mbo'annu pasal kahālan lahat.* If it is permissible to ask, O King, please have a search made in the written records.

**amu'-amu'** *v. ditr.* To petition a more powerful being. *Mbal ta'amu'-amu' bang saitan-mungkil.* A *mungkil* spirit cannot be petitioned. *Supaya sigām maka'amu'-amu'an sultan kahāpan.* So that they might seek favor for the king. (*Thesaurus:* **ampun-ampun, harap₂, pagduwa'a, pinta-pinta, pudji 1.1, sambahayang, ta'at 1.1**)

**amu'₂** *n.* A species of monkey. (*Thesaurus:* **kuyya', uwang**)

**amu' taral** *n. phrase* Person with ugly looks.

**amulawan** (var. **hamulaun; hamulawan**) *n.* Molave or ironwood. *Vitex parviflora.* *Ahāp amulawan nihinang busay, atatas ma tahik.* Ironwood is good for making paddles, it lasts in seawater. (*cf:* **agdaw, kayu-soha'**)

**-an₁** *aff.* Locative voice suffix: attaches to transitive verbs, identifying the location of the event as the subject of the clause. *Ina'an ma tongod bay pagbono'an Jipun maka Milikan.* There in the place where the Japanese and Americans fought a battle. *Maina'an pa'in ma pagkakanan, nilabot iya e' si Bo maka pai sinanglag.* There in the dining place, Bo gave her roasted grain to eat.

**-an₂ 1)** *aff.* Applicative suffix: attaches to verbs, indicating the addition of a new undergoer (often a beneficiary or recipient) to the clause. *Angamu'an iya sokal ina'na.* She is requesting sugar for her mother. *Buwananku onde'-onde' būk.* I will give the children schoolbooks. **1.1)** *aff.* With transitive -an verbs, this suffix must be used whenever there is a definite undergoer present in the clause, regardless of the verb's voice. *Bay ni'bbahan si Arung ma luma'.* Oldest Daughter was left behind in the house.

**-an₃** *aff.* Adjective suffix: indicates inherent quality. *Lanahan iya itū, sali' pulitik.* He is a smooth speaker, like a politician. *P'ttung bahi'an, ato'a na sidda. Akeyat isina.* Mature bamboo, very old. Its inside is red.

**aN-** **1)** *aff.* Actor voice prefix: attaches to transitive verbs, identifying the actor as the subject of the clause. *Am'lli aku kait duwa aheya pangait sanyawa onde'-onde'.* I will buy two safety pins, large ones, to fasten the baby's panties. *Angalop aku ka'a.* I come into your presence. **2)** *aff.* Intransitive prefix: attaches to verbs whose single argument is actor-like. *Angabal tahik, sōng t'bba.* The sea is roaring; it will soon be low tide. *Anubus du pa'in panganak inān ma hinang kamatto'ahan.* The children consistently follow the traditional activities of the forebears.

**anā** *intrj.* 'Look!' 'See that!' 'Alas!' *Anā, magpiha na ma dilaut, ma busayna.* Look at that. He is searching out at sea, for his paddle. *Anā, bang anangis na onde' inān, magta'ut na pa'in l'lla inān bang h'ndana maghinang.* Look at that! When that child cries, the man there keeps bouncing the cradle when his wife is busy. *Magsait na pa'in, sigi-sigi magsait. Anā, mbal na takole' sinaitan.* They bailed, they kept on bailing. Alas, it could not be bailed. (*Thesaurus:* **agkā', allā, arī, arōy, aruhuy, asē, ayī, dā'₁, ē**)

**anak₁** **1)** *n.* A child; offspring. (*Thesaurus:* **mpu, onde' 1, tubu' 1**) **1.1)** *v. tr.* -an To give birth; to reproduce. *Bang bay angiram si Mā, ab'ttong, sōng anganak.* When Ma had conceived she became pregnant, and will give birth. **2)** *v. advrs.* -in- Producing offspring. *Halam aniya' ma sigām d'nda tamanang, hatina ya mbal nianak.* They have no women who are barren, women, that is, who do not produce children.

**anak-anak₁** *n.* Children in a general sense, as distinct from offspring. (*Thesaurus:* **kamanahutan, makannak, onde'-onde'**)

**anak-bala'** *n.* An annoying child; a brat. {idiom}

**anak-ballo'** *n.* A step-child.

**anak-binowa** *n.* A child from a previous marriage.

**anak-ka'bbahan** *n.* An orphan or abandoned child.

**anak-kamanakan** *n.* Nephew; niece. *Magkaliru'an kita ma anak-kamanakanta, sali' kita magdohon.* We ache for our [related] young people, grieving for them.

**anak-kampung** *n.* Extended family in the same community. *Saga anak-kampungna mbal na pinabayad buwis parinta.* His extended family will not have to pay the government taxes. *Tantu aniya' bala' tum'kka ni nakura' kami sampay ni anak-kampungna.* Some trouble will certainly happen to our boss and his wider family.

**anak-kasi** *n.* A child born out of wedlock. {euphemism} (*syn:* **harambiyara' 1**)

**anak-kusa'** *n.* A brat. {idiom}

**anak-duru'an** *n.* A nursing child.

**anak-etek** *n.* An adopted child. {idiom}

**anak-h'lla** *n.* A woman's husband and children.

**anak-h'nda** *n.* A man's wife and children. *Magdeyo'an di Nabi Nū maka anak-h'ndana sampay ayuwanna.* The prophet Noah and his family including daughters-in-law disembarked. *Sali' kita angandakayu'an anak-h'nda a'a.* Like someone uniting with a man's wife or daughters.

**anak-ilu'** *n.* An orphan.

**anak-mpu** *n.* Children and grandchildren.

**anak-mulid** *n.* A student of a guru.

**anak-mussa'** *n.* Beloved children. {idiom}

**anak-paindam** *n.* A newborn child who lives only briefly. {euphemism}

**anak-sahili'** *n.* A child who provokes parents to anger. {idiom}

**anak-tabowa** *n.* A child from a previous marriage.

**anak-ubus** *n.* A child dedicated to the ancestor or healer responsible for its recovery; a memorial child. *Bang aniya' sali' asaki, ai na ka onde'-onde', ai na ka matto'a, bo' binowa ni a'a taga jīn, ati bo' kauli'an, niōnan na anak-ubus.* For example, if someone, child or adult, is ill and is taken to someone with a healing djinn and is healed, that person is called *anak-ubus* [memorial child]. *Magpaubus ni sigā ya taga jīn. Bang kauli'an subay da'a magl'kkat. Anak-ubus ko' hē'.* As a last resort, the one with a healing djinn goes to the [sick woman]. When healed [she and the healer] should not part. She is a memorial child [to the healer]. *Pagjakat itu ni pangkat anak-ubus.* This obligatory contribution is to an ancestor who is always remembered. *Anak-ubus si La ma Milikan, bay kauli'an ma deyomanna.* La is to be remembered forever as the Westerner's child; she was healed while in his care.

**paganak** *v. intr.* aN- **1)** To become as a child to someone. *Maganak aku ma ka'a.* I will be as your child. **1.1)** *v. tr.* -an To produce offspring, in a specific or general sense. *A'a aku'il tape'na, halam bay makal'ngngan sangay min kapaganak ma iya.* A person whose leg was crippled, hadn't been able to walk since he was born. *Bang balu masi gi' abata' subay magh'lla pabīng maka maganak.* Widows who are still young should marry again and have children. *Bay aku tagna' pinaganakan, ariki'-riki' gi'...* When I was just born, still very small... *A: "Painay ru si De maganak?" B: "Bay ru niā'an panday."* A: "How is

De going with her birthing?" B: "The midwife has been called for her."

**kapaganak** *n.* The act or moment of giving birth. *A'a aku'il tape'na, halam bay makal'ngngan sangay min kapaganak ma iya.* A person whose leg was crippled, who hadn't been able to walk since he was born. *Min llaw kapaganak ma iya sampay ni waktu kamatayna.* From the day of his birth to the time of his death. *Llaw kapanganakna, llaw kapanganak ma ka'a.* The day she gave birth, the day you were born.

**paganak-sulay** *n.* 1) Breech birth. **1.1)** *v. tr.* -*an* To give birth to a child by breech delivery.

**panganak** *n.* Children in a collective sense; one's offspring. (*cf:* **kamanahutan**)

**taganak** *n.* Someone who has rights and responsibilities over a younger person.

**anak₂** *n.* A segment or partition of a larger whole.

**anak-bagid** *n.* A match for igniting.

**anak-bulsa** *n.* An inner pocket.

**anak-kunsi'** *n.* A key to a lock. (*cf:* **kandaru 1, kunsi' 1**)

**anak-mama'an** *n.* Compartments of a betel-nut box. (*Thesaurus:* **loka'-loka', mama'an, salappa'**)

**anak-pana'** *n.* An arrow.

**anak-tangan** *n.* Fingers. *L'lla aheya to'ongan, nnom heka anak-tanganna maka nnom anak-tape'na.* A very large man, with six fingers and six toes. (*Thesaurus:* **anak-tape', gulamay 1;** *wh:* **tangan 1**)

**anak-tape'** *n.* Toes. (*Thesaurus:* **anak-tangan, gulamay 1;** *wh:* **tape'₁**)

**anak-tikam** *n.* The numbered markers used on a gaming board.

**anak₃** *n.* 1) The interest on an investment. (*Thesaurus:* **laba, untung₁ 1**) **1.1)** *v. tr.* -*an* To earn interest on a loan. *Ananda' aku sangpū' pilak ni si Om. Na anganak dakayu' pilak.* I pawn something at Om's for ten pesos. The loan then earns one peso. *Bang kita sinukuran gusi', bo' kita makaisi dakayu' pilak, anganak ko' inān.* If we have the good fortune of getting a magic money box, and we put one peso into it, it will make a profit.

**anak₄** *v. tr.* -*an* To multiply or spread, of an infection. *Binaha'an kitā, tinumbulan, sali' anganak.* We are afflicted by swellings, multiplying, as though producing offspring. (*cf:* **tumbul**)

**anak d'nda** *n. phrase* Daughter.

**anak l'lla** *n. phrase* Son. *Halam gi' aniya' anakku l'lla.* I don't yet have a son.

**anak manuk** *n. phrase* Chick.

**anak sapi'** *n. phrase* Calf.

**anak-anak₂** *v. intr.* aN- To take offense; to be irritated. *Da'a ka atumpalak, da'a ka anganak-nganak.* Don't be offended, don't be irritated. (*Thesaurus:* **ambul-dā', kagit atay 1, la'at atay, tumpalak 1**)

**anak-bāt** *n.* Anchovy. *Stolephorus spp.*

**anak-bobohan** *n.* Anemonefish or clownfish. *fam. Pomacentridae.*

**anak-lason** *n.* Clownfishes. *Amphiprion ocellaris (Ocellaris clownfish); A. frenatus (Tomato clownfish).*

**anad** *v. tr.* 1) To learn a skill or lesson. *Anganaran aku dīku, anadku ma kasehe'anku.* I learn by myself, I learn from others. *Ahunit ilu nianad.* That's hard to learn. (*Thesaurus:* **adji' 2, istadi, istadi, ta'u₁ 1.2**) 2) To train an animal.

**anagtol** *adj.* zero Durable. *Anagtol, hatina asandal kayuna. Minsan ai, basta asandal.* Durable, meaning that its wood is long-lasting. No matter what, so long as it is durable. *Bay aku pariyata' ni lansa, sabab aheka tamban daing niā' e' sigām. Ati bangka'ku inān, parugtul ni lansa. Anagtol lansa ina'an.* I went aboard the launch, because they had caught a lot of sardines. And that canoe of mine, it banged into the launch, which was solidly built. *Abuhat kumkum ina'an, sabab anagtol basi'na.* That backhoe is heavy, because its steel is solid. (*Thesaurus:* **kamdos₂, kumpay, galak₂, pagon₁ 1.1, taggu₁, tatas 1.1, togob₁**)

**anambahina** *adv.* To a greater degree; even more so. *Ageret badju'ku. Bowaku magbola, na paheya gese'na, anambahina paluha gese'na.* My shirt is torn. I wear it to play ball, then the tear gets bigger, its torn bit widens even more. *Bay aku sinoho' am'lli daing, ahalu' tab'lliku. Na sinoho' pinapole', sinoho' am'lli daing saddi. Makab'lli pa'in aku daing bawis, yuk manoho' hē', "Anambahina ilu-i!"* I was told to buy some fish and what I bought was not fresh. So I was told to return and buy different fish. When I had bought some rabbit fish, the person who sent [me] said, "That is even worse!" *Anambahina ap'ddi' atayna.* He is even more annoyed [lit. his liver is even more painful]. (*cf:* **tamba;** *Thesaurus:* **bangkinna...bangkinna, kalap, labi-labi, luba', luhūy, paligay, ya lagi'na**)

**anamū** *adj.* zero Rough, of a surface. *Anamū pahāp p'ttung ilū.* The surface of that bamboo is very rough. *Niluhu manamū inān.* Those projecting fibers are singed off.

**anay** *n.* Termites; ants. (*Thesaurus:* **boke', bukbuk 1, lutus**)

**andag** *v. tr.* To open bargaining by asking the price. *Bay kami angandag ma tinda, atilaw halga'.* We opened the buying process in the store, asking the price. (*Thesaurus:* **halga' 1.2, jawab₁, ladjaw, paragang**)

**pagpa'andag** *v. intr.* aN- To be active in getting potential customers to make an offer.

**pa'andag** *v. tr.* -*an* 1) To offer something for sale. (*Thesaurus:* **dagang, lilung, litu, pab'lli, pagsoroy, samsuy**) 2) To offer a woman in marriage.

**andal** *v. tr.* -*an* To increase the speed of an engine.

*Ka'andalan du malkina ilū, mbal abustak.* That motor can be speeded up, it won't fall apart. *Pa'andalun malkina ilū.* Make that engine go faster.

**andalaho'** *n.* A rainbow. (*Thesaurus:* **bāngaw, biradali 2, salindugu'** 1)

**andalan** *n.* The ringworm bush. *Cassia sp. Andalan itu tapanambal pohak. Andalan* can be used to treat ringworm. (*syn:* **halu'-halu'**₂)

**andarol** *n.* The wheeled frame for teaching children to walk.

**anday-anday** *see:* **anday-andayan, paganday-anday**

**anday-andayan** *n.* Something to be mocked. *Nihinang anday-andayan, sinōngan kaiya'anna.* Made something to be mocked, his shame made greater.

**andig** *see:* **pagpa'andig, pa'andig**

**andol** 1) *v. intr. aN-* To rely on or trust someone. *Bang aniya' pinabeya' ma ipalta, angandol kita ma iya.* When anything is sent with our brother-in-law, we have confidence in him. (*Thesaurus:* **kamdos**₁, **sangdol** 1.1) 2) *v. ditr.* To entrust something to another person. *Pangandolku ai-aiku itū ma ka'a.* I entrust these things of mine to you. *Bang ka ganta' bilahi angitung bang pila panambanu ma aku, kata'uhannu magtūy bang aku kapangandolan atawa mbal.* If for instance you wanted to count how much you paid me, you would know immediately whether or not I am to be trusted.

**pagandol-andol** *v. intr. aN-* To be mutually confident; to trust each other. *Magandol-andolan kita, hatina angandol kita sali'-sali'.* We trust each other, meaning to say that we trust equally.

**pangandolan** *n.* Someone who can be trusted or relied on.

**andom** *n.* 1) A dark cloud, often bringing rain. (*Thesaurus:* **gabun, haya'**₂, **tai'-baliyu, turung-balu 2**) 1.1) *v. intr. aN-* To cloud over. *Angandom Būd Datu'.* Mount Datu is clouding over. 1.2) *v. advrs. ka-...-an* To be clouded over. *Asidda ka'andoman Būd Kota'batu inān. Daka angay būdta itū mbal ka'andoman.* Mount Cotabato there is totally covered with cloud. Goodness knows why this mountain of ours is not clouded.

**pagandom-andom** *v. intr. aN-* To be intermittently clouded over. *Asidda pagandom-andom lahat itu, sali' bay andom bo' halam isāb.* This place is forever clouding over, like there was cloud and then there wasn't.

**anduk** *var. of* **handuk**

**anduhat** *n.* Fusilier fish.

**andu'-andu'** *v. intr. aN-* To feel shame for oneself or pity for another. *Buwat kita pinakaiya' ma kaheka'an a'a. Pinah'llingan kita bo' pah'lling mbal ahāp. Na angandu'-andu' deyom atayta, minsan halam aniya' bohe' mata.* Like when we are shamed in front of a crowd. We are abused

verbally and what's said is not good. Then we feel bad inside, even though there are no tears. *Angandu'-ngandu' iya pasalan yampa sigām makapag'nda' sat'ggol he'-i na.* He was emotionally moved because they had just now seen each other, after such a long time. *Angandu'-ngandu' kita, sali' mandā'-dā'.* We are feeling it deeply, as though left out. (*Thesaurus:* **ase', ndū'**)

**ani** *n.* Harvest.

**anihan** *n.* Harvest (specifically of grain). *Subay bowahunbi kamemon jakatbi ya bay min anihanbi sakahaba' tahun.* You should bring all your tithes from what you reaped every year.

**pagani** *v. tr.* To harvest grain (particularly of rice). *Pinasuku' ma Pira'un bahagi' lima min ai-ai pinagani ma deyom lahat.* The fifth part of anything harvested in the land became the property of the Pharaoh. *Subay ta'abut musim pagani pai bo' kabayaranku.* The season for reaping rice should come before I can pay. (*cf:* **k'ttu'**)

**anib** *n.* 1) Danger from unfriendly human activity. 1.1) *adj. a-* Dangerous. *Da'a kām kaleya, sali' aheka mundu. A'anib lahat, aheka panangkaw.* Don't go inland, it is as if there are many bandits. The place is dangerous, there are many thieves. (*cf:* **piligdu 1.1**)

**ka'aniban** *n.* Danger from unfriendly people.

**hinanib** *n.* 1) Weapons carried for defense or attack. (*Thesaurus:* **almas, pakokos, pangatu, takos** 1) 1.1) *v. intr. aN-* To wear a weapon for defense. *Sōng angahinanib mundu pi'itu.* Bandits are coming this way, armed.

**anibung** *n.* A species of palm, a source of good quality flooring. *Oncosperma sp.*

**animu** *v. tr. -an* To deceive someone. *Ebot-ebot da'a ka ameya' nianimuhan e' a'a ilū, hal ko' ka'a ilu niakkalan.* Be careful not to be enticed by that person, he will just deceive you. *Da'a ka ameya' nianimuhan e' a'a ilū, hal ko' ka'a ilu niakkalan.* Be careful not to be enticed by that person, he will just deceive you.

**anjibi** *n.* 1) Dye. 1.1) *v. tr.* To dye a specific color. *Nianjibi bilu.* Dyed blue.

**anok** *adj. a-* 1) Left over a heat source to complete cooking. 1.1) *v. intr. pa-* To cook slowly. *Pina'anok-anok lagi'.* Let it sit over the heat a bit longer yet. (*Thesaurus:* **alung 1**)

**anom** (*var.* **anyam**) *v. tr.* To weave or plait. *Paganomku p'ttung itū makahinang aku duwa bubu. Mbal maka'anoman duwa bubu p'ttung ina'an.* When I have woven this bamboo I will be able to make two fish traps. That other bamboo will not be enough to make two traps. *Asidda panganganom tepo d'nda ina'an.* That woman is very committed to weaving mats. *Makatuli pa'in si Samson, niā' e' si Delila pitu' sapiran bu'unna bo' nianyam ni kakana'.* When Samson had fallen asleep, Delila took seven braids of his hair to be woven into some fabric. (*Thesaurus:* **ayum-ayum, huwit-huwit 1.1, t'nnun**)

**paganom** *v. tr.* To weave things as a way of making a living. *Mbal makapaganom bubu si Mma' ma pantān luma' kami apa aniya' asaki.* Father is unable to weave his fish traps on the porch of our house because someone is ill.

**ansak** *n.* A basket woven from coconut leaflets. *Ansak pagguna e' Sama, tinemposan diyata'na, tahinang atibulung.* The coconut leaf baskets used by Sama have the top cut off and [the rim] made circular. (*gen:* **baka'₁**)

**ansel** *n.* **1)** An answer in a school context. **1.1)** *v. tr.* *-an* To answer a question. *Bang kita nilinganan ni mastal, bo' kita mbal maka'ansel, na kaiya'-iya'an kita.* When we are called by the teacher and we can't answer, then we are shamed.

**ansom** *var. of* **hansom**

**ansong** *v. intr.* *aN-* To be daydreaming. (*Thesaurus:* **ddop, lāp-lāp, mutamad, pagdabdab, uppi 1**)

**ansuwang** *var. of* **gansuwang**

**antag** *var. of* **atag₁**

**antil 1)** *n.* An infection of the ears. (*cf:* **tolek 1.1**) **1.1)** *v. tr.* *-an* To clear the ears of pus. *Pikiantil aku ma ina'ku, danakanku.* I get my mother or my sister to clean out my ears. **2)** *v. advrs.* *-in-* Suffering from infection of the ears. *Niantil aku, nila'anan tolekku he' ina'ku.* I have an ear infection, my mother removes the discharge.

**antin** *see:* **pangantin**

**anting-anting** *n.* **1)** Long pendant earrings. *Anting-anting patonton, aretes nsa' aniya' tontonna, hal pinasōd ni tainga. Sali' du maka subang. Anting-anting* hang down, *aretes* have nothing hanging, they are just inserted in the ear. Same as *subang. Bang aku ni pagkawinan sangonku anting-anting itū ni talingaku.* When I go to a wedding I attach these earrings to my ears. *Da'a bowahun anting-anting ilu apa pa'anting-antingku.* Don't take those long earrings because I am going to use them [as earrings]. (*Thesaurus:* **aretes, bāng₂, domelo, pinting, subang**) **1.1)** *v. advrs.* *ka-...-an* To wear pendant earrings. *Pa'anting-antinganku anakku. Mbal gi' ka'anting-antingan si Li, halam bay nilowangan talingana.* I will have my child wear earrings. Li cannot be wearing earrings yet, her ears haven't been pierced. **2)** An amulet worn as protection against unseen spirit beings. *Taga anting-anting, hatina taga ilmu'.* He has an *anting-anting* charm, in other words he has spiritual power. (*gen:* **tambang₃ 1**)

**antugan** *var. of* **kalitan-antugan**

**antu'ang** *var. of* **kima-antu'ang**

**antung** (*var.* **atung**) *v. intr.* *pa-* To float motionless in one place despite current flow. *Buwat daing pa'antung-antung ma kabatuhan bang aniya' s'llog. Saddī palaran. Bang pa'antung mbal maghibal, mbal kita tabowa ma s'llog.* Like fish staying in the same place among the coral when there is a current. Drifting [*laran*] is different. With

*antung* there is no movement, one is not carried along on the current. *Buwat sikuhan pa'atung maina'an.* Like the *sikuhan* fish, which stays there in the one place. *Bang aniya' ai-ai ahūg ni tahik mbal palaran. Pa'antung na ma baina.* When something heavy falls into the sea it doesn't drift, just stays where it was. *Buwat sikuhan pa'atung maina'an.* Like the *sikuhan* fish, staying in place without moving. (*cf:* **atol**)

**antup** *v. tr.* *-an* To threaten someone with harm. *Antupanta ka. Ka'a bono'ku.* I warn you. I will kill you. (*syn:* **hansom**)

**antuwilas** *n.* **1)** Filigree buttons. **1.1)** *v. tr.* *-an* To decorate with filigree buttons. *Niantuwilasan pamakayna, ya badju'na batawi'.* His clothes are decorated with buttons, his traditional *batawi'* shirt, that is.

**anu** (*var.* **manu**) *n.* **1)** Anything for which the proper word is unknown or cannot readily be remembered; thingummy. *Anuhun kono' ma aku.* Do whatsit to it for me. *Pansul ya panganuhan bohe' inān.* A pipe is that whatsit for water. *Bay ta'nda' kami si Anu amowa busay.* We saw What's-his-name carrying a paddle. *Buwat kita anganuhan tapi' pelang.* Like us doing something-or-other to the planks of a canoe. *Am'lli aku bawang panganuku daing.* I will buy some garlic to do whatever to the fish. **2)** Something owned, a possession. *Anuku ko' itū.* This thing is mine. (*cf:* **suku'**) **3)** Euphemism for bodily parts or functions. {euphemism} *Arōy tuwan, ap'ddi' anuku.* Ouch, friend, my thing is painful.

**paganu-anu** *v. intr.* *aN-* To be engaged in doing an unspecified variety of things. *B'nnal isāb ata'u aku aganu-anu magtukangan.* It's true that I do know how to do this and that, doing skilled work.

**anughala'** *n.* **1)** Divine blessing. *Kalu aniya' anughala' min Tuhan.* There may perhaps be a blessing from God. (*Thesaurus:* **apuwa, barakat 1, hirayat, lidjiki' 1, pahala'**) **1.1)** *v. tr.* *-an* To bless someone. *Jari bang ka nianughala'an na e' Tuhan, ndū', da'a aku kalipatun.* So when God confers great blessings on you, please don't forget me.

**anupin** *n.* Snapper species. *Lutjanus spp.* (*gen:* **kutambak**)

**anyak-anyak** *v. tr.* *-an* To specify what is expected or required. *Maganyak-anyak dahatus panyām, limampū' tamu, dahatus oko'-oko', t'llu bungkal tabaku' maka lima koleng naylon jukup maka p'ssina maka kowatna. Duwa kadjang niambung-ambung.* One hundred rice cakes were specified, fifty containers of boiled rice, one hundred cooked sea urchins, three balls of tobacco and five coils of nylon complete with fish hooks and traces. Two fine leaf awnings. *Tinugila' dakayu'-kayu', nianyak-anyak, niōnan dakayu'-dakayu', tinutat.* Specified one by one, named individually, listed. (*Thesaurus:* **sokat₁ 1, tugila'**

1.1, tutat 1.1)

**anyam** *var. of* **anom**

**anyil** *n.* 1) Laundry bluing. 1.1) *v. tr. -an* To add bluing to water.

**āng-āng** *var. of* **alang-alang**

**angan** *n.* Reef edge, the place where shallow and deep water meet.

**angan-angan** *adv.* Hopefully. *Alamat sulat itu deyo' min kami magtai'anak angan-angan tudju ni ka'am.* This letter comes from our family, hopefully to you all.

**angas** *var. of* **engas-engas**

**angay** (*var.* **niangay**) *interrog.* Why? For what purpose? *Angay ka pi'itu waktu sangom?* Why do you come here at night time? *"Angay aku putingannu?" yuk sultan. "Angay aku halam pata'unu in iya h'ndanu?"* "Why did you lie to me?" said the sultan. "Why didn't you let me know she is your wife?" (*Thesaurus:* **ai, buwattingga 1.1, magay, maingga, sai, sumiyan**)

**angay-angay** *n.* Anything. *Halam gi' angay-angay.* Nothing has happened yet. (*cf:* **mina'-mina' 1**)

**angkan** (*var.* **hangkan**) *n.* 1) The reason for some action or condition. *Angkanna, magtapis kitam karut ma hawakantam.* That's the reason why we wore sacks around our waists. 1.1) *conj.* That is why; wherefore. *A: "Angay ka angkan alēt?" B: "Bay aku amangan."* A: "What is the reason for your being late?" B: " I was eating." *Budjang na iya, hangkan nilaha' na.* She is a teenager now, that's why she is menstruating. *Talilap aku hangkan halam tasayuku ulan.* I was overcome by sleep, that's why I was unaware of the rain.

**angkap** *n.* 1) The extra level or story of a building. *Yukku, "Subay aniya' luma' bo' aniya' angkap."* *Yuk dangan, "Taga angkap isāb kappal."* I said, "It must be a house to have a story." Another said, "Ships too have a second level." *Luma' i Pa, t'llu angkapna.* Pa's house has three stories. 1.1) *v. tr. -an* To provide a building with a second story. *Ka'angkapan luma' saisig ina'an, mbal bahā' agka'at saisigna?* That house with woven cane walling is built with upper floors, won't its walling wear out?

**pagangkap** *v. intr. aN-* 1) To be built with multiple storys or floors. *Asidda magangkap luma' Bisaya'.* The houses of Christian Filipinos very often have more than one story. 1.1) *v. tr.* To build a second story. *Am'lli aku papan somel pagangkapku luma' kami.* I will buy milled planks for building a story on our house.

**angkas₁** *n.* 1) Fibrous residue; sediment. *Aniya' angkas tī. Subay neskape bo' nsa' angkasna.* There are fibres in tea. It must be Nescafe to have no fibres. *Bang tibu'uk bo' nili'is, aniya' angkasna, ahunit nili'is.* When non-toxic species of cassava are grated, there are rough bits, difficult to grate. (*Thesaurus:* **akal, hali₁ 1, p'tti', sapal, tai'-lahing**) 1.1) *v. intr. aN-* To leave a residue.

*Ahāp tī ilū, mbal angangkas. Halam angkasan.* That tea is good, it doesn't leave any sediment. No sediment.

**angkas₂** *v. intr. pa-* To ride pillion. *Atagi si Ja pa'angkas ma motol.* Ja loves riding pillion on a motorcycle.

**angkat₁** *v. intr. pa-* 1) To rise above a surface. *Mbal pa'angkat tape'ta, pasapu ni tana'.* Our feet don't lift up, they sweep along the ground. *Bang aku bay abuhaw, la'ananku banog i' maka dambila' katig. Pehē'ku ni deyo' taddas pelang ati bo' pabuhat pariyata', pa'angkat na man kulit tahik.* When I capsized I removed the sail and the outrigger on one side. I put it under the keel of the canoe so it lifted up and rose above the surface of the sea. 1.1) *v. tr.* To raise something up. *Tinangon maka katig min deyo' abō' niangkat min kulit tahik.* Support it from below with an outrigger so it is raised above the surface of the sea. *Bang saupama kita anganggonteng, na wa'i angahūg sau. Pat'kkad na, angkatanta na. Puwas e' pat'kkaranta isāb. Pat'kkad pa'in, balutanta. Amalut pa'in hē', landahanta ko mbal apigtal sau hē.* For example we are fishing from a stationary position, then we drop the anchor. When it touches bottom we pull it up again. After that we let it touch again and when it touches we hold [the rope]. As we hold it we let out some slack so the anchor isn't tied too tightly. (*Thesaurus:* **bayaw, buhat₁ 1.2, tangon 1.1**)

**angkat₂** *v. tr.* To disinter buried remains.

**angkud** *var. of* **angpud**

**anggalis** *n.* The English language. (*syn:* **ingglis**)

**anggap** *v. tr. -an* 1) To do something completely. *Nianggapan itū, na sali' bay dakayu' bo' dakayu'. Pahilala'ku kamemon, buwat pelangku, pelang si Mi. Yukku, "Mbal na ta'anggapku amahalila', sali' mbal ta'ambatku." Anggap* is like one thing after another being completed. I was caring for everything, like my canoe and Mi's. I said, "I am unable to care fully for them [both]. It's like I cannot get it all done." *Pinatuntul: nihinangan lutu' a'a matulak, bo' mbal ta'anggap e'na.* Getting people ready for work: food prepared for people leaving, but she can't get it all done. *Bang aniya' nianggapan he'na sampay ni kakohapan, ahusa' iya.* If he keeps working at something until late afternoon, he gets exhausted. *Ka'anggapan e' si Mo kamemon hinang ma deyom luma'.* Mo manages to get all the housework done. (*Thesaurus:* **aguwanta 1.1, ambat 1.1, anggop₂, bāng-bāng₁, bogbog₂, kole', gaga, lakap, tigayu'**) 1.1) *v. intr. pa-* To keep at some task; to persist. *Buwat ma pagongka'an, pa'anggap iya, amogos dīna palamugay.* Like at a game, he pushes in, forcing himself to get involved.

**anggauta'** *n.* Vigor; virility. *Bang kita magh'nda niā' anggauta'ta, kala'anan kosogta.* When we get a wife our virility is taken, our strength is removed. *Magtuyu' na pa'in kita, baba akosog* *anggauta'ta.* Let us persist, while our vigor is still strong. (*cf:* **basi'-dongan**)

**anggi** *v. tr.* To love one's relatives. *Minsan amatay danakan, masi nianggi.* Even though a sibling has died he is still loved. *Minsan magtiman matto'ana masi nianggi he' nggo'na. Nianggi, pinabilahi pehē'.* Even though his parents are divorced he is still loved by his mother. Loved, persuaded to go there.

**paganggi** *v. intr.* aN- To feel mutual affection, of close relatives. *Maganggi, buwat magkaki magkalasa. Minsan wa'i amatay danakan masi nianggi.* Having mutual affection, like cousins loving each other. Even though a brother has died he is still loved. *Buwat kami magdanakan, aku binowa he' si Ina', ka'a binowa he' Mma'. Na bang aniya' h'lla-h'nda kami sali'-sali', maganggi kami sabab magdanakan, minsan bay magtiman matto'a kami.* Like us siblings, Mom taking me, Dad taking you. Then when we both have husbands or wives, we are attached to each other because we are siblings even though our parents have divorced. (*Thesaurus:* **kasi 1, gumbala', lasa₂ 1.1, s'lli 1.1**)

**pa'anggi** *v. tr.* To win someone's affection, as a divorced parent may do to a child for whom he or she does not have custody.

**anggil** *n.* 1) Likeness; similarities in appearance. *Da'anggil luwaku maka saga danakanku.* My appearance is similar to that of my brothers and sisters. 1.1) *v. intr.* pa- To look like something. *Sawasa' itū sali' pa'anggil ni bulawan.* This alloy sort of looks like gold.

**paganggil** *v. intr.* aN- To share a common feature of appearance or meaning. *Maganggil itū sali'-sali' ōn. Anggil* is when names are similar. *Maganggil du tomtom maka entom. Tomtom* and *entom* are words with similar sounds and meaning. *Sunduknu maka damba'nu, sali' maganggil.* Your cursed [paddle] and your cursed thing, they are sort of the same. (*cf:* **pagagid**)

**anggop₁** *v. intr.* pa- To face something directly; to be opposite. *Pa'anggop luma' kami ma luma' si Go.* Our house faces that of Go. *Pa'anggop luma' kami ni disi Anu.* Our house faces that of What's-his-name's family. (*Thesaurus:* **alop₁, arap, atubang 1, bayhu' 1.1, harap₁ 1.2**)

**anggopan** *n.* Location across from a point of reference.

**paganggop** *v. intr.* aN- To face each other across a space; to be spatially opposite. *Luma' kami maganggop maka luma' disi Im.* Our house and the house of Im and his family face towards each other. *Ya tinda maganggop maka jambatan.* The shop that is opposite the wharf. (*cf:* **pagbayhu'**)

**anggop₂** *v. tr.* To do something single-handedly. *Takole' nianggop he'na dangan-danganna, halam aniya' anehe'an iya.* He can do it single-handed on his own, no one accompanying him. *Aku na*

*anggop, angandoble.* I am the one to do it, doing twice as much. (*Thesaurus:* **aguwanta 1.1, anggap 1, bāng-bāng₁, bogbog₂, kole', gaga, tigayu'**)

**anggul** *n.* Grapes; raisins.

**angil** *v. intr.* aN- To smell bad due to decay or over-ripeness. (*Thesaurus:* **angsod, bbu 1.1, hangsu 1.1, pulag-pulag, tunug 1.1**)

**pagangilan** *v. intr.* aN- To show signs of ripening, of various fruit, including bananas. (*Thesaurus:* **b'ngkol₂, lāg, pagdauman**)

**angin** *v. tr.* To compel someone to act in a particular way. *Niangin aku maghinang kala'atan.* I was forced to do wrong. (*Thesaurus:* **abiyug, agpot 1, egot-egot, logos 1, panhot, p'ggong, poleggaw**)

**angit** *see:* **ma'angit**

**angol** *adj.* a- Dazed by shock or physical blow. *A'angol itu sali' ap'ddi' kōk, auling mata, bo' halam pali'an. Mbal sali' makasikad. Angol* is like having a sore head, dizzy eyes, even though there is no wound. Sort of unable to be energetic. *Belle'ku ya lundu' timbak, ya ma'angol.* I will dive for the fish stunned by dynamite, the dizzy ones. (*Thesaurus:* **baliyang, bo'ay, lango 1.1, pagboyokan, pagtunggang-kīng, uling**)

**angpud** (*var.* **ampud; angkud**) *adj.* a- 1) Ablaze; burning. *Gansuwang hē', ya kakanna g'llom. A'angkud kono' bang kat'ppi'-t'ppi'an keyat.* The food of those *gansuwang* is caulking fiber. They are said to be afraid of fire, and burn up when approached with flame. 1.1) *v. tr.* To set fire to.

**angsa'** *n.* A large bird such as a turkey or goose.

**angsod** *n.* The smell of decay or rot. *Minsan wanni, bau angsod yuk kasehe'an, bo' mbal abuhuk, tu'ud bauna.* Even *wanni* [a kind of mango], some say it smells rotten, but it is not rotten, that is simply the way it smells. *Bau buhuk, bau angsod na. Aniya' daing ma mohang ilū.* The smell of rot, of something decaying. There are some fish there in the bilge. (*Thesaurus:* **angil, bbu 1.1, hangsu 1.1, pulag-pulag, tunug 1.1**)

**angut** *v. tr.* To set one's mind on a desired outcome. *Angutku isāb nihati mpat halimaw hē.* I really want to have those four tigers explained [to me]. *Ya hē' niangut, lling Sama. Halam makaliyu ni saddī, ya hē' na pa'in niangut.* That is what he really desires, the Sama language. [He] hasn't switched to anything else, that's what he is set on. *Niangut siba'.* Courtship gifts are treasured. (*cf:* **gawi 1**; *Thesaurus:* **go'on 1, niyat 1, pagbo'ot, tamsil, tu'ud₁ 1.1, tuntut₂**)

**pagangut** *v. tr.* To be set firmly on a specific outcome. *Ahāp bay timpu Milikan, angkan pinagangut Milikan amarinta.* The American era was good. That's why we had our heart set on the Americans governing.

**āp-āp** 1) *n.* A fungus-type skin disease marked by loss of color. (*Thesaurus:* **kamuti', limuti',**

**nilastung, panaw** 1) 2) *v. advrs.* -*in*- Affected by depigmentation of the skin. *Niặp-ặp buli' k'llongna.* The nape of his neck has white patches.

**apā** *intrj.* 'Just too much!' Excessive. *Apā ka'a ilu amūng-mūng na pa'in.* You're just too much, talking on and on. *Apā! Aniya' a'a.* Hey! There are people about. *Apā ka'am ilū asidda ba magbono'.* You are too much, so quick to fight!

**apa** *conj.* Because; for the stated reason. *Nijagjag luma' ilu, nirarut sampay hāg apa ilu'un na mundu.* The house is being dismantled, even the posts are being pulled up because bandits are about to arrive. *Salinanku badju'ku apa itiya' abase'.* I'll change my shirt because here it is all wet. (*Thesaurus:* **kalna'** 1.1, **pagka, po'on₂, sabab₁** 1.1, **sangga'ina, saukat**)

**apad-apad** *v. intr.* *aN*- To be overloaded, of a boat or vehicle. (*Thesaurus:* **apang, llop** 1, **togob₂**)

**apalal** *n.* Typical behavior; the way someone is by nature. *Ya na tu'ud apalalna. Ya na addatna.* That is simply his nature. His customary behavior. (*cf:* **sadsaran**; *Thesaurus:* **addat-tabi'at, kaulpi'il, palangay**)

**apam** *n.* 1) A pancake or waffle. (*cf:* **mamun**; *spec:* **balatu, daral, dinglu'** 2, **doppeng, jā, nīggang, okoy, panyām, tinompe'**) 1.1) *v. intr.* *aN*- To make pancakes.

**apang** (var. **atang**; **epang**) *v. intr.* *aN*- To be reaching the limits of a liquid (of a container or boat). *Mbal angapang ni bihing tapi'.* It is not loaded to the lower edge of the [hull] planking. *Sali' a'llop. Wa'i angatang pelang. Ap'nno' he' bohe', tahik, daing.* Like the word *llop*. The canoe has become low in the water, being full of water, sea water, or fish. *Sali' sin'llop, basta aheka duwa'anna angatang.* Like being flooded, whenever it has a lot of freight it goes low in the water. *Mbal makaepang papan itu, tūranku na.* This board won't match [the others], I'll send it back. (*Thesaurus:* **apad-apad, llop** 1, **pagsamaongkop** 1.1, **samaintib, togob₂**)

**pagapang** *v. intr.* *aN*- To be of matching thickness. *Bang mbal dasali' bihing pelang maka tapi', mbal magepang. Bang akapal dakayu' anipis dakayu'.* When the edge of the canoe [hull] is not the same as the upper strake, they aren't of matching thickness. Where one is thick the other is thin.

**aparadol** var. of **paradol**

**apas** *v. intr.* *pa*- 1) To follow swiftly; to be in pursuit. *Bang pa'apas paragan, bang paurul pal'ngngan.* When pursuing we run, when following we walk. 1.1) *v. tr.* To chase someone. *"Papatayku na ka'a, apasta ka to'ongan."* *Bissala astol ko' hē'.* "I will kill you, I will chase you utterly." That's the language of anger. (*Thesaurus:* **pagiku-iku, sunud** 1.1, **sunu', turul** 1)

**api** *n.* 1) A fire. *Bang aniya' kaluma'an taga api,*

*angā' kami pehē' ni luma' dakayu'.* If someone in the village has fire, we go to that house to get it. 1.1) *v. tr.* -*an* To increase a flame by adding fuel. (*cf:* **siglat** 1.1)

**apiki** *adj. zero* 1) Getting close to a time or location. *Apiki ni waktu.* Almost time. (*cf:* **pagsinta', tapa'ut**) 1.1) *v. intr.* *pa*- To approach something closely. (*Thesaurus:* **pagtongop, sekot** 1.2, **sigpi', t'ppi'** 1) 1.2) *v. tr.* To place something near a limiting point. *Da'a apikihun ni bihing.* Don't put it near the edge. 1.3) *v. tr.* -*an* To get physically close with the intent of doing harm. *Bang kami ka'apikihan he' bangsa inān, patā kami alahi.* If someone from that ethnic group closes up with us, we run far away. *Bang aniya' sehe'nu magsuntuk bo' ka'apikihannu, magtūy lubakun pehē'.* *Da'a ka angagad sinuntuk.* If you are going to box someone, and you have closed in with him, sock him one. Don't wait to be punched. *Niapikihan, sali' pineyanan. M'ssa' aniya' daing, m'ssa' aniya' a'a, bang ka angispāy daing bo' ka'apikihannu, larukin na timbak.* Approached closely, like being watched. Whether fish or people, if you see fish and have come right up close to them, throw the dynamite.

**apil** *v. tr.* -*an* To prepare a betel chew. *Yukku ma h'ndaku, "Apilin aku dakayu'."* I said to my wife, "Prepare me a betel nut chew." *Minsan aniya' h'nda angapilan kita dīta.* Even if we have a wife we prepare our own chew.

**apipila'** *n.* Common red ants, likely to bite. *Momemenium pharaonis.* (*gen:* **s'mmut** 1)

**apis** *n.* 1) A mesh fence. (*Thesaurus:* **ād** 1, **buluyan, koral** 1, **kumbangan, kumbisan, likusan, sasak** 1) 1.1) *v. tr.* To enclose something in a fence. *Apisku sumping bo' mbal tasōd he' kambing.* I fence the flowers so that the goats can't get in. *Paluma'an sultan sidda aheya, bay niapis.* The very large house-complex of the sultan has been fenced off. *Makajari tandawan niapis maka basi'.* Windows can be protected with iron rods. *Hinangku sasak pangapisku sumping.* I will build a fence to protect the flowers.

**apit** (var. **hapit₂**) *adv.* Almost but not quite. *Apit iya tatimbak daipara magtūy makatapuk.* He was almost shot, but fortunately was immediately able to hide. (*Thesaurus:* **agon mbal, arāk, himan-himan**)

**apol** *adj. zero* Coagulated, of blood. *Kakoholan laha' apol, asidda na.* Clotted blood being coughed up, his condition serious. (*cf:* **laha'₁** 1)

**appa'** *voc. n.* Address form for a person of high rank. *Itiya' na kami amole', Appa'.* We're going home now, Sir. (*cf:* **ampun₂**)

**appang** var. of **agpang**

**appu'** *v. intr.* *aN*- To spurt or surge up under pressure. *Angappu' na buwas ilū, sali' palasay na he' bohe'na. La'anin turungna. Minsan daing* *angappu' du basta pasubu bohe'na.* That rice is breaking up, like it's awash with water. Remove the lid. Even fish will break up if the water [around it] boils up. *Bang kahumbu angappu', pahusbu bohe'na min diyata' kōkna.* When a whale blows, its water spurts out from its head. (*Thesaurus:* **sasay, sauk 2, s'pput, suput₁**)

**appu' atay** *v. intr. aN-* To seeth with rage; to be furious. {*idiom*} *Angappu' atayna.* He is very angry [lit. his liver is boiling over].

**appula** (var. **akkula**) *v. tr.* To hold on to something of special importance. *Akkula, binowa pi'ingga-pi'ingga, mbal ni'bbahan. Akkula,* taken everywhere, not left behind. *Bang kita abuhaw, busay ya niappula.* If our canoe swamps, it is the paddle that's hung on to. (*Thesaurus:* **abin, habit**)

**apug** *n.* Betel nut chew. *Apug itū tabaku', buyu', bangkit, tagambil, dantilad. Bang bay nihinang ya he' niōnan apug.* Betel chew is made up of tobacco, pepper leaf, lime, resin, betel nut. When it is put together it is called *apug. Bang kita sinagda he' saitan subay nihinang apug pamuwista. Atawa ma pagkawinan, binuwanan apug pagmama'.* When we are oppressed by demons betel chew should be prepared as our tribute. Or at a wedding, a betel nut preparation is given [guests] for chewing.

**apu'-apu'** *v. tr.* To improve relations with someone who is offended. *Minsan aniya' ap'ddi' atayna niapu'-apu', niamu.* Even if there is someone with hurt feelings he is consoled, appeased. (*Thesaurus:* **aluk, dindang-dindang, sayudja' 1**)

**apus** var. of **hapus₁**

**apuwa** *n.* Physical health and vigor, appreciated as a gift from a divine source. *Lidjiki' itū binuwanan kita usaha, apuwa itu binuwanan kita kahāpan baran. Lidjiki'* refers to the provision of a livelihood; *apuwa* refers to the gift of physical health. *Amudji ni Tuhan, sali' angamu' apuwa.* Giving praise to God, sort of asking for good health. *Paminta-mintahan itu pangamu' apuwa ni mbo'.* This request ceremony is for asking an ancestor to grant us physical health. (*Thesaurus:* **anughala' 1, barakat 1, hirayat, lidjiki' 1, pahala'**)

**Arab** *n.* Ethnic Arab; someone of Arabic origin.

**arāk** *adv.* About to (but didn't). *Arāk alungay bangka'nu.* Your canoe was almost lost [but wasn't]. *Ya na d'nda bay pakilāku ma ka'am maka arāk pikilanku kinawinan.* That was the woman I introduced you to and had thought to marry. *Kaleya kita, arāk kita sangoman.* Let's go inland, we're close to being benighted. *Arāk pina'nda'an tungkangku ni ka'a, abila'.* I had thought of showing you my cooking pot, it's broken. (*Thesaurus:* **agon mbal, apit, himan-himan**)

**arakala'** *adv.* Likely, of an unfavorable outcome.

*Angay halam bay sipitbi s'mmek ilu? Arakala' aniya' baliyu paleyang ko' ilu.* Why did you not pin those clothes? If [as is likely] there is wind, they will blow away. *Ya mbal kakautku inān arakala' aniya' goyak maka baliyu bo' makatīg paraw inān, pakkom aku.* The reason I'm not going to sea is that if, as is likely, there is rough weather and wind and the canoe there tips over, I will capsize. *Da'a bbahin busay mailu. Arakala' tinangkaw.* Don't leave the paddle there. It is likely to be stolen.

**aradju** *n.* 1) An old-fashioned radio. 1.1) *v. intr. aN-* To communicate by radio. *Angaradju kitām ni Siasi min Tianggi bo' sigām makahati.* We radioed to Siasi from Jolo so that they would understand.

**arai'** (var. **marai'**) *adv.* 1) Perhaps; possibly. *Marai' halam taentombi bay hinang mma'ku ma pasalanbi.* You may not perhaps have remembered what my father did on your behalf. *Bang a'a saddī ya pameya'annu, aniya' arai' angala'at ka'a.* If you go with anybody else, there could be someone who does you harm. *A:* "*At'kka na si Mma'?*" *B:* "*Arai' halam.*" A: "Has Dad arrived yet?" B: "Possibly not." "*Makasampay lahat du bahā' sigām?*" *B:* "*Marai'.*" A: "Have they reached land yet?" B: "Perhaps." *Itiya' aku magsungi'-sungi', marai' aniya' sassingku.* Here I am with diarrhea, maybe I've got worms. *Magl'ggon lahat, marāi' pangulan na.* It is thundering continuously, maybe it is the rainy season already. 2) Imminent; about to happen. *Aku itū arai' na ta'abut.* As for me, my time has almost come. *Marai' na waktu in aku mbal ta'nda' e' saga a'a ya mbal angisbat Tuhan.* The time is close when I will not be seen by people who do not reverence God. *Magl'ggon lahat, marāi' pangulan na.* It is thundering continuously, the rainy season is close.

**ara'-ara'** *adj. zero* 1) Shaking with fear. *Pina'ara'-ara' he' ina'na. Pinakitāw sali'.* Caused to tremble by his mother. Sort of made afraid. (*Thesaurus:* **k'ddil-k'ddil, kogkog, korog-korog, oro'-oro'₁, pidpid**) 1.1) *v. intr. aN-* To be trembling. *Angara'-ngara' si Ba, sali' amidpid.* Ba gets very scared, kind of shaking.

**aral** *v. intr. aN-* To be shameless.

**arap** *v. intr. aN-* To keep one's mind on God. *Angarap na pa'in kitam ni Tuhan.* Let us always keep our focus on God. (*Thesaurus:* **alop₁, anggop₁, atubang 1, bayhu' 1.1, harap₁ 1.2**)

**arapun** *adv.* Better that; would have been preferable. *Arapun pinuwad bo' mbal tinangkaw.* Better to have been cut down than be stolen. *Arapun ma tongod mma'ku, wa'i iya pina'admit ma ispital llaw itu ma Sambo.* What's fortunate about my father, he was admitted to hospital in Zamboanga today. (*Thesaurus:* **daipara, gōm, sapād-pād**)

**arapun du pa'in** *conj.* If it had been the case.

**araru** *n.* 1) A plow. **1.1)** *v. tr.* -an To plow a field. *Angararuhan aku huma.* I will plow the farmable land. *Pa'araru bahā' tana' matuwas itū?* Is this hard soil in fact plowable? *Sapi' magararu tana' ya tinanoman panggi' kayu ma deya, atawa batung.* Cattle are plowing land away from the coast, to be planted in cassava or peanuts.

**aretes** *n.* Earrings inserted into the ears. *Anting-anting patonton. Aretes nsa' aniya' tontonna, hal pinasōd ni tainga. Sali' du maka subang.* Anting-anting earrings hang down. *Aretes* have nothing hanging, they are just inserted in the ear. They're just like *subang. Bang dalos aretes, mbal ahūg pareyo'.* If the earrings are connected [to the ears], they don't fall down. (*Thesaurus:* **anting-anting 1, bāng₂, domelo, pamulawan, pansi, pinting, singsing, subang**)

**arī** *intrj.* Exclamation of surprise or uncertainty. *Tinilaw iya magtūy e' si Isa'ak, "Arī, sai sa ka'a ilu?"* Isaac promptly asked him, "Hey, who are you?" *Arī! Asal iya ilu, mbal ka'asahan.* Really! That's how he is, nothing to be expected from him. (*Thesaurus:* **agkā', allā, anā, arōy, aruhuy, asē, ayī, dā'₁, ē**)

**ari-ari** *v. tr.* 1) To groom or beautify someone. *Bang aniya' kinawin anakku, pa'ari-ariku si An inān apa asidda ata'u.* If I have a daughter getting married, I'll have An there beautify her because she really knows how. *Niari-arihan, sinoso'an, sin'ssol kilayna, bo' aborak. Magginallang, magsin'mmek ahāp, magsinudlay.* Made beautiful, the hairline shaved, the eyebrows trimmed, and then powdered. Wearing bracelets, dressed in fine clothes, combs in the hair. *Bay niukil-ukilan, magsulang-saingsing ari-arihanna.* It was carved so that its decorative pattern is reversed. (*Thesaurus:* **atal, pagalis-alis**) **1.1)** *v. tr.* -an To decorate important things such as houses or vehicles.

**ari-arihan** *n.* Decoration; embellishment. *Bay niukil-ukilan, magsulang-saingsing ari-arihanna.* It was carved so that the decorative pattern is reversed.

**pangari-ngari** *n.* Things used as decoration.

**ariplano** *n.* An airplane. *Waktu tagna', aniya' bay paglalandingan ariplano ma Bakal sagō' halam na buwattina'an, magka'at na.* At early times, there was a place for airplanes to land at Bakal, but there is none now, destroyed now. (*syn:* **plēn**)

**aro'** *v. intr. pa-* 1) To go close, hoping to hear or be included. *Da'a ka pa'aro' bang magsuli-suli matto'a bo' halam lamudnu.* Don't hang around when the elders are talking but it's not your business. (*Thesaurus:* **harung-harung, sahubu, timuk 1.1**) **1.1)** *v. intr. aN-* To draw near as children do when there is food. (*cf:* **alung 2, donga'**) **1.2)** *v. tr.* -an To look at closely. *Aro'in bo' ka ata'u.* Look closely so you will know [how].

**pa'aro'-aro'** *adv.* Watched closely.

**arōy** (var. **adōy**) *intrj.* 'Oh dear; good grief; alas.' *Arōy! Wa'i na as'bbang buli' pelang ē'.* Alas! The rear of the canoe there has broken off. (*Thesaurus:* **agkā', allā, anā, arī, aruhuy, asē, ayī, dā'₁, ē**)

**pagarōy** *v. tr.* -an To groan about chronic pain or discomfort. *Ai pagarōyannu?* What are you groaning about? (*syn:* **pagaruhuy**)

**aru** *v. ditr.* To seek someone's advice or permission. *Angaru aku ni iya ai-ai mbal kinata'uhan he'ku.* I consult with him on anything I don't know about. *Angaru aku bang makajari pina'awal gadjiku bo' supaya aniya' panabangku pagbalanja' ma luma' hinabuku maka si La ma Sambo.* I am asking for your consideration, whether it might be possible for my salary to be paid early so I can have something for helping with house costs while La and I are in Zamboanga. *Wa'i na amole' si Kuya' Ji, angkan halam aniya' maitu kapangaruhan.* Uncle Ji has gone home, that's why there is no one here to ask advice from. *Aruhun kono' si Mu, kalu bilahi animpay banog apa mbal kata'uhanku.* Just ask Mu's advice, he may be willing to lay out the sail cloth because I don't know how.

**pangaru** *v. tr.* To consult with (or appeal to) someone of higher status.

**aru-aru** *v. tr.* To reduce sail by folding. *Tinuklug niaru-aru. Da'a pasangdanun banog ilu, piligdu magka'at kita ma dilaut. Aru-aruhun sadja.* Fold the sail partway down on its pole. Don't leave the sail like that, we're in danger of suffering damage at sea. Just fold the sail partly down. *Niaru itū tinuklug tonga'-tonga'. Aru* means having the sprit at the half-way position.

**aruhuy** (var. **arūy**) *intrj.* 'Ow; ouch!' *Arōy, wa'i na as'bbang buli' pelang ē'.* What a pain! The stern of the canoe there is broken off. (*Thesaurus:* **agkā', allā, anā, arī, arōy, asē, ayī, dā'₁, ē**)

**pagaruhuy** *v. intr. aN-* To cry out in pain. *Bay asaki, magaruhuy. Sali' iya aglingan saga nggo', mma'.* He was sick, crying out in pain. He sort of calls out mother, father. (*syn:* **pagarōy**)

**arung** *voc. n.* Address term for a younger female. (*Thesaurus:* **dayang, neneng-neneng, nne', nneng 1, nnong**)

**arūy** var. of **aruhuy**

**asa** *n.* 1) Hope; positive outlook. **1.1)** *v. tr.* To be hopeful (but not sure) of a good outcome. *"Amole' aku salung," yuk dangan. Yuk dangan, "Ōy, da'a asa-asata llaw. Arakala' aniya' at'kka ni kita kala'atan."* "I'll go home tomorrow," says one. Says another, "Hey, let's not count on tomorrow. Something bad will likely happen to us." *Angasa-ngasa saga a'a bang aku mbal tabeya'.* The people will be hoping in vain if I am not included. (*Thesaurus:* **kiri-kiri, holat 1, lagad 1.1**)

**pa'asa-asa** *v. tr.* To raise someone's hopes,

however uncertain the outcome.

**pangasa** *n.* 1) Hope. 1.1) *v. tr. -an* To put confidence in someone. *Pangasahinbi Tuhan. Iya ya pangasahan he' kamemon palbangsahan.* Put your trust in God. He is the hope of all nations.

**pangasahan** *n.* The object or basis of one's hope.

**asa'** *v. tr.* To whet or hone a cutting tool. *Asa'un laringnu ilū bo' angōk.* Hone that knife of yours so it cuts. (*cf:* **gisgis** 1.1)

**asa'an** *n.* A sharpening stone.

**asa'an mangsi'** *n. phrase* A high quality whetstone, from Mangsi' Island. *Aniya' ma iya asa'an Mangsi', umbul satu kono'.* He has a whetstone from Mangsi' Island, said to be firstclass.

**asāl** *adv.* By nature or long habit. *Asāl mbal bilahi sinoho'.* He has always disliked being told what to do. *Panubu' sigām ilū asāl maga'agama.* Their family line has always been faithfully religious. *Akiyu' bowa'na, asāl min ka'asalna.* His mouth is twisted, like that from his very beginning. *Pasakaum sigām ma saga a'a ya asāl maglahat maina'an.* They joined the community of the people who had resided there from long ago. (*cf:* **tu'ud₁** 1)

**ka'asāl** *n.* The natural or original state of a person or thing.

**asal** *adv.* Afternoon prayer time for Muslims. (*Thesaurus:* **aisa, luhul₁, magrib** 1, **subu₂** 2)

**asang₁** *n.* 1) The throat and vocal cords. *Min deyom to'ongan asangta, ma luwasan k'llongta.* Our vocal cords are right inside, our necks are outside. 2) Gills of a fish.

**asang₂** *v. intr. aN-* To cry with mouth wide open. *Angasang, bineya'an p'ddi' atay.* Crying with open mouth, carried away by anger. (*Thesaurus:* **kula'ak, galit, gasud, olang** 1.1, **pagalud, pahit**)

**asang-selo** *v. intr. aN-* To cry uncontrollably, with mouth wide open. (*Thesaurus:* **lihing, llad, tangis** 1.1)

**pangasang** *n.* A child notorious for crying with its mouth wide open.

**asang-lumahan** *n.* Various jobfishes. *Aphareus rutilans.*

**asē** *intrj.* 'Yuck!' (*Thesaurus:* **agkā', allā, anā, arī, arōy, aruhuy, ayī, dā'₁, ē**)

**ase'** *v. tr. a-, ka-..-an, -an* To show someone mercy or pity. *Kina'ase'an kita he'na.* He will treat us with mercy. (*Thesaurus:* **andu'-andu', ndū'**)

**ase'-ase'** *v. intr. maka-* To be heart-rending; to stir sympathy or pity. *Ndū', maka'ase'-ase', alungay pamulawanna.* Oh dear, how sad, she has lost her jewelry. *Ndū', maka'ase'-ase' saga d'nda ab'ttong ma masa ina'an-i.* Oh dear, how sad it will be for pregnant women at that time.

**ma'ase'** *v. intr. zero* Merciful; considerate.

**pagmatiase'** *v. intr. aN-* To plead for mercy or sympathy.

**patiase'un** *adj.* Deeply compassionate; merciful.

**asig** *var. of* **lasig**

**asin** *n.* 1) Salt. (*cf:* **timus-timus**) 1.1) *v. tr.* To preserve with salt. *Subay niasin agal-agal bo' bin'lli.* Agar [a kind of seaweed] must be sprinkled with salt in order to be purchased. *Na Babū', am'lli ka daing niasin?* Now then Madam, are you buying salted fish? 1.2) *v. tr. -an* To add or apply salt. *Subay niasinan daing itū bo' ahāp nanamna.* This fish should have salt added so its flavor is better.

**asin-asin** *n.* A salt-like substance.

**asin-budbud** *n.* Fine salt.

**asip** *v. tr.* To notice and respond to something seen or heard. *Bang kita nilinganan subay kita angasip, da'a kita amabiyal.* When we are called we should take notice, not ignoring it. *Angay kām mbal angasip bang kām pinandu'an.* Why don't you pay attention when you are being taught? *Bang aniya' pariyata' ni luma'ta, subay kita angasip atawa anagina.* When someone comes up into our house, we should acknowledge them or welcome them in. (*Thesaurus:* **beya'-beya'₁** 1.1, **hirup₁, ikut**)

**aslag₁** *adj. a-* Full grown. *Kamanahutan itū mbal ameya' gara', anak tahun itū. Subay kami a'aslag.* The young ones can't take advice, the youth of today. We have to be to grown up.

**aslag₂** *adj. a-* 1) Large in cross-section. *Daing a'aslag bay ta'ā'nu?* Was it a very big fish that you caught? *Aniya' budjakna da'aslag batangna maka batang pagt'nnunan kakana'.* He had a spear whose shaft was the same size as the beam of a weaving frame. (*ant:* **nahut**; *Thesaurus:* **heya** 1.1, **mehe**) 2) Wide, of the mesh of a fishnet. (*syn:* **mata₂**)

**asok** *v. intr. pa-* 1) To get inside something. *Niasok maka sinōd sali' du. Manjari yukta ni anak, "Pa'asok ka." Mbal manjari niōnan "pa'asok ka" ni a'a saddi. Ataksil.* Asok and sōd are the same. We can say to a child, "Get in [under the cover with me.]" It is not proper say "come in" to anyone else. You'll be fined. (*Thesaurus:* **deyom** 1.1, **isi₁** 1.1, **sōd** 1) 1.1) *v. tr.* To put something into a container. *Mbal niengkotan panggal, sinagaran na. Subay na niasok e' pellok bo' niā'.* A trap is not tied, just left there. It must be entered by fish [wrasses] and then taken up. *Magbinungkus maka hōs bo' asokta tambal mareyom banga'.* Wrapped in a sarong and then we put the steamed medicine in a clay pot. (*Thesaurus:* **batuk₁** 1.1, **sangon₁** 1)

**pagasok** *v. tr.* To stack together a number of things that fit into a container. *Pagasokun labban bo' mbal agubin.* Pack the cartons inside each other so that they aren't bulky and awkward.

**assang** *n.* A species of dove. *fam. Columbidae.* (*cf:* **balud**)

**astag pirulla** *intrj.* God forbid (a plea for mercy).

**astana'** *n.* A palace or palatial building. *Astana' itū paluma'an sultan, sidda aheya, bay niapis, niād* *inān.* An *astana'* is the place where a sultan lives, very big, enclosed, fenced there.

**astol 1)** *n.* Anger; irritation. **1.1)** *v. intr. aN-* To feel anger towards someone. *Sali' ka angahinang luma'-luma' bo' wa'i paleyang e' baliyu, ya atopna. Na agtūy ko' itū ka angastol. Yuknu, "Ya na itu baliyu akalarak luma'-luma'" Ya ī'-i dikayu' angastol.* Like you playing houses when the wind sends it flying, its roof. Then you immediately get angry and say, "This is the wind that wrecks play houses." That's one case of getting angry. *Luwal ka angastolan dīnu.* You are just making yourself angry. (*Thesaurus:* **la'at-s'mmu, p'ddi' atay 1) 2)** *v. advrs. -in-* To be stirred to anger. *Bang aku niastolan lubakanku si Anu.* When I am angry I whip What's-his-name. (*Thesaurus:* **katol atay**)

**astol atay** *v. tr. a-, ka-..-an, -an* To be deeply angry with someone. {idiom} *Aniya' kina'astolan atayna ni ka'a.* There is someone deeply angry with you.

**asu-asu** *n.* **1)** Steam; vapor. **1.1)** *v. intr. aN-* To give off steam or smoke. *Angasu-ngasu paningkō'anna. Angasu-ngasu isāb daing.* The place where he sat was emitting smoke. Some fish emit vapor too. (*Thesaurus:* **humbu 1.1, husbu 1.1, limbōn**) **1.2)** *v. tr. -an* To treat (medically) by fuming. *Bang kono' pinokot-pokot, subay pinasu-asuhan maka hiyu.* It's said that when we come out in lumps on the skin, we should be fumed with incense sticks.

**ata** *n.* Person who lives with a family and does routine work. (*Thesaurus:* **banyaga' 1, bata'an, sosoho'an**)

**pagpa'ata** *v. intr. aN-* To submit oneself to being a slave.

**pagpatiata** *v. intr. aN-* To submit oneself to being a slave.

**ata-** *aff.* Prefix indicating the emphatic nature of a predicate. Occurs with a small number of stems. *Atapusu' biyabas inān.* The guavas are coming away plucked. *Atakiyum saga makannak.* The children are smiling and smiling. *Atatittowa si Oto'.* Oldest Son is laughing uncontrollably.

**atāk** *n.* **1)** A military attack. *Kasalipan maka karatu'an mareyom foxhole sigām, parohay si Anu amalos. (Dohay itū aniya' atāk pabīng.)* With the salips and the datus in their foxholes, What's-his-name attacked in revenge. (This word dohay implies a return attack.) **1.1)** *v. tr.* To attack or assault an enemy. *Angatāk sundalu min deya maka min dilaut.* The soldiers attacked from the land and from the sea. *Niatāk kami marilaut Pandami'.* We were attacked offshore from Pandami'. (*Thesaurus:* **dogpa' 1.1, dugpak 2, gubat, sakat₁**)

**atakabbul** (derivative of **kabbul**) *adj. zero* Confident or arrogant in regard to one's assertions about the future. *Atakabbul a'a hē', ya magtūy sinulat he' Tuhan, yuk-i, "B'nnal a'a inān."*

*Bang mbal kinale he' Tuhan, putingan.* That man is sure of himself. God promptly records his words and says, "That man is truthful." If God doesn't listen to him, he is a liar. *Atakabbul, tinuhug e' Tuhan bang ah'lling.* Speaking confidently [about the future], his words stored by God on a string.

**atag₁** (var. **antag; tag**) *n.* **1)** A place; location. *Wa'i ma atag ingga?* Where is its location? *Ina'an ma atag kami.* There at our place. *Ma tag ingga? Halam maitu.* Whereabouts? It isn't here. **1.1)** *v. intr. pa-* To stay in some location. *Pa'atag aku ma ka'am.* I will stay where you are. *Taptap iya niumbangan e'na, ya pa'atag ma po'on kayu akeyat.* He will always be cared for by him, the One who locates in the burning tree. (*Thesaurus:* **paglahat 1.1, t'nna' 1.1, tongod₂ 1.2**)

**pa'atagan** *n.* The location of something; a place where someone stays; a lair. (*Thesaurus:* **jadjahan, lugal 1, pat'nna'an**)

**pangatag** *n.* People near one's house; neighbors.

**atag₂** *n.* A girlfriend. *Taga atag na si Oto'.* Oldest son now has a girlfriend. (*cf:* **tunang 1**)

**atag₃** *v. advrs. ka-...-an* To be treated in the same way as others. *Buwat magbuwan, luma' inān kabuwanan, dakayu' inān halam. Na ya dakayu' halam kaniya'an, halam ka'atagan.* Like when things are being given, that house has been given something, [but] that other one hasn't. So the one house has not received anything, isn't treated as others.

**ata'** *n.* Coarse fragments in pounded grain; grit. *Ata', ya kapin panapungan.* Grit, that is left after pounding. (*Thesaurus:* **tapung 1, tirigu 2**)

**atal** *v. tr.* To apply lipstick. (*syn:* **lipistīk 1.1;** *Thesaurus:* **ari-ari 1, pagalis-alis**)

**atang** var. of **apang**

**atap** *n.* The gap between asking price and what a buyer offers. (*Thesaurus:* **lampak₂ 1, samaunjuk**)

**pagatap** *v. intr. aN-* **1)** To match, of asking price and money offered. *Magatap, magtongod halga'na maka sīn pam'lli.* Matching, the value of something and the money to buy it. **1.1)** *v. tr.* To have things matching. *Pinapagatap, pinapagdasali'.* Made to match; made to be the same.

**pa'atap** *v. tr.* To match the price asked by the seller with the money available to the buyer.

**atarasaw** (var. **atrās**) *adj. zero* Late; tardy. *Bang kami animbak ni Tapa'an ameya' kami man donson. Al'kkas binayan, mbal atarasaw bang aniya' daing binowa ni M'ddas.* When we go dynamiting to Tapa'an we go in a boat with an outboard motor. It is a fast conveyance, we are not late when we have fish to take to Siasi. (*Thesaurus:* **damuli 1, lēt, tanggollayan**)

**atas₁** *adv.* Preferably; instead. *Atas alungay sīnku.* It was inevitable that my money was lost. *Dayas-dayasan, sali' aheka kinakanna. Atas* *pinagtimanan ya takapin inān, apa a'sso.* Abundant, lots of food. But instead, because [he] was full, the left-overs were thrown out. *Yuk ina' ma onde', "Anak, da'a ka paluwas sangom ilu." Atas iya palaksu min ād.* Mother says to the child, "Son, don't go out tonight." Instead he jumped the fence. *Buwat saga nilagut aku, abakat bo' mbal angalaha', na yuk kasehe'an, "Angay ka mbal niōk to'ongan ilū?" Na yukku, "Atas angalahod."* Like when I was cut with a knife, wounded but not bleeding, the others said, "How come you weren't seriously cut?" So I said, "A bruise will come up instead." *Atas bay ningā' e'na sīn ya suku' a'a miskin.* Instead he took money that belonged to a poor man. (*cf:* **tahan₁ 1.1**)

**pangatasan** *n.* A preferred outcome.

**atas₂** *adj. zero* **1)** Responsible; blameable. *Bang aniya' bay pinabeya' e' a'a, pinabeya' ma siyaliku bo' alungay, aku atas.* If a man sends something with my younger sibling and it is lost, I take responsibility. *Atas iya magpaganti' ma siyali sigām.* He was responsible to take the place of their youngest brother. (*Thesaurus:* **abunaw, bahala'₁, kuwiraw, lawag-baran, siyal, tanggung₂**) **1.1)** *v. tr.* -an To accept responsiblity or blame for some outcome. *Bang alungay kapaku itū, angatas si Aj.* If this axe of mine is lost, Aj takes the responsibility for it. *Pangatasan sigām magmula bang pa'in mbal magta'at ni tuhan saddī.* They accepted being destroyed so long as they did not worship any other god. *Ta'atas he'na angala'ugan sehe'na mampa'in iya maka'ā' sīn.* He takes it on himself to assault his companion so long as he can get money.

**atas-pikil** *adj. zero* Responsible for some intended action. *Tantu kami ya atas-pikil anukbalan iya ni ka'a.* We will definitely be responsible to hand him over to you.

**pagatas-pikil** *v. intr.* aN- To have the responsibility of deciding. *Arakala' itu asōng e' tambal itū, ka'a ya magatas-pikil ai-ai pamūngan.* Since this [illness] is likely to progress with this treatment, you are the one to decide what is to be said. *Ka'am matto'a ya magatas-pikil.* You elders are the responsible ones.

**pangatas** *n.* Resources for discharging a debt or liability.

**ataw-ataw** *n.* **1)** The ripples on a water surface. *Buwat ma kulit tahik, bang yukta t'ddo' ta'nda' to'ongan. Bang ataw-ataw mbal na ta'nda'.* Like the surface of the sea, when we say it is calm, things are seen clearly. When there are ripples, things are not seen. **1.1)** *v. tr.* To ruffle a water surface. *Bay ataw-atawku tahik, manjari mbal tapag'nda'anku sīn.* I stirred up the sea, so I couldn't see the money. *Oto', da'a ataw-atawun bohe' ilū.* Son, don't ruffle that water.

**atawa** *conj.* Either; or. *Bang ka pinapene', ai ahāp,*

*alta' atawa pangiskul?* If you are given a choice, what is best, riches or schooling? *Am'lli aku buwahan atawa daing?* Shall I buy lansones or fish?

**atay₁** *n.* Liver.

    **inu-inu atay** *adj.* a- To take offense; take personally. {idiom} *Da'a pa'in kām mandā'-dā', da'a na ainu-inu ataybi.* Please don't be offended, don't take it personally.

**atay₂** *n.* The emotional center of a range of emotions (similar to the heart in English). *Halam aniya' tau'ku ma deyom atay.* I do not hold anything in my heart. *Nna'un to'ongan ma deyom ataynu.* Store it securely in your heart [i.e. commit it to memory].

    **appu' atay** *v. intr.* aN- To seeth with rage; to be furious. {idiom} *Angappu' atayna.* He is very angry [lit. his liver is boiling over].

    **astol atay** *v. tr.* a-, ka-..-an, -an To be deeply angry with someone. {idiom} *Aniya' kina'astolan atayna ni ka'a.* There is someone deeply angry with you.

    **atay kambing** *v. intr.* aN- To have an insatiable sexual appetite. {idiom} *Da'a kām angatay kambing.* Don't behave like a goat, always eager for sex.

    **atay-batu** *n.* A hard or brave heart, unmoved by fear or pity. {idiom}

    **atay-pote'** *n.* Innocence; purity of intentions. {idiom} *Pamuwanku ka'a, Tuwan, hilas atay-pote'.* My gift to you, friend, freely given from a pure heart.

    **bakat atay** *adj.* a- Suffering emotional hurt. {idiom} *Abakat atayku pasal panipu e' bagayku lissi.* I am hurt emotionally because of being betrayed by my closest friend.

    **kabid atay** *adj.* a- Emotionally troubled. {idiom}

    **pagkabid-atay** *v. intr.* aN- **1)** To be unsettled in one's mind. **1.1)** *v. tr.* To let one's mind become unsettled. *Anawhid sadja kita, mbal pagkabidta atayta.* We just make a settled decision, we don't let our minds become unsettled.

    **kagit atay** **1)** *v. intr.* pa-/a- To be offensive. {idiom} *Ē! Amakagit atay ko' ilū.* Hey! That [behavior] is very offensive. (*Thesaurus:* **ambul-dā', anak-anak₂, la'at atay, tumpalak 1**) **2)** *v. tr.* a-, ka-..-an, -an To be feeling the force of someone's displeasure. {idiom} *Hinangunbi ai-ai bay panoho'an ka'am bo' kam mbal kinakagitan e'na atay.* Do whatever you are told to do so you don't experience his anger.

    **katol atay** *adj.* a- Irritating; annoying. {idiom} *Makakatol atay to'ongan saga onde'-onde' itū nilāng.* It is very irritating getting these children to stop. (*Thesaurus:* **astol 2**)

    **keyas atay** *v. intr.* pa- To ease, of the intensity of some grief or disappointment. {idiom} *Pakeyas atayta, halam na bay susa.* Our sadness has eased, the past sorrow is no more.

    **kibad atay** *adj.* a- Emotionally tense due to

anxiety or shock. {idiom} *Pakibad deyom atayku, sali' mandā'dā'.* I am emotionally distracted, sort of feeling hurt. *Bay kami angusaha panit, yukku, "Angā' na ka palsuku'annu." Yuknu, "Da'a na pakibarun deyom ataynu ilu. Aniya' du tungbasna."* I had been catching tuna and said, "Take your share." You said, "Don't worry yourself about it. There will be no doubt be compensation." *Magkakibad deyom atayku sabab siyaliku laha'an, bay binono'. Sali' ameya' ginhawaku to'ongan.* My emotions are shaken because my younger brother is bleeding, he was hit. It is like my whole inner being is involved. (*Thesaurus:* **pagsorol, sukkal 1, susa 1**)

**k'bbal atay** *v. advrs.* ta- Suffering sudden grief or shock. {idiom} *Buwat aniya' ahūg onde'-onde', ati kuppata, manjari tak'bbal atayta.* For example when a child falls and we jump into the sea after it, we experience severe shock. *Tak'bbal atayta, takuddat to'ongan.* Deeply distressed, greatly shocked.

**deyom-deyom atay** *n. phrase* Something fixed securely in one's memory, especially a grudge. {idiom} *Kata'uhanku deyom-deyom ataynu. Ah'lling ka kono'.* I know what you are holding back. Please speak up. (*Thesaurus:* **akon-akon, agmol 1, buli'an₂, koto'-koto', lagod-lagod**)

**ganggu' atay** *adj.* a- Anxious; apprehensive. {idiom} *Mbal pangandolku, aganggu' atayku.* I won't rely [on him], I am anxious. (*Thesaurus:* **kanaw-kanaw, kawang, hanggaw₁ 1**)

**haggut atay** *adj.* a- Inwardly calm; unperturbed. {idiom}

**handok atay** *adj.* a- **1)** Reassured after being emotionally stressed. {idiom} **1.1)** *v. intr.* pa- To become calm or less distressed, of a person who has experienced shock or fright. {idiom} *Handok atay itū ai-ai basta takuddat kita, atawa asusa llum-patay. Buwat aniya' sōng amatay, bo' pabīng, na pahandok atayta.* This emotional relief refers to anything has shocked us, or caused anxiety as to life or death. It is like being close to death but reviving, our emotions calmed. *Pahandok atayta, tabāk na bay malungay.* We are comforted, the thing that was lost is found.

**handul atay** *v. advrs.* ta- Affected by grief, but without audible weeping. {idiom} *Tahandul deyom atay, mbal anangis, sagwā' patū' bohe' matana, suma'an akeyat mata.* Grieving quietly, not crying audibly, but our tears flowing down, or sometimes our eyes becoming red. *Sali' anangis ma deyom atayta. Buwat aniya' kalasahanta halam na ma kita, na makahandul-handul atay.* It's like crying inside. Like when someone we love is no longer with us, then we feel grief deep in our hearts. (*Thesaurus:* **pagdohon, pagdukka' 1.1, paglemong 1.1, paglindu**)

**hansul atay** *adj.* a- Deeply moved emotionally. {idiom} *Ahansul pangatayanna.* He is deeply

moved. *Magtūy ahansul atayna sultan-i maka he'na angolang, "Oto'ku! Oto'ku!"* Right then the sultan's heart was broken, and he cried, "My son! My son!"

**hāp atay** *adj.* a- Cheerful; in a good mood. {idiom} *Makahāp atay ko' ilū.* That makes us cheerful.

**heya ma atay** *v. tr.* To esteem. {idiom} *Halam aku bay paheyana ma atay.* He didn't treat me as being important. *Mura-murahan magpakasampay in niyat kami ni ka'am, paheyabi du isāb ma atay.* May it be that our commitment to you will be fulfilled, you too treating it as important.

**holat deyom atay** *adj.* a- Experiencing suppressed excitement. {idiom}

**la'at atay** *adj.* a- The feeling of offense or emotional hurt. {idiom} *Ōy, makala'at atay ko' ilū.* Hey, that is offensive. *Da'a kām angahinang ai-ai ya makala'at pangatayan sigām kasehe' itū.* Don't do anything that annoys the rest of them. (*cf:* **akon-akon**; *Thesaurus:* **ambul-dā', anak-anak₂, kagit atay 1, tumpalak 1**)

**lanu' atay** *adj.* a- Cordial; with no hard feelings. {idiom} *Alanu' atayna, halam aniya' koto'-koto' mareyom atayna.* Gentle in manner, no resentment in her heart.

**langa atay** *adj.* a- Proud; haughty. {idiom} *Magabbu-abbu, sali' alanga atayna.* Showing off his status, kind of haughty.

**leyang atay** *v. intr.* pa- To be startled. {idiom} *Ahūg tibu'uk, paleyang magtūy atayku.* Some cassava fell, I was immediately startled [lit. my liver flew up]. (*Thesaurus:* **k'bbal, kobla', kuddat, himatta'**)

**lunuk atay** *adj.* a- Placated; mollified; approachable. {idiom} *Alunuk na atay. Palabay na bay map'ddi' atay hē'.* He is mollified now. What upset him has passed. *A: "Pamagay daing ilū?" B: "Pamalunukku atayna."* A: "What is that fish for?" B: "It's to make him pleased with me again [lit. for my softening of his liver]." *Pinalunuk pangatayanna.* He was made to feel well-disposed.

**padlak ni atay** *v. intr.* aN- To come to one's mind. *Yampa amadlak ni atayku.* It has just now come to mind. (*Thesaurus:* **entom 1.2, magtak, sangpit, suligpat, tambung, tasdik, tomtom 1.1**)

**pagk'bba-k'bba atay** *v. intr.* aN- To be experiencing rapid heartbeat, as a symptom of distress or shock. {idiom} *Magk'bba-k'bba atayku bang aku angandusa.* I am deeply distressed when I do something bad. *Magk'bba-k'bba deyom atayta sabab aniya' katāwanku.* My pulse races because I am afraid of something.

**pasu' atay** *adj.* a- Angry; furious; in a temper. {idiom} *Saga a'a apasu' pangatayna ma bangsata.* People who are violent towards our ethnic group. (*Thesaurus:* **masu'**)

**p'ddi' atay** *adj.* a- **1)** Angry about something.

{idiom} *Ap'ddi' atayku ma si Oto'.* I am angry with Older Brother. *Sali' bay magbono' maglakibini, sali' amowa sīn matto'a l'lla hē' pangayu' bo' mbal amasi ap'ddi' atay matto'a d'nda.* Like a married couple having a fight, the father of the man bringing a compensation gift so that the father of the woman does not continue to be angry. *Sali' hāl aningkō', maka sali' ap'ddi' atayna bang anoho'.* He just sort of sits and gives orders as though he is angry. (*Thesaurus:* **astol** 1.1, **la'at-s'mmu**) **1.1)** *v. intr.* aN- To become angry. {idiom} *Magdugal kita bay ai-aita, bay nna'ta, bo' wa'i alungay. Am'ddi' atayta.* We are really annoyed about our things which we had put away but which are now lost. We have become angry. **1.2)** *v. tr.* a-, ka-..-an, -an To be annoyed at someone; to feel angry with. {idiom} *Ya makap'ddi'an atayna bay sigā maglegot.* What made him angry was them playing dice.

**pagp'ddi' atay** *n. phrase* **1)** Irritability; anger. *Palabayta na ya pagp'ddi' atayta bay. K'llo'ta imam mikisugsug kita tawbat.* We put behind us what we had been angry about. We get the imam to pray the forgiveness prayer over us. **1.1)** *v. tr.* To be angry about something.

**pote' atay** *adj.* a- Innocent; blameless. {idiom}

**sabali-bali man atay** *adj.* zero Slipped from one's mind. {idiom} *Buwat aniya' tab'llita ai-ai bo' tapat'nna', ati bo' kita makal'ngngan. Pamat'nna'anta inān halam kabiyasahan. Yukta, "Sabali-bali min atayku."* Like when we've bought something and put it down and then walked off. The place where we put it is unfamiliar. We say, "It went right out of my mind." *Sabali-sabali man atayku suru' hē', sali' takaipat bahā', nsa' bay taentom.* That spoon slipped my mind, forgotten perhaps, beyond recall.

**pagda'atay** *v. intr.* aN- To be on informal or intimate terms with each other, as people in the same household. (*Thesaurus:* **pagsamod**, **pagsōd-addat**)

**pangatayan** *n.* The psychological seat of emotions; a person's psyche.

**atay dugu-dugu** *n. phrase* Edible entrails of some species of trepang.

**atay-atay** *n.* The opening of a woven fish trap. *Kinahiran daing min atay-atay bubu.* The fish were moved [with a stick] through the opening of the *bubu* trap.

**ati** *conj.* Then; so then; and then; and now. *Angindam ka sīn, ati mbal pa'in kabayarannu?* You borrow money, and now you can't pay? *Bang kami magbono' maka si Nu ati anangis iya, na nirapitan sidda he' Ina'.* When Nu and I fight and he cries, then Mom takes his side, totally. *Sinagaran ati pinataguntun.* Just let go and allowed to hang down. (*cf:* **ampa₁**; *Thesaurus:* **manjari₂**, **nā** 1, **sakali₂**)

**atis** *n.* The sugar-apple. *Annona squamosa.*

**atiya'** var. of **itiya'**

**atol** *v. intr.* pa- To stay put in one place. (*cf:* **antung**)

**pagatol-atol** *v. intr.* aN- To stay together in one location. *Magatol-atolan saga pelang.* The canoes are staying together in the same spot.

**atop** *n.* **1)** The roof of a building. *"Ndiya aku dambila' sairap-sairap ilū," yuk Sultan, "hinangku atop."* "Give me half of that piece of woven walling," said the Sultan, "to make a roof with." (*cf:* **sapaw** 1; *Thesaurus:* **layang-layang**, **ungkup**) **1.1)** *v. tr.* -an To roof a building. *Luma' labban niatopan karut.* A cardboard house roofed with sacking. **2)** A section of nipa thatch. *Wa'i ahūg dakayu' atop. Halam bay kaengkotan.* One unit of thatch has fallen. It was not tied down. (*cf:* **pa'ud** 1, **silang₂**)

**atop mital** *n. phrase* Corrugated iron roofing.

**atrās** var. of **atarasaw**

**atu** *n.* **1)** An opponent. **1.1)** *v. tr.* -an To react to what another does, as to fight back. *Bang kita bay na magbono' bo' ka mbal angatu ma aku, lagutta ka maka lahut.* When you and I had been fighting and you couldn't defend yourself, I struck you with my large knife. You bled. *Pila atuhanku? Aheka sigā, aku dangan-danganku.* How many was I fighting off? They were many, I was on my own. *Alō, bang pasah'mpu ba'anan a'a, na mbal tagaga niatuhan.* Wow, when lots of people cooperate, then they can't be counter-attacked.

**pagatu-atu** *v. tr.* To fight with each other. *Pinagmanuk-manuk, sali' onde'-onde' pinagatu-atu.* Made to behave like fighting cocks, as children set to fighting each other.

**pangatu** *n.* A defensive weapon. (*Thesaurus:* **almas**, **hinanib** 1, **pakokos**, **takos** 1)

**atubang** *v. intr.* pa- **1)** To face towards something. *Manjari pa'atubang sigām magbono'.* So then they faced them to engage in battle. (*Thesaurus:* **alop₁**, **anggop₁**, **arap**, **bayhu'** 1.1, **harap₁** 1.2) **1.1)** *v. tr.* To confront someone. *A'abag pahāp angatubang daing itū.* The strings of fish facing this way are excellent. *Asukkal landu' pangatayan sigām angkan halam makatawakkal angatubang saga banta.* Their hearts were very troubled, which is why they didn't dare confront the enemies.

**pagatubang** *v. intr.* aN- To be face to face.

**atung** var. of **antung**

**auliya'** *n.* A person with divine gifts of wisdom. *Auliya' itū niōnan tulun. Ai-ai niamu' ilu'un na.* An *auliya'* is spoken of as a divinely gifted person. Whatever [he] asks for is there promptly. *Auliya' ataha' p'ngngotna, ta'abut hawakanna, sali' bay ma deyom tana'. Kinata'uhan he'na kamemon. Manusiya' isāb.* An *auliya'* has a long beard reaching to his waist, like something that has been in the ground. He knows everything. He's also human. (*Thesaurus:* **langtas 1, tugu, tulun₁ 1**)

**aut** *n.* **1)** Impurities in water. *Aniya' suru' arāk sinassaw ma deyom aut.* A spoon was about to be groped for in murky water. *Aniya' sīn arāk sassawku ma deyom aut. Yuk Ina', "Bang aniya' sīn ahūg nireyom bohe' angaut, mbal tapiha."* I was about to grope for a coin in murky water. Mother said, "If money falls into dirty water, it can't be found." (*Thesaurus:* **lagod₁, lobog 1**) **1.1)** *v. intr. aN-* To become discolored. *Bang aniya' sīn ahūg bo' angaut, mbal tapiha.* If money falls [into the sea] and it is dirty, it can't be found.

**awak-awak** *n.* A type of kite. (*Thesaurus:* **birarul, pindun, taguri'**)

**awal₁** *adv.* In times past; long ago. *Bay awal, jāman bay kami magkalga'.* Way back, in the times when we were working as porters. *Min awalna to'ongan.* From its long past. (*cf:* **ahil, timpu 1**; *Thesaurus:* **awal-jāman, awal-tagna', masa-awal, musim tagna'**)

**awal ni ahil** *adv. phrase* From time long past to the present. *Min awal ni ahil na pa'in aku ya magpatireyo' ma iya.* For a long time [lit. from the past to the future] I have been the one to abase myself before him. *Sangay min awal sampay ni ahil, halam bay buwattē' hekana.* From ancient times until the distant future, there has never been such a profusion. (*Thesaurus:* **jāman, masa 1, taem, timpu 1, waktu 1**)

**awal-jāman** *n.* Time long past. *Yuk mbo'ku, halam kono' dragadik tempo awal-jāman ē'.* My grandparent said there were no drug addicts in the olden times. (*Thesaurus:* **awal-tagna', awal₁, masa-awal, musim tagna'**)

**awal-tagna'** *n.* Ancient times; long ago. *Sa'angay min awal-tagna'.* Ever since the long-ago beginning. (*Thesaurus:* **awal-jāman, awal₁, masa-awal, musim tagna'**)

**awal₂** *adj. a-* **1)** Early; in good time. *A'awal ya t'kka sigām.* Their arrival is earlier than expected. **1.1)** *v. intr. aN-* To be early; to be in good time. *Ahāp angawal.* It's good to be early. *Angaru aku bang makajari pina'awal gadjiku bo' supaya aniya' panabangku pagbalanja' ma luma' hinabuku maka si La ma Sambo.* I am appealing [to you] that it might be possible for my salary to be paid early so I can have something for helping with house costs while La and I are in Zamboanga. (*cf:* **k'llaw**) **1.2)** *v. tr. -an* Do something beforehand. *Awalanku pangahakaku itū bo' supaya kam mbal takuddat.* I will tell you before it happens so you are not startled.

**pangawal** *n.* A time set for some activity or result.

**awam** *adj. a-* Ignorant of; uninformed. *Bang aniya' amatay kaukaki si Mma', halam bay nihaka'an si Ina'. A'awam na iya.* When cousins of Father died, Mother was not informed. She is ignorant

of it now. *Buwat aniya' alungay ai-aita, asal angahaka na kita ni pangatagta atawa ni botang lahat bo' supaya sigām mbal a'awam. Kita kalungayan ya amasasā.* When something of ours is lost, we naturally let our neighbors or the community leaders know so they are not unaware. As those who have suffered the loss, we are the ones to let people know.

**pagawam** *v. intr. aN-* To pretend to be ignorant or unaware of some situation. *Magawam-awam dīna halam makatangkaw, bo' mbal tajīl.* He pretended personnel ignorance [about] having stolen anything, in order not to be jailed. *Sali' magawam, magp'ddi'-p'ddi' sali'.* Acting unaware [of illness], with pain sort of coming and going.

**awat** *adj. a-* **1)** Having an advantage over someone. *Ka'a am'lli t'llumpū' sīn, mbal niā'. B'lliku dambila'. Agsāy ka'a-i ah'lling. "A'awat ka'a-i am'lli sinaukat aheka sīnnu."* You would buy for thirty centavos, but didn't get it. I bought for fifty centavos. Then you said, "You had the buying advantage [over me] just because you have a lot of money." **1.1)** *v. intr. pa-* To go ahead of someone. *"Pa'awat ka,"* yukna, *"pariyata'an."* "Go further ahead," he said, "up-current." **1.2)** *v. tr. -an* To outstrip or outdo someone. *Angawat itū, buwat kita angusaha bo' duwa ya hūgku bang kita magpanonda'.* Awat is like when we are at work and I drop two lines when we are trolling. *Awat-awatanku na pa'in sudju pariyata'an itū.* I keep getting ahead going upstream here. (*Thesaurus:* **labi 1.2, lakbaw 1**)

**pagawat** *v. tr. -an* To compete in order to get the advantage over one another. *Sīn ya pinagawatan e' sigā.* Money is what they competed over.

**pa'awat** *v. tr.* To outbid another bidder.

**awil** *see:* **ta'awil**

**Awrusalam** *n.* Jerusalem.

**awtu** *n.* Automobile or car.

**ayak** *v. tr.* To sift powdery material such as flour. *Ayakun dahū, aheka s'ggit.* Sift it first, there's a lot of rubbish. (*cf:* **sā'₂**)

**ayakan** *n.* A sieve or strainer. *Aniya' pangayakan, subay anahut-nahut minnitu.* There is a sieve, it should be finer than this. (*cf:* **sā'an 1**)

**pangayakan** *n.* A sieve or strainer.

**ayad** *v. tr. -an* To treat something with care. *Niayaran e'na pasal pusaka'.* She treated it carefully because it was something inherited. (*Thesaurus:* **ayuput, hamumu', ipat, pahilala' 1, paintul, paipid, payakun, talkin, ulip, upiksa', ussap 1**)

**ayad-ayad** *v. intr. pa-* To be careful in what one does. *Pa'ayad-ayad ka bang ka amayan pelang bo' ngga'i ka pelangnu, ko da'a magka'at.* Be careful when you use a canoe as a conveyance and it's not your canoe, so as not to damage it. (*cf:* **kamaya'-maya' 1.1**)

**ayan** *n.* The space above earth; the firmament; outer space. *Paletop bohe' niriyata' ayan.* The water rose up into space. (*Thesaurus:* **alam₁, dunya, langit**)

**ayas-ayas** *n.* The drying racks at the outer end of the outrigger boom supports, of a traditional canoe. (*cf:* **ampang**)

**ayat** *n.* A short length of text, especially of a religious text such as the Holy Koran or the Holy Bible. *Amassa kita da'ayat patiha'.* We recited a single stanza of the opening section of the Holy Koran. *Nda'unbi kaheya puyu'-puyu' pangisihan ayat Kitab ya pin'kkos ma l'ngngon sigām.* See how big the Scripture packets are that are tied to their arms. (*Thesaurus:* **bāb, jūd**)

**aykalas** *n.* 1) Foolhardy courage; daring. *Oy! Ka'a ilu amowa aikalas, sali' amiha kamataynu.* Hey! You with your foolhardy courage. It's like you are seeking your death. *Bang am'mmong-m'mmong mbal du kita ainay, sa' bang kita angaikalas...* If we are somewhat inconspicuous nothing will happen to us, but if we are foolishly brave... (*Thesaurus:* **bahani 1, esog 1.1**) **1.1**) *v. intr.* aN- To be daring; to be risk-taking. *Angaikalas kita, sali' kita aesog.* We display our courage, like we are so brave.

**ayī** *intrj.* Expression of emphasis on what is being said. *Ayī, asaltun pahāp ka'a ilū.* Wow, you are so perfect! (*Thesaurus:* **agkā', allā, anā, arī, arōy, aruhuy, asē, dā'₁, ē**)

**aymuka** *n.* Facial expression. *Asawa aymukana.* He looks friendly [lit. his face is bright]. (*Thesaurus:* **bantuk, bayhu' 1, dagbos, jantang-jari, lahi₄, luwa 1, pangli' 1**)

**aymulla** *n.* The deceased, a euphemism used to avoid naming the dead. *Bay a'llum lagi' si Aymulla hē'.* When the departed referred to was still alive. (*cf:* **matay₁ 1**; *Thesaurus:* **lipulmi'ad, maruhum, nahanat, wapat**)

**ayron** *adj.* zero Powerful, of someone's physique. *Ayron pahāp a'a ina'an amusay, sali' bastigan.* The man paddling there is a real iron man, like an athlete. (*Thesaurus:* **basag 1, bastig, kosog 1.1, kulasog 1.1, kuwat-anggauta', landos 1, paslod 1.1**)

**pagayron** *v. intr.* aN- To display an impressive degree of strength. *Maka'nda' kita a'a amuhat ai-ai, basi' aheya ka, batu ka, batang kayu, basta aheya, ōnanta magayron.* When we see a man lifting something, a steel [girder], a rock, or a wooden beam, anything large, we call him 'Iron Man'.

**ayuk-ayuk** *v. tr.* To stimulate fighting cocks by holding them beak to beak. (*Thesaurus:* **manuk-sigun, pagbulang, pagtakbi', pagtūkan**)

**ayu'** *v. ditr.* To compensate someone for causing physical or emotional harm. *Bang aku bay makabuwan dusa, subay aniya' sīn nde'anku pangayu'.* If I am the one who has committed an offense, I should hand over a sum of money by way of compensation. *Sali' bay magbono' maglakibini, sali' amowa sīn matto'a l'lla hē' pangayu' bo' mbal amasi ap'ddi' atay matto'a d'nda.* Like a married couple having a fight, the father of the man bringing a compensation gift so that the father of the woman does not continue to be angry. (*Thesaurus:* **bangun₂ 1, diyat, masangka**)

**pangayu'an** *n.* Cash or goods paid in compensation for an offense or injury.

**ayum-ayum** *v. tr.* -an To mend a hole by darning. *Subay niayum-ayuman bo' mbal pasōng lowang ilū.* The hole should be darned so it doesn't get any bigger. (*Thesaurus:* **anom, huwit-huwit 1.1, lalipan-lalipan, sulsi, t'nnun**)

**ayun** *n.* Agreement.

**pagta'ayun** *v. intr.* aN- To be in accord with each other. (*Thesaurus:* **amu₂ 1.1, beya'₃ 1, dakayu'₂ 1, manghalapi, sulut 1, tayudtud**)

**ayuput** *v. tr.* To provide for someone's needs. *Itiya' kami niayuput pahāp e' saga mato'aku angkan asambu pamaranan kami.* Here we are very well cared for by my parents-in-law, which is why our bodies are getting plump. (*syn:* **ayura 1**; *Thesaurus:* **ayad, hamumu', ipat, pahilala' 1, paintul, paipid, payakun, talkin, ulip, upiksa', ussap 1**)

**ayura** 1) *v. tr.* To treat a person or thing with care and persistence. *Niayura kita he' matto'ata, sali' kita pinahilala' to'ongan sat'ggol mbal pahali sakita.* We are well cared for by our parents, the same as being fully looked after for as long as our sickness is not over. *Ayurata daing, hella'ta painut.* We treat a fish gently, pulling it up little by little. (*syn:* **ayuput**) 2) *v. ditr.* To intercede for someone in need of care. *Bang aniya' ma kita a'a asakki subay ayurata ni mbo'.* If we have someone who is sick we must request help for them from the ancestors.

**ayuwan** *n.* Spouse of one's child, nephew or niece.

**pagayuwan** *v. intr.* aN- To be related as ego to spouse's parent, or as ego to child's spouse. *Magayuwan kami maka si Ga.* We are parents-in-law to Ga.

**ayuwan min pagkakihan** *n. phrase* Spouse of nephew or niece's child.

**ayuwan min pang'mpuhan** *n. phrase* Spouse of grandchild or of sibling's grandchild.

# B b

**bā** *ptl.* 1) Mild emphasis marker. *Aluhay bā, takole'nu du.* Quite easy, you can certainly do it. 2) Question marker. *Buwat ni'nde'an ni aku gadjiku. Tilawnu, "Jukup bā ilū?" "Aho'," yukku, "ustu."* Like when my wages are handed over to me. You ask, "Is that complete?" "Yes," I say, "it's enough." (*Thesaurus:* **ka₁, du 1, sa**)

**bāb** *n.* A chapter or heading in printed material. (*Thesaurus:* **ayat, jūd**)

**baba** *conj.* During; while. *Inumun kahawa itū baba apasu'.* Drink this coffee while it is hot. *Dugpakku iya baba iya minale' gi'.* I will attack him while he is tired. (*Thesaurus:* **sabu 1, sinabu 1**)

**babak** *v. tr.* To startle fish into movement. *Sali' kita amuwang, sakali aniya' palabay ma pamuwanganta i'. Yukta, "Da'a babakun daing."* We are fishing with hook and line, for example, and then someone passes by the place where we are fishing. We say, "Don't scare off the fish."

**babakan** *n.* Various pufferfishes. *fam. Tetraodontidae. Bang aniya' babakan, ya hē' pandoga habagat.* When there are pufferfish, that is the signal for the southwest monsoon. *Am'lli aku p'ssi. Halam aniya' p'ssiku, wa'i bay al'ngngat he' babakan.* I'll buy some fish-hooks. I don't have any, they've all been pulled out of shape by pufferfish.

**babag** *n.* 1) A main structural crosspiece, as the floor bearer of a house or the spine of a kite. *Ahogot babag luma'nu, mbal ah'bba' bang akosog baliyu.* The floor beams of your house are firm, it won't fall when the wind is strong. *Babag ina'an, ya to'od ōnna hobong.* That beam there, its name is simply *hobong.* (*Thesaurus:* **dagan₁, hobong, salsal, taytayan tikus**) 1.1) *v. intr.* pa- To lie across something. *Da'a ka pababag.* Don't lie crosswise. 1.2) *v. tr.* -an To fit a crosspiece to a structure. (*cf:* **sulad 1**) 2) Barrier across a path, bar across a doorway. (*Thesaurus:* **agpang 1, lapad**) 2.1) *v. tr.* To bar access; to bring closure to some activity. *Amabag gara' bang pinaghona'-hona'an agaggat. Binabag e' dangan, mbal pagbeya'an.* The plan is blocked when it is discussed combatively. One person blocks it, and it isn't agreed on.

**pagbabag** (var. **pagbalabag**) *v. intr.* aN- To lie cross-wise to the length of something.

**pagbaubabag** *v. intr.* aN- To lie in random directions, in contrast to lying parallel. *Ya du bang magtulihan magbaubabag, sinō' magleson.* Likewise when everyone is sleeping cross-wise, they're told to straighten up. (*Thesaurus:* pagtangday, tihin)

**pababag** *adv.* 1) Crosswise; athwart. 1.1) *v. tr.* To steer a canoe so that it is transverse to the line of wave movement. *Da'a pababagun, abuhaw kita.* Don't go transverse to the direction in which the sea is running, we will ship water.

**baba'** *v. tr.* 1) To carry something on one's back. *Baba'un gi' onde' ilū ma aku ni nāsuri.* Carry that child on your back for me, to the nursery. (*Thesaurus:* **balung 1, tanggung₁, tumpay, usung**) 1.1) *v. intr.* pa-/a- To ride on someone's back. *Ababa' ka ni bukutku.* Ride on my back.

**baba'an₁** *n.* The handle of a container. *Angamu' aku mital baba'anan ilū.* I'm asking for that can with a handle. (*Thesaurus:* **patihan, puhan 1, tangkay 2**)

**baba'an₂** *n.* Spotted pomadasid, a fish species. *Pomadasid sp.*

**babal₁** *v. tr.* To heat metal in a furnace or forge. (*Thesaurus:* **sasal, subu₁ 2, tawtaw**)

**babalan** *n.* Metal tools and weapons made in a forge. *Ya laring babalan ilū.* That forged knife there.

**pagbabal** *v. tr.* To make a living working metal in a forge. *Magbababal a'a itū.* This man is a blacksmith [or metal-worker].

**babal₂** (var. **b'bbal**) *v. tr.* To train younger children in right behavior, a process that involves warning and inducement. *Subay a'a to'a amandu' ni ariki' bo' niōnan amabal.* An old person should be teaching a child for it to be called *babal. Bay binabal si Sa min kariki'-diki'na.* Sa has been brought up well from her early childhood. (*Thesaurus:* **bi'at 1.1**)

**babantugun** (derivative of **bantug**) *n.* A person who is famous or notorious. *Babantugun si Banana.* Banana [a well-known swimmer] was a famous person.

**babarapa** *n.* This and that; things of all sorts. (*Thesaurus:* **kaginisan, inda wa barapa ginis, indalupa 1, mussak-massik**)

**babas** var. of **b'bbas**

**babat** *n.* The abdomen; belly. *Aheya babatna kuting ilū.* That cat's stomach is large. (*Thesaurus:* **badding-badding, b'ttong₁ 1, tungul 1**)

**babauluhan** (derivative of **baulu**) *n.* A metal mold, usually of brass, in which small egg-based cakes are baked.

**babaw₁** *n.* Rat or mouse. (*syn:* **ambaw**)

**babaw₂** *adj.* a- Shallow, of tide. *Subay kohap sabab ababaw tahik.* Should be afternoon because the tide will be low then.

**babaw-dunya** *n.* The earth's surface as the sphere

of living things. *Sat'ggolta a'llum ma babaw-dunya itū.* As long as we live here on earth. *"Subay," yukna, "b'nnal-b'nnal du, iya na tuhan ma babaw-dunya itu."* "It must be [accepted as] true," he said, "that he is the god of the whole world."

**babaw-tana'** *n.* The surface and subsoil of a land area. *Aniya' kono' bay takali e' sigām ba'ul bulawan ma babaw-tana'.* It is said that they dug up a golden chest from the ground. (*cf:* **kuwit 1, lapis₁ 1**)

**kababawan** *n.* A shallow area of sea floor. *Temang itū ma llot timbang maka kababawan. Temang* [a flattish area of sea-floor] is between deep and shallow water. *Makal'bbos pa'in pelang min diyata' kababawan, palaran-laran na kami pahali.* Once the canoe was lowered into the water from the shallows, we just drifted, resting. (*Thesaurus:* **kahanggalan, kat'bbahan, katoho'an**)

**babawan** *n.* A species of fish esteemed for its firm white flesh. *fam. Carangidae.* (*gen:* **kutambak**)

**babay** *n.* A species of fish (unclassified).

**babbal** *n.* A person who suffers from mental impairment. *Ndū', babbal pahāp ka'am ilū.* Goodness, what dummies you are.

**kababbalan** *n.* Mental deficiency; idiocy. *In a'a asabal alalom panghatina, sagō' ya a'a al'kkas angamasu' ama'nda' kababbalanna.* The patient man has deep understanding, but the guy who is quick to lose his temper shows his idiocy.

**babbel** *v. tr.* -an To bob one's hair. *Bay binabbelan bu'un si Nu. Ata'u ka amabbel? Babbelin aku.* Nu's hair has been bobbed. Do you know how to do it? Bob mine for me. (*cf:* **gunting 1.2**)

**babet** *n.* A diving weight. *Bang aku atuhun ma deyo' lalom limampū' subay aku ameya' ma babet ko' al'kkas pareyo'.* When I am diving to a depth of fifty fathoms I must go with a weighted bar in order to get down quickly.

**babu'** *n.* 1) Female relative of parents' generation. *Subay ka pahapit maī' ma luma' babu'ku.* You should call in there at my aunt's house. (*cf:* **bapa' 1, si'it**) 1.1) *voc. n.* Address term for parent's sister or cousin, and for any senior woman. (*cf:* **ina', mamang₁, mma', papang**)

**bāk₁** *v. tr.* To find something by chance. *Nilahu' bulan, na subay nilisagan min kaluma'an. Nilisagan na turung kaldero mital, kulintangan, agung, ai-ai na tabāk-bāk i'.* There is a lunar eclipse, well then, things should be struck for it. Pot lids, brass ensemble, large gongs, whatever comes to hand. A: *"Bay kami makabāk pitaka."* B: *"Maingga tabākbi?"* A: "We happened to find a wallet." B: "Where did you find it?" *Nilahu' bulan, subay nilisagan turung kaldero mital, kulintangan, agung, ai-ai na tabāk-bāk i'.* When there is a lunar eclipse, things should be struck for it, things like pot lids, gongs, whatever comes to hand.

**bāk₂** *v. tr.* To meet and welcome someone as they arrive. *Kalu-kalu kami bināk e' luma' itū.* Perhaps we will be met by the people of this house. (*Thesaurus:* **abang, langgal₂ 2, pagsamban, sampang 1**)

**pagbāk** *v. tr.* To meet together; to come face to face. *Akulingkung pahāp l'ngngan sehe'ta hē', mbal tabākta. Subay na kita ma pameya'an atawa ma luma' bo' makapagbāk.* The path of that companion of ours is so erratic that we cannot find him. We will need to be at the boat or at the house for us to meet up [with him]. *Bang aku magbāk maka bitu'anunku, buli'-buli'ku mataku.* When I came face-to-face with my former spouse, I turn my face away from her. *Tūk, man dambila' dahatus man dambila' dahatus, hatina magbāk dahatus.* A bet, one hundred from each side, in other words the ₱100 bids coming together.

**pagbākan** *n.* A location where people meet. *Ariki' lahat ya pagbākantam itū.* This place where we are meeting is limited.

**bakakka** *n.* Kingfisher. *gen. Alcedo.*

**bakag₁** *n.* A cardboard carton. (*Thesaurus:* **ba'ul₁, kalton, labban, maleta, tu'ung**)

**bakag₂** *adj.* a-/-an Swollen, of stomach, due to gas or indigestion. *Abakag b'ttongta bang kita bay amangan pinutu bo' sangom na.* Our stomach gets swollen if we eat steamed cassava and it's night already. *Subay a'a sakihan bo' bakagan, sali' bago', sali' an'gga b'ttong.* A person must be an invalid to have a swollen stomach, like a distended belly, like a stomach stuffed full. (*Thesaurus:* **bago' 1, baha' 1, butig 1, ikat 1.1, pagbutud, p'ngkong 1**)

**baka'₁** *n.* A marketing basket woven of bamboo or rattan, has a rigid handle. *Buwat ambung, subay aniya' baba'anna.* It is like an *ambung*, but it should have a handle. (*cf:* **ambung 2**; *spec:* **ansak, balatak, baluyut, basket, kalanjangan, kampil, kanasto, japang, salingkat, sugub, tampipi', tiklis**)

**baka'₂** 1) *n.* Tartar; yellowish build-up on teeth. (*Thesaurus:* **balakang 1, kiki' 1**) 2) *v. advrs.* -in- Stained yellow, of teeth.

**bakal** *v. tr.* To plant out seedlings or cuttings. (*Thesaurus:* **tanom₁ 1, tugbal**)

**bakas-bakas** *n.* The final phase of a repeated sequence, especially of tide.

**bakat** *n.* 1) A wound caused by cutting. 1.1) *adj.* -an Suffering from a cut into the flesh. *Lagutta ka maka lahut. Bang ka nilappet maka kayu mbal bakatan.* I'll slash you with a knife. If someone is smacked with a piece wood, he is not wounded. (*Thesaurus:* **bu'ag, langgahi', pali' 1**) 1.2) *v. tr.* -an To wound someone by cutting. *Amakatan aku dīku.* I cut myself. *Ngga'i ka buwat kappo' maka bawis ya bisana bang makabakat.* It [the katol-katol fish] is not like stonefish or rabbitfish in the pain of the wound it causes.

**1.3)** *v. advrs.* **ka-...-an** To be wounded by cutting. *Kabakatan ni bila' kassa'.* Cut by broken glass.

**bakat atay** *adj.* **a-** Suffering emotional hurt. {idiom} *Abakat atayku pasal panipu e' bagayku lissi.* I am hurt emotionally because of being betrayed by my closest friend.

**pagbakat** *v. intr.* **aN-** To break out in multiple sores.

**bakbak** *v. tr.* To cut up fish for bait. *Bakbakanta daing nihinang umpan.* We cut up fish to make bait.

**bakbakan** *n.* A species of tree (unclassified) useful for canoe hulls.

**bakkas** *n.* The physical evidence of some activity. *Abakkas du pa'in hinangnu.* There are always traces of your work.

**bakkaw** *var. of* **bangkaw**

**bakkel** *n.* **1)** The abrasive skin of scale-less fish such as rays. (*Thesaurus:* **lapu-lapu 1, tai'-bamban**) **1.1)** *v. tr.* **-an** To remove the abrasive skin of certain fish species. (*Thesaurus:* **kagis 1, keke₁, l'ngnges 1.2**)

**bakkid** *n.* Various breams. *Pentapodus setosus; Pentapodus parariseus. Saga bakkid-bakkid bay pin'ssi-p'ssi e' kami.* Various breams that we caught on small hooks.

**bakkug** *var. of* **bangkug**

**baki'** *n.* Striped eel catfish. *Plotosus anguillaris. Bay aku am'lli daing taga sisik, mangku'. Baki' halam aniya' sisikna, mbal takilaw.* I bought skip-jack tuna, a fish with scales. Catfish have no scales and cannot be eaten raw. (*gen:* **taote'**)

**bakiya'₁** *n.* Wooden slippers or clogs. *Alahang magsulug bakiya' buwattina'an, luwal bay timpu Kastila'.* People rarely wear wooden-soled slippers nowadays, it was only back in Spanish times. (*Thesaurus:* **sinelas, takon, taumpa'**)

**bakiya'₂** *v. tr.* To sew using back-stitch. *Apagon tahi'an bakiya' min tahi'an malkina.* Back-stitch is more durable than machine stitching. (*Thesaurus:* **bagsak₂, dahut, la'it, tahi'**)

**baklaw** *n.* An amulet (for personal protection). *Baklaw, ya ginantung ma k'llong, ya hampan onde'-onde'. Bang matto'a subay buku, hadjimat, habay-habay.* A baklaw is the one that hangs around the neck, that protects a child [from sorcery]. In the case of adults it should be an amulet round the wrist, or words from the Holy Koran, or a charm round the waist. (*gen:* **tambang₃ 1**)

**baklay** *v. intr.* **aN-** To travel by foot. *Hal kita amaklay bang t'bba.* When the tide is low we just travel along the shore. *Jari magpamaklay sigām min kohap sampay ni kasubuhan.* So they hiked from afternoon to morning. (*Thesaurus:* **baybay₁, l'ngngan₁ 1.1, pasiyal**)

**bakokang** *n.* A type of ulcer. (*cf:* **dugsul 1**)

**bakol** *n.* The thumb; big toe.

**bakot** *v. tr.* **-an** To correct the direction in which one is travelling. (*Thesaurus:* **malim 1.1, tuhung, tuli' 1.1, tullus 1.2, ulin**)

**bakti'** *n.* **1)** A gift from a student of religion to his teaching guru. **1.1)** *adj.* **a-** Showing appreciation to one's religious teacher. *Subay kita maghusa' pina'an ni guruta. Subay kita abakti'.* We should work hard there regarding our teacher of religion. We should be appreciative.

**pagbakti'** *v. intr.* **aN-** To show appreciation to one's religious teacher by doing household chores. *Magbakti' kita ni guru. Sat'ggol kita mbal makatammat, subay kita maghusa' pina'an amowa bohe'-kayu.* We show appreciation to [our] religious teacher. So long as we haven't graduated we should work hard taking water and firewood there [to him].

**baktulan** *n.* Reputation. *Ya na itu baktulanna.* This is his reputation. (*Thesaurus:* **bowahan, l'ngnganan₂, pakang₁, palantara 1, tebong**)

**bakukku** *n.* Harlequin sweetlips (a perch-like fish). *Plectorhynchus chaetodontoides.*

**bakul** *n.* A small lidded basket of woven cane. *Aniya' atibulung, aniya' pasagi'. Subay aniya' turungna.* There are round ones, there are square ones. They are meant to have a cover.

**bakul-bakul** *n.* A trinket container of closely woven bamboo or rattan.

**bakung** *var. of* **pandan-bakung**

**bakwet** *n.* An evacuee. *Ati'il kami ma pagkakan buwat bakwet.* We are suffering from lack of food, like evacuees.

**pagbakwet** *v. intr.* **aN-** To be displaced from one's home area, as due to a natural disaster or civil unrest. (*Thesaurus:* **lalat₁ 1.1, pagdo'ag**)

**badbad** *adj.* **a-** **1)** Unfolded or unfurled. *Abadbad, sali' ap'kkal, bang bay alūn.* It's unfurled, sort of coming apart when it has been rolled up. *Abadbad bu'unna.* Her hair has lost its curl. **1.1)** *v. tr.* To unroll from its folded state, as a sail or mat. *Badbarun na banog apa aniya' baliyu.* Unfurl the sail because there is wind. (*cf:* **b'llat 1.1**)

**badding-badding** *adj.* **zero** Protruding, of the abdomen. {vulgar} (*Thesaurus:* **babat, b'ttong₁ 1, tungul 1**)

**badja'** *n.* **1)** A dredging rake or hook. **1.1)** *v. tr.* To locate something using a hooked implement. *Magbadja' kami. Ya binadja' bahan abō' niā' bubu bay pagpalit kami.* We use a hook. What was hooked was the length of vine to get the trap we were checking. *Ya binadja' bahan abō' niā' bubu bay pagpalit kami.* A length of vine was used with a hook to retrieve the trap we were fishing with. (*cf:* **palit₂**)

**badja' sau** *n. phrase* A hooked anchor used to grapple deepwater traps.

**badjang** *n.* A slender and durable species of cane, a source of thatching ties. (*Thesaurus:* **bamban₂, hidjuk, lanut, lupis**)

**badjangan** *n.* A species of grouper. *Bang kami*

*am'ssi ni Paluwas-pata anongod kami mana-mana, ya badjangan ē'. Sali' tapog atawa tandukan.* When we go fishing near Paluwas-pata we locate ourselves over the *mana-mana*, the groupers. Like *tapog* or *tandukan* groupers. (*syn:* **mana-mana**; *gen:* **kuhapo'**)

**Badjaw** *n.* A name sometimes used to refer to the Sama Dilaut (sea-oriented Sama).

**badji** *v. tr. -an* To throw something vigorously. *Badji itū akalap min bantung, pinatā to'ongan. Badji* is more than just throwing, it is making something go a long way. *Ōy, badjihanta ka.* Hey, I'll throw you out! (*Thesaurus:* **bantung 1.1, buwang₁ 1, laruk, timan₁**)

**badji-gandang** *n.* Beach Lettuce, a useful small tree of sandy foreshores. *Scaevola frutescens. Ahāp pangayu badji-gandang itū bang atoho'. Tahinang hāg bang aheya. Patomo' ma tana'.* This *badji-gandang* is good for firewood when dry. When it is big enough it can be made into house posts. It grows on land. *Angā' kita badji-gandang man kanusahan, mbal tab'lli.* We get *badji-gandang* from the outer islands, it can't be purchased.

**badju** *n.* A storm of typhoon-like severity. *Bang alandos badju makal'bbos luma'.* When a typhoon is strong it causes houses to collapse. (*Thesaurus:* **baliyu 1, hunus 1, simpal**)

**badju'** *n.* A garment worn on the upper body; clothing in general. *Amuwan ka badju', agese' ma aku.* Give me a shirt, the one I have is torn. (*Thesaurus:* **jaket, polo**)

**badju'-bandung** *n.* A traditional long-sleeved shirt or blouse.

**badju'-batawi'** *n.* A traditional shirt of black cloth, decorated with gold buttons. *Niantuwilasan pamakayna, ya badju'na batawi'.* His clothes are decorated with buttons, his *batawi'* shirt, that is.

**badju'-ma'as** *n.* A traditional shirt with long tight sleeves and no collar.

**badju'-sablay** *n.* A long-sleeved blouse worn together with a sarong. (*cf:* **supa₂**)

**badju'-samda** *n.* A traditional shirt with long tight sleeves and no collar.

**badju'-supa** *n.* A traditional tight-sleeved shirt formerly worn by men. *Badju'-supa itū buwat badju'-sablay, bo' asigpit ma l'ngngon.* This *supa* type shirt is like a *sablay* blouse, but with tight sleeves.

**pagbadju'** *v. intr. aN-* To wear a shirt. *Magkarukka'an aku, amehē'an aku dīku abu, maka magbadju' karut.* I was in great distress, I put ashes on myself and clothed myself in sacking. *Paghinumag, sali' badju' ala'at. Bang kita angusaha ngga'i ka badju' ahāp. Magbadju' ahāp subay aniya' pagkawinan.* Work gear, like worn-out shirts. When we are earning our living it's not good shirts [that we wear]. There must be a wedding for us to wear good clothes.

**pagbinadju'** *v. intr. aN-* To wear a shirt or blouse.

**badlis** *n.* A row of planted items. *Dabadlis panggi' kayu.* A single row of cassava. (*Thesaurus:* **diril-diril, dirit₁ 1, sapan₁ 1, tād, tagik**)

**badlisan** *n.* Things planted in rows. *Ma badlisan, ma tāran, ya lagi'na bang niyug.* By the planted row, by the line, especially of coconuts. *Paririt badlisan niyug.* The rows of coconut palms form lines.

**baek** *n.* A bicycle.

**pagbaek** *v. intr. aN-* To ride a bicycle. *Tinagi-tagi to'ongan aku magbaek.* I am very fond of riding a bicycle.

**bāg** *n.* A Western-style carry-bag, in contrast to hand-woven bags. *Tampupuhun bāg ilu bo' mbal abustak.* Lift that bag from underneath so it doesn't burst.

**baga** *n.* 1) Live coals; embers. *Apakpak bagana, angkan atunu' luma'.* Its live coals fell down, that's why the house burnt. (*syn:* **bale₅**; *Thesaurus:* **dūk₂ 1, unggun 1**) 1.1) *v. intr. aN-* To form live coals. *At'ggol ilu amaga.* That [wood] will produce live coals for a long time.

**bagahak₁** (*var.* **bugahak**) *n.* Various coral fishes.

**bagahak₂** *n.* A greedy person. (*Thesaurus:* **boslad, buhawi'₁, butu', kanam, kaway 1.1, dahaga', damba'₁ 1.1, lagak 1.1, tanggal₁**)

**bagahak-lanus** *n.* Brown-marbled grouper; Blotched rock cod. *Epinephelus fuscoguttatus.*

**baga'ang** *n.* Molars. *Nilarutan baga'angna pasal ahalu' na maka ap'ddi'.* His molars are pulled out because they have become rotten and painful. (*Thesaurus:* **bangkil₂, empon 1, sengel, taling**)

**baga'ud** *see:* **pagbaga'ud**

**bagala** *see:* **pagbagala**

**bagambul** *var. of* **kalitan-bagambul**

**bagangan** *n.* Various breams (Grey large-eye; Gray bare-nose; Blue-lined large-eye). *Gymnocranius griseus; G. robinsonii.*

**bagas** *adj. a-* Forceful and rough, of waves or of speech. *Pa'agak du ka bang amissala, da'a ka abagas.* Be cautious when you speak, don't be rough. (*Thesaurus:* **kasla 1, labas₂ 1**)

**bagat** *v. tr.* To fasten securely, of a door or lid. (*Thesaurus:* **kandaru 1.1, kansing 1.1**)

**bagay 1)** *n.* A friend. (*ant:* **banta 1**; *Thesaurus:* **agay, beyang, bō, gge, panon**) **2)** *v. tr.* To befriend someone. *Manda' kami binagay e' saga a'a ma lahat ē'.* Fortunately we were befriended by the people of that place.

**bagay-bagay** *v. tr.* To treat someone as a friend; pretend to be friendly. *Binagay-bagay aku e' daka sai, sinuli-sulihan aku buwattitu-buwattina'an. Mbal pahali, gōm pa'in pinagko'ot bulsaku.* Someone, goodness knows who, acts like he's my friend, talking at me about this and that. He doesn't let up, instead he's reaching into my pocket.

**pagbagay** *v. intr. aN-* To relate as friends. *Bilahi aku magbagay maka Milikan.* I want to be friends with the Westerner. (*Thesaurus:* **paglundang-lundang, pagpanon**)

**patibagayun** *adj.* Extremely friendly.

**bagaybay** *n.* The newly opened flowers of the coconut palm. (*wh:* **niyug**)

**bagbag** *v. advrs.* ta- Broken into pieces. (*Thesaurus:* **lopot 1, māg-māg, tumu-tumu**)

**baggis** *adj.* a- Ridiculously quick. *Bang lum'ngngan al'kkas atawa bang amusay al'kkas, abaggis. Sali' magkayas-kayas dīna.* When [he] walks swiftly or paddles swiftly, it looks ridiculous. It is as though he is putting all his effort into it. (*Thesaurus:* **ka'is, kasay 1, kulakkus, l'kkas 1, samot 1, sapat₂ 1**)

**baggok** *n.* The bittern; brown heron. *fam. Ardeidae.*

**baggot** *v. tr.* To tie a component to a main part; to tie up a bundle. *Epo' itu sali' laring-laring atalom binaggot ni tape' manuk.* A spur is like a small sharp knife tied to the leg of the rooster. *Angā' aku lupis pamaggot tepo pinabeya' ni Sambuwangan.* I'll get some banana fiber for tying up a mat to be sent to Zamboanga. *"Na," yukna, "minsan manuk angukku'uk ilū, binaggot bowa'na anak datu' si'."* "Well now," he said, "even though that cockerel crows, the datu's son will have his mouth tied." (*Thesaurus:* **bīt₂, buka'₁ 1.1, engkot 1.1, gakut, pinate 1, sappit₁ 1, sihag₁ 1.1, tabul-tabul, tollen**)

**baggu'** *n.* Various cowrie species. *Cypreaea spp. Amihing-mihing tampe si Ji tudju ni Simulsiddi amiha baggu'.* Ji goes along the edge of the shore towards Simulsiddi, looking for cowries. (*syn:* **kuba₁**)

**baggu'-ettom** *n.* Dark-shelled species of cowrie.

**baggu'-lumpay** *n.* A species of cowrie.

**baggu'-sigay** *n.* A species of cowrie.

**baggungan** *n.* A marine monovalve, edible. *Cerith sp.* (*syn:* **bagumun**)

**bagid** *n.* A match for ignition; matchbox. *Indamin aku bagid panū'anku siga.* Lend me a match for lighting a cigaret. (*Thesaurus:* **dokot₂ 1.2, pakeyat, santik 1, sū' 1.2**)

**bagi'ad** *see:* **pagbagi'ad**

**bagimbin** *see:* **pagbagimbin**

**bagiyas** (*var.* **pagiyas**) *n.* 1) A woven trap for small fish and turtles. *Magpakahinang aku saga duwa bagiyas duwang'llaw.* I have the ability to make two woven traps in two days. (*Thesaurus:* **bubu₁, kiming, panggal 1, togong 1**) 1.1) *v. tr.* To trap small fish. *Pamagiyasanku ni Bakal, amagiyas aku pellok maina'an.* My trapping-place is towards Bakal. I trap wrasses there.

**bag'llal** (derivative of **g'llal**) *n.* 1) A local official or headman. *Buwat aku itū tahinang bag'llal ma tumpukku.* Like me being made a headman for my house-group. 1.1) *v. tr.* To appoint someone to a community leadership position. *Tabag'llal kita. Sali' kita magimam atawa a'a kita parinta.* We are appointed to office. Like serving as an

imam, or we are government appointees.

**bagnet** *v. tr.* To shock someone with an electric current. *Tabagnet iya, atunu' dambila' baranna.* He suffered an electric shock, half his body burnt. (*cf:* **batu-balan**)

**bagod** *n.* A disagreement.

**pagbagod** *v. intr.* aN- To argue an issue with each other. *Magbagod na pa'in, sali' anagga'. Buwat aku sinoho' am'lli, yukku, "Ngga'i ka itu bīlli, ina'an bīlli."* Arguing, sort of resisting. Like when I am told to buy and I say, "This is not the one to buy, that's the one." (*Thesaurus:* **pagagaw-besod, pagbengtod, pagdiskās, pagjawab 1.1, pagpayod 1.1, pagsalod, pagsu'al**)

**bagoggol** (*var.* **baguggul**) *v. intr.* pa- 1) Losing hair on one's head. (*cf:* **tugak**) 1.1) *v. tr.* -an To shave the head. (*Thesaurus:* **bagong₂, himangot 1.1, p'ngngot 1.2, s'ssol₁, soso'**)

**bago'** 1) *n.* A disease involving massive swelling of the abdomen. (*Thesaurus:* **bakag₂, baha' 1, bogon₁ 1, bongol 1, busul, butig 1, ikat 1.1, pagbutud, p'ngkong 1, talis'ssok 1**) 2) *v. advrs.* -in- Suffering from a massive abdominal swelling. *Taluwa' mbo' angkan binago'.* Affected by ancestors that is why the spleen is swollen. *Binago'. B'ttongta aheya, ngga'i ka kalog. Min b'ttong sa' tabowa pi'itu ni timbanganta. Binago'.* One's stomach is large, but not from worms. It is in the stomach but extends to one's flanks.

**bagong₁** *n.* Elephant's foot, a wild arum, eaten in hard times. *Amorphophallus campanulatus. Makakatol bagong itū, subay tin'ppa, nilamuran panggi'. Ak'ddot kinakan.* The Elephant's foot causes itching, it needs to be pounded and mixed with cassava. It is tough to eat.

**bagong₂** *v. tr.* -an To shave the hair of head or beard. *Binagongan hal tonga' p'ngngot sigām.* Only half their beard was shaved. (*Thesaurus:* **bagoggol 1.1, himangot 1.1, p'ngngot 1.2, s'ssol₁, soso'**)

**pagbagong** *n.* Something used for shaving or cutting hair. *Am'lli aku gelet pagbagong.* I am buying a razor blade for shaving.

**bagsak₁** *n.* Swampy land suitable for growing paddy rice.

**bagsak₂** *v. tr.* To sew a hem or seam with big stitches. *Binagsak na s'mmek, hal sala pinabalut.* The cloth is sewn with big stitches, just sort of holding it together. *La'itan binagsak.* A stitch using the *bagsak* technique. (*Thesaurus:* **bakiya'₂, dahut, la'it, tahi'**)

**bagting** *n.* 1) The sound of a bell ringing. (*cf:* **bēl**) 1.1) *v. tr.* To ring a bell. (*syn:* **tingting 1.1**)

**bagubu'** 1) *n.* Mildew; mold. 2) *v. advrs.* -in- Infected by mold, especially of cloth. *Binagubu' s'mmek bang abase' bo' mbal magtūy pinatoho'.* Cloth gets moldy when it is wet and not immediately dried. (*Thesaurus:* **kapu-kapu 1, tagimtim 1, tagutu' 1**)

**baguggul** *var. of* **bagoggol**

**bagul** *v. tr. -an* To dehusk a coconut. *Bagulin ma kita lahing ilū ati usalta bunutna panapa kihampaw itū.* Remove the husk of that coconut for us and we will use it to roast this sand ray. (*cf:* **bunut 1.1**)

**bagumbilya** *n.* Bougainvillea, a flowering climber. *Bougainvillea spp.*

**bagumun** *n.* A marine monovalve, edible. *Cerith sp.* (*syn:* **baggungan**)

**bagunbun** *n.* Airborne dust. *Alimpunus itū sali' linug, tabowa bagunbun pariyata'.* These whirlwinds are like an earthquake, carrying dust up into the air. (*cf:* **hamud-hamud**)

**bagung-lipunan** *n.* An unlawful military organization.

**baguy** *adj. a-* Going off but still edible, of fish. *Abaguy, sali' ahalu' na, sali' ma olangan ahalu' maka halam gi'.* Somewhat rotten, sort of between being rotten and not yet [rotten]. *Abaguy daing, atoho' he' llaw.* Fish no longer fresh, dried out by the sun. (*Thesaurus:* **balos₂, buhuk, buntu'₁ 1.1, halu' 1.1, langag, p'ngkak**)

**baha** *n.* The shoulder. *Pīs sinabit itū, pinarablay baha' man bahanu?* This woven scarf, is it to be draped over your shoulder? (*syn:* **punggu-baha**)

**baha-būd** *n.* The middle slope of a hill or mountain. (*Thesaurus:* **bīd, būd 1, lorosan, tukaran**)

**bahaba'** *n.* Russell's snapper, a fish species. *Lutjanus russelli.* (*gen:* **kutambak**)

**bahak** *v. intr. pa-* To lie down when resting or sleeping. *Angā' iya dakayu' batu paū'anna bo' yampa pabahak atuli.* He got a rock as his pillow and then lay down to sleep. *Pabahak iya ma gusung daka pilan sangom.* He lay on the sand for who knows how many nights. (*Thesaurus:* **lege**)

**pabahakan** *n.* A place for lying down or sleeping; a bed. (*Thesaurus:* **kantil₁, palangka'₂, palegehan, patulihan**)

**bahagi'** *n.* 1) A share or division. *Aniya' na nnompū' pilak bahagi' kami para dangan.* There was a share of sixty pesos for each one of us. (*Thesaurus:* **gihay, hampit, paglamit-lamit 1.1, sihak**) 1.1) *adj. a-* Divided into parts or shares. *Magtūy abahagi'-duwa bohe' inān, parambila'-ni-dambila'.* The water there quickly divided into two, from one side to the other. 1.2) *v. tr.* To divide something into parts or shares. *Binahagi'-bahagi' na.* Divided into multiple shares. 1.3) *v. tr. -an* To assign someone a share. *"Bahagi'in kita," yukna, "ina'an."* "Give us a share of that," he said.

**bahagi'-buyung** *n.* An uneven or inequitable distribution of shares. {idiom}

**bahagi'-tempang** *n.* 1) An uneven division of shares. 1.1) *v. intr. aN-* To distribute shares unevenly.

**pagbahagi'** *v. tr.* To share something with each other. *Bang kita magbeya' am'ssi, magbahagi' na.* When we go together fishing, [we] share. *Yuk sara', "Bang kabaya'anbi dangan-duwa, na magbahagi' kām pahāp. Magsalassay na kām."* The magistrate said, "If it is your wish, both of you together, then divide things well. Be agreed." *Bay aku pikisehe' aku ma si Sm, bo' mbal iya. Manjari kaut aku dangan-danganku ati tapuwa'ku lima pilak ma lān. Pagt'kkaku, yukku, "Bay tapuwa'ku lima pilak." Yuk si Sm, "Gōm bay aku ameya', magbahagi' kitā." "Na," yukku, "maglalin ka, bay na ka'a-i bowaku."* I asked Sm to accompany me but he wouldn't. So I went to the shore on my own and happened to find ₱5 on the path. On getting back I said, "I found five pesos." Sm said, "If only I had gone too. Let's share it." "Well," I said, "Take your turn, I would have taken you."

**bahā'** *ptl.* Question marker. *Yuk kuyya' ina'an, "Buwattingga na bahā' pang'llo'an bulawan itū?"* That monkey said, "What will it be like, this place where the gold is obtained?" *Na ai bahā' ma pikilannu, Bapa'? Aniya' bohe' bahā' ma nusa itu?* So what is it, Uncle, in your opinion? Might there be water on this atoll? *Aniya' bohe' bahā' ma nusa itu?* Is there water perhaps, on this atoll? *Sampay sultan asusa na bang ai na bahā' kinakan e' anakna.* The sultan too was anxious as to what his son had eaten. (*Thesaurus:* **kalu-kalu 1, siguru 1, ya aniya'**)

**baha'** 1) *n.* A swelling of body tissue. (*Thesaurus:* **bakag₂, bago' 1, butig 1, ikat 1.1, pagbutud, p'ngkong 1**) 2) *v. advrs. -in-* Suffering from swelling. *Binaha'an kita, am'ngkong.* We are affected by swelling, distended.

**baha'u** (var. **ba'ahu**) *adj. zero* 1) New; fresh. *Baha'u malkina ilu.* That motor is new. *Langkatku kamaligku goret-goret bo' hinangku kamalig baha'u, aheya lagi' min bay tagna'.* I will dismantle my broken-down shed and build a new one, bigger than the original one. (*cf:* **ndang, to'a 1.1**) 1.1) *adv.* Recently. *Baha'u aku at'kka.* I just arrived. *Tinapay baha'u bay hinangna.* Bread she has just made.

**pabaha'u** *v. tr. -an* To renew something; to restore something to its former state.

**bahal** *adj. a-* No longer new, but still usable. *Abahal na, at'ggol na, sagwā' pagguna na pa'in.* It's worn, a long time already, but still in use. (*Thesaurus:* **longa', ndang**)

**bahala'₁** *n.* A responsibility; a liability. *Bahala' ma ka'a bang itu alungay.* The responsibility is yours if this is lost. *Iya lagi' bahala' anganjaga.* He is still responsible to keep watch. *Bang aniya' hayop tatangkaw hinabuna ma deyoman a'a kapangandolan hē', na a'a inān subay angangganti' sabab iya ya bahala'.* If an animal is stolen while it is in the keeping of someone reliable, then that person has to replace it because he was responsible. (*Thesaurus:* **abunaw, atas₂ 1,**

kuwiraw, lawag-baran, siyal, tanggung$_2$)

**bahala'**$_2$ *n.* An idol or image as an object of worship.

**bahan** *n.* **1)** Generic term for vine-like plants; vines as a durable salt-tolerant tying material. *Wa'i palebod ma batu bahanna.* Its vine is wound round the rocks. *Aheka bahan mareya, amalut. Pi' ka amiha.* There are lots of vines inland, they cling. Go and look for some. (*spec:* **belle'-belle'** 1, **daplakan**$_2$, **nitu', tuwa** 1) **1.1)** *v. tr.* *-an* To tie something using vine as rope. *Bang aku angahūg bubu binahanan ni Serom, palebod ma batu bahanna.* When I set a vine-tied fish trap near Serom Island, its vine gets wound round the rocks.

**bahana'** *v. intr.* *aN-* To become manifest by making a noise or giving off a distinctive smell. *Aniya' amahana', buwat aniya' amatay, paligay asekot ni kita.* Something is making its presence known, like when someone dies, especially when it is close to us. (*Thesaurus:* **lutaw, pagbagala, panyata'**$_2$ 1, **pangguwa'** 1.1)

**bahani** *n.* **1)** Reckless courage. *Akosog bahanina, bang magsalla' angahūg saga duwampū', saga t'llumpū', saukat aheka sīn.* His daring is great, when he plays toss-the-coin he wagers twenty or thirty pesos, just because he has a lot of money. *Bahani buwat a'a magdabayan, buwat aku amole' sangom min Sibaud. Yuk a'a hē', "Bahaninu, amole' dangan-dangannu man bowa' Lapak."* *Bahani* is like people traveling in the same boat, like I do when going home at night from Sibaud. People say, "How brave you are to go across Lapak Bay on your own." (*Thesaurus:* **aykalas** 1, **esog** 1.1) **1.1)** *adj. zero* Courageous, with connotation of foolhardiness. *Saga a'a bahani.* Brave men. *Katamakan mailu taming saga a'a abahani.* The shields of the brave ones were defiled there. **1.2)** *v. intr.* *pa-* To behave bravely. *Da'a kām tināw. Pabahani kām angatu.* Don't be scared. Fight back bravely.

**bahangi** **1)** *adv.* Night as a period of 24 hours. *Maina'an kami amalabay bahangi.* We passed the night there. (*cf:* **dibuhi', salung**) **2)** *clf.* Count word for periods of 24 hours. *Aniya' na saga mpat bahangi.* It has been about four days. *Jari pitumbahangi ya t'ggol paghinang si Ya ma mma'na ma atag ina'an.* So seven nights was the duration of Ya's funeral ceremonies for his father, there in that place. **3)** *v. intr.* *aN-* To engage in night fishing. **4)** *v. tr.* *-an* To leave overnight, of uncooked fish. *Halam aniya' lauk, luwal daing-daing binahangi'an.* Nothing to eat with [the staple], only the small fish that were not cooked last night.

**bahangi-dibuhi'** *adv.* The night before last.

**bahangi-di'ilaw** *adv.* Two nights ago; the day before yesterday.

**bahangi-he'in** *adv.* Two days before yesterday.

**bahasa**$_1$ *n.* Language; speech. *Angalangguyud iya ma bahasa.* He drawls in his speech. *Bahasa Bisaya', bahasa Sūk, bahasa Milikan, bahasa kami Sama.* The languages of the Visayans, of the Tausug, of the Westerners, and of us Sama. (*Thesaurus:* **bā'**$_1$, **batbat**$_2$, **bissala** 1.1, **k'bbat**$_1$ 1, **h'lling**$_1$ 1.1, **pagmūng-mūng** 1.1, **sambat, yuk**)

**bahasa**$_2$ *adv.* As one might say; in a manner of speaking. *Akatis pa'in aku bay pinasiga, manjari na atilaw ipalku i' bahasa bang nsa' taga tunang.* When he had finished giving me a cigaret, my brother-in-law asked, as one does, if he did not have a sweetheart. *Aho', pinasugsug na e' imam, kinawin na bahasa.* Yes, joined in marriage by the imam, wedded as they say.

**pagbahasa** *v. tr.* To intend something other than the obvious or literal meaning of what is said; to speak figuratively or generally. *"Minsan kami makaleyang," yukna, "pinagbahasa taga kepet kami."* "Even though we could fly," he said, "having wings, as one might say." *Aheka manusiya' itū, pinagbahasa magduwa-t'llu hatus.* These many people, one could say two or three hundred. *Barang itū boras, tepo. Ya he' pinagbahasa barang, ya palamud maka sīn.* The *barang* referred to here are rattan mats, pandanus mats. These are things included with the [bride-gift] money.

**bahaya** *adj.* *a-* Envious; covetous. *Abahaya itū, sali' kita aheya matata ang'nda' pilak.* This word *bahaya* is like our eyes growing big looking at money. *Bahaya itū, aniya' ta'nda'nu alta' a'a sa'agon-agon k'llo'nu.* This word *bahaya* is when you see someone's valuables and are about to take them. (*Thesaurus:* **kaway** 1, **hangsaw** 1, **hawa** 1.1, **napsu** 1.1, **sawiya** 1, **sayap-sayap**)

**bahaya alta'** *adj. zero* Addicted to getting rich. {idiom} *Bahaya alta' iya inān, tabowa napsuna ma alta'na, yukna, "Ameya' aku pehē' magkali bulawan." Yukta, "Mbal at'ggol ka ilū, tabowa ni bahaya alta'."* He is addicted to acquiring wealth, influenced by his desire for possessions, saying, "I will go there to dig for gold." We say, "It won't be long before you are addicted to wealth." (*cf:* **beya' hawa**)

**bahembas** *adj.* *a-* **1)** Making small repetitive sounds. *Pagkuppa, magtūy abahembas bohe'.* On jumping in, the water immediately made a rippling noise. (*Thesaurus:* **bah'ssek** 1, **kerek-kerek, keyos**$_2$, **kulanas** 1, **kulessab, ganggu', ussab-ussab**) **1.1)** *v. intr.* *aN-* To cause repetitive small sounds. *Amahembas sangana kamemon bang taluwa' baliyu.* All of its branches begin to rustle when the wind blows them.

**pagbahembas** *v. intr.* *aN-* To make a repeated splashing noise. *Bang kita anū', sinoho' kita da'a magbahembas ko' da'a alahi daing.* When we go fishing with a lantern we are told not to make splashing noises so the fish don't move away. *Magbahembas, ya magt'bba' katig man duwambila', sali' mags'lle'.* Making a great splashing noise, outriggers crashing into each other, as though taking turns.

**bahi** *adj. a-* Going off, of cooked food. *Abahi ai-ai basta kakanta.* Anything can be *bahi*, so long as it something we eat. *Bang kita amangan kinakan abahi, sali' kita angutta'.* When we eat food that is going off, we kind of retch. (*cf:* **balos₂**)

**bahibū 1)** *n.* The body hair of humans. (*Thesaurus:* **bū 1, bu'un 1, bulbul 1**) **2)** *v. advrs. -in-* To be hairy. *Aniya' du isāb a'a binahibū minsan ngga'i ka milikan.* There are also people with body hair, even people who are not Westerners.

**bahi'** *adj. -an* Mature, of large bamboo. *P'ttung bahi'an, ato'a na sidda. Akeyat isina.* Mature bamboo, very old. Its inside is red.

**bahingaw** *v. tr.* To hear something moving about. A: *"Bay tabahingawnu pagtulak a'a magp'ssihan dibuhi'?"* B: *"Bay tabahingawku, tasayuku, ati atuli aku pabīng."* A: "Did you hear the departure of the men going fishing last night?" B: "I heard, I was aware of them, and I went back to sleep again." (*Thesaurus:* **kale 1, hīng-hīng, talengog**)

**bah'ssek** *n.* **1)** A faint noise. *Halam bah'ssek.* Not a sound. (*syn:* **bahonos 1**; *Thesaurus:* **bahembas 1, kerek-kerek, keyos₂, kulanas 1, kulessab, ganggu', ussab-ussab**) **1.1)** *v. intr. aN-* To make a brief faint noise. *Aniya' daing takaleta amah'ssek.* We can hear fish breaking the surface.

**baho'-baho'** *n.* A species of fish (unclassified).

**bahonos** *n.* **1)** The light sound of something moving. (*syn:* **bah'ssek 1**) **1.1)** *v. intr. aN-* To make a sound by moving. *Amahonos, buwat malabuhuk bang taluwa' baliyu. Sali' takaleta.* Rustling, like a pine tree when the wind hits it. It's as though we hear it.

**bahubuk** *n.* The sound of movement between water and something solid.

  **pagbahubuk** *v. intr. aN-* **1)** To make the sound of a solid object through water, as when wading or pulling a paddle. *Bang pakapo' atawa amusay, agbahubuk.* When wading or paddling [a canoe], a splashing sound is made. *Makabati' aku dai'-llaw, aheka magbusay saga a'a Sisangat magbahubuk.* I woke up at daybreak, a lot of Sisangat people were paddling [their canoes] and making the noise of splashing. *Magbahubuk, sali' magkaka. Agbahubuk bang magambit selo.* Making a splashing noise, like knocking sticks together. Making a splashing noise when driving needlefish [into a net]. **1.1)** *v. tr. -an* To smack water with a flat item.

**bahudji'** *n.* A heavy rope, cable or hawser. *Am'lli aku bahudji' pangengkotku ma kumpitku ko da'a tinangkaw.* I will buy an anchor chain to tie up my boat with so it won't be stolen. *Ya bahudji' itū ya basi', ina'an ya sau.* The *bahudji'* is the iron chain, that over there is the anchor. (*cf:* **kanyamun**)

**bahug** *adj. a-* **1)** Wet from immersion. **1.1)** *v. tr.* To

dunk food. *Bang aku amangan amahug aku, an'nno'.* When I am eating I dunk it, dipping it to get flavor. *Buwas binahug maka loho' bo' tas'llong magtūy.* Rice dipped into soup so it can be immediately swallowed. *Apu'aw sinanglag, akanat-kanat, subay binahug maka bohe' bo' magpikit.* The roasted cassava is crumbly, scattered, it should be moistened with water so it sticks together. (*Thesaurus:* **butag, dulis, t'nno', tublak₁ 1**)

**bahu'₁** *n.* The boom of a sail. *Sinangonan, sali' sinulugan bahu'na duwa, pinagdayawan.* Fitting together, both of its booms being slid into [the sail], assembled. *Ndia, sugpatanta ka'a bahu' ilū bay apōng.* Give it here, I will extend for you the boom that broke. *Ab'kkat palimping diyata', pahūs bahu' pareyo'.* The upper bolt-rope broke, the boom slid down.

**bahu'₂** *v. advrs. -in-* Reacting physically to the aroma of an unfamiliar place. *Binahu' si Sū. Mbal biyasa ma hamut lahat i'.* Sū reacts badly. He is not used to the smell of that place.

**bahurungan** *var.* of **buhungan**

**bai** *n.* A previous stage or condition; the way something was. *Minda' pinaludju' e' mma' si Ma, pinabīng ni baina.* Ma's father fortunately got negotiations going again, back to where they had been. *Pabīng ka ni bainu.* Go back to where you were. *Niumas na pa'in, nilotok, apinda min baina.* Touched repeatedly, handled, changed from its former condition. *Bang aniya' ai-ai ahūg ni tahik mbal palaran. Pa'antung na ma baina.* When anything falls into the sea it doesn't drift. It stays where it was. (*cf:* **takas**; *Thesaurus:* **bay**)

**baibad** *n.* **1)** A rejected suitor. *Bay aku anunang ni d'nda. Ta'abut magpah'nda magkimmat na alta'. Na akulang alta'ku, na halam aku makasōng ni d'nda. Baibad aku.* I was courting a girl. At the negotiation stage the bride-wealth was counted up, but my resources were insufficient, so I didn't proceed with that girl. I was a failed suitor. **1.1)** *adj. a-* Broken off, of a courtship. *A'a magtunang bay abaibad, pinaludju' bo' asugpat pabalik.* A couple of sweethearts who had broken it off, but were persuaded to get together again. **1.2)** *v. tr.* To reject the other person in a courting relationship. *Bang aniya' magtunang abō' l'lla hē' maka'nda' d'nda dakayu', nā binaibad d'nda bay dahū.* If a couple are in a courting relationship and the youth sees another girl, then the previous girl is rejected.

  **pagbaibad** *v. tr.* To break off a courting relationship with each other.

**baili** *n.* A species of low-growing grass. *Parang-parang baili itū mbal asagmot to'ongan.* This *baili* grass isn't really weedy.

**bait ul mukaddis** *n. phrase* Designation for Jerusalem in Islamic sources. *Ya ma lahat Tuhan bahā'.* The one in God's country perhaps.

**bā'**₁ *v. tr.* a-, ka-...-an, -an To speak to someone; to advise. *Bā'in pa'in ina'nu.* Just tell your mother. *Bā'anta ka, mbal manjari bang pinaghengkotan kamemon.* I tell you, it won't work to tie everything together. (*Thesaurus:* **bahasa**₁, **batbat**₂, **bissala 1.1, k'bbat**₁ **1, h'lling**₁ **1.1, pagmūng-mūng 1.1, sambat, yuk**)

**bā'-bā'** *n.* A message implied by some sign. *Bang aniya' tanda'ta haya', aniya' sadja bā'-bā'na.* When we see a cloud of the omen type, it always has a message.

**pagbā'**₁ *v. tr.* To inform someone about what is going on. *Pinagbā' na pa'in komandel pasal kagara'anbi.* The commander is always being informed about what you are planning. *Iya ya magbā'an sultan bang ai pagbissalanu minsan ka mareyom bilik patulihannu.* He is the one who tells the sultan what you say even when you are in your bedroom.

**pabā'** *v. tr.* -an To inform someone of an event that he should attend.

**pagpabā'** *v. intr.* aN- To inform people of a coming event.

**bā'**₂ *v. tr.* To suppose or imagine something that may not be true or real. *Bay angahūgan bām ni Serom, binā' aniya' a'a.* They dropped bombs on Serom, thinking there was someone there. *Bang kahōpan, bā'nu tinundun buwahan.* When [he] goes into his trance, you will be filled with pleasure [lit. you would think you were clustered with lansones fruit]. (*Thesaurus:* **pangannal**₂)

**pagbā'**₂ *v. intr.* aN- 1) To assume something; to be convinced without evidence. *Makabati' pa'in iya, pagbā'na dai'-dai' du iya makakuyas buwat bay tagna'.* When he woke he thought, wrongly, that he would immediately be able to get up as before. 1.1) *v. tr.* To assume something by mistake. *Pinagbā' e' sigām mbal to'ongan makasōd.* They thought mistakenly that they would surely be unable to enter.

**kabā'** *v. tr.* To assume wrongly about some fact or situation.

**bā'**₃ *n.* A pig; pork. *gen. Sus.* (*syn:* **bawi**)

**bā'-bā'an** *n.* A species of fish (unclassified).

**ba'ahu** var. of **baha'u**

**ba'an**₁ *n.* A group or cluster of living creatures, animals in particular. *Sinoho' sigām pauntas dahū maka in saga hayop pinaglawak-lawak damba'an maka damba'an.* They were told to cross over first and the animals were moved further away one group at a time. (*Thesaurus:* **botang**₁ **1, kapono'an, puntak 1**)

**ba'anan** (var. **bānan**) *adj. zero* All of a group or category. *Bang nda'nu ba'anan Jipun inān.* If you could have seen all those Japanese. *Buwat pelang nih'llop he' maut, mbal nihella' e' saddi. Pinatuwa' kita bo' halam na maina'an ba'anan sakapta.* Like a canoe sucked in by nothing other than a *maut* spirit. We ourselves were allowed to emerge but

all of our gear was no longer there. (*cf:* **kamemon 1**)

**pagba'an** *v. intr.* aN- 1) To assemble in large groups of living things; to swarm. *Suwala inān sali' suwala manusiya' magba'an.* The voice referred to was like the voice of people gathered in a large group. *Magba'an saga a'a ahiyul.* The excited people are massing together. 1.1) *v. tr.* To gather multiple items into separate groups. *Jari pinagba'an-ba'an saga sapi'.* So the cattle were formed into separate herds.

**ba'an**₂ *see:* **pagba'anan**

**ba'as** *n.* 1) The gleam of marine phosphorescence. (*cf:* **mata-tina'ung**) 1.1) *v. intr.* aN- To gleam with phosphorescence, as seawater may do when agitated. (*cf:* **pagbetong-betong**)

**ba'as-ba'as-llaw** *n.* The after-glow seen just after sunset. *Halam na aniya' llaw, hal ba'as-ba'asna. Sōng sū' palita'an na.* There is no sun anymore, just its after-glow. It is nearly lamp-lighting time.

**ba'at** *n.* 1) A message; a portent. (*Thesaurus:* **kabtangan, haka 1, hunub-hunub 1, pahati 1, sambatan, suli-suli 1**) 1.1) *v. intr.* pa- To mention something; tell. *Buwat ka'a sōng atulak bo' aniya' mareyom kabaya'anku bin'lli. Ma luma' pa'in aku, yuknu, "Ai la yuknu ma aku di'ilaw? Paba'at na ka."* Like when you were about to leave and I had something I wanted to have [you] purchase. When I was in the house you said, "What was it you said to me yesterday? Tell me about it."

**pagba'at** *n.* 1) An oracle; a prophetic utterance; a prediction. (*cf:* **nasa**) 1.1) *v. tr.* To make particular mention of something; to state something in regard to the future. *Bay pinagba'at he' nabi.* It was mentioned by a prophet.

**ba'i** *n.* 1) The relationship between the parents of a married couple. 1.1) *voc. n.* Address term to the parent of one's son-in-law or daughter-in-law.

**pagba'i** *v. intr.* aN- To be related to each other as the parents of a married couple. *Magba'i kami. Anakku si Ju ya h'lla anaknu.* We are ba'i to each other. My son Ju is the husband of your daughter.

**ba'id** *n.* 1) Permission to leave or proceed. 1.1) *v. intr.* aN- To ask permission of someone. *Tuwan Guru, itiya' aku ama'id amole'.* Teacher, I am asking your leave to go home. (*syn:* **puhun**)

**paba'id** *v. tr.* -an To grant someone permission. (*Thesaurus:* **pakuhi, papuhun, parūl 1.1, tugut 2**)

**pama'iran** *n.* A source of permission; a reason for permission.

**ba'is** *v. tr.* To desire someone sexually, with implications of immorality. (*Thesaurus:* **biga', ga'ira, puta, sundal 1**)

**pagba'is** *v. intr.* aN- 1) To behave in a sexually provocative manner. *Bang aniya' d'nda sidda magba'is-ba'is, sali' hinang puta.* If a woman acts in a sexually aggressive manner, it's like the behavior of a prostitute. **1.1)** *v. tr. -an* To desire someone sexually. *Buwat aniya' d'nda pinagba'isan e' a'a, nihawa iya.* Like when a woman is desired sexually by a man, she is longed for.

**ba'it** *n.* A forest tree (unclassified), the large seed cases of which were sometimes used as moneyboxes.

**ba'ugan₁** *n.* A species of tree (unclassified).

**ba'ugan₂** *n.* A curved rod; bow; spreader between lines. *Angalitag, sali' anahat maka kayu ba'ugan, ya pal'mbut inān.* Trapping game, like snaring [crustaceans] with a curved rod, a springy one. *Nihinangan ba'ugan bang duwa nihūg, bo' mbal magsa'ud.* We make a rod if there are two [lines] to drop, so they won't get caught up together. (*Thesaurus:* **palanggungan, papagan 1**)

**ba'u'u** *n.* A species of fresh water tortoise. (*cf:* **p'nnu**; *syn:* **kula-kula**)

**ba'ul₁** *n.* A wooden chest or suitcase. *Aniya' kono' bay takali e' sigām ba'ul bulawan ma babaw-tana'.* They reportedly dug up a golden chest from the ground. (*Thesaurus:* **bakag₁, kalton, labban, maleta, tu'ung**)

**ba'ul₂** *n.* A paddle blank. *T'llu maka dambila', ba'ulna sadja.* Three fifty, for the roughed-out paddle only.

**ba'ung** *n.* A money-box made of a coconut shell. *Sali' ba'ung-ba'ung ya panau'an sīn, ya gusi' hē'.* The *gusi'* referred to is like a coconut-shell container for keeping money in. (*gen:* **pagtau'an**)

**ba'ung-ba'ung** *n.* **1)** Small specks. *Arōy Būd Musu'-i, ba'ung-ba'ung.* Alas, there's Musu' Hill, just specks in the distance. **1.1)** *v. intr. pa-* To appear as small specks in the distance. *Sali' aniya' paba'ung-ba'ung maī' ma kalawakan.* There is something showing up out there, far off.

   **pagba'ung-ba'ung** *v. intr. aN-* To look like specks in the distance. *Būd magba'ung-ba'ung ē', atā kita. Pasōng kita, pasōng, na aheya na.* Those hills that look like dots, us being far away. As we get closer and closer they become large. (*Thesaurus:* **abu-abu₂, ahud-ahud 1.1, buraw, hanaw-hanaw**)

**bal-** *var. of* **bar-**

**bala-bala** *var. of* **sowa-bala-bala**

**balabak** *v. intr. aN-* To fall in mass or in large numbers. *Buwat buwa' kayu bang nijogjog, aheka ahūg. Amalabak hūgna.* Like fruit on the tree, when it is shaken many fall. The fall is in great quantity. *Aheka amalabak bang buwattē' baliyu.* A mass of fruit comes down when the wind is like that. (*cf:* **hūg₁**; *Thesaurus:* **lagonos 1, latak**)

**balakang 1)** *n.* The permanent yellow stain of the teeth. (*Thesaurus:* **baka'₂ 1, kiki' 1**) **2)** *v. advrs. -in-* Suffering from discoloration of the teeth. *Binalakang emponna, sali' maggaringan.* His teeth

are discolored, sort of turning yellow.

**balakat** *var. of* **barakat**

**balakkal** *var. of* **barakkal**

**balad** *n.* A board for spinning dice on. *Bang ato'on legot, subay pinat'nna' sīn ni deyom balad.* When betting in a dice game you must place money inside the gaming board.

**bala'** *n.* Disaster or serious trouble, often the result of offending a supernatural or divine being. *Bay na amuwas huwas-huwas. Halam aniya' magjallat iya. Apuwas na iya man bala'.* He has discharged the obligation. There is nothing now to encumber him. He is free from serious trouble. *Mura-murahan lappasan kita man bala'.* It is to be devoutly hoped that we will be safe from serious trouble. *Sali' sinukna'an a'A: "A'a du ka pamuwangkan ni bala' kamemon."* Like a person being cursed: "You are a person to be thrown away to every kind of disaster." *Ka'a ahāp addat, ma ka'a pahala'. Ma aku, hal bala'.* You have a good character, for you there are rewards. For me, just disaster. (*cf:* **mula₁, nahas 1**; *Thesaurus:* **kajahatan, kala'atan, mulka' 1, naja', pa'al 1, udjul₁ 1**)

**balambangan** *var. of* **tehe'-tehe'-balambangan**

**balan** *n.* Ferrous metal; metal that can be magnetized.

**balanda'₁** *n.* A sailing vessel rigged in traditional western style. *Nijudjal e'na jungal balanda', munda' balanda'.* He pushed the bow of the schooner, its prow.

**balanda'₂** *adj. zero* Dutch; of Dutch origin.

**balanja'** *n.* **1)** Generic term for basic supplies such as food, firewood, cigarettes. *Ta'ā' kami duwa hekana. Aniya' na pam'lli balanja'.* We have caught two [fish]. There is something now to buy supplies with. (*Thesaurus:* **kahirupan, ka'lluman, gastu 1, lutu'₁ 1, pagnapaka**) **1.1)** *v. tr. -an* To provide someone with basic necessities. *Halam kām bay kabuhatan amalanja'an aku.* You were not burdened with taking care of my needs. *Subay binalanja'an kamemon kagunahan sigām llaw-llaw ma waktu kapaghinang langgal ilū.* All their daily needs will be met for the time of building the prayer house. *Halam aniya' pamalanja'.* There is nothing for providing food.

**balang 1)** *n.* Fillets cut from large sea creatures such as shark or stingray. *Am'lli aku dambalang kalitan.* I will buy one fillet of shark. (*Thesaurus:* **balkehet, ballul 1, gali'₁, galing-galing**) **1.1)** *v. tr.* To cut a large sea creature up into fillets that run the length of its body. **2)** *clf.* Count word for long fillets of flesh.

**Balangingi'** *var. of* **Sama Bāngingi'**

**balaru'-balaru'** *n.* Eyes downcast in shyness or deference.

   **pagbalaru'-balaru'** *v. intr. aN-* To keep the eyes downcast, as a bride during the formal stage of waiting for the wedding ceremony.

**balasa** *v. tr.* To shuffle playing cards.

**balat** *v. advrs.* ka-...-an To be interrupted and kept from completing a task. *Kabalatan aku, daka ai bay pamissalaku.* I have been interrupted, goodness knows what I was saying. (*cf:* **jau'-jau', lamud₂ 1.1, pagsakutu**)

**balat-daya** (var. **barat-daya**) *n.* An offshore wind from the southwest to northwest quarter. (*gen:* **baliyu 1**)

**balatak** *n.* A large-meshed basket of rattan or bamboo laths, used for large items. (*gen:* **baka'₁**)

**balatin** *n.* A team game played on a marked court by children.

    **pagbalatin** *v. intr.* aN- To engage in playing balatin. (*syn:* **paghuru 1.1**)

**balatu** *n.* Various cakes and sweetmeats made locally. *Tin'ppa nihinang balatu, ya bāng-bāng panggi' kayu, sali' kolleng-kolleng.* [Cassava] pounded to be made into sweetmeats, the cassava cookies, like deep-fried twists. *Balatu, ya basta niragang-dagangan putili'-mandi, ya pullu'.* Local cakes that may be sold locally, like *putili'-mandi* [cassava cake flavored with grated coconut], like *pullu'. Panggi' kayu tin'ppa nihinang balatu, ya bāng-bāng panggi' kayu, sali' kolleng-kolleng.* Cassava pounded and made into cakes, cassava cookies, similar to deep-fried twists. (*gen:* **apam 1, mamun**)

**balaw** var. of **balo'**

**balayang** *n.* Varieties of paddy rice. (*cf:* **pai 1**)

**balbal** *v. tr.* To harm someone by sucking out vital fluids, the action of a spirit being. *Bang asaki a'a yukna, "Binalbal a'a inān, bay ma lahat dakayu', ya hē' po'onan sakina." Hatina bay binalbal.* When a person is sick they say, "That person has been harmed by a balbalan, he has been away in another place, that's the source of his sickness." In other words he has been attacked by a balbalan spirit. *Ya mangowak mariyata', ya hē' amalbal. Bang iya kasangdanan, amatay, bang mbal kasangdanan a'llum isāb.* The one that makes a cawing noise above, that's the one that sucks bodily fluids. If it continues uninterrupted [the victim] dies, if is interrupted he lives. (*Thesaurus:* **kowang, uwak**)

    **balbalan** *n.* A supernatural monster. *Balbalan, ya mangowak mariyata', ya hē' amalbal. Bang iya kasangdanan, amatay, bang mbal kasangdanan allum isāb.* Balbalan, the one that makes a cawing noise above, that's the one that sucks bodily fluids. If it continues uninterrupted [the victim] dies, if is interrupted he will live.

    **balbangsa** (derivative of **bangsa₂**) *n.* A person of noble birth or rank. *Kal'llahan buwat ka'a, pangluwahan balbangsa.* Men like you, having the appearance of nobility. *Saga a'a balbangsa maka saga magbabaya'.* Men of noble descent and those who exercise power.

**balbero** *n.* A barber.

**balkan** *adj.* -an Wealthy and socially privileged. *Dayahan isāb si Anu, a'a balkanan ya mbal alasa ma miskin. Ya pa'in niharap he'na hinangna.* What's-his-name is wealthy, a rich man who does not love the poor. All he looks at is his work. (*Thesaurus:* **daya, haldaya, mayaman, sayuman**)

**balkehet** (derivative of **kehet**) *n.* A slice of a whole piece. (*Thesaurus:* **balang 1, ballul 1, gali'₁, galing-galing**).

**balkon** *n.* The front veranda of a house. (*Thesaurus:* **pantān, salas, saurung**)

**balda** *v. tr.* To resist doing what one is told to do. *Ai-ai sinoho' he' mastal subay da'a binalda, subay bineya'-beya'.* Whatever the teacher tells you to do you should not dispute it, you should obey. *Balda itu subay aniya' lling. Bang aniya' llingnu mbal kami makabalda.* Something has to be spoken for *balda* [to be relevant]. If you say something we cannot go against it. (*Thesaurus:* **dangat 1, paggat, sagga' 1.1, sīng-sūd**)

**baldapat** (derivative of **dapat₁**) *n.* An unreliable person. *A'a baldapat mbal kapangandolan.* An unreliable person cannot be trusted.

**balde** *n.* A pail or bucket.

**baldusa** (derivative of **dusa**) *n.* A persistent sinner. *Tantu abinasa saga baldusa.* Sinners will surely suffer.

**bale₁** *n.* A matter of concern or importance. *Minsan aku mbal makahampit, nsa' du bale ma aku.* Even though I don't get to share, it is no concern of mine.

**bale₂** *v. tr.* To seek funding for a business enterprise such as a seasonal fishing venture. *Pabalehun aku sīnnu.* Let me have an advance of your money. *Bang aniya' niyugta, sali' kabbun ina'an, amale kita ni tinda. Pila-pila baleta, pina'ā'an kita sīn e' Lannang.* If one has coconuts, like that plantation, we seek an advance from the store. However much we need, the Chinese [shop-owner] will let us have the money.

**bale₃** *n.* 1) An upright stake or prop. (*Thesaurus:* **hāg 1, lusuk-lusuk, pangtu'ud, pipul, sambuwang, soha', sumpiyang, tuku 1, tungkud 1**) 1.1) *v. tr.* -an To support with stakes. *Bang aku angampas subay balehanku bo' mbal ah'bba apa alandos s'llog.* When I go fishing with the fence trap I should stake it so it doesn't fall down, because the current is strong. *Bang kita angambit subay bowata batu maka lubid. Pinatuntun batu pareyo', nihagul. Minsan k'llat pinabale-bale.* When we drive fish into a fenced area we need to take stones and cord. The stones are lowered and jigged up and down. Even ropes are supported by multiple stakes.

**bale₄** *adv.* In one's judgment or estimation. *Bale sangpū' hekana.* About ten in number [I guess]. *Bale waktu itu.* About this time [I suppose].

**bale₅** *n.* Coals; embers. (*syn:* **baga 1**; *Thesaurus:* **abu 1, buling**)

**balebol** *n.* A volleyball.

**pagbalebol** (var. **pagbolebol**) *n.* 1) The game of volleyball. 1.1) *v. intr. aN-* To play the game of volleyball. *Bang akatis pagbalebol, nihapus aku.* When the volleyball game is finished I am out of breath. *Bang kita bay magdugtul maka sehe'ta, buwat magbalebol ina'an.* When we collided with our mates, like when playing volleyball. (*cf:* **pagbola**)

**bale'** *v. advrs. -in-* Tired after physical activity. *Binale' gi' aku, bay na aku angā' bohe'.* I'm still tired, I have been fetching water. (*cf:* **male' 1.1**; *Thesaurus:* **binasa 1, b'kkat 2, husa', lumpu, paya**)

**bale'-bale'** *adj. -an* Exhausted. *Bay kam nirugpak e' sigām ma waktu kām bale'-bale'an maka nihapus ma l'ngngananbi.* They attacked you at a time when you were exhausted and out of breath on your journey.

**balguru** (derivative of **guru**) *n.* A religious scholar.

**bali-bali** var. of **mali-mali**

**balibag**₁ *v. tr.* To hit a target with something thrown. *Balibagta ka maka batu atawa kayu.* I will pelt you with a stone or a stick. (*Thesaurus:* **balleng 1.1, sigung, timbag**)

**balibag**₂ *see:* **pagbalibag**

**balik**₁ *adj. zero* 1) Recurrent or next, of a day of the week or some recurring event. *A: "Ahad itu?" B: "Ngga'i ka, Ahad balik."* A: "This Sunday?" B: "No, next Sunday." 1.1) *v. intr. pa-* To return to a previous point or place; recur. *Pabalik kita ni bay yukna insini'.* Let's go back to what you said earlier. *Tapabalikan Nasuli' itū apa ahāp, halam anganjahulaka'.* Nasuli [inland Mindanao] is a place to revisit because it is good, no one causing harm. (*Thesaurus:* **bing₂ 1**) 1.2) *v. tr.* To go back and get something. *Balikku pitakaku, bay ta'bba arai' ma bihing tigbaw.* I will go back for my wallet which may perhaps have been left beside the pool. 1.3) *v. tr. -an* To repeat something; return something to its owner. *Balikin kono', balikin he'nu amūng.* Say it again please, say again what you said. *Mbal kabalikan kalingkatna.* Her beauty cannot be repeated. *Lima pilak pinehē' ni matto'ana. Minsan hē'-i akatis, aniya' balikanna lima pilak.* Five pesos passed on to his parents. Even when that is used up, he has five pesos to do it again. (*Thesaurus:* **duwa 1.1, isab 2**)

**balik salawat** *v. tr. -an* To get back to the subject of conversation. {idiom} *Balikanku salawat.* Getting back to what I was saying. *Ya na salawat pagbalik-balikanku, aheya landu' pagmahaltabatku ma ka'am angkan kām patut pama'iran.* That's what I keep coming back to, I respect you very much, which is why you should be asked for permission.

**pagbalik** *v. tr.* To restore a relationship to its former state. *Bang aniya' bay magtiman maglakibini, pinapagbalik he' saga matto'a sigā.* When a married couple have separated, their elders get them back [to their married state]. *Mbal anatas kapagbalik sigām.* Their restoration will not endure.

**pabalik** *adv.* Again.

**balik**₂ *v. intr. aN-* To rebound, of a curse or something thrown. (*Thesaurus:* **bing₃, bitung, hili, likid, pagbintu, pagpatimpa, pelleng 1.2**)

**balikat** *n.* Good quality cloth used in sarongs. *Hōs tadjung balikat, buwat hōs tadjung, bo' a'aslag sapakna.* A balikat sarong, like an ordinary check sarong, but with large motifs.

**balikmata** *n.* Conjuring; tricks of magic.

**pagbalikmata** *v. intr. aN-* To do conjuring tricks; to perform sleight of hand. *Ata'u magbalikmata. Bigi ipil-ipil sina'oban maka turung kassa'. Pinatokod kita bang maingga.* He can do sleight of hand. An *ipil* seed is covered with a jar lid, and we are told to guess where it is.

**balidja** *v. tr. -an* To deceive someone by giving misleading information. *Buwat aniya' amab'llihan s'mmek. Aku amalidja ni kasehe'an bo' supaya hal aku. Kulli'anku kasehe'an ina'an.* For example, someone is selling clothes. I misinform the others so that I alone can buy. I deceive those others. *Atawa buwat aniya' ai-ai ahūg min luma'ta bo' ya patilawanta inān ya na bay makapuwa' iya. Binalidjahan he'na ngga'i ka kono' iya.* Or like when something has fallen from our house, but the person we ask is the one who picked it up. He says misleadingly that it was not [reportedly] him. (*Thesaurus:* **akkal 1.1**)

**balig** *adj. zero* Deviating from what is expected, as ungrammatical speech or uneducated behavior. *Bang kita sinoho' bo' saddī b'llita min bay panoho'an kita, yuk-i, "Balig sinoho' onde'-onde'."* If we are sent on an errand and buy something other than we were told to, they say, "The child doesn't know how to go on an errand." *Balig, basta asā' min kabontolan.* Improper, whenever something errs from what is correct. (*cf:* **akil-balig**)

**baligbig** *adj. a-* Asymmetrical; misshapen. (*cf:* **kamigmig 1**; *Thesaurus:* **kirus 1, pagkamihu, tempang**)

**pagbaligbig** *v. intr. aN-* To become misshapen. *Na, ya buwat man deyom kandang, buwat saga magbaligbig kōkna, sahili'. Asal man deyom kandang.* Now like [a child] still inside the womb, its head becoming sort of misshapen, something congenital. It's already that way inside the womb.

**balihan** *n.* A species of sea perch.

**baliman** (derivative of **iman**₁) *n.* A person characterized by strong faith in God; the community of the faithful.

**balimbing** *n.* The tree and fruit of the carambola or star apple. *Averrhoa carambola.* (*Thesaurus:* **kamyas, kisas**₁, **iba'**)

**balin** *v. intr. pa-* To do something other than what is usual. *Mbal aku ameya', ka'a ya pabalīn. Hatina* *ka'a ya ganti', pas'lle'.* I'm not going [fishing], you go for a change. In other words, you substitute, you take a turn. *Pinabalīn pelangna ma si Ji.* He transfers the use of his canoe to Ji.

**pagbalīn** *v. intr. aN-* **1)** To make a change that affects the two people or groups involved. *Kami asal magdamunda'. Pag'llaw dakayu' yuk kami, "Magbalīn na, abō' na pa'in aheka ta'ā'."* We normally go in the one canoe. One day we say [to each other], "Let's swap gear so we keep catching a lot." *Da'a magtiggan, magbalīn kita, magsaliyu sehe'. Ka'a-i ameya', h'ndanu ta'bba ka?* Don't go all together, let's have a change, changing workmates. Will you come [with us], your wife left behind? **1.1)** *v. tr. -an* To make changes to what is right or agreed on. *Da'a pagbalīninbi ya kabontolan sara', atawa ama'nda' pagtabang dapit.* Do not make changes to the rightness of the law, nor display support for an ally.

**pabalīn** *v. tr.* To transfer something to another person.

**baling** *n.* A paste of pickled shrimp, known as bagoong.

**baling-baling** *n.* A species of tiny shrimp.

**balis₁** *v. tr. -an* To open fire on someone. *Binalisan kami he' a'a. Binalisan itu bang ganta' tinimbak.* We were fired at by someone. *Balis* here refers to an imagined shooting. (*Thesaurus:* **kalsa, kital, surang**)

**balis₂** *var. of* **baris**

**balis₃** *n.* A species of forest tree, a source of good flooring material. *Kayu balis itū kayu talun. Ahāp pangalantay luma', akeyat esokna.* This *balis* tree is a forest tree. It is good for flooring a house, its heartwood is red.

**baliskat** (*var.* **baliskuwat**) *adj. a-* **1)** Upside down; reversed in order. *Bang ka anurungan garapun, yukna hē', "Ahāp na." Pag'nda'nu pabalik, abaliskat.* When you put the lid on the jar you said, "That's fine." On looking at it again, it was upside down. *Abaliskat kasehe'an kintas itū.* Some of these pages are the wrong way up. **1.1)** *v. tr.* To turn something upside down.

**baliskuwat** *var. of* **baliskat**

**baliyakaw** *v. tr.* To notice where something went. *Halam bay tabaliyakaw.* Hadn't seen what happened to it. *Magtūy tinelop-telopan bay mahūg ē', halam tabaliyakaw.* The thing that fell was promptly carried out of sight and could not be seen.

**baliyang** *v. advrs. ta-* Made giddy by height or sudden shock. *Ala'at palasahan si Lu bang binuwattē'. Yuk kami Sama tabaliyang laha'na, saga patunggang.* Lu will feel ill if treated like that. We Sama say that her blood experiences vertigo, [her head] dipping down. *Atawa bang kita angandāg ni puttuk-puttuk balunu', tabaliyang kita, sali' kita nihanggaw inān.* Or when we climb to the very top of the *balunu'* [mango] tree, we

experience vertigo, like we are scared. *Buwat kita ameya' ma ariplano, bo' mbal biyasa, na tabaliyang kita. Sali' kita auling matata, sali' kita lango goyak. Yuk kami Sama tabaliyang laha'na.* When we travel by plane and are not accustomed to it, then we suffer vertigo. It's like our eyes are unfocused, as if we are seasick. We Sama say that the blood is made giddy. (*Thesaurus:* **angol, bo'ay, lango 1.1, pagboyokan, pagtunggang-kīng, uling**)

**baliyu** **1)** *n.* Wind. *Alandos baliyu.* The wind is strong. (*spec:* **balat-daya, dalat, habagat, hilaga', satan, timul, tunggara', uttala', uttala'-lo'ok**; *Thesaurus:* **badju, hunus 1, simpal**) **1.1)** *v. advrs. ka-...-an* To be overcome or exhausted by paddling against the wind. *Kabaliyuhan kami amusay, alandos s'llog.* We are exhausted through paddling upwind, the current very strong. **2)** *v. advrs. ka-...-an* To be deprived of flavor by exposure to the air. *Panggi' kayu, aniya' sali' bay at'bbag, ya bay kabaliyuhan. Ya hē' nihinang hapit-hapit.* Cassava, some of it sort of tasteless, left exposed to the air. That's what is made into *hapit-hapit* [a sweet].

**pamaliyu** *n.* The windy season.

**baljanji'** (derivative of **janji'**) *n.* **1)** A religous vow made for safety or the recovery of good health. **1.1)** *v. tr. -an* To make a vow of religious commitment for the purpose of restoring good health or safety. **2)** A dedication ceremony involving the reading of the baljanji' section of the Holy Koran.

**ballabi-labi** (derivative of **labi**) *adj. -an* Much greater in abundance or value. *Lidjiki' ballabi-labihan min saga danakanna.* Blessings much greater than those of his brothers.

**ballak** *n.* A species of coastal tree, sand tolerant. *Tournefortia argentea. Kayu ballak buwat luwa amboway.* A *ballak* tree looks like an *amboway*. *Bang taluwa' sallak subay kayu ballak panambal.* If someone is affected by *sallak* [a sickness], the medicine is from the *ballak* tree.

**ballag** *adj. a-* Clearly seen. *Mbal sali' agabul pang'nda'ta. Magtūy du aballag, buwat ka'a mareyom patta', aballag ka.* It is like our vision is not blurry. It is immediately clear, like you in the photograph, you are clearly seen.

**ballas** **1)** *n.* Restitution for harm done. **2)** *v. tr. -an* To require recompense for harm done, the action of God. (*Thesaurus:* **tungbas 1.1**)

**ballay** *n.* A house in process of building. *Ballay itū luma' mbal gi' ajatu. Mbal niōnan ballay bang akatis na. Luma' na.* *Ballay* refers to a house that is not fully complete. It is not called *ballay* once it is finished. Then it is a house. (*Thesaurus:* **kubu'-kubu', luma', pamāy-bāy**)

**balleng** *v. intr. pa-* **1)** To move through the air in a curving movement. *Saukku bohe'. Pagsaukku makaballeng ni iya.* I scooped up some water. As I scooped, it flew through the air towards him.

**1.1)** *v. tr. -an* To hit a target by throwing something at arm's length. *Ballenganku siyaliku maka gayung.* I hit my younger brother with a dipper thrown at arm's length. (*Thesaurus:* **balibag₁, sigung, timbag**)

**balling** *n.* Various wrasses. *fam. Labridae.* (*cf:* **pellok**)

**ballit** *adj. a-* Moved out of sequence.

**ballo'** (var. **bollo'**) *adj. zero* Related fictively through adoption or re-marriage. *Ina'ku ballo'.* My stepmother. (*Thesaurus:* **eddok-eddok, tē'₁**)

**ballul** *n.* **1)** A long fillet cut from a shark or stingray. (*Thesaurus:* **balang 1, balkehet, gali'₁, galing-galing**) **1.1)** *v. tr.* To cut a large fish or ray into long fillets.

**ballum** *neg.* A negative answer to an assertion. {rare} *Ballum lagi'.* Not yet. *Ballum tantu, asarap-duwa.* Not certain, two possible outcomes. *Ballum tantu, m'ssa' tantu, daka at'kka daka ai.* Not definite, whether [they will] arrive or what. (*Thesaurus:* **ai po'on, duma'in, mbal 1.1, m'ssa', ngga'i ka**)

**balmula** *v. tr.* To restore something to its original state. *Da'a na balmulahunbi pabalik.* Do not build it again. *Bay atunu' Ma'asim sampay munisipiyo, na wa'i na binalmula pabalik kamemon halu'na i'.* Ma'asim and its municipal buildings was burnt, and now all of its ruins have been restored. (*Thesaurus:* **bangun₂ 2**)

**balobok₁** *v. intr. aN-* To blow air through the lips while under water. (*syn:* **balombong**)

**balobok₂** *n.* A species of fish valued for its firm flesh and mild flavor. (*cf:* **daing-pote'**)

**balo'** (var. **balaw**) *n.* A species of hardwood tree, the leaves and roots of which are used medicinally. *Premna or Shorea sp. Subay kulit balo' nihinang tambal ugam. Gamutna atuwas, nihinang puhan kalis.* The bark of the tree is used to treat furring on the tongue. Its roots are hard and are used for making a scabbard for a kris. *Subay kulit balo' nihinang tambal ugam. Gamutna atuwas, nihinang tipara atawa puhan kalis.* The bark of the tree is used to treat furring on the tongue. Its roots are hard and are used for making diving goggles or the scabbard for a kris.

**balombong** *v. intr. aN-* To blow a mixture of air and water out through the lips. *Amalombong kita tahik bay inumta. Ya du daing pote' ma deyo'.* We blow out seawater that we have drunk. White-fish do the same thing under water. (*syn:* **balobok₁**)

**balos₁ 1)** *v. tr. -an* To retaliate; to take revenge. *Bay aku sinuntuk e' si Sa, halam aku makabalos.* Sa punched me, but I didn't take revenge. *Tu'ud binalosan anakna.* He is simply taking revenge for [what happpened to] his son. *Maghona'-hona' sigām, arakala' binalosan e' si Yu ma pasalan bay tahinang sigām ma iya.* They considered that Yu would in all likelihood take revenge on them because of what they had done to him. (*Thesaurus:* **entom buddi, pagbuling-bata' 1.1, paluli**) **2)** *v. tr. -an* To make a counter-offer when bargaining. *Bay aku am'lli daing, nihalga'an sangpū' pilak, balosku lima.* I was buying fish. It was priced at ten pesos; I offered five pesos. **3)** *v. tr.* To move in a counter-direction. *Insini' bay sōn, bo' la'ang amalos.* Earlier it was sōn, the incoming tide, with la'ang, the outgoing tide, flowing back. *Asesek p'ttung itū, subay binalos man dambila'.* This bamboo is still holding, it needs to be cut from the opposite side. *Tupananta lling, subay aniya' pamalosta ahāp.* We make our words suitable, we should have a good response.

**balos-hulas** *v. intr. aN-* To require payment for work done (as required by custom). {idiom} *Bang amahinang ni panday subay aniya' tulahan ko da'a amalos-hulas.* If someone gets an expert to do something there must be some recompense lest his sweat demand revenge.

**pagbalos** *v. intr. aN-* To come together from opposite directions, as weather events. *Duwa tahik magbalos, tahik uttara' maka tahik satan.* There are two opposing sea-seasons, the season of the north wind and the season of the southwest monsoon.

**balos₂** *adj. a-* Turning sour or rancid. *Abalos gatas apa nihinang di'ilaw.* The milk is going sour because it was made up yesterday. *Da'a lotokun daing ilū abō' mbal kalīman. Abalos pa'in mbal takakan.* Don't handle that fish lest it be wasted. Once it goes off it's not edible. (*cf:* **bahi**; *Thesaurus:* **baguy, buhuk, buntu'₁ 1.1, halu' 1.1, langag, p'ngkak**)

**balosok** *n.* An incoming tide with exceptionally strong current. *Sōn subu. Min duwa na sōn, min duwa na balosok.* An incoming tide in the morning. When it comes in twice, the strong current occurs twice. (*cf:* **duwasay₂**)

**balot** *see:* **pagbalot**

**balowak** *v. advrs. ta-* Caused to retch or gag. *Sali' ai-ai bay ma deyom b'ttongta tautta'an. Buwat aniya' mbal ameya' ma napsuta, tabalowak kita.* As if whatever was in our stomach is vomited up. Like when something is not to our taste, and we are made to retch. *Atawa aniya' ta'nda'ta mbal tas'llongta, tabalowak kita. Bilahi kita angutta' bo' mbal.* Or we see something that we cannot tolerate, it causes us to gag. We want to vomit but don't. (*Thesaurus:* **pagsallowa', toya', utta' 1**)

**balsa** *n.* A raft or swimming float. (*Thesaurus:* **alul, plātbōt**)

**balu** *n.* **1)** Someone whose marriage has been ended by death, whether the surviving spouse or the deceased. *Ina'an baluku mareyom patta'.* That's my deceased wife in the photo. **1.1)** *adj. a-* Separated by the death of wife or husband. *"Otō'," yukna, "ipalnu si Ta abalu na."* "Son," he

said, "your sister-in-law Ta is a widow now."
**1.2)** *v. advrs.* -in- To suffer the death of one's
husband or wife.

**balu-assang** *n.* A person whose betrothed dies
before the marriage.

**balu-d'nda** (var. **d'nda-balu**) *n.* A widow.
*Maka'nda' du ka balu d'nda, ya bay soho'ku ka
pinakan ma iya.* You will see a widowed woman
to whom I have given orders that you are to be
fed. *Aniya' dakayu' d'nda balu ya bay tapah'llana
dakayu' min tumpukan kanabi-nabihan.* There was
a widowed woman who had taken as husband
one of the prophet community.

**pamalu** *n.* A woman who is often widowed.

**baluba 1)** *v. intr. aN-* To lose desirable features; to
fade in color. *Bang bulawan pinehē' ni tahik,
amasi luwa bulawan. Bang tumbaga amaluba.* If
gold is put in the sea its appearance is still like
gold. If brass, it changes color. *Amaluba talam
itu ni tumbaga, aniya' isāb amaluba ni pote'.* This
metal tray changes to a coppery color, there are
also some that turn white. (*Thesaurus:* **gagas,
lulu, padpad, papas**₁) **2)** *v. tr.* -an To change
what was promised. *Binalubahan janji'nu. Yuknu
salung, ati ngga'i ka.* Your promise changed. You
said tomorrow and it isn't so. *Mbal magbaluba
llingku, sali' mbal apinda.* My word will not
become less true, like it will not change.

**balubak** *v. tr.* -an To whip someone. *Kabalubakan
pa'in iya, na magtūy angalahod baranna.* Once he
was whipped, his body immediately showed
bruising. (*Thesaurus:* **daplos, lambot, lappet,
lubak**₁)

**balukakkad** *see:* **pagbalukakkad**

**balukad** *v. intr. pa-* To get up from a prone position
or state. *Makabalukad na ka min kasakihan.
Minsan mbal pahali, makakole' na lum'ngngan.*
You are able to get up from your sick bed. Even
though not well, you are able to walk. *Na mbal
na makabalukad, mbal na makatuwa', alembo.*
Well [he] can't rise up now, can't appear, is
drowned. (*Thesaurus:* **punduk 1**)

**balud** *n.* The pink-bellied Imperial Pigeon. *Ducula
poliocephala. Buwat balud, ang'mmu.* Coos like a
dove. (*cf:* **assang**)

**balu'** *adj. a-* Unsettled, of a local community. *Bang
sangom bo' aniya' bay tatangkaw, bo' sali'
ahiluhala' deyom paglūng, ya na hē' abalu'.* When
it is night and something has been stolen, and
there is a great disturbance in the neighborhood,
that is *balu'. Abalu' ma deyom paglahat.* It is very
unsettled in the district. (*Thesaurus:* **dongkag,
halubilu, hengo-hengo, hiluhala' 1.1, hiyul,
jabu 1, lengog 1.1, sasaw 1.1, sensong**)

**balunu'** *n.* A coarse variety of mango and its
odorous fruit. *Mangifera caesia. Minsan
mampallam, wanni, balunu', anadjuk. Bang mbal
niruplak, palanjal, yampa magdurū'-ero'.* Whether
common mango, odorous mango or horse

mango, all set fruit. If not damaged they develop
and then go on to the budding stage. (*Thesaurus:*
**kobkoban, mampallam, wanni**)

**balung** *v. tr.* **1)** To carry a person on one's
shoulders. *Balungku si Li ni Tōng Batu amandi ma
tahik.* I will carry Li on my shoulders to Rock
End to swim in the sea. (*Thesaurus:* **baba' 1,
tanggung**₁**, tumpay, usung**) **1.1)** *v. intr. pa-* To
ride on someone's shoulders.

**balung-balung** *n.* A field shelter. (*Thesaurus:*
**kamalig, lapaw, panggung, payad, pillayag**)

**balut 1)** *adj. a-* Adhering to a surface. *Tagimtim itū
bang abalut to'ongan, mbal ala'an to'ongan. Amasi
limpa'na.* When freckles are adhering firmly they
will never go away completely. The scars
remain. **1.1)** *v. intr. aN-* To cling to a surface.
*Bang aku kaut, hūgku sau bo' amalut ni batu.*
When I go out to sea I drop the anchor so it will
hold firmly to a coral rock. *Kabalutku ma si Id
inān insini' gi'. Yampa bbahanku, at'kka na si Ina'
man pam'llihan ai-ai.* My holding on to Id [a
toddler] was from earlier on. I had only just put
her down when Mom arrived from the places
where various things are purchased. *Ya paluwas
damuli wa'i amalut pahogot ma buli' tape'
siyakana.* The one that came out last was
holding firmly to the heel of his older sibling.
(*Thesaurus:* **kakkot, damil, pikit**₁ **1**) **1.2)** *v. tr.*
-an To hold something firmly. *Daipara makabalut
aku angkan halam ahūg pareyo'.* Fortunately I
held on which is why it didn't fall down.
*Magbayla kami, balutanku ma hawakan.* We
dance together, I hold [her] by the waist. *Daka
angay, sali' binalut na in bilahiku anganiyat
bissalaku ni ka'a.* Goodness knows why, it's like
my firm intention to send my message to you
gets held back. (*Thesaurus:* **komkom, kopkop 1,
ntan**₁ **1**) **2)** *v. intr. aN-* To be loyal to someone.
(*Thesaurus:* **lumut**₂ **1, lūt**₂ **1, uli, umid 1**)

**pamalutan** *n.* Something to hold on to; handles
by which a container may be lifted.

**balutbatu** var. of **bāt-balutbatu**

**balutu** (var. **bautu**) *n.* A large canoe of the pelang
type. *Balutu itū niukilan, sagō' mbal kaōnan
dapang bang halam bay pinansalan.* These *balutu*
canoes are decorated with carving, but they
can't be called *dapang* if the bow isn't decked.
(*Thesaurus:* **bangka', dapang, londay,
pallungan, pambot, paraw 1, pelang, pongag**)

**baluyut** *n.* A woven container of natural fibers.
*Ahāp silal nihinang baluyut.* Buri palm [leaves]
are good for making woven containers. (*gen:*
**baka'**₁)

**bām** *n.* A bomb or grenade. (*cf:* **timbak 1**)

**bamba** *see:* **pagbamba**

**bamban**₁ *v. tr.* To boil grated cassava meal in a leaf
wrapper. *Mbal binamban panggi' bang bay
pinatuwas.* Cassava is not boiled if it has been
allowed to go hard. (*gen:* **b'lla 1**)

**binamban** *n.* Boiled cassava meal, an alternative

form of starch staple.

**bamban₂** *n.* A species of slender cane used for tying thatch panels. *Badjang itū pagtahi' atop, batangna. Bamban bang ma lling kami Sama.* The leaf of the *badjang* cane is for tying thatch, its stalk. In our Sama language it is *bamban.* (*Thesaurus:* **badjang, hidjuk, lanut, lupis**)

**banak** *n.* Various gray mullets and goatfish. *fam. Mugilidae. Agpatay-patay banak-banak bo' isāb a'llum.* Young mullet play dead, but they are actually alive. (*cf:* **pugaw**; *spec:* **bonte, kepak₂**)

**banag** *n.* A dragonfly. *Banag, tasaggaw bang binalutan buli'na tinangkaw.* A dragonfly, it can be captured if you stealthily take it by the rear.

**bana'** *n.* Leafflower tree. *Glochidion sp.*

**bānan** var. of **ba'anan**

**banda'** *v. tr. -an* To warn someone on the basis of known dangers. *Banda'anku iya. Mbal pakaleyaku apa aniya' mundu.* I have been warning him. I won't let him go inland because there are bandits. (*Thesaurus:* **lāng, pamarā**)

**bandehaw** *n.* A shallow metal tray, usually enameled. (*cf:* **garul**; *Thesaurus:* **talam, tataklayan**)

**bandila'** *n.* A large flag or banner. *Bang nda'nu bandila' itū tauwa' baliyu uttala', ang'llay-ng'llay sadja.* If only you could see the flags blown by the north wind, just fluttering to and fro. (*Thesaurus:* **panji, sambulayang, tipas-tipas**)

**banding** *v. tr.* To examine something carefully. *Bandingun pahāp, tandingun pahāp, lilingun pahāp.* Inspect it well, look at it well, examine it carefully. (*Thesaurus:* **liling, tanding 1**)

**bandu₁** (var. **bantu₁**) *v. tr.* To put the same price on diverse items when selling. *Buwat saga ma tabu', ai-ai niragangan binandu kamemon. Hatina pinagdasali' halga'na.* Like at the market, a variety of things being offered for the same amount each. In other words making the asking price identical.

**bandu₂** *v. tr. -an* To plot against someone. *Binanduhan kita, minunduhan.* We are being plotted against, to be raided. *Bang aniya' taga ai-ai, buwat sali' mareyom kauman bo' ta'nda' he' sai-sai, binanduhan he' bay maka'nda'. Agara' angalangpas.* When anyone has various possessions and is in a community where anyone can see them, someone who saw them plots something. They plan to raid.

**bandung₁** *v. tr.* To lash a supporting piece alongside an object that is weak or damaged. *Binandung na hāg ni bihing paraw, tinapil saga. Mbal tinundan, mbal niruwa'.* The post is lashed alongside the canoe, like a splint. It isn't towed or taken on board. (*Thesaurus:* **hapid₁ 1.1**)

**bandung₂** *v. tr. -an* To encourage the performance of a reluctant singer, especially of one who sings the kata-kata epic. *Bandung-bandungin ba abō' paluwas tunisna.* Stir him up so the melody will come out. *Amandungan ka'a, ahāp kinale, sali' magmanuk-manuk.* Urging you to perform [the kata-kata], good to hear, like birds singing. (*cf:* **su'al-su'al**)

**Bandung** *n.* A coastal Indonesian city, known for its cloth goods.

**bannang** *n.* Strong thread or line. *Amole' na kitam. Kolengun bannang naylon. Patandan na kitam.* Let's go home. Wind up the nylon line. We'll head for shore. (*cf:* **lubid 1**; *Thesaurus:* **jiyay, tanud, tingkal**)

**bannang tinabid** *n. phrase* Twined thread in contrast to mono-filament nylon line.

**banog** (var. **banug**) *n.* A crab-claw sail. (*syn:* **sorekang**)

**pagbanog-banog** *n.* Toy sailboats. *Daun salirap nihinang pagbanog-banog.* Palm leaflets made into sailing toys.

**pabanogan** *adv.* Sailing under a banog-type sail.

**banog pelang** *n. phrase* A four-cornered sail with the the upper corner propped away from the mast by a sprit. (*cf:* **leha 1**)

**banol** *adj. a-* 1) Bruised internally due to repeated blows. *Bang butugta, na abanol na. Ap'ddi' ma deyom, sali' angisi-kulabutan isita hē'.* If we pummel [arm or leg], it becomes bruised. It is painful inside, our muscular tissue becomes lumpy like the meat of a cuttlefish. **1.1)** *v. tr.* To pound something in order to soften the flesh; to pound someone's body in order to bruise. (*Thesaurus:* **pangki', pogpog 1.1, t'ppa**)

**banos** *adj. a-* Plentiful; abundant. *Abanos na lahing.* There are plenty of coconuts. (*Thesaurus:* **besal, kansang 1, datay₂, dayas-dayas, dorot, heka 1.1, jayak, parat**)

**bansān** *n.* 1) A rudder. **1.1)** *v. tr. -an* To steer a boat with a rudder-like device. *Bang kita am'ssi ni Buli' Pongpong, bo' akatis na am'ssi, bo' aniya' baliyu, pinat'ngge na banog bo' ka amansān man buli'.* When we go fishing to Buli' Pongpong, and we finish fishing, and there is wind, the sail will be rigged and you will steer over the stern.

**bansil** *n.* 1) Teeth covered with gold. *Bansil dakayu', bansil duwa. Bang aheka, niōnan empon lapus.* One gold tooth, two gold teeth. If there are a whole lot, it's called a full set of [gold] teeth. **1.1)** *v. tr.* To fit a gold layer over a tooth.

**pagbansil** *v. intr. aN-* To have teeth capped with gold. *Si Mi magbansil bulawan.* Mi has her teeth gold-capped. *Magbansil lapus si Arung.* Oldest daughter has a full set of gold-covered teeth.

**bansing** *n.* A large ax. (*cf:* **kapa**)

**banta** *n.* 1) An enemy. *Bang aniya' bantanu, painsap ka ko da'a tinipu.* If you have an enemy be watchful lest you be attacked unsuspectingly. (*ant:* **bagay 1**) **1.1)** *v. tr. -an* To treat someone as an enemy. *Bang aniya' danakanku bo' ap'ddi' atayna ma aku, bo' aku sinuntuk, nihalus aku, sali' binantahan na.* If I have a sibling who is angry with me, and I get punched, I am seen as someone who may be fought with, treated as an enemy.

**pagbalbantahan** *v. intr.* aN- To relate to each other as enemies. *Magjingki-jingkihan, sali' magpalbantahan.* Mutually antagonistic, like being enemies.

**pagbanta** *n.* 1) A state of enmity. 1.1) *v. intr.* aN- To relate to each other as enemies. *Bang kami magbono' maka Sūk magbanta kami.* When we fight with a Tausug we become enemies to each other. *Aniya' kasehe'an magbanta isāb tīttopan buway. Yuk a'a magbono' hē', "Subay asugpat buway inān bo' kita magkahāp."* There are also some people in an enemy relationship who [formalize it] by cutting off a piece of rattan. Those enemies say, "That rattan will have to joined again for us to make peace." *Mahē' magtimuk, magkahāp maka bay banta. Magtūy aku parauhat pasiyum. Magkaki kami sampay ni dunya hē'-i.* Coming together there, becoming reconciled with one who had been an enemy. I immediately went up and kissed him. We [would be] cousins until the world to come. (*Thesaurus:* **pagkuntara**)

**palbantahan** *n.* Enemies in a collective sense.

**banta'** *v. advrs.* -in- Suffering from the recurrence of a sickness. *Bang aku bay asaki bo' aku magl'ngngan binanta' aku, sali' pabalik sakiku. Tinandog aku pabīng.* If I had been sick and I was out and about, I had a relapse, it was as though my sickness came back. I was feverish again. *Ya po'on asidda binanta' h'ndanu.* That's why your wife keeps getting sick so often. (*Thesaurus:* **boggat, sangti', timbalun₁** 1)

**bantang** *adj.* a- 1) Horizontal; level with. *Abantang pahāp kayu inān.* That wood is truly horizontal. *Subay abantang timbangan.* The beam-scale should be level. (*Thesaurus:* **kondo', kuru', domol** 1, **tondok** 1) 1.1) *v. tr.* -an To point horizontally at a target. *Magtūy kami binantangan.* We were immediately aimed directly at.

**pabantang** *adv.* 1) Horizontally. 1.1) *v. tr.* To hold or extend something horizontally. *Pinabantang e'na tungkudna ni kabohe'-bohe'an.* He held his walking-stick out horizontally towards the waters.

**bantilan** *n.* Posts used to raise a canoe above high tide level, for maintenance. *Bantilan, ya panangonan pelang. Bantilan*, the structure for supporting a canoe. (*syn:* **kalangan₂, tangonan**)

**bantingag** (var. **pantingag**) *v. tr.* To gather information about a region, person, or situation; to investigate. *Na, amapehē' kitām dahū saga kal'llahan amantingagan kitām lahat.* Now then, let's have some men go and check out the district for us. *Jari pinapehē' lima a'a aesog amantingag palahatan bo' kapaglahatan e' sigām.* So five brave men were sent there to spy out the land so they could settle in it.

**bantu₁** var. of **bandu₁**

**bantu₂** *see:* **pagbantu**

**bantuk** *n.* The shape of something; profile of a canoe or ship. (*Thesaurus:* **aymuka, bayhu'** 1, **dagbos, jantang-jari, lahi₄, luwa** 1, **pangli'** 1)

**bantukan** *n.* A pattern or plan to guide construction of something such as a house. (*Thesaurus:* **ladjawan, sengoran, simpayan, suntu'an**)

**bantug** *n.* 1) Fame; reputation. *Kīnnopan pagbuwan pangā'an bantug.* Added to the gifts in order to gain a reputation. (*Thesaurus:* **bawag, buhanyag, busling, hayag, hula-layag** 1, **tanyag** 1) 1.1) *adj.* a- Widely known; famous; notorious. *Abantug pehē' Sitti Bulkiya', aheka bay amatay.* Sitti Bulkiya [a passenger launch which capsized] is widely known, many died. 1.2) *v. intr.* pa- To become famous. 1.3) *v. tr.* To make something famous. *Pinaheya ma atay, sigā ya amantug, anuli-nuli ma pasal hinangna.* Considered important, them making it known, talking about what he had done.

**pagbantug-bantug** *v. intr.* aN- To brag about oneself. (*Thesaurus:* **pagabbu** 1.1, **pagheya-heya, pagmahatinggi, pagmalangkahi, pagpasanglit, pagtāp-tāp**)

**babantugun** *n.* A person who is famous or notorious.

**binabantug** *n.* Someone who has become famous or notorious.

**bantunan** var. of **bāt-bantunan**

**bantung** *v. tr.* 1) To strike a target with something thrown. *Bantungta maka kapa, pininsan ka.* I will hit you with a thrown axe, and you will be knocked out. *Bang aniya' a'a amatay tinanduk e' sapi' mandangan, ya sapi' inān subay binantung maka batu sampay amatay.* If someone dies from being gored by a bull, that bull should be stoned [by throwing] until it is dead. *Bang aku bantungnu maka papan ma bukutku, nialoman aku. Mbal na paluwas laha'.* When I am hit in the back with wood that you throw, I get bruised. No blood comes out. 1.1) *v. ditr.* To throw something in a particular direction. *Bay bantunganku bola kaut, pinalaran ma s'llog.* I throw the ball seawards, let it drift with the current. (*Thesaurus:* **badji, buwang₁** 1, **laruk, timan₁**)

**pagbantung** *v. intr.* aN- To throw something back and forth, as a game. *Magbantung bola bang ma iskul.* They throw balls to each other at school.

**bantut** *n.* 1) A transvestite. *Ya bantut inān, ya l'lla magd'nda-d'nda dīna, d'nda isāb magl'lla-l'lla dīna.* A *bantut* is a man who acts like a woman, or a woman who acts like a man. (*cf:* **pagl'lla-l'lla₂**) 1.1) *adj.* a- Effeminate, of a male. *Kalihi'an ka e' bapa'nu, angkan abantut.* You have got characteristics from your uncle, that's why you are effeminate.

**banug** var. of **banog**

**banusu** *n.* Cured tobacco in leaf form. (*Thesaurus:* **bungkal₃ 1, pasta, pikaroda, siga 1, sigupan, tabaku' 1**)

**banut** var. of **bunut**

**banwa** *n.* Historic title for a person of high rank. *Bang niōnan banwa mbal patanam, sultan ka, datu' ka.* Sultans or traditional chieftains are not accustomed to being called *banwa.*

**banyaga'** *n.* 1) A slave; a servant of low status. *Tahinang kita banyaga' he'na.* He made slaves of us. (*Thesaurus:* **ata, bata'an, sosoho'an**) 1.1) *v. tr.* To enslave someone. *Banyaga' kita bang pinagsoho', pa'ddas kita tabanyaga'.* We are slaves when we are often given orders, permanently enslaved.

  **pagbanyaga'** *v. intr. aN-* 1) To become slaves. *Mahē' kām amab'llihan dībi d'nda-l'lla ni saga bantabi supaya magbanyaga'.* There you will sell yourselves, both women and men, to your enemies to become slaves. 1.1) *v. tr.* To enslave someone. *Aniya' isab saga ka'anakan sigām d'nda bay pagbanyaga'.* Some of their daughters too were put into slavery. *Tabowa sigām paluwas min lahat pagbanyaga'an.* They were taken out of the land of slavery.

**bāng₁** *n.* The beginning of Muslim prayer.

  **pagbāng** *v. intr. aN-* 1) To prepare for prayer by cleansing the building and surrounding area of any evil. *Magbāng abō' halam aniya' saitan pasekot.* We carry out the *bāng* ceremony so that no demons come near. 2) To sing over a male child immediately following birth, in order to ensure that he grows in good health.

**bāng₂** *n.* Earrings held in the ear by a screw. (*Thesaurus:* **anting-anting 1, aretes, domelo, pinting, subang**)

**bang₁** (var. **mang**) *conj.* If; when. *Bang kami ma lahat kami, amangan kami panggi'.* When we are in our home place we eat cassava. *Nda'un ba, bang akulang pamikil.* See that, when intelligence is lacking. *Ā, bang nda'nu saga a'a magpangigal inān.* Ah, if you could see those people dancing. *Bang buwat si Anu inān, mbal aku ameya'-ameya'.* What's-his-name for example, I won't believe him. *Mang aku angindam barena bo' ka'a ilū mbal amaindam, yukku, "Ikutanta."* When I ask to borrow a drill but you won't lend it, I say, "I'll keep you in mind [regarding this]." *Magpalilu kita mang aniya' kono' ameya' ni lahat Sandakan. Yuknu, "Si Mma'." Yukku, "Ngga'i ka!"* We contradict each other when someone is reportedly going to Sandakan. You say, "Dad is." I say, "No he's not!" *Mang aniya' abangat sakina subay mbal makakakan ai-ai sukangna abō' mbal sinangti.* If someone's illness is serious he cannot eat anything that is forbidden to them lest they have a relapse. (*Thesaurus:* **abila, bangsi', basta, bo' na, gana, pagka, samantala', talkala'**)

**bang₂** *conj.* Conjunction introducing something said or known. *Tilawta ka bang ai bay pah'llingnu insini'.* I am asking you what it was you said earlier. *Kinata'uhan du bang sai ya bay amono'.* It is well known who did the killing. *Halam takaleta bang ai bay pinamūng pasal anak sigām.* We haven't heard what was said about their children.

**bang ba** *conj.* If perhaps; supposing. {idiom} *Bang ba aku pehē' binuwanan aku bahā'?* If I were to go there, would I be given some?

**bang bay** *conj.* If, of an unrealized hope or condition. {idiom} *Bang bay engkotannu pahogot, halam bay alatas.* If only you had tied it securely, it would not have come undone.

**bang hati'** *conj.* If indeed; if in fact. {idiom} *Bang hati' halam aniya' daing ma luma', subay ka ni tabu'.* If in fact there are no fish in the house, you had better go to the market. *Na bang hati' ahāp na, aku na angangguna iya paglituhanku na.* So if it turns out to be okay, then I will use it for my buying and selling business. *Na bang hati' ka kasulatan ma aku, buwanin aku paltanda'an.* If you are in fact pleased with me, give me a sign.

**bang ma** *conj.* In the opinion of. {idiom} *Bang ma aku, ya kakana' maglowang-lowang.* In my opinion it's the cloth with the holes. *Bang ma lapana kono'.* According to his physical senses, so it is said. *Bang ma si Mma' lumandu'an ahunit.* In Dad's opinion it is excessively expensive.

**bang makani-** *conj.* With regard to; in the case of. {idiom} *Bang makanilinggi', ajalang itu at'llag.* With regard to fishnets, this word *jalang* means widely spaced. *Bang makaniplaes, aramil he' gaha'.* In the case of pliers, stuck together with rust.

**bang pa'in** (var. **mam pa'in**) *conj.* Provided that; so long as; if only. {idiom} *Aho', makabola du ka bang pa'in akatis bay pahinangku ma ka'a.* Yes, you can play ball so long as what I had you do is completed. *Bang pa'in ataha' umulnu.* May your life be long. *Mampa'in ka binarakatan e' Tuhan. Mampa'in ka magkarayahan.* May you be favored by God. May you become wealthy.

**bang pasān** *adv. phrase* At times; occasionally. {idiom} *Buwat bay kitam ni Malaybalay ē', bang pasān aheka basket, bang pasān halam.* Like when we went to Malaybalay, at times there were lots of baskets, at other times none. *Asalut isāb si Yu bang pasān, angkan bilang mbal katulihan.* Yu is fretful at times, which is why [he] sometimes can't get off to sleep. *Ahāp isāb kahālan kami maitu, ya sadja bang pasān ala'at pagpangiramku.* Our situation here is good, except that the conception phase of my pregnancy is not good. (*Thesaurus:* **sasā', sumā'..sumā', suma'an..suma'an**)

**bang pina'amu** *conj.* Supposedly; to be frank. {idiom} *Bang pina'amu, halam sali'nu ma lahat itū!* Frankly, you have no equal in this place!

**bang sadja** *conj.* If only. {idiom} *Bang sadja aku ya bay maghuhukum.* If only I had been the judge.

**bang saupama** *conj.* If for example (not necessarily factual). {idiom} *Bang saupama, s'lle' puhu', magtiman ka maka ndanu.* If for example, perish the thought, you and your wife separate.

**bāng-bāng₁** *v. tr.* To endure or cope with something. *Mbal takole'-kole', mbal tapula'-pula', mbal tainay-inay, mbal tabāng-bāng buhatna atawa kosogna.* Couldn't do it, couldn't imagine it, couldn't do anything whatever. Couldn't manage its weight or its strength. *Mbal tabāng-bāng pasu' kahawana.* The heat of his coffee is unbearable. (*Thesaurus:* **aguwanta 1.1, anggap 1, anggop₂, bogbog₂, kole', gaga, tigayu'**)

**bāng-bāng₂** *n.* A cookie or cracker. *Kamemon na ai-ai tabowa kami na, saga bāng-bāng kinakan saga onde'-onde'.* We took all sorts of things, cookies for the children to eat. (*gen:* **mamun**)

**banga** *n.* The fishtail palm. *Caryota sp.*

**banga'₁** *v. intr. pa-* To open widely, of a mouth. *Pabanga' bowa'na ni ulan.* His mouth is opened to the rain. (*syn:* **bongat 1**; *Thesaurus:* **buka'₃, lungkad 1, sungkab, ukab 1.1**)

　**pabanga'** *v. tr.* To open one's mouth.

**banga'₂** *n.* A round clay pot with wide mouth. *Am'lli aku banga' pagmistangku buwasku.* I will buy a clay pot for making gruel of my rice. (*gen:* **pam'llahan**)

**bangasan** *n.* The banded barracuda. *Sphyraena jello.* (*cf:* **pangaluwan**; *gen:* **lambana' 1**)

**bangat** *adj. a-* Serious or grave, of an illness. *Asidda abangat saki ina'ku. Halam aniya' makatambalan iya.* My mother's sickness is severe. There is no one who can treat her. *Mang aniya' abangat sakina, subay mbal makakakan ai-ai sukangna.* When someone has a serious illness she should not eat any food that is to be avoided by her. (*Thesaurus:* **kansang 1.1, pangsan, sidda 2**)

**bāngaw** *n.* A rainbow. (*Thesaurus:* **andalaho', biradali 2, salindugu' 1**)

**bangka₁** *n.* Various cardinal-fishes, including the Ring-tailed cardinal and Band-tail cardinal. *Ostorhinchus aureus.*

**bangka₂** *n.* 1) The banker in gambling games. *Tinilaw bangka, "Angabunaw ka?"* The banker is asked, "Will you take the bet?" **1.1)** *v. intr. aN-* To act as banker. *Saupama ka'a ya amangka legot. Yukku, "Aniya' hād legot itū?"* For example, you are the banker in a dice game. I say, "Is there a limit [on the amount bet] in this dice game?"

**bangkak** *n.* Small bones; knuckle-bones. *Magpaletek iya bangkakna.* He cracks his knuckle-bones. (*Thesaurus:* **bokog, kowa' 1, to'olang**)

**bangka'** *n.* A basic dugout canoe; dugout base of a planked canoe. *Wa'i talaran bangka'ku, halam bay niengkotan.* My canoe has drifted away, it wasn't tied. (*Thesaurus:* **balutu, dapang,** londay, pallungan, pambot, paraw 1, peddas, pelang, pongag)

**pagbangka'-bangka'** *v. intr. aN-* To travel here and there, especially by dugout canoe. *Magbangka'-bangka' aku ni Tōng Batu amandi.* I will paddle down to Rock End and bathe.

**bangkas** *n.* Horseshoe crab. *fam. Limulidae.* (*gen:* **kagang**)

**bangkat₁** *v. tr. -an* To place one thing on top of another; stack. *Binangkatan itū, mpat duminu pamangkatku.* Things being stacked, [like] four dominoes for me to stack. (*Thesaurus:* **bingkis 1, pangkat₁**)

**pagbangkat-bangkat** *v. intr. aN-* 1) To form a stack with a series of items. **1.1)** *v. tr.* To arrange things in a stack. *Da'a g'mmosun daing-daing ilū. Da'a pinagbangkat-bangkat. Llawin ko' na pa'in atoho'.* Don't soak those little fish. Don't have them piled up in layers. Set them in the sun so they keep drying. *Pagdiritun bang ka amat'nna' ai-ai. Da'a pagbangkatun bo' mbal abila'.* Set things in rows when you are laying them out. Don't stack them lest they break. *Aheka batu pinagbangkat-bangkat nihinang halaman luma'.* Lots of coral rocks piled up to make a yard for the house. (*Thesaurus:* **pagsusun₁**)

**bangkat₂** *v. intr. pa-* To get up from sitting or lying down. *Pabangkat ka min paningkō'an bang ka binale' na magsulat.* Get up from the chair if you are tired from writing. (*Thesaurus:* **buhat₂, buladjang, punduk 1**)

**bangkat sa'am** *n. phrase* The upper planks of a canoe into which outrigger boom supports are fitted. (*gen:* **tapi' 1**)

**bangkaw** (*var.* **bakkaw**) *n.* Saltwater forest complex, of which mangrove shrubs are a member. *Hal kami ma bihing bangkaw alayo.* We just anchored by the edge of the mangroves.

**bangkaw-d'nda** *n.* Low-growing tree typical of mangrove swamps (lit. female mangrove). *Bruguiera spp.*

**bangkaw-l'lla** *n.* Low-growing tree typical of mangrove swamps (lit. male mangrove). *Rhizophera ceriops et al.*

**kabangkawan** *n.* Mangrove complex. *Bang halam larang-larang, pehē' saitan ni deyom kabangkawan.* If there is no shelter [made for it] the demon goes into the mangrove forest.

**pagbangkaw** *v. intr. aN-* To use the resources of the mangrove forest.

**bangkay** *n.* The dead body of a human being; corpse or cadaver. *Ap'nno' lowang inān he' bangkay.* That hole was full of corpses. (*Thesaurus:* **mayat, patay₁ 1**)

**bangkayawan** *n.* The spine of a thatch shingle, to which leaves are attached.

**bangkero** *n.* 1) A person who makes a living by ferrying people short distances. *Ameya' aku ma bangkero tudju ni jambatan si Pawpaw.* I go with the ferry person towards Pawpaw's wharf. **1.1)** *v. tr.* To ferry people in a small boat. *Wa'i na as'bbang buli' pelang ē', halam na aniya' pamangkerohan.* The rear of the canoe is damaged, there is nothing now for ferrying people.

**bangkil₁** *v. tr.* To remind someone of a favor shown to him in the past, causing him embarrassment. *Bang aniya' tapamuwannu aku, ati bo' kita makapagbono', bangkilnu na. Tabangkil na he'nu ya bay ma aku, pamakaiya' sali'.* If you gave me something and then we have a fight, you recall that favor. You recount what you did for me, to sort of shame me. *Buwat kita magsagga' bo' sali' mbal magampun-ampunan, na bang sali' aniya' pamakaiya'nu, tabangkilnu aku.* Like us being in conflict but not forgiving each other, then if you have something to shame me with, you remind me of it. (*syn:* **tumbi', tungbuy**)

**pagbangkil** *v. intr. aN-* **1)** To keep uttering the name of a deceased person. **1.1)** *v. tr. -an* To keep uttering the name of someone who has died. *Da'a na pa'in pagbangkilinbi si Mbo'.* Don't keep saying Grandfather's name.

**bangkil₂** *n.* A fang or canine tooth. (*Thesaurus:* **baga'ang, empon 1, sengel, taling**)

**bangkinna...bangkinna** (var. **mangkinna...mangkinna**) *adv. phrase* The more one thing; the more another. *Bangkinna kam sinoho' ni tabu', bangkinna kam mbal bilahi.* The more you are told to go to the market, the more you don't want to. *Ai ba, mangkinna sin'nsong, mangkinna paheya geret pelang ina'an.* So then, the more it was plugged, the more that tear in the canoe grew larger. (*Thesaurus:* **anambahina, kalap, labi-labi, luba', luhūy, paligay, ya lagi'na**)

**bangking** *n.* Various small beetles such as stink bugs and bed bugs.

**bangkit** *n.* Calceous lime in powder form, an ingredient of betel nut chew. *Sali' tapung ya bangkit itū. Bangkit is like rice flour. Paila'un bangkit, lamurin dulaw. Dulaw nili'is, pin'gga', ati bohe'na pamaila', manjari akeyat bangkit.* Add an ingredient to the [calceous] lime, mix in turmeric. The turmeric is grated, squeezed, and its liquid added so that the lime is red. (*gen:* **pagmama' 1**)

**bangko** *n.* A bank, as a financial institution. *Bang kita sali' sinukuran niōnan gusi' ilu, bang kita makaisi dakayu' pilak ma hatusan, buwat ma bangko inān. Sali' anganak inān.* Suppose we have the fortune of getting this [magical] chest, and we invest at one peso per hundred, as in a bank. It earns interest. *Bangko, ya patau'an sīn kamastalan, kalannangan inān.* A bank, the place where those schoolteachers and Chinese keep their money.

**bangkug** (var. **bakkug**) *adj. a-* **1)** Jolted, of a wound or some internal complaint. *Buwat kita lum'ngngan bo' pa'in kinalibubut, na abangkug kita.* If we go walking even though we have boils, then the movement will jolt us painfully. *Bang aniya' kalibubut ma pa'ata subay kita da'a magl'ngngan bo' mbal abakkug. Atawa bang aniya' ap'ddi' mareyom k'llongta bo' kita magkohol, abakkug, ap'ddi'.* When we have a boil on the thigh we shouldn't walk lest we get bumped. Or when we have pain in the throat and cough we are jolted and feel sore. *Buwat kita d'nda bang bay na maganak, amasi batu-batu mareyom itu. Sinoho' kita da'a magl'ngngan he ra'a abakkug.* Like with us women after giving birth, a clot still inside us here. We are instructed not to go walking lest the movement jolts painfully. (*Thesaurus:* **bakkug, bōg, sikmu', siggul, singku 1**) **1.1)** *v. tr.* To jolt something to cause pain. *Bang kalibubut, da'a bangkugun lamisahan.* If there is a boil, don't jolt the table.

**bangku'** *n.* The bench on which a person lies who is to be a spirit medium. *Bangku' itū paghinang ni duwata, palegehan ka, patingkō'an ka a'a sinangon.* This bench is for the *duwata* ceremony, a place for the medium to lie or sit when possessed. (*Thesaurus:* **kulsi, paningkō'an, siya**)

**bangkung** *n.* A heavy working knife. (*Thesaurus:* **bari', gayang, lahut, laring lahut, pira, sundang**)

**bangkungan** var. of **bāt-bangkungan**

**bangkuru** *n.* Morinda, a small tree and its edible fruit, used extensively for medicinal purposes. *Morinda citrifolia.*

**bangday** var. of **tangday**

**bangga'** **1)** *v. tr.* To hit something head on. **2)** *v. tr. -an* To intervene vigorously to prevent accidental violation of a taboo. *Bang aniya' mbo' pat'nna' ma kōkan, bo' lahi-lahi onde' ma t'ngnga', binangga'an. Taluwa' saki, pasu' sala.* If an ancestor is in place on the up-current side of the house, and a child is running about in the middle, he will be forcibly prevented. He'll get a sickness, or a fever or something. *Kabangga'an he' mbo', bang mbal niampun, amatay.* Someone abruptly stopped by a ritual ancestor will die if not forgiven.

**pagbangga'** *v. intr. aN-* To bang things together. (*Thesaurus:* **pagbanggul 1, pagdugtul**)

**bangga'-bangga'** *n.* Various boxfishes including the Longhorn cowfish. *Ostracion cornotus; Lactoria cornuta.*

**banggala** *n.* Heavy gauge paper used for wrapping. *Katas banggala, bang ma kami ya katas makapal, akapal man katas jimpaw. Banggala* paper, what we call the thick paper, thicker than kite paper. (*Thesaurus:* **katas, papel**)

**Banggali** *n.* An Indian; a Hindu.

**banggid** (var. **ganggid**; **langgid**) *adj. a-* **1)** Abraded; grazed. A: *"Bay abanggid he' ai?"* B: *"Hē' ma deya, daka ai."* A: "What was it scratched by?" B: "By

something inland, who knows what."
(*Thesaurus:* **geges, langgad 1, pares₁, sahumut-sahumut**) **1.1)** *v. tr.* **-an** To abrade the surface of something.

**banggud** *n.* **1)** Various wrasses including the Olive club-nosed wrasse, Bird wrasse. *Gomphosus varius.* **2)** Black-eyed thick-lip wrasse. *Hemigymnus melapterus.*

**banggul** *v. intr. pa-* To hit something with force; to bang into. *Bay kami makabanggul ni daka ai.* We banged into goodness knows what. (*syn:* **binggil**)

**pagbanggul** *v. intr. aN-* **1)** To bang together, of solid items. *Pinagbanggul kōk onde'-onde' bo' samap'ddi'.* The children's heads were bumped together so as to be equally painful. (*Thesaurus:* **pagbangga', pagdugtul**) **1.1)** *v. tr.* To bang things together.

**banghad** *n.* **1)** The bride-gift terms set down by the elders of a girl being sought in marriage. *"Pila,"* yukna, *"banghad si Li bang kinawin?" Ya sambungna, "Dakayu' luma' ahāp maka dangibu pilak."* "How much will the bride-gift be," he said, "when Li marries?" The answer, "One fine house and one thousand pesos." *Saupama atilaw d'nda si'itku-matto'aku, nihalga'an buwattitu-buwattina'an. Ya hē' bang ma kami banghad. Mbal gi' kaōnan ungsud.* For example my uncles and parents inquire about a girl, some amount like this or that is stated. That is what we call *banghad.* It is not yet called *ungsud.* (*Thesaurus:* **basingan, mahal₂, pagtinabawan, punggit 1, ungsud₁ 1**) **1.1)** *v. ditr.* To inform the suitor's elders of the bride-gift set for a marriageable girl. *Binangharan kita dangibu pilak.* We were quoted one thousand pesos as the bride-gift.

**bang'llus** *n.* Milkfish; bangus. *Chanos chanos.* (*cf:* **owa'₂**)

**banglut** *n.* A species of flowering shrub.

**bangsa₁** *n.* A distinct category or class of living things; race or nation. *Bangsa Sama kami.* We are of the Sama nation [or tribe]. (*Thesaurus:* **pihak, ummat 1**)

**bangsa magl'l'ngngan** *n. phrase* Category of spirit beings that walk about. {idiom} (*Thesaurus:* **duwata 1, hama'-hama' a'a, hibilis, jin 1, saitan, ya mbal ta'nda'**)

**bangsa-paleyang** *n.* Category of spirit beings that fly. {idiom}

**bangsa-pote'** *n.* White people; Caucasians. (*cf:* **Milikan**)

**kabangsa-bangsahan** *n.* Nations; ethnic groups. *Min waktu bay katagna' kabangsa-bangsahan sampay ni kabuwattina'an, yampa aniya' kabinsana'an buwattē'.* From the time when all nations began up until now, suffering like that has only just occurred.

**binangsa** *n.* Created as a distinct race or species.

**palbangsahan** *n.* Collective term for multiple ethnic groups.

**bangsa₂** *adj. a-/-an* High rank or good family background. *Abangsa ōnna. A'a bangsahan isāb presidente ma ōnna.* He has an honorable name. A president is of high rank due to his name. *Bang saupama anak datu' magh'nda a'a areyo', binowa pehē' ni astana' pinabangsa na iya, niusungan bulawan, pinas'mmekan.* For example, if the son of chieftain marries a commoner, she is taken to the palace and treated as someone well-born, carried in a golden chair and [finely] dressed.

**balbangsa** *n.* A person of noble birth or rank.

**bangsi'** *conj.* If only. *Buwat mma'ku amatay, yukku, "Bangsi' aku bay makamahē', makatingkō'."* Like when my father died, I said, "If only I could have being there, sitting with him." *Bangsi' aniya' ulan llaw ilu.* If only there was rain today. *Buwat sali' aniya' kampungku mahē', ma dampōng e' magtimbak. Sōng pa'in pehē' pulis inān, yukku, "Bangsi' aku makapehē' abō' lāngku, ati mbal na sigā tasaggaw."* Like some of my relatives being there on the other side, shooting each other. When the police were about to get there, I said, "If I could just have got there in order to stop them, then they would not have been arrested." (*Thesaurus:* **abila, bang₁, basta, bo' na, gana, pagka, samantala', talkala'**)

**bangun₁** *v. intr. pa-* **1)** To get up from a prone position. *Pabangun ka bang ka bay atuli.* Get up if you have been asleep. **1.1)** *v. tr.* To raise someone or something from a prone position. *Luma' baha'u bay binangun.* A house that had just been erected.

**bangun₂** *v. tr.* **-an 1)** To restore a damaged relationship by compensating the aggrieved party. (*Thesaurus:* **ayu', diyat, masangka**) **2)** To restore buildings damaged by time, war or natural force. *Pinagmulka'an e' Tuhan sai-na amabangun da'ira itū.* God will lay a curse on whoever has this city rebuilt. *Mpatpū' maka nnom tahun bay kapangahinang langgal itū. Tabangunnu pabīng bahā'?* This prayer house took forty years to build. Can you rebuild it? (*Thesaurus:* **balmula**)

**bangun₃** *v. tr.* **-an** To hand down to succeeding generations features such as name, traditions, skills, and physical features. *Tu'ud aku amangunan mma'ku, angkan aku magmatuyu' ma bay ntanna.* I am simply perpetuating my father's memory, which is why I am committed to carrying on his livelihood. *Aniya' sadja amangun bang a'a dayahan.* There is always someone to maintain the family name if people are wealthy. *Pamangun ōn, sali' buwat aku inān imam bo' aku amatay na. Na, bay ōnku pinasalin ni anakku.* Perpetuating a name, it's like me being an imam and I die. Then the name that was mine is transferred to my son.

**bangungngut** *v. advrs.* **-in-** Affected by a kind of

paralysis when waking during the night, a condition attributed to demonic activity. (*syn:* **bolelong**)

**bapa'** *n.* **1)** Parent's male sibling or cousin; any related male in parent's generation. *Ō Bapa', ameya' aku ni M'ddas am'lli aku ai-ai.* Oh Uncle, I am going to Siasi to buy various things. (*cf:* **babu'** 1, **si'it**) **1.1)** *voc. n.* Address term for male in parent's generation.

    **pagbapa'** *v. intr. aN-* **1)** To be related to someone as uncle; to refer to someone as uncle. **1.1)** *v. tr. -an* To treat someone as uncle. *Ka'a ya subay pagbapa'anku.* You are the one I should be treating as *bapa'*.

**baptaes** *v. tr.* To baptize someone by immersion or sprinkling.

**bar-** (var. **bal-**) *aff.* Derivational prefix that creates a noun referring to a person whose nature is characterized by the prefixed stem.

**bara** *n.* A crowbar. *Bara itu pangalugitku lantay.* This crowbar is what I use to pry up the flooring. (*Thesaurus:* **lalandak, pala, piku, sangkul** 1, **susuwat**)

**barakat** (var. **balakat**) *n.* **1)** Gifts and abilities from a divine source. (*Thesaurus:* **anughala'** 1, **apuwa, hirayat, lidjiki'** 1, **pahala'**) **1.1)** *adj. a-* Favored by God. *Bang ka'a sab'nnal-b'nnal man bihing batu itū, bang ka abarakat du, mampa'in patubud api itu.* If you are truly from the edge of this rock, if you do have power [from God] then may this fire flare up. **1.2)** *v. tr. -an* To confer divine favor on someone. *Sai-sai angandol ma Tuhan binarakatan he'na. Bang a'a mbal angandol, b'nnal iya tinabang, ngga'i ka na pa'in buwat a'a angandol ma iya.* Whoever trusts in God is favored by him. A person who doesn't trust will indeed be helped, but not like the person who trusts.

**barakkal** (var. **balakkal**) (derivative of **akkal**) *n.* **1)** A person of great intelligence and wisdom. *Ya pangita'u saga a'a balakkal.* The knowledge of the wise ones. *Bay pa'nda'annu balakkalnu ma a'a abengkok pikilanna.* You have shown your wisdom to people whose thinking is crooked. *Aheya labi pangita'u si Sulayman min saga a'a balakkal ma lahat Misil.* Solomon's wisdom was greater than that of the wise men of Egypt. (*cf:* **alim₁**). **2)** Extraordinary wisdom. *Bay pa'nda'annu balakkalnu ma a'a abengkok pikilanna.* You have shown your wisdom to people whose thinking is crooked.

**baran₁** *n.* **1)** The body of an animate creature; body or main part of a structure. *Tambal pamakosog baran.* Medicine to make the body strong. **2)** Physical condition or appearance of someone or something. *Ahāp baranna.* She is beautiful [lit. her body is good].

    **pamaranan** *n.* One's physical condition or appearance.

**baran₂** *n.* **1)** Oneself; one's person. *Aku baranku bay maka'nda'.* I myself saw [it]. *Maitu iya di'ilaw, baranna du.* He was here yesterday, himself. *Magpahāp ka barannu.* Improve yourself. (*Thesaurus:* **a'a, manusiya'** 1, **puhu'** 1) **1.1)** *v. tr.* To meet someone in person. *Mbal kita bilahi pinagtambuku-tambukuhan, subay binaran. Ya hē' niōnan subay kita minahaldika'.* We don't like being sent repeated messages, we should be contacted in person. That's what is called showing us honor. (*Thesaurus:* **pagtampal, solab₂**) **2)** Name for a girl being courted, used in song lyrics. *Si Baran tibung-tibung.* She with the plump figure.

    **pagbabaran** *n.* **1)** Personal qualities of dignity and integrity. *A'a inān ahāp isāb pagbabaranna. Mbal angakkal, pinagkalomanan e' manusiya'.* The dignity and integrity of that man are great. He doesn't cheat and is respected by people everywhere. **1.1)** *v. intr. aN-* To conduct oneself with dignity or a sense of importance. *Magbabaran-baran sali' anūd. Subay kam magbaran anūd apa bay indamanbi.* Behaving properly as when returning something [to source]. You should return it yourself because you borrowed it.

    **pagbabaran-baran** *v. intr. aN-* To attend personally to one's affairs. *Asal iya magbabaran-baran min bay kabata'na sampay ni kato'ana na.* He in fact has dealt personally with issues from his youth right up to his present old age. *Magbabaran-baran sali' anūd.* He returned it in person.

    **pagbaran** *v. intr. aN-* To do something in person, rather than send a representative. *Subay kita magbaran pehē'.* We should go there in person. *Ka'a to'ongan ya magbaran magnakura'an sigām ni pagbono'an.* You yourself personally are the one to be their leader on the battleground.

    **tagbaran** *n.* A person with the responsibility of care, as for an older relative or young woman.

**barang** *n.* Valuables other than money, of bride-wealth or other transactions. *Halam aniya' barang palamud.* No valuables other than money included. *Barang itū boras, tepo. Ya hē pinagbahasa barang, ya palamud ma sīn.* The *barang* referred to is a rattan or pandanus mat. Those items are referred to as *barang*, things put together with the money.

**baranggay** *n.* Village-level administrative unit of Philippine society.

**barapa** *see:* **babarapa, inda wa barapa ginis**

**baras-baras** *n.* Building materials consisting of unsawn tree branches less in diameter than a man's wrist. *Subay lansang ataha' pangalansangku baras-baras.* It has to be long nails for me to nail rough unsawn wood with. (*Thesaurus:* **hanglad** 1, **listun, papan₁, pasagi'** 1)

**barat-daya** var. of **balat-daya**

**barena** *n.* **1)** A carpenter's drill or brace. (*cf:* **sangkap** 1) **1.1)** *v. tr. -an* To drill a hole. *A: "Ai* *hinangnu ilu?" B: "Amarenahan aku kayu. Wa'i asegpong dambila', bay binarehanan aheya."* What are you doing there? I am drilling a hole in some lumber. The other part has broken out, it was drilled [too] large.

**barese-barese** *see:* **pagbarese-barese**

**bari'** *n.* A working knife used for cutting heavy items. *Bang ariki'-diki', laring-laring. Bang aheya, bari'.* When it is small it is a knife. When it is large it is a working knife. (*Thesaurus:* **bangkung, gayang, lahut, laring lahut, pira, sundang**)

  **bari'-pira** *n.* A large working knife.

**bari'-bari'** *n.* Various sweeperfish. *fam.* Pempheridae.

**barilis** *n.* A cylindrical metal container; a barrel. *Barilis ginulung-gulung hē' ma M'ddas he' kalgadol.* Barrels, rolled along by laborers over there in Siasi Town.

**baris** (var. **balis₂**) *n.* A mark above or below a letter to aid pronunciation. *Aniya' barisna man deyo' man diyata'.* It has vowel marks above and below. (*cf:* **batang-sulat, sulat 1.1**)

**baro** *n.* A cylindrical lidded container of metal or plastic.

**barung** *n.* A heavy-bladed fighting weapon. (*Thesaurus:* **kalis, punyal 1**)

**baruwang** *n.* A bear. *fam.* Ursidae.

**basak** *n.* Something worn out or broken down. *Hal basak karut ya niruwa'.* Only worn out sacks were loaded. *Basak luma' inān.* The ruins of that house. (*Thesaurus:* **jagjag 1, langkat 1, larak 1.1, lorak**)

**basag** *adj. a-* **1)** Strong, of a person or animal. *Abasag si Ji amowa bohe' duwa mital.* Ji is strong, carrying two [4-gallon] cans of water. (*Thesaurus:* **ayron, bastig, kosog 1.1, kulasog 1.1, kuwat-anggauta', landos 1, paslod 1.1**) **1.1)** *v. intr. pa-* To do with vigor. *Pabasag ka.* Be strong. (*Thesaurus:* **kuyaskas**)

  **pagbinasag** *v. intr. aN-* To put continuous effort into what one is doing. *Bang kām ganta' pasekot ni abal, subay kām magbinasag.* Suppose you get close to an area of strong current, you should work hard at paddling.

**basagan** var. of **sowa-basagan**

**basal₁** *n.* A rust-resistant metal. *At'ggol-t'ggol ginaha' basal itū, al'kkas al'ngngat.* This *basal* takes quite a long time to rust, it gets straightened out quickly.

**basal₂** *n.* A large shop; department store.

**basalsalan** (derivative of **salsal**) *adj. zero* Overloaded; overstressed. *Basalsalan pantān ilu.* That porch is overloaded. *Ya angkan nilutang pantān, bo' naylon ē' mbal basalsalan.* The reason the porch is made doubly strong, so the nylon [lashings] are not over-stretched. *Basalsalan makalandu' bang aheka tabowa.* Seriously overloaded when a great many [people] are

carried. *Basalsalan, minsan hāg, minsan a'a bang mbal magtōp hinang maka kosog.* Overloaded, whether of posts or people, whenever load and strength don't match.

**basbas** *v. tr. -an* To whittle or trim something to size or shape. *Basbasanku kōk katig itū ko' alampung.* I will trim this outrigger horn so it will be light. *Kayu bay binasbasan, bay kinulangan, ati yuk dangan, "Amasi atibaggol kayu inān."* Wood whittled and reduced in size and then someone else says, "That wood is still unevenly shaped." (*Thesaurus:* **katam 1.1, kirus 1.1, saplung 1.1, sapsap₂, sosok**)

**baska** **1)** *adj. a-* Soft but not squashy, of starch foods. *Ahāp tahakna, halam amata', halam apetak, abaska. Alunuk-lunuk to'ongan, sali' apīt.* It is well cooked, neither underdone nor squashy, just *baska.* Fully soft, almost sticky. (*Thesaurus:* **lunuk 1, lunyag, posak**) **2)** *v. tr.* To cook rice so that it is soft but still firm. (*gen:* **b'lla 1**)

**basket** *n.* A western-style basket with permanent rigid handle, woven of natural materials. (*gen:* **baka'₁**)

**basketbōl** *n.* The game of basketball. *Ma basketbōl, kalogdangan, halam minsan makasagid ni ring.* In basketball, right on target, not even brushing the hoop.

**base'₁** *adj. a-* Wet. *Abase' badju'ku he' ulan.* My shirt is wet from the rain. *Abase' baranna e' alu'.* His body was wet with dew. (*ant:* **toho'**; *Thesaurus:* **bugbug₁, bugga' 1, gamos 1, himāy, tomog**)

  **pagbase'** *v. intr. aN-* To live in a wet environment. *Sūk ya magtoho', kami magbase'.* Tausugs are the ones who inhabit the dry land, we inhabit the wet.

  **pagbase'an** *v. intr. aN-* To do something which involves getting wet, as wading. *Pal'ngngan kita ma tahik, magbase'anan kita.* We walk in the sea, we get thoroughly wet.

**base'₂** *adj. a-* Fresh in contrast to salted or dried, of fish.

**base'-bulan** *n.* The moon phase immediately after new moon. (*cf:* **kōpan, damlag 1.1**)

**base'-kayu** *n.* The sap of newly cut wood.

**basi'₁** *n.* **1)** Various ferrous metals such as iron or steel. *Mbal pagūng basi', pat'nde.* Iron doesn't float, it sinks. **1.1)** *adj. zero* Made of iron or steel. *Kappal basi' inān palayo ma llot M'ddas maka Siganggang.* That steel-hulled ship is anchored between Siasi and Siganggang.

  **basi'-basi'** *n.* Wire. *Taga galna' pinggan ilu, kagalna'an he' kuskus basi'-basi'.* That drinking glass has a crack in it, it has been blemished by a metal pot scourer. (*Thesaurus:* **korente 1.1, kowat, estenles-kitara**)

**basi'₂** *n.* **1)** The element of virility in human males; physical prowess. *Halam pahurus basi'na.* His virility has not slipped away from him. (*cf:* **hawas-basi'**) **1.1)** *adj. -an* Virile and immune to physical harm. *A'a basi'an, sali' kobolan.* A man of physical prowess, like he's magically invulnerable. (*Thesaurus:* **kobol 1.1, pagkal'lla, pangliyas, sihil 1**)

**basi'-dongan** *n.* The element in a human body responsible for rigor mortis. *Basi'-dongan itū, sat'ggol kita a'llum kosogta sali' ko'. Bang amatay atuwas na.* This *basi'-dongan*, as long as we are alive, it is our strength, so to speak. When we die it becomes stiff. (*cf:* **anggauta'**)

**basingan** *n.* The component of the bride-gift which goes to the girl's parents, usually a gold pin. *Yangkon takapin ma matto'a d'nda mahal maka basingan. Pinunggitan he' sigā min kar'ndahan limampū' pilak, ya hē' nihinang mahal maka basingan.* All that is left for the girl's parents are the *mahal* and *basingan.* They of the women's side require fifty pesos, that's the share of the bride's parents. (*Thesaurus:* **banghad 1, mahal$_2$, pagtinabawan, punggit 1, ungsud$_1$ 1**)

**basnig** *n.* A large motor-powered outrigger vessel, used for seine fishing. (*syn:* **palakaya**)

**bassa** *v. tr.* To read something. *Mbal aku makabassa, agabul e'ku ang'nda'.* I can't read, my eyesight is blurred.

**basta** *conj.* If; if at any time; whenever; provided that. *Basta kami angusaha mbal kami ameyad ma deya, subay ma pelang ma dilaut.* Whenever we are fishing for a living we do not dry the fish ashore, it needs to be done on the canoe out at sea. *Nsa' pagda'awa basta bangsa Jipun.* There was no arguing with Japanese. *Llaw, sangom, makajari kita angalamat, basta duma'in ugtu-llaw atawa tonga'-bahangi.* Day or night, it's okay for us to use divination, so long as it's not [right on] noon or midnight. *Luwal bang kami mbal am'ssi halam aniya'. Basta kami am'ssi aniya'.* It's only when we do not fish that there are no fish. So long as we fish there will be fish. (*Thesaurus:* **abila, bang$_1$, bangsi', bo' na, gana, pagka, samantala', talkala'**)

**bastig** *adj.* -an Physically strong; athletic. *Bastigan pahāp a'a ilu amusay.* That man is very strong in his paddling. (*Thesaurus:* **ayron, basag 1, kosog 1.1, kulasog 1.1, kuwat-anggauta', landos 1, paslod 1.1**)

**bastiru** *n.* An embroidery frame.

**bastun** *n.* A walking stick; a club as a weapon of defense. (*cf:* **kakakal, tungkud 1**)

**basu** *n.* A handle-less cup. (*Thesaurus:* **panginuman, sawan, tasa**)

**basung** *n.* A conical spool for twine or thread.

**bāt** *n.* A trepang or sea cucumber; also known as bêche-de-mere. *gen. Holothuria.* (*cf:* **daga' 2**)

**bāt-balutbatu** (var. **balutbatu**) *n.* A species of trepang, edible.

**bāt-bantunan** (var. **bantunan**) *n.* A species of trepang, edible.

**bāt-bangkungan** (var. **bangkungan**) *n.* A species of trepang, edible.

**bāt-bodbod** (var. **bodbod$_2$**) *n.* A species of trepang, edible.

**bāt-bohe'an** (var. **bohe'an**) *n.* A species of trepang, edible.

**bāt-kandong-kandong** (var. **kandong-kandong**) *n.* A species of trepang, edible.

**bāt-kangan** (var. **kangan**) *n.* A species of trepang, edible. (*syn:* **bāt-legetan, bāt-taumpa'**)

**bāt-kitut** (var. **kitut**) *n.* A species of trepang about 8cm long and as thick as a finger, edible.

**bāt-kumbatang** (var. **kumbatang**) *n.* A species of trepang, edible.

**bāt-kuting** (var. **kuting$_2$**) *n.* A species of trepang, edible.

**bāt-dugu-dugu** (var. **dugu-dugu**) *n.* A species of trepang, edible.

**bāt-duru'an** (var. **duru'an**) *n.* A species of trepang, edible.

**bāt-ettom** *n.* A species of trepang, dark-skinned.

**bāt-gamat** (var. **gamat$_1$**) *n.* A species of trepang, edible. *Bāt-gamat itu t'bbahan. Bay aku an'bba ni Bakal bāt-gamat, agtūy angahimāt.* The *bāt-gamat* referred to is strand food. I gathered some at Bakal, and it promptly went limp. *Bāt-gamat sidda angaluntang.* The gamut trepang gets very slimy.

**bāt-labuyu'** (var. **labuyu'$_2$**) *n.* A species of trepang, edible.

**bāt-legetan** (var. **legetan**) *n.* A species of trepang, edible. (*syn:* **bāt-kangan, bāt-taumpa'**)

**bāt-llaw** *n.* A species of trepang, edible.

**bāt-lubu** *n.* A species of trepang which exudes edible, sticky, thread-like strands. *Bāt-lubu itū taga tagok.* This trepang exudes sticky strands.

**bāt-nggo'-nggo'** (var. **nggo'-nggo'**) *n.* A species of trepang, edible. (*syn:* **bāt-sa'i**)

**bāt-pasan** *n.* A species of trepang, edible.

**bāt-pote'** *n.* A species of trepang, edible.

**bāt-saddo'** (var. **saddo'**) *n.* A species of trepang, edible.

**bāt-sa'i** *n.* A species of trepang, edible. (*syn:* **bāt-nggo'-nggo'**)

**bāt-sandulay** (var. **sandulay**) *n.* A species of trepang, edible.

**bāt-sandulay-l'ggon** *n.* A species of trepang, a sub-variety of sandulay.

**bāt-serol** (var. **serol**) *n.* A species of trepang, edible. (*syn:* **bāt-timpū**)

**bāt-taddik** (var. **taddik**) *n.* A species of trepang, edible.

**bāt-tagokan** (var. **tagokan**) *n.* Various edible trepang noted for their sticky entrails.

**bāt-talipan** (var. **talipan**) *n.* A species of trepang, edible.

**bāt-taumpa'** *n.* A species of trepang, edible. (*syn:* **bāt-kangan, bāt-legetan**)

**bāt-timpū** (var. **timpū**) *n.* A species of trepang, edible. (*syn:* **bāt-serol**)

**bat sabab** *conj.* Because; reason why. *Binowa na payung e' sigām pi'itu, duma'in na aku amowa, bat* *sabab l'ngnganku he' ang'nde'.* They brought the umbrella here, not me, which is why I walked here returning it. (*Thesaurus:* **bo' supaya, bo'₂, dok supaya, he da'a, supaya**)

**bata** *v. tr.* To scour metal to inhibit rust or discoloration. *Binata maka ns'llan ko' da'a ginaha'. Ginidgid.* Scoured with oil so it won't rust. Rubbed smooth. (*cf:* **kaskas₁**; *Thesaurus:* **lampasu, lanu' 1.2, ponglas**)

**batak₁** *v. tr.* To voice an opinion; to offer advice.

**batak₂** *v. tr.* To cover something with loose planks.

**bata'** *adj. a-* Young but mature, of a human. *Abata' lagi' iya, ma llot matto'a maka onde'-onde'.* He is still young, between middle age and childhood. (*Thesaurus:* **hoben, lumbu'-baha'u, onde'-baha'u**)

**bata'-bata'** *var. of* **saging-bata'-bata'**

**bata'an** *n.* A junior employee; an errand-boy. *Bang kita magbihing aningkō', bo' aku sinoho' he' si Mām, minsan du aniya' bata'anna, aku ya kaiddahan dahū, aku ya nilinganan.* When we are sitting side by side, and I am sent by Mum, even though she has an errand boy, I am specifically ordered first, I am the one she calls. (*Thesaurus:* **ata, banyaga' 1, sosoho'an**)

**batal** *adj. a-* Nullified, of the pure state required for formal worship. *Bang bay anambahayang si Mo ma langgal bo' pasagid ero', abatal na iya. Mbal na makasambahayang.* When Mo goes to pray at the mosque and a dog brushes against him, his [ritually pure status] is nullified. He cannot now pray. *Bang aniya' magsambahayang bo' aheka onde'-onde' asagaw, abatal.* If someone is praying and a lot of children are making a noise, [he] is made unfit to pray.

**pabatal** *v. tr.* To nullify the cultural rules prohibiting physical contact between a man and a woman. (*Thesaurus:* **kasal 1, kawin 1.1, paglahi 1.1, pasugsug**)

**batang₁** *n.* The central upright part of a plant; trunk of a tree in contrast to its branches. *Aniya' isāb sayul taga batang.* There are vegetables, too, that have stalks. (*cf:* **taroso**; *wh:* **kayu 1**)

**batang₂ 1)** *n.* Something long, more or less rigid, as the main component of a structure. **2)** *clf.* Count word for stick-shaped pieces. *Alutu' kami duwambatang t'bbu.* We had as provisions two sticks of sugar cane. *Ndiya, b'lliku siga, saga limambatang.* Give it here, I'll buy some cigarets, five pieces.

**batang-baran** *n.* The trunk of a human body; body of an animate creature as distinct from its limbs or tentacles.

**batang-buhungan** *n.* The ridgepole of a house.

**batang-k'llong** *n.* The larynx or voice box. (*syn:* **bunga-jakkum**)

**batang-ehe** (var. **ehe**) *n.* The shaft of a motor; the axle of a wheel assembly. (*cf:* **kapay**)

**batang-pana'** *n.* The curved bow of a speargun; the crosspiece of a kite. *Batang-pana' i' ma*

*mandal.* The bow there on a *mandal*-type kite.

**batang-sulat** *n.* A letter of the alphabet. (*cf:* **baris, sulat 1.1**)

**batang-tubu** *n.* The skeleton; skeletal framework of a body. (*Thesaurus:* **akal-baran, pagdayaw 1, paltubu-tubuhan 2, tangkorak**)

**batang-ūng** *n.* The bridge of the nose in humans.

**batangan** *n.* An outrigger boom. (*Thesaurus:* **katig 1, sa'am 1, tarik**)

**ma batangan** *adv. phrase* By the bundle, of rod-like objects such as poles or cigarettes. *Siga? Bīlli ma batangan.* cigarets? Bought by the piece.

**pagbatang-saging** *v. intr. aN-* To support a dead body before it is wrapped in shroud cloth, by laying it across the extended legs of seven men. *Sinalinan na in bay magbatang-saging, ya a'a pitu' puhu' magh'nnat inān.* The men who were holding the body on their legs are replaced, those seven men who had been sitting with their legs stretched out.

**binatang₂** *n.* Shop-rolled cigarets.

**batang-batang** *v. tr.* To impose restrictive conditions, the action of a magistrate towards a couple seeking divorce, or someone who is a first offender. *Buwat kami magtiman maka h'ndaku, pinat'nna'an kami hād. Ma deyom duwambulan subay da'a kami magh'nda ni saddī. Binatang-batang kami.* For example, if my wife and I divorce, then a limit of two months is imposed on us before we can remarry. We are placed under a restriction. *Buwat aku saupama anangkaw bo' ta'abut aku, binatang-batangan aku. Na bang aku anangkaw pabalik mbal minsan nihukum, nijīl sadja.* Like, for example, I steal and get caught, I am released on condition. Then if I steal again I will not even be charged, simply sent to prison. *Sinumbung kami maglakibini ni botang-lahat. Na magbisala na kami, na sai-sai makabāk bisala ahāp, ya anganda'ug. Magtimbul kami pabīng, nīntanan kami batang-batang.* The two of us, husband and wife, were reported to the community leader. So we talked, and whoever could say things well won [the argument]. We got together again, and restrictions were laid on us.

**batang-pai** *n.* A species of fish (unclassified).

**Batawi'** *n.* Batavia, an old name for Jakarta.

**batbat₁** *v. intr. aN-* To set out for a destination. *Wa'i amatbat min t'ngnga' lān.* He's on his way down the middle of the road. (*Thesaurus:* **l'ttu, tulak₁ 1.1**)

**batbat₂** *v. tr.* To say something; to utter. *Ya hē' batbatta.* That's what we said. (*Thesaurus:* **bahasa₁, bā'₁, bissala 1.1, k'bbat₁ 1, h'lling₁ 1.1, pagmūng-mūng 1.1, sambat, yuk**)

**batbatan** *n.* The essential part of something said. *Ya batbatan lling si Nu sali' halam. Hal suwala.* The real content of Nu's speech is non-existent. It is just talk. *Sali' po'onan lling ko' batbatan itū. Buwat batbatan lling si Nu, sali' halam, hal* *suwala. Batbatan* is like the origin of something spoken. Nu's speech for example, there's nothing in it, just talk.

**batik** *n.* The part of the constellation of Orion formed by the belt and sword. (*cf:* **bubu₂**)

**bati'₁** *adj. a-* **1)** Awake after sleeping. *Apu'aw karu'na, nsa' ahāp e'na atuli, akabati' na.* Her sleep is broken, she didn't sleep well, she has become awake. *Abati' na ka, alangkaw na llaw.* Wake up, the sun is high already. *Tagna' katuliku halam aku makasayu. At'ggol katuliku halam pagbati'ku. Kohap na pabīng.* When I first go to sleep I am not aware of anything. When my sleep is long-lasting I have no waking periods. It's afternoon again. **1.1)** *v. tr.* To waken someone. *Bang aku atuli, ni'ddikan aku e' siyaliku, tabati' na aku pabīng.* When I sleep my older brother steps on me, and I am woken up again. *Aho' sangom, bati'ku luma' ilū.* Yes it was night, I woke the house up. (*cf:* **pukaw**)

**pagbati'** *v. intr. aN-* To be waking up.

**himati'** *v. intr. aN-* To feel the movement of a child in the womb; to have contractions prior to birth. (*Thesaurus:* **b'ttong₂ 1**, **buka'-puhu'**, **iram**)

**bati'₂** *v. tr.* To stir up a liquid such as coconut oil, that has become viscous. *Subay nilunglungan kassa' ilū bo' tabati' ns'llan bay atuli.* The bottle should be shaken so the oil [that was left overnight] will become liquid again.

**batil** *n.* An antique metal container. *Yuk siyaka inān, "Buwangku batilku makania'a pagpanggal." "Na," yuk pasunu', "buwangku batilku makania'a pagbubu maka ni kōk kumay."* The older brother there said, "I will toss my container away to the basket trap fisherman." "Well," says the next brother, "I will toss my container there to the *bubu* trap fisherman, and to the head of the surgeon-fish."

**batin** *n.* **1)** Things kept private for reasons of modesty. *Ai-ai mareyom baran d'nda mbal kapa'nda'an, ya na hē' batin. Bang ta'nda' lahil batin, makatamparasa.* Anything in a woman's body that cannot be shown, that is *batin*. When such things are exposed to view it causes shame. **1.1)** *v. tr.* To keep something secret or private. *Pinalahil, halam binatin.* Caused to appear, not kept secret. *Bang a'a magkawin maka h'ndana', mbal maggapus, mbal magsiyum, bang halam bay binatin. Binatin, mbal nianu ni a'a kamemon.* When a man and his wife are married, they don't embrace, they don't kiss, unless it is in secret. It is kept private, not [displayed] to everyone.

**batiya'** *n.* A heavy basin used for washing clothes. *Batiya' pagdakdakan binowa ni bohe'.* A basin used for washing is taken to the water. (*Thesaurus:* **lumpang-lumpang, palanggana, pastan, undam**)

**batri** *n.* A voltaic battery.

**battik** *n.* Cloth hand-printed by the wax-dye method, or its machine-printed copy.

**battitu** *var. of* **buwattitu**

**batu₁** *n.* A naturally formed mass; a rock; a stone. (*Thesaurus:* **bussu'₁, lakit**)

**batu-balan** *n.* A magnet. (*cf:* **bagnet**)

**batu-batu₁** *n.* A pebble or small stone. *Jari pehē' iya ni sapa' amene' lima batu-batu alanu', pinat'nna' e'na ni deyom puyu'-puyu' ya asāl pagbowana.* So he went to the river to choose five smooth pebbles, placing them in the bag he always carried.

**batu-ettom** *n.* A hard rock, as distinct from coral.

**batu-lakit** *n.* A large rock; a boulder. *Aheya batu-lakit ma bihing tampe Siganggang.* The hard rock on the shore at Siganggang is large. *Jari aniya' batu-lakit niosolan e' Nabi Yusup, batu panganggindanan kubul si Sitti Rakiya.* So prophet Joseph erected a boulder-stone, a stone for marking Lady Rakiya's grave.

**batu-lantup** *n.* Pumice; buoyant rock.

**batu-manunggul** *n.* A sentinel rock exposed at low tides, standing alone.

**batu-patollok** *n.* A distinctive coral formation which stands alone in a sandy area of sea floor. (*gen:* **batu₂ 1**)

**batu-timbang** *n.* The measuring weight of a beam scale.

**batu₂** *n.* **1)** Coral formations in contrast to rocks and stones. (*spec:* **batu-patollok, dulang-kokok, lakas-lakas, langat-langat, munu-munu, sahasa', sāng-sāng, s'bbo, tangkapa'**) **2)** Solid coral formations, a source of building material. *Batu ya nihinang papagan luma'.* Coral rock that house foundations are built of.

**batu₃** *n.* A mile or kilometer. *Yukna, "Ala'an kām lawak sangpū' aka lima batu."* He said, "Go away, fifteen miles distance." (*Thesaurus:* **kilometēl, d'ppa 1, honga'₂, inses, maniku**)

**batu-batu₂** *n.* A clot of blood or tissue. *Buwat kita d'nda bang bay na maganak, amasi batu-batu mareyom itu. Sinoho' kita da'a magl'ngngan he ra'a abakkug.* Like with us women after giving birth, a clot still inside us here. We are instructed not to go walking lest the movement causes pain.

**batu-kawin** *n.* A token fee paid to the civil or religious leader who solemnizes a wedding. *Batu-kawin itū dakayu' pilak panamba imam bay manugsug hē'.* The *batu-kawin* is the one peso fee to the imam who traced the kinship connexions. (*cf:* **talmal**)

**batuk₁** *v. intr. pa-* **1)** To be installed; to set in place. *Pabatuk pa'in tambol lawang da'ira inān, amatay isāb anakna siyali.* When the door of that gateway was installed, his younger child also died. **1.1)** *v. tr.* To connect two parts. *Batukun tambuku badju'nu ilu, sali' sangonun.* Do up the button on your shirt, like [saying] put it into its place. (*Thesaurus:* **asok 1.1, sangon₁ 1**)

**batuk-batuk** *n.* A snap fastener. (*Thesaurus:* **kassup 1, kattup, dopon-dopon 1.1, tikkup**)

**batuk₂** *v. tr.* To look for something lost or left behind. *Bang aniya' bay takalipat subay binatuk bay pat'nna'an. Kalu masi.* If something has been forgotten, we should look for it in the place it was. Maybe it is still there. *Batukta ai-ai bay ta'bba.* We are looking for whatever was left behind. (*cf:* **piha 1**; *Thesaurus:* **jadja' 1.1, lalag, libu 1.1, nda' 1.1, salusu**)

**batul** *v. tr.* To lay out strands in preparation for weaving. *Batulun pandan ilū, sali' pinagsama-sama.* Lay out the pieces of pandanus, make them all the same. *Baha'u bay binatul lapisna.* Its backing has just been laid out. (*cf:* **ppi' 1**)

**batulan** *n.* A pattern for something to be woven. *Ai-ai anomta subay aniya' batulanna, bubu ka, tepo ka. Bang banog sukuran.* Whatever one weaves there should be a pattern for laying out the strands, whether it's a fish trap or a mat. With a sail there are measurements.

**batung₁** *n.* Peanuts. *Arachis hypogaea. Tinanoman panggi' kayu atawa batung.* Planted with cassava or peanuts. (*cf:* **tawsiyu**)

**batung₂** *n.* Various legumes with edible pods or seeds. *Phaseolus aureus & vidalis; Vigna sesquipedalis.* (*Thesaurus:* **monggo, taoge**)

**batung-hidjaw** *n.* Green beans; string beans.

**bau** *n.* 1) An odor, good or bad. *Ala'at bauna.* Its smell is bad. *Ē, bau kepet!* Yuk, the smell of armpits! 1.1) *adj. a-/-an* Odorous. *Bauhan talingana, niantil.* His ear smells, he has an infection. *Bō' baha'u nihinang bo' amasi isihan saga duwang'llaw, abau b'ngngog.* A newly made bamboo water-pole that still has something in it after two days smells foul. (*Thesaurus:* **b'ngngi, hamut 1.1, hangsu 1, langsa, langtu, mahali, p'ngngak**) 1.2) *v. tr.* To detect something by smell. *Amau aku ero' bay amatay.* I smell a dog that has died. (*Thesaurus:* **bbu 1, hamut 1.2**)

**bau langag** *n. phrase* The smell of a decaying body.

**bau p'llut** *n. phrase* The smell of old urine or rotting fish. *Oy! Bau p'llut ero' itū.* Ugh! This dog stinks of dead fish.

**bau tunu'** *n. phrase* The smell of burning.

**bau-** *see section 2.2.2.4* Prefix: **Cau-**

**bau-bau** *n.* Black spots in the skin. (*cf:* **tagimtim 1**; *Thesaurus:* **langking, tai'-lalat**)

**bauballi'** *n.* The payment made to a midwife for assisting at births other than the first. (*Thesaurus:* **bayad 1, tambahan, tiyandā, tulahan**)

**baud-baud** *n.* A toy consisting of a disc on two strings which are alternately pulled and relaxed.

**bau'-bau'** *see:* **pagbau'-bau'**

**baulu** *n.* Small cakes baked in a metal mold with a convex lid in which coals are placed for cooking. (*gen:* **mamun**)

**babauluhan** *n.* A metal mold, usually of brass, in which small egg-based cakes are baked.

**bautu** *var. of* **balutu**

**bautut** 1) *n.* A painful pus-filled swelling; boil or furuncle. *Bowa' kassa' pinehē' ni bautut, bo' pin'ppok na, ya matana ala'an. Subay ma patulihan.* The mouth of the glass is put on the boil, then it is struck sharply, its core coming out. [The sufferer] should be on a bed. (*Thesaurus:* **bularut, kalibubut 1**) 2) *v. advrs. -in-* Afflicted with boils.

**bawag** *v. tr.* To make something generally known. *Binawag suwi-suwi.* The talk has been made widely known. (*Thesaurus:* **bantug 1, buhanyag, busling, hayag, hula-layag 1, tanyag 1**)

**bawal** *n.* 1) Something prohibited by the authorities. 1.1) *v. tr.* To prohibit a specific activity.

**bawang** *n.* Garlic. *Allium sativa. Am'lli aku bawang panganuku daing.* I am buying garlic for doing something-or-other with fish. (*gen:* **pamapā**)

**bawi** *n.* A pig; pork. *gen. Sus.* (*syn:* **bā'₃**)

**bawi-bawi** *v. advrs. -in-* Suffering from seizures, as due to epilepsy. *Magduliyag, sali' a'a binawi-bawi.* Eyes rolling, like a person having an epileptic seizure. (*Thesaurus:* **belaw, kangog, sawan-sawan**)

**bawi'** *v. tr.* 1) To recoup a loss; to replace something lost. *Angkan tabawi' na bay kosog kabata'bi.* That's why the strength of your youth has now been restored. *Tabawi' bay lapis di'ilaw.* We have made up the loss we took [in trading] yesterday. *Angay halam bay bawi'bi paltana'anbi ma deyom t'llu hatus tahun ē'?* Why did you not recover your lands during those three hundred years? (*Thesaurus:* **puli**) 1.1) *v. tr. -an* To take back what one has said. *Saupama bay kita magb'lli, bay magsulut. Mbal manjari binawi'an bissala, mbal na manjari agpapole'. Bay na maghodhod to'ongan bissala ē'.* For example, we have been buying and have come to an agreement. It is not possible to go back on what has been said, not possible to return [goods]. The spoken words have made the deal secure in detail.

**pamawi'** *n.* A replacement for something lost or damaged; a sum of money paid to make up for a deficit.

**bawis₁** *v. intr. aN-* To suffer loss of consciousness when surfacing from a dive. *Amawis ma kulit tahik apa at'ggol na bay ma deyo'. Sali' alembo, amulibud ma kulit tahik.* He passed out at the surface because he had been a long time below. It's like he was drowned, turning end for end on the surface of the sea. (*Thesaurus:* **lipat₂, pinsan 1**)

**bawis₂** *n.* Rabbitfishes; spinefoots. *Siganus sp. Panggal itū pamanggal bawis maka b'llong.* The *panggal* trap is used for trapping rabbitfish and spinefoots.

**bawis-kallo'** *n.* Spiny or Scribbled rabbitfish. *Siganus spinus.*

**bawis-lambu** *n.* Streaked spinefoot. *Siganus javus.*

**bawis-pote'** *n.* White-spotted spinefoot; Rabbitfish. *Siganus canaliculatus.*

**bāy** *see:* **pamāy-bāy**

**bay** *ptl.* Past tense marker. *Al'ssin na, bay na ka amandi.* Clean now; you have bathed. *Bay kami min Sambuwangan.* We have [come] from Zamboanga. (*Thesaurus:* **bai**)

**baya-baya** *n.* A negative event; mishap or misadventure. *Magsalamat aku bang iya amole' ma halam baya-baya.* I will celebrate a thanksgiving if he gets home without harm. *Bang pa'in makasampay ni tanganbi ma halam baya-baya.* May it reach your hands without incident. *Salamat-baran bang apuwas min sabaya-baya, min susa.* Physical well-being when getting free from trouble, or from sorrow. *Da'a kemeng-kemengun bā. Sali' baya-baya ahūg.* Don't hold it with your fingertips. It's like you'll end up with it falling.

**baya-baya pa'in** *adv. phrase* Imminently; about to happen. *Baya-baya pa'in magkamatay, na ta'abut tambal.* When he was close to death, the medicine began to work. *Buwat a'a magismagol, baya-baya pa'in sigā ta'abut he' nabal, pinasōd he' sigā nireyom sowang.* Like smugglers, when the naval cutter is about to catch up with them, they get [their boat] into a mangrove channel. *Jari itu, baya-baya pa'in tonga' bahangi...* So then, just before midnight... (*Thesaurus:* **sōng₁ 2**)

**bayad** *n.* **1)** Payment for goods received, whether in cash or in the form of other goods. (*Thesaurus:* **bauballi', tambahan, tiyandā, tulahan**) **1.1)** *v. ditr.* To pay someone for something. *Bang aniya' utangnu, bayarin magtūy.* If you have a debt pay it immediately. *At'ggol na utang bo' waktu pagtambukuhan na. Sukutnu na aku bo' halam aniya' pamayaran.* My debt is longstanding and it is the time agreed on. You dun me but there is nothing to pay with. *Bang buwas bay utangannu, mbal na manjari bang bayarannu sīn. Subay buwas du isāb pamayadnu. Bang ka am'lli, pamayadnu sīn.* If it is rice that you have borrowed, then it is not proper if you pay with money. It has to be rice that you pay with. If you buy [something], it is money that you pay with. (*Thesaurus:* **gadji 1.1, hokas, lampak₁ 1.1, susuk, tinga 1.1, tulahan, tunay₂, tungbas 1**)

**pagbayad** *n.* **1)** Regular payment or dues. *In pagbayadna halam du isāb bay alipas bulan-bulan.* His monthly payment was never forgotten. **1.1)** *v. tr.* **-an** To pay off some purchase or debt in regular instalments.

**baya'** *n.* **1)** A desire for someone or something. *Kilāku mbal kasandalan baya'nu ma iya.* I

perceive that your desire for her is unbearable. (*Thesaurus:* **bilahi 1, ebog 1, helo₁ 1, lingit 1, napsu 1**) **1.1)** *v. tr.* **a-, ka-..-an, -an** To like or want something. *Ai-ai kabaya'anta mareyom junna itu hal palabay min kita.* Whatever we desire in this world simply passes away from us. *Kabaya'ku ma iya mbal na buwattehe'.* My desire for her is beyond anything. *Bang atoho' na pantalun, pinilinsa na. Na, bo' angalinig pantalun ē', na, kinabaya'an kita e' budjang!* When the trousers are dry they're ironed. Then those trousers gleam, and then the girls desire us! *Kinabaya'an e' si Sultan Sulayman saga d'nda liyu.* King Solomon desired foreign women. *Apuwas pa'in sigām bay maghulid, mbal na iya kinabaya'an e' h'llana.* After they had slept together she was no longer desired by her husband. *Ai kabaya'anbi? Bang kabaya'annu tana' tampal ni kowan, ma aku na tampal ni gibang.* What do you want? If you want the land on the right-hand side, then that on the left is for me.

**baya'-baya'₁** *v. tr.* To be attracted to or in love with someone. *Amaya'-maya' iya ma anak si Jo.* She is in love with the son of Jo. *Sai pamaya'-maya'annu?* Who are you in love with? *Kap'ddi'an aku, agkā'! Sali' kita anganjelus pamaya'-maya'.* I am in pain, alas! It's as though we are jealous in love.

**kabaya'an** *n.* What one wills or desires.

**pagbaya'₁** *v. tr.* **-an** To be in control; to exercise the right to choose. *Ka'a na pinagbaya' bang pila llaw t'ggolna.* You be the one to decide how many days the time should be. *Sali' magiyaitu-iyaina'an, sali' iya makapagbaya' ma aku.* Kind of doing this and that, and him making decisions affecting me. *Ē! Ka'a ilū magsultan bahā' ma kami? Pagbaya'annu kami?* Hey! Will you be king over us? Will you control us? *Bang aniya' makasugpatan akkalku hē', na makapagdūl-baya' na aku.* If something completes my contentment, then I able to do whatever I want. (*Thesaurus:* **kapatut, pagagi, pagkawasa, pagkuma'agi, pagnakura' 1**)

**pagbaya'₂** *v. intr.* **aN-** To be romantically attracted to each other. *Bang aniya' sehe'ta magbaya', kiddatanta.* If I and someone else are attracted to each other, we wink. *Da'a gi' bang buwat d'nda maka l'lla magbaya', bo' sali' at'ggol halam makapag'nda', bo' samaentom, na maglaman.* Especially when a woman and a man are in love but haven't seen each other for ages and are each thinking of the other, then they appear to each other. (*Thesaurus:* **istrōk**)

**hinbaya'** *adj.* **a-** Longing to have something.

**magbabaya'** *n.* The person who is in control, whose will gets done.

**baya'-baya'₂** *n.* One's personal choice. *Baya'-baya'nu na.* It's your business [or your choice]. (*Thesaurus:* **pagdūl-baya'**)

**bayan** *n.* 1) A means of transport. **1.1)** *v. tr.* To travel by some kind of boat. *Mbal tabayan bangka' itū, al'ssu'.* This canoe is unusable as a way of getting somewhere, it leaks. *Angindam aku pelang bayanku ni M'ddas am'lli ai-ai.* I will borrow a canoe as my conveyance to Siasi to buy things. *Bang bangka' halam katigna bo' mbal biyaksa magbayan, maglenggangg-lenggang.* When a canoe has no outriggers and one is not accustomed to travelling in one, it tips from side to side. *Bang buwat ka'am ameya' man Donson, al'kkas binayan, mbal atrasan.* When people like you go by outboard motor, travel is speedy, not left behind. *Sali' ase'ak ba pelang inān. Tabayan bo' mbal na.* That canoe is quite split. It was used for transport but not any more. (*Thesaurus:* **beya'₁, pagbiyahi, palaktas, sakay 1, tumpang, tundug 1.1**)

**bayanan** *n.* Generic term for various means of transport. *In kami binangsa Sama maglahat ma tahik, pelang ya bayanan kabiyaksahan kami.* For us ethnic Sama people who live on the sea, the *pelang* [a canoe type] is our customary means of transport. (*Thesaurus:* **pahinggaman, pameya'an₁, panumpangan**)

**bayaw** *v. tr.* To lift something up. *Binayaw pariyata', binuhat sali'.* Lifted up, like *buhat.* A: *"Bayawun!"* B: *"Ē, mbal pabayaw."* A: "Lift it up!" B: "Hey! It's not liftable." (*Thesaurus:* **angkat₁ 1.1, buhat₁ 1.2, tangon 1.1**)

**baybay₁** *v. tr.* *-an* To go along an edge; to follow a coastline. (*Thesaurus:* **baklay, bihing-bihing, l'ngngan₁ 1.1, pasiyal**)

**baybay₂** *adj. zero* 'To the contrary!' *Oy! Aku pellengannu? Baybay ka'a.* Hey! You blame me? It was you in fact.

**bayhu'** *n.* 1) Face; facial expression. (*Thesaurus:* **aymuka, bantuk, dagbos, jantang-jari, lahi₄, luwa 1, pangli' 1**) **1.1)** *v. intr. pa-* To face someone; to appear in person. *Bang magpah'nda subay pabayhu' matto'a sin l'lla ni matto'a sin d'nda.* When an engagement is being negotiated the elders of the man should go in person to see the elders of the woman. (*Thesaurus:* **alop₁, anggop₁, arap, atubang 1, harap₁ 1.2**)

**pagbayhu'** *v. intr. aN-* To be face to face. *Bay sinoho' si Ju amajatu iya magbayhu' maka sultan sagō' halam du iya pinajatu.* Ju was told to prepare things for him to have audience with the sultan, but he wasn't prepared. (*cf:* **paganggop**)

**pamayhu'an** *n.* A person's facial appearance.

**bayla** *n.* Western-style dancing.

**pagbayla** *n.* 1) Western-style dancing. (*cf:* **pagigal 1**) **1.1)** *v. intr. aN-* To dance with a partner, Western-style. *Magbayla kita. Balutanku ma hawakannu.* We dance, Western style. I hold you by your waist.

**baynat** *n.* Physical proof of some event. *Bang kita abakat bo' busulan, aniya' baynatna.* When we are

wounded and there is bruising, there is physical proof of it. *Niriyatan bang aniya' bay baynat. Binayaran laha'ta basta aniya' pa'alom ma kita.* Compensated when there had been evidence. Our blood is recompensed any time a bruise appears on us. (*Thesaurus:* **mattan 1, tanda'**)

**pagbaynat** *v. intr. aN-* 1) To act in a decisive way; confidently. *Ai-ai gustuta am'lli, b'llita sadja magbaynat.* Whatever we feel good about buying, we just buy decisively, confidently. **1.1)** *v. intr. aN-* To be evidently determined on a course of action. *Magbaynat pahāp si Ja ameya' ma Milikan.* Ja is clearly set on going with the Westerner.

**bba₁** 1) *v. tr. -an* To leave someone or something behind. *Bay ni'bbahan si Arung ma luma'.* Oldest daughter was left behind in the house. *Ta'bba na ka.* You'll be left behind. (*Thesaurus:* **pulaw₂, siya-siya 1**) 2) *v. tr. -an* To leave something of value to one's descendants. *Sali' bay aniya' ka'bbahan matto'a ai-ai na, ka'bbahan ma panubu' sigā.* It's like when elders have left something behind [on their death], whatever, it is left for their descendants. 3) *v. advrs. ka-...-an* To be abandoned by kin; orphaned.

**pag'bba** (var. **pagl'bba**) *v. intr. aN-* To take leave of each other, as people going different ways. *Na buwattē' ya kapag'bba si Nabi Ibrahim maka si Lot.* So that's how the parting of Abraham and Lot took place. *Buwat saga kita magbagay, magokat, mag'bba. Ka'a tudju ni ospital, aku ni tabu'.* Like you and me being friends and going different ways, saying goodbye. You head for the hospital, I to the market. *Magpaopēt, sali' magsapehak, magl'bba.* Going different ways, sort of diverging, taking leave of each other.

**bba₂** *v. intr. pa-* To come to an end, as a weather event or a sickness; cease an action. *Pa'bba na ulan.* The rain stops. *Pa'bba na ka!* Stop it! A: *"Pa'bba na sakinu?"* A: *"Sōng na."* "Is your sickness over?" A: "Just about." (*cf:* **b'bbas 1**)

**bba₃** (var. **l'bba**) *v. tr. -an* To release hold on something; to put something down. *Engkotanta kulambut ni tōng tonda'. Pagtinduk daing kasabitan na, sakali itū wa'i ang'bba.* We tie a dropper to the end of the trolling-line. When the fish strikes it is hooked, and then suddenly it lets go. *Da'a bbahin papan ilū ko da'a tagipit tape'ku.* Don't let that plank go lest my foot be pinned down. (*syn:* **mban**)

**bbet** *see:* **tabuli-bbet**

**bbos** var. of **l'bbos**

**bbot** var. of **l'bbot**

**bbu** *v. tr.* 1) To detect something by smelling it. *Bbuhun bohe' ilu. Bbuhin aku.* Smell that water. Smell it for me. (*Thesaurus:* **bau 1.2, hamut 1.2**) **1.1)** *v. intr. aN-* To give off an odor. *Ang'bbu, sali' abau.* Emitting an odor, like making a smell. (*Thesaurus:* **angil, angsod, hangsu 1.1, pulag-pulag, tunug 1.1**)

**bbung** *n.* Various species of dolphin or porpoise. *Order Cetacea.* (*cf:* **lomba-lomba**)

**bebang**₁ *n.* Various Butterflyfishes and Angelfishes. *Apolemichthys trimaculatus (Three-spot angelfish); Chaetodontoplus mesoleucus (Vermiculated angelfish); Chelmon rostratus (Beaked coralfish); Chaetodon xanthurus/C. adiergastos (Philippine chevron butterflyfish). Daing anōd bubu bebang itū.* The angelfish referred to are fish that enter a *bubu* trap. (*Thesaurus:* **taliruk, tibuk-lawi'an**)

**bebang-lās-lās** *n.* Spot-banded butterflyfish. *Chaetodon punctatofasciatus.*

**bebang**₂ *n.* A cattle tick.

**bebeya'an** (derivative of **beya'**₃) *n.* A supporter or adherent. (*Thesaurus:* **pitis-tendog**).

**beklo'** (var. **biklu'**) *v. intr. pa-* To deviate from a straight course. *Mbal aku makabeklo', al'kkas palisad.* I am not able to go off the path, I easily slip.

**beklo'an** *n.* An angle or junction of a road. *Bang kita lum'ngngan bo' lān abontol, aniya' isāb beklo'an.* When we are hiking and the path is straight, there are also bends.

**kabeklo'an** *n.* A sequence of bends and turns. *Sasuku magtulakan subay palabay min saga lān kabiklu'-biklu'an.* Anyone who left had to pass by paths that turned this way and that.

**pagbeklo'** *v. intr. aN-* To be winding and twisting, of a trail or highway. *Bang kita magpiknik ni Singkona magliputan kita, magbeklo'an sali'.* When we go to Cincona for a picnic we go by a roundabout way, turn after turn.

**bekos**₁ *n.* Transverse stripes, as seen on some snakes and fish. *Aniya' isāb sowa taga bekos.* There are also snakes that have stripes across their length. (*Thesaurus:* **pagb'kkos, pagg'llot-g'llot, pagg'ttos**)

**bekos**₂ *n.* A collar of a shirt or dress.

**beggong** *n.* A type of canoe without outriggers. (*Thesaurus:* **biruk, buti, kappal, kumpit, lansa, papet, sappit**₂**, tempel**)

**begod** var. of **b'ggod**

**be'ak** var. of **se'ak**

**bēl** *n.* A bell of a school or mosque. *Jabu-jabu, ya nilisag inān, tambul atawa bēl. Sinoho' patimuk saga ma'amun, atawa onde' iskul.* Jabu-jabu, the drum or bell that is struck. Tells the mosque congregation or school children to gather. (*cf:* **bagting 1**)

**belad** *v. advrs. -in-* Suffering from conjunctivitis, a painful infection of the eyes. *Da'a kusu-kusuhin matanu dok mbal binelad.* Don't rub your eyes lest they get conjunctivitis. (*Thesaurus:* **bussik 1, liblib, piting**)

**belas** *n.* Smalltooth sawfish. *Pristis microdon.*

**belaw** *v. advrs. -in-* Temporarily insane; possessed by a spirit being. *Binelaw iya, sali' aniya' saitan pasalin ni iya. Mbal ala'an.* He is insane, as if there is a demon taking him over. It won't

leave. (*Thesaurus:* **bawi-bawi, kangog, sawan-sawan**)

**pagbelaw** *v. intr. aN-* To behave irrationally, as due to grief or rage, or because of a mental disorder. *Hal magalud, hal amono', ya hē' pikilanna. Halam bay sinōd saitan, hinangna magbelaw.* He just cries out, just hits out [at people], that's the way he thinks. He hasn't been possessed by a saitan; acting crazy is just what he does.

**pabelaw** *v. tr.* To tease someone; to annoy. (*Thesaurus:* **bellod**₁**, jullit**₂**, juri 1.1, lawat**)

**belaw-belaw** *n.* Fish stunned by dynamiting, flopping about on the surface. (*Thesaurus:* **hantak**₂**, lundu'**)

**belle'**₁ *n.* White-fronted sea eagle; other avian raptors. *Magtūy pina'an Mbo' Belle' ni si Kulas.* So Grandfather Eagle went there to Kulas [a folk hero]. (*cf:* **sambula'an**)

**belle'**₂ *v. tr.* To collect dynamited fish by diving. *Angabay kita ma a'a animbak daing, amelle'.* We will accompany the dynamiters, gathering up fish. *Belle'ku ya lundu' timbak, ya ma'angol.* I will dive for fish stunned by dynamite, the dizzy ones.

**belle'-belle'** *n.* **1)** Large-leafed vine that grows up the trunks of trees. *Belle'-belle' aheka tanganna, magdirit.* The *belle'-belle'* vine has many runners, in parallel rows. (*gen:* **bahan 1**) **2)** Type of kite made from the large skeletal leaves of the *belle'-belle'* vine. *Belle'-belle' pinaghinang taguri' he' saga onde'-onde'. Belle'-belle'* leaves used by children to make kites.

**bellok** *n.* A species of snapper, said to be a full-grown form. *Lutjanus spp.* (*gen:* **kutambak**)

**bellod**₁ *v. tr.* To trick someone in fun. (*Thesaurus:* **jullit**₂**, juri 1.1, lawat, pabelaw**)

**bellod**₂ var. of **b'llod**

**belong** *n.* A species of bivalve with pearl-like shell and multiple surface curves.

**bembet** *v. tr.* To carry a load. *Magbembet sigā duwangan.* The two of them are carrying [something] together.

**benten** *v. tr.* To carry small items in one hand. *Onde'-onde' ya bay amenten bāgku ni jambatan.* The child who carried my bag to the pier. *Akumbang daing, halam aniya' pamentenan apa ap'nno' he' daing.* The fish are strung closely together, no way of carrying them with one hand because the [carrying string] is full. *Ya niōnan benten itū ai-ai manga sokal, manga būk, atawa manga lahing dakayu', ai-ai duma'in isāb abuhat.* This word *benten* applies to anything such as sugar, books, or single coconuts, anything that is not heavy. *Mbal tabowaku basket ē', bentenin aku gi'.* I can't carry that basket, please lift it up for me. (*Thesaurus:* **bengket, kopkop 1.1, pendet**)

**bentol** *adj. a-* Stale and powdery, of cassava. *Niranos panggi', pinat'nna' ma deyom ambung.*

*Abentol luhūy.* The cassava is pressed down and put into a basket. It quickly becomes stale and dry. *Abentol itu ak'ddot, ag'nnol-g'nnol sali'. Bang abentol mbal takompol, subay tin'ppa nihinang saga pullu', pinutu.* Stale [cassava] is tough in texture; somewhat chewy. When it is stale it can't be molded into a lump and should be pounded and made into cassava cakes, steamed. *Pa'agaw-agaw ni biyaning, ya hē' abentol.* Becoming yellowish, that's stale [cassava].

**bengkang** *var. of* **sengkang**

**bengke** *n.* Various flying-fishes. *Cypselurus, Cheilopogon, Parexocoetus spp.*

**bengke-gampal** *n.* Mirror-wing flying-fish; Bony flying-fish. *Hirundichthys sp.*

**bengket** *v. tr.* To raise or carry something using both hands. *Pabuhatun mital inān ma aku apa mbal takole'ku binengket.* Raise up that can for me [to my shoulder] because I cannot lift it with my hands. *Nira'ut, subay ka'a ya makabengket, subay ka'a ya pehē', mbal sigā. Ka'a ya angandarut.* The one in charge called on, you should be able to carry it, you should be the one to go there, they won't. You are the one to pull out [the tape]. (*Thesaurus:* **benten, kopkop 1.1, pendet**)

**bengkok** *adj. a-* **1)** Bent or curved out of line or from a plane surface. *Luwa tipay sa' abengkok.* The appearance of an oyster but curved. *Saga lān abengkok subay pinabontol, maka palabayan magtinggil-l'bbak subay pinalanu'.* Crooked paths should be straightened, and bumpy trails should be made smooth. (*Thesaurus:* **bunt'lled, kalluk 1, kello' 1.1**) **2)** Morally bent or warped. *Bay panda'annu balakkalnu ma saga a'a abengkok pikilanna.* You displayed your wisdom to people whose thinking was warped. *Bay bahā' aku katambahan he' saina ma ka'am bo' supaya abengkok hukumanku?* Have I taken bribes from any of you so my judgment would be bent?

**pagbengkok** *v. tr.* To change or corrupt the content of a something. *Pinagbengkok pandu' e' sigām.* They twist the teaching.

**bengkol₁** *n.* The reinforced rim of a circular basket. (*Thesaurus:* **lakal 1, legong, lengkol 1, lengkong 1, tibulung 1**)

**bengkol₂** *n.* A place in deep water where currents move strongly. *Ō ba hē', bengkol s'llog. Sali' abal.* Look there, the deep current. It's like an *abal* [the turbulent meeting of two currents].

**pagbengkol** *v. intr. aN-* To move, of currents in deep water. *Bengkol, hatina deyo' magbengkol, ma deyo' kalalomsan pat'nna'an tipay, ya deyo' taga unas. Bengkol,* the deeps where powerful currents move, the deep places where oysters live, the deeps that have sea-grass.

**benglod** *n.* Cracked pieces of rice grain. (*cf:* **biti'₂ 1, dorok**)

**bengog** (*var.* **bongog**) *n.* **1)** Someone who has

learning difficulties and lacks awareness of consequences of his actions. *Bang kita ma deyom iskul, bo' mbal pasōd ni deyom utukta, niranglay kita bengog.* When we are in school but [the lesson] doesn't penetrate, we are nicknamed *bongog.* (*Thesaurus:* **b'ggod, b'llod, bobo, dupang 1, hibang-hibang**) **1.1)** *adj. a-* Behaving without regard for consequences. *Sali' onde'-onde' iskul mbal ata'u ai-ai, ya hē' abongog.* Like school children who don't know anything, that's being slow to learn.

**bengtod** *see:* **pagbengtod**

**besal** *adj. a-* Abundant. (*Thesaurus:* **banos, kansang 1, datay₂, dayas-dayas, dorot, heka 1.1, jayak, parat**)

**besod** *v. advrs. -in-* Pulled at from each end.

**pagbesod** *v. intr. aN-* To argue or be at cross-purposes; to pull from two directions. *Magbesod, magpalilu. Bang ma a'a dangan, "Buwattē'." Damikiyan du isāb bang dangan, "Buwattina'an!"* Arguing, contradicting each other. One person [says], "It's like that!" Another person, in the same way, says, "Like that over there!" *Bang buwattē', magbesod angutta.* If that's how it is, then our goals are in conflict. (*syn:* **pagbengtod**)

**betong-betong** *see:* **pagbetong-betong**

**beya'₁** *v. intr. aN-* To travel by a conveyance of any kind. *Bay aku ameya' min pelang.* I came by outrigger canoe. *Pagsalung amole' na aku ni Siganggang, ameya' ma Sisabros.* Come tomorrow I will return to Siganggang, traveling by the launch Sisabros. (*Thesaurus:* **bayan 1.1, pagbiyahi, palaktas, sakay 1, tumpang, tundug 1.1**)

**dambeya'an** *n.* A single group.

**pameya'an₁** *n.* Generic term for conveyances such as road vehicles, riding animals, seagoing vessels or aircraft. (*Thesaurus:* **bayanan, pahinggaman, panumpangan**)

**beya'₂** *v. intr. aN-* **1)** To accompany (someone). *Ina', ameya' akū.* Mama, I'm coming too. (*Thesaurus:* **abay₁ 1.1, bunyug 1.2, dongan, sehe' 1.1, unung 1**) **1.1)** *v. tr. -an* To co-occur. *Asidda magl'ggon lahat, bineya'an ulan-ulan.* The weather is extremely thundery, accompanied by some rain. *Angasang si Oto', bineya'an p'ddi' atay.* Eldest son is crying hard, and angry with it.

**pagbeya'** *v. intr. aN-* To be companions or workmates. *Bang kami magbeya' angusaha maka sehe'ku, hilagku. Soho'ku pabasag amusay.* When I am going fishing with my companion, I tell him what to do. I tell him to paddle strongly. *Bang kita magbeya' angongka', yuk dangan, "Da'a ka pasōng, alumu ko' onde'-onde' ilū."* When we get together playing, one of us says, "Don't go any further, those children are revolting." *Agbeya' maka matto'ata ni tabu' am'lli panggi'.* Going to market with our parents to buy cassava.

**pagbeya'-beya'** *v. intr. aN-* **1)** To move together in concert or in rhythm; to interact as a group.

*Magl'mpet-l'mpet letehan, magbuwang-buwang, magbeya'-beya'.* The walkway springs up and down, keeps bouncing, moving in rhythm. *Bunyug itū magbeya'-beya' karuwa.* This word *bunyug* means two going together. *Bang kami pehē' ni M'ddas magbeya'-beya' kamemon.* When we go to Siasi town everybody goes along in a group. **1.1)** *v. tr.* *-an* To agree together regarding a plan or some official ruling.

**pabeya'** *v. tr.* To send something.

**pagsambeya'** *v. intr. aN-* To go together as a group. (*Thesaurus:* **pagdongan, pagdora', pagunung**)

**tabeya'** *v. intr. -um-* To be included with. (*cf:* **lapay 1.1**)

**beya'₃ 1)** *adj. a-* Convinced; persuaded by advice. *Abeya' aku he'nu.* You have convinced me. *Beya' isab aku ma gara'bi pasal desktop.* I concur with your advice regarding the desktop [computer]. (*Thesaurus:* **amu₂ 1.1, dakayu'₂ 1, manghalapi, pagta'ayun, sulut 1, tayudtud**) **1.1)** *v. intr. aN-* To obey or agree in response to pressure or influence. *Ameya' aku ma ka'a.* I'll come with you. *Apoyog na kayu, pat'ngge, halam gi' ah'bba'. Na bang taluwa' goyak alandos, na ameya' pah'bba'.* The standing tree leans over, not yet falling. Then when a strong storm hits it, it responds to the pressure and falls over. *Mbal ameya' siput itū.* This screw won't turn. **1.2)** *v. tr.* To persuade or compel someone to act. *Maglami-lami kita magduminu, tabeya' si Sa amange'.* We were playing dominoes and Sa was compelled to pee. *Mbal tabeya' kabilahi'anbi ilu.* What you want will not be accepted. **2)** *adv.* Responding to conditions. *Taluwa' punglu', beya' ni kamatay sa' amasi a'llum.* Hit by a bullet, drawn by death but still living.

**beya' hawa** *v. intr. aN-* To be selfishly attached to something. {idiom} *Ameya' hawana ma pilak inān, mbal amahagi'.* He is attached to that money of his, he doesn't share. (*cf:* **bahaya alta'**)

**beya'-beya'₁** *v. intr. aN-* **1)** To be in accord with what is said or commanded; to believe or obey. *Aho', ameya'-meya' aku.* Yes, I am convinced. (*Thesaurus:* **b'nnal 1.2, kahagad, halap₁, parassaya, siddik**) **1.1)** *v. tr. -an* To imitate or obey someone. *Subay aku beya'-beya'nu.* You should imitate me. *Bay ka nilinganan he' h'ndanu, mbal ka ameya'-ameya'.* Your wife called you [but] you didn't obey. (*Thesaurus:* **asip, hirup₁, ikut**)

**pagbebeya'an** *n.* A person whom one supports or follows, a religious or political leader. (*cf:* **mandul**; *Thesaurus:* **pagmakōk, pagmandangan, pagmete-mete, pagmunda'an**)

**pagbeya'an** *n.* A shared commitment or conviction. *Ma dohongan kita bang mbal du pagbeya'an gara'.* We are in limbo if the plan is not mutually committed to.

**bebeya'an** *n.* A supporter or adherent. (*Thesaurus:* **pitis-tendog**)

**pameya'an₂** *n.* Something to be imitated or followed; a pattern or sample.

**beya' isāb** *adv. phrase* Included with or accompanied by other things. *Aniya' sigām labi limampū' puhu', beya' isāb onde'.* There are more than fifty of them, including children. (*Thesaurus:* **lapay 1, malit**)

**beya'-beya'₂** *n.* Individual choice or responsibility. *Saupama aniya' dusata ma kasehe'anta, bang aniya' kajahatannu, beya'-beya'nu. Mbal aku palamud.* For example one of us has done wrong to others, if you suffer harm, it's your own fault. I won't get involved. *Bang ka pandu'anku, soho'ta ka ma luma'. Bang ka mbal magusaha, na beya'-beya'nu. Bang ka bininasa he' a'a, mbal aku pi'ilu.* When I teach you and tell you to stay at home, if you don't go to work, that's up to you. If someone mistreats you, I won't go there [to where you are].

**beyang** *voc. n.* Address term for a friend. (*Thesaurus:* **agay, bagay 1, bō, gge, panon**)

**pagbeyang** *v. intr. aN-* To be friends. *Bang ma Samehakan magbeyang.* Yakans are *beyang* with each other.

**= bi** *pron.* You plural; your (second person plural) [Set II]. *Ai hinangbi karuwangan?* What are the two of you doing? (*cf:* **ka'am, kām**; *Set:* **=ku, =na, =nu, =sigā, =sigām, =ta 1, =tabi, =tam**)

**bi-bī** *n.* **1)** The feeding call to ducks. (*Thesaurus:* **kuruk-kuruk 1**) **1.1)** *v. intr. aN-* To call ducks.

**bibang** var. of **gibang**

**bibas₁** *adj. a-* Rapid, of speech. *Abibas bowa'na, asapat, mbal kasambungan.* His speech is rapid, agile, cannot be answered. *Abibas si Le bang amisala.* Le is very quick when he speaks.

**bibas₂** *adj. a-* Forgotten about entirely; gone from the mind. *Bang aniya' alopas ma aku bo' nsa' na kata'uhanku, abibas na min deyom atayku. Sali' halam na.* If there is something of mine lost and I have no knowledge of it, it is completely forgotten from my mind. Like it no longer existed. (*Thesaurus:* **kalipat 1, liha-liha, lipas, panglupa**)

**bibingka** *n.* A roasted cake of cassava or glutinous rice.

**bibis** *v. advrs. -in-* Prone to miscarriage. (*Thesaurus:* **kawa'₂, labu' 1.1, pakpak 2, pulak 1.1**)

**bibissalahun** (derivative of **bissala**) *n.* An effective speaker; orator.

**bibitan** *n.* The warp beam of a loom.

**bibud** var. of **bulibud**

**bikannol** *see:* **pagbikannol**

**bikkin** *n.* A species of edible bivalve. *Cardita sp.*

**biklu'** var. of **beklo'**

**bīd** *n.* A small hill or undulation; a ridge between valleys. *Ubus bīd, ubus l'bbak.* Hills, then valleys.

(*Thesaurus:* **baha-būd, būd 1, lorosan, tukaran**)

**bīd-bīd** *n.* 1) Foothills; slopes. *Patukad iya ni bīd-bīd aningkō' mahē'.* He climbed a slope and sat down there. *Kaheka' kayu ma bīd-bīd būd.* The abundance of trees at the foothills of the mountain. **1.1)** *v. intr. pa-* To travel across undulating country.

**kabīd-bīran** *n.* Hilly country; foothills.

**pagbīd-bīd** *v. intr. aN-* To be alternating between ridges and valleys, as rolling country.

**bidda'** *n.* 1) Difference. *Sali' du hinanganna, halam aniya' bidda'na.* Its construction is the same, there is no difference. *Lubid atawa k'llat, nsa' bidda'.* Cord or rope, there's no difference. **1.1)** *adj. a-* Different from; other than. *Minsan abidda' mbal aku.* Even if it is different I still won't. **1.2)** *v. intr. pa-* To differ in some way. *Pabidda' pahāp s'mmek inān.* That fabric is really different [from other cloth]. (*cf:* **saddī 1**)

**pagbidda'** *v. intr. aN-* To be mutually different. *Da'a kam an'ppong ma t'ppongan ya magbidda' heyana.* Do not measure out from measures that vary in size.

**pagbidda'an** *n.* A difference; the basis of a difference. *Atā pagbidda'an.* Very different [lit. a remote difference].

**papagbidda'** *v. tr.* To make things distinct from each other.

**bidduli** *n.* A species of broad-leafed shrub, the leaf shoots of which are used as an ingredient to color cosmetic rice powder.

**bidjak** *adj. a-* 1) Characterized by persuasive, insincere speech. **1.1)** *v. tr. -an* To cajole or entice someone to do what is wrong. *Arūng, bidjakin si Samson ilū bo' tahakana bang m'nningga pangā'anna kosogna landu' aheya.* Young woman, coax Samson so he lets [you] know where he gets his great power from. (*Thesaurus:* **bowa₃, kuti-kuti, pilad, pitna**)

**pamimidjak** *n.* Someone in the habit of enticing or seducing.

**biga'** *adj. -an* Promiscuous or lustful, of a woman. *Sali' bang magbono' d'nda sali'-sali', magpakaiya' na kaginisan, niōnan biga'an, palaban, sundalan, palalu, pagkolet.* Like when women are fighting, they throw all kinds of insults around, calling [each other] promiscuous, sexually aggressive, a whore, a fornicator, an indecent toucher. (*Thesaurus:* **ba'is, ga'ira, puta, sundal 1**)

**pagbiga'-biga'** *v. intr. aN-* To be habitually or repeatedly promiscuous, of a woman. *Sidda magbiga'-biga' d'nda inān.* That woman is habitually promiscuous.

**biga'ung** *n.* Various terapons or terapon perches. *fam. Terapontidae.* (*syn:* **langāt**)

**biggal** *n.* 1) A block or wedge used to raise something above where it is placed. (*Thesaurus:* **bulatuk, pahanggal, s'ngngal, tanok 1**) **1.1)** *v. intr. pa-* To be propped up and not lying flat. *Pabiggal būk ina'an, aniya' katahanan man deyo'.*

*Mbal ahāp pat'nna'anna, mbal aratag.* That book there is propped up, lying on something underneath. Its location is not good, not flat. **1.2)** *v. tr. -an* To raise something by placing a block or wedge under it. *Biniggalan maka linsungan.* Propped up with a wooden mortar. *Siningalan abō' ahāp l'ngngan tanok, sali' biniggalan.* Propped up so the splitting wedge moves easily, same as *biggal*.

**bigguwal** *see:* **pagbigguwal**

**bigi₁** *n.* A seed; grains of cereal. *Niā' sala bigihan buwas man deyom b'ttong daing ilū ko' mbal makalango.* Things like grains of rice are removed from the gut of that fish so it won't cause nausea. (*cf:* **bisul**; *syn:* **binhi'**)

**bigi-jantung** *n.* The heart as the location of romantic feelings; a sweetheart. *Ahublut saru'un-du'un ya tunuk bay ma bigi-jantungku.* The thorn that was in my heart has been suddenly removed.

**bigi-tinanom** *n.* The seeds of planted things.

**bigi₂** *n.* The clitoris. (*cf:* **toro' 2**)

**bigi-buyung** *n.* The testicles. (*syn:* **pola-pola**)

**bigla'** *adj. a-* Done without care. *Buwat kahawasan, abigla' ta'ā'.* Like freight being unloaded, taken without much care.

**bigsi'** *adj. a-* 1) Very bad-tempered. *Bang kita abigsi', da'a gi' kampung, minsan anakta mbal pasekot ni kita. Kinatāwan kita.* When we are very bad-tempered, even our children, let alone neighbors will not come near us. We are feared. (*Thesaurus:* **b'nsi 1.1, b'ngngis 1, j'ngngit**) **1.1)** *v. tr.* To treat someone in a bad-tempered way. *Aniya' dakayu' a'a bay pat'nna' ma a'a asal ala'at. Asidda iya binigsi' he' sigā apa ngga'i ka na pa'in buwat matto'a-danakanna.* There was someone who lived with people who were simply bad. He was badly treated by them, for they were always so unlike his parents and siblings. *Angkan bigsi'ta iya sabab kab'nsihanta hinangna. Niā'an katikmuhanan.* The reason we were mean to him is that we hated what he did. That was taken as a pretext [for our behavior].

**bigtang** *v. intr. pa-* 1) To be suspended between two points. *Pamagay ina'an, ya pabigtang ina'an?* What's the purpose of those [decorative streamers], that are strung out there? **1.1)** *v. tr.* To stretch out a line. *Bigtangun k'llat ilu, niuli'an ko da'a magkulengkong.* Stretch out that line, straighten it so that it doesn't curl up into a tangle. (*Thesaurus:* **b'ttad 1.1, l'dduk 1.1, l'ngngat, lūk, tilud 1.1, uli'₂**)

**bihag** *v. tr.* To take someone captive, as a hostage or prisoner of war.

**bihang₁** *adj. a-* Ill due to supernatural influence. *Abihang, apa'in, asabab.* Causing illness, sickness, brought about by a non-physical cause. (*Thesaurus:* **labba'₂ 1, pa'in₃ 1, sabab₂ 1.1, semet, sila'-sila' 1.1**)

**bihang₂** *adj. a-* Rare; seldom. (*Thesaurus:* **bislang 1,**

**jalang₂, lahang, salat 1**)

**bihing₁** *n.* **1)** An edge; a fringe. *Tumbukan bihing hoŝku, ya na hē' amuwan pagon.* The edge of my sarong is double woven, that's what gives it durability. **1.1)** *v. intr.* pa- To go to the edge of something; to locate on an edge. **1.2)** *v. tr.* -an To form an edge on something. *Bihingin kono' si Oto' ilū bo' mbal ahūg.* Form an edge by Oldest Son so that he doesn't fall. *Am'lli aku bulda pamihingku l'ngngon badju'ku.* I will buy some lace to border the sleeves of my blouse with. (*Thesaurus:* **gibayan**)

**bihing langit** *n. phrase* The horizon; any remote location. {idiom} *Sai bahā' dapu luma' angitaw-ngitaw ma bihing langit ī', ma dilaut ī'?* Who is the owner of the house that glitters there on the horizon, out there at sea? (*cf:* **mpat pidju alam**)

**bihing-bihing** *v. intr.* aN- To walk along an edge, as a beach or the grass verge of a path. *Amihing-mihing tampe si Ja tudju ni Hambilan.* Ja is walking along the edge of the tidal limit towards Hambilan. (*Thesaurus:* **baybay₁**)

**bihing-bowa'** *n.* Lips; the outer edges of an opening such as a sack. *Alūs bihing-bowa'ku e' kahawa.* My lips are burnt by the coffee. *Pe'esin kono' bihing-bowa'nu.* Just rub it over your lips. *Samaintib du buwas maka bihing-bowa' mital.* The rice is level with the rim of the can.

**bihing₂** **1)** *n.* The location adjacent to anything. *Sinusul e' kami bihing kabangkawan ē'.* We made our way along the edge of the mangroves there. *Dilaut mbal sakit atā to'ongan min bihing. Na timbang alawak. Atā kaut timbang.* The sea is not very far from shore. *Timbang*, it is distant. *Timbang* is far out to sea. *Atiya' ma bihingku.* Here beside me. (*Thesaurus:* **kĭd₁** 1) **2)** *v. tr.* -an To be in contact with someone by lying alongside, implying sexual relations. *Binihingan e'na saga h'nda-tape' mma'na.* He lay with his father's minor wives.

**bihing-luma'** *n.* Neighbor. *Mbal sigām magsulut sabab angalindihan ya bihing-luma'na.* They don't get on because she aspires to outdo her neighbors. *Gōm lagi' ka ni sehe'nu magbihing-luma' min danakannu ya wa'i atā.* It is preferable [to go] to your friend who lives next door, rather than your brother who is far away.

**bihingan** *n.* The junction of land and sea; the tidal limit. (*Thesaurus:* **daplakan₁, gintana'an, hampilan, pari'an, susulan, tampe, tapiyan**)

**pagbihing-luma'** *v. intr.* aN- To live in adjacent houses. *Bay magbihing-luma' kami.* We used to live next door to each other.

**pagbihing₁** *v. intr.* aN- To be side by side.

**pagbihing₂** *v. intr.* aN- To unite sexually. *Ta'abutku h'ndaku magbihing maka l'lla saddī ma kara-kara. Magmalān aku magtūy.* I found my wife in the act of having sex with another man. I immediately reacted noisily. (*cf:* **pagdakayu'₁** 1)

**bihing tampe** *n. phrase* The highwater line on a beach.

**bihun** *n.* A type of fine rice noodle. *Pastil ko' itū, isina bihun maka manuk.* This is a pastry, its contents are noodles and chicken.

**bi'at** *adj.* a- **1)** Disciplined; well-behaved. **1.1)** *v. tr.* To train a child in right behavior. *Aniya' isāb a'a atuwas kōkna maka bula'ug ya mbal ameya' ma pandu' ina'-mma'na minsan du bay na bini'at.* There are also people who are stubborn and violent and who do not follow the teaching of their mother and father even though they have been brought up to behave well. (*Thesaurus:* **babal₂, papat 1.1, pitis₂ 1.1**)

**tabi'at** *n.* A person's characteristic behavior and disposition.

**bĭl** *n.* Beer. (*Thesaurus:* **alak, binu, toba'**)

**bilahi** *n.* **1)** A desire for something. *Alingas na iya maitu, bilahina amole' ni lahat sigām.* He is uneasy here now, his desire is to go home to their place. *Bilahi kita bo' halam aniya' pangabutta bay bilahita hē'.* We want something but haven't come across what we wanted. (*Thesaurus:* **baya' 1, ebog 1, helo₁ 1, lingit 1, napsu 1**) **1.1)** *v. tr. zero* To be willing to do. *Bilahi isāb ta'uku ya ma'anana.* I want also to know its meaning. *Bilahi ka patugpa' ni tahik?* Do you want to dive into the sea? **1.2)** *v. tr.* a-, ka-..-an, -an To like or want something or someone. *Abilahi'an aku badju' ilu.* I want that shirt [of yours]. *Si Rakiya iya alingkat, ahāp pamarananna, jari kinabilahi'an iya e' si Yakub.* Rachel was the beautiful one, her figure lovely, and she was the one Jacob desired. *Aniya' kono' kinabilahi'an, sagō' mbal kahaka'an.* There is something that is desired, it is said, but it is not to be told. **2)** Sexual or romantic desire. *Aheya bilahiku ma ka'a, mbal kasandalan.* My desire for you is very great, unbearable.

**pagbilahi** *v. intr.* aN- To be romantically attracted to each other. *Aniya' gandahan min kar'ndahan, sinō' na lum'ngngan. Sali' amapagbilahi.* An instruction from the women's side, telling [them] to proceed [with a marriage proposal]. Like being made to want each other. *Magtotos magbilahi maka mbal.* To be in full agreement whether they like each other or not.

**pabilahi** *v. tr.* To make someone willing to do something; to persuade.

**bila'** **1)** *n.* A break or crack in something rigid. *Bila' kassa', bila' pelang.* Broken glass, a broken canoe. (*cf:* **dambila'** 1) **1.1)** *adj.* a- Broken; shattered. *Abila' samin-matana.* His eye-glasses are broken. **1.2)** *v. tr.* To break something apart. *Bang bin'lla ma banga' isi sapi' inān, in banga' subay binila'.* If that beef is cooked in a clay pot, the pot should be broken. *Mbal manjari binila' p'ttung.* Bamboo can't be split. (*Thesaurus:* **b'kka' 1.1, lelek, se'ak 1, sepak**) **2)** *v. tr.* To divide a number of things into groups. *Binila' duwa isi hayop ina'an bo' yampa pinapagalop* *bila'anna. Sagō' halam binila' saga manuk-manuk, hal pinat'nna' sadja.* The animal flesh was divided into two and the pieces set out facing each other. But the chickens were not cut in two, simply put in place.

**karuwambila'** *n.* Both sides of a reference point. (*cf:* **katilibut**)

**pagkabila'-bila'** *v. intr. aN-* To break up into pieces.

**paruwambila'** (var. **paruruwambila'**) *adv.* On both sides; on all sides.

**bilal** *n.* The third ranking leader in a mosque comunity, below a hatib. (*cf:* **hatib, imam, muwallam**)

**bilalang** *n.* Various species of grasshopper. (*Thesaurus:* **ampan-dulu, tompang**)

**bilang₁** *adv.* Often; on many occasions. *Bilang asidda takalipatku bang ma'ai bay pat'nna'ku.* I often completely forget where I placed it. *Ala'at bang a'a makalandu' abbuhan, bilang halam bagayna.* It is bad when a person is excessively proud, he often has no friends. (*Thesaurus:* **daran, masuhul, maumu**)

**bilang₂** *n.* All people in a group or list. *Mbal aku magpataha' salawat itū. Bilahi sadja aku amahati ni ka'am bilang saga matto'a kami ma deyoman si Isa.* I won't make this a long message. I just want to inform all you senior people in the Jesus community.

**bilang₃** *adj. zero* The call 'All ready' in games of hiding or chasing. *Pikiembet na, bilang itū. Bilang* is a request to be chased. *Bang kami magembet na bo' magtaem sehe'ku inān, aku itū bilang na.* When we are playing hide and seek and my companions say time's up, I am ready.

**du-bilang** *adj. zero* The call "Not ready", in children's games.

**bilang-bilang** *n.* Portulaca, a succulent plant that grows in sand. *Sesuvium portulacastrum.*

**bilanggu'** *n.* **1)** Shackles, fetters. (*Thesaurus:* **karena 1.1, kili-kili, ekang-ekang 1.1**) **1.1)** *v. tr. -an* To shackle or handcuff someone.

**bilas** *n.* The relationship between people whose spouses are siblings or cousins. *A: "Danakannu h'nda si To?" B: "Mbal, bilasku. Danakanku si To."* A: "Is To's wife your sister?" B: "No, she's my sister-in-law. To is my brother." *Dambilasan kami maka si Hu.* We and Hu are brothers-in-law [i.e. our wives are sisters]. (*cf:* **ipal**; *syn:* **iras**)

**bildu'** *n.* A fine cloth interwoven with gold or silver threads. (*Thesaurus:* **buwal₂, dasu, lehag, lere-lere 1, pima, taplak₁**)

**bili-bili** (var. **kambing-bili-bili**) *n.* Sheep. *Ovis aries.*

**bilīb** *adj. zero* Convinced by persuasion or evidence. *Ōy, bilīb aku ma ka'a.* Hey, I believe you now. *Aniya' kono' taluwa' bakat, yukta "Ōy, mbal aku magbilīb. Subay aku anganyata' pehē'."* Someone is alleged to have been wounded, and

we say, "Hey, I don't believe that. I must go and see for myself." (*Thesaurus:* **amu₂ 1.1, kompolme, tuksu'**)

**bilik** *n.* **1)** A partitioned area of a house; room. *Ya bilik itu pagtulihan.* This room is a place for sleeping. (*Thesaurus:* **kumbis 1.1**) **1.1)** *v. tr.* To enclose someone in a partitioned area of a house. *Nilibun iya, sali' binilik. Mbal pinagluwas-luwas supaya mbal aettom.* She is kept out of sight, kind of confined to a room, not allowed to keep going out lest she be darkened [by the sun]. **1.2)** *v. tr. -an* To partition a house by the use of walling or curtains.

**billag** *see:* **pagkabillag**

**bilma'arup** *see:* **pagbilma'arup**

**bilsut** (var. **bisut**; **bulsit**) *adj. a-* Unlucky; jinxed. *Da'a ka ameya' ma aku, abisut ka. Mbal ka maka'ā' ai-ai.* Don't come with me, you are unlucky. You won't succeed in catching anything. *Da'a ka ameya' ma pagusaha itu, bulsit ka, ala'at sukudnu.* Don't get involved in this business, you are jinxed, your luck is bad. (*Thesaurus:* **nahas 1, paksa' 1, pawas 1.1, piyurus₂**)

**bilu** *n.* **1)** The color blue. *Lalom tegob-tegoban. Alalom to'ongan, sali' hal bilu-biluhan la.* Extreme depth. Very deep indeed, only blueness. (*gen:* **walna'**) **1.1)** *adj. zero* Blue in color. *Bang manggis bilu apa'it, bang akeyat amamis.* When mangosteens are blue they are bitter, when red they are sweet.

**bilu-bilu₁** *n.* A species of fish (unclassified).

**bilu-bilu₂** *n.* Jamaican verbena, a species of shrub, used medicinally. *Stachytarpheta jamaicensis.*

**bilu-bilu₃** *var. of* **panggi'-bilu-bilu**

**biluk** *v. intr. pa-* **1)** To change direction by moving a sail across; to tack. *Sōng sangom aniya' buwaya. Na pabiluk na kami, tināw na ba ē', piligdu.* When it was almost night there was a crocodile. So we changed direction, being afraid, could be dangerous. *Pabiluk itū mbal na kita angulin. Bang amiluk na kita, angulin.* In making the turn we don't steer. When we are already turned we steer [again]. **1.1)** *v. tr.* To change direction by tacking a sailboat. *Na, bang bay baliyu, animpasan amiluk pinatūt na.* Now, if there had been wind, [we] would have reset the sail, changed tack, and run before the wind. *Amiluk itū amasi angulin, pababag banog.* While changing tack we still steer [using a paddle], the sail is at right-angles. (*Thesaurus:* **agod, bintung 1, kabig, kauk, timpas**)

**pagbiluk** *v. intr. aN-* To change direction repeatedly; to zigzag. *Niapas e'na si Ja ma halam magbiluk-biluk ni kowan atawa ni gibang.* He pursued Ja without veering to right or left.

**pabiluk** *v. tr.* To cause a canoe under sail to change direction.

**bilu'uk** *n.* **1)** The immature fruit of the coconut palm. *Botong so' bilu'uk' halam isina, hal bohe'.*

An immature coconut lacking flesh, only water.
**1.1)** *v. intr.* *aN-* To be nearly full size but
without forming meat, of coconuts. *(Stages:*
**kambung-kambung, botong-botong, bilu'uk,
botong, gangkul, lahing, pangtusan)**

**bilulang** *n.* **1)** A species of tree which provides
timber with a grain of broad contrastive bands,
valued for furniture making. **1.1)** *v. intr.* *aN-* To
show contrastive bands of color. *Amilulang,
angaluwa bilulang.* Showing contrastive bands,
looking like *bilulang* wood.

**bimbang** *n.* **1)** Something for which one feels
concern or responsibility, and which one is
limited by. *Buwat h'ndanu, susa buwattē',
bimbang anak-h'llana, maka alawak lahat.
Daipara ngga'i ka kita ya magkabaya'an. Mbal
tatukuta langit.* Like your wife, so many worries,
anxious for her husband and children in distant
places. However, it is not we who have the say.
We [humans] cannot prop up the sky. (*cf:*
**gaggat 1, limbit 1**) **1.1)** *v. advrs.* *ka-...-an* To
be feeling concerned. *Bang aku pi'ingga-pi'ingga,
mbal bbahanku siyaliku. Atāw aku binono' he' saga
a'a. Kabimbangan aku.* Whenever I go some
place, I do not leave my younger sibling. I am
afraid of being shot by someone. I feel concern
for him. **1.2)** *v. tr.* *a-, ka-..-an, -an* To feel
burdened by responsibilities. *Kinabimbangan aku
e' anakku.* My children cause me to be
concerned for them. *Sinō' na mbal
kinabimbangan saga ai-ai sigām ya ta'bba ma lahat
sabab binuwanan du sigām ai-ai ahāp ma lahat
dakayu'.* They were told not to be bothered by
things left behind in the land because they
would be given good things in the other land.
*Abimbang iya ma ai-ai bay bbahanna.* He is
burdened by the things he left behind.

**kabimbangan** *n.* Responsibilities; concerns. *Bay
aku absen sabab aheka to'ongan sasaw maka
kabimbanganku.* I was absent because of very
many troubles and personal responsibilities.

**bimbing** *v. tr.* To slap someone's face lightly.
(*Thesaurus:* **b'ddak, sampak, sampiyal, tapling,
t'ppak₁**)

**bin** *n.* **1)** Loss of blood by a woman immediately
after giving birth, especially when the placenta
is not fully released. *Am'lli gi' aku samigēl
panambal d'nda baha'u bay anganak, saki bīn.* I
will buy San Miguel [beer] as a treatment for a
woman who has just given birth and is suffering
from hemorrhage. **1.1)** *v. advrs.* *ka-...-an* To be
suffering from bleeding in childbirth due to
incomplete separation of placental material. *A'a
bay maganak kabīnan, aniya' magka'at man
deyom baran, laha' lullun.* A woman
hemorrhaging having given birth, something not
right in her body, nothing but blood. *Kabīnan
aku, sali' aniya' tamuni halam kala'anan.* I am
hemorrhaging, it is as though some of the
placenta has not been expelled.

**binabantug** (derivative of **bantug**) *n.* Someone who
has become famous or notorious.

**binamban** (derivative of **bamban₁**) *n.* Boiled
cassava meal, an alternative form of starch
staple. *Suma'an ni'llawan binamban bo' nihinang
lapuk-lapuk. Bang atoho', nihuwal ni sokal, ni'isi
ma daun, pinab'llihan.* Alternatively boiled
cassava is dried in the sun to be made into
lapuk-lapuk. When it is dry, sugar is stirred into
it and it is placed in a leaf to be sold. *Aniya' isāb
binamban bagong.* There is also a starch food of
boiled Elephant's foot.

**binangsa** (derivative of **bangsa₁**) *n.* Created as a
distinct race or species. *Ya binangsa manusiya'
itū.* Those [of us] created as human beings. *In
kami binangsa Sama maglahat ma tahik, pelang ya
bayanan kabiyaksahan kami.* For us Sama people
living on the sea, the *pelang* [a canoe type] is
our customary means of transport. *Hinangun
buwattilu supaya aniya' anatas allum min ginisan
binangsa ai-ai kamemon.* Do that so there will be
some that survive from all living species
whatsoever. *A'a iya magipat binangsa basi'
kamemon.* He was a person responsible for all
metal things.

**binasa** *adj.* *a-* **1)** Suffering from physical, emotional
or mental punishment. *Bay aku angusaha bo'
akosog baliyu, sidda aku abinasa.* I had been
fishing, the wind was strong and I was
exhausted. *Buwat makannak angongka', manjari
aheka puhu'. Na pinamūng-mūngan he' ina'na,
yukna, "Analik-nalik kām, ngga'i ka sehe'bi ya
abinasa, ka'am apa ka'am ya amowa-mowa ni
luma' itū."* Like children playing, and there are a
lot of them. Then his mother scolds them,
saying, "Sort things out. It's not your playmates
who will feel the pain, it's you [pl], because you
are the one who persuaded them to come to this
house." (*Thesaurus:* **bale', b'kkat 2, husa',
lumpu, paya**) **1.1)** *v. tr.* To punish someone by
inflicting pain.

**kabinasahan** *n.* Suffering; hardship. *Kabinasahan
kamemon bay kalabayanku.* All the suffering I
have experienced. (*Thesaurus:* **kasigpitan,
kati'ilan**)

**binatang₁** *n.* A despicable creature. *Ka'a ilū
binatang!* You are just an animal.

**binatang₂** (derivative of **batang₂**) *n.* Shop-rolled
cigarets. *Pehē' ka am'lli siga binatang, da'a ka
am'lli pasta.* Go and buy some cigarets by the
piece, don't buy loose tobacco.

**binegal** *n.* Vinegar. *Isi tipay pinaglamugay maka
binegal ko mbal ahalu'.* The flesh of oysters mixed
with vinegar so it doesn't spoil. (*syn:* **suka'**)

**binhi'** *n.* Seed, especially for grain crops. (*syn:*
**bigi₁**)

**binolog** (derivative of **bolog**) *n.* A thick paste of
flour (wheat or rice) cooked with water. *Binolog
itū pamikit taguri', binugbug itū kinakan. Binolog* is
a paste for glueing kites, *binugbug* is a food.

**binsana'** *adj. a-* **1)** Suffering from over-exertion and muscular pain. *Bang aniya' nihinang he'na buwat saga luma' dangan-danganna, halam aniya' tabangna, abinsana'. Sali' magpatay to'olangna.* If he is building something such as a house on his own, with no help, he is over-exerted. It is as if his bones are dying. *Abinsana', niōnan he' kasehe'an abusā' na. Mbal kita makapagkesong, mbal kita sali' makapaglingi'.* Suffering pain from overwork, what some call *busā'*. We can't turn the head, cant look around. (*Thesaurus:* **bo'ol, bongso'** 1, **bugtu'₂** 1.1, **busā'** 1.1) **1.1)** *v. tr.* To discipline someone by inflicting pain. *Bininsana' kita he' matto'ata, sali' binono'.* We are punished by our parents, like being struck.

**bintak** *v. tr.* To pay a component of bride-wealth goods as a pledge of good faith. *Bang bay amintak ₱500, bo' magdupang d'nda, subay ang'nde' ₱1,000.* When ₱500 is paid in advance, and the woman behaves foolishly, they should return ₱1,000. (*Thesaurus:* **pagdamak, siba'** 1.1)

**bintadol** *n.* Fireworks, rockets in particular. (*cf:* **kulitis**)

**binta'** *v. ditr.* To travel to a trading post in order to replenish supplies, especially during an extended fishing expedition. *Aminta' aku ni lahat dakayu' bang aku kulang-kabus. Bohe' bininta'an luwal.* I get supplies from another place when I am short of essentials. It [may be] just water that is replenished. *Bang kita wa'i ma kanusahan, bo' kulang-kabus, na aminta' kita. Angā' suma'an am'lli.* When we are away at the outer islands and are short of supplies, then we go to a trading post. We get [and sometimes buy] what we need.

**bintan** *v. intr. maka-* **1)** To produce unhelpful habits. *Na bang aniya' hinangta subay jatuta. Da'a ni'bbahan, makabintan.* So then, if we have work to do we should do it well. It shouldn't be left undone, that leads to bad habits. **1.1)** *v. advrs. ka-...-an* To be habitually unproductive or unhelpful. *Kabintanan, sali' kabiyasahan. Kabintanan na aku, hal aku magl'ngngan ma luma', baran-baranku sadja. Alisu' aku magusaha.* I have bad habits, I simply walk around the house, just me on my own. I'm reluctant to earn a living. *Kabintanan na ka'am ilū, maglete ni kaluma'an a'a, ya angkan kām subay pinabukagan.* You are driven by habit, walking across to other people's houses, that's why you should be rebuked. (*Thesaurus:* **tagi** 1)

**bintanag** *n.* A species of tree, the bark of which provides material for tying and making containers. *Macaranga sp. Kayu bintanag, sali' du maka kayu pataw. Bintanag* wood, the same as *pataw* wood. (*cf:* **pataw₂**)

**bintang₁** *n.* A bowl-shaped brass container. (*Thesaurus:* **gangsa, garul, langguway,** tumbaga 2)

**bintang₂** var. of **b'ntang**

**bintas** *adj. a-* Unraveled; unstitched. *Abintas sanyawaku.* My underwear has come unstitched. (*syn:* **tastas₂** 1)

**binti'** *v. tr.* To kick an opponent's calf in a test of endurance. *B'ttisku aheya, bay bininti'.* The calf of my leg is big, it was kicked. *Binti'un a'a inā'an.* Kick that fellow in the calf. (*Thesaurus:* **sipa'** 1, **tagdok, tindak** 1)

**pagbinti'** *n.* **1)** A game of leg kicking. **1.1)** *v. intr. aN-* To play a game in which players kick each other's calves in turn. *Bay kami magbinti' insini'. Apares kōk tu'utku he' gusung.* We played the calf-kicking game earlier today. My knee was grazed by the sand.

**bintu** *v. intr. aN-* To shift responsibility to someone else. *Iya amintu ni aku, subay aku ameya'. Subay sali'-sali' minsan dangkuri' binowa.* She makes me responsible that I should conform. It should be even-handed even if very little is involved.

**pagbintu** *v. tr.* To argue together about who is responsible. *Bang sinoho', magbintu. Yukna, "Angay subay aku? Ina'an siyaliku."* When told to do something they argue. Says one, "Why me? My younger sibling is there." *Magbintu-bintuhan kami bang sai ya sinoho'.* We argue about who was told [to do it]. (*Thesaurus:* **balik₂, bing₃, bitung, hili, likid, pagpatimpa, pelleng** 1.2)

**bintul** *n.* A lump raised on the surface of skin.

**pagbintul** *v. intr. aN-* To form raised lumps or patches in the skin, as an allergic response. *Buwat aku bang kineket hama', magbintul.* Like me when I'm bitten by mosquitoes, lumps form.

**bintung** *v. intr. pa-* **1)** To be heading in a different direction. *Pabintungun munda'.* Bring the bow round. (*Thesaurus:* **agod, biluk** 1.1, **kabig, kauk, timpas**) **1.1)** *v. tr.* To redirect something. *Jari ya kamemon sapda itū binintung ni sasuku ya amissoko' ka'am.* So all of this curse will be transferred to whoever does you harm.

**binu** *n.* Wine; fermented liquors other than beer. (*Thesaurus:* **alak, bil, toba'**)

**binugbug** (derivative of **bugbug₂**) *n.* Porridge made by boiling starch meal, usually cassava. *Pin'kkal tibu'uk bo' binugbug, pinagtebla' bo' yampa nihūg ni kaldero angaes-ngaes bohe'na.* [Cooked] whole cassava shredded for making into porridge, crumbled and dropped into a pot whose water is boiling away.

**binuwa** *n.* **1)** A lullaby. *Bang kita angaluk onde', pinaruru' atawa pinagbinuwahan.* When we comfort a child she is nursed or has a lullaby sung to her. **1.1)** *v. tr. -an* To calm a child by singing a lullaby. *Binuwahin onde'-onde' ilu ko' atuli.* Sing a lullaby to that child so she sleeps.

**pagbinuwa 1)** *v. intr. aN-* To sing a lullaby over a child. *Magbinuwa siyakaku, anangis onde'-onde'.* My older sister is singing a lullaby, the child is crying. (*Thesaurus:* **kalang₁** 1, **kerol, dindang-**

dindang, tenes-tenes) 2) *v. tr.* To soothe a child by singing a lullaby. *Bang kita angaluk onde', pinaruru' atawa pinagbinuwahan.* When one comforts a child, it is given the breast or soothed with a lullaby.

**bīng₁** *adj. a-* 1) Inverted; overturned; misaligned. *Abulikat, sali' abīng matata. Niudju' kita. Bulikat* [means], our eyes sort of reversed. We are made fun of. (*Thesaurus:* **bulallit, sumpallit**) 1.1) *v. tr.* To overturn or invert something. *Subay binīng bo' ahāp tahakna.* It should be turned over to be well cooked.

**bīng₂** *v. intr. pa-* 1) To return to a location. *Pabīng ka pi'itu salung subu.* Come back here tomorrow morning. (*Thesaurus:* **balik₁** 1.1) 1.1) *v. tr.* To get something by going back to a former location. *Bīngku badju'ku, bay ta'bba ma pagbolahan.* I'm going back for my shirt, I left it at the volleyball court.

**pagbīng-bīng** *v. intr. aN-* To keep going to and fro.

**pabīng** *adv.* 1) Again. 1.1) *v. tr.* To return something to where it was previously. A: *"Ma'ai bola?"* B: *"Wa'i pinabīng ni bay baina."* A: "Where is the ball?" B: "It's been put back where it was before."

**bīng₃** *v. tr. -an* To shift responsibility or blame to someone else. *Ai-ai tum'kka ni siyali sigām inān, iya ya kabīngan.* Whatever happened to that younger brother of theirs, he would be held responsible. *Angagad ka, bīnganta ka.* You wait, I will turn it back on you. *Da'a bowahunbi ni luma'bi ai-ai sakkal supaya kam mbal kabīngan sapda ya asal na bay tapanapda ina'an-i.* Don't take anything disgusting to your house so that you will not be struck with the curse with which that thing had been cursed. *Yukna ma datu', "Tuwan, amu'ku ma ka'a, aku ya bīngin."* She said to the datu, "Sir, I beg you, let the blame fall on me." (*Thesaurus:* **balik₂, bitung, hili, likid, pagbintu, pagpatimpa, pelleng 1.2**)

**binga'** *n.* Baler volute (a monovalve shellfish). *gen. Melo.*

**binga'-binga'** *n.* A species of monovalve (unclassified).

**bingal** *n.* The protective lining of a grave wall. *Ya pangahampe'an ma kubul niōnan bingal. Ya du saga pilang-pilang, pinagōnan isāb bingal.* The lining for a grave is called *bingal.* Likewise the protective markers of women's graves, they too are called *bingal.* (*Thesaurus:* **hampe 1, hanig, lampik 1, lapis₁ 1**)

**bingaw** *adj. a-* Unable to think clearly; confused or dazed. *Bay aku sinampak, abingaw aku, ma llot alipat maka asayu.* I was struck on the face, unable to concentrate, between being unconscious and being aware. (*Thesaurus:* **buriru, lambang-mata 1, lengog kōk, ligoto'**)

**kabingawan** *n.* A state of confusion.

**bingkal** *adj. a-* Firm in consistency. *Abingkal biyaki'. Abingkal isāb buwas bay b'llabi.* Corn cakes are firm. The rice you cooked was firm too. *Mbal abingkal sungi'na, masi apetak.* His stools are not firm, still loose.

**bingkay** *n.* A decorative strip of colored cloth. (*Thesaurus:* **bulda 1, ingkahi 1**)

**bingki'** *n.* An earthenware jar, unglazed. (*Thesaurus:* **ka'ang, kasambagan, kibut, pipa, poga, tanāng, tangpad**)

**bingkis** 1) *n.* A stack of similar items. (*Thesaurus:* **bangkat₁, pangkat₁**) 2) *clf.* Count word for items in a stack. *Dabingkis atop, dabingkis ambūng bang wa'i ma pendetanta.* One stack of thatch, one stack of sago meal when it is in our hands.

**pabingkis** *v. tr.* To stack flat items of a similar shape.

**bingkug** *v. tr.* To stir up an issue that has already been settled. *Buwat palkala', biningkug pabīng. Bay na halam, apuwas na, parahāl pinarokot pabīng.* Like a dispute, it is revived again. It had come to nothing, it was over and done with, but unfortunately it was made to flare up again.

**bingkung** *n.* A species of bivalve, edible.

**binggal** *see:* **pagbinggal**

**binggil** *v. intr. pa-* To hit something with force; to bang into. *Bay pabinggil ni batu, tabowa he' goyak.* It hit against the rocks, impelled by the waves. (*syn:* **banggul**; *Thesaurus:* **daplig 1, dugtul, sampig, sangku'**)

**pagbinggil** *v. intr. aN-* 1) To knock things together repeatedly. 1.1) *v. tr.* To knock things together, especially breakable items such as plates.

**bira** 1) *v. tr.* To pull something. *Birahun k'llatna.* Pull on its rope. (*Thesaurus:* **konot₂, ga'ut, ganggut, guyud 1, hella', paglagedled 1**) 2) *v. tr. -an* To pull at the bow of a spear-gun. *Bang kita amirahan pana', kawat itū pangahawid goma.* When we pull back the bow [of a spear-gun], the hook here is for holding the rubber.

**biradali** *n.* 1) A winged maiden of the sky. *Bang aniya' salindugu' bo' ulan-ulan, aniya' bidadali amandi.* If a rainbow appears during light rain, there are celestial maidens bathing. *Biradali, ahāp d'nda so' taga pikpik.* Biradali, beautiful women but with wings. *Talli-talli, ma'ai luma' kami? Wa'i ma bidadali.* Talli-talli, where is our home? There with the sky maidens. 2) A rainbow. (*Thesaurus:* **andalaho', bāngaw, salindugu' 1**)

**birang** 1) *n.* A long roll of netting. (*cf:* **lantaw 1**; *Thesaurus:* **koleng₁ 1, lebod 1, pasangan₁, tongko' 1, towa'**) 2) *clf.* Count word for rolls of net. *Duwambirang linggi' atawa lantaw.* Two rolls of *linggi'* or *lantaw* [both long nets]. *Dambirang basta dampasangan.* One *birang* whenever it is a single roll or coil.

**birarul** *n.* A type of kite, flown for recreation. (*Thesaurus:* **awak-awak, pindun, taguri'**)

**biring** *n.* The mantle of a squid and other cephalopods.

**biruk** *n.* A canoe without outriggers. (*Thesaurus:* **beggong, buti, kappal, kumpit, lansa, papet, sappit₂, tempel**)

**biruk kapituhan** *n. phrase* A very large canoe of the biruk type.

**bisa** *adj. a-* 1) Intensely painful; severe; potent. *Bay keket ero' di'ilaw, amasi abisa.* Bitten by a dog yesterday, still very painful. *Na pagka buwattē' kabisa gotom apinda kami pi'itu.* Since the famine was so severe, we transferred here. *Abisa ilmu'na.* His supernatural knowledge is mighty. (*Thesaurus:* **paglera-lera, p'ddi'** 1.1, **p'llat** 1.1) 1.1) *v. advrs.* ka-...-an To be affected adversely by the strength or venom of some event. *Bay aku abakat, kabisahan aku.* I was wounded and felt it severely. *Anangis na, angalud na, kabisahan.* Crying away, crying loudly, really feeling something.

**bisala** var. of **bissala**

**Bisaya'** *n.* 1) Visayan-speaking peoples; a member of a Visayan ethnic group. *Ā, kamemon na manusiya', Sūk na, Sama na, Bisaya' na, Lannang na, magto'on wahoy inān.* Oh, every kind of people, Tausug, Sama, Visayan, Chinese, all playing the *wahoy* game. 2) Christian Filipinos in general; Christian Filipinos from Zamboanga or the Central Philippines, as distinct from Tagalogs.

**Bisaya'-bukut** *n.* Christian Filipinos living in the Zamboanga hinterland.

**Bisaya'-Sambuwangan** *n.* Christian inhabitants of Zamboanga City; Chavacano.

**bisbis₁** *v. tr.* To nibble something; to eat something crumb by crumb. *Bang kita angahūg p'ssi bo' hella'ta, halam na magumpan. Bay binisbis he' daing-daing.* When we drop our hooks and pull them up the bait has gone. Small fish have nibbled it. *Aheka amisbis umpan bang aku angahūg gonteng.* Lots [of fish] nibble the bait when I drop multiple hooks.

**bisbisan** *n.* Small fish which steal bait. *Ya niōnan bisbisan laipapa maka tambak.* Fish called bait-nibblers are *laipapa* and *tambak.*

**pagbisbis-bisbis** *v. intr.* aN- To nibble away at something. *Magbisbis-bisbis ma kinakan, pinagdangkuri'-dangkuri' buwat onde'-onde'.* Picking at the food, breaking it up into little bits, as children do.

**bisbis₂** *v. tr.* To consider alternatives carefully before making a decision. *Bisbisun bang ingga ya kabontolan.* Weigh options up carefully [to determine] which is the right thing. *Bisbisun kono' ingga kahāpan hona'-hona'. Sinila'.* Please consider carefully which ideas are useful. Identifying [options].

**biskuwit** (var. **biskwit₂**) *n.* A cracker; a biscuit.

**biskwit₁** var. of **panggi'-biskwit**

**biskwit₂** var. of **biskuwit**

**bisita** *n.* 1) A visitor; a guest. *Da'a jahulaka'inbi a'a itū pagga bisitaku iya.* Don't harm this man because he is my guest. 1.1) *v. tr.* To visit someone. (*Thesaurus:* **liyud, tibaw** 1.2, **tulaga', tuwa'** 2)

**bislang** *adj. a-* 1) Occurring rarely; seldom. *Abislang na aku magpi'itu, sali' at'ggol magpi'itu.* It is rare now that I come here, a long time since coming here. (*Thesaurus:* **bihang₂, jalang₂, lahang, salat** 1) 1.1) *v. advrs.* ka-...-an To be affected by rare occurrence.

**bisnis** *n.* The trade across international boundaries; smuggling.

**pagbisnis** *v. tr.* To obtain goods by smuggling; to trade in contraband goods. *Angkan du aheka untung bang aniya' magbisnis.* That is why there is a lot of profit when someone is engaged in smuggling. (*cf:* **pagismagol**)

**bissala** (var. **bisala**; **bissara**) *n.* 1) Speech; language. *Bilahi iya anganad bisala Sinama.* She wants to learn the Sinama language. 1.1) *v. tr.* To utter something. *Bang pa'in ka amissara agak-agak.* If you would just speak carefully. (*Thesaurus:* **bahasa₁, bā'₁, batbat₂, k'bbat₁** 1, **h'lling₁** 1.1, **pagmūng-mūng** 1.1, **pagpina'in** 1.1, **sambat, yuk**) 1.2) *v. tr.* -an To scold or criticise for something. *Binisalahan itū sali' pinandu'an atawa nihukum.* Being spoken to is sort of like being taught or judged. *Bay kami binisalahan e' mastal. Aheka kono' sā' kami.* The teacher scolded us. According to him we had many mistakes.

**pagbissala** *n.* 1) What someone says, in a general sense. *Iya ya magbā'an sultan bang ai pagbissalanu minsan ka mareyom bilik patulihannu.* He is the one who tells the sultan what you say even when you are in your bedroom. 1.1) *v. tr.* -an To engage in formal discussion. *Buwat ka'a-i ata'u magbissala, aku mbal.* Like you who know how to engage in a discussion, and I don't. *Ta'abut pagpah'nda, bang ya bay pagbisalahan maka mma' d'nda hē' t'llu hatus, nā, pehē'ta t'llu hatus.* When we get to the marriage stage, if ₱300 was the outcome of discussions with the woman's father, then we hand over ₱300. *Sinumbung kami maglakibini ni botang-lahat. Na magbisala na kami, na sai-sai makabāk bisala ahāp, ya anganda'ug.* We two, husband and wife, were reported to the community leader. So we talked, and whoever could speak best won [the dispute].

**bibissalahun** *n.* An effective speaker; orator.

**bissala talus** *n. phrase* A prophetic message.

**bissara** var. of **bissala**

**bista₁** *v. tr.* To give thought to something; to analyze. (*Thesaurus:* **kira-kira, kumpas₁, tē'₂**)

**pagbista** *n.* 1) Accounting; reckoning (financial). *Halam bay niamu'an pagbista min saga a'a kapangandolan.* No accounting was asked for from the trustworthy people. 1.1) *v. intr.* aN- To keep a financial record; to worry about details. *A: "Pila sīn itū?" B: "Da'a ka magbista."* "How much is this?" B: "Think nothing of it."

**bista₂** *adj. a-* **1)** Careful rather than generous. (*Thesaurus:* **kaikit₁, kigit, kimmat 1, k'mmit 1, kudkud, kuriput 1, kussil, giging, iskut, sumil₁**) **1.1)** *v. tr.* To compute something; to calculate. *Buwat aniya' utangku ni ka'a, binista.* Like when I owe you something, it gets added up.

**bistira** var. of **bistiru**

**bistiru** (var. **bistira**) *n.* A western style dress. *Ya bistiru si Mām aheka tambukuna.* The school-mistress's dress has many buttons. (*Thesaurus:* **palda, saya-saya**)

**bistu** *adj. a-* **1)** Widely known or observed. **1.1)** *v. tr.* To make something widely known. *Bang d'nda maka l'lla maglundang-lundang, tabistu du. Minsan aku, tabistu he' a'a aniya' sehe'ku magbaya', d'nda.* If a woman and a man have a close friendship, it will become widely known. Even myself have been reported by someone as having a romantic relationship with a woman. *Da'a pinabistu ni nakura'.* Don't let it be reported to the boss.

**bisu** *n.* **1)** A deaf person. **1.1)** *adj. a-* Deaf; hard of hearing. (*Thesaurus:* **halong, lantak, palpal 1**)

**pagbisu-bisu** *v. intr. aN-* To be deliberately deaf to what is being said. *Sagō' halam bay bineya' pandu' itū e' sigām, gōm pa'in magpabisu-bisu dī sigām.* But they didn't follow this teaching, instead making themselves deaf [to it]. (*cf:* **pabiyal**)

**misu-misu** *v. intr. pa-* To feign deafness; to ignore what is being said or done.

**bisul** *n.* The large soft seeds of lansones. *Lansium domesticum. Kamemon kayu taga bigi, hal buwahan ya taga bisul.* All trees have *bigi* [seeds], but only lansones have *bisul.* (*cf:* **bigi₁**)

**bisut** var. of **bilsut**

**bit₁** *n.* A cursing substitute for something referred to in anger. *Ndiya na gi' ba bītnu ilū! Abisu ka!* Hand me that cursed whatsit of yours! You must be deaf! (*gen:* **sukna' 1.1**)

**bit₂** *v. tr.* To lash slats to a framework, as when building a floor or deck. *Bang ka angalantay luma' bo' lantay p'ttung, bītun maka buway ko' abontol.* When you put flooring on the house and the flooring is bamboo, lash with rattan so it will be straight. (*Thesaurus:* **baggot, k'kkod, engkot 1.1, gakut, laggos, sigid, tabul-tabul, tollen**)

**bitad** var. of **b'ttad**

**bital-bital** *n.* Achilles tendon or Calcaneal tendon.

**bitawali'** *n.* A species of plant, used medicinally.

**bitay** *v. intr. pa-* To be suspended; to hang down.

**pagbitay** *v. intr. aN-* **1)** To hang from something by the arms or feet, as a bat from a tree or a person from a beam. **2)** To move along a beam

by alternating one's grip.

**kulambitay** *v. intr. pa-* To climb across from one thing to another.

**biti'₁** *n.* Cakes of popped rice or corn, usually sugared. *Am'lli aku biti' kakanku.* I will buy some popped rice to eat. (*Thesaurus:* **ampaw, bulitik₂, gagati'**)

**biti'₂** *n.* **1)** A chip or flake from something brittle. (*cf:* **benglod, dorok**) **1.1)** *adj. -an* Chipped; flaked. *Bay sinambi'an olenku biti'an.* I exchanged my chipped marble. **1.2)** *v. tr. -an* To chip flakes off something with a blow. *Bang saupama magtrāp olen, biti'anku olennu maka olenku ati magbiti'.* For example, when playing 'trap the marble'. I strike a flaking blow at your marble and they produce chips.

**pagbiti'** *v. intr. aN-* To be disintegrating by chipping or flaking.

**bitil-bitil** *v. tr.* To fasten building material in a temporary manner.

**bitu-bitu₁** *adj. -an* Infinitely; utterly. *Ma dilaut kaladjun, sali' mbal ta'nda' lahat, ma timbang bitu-bituhan.* Far out at sea, can't see the land, in the darkest ocean depths. *Sipat nalka', lendom bitu-bituhan.* A feature of hell, utter darkness.

**bitu-bitu₂** *n.* Small fragments or sparks. *Bang angaluhu pelang paleyang bitu-bituna. Amasi sali' taga api.* When singeing a canoe hull, the sparks fly. It seems as though they still have fire. *Bitu-bitu api amulagsik.* Sparks from a fire flying through the air.

**pagbitu-bitu** *v. intr. aN-* To appear like specks in the distance, of large items. *Ya timbang ta'nda'ta hal bitu-bitu. Kayuna magbitu-bitu.* The distant seas where we see [land] as nothing more than specks. Its trees just showing like specks on the horizon.

**bitu'anun** *n.* A person separated from his or her spouse by divorce; an ex wife or husband. (*cf:* **timan₂**)

**bitu'un** *n.* A star as a fixed luminous point in the night sky. *Pahangad ka ni langit bo' ka mag'nda' bitu'un magsinglab.* Look up to the sky to see the stars twinkling. *Tauppiku llaw maka bulan sampay saga bitu'un sangpū' maka ssa hekana.* I dreamed of the sun and the moon and eleven stars as well. (*syn:* **mamahi, pote'an**; *spec:* **bubu₂, maga, tunggal-bahangi**)

**bitung** *v. tr.* To turn something back towards its origin. *Binitung ni iya bay kala'atanna.* His evil-doing was turned back on him. (*Thesaurus:* **balik₂, bīng₃, bulibud 1.1, hili, likid, pagbintu, pagbuli'-munda', pagpatimpa, pelleng 1.2**)

**biyabas** *n.* The guava tree and its fruit. *Psidium guajava. Kaleya aku amusu' biyabas.* I'll go inland to pick some guavas. *Borak pinaglamud buwas maka ugbus biyabas.* Cosmetic powder of rice mixed with guava shoots.

**biyaki'** *n.* **1)** A sweet cake of grated corn maize,

wrapped in a section of husk before boiling. *Angugut aku lahing panganggata' biyaki'.* I am grating coconut to make cream for *biyaki'* cakes. *Angā' aku daun kaleya pangahinangku biyaki'.* I will get some leaves inland for making *biyaki'.* (*cf:* **durul, gandum**; *gen:* **mamun**) **1.1)** *v. tr.* To make sweet corn cakes.

**biyaksa** (var. **biyasa**) *adj. zero* **1)** Accustomed to; familiar with. *Biyasa na ameya' ni timbang anonda' panit.* [He] is accustomed to go out to open sea to troll for tuna. *Bang bangka' halam katigna, bo' mbal biyaksa magbayan, maglenggangg-lenggang.* When a canoe has no outriggers, and one is not accustomed to traveling [like that], it tips from side to side. *Biyaksa na kitam maitu ma Siganggang.* We feel at home now here at Siganggang. *Buwat kita ameya' ma ariplano, bo' mbal biyasa, na tabaliyang kita.* It's like when we travel by plane but are not used to it, then we suffer from vertigo. (*cf:* **tanam₁ 1**) **1.1)** *v. advrs.* **ka-...-an** To be accustomed to; habituated. *Kabiyaksahan isab sigām maghinang kalumu'an d'nda maka l'lla.* They are also accustomed to doing immoral things, men and women. *Kabiyaksahan kām maghāp palasahan maka angandūlan napsubi.* You are addicted to making yourelves comfortable and indulging your desires.

**kabiyaksahan** (var. **kabiyasahan**) *n.* Customary behavior; habit. *Yuk siyaka ma siyali, "Nneng, halam na aniya' l'lla ma lahat itu tahinangta h'lla buwat kabiyaksahanta manusiya'."* The older sister said to the younger, "Dear, there are no men in this place for us to marry as is our human custom."

**pabiyaksa** *v. tr.* To familiarize or train someone.

**biyahero** *n.* A passenger; a traveler. *Ma katapusanna, pagka mbal na kasandalan pasu' inān, anantang biyahero itū bo' pakuppa ni tigbaw ya bay maina'an.* Finally, since the heat was unbearable, the traveler stripped off and dived into the pool that was there.

**biyahi** *n.* Travel; a journey.

**pagbiyahi** *v. intr.* **aN-** To travel; to undertake a journey. (*Thesaurus:* **bayan 1.1, beya'₁, palaktas, sakay 1, tumpang, tundug 1.1**)

**biyal** *see:* **pabiyal**

**biyaning** *n.* **1)** The color yellow. (*syn:* **kuning**; *gen:* **walna'**) **1.1)** *adj. zero* Yellow in color. **1.2)** *v. intr.* **aN-** To become yellow. *Bang kita sinangti', gaddung e'ta ang'nda', amiyaning kita, humantak ma labayan.* When we take a turn for the worse we see green, become yellow and collapse heavily on the path.

**biyas** *adj.* **a-** Shamed in a public context. *Nihukum kita duwangan. Aku araran nihukum. Na ka'a ya kabeya'an, aku abiyas.* The two of us are involved in a court case. As for me, I have often been judged. Well, your evidence is believed and I am humiliated. *Hinang makabiyas matto'a,*

*hinang makaiya'-iya'.* Actions that bring shame to our parent, actions that cause embarrassment. *Bang aniya' anuta bay patundug bo' niā' he' a'a halam ama'id. Na ta'abutta na, yukta, "Mbal abiyas a'a itū!"* When something of ours [a canoe] has come onshore and someone takes it, not asking permission. Then we catch up with him and say, "This fellow has no shame." *Nihukum kita duwangan, na ka'a ya kabeya'an, aku abiyas.* The two of us are involved in a court case, you are agreed with, and I am humiliated. (*Thesaurus:* **iya', maru 1.2, paki' 1, tamparasa**)

**biyasa** var. of **biyaksa**

**biyobog** *adj.* **a-** Mushy in consistency. (*Thesaurus:* **k'ddos, lodjag 1, lonyat, petak 1, tonyak**)

**biyu-biyu** *see:* **pagbiyu-biyu**

**biyul** *adj.* **a-** Discordant; hard to listen to. *Abiyul honel.* The mouth organ has a discordant sound.

**biyula** *n.* **1)** A stringed instrument such as a violin. *Bang angindam biyula si Be, mbal amas'lle' si Sa.* When he borrows Be's violin, Sa won't let anyone have a turn. (*cf:* **kitara**) **1.1)** *v. tr.* **-an** To accompany a song on a stringed instrument. *Biniyulahan saga magbayla inān.* Those dancers are accompanied with violin.

**pagbiyula** *v. intr.* **aN-** To play a stringed instrument. *Aniya' isāb min dahū'an sigām saga magbibiyula maka magsusuling maka a'a magtaroro'an tambul-tambul.* In front of them also were players of stringed instruments, and flute players, and people beating time on tambourines.

**b'bbak** *adj.* **a-** Torn open; ripped, of fabric. *Pantalun ya ab'bbak.* It is trousers that get torn. *Buwat taguri' bang kakosogan baliyu, bo' sali' asāl bay abase', na ab'bbak min bay mabase'.* Like a kite when the wind strengthens and it has already been wet, now tearing away from the part that had been wet.

**b'bbal** var. of **babal₂**

**b'bbas** (var. **babas**) *adj.* **a-** **1)** Diminished in volume or intensity. *Ab'bbas na bay p'ngkong.* What was swollen has reduced to normal size. *Aheka bohe' mariyata' karut. Pagbabas ulan, na pasobsob na, ah'llop pareyom.* There is a lot of water on the sacks. When the rain ceases, it will soak in, going inside. (*cf:* **bba₂**; *Thesaurus:* **k'llos, k'ppel, k'ppeng, k'ppos 1.1**) **1.1)** *v. tr.* To reduce swelling by squeezing.

**b'kka'** *adj.* **a-** **1)** Split open; cracking. *Ab'kka' pelang, taluwa' llaw.* The canoe is splitting, damaged by the sun. (*Thesaurus:* **l'ssa', posat**) **1.1)** *v. intr.* **aN-** To break up, due to pressure or too much heat. *Am'kka' na p'ttung bay puwadku.* The bamboo I chopped down is splitting apart. *Bang pa'in am'kka tibu'uk ilū, engketin. Da'a pinapodjak.* As soon as that cassava is splitting, take it off the heat. Don't let it become crumbled. (*Thesaurus:* **bila' 1.2, lelek, se'ak 1, sepak**)

**pagb'kka'** *v. intr. aN-* To become split or cracked, as fruit or parched soil. *Bang ahūg mampallam magb'kka' kulitna, apogpog isina. Bang p'ssilta magtūy paluwas bohe'na minsan bay amata' lagi'.* When mangos fall their skin [always] splits, and the inside is bruised. When we squeeze it, its juice comes out freely even though it is still unripe. *Magb'kka' katana'an.* The soil is becoming cracked.

**b'kka'an** *n.* Weak currents at certain phases of moon. *B'kka'anan, sali' halam s'llog. B'nnal aniya' s'llog, bo' hal pabuway-buway. Subay sangpū' maka duwa bulan sampay ni sangpū' maka mpat.* The *b'kka'an* phase is like there is no current. There is a current, in fact, but it is slow-moving. It has to be from the 12th night of the moon to the 14th. (*cf:* **bulagas**)

**b'kkat 1)** *adj. a-* Broken; snapped, of flexible items such as twine or light chain. *Bang ab'kkat buway alatas du katig.* When the rattan breaks the outrigger becomes disconnected. (*Thesaurus:* **piyurus₁, pugtul**) **1.1)** *v. tr.* To break a flexible item. **2)** *v. advrs. ka-...-an* To be exhausted from physical exertion. *Bang kita palūd min deya amowa panggi' kayu, kab'kkatan kita, maghangu-hangu.* When we come down from inland carrying cassava we are completely exhausted, gasping for breath. (*Thesaurus:* **bale', binasa 1, husa', lumpu, paya**)

**b'kkat napas** *v. intr. a-* To cease breathing (the moment of death). {euphemism, idiom}

**pagb'kkat-b'kkat** *v. intr. aN-* To break repeatedly, of line or thread. *Alagtu' pahāp tanod itū, hal agb'kkat-b'kkat.* This thread is of really poor quality, it just keeps breaking.

**b'kkos** *n.* A crease in the skin.

**pagb'kkos** *v. intr. aN-* To have creases in the skin, due to plumpness or repeated flexing of a joint. *Bay onde'-onde' lagi' si Gi, bay agb'kkos l'ngngonna.* When Gi was still a baby her arms were creased with plumpness. (*Thesaurus:* **bekos₁, pagg'llot-g'llot, pagg'ttos**)

**b'ddak** *v. tr.* To smack someone with an open palm. (*Thesaurus:* **bimbing, sampak, sampiyal, tapling, t'ppak₁**)

**pagb'ddak** *v. tr.* To smack one another repeatedly. *Pinagb'ddak maka ū'an.* Smacked repeatedly with pillows.

**b'ddu'** *adj. a-* Distended and discolored, of the eyes. *Ab'ddu' na mataku, bay aku anganjaga ma pagtangisan, am'ngkong na.* My eyes are bloated, I have been sitting up all night at a wake, and they are swollen. *Bang ni daing, aniya' buwat saga daing a'aslag bay labayan bahangi, ab'ddu' du isāb matana.* In the case of fish, when large fish have been kept overnight, the eyes may be bloated too.

**b'ggod** (var. **begod**) *adj. a-* Ungrammatical and lacking fluency. *Amissala kita, bang mbal abontol bissalata niōnan begod.* We speak, if our speaking is not correct it is called *begod. Ab'ggod gi' ka.* You are still not fluent. (*Thesaurus:* **bengog 1, b'llod, bobo, dupang 1, hibang-hibang**)

**b'ggo'** var. of **boggo'**

**b'lla** *v. tr.* **1)** To cook food, a generic term for most methods. *Pamab'llahun daing itū ma a'a sabab aniya' bīlla.* Have this fish cooked by someone [else] because there are things being cooked here. *Da'a kam am'lla kambing abata' ya halam gi' talutas.* Don't cook a young goat that hasn't been weaned yet. (*cf:* **panggang₁, tapa 1**; *spec:* **bamban₁, baska 2, bolog, bugbug₂, k'tti' 1.1, kuddang, gisa, guling, landang-landang 1.1, mistang 1.1, paksiyu, palam, pangat, putu₂, suwan-suwan, tula'**) **2)** To cook food by boiling.

**pagb'lla** *n.* **1)** The action or time of cooking. *Akatis pa'in kita magb'lla pat'nna'anta na buku po'on kayu pangunggun. Ta'abut pagb'lla pabīng, na asāl aniya' apita.* When we finished cooking, we place a knotty root [on the fire]. When it is cooking time again, we already have fire. **1.1)** *v. tr. -an* To be involved in the cooking of food. *Bang saupama kitam amangan: bang magb'lla subay maglamu-lamu.* Us eating, for example: if someone does the cooking they should share the supplies. *Bay kita pinayakan he'na, bay kita pinagb'llahan e'na.* She took good care of us, she did the cooking for us.

**pagb'llahan** *n.* The place where a cooking fire is contained, as a clay oven or a fire-table. (*Thesaurus:* **lapohan, pilang, sukul₂**)

**pam'lla** *n.* The time taken to cook a meal. (*cf:* **paniga**)

**pam'llahan** *n.* Generic term for cooking containers. (*spec:* **banga'₂, kaha', kaldero, kasirola, kawa'₁, kawali', kenseng, lenga', l'ppo', paliyuk, pasu₁, sanglagan, simpi', tungkang**)

**b'llad 1)** *n.* A sheet of something flat and rigid. (*Thesaurus:* **b'llat 1, kintas 1, gekap 1, lamba₂**) **2)** *clf.* Count word for sheets. *Pilamb'llad papan?* How many sheets of flat wood?

**b'llat 1)** *n.* Sheets of something thin and flexible. (*Thesaurus:* **b'llad 1, kintas 1, gekap 1, lamba₂**) **1.1)** *v. tr.* To unfold something rolled or folded. *Bang bay ma deyom maleta badju'ku, ukabku maleta, b'llatku pabadju'ku.* If my shirt has been in a suitcase, I open the suitcase and unfold it to wear. *B'llatun gi' tōng mantanu ma aku.* Unfold the end of your blanket over me. *Bin'llat bay patakkop.* What had been fastened was unfolded. (*cf:* **badbad 1.1**) **2)** *clf.* Count word for items that can be rolled or folded.

**b'lli** *v. tr.* To buy something; to purchase. *Ai b'llinu?* What are you buying? *B'llihannu aku taumpa'?* Are you buying shoes for me? (*cf:* **muddal 1**)

**b'llihan** *n.* The proceeds of a sale. *Ya sapi' a'llum subay pinab'llihan, ati b'llihanna binahagi' duwa* *ma duwangan tag-dapu hē'.* The living cows should be sold, and the proceeds divided between those two owners.

**pagb'lli** *v. intr. aN-* To be engaged in buying. *Saupama bay kita magb'lli, bay magsulut. Mbal manjari binawi'an bissala, mbal na manjari agpapole'.* For example, we were buying things and had reached agreement. It is not possible to go back on what was said, nor is it possible to return [goods].

**pab'lli** *v. ditr.* To offer something for sale; to sell something. (*Thesaurus:* **dagang, lilung, litu, pagsoroy, pa'andag 1, samsuy**)

**pagpab'lli** *v. intr. aN-* To get people to buy things.

**pam'lli-m'lli** *n.* Various minor purchases.

**b'llod** (var. **bellod**₂) *adj. a-* Slow to learn; hard to teach. *Ab'llod kita ma pagguruhan.* We are slow learners in religious instruction. (*Thesaurus:* **bengog 1, b'ggod, bobo, dupang 1, hibang-hibang**)

**b'llong** *n.* Gold-spotted spinefoot. *Siganus guttatus. Anū' kami b'llong pangumpan salung.* We catch spinefoots to use as bait tomorrow.

**b'llong-sulatan** *n.* Gold-lined spinefoot. *Siganus lineatus.*

**b'llu'** *n.* A large acacia-like tree and its edible fruit.

**b'llung** *see:* **pagtab'llung**

**b'nnal** *n.* 1) Truth; evidence. *Ya b'nnalna, mbal iya ata'u.* The truth of the matter is that he doesn't know how. *Binalutan badju'na pangā'anna b'nnal ni h'llana.* She held his shirt as something to bring as evidence to her husband. 1.1) *adj. zero* True; evident. *Ilu b'nnal ba!* That's so true! *"Ā," yukna, "b'nnal-b'nnal du."* "Ahah," he said, "that's quite true." *Ab'nnal du bay amabeya' sīn ni M'ddas pam'lli daing.* It's true that [we] sent money to Siasi for buying fish. 1.2) *v. tr.* To accept as true; to believe something. *Halam aku bay bin'nnal.* I wasn't believed. *Sasuku mbal am'nnal ma bay janji'na.* Whoever does not believe what he promised. *Angandol, sali' kita angagad, am'nnal sali' amaratsaya, subay aniya' lling.* Trust is like waiting for something. Believing is like accepting as true, it requires something to be spoken. (*Thesaurus:* **beya'-beya'₁ 1, kahagad, halap₁, parassaya, siddik**)

**kasab'nnalan** *n.* The truth.

**pagb'nnal** *v. intr. aN-* To have a relationship of mutual trust. *Angaku aku magtaluhan ma ka'a, sali' magb'nnal-b'nnal duwangan.* I accept your wager, it's like two people trusting each other.

**pagpasab'nnal** *v. intr. aN-* 1) To accept or speak the truth. 1.1) *v. intr. aN-* To make a confession. *Magpasab'nnal pasal bay kahinangan sigām ala'at.* They are owning up to the bad things they had done.

**pagsab'nnal** *v. tr. -an* To tell the truth about something; to confess something. (*cf:* **pagnaik-saksi'**)

**pam'nnalan** *n.* Things generally believed.

**pasab'nnal** *v. tr.* To speak the truth about something; to confess regarding some action, good or bad.

**sab'nnal-b'nnal** *adj. zero* True; genuine; consistent with facts. (*Thesaurus:* **pasti'₁**)

**b'nnod** *n.* 1) Numbness, as due to staying in one place for a long time. 1.1) *v. advrs. -in-* Caused to suffer from cramp or numbness. *Bang aku atuli bin'nnod tape'ku.* When I sleep my leg becomes numb. (*Thesaurus:* **ulapid**) 1.2) *adj. a-* Numb, as from sitting. *Na ab'nnod aku aningkō'.* So I was getting numb from sitting.

**b'nsi** *n.* 1) Dislike; antipathy; aversion. *Makalandu' b'nsiku ma bangsa ina'an.* My dislike of that ethnic group is intense. 1.1) *adj. a-* Hating; disliking; holding in aversion. *H'llaku sidda akab'nsi-b'nsi, sidda anganjawab, mbal kapandu'an.* My husband makes me dislike him very much, always arguing, unteachable. *Sidda aku ab'nsi ma onde' inān. Nda'un, minsan bay lāngku, masi pinagpōng-pōng e'na sumping.* I really dislike that child. Look, even though I've told him not to, he keeps breaking off the flowers. (*Thesaurus:* **bigsi' 1, b'ngngis 1, j'ngngit**) 1.2) *v. tr. a-, ka-..-an, -an* To hate or dislike something or someone. *Sapadpad pamuwan si'itku, gōm na ni a'a, sabab kinab'nsihan aku he'na. Ya pagka kita kinala'atan e' si'it.* Better to give to some stranger rather than to my uncle, because he dislikes me intensely. *Kinab'nsihan na kami he' sigām.* We are hated by them now.

**pagkab'nsihan** *v. tr.* To dislike or hate someone.

**b'ntang** (var. **bintang**₂) *v. tr.* To fish with multiple hooks and a set line. *B'ntang, nilarukan tonda' maka p'ssi. Pasagarannu, halam aniya' anunggu', hal niengkotan ni hāg.* With *bintang* fishing, the lines and hooks are thrown in. You just leave them, no one watching, just tied to a post.

**b'ngka** *n.* 1) Various perches. *Lates calcarifer.* 2) Various Sand perches. *Psammopercus waigiensis.*

**b'ngkak** *v. intr. aN-* To bloat; to distend, of a dead body. (*Thesaurus:* **boskag, butud, tting**)

**b'ngka'** *n.* White trevally or Striped jack. *Pseudocaranx sp.*

**b'ngkol**₁ (var. **bongkol**) *n.* 1) Something stuck in the throat. 1.1) *v. advrs. ka-...-an* Affected by food stuck in the throat. *Subay kita pahantap amangan ai-ai. Subay kita anginum bohe' dahū bo' mbal kab'ngkolan.* We should carefully eat things. We should drink water first so food doesn't get stuck. (*Thesaurus:* **siplat, s'ddok**)

**b'ngkol deyom atay** *adj. a-* Irritated; in a bad mood. {idiom}

**pagb'ngkol 1)** *v. intr. aN-* To be annoyed; to be upset about. *Hal magmusmud, hal magb'ngkol mareyom atayna.* Just grumbling, inwardly annoyed. *Magb'ngkol, sali' ap'ddi' atayna ma aku,* *bay kami magbono'. Subay karūlan p'ddi' atayna, pinahāp. Pagb'ngkol*, like he is annoyed at me and we had a fight. His irritation needed to be expressed and things put right. **2)** *v. tr. -an* To be inwardly seething about something. *Magb'ngkol, aniya' kinas'ngngotan he'na. Aniya' mbal tapaluwas min atayna.* He is seething, upset about something. There is something that cannot let out of his heart.

**b'ngkol₂** *v. intr. aN-* To become ripe. *Am'ngkol wanni, tahak mint'dda, nsa' alagak.* The odorous mangoes are getting somewhat ripe, the first ripening, not over-ripe. (*Thesaurus:* **lāg, pagangilan, pagdauman**)

**b'ngnga'** *v. intr. pa-* **1)** To become straightened out from normal curved shape. *Wa'i ab'ngnga' p'ssi. Ya ru engkot lilusnu, wa'i pab'ngnga'.* The fishhook has straightened out. Your watch strap too has lost its [curving] shape. *Mbal pab'ngnga' bowa'na.* Its opening won't straighten. (*Thesaurus:* **būk₁ 1, kulluk 1**) **1.1)** *v. tr.* To enlarge the curve of something. *Mbal pab'ngnga' bowa'na.* Its gap won't open further.

**b'ngngi** *adj. a-* Strongly fragrant. (*Thesaurus:* **bau 1.1, hamut 1.1, hangsu 1, langsa, langtu, mahali, p'ngngak**)

**b'ngngis** *adj. a-* **1)** Stern; forbidding; severe. *Sidda ab'ngngis matto'a d'nda inān.* The parents of that girl are very stern. *Bang kita ab'ngngis, saga kinatāwan kitā.* If we are stern, we will be sort of feared. (*Thesaurus:* **bigsi' 1, b'nsi 1.1, j'ngngit**) **1.1)** *v. intr. aN-* To be unfriendly. *Maglaku-laku, sali' am'ngngis.* Acting like he's boss, sort of behaving sternly. **1.2)** *v. tr. -an* To treat someone sternly. *Ōy da'a aku k'llitun, da'a aku kab'ngngisin, halam aniya' dusaku ma ka'a.* Hey, don't treat me fiercely, don't be harsh towards me, I have done you no wrong.

**b'ngngog** *adj. zero* Foul-smelling, of liquid that has been stored too long. *Sali' akahang botong ilu, sali' bau b'ngngog.* That young coconut is rather rancid, it has the smell of long-stored water. *Bō' baha'u nihinang bo' amasi isihan saga duwang'llaw, abau b'ngngog.* A newly made bamboo water-pole that still has something in it after two days smells foul. (*cf:* **kahang**)

**b'ngngo'** *n.* A species of squirrelfish. *Adioryx spp. B'ngngo' saddī, tihik-tihik saddī, bo' mbal magbidda' to'ongan. B'ngngo'* is different from *tihik-tihik* [another squirrelfish] but not very different. (*gen:* **tihik-tihik 1**)

**b'ttak** *v. tr.* To measure a section of land using a marked line. *Bin'ttak, nihukud bahā' tana'. Buwat metrosan.* Measured as to area, a unit of land perhaps. Like [measuring] its square meterage.

**b'ttad** (var. **bitad**) *adj. a-* **1)** Pulled tight; made taut. *Atayo lubid, halam abitad.* The rope is sagging, not stretched tight. *Pinabitad, niengkotan karuwampōng.* Made tight, tied at both ends. **1.1)** *v. tr.* To stretch something long

in order to take out its kinks. *Binigtang k'llat bo' yampa bin'ttad.* The rope is laid out between two points and then stretched to remove kinks. (*Thesaurus:* **bigtang 1.1, l'dduk 1.1, l'ngngat, lūk, tilud 1.1, uli'₂**)

**b'ttas** *v. tr. -an* To unpick or dismantle something woven or sewn. *Ai-ai la'itan bīttasan.* Anything sewn can be unpicked. *Sali' kita angahinang linggi', ingga mata linggi' ab'kkat, subay bin'ttasan bo' yampa nianom pabīng.* Like when we are making a long net, whenever a section of mesh is broken it should be undone and then re-woven. *B'ttasin, sinō' pinōngan, da'a sinugpat.* Dismantle it, told to cut it off, not to have a section added.

**b'tteya** *adv.* Similar in size. *B'tteya iklug.* About the size of an egg. *B'tteya pisut-pisut ko' ka'a ilū.* You're only as big as a *pisut-pisut* nut.

**b'ttik** *n.* **1)** A color; a hue. *Ina'an na sali' b'ttik gaddung, b'ttik dulaw, b'ttik keyat, b'ttik pote'.* There were colors there like green, yellow, red, and white. (*Thesaurus:* **agaw-agaw, kolol 1, walna'**) **1.1)** *adj. -an* Dotted or speckled with color. (*Thesaurus:* **kabang 1.1, kelong-kelong₁, jali' 1.1, manas, palang**)

**b'ttina'an** var. of **buwattina'an**

**b'ttingga** var. of **buwattingga**

**b'ttis** *n.* The muscle of the lower leg; calf of leg. *B'ttisku aheya, bay bininti'.* My calf is enlarged, it was kicked in a kicking game.

**b'ttong₁** *n.* **1)** The belly or abdomen; a convex curve or bulge. (*Thesaurus:* **babat, badding-badding, tungul 1**) **1.1)** *v. advrs. -in-* Bulging or curving outwards. **1.2)** *v. intr. aN-* To bulge, become outwardly curved. *Am'ttong bihing busay.* The edge of the paddle bulges out of proper shape. (*cf:* **gombel**)

**b'ttong₂** *adj. a-* **1)** Pregnant, of the post-conception stage. *Ab'ttong na danakanku.* My sister is now fully pregnant. *Bang kita bay angiram, ab'ttong, sōng anganak. Yampa abontol helona bang atonga' na kab'ttongna.* When we have conceived, we become pregnant, about to give birth. Our saliva is only right when the [visible] pregnancy is about halfway. (*Thesaurus:* **buka'-puhu', himati', iram**) **1.1)** *v. tr.* To cause a woman to be with child. **1.2)** *v. tr. a-, ka-...-an, -an* To carry a child in the womb. *Aniya' na kinab'ttongan.* She has become pregnant [i.e. the conception phase is complete].

**pagb'ttong** *n.* Pregnancy at the stage where it is visually obvious. *Halam makalanjal pagb'ttongna sabab bay kalabu'an.* Her pregnancy did not proceed because of a miscarriage.

**b'ttong₃** *n.* A wide bay. *Pagk'llat subu anonda' na isāb kami ni b'ttong Bintaulan.* Come morning we trolled again towards Bintaulan Bay. (*Thesaurus:* **lo'ok, suba'**)

**blāp** *v. tr.* To deceive someone in fun; to bluff. *Da'a blāpun.* Don't tease him.

**bō** *voc. n.* Friend; pal; mate. (*Thesaurus:* **agay, bagay 1, beyang, gge, panon**)

**boben** *n.* 1) A bobbin for thread or line. 2) A yo-yo toy. *Boben, ya pinagbuwang-buwang.* A yo-yo, the thing that is bounced up and down.

**bobo** *n.* A person of limited intellect. (*Thesaurus:* **bengog 1, b'ggod, b'llod, dupang 1, hibang-hibang**)

**bobok** *n.* 1) A small marine crustacean. *Bobok, aheka mareyom pelang a'a magampas.* Lots of *bobok* in the bilge of the canoes of the fence fishers. (*cf:* **k'llut-k'llut**) 1.1) *v. tr.* To be infested with marine parasites.

**bobohan** *n.* An edible species of sea anemone, found in deeper water. *Actinia spp.*

**bobono'** (derivative of **bono'**) *n.* A fighter; a warrior. (*Thesaurus:* **militari, sundalu**).

**bobos** *adj. a-* Falling out through the bottom of a container. (*Thesaurus:* **l'bbot, mman**)

**bobotang-lahat** var. of **botang-lahat**

**bokko'** (var. **boko'**) *n.* Green turtle or leatherback. *Chelonia japonica.* (*Thesaurus:* **laggutan, payukan, p'nnu, tohongan**)

**bokko'-labi'-labi'** *n.* A species of leatherback turtle.

**boke'** *n.* A boring insect which infests sugar cane. (*Thesaurus:* **anay, bukbuk 1, lutus**)

**boklang** (var. **botlang**) *adj. a-* 1) Separated permanently. *Abotlang ai-ai t'bba'ta, buwat tahik, mbal na pabing ni bayna.* Whatever we hit [with something flat], like the sea, will be parted. It will never return to its former state. (*Thesaurus:* **bugtu'₁, butas 1, l'kkat₂ 1, logtas, okat₂ 1**) 1.1) *v. tr.* To part things or people permanently. *Buwat bay a'a maglakibini maganggop pinabalu he' Tuhan, ngga'i ka min kabaya'an manusiya'. Tuhan ya amoklang.* Like a "face-to-face" married couple whom God has caused to be widowed, not from their human wish. It is God who separates them. *Binoklang onde'-onde' min matto'ana.* A child parted from his parents.

**boklas** *n.* 1) The morning of the third day after a death. *Ya subu hinang t'llu, niōnan boklas t'llu.* The morning of Day 3 [of the mourning sequence], called *boklas* three. 1.1) *v. tr. -an* To terminate the intermediate stages of something.

**bokog** *n.* A bone; a fish bone. *Ilak ē', aheya bokogna.* The rudder fish has large bones. (*Thesaurus:* **bangkak, kowa' 1, to'olang**)

**boko'** var. of **bokko'**

**bokol** *n.* 1) The thumb. (*syn:* **nggo'an-tangan**; *wh:* **tangan 1**) 2) Big toe. (*wh:* **tape'₁**)

**boksen** *n.* The sport of boxing.

**pagboksen** *v. intr. aN-* To box each other, western style. *Buwat kami magboksen maka si Sa. Na yukna, "Mbal ka arai' maka'atu. Na tatalta ka min t'dda."* Like when I am boxing with Sa. He says, "You probably won't be able to fight back. Now I am going to hit you once." (*cf:* pagsuntuk)

**bodbod₁** *adj. a-* 1) Wrapped around with rope or line. *Abodbod he' tonda'.* Wrapped around by a long line. 1.1) *v. tr.* To wrap around something several times. (*Thesaurus:* **kokos₁ 1, koleng₁ 1.1, lengke, longon**)

**pagbodbod** *v. tr.* To wrap around something. *Da'a pagbodborun.* Don't wrap it round and round.

**bodbod₂** var. of **bāt-bodbod**

**bodde'-bodde'** *adj. a-* Plump; chubby. (*cf:* **goldo-goldo**)

**bōg** *adj. a-* Jolted or knocked and causing pain. *Abōg pa'aku, sali' abakkug.* My thigh hurts from being bumped, like *bakkug* [jolted]. (*Thesaurus:* **bakkug, bangkug 1, sikmu', siggul, singku 1**)

**pagbōg** *v. intr. aN-* To continue jolting, causing a tender area of tissue to experience a recurrence or increase of pain. *Da'a sinoho' magbōg. Da'a na maghengko-hengko.* Told not to keep jolting. Don't keep moving about.

**bogbog₁** 1) *n.* Support in a discussion or disagreement. *Matto'a ya makaga'os, ga'os bogbog.* An elder is the one with influence, the influence of support. 1.1) *v. tr. -an* To support someone in a dispute or conflict. *Bang ya magtiman si Se, na amogbog si Nu ni saga danakanna.* When it is Se who is invoved in divorcing, then Nu sides with his siblings. *Ai-ai na ahāp subay binogbogan, ai-ai na ala'at sulakta.* Whatever is good should be supported, whatever is bad we reject. (*Thesaurus:* **dapit, ga'os 1.2, gapi' 1.2, tapil 2**) 2) *v. tr. -an* To maintain one's commitment to a relationship or a religion. (*cf:* **pagagama**)

**bogbog₂** *v. tr.* To be able to do or manage something. *Mbal aku makabogbog itu.* I am not able to do this. *Sali' mbal tabogbog ai-ai binowa.* It's like being unable to carry something. (*Thesaurus:* **aguwanta 1.1, anggap 1, anggop₂, bāng-bāng₁, kole', gaga, tigayu'**)

**boggat** *v. advrs. -in-* Ill from the recurrence of a sickness. (*Thesaurus:* **banta', sangti', timbalun₁ 1**)

**bogge'** *n.* Triggerfish or filefish.

**boggo'** (var. **b'ggo'**) *n.* A small dugout canoe without outriggers.

**bogon₁** *n.* 1) A swelling in the neck; goiter. *Aniya' pabutig ma k'llongna, niōnan bogon.* There is something growing in his neck, it's called a goiter. (*Thesaurus:* **bago' 1, bongol 1, busul, talis'ssok 1**) 1.1) *v. advrs. -in-* Afflicted with goiter.

**bogon₂** see: **pagbogon**

**bogon-bogon** *v. advrs. -in-* Suffering from uncontrollable shaking, especially of the hands. *Buwat tanganta amidpid, mbal pahali, binogon-bogon kita.* Like our hands are shaking and don't stop, we suffer from *bogon-bogon*.

**bohe'₁** *n.* 1) Water; liquid; fluid. *Bowahun bō'*

*pangisihan bohe'.* Bring a bamboo container for water. *Saguhan, ya pasū bohe'ta, ya isita ahalu', amohe'.* Producing serum, our bodily fluid dripping down, our flesh rotting and turning to liquid. (*cf:* **tahik**₁ 1.1) 1.1) *v. tr.* -an To add water to something; to irrigate. 1.2) *v. intr.* aN- To liquify. *Ya isita ahalu', amohe'.* Our flesh is rotting, producing fluid. 2) A body of fresh water. *A: "Maingga si Oto'?" B: "Maī' ma bohe'."* A: "Where is Older Son?" B: "There at the water source."

**bohe'-kali** *n.* A reservoir or well for water. *Aniya' ta'nda'na bohe' kali bay tinaplokan maka batu aheya.* He saw a cistern [dug into rock] covered with a large rock. *Ina'an isāb ma luwasan lungsud bohe' kali bay nihinang he' si Yakub.* There too, outside the town, was the well that Jacob had dug.

**bohe'-kunsuy** *n.* Water boiled for reasons of hygiene. *Bohe'-kunsuy, bohe' pinasu' ati pinaringin.* *Kunsuy,* water which has been heated and then allowed to cool.

**bohe'-mata** *n.* Tears (from the eye).

**bohe'-pagpalutu'** *n.* Water sprinkled over a corpse as part of a ritual. (*syn:* **bohe'-tinangas**)

**bohe'-pansul** *n.* Water from a faucet. *Sayuman iya, aniya' bohe'-pansul mareyom luma'na.* She is so fortunate, her house has water from a faucet.

**bohe'-pangandung** *n.* A small body of water formed in a natural hollow. *Bang saupama aniya' bohe' ma būd bo' ariki', ya hē' tapangōnta pangandung, ya tapamandihan.* If for example there is water up in the hills, something small, we call that *pangandung,* water that can be used for bathing.

**bohe'-patugpa'** *n.* A waterfall.

**bohe'-sasahan** *n.* Water that is flowing; a stream.

**bohe'-tinangas** *n.* Water sprinkled over a corpse as part of the preparation for burial. (*syn:* **bohe'-pagpalutu'**)

**pagbohe'** *v. intr.* aN- To emit liquid or juice. *Abulag aku, sidda magbohe'an.* I am temporarily blinded, [my eyes] watering profusely. *Mandā'-dā' atayku, anangis aku bo' halam magbohe'an matāku.* My feelings are hurt, I cry but my eyes produce no tears. *Bang ka angehet mangga bo' agbohe'-bohe' mangga-i, kinakan maka bowa'nu sadja.* When you cut a ripe mango and the mango emits juice, it is simply eaten with your mouth.

**pagbohe'-bohe'an** *n.* A small pool such as children play in. *Tigbaw, ariki'-diki' pagbohe'-bohe'an onde'-onde'.* A freshwater pool, a small play pond for little children.

**pagbohe'an** *n.* A water source; a well. *Ya du saga pagbohe'anna, ngga'i ka ka'am ya bay angali'.* Likewise with its wells, it was not you who dug them.

**bohe'**₂ *n.* Semen; one's father (fig.) *Duwa bohe' sigā, dakayu' pangisihan.* They have two fathers [lit.

two semen] but one mother [lit. one container]. (*cf:* **pangisihan**₂)

**bohe' duru'** *n. phrase* Mother's milk. *Saddī gatas, saddī gata', saddī bohe'-duru'.* Animal milk, coconut cream, breast milk, all different.

**bohe'an** var. of **bāt-bohe'an**

**bohelo** var. of **buhelo**

**bō'** *n.* A bamboo pole with the inter-nodes removed, used for carrying water. (*cf:* **p'ttung**; *Thesaurus:* **honga'**₁, **loka'**, **saud**₁, **tumpung**)

**bo'**₁ (var. **abō'**₁) *conj.* But or yet, marking a modification of a general statement. *Pahi, bo' ngga'i ka isāb pahi.* A stingray, but not precisely a stingray. *Yuk kuyya', bo' alawak gi', yukna, "Lahat yampa ta'nda' būd."* Monkey, still far off, said, "A land whose mountains are just now visible." *At'ggol na utang bo' waktu pagtambukuhan na. Sukutnu na aku bo' halam aniya' pamayaran.* The debt is longstanding but it is the time agreed on. You dun me but there is nothing to pay with. (*Thesaurus:* **manda'**, **saguwā'**, **sa'**)

**bo'**₂ (var. **abō'**₂) *conj.* In order to; so that. *Tau'un pahogot bo' mbal alungay.* Store it securely so it doesn't get lost. *Sū'anku palita'an abō' mbal angal'ddom.* I shall light the lamp so that it is not dark. (*Thesaurus:* **bat sabab, bo' supaya, dok supaya, he da'a, supaya**)

**bo'**₃ *conj.* If; when. *Bang kaut bo' alandos goyak, alatas katig.* When going out to sea, and [when] it is very rough, the outriggers come unlashed.

**bo' na** *conj.* At the time when. *Bo' na kami maggara' atulak ni Sambuwangan.* At the time when we planned leaving for Zamboanga. *Nsa' atapus suli-suli sigā bo' na pī' nirugsu'an.* Their conversation had not finished, when he was stabbed right there. (*Thesaurus:* **abila, bang**₁, **bangsi', basta, gana, pagka, samantala', talkala'**)

**bo' arapun** *conj.* However; nevertheless. *Sali' ahunit isāb pasal aheka kami maka ahalga' sukay, bo' arapun, halam du aniya' ahunit ma Tuhan.* It's kind of expensive too because there are a lot of us and travel is expensive. However, nothing is difficult for God. *Bo' arapun nihinang e'na ma waktu sangom sabab tināw iya ma saga kampungna ya maglahat ma kauman inān.* Instead he did it at night because he was afraid of his relatives who were living in that community. *Bo' arapun ma takdil kahālan ina'ku maka saga danakanku, ahāp du isāb sigām.* However, in regard to my mother and siblings, they are fine.

**bo' mbal** *conj.* In order not to; lest. *Da'a ddol-ddolin soha' ilū bo' mbal apōng.* Don't force that mooring stake in lest it break in two. *Subay tinau' pahogot bo' mbal alungay.* It should be stored securely so it doesn't get lost. (*Thesaurus:* **ko da'a, he da'a**)

**bo' pa'in** *conj.* However; except that; even though. *Buwat kita lum'ngngan bo' pa'in kinalibubut, na* *abangkug kita.* If we go walking even though we have boils, then the movement will jolt us painfully. *"Arī," yukna, "magharap aku maka Tuhan bo' pa'in itiya' aku masi a'llum."* "Wow," he said, "I come face to face with God, yet here I am still alive!"

**bo' supaya** var. of **supaya**

**bo' yampa** *conj.* And then; thereupon. *Subay na makala'an min goyak bo' yampa pasaitan kami.* We had to get free of the rough water first, and then we bailed it. *Subay kinose'an lai' bo' yampa ka angongka'.* The dishes must be washed before you play. (*Thesaurus:* **malaingkan, minsan, ya pa'in**)

**bo'ay** (var. **lo'ay**) *v. advrs. -in-* Made ill as a result of eating poisonous parts of certain seafoods. *Bang kita amangan t'bbahan, bo' halam bay ahāp he'ta angadjal, nilo'ay kita.* If we eat strand food but our preparation has not been well done, we are nauseated and caused to vomit. (*Thesaurus:* **angol, baliyang, lango 1.1, pagboyokan, pagtunggang-kīng, uling**)

**pagbo'ay** *v. intr. aN-* To suffer persistent acute nausea and vomiting. *Magbo'ay-bo'ay, sali' kita nilango he' buntal. Magboyokan kita.* Vomiting, like we are made seriously dizzy by the pufferfish. We are nauseated.

**bo'ol** *v. advrs. ka-...-an* To be suffering muscular strain. *Kabo'olan sigā amat'ngge banog.* They are physically strained in putting up a sail. *Kabo'olan aku ananggung duwa mital bohe'.* I am strained carrying two cans of water. *Kabo'olan ma k'llongna, aniya' pasagnat kinakan.* He is strained in his throat; there is food stuck there. (*Thesaurus:* **binsana' 1, bongso' 1, bugtu'₂ 1.1, busā' 1.1**)

**bo'ot** *n.* Something given to win favor. (*Thesaurus:* **k'llo' bo'ot, mamhu'**)

**pagbo'ot** *v. tr. -an* To desire something greatly; to set one's heart on something. *Lilus ya pagbo'otanku.* A watch is what I want most of all. *Magbo'ot, sali' magtuyu', aniya' pinagbo'otan ni ka'a.* Setting one's heart on something, being determined, wanting something very much from you. (*Thesaurus:* **angut**)

**bola** *n.* A ball.

**pagbola** *v. intr. aN-* To play ball of various kinds. *Si Sa abulag, bay magbola, kapē'an gusung matana.* Sa is blinded, he was playing ball and sand got into his eyes. *Yuk matto'a, "Abila onde' ilu saga tarugtul he' magbola ilū, dusanu sabab ka'a ya bay amowa iya pareyo'."* The parent said, "If that child happens to be hit by the ball players there, it will be your fault because it was you who took him down [onto the shore]." *Bang ka binowa magbola he' kasehe'annu, subay ka alistu ma laslaen ko' mbal kahūgan bola.* When you are persuaded by your mates to play volleyball, you must be quick on the backline so you're not hit by a falling ball. (*cf:* **pagbalebol 1.1**)

**bola-bola** *n.* **1)** Muscular cramp. **1.1)** *v. advrs. -in-* Suffering muscular cramp. *Binola-bola aku, arāk pat'nde.* I had the cramp, I might have sunk.

**bolag** *adj. -an* Cowardly; lacking courage. *Bolagan isāb ka'a ilu, patāw ka.* You're cowardly too, you are a fearful person. (*Thesaurus:* **dalan 1.1, damag, gawa, g'mma, gupu, leya'-leya', tāw 1.1, umagad 1.1**)

**bola'** *n.* A narrow lath, commonly made of bamboo. (*Thesaurus:* **gipis 1, lantay 1, ligpit 1**)

**bolbo₁** *n.* A wooden stringer that caps the plywood side panel of a canoe. (*syn:* **dingding-hangin, lipi-lipi**)

**bolbo₂** *n.* A western-style speedboat. (*syn:* **ispidbut**)

**bole** *n.* A stalk of bananas. *Kilāku ahāp bolehanna. Am'lli aku dambole.* I reckon the entire stalk of bananas is good. I will buy one stalk. *Bay nda'ku bole saging inān, asidda bongkahan sagingna.* I looked at that stalk of bananas, its bananas are quite under-ripe. (*cf:* **s'kkatan**; *Thesaurus:* **botod, la'al, okol, tangkay 1, tongol**)

**bolebog** *v. tr.* To mix liquid or solid ingredients by stirring. (*cf:* **gawgaw**)

**bolelong** *v. advrs. -in-* Experiencing paralysis when waking during the night, attributed to demonic activity. (*syn:* **bangungngut**)

**bolles** *n.* Striptease.

**pagbolles** *v. intr. aN-* To be semi-naked, of adults, as in striptease dancing.

**bollo'** var. of **ballo'**

**bolobok** *see:* **pagbolobok**

**bolog** *n.* To boil starchy material until it becomes paste-like. *Bolog itū apīt to'ongan, buwat bay nihinang e' si Mām.* The bolog referred to is very sticky, like the stuff Ma'am makes. *Bang ma kami a'a Musu', ya panggi' itū binugbug, buwas ministang. Bang ma a'a Sisangat, panggi' ya binolog maka buwas ya binugbug.* With us Musu' people, cassava is used to make binugbug porridge, and rice for mistang porridge. With Sisangat people, cassava is cooked to make paste, and rice is made into binugbug. (*gen:* **b'lla 1**)

**binolog** *n.* A thick paste of flour (wheat or rice) cooked with water.

**bolpen** *n.* A ball-point pen. (*cf:* **pinsil**)

**bonok-bonok** *n.* Persistent light rain. (*cf:* **pitik-pitik 1, ulan 1.1**)

**pagbonok-bonok** *v. intr. aN-* To rain lightly and persistently; to drizzle.

**bono'** *n.* **1)** Conflict; war. *Tagna' bono' bay kami apinda pehē' ni pū'.* At the start of the war we relocated to the outer islands. *Subay sigām kapandu'an amono' sabab ya kaheka'an sigām halam bay makalabay bono' ma waktu tagna'.* They should be taught to fight because most of them have not previously experienced war.

*Buwattē' du isāb a'a patibono'un bang amarokot bono'.* A fight-prone person is also like that when he causes fighting to flare up. **1.1)** *v. tr.* To hit someone with force; to kill or disable. *Buwat onde'-onde' bang sōng binono' he' matto'ana, bo' ta'nda' aniya' pamono' iya buwat saga lantay, anangis na, angaraw-ngaraw alahi.* Like when a child about to be beaten by his parent, sees that there is something like a bamboo slat for beating him with, he cries and looks anxiously for a way to escape. (*Thesaurus:* **papatay 1**, **pinsan 1.1**)

**pagbono'** *n.* **1)** A conflict; fighting. *Entomun bay masa pagbono'ta ma Siganggang.* Remember the times of our conflict at Siganggang. *Aho', kasakupan pagbono' sigā. Bay kamahē'anku bay pagbono' sigā.* Yes, their fight was witnessed. I was present at the time of their fight. **1.1)** *v. intr.* *aN-* To be mutually engaged in conflict. *Sali' magbono' mbal magkole', magbugbug na magbono'. Mbal kasekotan, mbal tasapad, sinagaran na hal.* Like people fighting each other and neither prevailing, dying together as they fought. Cannot be approached, cannot be restrained, simply left to carry on unchecked. *Bang magbono' na, mbal kahawiran. Subay pinasagaran.* When they are already fighting they cannot be restrained. They should just be left alone. *Sinakat magbono'. Bang kita pinahimulas magbono' na.* Attacked for the purpose of fighting. When we are accused of cowardice, we fight. **1.2)** *v. tr.* *-an* To make something the reason for a fight. *Na wa'i na agtūy isāb magbono'an suru' isāb Mbo' Munari maka Mbo' Belle'.* There they were again, Grandfather Herald-bird and Grandfather Sea-Eagle, fighting over a spoon. *Ai pagbono'anbi ilū? Pasal bay magsalla'?* What was the reason for your conflict? Over a gambling game?

**pagbono'an** *n.* A battleground; a place of fighting. *Halam gi' sinapang, maglagut sadja bang ma pagbono'an.* Before there were guns, people just slashed each other when they were on a battleground.

**bobono'** *n.* A fighter; a warrior. (*Thesaurus:* **militari**, **sundalu**)

**pamomono'** *n.* A person who habitually commits murder.

**patibono'** *adj.* Addicted to violence.

**bonte** *n.* A species of mullet, deep-bellied. *fam. Mugilidae.* (*gen:* **banak**)

**bontol** *adj. a-* **1)** Correct; straight; ethical. *Bang mbal abontol subay tinilud.* If it is not straight it should be straightened. *Pagkatambahan saga huwis bay masa awal, mbal isāb bay abontol pangahukum sigā.* The judges of long ago were involved in bribery and their judging was not honest. (*cf:* **adil**, **hāp 1.1**) **1.1)** *v. intr.* *aN-* To move in a straight line. *Mbal amontolan, patalilli'*

*man bay kahūganna.* It won't go straight, it goes obliquely from where it fell.

**pagbontol** *v. intr.* *aN-* To speak straightforwardly to each other; to get to the heart of things in discussion.

**pabontol** *adv.* **1)** Correctly; moving in a straight line. **1.1)** *v. tr.* To set something straight or correct. *Bang saupama magtiman, na magsalassay pahāp-hāp, magpa'amu ni sara', saga pinabontol.* Divorcing for example, settling things well, speaking frankly to the magistrate, getting things done correctly. *Pabontolunbi itikadbi tudju ni Tuhan.* Make right your consciences towards God.

**bōng** (var. **abong**) *adj. a-* Blurred or unfocused, of one's vision. *Auling mataku, angkan abōng he'ku ang'nda'. Sali' magtunggang-kīng ai-ai ta'nda'ta.* My eyes are unfocused, that is why my seeing is blurry. As though whatever I look at is out of focus. (*cf:* **uling**)

**pagbōng** *v. intr.* *aN-* To have difficulty focusing one's eyes. *Magabong e'ku ang'nda'. Sali' duwa ta'nda'ku, auling mataku sali'.* My vision becomes unfocused, like I am seeing double, my eyes sort of dizzy.

**bongat** *v. intr.* *pa-* **1)** To be open, of mouth. *Bang kita amissala, pabongat bowa'ta.* When we speak our mouths open. (*syn:* **banga'₁**) **1.1)** *v. tr.* To open one's mouth. *Bongatun bowa'nu bang aniya' pah'llingnu, bongatun bo' tahatiku.* Open your rmouth if you have something to say, open it so I can understand.

**bongka** *adj. -an* **1)** Semi-ripe or partly cooked. *Amasi bongkahan deyom iklug.* The inside of the egg is still somewhat raw. *Bay nda'ku bole saging inān, asidda bongkahan sagingna.* I looked at that stalk of bananas, its bananas are quite under-ripe. **1.1)** *v. intr.* *aN-* To become partly healed. *Yampa amongka bakatna.* His cut is only now starting to heal.

**bongkol** var. of **b'ngkol₁**

**bonglay** *n.* **1)** Epidemic illness; plague. *Bang aniya' bonglay at'kka ni lahat, analamat kām.* If a plague comes to your place, carry out the health ritual. *Paniya' du kono' saga linug aheya maka gotom maka saki bonglay ma kaluha'an dunya.* It is said that major earthquakes and famine and epidemic illness will occur around the world. (*syn:* **musiba**) **1.1)** *adj. a-* Widespread, of a sickness. *Abonglay a'a kamemon he' saki kolera itū.* All the people are affected by this cholera.

**bongog** var. of **bengog**

**bongol** *n.* **1)** A tumor or goiter. (*Thesaurus:* **bago' 1**, **bogon₁ 1**, **busul, talis'ssok 1**) **1.1)** *v. advrs.* *-in-* Suffering from a growth in the throat. *Binongol k'llongta, atibulung ma ituta. Bang aheya abuhat, subay nioperahan.* Our throat is swollen, something ball-shaped here. When it gets big it is heavy, and needs to be surgically removed. *"Bang pa'in ka binongol-bongol!" Sali' sinukna'an.*

"May you get tumors!" Like someone being cursed.

**bongso'** *adj. a-* **1)** Suffering from internal injuries. *Bang kita ananggung ai-ai bo' araran, magkabongso' isāb.* When we carry things, and do it often, it can lead to internal injuries. *Bang aku pakuppa man diyata' luma', abongso' aku. Apisu', magdalisu', ta'ā' saki.* If I jump from the top of the house I suffer internal damage. I suffer a sprain, dislocation, which becomes a sickness. (*Thesaurus:* **binsana'** 1, **bo'ol, bugtu'₂** 1.1, **busā'** 1.1) **1.1)** *v. advrs. ka-...-an* To be suffering from internal injuries due to strain or a blow. *Kabongso'an aku magkalga.* I am ruptured from working as a porter.

**bongtas** *n.* **1)** Death by starvation. *Bongtas itū lingantu to'ongan, buta pinunung, halam bay makakakan.* *Bongtas* means seriously hungry, blind from lack of nourishment, having not eaten anything. **1.1)** *adj. a-* Starving to death. *Abongtas ilū amatay. Halam takakan, minsan dangkuri'.* Died from starvation. Nothing to eat, not even a little. (*Thesaurus:* **gustang, hanu, lingantu** 1.1, **otas, punung**)

**borak** *n.* **1)** Powder used to improve the condition of the skin or to protect it from the darkening effect of the sun. *Borak, pinaglamud buwas maka ugbus biyabas.* Cosmetic powder, rice [flour] mixed with guava leaf shoots. (*cf:* **lipa', tula-tula**; *Thesaurus:* **polbos, tabun-tabun**) **1.1)** *v. tr.* To apply powder to the face. *Sinoso'an na d'nda ina'an, binorak na.* That woman has had her hairline trimmed, and powder has been applied.

**pagbinorak** *v. intr. aN-* To be coated with cosmetic powder. *A: "Ingga tunangnu?" B: "D'nda magbinorak inān."* A: "Which is your girlfriend?" B: "The girl there wearing face powder." *Bang budjang magbinorak, nilipa' tape', tangan, kamemon sambil pa'a.* When teenage girls used cosmetic powder, the feet and hands are treated, everything including the thighs.

**boras** *n.* A durable mat of rattan strips. (*cf:* **tepo**)

**borega** *n.* A warehouse; a store-shed. *Borega ap'nno' e' lahing, atop mital isāb.* A storehouse full of copra, has a metal roof too.

**boro** *n.* **1)** Fish preserved by soaking in brine and drying in the sun. *Ya boro itu daing anahut buwat manga kasig, pinahagom ma bohe' asin bo' yampa pina'llawan.* The fish known as *boro*, anchovy for example, are immersed first in brine and then sun-dried. **1.1)** *v. tr.* To preserve small fish by soaking in brine and drying. *Buwat kasig niasinan, asin asal binohe'an. Ubus niasinan, pinatoho' ni diyata' tasikan. Ya hē' binoro.* Like pilchards salted with salt naturally moistened. After salting, they are dried on racks. That's the *boro* process. (*Thesaurus:* **gamos** 1.2, **pagtasik**)

**boro-boro₁** *adj. zero* Long-haired, of a ram-goat.

**boro-boro₂** *see:* **pagboro-boro**

**bōs** *n.* A boss; a foreman. *Kinaslahan aku he' bōsku, bay bbahanku hinangku.* My boss scolded me, I had stopped doing my work. (*Thesaurus:* **kapala, kapatas, mandul, nakura'**)

**boskag** (var. **buskag**) *v. intr. aN-* To swell to the full. *Sali' pasulig ginuna e' d'nda pinalamud ni tirigu. Pagaddun pa'in, abuskag kamemon addunan.* Like the rising agent women use and mix in with flour. Once it is kneaded the entire dough swells up. (*Thesaurus:* **b'ngkak, butud, tting**)

**boslad** *v. tr. -an* To eat greedily even though not contributing to the meal. *Pagustangun b'ttongnu ilū bo' ka amole' amoslad!* Deprive that stomach of yours of food and go home to eat greedily! *Na, amoslad na ka!* There, fill your gut! (*Thesaurus:* **bagahak₂, buhawi'₁, butu', kanam, kaway** 1.1, **dahaga', damba'₁** 1.1, **lagak** 1.1, **tanggal₁**)

**boslaran** *n.* Food eaten by someone who has not contributed, a word used in anger. *Pehē' ka am'lli boslarannu.* Go and buy your wretched food. *"Niā' na boslarannu." Sali' kinakan pinagambahan, sali' judju'.* "Get your darned food." It's like food promised excessively, like over-giving. (*Thesaurus:* **dahalan, tanggalan**)

**bōt₁** *n.* **1)** The endosperm (sprout) of a coconut. (*syn:* **tabul₂**; *wh:* **niyug**) **1.1)** *v. intr. aN-* To form an endosperm, as a mature coconut. *Angamōt, amangtusan.* Forming the endosperm, sprouting.

**bōt₂** *v. advrs. -in-* Suffering a prolapse of the uterus.

**botang₁** **1)** *n.* A heap or pile of small objects. (*Thesaurus:* **ba'an₁, kapono'an, puntak** 1) **2)** *clf.* Count word for piles of small items. *Pila sīn dambotang kamatis ilū?* How much is one pile of those tomatoes?

**ma botangan** *adv. phrase* By the pile.

**botang₂** *v. tr.* To appoint an official or leader at the community level. (*cf:* **g'llal** 1.1)

**botang-lahat** (var. **bobotang-lahat**) *n.* **1)** An appointed official. *Buwat magbalebol, magsugal saga, na pinamarahan kami e' botang-lahat, sinō' kami da'a.* Like playing volleyball or cards, made to stop by the local official, told not to do it. (*Thesaurus:* **maharadja, panghulu'** 1, **panglima**) **1.1)** *v. tr.* To appoint someone to local leadership.

**botang-matto'a** *n.* **1)** A person appointed or recognized as a senior community leader. *Panghulu'ta, sali' tuhanta, buwat botang-matto'a.* Our senior leader, like a god to us, like an official elder-leader. **1.1)** *v. tr.* To appoint or install a local official. *Botang-matto'a buwat si Anu inān binotang-matto'a ma lahat.* A recognized village leader like What's-his-name, appointed to be leader for the district. *Beya' iya ma saga binotang-matto'a ma paglahat.* He was included with those appointed to leadership in the district.

**botlang** var. of **boklang**

**botod** *n.* The semi-rigid main stalk of palm-like plants. (*wh:* **pandan**; *Thesaurus:* **bole, la'al, okol, tangkay 1, tongol**)

**botod-pandan** *n.* The woody central stem of a pandanus plant, used medicinally.

**boto'₁** *n.* A projection used as a handle. *Ndiya kaldero boto'an ilū.* Give me that pot with the handle.

**boto'₂** *n.* The penis.

**boto'-boto'₁** *n.* A waterspout; a whirlwind over water. *Boto'-boto' itū baliyu.* This kind of *boto'-boto'* is a wind. (*Thesaurus:* **alimpunus, buhawi'₂ 1, kawas-kawas**)

**boto'-boto'-goyak** *n.* Sudden waterspouts and surges. *"Alōy!" yuk-i, "Pak'tta kām ni dilaut minsan du boto'-boto'-goyak."* "What!" he said, "Are you heading out to sea even though there are water-spouts?"

**boto'-boto'₂** var. of **tayum-boto'-boto'**

**boto'-boto' mata** *n. phrase* Inflammation of the eyelid; a stye. *Si Je taga boto'-boto' matana.* Je has a stye on his eye.

**boto'-goyak** *n.* 1) A species of mollusk, notable for its chalky shell. 2) Red slate pencil sea urchin. *Heterocentrotus mamillatus.* (*Thesaurus:* **indangan₂, oko'-oko', s'llang₂, tayum, tehe'-tehe'**)

**botong** *n.* The mature unripe fruit of the coconut palm. (*Stages:* **kambung-kambung, botong-botong, bilu'uk, botong, gangkul, lahing, pangtusan**)

**motong** *v. intr. aN-* To mature beyond the bilu'uk stage, of a coconut.

**botong-botong** *n.* The immature fruit of the coconut palm, between setting fruit and the new nut stages. *Botong-botong itū yampa anagna', mbal gi' bilu'uk. Botong-botong* has just begun, not yet at the *bilu'uk* stage. (*Stages:* **kambung-kambung, botong-botong, bilu'uk, botong, gangkul, lahing, pangtusan**)

**bowa₁** *v. ditr.* To convey something from one place to another. *Bowahun na ya s'mmek ilū pasōd.* Bring those clothes there inside. *Mbal makabowahan aku matto'aku bang iya bay pi'ingga-pi'ingga.* My father is unable to bring me anything when he has been to some place or other. *Ai-ai aloka. Manjari ma laring, manjari ma engkot, tabowa kamemon.* Anything loose. Can use it for a knife, or for a tie, it can all be brought. *Tabowa iya palamud ma sigām magbissala kaligawan.* He was brought along with those who were speaking words that made no sense.

**kabowahan** *n.* Portable posessions.

**pagbobowa** *v. intr. aN-* To be a carrier of information; a messenger. *Manjari pehē' saga magbobowa lapal ni kauman palahatan si Sa.* So messengers went to the village where Sa was living. *Aniya' magbobowa habal pina'an ni sultan angahaka'an iya.* A messenger went there to the king to inform him. *Apalo' du pa'in ka magbobowa lapal ni kala'atan.* You are especially reluctant to convey bad news.

**pagbowa** 1) *v. intr. aN-* To transport or carry something. 2) *v. tr.* To convey something as a matter of routine. *Aheka parangkang ma Silibis agbowa lahing.* There are many Buginese vessels in the Celebes transporting copra. *Lima batu-batu alanu', pinat'nna' e'na ni deyom puyu'-puyu' ya asal pinagbowa e'na ma waktu kapangipatna saga bili-bili.* Five smooth pebbles placed inside the little bag he always carried when he was caring for sheep. *Halam aku bay magbowa pakokos pagka asa'ut panoho'an sultan.* I wasn't carrying weapons because the sultan's orders were urgent.

**pagbowa-bowa** *v. tr.* To carry several things at one time. *Bay iya ni tabu', aheka na pinagbowa-bowa.* She has been to the market and is bringing lots of things.

**pagbowahan** (var. **pamowahan**) *n.* A person known for healing powers, whose house may be a place to stay for treatment. *Bang matto'a ya kasangonan inān subay du isāb pagkahina matto'a anitta, a'a pagbowahan.* If it is an elder who is possessed it should be a fellow elder who calls [on the spirits], a person who is a healer. *Bang aniya' asaki, si Mbo' Di pagbowahan he' a'a kamemon. Pahali du he'na.* If people are sick it is to Grandfather Di that everyone brings them. They become well through him. *Alibu na pagbowahan, na halam kauli'an, pinelleng ni ka'a.* All the healers have been sought out, and [he] is not healed, so he is being returned to you. *A'a pamowahan ya a'a pasangon.* The healer is the person involved in spirit possession. *Aniya' bay asaki, atale'ed na pamowahan.* Someone was sick, taken to healers in diverse places. (*Thesaurus:* **doktol, pananambal**)

**pagpakabowa** *v. tr.* To be able to bring the specified item.

**tagbowahan** *n.* A person with formal responsibilities for the wearing or carrying of something.

**bowa₂** *v. intr. aN-* To function as it is intended to. *Mbal amowa paggombahan itu.* This pump here is not working properly.

**magbobowa** *n.* The person in charge of an event.

**bowa₃** *v. tr.* To influence or coerce someone. *Bilahi kami amowa ka'a mag'nda'.* We want to have you meet [with us] face to face. *Subay na salung tabowa kita am'ssi, llaw-llaw Hambilan.* Tomorrow we'll be obliged to go fishing, it's a Hambilan market day. *Anak, da'a ka magpabowa ma a'a jahulaka'.* Child, don't let wicked people persuade you. *Bilahi kami amowa ka'am mag'nda'.* We want to have you meet [with us] face to face. *Tabowa iya palamud ma sigām magbissala kaligawan.* He was persuaded to join with them in speaking nonsense. (*cf:* **logos 1**; *Thesaurus:* **bidjak 1.1, kuti-kuti, pilad, pitna**)

**bowa-bowa** *adj. a-* Easily tempted. *"Ka'a na," yukna, "makabowa-bowa."* "You are the one," he said, "who tempts me" (*cf:* **talik-talik**)

**kabowa** *conj.* By reason of; because of.

**pagpabowa** *v. intr. aN-* To let oneself be influenced.

**bowa₄** *v. intr. aN-* To show one's nature through one's actions. *Amowa bahanina.* He behaves with foolish courage [lit. carries his foolhardiness]. *Oy! Ka'a ilu amowa aikalas, sali' amiha kamataynu.* Hey! You're showing foolhardy courage, as though seeking your death.

**bowa b'ttik** *v. tr.* To behave in bizarre and unacceptable ways. {idiom}

**bowahan** *n.* Typical behavior or manner, of person or thing. *Bowa-bowahanna, ai na ka manusiya', ai na ka panyap. Bowahan ai-ai ma ginisan ongka'.* Its way of behaving, whether of human beings or equipment. Any sort of tune in various amusements. (*Thesaurus:* **baktulan, l'ngnganan₂, pakang₁, palantara 1, tebong**)

**bowa mo'ot** *v. tr.* To bring a gift that will win favor. (*syn:* **k'llo' bo'ot**)

**bowa'₁** *n.* **1)** The mouth as a body part. *Temposanku bowa'nu.* I'll cut your mouth off [a threat]. **2)** The mouth as the organ of speech. *Alabas ah'lling: saupama magbono'. Min sangpū' aku ah'lling, min duwa iya ah'lling, bowa'ku ya kalabasan.* Forceful in speaking: arguing, for example. I spoke ten times, he spoke twice, it was my speech that was dominated. *"Ya na ko' ilū kaladja'anbi. Halam bay asaki, magtūy taluwa' saki. Ai bang ngga'i ka man bowa'bi, man hinangbi?"* "That's typical of you. She wasn't sick and now, suddenly, she is hit with a sickness. Where is that from, other than your speech or your action?" *Halam bay asaki, magtūy taluwa' saki. Ai bang ngga'i ka man bowa'bi, man hinangbi?"* You weren't sick and suddenly you are hit with a sickness. Where is that from, if not from your speech or your behavior?"

**bowa'-bakakka** *n.* Woman who uses lipstick (lit. kingfisher mouth). {idiom}

**bowa'-bowa'** *adj. a-* Talkative; garrulous.

**bowa'-tai'** *n.* Look of displeasure or disgust. {idiom}

**ma bowa'an** *adv. phrase* By the length from the mouth to the tip of one arm.

**pabowa'** *v. intr. aN-* To raise one's voice.

**bowa'₂** *n.* An opening that permits entry, as the mouth of a river or barrier reef.

**bowa'-angan** *n.* The seaward edge of a reef. *Luma' kami bay ma bowa'-angan.* Our house was by the edge of the reef.

**bowa'-goyak** *n.* The crest of a wave about to break. *Bowa' goyak angahisi' sadja, apote'.* The crest of the wave is gleaming white. (*cf:* **mata-goyak**)

**bowa'-lawang** *n.* A doorway.

**boyok** *see:* **pagboyokan**

**brās** *n.* A paintbrush.

**brussa** *var. of* **brutsa**

**brutsa** (*var.* **brussa**) *n.* A small brush.

**bū** *n.* **1)** The hair of animals; body hair of humans; spines of sea urchins. *Bang ka saupama magkawin maka kakinu, mbal a'llum būnu.* For example, if you marry your cousin, your hair will not flourish. *Kohek-kohekin tehe'-tehe' ilū mareyom basket, supaya ala'an būna.* Shake those sea urchins in the basket, so the spines come away. (*Thesaurus:* **bahibū 1, bu'un 1, bulbul 1**) **1.1)** *v. advrs. -in-* Covered with stiff hair or spines.

**bū-kangag** *n.* The green color of a parrot. (*gen:* **walna'**)

**bū-langal** *n.* A beard; whiskers. *Angamu' aku basi' paghimangotku bū-langalku.* I'm asking for a bit of metal for plucking out my whiskers. *Nirarut bū-langal si Le.* Le's whiskers have been tugged at. (*Thesaurus:* **mantis, misay 1, p'ngngot 1**)

**bū-mata** *n.* An eyelash. (*cf:* **kilay**; *syn:* **pelok**)

**bubu₁** *n.* A large, woven, box-shaped fish trap. *Bang aku angahūg bubu binahan ni Serom, palebod ma batu bahanna, mbal pala'an.* When I drop a vine-linked fish trap at Serom Island, its vine coils round the rocks and won't come away. (*cf:* **dakan 1**; *Thesaurus:* **bagiyas 1, kiming, panggal 1, togong 1**)

**pagbubu** *v. tr.* To be engaged in catching fish with a bubu-type trap.

**bubu₂** *n.* The constellation of Orion. (*cf:* **batik**; *gen:* **bitu'un**)

**bubu kapang** *n. phrase* A woven fish trap with an open base.

**bubuk₁** *n.* A species of fish.

**bubuk₂** *n.* A dip of chili pepper and salt with a base of grated coconut. (*Thesaurus:* **kilaw 1, lawal 1.1, pan'nno'an, tinu'anan**)

**bubuhan** *n.* A species of fish. *Bang aku am'ssi parilaut angahūg aku p'ssi bo' umpananku bo' ta'ā'ku daing bubuhan.* When I fish out at sea I drop baited hooks so I can catch *bubuhan* fish.

**bubuhatan** (derivative of **buhat₃**) *n.* Refreshments served at a feast.

**bubu'** *v. tr. -an* To pour water on, as to extinguish a fire. *Binubu'an api, sali' tinumpahan.* The fire is extinguished, like [water] poured on. (*Thesaurus:* **busug 1.1**)

**bubul** *v. tr. -an* To repair a hole; to fill a gap. *Binubulan, bang hibarat tupak, tinupakan, sali' pinuna'an.* A gap repaired, comparable to *tupak*, something patched, like filling the gaps. (*Thesaurus:* **puna', s'llap₁**)

**bubulangun** (derivative of **bulang**) *n.* A fighting cock. *Manuk sigun, bubulangun.* A *sigun* chicken, a cock-fighting bird.

**bubungan** *n.* A covering along the ridge of a roof. *Luma' si Ke atop. Bang taluwa' baliyu, amaspas bubungan sigām.* The roof of Ke's house is palm leaf thatch. Their ridging flaps when the wind hits it. (*cf:* **buhungan, kura'-kura'**₂)

**bubut** *v. tr.* To extract something by pulling. *Bubutun soha' ilū.* Pull out that mooring stake. (*Thesaurus:* **bugnus**₂, **darut 1.1, hublut 1, tugnus**₁ **1**)

**būk**₁ *adj. a-* **1)** Bent to shape. *Basta abūk pareyom, da'a k'mmogun p'ssi. Basta ai-ai paggi'ikannu alunuk.* Whenever a fishhook is bent inwards, don't squeeze it closer. [This applies to] anything soft that you tread on. (*Thesaurus:* **b'ngnga' 1, kulluk 1**) **1.1)** *v. tr.* To bend something to a desired shape.

**būk**₂ *n.* A book in a general sense, as distinct from religious writings. (*Thesaurus:* **nōtbūk**)

**buka** *v. intr. aN-* To break the fast during the month of Ramadan, especially of the first meal after sunset. (*cf:* **pagsahul**)

**bukakkal** *n.* The dome of a skull. *Daing bang taluwa' bukakkal kōkna amatay.* When the top of a fish's skull is struck it dies. (*Thesaurus:* **kulakob, peya'-peya' kōk**)

**bukag** *adj. a-* Loud; noisy; raised, of voice. *Bang bay tabayanku pelangnu am'ssi, bo' halam aku bay ama'id min ka'a, abukag ka ni aku.* When I used your canoe for fishing, and I hadn't asked permission from, you raised your voice at me. (*Thesaurus:* **hibuk, hidjul, sagaw**)

**pabukag** *v. tr. -an* To berate someone loudly. (*Thesaurus:* **dugal 1.1, pah'lling**₂, **pamūng-mūng, pugpug 1, s'ndal 1, tutul**)

**buka'**₁ *n.* **1)** Lashing techniques for binding wood. *Aniya' buka' sappit, buka' sinag, buka' pinate.* There is the 3-cord lashing, the sennit lashing, the anti-split lashing. **1.1)** *v. tr. -an* To bind wood to prevent splitting. *Subay binuka'an puhanna ko da'a aseplat.* The handle should be bound so it doesn't split. (*Thesaurus:* **baggot, pinate 1, sappit**₁ **1, sihag**₁ **1.1**)

**buka'**₂ *n.* A ball of woven rattan strips, used in the game of sipa'. (*cf:* **pagsipa' 1**)

**buka'**₃ *v. tr.* To display a playing card; to open a letter. *Buka'un sugalnu ilū bang pila ka.* Show your hand and see how much you have. *Yampa aku makabuka' imelku.* I've just opened my e-mail. (*cf:* **s'ngngat**₁; *Thesaurus:* **banga'**₁, **lungkad 1, sungkab, ukab 1.1**)

**buka'an** *n.* An opening which reveals contents. *Ya buka'anna itū atibulung.* Its opening was circular.

**buka'-llaw** *n.* Daybreak.

**pagbuka' llaw** *v. intr. aN-* To be breaking, of a new day. *Ta'abut e' sigām Bunggaw pagbuka' llaw.* They reached Bonggaw as day was breaking. *Jari magpamaklay sigām min kohap sampay ni kasubuhan ati ta'abut lahat ē' pagbuka' llaw.* So they hiked from afternoon to morning and reached that place at daybreak.

**buka'-puhu'** *v. intr. aN-* To stir in the womb. (*Thesaurus:* **b'ttong**₂ **1, himati', iram**)

**bukal** *v. intr. aN-* To bubble up, as boiling liquid. *Nda'un bohe', kalu amukal na.* Look at the water, it may be boiling already. (*Thesaurus:* **buwal**₁, **laga'**₁ **1.1, lere', ogok-ogok**)

**bukalkal** *v. intr. aN-* To bubble up as though boiling. *Magbuwal, sali' amukalkal.* Bubbling up, like it's boiling.

**pabukal** *v. tr.* To heat a liquid until it bubbles.

**bukān** *n.* Tuskfish, a species of wrasse. *fam. Labridae.*

**bukaskas** *v. intr. pa-* To throw a covering off without folding it. *Da'a pabukaskas min patulihannu, momosun pahāp.* Don't get up hurriedly from your bed, arrange it properly. *Ya niōnan pabukaskas hē', ya mbal tapahāpta bay patulihanta hē'.* What's called *pabukaskas* is when we haven't straightened up where we slept. (*syn:* **kuyaskas**)

**bukay** *n.* The Crested cockatoo. *Cacatua sp. Bukay, manuk-manuk ya taga punjung buli' kōkna. Bukay,* the bird that has a tuft on the back of its head. (*gen:* **agap**₁)

**bukay-bukay** *n.* Peacock and Keel-headed wrasses. *Iniistius pavo. Bang ta'ā' daing bukay-bukay, bowaku ni tabu' panambi' saging.* When a wrasse is caught I take it to the market to trade for bananas.

**bukayu'** *n.* **1)** A candy of grated coconut and sugar. *Bukayu' itū botong bay sinokalan. Bukayu'* is young coconut that has had sugar added to it. (*Thesaurus:* **halluwa 1, hinti' 1, hinuwal 1**) **1.1)** *v. tr.* To make a candy of grated young coconut. *Jangatun botong ilū binukayu'.* Grate that young coconut to be made into *bukayu'.*

**bukbuk** *n.* **1)** The fine droppings of various wood-boring insects. *Tabiya', la'ananta bukbuk min matanu ilū.* Excuse me, I'll remove that speck in your eye. (*Thesaurus:* **anay, boke', lutus**) **1.1)** *v. advrs. -in-* Infested with wood-boring insects.

**bukis**₁ *v. intr. aN-* To show light just before daybreak. *Hal amukis sobangan.* The eastern sky is only just showing light. (*Thesaurus:* **abay-subu, dai'-llaw, pagmanis-manis sobangan, pote' sobangan, subu**₂ **1**)

**pagbukis-bukis** *v. intr. aN-* To be breaking, of the first light of day. *Magbukis-bukis sobangan, bang ma kasehe'an magmanis-manis sobangan. Yampa akeyat sobangan inān.* The east becoming light, for others it is the east becoming beautiful. The east just showing light.

**bukis**₂ *adj. a-* Clearly seen, of something previously hidden. *Tu'ud abukis min ka'a apa halam aniya' saddi. Angkan aniya' bissala.* It has clearly come from you since there was no one else. That's why there is talk.

**pabukis** *v. tr.* To reveal something previously concealed.

**buklas**₁ *v. tr. -an* To symbolically slash a person's palm lines in order to modify his or her fate.

*Binuklasan kulista.* Our fate [lit. our palm lines] is ritually slashed. (*cf:* **kulis**)

**buklas**₂ *adj. a-* 1) Come undone, of a knot or lashing. (*syn:* **puklas** 1) 1.1) *v. tr. -an* To undo a lashing.

**buku**₁ *n.* 1) A knot at the end of a cord or line. (*cf:* **engkot** 1, **p'kkos tuwa**) 1.1) *v. tr. -an* To tie something with a knot; to stop a rope with a knot. *Bukuhin bo' mbal ap'kkal.* Knot it so it doesn't unravel.

**buku**₂ *n.* A node in plants such as bamboo or cane. *Atilud dalos, halam aniya' bukuna.* Straight right through, no nodes.

**buku**₃ *n.* An amulet worn around the waist. (*gen:* **tambang**₃ 1)

**buku-buku**₁ *n.* Ankle or wrist bones. (*cf:* **buku-tangan, buku-tape'**; *syn:* **bunga-bunga**)

**buku-buku**₂ *n.* A helix-shaped monovalve (unclassified), edible.

**buku-tangan** *n.* Wrist bones. (*cf:* **buku-buku**₁, **buku-tape'**)

**buku-tape'** *n.* Ankle bones. *Paluhanu labayanku bo' supaya mbal patabid buku tape'ku.* You widened my path so that my ankles would not be twisted. (*cf:* **buku-buku**₁, **buku-tangan**)

**bukut**₁ *n.* The back or obverse part, as the back of person or animal, the back of a hand, the upper surface of foot, the far side of a building or geographical feature. *Hē' ma bukut tinda.* There behind the store. *Ababa' ka ni bukutku.* Ride on my back. *Al'bbo bukut danaw.* The rear of the pond is boggy. (*Thesaurus:* **dambila'** 2, **liyu**₂ 1)

**bukut-siku** *n.* The point of the elbow.

**bukutan** *n.* 1) The space behind a person or building. *O'ō, ina'an sasapu ma bukutannu.* Look, there's the broom behind you. 2) Upper part or back of a woven fish-trap. *Subay sali'-sali' tilasna bang dakan atawa bukutan.* The bamboo strips should equal in width for the base or the back.

**pasibukut** *v. tr.* 1) To disregard a warning; to reject advice. (*Thesaurus:* **pagin'mbal** 1, **pagmari'**, **sulak**₂, **taikut** 1.1) 2) To break off a relationship.

**bukut**₂ *n.* The period immediately after a person's departure. *Bay tauwa' sakki ma bukutbi.* She was struck by illness when you had gone. (*cf:* **absen, likut** 1)

**būd** *n.* 1) A mountain; hill. *"Alawak gi'," yukna, "lahat, yampa ta'nda' būd. Piligdu na."* "Still a long way off," he said, "is the land whose mountains are only just seen. Dangerous." (*Thesaurus:* **baha-būd, bīd, lorosan, tukaran**) 1.1) *v. intr. pa-* To form a pile or a hillock. *Ahangka', sali' ap'nno' pabūd.* Spilling over, full and piled up. *Pabūd bo' isāb pal'bbak.* Forming a hill and then forming a valley. (*Thesaurus:* **kuta'**₂, **g'bbus** 1, **hunsuk, hungku'**, **pagbullud**)

**kabūd-būran** *n.* Hilly area; a mountain range.

**budbud** *adj. zero* 1) Finely ground, of substances such as tea, sugar or salt. *Tī budbud, asin budbud, sokal budbud.* Powdered tea, fine salt, caster sugar. (*cf:* **tigtig** 1) 1.1) *v. tr. -an* To sprinkle something with powder.

**buddi** *n.* 1) A remembered act of kindness, and the responsibility to reciprocate it. *Aheya buddi kami ma ka'a, Tuwan sultan.* O Sultan, our sense of gratitude to you is great. *Ya buddi itū ahāp kasuddahanna. Buddi* here [means] his nature is good. 1.1) *adj. a-* Kind; respectful; aware of responsibility to repay in kind. *Abuddi, sidda pamumuwan, sidda pangangaddat.* Kindly, very generous, very respectful.

**pagbuddi** *v. intr. aN-* To express in practical ways one's sense of obligation and love. *Magbuddi maka kasilasaku ma pang'mpunu.* I will repay kindness and show love to your grandchildren.

**budjak** (var. **ludjak**) *n.* 1) A spear used as a weapon. *Na bang aniya' ala'at, hiyakku maka budjak.* Now if there are bad people, I spear them with a spear. (*cf:* **sahapang** 1) 1.1) *v. tr.* To impale someone with a spear. (*Thesaurus:* **kudjut, dukduk, dugsu', punyal** 1.1)

**budjal-budjal** *adj. zero* Crumbly. (*Thesaurus:* **gokal, lomo** 1, **p'kkal** 1, **podjak** 1, **sughay**)

**budjang** *n.* A single girl of marriageable age; a maiden. *Nda'unbi, palabay na saga budjang.* Look, girls are going by. *Suli-suli mbal ahāp ya yuk-i, "Ngga'i ka na budjang ya d'nda bay tapah'ndaku itū."* Talk that was not good, which said, "This woman that I took as wife was not a virgin." (*Thesaurus:* **daga-raga, subul**)

**budjang-budjang** *n.* A girl in her early teens. *Bang aku mareyom iskul sidda aku angistrōk ma klasmetku budjang-budjang.* When I am in school I am smitten by my classmate, a young teen girl.

**Budjang Bo'an** *n. phrase* The name of an important spirit of the Siasi Lagoon area.

**Budjang Da'u** *n. phrase* The name of an important guardian spirit of the Siasi Lagoon area.

**budjaw** *v. tr.* To make chickens or flies go away. (*Thesaurus:* **dūy, siga'** 1.1, **singga'-singga', sū**₁ 1.1, **t'ggal**)

**budjul**₁ *n.* A firm lump or knob under the skin.

**budjul**₂ *n.* The central raised boss of a gong. *Bang tinitik budjul kulintangan magpangigal saga a'a.* When the boss of the gong is struck the people dance.

**bugahak** var. of **bagahak**₁

**bugbug**₁ *adj. a-* Drenched; totally wet. *Abugbug tepo, sali' abase' kamemon.* The mat is soaked, like it is all wet. *Abugbug pahāp onde' ilū he' mange'.* That child is absolutely soaked with urine. (*Thesaurus:* **base'**₁, **bugga'** 1, **gamos** 1, **himāy, tomog**)

**bugbug**₂ *v. tr.* To make a porridge by crumbling starch food into boiling water. *Bo' kita am'gga' bohe'na tahinang hali, binugbug, tinompe'.* So we squeeze out its liquid forming a starchy residue to be made into porridge and cooked in a pan. (*gen:* **b'lla** 1)

**binugbug** *n.* Porridge made by boiling starch meal, usually cassava.

**bugbug₃** *see:* **pagbugbug**

**bugga'** *adj. a-* 1) Drenched; totally wet. (*Thesaurus:* **base'₁, bugbug₁, gamos 1, himāy, tomog**) 1.1) *v. intr. aN-* To become wet. *Amugga' tepo itū, bay kamange'an.* This mat is soaked, it has been urinated on.

> **pagbugga'-bugga'** *v. intr. aN-* To form lumps (of dampened cassava meal).

**buggul** *n.* 1) A bulbous projection or protrusion, as the hump of a camel, the bow of a ship, the back of someone with a spinal deformity. *Pajungal buggul kappal.* The bulbous bow of a ship projects forward. 1.1) *adj. a-* Hump-backed. *Abuggul si Anu ma pagkalgahan.* What's-his-name is hump-backed from the carrying of loads. (*Thesaurus:* **kuba₂, dukkug 1**)

**bugis** (var. **ugis**) *n.* An albino; someone suffering from depigmentation of the skin.

**bugnus₁** *v. intr. pa-* To straighten up from a sitting position. *Bay kita pakuru'. "Pabugnus na ka," yukna. Atawa bay kita aningkō', "Pabugnus ka an'ngge."* Our heads were bowed. "Straighten up," he said. Or we were sitting [and he said] "Straighten up and stand."

**bugnus₂** *v. tr.* To jerk out something growing or driven into the ground. *Binugnus ai-ai bay niosolan.* Anything pulled up that has been driven into the ground. (*Thesaurus:* **bubut, darut 1.1, hublut 1, tugnus₁ 1**)

**bugnus₃** *n.* A call to an octopus, telling it to come out of hiding. *Buwat kuhita', yukta, "Bugnus, bugnus, bugnus."* An octopus for example, we say, "Come out, come out, come out."

**bugsak** *v. tr. -an* To throw a circular net. *Subay aniya' tamban bo' binugsakan laya.* There must be herrings for a circular net to be thrown. (*cf:* **laya 1.1**)

**bugtang** *adj. a-* Dead instantly as a result of a blow. *Sali' bang bay taluwa' timbak, dangan i' abugtang, dangan i' ahalol.* Like [two] hit by gunfire, one killed instantly, the other wounded. *Kagong bugtang, ya sala mbal takakan.* Dead crabs, the ones not to be eaten. *Abugtang, amatay pakkom. Makajari isāb daing niōnan bugtang bo' alahang. Buwat du hantak bang daing.* Struck a blow, dying face down. It's possible also for fish to be described as *bugtang*, but it is unusual. With fish [the word] is more likely to be *hantak* [stunned by dynamiting]. (*Thesaurus:* **bugtu' napas, butawan 1.1, halol, matay₁ 1, sagpe' 2, tubag**)

**bugtu'₁** *adj. a-* Separated conclusively. (*Thesaurus:* **boklang 1, butas 1, l'kkat₂ 1, logtas, okat₂ 1**)

> **bugtu' napas** *v. intr. a-* To have stopped breathing. {idiom} *Abugtu' napasna.* He has just died. (*Thesaurus:* **bugtang, butawan 1.1, halol, matay₁ 1, sagpe' 2, tubag**)

**bugtu'₂** *v. tr.* 1) To break something apart. 1.1) *v.*

*advrs. ka-...-an* To be damaged internally as a result of overtaxing one's physical ability. *Kabugtu'an sigā amat'ngge banog.* They ruptured themselves putting the sail up. (*Thesaurus:* **binsana' 1, bo'ol, bongso' 1, busā' 1.1**)

**buhanyag** *v. intr. pa-* To spread widely, of news or information. (*Thesaurus:* **bantug 1, bawag, busling, hayag, hula-layag 1, tanyag 1**)

**buhat₁** 1) *n.* The weight of something. *A: "Pila buhatna?" B: "Mbal kata'uhanku, subay tinimbang."* A: "What is its weight?" B: "I don't know, it will have to be weighed." 1.1) *adj. a-* Heavy (of weight). *Abuhat to'ongan mital bohe' bang ap'nno'. Mbal na tapareyo'.* A can of water is heavy when it is full. It can't be lowered. (*ant:* **lampung₁ 1**) 1.2) *v. tr.* To lift something heavy. *Aku itū lum'ngngan kaut amowa karut. Yuk sehe'ku inān, "Buhatin aku gi'." Yukku inān, "Pikibuhat ni a'a dangan inān, itiya' na aku amowa."* I'm walking seawards carrying a sack. My companion there says, "Please lift mine up for me." I say, "Ask that other fellow to lift it, I'm already carrying something." *Niusung, buwat pangantin d'nda binuhat.* Carried in a sitting position, the way a bride is lifted up. (*Thesaurus:* **angkat₁ 1.1, bayaw, tangon 1.1**) 1.3) *v. advrs. ka-...-an* To be overloaded; weighed down. *Anambatan iya. "Arōy," yukna, "kabuhatan aku sidda."* He voices [a complaint]. "Good grief!" he says, "I am seriously over-burdened." 2) *adj. -an* Burdened or uneasy about some enterprise. *Buhatan aku pal'ngngan. Hatina, da'a ka pal'ngngan, aniya' nahas.* I don't feel easy about going. In other words, don't go, there is something ominous.

**buhat-puhu'** *n.* The stage of pregnancy when a woman feels heavy. *Atibulung na kandangku jari buhat-puhu' na aku.* My womb is spherical now and so I'm feeling heavy.

**pabuhat** *v. tr.* To increase the weight of something.

**buhat₂** *v. intr. pa-* To get up from sitting or lying position. *Ahatul itū, mbal ah'lling-lling. Bang sinoho', magtūy du pabuhat man paningkō'an.* Being well-behaved, doesn't make a fuss. When told to do something he gets up immediately from his seat. (*Thesaurus:* **bangkat₂, buladjang, punduk 1**)

**buhat₃** *v. tr. -an* To serve refreshments to guests. (*Thesaurus:* **labot, latal 1.1**)

**bubuhatan** *n.* Refreshments served at a feast.

**magbubuhat** *n.* A person who waits on guests; a waiter.

**buhaw** *adj. a-* Filled with water, though not capsizing or sinking, of a boat. *Basta bay na abuhaw, alogdang na iya.* When it has filled with water, then it sinks. *Kallusin na, abuhaw. Saddī asait, hal ango'ot.* Dash out the water, it [the canoe] is taking water. Bailing is different, it is just dipping it up. *Bang aheya pelangta mbal* *abuhaw minsan agoyak.* If our canoe is large it won't take on water even if [the sea] is rough. (*Thesaurus:* **logdang₂, t'nde 1, t'nnob 1**)

**buhawi'₁** *v. advrs. -in-* Greedy; gluttonous. *Binuhawi', sali' lagak, pila-pila heka kinakan, akatis na pa'in. Buhawi'* is like being greedy, no matter how much food there is, it is always finished off. (*Thesaurus:* **bagahak₂, boslad, butu', kanam, kaway 1.1, dahaga', damba'₁ 1.1, lagak 1.1, tanggal₁**)

**buhawi'₂** *n.* **1)** A sudden swirling movement of wind or water. *Buhawi', kawas-kawas ya ameya' ma kōk baliyu.* Whirlwind, the gusty wind that comes with the onset of a seasonal wind. *Bang s'llog alandos makalandu', yukta, "S'llog ai itū?" Yukta, "Buhawi'."* When there is an exceedingly strong current we say, "What current is this?" And we say, "It's a whirlpool." (*Thesaurus:* **alimpunus, boto'-boto'₁, kawas-kawas**) **1.1)** *v. advrs. -in-* Affected by an unexpected swirl or squall of wind. *Buwat haus, pelang magbulibud, binuhawi'.* Like conflicting currents, the canoe turning end for end, tossed by a whirlpool.

**buhelo** (var. **bohelo**) *n.* **1)** Saliva. *Sali' magtagok buhelona, sali' angaludja'.* Like when his saliva thickens, like when he is spitting it up. *Ya bohelota am'ttak. Ya ludja'ta inān apīt bo' nihinang bohelo.* Our spittle dripping down. Our saliva getting thick and becoming spittle. (*cf:* **pila';** *Thesaurus:* **helo₂, laway₁ 1, ludja' 1, pagtagak**) **1.1)** *v. intr. aN-* To salivate or dribble; to water, of the inside of the mouth at the sight of food or during toothache.

   **pagbuhelo** *v. intr. aN-* To drool continually; to dribble, as a child when teething. *A'a to'a bang mbal magmama', magbuhelo.* If old people don't chew betel, they dribble a bit.

**buhuk** *adj. a-* Smelling of decay. *Bau buhuk, bau angsod na. Aniya' daing ma mohang ilū.* The smell of rot, something decaying. There are fish there in the bilge. (*Thesaurus:* **baguy, balos₂, buntu'₁ 1.1, halu' 1.1, langag, p'ngkak**)

**buhul₁** *v. tr.* To make a vow to someone, human or supernatural. *Binuhul lling jīn inān.* The promise spoken by that djinn spirit was kept. *Bay aku makabuhul ma iya.* I made a commitment to him.

**buhul₂** *v. tr.* To postpone; defer. *Binuhul sali' tinanggu-tangguhan. Buhul* is like deferring something. (*Thesaurus:* **lehod 1, pagmahuli-llaw, tanggu 1**)

   **pagbuhul** *v. intr. aN-* To keep deferring things. *Magbuhul-buhul na pa'in ka, na wa'i ta'abut.* You kept putting it off, and now it has happened.

**buhungan** (var. **bahurungan**) *n.* The ridge of a house as viewed from outside. *Luma' ungkup, alanga buhunganna.* A traditional house, its ridge high. *Bahurungan itū ma deyom luma', bubungan itū man diyata'.* The ridgepole is inside the house, the ridge of the roof is on top. (*cf:* **bubungan, kura'-kura'₂**)

**bu'ag** *adj. a-* Suffering from an internal injury. *Bang kita aniya' pali'an, tauwa' kita punglu', ariki' min luwasan aheya min deyom. Ya hē' abu'ag.* If one of us has a wound, hit by a bullet, [the hole] is smaller on the outside than inside. That's what *bu'ag* is. (*Thesaurus:* **bakat 1.1, langgahi', pali' 1**)

**bu'un** *n.* **1)** The hair of the human head. *Ataha' bu'unna, alabung isāb, ta'abut lo'akanna.* Her hair is long, it's abundant too, reaching to her elbows. *Ginanggut he'na bu'un ina'na.* She pulls her mother's hair. (*Thesaurus:* **bahibū 1, bū 1, bulbul 1**) **1.1)** *v. advrs. -in-* Having a good head of hair. *D'nda binu'un sidda, tusayan.* A woman with abundant hair, hanging low down her back.

**bu'ung-bu'ung** *see:* **pagbu'ung-bu'ung**

**bu'us** *adj. a-* **1)** Tipped out unintentionally; spilt. *Da'a patunggangun tu'ung itū ko da'a abu'us.* Don't tilt the box lest stuff tips out. (*Thesaurus:* **huddud 1**) **1.1)** *v. tr. -an* To tip something out. *Bay binu'usan he'na bohe', ni'isi ni undam pangose'.* She tipped out the water, put it into a basin for washing.

**bulak** *adj. a-* **1)** Immature, of plants, fruit, or young humans. *Amata' gi' wanni, abulak.* The *wanni* mango is unripe, it is immature. *Pangalaggosku bubu itū p'ttung abulak.* It is young bamboo that I use for lashing a *bubu* trap. *Pinah'lla'an si Anu minsan abulak lagi'.* What's-her-name is married even though she is still immature. **2)** Not fully cooked.

   **kabulakan** *n.* Immature stage of plant or animal growth. *Aniya' pola kabulak-bulakan, aniya' isāb pola ato'a.* There is betel nut in the immature stage, there is also mature betel nut.

**bulakay** var. of **bulaksay**

**bulakka₁** *n.* Yellow-cheeked or Orange-dotted tuskfish. *Choerodon anchorago.*

**bulakka₂** *n.* Coral hogfish. *Bodianus mesothorax.*

**bulaksay** (var. **bulakay**) *adj. a-* **1)** Disarranged by sudden movement. *Abulakay kinakanku e' siyaliku apa bay maglahi-lahi mareyom luma'.* My food was scattered by my younger siblings because they were running about inside the house. (*Thesaurus:* **kanēs-nēs, teges-teges**) **1.1)** *v. intr. aN-* To be sent flying by sudden movement. *Buwat tamban sinihag he' daing aheya, agtūy amulakay tamban.* Like anchovies scattered by a large fish, the anchovies immediately scatter. *Angaledje itu sali' amulakay ni baranta.* Spreading stuff, like scattering it over ourselves. **1.2)** *v. tr. -an* To upset or scatter someone with a sudden movement. *Binulaksayan gusung, amatay anapu.* Sand being scattered, worn out with sweeping. *Bang ap'ddi' atayku, bulaksayanku sugal saga bo' aku lum'ngngan.* When I get annoyed I scatter the cards, for example, and go for a walk.

**buladjang** *v. intr. pa-* To spring up from a sitting position. *Pabuladjang iya man paningkō'anna, pabuhat maka lahi-lahi.* He sprang up from where he was sitting, got up and ran off. (*Thesaurus:* **bangkat₂, buhat₂, punduk 1**)

**bulag** *adj. a-* Blinded temporarily by having something in the eye. *Wa'i abulag si Sa bay magbola, kapē'an gusung matana.* Sa is blinded playing ball. Sand got into his eyes. *Alegsok matanu bang ang'nda', sali' abulag.* Your eyes are blind when you look, as though there is something in them. (*Thesaurus:* **lempon, pē'₄, puling 1.1**)

**bulagas** *n.* Strong currents and wide tidal range associated with spring tides. *Bang aranta' bulan, yuk kami bulagas s'llog, alandos s'llog.* When the moon is bright we say the currents are *bulagas*, they are strong. (*cf:* **b'kka'an**)

**bulagtok** *n.* A species of bream (unclassified).

**bulahaw** *adj. a-* Semi-blind; purblind. *Sali' aniya' duwa lapis matata. Ma olangan maka'nda' maka mbal na, ya hē' bulahaw.* It is as if our eyes have two layers. Halfway between being able to see and not being able, that's *bulahaw. Abulahaw mata, sali' abulag. Minsan asekot mbal ta'nda'.* Our vision dim, sort of blinded. Even something up close is not seen. (*Thesaurus:* **gabul**)

**bula'-bula'** *n.* **1)** Froth; foam; lather. **1.1)** *v. intr. aN-* To produce foam. *Buwat kagong angalimumu, bowa'na amasi amula'-mula', kata'uhanta ala'an isina.* Like a crab losing substance, its mouth still foaming, we know that its flesh is going away.

**pagbula'-bula'** *v. intr. aN-* To produce bubbles or foam from one's mouth. *Magbula'-bula' onde'-onde'.* Children blowing bubbles.

**bula'ug₁** *n.* Chinese emperor, species of bream. *fam. Lethrinidae.* (*gen:* **kutambak**)

**bula'ug-piring** *n.* Gray large-eye bream. *Gymnocranius griseus.*

**bula'ug₂** (derivative of **la'ug**) *n.* A vindictive or belligerent person. *Ala'at kasuddahanna, bula'ug a'a inān, magbono'.* The character of that bully is bad, he kills.

**bulallay** *v. intr. pa-* To turn over from usual level position. *Bang atop taluwa' baliyu, pabulallay kamemon.* When the thatch is hit by the wind it all flips over.

**bulallit** *v. intr. pa-* To turn over from usual level position. *Pakayang-kayang atopna, pabulallit e' baliyu.* Its thatch flips over in the wind, overturned by the wind. *Bay pakkom, paleyak pabīng. Atawa bay paleyak bo' pakkom pabīng he' baliyu atawa he' s'llog.* Capsized and right-side up again. Or it was right way up and capsized again due to wind or current. (*Thesaurus:* **bīng₁ 1, sulang-saling, sulay₂, sumpallit, sunsang, susun-buyu'**)

**bulan₁** *n.* The moon. (*Thesaurus:* **bulan baha'u, damlag 1**)

**bulanan** *n.* The month in which an event occurs, as the birth of a child; the fruiting of a tree; the onset of a seasonal weather phase. *Halam gi' ta'abut bulananna.* Her time for delivery has not yet arrived.

**bulan₂ 1)** *n.* Month. *Pilambulan bay ab'ttong?* How many months pregnant was she? **2)** *clf.* Count word for nights of the month. (*spec:* **deyom-bulan, duwa kasobangan, ganap t'llumpū', matay-bulan, min lima abase', mint'dda abase', sahali-bulan, sangpū' maka mpat kasobangan**)

**bulan-bulan₃** *adv.* Every month.

**bulan₃** *v. tr.* To catch fish by moonlight. *Yuk kasehe'an, "Ahāp na kitabi amulan buwattī'."* The others say, "It would be good for us all to go moon-fishing right now."

**pagbulan** *v. intr. aN-* To catch shallow-water sea foods during the bright phase of the moon. *Na tagna'anta jāman kami isāb magbulan itū. Magbulan-bulan seso'.* Let's begin our moon-fishing season. We will 'moon-catch' *seso* snails.

**bulan₄** *v. advrs. -in-* To be menstruating. (*Thesaurus:* **laha'₁ 2, tindaw**)

**bulan baha'u** *n. phrase* The new moon. (*Thesaurus:* **bulan₁, damlag 1**)

**Bulan Hadji'** *n. phrase* The month in which pilgrims make their pilgrimage to Mecca. (*syn:* **Julhadji'**)

**Bulan Hailaya** *n. phrase* The Sulu name for the month following Ramadan. (*cf:* **hailaya;** *syn:* **Sawwal**)

**Bulan Muharram** *n. phrase* The first month of the Islamic year. (*Set:* **Julka'idda, Julhadji', Jumadir Ahil, Jumadir Awal, Rabiul Ahil, Rabiul Awal, Radjab, Ramadan, Saban, Sappal, Sawwal**)

**Bulan Puwasa** *n. phrase* The ninth month of the Islamic year, during which the fast is observed. (*syn:* **Ramadan**)

**bulan sobang** *n. phrase* The coming lunar month, beginning at the next new moon.

**bulan-bulan₁** *n.* **1)** Malabar cavalla or Naked-shield kingfish. *Carangoides malabaricus.* **2)** Tarpon. *Megalops cyprinoides.*

**bulan-bulan₂** *n.* Moon snail, an edible monovalve.

**bulang** *v. tr.* To set cocks to fighting. *Am'lli aku manuk pamulangku ni bulangan bang Ahad.* I will buy a chicken to fight with at the cockpit on Sunday.

**bulangan** *n.* A cockpit (where cocks are set to fighting).

**pagbulang** *v. intr. aN-* To fight, of cocks fitted with artificial spurs. *Magbulang na manuk ya magtakbi' ina'an. Angalaha' pē'na bay tinuttuk e' manuk dakayu'.* The cock is fighting, the one without metal spurs. Its comb is bleeding, pecked by the other bird. *Bang magbulang angalaha'.* When [cocks] fight they bleed.

(*Thesaurus:* **ayuk-ayuk, manuk-sigun, pagtakbi', pagtūkan**)

**bubulangun** *n.* A fighting cock.

**papagbulang** *v. tr.* To provoke people to mutual aggression; to get two people to fight.

**bulangkayat** *adj. a-* Disordered and unusable. (*Thesaurus:* **g'ppa', gubal, hogal, lubu₂ 1, tunas 1**)

**bularut** *n.* A carbuncle or unusually large boil. *Kalibubut bularut sīnsong maka banut, buwat ma kalangan onde'.* A huge boil plugged with coconut husk, as in the children's song. (*Thesaurus:* **bautut 1, kalibubut 1**)

**bulas₁** *n.* Cowardice. *Atukas, sali' kita pinahimulas, sinoho' pasekot magbono', yuk-i, "Bulasnu ilū."* Challenged, like being accused of cowardice, told to come close and fight, saying, "You are such a coward!" (*cf:* **himulas, tukas 1.1**)

**bulas₂** *n.* Smegma, a genital secretion.

**bulat** *v. intr. pa-* To come into the world, as at birth. *Pabulat ka ni babaw-dunya itū.* Come out into the world. (*Thesaurus:* **luwas₁ 1, tukaw, tuwa' 1**)

**bulatas** var. of **latas₁**

**bulatuk** *v. tr.* To cut a groove in wood to facilitate the insertion of a splitting wedge. *Binulatuk amulawan nihinang busay.* The [piece of] molave wood is grooved to be made into a paddle. *Ya pamulatuk pang'ntan, bari', kapa. Puwas bay binulatuk, tinanok.* The thing for making a groove is a tool such as a working knife, an axe. After grooving it is wedged apart. (*Thesaurus:* **biggal 1, pahanggal, s'ngngal, tanok 1**)

**bulawan** *n.* 1) Gold. (*Thesaurus:* **estenles, luyang, pilak 1, pittang, sawasa', tumbaga 1**) 1.1) Gold jewelry.

**bulawan-pote'** *n.* White gold, an alloy of gold and at least one 'white' metal such as silver or nickel.

**pagpamulawan** *v. intr. aN-* To display one's gold, especially in the form of gold-covered teeth.

**pamulawan** *n.* Jewelry of all kinds. (*Thesaurus:* **aretes, pansi, singsing**)

**bulbul** *n.* 1) The feather of a bird; fur of an animal. *Am'lli aku bulbul manuk panonda'ku ni timbang, anonda' mangku'.* I buy chicken feathers for trolling in the open sea, trolling for bonito. *Aniya' gilingan bulbul, aniya' du isāb gilingan naelon.* There are feather spinners, and there are also spools for nylon line. (*Thesaurus:* **bahibū 1, bū 1, bu'un 1**) 1.1) *adj. -an* Woolly or fluffy. *Manta bulbulan bay pamuwanku ma si Mo.* A fluffy blanket that I gave to Mo. 1.2) *v. tr. -an* To pluck feathers from a slaughtered chicken. (*cf:* **lasuwa**)

**bulda** *n.* 1) An embroidered fringe on clothes or pillowcases. (*Thesaurus:* **bingkay, ingkahi 1**) 1.1) *v. tr. -an* To attach a decorative border or fringe. *Punda ū'an ilu bay binuldahan, buwat ma bihing samda.* The pillowslip there has been decorated with a fringe, like the hem of a blouse.

**buli-buli** *adj. zero* Determined on; committed to doing. *Buli-buli pikilanku. Bang halam ka maina'an, manjari aku itu amikilan anganggganti' ma ka'a. Mbal magla'an pikilanku.* My mind is made up. If you are not there, then I will think about replacing you. My mind will not move away [from this].

**pagbuli-buli** *v. intr. aN-* 1) To remember without fail. 1.1) *v. tr. -an* To keep something securely in mind. *Buwat aku sinukut, yuk manukut ē', "Magbuli-buli ka amiha'an aku."* Like when someone reminds me of my debt, he says, "Remember for sure to find it for me." *Ebot-ebot Tuwan, pagbuli-bulihinbi kami supaya pasambu hinang itū.* Sir, don't forget. Keep us firmly in mind so that this project flourishes.

**pagsabuli-buli** *v. tr.* To be committed to some action.

**sabuli-buli** *adv.* Securely; definitely; permanently. (*syn:* **sakuli-kuli**)

**bulibud** (var. **bibud**) *v. intr. aN-* 1) To turn through 180 degrees. *Amawis a'a ma kulit tahik apa at'ggol bay mareyo'. Sali' alembo, amulibud ma kulit tahik.* He passed out at the surface because he was a long time below. It's like he had drowned, turning end for end on the surface of the sea. (*cf:* **buli'-munda'**) 1.1) *v. tr.* To turn something round to face in the opposite direction. *Buliburun pelang ē', tudju pi'itu munda'na bo' mbal magka'at sangpad.* Turn that canoe around, its bow facing in this way so its prow will not be damaged. *Buwat pelang bay niengkotan dahū munda'. Subay binibud dahū buli', ati buli' na ya niengkotan.* Like a canoe that had been tied bow forward. It should be turned so the stern is forward, so the stern is what is tied. *Na biburun pelang ilū ko ra'a tarugtul apa ilu pababag.* So turn that canoe around so it doesn't get knocked, because it's lying cross-wise. (*Thesaurus:* **bitung, pagbuli'-munda'**)

**pagbulibud** *v. intr. aN-* To keep turning end for end. *Tininduk kita he' kandelan, ati binowa paraw palahi-lahi, magbibud buli'-munda'.* A large shark takes our lure and the canoe is made to race away, stern and bow turning end for end.

**bulik** *n.* The green tree lizard. *Bronchocela cristatella. Buwat tokke' bo' angalinig. Gaddung, biyaning.* Like a gecko but shiny. Green, yellow.

**bulikat** *adj. a-* Open but not looking forward, of eyes. *Buwat aniya' lum'ngngan, amasi abati', magtūy tagi'ik dangan. Yukna, "Angay ka'a-i, ap'ssok? Halam ka maka'nda'? Kilaku abulikat matanu."* Like someone walking around still awake, when someone else is suddenly stepped on, and says, "What's up, are your eyes looking out the back of your head that you cannot see? I reckon your eyes must be sightless." *Abulikat,* *sali' abīng matata. Niudju' kita. Abulikat*, our eyes sort of reversed. We get mocked [for it]. (*Thesaurus:* **p'ssok**)

**buli'**₁ *n.* **1)** The lowest part of something, as the bottom of a container, or the sea floor. *Tabāk na ma buli' ba'ul.* Found already in the bottom of the chest. *Angambay kita ma buli' tahik amiha tipay.* Swimming along the sea floor looking for pearl oysters. **2)** Stern or rear, as the stern of a canoe, the rump of an animal, the buttocks of a human, the extremity of an island. *Buwat pelang bay niengkotan dahū munda'. Subay binibud dahū buli', ati buli'na ya niengkotan.* Like a canoe that has been tied bow forward. It should be turned so the stern is forward, and its stern tied.

**buli'-buli'** *v. intr.* aN- To work from a place in the stern of a vessel or vehicle. *Dakayu' ma dambila', dakayu' isāb ma dambila'. Dangan amansān amuli'-muli'.* One rows from one side, another rows from the other side. One steers, working over the stern.

**buli'-k'llong** *n.* The nape of the neck.

**buli'-jalum** *n.* The eye of a needle.

**buli'-munda'** (var. **buwi'-munda'**) *adv.* Reversing end for end. {idiom} *Tininduk kami e' kandelan ati binowa paraw palahi-lahi magbibud buwi'-munda'.* A large shark takes our lure and the canoe is made to race away, stern and bow turning end for end. (*cf:* **bulibud 1**)

**pagbuli'-munda'** (var. **pagbuwi'-munda'**) *v. intr.* aN- To be turning end for end. *Magbuli-munda'? Bistahun na katig, munda' pabalik ni buli'.* Turning end for end? Consider an outrigger, the bow end turning back to the stern. (*Thesaurus:* **bitung**, **bulibud 1.1**)

**buli'-pugay** *n.* The nape of the neck.

**buli'-siku** *n.* The point of the elbow joint.

**buli'-tape'** *n.* The heel.

**buli'an**₁ *n.* Location to the rear of something. *Ilu ma buli'anna.* There it is behind him.

**buli'**₂ *n.* **1)** Something hidden from sight or hearing. **1.1)** *v. tr.* -an To conceal something so it is not seen or heard.

**buli'-akkal** *n.* A concealed intention. *Araiyus anakku. Ai-ai pamandu'ta iya angaho'. Manjari pagl'ngnganna saddī buli'-akkal.* My child is perverse. Whatever we teach him he agrees with. However, as he walks off he has something else in mind. (*cf:* **limbung 1**)

**buli'-buli' mata** *v. tr.* To look at someone obliquely, avoiding eye contact. {idiom} *Bay aku magbāk maka bitu'anunku, buli'-buli'ku mataku.* I came face-to-face with my former spouse, looked at her obliquely. *Hal amuli'-muli' mata iya itū.* She simply averts her gaze. (*Thesaurus:* **keles**, **kibad**, **lingi' 1**, **pagkesong**)

**buli'an**₂ *n.* Something kept unsaid, as a grudge or reservation. *Taga buli'an llingna, mbal to'ongan. Bowa'na angaho', deyom atayna mbal.* There is a reservation in what he says, it is not genuine.

His mouth says yes, his heart doesn't. (*Thesaurus:* **akon-akon**, **agmol 1**, **koto'-koto'**, **deyom-deyom atay**, **lagod-lagod**)

**pagbuli'-buli'** *v. intr.* aN- **1)** To be motivated by a goal in one's mind, as a youth making gifts to a girl's parents. **1.1)** *v. tr.* -an To have some action in mind. *Bang ka'a binuwanan ai-ai subay aniya' pagbuli'-buli'annu.* If someone gives you something, you ought to have something in mind [as repayment].

**buliluk** *n.* A swirling movement at the intersection of ocean currents; small whirlpools forming at the stern of a moving vessel. *Buliluk sōn, buliluk s'llog.* Whirlpools of incoming tide, whirlpools of the current. (*cf:* **pusal**₁ **1**)

**pagbuliluk** *v. intr.* aN- To form swirling currents or whirlpools at the reversal of tides. *Bang kita pakapo' bo' angebol kita, aheka ma buli'anta magbuliluk sala.* When we wade and move vigorously, a lot of whirlpools sort of form behind us.

**bulintus** *v. tr.* To strike a triangular sail, wrapping sail round mast and hinged boom. *Bang banog binulintus. Bang lamak nilūn.* If it is a triangular sail it is wrapped around the mast. If it is a square sail it is rolled [around its lower boom].

**buling** *n.* Charcoal; soot. *Buwat si Li di'ilaw, bay magborak maka buling.* Like Li yesterday, powdering her face with soot. *Taga buling lapohan ina'an.* That stove has soot on it. (*Thesaurus:* **abu 1**, **bale**₅)

**buling-bata'** (var. **huling-bata'**) *n.* **1)** Something that cannot be forgotten; a remembered offense. **1.1)** *v. tr.* To keep in mind something to be repaid. *Buling-bata', bay aku karahu'annu. Makahiyak ka pahi, bay aku makatabang. Binuwanan du aku duwa-t'llu tudlu', na ya hē' binuling-bata' he'ku.* Something never forgotten, [like] the time you got the advantage of me. You speared a large ray, and I helped. I was given just two or three fingers of the meat. That's what I will not forget.

**pagbuling-bata'** *v. intr.* aN- **1)** To remember kindness shown or harm done. **1.1)** *v. tr.* To keep in mind an act of kindness or harm done until such time as the action can be reciprocated. *Pagbulingun-bata' salama-lama, ahāp-ala'at.* Keep it in your memory forever, good and bad alike. (*Thesaurus:* **balos**₁ **1**, **entom buddi**, **paluli**)

**bulinga** *n.* Yellow fat-like tissue in various living creatures; the yolk of an egg. *Ai-ai makanisattuwa taga bulinga.* Whatever has to do with great creatures contains yellowish tissue. *Bulinga sugpatan utuk.* The tissue that is an extension of the brain. *Bulinga kalitan, bulinga malu-malu, buwat isina mabiyaning ī', atibulung bo' apera'.* The fatty tissue of a shark or *malu-malu*, like its yellowish flesh, round but flattish.

**bulitik**₁ (var. **buttik**) *n.* Various natural gums and resins. *Agathis alba, Dipterocarpus spp. Ahāp tarul* *man buttik. Makalu'ug buttik.* Mango gum is preferable to *buttik* [gum from forest trees]. Getting *buttik* is exhausting. (*cf:* **tarul**)

**bulitik₂** *n.* Popped rice or corn, often sweetened with syrup to form cakes. (*Thesaurus:* **ampaw, biti'₁, gagati'**)

**bulitin** *n.* A game in which flat discs are shot on a square board. (*Thesaurus:* **kulang₂, pūl, tako, tira**)

    **pagbulitin** *v. intr. aN-* To play a game like pool, using discs rather than balls. *Buwat magbulitin inān, bang aniya' anira ni ngga'i ka kulangna, pabelawta iya.* Like playing pool, if someone hits a disc that isn't his, we tease him.

**buliyang** *v. intr. pa-* To wake up and begin eating immediately.

**bullat** *n.* A species of bream.

**bullaw** var. of **bunglaw**

**bullud** *n.* A hill-like formation.

    **pagbullud** *v. intr. aN-* To form a hill, of ocean waves. *Bang kami atulak ni Basilan, ma tonga'an pa'in, magbullud goyak.* When we leave for Basilan, halfway across, the waves grow like hills. (*Thesaurus:* **būd 1.1, kuta'₂, g'bbus 1, hunsuk, hungku'**)

    **pagbullud-bullud** *v. intr. aN-* To bounce up and down on a series of bumps or ridges. *Kamemon taraysikul magbullud-bullud ma labayan.* All passenger-tricycles bounce up and down on the road. (*Thesaurus:* **pagbuwang 1.1, paghandok, paghuntak, pagtongket-tongket, pagumpak-umpak**)

**bullu'** *n.* A species of large fish. *Daing bullu' itū makaobe'.* The *bullu'* fish causes sore gums.

**bullung** (var. **bulung**) *n.* A spherical glass float for supporting large seine nets. (*syn:* **bungga'₁, kassa'-bullung**)

**bulsa** *n.* A pocket sewn into clothing. *Nsa' aniya' sīn minsan dakayu' ma bulsaku.* There's not even a single coin in my pocket.

**bulsit** var. of **bilsut**

**bulu** *n.* Barrel of a firearm. *Bang kita niholdap he' mundu, pinatudju ni kita bulu timbak inān.* When we are held up by bandits, the barrel of the gun is aimed at us.

**bulung** var. of **bullung**

**buluy** *see:* **buluyan, pabūy, pagbuluyan**

**buluyan** (var. **būyan**) *n.* An enclosed area where livestock can move freely. *Sapi' ma buluyan, sapi' magpananduk.* Cattle in free runs, cattle that can use horns. (*Thesaurus:* **ād 1, apis 1, koral 1, kumbangan, kumbisan, likusan, sasak 1**)

    **pagbuluyan** *n.* An enclosure in which chickens or domestic animals are kept. *Pagbuluyan manuk, sali' ahawan, bay sinasak.* A chicken run, kind of clear, fenced.

**bumbum** var. of **bunbun**

**bunag** *n.* A span, defined as the distance between spread thumb and index finger. (*Thesaurus:* **h'kka 1, pāt 2, sa'ang₂**)

**buna'** *n.* Various batfishes. *Platax sp.*

    **buna'-halo** *n.* Chinese pomfret, a fish species. *Pampus chinensis.*

**bunbun** (var. **bumbum**) *n.* 1) Fine sand. (*Thesaurus:* **kalangan₃, kapote'an, gusung, igang₁**) 1.1) *v. tr. -an* To cover something with earth or sand. (*Thesaurus:* **kubul 1.1, pagl'bbong**)

**bundan** *adj. zero* Beard of male goat.

**bundu'** *n.* The area of body below the navel.

**buntal** *n.* Generic term for various pufferfish and porcupinefish. *fam. Tetraodontidae, fam. Diodontidae.* (*cf:* **luku'₁**)

**buntal-buntal** *n.* A species of pufferfish.

**buntal-kakas** *n.* A species of pufferfish.

**buntal-daing** *n.* A species of pufferfish.

**buntal-ero'** *n.* A species of pufferfish.

**buntal-itingan** *n.* A species of porcupinefish.

**buntal-petak** *n.* A species of pufferfish.

**buntal-pillu'an** *n.* Various smooth-skinned pufferfishes.

**buntal-s'llang** *n.* A deepwater species of pufferfish.

**buntal-tingga'** *n.* A species of pufferfish, lead-colored and inedible.

**buntal-unas** *n.* A shallow water species of pufferfish.

**bunt'lled** *n.* A complex bend or curve. *Bunt'lled, sali' kello' magtabid.* A complex curve, like a winding bend. (*Thesaurus:* **bengkok 1, kalluk 1, kello' 1.1**)

    **pagbunt'lled** *v. intr. aN-* To curve on more than one plane, as a length of wood or bamboo, or the twisting motion of fish. *Magbunt'lled, buwat a'a magl'dduk. Buwat kaitan isāb magbunt'lled du mareyo'.* Curving and twisting like a person stretching. Like a shark does too, down below.

**buntu'₁** *v. advrs. -in-* 1) Beginning to decay, of flesh. 1.1) *v. intr. aN-* To break down, of bodily tissue. *Amuntu' pa'aku, bang p'ssilta amote'.* My thigh is turning bad, if we press it shows white. *Amuntu' tanganku, bay aranglus he' espalton.* My hand is ulcerating, it was scalded by hot bitumen. (*Thesaurus:* **baguy, balos₂, buhuk, halu' 1.1, langag, p'ngkak**)

**buntu'₂** *v. tr.* To catch fish overnight, in contrast to early morning. *Sūng na kita amuntu', tulak kohap, amole' salung.* Let's go fishing overnight, afternoon departure, come home tomorrow. *Daing binuntu', bang mbal ta'abut amaragang, palabay na baha'una.* Fish caught overnight, if it doesn't make it to sell, its freshness will have passed.

**buntu'-buntu'** *v. advrs. -in-* Suffering from edema or beri-beri. *Binuntu'-buntu'an, buwat d'nda ab'ttong.* Suffering from edema, like a woman who is pregnant.

**buntul** *see:* **pagbuntul**

**bunut** (var. **banut**) *n.* 1) The fibrous husk of a coconut. *Aniya' na bunut paglampasu' lantay.* We now have a coconut husk for polishing the floor. *Angā' aku bunut panapaku daing.* I will get some coconut husks to roast the fish with. (*wh:* **niyug**) **1.1)** *v. tr.* -*an* To remove the husk from a mature coconut in order to open the shell. *Solab pamunut lahing.* A spike for de-husking coconuts. (*cf:* **bagul**)

**bunut-bunut** *v. tr.* To clean something by scrubbing. *Tape'-tangan binunut-bunut.* Hands and feet thoroughly scrubbed. (*Thesaurus:* **kuskus 1.1, dalug₁, gisgis 1.2, lukup, lupag, susut**)

**bunyi** *see:* **bunyi-bunyihan dunya, kabunyihan, pagbunyi-bunyi**

**bunyi-bunyihan dunya** *n. phrase* All the things that make life enjoyable. *Bunyi-bunyihan dunya, kalalamihan dunya, kakaya'an dunya.* Life's pleasures, the enjoyable things of this world, the valued things of the world.

**bunyug** *n.* **1)** A group formation. *Bunyug itū magbeya'-beya' karuwa.* This word *bunyug* means two [things] moving together. **1.1)** *v. intr. pa-* To go together with someone. *In ka'a ilū kapangandolan, angkan kasulutan sidda aku bang ka ganta' pabunyug ma aku maka saga sundaluku.* You are to be trusted, which is why I would be very pleased if you could perhaps come along with me and my soldiers. **1.2)** *v. tr.* -*an* To accompany someone. *Bunyuganta ka dugu'-nyawa.* I will accompany you, body and soul. (*Thesaurus:* **abay₁ 1.1, beya'₂ 1, dongan, sehe' 1.1, unung 1**)

**pagbunyug** *v. intr. aN-* To act as a single group made up of multiple members. *Na bang aniya' kinawin, magbunyug aku maka bagayku.* Now when there is a wedding, I and my friend go together. *Bang kami lum'ngngan, magbunyug-bunyug.* When we are out walking, we go in groups. *Saga ampan dulu halam aniya' nakura'na, sagō' bang sigām parugpak magbunyug kamemon.* Locusts don't have a chief, but when they attack [a place] they combine as a single group.

**būng** *n.* Various species of floating jellyfish. *Būng itū bang kita amandi, angeket abisa.* When we go swimming, floating jellyfish sting painfully. *"Na maina'an na," yuk sultan, "mussa' būng inān, na mussa' ulan, mussa' telop-telop," yukna.* "Over there now," said the sultan, "are those jellyfish pearls, and those rain pearls, the finest pearls ever." (*spec:* **ubul-ubul**)

**būng-leha** *n.* Pacific man-of-war or Australian bluebottle. *Physalia physalis.*

**būng-sabay** *n.* Jellyfish species with trailing strands that can sting a human.

**bunga₁** *n.* The betel palm. *Areca catechu. Bunga ya taga buwa' pagmama'. Banga ya sali' halam buwa'an. Bunga* is the [palm] that has fruit for a betel chew. *Banga* [the fishtail palm] is virtually without fruit. (*Thesaurus:* **dantilad, l'mmaw,** lugus, pola**)

**bunga₂** *n.* A decorative motif in woven materials. (*cf:* **sumping 1**)

**bunga-ammas** *n.* A diamond or flower-like motif in a mat pattern.

**bunga-bunga** *n.* Ankle or wrist bones. (*syn:* **buku-buku₁**)

**bunga-jakkum** *n.* The larynx or voicebox. {idiom} (*syn:* **batang-k'llong, buwa'-jakkum**)

**bungang-kahuy** *n.* Edible fruit in general. *Bungang-kahuy itu kaginisan buwa' kayu. Bungang-kahuy* refers to fruit of all kinds. (*cf:* **buwa'₁ 1**)

**bungkak** *n.* Various trevallies. *Seriolinae; Selaroidae.*

**bungkal₁** *v. intr. pa-* **1)** To get up from a prone position. (*Thesaurus:* **punduk 1**) **1.1)** *v. tr.* To raise something by hauling. *Bang sali' aniya' tino'onanta buwat panggal atawa bubu, bungkalta, palitta.* Like when there is something we have covered with coral rock, a basket trap or a box trap for example, we haul it up, bringing it to the surface. *Binungkal, sali' pinunduk bang bay atuli, sali' nihella' pariyata'.* Woken right up, made to sit up if they had been sleep, sort of hauled upwards.

**bungkal₂** *adj. a-* **1)** Disturbed or stirred up by vigorous movement. *Abungkal sakina he' tambal, aho' paluwas na sakina kamemon. Tagna' tambalanta mbal paluwas, ta'abut kaminduwana paluwas. Magtaluwa' maka tambalna.* Her sickness is stirred up by the medicine, yes, her entire illness has come out. It didn't come out when we first medicated it, but the second time it did. The illness and the treatment interacted properly. **1.1)** *v. intr. pa-* To be stirred up. *Pabungkal na gusung ma sabab kapay.* The sand is stirred up by a [passing] propellor. **1.2)** *v. tr.* To stir a mixture by bringing stuff up from the bottom. (*Thesaurus:* **keyol 1.1, kuwal, gawgaw**)

**bungkal₃** **1)** *n.* A ball of tobacco leaf. (*Thesaurus:* **banusu, pasta, pikaroda, siga 1, sigupan, tabaku' 1**) **2)** *clf.* Count word for balls of tobacco leaf. *T'llu bungkal tabaku'.* Three bundles of leaf tobacco.

**bungkas** *adj. a-* Pulled away from a location by force. *Abungkas durukan paraw, paokat pariyata'.* The mast block of the canoe has become detached, lifting away from [the hull]. *Abungkas atop e' baliyu. Aniya' isāb dakayu' tandawan abungkas.* Thatch panels were blown away by the wind. One of the window panels was also detached. (*Thesaurus:* **sisa**)

**bungku'₁** *v. tr.* To lift something with one's back, pushing up from a crouching position. *Bungku'un pelangnu min deyo' taddas.* Get your back under the keel to lift your canoe.

**bungku'₂** *v. intr. pa-* To knock one's feet against an obstruction. *Pabungku' magtūy, sali' pasukkut tōng tape'ku.* Promptly knocking against it, the end of my foot sort of connecting with it. (*Thesaurus:* **langgal₂ 1, santuk, sukkut**)

**bungkus** *adj.* a- 1) Covered or wrapped in a cloth. *Abungkus ka.* Cover yourself up. (*Thesaurus:* **pulipus 1, putus 1.1, tambun 1.1**) 1.1) *v. tr.* -an To enclose something by wrapping it in cloth. *Nihella' baranna, nila'anan min t'ngnga' lān tudju ni kapantayan bo' yampa binungkusan maka s'mmek.* His body was dragged, removed from the middle of the road to the flat area and then wrapped in a cloth.

**pagbinungkus** *v. intr.* aN- To enclose oneself in a cloth, as when inhaling fumes. *Magbinungkus ka maka hōs, asokta na tambal mareyom banga'.* Wrap yourself up with a sarong, we will put some medicine inside, in a wide-mouthed pot.

**bungga'₁** *n.* A spherical glass fishing float. (*syn:* **bullung**)

**bungga'₂** *n.* A treasure chest; the treasure itself. *Aniya' bungga' bay tatau' kambo'-mbo'annu?* Do you have treasure that your ancestors stored? (*gen:* **pagtau'an**)

**bunggu'** *n.* Six-bar grouper or Six-banded rock cod. *Epinephelus sexfasciatus.* (*gen:* **kuhapo'**)

**bunggu'-luha-mata** *n.* Black-tipped or Red-band rock cod. *Epinephelus fasciatus.*

**bunglaw** (var. **bullaw**) 1) *v. tr.* -an To rinse something by immersing it or pouring water over it. *Bang kita amandi ni tahik subay kita amullaw ni bohe'.* When we swim in the sea we should rinse in fresh water. *Ai pamunglawan s'mmek?* What is there to rinse the clothes in? *Bullawin dayang, masi sabun.* Rinse it dear, the soap is still there. (*Thesaurus:* **kula'up, gūm-gūm, saplut₁**) 2) *v. intr.* aN- To freshen the mouth after eating.

**pamunglaw** (var. **pamullaw**) *n.* Something eaten or drunk after a meal to freshen one's mouth.

**bungsu** *adj. zero* Last-born. *Siyalita min kamemon, bungsu ko' hē'.* Our youngest sibling of all, he is the *bungsu.*

**kabungsuhan** *n.* The youngest or last-born child. (*syn:* **katapusan 2**)

**bungsud** *n.* A permanent fish trap or corral, built in water 2 to 3 fathoms deep. *Bungsud, aniya' pamantawan.* A *bungsud* has a tower [for observing fish]. (*cf:* **ampas 1**)

**pagbungsud** *v. intr.* aN- To make a living by catching fish in the large, permanent fence traps known as bungsud. *Linukan magbubungsud saga kamatto'ahan ma Tinutu'.* The old people in Tinoto used permanent fence traps, an inherited skill.

**bungug** *n.* A species of fish.

**bungug-tapikan** *n.* A species of fish, distinct from bungug.

**buraw** *adj.* a- Clouded; difficult to see into or through. *Aburaw samin inān, bay ahūg ni tahik. Aburaw isāb langit, aheka tai'-baliyu sali'.* That mirror is blurred, it fell into the sea. The sky too is blurred, like when there is a lot of high cloud. *Aburaw pagtaep itū, halam bay kinosog.* This typing is faint, it wasn't done strongly. (*Thesaurus:* **abu-abu₂, ahud-ahud 1.1, hanaw-hanaw, pagba'ung-ba'ung**)

**buriru** *adj.* a- Confused and unable to think clearly; temporarily deranged due to emotional shock. *Aburiru kōkku wa'i amatay h'ndaku. Abalu na aku. Bay turungan kōkku maka hōs.* My head is confused because my wife has died, and I am widowed. I covered my head with a sarong. *Ya buriru itū sali' magkarupangan. Buriru* is like behaving irrationally. (*Thesaurus:* **bingaw, lambang-mata 1, lengog kōk, ligoto'**)

**buruk** *n.* 1) An itchy condition of the scalp symptomized by scaling and pitting. 1.1) *v. advrs.* -in- Afflicted with itchy scalp. *Binuruk, kinakan isi kōkta he' kutu.* Itchy scalp, the flesh of our head eaten by lice. *Aliput kōkna e' katol, binuruk sali'.* His head is covered with an itchy condition, as though having *buruk.* (*Thesaurus:* **gulis-manuk 1, hagikgik, tai'-kōk**)

**burut** *v. intr.* pa- To pout. (*cf:* **k'mmi'**)

**būs** 1) *n.* A roll or bolt of cloth. *Bang aniya' amatay, billihan saput ni M'ddas, saga tonga' būs. Aniya' saga duwampū' maka lima metro ma dabūs s'mmek.* When someone dies shroud cloth is purchased [for him] in Siasi Town, about half a roll. There are about 25 meters in one bolt of cloth. 2) *clf.* Count word for rolls of cloth.

**ma būsan** *adv. phrase* By the roll, of cloth. (*cf:* **ma gulungan**)

**tibūsan** *n.* A bolt of cloth.

**busā'** *n.* 1) A sprain or dislocation of a bodily organ. *Asidda pat'kka busā' itū, aniya' sabita mareyom baranta.* This *busā'* condition keeps coming back, with an awareness of something [amiss] in our body. *Akosog bongso' min busā'. Bongso'* [internal injuries] are more serious than *busā'.* 1.1) *adj.* a- Sprained; dislocated; ruptured. *Abusā' aku, bay aku amowa kayu aheya. Mbal aku makakole' magl'ngngan. Subay palege ma luma'. Subay isāb tinilik.* I am ruptured, I carried a large piece of wood. I am not able to walk. I have to lie down at home. I should also be treated by a healer. *Abinsana', niōnan he' kasehe'an abusā' na.* Suffering pain from overwork, what some call *busā'.* (*Thesaurus:* **binsana' 1, bo'ol, bongso' 1, bugtu'₂ 1.1**)

**busā' k'llong** *adj.* a- Suffering from a crick in the neck. *Mbal kita makapagkesong, mbal kita sali' makapaglingi'. "Abusā' k'llongku," yukta.* We are not able to turn our heads this way and that, unable to look from side to side. "My neck has a crick in it," we say.

**busā' jantung** *adj.* a- Suffering from a stabbing pain in the diaphragm. *Abusā' kono' jantungna.* He is suffering from diaphragm cramp.

**busa'ing** *n.* A species of tree which grows in saline conditions. *Busa'ing itū patomo' ma pisak, ta'abut he' tahik. Nihinang hāg, pagdayaw pelang.* This *busa'ing* tree grows in the mud, reached by tide. Posts are made from it, or canoe parts.

**busay** 1) *n.* The paddle for propelling a canoe. **1.1)** *v. intr. aN-* To paddle a canoe using two hands on the paddle. *Mbal aku ata'u amusay.* I don't know how to paddle. (*Thesaurus:* **kelle 1.1, dayung 1.1, epe, luwad, tindayung**) **1.2)** *v. tr.* To reach an objective by paddling. *A: "Ai binusay, pelang?" B: "Ngga'i ka. Ya lahat binusay."* A: "What is paddled, the canoe?" B: "Not so. It is the place that is reached by paddling." **2)** *v. intr. aN-* To go on a journey; metaphorically, to die. *Wa'i na si pastor Ed amusay dahū.* Pastor Ed has already passed away, gone first.

**busay lahat** *v. tr.* To travel to other places. {idiom} *Basta angaliyu lahat niōnan amusay lahat.* Whenever it involves going from one place to another it is called *busay lahat. Aheka lahat bay kabusayanna.* He has visited many places [traveled widely].

**busayan** *n.* A journey. *Buwat si'itku hē', tambuku sigā Maulud amole'. Na halam gi' tapole', alanat busayan sigā.* Like my uncles, sending word that they would be home by the month of Maulud. Well, they still haven't got home, their journey is prolonged.

**pagbusayan** *v. intr. aN-* To go from place to place as a way of life.

**buskag** var. of **boskag**

**buskaw** *v. advrs. ka-...-an* To cause to splutter. *Bay aku kabuskawan e' kahawa. Landu' apasu'.* I was caused to splutter by the coffee. Much too hot!

**busling** *adj. a-* Widely known; of public knowledge. *Abusling ni a'a kamemon bay na pinole' si Anu he' d'nda Sūk.* Everyone knows that a Tausug girl came to What's-his-name's bed. (*Thesaurus:* **bantug 1, bawag, buhanyag, hayag, hula-layag 1, tanyag 1**)

**buslut** *adj. a-* Leaking; bursting open. (*Thesaurus:* **l'ssu', mman**)

**bussik** *adj. a-* 1) Suffering from a painful discharge of the eye. *Abussik mataku, halam aku makatuli dibuhi'.* My eye has a painful discharge, I couldn't sleep last night. (*Thesaurus:* **belad, liblib, piting**) **1.1)** *v. tr. -an* To cause the eyes to produce a discharge.

**bussu'₁** *n.* A hard, dark, non-coral rock. *Angā' aku bussu' panahanku bubuku bo' mbal talaran minsan alandos s'llog.* I get a *bussu'* rock to weigh down my fish trap so it won't drift even when the current is strong. (*Thesaurus:* **batu₁, lakit**)

**bussu'₂** *n.* A species of edible bivalve. *Takakan isāb bussu', bo' alangsa. Bussu'* are edible but they have a strong smell.

**bustak** *adj. a-* Disintegrating or bursting open, as a bomb or a container. *Ka'andalan malkina itū, mbal abustak.* This engine can be speeded up, it won't disintegrate. *Wa'i abustak tting-tting, bay pinaheya'an.* The balloon has burst, it was made

very large. *Bang pa'in abustak b'ttongku.* May my stomach burst [if I am lying].

**bustakan** *n.* An explosion; the moment of bursting. *Magay timanannu pasagnatnu? Sunduknu ni Mimul! Paligay pangā'nu bustakannu ko' abustak b'ttongnu pariyata'.* What were you doing throwing away your grappling hook? [May it be] your grave marker at Mimul! Even more, may you get your explosion with your stomach bursting upwards!

**bustan** *adj. a-* Extra good, of the way something looks or sounds. *Abustan llingna, b'nnal sadja, halam tasoway.* His speech is excellent, always true, no fault to be found.

**kabustanan** *n.* The appearance of something attractive, as the lines of a canoe or someone's figure. *Ya na luwana, ya na hantangna. Sali' hurupna, sali' kahāpna, sali' kabustananna, sali' kahāpanna to'ongan.* That's how she looks, that's her appearance. Like her voice, her goodness, her physical beauty, all her good qualities.

**busu** *n.* Diving apparatus using piped air.

**busug** *v. tr.* 1) To pour water on; to irrigate a field. *Angindam mital si Mām pamusug jambangan.* The schoolmistress is borrowing a can for watering the flowers. (*cf:* **sumpit 1.1**) **1.1)** *v. advrs. ka-...-an* To have water poured over. *Da'a na kam pasalud min deyo' luma' bo' mbal kam kabusugan he' bohe' pasu'.* Don't pass beneath the house lest you get hot water poured on you. (*Thesaurus:* **bubu'**)

**busul** *n.* Swelling or bruising caused by a blow. *Bang kita abakat bo' busulan, aniya' baynatna.* When we are wounded and swelling occurs, there is proof. (*Thesaurus:* **bago' 1, bogon₁ 1, bongol 1, talis'ssok 1**)

**busung** *v. advrs. -in-* Experiencing trouble or misfortune from elders or spirit beings one has offended. *Da'a latahun matto'a inān, binusung ka. Aniya' ilmu'na.* Don't tease that old man, you will be punished. He has spiritual power. *Binusung aku he' mbo'ku apa bay sipa'anku.* I will suffer retribution from my grandfather because I hit him with my foot. (*cf:* **kisas₂**)

**busuwag** *v. intr. pa-* To spill or tip over. (*Thesaurus:* **pisik-pisik, tata', titi'**)

**buta₁** *adj. a-* Blind; sightless. *Saddī abuta maka alapis. Abuta itū sali' alendom, mbal maka'nda'. Buta* is different from having a cataract. *Buta* is like things being dark, not able to see. (*Thesaurus:* **lakap-manuk, legsok₂, palu' 1.1**)

**buta-punung** *v. advrs. -in-* Blind from lack of food and water. *Lingantu to'ongan, buta pinunung, halam bay makakakan.* Seriously hungry, blind from lack of nourishment, hadn't eaten anything.

**buta₂** *n.* 1) A person who conceals his choice in a game of cards or dominoes. *Ka'a-i buta bo' aku alas, kabayarannu aku kamemon.* You conceal your call and I have an ace, you can pay me the lot. **1.1)** *v. tr.* To hide one's call in a game. *Buwat kita magduminu, saga yukbi, "Binuta."* Like us playing dominoes, and you say, "It's hidden."

**buta-buta** *n.* A tree species. *Kayu buta-buta, tahinang hāg batangna. Kulitna tahinang pigi', sali' borak kalas.* The *buta-buta* tree, its trunk can be used for making posts. Its bark is grated to give a pinkish tinge to cosmetic rice paste. (*syn:* **tambu-tambu₃**)

**butag** *v. tr.* To dip food into something tasty, as a cracker into coffee, or boiled bananas into sugar. (*Thesaurus:* **bahug 1.1, dulis, t'nno', tublak₁ 1**)

**butas** *adj. a-* **1)** Separated, of a former relationship. *Manjari Kuyya' wa'i tinimanan, maka'ase'-ase' na, abutas na, halam na.* So then Mr Monkey was rejected, a pitiful thing, separated now, no more of him. (*Thesaurus:* **boklang 1, bugtu'₁, l'kkat₂ 1, logtas, okat₂ 1**) **1.1)** *v. tr. -an* To separate from a spouse; to wean a child.

  **pagbutas** *v. intr. aN-* **1)** To be separated, of things usually joined. **1.1)** *v. tr.* To separate two things that had been joined. (*Thesaurus:* **pagokat**)

**butawan** *v. tr. -an* **1)** To release something from restraint or control. *Sali' ni'bbahan, buwat taguri' mbal na balutanta, butawanta.* Like we leave it, like a kite that we do not hold onto, we let it go. *Butawanin daing ilū ko' da'a kita taloson.* Let that fish go so we don't get carried away by the current. (*Thesaurus:* **luklus 2**) **1.1)** *v. intr. aN-* To become detached, as a person's spirit from his body at death. *Amutawan nyawana, halam na ma baran.* His spirit has separated, no longer in his body. (*Thesaurus:* **bugtang, bugtu' napas, halol, matay₁ 1, sagpe' 2, tubag**)

**buti** *n.* A western-style rowboat. (*Thesaurus:* **beggong, biruk, kappal, katel-katel, kumpit, dinggi-dinggi, lansa, papet, sappit₂, tempel**)

  **pagbuti** *v. intr. aN-* To get about by rowboat.

**butig** *n.* **1)** A swelling or bruise. (*Thesaurus:* **bakag₂, bago' 1, baha' 1, ikat 1.1, pagbutud, p'ngkong 1**) **1.1)** *adj. -an* Affected by swelling. *Lampinig itū angeket abisa ati butigan kita. Mbal paluwas laha'.* Wasps bite painfully and we experience swelling. No blood comes out. *Bang bay maglahi-lahi si Le mareyom luma' bo' magdugtul ni siya, butigan kōkna.* When Le was running around the house and ran into a chair, her head had a swelling. **1.2)** *v. intr. pa-* To swell or form a lump in fleshy tissue. *Aniya' pabutig ma k'llongna, niōnan bogon.* There is something growing in his neck, it's called a goiter. *Ai pabutig mareyom?* What is swelling inside?

  **pagbutig-butig** *v. intr. aN-* To form multiple small lumps beneath the skin.

**butig-butig** *adj. zero* Lumpy and coarse, of something easily broken. *Sokal butig-butig.* Unrefined sugar.

**butingga'** *n.* Various pufferfishes.

  **butingga'-lumahan** *n.* Half-smooth golden pufferfish. *Lagocephalus spadiceus. Butingga'-lumahan buwat buntal ang'tting bo' halam sisikan. Makapatay a'a. Sali' agb'ttik. Aniya' isāb dī butingga'.* The *butingga' lumahan* is like a pufferfish that inflates, but without scales. It can kill people. It is sort of multicolored. There are also true pufferfish.

**but'ngngel** *n.* Larvae of various insects; a caterpillar. (*Thesaurus:* **kalog 1, iyas 1, sassing 1, ulat₁**)

**buttik** var. of **bulitik₁**

**butud** *v. intr. aN-* To become distended, as a decomposing body. *Amutud na ba, sali' am'ngkak.* It is so bloated, so distended. (*Thesaurus:* **b'ngkak, boskag, tting**)

  **pagbutud** *v. intr. aN-* To become covered with lumps over an expanse of the body. *Magbutud baranku, bay kineket he' hama'. Basta magbutig-butig.* Multiple lumps have come up on my body, bitten by mosquitoes. So long as there are many lumps. (*Thesaurus:* **bakag₂, bago' 1, baha' 1, butig 1, ikat 1.1, p'ngkong 1**)

  **himutud** *v. intr. aN-* To become distended, as a corpse.

**butug** *v. tr.* To strike someone with the front of the fist, on anywhere but the face. (*Thesaurus:* **g'bbuk, suntuk 1.1, tibu', tikbung**)

  **pagbutug** *v. tr.* To be involved in punching. *Magbutug na kita baranta suma'an magdarut kita saga kōkta.* We punch each other, and sometimes pull hair out from each other's heads.

**butu'** *v. tr.* To eat food greedily, as a pig does. *Amutu' ka pehē'!* Eat away, pig! *Ananggal na ka, amoslad na ka, amutu' na. Ina'an tanggalannu ai-ai na pa'in pagamahannu.* Gulp it down, eat it greedily, eat like a pig. There you are wolfing whatever it is you are so cranky about. (*Thesaurus:* **bagahak₂, boslad, buhawi'₁, kanam, kaway 1.1, dahaga', damba'₁ 1.1, lagak 1.1, tanggal₁**)

**butu'an** *n.* Slops; food for animals.

**butul** *n.* A narrow-necked bottle. (*Thesaurus:* **kassa' 2, garapun**)

**butun₁** *n.* The weight on a heaving line.

**butun₂** *n.* The powder-puff tree. *Barringtonia racemosa.*

**butun₃** *n.* Floats of buoyant wood used to support the upper edge of a net. *Butun itū bo' mbal pat'nde lantaw. Nihinang min lambus.* Floats are [used] so the fishnet does not sink. Made from the *lambus* tree. (*syn:* **pataw₁**)

**buwa₁** *n.* Large gongs, generally hung in pairs with the bosses facing inwards. (*Thesaurus:* **agung 1, kulintangan, gandang 1, titik 1**)

**buwa₂** *v. tr.* To bounce a baby in its hammock. (*Thesaurus:* **ta'ut**)

**buwahan₁** *n.* A hammock for a baby, consisting of a tube of cloth suspended from springy poles.

  **pagbuwahan** *v. intr. aN-* **1)** To rock in a

suspended hammock. **1.1)** *v. tr.* To rock a baby in a suspended hammock. *Bang kita angaluk, pinaruru' atawa pinagbinuwahan.* When we console [a child], it is nursed or it is rocked to sleep.

**buwak-buwak** *v. intr.* *aN-* To make the sound of bubbling or boiling water. *Amuwak-muwak goyak ma deyo' luma'.* The waves beneath the house make a bubbling sound.

**buwad** *v. tr.* To dry something by exposure to sun or wind, as clothes hung to dry, or fish spread to cure. (*Thesaurus:* **patoho', puhi, tumbal 1.1**)

**buwahan₂** *n.* The lansones tree and its sweet fruit. *Lansium domesticum. Bang bay aniya' buwahan, bay ru aku angahaka.* If there had been lansones I would have said so.

  **buwahan-kubing** *n.* An inferior variety of lansones.

  **buwahan-kuyya'** *n.* Monkey lansones, a species of tree different from the lansones.

**buwa'₁** *n.* **1)** Fruit (generic). (*cf:* **bungang-kahuy**) **1.1)** *adj.* *a-* Fruit-bearing. *Saging a'anu i', abuwa'.* The banana there at same stage or other, fruiting. (*cf:* **duplak**)

  **buwa'-jakkum** *n.* The larynx; voice box; Adam's apple. {idiom} (*syn:* **bunga-jakkum**)

  **buwa'-unas** *n.* The fruit-like growth on a shallow water seagrass. *Kamemon buwa' ahūg pareyo', buwa'-unas ahūg pariyata'.* All fruit falls downwards, but the fruit of the sea-grass falls upwards. (*cf:* **eral-eral₂**)

  **pagbuwa'** *v. intr.* *aN-* To produce fruit. *Yampa magbuwa' liyabanos itū.* This soursop tree is producing fruit for the first time. (*Thesaurus:* **pagduru'-ero', tadjuk, tungkalling**)

**buwa'₂** *see:* **pabuwa'**

**buwa'-buwa'** *n.* **1)** Various skin complaints symptomized by itching, small swellings, blisters or eruptions. *Aniya' isāb buwa'-buwa' tabowa min deyom kandang.* There are also skin problems from in the womb. (*Thesaurus:* **abas 1, kagutgut 1.1, katol 1.2, ugud**) **1.1)** *v. advrs.* *-in-* Suffering from some skin problem. (*Thesaurus:* **ampogod 1, samuwa' 1.1**)

  **buwa'-buwa'-hulas** *n.* **1)** Perspiration rash, a skin condition due to long exposure to the sun. **1.1)** *v. advrs.* *-in-* Suffering from perspiration rash.

  **buwa'-buwa'-llaw** *n.* **1)** Prickly heat, a skin condition symptomized by redness, chafing and itching, a reaction of small children to high daytime temperatures. **1.1)** *v. advrs.* *-in-* Suffering from prickly heat.

  **buwa'-buwa'-sangom** *n.* **1)** Scabies, a contagious skin disease, common in the folds between fingers and toes or in the groin, itching intensely at night. **1.1)** *v. advrs.* *-in-* Suffering from scabies. *Binuwa'-buwa' sangom aku sidda. Ai panambal?* I suffer terribly from scabies. What medicine is there for it?

**buwal₁** *v. intr.* *aN-* To flow or swirl vigorously upwards. *Angay bang kita amusay, mbal mamuwal i'?* Why is it that when we paddle [the canoe], it doesn't swirl upwards? *Amuwal itū, pabuhat pariyata' bohe'na, tahikna, ai-aina. Buwal* means that its water, its sea-water, its whatever, is rising. (*Thesaurus:* **bukal, laga'₁ 1.1, lere', ogok-ogok**)

**buwal₂** *n.* Various sorts of patterned light cloth used to make women's blouses. (*Thesaurus:* **bildu', dasu, lehag, lere-lere 1, pima, taplak₁**)

  **buwal-mayaman** *n.* A fine cloth used for blouses. *Buwal-mayaman, ōn s'mmek aheka ginisanna. Mayaman* cloth, the name of a fabric with many varieties.

**buwal kayapu'** *n. phrase* A fine silk cloth used for blouses.

**buwan₁** **1)** *n.* Something given. *In buwan ma kasipukan, maka'aluk pasu'-atay.* A gift in secret soothes hard feelings. **1.1)** *v. ditr.* To give something to someone. *Guntingin aku, buwananta ka duwampū' sīn.* Cut my hair for me, I will give you twenty centavos. *Buwananku onde'-onde' būk.* I will give the children schoolbooks. *Mbal tapamuwan pantalunku itū apa dakayu' du. Kalu-kalu bang bay magkaruwa, bay na pamuwan ni ka'a dakayu'.* These trousers of mine cannot be given away because I have only the one [pair]. Perhaps if there had been two I would have given you one. (*Thesaurus:* **pasuwa'**) **2)** *v. advrs.* *ka-...-an* To be given something. *Sasuku angā'an aku magkalang kabuwanan du tambahan.* Whoever gets me a singer will definitely be given some remuneration. *Bang aniya' onde'-onde' angamu' ai-ai, pak'mmi'. Bang kabuwanan, mbal na pak'mmi'.* When a small child asks for something, she pouts. If she is given she no longer pouts.

  **buwan dusa** *v. intr.* *aN-* To commit an offense against someone. {idiom} *Bang aniya' pagkahinu ganta' makabuwan dusa ma ka'a, subay iya tō'annu bang ai dusana.* If one of your fellows happens to wrong you, you should point out what his offense is. *Bay na aku makabuwan dusa ma ka'a.* I have sinned against you [lit. given sin to you].

  **buwan napas** *v. tr.* To give one's last breath. {idiom}

  **pagbuwan** *v. intr.* *aN-* **1)** To give to each other generously. **1.1)** *v. tr.* *-an* To give generous gifts to someone. *Pinagbuwanan e'na kara'ugan aheya.* He gives [them] many great victories.

  **pagbuwan-biyuwani** *v. intr.* *aN-* To give to one another repeatedly. *Magkalamihan sigām sampay magbuwan-biyuwani.* They enjoyed themselves and exchanged gifts with each other.

  **pagbuwan-buwan** *v. intr.* *aN-* To give to each other.

**pamuwan** *n.* **1)** Something given; a gift. **1.1)** *v. tr.* To make a gift of something. *Da'a pamuwanun badju'nu, ageret ko' ilū.* Don't give your shirt, it's so torn. *Huma bay panganjanji'na ya pinamuwan ma ka'am sampay ka'mbo'-mbo'anbi.* The farm he promised, which is to be given to you and your descendants.

**buwan₂** *v. tr.* To bring about a desired or expected result. *Tumbukan bihing hōsku, ya na hē' amuwan pagon.* The edge of my sarong has holes punched in it, that's what makes it durable. *Ya na hē' makabuwan kalengogan.* That's what caused the disturbance. *Ya anastas magkawin imam. Iya na amuwan katobtoban.* The one bringing the wedding ceremony to an end is the imam. He is the one to bring about completion. *Soho'bi kami, hatina amuwan gara'.* Telling us what to do, in other words giving advice.

**buwani** *n.* Various species of honey bee. (*Thesaurus:* **kabulig, lampinig, tabungay, teya'-teya'**)

**buwang₁** *v. ditr.* 1) To cast something (into the sea). *Yuk siyaka inān, "Buwangku batilku makania'a pagpanggal." "Na," yuk pasunu', "buwangku batilku makania'a pagbubu maka ni kōk kumay."* The older brother said, "I will toss my container towards the *panggal* trapper." "Well then," said the next one, "I will toss my container towards the *bubu* trapper, and to the head of the surgeon-fish." (*Thesaurus:* **badji, bantung 1.1, laruk, timan₁**) 1.1) *v. tr.* To fish with a line cast from the land. *Amuwang ma bihing bowa'-angan, nilarukan tonda' niumpanan omang.* Fishing at the edge of the reef, throwing a line baited with hermit crab.

**buwang₂** *v. intr. pa-* To move quickly upwards for a short distance; to bounce up. *Palaksu-laksu, pabuwang-buwang.* Jumping and jumping, moving up and down.

**pagbuwang** *v. intr. aN-* 1) To bounce up repeatedly. *Magkallit tape'na, magbuwang-buwang sali'.* His feet kick up behind, sort of bouncing. *Saupama pambot akosog paragan bo' aniya' goyak, magbuwang-buwang.* A pumpboat, for example, running powerfully when there is rough water, bouncing [across waves]. *Alegsak tana'. Bang kita lum'ngngan, pisak magbuwang-buwang, al'mmis kita.* The ground is squelchy. When we walk, mud keeps flying up and we are dirty. 1.1) *v. tr.* To move something up and down. *Boben, ya pinagbuwang-buwang.* A yo-yo, the toy that is bounced up and down. (*Thesaurus:* **pagbullud-bullud, paghandok, paghuntak, pagtongket-tongket, pagumpak-umpak**)

**buwang₃** *v. tr.* To stir cooking food with a scooping motion. (*Thesaurus:* **ggang, huwal, sanglag, tompe'**)

**buwangkan** *n.* Something not valued; a reject. *Buwangkan buwat aku itu mbal kalomanannu, so' buwat Milikan inān subay kinalomanan.* A reject like me you don't respect, but someone like that Westerner has to be respected.

**pamuwangkan** *n.* Something abandoned or thrown away.

**buwangkan... buwangkan** *conj.* Contrasts two options, of which one is rejected, and the other merely tolerated. *Buwangkan na mpatpū' mbal katawakkalan, buwangkan hal saga duwampū' ī', tapaindam du.* Couldn't risk forty pesos, but since it's only twenty pesos I can lend it. *Buwangkan tapamuwanku ka'a, sagwā' bang hal pamaindam...* Giving it to you is out of the question, but if it is only a matter of a loan... *Buwangkan na daing, bang panggi' aniya'.* Fish is impossible, if it's cassava [you want] there is some.

**buwas** *n.* Husked rice, raw or cooked. *Mām, angindam kami buwas, dasawan pa'in. Ginanti'an du.* Ma'am, we want to borrow some [raw] rice, just one cup. It will be replaced.

**buwas-kinakan** *n.* Cooked rice. (*Thesaurus:* **kinakan 2, gulami, pai 1.1**)

**buwas-kuning** *n.* Rice colored and flavored with turmeric. (*cf:* **dulaw**)

**buwas-gandum** *n.* Corn maize, cracked or coarsely ground. *Buwas gandum ya pinaghinang durul. Amene' ka, ai sinokalan, ai nilahingan.* Corn rice is made into steamed corn-cakes. Your choice, whether it should be made with sugar or with grated coconut.

**buwas-pai** *n.* Unhusked rice.

**buwat** *adv.* 1) Similar in size, manner, appearance. *Saga buwat heya duwa luma'.* About the size of two houses. *Buwat bay yukku.* Just like I said. *Buwat ka'a maka saga dauranakannu.* Like you and your siblings. *Buwat luwa halimaw.* Like the appearance of a tiger. (*cf:* **muwat**; *Thesaurus:* **damikiyan 1, gin, sala 1, sali' 1.3**) 1.1) *n.* The likeness or equivalent of something. *Halam aniya' buwatna.* He has no equal.

**buwatna'an** var. of **buwattina'an**

**buwattehe'** var. of **buwattē'**

**buwattē'** (var. **buwattehe'**) *adv. dem.* 1) Like that, in that manner; then (of time). *Pi'itu ka salung buwattē'.* Come tomorrow about then. (*Set:* **buwattilu 1, buwattina'an 1, buwattitu 1**) 1.1) *v. tr.* To leave as is, without further action. *Bang buwattē'nu, halam du bay apōng.* If you did it like that, it wouldn't have broken. *Buwattē'in na.* Leave it as it is [that's fine].

**pagkabuwattē'** *v. intr. aN-* To happen in such a way.

**buwattilu** *adv. dem.* 1) Like that, in that manner; near the person spoken to. *Aniya' isāb badju'ku buwattilu luwana.* I have a blouse like that [the one you have on] in appearance. *Da'a ntanin buwattilu ko da'a abila'.* Don't hold it that way lest it break. (*Set:* **buwattē' 1, buwattina'an 1, buwattitu 1**) 1.1) *v. tr.* To do something in that way.

**buwattina'an** (var. **b'ttina'an**; **buwatna'an**) *adv. dem.* 1) Now; this present moment. *Alahang na maglugu' b'ttina'an, luwal dakuman kahaba' bulan Maulud.* Religious chants are rarely sung these days, only during every month of Maulud. (*Set:* **buwattē' 1, buwattilu 1, buwattitu 1**) **2)** Like that; in that manner. *Na palaran na s'llog buwatna'an.* So the tide is flowing like that.

**buwattingga** (var. **b'ttingga**) *interrog.* **1)** Like what? How? In what way? *Buwattingga tape'nu, gge?* How is your foot, friend? *Buwattingga he'ku aganak bang buwattitu kato'aku?* How can I produce a child when my age is like this? **1.1)** *v. tr.* To do something in what way? *Binuwattingga daing itū?* How is this fish to be prepared? (*Thesaurus:* **ai, angay, magay, maingga, sai, sumiyan**)

**buwattingga-buwattingga** *interrog.* In any way whatever; no matter how.

**buwattitu** (var. **battitu**) *adv. dem.* **1)** Now, of time; this present moment. (*Set:* **buwattē' 1, buwattilu 1, buwattina'an 1**) **1.1)** *adv. dem.* In this way; looking like this. *Sulatun buwattitu.* Write it like this. *Buwattingga? Buwattitu?* Like what [or how]? Like this? *Aniya' mussa' ta'nda'ku b'ttitu heyana.* I saw a pearl like this in size. *Sali' aiya'-iya'an dī kami na, ah'lling battitu.* We are sort of ashamed of ourselves talking like this. **1.2)** *v. tr.* To do something this way. *Subay binuwattitu bo' amupput. Buwattē'un na ba!* It should be done like this in order to fire [of an engine]. Just do it that way! *Halam ganta' bay makaniai-ai, taggaha' makabuwattitu.* Let's say nothing whatsoever happened, and suddenly it became like this.

**buwattitu-buwattina'an** *n.* Like this and like that (various unspecified things). (*cf:* **itu-ini**)

**kabuwattituhan** *n.* The present; here and now. *Min kariki'-diki'ku sampay ni kabuwattituhan.* From my childhood until the present time. *Angkanna aniya' saga panubu'na maglahat maitu sampay ni kabuwattituhan.* That's why there are descendants of his living here up to the present time.

**buway** *n.* Rattan. *Calamus spp. Aniya' kasehe'an magbanta isāb tittopan buway. Yuk a'a magbono' hē', "Subay asugpat buway inān bo' kita*

*magkahāp."* There are also people in an enemy relationship who [formalize it] by cutting off a piece of rattan. Those enemies say, "That rattan will have to be joined again for us to make peace."

**buway-buway** *v. intr. pa-* To flow slowly, of tide when nearing slack water. *B'nnal aniya' s'llog, bo' hal pabuway-buway.* True there is a current but it is just flowing slowly.

**buwaya** *n.* Crocodile. *Crocodylus porosus. Angalagad ka, sōng sangom aniya' buwaya.* Wait a bit, when it is almost night there will be a crocodile.

**buwaya-buwaya munda'** *n. phrase* A stylized crocodile carved on the prow of a pelang-type canoe.

**buwi'-munda'** var. of **buli'-munda'**

**buwis** *n.* **1)** The tax or tribute paid to an authority. *Saga anak-kampungna mbal na pinabayad buwis parinta.* His extended family will not have to pay the government taxes. **1.1)** *v. ditr.* To pay tribute or toll, especially to a supernatural being to ward off its harmful influence. *Bang kita taluwa' ni tōng lahat subay kita amuwis ni saitan. Bang sinagda he' saitan subay nihinang apug pamuwista.* If we are afflicted by [the thing] at Land's End we should pay tribute to the *saitan* spirit there. When a *saitan* troubles us a complete betel nut chew should be prepared as our tribute. (*Thesaurus:* **lamas, paglabot 2, tanggap 1.1, ungsud$_2$**)

**buwis deyo'** *n. phrase* The tribute paid to a sea spirit. {idiom}

**būy** *see:* **būyan, pabūy**

**būyan** var. of **buluyan**

**buyu'** *n.* The pepper vine or betel vine, the leaf of which is used to wrap the betel nut chew. *Piper betle.* (*cf:* **halug 1**)

**buyung$_1$** **1)** *n.* The scrotum. **2)** *voc. n.* Affectionate nickname for a little boy. *"O Buyung, magay ka?"* "Hey boy, what are you up to?"

**buyung$_2$** *n.* The mantle of a gas lamp. (*syn:* **mantel**)

# K k

**kā** *pron.* You (second person singular) [Set I]. *Amandi kā llaw-llaw.* You bathe every day. (*cf:* =**nu, ka'a**; *Set:* **akū, kām, kamī, kitā 1, kitabi$_1$, kitām, iyā, sigā$_1$, sigām$_1$**)

**ka$_1$** *ptl.* Question marker. *Aniya' ka ilu?* Is there any there? *Taga hād du ka legot? Bang halam aniya' hād tumbaku.* Does the dice [game] actually have a limit? If there is no limit, I'll bet the maximum. (*Thesaurus:* **bā 2, du 1, sa**)

**ka$_2$** *conj.* Connects alternatives in a series. *Ai na ka*

*Sūk, ai na ka Sama, ai na ka Milikan, magsakihan sadja.* Whether Tausug, Sama, or Westerner, all get sick. *Nilambot du aku e' mma'ku. Busay ka, atawa papan ka, atawa lantay.* I get smacked by my father. Could be a paddle, a board or a flooring slat.

**ka$_3$** var. of **maka$_3$**

**ka-$_1$** (var. **ika-**) *aff.* Ordinal prefix: attaches to any count numeral to indicate position in a numbered sequence (e.g. first, second, third).

*Ika'nnomna si Anu.* What's-his-name was his sixth [son]. *Ikaruwana, buwat angahinang ka tupara.* The second thing, as when you are making diving goggles.

**ka-₂** *aff.* Derivational prefix that attaches to a stative verb to form a noun. *Kalungay siyaliku halam aku bay ma luma'.* I wasn't home at the loss of my younger sibling. *Kalasa d'nda inān ma aku, minsan saga matto'ana tatiman na e'na.* Such was the love of that woman for me, she would even disavow her parents.

**ka-₃** var. of **ta-**

**ka-..-an₁** *aff.* Derivational circumfix that attaches to a noun to form a collective noun. *Gangsa itū tumbaga bay kamatto'ahan.* The *gangsa* referred to is a copper vessel from the time of the forebears. *Bang halam larang-larang, pehē' saitan ni deyom kabangkawan.* If there is no shelter [made for it] the demon goes into the mangrove forest.

**ka-..-an₂** *aff.* Adversative circumfix: attaches to a verb to indicate an event (usually negative) which occurs to a participant apart from his or her control. *Bang kami ka'apikihan he' bangsa inān, patā kami alahi.* If someone from that ethnic group closes up with us, we run far away. (*cf:* **-in-** 1.1, **ta-** 1.1)

**kabag** *adj. a-* 1) Prominent, of ears. *Akabag talingana, sali' alambu.* His ears stick out, sort of wide. **1.1)** *v. intr. pa-* To stand out from a surface, as ears.

  **kabag talinga** *v. intr. pa-* To catch someone's attention (lit. make one's ears stand out). {idiom}

**kabā'** (derivative of **bā'₂**) *v. tr.* To assume wrongly about some fact or situation. *Kabā'ku alungay pitakaku bo' halam.* I thought I had lost my wallet, but hadn't. *Ampunun aku, kabā'ku halam taga a'a.* Forgive me, I tassumed there was no one here. *Mbal sigām am'nnal ma haka d'nda inān sabab kinabā' hal magligaw.* They won't believe that woman's account because they think, mistakenly, that she is raving.

**kaba'** *n.* Tails, the side of a coin marked with a coat of arms. *Kaba' ya sīn taga sāp, halam taga a'a.* Kaba' is the side of a coin with the mark, the [side] without a human head on it. (*Thesaurus:* **kara, kurus**)

**kaba'-kaba'** *n.* A moth or butterfly.

**kabalaw** var. of **kabelaw**

**kaban** *n.* 1) A coffin. (*cf:* **lalungan**) 2) Cursing equivalent for a canoe. *Kabannu! Angay halam engkotannu bangka'?* Your coffin! Why didn't you tie the canoe up? (*gen:* **sukna'** 1.1)

**kabang** *n.* 1) Variegated coloring, of cloth or plumage. **1.1)** *adj. a-* Many-colored; variegated. *Badju'nu ilū akabang. Ilu na kolol kaginisan.* Your shirt is many-colored. All kinds of colors are there. (*Thesaurus:* **b'ttik** 1.1, **kelong-kelong₁**, **jali'** 1.1, **manas, palang**)

**kabasi'** *n.* Vegetable squash. *Cucurbita maxima.* *Am'lli aku kabasi' sinayul maka pundang.* I shall buy some squash to be used as a vegetable with dried fish.

**kabba** *v. tr.* To lose something from one's grasp. *Kinomkoman ko' mbal takabba.* Held securely in the hand so as not to let slip. *Wa'i atanak, wa'i takabbata daing, wa'i ala'an.* It's dropped, we've let the fish slip, it's gone. (*Thesaurus:* **larus, tanak** 1)

**kabbat** (var. **k'bbat₂**) *v. tr.* To close something securely, as a door or a wrapping. *Kinumbis, kinabbat luma'.* The house is shut up, closed securely. (*Thesaurus:* **takkop** 1, **tambol** 1.2)

**kabbul** *v. tr.* To fulfill a prediction or request, something only God can do. A: "*Makak'llo' kita llaw itu.*" B: "*Na, mampa'in kinabbul bowa'nu.*" A: "We will catch something today." B: "May God fulfil what comes out of your mouth." *Sali' kita ah'lling pangkal ni Tuhan. Yukta ni Tuhan, "Ō Tuhan, papatayun na aku llaw itu." Na bang sinulat he' Tuhan, amatay na. Takabbul bowa'ta.* As when we speak disrespectfully to God. We say to him, "O God, let me die today." Then if it is recorded by God, we die. What we said will be fulfilled.

  **atakabbul** *adj. zero* Confident or arrogant in regard to one's assertions about the future.

**kabbun** *n.* Plantation or orchard of fruit-producing trees. *Kabbun itū bang aheka to'ongan buwa' kayu maka niyug, bo' aluha, ya na hē' ōnna, kakabbunan.* A *kabbun* is when there are very many fruits and coconut palms, a wide area, that is its name, a plantation. (*Thesaurus:* **kati'an, gulangan, talun** 1)

**kabkab** *n.* 1) Something used as a fan. **1.1)** *v. tr. -an* To fan something in order to create movement of air or water. *Bang kita ma deyom luma', pinasu', angabkaban kita dīta maka labban.* When we are inside a house, feeling hot, we fan ourselves with a piece of cardboard. *Kinabkaban gusung maka pisak ko tahinang k'bbong-k'bbong.* The sand and mud are fanned so that a hollow is created. (*Thesaurus:* **kaskas₂, kayab** 1.1, **kayas** 1, **kaykay**)

**kabel-kabel** *n.* Decorative triangular flaps on the lower edge of a sail. (*Thesaurus:* **gores** 1, **jabel, jebel-jebel** 1.1)

**kabelaw** (var. **kabalaw**) *n.* A species of small bat. *Wa'i pasōd kabelaw ni sipsipan atop.* The bat has gone into the gap in the thatch. (*cf:* **kabog**)

**kabeto'** *n.* A species of small conch. *Strombus spp.*

**kabid** *see:* **atay₂**

**kabig** *v. intr. pa-* To veer sharply from a course. *Pakabigun munda' ni luma' disi El.* Turn the prow towards El's house. (*Thesaurus:* **agod, biluk** 1.1, **bintung** 1, **kauk, timpas**)

**kabili** *v. tr.* To castrate an animal or human.

**kabinet** *n.* A cabinet; a cupboard. *Pagpugaran*

*kamahung lo'ok-lo'ok kabinet inān.* The inside corners of that cabinet are a nesting-place for cockroaches. (*Thesaurus:* **paradol, perol**)

**kabit₁** *n.* 1) A hook-shaped fastener. (*Thesaurus:* **sagnat** 1) 1.1) *v. tr.* To fasten something by inserting a hook into an eyelet.

   **kakabit** *n.* A hook for fastening items.

**kabit₂** *n.* The game of toss-the-coin.

   **pagkabit** *v. intr. aN-* To play a game in which coins are tossed and their fall observed. *Bay aku magkabit ma Sisangat, tara'ug aku duwampū' sīn.* I played tossing coins at Sisangat and I lost twenty centavos. *Bang saupama magkabit ba, abō' ya sīn ma aku asekot-sekot ni manohan, angaikit, na mbal na magparūl.* Playing toss-the-coin for example, and my coin very close to the mark, [the opponent] is mean and won't let me in. (*Thesaurus:* **agad₂, pagsalla'** 1.1, **pagtalang, sulang₂, tingka**)

**kabiyasahan** *var. of* **kabiyaksahan**

**kablangan** *n.* The open sea. *Kablangan itū halam aniya' kapū'-pū'anna, timbang na. Kablangan* has no islands, it is open sea. (*Thesaurus:* **kaladjun, dilaut, s'llang₁, timbang₂**)

**kablit₁** *v. tr.* To bring together the extremities of something.

   **pagkablit** *v. intr. aN-* To be joined along butting edges.

   **papagkablit** *v. tr.* To join two long items end to end.

**kablit₂** *adj. -an* To be close to an expected time or amount. *Kablitan na ni siyam, atawa ni sangpū'.* Almost up to her 9th or 10th month. (*Thesaurus:* **abut₂** 1, **sampay** 2, **t'kka₁** 1.1)

**kabog** *n.* A fruit bat. *Order Chiroptera. Kabog, kinakan he' Bisaya'. Amangan bungang-kahuy, daluwa maka ambaw.* Fruit bats, eaten by Visayans. It eats fruit, and looks like a rat. (*cf:* **kabelaw**)

**kabombong** *n.* Spiders of all species. (*syn:* **lawa'** 1)

**kabowa** (derivative of **bowa₃**) *conj.* By reason of; because of. *Angalogmay iya kabowa tāwna. Amidpid isāb.* He is drained of strength because of his fear. And trembles too. *Magtūy iya anangis pakosog kabowa kagit atayna.* He promptly cried loudly, by reason of his anger. *Nda'un kabowa tāwna, makaragan nsa' baya.* Look how his fear affects him, running without thinking.

**kabtang** *v. tr.* To express something in words, especially in a formal context. *Bang aniya' kami magbono', yukna, "Ai kabilahi'annu, magbono'?" Yukku, "Angabtang sadja ka min t'dda, buwananta ka dakayu' suntuk."* If some of us are fighting, he says, "What do you want, to fight?" I say, "Utter a single word and I will give you a punch." *Mbal lagi' kono' makahibal, sagō' makakabtang na iya minsan mbal to'ongan lagi' klaro.* Reportedly unable to move, but he can speak even though it is not yet very clear. (*Thesaurus:* **kallam** 1)

   **kabtangan** *n.* Something spoken; a unit of speech. *Ya ina'an kabtangan bay pang'bba e'na ma anakna l'lla kasangpū' maka duwa.* Those are the words he left for his twelve sons. (*Thesaurus:* **ba'at** 1, **habal, haka** 1, **himumūngan, hunub-hunub** 1, **lapal** 1, **pahati** 1, **sambatan, suli-suli** 1)

**kabubu** *n.* A species of cleaner fish that accompany groupers.

**kabug-kabug** *see:* **pagkabug-kabug**

**kabulan** *n.* The fluid that separates from the oil of grated mature coconut. (*Thesaurus:* **gata'** 1, **p'tti'**)

**kabulay** *n.* 1) The curling strands of hair hanging down on each side of the face; the mane of a horse. *Aniya' d'nda taga kabulay, patonton bu'unna.* There are women with side bangs, whose hair hangs down. 1.1) *v. tr. -an* To arrange hair to curl down on each side of the head. *Kinabulayan bang kinawin.* Hair made to curl down the side of her face when she gets married.

**kabulig** *n.* A wasp or other flying insect capable of inflicting a painful sting. *Kabulig itu luwa tabungay. Angeket abisa, arai' aheya kabulig. Kabulig* is like a hornet. It has a potent sting, and maybe larger [than a hornet]. (*Thesaurus:* **buwani, lampinig, tabungay, teya'-teya'**)

**kabuni-bunihan** *var. of* **kabunyihan**

**kabunyihan** (*var.* **kabuni-bunihan**) *n.* All the things that give prestige to a house. *Kulang kabunyihan luma'nu itū, subay buwat luma' si Pa.* Your house is lacking in furnishings, it should be like the house of Pa [a wealthy merchant]. *Kabunyi-bunyihan deyom langit maka deyom ahirat, sali' kakaya'-kaya'an.* The entire range of things in the sky, in the afterworld, and anything whatever on earth, the whole array. (*Thesaurus:* **kakaya'an, kalangkapan₁, kapanyapan, pahandang** 1, **pinduwa'**)

**kabus** *v. advrs. -in-* Lacking in regard to essential items. *Am'lli kita balanja' apa kinabus na ma kinakan.* We will buy supplies because we are short of food. (*cf:* **kulang-kabus, kulang₁** 1; *Thesaurus:* **kettak, ipis** 1, **pihit, pulubi**)

**kabut-kabut** (*var.* **kiyabut-kiyabut**) *n.* Tactless or thoughtless behavior. *Mbal pinikil ya ai paluwas h'lling min bowa'na, makap'ddi' ni kasehe'an atawa mbal. Ya hē' kiyabut-kiyabut.* Not thinking about the words coming out of his mouth, whether or not they're hurtful to others. That's *kiyabut-kiyabut.*

**kaka** *n.* Short planking across the hull of a canoe.

   **pagkaka** *v. intr. aN-* To repeatedly knock two pieces of wood together to make a noise. *Bang magambit kita, magkaka maka kakal, busay, papan.* When we are driving fish together we make a noise with pieces of wood, or a paddle, or a plank.

**kakabit** (derivative of **kabit₁**) *n.* A hook for fastening items.

**kakakal** (derivative of **kakal**) *n.* A heavy stick used to beat something. *Minsan du aniya' budjak ma tanganna a'a bangsa inān, niatuhan iya e' si Be maka kakakal.* Even though the man of that ethnic group had a spear in his hand, Be fought him off with a cudgel. (*cf:* **bastun, tungkud 1**).

**kaka'** (var. **ka'**) *voc. n.* Address term to older relative, male or female, of the same generation as oneself.

**kakal** *v. tr.* To club or bludgeon someone. *Subay bay kinakal atawa bay nirugsu' bo' atubag.* It must have been clubbed or stabbed in order to die completely. (*Thesaurus:* **papas₂**)

**kakakal** *n.* A heavy stick used to beat something. (*cf:* **bastun, tungkud 1**)

**kakan** [Note: this irregular verb has two forms. Kakan is used with undergoer voice, passive voice, and locative voice. Mangan is used with actor voice and conveyance voice.] *v. tr.* **1)** To eat something. *Angadjal lagi' kami dakayu' anak kambing bo' aniya' kakannu.* We will just prepare a young goat so you'll have something to eat. *Bang kam ganta' sinagina e' a'a, kakanunbi ai-ai ya pinat'nna'an ka'am e' sigām.* If you happen to be welcomed in by someone, eat whatever they place in front of you. *Anabsab saga ni pilang, kalu aniya' panggi' kayu. Bang aniya' takakan, kakanta na, halam aniya' pagtilaw.* We sort of felt around in the fireplace, there might be some cassava. If there is food we eat it, no questions asked. *Subay na ka aubus amangan.* Should be when you have finished eating. *Al'kkas aku amangan.* I eat quickly. *Amangan maka agkakan sali' du. Mangan* and *kakan* [eat] are the same. (*cf:* **papa'**; *Thesaurus:* **inta', lallan, l'kkob, pakan**) **2)** To consume or corrode something, as through disease or decay. {idiom} *Ya na hē' i saki amangan isita.* That is the disease that consumes our flesh. *Wa'i kinakan isina e' saki giti'.* His flesh has been eaten away by tuberculosis. **3)** To penetrate by cutting into. {idiom} *Akapal kulit karuhung, bang lagutnu mbal amangan lahut.* The skin of the whale shark is thick, when you slash it the knife doesn't penetrate.

**kakan h'lla/h'nda** *v. tr.* To cause the sickness of one's husband or wife, an outcome of one's personal bad luck. {idiom} *Amangan h'ndana, amangan h'lla, amapatayan saga.* Consuming his wife, her husband, as though causing their death. (*cf:* **papatay 1.1**)

**pagkakan** *n.* **1)** Food in a general sense; staple items of diet. *Ai na pa'in pagkakanbi mahē' ma lahat Milikan?* What was it that you ate there in the Westerner's country? *Bang aniya' pagkawin pinat'nna'an lalabotan saga a'a magluruk, saga pagkakan, saga pagmama', pagsiga.* When there is a wedding the guests are presented with items of hospitality, food, betel chew ingredients, cigarets. *Angkan angentom aku lahat, luba'-labina*

*na pagkakan Sama!* That's why I am homesick, especially for Sama food! *Saga pagkakan alanab maka saga inuman amamis.* Rich food and sweet drinks. **1.1)** *v. intr.* aN- To be engaged in eating. *Itiya' lagi' magkakan.* Still here, busy eating. *Bang kita bay man kapū'an, am'lli kita gastu ni pasal apa halam kita bay makapagkakan.* When we have been to the islands we buy supplies at the store because we had not been eating.

**pagkakanan** *n.* A place for eating, such as a table, a dining room, an area of floor covered with a mat. (*cf:* **pamanganan**)

**kapamangan** *n.* The means of obtaining food, as money or trade.

**kinakan** *n.* **1)** Food in general. (*Thesaurus:* **talopa'**) **2)** Cooked rice. (*Thesaurus:* **buwas-kinakan, gulami, pai 1.1**)

**pamangan** *n.* The utensils with which food is eaten (e.g. a spoon, fingers, a section of green coconut husk).

**pamanganan** *n.* The containers from which food is eaten (e.g. a plate or bowl). (*cf:* **pagkakanan**)

**patikakanun** *adj.* To be forever eating.

**kakana'** *n.* Textiles; cloth of various types. *Pinasulugan iya juba ahalga' kakana'na.* He was clothed in a gown of expensive cloth. *Billi e'na kakana' panaput.* He bought cloth for a shroud. (*Thesaurus:* **s'mmek 1**)

**kakās** (derivative of **kās**) *n.* An implement for gathering up loose items; a rake.

**kakas** *n.* **1)** A fungal disease of the skin, commonly called ringworm. (*syn:* **kulap 1, pohak 1**) **1.1)** *v. advrs.* -in- Suffering from ringworm.

**kakasi** (derivative of **kasi**) *n.* **1)** A darling; a loved one. *Bang kono' amadlak ni atay saga kakasitam ma lahat alawak, sali' aniya' kasusahanta.* It is said that when our loved ones in a distant place come to mind, it's as though we experience sorrow. **1.1)** *v. tr.* -an To love someone. *Kakasihinbi saga a'a banta.* Love the people who are enemies.

**kakati'** *v. tr.* To relieve joint pain by holding a metal object to it. *Bang aniya' nihantu, kakati'un.* If someone is affected by *hantu* spirits, hold something made of metal near the painful parts. (*syn:* **hantu 1.2**)

**kakaw** *n.* The cacao tree and its fruit. *Theobrama cacao.*

**kakaya'an** *n.* An entire array, of things, equipment, furnishings, personal effects. *Buwat si Aj minsan mbal pi'ingga, amaluwas kakaya'anna, lilus, s'mmek, badju'.* Like Aj even though not going anywhere, brings out all his gear, watch, clothes, shirt. *Kabunyi-bunyihan deyom langit maka deyom ahirat, ai-ai isāb mareyom junna, sali' kakaya'-kaya'anna.* The entire range of things in the sky, in the afterworld, and anything whatever on earth, the whole array. (*Thesaurus:* **kabunyihan, kalangkapan₁, kapanyapan,**

pahandang 1, pinduwa')

**kakayaw** *v. tr.* To relieve itching of the skin by scratching. *Kakayawun kono' bukutku.* Please scratch my back. (*Thesaurus:* **kakkut, kamas, katol 1.1**)

**kakkal** *adj. zero* Permanent; enduring. *A'a mbal sali' magl'ngngan, magusaha. Kakkal ma luma'.* A person who doesn't walk about, doesn't go fishing. He's permanently in the house. *Otō', kakkal du ka ma aku, maka suku'nu asal kaniya'ku itū kamemon.* Son, you are always with me, and everything I have belongs to you. (*Thesaurus:* **d'ddos, dorog₁, taptap 1, tattal, t'ttog 1**)

**pagkakkal** *v. intr. aN-* To be permanently present. *Sinaitan-sowa ina' si Mi mbal ala'an, mahē' na magkakkal.* Mi's mother has a snake spirit that doesn't go away, it's there permanently.

**kakkang₁** *adj. a-* Pulled up tightly, of clothing. *Akakkang pantalun a'a hē'. Ahogot.* That guy's trousers are pulled up tight. Securely.

**kakkang₂** *n.* The bit of a horse's bridle.

**kakkot** *v. intr. aN-* To adhere to a surface, as rice to the pot it is cooked in. *Angakkot daing ilū bang akulang ns'llan.* That fish sticks if the oil is lacking. (*Thesaurus:* **balut 1.1, damil, pikit₁ 1**)

**kakkut** *v. tr.* To damage a surface by scratching. (*Thesaurus:* **kakayaw, kamas, katol 1.1**)

**pagkakkut** *v. intr. aN-* To be constantly scratching. *Kam'ssangan si Li bang mbal amandi. Sidda magkakkut.* Li has a rash [from seawater] if she doesn't bathe. She scratches a great deal.

**kaki₁** *n.* The color khaki.

**kaki₂** *n.* A cousin (the child of one's parent's sibling or cousin).

**pagkakihan** *n.* Cousin relationship. *Ipalku iya min pagkakihan.* He is my brother-in-law by cousin relationship.

**kaukaki** *n.* Cousins, collectively.

**dangkakihan** *n.* 1) Cousin relationship. 2) Closely related in meaning (fig.)

**kaki minduwa** *n. phrase* Second cousin. *Kakiku ko' inān, kakiku minduwa.* That's my cousin, my second cousin.

**kaki mint'dda** *n. phrase* First cousin. *Kakiku iya mint'dda.* She is my first cousin.

**kaku'** *adj. a-* Slow to respond. *Bang yukku, "Ndiya lahut." Akaku' pahāp ang'nde' ni aku. Na wa'i alahi daing.* Suppose I say, "Give me the knife." [He is] so slow in handing it to me. So the fish gets away. (*Thesaurus:* **aggal 1, hinay-hinay, lahan 1, lallay, pagene'-ene'**)

**kadkad** *adj. a-* 1) Stripped of everything; ransacked. *Akadkad na kami sababna hal bay pagbowahan aku.* We are stripped of resources because they have been used solely for taking me to healers. (*cf:* **kugud**) 1.1) *v. tr.* To search thoroughly; to ransack. *Halam aniya' minsan takadkad.* There is nothing, even though

searched for thoroughly. (*syn:* **kulakkad 1, lungkad 1**)

**kaddaw** *adv.* Hopefully; may it be as hoped or predicted. *Kaddaw ka amatay!* May you die! (*Thesaurus:* **gōm na pa'in, mura-murahan**)

**kadday** *n.* A roadside stall selling ready-cooked food and drinks. *Maginum a'a inān ma kakaddayan, sali' halam aniya' luma'na.* That man takes his refreshment at wayside eating places, as if he had no house. (*Thesaurus:* **estawran, pasal₂ 1, tabu' 1, tinda, tiyanggi**)

**kadde'-kadde'** *n.* Various fan-shaped marine bivalves, commonly called scallops. *fam. Pectinidae.*

**kaddom** var. of **k'ddom₁**

**kādja** *see:* **pagkādja**

**kadjalangking** *n.* A scorpion. (*syn:* **jalalangking**)

**kadjang** *n.* A covering or awning as shelter from sun or rain when travelling by canoe. *Sapaw itū kadjang, ya pinagbowa ni kapū'an ilū paturung ulan maka llaw.* An awning is a *kadjang*, commonly taken to the fishing islands for shelter from rain or sun. (*Thesaurus:* **ambung-ambung₂ 1, sapaw 1, sayap 1**)

**kadjang-kadjang** *n.* The prominence of ribs due to illness or starvation. (*Thesaurus:* **giyak, usuk**)

**kadjap** *see:* **sakadjap**

**kagadol** var. of **kalgadol**

**kagang** (*var.* **kagong**) *n.* Generic term for all species of crab. (*spec:* **bangkas, kalimango, kangkang₂, omang 1, panawan, sangbaw**)

**kagang-batu** *n.* Rock crab.

**kagang-kampay** (*var.* **kampay**) *n.* A species of small crab found among rocks and on house posts, inedible. *Kampay itū kagong, ya kaheka'an kampay itū buwat ma Tōng Batu, saga ma hāg luma'.* The *kampay* is a kind of crab, most abundant at Rock Point and on house posts.

**kagang-kullu'** (*var.* **kullu'**) *n.* The coconut crab. *Birgus Latro.*

**kagang-kumkum** (*var.* **kumkum₁**) *n.* A species of crab which burrows into sand.

**kagang-pēk** (*var.* **pēk**) *n.* A species of mud crab with a single long claw. *Anaggaw gi' aku pēk ni bangkaw, binowa ni si Lu.* I'll just catch a mud crab in the mangroves, to be taken to Lu. *Kagong-pēk ya kinalut. Pēk* crabs are the ones that are dug up.

**kagang-pulamata** (*var.* **pulamata**) *n.* A species of crab distinguished by its red eyes.

**kagang-sisu'an** (*var.* **sisu'an**) *n.* A species of crab valued for its edible meat. *Kagong-sisu'an sali' buwat isi keyot. Sisu'an* crabs, its meat like that of crayfish.

**kagang-sukay** (*var.* **sukay₂**) *n.* A species of crab, edible.

**kagang-tika'-tika'** (*var.* **tika'-tika'**) *n.* A species of crab, the fiddler crab. *Bay aku sinakket e' kagong-tika'-tika'.* I got nipped by a fiddler crab.

**kagat** *see:* **pagkagat**

**kagaw** *n.* Minute creatures, especially those that cause disease or infection; germs.

**kagayan** *n.* **1)** The twist technique in mat-weaving. **1.1)** *v. advrs.* -in- Woven with a twist design, of mats. **1.2)** *v. tr.* To weave a mat using the twist technique. (*Thesaurus:* **huyap-huyap 1, tabid₂**)

**kagkag** *v. intr.* aN- To become thin; to lose weight. *Angagkag sidda si Anu, sinaki tibi.* What's-his-name is becoming very thin, sick with tuberculosis. (*Thesaurus:* **kayog 1, kittay, koskos, kulagkag, giti' 1, higtal, titis 2**)

**kagingking** *n.* Slender branchlets from the top or base of bamboo. *Bang kayu sanga, bang p'ttung atawa kayawan kagingking.* The branch of a tree is *sanga*. The branch of a large bamboo or *kayawan*-type bamboo is *kagingking.* A: "Kagingking itū p'ttung bo' ariki'." B: "Pamagaynu?" A: "Pangādku luma'." A: "This *kagingking* is bamboo, but it is small." B: "What do you use it for?" A: "I use it for a fence round the house." (*Thesaurus:* **kayawan, kayuwan, daumu'an, p'ttung, t'mmang**)

**kagingkul** *n.* The noise of things clinking or clattering.

  **pagkagingkul** *v. intr.* aN- To make the clattering noise of things banging together. *Takale magkagingkul mareyom luma'. Aniya' angā' kabasi' min kaldero.* The sound of things banging together is heard in the house. Someone is getting squash from the cooking pot.

**kagis** *v. tr.* **1)** To remove something from a surface by inserting a blade under it. (*Thesaurus:* **bakkel 1.1, keke₁, l'ngnges 1.2**) **1.1)** *v. tr.* -an To clean a surface by scraping, away what adheres to it. *Kagisin ba lantay ilū apa aheka lansuk.* Scrape the floor off because there is a lot of wax.

**kagit** (*var.* **kagut**) *adj.* a- Angry; irritated. *Akagut itū sali' aniya' kap'ddi'anta atay ma pagkahita. Kagut* is like when we are angry towards our fellow man. *Pangimbū ya makapakagit h'lla.* It is jealousy that makes a husband angry.

  **kagit atay 1)** *v. intr.* pa-/a- To be offensive. {idiom} *Ē! Amakagit atay ko' ilū.* Hey! That [behavior] is very offensive. (*Thesaurus:* **ambul-dā', anak-anak₂, la'at atay, tumpalak 1**) **2)** *v. tr.* a-, ka-..-an, -an To be feeling the force of someone's displeasure. {idiom} *Hinangunbi ai-ai bay panoho'an ka'am bo' kam mbal kinakagitan e'na atay.* Do whatever you are told to do so you don't experience his anger.

**kag'llal** (derivative of **g'llal**) *n.* Official status; an appointment in the civil service. *Hal angugut konsehal inān, saukat taga kag'llal.* That councillor simply burdens people with his demands, just because he has status.

**kagod** (*var.* **kagud₂**) *v. tr.* **1)** To scrape out what's left in a pot or shell. *Kagurun lagi' botong ilu, kalu amangan gi'.* Scrape out that green coconut, someone may still eat it. *Bang ma botong,* *kinagod bo' nila'anan isina. Atawa buwas atutung min kaldero.* With a green coconut, it is scraped to remove the flesh. Or burnt rice [scraped] from a pot. **2)** To scrape a side, as a canoe squeezing through a narrow gap. *Bang aniya' bangka' ma dahū'an bo' agon mbal palabay, kagodbi dai'-dai'.* When there is a canoe ahead and it is nearly impossible to pass, you scrape it briefly.

**kagong** *var. of* **kagang**

**kagud₁** *var. of* **kugud**

**kagud₂** *var. of* **kagod**

**kagut** *var. of* **kagit**

**kagutgut** *n.* **1)** An itchy skin condition marked by blisters. **1.1)** *v. advrs.* -in- Afflicted with an itchy skin infection. (*Thesaurus:* **abas 1, buwa'-buwa' 1, katol 1.2, ugud**)

**kaha₁** *n.* A strongbox for storing valuables. *Kaha, buwat perol pangisihan pilak.* A safe, like a cupboard for holding money. (*gen:* **pagtau'an**)

**kaha₂ 1)** *n.* Cigarets in packet form. *Siga bīlli ma kaha'an.* Cigarets bought by the packet. (*Thesaurus:* **kustal 1, pākete, papan₂**) **2)** *clf.* Count word for packets of things. *B'llihin aku dangkaha siga.* Buy me one pack of cigarets.

**kahaba'** *adv.* Each or every, of recurring events or conditions. *Kahaba' llaw, kahaba' sangom.* Every day and every night. *Tatugila' bang sai dakayu' a'a ma sakahaba' sangpū' puhu' subay pinene'.* It was specified which individual should be chosen from every [grouping of] ten people. *Angahimati' na h'ndaku kahaba' sangpū' minit.* My wife is having contractions every ten minutes. *Kahaba' iya lingantu halam iya paruwa-ruwa angalungkad.* Whenever he is hungry, he has not hesitated to open [some food].

  **kahaba'-kahaba'** *adv.* Each succeeding time. *Anambahayang du aku kahaba'-kahaba' Juma'at.* I pray every Friday.

**kahak** *v. tr.* To bring up mucus by clearing the throat.

  **pagkahak** *v. intr.* aN- To clear one's throat; to bring up phlegm. *Bang kami amangan bo' ka magkahak, ala'at.* When we are eating and you hawk phlegm, that's improper. (*cf:* **kehem, panggahak**)

**kahad** *adj.* a- Tasting acrid or metallic, as unripe citrus or fruit cut with a metal blade. *Sali' akahad botong ilū, sali' bau b'ngngog.* That green coconut is kind of bitter, smells like it has been kept too long. (*Thesaurus:* **pa'it 1, p'kkat, p'ddas, p'llod**)

**kahagad** *v. tr.* zero To believe or obey someone. *Kahagad kami ka buwat kahē' kami magkahagad ma si Nabi Musa.* We will obey you as we obeyed the Prophet Moses. (*Thesaurus:* **beya'-beya'₁ 1, b'nnal 1.2, halap₁, parassaya, siddik**)

  **pagkahagad** *v. intr.* aN- To believe or obey.

**kaha'** *n.* A cooking pan with a single handle. *Pat'nna'un ns'llan lahing mareyom kaha'* *paglandang-landang tulay.* Put some coconut oil in the pan for frying herrings. (*gen:* **pam'llahan**)

**kahālan** (var. **kahaliluwalan**) *n.* Circumstances; the way things are. *Kinata'uhan e' Tuhan bang ai kahālanbi.* God knows how things are with you. *Atiya' aku amahati pasalan kahālanku.* I will now explain about my circumstances. *Halam tapagpamagayna kahālan ina'an i.* He had no concern for what was happening there. *Ya na tu'ud apalalna, kahaliluwalanna.* That is just how he is, the way things are with him. (*Thesaurus:* **pakaradja'an**)

**kahaliluwalan** var. of **kahālan**

**kahamkam** *n.* A shallow water marine plant with buoyant fruit-like appendages.

**kahandak** *n.* 1) Will or arbitrary decision, especially of God's involvement in human affairs. *Ya na tu'ud kahandak Tuhan.* That's simply God's will. (*Thesaurus:* **karal 1, kulis, ganta'an₁, indika 1, piguhan, sukud₂ 1**) **1.1)** *v. tr.* *-an* To grant someone a favor, the action of God. *Daipara kinahandakan kami e' Tuhan, angkan niōnan anak kami pangahandak.* Fortunately God showed us favor, which is why [he] is named child of God's favor.

**kahantang** (var. **hantang**) *n.* What can be seen; the look of something. *Aniya' tahik sali' hantang dinding min bihing sigām karuwambila'.* There was sea that looked like a wall on both sides of them. *Ya dahū paluwas, akeyat-keyat kuwitna maka bahibu'an baranna kamemon sali' kahantang kakana' akasap.* The first to emerge, his skin was reddish and his entire body was hairy, having the appearance of coarse cloth. *Mbal ba a'a itū buwat bay kahantang kayu pinuwas min api?* Isn't this person like wood taken away from a fire? *O'ō, tuwan, aniya' na gabun tapantawku min diyata', kahantang pād-tangan a'a.* Look, sir, I can see a cloud up there now, like the palm of a man's hand in appearance.

**kahang** *adj.* *a-* Rancid-smelling, as of a coconut open to the air for several days. *Bau kahang ns'llan lahing itu, mbal tapagguna.* This coconut oil smells rancid, it can't be used. (*cf:* **b'ngngog**)

**kahanga** *n.* Various spider conchs. *fam. Strombidae.*

**kahanga-nabal** *n.* A spider conch with heavy flange.

**kahanga-selo** *n.* A large finger conch.

**kahāp** (derivative of **hāp**) *n.* Goodness; kindness. *Nilarukan saga s'mmek saga taumpa', ya kahāp Milikan.* Clothes and shoes were thrown [to us], the kindness of the Americans.

**kahawa** *n.* The coffee plant and its fruit; the beverage. *Coffea arabica.* *Na bang ka'a ilū anginum kahawa, aku pi'itu na pa'in anginum.* So when you are drinking coffee, I am in the habit of coming to get a drink. (*syn:* **kape**; *Thesaurus:* **neskape, tī**)

**kahemon** var. of **kamemon**

**kahentong** *n.* The egg shell, a white cowrie-like monovalve. *Ovula ovum.*

**kahi** *see:* **pagkahi**

**kahid** *v. tr.* 1) To move or reach something with the tip of a stick. *Bang aniya' s'mmek ahūg pareyo' kahidta pariyata'. Kahidta maka bola'.* If a garment falls down we lift it with something long. We get it with a bamboo slat. (*Thesaurus:* **kawit₁, kuhit, sungkit**) **1.1)** *v. tr.* *-an* To move something away with a stick. *Kinahiran daing min atay-atay bubu.* The fish were moved with a stick away from the opening of the *bubu* trap.

**kahig** *v. tr.* To scratch or rake the surface of the soil. (*Thesaurus:* **kās, kikis, hīs 1.1**)

**kahimul-himulan** *n.* A community assembly at a formal event such as a wedding or litigation. *Basta aheka a'a, kahimul-himulan a'a, sali' kalasigan.* When there are many people, people assembling for an event, like a celebration. *Kahimul-himulan, subay aniya' palkala', buwat saga ni pagkawinan, buwat maggunting, magtammat. Basta aheka a'a, kahimul-himulan a'a.* A public gathering, one which has a focus, such as a wedding, or a hair-cutting ceremony, or a graduation. Whenever there are many people, that is a *kahimul-himulan.*

**kahinapusan** (derivative of **hinapusan**) *n.* The final item in a series. *Buwat kita lum'ngngan kat'llu, aku itū kahinapusan, karamulihan to'ongan.* Like the three of us walking, and I am the last of all, left well behind. *Ma kahinapusanna, ah'lling saga po'on kayu ni dampo'on kayu itingan, "Na, ka'a na ya magsultanan kami."* At the conclusion, the trees said to a single thorn tree, "So then, you are the one to be king over us."

**kahirupan** *n.* Essentials for maintaining life. *Amiha kahirupan baran, buwat saga kinakan, bohe', s'mmek, pangayu, maka pelang.* Looking for bodily necessities such as food, water, clothing, firewood, and canoe. (*Thesaurus:* **balanja' 1, ka'lluman, gastu 1, lutu'₁ 1, pagnapaka**)

**kahukaw** (derivative of **hukaw**) *v. tr.* *-an* To resist being sexually intimate. *Ka'am maglakibini, da'a kahukawinbi batin.* You who are married, do not resist being intimate with each other.

**kahūgan** var. of **kahulugan**

**kahulugan** (var. **kahūgan**) *n.* The meaning of something said or written. *Niusal, buwat sapantun nihinang pabalik. Aheka kahuluganna.* The word *niusal,* for example, means something done again. It has many meanings. (*Thesaurus:* **hantang-hatulan, hati 1, hatulan 2, ma'ana₁ 1**)

**kahumbu** *n.* A whale. *Order Cetacea.* (*gen:* **sattuwa**; *Thesaurus:* **gadjamina, layul**)

**kaikit₁** *adj.* *zero* Ungenerous or stingy. (*Thesaurus:* **bista₂ 1, kigit, kimmat 1, k'mmit 1, kudkud, kuriput 1, kussil, giging, iskut, sumil₁**)

**kaikit₂** *adj. zero* 1) Sneaky; deceitful. *Si No itū mbal ala'an bang kaikit na. Halam aniya' sīnna.* No won't withdraw [from a game] when he's being tricky. He has no money. (*Thesaurus:* **akkal 1.1**) 1.1) *v. tr.* To win a game by trickery. *Bang saupama magkabit bo' ya sīn ma aku ina'an asekot-sekot ni manohan, abō' angaikit na, mbal na magparūl.* Playing toss-the-coin for example, and my coin is there quite close to the mark, and then he is playing his tricks, he won't allow me to win.

**kailū** *see:* **ndū' kailū**

**kaiman** *var. of* **kaliman**

**kaipat** *var. of* **kalipat**

**kait** *n.* 1) A fastener for a brooch; a safety pin. (*cf:* **alperel**) 1.1) *v. tr.* To fasten something with a safety pin. *Am'lli aku kait duwa aheya pangait sanyawa onde'-onde'.* I will buy two safety pins, large ones, to fasten the baby's panties.

**kaitan** *var. of* **kalitan**

**ka'** *var. of* **kaka'**

**ka'a** *pron.* You (second person singular) [Set III]. *Ka'a ko' ilū.* So it's you [a conventional greeting]. *A: "Ma sai kahawa itū?" B: "Ma ka'a."* A: "Who is this coffee for?" B: "For you." *Ndiya, sugpatanta ka'a bahu' ilū bay apōng.* Give it here, I will extend for you the boom that broke. (*cf:* =**nu, kā**; *Set:* **aku₂, ka'am, kami, kita, kitabi₂, kitam, iya, sigā₂, sigām₂**)

**ka'am** *pron.* You (second person plural) [Set III]. *Ka'am ilū, subay angasip.* You there, you had better pay attention. (*cf:* =**bi, kām**; *Set:* **aku₂, ka'a, kami, kita, kitabi₂, kitam, iya, sigā₂, sigām₂**)

**ka'ang** *n.* A glazed earthenware jar with wide mouth. (*Thesaurus:* **bingki', kasambagan, kibut, pipa, poga, tanāng, tangpad**)

**ka'asāl** (derivative of **asāl**) *n.* The natural or original state of a person or thing. *Akiyu' bowa'na, asāl bay ka'asālna hē'.* His mouth is twisted, the way it was from his very beginning.

**ka'at** *n.* 1) Damage or harm to something. *Aheya pahāp ka'atna.* Its damage is severe. 1.1) *v. advrs.* ka-...-an To be destroyed completely; trashed. *Bang kita kaut bo' sali' kaka'atan ai-ai bay bowata, yukna ma luma', "Anginsā' ka m'nnilu. Beya'-beya'un pandu'ku."* When we go out to sea and everything we brought is destroyed, those who stayed home say, "Learn a lesson from that. Follow my teaching."

**pagka'at** *v. intr.* aN- To become damaged. *Buliburun pelang i' tudju pi'itu munda'na bo' mbal magka'at sangpad.* Turn the front of that canoe round towards here so that the raised prow won't be damaged. *Sali' ai-ai bay magka'at ya alopas. Kaiman ka ya ai-aiku ī'.* Like whatever was broken is lost. Those things of mine are sadly wasted. *Magka'at na saga po'on kayu tamakahāp. Bay badju.* The finest trees were ruined. There was a storm.

**paka'at** *v. tr.* To destroy or misuse something.

**ka'ina-tagna'** *n.* Former times; long ago. *Ya pangannalku, ina'an kitām magbalharap magsuli-suli sali' ka'ina-tagna'.* In my thoughts we are there talking together, face to face, as we used to.

**ka'inagon** *see:* **pagka'inagon**

**ka'is** *adj.* a- Moving at a near run. *Aka'is pahāp a'a hē' lum'ngngan.* That fellow is a very brisk walker. (*Thesaurus:* **baggis, kasay 1, kulakkus, l'kkas 1, samot 1, sapat₂ 1**)

**ka'llum** (derivative of **llum**) *n.* Life, as a state of being.

**ka'llum-kamatay** *n.* Life and death as the span of human existence. *Ka'llum-kamatay, ameya' aku ma ka'a.* In life or in death, I will go with you.

**ka'mbal** (derivative of **mbal**) *n.* Negativity of response or attitude. *B'nnal aniya' ka'mbalna, ya mbal kasulutan.* True he has reservations, not being in agreement.

**ka'ob** *see:* **pagka'ob**

**ka'ssa** (derivative of **ssa₃**) *n.* The first item in a series.

**ka'ullang** *n.* Shrimp; prawn. *Anaggaw aku ka'ullang ni sowang-sowang.* I will capture shrimps in the mangrove channels. (*cf:* **ullang 1**; *syn:* **ulang 1**)

**kalabusu** *n.* 1) Jail; prison. *Bang aku mareyom jīl, aku haumnu. Binowa aku paluwas min kalabusu.* If I am in jail, you arrange for my release. I am brought out of the prison. 1.1) *v. tr.* To imprison someone. (*Thesaurus:* **jīl 1.1, pilisu 1.1**)

**kaladja'an** *var. of* **karadja'an**

**kaladjun** *n.* The remotest ocean. {archaic} *Ma dilaut kaladjun, atala dilaut, mbal na ta'nda' lahat.* The wide open sea, far out at sea, where no land is seen. (*Thesaurus:* **kablangan, dilaut, s'llang₁, timbang₂**)

**kalagihan** *n.* 1) Purpose, use or need for something. *Bang nsa' aniya' kalagihanbi pōng kayu ilu, arāk amu'ku.* If you have no use for that offcut of wood, I was thinking of asking for it. (*Thesaurus:* **kapunyahan, kapūsan, guna 1.2**) 1.1) *v. tr.* a-, ka-..-an, -an To make use of something. *Ai-ai tinimanan, ai-ai mbal na kinalagihan.* Anything thrown away, another no longer usable.

**kalamansi** *var. of* **kalamonden**

**kalamonden** (var. **kalamansi**) *n.* Calamansi (or calamondin) tree and its fruit. *Citrus microcarpa. Kalamonden maka muntay, saddī.* Calamansi and lemons are different. (*gen:* **muntay**)

**kalamunggay** *n.* Moringa, a small tree and its edible leaves and pods. *Moringa oleifera.* (*syn:* **kilul**)

**kalanjang** *n.* A unit of sago meal, the amount pressed into a kalanjangan basket.

**kalanjangan** *n.* A tall cylindrical basket of open-woven rattan. (*gen:* **baka'₁**)

**kalang**₁ *v. tr.* 1) To sing a song. *Ai kabaya'anbi kinalang?* What do you want to have sung? (*Thesaurus:* **kerol, dindang-dindang, pagbinuwa 1, tenes-tenes**) 1.1) *v. tr. -an* To sing over someone. *Aniya' kono' nnom budjang-budjang bay pina'an angalangan iya.* There were reportedly six girls who went there singing over him.

**kalangan**₁ *n.* A song. (*Thesaurus:* **langan**₂ 1, **lugu'** 1, **sa'il**)

**pagkalang** *v. intr. aN-* To be singing a song. *Sasuku angā'an aku magkalang kabuwanan du tambahan.* Whoever gets me a singer will definitely be given some remuneration.

**kalang**₂ *n.* Coral broken into fine fragments; gravel. (*syn:* **kalangan**₃)

**kalang-belle'** *n.* A hard-shelled seed case used in children's games.

**kalangan**₂ (var. **galangan**) *n.* A structure for supporting canoes above sea level so the hull can be cleaned. (*syn:* **bantilan, tangonan**)

**kalangan**₃ (var. **kāngan**) *n.* Coral broken into fine fragments; gravel. *Kāngan itū bay sahasa'. A'aslag man gusung bo' apote' du isāb. Aho', aniya' isāb gaddung, ya sali' nilumut.* This *kangan* was formerly finger coral. It is coarser than sand but it is just as white. Oh yes, and there is green [gravel] too, sort of moss-grown. (*syn:* **kalang**₂; *Thesaurus:* **bunbun 1, kapote'an, gusung, igang**₁)

**kalangkapan**₁ *n.* Equipment needed for a project or enterprise. *Bang ka ni M'ddas am'lli ka kalangkapan ai-ai, sakap ai-ai.* When you go to Siasi you buy gear of every kind, complete. *Aheka kalangkapannu, nsa' kulang, jukup.* You have so much gear, lacking nothing, complete. (*Thesaurus:* **kabunyihan, kakaya'an, kapanyapan, pahandang 1, pinduwa'**)

**kalap** *adj. a-* More so; to a greater degree. *Agsāy aku ah'lling, "Asā' ka." Magtūy yuknu, "Ya du ka'a, akalap ka min aku."* I promptly say, "You're wrong." Then you say, "So are you, more so than I am." *Akalap, sali' bang mareyom iskul ata'u iya min kamemon.* More so than [others], like in school, knowing more than them all. *Akalap lagi' kala'atan sigām min bay kahinangan kamatto'ahan sigām.* Their wrongdoing is worse than what their forebears used to do. (*Thesaurus:* **anambahina, bangkinna...bangkinna, labi-labi, luba', luhūy, paligay, ya lagi'na**)

**kalapiya** *n.* Rubber tree; various tree species with rubbery sap. *Palaquium spp. Anagok kalapiya itū bang kinehet.* This rubber tree forms sap when cut. (*cf:* **goma**₁ 1)

**kalas** *n.* The color pink. (*gen:* **walna'**)

**kalasussu** *n.* A shell case; a cartridge. (*cf:* **punglu'**)

**kalaut** var. of **kaut**

**kalaw** *n.* The Sulu hornbill. *Anthracoceros montani.*

**kalbaw** *n.* 1) The Asian water buffalo; carabao. *Bubalis bubalis.* (*cf:* **sapi'**) 1.1) *v. intr. aN-* To ride on a water buffalo. *Ameya' aku magguyud sapi', maka si Ha angalbaw.* I will go along pulling the cow, and Ha will ride the water buffalo.

**kalbin** *n.* A carbine; any older type of rifle. *Ina'an saljen niabing, an'ngge maka kalbinna.* There was the sergeant getting in the way, standing there with his rifle. (*Thesaurus:* **kanyun 1, garan, lantaka 1, musil, pistul, sinapang**)

**kalkula** *v. tr.* To make a detailed list. *Niuki', hatina kinalkula kamemon.* A sequence completed, in other words a detailed list. (*Thesaurus:* **kira, itung**₁, **jumla 1, saipuwa**)

**kaldang** *n.* Stilts for walking.

**kaldero** *n.* A metal cooking pot with a stirrup handle. *Wa'i al'ssu' kaldero, mbal na tapam'llahan daing.* The metal pot has developed a hole, it can't be used for boiling fish. (*gen:* **pam'llahan**)

**kale** *v. tr.* 1) To hear something. *Mbal paluwas llingna, sali' nihegom-hegom mareyom atayna. Mbal takale ni a'a kamemon.* He doesn't say anything, it's as though he keeps it in his heart. It isn't heard by everyone. *Bang abisu, mbal makakale.* If someone is deaf he cannot hear. (*Thesaurus:* **bahingaw, hīng-hīng, talengog**) 1.1) *v. intr. pa-/a-* To listen to what is being said. *Da'a kam asagaw. Pakale kam.* Don't be noisy. Be listening.

**pagkale** 1) *v. intr. aN-* To be listening attentively. 2) *v. tr.* To pay attention to what one hears. *Pagkalehun kono'.* Please be attentive.

**pakale** *v. tr.* To have someone listen; to make something known.

**pangale** *n.* Something heard or overhead.

**kalesa** *n.* A vehicle drawn by a draft animal. *Nsa' pa'in at'ggol, ta'nda'ku huwis ameya' min kalesa.* It wasn't long before I saw a judge coming on a horse-drawn carriage. (*Thesaurus:* **karita'**)

**kaleya** *adv.* 1) In a landwards direction. (*Thesaurus:* **kaut 1, lūd, takod 1, tukad**₁ 1) 1.1) *v. intr. zero* To go in a landwards direction. *Kaleya aku angā' daun biyabas.* I am going inland to get some guava leaves. *Banda'anku iya. Mbal pakaleyaku apa aniya' mundu.* I will warn him. I won't let him go inland because there are bandits. 1.2) *v. tr.* To get something by going inland. *Angaleya kami panggi' kayu ni deya Hambilan.* We get cassava by going inland to the hinterland of Hambilan.

**kalga** *v. intr. aN-* To carry loads for a living; to work as a porter. *Ni M'ddas aku angalga.* I am going to Siasi Town to earn money carrying things. *Si Sa bay angalga, agaranku ma jambatan.* Sa was stevedoring, I waited for him at the wharf.

**pagkalga** *v. intr. aN-* To carry loads for a living. *Mbal na aku makakole' magkalga.* I am no longer able to work as a porter.

**pagkalgahan** *n.* The work or occupation of carrying loads. *Abuggul si Anu he' pagkalgahan.* What's-his-name is hump-backed from the carrying of loads.

**kalgadol** (var. **kagadol**) *n.* A person who carries loads for a living. *Bariles ginulung-gulung hē' ma M'ddas he' kalgadol.* Barrels are rolled along there in Siasi by the porters.

**pagkalgadol** *v. intr.* aN- To work as a carrier.

**kali** (var. **kali'**) *v. tr.* To dig a hole. *Aniya' maina'an pagbohe'an baha'u bay kinali e' saga sosoho'an si Isa'ak.* There was a new water-hole there that had been dug by Isaac's workers. (*cf:* **kalut**)

**Kalibugan** *n.* Kolibugan, a Subanon subgroup from the Zamboanga Peninsula who have converted to Islam.

**kali-kali** (var. **kāy-kāy**) *n.* The lucine clam, an edible bivalve found about six inches deep in exposed sand. *fam. Tellinidae. Bang t'bba angalut kami ni gusung kāy-kāy.* When it is low water we dig in sandy places for lucine clams.

**kalibubut** *n.* 1) A boil or carbuncle. *Taga nana' kalibubut itū.* This boil has pus in it. (*Thesaurus:* **bautut 1, bularut**) 1.1) *v. advrs.* -in- Suffering from boils.

**kali'** var. of **kali**

**kali'awan** var. of **kaliyawan**

**kalima** *n.* Confessional statements derived from the Holy Koran. *Bang kita magsapda ma Kora'an yukta duwa'a kalima.* When we swear an oath on the Holy Koran, we say it is a *kalima* prayer.

**kaliman** (var. **kaiman**) *adj. zero* Wasted or lost, regrettably. *Kaliman pelang ya bay tinimanan he' a'a palaran ma dilaut. Asidda iya arupang. Halam pagbayanna ni M'ddas.* The canoe was sadly wasted, the one thrown away by someone to drift out at sea. He is really stupid. He has no transport to Siasi. *Sali' ai-ai bay magka'at ya alopas. Kaiman ka ya ai-aiku i'.* Like whatever was broken being lost. Those things of mine are sadly wasted. *Kaliman aku, wa'i alungay lilusku.* I am devastated, my watch is lost. (*syn:* **kaugun**)

**kalimango** *n.* Mangrove crab species. (*gen:* **kagang**)

**kalimango-pagung** *n.* A species of large, deepwater crab.

**kalimbit** (derivative of **limbit**) *n.* A responsibility which limits one's freedom. *Bang aku atulak ni Bukidnon halam aniya' kalimbitku.* When I leave for Bukidnon I will have nothing to distract me. *Alimaya itū sali' halam aniya' kalimbitku.* Feeling free is like my having no responsibilities.

**kalintaw** *adj.* a- Irritated; becoming annoyed. *Akalintaw, bay kami maglata.* Getting annoyed, we had been joking. (*Thesaurus:* **dole' 1, dugal 1, giyagas, jural, mata-mata₁, p'ggot-p'ggot, s'ngngot₁ 1, sunggud**)

**kalintawan** *n.* A source of irritation. *Bang a'a mbal kasulutan, buwat aniya' kalintawanna, an'kket iya.* When a person is not pleased, when there is something he is irritated about, he stands with hands on hips.

**pakalintaw** *v. tr.* To provoke or anger someone.

**pagpakalintaw** *v. tr.* To be provoking each other to anger.

**kalipat** (var.**kaipat**) (derivative of **lipat₂**) *v. tr.* 1) To forget something. *Ndū', da'a aku kalipatun.* Please, don't forget me. *Mbal itu takalipat e' saga panubu' sigām.* This will not be forgotten by their descendants. *Da'a ka ahaman-haman bang ka anau' ko' da'a alungay. Sali' da'a takalipatun.* Don't be thoughtless when you store something to keep it from being lost. Like [saying] don't forget it. *Halam aniya' bay takalipatku atawa taikutanku minsan ai.* I have neither forgotten nor rejected anything. *Magbono' Belle' maka Munari. Ya ko' i' bay takalipatku.* Eagle and *Munari* Bird were fighting. That's the bit I forgot. *Panglupa aku, wa'i takalipat.* I am absent-minded, it is totally forgotten. (*Thesaurus:* **bibas₂, liha-liha, lipas, panglupa**).1.1) *v. tr.* -an To forget something one was told to remember. *Na kamaya' kam to'ongan, da'a takalipatinbi ya bay pananggup mastal inān.* Now be very careful, don't forget the schoolmaster's warning.

**kalis** *n.* A weapon with a wavy blade; a kris. (*Thesaurus:* **barung, punyal 1**)

**kalitan** (var. **kaitan**) 1) *n.* Generic term for various shark species. (*spec:* **mangkesol, talom-badji**) 2) *v. intr.* aN- To fish for sharks. 3) *v. advrs.* -in- Eaten by a shark. *Bang ta'ā' daing bo' tininduk he' daing dakayu', kinalitan.* When a fish has been caught and it is taken by another fish, it has been sharked.

**kalitan-antugan** (var. **antugan**) *n.* Grey reef shark, a Requiem shark. *Carcharhinus amblyrhynchos.*

**kalitan-bagambul** (var. **bagambul**) *n.* Oceanic whitetip shark, a Requiem shark. *Charcharinus longimanus.*

**kalitan-batu** *n.* A species of coral shark.

**kalitan-bohe'** *n.* A species of shark (unclassified).

**kalitan-kallang-kallang** (var. **kallang-kallang**) *n.* Blue shark, a requiem shark species.

**kalitan-kamansihan** (var. **kamansihan**) *n.* A species of sand shark.

**kalitan-kuting** *n.* Wobbegong shark, a bottom-dwelling shark. *fam. Orectolobidae.*

**kalitan-gamat** (var. **gamat₂**) *n.* Blue shark, considered to be a variety of kalitan-kallang-kallang. *Prionace glauca.*

**kalitan-itingan** *n.* Various sea-catfishes, including the Spotted catfish and the Giant catfish. *Arius maculatus, A. thalassimus.*

**kalitan-lalu'u** (var. **lalu'u**) *n.* Bull shark. *Carcharinus leucus.*

**kalitan-lokay** *n.* Thresher shark. *Alopias vulpinus.*

**kalitan-mangali** *n.* Tiger shark. *Carcharodon carcharias.*

**kalitan-mela'** (var. **mela'**) *n.* Sand shark, a species which partly submerges in the sand. *fam. Odontaspididae.*

**kalitan-pamingkungan** (var. **pamingkungan**) *n.* Hammerhead shark. *Sphyrnidae zygaena.*

**kalitan-pinanaw** (var. **pinanaw**) *n.* A species of shark.

**kalitan-pipi** (var. **pipi₃**) *n.* A species of shark.

**kalitan-salimbūng** (var. **salimbūng**) *n.* A species of shark.

**kalitan-sosop** (var. **sosop**) *n.* Tawny nurse shark; Carpet shark. *Nebrius ferrugineous.*

**kalitan-t'kke'** (var. **kalitan-tokke'**) *n.* Epaulette shark, a shark-sucker. *fam. Echineidae (tentative).*

**kalitan-tutungan-s'llang** (var. **tutungan-s'llang**) *n.* Blacktip shark, a deepwater species. *Carcharias melanopterus.*

**kalitan-tutungan-t'bba** (var. **tutungan-t'bba**) *n.* Blacktip reef shark. *fam. Odontaspididae.*

**kalitan-ulagu** (var. **ulagu**) *n.* A species of shark.

**kalitan kallang-kallang pipi** *n. phrase* Oceanic whitetip shark, a Requiem shark. *Isurus oxyrinchus.*

**kalitan-tokke'** var. of **kalitan-t'kke'**

**kaliyagge'** *n.* A worthless, socially outcast person.

**kal'mmut** var. of **kammut**

**kalla'₁** *adj. a-* Being wasteful in the use of scarce resources. *Da'a ka akalla' ma umpan ilū apa akulang umpan.* Don't be wasteful with the bait because there is a shortage.

**kalla'₂** *n.* A funeral meal.

**kalla'an** *n.* 1) Food eaten by mourners after a burial. 2) A cursing equivalent for food eaten greedily. *Da'a ka amangan pagkalla'annu ilū. Angagad ka.* Don't go eating your own burial meal. Wait a bit.

**pagkalla'** *v. intr. aN-* To be engaged in the ceremonies and communal meal that mark the end of the funeral sequence. *Bang at'kka min pagkubulan, ya hē' niōnan magkalla', sali' magjamu a'a kamemon. Bang halam gi' kinubul, yuk kami, "tulun-tana'".* When [people] arrive from the burial ground, that's called *kalla'*, that's when all the people feast. If the interment has not yet taken place we call it, "down into the earth".

**kallam** *v. tr.* 1) To speak formally, especially of making a promise or vow. *Bay aku angallam ni Tuhan, sali' bay anganajal.* I made a commitment to God, like making a vow. (*Thesaurus:* **kabtang**) 2) Enunciation of Arabic letters. *Pangallam isāb tudju batang sulat ilū, nihidja'.* Kallam also refers to those [Arabic] letters being spelled out.

**kallang-kallang** var. of **kalitan-kallang-kallang**

**kallari'** *n.* A variety of taro of which only the corm is eaten. *Colocasia esculenta.* (*Thesaurus:* **kapeta', hupi' 1, tuwad**)

**kalling** *n.* The starfish, a generic term for several varieties. *fam. Acanthasteridae.*

**kalling-sahanay** (var. **sahanay**) *n.* The crown-of-thorns starfish. *Acanthaster planci.*

**kallit** *v. tr.* To lift something into the air in a burst of energy. *An'ngge si Hu, bay pah'bba'ku tape'na, bay kallitku.* Hu stood up, I caused his foot to fall, I had lifted it up into the air.

**pagkallit** *v. intr. aN-* To be flailing or threshing, as the tail of a fish, or the legs of a happy boy. *Mangkesol, ya magkallit tape'na. Yukta, "Kakalun, asagut naelon."* Coral sharks, the ones that thresh their tails. We say, "Club it, the line will get tangled." *Magkallit tape'na, magbuwang sali'.* His feet lifting up, sort of bouncing into the air.

**kallo'** *n.* A species of heron or egret. *Bo' na maggara' kallo' maka kuyya'.* The heron and the monkey then discussed [the plan]. *Kallo'-kallo' pote' ariki', bang t'bba aheka. Aniya' isāb ettom.* Small white egrets, a lot of them at low tide. There are black ones too.

**kalluk** *adj. a-* 1) Crooked; out of alignment. (*Thesaurus:* **bengkok 1, bunt'lled, kello' 1.1**) 1.1) *v. intr. pa-* To bend out of alignment. *Mbal na makabontol an'ngge, asidda na ataha' t'bbu. Pakalluk na pareyo'.* The sugar cane cannot stand up straight, it is too long. It has bent downwards.

**pagkalluk-kalluk** *v. intr. aN-* To curl and straighten one's fingers.

**kallu'** *v. advrs. -in-* Suffering from a congenital condition involving speech and motor control.

**kalluman** var. of **ka'lluman**

**kallus₁** *v. intr. zero* 1) To push when excreting. *Bang onde'-onde' a'sso to'ongan, yukta, "Kallus, kallus, makagām-gāman na."* When a toddler is over-full, we say, "Push, push, it's getting better." 1.1) *v. tr. -an* To press the stomach with a flat object to aid excretion. *An'gga b'ttongna, a'sso he' kinakan. Subay kinallusan maka luwag sinungi'an ni lowang.* His stomach is engorged, full of food. It should be pressed with a ladle, then excreted through the toilet-hole. (*Thesaurus:* **hilut, salimpak**)

**kallus₂** *v. tr. -an* To dash water from the hull of a canoe. *Kallusin na, abuhaw. Saddī asait, hal ango'ot.* Dash out the water, [the canoe] is taking water. Bailing is different, it is just scooping. (*Thesaurus:* **k'llut 1.1, lodjat₂ 2, sait**)

**kalna'** (var. **sabab-kalna'**) *conj.* 1) Because. *Bowahunbi isāb sīn nilipat duwa min bay pam'llibi tagna' hē', kalna' in sīn bay tabākbi subay pinabalik ni sigām.* And take twice the money you paid originally, because the money you found should be returned to them. 1.1) *n.* Reason; cause. (*Thesaurus:* **apa, pagka, po'on₂, sabab₁ 1.1, sangga'ina, saukat**) 1.2) *v. intr. maka-* To be the cause of something. *S'ssagta ya bay pangkat dahū bang iya bay makakalna' i'.* We consult the former ritual ancestor as to whether he caused [that situation].

**kaloka'** *n.* A very large octopus of the open sea, multi-colored and inedible, rarely seen. *fam. Cephalopod.* (*gen:* **sattuwa**; *Thesaurus:* **kuhita' 1, ngget**)

**kalog** *n.* **1)** Various worms. (*Thesaurus:* **but'ngngel, iyas 1, sassing 1, ulat₁**) **1.1)** *v. advrs.* -*in*- Suffering from intestinal worms.

   **kalog-tana'** *n.* An earthworm.

**kalo'ong** *n.* **1)** The chambered nautilus. *Nautilus pompilius.* (*cf:* **sugit-sugit**) **2)** A scroll or spiral.

**kalompang** *n.* The lower back of a human being.

**kaloposan** *var. of* **longpos**

**kalsa** *v. tr.* To cock a gun in readiness to shoot. *Ai pinagkalsa ilū?* What is being aimed at? (*Thesaurus:* **balis₁, kital, surang**)

**kalsara** *n.* A main road; a highway. *Ma kalsara Taglibi maka Tiyanggi.* The main road between Taglibi and Jolo Town. (*Thesaurus:* **labayan, lān, pal'ngnganan**)

**kalsinsilyu** *var. of* **kansinsilyu**

**kalsitin** *n.* Socks; hose. *Bay binuwanan si Ja kalsitin he' paipatanna.* Ja was given socks by the person in whose care he works. (*syn:* **medyas**)

**kalton** *n.* A carton. *Tinugila'an kami mpat hatus pilak maka duwa karut buwas maka dakalton siga, maka...* The list required of us was four hundred pesos, two sacks of rice, a carton of cigarets, and... (*Thesaurus:* **bakag₁, ba'ul₁, labban, maleta, tu'ung**)

**kalu gi'** *ptl.* Maybe; possibly, of a future event. (Hypothetical modality marker). *Kalu gi' iya amatay ma pagbono'an ati saddī gi' ya makapah'nda ma tunangna.* He may perhaps die on the battlefield and someone else may marry his wife-to-be.

**kalu-kalu** *adv.* **1)** Perhaps; maybe, expresses uncertainty. *Yukna, "Jo, pi'itu ka." Ya sambungna, "Tilawku gi' si Ina', kalu-kalu bilahi."* He said, "Hey Jo, come here." He answered, "I'll just ask Ma, she may be agreeable." *Kalu-kalu itu mbal kata'uhanta bang at'kka atawa mbal.* This word *kalu-kalu* means we don't know whether it will arrive or not. (*Thesaurus:* **bahā', siguru 1, ya aniya'**) **1.1)** *v. tr.* To express a conjecture about something. *Ngga'i ka tantu, hal kinalu-kalu.* Not certain, simply conjectured. *Tahunub-hunubku aniya' bono', hē'-i kinalu-kalu lagi'.* I spread the rumour that there was a battle, [but] that was still a conjecture.

**kalukassa** *see:* **pagkalukassa**

**kalu'a** *n.* A co-wife; a co-wife relationship. *Ya ina'an anak bay tinimanan e' kalu'ana.* That was the child her co-wife rejected.

**kalulay** *n.* **1)** Post-delivery stretch marks on a woman's stomach. **1.1)** *v. advrs.* -*in*- Showing stretch marks on the stomach.

**kalung** *v. tr.* To carry something in both arms. *Kinalung-kalung onde', sinauk maka hōs.* The

child carried in both arms, gathered up in a sarong. (*Thesaurus:* **golgol, golpe₂**)

**kalut** *v. tr.* To dig in the ground, as to remove soil or find something. *Angalut aku tana' nihinang bohe'.* I will dig out the dirt to make a water hole. *Bilahi aku angalut lowang aluha man lowang akiput.* I would rather dig a wide hole than a narrow one. (*cf:* **kali**)

   **pagkalut** *v. tr.* To be engaged in digging, as to find something. *Magpangalut saga a'a Sibaud inān ma gusung, daka ai pinagkalut e' sigā.* Those Sibaud people are always digging in the sand, who knows what they are digging for.

**kaluwa'** *v. advrs.* -*in*- Suffering from an intestinal disorder characterized by diarrhea. (*Thesaurus:* **pagloros-loros, pagsungi'-sungi'**)

**kaluy** *n.* Blue-spotted grouper; leopard coral-trout. *Cephalopholis taeniops.* (*gen:* **kuhapo'**)

**kaluy-b'ttikan** *n.* Dusky-tailed grouper or Bleeker's grouper. *Epinephelus bleekeri.*

**kaluy-magkangiyan** *n.* Coral cod. *Plectroplanus sp.*

**kaluy-mantis** *n.* Brown-striped snapper. *Lutjanus spp.* (*gen:* **kutambak**)

**kām** *pron.* You (second person plural) [Set I]. (*cf:* = **bi, ka'am**; *Set:* **akū, kā, kamī, kitā 1, kitabi₁, kitām, iyā, sigā₁, sigām₁**)

**kama** *n.* A thin mattress. (*Thesaurus:* **kasul, l'ppus 2, tilam**)

**kamahung** *n.* A cockroach. *Yuk onde'-onde', "Kamahung itū, bang kita atuli bo' halam asanyawa, kineket boto'ta."* Children say, "With cockroaches, if we sleep without undershorts, our penis gets bitten."

**kama'atay** (derivative of **ma'atay**) *v. advrs.* -*in*- Assumed; supposed. *Kinama'atay hē'-i, niwaham e'na sala.* That's something merely assumed, sort of guessed at.

**kamal** *adj.* *a*- Voiceless, a stage of sickness where speech is no longer possible. *Bang abangat sakina akamal na. Mbal na makapamūng, hal ang'nda'.* When his sickness is very severe he is voiceless. He can no longer talk, he just looks. *Akamal, sali' mbal makapah'lling. Sali' agohom, hal ang'nda' bang nilinganan.* Voiceless, as though not able to speak. Makes indistinct noises, just looks when called. *Mbal kita makapah'lling ni alim, sali' halam aniya' pangita'u. Sali' kamal kita.* We are unable to speak to a Wise One, it is like we have no understanding. Like we are deprived of speech. (*Thesaurus:* **kokam₂ 1.1, kowam 1, pamorok, umaw 1.1**)

   **pagkamal** *v. tr.* To deprive someone of the ability to speak. *Pinagkamal-kamal si Nu, mbal anaul bang nilinganan.* Nu is sometimes robbed of his power of speech, he doesn't answer when called.

**kamalig** *n.* A building or roofed shelter, used for storage or as a workplace. *Kamalig itū luma' saga pagpat'nna'an banog atawa pagtapi'an. Aniya' isāb* *buwat saurung.* A *kamalig* is a building for things like sail storage or planking of a boat. There are also some like a porch. (*Thesaurus:* **balung-balung, lapaw, panggung, payad, pillayag**)

**kamali'** *see:* **pagkamali'**

**kamama'u** *n.* The pelvic area; lower abdomen. (*Thesaurus:* **alopan₂, harapan₂, munda'an₂**)

**kamanakan** *n.* The offspring of close kin of the same generation; nephew or niece.

**kamansihan** var. of **kalitan-kamansihan**

**kamansi'** *n.* Breadfruit. *Artocarpus communis.*

**kamansili'** *n.* Manila tamarind. *Pithecolobium dulce.*

**kamanyan** *n.* Incense. *Bang kita anunu' kamanyan ma api bo' ma tugtugan, na bo' akeyat na, magkattek-kattek na.* When we burn incense over the fire, in a censer, and when it is alight it makes a crackling noise. *Peya' isihan abu maka kamanyan.* A coconut shell containing ashes and incense. (*Thesaurus:* **hiyu, laksi'**)

**kamang** *n.* **1)** Dwarf flathead. *Elates ransonnettii. Kamang itū daing pak'ppang mareyo', al'kkas bang alahi. Taga s'kke'.* The *kamang* is a fish that lies flat on the bottom, and escapes with great speed. It has a pronounced dorsal ridge. **2)** Bar tailed flathead. *Platycephalus indicus.* **3)** Variegated lizardfish. *Synodus variegatus.*

  **kamang-buhuk** *n.* **1)** Picnic sea bream. *Acanthopagrus berda.* **2)** Yellow-fin sea bream. *Acanthopagrus latus.*

**kamara** *n.* **1)** The side planking of a canoe. (*gen:* **tapi'** 1) **1.1)** *v. tr.* To fasten the planking of a canoe. *Kinamara kayu itū, pinahāp bangkatna.* The strakes are fastened, improving the way they fit.

**kamas** *v. tr.* To damage or hurt by scratching. *Bay aku kinamas e' kuting.* I was scratched by a cat. *Kukkuta ya pangamas.* It is our fingernails that we scratch with. (*Thesaurus:* **kakayaw, kakkut, katol** 1.1)

  **pagkamas** *v. intr.* aN- To inflict wounds on each other by scratching with nails (of women fighting). *Wa'i na sigā magluray maka magkamas saga.* There they are pulling each other's hair and clawing at each other.

**kamasu'** *n.* The spice imperial pigeon. *Ducula myristicivora.*

**kamat** *n.* **1)** A prayer for the health and physical form of a newborn girl. *Subay akatis magsambahayang subu bo' yampa aniya' kamat niruwaha'an.* The dawn prayer should be over before the prayer for a newborn girl is offered. **1.1)** *v. tr.* -an To pray the kamat prayer over a female child.

**kamatis** *n.* Tomato. *Lycopersicum esculentum.*

**kamatti** *n.* Purpose; intention. *Angay ka sali' yampa makapi'itu? Ai kamattinu?* Why have you come here now for the first time? What is your intention? *Ainu-inu kita pagka aniya' maitu na ma luma', ati yukta, "Ai kamattinu pi'itu?"* We are puzzled when someone is here in the house and we say, "What is your purpose in coming here?" (*Thesaurus:* **gawi** 1, **hadjat₁, maksud** 1, **tiranan**)

**kamattihan** *n.* **1)** The outcome of some plan or action. *Buwat kita maggara' ahinang luma'. Na, ya kamattihanna luma' na. Aniya' kat'kkaran, kat'nna'an.* As when we make plans to build a house. The end result purpose [of the planning] is a house. It has a conclusion, an outcome. *Kaiya'an maka kalala'atan ya kamattihanna.* Shame and hard times are his end result. *Buwat kita magpasarap ma lahat ngga'i ka kabiyasahanta bo' aniya' makanikita, ya na hē' kamattihanta.* It's like when we risk going to an unfamiliar place and something happens to us, that is our fate. (*Thesaurus:* **kaluwasan, kamaujuran, kat'kkahan₂, katobtoban, katumariyahan, pamole'an** 2) **2)** The final ceremony of the funeral sequence. *Pagpudji ma a'a amatay basta puwas min hinang mpatpū', ya na kamattihanna ilū.* Prayers for a person who has died, provided it is after the forty-day ceremony, that's his final stage.

**kamaujuran** *n.* The goal or outcome of an action. *In sapda halam aniya' kamaujuranna sapantun manuk-manuk halam aniya' kataptapanna, atawa pana' halam aniya' tudjuhanna.* A curse without a goal is like a bird with no permanent place, or an arrow without a target. (*Thesaurus:* **kaluwasan, kamattihan** 1, **kat'kkahan₂, katobtoban, katumariyahan, pamole'an** 2)

**kamaupa'atan** var. of **kamaupakkatan**

**kamaya'** *v. tr.* -an To treat something cautiously. *Kamaya'in ba, aguya' ko' ilu.* Be careful with it, that one is fragile. *Kamaya'in daing ilū ko da'a pakawas. Subay mbal sakit tinugutan.* Be careful with that fish so it doesn't get away. The line shouldn't be slackened too much. (*Thesaurus:* **amay-amay** 1, **ebot-ebot** 1.1, **hubaya-hubaya**)

**kamaya'-maya'** *adv.* **1)** Carefully. *Amissara ka kamaya'-maya'.* Speak carefully. **1.1)** *v. intr.* zero To be careful. *Kamaya'-maya' ka ko ra'a abu'us.* Be careful so that it doesn't spill. (*cf:* **ayad-ayad**)

**kamayu** *v. advrs.* -in- Affected by swelling and redness of the skin. *Kinamayu si Ji, bay am'lla bo' kayu batang ya pangayuna. Bang kayu deya, mbal du.* Ji has a [breast] infection. She was cooking and used floating wood for firewood. If it had been wood from inland it would not have happened. (*Thesaurus:* **ipit** 1.1)

**kamayung** *n.* The high prow of a paraw-type canoe, a separate structure attached to the stem. *Pahapat, paghinang kamayung, ya sugpat munda' paraw.* Pahapat tree is used for making the high prow, the extension to the front of the canoe. (*Thesaurus:* **pamalung, sangpad**)

**kambal** *n.* **1)** A reinforcing strip affixed to the outer edge of the planked section of canoe hulls. **1.1)**

*v. tr. -an* To fit a canoe with a reinforcing strip. *Pangambalin ba pelang.* Use it for reinforcing the planking of the canoe.

**kambang** *n.* A species of edible sea anemone, with red and white varieties. *Actinia spp.* (*Thesaurus:* **kombo'-kombo', lason, lo'on, pari-pari**)

**kambangtuli** *n.* The katuray, a broad-leafed leguminous tree. *Sesbania grandiflora.* *Kambangtuli: bang bay tagna' hē', pagsusut tonda' tingkal, bay halam gi' aniya' naelon. Sinusutan bo' atuwas, mbal ap'kkal ma deyom tahik.* *Kambangtuli*, in former times it was used for scrubbing fiber line, before there was nylon. It was scrubbed to make it hard, and would not unravel in the sea.

**kambay** 1) *v. tr.* To signal someone by waving one's arms. *Kinambay kita, sinō' pahondong.* Someone waved at us, telling us to stop. *Pangambayun tangannu ilū.* Use your arm for waving. (*Thesaurus:* **lambe₁ 1.1, mita, paglabad 1.1, sayang₂, sinyal 1.1**) 2) *v. intr. aN-* To move the arms as in swimming, especially of breaststroke. *Angambay ma buli' tahik amiha tipay.* Swimming along the sea floor looking for pearl oysters. *Angambayan aku dīku, halam aniya' pameya'anku pareyo'.* I swim [as though] waving to myself, having no device for going down in the sea. (*Thesaurus:* **pagkutebba', pagkutibbung**)

**kambing** 1) *n.* A goat. *Capra aegagrus hircus.* 2) *v. intr. aN-* To be sexually aggressive, i.e. like a male goat. *Angambing ka, sali' ka amaya'-maya'.* You are being a goat, as though you were rutting.

**kambing-boro-boro** *n.* Long-haired goat.

**kambing-bundan** *n.* Male goat with a long beard.

**kambing-bili-bili** var. of **bili-bili**

**kambing-kambing** *n.* Moorish idol, a fish species. *Zanclus cornutus.* (*syn:* **kayung-kayung**)

**kambot** *n.* 1) A belt around the waist. (*Thesaurus:* **kandit, sabitan, sambung₂, sintoron**) 1.1) *v. tr. -an* To secure something with a belt. *Subay kinambotan sauwalnu ilū.* Those wide trousers of yours should be held up with a belt.

**kambung-kambung** *n.* A very young coconut at the stage between the setting of the fruit and the new nut stage. *Ya kambung-kambungna bang buwa'-buwa' niyug. Malaingkan pa'aslag du isāb.* Its *kambung-kambung* stage is the mini-fruit of the coconut. It does grow, however. (*Stages:* **kambung-kambung, botong-botong, bilu'uk, botong, gangkul, lahing, pangtusan**)

**kambuyan** see: **pagkambuyan**

**kamdos₁** *v. intr. aN-* To place confidence in someone or something. *Angamdos ka ma barannu saukat na ka taga alta'.* You trust in yourself merely because you are wealthy. (*Thesaurus:* **andol 1, sangdol 1.1**)

**kamdos₂** *adj. a-* Hard-wearing, of cloth or canoes.

(*Thesaurus:* **anagtol, kumpay, galak₂, pagon₁ 1.1, taggu₁, tatas 1.1, togob₁**)

**kamemon** (var. **kahemon**) *n.* 1) All of something; entire number or amount. *Buwat tambal, yukna, "Na pe'esin ni kamemonnu ya map'ddi' ilū."* Ointment for example, he says, "So rub it all over you, wherever it hurts." *Ndiya, b'lliku na kamemonna.* Let's have it, I will buy all of it. (*cf:* **ba'anan**) 1.1) *adj. zero* All; every. *Maguyun kamemon a'a ya magtipun ma waktu inān.* All the people gathered at that time were in agreement. *Ya ōn Sitti Hawa itū bahasa Hibrani, hatina 'llum' sabab ina' iya ma bangsa manusiya' kamemon.* The name Sitti Hawa is Hebrew, its meaning is 'alive' because she is the mother of all human beings. (*Thesaurus:* **lullun 1, sabarang**)

**pagkamemon** *v. intr. aN-* To do all kinds of things at the same time. *Magsilap, sali' ah'lling magpehē'-pehē', ah'lling magkamemon.* Talking incoherently, sort of talking at random, talking about everything.

**pakamemon** *v. tr.* To use all of something.

**kamemon pinapanjari** *n. phrase* Everything created.

**kamī** *pron.* We, excluding the one spoken to (first person plural, exclusive) [Set I]. *Amole' na kamī.* We are going home now. (*cf:* = **kami, kami;** *Set:* **akū, kā, kām, kitā 1, kitabi₁, kitām, iyā, sigā₁, sigām₁**)

**kami** *pron.* We, excluding the one spoken to (first person plural exclusive) [Set III]. (*cf:* = **kami, kamī;** *Set:* **aku₂, ka'a, ka'am, kita, kitabi₂, kitam, iya, sigā₂, sigām₂**)

= **kami** *pron.* We, our, excluding the one spoken to (first person plural, exclusive) [Set II]. (*cf:* **kamī, kami**)

**kamigmig** *adj. zero* 1) Asymmetrical; lopsided. (*cf:* **baligbig**) 1.1) Mentally deficient.

**pagkamigmig** *v. intr. aN-* To be asymmetrical; lopsided. *Magkamigmig, aheya asal parambila', sala magbalabag. Magkamihu maka magkamigmig sali' du.* Unbalanced, one side just naturally big, sort of across the length. The same in meaning as *pagkamihu.*

**kamihu** see: **pagkamihu**

**kaminduwa** (derivative of **minduwa**) *n.* 1) The second occurrence of some event. *Abungkal sakina he' tambal, aho', paluwas na sakina kamemon. Tagna' tambalanta mbal paluwas, ta'abut kaminduwana paluwas. Magtaluwa' maka tambalna.* Her sickness is stirred up by the medicine, yes, her entire illness has come out. When we first medicated it didn't come out, but on its second time it did. *Abungkal sakina he' tambal, aho', paluwas na sakina kamemon. Tagna' tambalanta mbal paluwas, ta'abut kaminduwana paluwas.* Her sickness is stirred up by the medicine, yes, her entire illness has come out. When we first medicated it didn't come out, but on its second time it did. 1.1) *v. tr. -an* To do something twice or for the second time. *Bang aku sinoho' he' a'a, taramint'dda du. Mbal kaminduwahan.* If someone tells me to do something, it only happens once. Not happening a second time.

**kamint'dda** (derivative of **mint'dda**) *n.* The first occurrence of something. *Kamint'ddanu itu-i?* Is this your first time?

**kamint'llu** (derivative of **mint'llu**) *n.* **1)** The third time or occasion of some action. *Kamint'lluna na.* His third time already. **1.1)** *v. tr.* *-an* To do something three times, or for the third time. *"Kamint'lluhinbi gi' ilu bu'usinbi,"* yukna, maka nihinang e' sigām.* "Pour it out three times," he said, and they did it.

**kamisita** *n.* An undershirt. *Aniya' kamisitaku pangalgaku ni M'ddas.* I have an undershirt for when I am working as a porter in Siasi Town.

   **kamisita-sagnat** *n.* An undershirt with narrow shoulder straps.

**kamisun** *n.* A full-length slip or petticoat.

**kammut** (var. **kal'mmut**) *n.* A tiny insect that can inflict a painful bite; a gnat. *Kammut itū ariki'-diki' to'ongan. Angeket abisa. Aniya' pote', aniya' isāb ettom.* This gnat is very small. It bites painfully. There are white ones, and black too. (*Thesaurus:* **damuk, hama', hamug-hamug, hanglop**)

**kamot** *v. tr.* To determine something by divination, as the location of something lost, or the cause of a sickness. (*Thesaurus:* **alamat₁, limal, pag'nda'₂, putika'**)

**kampat** *see:* **pagkampat**

**kampay** var. of **kagang-kampay**

**kampēn₁** *n.* **1)** A political campaign. **1.1)** *v. intr.* *aN-* To campaign for election.

**kampēn₂** *v. tr.* To organize fishermen for a commercial fishing venture, providing capital and advance funds. *Ya angampēn kami tagna' si Pi.* The first one to organize us was Pi.

**kampil** *n.* A produce basket of coarsely woven coconut leaves. (*gen:* **baka'₁**)

**kampung₁** *n.* Kin in a general sense; a relation. A: *"Sugsugnu?"* B: *"Ngga'i ka, kampungku."* A: "Your relative?" B: "Not really, just a connection." *Buwat sali' aniya' kampungku mahē', ma dampōng ē', magtimbak. Sōng pa'in pehē' pulis inān, yukku, "Bangsi' aku makapehē' abō' lāngku, ati mbal na sigā tasaggaw."* Like some of my relatives being there, on the other side, shooting each other. When the police were about to get there, I said, "If only I had been there in order to stop them, then they would not have been arrested."

   **kakampungan** *n.* A person's wider kindred. *Bang magkawin na, subay tina'abbit kakampungan.* When a wedding is on, the relatives should be invited. (*Thesaurus:* **lūng-kampung, sugsugan**)

**kampung₂** *n.* A village or village section, typically inhabited by an extended kin group. (*Thesaurus:*

**kaluma'an, le'od₁, libug, lūng 1, nibung, tumpuk 2)**

**pagkampung** *v. intr.* *aN-* To become a kin-based sector in a village. *Magsuring-saingsing, sali' mbal maglawak, magkampung.* Growing and spreading, not getting further apart, but becoming a community.

**kamun** *n.* Mantis shrimp, a type of crustacean similar to a large shrimp but with retractable blade-like appendages. *Order Stomatopoda.* (*Thesaurus:* **keyot₁, lattik₁, pama'**)

**kamut** *v. tr.* To pick up loose material in one or both hands.

**kamuti'** (var. **lamuti'**; **pamuti'**) *v. advrs.* *-in-* Suffering from progressive and irreversible depigmentation of the skin. (*Thesaurus:* **āp-āp 1, limuti', nilastung, panaw 1**)

**kamyas** *n.* The star apple tree and its fruit. *Averrhoa bilimbi.* (*Thesaurus:* **balimbing, kisas₁, iba'**)

**kanam** *v. tr.* To consume every thing available without restraint. (*Thesaurus:* **bagahak₂, boslad, buhawi'₁, butu', kaway 1.1, dahaga', damba'₁ 1.1, lagak 1.1, tanggal₁**)

**pagkanam** *v. tr.* *-an* To do something without restraint. *Saupama maghinang ka, sinoway ka e'na inān. Jari ap'ddi' deyom ataynu, wa'i paka'atnu ya bay hinangnu. Niōnan pinagkanaman.* As an example: you are making something and it is criticized by the other. Then you get angry and smash what you have made. The name for that is *pagkanam. Hal sigām pinagkanaman e' bānan kuntara.* They were simply overwhelmed by the rage of their enemies. *Bang aniya' a'a ma parinta e'na magkanam, magagaw na, a'a nsa' maina'an sinaspēk.* When someone in authority acts without restraint, struggling for control, a person who wasn't there gets accused. (*Thesaurus:* **pagtabang 1, pila 1.1**)

**kanasto** (var. **kanastru**) *n.* A large open-weave rattan basket. (*gen:* **baka'₁**)

**kanastru** var. of **kanasto**

**kanat** *adj.* *a-* **1)** Scattered, of items that should be together. *Gomgomin ai-ainu ilū bo' mbal akanat.* Hold onto your things so they aren't scattered. (*Thesaurus:* **pāg, pulak-palik 1, sihag₂ 1**) **1.1)** *v. tr.* To scatter things. *Bang aholemang onde', bo' aniya' ta'nda'na pagsipit s'mmek, kinanat he'na.* When a child is mischievous, and sees some clothespins, she scatters them.

   **kaukanat** *adj.* *a-* Scattered widely.

**kanat-kanat** *n.* Coins; loose change. *Aniya' pinta sangpū' sinambi'an ni tinda-tinda maka kanat-kanat.* There is a ten peso bill changed at the shop for small change.

**kanaw-kanaw** *adj.* *a-* Apprehensive; anxious. *Akanaw-kanaw aku, arāk mbal sinagaran he' mastal.* I was anxious, I might not be given permission by the teacher. (*Thesaurus:* **kawang,**

**ganggu' atay, hanggaw₁ 1)**
**pagkanaw-kanaw** *v. intr. aN-* To become
apprehensive; anxious. *Bang sali' aniya' si'itku*
*bay angusaha atulak dai'-llaw, halam tapole'*
*sampay kohap, magkanaw-kanaw deyom atayta.*
Suppose an uncle of mine had gone out fishing
early in the morning and hadn't returned by
afternoon, we would become anxious.
**kanaway** *n.* A northwest wind.
**kandaman** *n.* 1) Glass big-eye, a fish species.
*Heteropriacanthos cruentatus.* 2) Red big-eye, a
fish species. *Priacanthus macracanthus.*
**kandaman-lawi'an** *n.* Purple spotted big-eye, a
fish species. *Priacanthus tayenus.*
**kandang** *n.* The womb. *A'a bay abuta asāl man*
*deyom kandang.* A person blind in fact from the
womb. (*syn:* **kulun, kuta'-kuddarat**)
**kandang ahirat** *n. phrase* The secure abode of the
after-life. {idiom} *Tuhan na amuwanan sigām*
*barakat min dunya itu sampil na ma kandang*
*ahirat.* God will give them power in this present
world and beyond to the abode of the afterlife.
**pakandangan** *n.* The grave (fig., lit. the ultimate
womb). {idiom}
**kandaru** *n.* 1) A padlock; a mortise lock. (*cf:* **anak-
kunsi', kunsi' 1**) 1.1) *v. tr.* To secure a door or
lid by locking. (*Thesaurus:* **bagat, kansing 1.1**)
**kandayan** *var.* of **kandelan**
**kandelan** (*var.* **kandayan**) *n.* The Pacific sailfish, a
large fish with a long sword-like projection of
the upper jaw. *Istiophorus platypterus. Tininduk*
*aku he' kandelan ati binowa parawku palahi-lahi*
*magbibud buli'-munda'.* I hooked a sailfish and
my canoe was carried racing away, turning end
for end.
**kandi'is₁** *n.* A species of tree and its tart but edible
fruit, known in the Philippines as kamandiis.
*Garcinia rubra.* (*cf:* **manggis**)
**kandi'is₂** *n.* A dimple; a cleft in the chin. *Aniya'*
*kandi'isna maitu bang iya anittowa.* She has a
dimple here when she smiles.
**kandit** *n.* A sash; a belt. (*Thesaurus:* **kambot 1,**
**sabitan, sambung₂, sintoron**)
**kandong-kandong** *var.* of **bāt-kandong-kandong**
**kandung₁** *v. intr. pa-* To accumulate in a hollow, of
water. *Aniya' bohe' pakandung maina'an, aheka*
*ambakna.* The water is ponding over there, lots
of frogs. (*Thesaurus:* **danaw, halo-halo, tangki,**
**tigbaw**)
**pakandungan** *n.* A place where water collects or
ponds.
**pangandung** *n.* A freshwater pool. (*cf:* **danaw**)
**kandung₂** *v. tr.* To carry something in a cloth.
*Amusu' aku biyabas. Bang halam pangisihanku*
*kandungku ma badju'ku.* I gather guavas. If I
have no containers I carry them in my shirt.
*Mbal takandung api.* Fire cannot be carried in a
cloth.
**kanēs-nēs** *adj. a-* Scattered untidily; strewn.

*Akanēs-nēs buwas e' manuk. Minsan onde'-onde'*
*magkanēs-nēs isāb bang asungi'.* The rice is spread
everywhere by the chickens. Even little children,
they make an untidy mess when they poo.
*Ngā'un na sikanēs-nēsan inān.* Grab that stuff
scattered everywhere. (*Thesaurus:* **bulaksay 1,**
**teges-teges**)
**kanit** *adj. a-* 1) Peeling; delaminating. *Bay akanit*
*tape'ku, bay alūs he' bohe' pasu'.* My foot was
peeling, it was scalded by hot water. *Buwat saga*
*pulaybūd ase'ak he' llaw, akanit he' tahik.* Like
plywood, split by the sun, delaminated by seawater. (*Thesaurus:* **gagus, lakles, laknit 1,**
**oplak 1**) 1.1) *v. tr. -an* To separate something
from its skin. *Kinanit mata-daing ma tanganku,*
*kinanit isāb buwahan.* The blisters on my hand
can be squeezed out, so too can lansones fruit.
(*Thesaurus:* **kisak, kupas, hagut, hampa' 1.1,**
**lapes**)
**pagkanit** *v. intr. aN-* To be flaking off, as scurf.
*Gulis-manuk mbal amali', hal magkanit-kanit.*
Scurf doesn't become a wound, it just flakes off.
**kaniya-kaniya** *adv.* Each one individually. *Aniya'*
*almas sigām kaniya-kaniya.* They each of them
have weapons. (*Thesaurus:* **paggintil, pinig,**
**tabul₁ 1.1, tarangan-tarangan, topod 1**)
**pagkaniya-kaniya** *v. intr. aN-* 1) To behave
individually and separately, as members of a
group. *Aheka kami magdanakan, na dangan maka*
*dangan magkaniya-kaniya dīna.* There are a lot of
us brothers, so each of us act as individuals.
*Pininig, binuwanan magkaniya-kaniya.* Treated
separately, given individually. 1.1) *v. tr.* To treat
things or people individually. *Sila'unbi d'nda*
*maka l'lla, pinagkaniya-kaniya.* Deal with women
and men separately, treating them individually.
**pakaniya-kaniya** *adv.* Individually; one by one.
**kaniya'** (derivative of **niya'₁**) *n.* Possessions or
property, implying more than average. *Taga*
*kaniya' a'a inān.* That man owns quite a lot.
(*Thesaurus:* **alta' 1, karaya 1, pagsauragal 1.1**).
**kaniyang-kaniyang** *v. intr. aN-* To open the eyes
wide in a terrified or terrifying way. *Tinggaung,*
*anganiyang-nganiyang matana, ataha' kukkuna.*
The civet cat, its eyes glare frighteningly, its
claws are long. (*Thesaurus:* **diyag, d'llag 1,**
**pagduliyag**)
**kanji'** *n.* Starch dressing which gives stiffness to
new cloth. *Mbal amaluba, ala'an sadja kanji'na. It*
isn't fading, its starch dressing has simply gone.
(*Thesaurus:* **almirul 1, sakkul**)
**kannal** *v. tr.* To keep something in mind; to care
about something or someone. *Angannal kita, sali'*
*amikilan. Ang'nda' kahāpan, ang'nda' kala'atan.*
We are keeping something in our minds, like
thinking it over. Looking at the good and the
bad. *Angannal sigā ma kita, amasi kita taentom*
*he' matto'ata. Mbal kita ni'bbahan, kinannal kita,*
*kinalasahan. Sali' bang kita magl'ngngan bo'*
*apuwas min pagkakanan, bay tinau'an he'*

*matto'ata. Ya hē' mangannal-i.* They are thoughtful towards us, our parents still remember us. We are not abandoned, we are kept in mind, loved. Like when we were out walking and miss being at the meal, our parents kept something back for us. That's *kannal.* (*Thesaurus:* **dalil 1.1, dongdong, pagka'inagon, pikil 1.1, tali' 1.1**)

**pagkannal-susun** *v. intr. aN-* To be in a regretful frame of mind.

**pangannal**₁ *n.* Conscious thought; awareness. (*Thesaurus:* **sakup**₁ 1, **sayu 1.1, sipat**₁ 1, **sipat**₁ 1.1, **tahu, tilas**₁)

**pangannal**₂ *v. tr.* To think mistakenly about something. (*Thesaurus:* **bā'**₂)

**kanop** *v. advrs. ta-* Becoming submerged below the surface of a liquid; disappearing below the horizon. *Takanop diyata' būd.* The tip of the mountain has vanished over the horizon. *Buwat kita bay aningkō' ma gusung, bay t'bba. Bang ta'abut na tahik bo' abase' na buli'ta, takanop na bay paningkō'anta.* Like if we were sitting on the sand when it was low tide. When the sea reaches it, and our bottoms are wet, the place where we were sitting is submerged. (*Thesaurus:* **letop 1, limun 1, lonob 1**)

**pagkanop-bulan** *v. tr.* To celebrate the moment when new moon and sun set the same time. *Panganop bulan itū bang ma kami, sali' pangagad bulan, buwat a'a amuwasa subay am'lli buwas, sokal.* The moon observance for us is the time of waiting for the moon [to appear], as when people who are fasting need to buy rice and sugar.

**kansang** *adj. a-* 1) Prolific; increasing rapidly. (*Thesaurus:* **banos, besal, datay**₂, **dayas-dayas, dorot, heka 1.1, jayak, parat**) 1.1) *v. intr. pa-* To proliferate, as the marks of an infection. *Pakansang gōm pa'in, mbal na patambal.* It increases even more, and cannot be treated [with medicine]. (*Thesaurus:* **bangat, pangsan, sidda 2**)

**kansinsilyu** (var. **kalsinsilyu**; **gansinsilyu**) *n.* Men's undershorts. (*Thesaurus:* **kindut, kudji-kudji, kullat, sanyawa**)

**kansing** *adj. a-* 1) Securely closed, as a door or teeth. *Buwat si Ina' bay nilango tingga'-tingga' lumahan, akansing emponna.* Like the time when Mother was poisoned from eating false-mackerel, her teeth clamped tight together. 1.1) *v. tr.* To secure a door or lid by inserting a bolt or bar. (*Thesaurus:* **bagat, kandaru 1.1**)

**kansiya** *n.* A money-box, especially one made of a large seed of the ba'it tree. (*gen:* **pagtau'an**)

**kantil**₁ *n.* A sleeping platform or raised bed. (*Thesaurus:* **pabahakan, palangka'**₂, **palegehan, patulihan**)

**kantil**₂ *n.* An underwater cliff or ledge. (*Thesaurus:* **deyo'**₂ 1, **pampang, temang, titib**)

**kanting**₁ *n.* The serrated spinal ridge of fish such as

the Yellow-fin tuna. (*Thesaurus:* **sēk, s'kke, tare'** 1)

**kanting**₂ *n.* The achilles tendon or heel cord; Calcaneal tendon.

**kanu'us** *n.* Various species of squid. *fam. Sepiolidae.* (*gen:* **lansongan**)

**kanyamun** *n.* An anchor cable; a hawser. (*cf:* **bahudji'**)

**kanyun** *n.* 1) A cannon; naval gun; artillery weapon. (*Thesaurus:* **kalbin, garan, lantaka 1, musil, pistul, sinapang**) 1.1) *v. tr.* To shoot someone with a naval gun or cannon. *Aniya' mundu bay kinanyun.* Some pirates were shelled.

**kangag** *n.* A species of green parrot. (*gen:* **agap**₁)

**kāngan** var. of **kalangan**₃

**kangan** var. of **bāt-kangan**

**kangkang**₁ *v. intr. aN-* 1) To spread one's fingers in shock or pain. *Angangkang kita, sali' aniya' yampa ta'nda'ta.* We spread our fingers, as though there was something we had never seen before. *Angay a'a angangkang sadja itu?* Why is this person just spreading his fingers? (*cf:* **pagkabug-kabug**) 1.1) *v. tr. -an* To spread the fingers in order to frighten. *Kinangkangan onde'-onde' bahasa pinakitāw.* Fingers spread to frighten children.

**kangkang**₂ *n.* An edible shallow-water crab. (*gen:* **kagang**)

**kangkung** *n.* Kangkong; water bindweed, the plant and its edible stalks and leaves. *Ipomoea reptans* or *I. aquatica.*

**kangog** *v. advrs. -in-* Demented, especially as a symptom of rabies. *Aniya' isāb ero' kinangog, ya mangeket inān.* There are demented dogs too, those ones that bite. (*Thesaurus:* **bawi-bawi, belaw, sawan-sawan**)

**kango'** *n.* Pink-necked green pigeon. *Treron vernaus.*

**kapa** *n.* An ax; a hatchet. *Kapa itū pamuwad kayu aheya.* The axe here is for cutting down large trees. *Milikan gabul mata, tin'tta' maka kapa, kak'llo'an pitaka.* Blue-eyed American, chopped with an axe, had his wallet taken. (*cf:* **bansing**)

**kapa-kapa** *n.* A species of fish.

**kapagagi** *n.* Authority over. *Waktu isāb kapagagi si Anu ma lahat itū.* The time also of What's-his-name's rule over this district. (*cf:* **kuma'agi, pagagi**)

**kapaga'a** (derivative of **a'a**) *n.* Everything to do with one's status as a human being.

**kapaganak** (derivative of **paganak**) *n.* The act or moment of giving birth. *A'a aku'il tape'na, halam bay makal'ngngan sangay min kapaganak ma iya.* A person whose leg was crippled, who hadn't been able to walk since he was born. *Min llaw kapaganak ma iya sampay ni waktu kamatayna.* From the day of his birth to the time of his death. *Llaw kapanganakna, llaw kapanganak ma ka'a.* The day she gave birth, the day you were born.

**kapagdakayu'** (derivative of **dakayu'₂**) *n.* Unity. *In tungkud dakayu' inān niōnan tungkud kapagdakayu'.* That other staff was called "the Staff of Unity." *Bang kam maglasa-liyasahi ahogot du kapagdakayu'bi atay.* When you love each other your inner unity will be secure.

**kapagd'nda** (derivative of **d'nda**) *n.* 1) Femininity.**1.1**) *n.* Female genitalia.

**kapagl'lla** (derivative of **l'lla**) *n.* 1) Masculinity.**1.1**) *n.* Male genitalia.

**kapagsultan** (derivative of **sultan**) *n.* The status of kingship; a kingdom. *Anatas kapagsultanna.* His sultanate lasted long.

**kapal** *n.* 1) Thickness; the gauge of something flat. **1.1**) *adj.* a- Thick through, as paper, planking or cloth. *Akapal sawan palastik, minsan nihantak mbal abila'.* Plastic drinking glasses are thick, even when dropped they do not break. (*cf:* **gayad**; *ant:* **nipis**)

**kapala** *n.* A leader; the head of an organization. {rare} (*Thesaurus:* **bōs, kapatas, mandul, nakura'**)

**kapalling** (derivative of **palling**) *n.* A children's toy with vanes that spin around a central axle when struck by the wind; a pinwheel.

**kapalu** *n.* Gobie species. *fam. Gobiidae.*

**kapamanjari** (derivative of **jari₁**) *n.* The state of something in its created form. *Saga kabatuhan ahāp kapamanjarina.* Rocks that are good in their created form.

**kapamangan** (derivative of **kakan**) *n.* The means of obtaining food, as money or trade.

**kapan** *clf.* Count word for the strips of cloth used to wrap a corpse.

**kapang₁** *n.* 1) The shipworm or teredo, a bivalve mollusk which bores into wood immersed in sea water. *Teredo spp. Kapang sali' s'ggit-man'ggit amalut ma hāg, sali' l'ssik-l'ssik tehem amalut. Kapang,* a kind of rubbishy growth that clings to posts, or like clinging barnacles. (*syn:* **tambelok** 1; *gen:* **tahemtem** 1) **1.1**) *v. advrs.* -in- To be damaged by ship-worm. *Bay kinakan he' tehem, ya hē' kinapang.* Eaten by barnacles, that's the meaning of *kapang. Kinapang, luwa imbaw-imbaw amikit ma hāg.* Damaged by shipworms that look like a tiny clam fastened to a housepost.

**kapang₂** *n.* To lie face down. *Pakapang onde' ma bihing lawang, mbal gi' makalē.* The baby lies on its stomach by the door, not yet able to crawl. (*syn:* **k'ppang** 1)

**kapatas** *n.* A foreman; a tally clerk. *Kapatas iya, amista iya, alanga isāb gadjina.* He is a foreman, he keeps the records, his wages are high. (*Thesaurus:* **bōs, kapala, mandul, nakura'**)

**kapatut** (var.**kapatutan**) (derivative of **patut**) *n.* Inherent or conferred right to act or claim certain privileges. *Panglima ya tag kapatut ma kaluma'an kami itū.* The *panglima* is the one with authority in this village of ours. *Bang aniya' a'a, l'lla, amatay bo' ta'abut kinawin anakna, na bo' magsagga' balu hē', ya bay siyaka atawa siyali aymulla inān angamu' kapatut, subay binuwanan ungsud.* If someone dies, a man, and the time comes for his daughter to be married, then if the widow disputes [her share], the older or younger brother of the deceased will ask for [his] rights, he should be given the *ungsud* [the parental share of the bride]. *Si Gr taga kapatut ma Nasuli', iya ya magkuma'agi ma saga ipatan.* It is Gr who has the authority at Nasuli, he is the one who has responsibility for the female workers. (*Thesaurus:* **pagagi, pagbaya'₁, pagkawasa, pagkuma'agi, pagnakura'** 1).

**kapatutan** var. of **kapatut**

**kapay** *n.* The propeller of a plane or ship. *Bang tagna' pinaka'llum kapay ariplano magtumballeng.* When the propeller of an airplane is first started it moves unevenly. (*cf:* **batang-ehe**)

**kapaya** *n.* The papaya or pawpaw. *Carica papaya.* *"Kapaya ī'," yuk-i, "atomo'. Laurun pi'itu."* "That pawpaw," he said, "is growing. Replant it over here."

**kape** *n.* The coffee plant and its fruit; the beverage. *Coffea arabica.* (*syn:* **kahawa**; *Thesaurus:* **neskape, tī**)

**kapeta'** *n.* An edible variety of taro. (*Thesaurus:* **kallari', hupi' 1, tuwad**)

**kapi** *v. tr.* To copy something written.

**kapi-kapi** *n.* The third series of side planks above the hull of a pelang-type canoe. *Aniya' isāb kapi-kapi diyata' pasunu', ya anu pote'-pote' isāb, bo' aniya' durung-sa'am.* An upper plank also follows, the whitish one, and then the outrigger boom plank. (*gen:* **tapi'** 1)

**kapil** *n.* 1) A religious renegade or apostate, one who does not observe the tenets of Islam. *Bang ma kami, kapil isāb a'a mbal angungsud.* With us, a person who does not observe the bride-wealth [custom] is also a renegade. **1.1**) *adj.* a- Irreligious. *Asabul, akapil a'a ina'an, mbal amuppu'.* That fellow is dirty, irreligious, he doesn't clean himself properly. (*cf:* **multad, munapik**)

**kapin** *n.* 1) A remainder; a surplus. **1.1**) *v. tr.* To keep something for later. *Kilaku halam aniya' pinta takapin.* I reckon there is no paint left. *Ma aku na, ā, bang aniya' angapin?* That's for me, is it, if there is anything over? *Halam aniya' kinapinan, niuki'-uki' ni manahut-nahut.* Nothing was kept back, it was counted in full, to the smallest detail. *Kapinin aku dakayu' undam.* Keep a basinful for me. *Mma', halam bahā' aniya' lidjiki' bay kapinannu aku?* Dad, haven't you reserved a blessing for me? (*Thesaurus:* **halli'₂, tau'** 1.1)

**kakapinan** *n.* A remnant; left-overs.

**kapis** *n.* A heavy cloth used mainly for sails. (*Thesaurus:* **ispowen, ispowen, lona, ma'ung, mantaluna, patig, tolda, wigan**)

**kapitan** *n.* A military captain; barrio captain. (*cf:* **kapten**; *Thesaurus:* **komandel, jeneral, tininti**)

**kapitera** *n.* A teapot or coffee pot. (*Thesaurus:* **kapsiyu, patikuwan, sili'**)

**kapiyalu** *n.* 1) Sunstroke; heat exhaustion. (*cf:* **panggang₂** 1) 1.1) *v. advrs. -in-* Affected by sunstroke. *Buwat kita an'bba ni kapasu'an. Pagt'kkata kinapiyalu kōkku, sali' ap'ddi'.* Like when we are collecting sea foods in shallow water until the hot time [of day]. When we get home my head is affected by sunstroke, like a headache.

**kapog** *adj. a-* Hard and stale, of toasted cassava meal kept too long. *Akapog sinanglag. Takakan du isāb minsan atuwas. Mbal akapog bang buwas, abalos.* Pan-roasted cassava meal becomes *kapog.* It is edible even though hard. Cooked rice does not become *kapog,* it ferments.

**kapo'** *v. intr. pa-* 1) To wade through water. *Bay pakapo' si Arung ni tahik, abase' lampinna.* Eldest daughter has been wading in the sea, her diaper is wet. *Ā bang takalenu magbahubuk na, magkapo' na!* Oh, if you could have heard all the water splashing, all the wading! *Kamaya'-maya' ka pakapo', aniya' mamuhuk.* Be careful wading, there are long-spined sea urchins there. (*cf:* **ubug₁** 1) 1.1) *v. tr.* To reach by wading. 1.2) *v. ditr.* To convey something by wading.

**kappal** *n.* A ship or large launch, typically a vessel with a metal hull and more than one deck. *Pareyo' na kami min luma' i tudju ni kappal.* We went down from the aforementioned house towards the ship. (*Thesaurus:* **beggong, biruk, buti, kumpit, lansa, papet, sappit₂, tempel**)

**kappo'₁** *n.* Generic term for various stonefish and anglerfish, and for some unrelated species. *fam. Scorpaenidae.*

**kappo'-s'mmek** *n.* The cloth stonefish. *Kappo'-s'mmek itū mbal makabakat.* The cloth stonefish does not cause harm.

**kappo'-tinggil-batu** *n.* The spotfish; frogfish. *Antennatus mummifer.*

**kappo'-tumbaga** *n.* The Copper stonefish. *Abisa kappo'-tumbaga, bay abakat si Ja.* The copper stonefish is very painful, Ja was wounded [by one].

**kappo'-ulak** *n.* A sargassum fish. *fam. Antennariidae.*

**kappo'-unas** *n.* A fish species, probably a stonefish.

**kappo'₂** *v. tr. -an* To be decorated ornately, of shirts or blouses. *Badju' kinappo'an, ya badju' matto'a. Taga tambuku sangpū' maka duwa ya pitis-pitis inān.* A shirt made in the *kappo'* style, an old person's shirt. It has twelve buttons, those filigree ones.

**kapsiyu** *n.* A teapot or coffee pot. (*Thesaurus:* **kapitera, patikuwan, sili'**)

**kapten** *n.* A ranking official in the Philippine barangay system. *Taga ranggo, buwat baranggay kapten, a'a pinagaddatan.* Having an official rank, like a barangay captain, a person to be respected. (*cf:* **kapitan**)

**kapu-kapu** *n.* 1) Mold; mildew. (*Thesaurus:* **bagubu'** 2, **tagimtim** 1, **tagutu'** 1) 1.1) *v. advrs. -in-* Moldy, as of dried foodstuffs. *Kinapu-kapu kanu'us inān.* That dried squid is mildewed.

**kapuk** *n.* 1) The kapok or cotton tree. *Ceiba pentandra.* 2) Cotton fiber used for mattress filling. (*syn:* **gapas**)

**kapūd-pūran** *n.* The ultimate stage or item in a series. *Kapūd-pūran ahāp.* The very best. *Katapusan siyali, ya na kapūd-pūran.* The youngest of all, that's the final one. (*Thesaurus:* **katapusan** 1, **tabtaban, tobtoban**)

**kapū'an** *var. of* **kapū'-pū'an**

**kapul** *n.* 1) Embalming spices; camphor. 1.1) *v. tr.* To embalm someone. *Bang kinapul mbal al'kkas abuhuk patayna, subay saga dambulan.* When embalmed his corpse does not decay rapidly, it should take about a month. *Kinapul bangkayna bo' yampa ni'isi ni deyom lalungan.* His corpse was embalmed and then put into a coffin.

**kapunyahan** *n.* Purpose or use for something. *Mbal aku makapaindam, aniya' kapunyahanku.* I cannot lend it, I have a use for it. *Kapunyahan, ya tapaglagi kamemon. Kapunyahan,* everything that is made use of. (*Thesaurus:* **kalagihan** 1, **kapūsan**)

**kapuy** *adj. a-* Lacking strength or force. *Akapuy he'na magnapas.* He is breathing weakly. *Akapuy na goyak.* The waves have lost their force. (*cf:* **lamma** 1; *Thesaurus:* **logmay-lamma**)

**kara** *n.* The side of a coin marked with a human head. (*syn:* **ta'u₃**; *Thesaurus:* **kaba', kurus**)

**kara-kara₁** *v. advrs. -in-* Done repeatedly without let-up. *Tinimbak kinara-kara, sali' huru-huru.* Shot at without pause, similar to *huru-huru. Sinukut, mbal pinara'awa. Sinoho' amayad utangna, ya hē' niōnan kinara-kara.* Dunned for debt, not allowed to make excuses. Told [repeatedly] to pay what he owes, that's called *kara-kara.* (*Thesaurus:* **daran-daran** 1.1, **pagabut-abut, pagkuwat, sigi-sigi** 1, **toldas**)

**kara-kara₂** *n.* The moment and location at which an offense occurs; the very act of doing something. *Bang halam ta'abut ma kara-kara, bo' hal tinuhuma bay anangkaw, mbal bīnnal.* If he wasn't caught in the act, and it was only rumored that he was stealing, it is not believed. *Ta'abutku h'ndaku magbihing maka l'lla saddī ma kara-kara. Gese'ku na hōs, bowaku ni sara'. Magmalān aku.* I found my wife in the act of having sex with another man. I tore my garment and brought her to the judge. I made an outcry about it. *Bang kita ameya' ma a'a ala'at hinangna, siyal kita ma baranta bang kita ta'abut.* If we accompany someone whose activities are bad, we are personally to blame if we are caught in the act. (*cf:* **agpot 1.1**)

**karadja'an** (var. **kaladja'an**) *n.* Characteristic behavior, of a person, sickness, or weather event. *Bang kita mbal ameya' pituwa, hal paluwasta karadja'anta ala'at.* If we will not obey instructions, we will just display our [intrinsically] bad behavior. *Ala'an ka, ala'at kaladja'annu.* Go away, your behavior is terrible. *Ya na ko' ilū kaladja'an sakki. Ubus pabīng bo' ala'an, ubus pabīng bo' ala'an. Ubus kita ahāp, ubus kita ni ala'at. Sali' magpuli-bahasa ya saki hē'.* The nature of illness. It recurs and then goes away, again and again. One day we're doing better, the next day we're fine, the next day we're getting worse. That illness is like someone pretending to be friendly.

   **pakaradja'an** *n.* An occurrence or event of significance. (*Thesaurus:* **kahālan**)

**karal** *n.* **1)** Destiny or fate decreed by God, not by chance. *Bang ka amatay ma deyom luma' ma halam aniya' sababna, karal min Tuhan. Minsan ka ma pal'ngnganan bang ka humantak bo' amatay, karalnu du.* If you die at home with no cause, that is a decree from God. Even if you are on the road when you fall and die, that is the fate decreed for you. *Da'a ka anganjanji', mbal kata'uhannu karalnu.* Do not make promises, you do not know what your fate is. (*Thesaurus:* **kahandak 1, kulis, ganta'an₁, indika 1, piguhan, sukud₂ 1**) **1.1)** *v. tr. -an* To assign someone's fate. *Aniya' panata' ni kita, sali' kita kinaralan.* Something appears to us, as though we are assigned a fate.

   **pangaral** *n.* Something destined.

**karaluma'** (derivative of **luma'**) *n.* All the members of one house. *Asensong karaluma'.* The entire household was unsettled.

**karaw-karaw** *v. intr. aN-* To keep looking for a way of escape. *Buwat onde'-onde' bang sōng binono' he' matto'ana, bo' ta'nda' aniya' pamono' iya buwat saga lantay, anangis na, angaraw-ngaraw alahi.* Like when a child about to be beaten by his parent sees something like a bamboo slat to be used for beating him, he cries and looks anxiously for a way to escape. *Angaraw-ngaraw daing, sali' amidpid.* The fish keeps looking for an opening, sort of trembling.

**karaya** (derivative of **daya**) *n.* **1)** Wealth; financial security. (*Thesaurus:* **alta' 1, kaniya', pagsauragal 1.1**).**1.1)** *adj. -an* To be becoming wealthy. *Minsan miskin makajari karayahan.* Even a poor person can become wealthy.

**karboredor** *n.* A carburetor.

**karena** *n.* **1)** A chain. **1.1)** *n.* Fetters such as chain or handcuffs. (*Thesaurus:* **bilanggu' 1, kili-kili, ekang-ekang 1.1**) **1.2)** *v. tr. -an* To fetter

someone.

**kari-kari** *n.* **1)** Curry (the spice). **1.1)** *v. tr.* To cook food seasoned with curry.

**karita'** (var. **karitun**) *n.* A two-wheeled cart used for transporting heavy items, pulled by men or animals. (*Thesaurus:* **kalesa**)

**karitun** var. of **karita'**

**kariyan** *n.* The black-fin crevalle. *Alepes melanoptera, fam. Carangidae.*

**kariyasali** *n.* A congenital condition such as a deformity or chronic illness. *Asal kariyasalina, pinabeya' he' Tuhan.* That is just the way he was born, something sent by God. (*cf:* **sahili'**)

**karpentero** *n.* A carpenter; builder.

**karuk** *see:* **kumarukan**

**karuhung** *n.* A species of fish, very large and with a thick skin; probably a whale shark. *Rhincodon spp. Karuhung itū daing, buwat heya kalitan, bo' anipis tape'na. Akapal kulitna, bang lagutnu mbal amangan lahut. Alunuk du bang bay bīlla.* The *karuhung* is a fish about the size of a shark, but its tail is slender. Its skin is thick, if you slash it the knife won't penetrate. It is soft though if it has been boiled.

**karu'** *n.* **1)** Drowsiness. *Apu'aw karu'na, nsa' ahāp e'na atuli. Akabati' na.* Her nodding off was broken, she didn't sleep well. She has woken up now. *Hal lapongan-lapongan karu'.* Just the semi-wakefulness of drowsiness. **1.1)** *v. advrs. -in-* Sleepy; overcome by drowsiness. *Kinaru' na si Nneng, wa'i na atuli.* Daughter is overcome by drowsiness, she's off to sleep. (*Thesaurus:* **lambung tuli, lilap, tuli₁ 1.1**)

**karusa** *n.* A sledge drawn by a draft animal. *Karusa itū pangisihan, ginuyud ma kalbaw.* This *karusa* is a container, pulled by a water buffalo.

**karut** *n.* **1)** Sacking or burlap; a bag made of sacking. *Bang aku tilawnu bang ai kaungsuran Sama, ya sambagku, "Pilak maka karut, buwas maka maligay."* If you ask me what the Sama bride-wealth is, my answer is, "Money and sacks [of goods], rice and ceremonial model houses." **1.1)** Coarse cloth of woven abaca fiber.

**karuwa** (derivative of **duwa**) *n.* **1)** Both, of things. *Ndiya karuwa ilū.* Give me both of them. **2)** Second in a series.

**karuwambila'** (derivative of **duwa, bila'**) *n.* Both sides of a reference point. *Na aniya' pampang min karuwambila' lān ya palabayan sigām.* Now there were cliffs on each side of the road along which they were passing. *Apengka' ma tape'na karuwambila'.* Lame in his feet on both sides. (*cf:* **katilibut**).

**karuwampōng** (derivative of **pōng, duwa**) *n.* Both ends of something. *Kubu', tanda'ta hobongna paluwas ma karuwampōng.* A hut, we could see its roof beam protruding at both ends.

**kās** *v. tr.* To gather with a sweeping motion; to rake. (*Thesaurus:* **kahig, kikis, hīs 1.1**)

**kakās** *n.* An implement for gathering up loose items; a rake.

**kasajahitra'an** var. of **sajahitra'**

**kasā'** (derivative of **sā'**₁) *n.* Dislocation, of bones.

**kasa'** *n.* White cloth used for a shroud. (*Thesaurus:* **kuku-pote', salimput 1, saput 1, talkun, tatap 1**)

**kasal** *n.* **1)** Christian marriage in contrast to marriage by Islamic custom. *Kasal itū buwat ma saga a'a pote', mbal magtiman-timan. Kasal* marriage is like that of westerners, no divorcing. (*Thesaurus:* **kawin 1.1, pabatal, paglahi 1.1, pasugsug**) **1.1)** *v. tr.* To marry a couple under civil law.

**kasambagan** *n.* A water jar dedicated to ritual ancestors on the birth of a first child. *Niagap ni kasambagan, ni poga. Puwas ē' pininta-pinta ma mbo'.* Felt around for the presentation jar, for the water jar. After that the ritual ancestor is called on. (*Thesaurus:* **bingki', ka'ang, kibut, pipa, poga, tanāng, tangpad**)

**kasap** *adj.* a- Rough and abrasive, of a surface. *Angalenges, akasap sali', ya buwat kulit kumay ina'an.* Grainy, sort of scratchy, like the skin of surgeon fishes. *Bang aku bay man dilaut bo' alandos goyak, pagt'kkaku ni luma' halam aku bay amandi. Tinuli pa'in aku, akatol na baranku, akasap kamemon.* When I have been at sea and it has been very stormy, on getting to the house I do not bathe. Having dropped off to sleep my body is scratchy, rough all over. (*Thesaurus:* **gasang, l'ngnges 1.1, s'ppal**)

**kasat** *adj.* a- Inferior in flavor, of cassava. *Sali' akasat gipitan, sali' halam apinsal to'ongan.* Like the flavor of squeezed cassava meal, as when [the press] is not fully tightened.

**kasaw** *n.* Thatch poles which run across the purlins, parallel to the rafters to which thatch is tied. *Palanta'un lagi' kasaw ilū.* Spread those thatch poles there further apart. (*Thesaurus:* **lubing-lubing, palimba'an**)

**kasay** *adj.* a- **1)** Quick in movement. (*Thesaurus:* **baggis, ka'is, kulakkus, l'kkas 1, samot 1, sapat₂ 1**) **1.1)** *v. intr.* pa- To move quickly. *Pakasay ka bang ka lum'ngngan.* Be brisk when you walk.

**kaskas**₁ *v. tr.* -an To polish items made of precious metal, using a brush. (*cf:* **bata**)

**kaskas**₂ *v. tr.* -an To move water with a vigorous digging motion, as when paddling a canoe or making a clear area in the water. *Bang alandos baliyu mbal tasagga', subay kaskasanta bo' patandan.* When the wind is strong we can't make headway against it, we must paddle hard to reach land. *Bohe' ilū subay kinaskasan atawa kinabkaban ko da'a angaut.* That water must be swished or fanned so it is not dirty. (*Thesaurus:* **kabkab 1.1, kayab 1.1, kayas 1, kaykay**)

**kasko** *n.* The hull of a boat in contrast to its superstructure. *Bang kaskona akapal, nihinang diretso lowang.* If its hull is thick the [mast] hole is made directly into it. *Kasko, sali' buwat paraw inān, ya bangka'na ina'an.* The basic hull, like that paraw-type canoe, its dugout section. (*syn:* **damas**)

**kasehe'** (derivative of **sehe'**) *n.* A part of a larger collection. *Magutta' na kasehe' isāb saga a'a.* The rest of the people also vomited. *Kasehe' panulung, kasehe' pinab'llihan bo' mbal alapis.* Some [of the fish] are for giving to the needy, some are to be sold so as not to make a loss. *Talappas isab min komkoman bangsa Jipun saga paglahat kasehe' ya ma jadjahan ina'an-i.* Other places in that district were set free from the control of the Japanese. *Na kasehe' itū magtulihan.* So these others are sleeping.

**kasī** *n.* A freshwater eel species. *Synbranchus bengalensis.* (*Thesaurus:* **endong, tagō'**)

**kasi** *n.* **1)** Love; affection. (*Thesaurus:* **gumbala', lasa₂ 1.1, paganggi, s'lli 1.1**) **1.1)** *adj.* a- Loving; affectionate. *Akasi na aku alasa ma h'ndaku.* I now love my wife dearly.

**kasi-lasa** *n.* Love and affection. *Anangon na ka kasi-lasa ni kami.* Pour your loving affection on us.

**pagkasi-lasa** *n.* **1)** Mutual affection; love for each other. **1.1)** *v. intr.* aN- To be loving towards each other.

**kakasi** *n.* **1)** A darling; a loved one. **1.1)** *v. tr.* -an To love someone. *Kakasihinbi saga a'a banta.* Love the people who are enemies.

**kasig** *n.* A sardine or pilchard species. *Sardinella spp. Si Su bay nilango e' luku' maka kasig maka buwas.* Su was giddy from [eating] pufferfish with pilchards and rice. *Aho', saga dahatus mital makak'llo' kami kasig.* Yes, we obtained some hundreds [4 gallon] cans of pilchards. (*cf:* **toloy**)

**kasilyas** *n.* Toilet facilities; comfort room.

**kasirola** *n.* A metal cooking pot. (*gen:* **pam'llahan**)

**kasisayang** var. of **kuseseyang**

**kasiyag-labit** *n.* The right to be involved (usually in a negative context). *A'a inān sidda palamud ma palsagga'an kami magtautali'-anak minsan halam aniya' kasiyag-labitna.* That fellow get so involved in our family disagreements, even though they are none of his business. *Ai lamudbi (atawa kasiyag-labitbi) ma Tuhan bangsa Isra'il?* What rights (or involvement) do you have in the God of the Israelite people?

**kasla** *adj.* a- **1)** Rough; abusive, of speech. *Da'a ka akasla bang ka amissala, makaiya'-iya'.* Don't raise your voice angrily when you speak, it is shameful. (*Thesaurus:* **bagas, labas₂ 1**) **1.1)** *v. tr.* a-, ka-..-an, -an To address someone roughly or rudely. *Akaslahan aku iya ati yukna, "Abagas pahāp, ka'a ilū."* I spoke abusively to him and he said, "You are very rough in your speech." **1.2)** *v. tr.* -an To scold someone. *Kinaslahan aku he'* *bōsku, bay bbahanku hinangku.* My boss scolded me, I had stopped doing my work.

**kaslog** (var. **kaslug**) *adj.* *-an* Tough and sinewy, of food or the muscles of a working man. *Kaslogan ko' ka'a ilū.* What a husky fellow you are.

**kaslug** var. of **kaslog**

**kasob** *n.* Dense growth; a thicket. *Bahan maglē ma deyom kasob, bang mbal ta'nda'ta bo' tasagidta kakatolan kita.* Vines are spreading inside the thicket, if we don't see them and brush against them we will be itchy all over. *Kasob itū asembol. Bang ala'at llawta aheka kuyya', aheka sowa, mareyom. Kasob* means crowded growth. If we have a bad day there are many monkeys and snakes in there. (*cf:* **sagbot 1, s'ggit 1**)

**kassa'** *n.* 1) Glass (the material). *Timanin bila' kassa' ilū ni dilaut bo' mbal makabakat bang nihūg ma luma'.* Discard that broken glass out at sea so it doesn't wound someone when thrown from the house. (*cf:* **samin 1**) 2) A glass container such as a bottle or pitcher. (*Thesaurus:* **butul, garapun**)

**kassa'-bullung** *n.* A glass fishing float. (*syn:* **bullung**)

**kassa'-kassa'** *v. intr.* *aN-* To form blisters as a result of burning. (*Thesaurus:* **danglus, l'ttup 1, lungkab, lūs₁ 1, lutup, mata-daing 1, tambu-tambu₂**)

**kassup** *n.* 1) A large snap fastener. *Tambukuhin kassup-kassup badju'nu ilu.* Do up the snap fastener there on your shirt. (*Thesaurus:* **batuk-batuk, kattup, dopon-dopon 1.1, tikkup**) 1.1) *v. tr.* To secure with a snap fastener.

**Kastila'** *adj.* zero Spanish. *Bay timpu Kastila' lagi'.* When it was still the Spanish times.

**kasul** *n.* The quilted decoration of a mattress cover. (*Thesaurus:* **kama, l'ppus 2, tilam**)

**kinasulan** *adj.* zero Decorated by quilting, of bedding.

**kasuy** *n.* Cashew, the tree and its edible drupes. *Anacardium occidentale.*

**kāt** *n.* The Humphead or Napoleon wrasse. *Cheilinus undulatus.* (*syn:* **maming 1**)

**kāt-buggulan** *n.* A mature hump-head wrasse.

**kata-kata** *n.* A traditional narrative song in epic form.

**pagkata-kata** *n.* 1) An epic story in poetic form. 1.1) *v. intr.* *aN-* To sing a kata-kata epic over someone. *Bang aniya' amatay aniya' du magkata-kata saga matto'a l'lla ata'u.* When someone dies there are older men who know how to sing the epic story. *Sali' aniya' magkata-kata, na bang sōng-sōng na kahōpan yuk-i̧, "Da'a na kam magolang-olang, da'a gi' kam anasat apa ilu iya yampa kahōpan."* Suppose someone is to sing the epic story, well when he is about to be possessed, someone says, "Don't shout, don't stir him up yet because he is only just now becoming possessed." *Bang kita ma dilaut, bo' kita sōng tinuli, nā, maglanga'-langa' kita*

*pangalāng tuli. Sali' magkata-kata. Saddī tenes-tenes.* When we are out at sea, and we are becoming sleepy, we chant to stop sleeping. It is like *kata-kata. Tenes* singing is different. (*Thesaurus:* **kissa 1, istori 1, paglanga'-langa', salsila 1**)

**kata'** *v. intr.* *aN-* To utter the words of a curse.

**palkata'an** *n.* The words of a formal curse. (*Thesaurus:* **duti, hikmat, hinang-hinang₁, h'lling₃, pantak 1.1, sihil 1.1**)

**kata'-kata'** *n.* Small waves; light chop on sea. *Bang kita ni tabu' bo' man atag si Ju, maina'an i' kata'-kata'. Mbal alandos goyak, kata'-kata' sadja.* When we go to market and are just out from Ju's wharf, it's choppy there. Not very rough, just choppy. (*Thesaurus:* **alun-panjang, goyak 1, lumbag, sahal₁ 1.1, sampoyak**)

**kata'u** (derivative of **ta'u₁**) *n.* Knowledge.

**katam** *n.* 1) A plane (the woodworking tool). *Katam itū pamalanu' pasagi'.* The *katam* referred to is used for smoothing sawn lumber. 1.1) *v. tr.* To plane something. *Kayu asugat sidda, mbal pakatam.* Very cross-grained wood, can't be planed. (*Thesaurus:* **basbas, kirus 1.1, saplung 1.1, sapsap₂, sosok**)

**katama** *v. intr.* *aN-* To cut effectively, of a blade or pointed implement. *Mbal angatama laring itu.* This knife won't cut. *Subay kinatamahan, tinigad.* It should be cut right into, slashed. (*Thesaurus:* **duklat 1, ōk 1, utab**)

**katas** *n.* Paper. (*Thesaurus:* **banggala, papel**)

**katas-balan** *n.* Sandpaper; emery paper.

**katas-banggala** *n.* Heavy paper for wrapping.

**katas-daing** *n.* The translucent web between the spines of some fish. *Ma t'ngnga' iting, ya katas-daing inān, ya hē' niōnan ebed-ebed.* Between the spines, the fish-paper, that's what is known as *ebed-ebed.*

**katas-habal** *n.* A newspaper. *Na papehē'ta ni si Ch, asal pa'in llaw kasaggawna magtūy du kata'uhanku ma katas-habal.* Referring back now to Ch, on the very day of his capture I immediately knew about it from the newspaper.

**katas-jimpaw** *n.* Light paper suitable for kite-making. *A: "Halam aniya' katas-jimpaw?" B: "Buwattingga jimpaw, anipis?" A: "Ngga'i ka anipis to'ongan."* A: "Isn't there any kite paper?" B: "What kind of kite paper? Thin stuff?" A: "Not too thin."

**katat** *adj.* *a-* Chewy even after boiling, of some varieties of cassava. *Bang kineket mbal pakeket, akatat.* When you bite it, it is unbiteable, it is chewy. (*Thesaurus:* **kelot, ketot, k'llit 1, k'ttul**)

**kataw** *adj.* *a-* 1) Ruffled, of a water surface. *Akataw, sali' amukal.* Ruffled, as though boiling. 1.1) *v. intr.* *aN-* To cause a water surface to become ruffled. *Da'a kam angataw-ngataw mailu.* Don't make the water ruffled there.

**pakataw** *v. tr.* To disturb the surface of water.

**katay** *see:* **pagkatay**

**katkat** var. of **gatgat**

**katel-katel** *n.* A Western-style launch; marine runabout. *Katel-katel inān, ya niōnan anak-anak nabal, al'kkas.* That launch, the one called a baby gunboat, very speedy. (*Thesaurus:* **buti, dinggi-dinggi**)

**kati** *v. tr.* To fish using live bait. *Am'ssi aku parilaut angati kalitan.* I will fish out at sea catching shark [with live fish as lure]. *Bang aku angulaet ni timbang, angati aku panit.* When I fish out at sea by pressure lantern light, I catch tuna with live bait. (*Thesaurus:* **sangkaliya'**)

**katihan** *n.* Live bait; the gear for fishing with live bait. *Pabeya' kita ma s'llog, magpalaran kita. Katihan inān niengkotan ma limba' atawa ma panga. Daing a'llum pangumpan.* We go along with the current, we drift. The gear for live-bait fishing is tied to the cross-piece [of canoe] or to a forked support stick. Live fish are used for bait.

**katig** *n.* 1) Outrigger. *Bang kaut bo' alandos to'ongan goyak, alatas saga katig. Mbal anandal pelang.* If out at sea and it is really very rough, the outrigger lashing gives way. The canoe does not survive. (*Thesaurus:* **batangan, sa'am 1, tarik**) 1.1) *v. tr.* -an To attach outriggers. *Pagka kami pinaghodjog-hodjog, apōng pangatig ī'.* Because we were repeatedly jolted, the pieces used as outriggers there broke.

**kati'an** *n.* A forested area. *Komeng itū sali' saitan ma deya, ma deyom kakati'anan.* These *komeng* spirits are like inland demons, inside the forests. *Mbal kapusu'an biyabas kati'an inān apa aheka sowana.* Guavas can't be harvested in that wooded area because it has many snakes. (*Thesaurus:* **kabbun, gulangan, talun 1**)

**katilaw** (derivative of **tilaw**) *adj.* a- Persistent in asking questions, implying disbelief. (*Thesaurus:* **jakki 1, sumariya, tanya₂**).

**katilingkal** *n.* The circumference; the area surrounding a point of reference. *Atanyag ōn sigām ma katilingkal dunya.* Their name was famous around the world. (*Thesaurus:* **katilibut, sakalingkal**)

**katis₁** *adj.* a- 1) Used up, of some commodity. *Akatis na tambal panaw bo' halam kauli'an.* The depigmentation medicine is used up but it isn't healed. *Mbal du ka kakatisan tirigu ma deyom bintang, maka mbal du ka isab katitisan dakassa'-kassa' ns'llan.* The flour in the lidded jar will not be used up, and the oil in the little bottle will not be dried up. (*Thesaurus:* **hagin 1, puspus₂**) 1.1) *v. tr.* To use something up. *Bay kinatis-katis e'na kinakan.* He's about finished off the cooked rice.

**katis₂** *adv.* 1) After; then. *Akatis pa'in anginum magtūy iya bay angutta'.* After drinking, she promptly vomited. *Akatis pa'in he'na amissala, magpole'an na saga luruk.* When he had finished speaking the guests all went home. (*Thesaurus:*

**puwas₂, ubus₂**) 1.1) *adj.* a- Finished; concluded. *Jari akatis na kamemon kahinangan ma ba'anan kahāgan inān.* So the work on all those posts was over and done with. (*Thesaurus:* **sangkol, talus₁ 1.1, tammat 1.1, tapus 1.1, ubus₁ 1.1**)

**katoha'an** var. of **kato'ahan**

**katol** *n.* 1) An itchy condition of the skin. *Aliput kōkna he' katol, binuruk sali'.* His head is covered with an itchy condition, it's like *buruk*. (*Thesaurus:* **m'ssang 1**) 1.1) *v. tr.* To scratch to relieve an itch. *Katolun kono' bukutku, aheka buwa'-buwa'.* Scratch my back please, there are lots of little lumps. (*Thesaurus:* **kakayaw, kakkut, kamas**) 1.2) *v. advrs.* ka-...-an To be suffering from itching. *Bahan maglē ma deyom kasob, bang mbal ta'nda'ta bo' tasagidta kakatolan kita.* A vine that creeps along inside a thicket, if we don't see it and brush against it, we experience itching. (*Thesaurus:* **abas 1, buwa'-buwa' 1, kagutgut 1.1, ugud**)

**katol atay** *adj.* a- Irritating; annoying. {idiom} *Makakatol atay to'ongan saga onde'-onde' itū nilāng.* It is very irritating getting these children to stop. (*Thesaurus:* **astol 2**)

**pagkatol** *v. intr.* aN- To become a source of itching. *Bang bullawannu anaknu mbal du ko' ilū magkatol.* If you rinse your child off, that won't become an itchy condition.

**katoltol** *adj.* zero Intensely itchy.

**katol-katol** *n.* The sailfish tang; various Surgeonfish species. *Zebrasoma sp. Ngga'i ka buwat kappo' maka bawis ya bisana bang makabakat. Saddī min kuput maka palig. Akapal-kapal kulit kuput itū.* It [katol-katol] is not like stonefish or rabbitfish in the pain of the wound it causes. It is different also from *kuput* and *palig* [other surgeonfish]. The skin of the *kuput* is thicker. (*gen:* **kumay**)

**katoltol** (derivative of **katol**) *adj.* zero Intensely itchy.

**katom** *n.* A sac in some clam species which contains a poisonous secretion.

**kattek** *v. intr.* aN- To rattle; to crackle. *Pal'ddet ka bo' angattek to'olangnu. Pakattekun isāb kukkunu.* Bend backwards till your bones make a crackling noise. Make your knuckles crackle too. *Bang kita anunu' kamanyan ma api, bo' ma tugtugan, na bo' pinehē' ni sibayan, akeyat na, magkattek-kattek na, ya hē' niōnan magmula.* When we burn incense over the fire and it's in the censer, and when it is put up on the ancestor ledge, burning already, and it makes a crackling noise, we call that dangerous.

**kattup** *v. tr.* To click or snap into place, as the halves of a fastener or parts of a puzzle. *Buwat kandaru bay ukab, tinambol. Hatina kinattup pabīng.* Like a lock that was open being closed. Meaning it is clicked shut again. (*Thesaurus:* **batuk-batuk, kassup 1, dopon-dopon 1.1, tikkup**)

**katuk**₁ *adj. zero* Resolved, of problems in a courting relationship. *Amakatuk kita l'lla maka d'nda, amajatu sali'.* We get a man and a woman to sort things out, sort of making progress.

**pagkatuk** *v. intr. aN-* To be committed to getting married, of a courting couple. *Pinajatu anakna d'nda, pinapagkatuk maka l'lla.* She is putting things right for her daughter, getting her to be committed to a man. *Ya subul maka budjang ē', pinapagkatuk e'na inān supaya magdakayu'.* The teenage boy and the girl there, he is making their commitment definite so they can get married. *Buwat tunang bay magl'kkat, makapagkatuk na.* Like sweethearts who were separated, back together again.

**katuk**₂ *n.* 1) Mental instability. *Buwattē' bang pat'kka katukna.* He is like that when his mental condition comes on him. *Onde'-onde' itū taga katuk. Kulang-kulang iya.* This child has a mental problem. He is simple-minded. **1.1)** *adj. a-* Mentally unwell at times.

**katumariyahan** *n.* An outcome or result. *Buwat bay pinah'nda, bo' mbal bilahi d'nda, yuk matto'ana, "Mbal ka bilahi? Daka ai katumariyahannu ilū! Ya kabaya'annu subay maghinang kala'atan!"* For example, a girl is engaged to marry but does not want to do so, and her parents say, "You don't want to? Goodness knows what will become of you. All you want is to do bad things!" *Bang aminda pikilan Tuhan, ai katumariyahanna?* If God changes his mind, what will the outcome be? *Amatay kita magsabbut ni batu. Halam aniya' katumariyahanna.* We will wear ourselves out calling on a rock [for help]. Nothing comes of it. (*Thesaurus:* **kaluwasan, kamattihan 1, kamaujuran, kat'kkahan**₂**, katobtoban, pamole'an 2**)

**katumbal** *n.* The Black-spot or Thumbprint emperor fishes. *Lethrinus harak.* (*gen:* **kutambak**)

**katumbang** *n.* A species of fish. *Niobe' onde'-onde' e' katumbang apa asidda anaba'.* Children get ulcers by [eating] *katumbang* fish because it is so very tasty.

**kau-** *see section 2.2.2.4 Prefix:* **Cau-**

**kauk** *v. tr.* To change direction by paddling at right-angles to the line of travel. *Angauk ka, aniya' hapitta pina'an.* Paddle crossways, we have something to call in for there. *Kaukun kita ko da'a pasampig ni luma'. Angauk kita man pelang, pelang ya pangaukanta.* Change our direction so we don't run into the house. We change course from the canoe, the canoe is what we make the change from. (*Thesaurus:* **agod, biluk 1.1, bintung 1, kabig, timpas**)

**kaukaki** (derivative of **kaki**₂) *n.* Cousins, collectively. *Manjari saga kaukakina ina'an magtulakan na ni lahat Bisaya'.* So all his cousins are leaving for the Visayas [Central Philippines].

**kaukampung** *n.* Relatives in a collective sense. *Aniya' dakayu' min kaukampung d'nda hē' paganti' amarinta.* One of that woman's kinsmen replaced her in governing.

**kaukanat** (derivative of **kanat**) *adj. a-* Scattered widely. *Kaukanat itū, minsan bay atimuk akanat pabīng, sidda aheka tangan si Li.* Widely scattered: even though it was all gathered, it is scattered, Li has such busy hands.

**kaukati** *n.* 1) An infection of the bladder or lower stomach, symptomized by pain and frequent urination. (*cf:* **kima-kima**) **1.1)** *v. advrs. -in-* Affected by a bladder infection.

**kaugun** *adj. zero* Wasted or lost, regrettably. *Abu'us kassa' ati kaugun bay pangisihanna.* The bottle is overturned and its contents lost. *Kaugun isāb tana' kami bang halam aniya' makapajatu iya.* Our garden land is wasted if there is no one to make it productive. (*syn:* **kaliman**)

**kaul** *n.* What a person is, at heart. *Kata'uhannu sogō' mbal hinangnu, ya ilū kaul.* You know [what to do] but you don't do it, that's the real person. *Ala'at kaulna, hatina panipu iya.* His *kaul* is bad, which means he is given to treachery.

**kaul-pi'il** (var. **kaul maka pi'il**) *n.* A person's character or status as shown through speech and action. *Angkan tapusku bo' mbal aniya' la'at ma deyom kaul-pi'il.* That's why I brought [the discussion] to an end so there would be nothing amiss in either speech or action. *Ahantap, mbal angala'ug, hatina ahāp addat, ahāp kaul-pi'il.* Well-behaved, not violent, in other words of good character, good in speech and action. *A'adil iya ma kaul maka pi'il, mbal magdusa.* He is righteous in word and deed. He commits no offense. *Ahāp kaulnu maka pi'ilnu, bang ma kasehe'an ahāp addat maka tabi'at.* Your inner intention and your spoken word are both good. As others put it, your behavior and your upbringing are good. (*Thesaurus:* **addat-tabi'at, apalal, palangay**)

**pagkauli-pi'ili** *v. intr. aN-* To behave appropriately in speech and character. *Aniya' pamahinangta ma dakayu' tendogta. Iya ya magkauli-pi'ili ma ai-ai bay pamat'nna' iya.* We assign a job [for example] to one of our workers. He is the one who will behave appropriately regarding whatever is assigned to him.

**kaul maka pi'il** var. of **kaul-pi'il**

**kaum** (var. **kauman**) *n.* A social unit within a residential area, of people with kinship ties. *Kaum itū, sali' deyom paglahat. Kaum* is like a [grouping] within a geographical unit.

**sakaum** *v. intr. pa-* To form a single community together with the people of another kin group.

**pagsakaum** *v. intr. aN-* To form a single community, of people from diverse backgrounds. *Magsakaum, sali' magdakayu' a'a Butun maka a'a Siganggang, bay tinambukuhan e'* *mayul.* Forming a single community, like the people of Butun coming together with the people of Siganggang, told to do so by the mayor.

**kauman** var. of **kaum**

**kaumpang** *n.* The Stinky Sterculia tree. *Sterculia foetida.*

**kausun** *n.* The color brown. *Aheka kaginisan ellog. Aniya' bilu, aniya' pote', aniya' ettom, aniya' kausun, aniya' gaddung.* There are many kinds of wading birds, blue ones, white ones, black, brown, and green. (*gen:* **walna'**; *Thesaurus:* **loho'-ubi, sakulati 2**)

**kaut** (var. **kalaut**) *adv.* **1)** Seawards. *Dilaut mbal sakit atā to'ongan min bihing. Na timbang, alawak, atā kaut.* Open sea is not very far at all from the coast. *Timbang is distant, far out to sea. Hē' na alahi kalaut.* Away it goes escaping seawards. (*cf:* **gintana'an**; *Thesaurus:* **kaleya 1, lūd, takod 1, tukad₁ 1**) **1.1)** *v. intr.* zero To go in a seaward direction from inland or shore. *Kaut aku am'ssi ni bukut Sileheman.* I am heading out to sea to the far side of Sileheman. *Ya mbal kakautku inān arakala' aniya' goyak maka baliyu bo' makatīg paraw inān, pakkom aku.* The reason I'm not going to sea is that if, as is likely, there is rough weather and strong wind so that the canoe there leans over, I will capsize. *Kaut kita salung. Ubus kaut, ubus kaleya.* We go to sea tomorrow. Out to sea, then back to land. **1.2)** *v. tr.* To reach something by going out to sea. *Aniya' kautku gi' buwat bubu.* I still have something such as a fishtrap to go out to sea for.

**pagkaut** *v. intr.* aN- To fish out at sea. *Sampay buwattina'an mbal lagi' iya makapagkaut.* Right up to the present time, he is still unable to go to sea [for fishing].

**pakautan** *n.* The place out at sea where one intends to fish.

**kawa'₁** var. of **kawali'**

**kawa'₂** *v. advrs.* ka-...-an To lose a baby through miscarriage. (*Thesaurus:* **bibis, labu' 1.1, pakpak 2, pulak 1.1**)

**kawal** var. of **kawil**

**kawali'** (var. **kawa'₁**) *n.* A large iron cooking pan with two lugs for handling. *Buwat kaha' bo' aheya. Duwa talingana, halam boto'an.* Like a *kaha* but big. It has two lugs, no projecting handle. (*gen:* **pam'llahan**)

**kawang** *adj.* a- Apprehensive or nervous about an activity. *Akawang atayna bang hal buwattē', sali' mbal makatawakkal.* He is nervous [lit. his liver is apprehensive] on such occasions, as though he dare not risk it. *Akawang aku ni M'ddas bang halam aniya' sehe'ku.* I'm anxious about going to Siasi Town if I don't have a companion. (*Thesaurus:* **kanaw-kanaw, ganggu' atay, hanggaw₁ 1**)

**kawas** *v. intr. pa-* To make a sudden vigorous movement in order to escape. *Kamaya'in daing ilū ko da'a pakawas. Subay mbal sakit tinugutan.* Be careful with that fish so that it doesn't get away. The line shouldn't be slackened overmuch.

**kawas-kawas** *n.* A sudden strong gust of wind across a body of water. *Patanam ka, piligdu kita taluwa' kawas-kawas. Kalu mbal pakkom.* Be ready, fearing that a squall may hit us. We may not tip over. (*Thesaurus:* **alimpunus, boto'-boto'₁, buhawi'₂ 1**)

**pagkawas** *v. intr.* aN- To make brief but powerful efforts to escape. *Bang aku angahella' daing, magkawas kosog daing. Ubus akosog ubus mbal.* When I am pulling in a fish its strength is fitful. Strong one minute, none the next.

**pagkawas napas** *v. intr.* aN- To make efforts to breathe, as a person close to death. {idiom} *Magkawas napasna hal, ala'at sadja palasahan.* He breathes only by bursts of effort, still feeling unwell.

**kawasa** *n.* **1)** Authority; power; ability from a higher source. *Bang aku miskin halam na aniya' sali' takakanku, halam aniya' tabayanku magusaha, binuwanan aku kawasa e' Tuhan, binuwanan kita kosog.* When I am poor and have nothing to eat, and no canoe to go fishing in, God gives me power, gives us strength. (*cf:* **parinta 1**) **1.1)** *adj.* a-/-an Powerful; mighty.

**pagkawasa** *v. intr.* aN- To exercise authority or power. *Bang aniya' magkawasa Tuhan, taima' sadja kita ilū.* If there is a God who has power, we will be accepted. (*Thesaurus:* **kapatut, pagagi, pagbaya'₁, pagkuma'agi, pagnakura' 1**)

**kaway** *v. advrs.* -in- **1)** Driven by greed. *Kinaway pahāp a'a inān, bā'nu halam bay makakakan dambulan.* How greedily that person is acting, you would think he hadn't eaten for a month. *Kinaway ma s'mmek, kinaway ma tambal.* Greedy for clothes, greedy for medicine. (*Thesaurus:* **bahaya, hangsaw 1, hawa 1.1, napsu 1.1, sawiya 1, sayap-sayap**) **1.1)** *v. tr.* -an To eat without concern for others. *Kinawayan e'na bāng-bāng.* He gobbled up the cookies. (*Thesaurus:* **bagahak₂, boslad, buhawi'₁, butu', kanam, dahaga', damba'₁ 1.1, lagak 1.1, tanggal₁**)

**kawil** (var. **kawal**) *n.* A large fishhook used when trolling for fish such as tuna. *Kawil itū p'ssi aheya pangati daing aheya. Kawil* are large hooks used with live bait for large fish. (*Thesaurus:* **p'ssi 1, sabit₁ 2**)

**kawin** *v. tr.* -an **1)** To become married to someone. *Luhūy kawinanna si Anu.* What's worse he married What's-her-name. **1.1)** *v. tr.* To declare someone married. *Bang si Ja kinawin, taga maligay.* When Ja is married he will have a model ceremonial house. (*Thesaurus:* **kasal 1,**

**pabatal**, **paglahi 1.1**, **pasugsug**) **1.2**) *v. intr.*
*pa-* To marry into a kin group. *Da'a kam pakawin
ni sigām*. Do not marry into them [their family
line].

**pagkawin** *n.* **1**) A wedding event; a marriage.
*Buwat pagkawin, nilabot a'a paluruk*. Like a
wedding, the people who attend are given
refreshments. **1.1**) *v. intr.* *aN-* To get married.
*Sabab hatina bang ma kami, hatina magkawin
bulan maka llaw*. Because for us it means, it
means that Moon and Sun are getting married.
*Buwat magkawin, bay na tīmmu*. Like being
married, joined physically.

**pagkawinan** *n.* The place where a wedding is
being celebrated. *Buwat aniya' paluruk ni
pagkawinan, asal aheka a'a. Luba' gi' bang
maggabbang*. It's like when guests go to a
wedding venue, lots of people, naturally.
Especially so if there is to be marimba music.

**kawit₁** *v. tr.* To raise something by lifting it on the
end of a stick. *Bang aniya' ahūg buwat s'mmek
subay kinawit pariyata'*. If something such as
clothing falls [into the sea] it needs to be lifted
up with a stick. (*Thesaurus:* **kahid 1, kuhit,
sungkit**)

**kawit₂** *n.* **1**) A gangrenous disease symptomised by
widespread infection on hands, feet or in the
pubic area. (*Thesaurus:* **ka'mbo'an, kolera, ipul
1, pangkot 1, ttus-ttus 1, upāng 1**) **1.1**) *v.
advrs.* *-in-* Suffering from widespread infection
or gangrene. *Angay ka? Kinawit tape'nu?* What's
wrong with you? Have your feet rotted off?
[Said in irritation to someone walking
carelessly.]

**kawit-pupud** *n.* **1**) The loss of fingers or toes as a
secondary effect of Hansen's disease. **1.1**) *v.
advrs.* *-in-* Suffering the loss of fingers or toes
due to disease.

**kāy-kāy** *var.* of **kali-kali**

**kaya** *v. tr.* To achieve or manage something.
*Pin'nno'an karut sigām kamemon, pila-pila ya
takaya binowa e' sigām*. All of their sacks were
filled, as many they could manage to carry.

**kaya-kaya** *see:* **pagkaya-kaya**

**kayab** (*var.* **keyab**) *n.* **1**) Something used as a fan.
**1.1**) *v. tr.* *-an* To fan something in order to
create movement of air or water. *Kayabin aku
apa ilu apasu' baranku*. Fan me because my body
is hot. (*Thesaurus:* **kabkab 1.1, kaskas₂, kayas
1, kaykay**)

**pagkayab** *v. intr.* *aN-* To flap this way and that.
(*Thesaurus:* **k'llay-k'llay, pagk'llab, pagkotek-
kotek, pagp'llay 1, paspad 1**; *syn:* **kayang-
kayang**)

**kayab-kayab** *n.* A species of scallop or fan shell.
*fam. Pectinidae.*

**kayang-kayang** *v. intr.* *pa-* To be flapping, of
something that should be fastened. *Pakayang-
kayang atopna, pabulallit e' baliyu. Bang mbal
tapahāp, magka'at*. The thatch is flapping, turned

wrong way up by the wind. If it is not repaired
it will be ruined. *Buwat kadjang atawa leha
tabowa he' baliyu, magkayang-kayang, magjabjab.*
Like an awning or a sail caught by the wind,
blowing about and flapping. (*syn:* **pagkayab**)

**kayapo'** *n.* Water lettuce, a leafy plant that grows
in swampy soil, used medicinally. *Pistia
stratiotes.*

**kayas** *v. intr.* *pa-* **1**) To move energetically. *Buwat
saga amusay, yukta, "Pakayas ka amusay. Kayasin
busaynu ilū."* Like when paddling, we say, "Be
energetic when you paddle. Swing that paddle
of yours." (*Thesaurus:* **kabkab 1.1, kaskas₂,
kayab 1.1, kaykay**) **1.1**) *v. tr.* *-an* To sweep
something vigorously, as rubbish from a
surface. *Kinayasan busaynu amowa bohe'
pariyata'*. Swing your paddle to bring water to
the surface. *Bang aheka s'ggit ma deyo' luma'
subay kinayasan bo' ahawan*. When there is a lot
of rubbish under the house it should be swished
away so as to be clear.

**pagkayas** *v. intr.* *aN-* To make a display of one's
energy. *Bang lum'ngngan al'kkas atawa bang
amusay al'kkas, abaggis. Sali' magkayas-kayas
dīna*. When he walks rapidly or paddles rapidly,
he is showing off. It's like he is making himself
be energetic.

**kayawan** *n.* Various bamboos, both spiny and non-
spiny species. *Bambusa spp.* (*Thesaurus:*
**kagingking, kayuwan, daumu'an, p'ttung,
t'mmang**)

**kaykay** *v. tr.* To fan sand away in order to see
something clearly. *Kaykayun gusung bang ka
amiha t'bbahan*. Fan the sand away when you
search for strand food. (*Thesaurus:* **kabkab 1.1,
kaskas₂, kayab 1.1, kayas 1**)

**kayog** *adj.* *a-* **1**) Thin, of a person's physical
condition. *Agiti' na barannu, sali' akayog bā*. Your
body is thin, just like *kayog*. (*Thesaurus:* **kagkag,
kittay, koskos, kulagkag, giti' 1, higtal, titis
2**) **1.1**) *v. intr.* *aN-* To become thin.

**kayu** *n.* **1**) A tree, a generic term for many trees and
shrubs (distinct from coconuts and palms). (*pt:*
**batang₁, daun, engas-engas, gamut, po'on₁ 1,
sanga 1, seket**) **2**) Wood in general. **2.1**) *v. tr.*
*-an* To put wood on a fire. *Kayuhinbi api ilu*. Put
some wood on that fire.

**kakayuhan** *n.* A collection of trees; a grove or
copse.

**kayu-soha'** *n.* A species of hard, dark wood;
molave. *Vitex sp.* (*cf:* **agdaw, amulawan**)

**pangayu** *n.* Firewood. (*cf:* **tagay**)

**kayu batang** *n.* *phrase* Wood in log form, found
floating. *Kinamayu si Ji, bay am'lla bo' kayu
batang ya pangayuna*. Ji has a [breast] infection.
She was cooking and used floating wood for
firewood.

**kayung-kayung** *n.* Moorish idol, a fish species.
*Zanclus cornutus.* (*syn:* **kambing-kambing**)

**kayuwan** *n.* A species of thin-walled bamboo. (*Thesaurus:* **kagingking, kayawan, daumu'an, p'ttung, t'mmang**)

**kka** *adj. a-* **1)** To come untied, of a knot. *Anugpat aku lubid, sali' a'kka, sali' halam ahogot panugpatna.* I added a length to the line, it sort of came untied, the extension wasn't secure. *Ndiya laring, mbal pa'kka engkotna itū.* Hand me the knife, the knot of this thing won't come undone. **1.1)** *v. tr. -an* To untie something. *Halam maina'an kulambut. Sali' bay a'kka minsan halam aniya' ang'kkahan iya.* The dropper was not there. It is as though it had come undone, even though nobody had untied it. (*cf:* **tustus**; *Thesaurus:* **hubad, latas₁, p'llus 1, puklas 1**)

**kkat** *var. of* **l'kkat₂**

**kebak** *var. of* **kobak**

**kebang** *n.* **1)** Fruit partly eaten by an animal or bird. A: "*Kebang ai?*" B: "*Kebang mampallam.*" A: "What kind of damaged fruit is it?" B: "Damaged mango." (*Thesaurus:* **k'bbang, kobak 1, kobet 1.1, sembong, t'bbe' 1.1**) **1.1)** *v. tr. -an* To cut out a damaged part from fruit. *Kebangin maka laring. Nila'anan bay keket kabog.* Use a knife to cut out the damaged piece. Remove the part bitten by the bat.

**kebed-kebed₁** *n.* A decorative edging or trim to a garment.

**kebed-kebed₂** *see:* **pagkebed-kebed**

**keke₁** *v. tr. -an* To scrape a thick tough layer off rays or sharks, or off the hull of a boat. *Buwat gaha', kineke.* Scraped off, like rust. *Aniya' kaitan bin'lla. Yuk Ina', "Kekehin ba kuwitna ilū bo' ahāp niadjal."* There was shark to be cooked. Mother said, "Scrape its skin off so it's good to be fixed for cooking." (*Thesaurus:* **bakkel 1.1, kagis 1, l'ngnges 1.2**)

**keke₂** *adj. a-* All dead. *Akeke kamemon.* All dead.

**keket** *v. tr.* **1)** To bite or snap at something. *Kineket e' si Ba tangan siyakana.* Ba bit her older sister's hand. (*Thesaurus:* **k'ttob 1, k'ttop₁**) **1.1)** *n.* An imprint left by teeth or the bite of an insect. A: "*Ai makabakat ilū?*" B: "*Bay keket ero'.*" A: "What caused that wound?" B: "It was a dog bite." **2)** To sting or bite, of insects such as a bee or mosquito.

**keha** (*var.* **peha**) *see:* **pagkeha**

**kehab** *adj. a-* Gaping, of the opposing edges of something normally joined. A: "*Angay akehab b'ttisnu ilu? Bay ka nilagut?*" B: "*Bay aku ahūg min diyata' luma'.*" A: "Why is your lower leg cut open? Were you slashed?" B: "I fell from the top of the house."

**kehe** *n.* **1)** A hollow place or cleft under an overhanging rock or coral formation. *Wa'i ma lowang kehe patapuk.* Away there in that cleft, hiding. (*Thesaurus:* **lowang 1, p'llong, songab 1**) **1.1)** *v. intr. aN-* To open up into a recess under coral or rock. *Angehe batu ilū.* That coral rock opens out into a cleft.

**kehe'-kehe'** *v. intr. aN-* **1)** To laugh excitedly so that teeth are displayed. *Angehe'-ngehe', sali' pinakisi' emponna.* Laughing excitedly, sort of exposing his teeth by drawing back the lips. (*Thesaurus:* **kisi', kiya'-kiya'**) **1.1)** *v. tr. -an* To laugh excitedly at something. *Ai pangehe'-ngehe'annu? Ai kalasigannu?* What are you laughing about so excitedly? What are you happy about?

**kehem** *adj. a-* Making the sound of clearing one's throat. *Akehem si Lo.* Lo is making a coughing noise. *Bang ma tonga' bahangi, aniya' takalenu akehem, "Ahēm," buwattē'.* In the middle of the night you hear someone making a coughing noise, "Ahem," like that. (*cf:* **pagkahak, panggahak**)

**kehet** **1)** *v. tr.* To slice pieces from a larger item. *Kehetun ma aku wanni itū. Bay na kinuwitan bo' kinehet.* Slice that odorous mango for me. It has been peeled to be sliced. *Pinggangan, bay kinehet kulitna bo' ala'an.* A triggerfish, its skin has been cut in order to remove it. (*Thesaurus:* **hīk, hilap, pagsalik-salik**) **2)** *clf.* Count word for slices of something to be eaten.

**balkehet** *n.* A slice of a whole piece. (*Thesaurus:* **balang 1, ballul 1, gali'₁, galing-galing**)

**kehet-boto'** *n.* A species of crevalle. *fam. Carangidae.*

**kelas** *adj. zero* Bald due to scarring of the skull. *Ungas halam aniya' bakatna. Kelas itū bang sali' abakat, aniya' limpa'na.* There is no wound with *ungas* baldness. *Kelas* is when there is some kind of wound which leaves a scar. (*Thesaurus:* **lengas₂, penggas, ungas**)

**keleng** *v. intr. pa-* To turn the head away. *Pakeleng buwattē', mbal bilahi pinasiyum.* Turning her head like that, unwilling to have to kiss. (*Thesaurus:* **elong-elong mata, paglinga-linga**)

**pagkeleng** *v. tr. -an* To shake or turn one's head back and forth, as when signalling refusal. *Mbal bilahi. Itiya' magkelengan.* He isn't willing. Here he is shaking his head.

**keles** *v. intr. pa-* To turn the gaze away from someone, avoiding contact. *Buwat magbissala, mbal kita maka'atu, subay kita pakeles.* Like when talking together and we can't respond, we have to turn our head away. (*Thesaurus:* **buli'-buli' mata, kibad, lingi' 1, pagkesong**)

**kelle** *n.* **1)** A paddle with blades on each end of a shaft. **1.1)** *v. intr. aN-* To propel a canoe using a two-bladed paddle. *Agtūy isāb angelle dapistulan man bihing deya. Agtūy tininduk tangi'.* We promptly paddled a pistol-shot [50 meters or so] from land. And right away hooked a Spanish mackerel. (*Thesaurus:* **busay 1.1, dayung 1.1, epe, luwad, tindayung**) **1.2)** *v. tr.* To reach something by paddling.

**kello'** *n.* **1)** A bend or twist. *Bunt'lled, sali' kello' magtabid.* Curved and twisted, like a bend that winds. (*Thesaurus:* **lompeng 1**) **1.1**) *adj. a-* Bent out of shape or alignment. *Bang bay basi' akello' subay tinilud.* If it was wire that was bent, it should be straightened. (*Thesaurus:* **bengkok 1**, **bunt'lled**, **kalluk 1**)

**pagkello'-kello'** *v. tr.* To make a number of mistakes in marking or following a line. *Bang ka anganggudlis, da'a pagkello'-kello'un.* When you are scribing a line don't bend it this way and that.

**kelong-kelong**₁ *adj. zero* Banded with alternate dark and light strips. *Bū manuk-manuk basta magkabang, niōnan manas kelong-kelong.* Bird feathers, if they are banded, may be described as striped dark and light. (*Thesaurus:* **b'ttik 1.1**, **kabang 1.1**, **jali' 1.1**, **manas**, **palang**)

**kelong-kelong**₂ *n.* Four-lined therapon, a small fish which shelters among floating weeds. *Pelates quadrilineatus.*

**kelot** *adj. a-* Hard despite long boiling, of starchy root crops. (*Thesaurus:* **katat**, **ketot**, **k'llit 1**, **k'ttul**)

**kembo'** *n.* **1)** Dice. **1.1)** *v. tr.* To shake items in a container. *Kinembo' bohe' mareyom kassa'.* Water shaken inside a glass jar. (*Thesaurus:* **kohek-kohek**, **genggok**, **letok**)

**pagkembo'** *v. intr. aN-* To play a dice game.

**keme** *adj. a-* Disabled by injury. *Akeme kita bang kineket he' kalitan, ya mbal kita makasikad.* We are disabled if bitten by a shark, which is why we are unable to act energetically. *Bang kita abakat ma tanganta mbal kita makabalut pahogot. Akeme kita.* If we are cut in the hand we cannot hold anything securely. We are disabled. *Bay ap'ddi' k'llongnu, akeme ka ang'nda'.* Your neck was painful, you were disabled as you looked about. (*Thesaurus:* **ku'il**, **pagtamengka'**, **pagtongka'**, **pukul 1**)

**kemeng-kemeng** *v. tr.* To hold with the fingertips. *Da'a kemeng-kemengun bā. Sali' baya-baya ahūg.* Don't hold it with your fingertips. It's like you'll end up with it falling.

**kemol** *adj. a-* Indistinct and nasal, of speech. *Akemol llingna, pinaluwas min ūng.* His voice is indistinct, produced through the nose. (*Thesaurus:* **ponga'**, **s'ngngog**, **tanga'**₂, **terol**)

**kempot** *adj. a-* Closely spaced, in time or space. *Akempot d'nda hē', akempot he'na maganak. Baha'u bay maganak, magtūy ab'ttong pabalik.* That woman gives birth in quick succession. She has only just given birth and is promptly pregnant again. *Akempot honga'na p'ttung inān.* That bamboo has closely spaced nodes. (*Thesaurus:* **lapat 1.1**, **pagd'ppak 1**, **saplut**₂, **sonson**)

**kende** *n.* **1)** Candy; sweets. *Am'lli gi' aku kende bo' aku kamamisan.* I will buy some candy so I get the sweetness. **1.1)** *v. tr.* To make a sweetmeat of fruit juice. (*cf:* **liking 1**)

**kenog-kenog** *v. intr. aN-* To shiver or tremble due to intensity of emotion. *Bang aku kinōgan atawa angastol angenog-kenog isiku.* When I am happy or angry, my body quivers.

**kenseng** *n.* A metal cooking pot. (*gen:* **pam'llahan**)

**kengkeng** *n.* Little finger or little toe. (*wh:* **tangan 1**)

**pagkengkeng pagbokol** *n. phrase* Bias or prejudice. {idiom} *Nsa' pagkengkeng nsa' pagbokol, timbang-bibitan.* No discrimination [lit. neither little toe nor big toe], treated impartially.

**kepak**₁ *var. of* **sepak**

**kepak**₂ *n.* The Red-tailed mullet. *fam. Mugilidae.* (*gen:* **banak**)

**kepet**₁ *n.* A wing; a large fin. *Bang nijabjaban kepet linggisan, paleyang na.* When the frigate bird flaps its wings, it flies away. (*syn:* **pikpik**₁ **1**)

**kepet**₂ *n.* The armpit. *Bauhan kepetna.* His armpits smell. (*syn:* **pikpik**₂)

**ma kepet** *adv. phrase* By the distance from the armpit to the tip of the same arm.

**kerek-kerek** (*var.* **kulerek-kulerek**) *v. intr. aN-* To make a rattling or rustling sound in the ear. *Mbal ap'ddi' deyom talingaku, hal angerek-ngerek. Aniya' ma deyom, buwat aniya' makasōd langaw.* My ear is not painful, it just buzzes. There is something in it, as if a fly has gone in. (*Thesaurus:* **bahembas 1**, **bah'ssek 1**, **keyos**₂, **kulanas 1**, **kulessab**, **ganggu'**, **ussab-ussab**)

**kerol** *v. intr. aN-* To sing carols. *Yuk si Mma' aniya' kono' nnom budjang-budjang bay pina'an angerol angalangan iya.* Father said that six young teenage girls had gone there caroling, singing to him. (*Thesaurus:* **kalang**₁ **1**, **dindang-dindang**, **pagbinuwa 1**, **tenes-tenes**)

**kesom** *adj. a-* Tasteless, of something expected to be sweet. *Akesom t'bbu itū, angesok deyomna.* This sugar cane is tasteless, it has turned pithy inside. (*Thesaurus:* **imu' 1**, **lanab**, **l'ssom 1**, **mamis**₁ **1.1**, **sarap**₁, **taba' 1**)

**kesong** *see:* **pagkesong**

**kessek** *var. of* **pessek**

**ketok** *var. of* **letok**

**ketong** *n.* Various soldierfishes, including the Scarlet soldierfish and One-bar squirrelfish. *Myripristis pralinia.* (*gen:* **tihik-tihik 1**)

**ketot** *adj. a-* Hard, of boiled cassava. (*Thesaurus:* **katat**, **kelot**, **k'llit 1**, **k'ttul**)

**ketsap** *n.* Ketchup, a tomato-based sauce.

**kettak** *adj. a-* Destitute; penniless. (*Thesaurus:* **kabus**, **ipis 1**, **pihit**, **pulubi**)

**keyab** *var. of* **kayab**

**keyas** *v. intr. pa-* To diminish in force, of wind or rain. *Pakeyas, buwat ulan hal paleyang. Mbal ano'ongan.* Coming to nothing, like rain that simply blows away. Doesn't set in fully. (*Thesaurus:* **kō' 1.1**, **kontay**₂, **hulaw**, **patokang**, **tugut 1**)

**keyas atay** *v. intr. pa-* To ease, of the intensity of some grief or disappointment. {idiom} *Pakeyas atayta, halam na bay susa.* Our sadness has eased, the past sorrow is no more.

**keyat₁** *n.* 1) The color red. (*gen:* **walna'**) 1.1) *adj. a-* Fair, brown or blonde, of hair color.

**keyat₂** *n.* 1) A flame; a blaze. *Wa'i pasuleyab keyatna ni s'ggit.* Its flame has flared up in the trash. 1.1) *adj. a-* Alight; ignited; burning. *Aradju bang pinah'lling, akeyat du ma deyom.* The radio when turned on, glows inside. (*cf:* **tunu'₁** 1.1; *Thesaurus:* **dallet** 1, **dokot₂** 1.1, **lāb** 1, **suleyab** 1)

**pakeyat** *v. tr.* To ignite something; to turn a light on. (*Thesaurus:* **bagid**, **dokot₂** 1.2, **santik** 1, **sū'** 1.2)

**pagpakeyat** *v. tr.* To light lamps.

**keyok** var. of **eyok**

**keyol** (var. **kowel**) *v. tr. -an* 1) To move the hands with a stirring motion. *Keyol-keyolin tangannu, tindak-tindakin tape'nu.* Move your hands and stamp your feet in time. 1.1) *v. tr.* To stir food as it cooks. *Keyolun abō' tananam mamis sokal.* Stir it so the sweetness of the sugar can be tasted. *Kowelun sinanglag bo' mbal atunu'.* Keep turning the cassava meal so it doesn't burn. (*Thesaurus:* **bungkal₂** 1.2, **kuwal**, **gawgaw**)

**pakeyol** *v. tr.* To get the hands moving rhythmically.

**keyos₁** *v. intr. pa-* To turn one's upper body to be side on. *Bang ka niopera, mbal ka makakeyos magdai'-dai'.* If you have surgery you will not be able to turn over in a hurry. *Da'a pakeyosun barannu.* Don't make your body turn.

**pagkeyos** *v. intr. aN-* To twist the upper body this way and that. *Bang ap'ddi' hawakanta, mbal kita makapagkeyos.* When our waist is painful, we are unable to turn this way and that.

**keyos₂** *v. intr. aN-* To make the sound of something moving through undergrowth. *Angeyos, buwat sowa ma deyom sagmot, atawa buwat pantalun baha'u.* Making a rustling sound, like a snake in the undergrowth, or like brand-new trousers. (*Thesaurus:* **bahembas** 1, **bah'ssek** 1, **kerek-kerek**, **kulanas** 1, **kulessab**, **ganggu'**, **ussab-ussab**)

**keyot₁** (var. **eyot**) *n.* A lobster-like crustacean, a deep water species. *Keyot itū ahunit piniha, subay ma dilaut. Arāk luwa kamun sagwā' ngga'i ka isāb.* These *keyot* are difficult to find, it has to be out at sea. One might have said they are like *kamun* shrimps, but that's not really so. (*Thesaurus:* **kamun**, **lattik₁**, **pama'**)

**keyot₂** var. of **kowet**

**kibad** *v. intr. pa-* To look away from something. *Pakibad itu sali' binuli'-buli' mata, sali' palingi'. Kibad* is like averting one's eyes, like looking back. (*Thesaurus:* **buli'-buli' mata**, **keles**, **lingi' 1**, **pagkesong**)

**kibad atay** *adj. a-* Emotionally tense due to anxiety or shock. {idiom} *Pakibad deyom atayku, sali' mandā'dā'.* I am emotionally distracted, sort of feeling hurt. *Bay kami angusaha panit, yukku, "Angā' na ka palsuku'annu." Yukmu, "Da'a na pakibarun deyom ataynu ilu. Aniya' du tungbasna."* I had been catching tuna and said, "Take your share." You said, "Don't worry yourself about it. There will be no doubt be compensation." *Magkakibad deyom atayku sabab siyaliku laha'an, bay binono'. Sali' ameya' ginhawaku to'ongan.* My emotions are shaken because my younger brother is bleeding, he was hit. It is like my whole inner being is involved. (*Thesaurus:* **pagsorol**, **sukkal** 1, **susa** 1)

**kibi'** *adj. a-* Twisted, of the lips. (*Thesaurus:* **kiyu'**, **tabid bowa'**)

**kibi'-kibi'** *v. tr. -an* To threaten someone by grimacing with lower teeth showing. (*syn:* **kiya'-kiya'**)

**kibit** *v. intr. pa-* 1) To be partly open, exposing contents. *Yampa pakibit pandoga. Bay bagunan, ariki' kata'nda'anna, hal pakibit.* The navigation marker has just now come into view. It had been clouded over, a small part visible, just showing a little. *Bang aku anittowa, pakibit emponku, patuwa' dangkuri'.* When I laugh my teeth are exposed, sticking out a little. 1.1) *v. tr.* To partly open a door or lid. *Kibitta lawang itū.* Let's just open the door a bit.

**kibit-dawa** *adv.* Within moments of happening. {idiom} *Kibit-dawa ka'a ilū ta'bba.* You are within seconds of being left behind.

**kiblat** *n.* The direction of Mecca; the direction a Muslim faces in prayer.

**kibut** *n.* An earthenware jar, generally unglazed, used for holding water. (*Thesaurus:* **bingki'**, **ka'ang**, **kasambagan**, **pipa**, **poga**, **tanāng**, **tangpad**)

**kikkit** var. of **kitkit**

**kiki'** *n.* 1) A stain on the teeth; tartar. *Aniya' sali' aettom amalut ma empon atawa biyaning. Halam kita magtupras.* There is something sort of black or yellow sticking to the teeth. We haven't used a toothbrush. (*Thesaurus:* **baka'₂** 1, **balakang** 1) 1.1) *v. advrs. -in-* Stained, of teeth. *Kiniki' baka' iya.* His teeth are stained yellow.

**kikis** *v. tr.* To rake the top of a pile in order to level it. (*Thesaurus:* **kahig**, **kās**, **hīs** 1.1)

**kīd₁** *n.* 1) The side of a structure or body. (*syn:* **timbangan₂**; *Thesaurus:* **bihing₂** 1) 1.1) *v. intr. pa-* To lie on one's side. (*Thesaurus:* **lengag**, **pasindik**, **patiring**, **sīp**)

**kīd-tuktuk** *n.* The temple (side of one's head). *Nirugsu'an iya ma kīd-tuktukna bo' alopot kōkna.* He was stabbed in the side of his brow so that his head was shattered.

**kīran** *n.* The side part of a structure.

**kīd₂** *v. intr. pa-* To tilt to one side. *Pakīd pelang, sali' alenggang.* The canoe is tilting to one side, sort of tipping. (*Thesaurus:* **kīng** 1.1, **lemba**, **lenggang**, lihid, paglilip-lilip, poyog 1, tĭg)

**kidkid** (var. **kigkid**) *v. tr.* To smooth a wooden surface by sanding. *Ahāp kulit pahi pangidkid busay.* Stingray skin is good for smoothing paddles. (*Thesaurus:* **gidgid**)

**kiddat₁** *v. tr.* -an To signal someone by winking or raising the eyebrows. *Bang aniya' sehe'ta magbaya', kiddatanta.* If I and someone else are attracted to each other, we signal with our eyes. *Bay ka ta'nda'ku angiddatan d'nda.* I saw you winking at a girl.

**kiddat₂** var. of **kindat**

**kidjang** *n.* 1) The wing of a celestial being. (*Thesaurus:* **pikpik₁** 1, **tuntun₂**) 1.1) *v. intr. aN*- To spread the wings for flight or display. *Angidjang la'a, sali' bidadali.* Just gliding along, like a sky maiden. (*cf:* **leyang 1**)

**kidjib** (var. **kinyib**) *v. tr.* -an To obtain something by fraud. *Pangingidjib ko' ka'a!* You're such a cheat! (*Thesaurus:* **akkal 1.1**)

**kidjiban** *n.* Something obtained by fraud.

**pagkidjib** *v. intr. aN*- To behave resentfully or deceitfully with regard to people closely related. *Magkidjib itū sali' magdanakan magla'at-la'at.* *Kidjib* is like siblings behaving maliciously towards each other.

**kidjut** *n.* Involuntary movement of the muscles; a twitch. (*syn:* **kirut-kirut**)

**kidjut-kahibal** *n.* The many small tasks that demand attention. {idiom} *Aheka pahāp kidjut-kahibalbi.* You have so many things to do.

**pagkidjut** *v. intr. aN*- To make brief muscular movements; to twitch. *Magkidjut bahaku bang aku angigal.* My shoulders lift briefly when I am dancing. (*Thesaurus:* **k'bbut**, **pagkirut-kirut**, **pagkurat**)

**kidnap** *n.* 1) The act of kidnapping. 1.1) *v. tr.* To kidnap someone. *Bang aniya' a'a ta'abut angidnap saga pagkahina bo' nihinang banyaga' atawa pinab'llihan, ya a'a bay angidnap hē' subay pinapatay.* If a man is caught kidnapping his fellow-human for the purpose of enslaving or selling, that man should be killed.

**pagkidnap** *n.* 1) Kidnapping as a business. 1.1) *v. intr. aN*- To capture people for the purpose of making money. *Ya tinuntut he' a'a magkikidnap subay pilak.* What the kidnappers demand is money. (*Thesaurus:* **agaw 1.1**, **saggaw**)

**kigkid** var. of **kidkid**

**kigit** *adj. a*- Stingy; ungenerous. *Da'a kam am'lli ni paltira si Se apa sidda akigit.* Don't buy from the middleman Se, because he is very stingy. *Bang aku angamu' ai-ai ni ka'a, bo' aku mbal buwanannu, akigit ka.* If I ask you for something but you don't give it, you are mean. (*Thesaurus:* **bista₂** 1, **kaikit₁**, **kimmat 1**, **k'mmit 1**, **kudkud**, **kuriput 1**, **kussil**, **giging**, **iskut**, **sumil₁**)

**kihaka** (derivative of **haka**) *v. tr.* To ask someone for information. *Aniya' kampungna amatay ma Tabawan. Halam iya makata'u angkan iya mikihaka.* A relative of his has died in Tabawan. He hadn't known, so he asks for information. (*Thesaurus:* **hati 2**, **hodhod**, **sisi 2**, **tilaw 1.1**, **tilosa 1.1**).

**pagkihaka** *v. intr. aN*- To ask someone for information. *Magkihaka sigām dangan maka dangan.* They asked each other for information.

**kihampaw** *n.* Generic term for various stingrays, including the Blue-spotted or fantail ray. *fam. Dasyatidae.*

**kihampaw-bās** *n.* Sand ray, gray in color.

**kihampaw-batu** *n.* Rock ray, has blue spots.

**kīl** *v. tr.* To strike a volleyball with a powerful downward blow. *Palaksu gi' aku angīl.* I jump up in order to 'kill' the volleyball. (*cf:* **tūs**, **walup**)

**kilā** *v. tr.* 1) To recognize someone by sight or hearing. *Pīddahan na palita'an mareyom luma' sultan. Kinilā na ba. Pag'nda' itū, duma'in ka pahi. L'lla na.* The lights in the sultan's house were extinguished. [The thing] was identified. On looking, it wasn't a stingray. It was a man. (*Thesaurus:* **panhid**, **pangli' 1.1**) 2) To come to a conclusion based on limited information. *Kilāku aniya' sattuwa talun bay angā' iya.* I conclude that some wild animal got him.

**pagkilā** (var. **pagkilāhi**) *v. intr. aN*- To be acquainted with someone; to know each other by sight. *Ta'nda' pa'in iya he' saga a'a bay magkilāhi maka iya, magtilaw-tilawan sigām dansehe'an.* When people who were familiar with him saw him, they asked questions of each other. (*Thesaurus:* **pagkata'u**)

**pakakilāhan** *n.* The means of recognizing someone.

**pakilā** *v. tr.* To introduce; to make someone known.

**kila-kila** var. of **kira-kira**

**kilā-luku** *n.* A sickness of very small children, symptomized by enlargement of the skull. (*syn:* **kulang-kilā**)

**kilaw** *v. tr.* 1) To eat raw food, especially fish, with a relish. *Kinilaw itū sali' ni'inta', nsa' bĭlla.* Eaten with relish is like being eaten raw, not cooked. *Si Sa bay angandāg mampallam binowa ni luma' pangilawna kasig, kal'ssoman. Pahi mbal takilaw.* Sa climbed to get a mango to take home as a relish for raw pilchard, to be made sour. Manta rays cannot be eaten raw. (*Thesaurus:* **bubuk₂**, **lawal 1.1**, **pan'nno'an**, **tinu'anan**) 2) To prepare fish with a spicy marinade.

**kinilaw** *n.* Raw fish prepared with a relish.

**kilay** *n.* Eyebrows. *Bang aku ameya' ni pagkawinan subay aku sinoso'an kilayku.* If I go to a wedding I should have my eyebrows trimmed. (*cf:* **bū-mata**)

**kilkil** *n.* A species of coastal tree, the source of an easily worked yellowish wood. (*syn:* **kosok₂**)

**kili-kili** *n.* A chain. *Aniya' kili-kili bahudji', aniya' isāb kili-kili bulawan.* There are anchor chains, and there are gold chains [jewelry]. (*Thesaurus:* **bilanggu' 1, karena 1.1, ekang-ekang 1.1**)

**killaw** var. of **pillaw**

**killut-killut** (var. **kilut-kilut**) *adj. zero* Wrinkled and shaking from long immersion in cold water. *Subay kita bay ma bohe', akillut-killut kita ma deyom tahik.* We must have been in water, wrinkled from being in the sea. *Killut-killut tanganta, sali' magkonot.* Our hands are shriveled from immersion, sort of wrinkled. *Killut-killut bang at'ggol ma tahik, ai na ka tangan ai na ka tape'.* Skin wrinkles when in the sea for a long time, whether it is hands or feet. (*Thesaurus:* **kilorot, konot₁ 1.1**)

**kilometēl** *n.* A kilometer. (*Thesaurus:* **batu₃, d'ppa 1, honga'₂, inses, maniku**)

**kilorot** *adj. a-* Crumpled. *Buwat katas baha'u bay keket ambaw, na akilorot.* Like paper recently chewed by rats, that's *kilorot.* (*Thesaurus:* **killut-killut, konot₁ 1.1**)

**kilu** *n.* 1) A kilogram. 1.1) *v. tr.* To measure something by weight. (*cf:* **timbang₁ 1**)

  **kiluhan** *n.* A spring scale for weighing small items. (*cf:* **timbangan₁**)

  **ma kiluhan** *adv. phrase* By the kilo.

**kilu-kilu** var. of **kuli-kuli**

**kilul** *n.* The malunggay or horse-radish tree, has edible leaves. *Moringa oleifera.* (*syn:* **kalamunggay**)

**kilut-kilut** var. of **killut-killut**

**kima** *n.* Various species of giant clams. *Tridacna spp. Kima-kuyya' sali' luwa batu, kima-s'llot-s'llot ma deyom batu.* The *kuyya'* clam looks like a rock; the *s'llot-s'llot* clam is found in rocks.

  **kima-antu'ang** (var. **antu'ang**) *n.* A species of giant clam.

  **kima-kuyya'** *n.* A species of clam that looks like a rock.

  **kima-lapiran** *n.* A species of clam.

  **kima-s'llot-s'llot** *n.* A species of small clam which grows in the clefts of coral rocks.

**kima-kima** *v. advrs. -in-* Suffering from the need to urinate frequently; polyuria. (*cf:* **kaukati 1**)

**kimbing** var. of **kinbing**

**kimig** *n.* 1) An irregularity in the shape of spherical or nearly spherical objects. 1.1) *adj. a-* Irregularly shaped. *Akimig isāb kōkna ilu.* Its head is asymmetrical.

**kiming** *n.* A box-shaped trap for weed-eating fish. (*cf:* **gau**; *Thesaurus:* **bagiyas 1, bubu₁, panggal 1, togong 1**)

**kiming-kiming** *n.* A box-shaped cage of woven bamboo, for live birds. *Kiming-kiming panau'an manuk-manuk, buwat pagiyas.* A cage like a *pagiyas*, for keeping birds alive in.

**kimmat** 1) *adj. a-* Over-cautious (and mean) in counting or measuring out amounts. (*Thesaurus:* **bista₂ 1, kaikit₁, kigit, k'mmit 1, kudkud, kuriput 1, kussil, giging, iskut, sumil₁**) 2) *v. tr.* To estimate the amount of something, especially with regard to bride-gift goods. *Ta'abut pinah'nda'an, yuk matto'a l'lla ya kinawin inān, "Kimmatin aku alta'ta. Kalu maka'abut dakayu' d'nda."* When the time comes for the betrothal, the elder of the man being married, says, "Estimate for me our resources. Maybe it will suffice for one woman."

**kimu'** *v. tr.* To wash the soiled part of a garment without immersing the whole. (*Thesaurus:* **dakdak 1, pakang₂, pukpuk**)

**kimut-kimut** *v. intr. pa-* To mumble or mutter.

  **pagkimut-kimut** *v. intr. aN-* To move the lips as though speaking. *Hal bowa'na ta'nda' ah'lling. Mbal pinakale ni sehe'na, hal magkimut-kimut.* Only his mouth is seen speaking. He doesn't let his companions hear, he just moves the lips.

**kinakan** (derivative of **kakan**) *n.* 1) Food in general. (*Thesaurus:* **talopa'**). 2) Cooked rice. (*Thesaurus:* **buwas-kinakan, gulami, pai 1.1**).

**kinam** *v. tr. -an* 1) To try something by tasting; to experience the effects of some event (fig.) *Kinamin daing ilū bang ahāp ssana.* Sample that fish [to know] if its taste is good. *Anambung si Jo, "Bay t'nno'anku tōng tungkudku ni gula' buwani bo' bay kinamanku dangkuri'."* Jo replied, "I dipped the end of my staff in the honey and tasted a little bit." (*Thesaurus:* **ssa₁ 1.3, sulay₁ 2, timtim 1.1**) To experience the effects of some event (fig.) *Angkan mbal na takinambi kahāpan ya arāk pamuwanku ma ka'am.*

  **pagkinam** *v. tr. -an* To sample food for its flavor. *Bang ma pagkinamku sarang asinna.* According to my sampling it has enough salt.

**kinasulan** (derivative of **kasul**) *adj. zero* Decorated by quilting, of bedding. *Aniya' ma sigām tilam kinasulan.* They have a mattress fitted with a decorated cover.

**kinbing** (var. **kimbing**) *v. tr.* To twist someone's ears, as a punishment. *Kininbing-kinbing si Ju he' mastal bang bay absen.* Ju had his ears twisted by the teacher when he was absent. (*Thesaurus:* **k'bbit, hita' 2.1**)

**kinkin** *v. tr.* To roll or fold up one's sleeves or trouser cuffs. *Kininkin pariyata' sanyawana.* His shorts were rolled right up.

**kindang** *n.* A sarong tied over one shoulder (of a woman).

  **pagkinindang** *v. intr. aN-* To wear a sarong tied over one shoulder. *D'nda ya magkinindang inān.* The woman over there wearing her sarong *kindang* style.

**kindat** (var. **kiddat₂**) *n.* A cuttlefish species, small. *Order Sepiolida.* (*cf:* **kulangkung**; *gen:* **lansongan**)

**kindut** *n.* Briefs (underwear). (*Thesaurus:* **kansinsilyu, kudji-kudji, kullat, sanyawa**)

**kinilaw** (derivative of **kilaw**) *n.* Raw fish prepared with a relish.

**kinosog** (derivative of **kosog**) *v. intr. aN-* To

contribute energy or moral support to some activity. *Bang kita am'ssi kaut bo' llaw, ta'abut Tapol subay kita anginosog.* When we are fishing at sea during the day and we reach Tapul Island, we need to put effort into it. *Bang aku saupama kinawin, si'itku ina'an anginosog.* When I get married, for example, those uncles of mine will support me. (*cf:* **ga'os 1.2**).

**kinsan** *n.* An edible species of sea anemone. *Actinia sp.*

**kintas 1)** *n.* A sheet of something flat and foldable, as paper. (*Thesaurus:* **b'llad 1, b'llat 1, gekap 1, lamba₂**) **2)** *clf.* Count word for foldable items. *Ndiya, b'lliku t'llu kintas katas-balan.* Please, I will buy three sheets of sandpaper.
**ma kintasan** *adv. phrase* By the sheet.

**kinyib** var. of **kidjib**

**kīng** *n.* **1)** A tendency to lean away from the vertical. *Taga kīng taguri' saga bang mbal abontol nīnda' mariyata'.* Things like *taguri'* kites have a tilt when they are visibly off-vertical up in the air. **1.1)** *v. intr.* pa- To incline from the vertical. (*Thesaurus:* **kīd₂, lemba, lenggang, lihid, paglilip-lilip, poyog 1, tīg**)

**kingkoyan** *n.* **1)** A style of hair or tailoring distinguished by its sharply defined ridges or pleats. *Pahāpun kingkoyannu ilū.* Improve that *kingkoy* style of yours. **1.1)** *v. tr.* To style hair or clothes with well-defined ridges.

**kiparat** *see:* **pagkiparat**

**kiput** *adj.* a- Restricted, of openings such as a road or passageway. *Akiput asal lugal bay pagbono'an ē'.* The place where the fighting took place was in fact narrow. *Magsaddi tina'i. Tina'ibi akiput-kiput, tina'i kami aluha.* Digestive organs differ. Your digestive organs are quite constricted, ours are broad. (*cf:* **luha 1**; *Thesaurus:* **diki' 1, nahut**)
**kiput alam** *v. tr.* To modify distances or meteorological conditions by magical means. {idiom} *Ata'u angiput alam. Minsan bay aluha takiput, bay tambang tahinang ababaw, bay alawak tapasekot.* He knows how to reduce natural things. What was wide is restricted, high tide is made shallow, distances are made to be close.

**kira** *v. tr.* To estimate an amount. *Sakap na amono' saga l'lla min umul duwampū' pariyata' bang kinira.* Males from an estimated age of twenty or more are ready fight. (*Thesaurus:* **kalkula, itung₁, jumla 1, saipuwa**)

**kira-kira** (var. **kila-kila**) *v. tr.* To give serious thought to possible options. *Bang kita am'lli, pene'ta dahū bang ai ya kabaya'anta. Amikil ahāp maka ala'at, ya hē' angira-ngira.* When we buy, we choose first what we want. We then consider the good and the bad. That's what *kira-kira* means. *Kila-kilahun kono'. Kalu mbal makainay baran.* Please give a considered opinion. Perhaps

it will cause no physical harm. *Kilā-kilāku, sali' papataku, sali' kita talus-talus.* I consider the possibility, sort of predict something, as though we could see what is not yet known. (*Thesaurus:* **bista₁, kumpas₁, tē'₂**)

**pagkira-kira** *v. tr.* -an To think through the implications of a proposed action. *Buwat disi Ha magpaopera, yuk sigā, "Tuwan, buwattingga? Pagkila-kilahin kami sabab halam aniya' sīn."* Like Ha and the others requesting surgery, saying, "Sir, how will it be? Think it through for us because there is no money."

**kiramin-katibin** *n.* The heavenly book in which the records of each person are kept. *Kiramin-katibin, ya na sulatan Tuhan.* The kiramin-katibin is the writing of God. (*Thesaurus:* **kitab, Jabul, Kitab Tawrat**)

**kiraw** *adj.* a- Blinking; flashing on and off. (*Thesaurus:* **kitaw-kitaw, illap, inggat, pagpillaw-pillaw, pagsinglab, tingaw-tingaw**)
**pagkiraw** *v. tr.* To cause something to flash, as a mirror used for signaling. *Bang aniya' baliyu bo' aniya' ta'nda' boto'-boto', pinagkiraw samin.* When it is windy and we see a whirlwind, a mirror is flashed at it.

**kiri-kiri** *adj.* a- Excited as a result of good fortune or some anticipated good. *Akiri-kiri aku, bay aku anganda'ug. Sali' aku akōd.* I am excited, I won. It's like I am happy. (*Thesaurus:* **asa 1.1, holat 1, lagad 1.1**)

**kirik-kirik** *v. tr.* To tickle someone in order to make them laugh. *Agiluk aku bang aku kinirik-kirik, minsan du bay anangis.* I am giggly when I am tickled, even though I had been crying. (*cf:* **giluk 1.1**)

**kirida** *n.* A mistress or paramour.

**kirus** *adj.* a- **1)** Misshapen by being smaller on one side. *Paloddos dambila', sali' atimpang, akirus dampōng.* Too small on one side, asymmetrical, one half of it misshapen. (*Thesaurus:* **baligbig, pagkamihu, tempang**) **1.1)** *v. tr.* -an To trim the shape of something. *Bay aheya, bay kinurusan, bay pinīsan, buwat s'mmek, pelang.* It was large, made smaller, a piece snipped off, such as cloth or a canoe. *Kirusanta, diki'anta.* We reshape it, make it smaller. (*Thesaurus:* **basbas, katam 1.1, saplung 1.1, sapsap₂, sosok**)

**kirut-kirut** *n.* A twitch or tic. (*syn:* **kidjut**)
**pagkirut-kirut** *v. intr.* aN- To twitch, as from a muscular tic. (*Thesaurus:* **k'bbut, pagkidjut, pagkurat**)

**kīs₁** *v. tr.* To cut something into small pieces. *Kinīsan pamakay sigām.* Their clothing was cut to shreds. *Pagbalikna, kinīs-kīs e'na saga buwa' ē' ati pinat'nna' ma l'ppo'.* On her return she cut up that fruit and put it in the pan. (*syn:* **pīs₂ 1**)

**kīs₂** *n.* A legal offense; a court case. *Aheya na kīs a'a inān ma parinta. Bay iya amono'. Taga kīs na iya, taga kala'atan.* That man has a legal case against him. He killed someone. He has a case to answer, he has committed an offense. *Aniya' kīsnu, aniya' kala'atannu.* You have a case to answer, you have [committed] an offense. (*cf:* **palkala' 1**)

**kīs₃** *n.* A case or packet of small items. *Tinugila'an kami mpat hatus pilak maka duwa karut buwas maka dakalton siga, dangkīs kulitis saga.* The list required of us was four hundred pesos, two sacks of rice, a carton of cigarets, a packet of firecrackers, and so on.

**kīs₄** *n.* 1) A knife used to clean the nails of a dead body in preparation for burial. (*Thesaurus:* **janap, laring, pisaw**) 2) A cursing equivalent for any cutting tool. *Angay kīsnu?* What's up with that cursed tool of yours? (*gen:* **sukna' 1.1**)

**kisak** *v. tr.* **-an** To remove the skin of something. (*Thesaurus:* **kanit 1.1, kupas, hagut, hampa' 1.1, lapes**)

**kisal-kisal** *v. intr.* **pa-** To move a short distance. *Pakisal-kisal ka, pahigin-higin min bainu.* Move a bit, shift on from where you were. (*Thesaurus:* **hense, higin, ingsud, sigput**)

**kisas₁** *n.* The canistel or eggfruit tree and its fruit. *Lucuma nervosa.* (*Thesaurus:* **balimbing, kamyas, iba'**)

**kisas₂** *n.* Supernatural retribution for an offense against social norms, as when someone makes fun of another's physical defect. (*cf:* **busung**)

**kisi'** *v. intr.* **pa-** To draw back the lips and expose one's teeth. *Pinakisi' emponna, sali' pinatampal.* His teeth drawn back, sort of made obvious. (*Thesaurus:* **kehe'-kehe' 1, kiya'-kiya'**)

**kissa** *n.* 1) A story; a tale. *Kissa-kissa ya ngga'i ka b'nnal.* Minor stories that are not true. (*Thesaurus:* **istori 1, pagkata-kata 1.1, paglanga'-langa', salsila 1) 1.1**) *v. tr.* To relate a story or folktale. *Kinissa du pasal bay hinang d'nda itū, pangentoman ma iya.* The story about this woman's action will be told, in memory of her.

**pagkissa** *v. intr.* **aN-** To tell traditional stories. *Magkissa iya bay kama'asan.* He tells stories about the old ones [of long ago].

**kissat** *v. intr.* **pa-** To squirt out or flare up. *Ē' na pakissat llaw, hatina paluwa' na bā.* There's the sunlight bursting through, appearing, in other words. *Buwat saga pelang patongod ma panimbakan, bo' aniya' angissat bohe' min deyom pelang hē', ase'ak he' timbak.* For example canoes located over a dynamiting location, and there is water shooting up from inside those canoes, split open by the explosion. *Buwat bohe' ma tuburanna, ta'nda' pakissat pariyata'.* Like water coming up from its source, seen surging up. (*Thesaurus:* **pigsik₁ 1, p'ssik 1.1, pulagsik, sahupput, sumpit 1**)

**kisul** *n.* Aromatic ginger or galangal, the root of which is used medicinally and for flavoring. *Kampferia galanga.* (*cf:* **lu'uya**)

**kīt** *n.* A percussion cap for firing explosives. *Kah'llingan iya kīt.* He was hit by the blast of a percussion cap.

**kīt-kīt** *n.* A species of fish.

**kitā** *pron.* 1) We two, us (first person dual, inclusive) [Set I]. (*cf:* **=ta 1, kita**; *Set:* **akū, kā, kām, kamī, kitabi₁, kitām, iyā, sigā₁, sigām₁**) 2) Someone or anyone; indefinite pronoun. *Binaha'an kitā, tinumbulan, sali' anganak.* One might be affected with swelling, growing more boils, sort of producing young.

**kita** *pron.* We two, us (first person dual, inclusive) [Set III]. (*cf:* **=ta 1, kitā 1**; *Set:* **aku₂, ka'a, ka'am, kami, kitabi₂, kitam, iya, sigā₂, sigām₂**)

**kitab** *n.* A sacred book, especially the Holy Koran or the Holy Bible. (*Thesaurus:* **kiramin-katibin, Jabul, Kitab Tawrat**)

**Kitab Injil** (var. **Injil**) *n. phrase* The New Testament of the Holy Bible; the Book of the Evangel.

**Kitab Tawrat** (var. **Tawrat**) *n. phrase* The five books of Moses in the Old Testament of the Holy Bible. (*Thesaurus:* **kiramin-katibin, kitab, Jabul**)

**kitabi₁** var. of **kitām**

**kitabi₂** var. of **kitam**

**kital** *v. tr.* To take aim on a target, such as to fire a weapon, to punch someone, to shoot a ball. (*Thesaurus:* **balis₁, kalsa, surang**)

**kitām** (var. **kitabi₁**) *pron.* We, us, including the one spoken to (first person plural, inclusive) [Set I]. *Atuli na kitām.* Let's all sleep. (*cf:* **=tam, kitam**; *Set:* **akū, kā, kām, kamī, kitā 1, kitabi₁, iyā, sigā₁, sigām₁**)

**kitam** (var. **kitabi₂**) *pron.* We, us, including the one spoken to (first person plural, inclusive) [Set III]. (*cf:* **=tam, kitām**; *Set:* **aku₂, ka'a, ka'am, kami, kita, kitabi₂, iya, sigā₂, sigām₂**)

**kitara** (var. **gitara**) *n.* A guitar. (*cf:* **biyula 1**) **pagkitara** *v. intr.* **aN-** To play a guitar.

**kitaw-kitaw** *v. intr.* **aN-** To sparkle or flash; to flicker or twinkle, as stars or distant lights. *Yukna, "O Mma', sai bahā' dapu luma' angitaw-ngitaw ma bihing langit ē', ma dilaut ē'?"* He said, "Father, who is the owner of that house sparkling there on the horizon, out at sea?" (*Thesaurus:* **kiraw, illap, inggat, pagpillaw-pillaw, pagsinglab, tingaw-tingaw**)

**kitkit** (var. **kikkit**) *v. tr.* To nibble or gnaw at something, as small creatures do. *Bay kinitkit he' ogos.* Gnawed by a parrot fish [said of a poor haircut]. *Bay kinkkit umpan he' ogos.* A parrotfish has nibbled at the bait. (*Thesaurus:* **pagkuri'-kuri', pagliblib-liblib 1.1**)

**kitlan** (var. **itlan**) *n.* 1) Tar; pitch (resin). (*cf:* **espalton**) **1.1**) *v. tr.* To apply tar or bituminous paint to a surface. *Kitlanku parawku abō' mbal ang'mman.* I will apply tar to my canoe so it doesn't leak.

**kittay** *adj.* **a-** Very thin, of a person's physical condition. *Akittay na bagayku, angagkag.* My friend is so gaunt, becoming thin. (*Thesaurus:* **kagkag, kayog 1, koskos, kulagkag, giti' 1, higtal, titis 2**)

**kittup** *adj. a-* **1)** Closed firmly together, as the lips, edges of a wound, or bivalve shells. *Pakittupun bowa'nu.* Close your mouth tightly. (*Thesaurus:* **k'ntom, t'mmu 1.1**) **1.1)** *v. intr. aN-* To close up by bringing edges together. *Basta panagatunan kamemon, akittup. Pakittup bowa' kima.* In the case of all shellfish, they close up. The great clams close up.

**kitut** var. of **bāt-kitut**

**kiyabut-kiyabut** var. of **kabut-kabut**

**kiya'-kiya'** *v. tr. -an* To threaten someone by grimacing with lower teeth showing. (*syn:* **kibi'-kibi'**; *Thesaurus:* **kehe'-kehe' 1, kisi'**)

**kiyal** *v. intr. pa-* To look at something bright through narrowed lids. *Pakiyal kita apa apasu' llaw ati asilaw kita.* We squint because the day is hot and we are dazzled.

**kiyam** *v. tr.* To prepare a body for burial by laying its hands across the chest.

**kiyama** var. of **kiyamat**

**kiyamat** (var. **kiyama**) *n.* **1)** The afterworld; the final destruction of the world; judgment day; the realm of the dead. *Amole' du kita ni deyom kiyama, ya hē' dunya ahirat.* We shall go home to the afterworld, to the place where the dead dwell. *Ma kiyama hē' duwA: nalka' maka sulga'.* In the afterworld there are two options: hell and heaven. *Ya niōnan llaw kiyamat itū, ya llaw paglangkat dunya.* The day called *kiyamat* is the day when the world is dismantled. **1.1)** *adj. a-* Experiencing final judgment. *Bang pasayang ya pikpik galura', magtūy akiyamat dunya. Ya hamiyuna, m'nnē' magtambol dunya.* When the winged horse spreads its wings in flight, then the earth will experience final judgment. Its turbulence will bring about the closing up of the world.

**kiyap** *v. intr. pa-* To open wider, of a crack. *Buwat buli' pelang, pakiyap bang taluwa' goyak.* Like the stern of a pelang-type canoe, splitting more when struck by rough seas.

**kiyas** *v. intr. aN-* To keep from doing what others do, so as not to be blamed. *Buwat anakku mbal papandu', yukku, "Bang ka'a ilū makaka'at, angiyas aku."* When a child of mine is not teachable, I say, "If you come to grief I am not to blame." *Angiyas aku man palkala' ilū, mbal aku lamud.* I disassociate myself from that matter, I am not involved. (*cf:* **puwas₁ 1**)

**kiyat** *n.* A root crop eaten in times of scarcity.

**kiyomol** *adj. a-* Stuffed full of food, of one's mouth. *Bang kita amapa', aheka ma deyom bowa'ta, akiyomol bowa'ta.* When we are chewing something and a lot of food is in our mouth, our mouth is stuffed full. *Akiyomol, sali' as'ppul deyom bowa'na, mbal makalapal.* Stuffed full, like his mouth being overfull, unable to utter words.

(*Thesaurus:* **k'mmol, l'sso, s'gga**)

**kiyu'** *adj. a-* Wry, of mouth. *Akiyu' bowa'na, asāl min ka'asalna.* His mouth is twisted, like that from his very beginning. (*Thesaurus:* **kibi', tabid bowa'**)

**kiyul-kiyul** *v. intr. aN-* To make the noise of many talking in a confined space.

**kiyum** **1)** *v. intr. a-* To be smiling. *Saukat na ka taga lilus, mbal na ka pahali akiyum.* Just because you have a watch, you don't stop smiling. *Atakiyum saga makannak.* The children are overcome with laughter. **2)** *v. tr. -an* To smile at someone. *Aniya' d'nda kiyumanku.* There is a girl I smile at. *Takiyum aku.* I am caused to smile. (*Thesaurus:* **kohok-kohok, dahaggay, tittowa 1.1**)

**k'bba-k'bba** *v. advrs. -in-* Made apprehensive or uneasy. *Kin'bba-k'bba aku pag'nda'ku aheka sundalu.* I was worried when I saw a lot of soldiers. *Kin'bba-k'bba to'ongan aku sat'ggol halam gi' tapole' min dilaut disi Mma'.* I was very apprehensive as long as Father and his companions didn't return home from sea.

**pagk'bba-k'bba atay** *v. intr. aN-* To be experiencing rapid heartbeat, as a symptom of distress or shock. {idiom} *Magk'bba-k'bba atayku bang aku angandusa.* I am deeply distressed when I do something bad. *Magk'bba-k'bba deyom atayta sabab aniya' katāwanku.* My pulse races because I am afraid of something.

**k'bbal** *v. advrs. ta-* Shocked or troubled. *Tak'bbal, sali' kita asusa, ya kasusahanta marilaut kalu kita alembo.* We were shocked, troubled, our anxiety out at sea was that we might drown. (*Thesaurus:* **kobla', kuddat, himatta', leyang atay**)

**k'bbal atay** *v. advrs. ta-* Suffering sudden grief or shock. {idiom} *Buwat aniya' ahūg onde'-onde', ati kuppata, manjari tak'bbal atayta.* For example when a child falls and we jump into the sea after it, we experience severe shock. *Tak'bbal atayta, takuddat to'ongan.* Deeply distressed, greatly shocked.

**k'bbang** (var. **s'bbang**) *adj. a-* Damaged by the removal of a significant part. *Ak'bbang a'a, bay kineket he' ero'.* The man had a piece removed, he was bitten by a dog. *Wa'i na as'bbang buli' pelang ē', halam na aniya' pamangkerohan.* The rear of the canoe has a piece removed, there is nothing now for ferrying people. (*Thesaurus:* **kebang 1, kobak 1, kobet 1.1, sembong, t'bbe' 1.1**)

**pak'bbang** *v. tr.* To spoil something by cutting out a piece of it.

**k'bbat₁** *v. intr. pa-* **1)** To put one's thoughts into words. *Bang aniya' ai-ai amu'ta, yukta, "Pak'bbat na kita."* When we have something to ask for we say, "Let's speak up." (*Thesaurus:* **bahasa₁, bā'₁, batbat₂, bissala 1.1, h'lling₁ 1.1, pagmūng-mūng 1.1, sambat, yuk**) **1.1)** *v. tr.* To voice something. *Ang'bbat na ka, angaho' ka.* Say the words, say yes.

**kak'bbatan bowa'** *n. phrase* Words in contrast to actions. {*idiom*} *Hal kak'bbatan bowa', nileyangan. Sali' panukna' ba.* Simply words sent flying through the air. Sort of like a curse.

**k'bbat₂** *var. of* **kabbat**

**k'bbit** *v. tr.* To pinch something with the fingertips. *Bay aku kin'bbit e' siyaliku, abisa.* My younger sister pinched me, very painful. *Da'a k'bbitun onde' itu.* Don't pinch the child. *Bay ang'bbit baranku si Lo.* Lo pinched my body. (*Thesaurus:* **kinbing, hita' 2.1**)

**k'bbong** (var. **kobong**) *v. intr.* pa- Deeply concave, as a dish. (*Thesaurus:* **ku'ub, layas, pedda' 1**)

**k'bbong-k'bbong** *n.* A depression in sand or soil in which water collects; a pool. *Kinabkaban gusung maka pisak ko tahinang k'bbong-k'bbong.* Fan the sand and mud to make a little pond. (*Thesaurus:* **kohak-kohak, halo-halo, powak**)

**tik'bbong** *adj.* a- Deeply concave, as a bowl.

**k'bbot** *adj.* a- 1) Securely enclosed; wrapped up. *Tambolun lawang luma'nu bo' ka mbal nihaggut. Ak'bbot na. Minsan ka mbal na ahōs mbal na ka nihaggut.* Close the windows of your house so you won't be cold. Snug. Even though you are no longer wearing a sarong you won't be cold. **1.1)** *v. tr.* To enclose or wrap something securely. *Bang kita nihaggut mbal kita kala'anan hōs man baranta. Subay kita hal kībbot.* When we are cold the sarong isn't removed from our bodies. We should simply be wrapped up snugly. (*Thesaurus:* **k'mmos 1, p'kkos 1.1, putus 1.2**)

**k'bbut** *n.* A muscular twitch. (*Thesaurus:* **pagkidjut, pagkirut-kirut, pagkurat**)

**pagk'bbut-k'bbut** *v. intr.* aN- To beat rhythmically, as a pulse. (*cf:* **galak₃**; *Thesaurus:* **pagkowap-kowap, pagdutdut, paglaggut-laggut, pagsignat-signat, panag-panag 1**)

**k'kkod** *v. tr.* To bind with a series of half-hitches. *Kīkkod isāb tai' p'ttung pangaluhu.* Scraps of bamboo too are bound for singeing canoe hulls. (*Thesaurus:* **bit₂, laggos, sigid**)

**k'kkop** *var. of* **kopkop**

**k'ddaw** *see:* **pagk'ddaw-k'ddaw**

**k'dde'** *v. intr.* pa- To bend back against normal alignment. *Pahāpun e'nu angahambin onde' ilū bo' mbal pak'dde'.* Hold that baby properly so that its head doesn't tip back. (*syn:* **l'ddet 1**)

**k'ddil-k'ddil** *v. intr.* aN- To shudder or shake, as due to fear or sickness. *Ang'ddil-ng'ddil kōkku he' pasu'.* My head is shaking from fever. (*Thesaurus:* **ara'-ara' 1, kogkog, korog-korog, oro'-oro'₁, pidpid**)

**k'ddom₁** (var. **kaddom**) *v. intr.* pa- 1) To close one's eyes. *Pak'ddom mata si Ke bang atuli.* Ke shuts his eyes when asleep. *Da'a ka ang'nda'. Pak'ddomun matanu bo' ka makatuli.* Don't look. Close your eyes so you can sleep. (*ant:* **k'llat₁**) **1.1)** *v. intr.* aN- To keep the eyes closed. *Ang'ddom kām!*

Keep your eyes closed!

**k'ddom₂** *v. tr.* To do something without further thought. *K'ddomun pehē', pagtawakkalun, pasibukutun, buwat tepo ilū pagsusunan.* Take it as it is, take the risk, put it out of mind, like the mat there that [you] feel bad about. (*Thesaurus:* **halus₁, pagpasukud, pagsusaed, samba 1, sarap₂ 1, tawakkal**)

**k'ddos** *adj.* a- Squashed flat; mushy. *Ak'ddos ūngna.* His nose is flattened. *Ak'ddos itū sali' apetak, sali' ah'mmel to'ongan.* This word k'ddos is like something squashed, or something really flabby. (*Thesaurus:* **biyobog, lodjag 1, lonyat, petak 1, tonyak**)

**k'ddot** *adj.* a- Tough in texture; spongy. *Ak'ddot pinapa' kanu'us ē'.* That squid is tough to chew. *Buwat tibu'uk-silal, ak'ddot, tabowa emponta.* Like silal cassava, very tough, affecting our teeth. *Makakatol bagong itū, subay tin'ppa, nilamuran panggi'. Ak'ddot kinakan.* This Elephant's foot is itchy, has to be pounded and mixed with cassava. It is tough to eat. (*Thesaurus:* **k'nnol, p'ssil 1**)

**k'ddot-k'ddot** *v. intr.* pa- To gain physical toughness by moderate exercise before returning to work. (*syn:* **k'llit-k'llit**)

**k'llab** *v. intr.* aN- To flap.

**pagk'llab** *v. intr.* aN- To flutter or flap in the wind. *Bang aku amat'ngge s'mmek atawa panji magk'llab bihingna.* When I put cloth or a flag up, its edges flap. *Panji itū magk'llab-k'llab lullun.* These flags are all flaping in the breeze. (*Thesaurus:* **k'llay-k'llay, pagkayab, pagkotek-kotek, pagp'llay 1, paspad 1**)

**k'llap** (var. **kullap**) *v. intr.* pa- To look at something with a single glance. *Hal aku bay pakullap pehē'.* I just glanced briefly in that direction. (*Thesaurus:* **idlap 1.1, laman 1.1**)

**pagk'llap** *v. intr.* aN- To blink repeatedly due to shock or distress. *Hal magkullap-kullap, buwat a'a sakki atawa a'a mareyom jīl.* Just blinking, like someone who is sick or inside a jail.

**k'llas** *n.* 1) Stubbornness; rigidity. *Ē, k'llas-k'llasnu!* How stubborn you are! **1.1)** *adj.* a- Unyielding; stubborn (fig.) (*Thesaurus:* **alod₁, gagga, tuwas 1**)

**k'llat₁** *v. intr.* pa- To open by parting, as the eyelids on waking up or the skin of a snake as it molts. *Sali' pak'llat kuwit sowa. Amalut ma puhu'na.* Like the skin of a snake splitting open. It sticks to its body. *Asilaw aku, mbal pak'llat mataku.* I am dazzled, my eyes won't open. (*ant:* **k'ddom₁ 1**)

**pagk'llat** *v. intr.* aN- To ease, of prolonged rain; to break, of cloud cover. *Ulan halam magk'llat. Min subu-subu sampay ni kakohapan halam hali'an. Sigi-sigi na pa'in magulan.* The rain never let up. From early morning until afternoon there was no break. It just kept on raining.

**pak'llat** *v. tr.* To open one's eyes.

**k'llat₂** *n.* 1) Cordage; rigging ropes. *Am'lli ka k'llat* *pangengkotnu pelangnu bo' mbal talaran.* Buy a rope to tie your canoe with so it doesn't get carried away by the current. (*Thesaurus:* **lubid 1, tangbid**) **1.1)** *v. tr. -an* To fasten a rope or line. *Halam na bay k'llatanku banog ē' maina'an. Nilūnan na banog.* I didn't attach the sheet to the sail. The sail was just furled.

**k'llat-deyo'** *n.* The boom sheet (rope) of a sail. (*cf:* **pengka-pengka**)

**k'llat llaw** *v. intr. pa-* To appear above the horizon, of the rising sun.

**k'llat subu** *v. intr. pa-* To appear, of daylight. *Pagk'llat subu atulak kami kaut.* As morning apppeared we left for the open sea.

**k'llaw** (derivative of **llaw₁**) *adj. a-* Active early in the day. *Ak'llaw anak Milikan magbalebol. Halam gi' minsan patuwa' llaw, magbalebol.* The American children play volleyball early in the day. The sun hasn't even risen, and they're playing volleyball. *Pak'llaw pahāp ka'a ilu!* How early you are! (*cf:* **awal₂ 1.1**).

**k'llay-k'llay** *v. intr. aN-* To wave or flap in the wind, of cloth. *Bandila' tauwa' baliyu uttala' ang'llay-ng'llay sadja.* Flags blown by the north wind just keep fluttering away. (*Thesaurus:* **pagkayab, pagk'llab, pagkotek-kotek, pagp'llay 1, paspad 1**)

**k'lli'** *adj. a-* Damaged by the heat of the sun. *Ak'lli' sumping ilū he' llaw.* Those flowers are scorched by the heat of the sun. (*cf:* **sobsob 1.1**)

**k'llip** *v. intr. pa-* To lower or droop, of eyelids. *Pak'llip-k'llip mataku bang aku atuli.* My eyes droop when I'm sleepy. *Pak'llip mataku, tuli kuyya'.* My eyelids come down, just monkey sleep. (*Thesaurus:* **luyu', piru'**)

**k'llis** *v. intr. aN-* To make the trickling sound of water. *Ulan na, ang'llis bohe' ma deyom tangki.* Raining at last, water trickling inside the tank.

**k'llit** *adj. a-* **1)** Hard; unyielding, of physical substance or tissue. (*Thesaurus:* **katat, kelot, ketot, k'ttul**) **2)** Unyielding, of personality; ungenerous. *Bang anganda'ug si Ja saga dakayu' pilak bo' aku mbal binuwanan, ak'llit si Ja.* When Ja wins a peso and I'm not given any, he is ungenerous. **2.1)** *v. tr.* To resist someone's attempts to be friendly. *Ōy, da'a aku k'llitun, da'a aku kab'ngngisin, halam aniya' dusaku.* Hey, don't treat me with rejection, don't treat me harshly, I have done nothing wrong.

**pagk'llit-k'llit** *v. intr. aN-* To be unresponsive to friendliness. *Magk'llit-k'llit, araran ma saga onde'-onde' sabab akulang panghati sigām. Makajari isāb ma kita ato'a na, sagō' alahang na, makaiya'-iya'.* Resisting friendly overtures, a frequent response from children since their understanding is small. Can apply to us adults too but it is uncommon then, and embarrassing.

**k'llit-k'llit** *v. intr. pa-* To rebuild strength or toughness by moderate exercise. *Buwat aku bay asaki. Kauli'an pa'in aku, bo' palabay dambila'*

*bulan, ameya' aku kaut. Mbal bilahi disi Mma'. Yukna, "Pak'llit-k'llit gi' kā ma luma'."* Like when I was sick. When I had recovered and half a month had passed, I wanted to go to sea [fishing]. Father and others weren't willing. He said, "Just build up your strength at home." *Subay kita angayaran baranta, subay kita pak'llit-k'llit. Da'a isāb amangan atuwas.* We should care for ourselves, we should increase our physical toughness. We shouldn't eat hard foods. (*syn:* **k'ddot-k'ddot**)

**k'llob** *v. tr. -an* To trim fingernails. *K'llobin kukkunu ilū, nila'anan ya mataha' inān.* Trim your nails, take off those long ones. (*syn:* **t'ttop 1**)

**k'llo'₁** *v. tr.* To obtain something; to fetch. *Oto', k'llo'in aku bohe'.* Son, fetch me some water. *Nsa' ai-ai tak'llo'.* Didn't catch a thing. *Halam kami makak'llo' umpan.* We didn't get any bait. (*syn:* **hā', ngā'**)

**k'llo' bo'ot** *v. tr.* To bring a gift to win favor. {*idiom*} *Sali' kita anunggu'-tunang, ang'llo' aku bo'ot ni sigā dok kita kinabilahi'an.* It's like when I have sweeheart relationships, I bring a gift to them so that I will be approved. *Ang'llo' ka bo'ot bo' tataima' ai-ai soho'nu.* You take a gift so that whatever you send for will be agreed to. (*Thesaurus:* **bo'ot, go'on 1, mamhu', mohot 1**; *syn:* **bowa mo'ot**)

**k'llo'₂** *v. intr. a-* To leave a place; to move away. *Ak'llo' ka m'nnilu.* Get away from there. (*Thesaurus:* **hemos 1, la'an 1, tanggal₂, tungkas**)

**k'llong** *n.* The neck; the throat; the organ of voice. *Aladju k'llongna bang maglugu'.* Her voice is far-reaching when she sings a *lugu'* song. *Min deyom to'ongan asangta, ma luwasan k'llongta.* Our lungs are right inside, our throat and neck are external. (*cf:* **gonggongan**)

**k'llong-suling** *n.* A melodious voice. *K'llong-suling ma iya.* She has a melodious voice.

**k'llong-k'llong** *n.* A tree species of the mangrove complex.

**k'llos** *adj. a-* Shrunken in size due to drying. *Bang aku bay magpatahak mampallam mata' bo' mbal atahak, ak'llos na.* When I was ripening green mangoes when they weren't ripe, they shriveled. *Ya makak'llos daunna halam ulan.* What caused its leaves to shrivel was the lack of rain. (*Thesaurus:* **b'bbas 1, k'ppel, k'ppeng, k'ppos 1.1**)

**k'llot** *v. tr.* To cut something up into pieces. *Guling itū pinagt'ttok-t'ttok, kin'llot panahut.* This stir-fry is chopped up, sliced finely. (*Thesaurus:* **gōt-gōt 1, ladjang, pabuwa', padja', tama', t'ttok 1.1**)

**pagk'llot** *v. tr.* To slaughter a group of people by cutting. *Bay pinagā' ba'anan anak sultan, maka pinagk'llot kōk sigām pitumpū' hekana.* The sons of the sultan, seventy of them, were sent for and their heads cut off.

**k'llung-k'llung** *adj. a-* Dried out, of a water

container or channel. (*Thesaurus:* **lengas₁, panggang₂ 1, t'ggang₁**)

**k'llut** *adj. a-* **1)** Bailed dry. *Patogang itū, ak'llut maka mbal, basta paleyak na.* In upright position, bailed dry or not, as long as it is facing up. **1.1)** *v. tr. -an* To bail a canoe. (*Thesaurus:* **kallus₂, lodjat₂ 2, sait**)

**k'llut-k'llut** *n.* The gill lice found in the mouths of certain fish. (*cf:* **bobok 1**)

**k'mbal** *n.* A twin. *Manjari itū d'nda inān maganak na. Paganak d'nda inān, duwa k'mbal.* So then that woman gave birth. On giving birth there was a pair of twins. *Pagh'ndana damuli dakayu' si', makabāk anak duwa k'mbal.* Upon marrying this later wife, she came to have twins.

**k'mbal-bohe'** *n.* The amniotic fluid. (*Thesaurus:* **panubigan, tutuban**)

**k'mbal-saitan** *n.* The spirit counterpart of a newborn child.

**k'mbang** *adj. a-* **1)** Softened by soaking. *Ak'mbang kanu'us bang at'ggol ma bohe'.* Squid gets soft when it's a long time in water. *Pa'alungun buwas ilū ko da'a ak'mbang.* Put that rice on to cook so it doesn't get soft through soaking. **1.1)** *v. tr.* To soften something by soaking. *Subay kimbang bo' alunuk.* It should be soaked to become soft. (*Thesaurus:* **hagom 1.1, h'ggom 1.1, t'nde 1.1**)

**k'mbong** *n.* A tubular skirt tied above the breasts. **pagkin'mbong** (var. **pagkimbong**) *v. intr. aN-* To wear a sarong tied above the breasts.

**k'mmi** *n.* The remora or suckerfish. *Echeneis naucrates.* (*cf:* **langa-langa**)

**k'mmi'** *v. intr. pa-* To purse the lips in disapproval; to pout. *Bang aniya' onde'-onde' angamu' ai-ai, pak'mmi'. Bang kabuwanan, mbal na pak'mmi'. Bang mbal binuwanan, na anangis tūy.* When a small child asks for something, she pouts. If she is given [it], she no longer pouts. If not given, she cries openly. *Pak'mmi' kitā, agamā halam pinakan.* We make a face, we whine at not being fed. (*cf:* **burut**)

**pagk'mmi'** *v. intr. aN-* To pucker up one's face, as someone about to cry. *Magk'mmi'an si Jo.* Jo keeps puckering up her face [to cry].

**k'mmit** *adj. a-* **1)** Sparing of some resource; ungenerous. *Da'a paluwa'un sīnnu ilū kamemon. Subay ka ak'mmit. Ahunit sīn niusaha.* Don't bring out all your money. You should be sparing with it. Money is hard to acquire. *Ak'mmit pahāp a'a inān, mbal amaindam.* That man is mean, he won't lend things. (*Thesaurus:* **bista₂ 1, kaikit₁, kigit, kimmat 1, kudkud, kuriput 1, kussil, giging, iskut, sumil₁**) **1.1)** *v. tr.* To use something sparingly. *K'mmitunbi bang kam amangan sabab halam aniya' saddi. Ya du ilu.* Be sparing as you eat because there isn't any more. That's it there. (*cf:* **inut**)

**k'mmog** *adj. a-* **1)** Squashed together, as a can, or a loaf of bread. *Da'a gi'ikin ai-ai alunuk ko' mbal*

ak'mmog. Don't step on anything soft lest it be squashed. (*Thesaurus:* **k'ppi'₂, kummi', h'bbong, logpok 1**) **1.1)** *v. intr. pa-* To come together as a result of squashing. **1.2)** *v. tr.* To bring opposing edges together by squeezing. *K'mmogun mital bay k'ppi'ku.* Squash the can that I collapsed. *K'mmogun bowa'na bo' tapainum tambal.* Squeeze his mouth shut so he can be given the medicine. (*Thesaurus:* **k'ppi'₁ 1.1**)

**k'mmol** *adj. a-* Stuffed full, of the mouth. (*Thesaurus:* **kiyomol, l'sso, s'gga**)

**k'mmos** *adj. a-* **1)** Wrapped up in a cloth, of someone who is feeling cold. *Bang aniya' tinandog subay hal ak'mmos maka hōs.* If a person has a fever he should just be wrapped up with a sarong. (*Thesaurus:* **k'bbot 1.1, p'kkos 1.1, putus 1.2**) **1.1)** *v. intr. pa-* To be wrapped in a sarong. *Wa'i pak'mmos si Ina', tinandog kono'.* Mother's all wrapped up, says she's feverish.

**k'nna** *v. intr. pa-* To cease, of some activity or noise. *Minsan ulan, pak'nna-k'nna du isāb.* Rain too ceases somewhat. (*Thesaurus:* **h'ddok, h'nnok, tepok**)

**k'nnol** (var. **g'nnol**) *adj. a-* Spongy; resilient, as chewy food, or a mattress. *Kanu'us abase' itū ak'nnol-k'nnol, sali' gapas pinapa'.* This fresh squid is kind of spongy, like kapok fibre being chewed. *Kag'nnolan ū'an itū mbal na buwattē'.* This pillow can be squeezed, nothing like it before. *Ag'nnol atawa ak'ddot pinapa' kanu'us-kanu'us itū.* These little squid are tough to be chewed. (*Thesaurus:* **k'ddot, p'ssil 1**)

**k'nnop** *n.* **1)** Something added to an amount or list. **1.1)** *adj. a-* Having reached a full complement or stage. *Pagga pa'in ak'nnop dambulan amole' na kami.* A full month having passed, we returned home. **1.2)** *v. tr. -an* To add something to a total. *K'nnopin lagi' bohe'.* Add some more water. *Am'lli aku panggi' kayu pang'nnopku lutu' inān.* I will buy some cassava to supplement the food for my trip. *Subay at'kka matto'aku bo' yampa ni'nde'an sīn ni sara'. Subay kita ang'nnop ma sara' sabab kita pinuwasan man kasusahan.* My parents had to arrive before the money could be paid to the judge. We had to add [an amount] for the judge because we had been delivered from a serious problem. (*Thesaurus:* **ganap 1.2, jukup 1.2, tubil**)

**k'nnos** *v. intr. pa-* To remain still in order to avoid detection. *Sali' kanu'us mbal ah'lling-h'lling, hal pak'nnos. Atawa bawis pak'nnos ma ungus.* Like a squid that doesn't make a sound, just keeps still. Or like a rabbitfish staying motionless on the sandy bottom. *Aemon itū, sali' bang kita anū' mareyom kulaet, sali' mbal alahi. Pak'nnos sadja.* Emon is like when we are fishing by lantern light and [the fish] don't move away. They just stay there unmoving.

**k'nnum** *v. tr.* To hold something in the mouth without biting on it. *Hal sali' k'nnumta aes bang* *aniya' p'ddi' emponta.* We just hold ice in our mouth when we have a sore tooth. (*Thesaurus:* **tanga'₁, tanghab₂**)

**k'ntom** *v. intr. pa-* To come together, of lips or the matching edges of a wound. *Pak'ntom bihing bakat.* The edges of the wound are knitting. (*Thesaurus:* **kittup 1, t'mmu 1.1**)

**k'ngngik** var. of **ngngik**

**k'ppang** *v. intr. pa-* **1)** To lie face down. *Si Pa bay ariki'-diki' gi', pak'ppang. Mbal makat'ngge.* When Pa was still small, she lay face down. Couldn't stand. *"Sagarin na,"* yuk Nneng Pagi-pagi, *"pak'ppang na pa'in aku ma danaw."* "Never mind," said Stingray Maiden, "I'll keep on lying face down in the pond." (*syn:* **kapang₂**; *Thesaurus:* **kutung, da'ub, pakkom 1**) **1.1)** *v. tr. -an* To land face down on something. *Bang aniya' makaesog, magtūy kīppangan.* If anyone can be brave enough, it will be promptly belly-flopped onto.

**k'ppay** *v. tr.* To move smoothly, without friction. *Hal kīppay-kīppay he'na amusay min kaluma'an bang anangkaw.* He just keeps paddling with easy strokes through the village when he is stealing.

**pagk'ppay-k'ppay** *v. intr. aN-* **1)** To trim sails to make the best use of conditions. **1.1)** *v. tr.* To move rigging this way and that to make good use of conditions. *Pinagk'ppay-k'ppay leha.* The [square] sail is turned this way and that.

**k'ppel** *adj. a-* Deflated; empty of contents. *Ak'ppel leha ilū, halam isihan baliyu.* That sail is slack, it has no wind in it. *Buwat saging aheya kulitna bo' akulang isina, yukta, "Ak'ppel."* Like a banana with plenty of skin but not much inside, we say that it is *k'ppel. Ak'ppel silikan baek bang halam bay pināman.* The cycle tire is flat when it has not been pumped up. (*Thesaurus:* **b'bbas 1, k'llos, k'ppeng, k'ppos 1.1**)

**k'ppeng** *adj. a-* Lacking content, of fruit or muscle. *Nsa' na magisi, ak'ppeng. Buwat saging abulak.* It has no content, fleshless. Like an immature banana. (*Thesaurus:* **b'bbas 1, k'llos, k'ppel, k'ppos 1.1**)

**k'ppes** var. of **k'ppos**

**k'ppi'₁** *v. intr. pa-* **1)** To lie flat against a surface. *Pak'ppi' talinganu.* Your ears lie flat against your head. **1.1)** *v. tr.* To fold up something that is designed to do so. *Bang aku bay magsulat ma iskul ma nōtbūk, bo' aku akatis, k'ppi'ku na.* When I was writing in my notebook at school, and I had finished, I closed it up flat. (*Thesaurus:* **k'mmog 1.2**)

**k'ppi'₂** *adj. a-* Bent out of shape; buckled. *Ak'ppi', sali' akummi', ai na ka mital, bandehaw, atawa barilis.* Buckled, like *kummi'* [bent out of shape], whether metal cans, tin trays, or steel drums. *Ak'ppi', ai na ka mital, bandehaw, atawa barilis.* Buckled, whether metal cans, tin trays, or steel drums. (*Thesaurus:* **k'mmog 1, kummi', h'bbong, logpok 1**)

**k'ppit** *v. tr.* To hold something securely under the armpit. *Bay k'ppitku būkku itū.* I held this book of mine under my armpit.

**pagk'ppit** *v. intr. aN-* To have hands tucked under opposite armpits. *Magk'ppit tangan.* Tucking hands under opposite armpits.

**k'ppong** (var. **k'ppung**; **kuppung**) *n.* A well or pit for water.

**k'ppos** (var. **k'ppes**) *adj. a-* **1)** Emptied of contents; deflated. **1.1)** *v. intr. pa-* To reduce, of swelling or inflation. *Buwat bay butigku, bay aheya, pak'ppos na.* Like the swelling I had, it was big, but it has gone down now. *Pak'ppes na b'ttongna, bay aheya, bay ang'tting sala.* Her stomach has got smaller, it had been large, had been sort of inflated. (*cf:* **tayo**; *Thesaurus:* **b'bbas 1, k'llos, k'ppel, k'ppeng**)

**k'ppung** var. of **k'ppong**

**k'ssang₁** *adj. a-* Clean and smooth to the touch, as freshly laundered clothes. *Ahāp na kulitna, halam akatol. Ak'ssang badju'ta.* Its surface is good, not itchy. Our shirt is smooth. (*Thesaurus:* **lanu' 1, langis 1, l'ssin, sussi 1.1**)

**k'ssang₂** *adj. a-* Lacking in flavor; bland. (*syn:* **k'ssaw**; *Thesaurus:* **k'ssaw, t'bbag**)

**k'ssap** *v. intr. aN-* To sample something with the tip of the tongue. *Ang'ssap-ng'ssap, sali' aniya' ta'ssata.* Testing with the lips, as though we are tasting something. (*syn:* **pag'ttap-ttap**)

**k'ssaw** *adj. a-* Lacking flavor; bland. *Ak'ssaw, halam asin, halam pamapā, halam na nanamna ai-ai.* Bland, no salt, no spices, having no flavor whatever. (*syn:* **k'ssang₂**; *Thesaurus:* **k'ssang₂, t'bbag**)

**k'tta** *v. intr. a-* **1)** To set out for a destination. *Ak'tta kita parambila' Hambilan.* We are setting out across the channel to Hambilan. (*Thesaurus:* **laktas, lintas, untas 1**) **1.1)** *v. tr.* To reach a place by setting out. *Bay kami ang'tta lahat Nasuli' itū.* We set out [from our home place] to reach Nasuli.

**k'ttang** (var. **kotang**) *adj. zero* **1)** Slack, of tidal flow. *K'ttang du bang halam s'llog.* It's slack water when there is no current. **1.1)** *v. intr. pa-* To come to the end of a major phase. *Pakotang he'na magnapas.* He ceases to breathe.

**k'tti'** *adj. a-* **1)** Reduced to almost nothing, as water in a well. **1.1)** *v. tr.* To cook rice just until the water is nearly absorbed. (*gen:* **b'lla 1**)

**k'ttil** var. of **k'ttul**

**k'tting** var. of **tting**

**k'ttob** *v. tr.* **1)** To sever something by cutting or biting through. *Bang aku am'ssi, bo' at'ggol na ma deyo', kittob e' daing.* When I am fishing and it's been down a long time, it has been bitten through by fish. *Nda'un pīs-pīs kakana' bay k'ttobku min jubanu.* See the pieces of cloth I cut from your gown. (*Thesaurus:* **keket 1, k'ttop₁**) **1.1)** *v. tr. -an* To cut something off from a main part. *K'ttobanku min panubu'na kamemon* *kal'llahan, ai na ka a'a banyaga' atawa a'a aluhaya.* I will cut off all the men from his descendants, whether slave or free men.

**k'ttol** *adj. zero* Extremely cold. *K'ttol itū ahaggut to'ongan, anuwas-nuwas sala. K'ttol* means very cold, kind of becoming hard. (*Thesaurus:* **dingin 1, haggut 1.2, hagpay 1, t'nne 1**)

**k'ttop₁** *v. tr.* To crush hard or brittle food using the teeth. (*Thesaurus:* **keket 1, k'ttob 1**)

**k'ttop₂** *adj. a-* 1) Clenched, of teeth. *A: "Ai ka'astolannu?" B: "Halam, tu'ud aku ak'ttop."* A: "What are you angry about?" B: "Nothing, I simply have my teeth closed tight." 1.1) *v. tr.* To close the teeth against laughter, speech, or the insertion of something that is not wanted.

**k'ttop-le'e** *v. tr.* To show intense anger by clenching teeth. {idiom} *Ap'ddi' makalandu' atay sigām ya angkan sigām ang'ttop-le'e tudju ni iya.* They were extremely angry which is why they clenched their teeth towards him.

**k'ttu'** *v. tr.* To reap rice by cutting its seed-bearing stalks. *K'ttu' bang pai, hagpe' bang gandum. K'ttu'* is the word for reaping rice, *hagpe'* is for corn. (*cf:* **pagani**)

**k'ttu' nyawa** *v. tr.* To terminate someone's life. {idiom} *K'ttu'un na nyawaku apa mbal na pasandalku.* End my life because I can no longer bear [the pain].

**k'ttul** (var. **k'ttil**) *adj. a-* Hard, of boiled root staples such as cassava. *Ak'ttul tibu'uk, ai-ai na bīlla. Mbal ahāp isina bang bay na tab'lla, minsan painay he'ta am'lla, minsan pinalaga'.* Cassava cooked whole is hard, anything boiled. Its flesh is no good after it has been boiled, no matter how we cook it, even when it is cooked for a long time. (*Thesaurus:* **katat, kelot, ketot, k'llit 1**)

**k'ttung** *v. intr. pa-* To be tightly hunched, as someone trying to stay warm. *Aniya' pak'ttung ilū, a'a sali' nsa' magbadju'.* There's something hunched up there, a guy with no clothes on. *Bang ka patuhun ang'ttung napasnu, sali' ka anuwas-nuwas.* When you dive deeply you hold your breath tight, like you are becoming stiff.

**klaro** *adj. zero* Clearly understood. *Mbal lagi' kono' makahibal, sagō' makakabtang na iya minsan mbal to'ongan lagi' klaro.* Reportedly unable to move yet, but he is able to speak even though not clearly understood.

**klasmēt** *n.* A classmate. *Bay pa'in aku mareyom iskul, sidda aku angistrōk ma klasmetku bang aniya' d'nda budjang-budjang.* Back when I was in school, I was often infatuated with my classmates when they were teenage girls. (*Thesaurus:* **sehe' 1**)

**ko** (var. **ko'₂**) *conj.* In order to; so that. *Kose'in pahāp ko' pala'an l'mmisna.* Wash it well so the dirt on it comes off. *Kinabkaban gusung maka pisak ko tahinang k'bbong-k'bbong.* The sand and mud are fanned so that a hollow is created.

*Tahananku katas ko' mbal paleyang apa alandos baliyu.* I will weigh the paper down so it doesn't blow away, because the wind is strong. *La'ananku dambila' katig pehē'ku nireyo' taddas ati ko' pabuhat pariyata'.* I will remove half of an outrigger boom and put it beneath the keel so that it will move higher. (*cf:* **ko da'a**)

**ko da'a** *conj.* In order not to. *Am'lli aku bahudji' pangengkotku ma kumpitku ko da'a tinangkaw.* I will buy a cable for tying up my cargo vessel so it is not stolen. *Da'a henggolun lām ilū ko da'a ahūg pareyo'.* Don't shake that lamp lest it fall down. (*cf:* **ko**; *Thesaurus:* **bo' mbal**)

**kobak** (var. **kebak**) 1) *adj. a-* Damaged by the removal of large chunks. *Saliyuhanta ka pisita ni landing. Akebak landing itū.* I'll trade your paper bills for coins. These bills are damaged [by removal of a part]. *Bang keket ero', subay kobak. Bang kehet laring, subay kebak.* When it's a dog bite, *kobak* is the word. When it is something cut out with a knife, it is *kebak*. (*Thesaurus:* **kebang 1, k'bbang, kobet 1.1, sembong, t'bbe' 1.1**) 2) *v. advrs. ka-...-an* To be suffering a severe drain on resources. *Sali' alta'ta ala'an. Akobak atawa kakobakan alta'ta.* As when our resources are gone. Our resources drained or eaten into.

**kobal-kobal** *n.* Various scad species, including Torpedo kingfish, Hard-tailed scad, Finny scad, Mackerel jack. *fam. Megalaspis cordyla.*

**kobkoban** (var. **kokobkobun**) *n.* An immature mango. *L'kkobku na mampallam kokobkobun itū.* I will gobble up this immature mango. (*Thesaurus:* **balunu', mampallam, wanni**)

**kobet** *v. tr. -an* 1) To remove a part of something by pinching it out. *Aniya' bay atibu'uk, jari kobetanta.* Something was entire, then we removed a part. *Kinobetan apam bo' pamuwan ni onde'-onde'.* The pancake had a piece removed for giving to the children. 1.1) *v. intr. a-* Gapped by the removal of a part by pinching or biting. *Lamisahan inān akobetan dīna.* That table has become chipped of its own accord. (*Thesaurus:* **kebang 1, k'bbang, kobak 1, sembong, t'bbe' 1.1**) 1.2) *v. tr.* To grip and twist something, causing pain. *Maglaka'-laka' ka? Kobetta ka, Oto'.* Are you talking dirty? I'll twist your mouth, Son.

**kobla'** *v. tr. a-, ka-...-an, -an* To startle or shock. *Kinobla'an aku bang aniya' a'a pariyata' halam bay tinitik lawang.* I am startled if someone comes up [onto the porch] without knocking on the door. (*Thesaurus:* **k'bbal, kuddat, himatta', leyang atay**)

**kobol** *n.* 1) Magical immunity to harm from bullets or a bladed weapon. *Bang aniya' ata'u amono' a'a kobolan, amatay du isāb minsan painay kobolna.* If one knows how to kill a person immune to harm, he will indeed die no matter how immune. 1.1) *adj. -an* Magically immune to the penetration of blade or bullet. *A'a kobolan,*

*a'a basi'an, mbal iya nihalus he' ai-ai, mbal niōk.*
A person immune to attack, invulnerable, not to
be threatened by anything, not to be cut into.
(*Thesaurus:* **basi'₂ 1.1, pagkal'lla, pangliyas,
sihil 1**)

**pagkobol** *v. intr. aN-* 1) To be protected by
magical means against the penetration of blade
or bullet. 1.1) *v. tr. -an* To prevent the
penetration of bullets or blades, by magical
means. *Mbal tapagkobolan bang punglu'
Samehakan.* Yakan bullets cannot be protected
against by magical means.

**kobol-kobol** *v. intr. aN-* To swarm, as flies. *Alō,
kami bay mahē' ma kubul, angobol-ngobol
sundukna e' langaw.* Gross! When we were there
at the grave, the grave-pole was swarming with
flies. (*Thesaurus:* **kulatap, t'bbud₂**)

**kobong** var. of **k'bbong**

**kobong-kobong** *n.* A simple kite made from a sheet
of paper.

**kobos** *v. tr. -an* To improve the shape of something
by trimming. (*Thesaurus:* **kulang₁ 1.3, dagdag₁,
diki' 1.2, hilang, putung, sulak₁**)

**kōk** *n.* 1) The head part of a body. *Kōk si Ja bay
ginuntingan e' si Mu.* Ja's head has been shorn by
Mu. 2) The upper section of a tool or paddle.
*Angamu' aku pōng papan nihinang kōk busay.* I'm
asking for a remnant of wood to make into a
paddle handle. 2.1) *v. tr. -an* To fit a headpiece
to a tool. *Angōkan aku busayku.* I'm putting a
cross-piece on my paddle shaft.

**kōk-atay** *n.* The diaphragm; lower rib cage.
*Ap'ddi' kōk-atayku, mbal aku makal'ngngan, hal
aku magalud.* My upper abdomen hurts, I can't
walk, I just keep crying out.

**kōk-baliyu** *n.* The initial onset of a wind phase.
*Buhawi', kawas-kawas ya ameya' ma kōk-baliyu.*
Whirlwinds, the squalls that come with a change
in the wind phase. *Yampa patumbuk kōk
habagat.* The south-west monsoon has just
started to blow. (*cf:* **tape'-baliyu**)

**kōk-batu** *adj. zero* Stubborn; inflexible. {idiom}

**kōk-bundu'-bundu'** *n.* The junction of the navel
and pubic area of the body.

**kōk-busay** *n.* The hand grip of a canoe paddle.

**kōk-tu'ut** *n.* 1) The front of the knee. *Ni'ikat kōk-
tu'utna.* His knee is swollen. (*Thesaurus:* **tu'ut**)
1.1) *v. intr. aN-* To kneel.

**kōkan** *n.* 1) The upstream side of a house relative
to the incoming tidal flow. *Sohonayan s'llog
maka diyata'an s'llog, hatina kōkan s'llog.* The
area upstream in relation to the current, the
upper side currrent, in other words the head of
the current. *Sibayan, ya pagpat'nna'an mbo',
ba'ul, maleta, basta ma kōkan.* The *sibayan*, the
location of the chest or suitcase into which a
ritual ancestor comes, on the upstream part of
the house. (*Thesaurus:* **diyata'an₁ 1, sibayan,
tape'an**) 2) The shelf on the upstream side of a
house reserved for ritual ancestors. *Sibayan, ya*

*pagpat'nna'an mbo', ba'ul, maleta, basta ma
kōkan.* The *sibayan*, the location of the chest or
suitcase into which a ritual ancestor comes, on
the upstream part of the house.

**pagmakōk** *v. intr. aN-* To take the lead over a
group; to represent a group. (*Thesaurus:*
**pagbebeya'an, pagmandangan, pagmete-
mete, pagmunda'an**)

**kokam₁** *n.* A species of tarsier or lemur. *Al'pput
mata kokam.* The tarsier's eyes stick out.

**kokam₂** *n.* 1) A charm spoken to protect against
hostile speech or the ability to bite. *Bang
kata'uhanta kokamna mbal du. Makapaglamugay
kita minsan buwaya aheya, bang tausulta bay awal
mbo'ta manusiya'.* If we know its charm nothing
will happen. We can mix even with large
crocodiles, provided we follow the traditions of
our human ancestors. 1.1) *v. tr.* To prevent
something from biting or a person from
speaking, by shutting the mouth. *Kinokam
bowa'na bo' mbal pabanga'.* Closing its mouth
[reciting a charm] so it doesn't open.
(*Thesaurus:* **kamal, kowam 1, pamorok, umaw
1.1**)

**kokko'** *v. advrs. -in-* Claw-like, as the feet of
chickens, or the digits of people with Hansen's
disease. (*cf:* **pupus**)

**kokobkobun** var. of **kobkoban**

**kokok** *n.* 1) A spirit being of forest areas. *Kokok,
sali' saitan ma deyom talun. Bang kita pal'ngngan
dangan-dangan ma deya kinongkong kita.* A *kokok*
is something like a *saitan*-spirit in the forest. If
we walk alone ashore we [may] sort of curl up
in the fetal position. (*Thesaurus:* **komeng, hantu
1**) 1.1) *v. advrs. -in-* Affected by a kokok spirit.
*Kinokok ko' ka'a ilū anittowa. Mbal na pa'in
ala'an min panittowahan.* You are bewitched
laughing so much. You never get away from
laughter.

**kokola** *n.* Various aerated drinks; soft drinks. (*syn:*
**pipsikola**)

**kokos₁** *v. intr. pa-* 1) To coil around something.
(*Thesaurus:* **bodbod₁ 1.1, koleng₁ 1.1, lebod 1,
lengke, longon**) 1.1) *v. tr.* To hold something by
coiling. *Bang kita kinokos e' sowa-panga'an i',
amatay kita.* If that python coils around us we
will die.

**kokos₂** see: **pakokos**

**kōd** *adj. a-* Happy; joyful. *Landu' to'ongan akōd
pangatayanna pang'nda'na ma siyalina inān.* His
heart was extremely happy on seeing his
younger brother. *Ilu na si Ina' at'kka min tabu',
bay am'lli kinakan. Akōd aku, makakakan na.*
There's Mom arriving from the market, she's
bought food. I'm glad, I'll be able to eat now.
(*Thesaurus:* **kōg 2, koyag 1, lami, lasig 1,
paglangog**)

**kodak** *n.* A camera. (*syn:* **patta' 1.1**)

**kodjel** *v. tr.* To disturb or move something by
touching or poking. *Bang kita nilinganan bo'*

*halam tasayuta, yuk a'a, "Kodjelun ba ilū."* When we are called but aren't aware of it, someone says, "Give him a poke." (*Thesaurus:* **kohed 1, kublit, tangku'-tangku'**)

**pagkodjel** *v. intr. aN-* To move restlessly due to fever or illness. *Angalimasu' deyom baranku iya. Ya magkodjel baranku.* It's the inside of my body that is too hot. It is my body that moves restlessly.

**kōg 1)** *adj. a-* Happy. *Akōg a'a inān ma kahinangan ibilis.* That person is pleased with the activities of devils. **2)** *v. advrs. -in-* Happy; joyful. *Kinōgan si Oto' bang ta'nda'na tunangna.* Oldest Son is made happy when he sees his girlfriend. (*Thesaurus:* **kōd, koyag 1, lami, lasig 1, paglangog**)

**kōg maka baya'** *n. phrase* Full approval of an offer. {idiom}

**pagkōg-kōg** *v. intr. aN-* To be rejoicing; to celebrate. *Magkōg-kōg sigām maglami-lami.* They were very happy, celebrating.

**pagkōg-koyag** *v. tr. -an* Joy; happiness. *Aheya pagkōg-koyagan sigām.* Their joy was great.

**kogkog** *v. intr. aN-* To shiver violently. *Angogkog aku he' haggut.* I am shivering from the cold. (*Thesaurus:* **ara'-ara' 1, k'ddil-k'ddil, korog-korog, oro'-oro'₁, pidpid**)

**kohak-kohak** *n.* A hollow in sand or soil. (*Thesaurus:* **k'bbong-k'bbong**)

**kohang** *n.* A species of bivalve similar to a cockle, edible. *fam. Lucinidae. Kaheka'an kohang maina'an ma Sablay.* The most cockles are there at Sablay.

**kohap** *adv.* **1)** Afternoon; the period from about 2 p.m. to sundown. *A: "Sumiyan kām atulak?" B: "Subay na kohap, saga buwattē' luwa llaw."* A: "When do you leave?" B: "Should be this afternoon, when the sun's height is like that." *Inggay yukku-i, "Da'a na ka ni bohe' apa angulan du pagkohap."* Didn't I say to you, "Don't go for water because it rains in the afternoons." (*cf:* **subu₂ 1**; *Thesaurus:* **abay-kohap, lekot-lendom, lempos, logob-logob, magrib 2, sū'-palita'an**) **1.1)** *adj. -an* Overtaken by the onset of late afternoon. *Pinal'ngngan l'lla inān, pinabatal na, ko da'a kohapan bay maglurukan.* The man was told to proceed, and was ritually joined with the bride, so the people attending wouldn't be overtaken by evening.

**kohap-īn** *adv.* The previous afternoon or evening. *A: "Sumiyan kat'kkabi?" B: "Kohap-īn."* A: "When did you arrive?" B: "Yesterday afternoon." *Bay indamannu kohap-īn.* You borrowed [it] yesterday afternoon. (*Thesaurus:* **insini', subu-si'**)

**pagkohap** *v. intr. aN-* To do something later in the afternoon. *Kalanasan deyom luma' itū, kalanasan he' manusiya'. Na magagaw kamemon, ati yukta, "Gōm pa'in magkohap-kohap."* This house is packed full, full of people. Everyone is

grabbing at things, so we say, "Better to do it later this afternoon."

**kohek-kohek** *v. tr. -an* To shake things together in water. *Kohek-kohekin tehe'-tehe' ilū mareyom basket, supaya ala'an būna.* Shake those sea urchins in the basket, so the spines come away. (*cf:* **hokkok**; *Thesaurus:* **kembo' 1.1, genggok, letok**)

**kohed** (var. **koheg**) *v. tr.* **1)** To poke someone with fingertips or a pointed implement. *Bay aku kinohed he' si Mi insini', makalingi' aku.* I was poked by Mi just now, and looked round. (*Thesaurus:* **kodjel, kublit, tangku'-tangku'**) **1.1)** *v. tr. -an* To remove something by poking it with a pole or stick. *Kohegin kono' s'ggit ilū maka tōng busaynu.* Please push that rubbish away with the end of your paddle.

**kohed-kohed** *v. tr.* To make repeated marks with the fingers.

**koheg** var. of **kohed**

**kohok-kohok** *v. intr. aN-* To laugh through the nose. (*Thesaurus:* **kiyum 2, dahaggay, tittowa 1.1**)

**kohol 1)** *n.* A cough. **1.1)** *v. advrs. -in-* Affected by persistent coughing. **2)** *v. advrs. ka-...-an* To be brought up into the mouth by coughing. *Kakoholan laha' apol, asidda na.* Clotted blood being coughed up, his condition serious.

**pagkohol** *v. intr. aN-* To cough; to clear the throat by coughing. *Agkohol, akatol deyom k'llong.* Coughing, the inside of the throat itchy. *Bang aniya' ap'ddi' mareyom k'llongta bo' kita magkohol, abakkug.* When something is painful in our throat and we are coughing, the movement causes pain.

**kohot** *adj. a-* Hoarse; unable to speak freely due to infection or exhaustion. *Bang aniya' amatay bo' magalud, akohot k'llongta.* When someone dies and there is loud weeping, our throats are hoarse. (*Thesaurus:* **gohom 1, lagaw, pehet**)

**kō'** *n.* **1)** A decrease; reduction; discount. *Halam aniya' kō'na?* Is there no discount? **1.1)** *v. intr. pa-* To diminish in amount or force; to ebb. *Buwat kita angusaha, ma deyom dambulan aheka usahata. Ta'abut karuwana, pakō' na.* Like when we go fishing, for a month we make a good living. In the second month it diminishes. *Bay latap pajulut kaut pabīng, pakō' itū, pakulang-kulang.* The flooding has receded seawards once more, diminishing, becoming less. (*Thesaurus:* **keyas, kontay₂, hulaw, patokang, tugut 1**) **1.2)** *v. tr. -an* To reduce the amount or size of something. (*Thesaurus:* **kulang₁ 1.3, loddos 1, lō'**)

**ko'₁** *ptl.* Mild emphasis marker. *Man b'ttong sampay ni tape', ponod ko'. Hal isi.* From stomach down to the feet, it is all solid. Nothing but flesh. *Ahāp na ko' ilū, ameya' ka man bangkero ilū ni M'ddas.* That's fine then, go to Siasi Town by means of that ferry.

**ko'**₂ var. of **ko**

**ko'ot** *v. intr. pa-* 1) To reach with the hand into a space or substance. *Pako'ot aku ni deyom tahik angā' sīn apa bay ahūg man lantay luma'.* I put my hand into the sea to get the money because it had fallen through the flooring of the house. 1.1) *v. tr.* To get something by inserting a hand. *Kino'ot d'llang-d'llang bo' ala'an kowa' mareyom k'llong.* The uvula area is reached into so that the fish bone in the throat comes away. *Bang bubu kinahiran, bang panggal kino'ot.* A *bubu* trap is accessed with a pole, a *panggal* is reached into by hand. *Aniya' onde'-onde' ango'ot gusung.* Some children are feeling around in the sand. *Kallusin na, abuhaw. Saddī asait, hal ango'ot.* Dash out the water, [the canoe] is taking water. Bailing is different, it is just scooping.

**pagko'ot bohe'-pasu'** *v. tr. -an* To demonstrate one's innocence by inserting a hand into boiling water.

**pagko'ot-ko'ot** *n.* 1) A lottery or draw. 1.1) *v. tr. -an* To draw lots by taking a marker from a container. *Pagko'ot-ko'otinbi bang sai ma kami maka si Jo ya bay makarusa.* Draw lots as to which one of us [Jo or I] has commited a sin.

**kōl** *n.* 1) A call indicating agreement. 1.1) *v. tr.* To accept an offer or challenge. *Bang kita binangharan, makakōl kita ungsud hē'.* When are quoted a bride-wealth we accept the bride-wealth demands. *Tino'onan duwa pilak. Yuk a'a hē', "Makakōl ka?" (Sali' "makaesog ka?")* Two pesos are put down as a bet. The fellow who does it says, "Can you accept that?" (Like saying "are you game for it?") (*Thesaurus:* **hapus**₁ **1.1, pagtinggi, talu**₁**, tumba**₂ **1.1**)

**kola** *v. tr.* To bleach cloth. *Bay kinola ni deyom sabun bo' yampa tiniti' maka bohe'.* It was bleached in soap and then sprinkled with water. *Kolaku pantalunku ma deyom undam.* I will bleach my trousers in a basin.

**kola'** *n.* 1) A pleat or crease in cloth. *Buwat badju' aheka kola'na.* Like a blouse with many pleats. (*Thesaurus:* **kumpi' 1, la'up 1**) 1.1) *adj. a-* Pleated; creased. *Akola', sali' kinonotan.* Pleated, kind of wrinkled. 1.2) *v. tr.* To pleat or crease cloth.

**kolebok** *see:* **pagkolebok**

**koledje** *see:* **pagkoledje**

**kolehek** *v. tr.* To pick out something with the fingertips. *Kinolehek-kolehek, nila'anan iting ē'.* Picking away, removing those prickles. *Kinolehek talingata.* Something picked out of our ear. (*cf:* **kuri' 1.1**)

**kole'** *v. tr.* To achieve something through physical or moral strength, or through financial resources. *Makannak itū mbal takole' nilāng.* These kids cannot be made to stop. *Bang onde'-onde' angal'bbos bangka' dangan-danganna, mbal takole'na.* If a child goes to launch a canoe on his own, he can't manage it. *Mbal kita makakole',*

*makalandu' abuhat bay bowata.* We cannot do it, the thing we were carrying is much too heavy. (*Thesaurus:* **aguwanta 1.1, anggap 1, anggop**₂**, bāng-bāng**₁**, bogbog**₂**, gaga, tigayu'**)

**kole'-kole'**₁ *v. tr.* To be somewhat able, as when convalescing from an illness. *Yampa aku makakole'-kole'.* I'm only now feeling able to do a bit.

**kole'-kole'**₂ *v. tr.* To influence or persuade someone. *Yukku, "Subay na Ahad ba." Yuk si Ji, "Atiya' na aku pehē'." Yukku isāb ma iya, "Pehē' ka bang ka mbal takole'-kole'. Aku atāwan si Mma', ingga na aku llaw Ahad."* I said, "It should [wait until] Sunday." Ji replied, "I'm on my way there now." I then said to him, "Go then if you can't be persuaded otherwise. As for me, I am afraid of Dad, so it will have to be Sunday."

**pagkole'** *v. intr. aN-* To strive for dominance over another person. *Sali' magbono' mbal magkole'. Mbal kasekotan, mbal tasapad, sinagaran na hal.* Like [two] people fighting each other and neither prevailing. Could not be approached, could not be restrained, simply left to carry on. *Magagaw-besod, mbal sigā magkole'.* Arguing without resolving the issue, neither winning. *Buwat kami bay maghukum ni mastal, mbal magkole'. Maglagadlad ni sara' M'ddas, ni Sūk.* Like us taking a dispute to the schoolmaster, but nothing being resolved. The case goes on to the court in Siasi town, or to Jolo City.

**koleng**₁ 1) *n.* A roll of something. (*Thesaurus:* **birang 1, lebod 1, pasangan**₁**, tongko' 1, towa'**) 1.1) *v. tr.* To wind a line into a coil or on a spool. *Angoleng aku naelon, amole' na kami patandan kaleya.* I am winding up the line, we are going home to shore. (*Thesaurus:* **bodbod**₁ **1.1, kokos**₁ **1, lengke, longon**) 2) *clf.* Count word for rolls or coils. *Dantongko' basi'-basi', dangkoleng.* One coil of light wire, one *koleng*.

**kolengan** *n.* A reel or spool. *Kayu ya kolengan salban.* The spool of *salban* thread was wooden.

**ma kolengan** *adv. phrase* By the reel or coil.

**pagkoleng** *v. intr. aN-* To coil around an object. *Magkolengan na sowa inān ma bihing batu.* That snake is coiled around the edge of the coral rock.

**koleng**₂ *v. intr. pa-* To lie with knees drawn up, as someone who feels unwell.

**koleng-koleng** *n.* The Seram blenny, a small striped fish. *Salarias ceramensis.*

**koleng-punsul** *n.* The Jewelled blenny; the Banded blenny. *Salarias fasciatus.*

**kolepak** *see:* **pagkolepak**

**kolera** *n.* Cholera; any epidemic disease with diarrhea as the most obvious symptom. *Bang pa'in ka taluwa' kolera.* May you be struck down with an epidemic disease. (*Thesaurus:* **ka'mbo'an, kawit**₂ **1, ipul 1, pangkot 1, ttus-ttus 1, upāng 1**)

**kolesek** (var. **kulesek**) *v. intr. aN-* To thrash about in large numbers. *Subay na angolosek daing bo' yampa nihella' linggi'.* The fish must be threshing about together before the seine net is hauled in.

**pagkolesek** *v. intr. aN-* To make the noise of many fish trapped in a net. *Na magkolesek linggi' kami e' ba'anan daing.* So our trawl net made a great noise due to the mass of fish. (*cf:* **kularak**)

**kolet** *v. tr.* To arouse a woman by touching. {obscene}

**pagkolet** *n.* A person addicted to sexual touching.

**kollek-kollek** *v. tr.* To disarrange something by using the fingers; to scribble letters. *Bang aku magsulat, kollek-kollekku apa mbal aku ata'u anulat.* When I write I scribble it because I don't know how to write. *Kinollek-kollek pomedku he' onde'-onde', sali' pinaka'at.* My pomaded hair is messed up by a child, sort of ruined.

**kolleng** *v. tr.* To twist dough into decorative shapes before cooking. (*Thesaurus:* **lubid 1.1, pinsal 1.1, tabid₁ 1**)

**kolleng-kolleng** *n.* A cassava cake twisted into various shapes, fried in oil and glazed with a sugar mixture. *Saddi kolleng-kolleng, saddi doppeng. Doppeng ya hal pinera' atawa pinidju. Kolleng-kolleng* and *doppeng* are different. *Doppeng* are simply flattened or cut into wedges. (*gen:* **mamun**)

**kolol** *n.* 1) A color or tint. *Ginisan kolol, yuk kami ginisan b'ttik.* Kinds of color, what we refer to as kinds of *b'ttik.* (*Thesaurus:* **agaw-agaw, b'ttik 1, walna'**) 2) A colored crayon or pencil. *Dakayu'-dakayu' kolol ma dangan onde', pinagtabul-tabul.* A single pack of crayons for each child, all treated equally.

**kolong** *adj. -an* 1) Curly-haired. **1.1)** *v. tr.* To curl the hair.

**kolong-kolong** *adj. a-* Spiraling, as hair or vines. *Palebod bahan ma sagbot. Sali' togel bawi akolong-kolong.* The vine coils round the brushwood. Curly like a pig's tail.

**kolorom** *adj. zero* Unseen; illegal; done under cover. *Kolorom itū sali' nilimbungan man parinta. Kolorom* is something hidden from the authorities. *Ataddang itū legal, mbal kolorom.* This word *taddang* means legal, not counterfeit. (*cf:* **sipuk**; *ant:* **taddang**)

**pagkolorom** *v. intr. aN-* To do something illegally or in secret. *Magtampalan, da'a magkolorom, da'a maglimbung-limbung.* Do it openly, don't do it in secret, don't conceal.

**komandel** *n.* The commanding officer of a military unit. *Pinagbā' na pa'in komandel pasal kagara'anbi.* The commander is always being informed about what you are planning. (*Thesaurus:* **kapitan, jeneral, tininti**)

**komay** *adj. a-* Seriously weak, as from sickness or over-exertion. *Akomay, mbal maka'ahatan dīna.* Very weak, unable to do anything on his own. (*Thesaurus:* **lamma 1, loyot, pilay**)

**kombo** *n.* 1) A set of homemade hand drums. **1.1)** *v. tr.* To play hand drums.

**kombo'-kombo'** *n.* A species of sea anemone, yellowish in color, edible. *Actinia spp.* (*Thesaurus:* **kambang, lason, lo'on, pari-pari**)

**komkom** (var. **gomgom; gonggong**) *v. tr. -an* To grasp something securely. *Gomgomin ai-ainu ilū bo' mbal akanat.* Hold onto your things so they don't get scattered. *Kinomkoman sīn bo' mbal takabba.* The money is gripped securely lest it happen to fall. *Gonggongin ma pangatayannu in saga panoho'anku, pasal ya hē' makapataha' umulnu mareyom magtahunan.* Hold my instructions securely in your heart, because that is what will extend your lifespan for years. *Gonggongin ma pangatayannu in saga panoho'anku.* Keep my instructions in your heart. (*Thesaurus:* **balut 1.2, kopkop 1, ntan₁ 1**)

**komkoman** *n.* 1) The grasp of someone's hand. 2) The sphere of someone's control or authority. *Itiya' kām ma deyom gomgomanku.* Here you are under my protection. *Ma deyom komkomanbi na kami angkan hinangunbi ma kami bang ai makasulut ma ka'am.* We are under your control now so do to us whatever pleases you. *Angatu du ka ati makal'ppa min komkomanna.* You will fight back and escape from his control. (*Thesaurus:* **deyoman 2, milikan, okoman, pang'ntanan₁**)

**pagkomkom** *v. intr. aN-* To make a fist.

**komeng** *n.* A spirit being of forested areas. *Komeng itu sali' saitan ma deyom talun, sali' saitan kokok inān. Ma deya, ma deyom kakati'anan.* These *komeng* spirits are like demons in the forest, like those *kokok* spirits. Inland, in the jungle areas. (*Thesaurus:* **kokok 1, hantu 1**)

**komo'₁** *v. intr. pa-* To sit with the knees drawn tightly up and arms around knees. (*Thesaurus:* **kongkong 1, kulangkang 1, kullung, pagkorel-korel**)

**komo'₂** *v. intr. pa-* To form a crease or wrinkle. *Apu'ut tarukna, pasasa banog, pakomo'.* The mast is too short, the sail sags and a wrinkle develops. (*Thesaurus:* **g'mmot 1, go'ok 1.1, loko' 1**)

**komot-komot** (var. **gomo'-gomo'**) *v. tr.* To crumple something into a wad. *Bang katas, kinomot-komot atawa gino'ok-go'ok. Bang baranta taluwa' ulan, magkonot.* Paper is crumpled or wadded. If it is our body that is wet by rain, it becomes wrinkled. *Bang katas, kinomot-komot atawa gino'ok-go'ok.* Paper is crumpled or wadded.

**kompani** *n.* A military unit; the field location of such a unit.

**kompol** *v. tr.* To mold something into a solid form. *Bang abentol mbal takompol.* Something dried to a powder cannot be molded into a shape. (*Thesaurus:* **pongkol, tambu 1, tampa 1**)

**kompolan** *n.* A cohesive group of people. *Ina'an ma kompolan si Bapa' Si.* There in Uncle Si's community. (*Thesaurus:* **kaheka-heka'an,**

dansehe'an, **padjuhan**, **palti**, **umpigan**)

**kompolme** *adj.* *zero* Persuaded; convinced. *Kompolme, aniddik aku ma ka'a bang aku haka'annu. Angahalap aku ma ka'a. Kompolme,* that is, I agree with you when you tell me something. I believe you. (*Thesaurus:* **amu₂ 1.1, bilīb, tuksu'**)

**kondo'** *v. intr.* *pa-* To incline the head in order to see something below. (*Thesaurus:* **bantang 1, kuru', domol 1, tondok 1**)

**konog-konog** *v. intr.* *aN-* To make a deep rumbling sound, as of thunder, distant gunfire, or the sounds of digestion. *Buwat timbak atawa l'ggon ah'lling, angonog-ngonog mareyom paglahat.* Like when gunfire or thunder sounds, it rumbles around the district. *Angonog-ngonog deyom dunya.* The depths of the earth reverberate. (*Thesaurus:* **kulattub, llub, pagbolobok, paglagonggok, paglagublub**)

**kono'** *ptl.* **1)** Indicates that the speaker does not vouch for the accuracy of what he is saying. (Evidential marker, hearsay). *Ka'a kono' bay makapuwa' busayku.* They say that you found my paddle. *H'ndanu kono' bay maganak.* Your wife, I am told, has given birth. *Aniya' kono' bay takali e' sigām ba'ul bulawan ma babaw tana'.* It is reported that they had dug up a golden chest from the ground. **2)** Politeness marker. *Amalabay ka kono'.* Allow [me] to pass, please. (*Thesaurus:* **da'a busung, lagi' 3, pa'in₂ 2**)

**konot₁** *adj.* *a-* **1)** Wrinkled or stretched out of shape. *Bay aku akonot kuwitku. Na b'ttina'an angutad aku, ahāp-hāp na palasahanku.* I was wrinkled as to my skin. But I'm becoming wrinkle-free now, feeling somewhat better. **1.1)** *v. tr.* To wrinkle, of the skin, as in old age or as a result of long immersion. (*Thesaurus:* **killut-killut, kilorot**)

**pagkonot** *v. intr.* *aN-* To become wrinkled, as the brow when frowning, or skin after long immersion. *Bang magkonotan lendo'ta, lumandu'an ap'ddi' atayta.* When our forehead keeps wrinkling, we are excessively angry. *Kilut-kilut tanganta, sali' magkonot maka sali' amidpid.* Our hands are shrivelled from long immersion, sort of wrinkled and trembling. *Bang baranta taluwa' ulan, magkonot.* If it is our body wet by the rain, it wrinkles.

**konot₂** *v. tr.* To pull at something flexible, like a net. (*Thesaurus:* **bira 1, ga'ut, ganggut, guyud 1, hella', paglagedled 1**)

**konsehal** *n.* A councilor in the Philippines barrio system. *Buwat magsagga', nihukum e' konsehal, mbal takole'. Pasōng ni kapitan, mbal. Pasōng ni mayul.* Like a dispute, brought to a councilor, to no avail. Goes on to the barangay captain, no better. Goes on to the mayor.

**konsemisun** *n.* Romantic love that is not returned.

**pagkonsemisun** *v. intr.* *aN-* To keep loving someone even after a courtship has been

formally broken off.

**kontay₁** *v. intr.* *pa-* To stretch out of shape in more than one dimension. (*cf:* **hinit 1**)

**pagkontay** *v. intr.* *aN-* To be pulled out of shape in several directions. *Magkontay tepo itu, paheya sala.* This mat is stretching out of shape, sort of expanding.

**kontay₂** *v. intr.* *pa-* To abate, of a current. *Yuk si Ina', "Pakontay-kontayun gi' s'llog ilū bo' ka yampa ak'tta."* Mother said, "Let the current slacken a bit before you set out." (*Thesaurus:* **keyas, kō' 1.1, hulaw, patokang, tugut 1**)

**kontra** *var. of* **kuntara**

**kongkong** *v. intr.* *pa-* **1)** To curl up, of one's body, limbs, or digits. *Pakongkong he' haggut. Mbal makah'nnat, amigtal ugatna.* He's all curled up with the cold. Can't straighten out, his sinews pulled taut. *Ai-aita mbal pah'nnat, hatina pakongkong, mbal a'llum ugatta. Sali' halam aniya' pangannalta.* Whatever part of us doesn't straighten out, it is curled up, our sinews dead. It is as though we no longer have the power of thought. (*Thesaurus:* **komo'₁, kulangkang 1, kullung, pagkorel-korel**) **1.1)** *v. tr.* To make someone curl up, the action of kokok spirits. *Bang kita pal'ngngan dangan-dangan mareya bo' aniya' kokok, sali' kita kinongkong.* When we re walking inland on our own and kokok spirit is there, it is as though we are caused to curl up.

**kopal-kopal** *n.* Hoya species of the sandy foreshore, used medicinally. *Hoya spp.*

**kōpan** *n.* The night after full moon. (*cf:* **base'-bulan, damlag 1.1**)

**kopang** (*var.* **koppang**) *n.* The Asian green mussel. *Perna viridis.* (*syn:* **tahōng**)

**kopkop** (*var.* **k'kkop**) *v. intr.* *pa-* **1)** To be firmly attached to. *Ya sahasa' pak'kkop ma ungus, ya na s'bbo.* The branching coral that is firmly embedded in the sand, that is s'bbo. (*Thesaurus:* **balut 1.2, komkom, ntan₁ 1**) **1.1)** *v. tr.* *-an* To hold something in a clenched fist. *Kinopkopan ko da'a alungay.* Held in the fist so it doesn't get lost. (*Thesaurus:* **benten, bengket, pendet**)

**kopeng** *v. intr.* *pa-* To flop over, of something normally rigid. *Pakopeng talingana, patonton.* His ears flop and droop down. *Buwat saruk-saruk tepo, bang taluwa' llaw pakopeng.* Like a makeshift hat made of a woven mat, when the sun hits it flops down. (*cf:* **lompeng 1**; *Thesaurus:* **lapping-lapping, sondong, toyok**)

**kopo'** *v. intr.* *pa-* To crouch down; to cower. *Minsan sundalu sidda aesog, pakopo' tināw.* Even the bravest soldiers will crouch down in fear.

**koppang** *var. of* **kopang**

**Kora'an** *n.* The Holy Koran; the Islamic scriptures.

**koral** *n.* **1)** An enclosure for large animals; a corral. (*Thesaurus:* **ād 1, apis 1, buluyan, kumbangan, kumbisan, likusan, sasak 1**) **1.1)** *v. tr.* To enclose animals in a fenced area.

**korel-korel** *see:* **pagkorel-korel**

**korente** *n.* 1) Electricity. 1.1) A wire which carries an electric current. (*Thesaurus:* **basi'-basi'**, **kowat, estenles-kitara**)

**koro-koro** *adj. zero* 1) Used without care. *Koro-koro: maghinang sadja, magdai'-dai' sadja, mbal ahantap.* Wasteful: just working away, doing it in a hurry, not careful. 1.1) *v. tr.* To consume a resource by rapid or frequent use. *Ka'a itū, nikoro-koro na he'nu bang aniya' sīn.* As for you, if there is money you soon use it up.

**korog-korog** *v. intr. aN-* To tremble as with cold or fright. *Angorog-ngorog baranta; bihing-bowa'ta isāb.* Our body trembles; our lips too. (*Thesaurus:* **ara'-ara' 1, k'ddil-k'ddil, kogkog, oro'-oro'₁, pidpid**)

**korona** *n.* Decorative headgear; a crown. (*Thesaurus:* **panumping, tumanggal**)

**koskos** *v. intr. pa-/aN-* To lose weight or muscular tissue, as due to sickness. *Bay aku asaki manjari angoskos isiku.* I was sick and lost weight. *Barannu bay al'mmok, pakoskos.* Your body was fat, now it has become thin. (*Thesaurus:* **kagkag, kayog 1, kittay, kulagkag, giti' 1, higtal, titis 2**)

**kose'** *v. tr. -an* To wash things other than clothes. *Pahāpun e'nu agkose' mampallam ilū.* Make a good job of washing those mangoes. *Kose'anta ka'a lai' bay pamanganannu.* I will wash for you the plate you ate from. (*cf:* **pandi 1**)

  **pagkose'an** *n.* Washing facilities for things other than clothes. *Bay alungay suru', bay piha kami mareyo' pagkose'an lai'.* A spoon got lost, we found it underneath the dishwashing place.

**kosok₁** *v. tr.* To rub or crumple something vigorously. *Bay na alubi, na pinasobsob lagi' ya p'tti' bo' yampa amandi. Kinosok isāb bu'un.* The shampoo has been applied, then the coconut oil is just allowed to soak before taking a bath. The hair is also rubbed vigorously.

**kosok₂** *n.* A species of coastal tree, a source of easily carved white wood. (*syn:* **kilkil**)

**kosog** *n.* 1) Strength, of a substance, or of a person's ability. *Buwat aku itū alahang angusaha. Ya kosogku magl'ngngan.* Like me, seldom working for a living. What I am best at is roaming around. 1.1) *adj. a-* Strong, of persons; powerful, of a voice or machine. *Mbal akosog malkina inān.* That motor is not strong. (*Thesaurus:* **ayron, basag 1, bastig, kulasog 1.1, kuwat-anggauta', landos 1, paslod 1.1**) 1.2) *v. tr.* To deal vigorously with something. *Kakkutun bukutku. Aheka buwa'-buwa', kosogun.* Scratch my back. There are lots of itchy lumps, do it energetically. 1.3) *v. tr. -an* To do something with force, as paddling or hammering. *Kosogin, hangbosin.* Hit it hard, use force on it. (*Thesaurus:* **hangbos₂**)

  **pagkosogan** *v. intr. aN-* To engage in a contest of strength. *Dangan magduminu inān binowa magkosogan. Yuk-i, "Hapa'in to'ongan ina'an i bo' mbal makalabay."* One domino player is challenged to engage in a contest. Someone says, "Block that one so it can't pass." (*Thesaurus:* **pagda'ug, pagegot-egot, pagta'as-ta'as**)

  **kinosog** *v. intr. aN-* To contribute energy or moral support to some activity. (*cf:* **ga'os 1.2**)

  **pakosog** *adv.* Vigorously; energetically. (*Thesaurus:* **kuwat, kuyas 1, matay₂, paspas₁, puspus₁, sikad 1**)

**kotang** *var. of* **k'ttang**

**kotek** *v. tr.* To snap fingers.

  **pagkotek-kotek** *v. intr. aN-* To move to and fro, as wings, flippers or fins. *Bang paleyang manuk-manuk magkotek-kotek kepetna.* When a bird flies it flaps its wings. (*Thesaurus:* **k'llay-k'llay, pagkayab, pagk'llab, pagp'llay 1, paspad 1**)

**koto'-koto'** *n.* Hard feelings against another person; resentment. *Hanus, hatina alanu' atayna, halam aniya' koto'-koto' deyom atay.* Peaceable, meaning that his attitude is cordial, no resentment in his heart. (*Thesaurus:* **akon-akon, agmol 1, buli'an₂, deyom-deyom atay, lagod-lagod**)

**kowa'** *n.* 1) A fish bone stuck in the throat. *Kino'ot d'llang-d'llang bo' ala'an kowa' ma deyom k'llong.* Reached down to the uvula so the fish bone will come away from the throat. (*Thesaurus:* **bangkak, bokog, to'olang**) 1.1) *adj. -an* Suffering from a fish bone stuck in the throat. *Kowa'an aku he' to'olang daing.* I am stuck in the throat with a fish bone.

**kowam** *adj. a-* 1) Deprived by shock or illness of the power of speech. *Akowam sadja aku, sali' alungay pangannalku.* I am just dumbfounded, as if my mind has gone. *Akowam, mbal na makapah'lling, abangat sakina.* Mute, no longer able to speak, her sickness so serious. (*Thesaurus:* **kamal, kokam₂ 1.1, pamorok, umaw 1.1**) 1.1) *v. tr.* To deprive someone of the power of speech. *Kinowam kita. Saitan ya angowam, niā' bay bissalata.* We are deprived of speech. It is a *saitan* spirit that has deprived us, what we had said being taken away.

**kowan** *n.* The right-hand side. *Ilu du ma tangannu kowan.* There it is in your right hand. (*ant:* **gibang**)

**kowang** *v. tr.* To remove a person's vital organs, the action of a balbalan spirit. (*Thesaurus:* **balbal, uwak**)

**kowang-kowang** *n.* The spotted grouper. *Epinephelus sp.* (*gen:* **kuhapo'**)

**kowap-kowap** *see:* **pagkowap-kowap**

**kowat** *n.* Non-ferrous wire. (*Thesaurus:* **basi'-basi'**, **korente 1.1, estenles-kitara**)

  **kowat-kowat** *n.* The multiple hooks of a squid lure.

**kowel** *var. of* **keyol**

**kowet** (*var.* **keyot₂**) *n.* The umbilical cord. *Sambon* *anakna, saga keyotna pinalebod ma baranna. Bang sukud ala'at amatay anakna.* Her child is a *sambon* [entangled] birth, its umbilical cord wrapped around its body. If fate is adverse her child will die. *Huwit-huwit pang'ttob kowet.* A [sliver of] fine bamboo for severing the umbilical cord. (*cf:* **ponsot**)

**koyag** *n.* 1) Joy; happiness. (*Thesaurus:* **kōd, kōg 2, lami, lasig 1, paglangog**) 1.1) *adj.* a- Happy; joyful. *Akoyag aku.* I am happy.

  **kakoyagan** *n.* Joy; happiness. *Taga kakoyagan du a'a bay ananom maka bay amusu'.* The person who has sown and reaped has joy. *Bang kita amuwan, labi gi' kakoyaganta min a'a binuwanan.* When we give, our joy is greater than the person who is given something. *Aheya kakoyagan ma Hailaya ilu sabab maglasig-lasig a'a, buwat saga magbola, magkakan, magpangongka' saga a'a.* There is great happiness during that Holiday because people are having fun, with the people playing ball, eating, and celebrating together.

**koyang** *n.* A slender stick such as a toothpick. *Bang ni'isihan lapuk-lapuk ma daun, subay taga koyang tinugsukan bo' mbal ap'kkal.* When cassava candy is wrapped in a leaf it should have a toothpick inserted so it doesn't unwrap. (*cf:* **lituk 1**)

**krismas** *n.* Gifts distributed around the time of the Christmas festival. *Atabul tarangan-tarangan, sali' aniya' bay krismas sigā, atabul sigā.* Each of them receiving an equal share, as if they had received a Christmas gift, treated equally.

**Kristyan** *n.* A Christian; a lowland Filipino. (*cf:* **Almasihin**)

**krus** *n.* A crucifix.

=**ku** *pron.* I, me; my (first person singular) [Set II]. *Buwananku onde'-onde' būk.* I give books to the children. *Bay pa'in halam aniya' būkku, bay aku binuwanan e' mastal.* When I had no book [lit. my book did not exist], the teacher gave me one. (*cf:* **akū, aku₂**; *Set:* =**bi,** =**na,** =**nu,** =**sigā,** =**sigām,** =**ta 1,** =**tabi,** =**tam**)

**kuba₁** (var. **kubba**) *n.* Various cowries. *Kuba halam isina pagongka' pagtimbag.* Empty cowries used for playing a throwing game. (*syn:* **baggu'**)

**kuba₂** *adj.* a- Hunched or rounded, of the back of some object or person. *Bukut jīp ina'an, akuba-kuba.* The back of that jeep [a VW] is sort of rounded. (*Thesaurus:* **buggul 1.1, dukkug 1**)

**kubal** *n.* 1) The hard part of a tree, just below the outer layers. *Ahāp na lahi ni kubal. Esokna apōng-pōng. Kubal ya asekot ni kulit kayu, ya matuwas.* It's good near the hardwood. Its pith just breaks up. The hardwood is close to the bark, that's the hard stuff. (*Thesaurus:* **esok, sapan₂, tupas₂**) 2) A callus, as on hands or feet. *Bang aheka bay kabalutanta angapal dahū bo' yampa sali' akanit. Ya akanit kubal tangan, atuwas kulit tanganta.* When we have been holding a lot of things, thickening [of the skin] takes place before it peels. It is the callus that peels, the skin on our hands is tough.

**kubba** var. of **kuba₁**

**kubing₁** *n.* Various beetles, including a bed-bug, coconut borer or rhinoceros beetle. *Kubing itū t'llu tandukna, dakayu' ma diyata'.* This beetle has three horns, one on the top.

**kubing₂** *n.* The High-finned grouper, a brightly colored fish with a large mouth. *Epinephelus maculatus.* (*gen:* **kuhapo'**)

**kublit** *v. tr.* To touch something with the finger tips, as a way of getting attention. *Minsan aku patukad, Tuwan Putli' sī hal bay kinublit maka tanganna.* Even though I was going uphill, Sir Putli' here was merely poked with his hand. (*Thesaurus:* **kodjel, kohed 1, tangku'-tangku'**)

  **pagkublit-kublit** *v. tr.* To strum or pluck a musical instrument using one's fingertips. *Angulanting, buwat kula'ing ya pagkublit-kublitta inān.* Making a rhythmic sound like a jaw harp, the one we strum with our fingertips.

**kubu-kubu** *see:* **pagkubu-kubu**

**kubu'-kubu'** *n.* A basic building with one small room. *Kubu'-kubu' itū sat'ggol halam gi' aniya' kapanyapanna. B'nnal atopan, dindingan, b'nnal atiggup saguwā' ngga'i ka gi' luma'.* It's a shack so long as it lacks the full equipment. True it has thatch and walls, and it is closed in, but it is not yet a house. *Luma' kubu'-kubu', mbal pahinang duwa bilik.* A kubu'-kubu' house, it won't make two rooms. (*Thesaurus:* **ballay, luma', pamāy-bāy**)

**kubul** *n.* 1) A grave. (*Thesaurus:* **kuddaman, dinding-hali, gumi 2, paliyangan**) 1.1) *v. tr.* To bury a body. *Aniya' bay amatay a'a, bay kinubul di'ilaw.* A person died and was buried yesterday. (*Thesaurus:* **bunbun 1.1, pagl'bbong**)

  **kakubulan** *n.* A cemetery; a collection of graves.

**kukkaga'uk** (var. **kukkugu'uk**; **kukku'uk**) *v. intr.* aN- To crow, as a rooster. *"Na," yukna, "minsan manuk angukku'uk, ilu binaggot bowa'na anak datu' sī'."* "So then," he said, "even though the rooster crows, this nobleman's child will have his mouth bound up."

**kukku₁** (var. **kuku₂**) *n.* A fingernail or toenail; a claw.

**kukku₂** *n.* 1) The curved tip of an outrigger boom or anchor tine. 1.1) *v. tr.* -an To form an upward curve at the end of rod or beam. *Hal kinukkuhan la batang sau.* The anchor tine is just curved upward.

  **kukku-badja'** *n.* The prongs of a dredging rake.

**kukkugu'uk** var. of **kukkaga'uk**

**kukku'** *v. intr.* pa- To curl up to conserve warmth.

**kukku'uk** var. of **kukkaga'uk**

**kukkus** *n.* A sea fan with an abrasive surface, useful for scrubbing.

**kukkut** *n.* The Long-finned rock cod. *Epinephelus megachir, E. quoyanus.* (*gen:* **kuhapo'**)

  **kukkut-kangan** *n.* Short-pectoralled honeycomb

grouper.

**kuku₁** var. of **kuku'**

**kuku₂** var. of **kukku₁**

**kuku-pote'** *n.* White cotton cloth, the material for a burial shroud. *Pin'kkos maka kuku-pote' kamemonna, baranna, kōk harap ni tōng tape', tanganna buwat anambahayang.* All of him wrapped in white shroud cloth, from head to tip of feet, hands [folded] as in prayer. (*Thesaurus:* **kasa', salimput 1, saput 1, talkun, tatap 1**)

**kukuhit** (derivative of **kuhit**) *n.* An implement for harvesting fruit high in a tree. *Kuhitta lahing maka kukuhit, ya taga sanggot ina'an.* We reach coconuts with a *kukuhit*, the one with a curved blade attached. (*cf:* **sanggot₁ 1**).

**kuku'** (var. **kuku₁**) *v. tr.* To knock on something. *Kukuhun bilu'uk ilū, kalu angamotong na.* Tap that green coconut, perhaps it is becoming mature.

**pagkuku'** *v. intr.* aN- To make a noise by tapping with one's fingertips. *Aho' sangom, bati'ku luma' ilū. Magkuku' buwattili'.* Yes it was night, I woke the house up. I knocked like that.

**kukumit** *n.* The person responsible for the management of resources. *Buwat pagguluhan, aku ya kukumitna, sali' tendog.* Like in a religious class, I handle the funds, as an adherent.

**kukus** *v. tr.* -an To wipe something off a surface using a cloth. (*Thesaurus:* **pu'us, sapu 1.1, tarapu 1.1**)

**kukuwa** *n.* A cigaret holder; a tobacco pipe. (*syn:* **kuwako**)

**kūd** *n.* Sand or bank exposed by a receding tide. *Aheka panagatun ma diyata' kūd.* There are lots of shells on the exposed sandbar. (*cf:* **punsu**)

**kudkud** *adj.* a- Ungenerous. (*Thesaurus:* **bista₂ 1, kaikit₁, kigit, kimmat 1, k'mmit 1, kuriput 1, kussil, giging, iskut, sumil₁**)

**kuddam** *v. tr.* To enclose something securely. *Kinuddam, wa'i ma tau'an, mbal ta'nda'.* Closed securely, away in storage, can't be seen. (*Thesaurus:* **kumbis 1.1**)

**kuddaman** *n.* A secure place; the grave as a permanent resting place. (*Thesaurus:* **kubul 1, dinding-hali, gumi 2, paliyangan**)

**kuddang** *v. tr.* To cook a mixture of cassava and fish liver. (*gen:* **b'lla 1**)

**kuddarat** *n.* Mysterious power.

**kuddat** *v. tr.* To startle or shock someone. *Buwat kami soho'nu pariyata'. Kuddatnu kami magtūy.* Like when you tell us to come on up. You startle us. *Takuddat aku, ahūg tibu'uk, paleyang atayku.* I was startled, some cassava fell, I started. *Aniya' sali' palē ma baranta bo' halam ta'nda'ta, makakudjal kita. Sali' kita takuddat.* Like there was something crawling on our body that we did not see, we move quickly. Like we are startled. (*Thesaurus:* **k'bbal, kobla', dalihag, himatta', leyang atay**)

**kudjal** *v. intr.* pa- To move suddenly, as when startled or bitten. *Aniya' sali' palē ma baranta bo'*

*halam ta'nda'ta, makakudjal kita. Sali' kita takuddat. Yaru bang kita kinirik-kirik.* Something is sort of crawling on our body but we don't see it, and we move suddenly. It's like we are startled. Like that too when we are tickled.

**kudji-kudji** *n.* Underpants; panties. (*Thesaurus:* **kansinsilyu, kindut, kullat, sanyawa**)

**kudjut** *v. tr.* To kill someone with a single blow of a bladed weapon. *Kudjut itū, ginantung dahū bo' nilagut. Kudjut* is being hung up first and then slashed with a bladed weapon. (*Thesaurus:* **budjak 1.1, dukduk, dugsu', punyal 1.1**)

**kugud** (var. **kagud₁**) *adj.* a- Reduced to nothing from previous abundance. *Sinugpakan, yuk-i, "Bang pa'in akugud ai-ainu kamemon!"* Taunted [for being wasteful], saying, "May all you have come to nothing!" *Buwat ka'a angongka' bo' aubus na sīn ma bulsanu, yukta, "Akugud na ka."* Like when you gamble and the money in your pocket is all gone, we say, "You're broke." (*cf:* **kadkad 1**)

**kugut₁** *v. tr.* To grate something that is hard. *Angugut aku lahing panganggata'ku biyaki'.* I am grating coconut to get cream for *biyaki'* cakes. (*Thesaurus:* **jangat, li'is**)

**kugutan** *n.* A grater consisting of a semi-circular blade with a serrated edge.

**kugut₂** *v. tr.* To make excessive demands on someone. *Hal angugut konsehal inān, saukat taga kag'llal.* That councillor simply burdens people with his demands, just because he has an appointed position.

**kuhapo'** *n.* Various groupers and rock cods. *Cephalopholis spp.* (*cf:* **kulapu**; *spec:* **badjangan, bunggu', kaluy, kowang-kowang, kubing₂, kukkut, kuhatong, layu-manuk, longgang, man'llon-baggu', mbuk-mbuk, obon, tandukan, tangal**)

**kuhapo'-abu** *n.* The Summan grouper; Starry grouper; White-spotted rock cod. *Epinephelus summana.*

**kuhapo'-batang** *n.* A species of rock cod. *Cephalopholis sp.*

**kuhapo'-b'kkosan** *n.* The Brown-banded rock cod. *Cephalopholis pachycentron.*

**kuhapo'-b'ttikan** *n.* The Coral hind or Vermilion Hind, the Coral rock cod. *Cephalopholis miniatus.*

**kuhapo'-bunggu'** *n.* The Yellow-spotted rock cod. *Epinephelus areolatus.*

**kuhapo'-kabangan** *n.* The Comet grouper or Contour rock cod. *Epinephelus morrhua.*

**kuhapo'-kubing** *n.* The Humpback sea bass or Barramundi cod. *Cromileptes altiveli.*

**kuhapo'-jali'an** *n.* The Blue-line coral cod. *Cephalopholis boenak.*

**kuhapo'-samehakan** *n.* The Dampiera dottyback (lit. Yakan rock-cod). *Labracinus spilopterus.*

**kuhapo'-sunu** *n.* The Red coral trout, one of the fish known as lapu-lapu. *Plectroplanus sp.*

**kuhatong** *n.* The Giant grouper, a species considered to be more dangerous than a shark. *Epinephelus lanceolatus. Kuhatong, bang kita anuhun tin'llon kita. Sidda angeket.* Giant grouper, when we go diving we get swallowed. It bites fiercely. (*gen: kuhapo'*)

**kuhatong-palupalu** *n.* A species of grouper. *Epinephelus sp.*

**kuhi₁** *adj. a-* 1) Willing; agreeable. *Akuhi ka ameya' ma aku.* You are willing to accompany me. 1.1) *v. intr. pa-* To behave compliantly. *"Angay ka'a-i mbal pakuhi?" Buwat aniya' sinoho' pabuhat min paningkō'anna bo' mbal bilahi.* "Why won't you comply?" Like someone asked to get up from his seat, but is unwilling.

**pakuhi** *v. tr. -an* To give someone permission; to grant a request. (*Thesaurus: paba'id, papuhun, parūl 1.1, tugut 2*)

**kuhi₂** *v. tr.* To report someone for a fault. *Takuhi aku, ya pasal kami magbaya' maka d'nda hē'.* Someone has reported on me about that girl and me being in love. *Bay aku takuhi ang'ntan d'nda inān.* I've been reported for touching that girl. *Ai-ai bay hinangku takuhi aku he'na.* Whatever I have done he informs on me. (*Thesaurus: pagmahi, pagmalān, pagpuhun 1.1, sumbung, tuntut₁*)

**kuhit** *v. tr.* To hook or catch something using a long-shafted implement. *Kuhitun s'mmek, hē' na palaran.* Catch that cloth, it's drifting away. *Kuhitta lahing maka kukuhit, ya taga sanggot ina'an.* We reach coconuts with a *kukuhit*, the one with the curved blade attached. (*Thesaurus: kahid 1, kawit₁, sungkit*)

**kukuhit** *n.* An implement for harvesting fruit high in a tree. (*cf: sanggot₁ 1*)

**kuhita'** *n.* 1) Generic term for various species of octopus. *gen. Octopus.* (*Thesaurus: kaloka', ngget*) 1.1) *v. tr.* To catch an octopus by enticing it to come out from concealment.

**kuhita'-batu** *n.* The Rock octopus.

**kuhita'-gamat** *n.* An octopus species whose tentacles break on handling.

**kuhita'-ungus** *n.* The Sand octopus.

**kuhut** *n.* 1) An instrument with a blunt point for removing lice from the hair. *Kuhut itū lantay pagkutu.* The *kuhut* referred is a bamboo tool for removing lice. (*Thesaurus: sūd, suray 1*) 1.1) *v. tr.* To remove lice eggs from the hair. (*Thesaurus: kutu 1.1, siksik, t'bbok₂*)

**ku'il** *adj. a-* Disabled by the loss of hands or feet. *Bay iya taluwa' timbak-daing hangkan iya aku'il.* He was hit by fish dynamite that is why he is crippled. *Mbal makarai'-dai' angahinang abuhat. Aku'il iya, mbal al'kkas, mbal akosog.* He can't do heavy work promptly. He is disabled, neither quick nor strong. *Ai makaku'il ka'a, mbal maka'ntan ai-ai, mbal makahogot?* What has made you crippled, not able to hold anything,

not able to make it secure? (*Thesaurus: keme, pagtamengka', pagtongka', pukul 1*)

**ku'ub** *v. intr. pa-* Shallowly concave, as a dinner plate. (*Thesaurus: k'bbong, layas, pedda' 1*)

**kula-kula** *n.* A species of fresh-water tortoise. (*syn: ba'u'u*)

**kulabutan** *n.* Cuttlefish. *Order Sepiolida.* (*gen: lansongan*)

**kulakkad** *v. tr.* 1) To look for something among a lot of things. *Kinulakkad kamemon, sampay buli' ba'ul. Ni'nda' kamemon, piniha to'ongan.* Everything turned over, right down to the bottom of the box. Everything looked at, thoroughly searched. (*syn: kadkad 1.1, lungkad 1*) 1.1) *v. intr. pa-* To be sorted through. *Mbal pakulakkad ai-ai mareyom paradol apa bay kinunsi'.* It isn't possible to go through the things in the cupboard because it has been locked.

**kulakkus** *v. intr. aN-* To do in the shortest possible time. *Angulakkus kaut bang takbil magusaha, halam pa'in maka'ā'.* Heading swiftly out to sea to fish, but not catching anything. *Buwat saga a'a bay mareyo', na halam aniya' haronan, angulakkus man hāg.* Like a person who was below the house, and there was no ladder, he went up quickly by way of a post. *Pakulakkus na pa'in onde'.* Kids keeping climbing all over. (*Thesaurus: baggis, ka'is, kasay 1, l'kkas 1, samot 1, sapat₂ 1*)

**kulakob** *n.* Skull, a cursing equivalent for spherical items. (*Thesaurus: bukakkal, peya'-peya' kōk, tangkob₂*)

**kulaet** *n.* 1) A pressure lantern. (*Thesaurus: laet, lām, lampu, palita'an, plaslaet 1, sū' 1*) 1.1) *v. intr. aN-* To fish by the light of a pressure lantern. *Na i' makasampig kami ni a'a angulaet i'.* So there we were coming alongside that man fishing by lantern light.

**pagkulaet** *v. intr. aN-* To fish by the light of a pressure lantern. *Pagbusay kami, parunggu' na kami ni a'a magkulaet ē'.* After paddling, we moored by the people using pressure lanterns.

**kulagkag** *adj. a-* Emaciated; gaunt. (*Thesaurus: kagkag, kayog 1, kittay, koskos, giti' 1, higtal, titis 2*)

**kulagpak** *v. intr. aN-* To make the noise of things striking hard. (*Thesaurus: kutub, huru-huru*)

**kula'ak** (var. **kule'ek**) *v. intr. aN-* To cry loudly; to shriek. *Asidda angula'ak onde'-onde' inān bang halam ma luma' ina'na.* That child cries really loudly when his mother is not in the house. *Buwat kita ni M'ddas ati lingananta, bo' wa'i na atala. Lingananta, subay kita angula'ak bo' takale.* Like when we go to Siasi and call out, but are far away. We call out, but have to shout really loudly to be heard. *Angule'ek, sidda anangis.* Making a loud noise, crying very hard. (*Thesaurus: asang₂, galit, gasud, olang 1.1, pagalud, pahit*)

**kula'ing** *n.* A jaw harp made of bamboo. *Angulanting buwat kula'ing pagkublit-kublitta inān.* Making a rhythmic sound like a jaw harp that we strum with finger tips. (*cf:* **honel**)

**kula'up** *adj. a-* Rinsing one's face on getting up from sleep. *Bang kita bay atuli subay akula'up bo' halam belad maka bohe' atawa tahik. Agūm-gūm isāb ka, nila'anan bau bowa' hē'.* When we have been asleep we should rinse our face with water or sea-water so as to prevent eye infection. Rub teeth and gums too, to remove that mouth smell. (*Thesaurus:* **bunglaw 1, gūm-gūm, saplut₁ 1**)

**kulallit₁** *n.* A monovalve like a small helmet shell in shape. (*syn:* **eral-eral₁**)

**kulallit₂** *see:* **pagkulallit**

**kulam** *n.* A pond or container for live fish.

**kulambal** (var. **kuwambal**) *n.* The Pearly monocle bream and gold-lined sea bream. *Gymoncranius spp.*

**kulambal-bagangan** *n.* A species of bream.

**kulambitay** (derivative of **bitay**) *v. intr. pa-* To climb across from one thing to another. *Pakulambitay onde' itū.* This child climbs from one thing to another.

**kulambu'** *n.* **1)** A partition or enclosure of netting or cloth. (*cf:* **dinding 1**; *Thesaurus:* **kultina, langsay, luhul₂**) **1.1)** *v. tr. -an* To partition a room using curtains. **2)** A mosquito net. (*syn:* **muskitero**)

**kulambut** *n.* A dropper between a hook and the main fishing line. *Pagtinduk daing, kasabitan na, sakali itū wa'i ang'bba. Pag'nda'ta ni tōng tonda' bay pangengkotan kulambut, halam maina'an.* On striking the fish is hooked, but lets it go. When we see the end of the line where the dropper was tied, it is not there.

**kulambuwan** *n.* A species of fish.

**kulampera'** *n.* Generic term for various flatfish species.

**kulampera'-daing** *n.* The female of the Leopard flounder or Oriental sole. *Bothus pantherinus; Brachinus orientalis.*

**kulampera'-langohan** *n.* The male of the Leopard flounder or Oriental sole. *Bothus pantherinus; Brachinus orientalis.*

**kulampera'-s'llang** *n.* The Four-lined tongue-sole or the Deep-water flatfish. *Cynoglossus bilineatus.*

**kulampera'-tabaku** *n.* The Peacock sole. *Pardachirus pavoninus.*

**kulanas** *n.* **1)** The faint sound of something small moving. *Kulanas ambaw ko hē'.* That's the rustling of a rat. (*Thesaurus:* **bahembas 1, bah'ssek 1, kerek-kerek, keyos₂, kulessab, ganggu', ussab-ussab**) **1.1)** *v. intr. aN-* To make a rustling sound.

**kulanting** *v. tr.* **1)** To beat time on the end gong of a kulintangan set. (*Thesaurus:* **lisag₂ 1.1, tagunggu', taletek, taratu' 1.1, taroro', tigi'-**

**tigi'₂, tuntung**) **1.1)** *v. intr. aN-* To beat time. *Angulanting buwat kula'ing pagkublit-kublitta inān.* Making a rhythmic sound like a jaw harp that we strum with finger tips.

**pagkulanting-kulanting** *v. tr.* To play a wooden version of a kulintangan.

**kulang₁** *n.* **1)** Whatever is lacking. *Halam aniya' kulangna.* It was not short of anything. (*cf:* **kabus, kulang-kabus**) **1.1)** *adj. a-* Lacking; insufficient; fewer than. *Ma waktu ina'an, akulang gi' pana'u kami pasal Allahu-Ta'ala.* At that time our knowledge of God was lacking. *Akulang olen si Jo, bay tinangkaw e' si Anu.* Jo has fewer marbles, they have been stolen by What's-his-name. *Kulang-kulang duwantahun.* A bit less than two years. **1.2)** *v. intr. pa-* To decrease in number, volume, severity or intensity. *Pakulang na buwas.* The rice is getting less. (*Thesaurus:* **l'ddos 1.1, lō'**) **1.3)** *v. tr. -an* To reduce something in amount, size, or number. *Ya dakuman kinulangan gadjinu.* The only thing to be reduced is your wages. *Da'a itu k'nnopinbi atawa kulanginbi.* Don't increase or reduce this [amount]. (*Thesaurus:* **kobos, kō' 1.2, dagdag₁, diki' 1.2, hilang, loddos 1, lō', putung, sulak₁**)

**kulang-akkal** *adj. a-* Suffering from mental stress or disorder. *Kulang-akkal itū arupang-dupangan, kakulang-kulangan.* This word *kulang-akkal* means afflicted by some foolishness, suffering some lack.

**kulang-kabus** *adj. zero* Short of basic supplies. *Aminta' aku ni lahat dakayu' bang aku kulang-kabus.* I get supplies from another place when I am short of essentials. (*cf:* **kabus, kulang₁ 1**)

**kulang-kilā** *n.* A sickness of very small children, symptomized by enlargement of the skull. (*syn:* **kilā-luku**)

**kulang-kulang** **1)** *adj. zero* Somewhat lacking; somewhat less than. *Onde'-onde' itū taga katuk, kulang-kulang iya.* This child has a mental problem, he is lacking something. *Kulang-akkal itū arupang-dupangan, kakulang-kulangan.* This word *kulang-akkal* means afflicted by foolishness, somewhat deficient. **2)** *v. advrs. ka-...-an* To be lacking normal mental functions. *Kulang-akkal itū kakulang-kulangan.* This *kulang-akkal* condition is to be lacking normal mental functions.

**kulang-labi** *adv.* More or less; approximately. *Kulang-labi lisag sangpū'.* Approximately ten o'clock. (*syn:* **saga 3**)

**pagkulang** *v. intr. aN-* To be less than what is needed. *Lapus mbal maglabi, mbal magkulang. Buwat papan pelang, alapus munda'-buli, sarang to'ongan. Lapus* means not having too much nor being short of anything. Like the planking of a canoe, complete from stem to stern, exactly enough. *Saga a'a bay animuk aheka mbal maglabi, maka saga a'a isab bay animuk ariki' mbal magkulang.* The people who collected a lot didn't have an excess, and those who collected a few didn't lack.

**kulang₂** *n.* The numbered discs for the game of pool. *Bang kita anira ni ngga'i ka kulangta, pabelawta ya sehe'ta.* When one of us strikes a disc that is not his own, we tease that mate of ours. (*Thesaurus:* **bulitin, pūl, tako, tira**)

**kulangkang** *v. intr. aN-* **1)** To curl up, as a leaf or fish drying out. *Angulangkang sīn bay parangka.* The [paper] money drying by the fire has curled up. (*Thesaurus:* **komo'₁, kongkong 1, kullung, pagkorel-korel**) **2)** To project at an unnatural angle. *Angulangkang, sali' paperat tape'ta, anuwas-nuwas kita, amatay.* Projecting unnaturally, like our legs sticking out, we ourselves becoming rigid, dying.

**kulangkung** *n.* Cuttlebone, the boat-shaped chalky shield of a cuttlefish. (*cf:* **kindat**)

**kulap** *n.* **1)** A disease symptomised by chronic drying and flaking of the skin. *Ichthyosis.* (*syn:* **kakas 1, pohak 1**) **1.1)** *v. advrs. -in-* Afflicted with a disease of dry, flaking skin.

**kulapa'** *n.* The pithy stem of sago palm fronds, used for light construction purposes. *Bang kulapa' a'llum, tahinang dinding luma', maligay, pataw linggi'.* Green stems can be made into walls for a house, for a bride-wealth house, for net floats.

**kulapu** *n.* Generic term for various groupers. *fam. Serranidae.* (*cf:* **kuhapo'**)

 **kulapu-tangal** *n.* Blacktip grouper or Redbanded grouper. *Epinephelus fasciatus.* (*syn:* **kutkut-keyat**)

**kularak** *v. intr. aN-* To make the sound of a large number of trapped fish. *Bang aheka daing ma deyom bubu atawa panggal, angularak.* When there are lots of fish in the box or basket trap they make a thrashing sound. (*cf:* **pagkolesek**)

**kulasog** *n.* **1)** Physical strength. **1.1)** *adj. a-* Strong; powerful; vigorous. (*Thesaurus:* **ayron, basag 1, bastig, kosog 1.1, kuwat-anggauta', landos 1, paslod 1.1**) **1.2)** *v. intr. aN-* To exert one's physical strength. *Pagta'u si Ya ilu na at'kka si Yu, magtūy iya pakulasog papunduk.* When Ya knew that Yu was arriving, he quickly exerted himself to sit up.

**kulatap** *v. intr. aN-* To occur in large numbers over a wide area. (*Thesaurus:* **kobol-kobol, t'bbud₂**)

**kulatay** *v. intr. pa-* To cross from one elevated location to another. *Pakulatay kita, palatun min dakayu' ni dakayu', kayu ka atawa luma'.* We *kulatay*, we cross from one high place to another, whether trees or houses. (*Thesaurus:* **lete, pagsulakat, taytay 1**)

 **pagkulatay** *v. intr. aN-* To keep going from one place to another instead of staying at home. *Magkulatay na pa'in ka. Mbal amole' luma', mbal at'ttog.* You are always visiting some place. You don't go home, don't stay put.

**kulattub** (var. **kulattup**) *v. intr. aN-* To make the noise of something exploding. *Bang aku bay am'lla bo' pangayuku abase', angulattub.* When I was cooking and the firewood was wet, it exploded. (*Thesaurus:* **konog-konog, llub, pagbolobok, paglagonggok, paglagublub**)

**kulattup** var. of **kulattub**

**kulban** *n.* **1)** An animal slaughtered as a religious sacrifice. *Bay iya anukbal kukulbanan aheka makalandu'.* He presented a great number of sacrificed animals. (*syn:* **hakika' 1.1**) **1.1)** *v. tr.* To perform the sacrifice rite.

**kule'ek** var. of **kula'ak**

**kulenseng** *n.* The clatter of metal items together.

 **pagkulenseng** *v. intr. aN-* To make the noise of metal items being rattled together.

**kulengkong** (var. **kulingkung**) *adj. a-* **1)** Meandering; circuitous, of a trail. *Akulingkung pahāp l'ngngan sehe'ta hē', mbal tabākta.* Our companions' path is so meandering, we can't find them. It will have to be when we are on a boat or in the house that we meet up. **1.1)** *v. intr. aN-* To go by a circuitous route. *Angalingkung, sali' angalibut.* Going the long way around, like circling around. **1.2)** *v. tr. -an* To arrange something by twisting. *Bay kinulengkongan bu'un d'nda inān.* That woman's hair has been twisted into place.

 **pagkulengkong** *v. intr. aN-* To be curled or twisted in multiple directions. *Bigtangun k'llat ilū abō' niuli'an, ko da'a magkulengkong.* Stretch out that line so it will be straightened, so it doesn't get curled up.

**kulerek-kulerek** var. of **kerek-kerek**

**kulesek** var. of **kolesek**

**kulessab** *n.* The rustling sound of things moving about. (*Thesaurus:* **bahembas 1, bah'ssek 1, kerek-kerek, keyos₂, kulanas 1, ganggu', ussab-ussab**)

 **pagkulessab** *v. intr. aN-* To make a rustling noise, as rats in thatch or creatures in undergrowth. *Ai magkulessab ilū?* What's making that rustling noise?

**kulgaw** *v. tr.* To block a move in games such as dominoes. *Kinulgaw kita he' si Bapa' Am bang magduminu.* Uncle Am blocks us when we play dominoes. (*Thesaurus:* **seraw**)

**kuli-kuli** (var. **kilu-kilu**) *adj. -an* **1)** Securely, of storage. *Subay kilu-kiluhan nīnna'.* It must be stored securely. **1.1)** *v. tr. -an* To store something very securely. *Kinuli-kulihan tinau'. Minsan abalos tinau' na pa'in.* Securely stored. Even though it is rancid it is still stored. *Kilu-kiluhin sīn ilū ma buli' ba'ul. Da'a pareyo'un minsan dakayu' pilak.* Store that money securely in the bottom of the chest. Don't reduce it, even by a peso. (*Thesaurus:* **nna', tau' 1**)

 **sakuli-kuli** *adv.* Securely stored or hidden. (*syn:* **sabuli-buli**)

**kulibut** *v. intr. pa-* To bypass something by going around it. (*Thesaurus:* **libut 1.1, liku', likuwad 1**)

**kuligkig** *v. tr.* To dominate someone verbally. *Buwat aku ni lahat a'a, niamu' aku amasiga. "Ōy," yukku, "aku kuligkigbi. Subay aku pasigabi."* As when I go to someone's place and they ask me to give them cigarets. "Hey!" I say, "You're talking me into it. It should be you giving me a smoke." *Anguligkig a'a ni kita. Lum'ngngan aku, binagay-bagay aku, sinuli-sulihan aku buwattitu-buwattina'an. Mbal pahali, gōm pa'in pinagko'ot bulsaku.* People talking to us persuasively. I am walking along and he treats me friendly like, talking at me about this and that. He doesn't let up, instead he's reaching into my pocket.

**kuligi'₁** *n.* 1) A person who takes little care of his appearance. *Kuligi', al'mmis baranna.* A scruffy person, his body dirty. **1.1)** *v. advrs. -in-* Careless with regard to personal hygiene, grooming, and general tidiness. *E'na kuligi'! Mbal minsan ka amandi ilū.* Grossly untidy! You don't even bathe! (*Thesaurus:* **patabak**)

**kuligi'₂** *v. advrs. -in-* Suffering from a skin infection with suppurating lumps. *Kinuligi' aku he' hama'. Paburut kulit tangan, paluwas isina.* My skin is infected by mosquito bites. The skin of the hand puckers up, its contents come out.

**kulilla'** *n.* A species of fish.

**kulimad** var. of **limad-limad**

**kulina** *v. intr. aN-* To pass on to one's descendants, of a medical condition. *Saupama aniya' asaki, pagsaki, aku-i amūng, "Angulina ni saga anakna maka mpuna."* Someone ill, for example, chronically ill, and I say, "It will be passed on down to his children and grandchildren." (*cf:* **lamin 1, paglemed**)

**kulindara** *v. tr. -an* To trim a square sail by bringing the outer corner down to boom level. *Yaboho' aku angulindara ma olangan Tapa'an na. Alandos baliyu, kinulindarahan supaya al'kkas tapole'.* I only trimmed the [square] sail when we reached the Tapa'an gap. The wind was strong, and the sail was trimmed in order to get home quickly. *Bang alandos baliyu bo' kita aleha, ah'lling kasehe'an, "Pinasangdan leha itū ma landos baliyu itū?" Ah'lling man buli' inān, "Da'a pasangdanun, kulindarahun ko da'a kita magka'at."* When the wind is strong and we are sailing under a square sail, someone says, "Shall we leave the sail unchanged with the wind strong as it is?" The one in the stern says, "Don't leave it as it is, trim the sail so we don't get damaged."

**kulintangan** *n.* A set of eight brass gongs. (*Thesaurus:* **agung 1, buwa₁, gandang 1, titik 1**)

**kulintas** *n.* The canna lily, used medicinally. *Canna spp.*

**kulinting** *v. intr. aN-* To cover; to smother in. *Bang paluruk ni pagkawinan, subay angulinting e' bulawan maka saga pamakay angillap bo' kaōnan dayahan, minsan mbal tinōp.* When someone goes to a wedding, they must be covered with gold jewelry and shiny clothing so as to be called rich, even though it doesn't suit them.

**kulingkung** var. of **kulengkong**

**kulis** *n.* Palm lines, believed to be indicators of one's fate. (*cf:* **buklas₁**; *Thesaurus:* **kahandak 1, karal 1, ganta'an₁, indika 1, piguhan, sukud₂ 1**)

**kulis pelang** *n. phrase* The qualities of a canoe that affect its performance and safety.

**kulisa'** var. of **lisa'**

**kulisi'₁** *n.* The lorikeet. *fam. Psittacidae.*

**kulisi'₂** *n.* The Butterfly bream.

**kulit₁** *n.* The color orange. (*gen:* **walna'**)

**kulit₂** var. of **kuwit**

**kulitis** *n.* Firecrackers. *Na aheka na agtimbak maka ba'anan kulitis.* So there were a lot of people making explosions with a great many firecrackers. (*cf:* **bintadol**)

**kul'ddeng** see: **pagkul'ddeng**

**kullap** var. of **k'llap**

**kullat** *n.* Briefs (underwear). (*Thesaurus:* **kansinsilyu, kindut, kudji-kudji, sanyawa**)

**kulli'** *n.* 1) An untruth uttered to influence opinion against someone. *Ang'llo' ka kulli' bo' a'a makapagbono'.* You're promoting a lie so people will fight each other. *Kulli' itu, sali' amisala kita puting tudju ni iya.* This word *kulli'* is like when we speak lies about her. (*Thesaurus:* **akkal 1.1**) **1.1)** *v. tr. -an* To achieve an aim by saying something that is not true. *Kulli'-kulli'anku, sali' akkalanku.* I speak untruths about [him], it's like I am deceiving [someone]. *Kinulli'an buwattē', yuk-i, "D'nda ya mbal bilahi."* Maligned like that, saying [falsely], "It's the woman who is reluctant."

**kulling** *v. tr.* To wipe up remnants using one's fingers. *Pangungulling si Arung itū.* Eldest Daughter habitually wipes [the plate] clean with her fingers. (*Thesaurus:* **linug₂, timud 1.1**)

**kullu-kullu₁** *n.* A species of sea bird, seen perched on floating logs. (*cf:* **haus-bō'**)

**kullu-kullu₂** *v. intr. aN-* 1) To hold up and rob; to commit piracy. *Arāk kami sinaggaw sabab niōnan kami itū bay kono' angullu-ngullu.* We were about to be arrested because we were named, allegedly, as having committed piracy. (*Thesaurus:* **langpas, mundu 1.1, musu**) **1.1)** *v. tr. -an* To plunder someone of their goods.

**pagkullu-kullu** *v. intr. aN-* To make a living by piracy. *Magkullu-kullu, angamundu, ameya' min parangkang.* Committing piracy, robbing, travelling in large sailboats.

**kulluk** *adj. a-* 1) Out of shape. (*Thesaurus:* **b'ngnga' 1, būk₁ 1**) **1.1)** *v. tr.* To bend stiff material to the desired shape. *Kinulluk basi' sau.* The metal part of the anchor bent to shape.

**kullu'** var. of **kagang-kullu'**

**kullung** v. intr. pa- To curl up in a confined space for shelter or warmth. *Bang aniya' nanamta, nihaggut-haggut kita, maumu kita pakullung.* When we have a sick feeling and suffer a chill, we often curl up. (*Thesaurus:* **komo'**₁, **kongkong 1, kulangkang 1, pagkorel-korel**)

**kulsi** n. The seat on which a sultan sits; a throne. (*Thesaurus:* **bangku', paningkō'an, siya**)

**kultina** n. A curtain; drapes. *Makasangon luhul, ya na kultina.* Setting up the canopy, the curtain that is. (*Thesaurus:* **kulambu' 1, langsay, luhul**₂)

**kuluk** n. The Schooling bannerfish; the False Moorish idol; the Spotted surgeonfish. *Heniochus singularis et al.*

**kulun** (var. **kulunan**; **kūn**) n. The womb; the lining of the womb. *Aniya' patomo' sakki ma kulunanna.* There is a sickness growing from the lining of her womb. *Mareyom kūn itū, amowa kita saikula.* Within the womb, we carry the amniotic sac. (*syn:* **kandang, kuta'-kuddarat**)

**kulunan** var. of **kulun**

**kuma'agi** n. The exercise of authority. (*cf:* **kapagagi, pagagi**)

  **pagkuma'agi** v. tr. To exercise authority over someone. *Pinagkuma'agi, hal kita pinagsoho'-soho' dakayu' maka dakayu'.* Subject to authority, simply given one order after another. *Subay aku magkuma'agi.* I am the one who should be in charge. (*Thesaurus:* **kapatut, pagagi, pagbaya'**₁, **pagkawasa, pagnakura' 1**)

  **pagkuma'agihan** n. The authority figure of a community. *Buwat ma luma' kami, h'ndaku maka ayuwanku, aku ya pagkuma'agihan sigām.* Like in our house, for my wife and my son-in-law, I am the authority for them.

**kumala'** n. A fabled red jewel, said to be found in the mouths of creatures such as crocodiles. *Kumala' itu bang ma kami, maumu aheka ma kabangkawan, aheka a'a amatay maka lalunganna. Bang aniya' makaesog, magtūy kīppangan buwaya hē'.* This *kumala'* jewel is [found] in remote islands, in the mangroves where there are many corpses with their coffins. If anyone is brave enough the crocodile is immediately leapt onto, face down. *Aniya' kumala' ambaw, aniya' isāb kumala' sowa. Ahāp kumala' sowa.* There are rat *kumala'* and a snake *kumala'* too. The snake one is better. *Pagk'ppang pa'in, sali' sowa, tinilaw kita bang ai amu'ta. "Ya hē ma deyoman hē'," yukta. Magtūy palatun ni kita kumala' mareyom baranna pamasukud ni kita. Yuk a'a kamemon, "Taga kumala' a'a ina'an, minsan ai pamono' iya."* Having leapt onto it, it is like a snake, and we are asked what our request is. "That thing there inside," we say. The *kumala'* jewel promptly comes across to us. Everyone says, "That man has a *kumala',* no matter what is used to kill him."

**kuman**₁ n. Various louse-like insects which infest clothing. *Bang ma hōs, tuma. Kuman itū ya makeyat, ina'an ma deyom ba'ul. Tuma* lice are in sarongs. *Kuman* are the red ones, the ones there inside the box. (*Thesaurus:* **kutu 1, limad-limad, lisa' 1, tuma 1**)

**kuman**₂ see: **dangkuman**

**kumarukan** adj. zero Excessively abundant or numerous. *Kumarukan a'a bang aniya' magkawin, sabab ina'an patimuk min lahat dakayu' maka dakayu'. Kumarukan hekana.* There are too many people when there is a wedding because they come from all over. Their number is excessive. *Kumarukan karayana, kumarukan isāb susana.* His wealth is far too great, his troubles too are too many. (*Thesaurus:* **karalaman, dumasiyaw, landu'**₂ **1, mamarahi, sidda 1, to'od**)

**kumay** n. Various Surgeonfishes and Unicornfishes. gen. *Naso. Angalenges, akasap sali', ya buwat kulit kumay ina'an.* Grainy, sort of scratchy, like the skin of surgeonfishes. (*spec:* **katol-katol, kuteteng, gallangan, igang**₂, **indangan**₁, **mungit, palig, saliyaw, sore, tahella', tampellas**)

**kumay-kabog** n. The Bignosed unicornfish. *Naso vlamingii.*

**kumay-lamba** n. The Longhorn unicornfish. *Naso unicornis.*

**kumay-manuk** n. The Sleek unicornfish. *Naso hexacanthus.*

**kumay-tandukan** n. The Bluespine unicornfish. *Naso uniocrnis.*

**kumay-t'llong** n. The Bar-cheeked unicornfish; the Clown tang. *Naso lituratus.*

**kumba'** n. A tough spherical organ in the intestines of certain fish.

**kumba'id** v. ditr. To ask permission when about to do something. *Angumba'id kita ni a'a sampay ni tuhan, ai-ai kabaya'anta nihinang.* We ask permission of people or of God regarding whatever one wants to do.

**kumbang** adj. a- **1)** Arranged so that there are no gaps. *Akumbang daing, halam aniya' pamentenan apa ap'nno' he' daing.* The fish are strung closely together, no way of carrying them with one hand because it is full. **1.1)** v. intr. pa- To move in the direction of closing a gap. *"Pakumbang kām minnilu," yukna. Magtūy nilengkong na daing he' mangambit ē'.* "Come together there," he says. And those fish were promptly enclosed by the fence fishermen. **1.2)** v. tr. To bring together ends or edges so as to close a gap. *Bang daing tinuhug kinumbang, mbal agon tabententa.* When fish is strung so as to form a circle on the string, one can hardly carry it. *Kumbangun leha inān, ai-ai ageret.* Bring the edges of that sail together, whatever is torn.

**kumbangan** *n.* An area enclosed by a fence, or by closing the outlet of a marine lagoon. (*Thesaurus:* **ād 1, apis 1, buluyan, koral 1, kumbisan, likusan, sasak 1**)

**pagkumbang** *v. intr. aN-* To be butted together, of ends or edges. *Magkumbang, magabut tōng duwampōng bo' mbal makalabay daing.* Brought together, the two ends [of a fish fence] meeting so fish cannot get past.

**kumbatang** *var. of* **bāt-kumbatang**

**kumbis** *adj. a-* 1) Tightly closed. *Akumbis luma' disi Ju.* Ju's house is tightly closed. **1.1)** *v. tr.* To enclose something; to shut something in completely. (*Thesaurus:* **bilik 1, kuddam, lekom, libun, tiggup 1**)

**kumbisan** *n.* A secure enclosure. (*Thesaurus:* **ād 1, apis 1, buluyan, koral 1, kumbangan, likusan, sasak 1**)

**kumkum**₁ *var. of* **kagang-kumkum**

**kumkum**₂ *n.* A backhoe or grubber. *Abuhat kumkum ina'an, sabab anagtol basi'na.* That backhoe is heavy, because its steel is solid.

**kummaw** *n.* A species of fish.

**kummi'** *adj. a-* Buckled out of shape, of metal items. (*Thesaurus:* **k'mmog 1, k'ppi'₂, h'bbong, logpok 1**)

**kumpas**₁ *v. tr.* To consider something; to have an opinion about something; to estimate. *Kumpasku halam na.* I reckon there isn't any more. *Kumpasnu, ahāp atawa ala'at?* What do you think, is it good or bad? *Takumpasna sali' sōng na iya amole' ni hadarat Tuhan.* She reckons that it's like she is about to go home to the presence of God. (*Thesaurus:* **bista₁, kira-kira, tē'₂**)

**kumpasan** *n.* An opinion; a judgment. *Ma kumpasanku isāb.* In my opinion, at least.

**kumpas**₂ *n.* A direction-finding compass. (*syn:* **padduman**)

**kumpay** *adj. zero* Durable, of some ferrous parts. *Basi' kumpay, basi' ahāp, basi' balan.* Durable iron or steel, good iron, steel. (*Thesaurus:* **anagtol, kamdos₂, galak₂, pagon₁ 1.1, taggu₁, tatas 1.1, togob₁**)

**kumpi'** *n.* 1) A folded hem or cuff of a garment. *Pa'ari-arihun kumpi' juba.* Decorate the hem of the robe. (*Thesaurus:* **kola' 1, la'up 1**) **1.1)** *v. tr. -an* To form a hem or cuff.

**kumpit** *n.* A broad-beamed wooden vessel used for general-purpose transportation. *Kumpit, ya pagdayungan.* A *kumpit*, the boat oars are used with. (*cf:* **pelang**; *Thesaurus:* **beggong, biruk, buti, kappal, lansa, papet, sappit₂, tempel**)

**kūn** *var. of* **kulun**

**kundul** *n.* The wax gourd. *Benincasa hispida.*

**kuning** *n.* The color yellow. (*syn:* **biyaning 1**; *gen:* **walna'**)

**kunit** *v. tr.* To apply a salve of coconut oil and turmeric. *Kinunit, baha'u bay maganak. Subay bowata panday magsalu. Mbal gi' kita amangan. Pinabeya'an kita ns'llan lahing maka dulaw ni lowatanta kamemon.* A salve applied, having recently given birth. We should have the midwife in to share a meal, though we do not eat yet. Coconut oil and turmeric are applied to all our inner joints.

**kunit-kunit** *n.* A species of swamp tree with durable pale-gold wood, used for house posts. (*syn:* **puntik**)

**kunnig** *n.* The imperial volute. *Aulica imperialis.*

**kunsi'** *n.* 1) A mortise lock or padlock; a key. (*cf:* **anak-kunsi', kandaru 1**) **1.1)** *v. tr.* To lock a door. 2) A key. *Amu'in kita kunsi', ukayta bodega.* Request a key for us, we will open the storage shed.

**kunsuy** *adj. zero* Sterilized, of water.

**kuntara** (*var.* **kontra**) *n.* 1) An enemy, especially in a military context. **1.1)** *v. tr.* To oppose an enemy.

**pagkuntara** *v. intr. aN-* To relate as enemies. *Magkuntara Milikan maka Jipun.* Americans and Japanese were enemies. (*Thesaurus:* **pagbanta 1.1**)

**kuntaw**₁ (*var.* **puntaw**) *n.* A dustpan.

**kuntaw**₂ *n.* A martial arts form indigenous to Southeast Asia.

**pagkuntaw** *v. intr. aN-* To be engaged in the martial art form known as kuntaw. (*cf:* **pagsilat**)

**kūng-kūng** *n.* Small decorative bells, typically on anklets or harness. *Aniya' kūng-kūngna bulawan.* She has golden anklet bells.

**kungkung** *var. of* **jungkung**

**kungsi** *n.* People in a close partnership relationship; confederates. *Kungsi si Ka maka a'a Pata'.* Ka and the men of Pata were confederates.

**pagkungsi** *v. intr. aN-* To join together for trade or mutual support. *Magkungsi kita karuwangan, ka'a ya ata'u angahapid, mbal aku angahaka.* The two of us get together. You know how to conceal a card, and I won't tell.

**kupas** *v. tr. -an* To remove skin by peeling or stripping. *Akatis pa'in kinupasan t'bbu inān, tinamus e' onde'.* After the sugarcane was peeled, the children sucked at it. (*Thesaurus:* **kanit 1.1, kisak, hagut, hampa' 1.1, lapes**)

**kuppa** *v. intr. pa-/-um-* 1) To jump down onto something. *Bay aku kumuppa ni siya bang angal'ddom deyom luma'.* I landed on a chair when the house was dark inside. *Bay ahūg si Nu, bay makakuppa ni tunggul.* Nu fell, he jumped down onto a stump. (*Thesaurus:* **laksu₁, sulakat, tugpa' 1**) **1.1)** *v. tr.* To reach something by jumping down. *Kuppahun onde'-onde' ilū, pal'kkas ka.* Jump down to that child, be quick.

**kuppiya** *n.* A small brimless cap or fez worn by Muslim men.

**kuppung** *var. of* **k'ppong**

**kupul** *v. tr.* To speak presumptuously about things which are outside one's knowledge or control. *Bang yukku, "Kaut aku salung, maka aniya' ai-ai ta'ā'ku," saguwā' mbal tatantu. Angupul kita bang* *ah'lling buwattē'.* If I say, "I will go out to sea tomorrow, and I will catch something," but that is not certain. When we speak like that we speak presumptuously. *Magtaluhan itū sali' angupul b'nnal.* Betting is like claiming to be true. (*Thesaurus:* **pa'al 1.1, talus₂**)

**kuput** *n.* The Leatherjacket; a Surgeonfish. (*cf:* **p'ggot**)

**kura'** *n.* 1) A horse. *Kura' pote' pangura'an ma sulga'.* A white horse on which to ride in heaven. (*syn:* **mandu-mandu**) 1.1) *adj. a-* Riding a horse. *Kura' iya, kōkna a'a, ataha' bu'unna. Onde'-onde' akura' ma iya.* It is a horse, its head human, its hair long. A child is riding it. 1.2) *v. intr. aN-* To ride on the back of an animal or large bird. *"Sakapinbi aku kura' apa pangura'anku." Aniya' pa'in, angura' na iya bo' turulna bantana.* [He said] "Get a horse ready for me because I would ride." Once ready he mounted and pursued his enemy.

**kura'-asnu** *n.* A donkey; a mule.

**kura'-kura'₁** *v. intr. pa-/aN-* To crawl on all fours. *Angura'-ngura' si Gi bang mbal gi' makal'ngngan.* Gi goes on all fours when she is not yet able to walk. (*cf:* **lele 1**)

**kura'-mandu-mandu** *n.* A powerful combative horse. *Kura'-mandu-mandu, kura' paglomba', aesog maka ab'ngngis.* A *mandu-mandu* horse, races competitively, brave and fierce. *Bang yukta kura' mandu-mandu, aesog.* When we say a horse is *mandu-mandu*, it is brave [in fighting].

**kura'-kura'₂** *n.* Crossed pieces of wood a meter or so in length which hold down the capping over the ridge of a house. (*cf:* **bubungan, buhungan**)

**kurat** *n.* An involuntary muscle movement; a tic.

**pagkurat** *v. intr. aN-* To experience involuntary muscular movement or contraction, often with brief pain. *Magkurat tape'na bang sangom.* His foot twinges at night. *Magkurat, magsignat sali', kōkta atawa baranta.* Twitches, sort of throbs, in the head or body. (*Thesaurus:* **k'bbut, pagkidjut, pagkirut-kirut**)

**kuridas** (var. **kuwidas**) *v. tr.* To contract to buy in bulk regardless of variations in quality. *Buwat kita angalitu daing, ka'am ya taga daing, magt'llumpū' damunda' anahut a'aslag. B'lliku ni ka'am duwa-duwa pilak, kuridasku.* Like when one is trading for fish, and you have thirty [fish] in one boat, large and small. I buy them from you at two pesos each, buying in bulk. (*cf:* **padjak₂**; *Thesaurus:* **pakkiyaw, pono' 1.1, sampul-baul, tighan 1.1**)

**kuri'** *n.* 1) A tiny amount; a pinch of something. 1.1) *v. tr.* To pick out tiny objects or fragments with the finger tips. *Kuri'ta, sali' la'ananta dakayu'-dakayu'.* We pick it out, removing it one bit at a time. (*cf:* **kolehek**)

**pagkuri'-kuri'** *v. intr. aN-* To do things in stages or small increments. (*Thesaurus:* **kitkit, pagliblib-liblib 1.1**)

**dangkuri'** *n.* A tiny amount of something. (*cf:* **salat 1**; *Thesaurus:* **dangk'tti', sidda 1.1**)

**pagdangkuri'** *v. tr.* To use something in small amounts. *Da'a paruwasayun, subay pinagdangkuri'.* Don't consume it lavishly, it should be used in small amounts. *Magbisbis-bisbis ma kinakan, pinagdangkuri'-dangkuri' buwat onde'-onde'.* Picking at the food, breaking it up into little bits, as children do.

**kuri'an** 1) *n.* A package or bundle of uncut cloth. *Bīlli ma kuri'an, halam bay ahudjag.* Bought by the package, hadn't been opened and separated. 2) *clf.* Count word for bundles of uncut cloth.

**kuriput** *adj. a-* 1) Stingy; limited in amount. *Kata'uhanku asāl in ka'a akuriput.* I knew already that you were stingy. (*Thesaurus:* **bista₂ 1, kaikit₁, kigit, kimmat 1, k'mmit 1, kudkud, kussil, giging, iskut, sumil₁**) 1.1) *v. advrs. ka-...-an* To be limited as to the amount given. *Ilmu' Tuhan, mbal kakuriputan.* God's knowledge and power are unlimited.

**kurubata'** *n.* A necktie; a cravat.

**pagkurubata'** *v. intr. aN-* To wear a necktie. *Ahāp l'lla, magkinurubata'.* A fine lad, wearing a tie.

**kuruk-kuruk** *n.* 1) The call to hens at feeding time. (*Thesaurus:* **bī-bī 1**) 1.1) *v. intr. aN-* To make a clucking sound.

**kuru'** *v. intr. pa-* To bend forward with head down. *Bungku'ta maka bukutta. Sali' kita pakuru'.* We lift it up with our backs. We are sort of bent over. *Pakuru' itū aniya' ko'otta atawa hinangta. Patukku' halam aniya' hinangta, hal kita magkarukka'an.* This word *kuru'* is when we are picking something up or doing something. *Tukku'* [bowing head] does not involve doing an action, we are simply feeling sad. *Pakuru' itū aniya' ko'otta atawa hinangta. Kuru'* is when we are picking up or making something. (*Thesaurus:* **bantang 1, kondo', domol 1, tondok 1**)

**kurung** *n.* The shin. *Bay aku lumossok, apares kurungku.* I put my foot in a hole and my shin was grazed.

**kurus** *n.* The tails side of a coin. *Kurus maka kara, kaba' maka ta'u.* Tails and heads, or *kaba'* and *ta'u.* (*Thesaurus:* **kaba', kara**)

**kūs-kūs** *n.* 1) Various edible volutes. *Cymbiola aulica et al.* 2) The bat volute. *Cymbiola vespertilio.*

**kūs-kūs-keyat** *n.* The Red bat volute. *Voluta aulica.*

**kusa'** *n.* A deer. (*cf:* **usa**)

**kuskus** *n.* 1) A stiff brush for scouring a surface. *Kagalna'an pinggan he' kuskus basi'-basi'.* The bowl has surface damage from a wire brush. (*cf:* **eskoba 1**) 1.1) *v. tr. -an* To scour a surface to clean. *Kuskusin lantay itū. L'mmi' itū mbal tabowa e' sasapu. Subay kinuskusan.* Scrub this floor. This grime won't come away with a broom. It should be scrubbed. (*Thesaurus:*

bunut-bunut, dalug₁, gisgis 1.2, lukup, lupag, susut)

**kuseseyang** (var. **kasisayang**) *adj. a-* **1)** Energetic; enthusiastic. *Subay bang dai' llaw, subay kita akuseseyang ma ai-ai nihinang, sabab aheka ta'nda'ta kasehe'an angusaha.* Early in the day we should be energetic doing whatever, because we see many others at work. **1.1)** *v. intr. aN-* To do with energy and commitment. *Angay anangis saga anakbi, anguseseyang sadja itū? Asagaw, ahidjul.* Why are these children of yours crying with such commitment? Noisy, making a din.

**kusina** *n.* A kitchen. *Ta'nda'ku na h'ndaku, ilu magsanglag ma kusina.* I can see my wife now cooking cassava meal there in the kitchen.

**kusing** *n.* A washer, i.e. a metal disc with a central hole.

**kussay** *n.* Scallions or spring onions.

**kussil** *adj. a-* Stingy; unhelpful. *Ai-ai panoho'an, mbal to'ongan iya. Akussil, ak'llit, akigit.* Whatever the instructions, he absolutely won't [do them]. He is totally unhelpful, uncooperative, mean. *Akussil pahāp a'a inān pangamu'an.* That person is really unhelpful when something is requested. (*Thesaurus:* **bista₂ 1, kaikit₁, kigit, kimmat 1, k'mmit 1, kudkud, kuriput 1, giging, iskut, sumil₁**)

**kussu'** *v. tr.* To poke into something, as when making a hole or testing whether food is cooked. *Kussu'in na badju' ina'an bo' lowangin na kīdna.* Poke into that blouse to make a hole in its side. (*Thesaurus:* **langgit 1, sudlat 1.1, suruk, tugsuk 2.2**)

**kussung** *n.* Various gobies including the Shadow goby. *Order gobiiformes; Acentrogobius nebulosus.*

**kusta** *n.* **1)** Multi-colored check pattern in cloth. *Mantaluna ya kakana' pote', maka kusta ya ba'anan tadjung.* Muslin, that white cloth, and the checkered stuff, all those sarongs. (*Thesaurus:* **diyandi, tabanas 1.1, tadjung**) **1.1)** *v. tr.* To weave a mat with a multi-colored check pattern. *Anganom aku tepo kinusta-kusta pab'llihanku.* I will weave a mat using a check pattern and I will sell it.

**kustal** *n.* **1)** A packet made of folded paper. *Bang aniya' kustal atawa dampapan kulitis, b'lliku duwa hekana.* If there are packets or packs of firecrackers I will buy two. (*Thesaurus:* **kaha₂ 1, pākete, papan₂**) **1.1)** *v. tr.* To wrap something in paper. *Ai-ai nilupi' buwatna'an, kinustal.* Anything folded up like that is said to be *kustal.*

**kustaw** *v. tr.* To misuse money entrusted to one's care; to embezzle.

**pangungustaw** *n.* A person who misuses money entrusted to his care; an embezzler.

**kusu** *n.* **1)** A hole in the upper planking of a canoe into which the outrigger cross-boom is inserted. *Aloka na kusu batangan.* The outrigger boom hole is loose-fitting. **1.1)** *v. tr. -an* To make a hole in the upper planking of a canoe. *Bang ka angusuhan batang, pahāpun lengkongna ko mbal abila'.* When you make a hole for the outrigger boom, form an even circle so it won't break. *Kinusuhan panapi' pelang panulugan batangan.* The upper planking of the canoe has holes made in it for inserting the outrigger booms.

**kusu-kusu** *v. tr.* To rub something vigorously as clothes or eyes. *Angusu-ngusu matana apa binelad.* Rubbing his eyes because they suffer from conjunctivitis. (*Thesaurus:* **helog, sikat**)

**kutad** *adj. a-* **1)** Wrinkle-free. *Bay aku akonot kuwitku. Na b'ttina'an angutad aku, ahāp-hāp na palasahanku. Mura-murahan aku amangan kohap-subu na, angkan akutad na isiku itū.* I was wrinkled as to my skin. Right now I am wrinkle-free and feeling much better. Hopefully I will be eating afternoons and mornings now, which is why my body is sleek. **1.1)** *v. intr. aN-* To become wrinkle-free. *Bay aku akonot kuwitku. Na b'ttina'an angutad aku, ahāp-hāp na palasahanku.* **1.2)** *v. tr.* To remove wrinkles from cloth by ironing or pressing. (*syn:* **hotad₁**)

**kuta'₁** *n.* **1)** A fortified city or military outpost. **2)** A safe for storing valuables. *Kuta' itū panau'an alta', mbal tatuli' he' mundu.* This safe is for keeping wealth in, bandits can't find it. (*gen:* **pagtau'an**)

**kuta'-kuddarat** *n.* The womb or uterus. (*syn:* **kandang, kulun**)

**kuta'₂** *v. intr. pa-* To form a large mass or pile. *Aheka daing pakuta' ma M'ddas.* Masses of fish piled up in Siasi Town. *Pakuta' panggi' kayu ma jambatan, at'kka min Tiyanggi.* Cassava is piled up on the wharf, arrived from Jolo. (*Thesaurus:* **būd 1.1, g'bbus 1, hunsuk, hungku', pagbullud**)

**kutambak** *n.* Various emperors and snappers. *Lutjanus nebulosus.* (*spec:* **aha'an, anupin, babawan, bahaba', bellok, bula'ug₁, kaluy-mantis, katumbal, dapak, lahusu' 1, mangagat, maya-maya₂, saging-saging₁, tambangaw**)

**kutambak-balihan** *n.* A species of snapper.

**kutambak-bulagtok** *n.* A species of snapper.

**kutambak-t'bba** *n.* The Yellow-spotted emperor snapper. *Lethrinus kallopterus (Bleeker).*

**kutkut-keyat** *n.* The Blacktip grouper. *Epinephelus fasciatus.* (*syn:* **kulapu-tangal**)

**kutebba'** *see:* **pagkutebba'**

**kuteteng** *n.* The Headband surgeonfish. *Acunthurus leucopareius.* (*gen:* **kumay**)

**kuti-kuti** *v. tr. -an* To persuade or seduce someone to do something against their will. *Kinuti-kutihan, sali' binissalahan. Buwat si Ma budjang, sinō' bilahi ma si So.* Persuaded and urged on by words. Like Ma, a maiden, being told to be in love with So. *Buwat saupama kamanakanku si La, binowa maglahi e' a'a, tinambahan iya sīn. Mbal tahinang h'nda, hal kinuti-kutihan.* Like, for example, my niece La, persuaded to elope with a man and given money for it. Not taken as a wife, simply seduced. (*Thesaurus:* **bidjak 1.1, bowa₃, pilad, pitna**)

**kutibbung** *see:* **pagkutibbung**

**kuting₁** *n.* A cat, a kitten; other small mammals.
　**kuting-balanda'** *n.* A rabbit.
　**kuting-kubing** *n.* The Philippine civet cat. *Paradoxorus philippinensis.* (*syn:* **tinggaung**)

**kuting₂** var. of **bāt-kuting**

**kuting-kuting₁** *n.* Sun-dried cassava tubers. (*Thesaurus:* **ta'adjil 1, tumbal 1**)

**kuting-kuting₂** *n.* Olive shells (generic). *Oliva spp.*

**kuttung** *adj.* *zero* Working hard with little hope of being successful. *Kuttung iya amusay, halam makatandan. Kuttung iya maghinang, halam aniya' kasōnganna.* He paddled hard but couldn't reach shore. He worked and worked but made no progress. (*Thesaurus:* **llet 2**)

**kutu** *n.* **1)** Head lice. *Binuruk, kinakan isi kōkta he' kutu.* Scaly and pitted, one's head bitten by head lice. (*Thesaurus:* **kuman₁, limad-limad, lisa' 1, tuma 1**) **1.1)** *v. tr.* -*an* To delouse someone. *Bang aku kinutuhan tībbokan kutu bo' amatay.* When I am deloused the lice are squashed so they die. (*Thesaurus:* **kuhut 1.1, siksik, t'bbok₂**)

**kutu-bebang** *n.* Body lice (distinct from those on the head or pubic area). *Kutu-bebang, ya ma kepetnu. Bebang* lice, the ones in your armpits.

**kutu-kutu 1)** *n.* Various minute marine organisms. **2)** *v. advrs.* ka-...-an To be bitten by kutu-kutu lice. *Ala'an ka, onde', kakutu-kutuhan ka.* Move away, child; you'll be bitten by sea urchin lice.

**kutu-kutu-buwaya** *n.* Crocodile lice, tiny marine organisms about the size and appearance of millet, found floating on the sea surface.

**kutu-kutu-tahik** *n.* A species of sea plant growing in shallow water, the long strand-like leaves of which pop when pressed between the nails.

**kutu-kutu-tehe'-tehe'** *n.* Sea urchin lice, tiny marine organisms capable of an irritating bite.

**pagkutu** *n.* **1)** A tool for removing head lice. *Kuhut itū lantay pagkutu.* The *kuhut* referred is a bamboo tool for removing lice. **1.1)** *v. intr.* aN- To remove lice from each other's hair.

**kutub** *v. intr.* aN- To emit the rhythmic sound of a distant activity. *Bang aniya' magbola mahē', bo' mbal ta'nda'ta bo' takaleta angutub-ngutub. Atawa bang aniya' magpasāk kayu mareya.* As when someone is playing volleyball yonder and we don't see it but we hear the distant sound. Or when someone is splitting wood inland. *Sali' aniya' agt'tta', agbola, agt'ppa, bo' halam ta'nda'ta. Yukta, "Angutub pahāp."* Like someone chopping wood, playing ball, pounding rice but not actually seen. We say, "What a noise." (*Thesaurus:* **kulagpak, huru-huru**)

**kutung** *v. intr.* pa- To be face down, as an overturned bowl or a capsized canoe. *Pakutung, pakkom na, ngga'i ka pasip.* Face down, overturned, not lying on one side. *A'a inān atuli pakutung.* That guy is sleeping face down. (*Thesaurus:* **k'ppang 1, da'ub, pakkom 1**)

**kutut** *n.* A species of fish, similar in appearance to a piper. (*cf:* **lahusu' 1**)

**kuwako** *n.* A tobacco pipe. (*syn:* **kukuwa**)

**kuwa'-kuwa'** *adv.* Excessively long, of a period of waiting. *Kuwa'-kuwa' na aku angalagaran lahut ilu.* I've been waiting for that knife for a long time. *Pinarupang aku he'na, angagad aku kuwa'-kuwa'.* He played a trick on me, I waited for ages. (*Thesaurus:* **lanjut 1, panjang, taha' 1.1, t'ggol 1.1**)

**kuwal** *v. tr.* To stir food in a pan, as to mix it or coat it with a glaze. *Bang ka am'lla buwas, kuwalun maka luwag.* When you cook rice, turn it over with a ladle. (*Thesaurus:* **bungkal₂ 1.2, keyol 1.1, gawgaw**)

**kuwambal** var. of **kulambal**

**kuwat** *n.* Vigor; stamina. (*Thesaurus:* **kuyas 1, matay₂, pakosog, paspas₁, puspus₁, sikad 1**)
　**kuwat-anggauta'** *n.* Physical energy; stamina. (*Thesaurus:* **ayron, basag 1, bastig, kosog 1.1, kulasog 1.1, landos 1, paslod 1.1**)
　**kuwat-kuwat** *adv.* **1)** Persistently; without let-up. *Kuwat-kuwat na kita pinatuntul he' matto'ata man luma' bang kita angusaha. Ta'abut ma dilaut ya hinangta maglata. Aholat saga matto'ata ya yuk-i, wa'i kita angusaha bo' wa'i maglata.* When we head out from home to work we are consistently well-prepared by our parents. Yet when out at sea what we do is have fun. Our parents are expectant thinking we are at work but we are in fact playing around. **1.1)** *v. tr.* -an To persist in some action. *Da'a kuwat-kuwatin binasanu ma onde'-onde' ilu. Amatay, piligdu.* Don't keep on with your punishment of that child. He will die, I fear. *Anguwat-nguwat dīna, ai-ai nihinang kinuwat-kuwatan na pa'in.* Making himself keep at it, whatever is to be done is persisted at continually.

**pagkuwat** *v. intr.* aN- To work with steady persistence. *Magkuwat iya ilū an'tta' kayu.* He works away there at cutting firewood. (*Thesaurus:* **kara-kara₁, daran-daran 1.1, pagabut-abut, sigi-sigi 1, toldas**)

**pakuwat** *adv.* Doggedly; persistently.

**kuway** *v. tr.* To turn a skipping rope. *Kinuway k'llat man tōng duwampōng. Aniya' dangan inān palaksu pareyom.* That rope is turned from both ends. There is another person who jumps in.
　**pagkuway** *n.* **1)** The game of skipping rope. **1.1)** *v. intr.* aN- To skip rope. *Bang aniya' onde'-onde' magkuway, na kalambotan aku paglabayku. Sali' nileboran baranku itū, magtūy lahoran.* If the children are skipping, then I get smacked in passing by. [The rope] sort of wraps around my

body, and I immediately showed bruising.

**kuwidas** var. of **kuridas**

**kuwiraw** *adj. zero* Responsible or liable for. *Bang aniya' bay angindam tukulnu, bo' aku pehē' angā', mbal iya. Yukna, "Ka'a-i kuwiraw?"* If someone has borrowed your hammer, and I go to get it but he isn't willing. He asks, "Will you be responsible for it?" *Sali' maghukum maka a'a, bo' aku ya taga utang. Na sinukut aku, manjari halam aniya' pamayadku. Yuk dangan, ma'ase' ma aku, "Aku ya kuwiraw."* Like when we are in a legal dispute, and I am the one with the debt. Well I am asked to pay but I have nothing to pay with. Another person, feeling sorry for me, says, "I will go guarantor." (*Thesaurus:* **abunaw, atas₂ 1, bahala'₁, lawag-baran, siyal, tanggung₂**)

**kuwit** (var. **kulit₂**) *n.* 1) The outer layer, of skin, bark or shell. (*cf:* **babaw-tana', lapis₁ 1**) 1.1) *v. tr. -an* To remove the outer layer. *Subay pinggangan bo' kinulitan.* It must be a triggerfish, to be skinned.

**kuwit-lantay** *v. intr. aN-* To be short of resources. {idiom} *Anguwit-lantay aku.* I am broke [lit. down to floor level].

**kuwit-panagatun** *n.* Seashells.

**kuwit-sapi'** *n.* Leather.

**kuwit-tahik** *n.* The surface of the sea. *Aheka na makalandu' s'ggit ma kuwit-tahik.* There is an excessive amount of rubbish on the surface of the sea.

**kuwit-tana'** *n.* The surface of the ground. *Ai-ai palē ma kuwit-tana'.* Anything that crawls along the ground.

**kuwit-kuwit** var. of **kulit-kulit**

**kuyas** *v. intr. pa-* 1) To do with vigor or energy. *Pakuyas ka, da'a na pa'in ka hal ma luma', apa ilu ka bay asaki. Kalu akosog na barannu.* Be energetic, don't keep on staying in the house, because you have been ill. Perhaps your body is now strong. (*Thesaurus:* **kuwat, matay₂, pakosog, paspas₁, puspus₁, sikad 1**) 1.1) *v. tr. -an* To do something with vigor.

**kuyaskas** *v. intr. pa-* To move with vigor. *Bay kita abungkus maka ai-ai, sakali aniya' tasayuta angeket. Magtūy kita makakuyaskas.* We were wrapped up in whatever, when suddenly we sensed something biting. We immediately spring into action. *Bay ka asaki, yukta, "Pakuyaskas ka amangan." Sagō' masi ka angalamma-ngalamma, mbal gi' makakuyaskas.* You have been ill and we say, "Eat heartily." But you are still feeling weak, not yet able to be vigorous. (*Thesaurus:* **basag 1.1**; *syn:* **bukaskas**)

**kuyya'** *n.* A monkey, a generic term for all species but specific for the Philippine long-tailed macaque. *Macaca fascicularis philippensis. Aheka kuyya' ma Būd Bonggaw.* There are many monkeys on Mount Bongao. (*Thesaurus:* **amu'₂, uwang**)

# D d

**da-** (var. **daN-**) 1) *aff.* Numeral prefix meaning 'one'. Used with a small set of nouns and classifiers. *Saga dapam'lla t'ggolna.* The time [elapsed] is about one cooking period. *Dalapis katas.* One layer of paper. *Dang'llaw, dapitu', dambulan, dantahun.* One day, one week, one month, one year. (*Thesaurus:* **dakayu'₁ 1, dangan 1, issa, sa-, ssa₃**) 2) *aff.* Similative prefix meaning 'same', 'equivalent to', or 'identical with'. *Daheya tape' kami.* Our feet are the same size. *Dalahat kami.* We are from the same place. *Saga onde' ya bay daiskul maka anakku t'ngnga'an.* The children who were of the same school as my middle child. *Dangkakanan kami maka sigām.* We were at the same table with them.

**dabbana** *n.* A tambourine. *Ya dabbana ginuna bang aniya' magpama'ap atawa magduwa'a-salamat. Ya anitik, subay aniya' g'llalna ma kauman. Mbal manjari pagongka'an.* The tambourine is used when there is a forgiveness or thanksgiving ceremony. The player should have some status in the community. It is not for entertainment.

**dabdab** *v. advrs. -in-* To be disturbed by someone talking nonsense in their sleep. *Bang mbal abati' to'ongan, nirabdab.* When not fully awake, we are disturbed by sleep-talk.

**pagdabdab** *v. intr. aN-* To be talking in one's sleep; to be talking nonsense while awake. *Magdabdab, sali' mag'lling-lling bang atuli, bang taentomna na pa'in kahaba' llaw i'. Dabdab,* like talking while sleeping, or when he keeps remembering things day after day. (*Thesaurus:* **ansong, ddop, lāp-lāp, mutamad, uppi 1**)

**dablay** *adj. zero* Draped.

**parablay** *v. tr.* To drape a flexible item over something firm. (*Thesaurus:* **pagsalay₁, sablay**)

**dabtal** *n.* A supporting document such as title to land or house site.

**parabtalan** *n.* A supporting base for a task; a basis for an assertion. (*cf:* **pamataggalan**)

**dabung** *n.* Bamboo shoots. *Bang aku bay angā' p'ttung kaleya, kam'ssangan aku e' dabung.* When I was getting bamboo from inland, I suffered a rash from the shoots.

**daka** *neg.* 'Who knows (who, what, why, when,

where)!'; emphatically disclaims knowledge. (*cf:* **inday, sitta'a**)

**daka ai** *phrase* Who knows what? *Wa'i ni Tiyanggi am'lli daka ai.* He's gone off to Jolo to buy goodness knows what. *Ballum tantu, m'ssa' tantu, daka at'kka daka ai.* Not definite, whether [they will] arrive or what.

**daka angay** *phrase* Goodness knows why. *Daka angay, sali' binalutan na in bilahiku anganiyat bissalaku ni ka'a.* Goodness knows why. It's as if my firm intention to send my message to you has been held back.

**daka maingga** *phrase* Goodness knows where.

**daka painay** *phrase* Goodness knows how. *Daka painay kulaet itū, mbal palangkat.* Goodness knows [what to do] with this pressure lantern, it can't be dismantled.

**daka sai** *phrase* Goodness know who. *Pa'abay na daka sai maka kami.* Someone, goodness knows who, is sailing along with us. *Bay iya binono' he' daka sai.* He was killed by goodness knows who.

**daka sumiyan** *phrase* Goodness knows when. A: "*Sumiyan amole' disi Nu?*" B: "*Daka sumiyan, halam bay angahaka.*" A: "When will Nu and his crew come home?" B: "Who knows when. They didn't say."

**dakag** *adj. a-* Demanding; self-indulgent. *Arakag, subay nirūlan ni matto'ana bang ai-ai ta'nda'na subay bin'lli.* Demanding, has to be indulged by his parents when anything he sees must be purchased. *Bang s'mmek baha'u binowa amandi, minsan du aniya' s'mmek ndang, arakag.* If new clothes are used for swimming even when there are old clothes, that's indulgent. (*cf:* **dūl**)

**pagparakag** *v. intr. aN-* To be set on getting what one wants.

**parakag** *v. tr.* To harm someone's character by over-indulging him or her. (*Thesaurus:* **palangga' 1.1, parūl 1.1, patege'**)

**daka'** *n.* High, of spring tides. (*Thesaurus:* **lalom₁ 2, l'kkab, nso', sosob, tambang₁ 1**)

**dakan** *n.* 1) The base of a bubu-type fish trap. *Tinilas itū pinanahut-nahut nihinang bubu, sagō' subay sali'-sali' tilasna bang dakan.* The *tilas* process is [cane] made into fine strips and woven into a *bubu* trap, but the strips should be the same size for the base. *Pinagsuwa'-suwa'an dakanna maka bukutna maka p'ttung abulak.* Its base and its back are threaded together with green bamboo lacing. (*cf:* **bubu₁ 1.1**) *v. tr. -an* To attach the base of a bubu-type fish trap to its top. *Buwat bubu bang dakananta na, subay sīmmatan ko da'a magpinda matana.* Like a *bubu* trap we attach its base, it should be stiffened so the mesh size doesn't change.

**dakau'** var. of **dakayu'₁**

**dakayu'₁** (var. **dakau'**; **dikayu'**) 1) *num.* A specific one. *Aniya' isāb dakayu' llaw.* There was another day too. (*Thesaurus:* **da- 1, dangan 1, issa, sa-, ssa₃**) 2) *n.* The other one (of two or more).

*Amatay na dakayu' isāb.* The other one is dead too. *Pareyo' kami min kappal ē' tudju ni kappal dakayu'.* We will go down from that ship into the other one. 3) *clf.* Count word for individual items of things. *Dakayu' du daing-daing.* Just one little fish.

**dakayu' maka dakayu'** *adv. phrase* One by one. *Angkan yampa aku atekmod na, in dakayu' maka dakayu' bay kasusahan kami.* That's why I am only now telling you in detail, one by one, about our troubles.

**dakayu'-dakayu'** *adv.* One each. *Dakayu'-dakayu' kolol ma dangan onde', pinagtabul-tabul.* A single pack of crayons for each child, all treated equally.

**dakayu'₂** 1) *adj. a-* Unanimous; united. *Arakayu' na gara'.* The decision is now unanimous. (*Thesaurus:* **amu₁ 1.1, beya'₃ 1, manghalapi, pagta'ayun, sulut 1, tayudtud**) 2) *v. intr. pa-* To form a unit with; to partner. *Aniya' ta'nda'ta ma a'a ina'an, ya hē' sinapali he'ta. Sali' parakayu' kita ma iya.* We see something about that man, that's what we will be partners with. Like we combine with him.

**pagdakayu'₁** *v. intr. aN-* 1) To be united in common purpose; to form a single community. *Bay isab magdakayu' angatu ma saga banta sigām.* They also united to confront their enemies. *Magsakaum, sali' magdakayu' a'a Butun maka a'a Siganggang, bay tinambukuhan e' mayul.* Forming a single community, like the people of Butun coming together with the people of Siganggang, told to do so by the mayor. (*cf:* **pagbihing₂**) 1.1) *v. tr.* To bring people or things together.

**kapagdakayu'** *n.* Unity.

**dakayu'₃** *v. tr. -an* To unite physically with someone, as in marriage. *Sali' kita angandakayu'an anak-h'nda a'a.* As though someone were to become one with another man's wife or daughter.

**pagdakayu'₂** *v. tr. -an* To be united physically as in marriage. *Sakali itū magdakayu' na si nabi Yakub maka si Rakiya. Aheya sidda lasana ma iya.* So Jacob became one with Rachel. His love for her was very great.

**dakdak** *v. tr. -an* 1) To wash or launder fabric. *Aubus na bay dakdakannu ya s'mmek itū...* After you have washed these clothes... (*Thesaurus:* **kimu', pakang₂, pukpuk**) 1.1) *v. intr. pa-* To be washable, of fabric. *Mbal parakdak s'mmek itū apa abuhat.* This cloth is not washable because it is heavy.

**dakdakan** *n.* Laundry; a collection of things that have been washed. *Lupi'un kono' ba saga dakdakan ilū.* Please fold up that laundry.

**pagdakdak** *v. tr.* To be engaged in laundering clothes. *Bang magdakdak Milikan nihuwal he'na maka kayu.* When an American does her laundry she stirs it with a stick.

**dak'tti'** var. of **dangk'tti'**

**daklan-bulan** *n.* Blumea, a medicinal plant. *Blumea balsamifera.*

**dakop** *v. tr.* To capture or abduct a woman with a view to informal marriage. *Nirakop, magpūn-pūnan dī sigā.* Abducted, coming together of their own choice. (*Thesaurus:* **lahi₂, pole'₃**)

**pagdakop** *v. intr. aN-* To elope by mutual choice. *Magdakop itu bay maglahi. Ya pamole'an sigā sara'.* Eloping together is running off together. The magistrate is where they'll end up. *Ala'at magdakop bang lahu'an dunya.* It is bad to be eloping when the world is experiencing an eclipse.

**dakuman** *adv.* Solely; without exception. *Nsa' aniya' tahinang, hal kami an'bba dakuman.* There is no work to be done, we just collect seafood. *Amak'llat subu. Tahan dakuman kami amole'.* Waiting for daybreak. We are the only ones still to go home. (*Thesaurus:* **hal, la'a, luwal, puntul, sadja, samadjana, tunggal 1, yangkon**)

**dadarut** (derivative of **darut**) *n.* A tool for extracting teeth. *Bay pinagli'ad emponku e' dadarut empon.* My tooth was levered back and forth by a tooth extractor.

**dāg₁** *v. intr. aN-* 1) To climb. *Da'a kam angandāg m'nnilu, man haronan kam.* Don't climb up there, use the ladder. 1.1) *v. tr.* To reach something by climbing. *Dāgun na lahing ilū.* Climb for that coconut. *Sinō' nirāg ma kami, minsan, yukna, puttuk-puttukna, parāg kami.* We were given instructions for us to climb it, even, he said, its tip. We were to climb. *Mbal tapangandāgan kayu ilū he' saga kamanahutan apa halam aniya' sangana.* That tree can't be climbed by little kids because it has no branches. 1.2) *v. ditr.* To convey something by climbing. *Dāganku pa'in korente ni p'ttung inān.* I will climb carrying this wire up yonder bamboo.

**pagdāg-lurus** *v. tr.* To be able to go up and down a house ladder, especially of a small child or elderly person. *Sat'ggol kita masi magdāg-lurus, angamu'-ngamu' na pa'in kita napaka.* As long as we are still alive and active [lit. can still go up and down the ladder], we keep praying for the necessities of life.

**dāg₂** *n.* 1) The Masked spinefoot (a fish species). *Siganus puellus.* 2) The striped snakehead, a species of mudfish found in both brackish and freshwater environments. *Channa striatus.*

**dāg-lambu** *n.* The Barred Rabbitfish or Spinefoot. *Siganus virgatus.*

**dāg₃** *n.* The dried leaves of a banana plant. *Upak ē' ngga'i ka dāg saging.* Palm sheath is something other than dried banana leaf.

**daga** *adj. a-* Approaching maturity, of girls. *Araga, buwat kami itū.* Becoming teenage girls, like us.

**daga-raga** *n.* A teenage girl. *Buwat saupama d'nda, sōng aheya, daga-raga sōng iya, sōng na budjang.* A girl for example, becoming full-grown, she is about to be a teenager, a marriageable woman. (*Thesaurus:* **budjang, subul**)

**daga'** *n.* 1) Lung tissue; blood vessels, of animals and fish. 2) A reddish substance exuded by some sea cucumbers (trepang). {old-fashioned} *Sandulay-l'ggon, hal lubuna takakan. Aniya' isāb daga'na, sali' lubu keyat. Kuwitna sali' kuwit kura'.* The *sandulay l'ggon* trepang, of which only the *lubu* exudates can be eaten. It has *daga'* tissue as well, like red *lubu.* Its skin is like the skin of a horse. (*cf:* **bāt**)

**dagal** *adj. a-* Bulky; too big for some container. *Aragal ni'isi, sali' pahangka'.* Too big to fit, sort of spilling over. (*Thesaurus:* **sugmak**)

**dagan₁** *n.* The horizontal components of a construction; floor bearers, deck supports. (*Thesaurus:* **babag 1, hobong, salsal, taytayan tikus**)

**dagan₂** *v. intr. pa-* 1) To run, as an animal or human; to run, of a motor. *Daka angay malkina itū. Mbal ahāp daganna.* No idea what's up with this engine. It runs poorly. 1.1) *v. ditr.* To convey or retrieve something by running. (*syn:* **lahi-lahi 1, onse 1**) 2) To run through a vein, artery or pipe. *Tambal pamaragan laha'.* Medicine for getting the blood to flow.

**daganas** *var. of* **lagonos**

**dagang** *v. tr. -an* To sell things such as produce, food, or shop goods. *Pagt'kka kami ni Tiyanggi, niragangan na lahing mahē'.* On our arrival at Jolo Town our copra was sold there. (*Thesaurus:* **lilung, litu, pab'lli, pagsoroy, pa'andag 1, samsuy**)

**dagangan** *n.* Items for sale.

**pagdagang** *v. intr. aN-* To make a living from buying and selling goods. *Magdagang kami ma t'bbu mahē' ma Kalumpang bay timpu Jipun.* We were in the sugarcane trade there at Kalumpang, back in the Japanese era. *Lubid ettom, ahunit nihinang. Alahang a'a agdagang. Min kayu tuwa'.* A black rope, hard to make. It is rare for anyone to market it. It is from the *tuwak* palm. *Bang subu-subu, asidda magdagang si Gi putu-putu.* Early in the morning Gi is diligently selling steamed cakes.

**paragang** *v. tr.* To encourage someone to buy something. (*Thesaurus:* **andag, halga' 1.2, jawab₁, ladjaw**)

**dagbos** *n.* Appearance (facial); looks. (*Thesaurus:* **aymuka, bantuk, bayhu' 1, jantang-jari, lahi₄, luwa 1, pangli' 1**)

**dagdag₁** *v. tr. -an* To reduce an amount or proportion, of shares or ingredients. (*Thesaurus:* **kobos, kulang₁ 1.3, diki' 1.2, hilang, putung, sulak₁**)

**dagdag₂** *var. of* **jagjag**

**dagdag₃** *n.* A species of fish.

**daggaha** (var. **dagha**) *n.* The chest; thorax (the

front part of the body between head and abdomen). *Badju'-samda, taga ingkahi l'ngngonna maka daggahana.* A *samda* blouse with lace on its sleeves and upper front.

**daggot**₁ *v. intr. pa-* To run a canoe or boat up onto a beach. *Tampe itū bang ta'abut tahik, subay sali' paraggot mareya.* The foreshore when it is reached by the sea, [boats] should be up on the land. *Wa'i na si Anu paraggot kaleya, bo' kita itū halam makatandan. Yukta, "Hē' na si Anu paraggot ni bihing."* What's-his-name has made land already, while we haven't reached shore. We say, "There's What's-his-name already run up on the beach." (*Thesaurus:* **dunggu'** 1, **tandan**₁ 1, **t'kkad** 1, **tundug** 1)

**daggot**₂ *adj. -an* 1) Connected physically. *Musu' daggotan.* The section of Musu' village attached to land. (*Thesaurus:* **dalos** 1, **d'ppak** 1.1, **langkit** 1, **langkus** 1) 1.1) *v. intr. pa-* To be closely attached. *Paraggot na papan bay nilansang. Mbal na at'llag.* The nailed boards are closely attached. They are no longer widely spaced.

**dagha** *var. of* **daggaha**

**dagmit** *v. intr. pa-* 1) To go somewhere briefly. *Paragmit ka kono' pehē'.* Please go there for a short time. (*cf:* **sa'ut** 1.1) 1.1) *v. tr.* To do something for a brief period of time. *Hal bay dagmitku.* I did it for just a moment.

**dago'-dago'** *see:* **pagdago'-dago'**

**dago'os** *v. tr. -an* To persist at an activity until it is completed. *Bang magsagga', bo' aku halam taga dusa, dago'osanku ya a'a bay taga dusa hē', buwat saga ni Mayul, ni upis.* When there is a dispute but I am not at fault, I'll take the one who was in the wrong all the way to the Mayor's court. *Bang saki asigpit, subay nirago'osan to'ongan, subay binowa to'ongan ni a'a ata'u anambal.* When an illness is acute it should be treated persistently, it should be taken right to someone who knows how to treat it. *Nilibuhan, nirago'osan.* Looked everywhere, done with persistence. (*Thesaurus:* **akkul, sugsig** 1, **tebot, tuyu'** 1)

**dagpak** *var. of* **d'ppak**

**dagsa'** *v. intr. pa-/-um-* To hit a submerged obstacle. *Tabowa pelang paragsa' ni batu.* The canoe was carried along to hit the submerged rock. *Makasanglad, makaragsa', makahanggal, sali' du. Ya sadja magbidda' bang makasiyud. Sanglad, dagsa'* and *hanggal* all mean run aground. The only one that is different is *siyud,* to brush something and glide over it. *Buwat aku ma munda' halam taga busay, bo' nijudjalan pelang, yukku, "Da'a na paragsa'un."* Like when I am in the bow with no paddle, and the canoe is being pushed along vigorously, I say, "Don't let it hit the submerged things." *Palabayun kita man l'bbangan ilū bo' mbal dumagsa'.* Have us go through that gap so we don't run into something

submerged. (*Thesaurus:* **hanggal** 1.1, **sanglad, siyud**)

**dagsok** *var. of* **dasok**

**dagsol** *v. ditr.* To take a matter to court. *Bang mbal kasulutan he' bissala, subay angikiral ni M'ddas. Paragsol to'ongan kita ni po'on.* If [the issue] isn't resolved through discussion, it must be taken to Siasi Town. We take the case right to the top. *Bang aniya' magbono' maglakibini, bang mbal ameya'-meya' ma sara' luwasan (buwat saga panglima inān) na binowa ni opis, magdagsol ni opis.* If there is a married couple fighting and if they won't follow the law of the wider community (such as that of community judges) then they are brought to the civil court for judgement. (*Thesaurus:* **ikiral, paglagadlad, tukbal**₂)

**dagtol**₁ *v. intr. pa-* To put pressure on something. *Wa'i na pelang paragtol ni luma'.* The canoe is pushing hard against the house. *Saupama magbono' kami saga onde'-onde', saupama yuk-i, "Angatu ka ma aku, samaragtol kita ni dinding."* Us kids fighting, for example, and [one] says, "You want to get back at me, let's bang simultaneously into the wall." (*cf:* **d'ddol**)

  **pamaragtolan** *n.* Something capable of bearing weight or pressure, as a chopping block or mast support. (*Thesaurus:* **pasangdolan** 1)

**dagtol**₂ *n.* 1) The final word in a discussion. *Dagtol itū sali' kasangka'an bissala, sali' katobtoban bissala, ya kabontolanna.* This word *dagtol* is like the final word, the end of the matter, its proper state. 1.1) *v. intr. pa-* To reach a conclusion in a discussion. *Paragtol bissala, mbal sali' kabalikan, tapus na bissala.* The talk is concluded, cannot be repeated, the discussion over.

**dagtu'** *var. of* **hagtu'**

**dahaga'** *n.* A glutton. (*Thesaurus:* **bagahak**₂, **boslad, buhawi'**₁, **butu', kanam, kaway** 1.1, **damba'**₁ 1.1, **lagak** 1.1, **tanggal**₁)

**dahagbela'** *see:* **pagdahagbela'**

**dahaggay** *v. intr. pa-* To laugh loudly. (*Thesaurus:* **kiyum** 2, **kohok-kohok, tittowa** 1.1)

**dahal** *n.* 1) Someone who eats greedily without having contributed. *Ē, dahal ka.* You are a greedy sponger. (*Thesaurus:* **habbab**) 1.1) *v. advrs. -in-* Carried away by greed. *Buwat sali' nirahal kita, sinawiya kita ma ai-ai. Napsuhan kita, nihangsaw.* As though we are greedy, controlled by the desire for anything. We are lustful, greedy. 1.2) *v. tr. -an* To eat food greedily without having contributed anything. *Na angandahal ka pehē'.* Go on then and guzzle the lot!

  **dahalan** *n.* Food eaten by someone who has not contributed anything. *Dahalan ya kinakan, sali' kita anukna' ma kinakan, mbal pah'llinganta ahāp. Buwat buwas mbal niōnan buwas. Dahalan* refers to food [eaten by a greedy person]. It's as though we are cursing the food, not speaking well of it. Like rice not being called rice. *Ā, dahalannu.* There's your slops. (*Thesaurus:* **boslaran, tanggalan**)

**dahik** *v. tr.* To haul something from the sea. *Dahikun daing niriyata' pelang.* Pull the fish up into the canoe. (*Thesaurus:* **daldal, l'bbos 1.1, longsad₁**)

**dahing** *v. intr. aN-* 1) To cry out for help. *Bay aku angandahing ni parinta sagō' halam takale pangandahingku.* I cried to the government for help but my cries were not heard. **1.1)** *v. intr. pa-* To cry out to someone. *Sali' kasigpitan kita ma ai-ai, parahing na kita angamu'.* Like when desperately short of everything, we cry out, begging for help.

**pagdahing** *v. intr. aN-* To cry continually or repeatedly, as from pain or distress. *Buwat a'a pīngkongan, maingga-maingga palegehanna magdahing-dahing.* When someone has a swelling, no matter where he is lying he keeps crying out. *Saki timbalun, llaw-sangom magdahing. Sali' aglinganan saga nggo'.* Painfully ill, crying out night and day. Like calling for his mother. (*cf:* **agkā'**)

**pangandahing** *n.* A desperate cry for help.

**dahū** (var. **dahulu**) *adv.* 1) Earlier; previous. *Min bay dahū lagi' pamabeya'na sīn, asal bilahi aku amabeya'an iya sulat.* From the time when he first sent money I have in fact wanted to send him a letter. **1.1)** *adv.* Ahead in time or space. *Dahū na ka ni tabu' am'lli lara.* You go first to the market and buy chillies. *Kagisin lantay dahū bo' lanu'in.* Scrub the floor first and then polish it. *At'kka kappal dahū min kami.* The ship will arrive ahead of us. (*cf:* **sauna**; *ant:* **damuli** 1) **1.2)** *v. intr. pa-/-um-* To go before; to precede. *Bang aku ni M'ddas maka si Ina' bo' aku makarahū ni pelang, sagwā' wa'i iya pabīng. Aniya' takalipatna bay ma tinda, bay b'llina.* When I was in Siasi Town with Mom I went ahead to the canoe, but she went back. She had forgotten something in the store, something she had bought. **1.3)** *v. tr.* To bring something to the front. *Bang bay dahū buli' subay tarahū munda' bo' pinelleng.* If the stern was in front, the bow should be brought to the front in order to reverse direction.

**dahū-buli'** *adv.* Back to front.

**dahū-rahū** *n.* Former times; historical events. *Ang'ntan sigā ntan abō' ang'ntan saddi. Yuk a'a, "Da'a ka ang'ntan ilu ko da'a kam apaki'. Ang'ntan kam bay dahū-rahū i."* They observe ritual ancestors but observe different ones. Someone says, "Don't observe those ones lest you be shamed. Keep to the ones from time past."

**dahū'an** (var. **da'uhan**) *n.* 1) An area to the front; ahead. *Makatinggil ka ma da'uhanna. Saupama ka binissalahan puting, asal na ka'a wa'i ma dahū'an. Ka'a bay parahū ni sara'.* You got the advantage in front of him. You for example being accused

of lying, actually got in front. You got to the magistrate first. *Aniya' saga tabungay bay pinabeya' min dahū'anbi an'ggal sigām.* Hornets were sent in front of you to drive them out. *Aniya' ta'nda'ku buwat luwa halimaw an'ngge min dahū'anku.* I saw something like a great cat standing in front of me. *Nilikusan kami min dahū'an maka min bukutan.* We were closed in front and to the rear. (*Thesaurus:* **alopan₁, harapan₁, munda'an₁**; *ant:* **damulihan**) **1.1)** *n.* Someone's presence. *Magtūy iya paruwa'i min kura'na bo' pasujud min dahū'an sultan ē'.* He immediately got down from his horse and prostrated himself in the king's presence.

**parahū** *v. tr.* To advance a portion of the agreed-on bride-wealth.

**dahulu** var. of **dahū**

**dahun₁** var. of **daun**

**dahun₂** *n.* The numbers on a gaming board or dice. *Aniya' legot kapang hal dahun langa, aniya' isāb hal dahun deyo'. Ma balad.* There are weighted dice with only high numbers, and some with only low ones. On a gaming board.

**dahun-deyo'** *n.* The low-numbered squares on a gaming board (1 to 3). *Aniya' legot kapang hal dahun langa, aniya' isāb hal dahun deyo'. Ma balad.* There are weighted dice that [have] only high numbers, and there are those that have only low numbers. On a gaming board, that is.

**dahun-langa** *n.* The high-numered squares on a gaming board (4 to 6).

**dahungkung** *v. intr. pa-* To stumble and fall headlong.

**dahut** *v. tr. -an* To re-sew a garment in order to reduce its size and make it fit better. *Nirahutan la'a, apa aheya ma iya.* Resewn just a bit, because it is too big for him. (*Thesaurus:* **bakiya'₂, bagsak₂, la'it, tahi'**)

**dai'₁** *v. intr. zero* Come here (imperative). *Dai' ka kono' dai'-dai'.* Come here just for a moment. *Oto', dai' na ka.* Son, come here.

**dai'₂** *adj. a-* To happen shortly; to be about to. *Arai' na kami ala'an ni lahat dakayu'.* We are about to leave for another place. *Ab'ttong danakanku, marai' na.* My sister is pregnant, not far off.

**dai'-llaw** *adv.* The period just before sunrise. (*Thesaurus:* **abay-subu, bukis₁, pagmanis-manis sobangan, pote' sobangan, subu₂** 1)

**dai'-dai'** *adv.* 1) A brief period of time; just a moment. *Pi'itu ka dai'-dai'.* Come here for a minute. (*Thesaurus:* **puraw**) **1.1)** *v. intr. pa-* To hurry. *Parai'-dai' ka kono'.* Be quick, please. (*cf:* **jamput**) **1.2)** *v. tr.* To do something in a short time. *Mbal tarai'-dai' bang hinang buwattitu i.* Things cannot be hurried with jobs like this. (*Thesaurus:* **ambat 1, amot-amot 1.1, sa'ut 1.1, saunu'**) **1.3)** *ptl.* Development marker in narrative discourse, meaning 'to make a long story short', and signaling the end of a discourse unit. *Dai'-dai'ku nA: maglapahan na kayu,* *maglapahan na parang.* I'll make it brief: [he] cut down trees, cut the grass. (*Thesaurus:* **dalas 1.1**)

**dai'-dai'an** *adv.* Immediately; in a short time. *Mbal dai'-dai'an magka'at.* It won't be destroyed in a hurry. (*Thesaurus:* **agsāy, magtūy, sakadjap, saru'un-du'un, sigla' 1**)

**pagdai'-dai'** *v. intr. aN-* 1) To hurry. *Pariyata' ka magdai'-dai' apa pajalak na goyak ilu ni ka'a.* Get higher up in a hurry because those waves are going to break over you. **1.1)** *v. tr. -an* To do something hurriedly. *Palaktasun aku, aniya' pagdai'-dai'anku.* Give me a lift, I'm in a hurry over something.

**pagdai'-dai'an** *n.* A period or state of hurry. *Ma pagdai'-dai'an, ahūg pareyo' onde'-onde' inān angkan iya apengka'.* In the hurry the child fell, which is why he was lame.

**magdai'-dai'** *adv.* Hurriedly.

**daimanis** *n.* The fourth or ring finger. (*wh:* **tangan 1**)

**daina'** (derivative of **ina'**) *adj.* To have the same mother but different fathers. *Bang daina' kami maka da'mma', nsa' aniya' pagbidda'an, sala du magdanakan.* If we have the same mother and father, there is no difference between us, same as being siblings. (*cf:* **da'mma'**).

**dainding** *v. tr. -an* To protect someone against possible harm, the action of a deceased relative or other supernatural being. *"O mbo', daindingin kono' anak-mpunu itū."* "O grandfather, please protect these descendants of yours." *Niraindingan itū, sali' tinampan bang aniya' saki. "Daindingin saga anak-mpunu, da'a buwanin logmay-lamma."* Protected, as though shielded when there is some illness. "Protect your descendants, don't cause them to have serious loss of energy." (*cf:* **tampan 1.1**)

**daing** *n.* 1) Fish as a class (of cold-blooded aquatic vertebrates); specific fish of many kinds. **1.1)** *v. advrs. -in-* Damaged by fish. *Bay niraing bubu kami.* Our deep-water fish traps are 'fish-damaged'.

**pagdaing** *v. intr. aN-* To fish for a living. *Alaba bay pangā'an pagmunda' magdaing ni pū'.* What the fleet got fishing at the outer islands was profitable.

**pagdaingan** *n.* A fish market.

**pagdaraing** *n.* A person who makes a living by fishing.

**daing kohap** *n. phrase* Fish caught during the night and used or sold the following afternoon.

**daing niasin** *n. phrase* Fish preserved by salting. (*Thesaurus:* **lumay, peyad 1, pundang 1, sampila'₁ 1**)

**daing tangki** *n. phrase* Fish raised in a pond.

**daing-batu** *n. phrase* Various species of fish in the coral environment.

**daing-daing sahasa'** *n. phrase* The Coral goby.

**daing-pote'** *n.* Various Carangid fish valued for their firm white flesh. *fam. Carangidae. Ahāp*

*ssana daing mangsa'. Basta daing-pote' kamemon, ya magnakura' mangsa'.* The *mangsa'* fish has a good flavor. Of all the white-fish, *mangsa'* is the topmost. (*cf:* **balobok₂**)

**daing-pote'-langohan** *n.* The shadow kingfish. *Carangoides dinema.*

**daing-pote'-mangale'** *n.* The Golden toothless trevally; the Golden kingfish. *Gnathonodon speciosus.*

**daipara** *adv.* Contrary to expectation; better than expected; fortunately. *Daipara l'ppos, magkap'ddi'an kōk si Gi.* Just as well it was spongy material, or Gi would be experiencing a sore head. *Daluwa to'ongan maka langa-langa, daipara halam taga lakkop ma kōkna.* Looks the same as a remora except that it has no suction pad on its head. *Arāk patukbung taguri', daipara sinapatan, nihella'.* The kite would have dived [into the sea], but fortunately it was prevented, the line pulled. *Bay ulan, daipara aniya' payung.* It rained but fortunately there was an umbrella. (*Thesaurus:* **arapun, gōm, sapād-pād**)

**dairit** var. of **dirit₁**

**daiyus** *adj. a-* Perverse; shameless; grossly ill-behaved. *Araiyus anakku. Ai-ai pamandu'ta iya, angaho'. Manjari pagl'nganna, saddi buli'-akkal.* My child is perverse. Whatever we teach him he agrees with. However as he walks off he has something else in mind. *Bang ilu bineya'-bineya', makaraiyus ko' inān.* If that [advice] is followed it will result in something perverse. *Araiyus kita ma pagongka', minsan ai-ai bay pusaka'ta ngā'ta.* We are shameful in regard to gaming, we even take inherited valuables [to finance it]. *Buwat si Je kohap-īn angamu' angalalu h'nda si Mo, na bo' maina'an si Mo pakale. Makaraiyus lling buwattē' ma saga matto'a si Mo.* Like Je yesterday afternoon, asking to have sex with Mo's wife, and Mo there hearing it. Talk like that brings shame to Mo's parents.

**dā'₁** *intrj.* Exclamation of shock or disbelief. (*Thesaurus:* **agkā', allā, anā, arī, arōy, aruhuy, asē, ayī, ē**)

**dā'₂** see: **mandā'-dā'**

**da'a** *neg.* 1) 'Do not' (imperative negator). *Da'a hella'un.* Don't pull it. 2) None exists. *Bohe' sasahan itū sapa', sali' aniya' palaran. Bang pa'in da'a aniya' anasahan, tigbaw na.* Flowing water is a river, as though something is drifting. Provided there is nothing flowing, then it is a pond. (*syn:* **halam₁ 1, nsa' 1**; *Thesaurus:* **halam₁ 1**)

**da'a busung** *phrase* Please excuse me (lit. do no harm). {idiom} *Da'a busung. Da'a pa'in ap'ddi' ataynu ma aku pagka aniya' gi' amu'ku ni ka'a.* Excuse me. Please don't be angry with me; there is something else I am asking you for. (*Thesaurus:* **kono' 2, lagi' 3, pa'in₂ 2**)

**da'a gi'** *conj.* Especially; much rather; not only

so. {idiom} *Da'a gi' bang buwat d'nda maka l'lla magbaya', bo' sali' at'ggol halam makapag'nda', bo' samaentom, na maglaman.* Especially when a woman and a man are in love but haven't seen each other for ages and are missing each other, then they appear to each other. *Ahunit to'ongan pagusaha'an ma lahat, da'a lagi' ni kalawakan. Minsan ni kasekotan hal a'a binono' maka nilangpasan.* Making a living is very difficult throughout the region, not only in distant places. Even here close by, people are just being killed and raided. *Bilahi gi' aku anganak min duwa dang'llaw, da'a gi' kineket e' lalipan.* I would rather give birth twice in one day, much rather than being bitten by a centipede.

**da'a sakit** *adv. phrase* Don't overdo. {idiom} *Bu'un sigām subay nihatul, sagō' da'a sakit pina'alti.* Their hair should be kept tidy, but don't have it too beautiful.

**da'ak** *v. ditr.* To order someone to do some task. *Da'akku bata'anku.* I will instruct my servants. (*Thesaurus:* **gandahan, hilag, pagmanda 1, soho', sūg-sūg, uldin 1**)

**dara'akan** *n.* A messenger; a servant. (*syn:* **sosoho'an**)

**para'ak** *v. tr.* *-an* To inform the elders of the man about to be married that it is time to proceed to the bride's house (for the ceremony).

**da'awa** *n.* 1) A defense against an accusation. 1.1) *v. tr.* *-an* To defend oneself against an accusation. *Sinukut, mbal pinara'awa. Sinoho' amayad utangna.* Dunned for a debt, not allowed to make excuses. Ordered to pay his debts. *Kita ya anganda'awa ma a'a.* It is us who defend [ourselves] against someone. (*Thesaurus:* **paglugat, palilu, tawalli', tumagal 1.1**)

**pagda'awa** *n.* 1) An excuse or defense in response to a command or legal charge. *Nsa' pagda'awa basta bangsa Jipun.* There was no excuse with the Japanese. 1.1) *v. intr.* *aN-* To protest against a dispute, a command or ruling. *Aheka a'a magda'awa ma Sisangat, ahunit kala'anan minsan sinōd he' mundu, malaingkan talalat.* A lot of people in Sisangat were protesting [against an edict.] They are difficult to remove even though invaded by bandits. They can however be forced to flee.

**da'ayat** *n.* Citizens; populace; congregation of a local mosque or church. (*Thesaurus:* **mahadjana', mahalayak, majilis**)

**da'il** *see:* **pagpara'il**

**da'ira** *n.* 1) A population center. (*Thesaurus:* **lahat, lungsud, pasisil, tana'₂**) 2) A town plaza.

**da'mma'** (derivative of **mma'**) *adj.* To have the same father but a different mother. (*cf:* **daina'**).

**da'os** *v. tr.* *-an* To squeeze cassava meal between linked planks in order to remove liquid. *Bang angala'an bohe' panggi' subay nira'osan maka papan, ginipitan ni karut. Am'ttak bohe'na pareyo'.* When removing cassava fluid it should

be pressed with boards, squeezed through sacking. Its fluid drips down. (*cf:* **gipit 1**)

**da'ub** *v. intr.* *pa-* To lie face down, as a person sleeping, or a canoe. (*ant:* **daya'**; *Thesaurus:* **k'ppang 1, kutung, pakkom 1**)

**pagda'ub-daya'** *v. intr.* *aN-* To turn over and over repeatedly. (*cf:* **pagpakkom-leyak**)

**da'ug** *v. tr.* To defeat someone, as in a game, contest or war. *Tara'ug si Ji, araran anganda'ug si Ka.* Ji has been beaten, Ka often wins. *Magsusun aku wa'i tara'ug sīnku. Halam aniya' pam'lliku doppeng.* I regret losing my money in a contest. I have nothing to buy a pancake with. *Bang iya anganda'ug saga dakayu' pilak bo' aku halam binuwanan, ak'llit iya.* If he wins a peso or so but I am not given anything, he is stingy. (*cf:* **tiyuwas**)

**da'ugan** *n.* A victory; prize.

**pagda'ug** *v. intr.* *aN-* To strive together for supremacy. (*Thesaurus:* **pagkosogan, pagegot-egot, pagta'as-ta'as**)

**panganda'ug** *n.* Victory in a contest or conflict.

**da'uhan** *var. of* **dahū'an**

**da'ut** *v. tr.* To seek the presence of someone of higher status, when an issue is to be negotiated or litigated. *Bang aniya' d'nda amole' aku, subay matto'aku nira'ut.* If a girl comes to my bed at night [to compel marriage], my parents should be called on for support. *Ya sali' kita magluray, manjari da'utta sehe'ta magbono' supaya kita ma diyata'.* Like when we women are in a scrap, then we call on our companions to fight so that we may be on top. *Subay nira'ut tēp he' min kar'ndahan. Angkan nira'ut, bilahi akale. Maka ka'a barannu ya pinagda'ut, subay ka'a ya makabengket.* The bride's family simply must have the tape player brought over. The reason for getting it is that they want to hear it. And you personally are also called, you should carry it. *Buwat bissalana, bang aniya' bissala tudju ni kami. Hal sali' pang'llo'an bissala angkan nira'ut.* Like his words when he has something to say towards us. The reason for calling [on his help] is to get an opinion.

**dalam** *n.* An excess.

**karalaman** *adv.* Extremely; excessively. *Dupang karalaman a'a inān.* That man is utterly stupid. *Miskin kami karalaman.* We are totally destitute. (*Thesaurus:* **kumarukan, dumasiyaw, landu'₂ 1, mamarahi, sidda 1, to'od**)

**dalam isāb** *conj.* Even though; even while. *Dalam isāb kabaya'an kami usba-waris, tinilaw lagi' d'nda.* Even though we of the girl's kin on both sides are willing, the girl has yet to be asked. *Maglukun sangom. Abay kohap saga magtakbil na. Paglisag siyam akatis. Dalam isāb akatis, amasi isāb.* Celebrating at night. Early evening chanting praises, finishing at nine o'clock. Even though it is finished, it continues. *Dalam isāb buwattē' bay llingku ma ka'a, subay aku ampunnu.*

*Magsuli-suli gi' aku maka ndaku.* Even though what I said to you is like that, you should forgive me. I will talk some more with my wife. *"Dalam isāb ka,"* yuk imam, *"kinawin, mbal gi' pinabatal."* "Even though you are getting married," said the imam, "you are not yet released from the no-contact rules." (*Thesaurus:* **sasang**)

**dalam-duwa** *adj. zero* Undecided; of two minds. *Dalam-duwa at'kka Milikan kohap inān.* It is doubtful whether the Westerner will arrive this afternoon. *Tu'udna tu'ud, ngga'i ka dalam-duwa, ngā'ta.* Totally definite, no indecision, we simply take it. (*Thesaurus:* **duwa-abana, duwa-ruwa, paguntung-duwa, sarap-duwa**)

**dalan** *adj. zero* **1)** Faint-hearted, timid. *Bang magbono' aku dalan, sali' manuk bang alahi, angandalan.* When fighting I am faint-hearted, like a chicken running away, scared. **1.1)** *v. intr. aN-* To show timidity; to take fright. *Angandalan, angatu bo' atāw. Dalan-dalan du atuna.* Taking fright, fighting back though timid. His fight-back is half-hearted. (*Thesaurus:* **bolag, damag, gawa, g'mma, gupu, leya'-leya', tāw 1.1, umagad 1.1**)

**dalas** *adj. a-* **1)** Rapidly consumed; wasteful. *Aralas, al'kkas akatis.* Wasteful, quickly finished. (*cf:* **duwasay**₁) **1.1)** *v. tr.* Development marker in narrative discourse, meaning 'to make a long story short', and signaling the end of a discourse unit, always used with enclitic pronouns =ku or =ta. *Aheka tahā' sigā daing: kalitan-man'ssop, maka indangan, maka b'llong, maka longgang tahā' sigā. Dalasku, sigā amole na.* They caught a lot of fish: whitetip shark, surgeon fish, spinefoot and grouper. To make a long story short, then they went home. *Dalasta nA: tabāk na abay kami.* To make a long story short: our companions were found. (*Thesaurus:* **dai'-dai' 1.3, papu'ut**)

**dalat** *n.* A wind from off the land. *Dalat itū baliyu man būd tudju kaut.* Dalat is a wind from the mountain towards the open sea. (*gen:* **baliyu 1**)

**daldal** *v. tr. -an* To move something into the sea by dragging, or by lowering from a platform. *Pagdaldal kami pelang itū man diyata' kalangan, magtūy palowang ma t'ngnga'na.* When we had put the canoe down into the water off the drying rack, a hole immediately formed in the middle. (*Thesaurus:* **dahik, l'bbos 1.1, longsad**₁)

**daleyak** *var. of* **duleyak**

**dalig** *n.* **1)** New growth sprouting from beside the main stem or trunk of a plant. *Taga dalig, buwat kayu dapo'on du bo' duwa batangna.* Having a new growth, like a single tree with two trunks. **1.1)** *v. intr. aN-* To grow alongside. *Bang kita pīngkongan, bo' aniya' isāb p'ngkong dakayu', yukta, "Angandalig p'ngkong dakayu'."* When we have a swelling and there is yet another swelling, we say of it, "The one swelling is growing from the other."

**dalihag** *v. intr. pa-* To move in fright. *Buwat kami soho'nu pariyata', kuddatnu kami magtūy. Kami makaralihag, makabati', makapunduk.* Like when you tell us to get up, you suddenly startle us. We start up in fright, wake up, sit up. *Paralihag patā, sali' lahi-lahi patā.* We run off in fright, like running far away. (*Thesaurus:* **kuddat**)

**dali'it** *v. tr. -an* To resent someone else's wealth or well-being and seek to reduce what they have. *Nirali'itan ka ma alta'nu.* You are resented because of your wealth. *A'a mangandali'it itū sali' magnapsu. Buwat sali' aniya' ta'nda' e' sigā ma bihing luma' sigā, minsan sai-sai a'a. Ya nirali'itan a'a ya taga ai-ai hē'.* These people who resent others' good fortune are sort of covetous. It's like they have seen something in a neighboring house, no matter who. What they want to reduce are those people who have things. *Buwat saupama taga pelang aku ahāp, bo' sali' aniya' sehe'ku magjingki, nirali'itan aku he' sigām. Manjari nihinangan aku la'at, minsan aku halam bay magdusa.* Suppose I have a good canoe, and others have ill-will towards me and want to bring me down. So they do something bad to me, even though I have committed no wrong.

**dalil** *n.* **1)** Meaning, referent, or metaphorical sense of a word or statement. **1.1)** *v. tr.* To give careful thought as to the meaning of something. *Dalilunbi baran manusiya'. Baranta itū dakayu' du, bo' magginis pagdayawna.* Think about the human body. This body of ours is just one, but its parts are diverse. *Ai-ai b'llita subay kita angandalilan dahū, sali' amikilan.* Whatever we buy we should evaluate first, like giving thought to it. (*Thesaurus:* **kannal, dongdong, pagka'inagon, pikil 1.1, tali' 1.1**)

**dalilan** *n.* Careful thought or consideration. *Bang a'a am'lli ai-ai bay ta'nda'na, halam aniya' dalilanna.* When a person buys whatever he sees, not giving any thought to it.

**pamaralilan** (*var.* **pangandalilan**) *n.* A parable, example or metaphor that illustrates what is said; figurative language. (*Thesaurus:* **saupama 1, upamakun 1**)

**paralil** *v. tr.* **1)** To make an example of something. **1.1)** *v. intr. aN-* To cite something as an illustration or example. *Sagwā' amaralil si Hu pasal baranna.* But Hu was giving an illustration about himself.

**paralilan** *n.* An example; an illustration.

**dalima'** *n.* The pomegranate tree. *Ponica granatum.*

**daling** *n.* The comb of a bird. (*Thesaurus:* **label, pē'**₃)

**dalisu'** *v. intr. -um-* To suffer sprain or dislocation. *Bay aku dumalisu' bang aku ang'llo' bohe'.* I suffered a sprain when I was carrying water.

**pagdalisu'** *v. intr. aN-* To be dislocated or misaligned. *Bang apisu' magdalisu' to'olang.* When dislocated the bones are misaligned. *Magdalisu' deyom baranku.* Things are dislocated inside my body. *Bang aku pakuppa man diyata' luma', abongso' aku. Apisu', magdalisu', ta'ā' saki.* If I jump from the top of the house I suffer internal damage. I suffer a sprain, dislocated bones, resulting in sickness. (*Thesaurus:* **pagsā'**, **pi'ul**, **pisu'**, **pittay 1.1**, **possat**)

**dallet** *v. intr. aN-* **1)** To blaze up; to burst into flame. (*Thesaurus:* **keyat₂ 1.1**, **dokot₂ 1.1**, **lāb 1**, **suleyab 1**) **1.1)** *v. tr. -an* To ignite a fire. *Dalletin lapohan ilū.* Light the cooking fire. *Karalletan alkohol, halam ni'nda' ai-ai pa'alung.* The alcohol caught fire, the things placed to warm by the fire weren't seen.

**dalling** *n.* An entertainment form in which the dancers also sing. *Dalling itū igal bineya'an kalangan.* This *dalling* is dance accompanied by song.

  **pagdalling** *v. intr. aN-* To perform the dalling dance, an art form in which a performer both dances and sings.

**dallung** *n.* An alloy of bronze. *Tumbaga dallung billi ma Bulungan.* Items of copper bronze bought at Bulungan.

**dalos** (var. **daos**) *adj. zero* **1)** Connected physically. *Dalos Hambilan maka Siganggang.* Hambilan and Siganggang are connected [by land]. *Atanus kayu, atilud dalos.* Clear wood, unbroken, straight [grain] right through. *Bang dalos aretes mbal ahūg pareyo'.* If the earrings are attached [to the ears] they don't fall down. (*Thesaurus:* **daggot₂ 1**, **d'ppak 1.1**, **langkit 1**, **langkus 1**) **1.1)** *v. intr. pa-* To attach oneself to a house or its occupants. *Paralos kita ma luma' mananambal.* We will stay at the house of the healer. *Paralos kita buwat ma luma'ta, halam aniya' makala'an kita sabab luma'ta ru.* We are attached, as here in our house, no one can make us go away because it is our house, as a matter of fact. **1.2)** *v. tr.* To connect two items or parts. *Niralos na durukan.* The upper strake [of a canoe] has been connected. **1.3)** *v. tr. -an* To achieve something by being present in person. *Buwat saga aniya' anunggu' tunang, yukta, "Paraos na ka maili'. Daosin na maī'."* Like when someone is pursuing a courtship, we say, "Move in there [to her home]. Be there physically."

**dalosan** *n.* The lowest plank of a pelang-type canoe. (*syn:* **pamonod**; *gen:* **tapi' 1**)

  **pagdalos** *v. intr. aN-* To be physically connected. *Magdalos asal luma'na inān maka dinding kalabusu.* His house there was right next to the fence of the jail.

**dalug₁** *v. tr. -an* To do something thoroughly, as when cleaning a canoe or a house. *Dalugin pelang, nilukupan ati bo' sinaitan.* Maintain the canoe well, scrubbed and then bailed out. (*Thesaurus:* **bunut-bunut, kuskus 1.1, gisgis 1.2, lukup, lupag, susut**)

**dalug₂** (var. **talug**) *v. intr. aN-* To reappear in a different part of the body, of a pain or ache. *Bay ala'an tandogta analug ni kōk, ap'ddi' kōkta.* Our fever went away and settled in our head, so we have a headache. (*syn:* **tanog₂ 1**)

**daluma'** (derivative of **luma'**) *n.* The members of a single house. *Buwat duwa luma' magbihing, bo' tuman-tuman dakayu' luma' inān amole' salung, ati makasambeya' daluma' inān amole' isāb. Makapagbāk pa'in ma pagbākan, tinilaw "Angay kam amole'?"* Like two household-groups [fishing] near each other, then one of them is set on returning home, those of the same house also going. When they meet up at the departure place, they are asked, "How come you are going home?" *Buwat duwa luma' magbihing, bo' tuman-tuman dakayu' luma' inān amole' salung, ati makasambeya' daluma' inān amole' isāb.* Like two household-groups [fishing] near each other, then one of them is set on returning home, those of the same house also going.

  **pagdaluma'** *v. intr. aN-* To be living together in the same house. *Bay pa'in kami magdaluma' maka milikan ē', dangkakanan kami maka sigām.* When we were living in the same house with those Westerners, we ate at the same table.

**daluwa** (derivative of **luwa**) *adj.* Identical in appearance; looking alike. *Daluwa ka maka danakannu inān. Daluwa badju'nu maka badju' si Ig.* You and that sibling of yours are look-alikes. Your shirt and Ig's are identical. *Saddi luwa si Li maka luwa si Gi, mbal daluwa.* Li's appearance is diffenent from Gi's, they are not alike. (*cf:* **dasali'**).

  **pagdaluwa** *v. intr. aN-* To be identical in appearance.

**dama** *v. intr. pa-* **1)** To warm oneself by a fire. (*Thesaurus:* **dangka₂ 1, dangu 1, tapa 1.1**) **1.1)** *v. tr.* To dry something by the heat of a fire.

**damak** *see:* **pagdamak**

**damag** *v. advrs. -in-* Cowardly; fearful; terrified. *Niramag, bang aniya' pal'ngngan a'a, palahi kaut.* Timid, if someone comes visiting, [he] escapes seaward. (*Thesaurus:* **bolag, dalan 1.1, gawa, g'mma, gupu, leya'-leya', tāw 1.1, umagad 1.1**)

**damahē'an** (derivative of **hē'₁**) *n.* The same location. *Asidda aku pinabukagan minsan ngga'i ka tta'anna ni bohe' aku, asāl aku ni bohe'. Kabā'na damahē'an.* I was severely scolded though there was nothing intentional in my going to the water source, I was just going to the water as usual. She supposed I intended to be in the same place.

**damal** *adj. a-* Growing less bright, as a lamp.

**damas** *n.* The hull of a canoe in contrast to its upper planks. *Pelang halam bay tinapi', hal damasna.* A canoe with no added side-planks, just the hull. *A: "Pongag?" B: "Ngga'i ka, pelang damas-damas."* A: "A worn-out canoe?" B: "No, it's not, it's the hull of a canoe not yet completed." (*syn:* **kasko**)

**damba'**₁ *v. advrs.* -*in*- 1) Thoughtless and inconsiderate when eating. *Niramba', sali' hal amangan. Mbal sali' analu siyalina. Subay hal iya dangan-dangan.* Eats greedily, does nothing but eat. Won't share food with his younger sibling. He just wants to be eating alone. *Niramba' kita ma ai-ai, ma ai-ai, sali' nilagak.* One is selfish in regard to anything whatever, same as greedy. *Saupama aniya' t'llungan, duwangan ya amangan, dakayu' mbal. Niramba' karuwangan hē'.* Three people for example, two of them eating, one not. The two are selfish ones. 1.1) *v. intr.* aN- To eat greedily, without thought of others. (*Thesaurus:* **bagahak**₂, **boslad, buhawi'**₁, **butu', kanam, kaway 1.1, dahaga', lagak 1.1, tanggal**₁)

**damba'**₂ *n.* 1) A cursing equivalent for something lost or damaged through carelessness. *Ai ka soha', ai ka busay, "Angay timanannu damba'nu?"* Of a mooring stake or a paddle [one says], "Why did you throw that cursed thing of yours away." (*gen:* **sukna' 1.1**) 1.1) *v. tr.* To do some accursed thing. *"Angay damba'nu hūgnu?" Sali' panukna'.* "Why did you lose your danged change [from a purchase]?" Like a cussword. (*cf:* **sukna' 1**)

**dambeya'an** (derivative of **beya'**₁) *n.* A single group. *Magbinasa sigām dambeya'an.* They suffered as a single group.

**dambila'** *n.* 1) One half, especially of something divided in length. *Buwanin aku dambila' panitnu ilū.* Give me half of your tuna. *Dambila' atahak.* Half of it is ripe. (*cf:* **bila' 1**; *Thesaurus:* **dampōng, samalintonga', santonga'**) 2) The other side of something. *"Mbal kami," yuk sigām min dambila'.* "We disagree," said those from the other side. (*Thesaurus:* **bukut**₁, **liyu**₂ 1) 2.1) *v. intr.* pa- To cross to the other side of an intervening space. *Palatas ka parambila'.* Cross over to the other side.

 **dambila'-ni-dambila'** *adv.* From one side to the other. *Magtūy abahagi'-duwa bohe' inān, parambila'-ni-dambila'.* The water there promptly divided into two, from one side to the other.

**dambila' pilak** *n. phrase* Fifty centavos (lit. half peso). *Bay b'lliku dakayu' maka dambila' (pilak).* I bought it for one and a half (pesos).

**dambila'an** *n.* Something made up of two parts.

 **karambila'an** *n.* A cross-breed. *Nirūy e' sigām saga a'a karambila'an bangsa liyu min lahat ē'.* They drove out the cross-breed people from that land. *Tamanang kura' karambila'an itū.* These cross-breed horses cannot breed.

 **pagdambila'an** *v. intr.* aN- To be made up of two merged parts, as a person of mixed parentage, or speech that draws from diverse dialects. *Magdambila'an pahi maka manusiya'.* Half stingray and half human. *Buwat Sama Lipid magh'lling Sama, bo' magbagi'ad maka lling Sama.*

*Magdambila'an, sali' maglamud-lamugay. Bagi'ad* is like when Land Sama speak Sama, and they mix non-native words with the Sama. It's hybridized, different things being mixed together.

**damdam** var. of **dandam**

**damikkiyan** var. of **damikiyan**

**damikiyan** (var. **damikkiyan**) 1) *conj.* Likewise; similarly; in the same manner. *Magbesod, magpalilu. Bang ma a'a dangan, "Buwattē'." Damikiyan du isāb bang dangan, "Buwattina'an!"* Arguing, contradicting each other. According to one, "Like this!" In the same way another says, "Like that!" (*Thesaurus:* **buwat 1, gin, sala 1, sali' 1.3**) 2) *n.* Something equivalent or matching. *Damikiyanna du bang a'a taluwa' p'ddi' magsaleret, atawa magsularaw.* Likewise when a person is hit with pain, he writhes, or moves restlessly.

**damil** *adj.* a- Gummed or stuck firmly together. *Wa'i na aramil.* It has become stuck together now [of a canoe split repaired]. *Bang makaniplaes, aramil he' gaha', amikit he' gaha'.* With regard to pliers, fused together with rust, stuck with rust. (*Thesaurus:* **balut 1.1, kakkot, pikit**₁ 1)

**daminduwa** (derivative of **minduwa**) *v. tr.* To do something a second time. *Taraminduwa aku pinagbowa he' a'a.* It's the second time someone has influenced me.

**damint'dda** (derivative of **mint'dda**) *v. tr.* To do something once only. *Bang aku sinoho' he' a'a taramint'dda du. Mbal kaminduwahan.* If someone tells me to do something it happens only once. It won't happen a second time. *Mbal makabuwan minsan hal taramint'dda.* [He] won't give, even once.

**damlag** *n.* 1) Full moon. (*Thesaurus:* **bulan baha'u, bulan**₁, **matay-bulan**) 1.1) *adj.* zero Full, of the moon. *Na bang ta'abut bulan damlag.* Now when [we] get to full moon. (*cf:* **base'-bulan, kōpan**)

**damoseng** see: **pagdamoseng**

**dampal** var. of **sampal**

**dampeged-peged** *n.* An unusually small amount or extent. *Angay luma' ina'an dampeged-peged du dindingna?* Why does that house have such a small amount of walling?

**dampog** *n.* 1) A dark cloud formation. *Ngga'i ka ulan, dampog, ya tai' baliyu inān.* It's not rain or dampog, those cirrus clouds. 1.1) *v. intr.* aN- To become darkly overcast. *Angandampog lahat, sali' angulan. Angulan bang aniya' dampog.* The weather is becoming overcast, like it will rain. It rains when there are such clouds. (*Thesaurus:* **lempos, lendom 1.1, pagdo'om**)

**dampōng** (derivative of **pōng**) *n.* The end of something cut or broken across its length. *Buwat kita palete, dangan man dampōng dangan man dampōng, pa'aging sali' lum'ngngan.* Like when we go along the walkway, each [of us] from an end, unintentionally interrupting progress. (*Thesaurus:* **dambila' 1**, **samalintonga'**, **santonga'**).

**damuk** *n.* Tiny biting insects; gnats. (*Thesaurus:* **kammut, hama', hamug-hamug, hanglop**)

**damuli** *adj. zero* **1)** After in time; behind in space. *Ma llaw damuli.* At a later date. *Lāgi, damuli pa'in min latap, pasaplag ma dunya saga kabangsa-bangsahan kamemon.* What's more, after the flood people of all races spread across the world. (*ant:* **dahū 1.1**; *Thesaurus:* **atarasaw, lēt, tanggollayan**) **1.1)** *v. tr.* To overtake someone. *Na kami, taramuli na kami.* Us now, we're left behind.

**karamulihan** *n.* The last of a group or series. *Karamulihanna, patandan na sigām ni lahat paslangan.* At the last they arrived at the barren regions. *Min panubu'na kamemon sampay ni karamulihan kal'llahan, amatay lullun.* From all his descendants right up to the last of the men, all died.

**damuli punglu'** *adv. phrase* Swifter than a bullet. {idiom}

**damulihan** *n.* A location to the rear. (*ant:* **dahū'an 1**)

**damunda'** (derivative of **munda'₁**) *n.* A single boat. *Pasakay na duwangan ya bay sehe'na damunda' inān.* The two who had been his companions in that other boat now boarded.

**damunda'-munda'** (derivative of **munda'₁**) *n.* **1)** A single canoe traveling alone. *Hal si Oto' damunda'-munda'.* Just Eldest-son in his lonely canoe. *Saupama kita ma dilaut hal damunda'-munda'ta, s'lle' bale puhu' punung-punungan, tapalis kita.* For example we are out at sea, just one canoe, and God forbid, we are faint with hunger, we get carried far off course. *Pagtulakku ni kapū'an itū hal damunda'-munda'ku.* When I left for the islands recently I was just me in my canoe. (*cf:* **tukkal, tunggal-tunggal 1**). **1.1)** *v. intr. pa-* To travel by canoe on one's own. *Paramunda'-damunda' iya dīna, sali' parangan-dangan.* He is traveling by canoe on his own, going solo so to speak.

**daN-** *var. of* **da-**

**danakan** *n.* A sibling (brother or sister); a brother in a religious or fraternity sense. (*Thesaurus:* **siyaka 1, siyali 1**)

**pagdanakan** *n.* **1)** The relationship of siblings; brotherhood. **1.1)** *v. intr. aN-* To relate as siblings. *Magdanakan kami minsan saddī bangsa.* We are relating as brothers even though we are of different races.

**pagdanakan-danakan** *v. intr. aN-* To be in a fictive sibling relationship. *Makajari isāb magsubali ni kahāpan, buwat magdanakan-danakan magpanon.* It is possible also to swear an oath for good, like close friends declaring a fraternal relationship.

**pagdauranakan** *v. intr. aN-* To be united, as

people of the same religious community or people working together in common purpose. *In ka'am ilū magdauranakan kamemon, sabab dakayu' du gurubi luggiya'.* All of you are brothers because you have the one true religious teacher.

**dauranakan** *n.* **1)** Siblings in a collective sense. **2)** Members of a religious community or fraternity.

**danakan d'nda** *n. phrase* Sister (lit. female sibling).

**danakan l'lla** *n. phrase* Brother (lit. male sibling).

**danan** *n.* Boxfish species.

**danaw** (var. **lanaw**) *n.* A fairly large body of fresh water, not usually flowing; a lake or pond. *Yuk Tohongan, "Pak'ppang na pa'in aku ma danaw."* Said Mr. Turtle, "I will keep on diving into the pond." *Al'bbo bukut danaw.* The back of the lake is boggy. (*cf:* **pangandung, sapa'**; *Thesaurus:* **kandung₁, halo-halo, tangki, tigbaw**)

**dandam** (var. **damdam**) *v. tr. a-, ka-..-an, -an* To long deeply for someone or some thing. *Kinarandaman kono' si Anu he' Bisaya'.* What's-her-name, reportedly, is greatly desired by a man of the Christian community. *Kinarandaman, kinabilahi'an sala, ai-ai na, lilus ka, badju' ka, d'nda.* Longed for, desired, of various things: a watch, a shirt, or a woman.

**pagdandam-lindu** *v. tr. -an* To experience intense longing for a deceased or absent loved one.

**dandam-lindu** *see:* **dandam**

**dandiya'** *n.* A slug-like marine animal, inedible.

**dandiya' deya** *n. phrase* A common land slug.

**dandiya'-dandiya'** *n.* Sea anemone species. *Actinia spp.*

**danel** *n.* A foot race, a grade school activity.

**pagdanel** *v. intr. aN-* **1)** A running race. **1.1)** *v. intr. aN-* To compete in a foot race, a school activity. *Bay kami angongka', magdanel maka magembet.* We played, running races and playing tag. *Bay aku magdanel ma Sentral, bay aku pinunung halam aniya' takakanku.* I competed in a running race at Central School. I was famished, hadn't eaten anything. (*Thesaurus:* **paglomba, pagpasu 1.1**)

**daniyal** *n.* An edible monovalve species, helix-shaped.

**danos** *v. tr.* To combine loose material into a compact mass. *Niranos panggi' pinat'nna' ma deyom ambung. Abentol luhūy.* The grated cassava is pressed down and placed in a basket. It becomes even drier. *Niranos itu pinagtipun sali'. Danos* is like bringing material into one mass. (*Thesaurus:* **dasok 1.1, d'ppon, p'nnod 1**)

**dansasa'at** (derivative of **sa'at**) *n.* **1)** A moment of time. **1.1)** *adv.* Momentarily; very briefly. *Yangkon ina'an pat'nna' dansasa'at panalusan sadja semestel itū.* Only that, staying a little longer for the completion of this semester.

**dansehe'an** (derivative of **sehe'**) *n.* A group of

companions or friends. *Magsumbung dansehe'an bang halam makani'iskul dangan.* The group report on each other if one of them doesn't attend school. (*Thesaurus:* **kaheka-heka'an, kompolan, padjuhan, palti, umpigan**).

**danta'** *adj. a-* Clear; lucid; bright. *Min karanta'an hadaratna magl'tte' saga lāt.* Lightning flashed from the brightness of his presence. *Bang agarantam sampay aranta' na llaw, aniya' mulka' tumaluwa' ma kitam.* If we wait for it until the day is bright, disaster will strike us. (*Thesaurus:* **sahaya 1.1, sawa 1.1, sinag 1.1**)

**dantilad** *n.* The areca palm (betel) nuts in their unripe stage. (*Thesaurus:* **bunga₁, l'mmaw, lugus, pola**)

**dāng** *var. of* **dayang**

**dangan 1)** *num.* One, of persons. *Dangan du anakna.* He has just one child. *Anakna dangan.* Her one child. (*Thesaurus:* **da- 1, dakayu'₁ 1, issa, sa-, ssa₃**) **2)** *n.* One person... the other person. *Bilahi dangan bo' mbal bilahi dangan.* One wants to but the other doesn't.

   **dangan-dangan** *n.* **1)** Oneself alone. *Takole'ku dangan-dangan ku.* I can manage it myself. *Buwat aku sinoho' kaut ni Kompani, pikisehe' aku ma si Sa, bo' mbal iya. Manjari kaut aku dangan-danganku ati tapuwa'ku lima pilak ma lān.* Like when I was sent shorewards to the military post, and I asked Sa to accompany me but he wouldn't. So I went to the shore on my own and happened to find five pesos on the path. *Bang ta'bba dangan-danganna ma luma', anangis si Arung.* When she is left alone in the house, Daughter cries. (*cf:* **tunggal 1**) **1.1)** *v. intr. pa-* To travel on one's own. *Paramunda'-damunda' iya dīna, sali' parangan-dangan.* He is travelling by canoe on his own, going solo so to speak. **1.2)** *v. advrs. ka-...-an* To be left without a companion. *Tināw karangan-danganan.* He is afraid of being left alone. *Atilaw iya, yuk-i, "Angay ka karangan-danganan ilu? Angay halam sehe'nu?"* He asked, saying, "Why are you on your own there? Why don't you have a companion?"

   **dangan-duwa** *adv.* Individually and together, of an agreement. *Bang kabaya'anbi dangan-duwa, na magbahagi' kam pahāp.* If it's what you wish, one and all, then divide it up well. *Baya' sigā dangan-duwa magtiman.* It was the desire of both of them to separate.

   **dangan-parangan** *adv.* One person after another; one (item) per person.

   **tarangan-tarangan** *adv.* Individually. *Bang aheka magusaha ma takot Siganggang, tarangan-tarangan du amayan man paraw.* When a lot of people are fishing over Siganggang reef, each man individually in a *paraw* canoe. *Atabul tarangan-tarangan, sali' aniya' bay krismas sigā, atabul sigā.* Each of them receiving an equal share, like when they had a Christmas event, treated equally. (*Thesaurus:* **kaniya-kaniya, paggintil,**

**pinig, tabul₁ 1.1, topod 1**)

**darangan** *adj. zero* Limited to one person.

**dangat** *v. intr. pa-* **1)** To go in a direction contrary to wind or current. *Sinulayan parangat aku kaut, kalu tarangat he'ku s'llog, baliyu atawa goyak.* I will try to make it out to sea, perhaps I can make headway against current, wind or waves. (*Thesaurus:* **balda, paggat, sagga' 1.1, sīng-sūd**) **1.1)** *v. tr.* To oppose wind or current.

**dangay** *interrog.* How many? How much? (*syn:* **pila 1**)

**dangay-dangay** *n.* **1)** An uncounted or uncountable number. (*syn:* **pila-pila**) **1.1)** *adj. zero* Extreme, of some quality. *Dangay-dangay pasu'na.* Its heat was intense [lit. beyond measure].

**dangka₁** *v. tr.* To frighten someone with threats of harm or physical violence. *Buwat aniya' ah'lling, "Aesog aku." Bang angatu ya bay pinah'llingan inān, na palō' ya bay mah'lling i'. Yukta, "Na hal tu'ud angandangka."* Like someone saying, "I am fearless." When the fellow who was spoken to fights back, then the one who spoke backed down, saying, "We are just making threats." *Bay kami nirangka he' man dambila'.* We were intimidated by those on the other side. (*Thesaurus:* **alu'₁, hansom, sanggup**)

**dangka₂** *v. intr. pa-* **1)** To warm oneself at a fire. *Pag'nda'na ma bitu'anunna parangka ma api, magtūy nda'na pahāp.* On seeing his former wife warming herself at the fire, he immediately looked carefully at her. (*Thesaurus:* **dama 1, dangu 1, tapa 1.1**) **1.1)** *v. tr.* To hold something to the heat of a fire to dry it. *Dangkahun sīn katas bo' atoho'.* Hold paper money by the heat of a fire to dry.

   **parangkahan** *n.* A place for getting oneself warm.

**dangkakihan** (derivative of **kaki₂**) *n.* **1)** Cousin relationship. *Dangkakihan kami maka disi Ab.* We are cousins with Ab and the others. **2)** Closely related in meaning (fig.) *Dangkakihan nirelat maka sin'ssop.* Licking something and sucking on something are closely related words.

**dangkaheka** (derivative of **heka**) *n.* The same extended kin group.

**dangk'tti'** (var. **dak'tti'**) *n.* A single small piece. (*Thesaurus:* **dangkuri', sidda 1.1**)

**dangkuman** *n.* A small amount.

**dangkuri'** (derivative of **kuri'**) *n.* A tiny amount of something. *Dangkuri' du.* Only a very little. (*cf:* **salat 1**; *Thesaurus:* **dangk'tti', sidda 1.1**).

   **pagdangkuri'** *v. tr.* To use something in small amounts. *Da'a paruwasayun, subay pinagdangkuri'.* Don't consume it lavishly, it should be used in small amounts. *Magbisbis-bisbis ma kinakan, pinagdangkuri'-dangkuri' buwat onde'-onde'.* Picking at the food, breaking it up into little bits, as children do.

**danggu'-danggu'** *n.* A repeated to-and-fro movement.

**pagdanggu'-danggu'** *v. intr. aN-* To move alternately forward and back, as a person paddling a canoe, grating cassava, or moving on a swing. *Buwat si Ji bang amusay magdanggu'-danggu'.* Like Ji, when paddling he rocks backwards and forwards. (*Thesaurus:* **dundang**₁ **1, duyan, ombo'-ombo', pagnanu', tadjun**)

**dangin** *v. tr.* To involve community-members in a group activity. *Nirangin kami magosolan hāg.* We were called on to help in putting in house-posts. *Angandandin kita manusiya' angahinang panggung pagkawinan dok al'kkas aubus hinang itu.* We call on people to build a roofed shelter for a wedding so that the work is speedily finished. (*cf:* **sabi**₁**, tabang 1**)

**pagdangin** *v. intr. aN-* To work together as a community. *Magdangin maghinang.* Getting together and working. (*Thesaurus:* **pagsandu, pagtaku-taku 1**)

**pangandanginan** *n.* A place where cooperative work is being done; the project or focus of such work.

**dangirasan** (derivative of **iras**) *n.* The relationship between siblings-in-law. *Dangirasan sigā.* They share a sibling-in-law relationship. (*cf:* **pamikitan**).

**danglay** *n.* **1)** A nickname; a familiar name between friends or workmates. *Ōnna to'ongan si Jillian, danglayna si Lambetong.* Her real name is Gillian, her familiar name is Firefly. (*syn:* **g'llal 2**; *Thesaurus:* **isay, ōn**₁ **1, saingan**) **1.1)** *v. tr.* To give someone a familiar name or nickname. *Niranglay iya K'mbal.* He was nicknamed 'Twin'.

**danglog** *n.* The Philippine mahogany, a tree species. *gen. Shorea.* (*cf:* **manakayan**)

**danglus** (var. **hanglus**) *adj. a-* Suffering burns by fire or hot liquid. *Aranglus tape'na he' api. Aku itū bay aranglus he' binugbug.* Her foot is burnt by fire. As for me, I was burnt by [hot] gruel. (*cf:* **tutung**; *Thesaurus:* **kassa'-kassa', lungkab, lūs**₁ **1**)

**dangu** *v. intr. pa-* **1)** To warm oneself at a heat source. *Parangu ma bihing api, sali' kita pasekot ni lapohan.* Getting warm by the fire, like when we go close to the firebox. (*Thesaurus:* **dama 1, dangka**₂ **1, tapa 1.1**) **1.1)** *v. tr.* To dry something by the heat of a fire.

**daogdog** (var. **daugdug; dugdug**) *n.* Thunder; rumbling sound. (*Thesaurus:* **lāt, l'ggon, l'tte'**₁)

**pagdaogdog** (var. **pagdogdog**) *v. intr. aN-* To rumble, as a large crowd on the move. *Magdaogdog puhu', sali' aheka to'ongan maglundug. Aniya' sali' ajogjog lantay.* People moving en masse, like a great many crowding to see. The floor is kind of shaking. (*Thesaurus:* **pagtendek**)

**daos** var. of **dalos**

**dapa-rapa** *n.* An outboard motor, especially one with no decorative engine cover. (*cf:* **donson**)

**dapak** *n.* The Humpback red snapper. *Lutjanus gibbus.* (*gen:* **kutambak**)

**dapa'ut** var. of **tapa'ut**

**dapal** *v. advrs. -in-* Affected by blistering and white discharge, of the mouth and tongue. *Bang onde'-onde' baha'u bay nianakan, yukta, "Oy! Nirapalan pahāp bowa' onde' itu!"* When a baby is newly born, someone says, "Wow! This baby has really bad blisters in the mouth!" *Niugam dapal, aheka buwa'-buwa' ma deyom bowa'.* Infected with an oral disease, many blisters inside the mouth. (*cf:* **sampal 1, ugam 1.1**)

**dapang** *n.* A traditional outrigger canoe with fully planked upper hull, often elaborately carved, built up on its dugout base. *Dapang itu pelang bay niukilan. Bang balutu halam bay pinansalan, minsan aheya mbal kaōnan dapang.* This large outrigger canoe is decorated with carving. A *balutu* canoe that doesn't have a short deck in the bow cannot be called *dapang*, even if it is large. (*Thesaurus:* **balutu, bangka', londay, pallungan, pambot, paraw 1, pelang, pongag**)

**dapassuk** (derivative of **passuk**) *n.* A single group of people. *Na ka'am ilū dapassuk, kasehe' ilū dapassuk.* So you are one group, and you others are a group.

**dapat**₁ **1)** *n.* The failure to meet expectations or hopes. *Bay ka angamu' daing ni aku, yukku, "Bowaku salung." Na dapat ma aku bang aku halam makabowa. Ka'a angandapat.* If you ask me for some fish and I say, "I'll bring some tomorrow." Then it's my failure if I don't bring it. You are the one who is disappointed. **1.1)** *v. intr. aN-* To feel disappointed with what someone else has done. *Angarapat aku ma ka'a.* I am disappointed in you. **1.2)** *v. advrs. ka-...-an* To be disappointed in someone. *Karapatannu aku bang bay tambukuhannu subay lisag sangpū' bo' ka tinabang, ati halam aku pi'ilu.* You will be disappointed in me if you have told me it should be ten o'clock when you [need] help, and then I don't get there. *Min waktu lagi' kala'anna min okoman mma'na sampay ni kabuwattina'anan, halam iya karapatanku.* From the time he left his father's house until now, I have not felt disappointment in him. **2)** *v. advrs. ka-...-an* To be blamed; held responsible for. *Bang aniya' bay amu'ku ni ka'a, bo' aku buwanannu, bo' ka angahaka ganti'anku, asidda aku karapatan.* If I ask you for something and you give it to me, and then you say I am to replace it with a similar item, I am definitely to blame. *Karapatan kami e' Airline Ticketing, sabab sidda magpinda-pinda eskedyul kami.* We were held responsible by Airline Ticketing because our schedule kept changing so much.

**baldapat** *n.* An unreliable person.

**dapat**₂ *n.* An opportunity; a way forward; a possibility (usually with a negative). *Arōy.*

*Halam aniya' dapat.* Alas, we were unsuccessful. *Aniya' bay sīnku limampū' pilak arāk pam'lliku ai-ai ni M'ddas. Sakali bay pangongka'ku bo' tara'ug aku. Magsusun aku, yukku, "Halam aniya' dapatku."* I had fifty pesos intended for buying something in Siasi. I promptly used the money for playing but I was beaten. I regretted it and said [to myself], "I have no success."

**dapat-daya** *n.* Financial resources. {idiom} *Buwattina'an halam na tu'ud aniya' dapat-daya kami liyu min ka'am magtai'-anak niholat.* At the present time we have absolutely no financial resource apart from you and the family.

**dapdap** *n.* The coral tree, a colorful coastal species. *Erythrina sp.*

**dapig** var. of **dapit**

**dapit** (var. **dapig**) *v. tr. -an* To take someone's side in a dispute or conflict. *Niā' tapil bang b'nnal du aku angandapit ni ka'a.* Taken as support that I will truly take your side. *Bang kami magbono' maka si Nu ati anangis iya, nā nirapitan sidda he' Ina'. Paligay ah'lling aku, "Nirapitan na pa'in e' Ina'." Na luhūy iya anangis.* When I and Nu fight and he cries, Mother always takes his side. All the more so when I say, "Always supported by Mother!" *Sai-sai na pa'in kām angandapig ma aku?* Whoever of you will support me? (*Thesaurus:* **bogbog₁ 1.1, ga'os 1.2, gapi' 1.2, tapil 2**)

**dapitu'** *n.* A single week; one week. (*cf:* **pitu'an**)

**daplak** *v. intr. pa-* **1)** To splash against or over, of waves. *Pasampig ni luma' paraplak.* Reaching the house, splashing against it. **1.1)** *v. tr. -an* To move something by wave action. *Ai-ai pagūng niraplakan kaleya.* Anything floating is carried ashore.

**daplakan₁** *n.* The shoreline; the limit of wave action. (*Thesaurus:* **bihingan, gintana'an, hampilan, pari'an, susulan, tampe, tapiyan**)

**pagdaplak-daplak** *v. intr. aN-* To splash continually, of wave action. *Umpak-umpak itū ya tahik magdaplak-daplak. Umpak-umpak* refers to the sea continually splashing over.

**daplakan₂** *n.* The Goat's-foot vine. *Ipomoea pescaprae.* (*gen:* **bahan 1**)

**daplig** *v. intr. pa-* **1)** To knock hard against something while moving. *Bang pelangbi ilū paraplig ni luma' bo' ah'bba', ka'am ya angangganti'.* If that canoe of yours bangs against the house and it collapses, you will be the ones to make good the damage. *Ai-ai tanggungta makaraplig.* Whatever we carry on the shoulder can bang into [something]. (*Thesaurus:* **binggil, dugtul, sampig, sangku'**) **1.1)** *v. advrs. ka-...-an* To be struck by a moving object. *Karapligan ka he' lansa.* You'll be crushed by the moving launch. *Ala'an ka m'nnilu, man bohe' pasu', abō' mbal ka karapligan, abō' mbal alūs.* Get away from there, from the hot water, so you don't get

knocked into, so you aren't scalded.

**daplos** *v. tr. -an* To whip or beat a living creature. *Niraplosan sapi' apa alallay pal'ngngan.* Whip the cow because it walks slowly. *Nilambot, sali' niraplosan, busay ka atawa papan.* Hit with something, the same as being whacked with a paddle or a board. (*Thesaurus:* **balubak, lambot, lappet, lubak₁**)

**pagdaplos** *v. tr. -an* To beat or whip someone repeatedly.

**dapu** *n.* **1)** Ownership; possession. *Bay indamanku, ngga'i ka ma aku dapuna.* I borrowed it, its ownership is not mine. *Yuk sigām inān, "Kami ya dapu bohe' itū."* They said, "We are the proprietors of this water source." **1.1)** *v. tr.* To gain ownership rights over something. *Lahat ya song dapubi.* The land you are about to take possession of. *Palanjal sigām minnē' bo' nirapu saga katana'-tana'an ya pamasuku' ma sigām.* They went on from there and took possession of the lands that had been assigned to them.

**pagdapu** *n.* **1)** Ownership. **1.1)** *v. tr. -an* To dispute ownership rights over property. *Duwangan a'a magdapuhan alta' inān subay binowa ni paghuwisan bo' sinalassay.* The two men claiming ownership of those valuables should be taken to the magistrate to be sorted out. *Aniya' alungay daingku. Bang tabowa he' a'a, minsan ngga'i ka daluwa maka daingku, magdapu.* A fish of mine was lost. When a person carries it, even though it is not identical with my fish, we argue over ownership.

**papagdapu** *v. tr. -an* To acquire property, especially in the sense of simply taking it over without payment.

**tagdapu** *n.* Owner; proprietor.

**dapu'** *v. tr.* To beat a rhythm by tapping something firm. *Buwat aniya' magigal-igal, na nirapu'an ma papan.* Like when there are people dancing, the board is beaten to provide them with rhythm.

**dara'akan** (derivative of **da'ak**) *n.* A messenger; a servant. (*syn:* **sosoho'an**).

**daral** *n.* A pancake. (*gen:* **apam 1**)

**daran** *adj. a-* Frequent in occurrence; repetitive. *Araran sigā ilū pi'itu angamu' mital.* They frequently come here asking for a tin can. (*Thesaurus:* **bilang₁, masuhul, maumu**)

**daran-daran** *adv.* **1)** Habitually; repeatedly. **1.1)** *v. tr.* To do something repeatedly. *Niraran-daran, mbal agon pahali-hali.* Done [to someone] repeatedly, scarcely a break. (*Thesaurus:* **kara-kara₁, pagabut-abut, pagkuwat, sigi-sigi 1, toldas**)

**darangan** (derivative of **dangan**) *adj. zero* Limited to one person. *Pararangan du sīn itū, mbal tabahagi' ma kasehe'an.* This money is for one person, not to be shared with others.

**darut** (var. **larut**) *v. tr.* **1)** To tug something. *Nirarut bū langal si Ke.* Ke's whiskers have been tugged at. *Nijagjag luma' ilū, nirarut sampay hāg apa* *ilu'un na mundu.* The house there is being dismantled, even the posts pulled up because bandits are not far off. **1.1)** *v. tr. -an* To pull something out from its place. *Subay nirarutan emponnu, taga lowang na.* Your tooth should be pulled out, it has a hole. *Bang kita bay angosol, yukna, "Larutin ba soha' ilū."* When we had driven the mooring pole in, he said, "Pull that pole out!" (*Thesaurus:* **bubut, bugnus₂, hublut 1, tugnus₁ 1**)

  **pagdarut** *v. tr. -an* To pull at each other's hair or clothing. *Magbutug na kita baranta suma'an magdarut kita saga kōkta.* We punch each other and sometimes pull hair out of each other's heads.

    **dadarut** *n.* A tool for extracting teeth.

    **pangandararut** *n.* A dentist (lit. one who pulls things out).

**dasal** *v. intr. pa-* To spread over an area. *Momosun na ai-ai sikarasal-dasalan itu.* Tidy up these things strewn all over the place. (*Thesaurus:* **lakat, pagsilapug, pagsilapug, saplag 1**)

**dasali'** (derivative of **sali'**) *adj.* Identical. *Dasali' luwa sigām apa k'mbal.* Their appearance is identical because they are twins. *Empon maka baga'ang, emponta ya nilagnas bo' dasali'.* Front teeth and molars, it is our front teeth that are filed to make them even. (*cf:* **daluwa**).

  **pagdasali'** *v. intr. aN-* To be equal or identical, of two things.*Pinapagatap, pinapagdasali'.* Made to match; made to be the same.

**dasambal** (derivative of **sambal₁**) *adj.* Identical as to dimensions. *Dasambal pasagi' itū.* This milled lumber is equal in its dimensions.

**dasdas** *v. intr. pa-/-um-* To slip or slide off, of feet or wheels. *Arāk aku dumasdas ma batu. Takuddat aku.* I nearly slipped on the rock. I was startled. *Parasdas, ya bay kitam sangom angigal. Makarasdas tape'na, lumigid.* Slipping, like us dancing at night. Someone's foot slipped, going over an edge. *Sali' aku angandāg saloka', pag'ntanku pehē', parasdas aku pareyo'.* Like me climbing a coconut palm, holding on to it I slide down. (*cf:* **dusdus**; *Thesaurus:* **deklas, ligdas, ligid₂ 1, lisad, lisig, lumintiyad**)

**dasiyaw** *see:* **dumasiyaw**

**dasok** (var. **dagsok**) *adj. a-* **1)** Compressed into a container. *Sinanglag isāb, bang pasān apoka, mbal arasok.* Pan-roasted cassava meal too, at times it falls apart, not firmly packed. **1.1)** *v. tr.* To compress something into a container. *Buwat katas ma deyom tu'ung ilū, nihigin-nihigin nirasok.* Like the papers in that box, moved along a bit and stuffed in. (*Thesaurus:* **danos, d'ppon, p'nnod 1**)

**dasu** *n.* Fine satin cloth with a flower pattern. (*Thesaurus:* **bildu', buwal₂, lehag, lere-lere 1, pima, taplak₁**)

**dasuligan** (derivative of **sulig₁**) *adj.* Brought up together (as children). *Duma'in sigām dasuligan.*

They had not been brought up together.

**datag** *adj. a-* Flat or level, of a surface. *Bang lantayta magbigguwal mbal ahāp palegehan, sagō' bang papan aratag makahaluk tulita.* If we have irregular flooring it is not good to sleep on, but if [there are] flat wooden planks we sleep soundly. (*syn:* **pantay**)

  **karatagan** *n.* A flat region; a plain.

**datay₁** *adj. a-* Stale and unappetizing.

**datay₂** *adj. a-* Excessive; piled up. *Aratay daing ma M'ddas, mbal na takole' billi.* Fish are abundant in Siasi, unable to be bought. *Aratay itū aheka, pabūd.* A great many, piled up. (*Thesaurus:* **banos, besal, kansang 1, dayas-dayas, dorot, heka 1.1, jayak, parat**)

**datilis** *n.* The Jamaican cherry and its sweet fruit. *Muntingia kalabura.* (*syn:* **sokal-sokal**)

**datu'** *n.* A person of royal descent; a traditional leader. (*Thesaurus:* **dayang-dayang 1, salip, sultan**)

  **karatu'an** *n.* Traditional leaders as a class. *Sali' luma' karatu'an ya luma' ungkup itū.* These houses with outward-leaning gables are like the houses of traditional chiefs.

  **pagdatu'** *v. intr. aN-* To exercise the authority and rights of a traditional leader (datu). *Aniya' kono' sangpū' a'a min panubu'na makapagdatu' ma sinosōng.* It is said that ten men from his descendants will rule as *datu* in the future.

**Datu' Jumurain** *n. phrase* The ruler of the abode of the dead.

**datu'-datu'** *n.* A doll or manikin. *Am'lli aku datu'-datu' ni M'ddas pangongka'an siyaliku.* I buy a doll in Siasi for my younger sibling to play with. (*cf:* **munyeka, ta'u-ta'u₁**)

**dau-** *see section 2.2.2.4 Prefix:* **Cau-**

**daug 1)** *v. intr. aN-* To grow in clusters, with no gaps. *Angandaug na niyug inān.* Those coconut palms are growing clusters [of nuts]. (*Thesaurus:* **pingkit 1.1, pulingkit, puliting, pungut 1, tundun 1**) **2)** *clf.* Count word for clusters of fruit. *Dandaug pola.* One cluster of new betel nuts.

  **daugan** *n.* A dense cluster or bunch. *Ahāp dauganna, buwat botong sala magpulingkit.* Its bunch is good, sort of like young coconuts clustered together.

**daugdug** var. of **daogdog**

**dauhat₁** *adv.* **1)** Physically close to. *An'ngge ka parauhat.* Stand up close to. **1.1)** *v. tr.* To approach someone closely. *Bay aku nirauhat e'na.* He came right up to me. **1.2)** *v. intr. pa-* To go close to someone. *Mahē' magtimuk, magkahāp maka bay banta. Magtūy aku parauhat pasiyum. Magkaki kami sampay ni dunya hē' i.* Coming together there, becoming reconciled with a former enemy. I immediately went up and kissed him. We are cousins until the other world.

**dauhat₂** *v. intr. pa-* **1)** To move decisively and

vigorously. *Amusay kita parauhat ni tongod bay pam'ssihanta hē'.* Let us paddle hard right now to the spot where we were fishing before. *Parauhat kita pariyata'an, sali' angagga'-nagga'.* Let's push upstream, like fighting the current. *Mahē' magtimuk, magkahāp maka bay banta. Magtūy aku parauhat pasiyum.* Coming together there, making peace with someone who had been an enemy. I immediately went right [to them] and kissed. **1.1)** *v. tr.* To get something by going against the current. *Dauhatun na, ngā'un na.* Go upstream for it, get it.

**dauman** *see:* **pagdauman**

**daumpigan** *n.* A group coming together on a cooperative project. *Buwat aniya' magbono' bo' kami itū saga t'llungan. Yuk kami, "Asal ka'am ilū daumpigan."* It's like when there is a fight and there are about three of us. We say, "Because you are a united group."

**daumu'an** *n.* Various non-spiny bamboos. *Bambusa spp.* (*Thesaurus:* **kagingking, kayawan, kayuwan, p'ttung, t'mmang**)

**daun** (var. **dahun**₁) *n.* A leaf. *Aniya' daun saging bang amatay dāg.* There are [fresh] banana leaves when the dried leaves have finished. *Angā' aku daun kaleya pangahinangku biyaki'.* I will get some leaves inland for making *biyaki'.* *Daun jati' pagtimayukan.* Teak leaves for wrapping food taken home by guests. (*wh:* **kayu 1**)

**daun-kapay** *n.* A propeller blade.

**daun-salirap** *n.* Coconut palm leaflets, useful for weaving into temporary walling. *Daun salirap nihinang pagbanog-banog.* Palm leaflets made into sailing toys.

**daupang** *n.* A tree species, the flowers of which are used for the treatment of oral ulcers.

**dauranakan** (derivative of **danakan**) *n.* **1)** Siblings in a collective sense. **2)** Members of a religious community or fraternity.

**dauyunan** (derivative of **uyun**) *n.* **1)** An agreement; consensus. **1.1)** *adj.* Of the same mind.

**dawa** *n.* Millet, the plant and its edible grain. *Setaria italica.* (*syn:* **doha**)

**dawat** *n.* **1)** The lead in a pencil. *Dawat pinsil ya isina pagsulatan.* The lead of a pencil, its inside used for writing. (*cf:* **ing**) **1.1)** *v. tr.* -*an* To make a written mark on something. *Angay mbal angandawat bolpen itu?* Why doesn't this ball pen make a mark? *Da'a dawatin katasku.* Don't make marks on my paper.

**daya** *adj.* -*an* Affluent; wealthy. *Dayahan itu aheka sīn, buwat ka'am. Dayahan* is having a lot of money, like you. (*Thesaurus:* **balkan, haldaya, mayaman, sayuman**)

**daya-damuli** *n.* The rewards received in the afterlife. *Mbal pamagay e' sigā daya-damuli.* They care nothing for the rewards of the afterlife.

**karaya** *n.* **1)** Wealth; financial security.

(*Thesaurus:* **alta' 1, kaniya', pagsauragal 1.1**) **1.1)** *adj.* -*an* To be becoming wealthy. *Minsan miskin makajari karayahan.* Even a poor person can become wealthy.

**paraya** *n.* **1)** A person of wealth. **1.1)** *v. tr.* -*an* To make someone wealthy. *Da'a aku pamiskinin atawa parayahin.* Don't make me either rich or poor.

**daya'** *v. intr.* pa- To lie face upwards, as a person or canoe. *Paraya' kita, m'ssa' pakkom.* We lie face up, not face down. (*ant:* **da'ub**; *Thesaurus:* **hagtang, hantal, haya'**₁, **leyak, pagduleyak**)

**dayang** (var. **dāng**) *voc. n.* A term of affectionate address to a female. (*Thesaurus:* **arung, neneng-neneng, nne', nneng 1, nnong**)

**dayang-dayang** *n.* **1)** A woman of royal blood. (*Thesaurus:* **datu', salip, sultan**) **1.1)** *voc. n.* Address form to a woman of royal blood.

**dayas-dayas** *adj.* a-/-an Abundant, of life's necessities. *Dayas-dayasan, sali' aheka kinakan atas pinagtimanan ya takapin inān apa a'sso na.* Over abundant, like there's so much food that what's left might just as well be thrown out because [we] are full. *Ahāp palasahanku maka dayas-dayasan.* I was well and experienced abundance. (*Thesaurus:* **banos, besal, kansang 1, datay**₂, **dorot, heka 1.1, jayak, parat**)

**pagdayas-dayas** *v. intr.* aN- To occur in great abundance, of basic necessities. *Magdayas-dayas ma kinakan, ma bohe', ma daing, ma sīn.* There is a great abundance with regard to food, water, fish, money. *Pagsōd sigām pehē', ta'nda' e' sigām gula' buwani inān magdayas-dayas.* On going into that place, they saw a great abundance of that honey.

**dayaw** *see:* **pagdayaw, pangdayaw**

**dayung** *n.* **1)** An oar. **1.1)** *v. tr.* -*an* To row a boat using an oar or paddle against a fulcrum. *Nirayungan itū subay ma kumpit. Dakayu' ma dambila', dakayu' isāb ma dambila'. Dangan amansān amuli'-muli'.* Being moved by rowing must refer to a cargo launch. One [rower] on this side, another on that. One person steering, working over the stern. (*Thesaurus:* **busay 1.1, kelle 1.1, epe, luwad, tindayung**)

**dda** var. of **ssa**₃

**ddas** (var. **t'ddas**) *v. intr.* pa- **1)** To endure for a long period; to be delayed. *Mbal na pa'in kita pa'ddas allum. Magkasosōng ato'a kita, magkamamatay kita. Minsan kita pa'ddas maitu, amole' du ni ahirat.* We can never stay alive for long. As time goes on we get old, we go on to die. Even if we do remain here for a long time, we will eventually go home to the world beyond. *Bang aku angā' bohe' bo' ap'nno' na kibut, mbal na pa'in pa'ddas bang ni'inum.* When I fetch water and the jar is filled, it won't last long when it is being drunk. (*Thesaurus:* **lanat, lehod 1.1, t'ddas 1**) **1.1)** *v. tr.* To prolong or defer some action. *Bang aniya' angindam mitalnu, mbal pinole'an. Subay* *tin'ddas he'na. Subay ka'a-i angā'.* When someone borrows your water cans, they aren't returned. He wants to hang on to them, and you have to go get them. (*Thesaurus:* **pagli'i-li'i, tagga 1.1, tahāl**) **1.2**) *v. advrs.* **ka-...-an** To be affected by long delay. *Ka'ddasan kahawa itū, mbal na tainum.* This coffee has stood too long, it's undrinkable. *Ka'ddasan luma' kami apa halam gi' akatis. Halam aniya' sīn pam'lli atop.* Our house is long delayed, not yet completed. There is no money to buy roofing. *Wa'i na atuli ka'ddasan.* Gone off to sleep for ages. *Ka'ddasan kami ma pelang.* We are stuck here on the canoe.

**ddik** *v. tr.* **-an** To hold something down by placing a foot on it. *Bang aku atuli, nīddikan aku e' siyaliku. Tabati' aku pabīng.* When I am asleep my younger brother steps on me. I am woken up again. (*syn:* **paddik**; *Thesaurus:* **d'dda, gi'ik 1**)

**paddik** *v. tr.* **-an** To hold something down by stepping on it. (*syn:* **ddik**)

**pang'ddikan** *n.* Something that is walked on.

**ddok** *adj.* **a-** Sound, of sleep. *Addok tulina, ahaluk sali'.* He's sleeping soundly, like unbroken sleep. (*Thesaurus:* **haluk, pagon₂**)

**pag'ddok** *n.* The stage when one sleeps soundly. *Da'a kam asagaw, waktu pag'ddok na atuli.* Don't make a noise, it's time now for sleeping soundly.

**ddol-ddol** *v. tr.* **-an** To force something into a space unsuited for it. *Da'a ddol-ddolin soha' bo' mbal apōng.* Don't force the mooring stake in lest it break in two. *Mbal ka'ddol-ddolan jalum ilu.* That needle there cannot be forced into [the sailcloth].

**ddon** *v. tr.* **-an** To expel something by exerting downward muscular pressure, as when excreting or giving birth.

**ddong** *v. intr.* **aN-** To become erect, of a penis.

**ddop** *v. advrs.* **-in-** Suffering from nightmares or disturbed sleep. *Nīddop iya, sali' pin'kkol e' saitan.* He has a nightmare, as though being strangled by a *saitan* spirit. (*Thesaurus:* **ansong, lāp-lāp, mutamad, pagdabdab, uppi 1**)

**pag'ddop** *v. tr.* To suffer from nightmares. *Bang kita atuli ma deyo' hobong atawa ma hāg, maumu pinag'ddop, maumu mbal.* When we sleep beneath a crossbeam or near a house-post [some of us are] often troubled by nightmares, some are not.

**dduk** *var. of* **l'dduk**

**ddut** *n.* A thick-stemmed plant, a source of starch in famine times. *Ddut sali' bagong. Hal kīllo' lumbiyana, nili'is.* Ddut is like the elephant's foot plant. Only its starchy substance is taken. It is grated.

**dē** *v. advrs.* **-in-** To be made ill by the sight of a deceased relative's spirit. *Angkan magkasakihan si To, pasal nirē e' ina'na.* The reason To is sick, his deceased mother appeared to him.

**deklas** *v. intr.* **pa-** To slip off something slippery, as feet off a path. *Bang aku lum'ngngan kaleya bo' bay ulan-ulan, makareklas na, al'mmis na*

*pantalunku.* When I walked inland and there had been some rain, and I happened to slip, my trousers became dirty. (*Thesaurus:* **dasdas, ligdas, ligid₂ 1, lisad, lisig, lumintiyad**)

**dekoresyon** *n.* Decoration, of a building or public place.

**pangoresyon** *n.* Things used as a decorative feature.

**dēg** *var. of* **dē'**

**degsal** *var. of* **d'ssal**

**dē'** (*var.* **dēg**) *n.* **1)** A call to a child. **1.1)** *v. tr.* To call a child in a cajoling tone. *Nirē' onde'-onde' he' mbo'na d'nda.* The child is enticed by its grandmother. (*Thesaurus:* **lingan 1, owa'₁ 1, sabbut 1.1, tawag**)

**delat** *v. tr.* To take in something by licking; to lap up. *Ero' angandelat, manuk anginum.* Dogs lap up [liquid], chickens drink. *A: "Delatun itu." B: "Ai delatku?" A: "Aeskrīm."* A: "Lick this" B: "What am I to lick?" A: "Icecream."

**pagdelat** *v. intr.* **aN-** To take turns at licking something. *Magdelatan dī sigā karuwangan, mags'lle' sigā bo' dakayu' kende tab'lli.* The two of them licking, they take turns, having bought a single candy.

**delos** *var. of* **lilus**

**depan** *v. intr.* **pa-** **1)** To become flat, of something that was protruding. *Parepan na kalibubutku, sali' paratag.* My boil has become flat, sort of smoothing off. (*cf:* **pedda' 1.1**) **1.1)** *v. tr.* To make something flat. *Depanta pitsa nihinang pangongka'an.* We flatten bottle caps to be made into toys.

**depende** *adv.* Dependent on some factor or other.

**pagdepende** *v. tr.* To consider various aspects of an action.

**deplas** (*var.* **teplas**) *adj.* **a-** **1)** Cut or struck obliquely; to glance off a surface. *Ī' ateplas tanganku, bay pali'an e' bari'.* My hand has a shallow cut, slashed with a working knife. (*cf:* **sulempat**; *Thesaurus:* **diplay, dupli'as) 1.1**) *v. advrs.* **ka-...-an** To be cut at an angle. *Kareplasan tanganku.* My hand has a glancing cut. **1.2)** *v. tr.* To hit something at too flat an angle and glance off.

**deretso** *var. of* **diretso**

**deya** (*var.* **dileya**) *loc. n.* Inland, in contrast to sea and coastal plain. *Aniya' isāb ma dileya bo' duma'in ka ma tana', patanom, sali' kal'bbohan.* There are places inland that are not on soil, [one] sinks in, it's like a bog. *Ina'an ma deyata itū.* There on our landward side. *Aniya' patay bay ta'nda'na ma deya, ma liyu bohe'.* He saw a dead body inland, beyond the water [source]. *Hē' ma deya angā' bohe'.* There inland fetching water.

**kareyahan** *n.* Inland environment; land in contrast to the sea. *Ina'an iya maka saga tendogna magpustu ma kareyahan.* There he is with his followers, camped out in the hill country.

**deya-dilaut** *n.* Everywhere (lit. land and sea). *Bay pihaku deya-dilaut.* I searched everywhere, land and sea.

**deyag** *see:* **pagdeyag, parereyagan**

**deyo'**₁ *loc. n.* 1) The location or area below something. *Niugam man deyo' d'lla'nu.* Under your tongue is infected with white spots. *Bang aku bay abuhaw, la'ananku banog ē' maka dambila' katig. Pehē'ku ni deyo' taddas pelang ati pabuhat mariyata'.* If I capsize I remove the sail and the outrigger on one side. Then I put it beneath the keel of the canoe and it lifts up. (*ant:* **diyata' 1**) 1.1) *v. intr. pa-* To descend. *Pareyo' na kami.* We are going down [from the house]. (*Thesaurus:* **duwa'i, hollo**) 1.2) *v. tr.* To get something by going down for it. *Bay ahūg laringku; deyo'ku pa'in.* My knife fell down; I will get it by going down.

**deyo' pikpik** *n. phrase* Secure place underneath a bird's wing; a place of protection (fig.) {idiom} *Bang bowanu pehē' da'a na pal'ppahun min deyo' pikpiknu.* If you are taking it there don't let it escape from under your wing. *Sali' sapantun manuk d'nda bang magsabak anak-anakna ma deyo' pikpikna.* Poetically like a hen when she holds her chicks close under her wings.

**deyo'-deyo'**₁ *adj. a-* Short in stature. (*Thesaurus:* **pandak, p'ndok, pu'ut**)

**deyo'an** *loc. n.* Districts to the southwest of Central Sulu.

**pareyo'**₁ *adv.* In a downwards direction.

**pareyo'-pariyata'** *adv.* Entirely; fully. {idiom} *Lungbus aku pareyo'-pariyata' ma sakap bayanan.* I am fully equipped with canoe gear. (*Thesaurus:* **jukup 1, lungbus**)

**deyo'**₂ *n.* 1) The ocean floor. (*Thesaurus:* **kantil**₂, **pampang, temang, titib**) 2) The ruling spirit being of the deep sea.

**deyo'**₃ 1) *adj. a-* Humble as to social standing. *Sampay isāb saga ka'mbo'an kami, a'a areyo' du ko' ma bangsa kami.* Our ancestors too, they were low-status people in our ethnic group. 2) *v. intr. pa-* To abase oneself to someone, as when seeking forgiveness. *Pareyo' aku ni ka'a magpa'ampun. Siniyum tape'-tangannu.* I will abase myself before you to ask forgiveness, kissing your feet and hands. (*Thesaurus:* **pagkahāp, pagpa'ampun, ū'ū**) 2.1) *v. tr.* To make someone the object of a request for reconciliation. *Amatay nireyo' he' sehe'na, atuwas na pa'in.* His companion exhaustively sought reconciliation, but he remained obdurate.

**deyo'-deyo'**₂ *adj. zero* Low in social standing.

**pagdeyo'-addat** *n.* 1) An attitude of respect and humility. *Magsujud sigām ma si Esaw tanda' sin pagdeyo'-addat sigām ma iya.* They prostrated themselves before Esau as a sign of their humility towards him. 1.1) *v. intr. aN-* To display an attitude of respect.

**pagpatireyo'** (var. **pagmatireyo'**) *v. intr. aN-* To show humility by making oneself lower in worth or rank. (*Thesaurus:* **duku', luku'**₂, **luhud, sujud**)

**deyom** *loc. n.* 1) The inner part; the space contained by an enclosure. *Atiya' sīnnu ma deyom bulsaku.* Here is your money inside my pocket. *Ap'ddi' deyomna itū.* The inner part of it is sore. *Bang Milikan ya pihanu, ina'an iya ma deyom.* If it is the Westerner you seek, he is there inside. *Mbal panata' ni kita bang kita ma deyom asayu.* It won't appear to us while we are in a conscious state. *Ma deyom dambulan.* For the space of a month. (*ant:* **luwasan**) 1.1) *v. intr. pa-* To enter an enclosed space. *Pareyom ka kono'.* Please go in. (*Thesaurus:* **asok 1, isi**₁ **1.1, sōd 1**)

**deyom sipuk** *n. phrase* In secret; under cover. {idiom} *Ma buwattina'an aniya' a'a magkahinangan ai-ai mamarahi la'atna, sagō' ma deyom sipuk.* At present there are people doing things that are very bad, but in secret.

**deyom-bulan** *n.* The first day after new moon. (*gen:* **bulan**₂ **2**)

**deyom-deyom atay** *n. phrase* Something fixed securely in one's memory, especially a grudge. {idiom} *Kata'uhanku deyom-deyom ataynu. Ah'lling ka kono'.* I know what you are holding back. Please speak up. (*Thesaurus:* **akon-akon, agmol 1, buli'an**₂, **koto'-koto', lagod-lagod**)

**deyoman** *n.* 1) The space inside. 2) The sphere of someone's care or control. *Aku ya angatas sat'ggol ka ma deyomanku.* I will be responsible for your needs as long as you are in my care. (*Thesaurus:* **komkoman 2, milikan, okoman, pang'ntanan**₁)

**dī**₁ *ptl.* Reflexive marker. Attaches to Set II pronouns, meaning '-self', e.g. myself, yourself, him/herself. *Anapukan iya dīna. Amono' iya dīna.* He hides himself. He will kill himself. *Aniya' du batu agkalitib, aniya' isāb batu alitiban dīna.* There are indeed rocks that can wear each other down, there are also rocks that simply wear down of themselves. *Buwat kita amowa tinapay bo' arigpit, yukta, "Tu'ud arigpitan dīna"* Like when we carry bread and it gets squeezed together, we say, "It simply squeezed itself." *Angkanna bilahi na aku magh'nda'an dīku ati ala'an na aku min okoman sigām.* That's why I want to get married on my own and then I will leave their sphere of influence.

**dī**₂ *adj. zero* Assertion of quality or purity. *Dī bulawan ko' itū.* This is authentic gold. *Dī goma pantalunku.* My long pants have real rubber. *Mbal sali' agabul e'ta ang'nda', magtūy dī aballag.* Our sight is not sort of blurred, it is really clear all of a sudden.

**di** var. of **disi**

**dibay** *see:* **pagparibay**

**dibuhi'** *adv.* Last night. *Dibuhi' bay kami tinangkawan pelang e' si Al.* Last night we had a canoe stolen by Al. *Sidda ka anangis dibuhi'.*

*Halam aku bay makatuli.* You cried so much last night. I was unable to sleep. (*cf:* **bahangi 1**)

**dibusaw** var. of **libusaw**

**dikayu'** var. of **dakayu'₁**

**diki'** (var. **diki'-diki'**) *adj. a-* 1) Small; few. *Kabatuhan ariki' tana'na.* A rocky place with little soil. *Ariki' lahat ya pagbākantam itū.* This place where we are meeting is of limited size. *Pangalta' bay tataban sigā aheya-ariki'.* Goods big and small that they plundered. *Mala'u-la'u, ariki' a'ana, sali' bang mbal aheka ma lahat.* Lonely, few people, as when there are few inhabitants. *Ariki' gi' kā, Oto'. Da'a kā asusa, paheya ru.* You are still small, Son. Don't worry, you'll get bigger. *Bigi-tinanom ariki'-riki'.* Tiny seeds. (*ant:* **heya 1.1**; *Thesaurus:* **kiput, nahut**) 1.1) *v. intr. aN-* To become small or few; to diminish. *Angandiki', bay aheka ai-ai ati sali' halam na.* Becoming few, there used to be many things and now there are almost none. 1.2) *v. tr. -an* To reduce the size or amount of something. *Subay niriki'an banog apa ilu alandos baliyu.* The sail should be taken in a bit because there is a strong wind coming up. (*cf:* **sampila'₂**; *Thesaurus:* **kobos, kulang₁ 1.3, dagdag₁, hilang, putung, sulak₁**)

**kariki'an** *n.* The relative smallness of something. *Minsan la'a hal bantug ma kariki'an.* Even though it is just a boast of something small.

**pariki'** *v. tr. -an* To make something small by removing part of it.

**diki'-diki'** var. of **diki'**

**dikisa** *v. tr.* 1) To investigate things or persons. *Luma' inān dikisaku, kalu tinapukan he' sigā ai-ai bay malungay min aku.* I will search that house for evidence, maybe they have hidden the things that I lost. *Bang aniya' bay anangkaw, dikisata, tilawta, "Bay ka anangkaw?"* When someone has committed a theft, we interrogate them, asking, "Did you steal something?" 1.1) *v. tr. -an* To examine evidence. *Nirikisahan ai-ainu kamemon bang ka sinaggaw.* All your things examined when you are arrested.

**didjiki'** var. of **lidjiki'**

**digpit** *adv.* 1) Tightly fitting. *Nili'id, sali' sinekot parigpit.* Pressed hard, sort of snuggled up to. (*Thesaurus:* **sigpit 2, s'mpok 1, sukad**) 1.1) *v. intr. pa-* To squeeze together as people in a confined space. *Parigpit ka pi'itu.* Squeeze in here.

**pagdigpit** *v. intr. aN-* 1) To get close together, side by side. *Puhu' aheka sinō' magdigpit na kamemon.* Lots of people asked to sit close to each other. 1.1) *v. tr.* To put things close togther, edge to edge. *Pagdigpitun tiyadtad ilū.* Get that bamboo walling close together.

**di'ilaw** *adv.* Yesterday. (*Thesaurus:* **llaw itu, ma t'llu, salung, simuddai**)

**di'in-di'in** *v. tr.* To treat someone disrespectfully. *Niri'in-di'in kita he' tagdapu luma'. Mbal kita sali'*

*pinaheya ma atay.* The owner of the house does not treat us well. We don't matter to him. (*Thesaurus:* **halipulu 1.1, hampul-hampul 1, mahadja'**)

**dilam** *n.* An inexpensive gemstone. (*Thesaurus:* **intan, palmata 1, puntu' 1**)

**dilaut** *loc. n.* The sea in contrast to land and shore; open sea in contrast to sheltered water. *Dilaut mbal sakit atā to'ongan min bihing. Na timbang, alawak. Atā kaut timbang. Dilaut* [at sea] is not really distant from the shore. *Timbang* now, that is distant. *Timbang* is far out at sea. *Ma t'ngnga' kami dilaut alandos goyak.* When we were in the middle of the ocean the sea was very rough. (*Thesaurus:* **kablangan, kaladjun, s'llang₁, timbang₂**)

**karilautan** *n.* The ocean environment, in contrast to land.

**parilaut** *adv.* 1) Towards open sea. 1.1) *v. intr. zero* To go out to sea. *Alandos goyak itū, mbal kita makaparilaut.* This rough weather is extreme, we can't go out to sea.

**dileya** var. of **deya**

**dimpulag** *v. intr. pa-* To leave rapidly, as in fright or shock; to escape, as in fear. *Parimpulag, sali' maglahi'an.* Going in panic, as though escaping. *Tininduk kita, wa'i tananamta parimpulag.* Our bait is taken, we feel [the fish] racing away. *Atāw kita hē', makarimpulag kita alahi.* We were afraid then, we ran away in fear. (*cf:* **lumpat**)

**dindang-dindang** *v. tr. -an* To soothe a child by singing a lullaby. (*Thesaurus:* **aluk, apu'-apu', kalang₁ 1, kerol, pagbinuwa 1, sayudja' 1, tenes-tenes**)

**dinding** (var. **dingding**) *n.* 1) The exterior wall of a house. *Ginipis dinding bo' ahogot.* The wall is battened so it is secure. (*cf:* **kulambu' 1**) 1.1) *v. tr. -an* To divide a space by building a wall.

**dinding-hali** *n.* The boards which keep earth from moving onto the burial shelf as a grave is filled. (*Thesaurus:* **kubul 1, kuddaman, gumi 2, paliyangan**)

**dinsini'** var. of **insini'**

**dingding** var. of **dinding**

**dinggi-dinggi** *n.* A Western style rowboat or dinghy. (*Thesaurus:* **buti, katel-katel**)

**dingin** *n.* 1) Coldness, of temperature. (*ant:* **pasu'₁ 1**; *Thesaurus:* **k'ttol, haggut 1.2, hagpay 1, t'nne 1**) 1.1) *adj. a-* Cold in contrast to normal or hot, of water, air temperature or food. *Arōy, aringin!* Wow, it's cold!

**pangandingin** *n.* A season or period of cold weather.

**dinglu'** 1) *adj. zero* Diamond-shaped or triangular. *Bilahi aku apam nihīk dinglu'-dinglu'.* I love pancakes cut into triangular slices. 2) *n.* A pancake of sago meal cut into triangle and diamond shapes. *Asarap lumbiya dinglu'.* Triangle-cut sago cakes are delicious. (*gen:* **apam 1**)

**dipinaw** *adj. zero* Fine in texture, of brown sugar. (*Thesaurus:* **pilun, sokal 1**)

**dipisil** *adj. zero* Difficult; impossible. (*cf:* **hunit 1, mustahil**)

**diplay** *v. intr. pa-* To cut or strike at too flat an angle. *Bang kita anigad kayu pariplay bari'.* When we slash at the wood the knife glances off. *Da'a pariplayun gayang ilū.* Don't let that bush knife glance off. (*Thesaurus:* **deplas 1, dupli'as**)

**diretso** (var. **deretso**) *adv.* Directly, without delay or diversion. *Bang kaskona akapal, nihinang diretso lowang.* If its hull is thick, the [mast] hole is made directly into it.

**diril-diril** *n.* Parallel rows. (*Thesaurus:* **badlis, dirit₁ 1, sapan₁ 1, tād, tagik**)

  **pagdiril-diril** *v. tr.* To be arranged in rows. *Ya luwasan langgal inān bay pinahinangan ād min t'llu bangkat batu magdiril-diril.* The outside of the prayer house had a fence made for it from three layers of stone set out in rows.

**dirit₁** (var. **dairit**) *n.* **1)** A row of items, people or plants. (*Thesaurus:* **badlis, diril-diril, sapan₁ 1, tād, tagik**) **1.1)** *v. intr. pa-* To be laid out in lines or rows; to run parallel. *Sali' paririt badlisan niyug.* The rows of coconut palms sort of run parallel. **1.2)** *v. tr.* To arrange things in rows. *Niririt p'ttung tinundan, subay tinugutan binuwanan landahan.* Bamboo lengths are lined up for towing. They should be let out further, given some slack.

  **pagdirit** *v. intr. aN-* **1)** To set items in rows. *Abontol, sali' magdirit-dirit.* Straight, as though set out in rows. **1.1)** *v. tr.* To arrange things in parallel rows. *Pagdiritun bang ka amat'nna' ai-ai. Da'a pagbangkatun bo' mbal abila'.* Set things in rows when you are laying them out. Don't stack them lest they break.

**dirit₂** *n.* Epiphytic plant with very large leaves.

  **dirit-dirit** *n.* The skeletal leaf of the dirit plant after the green matter has decayed. *Dirit-dirit pinaghinang taguri' he' saga onde'-onde'.* Leaf skeletons made into *taguri'*-type kites by children.

**diskared** *adj. a-* Discouraged; lacking enthusiasm.

**diskās** *see:* **pagdiskās**

**disi** (var. **di**) *ptl.* Personal name marker, plural. Used before the name of a person plus his or her companions. *Wa'i magbono' disi Anu.* What's-his-name and his companions are fighting. *Pelang disi Al bay nilangpasan dibuhi' maka kapanyapanna.* The canoe of Al and others was taken by force last night with all its gear. *Ina'an magtambal ma luma' disi Sēl.* There getting treatment at Sir and his family's house. *A: "Yuk sai?" B: "Yuk di Mma'."* A: "Who said so?" B: "Father and others did." (*Thesaurus:* **si**)

**dita'i** *v. intr. zero* To go up onto or into, as a house by way of the ladder, or a vessel by a gangplank. *Dita'i ka ni luma' bang aniya' gawinu.* Go up into the house if you have a purpose.

(*ant:* **duwa'i**; *Thesaurus:* **diyata' 1.1, sakat₂**)

**diya** var. of **ndiya**

**diyag** *v. intr. pa-* To turn one's eyes upwards, a symptom of shock or sickness. *Pariyag itū buwat du par'llag ina'an, sali' kita amangguwa'.* This word is the same as *d'llag*, opening the eyes wide as we do when pretending to be a ghost. (*Thesaurus:* **kaniyang-kaniyang, d'llag 1, pagduliyag**)

**diyandi** *n.* Patterned calico; any fine check pattern. (*Thesaurus:* **kusta 1, tabanas 1.1, tadjung**)

**diyat** *v. tr. -an* To compensate someone for doing him a non-fatal injury. *Bang aniya' pali'an atawa busulan subay niriyatan.* If anyone is wounded or bruised he should be compensated. *Niriyatan bang aniya' bay baynat. Binayaran laha'ta basta aniya' pa'alom ma kita. Subay kita tinu'ud.* Compensated when there has been evidence. Our blood is compensated for any time a bruise appears on us. We must have been hurt deliberately. (*Thesaurus:* **ayu', bangun₂ 1, masangka**)

**diyata'** *loc. n.* **1)** Location or area above. *Hē' na ma diyata' langit.* There it is up in the sky. *Ya manuk-manuk ē' ma diyata' luma'.* The bird there on top of the house. *Ya mbal kasōng pelang sabab aheka ma diyata'na.* What keeps the canoe from progressing is so much [loaded] on to it. (*ant:* **deyo'₁ 1**) **1.1)** *v. intr. pa-* To ascend onto something. (*Thesaurus:* **dita'i, sakat₂**)

  **pagpariyata'** *v. tr.* To raise something, especially a flag.

  **pariyata'** *adv.* Upwards; in an upwards direction.

**diyata'an₁** *loc. n.* **1)** The area on the upstream side of a reference point. *Sohonayan s'llog maka diyata'an s'llog, hatina kōkan s'llog.* The area downstream in relation to the current and the area upstream, in other words the head side of the current. (*Thesaurus:* **kōkan 1, sibayan, sohonayan, tape'an**) **1.1)** *v. intr. pa-* To move upstream from a place.

  **pariyata'an** *n.* The direction from which an ocean current is flowing.

**diyata'an₂** *n.* The advantage in a contest. *Ata'u anabid lling. Ai-ai pinah'lling he' dangan ta'ā' sadja diyata'an he' dangan.* He knows how to twist words. Whatever one says the other takes advantage of. *Ta'ā' sadja diyata'anna bang maghukum maka sehe'na.* He invariably gets an advantage when he goes to law with his companion.

**diyuhan** *n.* The customary limit on something, as the limit on bride-wealth. *Mbal kita makajari paliyu min diyuhan mbo'.* It is not proper for us to go beyond the [bride-wealth] limit of the ancestors. (*Thesaurus:* **hād 1**)

**d'kkal** *v. intr. pa-* To be adequate or suited for one person only. *Par'kkal ma aku hinang itū. Dangan-dangan maghinang, halam aniya' anabangan aku.*

The work is adequate for me. Working alone, with no one helping me.

**par'kkal** *v. tr.* To reserve a specific item.

**d'dda** *v. intr.* pa- To come down hard on something. *Wa'i par'dda tu'ung ni lantay luma'.* The box has come down hard against the floor of the house. (*Thesaurus:* **ddik, gi'ik 1**)

**par'dda** *v. tr.* To place something firmly on a surface. (*cf:* **d'ssal**)

**d'ddol** *v. tr.* To lever something against a fulcrum. *Nir'ddol busay buwattē' bo' makasagga'.* The paddle is levered hard like that so as to make headway. (*cf:* **dagtol₁**)

**d'ddos** *adj.* zero Remaining in one place. *D'ddos kami maitu. Sali' mbal na magla'an-la'an.* We are settled here. No longer moving from place to place. (*Thesaurus:* **kakkal, dorog₁, taptap 1, tattal, t'ttog 1**)

**pagd'ddos** *v. intr.* aN- To remain unchanged in one place or condition.

**pagd'ddosan** *n.* A permanent location. *Ai-ai kabaya'anta mareyom junna hal palabay min kita. Pagd'ddosan lahat ē' i.* Whatever we desire on this earth passes away from us. That [other] land is where we stay permanently.

**d'llag** *v. intr.* pa-/aN- 1) To open one's eyes wide. *Ī' par'llag!* There! Staring at you! [Said of something a person is looking for.] *Buwattē' angand'llag si Ne.* Ne opens his eyes wide, like that. (*Thesaurus:* **kaniyang-kaniyang, diyag, pagduliyag**) 1.1) *v. tr.* To stare or glare at someone.

**d'lla'** *n.* The tongue. *Abakat d'lla'ku, tambalin kono'.* My tongue has been cut, please treat it.

**d'lla'-sapi'** *n.* Oval puff pastry known in Cebuano as otap.

**d'llang-d'llang** *n.* The uvula and adjacent areas of the mouth. *Kino'ot d'llang-d'llang bo' ala'an kowa' mareyom k'llong.* The uvula is reached into to remove the fishbone from inside the throat.

**d'llot** *adj.* a- 1) Pulled tight, as a knot or line. *"Ar'llot," yukta, bang kita tininduk.* "It's taut," we say, when our bait is taken. (*Thesaurus:* **pigtal 1, p'nggod 1, sandat 1**) 1.1) *v. tr.* To pull tight the threads of a knot or lashing. *Subay aniya' engkotanta, subay d'llotta ko da'a abuklas.* There should be something for us to tie to, it should be pulled tight so it doesn't come undone. *Mbal a'kka bang dīllot.* It won't come undone if pulled tight.

**d'nda** *n.* 1) A woman. (*cf:* **l'lla 1**) 1.1) *adj.* zero Female; feminine. *Sapi' d'nda ko' inān.* That's a cow over there.

**kar'ndahan** *n.* Womenfolk; the woman's side in marriage discussions.

**d'nda pagtatambahan** *n. phrase* A prostitute; a sex worker. {idiom} *Mbal bilahi saga danakanna si Di l'lla in iya nihinang d'nda pinagtatambahan.* Di's brothers did not want her to be treated as a prostitute.

**pagd'nda** 1) *n.* The mating season; the act of mating, of animals. *Aniya' bay tauppina ma waktu pagd'nda saga kambing.* He dreamed about something at the time when goats mate. 1.1) *v. intr.* aN- To be mating, as animals or birds. *Saga kambing l'lla ya magd'nda ilū, kabang lullun maka jali'-jali'an.* The male goats that were mating there were all variegated and striped. 2) *v. intr.* aN- To be having sex with women other than one's wife.

**kapagd'nda** *n.* 1) Femininity. 1.1) *n.* Female genitalia.

**pagkar'nda** *n.* The distinctive features of a woman.

**d'nda-balu** *var.* of **balu-d'nda**

**d'nnat** *n.* 1) Bloody pus. (*Thesaurus:* **nana', sagu**) 1.1) *v. intr.* aN- To discharge bloody pus.

**d'ngngo'** *v. intr.* pa- To avoid drawing attention to oneself. *Hal kita aningkō', mbal ah'lling-h'lling. Ya tu'ud lihita par'ngngo'.* We just sit, not saying a word. It is simply our inborn characteristic, to go unnoticed. (*Thesaurus:* **m'mmong, sandol 1.1, t'mmun**)

**d'ppa** *n.* 1) A fathom; the distance between the fingertips of outstretched arms. *A: "Piland'ppa lalom panimbakan tulay?" B: "Saga limand'ppa"* A: "How many fathoms deep is the place for dynamiting scad?" B: "Some five fathoms." (*cf:* **h'kka 1**; *Thesaurus:* **batu₃, kilometēl, honga'₂, inses, maniku**) 1.1) *v. tr.* To measure by the fathom, using outstretched arms. *Angand'ppa ka lubid.* Measure the rope using arm-lengths. *D'ppahun p'ttung ilū.* Use your arms to measure that bamboo there.

**ma d'ppahan** *adv. phrase* By the length between outstretched hands; by the fathom.

**d'ppak** (*var.* **dagpak**) *n.* 1) The physical contact between two items. *Papan itū ahāp d'ppakna.* The fit betwen these planks is good. 1.1) *v. intr.* pa- To make physical contact with something; to beach a boat. *Sangpū' maka mpat llaw kami yampa kami makaragpak ni Saluping. Sagō' halam na arai' bohe' kami.* We were fourteen days before we at last made land at Saluping. We had almost no water. (*Thesaurus:* **daggot₂ 1, dalos 1, langkit 1, langkus 1**)

**pagd'ppak** *v. intr.* aN- 1) To fit tightly together, of two flat surfaces. *Bang tangan, magd'ppak. Bang katas, maglapis.* Palms [together] are said to be *pagd'ppak*. Sheets of paper are *paglapis* [layered]. *Magd'ppak kaluma'an Sibaud.* The houses of Sibaud are packed wall-to-wall. (*Thesaurus:* **kempot, lapat 1.1, saplut₂, sonson**) 1.1) *v. tr.* To get flat items set in place. *Pinapagd'ppak tiyadtad ampa niligpit.* Bamboo panels set face-to-face before being battened in place.

**d'ppon** *v. tr.* To press something into a container or down onto a surface. *D'pponun pareyo' abō' s'ddong.* Press it down so it will fit. *Hal dīppon* *ukilan buwattē'.* Canoe carvings pressed down on like that. (*Thesaurus:* **danos, dasok 1.1, p'nnod 1**)

**d'ssal** (var. **degsal**) *v. intr. pa-* To sit with buttocks flat on ground or floor. *Da'a ka paregsal, al'mmi' hōsnu.* Don't sit flat on the floor, your sarong will get dirty. *Da'a ka aningkō' pa'engge-engge, par'ssal ka.* Don't squat, sit down flat. *Pahāpun e'nu amat'nna' karut buwas. Paregsalun bo' mbal paligid.* Put that sack of rice down firmly. Set it down flat so it doesn't slip over. *Aningkō' kita paregsal, sampay pa'ata pat'nna'. Aningkō' kita pahāp.* We sit down flat on the floor, our thighs touching as well. We sit properly. (*cf:* **par'dda**; *syn:* **lesseg**)

**dō** *intrj.* Expression encouraging caution. *Dō, dō!* That's it, that's it! *Mbal ka pat'ggal angalubakan anaknu. Yuk matto'anu, "Dō dō."* You don't smack your child for long. Your father says, "Gently now, gently."

**dō-rō** *see:* **pagdō-rō**

**doble** *n.* **1)** A pair in a card game. *Lubakin doble alas.* Put down a pair of aces. **1.1)** *v. tr.* To double the amount or dimension of something. *Sinarahakan d'nda inān. Minsan mbal bilahi, niroblehan.* That woman has been made the object of a *sarahakan* proposal. If they don't approve it will be doubled. *Aku na anggop, angandoble.* I'm the one to do it, doing twice as much. (*Thesaurus:* **lipat₁ 1**) **1.2)** *v. tr. -an* To overbid or outdo someone. *Angandoble kita ma a'a, pata'as kita min iya.* We will overbid someone, we will go above him.

**dok** var. of **dok supaya**

**dok supaya** (var. **dok**) *conj.* In order to; so that. *Sampay sultan asusa na bang ai na bahā' kin'llo' e' anakna ina'an dok supaya tataima'.* The sultan too was concerned about what that child of his should get in order to be accepted. *Lipayin tahik dok ta'nda'nu ai-ai min deyo'.* Create a clear space on the sea surface so you can see what is underneath. *Lukupin pelang itū dok ahāp luwana.* Scrub the canoe here so its appearance is good. *D'nda ab'ttong subay pinandi ma linsungan dok mbal ni'ila.* A pregnant woman should be bathed in a large grain mortar so [the baby] is not freckled. (*Thesaurus:* **bat sabab, bo' supaya, bo'₂, he da'a, supaya**)

**dokkog** var. of **dukkug**

**dokdok** *adj. a-* Finely woven, of cloth.

**dokdos** *v. intr. pa-* To slide down something rigid. *Parokdos aku pareyo' min saloka'.* I slide down by way of a coconut tree. *Parokdos medyasku.* My socks are sliding down. (*Thesaurus:* **dusdus, dūt, julut 1, loros, lurus₁ 1, luslus 1**)

**dokot₁** *n.* The hard crust of cooked rice adhering to a cooking pot. (*syn:* **l'kkot**)

**dokot₂** *adj. a-* **1)** Alight; aflame. **1.1)** *v. intr. pa-* To flare up, of a fire; to become serious, of a minor dispute. *Sinō' patepok ko da'a parokot.* Told to leave off [the argument] lest it flare up. *Buwattē' du a'a patibono'un bang amarokot bono'.* So too is the fight-prone person when he causes fighting to flare up. (*Thesaurus:* **keyat₂ 1.1, dallet 1, lāb 1, suleyab 1**) **1.2)** *v. tr. -an* To ignite something. *Nirokotan e' sigām api, sabab ulan na.* They lit a fire because it was raining. (*Thesaurus:* **bagid, pakeyat, santik 1, sū' 1.2**)

**dokot suli-suli** *adj. a-* Flaring up, of a dispute spread by talk. {idiom} *Arokot suli-suli, arongkag.* The dispute has flared up, things are tense.

**doktol** *n.* A doctor, especially a licensed practitioner of medicine. (*Thesaurus:* **pagbowahan, pananambal**)

**dogpa'** *v. intr. pa-* **1)** To act or speak impulsively; to interrupt. *Parogpa' itū sali' abigla' pat'kka. Dogpa'* is like something happening abruptly. *Parogpa' sadja iya ilū, mbal minsan amahati.* He just breaks [into a conversation], not even explaining. **1.1)** *v. tr. -an* To affect someone abruptly and with force. *Nirogpa'an kita, nilangpasan.* We were suddenly attacked, plundered. *Nirogpa'an dakayu' lahat. Niatāk kita he' ai-ai ala'at, susa, saki, mundu.* An entire region is abruptly invaded. We are attacked by various bad things, by trouble, by illness, by bandits. *Bay aku nirogpa'an e' saga pagkahiku.* I was set on suddenly by some of my fellows. (*Thesaurus:* **atāk 1.1, dugpak 2, gubat, sakat₁**)

**dogsol** *v. tr.* To push something or someone off an edge. *Bang kita atuli dogsolta ka. Ka'a ilu atā man tepo, subay hal aku dangan-dangan ahayang.* When we are sleeping I push you off. You are off the sleeping mat, I have to be the only one who is in the breeze. (*Thesaurus:* **tagang, tulak₂**)

**pagdogsol** *v. intr. aN-* To compete in a wrestling contest. *Aheka a'a bay ang'nda' si Ja sampay magdogsol na. Maggesges ya heka a'a ang'nda'-ng'nda' iya.* A lot of people saw Ja eventually push [his opponent] off [the platform]. The crowd pushed through in order to watch him.

**doha** *n.* Millet, the plant and its edible grain. *Setaria italica. Doha maka layagan, sali' buwa' gandum. Apu'ut-pu'ut man pai.* Millet and sorghum, like corn [maize]. Somewhat shorter [in growth] than rice. (*syn:* **dawa**)

**dohay** *v. tr.* To invade or attack as an act of revenge. *Kasalipan maka karatu'an mareyom 'foxhole' sigām, parohay si Anu amalos. Dohay itū aniya' atāk pabīng.* With the *salips* and the *datus* in their foxholes, What's-his-name attacked in revenge. This word *dohay* implies a return attack. (*Thesaurus:* **sakay 2**)

**dohon** *see:* **sandal-dohon, pagdohon**

**dohong** *v. intr. pa-* To desist; to come to nothing. *Sali' mbal kita makalanjal. Parohong bay paggara'.* Like when we are unable to proceed. The former plan came to nothing. *Parohong na baliyu, minsan kita atulak na.* The wind has dropped, even if we leave now [it will be all right].

**dohongan** *n.* A state of suspended activity. *Mbal na aku ni Sisangat. Ma dohongan na aku, halam na tabayanku.* I won't go to Sisangat now. I'm not doing anything, I have no means of transport. *Ma rohongan kita bang mbal du pagbeya'an sara'. Sali' kita mbal makalanjal, parohong bay paggara'.* We are in limbo if the legal judgment law is not followed. It is as though we cannot go ahead, what had been planned coming to nothing.

**do'ag** *adj. a-* Deserted, of a community where trouble has occurred. *Lahat Sisangat aro'ag makalandu'.* The village of Sisangat largely abandoned due to trouble. (*Thesaurus:* **p'ggal**)

**pagdo'ag** *v. intr. aN-* To be in process of evacuating or abandoning a settlement. *Magdo'ag, magla'an min lahat.* Getting out, leaving the district. (*Thesaurus:* **lalat₁ 1.1, pagbakwet**)

**do'om** *n.* Darkness.

**pagdo'om** *v. intr. aN-* To become overcast; to cloud over. *Magdo'om-do'om na lahat, song angulan.* The sky is growing dark, it will soon be raining. (*Thesaurus:* **dampog 1.1, lempos, lendom 1.1**)

**dolehag** *var. of* **duliyat**

**dole'** *v. advrs. -in-* 1) Irritated. (*Thesaurus:* **kalintaw, dugal 1, giyagas, p'ggot-p'ggot, s'ngngot₁ 1, sunggud**) 1.1) *v. intr. aN-* To behave irritably after an illness. *Angandole' pahāp a'a itū! Bay ka asakki?* How irritable this person is! Have you been sick?

**dollen** *n.* A species of conch, edible. *Strombus gibberulus. Bang halam aniya' bay lambi'-lambi', saga dollen inān pangomang.* If there had been no snails, *dollen* there would be for bait. (*syn:* **sikad-sikad**)

**dolmelo** *var. of* **domelo**

**dome-dome** *adj. a-* Physically feeble; lacking muscular strength. *A: "Angay ka arome-rome ilū?" B: "Ap'ddi' baranku."* A: "Why are you so weak?" B: "I am in pain." (*Thesaurus:* **layu-layu, longkoy, s'nnay, summil**)

**domelo** (*var.* **dolmelo**) *n.* Pendant earrings. (*Thesaurus:* **anting-anting 1, aretes, bāng₂, pinting, subang**)

**domeno** *var. of* **duminu**

**domol** *v. intr. pa-* 1) To look down by inclining the head. (*Thesaurus:* **bantang 1, kondo', kuru', tondok 1**) 1.1) *v. tr. -an* To see or seek something by looking down. *Domolin sīn ahūg pareyo'.* Mark the spot below where the money fell. *Domolinbi pahāp.* Look downwards for it, doing it well. *Sabu inān binissala e'na ni aku, makaromol aku maka halam aniya' tapah'llingku.* While he said that to me, I looked down and said nothing.

**pagdomol** *v. intr. aN-* To look carefully at something. *Pagdomol putika'an.* Looking at a divining device. *Pagdomolna halam maina'an si Yu, agsai gineret e'na badju'na tanda' sin pagdukkana.* Having looked down and seen that Yu was not there, he immediately tore his clothes as a sign of his distress.

**dompa'** *n.* A species of fish.

**dondon** *v. tr. -an* To abandon someone in difficulties. *Mbal kita nilembo bang nirondonan.* We won't be drowned [even] if left without help. *Bang talanggalku kuntaraku alembo, dondonanku.* If I come across my enemy drowning, I let him stay as he is.

**donson** *n.* An outboard motor. *Bang kami animbak ni Tapa'an, ameya' kami man donson, al'kkas binayan, mbal atarasaw bang aniya' daing binowa ni tabu'.* When we dynamite fish by Tapa'an Island, we go by outboard, travelling quickly, not late when we have fish to get to market. (*cf:* **dapa-rapa**)

**donga'** *v. tr.* To expect a share of food at mealtimes when one has no right to do so. *Asidda pangalung onde'-onde' inān ni luma'nu angandonga'.* That child is such a scrounger, turning up at your house at mealtimes. (*cf:* **alung 2, aro' 1.1**)

**dongan** *v. intr. pa-* To accompany. *Subay halam aniya' parongan ma ka'a. Minsan maingga-maingga ma sakalingkal būd itu, subay halam aniya' manusiya' ta'nda', luwal ka'a.* There should be no one accompanying you. No matter where it is around this mountain, there should be no people in sight, only you. (*Thesaurus:* **abay₁ 1.1, beya'₂ 1, bunyug 1.2, sehe' 1.1, unung 1**)

**pagdongan** *v. intr. aN-* To go together; to travel in company. *Magdongan kita pehē'.* Let's go there together. *Jari magdongan si Nabi Ibrahim maka anakna si Isma'il ni'islam ma dang'llaw du.* So the Prophet Abraham and his son Ishmael went together to be circumcised on the very same day. (*Thesaurus:* **pagdora', pagsambeya', pagunung**)

**dongkag** *adj. a-* Unsettled, as a community where there has been trouble. *Arokot suli-suli, arongkag. Abalu' deyom paglahat.* The news is spreading, things are unsettled. The district is in an uproar. *Abalu' ma deyom paglahat. Aniya' kalahiannu, arongkag ka.* The place is in an uproar. There's something you are escaping from, you are upset. (*Thesaurus:* **balu', halubilu, hengo-hengo, hiluhala' 1.1, hiyul, jabu 1, lengog 1.1, sasaw 1.1, sensong**)

**dongdong** *v. tr. -an* To give careful thought to something. *Halam bay karongdonganku mma'ku.* I have not reflected on my father's life. *Masi ya angandongdong bang ai hatina ya bay ta'nda'na inān.* He was still thinking about the meaning of what had seen there. *Subay nirongdongan pahāp lapal sigām.* What they were saying should be carefully considered. (*Thesaurus:* **kannal, dalil 1.1, pagka'inagon, pikil 1.1, tali' 1.1**)

**dopon** *v. tr.* *-an* To hold something firmly to prevent its movement or escape. *Ai-ai ntananta bo' aoseg, yukta "Doponin hē' da'a makalahi." Buwat kuting, sapi', manuk.* Whatever we are holding that wriggles, we say, "Hold it down so it can't escape." Like a cat, a cow or a chicken. (*Thesaurus:* **gipis 1.1, t'kkon**)

**dopon-dopon** *n.* 1) A snap fastener. 1.1) *v. tr.* To snap together the parts of a purse fastener. (*Thesaurus:* **batuk-batuk, kassup 1, kattup, tikkup**)

**doppeng** *n.* A flat three-cornered cake of cassava meal. *Magsusun aku, wa'i tara'ug sīnku. Halam aniya' pam'lliku doppeng.* I regret losing my money in a contest. I have nothing to buy a pancake with. (*gen:* **apam 1**)

**dora'** 1) *n.* One's equal in size, age or social development. 2) *v. tr.* To keep up with in growth or progress. *Mbal aheya man aku, dora'ku na pa'in, topad-sali'ku.* No bigger than I am, I stay equal with him, my peer. (*Thesaurus:* **sali' 1, samapasang, sibu' 1, suga-suga₂, tupan 1**)

**pagdora'** *v. intr.* *aN-* To travel at the same rate or by the same means. *Bang kami magdora' lum'ngngan, sali' magsambeya'.* When we walk together at the same pace, it's like we are accompanying each other. *Buwat kita man dilaut, magdora' kami abanog.* Like us coming from out at sea, travelling together under sail. (*Thesaurus:* **pagdongan, pagsambeya', pagunung**)

**dorok** *n.* Cracked particles of rice or corn. *Ai lagi' dorok-gandum, nihinang biyaki'?* What else but corn rice, made into *biyaki'* cakes? (*cf:* **benglod, biti'₂ 1**)

**dorog₁** *adj.* *a-* Permanent as to residence or location. *Ka'a mbal arorog ma lahat itū.* As for you, you do not stay in this district. (*Thesaurus:* **kakkal, d'ddos, taptap 1, tattal, t'ttog 1**)

**pagdorog** *v. intr.* *aN-* To be settled in one place. *Magdorog, sali' aningkō' ma luma', buwat ka'a magdorog maitu.* Staying in place, like sitting in the house, like you settling here.

**dorog₂** *n.* 1) Good looks; attractive physical form. *Buwat a'a ahāp dorogna. L'lla ka, d'nda ka, ahāp l'ngnganna.* Like someone whose appearance is good. Male or female, they move well. 1.1) *adj.* *-an* Physically attractive. *Dorogan d'nda hē', halam aniya' sinoway ma baranna.* That girl is beautiful, nothing about her person to find fault with. (*Thesaurus:* **alti, hansam, hāp baran, himpit, jalang₁, lingkat 1.1, manis 1.1, polma 1.1**)

**dorot** *adj.* *a-* Numerous; teeming. *Aheka, arorot, sali' kita mbal makalabay ya kaheka'an manusiya' itū.* Many, teeming, we can hardly get through due to the crowds of people. *Arorot daing ma tabu'.* There are lots of fish in the market. (*Thesaurus:* **banos, besal, kansang 1, datay₂,**

**dayas-dayas, heka 1.1, jayak, parat**)

**pandorot** *v. intr.* *aN-* To fall in abundance, as rain from eaves. (*cf:* **tampiyas 1**)

**dosdos** *v. intr.* *pa-* To collapse, of a structure. *Luma' inān bay niosolan, bay binabagan. Aubus bay nihinang, parosdos, al'bbo nireyo'.* That house had posts in, it had cross-beams in place. After that was done it collapsed, soft ground beneath.

**dosena** *n.* A dozen. *Darosena pa'in.* Just one dozen.

**doson** *adj.* *a-* 1) Feeling weighed down. *Aroson kita ma paningkō'an, sali' pahonhon tina'ita.* We are heavy from sitting down, as if our intestines had prolapsed. (*Thesaurus:* **gadgad₁, honhon, lomeng-lomeng**) 1.1) *v. tr.* *-an* To damage something by pressing heavily on it. *Nirosonan iya, ai-ai hē' makataluwa' ni iya. Ai-ai bay man diyata'na ya makamula iya.* He is crushed, whatever it was that hit him. It is something from above that has destroyed him.

**doyog** *var.* of **poyog**

**draeb** *see:* **pagdraeb**

**dragadik** *n.* A drug addict. *Yuk mbo'ku, halam kono' dragadik tempo awal-jaman ē'.* My grandparent said there were no drug addicts in olden times.

**draybel** *n.* A driver or chauffeur.

**du** *ptl.* 1) Indicates certainty. (Evidential marker). Frequently accompanies assertions of intention. *Sali' du.* It is just the same. *Amole' du kami salung kohap.* We will indeed be going home tomorrow afternoon. *Mbal du. Nsa' du aniya'.* Not really. There simply aren't any. (*Thesaurus:* **bā 2, ka₁, sa**) 2) Politeness marker. Softens the force of an assertion.

**du pa'in** *adv. phrase* More than average; always the case. *Katudju du pa'in a'a inān bang angahiyak daing. Taluwa' sadja.* How accurate that man is when he spears a fish. Always on target. *Kagaddung du pa'in sumping inān!* The greenness of that flower! *Kapang'ddil-ng'ddil du pa'in baranku itū.* How this body of mine is always shaking. *A: "Maka'ā' kām?" B: "Aniya' du pa'in palauk."* A: "Did you catch anything?" B: "There's always enough to flavor our cassava." *Mag'nda' du pa'in kitabi magtai'-anak.* We [incl.] members of the family keep seeing each other. *Hayak-hayakan aku aholat pat'nna' ma lahat itū, halam aniya' lengogna. Ai ka itū, aniya' du pa'in.* I was disappointed in my hopes of settling in this place, that it had no unrest. Whatever! There always is.

**du-bilang** (derivative of **bilang₃**) *adj.* *zero* The call "Not ready", in children's games. *Du-bilang mbal beya', bilang beya'.* *Du-bilang* means not ready [to play], *bilang* means ready.

**dublun** *n.* A gold coin used as jewelry; a large gold button. *Maginggat dublun bang taluwa' llaw.* Gold coins flash when the sun strikes them. (*spec:* **mata-kura', mata-jīp, pikit₃ 1**)

**dūk₁** *v. tr.* *-an* To persuade someone to act in a specific way. *Buwat ka'a-i ata'u magbissala, aku* *mbal, na ka'a dūkanku magbissala.* Like you who know how to discuss, and me who doesn't know, then you try to get me involved in a discussion. *Aku na pa'in dūkannu ni kala'atan.* I am the one you keep urging to [do something] bad.

**dūk₂** *n.* 1) Firewood available for burning. *Sōngin dūkna ilu.* Move the unburnt pieces [into the fire]. (*Thesaurus:* **baga** 1) 1.1) *v. tr. -an* To put available firewood on a fire. *Oy! Dūkannu aku ni baga nalka'?* Hey! Will you feed me to the coals of hell? *Nirūkan kayu ni api, pang'nnop kayu.* The wood was moved to the fire, adding to it.

**dukka'** *v. advrs. ka-...-an* To be sorrowing greatly.

**pagkarukka'an** *v. intr. aN-* 1) To be going through a period of intense grief. *Magkarukka'an aku, amehē'an aku dīku abu, maka magbadju' karut.* I went through intense grief, putting ash on myself and wearing burlap. *Aku ya marasahi magkarukka'an.* I am exhausted from grieving. 1.1) *v. tr.* To grieve for something. *Pinagkarukka'an ai-ai alungay min kita.* Anything we lose is something to be mourned. *Geretunbi badju'bi ati anulug kam badju' karut bo' pagkarukka'anbi si Ab.* Tear your clothes and put on burlap clothes so that you grieve for Ab.

**pagdukka'** *n.* 1) Grief over the death of a loved one. 1.1) *v. tr. -an* To grieve over the loss of a loved one or treasured possession. *Bang amatay bapa'ku asidda magdukka si Ina'.* If my uncle dies my mother will grieve very much. *Wa'i paluruk di mma' magdukka'an mayul.* Father and others have gone to mourn for the mayor. *Magbidda' to'ongan sigām bang kaudjulan sabab minsan magdukka' masi asawa pamayhu'an sigām.* They are very different when bereaved because even though they weep they look cheerful. *Da'a gese'unbi saga s'mmekbi tanda' kapagdukkabi.* Do not tear your clothes as a sign of your grief. (*Thesaurus:* **handul atay, pagdohon, paglemong** 1.1, **paglindu**)

**dukkug** (var. **dokkog**) *n.* 1) A hump-back due to spinal deformity. (*Thesaurus:* **buggul** 1.1, **kuba₂**) 1.1) *v. advrs. -in-* To suffer from a spinal hump. *Nirukkug anak si Ha.* Ha's son has a humped back.

**dukduk** *v. tr.* To stab something. (*Thesaurus:* **budjak** 1.1, **kudjut, dugsu', punyal** 1.1)

**dukla'** *v. intr. pa-* 1) To reach land. *Wa'i sigām parukla' ma tape' gusung.* There they were, making shore where the sand begins. (*syn:* **dunggu'** 1) 1.1) *v. tr. -an* To moor a canoe or boat. *Subay nirukla'an pelangnu.* Your canoe should be moored.

**duklat** *v. intr. pa-* 1) To penetrate flesh with a pointed object. *Buwat kita angahiyak pahi, "Wa'i paruklat," yukta.* For example, when we are spearing a stingray, we say, "It has gone in." *Tananamta paruklat ni tanganta. Pag'nda'ta abakat.* We feel it going into our hand. When we look it is wounded. (*Thesaurus:* **katama, ōk** 1,

**utab**) 1.1) *v. tr.* To drive a spear or thorn into something. *Taruklat tape'na.* His foot is pierced.

**duku'** *v. intr. pa-* To kneel face down in the Muslim position for prayer. (*Thesaurus:* **luku'₂, luhud, pagpatireyo', sujud**)

**dugal** *adj. a-/-an* 1) Annoyed; irritated. *Arugal kami, at'ggol na kami angalagaran ka'am.* We are annoyed, having waited a long time for you. (*Thesaurus:* **kalintaw, dole'** 1, **giyagas, p'ggot-p'ggot, s'ngngot₁** 1, **sunggud**) 1.1) *v. tr. -an* To scold someone irritably. (*Thesaurus:* **pabukag, pah'lling₂, pamūng-mūng, pugpug** 1, **s'ndal** 1, **tutul**)

**pagdugal** *v. intr. aN-* To be in an irritable state of mind. *Aniya' maina'an saga a'a magdugal kabowa kagit atay sigām.* There were people there in a bad mood because of their displeasure. *Magdugal kita bay ai-aita, bay nna'ta, bo' wa'i alungay. Am'ddi' atayta.* We are really annoyed about our things which we had put away but are now lost. We have become angry.

**dugdug** var. of **daogdog**

**dugpak** 1) *v. intr. pa-* To set in, of natural forces such as wind or rain. *Parugpak baliyu min Būd Lapak maka min Būd Siasi.* The wind struck from Mt. Lapak and from Mt. Siasi. (*cf:* **tumbuk₁** 1) 2) *v. tr.* To attack a place or person. *Dugpakku iya baba iya minale' gi'.* I will attack him while he is still tired out. *Nirugpak min dambila' maka min dambila'.* Struck at from one side and another. *Na bang buwttē', mintag ingga kita parugpak?* Well if that is so, where will we attack from? (*cf:* **dumpas**; *Thesaurus:* **atāk** 1.1, **dogpa'** 1.1, **gubat, sakat₁**)

**dugsu'** *v. tr. -an* To stab someone with a bladed weapon. *Na bo' kita nirugsu'an na, hal kita amatay pahantak.* So then if we have been stabbed, we just fall down dead. *Nirugsu'an iya ma kīd tuktukna.* He was stabbed in the side of his brow. *Puhan budjakna ya pangandugsu'.* The shaft of his spear was what he stabbed with. *Hublutun na kalisnu ilu bo' aku papatayun, pād-pād saga kapil itū angandugsu'an aku maka anganjahulaka'an baranku.* Draw your bladed weapon and kill me, rather than this heathen stabbing me and abusing my body. (*Thesaurus:* **budjak** 1.1, **kudjut, dukduk, punyal** 1.1)

**dugsul** *n.* 1) An ulcer or ulcerated sore. (*cf:* **bakokang**) 1.1) *v. advrs. -in-* Suffering from ulcers.

**dugtul** *v. tr.* To bang into something. *Bang ka ni Tiyanggi lum'ngngan ka, kamaya'-maya' ko da'a ka tarugtul e' jīp.* When you go to Jolo Market and are walking, be careful that you don't get struck by a jeepney. *Tarugtul pinggan dakayu' ni pinggan dakayu'.* One bowl banged by the other. (*Thesaurus:* **binggil, daplig** 1, **sampig, sangku'**)

**pagdugtul** *v. intr. aN-* To bang together head on. (*Thesaurus:* **pagbangga', pagbanggul** 1)

**dugu** *n.* A right-angle corner; an outer angle of a

structure. *Ina'an na ma dugu lamisahan.* There on the corner of the table. (*Thesaurus:* **lo'ok-lo'ok, pidju** 1)

**dugu-dugu** var. of **bāt-dugu-dugu**

**dugu'-nyawa** *adv.* Body and soul; in life and in death. {idiom} *Bunyuganta ka dugu'-nyawa.* I will accompany you, body and soul.

**Duhul Kudus** *n. phrase* The Holy Spirit of Christian theology.

**duhun** *v. intr. pa-* **1)** To worsen, of health or quality. *Bang aniya' amatay dakayu', paruhun dakayu'. Na luhūy magkarupangan sali'.* If one person dies, then another deteriorates. Then [the mother] promptly behaves even more irrationally. *Paruhun na pa'in pagbono' ma atag saga a'a Logos.* The fighting grew fiercer around the men of Logos. (*Thesaurus:* **tungkap₁**) **1.1)** *v. tr. -an* To make something worse. *Bang aniya' bay nilagut, yukna ni dangan ya bantana, "Lutangun, duhunin."* When someone is hacked with a fighting knife, he says to the one who is his enemy, "Do it again, make it even worse." (*cf:* **luba'**) **1.2)** *v. advrs. ka-...-an* To be worse than before. *Karuhunan bohe' angaut. Sali' pasōng min dahū.* The water gets even more dirty. It's like it becomes more so than it was originally. *Mang aniya' abangat sakina subay mbal makakakan ai-ai sukangna abō' mbal sinangti', sabab bang sinangti' karuhunan sakina.* If someone's illness is serious he cannot eat anything that is forbidden to him lest he have a relapse, because if he does his sickness will be even worse.

**duhun manduhun** *adv. phrase* Getting worse and worse. *Duhun manduhun ap'ddi' atay sigā.* Their anger becomes more and more intense.

**pagduhun** *v. intr. aN-* To become worse, of some condition. *Gom pa'in magduruhun tāwna.* His fear became even more extreme.

**paruhun** *v. tr.* To allow or cause a situation to become worse.

**du'un-du'un** *see:* **saru'un-du'un**

**dūl** *v. tr. -an* To fulfil needs, wants or requests. *Bang sinabbut Tuhan, "O Tuhan, dūlin aku."* As when praying to God [we say], "O God, meet my needs." *Angandūl kita ma halga'na.* We meet the asking price. *Magtangis iya pasal anakna bay amatay, halam bay karūlan ai-ai.* She is weeping for her child who has died without being indulged in any way. *Pakirūl ni Tuhan, angamu'-ngamu' ni iya hē' bang kita amudji.* We ask God for consideration, making request of him when we worship. (*cf:* **dakag**)

**pagdūl-baya'** *v. intr. aN-* To be in control; to do what one pleases. *Pinangandolan iya e' si Potepal maka binuwanan iya kapatut magnakura'. Iya ya magdūl-baya'.* Potiphar trusted him and gave him authority to be in charge. He was the one to exercise control. *Magdūl-baya' itu, ai-ai kabaya'anta sali' halam aniya' makalāng.* This

word magdul-baya' is about having whatever we want, with none able to prevent it. *Bang aniya' makasugpatan akkalku hē', na makapagdūl-baya' na aku.* If something completes my contentment, then I can do what I want. *Magdūl-baya' itu, ai-ai kabaya'anta sali' halam aniya' makalāng. Magdūl-baya', sali' kita makapagbaya' ma ai-aita. Dūl-baya'* is when no one can forbid anything we want. It is us [personally] having control over our possessions. *Bang aniya' makasugpatan akkalku hē', na makapagdūl-baya' na aku.* If something adds to my contentment, then I will be doing what I want. (*Thesaurus:* **baya'-baya'₂**)

**pagparūl** *v. tr.* **1)** To indulge one's desires. **1.1)** *v. intr. aN-* To be indulging oneself.

**pamarūl** *n.* A favor granted; permission given.

**parūl** *adj. zero* **1)** Over-indulged; spoilt. **1.1)** *v. tr.* To grant someone permission; to indulge someone. *Subay aku parūlnu angipat ba'anan hayopnu buwat bay dahū.* You must allow me to care for your many animals just as before. *Appa', angamu' aku junjung bang pa'in parūlnu ina'-mma'ku pahanti' ma deyomannu.* Your majesty, I ask a favor of you that you might permit my parents to stay in your care. (*Thesaurus:* **paba'id, pakuhi, palangga' 1.1, papuhun, parakag, patege', tugut 2**)

**dulang** *n.* A tray for festive foods. *Dulang taga panyām, taga buwas, taga saging, ni'isi ni deyom ligu atawa talam.* Festive trays have cakes, rice, bananas, put into a winnowing basket or tray.

**dulang-kokok** *n.* Saucer coral. *Aheka dulang-kokok ma Talusan dilaut.* There are many saucer corals on the seaward side of Talusan Point. (*cf:* **tangkapa'**; *gen:* **batu₂ 1**)

**dulaw** *n.* Turmeric, a rhizome used to color and flavor rice. *Curcuma domestica. Punjung itū buwas gandum atawa buwas to'ongan nilamugay maka lahing maka dulaw. Punjung* is corn rice or real rice mixed with grated coconut and turmeric. (*cf:* **buwas-kuning**; *gen:* **pamapā**)

**duleyak** (var. **daleyak**) *v. intr. -um-* To fall backwards and lie facing upwards. *Nsa' ahāp paningkō'ku, makaduleyak aku.* The way I'm sitting is not good, I could fall backwards.

**pagduleyak** *v. intr. aN-* To fall over and over, face up then face down. *Bang kita atuhun magduleyak kita. Ubus pakkom bo' paleyak inān.* When we dive we turn over and over, face down then face up. (*Thesaurus:* **daya', hagtang, hantal, haya'₁, leyak**)

**dulis** *v. tr.* To get food by dipping one's fingers into it. (*cf:* **sobo'**; *Thesaurus:* **bahug 1.1, butag, t'nno', tublak₁ 1**)

**duliyag** var. of **duliyat**

**duliyan** (var. **duwiyan**) *n.* Durian and the creamy flesh of its odorous fruit. *Durio zibethinus.*

**duliyat** (var. **dolehag; duliyag**) *v. intr. pa-* **1)** To roll one's eyes so that the white is visible. *Sali'* *saddī na matana. Peyanin matana, bang paruliyat amatay na.* It is as though his eyes are now different. Watch his eyes, if they are rolled back he is dead. **1.1)** *v. tr.* To roll one's eyes so the whites are visible; to glare. *Subay angastol a'a angandolehag matana.* A man whose eyes glare must be angry.

**pagduliyag** *v. intr. aN-* To be rolling one's eyes back, as when having a seizure. *Magduliyag, sali' a'a binawi-bawi.* Rolling one's eyes, like a person suffering an epileptic seizure. (*Thesaurus:* **kaniyang-kaniyang, diyag, d'llag 1**)

**dulu₁** *n.* A species of swarming locust. (*syn:* **ampan-dulu**)

**dulu₂** var. of **panggi'-dulu**

**duma'in** *neg.* 'Not so', of an assertion or assumption, offering or implying an alternative proposition. *Duma'in ka aku ya bay angindam pelangnu.* It wasn't me who borrowed your canoe. *Ka'a anak sundalu? Duma'in.* Are you the son of a soldier? No, I'm not. *Ata'u iya ama'amu-amu dīna minsan duma'in na baha'u badju'na.* He knows how to present himself well even though his clothes are not new. (*Thesaurus:* **ai po'on, ballum, mbal 1.1, m'ssa', ngga'i ka**)

**dumasiyaw** *adv.* Excessive; over the top. *Dumasiyaw pahāp kalanga pangadji'nu, ya na makabelaw ka'a ilu.* You're much too highly educated, that's what is making you crazy. *Da'a subay dumasiyaw paglami-lamita.* Our merry-making should not be overmuch. (*Thesaurus:* **karalaman, kumarukan, landu'₂ 1, mamarahi, sidda 1, to'od**)

**duminu** (var. **domeno**) *n.* The game of dominoes and its pieces.

**pagduminu** *n.* **1)** The game of dominoes. **1.1)** *v. intr. aN-* To play the game of dominoes.

**dumpās** var. of **dumpas**

**dumpas** (var. **dumpās**) *v. intr. pa-* To invade land or seize property using force. *Parumpas sapantun dunuk mbal tasagga'. Dumpas* is figuratively like a flood that cannot be resisted. *Ta'ndaku bili-bili hē' parumpas tampal ni s'ddopan.* I saw that sheep charging towards the west. *Hal parumpās ya a'a bay pasōd ē'.* The man that entered there simply burst in. (*cf:* **dugpak 2**; *Thesaurus:* **sabsab, t'ppas₁**)

**dundang₁** *adj. a-* **1)** Swaying rhythmically, as on a swing. *Guyu itu sampay ni deyo' tana', ameya' arundang saga kahunasan.* This turbulence goes right to the bottom, the sea grasses swaying in time. (*cf:* **ta'ut**; *Thesaurus:* **duyan, ombo'-ombo', pagdanggu'-danggu', pagnanu', tadjun**) **1.1)** *v. tr.* To set someone swinging. *Bang ka'am nirundang, asidda aladji'.* When you are made to swing, you go way up. *Oto', dundangun si Arung.* Son, give Daughter a swing.

**dundangan** *n.* A swing of suspended rope.

**pagdundang** *v. intr. aN-* To swing to and fro.

**dundang₂** *n.* A species of plant, used medicinally.

**dundang-pote'** *n.* A species of medicinal plant, white.

**dundunay** *n.* The Nicobar pigeon. *Caloenas nicobarica. Manuk-manuk dundunay, tapuk ni sampunay.* A pigeon hiding in the *sampunay* tree.

**dunuk** *v. tr. -an* To flood an area by water flowing down from higher ground. (*Thesaurus:* **latap 1.1, sakla', s'llop**)

**pagdunuk** *v. intr. aN-* To flood an area. *Magdunuk na lahat.* The land is under water.

**dunya** (var. **junna**; **junya**) *n.* The earth in contrast to sky and heaven; the sphere of human life and activity. *Dunya itu maka dunya hē'-i.* This world and that other one. *Duwa hekana pat'nna'an a'a. Bang a'llum ma dunya, bang amatay ma ahirat.* There are two places where men dwell. While they live it is the earth, when they die it is the afterworld. *Yamboho' tasipatku heka manusiya' mareyom junna.* I have only just grasped how many humans there are in the world. *Buwat aniya' nientom mma'ta, wa'i na amatay, yukta, "Ndū', bay mma'ku amatay hē', halam na ma junna."* Like when our father comes to mind [after] he is dead, we say, "Alas, my father who has died is no longer here on earth." (*Thesaurus:* **alam₁, ayan, langit**)

**dunya-ahirat** *n.* The world to come; the place where souls go after death. (*Thesaurus:* **sulga'**)

**dunggu'** *v. intr. pa-* **1)** To reach land from the sea. *Pagabut kami pa'in ni jambatan, parunggu' na kami ni ispidbūt si P.* When we arrived at the wharf we moored to P's speedboat. (*syn:* **dukla' 1**; *Thesaurus:* **daggot₁, tandan₁ 1, t'kkad 1, tundug 1**) **1.1)** *v. tr.* To moor or beach a vessel. *"Da'a kita," yukna, "tarunggu' ni Laminusa."* "Let's not be moored at Laminusa," he said.

**dungun** *n.* A tree species known for its hard black seedcase. *Aniya' tabākku buwa'-dungun.* I found a *dungun* seedcase.

**dupang** *n.* **1)** A person who is mentally deficient; someone considered to be stupid. *Sigā inān, Tuwan, tabiya' min ka'a, dupang.* Those people, sir, begging your pardon, are stupid. (*Thesaurus:* **bengog 1, b'ggod, b'llod, bobo, hibang-hibang**) **1.1)** *adj. a-* Stupid or mentally deficient; foolish. **1.2)** *v. tr.* To make a fool of someone. *Pi'itu iya supaya angandupang ka'a.* He's coming in order to fool you. (*Thesaurus:* **lakbu'₂**)

**karupangan** *n.* Foolishness in thought or action.

**pagkarupangan** *v. intr. aN-* To behave irrationally.

**parupang** *v. tr.* To deceive or hoodwink someone. (*Thesaurus:* **akkal 1.1**)

**duplak** *v. advrs. -in-* Damaged in the bud stage, specially of mangoes. *Minsan mampallam, wanni, balunu', anadjuk. Bang mbal niruplak, palanjal, yampa magduru'-ero'.* Whether common mango, odorous mango or horse mango, all set fruit. If not damaged they develop and then go on to the budding stage. (*cf:* **buwa'**₁ **1.1**)

**dupli'as** *v. intr. pa-* To strike at too oblique an angle, of a cutting implement or a paddle. *Busay parupli'as ma deyom tahik. Mbal amowa tahik.* The paddle shifts to a flat angle in the sea. It doesn't grip the water. *Ai-ai t'tta'ta, ai-ai pōngta, parupli'as.* Anything we cut up or cut off, it may be struck too obliquely. (*Thesaurus:* **deplas 1, diplay**)

**durukan**₁ *n.* A mast block; the block in a canoe that takes the downward strain of the mast. *Abungkas durukan paraw, paokat pariyata'.* The mast block of the canoe has become detached, lifting away from [the hull].

**durukan**₂ *n.* The background color of patterned cloth.

**duru'** *n.* 1) The breast, of humans; udder, of other mammals. (*Thesaurus:* **tampang, tete' 1**) **1.1**) *adj. -an* At the breast; breast-fed. *Anak duru'an lagi'.* A child still nursing. **1.2)** *v. intr. a-* To suckle from breast or feeding bottle. *Aruru' gatas anak sigām.* Their children drink milk [by sucking]. (*cf:* **s'ssop**)

  **paruru'** *v. tr.* To suckle a child; to breastfeed.

  **paruru'an** *n.* Something to suckle from, as a baby's feeding bottle. (*cf:* **sopon**)

**duru'-ero'** *n.* Newly formed fruit.

  **pagduru'-ero'** *v. intr. aN-* To set fruit in the very early stages, i.e. before petals fall. (*Thesaurus:* **pagbuwa', tadjuk, tungkalling**)

**duru'an** var. of **bāt-duru'an**

**durul** *n.* A steamed cake of corn-meal flavored with sugar or grated coconut. *Dorok gandum ya pinaghinang durul. Amene' ka, ai sinokalan, ai nilahingan.* Cracked corn is what is used to make *durul.* Make your choice, sugared or made with coconut milk. *Durul itū kinakan bang aniya' sīnku pam'lli. Sidda ahāp nanamna. Durul* are eaten when I have the money to buy them. Their taste is so good. (*cf:* **biyaki' 1, gandum**; *gen:* **mamun**)

**durung**₁ *v. tr.* To carry something on the head. *Durungun ligu ilū ni diyata' kōknu.* Carry that winnowing basket on top of your head. (*syn:* **lutu**₂)

**durung**₂ *n.* The strake of a canoe.

  **durung-diyata'** *n.* The upmost strake of a planked canoe. (*cf:* **lipi-lipi**; *gen:* **tapi' 1**)

  **durung-sa'am** *n.* The strake of a planked canoe that carries the outrigger boom supports. *Pote'-pote' isāb kapi-kapi diyata' bo' aniya' durung-sa'am.* The *kapi-kapi* layer is whitish, and then there are the planks that take the outrigger boom support. (*gen:* **tapi' 1**)

**dūs** var. of **dusdus**

**dusa** *n.* 1) An offense or fault against a divine being or a fellow human. *Buwat onde'-onde' binowa pareyo', bo' ya amowa pareyo' ya ina'an manganjaga. Yuk matto'a, "Abila ilu saga tarugtul he' magbola ilū, dusana."* Like a small child being taken down [onto the beach], the one who takes him down is the one to watch him. The parent says, "When he gets hit by the ball-players there, it will be your fault." (*cf:* **tamak 1**) **1.1)** *v. intr. aN-* To commit a sin or offense. *Magk'bba-k'bba atayku bang aku bay angandusa.* My heart pounds when I have committed a sin. **1.2)** *v. tr. -an* To sin against someone. *Ngga'i ka sadja sultan ya nirusahan, sagō' kamemon saga a'a ya ma lahat itu.* It is not just the sultan who will be sinned against, but all the people in this region.

**pagdusa** *v. intr. aN-* To commit an offense against or with someone. *Manjari nihinangan aku la'at, minsan aku halam bay magdusa.* So something bad is done against me, even though I have committed no offense. *Sagō' buwattina'an tuna'annu aku magdusa maka d'nda itu!* But now you accuse me of having sinned with this woman! (*syn:* **pagpakay-dusa**)

**baldusa** *n.* A persistent sinner.

**paldusahan** *n.* Sins, collectively.

**dusdus** (var. **dūs**) *v. intr. pa-* To slide down a tree or post. *Buwat parāg kita halam aniya' tangga' parāganta inān, hal kita parusdus pareyo'.* Like when we climb [a tree] and there are no climbing notches, we just slide down. (*cf:* **dasdas**; *Thesaurus:* **dokdos, dūt, julut 1, loros, lurus**₁ **1, luslus 1**)

**dusta'** *n.* 1) An offense against custom or manners. *Dusta' itū sali' halam aniya' addata. Dusta'* is like having no respect. **1.1)** *v. tr.* To accuse someone of lying or refusing to believe. *Ka'a ilū ala'at. Angandusta' ka. Sali' mbal angandol.* You are bad. You question [my truthfulness]. It's like you don't trust. *Sali' pinagputingan kita, ya hē' angandusta'.* It's like someone being accused of lying, that's what *dusta'* is.

**dūt** *v. intr. pa-* To slide down a slope, as a canoe down a wave or a sled down a hillside. *Bang kita amusay min pelang, bo' aniya' goyak, da'a na kita amusay, parūt sadja kita.* When we're travelling by canoe and it's rough, we don't have to paddle, we just slide along. (*Thesaurus:* **dokdos, dusdus, julut 1, loros, lurus**₁ **1, luslus 1, lūt**₁)

**pagdūt-dūt** *v. intr. aN-* To play a game of pulling each other on a sled-like object. *Bang aku magdūt-dūt maka onde', subay ma l'bbak bo' al'kkas.* When I go sledding with kids, it should be down a valley so it goes fast.

**dutay** *adj. a-* Soft or fleshy, of cloth or the muscle tissue of an old person. (*Thesaurus:* **h'mmel, lunuk 1.1**)

**dutdut** *v. tr.* To suck something, as to relieve pain. (*Thesaurus:* **ligid**₁, **s'ssop, tamus**)

**pagdutdut** *v. intr. aN-* To be throbbing. (*Thesaurus:* **pagk'bbut-k'bbut, pagkowap-kowap, paglaggut-laggut, pagsignat-signat, panag-panag 1**)

**duti** *v. tr.* To cast a spell for the purpose of causing someone serious harm. (*Thesaurus:* **hikmat,**

hinang-hinang₁, h'lling₃, **palkata'an, pantak 1.1, sihil 1.1**)

**duwa** *num.* 1) Two. *Hinangin aku busay duwa hekana.* Make me some paddles, two of them. **1.1)** *v. tr.* -*an* To do something a second time. *Mbal karuwahan.* It can never be repeated. (*Thesaurus:* **balik₁ 1.3, isab 2**)

**karuwangan** *n.* Both, of people. *Hē' na maglahi karuwangan.* The two of them have run off together.

**duwa-abana** *adj. zero* One of two options. *Duwa-abana itū bang mbal bilahi pinandu'an, suma'an ni ahāp, suma'an ni ala'at. Duwa-abana* is when someone is unwilling to be taught, the outcome is either good or bad. *Bang anakta mbal kapandu'an duwa-abana iya. Alahang iya ni kahāpan, humeka ni kala'atan.* If our child can't be taught there are two possibilities. It rarely turns out well, mostly turns out bad. (*Thesaurus:* **dalam-duwa, duwa-ruwa, paguntung-duwa, sarap-duwa**)

**duwangan** 1) *num.* Two, of people. *Pag'nda'ku niriyata', aniya' ta'nda'ku duwangan d'nda, tabowa paleyang e' baliyu.* On looking upwards I saw two women flying away, borne by the wind. *O'ō, itiya' duwangan anakku budjang.* Look, here are my two unmarried daughters. 2) *n.* Two persons. *Sakali palanjal na pehē' duwangan min sigām i.* Two of them promptly went off in that direction. *Yuk duwangan itū ni pulis, "Ōy, ngga'i ka kami ya bay anangkaw."* The two said to the police, "Hey, it wasn't us who stole."

**duwang-duwangan** *adv.* By twos; working in twos. *Buwat ka'am damunda', kami damunda', duwa-duwangan kām, duwang-duwangan isāb kami.* Like you in one canoe and us in another, the two of you, and the two of us.

**pagduwa-pikilan** *v. tr.* To be of two opinions; to be undecided. {idiom} *Angkan sinipat, angkan magduwa-pikilan na, ala'at hinangna.* The reason his thinking was changed, the reason he was now of two minds, is that his actions were bad. *Magduwa-ruwa pikilan saga huwis ē'.* The judges were of two minds.

**karuwa** *n.* 1) Both, of things. 2) Second in a series.

**pagkaruwa** *v. intr. aN-* To be a pair; to be a duplicate of.

**duwa kasobangan** *n. phrase* Second day after new moon. (*gen:* **bulan₂ 2**)

**duwa lawang tinda** *n. phrase* Department store (lit. two-door shop). {idiom} *Bang aniya' tabākta ambal buwat heya pa'ata, siguru kita duwa lawang tinda.* If we find some ambergris the size of our thigh, we'll be almost certain of [being worth] a two-door shop.

**duwa-bayhu'** *n.* Insincerity (lit. two faces). {idiom}
**pagduwa-bayhu'** *v. intr. aN-* To be insincere (lit. two-faced). {idiom}

**duwa-ruwa** *v. intr. pa-* To waver between two

courses of action. *Kahaba' iya lingantu halam paruwa-ruwa, magtūy angalungkad.* Every time he is hungry he does not dither, he promptly opens the container. (*Thesaurus:* **dalam-duwa, duwa-abana, paguntung-duwa, sarap-duwa**)

**pagduwa-ruwa** *n.* 1) Uncertainty; indecision; doubt. {idiom} *Halam aniya' pagduwa-ruwana, h'ndanu ko' ilū.* No question about it, she is your wife. **1.1)** *v. intr.* a*N-* To be undecided; to be of two minds. {idiom} *Ingga bahā' pagduwa-duwahanbi ma duwa itu?* Which of these two are you uncertain about?

**duwa'** *v. tr.* To load cargo into a conveyance (sea or land). *Mbal taruwa' ma bangka'.* It can't be loaded onto a dugout canoe. (*ant:* **hawas**)

**duwa'an** *n.* Cargo; things loaded onto a conveyance.

**pagduwa'** *v. tr.* To be busy loading freight into a vessel or vehicle. *Na dai'-dai'ku na, magduwa' na kami kasakapan, binowa ni Silibis.* Now I'll make it short, we loaded all the things needed for taking to the Celebes.

**duwa'a** *n.* 1) Prayer, a core component of many Islamic ceremonies. **1.1)** *v. tr.* -*an* To offer a prayer for someone's wellbeing. *Subay akatis magsambahayang subu bo' yampa aniya' kamat niruwaha'an.* The dawn prayer should be over before the blessing prayer for a newborn girl is offered.

**duwa'a-kokam** *n.* A prayer or charm for closing the mouth of something that might cause harm.

**duwa'a-salamat** *n.* A thanksgiving ceremony carried out in fulfillment of a vow made for the safety of someone feared lost.

**pagduwa'a** *v. tr.* -*an* To engage in prayer, whether privately or as a congregation. (*Thesaurus:* **amu'-amu', harap₂, pudji 1.1, sambahayang, ta'at 1.1**)

**pagduwa'a-salamat** *v. tr.* -*an* To celebrate a recovery from loss or danger. *Ya dabbana ginuna bang aniya' magpama'ap atawa magduwa'a-salamat.* Tambourines may be used when there is a forgiveness or thanksgiving ceremony.

**pagduwa'ahan** (var. **pagduwaha'an**) *n.* A prayer meeting; a place where people assemble for prayer. *Lima mama'an i' niaminan ma pagduwa'ahan, jukup kapanyapanna.* Those five betel nut boxes were blessed at the prayer place, complete with all their contents. *Lubuhunbi saga tampat ya pagduwa'ahan sigām.* Dismantle the shrines where they make their prayers.

**duwa'i** *v. intr. pa-* To descend. *Magtūy iya paruwa'i min kura'na bo' pasujud min dahū'an sultan ē'.* He quickly got down from his horse and prostrated himself before the sultan. (*ant:* **dita'i**; *Thesaurus:* **deyo'₁ 1.1, hollo**)

**duwampū'** *num.* Twenty. *Bay kami ka'ā'an duwampū' pilak.* We were fined twenty pesos [lit. had twenty pesos taken from us]. *Aniya' sipat duwampū', tape' maka tangan. Aniya' isāb sipat* *siyampū'.* There is a diagnostic life-sign #20, feet and hands. There is also a life-sign #90.

**duwasay**₁ *adj. a-* Extravagant or wasteful. *Da'a paruwasayun sīnnu ilū.* Don't use that money of yours wastefully. (*cf:* **dalas 1**)

**duwasay**₂ *v. intr. pa-* To rush out to sea, of the water in a river or inlet. (*cf:* **balosok**)

**duwata** *n.* 1) A class of supernatural beings who interact in various ways with humans. *Dabangsa du duwata maka jīn sagwā' aheka ōnna. Aheka ginisan duwata, magtagunggu', magigal, maglabot saga, magsalamat, magmama', magsiga.* They are the same species as djinn but have many names. There are many kinds of duwata, those [summoned by] beating gongs, by dancing, by providing a feast, by giving alms, by sharing betel nut, or by providing cigarets. *Duwata na mandusiya' bang aniya' jīn pasōd. Subay aniya' duwatana bo' taga jīn.* A human being is a *duwata* when a djinn has entered. He must have a *duwata* in order to be a djinn proprietor. *Duwata itū halam aniya' saddī lahatna, hal baran a'a. Duwata maka jīn buwat manusiya' magdaluma'.* Duwata have no place other than a human body. Duwata and djinn are like humans who live in the same house. (*cf:* **jīn 1**; *Thesaurus:* **bangsa magl'l'ngngan, hama'-hama' a'a, hibilis, jīn 1, saitan, ya mbal ta'nda'**) 1.1) *v. advrs. -in-* Possessed or entered by a duwata being.

**pagduwata** *v. intr. aN-* To be engaged in summoning a duwata spirit.

**duwiyan** *var. of* **duliyan**

**dūy** *v. tr.* To drive away things that threaten or annoy. *Arōy, buwattingga e'tam angandūy saga bangsa itū? Aga'os gi' sigām min kitam.* Alas, how shall we drive away these other tribes? They are more powerful than we are. (*Thesaurus:* **budjaw, siga' 1.1, singga'-singga', sū₁ 1.1, t'ggal**)

**duyan** *v. tr.* To set someone swinging. (*Thesaurus:* **dundang₁ 1, ombo'-ombo', pagdanggu'-danggu', pagnanu', tadjun**)

**duyung** *n.* 1) The dugong or manatee; also referred to as a sea-cow. 2) A mermaid.

**duyung-duyung** *n.* The long beam that supports a grave marker. (*Thesaurus:* **pilang-pilang, sunduk 1**)

# E e

**ē** *intrj.* Expression of disapproval. *A: "Ameya' ka?" B: "Ē, mbal aku!"* A: "Will you come along?" B: "Not on your life!" *Ē, angurut na ka!* Fall out then, darn it! (*Thesaurus:* **agkā', allā, anā, arī, arōy, aruhuy, asē, ayī, dā'₁**)

**ebed-ebed** *n.* The webbing between the spines of the pectoral or dorsal fins of a fish. *Ma t'ngnga' iting, ya katas-daing inān, ya hē' niōnan ebed-ebed.* In the middle of the spines, the fish-tissue, that is what is called *ebed-ebed*.

**ebod** (var. **ibud**) *n.* The whorl of hair on the crown of one's head; a cowlick. (*Thesaurus:* **mbun-mbun, pusal₂**)

**ebog** 1) *adj. a-* Attracted to. *Aebog aku ma ka'a, ka'a bay magalti'-alti' hē'. D'nda ya aebog, abaya'an ka'a.* I am attracted to you, you who have made yourself so handsome. It's the girl who is attracted, wanting to have you. (*Thesaurus:* **baya' 1, bilahi 1, helo₁ 1, lingit 1, napsu 1**) 2) *n.* Desire, in response to beauty. 2.1) *v. advrs. ka-...-an* To be moved by desire. *Aniya' d'nda kaebogonna.* There is a woman whom he desires.

**paebog** *v. tr.* To stir a desire; to attract someone.

**ebol** *v. intr. aN-* To move vigorously through water. *Bang kita pakapo' bo' angebol kita, aheka ma buli'anta magbuliluk sala.* When we wade and move vigorously, little whirlpools sort of form behind us. *Bang aheka onde'-onde' angebol mbal na ta'nda'bi ai-ai.* When a lot of children are wading you can't see anything. (*Thesaurus:* **llis, sahabal, samb'llong**)

**ebol-ebol** *n.* The drain hole in the base of a container. *Pelang nihinangan ebol-ebol pamalabayan tahik. Sin'nsong pabalik bang halam na tahik ma deyom mohang.* A canoe with a drain hole made for it to allow the seawater to go out. The hole is plugged again when there is no longer seawater in the hull.

**ebot-ebot** *adv.* 1) Without fail; at all costs. *Ebot-ebot. Pagbuli-bulihinbi kami supaya pasambu hinang itu.* Don't forget. Keep us firmly in mind so that this project flourishes. 1.1) *v. tr. -an* To tell someone to do without fail. *Niebot-ebotan aku, sinoho' am'lli minsan ahunit.* I was told to make sure of it and instructed to buy even if expensive. (*Thesaurus:* **amay-amay 1, kamaya', hubaya-hubaya**)

**ekang-ekang** *n.* 1) A fetter; a handcuff. 1.1) *v. tr. -an* To fetter or handcuff someone. *Bang a'a tajīl inān, kinarenahan sali', niekang-ekangan.* When a person there is jailed, he is sort of chained, fettered. *Sinō' iya niekang-ekangan bo' yampa ni'isi ni deyom kalabusu.* Orders were given for him to be shackled and then put in prison. (*Thesaurus:* **bilanggu' 1, karena 1.1, kili-kili**)

**eddok-eddok** *adj. zero* Fake; fictive. *Anak eddok-eddok ko' inān.* That child is adopted [i.e. not born to her]. (*Thesaurus:* **ballo'**, **tē'₁**)

**egot-egot** *v. tr.* *-an* To urge someone to follow instructions. *Bang kami angahella' paraw angegot-ngegot kami.* When we're dragging a canoe, we keep urging [someone]. (*Thesaurus:* **abiyug, agpot 1, angin, logos 1, panhot, p'ggong, poleggaw**)

**pagegot-egot** *v. intr.* *aN-* To strive to influence or compel each other. *Sinukayan si Mma'. Yukna, "Da'a." Magegot-egot sigā maina'an. Ubus ni'nde'an sīn ni si Mma' inān, ubus ni'nde'an sīn ni bagay kami.* Dad was paid for the ride. He said, "Don't [pay]." They strove with each other. First the money was handed to Dad, then handed back to our friend. *Magegot-egot kami bang kami maghella' maka si Ja.* Ja and I strive together when we pull at each other. *Magegot-egot itu bang aniya' bay niamu' he' dangan bo' mbal ni'nde'an he' dangan, maumu na makapagbono'.* Egot-egot is when one person asks for something and the other won't hand it over, then they often get to fighting. (*Thesaurus:* **pagkosogan, pagda'ug, pagta'as-ta'as**)

**ehe** var. of **batang-ehe**

**ehe'-ehe'** *v. intr.* *aN-* To neigh, of a horse.

**ē'** var. of **hē'₁**, **hē'₂**

**e'** var. of **he'**

**elle'-elle'** *intrj.* A call to draw attention to something.

**pagpaelle'-elle'** *v. intr.* *aN-* To draw attention to one's own physical attractions. (*Thesaurus:* **mata-mata₁, pagpa'nda'-pa'nda', pa'amu-amu**)

**ellog** *n.* A species of wading bird. *Aheka kaginisan ellog. Aniya' bilu, aniya' pote', aniya' ettom, aniya' kausun, aniya' gaddung.* There are many kinds of *ellog*. There are blue ones, white ones, black, brown, and green. *Ellog, ataha' tuka'na angeket.* Herons have long beaks and can bite.

**elo** *n.* 1) Ice. 1.1) *v. tr.* To preserve something in ice. *Aniya' daing nielo.* There is some frozen fish. (*cf:* **aes**)

**elod-elod** *v. tr.* *-an* To do something persistently but without success. *Si Oto' hal magelod-elod maina'an, mbal pakattup.* Oldest Son just kept working on it, but it wouldn't click shut.

**elom** var. of **erom**

**elong-elong** *adj.* *zero* Dazzling; causing one to avert eyes.

**elong-elong mata** (var. **selong-selong mata**) *v. intr.* *maka-* To be dazzling or impressive. {idiom} *Makaelong-elong mata, buwat kita ang'nda' ni ka'llawan, mbal ahāp e'ta ang'nda'.* Dazzling the eyes, like when we look at the sun and can't see well. *Makaselong-selong mata, sali' ai-ai yamboho' ta'nda'ta.* Dazzling the eyes, like something never seen before. (*Thesaurus:* **keleng, paglinga-linga**)

**pagelong-elong** *v. tr.* To shake one's head as in surprise or shock. *Bang kita saupama nihalga'an*

*bo' kata'uhanta ngga'i ka tu'ud halga'na, hal kita magelong-elong.* For example, when we are quoted a price and we know that is really not its value, we simply shake our heads in shock. *Bang ka kahunitan magelong-elong.* When you are experiencing difficulties you shake your head. *A'a yampa ta'nda'ta, pinagelong-elong.* Someone not seen before, someone to shake the head at.

**embet** *v. tr.* To chase someone in a game of tag. *Pikiembet na, bilang itū.* Please chase us now, saying *bilang* [ready].

**pagembet** *n.* 1) The game of tag. 1.1) *v. intr.* *aN-* To play games of chasing. *Bay aniya' pelang aheka marilaut, kitam saga onde'-onde', ah'lling kita, "Oy! Aheka magembet-embet."* There were lots of canoes out at sea, us kids, and we said, "Hey, lots of us chasing each other." *Bang kami magembet, maglibut-libut kami.* When we play chasing, we run round and round.

**emon** *adj.* *a-* Tame; unafraid of humans. *Aemon itū, sali' bang kita anū' ma deyom kulaet, sali' mbal alahi, pak'nnos sadja.* This word *emon* is like when we fish by lantern-light, they don't escape, just stay perfectly still. (*cf:* **adla**)

**empon** *n.* 1) A tooth; the front tooth in contrast to a molar. *Empon maka baga'ang, emponta ya nilagnas bo' dasali'.* Front teeth and molars, it's our front teeth that are filed to make them even. (*Thesaurus:* **baga'ang, bangkil₂, sengel, taling**) 1.1) *v. intr.* *aN-* To cut new teeth; to be teething. (*cf:* **s'mbut 2**)

**empon talus** *n.* *phrase* Wisdom teeth. *Ahalol si Mu sabab bay magpalarutan empon talus.* Mu is close to death because he had his wisdom teeth extracted.

**endong** *n.* Various marine eels. (*Thesaurus:* **kasī, tagō'**)

**ene'-ene'** *see:* **pagene'-ene'**

**enok** *see:* **paenok**

**ensol** (var. **esnol**) *see:* **pagensol-ensol**

**entom** *adj.* *a-* 1) Able to remember. *Kulang na aku aentom, bo' pa'in basta Hailaya.* I don't remember much, but it would have been around the Hailaya festival. 1.1) *v. intr.* *pa-* To come to one's mind. *Paentom ma atayna ya kamemon bay tahinang e' saga danakanna ma iya ma waktu hē'.* All that his brothers had done to him way back came into his mind. 1.2) *v. tr.* To recall with emotion; to long for. *Sidda aku angentom ma ka'a bang ka ma lahat dakayu'.* I miss you so much when you are in another place. *Daipara nientom aku e' Tuhan, ya bay pagtuhanan mbo'ku si Ibrahim.* Fortunately however, I was remembered by the God who had been the god of my ancestor Ibrahim. (*Thesaurus:* **magtak, padlak ni atay, sangpit, suligpat, tambung, tasdik, tomtom 1.1**)

**kaentoman** *n.* The faculty or act of remembering. *Amiha lagi' kaentoman.* I'm still trying to find it in my memory.

**entom buddi** *n. phrase* A sense of obligation for kindness shown or a favor done. {idiom} *Taentomku buddinu.* I remember your goodness to me. *Bang aniya' taentom ma kita e' sai-sai na pa'in, bang kita ahāp, buddi a'a ma kita.* If someone, whoever it may be, remembers us for our goodness [to him], that person will feel an obligation. (*Thesaurus:* **balos₁** 1, **pagbuling-bata'** 1.1, **paluli**)

**pangentom** *n.* What one remembers; a longing for the past.

**pangentoman** *n.* A memorial; a souvenir.

**pangentom llum** *n. phrase* Longing for someone still alive.

**samaentom** *adj.* To miss each other when apart, of two people.

**entos** *v. tr.* To extract juice by pressure. *Angentos t'bbu tahinang gula'.* Pressing the sugar cane to be made into syrup.

**engas-engas** (var. **angas**; **hengas-hengas**) *n.* Twigs; small branches. (*wh:* **kayu** 1; *Thesaurus:* **tagay**)

**engke'** *v. intr. pa-* To stand on tiptoe. *Subay ka paengke' bo' ta'nda'nu.* You have to stand on tiptoe so you can see it. *Da'a paengke'un tape'nu, par'ddahun ni papan atawa ni lantay.* Don't stand on the tips of your feet; put them down firmly on a board or on the floor.

**pagengke'-engke'** *v. intr. aN-* To hop from one foot to the other.

**engket** *v. tr. -an* To remove cooking food from the heat. *Subay ma lapohan bo' niengketan, sali' nila'anan min pam'llahan.* Must be on a cooking-fire to be removed, like taking it away from the cooking place. *Engketin na daing ilū bang angogok-ngogok na.* Take that fish off the heat when it is bubbling. (*cf:* **haun₁**, **luwag** 1.1)

**engkot** (var. **hengkot**) *n.* 1) A knot in a line. (*cf:* **buku₁** 1, **p'kkos tuwa**) 1.1) *v. tr. -an* To tie something; to secure something by tying. *Am'lli aku goma pangengkotanku karsitinku.* I buy rubber bands for tying up my socks. *Buwat tiyangsi' niā' min batang niyug, niā', nilapesan. Mbal magtūy tapangengkot magdai'-dai' ni ai-ai. Subay gi' tinabid-tabid bo' mbal maglopeng.* Like *tiyangsi'* obtained from the central rib of a coconut frond. It can't be used in a hurry for tying anything. It should be twined a bit first so it doesn't lose its shape. *Hengkotinbi pelang ilū ko da'a talaran parilaut.* Tie that canoe there so it isn't swept out to sea by the current. *Wa'i ahūg dakayu' atop halam bay kaengkotan.* A section of thatch that wasn't tied has fallen down. (*Thesaurus:* **baggot**, **bīt₂**, **gakut**, **tabul-tabul**, **tollen**; *ant:* **hubad**)

**engkot-buta** *n.* 1) A thumb knot or half-hitch. 1.1) *v. tr. -an* To secure a knot by making an extra hitch. *Binutahan engkot pelang abō' ahogot.* The canoe line was tied with a half-hitch so it would be secure.

**engkot-sintak** *n.* A knot that can be released by

pulling on one end of the line.

**pagengkot** *v. tr. -an* 1) To tie numerous items into a single bundle. *Bā'anta ka, mbal manjari bang pinaghengkotan kamemon.* I tell you, it won't work to have everything tied together. 1.1) *v. intr. aN-* To bond together in an enduring relationship. *Magengkot aku maka bagayku, minsan pinapatay.* I will stay closely bonded with my friend, even though we are killed.

**engge'-engge'** *v. intr. pa-* To sit in a squatting position. *Da'a ka aningkō' paengge'-engge', par'ssal.* Don't squat, sit down flat [on the floor].

**epang** var. of **apang**

**epe** *v. intr. aN-* To propel a canoe with one hand on the paddle, using a foot as a fulcrum. *Amusay na aku angepe-ngepe tudju ni Manubal.* I will paddle towards Manubal Island, using the one-hand technique. (*Thesaurus:* **busay** 1.1, **kelle** 1.1, **dayung** 1.1, **luwad**, **tindayung**)

**epet** *n.* The Rippled triggerfish; the Blue triggerfish. *Balistes fuscus.*

**epet-timbang** *n.* The Red-tooth triggerfish. *Odonus niger.*

**epo'** *n.* A metal spur lashed to the leg of a fighting cock. *Epo' itū, sali' laring-laring atalom binaggot ni tape' manuk. Epo'* are like little sharp knives, tied to the cock's feet. *Bay magbulang manuk, paleyang na. Taluwa' pa'in he' epo, apakpak pareyo'.* The cocks were fighting, flying up. When struck by a spur [they] fall down. (*cf:* **tahod**)

**epol** *n.* An apple.

**eral-eral₁** *n.* A species of edible monovalve, like a small helmet shell in shape. (*syn:* **kulallit₁**)

**eral-eral₂** *n.* The edible fruit of some seagrass. *Ya pasugpatan sumping unas ya niōnan eral-eral.* The extension of the sea-grass flower is called *eral-eral.* (*cf:* **buwa'-unas**)

**erēs** *v. tr. -an* To erase something written. (*Thesaurus:* **pahalam**, **papas₁** 1.1)

**eresel** *n.* An eraser (of print). *Subay tinau' pahogot ereselnu ilū bo' mbal alungay.* That eraser of yours should be stored securely so it doesn't get lost.

**ero'** *n.* 1) A dog. *Ilu na daing, kinakan he' ero'.* There's the fish, eaten by a dog. 2) Dog as a derogatory term for a human being. *Bang aniya' sali' magsuli-suli, ubus palabay sadja kita mbal minsan magtabiya'. Hatina hē' sali' niyatta ero' in manusiya'.* When there are people talking and we just go by them not even saying excuse me. In other words we regard humans as dogs. (*cf:* **hanjing-binatang**)

**ero'-keyat** *v. tr.* To be extremely aggressive or violent. {idiom} *Angero'-keyat itū, hatina aesog to'ongan. Mbal iya pasapad. Ero'-keyat* means extremely aggressive. He can't be restrained.

**pagero'-ero'** *v. tr.* To treat someone as if he was a dog. *Pinagero'-ero' kita, sali' kita nihalam-biyara'.* Treated like dogs, as though we are of unknown parentage. *Pinagero'-ero' si Mo, sinoho' angandarutan hãg luma'na.* Mo is treated like a dog, ordered to pull out the posts of his house.

**erom** (var. **elom**) *adj. zero* Dark or dusky, of skin or fur.

**eskedyul** *n.* A timetable; a schedule.

**eskoba** *n.* 1) A scrubbing brush; a broom. *Daun langkay nihinang eskoba pangeskoba luma' kami.* Dry palm fronds made into a broom for sweeping our house. (*cf:* **kuskus** 1) 1.1) *v. tr.* To sweep a floor.

**eskwela** var. of **iskul**

**esnol** var. of **ensol**

**esok** *n.* The woody part of a tree, whether pith or hard wood. *Taga esok nsa' bidda' kayu. Aniya' esokna man deyom, ya magpōng-pōng. Ahãp lahi ni kubal.* Trees of all sorts have *esok*. There is *esok* inside, the stuff that breaks up. The part towards the hardwood layer is good. (*Thesaurus:* **kubal** 1, **sapan**₂, **tupas**₂)

**esok-mata** *n.* Sclera, the white of the eye. (*wh:* **mata**₁ 1)

**esog** *n.* 1) Courage; bravery. 1.1) *adj. a-* Brave; fierce; aggressive. *Aesog sigãm maka abantug ma kalahat-lahatan.* They are brave and famous across the lands. (*Thesaurus:* **aykalas** 1, **bahani** 1) 1.2) *v. intr. pa-* To behave with courage. *Paesog kam angatu, sabab bang mbal tabanyaga' kitam.* Fight bravely because if you don't, we will be enslaved.

**espalton** *n.* Bitumen. *Palanay na espalton, apasu' he' llaw.* The bitumen melts, made hot by the sun. (*cf:* **kitlan** 1)

**espowen** var. of **ispowen**

**estawran** *n.* A restaurant or cafe where one sits down to eat. (*Thesaurus:* **kadday, pasal**₂ 1, **tabu'** 1, **tinda, tiyanggi**)

**estenles** *adj. zero* Stainless; non-rusting. (*Thesaurus:* **bulawan** 1, **luyang, pilak** 1, **pittang, sawasa'**,

**tumbaga** 1)

**estenles-kitara** *n.* A guitar string (metal). *Subay kono' sinangonan estenles-kitara.* It needs, he says, to have a stainless steel guitar string fitted. (*Thesaurus:* **basi'-basi'**, **korente** 1.1, **kowat**)

**estēp** *n.* The game of kick the block.

**pagestēp** *v. intr. aN-* To play a game in which a block is kicked from square to square on a marked field. (*cf:* **ulat**₂)

**etang-etang** *n.* The mid-rib of a coconut frond. (*cf:* **paipa'**₂; *wh:* **niyug**)

**etek** *n.* Duck species. *Etek ilū palangi ma tahik.* The duck there swims on the sea. *Sali' buli' etek bu'unna.* His hair is like a duck's butt. (*cf:* **patu'**)

**eto'-eto'** *n.* The climbing fern and its strong fiber. *Lygodium sp.* (*cf:* **nitu'**)

**ettom** *adj. a-* 1) Black (color); dark (complexion). *Lahoran, sali' angaluwa salindugu', ettom, pote', gaddung.* Bruised, sort of looking like a rainbow, black, white, green. (*ant:* **pote'** 1.1; *gen:* **walna'**) 1.1) *v. intr. aN-* To become dark.

**kaettoman** *n.* Dark coloring of a natural feature, typically rock. *Puhu, ya kaettoman bo' aratag.* Puhu, the formation that is black but flat.

**kaettoman-mata** *n.* The pupil of the eye. (*syn:* **ta'u-ta'u-mata**)

**pagettom** *v. intr. aN-* To become dark in color; to blacken. *Pelangku itu alangis, mbal magettom-ettom. Ahãp nīnda'.* This canoe of mine is well-cared for, it doesn't blacken. It looks good.

**eya'** *intrj.* A call to get a baby's attention. *Eya'! Mimi' ka! Halam maitu ina'nu.* Ha! You're all alone! Your mother isn't here.

**eyaw** *v. intr. aN-* To mew, as a cat.

**eyok** (var. **keyok**) *v. intr. aN-* To squawk, as a chicken being slaughtered. *Bay aku pin'kkol e' si Mi. Angeyok, aheya manuk!* Mi throttled me. I squawked, what a bird!

**eyot** var. of **keyot**₁

# G g

**gabbang** *n.* 1) A musical instrument with wooden keys (similar to a marimba or xylophone). *Lisagun kono' ba gabbang ilū.* Please beat time on that marimba. 1.1) *v. advrs. ka-...-an* To be entertained by marimba music. *Bay kalongsaran luma' disi anu inān, bay kagabbangan dibuhi'.* What's-his-name's house there has collapsed, [the house] that had the bamboo marimba performance last night.

**paggabbang** *v. tr.* To be engaged in playing a gabbang (a wooden-keyed xylophone). *Buwat aniya' paluruk ni pagkawinan, asal aheka a'a. Luba' gi' bang maggabbang.* It's like when guests go to a wedding venue, lots people, naturally.

And even more so, if there is to be *gabbang*-playing.

**gabla'** *v. tr. -an* To disturb a community by intimidation or disorderly behavior. *Ginabla'an lahat ma aniya' bay makasōd a'a ala'at. Sali' ahidjul, aniya' ni kahāpan, aniya' ni kala'atan.* The place is unsettled when bad people have come in. It's kind of noisy, sometimes good, sometimes bad.

**gabuk** *adj. a-* Damaged by termites. *Gabuk itū maglowang-lowang, malomo itū sali' bāng-bāng magkabila'.* *Gabuk* means riddled with holes, *lomo* is like cookies prone to break. *Buwat kayu bay agabuk, na bo' taluwa' baliyu hal palintuwad.*

Like a tree that was damaged by termites, when hit by wind it simply falls down.

**gabul** *adj. a-* Blurred; misty, of someone's vision. *Mbal aku makabassa, agabul e'ku ang'nda'.* I can't read, my eyesight is blurry. (*Thesaurus:* **bulahaw**)

**gabul-mata** *n.* Blue eyes. {idiom} *Milikan gabul-mata.* A pale-eyed Westerner.

**gabun** *n.* A cloud (generic). *Bang sangom bo' asawa bulan, aheya landungta. Aniya' isāb landung gabun.* At night when the moon is bright, one's shadow is large. There are cloud shadows too. (*Thesaurus:* **andom 1, haya'₂, tai'-baliyu, turung-balu 2**)

**gakit** *adj. zero* Twisted together, of parallel segments.

**gakut** *v. tr. -an* To tie something securely. *Gakutin bo' mbal abustak.* Tie it up well so that it doesn't burst. (*Thesaurus:* **baggot, bīt₂, engkot 1.1, tabul-tabul, tollen**)

**paggakut** *v. tr.* To lash together a number of things arranged in parallel. *Pinaggakut buwat duwa bayan pinaggimbal.* Lashed together, like two canoes placed side-by-side.

**gaddong** *n.* A wooden container for secure storage. *Gaddong, pangisihan panggi' kayu. Papan suma'an kayu nihinang.* A wooden container for storing cassava. Made of milled boards, or sometimes of [solid] wood. (*gen:* **pagtau'an**)

**gaddongan** *n.* A source of wealth or livelihood, as a farm or fishing ground. *Gaddongan hē' pangā'an alta'ku.* That farm/fishing area is the source of my wealth. *Aniya' isāb gaddongan ma dilaut. Sali' aniya' deyo' tatuli'ku. Ya gaddongan, sali' humaku.* There is a food source at sea too. Like a fishing spot I can find my way to. *Gaddongan is like my farm.* (*cf:* **pagusaha'an**)

**gaddung** *n.* **1)** The color green. *Bang kita sinangti', gaddung he'ta ang'nda'.* When we suffer a relapse, we see green. *Ya sowa-sowa lokay, ya magaddung, mariki'-diki' ilū.* The little *lokay* snake, the green one, the little one. (*gen:* **walna'**) **1.1)** *adj. zero* Colored green. *Balimbing itū agaddung, aniya' du isāb akeyat bang atahak.* These star-apples are green, and there are red ones too when ripe.

**gadgad₁** *v. intr. pa-* To settle heavily in the pit of one's gut. *Pagadgad deyom tina'ita, sali' agumun.* Our intestines have settled, sort of entangled. *Itiya' patimuk pi'itu tina'ita, sali' kita a'sso.* Our gut accumulating here, like when we are full from eating. (*Thesaurus:* **doson 1, honhon, lomeng-lomeng**)

**gadgad₂** *n.* A flow of water. *Pahondong gadgad bohe'.* The flow of water stopped.

**pagadgad** *v. tr.* To set something flowing with the current.

**gadja** *n.* An elephant. (*gen:* **sattuwa**)

**gadja-gadja** *n.* **1)** Mumps; any swelling of the glands of the neck. **1.1)** *v. advrs. -in-* Suffering from mumps or other swelling of the neck glands.

**gadjamina** *n.* The sperm whale, said to be the source of ambergris. *Physeter catodon (tentative).* (*cf:* **tai'-ambal**; *gen:* **sattuwa**; *Thesaurus:* **kahumbu, layul**)

**gadji** *n.* **1)** Regular remuneration, in the form of wages or salary. *Pila gadjinu?* How much are your wages? **1.1)** *v. tr. -an* To pay someone a regular wage. *Halam aku bay ginadjihan sabab halam kono' aniya' sīn panganggadji.* I was not paid wages because, he said, there was no money for paying them. (*Thesaurus:* **bayad 1.1, hokas, lampak₁ 1.1, susuk, tinga 1.1, tulahan, tunay₂, tungbas 1**)

**gagā** *v. tr.* To stuff something into a narrow aperture, as to prevent leakage. *Bang ang'mman pelang subay ginagā maka bulitik.* When the canoe leaks it should be caulked with resin. *Tagagā bowa'na.* His mouth plugged. (*Thesaurus:* **s'nsong, tambal₂**)

**gaga** *v. tr.* To achieve something by physical ability, financial resources, or strength of personality. *Da'a aku b'llihin pelang aheya. Mbal tagagaku bang alandos baliyu.* Don't buy a large canoe for me. I won't be able to control it in a strong wind. (*Thesaurus:* **aguwanta 1.1, anggap 1, anggop₂, bāng-bāng₁, bogbog₂, kole', tigayu'**)

**gaga'** *v. advrs. ta-* Hesitant in manner, of speech. *Tagaga' aku, sali' ahawal-hawal. Buwat aku ang'ntan, ang'ntan du, mbal du.* I'm hesitant, sort of uncertain. Like when I touch something, I touch it, then I don't. *Pinandi kita atay-batu bo' mbal tagaga' amissala ya ai-ai kapatutan.* One is bathed ritually to prevent being hesitant to speak whatever is appropriate. *Da'a ka tagaga' bang ka ah'lling.* Don't be hesitant when you talk. *Bang pandu'anku ka'a, sidda aku tagaga', sali' magpōng-pōng.* When I teach you I am very hesitant, [my speech] sort of breaking up. (*cf:* **mamang₂**)

**gaga'osan** (derivative of **ga'os**) *n.* Combative abilities. *Ai na ka saga nakura', ai na ka saga kawasa, ai na ka saga gaga'osan.* Whether leaders, or authorities, or powers of combat.

**gagal₁** *adj. a-* Labored and irregular, of breathing. *Agagal napasta, sali' ajogjog kōk-atayta bang kita agnapas.* Our breathing is labored, our sternum sort of shaking when we breathe. (*Thesaurus:* **paghagak, pagnapas, panggahak, ppo**)

**gagal₂** *adj. a-* Seriously distressed, of someone gravely ill or in deep grief. *Wa'i anaknu mahē', na agagal ka ma si Li.* Your child is far away, you are grieving for Li. *Bang a'a asekot na kamatayna, yukta, "Da'a na ka agagal ma deyom luma'. Halam gi' tahukum."* When a person is close to death, we say, "Don't be distressed here in the house. He hasn't been judged yet." *Sali' kita asaki, bang asidda-sidda agagal paltubuhanta* *itū.* Like when we are sick, when things are very serious, our whole being is distressed.

**gagam** *v. intr.* pa- To move stealthily under cover of darkness. *Pagagam-gagam, sali' palē, sali' kamaya'-maya'.* Moving stealthily, sort of crawling, being very cautious. *Buwat l'lla pagagam ni d'nda bang sangom, bo' ngga'i ka h'ndana.* Like a man making advances to a woman at night, but she's not his wife. (*Thesaurus:* **agap₂, tangkaw 1**)

**gagas** *adj.* a- Completely faded or evaporated. (*Thesaurus:* **baluba 1, lulu, padpad, papas₁ 1**)

**gagati'** *n.* Popped rice or corn. (*Thesaurus:* **ampaw, biti'₁, bulitik₂**)

**gagawi'** *n.* Wooden implements for handling food during cooking.

**gagga** *adj.* a- Stubborn; disobedient. *Agagga onde'-onde' inān; mbal pasoho'.* That child is disobedient, can't be told what to do. *Bang onde'-onde' duwa imbun-imbunna, yukta agagga.* If a child has two whorls on his head, we say he is stubborn. (*ant:* **hutu**; *Thesaurus:* **alod₁, k'llas 1.1, tuwas 1**)

   **kagaggahan** *n.* Stubbornness; obstinacy. *Kagaggahan onde', mbal buwattina'an!* The stubbornnesss of the child, nothing like it!

**gaggal** var. of **aggal**

**gaggat** *n.* **1)** A hindrance to carrying out a plan. *Buwat kita atulak am'ssi, bang aniya' nahas buwat aniya' asaki atawa magka'at, yukta, "Da'a kam palanjal, aniya' gaggat."* Like when we leave for fishing, when there is a misfortune like someone being sick or something damaged, we say, "Don't go, there is a hindrance." (*cf:* **bimbang 1, limbit 1.1**) **1.1)** *adj.* a- Hindered or thwarted.

**gaggut** var. of **ganggut**

**gaguk** *n.* A species of catfish. (*gen:* **taote'**)

**gagus** *adj.* a- Peeled off or flaked due to heat. *Bang magusaha oto'ku agagus he' llaw.* When my eldest son is working for a living his skin peels due to the sun. *Mbal agagus dawat bolpen.* The ink of a ballpen doesn't flake off. (*Thesaurus:* **kanit 1, lakles, laknit 1, oplak 1**)

   **kagagusan** *n.* Severe flaking of the skin, attributed to long exposure to the sun. *Kagagusan a'a inān, mbal buwattina'an, gagus man gagus.* The flakiness of that man's skin, never seen anything like it, flake upon flake.

**gaha'** *n.* **1)** Rust; oxidation. **1.1)** *v. advrs.* -in- Rusting; corroded. *Barilis mbal tapangisihan bohe', ginaha' na.* The barrel can't be used for storing water, it has become rusty. *Pittang, at'ggol-t'ggol ginaha', al'kkas al'ngngat.* Pittang [a non-ferrous alloy] takes quite a long time to rust but is quickly bent out of shape. **1.2)** *v. advrs.* ka-...-an To be discolored with rust. *Kagaha'an badju'ku.* My shirt is covered with rust.

**gahal** *adj.* a- Pale or faded, of paint.

**gahud** *v. tr.* To shape wood with a spokeshave.

   **gahud-gahud₁** (var. **hagud-hagud**) *n.* A spokeshave or draw-knife.

**gahud-gahud₂** var. of **ahud-ahud**

**ga'ib** *v. intr.* pa- To be present without being seen. *Hal paga'ib sadja, hal lling takaleta. Mbal tanda'ta. Palahil itū ta'nda'ta.* It is simply present, just a sound that we hear. We do not see it. The *palahil* referred to is something seen. *Bang ma kami mbo' paga'ib, saddi ya mbo' palahil.* For us [excl] there are non-visible *mbo'* [ancestors], distinct from visible *mbo'* [grandparents].

**ga'ira** *n.* A person who offends shamelessly against moral standards. (*Thesaurus:* **ba'is, biga', puta, sundal 1**)

**ga'os** *n.* **1)** The ability to achieve something purposed or planned. *Matto'a ya makaga'os, ga'os bogbog.* An elder is the one who has the ability to make things happen, the supportive ability. **1.1)** *adj.* a- Capable; powerful. *Saga a'a as'nnay makapah'llingan dī sigām, "Aga'os na aku!"* Weaklings may say to themselves, "I can do it!" **1.2)** *v. tr.* To provide someone with support or backing. *Bang aku ta'abut kinawin, gina'os aku e' siyali si Mma'.* When the time comes for me to marry, my father's younger brother will support me. (*cf:* **kinosog**; *Thesaurus:* **bogbog₁ 1.1, dapit, gapi' 1.2, tapil 2**)

   **kaga'osan** *n.* Ability to achieve results or win battles. *In kaga'osan sultan, ya na heka saga a'ana.* The power of a sultan is the number of his men.

**ga'osan** *n.* The ability to dominate or achieve a purpose. *Pila ga'osan mareyom Pilipin itū, aga'os lagi' Milikan.* However many powers there are here in the Philippines, Americans are more powerful. *Pinuwasan kami min ga'osan saga mundu hē'.* We were rescued from the power of those bandits. *Bangsa ga'osan asal bangsa ina'an.* That tribe is by nature a nation of power.

**pagga'os-ga'os** *v. intr.* aN- To strive together for mastery. *Saga a'a ina'an hal magga'os-ga'os dī sigām.* Those people just struggle with each other.

**gaga'osan** *n.* Combative abilities.

**ga'ud-ga'ud** *n.* The Gold-lined sea bream. *Rhabdosargus sarba.*

**ga'ud-ga'ud-pote'** *n.* The King soldier-bream. *Argyrops spinifer.*

**ga'ut** *v. tr.* To tug at something. *Bang aku magdundang, yukku, "Da'a ga'utun lubid itū! Ahūg aku."* When I am swinging I say, "Don't pull on thís rope! I will fall." (*Thesaurus:* **bira 1, konot₂, ganggut, guyud 1, hella', paglagedled 1**)

**pagga'ut** *v. intr.* aN- **1)** To pull at each other. *Magga'ut, maggo'on-go'on, maghella', bang kita sali' maglata.* We tug at each other, trying to go in different directions, pulling at each other, when we are having fun together. *Magga'ut maka sehe'ta magbono', arai'-arai' magabut na.* Friends pulling at each other, getting into a fight, on the point of connecting. **1.1)** *v. intr. aN-* To be working at cross-purposes.

**galak₁** *n.* **1)** A positive outlook; the expectation of a good outcome. *Bang sali' angalampung baranta, nā bilahi kita ni pagbono'an. Aniya' galakta.* If our body becomes sort of light, then we want to go to where the fighting is. We have a good feeling about it. *Halam aniya' galakku ameya' ni pū'.* I don't have a good feeling about going to the outer islands. *Ag'mma aku, sali' akawang deyom atayku aku ni M'ddas bang halam aniya' sehe'ku. Sali' aku binuwanan galak pinal'ngngan atawa mbal.* I am fearful, apprehensive about going to Siasi Town without a companion. It's like being given a sense of rightness about going ahead or not. (*Thesaurus:* **kagustuhan, pasa'atan**) **1.1)** *v. tr. a-, ka-..-an, -an* To regard something positively. *Kinagalakan, sali' kinabilahi'an, buwat s'mmek. Ai-ai kabaya'anta niōnan kinagalakan.* Something regarded positively, as though wanted, like clothing. Anything we want to have is spoken of as the thing we feel good about. *Ya badju' ina'an i kagalakanku to'ongan bin'lli.* That shirt there is the one I feel really good about buying.

**kagalakan** *n.* A positive feeling towards something.

**paggalak** *v. intr. aN-* To be in a positive frame of mind about something. *Subay kinata'uhan aniya' sukud bo' kita maggalak.* It has to be known that there will be good luck for us to be feeling positive.

**paggalakan** *n.* The expectation of a good outcome. *Bang kita kaut mbal paggalakan. Subay kinata'uhan aniya' sukud bo' kita maggalak.* When we go to sea there is no positive expectation. We need to realize that there will [only] be good fortune if we are in a positive frame of mind. *Bang kita kaut mbal paggalakan.* When we go to sea there is no positive expectation.

**galak₂** *adj. a-* Non-fading, durable. (*Thesaurus:* **anagtol, kamdos₂, kumpay, pagon₁ 1.1, taggu₁, tatas 1.1, togob₁**)

**galak₃** *n.* A heartbeat; a pulse. *Tatatab galakta he' mananawal bang kita sōng amatay.* The healer feels our pulse when we are close to death. *Galak, ya sali' agk'bbut-k'bbut itū.* Galak, this thing that is beating here. (*cf:* **pagk'bbut-k'bbut**)

**galangan** var. of **kalangan₂**

**galawang** *n.* A type of kite (for flying). (*cf:* **mandal**)

**galden** *n.* A garden as a school project. *Landu' ahunit hinang ma galden.* Work in the [school] garden is tough. (*cf:* **jambangan**)

**gali'₁** *v. tr. -an* To make long shallow cuts in flesh. *Subay daing aheya pinundang, sabab mbal atoho' bang halam ginali'an. Niulat du.* A big fish has to be cut into because it will not dry otherwise. It will get fly-blown. *Ginali'an daing bo' nilandang-*

landang. Fish are cut lengthwise for frying. (*Thesaurus:* **balang 1, balkehet, ballul 1, galing-galing**)

**gali'₂** *n.* A crack or fault-line in a surface. *Bang gali'an sōng abila'.* If it has a crack it will shortly break. (*Thesaurus:* **galna' 1, l'tta' 1**)

**galing-galing** *v. tr.* To cut lengthwise slits in the surface of meat or fish for salting. *Tulay bay galing-galingku, bay niasin.* The scads that I cut slits in have been salted. (*Thesaurus:* **balang 1, balkehet, ballul 1, gali'₁**)

**galit** *v. tr. -an* To roar or shout abusively at someone. *Buwat si Ba bang kita mbal ameya-meya', magtūy kita ginalitan.* Like Ba, when we don't obey him we get shouted at immediately. *Olanganku siyaliku bang mbal ameya' soho'ku. Galitanku.* I shout at my younger sibling when he doesn't obey my instructions. I roar at him. (*Thesaurus:* **asang₂, kula'ak, gasud, olang 1.1, pagalud, pahit**)

**paggalit** *v. tr. -an* To yell at someone repeatedly. *Pinaggalitan iya bang nilinganan. Minsan takale mbal angasip.* He is yelled at repeatedly when called. Even though he hears he doesn't respond.

**gallang** *n.* Bracelets of various types. *Am'lli gallang si Ni pamuwanna ma tunangna si Mo.* Ni is buying a bracelet as a gift for Mo, his fiancée.

**pagginallang** *v. intr. aN-* To wear a bracelet. *Magginallang, magsin'mmek, magsinuray.* Wearing bracelets, dressed in fine clothes, combs in the hair.

**gallang gakit** *n. phrase* A bracelet of twined silver strands.

**gallang labu** *n. phrase* A bracelet made from the cross-section of a cone shell, worn to protect the wearer from supernatural harm. (*gen:* **tambang₃ 1**)

**gallang lubid** *n. phrase* A bracelet made of twined gold or silver strands.

**gallang pilak** *n. phrase* A bracelet made of silver. *Gallang pilak itū, sinasal.* These silver bracelets, they are made by beating hot metal.

**gallang pitis-pitis** *n. phrase* A bracelet of linked small coins.

**gallang sulabay** *n. phrase* A bracelet, made of gold set with gems.

**gallang sulaw** *n. phrase* A bracelet made from the cross-section of a cone shell, worn to protect the wearer from supernatural harm.

**gallangan** *n.* The Black-barred surgeonfish. *Acunthurus nigricans.* (*gen:* **kumay**)

**galna'** *n.* **1)** A flaw or crack in a surface. *Taga galna' pinggan ilū, kagalna'an he' kuskus basi'-basi'.* That bowl has a crack, it has been blemished by a metal pot scourer. *Taga galna' sawan ilū.* That drinking glass has a crack. (*Thesaurus:* **gali'₂, l'tta' 1**) **1.1)** *adj. -an* Damaged by a crack or split. *Galna'an, angal'tta', mbal abila' to'ongan.* Damaged, cracking, not completely broken apart. **1.2)** *v. advrs. ka-...-an* To be flawed as a result of some harmful action. *Kagalna'an pinggan he' kuskus basi'-basi'.* The bowl has been blemished by a metal pot scourer.

**galon** *n.* **1)** A water storage container that can be carried in the hand. **2)** A gallon measure.

**galsa** (var. **gasa**) *n.* The porcelain heating element of a pressure lantern.

**galung 1)** *n.* A bundle of flexible items. (*cf:* **halug** 2) **2)** *clf.* Count word for bundles of flexible items. *B'llihin aku duwanggalung buway, ya buway pagsigid ilū.* Buy me two bundles of rattan, that rattan for tying the thatch.

**galura'** *n.* A mythical winged horse whose appearance will herald the closing up of the present world. *Kura' iya, kōkna a'a, ataha' bu'unna. Onde'-onde' akura' ma iya.* It is a horse, its head human, its hair long. A child rides it. *Bang pasayang pikpik galura' magtūy akiyamat dunya, minnē', min hamiyuna, agtambol dunya.* When the winged horse spreads its wings in flight the world will end. From that, from the turbulence [of its flight], the world will be closed up. (*Thesaurus:* **sambalani, sumayang-galura'** 1)

**gām-gām** *v. intr. pa-* To improve, of a difficult situation or the physical condition of a person who is ill. *Pagām-gām na, mbal gi' kauli'an.* Getting better already but not yet healed. *Buwat kita tara'ug aheya, saga ₱20, pagsubu, anganda'ug kita ₱15. Makagām-gām kita.* Like when we lose a lot, ₱20 or so, and next morning we win ₱15. We are doing better. *Bang onde'-onde' a'sso to'ongan, yukta, "Kallus kallus, makagām-gāman na."* When a toddler is over-full, we say, "Push, push, it's getting better." (*syn:* **gōm-gōm**; *Thesaurus:* **hāp-hāp, hikay, hoblas** 1, **lōng-lōng, siha'-siha', si'at**)

   **kagām-gāman** *n.* Improvement in health; a change for the better. (*cf:* **kahikayan**)

**gamat₁** var. of **bāt-gamat**

**gamat₂** var. of **kalitan-gamat**

**gamay** *n.* An edible seaweed, like bunches of tiny green grapes in appearance. *Caulerpa lentillifera.* (*syn:* **lato'**; *Thesaurus:* **agal-agal, gulaman**)

**gambahan** *see:* **paggambahan**

**gambil** var. of **gimbal**

**gamis** *n.* A long robe or undergarment worn by Muslim men. (*Thesaurus:* **juba, luku**)

**gamos** (var. **g'mmos**) *adj. a-* **1)** Soaked; wet through. *Agamos kami, bay tauwa' ulan.* We are soaked, caught in the rain. *Ag'mmos kayu ilu, bohe'an sali'.* This wood is soaked, sort of full of sap. (*Thesaurus:* **base'₁, bugbug₁, bugga'** 1, **himāy, tomog**) **1.1)** *v. tr.* To soak something; to leave something in a wet condition. *Da'a gimmos. Ai-ai abase' subay da'a tinau'.* Don't leave it wet. Anything wet should not be stored. **1.2)** *v. tr. -an* To soak something in brine to preserve it. *Da'a pinagbangkat-bangkat daing-daing ilū, da'a ginamosan.* Don't stack those fish

up in layers, don't pickle them. (*Thesaurus:* **boro** 1.1, **pagtasik**)

**gampal** *n.* Floating masses of dead vegetation. *Aheka gampal, aheka sagbot ma dilaut maggūngan, buwat ulak, unas.* There is a lot of *gampal*, a lot of weedy rubbish floating out at sea, like [dead] seaweed or seagrass. (*Thesaurus:* **pagung, ulak** 1)

**gampang** *n.* **1)** A barrier or protection against mishap. *Ya gampang itū ya sali' saga habay-habay bo' mbal tauwa' hinang-hinang. Gampang* is like a charm against harm from witchcraft. *Hinangun ād mailu. Minsan baliyu akosog, aniya' gampangna.* Build a fence there. Even if there is a strong wind there will be a protection. **1.1)** *v. tr. -an* To provide someone with protection against sorcery by wearing a charm; to resist some influence. *Bang aniya' l'lla angalindang budjang inān, yukna ginampangan bo' mbal tauwa' hinang-hinang.* If a man has put a love-spell on a single girl, she says she is protected against influence from sorcery. (*cf:* **hampan** 1; *gen:* **tambang₃** 1)

**gamut** *n.* A root. *Aniya' lima ginis gamut kayu nihinang tambal lu'ug.* There are five kinds of tree roots that are made into medicine for exhaustion. (*wh:* **kayu** 1)

**gamut-nonan** *n.* A plant used medicinally.

**gana** *conj.* Given certain conditions. *Gana buwattē', magtūy aniya' limampū' sundalu.* When that happened, immediately there were fifty soldiers. *Na gana sangom na, tatangday e'na anakna ati amatay.* Then when night came, she lay on her child and [he] died. (*Thesaurus:* **abila, bang₁, bangsi', basta, bo' na, pagka, samantala', talkala'**)

**gana-gana** *adv.* **1)** Future time. *Subay na gana-gana bo' kami pehē'.* It will have to be later on when we go there. *Gana-gana isāb p'llayku kulaet.* In a while I'll swing the lantern around. *Gana-gana anigangkul batu ilū, ya lling kakal.* In time that stone will make a tapping noise, the sound of a club hitting. (*syn:* **pasōng-sōng** 1) **1.1)** Almost certainly; most likely. *Bang ka'a-i mbal ameya' pandu', gana-gana magnikala'atan.* If you will not listen to advice, then you will inevitably come to grief. *Tagna'anna sadja ko' itu, gana-gana angahinang du sigām ai-ai kamaksuran sigām.* This is just its beginning, they will most certainly do whatever they plan. *Abila na ka anukul, gana-gana akello' kōk lansang.* Whenever you hammer, the head of the nail will inevitably get bent. (*Thesaurus:* **sumiyan-sumiyan, taka-taka, tiyap-tiyap**)

**ganap** *n.* **1)** Something added to a mixture or situation. **1.1)** *adj. zero* Complete. **1.2)** *v. tr. -an* Increase an amount or quantity. *Na buwattitu panganggganta'na ma ka'a, ganapanna ru kasusahannu.* So this is what he decrees for you, he will increase your troubles. (*Thesaurus:* **k'nnop** 1.2, **jukup** 1.2, **tubil**)

**ganap t'llumpū'** *n. phrase* The calendar day added to compensate for the difference in length of lunar and solar days. (*gen*: **bulan₂ 2**)

**ganda** *v. tr.* To give someone a name of special significance. *Ginanda na ōnnu, sali' ka'a pagōnan maka ngga'i ka ōnnu. Buwat ka'a si Ag, niōnan si Jumala.* A name given to you, as when you are named with a name that is not yours. Like you are Ag, but you are named Jumala. (*Thesaurus:* **ōn₁ 1.2, taga'-taga'**)

**gandahan** *n.* An instruction to proceed with a plan. *Amuwan gandahan min kar'ndahan, sinō' na lum'ngngan. Sali' hagda min sigām.* Giving the go-ahead from the woman's side, to proceed [with marriage talks]. It's like an order from them. *Si Bapa' Ke amuwan gandahan ni si Lu, sinō' atilaw pasal kabtangan.* Uncle Ke giving Lu instructions, telling her to make inquiries about words. (*Thesaurus:* **da'ak, hilag, pagmanda 1, soho', sūg-sūg, uldin 1**)

**paggandahan** *v. tr.* To give orders. *Ōy, mbal aku kapaggandahan!* Hey, I'm not to be ordered around!

**gandang** *n.* 1) An instrument for beating time on. *Gandang, basta panitikan.* A percussion instrument, anything for beating time on. (*Thesaurus:* **agung 1, buwa₁, kulintangan, titik 1**) **1.1)** *v. tr.* To beat time on an instrument. *Gandanginbi a'a magpangigal.* Beat time for the people dancing. (*cf:* **ganding 1**)

**gandang-gumbala'** *n.* Problems of many kinds. *Tuhan ya bay angalappasan aku ma kamemon gandang-gumbala'.* It was God who rescued me from all problems.

**ganding** *v. tr.* 1) To beat time to music or dance. *Angangganding ni p'ttung na ka, ni tu'ung na ka.* Beating time, on bamboo or a wooden box. (*cf:* **gandang 1.1**) **1.1)** *v. tr.* -an To accompany a performance with a rhythmic beat. *Anganggandingan aku tenes-tenes ni bihing gabbang.* I accompany the *tenes* singing, beating time against the bamboo marimba.

**gandum** *n.* Corn (maize); sweet corn. *Zea mays.* *Aheka magagaw, halam gandum tabuwanan kami.* A lot of people grabbing at it, no corn being given to us. (*cf:* **biyaki' 1, durul**)

**gansinsilyu** var. of **kansinsilyu**

**gansuwang** (*var.* **ansuwang**) *n.* A malevolent spirit being of huge size. *Gansuwang itū alangkaw, bang ma olangan tum'kkad, tape'na duwand'ppa taha'na.* The *gansuwang* is very tall, touching bottom when out at sea, his feet two fathoms long. *Gansuwang hē', ya kakanna g'llom. A'angkud kono' bang kat'ppi'-t'ppi'an keyat.* The food of those *gansuwang* is caulking fibre. They are said to be afraid of fire, and burn when approached with flame. (*Thesaurus:* **agasi, saitan-lagtaw**)

**ganta'₁** *adj.* a- 1) Moderate in what one does. (*Thesaurus:* **sukud₁, t'ppong 1**) **1.1)** *v. tr.* To measure or estimate an amount. *Bang kita amangan, subay ganta'ta bo' mbal ap'ddi' b'ttongta.* When we eat, we should be moderate so our stomach doesn't hurt. *Ganta'-ganta'un, da'a b'llahun kamemon. Halam aniya' binalikan.* Measure it out a bit, don't cook it all. None of it can be repeated. *Ginanta' itū, bang aniya' gadji saga sangpū' maka lima, subay sasarang sangpū'. Ya lima pinehē' ni matto'anna.* Being measured, like when a wage is ₱15, ₱10 should suffice. The ₱5 is passed on to his parents.

**ganta'₂** *v. tr.* To assign a destiny. *Ginanta' asal e' Tuhan bangsa dakayu' maka dakayu' bang buwattingga ya t'ggol sigām anatas ma dunya maka bang maingga paglahatan sigām.* God has already ordained for every ethnic group how long they will last on the earth and where they will live. *Na buwattitu pangangganta'ku ma ka'a, ganapanku to'ongan kasusahannu bang ka ab'ttong. Kap'ddi'an to'ongan isāb ka bang anganak.* So this is what I decree for you, I will greatly increase your troubles when you become pregnant. You will also experience much pain when you give birth.

**ganta'an₁** *n.* Inevitable or preordained state of affairs. *Aniya' onde' halam ta'abut ganta'an na, halam napasna.* There are babies who have not reached their allotted span, who have no breath. *Buwat aniya' nde'anku ni luma' a'a. Manjari tinilaw aku e' a'a, yukna, "Magay na isāb ka? Sabunu isāb aku?" Yukku, "Minsan duma'in ka ganta'anna ka'a sabuku, tu'ud aniya' nde'anku saddī."* Suppose I am returning something to a person's house, and someone asks me, "What are you doing? Are you trying to meet me?" I say, "Even though it's not inevitable that I should coincide with you, I simply had something else to deliver." (*Thesaurus:* **kahandak 1, karal 1, kulis, indika 1, piguhan, sukud₂ 1**)

**ganta'₃** *ptl.* Suppose; for instance; let's say. (Hypothetical modality marker). *Bang ka ganta' kineket e' sowa, subay s'ssopnu magtūy.* Suppose you are bitten by a snake, you should immediately suck the wound. *Halam ganta' bay ai maka ai, taggaha' hal palintuwad.* Though it seems nothing whatsoever had happened, he suddenly fell prostrate. *Buwat kita maglihan maitu ma Pasonangka' saga t'llu pitu'. Ganta' paghanti'-hanti'an ba.* Like when we stay temporarily here at Pasonangka, for three weeks or so. Temporary accommodation, as it were. *Ganta' kajīnan, yuk jīn ī', "O Sahabbat."* Imagine someone possessed by a djinn, and the djinn says, "Oh friend." *Ganta' itu sali' saupama, yuk-i, "Magsamp'kka' itu bang ganta' kita bay abase', magsamp'kka' maka ulan."* This word *ganta'* is like an example. Someone says, "This word *samp'kka'* [coinciding] is like when, for instance, we got wet. We coincided with the rain." *Subay ganta' tugpangta tahunna, bulanna, llawna, ligtung* *ē'.* We should, for instance, specify how many years, months, or days, the time period is to be.

**ganta'an**₂ *n.* The Albacore, a tuna species closely related to the Spanish mackerel. *Thunnus alalunga.*

**gantang** *n.* A unit of bulk dry measurement equivalent to three liters. (*Thesaurus:* **pansing 1, supa₁**)

**gantang mama'** *n. phrase* The set of ingredients for a betel nut chew. {idiom} *Subay dagantang mama' panamba.* In payment there should be a full betel nut chew set. *Subay dagantang mama' panamba, hatina daokat tabaku', dahalug buyu', dakayu' tagambil, bangkit, maka dantuhug pola.* In payment there should be a full betel nut chew set, i.e. one roll of tobacco, one bundle of pepper vine leaves, one lump of resin, some lime and one string of ripe betel nuts.

**ganti'** *n.* 1) A replacement similar in kind or value. *In aku itu ato'a na, sagō' ilu du saga anakku l'lla ma deyomanbi ganti'ku.* I am now old, but my sons are there among you in my place. 1.1) *v. intr. pa-* To be a substitute for. *Atas iya paganti' min siyali sigām magpa'ata bang pa'in iya tumabeya' amole' ma saga danakanna kasehe'.* He would be a substitute for their younger brother, becoming a slave. 1.2) *v. tr. -an* To replace one item for another. *Bang aniya' bay magka'at he'ta, bo' ngga'i ka anuta, subay ginanti'an.* When something is wrecked by our action, and it is not ours, it must be replaced. *Ganti'anku atop apa ang'mman.* I will change the thatch because it leaks. (*Thesaurus:* **salin₁ 1.1, saliyu 1.1, sambi' 1**)

  **ganti' nyawa** *n. phrase* Remuneration to traditional healer or midwife. {idiom} *Pagbowahan limampū' pilak. Tulahanna limampū' hē', subay aniya' ganti' nyawa. Bang pahali saki alopas ma jīn, bang mbal pahali binahagi' limampū' duwa.* Fifty pesos for the healer. That amount is his fee, a "compensation for life". If the illness is healed [the money] all goes to the djinn person, if it isn't healed the fifty is divided in half.

  **pagganti'** *v. intr. aN-* To change places. *Buwat sundalu aniya' saga duwa pitu' magbono' sigām. Sinoho' sundalu saddī magganti'.* Like soldiers who have been fighting for some two weeks. Other soldiers are ordered to change places with them.

**gantung₁** *v. intr. pa-* To be waiting for a decision or judgment. *Pinding, amasi sala pagantung.* Pending, still sort of waiting for a decision. (*cf:* **pinding**)

**gantung₂** *v. intr. pa-* 1) To be hanging. *Sikagantungan pang'ntan.* Implements hanging in large numbers [said of kitchenware hanging on a wall]. *Sikagantungan pang'ntan.* Implements hanging in large numbers. 1.1) *v. tr.* To hang

something from a hook. *Aniya' manggis bay gantungku.* I suspended some mangosteens. (*Thesaurus:* **gulantung, sagnat 1.1, sa'ud₁ 1.1**)

  **paggantung-bitay** *v. intr. aN-* To be hanging from something by arms or feet.

**gantung-li'ug** *n.* A necklace; a charm hanging from the neck.

**gangat** *n.* 1) A hook-shaped item. *Gangat, ai-ai pakalluk, buwat anu ma kamisun.* Something hook-like, anything that curves back, like the thing on a petticoat. 1.1) *v. tr.* To move something using a hook. *Ngā'un ba kawil ilū, gangatun ni bowa'na.* Grab that shark hook, and gaff it in the mouth. *Ngā'un na sau, tapanganggangat du sau. Gangatun ba pareyo'.* Grab the anchor, an anchor can be used as a hook. Hook what's down below.

**gangkul** *n.* A partly ripened coconut. *Ma llot botong maka lahing.* Between the unripe and ripe stages of a mature coconut. (*Stages:* **kambung-kambung, botong-botong, bilu'uk, botong, gangkul, lahing, pangtusan**)

**ganggang** var. of **panggang₂**

**ganggas** *adj. a-* Dried out, of hair or foliage. *Atoho' bu'unku, nsa' bay talubi lahing, aganggas.* My hair is dry, it hasn't been shampooed with coconut cream, it's dried out. (*cf:* **tigangkal**; *Thesaurus:* **gosang-gosang, larang**)

**ganggid** var. of **banggid**

**ganggu'** *v. intr. a-* To make a slight sound; to rustle. A: *"Angay bahā' aganggu' luma', halam sai-sai?"* B: *"Aganggu' he' baliyu."* A: "Why does the house creak, nobody is there?" B: "The wind is making it creaky." (*Thesaurus:* **bahembas 1, bah'ssek 1, kerek-kerek, keyos₂, kulanas 1, kulessab, ussab-ussab**)

**ganggu' atay** *adj. a-* Anxious; apprehensive. {idiom} *Mbal pangandolku, aganggu' atayku.* I won't rely [on him], I am anxious. (*Thesaurus:* **kanaw-kanaw, kawang, hanggaw₁ 1**)

  **pagganggu'** *v. intr. aN-* To make a slight noise. *Da'a kam magganggu'.* Don't make a noise.

**ganggut** (var. **gaggut**) *v. tr.* To pull sharply on something hanging down. *Ginanggut bu'un si Li. Anangis, kap'ddi'an.* Li's hair is pulled. She cries, feeling pain. *Buwat lilusku ginaggut, arāk tinangkaw. Ai-ai pagantung makajari ginanggut. Bang sagmot, nirarut.* Like my watch being tugged at, almost stolen. Anything that hangs down can be *ganggut* [pulled down]. As to weeds, they are *darut* [uprooted]. *Tagaggut aku, takuddat.* I was pulled sharply, startled. (*cf:* **pagluray**; *Thesaurus:* **bira 1, konot₂, ga'ut, guyud 1, hella', paglagedled 1**)

  **pagganggut** *v. tr.* To pull sharply on clumps of things that hang loose. *Pagkaleku ma saga susumbungan itū, magtūy gese'ku badju'ku maka jubaku, bo' pagganggutku bu'unku maka p'ngngotku.* On hearing these reports I promptly tore my shirt and my gown, and pulled at my hair and my beard.

**gangotan** *n.* A pouch sewn inside the waistband of trousers. *Wa'i na tau'ku ni gangotanku.* I have it hidden in my inside pocket.

**gangsa** (var. **gangsa'**) *n.* A brass bowl, known only from old stories. *Gangsa itū tumbaga bay kamatto'ahan.* The *gangsa* referred to is a copper vessel from the time of the forebears. (*Thesaurus:* **bintang₁, garul, langguway, tumbaga 2**)

**gangsa'** var. of **gangsa**

**gapas** *n.* Kapok, the fiber obtained from the cotton tree; any cotton fiber used for filling. (*syn:* **kapuk 2**)

**gapi'** *n.* 1) An ally in a conflict; a supporter. 1.1) *v. intr. pa-* To be a support in a conflict situation. *Pagapi' asāl sigām magdanakan itū ma si B.* These three brothers simply provided support for B.

  **paggapi'** *v. intr. aN-* To be mutually supportive, as workmates or members of a team. *Maggapi' kami am'ssi, magbeya' sali'.* We fish together, like accompanying each other. *Buwat kami magbola, maggapi' duwa-duwa, magtapil sali'.* Like when we play volleyball, we team up in pairs, sort of strengthening each other.

**gapus** *v. tr.* To put one's arms around something or someone as when embracing or lifting. (*Thesaurus:* **giba 1.1, hambin 1.1, mpit, pipi₁, sangbay**)

**gara'** *n.* 1) A matter of business; a topic of discussion. *Magsuli-suli kām pahāp bo' aniya' katibu'ukan gara'bi.* Talk things over properly so there will be unity in your business matters. *Ai gara', ggē?* What's up friend [lit. what is the business]? (*Thesaurus:* **palkala' 1, parak**) 1.1) *adj. a-* To be in the planning stage. *Agara'an iya dīna, sōng agara' kaut.* Planning just to himself, planning on going to sea shortly. *Mareyom agara' lagi'.* Still in the planning stage. 1.2) *v. tr. -an* To give someone advice or counsel; to suggest a plan. *Bang halam aniya' sehe'nu gara'anta ka.* If you have no companion I will advise you. *Panganggara'anku pelangku itū ni a'a taga banog.* I will discuss this canoe of mine with a man who has a sail.

  **kagara'an** *n.* A discussion about a possible course of action; a conference. *Bang aniya' kagara'an, subay magisun-isun onde'-matto'a.* When there is a planning meeting, children and parents should discuss things together. *Ya kagara'an inān makasulut ma kamemon pagmatto'ahan ya bay maina'an.* That decision pleased all the elders who were there.

  **paggara'** *n.* 1) A plan or scheme. *Sali' mbal kita makalanjal, parohong bay paggara'.* Like when we are unable to proceed, the plan having come to nothing. *Ya paggara' sigām, bang makajari, pinasanglad kappal pina'an ni gusung.* Their plan, if possible, was to let the ship run aground there

onto the sand. 1.1) *v. tr. -an* To be involved in making action plans. *Maggara' kita am'ssi dai' llaw ilū.* We are planning to go fishing early tomorrow. *Song binono', pinaggara'-gara'. Buwattina'an hal magisun-isun, hal magbantu.* About to be killed, being plotted against. Right now it is just in the planning stage, just plotting.

**garan** *n.* A type of repeating rifle. (*Thesaurus:* **kalbin, kanyun 1, lantaka 1, musil, pistul, sinapang**)

**garapun** *n.* A jar; a wide-mouthed glass container with a lid. *Garapun itū pangisihan bāng-bāng, na ya kassa' itū pangisihan pipsikola.* This wide-mouthed jar is for holding cookies and this bottle is for soft-drink. (*Thesaurus:* **butul, kassa' 2**)

**garing** *n.* 1) Ivory; the creamy color of ivory. *Garing itu apote' buwat gallang labu. Garing* is white like a shell bracelet. 1.1) *v. advrs. -in-* Yellowed through age or long storage. *Ginaring na ma panau'an, atawa ginaha' ma panau'an, atawa anumbaga.* Becoming yellow in storage, or rusty, or coppery.

  **garing-garing** *v. tr.* To do fine engraving work on ivory. *Mbal aku siguru bang ai pagbidda'anna niukilan maka ginaring-garing, sagō' buwattē'.* I am not sure what the difference is between carving and *garing-garing*, but it is that sort of thing.

  **paggaring** *v. intr. aN-* To become permanently yellowed, of teeth. *Binalakang emponna, sali' maggaringan.* His teeth are discolored, sort of turning yellow all over.

**garul** *n.* A lidded brass container. *Anginggat la, buwat garul ma ina'ku. Bang baha'u, na luwa bulawan. Pinagbase' maka tahik, agtūy anumbaga.* Merely gleaming, like the brass container that my mother has. When new it looked like gold, after being wetted with seawater it quickly became coppery. (*cf:* **bandehaw**; *Thesaurus:* **bintang₁, gangsa, langguway, tumbaga 2**)

**garus** *adj. a-* Wearing out; frayed. *Buwat badju'nu, nsa' na bihingna, ala'an kumpi'na, agarus na.* Like your shirt, it has no edge, its hem has come off, wearing out.

**gās₁** *v. tr.* To prepare land for planting by clearing and burning. *Tinunu' dahū, mbal niararu, hal tinanoman, ya hē' ginās.* Burnt first, not plowed, just sown, that is swidden farming.

**gās₂** *n.* Kerosene for lamps or stoves. *Mbal ka am'lli lapohan pabalik, sabasag hal gās ya billi pabalik.* You will not buy another stove, it's only kerosene that will be bought again. (*Thesaurus:* **gasulin, ns'llan gās**)

**gasa** var. of **galsa**

**gasang** *adj. a-* Coarse and gritty, of food or soil. *Mbal ahāp tinanoman, agasang tana'na.* Not good for planting in, its soil is stony. *Agasang, sali' buwas apīt-pīt.* Gritty, like rice with insufficient water. (*Thesaurus:* **kasap, l'ngnges 1.1, s'ppal**)

**gasing** *n.* A spinning top. *Gasing, ya palegot inān,*

*taga lubayan.* A top, that spinning thing, with its special cord. *Magtimbag kita maka gasing.* We play 'hit the target' with a top. (*syn:* **talungkup**)

**gastu** *n.* 1) The expenses or costs of family or community life. *Bang kita bay man kapū'an, am'lli kita gastu ni pasal apa halam kita bay makapagkakan.* When we have been to the islands, we buy supplies at the store for we had not been eating. *Bang aniya' ma ka'am ganta' angahinang luma', subay iya amikil-mikil dahū bo' tabista bang pila gastuna.* If any of you wants to build a house, he should think about it first to figure out what the costs will be. (*Thesaurus:* **balanja'** 1, **kahirupan, ka'lluman, lutu'**₁ 1, **pagnapaka**) 1.1) *v. tr. -an* To buy essentials for someone. *Ka'a ya anganggastuhan kami, kinakan, s'mmek.* You are the one to spend money on supplies for us, food, clothing.

**gasud** *v. tr. -an* To get someone's attention by shouting. *Bay kami ginasuran e' pulis, da'a sinō' palanjal.* A policeman shouted at us, telling us not to go on. (*Thesaurus:* **asang**₂, **kula'ak, galit, olang** 1.1, **pagalud, pahit**)

**gasulīn** (var. **gasulina**) *n.* Gasoline. *Asinu' amangan gasulina.* Economical in its consumption of gasoline. (*Thesaurus:* **gās**₂, **ns'llan gās**)

**gasulina** var. of **gasulīn**

**gata'** *n.* 1) Coconut milk, the liquid expressed from grated mature coconut, used for cooking or shampoo. (*Thesaurus:* **kabulan, p'tti'**) 1.1) *v. tr. -an* To flavor food with coconut milk. *Am'lli aku lahing kinugut panganggata'ku daing niasin.* I will buy a ripe coconut grated for coconut cream [to flavor] salted fish.

**gatang** (var. **giyatang**) *n.* A species of fish, multicolored. *Pamana'ku gatang agon magb'kkos.* For spearing a *gatang* that was almost banded [with color].

**gatas** *n.* 1) The milk from animals in contrast to milk from a human mother. 1.1) *v. tr. -an* To add milk to something. *Kagatasan na kahawaku, aniya' bay anganggatasan iya.* My coffee has had milk added, someone put milk in it.

**gatgat** (var. **katkat**) *n.* 1) A saw, the carpenter's tool. *Am'lli aku gatgat ni M'ddas panganggatgatku papan.* I will buy a saw in Siasi to cut a board with. *Kagonsanan ya t'ngnga' katkat.* The middle of the saw is the effective part. 1.1) *v. tr.* To cut something with a saw.

**gatgat-basi'** *n.* A hacksaw.

**gau** *n.* The tapered entry funnel of a woven trap, which allows fish to enter but not emerge. *B'nnal isāb, ata'u aku aganu-anu, magtukangan. Sagō' ya gauna mbal kata'uhanku.* True, I know how to do various things, as a craftsman. But the funnels [of a fishtrap], that I don't know. *Na hati isāb tilas gau itū, anahut.* With regard to the materials for weaving a *gau* funnel, they are very fine. (*cf:* **kiming**)

**gau-** *see section 2.2.2.4 Prefix:* **Cau-**

**gauga'** var. of **muntay-gauga'**

**gaugari'** *n.* 1) A file; a rasp (the shaping tool). 1.1) *v. tr.* To shape something using a file or rasp. (*cf:* **lagnas**)

**gaunggang** *adj. zero* Hollow; empty. *Batang kapaya gaunggang du, taga lowang.* The trunk of a papaya is hollow, it has a hole. *Gaunggang tōb man b'ttong pariyata' sampay ni k'llong. Bang mbal isihan pak'ppos. Man b'ttong sampay ni tape', ponod. Hal isi.* The *gaungang* is from the belly up to the neck. It flattens if nothing is in it. From belly to feet it is solid, just flesh. (*cf:* **lagonggang**; *ant:* **ponod** 1.1)

**gawa** *adj. a-* Afraid; apprehensive. *Da'a ka agawa, da'a ka atāw.* Don't be scared, don't be afraid. (*Thesaurus:* **bolag, dalan** 1.1, **damag, g'mma, gupu, leya'-leya', tāw** 1.1, **umagad** 1.1)

**kagawahan** *n.* The sense of fear or misgiving. *Halam aniya' kagawahanku pagga ka'a ya sehe'ku.* I have nothing to fear since you are my companion. *O Tuhan, ya na ko' itu bay kagawahanku mahē' lagi' aku ma lahatku.* O God, this is what I was anxious about back there in my own land.

**gawat** *n.* A lug or hook for securing a flexible item. *Buwat sintoron taga gawat pangahengkot iya.* Like a belt having a prong for fastening it. *Bang kita amirahan pana', gawat itū pangahawid goma.* When we pull back the bow [on a spear-gun] the *gawat* is for holding the rubber in place. (*cf:* **gehe**)

**gawatan** *n.* A metal catch for securing a hinged lid.

**gawgaw** *v. tr.* To stir a liquid or wet mixture. *Gawgawku kahawaku bo' amamis.* I stir my coffee so it's sweet. *Ginawgaw gatas maka giling-giling ina'an.* Milk mixed with that spnning thing. (*cf:* **bolebog**; *Thesaurus:* **bungkal**₂ 1.2, **keyol** 1.1, **kuwal**)

**gawi** *n.* 1) A purpose; a matter of business. *Aniya' gawiku ma ka'a, gawi aheya.* I have business with you, important business. *Buwat aniya' taga gawi ni ka'a, bo' pataikut ka, na m'ssa' iyuk a'a inān.* Like when someone has something to talk to you about, but you ignore him, then that person is of no importance to you. (*cf:* **angut**; *Thesaurus:* **kamatti, hadjat**₁, **maksud** 1, **tiranan**) 1.1) *v. tr.* To purpose some action.

**gawil** *v. tr.* To carry a small item wherever one goes. (*Thesaurus:* **habit, hangkut, pagbaga'ud**)

**gayad** *adj. a-* Thick, as of cloth or roofing thatch. *Akapal atopna, agayad. S'mmekku isāb agayad. Bang papan akapal.* Its thatch is thick, *gayad.* My clothing too can be *gayad.* With wood the word is *kapal.* (*cf:* **kapal** 1.1)

**gayang** *n.* A long-bladed working knife. *Gayang itū sali' du maka bari'.* A *gayang* is the same as a *bari'.* (*Thesaurus:* **bangkung, bari', lahut, laring lahut, pira, sundang**)

**gayung** *n.* 1) A container for dipping up a liquid.

(*Thesaurus:* **sauk 1, tambu' 1**) **1.1**) *v. tr.* To dip up liquid using a container. *Makajari isāb sawan panganggayungta.* A drinking glass too can be used for us to dip with.

**gekap 1**) *n.* A sheet or piece of something flat. (*Thesaurus:* **b'llad 1, b'llat 1, kintas 1, lamba₂**) **2**) *clf.* Count word for flat items. *Buwanin aku katas, danggekap pa'in.* Give me some paper, just one sheet. *B'llihin aku danggekap juwalan.* Buy me a strip of fried banana.

  **ma gekapan** *adv. phrase* By the sheet. *Katas itu subay bin'lli ma gekapan.* This paper must be purchased by the sheet.

**gege** var. of **gesges**

**geges** *adj. a-* Abraded, of a surface such as skin. *Ageges he' kuwit kaitan.* Abraded by the skin of a shark. (*Thesaurus:* **banggid 1, langgad 1, pares₁, sahumut-sahumut**)

**gehe** *n.* The barb of a spear or hook. (*cf:* **gawat**)

**gele-gele** (var. **lege-lege**) *v. tr.* To roll dough into long strips. *Nilege-lege buwattilu bo' binugbug, buwat saga tabid.* Rolled out like that to be dropped in boiling water, like donut twists.

**gelet** *n.* A safety razor blade. *Am'lli aku gelet pagbagong kōknu.* I'll buy a razor blade for shaving your head.

**gelle-gelle** *n.* The Bullet tuna or mackerel. *Auxis rochei.*

**gellok** (var. **geyok**) *n.* Various wrasses. *fam. Labridae.* (*syn:* **tallad**)

  **gellok-bangkitan** *n.* The Red-banded wrasse.

  **gellok-t'bba** *n.* A species of wrasse, white, found in shallow water.

  **gellok-unas** *n.* A species of wrasse, black.

**gensang** var. of **pensang**

**genggok** *v. tr.* To mix contents by shaking. *Bang ka angahinang gatas subay ginenggok.* When you make milk [from powder] it should be shaken in a container. (*Thesaurus:* **kembo' 1.1, kohek-kohek, letok**)

  **paggenggok** *v. intr. aN-* To rattle inside a container. *Magpanag-panag kōkku, sali' maggenggok.* My head is throbbing, like something rattling around inside. *Bang aniya' onde'-onde' amowa labban bo' maggenggok deyomna. Bang ngga'i ka pinsil, bāng-bāng.* When a child is carrying a carton and something is rattling inside it. If it's not a pencil, it'll be a cookie.

**geret** (var. **peret**) *n.* **1**) A tear or rip, of clothing or the hull of a canoe. *Ai ba, mangkinna sin'nsong, mangkinna paheya geret pelang inān.* Guess what, the more it was caulked, the bigger the hole in that canoe became. (*syn:* **gese' 1**) **1.1**) *adj. a-* Torn. **1.2**) *v. tr.* To tear something. *Geretunbi badju'bi pagkarukka'anbi siyalibi.* Tear your shirts in your grief for your brother.

  **pagkageret** *v. intr. aN-* To be easily torn.

**gese'** (var. **geset**) *n.* **1**) A tear or rip in fabric. (*cf:*

**jebel-jebel 1.1**; *syn:* **geret 1**) **1.1**) *adj. a-* Torn; ripped apart. *Takaleta wa'i ag'llek banog. Aniya' pasa'uranna, ya angkan agese'.* We heard the sail tearing. Something had snagged it, that's why it tore. **1.2**) *v. tr.* To tear something. *Ta'abutku h'ndaku magbihing maka l'lla saddī ma kara-kara. Gese'ku na hōs, bowaku ni sara'. Magmalān aku.* I found my wife in the act of having sex with another man. I tore my garment and brought her to the judge. I made an outcry about it.

**paggeset-geset** *v. tr.* To tear fabric into strips. *Saru'un-du'un du, agtūy nihurusan he' nabi tapis jubana bo' pinaggeset-geset min sangpū' aka duwa.* That very moment the prophet took off a piece of his gown and tore it into twelve strips. *Sambutin sangpū' solag s'mmek itu ya bay paggeset-gesetku.* Take these ten pieces of cloth I have torn off.

**geset** var. of **gese'**

**gesges** (var. **gege**) *v. tr.* To move or carry something away. *Sali' ak'tta ni M'ddas, tagesges he' la'ang.* Like setting out for Siasi, moved along by the outgoing current. *Na, angay gegenu bangka'nu itū?* Why are you pushing this canoe of yours? *Saga ai-ai pat'nna', ginege pehē'.* Things sitting there, pushed away. (*Thesaurus:* **laran, loson, paghadjul-hadjul, palis₁, pespes 1.1**)

**paggesges** *v. intr. aN-* To push through a crowd. *Aheka a'a bay ang'nda' si Ja sampay magdogsol na. Maggesges ya heka a'a ang'nda'-ng'nda' iya.* A lot of people saw Ja eventually push [his opponent] off [the platform]. The crowd pushed through in order to watch him.

**gesong** *adj. a-* Wakeful during the night, as by the need to urinate. *Agesong kita amange'.* We wake at night to urinate.

**getos** var. of **g'ttos**

**geyok** var. of **gellok**

**ggak** *v. intr. aN-* To belch; burp; retch. *Bang kita amangan bo' ang'ggak, hatina anawad gi'.* When we eat and belch, it means we are asking for more.

**ggang** *v. tr.* To toss cassava or sago meal during roasting, until it forms a cohesive mass. (*Thesaurus:* **buwang₃, huwal, sanglag, tompe'**)

**niggang** (var. **ni'ggang**) *n.* Cassava meal in cake form. (*gen:* **apam 1**)

**gge** *voc. n.* Term of address for a friend. *Asiga ka, gge?* cigaret, friend? *Ō gge, pi'ingga ka?* Where you going, mate? (*Thesaurus:* **agay, bagay 1, beyang, bō, panon**)

**ggok** *v. intr. aN-* To take water in one's mouth when swimming. *Ang'ggok ko' ka'a ilū.* You're swallowing water. (*Thesaurus:* **inum 1, t'ggok, tunghab 1.1**)

**ggom** var. of **h'ggom**

**ggot** var. of **l'ggot**

**gguk** *v. intr. aN-* To make a noise in one's throat while mouth is closed.

**giba** *v. intr. pa-* **1**) To climb into someone's lap.

*Pagiba onde'-onde' ni kita.* The children come to our lap. **1.1)** *v. tr.* To hold someone on one's lap. *Anganggiba aku si La, anakku mussa'.* I hold La in my lap, my favorite child. (*Thesaurus:* **gapus, hambin 1.1, mpit, pipi₁, sangbay**)

**gibang** (var. **bibang**) *n.* The left-hand side. *Tampal ni bibang.* Towards the left. (*ant:* **kowan**)

**gibayan** *n.* The wide capping along the gunwales of a launch. *Aningkō' ka ma gibayan lansa ilū.* Sit on the gunwales of the launch. (*Thesaurus:* **bihing₁ 1.2**)

**gidgid** *v. tr.* To scour a surface to clean or brighten it. *Ginidgid maka batu bo' ala'an gaha'na.* Scoured with a stone to remove its rust. (*Thesaurus:* **kidkid**)

**paggidgid** *v. intr.* aN- To chafe or grind together. *Sali' bang poga magbihing karuwa, bo' ma deyom pelang, bo' goyakan, magta'is, sali' maggidgid.* Like when two water jars are put next to each other in the canoe and it is rough, they sort of grind together. (*Thesaurus:* **pagleges, pagta'is**)

**panganggidgiran** *n.* A grindstone or grind wheel.

**giging** *adj.* a- Ungenerous; stingy. *Sali' akigit, ahukaw amuwan.* Kind of stingy, reluctant to give. (*Thesaurus:* **bista₂ 1, kaikit₁, kigit, kimmat 1, k'mmit 1, kudkud, kuriput 1, kussil, iskut, sumil₁**)

**gihay** *v. tr.* To divide tasks or things among a number of people. *Gihay itū, sali' binahagi'.* *Gihay* is like something being divided into parts. (*Thesaurus:* **bahagi' 1, hampit, paglamit-lamit 1.1, sihak**)

**paggihay** *v. intr.* aN- **1)** To be divided up into separate sub-groups. *Yuk si Ku inān, "Maggihay kita bang ka mbal angandarut unas itū. Ma aku itū, darutku."* Ku said, "Let's split up if you are not going to pull up this sea-grass. For my part I am going to pull some." (*Thesaurus:* **gintil 1.1, lilay, sila' 1.1, silang₁ 1.1, sisig**) **1.1)** *v. tr.* To divide something into several parts. *Pinaggihay po'on sumping.* The clump of flowers is divided up.

**gi'** var. of **lagi'**

**gi'ik 1)** *v. tr.* To step or trample on something. *Bay tagi'ikku t'bbu ma tabu', apōng.* I stepped on some sugarcane at the market, it broke. (*Thesaurus:* **ddik, d'dda 1.1**) **1.1)** *v. tr.* -an To hold something down by placing a foot on it. *Gi'ikin bang aku anganggatgat, ko' da'a magkodjel-kodjel.* Hold it down with your foot when I am sawing, so it doesn't move. **2)** *v. tr.* -an To feel with the feet for things concealed in sand. *Ginindasan itū sali' gini'ikan, bo' Sama Lipid. Ginindasan saga kohang.* *Gindas* is the same as *gi'ik*, the inshore Sama equivalent. Cockles are located by feeling with the feet.

**gil** *v. tr.* To whet or sharpen a blade. *A: "Gīlun laring itū." B: "Halam pangasa'an pangL'ngil iya?"* A: "Sharpen this knife." B: "Is there no whetstone to sharpen it on?"

**gila** *v. advrs.* -in- Experiencing sexual excitement. *Bang d'nda ginila, biga'an.* If a woman gets sexually excited, she is [said to be] promiscuous.

**gilay** *adj.* a- **1)** Torn apart; shredded. (*cf:* **pensang 1.1**) **1.1)** *v. tr.* To tear something apart. *Ginilay-ginilay ai-ai takeketna.* Whatever he bit was torn into shreds.

**giling** *v. tr.* -an To keep something revolving or turning. *Bang ajabjab atawa ginilingan, ah'lling.* When it flaps or is rotated, it makes a noise.

**giling-giling** *n.* An implement with a basic rotary motion, as an egg-beater or mill. *Ginawgaw gatas maka giling-giling inān.* The [powdered] milk is mixed up with that rotating beater.

**gilingan** *n.* Something that turns on an axle or shaft. *Aniya' du isāb gilingan naylon.* There are also spools for nylon line. *Aniya' gilingan bulbul, aniya' du isāb gilingan naelon.* There are feather spinners, and there are nylon spinners too.

**paggiling** *v. tr.* To process something by turning or rolling. *Batu ya paggilinganbi tirigu.* The stones are what you grind flour with. (*Thesaurus:* **legot 1, pusal₁ 1.1**)

**gillo'ak** *n.* A counterfeit or fake. *Ngga'i ka to'ongan. Bay aku am'lli ni tindahan, pagsōngku sīn hē', pag'nda' e' tindera, "Gillo'ak sīnnu ilu."* It is not genuine. I bought something at the shop. On handing over the money, and the shop assistant seeing it, said, "That money of yours is counterfeit." (*Thesaurus:* **palsu, paltik**)

**gillu'-gillu'** *adj.* zero Fictious; joking. *Tuwan gillu'-gillu'.* A pretend nobleman. *Sali' ula-ula panoho'an gillu'-gillu'.* A kind of joke, a pretend instruction. (*Thesaurus:* **sainala, ula-ula**)

**giluk** *adj.* a- **1)** Ticklish; reacting to touch. **1.1)** *v. tr.* To tickle or provoke someone to react physically. *Giniluk aku, yukku, "Da'a aku gilukun apa agiluk aku."* I am tickled and say, "Don't tickle me because I am ticklish." (*cf:* **kirik-kirik**)

**gimbal** (var. **gambil**) *n.* **1)** A support provided by placing something strong alongside. (*Thesaurus:* **tapil 1.1**) **1.1)** *v. intr.* pa- To prevent damage by coming alongside something strong or secure. *Pagambil ka ma katig ilū. Saddī patundan.* Get support by coming alongside that outrigger. Getting a tow is something different. **1.2)** *v. ditr.* To place one structure alongside another for the purpose of support. *Anganggimbal aku pelang ni pelang dakayu'.* I place one canoe alongside another for support.

**paggimbal** *v. intr.* aN- **1)** To be placed together, parallel, for mutual support. *Maggimbal pelang karuwa, sali' magtapil.* The two canoes brought alongside each other, like supporting each other. **1.1)** *v. tr.* To bring long items together for mutual support, of canoes or building materials. *Pinaggambil, pinagengkot, buwat pelang pinab'llihan.* Placed together hull to hull, tied together, like canoes for sale. *Pinaggakut buwat duwa bayan pinaggimbal.* Lashed together, like two canoes placed side-by-side. (*Thesaurus:* **hapid₁** 1, **lantay-lantay** 1)

**gimi'-gimi'** *adj. a-* Between wet and dry, of clothing.

**gimut** *n.* The moment of some occurrence. *Gimutna, ya hinabuna.* Its occurrence, when it is happening. (*Thesaurus:* **sinabu** 1)

**gin** *adv.* Similar in size, appearance, or manner. (*Thesaurus:* **buwat** 1, **damikiyan** 1, **sala** 1, **sali'** 1.3)

**gindan** (var. **indan**) *n.* 1) A reference point or distinguishing feature, such as a landmark. (*cf:* **pamahingan, pandoga** 1) 1.1) *v. tr. -an* To mark position with a visible physical marker or by noting reference points. *Bang sali' kita amuwang, subay ginindanan bo' tatuli', bo' kita amuwang pabalik.* When we cast a line from the shore, it should be marked so it can be found, so we can throw a line there again. *Ai-ai bay alungay bo' sangom, na gindananta bo' piniha llaw salung.* Whatever was lost at night, we make a note of the location so it can be found the following day.

**gindanan** *n.* Identifying features. *Takilāku gindananna.* I recognised his facial features.

**gindas** *v. tr.* To find or feel something with the feet. *Ananggindas kita bāt, kohang saga.* We feel with our feet for things like trepang and cockles. (*Thesaurus:* **agap₂, sadsad** 1.1, **sanaw, sassaw**)

**ginhawa** *n.* The inner elements of a person as distinct from the outer body. *Magkakibad deyom atayku, sabab siyaliku laha'an, bay binono'. Sali' ameya' ginhawaku to'ongan.* My inner person is shaken because my younger brother is bleeding, he was struck. It is like my whole inner being is involved. (*Thesaurus:* **nyawa, panalengog, sumangat** 1, **umagad** 1)

**ginhawa-baran** *n.* One's entire being, body and soul. *Mbal panawakkal ginhawa-baranku itū ameya' ni kala'atan.* This whole being of mine does not dare to get involved in bad things.

**ginis** (var. **jinis**) *n.* 1) A species; kind; sort; variety. *Si Jy agamā, halam kabuwanan bawis. Ai-ai pagamāhanna mbal daginis.* Jy is angry, he wasn't given rabbit fish. It is not just one kind of thing that riles him. 1.1) *v. tr. -an* To provide a variety of sorts and colors.

**kaginisan** *n.* A variety or assortment of things in a class. *Aheka kaginisan a'a, aniya' Sama, Milikan, Jipun, aniya' Lannang.* There are many kinds of people, Sama, Westerners, Japanese, Chinese. (*Thesaurus:* **babarapa, inda wa barapa ginis, indalupa** 1, **mussak-massik**)

**ginisan** *n.* A variety; an assortment.

**pagginis** *v. intr. aN-* 1) To be of various kinds. *Magginis būng.* Floating jellyfish are of various kinds. 1.1) *v. tr.* To make variations of some basic type. *Hukuman Tuhan pinagginis he'na bangsa saitan. Bay tagna' ahāp, sinaddīhan na*

*pikilan he' sigām.* It was a judgment of God that he should cause *saitan* spirits to be of many kinds. At first they were good, and then they changed their thinking.

**indaginis** *n.* Things of all kinds; things in great variety. (*cf:* **inda wa barapa ginis**)

**pagkaginisan** *v. intr. aN-* To be of various kinds.

**ginsil** *v. tr.* To move something along by sliding or pushing. *Agtūy ginsilku tambol inān.* Immediately I slid the door along.

**pagginsil** *v. intr. aN-* To be sliding about from one place to another. *Dunya itū pajogjog maka alinug, ya saga hāg sulga' magginsilan.* The earth shaking and quaking, the posts of heaven sliding about.

**gintana'an** (derivative of **tana'₁**) *n.* Dry land in contrast to sea and inter-tidal zones. (*cf:* **kaut** 1; *Thesaurus:* **bihingan, daplakan₁, hampilan, pari'an, susulan, tampe, tapiyan**).

**gintil** *v. intr. pa-* 1) To separate oneself from the community of which one has been part. *Hē' na pagintil min maskid kami.* He has separated himself from our mosque. 1.1) *v. tr.* To sort diverse items into separate groups. *Gintilun s'mmek ilū, bang badju' subay ma badju'.* Sort those clothes, shirts should be together with shirts. (*Thesaurus:* **lilay, paggihay** 1, **sila'** 1.1, **silang₁** 1.1, **sisig**)

**paggintil** *v. tr.* To treat things or people in individual ways. *Paggintilun anaknu.* Treat your children individually. (*Thesaurus:* **kaniya-kaniya, pinig, tabul₁** 1.1, **tarangan-tarangan, topod** 1)

**gintu'** *n.* A species of eel-like fish.

**ginulang** *n.* The Whiteline triggerfish. *Balistes bursa.*

**gipis** *n.* 1) A strip of wood or bamboo used to hold thatch or walling in place. (*Thesaurus:* **bola', lantay** 1, **ligpit** 1) 1.1) *v. tr.* To hold something in place with battens. *Bang ka magluma' subay gipisnu atop ko da'a paleyang e' baliyu.* When you build a house you should fasten slats to the thatch so it isn't sent flying by the wind. *Ginipis dinding bo' ahogot.* The wall battened to make it secure. (*Thesaurus:* **dopon, t'kkon**)

**gipit** 1) *v. tr.* To apply pressure to something. *Da'a bbahin, tagipit tape'ku.* Don't put it down, my foot will be squashed. (*cf:* **da'os**) 1.1) *v. tr. -an* To squeeze liquid out by applying pressure. *Panganggipitun hallu ilū.* Use that pestle to express the cassava liquid. 2) *clf.* Count word for packages of pressed cassava meal. *Am'lli aku danggipit panggi'.* I am buying one package of cassava meal.

**ma gipitan** *adv. phrase* By the package, of pressed cassava meal.

**gisa** *v. tr.* To cook vegetables by frying briefly and adding water. (*gen:* **b'lla** 1)

**gisa'-gisa'** *v. tr.* To thresh grain by treading on it.

*Bang sapi' anganggisa'-gisa' pai, da'a baggotun bowa'na.* When a cow is treading on the rice, don't tie up its mouth. *Aheka pai ma paggisa'an.* Lots of [harvested] rice in the threshing place.

**gisgis** *n.* 1) An implement for cleaning or smoothing by abrasion. **1.1)** *v. tr.* To shape or sharpen something by abrading. *P'ssi isāb ginisgisan bo' pinatalom, buwat bila' poga panganggisgisan iya.* Fishhooks too are abraded to make them sharp, with a bit of broken pottery used for rubbing against. (*cf:* **asa'**) **1.2)** *v. tr. -an* To remove something by rubbing or abrading. *Buwat kita nilagnas, na ya hē' ginisgisan kita maka gaugari'.* Like us having our teeth filed, well that is us being abraded with a metal file. (*Thesaurus:* **bunut-bunut, kuskus 1.1, dalug₁, lukup, lupag, susut**)

**gisgis empon** *n. phrase* A toothbrush. (*Thesaurus:* **sangbawa, sipilyu 1, tupras**)

**gitara** *var. of* **kitara**

**giti'** *adj. a-* 1) Thin, of body shape. *Agiti' na baranna, saki kayog ba.* Her body is thin now, definitely a wasting sickness. (*Thesaurus:* **kagkag, kayog 1, kittay, koskos, kulagkag, higtal, titis 2**) **1.1)** *v. intr. pa-/aN-* To become thin.

**giyak** *n.* The cross-pieces of a structure, as the frame of a kite or the ribs of a boat. (*Thesaurus:* **kadjang-kadjang, usuk**)

**giyagas** *v. intr. aN-* To give expression to one's irritation. *Anganggiyagas, sali' ap'ddi' atayna, sali' aesog.* Showing irritation, sort of angry, kind of fierce. *Bang kita mbal anganggiyagas mbal ala'an saga onde'-onde' itū.* If we don't act in an angry way these children won't leave. (*Thesaurus:* **kalintaw, dole' 1, dugal 1, p'ggot-p'ggot, s'ngngot₁ 1, sunggud**)

**giyagay** *n.* The dried flower bract of a coconut palm. (*wh:* **niyug**)

**giyam** *n.* A tree species.

**giyatang** *var. of* **gatang**

**g'bbuk** (*var.* **gubbuk**) *v. tr.* To punch someone's body with the front of a fist. *Gin'bbuk ni bukutna, kap'ddi'an. Sali' binutug pakosog.* Punched on his back, made to hurt, in pain. Like being struck hard. (*Thesaurus:* **butug, suntuk 1.1, tibu', tikbung**)

**g'bbus** *v. intr. pa-* 1) To form a pile, as trash. (*Thesaurus:* **būd 1.1, kuta'₂, hunsuk, hungku', pagbullud**) **1.1)** *v. tr. -an* To cover something by piling things on top.

**g'llal** *n.* 1) A title denoting an official position. *Taga g'llal, binuwanan ōn, buwat imam, panglima, maharadja.* Having a title, given a name such as imam, local headman, court official. **1.1)** *v. tr.* To appoint someone to an official position. *Tagna', sultan ya anangg'llal. Buwattina'an alubu.* Originally it was the sultan who made the appointments. That has broken down now. *Aniya' sehe'na angahukum, saga t'llungan bay*

*gīllal isab.* He has companions who will judge, three or so who have also been appointed. (*cf:* **botang₂**) 2) An affectionate nickname. *Masi iya piha'an kami g'llal ma Sinama.* We are still seeking a pet name for him in the Sinama language. (*syn:* **danglay 1**)

**bag'llal** *n.* 1) A local official or headman. **1.1)** *v. tr.* To appoint someone to a community leadership position. *Tabag'llal kita. Sali' kita magimam atawa a'a kita parinta.* We are appointed to office. Like serving as an imam, or we are government appointees.

**kag'llal** *n.* Official status; an appointment in the civil service.

**g'llek** *adj. a-* Ripped off with the sound of tearing. *Takaleta wa'i ag'llek banog. Aniya' pasa'uranna, ya angkan agese'.* We heard the sail tear. There was something it snagged on, that is why it tore.

**g'llom** *n.* The tissue-like inner bark of certain trees, used for caulking. *Bang tinapi' pelang subay aniya' g'llom bo' mbal ang'mman.* When the canoe has planks put on there should be bark for caulking so it won't leak. *G'llom itū man po'on ngehat, lapisan sangpū' maka duwa.* This g'llom material is from the trunk of the ngehat tree, it has twelve layers. (*cf:* **ngehat**)

**g'llot** 1) *n.* Lines or creases on a surface. *Bang d'nda g'llotan ma k'llong, pamalu.* A woman with a creased neck is frequently widowed. **1.1)** *v. tr.* To make cuts in a surface. **1.2)** *v. tr. -an* To cut a notch into a pole. 2) *v. tr.* To superincise the penis. {*vulgar*} (*cf:* **pags'lle**)

**pagg'llot-g'llot** *v. intr. aN-* To form multiple deep creases, as the wrists of a chubby baby. *Bang aniya' onde'-onde' al'mmok to'ongan, magg'llot-g'llot l'ngngonna.* When a baby is very fat, its arms are deeply creased. (*Thesaurus:* **bekos₁, pagb'kkos, pagg'ttos**)

**g'mma** *adj. a-* Having a deep and unexplained fear. *Ag'mma sumangatku bang aku lum'ngngan kaleya, sali' aniya' a'a. Sali' atāw deyom baranku, sali' nyawaku itū atāw.* My spirit is troubled when I walk inland, there might be someone there. It is as if I am afraid deep inside, as if my spirit is fearful. *Ag'mma aku, sali' akawang deyom atayku bang aku ni M'ddas bo' halam aniya' sehe'ku. Sali' aku binuwanan galak pinal'ngngan atawa mbal.* I am fearful, deeply apprehensive about going to Siasi Town when I have no companion. It's like having a positive feeling whether or not to go. (*Thesaurus:* **bolag, dalan 1.1, damag, gawa, gupu, leya'-leya', tāw 1.1, umagad 1.1**)

**g'mmel** *adj. a-* Discordant, of a cracked gong or a voice. *Ag'mmel llingna, buwat saga agung, kulintangan, ndang na.* His voice is unpleasant, like a big gong or a gong set, when getting worn. *Buwat saga agung, bang anageseng bo' tiktikta min t'dda, aniya' duwa-t'llu llingna.* Like gongs, making a tinny sound. When we hit them once there are two or three sounds. (*cf:*

tagenseng)

**g'mmol₁** *adj. a-* Muffled, of a sound. *Ala'at h'llingna organ. Ag'mmol, mbal alagting.* The sound of an organ is unpleasant. It's muffled, not clear. *Angay suwalanu ag'mmol ilū.* Why is that voice of yours muffled?

**g'mmol₂** *adj. a-* Stored while damp, of laundered clothes. *Badju' ilū halam lagi' atoho' sogo' bay na tamomos min sablayan, angkan ag'mmol na.* That blouse is not dry yet but it has been put away off the hanger, that's why it is damp.

**g'mmos** var. of **gamos**

**g'mmot** (var. **gomot**) *adj. a-* **1)** Crumpled, of something that should be flat or folded. *Ai-ai agomot subay hūsta.* We should smooth [with our hands] anything that is crumpled. (*Thesaurus:* **komo'₂, go'ok 1.1, loko' 1**) **1.1)** *v. tr.* To crumple or wad something. *Da'a g'mmot-g'mmotun pantalunnu ilū.* Don't keep crumpling those pants of yours. *Buwas atawa ai-ai na ba niumas, ya pinaggomot inān sali'.* Rice or anything that has been handled a lot, things that are is sort of wadded up. *Pagomot du bang ginomot.* It becomes crumpled when it is wadded up. *Bang aniya' ganta' ntananku, buwas atawa ai-ai na ba niumas, ya pinaggomot inān sali'.* If there is something, say, that I hold, like rice or anything that is handled a lot, things that are sort of wadded up.

**g'nnol** var. of **k'nnol**

**g'nting** *adj. a-* Slender; lithe. *D'nda ag'nting hawakanna.* A woman whose waist is slender. (*Thesaurus:* **lampin₁, nipis, nipnip, tayang**)

**g'ppa'** *adj. a-* Ruined; falling apart. (*Thesaurus:* **bulangkayat, gubal, hogal, lubu₂ 1, tunas 1**)

**g'ppang** *n.* The removable planking of a canoe hull. (*cf:* **s'ngkol 1**; *gen:* **tapi' 1**)

**g'tta'** *adj. a-* Sticky, as sap from a rubber tree. (*Thesaurus:* **pekot, pīt, tagok 1**)

**g'ttok-g'ttok** *v. tr.* To shape something roughly using short chops. (*Thesaurus:* **pīs₂ 1**)

**g'ttos** (var. **getos**) *adj. a-* Creased, as flesh or paper. *Bang niengkotan tanganku maka lupis, agetos tanganku.* When my hand is tied with banana fibre my hand is creased. *Kag'ttosan tanganku he' goma.* My hands are deeply creased by rubber bands.

  **pagg'ttos** *v. intr. aN-* To form multiple creases due to fat under the skin. *Magg'ttos kal'mmokan si Sa.* Sa's plumpness forms creases. (*Thesaurus:* **bekos₁, pagb'kkos, pagg'llot-g'llot**)

**gokal** *adj. a-* Incohesive; crumbly. *Agokal, sali' ap'kkal, basta ai-ai bay atibu'uk.* Incohesive, sort of crumbly, of anything that was previously a single lump. (*Thesaurus:* **budjal-budjal, lomo 1, p'kkal 1, podjak 1, sughay**)

**gōd-gōd** var. of **gōt-gōt**

**godgod** var. of **hodhod**

**gohom** *adj. a-* **1)** Poorly articulated, of one's speech. *Akamal, sali' mbal makapah'lling. Sali'* agohom, hal ang'nda' bang nilinganan. Speechless, like being unable to speak. Words sort of badly spoken, he just looks when called. (*Thesaurus:* **kohot, lagaw, pehet**) **1.1)** *v. advrs. ka-...-an* To be labored or distorted, of someone's speech. *Kagohoman a'a inān mbal na buwattē'.* That person's speech is so distorted, nothing like it. *Kagohoman aku he' bohe' bay inumku.* I have become unable to speak clearly due to the water that I drank.

**gō'** var. of **nggo'**

**go'ok** *adj. a-* **1)** Crumpled or creased, as unironed clothes. *Ago'ok ma lupi'an.* Crumpled in the process of folding. **1.1)** *v. tr.* To crease or crumple something. *Buwat pantalun bay pilinsahanta, subay da'a gino'ok-go'ok.* Like long pants we are ironing, they should not be crumpled. (*Thesaurus:* **komo'₂, g'mmot 1, loko' 1**)

**go'on** (var. **go'ot**) *n.* **1)** Something greatly desired. *Aniya' go'onku ma iya.* He has something I really must have. (*Thesaurus:* **angut, k'llo' bo'ot, mohot 1**) **1.1)** *v. tr. -an* To be determined to get what someone else has. *Gino'onan d'nda inān minsan taga tunang asal.* That girl is greatly desired even though she has a suitor already. *Bang aniya' kinabaya'an, kago'onan na e'na ma iya na. Mbal maka'ppa.* If something is really wanted, he sets his heart on it that it might be his. It doesn't get away from him.

  **paggo'on-go'on** *v. intr. aN-* To be working at cross-purposes; to be pulling in different directions. *Magga'ut, maggo'on-go'onan, buwat kita sali' maglata.* Tugging at each other, aiming at different goals, like when we are fooling around. *Buwat aku magbusay maka si Gi, iya amusay tudju ni T'lling, aku tudju ni M'ddas. Maggo'on-go'on.* Like when I paddle with Gi. She paddles towards T'lling, I towards Siasi. We are at cross-purposes.

**go'ot** var. of **go'on**

**goldo-goldo** *adj. a-* Attractively plump. *Agoldo-goldo itū bang ameya'-meya' deyo'-deyo'ta maka l'mmokta. Goldo-goldo* is when our short stature matches our plumpness. (*cf:* **bodde'-bodde'**; *Thesaurus:* **hambug 1, littub, l'mmok 1.1, poko-poko, subuk, tibung-tibung**)

**golgol** *v. tr.* To hold or restrain someone by placing arms around him. *Da'a golgolun onde'-onde' ilū.* Don't hold that child. (*Thesaurus:* **kalung, golpe₂**)

**gollay** *v. intr. pa-* To dangle loosely, as the tail of a dog, or sagging breasts. (*cf:* **gottay**)

**golpe₁** *adj. a-* **1)** Overwhelmed by the number of things to be dealt with at one time. *Agolpe bang angā' daing, aheka ta'ā'na.* Over-busy when fishing and catching a great many. **1.1)** *v. tr.* To cope with many items at one time.

**golpe₂** *v. tr.* To restrain someone by holding in both arms. (*Thesaurus:* **kalung, golgol**)

**gōm** *adv.* Contrasting between two options, generally from the standpoint of the more preferable. *Gōm na bay nde'anku ya bay indamanku itū ko da'a alungay.* I should have returned this thing that I borrowed so it didn't get lost. *Aheka sīn sigām, gōm kami halam.* They have plenty of money, we by contrast have none. *Gōm ba buwas pai, as'ppal itū.* Real rice is preferable, this stuff is coarse. *Yuk Kuyya', "Gōm ba kami ameya' na."* Monkey said, "We'd better go along." *Pagt'kkaku ni luma', yukku, "Bay tapuwa'ku lima pilak." Yuk siyaliku, "Gōm bay aku ameya', magbahagi' kitā." "Na," yukku, "Maglalin ka, bay na ka'a-i bowaku."* On arrival at the house I said, "I happened to find five pesos on the path." My younger brother said, "I wish I had come along, we would share it." "Well now," I said, "Wait your turn, I would have taken you." (*Thesaurus:* **arapun, daipara, sapād-pād**)

**gōm na pa'in** *phrase* May it be as you say. {idiom} (*Thesaurus:* **kaddaw, mura-murahan**)

**gōm pa'in** *adv. phrase* Instead; in preference to; by contrast. *Halam aku bay makahampit, gōm pa'in niudju'.* I did not get a share, I was made fun of instead. *Bang kita bay anangkaw sīn bo' pangongka'ta, na bo' kita tara'ug, mbal kita nirūlan e' Tuhan. Gōm pa'in mbal ahāp baranta.* When we have stolen some money and are using it for gambling, and then we get beaten, God won't favor us. Our bodies are unwell instead.

**gōm-gōm** *v. intr.* pa- To improve, of weather or the condition of a someone who is sick. (*syn:* **gām-gām**)

**goma₁** *n.* 1) Rubber; rubber band; elastic. *Am'lli aku goma pangengkotku kalsitin.* I'll buy some elastic to secure my socks. (*cf:* **kalapiya**) **1.1)** *v. tr.* -an To attach an elastic band to clothing. *Ginomahan pantalunku.* My trousers have elastic [waistband] included.

**goma₂** *n.* An inflatable tire. *Pal'ppok gomana.* Its tire is flat. (*cf:* **silikan, tape'₁**)

**gomba** (*var.* **gumba**) *v. tr.* -an To pump air into something. *Gombahin kulaet ilū, Oto'.* Pump that pressure lantern, Son. (*syn:* **pām**)

**gombahan** *n.* A pump for moving fluid or air.

**gombel** *v. advrs.* -in- Having a prominent stomach. *Ginombel aku, sa'angay min kabudjangku. Bin'ttong.* I have had a large stomach ever since I was a young woman. Curving out. (*cf:* **b'ttong₁ 1.2**)

**gomgom** *var. of* **komkom**

**gomo'-gomo'** *var. of* **komot-komot**

**gomot** *var. of* **g'mmot**

**gonsan** *v. intr.* a- To be adequate or effective for the task, of a tool. *Pang'ntan ya makagonsan. Buwat laring-laring, mbal du makagonsan bang a'aslag kayu. Mbal sali' amangan, mbal makatanam apa ariki'.* It's the tool that can do the job adequately. Like a little knife, it won't be adequate if the wood is large. It's like it won't bite [into the material], it is unhandy because it is small.

**kagonsanan** *n.* The effective part of a cutting tool. *Kagonsanan ya t'ngnga' katkat.* The middle of the saw is the cutting part.

**gonteng** *n.* 1) A line with multiple hooks attached. *Aheka amisbis umpan bang aku angahūg gonteng.* Lots [of fish] nibble the bait when I drop multiple hooks. **1.1)** *v. tr.* To fish a location using a stationary line and multiple hooks. *Takot ya ginonteng, daing ginontengan.* The reef is reached by stationary fishing; the fish is caught by [this technique]. **1.2)** *v. tr.* -an To catch fish using a stationary line and multiple hooks. *Bang anganggonteng, suma'an mpat, suma'an lima, suma'an t'llu p'ssina.* When we fish with multiple hooks, we sometimes use four, sometimes five, sometimes three hooks. *Bang saupama anganggonteng kita, na angahūg sau.* Fishing from a fixed position, for example, we drop the anchor. (*Thesaurus:* **laway₂ 1.1, manit, pamalastik, paranas, p'ssi 1.1, tonda'₁ 1.1**)

**gonggong** *var. of* **komkom**

**gonggongan** *n.* The windpipe; the forward part of one's neck. *Da'a ka amalut ma gonggonganku Rāng, ap'ddi'.* Don't cling to my neck, Honey, it hurts. (*cf:* **k'llong**)

**gora'₁** *n.* 1) A defect or blemish. *Taga gora' angkan apōng.* It had a defect, therefore it broke. (*Thesaurus:* **powera 1, salla'₁ 1, sassat, tamak 1**) **1.1)** *adj.* a- Blemished.

**gora'₂** *adj.* a- 1) Teeming; occurring in large numbers. *Bang timbak daing, agora' patay daing. Ya ru bang magbono' manusiya', agora', yuk-i.* With dynamiting fish, there are a great many dead fish. Likewise when humans are fighting, many dead, they say. *Bay ka am'lli listun, agora' listun Tiyanggi, sali' aheka tab'llinu.* You bought milled lumber, so much timber in Jolo Town, it's as though you bought a lot. **1.1)** *v. tr.* To take in large amounts; to ransack. *Gora'tam ai-ai sigām.* Let's take everything they have. (*Thesaurus:* **longpos, taban**)

**kagora'an** *n.* An abundance of possessions. *Ingga taga kaniya', ya hē' aheya kagora'an a'a, sali' aheka kabowahan.* Whenever one has wealth, that is a man's abundance, as when he has many things to take with him.

**gores** (*var.* **goret**) *adj.* a- 1) Torn and wearing out, of clothing or a building. *Agoret-goret luma'na, lowang man lowang, geret man geret, sumpal man sumpal.* His house is in disrepair, hole upon hole, tear upon tear, patch upon patch. (*Thesaurus:* **kabel-kabel, jabel, jebel-jebel 1.1**) **1.1)** *v. tr.* To let something become too worn to be usable. *Karuhunan pahāp dinding ilu-i, da'a na pa'in goresunbi.* That wall has been that way for a long time, don't let it get any worse.

**goret** *var. of* **gores**

**gosak-gosak** *adj. a-* 1) Jumbled together; all mixed up. **1.1)** *v. tr.* To pile things together without sorting.

**gosang-gosang** *adj. a-* Tangled or disheveled, as uncombed hair or weaving threads. (*Thesaurus:* **ganggas, larang**)

**gōt-gōt** (var. **gōd-gōd**) *v. tr.* 1) To cut through something with repeated movements. (*Thesaurus:* **k'llot, ladjang, pabuwa', padja', tama', t'ttok 1.1**) 2) To draw a bow across a stringed instrument.

**gotom** *n.* 1) Famine. *Minsan ma waktu gotom, maka'ssohan kinakan sigām.* Even in times of famine their food fully satisfied them. **1.1)** *v. advrs. -in-* Suffering from famine, of a district and its people. *Ginotom na lahat. Halam aniya' kinakan tab'lli minsan aheka sīnta.* The land is suffering from famine. There is no food to be bought even though we have plenty of money.

**gotong** *v. tr.* To cut or divide something by cutting across, as wood into firewood, fish into cutlets. *Ginotong, buwat daing pinabuwa'.* Cut cross-ways, like fish cut into pieces. (*Thesaurus:* **hanggol 1.1, p'ppot 1**)

**paggotong** *v. tr.* To cut into several short lengths. *Kayu pinōng, pinaggotong dahanggol-dahanggol.* Wood cut in half, cut cross-ways into individual sections.

**gottay** *adj. a-* Distended, of breasts. *Agottay duru'na, ataha'. Gollay itu sali' magballeng.* Her breasts are distended and long. *Gollay* is hanging loosely and swinging. (*cf:* **gollay**)

**goyak** *n.* 1) Roughness, of the sea. (*cf:* **guyu 1**; *Thesaurus:* **alun-panjang, kata'-kata', lumbag, sahal₁ 1.1, sampoyak**) **1.1)** *adj. a-* Wavy; choppy. **1.2)** *v. tr. -an* To toss something about in rough seas. *Ginoyakan na pa'in kami.* We were continually tossed about by the storm. **1.3)** *v. advrs. ka-...-an* To be experiencing rough seas. *Kagoyakan kita, kagoyakan mbal na buwattē'.* We were experiencing wild seas, wild like never before.

**kagoyakan** *n.* Turbulence at sea. *Buwat pelang magsaligsig min deyom kagoyakan.* Like a canoe skimming through rough seas.

**goyakan** *n.* An expanse or locale of rough seas. *Bang ma goyakan maghantak pelang ni tahik.* When in a stormy area the canoe hits the sea hard.

**paggoyak** *v. tr. -an* To push something about by the force of a storm. *Pinaggoyakan pelang, mbal makabusay a'ana.* The canoe is tossed about by a storm, its crew unable to paddle.

**gradwet** *n.* A graduate from a course of (secular) training.

**paggradwet** *v. intr. aN-* To qualify for a degree or diploma on completing a course of study. (*cf:* **tammat 1**)

**gubal** *adj. a-* Falling apart due to lack of repair. *Sōng ajagjag, mbal na aponod, yukta agubal.* About to fall apart, no longer solid, we say it is *gubal.* (*Thesaurus:* **bulangkayat, g'ppa', hogal, lubu₂ 1, tunas 1**)

**gubang** *n.* A small dugout canoe. {archaic}

**gubat** *v. tr.* To attack a military objective. *Da'a kam anganggubat min dahū'an, sagō' libutinbi bo' tagubatbi sigām min bukutan.* Don't attack from the front, go around instead so you can attack them from behind. (*Thesaurus:* **atāk 1.1, dogpa' 1.1, dugpak 2, sakat₁**)

**gubbuk** var. of **g'bbuk**

**gubin** *adj. a-* Bulky and awkward in movement. *Gubin itū ai-ai asembol, abuhat. Gubin* is anything in the way, or heavy [to move]. *Na mbal aku ameya'. Agubin sidda aku, aheya b'ttongku.* No I won't go along. I am so awkward, my belly so big. *Makagubin ka'a itū, Oto', pasal maghambin ma ka'a. Dok ka mbal makagubin, ta'bba na ka.* You're awkward Son, because [I'm] carrying you. So you don't make things awkward, you'll be left here.

**gublis** var. of **gudlis**

**gubnul** *n.* A governor or official of similar high rank. *Tana' ya pinapagdapuhan e' gubnul.* Land taken possession of by the governor. *Bay kami magisun kamemon, kagubnulan, saga nakura', bag'llal, a'a pagpangaruhannu maka saga wakil.* We have all discussed this, governors, leaders, civil officials, people from whom you get advice, together with the deputies.

**paggubnul** *v. intr. aN-* To serve as governor.

**gudlis** (var. **gublis**) *v. intr. pa-* 1) Creating a long mark across a surface by moving something firmly across it. *Selo ataha' pagudlis.* A garfish makes a long furrow [across the sea]. *Sin'ngngat tapi' pelang bo' mbal akello'. Ya hē' pagudlis.* The canoe strake is inscribed with a line to prevent being misaligned. That is *gudlis.* **1.1)** *v. tr. -an* To scribe a line on a surface as when marking sailcloth. *Gudlisanta buwattē', sali' hinanganta ganta' pandoga.* Let's mark it like that, as though, let's say, we are establishing it as a landmark. *Bang a'a maghuma, ginudlisan du he' sigā pamat'nna'an tinanom sigā.* People who farm mark out where they place their plants. *Bang ka anganggudlis, da'a pagkello'-kello'un.* When you scribe a line don't make a lot of bends. (*Thesaurus:* **guhit 1.1, sangat 1.1**)

**gugul** *n.* 1) A trawl net. (*Thesaurus:* **lantaw 1, laya 1, linggi' 1, pokot₁ 1, sinsoro 1, siyul 1**) **1.1)** *v. tr.* To fish by trawl-netting. *Pagga pa'in kohap na lahat, ya du isāb anganggugul na kami ni Tausan.* When it is evening, then we also trawl for fish towards Tausan.

**guhit** *n.* 1) A line drawn on something. **1.1)** *v. tr. -an* To mark something with a line. *Guhitin manohan maka sīn.* Mark the playing area with coins. (*Thesaurus:* **gudlis 1.1, sangat 1.1**) **1.2)** *n.* Intervals marked on a scale. *Minsan lling a'a buwattina'an, bo' kita ah'lling palabi llingna* *(minsan palabi dangguhit), ya hē' niōnan magambahan.* If a person says something like that, then we say something beyond what he said (even a single interval beyond) that is called being deceptive.

**gu'ud** *n.* The upper end of sugar cane, where the leaves begin. *Ma aku gu'udna.* The *gu'ud* part is mine. (*cf:* **t'bbu**)

**gu'ud-t'bbu** *n.* The Pacific squaretail (fish species).

**gula'** *n.* Syrup.

**gula' buwani** *n. phrase* Honey (lit. bee syrup).

**gula' tuwak** *n. phrase* The syrup from the sap of the tuwak palm (toddy palm).

**gulaman** *n.* An edible seaweed species. (*Thesaurus:* **agal-agal, gamay**)

**gulamay** *n.* 1) The digits of hand or foot; fingers or toes. *Apaklus min tanganku bay balutanku. Yuk sehe'ku, "Ōy, halam aniya' gulamaynu?"* What I was holding slipped from my hand. My companion said, "Hey, don't you have any fingers?" (*wh:* **tangan** 1; *Thesaurus:* **anak-tangan, anak-tape'**) 2) The tentacles of an octopus. (*cf:* **janggut** 1, **labu**₄)

**gulami** *n.* Rice stalks; chaff. (*Thesaurus:* **buwas-kinakan, kinakan** 2, **pai** 1.1)

**gulandi'** *n.* 1) A sickness symptomized by swelling and ulceration of the glands in the neck, armpits or groin. 1.1) *v. advrs. -in-* Suffering from glandular swelling and ulceration.

**gulantung** *v. intr. pa-* To hang at arm's length from some support. *Da'a ka pagulantung bo' ka mbal papittay.* Don't dangle lest you suffer dislocation. (*Thesaurus:* **gantung**₂ 1.1, **sagnat** 1.1, **sa'ud**₁ 1.1)

**gulangan** *n.* A forested upland area. *Basta būd, niōnan gulangan. Būd to'ongan aheya kayuna.* Wherever there is a mountain it is called jungle. A true mountain has big trees. (*Thesaurus:* **kabbun, kati'an, talun** 1)

**guleyak** *n.* A rattle made of stones inside a container. *Maggilingan kita leha, pinat'nna' ma jambuna guleyak. Guleyak ē' bay ni'isihan batu-batu. Bang pinagtangkug-tangkug ah'lling. Manisna, pagbantuganna.* We rotate the boom of the square sail, and a rattle is attached to its decorative tuft. This rattle has been filled with pebbles. It makes a noise when shaken. It is [the canoe's] adornment and self-advertisement.

**guling** *v. tr.* To cook vegetables by frying briefly then adding water and herbs. (*gen:* **b'lla** 1)

**gulis-manuk** *n.* 1) A skin condition characterized by flaking of the scalp. *Saddī buruk min gulis-manuk. Gulis-manuk mbal amali', hal magkanit-kanit. Buruk* [scalp itch] is different from *gulis manuk* [scurf]. The latter won't become a wound, it just flakes off. (*Thesaurus:* **buruk** 1.1, **hagikgik, tai'-kōk**) 1.1) *v. advrs. -in-* Suffering from a scurf-like condition.

**gulu** *var. of* **guru**

**gulung** 1) *v. tr.* To roll up something flexible.

(*Thesaurus:* **lūn** 1.2) 2) *clf.* Count word for rolls of flexible material such as cloth.

**ma gulungan** *adv. phrase* By the roll, of cloth. (*cf:* **ma būsan**)

**gulung-gulung** *v. tr.* To move something by rolling, of a wheel or ball. *Bariles ginulung-gulung hē' ma M'ddas, he' kalgadol.* Barrels are rolled along over there in Siasi, by laborers.

**paggulung-gulung** *v. intr. aN-* 1) To turn on a shaft; to roll along. (*Thesaurus:* **paglegot** 1, **pagpalling**) 1.1) *v. tr.* To roll or turn something over and over.

**gūm-gūm** *v. intr. a-* To cleanse mouth by rubbing gums and gargling. *Agūm-gūm ka bang ka abati', nila'anan bau bowa' hē'.* Rub your teeth when you wake up, that mouth odor will be removed. (*Thesaurus:* **bunglaw** 1, **kula'up, saplut**₁ 1)

**gumamela** *n.* The hibiscus, a flowering plant. *Hibiscus rosasinensis.*

**gumba** *var. of* **gomba**

**gumbala'** *v. tr. -an* To show someone care and affection. *Minsan mbal gumbala'annu, anaknu du.* Even though you do not show care and affection, she is still your child. (*Thesaurus:* **kasi** 1, **lasa**₂ 1.1, **paganggi, s'lli** 1.1)

**gumi** *n.* 1) The earth as the place of one's abode after death. *Bang bay na kinubul, wa'i na ma deyom gumi.* Once [a body] has been buried it is there in the earth. 2) A grave. *Aheka gumi ma Mimul atawa ma Tangonan.* There are many graves at Mimul or at Tangonan. (*Thesaurus:* **kubul** 1, **kuddaman, dinding-hali, paliyangan**)

**gumun** *adj. a-* Seriously tangled, of thread or digestive organs. *Agumun tanud bay pamuwannu aku, asagut sali', mbal na pausay.* The thread you gave me is badly tangled, sort of snarled, no longer able to be unraveled. *Pagadgad deyom tina'ita, sali' agumun. Ya hē' isāb busā'.* Our bowels move around, sort of tangled. That's also what rupture does. (*Thesaurus:* **lokot, sagut** 1, **tulabid**)

**guna** *n.* 1) Use; value; worth. *Bang kita onde'-onde', halam aniya' gunata bang mbal pasoho'.* As children we have no use if we can't be told what to do. *Magkamundal-mandil, magkangī'-ngī. Bay kita ahāp, halam na aniya' kagunahanta.* Going from one place to another, and coming to a bad end. We were good people, but now we are worthless. (*Thesaurus:* **pūs**) 1.1) *v. tr.* To make use of something. *Na bang hati' ahāp na, aku na angangguna iya paglituhanku na.* So if it turns out to be okay, then I will use it for my buying and selling [fish]. (*Thesaurus:* **pakay**₁, **pasang**₁, **usal**) 1.2) *v. tr. a-, ka-..-an, -an* To need something. *Ka'a barannu ya kinagunahan.* It's you personally who is needed. (*Thesaurus:* **kalagihan** 1)

**kagunahan** *n.* An item of use to someone. *Niruwa' e' sigām ni kappal ai-ai kagunahan kami palutu'.* They loaded onto the ship all the things we need for travelling supplies. *Ai kagunahannu ma pōng papan itū?* What do you need this cut-off piece of lumber for?

**pagguna** *v. tr.* To make use of something for a specific or habitual purpose. *Da'a indamin katamku itū, paggunaku. Ya ru bang niamu' ai-aiku atawa buwat papel itū.* Don't borrow this plane of mine, I am using it. It's like that too when my things or this paper are asked for. *Magguna aku ma lahut itū.* I use this knife [all the time]. *Aho', makajari, paggunahun na.* Yes, okay, use it. *Ansak, pagguna e' Sama, tinemposan diyata'na, tahinang atibulung.* A coconut leaf basket regularly used by Sama, its top cut off and made circular.

**gunta'** *adj. a-* Overworked; overloaded.

**gunting** *n.* 1) Scissors. 1.1) *v. tr.* To cut something with scissors. 1.2) *v. tr. -an* To cut off hair or wool using scissors. *A: "Sai pagguntingan kōknu?" B: "Si Mu. Bu'un si Ja bay ginuntingan e' si'itna."* A: "Whose place did you get your hair cut at?" B: "At Mu's. Ja's hair was cut by his uncle." (*cf:* **babbel**)

**paggunting** *n.* The ceremonial first cutting of a child's hair, normally in its first year.

**guntul** *n.* The Green jobfish. *Aprion virescens.*

**gunu'** *n.* Anchovy, various species. *fam. Engraulidae.*

**gunyak-gunyak** *v. tr.* To mock someone. *Angay ka manggunyak-gunyak ilū? Bang ka'a Tuhan, pindahin aku. Bang m'ssa', da'a ka angudju'-ngudju' apa sali'-sali' kita manusiya'.* Why are you mocking? If you are God, change me. If not, don't ridicule me because we are both human beings. (*Thesaurus:* **paganday-anday, pagtunggīng, udju'**)

**gūng** *v. intr. pa-* To float on the surface of a liquid. *Bang aheka daing amatay sikagūngan ameya' palaran ma s'llog, ma ulak, bo' halam aniya' makapatay, yukta, "P'llut!"* When many fish are floating, drifting with the current and the weed, but nothing [obvious] has killed them, we say, "Plague!" (*cf:* **Sama Pagūng**; *syn:* **lantup**; *ant:* **t'nde 1**)

**pagūng** *v. tr.* To cause something to float.

**sikagūngan** *adj.* Floating in great numbers or mass.

**gunggus** *v. tr. -an* To clean a container by shaking an abrasive inside it. *Buwat kassa' taga l'mmis deyomna, subay ginunggusan aheka sabun atawa gusung.* Like a bottle with dirt inside it, must be cleaned by shaking lots of soap or sand. (*cf:* **lunglung**)

**gupu** *adj. a-* Becoming distressed so that speech and clear thought are temporarily lost. *Sali' kita agupu, sali' kita arupang bang aniya' kasusahanta. Halam aniya' llingta. Buwat kamatayan, kalungayan.* We get distressed and foolish, when trouble strikes us. We have no words, like when

we are bereaved or have suffered a loss. *Ginupu kita bang kita angongka' ma kaheka-heka'an a'a.* We are made nervous when we perform among lots of people. (*Thesaurus:* **bolag, dalan 1.1, damag, gawa, g'mma, leya'-leya', tāw 1.1, umagad 1.1**)

**guri'** *v. tr. -an* To have such antagonism towards someone that one considers doing him harm.

**guru** (var. **gulu**) *n.* 1) A teacher of religion or mystic skills. (*cf:* **mastal, mulid**) 1.1) *v. tr.* To acquire knowledge from a religious teacher or expert in mystic lore. *Mbal kita ainay bang aniya' punglu' makatudju ni baranta sabab aniya' ilmu' bassata ma deyom atayta bang asal bay ginulu.* Nothing happens to us when a bullet hits our body, because we have magical protection that we recite in our minds, if we have in fact learnt them.

**pagguru** *v. intr. aN-* To become the student of a teacher of religion. *Si Imam Mu ya pagguruhanku.* Imam Mu is the one I follow as my teacher.

**balguru** *n.* A religious scholar.

**gusi'** *n.* A container for storing money, especially one that multiplies what is put into it. *Tau'un pahogot. Sali' gusi' pamalidjiki' ma kita.* Keep it secure. It's like a magic money box bringing us good fortune. *Bang kita sinukuran gusi', bo' kita makaisi dakayu' pilak, anganak ko' inān.* If we have the good fortune of getting a magic money box and we put one peso into it, it will make a profit. (*gen:* **pagtau'an**)

**gustang** *adj. a-* Needing refreshment after physical exertion. *Agustang na iya. Bay angā' bohe', halam bay makakakan.* He needs refreshments. He fetched water, and hadn't eaten. *Pagustangun b'ttongnu ilū bo' ka amole' amoslad!* Make that stomach of yours hungry and go home to eat greedily! (*Thesaurus:* **bongtas 1.1, hanu, lingantu 1.1, otas, punung**)

**gustu** *n.* 1) A positive feeling about a decision. 1.1) *v. tr.* Convinced that a choice will turn out to be good. *Ai-ai gustuta am'lli, b'llita sadja magbaynat.* Whatever we feel good about buying, we just buy, resolutely. *Bang ma paglegotan, anganggustu ka to'ongan bang maingga karuwa umbul inān. Bang gustuta dahū lima, to'onanta.* At the gaming board, concentrate on where the two numbers are. If we feel good about a 5 appearing first, we put our money down.

**kagustuhan** *n.* A positive feeling about something. *Pasa'atan sali' kagustuhan, buwat sali' kita amowa si Sa inān ni sapa'. Yukna, "Halam gi' pat'kka pasa'atanku ni sapa'." Pasa'atan* is like *kagustuhan,* like when we were taking Sa to the creek. He said, "I don't yet have a good feeling about going to the creek." (*Thesaurus:* **galak₁ 1, pasa'atan**)

**gusuk** var. of **usuk**

**gusung** *n.* Sand; a sandy beach. (*syn:* **ungus;**

*Thesaurus:* **bunbun 1, kalangan₃, kapote'an, igang₁**)

**guya'** *adj. a-* Flimsy; insubstantial, of cloth or metal. *Aguya' maka anipis-nipis na badju' si Mma'.* Dad's shirt is already worn out and thin. *Mital aguya', al'kkas magka'at.* Light metal, soon wrecked. (*cf:* **p'ddut**)

**guyu** *n.* 1) The turbulence of water below the surface. *Guyu itū sampay ni tana' deyo', ameya' arundang saga kahunasan.* This word *guyu* is the turbulence of sea water that reaches right to the seabed, the sea grasses swaying with it. (*cf:* **goyak 1**; *Thesaurus:* **abal 1.1, haus 1, sahabal**) **1.1)** *adj. a-* Turbulent.

**pagdaguyu** *v. intr. aN-* To move together restlessly; to jostle. (*Thesaurus:* **lensa, tangkug 1**)

**guyud** *v. tr.* 1) To move something by pulling. *Guyurun pi'itu buli' pelang ilū bo' mbal talaran bang alalom.* Pull the stern of the canoe this way so it won't drift away when the tide is full. (*Thesaurus:* **bira 1, konot₂, ga'ut, ganggut, hella', paglagedled 1**) 2) To seize a woman and compel her to marry. (*cf:* **lalas, saggaw-sangom**)

**pagguyud** *v. intr. aN-* To pull or tow each other. *Makapagguyud kami maka ipalku.* My brother-in-law and I towed each other.

# H h

**habagat** *n.* Monsoon; lesser winds from the southwest. *Tulakta tudju s'ddopan sagō' baliyu habagat.* Our heading is southwest, but the wind is the southwest monsoon. *Bang aniya' babakan, ya hē' pandoga habagat.* When there are pufferfish that's the sign of the coming southwest monsoon. (*gen:* **baliyu 1**)

**habal** *n.* News from elsewhere. *Ya ru ilū habalku buwattina'an.* That's my news for the present. *Pagkale kami ma habal itū, magtūy kami kinōgan sidda.* On hearing this report we were very happy. *Taluwa' kami habal ma dilaut. Tinandog atawa ap'ddi' b'ttong, hal kami magpagūng.* A sense of trouble hit us at sea. We have a fever or a stomach ache, and we just float aimlessly. *Taluwa' kita habal, taluwa' kita sukkal.* We are struck with a feeling of concern, we are struck with trouble. (*Thesaurus:* **kabtangan**)

**habay-habay** *n.* A protective charm worn across the chest. *Maitu ma hawakan hadjimat, ya habay-habay maitu ma dagaha.* A *hadjimat* amulet is [worn] here at the waist, a *habay-habay* is here on the chest. (*gen:* **tambang₃ 1**)

**paghabay-habay** *v. intr. aN-* To wear a protective charm around one's upper body. *Bay maghabay-habay si Imam Ma. Bay atunu' luma' sigām.* Imam Ma had been wearing his protective charms. Their house had burnt down.

**habbab** *v. tr. -an* To eat without concern for others who are hungry. *Buwat salingkal buwahan, na nihabbaban kamemon, halam aniya' takapin.* Like a *salingkal* basket full of lansones, then eaten up completely, nothing left. (*Thesaurus:* **dahal 1**)

**habba'** var. of **h'bba'**

**habit** *v. tr.* To carry something on one's person, wherever one goes. *Nihabit onde'-onde', binowa na pa'in e' ina'na pi'ingga-pi'ingga, mbal ni'bbahan.* A child, carried around by its mother wherever [she] goes and never put down.

(*Thesaurus:* **abin, appula, gawil, hangkut, pagbaga'ud**)

**habog** *adj. a-* Broad, of tobacco leaves. (*Thesaurus:* **lambu 1.1, lampo' 1.1, luha 1.1**)

**habuggu'** var. of **abuggu'**

**hāk** *n.* Something acquired without the explicit consent of the owner or producer, especially of food. *Bang kita pinakan ngga'i ka hilas, na makakakan kita hāk, ya hulas-sangsā' a'a.* If we are fed without goodwill, then we are eating *hāk*, a man's toil and sweat.

**paghāk** *v. intr. aN-* 1) To be deeply and enduringly offended at someone who had been a friend. **1.1)** *v. tr. -an* To reject someone as disgusting. *Bang ka'a-i mbal anaima', paghākanta ka.* If you will not accept it, I will treat you as something disgusting. *Ya paghākan ludja'anta.* We spit out someone considered to be disgusting.

**haka** (var. **haka'**) *n.* 1) News; information. (*Thesaurus:* **ba'at 1, kabtangan, hunub-hunub 1, pahati 1, sambatan, suli-suli 1**) **1.1)** *v. ditr.* To communicate or confess something to another person. *Buwat aniya' alungay ai-aita, asal angahaka na kita ni pangatagta bo' supaya sigām mbal a'awam.* When something of ours is lost, we naturally let our neighbors know so they are not unaware. *Aniya' lagi' tuwi' takalipatku nihaka.* Oh, there is something else I forgot to tell. *Yampa pinakale ni talingata; bang ka bay angahaka di'ilaw.* Only reaching my hearing just now; if only you had told me yesterday. *Bang ningā' saga buwahan, bay ru aku angahaka.* If lansones had been taken I would have admitted it. (*Thesaurus:* **palapal, pata'u, tubad**)

**kihaka** *v. tr.* To ask someone for information. (*Thesaurus:* **hati 2, hodhod, sisi 2, tilaw 1.1, tilosa 1.1**)

**pagkihaka** *v. intr. aN-* To ask someone for

information. *Magkihaka sigām dangan maka dangan.* They asked each other for information.

**haka'** var. of **haka**

**hakika'** *n.* 1) An animal sacrifice, typically of a goat or sheep. (*cf:* **sumbali'**) 1.1) *v. tr.* To slaughter an animal as a sacrifice. *Nihakika' bang aniya' amatay matto'a, sinumbali'an kambing.* An animal is sacrificed when an old person dies, a goat is slaughtered for him. (*syn:* **kulban 1**)

**hakim** *v. tr.* *-an* To apply a law unjustly. *Sali' si Nabi Da'ud, bay nihakiman e'na h'nda si Uriya.* Like the Prophet David, who used legal means to get for himself the wife of Uriah.

**hakin** *adj.* *zero* To be sitting cross-legged. (*Thesaurus:* **milang, pagsengkang, pagsiningkulang**)

  **pagnihakin** *v. intr.* *aN-* To sit with legs crossed and upper leg swinging.

**hakos** *adj.* *a-* Dressed for the occasion, as a soldier in battle-dress or a youth in courting clothes. *Ahakos, sali' kita as'mmek, magsinawwal, magbinadju', magpinīs, magkinuppiya', magtinakos saga. Ya buwat sundalu, ahakos na s'mmek sigā.* Dressed for the occasion, well-clothed, wearing wide Sulu trousers, a shirt, a shoulder cloth, a cap, armed perhaps. Like soldiers, wearing full uniform. (*cf:* **pagtinakos**)

**hakpan** *n.* Shorts or pajamas for women. (*Thesaurus:* **sauwal, solpan**)

**hakup** var. of **akup**

**hād** *n.* 1) A stated limit on space, time or financial resources. *Buwat kami magtiman maka h'ndaku. Pinat'nna'an kami hād. Ma deyom duwambulan subay da'a kita magh'lla, magh'nda ni saddī.* Like my wife and I divorce. We have a time limit placed on us. For two months we mustn't marry someone else. *Buwat tilawku ma bangka', yukku, "Aniya' hād legot itū?" Ya sambungna, "Subay taga balad bo' taga hād."* Like when I ask the banker, saying, "Is there a limit [on bets] in this dice game?" His answer, "There has to be a gaming-board for limits to be set." (*Thesaurus:* **diyuhan**) 1.1) *v. tr.* To allow someone opportunity, as in a contest. *Bang aniya' sehe'nu magsuntuk bo' ka'apikihannu, da'a hārun ba. Magtūy lubakun pehē', da'a ka angagad sinuntuk.* When you have an opponent in boxing and you are about to close with him, don't give him time. Get going immediately, don't wait to be punched. 1.2) *v. tr.* *-an* To assign someone a limit on time or space. *Nihāran ka dapitu' maitu.* You have a limit of one week here. (*Thesaurus:* **sangka' 1.1, tobtob 1.2**)

  **paghād** *v. tr.* *-an* To set limits on the scope of something. *Pinaghāran sigām ma liyuhan sapa'.* They were confined to the other side of the river.

    **mahād** *adv.* 1) In accord with constraints or limits set by an authority. 1.1) *v. tr.* *-an* To set limits on some activity or scope. *Magbislangan dang'llaw ni*

duwa, minahāran maka niorahan. Doing something infrequently, for a day or two, the extent and times set [by a magistrate].

  **pangahād** *n.* Limits or restrictions imposed by a court order.

**hadarat** (var. **hadjarat**) *n.* The presence of a divine being. *Ya sambung mala'ikat, "Aku itu si Jibra'il, ya pat'nna' na pa'in ma hadarat Tuhan."* The angel's answer, "I am Gabriel, who dwells in the presence of God." *Takumpasna sali' sōng na iya amole' ni hadarat Tuhan.* She figures that she is about to go home to the presence of God. (*cf:* **alopan₁**; *Thesaurus:* **matahan, pajātan**)

**haddad** var. of **huddud**

**hadil** *v. intr.* *pa-* To be present at an event. *Bang makasulut ma ka'a, tuwan sultan, pahadil pa'in ka llaw itu ni pagjamu ya sakapku.* If it pleases you, oh Sultan, please come today to the feast I have prepared. *Palabay pa'in duwantahun, bay pinaba'an e'na ya kamemon kal'llahan anak sultan supaya angahadil.* When two years had passed he invited all the sultan's male children to attend [the event]. *Pahadil kita, pasabu kita ma aniya' palhimpunan.* We will attend; we will be there when there is a gathering. (*Thesaurus:* **luruk 1.1, taddung, tupuk**)

**hadja₁** *n.* A woman who makes the pilgrimage to Mecca in fulfillment of one of the five pillars of Islam.

**hadja₂** var. of **sadja**

**hadjarat** var. of **hadarat**

**hadjat₁** *n.* The purpose of some action. *Ai hadjatbi pi'itu?* What is the purpose of your coming here? (*Thesaurus:* **kamatti, gawi 1, maksud 1, tiranan**)

**hadjat₂** *v. advrs.* *-in-* Affected by mild fever which has no external symptoms. *Nihadjat, luwasanna halam nihaggut, hal deyomna.* Affected by a fever, not experiencing chills externally, just inside. *Sali' kita tinandog bo' ngga'i ka tandog to'ongan, hal kita nihadjat. Sali' kita tinandog-tandogan.* Like being feverish but not a real fever, just a hadjat. It's as though we are being shaken. (*Thesaurus:* **hōb-hōb, l'mmun, tandog 1, tatat**)

**hadji'** *n.* A man or boy who makes the pilgrimage to Mecca in fulfillment of one of the five pillars of Islam.

  **paghadji'** *v. intr.* *aN-* To make the pilgrimage to Mecca. *Makka, lahat paghadji'an.* Mecca, the place of pilgirimage.

**hadjimat** *n.* A charm comprising words of the Holy Koran wrapped in a cloth container and worn on the body. *Hadjimat to'ongan, ya ganta' panampan. Pakambotta ni hawakan, atawa pagantungta ni k'llong.* A real charm, protection against possible harm. We fasten it on a belt around the waist, or hang it around the neck. (*gen:* **tambang₃ 1**)

**hadjul-hadjul** *see:* **paghadjul-hadjul**

**hāg** *n.* 1) A post of a house or fence. *Bay aku anigbas kayu, hinangku hāg.* I cut down a tree and will make a post of it. *Nirangin kami magosolan hāg.* We were called on to cooperate in putting in posts. (*Thesaurus:* **bale₃ 1, lusuk-lusuk, pangtu'ud, pipul, sumpiyang, tuku** 1) 1.1) *v. tr. -an* To provide a structure with posts. *Am'lli aku hāg pangahāgku luma'.* I am buying posts for building my house.

**kahāgan** *n.* Structures involving posts. *Jari akatis na kamemon kahinangan ma ba'anan kahāgan inān.* So all the work on those various post structures was over and done with.

**hāg analus** *n. phrase* The main house posts, generally on corners, that run through right up to the tops of the walls. *Bang ka ahinang luma' subay hāg analus man mpat pidju' luma'.* When you are building a house there should be main load-bearing posts on the house's four corners.

**hagak** *n.* Noisy breathing.

**paghagak** *v. intr. aN-* To be struggling to breathe. *Bay aku agon pat'nde, pagdiyata'ku, hāl aku maghagak.* I nearly sank, on coming up I was simply gasping for breath. (*cf:* **paghagok**; *Thesaurus:* **gagal₁, pagnapas, panggahak, ppo**)

**hagas-hagas** *v. tr.* To whisper something. (*Thesaurus:* **higung-higung, singu'-singu'**)

**paghagas-hagas** *v. intr. aN-* To talk together in whispers.

**hagda** (*var.* **sagda₂**) *adj. a-* 1) Gruff; curt, of speech. *Sali' hal aningkō', maka sali' ap'ddi' atayna bang anoho'. Ya hē' niōnan ahagda.* He just sort of sits and gives orders as though he is angry. That's what we call being *hagda.* 1.1) *v. tr.* To chide or correct someone gruffly. *Angahagda aku sehe'ku. Soho'ku amat'ngge banog.* I give orders to my companion. I tell him to raise the sail. *Sagdahan ya a'a alalom nahuna ati kinalasahan ka e'na.* Correct a thoughtful person and he will love you.

**hagda-hagda** *v. tr.* To make someone ill by invoking the baleful influence of beings such as ancestors, ghosts or spirits. (*syn:* **sagda₁**)

**hagdan-hagdan** *v. advrs. -in-* Woven with a decorative strip along each side of a long mat. (*syn:* **sasa-dandan**)

**haggut** 1) *n.* Cold, as a state of the atmosphere or environment. *A: "Ō Kulas, nihaggut gi' ka?" K: "Aho', mbal kasandalan haggut itū."* A: "Oh Kulas, are you still cold?" K: "Yes, this cold is unbearable." 1.1) *adj. a-* Cold, of the temperature, of water, food, wind, etc. *Halam aku makatuli dibuhi', sidda ahaggut.* I couldn't sleep last night, it was really cold. 1.2) *v. advrs. -in-* Affected by cold. *Bay si Ji anuhun tulay, nihaggut baranna.* Ji dived for herrings, and his body got cold. (*Thesaurus:* **k'ttol, dingin 1, hagpay 1, t'nne** 1) 2) *v. advrs. -in-* To be shivering, as when feverish. *Bang aniya' nanamta, nihaggut-haggut kita, maumu kita pakullung.* When we feel unwell and suffer a bit of a chill, we often curl up.

**haggut atay** *adj. a-* Inwardly calm; unperturbed. {idiom}

**haggut-pasu'** *n.* A wide range of conditions, good and bad. {idiom} *Magdorog, sali' aningkō' ma luma', buwat ka'a magdorog maitu. Sandalanku haggut-pasu'.* Staying in some place, like sitting in the house, like you settling here. I endure the good and the bad [lit. heat and cold] of life.

**haggut-tangan** *adj. a-* Skilled in growing things or keeping livestock. {idiom} (*syn:* **hagpay-tangan**)

**hagikgik** *n.* A scaly infection of the head; dandruff. (*Thesaurus:* **buruk 1.1, gulis-manuk 1, tai'-kōk**)

**hagin** *adj. a-* 1) Consumed, of supplies; used up. *Buwat ai-ai taga isi bo' akatis na bay isina, ahagin na.* Anything that has contents, for example, when everything it contained is used up, that's *hagin.* (*Thesaurus:* **katis₁ 1, puspus₂**) 1.1) *v. tr. -an* To use all that is available, of basic resources like water, food, firewood. *Bang ap'nno' dabariles bohe' bo' halam aniya' ma poga, na nihaginan min bariles bo' supaya aniya' ma poga.* When a barrel is full of water and there is none in the water jar, then it is used up from the barrel so there is some in the water jar. 1.2) *v. advrs. ka-...-an* To be used up; consumed. *Bay ap'nno' garapun he' bāng-bāng, bay na kahaginan, bay na kinakan, bay na niā'.* The jar had been full of cookies, they have all been consumed, eaten, they have been taken out.

**hagmak** *v. tr. -an* To do something without proper care. *Hagmakin banog apa ilu hunus.* Strike the sail [without rolling and lashing it] because a squall is coming. (*Thesaurus:* **patabak**)

**pahagmak** *v. tr.* To leave things uncared-for. (*syn:* **pagumak**)

**hagok** *n.* The sound of snoring.

**paghagok** *v. intr. aN-* To produce a snoring noise. *Maghagok, magnapas paheya.* Making a snoring noise, breathing heavily. *Maghagok sali' koholna.* His cough is sort of snoring. (*cf:* **paghagak**; *Thesaurus:* **panggahak**)

**hagom** *v. intr. pa-* 1) To remain in a liquid for a long time. *Wa'i bay pahagom si Arung. Pamahagomanku iya wa'i ma tahik.* Eldest daughter has been having a long soak. The sea is where I have her soak. 1.1) *v. tr. -an* To soak something, as to soften or cure it. *Bang aniya' abakat, bo' pagnana', nihagoman ni tahik atawa ni bohe'.* If someone has a wound from cutting and it is producing pus, it is soaked in seawater or freshwater. (*Thesaurus:* **k'mbang 1.1, h'ggom 1.1, t'nde 1.1**)

**paghagom** *v. tr. -an* To soak something thoroughly. *Nirakdakan s'mmek, buwat saga paghagom-hagomanta ni undam.* The clothes are washed, like when we soak them thoroughly in a basin.

**hagpay** *n.* 1) Coldness. (*Thesaurus:* **k'ttol, dingin 1,**

**haggut 1.2, t'nne 1) 1.1)** *adj. a-* Cold, in contrast to normal temperature. *Ninanam baranna bang ahagpay.* Checking his body, whether it is cold.

**hagpay-tangan** *adj. a-* Skilled in growing plants or keeping livestock. {idiom} (*syn:* **hagguttangan**)

**hagpe'** var. of **sagpe'**

**hagtang** *v. intr. pa-* To be lying face upwards. *Sikahagtangan ba'anan lagtaw inān.* All those many giants were lying flat on their backs. *Ina'an pahagtang ma kōkan.* Lying there on the upstream side of the house. (*Thesaurus:* **daya', hantal, haya'₁, leyak, pagduleyak**)

**hagtu'** (var. **dagtu'**) *v. tr.* To tug sharply on the end of a line such as a tether or anchor cable. *Sali' ai-ai bay engkotanta, nihagtu' bo' apuwas.* Like anything we have tied, tugged in order to come loose. *Da'a dagtu'un badju' ilu bo' mbal ageret.* Don't tug at that shirt lest it tear. *Bang kami magtuhun kaut bo' aniya' patuhun dangan bo' niengkotan maka lubid, subay angandagtu' bo' yampa nihella'.* When we are diving out at sea and one of us is diving tied with a rope, he must tug and be pulled up. (*Thesaurus:* **hagul, hantuk, hangku'**)

**paghagtu'** *v. tr.* To jerk something sharply; to snap finger joints by tugging on the fingertips. *Pinaghagtu'-hagtu', buwat amuwang.* Jerked repeatedly as when fishing with hook and line.

**hagud-hagud** var. of **gahud-gahud₁**

**hagul** *v. tr.* To repeatedly raise and lower a weighted line. *Bang kita angambit subay bowata batu maka lubid pangahagul. Pinatuntun batu pareyo' bo' nihagul.* When we catch fish by driving we should take stones and rope for jigging. The stones are suspended on a line and jigged up and down [to herd fish]. (*Thesaurus:* **hagtu', hantuk, hangku'**)

**paghagul** *v. intr. aN-* To move up and down repeatedly, as a restless child. *Buwat sali' kita an'ngge, yukta, "Da'a ka maghagul apa itiya' aku magsulat. Da'a ka magjogjog inān."* Like when one of us stands up, we say, "Don't keep getting up and down because I'm writing. Don't shake things there." *Pahandok itu sali' mint'dda. Maghandok, maghagul sali'. Pahandok* is just one bounce, *maghandok* is repeated bouncing, like *maghagul.*

**hagupit** *n.* The sandpaper shrub, a plant with rough leaves useful for smoothing wood. *Ficus sp.*

**hagut** *v. tr. -an* To remove the outer layer of plants such as pandanus, abaca, banana. *Nihagutan, sali' nila'anan dalapis, buwat pandan, lanut. Hagut* is like one layer being removed, as pandanus or abaca. (*Thesaurus:* **kanit 1.1, kisak, kupas, hampa' 1.1, lapes**)

**hahāy** var. of **ahāy**

**hailaya** *n.* A religious festival. (*cf:* **Bulan Hailaya**)

**Hailaya Hadji'** *n. phrase* The celebration on the 10th day of the month Julhadji'.

**Hailaya Puwasa₁** *n. phrase* The celebration at the end of Ramadan, thirty days after the beginning of the fast; on the day Aid ul Pitri. (*syn:* **Aid ul Pitri**)

**Hailaya Puwasa₂** *n. phrase* Sulu name for the month when the pilgrims return from Mecca.

**hain** (var. **ahin**) *v. ditr.* To pour a liquid from one container to another. *Nihainan bohe' bay ma mital, nihainan ni kibut. Hatina pinasaddī pangisihan.* The water that had been in the metal can is poured into the water-jar. In other words the container is changed. (*Thesaurus:* **huddud 1.1, tumpa 1.1, tuwang, tuyung**)

**hairat** var. of **ahirat**

**hait** (var. **ahit**) *v. tr. -an* To prepare plant material for weaving by removing superfluous matter. (*Thesaurus:* **ambuhut, salimi, tai' 1.1, tilas₂**)

**hā'** var. of **ā'**

**hāl** *see:* **kahālan, hāl-hāl**

**hal** *adv.* Only; merely; simply. *Bang aku hal amangan daing, bo' halam aniya' lauk, sinassing aku.* If I eat only fish and there is no staple to go with it, I get pinworms. *Atulakan iya dīna. Hal iya, halam aniya' sehe'na, halam aniya' isāb amatulak iya.* He departs on his own account. Just him, no companion, no one sending him off. *Nsa' aniya' sinapang saddī, hal tamson.* No other weapon, only a Thompson [machine gun]. *Ai-ai pamissalanu ma aku, ahāp-ala'at, hal aku angaluluy.* Whatever you say to me, good or bad, I simply accept. (*Thesaurus:* **dakuman, la'a, luwal, puntul, sadja, samadjana, tunggal 1, yangkon**)

**hāl-hāl** *adj.* zero Aloneness; the condition of being unaccompanied. *Mbal ka makalingus, hāl-hālnu?* Aren't you lonely, being on your own?

**halahuwalam** *intrj.* Absolutely no idea (only God knows). (*cf:* **inday**)

**halal 1)** *v. tr.* To eat what is allowed by Islamic dietary laws. (*Thesaurus:* **halam-mutallak, halus₂, haram 1, sumbang**) **1.1)** *adj.* zero Permitted for consumption under Islamic dietary laws. **2)** *adj.* zero Suitable as a marriage partner, i.e. not forbidden by incest restrictions. **2.1)** *v. tr.* To accept someone as a suitable marriage partner.

**halal-kawin** *n.* Marriage that is formally celebrated.

**halam₁** (var. **alam₂; hām**) **1)** *neg.* None; there is none (existential clause negator). *Halam aku taga sairola.* I have no certificate. *A: "Aniya' dambila' pilaknu?" B: "Halam."* A: "Do you have fifty centavos?" B: "No." *Atagi sidda angambil-hati minsan bissara hām kapusanna.* [She is] addicted to making wrong assumptions even when it's talk with no special purpose. (*syn:* **da'a 2, nsa' 1**; *Thesaurus:* **da'a 2**) **1.1)** 'Not', of a realised assertion or action (realis clause negator). *A: "Bay tangkawnu lilusnu ilū?" B: "Ōy, halam aku bay anangkaw."* A: "Did you steal that watch of yours?" B: "Hey. I haven't stolen." *A: "Ma'ai bangka'?" B: "Halam ta'nda'ku."* A: "Where is the canoe?" B: "I haven't seen it." *Alam iya ōnan kami ōn Sinama sagō' masi iya piha'an kami g'llal ma Sinama.* We haven't given him a Sama name but we are still seeking a Sama nickname for him. (*cf:* **mbal 1.1**; *syn:* **nsa' 1.1**) 2) *v. intr. pa-* To become nothing. *Apadpad lasata, linduta, sali' pahalam.* Our love and our longing felt no more, sort of fading to nothing. *Buwat kita bay aheka ai-aita, manjari ma sosōng tahun pahalam na pa'in, pahalam. Paloddos ai-ai.* Like us [incl] having lots of things, but then as the years pass they keep on vanishing. Things grow less and less.

**halam ugat** *adj. zero* Lacking in physical strength. {idiom} *Halam aniya' ugatna, mbal makabuhat.* He has no muscular strength, can't lift anything.

**pahalam** *v. tr.* To negate or erase something; to reduce something to nothing. (*Thesaurus:* **erēs, papas₁ 1.1**)

**halam₂** var. of **haram**

**halam aniya'** (var. **hāmaniya'**) *v. intr. zero* There is none; none. *Talingus-lingus aku sabab halam aniya' sehe'ku.* I feel lonely because I have no companion. *Halam aniya' daing ma luma'.* There is no fish in the house.

**halam baya'** *adv. phrase* Spontaneously; unintentionally. {idiom} *Tabowa e' kōdna, makalaksu iya halam baya'.* He jumps up spontaneously, carried away by his joy. *Nda'un kabowa tāwna, makaragan nsa' baya'.* Look how his fear affects him, running without thinking.

**halam pa'in** *adv. phrase* Not much later; before. *Halam pa'in at'ggol, pinat'nna' iya maggubnul.* Not much later, he was installed as governor. *Na, halam pa'in at'kka disi Sa, magkanat-kanat na saga sundalu.* So before Sa and the others had arrived, the soldiers dispersed.

**halam-mutallak** *adv.* Absolutely unfit for human consumption. *A: "Aniya' bohe'? Angamu' aku." B: "Halam-mutallak, halam ero'." (Bang aniya' mbal tahalal.)* A: "Do you have any water? I'm asking for some." B: "Absolutely unclean, the uncleanness of a dog." (Said of something ritually unacceptable.) (*Thesaurus:* **halal 1, halus₂, haram 1, sumbang**)

**halaman** *n.* A cleared space or yard about a house. *Halaman itū sali' halam aniya' sembolna.* This yard is like it has nothing untidy about it.

**halambiyara'** var. of **harambiyara'**

**halap₁** *v. intr. aN-* To believe what someone says. *Mbal aku paratsaya ma ka'a, sali' aku mbal angahalap.* I do not have faith in you, it's like I don't believe [what is said]. (*Thesaurus:* **beya'-beya'₁ 1, b'nnal 1.2, kahagad, parassaya,** siddik)

**halap₂** var. of **hāp**

**halapi** *see:* **manghalapi**

**haldaya** *adj. zero* Wealthy; prosperous. *Tuhan ya bay angala'an kahaldaya si Laban bo' apinda ni si Yakub.* It is God who removed Laban's wealth in order to transfer it to Jacob. *Minsan sultan Sulayman maka kahaldayana ma masa awal ē', mbal du maka'atu lingkat pamakayna ma dakayu' sumping itū.* Even King Sulayman and his great wealth long ago, the splendor of his clothes would not compare with one of these flowers. (*Thesaurus:* **balkan, daya, mayaman, sayuman**)

**halga'** *n.* 1) Value; price; expense. *Pila halga'na ilū?* What is the price of that? *A'a mbal magta'at ma Tuhan sali' halam aniya' halga'na.* A person who does not pray to God is like someone with no value. (*cf:* **hunit 2.1, luhay₁ 1.1**) 1.1) *adj. a-* Expensive. 1.2) *v. tr. -an* To state a price when opening a bargaining sequence. *Aho', sinoho' nihalga'an duwa ina'an. Wa'i na halga'anku sangpū' maka walu'.* Yes, asked to put a price on those two. I have priced it as ₱18. *Bay aku am'lli daing nihalga'an dakayu' pilak, balosku dambila'. "Aho'," yukna, "ngā'un na."* I was buying a fish priced at one peso, and I offered half that. "Yes," he said, "take it." (*Thesaurus:* **andag, jawab₁, ladjaw, paragang**)

**pahalga'** *v. tr.* To treat someone or some thing as special.

**hali₁** *n.* 1) The usable starch residue from the liquid expressed when cassava is grated. *Bay na ginipitan panggi', sinaud bohe'na. Ubus ya bohe' ī' pinato'ong mareyom undam. Binu'usan bohe'na, ya ta'bba ē', ya na halina. Tahinang amirul, atawa binugbug, atawa nilandang.* When the cassava has been squeezed, its liquid is caught. The liquid is left to settle in a basin. Its water is then tipped out and what is left is the *hali.* It is made into laundry starch, or cooked as porridge, or fried. (*Thesaurus:* **akal, angkas₁ 1, p'tti', sapal, tai'-lahing**) 1.1) *v. tr.* To express the toxic liquid from grated cassava.

**mahali** *adj. zero* Having the characteristic smell and flavor of newly squeezed cassava meal; strongly odorous, of certain fish. (*Thesaurus:* **bau 1.1, b'ngngi, hamut 1.1, hangsu 1, langsa, langtu, p'ngngak**)

**hali₂** *v. intr. pa-* To improve in health; to heal. *Pahali na bakatna.* Her wound is getting better. (*syn:* **uli'₁ 1**)

**hali₃** *v. intr. pa-* To take a break from some activity. *Pahali na kām maglata.* Stop teasing each other. *Pahali gi' aku dai'-dai'.* I'll take a break for a minute. *Alanat pahāp ulan, mbal pahali.* This rain is so persistent, it doesn't slacken off. (*cf:* **h'ddok**; *Thesaurus:* **hogga' 1, hondong 1, honglo' 1**)

**kahali'an** *n.* A period of rest from work. *Asidda patihinangun d'nda inān, sali' ya na kahali'anna* *amangan maka atuli.* That woman is so committed to her work, it is as if her only rest is when she eats and sleeps.

**hali-hali** *v. intr. pa-* To rest; to take time off. *Pahali-hali lagi' aku, subay na salung bo' kita am'ssi, llaw tabu' Hambilan.* I am still resting, it should be tomorrow that we will go fishing, the day of the Hambilan market. (*cf:* **hotay**)

**hali'an** *n.* A break in activity.

**hali-gaha'** *n.* The rusty discoloration of water.

**haliluwal** *see:* **kahaliluwalan**

**halimaw** *n.* A great cat such as a tiger or lion. *Aniya' inān pinakahalimaw bo' pa'in katas.* There was something there made to look like a tiger, but it was just paper. (*cf:* **layon;** *gen:* **sattuwa**)

**halimpunus** var. of **alimpunus**

**halin** *adj. a-* Well-groomed; dressed for a public event. *Ahalin, sali' patuwa' manista. Ahāp luwata.* Groomed, our beauty emerging. We look good. *Buwat kita ahalin ma pagkawin, halam ah'lling-h'lling, hal ang'nda'-ng'nda'.* Like us dressing up for a wedding, not saying anything, just watching.

**halipa** *n.* A religious official of high rank. *Hinang halipa itū amahāp ai-ai bang aniya' magka'at ma luma' Tuhan. Halipa itū binotang matto'a. Ai-ai paghinang, ya hē' subay anguldin.* The work of the *halipa* is to fix whatever is damaged in the house of God. A *halipa* is appointed as a community leader. Whatever the event, he is the one to give the orders.

**halipulu** *adj. zero* **1)** Lacking in the expected courtesies. *Halipulu pahāp ka'a ilū, sali' halam aniya' addatnu.* How rude you are, as if you have no manners. *Bang aniya' magsuli-suli bo' halam lamudnu, da'a ka pajau'-jau' sabab ilu-i halipulu.* If some people are talking together and you are not involved, don't interrupt, because that is impolite. **1.1)** *v. tr.* To treat someone with a serious lack of good manners. *Sali' kita niharambiyara', nihalipulu.* It is as though we are treated as persons without a father, shown no courtesy. (*Thesaurus:* **di'in-di'in, hampul-hampul 1, mahadja'**)

**haliyu** *adv.* Other than; with the exception of. *Tu'ud halam aniya' saddī kapangamu'an tabang haliyu min si Ja.* There is simply no one to ask help from other than Ja.

**hallal** *v. intr. pa-* To hang or flop down below acceptable limits, of clothing. *Bang banog pasasa, bang buwat sauwal, pantalun, sanyawa pahallal. Subay kinambotan.* For sagging sails the word is *sasa.* For things like traditional trousers, western-style trousers, shorts, the word is *hallal.* They need holding up with a belt. (*Thesaurus:* **hellel, sasa₂, tonton 1**)

**halli'₁** *v. intr. pa-* **1)** To be cautious. *Pahalli' ka, ya aniya' mundu.* Take care, there may be bandits. **1.1)** *v. tr. -an* To be wary of anything that might be harmful. *Painsap ka, aniya' nihalli'an, aniya'*

*kinatāwan.* Be alert; there is something to be guarded against, something to be feared. *Pal'ppi ka mareyom lahat ilu ko ra'a ka taluwa' kajahatan. Sali' painsap, aniya' nihalli'an.* Behave with caution in that place so you aren't hit with trouble. Just be on guard, there are things to be wary of. (*Thesaurus:* **insap, liyal, l'ppi, llog 1.1**)

**halli'₂** *v. ditr.* To keep something in reserve for the benefit of someone else. *Halli'anta sai-sai wa'i makalikut. Da'a kita magdai'-dai', tagarantam.* We'll keep some [food] back for those who are absent. Let's not hurry, we'll wait for them. *Angahalli' ka pamayad sigā, da'a pam'llihun kamemon ilū.* Keep some in reserve for paying them, don't use it all for buying that. *Bang aniya' a'a bay ni lahat dakayu' pina'an ni luma' kami, bo' aheka puhu' ma luma', asal bay nihalli'an palegehan sigā.* When there were people coming to our house after being abroad, and there are many in the house, sleeping places have already been reserved for them. (*Thesaurus:* **kapin 1.1, tau' 1.1**)

**hallu** *n.* A pestle, especially for pounding rice. *Hallu itū pan'ppa buwas.* The *hallu* referred to is for pounding rice. (*cf:* **linsungan**)

**halluwa** *n.* **1)** A confection of pounded grain flavored with sugar and coconut milk. (*Thesaurus:* **bukayu' 1, hinti' 1, hinuwal 1**) **2)** Cursing equivalent for food offered in sarcasm or anger. *Ā, ngā'un, halluwanu!* Here, take it, your delicious pudding! (*gen:* **sukna' 1.1**)

**halo-halo** *n.* A pond or pool ashore or on intertidal flats. *Halo-halo itū taga tahik-tahik halam aniya' t'bbana.* A *halo-halo* has some sea-water but no tidal movement. *Paka'llumta daing bang ariki'-diki'. Subay nihinangan halo-halo ko' al'kkas pasulig.* We keep some fish alive if they are small. They need to have a pool made for them so they will grow quickly. (*Thesaurus:* **kandung₁, k'bbong-k'bbong, danaw, powak, tangki, tigbaw**)

**paghalo-halo** *v. intr. aN-* To form pools due to heavy rain. *Maghalo-halo na he' bohe', makalandu' atomog.* Pools are forming from the rain, the ground absolutely soaked.

**haloblāk** *n.* A cement building block. *Sali' haloblāk kulang timplana, apoka na.* Like hollow-blocks lacking in solids, easily broken. (*Thesaurus:* **semento 1, tisa'**)

**halol** *adj. a-* Critically wounded. *Sali' bang bay taluwa' he' timbak, dangan i' abugtang, dangan i' ahalol. Beya' ni kamatay sa' amasi allum. Hal sali' pama'asa-asa.* Like when people are shot, one dies instantly, the other is mortally wounded. Close to death but still alive. Hope is all that is left. *Ahalol si Mu sabab bay magpalarutan empon talus.* Mu is close to death because he had his wisdom tooth extracted. (*Thesaurus:* **bugtang, bugtu' napas, butawan 1.1, matay₁ 1, sagpe' 2, tubag**)

**halong** *adj.* *a-* Muffled and unclear, of speech. *Ahalong e'ku akale. Takaleku dambila', dambila' halam. Sali' aku abisu-bisu.* I hear imperfectly. I hear one half [of what is said] but not the other. I am sort of deaf. *Ahalong bissalana, sali' halam makaisi ni ta'uta.* His words weren't clearly heard, they didn't get into our conscious awareness. (*Thesaurus:* **bisu 1.1, lantak, palpal 1**)

**halu 1)** *n.* Disorders of the blood such as jaundice. **1.1)** *v. advrs.* *-in-* Displaying signs of jaundice. **2)** *v. advrs.* *-in-* Feeling faint at the sight of blood. *Nihalu bang ang'nda' laha', halam makasayu.* He felt faint when he saw blood, not aware of anything.

**halubilu** *n.* Social chaos or disorder. (*Thesaurus:* **balu', dongkag, hengo-hengo, hiluhala' 1.1, hiyul, jabu 1, lengog 1.1, sasaw 1.1, sensong**)

**haluk** *adj.* *a-* Sound or uninterrupted, of sleep. *Ahaluk, hatina atuli sadja na, buwat ma tonga' bahangi.* Sound asleep, meaning that he's simply sleeping now, like in the middle of the night. (*Thesaurus:* **ddok, pagon₂**)

**halug 1)** *n.* A bundle of leaves. (*cf:* **buyu'**) **2)** *clf.* Count word for bundles of pepper-vine leaves. *Dahalug buyu'.* One bundle of betel pepper leaves. (*cf:* **galung 1**)

**halu'** *n.* **1)** Decay; rot. *Buwat buwa' kayu bang aniya' bay angeket iya, buwat ambaw, tokke', kabog. Tinemposan ya bay kineket ē', bang aniya' halu'na.* As with fruit when something such as a rat, a gecko or a bat has bitten it. The bitten section is cut out if it has any decay. **1.1)** *adj.* *a-* In an advanced stage of decay, of food. *Ya kima ina'an ahalu', mbal takakan.* That giant clam is rotten, cannot be eaten. (*Thesaurus:* **baguy, balos₂, buhuk, buntu'₁ 1.1, langag, p'ngkak**) **1.2)** *v. intr.* *aN-* To become rotten. *Taluwa' sigām bonglay. Angahalu' d'lla' sigām mareyom bowa'.* They were struck by a plague. Their tongues rotted in their mouths.

**halu'-halu'₁** *n.* Dried bay leaf (laurel leaf), used as a spice to flavor meat or fish. (*gen:* **pamapā**)

**halu'-halu'₂** *n.* The ringworm bush, a leguminous shrub. *Cassia alata.* (*syn:* **andalan**)

**halul-akkal** *adj.* *zero* **1)** Intelligent; quick thinking. **1.1)** *v. tr.* To outwit someone. *Nihalli'an e' si Yu anakna kasiyalihan, nihalul-akkal.* Yu was cautious of his youngest son, having been tricked by him.

**halulay** *v. tr.* To get two people reconciled after an estrangement.

  **paghalulay** *v. intr.* *aN-* To be reconciled, of a separated couple. (*syn:* **pagkahāp**)

**halus₁** *v. tr.* To accept or dare the risks of an action. *Buwat piligdu lahat, na angahalus aku man labayan itu lum'ngngan. Haluku na palabay.* Like when the district is dangerous, I dare to go by this path. I take the risk of passing. *Am'lli aku daing ni kakiku, bang halga' dambila' bayaranku.*

*Pagkohap na, pinabīng ni aku saga duwampū' maka lima sīn. Yuk bay pam'llianku, "Ngā'un na santonga' itū. Nihalus na santonga'. Mbal makahalus pinapole' kamemon."* I buy fish from my cousin and pay fifty centavos for it. Come afternoon, twenty-five centavos is returned to me. The person I bought from says, "Take half the money. I dare [to give] half. I don't dare return it all." *Mbal tahalus pangandinding papan itū.* This planking is not to be risked for use as walling. (*Thesaurus:* **k'ddom₂, pagpasukud, pagsusaed, samba 1, sarap₂ 1, tawakkal**)

**halus₂** (var. **harus**) *v. tr.* To accept as suitable, of relationships such as marriage or fighting. *Tahalusku Sūk apa ngga'i ka danakan. Mbal magsimbug laha', ngga'i ka dapaluwasan.* It is acceptable for me to fight with a Tausug [kid] because we're not brothers. Our blood-lines aren't mingled, we are not from the same source [i.e. mother]. *Bang aniya' danakanku bo' ap'ddi' atayna ma aku, bo' aku sinuntuk, nihalus aku, sali' binantahan na.* If I have a sibling who is angry with me, and I get punched, I am recognized as someone who may be fought with, treated as an enemy. *Ya hē' makaharus kita, bang d'nda ya amono'. Kapilluwangan kita.* That is what makes us available, when it's a woman who fights. We are vulnerable to our defenses being breached. *Danakanna inān budjang gi', angkan ahunit to'ongan pinikilan bang taharus e'na.* His sister was still a virgin, so it was difficult to think how he might treat her appropriately. (*Thesaurus:* **halal 1, halam-mutallak, haram 1, sumbang**)

**paghalus** *v. intr.* *aN-* To be in an appropriate marriage. *Bang kami maka kakiku magkawin mbal maghalus, magsugsug dahū. Bang kakiku min t'llu makajari nihalus, sali' magtimbul na.* If my cousin and I [might be] marrying inappropriately, we trace kin links first. If she is my third cousin a union is considered acceptable, we can now be married.

**haluy** *n.* **1)** Looseness, of clothing. **1.1)** *adj.* *a-* Loose-fitting. *Ai-ai aloka. Manjari ma laring, manjari ma engkot.* Anything loose. Can apply to a knife, or to a knot.

**hām** var. of **halam₁**

**hama'** *n.* A mosquito. *fam.* Culicidae. (*Thesaurus:* **kammut, damuk, hamug-hamug, hanglop**)

**hama'-hama' a'a** *n. phrase* A house-based spirit who calls people by name, inviting them to come in. *Bang iya ala'an min luma', ma deyom hē' aniya' hama'-hama' a'a. Bang sangom, makakale ka magalud. "Pareyom ka pi'itu."* When he leaves the house, a *hama'-hama'* spirit is there inside. At night you hear it shouting out, "Come here inside." (*Thesaurus:* **bangsa magl'l'ngngan, duwata 1, hibilis, jīn 1, saitan, ya mbal ta'nda'**)

**haman-haman** *adj.* *a-* **1)** Forgetful and neglectful of commitments. *Bang ka sinoho' ni M'ddas bo' mbal* *taentomnu am'lli ai-ai, ahaman-haman ka.* If you are sent to Siasi and you don't remember to buy whatever, you are neglectful. *Da'a ka ahaman-haman bang ka anau' ko' da'a alungay. Sali' da'a takalipatun.* Don't be thoughtless when you store something so it isn't lost. Like [saying] don't forget it. (*Thesaurus:* **palehom, sumadja**) **1.1)** *v. tr.* To treat something without proper care. *Da'a haman-hamanun ai-ai. Tau'un pahogot.* Don't neglect things. Store them securely.

**hāmaniya'** *var.* of **halam aniya'**

**hambak** *v. tr.* **-an** To arrange one's hair in a knot so that a thick tail hangs down. (*Thesaurus:* **hampal, pugay 2, sapid 1.1, simbōng 1.1, toket 1.1, tusay**)

**hambawan** *n.* A rigging rope attached to the peak of a sail or to the upper boom, used for raising or lowering the sail; a halyard. *Kamaya'in ko mbal aleges hambawan bang nihella'.* Be careful with it so the halyard doesn't chafe when it is pulled. A: *"Tinustusan, pinahagmak pareyo'."* B: *"Tinustusan tabul-tabul?"* A: *"Aho', sampay hambawan."* A: "Unlash the sail, bring the sail-mast assembly down." B: "Unlash the sail itself?" A: "Yes, and the halyard as well."

**hambin** *v. intr.* **pa-** **1)** To press against a mother's body or hip, the action of a small child. *Aheka sidda anakna d'nda inān, saga sangpū' marai'. Aniya' na pahambin, aniya' isāb anangis, aniya' pa'apas.* That woman has many children, ten perhaps. Some hang on her hip, some cry, and some chase after her. **1.1)** *v. tr.* To hold a child against one's body using one arm. *Pahāpun e'nu angahambin onde' ilū bo' mbal pak'dde'.* Be careful how you hold that child lest it bend back too far. (*Thesaurus:* **gapus, giba 1.1, mpit, pipi₁, sangbay**)

**paghambin** *v. intr.* **aN-** To carry a child close to one's body. *Makagubin ka'a itū, Oto', pasal maghambin ma ka'a.* You're getting in the way, Son, because of carrying you.

**hambug** *adj.* **a-** **1)** Large in cross-section; fat or plump. *Ahambug pataklayannu.* Your forearm is big. *Ahambug pahāp t'bbu ilu.* That sugarcane is very big. (*Thesaurus:* **goldo-goldo, littub, l'mmok 1.1, poko-poko, subuk, tibung-tibung**) **1.1)** *v. tr.* To become fat. *Angahambug baran d'nda ina'an, al'mmok sali'.* That woman is getting plump, kind of fat.

**hambul** *v. tr.* To throw rice to show pleasure or congratulations. *Hambulanta ka buwas bang takawinnu d'nda inān.* I will throw rice on you if you can marry that girl.

**hami'-hami'** *adj.* **-an** Moist, of clothes not properly aired, or wet with perspiration. *Da'a gi' sulugun s'mmek ilū, hami'-hami'an lagi'. Mbal isāb abase' to'ongan.* Don't put those clothes on yet, they are still wet. They're not completely wet though. *Kepetku hami'-hami'an lagi'.* My underarms are still damp. *Hami'-hami'an badju', aheka lobagna,*

*aheka autna. Subay dakdakanta.* The shirts are damp, lots of stains, lots of dirt. We should launder [them]. (*Thesaurus:* **himāy**)

**hamiyu** *n.* **1)** The side effects of some force or power, as the blast of an explosion or the tail of a typhoon. *Mbal ta'nda' saitan. Hal hamiyu ya pasangon.* Saitan spirits are not visible. It's just the effect [of them] that enters [humans]. *Bang pasayang pikpik galura' magtūy akiyamat dunya. Minnē', min hamiyuna, agtambol dunya.* When the winged horse spreads its wings in flight, the world will end. From that, from the turbulence [of its flight], the world will be closed up. (*Thesaurus:* **sabat₂, samba 1.1, sambut 1.1**) **1.1)** *v. advrs.* **ka-...-an** To be impacted by some powerful event or presence. *Bang aniya' animbak bo' ah'lling ma diyata', ya amalutan timbak inān amatay, ati man buli' inān kahamiyu'an.* If someone is dynamiting and it goes off above water, the one holding the dynamite dies and the one at the stern is hit by the blast.

**Hammis** *n.* Thursday. (*Thesaurus:* **Ahad, Alba'a, Isnin, Juma'at, Sabtu', Salasa**)

**hampa'** *n.* **1)** The husk of grain. **1.1)** *v. tr.* **-an** To remove the husk of grain. *Hampa'anta pai atawa gandum.* We dehusk rice or corn. (*Thesaurus:* **kanit 1.1, kisak, kupas, hagut, lapes**)

**hampal** *n.* Hair worn loose rather than in a knot. (*Thesaurus:* **hambak, pugay 2, sapid 1.1, simbōng 1.1, toket 1.1, tusay**)

**paghinampal** *v. intr.* **aN-** To wear one's hair loosely bound. *Maghinampal, pin'kkal sadja bu'unta, mbal sinimbōng.* Wearing hair loose, one's hair just left unbound, not formed into a knot. *Na ī' na d'nda aningkō' maghinampal bu'unna ma buli' adjung.* So there was the woman sitting at the stern of the *adjung* [a ship of folklore], hair loosely bound.

**hampan** *n.* **1)** A shell bracelet or amulet worn as protection against sorcery or harm of a supernatural nature. (*cf:* **gampang 1.1**; *syn:* **tampan 1**; *gen:* **tambang₃ 1**) **1.1)** *v. tr.* **-an** To guard someone against harm from human or other beings. *Ilmu' ya pangahampanku baranku bo' mbal tauwa' saitan atawa punglu' manusiya'.* Esoteric knowledge is my personal defense so I cannot be harmed by demons or human bullets. *Nihampanan onde'-onde' bo' mbal sinekot e' saitan atawa saki.* Children protected against being approached by *saitan* or sickness. *Anak-anak nihampanan bo' mbal nilabha'an.* Little children protected by a charm against harm of a supernatural source.

**paghampan** *n.* **1)** Protection against sorcery or attack from a spirit being. **1.1)** *v. tr.* **-an** To protect someone against harm from spiritual entities. *Gallang itū paghampanan onde'-onde' bo' mbal sinagda e' a'a. Baklaw ya ginantung ma k'llong.* Bracelets are for the protection of children so no one can cause them to be sick. An amulet is the one hung around the neck.

**hampat** var. of **hangpat**

**hampe** (var. **ampe**) *n.* **1)** A protective layer or lining. (*Thesaurus:* **bingal, hanig, lampik 1, lapis₁ 1**) **1.1)** *v. tr.* -an To install a protective layer around something or between layers. *Pangahampe'an kubul, ya pilang-pilang ē'.* They are for the protection of a grave, those planks. *Bang sali' buwat jā-i bay bowa kami, niampehan maka katas ko' mbal ang'ssa mital.* Like those rice cookies that we took, layered in paper so as not to have the metallic taste of the can.

**hampi'** (var. **ampi'**) *n.* **1)** A wrap-around sarong. **1.1)** *v. intr.* a- To wear a sarong in the male style, the top rolled down to hold it in place. *Bang halam na aniya' pantalunku, bay nirakdakan kamemon, na a'ampi' na aku.* When I have no trousers, all of them having been laundered, then I wear something man-style. *Bang d'nda asiyag, bang l'lla a'ampi'.* A woman wears a skirt *siyag* style, a man wears it *ampi'* style. (*Thesaurus:* **hōs 1.2, pagkīmbong, pagsina'ul, pindung, siyag 1.1**)

**paghinampi'** *v. intr.* aN- To wear a sarong, male style. *Maghinampi' aku bang sangom.* I wear my sarong man-style at night.

**hampilan** *n.* The land above the tidal limit. *Hampilan itū basta mbal ma tampe. Buwat du gintana'an.* Land above the tide is anything above highwater. The same as dry land. (*Thesaurus:* **bihingan, daplakan₁, gintana'an, pari'an, susulan, tampe, tapiyan**)

**hampit** *v. intr.* aN- To receive a share of someone's profit or earnings. *Na, magsukul-sukul kami makahampit du pa'in kami usahabi.* So then, we say thank-you that we keep getting a share of your labors. (*Thesaurus:* **bahagi' 1, gihay, paglamit-lamit 1.1, sihak**)

**pahampit** *v. tr.* To give someone a share.

**hampul-hampul** *adj. zero* **1)** To be neglectful of the responsibilities implied by kin and community relationships. *Hampul-hampul e'nu maganak ma aku, sali' duma'in ka to'od.* You're neglectful of the way you are a child to me, as if you weren't really one. (*Thesaurus:* **di'in-di'in, halipulu 1.1, mahadja'**) **1.1)** *v. tr.* To fail to treat things with the necessary care. *Da'a hampul-hampulun listun ilū, aniya' kagunahanku.* Don't treat that sawn lumber roughly, I have a use for it. *Nihampul-hampul lilus e' si Je.* Je mishandled the watch.

**hamput** *v. tr.* To impel something by a forward jerk of the pelvis, as the half coconut in the game of luhu'. (*syn:* **limbuku'**)

**paghamput** *v. intr.* aN- To move the hips rhythmically, as in copulation.

**hamud-hamud** *n.* Dust; air-borne trash. (*cf:* **bagunbun**)

**hamug-hamug** *n.* A small biting insect. (*Thesaurus:* **kammut, damuk, hama', hanglop**)

**hamul** *see:* **tahamul**

**hamulaun** var. of **amulawan**

**hamulawan** var. of **amulawan**

**hamumu'** (var. **himumu'**) *v. tr.* To keep something in good order. *Bang aniya' pina'bba ma kita, subay hamumu'ta supaya kita pinaindaman pabīng.* When something is left with us we should take good care of it so that we may be allowed to borrow it again. (*Thesaurus:* **ayad, ayuput, ipat, pahilala' 1, paintul, paipid, payakun, talkin, ulip, upiksa', ussap 1**)

**hamut** *n.* **1)** A smell or odor, generally pleasant. (*cf:* **tunug 1**) **1.1)** *adj.* a- Fragrant. *Bang kita bay asaki bo' makahamut kinakan ahamut, sinangti'.* If we were sick and happened to smell food with a strong odor, we would suffer a relapse. (*Thesaurus:* **bau 1.1, b'ngngi, hangsu 1, langsa, langtu, mahali, p'ngngak**) **1.2)** *v. tr.* To detect something by smell. *Hamutun sumping inān.* Smell those flowers. (*Thesaurus:* **bau 1.2, bbu 1**)

**pahamut** *v. tr.* To apply perfume or deodorant; to anoint.

**hanaw-hanaw** *adj. zero* Unclear due to atmospheric haze. (*Thesaurus:* **abu-abu₂, ahud-ahud 1.1, buraw, pagba'ung-ba'ung**)

**hanay-hanay** *n.* A tune played on the kulintangan ensemble.

**handak** *see:* **kahandak, pangahandak**

**hande-hande** *n.* A mackerel species. *fam.* Scombridae.

**handok₁** *v. intr.* pa- **1)** To move the feet vigorously. *Pahandok itū sali' mint'dda. Maghandok, maghagul sali'.* Pahandok is just one bounce, *paghandok* is repeated bouncing, like jigging [for fish]. **1.1)** *v. tr.* -an To move something by vigorous movement of feet. *Da'a handokin bangka' ilū ko da'a abuhaw.* Don't upset the canoe with foot movement lest it be swamped.

**paghandok** *v. intr.* aN- To bounce repeatedly. *Paghandok pelang buwattē', agtūy apōng batangan.* With the canoe bouncing like that, the outrigger boom will quickly break. *Bang angamu'-amu' ai-ai si Lu ni ina'na bo' mbal kabuwanan, maghandok.* When Lu asks anything from her mother and isn't given it, she bounces up and down. (*Thesaurus:* **pagbullud-bullud, pagbuwang 1.1, paghuntak, pagtongket-tongket, pagumpak-umpak**)

**handok₂** *see:* **atay₂**

**handuk** (var. **anduk**) *v. intr.* pa- To bow the head. *Buwat a'a alanga bo' areyo' lawang, subay iya pa'anduk bo' mbal sumantuk kōkna.* Like a tall man when a doorway is low, he has to bow so that he won't hit his head. *Buwat magaddat, pa'anduk ni a'a alanga.* Like showing respect, bowing the head to someone of higher status. *Pa'andukun kōknu.* Duck your head. (*Thesaurus:* **tango'**) **1.1)** *v. intr.* aN- To nod the head as a sign of assent.

**handul** *see:* **atay₂**

**hanig** *n.* A mattress cover. (*Thesaurus:* **bingal, hampe 1, lampik 1, lapis₁ 1**)

**hanjing** *n.* An unpleasant creature; vermin.
**hanjing-binatang** *n.* 'Wretched creature!' (*cf:* **ero' 2**)

**hansam** *adj. a-* Handsome; well-groomed. *Maghansam-hansaman sigā bang sai ahansam.* They compete in their good looks as to who is the handsomest one. (*Thesaurus:* **alti, dorog₂ 1.1, hāp baran, himpit, jalang₁, lingkat 1.1, manis 1.1, polma 1.1**)
**paghansam-hansam** *v. intr. aN-* To compete for the best looks.

**hansom** (var. **ansom**) *v. tr. -an* To threaten someone with physical harm. *Niansoman, luwal sōng sinuntuk, pinakitāw sala.* Threatened, used only when about to be punched, sort of made afraid. (*syn:* **antup**; *Thesaurus:* **alu'₁, dangka₁, sanggup**)

**hansul₁** *adj. a-* **1)** Reduced to a near liquid state, as by decay or destructive force. *Ahansul na daing itū, abuhuk.* This fish is breaking up, rotten. *Nihūgan bām Kalari'an, halam isāb anandal. Ahansul saga sundalu Jipun.* Calarian had a bomb dropped on it and didn't survive. Japanese soldiers died in large numbers. **1.1)** *v. tr.* To reduce something from a solid state to a liquid. *Nihansul, buwat saga tingga' nihinang lambat.* Melted down, like lead being made into sinkers.

**hansul₂** *see:* **atay₂**

**hantak₁** *v. intr. pa-/-um-* **1)** To fall heavily onto a surface. *Bang kita saupama nirugsu'an, na hal kita amatay pahantak.* If we for example are stabbed, then we simply fall down dead. *Bang kita sinangti', amiyaning kita, humantak ma labayan.* When we take a turn for the worse, we become yellow and collapse heavily on the path. (*Thesaurus:* **h'bba', ligad, lintuwad 1, pungkad, timpuwad 1**) **1.1)** *v. ditr.* To throw something down hard. *Apagon samin sawan itū, mbal abila' minsan nihantakan ni simento.* The glass of this drinking tumbler is strong, it doesn't break even when thrown down on to a concrete surface. *Bay kahantakan batu tape'na.* His foot had a stone fall on it. *Bang aniya' ai-ai abila' mbal lulus para'akkal bang halam aniya' bay makahantak.* If anything is broken it would never have happened if nothing had caused it to fall hard.
**paghantak** *v. tr. -an* To strike repeatedly on an underlying surface, as a canoe prow on a rough sea. *Onde' ilu, saukat halam binowa ni tabu' hal maghantakan dīna ni lantay.* That child, just because he wasn't taken to market, keeps banging himself hard on the floor.
**pagpatihantak** *v. intr. aN-* **1)** To humble oneself before a girl's elders, initiating a proposal of marriage that bypasses the usual negotiations and risks all on a single offer. (*cf:* **pagpatialop, pagsarahakan**) **2)** To throw oneself down, as to avoid detection.
**pahantak** *adv.* Falling down hard.

**hantak₂** *n.* Fish killed by dynamiting. *Animbak si Anu, aheka hantak tulay.* What's-his-name is dynamiting, there are many dead *tulay* fish. (*Thesaurus:* **belaw-belaw, lundu'**)

**hantal** *v. intr. pa-* To lie face up, as someone sleeping or dead. (*Thesaurus:* **daya', hagtang, haya'₁, leyak, pagduleyak**)

**hantang** var. of **kahantang**

**hantap** *adj. a-* **1)** Done in a proper and effective way. *Bang kita at'kka minningga-minningga, subay ahantap ma deyom luma'. Subay halam aniya' anassaw.* When we arrive from anywhere, things should be tranquil in the house. There shouldn't be anything to disturb. *Ahantap, mbal angala'ug, ahāp addat, ahāp kaul-pi'il.* Well-behaved, doesn't behave violently, has good manners, good in word and thought. *Subay na atalus hinang magdukka sin bay saga kamatayan, hatina, ingga na ahantap kamemon.* The ceremonies of the mourners grieving for the dead should be fully completed, that is to say, when everything is properly done. **1.1)** *v. intr. pa-* To behave in an orderly way. *Bang kita amangan subay kita pahantap ai-ai. Subay kita anginum bohe' dahū bo' mbal kabongkolan.* When we eat we should be orderly. We should drink water first so that food doesn't stick in the throat.

**hanti'** *v. intr. pa-* **1)** To stop over briefly in the course of a journey. *Na, ina'an disi Sa'ul maka anakna si Jonatan pahanti' ma tape' būd.* Well, there was Saul and his son Jonathan stopping briefly at the base of the hill. *Minsan danjām atawa daminit, basta kita bay magsuli-suli atawa amangan ma restauran, atawa atuli, ya hē' hanti'.* Whether it is one hour or one minute, whenever we have had a discussion or eaten in a restaurant or slept, those are [examples] of *hanti'*. (*Thesaurus:* **lihan 1, pustu 1.1, tingan, tingkap**) **1.1)** *v. tr. -an* To take a break in a journey in order to do something else. *Angahanti'an aku sehe'ku, hatina angalagaran aku iya.* I stay overnight for my companion; waiting for him, that is.
**paghanti'an** *n.* A stopping place on journey. *Buwat kita maglihan maitu ma Pasonangka' saga t'llu pitu'. Ganta' paghanti'-hanti'an ba.* Like when we stay temporarily here at Pasonangka for three weeks. A sort of temporary accommodation, as it were.

**hantu** *n.* **1)** A spirit being that causes minor ailments such as joint pain. (*Thesaurus:* **kokok 1, komeng**) **1.1)** *v. advrs. -in-* Made mildly unwell by hantu spirits. *Nihantu si Ja, kap'ddi'an, bay tinawalan he' mma'na.* Ja was affected by a spirit and experiencing pain, his father said a healing charm over him. (*cf:* **labba'₂ 1.1**) **1.2)** *v. tr. -an* To remove the symptoms caused by hantu spirits. *Buwat si Al ata'u angahantu. Bay*

*aku hantu'anna maina'an ma luma' dilaut bo'
amasi sakiku.* Like Al, who knows how to deal
with *hantu* spirits. He treated my *hantu*
condition there at the seaward house, but my
sickness remains. (*syn:* **kakati'**)

**hantuk** *v. tr.* To move a fishing lure with a gentle
up and down motion. (*Thesaurus:* **hagtu', hagul,
hangku'**)

**hanu** *v. intr.* *aN-* To become exhausted. *Angahanu
aku, bay aku angahangkut bohe'.* I am becoming
exhausted, I have been carrying water.
(*Thesaurus:* **bongtas 1.1, gustang, lingantu 1.1,
otas, punung**)

**hanunus** *var. of* **hanunut**

**hanunut** (*var.* **hanunus**) *adj.* *a-* Soothing and non-
combative, of speech. (*syn:* **hanus**)

**hanus** *adj.* *a-* Calming and positive, of speech.
*Ahanus ka maggara', da'a ka magsagga'-sagga'.* Be
gentle in discussion, don't keep getting into
arguments. (*syn:* **hanunut**)

  **kahanusan** *n.* Words intended to soothe and
unite. *Yukna, "Ōy, llingku itū ni kahanusan, bo'
llingnu ilū ni kala'atan."* He said, "Look, these
words of mine are intended for goodwill, but
your words are intended for trouble." *Kahanusan
deyom atayku, halam aniya' koto'-koto' deyom
atay. Pamuwanku ka'a badju' itū.* I am inwardly
calmed, having no hard feelings. I am giving
you this shirt.

**hanut** *v. intr.* *pa-/-um-* To be carried away by a
current. (*syn:* **laran**)

**hangad** *v. intr.* *pa-* To look upwards. *Bay aku
pahangad, kapakpakan s'ggit mataku, abulag aku.* I
looked up, fine rubbish fell into my eyes and I
was temporarily blinded. *Pahangad ka ni langit
bo' ka maka'nda' bitu'un magsinglab.* Look up
towards the sky so you can see the stars
twinkling. *Pahangarun kōknu tinambalan.* Tilt
your head up to be medicined. (*Thesaurus:*
**tongas**)

**hangat** *v. advrs.* *-in-* Affected by having too much of
something. *Nihangat aku ma pal'ngnganan, subay
aku makainum bohe'.* I have overdone my
walking about, I must have a drink of water.
*Bang kita makakakan ai-ai amamis, nihangat.
Buwat bay aku amangan durul, sidda amamis.
Makahangat mamisna.* When we have eaten
anything sweet, it becomes too much. Like when
I ate sweet corn-cake and it was excessively
sweet. Its sweetness caused [me] to react.

**hangbos**₁ *adj.* *a-* Conclusive and to the point, of
something said. *Ahangbos suli-suli, mbal na
taisab.* The discussion is conclusive, and will not
be repeated. *Ahangbos, ya kat'kkaran lling.* To
the point, the essence of what is being said.
(*Thesaurus:* **tumlang 1**)

**hangbos**₂ *v. tr.* *-an* To hit something forcibly into or
against something hard. *Nihangbosan munda'
pelang bang kalandosan baliyu maka goyak,
minsan kita ma pabanogan.* The prow of the

canoe is hit hard when struck by strong wind
and waves, even when we are under sail.
*Kosogin, tukulin pakosog, hangbosin.* Be forceful,
nail it with force, hit it home. (*Thesaurus:* **kosog
1.3**)

**hangka'** *var. of* **sangka'**

**hangkan** *var. of* **angkan**

**hangku'** *v. tr.* To control or move something by
pulling sharply on a line. *Subay sapi', kalbaw,
nihangku'.* It must be a cow or a buffalo that is
controlled by pulling [a tether]. (*Thesaurus:*
**hagtu', hagul, hantuk**)

  **paghangku'-hangku'** *v. tr.* To tug something
repeatedly. *Buwat sau, paghangku'-hangku'un
buwattē' bo' apuwas.* Like an anchor, keep pulling
at it sharply like that so comes free.

**hangkut** *v. tr.* To convey something by carrying.
*Angahangkut gi' aku bohe' kaleya, halam aniya'
bohe' kami.* I'll just carry some water from
inland, we have no water. (*Thesaurus:* **gawil,
habit, pagbaga'ud**)

**hanggal** (*var.* **sanggal**) *n.* **1)** An object that projects
or protrudes above a surface. **1.1)** *v. intr.* *pa-* To
run aground on something projecting above the
sea floor, as a rock or a sand bar. *Aniya'
makahanggal mariyata' t'bba.* Someone has run
aground on the shallows. *Makasanggal,
makaragsa', makahanggal, sali' du. Ya sadja
magbidda' bang makasiyud. Sanggal, dagsa'* or
*hanggal,* they're the same thing. The only one
that differs is *siyud* [to run lightly over
something]. (*Thesaurus:* **dagsa', sanglad, siyud**)

  **kahanggalan** *n.* A marine shallow with ridges
that limit the movement of a vessel. *Wa'i kami
makasiyud ni kahanggal-hanggalan atawa ma
punsu.* We had touched bottom on a shallow
ridge or a sand mound. *Sagō' makaragsa' sigām ni
kahanggalan. Amalut munda' kappal, mbal
pajudjal, maka buli'na he' abagbag e' goyak.* But
they ran aground on shallow bottom. The bow
stuck fast, couldn't be moved, and the stern was
battered by the waves. (*Thesaurus:* **kababawan,
kat'bbahan, katoho'an**)

**pahanggal** *v. tr.* To prop something up by placing
a chock under it. (*Thesaurus:* **biggal 1, bulatuk,
s'ngngal, tanok 1**)

**hanggaw**₁ *adj.* *a-* **1)** Apprehensive; anxious.
*Ahanggaw aku ni bohe' bang angulan-ulan apa
angalu'ud lān.* I am apprehensive about going to
the water-hole when it is raining just a little,
because the path is slippery. (*Thesaurus:* **kanaw-
kanaw, kawang, ganggu' atay**) **1.1)** *v. advrs.*
*-in-* To be overcome by anxiety. *Atawa bang kita
angandāg ni puttuk-puttuk balunu', tabaliyang kita,
sali' kita nihanggaw.* Or when we climb to the
very top of that *balunu'* mango tree, we come
over dizzy, sort of anxious.

**hanggaw**₂ *var. of* **hunggaw**

**hanggol** *n.* **1)** A length of wood cut off a main part.
*Kayu pinōng, pinaggotong dahanggol-dahanggol.*

Wood is cut in half, cut cross-ways into individual lengths. **1.1)** *v. tr.* To cut something into lengths. (*Thesaurus:* **gotong, p'ppot 1**)

**hanggom** *v. tr.* To keep something for oneself.

**hanggup** *v. tr.* To inhale something.

**hanglad** *n.* **1)** Building materials of unsawn round-wood, usually from two to four inches in diameter. (*Thesaurus:* **baras-baras, listun, papan₁, pasagi' 1**) **2)** Poles running across the purlins of a roof (parallel to rafters) to which thatch shingles are tied.

**hanglop** *n.* Chicken lice; red mites. (*Thesaurus:* **kammut, damuk, hama', hamug-hamug**)

**hanglus** var. of **danglus**

**hangpat** (var. **hampat**) *adj. a-* **1)** Clear and intelligible. *Ahangpat e'na ah'lling, mbal al'kkas. Ata'u to'ongan ah'lling.* His speech is clear, not hurried. He really knows how to talk. *Pahangpatun e'nu ah'lling bo' takaleku.* Make your speech clear so I can hear it. *Kosog-kosogun e'nu amūng bo' ahangpat.* Make your speaking louder so it is clear. (*Thesaurus:* **hapal 2, hurup 1.1, ladju, lagsing, nyala-nyala, tanog₁**) **1.1)** *v. tr.* To express something clearly; to enunciate. *Bay angahangpat to'ongan saga kanabihan pasal kasalamatan itū.* Prophets explained clearly about this deliverance. *Daka ai, nsa' tahangpatku.* No idea, I didn't hear it clearly. **1.2)** *v. tr. -an* To hear with comprehension. *Halam kahangpatanku.* I didn't understand it well. *Aheya kasensongan angkan mbal kahangpatan e' nakura' hē' bang ai to'ongan sababanna.* There was a great uproar which is why the boss couldn't figure out what the real cause was.

**hangsaw** *v. advrs. -in-* **1)** Seduced by greedy desire. *Bang sali' nirahal kita, sinawiya kita ma ai-ai, napsuhan kita, nihangsaw.* Like when we are greedy, controlled by our appetites, full of lust, that's *hangsaw*. (*Thesaurus:* **bahaya, kaway 1, hawa 1.1, napsu 1.1, sawiya 1, sayap-sayap**) **1.1)** *v. tr. -an* To long greedily for something. *Ai-ai na pa'in ta'nda'na, subay nihangsawan e'na.* Whatever he sees he has to long greedily for.

**hangsu** *adj. a-* **1)** Odorous; giving off fumes. (*Thesaurus:* **bau 1.1, b'ngngi, hamut 1.1, langsa, langtu, mahali, p'ngngak**) **1.1)** *v. intr. pa-* To emit odor or fumes. *Bang kita am'lla bo' kita pasekot ni pam'llahan, pahangsu ni kita.* When we are cooking and go close to the stove, the smell comes to us. *Patunug, sali' pahangsu bauna, bau deya, hamut sumping, kaginisan.* Giving off a smell, emitting its odor, the smell of the land, the fragrance of flowers, all sorts of things. (*Thesaurus:* **angil, angsod, bbu 1.1, pulag-pulag, tunug 1.1**)

**pahangsu** *v. intr. aN-* To emit odor or fumes.

**hangtad** (var. **h'ttad**) *v. intr. pa-* To lie stretched out flat. *Bang sali' am'ngkong tape'ku mbal na makah'ttad.* When my foot is sort of swollen it

can no longer straighten out. (*cf:* **h'nnat 1**)

**ma hangtaran** *adv. phrase* By the length of something laid out flat. *Sinukud ma hangtaranna, ai na duwand'ppa, ai labi dand'ppa, ni'ppi'an.* Measured by length when stretched out flat, two fathoms or just over one fathom, with a woven hem.

**pahangtad** *v. tr.* To lay something out full length.

**hangu-hangu** *see:* **paghangu-hangu**

**hāp** (var. **halap₂**) *n.* **1)** Goodness; advantages; benefits. *Ya hāpna halam niōk.* The good thing about it is that it was not cut into. **1.1)** *adj. a-* Good, morally or in terms of quality. *Ahāp baranna, ahāp l'lla.* He is good-looking, a fine fellow. (*cf:* **adil, bontol 1**) **1.2)** *v. tr. a-, ka-..-an, -an* To treat someone positively. *Arāk kami patay otas, manda' kami kinahāpan e' a'a ma lahat inān.* We might have died of hunger, but fortunately the people of that place treated us kindly. *Bay kām kahāpanku.* I treated you well. *Buwat aniya' maglakibini ati magbono', ah'lling dakayu' matto'a yukna, "Da'a kahāpinbi h'llanu bang halam aniya' tabowa."* Like when there is a married couple and they are fighting, and an elder says, "Don't make up with your husband unless he brings some gift." **1.3)** *v. tr.* To treat well. *Bang aku mbal nihāp, gōm aku ala'an.* If I am not well-treated I might as well leave.

**kahāpan** *n.* Favorable conditions; advantage; blessing. *Daipara aniya' kahāpan min Tuhan, pinuwa' kami ma dilaut.* Fortunately God granted us favor, we were picked up out at sea.

**hāp atay** *adj. a-* Cheerful; in a good mood. {idiom} *Makahāp atay ko' ilū.* That makes us cheerful.

**hāp baran** *adj. a-* Physically attractive; shapely. {idiom} (*Thesaurus:* **alti, dorog₂ 1.1, hansam, himpit, jalang₁, lingkat 1.1, manis 1.1, polma 1.1**)

**hāp d'nda** *adj. a-* Good-looking; attractive, of a woman. {idiom} *Ahāp d'nda si Lo.* Lo is a good-looking woman.

**hāp l'lla** *adj. a-* Attractive; handsome, of a man. {idiom}

**hāp-hāp** *v. intr. pa-* To improve, of health or circumstances. *Yampa pahāp-hāp kahālanna.* His circumstance are only just now improving. (*Thesaurus:* **gām-gām, hikay, hoblas 1, lōng-lōng, siha'-siha', si'at**)

**kahāp** *n.* Goodness; kindness.

**pagkahāp** *v. intr. aN-* To become reconciled after a disagreement. (*Thesaurus:* **deyo'₃ 2, pagpa'ampun, ū'ū; syn: paghalulay**)

**pahāp-hāp** *v. tr.* **1)** To treat someone well in order to get their approval. **1.1)** *adv.* Well; in a good manner. *Angkan ayarinbi to'ongan pahāp-hāp, sampay ta'abut waktu kapagtimbang.* That's why you should treat it very well until it's time for weighing.

**pahāp₁** *adv.* Indeed; truly; really. (*Thesaurus:*

to'ongan 1.1)

**pahāp₂** *v. tr.* **1)** To improve or repair something. **2)** To do something well.

**pamahāp** *n.* Something for the good or benefit of.

**sangkahāpan** *adv.* Well done; appropriately.

**hāp palasahan** *n. phrase* The feeling of good health.

**hāp sukud** *n. phrase* Good luck or fortune. *Ahāp sukudnu, halam taluwa' kōknu.* Your luck is good, your head wasn't hit.

**hapa** *n.* **1)** Milt (the semen of a fish). (*Thesaurus:* **pehak 1, pulling**) **1.1)** *v. intr.* **aN-** To produce milt. *Bang angahapa, mbal amehak.* If a fish produces milt, it won't produce roe.

**hapa'** *n.* **1)** A hold-up. *Ya mbal kasōngku pehē', aniya' hapa', aniya' katāwanku.* The reason for my not going further that way is that there was a hold-up, something I fear. **1.1)** *v. tr.* **-an** To prevent someone from proceeding on his way. *"Bang ka makatugpa'," yuk Tohongan ni Kuyya', "hapa'anta na ka."* If you jump down," said Turtle to Monkey, "I will stop you from going on." **1.2)** *v. tr.* **-an** To block a move in a game. *Buwat duwangan magduminu, magkosogan. Yuk dangan, "Hapa'in to'ongan ina'an-i, bo' mbal makalabay."* Like two playing dominoes, competing. Someone else says, "Block that move totally, so he can't pass." (*Thesaurus:* **ambus, holdap, ingu, sipi₁ 1.1, tipu 1.1**)

**hapal 1)** *n.* Clarity of speech. **2)** *adj.* **a-** Clear; distinct, of someone's enunciation. *Ahapal Innglisna, sali' takaleta pahāp.* His English is clear, it's like we can hear it well. *Aladju suwalana, sali' ahapal.* Her voice carries well, sort of clear. (*Thesaurus:* **hangpat 1, hurup 1.1, ladju, lagsing, nyala-nyala, tanog₁**)

**hapid₁** *n.* **1)** A supportive splint. (*Thesaurus:* **lantay-lantay 1, paggimbal 1.1**) **1.1)** *v. tr.* **-an** To strengthen a weak or damaged item by fastening a splint alongside. *Ap'ggos pa'in bahu' banog ma dilaut, na bang aniya' pangahapid, mbal anūy.* If a boom cracks at sea, then if there is something to serve as splint, it will not break completely. *Hapiranta isāb bang aniya' saga apōng batangan, hapiranta maka soha'.* We also support an outrigger boom that breaks, strengthening it with a mooring pole. (*Thesaurus:* **bandung₁**)

**hapid₂** *v. tr.* To hide or palm a card or domino. *Ōy, hal hapidnu alas.* Hey, you are just palming the aces.

**hapit₁** *v. intr.* **pa-** **1)** To visit someone en route. *Pahapit kami min Sūk tudju ni Bukidnon.* We call in at Jolo Town en route to Bukidnon. **1.1)** *v. tr.* To get something en route.

**paghapit-hapit** *v. intr.* **aN-** To call in at place after place. *Saga lahat paghapit-hapitan lansa.* The places where the [passenger] launch calls in at. *Patūy ka, da'a ka maghapit-hapit, saga ang'nda' ma pangongka'an.* Go straight there, don't keep stopping and watching games and so on.

(*Thesaurus:* **l'ppad-l'ppad 1**)

**hapit₂** var. of **apit**

**hapit-hapit** *n.* A confection of cassava meal or rice flavored with sugar and grated coconut. *Panggi' kayu, aniya' sali' bay at'bbag, ya bay kabaliyuhan. Ya hē' nihinang hapit-hapit.* Cassava, if some has become somewhat tasteless, left exposed to the air, that's what is made into *hapit-hapit*. (*Thesaurus:* **suman, wadjit**)

**haplus** *v. intr.* **pa-** **1)** To move freely along some object. **1.1)** *v. advrs.* **-in-** To be healed after circumcision so that the skin is free to move.

**hapus₁** (var. **apus**) *adj.* **a-** **1)** Accepting, of a financial offer. *Buwat ka'a bangka ma pagsalla'an. Pat'nna'ku dakayu' pilak bo' tilawku ka'a, "Ahapus na?" Yuknu, "Hapus."* Suppose you are banker in a gambling place. I put down one peso and I ask you, "Do you accept?" You say, "Accepted." *Kōl itū bang ma kami, hapus sadja.* For us this word *kōl* just means 'accepted fully'. (*Thesaurus:* **pikit₃ 2**) **1.1)** *v. tr.* To accept an offer or bid. *Pila-pila badju' itū, nihalga'an lima pilak. Angahapus sadja aku, mbal amalos.* No matter how many shirts there are here, they are priced at five pesos. I accept right away, not bargaining. (*Thesaurus:* **kōl 1.1, pagtinggi, talu₁, tumba₂ 1.1**)

**hapus₂** *v. advrs.* **-in-** Out of breath due to exertion. *Bang akatis magbalebol nihapus na aku.* When we finish playing volleyball I am puffed. *Angahawak aku bang aku nihapus.* I rest with hands on hips when I am winded. *Bay kam nirugpak e' sigām ma waktu kam nihapus ma l'ngngananbi.* You were attacked by them at a time when you were out of breath on your journey. (*Thesaurus:* **lumu, paghangu-hangu, pagh'ngka-h'ngka, paghongat-hongat, puha**)

**haram** (var. **halam₂**) *n.* **1)** Things, actions, relationships that are ritually unclean and forbidden by Islamic law. *Mbal aku makakakan ambaw, apa haram.* I cannot eat rat, for it is an unclean food. *D'nda hē' halam gi' palabayan haram.* That woman has not yet experienced a period. *Paluwasan haramta.* A place for discharging our bodily wastes. (*Thesaurus:* **halal 1, halam-mutallak, halus₂, sumbang**) **1.1)** *adj. zero* Ritually unclean and prohibited by Islamic law and practice. *Sīn itu haram bang ma agamata sabab bay tambahan pamapatay a'a.* This money is unclean according to our religion because it was the fee for killing someone. *Bang nilaha' d'nda mbal makajari anambahayang apa haram.* When a woman is menstruating she cannot take part in congregational prayer because she is ritually unclean. **1.2)** *v. tr.* To discharge bodily wastes. *Taharamta, tasungi'ta.* We evacuate waste, we excrete.

**pagharam** *v. intr.* **aN-** To empty one's bowels. *Magharam gi' aku.* I'll just have a bowel movement. (*cf:* **sungi' 1**)

**harambiyara'** (var. **halambiyara'**) *n.* 1) An illegitimate child whose father is not known. *"Ē! Halambiyara' itū, mamarahi tuwas kōknu!"* "You son-of-a-b, you are so stubborn!" (*syn:* **anak-kasi**) 1.1) *v. tr.* To treat someone as though he was illegitimate. *Sali' kita nihalambiyara', nihalipulu.* It is as though we are treated as persons without a father, shown no courtesy. *Pinagero'-ero' kita, sali' kita nihalambiyara'.* Treated like dogs, as though we are bastards of unknown parentage.

**harap₁** *n.* 1) The front; foreground. 1.1) *adv.* In the direction of; towards. 1.2) *v. intr. pa-* To face towards something. *Bang aku paharap ni mata llaw, sali' aku asilaw.* When I face towards the sun I become sort of dazzled. *Sali' du papan magka'ob, samaharap buwat lai'.* Just like planks facing together, facing each other like plates. (*Thesaurus:* **alop₁, anggop₁, arap, atubang 1, bayhu' 1.1, sabung**) 1.3) *v. tr.* To fix attention on something. *Angaharap lagi' aku hinangku, bang mbal angaharap mbal akatis.* I focus on my work, if I don't focus it doesn't get finished. (*cf:* **nda' 1**)

**harapan₁** *n.* Someone's presence; the area in front. (*Thesaurus:* **alopan₁, dahū'an 1, munda'an₁**)

**harapan₂** *n.* The genital area of a person's body. *Subay mbal ta'nda' harapan a'a.* A person's genitals should not be seen. (*Thesaurus:* **alopan₂, kamama'u, munda'an₂**)

**pagbalharap** *v. intr. aN-* To have a close face-to-face relationship. *Ya pangannalku, ina'an kitām magbalharap magsuli-suli sali' ka'ina-tagna'.* In my thoughts we are there talking together, face to face, as we used to.

**pagharap** *v. intr. aN-* To be face to face with someone. *Bang kita aningkō', subay kita magharap bo' magsuli-suli.* When we are seated, we should be face to face in order to talk together. (*Thesaurus:* **pagalop, pag'nda'₁, paglambung, pagtampal**)

**harap₂** *v. tr.* To call out to God; to invoke a ritual ancestor. (*Thesaurus:* **amu'-amu', pagduwa'a, pudji 1.1, sambahayang, ta'at 1.1**)

**pagpaharap** *v. ditr.* To present a newborn child to a ritual ancestor.

**harat** *n.* 1) Tartness; astringency. 1.1) *adj. zero* Tart or astringent, as lemon peel when cut with a metal implement. *Aharat, buwat kulit muntaygadja.* Astringent, like the peel of a pomelo.

**haris** *v. ditr.* To convey a message to someone, the action of a supernatural being. *Angaharis duwata ni manusiya'. Yukta, "Angaharis ka bang ai nihinang." Manjari amalman na.* Duwata spirits communicate with humans. We say [to it], "Speak to us about what is to be done." So then it speaks. (*Thesaurus:* **palman 1.1**)

**pagharis** *v. intr. aN-* To converse one another, especially about religious matters. *Buwat kita magsuli-suli, magharis kita.* Like when we are talking, speaking together seriously. (*Thesaurus:* **pagbilma'arup, pagistori-istori, pagsuli-suli**)

**harok** var. of **h'ddok**

**haron** *n.* 1) A stepped device for getting from one level to another, as a house post, stairway, or ladder. 1.1) *v. tr.* To reach something by going up or down a ladder. *Haronun lagi' ya pagūng ilu.* Just go down the ladder to reach that floating thing. 1.2) *v. tr. -an* To convey something by way of a ladder. *Buwas ilū haronin, da'a bbahin.* That rice, carry it by way of the ladder, don't set it down. 1.3) *v. tr. a-, ka-..-an, -an* To provide a house with ladder. *Haronanku luma'ta itū apa piligdu bang aheka paluruk.* I shall provide our house with a ladder because it could be dangerous if a lot of people are visiting.

**haronan** *n.* A ladder or stepped path.

**harung-harung** *v. tr. -an* To gather around a focus of interest. *Ai na pa'in niharung-harunganbi ilu?* What is going on that you're all gathered around? *Sikaharung-harungan saga a'a.* People are gathering in crowds. (*Thesaurus:* **aro' 1, sahubu, timuk 1.1**)

**sikaharung-harungan** *adj.* Assembled in a great crowd.

**harus** var. of **halus₂**

**hasang** *conj.* During.

**hatam** *n.* 1) The final chapter of the Holy Koran, and the prayer offered when a reader reaches this stage. 1.1) *v. tr. -an* To complete the final stage in reading the Holy Koran, when one can read with some fluency. (*Thesaurus:* **tammat 1**)

**paghatam** *v. intr. aN-* To celebrate the stage in religious studies when a student is able to read the Holy Koran. *Bang ta'abut jūran, maghatam kitam, maghinang tonga'.* When we reach the last sura, we celebrate, [having done] half.

**hātan** *n.* A person's manual activity, especially his handwriting or signature. *Takilāku hātanna.* I recognise his handwriting. (*cf:* **sulatan**)

**hati** 1) *n.* The meaning of something said or written. *Ai hatina ya bay yukna? Halam tahatiku.* What does it mean, that which he just said? I didn't understand it. (*Thesaurus:* **kahulugan, hantang-hatulan, hatulan 2, ma'ana,** 1) 1.1) *v. intr. pa-* To understand what something means. *Pahati kām pahāp.* Understand [it] well! 1.2) *v. tr.* To understand or suppose something. *Halam tahatiku.* I did not understand. *Hatiku aniya' sassingku.* I figure I have pinworms. 1.3) *v. tr. a-, ka-..-an, -an* To come to an understanding of something. *Lling yampa kinahati'an.* Words that are only just now understood. (*Thesaurus:* **pagsabut**) 2) *v. tr.* To get or convey information. *Hati'un kono' pehē' bang ai sababan sigā angkan magbono'.* Please go there and find out what their reason is for fighting. *Angahati sadja aku bang manjari ya bay pangaruku hē'.* I am just inquiring whether what

I asked your advice about is possible. *Halam kami bay nihati pasal song magkawin, minsan kami magkampung.* We were not notified of the wedding being about to take place, even though we are village-mates. (*Thesaurus:* **kihaka, hodhod, sisi 2, tilaw 1.1, tilosa 1.1**)

**paghati** *v. intr. aN-* Having a shared understanding of a matter.

**paghati'an** *n.* A mutual understanding. *Asal min paghati'an sigām angkan buwattē' ya pangalupit.* An understanding between them, in fact, which is why the divorce compensation was like that.

**pahati** *n.* 1) A notice or information sheet. (*Thesaurus:* **ba'at 1, kabtangan, haka 1, hunub-hunub 1, sambatan, suli-suli 1**) 1.1) *v. tr.* To inform someone. *Pahati'un kono' aku bang ai hatina inān.* Please explain to me what the meaning of that was. *Bay aku makapamahati ni Siasi.* I had informed those in Siasi about various things.

**panghati** *n.* How one understands something; comprehension. (*Thesaurus:* **alab-alab, himangkan, ingat, pamapatahan, ta'u₁ 1**)

**hatib** *n.* The second-ranking leader in a mosque community, below an imam and above a bilal. (*cf:* **bilal, imam, muwallam**)

**hati'** *ptl.* Indicator of mild surprise. (Deontic modality marker.) *Na, bang hati' buwattē', magtūy kata'uhanku in kasi-lasanu ma nakura'ku aheya to'ongan.* Well then if that's how it is, I will know immediately that your affection for my boss is very great. *Angkan pinagsambatan maina'an, yuk-i, "Nabi hati' si Sa'ul?"* That's why it is said in that place, "Is Saul really a prophet?"

**hatina** *conj.* Meaning to say; as much as to say; in other words. *Pagjamuna ma anakna, hatina in bay saki pahali na.* The feast he put on for his son, as much as to say that his recent sickness is healed.

**hatul₁** *v. tr. -an* To arrange or distribute things in an orderly way. *Kapangandolan ai-ai pangahatul e' Tuhan.* Whatever God has arranged can be trusted. (*Thesaurus:* **patuntul, temo-temo, uki'-uki'**)

**hatulan** *n.* 1) The proper arrangement of things or events. *Ai na pa'in saga hatulan panunuran kami ma onde' itu ma kapaga'ana?* What are the arrangements we are to follow in regard to this child and his personal development? *Ya ru ilu hatulan pangā'an pangita'u e' a'a bilahi pinandu'an.* That is the way for someone who wants to be taught to get knowledge. 2) The intent of an utterance. (*Thesaurus:* **kahulugan, hantang-hatulan, hati 1, ma'ana₁ 1**)

**paghatul-hatul** *v. tr.* To keep rearranging things. *Angay ka maghatul-hatul? Ngga'i ka ai-ainu.* Why do you keep rearranging things? They're not your things. (*cf:* **paghirang**)

**hatul₂** *adj. a-* Exemplary in character or behavior. *Ahatul itu mbal patil'ngnganun, mbal ah'lling-h'lling, mbal magbono'.* Bang sinoho', magtūy du pabuhat man paningkō'an. Bang palege, palege sadja.* Hatul means not habitually walking about, not talking, not fighting. When told to do something gets up immediately from where he was sitting. When lying down, he just lies there. *Aniya' isāb matto'a ahatul, aniya' isāb ala'at.* There are adults too who are exemplary, and bad ones as well. (*Thesaurus:* **addat 1.1, hongpot, pantun 1, papat 1, p'mpon 1, saldik, saltun 1**)

**hatus** *num.* Hundred. *O Ina', ya dangibu maka dahatus pilak bay tinangkaw min ka'a, aku ya bay angā'.* Mother, the one thousand and one hundred pesos that was stolen from you, I am the one who took it. (*Thesaurus:* **ibu, laksa' 1**)

**ma hatusan** *adv. phrase* By the hundred. *Bang kita makaisi dakayu' pilak ma hatusan, buwat ma bangko inān, sali' anganak inān.* When we put in single pesos by the hundreds, as into the bank, they will earn interest.

**hau-** *see section 2.2.2.4 Prefix:* **Cau-**

**haum** *v. tr.* To arrange someone's release from jail. *Bang aku ma deyom jīl, aku haumnu. Binowa paluwas min kalabusu.* If I am in jail, you arrange for my release, getting me out of prison. (*Thesaurus:* **jamin, l'kkat₁ 1.1, luyal 1.1, piyansa**)

**haun₁** (var. **ahun₁**) *v. tr. -an* To serve up food. *Ahunin bang atahak na.* Remove [the food] when it is cooked already. *Niahunan ni lai' pagsama-sama. Luwag itu pangaun.* Served up into individual plates. This ladle here is for serving. *Jari nihaunan e'na loho' ē' ni sigām.* So she served up that soup to them. (*cf:* **engket, luwag 1.1**)

**haun₂** (var. **ahun₂**) *v. ditr.* To rescue someone from danger. *Waktu bay kapangahaunnu ma saga a'anu min lahat Misil.* The time when you rescued your people from the land of Egypt. *Tahaun saga miskin min kasigpitan sigām.* Poor people will be rescued from their hardship. (*Thesaurus:* **lappas₂ 1, liyus 1.2, puwas₁ 1.1**)

**haup** *see:* **paghaup, paghaupan**

**haus** *n.* 1) An area of disturbed water where currents interact and flow strongly downward. *Buwat haus, pelang magbulibud, binuhawi'.* Like currents fighting, the canoe turning end for end, tossed by a whirlpool. (*Thesaurus:* **abal 1.1, guyu 1, sahabal**) 1.1) *v. intr. aN-* To become disturbed, of the sea in an area where currents interact. *Subay bulan Maulud bo' angahaus, ati alahang kita kaut.* It is in the month Maulud that the sea forms dangerously rough areas, and then we rarely go out to sea.

**haus-bō'** *n.* A species of bird, about as big as a domestic chicken, said to live entirely at sea. (*cf:* **kullu-kullu₁**; *gen:* **manuk-manuk 1**)

**hāw-hāw 1)** *n.* The faint outline of something, as a landmark in the distance. *Yampa tanda'ta hāw-hāwna, sōng ta'nda' lahat.* When we begin to see its faint outline, land will soon be seen. *Aniya' isāb lahat tegob-tegoban, mbal ta'nda' kakayu-kayuhanna. Minsan hāw-hāwna mbal ta'nda'.* There is a far-off place too, its trees not visible. Even its outline cannot be seen. **2)** *v. intr.* maka- To do something in a limited way, as to read a little, or to paddle a canoe in an amateur way. *Makahāw-hāw si Hi magbinisaya'. Mbal ata'u to'ongan, sagwā' makahāw-hāw.* Hi speaks a bit of Cebuano. He doesn't know it well but can talk it a little. *Makahāw-hāw kita, ata'u diki'-diki' bang takdil ni magbassa.* We do it a bit, we know a little with regard to reading.

**hawa** *n.* **1)** Intense longing; covetous desire. *Aniya' hawaku am'lli ai-ai inān. Labi min baya'.* I have a strong desire to buy whatever is there. things. It's more Stronger than just wanting. *Hawata na, ai-ai ta'nda'ta subay tab'llita. Subay kita karūlan ya matata ang'nda' bo' am'lli.* Our desire is that we want to buy everything we see. We want to indulge whatever our eyes see, and buy [it]. *Ameya' hawanu ma pilak inān, mbal na ka amahagi'.* Your desire stays with that money, you will not share it. **1.1)** *adj.* a- Covetous; lustful. *Da'a ka makalandu' ahawa ma alta'.* Don't be too covetous for wealth. (*Thesaurus:* **bahaya, kaway 1, hangsaw 1, napsu 1.1, sawiya 1, sayap-sayap**) **1.2)** *v. advrs.* -in- Motivated by lust. *Buwat aniya' d'nda pinagba'isan e' a'a, nihawa iya.* Like when a man desires a woman sexually, he is moved by lust. **1.3)** *v. tr.* -an To desire something intensely. *Da'a hawa'in ai-ai a'a ilū.* Don't set your heart on whatever that fellow has. *Hawata na, ai-ai ta'nda'ta subay tab'llita. Subay kita karūlan ya matata ang'nda' bo' am'lli.* Our desire is for everything we see to be purchased. Everything our eyes see has to be indulged, so we buy them.

**hawak** *v. intr.* aN- To stand with hands on hips. *Angahawak aku bang nihapus.* I rest my arms on my hips when I am winded.

**hawakan** *n.* The waist. *Magbayla kami, balutanku ma hawakan.* When we dance the western way I hold [her] by the waist.

**hawal** *n.* **1)** Uncertainty. *Kabaya'anku to'ongan, halam aniya' hawalna.* What I really want, without a doubt. **1.1)** *adj.* a- Hesitant; not sure whether to trust; tentative. *Ahawal sala bang kita patuhun. Kalu aniya' angeket.* We are sort of afraid when we dive. There might be something that will bite. *Bang pabeya'ku ma a'a ina'an bo' ngga'i ka ai-aiku, ahawal-hawal aku amabeya'. Sali' mbal aku angandol. Atāw aku ai-aiku alungay.* If I send [something] with that man and it is not my things, I am somewhat hesitant about sending. It is as though I don't trust. I am afraid my things may be lost.

**hawan** *adj.* a- **1)** Clear of rubbish; smooth, as an area of ground. *Bang aheka s'ggit ma deyo' luma', subay kinayasan bo' ahawan.* When there is a lot

of rubbish under the house it should be cleared away so it is clean. **1.1)** *v. tr.* -an To clear away rubbish from an open area.

**hawas** *v. tr.* -an To unload something; to remove contents. *Bang ka bay at'kka min Bukidnon bo' aku linganannu sinoho' angahawas ni diyata' luma'nu.* When you arrive from Bukidnon and you call me, I'm told to unload [things] into your house. (*ant:* **duwa'**)

**hawas-basi'** *v. tr.* -an To conduct the ritual of removing the effects of rigor mortis. *Subay nihawasan-basi' bo' yampa nilukbu'.* The rigidity of death should be dealt with before the body is laid out. *Nilukbu' tanganta, tape'ta, bang apuwas na bay nihawasan basi'.* Our hands and feet are manipulated after rigor mortis has been dealt with. (*cf:* **basi'₂ 1**)

**hawid** *v. tr.* -an To hold someone firmly in order to restrain him from fighting or self harm. *Bay ni'ddop si Nu, mbal tahawid. Nileya'-leya' asal.* Nu had a nightmare and couldn't be restrained. Terrrified in fact. *Bang magbono' na, mbal kahawiran. Subay pinasagaran.* When [people] are already fighting they cannot be restrained. They should just be left alone.

**hayak-hayak** *adj.* -an Having expectations that are not fulfilled. *Hayak-hayakan aku aholat pat'nna' ma lahat itū, halam aniya' lengogna. Ai ka itū, aniya' du pa'in.* I was disappointed in my expectations of settling in this place, no unrest. Guess what, there always is. *Hayak-hayakan aku luma' ilū bay tinambol e'nu, angkanna kita katangkawan.* I was hoping that you would close the house, so that's why we were burgled. (*cf:* **pagambahan 1**)

**hayag** *v. intr.* pa- To spread widely, of information. (*Thesaurus:* **bantug 1, bawag, buhanyag, busling, hula-layag 1, tanyag 1**)

**haya'₁** *v. intr.* pa- To lie on one's back. (*Thesaurus:* **daya', hagtang, hantal, leyak, pagduleyak**)

**haya'₂** *n.* A single horizontal cloud in a clear sky. (*Thesaurus:* **andom 1, gabun, tai'-baliyu, turung-balu 2**)

**hayang** *adj.* a- **1)** Airy or breezy; roomy. *Bang kita atuli dogsolta ka, ka'a ilū atā man tepo. Subay hal aku dangan-dangan ahayang.* When we are sleeping I push you off; you are far from the sleeping mat. I alone should feel the breeze. *Saupama nijīl kami bo' aniya' kasipihanku palahi'an, magtūy aku pal'ssut lahi-lahi. Ahayang na aku.* For example, we are jailed and I spy a way of escape, I promptly slip out and run away. I am in the open air again. **1.1)** *v. intr.* pa- To locate in a breeze in order to cool off. *Bang kita bay kapasu'an, pahayang-hayang.* After we have been in the heat, we cool off in the breeze. **2)** Exposed to the air. *Ahayang sinanglag, bay na sinanglag llaw itu bo' tinau'. Salung akapog, akasat, sali' magpikit. Takakan so' atuwas.* Pan-roasted cassava kept overnight and exposed to the air. By tomorrow it is stale, poor in flavor and sort of sticking together. It is edible but hard. *Pehē' ka, b'llatun daing ilū bo' ahayang. Ilu na llaw. Bang ahayang, yukta ahāp na toho'na, atuwas na.* Off you go, spread that fish out so it is exposed to the air. The sun's there now. When it is aired we say its dryness is good and hard.

**kahayang-hayangan** *n.* An airy place; a breezeway. *Si Sel bay ni M'ddas kapasu'an e' llaw. Aningkō' ma jala-jalana kahayang-hayangan.* Sir went to Siasi and got overheated in the sun. He is sitting in his trellised breezeway.

**hayang pangatayan** *n. phrase* 1) Freedom from cares or tension. {idiom} *Bang pa'in ka binuwanan hayang pangatayan.* May you be emotionally refreshed. **1.1)** *adj.* a- Care-free. *Ahayang pangatayanku.* I feel better in my heart [lit. my liver is refreshed].

**pahayang** *v. tr.* To place something or someone where it is breezy.

**haybol** *v. tr.* To mix two or more liquids together. *Ai-ai nilamuran, buwat duwa ginis pinta nihaybol, pinaila'.* Anything added, like two kinds of paint shaken together, a liquid component added. *Haybolun mastik ilu.* Mix up that epoxy. (*Thesaurus:* **lamud₁ 1.1, lamugay 1.1, pagsagol 1.1, paila', simbug 1, templa 1.1**)

**haylan** *adj.* a- Amazed at; fascinated by. *Ahaylan to'ongan dayang-dayang itū pagta'una ma pangita'u si Sulayman.* The princess referred to was amazed on experiencing the wisdom of Sulayman. (*Thesaurus:* **ili-ili, inu-inu 1, jaip, littā 1**)

**hayop** *n.* Four-footed animals in general; domestic animals in particular. *Hayop itū saga sapi', kura', kambing, ero', kuting. Hayop* includes things like cows, horses, goats, dogs, and cats.

**hē** *intrj.* Exclamation indicating exasperation. *Hē, tittowana ī'!* Good grief, that laugh of his! *Hē! S'lle' bale puhu'! Bang pa'in aku sinagga' e' Tuhan bo' mbal makamula a'a bay pene'na nihinang sultan.* Whoa! Perish the thought! May God prevent me from harming someone he has chosen to become king.

**he da'a** *conj.* So that not; in order not to. *Amalut ka pahogot he da'a ahūg.* Hold on firmly so you don't fall. *Bang kita ni Sisangat subay amusay akuwat he da'a tabowa he' s'llog.* If we're off to Sisangat we have to paddle vigorously so as to not be carried by the current. (*Thesaurus:* **bat sabab, bo' mbal, bo' supaya, bo'₂, dok supaya, supaya**)

**hebi** *n.* A species of tree and its edible fruit.

**heka** (var. **heka'**) *n.* 1) The number or quantity of things. *Pila heka anaknu?* How many children do you have? **1.1)** *adj.* a- Many; much. *Aheka bohe' mareyom tangki.* There is a lot of water in the tank. *Aheya kasusahan ma M'ddas ma pasalan saki kolera, aheka' amatay.* There was a serious situation in Siasi Town because of a cholera

outbreak, many dying. (*Thesaurus:* **banos, besal, kansang 1, datay₂, dayas-dayas, dorot, jayak, parat**) **1.2)** *v. advrs.* ka-...-an Overcome by force of numbers.

**kaheka-kataha'an** *n.* Abundance and extent. *Ya kaheka-kataha'anna.* Its abundance and extent.

**kaheka-heka'an** *n.* Abundance; crowds. *Ginupu kita bang kita angongka' ma kaheka-heka'an a'a.* We are nervous when we perform among crowds of people. (*Thesaurus:* **kompolan, dansehe'an, padjuhan, palti, umpigan**)

**kaheka'an** *n.* A large number; majority. *Kaheka'an kohang maina'an ma Sablay.* The majority of clams are there at Sablay. *Kaheka'an pisang ma Bukidnon.* The bulk of pineapples are in Bukidnon.

**kamaheka'an** *n.* A great many. *Magtūy iya amabeya' saga kamaheka'an sundaluna.* He promptly sent a great number of his soldiers.

**heka bowa'** *adj.* a- To have a lot to say; to be wordy. {idiom} *Abiyas, aheka bowa'na ma pagbono'.* Shameless, with a lot to say in a fight.

**heka min heka** *adv. phrase* More often than usual; no matter how many. {idiom} *Heka man heka, sinokat walumpū' pilak e' tag anak.* Regardless of what was usual, eighty pesos was demanded by the bride's carers. *Heka man heka Milikan, nsa' aniya' ahāp min si Lu sidda amisita ma aku.* However many Americans, there are none better than Lu visiting me so often.

**heka tangan** *adj.* a- Habitually touching things. {idiom} *Magkoledje itū aheka ntananna, sali' aheka tanganna.* Handling everything, touching lots of things, like having a lot of hands.

**dangkaheka** *n.* The same extended kin group.

**pagkaheka'an** *n.* 1) An extended kin group. **1.1)** *v. intr.* aN- To be an extended kin group. *Sugsug isāb kami, magkaheka'an.* We're connected, we are a wider kindred.

**paheka** *adv.* Much; plentifully.

**heka'** var. of **heka**

**hegom-hegom** *v. tr.* To keep information or opinions secret. *Mbal paluwas llingna, sali' nihegom-hegom ma deyom atayna. Mbal takale ni a'a kamemon.* His words don't get spoken, they're sort of kept secret inside him. They are not heard by everyone. (*Thesaurus:* **limbung 1.1**)

**hē'₁** (var. **ē'**; **hele'**; **ī'**; **ili'**) 1) *dem.* That over there, referring to something far from both speaker and hearer; precise location reference [Set II]. *Hē' mahē' luma' mastal.* There over there is the school-teacher's house. *Ī' mariyata' atop.* There on the roof. *Ya na hē' makalemed.* That is what contaminates. (*Set:* **ilu 1, ina'an 1, itu 1**) **1.1)** Refers back to an entire discourse or a large section of a discourse. 2) *ptl.* Perfect aspect marker. Indicates that the state or action described has begun and is still relevant or current, though remote from speaker and hearer. *A: "Ma'ai si Ab?" B: "Hē' na atulak ni kapū'an."* A: "Where is Ab?" B: "He has left for the outer islands [and is still there]." (*cf:* **wa'i**) **damahē'an** *n.* The same location.

**hē'₂** (var. **ē'**; **hele'**; **ī'**; **ili'**) *dem.* 1) That over there, referring to something far from both speaker and hearer; precise location reference [Set I]. *Ma deyom mohang ē'.* In the bilge there. *Maglimbahod ī', buwat sali' a'a ab'ttong palege na pa'in bo' ngga'i ka gi' bulananna.* That [word] limbahod, is like a pregnant woman who keeps lying down even though it's not yet her time. *Mahē' aku aningkō', ma tōng Santa Ana. Ya Santa Ana hē', gusung gi'.* I was sitting there at the Santa Ana point. By the way, Santa Ana was still sandy then. *Pareyo' na kami tudju ni Tinda-Laud ī'.* We went on down towards Tinda-Laud there. (*Set:* **ilū 1, inān 1, itū 1**) 1.1) Signals that a character in a story is involved in a critical event or episode. *Lling hē', ahūg pareyo' ambak hē'. Amatay iya.* At that word, the frog fell through the air [into the fire]. He died.

**he'** (var. **e'**) *ptl.* 1) Actor marker, used to mark the demoted actor of a passive construction. *Buwattingga he'ta angahinang taguri'?* How do we make a kite? *Pa'ambat kahe'nu amangan.* Do your eating without interruption. *Bay aku kineket e' ero'.* I was bitten by a dog. *Aniya' tai'-ambal bay tabāk he' a'a.* Some ambergris has been found by someone or other. *Bay magbulang manuk paleyang, na taluwa' pa'in he' epo', apakpak pareyo'.* Fighting cocks flying up, then when one is wounded with a spur it falls down. (*syn:* **ni₂ 1**) 1.1) Agent marker, used to mark the agent by which a state or situation is brought about.

**he' angay** *neg.* Vigorous contradiction or denial of something that has been asserted or implied. *A: "Mbal kita pinaindaman." B: "He' angay! Taga utang iya ma aku."* A: "He won't lend it to us." B: "Why in the world not! He is in debt to me." *He' angay. Aheka isāb ta'nda'ku.* That's not so! I definitely saw a lot.

**heldo** *v. tr.* *-an* To style hair in a modern style. **heldo'an** *n.* A modern hair style; permanent wave. *Kabaya'anku bay heldo'an si Ib.* What I used to want was a hairdo like Ib.

**hele'** var. of **hē'₁, hē'₂**

**hella'** *v. tr.* To pull something along. *Bang am'ssi si Mu ni Serom, tininduk he' dapak agtūy nihella' he'na.* When Mu went fishing to Serom, a paddle-tail [fish] took his bait and he promptly pulled it up. *Bang kita makapah'lling, yukta, "Bay palagtik d'lla'na," D'llata palagtik, mbal pagkahella'an, mbal taisaban.* When someone has said something we say, "His tongue has clicked." Our tongues cannot be pulled back, our words cannot be repeated. (*Thesaurus:* **bira 1, konot₂, ga'ut, ganggut, guyud 1, paglagedled 1**) **paghella'** *v. intr.* *aN-* To pull at each other, as in a

tug-of-war.

**hellel** *v. intr.* *pa-* To protrude and dangle, as a tongue or the foot of a large monovalve shell. *Pahellel isina, buwat kulallit, kahanga.* Its foot was hanging out, like a helmet shell or a conch. (*Thesaurus:* **hallal, sasa₂, tonton 1**)

**helmet** *n.* A military helmet. *Helmet, ya saruk sundalu.* A helmet, a soldier's head covering. *Buwattingga luwa helmet? Sali' tibulung. Bang nilagpi' ah'lling. Mbal niōk e' punglu'. Bang tinimbak, pasalisig punglu'.* What is the appearance of the helmet? Roundish. When flicked it makes a noise. It is not penetrated by a bullet. When shot at the bullet glances off.

**helo₁** *n.* 1) A strong desire, sexual or otherwise. *Mbal bilahi magkawin, halam gi' aniya' helona.* Does not want to get married, she has no desire yet. (*Thesaurus:* **baya' 1, bilahi 1, ebog 1, lingit 1, napsu 1**) 1.1) *v. tr.* *a-, ka-..-an, -an* To want something very much. *Ahelo'an aku kamisita.* I really want a T-shirt.

**helo₂** *n.* An increased flow of saliva, as caused by nausea or appetite. *Abontol helota bay atonga' kab'ttongta.* Our saliva flow is regular when we are half-way into our pregnancy. (*Thesaurus:* **buhelo 1, laway₁ 1, ludja' 1, pagtagak**) **paghelo** *v. intr.* *aN-* To be experiencing a strong desire for something, marked by increased salivation and nausea. *Bang ganta' maghelo h'ndanu ma ai-ai. Ai-ai ta'nda'na bang aniya' kanapsuhanna, subay b'llina.* Suppose your wife feels desire for something or other. Whatever she sees and has a desire for, she must buy.

**helog** *v. tr.* *-an* To scrub grime off the skin. (*Thesaurus:* **kusu-kusu, sikat**)

**hemol** *adj.* *a-* Blurred or slurred, as the speech of someone who is very ill.

**hemos** *v. intr.* *pa-* 1) To depart from; to get going on one's way. *Abay kohap, masi paluwas llaw bo' sōng sangom. Pahemos-hemos na kām.* Late afternoon, the sun is still out but it will soon be night. Get going now. (*Thesaurus:* **k'llo'₂, la'an 1, tanggal₂, tungkas**) 1.1) *v. tr.* To take something away. *Agtūy nihemos kamemon.* Everything promptly taken away.

**hendog-hendog** *n.* Adult maturity; coming of age. *Sangay min bay kahendog-hendogku.* Ever since I grew up to adulthood. (*Thesaurus:* **lasag, pata'₁, sangpot 1, sibuwa, to'a 1.1**)

**henned** *v. tr.* To massage a bruised area to reduce swelling. *Nihenned, sali' kita butugan, bo' sinapuhan maka bu'un, buwat bu'un h'ndata.* Henned is like when we have a bruise, and it is rubbed gently with hair, like the hair of one's wife. (*syn:* **p'nnod 2**)

**henok** var. of **h'nnok**

**hense** *v. intr.* *pa-* To move away a little distance. *Pahense ka bo' mbal ajogjog sulatan itū.* Move away so that this writing doesn't get jolted. (*Thesaurus:* **kisal-kisal, higin, ingsud, sigput**)

**paghense** *v. intr. aN-* To move about restlessly. *Da'a kām maghense, bilahi aku atuli.* Don't move about, I want to sleep. (*Thesaurus:* **pagkebed-kebed, paghibal-hibal, paglinggayu', pagoseg-oseg**)

**hengas-hengas** var. of **engas-engas**

**hengko** *adj. a-* Unstable. *Bang pelang ma tangonan, bang aniya' goyak maka baliyu, ahengko.* When the canoe is up on the supports, if there are waves and wind, it will be unstable. (*Thesaurus:* **henggol 1, hodjog 1, jogjog 1, oseg 1**)

    **paghengko-hengko** *v. intr. aN-* To move about restlessly. *Da'a sinō' magbōg, da'a maghengko-hengko.* Told not to jolt, not to be moving about.

**hengkot** var. of **engkot**

**henggol** *adj. a-* 1) Shaky; insecurely fixed. (*Thesaurus:* **hengko, hodjog 1, jogjog 1, oseg 1**) 1.1) *v. tr.* To loosen something; to make something shaky. *Da'a henggolun lām ilū ko da'a ahūg pareyo'. Abila' saminna.* Don't shake that lamp lest it fall down. Its glass will break.

    **paghenggol** *v. intr. aN-* To move about insecurely or restlessly. *Sali' magloka-loka, maghenggol.* Sort of loose-fitting, moving about.

**hengo-hengo** *adj. a-* Unsettled; in a disturbed state. *Ahengo-hengo sali' bay kat'kkahan, buwat kami at'kka min Sambo. Ahengo-hengo na deyom luma', asasaw sali'.* In an uproar, as when we are affected by some event, like when we arrived from Zamboanga. The house was in an uproar, disturbed so to speak. *Sinoho' amanyabut, yukna, "Da'a gi' ka anangis. Piligdu nyawa hē' ahengo-hengo."* [He] was told to recite the creed, saying, "Don't start crying. The danger is that the life-essence may be unsettled." (*Thesaurus:* **balu', dongkag, halubilu, hiluhala' 1.1, hiyul, jabu 1, lengog 1.1, sasaw 1.1, sensong**)

**hengol** *adj. a-* 1) Disturbed by sudden or clumsy movement. *Aheka pahāp amahengol ma deyom luma' itū.* There are so many things causing disturbances here in the house. 1.1) *v. tr.* To disturb something by moving or bumping.

**herot** *adj. a-* Densely packed; close-growing. *Aherot katolna.* He has eczema all over. *Aherot bangkawna, mbal taitung.* Its mangrove forest is dense, beyond counting. (*cf:* **timbakkol**)

**heya** *n.* 1) The size of something. *Buwattilu heyana, saga.* Its size is about like that. 1.1) *adj. a-* Large. *Bang ariki'-diki' nih'nnat tanganna bo' aheya alantik.* When small her hands are manipulated so that when they are big they will curve back [for dancing]. *Min kariki'-diki'ku ni kaheyaku.* From when I was small to when I was big. *Ka'a ya makalabay maka makamata ma kaheya kawasana.* You have experienced and witnessed the extent of his authority. (*Thesaurus:* **aslag₂ 1, mehe**; *ant:* **diki' 1**) 1.2) *v. intr. pa-/-um-* To become larger. *Magkontay tepo itu, paheya sala.* This mat is stretching out of shape, sort of expanding. *Humeya humeya.* Growing bigger and bigger.

**kaheya'an** *n.* A more public sphere or level. *Maglekles, magnikaheya'an. Buwat magsagga', nihukum e' konsehal, mbal takole'. Pasōng ni kapitan, mbal. Pasōng ni mayul.* Going further and further, extending to the public sphere. Like a dispute brought to a councilor, to no avail. Goes on to the barangay captain, no better. Goes on to the mayor.

**heya ma atay** *v. tr.* To esteem. {idiom} *Halam aku bay paheyana ma atay.* He didn't treat me as being important. *Mura-murahan magpakasampay in niyat kami ni ka'am, paheyabi du isāb ma atay.* May it be that our commitment to you will be fulfilled, you too treating it as important.

**heya mata** *adj. a-* Looking at with longing. {idiom} *Sali' kita aheya matata ang'nda' pilak, heyana ī'!* Like us looking at the money with bulging longing eyes, so much!.

**heya pisut-pisut** *n. phrase* To be trivial in size or amount. {idiom} *B'tteya pisut-pisut ko' ka'a ilu.* You're so insignificant [lit. like a *pisut* nut].

**pagheya-heya** *v. tr.* To make something important. *Tu'ud magheya-heya dīna.* He's simply making himself big. (*Thesaurus:* **pagabbu 1.1, pagbantug-bantug, pagmahatinggi, pagmalangkahi, pagpasanglit, pagtāp-tāp**)

**paheya₁** *adv.* To a great degree.

**paheya₂** *v. tr.* To enlarge something; to make something important.

**samaheya** *adj.* To be of the same size.

**heya-diki'** *adj. a-* Big and small. *Wa'i apakpak kapanyapanna aheya-ariki'.* All of his tools, large and small, have fallen down.

**hibal** *adj. a-* 1) Restless; unsettled. 1.1) *v. tr.* To disturb something by moving it about. *Da'a na hibalun lām ilū.* Don't move that lamp about. *Hibalun pangatayan saga banta sigām supaya ma'ase'.* Stir the hearts of their enemies that they may be merciful. *Binalanja'an du e'na saga h'nda-h'ndana sagō' halam bay nihibal he'na.* He provided for his minor wives but he did not disturb them.

**paghibal-hibal** *v. intr. aN-* To move restlessly. *Da'a na ka maghibal-hibal mailu-ilū.* Don't keep wriggling around there. (*Thesaurus:* **pagkebed-kebed, paghense, paglinggayu', pagoseg-oseg**)

**hibang-hibang** *adj. zero* Mentally slow. (*Thesaurus:* **bengog 1, b'ggod, b'llod, bobo, dupang 1**)

**hibarat** var. of **ibarat₂**

**hibilis** (var. **ibilis**) *n.* A demonic being. *Bang ma kami halam aniya' alanga min kamemon, buwat ma hibilis. Aheka isāb bangsa hibilis.* With us there is no one person above all the rest, as there are with demonic beings. There are many tribes of demons. *Akōg a'a inān ma kahinangan ibilis.* That person is pleased with the activities of devils. (*Thesaurus:* **bangsa magl'l'ngngan, duwata 1, hama'-hama' a'a, jīn 1, saitan, ya mbal ta'nda'**)

**Hibrani** *n.* An ethnic Hebrew; a descendant of Abraham through Isaac.

**hibuk** *adj.* a- Noisy. (*Thesaurus:* **bukag, hidjul, sagaw**)

**hīk** *v. tr.* To cut small pieces off a larger whole. *Angkan na hīkku s'mmek bat sabab akalabi.* The reason I have cut bits off the garment is that it is over-large. *Bang gandum atuwas pinagt'ttok-t'ttok dahū ampa nihīk-hīk.* When the corn is hard it is first cut into small pieces and then sliced thinly. (*Thesaurus:* **kehet 1, hilap, pagsalik-salik**)

**hīk-hīk** *n.* Snippets; shavings.

**paghīk-hīk** *v. tr.* To cut something up into small pieces. *Pinaghīk-hīk isina bo' tinunu' kōkna.* The flesh is cut up finely and the head burnt.

**hikay** *v. intr.* pa- To improve in condition, of sickness. *A: "Si Mbo', halam pahikay-hikay sakina?" B: "Angay? Pahikay-hikay na apa makal'ngngan na."* A: "Has Grandad's sickness not improved?" B: "Why not? It's improved already because he is already able to walk." (*Thesaurus:* **gām-gām, hāp-hāp, hoblas 1, lōng-lōng, siha'-siha', si'at**)

**kahikayan** *n.* Improvement in the condition of a sick person. (*cf:* **kagām-gāman**)

**hikmat** *n.* A magic spell or hypnosis used to influence the way someone behaves. *Buwat a'a magkuntaw inān, minsan buwattingga he' anudju iya maka ai-ai, katangkisan sadja. Aniya' hikmatna.* Like that fellow doing martial arts, no matter what you aim at him with, he simply dodges it. He has a magic spell. *Ni'llingan kita, pinat'nna'an kita hikmat.* We are targeted with a charm, a spell laid on us. (*Thesaurus:* **duti, hinang-hinang₁, h'lling₃, palkata'an, pantak 1.1, sihil 1.1**)

**hidja** *v. tr.* To spell out syllables as when learning to read.

**paghidja-hidja** (var. **paghijajā**) *v. tr.* To read hesitantly, as a person still learning. *Angalansal na bang amassa, mbal maghidja-hidja.* He reads fluently now, not hesitating.

**hidjab** *n.* A veil.

**paghidjab** *v. intr.* aN- To talk together in secret, as a couple planning an elopement. *Maghidjab, sali' kita magduwang-duwangan magsuli-suli.* Talking privately, like the two of us talking together. *Maghidjab itū, buwat a'a maglahi.* Plotting privately, like people eloping.

**hidjaw** *adj.* zero Yellow, of chicken legs. *Subay manuk hidjaw tape'na pagkulban ni saitan deya.* It should be a chicken with yellow legs that is offered to the land demon. (*gen:* **walna'**)

**hidjuk** *n.* A durable black cord made from the outer layer of the tuwak palm. *Lubid ettom, ahunit nihinang. Alahang a'a agdagang. Min kayu tuwa'.* Black rope, hard to make. People selling it are rare. It is from the *tuwak* palm. (*Thesaurus:* **badjang, bamban₂, lanut, lupis**)

**hidjul** *adj.* a- Noisy; rowdy. *Magkolebokan a'a inān,*

*sali' ahidjul maina'an, magpiha onde'-onde' alungay.* Those people are milling around, making a noise, looking for a lost child. (*Thesaurus:* **bukag, hibuk, sagaw**)

**paghidjul** *v. intr.* aN- To make a noise, as a crowd of people milling about. *A: "Ai paghidjulanbi ilu?" B: "Pasal bay magsalla'."* A: "What are you making a noise about there?" B: "It's about a [recent] game of two-up."

**higin** *v. intr.* pa- To move a short distance. *Saupama atuli, yukku, "Pahigin ka pehē', Ib, da'a magligpit."* For example when sleeping, I say, "Ib, move that way a bit, don't lie with your legs across me." (*Thesaurus:* **kisal-kisal, hense, ingsud, sigput**)

**pahigin** *v. tr.* To make something move a small distance.

**higtal** *adj.* a- Gaunt, of body shape. *Ahigtal, angagkag, halam taga isi.* Gaunt, thin, without any flesh. (*Thesaurus:* **kagkag, kayog 1, kittay, koskos, kulagkag, giti' 1, titis 2**)

**paghigtal** *v. tr.* To stretch one's body. *Maghigtal aku dīku.* I stretch myself.

**higung-higung** *v. tr.* To say something in a whisper. (*Thesaurus:* **hagas-hagas, singu'-singu'**)

**hīl** *v. tr.* To acknowledge someone's presence. *Saupama lum'ngngan ni Lihondo, na halam kami bay nihīl.* Walking to Rio Hondo for example, we weren't acknowledged. *Da'a na hīlun, da'a sinagina.* Don't acknowledge him anymore, don't have him welcomed. *Nihīl kita, minsan kita pi'ingga-pi'ingga kinabaya'an kita he a'a.* We are greeted, no matter where we go people appreciate us. (*Thesaurus:* **owa'₁ 1.1, paidda, sagina, sahawi 1**)

**hilag** *v. tr.* To encourage someone to be energetic. *Bang kami magbeya' angusaha maka sehe'ku, hilagku. Soho'ku pabasag amusay.* When I am going fishing with my companion, I urge him to be energetic. I tell him to paddle strongly. (*Thesaurus:* **da'ak, gandahan, pagmanda 1, soho', sūg-sūg, uldin 1**)

**hilaga'** *n.* A northwest wind. (*gen:* **baliyu 1**)

**hilala'** *see:* **pahilala'**

**hilala'ungan** *n.* A significant utterance. *Yampa kami magsambung-siyambungi hilala'ungan.* We have only now begun exchanging words of any significance. (*syn:* **himumūngan**)

**hilang** *v. tr.* -an To reduce the amount of something. *Halam bay kahilangannu isina ilū?* You haven't taken some out of it, have you? (*Thesaurus:* **kobos, kulang₁ 1.3, dagdag₁, diki' 1.2, putung, sulak₁**)

**hilap** *v. tr.* To cut fish or beef in thin slices. *Angay daing angkan nihilap? Bo' supaya aheka bo' anipis, bo' sarang ma bowa'ta.* Why is fish sliced this way? So there will be plenty though thin, so it will fit into our mouths. (*Thesaurus:* **kehet 1, hīk, pagsalik-salik**)

**hilas** *adj. zero* Given without reservation. *Ā, ma ka'a na. Hilas du min deyom atayku.* Here, this is for you. It is given out of the free generosity of my heart. *Kasi-lasa hilas min kami maglakibini.* Open-hearted love from the two of us [husband and wife]. *Hilas itū sali' halam aniya' mareyom atayta ma damuli. Hilas* is when there is nothing in our hearts about a later [repayment]. (*cf:* **lilla'**)

**paghilas** *v. tr.* To give freely with no expectation of a reciprocal gift. *Bang bay aniya' pamuwan, paghilasku ma ka'a.* If there had been anything to give, I would have given it to you freely.

**hili** *v. tr. -an* To blame someone for failing to do his share of work. *Nihili'an aku bang sali' alallay he'ku maghinang.* I get blamed when I work slowly. (*Thesaurus:* **balik₂, bīng₃, bitung, likid, pagbintu, pagpatimpa, pelleng 1.2**)

**paghili-hili** *v. intr. aN-* To shift the responsibility to one another. *Magbintu, sali' maghili-hili. Buwat yuk dangan, "Pehē' ka," ati yuk dangan, "Ōy, pehē' ka."* Arguing, passing the buck. Like when one person says, "You go," and the other one says, "No, you go!" (*Thesaurus:* **pagampa-ampa**)

**hiluhala'** *n.* **1)** Widespread confusion. **1.1)** *adj. a-* In a disturbed state; stirred up. *Na ahiluhala' na maina'an h'ndana inān.* Well that wife of his was making trouble there. (*Thesaurus:* **balu', dongkag, halubilu, hengo-hengo, hiyul, jabu 1, lengog 1.1, sasaw 1.1, sensong**) **1.2)** *v. tr.* To cause an uproar. *Biyaksa isāb sigām angahiluhala' maka amuwan sasaw.* They are accustomed to spreading confusion and causing trouble.

**hilut** *v. tr.* To massage someone. *Atiya' aku alēt. Wa'i bay nihilut h'nda si Hu he' panday.* Here I am, late. Hu's wife has been massaged by the midwife. *Makajari isāb l'lla nihilut bang ap'ddi' b'ttongna.* A man may be massaged too, when his stomach is sore. (*Thesaurus:* **kallus₁ 1.1, salimpak**)

**himan-himan** *adj. -an* Almost but not quite. *Himan-himanan mbal ta'abut panday.* The midwife was almost not reached [in time]. (*Thesaurus:* **agon mbal, apit, arāk**)

**himanta'u** var. of **hinabta'u**

**himangkan** (var. **imangkan**; **mahingkan**) *v. tr.* To have knowledge or experience of some thing. *Halam tahimangkan kami ai ka at'kka, ai ka halam. Sali' mbal kinata'uhanan.* We had no knowledge as to whether [they were] arriving or not. It just wasn't known. *Kinakan ya halam bay taimangkan e' kamatto'ahanbi.* Food that your forebears never experienced. (*Thesaurus:* **alab-alab, ingat, pamapatahan, panghati, ta'u₁ 1**)

**himangot** *n.* **1)** Tweezers made of metal or bamboo. **1.1)** *v. tr. -an* To remove facial hair by plucking. *Angamu' aku basi' paghimangotku bū-langalku.* I'll request a bit of metal for plucking out my beard. *Angahimangotan iya p'ngngotna.* He plucks out his whiskers. (*Thesaurus:* **bagoggol 1.1, bagong₂, p'ngngot 1.2, s'ssol₁, soso'**)

**himāt** *v. intr. aN-* To become floppy or limp. *Bay aku an'bba ni Bakal maka'ā' gamat, sakali maglūng-lūngan ma deyom mohang, angahimāt.* I was collecting strand food at Bakal and had got some *gamat* trepang, which sloshed around inside the hull, all floppy. *Angahimāt na baranna, hal bohe' tasungi'na.* His body has become limp now, all he excretes is water. (*Thesaurus:* **hoyon, sampoyan**)

**himāt pangatayan** *n. phrase* Soul-deep despair. {idiom} *Angahimāt sala pangatayanku pagka halam aniya' pangasa.* I was in a kind of deep despair because there was no hope.

**himati'** (derivative of **bati'₁**) *v. intr. aN-* To feel the movement of a child in the womb; to have contractions prior to birth. *Angahimati' kahaba' sangpū' minit.* Having contractions every ten minutes. (*Thesaurus:* **b'ttong₂ 1, buka'-puhu', iram**).

**himatta'** *v. advrs. ka-...-an* To be shocked to the point of incredulity, as by some terrible news. *Aniya' sehe' agsuli-suli, na manjari wa'i na amole' dangan. Na buwat taluwa' l'tte, amatay. Na kahimatta'an bang kahaka'an.* Some companions were talking and one left for home. Then [one] was struck by lightning and died. Then those who were told about it were shocked. *Kahimatta'an, sali' aniya' makanipikilanta, b'nnal maka ngga'i ka.* Shocked, like when something comes into our minds, whether true or false. (*Thesaurus:* **k'bbal, kobla', kuddat, leyang atay**)

**himāy** *adj. a-* Slightly damp, as clothes hung out to dry. *Ahimāy, ma llot abase' maka atoho'. Sōng atoho'. Himāy* is between wet and dry. Nearly dry. *Sali' s'mmek pina'llawan, yukta, "Nda'un ilū bang ahimāy na, atawa atoho'."* Like when clothes are put out to dry in the sun, we say, "See if they are still a bit wet, or dry." (*Thesaurus:* **base'₁, bugbug₁, bugga' 1, gamos 1, hami'-hami', tomog**)

**himbulas** var. of **himulas**

**himoway** *v. tr. -an* To criticize or belittle someone. (*Thesaurus:* **pastul, poway-poway, sā'₁ 1.3, salba₁, salla'₁ 1.2, salu'-salu', soway**)

**himpit** *adj. a-* Attractive and in good taste; elegant. *Ahimpit tapi'an pelang, mbal na agon kabalikan.* The planking of the canoe is beautiful, it can hardly be repeated. (*Thesaurus:* **alti, dorog₂ 1.1, hansam, hāp baran, jalang₁, lingkat 1.1, manis 1.1, polma 1.1**)

**himpun** see: **paghimpun, palhimpunan**

**himuggu'** *v. tr. -an* To be jealous of something. *Ai pangahimuggu'annu?* What are you jealous of? (*Thesaurus:* **abuggu', iggil 1.1, imbū, jelus, jingki 1, lindi 1**)

**himul-himul** see: **kahimul-himulan**

**himulas** (var. **himbulas**) *n.* Vulgar or insulting things said as a challenge. (*cf:* **bulas**₁, **tukas 1.1**)

**pahimulas** *v. tr.* To accuse someone of cowardice.

**himumu'** var. of **hamumu'**

**himumūngan** (derivative of **mūng**) *n.* Significant things said in order to provoke a response. *Bay ai-ai himumūngan, bay sala magbono', bay diki'-diki' ati paluha. Bay yuk dangan, "Paddamunbi."* Various provocative things had been said, there had been a kind of fight, something initially small had spread more widely. Someone said, "Keep it to yourselves." *Kōk-ero' bahā' aku itū ya angkan buwattilu himumungannu!* Am I a dog's head that you should speak in such a provocative way? (*Thesaurus:* **kabtangan**; *syn:* **hilala'ungan**).

**himutud** (derivative of **butud**) *v. intr. aN-* To become distended, as a corpse.

**himuya** *v. intr. aN-* **1)** To stir in one's sleep, as someone about to waken. *Angahimuya sadja sigā.* They are just stirring in their sleep. *Sali' ap'ddi' mange'ta atawa tai'ta, angahimuya kita.* Like when our bladder or our bowel is overfull, we become wakeful. **1.1)** *v. tr. -an* To disturb someone who is resting or sleeping. *Nihimuya'an kita, bang sali' ap'ddi' mange'ta.* We are woken from sleep, like when we have a painful need to urinate.

**hinabta'u** (var.**himanta'u**) (derivative of **ta'u**₁) *n.* Knowledge or awareness of something. *Halam aniya' hinabta'uku abilahi'an aku d'nda.* I had no idea I was in love with some girl. *Nsa' himanta'uku niakkalan aku he' a'a inān.* I was not aware that I was being cheated by that fellow. *Halam aniya' himanta'uku bang ilu-i. (Hatina mbal kasakupan.)* I have no knowledge if that is so. (In other words it's not clearly known.) (*cf:* **pangita'u**).

**hinabu** var. of **sinabu**

**hina'** *v. tr.* To insult or shame. *Nihina' aku, pinagtunggangkīng.* I am shamed, made a mockery of. *A'a Hibrani bay pinapi'itu angahina' kitam.* A Hebrew person sent here to insult us.

**pangahina'** *n.* An insulting act.

**hinanib** (derivative of **anib**) *n.***1)** Weapons carried for defense or attack. *Bang kita pal'ngngan kaleya subay aniya' hinanibta, pakokosta.* When we travel inland we should have something for defence, we should carry a weapon. (*Thesaurus:* **almas**, **pakokos**, **pangatu**, **takos** 1).**1.1)** *v. intr. aN-* To wear a weapon for defense. *Sōng angahinanib mundu pi'itu.* Bandits are coming this way, armed.

**hinansong** *n.* **1)** Breath. *Amahāp hinansong kami.* Getting our breath back. *Pasimay napasta, sali' apōng hinansongta.* Our breathing stops, it's as though our breath is broken. (*syn:* **napas**) **1.1)** *v. intr. aN-* To take a breath. *An'gga b'ttongna, a'sso he' kinakan, mbal makahinansong sala, subay*

*kinallusan maka luwag, sinungi'an ni lowang.* His stomach is gorged, full of food, kind of unable to breathe, [the mass] having to be pressed hard with a ladle and excreted down a hole.

**paghinansong** *v. intr. aN-* To be breathing. *Mbal maghinansong bang kami amatay.* We do not breathe when we die.

**hinang**₁ *n.* **1)** Work; activity; what one is doing. *Aniya' hinangku.* I have work [to do]. **1.1)** *v. intr. pa-* To be able to be used as or made into. *Luma' kubu'-kubu', mbal pahinang duwa bilik.* A kubu'-kubu' house, it won't make two rooms. **1.2)** *v. tr.* To build, do or make something. *Bang kita angali'is panggi' kayu, bo' kita am'gga' bohe'na, tahinang hali, binugbug.* When we grate cassava and squeeze out its liquid, it is made into a starchy residue and cooked as a porridge. *Angahinang kami luma' ma bowa'-angan.* We are building a house at the edge of the reef. *Bang aniya' mastalku pikihinang ōn mbal gi' aku ata'u.* When a teacher of mine asks me to do [my] name, I don't yet know how. *Bang aku amangan buwas bo' mbal ala'an, tahinang tangkekel.* If I eat rice and [grains of it] aren't removed, they become cysts. *Ginuna e'na sīn itū panamba saga a'a bula'ug tahinang tendogna.* He used this money to pay some bullies to become his workers. **1.3)** *v. tr. a-, ka-..-an, -an* To produce something through regular work routines. *Aniya' kinahinangan inān magabut-abut, bo' dakayu' maka dakayu'.* There were things being produced there, repeatedly, one thing after another.

**kahinangan** *n.* Things done by habit or practice; activities characteristic of an individual. *Akalap lagi' la'at sigām min bay kahinangan kamatto'ahan sigām.* Their wrongdoing is worse than what their forebears used to do.

**hinangan** *n.* A style of doing or making something. *Papi'ituhun si Arung angaddunan aku tinapay ahāp, bo' aku makakakan min hinanganna.* Have Older Sister come to mix some good bread for me, so I may eat from her style of making it. *Hinangan Jipun.* Of Japanese manufacture.

**paghinang**₁ *n.* **1)** Materials for building or making things. *Pagdayaw itū kayu paghinang luma': hāg, papan, hobong, kamemon ai-ai.* Pagdayaw includes timber for building a house: things such as posts, boards, crossbeams, everything. **1.1)** *v. intr. aN-* To make a living from building or making things. *Bang sakalina maghinang, maghinang to'ongan, agon mbal kasekotan.* When his commitment is to work he really works; can scarcely be approached. *Sakup iya, sakup iya am'ssi kaut, anonda', amubu, maghinang ma deya.* He is well informed, knows all about fishing with hook and line, trolling, trap fishing, and about working ashore. **1.2)** *v. tr.* To make things out of basic materials. *Dirit-dirit pinaghinang taguri' he' saga onde'-onde'.* Leaf skeletons made into little kites by children. *Tiyup-tiyup pinaghinang min pilak atawa bulawan.* Wind instruments made from silver or gold.

**paghinang₂** *v. intr. aN-* To engage in sexual intercourse. {coarse}

**pagkahinangan** *v. intr. aN-* To behave in a particular way.

**pagpakahinang 1)** *v. tr.* To be capable of doing the stated action. **2)** *v. intr. aN-* To be able to be used.

**patihinangun** *adj.* Very hard-working.

**hinang₂** *n.* An activity or event involving supernatural beings.

**hinang-kalla'** *n.* The ceremonies carried out on the day of a burial, concluding with a meal eaten after the interment. *Bang ma kami hinang-kalla' bo' hinang t'llu.* For us it is the burial ceremony, and then the third-day ceremony. (*cf:* **tulun-tana'**)

**hinang-kalun** *n.* **1)** A ceremony of thanksgiving for one's livelihood. **1.1)** *v. intr. aN-* To carry out the kalun ceremony.

**paghinang-kalun** *v. intr. aN-* To engage in a thanksgiving ceremony for the supply of natural resources.

**hinang-hinang₁** *v. tr.* To influence or affect someone by means of witchcraft. *Nihinang-hinang kita, ata'u du a'a mangahinang-hinang-i. Yukta, "Tinubu a'a hē'."* We are harmed by witchcraft. The person doing the witchcraft is very experienced. We say, "That person has inherited powers." (*Thesaurus:* **duti, hikmat, h'lling₃, palkata'an, pantak 1.1, sihil 1.1**)

**hinang-mbo'** *n.* Ceremonies involving ritual ancestors.

**hinang-pitu'** *n.* The seventh-day ceremony of the funerary series.

**hinang-tapus** *n.* The final ceremony of the funerary series.

**hinang-t'llu** *n.* The third-day ceremony of the funerary series, the day after the burial.

**paghinang-bulan** *n.* **1)** A religious ceremony celebrating the appearance of the new moon, especially significant at the beginning of Ramadan. **1.1)** *v. intr. aN-* To be engaged in a religious ceremony involving the new moon. *Bang maghinang-bulan, aheka maghinang sinuwan-suwan.* When we are involved in the new moon ceremonies a lot of people cook soya sauce recipes.

**paghinang-maut 1)** *n.* A ceremony to appease the death spirit. *Pagt'kkata ni luma', asaki kita duwa-t'llu ng'llaw. Bang maghinang-maut mbal na.* On arriving home we are sick for two or three days. If we appease the *maut* spirit, [the sickness] is no more. **2)** *v. tr.* To placate a maut spirit with the appropriate ceremony. *Saitan maut amapatay bang mbal nihinang.* A maut spirit will kill if it is not placated with the ceremony. *Sali' bang maghinang maut, ya niā' he' imam niōnan*

*tulahan.* When for example someone performs the *maut* ceremony, the imam's payment is called *tulahan.*

**paghinang₃** *n.* **1)** A religious ceremony. **1.1)** *v. intr. aN-* To be engaged in a ceremony involving a supernatural being (e.g. God, a ritual ancestor, or a saitan spirit). *Magpole'an na sigām maghinang bulan.* They are all going home to carry out the new moon ceremony.

**paghinangan** *n.* A place where religious activities are conducted. *Buwat saupama mareyom paghinangan bo' akatis na, niā' dakayu' panyām, saga t'llu saging min dakayu' dulang. Nilatag na dulang.* In a place for example where a ceremony has been held and is concluded, one rice cake is taken, three bananas or so, from a single food tray. The tray is passed around.

**hinang-hinang₂** (var. **pahinang**) *v. tr.* To do something as a pretense. *Ai kono' makap'ddi' kōkna? Hal pinahinang e'na.* What has given her a headache? She is just pretending. *Hal hinang-hinangnu bissala ilū.* You are just making that statement up. *A: "Bang aniya' daing ahūg ni lantay, mbal kinakan e'na." B: "Angay buwattē'?" A: "Tu'ud pinahinang-hinang."* A: "When some fish falls onto the floor, he won't eat it." B: "Why's that?" A: "Just done deliberately." *Pahali ka. Hal pinahinang tangisnu.* Stop it. Your crying is just pretended. (*Thesaurus:* **pagbau'-bau', pagdō-rō, paglaku-laku, pagnaho'-naho'**)

**hinapusan** *n.* The last item in a series. *Hinapusan, ya karamulihan kita kat'llu, aku itū kahinapusan, karamulihan to'ongan.* Last in line, the final one of us three, I am the last one, the very last. (*cf:* **tapus 1**)

**paghinapusan** *v. intr. aN-* To be at the last item in a series. *Aku ya maghinapusan ma kami magdauranakan.* I am the last [surviving] of us siblings.

**kahinapusan** *n.* The final item in a series.

**hinasang** var. of **sasang**

**hinasil** *n.* The four basic elements of which all things are made, and to which a body returns after burial. *Mpat hinasil ya palnyawahan itū. Bang mbal ap'nno' deyom sumsumanta, na maganu-anu.* Four elements [make up] our spiritual components. If our marrows are not filled [with them] something or other will happen.

**hinay-hinay** *v. intr. pa-* To act without haste. (*Thesaurus:* **aggal 1, kaku', lahan 1, lallay, pagene'-ene'**)

**hinbaya'** (derivative of **baya'**) *adj. a-* Longing to have something.

**hinit** *adj. a-* **1)** Elastic; stretchable. *Nihinit goma, ahinit asāl.* Rubber bands are stretched, they are naturally stretchable. (*cf:* **kontay₁**) **1.1)** *v. tr.* To stretch something.

**hinti'** *n.* **1)** A confection of grated coconut fried with sugar. *Bang aniya' pullu' niragangan ma* *tabu' Hambilan, b'llihin aku ya taga hinti' deyomna.* If cassava meal cakes are being sold at the Hambilan market, buy me those that have *hinti'* inside. (*Thesaurus:* **bukayu' 1, halluwa 1, hinuwal 1**) **1.1)** *v. tr.* To make coconut candy. **1.2)** *v. tr.* **-an** To add coconut candy to cooked foods.

**hinu-hinu₁** *n.* Light blue color; turquoise. (*gen:* **walna'**)

　**paghinu-hinu** *v. intr.* **aN-** To display iridescence. *Maghinu-hinu buwat kulit kanu'us.* It is iridescent like the skin of a squid.

**hinu-hinu₂** *n.* A dark-skinned variety of cassava. *Tibu'uk hinu-hinu, ya sali' ettom kulitna.* The *hinu-hinu* variety of non-toxic cassava, the one that has blackish skin.

**hinugun** var. of **saging-hinugun**

**hinuwal** (derivative of **huwal**) *n.* **1)** A confection of sugared coconut. (*Thesaurus:* **bukayu' 1, halluwa 1, hinti' 1**). **2)** Cursing equivalent for food offered in sarcasm or anger. *Ā, ngā'un na hinuwalnu.* Here. Take your precious food!

**hīng 1)** *adj.* **a-** Aware of something through sight or sound. *Da'a ka ahīng ma lingkatna.* Do not be drawn by her beauty. *Ahīng talingaku.* My ears are open to hear. **2)** *v. intr.* **aN-** To be aware of what is going on around one. *Bang aku ma deyom iskul sidda aku angahīng ma klasmetku bang aniya' d'nda budjang-budjang.* When I am in school I am very aware of my classmates when one of them is coming into her teens.

　**hīng-hīng** *v. intr.* **pa-** To turn the head in order to hear or see better. *Pahīng-hīng kita ang'nda', atawa pahīng-hīng kita akale. Pinahīng-hīng talingata.* We turn to look, or turn to hear, our ears turned towards something. (*Thesaurus:* **bahingaw, kale 1, talengog**)

**hingas** var. of **lingas₁**

**hingbū** var. of **imbū**

**hinggam** *see:* **pahinggaman**

**hirang** *see:* **paghirang**

**hirayat** *n.* Good fortune from a higher source; divine favor. *Bay kami magsassay ni kubul, halam aniya' hirayat.* We sought help at the grave, but got no favorable result. *Aniya' hirayat he' Tuhan ma ka'a. Hatina bay ka asaki sagwā' halam pinapatay he' Tuhan.* You have a favor from God. In other words you were sick but God did not let you die. (*Thesaurus:* **anughala' 1, apuwa, barakat 1, lidjiki' 1, pahala'**)

**hiritan** *n.* The throttle of an engine.

**hirup₁** (var. **irup**) *v. tr.* To take notice of advice given or something overheard. *A'a iya subay pinalok bang magsuli-suli. Nihirup, niasip iya.* He is a person who should be shown respect when talking with him. Heeded, paid attention to. *Bang aniya' bissala ala'at da'a kam angirup.* When there is bad language don't take any notice. *Da'a sinō' to'ongan ni'irup. Da'a kalehin, ala'an ka.* Told firmly not to take any notice. Don't

listen to it, just go away. (*Thesaurus:* **asip, beya'-beya'₁ 1.1, ikut**)

**hirup₂** *see:* **kahirupan**

**hīs** (var. **hūs₂**) *v. tr.* **1)** To smooth with a sweeping motion. *Ai-ai agomot subay hūsta.* We should smooth [with the hands] whatever is crumpled. *Hūsun sīn ilū kamemon.* Rake together all that money [the winnings]. **1.1)** *v. tr.* **-an** To move loose items with a sweeping motion; to rake off the surplus grain on a measure. *Na aheka makapamūng pagga sīn kami nihīs. Tak'llo' sadja. Mbal pinole'an kasehe'an.* A lot of people commented since it was our money that was raked in. Just taken, the balance not returned. *Hūsin paluwas supaya alanu'.* Sweep it out so it will be clean. (*Thesaurus:* **kahig, kās, kikis**)

**hīs-da'ug** *n.* A call in playing coin games, betting on a heads-up fall of two coins.

**hīs-daya'** *n.* A call in coin games, betting on a tails-up fall of the two coins.

**hisi'** *v. intr.* **aN-** To show a gleam of white, as a wave crest or teeth. *Bowa' goyak angahisi' sadja, apote'.* The crest of the wave is gleaming white.

**hisu'** *v. tr.* To relieve joint pains by reciting a charm. *Bang aniya' apisu' baranna subay nihisu' e' a'a ata'u anilik.* If someone has pain in his joints he should be treated with a *hisu'* charm by someone skilled in healing charms. (*cf:* **pisu'**; *Thesaurus:* **tawal 1.1, tilik**)

**hitad** *see:* **paghitad**

**hita'** *n.* **1)** The groin and its joints. **2)** To treat pains in the thigh area by reciting a charm. **2.1)** *v. tr.* To pinch flesh on the inside of the thigh. (*Thesaurus:* **kinbing, k'bbit**)

**hiyak** *v. tr.* To thrust a spear or spike into something. *Sahapang pangahiyak daing, tayum, sangkil ya pangahiyak pahi. Na bang a'a ala'at, hiyakku maka budjak.* A three-tined spear is used to spear fish and sea urchins, it's a single-pronged spear that is used to spear stingrays. Now if there is a bad person, I drive a fighting spear into him. (*Thesaurus:* **tagbak₁**)

**hiyu** *n.* Incense in the form of a stick. *Hiyu itū buwat heya koyang sasapu. Ahamut bang sinū'an.* Incense sticks are about as big as a the bristles of a broom. They are fragrant when ignited. *Buwat saki nirampal, tinangas maka kamanyan atawa hiyu.* When someone has measles he is treated with the fumes of solid incense or a joss stick. (*Thesaurus:* **kamanyan, laksi'**)

**hiyul** *adj.* **a-** Rushing about excitedly, of a group of people. *Buwat aniya' magbono' ma deyom tabu'. Inggay ahiyul?* Like there is fighting in the market. Wouldn't that be *hiyul*? *Saga a'a paluruk ni pagtenesan, yuk-i, "Ōy, da'a kām ahiyul."* People gathering where the *tenes* singing is, and [someone] saying, "Hey, don't get excited." (*Thesaurus:* **balu', dongkag, halubilu, hengo-hengo, hiluhala' 1.1, jabu 1, lengog 1.1, sasaw 1.1, sensong**)

**hiyup** *v. tr.* To ingest a liquid by slurping its surface. (*Thesaurus:* **h'llop 1.1, h'llop 1.1, horot, huttut**)

**paghiyup** *v. tr.* To slurp up hot liquids. *Saga loho' ya pinaghiyup, basta ai-ai apasu'.* It's soups that are normally slurped up, anything hot.

**h'bba'** (var. **habba'**) *v. intr. a-* To collapse, of a structure. *Bang aku angampas subay balehanku bo' mbal ah'bba', apa alandos s'llog.* When I fish using a fence trap I have to support it with stakes so it doesn't fall, because the current is strong. *Bang alandos badju ah'bba' luma'.* When typhoon winds are strong, houses collapse. *Ah'bba' bu'unna kasehe'an, an'ngge kasehe'an.* Some of his hair has fallen over, some is standing up. (*Thesaurus:* **hantak₁ 1, ligad, lintuwad 1, l'bbos 1, pungkad, timpuwad 1**)

**h'bbol** *adj. a-* Wobbly like a jelly. *Tana' ina'an (gusung bangkaw), sidda ah'bbol bang pal'ngnganan.* That ground (mangrove sand), is very unstable when walked over. *Magh'bbol-h'bbol utukta, subay pinikit-pikit.* When our brains are quivering we need to have a plaster stuck on.

**h'bbong** *adj. a-* Squeezed out of shape or alignment. *Buwat tinapay nsa' isina min t'ngnga', na niōnan pah'bbong.* Like a loaf of bread that has nothing in the middle, well that is called *h'bbong*. (*Thesaurus:* **k'mmog 1, k'ppi'₂, kummi', logpok 1**)

**h'kka** *n.* 1) A span, the distance between the tip of a thumb and a middle finger. (*cf:* **d'ppa 1**; *Thesaurus:* **bunag, pāt 2, sa'ang₂**) 1.1) *v. tr.* To measure a distance in spans.

**h'ddok** (var. **harok**) *v. intr. pa-* To fall silent. *Buwat aniya' magsuli-suli, makasekot pa'in aku pina'an, na mag'bba na. Pah'ddok magtūy.* Like when people are talking, when I get close they all stop. They immediately fall quiet. (*cf:* **hali₃**; *Thesaurus:* **k'nna, h'nnok, tepok**)

**h'ggom** (var. **ggom**) *v. intr. pa-* 1) To soak in a liquid. *Itiya' si Arung pah'ggom ma tahik.* Here's Eldest Daughter immersed in the sea. 1.1) *v. tr. -an* To immerse something in a liquid, as when softening or curing it. *Ggomin tōng pinsil ni īng.* Soak the end of the pencil in the ink. (*Thesaurus:* **k'mbang 1.1, hagom 1.1, t'nde 1.1**)

**pagh'ggom** *v. tr. -an* To dip something in and out of a liquid.

**h'lla** (var. **lla**) *n.* A husband. *Aho', kalasahanku h'llaku.* Yes, I love my husband. (*cf:* **h'nda, paghola'**)

**pagh'lla** *v. tr. -an* To take a man as one's husband. *Bang pa'in kam isab nirūlan e'na makapagh'lla, maka kaniya'an kam kahāpan ma deyoman sigām.* May he favor you with getting a husband and be provided with good things in their society. *Pagtiman kami pinat'nna'an kami hād. Ma deyom duwambulan subay da'a kita*

*magh'lla, magh'nda ni saddī.* On being divorced a restriction was laid on us. We were not to marry another man or woman for two months.

**pah'lla** 1) *v. tr.* To take someone to be one's husband. 2) *v. tr. -an* To provide someone with a husband.

**h'lling₁** (var. **lling**) *n.* 1) Something heard or said; birdsong; noise in general. 1.1) *v. intr. a-* To produce a sound; to speak or utter. *Ah'lling sultan, yukna, "Abunnawas, sinokat ka angungsud dakayu' luma' bulawan."* The sultan spoke and said, "Abunnawas, you are required to provide one gold house as bride-price." *Ah'lling ka min t'dda, ati suntukta ka.* Speak just once and I will punch you. (*Thesaurus:* **bahasa₁, bā'₁, batbat₂, bissala 1.1, k'bbat₁ 1, pagmūng-mūng 1.1, sambat, yuk**) 2) The distinctive speech or dialect of a community. 2.1) An individual's manner or style of speaking a language. *Ya hē' niangut, lling Sama. Halam makaliyu ni saddī.* That's what he really desires, the Sinama language. He hasn't switched to anything else. (*Thesaurus:* **lagam, suwala 1**)

**h'lling-k'llong** *n.* An involuntary sound such as snoring or wheezing.

**h'lling-h'lling** *adj. a-* Talkative. *Ahatul iya itu, mbal ah'lling-lling.* He is very well-behaved and doesn't answer back.

**pagh'lling** *v. intr. aN-* To speak a language; to make a noise repeatedly or continually. *Ag'lling daggahana.* His chest makes a noise. *Buwat Sama Lipid magh'lling Sama, bo' magbagi'ad maka lling Sama. Magdambila'an, sali' maglamud-lamugay.* Like land-oriented Sama speaking Sama and including non-native words with the Sama words. It's hybridized, sort of mixed up.

**pag'lling-lling** *v. intr. aN-* To be talking continuously or irrationally. *Binelaw a'a mag'lling-lling ina'an.* That guy who is talking wildly and incessantly is crazy. *Ni'mmaw, sali' a'a bay asaki mag'lling-lling.* Fussing, like someone talking and talking after being sick.

**pah'lling₁** *v. tr.* To cause something to make a sound, as by playing a musical instrument or a recording.

**pah'lling₂** *v. tr. -an* To speak to or about someone, generally with the connotation of scolding. (*Thesaurus:* **dugal 1.1, pabukag, pamūng-mūng, pugpug 1, s'ndal 1, tutul**)

**h'lling₂** *v. tr. a-, ka-...-an, -an* 1) To detonate or explode, especially of the dynamite used to kill fish. *Bang aniya' animbak bo' ah'lling ma diyata', ya amalutan timbak inān amatay.* If people are dynamiting and it explodes above water, the one holding the dynamite dies. *Bang tumakbil ni timbak kulitis aheka apalsu. Angkan mbal ah'lling apugtul sumbuhanna.* With regard to firecrackers, many are faulty. The reason they don't explode is that the wick is broken off. 1.1) *v. advrs. ka-...-an* To be affected by an explosion. *Kah'llingan* *sigām timbak ma diyata'.* They were affected by an above-water explosion.

**h'lling**₃ (var. **lling**) *v. tr. -an* To influence someone by magical means. *Ni'llingan kita, pinat'nna'an hikmat.* We are targeted with a charm, a spell laid on us. (*Thesaurus:* **duti, hikmat, hinang-hinang**₁, **palkata'an, pantak 1.1, sihil 1.1**)

**pah'lling**₃ *v. tr. -an* To cast a spell on someone in order to influence him or her to behave in a desired way.

**h'llop** *v. intr. pa-* **1)** To slip down into a cavity such as nose or throat. *Hē' na olen pah'llop ni deyom ūngna.* A marble has slipped right into his nose. *Aheka bohe' mariyata' karut. Pagbabas ulan, na pasobsob na, pah'llop pareyom.* There is a lot of water on the sacks. When the rain ceases, it will soak in, right inside. **1.1)** *v. tr.* To ingest something by sucking; to inhale smoke. *Tah'llop sigā he' s'llog alandos. Aniya' isāb tah'llop he' kaitan.* Sucked down by a powerful current. There are also some sucked down by a shark. *Buwat pelang nih'llop pareyo' he' maut, mbal nih'llop he' saddi. Pinatuwa' kita bo' halam na maina'an ba'anan sakapta.* Like a *pelang*-type canoe drawn down by a death-spirit, drawn down by nothing less. We are allowed to reappear but none of our equipment is there. (*Thesaurus:* **hiyup, hiyup, horot, huttut**) **1.2)** *v. tr. -an* To draw something in by the motion of water, as in a whirlpool. *Bang pa'in ka nih'llopan!* May you be drawn down [by a whirlpool]!

**h'mmel** *adj. a-* Flabby, from the loss of flesh or tissue. *Sali' ak'llos, buwat bola ma llot abustak maka mbal.* It's like losing bulk through drying, like a ball midway between bursting and not quite. *Ah'mmel to'ongan, palabay na tahakna.* It's completely soft, its ripeness is past. (*Thesaurus:* **dutay, lunuk 1.1**)

**h'mmok** *v. intr. pa-* To collapse under external pressure. *Buwat sali' tilam inān, pag'nda'ta ahāp, paglege ah'mmok.* Like that mattress, it's fine when we look at it, but when lying on it, it goes flat. *Da'a ka pagi'ik mailu, pah'mmok papan apōng.* Don't step there, the board will give way and break.

**h'nda** (var. **nda**) *n.* A wife. *Itu bay sinulat insini' he' ndaku.* This was written earlier by my wife. (*cf:* **h'lla, paghola'**)

**h'nda-h'nda** *n.* A minor wife; a concubine. (*syn:* **h'nda-tape'**)

**h'nda-po'on** *n.* The first and senior wife in a polygamous household.

**h'nda-tape'** *n.* A minor wife; a concubine. *T'llu hatus isāb heka'na h'ndana tape'.* He also had three hundred minor wives. (*syn:* **h'nda-h'nda**)

**pagh'nda** *v. tr. -an* To take a woman as one's wife. *Angay gi' ka subay magh'nda'an bangsa ina'an-i, bangsa kapil lagi'?* Why should you take a person of that ethnic group as wife, a pagan

what's more? *Pagtiman kami pinat'nna'an kami hād. Ma deyom duwambulan subay da'a kita magh'lla, magh'nda ni saddi.* On being divorced a restriction was laid on us. We were not to marry another man or woman for two months. *Magh'nda na kita.* Let's get married. *Mag'nda aku ma lahatbi.* I will get a wife in your country.

**pagpah'nda** *n.* **1)** The process of providing a man with a wife. (*Thesaurus:* **pagtunggu'-tunang, tagad-kawin**) **1.1)** *v. intr. aN-* To be involved in getting a wife for a man.

**pah'nda 1)** *v. tr.* To take someone to be one's wife. **2)** *v. tr. -an* To provide someone with a wife.

**h'nnat** *v. intr. pa-* **1)** To stretch one's body or limbs, as on awaking. (*cf:* **hangtad**; *Thesaurus:* **l'dduk 1, nned, pagkul'ddeng, paghitad, pagle'od**) **1.1)** *v. tr.* To manipulate one's hands or limbs. *Bang ariki'-diki' onde' nih'nnat tanganna bo' aheya alantik.* When the child is small we stretch her hands so that when big they will curve fully [for dancing].

**paghin'nnat** *v. intr. aN-* To sit (on a mat) with legs stretched out in front.

**h'nnok** (var. **henok**) *v. intr. pa-* To become silent in contrast to talking. (*Thesaurus:* **k'nna, h'ddok, tepok**)

**h'ngka-h'ngka** *see:* **pagh'ngka-h'ngka**

**h'nggol** *v. tr.* To partition an area.

**h'ngngek-h'ngngek** *see:* **pagh'ngngek-h'ngngek**

**h'ttad** var. of **hangtad**

**hōb-hōb** *v. advrs. -in-* Caused to tremble or shake, as by fever. *Bay amandi si Jy, nihaggut baranna, nihōb-hōb.* Jy bathed, his body became cold and his body shook. (*Thesaurus:* **hadjat**₂, **l'mmun, tandog 1, tatat**)

**hoben** *adj. zero* Youthful. (*Thesaurus:* **bata', lumbu'-baha'u, onde'-baha'u**)

**hoblas** *v. intr. pa-* **1)** To ease up or improve temporarily. *Minsan halam pahali, ala'an tandog, pabalik salung. Pahoblas bay pasu'ta.* Even though it isn't cured, the fever leaves but comes back the next day. Our former temperature eases for a while. *Lum'ngngan na kitā, pahoblas na ulan, aniya' ganta' palabayanta.* We are walking, the rain eases for a bit, as though we might have a way through. *Pahoblas bay pasu'ta. Minsan halam pahali, ala'an tandog. Pabalik salung.* Our fever eases for a while. Though not cured, the shakes are gone. Back again tomorrow. (*cf:* **hoka'**; *Thesaurus:* **gām-gām, hāp-hāp, hikay, lōng-lōng, siha'-siha', si'at**) **1.1)** *v. advrs. ka-...-an* To be experiencing improvement in the symptoms of an illness. *Buwat kita bay tinandog, kahoblasan kita.* Like when we had a fever and experienced some improvement.

**hobong** *n.* The crossbeams connecting house posts at the top of a wall. *Babag ina'an, ya to'od ōnna hobong.* The cross-beam there, its name is in fact *hobong. Bang kita atuli ma deyo' hobong atawa*

*ma hāg, maumu pinag'ddop, maumu mbal.* When
we sleep beneath the crossbeam or by the
house-post, we sometimes have nightmares, and
sometimes don't. (*Thesaurus:* **babag 1, dagan₁,
salsal, taytayan tikus**)

**hoka'** *v. intr. pa-* To reduce the intensity of a
sequence of events. *Buwat aniya' magbono', mbal
katiyara'an, mbal sali' pahoka'.* Like people
fighting each other, unable to be controlled, not
easing up. (*cf:* **hoblas 1**)

**kahoka'an** *n.* A break in a long-running event.
*Buwat baliyu bo' ulan na pa'in. Yukta, "Angay
ulan itū halam aniya' kahoka'anna?"* Like when
there is wind but it keeps raining. We say, "Why
are there no breaks in this rain?" (*Thesaurus:*
**hondong 1**)

**hokas** *n.* Something given as recompense for the
services of an expert. *Ya hē' hokasna, dakayu'
badju'.* That's her remuneration, one blouse.
(*Thesaurus:* **bayad 1.1, gadji 1.1, lampak₁ 1.1,
susuk, tinga 1.1, tulahan, tunay₂, tungbas 1**)

**pahokas** *v. tr. -an* To remunerate someone for a
service done.

**hokkok** *v. tr. -an* To shake things in water in order
to remove suds or dirt. *Mbal ka? Hokkokanta na
ka.* You refuse? I'll dunk you. *Ka'a-i
pinaghokkokan! (Sali' pinaghantak-hantakan
mareyom tahik.)* You will be dunked repeatedly!
(Like being pushed down repeatedly in
seawater.) (*cf:* **kohek-kohek**)

**hodhod** (var. **godgod**) *v. tr.* To ask someone for
details. *Hodhorun to'ongan bang pila halga'na
ai-ai tab'lli e'na.* Find out for sure how much he
paid for everything. (*Thesaurus:* **kihaka, hati 2,
sisi 2, tilaw 1.1, tilosa 1.1**)

**paghodhod** *v. intr. aN-* To be in full agreement
on a deal. *Saupama bay kita magb'lli, bay
magsulut. Mbal manjari binawi'an bissala, mbal na
manjari agpapole'. Bay na maghodhod to'ongan
bissala ē'.* For example, we have been buying
and have come to an agreement. It is not
possible to go back on what has been said, not
possible to return [goods]. We were in full
agreement when we talked.

**hodjog** (var. **hodjo'**) **1)** *adj. a-* Shaky, unstable.
*Bang aniya' luma' halam ahogot, hāgna ahodjog.* If
a house is not firm, its posts are shaky.
(*Thesaurus:* **hengko, henggol 1, jogjog 1, oseg
1**) **2)** *v. tr.* To make something shake by
applying force.

**paghodjog-hodjog** *v. tr.* To jolt something,
making it unstable. *Pinaghodjog-hodjog pelang
ina'an. Bang ahūg man kalangan ina'an subay
magganti'.* That outrigger canoe is being
repeatedly jolted. If it falls from the drying rack
there, [you will] be obliged to make good the
damage.

**hodjo'** var. of **hodjog**

**hogal** *adj. a-* Falling apart, of a poorly tied knot or
the framing of a house. *Halam ahogot simbōngna,*

*ahogal.* Her hair knot is loose and will soon fall
apart. (*Thesaurus:* **bulangkayat, g'ppa', gubal,
lubu₂ 1, tunas 1**)

**hogga'** *v. intr. pa-* **1)** To stop doing what one was
doing. *Bay aku lahi-lahi, sakali bay aniya' ahūg
min aku. Pahogga' aku.* I was running when I
suddenly dropped something. I stopped. *Bang ka
ang'nda' ai-ai, da'a ka pahogga' tūy.* When you
see something or other, don't stop completely.
(*Thesaurus:* **hali₃, hondong 1, honglo' 1**) **1.1)**
*v. tr. -an* To stop someone or something.

**hogga'an** *n.* An interruption or pause in a series
of actions.

**paghogga'** *v. intr. aN-* To be speaking or singing
with repeated pauses. *Tamamang suwalata, ai-ai
pah'llingta maghogga'-hogga' kita. Buwat angalang
isāb, ya sali' maghogga'-hogga', ya amidpid bowa'.*
Our voices are uncertain, whatever we say is
produced in short bursts. Or like singing,
stopping repeatedly, mouth trembling.

**hogot** *adj. a-* Firm; secure. *Ahogot pahāp pangengkot
pelang itū. Bang ni'kkahan mbal pa'kka.* This
canoe is tied so securely. Though one unties it, it
will not come undone. *Mbal tabowa luma' inān
sabab hāg ya makahogot iya, hatina atatal he'
hāg.* That house won't be carried away because
the posts make it secure, meaning to say it is
made firm by posts. *Ginipis dinding bo' ahogot.*
The walling is battened so it is firm.

**hogot nyawa** *v. tr.* To cause someone to have a
brave heart. {idiom} *Tuwan Putli', pahogotun itū
nyawa kami.* Honored Putli', encourage these
hearts of ours.

**pahogot** *adv.* Firmly; securely.

**ho'on-ho'on** *v. tr.* To keep one's thought to
oneself. *Taho'on-ho'on ma deyom atayku, sali'
tinuhuma ma deyom atay.* My thoughts kept to
myself, like suspecting inwardly. (*syn:* **hōm-
hōm**)

**hola'** *see:* **paghola'**

**holat** *adj. a-* **1)** Hopeful; expectant. *Aholat na aku,
kab'llihan aku badju' salung.* I expect to have a
shirt bought for me tomorrow. *Beya' ni kamatay
sa' amasi allum, hal sali' pama'asa-asa. Sali' kita
pinaholat-holat.* Like dying but still alive, just
being somewhat hopeful. It's as though we have
been caused to expect something better.
(*Thesaurus:* **asa 1.1, kiri-kiri, lagad 1.1**) **1.1)**
*v. tr.* To expect something. *Pautangin minsan
halam aniya' bayad niholat. Paglūngnu du.* Give
him a loan even though no payment is expected.
He is your relative, really. *Buwattina'an halam
na tu'ud aniya' dapat-daya kami liyu min ka'am
magtai'-anak niholat.* At the present time we
have absolutely no financial resource to hope for
other than from you and the family. *Mbal gi'
taholat si Mu apa halam gi' at'kka man T'bba-Bās.*
Not yet expecting Mu because he hasn't arrived
yet from Bās shallows.

**kaholatan** *n.* A reason to be hopeful; expectation

of something good. *Bang bay allum masi si Ne, aniya' kaholatan, minsan dakuman diki'-diki'.* If Ne had been alive there would have been something to expect, however small.

**holat deyom atay** *adj. a-* Experiencing suppressed excitement. {idiom}

**holdap** *v. tr.* To hold someone up; to stop someone in order to rob them. *Agtūy kami niholdap. "Ma sai," yukna, "lansa." Yukku, "Ma hadji'."* We were promptly held up. "Whose launch is this?" he said. "It belongs to a *hadji*," I replied. (*Thesaurus:* **ambus, hapa'** 1.2, **ingu, sipi**₁ 1.1, **tipu** 1.1)

**holega** var. of **hulega**

**holemang** var. of **hulemang**

**holen** var. of **olen**

**hollo** *v. intr. pa-* To descend freely, as a person going down a ladder or getting down from a boat. *Pahollo ka min buli' ilū, pakapo' atawa patuhun.* Slip down from the stern there, wade or dive. *Hal pahollo bang atuhun.* Just going down freely when diving. (*Thesaurus:* **deyo'**₁ 1.1, **duwa'i**)

**hōm-hōm** *v. tr.* To keep an opinion to oneself. (*syn:* **ho'on-ho'on**)

**hompot** var. of **hongpot**

**hona'-hona'** *n.* The ability to think; to have something in mind. *Bang buwat a'a dupang, halam aniya' hona'-hona'na.* How it is with a foolish person, he has no capacity to think. (*Thesaurus:* **pikil** 1)

   **paghona'-hona'** 1) *v. intr. aN-* To give thought to a situation. *Maghona'-hona' sigām arakala' binalosan e' si Yusup ma pasalan bay tahinang sigām ma iya.* They thought Joseph would in all likelihood take revenge on them because of what they had done to him. 2) *v. tr. -an* To influence someone by reasoning. *Mbal kapaghona'-hona'an a'a itū.* This fellow can't be reasoned with. *Aku ya pinaghona'-hona'an na pa'in.* I am constantly the target of [someone's]thinking.

**hondong** *v. intr. pa-* 1) To stop or pause doing something. *Ulan, bay na pahondong.* The rain had already stopped. *Sigi-sigi angalaha'. Mbal pahondong laha'.* Bleeding continuously. The blood doesn't stop. (*Thesaurus:* **kahoka'an, hali**₃, **hogga'** 1, **honglo'** 1) 1.1) *v. tr. -an* To discontinue some action. *Yampa nihondongan he' ero', bay na takeket.* The dog had just given up [biting him], but he was already bitten. *Mbal kam nihondongan e' saga tendogku niapas sampay ni kasubuhan.* You will not be relieved of being pursued by my men until morning.

   **kahondongan** *n.* A place or time of resting from some activity. *Kahondonganna t'ngnga' lān.* The center of the road is where he stops.

**honel** *n.* A mouth organ (harmonica). (*cf:* **kula'ing**)

**honhon** *v. intr. pa-* To suffer from an abdominal disorder; to rupture internally. *Pahonhon kamemon pareyo' ni atag ponsotku.* Everything is pressing down to where my navel is. *Ya makahonhon ya ai-ai bowata mabuhat.* What causes a rupture is anything heavy that we carry. *Aroson kita ma paningkō'an, sali' pahonhon tina'ita.* We feel weighed down from sitting, as if our intestines had prolapsed. (*Thesaurus:* **doson** 1, **gadgad**₁, **lomeng-lomeng**)

**honga'**₁ *n.* The dividing nodes of bamboos; the section between the nodes. *Si Nneng Pagi-pagi inān, duwa honga' du p'ttung binowa he'na.* Stingray Maiden was carrying just two sections of large bamboo. *Akempot honga'na p'ttung inān.* The nodes of that bamboo are closely spaced. (*Thesaurus:* **bō', loka', saud**₁, **tumpung**)

**honga'**₂ *n.* The distance from chest to fingertips, equal to one half d'ppa (fathom). (*Thesaurus:* **batu**₃, **kilometēl, d'ppa** 1, **inses, maniku**)

**hongat** *v. intr. pa-* To pause in order to catch one's breath.

   **paghongat** *v. intr. aN-* To pause briefly. *Mbal maghongat ulan, sigi-sigi na pa'in.* The rain doesn't pause for a moment, just keeps on going.

   **paghongat-hongat** *v. intr. aN-* To breathe fitfully or shallowly. *Hal maghongat-hongat bang aniya' saki abangat. H'ngka-h'ngka, buwat a'a sinongot.* If someone has a serious illness he just breathes shallowly. Panting, like someone having an asthma attack. (*Thesaurus:* **hapus**₂, **lumu, paghangu-hangu, pagh'ngka-h'ngka, puha**)

**honglo'** *v. intr. pa-* 1) To pause in what one is saying. (*Thesaurus:* **hali**₃, **hogga'** 1, **hondong** 1) 1.1) *v. tr.* To interrupt what is being said or sung. *Honglo'-honglo'un tēp ilū.* Pause the tape-recorder there.

**honglo'an** *n.* A pause or gap in speech.

**hongpot** (var. **hompot**) *adj. a-* Well-behaved; demure; courteous. *Bang kita at'kka minningga-minningga, subay pahompot. Da'a kita magdai'-dai'.* Like when we arrive from some place or other, we should be courteous. Not in a hurry. *Ahongpot, mbal asabul, mbal patil'ngnganun, mbal amono' ma kasehe'an.* Exemplary, not behaving offensively, not wandering about, not fighting others. (*Thesaurus:* **addat** 1.1, **hatul**₂, **pantun** 1, **papat** 1, **p'mpon** 1, **saldik, saltun** 1)

**hōp**₁ 1) *v. intr. pa-/-um-* To go into a container. *Buwat pansulan inān ya panumpahanku bohe', wa'i pahōp pareyom.* Like that waterpipe into which I pour water, it goes straight into [the container]. 1.1) To enter one's mind. *Pahōpun ni deyom pikilannu.* Let it penetrate your mind. *Buwat duwangan bo' dangan amandu' ati dangan ē' pinandu'an, na bang pahōp na pandu' ni pikilan, yampa humōp ni utukna.* Like two people, one teaching and the other being taught. Then when the teaching has got into the thinking, it then enters his brain. *Buwat a'a pinandu'an, na bang pahōp na pandu' ni pikilan, yampa humōp ni* *utukna.* Like someone being taught, when the teaching gets into his thinking, only then does it enter his brain. **1.2)** To soak into fabric. **2)** *v. advrs.* ka-...-an To be possessed by a spirit being. *Sali' aniya' magkata-kata, na bang sōng-sōng na kahōpan, yuk-i, "Da'a na kam magolang-olang. Da'a gi' kam anasat apa ilu iya yampa kahōpan."* For example when an epic song is going on, when the person is about to be possessed, someone says, "Don't shout anymore. Don't make a disturbance yet because he is only just now being possessed." *Sali' yampa aniya' patongap ni iya. Bang kahōpan bā'nu tinundun buwahan.* Its as if something had only just entered him. When he is possessed you would have great pleasure. *Sali' aniya' a'a magkata-kata, na bang sōng-sōng na kahōpan, yuk-i, "Da'a na kam magolang-olang."* For example, someone is to sing the *kata-kata* epic, when he is about to be possessed, someone says, "Don't shout anymore." (*Thesaurus:* **sangon₂ 1, tongop₁ 1**)

**hōp baya'** *v. intr.* pa- To enter one's mind, of amorous desire. {idiom} *Pahōp baya' si Samson ma dakayu' d'nda, ōnna si Delila.* Samson fell in love with a woman, name of Delila.

**hōp₂** *v. advrs.* ka-...-an To be ecstatic with pleasure. *Kahōpan itu palabi min kinōgan. Kahōpan* is more than being happy. *Ka'amuhan aku, sali' kahōpan ang'nda' ma sini.* I am very pleased, thrilled to be watching a movie. (*syn:* **hūg bulan**)

**hopay** *adj.* a- To come to an end, of a bad weather event or a difficult stage in negotiations. *Ahopay na saga magbono', ahopay isāb goyak.* The fighting is over, the rough seas have abated. (*cf:* **tapus 1**)

**horot** *v. tr.* To take something into the mouth without chewing, or into the nose by inhaling. *Hal nihorot aeskrīm he' si Li.* Li just slurps up the ice cream. *Buwas ilū hal nihorot, sali' mbal pinapa'.* That rice is simply swallowed, kind of unchewed. (*Thesaurus:* **hiyup, h'llop 1.1, huttut**)

**hōs** (var. **ōs**) *n.* **1)** A sarong, the cloth tube worn as an informal, all-purpose garment. (*Thesaurus:* **manta 1, se'ob**) **1.1)** *adj.* a- To wear a sarong. *Tambolun lawang luma'nu bo' ka mbal nihaggut. Minsan ka mbal na ahōs mbal na ka nihaggut.* Close the windows of your house so you won't be cold. Even though you are no longer wearing a sarong you won't feel cold. **1.2)** *v. tr.* a-, ka-...-an, -an To clothe someone with a sarong. *Mbal makahōsan aku apa ariki'.* It will not serve me as a sarong because it is small. (*Thesaurus:* **hampi' 1.1, pagkīmbong, pagsina'ul, pindung, siyag 1.1**)

  **paghinōs** (var. **pagnihōs**) *v. tr.* To wear a sarong.

**hota** *see:* **paghota**

**hotad₁** *v. tr.* To remove wrinkles or kinks by ironing or placing under a weight. (*syn:* **kutad 1.2**)

**hotad₂** var. of **hotay**

**hotay** (var. **hotad₂**) *v. intr.* pa- To stretch out, of one's body; to take a rest by lying down. *Buwat kita mareyom maghinang, pahinotay, pahali.* Like when we are at work, lying stretched out, resting. *Ala'an ka m'nnilu, pahotay-hotayanku.* Move away from there, it's my place for having a lie-down. *Pahotad-hotad lagi' aku, pahali-hali.* I will just lie down, rest a bit. *Ap'ddi' tangkalku, subay aku pahotad.* My lower back is hurting, I should lie down full-length. (*cf:* **hali-hali**)

**hotel** *n.* A hotel or motel.

**howa'** var. of **owa'₁**

**hōy** var. of **ōy**

**hoyon** *adj.* a- Lacking muscular strength or tone as a result of exhaustion. *Sali' kita angahimāt. Mbal to'ongan makakole'. Ahoyon kita.* It's as if we have lost physical strength. Can do absolutely nothing. We are limp through exhaustion. (*Thesaurus:* **himāt, sampoyan**)

**hubad** *v. tr.* -an To untie a knot. *Mbal aku tōp minsan angahubaran engkot taumpa'na.* I am not fit even to untie the laces of his shoes. (*ant:* **engkot 1.1**; *Thesaurus:* **kka 1.1, latas₁, p'llus 1, puklas 1**)

**hubang-hubang** *see:* **paghubang-hubang**

**hubaya-hubaya** *intrj.* A call to be careful, thoughtful, diligent. *Buwat aniya' soho'ta am'lli buwahan. "Hubaya-hubaya, am'lli ka to'ongan."* Like when we send someone off to buy lansones. We say "Don't forget now, make sure you buy some." *Hubaya-hubaya, ebot-ebot, ma imamnu, pasampayun llingku itu ni iya.* Don't forget, it's for your imam, make sure my message gets to him. (*Thesaurus:* **amay-amay 1, kamaya', ebot-ebot 1.1**)

**hublut** *v. tr.* **1)** To pull something from where it was fastened or growing. *Ahublut na tunuk bay ma jantungku.* The thorn [emotional pain] was pulled out of my heart. (*Thesaurus:* **bubut, bugnus₂, darut 1.1, tugnus₁ 1**) **2)** To withdraw a weapon from its sheath or holster. *Nihublut lahut-lahut ina'an e' si Kulas. inān.* Kulas took out his little knife. *Na paghublut a'a ina'an, magtūy amatay kamemon.* Well when that man unsheathed [his weapon] they all promptly died.

**hukaw** (var. **huskaw; uskaw**) *n.* **1)** Aversion or deep dislike for something. *Ya hukawku pinagsaggaw-saggaw he' mastal. Wajib angiskul.* My deep dislike is for being rounded up by schoolteachers. We have to go to school. *Hukawku angiskul mbal na buwattē'.* My dislike of going to school is beyond reason. (*Thesaurus:* **lisu', takal**) **1.1)** *adj.* a-/-an Unwilling to do something. *Buwat aniya' bay maglakibini bo' halam du at'ggol pagpūn sigā, bo' sali' ahukaw d'nda. Min d'nda ya angalupit, ang'nde' alta'.* For example a married couple who haven't been together very long, and the woman is reluctant.

It's the woman's side who pay compensation, returning the valuables. *Atakal ka anulat, uskawan sali', alisu'.* You are averse to writing, you don't like doing it, you're lazy.

**kahukaw** *v. tr. -an* To resist being sexually intimate.

**pagkahukaw** (var. **pagkahuskaw**) *v. intr. aN-* To be mutually reluctant regarding sexual intimacy, of a married couple.

**hukud** var. of **sukud**₁

**hukum** *v. tr.* To pass a legal judgement on someone. *Bang a'a niampun e' Tuhan mbal nihukum, mbal pinapatay.* A man whom God has forgiven will not be judged, not put to death. *Si Ti maka si Ta bay magsaggaw. Sinara' na sigām nihukum.* Ti and Ta eloped. The verdict was that they should be judged. (*cf:* **sara' 1.1**)

**hukuman** *n.* A judgment; a verdict. *"Bang hukuman manusiya', mbal aku," yukna, "bilahi."* "If it is human judgment," he said, "I do not want it."

**hukuman kudjut** *n. phrase* A judgment made without discussion or appeal. {idiom} *Halam aniya' sakkina, amatay sadja. Yuk kami, hukuman kudjut.* There was no sickness. He just died. We call it summary judgment.

**paghukum** *n.* **1)** The act of judging; a judgement or ruling. *Anagna' na paghukum, bo' niukab na saga būk.* The judging has begun, and the books are being opened. **1.1)** *v. intr. aN-* To carry out the duties of a judge. *Subay abontol e'nu maghukum maka magmandul.* You should be upright in judgement and in administration. *Ya a'a paghukuman, ina'an bay gin'llal he' mayol.* The man who represents the law has been appointed by the Mayor. **1.2)** *v. tr. -an* To engage in a legal dispute. *Sali' maghukum maka a'a, bo' aku ya taga utang. Na sinukut aku, manjari halam aniya' pamayadku. Yuk dangan, ma'ase' ma aku, "Aku ya kuwiraw."* Like being in a legal dispute with someone, and I am the one with the debt. I am required to pay but I have nothing to pay with. Another person, feeling sorry for me, says, "I will go guarantor." *A: "Pasal ai?" B: "Pasal kami bay maghukum ni upis."* A: "About what?" B: "About us having gone to the town hall to get a legal ruling." *Kalongkopan sadja kami bang maghukum. Mbal kita maka'atu ma bissala atawa ma pamikil.* We always get the worst of it in a legal argument. We can't compete, in speech or thought. *Ē' maghukum si Du maka si Tri pasalan panau'na ma bangku.* Du and Tri have gone to court over his bank deposit. **1.3)** *v. intr. aN-* To refer a matter to an official entity for resolution. *Buwat kami bay maghukum ni mastal, mbal magkole'. Maglagadlad ni sara' M'ddas, ni Sūk.* Like us taking a dispute to the schoolmaster, but not achieving anything. The case goes on to the court in Siasi town, or to Jolo.

**maghuhukum** *n.* A judge; one who judges.

**huddud** (var. **haddad**) *v. intr. pa-* **1)** To spill or gush out through a narrow opening. *Bay pahuddud sīn kanat min bulsaku.* Loose coins spilled out of my pocket. *Pahaddad sali' tina'ita.* Our intestines sort of gush out. (*Thesaurus:* **bu'us 1**) **1.1)** *v. ditr.* To pour or tip something from one container to another. *Nihudduran, sali' tinumpahan ni pangisihan dakayu'. Subay tinutat sehe'na pi'ingga-pi'ingga.* Transferred by pouring, like being tipped into another container. Its accompanying word, wherever it is going, should be specified. *Nihudduran, sali' tinumpahan ni pangisihan dakayu'.* Transferred by pouring, like being tipped into another container. (*Thesaurus:* **hain, tumpa 1.1, tuwang, tuyung**)

**hudjag** *adj. a-* Divided up into separate parts. *Bay b'lliku ma kuri'an ma halam ahudjag.* I bought them by the dress-length before they were divided up.

**hudjat** *v. tr.* To liquify, as ice or congealed fat. (*Thesaurus:* **lanay**₂, **tadjul, tunaw 1**)

**hudjidjat** *n.* An individual's inherent qualities of mind and character. *Ahāp hudjidjatna, ataha' akkalna.* His personality is good, he is intelligent. *Aniya' mundu ma dambila' ina'na, aniya' du isāb tubu'na mundu. Ya ilu hudjidjatna.* There are outlaws on his mother's side, he has descendants too who are outlaws. That is his basic orientation. *Ya rū isāb bang jiniral, aniya' isāb hudjidjat tubu'na militari.* Like that too with a general, he has offspring whose natural inclination is the military. (*Thesaurus:* **kalakuhan, kasuddahan, jaguni', jari**₄ **1, jāt**₁**, sadsaran**)

**hūg**₁ (var. **hulug**) *v. intr. a-* **1)** To fall freely through space. *Hal ahūgan dīna.* Just falling of itself. (*cf:* **balabak**; *Thesaurus:* **pakpak 1, togge'**₁**, tukbung 1, tulelle, tumba**₁**) 1.1)** *v. tr.* To drop something. *Hūgun batu inān.* Drop that rock. *Hūgin aku bari'.* Drop me the knife. *Apug itū nihūg ni saitan, buwat ni duwata' ma a'a kasangonan inān.* The betel nut chew is dropped down to a spirit being such as the duwata of the man who has become possessed.

**hūg bulan** *v. advrs. ka-...-an* To be thrilled at good fortune; ecstatic. {idiom} *Kahūgan aku bulan, bay aku kab'llihan lilus he' si Mma'.* I am thrilled, Dad has bought a watch for me. (*syn:* **hōp**₂)

**paghūg** *v. intr. aN-* To drop fishing gear into the sea. *Bang kita makatuli' deyo' taga daing, al'kkas kita maka'ā'. Paghūg, pagsintak, paghella'.* When we find a depth that has fish we soon get some. Dropping [the hook], striking, pulling up [the fish].

**hūg**₂ *n.* **1)** The change from a financial transaction. *Wa'i alungay hūgna.* The change [from the purchase] is lost. **1.1)** *v. tr.* To hand over the change from a purchase. *Hūgin aku dambila' pilak.* Give me fifty centavos in change.

**hūg₃** *v. tr.* To place a bet. *Akosog bahanina, bang magsalla' angahūg saga duwampū', saga t'llumpū', saukat aheka sīn.* His daring is great, when he plays toss-the-coin he wagers ₱20 or ₱30, just because he has a lot of money.

**hūg ma'ana** (var. **hulug ma'ana**) *v. tr. -an* To explain the meaning of something said or written. {idiom} *Ata'u si Ma angahūgan ma'ana.* Ma knows how to give the meanings of words.

**hugiyap** var. of **ugihap**

**huhulmatan** (derivative of **hulmat**) *n.* A gift presented to a person of high rank. (*cf:* **tanggap 1**).

**hula-layag** *adj. a-* 1) Widely known. *Ahula-layag ni a'a kamemon, sali' abantug ni a'a kamemon.* Widely known by everyone, like being famous to all people. (*Thesaurus:* **bantug 1, bawag, buhanyag, busling, hayag, s'ssag 1.1, tanyag 1**) 1.1) *v. intr. pa-/a-* To become widely known. *Pahayag pandu'bi, sali' pahula-layag.* Your teachings are spreading, becoming more widely known.

  **pahula-layag** *v. tr.* To make a body of information widely known.

**hulak** *adj. a-* 1) Occurring repeatedly over of time. *Ahulak na sinulayan, timpu bay nilabayan.* Attempted over a period of time, in an era now past. 1.1) *v. tr. a-, ka-..-an, -an* To enjoy something to the full, over a period of time. *Buwat lilus, bang dambulan du ma kita, ati alungay atawa magka'at, na halam kahulakanta.* Like a watch, if we have it just one month and then it is lost or broken, then we haven't enjoyed it fully. *Buwat a'a maglakibini yampa taga anak l'lla. Nianakan pa'in bo' mbal gi' makalē, na amatay na. Na onde' hē' halam kahulakan e' matto'a.* Like a couple who have just had a son. After he was born, before he could crawl, he died. So the parents did not get to enjoy that child. *Halam bay kahulakanna, sali' halam kahampitan.* She didn't get to experience it, didn't get to share, so to speak.

**hulas** *n.* 1) Sweat; perspiration. 1.1) *v. advrs. -in-* To perspire. *Nihulasan si Anu inān.* What's-his-name is perspiring.

**hulaw** *v. intr. pa-* To allow natural forces to diminish in intensity, such as wind, current, rain or heat. *Pahulawta gi' ko ra'a alūs bowa'ta.* We'll let it cool a bit so our mouths aren't burnt. (*Thesaurus:* **keyas, kō' 1.1, kontay₂, luhaw-luhaw, patokang, tugut 1**)

**hulay** see: **paghulay**

**hulega** (var. **holega**) *v. intr. a-* To move freely from place to place. *Mbal gi' aku makahulega ni lahat dakayu' bang aniya' palbantahan.* I am not free yet to move to another place, while there are enemies.

**hulemang** (var. **holemang**) *adj. a-* 1) Meddlesome;

given to fiddling with things. *Aholemang pahāp l'lla itū.* This fellow is so meddlesome. *Da'a hampul-hampulun si Gi sabab ya du ilu onde'-onde' mbal aholemang.* Don't be hard on Gi because she is in fact a child who doesn't meddle. 1.1) *v. tr.* To fiddle with things. *Da'a hulemangun sīnnu ilū. Da'a pag'ntan-ntanin.* Don't meddle with your money. Don't keep handling it. (*Thesaurus:* **lotok 1.1, pagkoledje, umas**)

**hulid** (var. **ulid**) *v. intr. pa-* 1) To sleep next to someone. *Pahulid ka ni siyakanu.* Sleep next to your older sibling. 1.1) *v. tr.* To hold someone while sleeping. *Hulirun pahāp bo' atuli.* Hold her carefully so she goes to sleep. *Bang pa'in ka kasulutan ma pangulidna.* May you be content with her embrace.

  **paghulid** *v. intr. aN-* 1) To sleep in each other's arms, as mother and child or a married couple. 2) To have sexual intercourse. {euphemism}

**huling-bata'** var. of **buling-bata'**

**hulma** var. of **hulma'**

**hulma'** (var. **hulma**) *n.* The date palm and its fruit. *Phoenix dactylifera. Hulma, ya kinakan ma paghadji'an.* Dates, the food eaten on the hajj.

**hulmat** *v. tr.* 1) To show someone respect or honor. *Sali' bang aniya' pariyata' subay hulmatta, subay sinagina. Yukta, "Pasōd ka."* Like when someone comes up into the house, we should show him respect, he should be welcomed in. We say, "Come in." *Buwat si Ji amaya'-maya' ma d'nda, amuwan-muwan sadja ni matto'ana, angahulmat-ngahulmat, amahāp-mahāp sali'.* Like Ji when he is in love with a girl, he keeps giving things to her parents, keeps showing them honor, keeps making them feel good. (*Thesaurus:* **mahaldika', pagmahaltabat, pudji 1.2, sanglit 1.2**) 1.1) *v. tr. -an* To present someone with a gift as a way of honoring them.

  **paghulmat** *v. intr. aN-* To be engaged in the courting strategy of giving frequent gifts to win the favor of the girl and her parents. *Maghulmat itū bang buwat si Jo amaya'-maya' ma d'nda, amuwan-muwan sadja ni matto'ana.* This word *paghulmat* is like when Jo fancies a girl, giving frequent gifts to her parents. *Maghulmat bang aniya' d'nda maka l'lla magbaya'.* Exchanging gifts when a girl and a lad fancy each other.

  **huhulmatan** *n.* A gift presented to a person of high rank. (*cf:* **tanggap 1**)

**hulug** var. of **hūg₁**

**hulug ma'ana** var. of **hūg ma'ana**

**huma** (var. **uma**) *n.* An upland farm, in contrast to paddy fields. *Aniya' a'a lūd bay min pagumahanna.* Someone who has come down from his hill farm. *Gaddongan, sali' humaku, ya pangā'anku alta'.* A natural resource, like my farm, where I get my wealth.

  **paghuma** *v. intr. aN-* To be engaged in farming. *Wa'i aniya' a'a maghuma mareya.* There is someone farming inland.

**paghuhuma** *n.* A person who farms for a living.

**humag** *see:* **paghinumag**

**humbu** *n.* 1) Smoke; vapor. 1.1) *v. intr. aN-* To emit smoke or vapor. *Kahumbu, ya sali' angahumbu pariyata', sali' anahupput.* A whale, which sort of emits smoke, like squirting it out. (*Thesaurus:* **asu-asu 1.1, husbu 1.1, limbōn**)

**humilan** *var. of* **sumiyan**

**humiyan** *var. of* **sumiyan**

**hūn** *see:* **paghūn**

**hunas** *var. of* **unas**

**hundaw** *var. of* **hunggaw**

**hunit** *n.* 1) Difficulty. (*cf:* **dipisil, mustahil**) 1.1) *adj. a-* Difficult. *Ahunit kauli'an bakatna.* His wound is difficult to heal. *Oy nā! Ahunit ko' ya pangamu'nu ilū.* No way! What you're asking for is very difficult! *Maglahi'an sigām ni kabūd-būran bo' angahinangan dī sigām kubu'-kubu' ma saga songab batu maka ma saga tapukan ya ahunit sinōd.* They escaped to the hills and made huts for themselves in caves, and in hiding places that were hard to get into. 2) Expense. *Bayarin pehē' minsan buwattilu hunitna.* Pay up even though its price is like that. 2.1) *adj. a-* Expensive. *Ahunit daing, alandos goyak.* Fish is expensive, the sea is rough. (*cf:* **halga' 1, luhay₁ 1.1**) 2.2) *v. advrs. ka-...-an* To be affected by the high cost of something. *Kahunitan aku am'lli daing.* I am affected by the cost of buying fish.

**hunsuk** *v. intr. pa-* To pile up due to abundance. *Pahunsuk itū aheka, buwat du lahing. Atawa buwat karut ma jambatan. Pahunsuk* implies a large number, like coconuts. Or like sacks on the wharf. *Pabūd, pahunsuk, pakuta'. Sali' du kat'llu itū.* Forming a mound, piling up, heaping. These three are the same. (*Thesaurus:* **būd 1.1, kuta'₂, g'bbus 1, hungku', pagbullud**)

**huntak** *v. intr. pa-* To bounce up and down.

**paghuntak** *v. intr. aN-* To bounce vigorously and repeatedly over a rough surface. *Buwat awtu di'ilaw pameya'anta tudju kaut, hal sali' maghuntak-huntak, mbal al'kkas.* Like the car we traveled in yesterday going towards the shore, it just kept bouncing up and down, not fast. *Maghuntak-huntak he' goyak, sali' magtongket-tongket.* Bouncing up and down due to the choppy waves, like riding a teeter-totter. *Sinauk pelang kami he' goyak. Buwat kami abanog, paghuntak pelang pasōd goyak.* Our canoe took water from the choppy sea. Like when sailing, the canoe bouncing up and down and the waves coming in. (*Thesaurus:* **pagbullud-bullud, pagbuwang 1.1, paghandok, pagtongket-tongket, pagumpak-umpak**)

**hunub-hunub** *n.* 1) A report; a rumor. *Aniya' takale hunub-hunub amusay, buwat du ni Sambuwangan.* A rumor has been heard of a trip, like someone going to Zamboanga. (*Thesaurus:* **ba'at 1, kabtangan, haka 1, pahati 1, sambatan, suli-suli 1**) 1.1) *v. tr.* To spread information.

*Tahunub-hunubku aniya' bono', hē'-i kinalu-kalu lagi'.* I spread the word that there was a battle, [but] that was still a conjecture. (*Thesaurus:* **taha, tuhuma 1, tuna', waham**)

**hunus** *n.* 1) A sudden onset of strong wind, with or without rain; a squall. *Bang hunus bo' halam busaytam, palaran kitā.* When there is a squall and we have no paddle, we drift. (*Thesaurus:* **badju, baliyu 1, simpal**) 1.1) *v. intr. aN-* To become squally.

**hungku'** *v. intr. pa-* To pile up because of volume or abundance. *Pahungku' pariyata', buwat saga lahing atawa buwa' kayu pinatimuk ma deya itū.* Piled up high, like coconuts or fruit gathered together inland from here. (*Thesaurus:* **būd 1.1, kuta'₂, g'bbus 1, hunsuk, pagbullud**)

**hunggaw** (var. **hanggaw₂**; **hundaw**) *v. intr. pa-* 1) To see something by moving one's head. *Pahanggaw kono' ka ma tandawan ilū bang sai pariyata'. Kalu ilu Sama atawa Sūk.* Peep out the window there to see who is coming up. Could be a Sama or a Tausug. 1.1) *v. tr.* To look closely or intently at something. (*Thesaurus:* **liling**)

**paghunggaw** *v. intr. aN-* To be constantly looking out through an opening. *Maghunggaw-hunggaw na pa'in, patīk min tandawan buwat nilinganan.* Forever looking out, peeping from the window as though called to.

**hungun** (var. **sungun**) *adj. a-* Willing to do what is asked; cooperative. *Ahungun sadja sinoho', bilahi sadja.* Always willing to be told what to do, always agreeable. *Anusutan pelang, ang'llawan banog, anangon gi'. Ahungun amahilala'.* Scrubbing the canoe hull, drying the sail, even putting the canoe on the drying rack. Willing to take care of things. (*syn:* **hutu**)

**hupi'** *n.* 1) Taro, an edible tuber. *Colecasia esculentum.* *Sayul hupi' ahāp ssana bang daing niasin lamudna maka gata'.* Taro leaves taste good when cooked with salted fish and coconut milk. (*Thesaurus:* **kallari', kapeta', tuwad**) 2) The swamp taro. *Cyrtosperma merkusii.*

**hupi'-badjang** *n.* The Elephant's ear, an edible plant with large leaves. *Alocasia macrorrhiza.* *Daun-badjang, ya daun hupi'-badjang ilū.* Wild taro leaves, the leaves of that Elephant-ear.

**hupit-hupit** *v. tr. -an* 1) To instruct or advise someone how to behave. *Bang maglakibini baha'u subay nihupit-hupitan he' matto'a.* Newlyweds should be instructed by an elder. (*Thesaurus:* **pandu' 1, pintulu' 1, pitis₂ 1**) 1.1) To seduce or suborn someone. *Palawak kam min pangahupit-ngahupit sin d'nda magpangaliyu-lakad.* Keep away from the seductive talk of women who commit adultery. *"Sai bay makahupit-hupitan ka'a?" (Sali' kita bay amowa d'nda maglahi, bo' putingan.)* "Who told you how to do that?" (Said when we had persuaded a girl to elope, but were not sincere.)

**huru** *n.* A children's game played by two teams trying to evade each other on a marked court.

**paghuru** *n.* 1) A game of huru. 1.1) *v. intr. aN-* To be engaged in playing the game of huru. *Magbantung na, maghuru na. Manjari itū na, aniya' na sowa talanggal kami.* Throwing to each other, playing *huru.* So here now we have come across a snake. (*syn:* **pagbalatin**)

**huru-huru** *n.* A rapidly repeated action or sound. (*Thesaurus:* **kulagpak, kutub**)

**paghuru-huru** *v. intr. aN-* To make sharp, repetitive sounds, as of gunfire. *H'lling masinggan ina'an, maghuru-huru.* That noise of machine-guns, making repetitive sounds.

**pahuru-huru** *v. intr. aN-* To move swiftly and in large numbers.

**hurup** *n.* 1) Clarity of enunciation, especially in reading the Holy Koran. *Ahāp hurupna, sali' alangguyud bissala, alanu' kinale.* The enunciation is good, the words drawn out, nice to listen to. 1.1) *adj. a-* Clearly enunciated. *Ai-ai pamissalata bo' halam sā'na maka sali' ahapal bowahan, ya hē' niōnan ahurup.* Anything we say without mistakes and with clear intonation, that is *hurup.* (*Thesaurus:* **hangpat 1, hapal 2, ladju, lagsing, nyala-nyala, tanog₁**)

**paghurup** *v. intr. aN-* To sound out the individual letters of written material. *Kami itū hal maghurup.* We just sound out the letters.

**hurus** (var. **hūs₁; urus**) *v. intr. pa-* 1) To slip out from a wrapping or a supporting framework. *Bang iya bilahi amangan kabasi' bo' halam karūlan, na bang amatay na, saga pinahilala', sinaput, paurus iya min saputna bang sangom. Takale magkagingkul ma deyom luma', angā' kabasi' min kaldero.* If he wants to eat squash and isn't allowed, then when he dies and is laid out, shrouded, he will slip out of his shroud during the night. He will be heard clattering inside the house, getting squash from the pot. *Halam pahurus basi'na, halam pala'an.* His rigor has not slipped off him, it has not gone away. *Ab'kkat ya palimping diyata', pahūs pareyo'.* The upper bolt rope breaks and [the sail assembly] slips down. *Pahūs isita, sali' kita anganggiti'.* Our flesh slips away, as though we are becoming thin. 1.1) *v. tr. -an* To remove clothes. *Manjari itū niurusan badju'na.* So then he removed his shirt.

**hūs₁** var. of **hurus**

**hūs₂** var. of **hīs**

**husa'** *adj. a-* Physically exhausted due to prolonged effort. *Ahusa' si Sa angahangkut bohe' bang binale'.* Sa is exhausted carrying water when he is tired. (*Thesaurus:* **bale', binasa 1, b'kkat 2, lumpu, paya**)

**paghusa'** *v. intr. aN-* To become exhausted due to prolonged effort. *Magbakti' kita ni guru. Sat'ggol kita mbal makatammat, subay kita maghusa' pina'an amowa bohe'-kayu.* We show appreciation to [our] religious teacher. So long as we haven't graduated we should work hard taking water and firewood [to him].

**husay** var. of **usay**

**husbu** (var. **usbu**) *n.* 1) Steam; water vapor. 1.1) *v. intr. pa-* To produce or give off steam. *Bang kahumbu angappu', pahusbu bohe'na min diyata' kōkna. Minsan daing, angappu' du basta pahusbu bohe'na.* When a whale blows, the water vapor comes out from its head. Fish too may be said to 'blow' whenever their fluid spurts out. (*Thesaurus:* **asu-asu 1.1, humbu 1.1, limbōn**)

**huskaw** var. of **hukaw**

**hustu** var. of **ustu**

**hutba'** *n.* A sermon; a book of sermons. *Amassa hutba' imam, saga kalangan nabi. Binassa hutba' itū sali' nōtbūk, ngga'i ka Kora'an.* The imam reads the sermon, songs of the prophets perhaps. The sermon being read is from a notebook, not the Holy Koran.

**paghutba'** *v. tr.* To read a sermon to a congregation. *Maghutba' itū an'ngge dangan-danganna.* The one reading the sermon stands up on his own.

**huttut** *v. tr.* To draw something in by suction. *Angay na pa'in huttutnu s'ppunnu ilū?* Why do you keep sniffing up your mucus? (*Thesaurus:* **hiyup, h'llop 1.1, horot**)

**hutu** *adj. a-* Enthusiastic; diligent. *Ahutu sinoho', sali' ahungun.* Keen to be given a job, like being *hungun. Pabistuku si Ki inān ahutu sinoho'. Ai-ai soho'ku bilahi sadja.* In my experience Ki is willing when asked. Whatever I tell him to do he always responds positively. (*syn:* **hungun**; *ant:* **gagga**)

**huwal** *v. tr.* To stir something in a cooking container in order to mix it, or to coat it with oil or a sugar glaze. *Nihuwal buwas maka ns'llan ma deyom kaha' bo' mbal abalos buwas i'.* Mix the rice with oil in a frying pan so the rice doesn't go sour. *Suma'an ni'llawan binamban bo' nihinang lapuk-lapuk. Bang atoho' nihuwal ni sokal.* Or at times boiled cassava is sun-dried to be made into candy. When dry it is stirred and coated with sugar. (*Thesaurus:* **buwang₃, ggang, sanglag, tompe'**)

**hinuwal** *n.* 1) A confection of sugared coconut. (*Thesaurus:* **bukayu 1, halluwa 1, hinti' 1**) 2) Cursing equivalent for food offered in sarcasm or anger.

**huwang₁** *n.* 1) A space or section designated for a specific person. *Ī' ma si Ma dahuwang, dahuwang isāb ma kami.* There is Ma's own personal part, and one part is for us. *Ya kumpit inān bay sin'ngkol mpat huwang.* That *kumpit* boat is separated into four parts. *Ya ilu huwangnu, patulihannu.* That's your place, where you sleep. (*cf:* **suhutan**) 1.1) *v. intr. aN-* To take the place reserved for one. *Angahuwang ka min t'ngnga' ilū.* Take your place there in the middle [of the canoe].

**huwang₂** *n.* An activity or skill for which a specific individual is known. *Ya na huwangnu magsulat, ya na huwangku magp'ssi.* Your skill is to write, my skill is to fish with hook and line. (*cf:* **ingat-kapandayan**)

**huwas-huwas** *n.* An obligation to pay a debt or refute an accusation. *Bay na amuwasan huwas-huwas, buwat bay angutang bo' amayad na. Apuwas na man iya huwas-huwas bo' halam aniya' magjallat iya.* He has discharged his obligation, like someone who has been in debt but has now paid. He is free now of the obligation so that there is nothing to hold him back.

**paghuwas-huwas** *v. intr.* aN- To undergo a ritual test as a way of proving one's innocence. *Subay ka maghuwas-huwas magko'ot bohe' pasu'.* You must put your hand into hot water to prove your innocence. *Bang kita tinuna'an bay anangkaw, na magpayod kita. Maghuwas-huwas kita, sali' kita anaksi' ni Tuhan.* When we are accused of having stolen something, we protest. We must prove otherwise, as though we are calling on God as witness.

**huwis** *n.* A judge in the state's legal system. (*Thesaurus:* **abugaw, po'on-sara', sara' 2**)

**huwit-huwit** *n.* 1) Strips from the durable outer layer of bamboo. 1.1) *v. tr.* To prepare bamboo into strips for fine weaving. (*Thesaurus:* **anom, ayum-ayum, t'nnun**)

**huyap-huyap** *n.* 1) A mat-weaving pattern which utilizes the twist technique. (*Thesaurus:* **kagayan 1.2, tabid₂**) 1.1) *v. tr.* To weave a mat with the huyap-huyap pattern.

**huyungan** *n.* A funnel for guiding a liquid or powder into a narrow-mouthed container.

# I i

**i₁** *ptl.* 1) Demonstrative clitic, attaches to noun phrases to mark mild emphasis. *"Onde' itu, pinakan wanni, mapasu' itu?" Bang ma si Mma', "Ilu i subay mamangan ilu."* "Shall we feed this child mango, this feverish one?" Father said, "He should be the one to eat it." 1.1) Peak marker, attaches to noun phrases to indicate the peak or climax of a narrative. *Ya llingna hē', ahāp kono' aku i pinabuwa' kinakan. Aku i anittowa. Balutanku busayku i. Halam bbahanku.* He said it would be better if I were chopped up like food. I smiled. I held tightly onto my paddle. I didn't let go of it.

**i₂** *var. of* **si**

**iba'** *n.* The kamias, a fruit of the carambola group. *Averrhoa bilimbi.* (*Thesaurus:* **balimbing, kamyas, kisas₁**)

**ibarat₁** *n.* Religious duties enjoined on a Muslim by the teachings of the Holy Koran.

**pagibarat** *v. intr.* aN- To be faithful in carrying out religious duties.

**ibarat₂** (*var.* **hibarat**) *conj.* With reference to; for example. *Sali' ibarat kita angahinang paraw. Hinangta suntu'an paraw.* As when, for example, we are making a *paraw* type canoe. We make a *paraw* pattern. *Ibarat kakana', apinda walna'.* Like cloth, its color changing. *Tu'ud aheka makalandu', buwat ibarat gusung ma bihing tahik mbal taitung.* Simply an exceedingly great number, comparable to the uncountable sand on the seashore. *Binubulan, bang hibarat tupak, sali' pinuna'an.* Being repaired, with a patch, for example, like filling a gap. (*Thesaurus:* **sapantun, saupama 1.1**)

**ibilis** *var. of* **hibilis**

**ibis** *n.* The Balabac barb, a small inshore fish caught by children with a hook and line. *Puntius ivis.*

**Ibrahim** *var. of* **Nabi Ibrahim**

**ibu** *n.* Thousand, as a counting unit. *Dangibu pilak bay pam'lli kami bangka'.* The thousand pesos we paid for a canoe. *Duwangibu pilak.* Two thousand pesos. (*Thesaurus:* **hatus, laksa' 1**)

**ibu-ibuhan** *adv.* By the thousand.

**pagibu-ibuhan** *v. intr.* aN- To occur in thousands. *Magibu-ibuhan saga bām.* Bombs occurring in thousands.

**ibud** *var. of* **ebod**

**ika-** *var. of* **ka-₁**

**ikat** *n.* 1) Large swellings in the soft tissue of the body. 1.1) *v. advrs.* -in- Suffering from a large swelling in the soft tissue of the body. *Ni'ikat kōk-tu'utna.* Her knee is affected with swelling. (*Thesaurus:* **bakag₂, bago' 1, baha' 1, butig 1, pagbutud, p'ngkong 1**)

**ikat-liyabod** *n.* A swelling, long ridge-like form, typically occurring across the back of the neck.

**ikiral** *v. intr.* aN- To refer a legal case to a higher court. *Bang mbal kasulutan he' bissala, subay angikiral ni M'ddas. Paragsol to'ongan kita ni po'on.* If [the issue] isn't resolved through discussion, we should take it to Siasi Town. We take the case right to the top. (*Thesaurus:* **dagsol, paglagadlad, tukbal₂**)

**iklug** *n.* An egg of a bird. *Nt'llo itū tohongan, iklug i' manuk.* A turtle egg is nt'llo, a chicken egg is iklug. (*cf:* **nt'llo 1**)

**iku-iku** *see:* **pagiku-iku**

**ikut** *v. tr.* To keep something in mind. *Bang aniya' sali' pandu' matto'a, pandu' ni kahāpan, ngga'i ka* *ni kala'atan, subay ikutta. Subay nna'ta ma deyom pikilanta.* When there is advice from elders, advice for good, not for bad, we should heed it. We should store it in our minds. *Mang aku angindam barena bo' ka'a ilū mbal amaindam, yukku, "Ikutanta."* When I ask to borrow a drill but you won't lend it, I say, "I'll keep it in mind regarding you." (*Thesaurus:* **asip, beya'-beya'**₁ **1.1, hirup**₁)

**idda** *n.* 1) Deadline for payment; a time limit. *Alōb e' padjak singsingku, sa'agon palabay min idda bo' halam aniya' pangal'kkat.* My ring held in pawn as security, and the time limit about to pass but nothing to redeem it with. *Idda, ya hē' paltanda'an to'ongan, halam saddī. Idda,* that is a clear signal, with no option. **1.1)** *v. tr.* *-an* To set conditions such as time of appointment or completion of a task. *Angagad ka ni'iddahan.* Wait until you're told [when to go]. *Iddahin kita bang pilang'llaw. Sali' tutatin aku.* Tell us how many days. It's like saying to tell me the specifics. *Bang kita magbihing aningkō', bo' aku sinoho' he' si Mām Jo minsan du aniya' bata'anna, aku ya kaiddahan dahū, aku ya nilinganan.* When we are sitting together, and I am sent to do something by Ma'am Jo, I am the one who gets singled out first, I am the one who is called. *Ni'iddahan kita subay kita atuli, bay ni'iddahan e' Tuhan. Sali' aniya' mareyom patulihanta hē' pasekot ni kita. Yukna, "Bogbogin." Sali' aniya' palman min Tuhan ni kita.* We need to be asleep to be given an *idda* task, chosen specifically by God. It's like someone approaching us during our sleep, saying, "Obey." It's like a divine word to us from God. (*Thesaurus:* **ligtung, ora, pagtaratu, tugna', tugun 1.1, waktu 1.1**)

**iddahan** *n.* The time set for some event or activity. *Iddahannu duwang'llaw. Subay Sabtu' bo' magtenes, ya hē' pangiddaku ma ka'a.* Your appointment is two days away. Saturday is when you sing the *tenes* songs. That's the time I have set for you.

**idji'** *var.* of **udju'**

**idjin** *n.* An agent.

**pagidjin** *v. intr.* *aN-* To act as an agent. *Bang aniya' llingnu, aku sosoho'annu, magidjin aku ma ka'a. Palatunku llingnu ni sai ni sai.* If you have a message, I am your messenger, I serve you as agent. I will convey your word to whomever.

**idlap** *v. intr.* *pa-* 1) To see something out of the corner of one's eye. *Paidlap, sali' mag'nda', sali' palingi'-lingi'. Idlap* is like seeing things indirectly, like looking this way and that. *Mbal ang'nda' pabontol, paidlap asāl.* He doesn't look straight ahead, he just naturally looks to the side. **1.1)** *v. tr.* To look briefly at someone. *Bang aniya' magbaya' d'nda maka l'lla, ni'idlap d'nda.* When a man and woman are courting, the man glances at the woman. (*cf:* **nda' 1**; *Thesaurus:* **k'llap, laman 1.1**)

**igal** *n.* 1) A traditional dance style. *Apolma igalna.* Her dancing is graceful. **1.1)** *v. intr.* *aN-* To engage in traditional Sama dancing.

**pagigal** *n.* 1) Dances in the traditional style, in which the sexes do not dance together. (*cf:* **pagbayla 1**) **1.1)** *v. intr.* *aN-* To dance, traditional style.

**igang**₁ *n.* A coarse gravel-like material consisting of coral fragments. (*Thesaurus:* **bunbun 1, kalangan**₃**, kapote'an, gusung**)

**igang**₂ *n.* The Brown surgeonfish. *Acanthurus nigrofuscus.* (*gen:* **kumay**)

**iggil** *adj.* *a-* 1) Spitefully jealous of another's good fortune. *Aiggil isāb kakina.* His cousin is also spitefully jealous. **1.1)** *v. tr.* To covet someone's property out of envy. *Sali' aheka alta' ma dangan, ni'iggil he' dangan, subay ma iya.* Like someone has lots of wealth, it is coveted by someone else, he must have it. (*cf:* **ihid**; *Thesaurus:* **abuggu', himuggu', imbū, jelus, jingki 1, lindi 1**)

**pagiggil** *v. intr.* *aN-* To be spitefully jealous of each other. *Magugpang, magiggil.* Keeping up with each other, jealous of each other.

**igira** *n.* A species of tree (possibly a fig).

**igut** *n.* The tailbone or coccyx, the projection at the base of the spine in vertebrates. *Igut, ya ma tongod tombongta.* The *igut,* the bump in our rectal area.

**ihid** *v. tr.* *-an* To envy someone for his possessions or skills. *Ni'ihiran aku ma alta'ku, sali' aku kinab'nsihan. Buwat si Ng, ai-ai ta'nda'na ma aku, subay iya bin'llihan he' matto'ana.* I am envied because of my wealth, as though I am hated [for it]. Ng for example, whatever he sees me having, he must have his parents buy it for him. *Angalihi aku ni ka'a, ai-ai hinangnu lihi'anku, sali' angihid.* I imitate you, whatever you do I do too, as though I am envious. (*cf:* **iggil 1.1**)

**ī'** *var.* of **hē'**₁**, hē'**₂

**ila** *n.* 1) A birthmark. *Angalom aku, sali' angal'ddom baranku, sali' ni'ila aku. Aniya' ila akeyat, aniya' isāb ettom. Aniya' ila magtumpak-tumpak.* I am becoming red, as though my body is getting dark, as though I have been birthmarked. There are red birthmarks, and black ones too. There are spotted birthmarks. **1.1)** *v. advrs.* *-in-* Marked at birth with a blemish. *Ingga sasuku saga a'a ab'ttong subay pinandi ma linsungan dok mbal ni'ila.* All pregnant women, no matter who, should be bathed in a rice mortar so [the baby] will not have a birthmark.

**ilak** *n.* Various sea chubs and drummers. *Kyphosus lembus.*

**ilak-pampang** *n.* The Ashen drummer, a fish species.

**ilak-tawas** *n.* A species of chub.

**Ilanun** (*var.* **Lanun**) *n.* Maranao or Maguindanao, Muslim people groups of Central Mindanao.

**ilat** *var.* of **illat**

**ilaw** *n.* 1) A light source. (*cf:* **tanju'**) 1.1) *v. tr.* *-an* To illuminate something.

**ili-ili** *v. intr.* maka- To cause wonder or astonishment. *Makaili-ili ma pang'nda' a'a.* Wonderful for people to see. (*Thesaurus:* **haylan, inu-inu 1, jaip, littā 1**)

**ili'** var. of **hē'₁, hē'₂**

**illag** *v. tr.* *-an* 1) To avoid something that may harm. *Illagin a'a inān apa ala'at kasuddahanna. Asidda ang'ntan.* Be wary of that person because his character is bad. He does a lot of touching. *Sali' tigbas, pak'ppang buwattē', magtūy alahi angillag.* Like the *tigbas* fish, lying face-down thus, then immediately escapes, avoiding harm. *Ni'illagan, sali' kinatāwan, pinaghalli'an.* Treated warily, like something feared, handled with caution. *Illagin kar'ndahan magpangabiyug.* Be on guard against women who are in the habit of seduction. (*Thesaurus:* **llog 1**) 1.1) *v. tr.* a-, ka-..-an, -an To be treated as something to be avoided. *Kinaillagan si Ug apa asidda amono'.* Ug is avoided because he hits so much.

**illap** *v. intr.* aN- To flash or glisten. *Angillap kulit langohan, magsinglab sali'.* The skin of the kingfish glistens, sort of flashing. (*Thesaurus:* **kiraw, kitaw-kitaw, inggat, pagpillaw-pillaw, pagsinglab, tingaw-tingaw**)

**illat** (var. ilat) *v. intr.* pa- To be shy or wary regarding one's personal space. *Paillat ka. Da'a ka pasekot.* Be cautious of your personal pace. Don't get close.

**illig** *v. tr.* To corral a group of things, such as chickens or fish. (*Thesaurus:* **lakod, s'ssol₂ 1.1**)

**ilmu'** *n.* 1) Esoteric or magical knowledge. *Bang nilagut bo' mbal niōk aniya' ilmu'.* If someone is attacked with a knife but isn't cut, there is supernatural power involved. *Bang aniya' d'nda kabaya'anta, na lindangta. Bang taluwa' ma ilmu' pangalindanganta mbal makasandal. Lum'ngngan ni luma'ta.* If there is a woman we desire, we use a love charm on her. When she is hit by the magical power of our love enchantment, she cannot endure. She will walk to our house. *Bang ahūg pareyo' bo' mbal apōng to'olang, na taga ilmu'.* When [someone] falls down and no bones are broken, then he has magical power. *Ilmu' Tuhan mbal kakuriputan.* Special knowledge from God is not restricted. (*cf:* **putika'**; *Thesaurus:* **ingat, langkat-samat, salawat₁**) 1.1) *v. tr.* *-an* To influence someone by the use of magical power. *Mbal makabissala, bay ni'ilmu'an.* He is unable to speak, he has been affected by some magical power.

**ilū** *dem.* 1) That by you, referring to something near hearer but far from speaker [Set I]. *Ndiya ma aku busay ilū. Busay ilū.* Hand me that paddle, the paddle there by you. *Na ndiya na ba ya bay binila' e'nu ilū.* Hand over that one that you have just divided in half. (*Set:* **hē'₂ 1, inān 1, itū 1**) 1.1) That (mutually understood), referring to

specific shared knowledge between speakers. *"Ndiya na ba saga ma buli'-sikunu," (apa anu, bohe' buwahan ilū pasū, ā, Ja?).* "Hand over the ones [dripping] down your elbows" (because [you know how] the lanzones juice drips down, Ja).

**ilu** 1) *dem.* That by you, referring to something near hearer but far from speaker [Set II]. *Na ilu ko' ilū angiskul arai' si Bi inān.* So that's probably Bi there going off to school. *Pat'nna'un ma lamisahan ilū.* Place it on that table there [by you]. (*Set:* **hē'₁ 1, ina'an 1, itu 1**) 1.1) 'That is'. (A demonstrative that functions as a predicate and identifies the person or thing being talked about.) *Agpala'u kami tinimbak. Ilu du si Ki, ilu kakiku l'lla.* It was when we were living on boats, we were shot at. [Myself and] Ki, that is--my male cousin, that is. (*cf:* **itiya', itu 1.1**) 2) *ptl.* Prospective aspect marker. Indicates imminent arrival or occurrence. *Ilu na kappal.* The ship is almost here.

**ilud-ilud** *v. intr.* aN- To bellow or moo, of bovine animals. (*syn:* **ngngong**)

**ilu'₁** *adj.* a- 1) Wasted or shrivelled, of a body part. *Si Bapa' Al inān, ailu' tanganna dambila', bay ahūg pareyo'. Mbal paheya dambila'na.* Uncle Al there has a withered arm, he had a fall. His one side will not become big. 1.1) *v. intr.* aN- To waste away; to shrivel. *Angilu' si Arung, halam aniya' bohe' duru' ina'na.* Oldest Daughter is wasting away, her mother has no milk.

**ilu'₂** *n.* 1) An orphan due to the loss of one parent or both. *Ilu' iya, ilu' logtas, halam aniya' matto'ana.* She is an orphan, fully orphan, having no parents. 1.1) *adj.* a- Orphaned.

**ilu'-logtas** *n.* An orphan both of whose parents have died. *Ilu'-logtas kita bang amatay mma'ta maka ina'ta.* We are orphans when our father and mother have both died.

**imam** *n.* The leader of a mosque community, assisted by hatib and bilal. *Bang aku angungsuran sarakka siyaliku, pasampayku ni imam.* When I give alms on behalf of my younger brother, I hand it over to the *imam*. (*cf:* **bilal, hatib, muwallam**)

**pagimam** *n.* 1) The status or work of an imam. *Binangsa purukan hali-Kura'an bang tudju ni pagimam.* People of a descent group skilled in the Holy Koran, with regard to *imam* status. 1.1) *v. intr.* aN- To do the work of an imam. *Magkapakil, magkaimam, ahāp salawatna.* Able to serve as a leader in a mosque community, as an imam, their spiritual power is good.

**iman₁** *n.* 1) Forbearance; patient endurance; religious consistency. *Jari pahogot sigā ma iman, sali' pasogsog ni Tuhan.* So they became firm in faith, committing themselves to God. 1.1) *v. tr.* *-an* To endure. *Minsan alandos goyak, da'a na kita amūng, subay imananta.* Even though the sea is very rough we should not talk, we should just endure it. (*Thesaurus:* **pagsabal**, **sandal 1.1**, **tahan-tahan**, **tangka'**, **tatas 1.2**)

**baliman** *n.* A person characterized by strong faith in God; the community of the faithful.

**pangimanan** *n.* The source or basis of one's religious trust.

**iman**₂ *adj.* *a-* Satisfied with one's situation in life. *Aiman, aheka alta'na, mbal angamu' ni pagkahi.* He is content, he has plenty of money, doesn't ask anything of his fellows.

**imangkan** *var. of* **himangkan**

**imba-imba** *see:* **pagimba-imba**

**imbaw** *n.* Tellin clam species. *fam. Tellinidae.* *Imbaw itū paloblob ma deyom pisak. Imbaw* clams burrow into the mud.

**imbū** (*var.* **hingbū**) *v. tr.* *-an* To be jealous of someone's affections or possessions. *Badju'na ya pangimbūhanku.* It is his shirt I am jealous of. *Angimbū bang d'nda, bo' h'llana araran pal'ngngan ni d'nda dakayu'.* A woman is jealous when her husband frequently visits another woman. *Bay b'llihannu taumpa' dakayu' inān. Jari na, duwangan inān angimbū. "Angay sigā nsa' bin'llihan, pagga dakayu' inān bay kab'llihan?"* You bought shoes for one of them. Then the other two were envious, "Why weren't they bought anything, when that other one there had something bought for her?" (*cf:* **imu'-imu'**; *Thesaurus:* **abuggu'**, **himuggu'**, **iggil 1.1**, **jelus**, **jingki 1**, **lindi 1**)

**pangimbū** *n.* Jealousy.

**imbun-imbun** *var. of* **mbun-mbun**

**īmēl** *n.* E-mail. *Aheya to'ongan kōdku ma lapalnu. Yampa aku makabuka' īmēlku.* I was very happy with your message. I had just opened my e-mail.

**impasal** *var. of* **pasal**₁

**imu'** (*var.* **maimu'**) *n.* 1) Sweetness. (*Thesaurus:* **kesom**, **lanab**, **l'ssom 1**, **mamis**₁ **1.1**, **sarap**₁, **taba' 1**) 1.1) *adj.* *a-* Sweet tasting. *Aniya' panggi' kayu aimu', aniya' isāb a'ssom.* There is sweet cassava, and there is also sour.

**imu'-imu'** *v. tr.* *-an* To provoke envy by flaunting one's possessions. *Subay aniya' binowa he' onde'-onde' ai-aina, ati onde'-onde' dakayu' inān halam amowa ai-ai. Ya hē' ni'imu'-imu'an, sali' pinakaiya'.* One child must bring all his things, and the other child doesn't bring anything. That's an example of stirring up envy or causing shame. *Ni'imu'-imu'an, sali' anuna kamemon subay ma iya.* Moved to envy, as though he should have all [the other] person's things. (*cf:* **imbū**)

**imun** *see:* **pagimun-imun**

**imut** *v. tr.* To pick up scraps. *Ni'imut he' si Ib bang aniya' l'bbi kinakan.* If there are scraps of food about Ib picks them up. *Angimut aku kayu pam'llaku sinanglag.* I shall gather wood for me to cook cassava meal with. *Angimut-ngimut onde'-onde' bang pat'nna' ma lantay.* Babies pick stuff up when put down on the floor.

(*Thesaurus:* **puwa'**)

**īn** *ptl.* Recent past tense marker.

**in** *ptl.* Elevated register marker, marks the subject of the clause in formal speech. *In si Da'ud itū bay magipat bili-bili.* This David, he used to look after sheep. *Sagō' pahatihun ni si Yu īn panoho'an.* But communicate the command to Yu. *Magtūy patimuk in kasehe'an bangsa Samehakan ma bihing tampe.* The remaining Yakan people promptly gathered on the shore. *Mbal ba, ka'a in talus magpang'nda' kahālan ma sinosōng?* Is it not the case that you are the seer who foresees future events?

**-in-** 1) *aff.* Passive voice infix: attaches to transitive verbs, identifying the undergoer as the subject of the clause, and demoting the actor to oblique status. *Bang kami niholdap he' mundu sinurangan kami timbak. Tudju ni kita bulu timbak inān.* When we are held up by bandits we have a weapon pointed at us. The barrel of that gun aimed in our direction. 1.1) *aff.* Adversative infix: attaches to a verb to indicate an event (usually negative) which occurs to a participant apart from his or her control. *Sinumu akū amangan saldinas.* I am fed up with eating sardines. *Papu'utta na, ilu kam tinuli.* I'll cut it short, you're getting sleepy. (*cf:* **ka-..-an**₂, **ta-1.1**)

**-in** *aff.* Imperative applicative undergoer voice suffix: indicates a command, and identifies the undergoer as the subject of the clause. [Note: This affix is used when there is an undergoer added to the clause by the applicative suffix -an. The suffix -in replaces the combination of applicative -an and imperative -un.] *Balutin kayawan ilu.* Hold on to that bamboo. *"Paindamin na aku saga dahatus pa'in." Pinaindaman aku duwahatus.* "Lend me about one hundred or so." They lent me two hundred.

**ina'** *n.* Mother. (*cf:* **babu' 1.1**, **mamang**₁, **mma'**, **mma'**, **papa**₂, **papang**; *syn:* **nggo' 1**, **sa'i**)

**daina'** *adj.* To have the same mother but different fathers. (*cf:* **da'mma'**)

**ina'-baki'** *n.* The catfish eel. (*syn:* **nggo'an-baki'**; *gen:* **taote'**)

**ina'an** 1) *dem.* That over there, referring to something far from both speaker and hearer; vague location reference [Set II]. *Ina'an i suku' si Bowa'.* That one, it belongs to Mr. Mouth. *Bang yuk Tuhan, "Mailu kā," na maina'an na aku.* If God says, "Go over there," then I go over there. (*Set:* **hē'**₁ **1**, **ilu 1**, **itu 1**) 1.1) Refers back to an entire sentence or proposition within a discourse. *"Subay ka'a i ameya' magk'tta ni jadjahan anu." Ya ina'an abeya'.* "You ought to head out to what's-the-place." That's what he did. 2) *ptl.* Aspect marker indicating that an event remote from the speaker has begun and is still current. *Ina'an amatay si Anu.* What's-his-name has died already.

**inān** *dem.* 1) That over there, referring to something far from both speaker and hearer; vague location reference [Set I]. *Aheka tinda ma lungsud inān.* There are many shops in that city. (*Set:* **hē'₂ 1, ilū 1, itū 1**) 1.1) Default demonstrative for referring to something previously mentioned. *Subay aniya' binowa he' onde'-iskul ai-aina, ati onde'-onde' dakayu' inān halam amowa ai-ai, ya hē' pinakaiya'.* The school children are supposed to bring something of their own, but the child in question hasn't brought anything, he's the one made to feel shame. *Paglūd kami ni pelang inān, bay na niruwa' p'ttung inān ni pelang he' si Mma'.* When we had gone downhill to the canoe, Dad loaded the bamboo onto the canoe.

**inay** *v. intr. a-* 1) To happen. *Da'a ka tināw, mbal du ainay.* Don't be frightened, nothing will happen. 1.1) *v. intr. -um-* To do something in a specific way. *Uminay ka magkabuwattē'?* What are you doing to get in that state? 1.2) *v. tr.* To treat something or someone in what way. *Ni'inay daing itu? Nilandang-landang?* What's to be done with this fish? Is it to be fried?

**inay-inay** *v. tr.* To do something. *Halam bay inay-inayku. Angay aku subay tinuna'an?* I haven't done anything. Why should I be under suspicion? *Angalaha'an iya dīna, halam iya bay ni'inay-inay he' a'a, tu'ud angalaha'an dīna.* He is bleeding on his own, no one has done anything to him, he is simply bleeding spontaneously.

**pagpainay-painay** *v. intr. aN-* To do anything whatever.

**painay** *interrog.* What? How?

**sapainay-painay** *adv.* No matter what. *Sapainay-painay, niōnan angeyok.* No matter what, it's called *angeyok.*

**inda wa barapa ginis** *n. phrase* Things of various kinds. *Inda wa barapa ginis.* All sorts of things. (*cf:* **indaginis**; *Thesaurus:* **babarapa, kaginisan, indalupa 1, mussak-massik**)

**indaginis** (derivative of **ginis**) *n.* Things of all kinds; things in great variety. *Bang ta'nda'nu sawa indaginis na, ai mbal ta'nda'nu mareyom astana' i'.* If only you could see those lights of so many kinds, what would you not see there inside the palace? (*cf:* **inda wa barapa ginis**).

**indalupa** 1) *adj. zero* Of many kinds; in great variety. *Indalupa itu kaginisan, buwat balatu indalupa ginis. Indalupa* means all sorts, such as cakes of all kinds. *Magsauragal, aheka na indalupa-kaginisna.* Enjoying abundance, having an abundance of all sorts of things. *Buwat saupama siyaliku pinah'nda, ungsudna t'llu ngibu. Hal pam'lli indalupa-kaginisan, maleta, s'mmek saga. Halam aniya' pūsna tahampitku.* My younger sister for example, getting married, her bride-wealth ₱3000. Just to buy this and that, suitcase, clothes and so on. I got nothing of worth as my share. (*Thesaurus:* **babarapa,**

**kaginisan, inda wa barapa ginis, mussak-massik**) 2) *v. tr. -an* To get in great variety. *Niadjak-adjak e'na; ni'indalupahan.* To get things of all sorts; to get the entire range.

**indam** *v. ditr.* To borrow something from someone. *Buwat aniya' angindam gaugari' ni ka'a, bo' halam ni'nde'an. Yuk bay mangindam i', "Kalu mbal nientom."* Like when someone borrows a file from you but doesn't return it. The person who borrowed says, "Maybe it won't be remembered." *Halam bay angindam, tinangpas min ka'a.* He didn't borrow, it was taken from you without permission. (*Thesaurus:* **sambi' 1.1, sanda'-sanda', s'nnad, utang 1.1**)

**paindam** *v. ditr.* To lend something to someone.

**indan** var. of **gindan**

**indangan₁** *n.* Surgeonfish; Achilles tang. *Acantharus bleekeri. Daing sōd bubu indangan itū.* Fish that go into a *bubu* trap, these Surgeonfishes. (*gen:* **kumay**)

**indangan₂** *n.* A species of long-spined sea urchin, edible. (*Thesaurus:* **boto'-goyak 2, oko'-oko', s'llang₂, tayum, tehe'-tehe'**)

**inday** *neg.* 'I don't know'; disclaims knowledge in response to a question. *Indayku ka'a.* I don't know what you ask. (*cf:* **daka, halahuwalam, sitta'a**)

**indika** *n.* 1) A summary decree or decision. *Bang sali' kita angusaha yukta, "Ō Tuhan, buwanin kita daing." Subay ka angagad indikana.* When we are out fishing for example, we say, "O God, give us fish." You have to wait for his decision. *Bang indikahan presiden, amowa kami tai'.* If it is the President's command, we will carry excrement. (*Thesaurus:* **kahandak 1, karal 1, kulis, ganta'an₁, piguhan, sukud₂ 1**) 1.1) *v. tr. -an* To impose a binding decision on someone. *Yukna, "Angagad ka pangindikahanku, tininduk atawa mbal."* [God] says, "Wait for what I ordain for you, whether your bait will be taken or not."

**inig** var. of **linig**

**Injil** var. of **Kitab Injil**

**inrol** *n.* 1) School enrolment. 1.1) *v. ditr.* To enrol for school or course of study.

**paginrol** *n.* Enrolment at a school. *Halam du isāb jukup, aniya' lagi' tinggalna ma paginrolna.* It wasn't complete either, there was a shortage in her enrolment fees.

**insa Allah** *intrj.* An expression of submission to God's will.

**insā'** *v. intr. aN-* To learn a lesson from. *Bang kita kaut bo' sali' kaka'atan ai-ai bay bowata, yukna ma luma', "Anginsā' ka m'nnilu. Beya'-beya'un pandu'ku."* When we go out to sea and everything we brought is destroyed, the one at home says, "Learn from that. Follow my teaching." *Ya anginsā' ma kakana': tagna' niukab, būsanna ₱2.50. Pasōng-sōng, ₱2.30. Bang sōng na to'ongan, duwa-ruwa pilak (₱2.00).* The thing to learn about (buying) cloth: when a bolt is first opened it is ₱2.50 a meter. Later it is ₱2.30. Later still it is ₱2.00. (*Thesaurus:* **l'gga 1.1, mintāng**)

**insap** *v. intr.* pa- To be alert to danger. *Bang aniya' bantanu, painsap ka ko da'a tinipu.* If you have enemies be careful so you don't get ambushed. *Painsap ka, ilu aniya' mundu. Bang ka ni bohe' magliling-liling ka. Piligdu nilagut ka ma halam ta'nda'nu.* Be alert, there are bandits about. When you go to the water hole, be on guard. The concern is that you may be slashed without seeing it coming. (*Thesaurus:* **halli'₁ 1.1, liyal, l'ppi, llog 1.1**)

**inses** *n.* An inch, as the unit of length. *Dainses pa'in.* Just an inch. (*Thesaurus:* **batu₃, kilometēl, d'ppa 1, honga'₂, maniku**)

**insini'** (var. **dinsini'**) *adv.* Time just previous. *Ya itu bay sinulat e'na insini' kohap.* This is what he wrote earlier this afternoon. *Bo' kam mbal takuddat, aniya' habal min si Ate Jo in si Bapa' La wa'i na amole'-lahat dinsini' subu.* So you're not shocked, there was a message from Auntie Jo that Uncle La went home [died] this morning. (*Thesaurus:* **kohap-in, subu-sī'**)

**ins'llan** var. of **ns'llan**

**inta'** *v. tr.* To eat uncooked or unripe food without any complementary starch. *Tainta' du tibu'uksilal bo' ak'ddot. Silal* cassava can be eaten on its own, but it is tough and stringy. (*Thesaurus:* **kakan 1, kakan 1, lallan, l'kkob, pakan**)

**intan** *n.* Precious or semi-precious stones; diamonds. (*Thesaurus:* **dilam, palmata 1, puntu' 1**)

**intib** *see:* **samaintib**

**intul** *see:* **paintul**

**inu-inu** *adj.* a- 1) Surprised by; amazed at; wondering. *Bang kita ni lahat saddī bo' mbal takilā he' a'a ma lahat inān, ainu-inu sigā.* When we go to some other place and the people of that place do not recognize us, they wonder [who we are]. *Ainu-inu kita pagka aniya' maitu na ma luma' ati yukta, "Ai kamattinu pi'itu?"* We are puzzled when someone is here in the house and we say, "What is your purpose in coming here?" (*Thesaurus:* **haylan, ili-ili, jaip, littā 1**) 1.1) *v. tr.* a-, ka-..-an, -an To be amazed at something. *Aubus pa'in e'na amissala, kinainu-inuhan pamissalana e' ba'anan a'a bay maina'an.* When he had finished talking, the people who were there were amazed at what he had said. 1.2) *v. advrs.* ka-....-an To be amazed by something wonderful or miraculous. *Aniya' hinang kainu-inuhan bay ta'nda' kami mahē'.* We saw some amazing things done there. *Kalittāhan aku, sali' ai-ai yampa ta'ndata, minsan lapal yampa takale. Kainu-inuhan to'ongan.* I am astonished, like something I have only just seen, even a message only just heard. Really amazed at it.

**inu-inu atay** *adj.* a- To take offense; take personally. {idiom} *Da'a pa'in kām mandā'-dā', da'a na ainu-inu ataybi.* Please don't be offended, don't take it personally.

**inum** 1) *v. tr.* To drink something. *Pati'inumun toba' si Ak ina'an.* Ak is much given to drinking palm toddy. *Panginginum bohe' onde'-onde' inān. Kalu asaki.* That child habitually drinks so much water. He may be ill. (*Thesaurus:* **ggok, t'ggok, tunghab 1.1**) 1.1) *v. tr.* -an To drink something for a specific purpose. *Bay aku kabongkolan, manda' bay inumanku bohe'.* I had something stuck in my throat, but fortunately I drank some water for it. 1.2) *v. tr.* To take medicine. *Sinoho' aku amainum sigā lagi' tambal ma deyom dambulan maka tonga'.* I was told to keep giving them medicine for one and a half months. 2) *v. intr.* aN- To eat a small meal before starting the day's work.

**paginum** 1) *v. intr.* aN- To drink together habitually. *Magsamod sigām maginum toba'.* They get together as mates to drink palm toddy. *Magi'inum disi Anu.* What's-his-name and his mates are habitual drinkers. 2) *v. tr.* To drink something habitually. *Marat, ya pinaginum, makalango. Marat,* the substance drunk habitually, is intoxicating.

**panginuman** (var. **pagi'inuman**) *n.* A drinking container of any kind. (*Thesaurus:* **basu, sawan, tasa**)

**pati'inumun** *adj.* To be a committed drinker.

**inut** *v. tr.* To use a resource in small amounts; to eke out a limited supply. *Da'a palandosun, subay ni'inut-inut.* Don't force it; it should be done little by little. (*cf:* **k'mmit 1.1**)

**painut-inut** *adv.* In small increments; gradually.

**inyaya** *v. tr.* To oppress someone by depriving them of life's necessities. *Ni'inyayaA: nila'at kita, binono' saga. Inyaya:* harshly treated, beaten, etc. (*Thesaurus:* **pa'alu', paulan, tanya₁**)

**īng** *n.* Ink. *Ggomin tōng pinsil ni īng.* Dip the end of the pencil in the ink. (*cf:* **dawat 1**)

**ingan** var. of **lingan**

**ingat** *n.* Knowledge, religious or esoteric. *Mbal pangaral kita dayata, saguwā' ya pangaral kita ingat.* Our wealth is not our destiny, it is spiritual knowledge. *Mbal tapagmairan ingatnu.* Your religious knowledge is not to be displayed publicly. (*Thesaurus:* **alab-alab, himangkan, ilmu' 1, langkat-samat, pamapatahan, panghati, salawat₁, ta'u₁ 1**)

**ingat-kapandayan** *n.* An individual's combination of knowledge and skill. (*cf:* **huwang₂**)

**ingkahi** *n.* 1) A border on a garment of lace or crochet-work. *Buwat bistiru si La taga ingkahi l'ngngonna. Ya lagi'na bang buwat saga badju' samda.* Like the lace on the sleeves of La's blouse. Even more so with *samda*-type blouses. (*Thesaurus:* **bingkay, bulda 1**) 1.1) *v. tr.* -an To decorate something with lace. *Ya pinagb'lli ma M'ddas pagingkahi. Bulda itu ma punda ū'an, binuldahan.* That which is bought in Siasi Town for decorating with lace. *Bulda* is for pillowcases, [they are] embroidered.

**ingkug** *n.* The cucumber species. *Cucumis melo.* (*cf:* **maras**)

**ingga** *interrog.* Which one? Whichever? Whoever? Whenever? *Ya ingga luma'nu?* Which house is yours? *Ingga sali' makalabay bibi'atan kamatto'ahan, ya saga bay maggulu.* Whenever someone has sort of experienced the instructions of the elders, those who have studied under a teacher.

**ingga na** *adv. phrase* When the time comes, of an event or circumstance. *Buwat ma dilaut, yukta, "Bati'un pa'in aku. Ingga na aku bay apiru'-piru', pas'lle' pa'in ka."* Like when out at sea, when we say, "Just wake me up. As soon as I have had some shut-eye, you get to have a turn." A: *"Ingga na aku akatis bay amangan."* B: *"Ingga na salung, bang buwattē'."* A: "When I have finished eating." B: "When tomorrow comes, in that case." *Hal pinalabay bay p'ddi' matata hē'. Buwat ma dilaut, yukta, "Bati'un pa'in aku. Ingga na aku bay apiru'-piru', pas'lle' pa'in ka."* Just letting the eye-strain pass. Like when out at sea, when we say, "Just wake me up. As soon as I have had some shut-eye, you get to have a turn."

**ingga sasuku** *n. phrase* Anyone, no matter who or what. {idiom} *Ingga sasuku saga a'a ab'ttong subay pinandi.* All pregnant women, no matter who, should be bathed.

**ingga-ingga** *n.* Anything whatever. *Ingga-ingga ya kabaya'annu, ka'a ya pinagbaya'.* Whichever you like, you're the one to decide.

**inggat** *v. intr.* aN- To sparkle, as something polished or bright. *Anginggat la, buwat garul ma ina' si Be. Baha'u iya, na luwa bulawan, pinagbase' maka tahik agtūy anumbaga.* Simply gleaming, like the brass container that Be's mother has. When new it looked like gold, after being wetted with seawater it quickly became coppery. *Maginggat doblon bang taluwa' llaw.* Gold pieces shine when sunlight strikes them. (*cf:* **sawa 1.1**; *Thesaurus:* **kiraw, kitaw-kitaw, illap, pagpillaw-pillaw, pagsinglab, tingaw-tingaw**)

**inggatan** *n.* The Banded trevally; the Cleft-belly kingfish. *Atropus atropos.*

**inggay** *intrj.* Reminder of a prior statement or commitment. *Inggay yukku ma ka'a, abila' du?* Didn't I say to you that it would split? *Inggay yukku-i, "Da'a na ka ni bohe' apa angulan du pagkohap."* Na nda'un ba, halam na aniya' pangisihanta bohe' ulan ē'.* Didn't I say to you, "Don't go for water because it rains afternoons." Now look, we have no container for the rain. *Inggay pauli' du pengka'na?* Hasn't his lameness

been healed? *Inggay yukna wa'i mahē'?* Didn't he say it was there a long way off?

**ingglis** *n.* The English language. (*syn:* **anggalis**)

**ingsud** *v. intr.* pa- To move a short distance; to shift position slightly. *Paingsud ka min paningkō'annu ilū. Da'a ka isāb ala'an.* Move a bit from where you are sitting. But don't go away. *Bang alallay he'ta lum'ngngan, sali' paingsud-ingsud saga dah'kka bo' dah'kka.* When we are walking along slowly, inching along one handspan after another. *Bang aku makaingsud ni bohe', aniya' dahū min aku.* When I make slow progress toward the water hole, there are others before me. (*Thesaurus:* **kisal-kisal, hense, higin, sigput**)

**ingu** *v. tr.* -an To lie in wait for someone with a view to doing harm. *Bang kita bay magbono' ati yukta magkahāp na kita, manjari tinau' ma deyom atayna ko pinapatay. Ni'inguhan aku.* When we have been fighting and we say that we are reconciled, then he keeps it in his mind [for me] to be killed. I am ambushed. *Angingu si Ub, bilahi angamu' sīn.* Ub lies in wait [for people], wanting to ask for money. (*cf:* **lingu 1.1**; *Thesaurus:* **ambus, hapa' 1.2, holdap, sipi₁ 1.1, tipu 1.1**)

**ipal** *n.* The relationship between an individual and his wife's sibling or cousin; between his wife and his own sibling or cousin. *"Otō'," yukna, "ipalnu si Ta abalu na."* "Son," he said, "your sister-in-law Ta is a widow now." (*cf:* **bilas**; *gen:* **pamikitan**)

**ipang-ipang** *n.* The female attendants of a woman of royal blood. (*Thesaurus:* **pangantin**)

**ipat** *v. tr.* To take care of someone or something. *Aniya' isāb etek bay ipatku.* I also cared for ducks. *Nianggap he' d'nda ina'an hinangna mareyom luma' sampay saga angipat onde'-onde'.* That woman gets all her housework done as well as taking care of the children. (*Thesaurus:* **ayad, ayuput, hamumu', pahilala' 1, paintul, paipid, payakun, talkin, ulip, upiksa', ussap 1**)

**ipatan** *n.* A person resident in one's care, especially someone who helps with housework. *Buwat ipatanta, ya pamahinang ma iya ananggung bohe', ati subay bilahi saddī hinang minnē'. Yuk pat'nna'an hē', "Samantala' hinang ilu ya bay pamahinang ma ka'a-i, hinangun to'ongan na!"* Like our live-in worker; the work assigned to him is fetching water, but he must prefer some other work. The person he stays with says, "Since fetching water is your assigned work, get on and do it!"

**pagipat** *v. tr.* To be responsible for the care of specific things. *Ya si Je itū a'a magipat binangsa hayop kamemon, binangsa basi' kamemon.* Je was the person responsible for all domestic animals and all things made of iron.

**ipil** *n.* The Moluccan ironwood, a source of durable timber. *Intsia bijuga.*

**ipis** *adj.* **a-** **1)** Seriously lacking some essential. *Aipis aku ma sukay, sali' kakulangan aku.* I am lacking [enough] for the fare, it's like I am suffering from a shortfall. (*Thesaurus:* **kabus, kettak, pihit, pulubi**) **1.1)** *v. advrs.* **ka-...-an** To be affected by the lack of something essential. *Kabus ba sidda. Amab'lli kami bang kaipisan.* Absolutely nothing left. We sell stuff when seriously lacking.

**ipit** *n.* **1)** A sickness (possibly yaws) symptomized by widespread skin eruptions. *Mampa'in ka sinaki ipit.* May you be afflicted with ulcers. **1.1)** *v. advrs.* **-in-** Suffering widespread skin eruptions. (*Thesaurus:* **kamayu**)

**ipul** *n.* **1)** Hansen's disease (leprosy) and other diseases of the skin believed to be incurable. *Mampa'in sigām pinagmulka'an bo' aniya' na pa'in ma sigām a'a taluwa' dugsul maka kaginisan ipul.* May they be punished so they continually have people afflicted with ulcers and various kinds of skin disease. (*Thesaurus:* **ka'mbo'an, kawit₂ 1, kolera, pangkot 1, ttus-ttus 1, upāng 1**) **1.1)** *v. advrs.* **-in-** Suffering from leprosy or similar diseases.

**iral** *v. tr.* To aim at a target. *Aniya' matto'a magpahāp kulaet, aniya' anakna angalarak pistul. Sakali ya amūng anak, "Sulaytanta iral-iralta mma' inān bang mundu." Na i' pinassik. Tauwa' mma'na.* There was an older man fixing his pressure lantern, and his son dismantling a pistol. Then the son said, "Let's try aiming at father as though a bandit." So the trigger was pulled and the father was hit.

  **iralan** *n.* A target; a military objective.

**iram** *v. intr.* **aN-** To be going through the early months of a pregnancy, before the pregnancy is visibly perceptible. *Aubus bay angiram si Anna ab'ttong na, sōng anganak.* When Anna had finished the first months she was visibly pregnant and would soon give birth. *Ahāp isāb kahālan kami maitu, ya sadja bang pasān ala'at pagpangiramku.* Our situation here is good, except that my first months of pregnancy are hard at times. (*cf:* **laha'₃, onde' 2**; *Thesaurus:* **b'ttong₂ 1, buka'-puhu', himati'**)

  **iram-kalitan** *n.* Early stage of pregnancy marked by mood swings and irritability (lit. shark conception). {idiom} *Iram-kalitan, buwat d'nda magbono' maka h'llana bang ma luma', angentom bang makalikut.* Shark phase of pregnancy, like a woman who fights with her husband when he is home and misses him when he is absent.

  **iram-sapi'** *n.* Early stage of pregnancy marked by energy and good health (lit. cow conception). {idiom}

  **pangiram** *n.* The early stage of pregnancy.

  **pangiraman** *n.* Foods craved by a pregnant woman during the early stage of her pregnancy. *Na bo' na kono' nileyang pangiraman.* So then, as the story goes, the craved food was attained by flying. *Am'lli aku tagbak pangiraman h'ndaku.* I will buy wild ginger fruit for my wife's pregnancy craving.

**iras** *n.* The relationship between people whose spouses are siblings or cousins. (*syn:* **bilas**)

  **dangirasan** *n.* The relationship between siblings-in-law. (*cf:* **pamikitan**)

**iring** *n.* A partner of one's own age, in activities such as dancing. *Bay aku angigal dibuhi', aniya' iringku. Subul sali-sali'.* I danced last night, had a partner. Both of us single males. (*Thesaurus:* **limbang 1, ugpang 1, umbuk 1**)

  **pagiring-iring** *v. intr.* **aN-** To match each other, in size or social maturity. *Magiring-iring heya sigā.* Their size continues to be the same.

**iris** *v. tr.* **-an** To pay compensation for getting custody of a child whose parents divorce. *Buwat si Ja taga anak d'nda, ati baya' sigā dangan-duwa magtiman. Onde' inān ni'irisan he' man kal'llahan. Limampū' pilak pangiris.* Like Ja, who had a daughter, and the two of them agreed to divorce. Custody of the child was secured by the man's family, and fifty pesos was the compensation [paid to the woman's family]. *Manjari l'lla atawa d'nda angiris. Bang duwangan sigām bilahi angiris, subay magsulut.* The man or the woman may pay to get custody. If they both want to, then they need to come to an agreement. *Kairisan d'nda bang l'lla ya bay magmahal.* The woman is compensated when the man gets custody, since it was the man's side who chose to pay the *mahal* component of the bride-wealth. (*cf:* **lupit**)

**irup** *var.* of **hirup₁**

**Isa** *n.* Jesus, the Jewish religious teacher whose life, death and resurrection as recorded in the New Testament are the basis of the Christian faith, and who is recognized by Islam as an important prophet. (*syn:* **Isa Almasi**)

**Isa Almasi** *n. phrase* Jesus Christ; Jesus the Messiah; the Prophet Jesus. (*cf:* **Almasi**; *syn:* **Isa**; *Thesaurus:* **Almasihin**)

**isāb** *adv.* Also; again; likewise. *Aku isāb amole' salung.* I also will go home tomorrow. *Magutta' na kasehe' isāb saga a'a.* The rest of the people also vomited. *He' angay, aheka isāb ta'nda'ku.* That's not so, I definitely saw a lot.

**isab** **1)** *v. intr.* **pa-** To recur, as a chronic sickness. **2)** *v. tr.* **-an** To repeat an action. *Miki'isab, bo' palabay na.* Asking for a repetition, but [the moment] has passed already. *Bang kita makapah'lling, yukta, "Bay palagtik d'lla'na." D'lla'ta palagtik, mbal pagkahella'an, mbal taisaban.* When someone has said something we say, "He blurted it out [lit. his tongue flicked]." Our tongues cannot be pulled back, what's said cannot be undone. *Ni'isaban e'na bay pah'llingna tagna'.* He repeated his original statement. (*Thesaurus:* **balik₁ 1.3, duwa 1.1**)

**isay** *n.* A person with the same name as oneself. *Isay itū sali'-sali' ōn. Yukta, "O Isay." Isay* means having the same name. We say, "O Namesake." (*Thesaurus:* **danglay 1, ōn₁ 1, saingan**)

**isbat** *v. tr.* To treat something with proper care and diligence. *Bang pelang nil'bbos bo' halam niluhu he' kami, yuknu, "Halam isbatnu." Halam bay nijagahan.* If a canoe is launched but we didn't singe it, you say, "You didn't take care of it." It hadn't been looked after. *Bay pinakeyat palita'an bo' halam bay taisbat.* The lamp was lit but not properly tended. *Panoho'an Tuhan subay ni'isbat na pa'in.* God's commands should be treated with great care. *Isbatun tana'nu.* Take good care of your farmland. (*Thesaurus:* **pagagama, pagma'aripat**)

**iskopeta** *n.* An air-gun or toy which uses compressed air to fire a slug.

**iskul** (var. **eskwela**) *n.* 1) A school, especially one in the state system. *Mbal makani'iskul si Ng sabab halam aniya' pinsilna.* Ng can't to school because he doesn't have a pencil. (*cf:* **madrasa**) 1.1) *v. intr. aN-* To be attending school. *Na ilu ko' ilū angiskul arai' si Me inān.* So that'll be Me there going off to school. *Bay aku angeskwela ma Matina, ta'anuku na suwalaku, takaleku ma talingaku, yukku, "Apehet na k'llongku." Ainu-inu aku, yukku, "Halam bay aku angolang."* I was attending school in Matina and something happened to my voice, I heard it in my ear and thought, "My voice is cracked." I was surprised and said, "I haven't been shouting." *Bay aku angeskwela ma Matina, ta'anuku na suwalaku, takaleku ma talingaku, yukku, "Apehet na k'llongku."* I was attending school in Matina and something happened to my voice, I heard it in my ear and thought, "My voice is cracked."

**pangiskul** *n.* Schooling or education, as provided by the state.

**iskut** *adj. a-* Ungenerous; tight-fisted; stingy. *Aiskut bang pangamu'an ai-ai. A'llog iya ma ai-aina, mbal amuwan. A'llog ma danakanna.* Tight-fisted when asked for anything. He is so careful of his things, won't give anything away. He is mean towards his siblings. (*Thesaurus:* **bista₂ 1, kaikit₁, kigit, kimmat 1, k'mmit 1, kudkud, kuriput 1, kussil, giging, sumil₁**)

**isi₁** *n.* 1) The contents (of a container). 1.1) *v. intr. pa-* To fit into a container. *Minsan nirasok, minsan pinaponod, mbal paisi sabab hekana.* Even though it is jammed in, even though packed solid, it won't go in, being so many. *Ahalong bissalana, sali' halam makaisi ni ta'uta.* His words weren't clearly heard, they didn't get into our conscious awareness. (*Thesaurus:* **asok 1, deyom 1.1, sōd 1**) 1.2) *v. tr.* To put something into a container. *Bang bīlla saging bo' atahak, ni'isi ni lai'.* When bananas are boiled and cooked, they are put onto a plate. *Amu'us aku bohe', isiku ni undam pangose' lai'.* I pour some water, then I

put it into a basin for washing plates. (*cf:* **akay**)

**isi-isi** *v. tr. -an* To put ideas into someone's mind. *Sai bay makaisi-isihan ka'a lling buwattē'?* Who put words like that in your mind?

**pangisihan₁** 1) *n.* A container. 2) *v. tr.* To use something as a container.

**pangisihan₂** *n.* Mother, in a figurative sense as the container through which a child is brought into the world. (*cf:* **bohe'₂**)

**isi₂** *n.* The substance or essence of something; the fleshy part of a living creature or vegetable. *Aniya' na daing, taga isi dakayu'.* There are some fish, and one has flesh on it. *Isi sigām du.* Their essential nature.

**isi-kulabutan** *v. intr. aN-* To form lumps in the fleshy part of an arm or leg. {idiom} *Bang butugta, na abanol na, sali' angisi-kulabutan isita. Anuwa-nuwas l'ngngon-tape'.* If we pummel [something] it is bruised, sort of lumpy [lit. like cuttlefish meat]. The muscle tissue of arms and legs forms hard lumps. *Angisi-kulabutan, sali' pabutig, sali' takuddat laha'ta maka ugatta. Isi-kulabutan* is like muscle tissue forming lumps, as though our blood and sinews had been traumatised.

**isi-lling** *n.* The core sense of an expression. {idiom} *Ta'ā' isi-lling, ya ma'anana.* The core sense of the word is grasped, its meaning.

**isi empon** *n. phrase* The gums of the mouth (gingivae). {idiom}

**isi sapi'** *n. phrase* Beef; the flesh of a bull or cow.

**islam** *v. tr.* 1) To circumcise. 1.1) To mark (by circumcision) the formal entry of a pubescent boy into the community of Islam. *Subay kām bay labay islam kamemon ampa kitam makajari magpikit-pikiti. Bang mbal ni'islam, mbal makajari.* You must all have undergone circumcision for us to be able to intermarry. If [you] haven't been circumcised, it is not possible. (*cf:* **sunnat**)

**pagislam** *v. intr. aN-* 1) To circumcise. 1.1) *v. intr. aN-* To circumcise a teenage boy as a formal sign of his entry into the community of Islam. *Magislam itū aheka puhu' maglisag agung.* With an *islam* ceremony there are lots of people and gongs being played.

**Islam** *n.* The religious faith of Muslims as revealed to the Prophet Muhammad and recorded in the Holy Koran.

**ismagol** *v. tr.* To obtain trade goods by smuggling.

**pagismagol** *v. tr.* To be engaged in smuggling as an occupation. *Am'lli aku lansa bo' aku magismagol pehē' ni Sandakan atawa ni Bolneo.* I will buy a launch so I can engage in smuggling away there in Sandakan or [Indonesian] Borneo. (*cf:* **pagbisnis**)

**Isnin** *n.* Monday. (*Thesaurus:* **Ahad, Alba'a, Hammis, Juma'at, Sabtu', Salasa**)

**ispara** *n.* A bayonet or western style sword. *Bay kono' sinangko' maka ispara ilū.* Reportedly stabbed with that sword. (*cf:* **sangko' 1**)

**ispāy** (var. **ispiya**) *n.* 1) A spy. (*cf:* **mata-mata₂ 1**) 1.1) *v. tr. -an* To be involved in espionage; to keep a watch on someone or something. *Bang ka angispāy daing, bang ka'apikihannu, larukin na timbak.* When you spot some fish, and you get up close, toss the dynamite in. *Ispāyin si Ji hē', piligdu anangkaw. Ispāyin, sali' peyanin.* Keep a watch on Ji, it is feared that he may be stealing. Watch him, keep a lookout.

**ispidbut** *n.* A western-style speedboat. (*syn:* **bolbo₂**)

**ispital** (var. **ospital**) *n.* A hospital. *Arapun ma tongod mma'ku, wa'i iya pina'admit ma ispital llaw itu ma Sambo.* Oh and about my father, he was admitted to the hospital in Zamboanga today.

**ispiya** var. of **ispāy**

**ispowen** (var. **espowen**) *n.* A type of heavy cloth used for sails. *Am'lli aku ispowen nihinang lamak.* I'll buy some heavy cloth to make a sail. (*Thesaurus:* **kapis, kapis, lona, ma'ung, mantaluna, patig, tolda, wigan**)

**Isra'ili** *n.* An Israeli citizen of Jewish descent. *Aheka Isra'ili ma lahat sigām.* There are many Israelis in their country.

**issa** *num.* One, used in counting sequentially. *Issa, duwa, t'llu...* One, two, three... *Angitung aku min ssa.* I count from one. (*Thesaurus:* **da- 1, dakayu'₁ 1, dangan 1, sa-, ssa₃**)

**istadi** *v. tr.* To study a lesson, specifically of material provided by the secular school system. *Pahāpun e'nu angistadi.* Improve your studying. (*Thesaurus:* **adji' 2, anad 1, anad 1, ta'u₁ 1.2**)

**istinja'** *n.* Ritual washing after defecation, urination, or sexual intercourse. (*Thesaurus:* **ail, junub, peppet, puppu'**)

**pagistinja'** *v. intr. aN-* To prepare for prayer by carrying out the prescribed cleansing.

**istori** *n.* 1) An account of some event, real or imagined; a story. *Istori hē' putingan sa.* That story was surely a lie. (*Thesaurus:* **kissa 1, pagkata-kata 1.1, paglanga'-langa', salsila 1**) 1.1) *v. tr.* To tell a story; to relate an event. *Bang taistori hē'-i, sali' kamemon a'a tatangis.* If that story was told most everybody would be moved to tears.

**pagistori-istori** *v. intr. aN-* To talk and plan together, as sweethearts or accomplices do. *Bang saupama magistori-istori maka d'nda. Magtaratu kami, iya lum'ngngan pehē', aku isāb lum'ngngan ati magsabu.* For example I discuss plans with a girl. We agree on a time, she will walk there yonder, I also will walk and we will meet up. (*Thesaurus:* **pagbilma'arup, pagharis, pagsuli-suli**)

**istrōk** *v. intr. aN-* To be infatuated with someone. *Bang angalinig pantalunta, kinabaya'an kita he' budjang, angistrōk kita.* When our trousers are shiny the maidens desire us, and we are infatuated with each other. (*Thesaurus:*

**pagbaya'₂**)

**istung** *n.* A faulty move in games of motor skill, as tripping while jumping rope.

**isun** *v. tr.* To involve someone in a discussion; to inform someone of the results of a discussion.

**kaisunan** *n.* A formal discussion. *Pagga pa'in itū apūn kaisunan min d'nda maka min l'lla, na magtilaw sokat na.* Since the counsel from the woman's side and from the man's side were as one, they began to ask about the bride-wealth.

**isunan** *n.* An agreement resulting from discussion. *Pagkalena ya bay daisunan disi Anu ma habal itū, magtūy iya alahi pehē'.* On hearing what What's-his-name and his companions had planned together in response to this news, he promptly got away from there.

**pagisun** *n.* 1) A plan or plot. *Arapun in pasal kapagisun angatu ma ka'a, ndū' tuwan, da'a aku tuna'un.* With regard to a plot to fight against you, good sir, do not accuse me. 1.1) *v. tr.* To talk things over; to plan something together. *Makapagisun kami maka si Ro insini'.* We discussed things together with Ro earlier. *Sōng binono', pinaggara'-gara'. Buwattina'an hal magisun-isun, hal magbantu.* About to be killed, being plotted against. Right now it is just in the planning stage, just plotting. *Bang sali' ka'a ilū kinawinan, subay magisun-isun matto'anu du maka kar'ndahan. Subay maggara' dahū.* If you are getting married, your parents and those from the girl's family must agree on plans. They need to discuss things first. *Bang aniya' kagara'an subay magisun-isun onde'-matto'a.* When there is a planning meeting young and old should discuss things together. (*Thesaurus:* **pagbamba 1.1, pagimba-imba, pagmiting, paru, plano**) 1.2) *v. tr. -an* To plot against someone. *Na, alawak-lawak gi' si Yusup, ta'nda' iya he' saga danakanna. Magtūy iya pinagisunan pinapatay e' sigām.* Now while Joseph was quite far away, his brothers saw him. They promptly plotted against him.

**itaw-itaw** *v. intr. aN-* To flash, as something shiny reflecting light. *Sai bahā' dapu luma' angitaw-ngitaw ma bihing langit ē', buwat mital taluwa' llaw?* Who is the owner of the house that sparkles on the horizon there, like sheet metal catching the sun?

**itikad** *n.* The way one thinks; inner conviction; conscience. *Daitikad.* Of one mind [in religious conviction]. *Abontol itikadku tudju ni Tuhan.* My conscience is clear before God.

**itikad-atay** *n.* Conscience; state of mind. *Magtūy magk'bba itikad-atay si Sultan Da'ud.* King David's conscience was promptly disturbed.

**pagitikad** *v. intr. aN-* To have one's mind directed towards God. *Ai-ai pinabeya'an kita, magitikad sadja kita ni Tuhan.* Whatever is sent to us, we will continue to keep our minds on God. *Kami itū magitikad tunggal.* We-excl have God alone in mind.

**iting 1)** *n.* A spiny projection; a thorn. *Bo' na ang'llo' tuklang, iting anu ilū, iting kamemon na.* And then got some spikes, those whatsit thorns, thorns of all sorts. *Abisa kappo' tumbaga itū, makabakat, taga iting.* The Cloth stonefish referred to is intensely painful, it wounds, has spines. (*Thesaurus:* **leget, tuklang, tunuk**) **2)** *v. intr.* aN- To stand up from the skin, of hair, as a sign of fear or alarm. *Bay angiting bahibūku.* My body hair stood on end [in terror].

**itiya'** (var. **atiya'**) *dem.* 'Here [it] is.' (A demonstrative that functions as a predicate and identifies the person or thing being talked about.) *Mbal gi' kami ni iskul, itiya' gi' kami maglampasu'.* We aren't going to school yet, we're still here polishing the floor. *A: "Ma'ai laring?" B: "Atiya' ma bihingku."* A: "Where is my knife?" B: "Here it is beside me." *Atiya' na aku angadjal.* I'm here preparing food. *Atiya' na aku pal'kkat apa ka'a ni tabu'.* Here I am heading in a different direction now because you are going to the market. *Atiya' gusuk ma deyom baranku.* Here are the ribs, inside my body. (*cf:* **ilu 1.1, itu 1.1, niya'₁ 1**)

**itlan** var. of **kitlan**

**itū** *dem.* **1)** This here, referring to something near speaker and hearer [Set I]. *Nijagjag luma' itū, nirarut sampay hāg, apa ilu'un mundu.* This house referred to will be dismantled, even the posts pulled out, because there are bandits on the way. (*Set:* **hē'₂ 1, ilū 1, inān 1**) **1.1)** Reference to a recently introduced central participant in a narrative. *Nā, amandu' pa'in, na ya aniya' dakayu' a'a, niōnan si Da. Nā, si Da itu, hatina, bay iya nihinang-hinang.* Now, while he was teaching, there was a person named Da. Now this Da, in fact, had been a victim of witchcraft.

**itu** *dem.* **1)** This here, referring to something near speaker and hearer [Set II]. *Sali' atangtang ituta, bay nilabba'an, sali' nihantu.* This part of us sort of shrivelled, weakened, like being affected by a *hantu* sprite. (*Set:* **hē'₁ 1, ilu 1, ina'an 1**) **1.1)** Here [it] is, with an emphasis on being near the speaker. (A demonstrative that functions as a predicate and identifies the person or thing being talked about.) *Takaleku si Lo angalingan, yukna, "Mamang, itu papangku."* I heard Lo calling out, saying, "Mama, here is my Daddy." *Itu na saga senten bay pah'llingku.* Here are the sentences I referred to. *Itu aniya' isāb kissaku.* Here's a story of mine. (*cf:* **ilu 1.1, itiya'**)

**itu-ini** (var. **itu-itū**) *n.* This and that (various unspecified things). *Buwat saga itu-itū amussak-massik.* Like this and that causing clutter. (*cf:* **buwattitu-buwattina'an**)

**itu-itū** var. of **itu-ini**

**itung₁** *v. tr.* To count. *T'llumpū' ka ssa ya heka saga sultan itū kamemon bang ni'itung.* There were eleven of all these kings, when counted. *Angitung aku min ssa.* I am counting from one.

*Bang ni'itung saga datu' bay ma lahat, t'llumpū' ya hekana.* When the chieftains who were in the land were counted, there were thirty of them. (*Thesaurus:* **kalkula, kira, jumla 1, saipuwa**)

**itungan** *n.* The number counted. *Pila itunganna?* How much was the count?

**itung₂** *v. tr.* To regard or include a person or thing as

being of a particular sort. *Da'a pa'in iya itungunbi sali' bantabi, sagō' banda'anbi iya sali' dakayu' danakanbi.* Please don't regard him as an enemy, but warn him as though he were a sibling of yours.

**iyā** *pron.* He, she, it, him, her (third person singular) [Set I]. *Daipara asa'ut tonga' bahangi, bowaku iyā ni ispital, ati saga t'llu pitu' kami maina'an.* Fortunately, late at night, I was prompt in taking her to the hospital, and we were there for three weeks. *Da'a na iyā buwanin.* Don't give him any. (*cf:* = **na, iya;** *Set:* **akū, kā, kām, kamī, kitā 1, kitabi₁, kitām, sigā₁, sigām₁**)

**iya** *pron.* He, she, it, him, her (third person singular) [Set III]. *Makajari si Le niōnan a'a sayuman, pinagaddatan e' a'a kamemon. Iya na pagbeya'-beya'an.* Le could be described as someone who is sayuman, respected by everyone. He is someone to follow. (*cf:* = **na, iyā;** *Set:* **aku₂, ka'a, ka'am, kami, kita, kitabi₂, kitam, sigā₂, sigām₂**)

**iya'** *adj.* a- Ashamed; embarrassed. *Halam kami kabuwanan gandum. Alahi kami, aiya'.* We weren't given any corn. We ran off, ashamed. (*Thesaurus:* **biyas, maru 1.2, paki' 1, tamparasa**)

**kaiya'an** *n.* Shame; humiliation; embarrassment. *Kaiya'anku, halam bīlli tepoku.* My embarrassment, my mat wasn't purchased. *Amūng na ya mato'aku, yukna, "Ai kaiya'annu? Asal du," yukna, "h'ndanu."* My father-in-law spoke up, "What are you embarrassed about? She is in fact," he said, "your wife."

**iya'-iya'** *v. intr.* a- Shameful; embarrassing. *Sali' aiya'-iya'an dī kami na, ah'lling battitu.* We are sort of ashamed of ourselves talking like this. *Makaiya'-iya' ya bay kahinanganbi tagna'.* The things you used to do were sources of shame.

**pakaiya'** *v. tr.* To make someone ashamed or deeply embarrassed.

**pagpakaiya'** *v. intr.* aN- To shame each other for something. *Sali' bang magbono' d'nda sali'-sali', magpakaiya' paglalu.* When two women fight, they shame each other as being promiscuous.

**iyan** *v. tr.* To mention something of no great significance. *Saupama kita marilaut hal damunda'-damunda'ta, s'lle' bale puhu', minsan ni'iyan, punung-punungan, tapalis kita.* For example we are out at sea, just our one canoe, perish the thought, and, forgive me for mentioning it, we are faint with hunger, carried far off course. *Minsan ni'iyan d'nda inān, bang ngā'ta, mbal makajari si Anu angā'. Subay mma'na, danakanna.* Regardless of what is said about that woman if we are to get her, What's-his-name can't be the one. It will have to be his father an his brothers.

**iyas** *n.* 1) A tiny maggot, thought to be the maggot

of the common blowfly at a very small stage. (*Thesaurus:* **but'ngngel, kalog 1, sassing 1, ulat₁**) 1.1) *v. advrs.* -in- Infested with tiny

maggots. *Daing ni'iyas, song niulat.* Fish infested with tiny maggots, soon to be fly-blown.

**iyuk** var. of **yuk**

# J j

**jā** *n.* A rice cookie made of strands of fried batter. *Jā, aniya' nilūnan, aniya' isāb nilupi'-lupi' buwattina'an. Jā* cookies, some are rolled, and others are folded like so. (*gen:* **apam 1**)

**Jaba** *n.* Java, a distant land of mythic status.

**jaba'** *n.* A non-toxic variety of cassava that can be boiled and eaten without being grated and squeezed. *Aniya' isāb tibu'uk jaba', aettom kulitna, sali' maglapis. Makajari bīlla.* There is also java cassava, its skin black and layered. It can simply be boiled.

**jabel** *v. intr.* pa- To hang in tatters or flaps, of cloth or flesh. (*Thesaurus:* **kabel-kabel, gores 1, jebel-jebel 1.1**)

  **jabel-jabel** *n.* 1) Tatters. 1.1) *adj.* a- Tattered.

**jabjab** *v. intr.* pa- 1) To flap, as the wings of a bird. *Ang'llub isab pikpik sigām bang pajabjab, sali' tagandak ba'anan kura'.* Their wings make a rumbling sound when they flap, like the pounding hooves of many horses. 1.1) *v. tr.* -an To flap or shake something repeatedly. *Bang nijabjaban pikpik linggisan, paleyang.* When the wings of the frigate bird are flapped, it flies off.

  **pagjabjab** *v. intr.* aN- To be fluttering or flapping continually, as sails or flags in the wind.

**jablut** *n.* Fibrous growths or segments. *Laput nangka', ya jablutna ma deyom, takakan.* Jackfruit segments, its inner fibrous parts can be eaten. *Subay at'ggol bohe' ma deyom pelang bo' aniya' tai'-bamban maka jablutna.* Water has to be in the canoe for a long time for it to have mossy growth with its fibres.

**jabu** *adj.* a- 1) Disturbed, as a community by troublemakers. *Tapanhid kami in a'a inān asal panganjabu.* We recognized those people as known troublemakers. (*Thesaurus:* **balu', dongkag, halubilu, hengo-hengo, hiluhala' 1.1, hiyul, lengog 1.1, sasaw 1.1, sensong**) 1.1) *v. tr.* To create trouble in a community.

**jabu-jabu** *n.* An instrument for calling people together, such as a drum or bell. *Jabu-jabu, ya nilisag inān, tambul atawa bēl. Sinoho' patimuk saga ma'amun, atawa onde' iskul.* Jabu-jabu, the drum or bell that is struck, telling the mosque congregation or school children to gather.

*Paglukum: bang ma kami tonga' gantang buwas, maka daing. Atonga' pa'in sambahayang pinah'lling jabu-jabu, tinimuk kinakan, magkakan na.* The *lukum* meal, for us a half ganta of rice, plus fish. Halfway through prayers the gong is sounded, the food brought together, and the eating takes place. (*Thesaurus:* **tambul**)

**Jabul** *n.* The poetic and prophetic sections of the Old Testament portion of the Holy Bible. (*Thesaurus:* **kiramin-katibin, kitab, Kitab Tawrat**)

**jakat** *n.* A tithe or religious tax. (*Thesaurus:* **pagsapa'at, pitla', sarakka 1**)

  **pagjakat** *n.* 1) The act of giving alms. *Pagjakat itu ni pangkat anak-ubus.* This obligatory contribution is to a ritual ancestor. 1.1) *v. intr.* aN- To give a regular religious tribute. *Subay ta'abut bulan sangpū' maka duwa bo' kita magjakat pitla' ni guruta atawa ni imam angamu' apuwa. Na amowa kita tonga' gantang buwas, pinehē'an iya.* It should be in the twelfth month that we pay religious tribute and alms to our teacher or imam, requesting a blessing. We take half a measure of rice to him there.

**Jakatla'** *n.* Jakarta (the Indonesian city). *Juhul maka Jakatla'.* Johore and Jakarta [semi-mythical places at the outer limit of the known world].

**jakki** *v. tr.* 1) To doubt the truth of someone's response. *Asidda anganjakki a'a inān ma aku. Mbal ameya'-meya' bang nihaka'an. Tinajakki aku.* That person really treats me as a liar. Will not believe when told. I am doubted as to my truthfulness. *Atajakki pahāp a'a itu! Mbal am'nnal ma aku.* What a doubter this fellow is! He will not believe me. *Sali' pinagputingan iya bay mangahaka'. Mbal ameya'-meya' nihaka'an. Sali' atajakki ma iya.* The person who reported [the information] accused of being a liar. [The accuser] unwilling to be informed, hard to convince. *Bang nihaka'an mbal ameya', sigi-sigi na pa'in atilaw, sali' atajakki ma aku.* When told he will not accept it, keeps on asking, sort of skeptical towards me. (*Thesaurus:* **katilaw, sumariya, tanya₂**) 2) To interrogate those involved in a court case; to investigate the details of claim or complaint. **3)** To interrogate someone newly dead, the action of the mungkalun angel.

**jakkum₁** *n.* The tree of hell referred to in the Holy Koran.

**jakkum₂** *see:* **bunga-jakkum**

**jaket** *n.* A western-style short coat or jacket. (*Thesaurus:* **badju', polo**)

   **pagnijaket** *v. intr. aN-* To wear a jacket.

**jadjahan** *n.* A locality; a neighborhood; a district. *Jadjahan kami.* Our house group. *Da'a na to'onin maitu apa jadjahan sigā, pano'onan sigā.* Don't place the fishtrap here because it is their territory, their trapping site. *Bay pamasuku' ma sigām magtumpuk-manumpuk in kamemon kaluma'an maka saga da'ira ma jadjahan inān.* All the villages and towns in that district were made their property, one kin group after another. (*Thesaurus:* **lugal 1, pa'atagan, pat'nna'an**)

**jadja'** *adj. a-* **1)** Widespread; sparsely distributed. (*cf:* **ladja' 1**) **1.1)** *v. tr.* To look for something across a wide range of places. (*Thesaurus:* **batuk₂, lalag, libu 1.1, nda' 1.1, salusu**)

**jaga** *n.* **1)** Someone who guards. *Pagnakura'an iya ma saga jaga ma deyom astana'.* He was in authority over all the guards in the palace. (*cf:* **tunggu' 1**) **1.1)** *adj. a-* Watchful; on guard; staying awake. *Ajaga ka, da'a ka atuli.* Be watchful, don't sleep. **1.2)** *v. tr. -an* To watch over something; to guard. *Jagahin onde'-onde' itū, Neng.* Watch these kids, Dear. *Bang pelang nil'bbos bo' halam niluhu he' kami, yukun, "Halam isbatnu." Halam bay nijagahan.* If a canoe is launched but we didn't singe it, you say, "You didn't take care of it." It hadn't been looked after. (*Thesaurus:* **alimata, papag, peyan, tunggu' 1.1**)

   **pagjaga** *v. intr. aN-* **1)** To stay awake through the night. **1.1)** *v. intr. aN-* To be present at a ceremony which involves being awake through the night. *Bang a'a tag luma' bay ata'u bang lisag pila ya kasakat panangkaw ni luma'na, tantu du iya magjaga bo' mbal tasōd.* If the house-owner man had known what time the thief would get in the house, he would surely have watched so the house wouldn't be entered. (*cf:* **tingkō' 2**)

   **pajajaga** *n.* One who stays awake; a watcher.

   **patijagahun** *adj.* To be persistently watchful.

**jagjag** (*var.* **dagdag₂**) *adj. a-* **1)** Disorganized; disarranged; dismantled. *Ajagjag, mbal na tapagguna.* Broken up, no longer usable. (*Thesaurus:* **basak, langkat 1, larak 1.1, lorak**) **1.1)** *v. tr.* To dismantle something; to reduce to disorder. *Nijagjag luma'tam, nirarut sampay hāg apa ilu'un mundu. Ilu apinda kitam pehē' ni Butun.* This house of ours will be dismantled, posts and all pulled out, because bandits are coming. We will shortly transfer there to Butun.

**jaguni'** *n.* Character; behavior. *Da'a kam anaksi'*

*puting ma munda'an sara' pangandapitbi ma a'a ala'at jaguni'na.* Do not give false evidence before the court in support of a person whose character is bad. (*Thesaurus:* **kalakuhan, kasuddahan, hudjidjat, jari₄ 1, jāt₁, sadsaran**)

**jahallis** *adj. a-* Ill-natured; addicted to evil. *Na, bang ta'abut waktu, aniya' paluwas sultan landu' jahallis maka ab'ngngis.* Now when the time comes, a very wicked and harsh king will emerge. (*Thesaurus:* **jahat, jahil 1, jahulaka' 1, la'at 1**)

**Jahannam** *n.* Gehenna, a division of hell.

**jahat** *adj. a-* Harmful; adverse. (*Thesaurus:* **jahallis, jahil 1, jahulaka' 1, la'at 1**)

   **kajahatan** *n.* An unfortunate event; serious trouble. *Kajahatan, sali' kanahasan, sali' bininasa bang ganta' aniya' dusata.* A calamity, some ominous event, like being punished for some offense we may have committed. *Pal'ppi ka mareyom lahat ilu ko ra'a ka taluwa' kajahatan.* Be cautious in that place lest you be hit with something really bad. (*Thesaurus:* **bala', kala'atan, mulka' 1, naja', pa'al 1, udjul₁ 1**)

**jahil** *adj. a-* **1)** Ill-natured; immoral; addicted to evil. *Basta ala'at kaul maka pi'il, hinang maka addat, ajahil. Sali' jahulaka'.* When words and thought, actions and customs are evil, that is jahil. Similar to jahulaka'. (*Thesaurus:* **jahallis, jahat, jahulaka' 1, la'at 1**) **1.1)** *v. tr.* To treat someone cruelly or viciously.

**jahira** *n.* A species of fish sometimes caught in a panggal trap.

**jahulaka'** *adj. zero* **1)** Cruel; inhumane. *Jahulaka' itū asidda amono'. Ala'at kasuddahanna, sali' abbuhan.* Jahulaka refers to someone who is always fighting. His character is bad, he's proud. *Jahulaka', ala'at min ala'at.* Evil, worse than bad. (*Thesaurus:* **jahallis, jahat, jahil 1, la'at 1**) **1.1)** *v. tr.* To treat someone cruelly; to cause someone harm. *Tapabalikan Nasuli' itū apa ahāp, halam anganjahulaka'.* Nasuli is a place to go back to because it is good, with no one who causes harm to others. *Nijahaluka' iya he' siyakana, pinaka'at.* Treated viciously by his older brother, destroyed. *Da'a jahulaka'inbi a'a itū pagga bisitaku iya.* Don't maltreat this man because he is my guest. **1.2)** *v. tr. -an* To maltreat someone's person or property. *Hublutun na kalisnu ilu bo' aku papatayun, pād-pād saga kapil itu angandugsu'an aku maka anganjahulaka'an baranku.* Draw your bladed weapon and kill me, rather than this heathen stabbing me and abusing my body.

**jaip** *adj. a-* Amazed at. *Ajaip pahāp aku itū. Baha'u bay atulak a'a inān, atiya' na at'kka.* I am really amazed. That person has just left, here he is back already. (*Thesaurus:* **haylan, ili-ili, inu-inu 1, littā 1**)

**jaitun** *n.* The olive tree and its fruit. *Olea europaea.*

**jajamuhan** (derivative of **jamu**) *n.* The food eaten

at a feast. *Jajamuhan sangom ma maskid, maglukun kami.* The evening feast at a prayer house, we celebrate a religious festival.

**jala-jala** *n.* A grid; a trellis. *Inān iya aningkō' ma jala-jalana kahayang-hayangan.* He is there sitting in his trellised breezeway.

**jalak** *v. intr. pa-* To break, of waves. *Pajalak na goyak tudju kaleya. Ubus pat'ngge, ubus pal'ngngan.* The waves are breaking towards land. First they stand up on end, then they move forward. *Pariyata' ka magdai'-dai' apa pajalak na goyak ilu ni ka'a.* Get higher up quickly because those waves are going to break over you.

**jalalangking** *n.* A scorpion. *Jalalangking, sali' manuk-manuk abisa angeket.* A scorpion, a kind of insect that stings painfully. (*syn:* **kadjalangking**)

**jalampa** *n.* A traditional type of canoe referred to in kata-kata epics. {archaic} *Jalampa maka adjung bay awal.* The *jalampa* canoe and the *adjung* were vessels of long ago.

**pagjalampa-jalampa** *v. intr. aN-* To travel by a jalampa-type canoe. {archaic}

**jalanan** *n.* A cause; a reason. *Ai jalananna angkan paniya' kala'atan?* What is the cause that evil has come to be? (*cf:* **sabab₁ 1**)

**jalani** *n.* The slipper plant, a thorny succulent. *Pedilanthus tithymaloides (probable). Jalani itū, kīllo' tagokna panambal.* Jalani, its sticky sap taken for use as medicine.

**jalang₁** *adj. a-* Well-shaped; attractive in form. *Ajalang, pasal addatna.* Attractive, referring to his character. (*Thesaurus:* **alti, dorog₂ 1.1, hansam, hāp baran, himpit, lingkat 1.1, manis 1.1, polma 1.1**)

**jalang₂** *adj. a-* Occurring at widely spaced intervals, of time or space. *Ajalang pahāp a'a itū magpi'itu.* It is only very occasionally that this man comes here. *Bang makanilinggi', ajalang itu at'llag.* When it comes to fishing nets this word *jalang* means widely spaced. (*Thesaurus:* **bihang₂, bislang 1, lahang, lanta', salat 1, t'llag**)

**jali'** *n.* **1)** A stripe or band of contrasting color. *B'llihanku sanyawa ginomahan jali'.* I will buy shorts made with striped elastic. **1.1)** *adj. -an* Striped; banded. (*Thesaurus:* **b'ttik 1.1, kabang 1.1, kelong-kelong₁, manas, palang**)

**pagjali'** *v. intr. aN-* To show stripes; to appear to be striped. *Kayu bilulang, ya kayu asal magjali'.* Bilulang wood, the wood that is naturally striped.

**jallat₁** *n.* A restriction involving a debt or a legal dispute. *Apuwas na kita man huwas-huwas, apuwas man jallat. Halam na aniya' makajallat.* We are free now of our obligations, free from legal requirements. There is nothing to hinder [us].

**jallat₂** *n.* **1)** A noose; a loop; a snare. *Tantu iya amuwasan ka'a min jallat ya pinat'nna'an ka'a.* He will surely extricate you from the trap that is set

for you. **1.1)** *v. intr. pa-* Caught in a loop of line. *Buwat kita maglata maka onde'-onde', na nilengkongan maka lubid. Na bo' nilarukan ni baranna ati hella'ta, agtūy pajallat.* Like when we are playing with a child and encircle him with a rope. Then we throw it around him and pull it, and he's quickly lassoed. **1.2)** *v. tr.* To catch something in a loop or noose. *Tambalin aku. Bay aku tajallat e' tonda'.* Treat my wound. I was caught in a loop of trolling line. *Tu'ud ko' ka'a ilū pasulay anganjallat aku.* You're obviously just trying to trap me.

**jalnang** *n.* A shrub, the seeds of which provide a bright red dye. (*cf:* **passal 1**)

**jalum** *n.* A needle. *Agese' badju'ku, bay angindam jalum ni si Babu' A pangal'ait.* My shirt was torn, so I borrowed a needle from Aunt A to sew it with.

**jalum-kuyya'** *n.* The dry-love or amor-seco grass. *Andropogon or Chrysopogon aciculatus.* (*syn:* **lukut-lappas**)

**jām** *n.* An hour. *Pilanjām bay t'ggolbi mahē' ma ospital?* How many hours were you there at the hospital?

**jāman** *n.* An extended period of time; an era. *Min awal jāman sampay ni ahil jāman itū.* From olden times until the present period. (*Thesaurus:* **awal ni ahil, masa 1, taem, timpu 1, waktu 1**)

**jama'** *adj. a-* Notorious. *Sali' a'a bay maginum, kapamūng-mūngan e'na kamemon. Ajama' na.* Like someone who has been drinking and talking freeely about everything. It's community knowledge now. *Sali' aniya' bay kala'atan, tatuna' kamemon. Ajama' kamemon.* Like when there has been some serious misbehavior and it's all out there. All widely known.

**pagjama'-jama'** (var. **pagjamba'-jamba'**) *v. tr. -an* To talk openly about things that should be kept secret.

**jama'a** *n.* A religious congregation, especially in the context of a mosque or a company of pilgrims. (*cf:* **ma'amun**)

**jamban** *v. intr. a-* **1)** To defecate, a polite equivalent of sungi'. *Ā, kalu wa'i gi' ajamban.* Oh, he may be on the toilet. (*Thesaurus:* **mange' 1, sungi' 1, tai' 2**) **1.1)** *v. tr. -an* To excrete something.

**pagjambanan** *n.* Toilet facilities. *Angkan sampay buwattina'anan, pinagusal e' saga a'a nihinang pagjambanan.* That is why, right up until the present, people use it as a toilet. (*cf:* **toylet**)

**jambangan** *n.* A decorative garden; ornamental plants. *Angindam aku mital pamusug jambangan.* I am borrowing a can for watering the flowers. (*cf:* **galden**)

**jambatan** *n.* A pier; a wharf. *Lagaranta ka ma jambatan si Paupau.* I will wait for you at Paupau's wharf.

**jambay** *n.* A decorative tassel or fringe. *Itiya' na būng ataha' jambayna.* Here is a jellyfish with its long strands. (*cf:* **tipas-tipas**; *Thesaurus:*

**jambili, jambu 1, jombay-jombay)**

**jambay-būng** *n.* 1) The venomous trailing tentacles of the bluebottle jellyfish. 2) Long trailing fringes attached to a kite as decoration. *Angahinang aku mandal hinangku jambay-būng abō' pinaleyang.* I will construct a kite. I will make it with trailing threads and fly it.

**jambeyaw** *see:* **pagjambeyaw**

**jambili** *n.* The decorative flaps of paper attached to the outer string on the sides of a kite. (*Thesaurus:* **jambay, jambu 1, jombay-jombay**)

**jambu** *n.* 1) A decorative tuft, as on the edges of a sail or kite. *Ballak nihinang jambu panganjambu leha ko ahāp ninda'.* Ballak fibre made into tufts to decorate a sail so it looks good. *Aniya' jambu-jambuna bistiraku.* My dress is decorated with pompoms. (*Thesaurus:* **jambay, jambili, jombay-jombay**) 1.1) *v. tr. -an* To decorate something with tufts.

**jamin** *v. tr. -an* To go guarantee for someone; to bail someone out of custody. *Niluyal ma kasehe'an, nijamin ma kami. Sali' nil'kkat.* Some say *luyal*, we say *jamin*. [Both mean] ransomed or set free. *Buwat bay a'a tajil, buwat sala lung-kampung kami, na aku anganjamin ma iya.* Like when a person is jailed, like from our neighborhood, I provide bail for him. (*Thesaurus:* **haum, l'kkat₁ 1.1, luyal 1.1, piyansa**)

**jampa** *v. tr.* To answer someone negatively or rudely.

**jamput** *v. tr.* To do something in undue haste. (*cf:* **dai'-dai' 1.1**)

**jamu** *n.* 1) A feast, commonly as part of a religious festival. 1.1) *v. tr. -an* To provide someone with a feast; to invite to a feast. *Nijamuhan kita e'na.* He provided us with a feast.

**pagjamu** *v. intr. aN-* To celebrate a feast together. *Pagjamuna ma anakna, hatina in bay saki pahali na.* The feast he put on for his son, meaning to say that his sickness was healed.

**jajamuhan** *n.* The food eaten at a feast.

**janap** *n.* A short working knife with a square end sharpened for weeding or digging. (*Thesaurus:* **kīs₄ 1, laring, pisaw**)

**janji'** *n.* 1) A promise; a commitment; a contract. *Bay bogbogannu janji'nu ni mma'ku.* You have kept your promise to my father. 1.1) *v. ditr.* To promise something to someone. *Tinuman bay panganjanji'na ma aku.* His promise to me was carried out. *Tuwan Sultan, bay sa ka anganjanji' ni aku anakku si Sulayman ya pas'lle' magsultan min ka'a.* Oh king, you promised me that my son Sulayman would be king after you.

**pagjanji'** *n.* 1) A mutual promise. 1.1) *v. intr. aN-* To make mutual promises; to be in a covenant relationship. *Ya tumpukan batu itu paltanda'an in kita duwangan bay makapagjanji' ma llaw itu.* This pile of stones is a sign that the two of us have made promises to each other today. *"Ta'abut*

*mpat llaw pagjanji'an," yuk-i ni sultan, "taima' kami."* "When the four days agreed on are over," said he to the sultan, "we will be accepted."

**baljanji'** *n.* 1) A religous vow made for safety or the recovery of good health. 1.1) *v. tr. -an* To make a vow of religious commitment for the purpose of restoring good health or safety. 2) A dedication ceremony involving the reading of the baljanji' section of the Holy Koran.

**pagpaljanji'an** *v. intr. aN-* To make a solemn promise to each other.

**paljanji'an** *n.* A formal promise or covenant.

**jantang** *n.* The essential characteristics of a person. *Jantangna, lahina. B'nnal ibarat hatulanna, ya jantangna to'ongan.* His *jantang*, his appearance. A reference in fact to his nature, his true essence.

**jantang-jari** *n.* The characteristic appearance of a person; facial features. *Ya na luwa jantang-jarina.* That's the way he looks and is. (*Thesaurus:* **aymuka, bantuk, bayhu' 1, dagbos, lahi₄, luwa 1, pangli' 1**)

**jantung** *n.* The heart as a physical organ.

**jangat** *v. tr.* To cut something into thin strips. *Jangatun botong ilū, binukayu'.* Grate that young coconut to be made into candy. (*Thesaurus:* **kugut₁, li'is**)

**jangatan** *n.* An implement for cutting vegetable material into slivers, consisting of a handle with a row of sheet metal loops or blades. *Am'lli aku jangatan panganjangat pandan nihinang tepo.* I will buy a strip-cutter to prepare pandanus for weaving a mat.

**jangka'an** *n.* 1) A boundary or limit; the line in throwing games beyond which a ball or marker is out. (*Thesaurus:* **manohan, tibtib**) 2) The predestined time of a person's death. *Tiyap-tiyap manusiya' aniya' jangka'anna.* It is inevitable that a human being has a limit to his life.

**jangki** *var. of* **jingki**

**janggay** *n.* 1) A metal fingernail extension which fits over the fingertips when dancing. 1.1) *v. tr. -an* To fit metal extensions to the fingernails.

**janggi'** *adj. -an* Striped gray and black, as of cats. *Kuting ya janggi'-janggi'an, basta kuting sadja.* A cat, the one with grey and black stripes, only of cats.

**janggut** *n.* 1) The hairlike projections of squid, cuttlefish or shrimp. (*cf:* **gulamay 2, labu₄**) 2) A goatee beard.

**jangngang** *adj. a-* Shapely; good, of a person's figure. *Buwattē' si Bapa', mbal na ajangngang baranna buwat tagna'. Parokkog na.* Uncle is like that, his body is no longer shapely as it used to be. He stoops now.

**japang** *n.* A basket of loosely woven mature coconut leaves. *Salingkat itū buwat du japang, sali' du hinanganna, halam aniya' bidda'na.* The *salingkat* referred to is like a *japang*, same construction, no difference. (*syn:* **salingkat;**

*gen:* **baka'**₁)

**jarayan** *n.* A back rest for the support of someone working long hours at a task.

**jari**₁ *v. intr. zero* **1)** For something to be possible or accepted. **1.1)** *v. tr.* To make something happen. *Saga a'a makamata ma bay tajari ma a'a sinōd saitan.* The people who witnessed what happened to the fellow possessed by a *saitan* spirit.

  **kapamanjari** *n.* The state of something in its created form.

**jari**₂ *v. intr. aN-* To worsen, of a sickness.

**jari**₃ *conj.* So then (a sentence or paragraph introducer). *Jari itu, pagka halam maina'an si Ku, amole' na kami.* So then, since Ku was not there, we went home. *Jari itu, makatuli pa'in si Samson, niā' e' si Delila pitu' sapiran bu'unna bo' nianyam ni kakana'.* So then, while Samson was sleeping, Delilah took seven plaits of his hair to be woven into cloth. *(syn:* **manjari**₂)

**jari**₄ *n.* **1)** The intrinsic nature of a person, usually in a negative sense. *Ala'at kajarihan saga a'a itū.* The character of these people is bad. *(Thesaurus:* **kalakuhan, kasuddahan, hudjidjat, jaguni', jāt**₁**, sadsaran) 1.1)** *v. advrs. ka-...-an* Destined to come to a bad end.

  **pagkajarihan** *v. intr. aN-* To behave in ways which reveal one's true character. *Sai sa makapikil magkajarihan angahinang la'at buwattilu?* Who could even consider displaying his nature by doing such bad things? *Saki bilasku inān, manusiya' bay magkajarihan amat'nna' saki.* My brother-in-law's illness, it was a human being whose nature was to impose an illness on someone.

**jāt**₁ *n.* The essential qualities or components of a person's nature. *(Thesaurus:* **kalakuhan, kasuddahan, hudjidjat, jaguni', jari**₄ **1, sadsaran)**

**jāt**₂ *see:* **pajātan**

**jati'** *n.* Teak. *Tectona grandis. Daun jati' ya pagtimayukan.* Teak leaves are used to wrap food for guests.

**jatti** *n.* Something beyond dispute. *Jatti ma iya kapanyapan inān.* That equipment is undisputedly his. *Anakku jatti.* My legitimate son. *(cf:* **lahasiya' 1, porol)**

  **pagjatti** *v. intr. aN-* To be the rightful owner of something. *A: "Jatti ma h'ndaku pamanganan ilu." B: "Ōy, ngga'i ka ma iya, aku ya magjatti."* A: "Those plates belong to my wife." B: "No way, they are not hers; I am the undisputed owner."

**jatu** *adj. a-* **1)** Satisfactory; functioning well; productive. *Halam ajatu iskul apa magsakihan mastal.* School is not satisfactory because the teachers get sick. *Ajatu na paggara'bi?* Is your discussion completed satisfactorily? *(cf:* **abag) 1.1)** *v. tr.* To do something completely and effectively. *Jatuhun hinangnu ilū.* Do that work of yours well. *Na bang aniya' hinangta, subay jatuta.*

*Da'a ni'bbahan, makabintan.* So if we have work to do we should carry through with it. Don't just put it down, it makes for unproductive behavior. *Amakatuk kita l'lla maka d'nda, amajatu sali'.* We get a man and a woman to commit to getting married, like clarifying the situation.

  **kajatuhan** *n.* Prosperity; a positive outcome.

  **pajatu** *v. tr.* To complete something satisfactorily.

**jau-** *see section 2.2.2.4 Prefix:* **Cau-**

**jauk** *n.* **1)** A sweetmeat made of cassava. *(syn:* **lapuk-lapuk) 1.1)** *v. tr.* To make a cassava sweetmeat.

**jau'-jau'** *v. intr. pa-* To interrupt rudely. *Palamugay kita, pajau'-jau'.* We join in, interrupting. *Saupama ka'a ilū soho'ku, na manjari itū pajau'-jau' ya dangan itū, supaya binuwanan.* For example I send you off, and then, this other one interrupts to be given something. *Bang aniya' magsuli-suli bo' halam lamudnu, da'a ka pajau'-jau' sabab ilu-i halipulu.* If some people are talking together and you are not involved, don't interrupt, because that is impolite. *(cf:* **balat, lamud**₂ **1.1, pagsakutu)**

**jawab**₁ *v. ditr.* To make someone a counter-offer when buying or selling; to bargain. *(Thesaurus:* **andag, halga' 1.2, ladjaw, paragang)**

**jawab**₂ *n.* **1)** An argument; a defense against a charge. *Angay iya ananggung jawab dangan-danganna?* Why does she take on herself the responsibility of responding [to an accusation]? **1.1)** *v. tr.* To contest someone's decision or statement. *Jinawab aku he' mastal.* The schoolteacher contradicted me.

  **pagjawab** *n.* **1)** A dispute; a disagreement. **1.1)** *v. tr. -an* To argue with someone; to bargain. *Buwat onde'-onde' aniya' kabilahi'anna bo' mbal ta'ā'na, magjawab iya maka matto'ana.* Like a kid who wants something but doesn't get it, he argues with his parents. *Halli'inbi saga a'a magjawab ma halam aniya' kagunahanna.* Avoid the people who argue for no purpose. *(Thesaurus:* **pagagaw-besod, pagbagod, pagbengtod, pagdiskās, pagpayod 1.1, pagsalod, pagsu'al)**

**jayak** *adj. a-* Plentiful. *(Thesaurus:* **banos, besal, kansang 1, datay**₂**, dayas-dayas, dorot, heka 1.1, parat)**

  **pagjayak** *v. tr.* To produce something in abundance. *Bang pinagjayak, na aheka, maglabi-labihan na.* When something is made in abundance, then there is very much of it, more than enough.

  **pajayak** *v. tr.* To produce in abundance.

**jebel-jebel** (var. **sebel-sebel**) *adj. a-* **1)** Tattered; torn in many places. **1.1)** *v. intr. aN-* To become tattered, of clothing or a lacerated wound. *Anebel-nebel, agese', buwat buli' pantalun halam bay tinupakan.* Hanging down in tatters, torn, like the backside of trousers that haven't been mended. *(cf:* **gese' 1**; *Thesaurus:* **kabel-kabel,**

gores 1, jabel)

**jēk** *voc. n.* A pal; a mate; a buddy.

**pagjēk** *v. intr. aN-* To be in a cordial but casual relationship. *Magjēk kami, sali' du maka 'prēn' ma Ingglis.* We are buddies, like English 'friend'.

**jego** *v. advrs. -in-* Marked by scribbled lines. *Nijego-jego bukutta, baranta. Bā'nu bay palēhan omang.* Our backs and bodies are marked. You would think they had been crawled on by a hermit crab.

**jelus** *v. intr. aN-* To be jealous of someone for romantic reasons. *Kap'ddi'an aku, agkā', sali' kita anganjelus pamaya'-maya'.* I am in pain, alas, as though being jealous in love. (*Thesaurus:* **abuggu', himuggu', iggil 1.1, imbū, jingki 1, lindi 1**)

**jeneral** (var. **jiniral**) *n.* A military officer of any rank higher than colonel. (*Thesaurus:* **kapitan, komandel, tininti**)

**Jengen** *n.* Alternative name for boat-dwelling Sama. {old-fashioned} *Nilangguyuran, buwat a'a Jengen, lling sigā.* Dragged out, like the speech of Jengen Sama. (*syn:* **pala'u**)

**Jibra'il** *n.* The archangel Gabriel.

**jikil** *n.* 1) A melodic chant from the book of Maulud. **1.1)** *v. tr. -an* To accompany a ceremony with melodic chanting. *Atawa kita maghinang amatay, atawa hinang maut, subay nijikilan.* Whether we are performing a mourning ritual, or placating the death spirit, it should be accompanied by chanting.

**pagjikil** *v. intr. aN-* To be engaged in congregational singing or chanting. *Hinang ai-ai na bā. Bang aniya' a'a patay niā' kapakilan magjikil.* Any kind of ceremony. If someone has died the religious assistants are fetched to do the *jikil* chant. *Magjikil kita tasbi'.* We chant using prayer beads.

**jīl** *n.* 1) A jail or prison. **1.1)** *v. tr.* To jail someone. *Pasal bay anangkaw onde'-onde' ilū, tajīl.* Because that child had been stealing, he was jailed. *"Ya na ilu," yukna, "lahat panganjīlan i'."* "There," he said, "is the place where [people] are imprisoned." *Buwat aku saupama anangkaw bo' ta'abut aku, binatang-batangan aku. Na bang aku anangkaw pabalik mbal minsan nihukum, nijīl sadja.* Like, for example, if I steal and get caught, I am released on condition. Then if I steal again I am not even charged, but simply put in jail. (*Thesaurus:* **kalabusu 1.1, pilisu 1.1**)

**jilaka'** *v. tr.* To cause someone grievous harm; to violate someone. *Bay iya nijilaka' he' saitan, sali' pinasakki.* He was seriously harmed by a *saitan* spirit, sort of made ill. (*Thesaurus:* **la'at 1.2, la'ug 1.1, pinjala' 1.1, pissoko', puhinga', sikla, usiba'**)

**jimban** (var. **simpan**) *n.* The counters used in the game of jacks.

**pagjimban** *n.* 1) The game of jacks (knucklebones). **1.1)** *v. intr. aN-* To play the game of jacks.

**jimpaw** *n.* A towel; a napkin. (*Thesaurus:* **panyu', sapu-tangan, tawel, tuwalya**)

**jīn** *n.* 1) Supernatural beings who can communicate through a human being in a trance state. *Magpaubus ni sigā ya taga jīn. Bang kauli'an subay da'a magl'kkat. Anak-ubus ko' hē'.* As a last resort, the one with a healing djinn goes to the [sick woman]. When healed [she and the healer] should not part. She is his daughter for life. *Bang jīn ahāp, makaka'llum, bang jīn ala'at makapatay. Kamemon jīn magsarap.* If a djinn is good it makes alive, if it is a bad djinn it kills. All djinns are unpredictable. *Ya po'onan jīn min duwata, min tag-jīn, min po'on kayu.* The origin of a djinn is a *duwata* spirit, from a djinn proprietor, or from a tree. (*cf:* **duwata 1;** *Thesaurus:* **bangsa magl'l'ngngan, duwata 1, hama'-hama' a'a, hibilis, saitan, ya mbal ta'nda'**) **1.1)** *adj. -an* Having enduring rights over a djinn. *A'a jīnan si mbo' Ab.* Grandfather Ab is a djinn proprietor. **1.2)** *v. advrs. ka-...-an* To be possessed by a djinn. *Magdamoseng a'a inān, mbal makat'nna' ma paningkō'anna, ya pasal kajīnan iya.* That person is dancing in ecstasy and can't remain in his place, due to being possessed by a djinn. (*Thesaurus:* **sangon₂ 1.1, sawi'**)

**jina** *see:* **pagjina**

**jiniral** var. of **jeneral**

**jinis** var. of **ginis**

**jingki** (var. **jangki**) *adj. a-* 1) Spitefully jealous. (*Thesaurus:* **abuggu', himuggu', iggil 1.1, imbū, jelus, lindi 1**) **1.1)** *v. intr. aN-* To display ill-will towards someone out of spite. *Anganjingki si Mo ma kami sabab anakna abilahi'an si Arung.* Mo is spiteful towards us because his son desires Eldest Daughter. (*cf:* **puhinga'**) **1.2)** *v. tr.* To harm someone out of spite. *Nijangki aku he' a'a inān, sali' nila'at aku.* I have been badly treated by that guy, like I've been harmed.

**pagjingki** *v. intr. aN-* To be mutually antagonistic. *Buwat saupama taga pelang aku ahāp, bo' sali' aniya' sehe'ku magjingki. Nirali'itan aku he' sigām. Manjari nihinangan aku la'at, minsan aku halam bay magdusa.* Supposing I have a good canoe, and someone has malice towards me and wants to bring me down. So they do something bad to me, even though I have committed no wrong. *Magjingki-jingkihan, sali' magpalbantahan.* Mutually antagonistic, like being in an enemy relationship.

**jinggam** var. of **singgam**

**jīp** *n.* 1) An all-purpose vehicle; a medium-sized people-carrier. *Nsa' pa'in at'ggol-t'ggol isāb, ameya' na kami man jīp min Malaybalay inān sudju Nasuli'.* And not much later, we went by jeep from Malaybalay towards Nasuli. **1.1)** A jeepney.

**Jipun** *n.* The country of Japan; an ethnic Japanese.

*Hinangan Jipun.* Of Japanese make.

**jiyara** *v. intr.* pa- To greet someone formally with a handshake or kiss. *Pajiyara kita ni a'a bang aniya' bay at'kka min paghadji'an. Suma'an pa'ampun kita, pama'ap kita.* When someone has arrived back from the pilgrimage we greet him formally. At other times we may be seeking forgiveness or reconciliation. (*Thesaurus:* **sekan**)

**pagjiyara** *v. intr.* aN- To greet each other formally with a handshake or kiss. (*cf:* **pagsalam**)

**jiyay** *n.* A brand of cotton thread originally obtained from US soldiers (GIs). (*Thesaurus:* **bannang, tanud, tingkal**)

**j'ngngit** *v. tr.* To treat someone with dislike or antagonism. *Sali' kita nij'ngngit, kĭllit, kinab'nsihan sala.* We are sort of treated with dislike, aversion, as though we are disliked intensely. (*Thesaurus:* **bigsi' 1, b'nsi 1.1, b'ngngis 1**)

**jōk** *v. tr.* To answer someone flippantly, especially in response to something said in seriousness. *Pandu'anta ka ni kahāpan, gōm pa'in aku jōknu.* I teach you for your good, and instead you are sassy towards me.

**jodjol** *v. intr.* pa- To persist in doing something in the hope of forming a useful relationship. *Minsan kita kinab'nsihan, pajodjol na pa'in. Minsan mbal niasip.* Even though they dislike us, we will keep on [visiting.] Even though [our presence] is not acknowledged.

**jogjog** *adj.* a- 1) Unstable; shaky. (*Thesaurus:* **hengko, henggol 1, hodjog 1, oseg 1**) 1.1) *v. tr.* To cause something to shake or become unsteady. *Halam aku bay makatalus amangan, sali' nijogjog kinakanku.* I had not finished eating when my food was sort of jolted. (*Thesaurus:* **siggul**)

**jogjog tana'** *n. phrase* An earthquake.

**jogjog deyom dunya** *adj.* a- Shaking, of a seismic event (an earthquake). (*Thesaurus:* **linug₁**)

**jolog** *v. intr.* pa- To stand out from others in a group, as someone who is different. *"Alō," yuk-i, "luwana. Mbal paraluwa ni sehe'na, pajolog."* "Wow," they say, "see that. He doesn't look the same as his companions, he is so obvious." *Minsan gi' nsa' lamudna, pajolog na pa'in iya, amalamud dīna.* Even though he has no involvement, he continues to stand out from the rest, getting himself involved. *"To'ana," yuk-i, "pajolog iya. Ameya' ma saga onde' baha'u."* "At his age," they say, "going where he doesn't fit in, joining in with the young men."

**jombay-jombay** *n.* The decorative tassels on the edge of a cloth or shawl. (*Thesaurus:* **jambay, jambili, jambu 1**)

**jompo'** *adj.* a- Bored or surfeited, especially with an item of food. *Ajompo' itū a'sso, halam galak amangan. Ajompo' iya ma pagkakan. Jompo'* means full from eating, having no desire to eat.

He does not feel like food. (*Thesaurus:* **lumad, sumu 1.1**)

**juba** *n.* A long outer garment of white cloth worn by men on formal occasions such as prayer. (*Thesaurus:* **gamis, luku**)

**pagnijuba** *v. intr.* aN- To wear a long gown of white cloth.

**jubul** *n.* The anus; the rectum. *Sinuruk kita he' a'a ma lowang jubulta.* Someone pokes us in the anal orifice. (*cf:* **tombong**)

**jukup** *adj.* a- 1) Complete; in total. *Ajukup na duminuku, bay na itungku.* My dominoes are complete, I have counted them. (*Thesaurus:* **lungbus, pareyo'-pariyata'**) 1.1) *v. tr.* To bring to completion. *Jinukup isāb ya takapin panganggastus, pamahāp langgal.* The remaining building materials were completed for repairing the prayer house. 1.2) *v. tr.* -an To add something in order to complete or make up a shortage. *Nijukupan na pa'in e'na kulang-kabus matto'a-danakanna.* He keeps on replenishing what his parents and siblings lacked. (*Thesaurus:* **k'nnop 1.2, ganap 1.2, tubil**)

**jūd** *n.* A major division of the Holy Koran; by extension, a major division of other religious books. (*Thesaurus:* **ayat, bāb**)

**judjal** 1) *v. intr.* pa- To project forward. *Jungal, ya pajudjal ma munda' balanda'.* A bowsprit, that which projects from the front of a sailing ship. *Bang pajudjal, tu'ud pasōngan dīna.* If [someone] moves out in front, he is simply promoting himself. *Sagō' makaragsa' sigām ni kahanggalan. Amalut munda' kappal, mbal pajudjal, maka buli'na hē' abagbag e' goyak.* But they happened to run aground on the shallow bottom. The bow stuck fast, couldn't be moved forward, and the stern was battered by the waves. 2) *v. tr.* -an To push something vigorously forward. *Judjalin bangka' inān.* Push that canoe ahead. *Buwat aku ma munda' halam taga busay, bo' nijudjalan pelang, yukku, "Da'a na paragsa'un."* Like when I am in the bow with no paddle, and the canoe is being pushed along vigorously, I say, "Don't let it hit anything under the water." (*cf:* **lodjat₂ 1**)

**judju'** *v. tr.* 1) To offend someone by doing more than was asked, or expected by cultural norms. *Panganjudju'ta iya ma hinangta, panganjuralta iya atawa pamakalintawta iya.* We do something that irritates him by its excess, we do [something] to provoke him or make him annoyed. 1.1) *v. tr.* -an To give someone excessively more than was asked or expected. *Bang aniya' badju' si Ji, bo' bay tasulugku, ap'ddi' atayna. Kin'nnopan gi' dakayu' badju'na, nijudju'an aku e'na.* If Ji has a shirt and I have put it on, he gets upset with me. He adds yet another of his shirts and gives it to me [out of annoyance]. *Yukku ma ka'a, "Amuwan ka katas, saga dakayu' sadja pangalampik sugal," ati bang aku buwanannu aheka, magjudju' ka. Sali' ka astolan.* If I say to you, "Give me some paper, just one piece to wrap my playing cards in," and you give me many sheets, you are behaving excessively. Sort of angry. (*syn:* **pagjuru' 1.1**)

**juhal** *v. intr.* pa- To protrude, of one or more teeth. (*Thesaurus:* **jungal 1.1, toro' 1.1, tungalu'**)

**Juhul maka Jakatla'** *n. phrase* Johore and Jakarta, the remotest places of the Sama world. {idiom} *Juhul maka Jakatla', sali' tapagliyu-liyu bang kita angamu'.* Johore and Jakarta, as though we have gone everywhere making a request.

**julangkang** *v. intr.* pa- To lie on one's back with feet in the air. *Pajulangkang, sali' tape'na pariyata', bukutna pat'nna' ma papan. Hal yangkon tape'na pariyata'.* Pajulangkang means his feet are up in the air, his back lying on the floor. Just his feet alone sticking up. (*cf:* **sulalla**)

**Julka'idda** *n.* The eleventh month of the Islamic year. (*Set:* **Bulan Muharram, Julhadji', Jumadir Ahil, Jumadir Awal, Rabiul Ahil, Rabiul Awal, Radjab, Ramadan, Saban, Sappal, Sawwal**)

**julenget** *v. intr.* pa- To project awkwardly, as of badly set teeth. (*Thesaurus:* **pagsalisi, pagsōng-suwa', pagsuwa'-s'llo', sulangat**)

**Julhadji'** *n.* The twelfth month of the Islamic year, the month in which pilgrims make their pilgrimage to Mecca. (*syn:* **Bulan Hadji'**; *Set:* **Bulan Muharram, Julka'idda, Jumadir Ahil, Jumadir Awal, Rabiul Ahil, Rabiul Awal, Radjab, Ramadan, Saban, Sappal, Sawwal**)

**jullit$_1$** *v. tr.* **1)** To see something out of the corner of one's eye. **1.1)** *v. intr.* pa- To look briefly to one side. *Ang'nda' sali' pajullit, palingi'.* Looking, kind of glancing, turning the head to see. (*syn:* **sulli'**)

**jullit$_2$** *v. tr.* To tease or annoy someone, as in play or to get attention. *Da'a jullitun onde' ilū.* Don't tease that child. (*Thesaurus:* **bellod$_1$, juri 1.1, lawat, pabelaw**)

**pagjullit** *v. intr.* aN- To engage in joking with each other.

**julut** *v. intr.* pa- **1)** To slide down a slope. *Buwat kita amowa lai' isihan kinakan, subay kita kamaya' ko da'a pajulut.* It's like when we are carrying a plate of food, we must be careful that it doesn't slide off. *Bay latap pajulut kaut pabīng.* What had been a flood slips out to sea again. *Ameya' kita pajulut ma goyak, sali' patūd ma goyak.* We slide with the waves, like running before the waves. (*Thesaurus:* **dokdos, dusdus, dūt, loros, lurus$_1$ 1, luslus 1**) **1.1)** *v. tr.* -an To cause something to slide down a slope.

**Jumadir Ahil** *n. phrase* The sixth month of the Islamic year. (*Set:* **Bulan Muharram, Julka'idda, Julhadji', Jumadir Awal, Rabiul Ahil, Rabiul Awal, Radjab, Ramadan, Saban, Sappal, Sawwal**)

**Jumadir Awal** *n. phrase* The fifth month of the Islamic year. (*Set:* **Bulan Muharram,** **Julka'idda, Julhadji', Jumadir Ahil, Rabiul Ahil, Rabiul Awal, Radjab, Ramadan, Saban, Sappal, Sawwal**)

**Juma'at** *n.* Friday. (*Thesaurus:* **Ahad, Alba'a, Hammis, Isnin, Sabtu', Salasa**)

**Jumala** *n.* The name of a folk character noted for the incongruous things he does. *Si Jumala, bang pakapo' magtaumpa', bang pal'ngngan binenten.* Jumala, he wears his shoes when wading, and carries them when walking on land.

**jumla** *adj.* a- **1)** Totaled, of a list of figures. *Ajumla, tabista kamemon.* Totaled, all counted. (*Thesaurus:* **kalkula, kira, itung$_1$, saipuwa**) **1.1)** *v. tr.* To add up a total.

**jumlahan** *n.* The total from adding a list of figures.

**junjung** (var. **jungjung**) *n.* **1)** Mercy or favor that is granted by a superior. **1.1)** *n.* A favor requested from a supernatural source. *Lidjiki' maka barakat ya junjung kami ni Tuhan.* Blessing and power are what we request from God. **1.2)** *v. ditr.* To request a favor from a supernatural source.

**junna** var. of **dunya**

**junub** *n.* Purification from bodily emissions in preparation for worship. (*Thesaurus:* **ail, istinja', peppet, puppu'**)

**junya** var. of **dunya**

**jūng-jūng** *n.* The Non-spotted halfbeak. *Hemiramphus far.* (*gen:* **pillangan**)

**jungal** *n.* **1)** A projection from a main part, as the prow of a sailing vessel. *Jungal, ya pajudjal ma munda' balanda'.* A bowsprit, the pole that projects out from the bow of a European-type schooner. **1.1)** *v. intr.* pa- To project from a main part, as teeth, an upper lip, or a protruding beam. *Pajungal emponna, paluwas sala.* His teeth stick out, sort of coming out. *Pajungal buggul kappal.* The bulbous bow of a ship protrudes [from its hull]. (*Thesaurus:* **juhal, toro' 1.1, tungalu'**)

**jungkak** *n.* A fish species with long white-tipped lower jaw, up to 20cm in length.

**jungkat** *v. intr.* pa- **1)** To move upwards suddenly, as though pushed from beneath. *Ameya' kita pajungkat, bay takuddat, sali' ameya' kita pabuwang.* We make a sudden upwards movement, startled, as if going to jump up. **1.1)** *v. tr.* To tip someone over by pushing from beneath. *Nijungkat, sali' binuhat buli'ta pariyata'.* Pushed from beneath, as though our bottom was lifted in an upwards direction. *Buwat aku patondok, nijungkatnu buli'ku, agsay yukku, "Da'a ka anganjungkat, aku itū ahūg pareyo'."* Like if I am facing down and you push my bottom upwards, I immediately say, "Don't make me jerk upwards, I'm likely to fall down." (*Thesaurus:* **pagtungkellat-tungkellat, togsok, tunggang**)

**pagjungkat-jungkat** *n.* **1)** A see-saw or teeter board. **1.1)** *v. intr.* aN- To move up and down repeatedly; to play together on a see-saw.

**jungkung** (var. **kungkung**) *n.* **1)** A traditional sailing vessel of the type sometimes referred to as a Chinese junk. **2)** A sailing toy made of a coconut leaflet and a piece of its central spine. *Sali' kita magpangongka1', ya daun salirap nihinang jungkung pagbanog-banog.* Like us playing together, coconut leaflets made into little boats for sailing.

**jungjung** var. of **junjung**

**jural** *v. tr.* To provoke a reaction, as by teasing or poking. *A'a inān magpanganjural.* That fellow is always behaving in a provocative way. *Panganjudju'ta iya ma hinangta, panganjuralta iya atawa pamakalintawta iya.* We do something that irritates him by its excess, we do [something] to provoke him or make him annoyed. (*Thesaurus:* **kalintaw, mata-mata₁**)

**juri** *adj. a-* **1)** Annoying; irritating. *Ajuri pahāp a'a itū.* This fellow is so annoying. *Ajuri itu amuwan na pa'in kala'atan, minsan malkina, minsan tudju ni manusiya'.* *Ajuri* is to keep on causing irritation, whether it's an engine or even a person. **1.1)** *v. tr.* To tease; to make fun of. (*Thesaurus:* **bellod₁, jullit₂, lawat, pabelaw**)

**juru'** *see:* **pagjuru'**

**juwalan** *n.* Bananas or sweet potato, sliced, fried and glazed. (*Thesaurus:* **libusaw 1, piritu**)

# L l

**lā** var. of **la'a**

**lāb** *adj. a-* **1)** Scorched by flames; caught in a fire. *Alāb tinapa he' tunu'.* The roasting fish is scorched by the flames. (*Thesaurus:* **keyat₂ 1.1, dallet 1, dokot₂ 1.1, suleyab 1**) **1.1)** *v. tr.* To burn off, as brush in preparation for sowing. *Nilāb kasagmotan.* The brush or weeds are burnt. (*Thesaurus:* **lablab 2, lapug, tunu'₁ 1.2**)

**paglāb** *v. intr. aN-* To burn field rubbish in preparation for planting. *Ta'nda' pa'in keyat mareya, yuk-i, "Maglāb mareya."* When the fire was seen inland, [someone] said, "Someone is burning rubbish inland."

**laba** *adj. a-* Financially profitable, of a sale. *Alaba bay pangā'an pagmunda' magdaing ni pū'.* What the fleet got while fishing at the outer islands was profitable. *Alaba daingta itū apa halam daing.* Our fish get a good price because there are no fish. (*cf:* **lugi' 1**; *Thesaurus:* **anak₃ 1, untung₁ 1**)

**labak** *v. tr. -an* To scatter things by throwing them down carelessly. *Da'a labakin s'ggit ilū maingga-maingga.* Don't throw that rubbish all over the place. (*Thesaurus:* **paglatag-latag, sabud, sabulak**)

**labad** *v. intr. pa-* To move back and forth. *Palabarun kono' he'nu anahi' ilū.* Please keep your sewing [machine] moving to and fro.

**paglabad** *v. intr. aN-* **1)** To wave to and fro. *Asidda maglabad-labad togel ero'.* The dog's tail wags a lot. **1.1)** *v. tr.* To wave something to and fro repeatedly. *Subay pinaglabad langkay bo' mbal ap'dda.* A coconut frond needs to be waved repeatedly so [the light] doesn't go out. (*Thesaurus:* **kambay 1, lambe₁ 1.1, mita, sayang₂, sinyal 1.1**)

**laban** *see:* **paglaban**

**labanos** var. of **liyabanos**

**labas₁** *v. tr. -an* To trim weeds and surplus growth. *Labasin saga daunna maka kanatin buwa'na.* Trim off its leaves and scatter its fruit. *Pangalabasun na sanggot ilū.* Use the sickle there for trimming. *Bang kayu nilabasan, ya sangana nila'anan.* When a tree is trimmed, its branches are removed.

**labas₂** *adj. a-* **1)** Forceful and compelling speech. *Alabas ah'lling, saupama magbono'.* Forceful in speaking, arguing, for example. (*Thesaurus:* **bagas, kasla 1, paul, talom bowa'**) **1.1)** *v. advrs. ka-...-an* To be overwhelmed by a superior force. *Min sangpū' aku ah'lling, min duwa iya ah'lling, bowa'ku ya kalabasan.* I spoke ten times, he spoke twice, and it was my speech that was dominated.

**labay₁** *v. intr. pa-* **1)** To pass by some place. *Palabay aku min t'ngna'.* I passed through the middle. *Sikalabay-labayan puhu'.* People continually passing to and fro. *Kalabayku min pū'-pū' Damay di'ilaw, halam munda'.* When I was passing by the islet of Damay yesterday, there were no boats. (*Thesaurus:* **likuwad 1.1, liyus 1.1, paglipuwas, pagsulabay, pintas 1, timbay 1**) **1.1)** *v. tr. -an* To bypass something. *Labayin pongag inān.* Go around that old canoe. *Palabayin sadja kami.* Just let us pass. *Labayan kubul ilu i, duma'in na ka ka'mbo'-mbo'anta.* Bypass that grave there, it's not our ancestor. *Bang amokot, nilabayan daing a'aslag bo' mbal ageret pokot.* When haul-netting, large fish are worked around so the net doesn't get torn.

**labay min** *adv. phrase* By way of; through the agency of; on the authority of. *Labay min mayul.* On the mayor's authority. *Mbal na taitung heka lidjiki' bay pamuwan e' Tuhan ma aku labay min sigām.* The blessings cannot be counted that God has given me through them.

**labayan** *n.* A way through; a path. *Pasiha' kita man labayan.* We went aside from the path. *Bang buwat sagmot p'llaynu, pasihaknu man sagmot*

*kasehe'an nihinang labayan.* When you run into
something like floating weeds, you separate it
from the other weeks to make a way through.
(*Thesaurus:* **kalsara**, **lān**, **pal'ngnganan**)

**paglalabayan** *n.* A main road with traffic coming
and going. *Angamu' kami palabay min lahatbi.
Hal kami min lān paglalabayan maka mbal kami
pasolekma' minnē'.* We ask [permission] to pass
through your district. We will only go by way of
the main road and will not diverge from there.

**paglaulabay** *v. intr.* aN- To be coming and going,
of many people. *Santili', hatina a'a pangangamu'
ni a'a maglaulabay. Santili',* referring to those
who continually beg from the crowds going to
and fro.

**palabayan** *n.* A passageway; a way through.

**labay₂** *v. intr.* pa- To pass, of a period of time or the
duration of an activity. *Palabay na ulan.* The rain
is over. *Tahun palabay.* The previous year.

**labay bahangi** *v. tr.* -an To let something settle
overnight, as the dregs in coconut liquid.
{idiom} (*Thesaurus:* **lihaw 1.1**, **pato'ong**, **patuli**)

**palabay** *v. tr.* To endure a period or phase of
activity.

**labay₃** *v. tr.* a-, ka-..-an, -an To experience
something; to undergo an experience. *Aniya' isāb
bay kalabayanku buwattē'.* I have experienced
something like that too. *Bang aku bitu'anun, iya
budjang, subay aniya' kalakaran. Hatina subay
aniya' k'nnopna sabab bay na aku makalabay.* If I
am a divorcee and she is a virgin, there should
be an extra [bride-gift] amount. In other words
there should be some addition because I have
already experienced [marriage]. *Kamemon sasat-
manasat ya kalabayanta itū mbal magbidda' maka
sasat ya maumu kalabayan e' manusiya'.* All the
troubles we are experiencing are no different
from the troubles commonly experienced by
human beings. *Aheka isab kasukkalan bay
kalabayanku.* I have experienced many sorrows.
(*Thesaurus:* **lapa₁**, **nanam 2**, **sabi₂**, **ssa₂**)

**kalabayan** *n.* Something experienced. *Si Hu itū,
asal aheka kata'una maka kalabayanna maghinang
ai ma hinang tumbaga.* This fellow Hu, he had a
lot of knowledge and experience in making
things of bronze.

**pagkalabayan** *n.* Things that people experience.

**labay ba'id** *n. phrase* Specific permission. *Ama'id
kami ni mastal, "Pakuhi'in aku am'ssi ni lahat
dakayu'." Basta labay ba'id ni iya.* We ask
permission of the teacher, "Allow me to go
fishing to another place." So long as we have
permission from him.

**labba'₁** *v. tr.* -an To treat someone badly, especially
by deceit. *T'llungan kami bay magbeya'
lum'ngngan ni pagkawin, paluruk. Mahē' pa'in
kami, amowa pasōd nireyom. Yukku, "Pi'ilu kam."
Yuk sigā, "Dahū ka." Na, dahū na aku. Halam sigā
pasōd, gōm pa'in wa'i ala'an. Na kalabba'an aku,
sali' aku niakkalan e' sigā.* Three of us went

together to attend a wedding. Once there, we
went to go in. I said, "You two go." They said,
"You first." So I went first. They didn't go in but
went away instead. So I am treated badly; they
sort of deceived me. *Buwat aku maka si Sa ni
Lihondo bo' aku ya makatuli'. Yukku ma iya,
"Dahū na ka ma lān ilū, amange' gi' aku." Bo' wa'i
aku ma lān dakayu', angalabba' aku ma iya.* Like
Sa and me going to Rio Hondo and I was leading
the way. I said to him, "You go first by that
path, while I take a pee." But I went by another
path, deceiving him. (*Thesaurus:* **akkal 1.1**)

**labba'₂** (var. **labha'**; **l'bba'**) *adj.* a- 1) Experiencing
muscle pain or weakness. (*Thesaurus:* **bihang₁**,
**pa'in₃ 1**, **sabab₂ 1.1**, **semet**, **sila'-sila' 1.1**) 1.1)
*v. tr.* -an To cause weakness or mild muscle pain,
thought to be the action of a spirit being. *Sali'
atangtang ituta, bay nilabba'an, sali' nihantu. Bang
kita amusay buwattē', ap'ddi'.* This part of us sort
of shrivelled, weakened, probably affected by a
*hantu* sprite. When we paddle in such a way it is
painful. *Asal hinang saitan angal'bba'.* Inflicting
weakness is in fact the work of a *saitan* spirit.
(*cf:* **hantu 1.1**)

**labban** *n.* A cardboard carton. *Labban pangisihan
s'mmek.* A carton for keeping clothes in.
(*Thesaurus:* **bakag₁**, **ba'ul₁**, **kalton**, **maleta**,
**tu'ung**)

**labbihi** *see:* **malabbihi**

**label** *n.* The wattles of a rooster. (*Thesaurus:*
**daling**, **pē'₃**)

**labha'** var. of **labba'₂**

**labi** *n.* 1) An extra number or amount. *Aheya isāb
labina.* What's left over is quite large. (*cf:* **l'bbi**)
1.1) *adv.* In a greater amount, number, or size.
*Labi t'llungibu pilak kono' pangal'kkat.* The
ransom is reportedly more than three thousand
pesos. *Labi dand'ppa taha'na.* More than a
fathom in length. 1.2) *v. intr.* pa- To go beyond
some limit or expectation. *Angay ka palabi min
bay panoho'an nakura'nu?* What do you mean by
going beyond what your boss told you?
(*Thesaurus:* **awat 1.2**, **lakbaw 1**) 1.3) *v. tr.* -an
To add an extra amount to something.

**labi-labi** *adv.* To a greater degree; especially.
*Labi-labi alingkat bang pininta.* It will be even
more beautiful when it is painted. *Buwat ai-ai
kabaya'anta bin'lli, pinagtaku-takuhan e'
danakanta bang mbal takole'ta. Labi-labi bang l'lla
ni pagh'nda.* Like anything we want to buy, our
siblings help us out if we can't manage it.
Especially so if it is a man getting married. *Labi-
labina mma' sigām.* Especially their father.
(*Thesaurus:* **anambahina**,
**bangkinna...bangkinna**, **kalap**, **luba'**, **luhūy**,
**paligay**, **ya lagi'na**)

**paglabi** *v. intr.* aN- To do too much of
something. *Lapus mbal maglabi, mbal magkulang.*
*Lapus* means not exceeding and not lacking.

**ballabi-labi** *adj.* -an Much greater in abundance

or value.

**labi-awla** *adv.* Especially; even more so.

**labi'-labi'** *n.* A species of leatherback turtle.

**labit** *n.* The fibrous burlap-like bark at the lower end of a coconut palm frond. *Aniya' kagunahanna, paggipitan panggi' bang halam karut.* It has its uses: squeezing cassava liquid when there is no sack. *Tuba ni'isi nireyom puyu'-puyu' labit ati ginuyud mareyom sowang.* Tuba [for stupefying fish] is put into a fibrous bark container and dragged through a channel. (*wh:* **niyug**)

**lablab** 1) *adj. a-* To be ablaze. 2) *v. tr.* To set a person or structure on fire. (*Thesaurus:* **lāb 1.1, lapug, tunu'₁ 1.2**)

**labog** *n.* The Medusa jellyfish. *Subphylum Medusozoa. Labog pamakan payukan.* It is the jellyfish that turtles eat.

**labot** *v. tr.* To entertain guests by providing refreshments, cigarettes or betel chew. *Bang aniya' bisita subay nilabot, buwat saga luruk ma pagkawin.* When there are visitors they should be served refreshments, like guests at a wedding. (*Thesaurus:* **buhat₃, latal 1.1**)

  **lalabotan** *n.* 1) Items given to show hospitality or respect, as food served at a feast. *Bang aniya' pagkawin pinat'nna'an lalabotan saga a'a magluruk, saga pagkakan, saga pagmama', pagsiga.* When there is a wedding the guests are presented with items of hospitality, food, betel chew ingredients, cigarets. 1.1) *n.* Offerings to a supernatural being.

  **paglabot** 1) *v. intr. aN-* To provide refreshments for visitors. *Maglabot bang aniya' palkala'.* Showing hospitality when there is an event. 2) *v. ditr.* To offer tributes to a supernatural being. *Maglabot ni tampat.* Presenting gifts at a shrine. (*Thesaurus:* **buwis 1.1, lamas, tanggap 1.1, ungsud₂**)

**labu₁** *n.* Various cone shells. *Conus spp.*

**labu₂** *n.* 1) An anchor. 1.1) *v. intr. pa-* To be at anchor, using bottom anchor or drift. *Ya palabuta ē' langkay, tinugutan saga sangpū' d'ppa ko' alallay nilaranan.* What we used as an anchor was a coconut frond, let out about ten fathoms so that we would be carried slowly by the current. (*Thesaurus:* **layo 1.1, tangkal₂ 1.1**) 1.2) *v. tr. -an* To anchor a boat. *Bay kami angalabuhan pelang ma tehetek Siliyala'.* We anchored the canoe at Siliyala' Reef.

**labu₃** *n.* The Asiatic white-flowered bottle-gourd. *Lagenaria leucantha.* (*cf:* **tambulig**)

**labu₄** *n.* The paired feelers of a squid or cuttlefish. (*cf:* **gulamay 2, janggut 1**)

**labu'** *v. tr. -an* 1) To induce the abortion of a fetus. 1.1) *v. advrs. ka-...-an* To suffer a miscarriage. *Halam makalanjal pagb'ttongna sabab bay kalabu'an.* Her pregnancy did not proceed because she suffered a miscarriage. (*Thesaurus:*

**bibis, kawa'₂, pakpak 2, pulak 1.1**)

**labung** *adj. a-* 1) Profuse in growth, as hair or grass. *Manuk labuyu', alabung bulbul.* Wild chickens, abundant feathers. *Alabung unas mareyom tigbaw, ataha' sampay asembol.* The watergrass in the freshwater pool is profuse, it is both long and dense. (*Thesaurus:* **libombo', tusay**) 2) Numerous and widespread. *Alabung kami itū, sali' aheka kami. Aniya' ma kami ma Sambuwangan, ma Pasangan, ma Siganggang, ma Sibaud, ma Sisangat.* We [Sama Dilaut] are widespread, there are many of us. There are some of us at Zamboanga, at Pasangan, at Siganggang, at Sibaud, at Sisangat.

**labuyu'₁** *n.* Wild chickens. *Manuk labuyu' itū, alabung bulbul. Manuk ma deyom talun.* These wild chickens have profuse feathers. Chickens in forest areas. (*Thesaurus:* **manuk 1, tukung**)

**labuyu'₂** *var. of* **bāt-labuyu'**

**lāk** *n.* Various top shells. *Trochus spp.*

**lakad** *v. intr. pa-* 1) To step over an intervening space, obstacle or limit. *Palakad gi' aku ni munda'.* I will just step over to the bow of the boat. (*Thesaurus:* **laktaw, lingka' 1, pitas₁, saliyu 1**) 1.1) *v. tr. -an* To overstep or bypass an intermediate item. *Saupama aniya' a'a palege bo' asigpit, na lakaranta.* For example, if people are lying down closely placed, then we step over them. *Da'a lakarin matto'anu, makabusung ko' ilū.* Do not step over your elder, that will bring misfortune. *Nilakaran dakayu' tangga' haron.* Overstepped one foothold on the entry ladder.

  **kalakaran** *n.* An amount over and above the norm. *Bang aku bitu'anun, iya budjang, subay aniya' kalakaran. Hatina subay aniya' k'nnopna sabab bay na aku makalabay.* If I am divorced and she is a maiden, there should be an extra amount. In other words there should be some extra bride-gift since I have already experienced [marriage].

**lakag** *n.* The morning star, the sign of approaching dawn. *Lakag, bitu'un patuwa' dai'-llaw. Lakag,* a star that appears just before dawn. (*syn:* **maga**)

**laka'-laka'** *see:* **paglaka'-laka'**

**lakal** *n.* 1) A circular band or frame, used to protect fragile items, or to hold a turban on one's head. (*Thesaurus:* **bengkol₁, legong, lengkol 1, lengkong 1, tibulung 1**) 1.1) *v. tr.* To weave a band around fragile items such as cups or bowls. *Angalakal itū sali' buwat kassa' abila', halam abila' to'ongan. Na subay nilakal maka lubid-lubid atawa buway. Lakal* is like when a glass is breaking, but not completely. It needs to be bound with woven cord or rattan.

**lakal-lakal** *n.* A slotted rack for storing plates on edge. *Ni'isi na lai' ni lakal-lakal abō' pasindikta.* The plates are put in the rack so we can stand them up.

**lakap** *v. tr. -an* To complete an entire task on one's own; to take an entire amount for oneself.

*Nda'un napsu si Anu inān, nilakapan e'na kamemon minsan mbal apatut ma iya.* Look at What's-his-name's greed, he takes the lot even though it doesn't suit him. *Mbal kalakapan hinang bang aheka anak.* The work cannot be completed when there are many children. (*Thesaurus:* **ambat 1.1, anggap 1**)

**lakap-manuk** *v. advrs. -in-* Suffering from impaired vision in low light. *Nilakap-manuk a'a inān.* That man has twilight blindness. *Nilakap manuk-manuk inān, asāl du isāb manuk-manuk.* That bird is blind [at night], that's just how it is with birds. (*syn:* **manuk 2**; *Thesaurus:* **buta₁, legsok₂, palu' 1.1**)

   **paglakap-manuk 1)** *v. intr. aN-* To be suffering from twilight blindness. **2)** *v. advrs. -in-* To be afflicted with twilight blindness. *Abay-kohap maka dai'-llaw mbal maka'nda'. Bang tonga' bahangi maka'nda'. Asal tubu'anan sigām pinaglakap-manuk.* At dusk or early morning he cannot see, but at midnight he can see. It is their family heritage to be affected by twilight blindness.

**lakas** *v. tr. -an* To strip dead leaves away from new growth, especially of plants such as sugar cane which are propagated by cuttings.

**lakas-lakas** *n.* Finger coral. *Aheka lakas-lakas ma bukut Manubal.* There is a lot of finger coral on the back side of Manubal. (*syn:* **sahasa'**; *gen:* **batu₂ 1**)

**lakat** *adj. a-* To spread across and cover a whole area. *Alakat na badju' e' laway, subay ginanti'an.* The shirt is covered with saliva, it should be changed. *Alakat tana' he' tai' sapi'.* The ground is covered with cow muck. *Bang onde' asungi' alakatan dīna sabab pahibal.* When a baby poos he smears it over himself because he moves around. (*Thesaurus:* **dasal, pagsilapug, saplag 1**)

   **paglakat** *v. intr. aN-* To spread over a surface area, as a crowd of people or an excess of fish. *Buwat daing ma tabu' M'ddas maglakat, aheka daing mbal ta'ambat bīlli.* Like fish in a Siasi market, an excessive number, so many fish that they cannot all be sold.

**lakay** *v. tr.* To make full use of resources; to pay out all the line on a spool. *Lakayun kamemon, ilmu' kamemon.* Make use of everything, of all the deep knowledge. *Lakayun k'llat inān bo' pat'kkad, pinakamemon.* Let that line run completely out so it reaches bottom, let it all go.

**lakbaw** *v. intr. pa-* **1)** To exceed or out-perform one's peers. *Bang sali'-sali' bay angiskul, heka man heka, ka'a-i makalakbaw man kasehe'an. Ka'a-i sambatan tahinang mastal.* When all go to school in the same way, you outperform the others time and again. The comment is made that you will become a school-teacher. (*cf:* **laktaw**; *Thesaurus:* **awat 1.2, labi 1.2**) **1.1)** *v. tr. -an* To gain an advantage, as in negotiating a business

deal. *Bīlli e' si Id lilus duwampū' maka lima. B'lliku t'llumpū', lakbawanku man iya. Lima pilak kalakbawan. Aku ya angalakbaw man pam'llina.* Id was buying a watch for twenty five [pesos]. I buy it for thirty, overbidding him. An overbid of five pesos. I am the one who goes beyond what he paid.

**lakbu'₁** *v. tr. -an* To cook something partially. *Lakbu'in isi sapi' ilū bo' palunuk.* Cook that beef partially so it will soften. *Nilakbu'an subay, ko da'a ahalu'.* Should be parboiled so as not to go bad.

**lakbu'₂** *v. tr. -an* To mislead someone deliberately, especially for the purpose of making him feel foolish. *Nilakbu'an kita. Sinoho' kita m'ssa' b'nnal. Sali' kita pinarupang.* We were misled. We were told to do something that wasn't true. We were sort of made to look foolish. *Ata'u isāb iya amarupang, anglakbu', matto'ana.* He is accustomed to deceiving, misleading, his parents. (*cf:* **akkal 1.1**; *Thesaurus:* **dupang 1.2**)

**lakkop** (var. **l'kkop₁**) *n.* **1)** The suction pad on the head of suckerfish such as a remora. *Daluwa to'ongan maka langa-langa, daipara halam taga lakkop ma kōkna.* Looks the same as a remora, except that it has no suction pad on its head. **1.1)** *v. intr. aN-* To have a suckerfish adhering. *Dakayu' du pahi angalakkop.* Just one kind of ray has suckerfish adhering to it.

**lakkop-lakkop** *n.* A species of suckerfish that cling to the gill slits of large rays. *Taga lakkop-lakkop pahi amalut ma asangna. Bin'lli e' saga Lannang.* Rays have suckerfish clinging to their gills. The Chinese buy them.

**lakdan-bulan** *n.* The camphor plant, a medicinal plant useful as a diuretic. *Blumea balsamifera.*

**laki** *n.* 'Lucky', a card game.

   **paglaki** *v. intr. aN-* To play the card game known as Lucky. *Kahaba' aniya' magjaga, aniya' isāb na pa'in maglaki.* Whenever there are people at a wake, there are always people playing the 'Lucky' card game as well. (*Thesaurus:* **pagpares 1, pagsugal**)

**lakibini** *n.* A married couple.

   **paglakibini** *v. intr. aN-* To be related to each other as husband and wife. *Maglakibini sigām, buwat ka'am d'nda maka l'lla.* They are a married couple, like you, a man and a woman. (*cf:* **tagubata'**)

**lakit** *n.* A hard non-coral rock. (*Thesaurus:* **batu₁, bussu'₁**)

**laklak** *adj. a-* Torn apart, causing extensive and irreversible damage. *Alaklak itū geret aheya to'ongan.* This word *laklak* means a very serious tear. *Alaklak agese' papantalunna, mbal na tatahi'.* The tear in his trousers is torn wide open, it can no longer be sewn up. *Agese' itū tajari du, alaklak itū mbal. Mbal to'ongan panga'anta.* If it is merely torn, something can be done with it, but not if it is *laklak*. It is totally beyond recovery. (*Thesaurus:* **pensang 1, saksak 1**)

**laklak alam** *v. tr.* **-an** To be torn apart, of the physical world. *Makalandu' kosogna anittowa, subay angalaklakan alam.* He laughs with such excessive force that the world must tear apart. *Tittowana makalaklak alam!* His laughter would split the world apart!

**lakles** *adj.* **a-** Peeling off; flaking. (*Thesaurus:* **kanit 1, gagus, laknit 1, oplak 1**)

**laknet** *var.* of **laknit**

**laknit** (*var.* **laknet**; **lanit**) *adj.* **a-** 1) Peeling or flaking off, as a scab from a wound, or skin after sunburn. *Alaknit kuwitna ni pasu' llaw.* His skin is peeling from the heat of the sun. *Alanit, ya sali' ala'an kulitna, buwat pulaybūd. Lanit,* its surface layer sort of coming away, like plywood. (*Thesaurus:* **kanit 1, gagus, lakles, oplak 1**) 1.1) *v. tr.* **-an** To peel off a surface layer.

**lakod** *v. tr.* To drive fish into a fence trap or net set in shallow water at low tide. *Bang angalakod, aniya' ampasna ati sin'ssol daing. Subay aniya' lubid nihella' bo' pasōd daing ni ampas atawa ni linggi.* With the *lakod* system there is a fence trap and fish are herded into it. A rope has to be pulled along so the fish go into the fence trap or a dragnet. (*cf:* **pagt'bba**; *Thesaurus:* **illig, s'ssol₂ 1.1**)

**laksa'** *n.* 1) Ten thousand as a counting unit. (*Thesaurus:* **hatus, ibu**) 1.1) *n.* Any very large number of items. 1.2) *adj.* **-an** Occurring in uncountable numbers.

**laksi'** *n.* An aromatic variety of incense. *Subay aniya' laksi' bang magpat'nna' pabahakan.* There should be some *laksi'* incense when preparing beds. (*Thesaurus:* **kamanyan, hiyu**)

**laksu₁** *v. intr.* **pa-** To jump to a different location. *Palaksu ampan.* The grasshopper jumped. *Tabowa e' kōdna, makalaksu iya halam baya'.* Carried away by his joy, he jumps without thinking. *Sikalaksuhan sigām min diyata' pussuk būd.* They will be leaping and leaping across the mountain peaks. (*Thesaurus:* **kuppa 1, sulakat, tugpa' 1**)

**laksu₂** *n.* Various mudskippers. *fam. Gobiidae.*

**laktas** (*var.* **latas₂**) *v. intr.* **pa-** To cross over a short distance. *Ameya' iya palaktas ma tempel.* He intends to cross the distance in a *tempel* motorboat. *Palaktas itū sali' pasampay ni dambila'.* This word *laktas* is like reaching the other side. *Palatas ka parambila'.* Cross to the other side. (*Thesaurus:* **k'tta 1, lintas, untas 1**)

**paglaktas** *v. intr.* **aN-** To be connected across a divide. *Ya pangannalku, ina'an kitām magbalharap magsuli-suli sali' ka'ina-tagna', sagwā' ma buwattina'an hal umagad la'a ya paglaktasantabi.* In my mind we were there talking together, face to face as before, but at the present time it is only our spirits that connect.

**palaktas** *v. tr.* To allow someone to travel as a passenger just to cross a channel. (*Thesaurus:* **bayan 1.1, beya'₁, pagbiyahi, sakay 1, tumpang, tundug 1.1**)

**laktaw** *v. tr.* **-an** To skip an intervening space or stage. *Bay iya makalaktaw pagiskulna.* She skipped a year in her schooling. *Bang kita amassa bo' mbal kata'uhanta, laktawanta, sali' nilabayan.* When we are reading but don't know [a section] we skip over it, sort of bypassing it. (*cf:* **lakbaw 1**; *Thesaurus:* **lakad 1, lingka' 1, pitas₁, saliyu 1**)

**laku** *n.* Behavior; disposition.

**kalakuhan** *n.* Character or characteristic behavior. *Makalandu' na kalakuhanna, mbal na tasipat.* His behavior is excessive, beyond understanding. (*Thesaurus:* **kasuddahan, hudjidjat, jaguni', jari₄ 1, jāt₁, sadsaran**)

**laku-tabi'at** *n.* Courteous behavior.

**paglaku-laku** *v. intr.* **aN-** To pretend to have rank, authority or prestige. *Sali' pinagmandahan he'na a'a kamemon, ya hē' maglaku-laku.* It's as though he bosses everybody, that is a case of claiming to the one in charge. *Maglaku-laku, sali' am'ngngis.* Claiming to be boss, sort of behaving sternly. *Kita-i ganta' ata'u, na aku maglaku-laku min ka'a. Yukku, "Aku beya'-beya'un." Sali' aku magnakura'-nakura' dīku bo' halam aku bay gin'llal.* Suppose we know something, and I claim to be above you, saying, "Obey me." It is as if I make myself out to be the boss when I haven't been appointed. *Sidda maglaku-laku dīna minsan mbal tinōp. Pinagmanda-mandahan e'na a'a kamemon, ya hē' maglaku-laku.* He makes much of himself even though it isn't appropriate. He orders everyone around, that is *laku-laku.* (*Thesaurus:* **hinang-hinang₂, pagbau'-bau', pagdō-rō, pagnaho'-naho'**)

**Ladja Sulayman** *n. phrase* Rajah Solomon, the name of an important spirit of the open sea. (*cf:* **a'a man deyo'**)

**ladja'** *adj.* **a-** 1) Unproductive; disappointing. *Aladja' pananoman.* The planted area is sprouting poorly. *Apinda kita ni deyo' saddī. Aladja'-ladja' bay pangusaha'an saga a'a, sali' halam aniya' ta'ā'.* We moved to another fishing spot. It was rather disappointing, people having been fishing there already and almost nothing caught. *Bay kami ni Paluwas-pata', ni deyo' marilaut Pata'. Aladja'-ladja' mahē', halam na ai-ai.* We went to the Pata' opening, to the deep offshore from Pata'. It was quite unproductive, nothing there. *Kaladja'-ladja'an saki. Ubus kita ni ahāp, ubus kita ni ala'at.* The frustration of sickness. We're fine at one stage and no good at the next. (*cf:* **jadja' 1**) 1.1) *v. advrs.* **ta-** Disappointed. *Talatag kamemon takot pam'ssihan, taladja'-ladja' kami na piniha.* [We] visited very fishing reef, but we were disappointed by what we found.

**ladjang** *v. tr.* To cut into pieces with a knife. *Bang kita pinaglagut-lagut niōnan niladjang.* If we are chopped up it is called *ladjang. Sukna': "Bang pa'in ka taladjang."* A curse: "May you be cut to pieces." (*Thesaurus:* **k'llot, gōt-gōt 1, pabuwa', padja', tama', t'ttok 1.1**)

**ladjaw** *v. tr.* To make an unreasonably low first bid. *Mbal kita ano'ongan bang kita am'lli ai-ai, hal kita angaladjaw.* We are not serious when we are buying anything, we just make low offers. *Ladjawta, hal sali' bin'lli akkal-akkal.* We make a low bid, simply pretending to buy. (*Thesaurus:* **andag, halga' 1.2, jawab₁, paragang**)

**ladjawan** *n.* A pattern; a sample. *Subay aniya' ladjawannna bang maghinang luma'.* There should be a plan when building a house. *Buwat nā'annu min suntu'an, atawa nā'annu ladjawan ya tupara hē'.* Like you got something from a pattern, or you got a pattern for those goggles. (*Thesaurus:* **bantukan, sengoran, simpayan, suntu'an**)

**ladji'** *adj. a-* Moved a long distance, of something thrown or pushed. *Bang bantunganku olen ni bangkaw, aladji'. Aladji' to'ongan, mbal tapiha.* When I throw a marble to the mangroves it goes far. Goes really far, can't be found. *Bang kita nirundang, asidda aladji'.* When we are pushed on a swing, we go a long way up.

**ladju** *adj. a-* Clear sounding; carrying a long way. *Aladju suwalana, sali' ahapal.* Her voice carries a long way, quite clear. *Aladju k'llongna bang maglugu'.* Her voice is far-reaching when she sings a *lugu'* song. (*Thesaurus:* **hangpat 1, hapal 2, hurup 1.1, lagsing, nyala-nyala, tanog₁**)

**ladju pikilan** *adj. a-* Clear-thinking, sharp-witted. {idiom}

**ladjuk** *n.* 1) The folded peak of a head scarf. 1.1) *v. tr. -an* To fold a cloth into peaks, as for a head scarf.

**laet** *n.* A household lamp. (*Thesaurus:* **kulaet 1, lām, lampu, palita'an, plaslaet 1, sū' 1**)

**lāg** (var. **lahag**) *adj. a-* Coloring up, of fruit. *Saging, bang sōng atahak, alāg na.* Bananas, when they are nearly ripe they change color. *Subay sinungkit na buwa' marang sabab alahag na, pād-pād amakpak.* Rather than just letting it drop, the marang fruit should be harvested with a sharp pole because it is coloring up now. *Alāg na wanni, mampallam, minsan saging. Magb'ttik na, sōng atahak.* The various mangos and even bananas are coloring up. They are showing color, almost ripe. *Subay sinungkit na buwa' marang sabab alahag na, pād-pād amakpak.* Rather than just letting it drop, the marang fruit should be speared-with-a-pole now because it is coloring up. (*cf:* **tahak 1**; *Thesaurus:* **b'ngkol₂, pagangilan, pagdauman**)

**laga** *n.* 1) A flame; a blaze. 1.1) *v. advrs. -in-* Burning up with fever.

**paglaga** *v. intr. aN-* To be burning in flames. *Baga maglaga-laga.* Flaming coals.

**lagak** *n.* 1) A person who eats greedily and without regard for others. *Lagak ka ma kinakan. Mbal ka anau'an kasehe'annu, subay hal ma ka'a.* You are a greedy person in regard to food. You save nothing for the others, it has to be for you only. 1.1) *v. tr. -an* To eat ravenously. *A: "Ma'ai kapin buwas?" B: "Wa'i bay nilagakan e'na."* A: "Where is the leftover rice?" B: " He has gobbled it up." (*Thesaurus:* **bagahak₂, boslad, buhawi'₁, butu', kanam, kaway 1.1, dahaga', damba'₁ 1.1, tanggal₁**) 1.2) *v. advrs. -in-* Overcome by greed, as to food. *Niramba' kita ma ai-ai, sali' nilagak.* We selfishly eat up anything, like being greedy.

**lagaklak** *v. intr. aN-* To make a rattling noise. *Angalagaklak deyom k'llongna bang atuli.* He makes a rattling noise in his throat when he is sleeping. (*cf:* **tigangkul 1**)

**lagad** (var. **agad₁**) *v. intr. pa-* 1) To wait patiently; to resign oneself. *Hal patannay, hal palagad nihukum.* He is near to death, simply waiting to be judged. *Angaluluy aku, sali' pasagaranku ai-ai pah'llingnu. Sali' aku hal palagad.* I am resigned, sort of accepting whatever you say. It is as though I am just waiting. *Hal iya patongngol, palagad ma kasehe'an.* He just sits doing nothing, waiting for the others. 1.1) *v. intr. aN-* To be waiting expectantly. *Angagad ka dai'-dai'.* Wait a moment. *Angandol sali' kita angagad. Amaratsaya sali' am'nnal, subay aniya' lling. Andol* [trust] is like when we wait expectantly. *Paratsaya* [believing in] is like accepting as true, it must involve speech. (*Thesaurus:* **asa 1.1, kiri-kiri, holat 1**) 1.2) *v. tr. -an* To await someone or some thing. *Wa'i ni tabu' si Ina', lagaranku ma jambatan.* Mother has gone to the market, I will await her at the wharf. *Maitu gi' aku angagaran ka'a sampay ka makabalik pi'itu.* I will wait for you here until you have got back. (*Thesaurus:* **lanti-lanti, langay, tagad**)

**lagadlad₁** *v. intr. pa-* To emerge from inside a person's body. *Palagadlad laha' min b'ttongna.* Blood flowed out from his stomach.

**lagadlaran** *n.* The product of a woman's womb. *A: "Anak itu ngga'i bay lagadlaran min deyom b'ttong ina'na, anak d'nda saddi." B: "Aho', anakku sagwā' duma'in ka paluwas min h'ndaku."* A: "This child was not an issue from the womb of her [supposed] mother, but the child of another woman." B: "Yes, she is my child, but not from my [present] wife."

**lagadlad₂** *see:* **paglagadlad**

**laga'₁** (var. **lagas**) *adj. a-* 1) Well-cooked; fully ripe. *Alaga' na wanni.* The *wanni* mangoes are fully ripe. *Palaga'un daing ilu min t'dda du, sali' bay angalere' abō' mbal sali' ma'angit ina'an.* Let that fish cook thoroughly just once, like it has boiled, so it doesn't have that sort of chlorine taste. *Pinalagas ai-ai atuwas, pinat'ggol hē' am'lla.* Let anything hard be well-cooked, left cooking a long time. (*Thesaurus:* **lasaw, tahak 1**) 1.1) *v.*

*tr.* To boil something thoroughly. *Laga'un na kahawa ilū panginuman.* Heat up that coffee for something to drink. *Buwat kalitan b'llata, subay nilagas ko' alunuk.* Like when shark is being cooked, it should be well-boiled so as to be tender. (*Thesaurus:* **bukal, buwal₁, lere', ogok-ogok**)

**laga'₂** *n.* **1)** A large tightly woven basket for unpounded rice. **2)** A unit of bulk for unpounded rice (about 30 liters).

**lagam** *n.* Voice or manner of speech as a distinctive feature of an individual. *Akulang lagamna.* He speaks quietly [lit. his voice lacks distinction]. *Takaleta lagamna, magtūy takilāta bang sai.* We heard his voice and immediately knew who it was. (*Thesaurus:* **h'lling₁ 2.1, suwala 1**)

**lagam-bowa'** *n.* Prattle; nonsense. *Nsa' ka bay inayku. Aheka isāb lagam bowa'nu.* I did nothing to you. You talk a lot of nonsense.

**laganas** var. of **lagonos**

**lagas** var. of **laga'₁**

**lagaw** *adj.* -*an* Rough and unpleasing, of someone's voice. *Lagawan k'llongku. Agohom sala, mbal alu'uy.* My throat is rough. It's sort of hoarse, not pleasant sounding. (*Thesaurus:* **kohot, gohom 1, pehet**)

**lagbas 1)** *v. intr. pa-* To pierce something right through. *Angalagbas parambila'.* Penetrating right through and out the other side. (*Thesaurus:* **lambang₁, latus, l'ppas 1.1, l'ssut**) **2)** *v. tr.* To join the patterned and backing parts of a woven mat by sewing through both. *Song nilagbas tepo ina'an e' si Pe, lapis maka deyomna.* That mat will be sewn together by Pe, its backing and its patterned part.

**lageklek** *v. intr. aN-* To produce the sound or sensation of something snagged and coming suddenly free. *Wa'i angalageklek man buli'ku, kilāku arai' agese'.* Something has snagged at my butt, I think it is probably torn. *Tananamta tonda' bay sumagnat bang lageklek. Bay palebod ni batu.* We felt the line was snagged when it suddenly came free. It had been wrapped around a coral rock.

**lagedled 1)** *adj.* a- Unsettled as to place of residence or work. *Alagedled pat'nna'an a'a hē', mbal na makat'ttog. Magpinda-pinda.* The location of those people is unsettled; unable to stay put. Always moving from one place to another. (*Thesaurus:* **laud 1, lintas, pagtagestes, pagtaleted**) **2)** *v. intr. pa-* To spread to a wider area, as fire or a disturbance. *Palagedled ni kasehe'an, buwat magbono' hal bay dangan, na pasōng.* Spreading to someone else, like a fight where there had been just one, but is now increasing. *Dūkin pahāp lapohan ilū bo' mbal palagedled keyat ilu ni salirap.* Add firewood carefully to that stove so the fire doesn't spread onto the wall panels. *Aniya' bay atunu' ma Lihondo, palagedled ni Mariki'.* There was a fire in

Rio Hondo, [it] spread to Mariki.

**paglagedled** *v. intr. aN-* **1)** To keep snagging while dragging across a surface. *Daka ai maglagedled man deyo' pelang ilū!* Whatever is that dragging along under the canoe there! *Aniya' takaleta ma luwasan, yukta, "Ai baha' maglagedled lantay?"* We hear something outside and say, "What is that scraping along the decking?" (*Thesaurus:* **bira 1, konot₂, ga'ut, ganggut, guyud 1, hella'**; *syn:* **paglagesles**) **1.1)** *v. tr.* To drag something over an uneven surface. *Da'a paglagedlerun, kalu aniya' ai-ai magkabila.* Don't drag it, there may be something breakable.

**lagesles** *v. intr. pa-* **1)** To move from one location to another, as when fishing. *Bang kita wa'i am'ssi, buwat kami magpanonda' halam maka'ā', na palagesles kita ni timbang dakayu'.* If we are out fishing, when we were trolling for tuna and not catching any, we move on to another deep area. (*Thesaurus:* **tagestes**) **2)** To drag along a rough sea floor, snagging but not catching. *Tabowa e' s'llog, palagesles sau, mbal amalut ni batu.* Carried by the current, the anchor catching briefly, but not holding to a rock. (*cf:* **lagid 1**)

**paglagesles** *v. intr. aN-* To keep catching and dragging across a rough surface. *Sali' alabu kita, ab'kkat na batu sau. sau ya maglagesles mareyo', pelang palaran.* Like when we lie at anchor and the anchor [binding] gives way. It is the anchor that catches and then lets go, the canoe drifts. *Lubid itū ya maglagesles. Aniya' sehe'na magsabod.* This rope is what is catching on something. It has a companion word: *sabod.* (*syn:* **paglagedled 1**)

**laggong** *n.* The cat's-eye turban, an edible monovalve shellfish. *Turbo spp. Sali' maka mata laggong.* [Wide-eyed], like the eyes of a turban shell. *Pehē' aku ni Kalang amuwa' laggong kakanku.* I will go to Kalang and find some *laggong* to eat. (*syn:* **sukkiyan**)

**laggos** *v. tr.* To bind two things together along their shared edge. *Bang ma bubu, p'ttung in pangalaggos, p'ttung abulak. Bang tepo, lanut.* With a woven fish trap, immature bamboo is used for its binding. With a mat it is abaca. (*Thesaurus:* **bīt₂, k'kkod, sigid**)

**laggut-laggut** see: **paglaggut-laggut**

**laggutan** *n.* A species of small turtle. (*Thesaurus:* **bokko', payukan, p'nnu, tohongan**)

**lāgi** *adv.* Moreover; what's more. *Aniya' lāgi kapandayanna angama'anahan ba'anan uppi.* What's more he had the ability to interpret various dreams. *Lāgi ina'an isāb saga kubul bay pangubulan ka'mbo'anku.* Moreover the graves where my ancestors were buried are there.

**lagi** see: **kalagihan, paglagi**

**lagid** *v. intr. pa-* **1)** To touch or visit something briefly in passing. *Tudju kita Sisangat, palagesles tudju ni Siganggang, sali' palagid.* We are headed for Sisangat, touching in at Siganggang, the same thing as *palagid*. *Aniya' daing halam palagid ni aku, wa'i pas'llu.* There was a fish that didn't touch me, just slipped through. (*cf:* **lagesles** 2) **1.1)** *v. tr. -an* To deliver something in passing.

**lagi'** (var. **gi'**) **1)** *ptl.* Still; yet; a bit more. Aspect marker indicating that an action or state is not yet completed, without regard to whether it has begun. *Halam lagi' kam kinaru'.* You haven't become sleepy yet. *Itiya' lagi' magkakan.* Still here, eating. *Aniya' gi' duwansolag.* There are still two pieces. *Angagad gi' ka, Ja. Halam gi' pamayad si Ina' itū.* Please wait a bit longer. Mother doesn't have the payment yet. *Halam gi' aku a'a.* I was not yet a person. (*cf:* **na**) **2)** *adv.* To a greater degree; more so. *Sapadpad alungay suru', ahāp lagi' bay pab'llihannu.* Rather than lose the spoon, it would be better to have sold it. **3)** *ptl.* Politeness marker. *Angagad gi' ka. Halam gi' amayad si Ina' itū.* Just wait a bit longer. Mother hasn't paid yet. *Pabalik lagi' bahā' kami ni pagbono'an anakay saga pagkahi kami?* Are we [excuse me asking] to go back to the battlefield and attack our companions? (*Thesaurus:* **kono' 2, da'a busung, pa'in₂ 2**)

**laginit** *see:* **paglaginit**

**laglag** *adj. a-* **1)** Dead en masse; exterminated. *Aheka alaglag ni timbak daing atawa punglu'.* Many have died from fishing dynamite or from bullets. *Kaheka'an sigām alaglag amatay.* The majority of them dead. **1.1)** *v. tr.* To exterminate an entire group of people. *Sinoho' binono' bangsa Sama, nilaglag.* Giving orders for Sama people to be killed, wiped out. (*Thesaurus:* **ligis₂, pagbugbug**)

**lagnas** *v. tr.* To file the front of upper teeth in preparation for the fitting of gold caps. *Bay nilagnas emponna bo' dasali'.* Her teeth were filed so they would be level. *Indamin aku gaugari' pangalagnas empon si Arung.* Lend me a file for filing Eldest Daughter's teeth. (*cf:* **gaugari'** 1.1; *Thesaurus:* **pangtad, solsol, tā'**)

**lagod₁** *n.* Minute particles in water. *Lagod bohe', ya s'ggit-man'ggit, ya mbal ta'nda'ta, ya he' lagodna.* Water particles, all the bits of rubbish, the stuff we can't see, that is its *lagod*. *Minsan bay bohe' asawa, aniya' na l'mmis mareyom, aniya' na lagod-lagodna.* Even water that was clear, there could be dirt in it, minute particles. (*Thesaurus:* **aut 1, lobog 1**)

**lagod₂** *n.* The jelly-like film on the inner surface of an immature coconut. *Aheka bay lagod-lagodna. Pagtohobta na akulang isina, wa'i kinakan he' lahu'.* It had a lot of soft unripe stuff. When we cut it open it had little meat, all eaten by the eclipse creature. (*syn:* **lu'ud₂**)

**lagod-lagod** *n.* A sense of resentment; a grudge. *Aheya lagod-lagodna, subay makabalos.* His resentment is great, he wants to get revenge.

(*Thesaurus:* **akon-akon, agmol 1, buli'an₂, koto'-koto', deyom-deyom atay**)

**lagonos** (var. **daganas**; **laganas**) *adj. a-* **1)** Falling down in numbers, noisily and heavily. *Alagonos kakayuhan bang akosog baliyu.* The trees fall heavily when the wind is strong. (*Thesaurus:* **balabak, latak**) **1.1)** *v. intr. pa-* To fall noisily and in number, as fruit from a tree. *Paghūg lahing, magtūy palaganas.* When a coconut is dropped, it falls heavily.

**lagonggang** *adj. a-* Loose-fitting, as over-large clothes. *Alagonggang na badju'na, sōng na agese'.* His shirt is loose, about to tear. (*cf:* **gaunggang**)

**lagonggok** *see:* **paglagonggok**

**lagot** *v. advrs. -in-* Limited to one position or activity for an extended period. *Nilagot kita ma paningkō'an, at'ggol aningkō' halam makatangkug.* We have been stuck in these chairs, sitting a long time without stirring.

**lagot-lagot** *n.* Something that irritates or tickles the throat. *Lagot-lagot, ya ma k'llongta bang apehet.* Something tickling, the thing in the throat when hoarse.

**lagpak₁** (var. **lalagpak**) *n.* A spring-loaded device such as a rat trap.

**lagpak₂** *v. tr. -an* **1)** To clap hands sharply together to make a noise. *Lagpakin tangannu.* Clap your hands. **1.1)** *v. tr.* To frighten birds or bats away with the use of a mechanical rattle.

**paglagpak** *v. intr. aN-* **1)** To clap hands. *Bang aniya' maggradwesyon bo' aniya' magkalang, maglagpak-lagpak magtūy.* When there is a graduation and someone sings, we promptly clap. (*cf:* **pagpapak**) **1.1)** *v. tr. -an* To applaud someone or some action by clapping hands.

**lagpi'** *v. tr.* To slap or flick something with force, using fingers or claws. *Kamun itū angalagpi' ma daing aheya. Minsan daing dand'ppa kabisahan.* The mantis shrimp slashes big fish with its claw. Even fish a fathom long can be wounded painfully. *Nilagpi' helmet sundalu bo' ah'lling.* The soldier's helmet was flicked to produce a noise. (*Thesaurus:* **lagtik 1**)

**paglagpi'** *v. intr. aN-* To play a game of manual dexterity that involves pinching and slapping each other's hand.

**lagsak** *v. tr.* To fasten something with a pin or bolt. *Aniya' ma ka'a lansang tumbaga pangalagsakku papan parawku inān?* Do you have some copper nails for me to fasten the plank of my *paraw* canoe with? (*cf:* **lansang 1**)

**lagsik** var. of **lagtik**

**lagsing** (var. **lagting₁**) *adj. a-* Sharp and clear, of sounds. *Alagsing lling gabbang inān, takale pi'itu.* The sound of the gong there is clear, it can be heard right here. *Palagsingun kono' ulehem ilū.* Please turn that player up. *Bang alagting suwalata makarayahan kita.* If our voice is sharp and clear we might become rich. *Ala'at h'llingna organ. Ag'mmol, mbal alagting.* The sound of an organ is unpleasant. It's muffled, not clear. (*Thesaurus:* **hangpat 1, hapal 2, hurup 1.1, ladju, nyala-nyala, tanog₁**)

**lagtang** *n.* **1)** A vine species, the source of a poison for stupefying fish. *Menispermaceous spp.* (*Thesaurus:* **tuba 1, tuwa 1**) **1.1)** *v. tr.* To stupefy fish using a poison from a vine. *Bang aku angalagtang ma jambatan si Ba, aheka bawis-bawis.* When I poison fish at Ba's wharf, there are many rabbitfish.

**lagtaw** *var.* of **saitan-lagtaw**

**lagtik** (var. **lagsik**; **lattik₂**) *v. intr. pa-* **1)** To move with a sudden release of tension, such as a flicked finger or a released spring. *Buwat bay litagku, palagsik pariyata', atawa pana' wa'i palagsik, papassik bā sali'.* Like my spring trap, flying up with force, or a spear shooting away under tension, also called *passik*. *Palagtik, buwat kita angahinang taguri' bo' apuwas tōngna, palattik.* *Lagtik* is like when we are making a kite and the end comes out, it flicks apart. *Buwat bay litagku, palagsik pariyata', atawa pana' wa'i palagsik, papassik bā sali'.* Like my spring trap, flying up with force, or a fish-spear released from tension. (*Thesaurus:* **lagpi'**) **1.1)** *v. tr.* To hit a target with something suddenly released from tension. *A: "Angay abakat tangannu, asidda angalaha'?"* *B: "Bay nilattik e' kamun. Bay aku anahat."* A: "Why is your hand wounded, bleeding so much?" B: "It was struck by the blades of a mantis shrimp. I was snaring it."

**lagtik d'lla'** *v. intr. pa-* To say something that cannot be taken back. {idiom} *Bang kita makapah'lling, yukta, "Bay palagtik d'lla'na, mbal pagkahella'an, mbal taisaban."* When someone has spoken, we say, "His tongue has moved-decisively, it cannot be pulled back, cannot be repeated." *Mbal kapindahan sabab makalagtik na d'lla'ku.* It cannot be changed because my word has been given [lit. my tongue is released from tension].

**paglagtik-lagtik** *v. intr. aN-* To be released from tension. *Tompang, ya manuk-manuk maglagsik-lagsik.* Grasshopper, the insect that flicks up repeatedly.

**lagting₁** *var.* of **lagsing**

**lagting₂** *n.* A mangrove forest tree, a source of moderately durable house posts. *Apagon kayu lagting.* The *lagting* tree is durable.

**lagtok** *v. tr. -an* To identify or use something correctly. *Kalagtokannu magtūy.* You immediately distinguish [them]. *Onde'-onde', minsan buwattingga iya pinalege, nilagtokan kita e'na. Ang'nda' iya ni kita.* A child, no matter how it is put down [to sleep], it knows exactly where we are. It looks our way. *Nilagtokan bo' mbal talabay e'na.* It is carefully observed so it isn't bypassed.

**lagtu'** *adj. a-* **1)** Fragile and easily broken. *Mbal tali'is bang alagtu' lahing.* When a ripe coconut is

fragile it cannot be grated. *Alagtu' na buway inān, mbal na tapangahengkot.* That rattan has become brittle, it can't be used for tying. *Kayu alagtu', minsan ariki' katikbi'an agtūy abila'. Mbal alagtu' kayu itu-itū.* Blemished wood breaks easily even with a small knock. This wood here [by contrast] is not fragile. (*Thesaurus:* **p'ggos, p'ssa' 1**) **1.1)** *v. intr. aN-* To become brittle through drying. *Mamis i' angalagtu' bang alanos na.* That sweet coconut variety becomes brittle once dry.

**lagublub** *n.* A rumbling sound, such as the running of hoofed animals.

**paglagublub** *v. intr. aN-* To make a rumbling noise, as the sound of digestive processes or horses running. *Maglagublub deyom b'ttongku.* My stomach is rumbling. (*Thesaurus:* **konog-konog, kulattub, llub, pagbolobok, paglagonggok**)

**lagunahan** *n.* A tune played on the brass ensemble.

**lagundi'** *n.* A tree, the fruit of which is believed to prevent aging. *Vitex spp. Buwa' lagundi' man pekkes-pekkes Duwa Būd inān. Bang aniya' amangan mbal magkatoto'a.* Lagundi fruit from the peak of Twin-Mountain Island. Anyone who eats it will not become old. *Yuk kamatto'ahan, "Subay ka bay kapamasuku'an bo' ka makabāk kayu lagundi'."* The old people say, "You must have been specially favored to find a *lagundi* tree."

**lagungkad** *see:* **paglagungkad**

**lagut** *v. tr.* To slash something; to wound someone with a bladed weapon. *Akapal kulit karuhung, bang lagutnu mbal amangan lahut.* The skin of a whale shark is thick, if you slash it the knife won't penetrate. *Lagutta ka maka lahut, bang nilappet maka kayu mbal bakatan.* I will slash you with a knife, if struck with something wooden there won't be a wound. (*Thesaurus:* **pagtebag-tebag, tadtad 1**)

**paglagut** *v. intr. aN-* **1)** To fight with bladed weapons. *Halam gi' sinapang, maglagut sadja bang ma pagbono'an.* Before there were guns, people just slashed each other on the battlefield. **2)** To conduct a healing ceremony that involves a symbolic slashing of the snake spirit responsible for the illness.

**lahag** *var.* of **lāg**

**laha'** **1)** *n.* Blood. *D'nda baha'u bay anganak, subay mbal amangan daing laha'an.* A woman who has given birth should not eat fish that has blood in it. (*cf:* **apol**; *Thesaurus:* **sallak 1.1**) **1.1)** *v. intr. aN-* To bleed. *Angalaha'an iya dīna, halam iya bay ni'inay-inay.* He bled all on his own, nobody did anything to him. *Sigi-sigi angalaha'. Mbal pahondong laha'.* Bleeding continuously. The blood doesn't stop. (*Thesaurus:* **lota', sungbu-sungbu**) **2)** *v. advrs. -in-* To be menstruating. *Budjang na iya hangkan nilaha' na.* She is a teenager now, that's why she is having a period. *Pilambulan na ka bay nilaha'?* For how many months have you been having your period? (*Thesaurus:* **bulan₄, tindaw**)

**laha'-llaw** *n.* The reddish glow sometimes seen about sunset, said to be a sign of coming bad weather or misfortune. {idiom}

**laha'₂** *n.* A bloodline; a genetic link. *Ahunit laha' salip min laha' sultan. Salip* blood is of greater worth than royal blood.

**laha'₃** *n.* The embryo of mammals. *Wa'i iya angalabu'an laha'.* She has aborted an embryo. (*cf:* **iram, onde' 2**)

**laha' tindaw** *n. phrase* A girl's first menses.

**lahal** *adj. zero* Adept; skilled. *Lahal na ka ma lahat a'a. Biyasa na ka maingga-maingga.* You are an expert in the inhabited lands. You are comfortable no matter where. *Lahal to'ongan iya ma hinangna, ata'u to'ongan maghinang.* He is expert in what he does, he really knows how to do things. (*Thesaurus:* **layam 1.1, panday 1.1, tullus 1**)

**lahan** *adj. a-* **1)** Very slow; dawdling. *Alahan itu alallay to'ongan, agak-agak sali'.* This word *lahan* means very slow, sort of walking with care. *Bang kita asaki, subay alahan-lahan he'ta lum'ngngan. Sali' hal pahali.* When we are sick, we should walk quite slowly. Just sort of resting. (*Thesaurus:* **aggal 1, kaku', hinay-hinay, lallay, pagene'-ene'**) **1.1)** *v. intr. pa-* To move very slowly, as in the initial period of convalescence. *Palahan itū, sali' hal kita ma luma'. Mbal kita maglunsulan, bay asakki.* This word *lahan* is when we simply stay in the house. We don't go walking about, having been ill.

**palahan-palahan** *adv.* Slowly, of singing.

**lahang** *v. intr. a-* To occur rarely, infrequently, unusually. *Buwat aku itū alahang angusaha. Ya kosogku magl'ngngan.* Like myself, seldom working. My strong point is walking about. *Ma waktu ina'an alahang manusiya' pinakalehan suwala Tuhan.* In those times human beings were seldom made to hear the voice of God. *Alahang na aniya' Milikan ni Sūk.* It is rare now for there to be Westerners coming to Jolo Town. *Alahang, sali' mbal araran kaut.* Seldom, not often going out to sea. (*Thesaurus:* **bihang₂, bislang 1, jalang₂, salat 1**)

**paglahangan** *v. intr. aN-* To be of rare occurrence. *Maglahangan du aniya' musibaku buwattitu.* It is rare for me to have a disaster like this.

**lahasiya'** *n.* **1)** A blood relative. *Anakku lahasiya', anak liksi, anak to'ongan.* My very own child, my true child, a genuine child. *Si Ab ya tapene' pagnakura'am sigām sabab in iya lahasiya' sigām lissi.* Ab was chosen as their leader because he was their close relative. (*cf:* **jatti, porol**; *Thesaurus:* **legsok₁, lissi, luggiya'**) **1.1)** *voc. n.* An affectionate vocative used to address close friends and relatives. *O lahasiya', pi'ingga ka?* Oh friend, where are you going?

**paglahasiya'** *n.* **1)** A group of people related by blood. **1.1)** *v. intr. aN-* To be related closely by blood. *Ndū' tuwan, da'a aku tuna'un atawa minsan saina ma kami maglaulahasiya'.* Please sir, do not accuse me or anyone else of our group of relatives.

**lahat** *n.* A location; a place of residence; a homeland or country of origin. *Bang kām mahē' ma lahatbi porol, hal patatas kono' ya pagkakanbi. B'nnal bahā'?* It is said that when you are there in your homeland you eat only potatoes. Is that true? (*Thesaurus:* **da'ira 1, lungsud, pasisil, tana'₂**)

**lahat-diyata'** *n.* The islands along the Sulu Archipelago to the southwest of Siasi and Jolo.

**paglahat** *n.* **1)** A geographical area; a place in which to reside or settle. *Arokot suli-suli, arongkag. Abalu' deyom paglahat.* The matter has spread [like fire], things are tense. The district is in an uproar. **1.1)** *v. intr. aN-* To reside in a place. *At'ggol kapaglahat maina'an disi Nabi Ibrahim.* The Prophet Abraham and his group stayed there for a long time. *Pilantahun kām maglahat maitu?* How many years will you live here? *Jari pinapehē' lima a'a aesog amantingag palahatan bo' kapaglahatan e' sigām.* So five brave men were sent there to spy out the land so they could settle in it. (*Thesaurus:* **atag₁ 1.1, t'nna' 1.1, tongod₂ 1.2**)

**paglahatan** *n.* The place where one lives.

**lahi₁** *v. intr. pa-/a-* To escape from control or confinement by moving swiftly away. *Wa'i makalahi tohongan ē'.* That tortoise has escaped. *Niramag, bang aniya' pal'ngngan a'a, palahi kaut.* Timid, if someone comes visiting, [he] escapes seaward. (*Thesaurus:* **l'ppa, s'llu 1.1**)

**lahi-lahi** *v. intr. pa-/a-* **1)** To run somewhere. *Palahi-lahi ka pehē' ni luma' palegehan onde'.* Run to the house where the child is lying. (*syn:* **dagan₂ 1.1, onse 1**) **1.1)** *v. tr.* To reach an objective by running. *Lahi-lahi'un luma' inān.* Reach that house by running. **1.2)** *v. ditr.* To convey something by running. *Lahi-lahi'anku daing itū kaleya.* I run inland with this fish.

**paglahi-lahi** *v. intr. aN-* To run.

**palahi** *v. tr.* **1)** To allow something to escape or run away. **1.1)** *v. tr. -an* To evade a pursuer. *Palahi'in mundu ko da'a ka binono'.* Escape from the bandits so as not to be killed.

**lahi₂** *v. tr. -an* To abduct someone; to run off with. (*Thesaurus:* **dakop, pole'₃**)

**paglahi** *n.* **1)** Elopement. **1.1)** *v. intr. aN-* To elope, an alternative way of getting married when the bride-wealth and/or disapproval of elders are obstacles. *T'llu pitu' min kalikutannu, ya na kapaglahi sigām.* Three weeks from your leaving the area, that's when they eloped. *Sai bay anūg-sūgan ka'a aglahi?* Who urged you to elope? *Buwa kamanakanna, binowa maglahi e' a'a, tinambahan iya sīn. Mbal tahinang h'nda, hal* *kinuti-kutihan.* Like her niece, persuaded to elope with a man and given money for it. Not taken as a wife, simply seduced. *Hē' na maglahi karuwangan.* The two of them have run off together. (*Thesaurus:* **kasal 1**, **kawin 1.1**, **pabatal**, **pagsaggaw-ubus**, **pasugsug**)

**lahi₃** *n.* A specific direction, such as a point of the compass. *Lahi pehē' Sambuwangan, lahi pi'itu Taluksangay.* Zamboanga is in that direction, Taluksangay in this other direction. (*Thesaurus:* **tampak 1**, **tampal 1**)

**lahi₄** *n.* The likeness or appearance of something. *Jantangna, lahina.* His physical features, the way he looks. (*Thesaurus:* **aymuka**, **bantuk**, **bayhu' 1**, **dagbos**, **jantang-jari**, **luwa 1**, **pangli' 1**)

**lahil** *v. intr.* pa- 1) To become visible. *Aniya' a'a bay lahil pi'itu, magtūy alungay. Hal alungay man mataku.* Someone became visible here and promptly vanished. Simply vanished from my sight. *Hal paga'ib sadja, hal lling takaleta. Mbal tanda'ta. Palahil itū ta'nda'ta.* It is invisibly present, just a sound that we hear. This word *palahil* is something we have seen. **1.1**) Newly born; to appear in the world at birth. *Aniya' bay palahil pi'itu onde'-onde' halam tape'an, hal kōkna maka baranna.* There was a child who was born with no feet, just its head and its body. (*cf:* **palahil**)

**lahil-batin** *n.* Exposure of what should be concealed, external genitalia in particular. *Bang ta'nda' lahil-batin, makatamparasa.* When genitals are seen it causes shame.

**lahing** *n.* 1) The mature ripe nut of the coconut palm; copra. (*wh:* **niyug**; *Thesaurus:* **l'kkop₂**, **putang**, **tongkop**) **1.1**) *v. intr.* aN- To ripen, of a coconut in its mature stage. **1.2**) *v. tr.* -an To add grated coconut to some food. *Putu-putu nilahingan maka sinokalan. Aniya' isāb nihinti'an.* Steamed rice cakes sprinkled with grated coconut and sugar. Some are sprinkled with coconut candy. *Buwas gandum ya pinaghinang durul. Amene' ka, ai sinokalan, ai nilahingan.* Corn meal made into corn-meal cakes. You choose whether to sugar it or coconut it. (*Stages:* **kambung-kambung**, **botong-botong**, **bilu'uk**, **botong**, **gangkul**, **lahing**, **pangtusan**)

**paglahing** *v. intr.* aN- To be engaged in reaping mature ripe coconuts; to make a living from coconut production. *Subay na aku maglahing bo' binayaran utang.* I'll have to be reaping coconuts to pay the debt.

**lahod** *adj.* -an 1) Discolored through superficial bruising. *Lahoran, sali' angaluwa salindugu', ettom, pote', gaddung.* Bruised, sort of looking like a rainbow, black, white, and green. *Bang aniya' onde'-onde' magkuway, na kalambotan aku paglabayku. Sali' nileboran baranku itū, agtūy lahoran aku.* When children are skipping, then I get smacked in passing. My body gets sort of wrapped around, and I immediately show bruising. (*Thesaurus:* **alom 1**) **1.1**) *v. intr.* aN- To show discoloration of the skin through bruising. *Kabalubakan pa'in iya, na magtūy angalahod baranna.* When he had been beaten, his body immediately showed bruising.

**lahu'** *n.* 1) A solar or lunar eclipse. *Botong aheka bay lagod-lagodna. Pagtohobta na, akulang isina. Wa'i kinakan he' lahu'.* A green coconut that had lots of flesh in it. When we opened it, it had hardly any. It had been devoured by an eclipse. *Ala'at magdakop bang lahu'an dunya.* It is bad to be eloping when the world is experiencing an eclipse. **1.1**) *v. advrs.* -in- Eclipsed, of sun or moon. *Bang ta'abut bulan damlag, buwat saupama nilahu' bulan, magtitik kitām.* When full moon has come, for example, and the moon is eclipsed, we beat things to make a noise. *Sangom minsan, pinandi bang tagna' nilahu' bulan.* Even though it is night, [people] are bathed when the lunar eclipse begins.

**lahusu'** *n.* 1) Various emperor fishes including the Trumpet, or Sweet-lipped emperor. *Lethrinus miniatus.* (*cf:* **kutut**; *gen:* **kutambak**) 2) The Blue-streak emperor. *Lethrinus choirorhynchus.* 3) The Red-throat emperor. *Lethrinus chrysostomus.*

**lahut** *n.* A large working knife; a machete or bolo. (*Thesaurus:* **bangkung**, **bari'**, **gayang**, **laring lahut**, **pira**, **sundang**)

**lai** var. of **lai'**

**lai'** (var. **lai**) *n.* A plate or dish. *O Arung, pi'itu ka angose' lai'.* Daughter, come and wash the dishes. (*Thesaurus:* **pinggan**, **suwit**)

**lai'-tapak** *n.* A saucer or small plate. *Aniya' isāb lai'-tapak buwat pagpat'nna'an sawan kahawa, ya lai' mariki'.* There are also plates like those for putting a coffee cup on, the little ones. (*syn:* **tapak-tapak**)

**lai'-lai'** *n.* An edible bivalve. (*syn:* **pindi' 1**)

**lailatul-kadal** *n.* The apparition of an angel or Muslim saint, seen by one who is specially favored by God. *Ya pamalidjiki' ma kita lailatul-kadal, buwat aniya' tapuwa'ta halam bay ta'nda'ta, saddī-saddī luwana. Ai-ai amu'ta nirūlan sadja kita.* We are given a sight of the *lailatul* as a special favor, for example we find something we have not seen before, something amazing in appearance. Whatever we ask for is granted. *Binuwanan kita kawasa, ya pamalsuku'an ma kita lailatul-kadal.* We are given spiritual power, we are endowed with a *lailatul-kadal* event.

**lain** var. of **lalin**

**laipapa** *n.* A species of small fish, notorious for stealing bait. *Ya niōnan bisbisan laipapa. Laipapa* are referred to as nibblers.

**lais** *v. intr.* pa- 1) To be flattened; to be smoothed, as hair. *Akosog baliyu, palais paldana.* The wind is strong, her skirt is flattened [against her body]. **1.1**) *v. tr.* To comb or flatten one's hair.

*Laista pariyata' ai-ai bay patonton.* We smooth upwards any [hair] that was hanging down. *Aniya' d'nda taga kabulay, patonton bu'unna. Aniya' isāb nilais-lais pariyata'.* There are women with side bangs, whose hair hangs down. There are also some combed in an upward direction. *Bang pinolmed kōkku subay nilais.* When hair-oil has been applied to my hair it should be combed flat. *Si Lais-lais punjung.* He of the combed forelock [from a love song]. (*cf:* **suray 1.1**) **1.2**) *v. advrs.* ka-...-an To be groomed, of one's hair. *Kalaisan iya, daipara aniya' lapis badju'na.* He has been groomed, fortunately his shirt has a covering layer.

**paglais-lais** *v. tr.* To be repeatedly combing one's hair. *Am'lli aku suray paglais-laisku.* I shall buy a comb to keep my hair neat.

**la'a** (var. **lā**) *adv.* Just; merely; only. *T'llu munda' la'a kami.* There are just three canoes of us. *A: "Bay na kam binuwanan kamemon?" B: "Aku lā, Mām."* A: "Have you all been given some?" B: "Just me still, Ma'am." *Lalom tegob-tegoban: alalom to'ongan, sali' hal bilu-biluhan lā.* A *tegob-tegob* depth: extremely deep, only its blueness remaining. *A: "Pila lā?" B: "Duwa la'a."* A: "How many left?" B: "Just two." *Bang aniya' lannang amatay, hinangan liyang dahū ati hal magkubul lā.* If a Chinese person dies, a grave-shelf is made and they simply bury [him]. *Duwansolag lā pinsil si Sel, wa'i tinangkaw nnom. Bay walu' solag hekana.* Only two of Sir's pencils left, six of them stolen. There were eight of them. (*Thesaurus:* **dakuman, hal, luwal, puntul, sadja, samadjana, tunggal 1, yangkon**)

**la'al** *n.* The thickened base of pandanus leaves. (*wh:* **pandan**; *Thesaurus:* **bole, botod, okol, tangkay 1, tongol**)

**la'an** *v. intr.* pa-/a- **1**) To depart from; to disconnect from. *Ōy makannak, ala'an kām man deyo' luma' inān.* Hey you kids, get away from under the house there. *Subay na makala'an min goyak bo' yampa pasaitan kami.* We need to get out from the rough water before we bail out [the canoe]. *Buwat saging alatak min s'kkatanna, ala'anan dīna.* Like bananas dropping from its hand, leaving of itself. *Pala'an kām mannilu ko da'a ka makasanggul.* Get away from there so you don't block [the ball]. (*Thesaurus:* **k'llo'₂, hemos 1, tanggal₂, tungkas**) **1.1**) *v. tr.* -an To remove something from a location. *Mbal kala'anan lansang ma papan inān.* The nails cannot be removed from that plank. *Bay aku abakat e' lahut, kala'anan aku laha' aheka.* I was wounded with a knife and I lost a lot of blood. *Aheka a'a magda'awa ma Sisangat, ahunit kala'anan minsan sinōd he' mundu, malaingkan talalat.* A lot of people in Sisangat argue [against an edict], they are difficult to remove even when invaded by bandits, though they can be relocated.

**la'an kaul** *v. intr.* a- To be speechless from shock. {idiom} *Ala'an bay kaulku.* I was speechless.

**pagla'an** *v. intr.* aN- To shift from a place or commitment. *Pagla'annu minnitu, makalanggal ka duwa a'a ma tongod bay pangubulan si Sitti Rakiya.* On departing from here, you will meet two people at the place where *Sitti Rakiya* was buried. *Buli-buli pikilanku. Bang halam ka maina'an, manjari aku itu amikilan angangganti' ma ka'a. Mbal magla'an pikilanku.* My mind is made up. If you are not there, then I will think about replacing you. My thinking will not shift.

**la'ang** *n.* **1**) The current associated with an outgoing tide. *Akosog sidda la'ang bang kohap ma tahik Siasi.* The outgoing tide is very strong in the afternoon in the Siasi waters. *Duwa s'llang, sōn maka la'ang. Insini' bay sōn, bo' la'ang amalos.* Two sea movements, *sōn* [incoming tide] and *la'ang* [outgoing tide]. It was an incoming tide earlier, but the outgoing tide now flows back. (*cf:* **abal 1.1, s'llog, tambang₁ 1.1**) **1.1**) *v. intr.* -um- To ebb, of tide. *Luma'ang na, sōng t'bba.* It is ebbing and will soon be low tide. (*Thesaurus:* **sōn**)

**la'at** *n.* **1**) The bad aspect of something; evil. *Ya la'atna halam maina'an h'llana.* The worst of it is that her husband wasn't there. (*Thesaurus:* **jahallis, jahat, jahil 1, jahulaka' 1**) **1.1**) *adj.* a- Bad, of physical condition or moral quality. *Ala'at isina itū.* Its flesh is bad [of fruit]. *Ala'at isāb a'a inān.* That person is evil. **1.2**) *v. tr.* To treat someone or something badly. *La'atbi du bay pangalāngku ka'am.* You reacted badly to my forbidding you. *Nila'at saga a'a inān, nilāng min usahana.* Those people are badly treated, prohibited from making their living. *Bang a'a saddī ya pameya'annu, aniya' arai' angala'at ka'a.* If you go with anybody else, there could be someone who will do you harm. (*Thesaurus:* **jilaka', la'ug 1.1, pinjala' 1.1, pissoko', puhinga', sikla, usiba'**) **1.3**) *v. tr.* a-, ka-..-an, -an To treat someone badly. *Sapadpad pamuwan si'itku, gōm na ni a'a, sabab kinab'nsihan aku he'na, ya pagka kita kinala'atan e' si'it.* Rather than gifting [it] to my uncle, better to give it to someone [else]. That's because the uncle hates us, in that we are badly treated by uncle. *Minsan du kita kinala'atan e' saga kakita hē', paloglog na pa'in.* Even though we are badly treated by our cousins, we persist in visiting.

**kala'atan** *n.* Wrong or evil actions. *Aheya na kīs a'a inān ma parinta. Bay iya amono'. Taga kīs na iya, taga kala'atan.* That man has an official case against him. He killed someone. He has a case to answer, he has some badness. *An'ppu iya mma'na maghinang kala'atan. Labi abuhat gi' kala'atanna itū min pagkahina.* He behaves like his father in doing evil. His evil was more serious than that of his contemporaries. (*Thesaurus:* **bala', kajahatan, mulka' 1, naja', pa'al 1, udjul₁ 1**)

**la'at atay** *adj. a-* The feeling of offense or emotional hurt. {idiom} *Ōy, makala'at atay ko' ilū.* Hey, that is offensive. *Da'a kām angahinang ai-ai ya makala'at pangatayan sigām kasehe' itū.* Don't do anything that annoys the rest of them. (*cf:* **akon-akon**; *Thesaurus:* **ambul-dā'**, **anak-anak₂**, **kagit atay 1**, **tumpalak 1**)

**la'at bowa'** *adj. a-* Indecent or vulgar, of speech. {idiom} *Ala'at bowa'na.* His speech is indecent [lit. his mouth is bad]. *Angalu'ud-lama' iya mareyom kauman, ala'at bowa'na.* He behaves in the community without shame, his speech vulgar. (*Thesaurus:* **lu'ug-lama' 1**, **lumu'**, **sabul 1.1**)

**la'at helo** *adj. a-* Feeling nauseated, especially with regard to the early stage of a pregnancy. {idiom} *Ala'at kono' helona, kilāku angiram na sōng.* She says she is nauseated, I figure she is becoming pregnant.

**la'at palasahan** *n. phrase* The feeling of being unwell. {idiom} *Ala'at na palasahanku.* I am feeling poorly now.

**la'at-ludja'** *adj. a-* Disgusted at something or someone. {idiom} *Ē! Makala'at-ludja' ko' ilū.* Yuk! That is disgusting.

**la'at-s'mmu** *adj. a-* Looking angry or displeased. {idiom} *Angay ala'at-s'mmunu ma aku?* Why are you looking displeased with me? *Bang aniya' amah'llingan aku, angalom bayhu'ku, sali' ala'at-s'mmuku.* When someone scolds me my face becomes dark red, I look angry. (*Thesaurus:* **astol 1.1**, **p'ddi' atay 1**)

**pagla'at-la'at** *v. intr. aN-* To behave badly towards each other. *Magkidjib itū sali' magdanakan magla'at-la'at.* Kidjib is about siblings behaving maliciously towards each other.

**pagnikala'atan** *v. intr. aN-* To come to a bad end as a consequence of present actions or attitudes.

**pala'at** *v. tr.* To harm someone by speaking ill of him.

**la'in-la'in** *adj. zero* Unusual; out of the ordinary. *Sali' aku la'in-la'in bang lum'ngngan. Makarugtul nsa' bidda'.* It's like I am unusually careless when I walk. I stumble over this and that. *La'in-la'in t'ggolnu bang ka lum'ngngan.* You take an unusually long time when you walk. (*Thesaurus:* **mahal-mahal, saddī-saddī**)

**la'it** *v. tr.* To sew cloth. *Agese' badju' si Ja, bay angindam jalum ni si Mām pangala'it badju'na.* Ja's shirt is torn, he borrowed a needle from Mam to sew it. (*cf:* **sulsi**; *Thesaurus:* **bakiya'₂, bagsak₂, dahut, tahi'**)

**la'itan** *n.* A sewing style or technique. *La'itan binagsak.* Sewing done with the *bagsak* technique.

**la'uk** var. of **la'up**

**la'ug** *adj. a-* 1) Physically aggressive. *Bi, da'a ka ala'ug, ā.* Bi, don't be aggressive, huh. **1.1)** *v. tr. -an* To assault someone; to treat someone viciously. *Asabul makalandu' saga mundu, hal angala'ug hinang sigām.* Bandits behave really badly, victimising people is their sole work. *Ta'atas he'na angala'ugan sehe'na mampa'in iya maka'ā' sīn.* He takes it on himself to assault his companion so long as he can get money. *Subay aheya baranna bo' mbal nila'ugan.* His body will have to be big for him not to be bullied. (*Thesaurus:* **jilaka', la'at 1.2, pinjala' 1.1, pissoko', puhinga', sikla, usiba'**)

**la'ug-sehe'** *v. tr. -an* To mistreat or take advantage of a companion. *Ata'u iya angalista, bo' sehe'na mbal. Bang angalista pokotan, bang bayad dakayu' pilak, amabā' iya dambila' pilak. Bay angala'ugan sehe'na.* He knows how to keep a record but his companion doesn't. When he is recording the catch of fish netted, when the rate is one peso he says it is half that. He has treated his workmate badly.

**bula'ug₂** *n.* A vindictive or belligerent person.

**la'un** *adj. a-* 1) Still single beyond the age when most people are married. *Subay na iya ala'un bo' yampa makabāk h'nda.* He had to be past marriageable age before finding a wife. **1.1)** *adj. -an* Confirmed in singleness. *Budjang la'unan na iya.* She is an old maid now.

**la'ung** *see:* **hilala'ungan**

**la'up** (var. **la'uk**) *n.* 1) A pleat in cloth. *Al'ssin la'up badju'na bang niukkilan.* The pleats in her blouse are neat when decorated. (*Thesaurus:* **kola' 1, kumpi' 1**) **1.1)** *v. tr. -an* To make a pleat in cloth.

**lalag** *v. intr. aN-* To roam about looking for things that might be useful. *Buwat saga onde' inān angalalag man deyo' luma' itū, amiha anangkaw. Aniya' isāb bay makalalag suru'.* Like those children roaming around under the house here, looking to steal. One of them in fact came across a spoon. (*Thesaurus:* **batuk₂, jadja' 1.1, libu 1.1, nda' 1.1, salusu**)

**lalagpak** var. of **lagpak₁**

**lalandak** (derivative of **landak**) *n.* A crowbar. (*Thesaurus:* **bara, pala, piku, sangkul 1, susuwat**).

**lalangga'** *n.* A species of tree ant, capable of inflicting a painful bite. *Aheka lalangga' ma amboway, bang angeket abisa.* There are many yellow ants on the *amboway* tree, very painful when they bite. (*gen:* **s'mmut 1**)

**lalap** *see:* **paglalap**

**lalas** *v. tr.* To abduct someone; to force a woman into a sexual relationship. *D'nda ya bay nilalas min deyom luma'na, maumu sali' buwat pinogos.* The woman who was abducted from her house, usually some sort of compulsion. *Lalas itū pasal budjang maka subul. Budjang binowa ni lahat dakayu' ati niurul e' saga matto'ana. Ya makataksil man kal'llahan sabab pinogos. Ngga'i ka baya' d'nda.* Lalas is to do with a teenage couple. The girl is taken to some other place and pursued by her elders. It is the boy's side who are fined because [she] was compelled. It was not what the girl wanted. (*cf:* **guyud 2, saggaw-sangom**)

**lalat₁** *v. tr.* **1)** To force someone to conform. *Saupama minunduhan kita ma Sisangat. Na talalat kita ni Siganggang. Ya makalalat mundu maka tāwta na hē'.* For example we are attacked by bandits at Sisangat, and are forced to go to Siganggang. What causes us to go are the bandits and our fear. *Aheka a'a magda'awa ma Sisangat, ahunit kala'anan minsan sinōd he' mundu, malaingkan talalat.* A lot of people in Sisangat resist [an edict], difficult to remove even when invaded by bandits. Nevertheless they can forced to move. *Talalat e' goyak, mbal kita makakole'.* Forced by the rough weather, we couldn't cope. **1.1)** *v. intr. pa-* To relocate in response to a an impending danger. *Palalat kita ni lahat dakayu' sabab aniya' badju.* We are compelled by fear to relocate because there is a typhoon. (*Thesaurus:* **pagbakwet, pagdo'ag**)

**lalat₂** *see:* **tai'-lalat**

**lalga** *v. intr. pa-* To set out for a destination. *Tonga' bahangi palalga na kami isāb minna'an sudju Tiyanggi.* At midnight we too set out from there towards Jolo. *Ta'abut pa'in lisag nnom kohap, yuk Saljen Nu, "Palalgahunbi na," yukna, "lansa ilu sudju ni Siasi."* Come 6.00 p.m., Sergeant Nu said, "Let that launch depart now for Siasi." (*Thesaurus:* **lanjal 1.1, laus 1, sōng₂ 1, unjal**)

**lali** *n.* The Dolphinfish; the Pompano. *Coryphaena equiselis.*

**lalin** (var. **lain**) *v. intr. aN-* **1)** To change location. **1.1)** *v. intr. pa-* To transfer to another location or container. *Na, ya saki ipul si Na ē' palalin na ni ka'a sampay ma saga panubu'nu salama-lama.* So the leprous condition of Na will transfer to you and to your descendants forever. **1.2)** *v. tr. -an* To transfer an item to another location or container. *Lainin ni lai' dakayu'.* Transfer it to another plate. *Nilainan duwa'anta ni lansa dakayu'.* Our goods are moved over to another launch.

**paglalin** *v. intr. aN-* To trade situation or circumstances with someone. *Buwat ma deyom iskul bo' aku ata'u, yuk kasehe'an, "Ata'u pahāp ka'a ilū!" Na yukta, "Maglalin aku ma ta'unu."* Like in school when I know [the answer], others say, "How clever you are!" So we say, "I'll swap brains with you [lit. I will take over your cleverness]." *Sali' si Tu bay maka'ā' bo' si Al halam maka'ā'. Yuk si Al, "Mayaman ka'a ilū." Yuk si Tu, "Maglalin ka, magsalin sukud."* Like when Tu had caught fish and Al had caught nothing. Al said, "You are so well off." Tu said, "Your time will come [lit. change your location, change your luck]." *Buwat aku sinoho' kaut ni Kompani, pikisehe' aku ma si Sm, bo' mbal iya.*

*Manjari kaut aku dangan-danganku ati tapuwa'ku lima pilak ma lān. Pagt'kkaku, yukku, "Bay tapuwa'ku lima pilak." Yuk si Sm, "Gōm bay aku ameya', magbahagi' kitā." "Na," yukku, "maglalin ka, bay na ka'a-i bowaku."* Like when I was sent shorewards to the military post, and I asked Sm to accompany me but he wouldn't. So I went to the shore on my own and happened to find five pesos on the path. On getting back I said, "I found five pesos." Sm said, "If only I had gone. Let's share it." "Well," I said, "Take your turn, I would have taken you." *Maglain, sali' ala'an ni lahat dakayu'.* Relocating, leaving for another district for example. (*Thesaurus:* **pagtagestes**)

**lalingu** *adj. zero* To become separated in a crowd. *Sali' kita bay lalingu. Yukku, "Si Mo?" Yuknu, "Ngga'i ka." Aku kasaman-samanan.* Like the two of us separated in a crowd. I said, "Is that Mo?" You said "No it's not." And I was disappointed.

**paglalingu** *v. intr. aN-* To be mutually confused about the whereabouts of each other, as people separated in a crowd. *Maglalingu itu magkalungay, sali' magsaliyu. Maglalingu sigām ma kaheka'an a'a sabab sin tunu'.* Maglalingu means getting lost, getting mixed up. They were lost in the crowd because of the fire. *Maglalingu kita dansehe'an, daka ma'ai bay sehe'ta.* Our group of companions got separated, who knows where one who had been our companion was.

**lalipan** *n.* A species of large centipede that can inflict a painful bite with its pincers. *Aheka lalipan ma luma' atop sairap.* There are lots of centipedes in houses with palm frond thatch. *Bilahi gi' anganak min duwa dang'llaw, da'a gi' kineket e' lalipan.* I would rather give birth twice in one day, than be bitten by a centipede. (*Thesaurus:* **liyabod, nne**)

**lalipan-tahik** *n.* A centipede-like sea creature about 2 cm long which leaves a bright phosphorescent trail. *Mixophilus spp. Bang aheka lalipan-tahik palangi kaleya, ya na hē' pandoga ulan.* When many sea centipedes swim towards land, that's a sign of rain. *Subay kam kamaya' bang an'bba bo' mbal takeket ni lalipan tahik.* You should be careful when collecting sea foods in the shallows lest you be bitten by sea centipedes.

**lalipan-lalipan** *v. tr.* To join the edges of a tear; to trim an edge with closely spaced parallel threads. (*Thesaurus:* **ayum-ayum, sulsi**)

**lallan** *v. tr.* To eat food without the usual starch or protein counterparts. *Bang pamaliyu, hal angalallan sinanglag sabab akulang daing.* When it is the windy season [they] just eat pan-roasted cassava alone because fish are scarce. (*cf:* **lauk 1**; *Thesaurus:* **kakan 1, kakan 1, inta', l'kkob, pakan**)

**lallay** *adj. a-* Slow-moving; lethargic. *Agaranku si Sa, bay angalga ma jambatan. Alallay iya.* I will wait for Sa, he had been carrying stuff at the

wharf. He's slow. (*Thesaurus:* **aggal 1, kaku',
hinay-hinay, lahan 1, pagene'-ene'**)

**paglallay-lallay** *v. intr. aN-* To dawdle. *Da'a ka
maglallay-lallay dīnu bang ka mbal kalingananku.*
Don't make yourself go slow when I haven't
called you. *Maglallay-lallayan kita bang
lum'ngngan, ni'nda' bang sai alallay.* We compete
for slowness when we walk, to see who is the
slow one.

**lalom₁ 1)** *n.* Depth, as the distance from the top to
the bottom of a liquid. *Labi saga sangpū' d'ppa
lalomna. Mbal aku makap'ddon bang buwattē'.*
More than ten fathoms or so deep. I cannot hold
my breath at that depth. **1.1)** *adj. a-* Deep, of a
liquid. **2)** *adj. a-* High, of tide. *Al'kkab na tahik,
sali' alalom.* The tide is full in, that is it is high
tide. *Alalom na tahik, mbal aku tum'kkad.* The
tide is high, I won't touch bottom. (*cf:* **t'bba 1**;
*Thesaurus:* **daka', l'kkab, nso', sosob,
tambang₁ 1**)

**kalaloman** *n.* Ocean depths; deep regions of the
sea.

**lalom bahangi** *adj. a-* Late at night. {idiom}

**lalom₂** *adj. a-* Profound, of mental capacity or a
concept. *Alalom isāb pangita'una maka
pamikilna.* His knowledge and his thinking are
deep. *Halam aniya' pangita'u, lalom palnahu'an,
ya manjari paliyu min Tuhan.* There is no
knowledge or deep intellect that can go beyond
God's.

**lalom ampun** *adj. a-* Total, of forgiveness.
{idiom} *Alalom ampunna ma ka'am.* His
forgiveness towards you is absolute. *Subay
alalom ampunta bang aheya kasā'anta.* Our
forgiveness should be comprehensive when our
[own] error has been great.

**lalu** *v. tr.* To have sexual intercourse with
someone. {vulgar} *Puspusku kabaya'anku, asal du
aku nirūlan he' si Mma'. Minsan aku, tabiya',
angalalu d'nda.* I will do whatever I want,
indulged as I in fact am by my father, even if
[pardon my language] I have sexual intercourse
with a woman. *Maglaka'-laka', pinakaiya' sali',
niamu' nilalu.* Insult [someone] by using obscene
language, causing shame, suggesting
intercourse.

**paglalu** *v. intr. aN-* To have sexual relations.
{vulgar} *Ala'at hinang si Anu maglaka'-laka'an
d'nda, pinakaiya' paglalu.* What's-his-name's
behavior is bad, insulting a woman, causing
shame by suggesting sex.

**palalu** *n.* Someone addicted to having sex.
{vulgar}

**lalu'u** var. of **kalitan-lalu'u**

**lalung₁** *n.* Generic term for various lionfishes.
*Pterois spp.*

**lalung-ettom** *n.* The Spotfin lionfish. *Pterois
antennata.*

**lalung₂** *n.* A cursing equivalent for a canoe. (*gen:*

**sukna' 1.1**)

**lalungan** *n.* A coffin. (*cf:* **kaban 1**)

**lām** *n.* A wick lamp, typically one with a glass. *Da'a
henggolun lām ilū ko da'a ahūg saminna.* Don't
shake that lamp lest its glass falls. (*Thesaurus:*
**kulaet 1, laet, lampu, palita'an, plaslaet 1,
sū' 1**)

**lama-lama** see: **salama-lama**

**lamak** *n.* A square sail with upper and lower yards,
rigged obliquely on a tripod mast. *Am'lli aku
espowen, hinangku lamak pangalamakku pelang.* I
will buy sail cloth, I will make a square sail as a
sail for the canoe. (*syn:* **leha 1**)

**laman** *v. intr. pa-* **1)** To become visible to someone
for a brief time, as when awake or in a dream
state. *Ya maumu bang kita atuli, aniya' palaman
ni kita.* It is most often when we are sleeping
that someone appears to us. (*Thesaurus:*
**lambung₁ 1, pagsagiyaw**) **1.1)** *v. tr.* To see
someone or something briefly, as when passing
by or when dreaming. *Buwat aniya' pihanu,
atilaw ka ma aku, "Halam bay talamannu
sehe'ku?"* Suppose you are looking for someone,
you say to me, "You haven't glimpsed my
companion, have you?" (*Thesaurus:* **k'llap, idlap
1.1**)

**paglaman** *v. intr. aN-* To catch a brief glimpse of
each other, literally or in spirit form. *Hal kami
bay maglaman, halam bay makapagsuli-suli.* We
just caught sight of each other, but we didn't
talk. *Da'a gi' bang buwat d'nda maka l'lla
magbaya', bo' sali' at'ggol halam makapag'nda',
bo' samaentom, na maglaman.* Especially when a
woman and a man are in love but haven't seen
each other for ages and are each thinking of the
other, then they appear to each other.

**lamas** *v. ditr.* To offer something to a supernatural
being, as for example a food offering to the
guardian spirit of a place. *Angalamas ni tunggu'
batu ma Pagatpat.* Making an offering to the
guardian of the rock at Pagatpat. (*Thesaurus:*
**buwis 1.1, paglabot 2, tanggap 1.1, ungsud₂**)

**lamba₁** *adj. a-* Long and widely spaced, of outrigger
booms. *Bang bangka'nu ariki'-diki', ataha'
batanganna, alamba. Bang mbal alamba al'kkas
pakkom.* If your dugout canoe is small, its
outrigger booms long and well-spaced, it will be
stable. If they are not it will capsize readily.
*Alamba batangan ilū ni munda', apu'ut ni buli'.*
Those outriggers are well-spaced forward, and
short at the stern.

**lamba₂** *clf.* Count word for flexible items. *Dalamba
daun saging, duwa lamba bu'un, t'llu lamba
bulbul.* One strip of banana leaf, two strands of
hair, three feathers. *Yuk sultan, "Minsan
dalamba bu'un ma kōk anaknu mbal tapaka'at."*
The sultan said, "Not even one strand of the hair
on your son's head will be harmed." *Makajari
dalamba katas, makajari isāb dalamba atop.* It's
possible [to say] a *lamba* of paper, a *lamba* of

thatch is also possible. (*Thesaurus:* **b'llad 1, b'llat 1, kintas 1, gekap 1**)

**lambahan** *n.* A unit for measuring the width of a mat. *Pila lambahan tepo inān?* How many units wide is that mat?

**lambana'** *n.* 1) Generic term for various barracudas, including the Big-eye barracuda. *Sphyraena forsteri.* (*spec:* **bangasan, pangaluwan**) 2) The snake mackerel. *Promethichthys prometheus.*

**lambana'-lengko'** *n.* The Great barracuda. *Sphyraena barracuda.*

**lambana'-tigul** *n.* The Obtuse barracuda. *Sphyraena obtusata.*

**lambang₁** *adj.* a- Hidden from view by an intervening item. *Dakayu' punglu' tinimbak dakayu' a'a, makalatun ni dakayu'. Alambang.* One person shot with a single bullet which goes [through] to another. Hidden [from the shooter]. *Aniya' maglapis daing, dakayu' paharap ni ka'a. Pagpassik pana', duwa. Alambang.* There are fish in layers, just one of them facing you. When the spear is released there are two. Hidden from view. *Bang ka amarena aniya' kayu nsa' tata'u mareyo', talapay. Alambang iya.* If you're drilling a hole and there is an unnoticed piece of timber underneath, it gets drilled as well. It is hidden from view. (*Thesaurus:* **lagbas 1, latus, l'ppas 1.1, l'ssut**)

**lambang-mata** *adj.* a- 1) Confused by the profusion of items on display. {idiom} *Minsan ala'at pina'nda'an ni iya, yukna ahāp. Aburiru pikilanna, alambang matana.* Even though what is shown him is bad, he thinks it is good. His thinking is muddled, his vision gets confused. (*Thesaurus:* **bingaw, buriru, lengog kōk, ligoto'**) 1.1) *v. advrs.* -in- To become confused by the wide range of choices. {idiom} *Nilambang-mata kita ma pamene'an ai-ai.* We have become confused by the choice of various things.

**lambang₂** *v. tr.* To strengthen a mast with a supporting pole.

**paglambangan** *n.* The rear supporting poles of a tripod mast.

**lambat** *n.* 1) A sinker on a fishing line. *Lambat itū bo' al'kkas pat'nde p'ssina, bo' al'kkas tininduk e' daing.* This sinker is so that its hooks will sink quickly, and so that the fish will strike quickly. (*cf:* **larung 1, tingga'**) 1.1) *v. tr.* To catch fish with a weighted line. *Ni Tōng T'lling aku angalambat saga bukay-bukay, saga pellok s'llang.* I'm going to T'lling Point to fish with a weighted line for keel-heads and other wrasses. *Am'lli aku tingga' hinangku lambat pangalambatku pehē' ni Sinundang.* I will buy some lead to make a sinker for fishing with a weighted line there at Sinundang.

**lambay** *n.* A ceremony held during the month Julhadji' and at the completion of Ramadan. *Lambay itū paghinang mareyom maskid hinabu bulan hadji'. Lambay* is a ceremony in the mosque during the month of the hajj.

**paglambay** *v. intr.* aN- To be engaged in the lambay (waving) ceremony.

**lambe₁** *v. intr.* aN- 1) To swing to and fro. *Subay niengkotan ni kambotna bo' supaya mbal angalambe.* It should be fastened to his belt so it doesn't swing to and fro. 1.1) *v. tr.* To get attention by waving to and fro. *Bang ka ni M'ddas, bo' ka wa'i ma olangan, lambeta ka. Aniya' pabeya'ku.* When you go to Siasi, and are already halfway across [the channel], I wave to you. I have something to send. (*Thesaurus:* **kambay 1, mita, paglabad 1.1, sayang₂, sinyal 1.1**)

**lambe₂** *n.* The Spiny or Sabre squirrelfish. *Sargocentrum sp.* (*gen:* **tihik-tihik 1**)

**lambeng-lambeng** *see:* **paglambeng-lambeng**

**lambetong** *n.* A firefly. *Ōnna to'ongan si Jillian, danglayna si Lambetong.* Her real name is Gillian, her familiar name is Firefly.

**lambi'** *n.* Generic term for various cerith snail species. *Cerithium spp.*

**lambot** *v. tr.* To strike something using an implement; to spank. *Bay aku nilambot e' mma'ku maka lubid. Busay ka, atawa papan ka, atawa lantay.* I was smacked by my father with a rope. Could be a paddle, a board or a flooring slat. *Aniya' onde'-onde' magkuway, na kalambotan aku paglabayku.* There were children skipping rope, then I got smacked on passing by. (*Thesaurus:* **balubak, daplos, lappet, lubak₁**)

**lambu** *n.* 1) The width or transverse dimension of an object. *Aniya' ba'ul lima h'kka taha'na, t'llu h'kka lambuna.* There was a box three spans long and two spans across. 1.1) *adj.* a- Broad, of something with edges but not walls. *Bang angahinang tepo, subay alambu ni kīd.* When a mat is being made, it should be wide along the sides. *Alambu lamisahanbi.* Your table is broad. (*Thesaurus:* **habog, lampo' 1.1, luha 1.1**)

**lambung₁** (var. **landung**) *n.* 1) The appearance of something in contrast to its physical reality; a reflection, apparition or shadow. *Anambung Kayu-itingan itu, yukna, "Bang aku to'ongan ya pene'bi magsultanan ka'am, pi'itu kam pasindung ma lambungku."* Thorn-tree answered and said, "If I really am the one you chose to be king over you, come here and shelter in my shadow." *Bang kita atanding ni samin, ta'nda'ta landungta.* When we look in a mirror, we see our reflection. *Bang sangom bo' asawa bulan, aheya landungta. Aniya' isāb landung gabun.* At night when the moon is bright, our shadow is large. There are shadows from clouds too. (*Thesaurus:* **laman 1, pagsagiyaw**) 1.1) *v. intr.* pa- To appear to someone in dream form. *Palambung, sali' magpa'nda'.* Like becoming visible. 1.2) *v.*

*intr. aN-* To cause a reflection or shadow; to produce a visual manifestation, as some spirit beings do. *Angalandung tanganku ma katas itū.* My hand casts a shadow on this paper.

**lambung tuli** *v. advrs. -in-* Dropping off to sleep. {idiom} *Lambung aku tinuli, minsan aku amasi magsuli-suli.* I am dropping off to sleep, even though I am still talking. *Bang kita baha'u bay atuli bo' abati' na, apiru' matata. Amasi lambung tinuli gi'.* When we have just gone to sleep and wake up, our eyelids are closed. We're still in sleep mode. (*Thesaurus:* **karu' 1.1, lilap, tuli₁ 1.1**)

**palambung** *v. tr.* To communicate something by means of a dream.

**lambung₂** *v. tr.* To catch sight of someone or something. *Talambungku pa'in luwana bay bitu'anunku, magtūy aku pabīng lahi-lahi.* When I caught sight of my divorced wife's face, I immediately turned back and ran away. *Pehē' ka, lambungun pehē' apa sōng atulak lansa.* Go and have a look because the launch is about to leave.

**paglambung** *v. intr. aN-* To catch a glimpse of someone. *Yukku, "Bang ta'nda'nu si Ti, soho'un pal'kkas." Na yukku, "Aho' tuwan, bang kami maglambung, haka'anta pa'in ka."* You said, "If you see Ti, tell him to be quick." Then I said, "Yes sir, if we catch sight of each other I will tell you." *Magtinampalan, magtūy dī maglambung, ya kamaumuhanna bang d'nda maka l'lla.* Coming face to face and promptly looking seriously at each other, the way it often is with a woman and a man. (*Thesaurus:* **pagalop, pagharap, pag'nda'₁, pagtampal**)

**lambus** *n.* Buoyant wood useful for making floats. *Lambus itū subay ma pahapat.* These *lambus* trees are where the *pahapat* [saltwater tree] grow. *Bay kariki'-riki'ku lagi', sidda kami ni bakkaw ang'llo' lambus nihinang bangka'-bangka'.* Back in my childhood we went often to the mangroves to get some *lambus* for making little canoes. (*cf:* **tongke'**)

**lambuyut** *n.* The slack in a line or tie. *Pabontolun lambuyut hengkot ilū, hella'-hella'un, pahogotun.* Fix the slackness of that knot, pull it a bit, make it secure. (*Thesaurus:* **loka, luslus 1.1**)

**lamekkat** *adj.* zero Slushy, as of deep mud. (*Thesaurus:* **legsak, lettak, l'bbo 1, pekat**)

**paglamekkat** *v. intr. aN-* To play in muddy puddles. *Basta angulan, atagi saga anak kamemon maglamekkat ma lanaw-lanaw.* When it's raining, the kids all love to wallow around in the puddles.

**lamesahan** var. of **lamisahan**

**lami** *adj. a-* Enjoyable; having fun. *Hailaya alami. Alami sidda ma M'ddas bang Hailaya pasal aheka magongka'.* A fun festival. It's very enjoyable in Siasi Town on a holiday because a lot of people are playing games together. (*Thesaurus:* **kōd,** **kōg 2, koyag 1, lasig 1, paglangog**)

**kalamihan** *n.* Festivity; enjoyment; entertainment. *Kalalamihan dunya, kakaya'an dunya.* The enjoyable things of the world, its possessions.

**paglami** *n.* 1) Merrymaking; celebrating. *Da'a subay dumasiyaw paglami-lamita.* Our merrymaking should not be excessive. **1.1)** *v. intr. aN-* To be having fun together. *Maglami-lami kami magdumino, tabeya' amange' si Hi.* We had such fun playing dominoes that it made Hi wet himself. *Agongka' sigām maka aglami-lami.* They were playing and having fun together.

**pagkalamihan** *n.* 1) A celebration or happy event. **1.1)** *v. intr. aN-* To celebrate together. *Magkalamihan sigām sampay magbuwan-biyuwani.* They were celebrating and giving gifts to each other.

**lamin** *v. intr. pa-* 1) To spread, of a sickness; to be contagious. *Sakina bay akalaminan aku. Aho', palamin du saki ilu.* His sickness infected me. Yes, that sickness does spread. (*cf:* **kulina, paglemed**) **1.1)** *v. tr. -an* To communicate a sickness to someone else. **1.2)** *v. advrs. ka-...-an* To be infected or ill from someone else's illness. *Wa'i iya kalaminan, kinohol.* He has been infected, coughing.

**lamisahan** (var. **lamesahan**) *n.* A table. *Dalamesahan sigām maka sultan.* They are at the same table as the sultan. *Magtipu-tipuhan duwa sultan inān, amangan dalamesahan sagō' sali'-sali' amikil kala'atan.* Those two kings behaved deceitfully, eating at the same table but both thinking bad things toward the other. (*cf:* **mesa**)

**lamit** *v. tr. -an* To share food with others. *Lamitin danakannu.* Give some to your brothers and sisters.

**paglamit-lamit** *v. intr. aN-* 1) To be distributed evenly. **1.1)** *v. tr. -an* To distribute resources evenly. *Bang aniya' dakarut buwas pamuwan min baranggay, pinaglamit-lamitan e' anak-kampung. Aheka-ariki' na, subay makahampit kamemon.* When a sack of rice is given by the barangay [official], it is distributed equally by the children of the community. A lot or a little, everybody should get some. (*Thesaurus:* **bahagi' 1, gihay, hampit, sihak**)

**lamma** (var. **l'mma'₂**) 1) *adj. a-* Weakened by sickness; disheartened. *Alamma iya bay luwa' min ospital.* He was weak when he came out of hospital. *Buwat aniya' bay sakita, buwat bay tinandog, na angal'mma' kita, sali' angalamma.* Like when we have had an illness, like malaria, then we become feeble, sort of downcast. *Saki ai-ai basta apasu', angal'mma' kita, mbal makakole'.* Any sickness if it involves a high temperature, we are weakened and can't do anything. (*cf:* **kapuy**; *Thesaurus:* **komay, loyot, pilay**) 2) *n.* Weakness; lack of energy or resolve. *Ya a'a ahogot pangatayanna maka'atuhan* *dīna min kalammahan.* The person whose heart is steadfast can defend himself from discouragement. **2.1)** *v. advrs. ka-...-an* To be weakened; dishearten. *Jari saga a'a kamemon ma kalahat-lahatan inān bay kalamma-lammahan e' punung.* So all the people in those regions were weakened by the lack of food. (*Thesaurus:* **paggambahan, saman-saman**)

**paglamma** *v. intr. aN-* To become weakened and disheartened. *Maglammahan sigām kamemon, magtāwan paluwas min pagtapukan sigām.* They all lost heart, afraid to come out from their hiding places.

**pagkalalamma** *v. intr. aN-* To become progressively weaker.

**pagkalammahan** *v. intr. aN-* To be low-spirited; disheartened.

**lampak₁** *n.* **1)** A cash payment; a deposit on a purchase. *Buwat kita arāk angutang bo' mbal pamautang, subay lampak.* Like us expecting to buy on credit, but it isn't to be given, it must be cash. **1.1)** *v. tr.* To pay for something in cash. *Lampakun na bang pila kaga'osannu ungsud.* Pay in cash however much of the bride-price you can manage. *Mpatpū' pilak bang nilampak, mpatpū' maka lima bang niutang.* Forty pesos cash up front, forty-five when credit is involved. (*Thesaurus:* **bayad 1.1, gadji 1.1, hokas, susuk, tinga 1.1, tulahan, tunay₂, tungbas 1**)

**lampak₂** *adj. zero* **1)** Matching or equalling, of bets in a gambling game. *Lampak na sīnnu.* Your bet is matched. *Buwat kita magsalla' bo' aku kapikitannu, yukku, "Pabeya'un dambila' pilak ilū. Lampak."* Like when we are playing toss-the-coin and you have staked me, I say, "Include that half peso. Matching." (*Thesaurus:* **atap, samaunjuk**) **1.1)** *v. tr. -an* To match the bid of another player.

**lampag** *adj. a-* Careless or clumsy in the use of something. *Alampag a'a itū mags'mmek, minsan baha'u agese'.* How careless this fellow is with his clothes, they are torn even though new.

**lampasu** *v. tr. -an* To polish a floor by skating it with a coconut-husk brush. *Halam gi' makina, tape' sadja pangalampasu lantay.* Before there were machines, feet alone were used to polish the floor. (*Thesaurus:* **bata, lanu' 1.2, ponglas**)

**lampek** (var. **lampet**) *n.* Various wrasses, including the Ragged-tail wrasse, the Two-spot Maori wrasse and the Cheek-lined Maori wrasse. *Oxycheilinus bimaculatus.*

**lampek-s'llang** *n.* **1)** The Scarlet-breasted wrasse, a deep-water species. *Cheilinus fasciatus.* **2)** The Black-lined Maori wrasse. *Cheilinus diagrammus.* **3)** The Snooty wrasse or Pointy-headed wrasse. *Cheilinus oxycephalus.* **4)** The Triple-tail wrasse. *Cheilinus trilobatus.*

**lampet** var. of **lampek**

**lampik** (var. **lappik**) *n.* **1)** A protective layer. *Bang ka magsulat subay aniya' lampikna pamatagalan katas.* When you're writing there should be a protective backing for the paper to rest on. *Lampik k'llongna ko da'a al'mmi' badju'na.* A protective cloth around his neck so his shirt doesn't get dirty. (*Thesaurus:* **bingal, hampe 1, hanig, lapis₁ 1**) **1.1)** *v. tr. -an* To protect something with a cover or underlying layer.

**paglampik** *v. tr. -an* To be careful in the choice of words in order to minimize hurt from something said. *Halam maglampik, halam magmaloman, magtūy ah'lling.* [He] isn't cautious in what is said, doesn't show respect, speaks right away.

**lampin₁** *adj. a-* Very thin in cross-section, as a person's waist or the flexible blade of a knife. *Subay laring alampin pangahait buway.* A thin knife is what should be used for removing the pithy material from rattan. (*Thesaurus:* **g'nting, nipis, nipnip, tayang**)

**lampin₂** *n.* **1)** A cloth for wrapping; a diaper. *Taga lampin si Gi apa ariki' lagi'.* Gi has a diaper because she is still little. *Pinutus b'ttongna maka lampin bo' mbal binakagan.* His stomach is wrapped with a cloth so it doesn't become swollen. **1.1)** *v. tr. -an* To wrap in a cloth.

**lampinig** *n.* Various species of wasp. *Lampinig itū angeket abisa, ati butigan kita. Mbal paluwas laha'.* This wasp stings severely and we have swellings as a result. There is no bleeding. (*Thesaurus:* **buwani, kabulig, tabungay, teya'-teya'**)

**lampo'** *n.* **1)** Width or depth, of foldable material such as cloth or netting. *Bang ma pokot, lampo'na min pataw tudju ni tingga'.* With a haul net its *lampo'* is the depth from floats to weights. **1.1)** *adj. a-* Wide, of cloth; deep, of nets. *Alampo' kakana', alambu.* The cloth is wide, broad. (*Thesaurus:* **habog, lambu 1.1, luha 1.1**)

**lampu** *n.* A wick lamp with a glass chimney. *Ma waktu awal jaman, lampu ya niusal ma deyom langgal.* In the old days, a wick lamp was used in the prayer-house. (*Thesaurus:* **kulaet 1, laet, lām, palita'an, plaslaet 1, sū' 1**)

**lampung₁** *adj. a-* **1)** Light in weight or density. *Alampung pahāp kapuk ilū.* This kapok [mattress filling] is so light. *Alampung baka itu bang halam taga isi.* This basket is light when it has nothing in it. (ant: **buhat₁ 1.1**; *Thesaurus:* **langgung₂, nintil 1, paglantun**) **2)** Light; undemanding, of a workload. *Minsan saga hinang alampung-lampung, mbal na tahinangna apa aku'il.* He can no longer do even light tasks, because he is crippled.

**lampung₂** *adj. a-/-an* Having a sense of ease or appropriateness. *Lampungan aku maghinang ma luma'.* I feel good about working in the house.

**lampung baran** *v. intr. aN-* Positive expectation; feeling good about things. {idiom} *Bang sali' angalampung baranta, na bilahi kita ni pagbono'an. Aniya' galakta.* When our body becomes sort of light, then we want to go to where the fighting is. We have a sense that it is propitious. *Alampung baranku ma tana' hē'.* I have a good feeling about that plot of land. *Alampung baranku pal'ngngan llaw itu.* I feel like going for a walk today.

**lamu-lamu** *see:* **paglamu-lamu, paglamu-lamuhan**

**lamuk** *n.* The flavoring components of a recipe, as fish or meat in a predominantly vegetable stew. *Bang magsayul subay aniya' lamukna minsan dakuman dangkuri'.* When cooking vegetables there should be something for flavor, however small. (*gen:* **pamapā**)

**lamud₁** *n.* **1)** Something added to a mixture, as in cooking. *Ns'llan lahing halam aniya' lamudna.* Coconut oil with no additives. **1.1)** *v. tr.* *-an* To add a component to a mixture. *Nilamuran sokal bo' bin'lla.* Sugar added and then cooked. *Ni M'ddas aku am'lli gatas pangalamudku kahawa.* I will go to Siasi town to buy milk for mixing with coffee. *Buwat aniya' anangis, sali' aniya' lling palamud ni tangis.* Like when someone is weeping and there are words sort of mingling with the tears. (*Thesaurus:* **haybol, lamugay 1.1, pagsagol 1.1, paila', simbug 1, templa 1.1**)

**lamud-borak** *n.* The ingredients added to home-made cosmetic powder. (*cf:* **pigi'₂ 1**)

**paglamud** *v. tr.* To mix things together; to combine several ingredients as when cooking. *Borak pinaglamud buwas maka ugbus biyabas.* Powder, rice [flour] mixed with guava leaf shoots. *Pamapā paglamud ma tinula'.* Spices for mixing together with a herb-flavored stew.

**paglamud-lamugay** *v. intr.* *aN-* To be mixed together so that it is difficult to distinguish the components. *Maglamud-lamugay bangsa sigām.* Their ethnic backgrounds are inextricably mixed. *Buwat Sama Lipid magh'lling Sama, bo' magbagi'ad maka lling Sama. Magdambila'an, sali' maglamud-lamugay.* Like Land Sama speaking Sama, and including non-native words with the Sama words. It's hybridized, sort of mixed up.

**palamud** *v. tr.* To add an ingredient to a mixture.

**lamud₂** *n.* **1)** Involvement in the activity of a group of people. *Ōy, halam aniya' lamudku ma hinang sigām!* Hey, I have nothing to do with their actions. **1.1)** *v. intr.* *pa-* To get involved with what someone else is doing. (*cf:* **balat, jau'-jau', pagsakutu**) **1.2)** *v. tr.* To involve someone. *Amakiyas aku, da'a aku lamurun.* I disassociate myself, don't involve me.

**lamugay** *n.* **1)** An addition to a mixture. **1.1)** *v. tr.* *-an* To add something to a mixture. (*Thesaurus:* **haybol, lamud₁ 1.1, pagsagol 1.1, paila', simbug 1, templa 1.1**)

**paglamugay** *v. tr.* **1)** To mix things together, combining several ingredients as when cooking. *Isi tipay pinaglamugay maka binegal ko' mbal ahalu'.* The flesh of the oyster is mixed with

vinegar so it won't become rotten. **2)** To interact, of diverse species of creatures. *Makapaglamugay kita minsan buwaya aheya, bang tausulta bay awal mbo'ta manusiya'.* We can even mix together with large crocodiles, if we follow the traditions of our ancestors.

**lamun** *n.* **1)** Myopia (short-sightedness). **1.1)** *v. advrs.* *-in-* Affected by shortness of one's vision. *Nilamun pag'nda'na, nilamun matana.* His vision, his eyes, are short-sighted.

**lamuruk** *n.* Various Silverbiddies or Mojarras. *Gerres sp.* (*syn:* **porok₁**)

**lamuti'** *var. of* **kamuti'**

**lān** *n.* A pathway, track or trail. *Pamagay ba'anan tumpukan hayop ya bay talanggalku ma lān ina'an?* What's the purpose of that mob of cattle I met on that trail? *Ahāp gi' kita pehē' ni iya, kalu-kalu kita katuli'anna lān pamiha'anta kakaddayan.* It is better for us to go to him, he may be able to show us the street where we may find roadside shops. (*Thesaurus:* **kalsara, labayan, pal'ngnganan**)

**kalān-lānan** *n.* Paths; roads; walkways. *Saguwa' bang saina paluwas min luma'nu ni kalān-lanan bo' tapapatay kami, na magsabal iya pagka dusana na tu'ud.* But if anyone goes out of your house into the streets and is killed by us, then he must accept it because it was his own fault.

**palānan** *n.* A place used as a path.

**lān pasiklut** *n. phrase* A path which narrows to an almost impassable trail.

**lana** *adj.* *-an* **1)** Unpleasantly smooth or ingratiating; oily (fig.) *Lanahan iya itū, sali' pulitik.* He is a smooth speaker, as in politics. **1.1)** *v. tr.* *-an* To compliment someone insincerely, for the purpose of getting some benefit. (*Thesaurus:* **pagmamhu', paili, puli-bahasa**)

**lanab** *adj.* *a-* Tasty; savory; rich in oil. *Saga pagkakan alanab maka saga inuman amamis.* Rich foods and sweet drinks. *Halam aku bay amangan pagkakan angalanab atawa saga sumbali'an.* I have not eaten rich food or animal meat. (*Thesaurus:* **kesom, imu' 1, l'ssom 1, mamis₁ 1.1, sarap₁, taba' 1**)

**lanab-lanab** *var. of* **tehe'-tehe'-lanab-lanab**

**lanas** *n.* **1)** Large numbers of things or people involved in some tragic event. **1.1)** *adj.* *a-* Affected in large numbers as a result of some disaster. *Aheya kasusahan ma M'ddas ma pasalan saki kolera, aheka' amatay. Alanas onde'-matto'a.* There was a serious situation in Siasi Town because of a cholera outbreak, many dying. A great number affected, of both children and adults. *Niambūs damba'anan bay atulak ni Cotabato ma pasalan eleksiyon. Alanas sigām kamemon.* An entire group was ambushed, [people] who left for Cotabato City for the elections. All of them caught up in it. **1.2)** *v. advrs.* *ka-...-an* To be overwhelmed by mass or number (of things or people). *Kalanasan deya he'* *ba'anan buwa'-buwa' kamemon kaginisan. Buwat mampallam mbal sali' ta'nda' daunna, hal ba'anan buwa'na na. Mbal sali' ta'ambat pinuwa' atawa kinakan.* The inland area is overwhelmed with fruit of all kinds. Like mangoes, it is as if you can't see the leaves, only the abundant fruit. It is as though they can neither be harvested nor eaten. *Kalanasan deyom luma' itū, kalanasan he' manusiya'. Na magagaw kamemon, ati yukta, "Gōm pa'in magkohap-kohap."* This house is packed full, full of people. Everyone is grabbing at things, so we say, "Better to do it later this afternoon."

**lanat** *adj. a-* Extended in time; delayed in taking place. *Alanat sidda bang angutang.* Long delayed when in debt. *Buwat si'itku hē', tambuku sigā Maulud amole'. Na halam gi' tapole', alanat busayan sigā.* Like my uncles, sending word that they would be home by the month of Maulud. Well they still haven't got home, their travels are prolonged. *Alanat pagbono' sigām.* Their fighting is drawn-out. (*Thesaurus:* **ddas 1, lehod 1.1, t'ddas 1**)

**lanaw** *var.* of **danaw**

**lanay₁** *n.* Silky or satiny fabric. *Lanay itū angalinig.* This *lanay* cloth is shiny. (*Thesaurus:* **punji, sutla'**)

**lanay₂** *v. intr. pa-* To melt due to heat. *Palanay na espalton, apasu' he' llaw.* The bitumen is melting, heated by the sun. *Aniya' bang tinunu' paledled, palanay.* There are things that spread out when burnt, liquefying. (*Thesaurus:* **hudjat, tadjul, tunaw 1**)

**landa** *v. tr. -an* To let out slack in a line. *Pat'kkad pa'in sau, balutanta. Amalut pa'in hē', landahanta ko mbal apigtal sau hē'.* When the anchor touches bottom we hold [to the rope]. As we hold it we let out some slack so the anchor isn't tied too tightly. *Bang saupama kita ananggonteng, na wa'i angahūg sau. Pat'kkad na, angkatanta na. Puwas e' pat'kkaranta isāb. Pat'kkad pa'in, balutanta. Amalut pa'in hē', landahanta ko mbal apigtal sau hē'.* For example we fish from a stationary position, and then we drop the anchor. When it touches bottom we pull it up again. After that we let it touch again and when it touches we hold [the rope]. As we hold it we let out some slack so the anchor isn't tied too tightly.

  **landahan** *n.* The slack in a line. *Niririt p'ttung. Subay tinugutan, binuwanan landahan.* The bamboo lengths are set out in rows [for towing behind a canoe]. They should be let out further, given slack.

**landak** *v. tr.* To prise something up with a sharpened pole or metal bar. *Atawa panagatun bang mbal ala'an min pa'ataganna, sali' landakta.* Or shellfish when it won't leave its lair, like we move it with a crowbar. *Subay bay nilandak bo' palarut.* It should have been prised up in order to

be pulled out. *Nilandak itū binuwanan lowang.* Doing something with a crowbar means a hole is involved. (*Thesaurus:* **li'ad, lugit, suwal 1**)

  **lalandak** *n.* A crowbar. (*Thesaurus:* **bara, pala, piku, sangkul 1, susuwat**)

**landag** *adj. a-* Fast-selling, as of something which is a good bargain. *Alandag, buwat ai-ai al'kkas tab'lli. Landag,* like things that are quickly purchased.

**landang** *n.* 1) Small balls of cassava or sago meal, prepared for steaming. *Ameya' atibulung landangna. Subay panggi' maka ambūng.* Its balls become round. Must be cassava or sago meal. **1.1)** *v. tr.* To toss cassava or sago meal so that it forms small balls as it cooks. *Nilandang panggi' kayu itū abō' tabugbug.* This cassava is formed into balls so it can be made into porridge. (*Thesaurus:* **pansī**)

**landang-landang** *n.* 1) Fried fish, especially as sold from food stalls. *Ahāp ssana bang landang-landang kasig.* Fried pilchards have a great taste. **1.1)** *v. tr.* To cook by frying in oil, of fish, meat, rice, or vegetables. *Pat'nna'un ns'llan lahing ma deyom kaha' paglandang-landang tulay.* Put coconut oil in the pan for frying herring. (*gen:* **b'lla 1**)

**landasan** *n.* 1) An anvil. *Aho', pangahinang bulawan, landasan pamaragtolan. Bang angahinang sundang atawa bari' isāb, ya rū landasan.* Yes, for working gold an anvil is the work-station. When making a machete or [other] working-knife, that too is a *landasan.* 2) Imminent punishment, used in threatening or scolding children. *Agarin landasannu!* Wait for what is coming to you!

**landeyok** *n.* The Blue-fin jack or trevally, the Blue kingfish. *Caranx melampygus.*

**landing₁** *n.* A landing field for aircraft; an airport.

  **paglandingan** *n.* A landing field for aircraft. *Waktu tagna', aniya' bay paglalandingan ariplano ma Bakal, sagō' halam na buwattina'an. Magka'at na.* In former times there was a landing-field at Bakal, but not any more. It is in disrepair.

**landing₂** *n.* Units of paper currency worth less than one peso. {obsolete} *Saliyuhanta ka pisita ni landing. Akebak landing itū.* I'll trade your paper bills for coins. These bills are damaged. (*Thesaurus:* **pilak 2, pinta₁, pisita, sīn, tustun**)

**landos** *adj. a-* 1) Strong or intense, of natural forces. *Alandos goyak itū, mbal kita makaparilaut.* These waves are very rough, we are not able to go out to sea. *Bohe' itū alandos tuburanna.* The inflow of this water is vigorous. *Taukab isāb taplok langit bo' patumbuk ulan alandos.* The stopper of heaven was opened so that heavy rain fell. (*Thesaurus:* **ayron, basag 1, bastig, kosog 1.1, kulasog 1.1, kuwat-anggauta', paslod 1.1**) **1.1)** *v. advrs. ka-...-an* To be driven by strong natural forces. *Bang paleyang tallung bo' kalandosan baliyu, anotog ma diyata', mbal maglensa.* When we fly a *tallung*-type kite and it is buffeted by the wind, it becomes steady higher up above, not diving around.

**palandos** *v. tr.* To do something with force.

**landu'**₁ *v. tr.* -an To follow through with a plan or committment. *Ngā'un, apa bay na makalandu' kono'.* Take it, because it's already underway [he says]. *Landu'in na sabab bay na kajanji'an.* Get on with it because it has already been promised. (*Thesaurus:* **lanjal** 1.2, **lubak**₂ 1, **pehē'**₂)

**landu'**₂ *adv.* 1) Very much; to a great degree. *Landu' kami bay angentom ka'am.* We longed for you very much. (*Thesaurus:* **karalaman, kumarukan, dumasiyaw, mamarahi, sidda** 1, **to'od**) 1.1) *adj.* a- Profound; sure and certain. *"Alandu' na," yukna, "tuyu'ku ma ka'a."* "My commitment to you," he said, "is deep."

**landu'an** *v. intr.* -um- To become excessive. *Lumandu'an na hekana.* The abundance of these things is too much already.

**landung** var. of **lambung**₁

**lanit** var. of **laknit**

**lanjal** *adj.* a- 1) Moving on; progressing. 1.1) *v. intr.* pa- To continue on towards a goal or expected outcome; to proceed on one's way. *Na ta'abut na tonga'an ī', amole' na aku pabīng. Sigām palanjal na.* Now when halfway was reached, I came back home again. As for them, they went on their way. *Bang akapal dinding, pasapat timbak. Mbal makalanjal pareyom.* If the walling is thick the bullet is stopped. It doesn't go right in. *Kapulakan siyakaku bay ab'ttong, halam na makalanjal kab'ttongna.* My older sister miscarrried at the pregnant stage, her pregnancy did not proceed. *Yuknu, "Nde'in sadja anakku ni tonga'an." Yukku, "Aho'." Na ta'abut na tonga'an ī', amole' na aku pabīng. Sigām palanjal na.* You said, "Just deliver my child to the halfway point." I said, "Yes." Now when halfway was reached, I came back home again. As for them, they went on their way. (*Thesaurus:* **lalga, laus** 1, **sōng**₂ 1, **unjal**) 1.2) *v. tr.* -an To carry on with something; to set something on its way. *Lanjalin na tēp ilū.* Set that tape there going. *Halam na nilanjalan e' sigām angapas saga mundu.* They did not continue their pursuit of the bandits. (*Thesaurus:* **landu'**₁, **lubak**₂ 1, **pehē'**₂)

**lanjang** *n.* 1) The height, of a person. *Kulang-labi dand'ppa maka tonga' lanjangna agasi' inān.* His height, that giant, was a fathom and a half, more or less. 1.1) *adj. zero* Tall (of one's body); lanky. *Ya l'lla lanjang inān.* That tall man. *Ahāp l'lla iya, arorog maka labi alanjang min kamemon pagkahina.* He is a fine man, attractive and taller than all his fellows. (*Thesaurus:* **langa** 1.1, **langkaw** 1.1, **langkawit**₁)

**lanji-lanji** *n.* A species of small field bird.

**lanjut** *n.* 1) Extended time, of one's life. (*Thesaurus:* **kuwa'-kuwa', panjang, taha'** 1.1, **t'ggol** 1.1)

1.1) *adj.* a- Long, of life. *Bang pa'in alanjut umulnu.* May your life be long. *Halam bay amu'na ni aku lanjut umul, karaya ma baranna, sagō' hal panghati ma pagsara' abontol.* He did not ask for length of life, or wealth for himself, but for an understanding of administering law in the right way.

**Lannang** *n.* Ethnic Chinese. *Bangko, ya patau'an sīn kamastalan, kalannangan inān.* A bank, the place where schoolteachers and Chinese keep their money. (*Thesaurus:* **makaw, sina'**₁, **taoke'**₁)

**lanos**₁ *adj.* a- Parched; withered; dried out. *Alanos atop, bay agaddung.* The thatch is withered, it was green. *Alanos pai e' llaw.* The rice is parched by the sun. *Aniya' pola kabulak-bulakan, aniya' isāb pola ato'a alanos na.* There is betel nut that is somewhat immature, there is also old betel nut gettting shrivelled. *Mamis ē' alagtu' bang alanos na.* That sweet coconut variety becomes brittle once it is dried out. (*Thesaurus:* **layu, lūs**₁ 2, **luyluy**)

**lanos**₂ *n.* A species of salt-water sponge. (*syn:* **l'ppus** 1)

**lansa** *n.* A passenger ferry; a launch. *Ilu na lansa, angalga kitām.* The launch is almost here, we will work as porters. *Am'lli aku lansa bo' aku magismagol pehē' ni Sandakan.* I will buy a lunch so I can engage in smuggling away there in Sandakan. (*Thesaurus:* **beggong, biruk, buti, kappal, kumpit, papet, sappit**₂, **tempel**)

**lansal** *v. tr.* To read fluently, without hesitation or error. *Angalansal na bang amassa, mbal maghidja-hidja.* Fluent now when reading, doesn't sound out the letters.

**lansang** *n.* 1) A building nail or bolt. *Am'lli aku lansang mpat inses pangalansangku luma'ku wa'i ma Siganggang.* I will buy four-inch nails for nailing my house over there in Siganggang. (*cf:* **lagsak**) 1.1) *v. tr.* To fasten something by nailing. *Angindam aku tukul pangalansangku papan.* I will borrow a hammer to nail a board. *Jari in baranna bay nilansang ma ād.* So its body was nailed to the fence.

**lansong** *n.* The ink or ink sac of cephalopods.

**lansongan** *n.* Sea animals which have an ink sac; a collective term for cephalopods such as squid, octopus, cuttlefish. (*spec:* **kanu'us, kindat, kulabutan, tabula**)

**lansuk** *n.* A candle; tallow; wax. *Bang aheka lansuk subay kinagisan.* If there is a lot of wax it should be scraped off. (*cf:* **talu**₂)

**lantak** *adj.* a- Profoundly deaf. *Wa'i na nilinganan, mbal anaul. Yukku, "Alantak talingana, mbal makakale."* He was called, didn't answer. I said, "His ears are very deaf, unable to hear." *Alantak pahāp ka'a ilū, apalpal.* You are so deaf, your ears plugged. (*Thesaurus:* **bisu** 1.1, **halong, palpal** 1)

**lantaka** *n.* 1) A brass cannon. (*Thesaurus:* **kalbin, kanyun** 1, **garan, musil, pistul, sinapang**) 1.1)

A bamboo cannon. (*syn:* **timbak p'ttung**)

**lanta'** *adj. a-* Widely spaced. *T'bbu itū alanta' honga'na.* This sugarcane has widely spaced nodes. *Ya alanta', saupama bang magtapi' bangka', halam apantay.* An example of *lanta'* is when fixing side-planks to a canoe and they are not even. (*Thesaurus:* **jalang₂, t'llag**)

 **palanta'** *v. tr.* To move things further apart.

**lantam** *see:* **palantaman**

**lantas** var. of **langtas**

**lantaw** *n.* **1)** A long net, set or trawled. *Aniya' linggi', aniya' lantaw, aniya' isāb pokot.* There are *linggi'* [long trawl nets], there are *lantaw,* and there are *pokot* [seine nets]. *Ya magtasik a'a maglantaw.* The people who preserve fish by pickling are *lantaw* fishermen. (*cf:* **birang 1**; *Thesaurus:* **gugul 1, laya 1, linggi' 1, pokot₁ 1, sinsoro 1, siyul 1**) **1.1)** *v. tr.* To catch fish with a lantaw net.

 **paglantaw** *v. intr. aN-* To make a living by fishing with long nets.

**lantay** *n.* **1)** A floor. *Anusut aku lantay ma luwasan.* I am scrubbing the floor outside. (*Thesaurus:* **bola', gipis 1, ligpit 1**) **1.1)** *v. tr. -an* To provide a house with a floor. *Nilantayan maka p'ttung.* Floored with bamboo.

 **palantayan** *n.* A low platform or mat on which a corpse is laid out.

**lantay-lantay** *n.* **1)** A support for something long; a splint. (*Thesaurus:* **hapid₁ 1, paggimbal 1.1**) **1.1)** *v. tr. -an* To support something with splints. *Nilantay-lantayan tape'na. Subay ta'abut kauli'an bo' makal'ngngan.* His foot is supported with splints. It needs to be healed before he can walk.

**lanti-lanti** *v. tr. -an* To await someone or some event. *Lanti-lantihanta lagi', kalu at'kka ru.* We'll just wait a bit, [they] may still arrive. *Lanti-lantihanta gi' saki inān.* Let's just wait for that illness to run its course. (*Thesaurus:* **lagad 1.2, langay, tagad**)

**lantik** *adj. a-* Curved against the normal position, of arms and the backs of hands. *Bang ariki'-diki' nih'nnat tanganna bo' aheya alantik.* When small her hands are stretched so that when large they will be well curved. *Bang angigal alantik sikuna.* When she dances her elbows curve back.

**lantun** *v. intr. pa-* To become excessive.

 **paglantun** *v. intr. aN-* To be going further and further. *Sali' bang limut, maglantun isāb bissala, hatina pakanat min dangan a'a ni dangan sampay tahinang pagbono'an na.* It's like negative talk, words too keep traveling, that is they keep spreading from one person to another until it becomes a conflict. (*Thesaurus:* **lampung₁ 1, langgung₂, nintil 1**)

**lantup** *v. intr. pa-* To float, as a ball or pumice. *Bang ahūg bola ni tahik, palantup.* If a ball falls into the sea, it floats. (*cf:* **langgung₂**; *syn:* **gūng**)

**lanu'** **1)** *adj. a-* Clean; smooth; attractive. *Maglampasu' maka abu ampa alanu'.* Scrubbing with ashes so it becomes smooth. *Ahāp hurupna, sali' alangguyud, alanu' kinale.* His enunciation is good, sort of drawn out, nice to listen to. (*Thesaurus:* **k'ssang₁, langis 1, l'ssin, sussi 1.1**) **1.1)** *v. tr.* To apply polish or a gloss. *Kagisin lantay dahū bo' lanu'un.* Scrape the floor off first, then apply polish. **1.2)** *v. tr. -an* To polish or groom something. (*Thesaurus:* **bata, lampasu, ponglas**) **2)** *v. tr. -an* To cleanse a body carefully for burial. *Nilanu'an baranna kamemon, kukkuna, sinusutan taingana, ūngna, emponna, kamemonna sampay manga buli'na.* Her whole body cleansed, nails, ears, nose, teeth, everything scrubbed clean including the anal area.

 **kalanu'an** *n.* Smoothness; gloss. *Agsay makasampig ma luma' mital, halam aniya' sabandingna, alingkat, ya kalanu'anna.* We promptly came up alongside a house with a metal roof, a house with no blemishes, beautiful, such smoothness.

 **lanu' atay** *adj. a-* Cordial; with no hard feelings. {idiom} *Alanu' atayna, halam aniya' koto'-koto' mareyom atayna.* Gentle in manner, no resentment in her heart.

**Lanun** var. of **Ilanun**

**lanut** *n.* Abaca; Manilla hemp. *Musa textilis. Lubayan itu tonda'-tonda' lanut panganggiling gasing. Lubayan* is a cord of abaca for spinning a top. (*Thesaurus:* **badjang, bamban₂, hidjuk, lupis**)

**lanyap** *v. intr. a-* **1)** To be removed out of sight; vanished suddenly. *Jari minnē' magtūy alanyap na sigām min pang'nda'na.* So at that point they vanished from his sight. **1.1)** *v. tr. -an* To cause something to disappear, an action of demonic entities. *Bang ap'ddi' atayku, bo' aniya' sukna'anku, yukku, "Bang pa'in ka alanyap. Bang pa'in ka nilanyapan he' saitan ma deya inān."* When I am angry and I curse someone, I say, "May you vanish. May that demon there on the land make you vanish." (*Thesaurus:* **talbang 1.1, tanggal₃ 1**)

**lanyaw** *n.* A stroll with no particular purpose. *Lanyaw pi'ingga na pa'in.* Always strolling off somewhere.

 **paglanyaw** *v. intr. aN-* To walk about with no particular purpose. (*Thesaurus:* **pagkambuyan, pagkatay, pagjambeyaw**)

**lāng** *v. tr.* To cause someone to desist; to forbid someone to do something. *Lāngun ba makannak inān.* Make those children stop. *Mbal tapangalutan gusung inān apa pangalāngan.* That sand can't be dug up because it is a prohibited place. (*cf:* **sanggup**; *Thesaurus:* **banda', pamarā**)

 **paglāngan** *n.* A prohibition or opposition to some action. *Subay mbal paglāngan bang aniya' bilahi* *ahinang magdanakan.* There should be no opposition when someone wants to form a sibling relationship.

**langa** *n.* 1) Height; altitude. *Hinangin olangan duwa h'kka langana ma llot diyata' dinding maka bihing atop.* Make a gap two spans in height between the top of the wall and the edge of the roof. 1.1) *adj. a-* High, in spatial terms or in social rank. *Abantug sigām maka alanga gi' min kamemon bangsa bay papanjarina.* They will be more famous and higher [in status] than all the nations that have been created. (*cf:* **ta'as 1;** *Thesaurus:* **lanjang 1.1, langkaw 1.1, langkawit₁**)

**langa atay** *adj. a-* Proud; haughty. {idiom} *Magabbu-abbu, sali' alanga atayna.* Showing off his status, kind of haughty.

**langa tai'** *adj. a-* Convinced of his own importance. {idiom} *Ilu'un na pareyo' alanga tai'na.* Here's his "majesty" disembarking.

**langa-llaw** *n.* The period of time around noon. *Binono' saga banta sigām sampay ta'abut alanga-llaw.* Their enemies were killed until the sun was high. (*Thesaurus:* **langkaw llaw, ugtu-llaw**)

**paglanga** *n.* To enjoy higher status than one's peers. *Paglanga-langa min pagkahi.* Making oneself more important than others. *Saitan magmahatinggi, maglanga-langa dīna.* A Saitan spirit who acts very high, making himself high.

**pagpalanga** *v. intr. aN-* To behave as though higher in status.

**langa-langa** *n.* A species of suckerfish, possibly a remora. *Daluwa to'ongan maka k'mmi, daipara halam taga lakkop.* It is just like a *k'mmi* [a remora] but without a sucker. (*cf:* **k'mmi**)

**langag** *v. advrs. -in-* Putrefying. *Bang aniya' amatay bo' pinasagaran e' pamilyana, nilangag.* If someone dies and is neglected by his family, he becomes putrid. (*Thesaurus:* **baguy, balos₂, buhuk, buntu'₁ 1.1, halu' 1.1, p'ngkak**)

**langa'-langa'** *n.* Traditional stories in metric form, chanted rather than sung. *Alu'uy lugu' min langa'-langa'. Lugu'* is more pleasant to listen to than *langa'-langa'.*

**paglanga'-langa'** *v. intr. aN-* To recite traditional stories in metric form. *Bang kita ma dilaut, bo' kita sōng tinuli, nā, maglanga'-langa' kita pangalāng tuli. Sali' magkata-kata. Saddi magtenes.* When we are out at sea, and we are becoming sleepy, we chant to keep from sleeping. It is like *kata-kata. Tenes* singing is different. (*Thesaurus:* **kissa 1, istori 1, pagkata-kata 1.1, salsila 1**)

**langal** *n.* The chin or jaw. *Aniya' p'ngngot-p'ngngot ma langalku.* There is a bit of a beard on my chin.

**langan₁** *v. intr. aN-* To be fretful due to pain or hunger. *Bang aniya' onde'-onde' angalangan, aniya' ap'ddi' atawa aruru'.* If a child cries fretfully something is hurting, or needs to

nurse. (*Thesaurus:* **mmaw 1, pagle'eng, s'ngngel 1, unga'**)

**langan₂** *n.* 1) Songs of various genres. (*Thesaurus:* **kalangan₁, lugu' 1, sa'il**) 1.1) *v. tr.* To accompany certain events with singing. *Bang aniya' ginuntingan ma langgal subay nilangan he' buwat h'nda si Am maingat.* When [a child] is to undergo the hair-cutting ceremony at the mosque it should be sung over by the likes of Am's wife, who has religious knowledge. *Maulud isāb, lugu' pangalangan iya.* Likewise with Maulud ceremonies, they are accompanied by *lugu'* singing.

**langāt** *n.* The Jarbua or Target therapon, a fish species. *Terapon jarbua.* (*syn:* **biga'ung**)

**langāt-pote'** *n.* The Large-scaled therapon. *Therapon theraps.*

**langat-langat** *n.* A species of coral. (*gen:* **batu₂ 1**)

**langaw** *n.* 1) A fly. *Minsan langaw paligid.* Even a fly would slip [of a slick surface]. 1.1) *adj. -an* Annoyed by flies. *Langawan na iya ma patulihan.* He is troubled by flies where he is sleeping. 1.2) *v. tr. -an* To prevent someone from sleeping soundly, as by flies or other irritants. *Nilangawan kami he' haggut bang ma Bukidnon.* We are prevented from sleeping by the cold when in Bukidnon.

**langay** *v. tr. -an* To wait for someone to catch up. *Langayanta gi' si Ig apa wa'i damuli.* Let's just wait for Ig because he is behind. (*Thesaurus:* **lagad 1.2, lanti-lanti, tagad**)

**paglangay-langay** *v. tr. -an* To wait for something inevitable, as for one's final fate. *Maglangay-langay la'a si Anu.* What's-his-name is just waiting for the end.

**langkan-langkan** *n.* The sheath which encloses a coconut flower bract. *Langkan-langkan itū ya sali' kumpit-kumpit.* The flower sheath referred to is [shaped] like a locally built launch. (*wh:* **niyug**)

**langkap₁** *see:* **kalangkapan₁**

**langkap₂** *adj. a-* Confused by too much sensory input. *Alangkap ūngku e' wanni.* My nose is overwhelmed by the smell of odorous mangoes.

**kalangkapan₂** *v. advrs. -in-* Overwhelmed by variety of options. *Kinalangkapan ka am'lli ai-ai saukat aniya' sīn ma deyom bulsanu.* You have become confused into buying various things just because there is money in your pocket.

**langkat** *adj. a-* 1) Dismantled; broken up into pieces. *Alangkat luma' Milikan. Halam bay pinahāp e' si Al, dalapis du tiyadtad.* The Westerner's house is falling to pieces. Al didn't do it well, only one layer of bamboo walling. (*Thesaurus:* **basak, jagjag 1, larak 1.1, lorak**) 1.1) *v. tr.* To dismantle something. *Da'a langkatun, masi tapagguna.* Don't break it up, it's still usable.

**langkat-samat** *n.* A person who is highly skilled in religious and ceremonial matters. *Langkat-samat,* *halam aniya' kulangna pareyo'-pariyata'. Iya na taga ilmu'. (Min pangadji'na, ata'u na, mbal asā'.)* *Langkat-samat*, lacking nothing from top to bottom. He is the one with esoteric knowledge. (From his study, knowing stuff, not making mistakes.) (*Thesaurus:* **ilmu' 1, ingat, salawat**$_1$)

**langkaw** *n.* 1) Height. *Sangpū' l'ngngon taha'na, sangpū' isāb langkawna.* Its length was ten arm-lengths, its height was also ten. **1.1)** *adj. a-* High, of buildings, or trees; tall, of people. *Aheya isāb saga luma'na maka tamakalangkaw isāb ādna.* Its houses were very large and its walls were exceedingly high. *Alangkaw sidda niyug.* Coconuts are very high. (*Thesaurus:* **lanjang 1.1, langa 1.1, langkawit**$_1$)

**langkaw llaw** *adj. a-* High in the sky, of sun. *Alangkaw na llaw, sūng na kitam angalga.* The sun's well up, off we go to work as stevedores. (*Thesaurus:* **langa-llaw, ugtu-llaw**)

**langkawit**$_1$ *n.* An unusually tall person. *Niudju' lanjangna, buwat si Mo niōnan langkawit.* Like Mo, mocked for his height, called a *langkawit.* (*Thesaurus:* **lanjang 1.1, langa 1.1, langkaw 1.1**)

**langkawit**$_2$ *n.* A species of fish, green, with large scales.

**langkay** *n.* 1) The dried fronds of a coconut palm. (*wh:* **niyug**) **1.1)** *v. intr. aN-* To curl up in process of drying, as coconut and pandanus leaves.

**langking** *n.* An artificial beauty spot placed on the face for cosmetic purposes. (*Thesaurus:* **bau-bau, tai'-lalat**)

**langkit** *adj. a-* 1) Connected, as houses by a bridge; uninterrupted, as a sequence of similar items or activities. *Bang alangkit kamemon pandan, makatandan kami lahat. Bang halam alangkit, al'kkat kamemon, halam makatandan.* When the pandanus bushes appear to be all connected, we are in reach of land. If they are not connected, all separate, we haven't reached land yet. (*Thesaurus:* **daggot**$_2$ **1, dalos 1, d'ppak 1.1, langkus 1**) **1.1)** *v. tr. -an* To do something without a break. *Da'a langkitin kaut.* Don't keep going to sea without a break. *Buwat aku makalangkit kaut, binale' aku. Lumpuhan, mbal na makakole'.* Like when I go fishing out at sea without a break, I get tired, I am exhausted and can't handle it. (*Thesaurus:* **mumut, pagabut-abut, pagambat-ambat 1**)

**langkob** *var. of* **lokob**

**langkop** *v. tr. -an* To plate a surface with a thin metal layer. *Bang mital al'ssu' nilangkopan maka mital baha'u, atawa binangkatan.* When a metal container has holes it is covered with new metal, or else overlaid. (*cf:* **sarul**)

**langkuk** *adj. a-* Curving up at the end, as the horn of a buffalo or the tip of an outrigger.

**langkus** *adj. zero* 1) Connected, as of houses, or of the letters in cursive writing. *Buwat luma' si Bu,*

*langkus maka luma' disi Ni, aniya' letehan.* Like the house of Bu it is connected with the house of Ni and others, there is a walkway. (*Thesaurus:* **daggot**$_2$ **1, dalos 1, d'ppak 1.1, langkit 1**) **1.1)** *v. intr. pa-* To go directly from one point to another. *Bang ka ni tabu' am'lli daing, palangkus ka ni Makaw angal'kkat pantalun.* When you go to the market to buy fish, go straight to the Chinese [tailor shop] and pay the money to get the trousers.

**langgad** *n.* 1) Damage to a surface. (*Thesaurus:* **banggid 1, geges, pares**$_1$**, sahumut-sahumut**) **1.1)** *adj. -an* Damaged, of a surface; abraded. **1.2)** *v. tr. -an* To abrade the surface or face of something. *Nilanggaran pelangku, bay aku makarugtul ni batu. Halam ta'nda'ku batu.* My canoe is damaged, I bumped against a coral rock. I didn't see the rock.

**langgahi'** *adj. a-* Cut superficially; lacerated. *Halam tinu'ud, manjari ta'abut he' tōng laring, alanggahi'.* Not deliberate, just touched by the end of a knife and cut. (*Thesaurus:* **bakat 1.1, bu'ag, pali' 1**)

**langgahit** *v. tr.* To hem a cloth border.

**langga'** *see:* **palangga'**

**langgal**$_1$ *n.* A building for communal prayer; a community mosque. (*cf:* **masjid**)

**langgal**$_2$ 1) *v. intr. pa-/-um-* To hit something head on. (*Thesaurus:* **bungku'**$_2$**, santuk, sukkut**) 2) *v. tr.* To meet or come across someone; to encounter something. *Makalanggal kami t'llu a'a bay niengkotan.* We came across three men tied up. *Ka'a ilū mbal pahali magl'ngngan-l'ngngan. Aniya' kamaupakkatannu, aniya' kala'atan talanggalnu.* You never stop going from place to place. You have a certian future, you will run into trouble. (*Thesaurus:* **abang, bāk**$_2$**, pagsamban, sampang 1**)

**paglanggal** *v. intr. aN-* To meet together when coming from opposite directions. *Aniya' kasampangan pinabeya'an si Es dahū gi' min kapaglanggal sigām duwangan.* Es sent an arrival gift ahead of their meeting together.

**langgal sara'** *n. phrase* 1) A legal offense. **1.1)** *v. tr.* To break a law.

**langgang** *var. of* **panggang**$_2$

**langgid** *var. of* **banggid**

**langging** *n.* The Malayan hairtail, a fish species. *Eupleuragrammus muticus.*

**langgit** *v. tr.* 1) To penetrate the surface of skin, as when vaccinating. *Nilanggit bo' mbal palsakkihan.* Vaccinated so he won't be sickly. (*Thesaurus:* **kussu', sudlat 1.1, suruk, tugsuk 2.2**) **1.1)** *v. tr. -an* To poke cooking food for the purpose of testing whether it is ready. *Langgitinbi pagkakan ilū.* Check that food [by piercing it].

**langgit mahal** *n. phrase* A fourth share of the bride-wealth. *Ma mahal t'llu ginisna. Aniya' lunggus mahal, aniya' tonga' mahal, aniya' langgit mahal (hatina bahagi' mpat).* With the *mahal* component of the bride-wealth there are three grades. There is the full amount, there is the half amount, and there is the quarter amount.

**langgom** *v. tr.* To harm a woman by causing distension of her stomach and a serious increase in menstrual flow (thought to be the action of some demonic entity). *Nilanggom kita he' saitan, sali' pinaheya laha'ta. Kīllo' ginhawa-baranta.* A demon harms us, increasing our flow of blood. Our physical strength is taken away.

**langgung₁** *n.* 1) A pair of things in close relationship. *Langgung itū sali' duwangan. Langgung* is about two people. 1.1) *adj. zero* In full sibling relationship. *Danakanku langgung.* My full brother [or sister].

**langgung-kilay** *n.* Eyebrows that join across the bridge of the nose (considered to be a feature of beauty).

**paglanggung** *v. intr. aN-* To be closely related, as siblings. *Langgung itū sali' duwangan. Maglanggung si Li maka si Gi. Bang bay halam si Gi, tunggal-tunggal si Li. Langgung* is about two people. Li and Gi are in full sibling relationship. If it wasn't for Gi, Li would be an only child.

**langgung₂** *adj. a-* Buoyant; supported above a surface. *Bang kayu alanggung buwat manakayan, alanga-langa pelang ma tahik.* When the wood is buoyant, like *manakayan*, the canoe rides high in the water. *Ariki' pat'nna' baranta ma kulit tahik. Am'kkig b'ttongta pariyata'. Alanggung b'ttongta, ang'tting sali'.* Only a little of our body is below the surface of the sea. Our stomach is distended upward. It protrudes, sort of puffed up. (*cf:* **lantup**; *Thesaurus:* **lampung₁ 1, nintil 1, paglantun**)

**palanggungan** *n.* A rectangular frame of wood which supports the gongs of a kulintangan set. (*Thesaurus:* **ba'ugan₂, papagan 1**)

**langguway** *n.* A brass bowl similar to a garul but without the supporting feet. *Aniya' langguway pinat'nna' ni kōkan, sali' garul atawa tumbaga.* A *langguway* is placed towards the sacred upstream side of a house, like a brass pot or a copper container. *Ligu, lling s'ddopan. Bang ma kami langguway. Ligu* [a tray] is a southern word. With us it is called a *langguway*. (*Thesaurus:* **bintang₁, gangsa, garul, tumbaga 2**)

**langguyud** *adj. a-* 1) Drawn out or drawled, of speech. *Alangguyud saga bissalana bang magsinama.* His words are dragged out when he speaks Sinama. 1.1) *v. tr. -an* To extend something lengthwise, of words or linked items. *Angalangguyud ma bahasa, ma pelang isāb ma pagtundanan. Langguyud* is about language, and also about canoes on a tow-line. *Nilangguyuran, buwat a'a Jengen, lling sigā.* Drawn out, as the Jengen Sama do, in their dialect.

**langi** *v. intr. pa-/-um-* 1) To swim. *Lumangi kita tudju ni jambatan.* Let's swim to the wharf. 1.1) *v. tr.* To reach something by swimming to it. *Langihun*

*ba si Arung.* Reach Eldest Daughter by swimming. 1.2) *v. tr. -an* To convey something by swimming. *Langihin papan ilu ni si Pra.* Swim that board over to Pra.

**paglangi** *v. intr. aN-* To swim for recreation or pleasure. *Alumu kita, bay maglangi.* We are winded, having been swimming. *Pas'lle'un maglangi si Arung.* Give Oldest Daughter a turn at swimming. (*cf:* **pagtindayung 2**)

**palangi** *v. tr. -an* To use something as an aid to swimming.

**palangihan** *n.* Something used as an aid to swimming.

**langis** *adj. a-* 1) Well-kept; groomed; sleek. *Buwat pelang, na bang ta'nda'ta sali' al'mmis-l'mmis, sinusutan, tinangon. Minsan bayanta alangis na.* Like a canoe, when we see it dirty, it is scrubbed and put up on a rack. Even if it is used as a conveyance it is well-kept. (*Thesaurus:* **k'ssang₁, lanu' 1, l'ssin, sussi 1.1**) 1.1) *v. tr.* To improve the appearance of something or someone. *Buwat si Sa bay amabeya' sīn pam'lliku polmed. Nilangis na bu'unku.* Like when Sa sent money for me to buy haircream. My hair is now groomed. 1.2) *adj. -an* Distinguished by well-groomed hair.

**langit** *n.* The sky; the heavens in contrast to the earth. *Pahangad ka ni langit bo' ka maka'nda' bitu'un magsinglab.* Look up towards the sky so you can see the twinkling stars. (*Thesaurus:* **alam₁, ayan, dunya**)

**lango** 1) *n.* Dizziness; intoxication. 1.1) *v. advrs. -in-* Suffering from loss of equilibrium or sobriety; giddy or intoxicated. (*Thesaurus:* **angol, baliyang, bo'ay, pagboyokan, pagtunggang-kīng, uling**) 2) *v. advrs. -in-* Nauseated, as from motion sickness or eating certain foods.

**lango-biyahi** *n.* Travel sickness.

**lango-goyak** *n.* Seasickness. *Mbal gi' makapasiyal pasal masi lango-goyak.* I can't go walking around yet because I'm still feeling seasick.

**paglalango** *n.* A drunkard. *Paglalango si Anu.* What's-his-name is a drunkard.

**palango** *v. tr.* To cause someone to be drunk.

**langog** *adj. a-* Joking; having fun.

**paglangog** *v. intr. aN-* To be joking and having fun together. *Aubus kami bay magkakan, na maglangog-langog ma diyata' pelang ē'.* After we had eaten, we had fun together there on the canoe. (*Thesaurus:* **kōd, kōg 2, koyag 1, lami, lasig 1**)

**langpas** *v. tr. -an* To plunder or raid someone. *Wa'i kalangpasan lansa bay min Sabah.* The launch that had come from Sabah was plundered. *Bang aniya' taga ai-ai buwat sali' mareyom kauman, bo' ta'nda' he' sai-sai, binanduhan he' bay maka'nda'. Agara' angalangpas.* If there is someone who has things, like someone in the village, and it's seen by someone or other, then a plot is hatched by the one who saw it. He plans to raid. (*Thesaurus:* **kullu-kullu₂ 1, mundu 1.1, musu**)

**langsa** *adj. a-* Strongly odorous, as fish freshly cut open. (*Thesaurus:* **bau 1.1, b'ngngi, hamut 1.1, hangsu 1, langtu, mahali, p'ngngak**)

**langsay** *n.* A canopy; a cloth screen; drapes. *Langsay itū ginuna sadja ma palkala' atawa ma karatu'an.* A *langsay* is used mostly for some significant event or for people of *datu'* rank. (*Thesaurus:* **kulambu' 1, kultina, luhul₂**)

**langtas** (var. **lantas**) *n.* 1) Special knowledge, especially of events remote in time or space. *Bang a'a tinubu e' salawat, b'nnal langtasna.* A person who has been endowed with supernatural powers, his ability to see the future is genuine. (*Thesaurus:* **auliya', tugu, tulun₁ 1**) 1.1) *adj. -an* Clairvoyant; having the ability to see the future.

**langtu** *adj. zero* Strongly odorous, as of freshly grated cassava and of certain fish. *Makas'bbol atay panggi' kayu malangtu bang aheka.* Strong-smelling cassava causes reflux when a lot of it [is eaten]. (*Thesaurus:* **bau 1.1, b'ngngi, hamut 1.1, hangsu 1, langsa, mahali, p'ngngak**)

**lāp-lāp** *v. advrs. -in-* Affected by somnambulism (sleep-walking). *Nilāp-lāp aku, lum'ngngan minsan halam abati'.* I move about in my sleep, walking even though not awake. (*cf:* **paglalap**; *Thesaurus:* **ansong, ddop, mutamad, pagdabdab, uppi 1**)

**lapa₁** *v. tr.* To feel the symptoms of some physical disorder. *Angkan iya mbal maka'abut makapi'itu, aniya' bay nilapa he'na.* The reason he wasn't able to make it here, he felt something wrong in his body. *Baranta ya pa'ahat bang halam na aniya' nilapa ai-ai mareyom baran.* Our bodies make careful moves when the symptoms are no longer felt. (*Thesaurus:* **labay₃, nanam 2, sabi₂, ssa₂**)

**lapa₂** *v. tr. -an* To clear weeds or shrubs by cutting them off at ground level. *Subay nilapahan, ataha' na sagmot.* They need to be cleared, the weeds have grown long. *Lapahin gi' halaman luma' kami, nilanu'an ya diyata'na.* Clear the weeds in the yard of our house, the upper part [the house] is made clean and tidy. (*cf:* **suwat**)

**lapak** *v. tr.* To join by lapping, as of wooden planks or the edges of a cloth seam. *Lapakin ba lowang inān bo' mbal lumossok saga kaonde'an.* Put overlapping planks on that hole so kids don't go through it.

**paglapak** *v. intr. aN-* To be joined by lapping, as of wooden planks or the edges of a cloth seam. *Pinapaglapak bo' mbal apitas.* The edges made to overlap so they don't tear away. *Papaglapakun duwa papan bo' mbal ang'mman pambot.* Make the two planks overlap so the boat doesn't leak.

**lapak-lapak** *n.* The sound of rapid gunfire.

**paglapak-lapak** 1) *v. intr. aN-* To make the sound of repeated gunfire. 2) *n.* To talk constantly.

**lapad** *n.* A low barrier erected to protect small children from harm. (*Thesaurus:* **agpang 1, babag 2**)

**lapal** *n.* 1) An utterance; a spoken message. *Aniya' lapal bay pinabeya' min ina'nu ma Sitangkay.* There is a message sent from your mother at Sitangkay. *Lapal, sali' lling, yuk-i, "Haka'un lapalku." Buwat si Ina' amabeya' tambuku.* A *lapal*, like a spoken message, saying, "Tell my message." Like Mom sending a list of requirements. (*Thesaurus:* **kabtangan**) 1.1) *v. intr. aN-* To utter; to form words. *Sali' pas'ppol deyom bowa'na, mbal makalapal.* His mouth stuffed [with food], unable to form words.

**lapal-duwa** *n.* Double talk; mixed messages. *Buwat du lapal-duwa bang mbal pamarūl ma kita.* It's just like double talk if he isn't permissive towards us.

**palapal** *v. tr. -an* To send someone a message. (*Thesaurus:* **haka 1.1, pata'u, tubad**)

**lapas** *see:* **palapas-palapas**

**lapat** *n.* 1) Firmness of a substance or mixture. *Saddī salang-sabot. Ngga'i ka isāb lapatna buwat doppeng inān, magt'llag-t'llag.* Fried cassava cake is different. It is not as compact as *doppeng* cakes, it has more gaps. 1.1) *adj. a-* Close-fitting; covering a surface without gaps. *Ahāp he'na angalantay, alapat sidda.* He did the flooring well, very close fitting. *Alapat he' kamunda'an.* Covered with canoes. *Akulang gi' alapat luma'nu, amasi at'llag.* Your house is insufficiently covered in, it still has gaps. (*Thesaurus:* **kempot, pagd'ppak 1, saplut₂, sonson**; *ant:* **t'llag**) 1.2) *v. tr. -an* To fit things closely together, as sections of a cover. *Talu itū pangalapatan pelang ko da'a ang'mman.* This wax is for making the canoe planking tight-fitting so it doesn't let water in.

**lapaw** *n.* A building with no walls. (*Thesaurus:* **balung-balung, kamalig, panggung, payad, pillayag**)

**lapay** *adj. a-* 1) Included with other items of the same kind. *Lapay sali' makalamud, makabeya'.* *Lapay* is like being included, going with. *Bang magbono' na pa'in, alapay kami minsan halam beya'.* When [they] keep fighting we are included even though we didn't go along with it. (*Thesaurus:* **beya' isāb, malit**) 1.1) *v. tr.* To include something. *Bang ka anabu', lapayin na kami sayul.* When you go to market, include some vegetables for us. *Bang ka amarena aniya' kayu nsa' tata'u pareyo', talapay. Alambang iya.* If you're drilling a hole and don't realize there is a piece of timber underneath, it gets included [in the drilling]. It was hidden. (*cf:* **tabeya'**)

**lapes** *v. tr. -an* To remove a surface layer or film. *Buwat katas akapal nilapesan, nila'anan dallapisna.* Like thick paper delaminated, one of its layers removed. *Buwat tiyangsi' bay waktu kamatto'ahan, niā' min langkay, nilapesan.* Like cord made from fibres in the time of the old people, taken from coconut fronds, removed from the bark. *Buwat buntal-buntal nilapesan, nila'anan kulitna. Atawa katas akapal nilapesan, nila'anan dallapisna.* Like the pufferfish the surface is stripped off, its skin is removed. Or like thick paper delaminated, one of its layers removed. (*Thesaurus:* **kanit 1.1, kisak, kupas, hagut, hampa' 1.1**)

**lapi'** *n.* A swinging movement from a fixed edge, as a door or window panel. *Lapi' pareyom, hatina aukab tambol. Lapi' paluwasan, hatina atambol.* Swinging inwards, meaning that the door is open. Swinging outwards, the door is closed.

**lapi'-lapi'** *n.* A panel that swings or folds out from a fixed edge to control the flow of air. *Ma kultina aniya' t'llu lapi'-lapi'na biyaning maka pote'.* The curtains there have three swinging panels, yellow and white.

**lapis₁** 1) *n.* A backing layer; a lining; a surface film. (*cf:* **babaw-tana', kuwit 1**; *Thesaurus:* **bingal, hampe 1, hanig, lampik 1**) 1.1) *v. tr.* -an To overlay something; to line a container. *A: "Bilahi ka tepo halam taga lapis?" B: "Mbal, subay nilapisan."* A: "Do you want a mat without a lining?" B: "No, it must be lined." *Bay nilapisan maka bulawan aponod ya deyoman bilik ina'an.* The inside of that room was overlaid with solid gold. 2) *clf.* Count word for layers of things. *Pitu' lapis langit.* The seven layers of the heavens. *Alangkat luma' si Anu, halam bay pinahāp he' si Ba, dallapis du tiyadtad.* What's-his-name's house is in need of repair, it wasn't well done by Ba, only one layer of flattened bamboo.

**pagduwallapis** *v. intr.* aN- To have two layers of cloth, as when sleeping. *Magduwallapis kami dibuhi' apa haggut.* We had two layers [of blankets] last night because of the cold.

**paglapis** *v. intr.* aN- To be together in layers, as paper in a pad. *Bang papan paraggot, tangan magd'ppak, katas maglapis.* Wooden planks butt together, hands lie flat together, paper forms layers. *Aniya' maglapis daing, dakayu' paharap ni ka'a. Pagpassik pana', duwa. Alambang.* There are fish in layers, just one of them facing you. When the spear is released there are two. Happened unintentionally.

**lapis₂** *n.* Something which comes between an observer and a distant objective. *Ma lapis Būd Siganggang kami.* We were out of sight behind Mt. Siganggang.

**lapis₃** *n.* 1) A repetition; a recurrence. *Ta'nda' e' sultan sangpū' lapis ya labi pangita'u sigām.* The king saw that their knowledge was ten times more. 1.1) *v. tr.* To double something; to repeat a number or amount.

**lapis₄** *adj.* a- Suffering from deterioration of the cornea, observed from the layer-like whitening of the pupil of the eye. *Saddī abuta maka alapis.* Buta [blind] and *lapis* [corneal damage] are different.

**lapis₅** *adj.* a- Unprofitable, of a business venture.

*Alapis po'onan dagangan. Halam makauntung.* The capital invested on the purchase was lost. Didn't make a profit. *Alapis kami, halam bay maka'ā'.* We took a loss, we didn't get anything.

**lapnas** *adj.* a- 1) Destroyed completely, by some disaster. (*Thesaurus:* **lognos, luhu'₂ 1, ponas, sapsay**) 1.1) To destroy something totally. *Makatāw-tāw waktu inān, sabab waktu pangalapnas Tuhan ma saga manusiya'.* That time will be terrifying because it is the time when God destroys mankind.

**lapod** (var. **sapod**) *v. tr.* To harvest fruit by shaking a tree or by throwing a stick. *Sūng kitam ni deya angalapod mampallam.* Lets go inland and shake down some mangoes. *Bay kami makapanapod mampallam dibuhi'.* We were able to knock some mangos down last night. (*Thesaurus:* **pusu'₁**)

**lapohan** *n.* A pottery firebox; a modern stove. *Taga buling lapohan inān.* That firebox has soot on it. *Am'lli aku lapohan ni M'ddas pagb'llahan kami.* I will buy a firebox in Siasi Town for us to cook on. *Buwat lapohan kami, bo' halam aniya' api, angā' kami pehē' ni luma' dakayu'.* Like our firebox when there is no fire [in it], we go get some from another house. (*Thesaurus:* **pagb'llahan, pilang, sukul₂**)

**lapong** *adj.* -an 1) Semi-blind. *Mma'ku to'a mbal agon maka'nda' pahāp. Sali' lapong-lapongan.* My grandfather can scarcely see well. He is semi-blind. 1.1) *v. advrs.* -in- Suffering impaired vision in low light; night blindness. *Magsasaw kita bang sangom, sali' mbal kita maka'nda'. Nilapong-lapong kita, mbal gi' makasayu to'ongan.* We are confused at night, as though we can't see. We are somewhat blinded, not yet fully awake.

**lappas₁** *n.* The abalone. *Haliotis asinina. Lappas-lappas, ya na pangiraman h'ndaku.* Abalone, that's what my wife craves during the conception phase.

**paglappas** *v. tr.* To earn an income from the harvesting of abalone. *Usaha sigām maglappas.* Their livelihood is collecting abalone.

**lappas₂** *adj.* -an 1) Delivered from disaster; death; hardship. *Lappasan sigām min bala', mura-murahan.* They will be delivered from disaster, it is hoped. *Makajari isāb bang a'a asigpit sinubalihan ni Tuhan, yukna, "Na Tuhanku, bang pa'in lappasan hinangku buwattitu-buwattina'an."* It is possible for a person experiencing difficulty to vow something to God, saying, "Oh my God, may whatever I do be kept free from harm." (*Thesaurus:* **haun₂, liyus 1.2, puwas₁ 1.1**) 1.1) *v. tr.* -an To deliver someone from disaster or death. *Bang kita nilappasan he' Tuhan, mbal kita binuwanan saki, mbal kita pinat'nna'an hukuman, mbal kita binono' e' a'a.* When God delivers us we are not given any illness, we are not brought to judgment, nor killed by people. *Mbal angalappas manusiya' ni manusiya' apa pagkahi.*

Humans do not deliver humans from harm because they are equals.

**lappet** *v. tr.* To smack someone with a flat implement. *Bay aku ni M'ddas pasal bay angalga, jari nilappet e' onde'-onde'.* I went over to Siasi Town because I was working as a porter, and then a kid hit me [with a stick]. (*Thesaurus:* **balubak, daplos, lambot, lubak₁**)

**lappik** *var.* of **lampik**

**lapping-lapping** *adj. zero* Folded over, of the upper part of the ear. (*Thesaurus:* **kopeng, sondong, toyok**)

**laptop** *n.* A portable computer; a laptop. *Aku'il laptopku sagō' mbal tatugila' bang ai salla'na.* My laptop is disabled but its defect cannot be determined.

**lapu-lapu** *n.* **1)** The surface growth on things that are continually wet. *Aheka magjabel-jabel lapu-lapu ma buntal bang pah'ggomta ni tahik. Subay ya hē' ya ala'an. Sali' hōs ma iya hē'.* A lot of growth hanging down from pufferfish when we soak it in saltwater. It needs to be removed. It is like its sarong, so to speak. *Lapu-lapuna, ya tai'-bambanna.* Its surface film, its mossy growth. (*Thesaurus:* **bakkel 1, tai'-bamban**) **1.1)** *v. tr.* -*an* To remove a surface film or layer. *Bang saupama pelang bay bayannu kaut, lapu-lapuhin. Ilu aheka al'mmis ma deyom mohang ilū, subay sinusutan tai'-bambanna.* A canoe for example that you have used out at sea, remove the film that has grown. There is a lot of dirty stuff in the hull, its moss needs scrubbing.

**lapuk** *adj.* -*a* Crisp, of foods. *Alapuk he'na maglandang-landang.* She fries things to a crisp. (*syn:* **lopok**)

   **lapuk-lapuk** *n.* A confection of cassavA: boiled, dried, sliced thin, fried crisp, and covered with syrup. *Suma'an ni'llawan binamban, bang atoho' nihuwal ni sokal bo' nihinang lapuk-lapuk.* Boiled cassava sometimes put in the sun and when dry tossed in sugar to make *lapuk-lapuk. Lapuk-lapuk itū atuwas, magpalere' mareyom bowa'.* This *lapuk-lapuk* is hard, it crackles in the mouth. (*syn:* **jauk 1**)

**lapug** *v. tr.* To burn off a pile of rubbish or brushwood. *Nilapugan ya ai-ai, aheka na tinunu'.* Anything being burnt off, a lot being burnt. (*Thesaurus:* **lāb 1.1, lablab 2, tunu'₁ 1.2**)

**lapus** *adj.* -*a* Complete, as every item of a set; fully covered, of a surface area. *Lapus mbal maglabi, mbal magkulang. Buwat papan pelang, alapus munda'-buli', sarang to'ongan. Lapus* means no extras and no shortages. Like the planks of a canoe, complete from prow to stern, just the right amount. *Alapus emponnu ilū, buwat empon si Ap, bulawan kamemon.* Your teeth are complete, like the teeth of the maiden Ap, all gold. *Alapus pahāp paha-paha si Ga he' daing.* Ga's canoe shelves are covered completely with fish.

**laput** *n.* The coarse dividing segments in large fruit such as jackfruit, edible but unappetising. *Laput nangka', ya jablutna ma deyom. Takakan.* The dividing segment of jackfruit, its fibrous bits. Can be eaten.

**laput-laput** *n.* A species of edible shellfish.

**lara** *n.* **1)** Chilli pepper. *Capsicum annuum.* (*gen:* **pamapā**) **1.1)** *adj.* -*a* Peppery; spicy; hot, as chilli. *Alara makalandu' loho' sinagol luku' inān.* That pufferfish liver soup is too spicy. **1.2)** *v. tr.* -*an* To season something with chilli. *Angā' aku lara kaleya pangalaraku daing.* I will get some chilli from ashore to make the fish spicy. **1.3)** *v. advrs.* ka-...-*an* To be affected by too much chilli pepper in food. *Bang kita kalarahan, magsularaw kita.* Whenever we get too much chilli pepper, then we writhe.

**lara sinayul** *n. phrase* The bell pepper; the capsicum. *Capsicum frutescens or annuum.*

**larak** *n.* **1)** The remnants of something that has fallen apart. **1.1)** *adj.* -*a* Damaged beyond repair; dismantled. *Alarak luma' bay taluwa' baliyu.* The house is destroyed, struck by the wind. *Badju' alarak, agese' na sali'.* A worn-out shirt, sort of torn. (*Thesaurus:* **basak, jagjag 1, langkat 1, lorak**) **1.2)** *v. tr.* To destroy something. *Da'a larakun mital ilū, nilangkopan sadja na.* Don't destroy that can, just have it patched.

**laran** *v. intr. pa-* To drift with a current or wind. *Magpalaran kami.* We let the current take us. *Pagūng-gūng na kami palaran.* We just float, drifting along. *Wa'i na talaran pelang.* The *pelang* has been carried away by the current. *Angā' aku bussu' panahanku bubu bo' mbal talaran minsan alandos s'llog.* I will get a rock to hold the fish trap down so it doesn't get carried away even though the current is strong. (*syn:* **hanut**; *Thesaurus:* **gesges, loson, paghadjul-hadjul, palis₁, pespes 1.1**)

**larang** *adj.* -*a* Disarrayed; unkempt, of hair. *Bang kita bay abati' man patulihan bo' mbal tapuwa'ta suray, alarang bu'unta. Ah'bba' kasehe'an, an'ngge kasehe'an.* When we have woken up from sleep but haven't found a comb, our hair is a mess. Some bits fare alling down, some are standing up. *Alarang kōkna, ariki' bu'unna, angiting.* Her head unkempt, her hair sparse, sticking up. (*Thesaurus:* **ganggas, gosang-gosang**)

**larang-larang** *n.* A platform built to hold items offered as tribute to a local guardian spirit. *Larang-larang aheka panjina, taga luma' ariki'-diki'. Larang-larang* has many flags, it has a small house on it. *Larang-larang itū pagluma'an saitan. Bang halam larang-larang pehē' ni kabangkawan.* A *larang-larang* is a house for *saitan* spirits. If there is no *larang-larang* they go into the mangroves.

**laras** *adj.* -*a* **1)** Done completely; used up. *A: "Bay na pinuwad kayu?" B: "Aho', alaras kamemon."*

A: "Has the tree been cut down?" B: "Yes, it's all done." **1.1)** *v. tr.* To consume the remnants of something. *A: "Buwattingga na takapin panggi' itū?"* B: *"Larasun na kamemon."* A: "What about this left-over cassava?" B: "Use it all up."

**laring** *n.* A small general-purpose knife. *Bang ariki', laring. Bang aheya, bari'.* If small it is a *laring*, if large it is a *bari'*. (*Thesaurus:* **kīs₄ 1, janap, pisaw**)

**laring lahut** *n. phrase* A large knife for cutting meat or fish. (*Thesaurus:* **bangkung, bari', gayang, lahut, pira, sundang**)

**laruk** *v. tr.* *-an* To throw something. *Larukanku ba'anan kunsi', halam makatudju ni ka'a, wa'i an'llu man lowang.* I threw the bunch of keys but they didn't go straight to you, they fell right through a hole. *Nilarukan saga s'mmek, saga taumpa', ya kahāp milikan.* Clothes and shoes are thrown [to us], the kindness of Westerners. *Larukin bola ilu ni aku.* Throw that ball to me. (*cf:* **timbag**; *Thesaurus:* **badji, bantung 1.1, buwang₁ 1, timan₁**)

**larung** *n.* **1)** A device for getting fish to move in the desired direction. *Hūgun na larung ilū, ai-ai na pat'nde.* Drop that weight, anything that will sink. *Larung binowa palangi pang'ssol daing, ma bungsud birahan maka ma ambitan, atawa ma pokot. Bang aniya' daing mbal to'ongan pasekot pasal tināwan larung.* A *larung*, something carried by a swimmer to herd fish into a fish corral, or fence, or into a net. If there are fish they will definitely not go close because they are scared of the *larung*. (*cf:* **lambat 1, tingga'**) **1.1)** *v. ditr.* To drop something heavy into water.

**larus** *v. intr.* *pa-* To lose tension or traction; to slip from one's grip. *Halam bay tinu'ud, magtūy palarus min tanganna.* It wasn't intentional, it suddenly slipped from his hand. (*Thesaurus:* **kabba, tanak 1**)

**paglarus-larus** *v. intr.* *aN-* To keep slipping, as a belt on a shaft, or as something held in one's grip. *Hal maglarus-larus pāmna.* Its pump keeps slipping off [the intake valve].

**larut** *var. of* **darut**

**lās-lās** *n.* Various coral fishes, including wrasses and butterflyfish.

**lās-lās-takot** *n.* The Indo-Pacific sergeant, a fish species. *Abudefduf vaigiensis.*

**lasa₁** *n.* Awareness or sense of health.

**pagpalasahan** *v. intr.* *aN-* To be feeling unwell. (*Thesaurus:* **pa'in₃ 1, saki 1.1**)

**palasahan** *n.* The way one feels, whether well or ill.

**lasa₂** *n.* **1)** Love for persons; affection. *Tuhan asal ya po'onan lasa.* God is indeed the origin of love. *Lasa-lasa sainala, hal lasa pinuwa'.* Pretend love, love just picked up in passing. **1.1)** *v. tr.* *a-, ka-..-an, -an* To have affection or love for someone. *Kinalasahan kitam e' si Babu' Anu buwat e'na alasahan saga anakna lissi.* Aunt Anu loves us the

way she loves her own children. *Kalasahin pagkahinu.* Love your fellow humans. *Kalasa a'a ina'an ma aku, minsan saga matto'ana tatiman na he'na.* That man's love for me is such that he even discards his parents. (*Thesaurus:* **kasi 1, gumbala', paganggi, s'lli 1.1**)

**kalasahan** *n.* Someone who is loved; loved ones.

**lasa pinuwa'** *n. phrase* A transient romantic affair. {idiom} *Hal lasa pinuwa', ngga'i ka dī lasa.* Just love picked up in passing, not real love.

**paglasa** *v. intr.* *aN-* To love each other. *Buwat balu bay magkalasa maka bay h'llana, sali' maglindu.* Like a widow who had come to be in love with her husband, she grieved.

**paglasa-liyasahi** *v. intr.* *aN-* To love reciprocally and continually. *Subay kām maglasa-liyasahi, sabab magdanakan kām, da'mma' kām, daina'.* You should love each other because you are siblings, you have one father and one mother. *Maglasa-liyasahi kitam.* We love each other.

**lasak** *v. tr.* To catch fish by herding into a submerged basket trap. *Angalasak kita tibuk, sissol maka tape'.* We will catch some *tibuk* [a slow-moving fish], herded in with our feet. (*cf:* **tibuk₂, ulan-ulan**)

**lasag** *adj.* *a-* Grown to full size. *Alasag na umulna.* She is fully of age. *Bay sali' aniya' maka'nda' kita, ariki'-diki' gi' kita. Ta'nda' pa'in kita pabīng, yuk maka'nda' kita, "Alasag pahāp ka'a ilū, Oto'."* Like when someone sees us when we are still small. When we are seen again, the one who saw us says, "Son, how big you've grown." *Ariki'-diki' gi' kita. Ta'nda' pa'in kita pabīng, yukna, "Alasag pahāp ka'a ilū, Oto'."* We were still small. When we are seen again, she says, "Son, how big you've grown." (*Thesaurus:* **hendog-hendog, pata'₁, sangpot 1, sibuwa, to'a 1.1**)

**lasaw** *adj.* *a-/-an* Over-ripe. *Lasawan bang atahak mariyata', palabay mamisna.* It becomes over-ripe when it is still on the tree, its sweetness passing. *Bang lasawan mbal takakan. Bang yukta alaga', takakan lagi'.* If it is *lasaw* it can't be eaten. If we say it is *laga'*, it is still edible. *Buwat buwahan maka duliyan bang at'ggol ma tau'an, alasaw. Bang yukta alaga', takakan lagi'.* Like lansones and durian a long time in storage, past their best. If we call it *laga'*, it is still edible. (*Thesaurus:* **laga'₁ 1, tahak 1**)

**lasay** *v. intr.* *pa-* To overflow a container. *Palasay na pangisihan bohe'.* The water container is overflowing. (*cf:* **s'ppaw**; *Thesaurus:* **lese₁, lipay₁, luput 1, sempok 1, uplut**)

**laskal** *adj.* *a-* Familiar with; accustomed to. *Sali' aku lum'ngngan ma Sambuwangan. Alaskal na aku magniSambuwangan, biyasa to'ongan.* Like me walking about in Zamboanga. I am familiar with going to Zamboanga, really accustomed to it.

**lasig** (*var.* **asig**) *n.* **1)** Cheerfulness; a sense of well-being. *Bang aniya' sehe'nu maglata, subay aniya'* *asigna. Bang d'nda bo' l'lla, mbal magtōp. Subay sali'-sali' d'nda.* If you are joking with someone, there should be fun in it. It's not appropriate between a woman and a man. They should both be women. (*Thesaurus:* **kōd, kōg 2, koyag 1, lami, paglangog**) **1.1)** *adj. a-* Merry; cheerful. *Bbahanku bahā' inumanku, ya makapalasig atay manusiya'?* Shall I give up my beverage, that cheers a man's heart?

**paglasig** *v. intr. aN-* To be joyfully celebrating an event together. *Magkalasigan sigām, aniya' bay at'kka min Saudi.* They are celebrating with joy, someone has arrived from Saudi Arabia. *Na maglasig-lasig na pa'in kami.* So we keep on having fun together.

**laslaen** *n.* The back line in court games such as volleyball. *Subay ka alistu ma laslaen ko' mbal kahūgan bola.* On the back line, you must be quick so as not to be hit by a falling ball.

**lason** *n.* A species of sea anemone, edible. *Actinia spp. Lason itū abisa angeket.* The *lason* referred to stings painfully. (*Thesaurus:* **kambang, kombo'-kombo', lo'on, pari-pari**)

**lassun** *n.* **1)** Poison. **1.1)** *v. tr.* To poison something or someone. *Aheka amatay ma Bohol, bay talassun.* Many died at Bohol; they were poisoned. *Bay nilassun mma' si Ja he' Bisaya', mahē' ma Libak.* Ja's father was poisoned by a lowland Filipino, there at Lebak.

**lastung** *see:* **nilastung**

**lasu'** *n.* The middle finger of a human hand. (*wh:* **tangan 1**)

**lasuwa** *v. tr. -an* To scald a chicken before cutting up the carcass and cooking it. *Nilasuwahan manuk bo' bin'lla.* The chicken is dressed and then cooked. (*cf:* **bulbul 1.2**)

**lāt** *n.* Lightning. *Taluwa' lāt kalbaw hē', magtūy amatay.* That carabao was hit by lightning and died immediately. (*Thesaurus:* **daogdog, l'ggon, l'tte'₁**)

**lata** *v. tr.* To make fun of someone. *Da'a latahun matto'a, binusung ka, aniya' ilmu'na.* Don't make fun of an old person, you will suffer retribution, he has supernatural ability. (*Thesaurus:* **pasu' gandum**)

**paglata** *v. intr. aN-* To be having fun together; to be teasing one another. *Maglata na pa'in saga ka'onde'an sampay na makapagsuntuk.* The children keep teasing each other until they get to fist fighting. *Pahali kām maglata.* Stop your fooling around. *Bang kita sali' maglata maka onde'-onde inān, na nilengkongan lubid, na bo' nilarukan ni baranna.* When we are kind of having fun with those kids, we form a loop of rope and throw it around their bodies. *Kuwat-kuwat na kita pinatuntul he' matto'ata man luma' bang kita angusaha. Ta'abut marilaut, ya hinangta maglata. Aholat matto'ata, ya yuk-i, "Wa'i kita angusaha," bo' wa'i maglata.* We are always sent

off for the day's fishing well prepared by our parents. When we get out to sea what we do is have fun. Our parents are hopeful, , "We are off earning our living," but in fact we are clowning around. *Sali' kita maglawat maglata. Kinodjel aku, yukku, "Ōy, da'a aku lawatun."* Like the two of us provoking each other, having fun. I get jolted and I say, "Hey, don't get me mad." *At'mmun, mbal maglata, mbal ah'lling-h'lling.* He is shy, doesn't joke, hardly talks.

**latak** *v. intr. aN-* To fall from a tree or palm, as ripe fruit growing too heavy for its stalk. *Buwat saging alatak min s'kkatanna, ala'anan dīna.* Like a banana dropping from the bunch, coming away of itself. (*Thesaurus:* **balabak, lagonos 1**)

**latag** *adj. a-* **1)** Spread over a wide area. *Alatag puhu'na he' katol.* His body is covered all over by eczema. *Aladja'-ladja', sali' alatag na bay pangusaha'an.* Unproductive, the fishing grounds having been widely covered. (*cf:* **taleted**) **1.1)** *v. tr.* To reach a range of places. *Talatagna kalahatan ma Pilipinas.* He reached every place in the Philippines. *Bay aku am'lli badju' bo' halam aniya' kabaya'anku ma tinda si Ak. Angalatag aku ni tinda kasehe'an.* I was buying a shirt but there was none that I liked in Ak's shop. I went all over to other stores. *Saga t'llu saging niā' min dakayu' dulang, nilatag na dulang ma paghinangan.* Three bananas or so taken from each food tray, the tray being taken around the place where the ceremony took place.

**paglatag-latag** *v. tr.* To spread things over a wide area. *Pinaglatag-latag iting kamemon ma po'on saging buwatti'.* All the thorns were spread widely around the base of the banana trunk. (*Thesaurus:* **labak, sabud, sabulak**)

**latal** *n.* **1)** Food served to guests on individual plates. *Latal itū, hatina bay na asal pinat'nna' pagkakan ma deyom tapak-tapak bo' ni'isi nireyom bandehaw.* This word *latal* means food set out beforehand on small plates and placed in a large tray. **1.1)** *v. tr. -an* To feed guests lavishly with individual servings. *Nilatalan, nilabot kamemon, pinat'nna'an lai', sawan, suru', jukup kamemon.* Lavishly entertained, everyone served, given a plate, cup, and spoon, fully complete. *Nilatalan, nilabot kamemon, pinat'nna'an lai', sawan, suru'. Nsa' aniya' kulangna, jukup kamemon.* Lavishly entertained, everyone served, given a plate, cup, and spoon. No shortage, fully complete. (*Thesaurus:* **buhat₃, labot**)

**paglatal** *v. tr. -an* To entertain guests in the traditional style of serving individual plates of food. *Bang kām magpakan ma llaw kawin, maglatal na sadja kām.* When you feed people on the wedding day, you just serve them individual plates.

**latap** *n.* **1)** Flooding due to rising water. **1.1)** *v. tr. -an* To inundate an area by rising waters. *Nilatapan deya Sambuwangan.* The Zamboanga hinterland was flooded. (*Thesaurus:* **dunuk, sakla', s'llop**)

**latas**₁ (var. **bulatas**) *adj. a-* Come undone, of a lashing or tie. *Bangka'na mbal na tabayan, abulatas na e' kapang.* His dugout is not usable, it has come untied by sea worms. *Alatas katig pelangku ma dilaut, alandos goyak.* The outrigger of my canoe came unlashed out at sea, it was very rough. *Atop, ab'kkat na tahi'na, alatas na iya.* Thatch, its stitching broken, now untied. *Minsan taingA: nsa' bulatas taingata, al'ppas.* Even ears: our ears aren't *bulatas*, they are pierced through. (*Thesaurus:* **kka 1.1, hubad, p'llus 1, puklas 1**)

**latas**₂ var. of **laktas**

**lato'** *n.* An edible seaweed, like bunches of tiny green grapes in appearance. *Caulerpa lentillifera.* (*syn:* **gamay**)

**lattik**₁ *n.* A small lobster-like crustacean. (*Thesaurus:* **kamun, keyot**₁, **pama'**)

**lattik**₂ var. of **lagtik**

**latun** *v. intr. pa-* **1)** To go from one location to another. *Magtūy palatun ni kita kumala' ya mareyom baranna, pamasukud ni kita.* The *kumala'* jewel which is inside his body promptly transfers to us, bringing us good fortune. **1.1)** *v. tr.* To go from one topic to another in conversation.
  **paglatun-latun** *v. intr. aN-* To keep going from one place to another. *Maglatun-latun kami.* We keep going from one island to another.
  **palatun** *v. tr.* To convey an item or person from one place to another.
  **pamalatunan** *n.* A person who carries messages or things between reference points.

**latus** *v. intr. pa-* To go right through something, as a bullet through flesh or a wall. *Daing bang pinana', palatus parambila' maka parambila'.* When a fish is speared, [the spear] penetrates from one side to the other. (*Thesaurus:* **lagbas 1, lambang**₁**, l'ppas 1.1, l'ssut**)
  **latus-lagbas** *adv.* Utterly; through and through. *Daipara Tuhan akawasa latus-lagbas taptap angandomolan iya min kapiligduhan.* Fortunately God is utterly powerful, always looking down [to keep] him from danger.
  **paglatus-lagbas** *v. intr. aN-* To affect something totally, going right through. *Tauwa' punglu', maglatus-lagbas.* Hit by a bullet, going right through.

**lau-** *see section 2.2.2.4 Prefix:* **Cau-**

**lauk** *n.* **1)** Basic foods that combine to make a complete meal, as fish or meat combine with cooked rice or cassava. *Bang aniya' buwas bo' halam aniya' daing, halam aniya' pangalauk.* If we have rice but no fish, we have nothing to complement it. *Bang kami amangan daing halam aniya' laukna, sinassing kita.* When we eat fish with no starch staple we get pinworms. (*cf:* **lallan**) **1.1)** *v. intr. a-* Using something as a complement to rice or cassava. *Alauk aku maka ta'uyu.* I will have soy sauce to complement [rice].

**laud** *v. intr. pa-* **1)** To move to a different location. *Wa'i palaud disi Je ni lahat dakayu'.* Je and family have transferred to another place. (*Thesaurus:* **lagedled 1, lintas, pagtagestes, pagtaleted**) **1.1)** *v. tr.* To transfer something to a different environment. *"Kapaya i'," yuk-i, "atomo'. Laurun pi'itu."* "That pawpaw," he said, "is growing. Replant it over here."

**laung** *adj. a-* **1)** Mistaken in what one asserts or understands. *Bang aku mbal alaung, ka'a Milikan ya bay maghinang luma' ma Siganggang.* If I'm not mistaken, you are the American who built a house at Siganggang. *Alaung aku, asā'.* I was mistaken, I was wrong. **1.1)** *v. advrs. ka-...-an* To be mistaken about something. *Kalaungan iya sugarul minsan duma'in iya bay anangkaw.* He was mistakenly treated as a rascal even though it wasn't him who had stolen. *Kalaungan akkal sigām.* Their thinking is mistaken.

**laus** *v. intr. pa-* **1)** To continue on one's way. *Bang aku ang'nde'an basket ni luma' si'itku, palaus aku ni pangongka'an. Mbal aku amole'.* When I take a basket back to my uncle's, I continue on to the festivities. I don't go home. (*Thesaurus:* **lalga, lanjal 1.1, sōng**₂ **1, unjal**) **1.1)** *v. tr.* To proceed with some action. *Sulut na, lausun na.* Deal. Proceed with [the purchase].

**laut** *see:* **kalaut, karilautan, dilaut**

**lawak** *adj. a-* Distant; remote. *Alawak makalandu' lahat Amerika hē', atawa ariplano, ina'an alawak ba min diyata'.* America is a very long way away, or an airplane, so far off, up high. (*syn:* **tā 1.1**; *ant:* **sekot 1**)
  **paglawak** *v. intr. aN-* To be far apart from each other, physically or in opinion. *Maglawak kita, mbal gi' magsulut.* We are far apart, not yet in agreement. *Buwat angusaha bang sali' maglawak, angalingan abay inān, yukna, "Pat'ppi' ka pi'itu."* Like when out fishing and we have become far apart, the fishing mate calls out, saying, "Come closer here."

**lawag-baran** *n.* Personal responsibility for offense given or damage done. *Buwat kita duwangan ni M'ddas, bo' aku angā' pelang a'a, nā lawag-baranku ya amowa.* Like the two of us going to Siasi, and I take another person's canoe, then I am responsible for taking it. (*Thesaurus:* **abunaw, atas**₂ **1, bahala'**₁**, kuwiraw, siyal, tanggung**₂)

**lawa'** *n.* **1)** A spider, a generic term for all species. (*syn:* **kabombong**) **2)** A large web spider reputed to have a painful bite.

**lawal** *n.* **1)** Fish eaten raw with a spicy relish. **1.1)** *v. tr.* To add a spicy relish to basic foods such as raw fish. *Ndiya lara maka suka', nilawal tamban itū.* Pass the peppers and the vinegar, relish is added to this herring. (*Thesaurus:* **bubuk**₂**, kilaw**

**1, pan'nno'an, tinu'anan**)

**lawan** *v. tr.* *-an* To keep watching something important or treasured. *Nilawanan d'nda, nilibun ko da'a niã' he' l'lla dakayu'.* A girl who was kept watch over, shut in so as not to be taken by another man. *Buwat aniya' ma tinda kinabilahi'an, sat'ggol halam sīnan a'a hē', angalawan gi' iya ma bay ta'nda'na hē'. Nīnda' na pa'in sa'agon-agon ta'ā'na, tab'llina.* Like something in a shop that is wanted, so long as the person lacks the money, he keeps watching out for what he has seen. Looked at again and again as though he had already got, already bought it. (*Thesaurus:* **liling, pandang, patong 1**)

**lawanan** *n.* A visual reminder of someone no longer present. *Sali' aniya' amatay. Ang'llo' kita dakayu' bay suku'na, nihinang lawanan.* Suppose someone has died. We get one of his possessions, make it a visual reminder. *Bang aniya' amatay siyakaku d'nda bo' aniya' lai'na ta'bba, nihinang lawanan. Buwattē' isāb bang patta'.* When my older sister dies and leaves one of her plates, it becomes a memento. A photo is like that too.

**paglawan** *v. intr.* *aN-* To gaze at each other. *Si Ju bay maglawan-lawan mahē' ma Malusu-tinggilan maka si Ma.* Ju and Ma were gazing at each other there at Malusu-tinggilan.

**lawang** *n.* **1)** A door or doorway. *Tambolin na lawang ilū, Nneng.* Close that door, dear. **2)** An opportunity. *Amiha na pa'in lawang pagbono'an.* Looking for an opportunity of getting into a fight.

**lawat** *v. tr.* To tease someone; to provoke someone to annoyance. *A: "Ina', angalawat disi Oto'."* B: *"Mbal du. Hal maglata."* A: "Mother, Eldest Son and others are teasing." B: "It's nothing. Just having fun together." *Kinodjel aku, yukku, "Ōy, da'a aku lawatun."* I get poked and say, "Hey, don't provoke me." (*Thesaurus:* **bellod₁, jullit₂, juri 1.1, pabelaw**)

**paglawat** *v. intr.* *aN-* To stir each other up in fun. *Sali' kita maglawat maglata. Kinodjel aku, yukku, "Ōy, da'a aku lawatun."* Like the two of us provoking each other, having fun. I get jolted and I say, "Hey, don't provoke me."

**laway₁** *n.* **1)** Saliva; spittle. (*Thesaurus:* **buhelo 1, helo₂, ludja' 1, pagtagak**) **1.1)** *v. advrs.* *-in-* Dribbling. *Nilaway si Anu bang pasān.* What's-his-name dribbles at times. **1.2)** *v. intr.* *aN-* To produce saliva.

**laway₂** *n.* **1)** Long-line fishing, a fishing technique using multiple baited hooks. *Aniya' laway pagūng, aniya' pat'nde. Ya laway pat'nde subay nilayohan. Bang pagūng ameya' kita palaran pi'ingga-pi'ingga.* There is a floating long-line technique and there is a sinking one. The sinking technique requires being anchored. When floating we just drift wherever. **1.1)** *v. tr.*

To catch fish using multiple baited hooks on a long line supported by floats. *Bang kita am'ssi pagūng kita, bang angalaway taga untang.* When we fish with a weighted hook we float, when we *laway* we have a floating line. (*Thesaurus:* **gonteng 1.2, manit, pamalastik, paranas, p'ssi 1.1, tonda₁ 1.1**)

**paglaway** *v. intr.* *aN-* To engage in long-line fishing. *Bang kita maglaway taga sau kita.* When we fish with the long-line system we have an anchor.

**lawayan** *n.* The Long-rakered trevally, the Heavy-jawed kingfish. *Ulua mentalis.*

**lāy-lāy** *n.* A lucine clam species. *fam. Tellinidae.*

**laya** *n.* **1)** A circular throw net with fine mesh. (*Thesaurus:* **gugul 1, lantaw 1, linggi' 1, pokot₁ 1, sinsoro 1, siyul 1**) **1.1)** *v. tr.* To throw a net or cloth with a spreading movement. *Angalaya aku tamban ni rilaut kaluma'an.* I catch herring with a thrown net out to sea from the village. *Nihaggut aku dibuhi', halam aniya' bay angalaya aku.* I was cold last night. No one spread a cover over me. (*cf:* **bugsak**)

**laya-laya** *n.* The fan coral. *Am'lli aku laya-laya pangoresyon luma'nu ma Niyusilan.* I will buy some fan coral to decorate your house in New Zealand.

**layagan** *n.* Sorghum, an edible grain. *Andropogon sorghum. Doha maka layagan, sali' buwa' gandum. Apu'ut-pu'ut arai' man pai.* Millet and sorghum are like maize grains. A bit shorter perhaps than rice.

**layam** *n.* **1)** A person skilled in a specific activity. **1.1)** *adj.* *a-* Expert; skilled. *Alayam itū ata'u to'ongan.* This word *layam* means really knowing. *Alayam ka am'ssi.* You are skilled at fishing. (*Thesaurus:* **lahal, panday 1.1, tullus 1**)

**layang-layang** *n.* The extended projections of the barge-boards of a house, decorated as formalized wings. (*Thesaurus:* **atop 1, ungkup**)

**layas** *v. intr.* *pa-* To be slightly concave, as a dinner plate. (*Thesaurus:* **k'bbong, ku'ub, pedda' 1**)

**laylay** *v. intr.* *pa-* To sag or flop down due to bulk or to loss of tautness. *Palaylay badju'nu, aheya makalandu'.* Your shirt is sagging down, it's much too large. *Palaylay, buwat b'ttong atawa d'lla' ero'.* Flopping down, like a stomach or a dog's tongue.

**layo** *adj.* *a-* **1)** Anchored. *Ma bihing bangkaw kami alayo.* We anchored by the edge of the mangroves. **1.1)** *v. intr.* *pa-* To lie at anchor. *Kappal basi' inān palayo ma llot M'ddas maka Siganggang.* That steel-hulled ship is at anchor between Siasi and Siganggang. *Pagabut kami ni Buli'-Lakit, na maī' na kami palayo-layo.* Having got as far as Rock Point, we anchored there for a while. (*Thesaurus:* **labu₂ 1.1, tangkal₂ 1.1**) **1.2)** *v. tr.* *-an* To anchor a vessel.

**paglayo** *v. intr.* *aN-* To be lying at anchor. *Paglayo* *na kami, agtūy tininduk dakayu' dapak.* On anchoring we promptly hooked into a humpbacked red snapper.

**layon** *n.* A lion. (*cf:* **halimaw**)

**layu** *adj. a-* Wilting, of plants. (*Thesaurus:* **lanos₁, lūs₁ 2, luyluy**)

  **layu-layu** *v. intr. aN-* To experience weakness and lassitude. (*Thesaurus:* **dome-dome, longkoy, s'nnay, summil**)

**layu-manuk** *n.* The Moon-tail rock cod; the Yellow-edged lyre-tail. *Variola louti.* (*gen:* **kuhapo'**)

**layul** *n.* A species of whale. (*Thesaurus:* **kahumbu, gadjamina**)

**lē₁** *v. tr.* To make advances to a woman under cover of darkness.

**lē₂** var. of **lele**

**lebod** *v. intr. pa-* **1)** To coil around something more or less solid, as a rope or snake around a body. *Palebod bahan ma sagbot. Sali' togel bawi akolong-kolong.* The vine coils among the weeds. It's curly like a pig's tail. *Palebod basi' inān ma taytayan-tikus.* That wire is curled around the upper plate of the wall. (*Thesaurus:* **birang 1, kokos₁ 1, koleng₁ 1, pasangan₁, tongko' 1, towa'**) **1.1)** *v. tr. -an* To form a coil; to wind around something. *Bang aniya' onde'-onde' magkuway, na kalambotan aku paglabayku. Sali' nileboran baranku itū, magtūy lahoran.* If some children are skipping, then I get smacked in passing. My body is sort of wrapped around, and I immediately show bruising. **1.2)** *v. advrs. ka-...-an* To be restricted by a coiled line. *Bang ka kaleboran e' lubid, puwasin maka tangannu.* If a rope gets looped around you, untangle it with your hands.

  **pangaleboran** *n.* A drum or reel on which to wind a line. (*syn:* **lengkehan**)

**lebre** *adj. zero* **1)** Free of charge. *Lebre lagi' balanja'na, lebre pagsigana, lebre pags'mmekna.* His supplies were free, his cigarets were free, and his clothing was free. **1.1)** *v. tr.* To waive payment or penalty; to release someone from custody. *Nilebre ka ma kappal bang amole'.* You will be allowed to travel free on the ship when you return home. *Na bang kita tinilaw, na makahati ma iya. Talebre kita e'na, yukna, "Da'a sangko'unbi a'a ilū."* Now when we were questioned, we understood him. He let us go, saying, "Don't bayonet those fellows."

**leke'-leke' llaw** *n. phrase* The hottest time of day, i.e. from noon to about 3 p.m. *Aku sinō' ni bohe', mbal aku. Yuk Ina', "Leke'-leke' llaw, atāw ka?"* I'm sent to get water, but I refuse. Mom says, "Broad daylight, and you're scared?" *Ōy! Asungi' ka buwattilu, leke'-leke' llaw!* Hey! You're excreting like that, in broad daylight!

**lekles** *adj. a-* Going beyond a limit, condition or intention. *Buwat pal'ngngan, yukku, "Ni luma' ina'an aku," bo' paliyu aku ni luma' dakayu'. Alekles l'ngnganku, alekles aku.* Taking a walk, for

example. I say, "I'm going to that house," but I go past that to another house. My walk goes beyond what is sensible; I go beyond it.

**paglekles** *v. intr. aN-* To spread beyond an original limit or intention. *Aglekles pohakna. Atawa bang ipul, aglekles ni saddī ma puhu'na.* His ringworm spreads. Or leprosy, it spreads to somewhere else on his body. *Maglekles, magnikaheya'an. Buwat magsagga', nihukum e' konsehal, mbal takole'. Pasōng ni kapitan, mbal. Pasōng ni mayul.* Going further and further, to a public sphere. Like a dispute brought to a councillor, to no avail. Goes on to the barangay captain, no better. Goes on to the mayor.

**lekom** *v. tr.* To enclose something by bringing together the ends of a net or fence. *Paghūgnu linggi' bo' pasōd na daing, subay nilekom bo' mbal na makalabay.* When you have lowered the net and the fish have gone in, it should be drawn shut so they don't get through [the opening]. (*Thesaurus:* **kumbis 1.1**)

**lekoman** *n.* An enclosure, specifically for holding fish that have been herded. *Buwat a'a magpangambit inān, bang aniya' daing tabowa patandan, bo' mareyom lekoman, na mbal makaluwas.* Like those people who catch fish by herding, when the fish are brought shorewards and are in the enclosure, they cannot go out.

**lekos** *n.* **1)** The circumference; the distance around. *Piland'ppa lekosna?* How many fathoms round is it? **1.1)** *adj. a-* Circuitous rather than direct, of speech. *Alekos ma bissala a'a.* Winding about, of someone's story. **1.2)** *v. intr. aN-* To wrap around the circumference of something. *Angalekos sowa ma kayu.* The snake wraps around the tree. **1.3)** *v. tr. -an* To measure the circumference of something by reaching around it. *Lekosun p'ttung bang pila h'kkana.* Measure the bamboo, how many handspans in circumference.

**lekot-lendom** *n.* The period just after twilight. *Lekot-lendom lahat ilū, maglunsulan na pa'in ka?* The place is dark, are you still walking about? (*Thesaurus:* **abay-kohap, kohap 1, lempos, logob-logob, magrib 2, sū'-palita'an**)

**ledje** *adj. a-* **1)** Spread unevenly over a surface; smeared. *Bang ma kami alakat, bang ma buwat Sama Dilaut aledje, sali' amulakay.* Our word is *lakat,* for ocean Sama it is *ledje,* like scattering [stuff]. **1.1)** *v. tr.* To besmear a surface. (*Thesaurus:* **ledled 1, l'ntap**)

  **pagledje** *v. intr. aN-* To smear a surface. *Bang onde'-onde' amangan mistang, magledje ni baranna.* When a child eats porridge, he smears it all over himself.

**ledled** *v. intr. pa-* **1)** To spread across a surface, as a flame or liquid. *Paledled keyat luma' sigā ni luma'ta, ati talapay isāb luma'ta tatunu'.* The flames from their house spread to ours, then our house was caught up in being burnt. *Aniya' bang* *tinunu' paledled palanay.* There are cases where something is burnt, it spreads out, liquefying. (*Thesaurus:* **ledje 1.1, l'ntap**) 1.1) *v. advrs.* ka-...-an To be completely enveloped. *Bay tunu' ma Tiyanggi, aheka luma' kaledleran.* The fire in Jolo Town, lots of houses were enveloped [in the spreading flames].

**lega-lega** *see:* **paglega-lega**

**legal** *adj. zero* Genuine, not a forgery. *Ataddang itū legal, mbal kolorom.* This word *taddang* means genuine, not counterfeit. (*cf:* **taddang**)

**lege** *v. intr.* pa-/-um- To lie down. *Lumege gi' aku.* I'll just lie down. (*Thesaurus:* **bahak**)

**palegehan** *n.* A place to lie down; a bed. (*Thesaurus:* **kantil₁, pabahakan, palangka'₂, patulihan**)

**lege-lege** *var.* of **gele-gele**

**leges** *adj.* a- Chafed; worn down through rubbing. *Kamaya'in ko mbal aleges hambawan bang nihella'.* Be careful so the halyard doesn't chafe when it is pulled.

**pagleges** *v. intr.* aN- To chafe or rub against something. *Patulakun kaut pelang ilū ko da'a magleges ni batu.* Push that canoe out to sea so it doesn't chafe against the rocks. (*Thesaurus:* **paggidgid, pagta'is**)

**leget** *n.* A sharp projection such as a thorn or spine. *Aniya' kayu legetan ataha' legetna, saga duwa inses legetna, niōnan puhung.* There are thorny trees with long thorns, thorns of about two inches, called *puhung. Kaginisan kayu legetan, basta itingan.* Various kinds of thorny trees, whatever has spikes. (*Thesaurus:* **iting 1, tuklang, tunuk**)

**pagleget** *v. intr.* aN- To appear as spikes on a distant horizon. *Magleget-leget lahat. Man kayu-kayuna patuwa', duwa, t'llu, mpat.* Land appears as spikes on the horizon. Its trees come into sight, two, three or four of them. *Pagabut t'llumbahangi itū aniya' lahat magleget-leget, kayu-kayuna patuwa' buwat Tapa'an.* When three nights had passed land appeared like spikes, its trees emerging as they do on Tapa'an atoll.

**legetan** *var.* of **bāt-legetan**

**legnok** *var.* of **legsok₁**

**legong** *adj.* a- Circular; spherical. *Alegong isāb bola, ya du isāb lilus alegong.* Balls are round, so too is a watch. *Salang-sabot, panggi' kayu bay nili'isan, alegong luwana. Salang-sabot,* grated cassava circular in shape. (*Thesaurus:* **bengkol₁, lakal 1, lengkol 1, lengkong 1, tibulung 1**)

**legot** *n.* 1) Rotation; revolution. (*Thesaurus:* **paggiling, pusal₁ 1.1**) 1.1) *v. intr.* pa- To spin on a shaft; to rotate around a central point. *Gasing, ya palegot inān, taga lubayan.* A top, the thing that spins, that has a whipping cord. 1.2) *v. tr.* To set something spinning, as a top. 2) A hexagonal die spun on a central shaft.

**legot-kapang** *n.* Loaded dice. *Legot-kapang, ngga'i ka tangkay payong, ngga'i ka to'olang. Ettom, bay*

*tanduk kalbaw.* A *kapang* dice is not from an umbrella strut, nor from a bone. It is black, from a buffalo horn.

**legot-legot** *v. intr.* pa- To form a spiral. *Pusal dakayu' itū, ebodta itū, sali' palegot-legot.* This crown here, this fontanel, it sort of spirals.

**paglegot** *v. intr.* aN- 1) To spin on a shaft, especially of spinning dice. (*Thesaurus:* **paggulung-gulung 1, pagpalling**) 2) To engage in betting on the fall of things such as spinning dice or a handful of rubber bands. *Si Sa wa'i maglegot goma.* Sa is off gambling rubber bands. (*cf:* **to'on₁ 1.1**)

**legot dunya** *n. phrase* The concerns, trials and temptations of everyday life. {idiom}

**legotoman** *n.* Edible vegetable products, including root crops, leaves and fruit. (*Thesaurus:* **l'mput deya, paltubu-tubuhan 1, sayul 1**)

**legpong** *adj.* a- Missing, of an item in a series. *Alegpong na matto'a d'nda inān.* That old woman has teeth missing. A: "*Angay katkat itū?*" B: "*Bay panganggatgat papan, alegpong na.*" A: "What happened to this saw?" B: "It was used for cutting a plank, and is now gapped." (*cf:* **l'bbang 1**)

**legsak** *adj.* a- Soft in consistency as through soaking; slushy. *Alegsak tana'. Bang kita lum'ngngan, pisak magbuwang-buwang, al'mmis kita.* The ground is soft. When we walk, mud flies up and we are dirty. (*Thesaurus:* **lamekkat, lettak, l'bbo 1, pekat**)

**legsok₁** (*var.* **legnok**) *adj. zero* Real, of kinship through birth rather than through adoption or residence; pure and unmixed, of language. *Dī legsok kampungku si Mu inān.* My village mate Mu is my real relative. *Anakku legsok, mpuku legsok.* My very own sons, my own grandchildren. *Kalegnokan lling Sama, kapatongan sidda, mbal alungay.* The pure Sama language, carefully watched, will not get lost. (*Thesaurus:* **lahasiya' 1, lissi, luggiya'**)

**legsok₂** *adj.* a- Blind (often used derisively). *Alegsok matanu bang ang'nda', sali' abulag.* Your eyes are blind when you look, as though there is something in them. *Angay ka'a bang ka lum'ngngan? Abuta ka? Alegsok ka?* What are you doing when you are walking? Are you blind? Are you sightless? (*Thesaurus:* **buta₁, lakap-manuk, palu' 1.1**)

**leha** *n.* 1) A square sail with upper and lower yard, rigged on a tripod mast. *Magkulindara aku leha bang alandos baliyu.* I adjust the sail when the wind is strong. (*cf:* **banog pelang**; *syn:* **lamak**) 1.1) *v. intr.* a- To sail under a square sail. *Aleha na kami tudju pi'itu ni Pilipīn.* We sailed [under a square sail] here to the Philippines.

**lehag** *adj.* a- Finely woven and almost transparent. *Alehag pahāp s'mmek bay b'llinu, sali' anipis-nipis.* The cloth you bought is finely woven, like something quite thin. *Alehag-lehag s'mmek itū,* *sali' atilag.* This cloth is finely woven, sort of transparent. (*Thesaurus:* **bildu', buwal₂, dasu, lere-lere 1, pima, taplak₁**)

**lehod** *n.* 1) A delay; a postponement. (*Thesaurus:* **buhul₂, pagmahuli-llaw, tanggu 1**) 1.1) *adj. a-* Slow in doing; dilatory. *A: "Mbal aku alehod." B: "Bang ka'a-i bay angutang ni aku, alehod ka amayad. Minsan ta'abut na janji'an, alehod."* A: "I will not procrastinate." B: "When you have borrowed from me, you delay paying. Even though the promised date has come, you delay." (*Thesaurus:* **ddas 1, lanat, t'ddas 1**) 1.2) *v. tr. -an* To subject something to delay. *Buwat aniya' angindam gaugari' ni ka'a bo' halam ni'nde'an, yuk bay mangindam i', "Kalu mbal nientom." Na, nilehoran gaugari'nu.* Like someone borrowing a file [the metal-working tool] from you and it hasn't been returned, the one who borrowed says [to himself], "It may not be remembered." Well, your file is delayed. 1.3) *v. advrs. ka-...-an* To be delayed. *A: "Ai kalehorannu? Ai kat'ggolannu?" B: "Alehod aku ma mato'aku d'nda."* A: "What is delaying you? What are you taking a long time over?" B: "I am being delayed by my mother-in-law."

**kalehoran** *n.* A cause of delay. *Ai kalehorannu?* What was the reason for your delay?

**paglehod** *v. tr. -an* To grant more time for the payment of a debt or return of something borrowed. *Bang bay angutang, pinaglehod-lehoran he' a'a bay pangutanganna inān. Sinukut pabīng.* When someone has borrowed something, he is given more time by the person from whom he borrowed. He is then dunned again.

**lehom** *v. tr.* To ignore what is going on; to be neglectful. *Pagsagaw karupangan, nilehom-lehom e' kauman min atay nsa' b'nnal. Minsan b'nnal, tinapukan, mbal pinahula-layag.* A foolish uproar, ignored by the community from false motives. Even if genuine, [the reasons] are hidden, not made known. *Na bang kām anganjanji' ni Tuhan bo' palehom-lehombi, katōngan kām dusa bang mbal suhulbi.* So when you make a vow to God and are neglectful about it, you will be found guilty if you don't fulfill it.

**palehom** *v. tr.* To neglect or ignore a responsibility or commitment. (*Thesaurus:* **haman-haman 1, sumadja**)

**le'e** *n.* The jaw. {archaic}

**le'eng** *see:* **pagle'eng**

**le'od₁** *n.* A cluster of houses whose residents are usually linked by kinship and identified by a leader of the cluster. *Pī' ka ni le'od si Anu.* Go over there to What's-his-name's house-group. (*Thesaurus:* **kaluma'an, kampung₂, libug, lūng 1, nibung, tumpuk 2**)

**le'od₂** *see:* **pagle'od**

**lele** (var. **lē₂**) *v. intr. pa-* 1) To crawl; to move along on the stomach, as a snake or a baby; to walk on short legs, as a turtle or centipede. *Yampa*

*makalē anak si Be.* Be's child is just now at the crawling stage. (*cf:* **kura'-kura'₁**) 1.1) *v. tr.* To reach something by crawling. *Ā, nilele na pa'in e' tohongan.* So then, he kept on being followed [crawled after] by the turtle.

**paglele** (var. **paglē**) *v. intr. aN-* To get about by crawling. *Apassut magl'ngngan, apassut maglele.* Adept at walking, at crawling. *Bahan maglē mareyom kasob, bang mbal ta'nda'ta bo' tasagidta, kakatolon.* A vine that creeps along inside a thicket, if we don't see it but brush against it, we will be itchy.

**lelek** *adj. a-* Split apart under pressure or weight. *Da'a ka aninggil ma pelang ilū bo' mbal palelek.* Don't stand on the canoe lest it split. (*Thesaurus:* **bila' 1.2, b'kka' 1.1, se'ak 1, sepak**)

**lemba** *v. intr. pa-* To pass the zenith, of a celestial body. *Bang palemba na mūpū, sōng na satan. Bang ma ugtu masi, uttala' masi.* When the Pleiades have passed the zenith, the south wind will soon begin. If they are still at the zenith, it's still the northeast monsoon. (*Thesaurus:* **kīd₂, king 1.1, lenggang, lihid, paglilip-lilip, poyog 1, tīg**)

**lembang** *adj. a-* Spoken with a pronounced accent. *Alembang e'na magsinūk.* She speaks Tausug with a strong accent.

**lembo** *adj. a-* 1) Drowned; taking water into the lungs. *Da'a ka pakuppa bo' ka mbal alembo.* Don't jump in so you avoid being drowned. *Aniya' onde'-onde' bay alembo ma Sisangat. Bay lum'ngngan, alalom tahik.* A child drowned at Sisangat village. She was walking and the tide was in. *Sali' aniya' onde'-onde' alembo, yuk a'a, "Oy! Onde'-onde' inān alembo patoyok."* Like when a child is drowning and someone says, "Hey! That child is drowning and is unconscious." 1.1) *v. tr.* To drown someone. *Bay kono' nilembo ni saitan tahik.* He was reportedly drowned by a sea demon.

**lemed** 1) *adj. a-* Contaminated by spreading or smearing. *Pabontolun pintura bo' mbal alemed.* Make the paint straight so it isn't smeared. (*Thesaurus:* **lemos₁ 1**) 1.1) *v. advrs. ka-...-an* To be contaminated; polluted. 1.2) *v. tr. -an* To smear or wipe across a surface. *Lemerin barannu maka ns'llan hamut itū.* Anoint your body with this perfumed oil. 2) *v. tr.* To promote similar behavior by contact or example, good or bad. *Aku saupama ala'at, t'llu kam ahāp. Talemed du aku ni kahāpan.* I for example am bad, and three of you are good. I am influenced towards the good. *Makalemed sadja ko' asāl hinang ahāp ilū.* That good behavior will naturally spread to others.

**paglemed** *v. intr. aN-* To be infectious or contaminating. *Maglemed saki buwattilu.* That kind of sickness is contagious. (*cf:* **kulina, lamin 1**)

**lemes** var. of **lemos₁**

**lemo-lemo** *v. tr.* To distract or divert someone's

attention. *Lemo-lemohun lagi' onde' ilū bo' mbal anasat ina'na maghinang.* Get that child to do something else so she doesn't bother her mother as she works. *Bang kita pal'ngngan ma tinda bo' aheka a'a, subay kita anganjaga bang aniya' angalemo-lemo kita mbal ka'akkalan.* When we're walking in a shop and there are a lot of people, we need to be watchful when someone distracts us so we don't get tricked.

**lemong** *see:* **paglemong**

**lemos₁** (var. **lemes**) *adj. a-* **1)** Smeared with some dirty substance. *Alemos kita he' tana'.* We are smeared with dirt. (*Thesaurus:* **lemed** 1) **1.1)** *v. tr. -an* To coat a surface with something dirty. *Nilemesan kita maka buling.* We are smeared with soot.

  **pangalemos** *n.* Someone known for lack of washing.

**lemos₂** *see:* **pagpangalemos**

**lempon** *v. advrs. ka-...-an* To be afflicted by having a foreign body in one's eye. *Kalemponan mata si Anu.* What's-her-name has something in her eye. (*Thesaurus:* **bulag, pē'₄, puling** 1.1)

**lempos** *adj. a-* Fully dark. *Abay kohap, alempos na. Sali' halam aniya' llaw ta'nda' minsan keyat-keyatna.* Evening, fully dark. Nothing seen of the sun, not even its afterglow. *Alempos na magalib. Da'a na asagaw, waktu pag'ddok atuli.* Dusk is now fully dark. Don't make a noise now, it is the time for sound sleep. (*Thesaurus:* **abay-kohap, kohap** 1, **dampog** 1.1, **lekot-lendom, lendom** 1.1, **logob-logob, magrib** 2, **pagdo'om, sū'-palita'an**)

**lendo'** *n.* The forehead; the temple (of the head). *Angalom lendo'ku, bay taluwa' he' batu.* My forehead is bruised, hit by a rock. *Bang magkonotan lendo'ta lumandu'an ap'ddi' atayta.* When our brow wrinkles we are very angry. *Sinoso'an kilayta maka lendo'ta.* Our eyebrows and our brows are trimmed. (*syn:* **tuktuk**)

**lendom** (var. **l'ddom**) *n.* **1)** Darkness; absence of light. **1.1)** *adj. a-* Dark, in contrast to bright. (*Thesaurus:* **dampog** 1.1, **lempos, pagdo'om**) **1.2)** *v. intr. aN-* To grow dark; to become overcast. *Angl'ddom Sama tu'ud, angalendoman Sama Lipid.* L'ddom is the Sama Dilaut word, lendom is the land-based Sama word. *Angal'ddom luma'tam bang halam aniya' palita'an. Atāw aku.* Our house becomes dark when there is no lamp. I am fearful.

  **kalendoman** *n.* Darkness.

  **lendom bitu-bituhan** *n. phrase* Utter darkness. {*idiom*} *Sipat nalka, lendom bitu-bituhan.* A distinguishing feature of hell, utter darkness.

  **lendoman** *n.* The dark phase of the moon, when it does not rise until midnight.

  **paglendom** *v. intr. aN-* To behave as though sightless.

**lenek** *v. intr. aN-* To make the crackling sound of something being heated quickly, as in hot oil.

*Bang tinunu' angalenek, angalere'. Buwat kita angalandang, ah'lling ē'. Nā, ya hē' angalenek.* When it is burnt it sizzles and bubbles. Like when we fry something, it makes a sound. That is *lenek. Angalenek tilag-tilag. Bay apīt, magtūy tahinang sali' bohe'. Atawa Puriko ang'ns'llan.* A plastic bag was melting. It was thick, and quickly became like water. Or like Puriko [a brand of cooking fat] turning to oil.

**lensa** *adj. a-* Unsettled; moving restlessly. *Da'a ka alensa bo' kitam mbal abuhaw.* Don't keep moving from side to side lest we take on water. (*Thesaurus:* **pagdaguyu, tangkug** 1)

  **paglensa** *v. intr. aN-* To move about unsteadily. *Bang paleyang tallung bo' kalandosan baliyu, anotog ma diyata', mbal maglensa.* When a *tallung*-type kite is flying and a strong breeze hits it, it becomes steady up above, not diving about.

**lentok** var. of **lentop**

**lentop** (var. **lentok**) *adj. a-* Prudent; carefully considered. *Alentop pikilan, ahogot, buwat pikilan a'a to'a.* Thoughtful, steady, like the thinking of an older person. *Alentok utukna, alalom pikilanna. Asal sali' tapikil e'na.* His brain is sharp, his thinking deep. He naturally thinks about things. *Bang a'a alentok, mbal kamunduhan, makalahi'an dīna.* A thoughtful man isn't attacked by bandits, he gets away on his own initiative.

**lengag** *v. intr. pa-* To incline the head to one side. *Palengag, sali' patiring kōkta. Lengag,* like turning our head side-on. (*Thesaurus:* **kīd₁** 1.1, **pasindik, patiring, sīp**)

**lenga'** *n.* A flat earthenware cooking pan. *Am'lli aku lenga'ku ni M'ddas pagsanglagan.* I will buy my flat dish in Siasi for dry-roasting cassava. (*gen:* **pam'llahan**)

**lengas₁** *adj. a-* Dried out or dying, of a plant exposed to sun or heat. *Alengas kayu, halam na magdahun pasal pasu' pang'llaw.* The tree is dry, no longer producing leaves due to the sun's heat. (*Thesaurus:* **k'llung-k'llung, panggang₂** 1, **t'ggang₁**)

**lengas₂** *adj. a-* Having a naturally high forehead, a sign of wisdom. *Alengas, a'a alangkaw tuktukna sagō' duma'in ungas. Lengas,* a person with a high forehead but not balding. *Pali-pali kamatto'ahan bang kono' alengas, hatina ata'u.* The folk-belief from the elders is that when a person has a high forehead he is knowledgeable. (*Thesaurus:* **kelas, penggas, ungas**)

**lengke** *v. tr.* To wind up a line on the hands or on a notched board. (*Thesaurus:* **bodbod₁** 1.1, **kokos₁** 1, **koleng₁** 1.1, **longon**)

  **lengkehan** *n.* A device for winding line, made of a flat board notched at each end. (*syn:* **pangaleboran**)

**lengkol** *n.* **1)** The stiffened rim of a circular container. *Ligu, basket taga lengkol.* A winnowing basket, a basket with a circular rim. (*Thesaurus:* **bengkol₁, lakal 1, legong, lengkong 1, tibulung 1**) **1.1**) *v. intr. aN-* To become circular. *Angalengkol bulan.* The moon becomes round. (*cf:* **salekolan**)

**lengkong** *n.* **1**) A circular shape. *Bang ka angusuhan batang, pahāpun lengkongna ko' mbal abila'.* When you make a hole for the outrigger boom, make it a good circle so it doesn't split. *Lengkong itū, lowangna atibulung.* The word *lengkong* here means that its hole is circular. (*Thesaurus:* **bengkol₁, lakal 1, legong, lengkol 1, tibulung 1**) **1.1**) *adj. a-* Circular in shape. *A: "Buwattingga luwa dunya?" B: "Alengkong, mbal ta'abut langit."* A: "What does the earth look like?" B: "It is round, and doesn't reach the sky." **1.2**) *v. intr. aN-* To become circular or spherical. **1.3**) *v. tr. -an* To form a loop; to enclose something in a circle. *Bang kita sali' maglata maka onde'-onde inān, na nilengkongan lubid, na bo' nilarukan ni baranna.* When we are kind of having fun with those kids, we form a loop of rope and throw it around their bodies.

**lenges** *var.* of **l'ngnges**

**lenggang** *v. intr. pa-* To tip from an upright position; to be unstable, of a canoe. *Totogun pelang dok mbal palenggang.* Steady the canoe so it doesn't tilt to one side. (*Thesaurus:* **kid₂, king 1.1, lemba, lihid, paglilip-lilip, poyog 1, tīg**)

**paglenggang** *v. intr. aN-* To tilt repeatedly from side to side. *Bang bangka' halam katigna, bo' mbal biyaksa magbayan, maglenggangg-lenggang.* When a canoe has no outriggers, and one is not accustomed to travelling [by boat], it keeps tipping from side to side.

**lengget** *n.* **1**) A notch or serration, as on a saw blade or the comb of a rooster. *Aniya' isāb lengget-lengget ma katkat.* There are serrations in a saw too. **1.1**) *adj. -an* Serrated; notched. *Aniya' surayna lenggetan.* She has a comb that is notched. *Manuk taga pē lengget-lenggetan.* A chicken with a serrated comb.

**lenghob** *v. tr. -an* To make a circular cut, as when forming a neckline or excising a snake bite. *Bang aniya' bay kineket sowa, subay nilenghoban.* If there is a person bitten by a snake, [the bite] should be cut out.

**lengog** *n.* **1**) A disturbance; confusion; trouble. *Landu' akagit atayku ma saga paglahat magmalangkahi halam aniya' lengog sigām.* I am seriously angry with the citizens who boast that they have no disturbances. **1.1**) *adj. a-* Disturbed, of social order or of thinking. *Bay alengog M'ddas, aheka magbono'.* Siasi town was in an uproar, lots of people fighting. (*Thesaurus:* **balu', dongkag, halubilu, hengo-hengo, hiluhala' 1.1, hiyul, jabu 1, sasaw 1.1, sensong**) **1.2**) *v. intr. aN-* To cause a disturbance. *Aho', bay kami magsalla' bo' angalengog si Si.* Yes, we were gambling on coins

and Si made a disturbance. *Bowahin iya pi'itu, ati mbal na iya angalengog ka'a pabalik.* Have him come here and he won't trouble you again.

**kalengogan** *n.* A disturbance among a crowd; an uproar. *Ya a'a magpangandupang makapaniya' kalengogan.* The person who behaves stupidly makes a disturbance happen.

**lengog kōk** *adj. a-* Mentally confused. {idiom} *Alengog sidda kōkku e' parakala' itū.* My head is really confused by this matter. (*Thesaurus:* **bingaw, buriru, lambang-mata 1, ligoto'**)

**pagkalengogan** *v. intr. aN-* To be in a state of civil unrest.

**lepa** *n.* A large single-hull canoe, often roofed and used as a houseboat by nomadic Sama. *Lepa ya pagbayanan a'a pala'u.* The *lepa* canoe is the conveyance of the boat-dwelling Sama. (*cf:* **Sama Jengen**)

**lepet** *adj. zero* Inconsistent; unreliable. *Lepet itū sali' a'a magputing. Yukta, "Yampa pinaluwas kaputingna." Lepet* is like a person given to telling lies. We say, "He has only now let his lying ways be seen."

**paglepet** *v. intr. aN-* To behave capriciously or unreliably. *Patay bohe' kami ma dilaut. Nā, yampa pat'nna' ulan ma luma' na. Yukta, "Yampa maglepet ulan."* We were parched out at sea. The rain only began when we got home. We said, "The rain only now shows its fickleness." (*Thesaurus:* **puting 1.1**)

**lera-lera₁** *n.* A fleshy jelly-like marine plant found growing on house posts. *Lera-lera, ya sali' amalut ma hāg inān, ya mangaluntang i'.* Lera-lera, the fleshy growth that kind of sticks to house-posts, producing a sort of froth. (*syn:* **solenggang**)

**lera-lera₂** *see:* **paglera-lera**

**lere-lere** *n.* **1**) A finely woven fabric. (*Thesaurus:* **bildu', buwal₂, dasu, lehag, pima, taplak₁**) **1.1**) *adj. a-* Translucent, as fine cloth. (*Thesaurus:* **tilag**)

**lere'** *v. intr. aN-* To boil to bubbling stage; to froth or foam. *Bang pat'kka sakina bawi-bawi, magtūy angalere' bowa'na.* When her epilepsy comes on, her mouth froths. (*Thesaurus:* **bukal, buwal₁, laga'₁ 1.1, ogok-ogok**)

**pagpalere'** *v. intr. aN-* To pop and crackle, as something brittle being chewed.

**lese₁** *v. intr. pa-* To overflow a container. (*Thesaurus:* **lasay, lipay₁, luput 1, sempok 1, uplut**)

**lese₂** *n.* A species of fish that lives in holes on the sea floor. (*cf:* **tamalengkeng**)

**lesen** *v. intr. pa-* To sit flat on a surface. *Garul tinape'an, mbal tinape'an langguway, palesen-lesen.* A garul [brass container] has feet, a langguway tray doesn't. It sits flat.

**leson** *adj. a-* Arranged in an orderly way so as to make the best use of space. *Ap'nno' pantān e' puhu'. Aleson isāb.* The porch is full of people. They are well packed in.

**pagleson** *v. intr. aN-* To arrange things to make the best use of space, for people sleeping or sitting in a crowded space. *Puhu' aheka sinō' magdigpit na kamemon. Magleson na kamemon, bo' makatingkō' kasehe'an.* Lots of people asked to sit close to each other. All move to make the best use of space so that others were able to sit. *Ya du bang magtulihan magbaubabag, sinō' magleson.* Likewise when people are sleeping cross-wise, they're told to make more room.

**lessad** *adj. a-* Removed from office; demoted. *Lumandu'an abbuna, alessad iya magtūy min pagmastalanna.* His pride was excessive; he was immediately demoted from his teaching position.

**lesseg** (var. **l'sseg**) *v. intr. pa-/-um-* To sit so that one's buttocks are right on the ground or floor. *Bang ameya' ma bangka' diki'-diki', subay palesseg bo' mbal palenggang.* When we go in a small canoe, we should sit right down with legs flat so as not to tip over. *Palesseg kita, aningkō' kita ma nsa' bidda' minsan al'mmis.* Let's sit on the ground, sitting wherever, even if it's dirty. *Aheka isab sigām magbinadju' karut maka palesseg ma abu.* Many of them wore sacking and sat right down on the ashes. (*syn:* **d'ssal**; *Thesaurus:* **tingkō' 1, tongngol**)

**pagnilesseg** *v. intr. aN-* To sit with buttocks and thighs flat on the floor.

**palesseg** *v. tr.* To put something down casually.

**palessegan** *n.* A place where someone sits without concern for cleanliness or decorum.

**lēt** *adj. a-* Late, especially in a school context. *Alēt na kami makapagtagna' magiskul dinsini'.* We were late for the opening of school earlier today. (*Thesaurus:* **atarasaw, damuli 1, tanggollayan**)

**lete** *v. intr. pa-* To cross by an elevated walkway. *Ang'ntan pahāp bang ka palete, bo' ka mbal ahulug.* Hold on well when you are crossing a walkway, so you don't fall. *Palete gi' aku ni luma' dakayu'.* I'll just walk across to the other house. *Buwat kita palete, dangan man dampōng, dangan man dampōng, pa'aging sali' lum'ngngan.* Like when we are crossing on a walkway, one from each end, sort of walking interruptedly. (*Thesaurus:* **kulatay, taytay 1**)

**letehan** *n.* A narrow walkway or bridge, commonly with a handrail. *Da'a ka tināw, ahogot du letehan luma' sigām. Dakayu' du p'ttung.* Have no fear, the bridge to their house is secure. It's a single length of bamboo. *Aniya' pamaletehan bo' ataha'.* There is a walkway for crossing over but it is long.

**paglete** *v. intr. aN-* To cross over by way of a beam or walkway. *Sowa isāb inān maglete na saga ni pelang min katig.* There's a snake there too, crossing over to the canoe apparently by way of the outrigger.

**letek** *see:* **pagpaletek, paletek**

**letok** (var. **ketok**) *v. tr.* To shake a container to determine whether it contains a liquid. *Bay niletok katig, aniya' tahik mareyom. Subay pinōngan ko' ala'an bohe'na ati alampung na.* The outrigger float was shaken, there was water inside it. It needs to be cut off to remove the water, and then it will be light. (*Thesaurus:* **kembo' 1.1, kohek-kohek, genggok**)

**pagletok** *v. intr. aN-* To indicate the presence of a liquid by sloshing, of a container. *Magletok gi' masi kulaet, masi ns'llanna.* The pressure lantern still sloshes, it still has kerosene.

**letop** *adj. a-* **1)** Covered with water, of a land feature or food in a pot. *Aletop lansa, ap'nno' he' tahik, nsa' aniya' paluwa'.* The launch is submerged, full of seawater, nothing showing. (*Thesaurus:* **kanop, limun 1, lonob 1**) **1.1)** *v. intr. pa-* To overflow with water. *Paletop bohe' ni diyata' ayan.* The water flooded to the top of the firmament.

**paletop** *v. tr.* To add enough water to cover food in a pot.

**lettak** *adj. a-* Saturated; marshy. *Alettak-lettak tana' bang bay binohe'an.* Soil is quite marshy when it has been watered. (*Thesaurus:* **lamekkat, legsak, l'bbo 1, pekat**)

**leya** *see:* **kaleya**

**leyak** *v. intr. pa-* To lie face upwards. *Bang paleyak atuli, sidda nīddop.* When she sleeps on her back, she is liable to have nightmares. (*ant:* **pakkom 1**; *Thesaurus:* **daya', hagtang, hantal, haya'₁, pagduleyak**)

**paleyak** *v. tr.* To turn something over so that it is face up.

**leya'-leya'** *v. advrs. -in-* Terrified; excessively frightened. *Nileya'-leya' iya atuli dangan-danganna.* He is frightened of sleeping alone. *Saddī lling, tu'ud nileya'-leya' ba'anan magh'lla-h'nda sabab heka kasusahan pagkalabayan ma waktu tagna'.* Changing the subject, many people considering marriage are simply terrified because of the many difficulties experienced at a previous time. *Bay ni'ddop si Nu, mbal tahawid. Nileya'-leya' asāl.* Nu had a nightmare, couldn't be restrained. Terrified in fact. (*Thesaurus:* **bolag, dalan 1.1, damag, gawa, g'mma, gupu, tāw 1.1, umagad 1.1**)

**leyang** *v. intr. pa-* **1)** To fly or soar, as a bird, airplane or kite. *Bang aniya' paleyang tallung abō' kalandosan baliyu, anotog ma diyata', mbal maglensa.* When a kite is flown and the wind is strong, it stays steadily up above, it doesn't change position. *Buwat manuk-manuk amiha kinakanna, magleyang-leyang.* Like birds looking for their food, flying here and there. (*cf:* **kidjang 1.1**) **1.1)** *n.* The manner of flying; the movement of a canoe over water. *Bang ma "estael pang-racing" to'ongan, bang buwattē' ahāp leyangna.* When it's true "racing style," when that's so, its movement is very good. **1.2)** *v. tr.*

-an To carry something to a target by flying, as in cursing. *Bang pa'in ka nileyangan!* May you be borne away! *Hal kak'bbatan bowa', nileyangan. Sali' panukna' ba.* Simply targeted by an utterance, to be sent flying through the air. Like a curse. **1.3)** *v. tr.* To reach something by flying. *Na bo' na kono' nileyang pangiraman.* So then the food craved during pregnancy was reached by flying.

**leyang atay** *v. intr. pa-* To be startled. {idiom} *Ahūg tibu'uk, paleyang magtūy atayku.* Some cassava fell, I was immediately startled [lit. my liver flew up]. (*Thesaurus:* **k'bbal, kobla', kuddat, himatta'**)

**leyat-leyat** *see:* **pagleyat-leyat**

**liban** *adj. -an* **1)** Elapsed, of time. **1.1)** *v. tr. -an* To allow a period of time to elapse. *Nilibanan pa'in dapitu', magtūy kami kaut pabing.* When a week had passed we promptly went to sea again.

**libat** *adj. a-* **1)** Cross-eyed (strabismus). *Kalibatna asāl min deyom kandang.* His cross-eyes are in fact from in the womb. **1.1)** *n.* A cross-eyed person.

**paglibat** *v. intr. aN-* To cross one's eyes. *Maglibat-libat dīna, katūyan du ko' inān.* He crosses his eyes, he will be completely cross-eyed.

**liblib** *v. advrs. -in-* Suffering from conjunctivitis or similar acute inflammation of the eyelids. (*Thesaurus:* **belad, bussik 1, piting**)

**liblib-liblib** *see:* **pagliblib-liblib**

**libombo'** (var. **libonbon**) *adj. a-* Luxuriant in growth, of plants or trees. *Alibombo' daun kayu, sali' aheka daunna.* The leaves of the tree are lush, like it has a lot of foliage. (*Thesaurus:* **labung 1, tusay**)

**libonbon** var. of **libombo'**

**libu** *adj. a-* **1)** Far-reaching, of a search for something. *Alibu sigām sampay Tapol pamatambalan.* They look everywhere including Tapol for something to use as medicine. *Alibu na he'ku katindahan, halam aniya' tab'lli.* I have searched all the shops, with nothing purchased. *Alibu na pagbowahan, na halam kauli'an, pinelleng ni ka'a.* All the healers have been sought out, and [he] is not healed, so he is brought back to you. **1.1)** *v. tr. -an* To look everywhere for something, as for medical help. *Yukna, "Libuhin na pangkat kamemon m'ssa'-bidda'."* He said, "Search out all the ritual ancestors no matter which." *Bang alatag na pangalibuhanbi, na pat'nna'in dīna.* When you have looked everywhere [for healing], then just leave him where he is. *Nilibuhan, nirago'osan.* Looked everywhere, done thoroughly. (*Thesaurus:* **batuk₂, jadja' 1.1, lalag, nda' 1.1, salusu**)

**libug** *n.* A cluster of houses, generally connected by walkways and occupied by members of a kindred. *Dalibug-libug kami.* We are from the same house-cluster. (*Thesaurus:* **kaluma'an, kampung₂, le'od₁, lūng 1, nibung, tumpuk 2**)

**paglibug** *v. intr. aN-* To reside in the same locality; to be neighbors.

**libun** *v. tr.* To enclose something to prevent it from being seen or exposed. *Nilibun, sali' binilik. Mbal pinagluwas-luwas supaya mbal aettom. Subay na pa'in apote'.* She is kept out of sight, kind of confined to a room, not allowed to keep going out lest she be darkened [by the sun]. She must stay pale. *Aniya' isāb buwa' kayu nilibun, niād ko da'a niā'.* There are also fruit that are enclosed, fenced in so as not to be taken. (*Thesaurus:* **kumbis 1.1**)

**libunan** *n.* An enclosed area.

**libusaw** (var. **dibusaw**) *n.* **1)** Pieces of cooking banana or sweet potato fried and coated with a sugar glaze. (*Thesaurus:* **juwalan, piritu**) **1.1)** *v. tr.* To coat items such as boiled sweet potato or fried cooking banana with a sugar glaze. *Bang binamban atoho', bo' nilibusaw, tahinang lapuk-lapuk.* When boiled cassava is dry and is fried and coated with a glaze, it becomes a crispy confection.

**paglibusaw** *n.* **1)** A method of cooking glazed bananas. *Asarap paglibusaw si Ig.* Ig's method of cooking glazed bananas is delicious. **1.1)** *v. intr. aN-* To cook glazed bananas, especially as a way of earning a living.

**libut** (var. **liput₂**) *adj. zero* **1)** Behind an intervening object. *Libut na min bukut hangkan halam ta'nda'.* Round the back now, that's why it isn't seen. **1.1)** *v. intr. pa-* To go around an obstruction. *Bang kami amusay ni Sisangat, palibut kami sudju Lapak.* When we paddle to Sisangat, we go around [a shallow] towards Lapak. (*Thesaurus:* **kulibut, liku', likuwad 1**) **1.2)** *v. tr.* To circumnavigate or go around something. *Liputta Būd Siganggang.* We circumnavigate Mt Siganggang.

**katilibut** *n.* The entire area surrounding a reference location. *Katilibut itū ma dakayu' lahat.* The area surrounding a particular place. *Angamata-mata ma katilibut paglahat.* Spying on the entire region. *Paheya na pa'in bono' sampay angabut na ni katilibut lahat inān.* The fighting kept increasing until it reached that entire land. (*cf:* **karuwambila'**; *Thesaurus:* **katilingkal, sakalingkal**)

**paglibut** *v. intr. aN-* To go around an obstacle or point of reference. *Bang kita magpiknik ni Singkona maglibutan kita, magbeklo'an sali'.* When we go to Cincona for a picnic, we go by a roundabout way, turn after turn. *Nilango na iya maglibut-libut ma pamiha'an sīn.* He is now dizzy from going around looking for money. *Bang kami magembet maglibut-libut kami.* When we play tag we run round and round.

**sakalibut** *n.* The entire region surrounding a reference location.

**likawan** *n.* Something that keeps coming into a person's mind. *Aheka likawanna bang magsuli-*

*suli.* He has a lot of diverse things in mind when you are talking with him.

**likid** *v. intr. pa-* To rebound, of a curse on its source. *Bang pantakta palikid ni kita, sali' paliyu ni kita.* When a spell we cast rebounds on us, it's as though it comes back to us. (*Thesaurus:* **balik₂, bīng₃, bitung, hili, pagbintu, pagpatimpa, pelleng 1.2**)

**liking** *n.* **1)** A sweetmeat made from the juice of ripe mangoes. (*cf:* **kende 1.1**) **1.1)** *v. tr.* To make such a sweetmeat of ripe mangoes.

**liksi** *var. of* **lissi**

**liku'** *v. intr. pa-* To go in different directions; to take another path. *Liku' min Tuhan; atawa liku' min lān.* Turning away from God; or getting off the track. (*Thesaurus:* **kulibut, libut 1.1, likuwad 1**)

**likup** *n.* **1)** A chisel-like tool for making holes in wood. (*Thesaurus:* **pa'at 1, patuk, sakal, sangkap 1, sosokan**) **1.1)** *v. tr.* To make a hole in wood using a tool with a cutting tip. *Pangalikup tapi', buwat barena, pangalowang.* For drilling into canoe strakes, like a brace and bit, for making holes.

**likus** *v. tr.* **1)** To enclose someone or something. *Bang aniya' kinawin subay nilikus d'nda, subay pinabatal l'lla bo' yampa ta'nda' d'nda.* When there is a wedding the bride must be enclosed in a room, and the groom should be made free of restrictions [between sexes]before seeing the bride. *Tinēt ba'anan sēk ma parang ati nilikus maka mital.* A lot of [shark] fins are spread out on the grass and enclosed in roofing iron. **1.1)** *v. tr. -an* To place an enclosure around someone. *Nilikusan kami min dahū'an maka min bukutan.* We were closed in to the front and to the rear.

**likusan** *n.* An enclosed partition; specifically, the enclosure in which a bride waits with her attendants. (*Thesaurus:* **ād 1, apis 1, buluyan, koral 1, kumbangan, kumbisan, sasak 1**)

**likut** *n.* **1)** Absence from one's home place. *Bay amatay ma likutnu, tuwan.* She died in your absence, friend. (*cf:* **absen, bukut₂**) **1.1)** *v. intr. pa-* To be away from one's home place. *Bang sali' aniya' bay tambukuta, buwat matto'ata, bo' aniya' bay sehe' sigā makapina'an ni luma' kami. Tinilaw sigā bang ma'ai si Mma'. Yukku, "Wa'i makalikut angusaha."* When we have sent someone a message, our elders for example, and someone who had been with them went to our house. The question was asked where Dad was. I said, "He is away working."

**kalikutan** *n.* Absence from home location. *T'llu pitu' min kalikutannu, ya na kapaglahi sigām.* Three weeks from your going away, that's when they eloped. *Buwatna si'itku wa'i atulak, na in dauranakanna maganak ma kalikutanna na.* The example of your uncle going away, and his siblings having children in his absence.

**likutan** *n.* The absence of someone from his usual location. (*cf:* **tulakan**)

**likuwad** *v. intr. pa-* **1)** To avoid an intervening object; to go around an obstacle; to circumnavigate something. *Bang bay buwat pelangnu ma dilaut, subay pinalikuwad min bukut pū' bo' da'a tinangkaw.* Like when your canoe is out at sea, you should go around the back of the island so it won't be stolen. *Palikuwad ka man dambila' luma'.* Go round by the side of the house. (*Thesaurus:* **kulibut, libut 1.1, liku'**) **1.1)** *v. tr. -an* To omit or bypass an intermediate item. *Nilikuwaran llaw-llaw.* Alternate days. (*Thesaurus:* **labay₁ 1, liyus 1.1, paglipuwas, pagsulabay, pintas 1, timbay 1**)

**paglikuwad** *v. intr. aN-* To pass each other without making eye contact. *Bay kami maglikuwad, halam bay mag'nda'.* We passed without noticing each other, didn't see each other.

**līd** *var. of* **lihid**

**liddas** *var. of* **ligdas**

**lidjal** *n.* A child who dies at birth after an extended time in the womb and who rapidly turns to stone. *Lidjal itū mbal ajukup, ala'at luwana, luwa munyeka ariki'. Bang pasōng llaw anumbaga. Bang ta'abut ganta'anna amatay. Mbal takubul. Subay ginantung ma luma', pinas'mmekan. Mbal abuhuk. Subay aniya' anunggu'an iya ma luma'. Saumul-umul buwattē'.* This lidjal [baby] is not complete, looks awful, with the appearance of a small doll. As days go by it turns coppery. Dies when its time comes. It is not buried. Should be hung up in the house, clothed. It does not decay and someone should guard it in the house. Like that forever.

**lidjiki'** (*var.* **didjiki'**) *n.* **1)** Blessing; good fortune of a material kind, especially the provision of daily supplies. *Kalu-kalu aniya' lidjiki' min Tuhan, pinahampit pa'in kami.* Maybe there will be blessing from God, we may be given a share in it. *Tau'un pahogot. Sali' gusi' pamalidjiki' ma kita.* Store it securely. It's like a magic money box for bringing us good fortune. (*Thesaurus:* **anughala' 1, apuwa, barakat 1, hirayat, pahala'**) **1.1)** *v. tr. -an* To bless someone with material benefits, usually with God as source. *Bang niulanan, nilidjiki'an.* When rained on, blessed with resources.

**ligad** *v. intr. pa-* To fall down flat. *Pagligadna na pa'in, dumahū kōkna ni semento magtūy kapali'an.* When he fell down, his head hit the concrete first and he sustained a wound. *Mbal du iya pat'ggol allum pagka buwattē' pagligadna.* He will not live long, having fallen down like that. (*Thesaurus:* **hantak₁ 1, h'bba', lintuwad 1, pungkad, timpuwad 1**)

**ligap** *n.* **1)** A distraction from the job in hand. *Tabowa ligapna, hangkan alungay sīn ī'.* [He was] influenced by his preoccupation with other things, hence the money was lost. **1.1)** *v. tr.* To give one's attention to something other than the job in hand. *Bang ka maghinang da'a ka angaligap saddī.* When you are working don't set your mind on other things. *Aheka niligap. Sinoho' kami am'lli-m'lli, puwas am'lli sinoho' na amole'. Am'lli kami bo' mbal amole', hal maglunsulan, ang'nda'-ng'nda' ma katindahan.* Distracted by lots of things. We are sent to buy this and that, and told to go home again after buying. We did the buying but didn't go home, just strolled about, looking at the shops.

**ligaw** *n.* Incoherence, of speech.

**kaligawan** *n.* Incoherent speech; babble. *Tabowa iya palamud ma sigām magbissala kaligawan.* He was influenced to participate with them in talking nonsense.

**pagligaw** *v. intr. aN-* To talk foolishly; to babble. *Magligaw e'na magkalang dinsini'.* He sang nonsense words earlier. *Magligaw, mbal ah'lling ahāp.* Babbling, not saying good things.

**ligay** *v. advrs. -in-* Encrusted with growth, as old buildings.

**ligaya** *n.* A record-player; a phonograph record. *Ligaya, ya amah'lling ina'an mareyom paggabbang.* A record player, the thing that plays during a bamboo marimba session. (*Thesaurus:* **plaka, ulehem**)

**ligayan** *n.* A tree species; a source of strong wood suitable for making outrigger booms.

**ligdas** (var. **liddas; liras**) *v. intr. pa-/-um-* To lose one's footing; to slip off. *Bang aku lum'ngngan man batu, paliddas tape'ku. Paligid itū, humantak kita.* When I am walking on the rocks, my feet slip off. *Ligid* means slipping down lower, as when we fall down hard. *Bay paligdas tape'na, wa'i patulelle' ahūg pareyo'.* His feet slipped and he fell down, arms flailing. (*Thesaurus:* **dasdas, deklas, ligid₂ 1, lisad, lisig, lumintiyad**)

**ligid₁** *v. tr.* To dissolve something by moving it around the mouth with the tongue. *Ni'inay tambal itū, pinapa' atawa niligid?* What's to be done with this pill, chewed or rolled around my mouth? (*Thesaurus:* **dutdut, s'ssop, tamus**)

**ligid₂** *v. intr. pa-/-um-* **1)** To fall over or down. *Bang alu'ud-lu'ud lān, bo' kita ni bohe', lumigid kita.* If the path is slippery and we go to fetch water, we slip off. *Bang lahi-lahi si Arung, paligid sumantuk ma lantay, anangis.* When Oldest daughter runs she slips down, banging her head and crying. *Bay aku paligid min pantān.* I fell from the decking. (*Thesaurus:* **dasdas, deklas, ligdas, lisad, lisig, lumintiyad**) **1.1)** *v. tr. -an* To push something out of the way. *Ligirin batu ilū, sinigayan.* Push that stone out of the way, get rid of it.

**ligis₁** *v. tr.* To crush something hard between solid objects in order to produce powder. (*Thesaurus:* **pedjet, pipis**)

**ligis₂** *adj. a-* Dead by violence, of the members of an entire group. *Bay sigām sinōd luma' tonga' bahangi bo' nilagut, aligis kamemon, halam kinapinan.* Their house was invaded in the middle of the night and they were slashed, everyone slaughtered, none left. (*Thesaurus:* **laglag 1.1, pagbugbug**)

**pagligis** *v. intr. aN-* To die together in large numbers, as the result of epidemic, disease or warfare.

**lig'tto'** *n.* A species of plant, the root of which is used medicinally. *Salacia integrifolia.*

**ligmun** var. of **limun**

**ligoto'** *adj. a-* Suffering from depression. (*Thesaurus:* **bingaw, buriru, lambang-mata 1, lengog kōk**)

**ligpit** *n.* **1)** A batten or lath. (*Thesaurus:* **bola', gipis 1, lantay 1**) **1.1)** *v. tr.* To hold roofing or walling in place by fastening with battens. *Pinapagd'ppak tiyadtad ampa niligpit.* The bamboo is beaten flat before battening it in place.

**pagligpit** *v. intr. aN-* To hold something down by laying heavy items across it. *"Pahigin ka pehē', Oto', da'a magligpit."* "Move that way, Son, don't lay [your legs] over me."

**ligtang** *n.* **1)** Mast stays (supporting ropes). **1.1)** *v. tr.* To stay the mast of a canoe with a rope from mast to outriggers.

**ligtung** (var. **ligtuwang**) *n.* A specified period of time. *Ligtungna duwa pitu'.* Her time [away] is two weeks. *Subay ganta' tugpangta tahunna, bulanna, llawna, ligtung ē'.* We should for example specify how many years, months, or days, the time period is to be. *Halam aku bay makakakan daligtung. Bay aku animpus dang'llaw.* I haven't eaten for one time period. I lasted one day. (*Thesaurus:* **idda 1.1, ora, pagtaratu, tugna', tugun 1.1, waktu 1.1**)

**ligtuwang** var. of **ligtung**

**ligu** *n.* **1)** A winnowing basket. *Am'lli aku ligu pagp'kkalanku panggi'.* I will buy a winnowing basket for breaking squeezed cassava up into fragments. **2)** A large tray. *Ligu, lling s'ddopan. Bang ma kami langguway. Ligu* [a tray] is a southern word. With us it is called a *langguway.*

**ligu'** *v. tr.* To wash a body in preparation for burial. *Niligu' dahū in mayat bo' pinutus maka kuku-pote'.* The body is first cleansed, then wrapped in white cloth.

**liha-liha** *v. advrs. -in-* Absent-minded; forgetful. *Asāl niliha-liha si Ji.* Ji is by nature forgetful. (*Thesaurus:* **bibas₂, kalipat 1, lipas, panglupa**)

**lihal** *see:* **palihalan**

**lihan** *v. intr. aN-* **1)** To live temporarily in a place, as for work. *Bang kami atulak ni kanusahan angalihan kami ni Tahu.* When we depart for the islands we stay at Tahu. (*Thesaurus:* **hanti' 1, pustu 1.1, tingan, tingkap**) **1.1)** *v. intr. pa-* To stay in temporary housing. *Luma' tolda ya palihanan kami ma timpu bono'.* Our accommodation in the war time was a tent.

**lihanan** *n.* A place where one camps for a period, as when fishing for a living.

**paglihan** *v. intr.* aN- To reside in a place for a limited period. *Saga tuwan, aku itu a'a liyu maglihan sadja ma deyomanbi.* Sirs, I am a stranger just living temporarily among you. *Buwat kita bay maglihan ma Pasonangka' t'llu pitu'. Ganta' paghanti'-hanti'an ba.* Like when we stayed for three weeks at Pasonanca. Temporary acccomodation as it were. *Ya na hē' waktu kapaglihan saga bangsa Isra'il ma paslangan.* That was the time when the nation of Israel stayed for a time out in the barren lands.

**paglihanan** *n.* A place to stay for a limited time. *Ya parunggu'an inān mbal ahāp paglihanan bang salta' timpu pamaliyu.* That harbor was not a good place to stay in during the windy season.

**palihanan** *n.* Temporary accommodation.

**lihaw** *adj.* a- 1) Clear, of a liquid. 1.1) *v. intr.* pa- To let a liquid settle and clarify. *Pinalihaw-lihaw gi', aniya' autna.* Let it settle a bit, there are specks of sediment. (*Thesaurus:* **labay bahangi, pato'ong, patuli**)

**lihi** 1) *n.* Desirable features acquired by imitating or observing those who have them. *Sinangbay he'na si Gi pangā'an lihi bo' supaya buwattē'.* She holds and sings to Gi in order to acquire features like hers [for the baby in her womb]. *Ya tu'ud lihita, par'ngngo'.* Our acquired feature is simply to speak rarely. *"Bang pa'in aku," yukna, "taga anak buwattē'." Panga'anna lihi ko' inān.* "May I have a child like that," she said. That's her way of getting the desired feature. (*cf:* **piguhan**) 1.1) *v. intr.* aN- To seek the desirable features or qualities of another person. *Angalihi aku ni ka'a, ai-ai hinangnu lihi'anku, sali' angihid.* I emulate you, doing whatever you do, like I am envious. 1.2) *v. tr.* -an To transfer to someone the desirable characteristics of another. *Kalu aku nilihi'an ai-ai hinangnu. Beya'anku sadja.* Perhaps I will acquire [your] characteristics in whatever you do. I simply copy them. 2) *v. advrs.* ka-...-an To have inherited characteristics passed on from a relative. *Kalihi'an ka e' bapa'nu angkan abantut.* You have got characteristics from your uncle, that's why you have feminine leanings.

**lihi-lihi** *n.* A shortcoming in the looks, quality or abilities of a person. *Halam aniya' lihi-lihina, halam aniya' kulang-kulangna.* He has no shortcomings, nothing at all is lacking.

**lihid** (var. **līd**) *v. intr.* pa- To tilt away from the vertical, as a heavenly body declining from its zenith. *Palīd na man ugtu.* [The sun] is past the noon position. *Pagdakdakku subu lagi', yampa tapole' palīd na man ugtu-llaw.* Doing the laundry since morning, I only got home when [the sun] had declined from noon. (*Thesaurus:* **kīd₂, kīng 1.1, lemba, lenggang, paglilip-lilip, poyog 1, tīg**)

**lihing** *v. intr.* pa- To fill with tears, of the eyes of someone about to cry. *Takalena pa'in kalangan, palihing magtūy bohe'-matana.* When she heard the singing her eyes were filled with tears. (*Thesaurus:* **asang-selo, llad, tangis 1.1**)

**li'ad** *v. tr.* To move something by applying leverage. *Bay nili'ad emponku e' magdadarut empon.* My tooth was levered out by the tooth extractor. (*Thesaurus:* **landak, lugit, suwal 1**)

**li'an** *v. advrs.* -in- Prone to rambling or incoherent speech, as when senile. *Amissalahan dīna matto'a inān. Nili'anan na.* The old man speaks to himself. He has become senile.

**pagli'anun** (var. **pagli'anan**) *v. intr.* aN- To talk to oneself in senility. *Magli'an-li'an sadja ina'ku to'a.* My grandmother just mutters to herself. *Hal magli'anun.* Just mumbling. (*Thesaurus:* **pagbarese-barese, pagsilap**)

**li'i-li'i** *see:* **pagli'i-li'i, pagsingkali'i-li'i**

**li'id** *v. intr.* pa- 1) To press hard against something. *Ōy, da'a ka pali'id ni aku.* Hey! Don't lean against me. (*Thesaurus:* **sandig 1, saray-saray**) 1.1) *v. tr.* To push something by leaning. *Da'a aku li'irun ba.* Don't push me [by leaning].

**pagli'id** *v. intr.* aN- To be leaning against each other. *Magli'id-li'id kuting ma anak Milikan ē'. Addat sigām.* The cat and the Westerner's child snuggle together. It's their habit.

**li'in** *n.* 1) An item of food prohibited because of sickness or ritual restrictions. (*cf:* **sukang 1**) 1.1) *v. intr.* aN- To observe restrictions on certain foods in order to heal or prevent a sickness, especially while a ritual ancestor is being invoked. *Buwat bang aniya' p'ngkongta bo' kita tinambalan, mbal kita makakakan daing keyat, subay kita angali'in.* Like when we have a swelling and are being treated, we cannot eat red fish, we must observe the restriction. 1.2) *v. tr.* -an To impose a dietary restriction for health reasons.

**li'is** *v. tr.* To grate fibrous vegetable material into small particles. *Gandum nili'is, ubus nili'is i', na base'-base'ta maka bohe'. Na amene' na kita, sokalanta, lahinganta.* Corn is grated, then after being grated we wet it a little with water. Then we choose whether to add sugar or grated coconut. *Gandum nili'is, ubus nili'is i', na base'-base'ta maka bohe'. Na amene' na kita, sokalanta, lahinganta. Apuwas i'-i, ni'isi ni kuwitna gandum abō' bin'lla na.* Corn is grated, then after being grated we wet it a little with water. Then we choose whether to add sugar or [grated] coconut. After that, it is put into the corn skin and boiled. (*Thesaurus:* **kugut₁, jangat**)

**li'isan** *n.* An implement for grating fibrous material, consisting of a metal sheet with multiple spikes.

**lilap** *v. advrs.* ta- Overcome by drowsiness. *Talilap aku hangkan halam tasayuku ulan.* I was overcome by drowsiness, that's why I wasn't aware of the rain. *Sali' aku aningkō' pasandig,* *sakali talilap aku tinuli.* Like me sitting, leaning against something, promptly overcome by sleep. (*Thesaurus:* **karu' 1.1, lambung tuli, tuli₁ 1.1**)

**paglilap** *v. intr. aN-* To drift off to sleep.

**lilay** *v. tr.* To distinguish among alternatives. *Lilayun usaha, ginihay, pinasaddī.* Arrange the work properly, divided up, separated out. (*Thesaurus:* **gintil 1.1, paggihay 1, sila' 1.1, silang₁ 1.1, sisig**)

**lili** *see:* **palilihan**

**liling** *v. tr.* To examine something carefully. *Bang kita ni M'ddas am'lli hōs subay nililing dahū, sabab aniya' ahāp, aniya' ala'at.* When we go to Siasi to buy a sarong we should examine it first, because there are good ones and bad. *Bang aku am'lli pelang ma Basilan ma Samehakan, subay aku angaliling dahū.* If I buy a canoe on Basilan from a Yakan, I have to inspect it first. *Pehē' ka patūy ni imam bo' palilingun barannu ma iya.* Go straight to the imam and have him examine your body. (*Thesaurus:* **banding, hunggaw 1.1, lawan, pandang, patong 1, pende**)

**pagliling** *v. intr. aN-* To look around cautiously. *Painsap ka, ilu aniya' mundu. Bang ka ni bohe' magliling-liling ka. Piligdu nilagut ka ma halam ta'nda'nu.* Be alert, there are bandits about. When you go to the water hole, be on guard. The fear is that you may be slashed without seeing it coming.

**lilip** *see:* **paglilip-lilip**

**lilla'** *adv.* Freely given; unreservedly. *Lilla' iya amatay ma bagayna.* He freely gave up his life for his friend. (*cf:* **hilas**)

**paglilla'** *v. tr.* To risk or surrender something of value, without holding anything back. *Maglilla' aku ma hukumannu.* I accept your verdict. *Paglilla'un ma aku.* Give it to me freely. *Bay paglilla'na kallumna waktu kapamono'na si Golayat.* He freely risked his life at the time of his killing Goliath.

**pangalilla'** *n.* Something given away, freely and totally.

**lilung** *v. tr.* To sell goods at auction; to sell things at bargain prices. (*Thesaurus:* **dagang, litu, pab'lli, pagsoroy, pa'andag 1, samsuy**)

**paglilung** *n.* 1) An auction; a bulk sale of goods. 1.1) *v. tr. -an* To sell goods in bulk. *Maglilung na bulawan ma padjak Tiyanggi.* Jewelry is currently being auctioned at the Jolo pawnshop. *S'mmek bay pags'mmek, ai-ai bay kapin min manusiya', paglilung e'na.* Clothing that has been used, anything people have cast off, he sells at bargain prices.

**lilus** (var. **delos**) *n.* A clock; a watch. *Saukat na ka taga lilus, mbal na ka pahali akiyum.* Just because you have a watch, you can't stop smiling.

**pagnililus** *v. intr. aN-* To wear a watch.

**lim** *see:* **kaliman**

**lima** *num.* Five. *Limang'llaw, limambulan,*

*limantahun.* Five days, five months, five years.

**paglima-waktu** *v. intr. aN-* To observe the five daily prayer times of Islam. (*Thesaurus:* **pagammal, pagsanittiya, pagta'at**)

**limad-limad** (var. **kulimad**) *n.* Newly hatched head lice. (*Thesaurus:* **kuman₁, kutu 1, lisa' 1, tuma 1**)

**limal** *v. tr.* To divine the unknown, as future events or the location of someone absent or of lost thing. *Nilimal itū sali' pinag'nda'.* Limal is similar to discerning the future. (*Thesaurus:* **alamat₁, kamot, pag'nda'₂, putika'**)

**paglimal** *v. intr. aN-* To divine something unknown. *Maglimal, sali' nih'kka tangan he' a'a talus.* Divining something, as with a hand-span measured by a seer.

**limampū'** *num.* Fifty.

**limanda** *see:* **paglimanda**

**limasu'** *adj. -an* 1) Over-heated due to fever. *Limasu'an baranna, subay pinainum tambal na magtūy bo' mbal katūyan ni'mmunan.* Her body is hot, she should be given medicine right away so she isn't completely feverish. (*Thesaurus:* **linganga, lingo'ot, pasu'₁ 1.1**) 1.1) *v. intr. aN-* To produce uncomfortable internal warmth. *Buwat aku bay tinandog, amole' ni palasahanku, magsalinggā aku, angalimasu' deyom baranku.* Like when I have malaria and it goes to where my symptoms are felt, I move restlessly and my internal body is painfully hot.

**limatok** *n.* A leech.

**limaya** *adj. zero* Free of responsibilities or worries. *Alimaya a'a bang halam utangna.* A man is free of worry when he has no debts. *Limaya baranku bang halam aniya' hinangku, hal aku ma luma'.* My body is at ease when I have no work to do, just myself in the house.

**kalimayahan** *n.* Freedom from restriction or stress.

**limayu'** (var. **linggayu'**) *v. advrs. -in-* Made uncomfortable from sitting too long in one position. *Magusaha kita, at'ggol kita tininduk. Na nilimayu' aku.* We are fishing, taking a long time to get a bite. I get uncomfortable from sitting in one position. *Nilimayu', sali' kita at'ggol aningkō', buwat ajaga, am'ssi. Sali' kita amale', magtoyo'an.* Limayu', like when sitting for a long time, like being on watch, or fishing. Like being weary, the head nodding.

**paglimayu'** *v. intr. aN-* To move restlessly due to discomfort from sitting too long in one position. *Minsan du maglinggayu' na ni karu', mbal na pa'in atuli.* Even though he is moving restlessly due to drowsiness, he still doesn't sleep. *Tinuli, maglinggayu' min paningkō'an.* Sleepy, fatigued from sitting up. (*Thesaurus:* **paglega-lega, paglimbahod, paglimpa, pagsalinggā, pagsularaw**)

**limbahod** *see:* **paglimbahod**

**limba'** *see:* **palimba'an, limba' pelang**

**limba' pelang** *n. phrase* Support poles to which the flooring or drying panels of a canoe are tied. *Limba' pelang itū pamahogotan ayas-ayas.* The tying poles of a canoe are for securing the drying racks.

**limbang** *n.* 1) A counterpart; the other member of a pair, as a marriage partner. (*Thesaurus:* **iring, ugpang 1, umbuk** 1) **1.1)** *adj. a-* Having a partner, specifically a marriage partner. *Halam aku alimbang.* I'm not married. **1.2)** *v. intr. pa-* To partner someone. *Buwat saupama ka'a taga h'nda, aniya' na limbangnu. Aniya' palimbang atuli.* You for example with a wife, you have a partner. You have someone to partner you as you sleep.

**limbang-sehe'** *n.* An associate; a co-worker.

**paglimbang** *v. tr.* To form a unit of two components; to be in a partner or spouse relationship. *Paglimbangun pelang ilū bo' mbal alungay.* Place those canoes together [and tie them] lest they get lost.

**paglimbang-kamatay** *v. intr. aN-* To be partners for life. {idiom} *Maglimbang-kamatay sigām minsan ai tumauwa' kasusahan.* They are partners for life no matter what sorrows fall.

**paglimbangan** *n.* A partnership; a marriage union. *Aku itu siyaka paglimbangan.* I am the oldest child of [this] marriage union.

**salimbang** *n.* A workmate.

**limbay** *v. tr.* To swing something at arm's length. *Palimbayta l'ngngonta karuwambila'.* We set both our arms swinging. *Da'a palimbayun basket.* Don't make the basket swing. *Hal bay nilimbayan e' sehe'na. Halam tinu'ud.* He was only swung at by his companion. Nothing serious.

**paglimbay** *v. intr. aN-* To swing arms in unison, of a group of people. *Buwat kita magl'ngngan, maglimbay.* Like us walking together, swinging [our arms]. (*cf:* **paglambeng-lambeng** 1.1)

**limbit** *n.* 1) A responsibility, especially for dependent family members. *Aheka limbitku.* I have many [children] to care for. *Angajanji' iya bang aniya' takdil l'lla bo' makasulut deyom pangatayanna ma halam limbitna, bang makapuwasan bu'unna min gamut nunuk inān, ya na nihinang h'lla e'na, yukna.* She promised that if there was a man who pleased her heart and had no obligations, if he could extricate her hair from the root of that strangler fig, he would be the one she would take as husband. That's what she said. *Bang aniya' l'lla halam limbitna, ya na ina'an nihinang h'lla e'na, yukna.* She said that if there was a man who had no family obligations, he was the one she would take as husband. **1.1)** *adj. a-* Burdened by a sense of responsibility. *Bang aku ala'an min luma', bo' halam aniya' anunggu', alimbit aku. Aheya ma atayku maka asusa aku.* If I leave the house and no one is watching it, then I feel responsible. It is important to me and I am worried. *Mbal kami*

*makajari pehē' kamemon, bo' mbal kami hal makalimbit ma ka'a.* We cannot all go there, lest we just make things difficult for you. (*cf:* **bimbang 1, gaggat 1**) **1.2)** *v. tr. -an* To cause someone to feel responsibility for something.

**kalimbitan** *n.* 1) A limitation due to one's responsibilites. *Mbal aku paluruk, aniya' kalimbitanku.* I won't go [to the wedding], there are things I feel responsible for. **1.1)** *v. advrs. ka-...-an* To feel restricted by responsibilities. *Kinalimbitan, kinabimbangan sali'.* Restricted [by responsibility], like being bothered by something.

**kalimbit** *n.* A responsibility which limits one's freedom.

**pagkalimbit** *v. intr. aN-* To be responsible for one's family members.

**limbokay** *see:* **paglimbokay**

**limbōn** *v. intr. aN-* To swirl around inside an enclosure, of steam or smoke. *Humbu amalikan ni kita, angalimbōn.* Smoke blows back at us, swirling around. (*cf:* **paglimbokay**; *Thesaurus:* **asu-asu 1.1, humbu 1.1, husbu 1.1**)

**paglimbōn** *v. intr. aN-* To experience churning in one's intestines, as from indigestion. *P'ddi' ai bahā' maglimbōn ma deyom baranku?* What sort of pain is this that is churning inside my body?

**limbu** *n.* 1) A physical feature that provides shelter or shade. *Buwat luma' si Pu katampalan he' baliyu, sali' halam aniya' limbuna.* Like Pu's house exposed to the wind, like it lacks shelter. **1.1)** *v. intr. pa-* To get in the way of light or wind. *Da'a ka palimbu, mbal aku maka'nda'.* Don't block [the light], I can't see. (*Thesaurus:* **lindung 1, pulipus 1.1, silung₁, sindung₁**) **1.2)** *v. intr. pa-* To take shelter behind an object. *Bang alandos s'llog, bang mbal makasagga', palimbu ka.* If the current is strong and you can't make headway, take shelter. **1.3)** *v. tr. -an* To cast a shadow on something by getting in the way of light. *Da'a limbuhin, Oto', itiya' aku amahāp kulaet.* Don't block the light, Son, I'm in process of repairing the pressure lantern. **1.4)** *v. advrs. ka-...-an* To be sheltered from the effects of a force such as wind or the thrust of a propeller.

**palimbuhan** *n.* A place of shelter.

**limbuku'** *v. tr. -an* To propel a coconut held between the thighs towards a target, a move in the game of luhu'. (*syn:* **hamput**)

**limbung** *adj. zero* 1) Something kept secret. *Limbung kaisunan sigā.* Their planning is kept secret. (*cf:* **buli'-akkal**) **1.1)** *v. tr. -an* To deceive someone by withholding information. *Aniya' buwat aku ina'an angamu' pinta, yukna inān, "Halam na," malaingkan masi. Hatina mbal pamuwanna pinta ina'an. Aku nilimbungan.* Like that time when I asked for some paint, and he said, "There isn't any," but in fact there is still some. It simply means he won't give that paint. I am deceived. *Ai untungna bang bono'ta siyalita* *itu bo' limbunganta kamatayna?* What's the profit if we kill our younger brother and conceal his death? (*Thesaurus:* **hegom-hegom**)

**paglimbung** *v. tr.* -an To keep things secret from one another. *Da'a ka maglimbung min aku.* Don't keep things back from me.

**limbunga** *n.* An inland tree species valued for its timber. (*syn:* **tima'al**)

**limogmog** *adj. a-* 1) Confusing; unresolved, of an issue being discussed. *Alimogmog kagara'an. Sali' mbal magtaluwa' kagara'an, mbal ausay sali'.* The discussion is inconclusive. There is no agreement, it isn't resolved. *Alimogmog na kita bang kita alasig.* We speak confusingly when we are having fun. 1.1) *v. tr.* To confuse someone. *Bay kita makaindam ni a'a. Limogmogta iya yukta, "Wa'i ma luma' a'a." Bo' pa'in itiya'.* We had borrowed something from someone. We confuse him by saying, "It's at someone's place." But it's actually right here.

**limomo** (*var.* **limumu**) *v. intr. aN-* To lose edible flesh, of some crab species when not cooked promptly after catching. *Angalimomo bang mbal magtūy tab'lla ina' kagong.* The female crab if not immediately cooked looses volume. *B'llahun agtūy sangbaw inān bo' mbal angalimumu. Buwat kagong bang amula'-mula' bowa'na, kata'uhanta ala'an na isina.* Cook that deep-sea crab immediately so it won't decrease in volume. Like a crab when its mouth is still foaming, we know its flesh is gone.

**limpa** *see:* **paglimpa**

**limpa'** *n.* 1) An imprint, as fingerprints, footprint or spoor; wheel-marks; scarring. *Tanda' limpa' tanganna, angkan kinata'uhan.* The print of his hand could be seen, which is how we knew. *Basta bay tauwa' laring, ya hē' ap'llod, ya limpa' laring.* Whenever something has been touched with a knife, that is *p'llod*, the imprint of a knife. 1.1) *v. intr. aN-* To leave a distinguishing mark. (*cf:* **m'ndal**)

**limpowak** *n.* An eddy or swirl, of wind.

**paglimpowak** *v. intr. aN-* To eddy around a sheltering feature, of wind. *Baliyu maglimpowak, baliyu min lahatta satan. Bang kita taluwa' limbu, magtūy baliyu minnē'. Pagpuwasta man limbu yampa isāb satan.* The wind eddying around, a wind southwest from our place. When we come under the lee, there's a wind from the other direction. As soon as we get out of the lee, it's the southwest wind again. (*syn:* **paglimbokay**)

**limumu** *var. of* **limomo**

**limun** (*var.* **ligmun**) *adj. a-* 1) Out of sight; invisible, as an island below the horizon. *Marilaut kami Duwa-bullud, alimun Tongkel.* When we are at sea off Duwa-Bullud Island, Tongkel is unseen, below the horizon. *Bay ma waktu kamatto'ahan kasehē'an, bang sigām magbono', amowa sigām habay-habay bo' aligmun.* In the time of some of our forebears,

when they fought, they wore charms to make them invisible. *Pagtalumpung itū aniya' na leha, alimun-limun ta'nda'. Apas kami na isāb.* On looking through the telescope there was a sail, disappearing from sight below the horizon. We still followed it. (*Thesaurus:* **kanop, letop 1, lonob 1**) 1.1) *v. tr.* -an To submerge something below the surface. *Nilimunan munda' paraw ko da'a ta'nda'.* The bow of the *paraw* canoe is below the surface and so cannot be seen.

**limut** *n.* 1) Critical speech. 1.1) *v. tr.* To speak ill of someone, especially in his absence. *Saupama taikutan kita, nilimut kita ni saga a'a.* If for example we are excluded, we are spoken ill of by people. *Bang sali' aniya' angamu' ni ka'a buwat saga lansang, yuknu, "Ka'a ilū angamu' lansang ni aku, mbal aku buwanannu daing." Angalimut sadja ka bang aku kabuwanan daing."* Like when someone asks you for something such as nails, and you say, "You ask me for nails, but you don't give me fish." You just criticize if I am given fish. (*Thesaurus:* **pagpa'andig, pagpara'il, pataggal-taggal, salig₃**)

**limuti'** *v. intr. aN-* To turn white. *Bang hati angalimuti' bū ma kuwit a'a inān, hatina ni'ipul.* If the body hair on someone turns white, it means that he is infected with a skin disease. (*Thesaurus:* **āp-āp 1, kamuti', nilastung, panaw 1**)

**linaw** *n.* The sea persimmon, a swamp tree. *Diospyros maritima.*

**lindang** *n.* 1) A love charm. (*cf:* **sulat-libun, suratan**) 1.1) *v. tr.* To attract a woman by means of a love charm. *Bay talindang, hangkan iya bilahi ma si Ab.* She was influenced by a love charm, that is why she desires. Ab. *Bang aniya' d'nda kabaya'anta, na lindangta. Bang taluwa' ma ilmu' pangalindanganta, mbal makasandal. Lum'ngngan ni luma'ta.* If there is some woman whom we desire, we put a charm on her. When she is struck by our charm's magic, she can't resist. She comes to our house. *Bang aniya' l'lla angalindang d'nda inān, yukna ginampangan bo' mbal tauwa' hinang-hinang.* If a man puts a love-spell on that woman, she says she is protected against influence from sorcery.

**lindi** *adj. a-* 1) Dissatisfied or envious of another's status or possessions. *Wa'i angandundang si Li, na alindi si Po.* Li is swinging away on the swing, so Po is jealous. (*Thesaurus:* **abuggu', himuggu', iggil 1.1, imbū, jelus, jingki 1**) 1.1) *v. tr.* -an To covet another person's status or possessions. *Mbal sigām magsulut sabab angalindihan ya bihing luma'na.* They are not in accord because she aspires to outdo her neighbours. *Lindihanta ka ma sabab badju'nu baha'u.* I envy you because of your new shirt.

**paglindi** *v. intr. aN-* To be mutually envious and competitive. *Buwat anakku d'nda inān, subay pagsambalnu bang b'llihannu ai-ai ko da'a* *maglindi-lindihan.* Like your two daughters, you have to treat them alike when you buy them anything, so they aren't jealous of each another.

**lindu** *n.* Longing for someone who is not present.

**paglindu** *v. intr.* aN- To be in a state of deep grief for someone who has died. *Buwat balu bay magkalasa maka bay h'llana, sali' maglindu.* Like a widow who was in love with her husband, she grieves for him. (*Thesaurus:* **handul atay, pagdohon, pagdukka' 1.1, paglemong 1.1**)

**paglindu-dandam** (var. **pagdandam-lindu**) *v. tr.* -an To experience intense longing for a deceased or absent loved one. *Pinaglinduhan-dandam, buwat balu bay magkalasa maka bay h'llana.* Deep longing, like a widow who was in love with her former husband. *Sali' angentom to'ongan, magdandam-lindu kita, buwat sali' aniya' amatay ma kita.* Missing [someone] very much, we long deeply, as when someone of ours has died.

**lindu-dandam** *see:* **lindu**

**lindung** *n.* 1) An area shaded from direct sunlight. *Ahāp aniya' lindung pahali-hali'an pole' min deya.* It is good to have a shady place to rest under on arrival home from inland. *Hinabu sigām amangan, si Ibrahim magbaran amuhatan sigām ma lindung kayu.* While they were eating Abraham himself served them in the shade of a tree. (*Thesaurus:* **limbu 1.1, pulipus 1.1, silung₁, sindung₁**) 2) A shadow; reflection; silhouette.

**linig** (var. **inig**) *n.* 1) Gloss; sheen. 1.1) *adj.* a- Shiny or glossy, of a surface. 1.2) *v. intr.* aN- To shine or glisten, of a surface. *Angalinig tuktukna bang nihulasan.* His forehead glistens when it is sweating. *Bang bay angamirul, na ni'llawan s'mmek ē'. Na, bang atoho' na, pinilinsa na. Na, bo' angalinig pantalun ē', na, kinabaya'an kita e' budjang!* When they have done the starching, the clothes are put out to dry. Once dry they're ironed. Then those trousers gleam and the maidens desire us! *Ya tapagguna e' sigām saga tumbaga angalinig, ya bay pagsasaminan saga kar'ndahan.* What they used was brassware that shone, used as mirrors by the womenfolk.

**linis** *adj.* a- Worn down and no longer functional. *Alinis na katas-balan itū.* This emery paper is worn smooth. *Makajari kita magkahāp, yukna, bang punduk kamatto'ahan, atawa bang patangkob langit, atawa bang alinis būd itu.* "It will be possible for us to be reconciled," he said, "when the ancestors rise [from their graves], or the sky is closed over, or this mountain is worn to nothing." (*Thesaurus:* **litib, pasaw, pupud 1.1**)

**linsungan** *n.* A large mortar for pounding rice. *Ingga sasuku saga a'a ab'ttong subay pinandi ma linsungan dok mbal ni'ila. Waktu isāb nilahu' bulan.* Whenever there is a pregnant woman she should be bathed in a mortar so the baby will not have birthmarks. At the time of a lunar eclipse, that is. (*cf:* **hallu**)

**lintang** *n.* 1) The protective framework of a clay firebox which protects nearby woodwork from catching fire. 1.1) *v. tr.* To enclose a clay firebox in an insulating framework. *Bay amu'ku p'ttung pangalintangku lapohan.* I asked for some bamboo to insulate the firebox.

**lintas** *v. intr.* pa- To relocate. *Palintas pehē' ni M'ddas, mbal na magbīng-bīng.* Transferring to Siasi, no longer going to and fro. *Buwat onde'-onde' bang ulan, pinalintas ni deyo' luma' dakayu'.* Like children when it rains, sent away [to shelter] beneath another house. (*Thesaurus:* **k'tta 1, laktas, lagedled 1, laud 1, pagtagestes, pagtaleted, untas 1**)

**lintasan** *n.* The extent or duration of a journey. *Ya lintasanna duwa-duwang'llaw.* The duration of the trip is two days or so.

**lintonga'** *see:* **samalintonga'**

**lintuwad** *v. intr.* pa- 1) To fall prostrate. *Buwat kayu bay agabuk, na bo' taluwa' baliyu, hal palintuwad.* Like a tree that has decayed, when it is hit by the wind it just falls down. *Halam ganta' bay ai maka ai, taggaha' hal patuwad.* When, let's suppose, nothing at all had happened, he suddenly fell prostrate. (*Thesaurus:* **hantak₁ 1, h'bba', ligad, pungkad, timpuwad 1**) 1.1) *v. tr.* -an To cause something to fall down flat. *Lintuwaranta ka, ameya' ka paligad.* I will push you over, down you'll fall.

**linukan** *n.* A skill or occupation handed down from the previous generation. *Linukan magbubungsud saga kamatto'ahan ma Tinutu'.* Fishing with permanent traps, an inherited skill of the older people in Tinoto.

**linug₁** *n.* An earthquake. *Dunya itu pajogjog maka alinug, ya saga hāg sulga' magginsilan.* The earth shook and quaked, the posts of heaven moving about. *Taggaha' sadja aniya' linug akosog, ajogjog papagan kalabusu inān.* Suddenly there was a big earthquake, and the foundations of the jail shook. (*Thesaurus:* **jogjog deyom dunya**)

**linug₂** *v. tr.* -an To remove dirt or scraps from plates by running water over them. *Nilinugan pamanganan yamboho' sinabunan.* The dishes are rinsed and after that washed with soap. (*Thesaurus:* **kulling, timud 1.1**)

**linga-linga** *see:* **paglinga-linga**

**lingan** (var. **ingan**) *v. tr.* -an 1) To call out to someone; to summon someone. *Linganin pa'in aku bang kām palabay.* Call to me when you are passing by. *Nilinganan saga tendogna.* His tenants were summoned. *Saupama angalingan. "Bay na ngā'nu ai-ai?" pangalinganna.* Someone calling, for example. "Have you caught anything?" is his call. (*Thesaurus:* **dē' 1.1, owa'₁ 1, sabbut 1.1, tawag**) 1.1) To call someone on the telephone.

**lingantu** *n.* 1) Hunger; appetite. 1.1) *adj.* zero Hungry; lacking food. *Halam bay aku amangan. Lingantu aku.* I hadn't eaten. I was hungry.

(*Thesaurus:* **bongtas 1.1, gustang, hanu, otas, punung**)

**kalingantuhan** *n.* The experience of hunger. *In a'a abontol mbal pinasagaran magkalingantuhan e' Tuhan.* God will not abandon a good man to experience starvation.

**linganga** *v. intr. aN-* To become hot and uncomfortable due to lack of ventilation. (*Thesaurus:* **limasu' 1, lingo'ot, pasu'₁ 1.1**)

**lingas₁** (var. **hingas**) **1)** *adj. a-* Troubled or uneasy at the strangeness of one's surroundings. *Alingas na iya maitu, bilahina amole' ni lahat sigām.* He is uneasy here now, he wants to go home to their own place. *Bang ngga'i ka luma'ta pagtulihan, bo' niā' kita atuli he' saga bagayta, alingas kita apa halam biyasa. At'ggol kita atuli.* If it is not the house we sleep in, but our friends take us to sleep over, we are uncomfortable because we are not accustomed. It takes ages to fall asleep. *Sali' aniya' ai-ai ya kulangta, aniya' kasusahanta, ap'ddi' akkalta. Hatina asalinggā kitā, ahingas.* As though we are short of something, we have worries, our minds are troubled. In other words we are very unsettled, troubled. (*Thesaurus:* **lingus-lingus**) **2)** *v. tr. a-, ka-..-an, -an* To miss someone who is absent. *Ahingasan aku bay bagayku.* I am lonely for my former friend. *Bang aku kinalingasan e' tunangku, alingas du isāb aku.* When I am missed by my sweetheart, I miss her too. *Masi iya kinalingasan he' saga a'a magp'p'ssi.* He is still missed by the line-fishing community. **2.1)** *v. intr. maka-* To produce a feeling of loneliness. *Makalingas lahat inān, sali' halam aniya' sehe'ta.* That place makes one lonely, like not having a companion.

**lingas₂** *adj. a-* Narrow in section, as the hull of an outrigger canoe. *Da'a na bang ya bangka' palingas, subay palayas.* Avoid a narrow-hulled dugout, it has to be broad in the beam. *Al'kkas pakkom bang alingas.* It capsizes easily if it is narrow-hulled.

**lingka'** *v. intr. pa-* **1)** To avoid something by stepping over it. *Palingka' aku man ka'a bang ka palege.* I will step over you if you are lying down. (*Thesaurus:* **lakad 1, laktaw, pitas₁, saliyu 1**) **1.1)** *v. tr. -an* To step over someone. *Bang aniya' palege subay da'a nilingka'an, subay kita palibut.* When someone is lying down they should not be stepped over, we should go around them.

**lingkal** *see:* **sakalingkal, katilingkal**

**lingkat** *n.* **1)** Beauty; elegance; good looks, of people and objects. *Da'a ka ahīng ma lingkatna.* Do not be drawn by her beauty. **1.1)** *adj. a-* Beautiful; handsome. *Luma' mital, halam aniya' sabandingna. Alingkat, tuwan, minsan langaw paligid.* A house with a metal roof, with no defects. Beautiful, my friend, even a fly would slip on it. *Bay halam alingkat, bang palingkatta, na alingkat to'ongan.* It wasn't beautiful before,

[but] if we beautify it then it will become very beautiful. (*Thesaurus:* **alti, dorog₂ 1.1, hansam, hāp baran, himpit, jalang₁, manis 1.1, polma 1.1**) **1.2)** *v. advrs. ka-...-an* To be affected by beauty. *Kalingkatan aku bang aku angahinang taguri'.* I am overwhelmed by beauty when I construct a kite.

**paglingkat-lingkat** *v. intr. aN-* To compete with each other in regard to beauty. *Maglingkat-lingkatan kita bang sai alingkat.* We are competing for beauty [to see] who is the beautiful one.

**lingkit** *n.* **1)** A link between items in a series, as the links of a chain. **1.1)** *v. tr.* To tie or string articles together to facilitate carrying. *Lingkitin daing ilū bo' mbal ahulug.* Tie the fish together so they don't fall. *Bang saging nila'anan man batangna, na nilingkit. Tabowata na pamint'dda bang nilingkit.* When bananas are removed from the main stem, they are tied together. Strung together they can be carried in one load. (*Thesaurus:* **surut, tōhan, tuhug 1**)

**paglingkit 1)** *v. intr. aN-* To be joined together. *Buwat lahing pinagengkot karuwa, na maglingkit.* Like two mature coconuts tied together, they are joined. **2)** *v. tr.* To join items by tying. *Niengkotan e'na togel ero' pinaglingkit duwa.* He tied dogs' tails together in pairs.

**lingku'** *adj. a-* Locked in a bent position, of knee or elbow. *Pagbati', alingku' tu'utku, mbal makal'ngngan.* On waking, my knee joint was locked so I couldn't walk.

**linggas** *adj. a-* Complete and without gaps, of things or actions. *Bang gandum alinggas, sangpū' maka lima sīn duwa halga'na. Bang mbal alinggas lima sīn dakayu'.* When the corn has kernels close together, it costs fifteen cents for two. If it is not close, five cents for one. *Alinggas emponnu, sali' alapat.* Your teeth are complete, sort of close together. *Kayu yakal itū alinggas toho'na.* The dryness of this *yakal* wood is complete throughout its length.

**linggatang** *n.* The Sunflower starfish, a shallow water animal that can give a painful sting. *Pycnopodia helianthoides. Linggatang itū luwa sumping amikit ma batu ka atawa ma unas. Abu-abu luwana.* Linggatang looks like a flower attached to rocks or sea grass. Greyish in appearance. (*cf:* **l'ppay**)

**linggayu'** var. of **limayu'**

**linggi'** *n.* **1)** A long trawl net, about one fathom deep and up to fifty fathoms long. *Aniya' linggi' saga dand'ppa lambuna, saga limampū' d'ppa taha'na.* There are trawl nets about one fathom wide and fifty fathoms long. *Paghūg linggi', ina'an sin'llu na e' banak, e' selo, e' pugaw.* When the net was lowered, mullet, longtoms, and *pugaw* slipped out. (*Thesaurus:* **gugul 1, lantaw 1, laya 1, pokot₁ 1, sinsoro 1, siyul 1**) **1.1)** *v. tr.* To catch fish with a long drag net. *Bay aku* *angalinggi' ni Tapa'an. Aheka banak, aheka pogan, aheka lamuruk, aheka togeng.* I went net fishing to Tapaan. Lots of mullet, *pogan, lamuruk*, and halfbeaks.

**paglinggi'** *v. intr. aN-* To fish with a long trawl net. *Paglinggi' kami, sinusul na bihing bangkaw.* Having netted some fish, we followed along the edge of the mangrove forest. *Paglinggi' kami, sinusul na bihing bangkaw, sowang, mahē' ma Tapa'an.* Having netted some fish, we followed along the edge of the mangrove swamps and the channels, out there by Tapa'an Island.

**linggisan** *n.* The frigate bird. *fam. Fregatidae. Bang nijabjaban kepet linggisan, paleyang na.* When the frigate bird flaps its wings, it flies off.

**lingi'** 1) *v. intr. pa-* To turn the head to see something to the side or rear. *Bang ka kaleya angā' panggi' kayu bo' halam aniya' sehe', palingi' ka ni buli'annu. Piligdu aniya' a'a paturul.* When you go inland to get cassava, and you don't have a companion, look around behind you. The danger is someone may be following. *Buwat aniya' nil'ngngan bo' kita palingi', ati parugtul kita.* Like when we are going to do something and we look back and bump into something. *Paglingi'na, ta'nda' aku e'na ati nilinganan aku.* On looking round he saw me and I was called. *Ang'nda' sali' pajullit, palingi'.* Looking kind of obliquely, turning the head to see. (*Thesaurus:* **buli'-buli' mata, keles, kibad, pagkesong**) 1.1) *v. tr.* To observe something by turning one's head. *Lingi'un du isāb ni bay panagna'annu.* Look back to where you started from. 2) *v. tr.* To turn to someone for help. {idiom} *Halam aniya' kalingi'anku bang halam na mato'aku ya pangutanganku.* There is no one to turn to, when my father-in-law is no longer present to borrow from. *Mbal na talingi'ku danakanku apa aniya' na anak-h'ndaku.* I can no longer turn to my brother [for help], because I have a wife and children now.

**paglingi'** *v. intr. aN-* To keep turning one's head to look in different directions. *Mbal kita makapagkesong, mbal kita sali' makapaglingi'. "Abusā' k'llongku," yukta.* We are not able to turn our heads this way and that, sort of unable to look from side to side. "My neck has a crick in it," we say.

**lingit** *v. tr. -an* 1) To desire something intensely. *Aheka angalingit ma ka'a.* Many people desire you. *Bang l'lla ya mbal bilahi ma d'nda, mbal du angalingit. Bang l'lla ya bilahi, na angalingit d'nda.* If the man is not keen on the woman she won't desire him. If the man is keen, then the woman will desire him. (*Thesaurus:* **baya'** 1, **bilahi** 1, **ebog** 1, **helo₁** 1, **napsu** 1) 1.1) *n.* Something intensely desired. *Aniya' isāb kakana' kalingitanku.* There is some cloth I have been wanting.

**lingo'ot** *adj. a-* Hot and uncomfortable due to

confined space; stuffy. *Bang kami atuli mareyom, alingo'ot.* When we sleep inside, it is hot and stuffy. *Si Ku ya sinō' pina'an ni dugu-rugu. Ya ina'an na malingo'ot-i, mapasu'-i. Na wa'i na iya anangis.* Ku is told to go into the corner. That's the stuffy place, the hot place. So off he's gone, crying. (*Thesaurus:* **limasu'** 1, **linganga, pasu'₁** 1.1)

**lingu** *v. intr. a-* 1) To be confused. 1.1) *v. tr.* To deceive or confuse someone; to take advantage of someone's ignorance. *Pilliyu a'a itū, pangalingu makalandu'.* This person is a rascal, such a deceiver. *Buwat aniya' magpangongka' duwangan, dangan ata'u, dangan mbal. Ya mbal ata'u talingu he' mata'u.* For example two people playing a game, one who knows how, one who doesn't. The one who doesn't know is tricked by the one who does. (*cf:* **ingu**; *Thesaurus:* **akkal** 1.1)

**lingus-lingus** *v. advrs. ta-* Lacking a companion; feeling lonely. *Asusa, talingus-lingus, halam aniya' sehe'na magsuli-suli.* Unhappy, feeling lonely, no companion to talk with. (*Thesaurus:* **lingas₁** 1)

**lipa'** *v. tr.* To apply cosmetic paste to the skin. *Bang budjang magbinorak, nilipa' tape', tangan, kamemon sambil pa'a.* When teenage girls used cosmetic powder, the feet and hands are treated, everything including the thighs. (*cf:* **borak** 1, **tula-tula**)

**paglipa'** *v. intr. aN-* To be in the habit of applying cosmetic paste. *Maglipa' saga kabudjangan Sibaud.* The young women from Sibaud apply cosmetic paste.

**lipas** *adj. a-* Forgotten; slipped from one's mind. *In pagbayadna halam du isāb bay alipas bulan-bulan.* His monthly payment was never forgotten. *Alipas min deyom atayna bay h'lling ē', sali' halam taentomna.* What was said has slipped from his mind, as though he hadn't remembered. (*Thesaurus:* **bibas₂, kalipat** 1, **liha-liha, panglupa**)

**panglipas** (var. **panglipat**) *n.* 1) An absent-minded person. (*syn:* **panglupa**) 1.1) *v. tr. -an* To forget something through absent-mindedness.

**lipat₁** *v. tr.* 1) To multiply something. *Nilipat min t'llu.* Multiplied by three. *Kin'nnopan gi' hekabi nilipat min ibu.* Your numbers will be increased a thousand-fold. (*Thesaurus:* **doble** 1.1) 2) To fold something in two, such as paper. (*Thesaurus:* **l'ppot, lupi'₁, peko'**)

**lipat₂** *adj. a-* Unconscious; unaware. *Buwat magbalebol inān, magdugtul si Te, na halam makasayu si Mo, alipat.* Like when playing volleyball, Te collided and Mo lost consciousness, totally unaware. *Sali' bang aku atuli, sali' aku alipat. Minsan aku nilagut atawa sinuntuk, mbal tananam.* Like when I am asleep I'm right out to it. Even if someone slashes me with a knife or punches me it still isn't noticed. (*Thesaurus:* **bawis₁, pinsan** 1)

**kalipat** (var. **kaipat**) *v. tr.* 1) To forget something. (*Thesaurus:* **bibas**₂, **liha-liha**, **lipas**, **panglupa**) 1.1) *v. tr. -an* To forget something one was told to remember. *Na kamaya' kam to'ongan, da'a takalipatinbi ya bay pananggup mastal inān.* Now be very careful, don't forget the schoolmaster's warning.

**lipay**₁ *v. intr. pa-* To overflow a container. *Palipay bohe' min bowa' poga.* The water is overflowing from the mouth of the water jar. (*Thesaurus:* **lasay, lese**₁, **luput 1, sempok 1, uplut**)

**paglipay** *v. intr. aN-* To keep overflowing the limits of a container or water-course. *Maglipay-lipay bohe' ulan, palasay min tangki.* The rainwater keeps running over, overflowing the tank.

**lipay**₂ *v. tr. -an* To clear a space on the surface of rippled or rubbish-covered water. *Lipayin tahik ilū dok ta'nda'nu ai-ai min deyo'-i. Sali' pinat'ddo'-t'ddo' maka busay.* Clear the sea there so you can see whatever is below. Sort of make a calm space with the paddle. *Bang aniya' bay ahūg s'ggit ni poga, na lipayanta dahū bo' yampa kita anauk. Ati ya tasaukta ya masawa ī'.* If rubbish has fallen into the water jar, then we clear the surface first and then we dip out. So what we dip out is the clear stuff.

**lipi-lipi** *n.* A wooden stringer that caps the plywood panel of a canoe side. (*cf:* **durung-diyata'**; *syn:* **bolbo**₁, **dingding-hangin**)

**Lipid** var. of **Sama Lipid**

**lipistĭk** *n.* 1) Lipstick. 1.1) *v. tr.* To apply lipstick. (*syn:* **atal**)

**lipulmi'ad** *adj. a-* Dead, a formal expression used only of humans. (*cf:* **matay**₁ 1; *Thesaurus:* **aymulla**)

**liput**₁ *adj. a-* Covered all over; infested. *Aliput kaluma'an itū e' sumping.* This village is covered with flowers. *Aliput kōkna e' katol, binuruk sali'.* His head is covered with an itchy condition, similar to *buruk.*

**liput**₂ var. of **libut**

**lipuwas** *v. intr. pa-* To pass without being noticed, as someone escaping from restraint. *Bay pagmohot-mohotantam supaya makalipuwas saga pagkahitam.* We made it our purpose so that our companions would escape.

**paglipuwas** *v. intr. aN-* To pass close by someone without seeing each other; to slip past. *Maglipuwas ma lān. Sigām tudju Sisangat, kami tudju Manubal.* We passed by on the road. They going towards Sisangat, we going to Manubal. (*Thesaurus:* **labay**₁ 1, **likuwad 1.1, liyus 1.1, pagsulabay, pintas 1, timbay 1**)

**liras** var. of **ligdas**

**liru'** 1) *adj. a-* Regretful; regretting some loss or failure to fulfill a commitment. *Bay aku min tabu', halam aniya' sīnku, anumpang aku ni a'a, atā luma'ku. Yukku ma iya, "Aliru' na ka'a." Yuk i', "Mbal du. Mags'lle'-s'lle' du."* I had been to market, had no money, asked a fellow for a ride, my house being far away. I said to him, "It's a nuisance for you [lit. you'll regret it." He said, "Not at all. Everyone has his turn." (*Thesaurus:* **susa 1.1, susun**₂ 1.1) 1.1) *v. tr.* To regret what has happened. *Liru'ku bang aniya' takodjel bo' ahūg. Aku subay pareyo', pangatasku, dusa.* I regret it when something I mess with falls [from the house]. I'm the one who should go down [to get it], it's my responsibility, my fault. 2) *v. tr. a-, ka-..-an, -an* To be regretful about things that cannot be changed. *Aniya' kinaliru'an, ya angkan ala'at s'mmuku.* There is something [I am] distressed about, that's why I look unhappy.

**pagkaliru'an** *v. intr. aN-* To grieve continually over someone's absence or death.

**lisad** *v. intr. pa-* To slip sideways. *Bang aku magbaek mbal aku magtūy makabeklo'. Al'kkas aku palisad.* When I am biking I can't suddenly turn aside. I quickly slip off. *Bay aku makalisad min batu.* I happened to slip off a rock. (*Thesaurus:* **dasdas, deklas, ligdas, ligid**₂ 1, **lisig, lumintiyad**)

**lisag**₁ *n.* O'clock; a marker of time in a 12/24-hour clock system. *A: "Lisag pila?" B: "Lisag duwa maka tonga'."* A: "What time is it?" B: "Two-thirty."

**lisag**₂ *n.* 1) A rhythm played on the brass gong ensemble. (*cf:* **taletek, taroro', titik 1.1**) 1.1) *v. tr.* To beat time on something; to strike a gong; to cause something to chime. *Lisagun kono' ba gabbang ilū.* Please beat time on that marimba. *Nilahu' bulan, na subay nilisagan min kaluma'an. Nilisagan na turung kaldero mital, kulintangan, agung, ai-ai na tabāk-bāk ī'.* There is a lunar eclipse, so there should be things beaten rhythmically in the villlage. Rhythm beaten on metal pot lids, brass ensemble, large gongs, whatever comes to hand. (*Thesaurus:* **kulanting 1, tagunggu', taletek, taratu' 1.1, taroro', tigi'-tigi'**₂, **tuntung**)

**paglisag** *v. intr. aN-* To beat time or play a rhythm. *Maglisag dakayu', angagung isāb dakayu'.* One person plays a rhythm, another beats the large gong.

**lisa'** (var. **kulisa'**) *n.* 1) Nits; the eggs of head lice. *Pediculus humanus capitis. Lisa' mbal palele ma kōk.* Nits don't crawl on the head. (*Thesaurus:* **kuman**₁, **kutu 1, limad-limad, tuma 1**) 1.1) *v. intr. aN-* To lay eggs, of lice. 1.2) *v. tr. -an* To remove nits.

**lisig** *v. intr. pa-* To slip off, of something placed too close to an edge. *Aningkō' kita ma bihing pelang, bo' mbal ang'nda' ni dahū'an, bo' makarugtul pelang inān. Na palisig kita.* We are sitting on the edge of the canoe but aren't looking to the front, when the canoe bangs into something head on. Then we slip off. *Da'a patipid-tipirun ko da'a palisig.* Don't place it close to the edge lest it slip off. *Mbal pasamod palig, wa'i palisig ni timbang.* Surgeon-fish don't occur [with these fish], they've slipped into the depths. (*Thesaurus:*

**dasdas, deklas, ligdas, ligid₂ 1, lisad, lumintiyad)**

**lisigan** *n.* A deep place below the surrounding sea floor. *Wa'i palig ma lisigan.* The surgeon-fish are down in the depths.

**lissi** (var. **liksi**) *adj.* zero Close, of kinship or friendship; personal, specific to an individual. *Anakku lissi.* My very own child. *Tahinang kami sali' a'a liyu, ngga'i na ka anakna lissi.* We are treated as strangers, no longer his own children. *Ka'am lissi ya bay makamata ma saga pagsulay aheya maka saga paltanda'an makatāw-tāw.* You personally witnessed the great tests and terrifying signs. (*Thesaurus:* **lahasiya' 1, legsok₁, luggiya'**)

**lista** *v. tr.* To keep a record. *Bang angalista pokotan, bo' bayad dakayu' pilak, amabā' iya dambila' pilak. Bay angala'ugan sehe'na.* When he is recording the catch [of fish netted], when the rate is one peso he says it is half that. He has treated his workmate badly.

**listahan** *n.* A list of items.

**palista** *v. tr.* To add names to a list.

**listun** *n.* Milled lumber of small dimensions, as for light framing. *Apagon listun luma' inān.* The lumber of that house is durable. (*Thesaurus:* **baras-baras, hanglad 1, papan₁, pasagi' 1**)

**lisu'** *adj.* a-/-an Averse to work, from laziness, boredom or lack of commitment. *A'a lisu'an halam katumariyahanna.* A lazy person has no future. *Ab'nsi na aku bang angiskul. Lisu'an aku.* I hate it when I go to school. I'm fed up with it. *In a'a lisu'an mbal amadja' tana'na ma waktu pagtanom.* The lazy fellow doesn't plow his land in the growing season. (*Thesaurus:* **hukaw 1, takal**)

**līt** *clf.* Count word for strings of corn cobs. *Bay kami am'lli gandum, dalīt.* We bought corn cobs, one string.

**ma lītan** *adv. phrase* By the string, of corn. *Pinab'llihan ma lītan sadja.* Sold only by the string.

**litag** *n.* 1) A spring trap; a snare. *Sahat ma tahik, litag itū ma katalunan.* Sahat traps are for the sea, these *litag* are for the forest. (*cf:* **sahat 1**) 1.1) *v. tr.* To snare animals, birds, crustaceans. *Nilitag, sali' anahat maka kayu ba'ugan, ya pal'mbut inān.* Snared, like snaring with a rod, the springy kind. *Angalitag aku kamun bo' aniya' palauk.* I will snare mantis shrimp so there'll be something to eat with the cassava.

**litib** *adj.* a- Worn down, as of teeth or rocks. *Aniya' du batu agkalitib, aniya' isāb batu alitiban dīna.* There are indeed rocks that can wear each other down, there are also rocks that simply wear down of themselves. (*Thesaurus:* **linis, pasaw, pupud 1.1**)

**pagkalitib** *v. intr.* aN- To wear down or erode.

**littā** *adj.* a- 1) Astonished; surprised. *Buwat aniya' a'a at'kka ni lahatta. Alittā kita, yukta, "Sai bahā'*

*a'a ina'an?"* Like when a person arrives at our place. We are surprised and say, "Who is that person?" (*Thesaurus:* **haylan, ili-ili, inu-inu 1, jaip**) 1.1) *v. advrs.* ka-...-an To be experiencing surprise or shock. *Kalittāhan itū, sali' ai-ai yampa ta'nda'ta, minsan lapal yampa takale. Kainu-inuhan to'ongan. Kalittāhan* is like anything we have only just seen, or even to a message we have just heard. It is something really amazing.

**littub** *adj.* a- Filled out or plump, as the features of a healthy person. *Halam gi' alittub onde' itū.* This child hasn't grown plump yet. (*Thesaurus:* **goldo-goldo, hambug 1, l'mmok 1.1, poko-poko, subuk, tibung-tibung**)

**litu** *v. tr.* -an To buy and sell things for profit, as agent. *Bay pam'lliku daing sangpū' pilak, bay lituhanku. Tab'lli du duwampū'. Na anguntung aku sangpū'.* I bought fish for ten pesos, and traded them. They were bought for twenty. So I made a profit of ten. *Buwat aku angalitu daing, bo' ka'am taga daing, b'lliku ni ka'am duwa-ruwa pilak anahut-a'aslag. Kuwidasku.* Like when I am trading fish and you have fish. I buy from you at two pesos each small or big. I buy in bulk. (*Thesaurus:* **dagang, lilung, pab'lli, pagsoroy, pa'andag 1, samsuy**)

**paglitu** *v. intr.* aN- To make a living by buying and selling.

**paglitu-litu bissala** *v. tr.* -an To exchange gossip, adding something.

**palilitu** *n.* A trader; a middleman. (*Thesaurus:* **paltira, tandero 1.1**)

**lituk** *n.* 1) A slender stick; the center rib of a palm leaf. *Ya lituk ilū tinuhug ma daun hupi' nihinang kadjang.* Those slender sticks are pushed through *hupi'* leaves to make a shade. (*cf:* **koyang**) 2) A broom made of tightly bound palm leaf ribs. *Am'lli aku lituk pehē' ni M'ddas pagsapuku deyom luma'.* I will buy a *lituk* broom there in Siasi for me to sweep the interior of the house.

**lituk bagid** *n. phrase* A matchstick.

**liyabanos** (var. **labanos**) *n.* The soursop or guyabano tree and its fruit. *Anona muricata.*

**liyabe** *n.* A tool for gripping; a wrench; pliers. (*Thesaurus:* **plaes**)

**liyabe-tubu** *n.* A tube wrench. *Liyabe-tubu itū pamahāp malkina.* This tube wrench is for fixing an engine.

**liyabod** *n.* A species of large millipede. (*Thesaurus:* **lalipan, nne**)

**liyal** *v. intr.* aN- To avoid a situation associated with a prior negative experience. *Buwat saga daing binubu atawa pin'ssi, na, bang mbal na pasōd atawa mbal na aninduk, yukta, "Ē! Angaliyal na daing ē'."* Like fish caught in a box trap or by hook and line, if they don't go in or don't bite, we say, "Hey! The fish have learned to avoid [us]." *Buwat si Ud asidda angala'ug ma si Na, na mbal pasekot. Angaliyal ma si Ud, kinaillagan si Ud apa asidda amono'.* Ud treats Na very badly, so he [Na]doesn't go near. He avoids Ud, wary of him because he hits so much. (*Thesaurus:* **halli'**₁ 1.1, **insap, l'ppi, llog** 1.1)

**liyang** *n.* **1)** A recess cut into the wall of a grave; a grave-shelf. *Bang aniya' amatay Lannang, hinangan liyang dahū ati hal magkubul la.* If a Chinese person dies, a grave cavity is made for him first and then he is simply buried [i.e. without boarding off the cavity]. **1.1)** *v. tr.* To prepare the wall recess in a grave. *Aubus na kām minnitu, pī' ni kubul, pagmakōkin na ya saga onde' ilū angaliyang-liyang.* When you have finished here, go to the burial and be in charge of the young ones preparing the recess.

**paliyangan** *n.* The grave as the final resting place of all mankind. (*Thesaurus:* **kubul** 1, **kuddaman, dinding-hali, gumi** 2)

**liyas** *see:* **pangliyas**

**liyaw** *adj. a-* **1)** Vanished; disembodied; spirited away. *Aliyaw sigām ma būd Siasi.* They have vanished up on Siasi mountain. *Bay pa'in ta'nda'nu, magtūy aliyaw.* When you had just seen it, it suddenly disappeared. **1.1)** *v. tr. -an* To cause something to disappear from the present world. (*Thesaurus:* **patawap** 1, **telop** 1)

**kaliyawan** (var. **kali'awan**) *intrj.* Exclamation expressing surprise or disgust. *Arōy! Kaliyawan!* Yuk! How disgusting!

**liyu**₁ *v. intr. pa-* **1)** To alternate the places where one stays. *Bang aku bay ma mato'aku dambulan, paliyu aku ni matto'aku isāb.* When I have been a month with my parents-in-law, then I go back to my parents again. **2)** To rebound, of a curse. *Bang pantakta palikid ni kita, sali' paliyu ni kita.* When we cast a curse it rebounds on us, like it comes back to us.

**pagliyu-liyu** *v. tr.* To alternate between two or more locations. *Juhul maka Jakatla' mbal tapagliyu-liyu.* Johore and Jakarta are not places one just visits

**liyu**₂ *n.* **1)** The far side of a solid object or barrier. *Hē' ma liyu Būd Datu'.* Yonder on the other side of Mt. Datu. (*Thesaurus:* **bukut**₁, **dambila'** 2) **1.1)** *v. intr. pa-* To go beyond an intervening object or limit. *Halam aniya' makaliyu min iya.* No one can surpass him. *Ahunit ko' inān, sagō' aniya' gi' kasusahanku paliyu minnē'.* That is indeed difficult, but I have troubles that exceed that. *Makaliyu-liyu pa'in si Da min diyata' būd, aniya' a'a tabākna.* When Da got a bit further than the hilltop, he found someone there. *Buwat pal'ngngan, yukku, "Ni luma' ina'an aku," bo' paliyu aku ni luma' dakayu'.* Taking a walk, for example. I say, "I'm going to that house," but I go beyond, to another house. **1.2)** *v. advrs. ka-...-an* To be capable of being surpassed, of some quality or condition. *In kasi-lasanu ma aku mbal kaliyuhan, palabi gi' min lasa kar'ndahan.* Your tender love for me cannot be exceeded, it is greater than the love of women. *Bang bay na*

*ah'lling huwis mbal kaliyuhan. Ya hē' anastas hukuman.* When the judge has spoken no one can say more. He is the one to conclude the proceedings.

**liyu-ahirat** *n.* The afterworld in contrast to the present one. (*Thesaurus:* **sulga'**)

**liyuhan** *n.* The area beyond a reference point. *Makajari na kami palanjal ni saga kalahat-lahatan ma liyuhanbi.* You may now proceed to the territories beyond where you are.

**liyu**₃ *adj. zero* Beyond; other than. *Liyu min kamemon.* Surpassing all others. *Malaingkan bang aniya' gi' anaknu liyu min sigām duwangan itu, suku'nu na.* However, if there is still a child of yours other than these two, he will be yours.

**liyu lagi'** *conj.* More than; apart from. *Liyu lagi' minnitu, bay na asal tasulat ma saga kitab kasultan-sultanan.* Anything apart from this has already been written in the book of the sultans.

**liyu-lakad** *v. intr. aN-* To commit adultery.

**pagliyu-lakad** *v. intr. aN-* To commit adultery. *Magpakay dusa bang a'a magliyu-lakad.* People who commit adultery are sinning. (*syn:* **pagjina**)

**pangaliyu-lakad** *n.* A habitual adulterer.

**liyud** *v. intr. pa-* To go somewhere for a brief stay or visit. *Buwat si La paliyud ni luma' dakayu'.* Like La paying a visit to another house. (*Thesaurus:* **bisita** 1.1, **tibaw** 1.2, **tulaga', tuwa'** 2)

**liyus** *adj. zero* **1)** To be spared mishap or misfortune. *Bang pa'in makasampay sulat itū ni ka'am ma halam baya-bayabi makaliyus isāb kām min bala'.* May this letter find you unharmed and free also from serious trouble. **1.1)** *v. intr. pa-* To pass by without harming or touching. *Bang kita binantung, ai-ai na pamantung kita, bo' katangkisanta. Halam kita taluwa', wa'i paliyus bay pamantung ē'.* Suppose we are being stoned, with anything whatever, and we dodge. We are not struck, the things thrown have gone right past. (*Thesaurus:* **labay**₁ 1, **likuwad** 1.1, **paglipuwas, pagsulabay, pintas** 1, **timbay** 1) **1.2)** *v. tr. -an* To bring someone through a difficult place or situation; to rescue. *Niliyusan na pa'in kitam min bala'.* We are continually brought safely out of trouble. (*Thesaurus:* **haun**₂, **lappas**₂ 1, **puwas**₁ 1.1)

**l'bba** var. of **bba**₃

**l'bbak** *n.* **1)** An extended depression in a surface, such as a valley, a corrugation, the inner joint of the elbow. *Aheka l'bbakna lān palabayan kami.* The road that we pass on has many ruts. *Bang aku magdūt-dūt maka onde', subay ma l'bbak bo' al'kkas.* When I go sledding with kids it should be down a valley so as to be quick. **1.1)** *v. intr. pa-* To form a hollow or groove. *Pabūd bo' isāb pal'bbak.* To form a mound and then a hollow.

**pagl'bbak** *v. intr. aN-* To be marked with grooves or corrugations. *Balimbing itū agaddung, aniya' du isāb akeyat bang atahak. Atibulung bo'* *magl'bbak.* The star apple is green, and there are red ones too when ripe. It is cylindrical but has grooves.

**l'bba'** var. of **labba'₂**

**l'bbang** *n.* 1) A gap or space, as between teeth. (*cf:* **legpong**) 1.1) *adj.* -*an* Gapped; lacking a tooth. *L'bbangan kita, sali' kita alegpong.* We have a space [between our teeth], it's like one is missing.

**l'bbangan** *n.* A gap through a reef or sandbank. *Palabayun kita man l'bbangan ilū bo' mbal dumagsa'.* Have us go through that gap so we don't run into something submerged.

**l'bbi** *n.* Food remaining after a meal. *Bang aku amangan, bo' aniya' onde'-onde' angalung, ya pamakanku iya l'bbiku.* When I am eating and a child comes asking for food, it's my leftovers that I give her to eat. (*cf:* **labi** 1)

**l'bbo** *adj.* *a-* 1) Soft; boggy, of soil or mud. *Al'bbo, buwat pisak inān, mbal kita makal'ngngan. Patanom tape'ta.* Boggy, like that mud, we can't walk on it. Our feet sink in. *Al'bbo bukut danaw.* The back of the lake is boggy. (*Thesaurus:* **lamekkat, legsak, lettak, pekat**)

**kal'bbohan** *n.* A marshy or boggy area. *Bay aku binuhat e'na min kal'bbohan.* He lifted me up bodily from the marsh.

**pal'bbo** *v. tr.* To cause something to be soft.

**l'bbong** *v. intr. pa-* 1) To form a hollow in a surface. 1.1) *v. tr.* -*an* To dig a hole for something.

**pagl'bbong** *v. tr.* To bury something by covering it with earth. *Buwat bay timpu Jipun, ba'anan patay hal pinagl'bbong.* As in the Japanese period, when many corpses were simply covered over [with earth]. (*Thesaurus:* **bunbun** 1.1, **kubul** 1.1)

**l'bbos** (var. **bbos**) *adj.* *a-* 1) Collapsed, as a house into the sea. *Pagkawin siyalina, al'bbos luma' sigām min heka paluruk. Arāk a'bbos isāb pantān.* When his younger sibling got married, their house collapsed from the many who attended. The porch nearly collapsed too. *Al'bbos na luma' sigām.* Their house has collapsed [into the sea]. (*Thesaurus:* **h'bba'**) 1.1) *v. tr.* To move something down into the water. *Onde'-onde' bang angal'bbos bangka' dangan-danganna, mbal takole'.* When a child is launching a dugout on his own, it can't be done. *Bay na ni'bbos pelang si Sel, bayan ni M'ddas.* Sir's canoe was launched as transport to Siasi Town. (*Thesaurus:* **dahik, daldal, longsad₁**)

**l'bbot** (var. **bbot**) *adj.* *a-* Having a hole which permits leakage. *Al'bbot mohang lansa, pasōd tahik.* The hull of the launch is leaking, water is coming in. (*Thesaurus:* **bobos, l'ssut**)

**l'kkab** *adj.* *a-* High or full, of tide. (*Thesaurus:* **daka', lalom₁, nso', sosob, tambang₁** 1)

**l'kkang** *n.* Dried serum from a sore or wound. *Saddī l'kkang, saddī tangkop.* Dried serum and a scab

are different things. (*Thesaurus:* **l'kkung** 1, **tangkop, taplok** 2)

**l'kkas** *adj.* *a-* 1) Quick in movement. *Al'kkas palangi si Ma, buwat si Banana.* Ma swims swiftly, like Banana [a famous swimmer from Sisangat]. *Pagpal'kkasna jīp magtūy makarugtul ni batu.* Having caused the jeep to speed up he immediately banged into a rock. *Ya mbal kasōng pelang, mbal kal'kkasna.* The canoe's lack of progress was due to its absence of speed. (*Thesaurus:* **baggis, ka'is, kasay** 1, **kulakkus, samot** 1, **sapat₂** 1) 1.1) *v. intr. pa-* To hurry; to do quickly. *Pal'kkas ka magdakdak.* Hurry up with the laundry.

**l'kkat₁** *v. tr.* 1) To redeem something from pawn. *Subay l'kkatku singsing bay sandahanku ni si Ot. Subay angal'kkat dangibu bo' sinagaran amole'.* I must redeem my ring that I pawned to Ot. I must redeem it for a thousand pesos in order to be allowed to [take it] home. (*Thesaurus:* **lōb** 1.1, **padjak₁, panau'**) 1.1) *v. ditr.* To pay release money for someone in jail or captivity. *Bang kita takidnap e' mundu subay kita nil'kkat limampū' ngibu.* When we are kidnapped by bandits we should be ransomed for fifty thousand. (*Thesaurus:* **haum, jamin, luyal** 1.1, **piyansa**)

**l'kkat₂** (var. **kkat**) *v. intr. pa-* 1) To become separate from a group or main part. *Atiya' na aku pal'kkat apa ka'a ni tabu'.* I'll head in a different direction now because you are going to the market. *Pal'kkatun iya min saga sehe'na ati bowahun iya ni dakayu' bilik bo' kam karangan-danganan magbissala.* Separate him from his companions and take him to another room so you can discuss things on your own. (*Thesaurus:* **boklang** 1, **bugtu'₁, butas** 1, **logtas, okat₂** 1) 1.1) *v. tr.* -*an* To detach something from its normal location. *Ni'kkatan tanganna.* His hand was detached [from what it was holding].

**pagl'kkat** *v. intr. aN-* To go off in different directions. *Bang kami angalga maka si Uj, magl'kkat kami, dakayu' tudju ni jambatan, dakayu' tudju ni posopis.* When Uj and I work as porters we split up, one going towards the wharf, the other towards the Post Office. *Magbanta na, magl'kkat na.* Enemies now, going different ways. (*Thesaurus:* **pagpaopēt, pagsapehak**)

**l'kkob** *v. tr.* To eat something together with parts normally removed, such as unpeeled fruit, or a cat eating a whole rat. *L'kkobun na sampay kaldero.* Gobble it up, cooking pot and all. (*Thesaurus:* **kakan** 1, **kakan** 1, **inta', lallan, pakan**)

**pagpangal'kkob** *v. tr.* To eat prey, bones and all. *Atalom to'ongan empon sigām, sapantun bangkil halimaw magpangal'kkob.* Their teeth are very sharp, like the fangs of a lion that devours its prey bones and all.

**l'kko'** *v. tr.* To fold flexible material across its

length. *Aniya' jā nilūn, aniya' isāb jā nil'kko'.* There are rice-cakes that are rolled, and there are also rice-cakes that are folded. (*cf:* **peko'**)

**pagl'kko'-l'kko'** *v. intr. aN-* To fold flexible material concertina-wise.

**l'kkop₁** var. of **lakkop**

**l'kkop₂** *n.* The harder layer of meat beneath the soft surface layer of a young coconut. (*Thesaurus:* **lahing 1, putang, tongkop**)

**l'kkot** *n.* The crust of cooked rice adhering to a cooking pot. (*syn:* **dokot₁**)

**l'kkung** *n.* 1) A crust on the skin, such as dried food or a scab over a wound. *L'kkung, ya pataplok ma bakat.* A scab, that which forms over a wound. (*Thesaurus:* **l'kkang, tangkop, taplok 2**) 1.1) *v. intr. aN-* To form a crust by drying. *Bang aniya' onde'-onde' bay amangan mistang, amalut ma bowa'na, nsa' bay kinose'an, angal'kkung bowa'na.* When a child has eaten rice gruel and it sticks to her mouth, when it hasn't been washed it forms a crust on her mouth. *Angay bowa' onde' mangal'kkung ilū?* What's up with that child's mouth, crusted so?

**l'ddang** var. of **logdang₂**

**l'ddet** *v. intr. pa-* 1) To bend back out of normal alignment. *Pal'ddet ka bo' angattek to'olangnu.* Bend your body till your bones make a cracking noise. (*syn:* **k'dde'**) 1.1) *v. tr.* To reach something by leaning over backwards.

**l'ddom** var. of **lendom**

**l'ddos** var. of **loddos**

**l'dduk** (var. **dduk**) *v. intr. pa-* 1) To stretch one's body, as on awakening. *Maghitad aku subu-subu, pal'dduk.* I stretch my body early in the morning, stretching. (*Thesaurus:* **h'nnat 1, nned, pagkul'ddeng, paghitad, pagle'od**) 1.1) *v. tr.* To straighten something rigid, as a wooden pole or heavy wire. *Bang p'ttung subay nīdduk bo' nihinang batangan.* Bamboo needs to be straightened for use as an outrigger boom. (*Thesaurus:* **bigtang 1.1, b'ttad 1.1, l'ngngat, lūk, tilud 1.1, uli'₂**)

**pagl'dduk** *v. intr. aN-* To stretch one's body in order to straighten out kinks and ease pain. *Maglimbahon, sali' taluwa' p'ddi', sali' magl'ddukan.* Moving restlessly, as though attacked with pain, stretching one's body.

**l'gga** 1) *n.* A cautionary experience. *Talkala' bay tatangkawnu anu inān, subay ka binuwanan l'gga ko da'a tabaliknu.* Since you have stolen whatever, you should be given a warning lesson so you don't do it again. 1.1) *adj. a-/-an* Persuaded by a negative experience not to repeat an action. *Buwat aku angutang ni ka'a, at'ggol-t'ggol aku amayad, bo' ta'abut dapitu' makabayad aku ni ka'a. Yukku, "Da'a ka al'gga pangutangan."* Like when I borrow from you and take rather a long time to pay, but a week later I pay you, saying "Don't be averse to lending." *L'ggahan na aku, bay aku niraplosan e' si Mma'.*

*Amintāng na aku.* I have learned my lesson, Father has given me a whipping. I learn from experience. *Buwat aku angutang ni ka'a, at'ggol-t'ggol aku amayad, bo' ta'abut dapitu' makabayad aku ni ka'a. Yukku, "Da'a ka al'gga pangutangan." (Sali' mbal amautang pabalik.)* Suppose I borrow from you and take quite a long time to pay, but a week later I pay you. I say, "Don't be averse to lending." (Like not allowing me to borrow again.) (*Thesaurus:* **insā', mintāng**) 2) *v. tr. a-, ka-..-an, -an* To learn a lesson from experience. *Al'gga na iya ma bay tumaluwa' ma anakna dahū.* He learned a lesson from what had happened to his previous son. *Aniya' kinapalo'an, aniya' kinal'ggahan.* There are things to hold back from, and things to learn a lesson from.

**pamal'ggahan** *n.* An experience from which one learns an important lesson.

**l'ggon** *n.* Thunder; a rumbling sound. (*Thesaurus:* **daogdog, lāt, l'tte'₁**)

**pagl'ggon** *v. intr. aN-* To thunder repeatedly or continuously. *Magl'ggon lahat, marāi' pangulan na.* It is thundering continuously, maybe it is the rainy season already.

**l'ggot** (var. **ggot**) *adj. a-* Exceptionally low, of tide. *Tahik bulagas, alandos sōn subu. Pagugtu-llaw, t'bba, a'ggot t'bbana.* At the *bulagas* stage of the tides the incoming current is strong in the morning. By noon it is low tide, extremely low. *Ahāp amuwa' sikad-sikad bang al'ggot t'bba.* It is good to gather *sikad* conchs when it is really low tide. *Bang aniya' onde'-onde' bay angongka' mareyo' bo' al'ggot t'bba, bo' sali'-sali' d'nda, magluray, magdarut.* When there are children playing below [the houses] when the tide is very low, and when they're girls, they fight physically, pulling each other's hair out. (*Thesaurus:* **mulilang, pipit₂ 1, t'bba 1**)

**l'ggotan** *n.* An area exposed by low tide. *Ya kaheka'an luma' ungkup ma l'ggotan Sambuwangan.* Most *ungkup*-style houses are on the tidal flats of Zamboanga.

**l'ggu'** *adj. a-* Browned but not burnt, of cooked food. *Da'a pal'ggu'un panyām ilū, subay ahāp tahakna.* Don't overcook those rice cakes, they should be cooked just right. *Al'ggu' basta ahūg ni ns'llan.* They will be browned so long as they drop into the oil.

**l'lla** *n.* 1) A man; a male. (*cf:* **d'nda 1**) 1.1) *adj. zero* Masculine; male.

**kal'llahan** *n.* Menfolk; the man's side in marriage negotiations. *Yuk man kar'ndahan, "Taima' ka." Yuk man kal'llahan, "Na humiyan pagpah'nda?" Bang yuk-i, "Salung magpah'nda," magtambuku kami llaw pagkawin.* The woman's side say, "You are accepted." The man's side say, "So when will the bride-wealth be presented?" If the answer is, "Tomorrow is the day for the bride-wealth," then we set the day for the wedding.

**pagl'lla** *v. intr. aN-* To have sexual relations with

men other than one's husband.

**pagl'lla-l'lla**₁ *v. intr. aN-* To pretend to be a tough guy; to act in a vain way. *Magl'lla-l'lla dīna, sidda abbuhan.* He is being macho, really arrogant. *A'abbu si Anu, magl'lla-l'lla, magtanding dīna.* What's-his-name is proud, showing how tough he is, watching himself in the mirror.

**pagl'lla-l'lla**₂ *v. intr. aN-* To behave as a man; to be a transvestite woman. (*cf:* **bantut 1**)

**kapagl'lla** *n.* 1) Masculinity. 1.1) *n.* Male genitalia.

**pagkal'lla** *n.* Magical masculinity, making the possessor immune to harm from attacks of various kinds. (*Thesaurus:* **basi'**₂ **1.1, kobol 1.1, pangliyas, sihil 1**)

**l'llok** *v. intr. pa-* 1) To withdraw from sight into a confined space. *Wa'i pal'llok sumbuhan palita'an.* The wick of the lamp has gone below the top of its tube. (*syn:* **loklok**) 1.1) *v. tr. -an* To conceal something below a surface. *Iklug ya nil'llokan maka katas, mbal na ta'nda'.* An egg concealed under paper, no longer visible.

**l'mbut** *adj. a-* Flexible; springy, of a pole or beam. *Subay pinal'mbut p'ttung ati ahāp pangasa'am katig pelang.* The bamboo should be made flexible and then it will be good for bracing a canoe outrigger. (*Thesaurus:* **l'mpet**)

**l'mma**₁ *adj. a-* Soft and easily chewed. *Subay pinabukalan at'ggol sapi' pangahinang tiyula' itu, ati pal'mma'.* The beef should be boiled a long time when making black stew, to make it really soft.

**l'mma**₂ var. of **lamma**

**l'mmaw** *n.* The areca palm nut, partly ripe. (*Thesaurus:* **bunga**₁**, dantilad, lugus, pola**)

**l'mmi'** (var. **l'mmis**) *n.* 1) Dirt. *Aniya' l'mmis mareyom mataku.* There is dirt in my eye. (*Thesaurus:* **lobag, lumut**₁ **2, moseng 1**) 1.1) *adj. a-* Dirty; grubby. *Bang humantak si Li ma gusung al'mmis na baranna.* When Li falls down on the sand her body gets dirty. *Alakat, ya al'mmi' sali' manga badju' atawa ya manga halaman. Ya mariyata' luma' subay sinapuhan.* Besmeared, dirty, like clothes or the yards of a house. The house above should be swept. *Al'mmi' baranna, mbal minsan amandi.* His body is dirty, doesn't even bathe.

**l'mmis** var. of **l'mmi'**

**l'mmok** *n.* 1) Fatty tissue. 1.1) *adj. a-* Fat; plump. *Si Sel bay akayog, bay pinabeya'an he' mma'na puding bo' al'mmok, bo' mbal asaki.* Sir was thin, he was sent pudding by his father so he would get fat and not be sick. (*Thesaurus:* **goldo-goldo, hambug 1, littub, poko-poko, subuk, tibung-tibung**)

**kal'mmokan** *n.* Corpulence; fatness. *Magg'ttos kal'mmokan si Sa.* Sa's fatness forms creases.

**l'mmuk** *n.* Moss-like sea plants, a source of baits for small fish traps. (*Thesaurus:* **taubang, unas**)

**l'mmun** (var. **mmun**) *v. advrs. -in-* Feverish. *Aniya'*

na t'llu pitu' ni'mmunan iya maka magutta'. *Tabiya' isāb.* It is three weeks now that she has been feverish and vomiting. Excuse my mentioning it. *Nīmmun aku.* I am fevered. (*Thesaurus:* **hadjat**₂**, hōb-hōb, tandog 1, tatat**)

**l'mmun-l'mmun** *n.* The Spider or Brittle starfish species. *Class Ophiuroidea.*

**l'mpet** (var. **l'ntet**) *adj. a-* Supple; springy; giving way under pressure. *Pal'mpet itū magbeya'-beya', magbuwang-buwang. Pal'mpet* just gives way, springing up and down repeatedly. (*Thesaurus:* **l'mbut**)

**pagl'mpet-l'mpet** *v. intr. aN-* To yield under pressure and springing back repeatedly. *Magl'mpet-l'mpet taytayan inān bang kita palabay.* That walkway buckles and springs back when we pass over it. *Bang aniya' letehan bo' magl'ntet-l'ntet, subay tinapilan.* When a walkway is springy, it should be braced.

**l'mput** (var. **lumput**) *n.* The leafy plants harvested from land or coastal shallows.

**l'mput deya** *n. phrase* Leafy food from the land. (*Thesaurus:* **legotoman, paltubu-tubuhan 1, sayul 1**)

**l'mput dilaut** *n. phrase* Edible plants of inshore shallows. (*Thesaurus:* **panagatun, t'bbahan**)

**l'nnas** *n.* Purity of color. *Minsan pinggan, makajari niōnan l'nnas pote' basta nsa' aniya' b'ttikna.* Even a dish can be called pure white so long as it has no colors. *L'nnas pote' badju'na.* His shirt is pure white. (*Thesaurus:* **lullun 1**)

**l'nnob** *v. intr. pa-* To sink down under the surface of something. *Ya pal'nnob itū sōng pat'nde. Pal'nnob* means about to submerge. (*Thesaurus:* **loblob, paglowak, senop, tanom**₂)

**l'nnu** (var. **nnu**) *adj. a-* Having the feeling that one's teeth are on edge; the feeling that something is crawling on one's skin (formication). *Ē, makal'nnu empon.* Eek, it sets my teeth on edge. *Bang aku ama'us t'bbu al'nnu isāb emponku.* When I chew sugarcane my teeth are on edge. *Mbal angeket langaw, hal al'nnu.* Flies don't bite, they merely feel crawly.

**l'ntap** (var. **l'ntip**) *v. intr. aN-* To spread across the surface of a liquid, especially of oil. *Sali' ns'llan lansa bang ma tahik, angal'ntap.* Like oil from a launch when it is in the sea, it spreads. (*Thesaurus:* **ledje 1.1, ledled 1**)

**l'ntet** var. of **l'mpet**

**l'ntip** var. of **l'ntap**

**l'ngngan**₁ *n.* 1) A walk or stroll. 1.1) *v. intr. pa-/-um-* To walk somewhere; to proceed to some location. *Lum'ngngan aku pehē' ni Butun ang'nda' manuk wa'i alungay.* I will walk to Butun to look for the chicken that has gone missing. (*Thesaurus:* **baklay, baybay**₁**, pasiyal**)

**l'ngnganan**₁ *n.* A journey; a trip. *Bang aniya' makamula ma iya ma l'ngnganan, paheya gōm pa'in karukka'anku.* If anything harms him on the journey, my distress will become even greater. *Bay kam nirugpak e' sigām ma waktu kam nihapus ma l'ngngananbi.* You were attacked by them at a time when you were tired on your journey.

**pagl'ngngan** *v. intr. aN-* To walk about. *Da'a kono' kām maglagungkad e'bi magl'ngngan ilū. Abati' kaluma'an.* Please don't make a clatter there with your walking about. The whole neighborhood will wake up. *Apassut magl'ngngan, apassut maglele.* Adept at walking, adept at crawling.

**pagl'ngngan-l'ngngan** *v. intr. aN-* 1) To be in the habit of going from house to house; to visit various people. *Ka'a ilū, pahali ka magl'ngngan-l'ngngan. Aniya' kamawpa'atannu, aniya' kala'atan talanggalnu, buwat sala ataksil halam tinu'ud.* You there, stop going from place to place. You will meet up with trouble, like for example being fined [for touching a girl] even if it is unintentional. *Palahan aku saga duwa-t'llung'llaw. Mbal aku makapagl'ngngan.* I move slowly for two or three days. I can't go walking about visiting. 2) To go about unseen, of some types of spirit beings.

**magl'l'ngngan** *n.* Spirit beings of various kinds who move unseen among humans; the travellers.

**pagpal'ngngan** *n.* 1) The stage in a wedding sequence when the groom's party goes to the house of the bride's family. 1.1) *v. intr. aN-* To manage a wedding event as master of ceremonies.

**pal'ngnganan** *n.* A walking path. (*Thesaurus:* **kalsara**, **labayan**, **lān**)

**patil'ngnganun** *adj.* Always walking about, never at home.

**l'ngngan₂** *n.* 1) An occurrence or occasion. *Ma l'ngngan itu sadja.* Only on this occasion. 1.1) *v. tr.* To attend to matters that require going elsewhere. *A: "Pi'ingga ka?" B: "Aniya' nil'ngngan."* A: "Where are you going?" B: "I have business to take care of." *L'ngnganku magpalungay ni lahat dakayu'.* My intention in travelling is to become lost in some other country. (*Thesaurus:* **pagmohot 1.1**, **puhung₁ 1**)

**kal'ngnganan** *n.* 1) Customary or habitual behavior. *Buwattitu kal'ngnganan budjang bang ta'abut na pinaharap ni sultan.* This was the usual practise for maidens when the time came to be presented to the sultan. *Magdai'-dai' saga onde' baha'u itū pasiha' min kal'ngnganan saga ka'mbo'-mbo'an.* These young men are in a hurry to abandon the ways of the ancestors. *Kal'ngnganan saga a'a ahāp ya panunurin.* [Let the] life-style of good people be what you pursue. 2) Matters of business to be taken care of; business responsibilities. *Buwat saupama aniya' kal'ngngananta, subay ambat-ambatta bo' al'kkas akatis, abō' kita makapuwas.* For example we have things to be attended to, we should apply ourselves to the task so it is quickly completed and we are free to go.

**l'ngnganan₂** (var. **pamal'ngngan**) *n.* The manner of doing things; the way things are done. *Buwattingga l'ngngananna?* How do such things proceed? (*Thesaurus:* **baktulan**, **bowahan**, **pakang₁**, **palantara 1**, **tebong**)

**pal'ngngan** *v. tr. -an* To lay down policy for one's followers or adherents. (*cf:* **pitis₂ 1**)

**l'ngngat** *adj. a-* Straightened out of proper alignment, usually involving force. *Am'lli aku p'ssi sabab wa'i bay al'ngngat p'ssiku e' babakan.* I will buy fishhooks because my fishhook got straightened by a pufferfish. (*Thesaurus:* **bigtang 1.1**, **b'ttad 1.1**, **l'dduk 1.1**, **lūk**, **tilud 1.1**, **uli'₂**)

**l'ngngaw-l'ngngaw** *adj. -an* Devoid of people. *Jari amusay sigām minnē' tudju ni lahat l'ngngaw-l'ngngawan, hal sigām sadja.* So they journeyed on from there to a deserted place, just them alone. (*Thesaurus:* **mala'u-la'u 1**, **tannay-tannay**, **t'nnaw-t'nnaw 1**)

**l'ngnges** (var. **lenges**) *n.* 1) The rough surface of shark and stingray skin (dermal denticles). *Aniya' kaitan bin'lla. Yuk Ina', "Kekehin ba kuwitna ilū bo' ahāp niadjal. La'anin l'ngngesna."* Shark was to be cooked. The mother said, "Scrape its skin off so it's ready to be prepared for cooking. Remove its rough surface layer." 1.1) *v. intr. aN-* To feel rough or abrasive to the touch, of shark or stingray skin. *Ya du angal'ngnges kaitan, kumay, peteg.* Sharks and leatherjackets too, are rough to the touch. *Angalenges, akasap sali', ya buwat kulit kumay inān. Lenges*, sort of rough, like the skin of a surgeonfish. (*Thesaurus:* **kasap**, **gasang**, **s'ppal**) 1.2) *v. tr. -an* To remove the denticles from the skin of a shark or stingray. (*Thesaurus:* **bakkel 1.1**, **kagis 1**, **keke₁**)

**l'ngngon** (var. **longngon**) *n.* 1) The arm from wrist to shoulder. *Man deyo' bahaku l'ngngonku.* My arm is below my shoulder. (*wh:* **tangan 1**) 2) The sleeve of a garment.

**l'ppa** (var. **ppa**) *v. intr. a-* To escape from restraint or captivity. *Bay aku makasaggaw daing, bo' wa'i makal'ppa pabīng. Halam ahogot e'ku amalut.* I caught a fish, but it escaped again. I hadn't got a firm grip on it. (*cf:* **pabūy**; *Thesaurus:* **lahi₁**, **s'llu 1.1**)

**l'ppahan** *n.* Freedom from restraint; a free-range area. *A'adla sapi', mbal pasaggaw. Subay na pa'in ma l'ppahan.* Cows are wild and can't be caught. They must always be in a free-range area.

**pal'ppa** *v. tr.* To let something go free; to release from restriction.

**l'ppad-l'ppad** *adj. a-* 1) Going in diverse directions. *Al'ppad-l'ppad, sali' pal'ngngan kaleya.* Heading in various directions, like when walking about inland. (*Thesaurus:* **paghapit-hapit**) 1.1) *v. tr.* To go to many destinations successively. *Bay na l'ppad-l'ppadku katindahan* *ma Balensya pamiha'an sumbuhan palita'an.* I have already gone to all the stores in Valencia looking for a lamp wick.

**l'ppang** *v. intr. aN-* To be just the right size of mesh (for the target fish species) in a trawl net. *Angal'ppang, hatina sarang to'od mata linggi'. Aheka tak'llo'ta bang angal'ppang linggi'. Mbal am'ssut, mbal amangsad.* The right size, the mesh size, in other words, being exactly right. We catch a lot when the mesh of the long net is right. [The fish] don't get through.

**l'ppas** *adj. a-* **1)** Appearing on the other side of an intervening object. *Al'ppas sulat parambila' katas.* The writing appears on the other side of the paper. **1.1)** *v. intr. pa-* To get through to the other side. *Pal'ppas na kami min kagoyakan aheya.* We got through very rough seas. (*Thesaurus:* **lagbas 1, lambang₁, latus, l'ssut**)

**l'ppay** *n.* Generic term for various stinging animals or plants, in the sea or on land. *Aniya' l'ppay ma tahik ataha' daunna, aniya' isāb ma deya. Angeket du sali'-sali'. Abisa l'ppay ma tahik min ma tana'.* There are *l'ppay* in the sea, long-leafed ones, and also on land. They both hurt. The ocean *l'ppay* are more potent than the land ones. (*cf:* **linggatang**)

**l'ppe** *n.* The Painted sweetlips, a fish species. *Plectorhynchus pictus.*

**l'ppet-kandel** *n.* The Ocean sunfish. *Mola mola.*

**l'ppi** *v. intr. pa-* To behave cautiously, alert for trouble. *Pal'ppi na pa'in, minsan aniya' bono'-i, magtūy makalahi.* Keep on being cautious, even when there is fighting we are able to escape immediately. *Pal'ppi ka mareyom lahat ilu ko ra'a ka taluwa' kajahatan. Sali' painsap.* Behave with caution in that place so you aren't struck by trouble. Just be on guard. (*Thesaurus:* **halli'₁ 1.1, insap, liyal, llog 1.1**)

**l'ppit** *v. tr.* **1)** To furl a sail by folding it around the collapsed boom and mast. **2)** To form an edge on to a woven article by folding. (*Thesaurus:* **ppi' 1, sapay 1**)

**l'ppok** *var. of* **logpok**

**l'ppog** *adj. a-* Buckled inwards from a surface. *Al'ppog na bayhu'na min pagsuntukan.* His face is dented from the boxing.

**l'ppo'** *n.* A spherical clay cooking pot with a narrow opening. (*gen:* **pam'llahan**)

**l'ppot** (*var.* **ppot**) *v. tr.* To fold flexible material into a tidy bundle, as a mat, or length of cloth. (*Thesaurus:* **lipat₁ 2, lupi'₁, peko'**)

**l'ppu** *v. tr.* To break something up with a crowbar. *Bang haloblāk aluhay nil'ppu.* Hollow-blocks are easy to break up.

**l'ppus** *n.* **1)** Various marine sponges. *Bapa'ku si' bay magusaha l'ppus.* My uncle used to make his living from marine sponges. (*syn:* **lanos₂**) **2)** Spongy material such as mattress filling. (*Thesaurus:* **kama, kasul, tilam**)

**l'pput₁** *v. intr. pa-* **1)** To protrude or bulge, as an eye from its socket. *Pal'pput mata kokam.* The tarsier's eyes stick out. (*cf:* **loleng, pangsut 1**) **1.1)** To develop hemorrhoids.

**l'pput₂** *see:* **pagl'pput, l'pputan**

**l'pputan** *n.* A liar.

**l'ssa** *var. of* **ssa₁**

**l'ssa'** *adj. a-* Cracked but not broken; showing the beginnings of a crack. *Bang pelang apanggang he' llaw, al'ssa'.* When a canoe is exposed to the sun, it cracks. *Magtīs kibut itū, sali' al'ssa'.* This jar leaks, as though it is cracked. (*cf:* **l'tta' 1**; *Thesaurus:* **b'kka' 1, posat**)

    **pagl'ssa'** *v. intr. aN-* To be showing signs of cracking. *Magl'ssa' bihingna, sali' magb'kka'.* Its edge is showing signs of cracking, like *b'kka'.*

**l'sseg** *var. of* **lesseg**

**l'ssik-l'ssik** *n.* A species of barnacle found on things floating in the sea. *L'ssik-l'ssik itū amikit ma batang palaran ma dilaut. Aniya' isāb amikit ma baran kahumbu.* These barnacles stick to floating logs. There are also some that stick to the bodies of whales. *L'ssik-l'ssik itū taga kulit duwa magka'ob. Apote', anumping bowa'na.* This kind of barnacle has two shells that close tightly together. It is white, and has a flower-like growth in its opening. (*gen:* **tahemtem 1**)

**l'ssin** *adj. a-* Clean; neatly or beautifully done. *Al'ssin la'up badju'na bang niukkilan.* The pleats on her blouse are beautiful when embroidered. *Al'ssin na ka, bay na ka amandi.* You're clean now, you've bathed. (*Thesaurus:* **k'ssang₁, lanu' 1, langis 1, sussi 1.1**)

**l'sso** (*var.* **sso**) *adj. a-* Full from eating. *Buwat makalandu' kinakanta, ya lagi'na bang al'sso.* Like when we have eaten excessively, especially when we are full. (*cf:* **p'nno' 1**; *Thesaurus:* **kiyomol, k'mmol, s'gga**)

**l'ssom** (*var.* **ssom**) *n.* **1)** Sourness. (*Thesaurus:* **kesom, imu' 1, lanab, mamis₁ 1.1, sarap₁, taba' 1**) **1.1)** *adj. a-* Sour, tart, as unripe fruit. **1.2)** *v. advrs. ka-...-an* To be affected by the sourness of something eaten. *Si Oto' bay angandāg mampallam binowa ni luma' pangilaw. Na kal'ssoman kami.* Oldest Son climbed to get mangoes to bring home for preparing raw fish. So we were affected by its sourness.

**l'ssu'** (*var.* **ssu'**) *adj. a-* Cracked or holed so that contents leak out. *Al'ssu' na kaldero, mbal na tapam'llahan buwas. Subay pinahāp maka simento.* The rice pot has a hole and cannot be used for cooking rice. It should be repaired with cement. *Magtūy tin'tta' pelang bo' al'ssu'.* The canoe was promptly pecked so it would leak. (*Thesaurus:* **buslut, mman**)

    **pagl'ssu'-l'ssu'** *v. intr. aN-* To allow liquid to flow out freely, as a container with many holes. *Sa'an itū taga tangkay buwat du isāb basket, magl'ssu'-l'ssu'.* A *sa'an* has a handle just like a basket, it lets liquid through.

**l'ssut** (var. **ssut**) *v. intr. pa-* To emerge from confinement through a small aperture. *Sumiyan ka bay makal'ssut?* When did you manage to get out [from jail]? *Saupama nijīl kami bo' aniya' kasipihanku palahi'an, magtūy aku pal'ssut lahi-lahi. Ahayang na aku.* For example, we are jailed and I spy a way of escape, I promptly slip out and run away. I am at ease again. *Wa'i makal'ssut manuk bay mareyom pagal, paluwas min gese'-gesena.* The chicken has escaped from its cage, getting out by way of its gaps. (*Thesaurus:* **lagbas 1, lambang₁, latus, l'bbot, l'ppas 1.1**)

**pal'ssut** *v. tr.* To convey something by a messenger, with implications of difficulty in getting it through.

**l'tta'** *n.* **1)** A flaw showing the beginning of a crack in something brittle. (*cf:* **l'ssa'**; *Thesaurus:* **gali'₂, galna' 1**) **1.1)** *v. intr. aN-* To show signs of splitting; to begin to crack. *Angal'tta' na munda' pelang, halam gi' abila'.* The canoe's prow is beginning to crack, not yet split.

**l'tte'₁** *n.* A flash of lightning accompanied by a thunderclap; a thunderbolt. *L'tte' itū ta'nda', takale, pasinglab, pasawa, magtūy l'ggon. L'tte'* is seen and heard, it flashes and lights up, and promptly thunders. (*Thesaurus:* **daogdog, lāt, l'ggon**)

**l'tte'₂** *v. tr.* To bend someone's fingers back against normal alignment, a mild punishment. *Bang bay magtalang, pagpole' ni luma' nil'tte' tangan kami.* When we have been playing toss-the-coin, on getting back home we have our fingers forced back.

**l'ttu** *v. intr. pa-* To set out for a remote destination. *Pal'ttu kami kaut.* We are heading far out to sea. *Buwattingga angkan kal'ttu lai' ni luma' sigām?* How was it that the plates went way off to their house? (*Thesaurus:* **batbat₁, tulak₁ 1.1**)

**l'ttup** *n.* **1)** A blister formed by prolonged pressure. *Aniya' l'ttup tanganku pagtukulku lantay luma' kami.* I have blisters on my hands from hammering the floor of our house. (*Thesaurus:* **kassa'-kassa', lutup, mata-daing 1, tambu-tambu₂**) **1.1)** *v. intr. aN-* To form blisters.

**lla** var. of **h'lla**

**llad** *v. intr. aN-* To cry soundlessly with open mouth. *At'ggol ang'llad onde' inān, angalom bayhu'na. Halam makatangis, hal pabanga'. Halam kita makakale tangis.* That child has been crying soundlessly for a while, its face has become very red. It hasn't managed to cry aloud, just has its mouth wide open. We haven't heard a cry. *Da'a na pa'in patangisun onde' ilu, bo' mbal ang'llad.* Don't keep making the child cry, lest it cry without breathing. (*Thesaurus:* **asang-selo, lihing, tangis 1.1**)

**llaw₁** **1)** *n.* Day in contrast to night. *Magpandan sadja d'nda itū llaw-sangom, angambuhut.* This woman works with pandanus day and night,

scraping it [for weaving]. **2)** *clf.* Count word for days as units of 24 hours. *Mpat ng'llaw atawa mpat llaw, sali' du.* Four *ng'llaw* or four *llaw*, they're the same thing. *Aniya' duwang'llaw palabay.* Two days have passed.

**ka'llawan** *n.* Daytime; daylight hours. *Ma llaw hē-i sampay ni ka'llawan dakayu'.* From that day until the following day.

**llaw-kalla'** *n.* The day of burial.

**llaw-llaw** *adv.* Daily. *Subay pilmi-pilmi magusaha, sali' llaw-llaw.* It is necessary to be always working, daily. *Amandi ka llaw-llaw bo' ka mbal pinohak.* Bathe every day so you don't get ringworm. (*cf:* **pilmi-pilmi**)

**k'llaw** *adj. a-* Active early in the day. (*cf:* **awal₂ 1.1**)

**llaw₂** **1)** The sun as the source of heat. *Apasu' llaw, mbal kasandalan.* The sun is hot, unbearable. **1.1)** *v. tr. -an* To expose something to the direct rays of the sun, as to dry it. *Wa'i pareyo' si Arung ang'llawan pantalunku.* Oldest Daughter has gone down to put my trousers in the sun. *Suma'an ni'llawan binamban bo' nihinang lapuk-lapuk bang atoho'.* Boiled cassave is at times dried in the sun to be made into *lapuk-lapuk* candy once it's dry. *Da'a g'mmosun daing-daing ilū. Llawin ko' na pa'in atoho'. Da'a pinagbangkat-bangkat.* Don't drench those little fish. Sun them so they become dry. Don't pile them up.

**pag'llaw** *v. intr. aN-* To expose oneself to the sun.

**pagpating'llaw** *v. intr. aN-* To expose oneself to the sun; to sunbathe.

**pang'llaw** *n.* The sunny season.

**llaw kapaganak** *n. phrase* The day of birth; birthday.

**llaw itu** *n. phrase* Today. *Minsan mbal atupus llaw itu, kalu atupus salung. Tupusku pa'in.* Even if it is not completed today, it may be completed tomorrow. I will complete it. (*Thesaurus:* **di'ilaw, ma t'llu, salung, simuddai**)

**llaw ni llaw** *adv. phrase* Day after day; one day after another.

**lleng** *v. intr. aN-* To be making a vibrating sound; to buzz; to hum. *Ang'lleng mandal itū bang taluwa' baliyu. Ya saga tabungay, ampan, ang'lleng du isāb.* This *mandal* kite will make a humming noise when the wind hits it. Hornets, locusts, they make a humming or buzzing noise too.

**llet** *v. advrs. -in-* **1)** Constipated. *Ni'llet kita asungi' bang kahunitan.* We are *llet* when we have difficulty defecating. (*syn:* **tobol**) **2)** Frustrated at not making progress after much effort. *Ni'llet ka'a ilū amusay. Anagga' s'llog bang ka mbal man bihing deya.* You will be frustrated with paddling. You will be fighting the current if you aren't close inshore. *Ni'llet kita amiha sīn. Minsan tangan-tape' amale' mbal papiha.* We are frustrated looking for the money. Even though hands and feet are exhausted, it's not to be

found. (*Thesaurus:* **kuttung**) **2.1**) *intrj.*
Exclamation indicating frustration.

**pag'llet** *v. tr. -an* To experience ongoing
frustration. *Ai-ai binowa mbal takole'; nīllet.*
*"Mag'lletan ka," yukna.* Anything being carried
but not managed; frustrated. Someone says,
"You're having a frustrating time."

**lling** var. of **h'lling₁, h'lling₃**

**llis** *v. intr. aN-* To make the hissing sound of an
object moving swiftly through water. *Ang'llis*
*tahik man buli' pelang.* The sea hisses aft of the
canoe. (*Thesaurus:* **ebol, sahabal, samb'llong**)

**llok** *v. intr. aN-* To make the sound of trickling
water. *Ang'llok pahāp bohe' ma sapa' inān.* The
water in that stream is really making a noise.
*Ang'llok bang amange'.* Urinating produces a
trickling sound.

**llog** *adj. a-* **1**) Cautious; watchful. *Bay aniya'*
*angindam lilusku, mbal paindamanku. A'llog aku,*
*atāw aku abila'.* Someone wanted to borrow my
watch, I wouldn't lend it. I'm cautious, I'm
afraid it will be broken. (*Thesaurus:* **illag** 1) **1.1**)
*v. intr. aN-* To be cautious, aware of
consequences. *Mbal ang'llog onde' ilū bang palahi-*
*lahi, mbal minsan pahogga'.* That child is heedless
[of obstacles] when she runs about, doesn't even
pause. *Ang'llog ka dīnu.* Watch out for yourself.
(*Thesaurus:* **halli'₁ 1.1, insap, liyal, l'ppi**) **1.2**)
*v. tr. a-, ka-..-an, -an* To treat something with
care or respect; to cherish. *Bang aniya' alungay*
*man kita, magdohon. Paligay bang bay ka'lloganta*
*sali' kita magdohon.* If something is lost to us, we
keep grieving. Especially when we had
cherished it, we go on grieving. *Batin itū ai-ai*
*kina'llogan mareyom baran d'nda.* Batin [private
parts] refers to whatever is treated with caution
in a woman's body. *Kina'llogan, sali' bang aniya'*
*niamu' mbal tapamuwan.* Treated with caution, as
when something is requested but can't be given.
*"Ka'llogin," yukna, "barannu."* "Be careful," she
said, "of yourself."

**llom** *v. tr.* To sit on eggs for a long time in order to
incubate them. (*syn:* **ōm**)

**pagka'lloman** *v. intr. aN-* To do something for a
long time.

**llop** *adj. a-* **1**) Becoming low in the water, as a
canoe loaded to the gunwales. *Allop na bangka'*
*ni heka duwa'anbi.* The canoe is low in the water
due to the number of your cargo items.
(*Thesaurus:* **apad-apad, apang, togob₂**) **1.1**) *v.*
*tr. -an* To overload a conveyance. *Ōy! Da'a llopin*
*pelang ilū sabab aheka na bay niruwa'.* Hey! Don't
overload that canoe because a lot has been
loaded onto it already.

**llot** *n.* A space or object separating two points or
stages. *Ma llot matto'a maka onde'-onde'.*
Between an adult and a child. *Bang kami ni*
*M'ddas palabay min llot taytayan.* When we go to
Siasi [by canoe] we pass between raised
walkways. (*cf:* **ōt**; *Thesaurus:* **olangan** 1,

t'ngnga')

**llotan** *n.* A space or interval between points.
*Aniya' ta'nda'ku ma uppiku mpat kalesa paluwas*
*min llotan duwa būd.* In my dream I saw four
horse-drawn carts coming from the space
between the two mountains.

**pag'llot** *v. intr. aN-* To locate between similar
things. *Bang kami atuli, mag'llot.* When we sleep,
we lie between [other people].

**pagpati'llot** *v. intr. aN-* **1**) To be in an
intermediate state. **2**) To serve as a mediator
between two parties.

**llub** *v. intr. aN-* To emit a resounding or throbbing
noise. *Tal'ngnget-l'ngnget, ya mang'llub ma kayu.*
Cicada, the thing that makes a throbbing noise
in the trees. *Ang'llub na pagtimbak.* The
dynamiting reverberates. *Asidda magbolobok*
*deyom b'ttongku. Kilāku aniya' saki ma deyom,*
*sali' ang'llub.* My stomach is really rumbling. I
think there is some sickness inside, sort of
gurgling. (*Thesaurus:* **konog-konog, kulattub,**
**pagbolobok, paglagonggok, paglagublub**)

**llum** *adj. a-* Alive. *A'llum gi' saga mato'ahanbi.* Your
parents-in-law are still alive. *Mbal na kami*
*magniyat in kami a'llum pabīng.* We no longer
expect to live again.

**ka'lluman** (var. **kalluman**) *n.* The means of
sustaining life; one's livelihood. (*Thesaurus:*
**balanja' 1, kahirupan, gastu 1, lutu'₁ 1,**
**pagnapaka**)

**llum helo** *adj. a-* Quickened or stimulated, of the
flow of saliva in response to the sight or taste of
something repulsive. {idiom} *A'llum heloku bang*
*aku ang'nda' patay, ya po'on aku angaludja',*
*angutta' saga.* I am nauseated when I see a
corpse, which is why I spit, sort of retch. *Ōy,*
*mbal a'llum helonu bang ka maka'nda' sowa*
*takot?* Oy, doesn't your saliva flow when you see
a reef snake?

**llum-patay** *n.* **1**) The condition between dead and
alive. **1.1**) *adj. a-* Dead or alive, with uncertainty
as to the outcome. *Bang bay taluwa' timbak bo'*
*a'llum-amatay, sali' ahalol. Pa'asa-asanu aku.*
When [I] was hit by an explosion and was
between dead and alive, gravely ill. You
reassured me.

**ka'llum** *n.* Life, as a state of being.

**ka'llum-kamatay** *n.* Life and death as the span of
human existence. *Ka'llum-kamatay, ameya' aku*
*ma ka'a.* In life or in death, I will go with you.

**paka'llum** *v. tr.* To keep something alive; to bring
something to life or action.

**pagka'llum** *n.* The quality of life.

**lōb** *n.* **1**) A sum of money that secures a loan or
opens a bargaining sequence for a valuable
item. *Buwat a'a magdagang mussa', bang mussa'*
*ahāp subay aniya' sīn pangukaban lawang, ati sīn*
*ē' lōb ma iya, minsan mbal tab'lli mussa'.* Suppose
a man is selling a pearl, if it is a good one there
must be a sum of money given as a "door

opener". Then that down payment becomes the property of the person selling, even if the pearl isn't bought. **1.1)** *adj.* a- Transferred to permanent ownership, especially of an item not redeemed from pawn within the time set. *Alōb e' padjak singsingku.* The pawnshop has kept my ring. (*Thesaurus:* l'kkat₁ 1, padjak₁, panau') **1.2)** *v. tr.* To retain possession of something borrowed or of something deposited as security. *Lōbku na sangkap bay indamanku min ka'a, mbal papole'ku. Ma aku na.* I will keep that chisel I borrowed from you, I shan't give it back. It's mine now.

**lobag** *n.* Ingrained dirt in skin or cloth. (*Thesaurus:* l'mmi' 1, lumut₁ 2, moseng 1)

**lobet** *adj.* a- Broken apart, of solid items. *Bay alobet dambila' pansal pelangnu. Apōng.* Half of the prow board of your canoe is broken. Broken in two. (*Thesaurus:* pate', pōng 1, punggul 2, teplong)

**loblob** *v. intr.* pa- To burrow or sink out of sight in mud or sand. *Imbaw itū paloblob ma deyom pisak.* These cockles burrow into the mud. *Patanom tape'ta, paloblob tobtob lo'atanta mareyom tana'.* Our feet go in, sinking in the earth as far as our knee joints. (*Thesaurus:* l'nnob, paglowak, senop, tanom₂)

**lobog** *n.* 1) Dirt suspended in a liquid. (*Thesaurus:* aut 1, lagod₁) **1.1)** *adj.* a- Containing sediment, of a liquid. *Mbal tainum bohe' alobog, makapagsungi'-sungi'.* Muddied water is not drinkable, it will cause diarrhea.

**lobot-lobot** *n.* A sea anemone species, edible.

**loka** *adj.* a- Loose-fitting. *Aloka na kusu batangan. Maglunsul na batangan parambila' maka parambila', apa aheya lowangna.* The hole for the outrigger support is loose. The support keeps on moving from one side to the other, because the hole is big. (*Thesaurus:* lambuyut, luslus 1.1)

**pagloka-loka** *v. intr.* aN- To move around within a space that was meant to be a snug fit. *Sali' magloka-loka, maghenggol.* Like it's moving around, shaky.

**loka'** *n.* A lidded container for small items, made of a single inter-nodal section of large bamboo. *Loka' itu taga turung, pangisihan p'ssi.* The *loka'* referred to has a lid, it is a container for fishhooks. (*Thesaurus:* bō', honga'₁, saud₁, tumpung)

**loka'-loka'** *n.* Small lidded containers for the individual ingredients inside a betel nut box. (*Thesaurus:* anak-mama'an, mama'an, salappa')

**lokay₁** *n.* The new leaves of a coconut frond, still in their protective sheath. (*wh:* niyug)

**lokay₂** var. of **sowa-lokay**

**loklok** *v. intr.* pa- To withdraw into a confined space. *Bang kita bay ma diyata' papan pelang, bo' aniya' katāwanta, paloklok kita nireyom mohang. Atapuk kita.* When we are on the deck planks of the canoe and we're frightened of something, we withdraw into the hull. We are hidden. *Paloklok kamun ni deyom lowang ma gusung.* The *kamun* shrimp goes into a hole on the sand. (*syn:* l'llok 1)

**lokob** (var. **langkob**) *v. tr.* -an To cover something completely. *Lokobin daing ilū, bo' al'kkas atahak.* Cover that fish so it will cook quickly. *Lokobin pagkakan bo' mbal nilangaw.* Cover the food so it doesn't get flies.

**lokob nyawa** *v. tr.* -an To extinguish the life-force of a human being, the action of a saitan spirit. {idiom} *Nilokoban nyawata, amatay na e' saitan. Sali' niroponan nyawata.* Our life-force is extinguished, killed by a *saitan* spirit. It is as though our life-force is pressed down.

**loko'** 1) *v. tr.* To wad clothes instead of folding them. *Niloko', ni'isi sadja, halam nilūn. Loko'* means just put in without being folded. (*Thesaurus:* komo'₂, g'mmot 1, go'ok 1.1) 2) *v. intr.* pa- To sit with the knees drawn up and hugged, a response to acute pain.

**lokom** *v. tr.* To eat with fingers, stuffing food into one's mouth. (*cf:* pagsobo')

**lokonan** *n.* The inner side of knee or elbow. (*Thesaurus:* lo'atan, peya'-peya' kōk-tu'ut, siku, tu'ut)

**lokot** *v. tr.* To allow kite lines to intertwine. *Da'a lokotun engkot taguri' ilu.* Don't let the strings of those kites intertwine. (*Thesaurus:* gumun, sagut 1, tulabid)

**lokot-lokot** *n.* An edible growth of multiple greenish strands found adhering in clumps to seagrass. *Lokot-lokot itū amikit ma unas. Lokot-lokot sticks to seagrass. Aheka sāng lokot tak'llo'.* Many *lokot* nests were gathered.

**loddos** (var. **l'ddos**) 1) *v. intr.* pa- To reduce in bulk or abundance. *Ai-ai akirus, paloddos dambila', sali' atimpang.* Things too small on one side, one half diminished in bulk, sort of uneven. *Buwat kita bay aheka ai-aita, manjari ma sosōng tahun pahalam na pa'in, pahalam. Paloddos ai-ai.* Like us [incl] having lots of things, but then as the years passed they kept on vanishing. Everything grew less and less. *Bang buwat usaha itū paloddos, halam minsan ta'abut po'on.* Getting smaller, like this business, not even reaching the capital outlay. (*Thesaurus:* kō' 1.2, kulang₁ 1.3, lō') 2) *v. tr.* -an To reduce the size or abundance of something. *Bay taga kaniya', sagwā' nil'ddosan e' Tuhan.* [They] had wealth, but God reduced it. *Buwat pelang aheya niloddosan, nila'anan tapi'na, nihinang pongag.* Like a big canoe reduced in size, its planking removed, made into a hulk.

**lodjag** (var. **lodjat₁**) *adj.* a- 1) Squashy; pulpy. *Bang lumandu'an atahak ai-ai, magkalodjat sadja.* If anything is really over-ripe, it just becomes squashy. (*Thesaurus:* biyobog, k'ddos, lonyat, petak 1, tonyak) **1.1)** *v. tr.* To reduce a substance to pulp, as fruits or cooked root crops.

**paglodjag** *v. intr. aN-* To become squashy, of fruit or root vegetables.

**lodjat₁** var. of **lodjag**

**lodjat₂** 1) *v. intr. pa-* To push a canoe vigorously away from a group of other vessels. *Bang saupama patundug ni jambatan, bo' alandos goyak, palodjat kita ko da'a magka'at.* Suppose we have docked at the pier and the waves are quite rough, we push off to avoid damage. (*cf:* **judjal** 2) 2) *v. tr. -an* To move a canoe vigorously forward and back, as to remove water from the hull. *Nilodjatan bangka' ko' ala'an bohe'na.* We move the dugout forward and back to remove the water. (*Thesaurus:* **kallus₂, k'llut 1.1, sait**)

**logdang₁** *adj. zero* 1) To be on target. 1.1) *v. advrs. ka-...-an* To be hit accurately. *Tinimbak sundalu, kalogdangan, diretso amatay.* The soldiers fired at, hit exactly, dying immediately. *Manjari isāb ma basketbōl, kalogdangan, halam minsan makasagid ni ring.* Can be used in basketball too, right on target, not even brushing against the hoop.

**logdang₂** (var. **l'ddang**) *adj. a-* Filled with water and sinking. *Min t'llu kami bay alogdang marilaut.* Three times we filled and sank out at sea. (*Thesaurus:* **buhaw, t'nde 1, t'nnob 1**)

**loglog** *v. intr. pa-* To persist in doing something despite lack of success. *Paloglog na pa'in iya itū minsan mbal tinaima'.* He persists in visiting even though he is not welcomed. *Minsan kita kinala'atan, paloglog na pa'in, buwat ni luma' saga si'itta, saga kakita hē'.* Even though we are badly treated we keep trying, like going to the house of our uncles and cousins for example.

**logmay** *n.* 1) The loss of energy; lassitude. 1.1) *adj. a-* Drained of strength. *Makalogmay bang kita mbal biyasa atuli ugtu-llaw.* It is exhausting if we are not used to sleeping in the middle of the day. 1.2) *v. tr. -an* To drain someone of strength. *Nilogmayan kitā.* We are deprived of strength.

**logmay-lamma** *n.* The feeling of total lack of energy. *Puwas bay amatay si Mma' to'a, pinah'lling e' panubu'na, "Daindingin saga anak-mpunu, ya binuwanan logmay-lamma."* After Grandfather had died his descendants said to him, "Protect your children and grandchildren, the ones who had been made drained of energy." *Niraindingan itū, sali' tinampan bang aniya' saki. "Daindingin saga anak-mpunu, da'a buwanin logmay-lamma."* "Protected, as though shielded when there is some illness. "Protect your descendants, don't cause them to have serious loss of energy." *Ya pangamu'ta, "Daindingin saga anak-mpunu, da'a buwanin logmay-lamma."* Our request is, "Protect your descendants, don't give them serious loss of energy." (*Thesaurus:* **kapuy**)

**lognos** *adj. a-* Demolished, as a collapsed house or a sunken boat. (*Thesaurus:* **lapnas 1, luhu'₂ 1, ponas, sapsay**)

**logo** *n.* A small woven trap placed at the end of a fish fence to catch escaping fish.

**logob-logob** *adj. a-* Semi-dark, as the period before dawn or after sunset. *Hinabu masi alogob-logob lahat magpakeyat kami palita'an.* While it is still dusk we light the lamps. *Logob-logob pa'in lahat ak'tta kami ni dambila'.* When it was dusk we set out for the other side. (*Thesaurus:* **abay-kohap, kohap 1, lekot-lendom, lempos, magrib 2, sū'-palita'an**)

**logos** (var. **pogos**) *v. tr.* 1) To use force on something contrary to its physical nature; to urge or compel a person against his or her will. *Da'a logosun gombahan ilū.* Don't force that pump. *Sagarin na, mbal palogos.* Let it be, it can't be forced. *Bay aku amogos dīku ang'ntanan l'mmi'.* I made myself handle dirty things. (*cf:* **bowa₃**; *Thesaurus:* **abiyug, agpot 1, angin, egot-egot, panhot, p'ggong, poleggaw**) 1.1) To rape. *Amogos kahukaw d'nda.* Urging [against] the woman's reluctance. *D'nda ya bay nilalas min deyom luma'na, pinogos.* A woman who was abducted from her house, forced [to engage in sex].

**logpok** (var. **l'ppok**) *adj. a-* 1) Dented; deflated; buckled. *Halam aniya' saddī minnitu? Alogpok ko' itū.* Is there nothing other than this? This is buckled. *Angay al'ppok mital itū?* Why is this metal can buckled in? (*Thesaurus:* **k'mmog 1, k'ppi'₂, kummi', h'bbong**) 1.1) *v. intr. pa-* To squeeze inwards so as to reduce size. *Pal'ppok bowa'ku, ato'a na aku.* My mouth is drawn in, I am old now. *Pal'ppok gomana.* Its tire is flat.

**logtas** *adj. a-* Gapped, of items normally connected. (*Thesaurus:* **boklang 1, bugtu'₁, butas 1, l'kkat₂ 1, okat₂ 1**)

**logtasan** *n.* A gap between two points. *Logtasan, buwat gallang mbal sarang, aniya' logtasanna.* Like a bracelet that isn't large enough, it has a gap.

**loho'** *n.* 1) The juice of something cooked; broth; soup. *Atigang na daing bin'lla, halam aniya' na loho'na.* The cooked fish is dry, it has no broth. (*Thesaurus:* **sindul 1**) 1.1) *v. tr.* To dip food in tasty liquid. *Binahug, niloho'.* Dipped into liquid, into soup. 1.2) *v. tr. -an* To cook soup. *Yukna ma ipatanna, "Pehē' ka angaloho' ma l'ppo' aheya ilū bo' aniya' takakantam."* He said to his house-help, "Off you go and make soup in that big pot so we have something to eat."

**loho'-ubi** *n.* Purple color; violet dye coloring. (*Thesaurus:* **kausun, sakulati 2**; *gen:* **walna'**)

**lō'** *v. intr. pa-* To reduce the severity of one's attitude; to be more gentle. *Palō', palunuk, pahali anganjawab.* Diminish, soften, stop arguing. *Yuk dangan, "Aesog aku." Bang angatu ya bay pinah'llingan inān, na palō' ya bay mah'lling ē'.* One says, "I'm tough!" When the one who was spoken to fights back, then the one who spoke changes his attitude. *Buwat kita angandag bo' nihalga'an na, yukta, "Ōy, mbal aku bang mbal lō'annu."* Like when we ask the price and are told what is being asked, and we say, "Hey, I won't be buying unless you come down a bit." (*Thesaurus:* **kō' 1.2, kulang₁ 1.2, kulang₁ 1.3, l'ddos 1.1, loddos 1**)

**lo'akan** var. of **lo'atan**

**lo'atan** (var. **lo'akan**) *n.* The inside of the knee joint; the inside of the elbow. *Alabung bu'unna, ta'abut lo'atanna.* Her hair grows profusely, reaching to the back of her knees. (*Thesaurus:* **lokonan, peya'-peya' kōk-tu'ut, siku, tu'ut**)

**lo'ay** var. of **bo'ay**

**lo'ok** *n.* An indentation of a coast; a cove or bay. *Aheka kagong ma deyom lo'ok.* There are many crabs in the bay. (*Thesaurus:* **b'ttong₃, suba'**)

**lo'ok-lo'ok** *n.* The inner corner of a rectangular enclosure. *Pagpugaran kamahung lo'ok-lo'ok kabinet inān.* The corner of that cabinet is where cockroaches nest. *A: "O Kulas, nihaggut gi' ka? Ilu na ka ma lo'ok-lo'ok ilū." B: "Na minsan na ba, mbal kasandalan haggut itū."* A: "Kulas, are you still cold? You are there in the corner." B: "Even so, this cold is unbearable." (*Thesaurus:* **dugu, pidju 1**)

**lo'od** *see:* **pagkalo'od**

**lo'on** *n.* A species of deepwater anemone, has stinging tendrils. (*Thesaurus:* **kambang, kombo'-kombo', lason, pari-pari**)

**loleng** *v. tr.* To gouge out an eye, sometimes used as a threat. *Lolengta ka matanu.* I'll gouge your eyes out. (*cf:* **l'pput₁ 1, pangsut 1**)

**lolog** *v. tr.* To openly seize or commandeer someone else's property. *Angalolog iya duma'in ai-aina.* He misappropriates things that are not his. *Saupama magi'ipat ka kambing, ubus nilolog min ka'a. Na kalongkopan na ka.* If for example you are a goat farmer, and they are taken from you. You are overwhelmed. (*Thesaurus:* **agaw 1.1**)

**loman** *adj. a-* **1)** Shy of someone; deferential. *Tamamang iya, sali' aloman anuli-nuli.* He is hesitant in speech, shy about talking. (*Thesaurus:* **pagkalo'od**) **1.1)** *v. tr. a-, ka-..-an, -an* To respect someone. *Subay ka kinalomanan to'ongan bo' ka pinab'llihan dahatus maka duwampū'.* You would have to be held in great respect for someone to sell it to you for one hundred and twenty pesos.

**pagloman** *v. intr. aN-* **1)** To be mutually respectful. *Magkalo'od, magloman-loman.* Mutually polite, mutually respectful. **1.1)** *v. tr. -an* To esteem someone; to treat someone with respect. *A'a inān ahāp isāb pagbabaranna. Mbal angakkal, pinagkalomanan e' manusiya'.* The dignity and integrity of that man are great. He doesn't cheat and is respected by people everywhere.

**pagmaloman** *v. intr. aN-* To show respect or courtesy.

**lomba** (var. **lomba'**) *v. tr. -an* To race someone. *Angalombahan aku a'a lahi-lahi inān.* I will race that running man.

**paglomba** *v. intr. aN-* To compete with each other; to race each other. *Bang Hailaya maglomba kamemon pambot.* At the Hailaya festival all the motor vessels race each other. *Bay aku ni Tiyanggi Sūk ang'nda'-ng'nda' ma ka'am maglomba-lomba.* I went to Jolo Town to watch you racing. *Kura' mandu-mandu, kura' paglomba', aesog maka ab'ngngis.* A powerful horse, a racing horse, aggressive and mean. (*Thesaurus:* **pagdanel 1.1, pagpasu 1.1**)

**lomba-lomba** (var. **lomba'-lomba'**) *n.* A porpoise; a dolphin. (*cf:* **bbung**)

**lomba'** var. of **lomba**

**lomba'-lomba'** var. of **lomba-lomba**

**lomeng-lomeng** *adj. a-* Slow-moving; lethargic; sluggish. *Alomeng-lomeng, aniya' ninanam.* Moving sluggishly, feeling some symptom. (*Thesaurus:* **doson 1, gadgad₁, honhon**)

**lomo** *adj. a-* **1)** Crumbling, as rotten wood or packs of grated cassava. *Alomo bāng-bāng itū.* These cookies are crumbly. *Alomo-lomo bay tapi', sali' kayu bā mbal na manjari.* The canoe strake was somewhat crumbly, like wood that is no long usable. (*Thesaurus:* **budjal-budjal, gokal, p'kkal 1, podjak 1, sughay**) **1.1)** *v. tr.* To crumble something.

**lompeng** (var. **lopeng**) *adj. a-* **1)** Buckled or bent from normal shape. *Mbal asandal, al'kkas alompeng sabab anipis.* It won't last long, it will soon buckle because it is thin. *Buwat busay, alopeng e' llaw. Atawa mital bubung, yukta, "Ai bay makalopeng? Kilāku bay pagi'ikan."* Like a paddle, warped by the sun's heat. Or of metal ridging, we say, "What caused this to bend? I reckon it got stood on." *Buwat pang'ntan bang makaniai-ai atuwas, mbal magtūy at'bbe', hal alopeng.* Like when a tool hits something hard, it doesn't get chipped immediately. It just gets bent. (*cf:* **kopeng;** *Thesaurus:* **kello' 1**) **1.1)** *v. tr.* To bend something against its normal alignment. *Lopeng-lopengun bo' apōng.* Bend it repeatedly so it breaks.

**paglompeng** *v. intr. aN-* To become distorted in shape. *Tiyangsi' itū niā' min batang langkay. Mbal magtūy tapangengkot magdai'-dai' ni ai-ai. Subay gi' tinabid-tabid bo' mbal maglompeng.* The *tiyangsi'* referred to is obtained from the central rib of a coconut frond. It can't be used in a hurry for tying anything. It should be twined a bit first so it doesn't lose its shape.

**lona** *n.* A tent or tent-like cloth shelter, especially in the context of Boy Scouts or school camping. (*Thesaurus:* **kapis, ispowen, ma'ung, mantaluna, patig, tolda**)

**londay** *n.* A type of outrigger canoe with no more

than one side plank attached to its hull. (*Thesaurus:* **balutu, bangka', dapang, pallungan, pambot, paraw 1, pelang, pongag**)

**lonob** (var. **lonod**) *adj. a-* **1)** Submerged, as by sinking or due to rising tide. *Alonob na tangonan, wa'i na palaran pelang.* The canoe rack is under water and the canoe has drifted away. (*Thesaurus:* **kanop, letop 1, limun 1**) **1.1)** *v. intr. pa-* To submerge below the surface.

**lonod** var. of **lonob**

**lonseng** *adj. a-* **1)** Poorly maintained, of a canoe. *Alonseng bayanan, mbal pinahilala', al'kkas magka'at.* The vessel is neglected, not cared for, it will soon break up. (*Thesaurus:* **patabak**) **1.1)** *v. tr.* To let something go uncared for. *Da'a lonsengun pelang ilu bā.* Hey, don't neglect that canoe!

**lonyat** *adj. a-* Mushy; squashy. *Alonyat, mbal tapuwa' he' tangan.* Squashy, can't be picked up in the hand. (*Thesaurus:* **biyobog, k'ddos, lodjag 1, petak 1, tonyak**)

**lōng-lōng** *v. intr. pa-* To improve, of weather conditions. *Bang kita taluwa' baliyu ma dilaut, bo' kita am'ssi, tahan-tahanta ma dilaut, kalu-kalu palōng-lōng.* When we are hit by the wind out at sea while fishing, we endure it out there, maybe the weather will improve. (*Thesaurus:* **gām-gām, hāp-hāp, hikay, hoblas 1, siha'-siha', si'at**)

**longa** *n.* Sesame seeds. *Sesamum orientale. Tapanambal du isāb longa. K'mbangta bo' painumta onde'-onde', bang ahagpay na.* Sesame seeds can also be used for medicine. We soak it and have children drink it once it is cold.

**longa'** *adj. a-* Old and worn but still usable if cared for. *Alonga', bang duhunanta magka'at. Tapahāp du.* It is worn; if we keep on using it will be ruined. It can be repaired though. (*Thesaurus:* **bahal, ndang**)

**longkang** (var. **longkong**) *v. intr. pa-* To accumulate, as water in a hollow. *Bohe' k'ppong hal palongkang, nsa' sasahanna.* Pond-water just accumulates, it has no current.

**longkong** var. of **longkang**

**longkop** *v. tr. -an* **1)** To conquer; overpower. *Mbal kami bilahi nilongkopan e' bangsa liyu.* We are unwilling to be defeated by foreigners. **1.1)** *v. advrs. ka-...-an* To be beaten in a contest, of words and wits, a legal dispute, or a military invasion. *Kalongkopan sadja kami bang maghukum. Mbal kita maka'atu ma bissala atawa ma pamikil.* We always get beaten in a legal argument. We can't compete, either in speech or thought. *Saupama magi'ipat ka kambing, ubus nilolog min ka'a. Na kalongkopan na ka. Niā' luma' atawa huma.* If for example you are a goat farmer, and they are taken from you. You are defeated, your house or farm taken from you. (*Thesaurus:* **agaw 1.1**)

**longkoy** *v. intr. aN-* To become flaccid and weak, of muscles; to lose all strength. *Angalongkoy, sali'*

*ala'an ugatta.* Becoming flaccid, as though our muscles have gone. (*Thesaurus:* **dome-dome, layu-layu, s'nnay, summil**)

**longgang** *n.* A species of grouper, medium size. (*gen:* **kuhapo'**)

**longngon** var. of **l'ngngon**

**longon** *v. tr.* To wind line onto a spool. (*Thesaurus:* **bodbod₁ 1.1, kokos₁ 1, koleng₁ 1.1, lengke**)

**longon-longon** *n.* The intestines. (*cf:* **tina'i**)

**longpos** (var. **kaloposan**) *v. advrs. ka-...-an* To be defeated and deprived of one's status and economic advantage. *Kalongposan sigām e' saga ata sigām.* They will be reduced in status and wealth by their own slaves. (*Thesaurus:* **agaw 1.1, gora'₂ 1.1, taban**)

**longsad₁** *v. tr.* To move something into the sea by lowering it from a platform or by dragging it from where it was beached. *Mbal talongsadku pelangku bang dangan-danganku.* I cannot launch my canoe if I am on my own. (*Thesaurus:* **dahik, daldal, l'bbos 1.1**)

**longsad₂** *v. advrs. ka-...-an* To be collapsed. *Bay kalongsaran luma' disi Anu inān, bay kagabbangan dibuhi'.* What's-his-name's house there has collapsed, [the house] that had the bamboo marimba event last night.

**lopa'** *v. tr.* To munch something while eating. *Bang daing ariki' minsan pinapa', mbal aku kowa'an. Talopa'ku.* With small fish, even when they are chewed, I don't get fishbones stuck in my throat. I munch them up. (*Thesaurus:* **pa'us, papa'**) **talopa'** *n.* That which is eaten; food of any kind. (*Thesaurus:* **kinakan 1**)

**lopas** *adj. a-* **1)** Lost or mislaid. *Wa'i alopas kamemon.* Everything lost. (*syn:* **lungay 1**) **1.1)** *v. tr.* To lose or mislay something. *Sanda'-sanda' sadja, mbal nilopas, mbal nilōb.* Just a brief loan, not to be lost, not to be pawned.

**lopeng** var. of **lompeng**

**lopok** *adj. a-* Crackly, of something munched. (*syn:* **lapuk**) **palopok** (var. **pahopok**) *v. intr. aN-* To crackle when compressed, as of something held tightly in the hand or between the teeth. (*cf:* **paletek**)

**lopot** *adj. a-* **1)** Destroyed; broken up. *Alopot-lopot basu paghūg ni lantay.* The glass breaks into pieces on falling to the floor. *Nirugsu'an iya ma kīd tuktukna bo' alopot kōkna.* He was stabbed in the side of his brow so that his head was shattered. *Bang kaut bo' alandos to'ongan goyak, alatas saga katig. Mbal anandal pelang ma goyak. Alopot-lopot.* When at sea and the waves are really rough, the outriggers are disconnected. A *pelang*-type canoe cannot cope with rough water. It will break up. (*Thesaurus:* **bagbag, māg-māg, tumu-tumu**) **1.1)** *v. tr.* To break something up. *Nilopot saga kibut ya bay bowa sigām.* The clay jars they had brought were broken up.

**lorak** *adj. a-* In disrepair, as buildings, canoes, or

clothing. *Alorak, ajagjag, mbal na tapagguna.* Falling apart, breaking up, no longer usable. *Sali' pelang bang alorak-lorak, na alonseng.* Like a canoe in need of repair, just neglected. (*Thesaurus:* **basak, jagjag 1, langkat 1, larak 1.1**)

**lorok** *v. intr. pa-* **1)** To plunge downwards from a surface. *Busay, hē' na palorok.* The paddle, it has plunged straight down [into the sea]. *Palorok ka pehē'.* Dive down there. (*Thesaurus:* **lurup, tuhun 1**) **1.1)** *v. tr.* To reach by diving. *Lorokun daing ē'.* Dive for that fish. **2)** To disappear from the land of the living. *Suring baha'u itū wa'i palorok kamemon.* All of this new generation have gone.

**loros** *v. intr. pa-* To slide down a slope. (*Thesaurus:* **dokdos, dusdus, dūt, julut 1, lurus₁ 1, luslus 1**)

**lorosan** *n.* The lower slope of a hill. (*Thesaurus:* **baha-būd, bīd, būd 1, tukaran**)

**pagloros-loros** *v. tr. -an* To pass loose stools, as in diarrhea. *Magloros-loros iya, bay pa'in makakakan sinanglag kapog.* He has diarrhea, having eaten cassava that was no longer fresh. (*Thesaurus:* **kaluwa', pagsungi'-sungi'**)

**losak** *adj. a-* Flattened by trampling or pounding. *Bang buwas tin'ppa, pinalosak, mbal na agon aniya' bigina.* When rice is pounded, beaten down flat, there are virtually no grains remaining.

**loson** *v. advrs. ta-* Carried along by a strong current. *Butawanin daing ko da'a kita taloson.* Let the fish go so we don't get carried away by the current. *Taloson kita ni s'llog alandos bang kita mbal abanog.* We get swept away by strong currents if we aren't under sail. (*Thesaurus:* **gesges, laran, paghadjul-hadjul, palis₁, pespes 1.1**)

**lospad** *v. intr. aN-* To become pale, as through shock or illness. (*Thesaurus:* **muntas, muras 1.1, pusiyat**)

**lossok** *v. intr. pa-/-um-* To put one's foot into a hole. *Magdauragan na pa'in ma pantān hangkan ko' wa'i lumossok.* Continually chasing one another around the landing, that's why his foot went through. *Bang lum'ngngan apōng lantay, lumossok.* When a bamboo slat breaks while walking, [he] goes through the hole. *Lapakin ba lowang inān bo' mbal lumossok saga kaonde'an.* Put overlapping planks on that hole so children don't go through it.

**pagpatilossok** *v. intr. aN-* To let oneself down into a hole.

**lota'** *v. intr. aN-* To bleed copiously, of a wound. *Buwat ka'a bay pali'an, yukta, "Ōy, angalota' tape'nu!"* Like when you were wounded, we said, "Hey, your foot is bleeding badly!" (*Thesaurus:* **laha'₁ 1.1, sungbu-sungbu**)

**lotok** *adj. a-* **1)** Damaged by handling, of food. *Alotok kinakan bang labayan bahangi, abalos,*

*bang aniya' isāb bay ang'ntanan iya.* The food is spoiled when kept overnight. It goes bad, especially when someone has handled it. **1.1)** *v. tr.* To handle food with bare hands. *Da'a lotokun abō' mbal kaliman. Abalos pa'in ilū mbal takakan.* Don't handle it lest it be wasted. If it goes off it can't be eaten. *Niumas na pa'in, nilotok, apinda min baina.* Repeatedly fiddled with, handled, changed from its original condition. (*Thesaurus:* **hulemang 1.1, pagkoledje, umas**)

**lowak** *n.* **1)** A depression in a surface. **1.1)** *v. intr. pa-* To be sunken, of the eyes. *Palowak matana bang magsungi'.* Her eyes are sunken when she has diarrhea.

**paglowak** *v. intr. aN-* To sink into a hollow, as feet into mud. (*Thesaurus:* **l'nnob, loblob, senop, tanom₂**)

**lowang** *n.* **1)** A hole in something more or less solid. *Bay na ka maka'nda' lowang kullu'? Aniya' aheka ma deyom bakkaw.* Have you seen the holes of *kullu'* crabs? There are many in the mangroves. *Bay aku sinuruk he' a'a ma lowang jubulku.* Someone poked me in my anal orifice. (*cf:* **s'bbo'**; *Thesaurus:* **kehe 1, p'llong, songab 1**) **1.1)** *v. intr. pa-* To develop into a hole. *Pagdaldal kami pelang itū man diyata' kalangan, magtūy palowang ma t'ngnga'na.* When we put the canoe down into the water off the drying rack, a hole immediately formed in the middle. **1.2)** *v. tr. -an* To make a hole in something. *Bay iya angā' ba'ul ati nilowangan e'na ma sa'obna.* He got hold of a box and made a hole in its lid.

**lowang-ūng** *n.* The nostril.

**paglowang-lowang** *v. intr. aN-* To form holes in something previously unblemished. *Gabuk itū maglowang-lowang, malomo itū sali' bāng-bāng magkabila'.* Gabuk [termite damage] forms holes, *lomo* is like cookies prone to crumble.

**loya'** *n.* A variety of jackfruit with pulpy flesh. *Artocarpus heterophyllus. Nangka' loya' itū aheka tagokna.* These *loya'* jackfruit have a lot of sticky sap. (*gen:* **nangka'**)

**loyot** *adj. a-* Lacking in muscular strength, as after a severe illness; flaccid. *Aloyot aku, sali' alunuk puhu'ku.* I lack muscle tone, my body is kind of soft. (*Thesaurus:* **komay, lamma 1, pilay**)

**lubak₁** *v. tr. -an* To beat or whip someone with an implement. *Ala'at du isāb bang makalandu' he'ta angalubakan anakta.* It is bad when we beat our children excessively. (*Thesaurus:* **balubak, daplos, lambot, lappet**)

**lubak₂** *v. tr.* **1)** To do something with force or enthusiasm. *Bang aniya' sehe'nu magsuntuk, bang ka'apikihannu, da'a hārun ba. Magtūy lubakun pehē'. Da'a ka angagad sinuntuk.* If you and a companion are boxing and you close in on him, don't give him time. Get going. Don't wait to be punched. (*Thesaurus:* **landu'₁, lanjal 1.2, pehē'₂ 1.1**) *intrj.* Go; get on with it. *Lubak na!*

Go for it!

**lubag** var. of **luba'**

**luba'** (var. **lubag**) *adv.* A greater degree of some condition or quality. *Buwat aniya' paluruk ni pagkawinan, asal aheka a'a. Luba' gi' bang maggabbang.* As when guests attend a wedding, there are lots people of course, and even more so if there is to be bamboo marimba music. *Abuggu'an h'ndana, luba' bang maka'nda' a'a magbulawan.* His wife is jealous, especially when she sees people wearing jewelry. *Yuk si Kaka', makajari sadja kono' aku ni Nasuli', luba'na na sat'ggol ina'an lagi' sigām masi.* Older Sister said it's quite okay for me to go to Nasuli', especially for as long as they are still there. (*cf:* **duhun 1.1, tungkap₁**; *Thesaurus:* **anambahina, bangkinna...bangkinna, kalap, labi-labi, luhūy, paligay, ya lagi'na**)

**luba'-labi** (var. **luba'-lagi'**) *adv.* To an even greater degree of something; especially so. *Angkan angentom aku lahat luba'-labina na pagkakan Sama!* That's why I am homesick, especially for Sama food!

**luba'-lagi'** var. of **luba'-labi**

**lubas** *n.* 1) Something that has lost flavor. *Buwat umpan, lubas na.* Like bait, something become tasteless. **1.1)** *adj. a-* Tasteless; lacking in flavour. *Alubas na, akatis na ya ssana. Buwat lahing, ya sapalna. Lubas sapal na.* Flavorless, its flavor gone. Like the residue of grated coconut. It's tasteless now.

**lubayan** *n.* The cord of a spinning-top. *Lubayan itu tonda'-tonda' lanut panganggiling gasing. Lubayan is a cord of abaca [hemp] used to spin a top. Ya palegot inān taga lubayan.* That spinning thing has an abaca cord.

**lubi** *adj. a-* 1) Engaged in applying shampoo. *Wa'i gi' iya alubi.* She is just putting shampoo on her hair. **1.1)** *v. tr.* To apply a shampooing agent to one's hair.

**palubi** *n.* A shampooing agent, commonly a mixture of coconut cream and water.

**lubid** *n.* 1) Twine or rope. *Angā' ka lubid bo' hengkotin sapi' ilū.* Get some rope and tie up that cow. (*cf:* **bannang**; *Thesaurus:* **k'llat₂ 1, tangbid**) **1.1)** *v. tr.* To twist strands into a single flexible line. *Ap'kkal k'llat, ya bay nilubid inān.* The rope is unravelling, the one there that was retwisted. (*Thesaurus:* **kolleng, pinsal 1.1, tabid₁ 1**)

**lubing-lubing** *n.* The bamboo laths to which nipa shingles are tied. (*Thesaurus:* **kasaw, palimba'an**)

**lubu₁** *n.* A string-like substance exuded by some species of trepang. *Sandulay l'ggon, hal lubuna takakan. Aniya' isāb daga'na, sali' lubu keyat. Kuwitna sali' kuwit kura'.* With *sandulay-l'ggon* trepang it is only its *lubu* that can be eaten. It has lung-stuff too, looks like red *lubu*. Its skin is like the skin of a horse.

**lubu₂** *adj. a-* 1) In disrepair due to the disarray of component parts. *Alubu kusina sigām, mbal na kapagb'llahan.* Their kitchen is in disrepair, it can't be used for cooking. *Alubu na pa'in batu inān.* Those rocks [of a wall] keep falling down. (*Thesaurus:* **bulangkayat, g'ppa', gubal, hogal, tunas 1**) **1.1)** *v. tr.* To dismantle something; to break it into small pieces.

**lūk** *v. tr.* To straighten out irregularities in something more or less rigid, as bamboo or wire. *Lūkun p'ttung ilu abō' ahāp pangalantay.* Straighten that bamboo so it is good for flooring. (*Thesaurus:* **bigtang 1.1, b'ttad 1.1, l'dduk 1.1, l'ngngat, tilud 1.1, uli'₂**)

**lukbu'₁** *v. tr.* To arrange the limbs of a dead person after rigor mortis has relaxed, in preparation for burial. *Nilukbu' tanganta, tape'ta, bang apuwas na bay nihawasan basi'.* Our hands and feet are arranged after rigor mortis has passed.

**lukbu'₂** (var. **tukbu'**) *v. intr. pa-/-um-* To stumble; to sink to one's knees. *Mbal kata'uhanna bang ai makalukbu' iya.* He won't know what made him stumble. *Ati palukbu' iya ma dahū'an tape' si Ja.* So he fell on his knees before Ja's feet.

**pagpatilukbu'** *v. intr. aN-* To fall on one's knees voluntarily, as an act of deep respect.

**lukdus** var. of **luklus**

**lukluk** *n.* Various owl species.

**luklus** (var. **lukdus**) *v. tr. -an* 1) To lower a sail down a mast by slackening its lashing. *Ya tabul-tabul niluklusan, tinugutan hambawan.* The lashing has been loosened, the halyard allowed to run free. *Lukdusin lubid ilū bo' makareyo'-deyo' engkotna. Makalandu' sidda alangkaw.* Loosen that rope so its knot comes down a bit. It is much too high. 2) To loosen clothing items that go around one's body. (*Thesaurus:* **butawan 1**)

**luku** *n.* A long gown of white cloth worn by Muslim women, especially during prayers. (*Thesaurus:* **gamis, juba**)

**luku-luku** *n.* A plant species, the dried leaves of which are used medicinally. *Ocimum sp. Luku-luku, daun ginantung. Nili'is isāb, ati pinainum ma a'a sinawan.* Luku-luku, its [dried] leaves hung up. It is also grated and given as a drink to a person suffering a seizure.

**luku'₁** *n.* Various pufferfishes, including the White-spotted puffer. *fam. Tetraodontidae, fam. Diodontidae.* (*cf:* **buntal**)

**luku'-babakan** *n.* The Narrow-lined toadfish, a species distinct from babakan. *Arothron immaculatus.*

**luku'-kakas** *n.* The Scribbled toadfish; the Map puffer. *Arothron mappa.*

**luku'-itingan** *n.* The Long-spine porcupinefish. *Diodon holocanthus. Nilango iya bay makakakan pehak luku' itingan.* He is sick from eating the roe of spiny pufferfish.

**luku'-sahapang** *n.* The Broad-barred toadfish. *Arothron hispidus.*

**luku'₂** *v. intr. a-* To bow down low as in prayer, or when relaxing. (*Thesaurus:* **duku', luhud, pagpatireyo', sujud**)

**lukun** (var. **rukun**) *n.* A primary tenet of Islam. *Lukun lima pasal sambahayang bangsa Islam.* The fifth tenet of the Islamic faith. (*cf:* **parukunan**)

**paglukun** (var. **paglukum**) *n.* **1)** The shared evening meal which celebrates major events of the Islamic calendar. *Paglukum bang ma kami tonga' gantang buwas, maka daing. Atonga' pa'in sambahayang, pinah'lling jabu-jabu, tinimuk kinakan, magkakan na.* The *lukum* meal, for us, is a half *ganta* of rice, plus fish. Halfway through the prayers the cymbal is sounded, the food is brought together, and the eating takes place. **1.1)** *v. intr. aN-* To share an evening meal together in celebration of a religious festival. *Maglukun sangom, buwat sali' balanja' sangom. Abay kohap saga magtakbil na. Paglisag siyam akatis.* Eating the *lukun* meal in the evening, the evening supply, as it were. At dusk we celebrate God's greatness. By nine o'clock it is over. *Panganop bulan, paglukum bulan, paglukum sambahayang.* Waiting for the new moon, the celebration of the moon, the celebration by prayer.

**lukup** *v. tr. -an* To clean a surface by scrubbing with a stiff brush. *Angalukupan aku pelang. Akatis pa'in bay angalukup tangonku na. Akatis bay tangonku amandi aku. Akatis pa'in aku bay amandi, asalin aku.* I am scrubbing a canoe. When I have finished scrubbing I put it up on the drying rack. When I have put it up I bathe. When I have bathed I change clothes. *Maglukup kitam luma' salung.* We will scrub the house tomorrow. (*Thesaurus:* **bunut-bunut, kuskus 1.1, dalug₁, gisgis 1.2, lupag, susut**)

**lulukup** *n.* An item used for scrubbing, such as a coconut husk.

**lukut-lappas** *n.* Dry-love or amor-seco, a grass with burr-like seeds. *Andropogon (or Chrysopogon) aciculatus.* (*syn:* **jalum-kuyya'**)

**lukyu** *n.* Garlic sprouts. *Lukyu itū pamapā.* The *lukyu* referred to here is a food flavoring. (*gen:* **pamapā**)

**lūd** *v. intr. pa-* To descend a slope; to go seawards. *Palūd bagayku min deya amowa lahing.* My friend came down from inland carrying coconuts. *Palūd kita kaut, amole' na man deya.* We go down toward the coast, returning from inland. (*Thesaurus:* **kaleya 1, kaut 1, takod 1, tukad₁ 1**)

**ludjak** var. of **budjak**

**ludja'** *n.* **1)** Saliva; loose phlegm. *Ya buhelota am'ttak, ya ludja'ta apīt.* Our spittle drips, our saliva is thick. (*Thesaurus:* **buhelo 1, helo₂, laway₁ 1, pagtagak**) **1.1)** *adj. zero* Salivating and spitting, as the physical response to something considered repulsive. *Ina'an na aludja' sultan i' apa manusiya' anganak kuting maka ero'.* There was the sultan, spitting because of a human giving birth to a cat and a dog. **1.2)** *v. intr. aN-* To produce saliva; to spit. *Sali' magtagok buhelona, sali' angaludja'.* His saliva becomes viscous, as though spitting. **1.3)** *v. tr. -an* To spit on someone as a way of showing rejection or contempt. *Niludja'an iya ma bayhu'na bo' sinukna'an.* He was spat at in the face and cursed.

**pagludja'** *v. tr. -an* To spit repeatedly at someone. *Pinagudju'-udju' iya e' bangsa inān sampay pinagludja'an.* He was mocked and spat at by those foreigners.

**ludju'** *v. intr. pa-* To resume marriage negotiations. *Paludju' pabīng apa bay na magtunang.* Resuming marriage discussions because they were already engaged.

**paludju'** *v. tr.* To revive negotiations that had been suspended.

**lugal** *n.* **1)** A place; a space for something. *Halam aniya' lugal ma lansa.* There was no room on the launch. (*Thesaurus:* **jadjahan, pa'atagan, pat'nna'an**) **1.1)** *adj. a-* Adequate or spacious, as a place to work or rest. *Alugal isāb paghinanganbi luma' ilū.* That's a spacious place for you to be building a house.

**lugat** *v. tr. -an* To oppose someone verbally; to contradict someone. *Pangalulugat sidda iya, hangkan halam aniya' bagayna.* He argues a lot, that is why he has no friends. *Angalugat iya ma kita. B'nnal Alba'a, bo' bang ma iya Sabtu'.* He argues with us. It really was Wednesday but according to him it was Saturday.

**paglugat** *v. intr. aN-* To be involved in a battle of contradictions. *Maglugat, sali' magagaw-bissala pariyata', sali' magta'as-ta'asan bang sai apatut.* Involved in an ever-growing war of words, like a kind of struggle as to who is fit [for the position]. (*Thesaurus:* **da'awa 1.1, palilu, tawalli', tumagal 1.1**)

**luggiya'** *adj. zero* Unique or personal to an individual. *Alta' itu luggiya' ma aku.* This wealth here belongs to me personally. *Bay ama'id iya min aku bo' pasa'ut amole' ni lahatna luggiya'.* He took his leave of me and returned promptly to his home place. *Aheya-heya pa'in onde'-onde' itu, ni'nde'an iya pehē' ni dayang-dayang ati tahinang sali' anakna luggiya'.* When this child was quite big he was delivered there to the princess and treated as her very own child. (*Thesaurus:* **lahasiya' 1, legsok₁, lissi**)

**lugi'** *adj. a-* **1)** Financially unprofitable; suffering a loss in a financial transaction. *Bang aku amab'llihan daing alugi' aku.* When I sell fish I lose money. (*cf:* **laba**; *Thesaurus:* **lussung**) **1.1)** *v. tr.* To cause someone to take a financial loss, as through hard bargaining. *Asidda aku lugi'nu.*

You cause me to take a big loss.

**pagkalugi'an** *v. intr. aN-* To suffer financial loss. *Magkalugi'an, magpaluntungan.* Losing money and making money. (*cf:* **paluntungan**)

**lugit** (var. **lu'it**) *v. tr.* To remove something by prising or gouging. *Bussu' ma gusung nilugit maka basi'.* The rock in the sand is pried out with a metal bar. *Buwat angahinang ka tupara, ang'nda' isāb kayu atuwas, buwat lugitnu-lugitnu kamemon, ya deyom hē'.* Like when you are making diving goggles, and looking for hard wood, you gouge it thoroughly, the inside bit. (*Thesaurus:* **landak, li'ad, suwal 1**)

**lugu'** *n.* 1) A genre of songs appropriate to ceremonial and religious occasions. *Angahinang iya lugu'-lugu' pangalemongna ma panonna.* He composed a *lugu'* as his lament for his close friend. (*Thesaurus:* **kalangan₁, langan₂ 1, sa'il**) **1.1)** *v. tr. -an* To accompany a ceremonial activity such as a burial with the singing of a lugu' song.

**paglugu'** *v. tr. -an* To sing formal ceremonial songs. *Alahang na maglugu' b'ttina'an, luwal dakuman kahaba' bulan Maulud.* Religious chants are rarely sung now, only during every month of Maulud.

**lugus** *n.* The nut of the areca (betel-nut) palm in its unripe stage. (*Thesaurus:* **bunga₁, dantilad, l'mmaw, pola**)

**lugus-magi** *n.* A species of palm, the nut of which is sometimes used as a substitute for the true betel nut. (*syn:* **pola-magi**)

**luha** *n.* 1) The breadth, of a space. *Saga t'llund'ppa luha salasna.* The width of its family room was about three fathoms. (*cf:* **kiput**) **1.1)** *adj. a-* Broad or wide, of a space. *Aluha luma' disi Saljen Ba, ahayang.* Sgt. Ba's house is wide and airy. (*Thesaurus:* **habog, lambu 1.1, lampo' 1.1**)

**kaluha'an** *n.* The entire breadth of an area. *Alengog na kaluha'an lahat.* The entire country is disturbed. (*cf:* **kasaplagan**)

**luha-limbay** *n.* A person who is not bound by social conventions (lit. free to swing about). {idiom}

**paluha** *v. tr.* To widen something already open.

**luhaw-luhaw** *adj. a-* Cooling off, of cooked food too hot to eat. *Pinaluhaw-luhaw gi' ma luwasan.* Let it cool down a bit outside. (*Thesaurus:* **hulaw**)

**luhay₁** *n.* 1) Relative cheapness, of things for sale. **1.1)** *adj. a-* Inexpensive. *Sidda aluhay daing ma M'ddas.* The fish in Siasi are really cheap. (*cf:* **halga' 1, hunit 2.1**)

**luhay₂** *adj. a-* 1) Easily done; simply achieved. *Engkotan taumpa'nu, Oto'. Aluhay ba, takole'nu du.* Tie your shoes, Son. It's easy, you can manage. (*cf:* **mura**) **1.1)** *v. advrs. ka-...-an* To be experiencing relative ease. *Ya b'nnalna, in d'nda Hibrani kaluhayan sidda bang maganak.* The fact is that Hebrew women have it very easy when

they give birth.

**luhay-luhay** *v. tr.* To do something easily. *Taluhay-luhaynu bahā' nihinang ayuwan sultan?* Would you find it easy to become the son-in-law of a sultan?

**luhaya** *adj. a-* Unrestricted as to movement; at liberty; relaxed. *Aluhaya, buwat hinangku halam aniya' asembol.* Unrestricted, like my work when there is nothing in the way. *Aluhaya itū, sali' magpasannang-pasannang kita, sali' halam aniya' ugatta.* This *luhaya* is like making ourselves totally relaxed, as though we no longer had sinews. *Bang wa'i makal'ngngan saga matto'aku, na minomos he' siyaliku. Pagt'kka matto'aku, ahāp na, aluhaya na.* When my parents have gone some place, then my younger sister sets things in order. On my parents' arrival things are good, uncluttered.

**kaluhaya'an** *n.* Freedom. *Ahāp bang sigām tugutanta maglahat maitu maka magusaha isab ma deyom kaluhaya'an.* It would be good for us to let them settle here and to make their living in freedom.

**luhu** *v. tr.* To singe the hull of a canoe to inhibit the growth of marine moss. *Angā' aku langkay pangaluhuku pelang.* I will get a dried coconut frond to singe the canoe with.

**luhud** *v. intr. pa-* To kneel with the body in an upright position. (*Thesaurus:* **duku', luku'₂, pagpatireyo', sujud**)

**luhu'₁** *n.* A game consisting of a series of movements which each successive player copies until one is disqualified by a mistake.

**pagluhu'** *v. intr. aN-* To play the game of luhu'.

**luhu'₂** *adj. a-* 1) Annihilated, of a community, as by illness, natural disaster, or war. *Halam aniya' takapin minsan dakayu', aluhu' na.* Not a single thing left, utterly destroyed. (*Thesaurus:* **lapnas 1, lognos, ponas, sapsay**) **1.1)** *v. tr.* To destroy an entire community.

**luhul₁** *adv.* The early afternoon prayer time. *Sowa basagan, bang kita kineket subu bo' halam katawalan, ta'abut pa'in waktu luhul amatay kita.* The *basagan* snake, if we are bitten in the morning, but not treated, then by the afternoon prayer time we'll be dead. (*Thesaurus:* **aisa, asal, magrib 1, subu₂ 2**)

**luhul₂** *n.* A decorative cloth canopy erected over a newly married couple or over a grave-shrine. *Buwat siyakaku bay asaki, bay kami ni Sisangat ni bay mma'na. Makasangon kami luhul, bo' mbal ala'an sakina. Ngga'i ka hē'-i.* Like when my older brother was sick, we went to Sisangat to where his father was [buried]. We put up a canopy [over the grave] but his sickness didn't go away. That wasn't it. (*Thesaurus:* **kulambu' 1, kultina, langsay**)

**luhūy** *adv.* To a greater degree, of some situation or condition. *Bay tinawalan, luhūy pasōng sakkina.* Incantations were said over him, but his sickness became even worse. *Niranos panggi', pinat'nna' mareyom ambung, luhūy abentol.* The cassava is squeezed, put in a basket, but becomes even more powdery. *Luhūy pakosog na pa'in kawasa pagnakura'na.* The power of his leadership kept growing still stronger. *Luhūy sigām sinukpakan e' Nabi Elija.* They were mocked even more by the prophet Elijah. (*Thesaurus:* **anambahina, bangkinna...bangkinna, kalap, labi-labi, luba', paligay, ya lagi'na**)

**lu'aw** *v. intr. pa-* 1) To go to see something. *Wa'i ma lahat dakayu' na, saupama amabeya' taligrama pi'itu, yukna, "Magsakihan danakannu." Na palu'aw kita pehē'.* Away in another country, for example, when they send a telegram saying, "Your siblings are sick." So we go to see [for ourselves]. (*Thesaurus:* **lundug 1.1, nyata' 1.1**) 1.1) *v. ditr.* To go in person to see something. *Lu'aw itū, luwal bang aniya' bay takalipatta ai-ai. Lu'awta pabīng ni bay pamat'nna'anta, sali' nda'ta pabalik.* This word *lu'aw*, used most likely when we have forgotten something. We search for it by going back to the place where we placed it, like seeing it again.

**lu'it** *var. of* **lugit**

**lu'ud₁** *adj. zero* 1) Slippery, of a surface. *Bang kita kaleya bo' lu'ud-lu'ud, humantak kita.* When we go inland and it's somewhat slippery, we fall down. 1.1) *v. intr. aN-* To become slippery. *Angalu'ud tana', mbal kal'ngnganan.* The ground has become slippery, it can't be walked on. *Deyom pelang itu angalu'ud, lumutan.* The inside of this canoe has got slippery, it's mossy.

**lu'ud₂** *n.* The jelly-like film on the inner surface of a coconut that is not yet fully ripe. (*syn:* **lagod₂**)

**lu'ug** *n.* 1) Loss of energy through over-exertion; a state of exhaustion. *Bang kita magusaha, bin'nnod baranta, subay niā'an tambal lu'ug. Aniya' lima ginis gamut kayu nihinang tambal lu'ug itū.* When we are out fishing and our bodies are numb with fatigue, we need someone to get us exhaustion medicine. There are five kinds of tree root used to make this exhaustion medicine. 1.1) *adj. -an* Exhausted; experiencing fatigue. *Lu'ugan si Oto' magkalga ni M'ddas.* Oldest Brother is exhausted working as a porter in Siasi. 1.2) *v. tr. -an* To cause someone to experience physical exhaustion. *Nilu'ugan sadja aku ni ispital, halam du maī' doktol.* I am exhausted going to the hospital, and the doctor isn't there.

**paglu'ug-liksa'** *v. intr. aN-* To be exhausted by prolonged physical strain. *Maglu'ug-liksa' matto'a amaiskul bo' na pa'in aniya' kasōngan anak sigām.* Parents wear themselves out sending children to school so that they might have a future. *Anggauta'ta, ya kosogta, maglu'ug-liksa'.* Our sinews, our strength, [they] feel the strain. (*cf:* **pagsangsā'**)

**lu'ug-lama'** *n.* 1) Language that is vulgar and offensive. *Angay ka? Hal ka amissala lu'ug-lama' ni aku.* What's up with you? You're saying crude things to me. (*Thesaurus:* **la'at bowa', lumu', sabul 1.1**) 1.1) *v. intr. aN-* To speak in a way intended to offend. *Angalu'ud-lama' iya mareyom kauman, ala'at bowa'na. Magesog-esog dīna.* He behaves in the community without shame, his speech vulgar. Acting so brave.

**lu'uy₁** *adj. a-* 1) Melodious; pleasant-sounding. *Alu'uy e'na amissala, sali' makahāp pangatayan.* He speaks gently, sort of making one feel at peace. *Alu'uy magkalang mastal kami d'nda.* Our lady teacher sings sweetly. 1.1) *v. advrs. ka-...-an* To be pleasantly affected by something heard. *Ōy, kalu'uyan aku!* Wow, I am so moved by the beauty of the sound!

**lu'uy₂** *adj. a-* Compassionate; gentle. *Patilu'uyun iya ma pagkahina.* He is compassionate to his fellow man. *Makalu'uy-lu'uy sidda palasahan sigām.* Their situation provokes great compassion.

**lu'uya** *n.* The ginger plant and its edible rhizome. *Zingiber officinale.* (*cf:* **kisul**; *gen:* **pamapā**)

**lullun** *adv.* 1) Entirely; all parts of a whole. *Lullun pote', halam aniya' lamudna. Atawa buwat lilusnu, lullun bulawan.* Entirely white, nothing mixed in. Or like your watch, gold all through. *Angkan du isāb pinagōnan Tuhan sabab ai-ai kasukkalan mareyom dunya itū, lullun aku tatabang e'na.* That's why he is called God, because whatever needs there are in this world he will help me in all aspects. *Panji itū magk'llab-k'llab lullun.* These flags all flapping in the breeze. (*Thesaurus:* **kamemon 1.1, l'nnas, sabarang, telnos 1**) 1.1) *adj. a-* Of the same sort. *Bang aku mags'mmek alullun pantalun maka badju', daluwa.* When I dress up pants and shirt are the same, looking alike. *Buwat bahagi', aniya' alullun min dambila'.* Like something shared, sometimes it is totally from one side.

**lulu** *v. intr. aN-* To lose color through washing, of cloth. *Kakana' ya angalulu.* It's the cloth that is losing its color. (*Thesaurus:* **baluba 1, gagas, padpad, papas₁ 1**)

**lulukup** (derivative of **lukup**) *n.* An item used for scrubbing, such as a coconut husk. *Ndiya ba lulukup.* Just hand me the scrubber.

**lulūnan** (derivative of **lūn**) *n.* A device for rolling cigarets. *Ōnna to'ongan pikaroda, sali' du pasta. Aniya' isāb lulūnanna.* It's real name is *pikaroda*, like leaf tobacco. There is a roller that goes with it.

**lulus para'akkal** *adv. phrase* Not to be thought about; absolutely unthinkable. {idiom} *Nsa' aniya' gunata maglitu bang kita mbal anguntung. Mbal lulus para'akkal.* There is no point in us trading if we don't make a profit. Simply unthinkable. *Bang aniya' ai-ai abila' mbal lulus para'akkal; bang nsa' aniya' bay makahantak.* If something is broken it could not have happened, unless something had caused it to fall. *Lulus* *para'akkal, hatina mbal taluwa' niakkal.* Never to be thought of, in other words, not fit to be thought about. *Lulus ka, yuk-i, para'akkal. Angay tak'llo' e' sigām ai-ai, sali' mbal kinahagad.* You are unbelievable, it was said. How come they got whatever? It can't be credited.

**luluy** *v. tr.* -an To accept without resentment or argument. *Bang aniya' bissalanu ni aku, bo' aku taga dusa, ai-ai na pamissalanu ma aku ahāp-ala'at, hal aku angaluluy.* If you have something to say to me, and I am at fault, whatever you say to me, good or bad, I simply accept. *Niluluyan sadja llingna, pinabeya'an sadja.* What he says is just accepted without question, simply go along with it. *Amaluluy aku, sali' pasagaranku ai-ai pah'llingnu. Sali' aku hal palagad.* I respond passively, sort of ignoring anything you say. It is as though I just wait.

**lumad** *v. advrs.* -in- Bored with some activity. *Makalumad na pinahilala' pelang ilū. Hatina makasumu.* Maintaining that canoe makes one bored. In other words it causes tedium. (*Thesaurus:* **jompo', sumu 1.1**)

**lumahan** *n.* The Indian or Long-jawed mackerel. *Rastrelliger kanagurta.* (*Thesaurus:* **sulay-sulay$_2$, tulay**)

**lumahan timbang** *n. phrase* The Blue or the Slimy mackerel. *Scomber australicus.*

**luma'** *n.* A house; any building that has walls and a roof. *Agpat'nna' aku luma' ma Siganggang.* I will set up a house at Siganggang. (*Thesaurus:* **ballay, kubu'-kubu', pamāy-bāy**)

**kaluma'an** *n.* A collection of houses; a village. (*Thesaurus:* **kampung$_2$, le'od$_1$, libug, lūng 1, nibung, tumpuk 2**)

**pagluma'** *v. intr.* aN- To live in or build a house. *Magluma' kami ma bihing bowa'-angan.* We live in a house on the edge of the reef. *Pahati'un sigām bang magluma', sināpan bo' ahāp nīnda'. Buwat kaluma'an Sabah.* Explain to them that when they build houses, they should be lined up so they are good to look at. Like the housing areas in Sabah.

**karaluma'** *n.* All the members of one house.

**daluma'** *n.* The members of a single house.

**pagdaluma'** *v. intr.* aN- To be living together in the same house. *Bay pa'in kami magdaluma' maka milikan ē', dangkakanan kami maka sigām.* When we were living in the same house with those Westerners, we ate at the same table.

**paluma'an** *n.* A housing complex.

**lumay** *n.* Fish split and dried in the sun. (*Thesaurus:* **daing niasin, peyad 1, pundang 1, sampila'$_1$ 1**)

**lumbag** *n.* A heavy swell due to stormy weather further out at sea. *Akosog lumbag dibuhi'.* The swell was heavy last night. (*Thesaurus:* **alun-panjang, kata'-kata', goyak 1, sahal$_1$ 1.1, sampoyak**)

**paglumbag** *v. intr.* aN- To be running with a heavy swell, of the sea.

**lumbayaw** *n.* A species of timber tree, one of several referred to as Philippine mahogany. *Tarrieta javanica.*

**lumbiya** *n.* The edible pith of the sago palm. *Metroxylon rumphii or sagus. Bang ntananta lumbiya angalu'ud sali' ma tanganta.* When we handle sago it is sort of slippery in our hands. *Lumbiya, ahāp ssana bang sinindul.* Lumbiya, it tastes good when it is made into *sindul* [a sweet drink]. (*Thesaurus:* **ambūng**)

**lumbu'** (var. **lungbu'**) *n.* The early stage of adulthood.

**lumbu'-baha'u** *n.* A youth, male or female, just coming into adulthood. *Ahalga' ungsud ma lungbu'-baha'u.* The bride-wealth for a teenage girl is expensive. *Onde' lumbu'-baha'u.* A mature youth. (*Thesaurus:* **bata', hoben, onde'-baha'u**)

**lumbu'-lumbu'** *n.* A young adult between puberty and early twenties.

**lumbus** var. of **lungbus**

**lumintiyad** *v. advrs.* -in- Prone to losing one's footing and slipping down. *Sali' bay lum'ngngan bo' magh'bba'-h'bba', yukta, "Nilumintiyad a'a inān."* Like someone who was walking and fell down repeatedly, we say, "That person is prone to slip and fall." (*Thesaurus:* **dasdas, deklas, ligdas, ligid$_2$ 1, lisad, lisig**)

**lumpang-lumpang** *n.* A basin or tub carved from a single piece of wood. {archaic} *"Na bbahinbi na aku," yuk si Nneng Pagi-pagi, "mailu ma lumpang-lumpang ilū. Magkotek-kotek na aku mailu."* "Just leave me," said Stingray Maiden, "there in the basin. I will be flapping my fins there now." (*Thesaurus:* **batiya', palanggana, pastan, undam**)

**lumpat** *v. intr.* aN- To move suddenly upwards, as frightened birds or a startled horse. *Sikalumpatan saga manuk-manuk bang atiyup baliyu akosog.* The birds scatter en masse and fly up when a strong wind blows. (*cf:* **dimpulag**)

**lumping** *n.* The cylindrical flower stalk of the lambus, a small tree of mangrove swamps. *Dahū lumping, ya paglustang ilū, ampa tongke'.* First the stalk, the one used for pea-shooters, then the fruit. (*cf:* **lustang 1**)

**lumpu** *adj.* -an Exhausted, worn out, from continuous activity. *Buwat kita makalangkit kaut, binale' kita. Lumpuhan, mbal na makakole'.* Like us going regularly to sea, we get tired. Exhausted, no longer coping. *Buwat aniya' bay magjaga, lumpuhan.* Like someone who has been holding vigil [over a dead person], tired out. (*Thesaurus:* **bale', binasa 1, b'kkat 2, husa', paya**)

**lumput** var. of **l'mput**

**lumu** *adj.* a- Out of breath from exertion. *Alumu kita, bay maglangi.* We are puffing, having been swimming. (*cf:* **simay₁** 1; *Thesaurus:* **hapus₂, paghangu-hangu, pagh'ngka-h'ngka, paghongat-hongat, puha**)

**lumu'** *adj. a-* Neglectful of community standards of hygiene, politeness, or morality. *Alumu' ko' ka'a ilū, ntanannu m'ssa'-bidda', magtūy ka ang'ntan ni kinakan.* You are so disgusting, handling all sorts of things, and immediately touching food. *Bang lai' at'ggol halam kinose'an, alumu'.* A dish that hasn't been washed for ages is filthy. (*Thesaurus:* **la'at bowa', lu'ug-lama'** 1, **sabul** 1.1)

  **kalumu'an** *n.* Morally filthy or disgusting behavior. *Landu' na kalumu'an manusiya', hangkan suma'an pinat'nna'an mulka' e' Tuhan.* People are so wicked that sometimes God has to impose judgment on them. *Halam nilāng e'na kalumu'an ya bay nihinang e' saga anakna, minsan du bay kata'uhanna.* He didn't stop the disgusting things done by his sons, even though he was aware of them. *Dusa sigām paghinang kalumu'an l'lla maka d'nda.* Their sin was men and women doing indecent things.

  **paglumu'** *v. intr. aN-* To be involved in things considered disgusting.

**lumut₁** *n.* **1)** A fibrous mossy plant which grows on rocks or wood immersed in seawater. *Anusutan aku pelang bang aheka lumut.* I will scrub the canoe when there is a lot of moss. *Angā' aku lumut pangumpanku panggal.* I'll gather some moss as bait for a small basket trap. **1.1)** *v. advrs. -in-* Covered with mossy growth, of a canoe that needs scrubbing. *Deyom pelang angalu'ud, lumutan.* The inside of the canoe hull is slippery, moss-covered. *Bang aniya' pahinggamanta sali' pelang bo' nilumut, subay sinusutan.* If we have a conveyance such as a *pelang* and it gets mossy, it must be scrubbed. **2)** Ingrained dirt in skin. (*Thesaurus:* **l'mmi'** 1, **lobag, moseng** 1)

**lumut₂** *adj. a-* **1)** Strongly attached to someone. *Alumut iya ma a'a alasahan iya.* He is very attached to people who love him. (*Thesaurus:* **balut** 2, **lūt₂** 1, **uli, umid** 1) **1.1)** *v. intr. pa-* To devote oneself to someone. *Ai-ai panoho'an, nihinang du he' a'a palumut ma iya.* Any instruction whatever is carried out by the person who follows him closely. *Onde' itū bilahi ameya' ma a'a palumutanna.* This child likes to be with a person he is devoted to.

**lūn** *adj. a-* **1)** Rolled up. *Abadbad, sali' ap'kkal, bang bay alūn.* Unfurled, sort of unravelling, of something that had been rolled up. **1.1)** *v. tr. -an* To roll flexible material into a compact bundle; to furl a sail. *Lūninbi na tepobi ilū, halam aniya' am'lli.* Roll up that mat of yours, nobody is buying. *Halam na bay k'llatanku banog ē' maina'an. Nilūnan na.* I had not attached the boom rope to the sail there at that place. It was furled. **1.2)** *v. tr.* To enclose something in a roll, as tobacco in a cigarette paper, or bedding

inside a mat. *Lūnun kono' pupud siga.* Just roll up that cigaret stub. (*Thesaurus:* **gulung** 1)

**lūn-lupi'** *adj. a-* Crinkled, as due to heat or burning. *Alūn-lupi kuwitku, bay alūs he' api.* My skin is puckered, burnt by fire.

**lulūnan** *n.* A device for rolling cigarets.

**lunab** *v. intr. aN-* To be chronically unhealed, of a wound or infection. *Angalunab, mbal ata'u kauli'an, buwat pali'ku itū. Ubus kauli'an bo' pabalik du.* Lunab, incapable of healing, like this cut of mine. It gets better, and then it recurs. (*syn:* **pagbu'ung-bu'ung**)

**lundang** *n.* A close friend of the same sex.

  **paglundang-lundang** *v. intr. aN-* To have a close friendship, especially with someone of the same sex. *Subay d'nda sali'-sali', atawa l'lla sali'-sali', bo' maglundang-lundang.* Both should be female, or both male, to have this close friendship. *Amasi iya maglundang-lundang maka bay h'ndana.* He is still good friends with his [former] wife. *Bang d'nda maka l'lla maglundang-lundang, tabistu du. Minsan aku, tabistu he' a'a aniya' sehe'ku magbaya', d'nda.* If a woman and a man have a close friendship, it will become widely known. Even I have been reported as having a romantic relationship with someone, a woman. (*Thesaurus:* **pagbagay, pagpanon**)

**lundug** *v. intr. pa-* **1)** To crowd around in order to see what is happening. *Palundug ka pehē'.* Go yonder and see. **1.1)** *v. tr.* To see something on the spot. *Pehē' ka lundugun.* Go and see for yourself. (*Thesaurus:* **lu'aw** 1, **nyata'** 1.1)

  **paglundug** *v. intr. aN-* To move as a crowd. *Magdaugdug puhu', sali' aheka to'ongan maglundug. Aniya' sali' ajogjog lantay.* Bodies moving en masse, like a great many crowding to see. The floor is kind of shaking. *Bang aniya' paluruk, bo' mbal ahāp pantān, yuk tagdapu, "Da'a kam maglundug pi'ilu. Ilu halam ahogot."* If there are people gathering for an event but the porch isn't in good shape, the owner says, "Don't gather there. It isn't securely fastened." (*Thesaurus:* **pagkubu-kubu, pagtimuk** 1.1)

**lundu'** *n.* Fish stunned by dynamite but still alive and floating on the surface. *Sūng kitam kaut, da'a na kitam anuhun hantak, amuwa' kitam lundu'.* Let's go to sea, let's not dive for the dynamited fish that have sunk, let's pick up the floating ones. *Belle'ku ya lundu' timbak, ya ma'angol.* I will dive for the fish stunned by dynamite, the stunned ones. (*Thesaurus:* **belaw-belaw, hantak₂**)

**lunsul** *adj. a-* **1)** In the habit of roaming around without purpose. *Atale'ed kita, alunsul.* We are all over the place, roaming around. **1.1)** *v. tr. -an* To reach an objective by strolling. *Nilunsulan e'na katindahan.* He strolled to the shops.

  **paglunsul** *v. intr. aN-* To move from one place to another; or just walk around. *Lekot-lendom lahat ilū, maglunsulan na pa'in ka?* The place is dark, and you're still wandering about? *Aloka na kusu batangan; maglunsul na batangan parambila' maka parambila'.* The hole of the outrigger boom is loose; the boom keeps moving from side to side. *Bilahi kami maglunsul ma M'ddas.* We like to stroll around Siasi town. (*syn:* **pasiyal**)

**luntang** *v. intr.* aN- **1)** To become slick or glutinous. *Buwat almidul inān angaluntang bang ginawgaw na.* Like starch, glutinous when it has been stirred. *Lera-lera, ya sali' amalut ma hāg inān, ya mangaluntang ī'.* *Lera-lera*, the growth that sort of sticks to houseposts, that becomes slimy. **2)** To produce froth, from the mouth of an animal or the opening of a shellfish. *Bang panagatun angaluntang hatina paluwa' na l'mmi'na. Bang a'a angaluntang hatina dupang.* When a shellfish froths it means its stuff comes out. When a man does it, it means he is crazy.

**lunuk** *n.* **1)** Softness; malleability. (*Thesaurus:* **baska 1, lunyag, posak**) **1.1)** *adj.* a- Soft; malleable; tender. *Sinangkulan itū, pinalunuk tana'.* Grubbing up [with a mattock], the soil made soft. *Kanu'us itū alunuk.* Squid is soft. *Buwat kalitan b'llata, subay nilagas ko' alunuk.* Like when we cook shark flesh, it should cooked for a long time to be tender. (*Thesaurus:* **dutay, h'mmel**)

**lunuk atay** *adj.* a- Placated; mollified; approachable. {idiom} *Alunuk na atay. Palabay na bay map'ddi' atay hē'.* He is mollified now. What upset him has passed. *A: "Pamagay daing ilū?" B: "Pamalunukku atayna."* A: "What is that fish for?" B: "It's to make him pleased with me again [lit. for my softening of his liver]." *Pinalunuk pangatayanna.* He was made to feel well-disposed.

**lunyag** *adj.* a- Soft in consistency by nature. *Alunyag, ya sali' mapetak inān, buwat kapaya atawa liyabanus. Lunyag,* squashy things like papaya or soursop. (*Thesaurus:* **baska 1, lunuk 1, posak**)

**lūng** *n.* **1)** A discrete sector of a settlement where people are related by birth or marriage. *Dalūng kam maka si Ma. Minsan saddī tumpuk, basta magsekot luma'bi.* You are in the same village sector as Ma, even though you are in a different house cluster; just so long as your houses are close. (*Thesaurus:* **kaluma'an, kampung₂, le'od₁, libug, nibung, tumpuk 2**) **2)** A person who lives (or once lived) in one's sector of a settlement.

**lūng-kampung** *n.* A kinsman in the broader sense of living in the same sector of a settlement; a village-mate. *Bang ma waktu kasigpitan, lūng-kampungta du kapangamu'anta tabang.* At times of shortage our local kin are the ones we can ask for help. *Ni Tiyanggi aku angalga. Wa'i aheka lūng-kampungku. Atuli na aku mahē'.* I am going to Jolo to work as a porter. There are many of my relatives there. I will sleep there. *Magsaddī*

*kami, lūng-kampung sadja.* We are a different kindred; just village-mates. (*Thesaurus:* **kakampungan, sugsugan**)

**lūngan** *n.* The sector of a settlement where a kin group live. *Ma aniya' alungay, an'ssag kita, atilaw kita sangkahāpan ni kalūnganta.* When something is lost we inform people, asking carefully of our village section. *Arapun kām magkarukka'an ma sabab aniya' a'a ma lūnganbi magkasumbang.* You should have been upset because there are people in your community committing incest.

**paglūng** *n.* **1)** A kin-based part of a village. **2)** Village-mates.

**pagdalūng** *v. intr.* aN- To be in the same community.

**lūng-lūng** *see:* **paglūng-lūng**

**lungay** *adj.* a- **1)** Lost; disappeared; no longer in sight. *Alungay lingantuku ma dilaut. Bang ma deya mbal kasandalan.* My hunger vanishes when at sea. On land it cannot be endured. *Kalungay siyaliku halam aku bay ma luma'.* I was not in the house when my younger brother disappeared. (*syn:* **lopas 1**) **1.1)** *v. tr.* To allow or cause something to be lost. *Mbal isab lungaynu ōnku min salsila kapanubu'an kami.* You will not let my name be lost from the stories [told by] our descendants.

**lungay sipat** *v. advrs.* ka-...-an To be out of one's mind due to grief or shock. {idiom} *Kalungayan sipat si Ina' pagka takalena.* Mother became confused with shock when she heard.

**palungay** *v. tr.* To cause something to disappear.

**lungbu'** var. of **lumbu'**

**lungbus** (var. **lumbus**) *adj. zero* Complete; entire. *Lungbus aku pareyo'-pariyata' ma sakap bayanan.* In regard to canoe equipment, I am complete from top to bottom. (*Thesaurus:* **jukup 1, pareyo'-pariyata'**)

**lungbus mahal** *n. phrase* The mahal component of bride-wealth goods that traditionally belongs to the bride's parents. {idiom} *Mbal na agon makaliyu d'nda man ina'na. Subay lungbus mahal.* The girl can scarcely be away from her mother. The parents' share of the bride-wealth needs to be paid in full.

**lungkab** *adj.* a- Burnt superficially; blistered from a burn. *Alungkab kuwitna bang kabu'usan bohe' pasu'.* His skin blistered when hot water was spilt over it. (*Thesaurus:* **kassa'-kassa', danglus, lūs₁ 1**)

**lungkad** *v. tr.* **1)** To open up a container and see its contents. *Kahaba' iya lingantu, halam paruwa-ruwa magtūy angalungkad.* Whenever he is hungry, he does not hesitate to open [a container]. *Lungkarun deyom ba'ul itū. Kalu ilu masi bay ni'nna'nu-i, bang halam bay tinangkaw e' saga onde'-onde'.* Open up this chest. What you stored may still be there, if the children haven't stolen it. (*syn:* **kadkad 1.1, kulakkad 1;** *Thesaurus:* **banga'₁, buka'₃, sungkab, ukab**

1.1) 2) To break up ground for planting. *Piku itū pangalungkad tana' atuwas.* This pickaxe is for opening up hard ground.

**lungkahad** *v. intr. pa-* To sit up abruptly from a lying or sitting position. *Palungkahad iya min paningkō'anna.* He sits up abruptly from his place. (*Thesaurus:* **punduk 1**)

**lunglung** *v. tr.* To shake a liquid with a lengthwise movement of its container. *Subay nilunglungan kassa' ilū bo' tabati' ns'llan bay atuli.* The bottle should be shaken to stir up the oil that was left overnight. *Subay nilunglung massuli' ilū bo' ala'an isina.* That ramose murex [a shell] should be shaken to remove its contents. (*cf:* **gunggus**)

**lungsud** *n.* A city or town, especially one that is the local seat of government. *Aluha sidda makalandu' lungsud Davao.* The city of Davao is very extensive. *Aparat kaluma'an ma kalungsuran.* The houses in cities are very numerous. (*Thesaurus:* **da'ira 1, lahat, pasisil, tana'$_2$**)

**lungtud** *n.* The second series of side-planks above the dugout hull of a pelang-type canoe. (*gen:* **tapi' 1**)

**lupa** *see:* **panglupa**

**lupag** *v. tr. -an* To clean something by scrubbing off dirt. (*Thesaurus:* **bunut-bunut, kuskus 1.1, dalug$_1$, gisgis 1.2, lukup, susut**)

**lupi'$_1$** *v. tr.* To form a fold in flexible material; to fold such material on itself. *Lupi'un kono' ba saga dakdakan ilū.* Please fold those washed clothes. *Mbal kalupi'anku s'mmek si Oto' apa ata'u du iya.* I can't be folding clothes for Eldest Son because he certainly knows how to do it. *Kakana' puyu' itū subay nilupi' duwa.* The cloth of this bag should be folded double. *Bay nilupi' pareyom bo' mbal patastas.* Folded in so as not to come unstitched. (*Thesaurus:* **lipat$_1$ 2, l'ppot, peko'**)

**lupi'$_2$** *v. tr.* To multiply something. *Subay bayaranna, subay nilupi' min mpat ya busay bay ngā'na hē'.* He should pay, the paddle he took should be multiplied by four.

**lupis** *n.* The fibrous outer layers of a banana stalk, useful as a tying material. *Angā' aku lupis pamaggot tepo pinabeya' ni Niyusilan.* I will get banana fibres to tie the mat to send to New Zealand. (*Thesaurus:* **badjang, bamban$_2$, hidjuk, lanut**)

**lupit** *v. ditr.* To compensate the deprived party when divorce takes place within a short time after marriage. *Buwat aniya' bay maglakibini, bo' halam du at'ggol pagpūn sigā, bo' sali' ahukaw d'nda. Min d'nda ya angalupit, ang'nde' alta', minsan mbal atupus.* It's like when a couple are married but haven't been together long, like when the woman is reluctant [to have sexual relations]. It is the woman's side that makes recompense, returning some of the valuables, though not the entire amount. (*cf:* **iris**)

**luput** *v. intr. pa-* 1) To overflow a container. (*Thesaurus:* **lasay, lese$_1$, lipay$_1$, sempok 1,**

uplut) 1.1) *v. tr. -an* To overfill a container.

**lūran** *n.* A downward slope; an incline.

**paglūran** *v. intr. aN-* To head downhill, of a group of people. *Wa'i maglūran saga sundalu ni sapa' anunggu'an kontra sigām.* The solders have gone down to the river, guarding against their enemies.

**lurang** *n.* The dried sheath of a coconut flower. (*wh:* **niyug**)

**luray** *see:* **pagluray**

**luruk** *n.* 1) A person who attends an event; a guest. *Aheka gi' masi luruk, akulang na pagkakan.* There are still a lot of visitors, not much food. 1.1) *v. intr. pa-* To go to an event such as a wedding, funeral or legal hearing. *Paluruk kitam ni pagkawinan.* We are attending the wedding. *Pinal'ngngan l'lla inān, pinabatal na ko da'a kohapan bay maglurukan.* The bridegroom is told to start moving, and the marriage is formalised so that those who attended are not overtaken by night. (*Thesaurus:* **hadil, taddung, tupuk**) 1.2) *v. tr.* To attend a gathering. *Bang magkawin subay tinagunggu'an ko niluruk e' saga a'a.* When there is a wedding there should be gongs played so people will attend.

**lurup** *v. tr.* To get something by diving. *Lurupun l'ppus inān.* Get those marine sponges by diving. (*Thesaurus:* **lorok 1, tuhun 1**)

**paglurup** *v. tr.* To dive for a living. *Pohak, ya maglurup na pa'in kita.* Ringworm, the result of our continual diving.

**lurus$_1$** *v. intr. pa-* 1) To slide down something more or less vertical, such as a tree or pole. (*Thesaurus:* **dokdos, dusdus, dūt, julut 1, loros, luslus 1**) 1.1) *v. tr.* To get something by sliding down a pole or post.

**paglurus-lurus** *v. intr. aN-* To slide repeatedly down a house post or ladder. *Bang onde'-onde' amandi ni tahik maglurus-lurus min haronan.* When children go swimming in the sea they keep sliding down the house ladder.

**lurus$_2$** *v. intr. pa-* To marry a woman from the kin group of a deceased wife. *Amatay pa'in h'ndana, palurus iya ni kamanakan h'ndana, min kabaya'an matto'ana.* When his wife had died, he married his wife's niece, with the good will of her elders.

**lūs$_1$** *adj. a-* 1) Suffering superficial injuries from a burn. *Bihing bowa'ku bay alūs e' kahawa.* My lips got burnt from the coffee. *Bay alūs si Hi ma pagtinapayan, bay angā' kaldero.* Hi was burnt by the oven, she took hold of the pot. (*Thesaurus:* **kassa'-kassa', danglus, lungkab**) 2) Parched from heat and lack of water, of plants. (*Thesaurus:* **lanos$_1$, layu, luyluy**)

**lūs$_2$** *v. intr. aN-* To lose weight.

**paglūs** *v. intr. aN-* To lose weght.

**lusay** *n.* Eelgrass. *Zostera marina.* (*cf:* **unas**)

**luslus** *v. intr. pa-* 1) To slip down, such as clothes off the body, someone sliding down a post. *Hengkotin pantalunnu ilū, bo' mbal paluslus.* Tie those trousers of yours, so they don't slip down. (*Thesaurus:* **dokdos, dusdus, dūt, julut 1, loros, lurus₁** 1) 1.1) *adj. a-* Loose and liable to slip down, of clothes. (*Thesaurus:* **lambuyut, loka**)

**lussung** *adj. a-* Incurring a loss; financially unprofitable. (*Thesaurus:* **lugi' 1**)

**pagkalussungan** *v. intr. aN-* To suffer a financial loss.

**lustang** *n.* 1) A tube, usually of bamboo, through which a pellet or dart is blown; a blowgun. (*cf:* **lumping**) 1.1) *v. tr.* To shoot something using a blowgun. *Angalustang manuk-manuk.* Shooting birds with a blowgun.

**paglustang** *n.* A tube for blowing pellets through.

**lusuk-lusuk** *n.* Upright supports, such as doorposts. *Sulatunbi isāb ōnbi ma lusuk-lusuk lawang luma'bi maka ma lawang ādbi.* Write your name too on the doorposts of your house and on the gates of your fence. (*Thesaurus:* **bale₃ 1, hāg 1, pangtu'ud, pipul, sumpiyang, tuku 1**)

**lūt₁** *v. tr.* To smooth a surface by pressing down and sliding along. *Bang nila'it subay nilūt, hatina sali' apigtal.* When it is sewn [the seam] should be pressed down smooth, sort of pulled tight. (*Thesaurus:* **dūt**)

**lūt₂** 1) *adj. a-* Emotionally attached to someone, as a small child to an older relative. *Alūt na ma aku si Se. Bang aku ala'an, anangis, subay ameya' ma aku.* Se is attached to me now. When I go away she cries; she wants to come with me. (*Thesaurus:* **balut 2, lumut₂ 1, uli, umid 1**) 2) *v. tr. a-, ka-..-an, -an* To love someone and long for their company. *Ahāp bang kita kinalūtan he' onde'-onde'.* It is nice to have a child want to be with us.

**lutang** *v. tr.* To make sure of a result by repeating an action or procedure. *Bay pintata min t'dda, nilutang pabalik bo' atogob.* We painted one coat and then did it again so it would be durable. *Bang aniya' bay nilagut, yukna ni dangan ya bantana, "Lutangun, duhunin."* When someone is hacked with a fighting knife, he says to the one who is his enemy, "Do it again, make it even worse." *Ya angkan nilutang pantān bo' naylon ē' mbal basalsalan.* The reason the porch is [lashed] twice is so that the nylon lashings are not strained.

**lutas** *v. tr.* To wean a child. *Nā, aheya-heya pa'in si Ib nilutas iya min ina'na.* So when Ib was a bit bigger he was weaned from his mother. *Sakali, aniya' bay ngā'na anak bili-bili halam gi' talutas.* Right after that he got a lamb that had not been weaned. *Da'a kam am'lla kambing abata' ya halam gi' talutas.* Don't cook a young goat that hasn't been weaned yet.

**lutaw** *n.* The ghost of a dead person, usually someone wicked or improperly buried, who may materialize to trouble the living. *Makatāw-tāw kami bang ta'nda' lutaw amangguwa' ma talun hē'.* We are frightened when we see the ghost of a dead person haunting the forest. (*Thesaurus:* **bahana', pagbagala, panyata'₂ 1, pangguwa' 1.1**)

**lutsa** *see:* **paglutsa**

**lutu₁** *v. tr.* To remove kernels from a corn cob by rubbing with the heel of one's palm. *Lututa isi gandum, la'ananta man batangna.* We hull the corn kernels, we remove them from the cob.

**lutu₂** *v. tr.* To carry something on the top of one's head. (*syn:* **durung₁**)

**lutu'₁** *n.* 1) Provisions for a journey or a fishing trip. *Am'lli aku panggi' kayu pang'nnopku lutu' inān.* I will buy some cassava to supplement my travel food. (*Thesaurus:* **balanja' 1, kahirupan, ka'lluman, gastu 1, pagnapaka**) 1.1) *adj. a-* Supplied with food for a trip. *Alutu' kami duwambatang t'bbu.* We were provisioned with two sticks of sugarcane.

**paglutu'** *n.* Provisions for a fishing trip. *Bang aku angā' panggi' kayu paglutu' ni kapū'an, subay aku patukad kaleya.* When I get cassava as provisions to the [fishing] islands, I have to go inland.

**paglutu'anan** *n.* A container for the provisions taken on a fishing expedition.

**palutu'** *v. ditr.* To provide someone with food for a journey or fishing expedition.

**lutu'₂** *adj. a-* Intense, of a color. *Gaddung mbal alutu'.* Green color that is not intense. *Palmata alutu' gaddungna.* A deep green jewel. (*cf:* **mata' 2**)

**lutup** *v. advrs. -in-* Blistered due as a result of pressure. *Nilutupan tape'na, asigpit taumpa'na.* His feet are blistered, his shoes are tight. (*Thesaurus:* **kassa'-kassa', l'ttup 1, mata-daing 1, tambu-tambu₂**)

**lutus** *v. advrs. -in-* Infested by a wood-boring insect. *Al'kkas nilutus bang bay na tapuwad.* Quickly infested with wood-borer once it is felled. (*Thesaurus:* **anay, boke', bukbuk 1**)

**luwa** *n.* 1) The characteristic appearance of something. *Ya saitan ta'nda'ku inān sali' luwa halimaw.* That demon I saw was sort of like a tiger in appearance. *Angay ala'at luwanu ilū?* Why are you looking so disagreeable [lit. why is your appearance bad]? *Luwa-luwanu! Ana'adjil ka aku.* Look at you! Your glory dazzles me! *Aniya' ta'nda'ku a'a pinakaluwa lagtaw.* I saw men who looked like lofty giants. (*Thesaurus:* **aymuka, bantuk, bayhu' 1, dagbos, jantang-jari, lahi₄, pangli' 1**) 1.1) *v. tr.* To look like something different from one's normal appearance. *Lahoran aku, sali' angaluwa salindugu': ettom, pote', gaddung.* I am bruised, looking rather like a rainbow: black, white, green.

**daluwa** *adj.* Identical in appearance; looking alike. (*cf:* **dasali'**)

**pagdaluwa** *v. intr. aN-* To be identical in appearance.

**pangluwahan** *n.* The external appearance of

something.

**luwad** *v. tr.* To row a canoe using a fulcrum. *Bang alandos baliyu, bo' aku mbal makakole' amusay, angaluwad aku man buli'.* When the wind is strong and I am unable to paddle, I row from the stern. (*Thesaurus:* **busay 1.1, kelle 1.1, dayung 1.1, epe, tindayung**)
> **pangaluwaran** *n.* A fulcrum; a rowlock.

**luwag** *n.* **1)** A large spoon or ladle, sometimes made from a section of coconut shell. *Bang ka am'lla buwas, kuwalun maka luwag. Luwag itu ya pangaun.* When you cook rice, stir it with a ladle. This ladle here is the one for serving. *Bang suru', pinedjetan. Bang halam aniya' suru' subay luwag.* With a spoon it is pressed down flat. If there is no spoon it will have to be a ladle. (*Thesaurus:* **paleta, sasanglag, sintib, suru' 1**) **1.1)** *v. tr.* To stir or dish up something with a ladle. (*cf:* **engket, haun₁**)

**luwa'** var. of **luwas₁**

**luwal** *adv.* Only; solely; uniquely. *Aheka tambal ma luma' itū, luwal tambal ipul halam aniya'.* There is a lot of medicine in this house, only leprosy medicine is lacking. *Ai-ai sinambat ni matto'a, luwal ka halam matto'a bo' mbal kabuwanan.* Anything hinted at by an elder, only if you were not an elder would it not be given. *Halam aniya' ata'u ma kamemon, luwal Tuhan.* No one other than God knows everything. *Luwal bang kami mbal am'ssi halam aniya'. Basta kami am'ssi aniya'.* Only when we do not fish are there no fish. So long as we fish there will be some. (*Thesaurus:* **dakuman, hal, la'a, puntul, sadja, samadjana, tunggal 1, yangkon**)
> **luwal bahā'** *adv. phrase* Most likely; except perhaps. {*idiom*} *Luwal bahā' salang-sabot, panggi' kayu bay nili'isan, alegong luwana.* Most likely *salang-sabot*, cassava that has been grated, and circular in shape. *Halam aku bay katōngan dusa, luwal bahā' ya bay pangalinganku ma tabu'.* I have not been found guilty, except perhaps what I shouted out at the market.

**luwas₁** (var. **luwa'**) *v. intr. pa-* **1)** To emerge; to appear. *Ta'abut pa'in maganak, manjari kuting ya paluwas, ngga'i ka manusiya'.* When the time came to give birth, it was a kitten that emerged, not a human. *Bang buwat ka'a-i lum'ngngan bo' halam ta'nda' he' anaknu. Pagluwasna, paturul ni ka'a bang ka ta'nda'. Na papulipus na ma ka'a, magtūy ka binalutan.* Like when you walk on somewhere and your daughter hasn't seen you. Having come out she follows you when you are seen. Then she shelters behind you, and you are promptly grabbed. *Bang paluwa' buwattē' bulan, ahāp bang ma kami.* When the moon rises like that, we say it is good. (*Thesaurus:* **bulat, tukaw, tuwa' 1**) **1.1)** *v. tr. -an* To bring

something to the outside. **1.2)** *v. advrs.* **ka-...-an** To be excluded from a place. *Ya sali' bay nggo' maka mma' kami, bay kaluwa'an pi'itu man Sisangat, lahat kami porol.* Like our mother and father, they came here having been excluded from Sisangat, our home place.

**kaluwasan** *n.* The outcome of events or discussions. *Bay kami makapagsuli-suli, ahāp isāb kaluwasanna.* We were able to talk together and the outcome was good. (*Thesaurus:* **kamattihan 1, kamaujuran, kat'kkahan₂, katobtoban, katumariyahan, pamole'an 2**)

**luwasan** *loc. n.* Outside. *Ina'an du ma luwasan iskul.* There outside the school. *Ina'an iya abahak ma luwasan bilik.* There he was lying outside the room. (*ant:* **deyom 1**)

**pagluwas-luwas** *v. intr. aN-* **1)** To keep emerging from some place. *Magluwa'-luwa' anak milikan min patulihanna.* The Westerner's child keeps coming out from where she sleeps. **1.1)** *v. tr.* To keep bringing someone out of doors. *Nilibun iya, sali' binilik. Mbal pinagluwas-luwas supaya mbal aettom. Subay na pa'in apote'.* She is kept out of sight, kind of confined to a room, not allowed to keep going out lest she be darkened [by the sun]. She must stay pale.

**paluwas** *v. tr.* To get something out of a container or storage place.

**paluwasan** *n.* A source, especially with regard to a woman as the source of one's existence.

**sikaluwasan** *adj.* Emerging in great numbers.

**luwas₂** *v. intr. pa-* To come from a sale before expenses are deducted, of the proceeds. *Bay po'on sangpū' pilak, paluwas lima pilak. Alapis kami.* The capital was ten pesos, and the take was five pesos. We lost money.

**luwas lling** *v. intr. pa-* To utter; to produce speech. *Mbal paluwas llingna, sali' nihegom-hegom ma deyom atayna.* Nothing is said, he sort of keeps it secret in his heart.

**luyal** *n.* **1)** A gift given to someone influential in the hope of getting their help. **1.1)** *v. tr.* To go guarantor for someone; to arrange for someone's release from custody on bail. *Niluyal ma kasehe'an, nijamin ma kami. Sali' nil'kkat.* Others say *luyal*, we say *jamin*. Similar to *l'kkat* [redeem]. (*Thesaurus:* **haum, jamin, l'kkat₁ 1.1, piyansa**)

**luyang** *n.* An alloy of tin and copper (tin being the major component). (*Thesaurus:* **bulawan 1, estenles, pilak 1, pittang, sawasa', tumbaga 1**)

**luyluy** *adj. a-* Withered. (*Thesaurus:* **lanos₁, layu, lūs₁ 2**)

**luyu'** *adj. a-* Drooping, of eyelids when one is drowsy. *Aluyu' matata, ma llot pak'ddom maka pak'llat.* Our eyes are heavy, midway between being closed and open. (*Thesaurus:* **k'llip, piru'**)

# M m

**ma** *prep.* **1)** At; in; on; by (indicating generic location). *Ma t'ngnga' kami dilaut alandos goyak.* When we were in the middle of the open sea it was very rough. *Ndiya ma aku.* Give it to me. (*Thesaurus:* **min 1, ni₁, tudju₁ 1**) **2)** Marker of a specific count unit. *Ni'itung ma tāran.* Counting by the row. **3)** For; belonging to; by means of (indicating beneficiary, possession, or instrument). *Tinahi' ma tangan.* Sewn by hand. *Tināw si Arung ma kuting.* Eldest Daughter is afraid of cats. (*Thesaurus:* **maka₁, para₂**)

**ma-** *aff.* Derivational prefix that creates a noun referring to someone or something described by the prefixed characteristic. *Ndiya maheya ilū.* Hand me that big one.

**ma + CLASS-an** *adv. phrase* By the (classifying noun).

**ma batangan** *adv. phrase* By the bundle, of rod-like objects such as poles or cigarettes. *Siga? Bĩlli ma batangan.* cigarets? Bought by the piece.

**ma botangan** *adv. phrase* By the pile.

**ma bowa'an** *adv. phrase* By the length from the mouth to the tip of one arm.

**ma būsan** *adv. phrase* By the roll, of cloth. (*cf:* **ma gulungan**)

**ma kepet** *adv. phrase* By the distance from the armpit to the tip of the same arm.

**ma kiluhan** *adv. phrase* By the kilo.

**ma kintasan** *adv. phrase* By the sheet.

**ma kolengan** *adv. phrase* By the reel or coil.

**ma d'ppahan** *adv. phrase* By the length between outstretched hands; by the fathom.

**ma gekapan** *adv. phrase* By the sheet. *Katas itu subay bin'lli ma gekapan.* This paper must be purchased by the sheet.

**ma gipitan** *adv. phrase* By the package, of pressed cassava meal.

**ma gulungan** *adv. phrase* By the roll, of cloth. (*cf:* **ma būsan**)

**ma hangtaran** *adv. phrase* By the length of something laid out flat. *Sinukud ma hangtaranna, ai na duwand'ppa, ai labi dand'ppa, ni'ppi'an.* Measured by length when stretched out flat, two fathoms or just over one fathom, with a woven hem.

**ma hatusan** *adv. phrase* By the hundred. *Bang kita makaisi dakayu' pilak ma hatusan, buwat ma bangko inān, sali' anganak inān.* When we put in single pesos by the hundreds, as into the bank, they will earn interest.

**ma lĩtan** *adv. phrase* By the string, of corn. *Pinab'llihan ma lĩtan sadja.* Sold only by the string.

**ma metohan** *adv. phrase* By the meter.

**ma pungutan** *adv. phrase* By the bunch. *Buwahan bĩlli ma pungutan.* Lansones purchased by the stalk.

**ma solagan** *adv. phrase* By the piece or segment. *Bĩlli ma solagan.* Bought by the piece. *Ubi-sowa, a'aslag solaganna.* Snake yam, its pieces quite big.

**ma tagikan** *adv. phrase* By the row. *Bang niyug ma tagikan, bang panggi' kayu ma tāran.* Coconuts go by the *tagikan,* cassava by the *tāran.*

**ma tahunan** *adv. phrase* By the year. *Nda'un, Mma', ma tahunan na aku maghinang ma ka'a sali' banyaga'nu.* Look, Dad, for years I have worked for you as if [I was] your slave. *Tahun bay palabay inān, bay magluma' maitu si Sa ĩ'. Ma tahunan, ngga'i ka ma bulanan.* Years past, Sa lived here in his house. For years, not for months.

**ma tāran** *adv. phrase* By the row, of planted things.

**ma tuhugan** *adv. phrase* By the string. *Daing bĩlli ma tuhugan.* Fish bought by the string.

**ma tundunan** *adv. phrase* By the cluster, of fruit that grows in bunches.

**ma atag 1)** *adv. phrase* Located at. **2)** *v. tr.* To stay for a time at a specific place. *Bang kami ni M'ddas, mina'atag luma' si Bapa' Em.* When we went to Siasi town we stayed at the house of Uncle Em. (*syn:* **mintag**)

**ma sai** *interrog.* Who is it for? *Ma sai kahawa itū? Ma aku?* Who is this coffee for? For me?

**ma t'llu** *adv. phrase* Three days ahead from the present. (*Thesaurus:* **di'ilaw, llaw itu, salung, simuddai**)

**mabolo** *n.* A species of tree and its edible fruit. *Diospyros discolor.*

**maka₁** *prep.* With; by; by means of (indicating instrument). *Bono'ku bantaku maka barung itū. Barung ina'an ya bay pamono'ku danakanna.* I will kill my enemy with this fighting knife. It is that knife that I used for killing his brother. *Maglampasu' kā maka abu ampa alanu'.* Scrub using ashes so it will be clean. *Pinagsuwa'-suwa'an dakanna maka bukutna maka p'ttung abulak.* Its base and its back are threaded together with green bamboo [strips]. (*Thesaurus:* **ma 3, para₂**)

**maka₂** *conj.* And; plus; together with (linking items of the same category). *Kami maka milikan.* We and the Westerner. *Ai pangiraman dayang-dayang? Manggis maka tagbak min Tawau.* What does the princess crave during early pregnancy?

Mangosteen and wild ginger fruit from Tawau. *Aku maka si Oto' maka saga kakiku.* I and Oldest Brother and my cousins. *Kami maka pagkahi kami onde' iskul.* We and our schoolmates.

**maka**₃ (var. **aka**; **ka**₃) *conj.* And; plus (in counting). *Sangpū' maka lima pilak.* Fifteen [lit. ten and five] pesos. *Ta'abut pa'in kasangpū' ka t'llung'llaw ma bulan panagna'an, magtulakan na sigām kamemon.* On reaching the thirteenth day of the first month, they all departed.

**maka-**₁ *aff.* Aptative actor voice prefix: attaches to transitive verbs, identifying the actor as the subject of the clause, and indicating that the actor is not completely in control of the event (e.g. circumstance, happenstance, or ability). *Bay mbal makal'ngngan.* Was unable to walk. *Daipara makabāk aku sīn pinta lima.* But fortunately I happened to find some money, a five peso note. *Sagō' at'ggol na pagpūn sigā, halam makabāk anak.* But when they had been married a long time, they didn't have a child. *Makatāw-tāw waktu inān, sabab waktu pangalapnas Tuhan ma saga manusiya'.* That time will be terrifying because it is the time when God destroys mankind. (*cf:* **ta-** 1)

**maka-**₂ *aff.* Intransitive prefix indicating that the subject produces the state described by the verb (often an emotional response). *Makalingas lahat inān, sali' halam aniya' sehe'ta.* That place makes one lonely, like not having a companion.

**makajari** *ptl.* 1) May be; permissible. (Deontic modality particle, permission). *Makajari aku angindam pelangnu?* May I borrow your canoe? *Ka'am kasehe'an ilū makajari na amole' pehē' ni mma'bi ma deyom kasalamatan.* The rest of you are now permitted to return in safety to your fathers. (*Thesaurus:* **manjari**₁ 1) 2) Might perhaps; possible. (Epistemic modality particle, possibility). *Minsan kami mbal makajari amole' sangom ilū, aniya' du patulihan maitu.* Even though it is not possible for us to get home tonight, there is a place to sleep here. (*Thesaurus:* **manjari**₁ 2)

**makalandu'** *adv.* Excessively; beyond what is reasonable or tolerable. *Da'a ka amowa, tuwan, bang abuhat makalandu' minsan pila pamuwan ma ka'a.* Don't carry it, friend, if it is too heavy, no matter how much you are given. *Makalandu' pahāp ka'a ilū!* You are really too much!

**makani-** *aff.* Prefix construction combining the aptative prefix maka- and the preposition ni. This prefix incorporates the meaning of the stem to derive a verb meaning 'to come to or happen to someone, to become, or to arrive at a place'. *Pinaentoman iya ai-ai bay makani'iya dakayu'-dakayu', hatina niuki'-uki' kamemon.* He was reminded of all that had happened to him, one by one. In other words it was all recounted. *Petong itū akiput matana, bang magnilantaw.* This word *petong* means small mesh, with regard to a

long net. *S'lle' bale puhu', pinatā e' Tuhan ya yuknu hē' bo' mbal makanika'a.* Perish the thought, may God banish what you were saying, that it may not happen to you. (*cf:* **makaniatay, ni**₁)

**makaniatay** *phrase* To come to mind; to occur to someone. {idiom} *Halam makaniataycu.* It didn't occur to me. (*cf:* **makani-**)

**makannak** *n.* Children in general or collectively. *Buwat makannak angongka', manjari aheka puhu'. Na pinamūng-mūngan he' ina'na, yukna, "Analik-nalik kām, ngga'i ka sehe'bi ya abinasa, ka'am apa ka'am ya amowa-mowa ni luma' itū."* Like children playing, and there are a lot of them. Then his mother scolds them, saying "Organise things, it's not your playmates who will get the pain, it's you [plural], because it's you who persuaded them to come to this house." *Bang aku amangan bo' aniya' angalung makannak, ya pamakanku iya l'bbiku.* When I am eating and a kid comes wanting food, what I give him are my leftovers. (*Thesaurus:* **anak-anak**₁, **kamanahutan, onde'-onde'**)

**makaw** *n.* Chinese, especially in a business context and in contrast to merchants of other ethnic backgrounds. *Sasalan makaw.* Of Chinese workmanship. (*Thesaurus:* **Lannang, sina'**₁, **taoke'**₁)

**Makka** *n.* Mecca, the goal of Muslim pilgrimage. *Makka ina'an lahat paghadji'an.* That place Mecca is the place to which pilgrims go. *Hal am'lli sahal ma Singgapura, halam bay makaniMakka.* All he did was buy a hadji's turban in Singapore. He hasn't been to Mecca.

**maki-** *var.* of **miki-**

**makina** (var. **malkina**) *n.* 1) A machine; an engine. *Ahāp pa'in malkina, amupput kami tudju kaut.* When the engine was working we motored seawards. (*cf:* **pupputan**) 1.1) *v. tr.* **-an** To provide something with an engine. *Am'lli aku makina pamakinaku ispidbut.* I will buy an engine to power my speedboat. 2) A sewing machine.

**makina tape'** *n. phrase* A pedal-powered sewing machine.

**makinilya** *n.* Barber's clippers.

**Maksina'** *n.* The name of some distant country; any far-off place. *Olangna itū takale ma lahat Maksina'.* His shouting can be heard way off in the land of Maksina.

**maksud** *n.* 1) Purpose; intention. *Aniya' kamaksuranna.* There is a purpose to it. *Aniya' maksudku ni ka'a (aniya' gawi, aniya' l'ngngan, aniya' mohot).* I have a reason for coming to you (a purpose, a goal, an intention). (*Thesaurus:* **kamatti, gawi** 1, **hadjat**₁, **tiranan**) 1.1) *v. tr.* To purpose or intend something. 1.2) *v. tr.* **-an** To deliver something to its intended destination. *Buwat soho'nu si Sa ni Tiyanggi, yukna, "Maksurin itū ni si Yo."* Like when you send Sa to Jolo City, you say, "Take this right to Yo." (*Thesaurus:*

nde', papole', pasampay, tukbal₁ 1, tūd₂, tulun₂ 1.1, tuyuk-tuyuk)

**makupa** (var. **mangupa**) *n.* The rose-apple tree and its red, bell-shaped fruit. *Eugenia javanica.* (*cf:* **tambis**)

**madjilis** var. of **majilis**

**madrasa** *n.* A Koranic school; the curriculum of such a school. *Angadji' kami madrasa.* We are studying the *madrasa* curriculum. (*cf:* **iskul** 1)

**mag-** (var. **ag-**) *aff.* Distributive actor voice prefix: attaches to a verb, identifying the actor as the subject of the clause, and indicating multiple occurrences of the action described (e.g. action that is frequent, habitual, repeated, performed by multiple actors, or in multiple locations). *At'kka pehē' ni Kagayan, mahē' matto'aku i magusaha llaw-sangom.* After we arrived there, that is where my parents worked, day and night. *Agtūy, magligid-ligid ya Buntal hē', ni gusung, magligid-ligid.* Suddenly, Pufferfish was rolling around in the sand, just rolling around.

**mag-..-in-** *aff.* Affix construction indicating that the actor is wearing the affixed item. *Sali' kita as'mmek, magsinawwal, magbinadju', magpinīs, magkinuppiya', magtinakos saga. Ya buwat sundalu, ahakos na s'mmek sigā.* We are clothed, wearing wide Sulu trousers, a shirt, a turban, a skull cap, weapons maybe. Like soldiers, they are uniformed. *Magpinantalun aku.* I will wear long pants.

**mag-+paN-** *aff.* Prefix indicating plural actors. *Magpangongka' aku maka kasehe'anku bang al'ggot t'bba.* I and the others all play together when the tide is really low.

**māg-māg** *adj. a-* Broken up into small pieces; shattered. *Amāg-māg kassa'ku, abila' kamemon. Angkan niōnan amāg-māg, mbal na manjari.* My bottle shatters, all broken. That's why it is called *māg-māg*, because it's no longer useful. *Amāg-māg bila' pelang, ya mbal na tabayan.* The split canoe is breaking up, the one that is no longer usable. (*Thesaurus:* **bagbag, lopot** 1, **tumu-tumu**)

**maga** *n.* The morning star, the sign of approaching dawn. (*syn:* **lakag**; *gen:* **bitu'un**)

**magalib** var. of **magrib**

**magay** *interrog.* To do what; to what purpose? *Magay inān?* What's going on there? *Sagō' ma buwattina'an, ina'an na iya amatay, magay gi' aku amuwasa?* But he has died already, so what is the point of me fasting? (*Thesaurus:* **ai, angay, buwattingga** 1.1, **maingga, sai, sumiyan**)

**magay-magay** *adj. zero* Caring about what happens (with a negative). *Magjuru'an kita dīta, mbal kita magay-magay.* We let ourselves behave excessively [in grief], we don't care what happens.

**pagmagay** *v. tr.* To be concerned for something (usually with a negative). *Halam tapagmagay he'na kahālan ina'an-i.* He was not concerned

about that state of affairs.

**pagpamagay** 1) *v. intr. aN-* To be concerned about what is going on (usually with a negative). 2) *v. tr.* To treat something as a matter of concern.

**pamagay** *n.* 1) A matter of concern. 1.1) *interrog.* For what purpose; to do what with? *Pamagaynu pōng papan itu? Arāk amu'ku.* What do you plan to do with these offcuts of wood? I had thought of asking you for them. *Pamagay lahing ilu?* What are those coconuts for?

**magbabaya'** (derivative of **baya'**) *n.* The person who is in control, whose will gets done. *Tuhan ya Magbabaya'.* God is the one in control.

**magbobowa** (derivative of **bowa₂**) *n.* The person in charge of an event. *Aku ya magbobowa.* I am the master of ceremonies.

**magbubuhat** (derivative of **buhat₃**) *n.* A person who waits on guests; a waiter. *Pinaluwas min kalabusu ya nakura' magbubuhat inuman.* The one in charge of the people serving drinks was brought out of jail.

**magka-** *aff.* Prefix indicating the possibility of the described condition. *Magkagaha' ko' ilū.* That is likely to rust. *Uminay ka magkabuwattilu?* What happened to you to be in such a state?

**magdai'-dai'** (derivative of **dai'-dai'**) *adv.* Hurriedly. *Tiyangsi' itū niā' min batang langkay. Mbal magtūy tapangengkot magdai'-dai' ni ai-ai. Subay gi' tinabid-tabid bo' mbal maglopeng.* The *tiyangsi'* referred to is obtained from the central rib of a coconut frond. It can't be used for tying anything in a hurry. It should be twined a bit first so it doesn't lose its shape.

**maghuhukum** (derivative of **hukum**) *n.* A judge; one who judges. *Tuhan ya Maghuhukum.* God is the Judge. *Saga maghuhukum maka saga pagnakura'an.* Judges and leading men.

**magi** *n.* A specific for a small group of palm-like plants.

**magl'l'ngngan** (derivative of **l'ngngan₁**) *n.* Spirit beings of various kinds who move unseen among humans; the travellers. *Saitan magl'l'ngngan magbaran ni kita bang pasangon.* Saitan beings of the 'walker' class come to us in person when they possess us.

**Magpapanjari** *n.* The Creator. *Bay tahun palabay aheya pagsukulan kami ni Magpapanjari in pagbayad si Mma' halam du isāb bay alipas bulan-bulan.* In the year past we had a great thanksgiving to the Creator, that Father's payment was never forgotten month after month.

**magpipiyansa** (derivative of **piyansa**) *n.* One who arranges bail for someone in custody.

**magp'p'ssi** (derivative of **p'ssi**) *n.* One who fishes for a living. *Masi iya kinalingasan he' saga a'a magp'p'ssi.* He is still missed by the people who make their living by fishing.

**magpuputika'** (derivative of **pagputika'**) *n.* An

expert in foretelling the future.

**magrib** (var. **magalib**) **1)** *n.* The fourth of the five daily prayer times of Islam, just after sunset. *Abay-kohap alempos na, magalib. Sali' halam aniya' llaw ta'nda', minsan keyat-keyatna.* Evening, fully dark, time for prayer. Nothing seen of the sun, not even its faint light. (*Thesaurus:* **aisa, asal, luhul₁, subu₂ 2)** **2)** *adv.* Late dusk or early dark. *Halam na aniya' llaw, hal ba'as-ba'as. Song sū'-palita'an na, ya na hē' magrib.* There is no longer any sun, only its glow. When it's almost lamp-lighting time, that's *magrib.* (*Thesaurus:* **abay-kohap, kohap 1, lekot-lendom, lempos, logob-logob, sū'-palita'an**)

**magsāy** var. of **agsāy**

**magtak** *v. intr.* a- To come into one's mind, of something that had been forgotten. *Yampa amagtak ni atayku.* It just now came into my mind. (*Thesaurus:* **entom 1.2, padlak ni atay, sangpit, suligpat, tambung, tasdik, tomtom 1.1**)

**magtai'anak** (var. **magtautai'anak**; **magtautali'anak**) *n.* A basic family unit of parents and children.

**magtautai'anak** var. of **magtai'anak**

**magtautali'anak** var. of **magtai'anak**

**magtūy** (var. **agtūy**) (derivative of **tūy**) *adv.* Immediately; without delay. *Bang am'ssi si Je ni Serom bo' tininduk he' dapak, agtūy nihella' he'na.* When Je is fishing towards Serom Island and a humpback red snapper takes his bait, he pulls it up right away. *Bang aniya' maggradwesyon bo' aniya' magkalang, maglagpak-lagpak magtūy.* When there is a graduation and someone sings, they promptly clap. *Magtūy iya maka saga a'ana min da'ira inān pehē' angatubang.* He and his men from the town promptly went there to confront [the opposition]. (*Thesaurus:* **agsāy, dai'-dai'an, sakadjap, saru'un-du'un, sigla' 1**).

**mahakutta'** *n.* A crown worn by a sultan. {rare}

**mahād** (derivative of **hād**) *adv.* **1)** In accord with constraints or limits set by an authority. **1.1)** *v. tr.* -an To set limits on some activity or scope. *Magbislangan dang'llaw ni duwa, minahāran maka niorahan.* Doing something infrequently, for a day or two, the extent and times set [by a magistrate].

**mahadja'** *v. tr.* To treat someone or something without respect. *Makajari isāb bang manusiya' bang sali' halam aniya' kagunahanna ma kita, minahadja'.* Can be used also of a person if he has no value to us, treated with contempt. (*Thesaurus:* **di'in-di'in, halipulu 1.1, hampul-hampul 1**)

  **pamahadja'** *n.* **1)** A person of no worth. **1.1)** *v. tr.* To treat someone as worthless. *Pamahadja'un na pehē', sali' nihampul-hampul.* Treat as worthless, like showing complete disregard for.

**mahadjana'** *n.* An entire population. *Buwat l'ppet-kandel yamboho' ta'nda' mata, pinagmata-matahan he' mahadjana' kamemon.* Like a Pacific sunfish, never seen before, gazed at in wonder by the whole population. (*Thesaurus:* **da'ayat, mahalayak, majilis**)

  **kamahadjana'an** *n.* A large assembly of people. *An'ngge iya ma kamahadjana'an a'a.* He stood up in the crowd of people.

**mahal₁** *adj.* zero Unthinkable.

  **mahal mustahil** (var. **mahal mustahab**) *phrase* Impossible yet it happened, of some event. {idiom} *Mahal mustahil ko' ka'a ilū.* You are really something.

  **mahal-mahal** *adj.* zero Outside the normal range of human experience, as something wonderful or grotesque. *Onde'-onde' lagi' si Mu ina'an, mahal-mahal lingkatna.* As a baby Mu was outstandingly good-looking. (*Thesaurus:* **la'in-la'in, saddī-saddī**)

**mahal₂** *n.* The portion of the bride-wealth goods that is considered to belong to the bride's parents. *Bay kami angungsud t'llu hatus. Na pinunggitan he' sigā min kar'ndahan limampū' pilak nihinang mahal maka basingan.* We presented the bride price of three hundred. Now the share demanded by the family on the woman's side was fifty pesos. That became the *mahal* and *basingan* components. *Mahal, ya mantaluna maka kusta. Ya hē' porol ma tag-dapu anak.* The *mahal* is that white cloth, and the checkered cloth. That's the property belonging entirely to the parents of the girl. (*Thesaurus:* **banghad 1, basingan, pagtinabawan, punggit 1, ungsud₁ 1**)

**mahal mustahab** var. of **mahal mustahil**

**mahalayak** *n.* An entire population. (*Thesaurus:* **da'ayat, mahadjana', majilis**)

  **pamahalayak** *v. tr.* To make news or information widely known. (*Thesaurus:* **nasihat, pablek**)

**mahaldika'** *v. tr.* To honor someone highly; to treat with the greatest respect. *Ai-ai amu'na subay bīllihan. Buwat anakta, subay mahaldika'ta anakta bang kalasahanta to'ongan.* Whatever he requests should be bought. Like our children, they should be greatly respected if we really love them. *Mbal kita bilahi pinagtambuku-tambukuhan, subay binaran. Ya hē' minahaldika'.* We don't like being sent messages all the time, we should be contacted in person. That's showing honor. (*Thesaurus:* **hulmat 1, pagmahaltabat, pudji 1.2, sanglit 1.2**)

  **kamahaldika'an** *n.* Honor; majesty. *Halam aniya' sultan ya makasibu' ni kamahaldika'an Sultan Sulayman.* There was no king who could compare with the majesty of King Solomon.

**mahali** (derivative of **hali₁**) *adj.* zero Having the characteristic smell and flavor of newly squeezed cassava meal; strongly odorous, of certain fish. *Mahali isāb panggi' kayu baha'u bay nili'is, sambil l'ssana, sambil bauna.* Freshly grated cassava is also *mahali*, which includes both its taste and its smell. *Mahali, ta'abut limang'llaw al'ssom. Ta'abut na sangpū' ng'llaw abentol. Ya hē' katapusanna.* Fresh-smelling then sour, after five days. After ten days it is dried out. That's the final stage. *Bang baha'u walu-walu mahali du.* When snakefish is fresh it is quite odorous. (*Thesaurus:* **bau 1.1**, **b'ngngi**, **hamut 1.1**, **hangsu 1**, **langsa**, **langtu**, **p'ngngak**).

**mahaltabat** *n.* Respect; honor; courtesy. *Palabay aku ma iskul, magsabu aku maka pinagpariyata' panji, jari pahondong aku, hatina amuwan mahaltabat ma panji bangsa.* I was passing by the school and coincided with the raising of the flag. So I stopped, paying respect, that is, to the national flag. *Ahāp mahaltabatna, sali' ahāp addatna.* His courteous behavior is good, like his manners being good.

**pagmahaltabat** *v. tr.* -an To show someone courtesy or respect. *Nabi hē' mbal pinagmahaltabatan he' lūng-kampungna.* That prophet was not respected by his fellow townsmen. *Kami itū pinagudju', bo' ka'am ya pinagmahaltabatan.* We are the ones to be ridiculed, while you are the ones to be treated with respect. (*Thesaurus:* **hulmat 1**, **mahaldika'**, **pudji 1.2**, **sanglit 1.2**)

**maharadja** *n.* An official who settles local disputes, of lower rank than panglima. (*Thesaurus:* **botang-lahat 1**, **panghulu' 1**, **panglima**)

**mahasussi** (derivative of **sussi**) *adj. zero* Totally pure; divinely holy. *Tuhanku mahasussi, datu'ku mahatinggi.* My God is great in holiness, my prince is high in rank. *Yuk sambung l'lla inān ma si Yu, "La'anin taumpa'nu, sabab mahasussi tana' ya pan'nggehannu ilū."* The answer of that person to Yu was, "Remove your shoes because the ground where you are standing is extremely holy."

**mahatinggi** (derivative of **tinggi₁**) *adj. zero* High, of social rank. *Ka'a ya Tuhan Mahatinggi, akawasa maka pinagmatāwan, ya Tuhan tuman ma saga paljanji'an kasi-lasanu.* You are the Exalted God, powerful and to be feared, the God who is constant in your promises of love.

**pagmahatinggi** *v. intr.* aN- To act as though superior, of someone trying to rise above his fellows. *Magmahatinggi iya, palabi iya min kasehe'an.* He puts himself above others, goes beyond the rest. *Saitan magmahatinggi, maglanga-langa dīna.* A saitan spirit who acts as though exalted, making himself high.

**mahē'** (var. **mai'**) *adv. dem.* Over there, far from both speaker and hearer, precise location reference. *Mahē' ma luma' disi Anu.* Over there in What's-his-name's house. (*Set:* **mailu 1**, **maina'an 1**, **maitu 1**)

**kamahē'an** *n.* 1) The location away from the speaker and hearer; precise location reference. 2) Physical presence. *Aho', kasakupan pagbono'*

*sigā. Bay kamahē'anku bay pagbono' sigā.* Yes, their fight was witnessed. I was present at the time of their fight.

**mahi** *see:* **pagmahi**

**mahil** *see:* **pagmahil**

**mahingkan** var. of **himangkan**

**mahit** var. of **pahit**

**mahot** *conj.* If in fact, of something to be regretted. *Mahot ka mbal bilahi, angay i' hinangnu?* If you will in fact regret it, why are you doing it?

**mahuli** *n.* Later in time. *Mahuli minna'an makabāk iya paghola' pabīng min kampung du bay h'llana.* After that she found a husband once more from among the relatives of her deceased husband.

**pagmahuli-llaw** *v. intr.* aN- To defer an action or result to a later date. *Mbal ka binuwanan magtūy, subay magmahuli-llaw.* You will not be given it right away, it must wait for another day. (*Thesaurus:* **buhul₂**, **lehod 1**, **tanggu 1**)

**maï'** var. of **mahē'**

**mailad** var. of **mairan**

**mailu** *adv. dem.* 1) There, by the person spoken to. *Ilu mailu, ilu ma deyom bulsanu.* Right there, there inside your pocket. *Niangay ka bilahi angahinang luma' mailu, ma bihing bowa'-angan?* Why do you want to build a house there, by the edge of the reef drop-off? (*Set:* **mahē'**, **maina'an 1**, **maitu 1**) 1.1) *v. tr.* To place or locate something beside the person spoken to. *Mailuhun na, aniya' na.* Keep it there by you, there is some [here] already. *Mailuhin dīna.* Leave him to himself.

**kamailuhan** *n.* The location of the person being spoken to; there by you.

**maimu'** var. of **imu'**

**maina'an** *adv. dem.* 1) There, far from both speaker and hearer, vague location reference. *Ina'an na maina'an.* There it is, over there. *Maina'an pa'in kami aniya' ta'nda' kami būd p'ttung.* While we were there we saw a mountain covered with bamboo. (*Set:* **mahē'**, **mailu 1**, **maitu 1**) 1.1) *v. tr.* To place something distant from speaker and hearer. *Mital inān minaina'an.* That can is to be placed over there.

**kamaina'anan** *n.* The location away from the speaker and hearer; vague location reference.

**maingkan** var. of **malaingkan**

**maingga** *interrog.* Where? *Maingga luma' mastal?* Where is the teacher's house? (*Thesaurus:* **ai**, **angay**, **buwattingga 1.1**, **magay**, **sai**, **sumiyan**)

**maingga-maingga** *adv.* Anywhere; any place; wherever. *Binuwanan iya kara'ugan e' Tuhan maingga-maingga lahat papehē'anna.* God gave him victory anywhere he went.

**mairan** (var. **mailad**) *n.* A public space; a town plaza. *Min kariki'-diki'ku sampay ni waktu itu, halam aniya' kapandayanku amissala ma mairan.* From my childhood and up to this time, I have no skill for speaking in public. (*cf:* **palasa**)

**pagmairan** (var. **pagmailad**) *v. intr.* aN- 1) To

appear in public view. *Manjari magmairan na pa'in si Gi ma matahan bangsa Isra'il.* So Gi continued to appear publicly in the sight of the Israeli people. *Buwat aniya' amatay, yukta, "Wa'i na magmailad ma sulga'."* Like when someone dies, we say, "Gathered for the great assembly in heaven." *Magmailad kamastalan ni M'ddas, aniya' miting.* The teachers are gathering formally in Siasi town, there is a meeting. **1.1)** *v. tr.* To make a public display of something. *Mbal tapagmairan ingatnu, mbal tabowa ni kaheka'an a'a.* Your religious knowledge should not be on public display, it is not something to be brought out to the crowds. *Manjari magmairan na pa'in si Gi ma matahan bangsa Isra'il.* So then Gi continued to appear publicly in the sight of the Israeli people. (*Thesaurus:* **paghimpun**, **pagtimuk 1**, **pulin**, **pūn 1.1**)

**mairan majilis** *n. phrase* A parade ground.

**maisa** *n.* Black or white pepper, in whole or ground form. *Piper nigrum.* (*gen:* **pamapā**)

**maitu** *adv. dem.* **1)** Here, by the person speaking. *Atuli kām maitu, aniya' tepo maka ū'an.* You sleep here, there are mats and pillows. (*Set:* **mahē'**, **mailu 1**, **maina'an 1**) **1.1)** *v. tr.* To place something near the person speaking. *Maituhun kono' kahawaku.* Please put my coffee here by me. *A: "Mailuhun lagi'." B: "Aho', maituku pa'in."* A: "Just put it there by you." B: "Yes, I'll just leave it here."

   **kamaituhan** *n.* The location of the person speaking; right here. *Angay angkan bowabi a'a itū bo' magbelaw-belaw ma kamaituhanku?* Why did you bring this man to act crazy here in my presence?

   **pamaitu** *v. tr.* To let or cause someone to remain by the person speaking.

**majilis** (var. **madjilis**) *n.* The general population; the public. (*Thesaurus:* **da'ayat**, **mahadjana'**, **mahalayak**)

**ma'adjul** *see:* **pagma'adjul**

**ma'ai** *interrog.* Where? *Yukku ma sehe'ku, "Ma'ai na suray i'?" Yukna, "Daka ma'ai. Ang'nda' ka ma barannu."* I said to my companion, "Where is that comb?" He said, "Who knows? Look for it yourself." *Ma'ai na ya bay yukun-i?* Where is the one you were talking about?

   **ma'ai-ma'ai** *adv.* Wherever; any place at all. *Ma'ai-ma'ai paglahatanbi wajib kām da'a amangan haram.* Wherever you settle you must not eat what is ceremonially unclean.

**ma'amun** (var. **ma'mun**) *n.* The initial phase of training in Islamic studies; the congregation attending a prayer house. *Ma'amun he' sali' panendog ma deyom maskid.* Ma'amun are like the adherents of a mosque. *Magsapa'atan saga ma'amun kamemon.* All the congregation give small gifts [to the officiating mosque leaders]. (*cf:* **jama'a**)

**ma'ana₁** *n.* **1)** The meaning of something seen or heard. *Ta'ā' isi lling, ya ma'anana.* Got the essence of what was being said, its meaning. *Magsaddī uppi sigām dangan maka dangan, maka saddī isāb ma'anana.* Each of their dreams was different, and its meaning was different too. (*Thesaurus:* **kahulugan**, **hantang-hatulan**, **hati 1**, **hatulan 2**) **1.1)** *v. tr. -an* To provide a meaning for something; to explain something. *Ka'a kono' ya ata'u angama'ana maka angahusay saga palkala' ahunit.* You, it is said, know how to explain meanings and to settle difficult issues.

**ma'ana₂** *v. tr. -an* To keep someone from proceeding. *Mina'ahan duwa-t'llung'llaw, sali' nilagad-lagaran.* Held back for two or three days, like being made to wait. *Mina'anahan kita he' a'a. Aniya' a'a ananggu-nangguhan kita.* Someone keeps us from going on. Someone is causing us to wait a bit.

**ma'angit** *adj. zero* Having a strong oily smell or taste, as certain fish. *Palaga'un daing ilū min t'dda du, sali' bay angalere' bo' mbal sali' ma'angit inān.* Boil that fish well just once, so that after it has boiled it won't have that oily taste. *Bang pamama' pola-magi e' kamatto'ahan ma'angit-angit.* If *pola-magi* is used by old people for chewing, its taste is unpleasantly fishy.

**ma'ap** *v. intr. pa-* To seek forgiveness from someone. *Aku na ya pama'ap ni ka'a bang aniya' h'lling ala'at bay tabissalaku.* I am the one to seek forgiveness from you if I have said something bad.

   **kama'apan** *n.* Forgiveness; remission of debt. *Amu'in kama'apan ni Tuhan bang ka bay makarusa.* Ask God for forgiveness if you have sinned.

   **pagma'ap** *v. tr.* **1)** To bring about formal reconciliation between people who have disagreed or quarreled. *Aniya' bangsa bang bay magbono', minsan bay pinagma'ap, nientom e' sigā, pinaluli bay pagbono'.* There is an ethnic group, who when they have fought, even though they have been formally reconciled, remember and keep in mind the fight. **1.1)** *v. tr. -an* To achieve reconciliation over a particular issue. *Pagma'apanta bang aniya' halam makasulut pangatayannu.* Let's forgive each other if there is something that doesn't suit you.

   **pagpama'ap** *v. intr. aN-* To engage in a forgiveness and reconciliation ritual.

**ma'aripat** *n.* An inward commitment to religious principles. *Magtawhid sadja ka ni ma'aripat, magitikad ka tunggal ni iya.* Be single-minded in maintaining your religious convictions, direct your mind only to him [God]. *Ma'aripat itū, sali' bang kita angamu'-ngamu' mbal paluwa' lling. Ma'aripat* is like when we are praying without uttering words.

   **pagma'aripat** *v. intr. aN-* To be in an attitude of devotion and right behavior. *Magma'aripat, sali' aniya' hinangta ni Tuhan, ya ai-ai makanibowa'ta* *pinta-pintata sudju ni iya. Sali' aniya' tinasdik ma deyom atay.* To have a *ma'aripat* attitude is like serving God with whatever comes to our minds in making requests to him. As when something comes into our hearts. (*Thesaurus:* **isbat, pagagama**)

**ma'as** *adj. zero* Of time long past; of old.
 **kama'asan** *n.* People of former times; old people. *Asannang makalandu' bay waktu kama'asan ī'.* It was really peaceful in those old times. *Barung kama'asan.* An old style fighting knife. *Magkissa iya bay kama'asan.* He tells stories from the time of the old people. (*cf:* **kamatto'ahan**)

**ma'ase'** (derivative of **ase'**) *v. intr. zero* Merciful; considerate. *Ma'ase' aku ma si Jo, wa'i alungay.* I pity Jo, he is lost. *Kalu iya mura-murahan ma'ase' ma ka'am.* Perhaps, hopefully, he [God] will be merciful to you.

**ma'atay** *n.* Something highly valued.
 **pagma'atay** *v. tr. -an* To think highly of something. *Aniya' pinagma'atay he'na.* There are things he is looking on with approval. *Tuhan-tuhan ya pinagma'atayan e' kar'ndahan bangsa liyu inān.* The gods that those foreign women think much of.
 **kama'atay** *v. advrs. -in-* Assumed; supposed.

**ma'mun** var. of **ma'amun**

**ma'ung** *n.* A heavy cloth; denim. (*Thesaurus:* **kapis, ispowen, lona, mantaluna, patig, tolda**)

**malabbihi** *adj. zero* Outdoing others. *Malabbihi, hatina paliyu min kasehe'. Malabbihi,* that is going ahead of the rest.

**malabuhuk** *n.* Various species of pine tree. *Aniya' isāb bay puwadku malabuhuk.* There were also pine trees that I cut down.

**malaingkan** (var. **maingkan**) *conj.* Notwithstanding; even though the contrary is asserted; nevertheless. *Mag'mbal-mbal dīna, malaingkan taga baya' du isāb iya ma l'lla inān.* She denies it to herself, though she does in fact have a desire for that man. *Aniya' buwat aku inān angamu' pinta, yuknu inān, "Halam na." Malaingkan amasi. Hatina mbal pamuwannu pinta inān.* Someone like me asks you for paint and you say, "None left." However there is still some left. The fact is that you won't give me that paint. *Bay aku ma M'ddas, aniya' pinabeya' ma aku. At'kka pa'in aku ni luma' tinilaw aku bang ma'ai bay pinabeya'. Angahaka aku, "Halam aku bay pinabeya'an." Yuk si Ina' inān, "Malaingkan bay ka pamabeya'an."* I was in Siasi and something was sent home with me. On reaching the house I was asked where the thing was that had been sent. I said, "Nothing was sent with me." Mother said, "Nevertheless you were sent with something." (*cf:* **saunahan**; *Thesaurus:* **bo' yampa, minsan, ya pa'in**)

**mala'ikat** *n.* An angelic being. *Aniya' isāb ta'nda'na saga mala'ikat magdeyo'-diyata'.* He also saw angels going upwards and downwards.

**mala'u-la'u** *n.* 1) A place with few people. (*Thesaurus:* **l'ngngaw-l'ngngaw, tannay-tannay, t'nnaw-t'nnaw 1**) 1.1) *adj. zero* Lonely; feeling isolated. *Mala'u-la'u, ariki' a'ana, sali' bang mbal aheka ma lahat.* Lonely, few people, as when there are few inhabitants. *Nsa' na makatimbul ni kampungna, mala'u-la'u na iya, karangan-danganan.* He no longer associates with his relatives, he is lonely, on his own.

**malān** *see:* **pagmalān**

**malangkahi** *see:* **pagmalangkahi**

**malapati** *n.* The brown dove or pigeon. *Phapitreron spp. Manuk-manuk malapati, bo' alahang ta'nda'ta.* A brown dove, something we rarely see.

**malapunti** *n.* 1) The Chinaman snapper. *Symphorus nematophorus.* 2) The Two-spot red snapper. *Lutjanus bohar.*

**malas** *see:* **pagmalas**

**malasahi** (var. **marasahi**) *adj. zero* To be exhausted after working hard. *Sidda kita malasahi, lu'ugan. Landu' kita amale'.* We are feeling really exhausted, worn out. We are very tired. *Aku ya marasahi magkarukka'an.* I am exhausted from grieving.
 **pagmalasahi** *v. intr. aN-* To experience serious fatigue or hardship. *Agmarasahi kita magusaha.* We experience fatigue earning our living.

**Malayu** *n.* A citizen of Malaysia; the Malay language. *Saga Malayu ī' amu'an kami sinambi' lahing ī'.* We requested those Malays to trade those coconuts.

**malbol** *n.* A flooring or roofing tile. *Luma' malbol, lantay malbol, ya hē' i du luma' dayahan.* Tiled house, tiled floor, that's what rich people's houses are like.

**malkina** var. of **makina**

**male'** *adj. a-* 1) Tired, as a result of prolonged effort. *Amale' aku bay magdakdak.* I am tired from washing clothes. 1.1) *v. advrs. -in-* To be affected by tiredness. *Asannang, halam aniya' hinangta. Mbal kita minale', sō' hal palege.* At ease, no work to do. We don't get tired, but just lie around. (*cf:* **bale'**)
 **pagmale'** *v. intr. aN-* To be in the habit of working to the point of exhaustion.

**maleta** *n.* A suitcase. (*Thesaurus:* **bakag₁, ba'ul₁, kalton, labban, tu'ung**)

**mali-mali** (var. **bali-bali**) *v. advrs. -in-* Dried out and unpalatable, of some fruits and root crops. *Bang kinupasan tibu'uk, bo' ta'abut duwang'llaw, minali-mali. Sali' abalos, bo' takakan masi.* If cassava is peeled, when two days pass it becomes dry. Sort of rancid, but still edible. *Binali-bali wanni, apote', sali' luwa tagok.* The *wanni* mangoes have defects in them, white stuff, looks a bit like sap.

**maligay₁** *n.* A model house about a meter high, used in various ceremonial activities. *Maligay itu* *panyām atopna, t'bbu lantayna, isina saging mareyom.* A *maligay* has rice cakes for its roof, sugar cane for its floor, its contents are bananas. *Ai kaungsuran Sama? Pilak maka karut buwas maka maligay.* What are the bride-wealth gifts of the Sama? Money, sacks of rice, and a ceremonial model house.

**maligay₂** *n.* 1) A pandanus mat woven using a folding technique to form 45 degree angles in complex patterns. 1.1) *v. tr.* To weave a mat with a maligay pattern. *Bay kami am'lli duwa tepo minaligay.* We bought two mats woven in the *maligay* style.

**malim** 1) *n.* A guide; a pilot (in the maritime sense). 1.1) *v. tr. -an* To lead someone to a destination. *Malimin aku ni tinda si Go.* Guide me to Go's store. *Tamalim kami pasiha'.* We were led on a detour. (*Thesaurus:* **bakot, tuhung, tuli'** 1.1, **tullus** 1.2, **ulin**) 2) *v. tr.* To appoint someone as leader or guide. *Ka'a ya tamalim e' sigā, tahinang magmunda'an.* They chose you to be their leader, the one going out in front.

**malit** *v. advrs. ka-...-an* To be included or involved in something adverse. *Kamalitan kakampunganku bay waktu pagbono' aktibis i'.* My village-mates were caught up in casualties during the time of the activists' war. *Kamalitan karuwangan bo' dakayu' katūyan.* Both of them were affected but one was totally involved [i.e. fatally]. (*Thesaurus:* **beya' isāb, lapay** 1)

**malpel** *v. tr. -an* To fit someone with false teeth (dentures).
   **pagmalpel** *v. intr. aN-* To wear false teeth.

**malu-malu bās** *n. phrase* The Bowmouth guitarfish or shark ray. *Rhina ancylostoma.*

**malu-malu solab** *n. phrase* The Giant guitarfish. *Rhina sp.*

**malul** *n.* A flower species.

**malulus** *see:* **pagmalulus**

**malumiyat** *n.* The Ribboned sweetlips, a fish species. *Plectorhynchus polytaemia.*

**mām** *voc. n.* A respectful address term for a woman in authority.

**mam pa'in** *var. of* **bang pa'in**

**mamahi** *n.* A star. (*syn:* **bitu'un, pote'an**)

**mama'** *n.* 1) Betel nut chew. *Bang aku ni tabu' b'llihanku mama' nggo'ku.* When I go to the market I buy betelnut chew for my grandmother. 1.1) *adj. a-* Chewing betel nut. *A: "Sō'un mbo'nu pi'itu amangan." B: "Wa'i gi' amama'."* A: "Tell your grandfather to come and eat." B: "He is still chewing betel nut."
   **mama'an** *n.* A container for the ingredients of the betel nut chew, usually made of brass or bronze. (*Thesaurus:* **anak-mama'an, loka'-loka', salappa'**)
   **pagmama'** *n.* 1) The ingredients for a betel nut chew. *Lalabotan ya pinat'nna'an saga a'a magluruk, buwat saga pagmama', pagsiga.* Items of

hospitality presented to the attendees, like betel chew ingredients, cigarets. (*spec:* **bangkit, pola, tagambil**) 1.1) *v. intr. aN-* To be an habitual chewer of betel nut. *Subay aku ato'a na bo' aku magmama'.* I have to be old before I become a chewer of betel nut.

**mamali** *var. of* **amamali**

**mamallas** *n.* The Whip-tailed threadfin bream. *Pentapodus nemurus.*

**mamang₁** *n.* An address term for mother or a senior female, used for women of the Chavacano community. (*cf:* **babu'** 1.1, **ina', mma', papang**)

**mamang₂** *v. advrs. ta-* Hesitant due to nervousness when singing or making a speech. *Tamamang, buwat angalang, ya sali' maghogga'-hogga', ya amidpid bowa'.* Hesitant, like when singing, stopping now and then, the mouth trembling. *Tamamang suwalata, ai-ai pah'llingta maghogga'-hogga' kita.* Our voice is uncertain, whatever we say we say erratically. *Yampa kita ni sara', minsan makalandu' ta'uta, subay mbal tamamang panganda'awata.* Facing the law for the first time, even though our fear is excessive, our defence should not be hesitant. (*cf:* **gaga'**)

**mamarahi** *adv.* More than enough; excessively. *Mamarahi pahāp ka'a ilū, bang aniya' lling takalenu, magtūy sulatnu.* You are too much, whenever you hear a word you write it down immediately. *Mamarahi dupangnu ilū, mbal ka ameya' pandu' matto'a.* You are much too foolish, you do not obey your parents' teaching. *Sali' kita amoway, sali' mamarahi. "Apalilihan pahāp a'a hē'."* It is like when we criticise, overstating things, saying, "That person is so easily swayed." (*Thesaurus:* **karalaman, kumarukan, dumasiyaw, landu'₂** 1, **sidda** 1, **to'od**)

**mamatun** *var. of* **sowa-mamatun**

**mamay** *see:* **pagmamay**

**mamhu'** *n.* A gift intended to win the favor of a potential benefactor. (*Thesaurus:* **bo'ot, k'llo' bo'ot**)
   **pagmamhu'** *v. intr. aN-* To give something of value in order to get a positive response to one's request. (*Thesaurus:* **lana** 1.1, **paili, puli-bahasa**)

**maming** *n.* 1) The Humphead or Napoleon wrasse (fish species). *Cheilinus undulatus.* (*syn:* **kāt**) 2) The Green humphead parrotfish. *Bolbometopon muricatum.*

**mamis₁** *n.* 1) Sweetness. *Kulang mamisna bahā'?* Is it lacking sweetness? 1.1) *adj. a-* Sweet-tasting. *K'nnopin sokal ma kahawaku bo' amamis.* Add more sugar to my coffee so it will be sweet. (*cf:* **pa'it** 1; *Thesaurus:* **kesom, imu'** 1, **lanab, l'ssom** 1, **sarap₁, taba'** 1) 1.2) *v. advrs. ka-...-an* To be affected by sweetness. *Am'lli gi' aku kende bo' aku kamamisan.* I will just buy some candy so I am affected by sweetness.

**mamis₂** *n.* A sweet-fruited variety of coconut, the

unripe fruit of which may be chewed together with its soft shell. *Mamis ī' angalagtu' bang alanos na.* That sweet coconut variety becomes brittle once it is dry.

**mampallam** *n.* The common mango and its fruit. *Mangifera indica. Bang aniya' tamban kami bo' kami bilahi amangan nilawal, am'lli kami mampallam.* When we have some herrings and want to eat them with a relish, we buy mangoes. *Bay aku binuwanan mampallam, bay tamusku.* I was given a mango, and I sucked its juice. *Minsan mampallam, wanni, balunu', anadjuk. Bang mbal niruplak, palanjal, yampa magduru'-ero'.* Whether common mango, odorous mango or horse mango, all set fruit. If not damaged they develop and then go on to the budding stage. (*syn:* **mangga**; *Thesaurus:* **balunu', kobkoban, wanni**)

**mamukan** var. of **sowa-mamukan**

**mamuhuk** var. of **tehe'-tehe'-mamuhuk**

**mamun** *n.* Sponge-like cakes of various kinds. (*cf:* **apam 1**; *spec:* **balatu, bāng-bāng₂, baulu, biyaki' 1, kolleng-kolleng, durul, panganan, pitis₁, pullu', putili'-mandi**)

**man** var. of **min**

**maN-** *aff.* Derivational prefix that creates a noun referring to someone who performed the action described by the prefixed verb. *Bang ma iya, "Ya ilu Tuhan mangahinang kita."* She said, "He is the God who made us." *Ilu i subay mamangan ilu.* Let him be the one to eat it.

**mana-mana** *n.* A species of fish. *Bang aniya' am'ssi ni Paluwas-pata anongod mana-mana.* When anyone fishes at Paluwas-pata they locate themselves above where the *mana-mana* are. (*syn:* **badjangan**)

**manakayan** *n.* Forest trees of several species known in the Philippines as lawan or Philippine mahogany, a valued source of timber for canoe hulls. *gen. Shorea. Am'lli aku pelang manakayan, kayu ahāp, akeyat, ahāp nihinang pelang.* I buy a canoe made of *manakayan*, good wood, red, good for making canoes. *Tasumpal pelang abō' magpakahinang. Bang manakayan, manakayan du isāb.* A canoe can be patched so it can be used. If it's made of mahogany, then [the patch] too is mahogany. (*cf:* **danglog**)

**manakayan-keyat** *n.* A species of forest tree, a red-timbered variety of Philippine mahogany.

**manakayan-pote'** *n.* A species of forest tree, a pale-timbered variety of the Philippine mahogany.

**manahut-nahut** *n.* Minute detail. *Halam aniya' kinapinan, niuki'-uki' ni manahut-nahut.* Nothing was kept back, it was related in full to the smallest detail.

**mana'ul** *n.* The white-bellied sea eagle. *Haliaeetus leucogaster.*

**mananahun** (derivative of **tahun**) *adv.* Persisting through many years, of a chronic illness.

**manananggal** (derivative of **tanggal₃**) *n.* A spirit being known for removing bodily organs from the living; also a word used in cursing.

**mananasat** (derivative of **sasat**) *n.* Spirit beings which trouble humans. *Bangsa mananasat, bangsa saitan.* The beings that trouble, the dangerous spirit beings. *Asāl ta'ssaku ma bulan inān, sinasat aku maka pinaka'at e' mananasat inyawaku.* That month I did in fact experience being tempted and having my spirit damaged by the tempter.

**manas** *n.* Multi-colored banding, of plumage. *Bū manuk-manuk, basta magkabang, niōnan manas kelong-kelong.* Bird feathers, so long as they are varicolored, may be described as banded dark and light. (*Thesaurus:* **b'ttik 1.1, kabang 1.1, kelong-kelong₁, jali' 1.1, palang**)

**manatad** *n.* The Indian bronze-wing dove. *Chaleophaps indica salve. Manatad inān manuk-manuk pinaglitag.* The *manatad* referred to is a bird that is [sometimes] trapped.

**manda** *n.* Orders or commands from a superior.

**pagmanda** *v. intr. aN-* **1)** To be bossy or overbearing towards someone. *Magmanda, sali' makapagbaya' ma aku, hatina sali' pahinggamanna bo' ngga'i ka anuna.* Being bossy, sort of having control over me, as if it was his transport but is wasn't. *Da'a ka magmanda bang aku lum'ngngan pi'ingga-pi'ingga. Beya'-beya'ku na, baya'-baya'ku.* Don't tell me what to do when I go some place or other. It's my choice, my decision. (*Thesaurus:* **da'ak, gandahan, hilag, soho', sūg-sūg, uldin 1**) **1.1)** *v. tr. -an* To give orders in an overbearing way. *Da'a aku pagmandahin apa ngga'i ka parawnu.* Don't order me around because it isn't your canoe. *Buwat aku tagdapu paraw ina'an bo' aniya' ameya' ma aku, na pinagmandahan aku he'na.* Like me being the owner of that canoe and someone travels with me, then I am bossed around by that person.

**manda'** (var. **mandi'; mandu'; minda'; mindi'**) *adv.* Contrary to what might have happened; but fortunately. *Bay aku kabongkolan he' sinanglag, manda' inumanku bohe'.* I was choking on cassava, but fortunately I drank some water for it. *Hal ka anangis, ya po'on ka'a-i binono'. Hal pamaralilan, mandi' hal binono', amangkaheng.* You just cry, that is why you are hit. That's just an example, good you were just hit and feel some pain. *Pagt'kka kami ni luma', mandu' kami ministangan e' a'a ma luma'.* Happily, having arrived at the house, the people of the house made rice gruel for us. *A: "Aniya' daingbi?" B: "Minda' kinakan insini'."* A: "Do you have any fish?" B: "It was in fact eaten earlier." (*Thesaurus:* **bo'₁, saguwā', sa'**)

**mandā'-dā'** *v. intr. zero* To feel hurt from being left out. *Ndū' dayang, da'a pa'in ka mandā'-dā' bang ka mbal pabeya'ku.* Dear girl, don't be offended when I don't bring you with me. *Da'a ka mandā'-dā', halam to'ongan aniya' tapamuwanku ka'a minsan dambigi buwas.* Don't be upset, I have absolutely nothing to give you, not even a grain of rice. *Mandā'-dā' atayku, anangis aku bo' halam magbohe'an mataku.* My feelings are hurt, I cry but my eyes produce no tears. *Mandā'-da', sali' pinah'llingan aku ala'at, yuk i, "Mbal kono' anabang maghinang, subay hal amangan."* Upset, as when something bad is said about me, he says, "Doesn't help with the work, just eats." (*syn:* **ambul-dā'**)

**mandal** *n.* A type of kite fitted with a cord that vibrates in the wind to make a sound. *Angahinang aku mandal, hinanganku jambay-būng abō' pinaleyang.* I am making a *mandal* kite and will make streamers for it so it can be flown. (*cf:* **galawang**)

**mandaling** *n.* A species of bird. {archaic}

**mandangan** *n.* A dominant male of large domestic animals such as a bull, carabao, goat or horse. *Mandangan basta hayop aheya, kalbaw mandangan, sapi' mandangan, kura' mandangan.* *Mandangan* applies to large domestic animals, a bull carabao, a bull, a stallion.

  **pagmandangan** *v. intr. aN-* To behave as if one was the dominant member of a group. *Ka'a ya magmandangan.* You're the boss. (*Thesaurus:* **pagbebeya'an, pagmakōk, pagmete-mete, pagmunda'an**)

**mandasiyang** *n.* The Philippine glossy starling. *Aplonis panayensis.*

**mandikakang** var. of **mandikakaw**

**mandikakaw** (var. **mandikakang**) *n.* Madre-de-cacao, a leguminous tree the leaves of which are used medicinally and in cosmetic powder. *Gliricidia sepium. Mandikakaw, basta pangalipa'.* Madre-de-cacao, used for cosmetic powder.

**mandi'** var. of **manda'**

**mandu-mandu** *n.* A horse. (*syn:* **kura' 1**)

**mandu'** var. of **manda'**

**mandul** *n.* A person responsible for ensuring that a project is carried out; a foreman or project manager. *Subay ka'a, apa ka'a ilū tahinang mandul kami.* You should do it because you have been appointed our foreman. (*cf:* **pagbebeya'an**; *Thesaurus:* **bōs, kapala, kapatas, nakura'**)

  **pagmandul** *v. tr. -an* To supervise a project; to act as foreman.

**mandusiya'** var. of **manusiya'**

**maneha** *n.* A manager.

  **pagmaneha** *v. tr. -an* To manage an event.

**manik** *n.* A decorative bead.

**maniku** (derivative of **siku**) *n.* A unit of measurement, the length from the tip of one hand to the opposite elbow. (*Thesaurus:* **batu₃, kilometēl, d'ppa 1, honga'₂, inses**).

**Manila'** *n.* The city of Manila.

**manipis** *n.* The Gold-spotted trevally. *Carangoides fulvoguttatus.*

**manis** *n.* 1) Beauty, especially of facial features or the design lines of a canoe. *Aheya manisna bang lipistik.* She looks pretty wearing lipstick. **1.1)** *adj. a-* Attractive; good-looking. *Amanis pinta paraw inān.* The paint of that canoe is attractive. *Bang ma kami, ya ganta' katōpan buwat aniya' amayan man pelang, ahāp sali' ni'nda', ya hē' amanis.* The pleasing thing for us is when someone travels by canoe, beautiful to look at, that is *manis.* (*Thesaurus:* **alti, dorog₂ 1.1, hansam, hāp baran, himpit, jalang₁, lingkat 1.1, polma 1.1**)

**kamanisan** *n.* Attractiveness of feature and manner.

**manis-buwahan** *n.* A desirable complexion midway between dark and pale. {idiom} *Manis buwahan, magpatīllot apote' maka aettom.* Lansones beauty, between light and dark.

**manis-erom** *n.* Dark-skinned beauty. *Buwat d'nda, aniya' manis erom, manis buwahan, magpati'llot apote' maka aettom.* With girls there is dusky beauty, and pale beauty, in between white and dark brown.

  **pagmanis-manis** *v. intr. aN-* To display one's looks.

  **pagmanis-manis sobangan** *v. intr. aN-* To be showing light just before daybreak (lit. to show the beauty of sunrise). (*Thesaurus:* **abay-subu, bukis₁, dai'-llaw, pote' sobangan, subu₂ 1**)

**palmanis** *n.* A magical formula for making someone beautiful.

**manit** (derivative of **panit**) *v. intr. aN-* To troll for tuna. (*Thesaurus:* **gonteng 1.2, laway₂ 1.1, pamalastik, paranas, p'ssi 1.1, tonda'₁ 1.1**).

**manitan** (derivative of **panit**) *n.* The equipment used in trolling for tuna.

**manja'** *see:* **pagmanja'**

**manjari₁** *ptl.* 1) Appropriate, acceptable and permissible. (Deontic modality particle, permission). (*Thesaurus:* **makajari 1**) 2) Possible, feasible, workable. (Epistemic modality particle, possibility). *Ōy, da'a gi' kām pi'itu, mbal manjari magtambal.* Hey, don't come here yet, medical treatment is not possible. (*Thesaurus:* **makajari 2**)

**manjari₂** *conj.* So then; now then (sentence or paragraph introducer). *Manjari itū aniya' na sowa talanggal kami.* So then we came across some snakes. (*syn:* **jari₃**; *Thesaurus:* **ati, nā 1, sakali₂**)

**manjari₃** *v. intr. zero* To become something; to happen. *Sangpū' manuk-manuk ma diyata' kayu. Paleyang dakayu', manjari siyam.* Ten birds up in a tree. One flies away, then there are nine.

**man'llon-baggu'** *n.* The Slender grouper; the White-lined rock cod. *Anyperodon leucogrammicus.* (*gen:* **kuhapo'**)

**mano** *n.* 1) The person whose turn it is to throw a counter in various games of skill. *Sai-sai mano dahū.* Whoever is the first to throw. (*Thesaurus:* **pagtaksi'** 1.1, **pamatu'**) 1.1) *v. intr. aN-* To throw a counter in games of skill such as marbles or toss-the-coin.

**manohan** *n.* An area marked out on the ground for certain games. *Bang sawpama magkabit ba, abō' ya sīnku inān asekot-sekot ni manohan, abō' angaikit na, mbal na magparūl.* Playing toss-the-coin for example, and my coin is quite close to the marker, but someone cheats and won't let me win. *Nihinang ma po'on hāg pagmanohan, pagtaksi'an.* Marked at the base of the post as an area for playing the game of *taksi'.* (*Thesaurus:* **jangka'an** 1, **tibtib**)

**mansay-mansay** *adj. a-* Flowing down over a surface, of a liquid. *Buwat aku abakat, amansay-mansay laha'. Sali' nihulasan.* Like when I am cut, my blood flows freely. Like sweating. *Amansay-mansay e' bohe', buwat tangki' palasay.* Flowing down with water, like a tank that's overflowing. (*Thesaurus:* **sasahan** 1.2, **tagudtud**)

**manta** *n.* 1) A bed-covering; a sheet or blanket. *Yuk-i, "Palege na ka ma tilam inān. Aniya' du manta pamantanu."* Saying, "Lie down on that mattress. There is a sheet for a bed cover." (*Thesaurus:* **hōs** 1, **se'ob**) 1.1) *v. tr. -an* To cover with a sheet or blanket. *Ngā'un manta itū pamantanu.* Take this sheet to use as a bed covering.

**manta bulbulan** *n. phrase* A woolen blanket.

**mantaluna** *n.* A coarsely woven white cloth; calico. *Mantaluna, ya kakana' pote', buwat karut-karut sokal. Mantaluna,* that white cloth, like the small bags for sugar. (*Thesaurus:* **kapis, ispowen, lona, ma'ung, patig, tolda**)

**mantega** *n.* A non-toxic variety of cassava with yellowish flesh and white inner skin.

**mantel** *n.* The mantle of a pressure lantern. (*cf:* **semento** 2; *syn:* **buyung**₂)

**mantika'** *n.* Cooking lard.

**mantis** *n.* A thin mustache that droops down each side of the mouth. (*Thesaurus:* **bū-langat, misay** 1, **p'ngngot** 1)

**mantiyanak** *n.* A brand of sarong.

**manu** var. of **anu**

**manuk** 1) *n.* The common domestic chicken. (*Thesaurus:* **labuyu'**₁, **tukung**) 2) *v. advrs. -in-* Suffering from impairment of vision in low light. (*syn:* **lakap-manuk**)

**manuk-bubulang** *n.* A fighting cock.

**manuk-d'nda** *n.* A hen. *Sali' sapantun manuk-d'nda bang pasabakna anak-anakna ma deyo' pikpikna.* Figuratively like a hen when she brings her chicks close to her body, beneath her wings.

**manuk-l'lla** *n.* A rooster.

**manuk-sigun** (var. **sigun**) *n.* A variety of fighting cock. *Manuk-sigun, bubulangun.* A *sigun* chicken, a cock-fighting bird. (*Thesaurus:* **ayuk-ayuk,**

**pagbulang, pagtakbi', pagtūkan**)

**pagmanuk-manuk**₁ *v. intr. aN-* 1) To behave like a fighting cock. 1.1) *v. tr.* To make someone behave like a fighting cock. *Pinagmanuk-manuk sali' onde'-onde' pinagatu-atu.* Made to act like fighting cocks, like children encouraged to fight each other.

**manuk-manuk** *n.* 1) Generic term for flying creatures other than domestic fowl. (*spec:* **haus-bō', paupit, saikukuwak, sambal**₂, **tukling**) 2) A term for minor spirit beings. {euphemism}

**manuk-manuk-manggis** *n.* An ornamental bird woven from fresh coconut leaflets. (*gen:* **taliyan**)

**manuk-manuk-tabug** *n.* A species of bird.

**pagmanuk-manuk**₂ *v. intr. aN-* To sing sweetly, like a bird. *Amandungan ka'a, ahāp kinale, sali' magmanuk-manuk.* Stirring you to perform [the kata-kata epic], so good to hear, like birds singing.

**manulus** *adj. zero* 1) Failing to be involved in some resource or plan. *Manulus kat'llu munda'. Hal disi Je maka'ā'.* The three canoes all failed to get a share. Only Je and his mates caught anything. *Buwat bissala, ai-ai na pinat'nna' ameya' na. Manulus hal min dambila'.* Like a discussion, whatever is laid down [we] agree with. The lack of involvement is from one side only. 1.1) *v. tr.* To deny someone a share in resources or benefits. *Buwat kakiku d'nda kinawin, bo' kami itū halam makahampit. Minanulus hal min dambila'.* Like when my female cousin got married and we didn't get a share. Just one side omitted.

**manumbuk** *n.* A swordfish; a marlin. *fam. Istiophoridae; Xiphias sp.*

**manunumbul** *n.* A species of plant, used medicinally.

**manurung** var. of **saging-manurung**

**manusiya'** (var. **mandusiya'**) *n.* 1) Mankind; humans in contrast to other orders of beings. *Magdasali' du kita. Saga mandusiya'ku, mandusiya'nu du isab.* You and I are the same. My humanness, is your humanness too. (*Thesaurus:* **a'a, baran**₂ 1, **puhu'** 1) 1.1) *v. advrs. -in-* Become a human being. *Halam gi' aku nimanusiya'.* I had not yet become a person [still a fetus].

**pagkamanusiya'** *n.* Humanity; the human condition.

**manyatakan** (derivative of **nyata'**) *adj. zero* Clearly visible, with connotations of certainty. *Manyatakan na bulan kohap itu.* The moon will certainly be seen this afternoon [and people will begin the month of fasting]. *Bang aniya' mailu a'a alalom panahu'anna, subay manyatakan ma kahāp tebongna in iya taga pangita'u.* If someone there has deep understanding, it should be clear from his good behavior that he possesses wisdom.

**mang** var. of **bang**₁

**manga** *ptl.* Plural marker. *Ahāp bohe'ta itu, at'bbag. Manga botong isāb at'bbag, nsa' ssana.* This water is good, savorless. Green coconuts too, they are savorless, no taste. (*syn:* **saga 1**)

**mangagat** *n.* The Dog snapper or the Pargo, a reef fish. *Sparidae sp.* (*gen:* **kutambak**)

**mangali** *n.* The Toothless cavalla, a species of trevally. *Caranx speciosus.*

**mangan** *see:* **kakan**

**mangapahan** *n.* The Thread-fin trevally; the Indian mirrorfish. *Alectis indicus.*

**mangat** *voc. n.* An address form for the spirit of a dead person, generally in the context of cursing. *Arūy mangat! Ngā'un na itū.* Oh spirit! Take this one. (*cf:* **sumangat 2**; *gen:* **sukna' 1.1**)

**mangkesol** *n.* The Brown-banded bamboo shark. *Mustelus antarcticus. Mangkesol, ya magkallit tape'na. Yukta, "Kakalun, asagut naelon."* A bamboo shark, the one that lashes its tail. We say, "Club it, the line will get tangled." (*gen:* **kalitan 1**)

**Mangkimahan** *n.* The name of a country ruled by beautiful women who are made pregnant by the wind and thus do not need men. *Nsa' aniya' l'lla ma lahat Mangkimahan, d'nda hē' alingkat. Ya harapan sigā angeket, ak'ttob anu l'lla. Ya baliyu amab'ttong, ya he' kahandak sigā arai'.* There are no men in the land of Mangkimahan, the women there are beautiful. Their genitals bite and men's get chopped off. The wind makes them pregnant, that perhaps is their destiny.

**mangkinna...mangkinna** var. of **bangkinna...bangkinna**

**mangku'** *n.* The Frigate mackerel; the Oceanic bonito. *Auxis thazard. Am'lli aku bulbul manuk panonda'ku mangku' ni timbang.* I will buy some chicken feathers for trolling for bonito in the open sea. (*Thesaurus:* **panit, poyan, sobad**)

**mange'** *n.* 1) Urine; the act of urinating. (*Thesaurus:* **jamban 1, sungi' 1, tai' 2**) 1.1) *v. intr. a-* To urinate. *Amange' gi' aku, ap'ddi' mange'ku.* I'll just have a pee, my bladder hurts. 1.2) *v. tr. -an* To urinate on something. *Da'a palegehin tepo itu, kamange'an.* Don't use this mat to lie on, it has been urinated on.

**mangel-mangel** (var. **mangil-mangil**) *adj. a-* Sounding faintly, as a call from a distance, or a persistent noise in the ears. *Sali' ma olangan takaleta maka halam. Yukku, "Pakale ka gi'. Aniya' takaleku angalingan amangel-mangel."* It's like [a sound] between hearing and not. I say "Keep listening. I hear someone calling faintly." *Amangil-mangil hal deyom talingaku.* There is a faint sound only inside my ears.

**mangga** *n.* A mango, especially one that is ripe. *Makahā' aku mangga ahūg min diyata'.* I got a mango that fell from above. (*syn:* **mampallam**)

**manggis** *n.* The mangosteen, a species of tree and its highly prized fruit. *Garcinia mangostana.*

*Am'lli aku manggis ni Sūk, kakanku. Bang manggis bilu apa'it, bang akeyat amamis.* I buy mangosteens in Jolo, and eat then. When mangosteens are blue they are bitter, when red they are sweet. *Yuk sultan, "Sai-sai makatauwa' manggis aheya, ma iya anakku siyaka. Bang manggis sarang-sarang, ya anak pasunu' ni siyaka. Bang manggis," yukna, "ariki', anak siyali."* The sultan said, "Whoever is able to hit the big mangosteen, he will have my elder daughter. If it is a medium-sized mangosteen, the next daughter. If," he said, "it is a small mangosteen, then the youngest." (*cf:* **kandi'is₁**)

**manghalapi** *v. intr. zero* To be in agreement with. *Aho', manghalapi aku.* Yes, I am confident. (*Thesaurus:* **amu₂ 1.1, beya'₃ 1, dakayu'₂ 1, pagta'ayun, sulut 1, tayudtud**)

**mangil-mangil** var. of **mangel-mangel**

**mangilāp** *n.* The Gold-spotted rabbitfish. *Siganus punctatus. Mangilāp itu aettom.* A *mangilāp* is [basically] black.

**mangilāp-ilahan** *n.* The Peppered spinefoot, a rabbitfish species. *Siganus punctatissimus.*

**mangilāp-lambu** *n.* The Blue-spotted or Ocellated-orange spinefoot. *Siganus corallinus.*

**mang'ntut** *n.* The Yellow-stripe goatfish; the Ochre-branded goatfish. *Upeneus sundaicus.*

**mang'ntut-pote'** *n.* A species of goatfish.

**mangsa'** *n.* 1) Generic term for various jacks and scads, including the African pompano. *Alectis ciliaris. Ahāp ssana daing mangsa'. Basta daing-pote' kamemon, ya magnakura' mangsa'.* The *mangsa'* fish has a good flavor. Of all the white-fish, *mangsa'* is the topmost. 2) The Indian threadfin or Threadfin mirrorfish. *Alectis indica.* 3) Yellow-stripe or Smooth-tailed trevally. *Selaroides leptolepsis.*

**mangsa'-tingga'** *n.* The Long-nose cavalla or kingfish. *Carangoides chrysophrys.*

**Mangsi** *n.* An atoll south of Balabak (Southern Palawan), a source of quality whetstones.

**mangupa** var. of **makupa**

**mapan** *n.* A Fusilier fish. *fam. Mullidae.*

**maparang** *n.* A species of shrub.

**marai'** var. of **arai'**

**marang** *n.* Marang (sweet jackfruit), the tree and its fruit. *Artocarpus odoratissima.*

**maras** *n.* A cucumber species. *Cucumis sativus.* (*cf:* **ingkug**)

**marasahi** var. of **malasahi**

**marat** *n.* 1) The physic-nut, a shrub used medicinally. *Jathropha multifida.* 2) Addictive drugs such as opium. *Marat, ya pinaginum, makalango.* Drugs, the substances taken habitually, are intoxicating.

**marī'** *see:* **pagmarī'**

**maru** *n.* 1) Shame, especially the shame of being ignored or snubbed. 1.1) *v. tr.* To shame someone by refusing to acknowledge them.

*Saupama magtiman kām, ubus makah'lla ni saddī. H'llana baha'u marunu.* You divorce, for example, and she marries another man. You shame her new spouse [by not acknowledging him]. **1.2)** *v. advrs.* **ka-...-an** To be shamed by being publicly ignored. *Buwat bay pamikitanku, kamaruhan sigā, angkan sigā ala'an man Siganggang.* Like my in-laws, they were humiliated, which is why they left Siganggang. (*Thesaurus:* **biyas, iya', paki' 1, tamparasa**)

**maruhum** *v. intr.* *zero* To die, of a high-born person. (*Thesaurus:* **aymulla, nahanat, wapat**)

**masa** *n.* **1)** A long period of time; an era. *Masa itū, sali' wa'i palabay, bay timpu masa.* This word *masa* is like something past, the *masa* era. *Entomun bay masa pagbono'ta maitu ma Siganggang.* Remember the times of our conflict here at Siganggang. (*Thesaurus:* **awal ni ahil, jāman, taem, timpu 1, waktu 1**) **1.1)** *adj. zero* Ancient, of times. *Bay timpu masa lagi'.* Back in ancient times. **1.2)** *v. tr.* To recall a long-past event. *Masahun bay pagbono'ta ma Siganggang.* Remember the fighting we had at Siganggang.

**masa-awal** *n.* Ancient or historic times; long ago. (*Thesaurus:* **awal-jāman, awal-tagna', awal₁, musim tagna'**)

**masangka** *v. tr.* To claim redress for an offense, as a condition for restoring a relationship. (*Thesaurus:* **ayu', bangun₂ 1, diyat**)

**pagmasangka** *n.* **1)** Redress, usually money, claimed for an offense. *Buwat aniya' maglakibini magbono', bo' d'nda hē' amole' ni matto'ana. Yuk min kal'llahan, "Ai pagmasangkanu?"* As when a married couple are fighting and the woman goes home to her parents. They of the man's side ask, "What do you claim as redress?" **1.1)** *v. tr.* To seek redress for an offense, as a condition for restoration of a relationship.

**maskid** *var. of* **masjid**

**masi** *adj.* **a-** **1)** Remaining; still present. *Bay aku am'lli sindul, amasi sīnku.* I purchased a *sindul* drink and I still have money. **1.1)** *adv.* Still; yet. *Masi gi' tambalna.* There is still some of his medicine. *Sagō' masi aletop dunya e' bohe', maka assang ē' mbal makabāk pat'ppakanna.* But the world was still submerged under water, and the pigeon could not find a landing-place for itself.

**masinggan** *n.* A machine gun. *H'lling masinggan ina'an, maghuru-huru.* The sound of that machine gun, rat-tat-tat.

**masjid** (var. **maskid**) *n.* A mosque; a Muslim house of prayer. (*cf:* **langgal₁**)

**massuli'** *var. of* **mastuli'**

**mastal** *n.* A teacher in the state school system. *Pinagagihan onde' iskul he' mastal, mastal ya kapagagihan he' prinsipal.* The school children are under the authority of the teacher, and the teacher is under the authority of the principal. (*cf:* **guru 1, mulid**)

**pagmastal** *v. intr.* **aN-** To be engaged in teaching

in the public school system.

**mastuli'** (var. **massuli'; matsuli'**) *n.* The ramose murex, a large marine mollusc. *Murex ramosus.*

**masuk** *v. advrs.* **ka-...-an** To be satisfied with an outcome. *Wa'i na sigām kamasukan, kasulutan.* They are delighted, satisfied. *Aho', kata'uhan kami kamasukan itū. Hatina halam aniya' lengog.* Yes, we know this word *kamasukan.* It means there is nothing to upset.

**masuhul** *adv.* Frequently; often; usually. (*Thesaurus:* **bilang₁, daran, maumu**)

**kamasuhulan** *n.* The frequent occurrence of something. *Ya na kamasuhulanna buwattē'.* That is how it usually is.

**masu'** *v. intr.* **aN-** To be in a bad temper. *Landu' angamasu' sultan inān.* The king was furious. (*Thesaurus:* **pasu' atay**)

**mata₁** *n.* **1)** The eye as the organ of sight. *Ap'ddi' mataku.* My eyes are sore. *Milikan gabul mata, tin'tta' maka kapa, ka'ā'an pitaka.* A Westerner with clouded eyes, struck with an axe, deprived of his wallet. *Alegsok matanu bang ka ang'nda', sali' abulag.* Your eyes are blind when you look, it's as though there is something in them. *Bang auling mata, pinoppok bawang maka buli' sawan ati pinehē' ni matana.* When someone is dizzy, garlic is crushed with the base of a cup, then applied to his eyes. (*pt:* **esok-mata**) **1.1)** *n.* One's vision; sight; that which one sees. *Aniya' a'a bay lahil pi'itu, magtūy alungay. Hal alungay man mataku.* Someone became visible here, and promptly vanished. Simply vanished from my vision. **1.2)** *v. tr.* To see something; to keep in view. *Mata Tuhan ya makamata ma katilingkal babaw-dunya.* The eyes of God that see the entire world. **1.3)** *n.* Something kept constantly in view. *Ya kamatahanku magbalebol.* What I keep watching is volleyball.

**mata-baliyu** *n.* The quarter from which a wind blows. *Mata-satan baliyu itū.* This wind is from the southerly quarter.

**mata-bulan** *n.* The face of the moon; the lunar orb.

**mata-kalibubut** *n.* The head or core of a boil. *Halam gi' paluwas mata-kalibubut.* The core of the boil has not come out yet.

**mata-kapa** *n.* The cutting edge of an axe. *Asombeng mata-kapa.* The edge of the axe is chipped.

**mata-kura'** *n.* An item of gold coin-jewelry (lit. horse's eye). (*syn:* **mata-jīp, pikit-mpat**; *gen:* **dublun**)

**mata-daing** *n.* **1)** A large blister. (*Thesaurus:* **kassa'-kassa', l'ttup 1, lutup, tambu-tambu₂**) **1.1)** *v. intr.* **aN-** To form a large blister. *Angamata-daing tanganna.* Large blisters are coming up on his hand.

**mata-duyung** *n.* A brand of perfume (lit. mermaid's eyes).

**mata-goyak** *n.* The crest of a wave just before it

breaks. *Mata-goyak, song amisik-misik, song abustak goyak.* A wave crest, about to burst, the wave about to break. (*cf:* **bowa'-goyak**)

**mata-jīp** *n.* A piece of gold coin-jewelry, about 35mm in diameter, stamped as US$10 (lit. jeepney headlights). (*syn:* **mata-kura'**, **pikit-mpat**; *gen:* **dublun**)

**mata-langit** *n.* The appearance of the sky in the meteorological sense. *Angal'ddom mata-langit.* The weather is becoming overcast.

**mata-llaw** *n.* The orb of the sun. *Bang aku paharap ni mata-llaw sali' aku asilaw.* When I look directly at the sun I am kind of dazzled.

**mata-mairan** *adv.* In public view. *Mbal iya bilahi amuwanan iya kaiya'an ma mata-mairan.* He did not want to cause her to be publicly shamed.

**mata-mata₁** *v. tr.* To provoke someone in order to draw attention to one's displeasure. *Buwat kap'ddi'anta matto'ata, ati ai-ai hinangta sali' mata-matata, pinalabay min matahanna.* Like when we are upset with our father, so whatever we do is to get him to notice, brought to his attention. *Pinaka'at e'na ai-aiku, aku ya minata-mata.* Various things of mine damaged by him, then I am the one being provoked. *Angamata-ngamata, sali' ama'nda'-ama'nda'. Mata-mata* is like making a show of something. (*Thesaurus:* **kalintaw**, **jural**, **pagpaelle'-elle'**, **pagpa'nda'-pa'nda'**, **pa'amu-amu**)

**mata-tina'ung** *n.* The blue phosphorescent organisms in seawater. (*cf:* **ba'as 1**)

**matahan** *n.* The area within sight of the person referred to. *Tapabantang e' si Harun tukkudna ma matahan Pira'un.* Aaron held out his staff in the presence of the Pharaoh. *Buwat kap'ddi'anta matto'ata, ati ai-ai hinangta sali' mata-matata, pinalabay min matahanna.* Like when we are upset with our father, so whatever we do is to get himt to notice, brought to his attention. (*Thesaurus:* **hadarat**, **pajātan**, **pajātan**)

**pagmata-mata₂** *v. tr.* -*an* To look at something in wonder. *Buwat l'ppet-kandel yamboho' ta'nda' mata, pinagmata-matahan he' mahadjana' kamemon.* Like a Pacific sunfish never seen before, gazed at in wonder by the whole population.

**mata₂** *n.* The mesh size of something woven. *Buwat bubu bang dakananta na, subay sīmmatan ko da'a magpinda matana.* Like a *bubu* [a large woven trap] when we attach the base, it should be stiffened so the mesh size doesn't change. *Sali' kita angahinang linggi'. Ingga mata linggi' ab'kkat, subay bin'ttasan bo' yampa nianom pabīng.* For example, if we are making a trawl net. Whenever there is a break in the mesh it should be cut out and then re-woven. *Angal'ppang, hatina sarang to'od mata linggi'. Aheka tak'llo'ta bang angal'ppang linggi'.* Matching size, the mesh size, in other words, being just right. We catch a lot when the mesh of the long net is right. (*syn:*

**aslag₂ 2**)

**mata-balud** *n.* A species of mullet. *fam. Mugilidae.*

**mata-mata₂** *n.* **1)** A spy. (*cf:* **ispāy 1**) **1.1)** *v. tr.* -*an* To get information by spying. *Aniya' saga a'a bay at'kka pi'itu sangom si' supaya angamata-mata ma paglahattam.* Some people arrived here this very night to spy on our land.

**pagmata-mata₁** *v. tr.* -*an* To engage in spying activities.

**mata-mata₃** *n.* A species of forest tree. *Kayu mata-mata ta'nda' ma gulangan.* The *mata-mata* tree, seen in inland forest.

**mata-mata₄** *see:* **samata-mata**

**mata-pilak** *n.* Bride-wealth items in the form of cash (in contrast to gold jewelry). *Subay mata-pilak sadja, halam aniya' barang palamud.* It [the bride-wealth] should be money only, with no sundry goods.

**mata'** *adj. a-* **1)** Unripe; uncooked. *Amata' maka abulak saddī. Amata' itū taga isi na.* Unripe and immature are different. Unripe refers to something fully grown. *Bang aku am'lli daing subay amasi amata'.* When I buy fish it should still be raw. (*ant:* **tahak 1**) **2)** Pale and lacking pigment, of a color. *Amata' kololna.* Its color is diluted. (*cf:* **lutu'₂**)

**mata'an** *n.* A family unit as defined by a wife and children (a term used to distinguish between the families of co-wives). (*Thesaurus:* **pagtali'anak 1, pamilya 1**)

**matalu** *n.* A species of shrub with spreading low growth.

**matay₁** *adj. a-* **1)** Dead or on the point of death. *Kitam manusiya' mbal na pa'in pa'ddas allum. Magkasosōng ato'a kita, magkamamatay kita.* We humans do not keep living. As time passes we become old, we go on to die. *Bo' kata'uhannu, amatay na si Ina'. Bahangi di'ilaw lagi' kamatayna.* So that you know, Mother has died. Her death was just the day before yesterday. (*cf:* **aymulla, lipulmi'ad**; *Thesaurus:* **bugtang, bugtu' napas, butawan 1.1, halol, sagpe' 2, tubag**) **1.1)** *v. advrs. ka-...-an* To be affected by a death; bereaved. *Kamatayan kami, mbal makapagkaut.* We have a bereavement, cannot go out to sea. (*cf:* **udjul₁ 1.1**)

**matay-bulan** *n.* The closing nights of the lunar month (lit. moon is dead). (*Thesaurus:* **damlag 1**; *gen:* **bulan₂ 2**)

**matay₂** *adj. a-* Putting exhaustive effort into some activity. *Amikakkul na pa'in, halam aniya' kasōnganna. Amatay-matayan dīna na pa'in magusaha.* Persisting at the work, to no avail. Putting total effort into earning a living at sea. *Amatay bowa'ta anabbut ni iya. Amatay kita magsabbut ni batu.* Our mouths are worn out from calling on him. We are exhausted from calling to a stone. *Amatay nireyo' he' sehe'na, atuwas na pa'in.* His companions exhausted themselves seeking reconciliation [lit. abasing themselves], but he remained obdurate. *Buwat anaknu mbal papapat. Amatay na pinapat.* Like your child not being teachable. Taught to exhaustion. (*Thesaurus:* **kuwat, kuyas 1, pakosog, paspas₁, puspus₁, sikad 1**)

**matibig** *n.* A species of fish with white flesh. *Carangid species.*

**mato'a** *n.* A parent-in-law; an aunt or uncle-in-law. *Mato'anu ya na mma' maka ina' h'ndanu.* Your *mato'a* are the mother and father of your wife. (*cf:* **matto'a 1**; *gen:* **pamikitan**)

**matsakaw** *n.* A slice of bread toasted until crisp. (*cf:* **tinapay**)

**matsuli'** var. of **mastuli'**

**mattan** *n.* **1)** Physical evidence in support of something; supporting facts. *Sali' halam aniya' mattanna tasaggaw he' sigām. Makara'awa kita.* It seems that they have seized no evidence. We will be able to deny the charges. (*Thesaurus:* **baynat, tanda'**) **1.1)** *adj. zero* Clearly true; persuasive because correct. *Pinamattan du kamemon bay tasulat e' saga kanabi-nabihan.* All that was written by the prophets was shown to be correct. **1.2)** *v. advrs.* ka-...-an To be convinced or satisfied by the evidence. *Bang mbal kamattanan ma sara' mastal, magdagsol ni upis.* If we are not satisfied with the headmaster's ruling, then we take the case to the [mayor's] office.
 **pamattan** *v. tr.* To pass on information truly and accurately.

**matti** *see:* **kamatti, kamattihan**

**matto'a** *n.* **1)** A parent. *Agbeya' kita maka matto'ata ni tabu' am'lli panggi'.* We go to market with our parents to buy cassava. *Mma'nu maka ina'nu ya matto'anu.* Your father and your mother, they are your *matto'a.* (*cf:* **mato'a**) **2)** A consanguineal (blood) relative of parent's generation; elders in general.
 **kamatto'ahan** *n.* Elders; forebears; people of the historic past. *Gangsa itū tumbaga bay kamatto'ahan.* The *gangsa* referred to is a copper vessel from the time of the forebears. (*cf:* **kama'asan**)

**matural** *adj. zero* Appropriate and to the point, of something said. *Matural e'na amabā' inān.* What he said there was to the point. (*Thesaurus:* **amu₁, patut, tōp 1.1**)

**mau-** *see section 2.2.2.4 Prefix:* **Cau-**

**maujud** *see:* **kamaujuran**

**Maulud** *n.* The celebration of the birthday of the Prophet Muhammad during Rabiul Awal, the third month of the Muslim year. (*cf:* **Rabiul Awal**)
 **pagmaulud** *v. intr.* aN- To engage in the religious activities of the month of Maulud.

**maumu** *adv.* Frequently; often; sometimes. *Bang kita atuli ma deyo' hobong atawa ma atag hāg, maumu kita pinag'ddop, maumu mbal. Sali' kita angolang, mbal tasayuta.* When we sleep below a

crossbeam or by a post, we sometimes have nightmares, sometimes don't. We shout out and aren't aware of it. *Da'a na kām magbeya'. Maumu ka'am ilū magbeya'.* Don't come with us. You often come with us. *Daing isāb ya an'gga he' kinakanna, ya maumu makapatay daing.* Fish too get choked on their food, that's what often kills fish. (*cf:* **suma'an..suma'an**; *Thesaurus:* **bilang₁, daran, masuhul**)

**kamaumuhan** *n.* The most common situation or cause. *Apenggas kōk, suma'an bay asaki, suma'an bay binagongan. Saki ya kamaumuhanna.* Partially bald, sometimes from being ill, sometimes from being shaved. Illness is its most common cause. *"Kamaumuhanna," yukna, "bang ma pagkawinan, pagkakan ahāp ya pamuhat dahū ma saga a'a maglurukan."* "The most common practice," he said, "at a wedding, is for good food to be served first to the guests."

**maupakkat** (var. **maupa'at**) *n.* An agreement made by a community.
 **kamaupakkatan** (var. **kamaupa'atan**) *n.* Certainty; inevitability, as to an outcome. *Ka'a ilū, pahali ka magl'ngngan-l'ngngan. Aniya' kamaupa'atannu, aniya' kala'atan talanggalnu, buwat sala ataksil halam tinu'ud.* You there, stop going from place to place. You have a certain future, you will meet up with trouble, like being fined for touching a girl even if it is unintentional. (*Thesaurus:* **tungga' 1.1**)
 **pagmaupakkat** *v. intr.* aN- To have come to a firm agreement about a course of action.

**maupa'at** var. of **maupakkat**

**maut** var. of **saitan-maut**

**maya** *n.* The Philippine rice bird or the Chestnut manikin. *Munia spp.*

**maya-maya₁** *n.* A dwarf.

**maya-maya₂** *n.* Various snapper species; the Humpbacked red snapper. *Lutjanus sp.* (*gen:* **kutambak**)

**maya'** *see:* **kamaya', kamaya'-maya'**

**mayaman** *adj. zero* Wealthy; fortunate. *Mayaman sali' dayahan. Magkamayaman si Pa inān. Mayaman* is like being rich. Pa [a successful merchant] enjoys wealth. *Buwat si Am inān halam bay maka'ā', yukna ma si Idd, "Mayaman ka'a ilū." Yuk si Idd, "Maglalin ka, magsalin sukud."* Like when Am had caught nothing and said to Idd, "You are so well off." Idd replied, "Change your location, change your luck." (*Thesaurus:* **balkan, daya, haldaya, sayuman**)

**mayat** *n.* A corpse prepared for burial. (*Thesaurus:* **bangkay, patay₁ 1**)

**maylang** *n.* Sulfur; brimstone.

**mayul** *n.* A mayor.

**mayung** *n.* The Yellow-margin triggerfish. *Pseudobalistes flavimarginatus.* (*syn:* **tombad**)

**mbal** *neg.* **1)** 'No', in answer to a question. *A: "Bilahi ka kahawa?" B: "Mbal." A:* "Would you like some coffee?" B: "No." (*cf:* **aho'** 1) **1.1**) *neg.* 'Not', of a statement or an unrealised assertion or action (irrealis clause negator). *Mbal aku ameya'-meya'.* I will not agree. *A: "Anatas daing itū ni kasalungan?"* B: *"Mbal anatas."* A: "Will this fish stay [fresh] until tomorrow?" B: "No, it won't last." *Taga buli'an llingna, mbal to'ongan. Bowa'na angaho', deyom atay mbal.* His words hold something back, it is not genuine. His mouth says yes, but his heart doesn't. *A: "Alingkat ka, nneng." B: "Da'a ka maglata, mbal aku alingkat, to'aku itū!" A: "Bay du ka alingkat ma waktu kabudjangnu." B: "Ē, halam aku bay alingkat."* A: "You are beautiful, dear." B: "Don't joke, I am not beautiful, at my age!" A: "You were certainly beautiful in your teens." B: "Lay off, I was not beautiful." *Jari mbal na angaku pinagbaya'an e' si Ad saga maglalahat maina'an.* So the people living there were no longer willing take orders from Ad. (*cf:* **halam**₁ **1.1**, **nsa' 1.1**; *Thesaurus:* **ai po'on**, **ballum**, **duma'in**, **m'ssa'**, **ngga'i ka**) **1.2**) *v. tr.* a-, ka-..-an, -an To say 'no' to something. *Ai-ai kina'mbalan e' Tuhan, subay sulakta.* Whatever God has said no to, we should shun.

**mbal du** *phrase* Never mind; don't be worried. {idiom} *Mbal du, dayang.* Don't worry, sweetheart [said to a frightened baby]. *Mbal du, hal pitik-pitik.* No matter, it's just a few drops.

**mbal lulus** *phrase* Never possible. {idiom} *Mbal lulus alapis, aniya' sadja.* [Fishing] is never a total loss, there is always something. *Mbal lulus magtanom a'a inān bang halam aniya' nilagaran.* That man would never plant unless there was something to expect.

**mbal na buwattē'** *phrase* Like nothing ever experienced; unthinkable. {idiom} *Kag'nnolan ū'an itū, mbal na buwattē'.* The squashability of this pillow, nothing was ever like it. *Hukawku angiskul mbal na buwattē'.* My dislike of going to school is just too much. *Baya'ku ma iya mbal na buwattē'.* My desire for her is unbearable.

**mbal pamagay** *phrase* Unconcerned about something which is usually a matter of concern. {idiom} *Mbal pamagay he'na daya damuli.* He is unconcerned about the riches to come.

**mbal sakit** *phrase* Not very; only moderately. {idiom} *Mbal na sakit pamaliyu.* Conditions are no longer very windy. *Ap'ddi' sagō' mbal sakit abisa.* It hurts but it is not acutely painful.

**mbal taitung umaw** *phrase* Uncountable. {idiom} *Mbal tasipat ba'anan bungang-kahuy, marang, duliyan. Mbal taitung umaw.* The abundance and variety of fruit could not be grasped, the sweet jackfruit, the durian. Beyond counting.

**mbal-mbal** *n.* A mental reservation; an attitude not consistent with what is being said. *Taga mbal-mbal ma deyom atayna.* He has a negative attitude in his heart.

**pag'mbal** *v. intr. aN-* 1) To say no to something. *Mag'mbal-mbal dīna, malaingkan taga baya' du isāb iya ma l'lla inān.* She denies it to herself, though she does in fact have feelings for that man. 1.1) *v. tr.* To reject something; to turn down an offer. *Ahāp kami pinag'mbal buwattina'an.* Better that we be rejected right now.

**ka'mbal** *n.* Negativity of response or attitude.

**pagin'mbal** *n.* 1) A refusal. (*Thesaurus:* **pagmari'**, **pasibukut** 1, **sulak**₂, **taikut 1.1**) 1.1) *v. tr.* To refuse or say no to something. *Sagō' magin'mbal iya maka mbal isāb iya bilahi pasalu ni saga pagmatto'ahan inān amangan pagkakan minsan hal dangkuri'.* But he refused and did not want to eat together with those elders, not eating even a little bit of the food.

**mbal agon** *var.* of **agon mbal**

**mbal ba** *phrase* Isn't that so? *Mbal ba min dakayu' panubu'an du kita?* Are we not from the same descent line? *Mbal ba a'a itu buwat bay kahantang kayu pinuwas min api?"* Isn't this man figuratively like wood taken from a fire? *Angay takalipatbi na ba bang sai bay makapapatay ma si Ab? Mbal ba, d'nda du ya bay angahūgan iya batu.* Why have you forgotten already who killed Ab? Wasn't it the woman who dropped a stone on him?

**mbal isāb** *phrase* Neither; nor. *Pagkatambahan saga huwis, mbal isāb abontol pangahukum sigā.* The judges could be bribed, and their legal judgements weren't straight either. *Mbal isāb aku amangan, anginum, minsan ai, t'ggolku maina'an.* I neither ate nor drank anything whatsoever while I was there.

**mbal manjari** *phrase* Not possible; not usable; unthinkable. *Angkan niōnan amāg-māg, mbal na manjari.* That's why it is described as utterly shattered, it is no longer usable. *Mbal manjari a'a inān.* That fellow is impossible. *Hōy, da'a na kām pi'itu, mbal manjari magtambal. Subay na kohap.* Hey, don't come here, it's not possible to get medical treatment. It must be this afternoon.

**mbal muwat** *phrase* Unequaled; incomparable. *Mbal muwat susun sigām.* Their regret is without equal.

**mbal na pa'in** *phrase* Will never be so. *Bang aku angā' bohe' bo' ap'nno' na kibut, mbal na pa'in pa'ddas bang ni'inum.* When I fetch water and the water jar is full, it will never last long when it is being drunk.

**mbal pa'in** *phrase* Even though it is not the case. *Angindam ka sīn, ati mbal pa'in kabayarannu?* You are borrowing money, even though you are not able to pay?

**mbal taliyu** *phrase* Unsurpassed; incomparable. *Kahāp d'nda inān mbal taliyu.* The beauty of that woman cannot be surpassed.

**mbal tasilang** *phrase* Immeasurable, of large numbers of people.

**mbal tasipat** *phrase* Inconceivable; beyond imagining. *Mbal tasipat! Abau to'ongan toylet lansa.* Unthinkable! The toilet on the launch was extremely foul-smelling. *Mbal tasipat ba'anan bungang-kahuy, marang, duliyan. Mbal taitung umaw.* The abundance of fruit was too much for the mind to take in, the sweet jackfruit and the durian. Beyond counting.

**mban** *v. tr. -an* To release hold on something; to leave something behind. (*syn:* **bba₃**)

**mbehek** var. of **mbehe'**

**mbehe'** (var. **mbehek**) *v. intr. aN-* To bleat, as a goat or sheep.

**mbo'₁** *n.* A grandparent, grandparent's sibling or cousin; any consanguineal (blood) relative of grandparent's generation; loosely, any relative in the second ascending degree (grandparent's generation) and above. (*Thesaurus:* **ntan₂ 1, palmula'an, pangkat₂**)

  **ka'mbo'-mbo'an** *n.* Forebears or ancestors, as a group. *Bay waktu ka'mbo'-mbo'an gi'.* Back in the time of the ancestors. (*cf:* **mu'min**)

  **mbo'-kengkeng** *n.* A great-great-grandparent or great-great-grandparent's sibling or cousin.

  **mbo'-tu'ut** *n.* A great-grandparent or great-grandparent's sibling or cousin.

  **pang'mbo'an** *n.* The individuals from whom one traces descent; one's ancestors.

**mbo'₂** *n.* A ritual ancestor; a class of supernatural beings around whom indigenous Sama religion is centered. No specific kinship link is involved. *Bang billa saging bo' atahak, ni'isi ni lai, binowa ni mbo', niampun-ampunan.* When the banana is boiled and cooked through, it is put into a plate and taken to the ancestor and a request made. (*syn:* **mbo' pinat'nna'**)

  **ka'mbo'an** *n.* Smallpox, a disease attributed to the influence of ritual ancestors. (*Thesaurus:* **kawit₂ 1, kolera, ipul 1, pangkot 1, ttus-ttus 1, upāng 1**)

  **mbo'-baggu'** *n.* The cowrie ancestor.

  **mbo'-bilu'uk** *n.* The green coconut ancestor.

  **mbo'-botong** *n.* The coconut ancestor.

  **mbo'-kahanga** *n.* The conch ancestor.

  **mbo'-gandum** *n.* The corn maize ancestor.

  **mbo'-langguway** *n.* The betel nut ancestor. (*syn:* **mbo'-mama'**)

  **mbo'-lokay** *n.* The coconut frond ancestor.

  **mbo'-mama'** *n.* The betel nut ancestor. (*syn:* **mbo'-langguway**)

  **mbo'-pai** *n.* The rice ancestor.

  **mbo'-panggi'** *n.* The cassava ancestor.

  **mbo'-saging** *n.* The banana ancestor. (*cf:* **saging-manurung**)

  **mbo'-t'kke'** *n.* The shark ancestor.

  **mbo'-wanni** *n.* The mango ancestor.

  **pag'mbo'** *v. intr. aN-* To invoke a ritual ancestor. *Ntanku mag'mbo' aku.* My inheritance is that I [should] invoke our ancestors. *Am'lli gi' aku saging maka lahing, mag'mbo' kami.* I will just buy bananas and ripe coconut, we are going to be invoking ancestors.

  **mbo' pinat'nna'** *n. phrase* A ritual ancestor, in contrast to a physical ancestor. (*syn:* **mbo'₂**)

**Mbo' Solebad** *n. phrase* An important guardian spirit in the Siasi Lagoon area, believed to be a giant who lives on Mt. Siganggang, on the island of Lapak.

**mbo'-adjani** *n.* A species of bird, known as rare and exotic.

**mbo'-mbo'-llaw** *n.* The hottest time of the day, a period from noon to about 3 p.m.

**mbuk-mbuk** *n.* The Peacock rock cod or the Peacock hind. *Cephalopholis argus.* (*gen:* **kuhapo'**)

**mbun-mbun** (var. **imbun-imbun**) *n.* The fontanel, the soft membranous gap on the head of a newborn baby. *Bang onde'-onde' kabus, mbal atikkup imbun-imbunanna minsan aheya.* When a child is premature, the fontanel will not close up even when he is big. (*Thesaurus:* **ebod, pusal₂**)

**mekanek** *n.* A mechanic, especially of a launch or ship.

**medyas** *n.* Socks; hose. (*syn:* **kalsitin**)

**mehe** *adj. a-* Large. (*Thesaurus:* **aslag₂ 1, heya 1.1**)

**mela'** var. of **kalitan-mela'**

**men** *voc. n.* An informal address term to a man.

**meres** *v. advrs. -in-* Suffering from ulceration of the membrane of the eye socket, as through prolonged conjunctivitis.

**mesa** *n.* A table or tray in a market stall. (*cf:* **lamisahan**)

**mete-mete** see: **pagmete-mete**

**meto** *n.* 1) A meter in length. *Bay bin'llihan kuku-pote', saga lima meto.* White shroud-cloth was bought for her, about five meters. 1.1) *v. tr. -an* To measure something in meters.

  **ma metohan** *adv. phrase* By the meter.

**metrosan** *n.* The dimensions in meters, of a block of land. *Nihukud bahā' tana', buwat metrosan.* An area of land perhaps being measured, like its size in meters.

**mikakkul** (var. **mikakkut**) *v. intr. aN-* To put persistent effort into a task. *Amikakkul ka min munda' ilū. Sinō' amusay pababag.* You in the stern work at it. Told to paddle at right angles [to the canoe].

**mikakkut** var. of **mikakkul**

**miki-** (var. **maki-**; **paki-**; **piki-**) *aff.* Prefix indicating a request. *Mikipabontol aku.* I ask to be corrected. *Si Mu na pikib'lli badju'.* Mu is now asking [someone] to buy a shirt. *Mikip'ngngot aku ma iya.* I am asking him to shave me. *Yuk sehe'ku inān, "Pabuhatin gi' aku." Yukku inān, "Pikibuhat ni a'a ina'an. Itiya' na aku amowa."* That mate of mine said, "Just lift the load up for me." I said, "Ask that guy there to lift it. I'm already carrying something here." *Sinoho' pikihinang luma', asensong na.* Told to ask for a house to be built, very noisy.

**milang** *v. intr. a-* To sit cross-legged, the formal position appropriate to ceremonial events. *Amilang pahāp! Itu kita magduwa'a, da'a ka ahidjul.* Sitting with legs nicely crossed! Here we are praying, don't be noisy. *Magl'lla-l'lla dīna, amilang minsan du mbal ata'u.* Behaving in such a manly way, sitting cross-legged even though he doesn't know how. (*Thesaurus:* **hakin, pagsengkang, pagsiningkulang**)

**milikan** *n.* The sphere of control, as the domain of a ruler or territorial authority. (*Thesaurus:* **komkoman 2, deyoman 2, okoman, pang'ntanan₁**)

**tagmilikan** *n.* A person having jurisdiction over a region.

**Milikan** *n.* A citizen of the United States; any English-speaking Westerner. (*cf:* **bangsa-pote'**)

**militari** *n.* Government forces; the military. *Magugpang militari maka rebelde.* The military and the rebels facing off against each other. (*Thesaurus:* **bobono', sundalu**)

**millat** *v. tr.* To break out the side of a plank when drilling dowel holes. *Likup ya amillat.* It's the hole-chisel that breaks out.

**mimbal** *n.* The pulpit or lectern in a mosque from which sermons are read.

**mimi'** *adj. zero* **1)** Separated from its mother, of a baby. *Eya'! Mimi' ka! Halam maitu ina'nu.* Ha! You're all alone! Your mother isn't here. **1.1)** *v. tr.* To tease a child about his mother's absence.

**min** (var. **man**) *prep.* **1)** From; via; by (indicating origin, route, or conveyance). *A: "Minningga kam." B: "Min Sambuwangan kami. Bay kami ameya' man lansa."* A: "Where are you from?" B: "We are from Zamboanga. We came by launch." *Bay kami pi'itu labay min tabu'.* We came here by way of the market. *Wa'i ahūg min bulsaku.* It fell out of my pocket. (*Thesaurus:* **ma 1, ni₁, tudju₁ 1**) **2)** Than; more than (indicating a ground for comparison). *Aheya na ka man siyakanu.* You are bigger than your older brother. *Hal aningkō' sandol. At'mmun min at'mmun.* Simply sitting without any attempt to join in. More than usually quiet. **3)** 'x' times (indicating number of occurrences). *A: "Min pila ka bay anginum tambal ilū?" B: "Min lima arai' bang ngga'i ka min nnom."* A: "How often have you taken that medicine?" B: "Five times perhaps, if not six times." *Man t'llu na aku bay angalinganan ka'a.* I have called you three times already.

**min lima abase'** *n. phrase* The fifth day after full moon. {idiom} (*gen:* **bulan₂ 2**)

**min pila** *interrog.* How often? *Min pila, min pila pabīng? Basta mbal takeket etek maka mbal tatittuk buwas.* How often, how often will it recur? So long as ducks don't bite and rice isn't pecked at.

**mina'-mina'** *adj. zero* **1)** Making progress towards the attainment of a goal (always with a negative). *Buwat saga amusay kita ni atā. Busayta inān, mbal gi' ta'nda' minsan būd. Halam gi' kita mina'-mina' ni kat'kkahanta.* As when we make a long journey. Paddling on, we can't see even a mountain. We are still nowhere near our destination. *Nsa' mina'-mina' atahak, at'ggol gi'.* Nowhere near cooked, a long time yet. (*cf:* **angay-angay**) **1.1)** *n.* Progress made towards a goal. *Halam kamina'-mina'anna lling Sama a'a hē'.* That fellow has not got anywhere near speaking the Sama language. *Halam ap'nno', halam kamina'-mina'an.* Not full, nowhere near.

**minda'** var. of **manda'**

**mindeyom** (var. **m'ndeyom**) *v. tr.* To do something from inside. *M'ndeyomun bang mbal ta'abutnu man luwasan.* Do it from the inside if you cannot reach it from the outside.

**mindi'** var. of **manda'**

**minduwa** *adv.* Twice; for the second time. (*cf:* **mint'dda, mint'llu**)

**kaminduwa** *n.* **1)** The second occurrence of some event. **1.1)** *v. tr. -an* To do something twice or for the second time. *Bang aku sinoho' he' a'a, taramint'dda du. Mbal kaminduwahan.* If someone tells me to do something, it only happens once. Not happening a second time.

**daminduwa** *v. tr.* To do something a second time.

**minna'an** (var. **m'nna'an**) *adv. dem.* From there, far from both speaker and hearer; vague location reference. (*Set:* **minnē', minnilu, minnitu**)

**minnē'** (var. **m'nnē'**) *adv. dem.* From there, far from both speaker and hearer; precise location reference. (*Set:* **minna'an, minnilu, minnitu**)

**minnilu** (var. **m'nnilu**) *adv. dem.* From there, near hearer. *Ya gara' kami pahapit m'nnilu pole' kami tudju ni Pilipin.* Our plan is to call in there [where you are] on our return towards the Philippines. *Paluwas kam minnilu bo' ka an'ngge maitu ma dahū'anku.* Come out from there and stand here in front of me. (*Set:* **minna'an, minnē', minnitu**)

**minningga** (var. **m'nningga**) *interrog.* Where from? *M'nningga pangā'annu laring ilū?* Where did you get that knife from? *A: "Minningga kam." B: "Min Sambuwangan kami. Bay kami ameya' man lansa."* A: "Where are you from?" B: "We are from Zamboanga. We came by launch."

**m'nningga-m'nningga** *adv.* From anywhere; from some place or other. *Bang aku bay m'nningga-m'nninga, pagt'kkaku ni luma' amalut saga siyaliku angamu' ai-ai ni aku.* When I've been somewhere, on my arriving home my younger siblings hold onto me, asking for this and that.

**minnitu** (var. **m'nnitu**) *adv. dem.* From here, near the person speaking. (*Set:* **minna'an, minnē',**

**minnilu**)

**minsan** *conj.* Even if; notwithstanding; no matter how. *Kasehe'an mbal angutta', minsan agoyak.* The others didn't vomit, even though it was rough. *Bang makalandu'-landu' buhatna, da'a ka amowa minsan pila pamuwan ka'a.* If its weight is somewhat excessive don't carry it, no matter how much you're given. (*Thesaurus:* **bo' yampa, malaingkan, ya pa'in**)

**minsan aina** *phrase* No matter what. (*cf:* **sandu₁**)

**mintag** *adv.* Located at. *Saga tendog si Da'ud, binagongan hal tonga' p'ngngot sigām, kinīsan pamakay sigām mintag t'ngnga' buli'.* David's retainers, half their beards shaved, their clothing cut to pieces at the middle of their buttocks. *Na bang buwattē', mintag ingga kita parugpak?* So in that case, where shall we attack? (*syn:* **ma atag 2**)

**mintāng** *v. intr. a-* To learn a lesson from experience. *Pinandu'an kita bo' kita mbal ameya' pandu', bo' saupama magmula baranta. Na amintāng ka m'nnilu.* We are taught but do not heed the lesson, and then, for example, suffer bodily harm. Then [someone says] learn from that experience. (*Thesaurus:* **insā', l'gga 1.1**)

**pamintāng** *v. tr. -an* To learn a lesson from some experience.

**pamintāngan** *n.* A lesson learned from experience.

**mint'dda** *adv.* Once only, of some event. *Mint'dda lagi'.* Just once more. *T'kkonun, mint'dda sadja.* Press on it; just once. (*cf:* **minduwa, mint'llu**)

**mint'dda abase'** *n. phrase* The first day after full moon. {idiom} (*gen:* **bulan₂ 2**)

**kamint'dda** *n.* The first occurrence of something.

**damint'dda** *v. tr.* To do something once only.

**pamint'dda** *adv.* 1) Done as a single action. 1.1) *v. tr.* To do something in a single action; to do all at once. *Kahunitan ka bang pinamint'dda, buhatna hē'.* You'll find it difficult if you do it all at once, with all that weight. *Pamint'ddaku sadja, mbal biningan.* I will do it with a single [blow], it will not be repeated.

**mint'llu** *adv.* Three times; for the third time. (*cf:* **minduwa, mint'dda**)

**kamint'llu** *n.* 1) The third time or occasion of some action. 1.1) *v. tr. -an* To do something three times, or for the third time. *"Kamint'lluhinbi gi' ilu bu'usinbi,"* yukna, maka nihinang e' sigām. "Pour it out three times," he said, and they did it.

**minul** *n.* A tree with clusters of tiny edible berries. *Antidesma ghaesembilla.*

**mīng-mīng** *n.* A call to cats.

**misay** *n.* 1) Mustache or side-whiskers. (*Thesaurus:* **bū-langal, mantis, p'ngngot 1**) 1.1) *v. advrs. -in-* Having mustaches or side-whiskers. *Minisay ka bang mbal pin'ngngotan.* You become whiskered when not shaved.

**miskin** *adj. zero* Poor; lacking the means to live at a socially approved standard. *Miskin disi Je. Halam aniya' sīnna pam'lli ai-ai. Lingantu.* Je and his family are poor. He has no money to buy things. Hungry. (*Thesaurus:* **tiksa' 1, ti'il**)

**pamiskin** *v. tr. -an* To cause someone to be poor.

**Misil** *n.* Egypt.

**mistang** *n.* 1) Rice cooked to a gruel-like consistency. *Tambal itu subay pinalamud ma mistang.* This medication should be mixed in with gruel. 1.1) *v. tr.* To cook rice gruel. *Am'lli aku banga' pagmistangku buwas.* I will buy a clay pot for cooking rice gruel. *Manda' pagt'kka kami ni luma', manda' kami ministangan e' a'a ma luma'.* Fortunately on reaching the house, the people of the house provided us with rice gruel. (*gen:* **b'lla 1**)

**misu-misu** (derivative of **bisu**) *v. intr. pa-* To feign deafness; to ignore what is being said or done. *Subay ka pamisu-misu.* You should ignore it.

**mita** *v. intr. a-* To sound a signal or whistle. *Amita saga jīp.* The jeepneys sound their horns. *Pagmita kappal, atulak na.* On sounding its signal the ship leaves. (*Thesaurus:* **kambay 1, lambe₁ 1.1, paglabad 1.1, sayang₂, sinyal 1.1**)

**mital** *n.* 1) Sheet metal; corrugated iron; metal as a substance. *Kapa ilū subay sinubuhan, da'a na tinunu' mital.* The axe there should be put in the fire, but not burning the metal. 2) A metal container or can. *Indamin aku mital.* Lend me a can.

**miting** *n.* An assembly called to talk about some issue. *Na magmailad ni M'ddas, aniya' miting.* Well they're congregating over in Siasi, there is a community discussion.

**miting-miting** *v. tr. -an* To arrange a meeting, as for a discussion or sexual liaison. *L'lla isāb magpalla'-palla' angamiting-ngamitingan ma d'nda.* Men too behave in sexually provocative ways, arranging assignations with women.

**pagmiting** *v. intr. aN-* To be engaged with others in a business meeting. *Bang bay atalus magmiting, magpole'an na.* When they had finished their meeting, they went home. *Bang aniya' magmiting, bo' niholdap na, apulag sigā.* If there are people in discussion and they are held up [by bandits], they scatter in all directions. (*Thesaurus:* **pagbamba 1.1, pagimba-imba, pagisun 1.1, paru, plano**)

**m'kkig** *adj. a-* Swollen; distended, of the stomach. *Am'kkig kita he' kinakanta.* We are distended from what we ate. *A: "Bay ka pi'ingga?" B: "Bay aku amandi."A: "Aheya b'ttongnu." B: "Am'kkig he' tahik."* A: "Where have you been?" B: "I've been swimming." A: "Your stomach is big." B: "It is swollen with seawater."

**M'ddas** *n.* Siasi township, as distinct from Siasi Island and mountain. *Am'lli aku lituk pehē' ni M'ddas pagsapuku deyom luma'.* I will buy a broom there in Siasi town for me to sweep the interior of the house with.

**m'mmong** *adj.* a- Unnoticed; inconspicuous. *Bang am'mmong-m'mmong mbal du kita ainay, sa' bang kita angaikalas...* If we are somewhat inconspicuous nothing will happen to us, but if we are foolishly brave... (*Thesaurus:* **d'ngngo', sandol 1.1, t'mmun**)

**m'mmos** (var. **momos**₁) *v. intr.* pa- 1) To behave in an orderly way; to be settled. *Oy! Saga makannak! Pam'mmos kam ni kōkan magtulihan.* Hey, you kids! Settle down on the upstream side and go to sleep together. *Pamomos kam, aniya' mundu ma deyo'.* Be quiet, there are bandits under the house. *Pam'mmos ka bo' mbal ta'nda'.* Behave quietly so as not to be seen. 1.1) *v. tr.* To restore household things to order; to tidy up. *Bang kām akatis bay magkakan m'mmosun ni deyom aparadol.* When you have finished eating, tidy things away in the cupboard. *Bang wa'i makal'ngngan saga matto'aku, na, minomos he' siyaliku. Pagt'kka matto'aku ahāp na, aluhaya na.* When my parents have gone somewhere, then my younger sister sets things in order. On my parents' arrival things are good, uncluttered.

**m'ndal** *v. intr.* aN- To show marks from a blow or burn. *Angam'ndal bukutku, akeyat he' llaw.* My back shows a mark, it got sunburnt. (*cf:* **limpa' 1.1**)

**m'ndeyom** var. of **mindeyom**

**m'nna'an** var. of **minna'an**

**m'nnē'** var. of **minnē'**

**m'nnilu** var. of **minnilu**

**m'nningga** var. of **minningga**

**m'nnitu** var. of **minnitu**

**m'ngngang** *see:* **pam'ngngang**

**m'ssa'** *neg.* Negates the certainty or importantance of a matter, in response to a question or suggestion. *A: "Atahak salung?" B: "M'ssa'."* A: "Ripe by tomorrow?" B: "No, maybe not." *M'ssa' tantu, daka at'kka daka ai.* Not definite, whether [they will] arrive or not. (*Thesaurus:* **ai po'on, ballum, duma'in, mbal 1.1, ngga'i ka**)

**m'ssa' aniya'** *phrase* Whether or not. {idiom} *Niapikihan, sali' pineyanan. M'ssa' aniya' daing, m'ssa' aniya' a'a, bang ka angispāy daing bo' ka'apikihannu, larukin na timbak.* Approached closely, like being watched. Whether fish or people, if you see fish and have come right up close to them, throw the dynamite.

**m'ssa' bidda'** *adv. phrase* Indiscriminately; without distinction. {idiom} *Amangan m'ssa'-bidda'.* Eating indiscriminately. *Kasawi'an iya, ah'lling m'ssa'-bidda', suma'an anumpa', suma'an anukna'-nukna'.* He talks randomly, talking nonsense; at times speaking crudely, at times cursing. (*syn:* **nsa'-bidda'**)

**m'ssa' du isāb** *phrase* Never mind. {idiom} *Na bang ka mbal, m'ssa' du isāb.* Oh well if you're not willing, it doesn't matter.

**m'ssa' iyuk** *phrase* Trivial; not worth mentioning. {idiom} *M'ssa' iyuk bakat bang binowa magusaha.* A wound is irrelevant when going fishing. *M'ssa' iyuk pandu' hē', halam pinaheya ma atay.* That teaching is of no value, not treated as important [lit. made large in the liver]. *M'ssa' iyuk sīn, wa'i daka pamagay e' a'a bula'ug.* Never mind the money, gone for the bully to do who knows what. *Buwat aniya' taga gawi ni ka'a bo' pataikut ka, na m'ssa' iyuk a'a inān.* Like when someone has something to talk to you about, but you ignore him, then that person is of no importance to you.

**m'ssang** *n.* 1) Irritation of the skin caused by contact with sand or the hair-like coating on some plants. (*Thesaurus:* **katol 1**) 1.1) *v. advrs.* ka-...-an To suffer from a rash due to the fine hairs of certain plants. *Bang aku bay angā' p'ttung kaleya, kam'ssangan aku e' dabung.* When I have been getting bamboo from inland I suffer a rash from the [hair-like growth on] the shoots. *Kam'ssangan si Li bang mbal amandi. Sidda magkakkut.* Li has a rash [from seawater] if she doesn't bathe. She does a lot of scratching.

**mma'** *n.* Father. *Bang ato'a na mma'ku, halam aniya' emponna.* When my father had become old, he had no teeth. (*cf:* **babu' 1.1, ina', ina', mamang**₁**, papa**₂**, papang**)

**pag'mma'** *v. intr.* aN- 1) To behave as a father. 1.1) *v. tr.* -an To treat someone as one's father. *Aku ya pag'mma'anbi bang kām tauwa' sukkal.* I am the one you treat as father when you are in trouble.

**da'mma'** *adj.* To have the same father but a different mother. (*cf:* **daina'**)

**mman** *v. intr.* aN- To leak, of a canoe. *Bang aniya' pelang taga bila' mbal aku am'lli. Ang'mman ko' inān.* If a canoe has a split I won't buy it. It is sure to leak. (*Thesaurus:* **bobos, buslut, l'ssu'**)

**mmaw** *v. advrs.* -in- 1) Fretful, as in convalescence. *Nīmmaw, sali' a'a bay asaki mag'lling-lling.* Fussing, like someone talking and talking after being sick. (*Thesaurus:* **langan**₁**, pagle'eng, s'ngngel 1, unga'**) 1.1) *v. intr.* aN- To talk irritably in convalescence. *Ang'mmaw sadja si Gi, mag'lling-'lling. Bay iya asaki.* Gi speaks irritably, talking on and on. She has been sick.

**mmu** *v. intr.* aN- To emit a muted vibrant sound; to moan softly; to coo. *Buwat balud, ang'mmu.* Cooing, like a dove.

**pag'mmu-mmu** *v. intr.* aN- To grumble quietly; to be mumbling. *Kami ina'an hal mag'mmu-mmu dakuman, sabab mbal na kami makakole'.* We were simply mumbling because we couldn't manage [what we were trying to do].

**mmun** var. of **l'mmun**

**mohang** *n.* The hollow part of something, as of a plate or of the inside part of a boat below deck level. *Pak'ppang si Lo ma deyom mohang.* Lo lay face down in the bilge. *Ya lai' halam aniya'* *mareyom, ya sali' halam mohangan ilū.* The plate with nothing in it, the one there with no hollow.

**mohot** (var. **mo'ot**) *n.* 1) Something given as an incentive. (*Thesaurus:* **k'llo' bo'ot, go'on** 1) 1.1) *v. tr.* To pursue a purpose with intensity. *Ya na ilu minohotku pi'itu.* That's the thing I am committed to in coming here. *Ya ai-ai kabaya'anku mbal aku makapagdūl-baya', apa aniya' mohotku.* I cannot succeed in whatever I want, because there are other things I am set on doing.

   **pagmohot** *v. intr. aN-* 1) To plot and plan. *Aniya' magmohot: magtuyu'-tuyu' ka bo' makapehē'.* Someone is plotting: you should be determined so you can go there. 1.1) *v. tr. -an* To plan a strategy or course of action. *A: "Pamagay ilū?" B: "Aniya' pinagmohotan."* A: "What's that for?" B: "Something is definitely being planned for it." *Bay pagmohot-mohotantam supaya makalipuwas saga pagkahitam.* We made it our firm purpose that our companions would manage to escape. (*Thesaurus:* **l'ngngan₂** 1.1, **puhung₁** 1)

**mo'ong** *n.* The Bicolor blenny, a fish species. *Ecsenius bicolor.*

**mo'ot** var. of **mohot**

**momok** *n.* Small pieces coming away from a main lump; shavings; crumbs. *Momok kayu, sali' obangna inān. Maka momok sinanglag, ya manahut-nahut inān, sali' s'ggitna.* Wood scraps, like its shavings there. And scraps of toasted cassava meal, those very little fragments, its rubbish. (*cf:* **obang**)

**momos₁** var. of **m'mmos**

**momos₂** *v. tr.* To end someone's life, the action of God. *Magtūy iya minomos e' Tuhan saru'un-du'un.* God quickly and immediately brought his life to a close.

**monggo** *n.* Mung, a small green bean either stewed or cooked after sprouting. *Phaseolus aureus.* (*Thesaurus:* **batung₂, taoge**)

**Moro** var. of **Murus**

**Moros** var. of **Murus**

**moseng** *n.* 1) Any powdery substance that makes one dirty, as soot, dirt or face-powder. *Onde'-onde' aheka mosengna, alumu'.* Children with lots of grime, disgusting. (*Thesaurus:* **l'mmi'** 1, **lobag, lumut₁** 2) 1.1) *adj. a-/-an* Grimed by some powdery substance.

**moto** *see:* **pagmoto**

**motol** *n.* A motorcycle.

**motong** (derivative of **botong**) *v. intr. aN-* To mature beyond the bilu'uk stage, of a coconut. *Kukuhun bilu'uk ilū, kalu angamotong na.* Tap that immature coconut, it may be maturing.

**mpat** *num.* Four.

   **mpat pidju alam** *n.* phrase The four corners of the earth; all over the world. {idiom} *Patimuk du isāb pina'an saga a'a min mpat pidjū alam ati*

*magtingkō'an maina'an magjamu.* People will assemble there from every part of the world and sit down to share a feast. (*cf:* **bihing langit**)

**mpatpū'** *num.* Forty.

**mpit** *v. tr.* To hold something against one's body, as a baby to the breast. (*Thesaurus:* **gapus, giba** 1.1, **hambin** 1.1, **pipi₁, sangbay**)

**mpu** *n.* A grandchild; a grandchild of one's sibling or cousin; descendants in general. (*Thesaurus:* **anak₁** 1, **onde'** 1, **tubu'** 1)

   **mpu-kengkeng** *n.* A great-great-grandchild; a great-great-grandchild of one's sibling or cousin.

   **mpu-tu'ut** *n.* A great-grandchild; a great-grandchild of one's sibling or cousin.

   **pang'mpu** *n.* Grandchildren.

   **pang'mpuhan** *n.* Descendants.

**mukali'** *n.* An expert who derives his knowledge from observation and experience rather than from religious study. *Mukali' ya mbal ata'u angadji' Kora'an, hal tatatab he' sigā. Mukali'* are those who do not know how to read the Holy Koran, they just learn [ritual] by observing what is happening.

**muddal** *n.* 1) Cash or goods exchanged in a financial transaction. *A: "Pi'ingga ilu?" B: "Kaleya am'lli panggi'." A: "Ai muddalnu?" B: "Daing."* A: "Where are you going?" B: "Inland to buy cassava." A: "What with?" A: "Fish." (*cf:* **b'lli**) 1.1) *v. tr.* To obtain something by barter or purchase. *Aniya' muddalna pehē' ni Tiyanggi.* He has something to trade there in Jolo Town.

**mudjidjat** *n.* A miraculous event or favor from a supernatural source. *Bang aniya' ka'mbo'anbi barakatan, aniya' paluwa' ni saga anak-mpu. Ya mudjidjat si Anu, kamemon anakna sampay pamikitanna, aheka taga pangiskul, k'llo' bay min iya. Ilmu' Tuhan, mbal kakuriputan.* If you have divinely favored forebears, something will come to the descendants. What's-his-name's miracle is that all his children and in-laws have education, derived from him. Special knowledge from God, given without limit. *Mudjidjat itū min Tuhan. Aniya' pinatauwa' ma dangan ahāp, aniya' pinatauwa' ma dangan ala'at. Ya ala'at mbal mudjidjat. Mudjidjat* [miracle] is from God. What happens to one person is good, what happens to another is bad. The bad stuff is not *mudjidjat. Mudjidjat saga anakna, mpuna tahinang mastal. Subay ka tulunan.* His children are favored, his grandchildren become teachers. You need to have inherited abilities. *Subay ka tulunan bo' pinataluwa'an mudjidjat.* You have to be supernaturally favored have a miracle happen to you.

   **pagmudjidjat** *v. intr. aN-* To display miraculous power.

**Muhammad** var. of **Nabi Muhammad**

**mu'min** *n.* The dead, viewed as beings to be invoked or placated. *Kamu'minan, ya na ka'mbo'-mbo'an.* The *mu'min* category of beings, they are the ancestors. (*cf:* **ka'mbo'-mbo'an**)

**mula**₁ *v. tr.* To harm or injure someone. *Mbal du at'ggol minula sigām maka kalis.* It won't be long before they are cut up with a kris. *Da'a ka anginum. Makamula baran ko' ilū.* Don't drink it. It will harm your body. (*cf:* **bala'**)

**pagmula** *v. intr. aN-* To be experiencing physical harm. *Bang ka lum'ngngan ni tabu' bo' ka man deya, kamaya'-maya' ko da'a magmula. Piligdu aniya' magmundu.* When you hike to the market by the inland route, be careful lest you come to harm. One fears that there may be men raiding. *Pinandu'an kita bo' kita mbal ameya' pandu', bo' saupama magmula baranta. Na amintāng ka m'nnilu.* We are taught but do not heed the lesson, and then, by way of example, suffer bodily harm. Learn from that experience. *Magmula ituku, magkowap-kowap.* This part [of my head] is damaged, it throbs and throbs.

**mula**₂ *see:* **balmula**

**mula'** (var. **ngula'**) *adj. zero* Newborn; just begun. *Onde' ngula', sidda anangis.* A very young child, always crying.

**palmula'an** *n.* Ancestors, especially those that are foundational in Sama folk history. (*Thesaurus:* **mbo'**₁, **ntan**₂ 1, **pangkat**₂)

**mulka'** *n.* 1) Anger of a supernatural being, of God in particular. *Taluwa' mulka' he' mbo' atawa he' Tuhan.* Struck supernaturally by ancestors or by God. (*Thesaurus:* **bala', kajahatan, kala'atan, naja', pa'al 1, udjul**₁ 1) 1.1) *v. tr. -an* To be wrathful with someone, generally involving harm to his person or property. *Mbal tabowa pi'itu bang amasi amat'nna' mbo', minulka'an kami.* He can't be brought here while we are invoking the ancestor, wrath will fall on us. *Ya makapatay iya bang minulka'an. Minulka'an: taluwa' saki, binelaw, tinunu' luma'.* What causes his death is when wrath comes on him. Wrath includes beings truck down by illness, losing one's mind,or a house being burnt.

**pagmulka'** *v. intr. aN-* 1) To impose supernatural penalties. 1.1) *v. tr. -an* To punish someone by imposing supernatural penalties. *Da'a kam angā' minsan ai na min saga tatabanan bo' supaya kam mbal pinagmulka'an.* Don't take anything at all from the loot lest you incur supernatural penalties. *Pinagmulka'an e' Tuhan sai-na amabangun da'ira itū.* God will lay a curse on whoever has this city rebuilt. *Bang kita anunu' amanyan ni api bo' ma tugtugan, na bo' pinehē' ni sibayan akeyat na, magkattek-kattek, ya hē' niōnan magmulka'.* When we ignite incense at the fire in the censer, and then it is placed burning on the ritual shelf making a crackling noise, that's called an act of wrath.

**mulid** (var. **mulit**) *n.* A student of religion who learns from a guru; a disciple. (*cf:* **guru 1, mastal**)

**mulilang** *adj. a-* Almost fully ebbed, of a tide about to turn. *Amulilang na tahik, sōng t'bba, sōng pabĭng s'llog.* The sea is almost fully ebbed, nearly low tide, soon the current will turn. (*Thesaurus:* **l'ggot, pipit**₂ 1, **t'bba 1**)

**mulit** var. of **mulid**

**mulliya** *n.* 1) Something set apart for special honor, as a holy day. 1.1) *v. tr.* To set something apart for special honor. *Llaw minulliya he' Tuhan, hatina pinahalga' he' Tuhan.* A day made special by God, meaning that it has been made of special value by God.

**mulsiku** (var. **musiku**) *n.* Band music; an orchestra; Western music.

**multa** *n.* 1) A fine imposed by civil authorities as penalty for an offense. (*Thesaurus:* **niya'**₂, **taksil 1**) 1.1) *v. tr. -an* To fine someone an amount. *Sali' kita bay angalanggal sara', bang aniya' pilak pagmultata paluwas sadja kita. Bang halam, tajīl kita.* Suppose we have committed an offense, if we have money to pay the fine we simply go free. If not, we are jailed.

**multad** (var. **mutad**) *v. advrs. -in-* Accursed because of failure to carry out religious duties with a pure heart. *Minutad iya he' napsuna. Ai-ai, labi-labi na ni d'nda.* He has become a renegade because of his desires. Anything at all, but especially desires for women. (*cf:* **kapil 1.1, munapik**)

**mumut** *adj. a-* Unduly persistent; continuing without relief. *Amumut bissalanu, mbal ka amas'lle' ma sehe'nu.* Your talk is continuous, you don't give your companions a turn. *Amumut pahāp he'nu magsulat. Sa'agon-agon akatis na ba.* You are extremely persistent in writing. It's as though it's finished up. (*cf:* **toldas**; *Thesaurus:* **langkit 1.1, pagabut-abut, pagambat-ambat 1**)

**muna-muna** *adj. zero* 1) Of primary importance, as someone who takes a prominent role in negotiations. *Ka'a ya muna-muna, minsan halam bay ah'lling taga ai-ai ilū, asal ka'a na.* You are most important, even though the people with the resources have not spoken, you are the one. *Muna-muna min kamemon, magsukul aku ni ka'a ma bay pabeya'nu.* Most important of all, I thank you for what you sent. *Tagna'anku na sulatku pinabowa, pinaleyang, ni ka'a. Ya balikna, muna-muna min kamemon, salam duwa'a ni ka'am.* I begin my letter that will be sent to you by air. However, most important of all, devout greetings to you. 1.1) *adv.* Importantly; especially. *Sagō' muna-muna kannalunbi kahandak Tuhan.* But think especially of the will of God. 1.2) *v. tr.* To treat something as most important. *Ya subay muna-munata kahinangan abontol maka iman.* What we should treat as most important are good actions and faith.

**pagmuna-muna** *v. tr.* To treat something as of primary importance. *Ya pinagmuna-muna ma jūd itu pandu' pasal kahālan saga a'a suku' Tuhan* *bang angisbat iya.* What is stressed as important in this sura is the teaching concerning the people belonging to God when they are devoutly committed. *Angay ka'a ya magmuna-muna dīnu, minsan ngga'i ka anaknu?* Why are you the one making yourself important, even though it is not your child? (*Thesaurus:* **sōng-sōng₂**)

**munapik** *n.* A hypocrite; someone who is neglectful of the religious duties he claims to observe. (*cf:* **kapil 1.1, multad**)

**munari** *n.* 1) A species of sea bird. *Aheya gi' belle' min munari, sali' etek. Apote' b'ttongna, ettom kepetna, abu-abu min diyata'na, apote' k'llongna.* The white-fronted sea eagle is bigger than the *munari.* It's like a duck, its underside is white, its wings are black, it is grey from above, its neck is white. 2) A bird-herald authorized to speak on behalf of an authority. {archaic} *Magtūy aniya' magbono' belle' maka munari.* Immediately there were an eagle and a *munari* fighting.

**munda'₁** 1) *n.* The front part of a canoe or vehicle. *Buliburun pelang i' tudju pī'itu munda'na bo' mbal magka'at sangpad.* Turn the canoe around with its bow in this direction so the decorative prow is not damaged. *Tininduk aku e' kandelan ati binowa paraw palahi-lahi magbibud buwi'-munda'.* A sailfish took my lure and the canoe was made to race away, stern and bow turning end for end. *Amalut munda' kappal, mbal pajudjal, maka buli'na hē' abagbag e' goyak.* The bow of the ship stuck fast, unmovable, and its stern was broken by the surf. 2) *clf.* Count word for counting canoes. *T'llu munda' kami.* There are three canoes of us. (*cf:* **puntu**)

**kamunda'an** *n.* An assembly of canoes in one place. *Alapat he' kamunda'an.* Covered with canoes.

**munda'an₁** *loc. n.* The area in front. *Bay ta'nda'ta man munda'anta a'a lum'ngngan na tudju ni kita. Na halam na ta'nda'ta a'a ina'an, ya ta'nda'ta hayop.* We saw in front of us a person walking towards us. Then we no longer saw that person, what we saw was an animal. (*Thesaurus:* **alopan₁, dahū'an 1, harapan₁**)

**munda'an₂** *n.* The genital area. (*Thesaurus:* **alopan₂, kamama'u, harapan₂**)

**pagmunda'₁** *n.* A group of canoes forming a fishing fleet. *Alaba bay pangā'an pagmunda' magdaing ni pū'.* What the fishing fleet caught at the outer islands was profitable. *Takale kami pagmunda' atulak magpangambit na, magpang'llo' daing na, saga magpana' na.* We heard the fleet leaving to catch fish by herding, to fish, to spear them.

**damunda'** *n.* A single boat.

**damunda'-munda'** *n.* 1) A single canoe traveling alone. (*cf:* **tukkal, tunggal-tunggal 1**) 1.1) *v. intr. pa-* To travel by canoe on one's own. *Paramunda'-damunda' iya dīna, sali' parangandangan.* He is traveling by canoe on his own,

going solo so to speak.

**munda'₂** *n.* A person who takes the lead, literally or metaphorically. *Bang aku tahinang munda' he' sigām.* If they made me the leader.

**pagmunda'₂** *v. tr. -an* To lead a group or community. *Ka'a ya magmunda' ma saga a'a itū.* You are the one to be leading these people.

**pagmunda'an** *n.* A person recognized as the leader for a specific enterprise. *Ka'a ya tamalim e' sigā, tahinang pagmunda'an.* You are the one they made guide, made to be the leader. (*Thesaurus:* **pagbebeya'an, pagmakōk, pagmandangan, pagmete-mete**)

**mundal-mandil** *see:* **pagkamundal-mandil**

**mundu** *n.* 1) An outlaw or raider. *Nijagjag luma' ilū, nirarut sampay hāg apa ilu'un na mundu.* The house there is being dismantled, even the posts being pulled out because bandits aren't far off. (*Thesaurus:* **panangkaw, pilliyu, sugarul**) 1.1) *v. intr. aN-* To engage in banditry. *Angalangpas itū sali' angamundu. Langpas* is similar to engaging in banditry. (*Thesaurus:* **kullu-kullu₂ 1, langpas, musu**) 1.2) *v. tr. -an* To plunder someone's goods. *Saupama minunduhan kita ma Sisangat, na talalat kita ni Siganggang.* Suppose we are attacked by outlaws in Sisangat, then we are forced to escape to Siganggang. *Bang a'a alentok, mbal kamunduhan, makalahi'an dīna.* A thoughtful man doesn't get attacked by bandits, he gets away on his own initiative.

**pagmundu** *v. intr. aN-* To be involved in raiding or plundering. *Bang ka lum'ngngan ni tabu' bo' ka man deya, kamaya'-maya' ko da'a magmula. Piligdu aniya' magmundu.* When you hike to the market by the inland route, be careful lest you come to harm. One fears that there may be men raiding. *Piligdu sangom inān, aniya' magmundu.* Risky tonight, there may be raiding.

**muntas** *v. intr. aN-* To pale, as through shock or illness. *Angamuntas si Mām, sali' asaki. Angamote' sala.* Mum is going pale as though sick. She turns sort of white. (*Thesaurus:* **lospad, muras 1.1, pusiyat**)

**muntay** *n.* Generic term for several citrus species and hybrids. *Citrus nobilis; citrus aurantia.* (*spec:* **kalamonden**)

**muntay-gadja** *n.* The pomelo or lukban. *C. maxima.*

**muntay-gauga'** (var. **gauga'**) *n.* A sweet variety of citrus.

**muntay-iklug** *n.* A lemon.

**muntay-lannang** *n.* A mandarin orange, smooth-skinned. (*syn:* **muntay-sina', muntay-taoke'**)

**muntay-liyabod** *n.* A mandarin orange, rough-skinned.

**muntay-muntay** *n.* A green-skinned variant of calamansi (calamondin).

**muntay-sina'** *n.* A mandarin orange. (*syn:* **muntay-lannang, muntay-taoke'**)

**muntay-suha'** *n.* A mandarin orange, green-skinned.

**muntay-taoke'** *n.* A mandarin orange of Chinese origin. (*syn:* **muntay-lannang, muntay-sina'**)

**munu-munu** *n.* An outcrop of dark coral rising from the sea floor at a depth of ten to twenty fathoms. (*gen:* **batu₂ 1**; *Thesaurus:* **puhu, takot, tahetek**)

**munyeka** *n.* A doll; a mannequin. (*cf:* **datu'-datu', ta'u-ta'u₁**)

**mūng** *v. intr. a-* To speak; to say. *Magkamamatay pa'in iya, amūng saga panday, yuk-i, "Ndū' nneng, da'a ka tināw."* As she was dying, the midwife said, "Dear woman, don't be afraid." *Amūng saga kamatto'ahan, yuk-i, "B'nnal bahā' bay soho'nu iya nilappet?"* The elders spoke, saying, "Is it true that you gave orders for him to be whipped?" *Kosog-kosogun e'nu amūng bo' ahangpat.* Make your speaking a bit louder so it is clear.

**mūng-mūng** *v. intr. a-* To speak roughly or critically; to berate.

**pagmūng-mūng** *v. intr. aN-* **1)** To be engaged in talking. **1.1)** *v. tr.* To refer openly to some issue or news. *Mbal pahali tapagmūng-mūng pi'ingga-pi'ingga lahat. Bay dangan du ata'u, aheka na ata'u.* It doesn't stop being spoken about some place or other. Just one person had known of it, now many know. (*Thesaurus:* **bahasa₁, bā'₁, batbat₂, bissala 1.1, k'bbat₁ 1, h'lling₁ 1.1, sambat, yuk**)

**himumūngan** *n.* Significant things said in order to provoke a response. (*Thesaurus:* **kabtangan**; *syn:* **hilala'ungan**)

**paghimumūngan** *n.* **1)** An utterance of significance; a pronouncement. **1.1)** *v. intr. aN-* To say things of significance. *Bay kami maka si Sa magbono'-bono' bo' pahali. Takaleku iya maghimumūngan ma aku.* Sa and I were fighting a bit, but stopped. I had heard him saying serious things about me.

**pamūng** *v. tr.* To say something; to utter.

**pamūng-mūng** *v. tr. -an* To berate someone; to scold. (*Thesaurus:* **dugal 1.1, pabukag, pah'lling₂, pugpug 1, s'ndal 1, tutul**)

**mungkalun** *n.* The Questioner who interrogates a person who has just died. (*cf:* **tanya₂**)

**mungkang** *n.* A worn-out canoe of the paraw type.

**mungkil** *n.* A person or domestic animal that rebels against control. *Saga mungkil ilū mbal pakale, aniya' isāb hayop.* A mungkil won't listen, there are domestic animals too [like that]. (*cf:* **saitan-mungkil 2**)

**mungit** *n.* A Surgeonfish. *Acanthurus nigrofuscus.* (*gen:* **kumay**)

**mungit-keyat-kepet** *n.* The Orange-epaulette surgeonfish. *Acunthurus olivaceus.*

**muparik** *n.* Someone who rebels against cultural standards.

**mūpū** *n.* The Pleiades (a star cluster in the Taurus constellation). *Aggal daing aninduk, ngga'i ka patahunanna. Tu'ud aglawanan mūpū.* Fish are slow to bite, it is not the season. Just waiting for the Pleiades to appear.

**mura** *adj. a-* Easy; easily achieved. *Amura kita nira'ug e' saitan.* We will be easily defeated by the *saitan* spirit. (*cf:* **luhay₂ 1**)

**mura-murahan** *adv.* Fervently desired, of the fulfillment of a prediction or hope. *Yuk l'lla inān, "Aniya' du pa'in. Kalu-kalu mura-murahan pinataha' umulna he' Tuhan."* The man said, "There is always something. One hopes, perhaps, that God will extend her life." *Yuk si Kiskisan inān, "Ā, paka'lluminbi na pa'in. Kalu-kalu mura-murahan..."* Kiskisan said, "Oh, keep it alive. Perhaps, hopefully..." *Mura-murahan lappasan kita man bala'.* It is to be devoutly hoped that we will be safe from serious trouble. (*Thesaurus:* **kaddaw, gōm na pa'in**)

**pagmura** *v. intr. aN-* **1)** To be generous in the sharing of one's possessions. **1.1)** *v. tr.* To share one's possessions with others. *Pagmura-murahun ai-ainu ni Juhul makaniJakatla', ni a'a kamemon. Hatina pagsarakkahun ni kalūng-kampungan sampay ni atā-asekot.* Deal generously with your possessions to people from Johore to Jakarta. In other words make donations to your kinfolk and neighbors, to those who are close and to those who are far off. (*Thesaurus:* **pagsarakka 1**)

**mural** *see:* **patay-mural**

**muras** *adj. a-* **1)** Bleached; depigmented. *Bang bay tinambalan maka tambal pohak, amuras k'llongna.* If [her neck] had been treated with ringworm medicine, her neck would be fairly white. (*Thesaurus:* **pote' 1.2**) **1.1)** *v. intr. aN-* To show the effects of depigmentation; to become pale. *Angamuras apote'.* Fading to white. (*Thesaurus:* **lospad, muntas, pusiyat**)

**Muru** *var. of* **Murus**

**Murus** (*var.* **Moro**; **Moros**; **Muru**) *n.* A Muslim Filipino.

**Musa** *var. of* **Nabi Musa**

**musalla** *n.* A prayer mat. (*Thesaurus:* **palmaddani', tudjara**)

**muskitero** *n.* A mosquito net. (*syn:* **kulambu' 2**)

**musiba** *n.* A widespread disaster such as epidemic sickness, typhoon, or famine; a personal disaster. *Maglahangan du aniya' musibaku buwattitu.* It is a rare occurrence for me to have a disaster like this. (*syn:* **bonglay 1**)

**musiku** *var. of* **mulsiku**

**musil** *n.* A bolt action rifle. (*Thesaurus:* **kalbin, kanyun 1, garan, lantaka 1, pistul, sinapang**)

**musim** *n.* A season (part of a year). *Ya na itu musim ma olangan kōk uttala' maka tape' satan.* This is the season between the onset of the north wind and the tail end of the southwest wind. (*Thesaurus:* **paliyama', tahun 1**)

**musim tagna'** *n. phrase* Time long past. {idiom}

(*Thesaurus:* **awal-jāman, awal-tagna', awal₁, masa-awal**)

**musiman maka tahunan** *n. phrase* A long period of time. {idiom} *Agon-agon ta'abut musiman maka tahunan bo' yampa aniya' lapal takalebi.* It's getting to be months, years, before you get to hear news.

**Muslim** *n.* A Muslim, a person who has embraced Islam.

**musmud** *see:* **pagmusmud**

**mussak-massik** *adj. a-* Profuse, of things in a house such as furnishings, utensils, and decorations. *Kapanyapan deyom luma', yukta, "Amussak-massik." Buwat saga itu-itū amussak-massik.* Of the various things in a house we say, "So cluttered." Like this and that all over the place. (*cf:* **kapanyapan**; *Thesaurus:* **babarapa, kaginisan, inda wa barapa ginis, indalupa 1**)

**mussa'** *n.* A pearl; the pearl oyster. *"Na maina'an na," yuk sultan, "mussa' būng inān, na mussa' ulan, mussa' telop-telop," yukna.* "Over there now," said the sultan, "are those jellyfish pearls, and those rain pearls, and the finest pearls ever." (*cf:* **tipay**)

**mussa'-gamat** *n.* A rare and valuable type of pearl.

**mustahab** *var. of* **mustajab**

**mustahak** *n.* The right to decide, especially in the context of marriage negotiations. *Sai bay makapogos ka'a? Ka'a ya tag-mustahak.* Who forced you [to let the girl marry]? You have the right to decide. *Ka'a tag-mustahak ma saga anaknu.* You have the right to make decisions about your children.

**mustahil** *adj. zero* Actually happening, though unlikely or impossible. *Mahal mustahil ko' ka'a ilū.* You are unbelievably special. *Sali' magsān-sān ya mustahil itū. Mustahil aheka ah'lling, mustahil halam.* This *mustahil* is something that occurs intermittently. At times many are talking, at times none. (*cf:* **dipisil, hunit 1**)

**mustajab** (var. **mustahab**) *adj. zero* Fulfilled, as a dream or prophesy.

**mustala** *adj. zero* Beautiful; lovely to see. *D'nda mustala si Gi.* Gi is a beautiful girl. *Bang anangbay si'itku onde'-onde', mustala.* When my aunt holds a baby and sings to it, it is lovely.

**musti-musti** *adv.* Doubtless; with absolute certainty. *Musti-musti kita mbal angandupang ma Tuhan.* We should certainly not play the fool with God. *Musti-musti mailu aku salung. Sali' sab'nnal-b'nnal.* I will definitely be here tomorrow. Like being totally certain. (*Thesaurus:* **pasti'₁, talhakit 1.1**)

**musu** *n.* A bandit. (*Thesaurus:* **kullu-kullu₂ 1, langpas, mundu 1.1**)

**mutad** *var. of* **multad**

**mutallak** *n.* Something completely worthless. *Mutallak itū ai-ai tinimanan, ai-ai mbal na kinalagihan.* This *mutallak* is anything thrown away, anything no longer usable.

**mutamad** *v. advrs. ta-* Experiencing a nightmare. *Bang kita tamutamad, ni'ddop kita. Ah'lling kita, halam ai-ai ma pikilanta.* When we suffer a nightmare our sleep is fitful. We talk, nothing whatever in our minds. (*Thesaurus:* **ansong, ddop, lāp-lāp, pagdabdab, uppi 1**)

**muwallam** *n.* A high-ranking religious official or imam. *Muwallam itū hatina jukup na kamemon, ma saga kitab.* The *muwallam* referred to is complete in everything, in all the religious books. (*cf:* **bilal, hatib, imam**)

**muwat** *adj. zero* Comparable; similar to. *Mbal muwat susun sigām.* Their remorse was unequaled. (*cf:* **buwat 1**)

**pagmuwat** *v. intr. aN-* To make something possible. *Aniya' anaknu bilahi'an anakna, hatina ka'a magmuwat bo' kinabaya'an e' kar'ndahan. Hatina ka'a ya magmatuyu'.* A son of yours fancies his daughter, which means that you do what is needed to have him approved by the girl's family. You are the one to be persistent.

# N n

**nā** *conj.* 1) Paragraph introducer meaning: 'so', 'so then', 'now', 'then', 'now then'. *Nā, pagga' halam sīnnu, subay ka magpa'ata ma aku.* All right, since you have no money, you had better work for me as an unpaid servant. *Bang d'nda sali'-sali', bo' aniya' pagsagga'an tahinang bono', nā bang magsekot makapagluray.* When both parties are women, and there is a difference of opinion that turns into a fight, when they get close to each other they may pull each other's hair. *Nā, ya na itu tana' bay pamasuku' ma saga bakwet.* So this is the land that was allotted to the evacuees.

(*Thesaurus:* **ati, manjari₂, sakali₂**) **1.1**) *ptl.* Development marker in narrative discourse that signals resumption of the event line after backgrounding or a disruption. *Minsan kita atulak, tinaggahan, sinoho' pinuwas gi' bay nahas. Mbal kita. Bang ma dilaut apōng taruk, agese' leha. Nā sinemet kita.* Even on the point of leaving, we are held back and told to let the effects of some misfortune pass. But we are unwilling. Out at sea, the mast breaks and the sail rips. So the ancestors have got back at us.

**na** *ptl.* Aspect marker indicating the situation or

action described is already in process. *Amole' na kami.* We are going home now. *Bay dangan du ata'u, aheka na ata'u.* Only one knew of it, now a lot know. *Mbal na sakit pamaliyu.* It is no longer very windy. (*cf:* **lagi'** 1)

=**na** *pron.* He, she, it; his, her, its (third person singular) [Set II]. *Aheya sakkina.* His sickness is severe. *Bay aku binuwanan sangpū' pilak he'na.* He gave me ten pesos. *Arāk angandāg mampallam, sagō' mbal ta'abutna.* He would have climbed the mango tree, but he couldn't reach it. (*cf:* **iyā, iya**; *Set:* =**bi,** =**ku,** =**nu,** =**sigā,** =**sigām,** =**ta** 1, =**tabi,** =**tam**)

**na ka..na ka** *phrase* Whether one thing or another. {idiom} *Angangganding ni p'ttung na ka, ni tu'ung na ka.* Beating time, on either a section of bamboo or on a wooden box.

**na pa'in** *adv. phrase* Ongoing; continually; always. (Continuous aspect marker.) *Mahē' na pa'in kami, halam aniya' pameya'an.* There we were, all the time, stuck with no transport. *Nihabit onde'-onde', binowa na pa'in e' ina'na.* The child is held close, always carried about by its mother. *Pehē' na pa'in kitā, buwat sali' pareyo', bo' mbal bilahi pareyo'an, sogsogta na pa'in. Kalu ma'ase'.* We keep going there, sort of humbling ourselves, but the one we show humility to is not willing, we keep on persisting. Perhaps he will be merciful.

**nabal** *n.* A naval vessel. *Arai' kita itū kinanyun he' nabal.* We were about to be shelled by a naval vessel.

**nabi** *n.* A religious prophet. *Amassa hutba' imam, kalangan nabi.* The imam read a sermon, the song of a prophet.

    **kanabi-nabihan** *n.* Prophets recorded in the Holy Koran and in the Holy Bible.

**Nabi Ibrahim** (var. **Ibrahim**) *n.* Abraham, the Hebrew patriarch.

**Nabi Muhammad** (var. **Muhammad**) *n.* Muhammad, the prophet of Islam to whom the Holy Koran was revealed.

**Nabi Musa** (var. **Musa**) *n.* Moses, the prophet who led the Hebrew people out of slavery in Egypt, and whose writings in the Torah (Kitab Tawrat) are sacred to the Jewish, Christian and Muslim religions.

**Nabi Nū** (var. **Nū**) *n.* The prophet Noah, builder of the Ark.

**nakura'** *n.* A person in charge; the captain of a ship. *Sagō' tabowa iya magkahagad ma bissala nakura' kappal maka tag-dapu.* But he was persuaded to agree with the instructions of the ship's captain and the owners. (*Thesaurus:* **bōs, kapala, kapatas, mandul**)

    **pagnakura'** 1) *v. tr.* -*an* To exercise authority over a group; to lead or command a group. *Sabab iya in magnakura'an sigām pauntas pehē'.* Because he was the one to lead them forward there. *Bay niakkalan e'na dok supaya iya ya makapagnakura'*

*ma lahat.* He tricked them so that he would be the one to hold power over the district. *Pagnakura'an iya ma saga jaga ma deyom astana'.* He was in authority over all the guards in the palace. (*Thesaurus:* **kaputat, pagagi, pagbaya'**₁, **pagkawasa, pagkuma'agi**) 2) *v. intr.* *aN*- To be the dominant or most significant of a series. *Basta daing pote' kamemon, ya magnakura' mangsa'.* Of all the white-fish, *mangsa'* is the topmost.

**naelon** (var. **naylon**) *n.* Nylon line. *Amole' na kita. Kolengun bannang naelon, patandan na kita amole'.* Let's go home. Wind up the nylon line, we'll head for shore, homewards. (*Thesaurus:* **tangsi'**₁ 1, **tonda'**₁ 1)

**naga** *n.* 1) A mythical dragon said to swallow the moon during an eclipse, and to be particularly dangerous to pregnant women on such occasions. *Anakna kamemon wa'i kinakan he' naga.* All of her children have been consumed by the *naga* spirit. 1.1) *v. advrs.* -*in*- Made ill by proximity to a dragon spirit. *Buwat a'a ninaga, ya botong maka giyagayna ginantung, tinigbasan bo' ala'an saki.* Like a person made ill by a dragon spirit, a young coconut and its dried flower are hung up, then slashed so his illness goes away.

    **pagnaga** *v. intr.* *aN*- To become a dragon, as large sea snakes are said to do when they move out to deep water.

**nahanat** *n.* The deceased, a euphemism used to avoid referring to by name. (*Thesaurus:* **aymulla, maruhum, wapat**)

**nahas** *n.* 1) Luck or fortune, usually negative; a portent of trouble to come. *Minsan kita atulak, tinaggahan, sinoho' pinuwas gi' bay nahas, mbal kita. Bang ma dilaut apōng taruk, agese' leha. Na sinemet kita.* Though we are leaving we are delayed, advised to get over a recent misfortune, but we dissent. Then out at sea the mast breaks and the sail splits. We are punished. *Aniya' nahas ni kahāpan, sali' lidjiki'. Aniya' isāb nahas ni kala'atan.* There is luck that brings something good, like a blessing. There is also luck that brings something bad. *Tauwa' kami nahas. Nahas itū sali' habal.* We were affected by a sense of impending trouble. *Nahas* is like a message. (*cf:* **bala'**; *Thesaurus:* **bilsut, paksa'** 1, **pawas** 1.1, **piyurus**₂) 1.1) *v. advrs.* *ka*-....-*an* To be affected by luck, good or bad. *Bang aniya' magka'at ai-ai ma parawbi, kanahasan ka.* When something is ruined, like things on your canoe, you are experiencing bad luck. *Aniya' nahas ala'at, aniya' isāb nahas ahāp, buwat kita magpaka'ā' daing aheka, "Kanahasan sigā," yuk kasehe'.* There is bad luck, there is also good luck, like when we happen to catch a great many fish and others say, "They are benefiting from good fortune."

**naho'-naho'** *see:* **pagnaho'-naho'**

**nahu** *n.* 1) Mental capacity; thought processes; intelligence. *Minsan ahāp nahuku bo' halam aniya' akkalku, ala'at.* Though my intellect is fine, if I am not shrewd, it is not good. *Ahāp nahu a'a inān, mbal ab'nsi ma pagkahina manusiya'.* That guy's understanding of things is good, he doesn't dislike his fellow men. **1.1)** *v. tr.* To know someone. *Sai anganahu aku, makanahu isāb ma mma'ku.* Whoever knows me will be able to know my father too.

**panahu'an** (var. **palnahu'an**) *n.* Intellect; the ability to think or reason. (*Thesaurus:* **akkal 1, pamikil**)

**nahut** *adj.* a- Small in cross-section, as rope or line; small in gauge, as the mesh of a net. *Subay pangayakan anahut-nahut m'nnitu.* It needs to be a sieve somewhat finer than this. *Ōy, anahut pahāp daing ilū dambila' pilak!* Hey, that's an extremely small fish for half a peso! (*ant:* **aslag₂ 1**; *Thesaurus:* **kiput, diki' 1**)

**kamanahutan** *n.* Little children or young people, as a group. *Kamanahutan itū mbal ameya' gara', anak tahun itū. Subay kami a'aslag.* The young ones can't take advice, today's youth. It must be us adults. (*cf:* **panganak**; *Thesaurus:* **anak-anak₁, makannak, onde'-onde'**)

**panahut** *adv.* Finely; into small pieces.

**naja'** *n.* Misfortune or disaster, dire but not necessarily terminal. *Bay kami kalabayan naja'. Aniya' naja' at'kka pi'itu sali' saki bonglay.* We have experienced disaster. A disaster came here, like a plague. (*Thesaurus:* **bala', kajahatan, kala'atarī, mulka' 1, pa'al 1, udjul₁ 1**)

**najal** *n.* 1) A vow or promise made to God, an ancestor, or a person of high status. **1.1)** *v. ditr.* To fulfill a vow made to a supernatural being for help in some crisis. *Ninajalan anakku ni Tuhan. Bang sōng amatay onde'-onde', bo' ta'abut he' tambal maka tawal, subay kita magnajal.* I make a vow to God on behalf of my children. When a child is close to death but responds in time to medicine and healing charms, we should fulfill a vow. (*Thesaurus:* **pagsapa 1.1, sapda 1, subali 1.1, suhud 1.2, wa'ad**)

**pagnajal** *v. intr.* aN- 1) To make a formal vow to a ritual ancestor as a response to some favor received. *Magnajal kita ni mbo' ko da'a taluwa' maut.* We keep our promise to the ancestor lest we be targeted by the death spirit. **1.1)** *v. tr.* -an To make someone's illness the object of a formal vow. *Bang aku bay asaki, bo' at'ggol bay kasakiku, pinagnajalan tinimbang ma bulan Hailaya.* When I was ill and my illness was long-lasting, a vow was made for me to undergo the weighing ceremony in the month of Hailaya.

**nā'** var. of **ā'**

**nalka'** *n.* Hell, the place where the wicked are sent in the afterworld. *Bang ala'at bay hinangta, tina'adjil kita. Pina'llawan kita mahē' ma ahirat, pina'alu'an. Pinehē' kita ni nalka'. Bang kita ahāp,* pinehē' *ni deyom sulga'.* If our deeds are bad we will be exposed to the elements. Put out in the sun there in the afterworld, subjected to the dew. Sent to hell. If we are good we will be sent to heaven. *Pinehē' ni kal'ddoman maka ni nalka'. Mahē' sadja saumul-umul, pi'ingga-pi'ingga goyak ameya'.* Sent to darkness and to hell. There forever, going wherever the storm waves go. (*Thesaurus:* **sulga'**)

**nalka'-jahannam** *n.* A compartment of hell prepared for the very wicked.

**nana'** *n.* Pus. *Bang kinalibubut si Ji, aheka nana'.* When Ji gets boils there is a lot of pus. (*Thesaurus:* **d'nnat 1, sagu**)

**pagnana'** *v. intr.* aN- To produce pus. *Bang aniya' abakat, bo' pagnana', nihagoman ni tahik atawa ni bohe'.* If someone has a wound from cutting and it is producing pus, it is soaked in seawater or freshwater.

**nanam** 1) *n.* The sense of taste or smell. *Nanam ahalu'. Salung ahalu' to'ongan.* Smelling of decay. By tomorrow it will be fully rotten. (*Thesaurus:* **ssa₁ 1**) **1.1)** *adj.* a- Tasty. *Bang aku am'lla daing ananam, tananamta ahāp.* When I cook tasty fish we can smell that it is good. *Bang kahawa bay halam ananam, k'nnopanta, gōm pa'in papa'it.* When the coffee was flavorless we added to it, but it became bitter instead. **2)** *v. tr.* To sense or experience something. *Bang aku atuli, sali' aku alipat. Minsan aku nilagut atawa sinuntuk, mbal tananam.* When I sleep it's like I'm right out. Even if I am slashed or punched, I don't notice. *Sinugpakan kita e' matto'ata. Yuk-i', "Na ka'a bay lāngku, mbal ameya'-meya'. Na nanamun na."* Our parents tell us we have ourselves to blame. They say, "There, I forbade you and you wouldn't heed. Now find out what it's like." (*Thesaurus:* **labay₃, lapa₁, sabi₂, ssa₂**) **2.1)** To experience a bodily symptom. *A: "Ai nanamnu ma barannu?" B: "Ap'ddi' b'ttongku."* A: "What do you feel in your body?" B: "My stomach is sore."

**pananam** *v. tr.* -an To make a person aware of something unseen.

**nanu'** *see:* **pagnanu'**

**nangka'** *n.* The jackfruit tree and its edible fruit. *Artocarpus heterophyllus. Duwansalik nangka', aniya' nangka' tignus, aniya' nangka' loya'.* Two segments of jackfruit. There is the *tignus* variety and the *loya'* variety. (*spec:* **loya', tignus**)

**napaka** *n.* The daily needs of a household. *Sat'ggol masi kita magdāg-lurus, angamu'-ngamu' na pa'in kita napaka maka salam-duwa'a.* So long as we are still alive and active, we will keep praying for daily needs and for peace.

**pagnapaka** *v. tr.* -an To provide the basic necessities for members of one's household. *"Dayang," yukna, "piha'anta ka pat'nna'an atotog bo' aniya' magnapaka ma ka'a."* "Dear girl," she said, "I will try to find a permanent home for you so there will be someone to provide for your needs." (*Thesaurus:* **aku**₁, **balanja'** 1, **kahirupan**, **ka'lluman**, **gastu** 1, **lutu'**₁ 1, **umbang**)

**napas** *n.* Breath; the air in one's lungs. *Bang aku patuhun mbal makatatas, akulang napasku.* When I dive I can't last long, my breath is limited. (*syn:* **hinansong** 1)

**pagnapas** *v. intr.* aN- To be breathing. *Maghagok, magnapas paheya.* Snorting, breathing heavily. *Halam na magnapas, amatay na.* He's no longer breathing, he's dead. *As'ppol ūngna angkan kahunitan magnapas.* His nose is blocked which is why he has difficulty breathing. (*cf:* **paghota**; *Thesaurus:* **gagal**₁, **paghagak**, **panggahak**, **ppo**)

**napsu** *n.* 1) A strong desire for something; appetite; lust. *Aniya' napsu ahāp, aniya' napsu ala'at.* There are good desires and bad desires. (*Thesaurus:* **baya'** 1, **bilahi** 1, **ebog** 1, **helo**₁ 1, **lingit** 1, **tawad** 1) 1.1) *adj.* a- Lustful; excessively desirous, as for a specific food or for sex outside of marriage. *Atawad, sali' anapsu.* *Bay na magsulut ati niamu' gi'.* Greedy for more, kind of lustful. They've already agreed [on a price] but still ask for more. (*Thesaurus:* **bahaya**, **kaway** 1, **hangsaw** 1, **hawa** 1.1, **sawiya** 1, **sayap-sayap**)

**kanapsuhan** *n.* A craving. *Bang angiram h'ndanu bo' aniya' kanapsuhanna, subay b'llinu.* If your wife is pregnant and craving something, you should buy it.

**napsu kabasi'** *n. phrase* An uncontrolled desire. {idiom}

**napsu-sawiya** *n.* An uncontrollable desire.

**pagnapsu** *v. intr.* aN- To jealously want what someone else has. *A'a mangandali'it itū sali' magnapsu, buwat sali' aniya' ta'nda' e' sigā ma bihing luma' sigā, minsan sai-sai a'a. Ya nirali'itan a'a ya taga ai-ai hē'.* These people who resent others' good fortune are sort of covetous. It's like they have seen something in a neighboring house, no matter who. What they want reduced are those people who have things.

**nasa** *n.* A portent; a sense of impending trouble. *Bay aku wa'i kaut bo' halam maka'ā' ai-ai, bay maganak h'ndaku. Taluwa' nasa aku.* I was away fishing but not catching anything, my wife had given birth. I have been hit with a portent. *Nasa itū aheka ginisanna, buwat aniya' maganak, aniya' problema.* There are many kinds of *nasa*, like the birth of a child, or the existence of some problem. (*cf:* **pagba'at** 1)

**pagnasahan** *n.* Events close at hand that warn of trouble elsewhere. *Bang kita angusaha kaut ati yukta niangay mbal sinōd bubuta, ya he' pagnasahan. Aniya' asaki ma luma'.* When we are working at sea and we wonder why no [fish] are entering our traps, that is a sign of trouble. Someone at home is sick.

**nasib** *v. tr.* -an To chant as part of a religious ceremony. *Imam inān amassa tawbat kupul, aku itū anganasib, kaheka'an inān angamin.* The mosque leader reads the sermon on forgiveness

for presumption, I sing the chant, while the congregation says the amen. *Sali' anganasib kita ma paghinangan, ilu parak ma paghinangan.* We chant in the assembly, that's the purpose of the assembly.

**nasihat** *v. ditr.* To proclaim something of general interest; to declare a message of religious or moral import; to preach a sermon. (*Thesaurus:* **pablek**, **pamahalayak**, **usihat**)

**pagnasihat** *v. tr.* To make information widely known. *Pagnasihatunbi lapal itū.* Make this message widely known.

**nata'** *var. of* **nyata'**

**nau-** *see section 2.2.2.4 Prefix:* **Cau-**

**naylon** *var. of* **naelon**

**nda** *var. of* **h'nda**

**nda'** *v. tr.* 1) To look at something; to see. *Halam aniya' ta'nda'ku, luwal s'ggit.* I can't see anything, only rubbish. *Agabul mata milikan, ahāp ni'nda'.* The Westerner's eyes are clouded, good to look at. *Pagk'llat subu dakayu', na halam na ta'nda' būd Musu' itū.* When another day dawned, Musu' peak here was no longer visible. (*cf:* **harap**₁ 1.3, **idlap** 1.1) 1.1) To look for something; to seek. *Nda'in aku pisaw.* Look for a small knife for me. (*Thesaurus:* **batuk**₂, **jadja'** 1.1, **lalag**, **libu** 1.1, **salusu**)

**nda'-kutu** *v. tr.* To delouse; to look for lice in someone's hair.

**nda'-nda'** *v. intr.* aN- To watch; to be a spectator. *Hal maglinga-linga, sali' mag'nda'-nda'.* Just looking this way and that, sort of looking around. (*Thesaurus:* **tatab**, **t'ntong**₂)

**pag'nda'-mata** *v. intr.* aN- To see each other face to face.

**pag'nda'**₁ *v. intr.* aN- To see or look at each other. *Bay kami maglikuwad, halam bay mag'nda'.* We passed without noticing each other, didn't see each other. *Da'a gi' bang buwat d'nda maka l'lla magbaya', bo' sali' at'ggol halam makapag'nda', bo' samaentom, na maglaman.* Especially when a woman and a man are in love but haven't seen each other for ages and are each thinking of the other, then they become visible to each other. *Mbal na makapag'nda' saga a'a Misil dansehe'an.* The people of Egypt could not see each other. (*Thesaurus:* **pagalop**, **pagharap**, **paglambung**, **pagtampal**)

**pag'nda'**₂ *v. tr.* To get information by divination. (*Thesaurus:* **alamat**₁, **kamot**, **limal**, **putika'**)

**pag'nda'an** *n.* Things used for divination. *Aniya' pag'nda'an ma si'itku. Bang aniya' asaki agtūy tinugpang aniya' amatay.* My uncle has the things needed for divining. If someone is sick he promptly identifies if someone will die.

**pagpa'nda'-pa'nda'** *v. intr.* aN- To make a display or show of something. (*Thesaurus:* **mata-mata**₁, **pagpaelle'-elle'**, **pa'amu-amu**)

**pa'nda'** *v. tr.* 1) To display something. 1.1) *v. ditr.* To show something to someone. *A'a inān hal* *ama'nda'an abbuna.* That fellow is just making a show of his pride. *Subay pama'nda'ku kosog-kawasaku supaya patanyag ōnku ni manusiya' kamemon ma sakalibutan dunya.* I must display my power so that my fame is known to people all around the world. **1.2)** *v. tr. -an* To seek repair for a damaged object, or treatment for a sick or injured person. *Arāk pina'nda'an tungkangku ni ka'a, abila'.* I almost showed you my cooking pot, it's broken.

**ndang** *adj. zero* Well-used; old, of things. *Basak karut maka suput ndang.* Worn-out sacks and old bags. *Bang s'mmek baha'u binowa amandi, minsan du aniya' s'mmek ndang, arakag.* If new clothes are used for swimming even though there are old clothes, that's indulgent. (*cf:* **baha'u 1, to'a 1.1**; *Thesaurus:* **bahal, longa'**)

**nde'** *v. ditr.* To return or deliver something to its intended destination. *Nde'in payung itū pehē' ni si Lo.* Take the umbrella back to Lo. *Bay pang'nde' kinakan insini' gi'.* It was earlier today that I delivered the food. *Angkan na ai-ai ni'nde'an itū, mbal na tabīng ni kita.* Therefore whatever is returned now to where it belongs will not be returned to us. *Yuknu, "Nde'in sadja anakku ni tonga'an." Yukku, "Aho'." Na ta'abut na tonga'an ī', amole' na aku pabīng. Sigām palanjal na.* You said, "Just deliver my child to the halfway point." I said, "Yes." So when [we] reached halfway, I came back home again. They went on their way. *Nde'anku daing apa halam bay makausaha.* I will deliver this fish [to them] because they haven't been out fishing. (*Thesaurus:* **maksud 1.2, papole', pasampay, tukbal₁ 1, tūd₂, tulun₂ 1.1, tuyuk-tuyuk**)

**ndiya** (*var.* **diya**) *v. tr. zero* 'Give me [that]'; a command to someone to give or hand something to the person who is asking. *Ndiya taumpa' ilū.* Give me those shoes. *Diya na sīn, Otō'.* Hand me the money, Son. (*cf:* **sōng₂ 1.1**)

**nduk** *v. tr.* To draw water from a source. (*Thesaurus:* **sagob 1.1, sauk 1.1, tambu' 1.1**)

**ndū'** *intrj.* An expression of sympathy, affection or entreaty. *Ndū', tugutin aku makauntas min sowang bo' ta'nda'ku lahat ahāp tana'na inān.* Please, let me cross the stream so I can see that land with its good soil. (*Thesaurus:* **andu'-andu', ase'**)

**ndū' kailū** *intrj.* An exclamation of pity or concern. {idiom}

**nē** *intrj.* An expression of scorn or derision.

**neneng** *n.* A species of shrub, used medicinally.

**neneng-neneng** *voc. n.* An affectionate term of address to a woman; sweetheart. (*Thesaurus:* **arung, dayang, nne', nneng 1, nnong**)

**neskape** *n.* Instant coffee. (*Thesaurus:* **kahawa, kape, tī, tī**)

**ni₁** *prep.* To; towards; into; in; until (indicating destination or end goal). *Palanjal ka ni t'ngnga'.* Proceed to the middle [of the house]. *Isihun ni bulsanu.* Put it into your pocket. *Min subu-subu ni kakohapan.* From early morning until afternoon. *Anakat-nakat ni ugtu bulan.* The moon is rising to its zenith. *Anakat-nakat ni ugtu bulan.* (*cf:* **makani-**; *Thesaurus:* **ma 1, min 1, tudju₁ 1**)

**ni₂** *ptl.* **1)** Actor marker, used to mark the demoted actor of a passive construction. *Aniya' a'a bay nilembo ni saitan tahik.* Someone was drowned by a sea demon. *Taloson kita ni s'llog alandos bang kita mbal abanog.* We get swept away by strong currents when we are not under sail. (*syn:* **he' 1**) **1.1)** Agent marker, used to mark the agent by which a state or situation is brought about. *Minsan du maglinggayu' na ni karu', mbal na pa'in atuli.* Even though he moves restlessly due to drowsiness, he continues to be sleepless.

**niangay** *var. of* **angay**

**niawa** *var. of* **nyawa**

**nibung** *n.* A cluster of houses, typically separated from others by an access channel. *Nibung, sali' kalibugan atawa kaluma'an.* A *nibung*, like a house-cluster or a village. (*Thesaurus:* **kaluma'an, kampung₂, le'od₁, libug, lūng 1, tumpuk 2**)

**niki'-niki'** (*var.* **niknik**) *n.* A tiny object or insect.

**niknik** *var. of* **niki'-niki'**

**nīggang** (*var.* **ni'ggang**) (*derivative of* **ggang**) *n.* Cassava meal in cake form. (*gen:* **apam 1**).

**ni'ggang** *var. of* **nīggang**

**nilastung** *n.* Superficial infection and whitening of the skin around the nails (paronychia); abnormal whitening of the hair. *Minsan iya abata' gi', aheka nilastungna. Niuban na iya, subul lagi'.* Even though he is still young, he has many white patches. He became bald while still a youth. (*Thesaurus:* **āp-āp 1, kamuti', limuti', panaw 1**)

**nintil** *adj. a-* **1)** Lightly built or loaded, as a canoe which floats high in the water. *Anintil-nintil pelang, alanggung, alanga pagūnganna. Minsan atā hē' ta'nda'ta na pa'in.* The canoe rides quite high in the water, buoyant, high in the way it floats. Even from a distance we can always see it. (*Thesaurus:* **lampung₁ 1, langgung₂, paglantun**) **2)** Slightly built, of a person's physique. *Anintil pahāp d'nda inān, sali' angayog, sali' ariki' pamarananan.* That woman is quite slender, sort of skinny, of small build.

**nipa'** *n.* The nipa palm, the leaflets of which provide a moderately durable material used for roofing and for hats. *Nipa fruticans. Ya kagunahan nipa' nihinang kadjang. Sani hal atop luma'.* The use of *nipa'* is to make awnings. *Sani* is for house thatch only. *Ahāp sani, asandal min nipa'.* *Sani* is good, more durable than *nipa'*. (*Thesaurus:* **sani, tigul**)

**nipa'-nipa'** *n.* **1)** The Common pike-conger, a species of eel. *Muraenesox bagio.* **2)** The Yellow pike-conger. *Congresox talabon.*

**nipis** *adj. a-* Thin, of flat items such as paper, cloth, or wooden planking. *Anipis atopnu hē'.* That thatch of yours is thin. *Buwat pelang ahāp kayuna, anipnip ma kulit tahik, ariki' pat'ndehanna. Atawa solab bari', anipnip, sali' anipis.* Like a canoe of good timber, it sits lightly on the surface of the sea, its immersion small. Or a knife blade, thin in section, sort of thin. (*ant:* **kapal 1.1**; *Thesaurus:* **g'nting, lampin₁, nipnip, tayang**)

**nipnip** *adj. a-* Narrow in cross-section; slender, of an object. *Buwat pelang ahāp kayuna, anipnip ma kulit tahik, ariki' pat'ndehanna. Atawa solab bari', anipnip.* Like a canoe [made] of good timber, it sits lightly on the surface of the sea, its immersion small. Or a knife blade, thin in section. *A: "Guntingnu ilū, panipnipun na ba." B: "Ā, subay anipnip?"* A: "Those scissors of yours, make them thinner." B: "Oh, should they be thinner?". (*Thesaurus:* **g'nting, lampin₁, nipis, tayang**)

**Nispu** *n.* The eighth month of the Islamic year, the month in which Sulu Muslims remember the dead and tend their graves. (*syn:* **Saban, Taiti'**)

**nitu'** *n.* The climbing fern vine; the scrambling fern. *Lygodium sp.* (*cf:* **eto'-eto'**; *gen:* **bahan 1**)

**niya'₁ 1)** *v. intr. a-* To exist; to be present. *Nsa' aniya' bayan kami.* We have no conveyance. *Aniya' saga a'a magsollet-sollet bay ta'nda'ku ma dilaut.* There were some people wearing loincloths whom I saw out at sea. *Halam aniya' siboyas ma tabu' Hambilan, subay kono' tabu' balik.* There are no onions at the Hambilan market, they say there should be some on the next market day. *Aniya' h'ndaku.* I have a wife [lit. exists my-wife]. *Aniya' kamisitaku pangalgaku ni M'ddas.* I have an undershirt for when I work as a porter in Siasi Town. (*cf:* **itiya'**) **1.1)** *v. intr. pa-* To come into existence; to happen. *Ai sababna angkan paniya' kala'atan?* What is the reason that evil has come into being? *D'nda ya makaniya' ma aku.* It was a woman who made it [happen] to me. **2)** *v. advrs. ka-...-an* To be benefited by gaining something; to be favored with something. *Buwat magbuwan, luma' ina'an kabuwanan, dakayu' inān halam. Na, ya dakayu' he' halam kaniya'an, halam ka'atagan.* Like when giving stuff out, that house there is given some, that other one gets nothing. So the other one referred to is not benefited, is not reached. *Buwat t'llungan magusaha, wa'i alikut dakayu', na halam iya kaniya'an, sali' pinahalam.* Like three people out fishing, and one is absent, then he does not get anything, it's as though he has ceased to exist. *Kaniya'an aku anak e' h'ndaku tape'.* My minor wife has favored me with a child. *Kaniya'an aku panghati sabab pandu'annu aku.* I have gained wisdom because you taught me.

**kaniya'** *n.* Possessions or property, implying more than average. (*Thesaurus:* **alta' 1, karaya 1, pagsauragal 1.1**)

**paniya'** *v. tr.* To cause something to exist or be present. (*Thesaurus:* **papanjari, ummat 1.1**)

**niya'₂** *v. advrs. ka-...-an* To be liable to a fine for an offense against physical contact between sexes. *Kaniya'an aku he' d'nda.* I am liable to a fine because of a woman. *Kaniya'an ko' ka'a ilu, ataksil.* You are to be fined, you are liable. (*Thesaurus:* **multa 1, taksil 1**)

**niyat** *n.* **1)** A fixed state of mind; a firm intention. *In niyat subay tatampan.* A definite commitment should be protected. *Mura-murahan magpakasampay in niyat kami ni ka'am, paheyabi du isāb ma atay.* May it be that our commitment to you will be fulfilled, you too treating it as important. *Ma'ase' iya ma sigām ati halam nilanjalan niyatna angamulka'an sigām.* He was merciful towards them did not carry out his intention of destroying them. (*Thesaurus:* **angut, tamsil**) **1.1)** *v. tr.* To regard something as being real; to be firmly committed to. *Niniyat anak bilibili inān sali' anakna mussa'.* He regarded that lamb as his favorite child. *Pikilin to'ongan, sali' niyatun.* Think seriously about it, set your mind on it. **1.2)** *v. advrs. ka-...-an* To be committed to doing something. *Kaniyatan buwat si Ko. Ai-ai panoho'an iya he' saga a'a mareyom Nasuli', ya hē' hinangna.* Committed, like Ko. Whatever the people of Nasuli tell him to do, that's what he does.

**pagniyat** *v. intr. aN-* To be sure about something. *Mbal na kami magniyat in kami allum pabīng.* We were not certain that we would live again. *Bilahi to'ongan magniyat ma ka'a, sali' amatay ma ka'a.* Wanting very much to be committed to you, like dying for you. *Angkan aku bay magniyat magtukbal lalabotan itū.* That's why I decided to present these offerings.

**niyug** *n.* The coconut palm and its fruit. *Cocos nucifera. Niyug maka kayu, mbal daginis.* A coconut palm and a tree are not the same kind of thing. (*syn:* **saloka'**; *pt:* **bagaybay, bōt₁ 1, bunut 1, etang-etang, giyagay, labit, lahing 1, langkan-langkan, langkay 1, lokay₁, lurang, paipa'₂, pangtusan, peya', tabul₂**)

**Niyusilan** *n.* New Zealand.

**nna'** *v. tr.* To store something; to put something away. *Lungkarun deyom ba'ul ē', kalu ilu masi bay nīnna'nu-i.* Open up the inside of that box, perhaps what you put away is still there. *Subay kilu-kiluhan nīnna'.* It should be stored with great care. *Nna'un to'ongan ma deyom ataynu.* Remember it well [lit. store it securely in your liver]. (*Thesaurus:* **kuli-kuli 1.1, tau' 1**)

**pang'nna'an** *n.* A storage place. (*cf:* **pagtau'an**)

**nne** *n.* A species of small centipede. (*Thesaurus:* **lalipan, liyabod**)

**nnek** *n.* A species of fish.

**nned** *v. intr. aN-* To stretch one's body on waking. (*Thesaurus:* **h'nnat 1, l'dduk 1, pagkul'ddeng, paghitad, pagle'od**)

**nne'** *voc. n.* An address term to a young woman or girl. (*Thesaurus:* **arung, dayang, neneng-neneng, nneng 1, nnong**)

**nneng** *voc. n.* 1) An address term to eldest sister or daughter. (*Thesaurus:* **arung, dayang, neneng-neneng, nne', nnong**) 2) An affectionate address term by a man to his wife.

**nnom** *num.* Six. *Ka'nnom puhu' atuhun pareyo'.* The six people diving into the depths.

**nnompū'** *num.* Sixty.

**nnong** *voc. n.* An affectionate address term to a woman or girl. (*Thesaurus:* **arung, dayang, neneng-neneng, nne', nneng 1**)

**nnu** var. of **l'nnu**

**nōtbūk** *n.* A notebook; a workbook. (*Thesaurus:* **būk₂**)

**nsa'** *neg.* 1) None; there is none (existential clause negator). (*syn:* **da'a 2, halam₁ 1**) 1.1) 'Not', of a realised assertion or action (realis clause negator). *Nsa' kami bay makalanjal.* We made no progress. (*cf:* **mbal 1.1**; *syn:* **halam₁ 1.1**)
 **nsa'-bidda'** *adj. zero* No difference; without distinction; indiscriminately. *Aniya' maghimumūngan ala'at, aniya' magtuna' nsa'-bidda'.* There are some saying bad things, and some making random accusations. (*syn:* **m'ssa' bidda'**)

**nsa' aniya'** *v. intr. zero* There are none. *"Na nsa' aniya'," yukku, "minsan saga pamayad panggi'."* "There is simply nothing," I said, "even to pay for cassava."

**nsa' lagi'** *neg.* Not yet. *A: "En, bay na kasapuhannu lantay?" B: "Nsa' lagi'."* A: "En, have you swept the floor?" B: "Not yet." *Budjang inān nsa' gi' taga tunang.* That girl doesn't have a suitor yet.

**ns'llan** (var. **ins'llan**) *n.* 1) Oil; liquefied fat. *Am'lli kam pehē' ns'llan pangisihan kulaet bo' asawa luma'tam.* Go over there to buy oil for filling the pressure lantern so our house will be lit up. 1.1) *v. intr. aN-* To turn into oil, as the wax of a melting candle. 1.2) *v. tr. -an* To lubricate by applying oil. *Subay ns'llanannu bo' ahāp legotna.* You should lubricate it so it turns well.

**ns'llan gās** *n. phrase* Kerosene. (*Thesaurus:* **gās₂, gasulīn**)

**ns'llan pahamut** *n. phrase* Perfumed oil.

**nso'** *adj. a-* Flowing or rising to high water, of tide. (*Thesaurus:* **daka', lalom₁ 2, l'kkab, sosob, tambang₁ 1**)

**ntan₁** 1) *v. tr. -an* To touch or hold something. *Da'a ntanin kaldero itū, mbal ta'ntanan apa apasu'.* Don't touch this pot, it can't be touched because it is hot. *Tanganku ya pang'ntanku kayu itū.* My hand is what I hold this wood with. *Ntananku lai' itu. Ka'a ya ang'ntanan ilu-i.* I am holding this plate. You're the one holding that one. (*Thesaurus:* **balut 1.2, komkom, kopkop 1**) 2) *v.*
*tr.* To form a courting relationship with a girl. *Mbal ta'ntanku budjang inān apa taga tunang.* I can't court that girl because she has a sweetheart already.

**pang'ntan** *n.* Hand tools; implements.

**pang'ntanan₁** *n.* Sphere of control or protection. (*Thesaurus:* **komkoman 2, deyoman 2, milikan, okoman**)

**tag'ntanan** *n.* A person in charge of an event; a master of ceremonies.

**ntan₂** *n.* 1) A ritual ancestor. *Mbal manjari tinimanan ntan kami.* It is not proper for us discard our ancestors. *Sinemet kita, sali' aniya' makataluwa' kita min ntanta.* We are harmed, as though something from our ritual ancestors is affecting us. (*Thesaurus:* **mbo'₁, palmula'an, pangkat₂**) 1.1) *v. tr.* To maintain and care for one's ritual ancestors. 2) Customary lifestyle, especially as handed down from one's forebears. *Ya ntan kami magbubu.* Our customary livelihood is catching fish in *bubu* traps. *Wa'i bay pinalessad min ntanna.* He has been deposed from his occupation. (*Thesaurus:* **pakas-pakas 1, pali-pali, pangkatan, purukan, tubus₂ 1, tuttulan, tuttulan, usulan, usulan**)

**pang'ntanan₂** *n.* Ritual ancestors in general.

**nt'llo** *n.* 1) An egg (of a bird). (*cf:* **iklug**) 1.1) *v. intr. aN-* To lay an egg.

**ntut** *v. intr. aN-* To pass or break wind. *Amulag-mulag bau ntut itū ni kamemon a'a.* The smell of this fart spreads to everybody. (*cf:* **pagboro-boro**)

**Nū** var. of **Nabi Nū**

**=nu** *pron.* You; your (second person singular) [Set II]. *Pahāpun e'nu agistadi.* Improve the way you study. *Angay matanu?* What's the trouble with your eye? (*cf:* **kā, ka'a;** *Set:* **=bi, =ku, =na, =sigā, =sigām, =ta 1, =tabi, =tam**)

**nubu-nubu** *v. intr. a-* To gush out from the mouth, as cigarette smoke or water from a drowned man.

**nunang** *n.* A species of tree, the sticky sap of which is used as glue. *Nunang, ya pamikit taguri'.* Nunang, the one used for gluing kites.

**nunuk** *n.* The strangler fig or banyan tree (balete). *Ficus benjamina. Nunuk, ya kayu taga saitan.* The balete, the tree that has *saitan* spirits.

**nusa** *n.* An island with no hills; an atoll. *Angā' kita badji'-gandang min kanusahan.* We get *badji'-gandang* timber from the outer islands. (*cf:* **pū'₁**)

**nyala-nyala** *adj. zero* Distinctive, of a sound or voice. *Anyala-nyala suwalana.* Her voice is clearly recognizable. (*Thesaurus:* **hangpat 1, hapal 2, hurup 1.1, ladju, lagsing, tanog₁**)

**nyata'** (var. **nata'**) *v. intr. pa-/aN-* 1) To appear in visible form. *Mbal panata' ni kita bang kita mareyom asayu. Subay mareyom uppi.* It won't appear to us when we are in a state of consciousness. It must be in a dream state. *Pauppi ni kita, sali' anganyata'.* Appearing to us in a dream, like manifesting itself. **1.1)** *v. tr.* To see something with one's own eyes; to witness something. *Nyata'un kono' saki si La.* Please see La's sickness for yourself. *Sūng ka kono'. Nyata'ta ya tampat bay sinuli-suli ma buli' Laminusa.* Just go. We will see with our own eyes the shrine that is said to be on the back side of Laminusa Island. *Si Imam Ma bay anata' bang magtiman.* Imam Ma was the witness when couples divorced. *Aniya' kono' taluwa' bakat, yukta "Ōy, mbal aku magbilīb. Subay aku anganyata' pehē'."* When someone is alleged to have been wounded we say, "Hey, I don't believe that. I have to go there and see for myself." (*Thesaurus:* **lu'aw 1, lundug 1.1**)

**pagnyata'** *v. intr.* aN- To become visible, of a spirit being. *Agtūy dī magnata' baranna.* His own person promptly appears.

**manyatakan** *adj. zero* Clearly visible, with connotations of certainty.

**panyata'**₁ *v. tr.* To disclose or make visible something not normally seen.

**nyawa** (var. **niawa**) *n.* The non-material component of a living creature; the life-principle or soul. *Ai mbal amatay ma baranta? Dakayu'-kayu' nyawa mbal amatay.* What is it that does not die in our body? The *nyawa* is the one and only thing that does not die. *Bang kita amatay malimaya nyawata, sali' mal'ngngan mareyom dunya itū.* When we die our nyawa is unrestricted, sort of walking about in this world. *Asāl ta'ssaku ma bulan inān, sinasat aku maka pinaka'at e' mananasat in nyawaku.* That month I did in fact experience being tempted and having my spirit damaged by the tempter. (*Thesaurus:* **ginhawa, panalengog, sumangat 1, umagad 1**)

**nyawa-lihan** *n.* The non-material component of the human personality, capable of detaching itself from the body. *Atuli ka, anguppi ka, na ya ilu nyawa-lihan ya anguppi ī'.* Sleeping or dreaming, that's the *nyawa-lihan*, the one that dreams. *Bang aniya' bay amatay, yamboho' ma hinang mpatpū' maka mpat llaw at'kka nyawa-lihanta ni Tuhan.* When someone dies, it is not until the 44th day of the funeral ceremonies that our soul gets to God.

**palnyawahan** (var. **panyawahan**) *n.* The physical location of a person's life-principle.

**nyuli'** *n.* A species of parrot, brilliantly plumaged. (*gen:* **agap**₁)

# Ng ng

**ngā'** var. of **ā'**

**-ngan** *aff.* Numeral classifier suffix used when enumerating people. *Dakayu'-dakayu' kolol ma dangan onde', pinagtabul-tabul.* A single pack of crayons for each child, all treated equally. *Magbembet sigā duwangan.* The two of them are carrying [something] together.

**ngau-** *see section 2.2.2.4 Prefix:* **Cau-**

**ngkon-ngkon** *n.* A limited number or quantity of something. *Ya tu'ud ngkon-ngkonna.* That is quite simply how much there is. (*Thesaurus:* **sabasag**)

**ngehat** *n.* A species of coastal shrub, valued as a remedy for fatigue and as a source of hard wood and caulking fiber. *Pemphis acidula.* (*cf:* **g'llom**)

**ngelo'** *n.* The hard palate (roof of mouth).

**ngga'i ka** *neg.* 'Not so', of an assertion or assumption, offering or implying an alternative proposition. *Bang ma aku ngga'i ka dī bulawan.* In my opinion it is not real gold. *Ngga'i ka ka'a ya bay soho'ku.* It's not you I told to go. (*Thesaurus:* **ai po'on, ballum, duma'in, mbal 1.1, m'ssa'**)

**nggek** *n.* A species of fish.

**ngget** *n.* A species of octopus. (*Thesaurus:* **kaloka', kuhita' 1**)

**nggo'** (var. **gō'**) *n.* **1)** Mother. *Minsan magtiman matto'ana masi iya nianggi he' nggo'na. Nianggi,* *pinabilahi pehē'.* Even though his parents are divorced he is still loved by his mother. Loved, persuaded to go there. (*syn:* **ina', sa'i**) **2)** Grandmother.

**nggo'an-bagid** *n.* A matchbox.

**nggo'an-tangan** *n.* The thumb. (*syn:* **bokol 1**; *wh:* **tangan 1**)

**nggo'an-tape'** *n.* The big toe or hallux. (*wh:* **tape'**₁)

**nggo'-nggo'** var. of **bāt-nggo'-nggo'**

**nggo'an-baki'** *n.* The catfish eel. (*syn:* **ina'-baki'**; *gen:* **taote'**)

**ngibu** *n.* Thousand as a unit of counting. *Duwangibu pilak.* Two thousand pesos.

**ngī'-ngī'** *see:* **pagkangī'-ngī'**

**ngngik** (var. **k'ngngik**) *v. intr.* aN- To emit a squeak, as a bat or mouse. *Ai mang'ngngik ē'?* What's that squeaking?

**ngngok** *n.* The Smooth flute-mouth, a fish species. *Fistularia sp.* (*cf:* **sikuhan**)

**ngngong** *v. intr.* aN- To make the noise of a cow or bull; to moo. (*syn:* **ilud-ilud**)

**pagin'ngngong** *v. intr.* aN- To make the sound of a cow or bull; to moo.

**ngula'** var. of **mula'**

# O o

**obang** *n.* The shavings from cutting or shaping wood. *Bang sinosokan kayu aheka obangna.* When wood is shaped with an adze there are lots of shavings. *Momok kayu, sali' obangna.* Particles of wood, its *obang.* (*cf:* **momok**)

**obe'** *n.* **1)** An oral ulcer. (*cf:* **ugam 1**) **1.1)** *v. advrs.* *-in-* Affected with oral ulcers, especially at the corners of the mouth. *Niobe' e' katumbang apa asidda anaba'.* Given ulcers by [eating] *katumbang* fish because it is so very tasty.

**obon** *n.* The Greasy grouper, a fish species. *Epinephelus tauvina.* (*gen:* **kuhapo'**)

**obon-deyom-halo** *n.* The Giant grouper or the Queensland grouper. *Epinephelus lanceolatus.*

**ōk** *v. tr.* **1)** To penetrate through a surface to the contents, of the blade of a weapon or the heat of a fire. *Bang ka lagutku bo' ka bakatan, na niōk ka e' lahut. Bang ka ganta' mbal niōk taga ilmu' ka.* If I slash you and you are wounded, then you are cut into with the knife. If perhaps you are not cut then you have magical protection. *Helmet itū mbal niōk e' punglu'. Bang tinimbak pasalisig punglu'.* A helmet isn't penetrated by a bullet. When someone fires at it the bullet glances off. *Asa'un laringnu ilū bo' angōk.* Sharpen that knife of yours so it will cut. *Bang kita bay na magbono' bo' ka mbal angatu ma aku, lagutta maka lahut. Angalaha' na, na ya hē' niōnan niōk.* If were fighting each other and you couldn't defend yourself against me, I would slash you with a big knife. Blood would flow, and that's called being cut into. (*Thesaurus:* **katama, duklat 1, utab**) **2)** To get through to one's understanding. *Atali' si Anu min aku. Mbal makaōk bissalana ma pikilanku.* What's-his-name is more quick-witted than I am. What he says does not penetrate my thinking.

**okat₁ 1)** *n.* The leaves of green tobacco formed into small bundles. **2)** *clf.* Count word for bundles of leaf tobacco.

**okat₂** *adj. a-* **1)** Separated, of things normally together. (*Thesaurus:* **boklang 1, bugtu'₁, butas 1, l'kkat₂ 1, logtas**) **1.1)** *v. intr. pa-* To separate from a main part. **1.2)** *v. tr.* To separate items normally or naturally together. *Aniya' ta'nda'ku batu bay niokat min būd.* I saw a stone that had been separated from the mountain.

**pagokat** *v. intr. aN-* To part from each other. *Buwat saga kita magbagay magokat. Ka'a tudju ni ospital, aku ni tabu'.* Like us who are friends going separate ways, you towards the hospital, I towards the market. *Magokat na, mag'bba na.* Parting, taking leave of each other. (*Thesaurus:*

**pagbutas 1.1**)

**oklak** var. of **oplak**

**oko'-oko'** *n.* Sea urchins boiled with rice inside. *Angā' aku tehe'-tehe' ni Siyambing hinangku oko'-oko'.* I will get sea urchins from Siyambing and cook some with rice in them. (*Thesaurus:* **boto'-goyak 2, indangan₂, s'llang₂, tayum, tehe'-tehe'**)

**okol** *n.* A cob of corn maize stripped of its kernels. (*Thesaurus:* **bole, botod, la'al, tangkay 1, tongol**)

**okom** *v. intr. pa-* **1)** To live in someone's house and benefit from its security. *Si Je sampay si Ka paokom ma ina'na.* Je and Ka are staying in her mother's house. **1.1)** *v. tr. -an* To include someone in one's household, taking responsibility for their well-being.

**okoman** *n.* The sphere of someone's protective responsibility. *Angkanna bilahi na aku magh'nda'an dīku ati ala'an na aku min okoman sigām.* That's why I want to have my own wife and then I will leave their sphere of influence. (*Thesaurus:* **komkoman 2, deyoman 2, milikan, pang'ntanan₁**)

**pagokom** *v. intr. aN-* To stay in each other's houses. *Magokom sali' magdanakan.* Staying in each other's houses like siblings. *At'ggol na tahun halam makapagokom sigām magdanakan.* It's many years now that the siblings have not lived in the same house.

**okos** *v. intr. aN-* To wrap around the circumference of a solid item. *Saddī lekos, saddī okos. Angokos bang ma sowa.* Lekos and okos are different. Okos [wrap around] is what a snake does.

**okoy** *n.* A fried dumpling or fritter containing bits of fruit or root vegetable. (*gen:* **apam 1**)

**ogok-ogok** *v. intr. aN-* To bubble, of a boiling liquid. (*Thesaurus:* **bukal, buwal₁, laga'₁ 1.1, lere'**)

**pagogok-ogok** *v. intr. aN-* **1)** To boil steadily. **1.1)** *v. tr.* To allow a liquid to boil. *Da'a gi'. Subay pinagogok-ogok lagi'.* Not yet. It should be allowed to boil a bit more.

**ogos** *n.* Generic term for various parrotfish.

**ogos-batahan** *n.* The Blue-barred orange parrotfish. *Scarus ghobban.*

**ogos-bukay** *n.* The Black-veined red parrotfish. *Scarus rubirviolaceous.*

**ogos-gaddung** *n.* **1)** The Bloch's parrotfish. *Scarus croicensis.* **2)** The Quoy's parrotfish. *Scarus quoyi.*

**ogos-lakit** *n.* **1)** The Globe-headed parrotfish. *Scarus globiceps.* **2)** The Six-bar wrasse. *Thalassoma hardwickii.*

**ohō** *intrj.* An expression of mild concern or surprise at some news.

**o'ō** *intrj.* A call to see what is being pointed out. *O'ō ba inān.* Look, over there! *O'ō, itiya' duwangan anakku budjang.* Look, here are my two teenage daughters.

**olang** *v. intr. aN-* **1)** To shout; to cry aloud. *Da'a ka angolang.* Don't shout. **1.1)** *v. tr. -an* To attract someone's attention by shouting; to show anger towards someone by shouting. *Bay kami niolangan e' mastal.* The schoolmaster roared at us. (*Thesaurus:* **asang₂, kula'ak, galit, gasud, pagalud, pahit**)

   **pagolang** *n.* **1)** Loud crying. **1.1)** *v. intr. aN-* To cry or shout loudly. *Magolang iya apa kap'ddi'an.* He is crying loudly because he is in pain. *Bang kita ma dilaut bo' magolang atawa maglata, sinila'-sila', pinaka'at kita, suma'an makanibaran suma'an makanipahinggaman.* When we are at sea and shout or joke, we get harmed [by a *saitan* spirit], damaged, sometimes to our persons, sometimes to our vessel.

**olangan** *n.* **1)** The space between two points. (*Thesaurus:* **llot, t'ngnga'**) **1.1)** The open water between islands. *Ma olangan pa'in kami, magtūy abuhaw.* When we were out in the middle [of the channel] we filled with water.

**olen** (*var.* **holen**) *n.* A marble (the hard ball used in children's games). *Bang bantunganku holen tudju ni bangkaw, aladji'.* When I throw a marble towards the mangroves it carries a long way.

   **pagolen** *v. intr. aN-* To play the game of marbles.

**olgan 1)** *n.* A musical instrument with a keyboard. *Ala'at h'llingna olgan. Ag'mmol, mbal alagting.* The sound of an organ is unpleasant. It is muffled, not clear. **2)** *v. intr. aN-* To play a keyboard instrument. *Yuk a'a angolgan ni d'nda angigal, "Pakowel-kowelun tangannu ilū, Dayang."* The keyboard player says to the girl who is dancing, "Get your hands moving rhythmically, honey."

**ōm** *v. tr. -an* To sit on eggs in order to incubate them. (*syn:* **llom**)

**omang** *n.* **1)** Various hermit crabs, useful for baiting small hooks. *Nilarukan tonda' niumpanan omang bay tettekku.* The line was thrown out, baited with the hermit crab I had cracked open. (*gen:* **kagang**) **1.1)** *v. tr. -an* To bait a hook. *Bang aniya' bay lambi'-lambi', saga dollen ina'an, pangomangku p'ssi.* If there had been cerith snails or those small conchs, they would have been bait for my hooks.

   **omang-tatus** *n.* A species of hermit crab.

**ombe-ombe** *n.* A species of fish that tolerates being kept alive in saltwater tanks. *Yamboho' ta'nda'ku daing tangki pinab'llihan, ombe-ombe maka kuhapo'-batang.* This is the first time I have seen live fish sold, *ombe-ombe* and rock cod.

**ombo'-ombo'** *v. tr.* To swing a child who is sitting on one's lower legs. (*Thesaurus:* **dundang₁ 1, duyan, pagdanggu'-danggu', pagnanu',**

tadjun)

**ompod** *var.* of **ongpod**

**ōn₁** *n.* **1)** The name of a person or thing. *Ai ōnna ilū.* What is the name of that thing? *Bang aniya' mastal pikihinang ōn, mbal gi' aku ata'u.* If a school-teacher asks for a name to be written, I don't yet know how. *Sai ōnnu?* What is your name? (*Thesaurus:* **danglay 1, isay, saingan**) **1.1)** *v. tr.* To name someone. *Bang aku taga mma' lannang angōn aku papang.* If I had a Chinese father, I would call him *Papang.* **1.2)** *v. tr. -an* To call or identify someone or something by name. *Bang buwattē' sawa bulan, niōnan damlag e' kami.* When the moon is that bright, we call it *damlag.* *Si Ko ya pangōn kami ma iya.* Ko is the name we give him. *Bang kita tatukul anak-tanganta magtūy kita akaōnan agkā'.* When we pound a finger, we immediately say *agka.* (*Thesaurus:* **ganda, taga'-taga'**)

   **pagōn** *v. tr. -an* To give something a name or a title; to mention something by name. *Saga pilang-pilang pinagōnan bingal.* The enclosure of women's graves are referred to as *bingal.* *In iya bay aningkō' angamu' sarakka ma bowa' lawang ya pinagōnan Lawang Alingkat.* He was sitting begging alms in the doorway spoken of as the Beautiful Door. *Angkan du isāb pinagōnan Tuhan sabab ai-ai kasukkalan mareyom dunya itū, lullun aku tatabang e'na.* And that's why he is called God because whatever needs there may be in this world, he will help me with all of them. *Ya undam tumbaga ya pinagōnan Tahik.* The brass basin that was called The Ocean.

**ōn₂** *n.* Reputation; renown. *Pinaheya ōnna.* His reputation is made greater.

**onde'** *n.* **1)** Offspring; a child. (*Thesaurus:* **anak₁ 1, mpu, tubu' 1**) **2)** A fetus in the second phase of gestation, when the pregnancy is perceptible. (*cf:* **iram, laha'₃**)

   **kaonde'-onde'an** *n.* Children, collectively.

   **onde'-baha'u** *n.* Early adulthood; late adolescence. *Saru'un-du'un kauli'an baranna maka palanu', sali' baran onde'-baha'u.* Her body was immediately healed and became smooth, like the body of a teenager. (*Thesaurus:* **bata', hoben, lumbu'-baha'u**)

   **onde'-matto'a** *n.* Young and old collectively. *Bang aniya' kagara'an subay magisun-isun onde'-matto'a.* When there is a planning meeting young and old should discuss things together.

   **onde'-onde'** *n.* A small child; a baby. *Niukab magtūy ambung e' dayang-dayang ati ta'nda' e'na onde'-onde' l'lla ma deyomna anangis.* The royal maiden quickly opened the basket and saw a baby boy inside, crying. (*Thesaurus:* **anak-anak₁, kamanahutan, makannak**)

   **onde'-onde' kabus** *n. phrase* A premature baby. *Bang onde'-onde' kabus, mbal atikkup imbun-imbunanna minsan aheya.* When a baby is premature, its fontanel does not close up completely even when it gets big.

**onse** *v. intr. aN-* **1)** To run. (*syn:* **dagan**₂ **1.1, lahi-lahi 1) 1.1)** *v. tr.* To pursue someone by running. *Bay onseku saga kuntaraku ati bono'ku.* I pursued my opponents and killed them.

**ongka'** *v. intr. aN-* **1)** To play; to play a game. *Bay kami angongka' magdanel maka magembet.* We were playing, running races and playing tag. *Bang kita bay anangkaw sīn bo' pangongka'ta, na bo' kita tara'ug, mbal kita nirūlan e' Tuhan. Gōm pa'in mbal ahāp baranta.* When we have stolen some money and are using it for gambling, and then we get beaten, God won't favor us. Instead our bodies become unwell. **1.1)** *n.* A festivity; an entertainment. *Aniya' ongka' sangom ilū.* There is an entertainment on tonight. (*syn:* **pagdeyag**)
  **pagongka'** *v. intr. aN-* To play or celebrate as a group. *Alami sidda ma M'ddas bang Hailaya, pasal aheka magongka'.* It's very enjoyable in Siasi Town on a holiday because a lot of people are playing games together.
  **pagpangongka'** *v. intr. aN-* To gamble or play games together.
  **pangongka'an** *n.* Things for playing with; toys.
  **pationgka'un** *adj.* Addicted to playing games, especially games that involve gambling.

**ongkop** *var. of* **ongpod**

**ongpod** (*var.* **ompod**; **ongkop**) *see:* **samaongpod, pagsamaongkop**

**opera** *v. tr.* To operate surgically on someone. *Buwat disi Hu magpaopera bo' mbal kapulakan.* Like Hu and others seeking an operation so as not to miscarry.

**opis** (*var.* **upis**) *n.* An office; a government office; a courtroom.

**oplak** (*var.* **oklak**) *adj. a-* **1)** Breaking away or cracking, of the surface of something more or less solid. *Bang akapal to'ongan, aoklak, sali' abila'. Buwat katig bangka'nu, aoklak e' llaw.* If it [the glue] is very thick it will *oklak*, sort of breaking apart. Like the outriggers of your canoe, cracking due to the sun. *Buwat pulaybūd aoplak kuwitna.* Like plywood, its outer layer peeling off. *Saupama ma tana' bang halam aniya' ulan, maumu aoklak. Minsan isāb ma semento, ma bangka', ma taumpa', ma pinta jīp. Ma sabab t'ggolna.* Soil for example, when there has been no rain, often cracks. Even concrete, or canoes, shoes, the paint on a jeepney. Because of its age. (*Thesaurus:* **kanit 1, gagus, lakles, laknit 1**) **1.1)** *v. tr.* To break away the outer layer of something. *Oplakta kuwit batang saging an'ngge.* We peel off the outer skin of a standing banana plant.

**ora** *v. tr. -an* To set a time for some planned event. *Ta'abut pa'in llaw bay pangora i', na ananggu simuddai.* When the agreed-on date arrived, [he] postponed it to the day after tomorrow. *Subay niorahan bo' mbal magsabali.* A time should be set to avoid misunderstanding. (*Thesaurus:* **idda 1.1, ligtung, pagtaratu, tugna', tugun 1.1, waktu 1.1**)

**oro'-oro'**₁ *v. intr. aN-* To shiver; to tremble. *Bay aku taluwa' ulan di'ilaw, asidda aku angoro'-oro'.* I was rained on yesterday and I shivered very much. (*Thesaurus:* **ara'-ara' 1, k'ddil-k'ddil, kogkog, korog-korog, pidpid**)

**oro'-oro'**₂ *intrj.* A taunt by children rejoicing in someone else's misfortune.

**ōs** *var. of* **hōs**

**oseg** *adj. a-* **1)** Unstable; unsteady, as something set on an uneven surface or not properly fixed in place. (*Thesaurus:* **hengko, henggol 1, hodjog 1, jogjog 1**) **1.1)** *v. tr.* To make something wobble. *Da'a osegun lām ilū.* Don't shake that wick lamp.
  **pagoseg-oseg** *v. intr. aN-* To be restless; to be unstable. *Da'a kam magoseg-oseg!* Stop your wriggling! *Pahāpun t'nna' lamisahan itū. Magoseg-oseg.* Fix the way this table is standing. It wobbles. (*Thesaurus:* **pagkebed-kebed, paghense, paghibal-hibal, paglinggayu'**)

**osok** *v. intr. a-* **1)** To stand upright in a firm substance, as a post in the ground or dowels in wood. *Angā' kita p'ttung atawa bola' pinaosok supaya panasak luma'.* Let's get some whole bamboo or laths to stick into the ground as a fence for the house. *Subay nihublut babag luma'na ati bo' iya pinaosok maka ginantung mahē'.* A house beam should be pulled out so that he is impaled and suspended there. **1.1)** *v. tr. -an* To insert a pole-like object into firm material.

**osol** *v. intr. pa-* **1)** To stand upright in the soil or sea-floor, of a pole or a post. *Ina'an paosol budjakna ma tana' min kōkanna.* There was his spear driven into the ground by his head. **1.1)** *v. tr. -an* To drive a post or stake into the soil or sea-floor; to provide a house with posts. *Osolin pelang ko da'a atā.* Drive a stake in for that canoe so it doesn't go any distance. *Osolanku luma' kami maka hāg analus.* I will make our house firm with strong corner-posts. *Luma' pamantawan ahogot pangosolanna.* A watch-tower with firm supporting posts.

**ospital** *var. of* **ispital**

**osto** *var. of* **ustu**

**ōt** *n.* A space between similar things. (*cf:* **llot**)
  **pagōt** *v. intr. aN-* To be located between similar things.
  **pagōt-bunga** *v. intr. aN-* To give birth to alternate sons and daughters.

**otas** *adj. a-* Famished. *Lingantu, halam bay makakakan, aotas.* Hungry, hadn't eaten, famished. (*Thesaurus:* **bongtas 1.1, gustang, hanu, lingantu 1.1, punung**)

**oto'** **1)** *n.* The oldest son; the older brother. *Halam ka bay ni'inay e' oto'nu.* Your oldest brother didn't do anything to you. **2)** *voc. n.* An address term for eldest son; a familiar address to any younger male. *Ya pangolangna, "Oto'ku, Oto'ku!"* His cry was, "Oh my son, my son!"

**owak** *n.* A crow; a raven.

    **owak-owak** *v. intr. aN-* To make the noise of a crow; to caw.

**owa'₁** (var. **howa'**; **oya'**) *intrj.* 1) A call to get the attention of a person some distance away, or to let people in a house know someone is approaching. (*Thesaurus:* **dē'** 1.1, **lingan 1, sabbut 1.1, tawag**) 1.1) *v. tr. -an* To hail someone by calling out, especially to someone in a house. *Bay kami niowa'an, pagtandaw itū, halam a'a.* We were hailed, but on looking out the window, no one was there. (*Thesaurus:* **hil, paidda, sagina, sahawi 1**)

**owa'₂** *n.* The milkfish (bangus), the mature female. *Chanos chanos.* (*cf:* **bang'llus**)

**ōy** (var. **hōy**) *intrj.* A call urging caution or attention. *Ōy, bangkero, ameya' aku.* Hey, ferryman, I am coming along. *Hōy, da'a na kam pi'itu. Mbal manjari magtambal.* Hey, don't come here now. It's not time for getting medicine. *Ōy nā! Ahunit ko' ya pangamu'nu ilu.* No way! What you're asking for is very difficult.

**oya'** var. of **owa'₁**

**oyo'-oyo'** *v. tr. -an* To shake something gently so that it trembles. *Buwat kita magtapi' bayanan, yukta, "Oyo'-oyo'in minnilu bo' pag'nda'an ahogot maka mbal ī'."* Like when we are planking a canoe, we say, "Shake it a little right there to see whether it is firm or not."

    **pagoyo'-oyo'** *v. intr. aN-* To sing with unsteady control of one's voice. *Ala'at pahāp suwala a'a maglugu' magoyo'-oyo' suwalana.* The voice of someone singing a *lugu'* chant is so bad when it quavers.

# P p

**pa-₁** *aff.* Intransitive prefix: attaches to verbs whose single argument is actor-like, especially verbs of motion. *Bang kitā mbal pasōd, na pinapatay kitā.* If we don't enter, we will be killed. *Pagka ka'a i lagak, mbal ka amuwan kinakan, pakuppa na ka mannilu!* Since you were being greedy, not giving us any food, why don't you just jump down from there!

**pa-₂** *aff.* Causative prefix. *Ya na d'nda bay pakilāku ma ka'am maka arāk pikilanku kinawinan.* That is the woman I introduced you to and had thought to marry.

**pa-₃** *aff.* Prefix that attaches to a stative verb, indicating a change of state. *Aku i pahāp d'nda, apote' na!* I became a more beautiful woman, [I was] white now! *Anginum iya tahik, paheka'-paheka'.* He drank sea water, more and more.

**pa-₄** *aff.* Directional prefix: attaches to locative nouns to indicate motion in the direction of the noun. *Pareyo'-pariyata', pehē'-pi'itu.* Moving up and moving down, going there and coming here. (*cf:* **pi-**)

**pa-₅** *aff.* Prefix indicating that the subject can be acted upon in the manner described by the verb (usually used with the negative mbal). *Mbal papandu' makannak itū, atuwas kōkna.* This child is unteachable, he is stubborn. *Ōy, ka'am ilū mbal pasoho' maghinang kabontolan.* Come on, you can't be told to do what is right.

**pababag** (derivative of **babag**) *adv.* 1) Crosswise; athwart. 1.1) *v. tr.* To steer a canoe so that it is transverse to the line of wave movement. *Da'a pababagun, abuhaw kita.* Don't go transverse to the direction in which the sea is running, we will ship water.

**pabahakan** (derivative of **bahak**) *n.* A place for lying down or sleeping; a bed. (*Thesaurus:* **kantil₁, palangka'₂, palegehan, patulihan**).

**pabaha'u** (derivative of **baha'u**) *v. tr. -an* To renew something; to restore something to its former state.

**pabā'** (derivative of **bā'₁**) *v. tr. -an* To inform someone of an event that he should attend. *Bay sigām pinabā'an buwat saga luruk, ma halam aniya' agon panayu sigām ma kahālan hē'.* They were invited as though guests, but with hardly any awareness of what was happening there. *Palabay pa'in duwantahun, bay pinaba'an e'na ya kamemon kal'llahan anak sultan supaya angahadil.* When two years had passed he invited all the sultan's male children to attend [the event].

**paba'id** (derivative of **ba'id**) *v. tr. -an* To grant someone permission. *Bay iya pinaba'iran e' nakura'na angkan halam na maina'an.* He had been given leave by his boss, which is why he was no longer there. (*Thesaurus:* **pakuhi, papuhun, parūl 1.1, tugut 2**).

**pabalik** (derivative of **balik₁**) *adv.* Again. *Pelang nihinangan ebol-ebol pamalabayan tahik. Sin'nsong pabalik bang halam na tahik ma deyom mohang.* A drain hole made for the canoe to allow the seawater to go out. The hole is plugged again when there is no longer seawater in the hull.

**pabalīn** (derivative of **balīn**) *v. tr.* To transfer something to another person. *Pinabalīn pelangna ma si Ji.* He allows Ji to use his canoe.

**pabanogan** (derivative of **banog**) *adv.* Sailing under a banog-type sail. *Nihangbosan munda' pelang bang kalandosan baliyu maka goyak,* *minsan kita ma pabanogan.* The prow of the canoe comes down hard when hit by strong wind and waves, even when we are under sail.

**pabantang** (derivative of **bantang**) *adv.* 1) Horizontally. *Ang'nda' kita pabantang ni munda'an.* We look horizontally towards the bow. 1.1) *v. tr.* To hold or extend something horizontally. *Pinabantang e'na tungkudna ni kabohe'-bohe'an.* He held his walking-stick out horizontally towards the waters.

**pabanga'** (derivative of **banga'**₁) *v. tr.* To open one's mouth. *Pabanga'un bowa'nu.* Open your mouth.

**pabatal** (derivative of **batal**) *v. tr.* To nullify the cultural rules prohibiting physical contact between a man and a woman. *Bang aniya' kinawin pinabatal na karuwangan ni imam.* When a couple are being married the two of them are declared unrestricted by a religious leader of the community. *Bang aniya' kinawin subay nilikus d'nda, subay pinabatal l'lla bo' yampa ta'nda' d'nda. Pinabatal isāb d'nda, binowa ni l'lla.* When someone is being married the woman should be kept out of sight, and the man should be ritually released from restrictions before the woman is seen. The woman too is released and brought to the man. *"Dalam isāb ka," yuk imam, "kinawin, mbal gi' pinabatal."* "Even though you are in the process," said the imam, "of being married, you are not released from the contact restrictions." (*Thesaurus:* **kasal 1**, **kawin 1.1**, **paglahi 1.1**, **pasugsug**).

**pabelaw** (derivative of **belaw**) *v. tr.* To tease someone; to annoy. *Hal amabelaw.* Just teasing. *Oto', da'a pabelawun.* Son, don't tease her. (*Thesaurus:* **bellod**₁, **jullit**₂, **juri 1.1**, **lawat**).

**pabeya'** (derivative of **beya'**₂) *v. tr.* To send something. *Angagad ka gi', magpatta' gi' aku bo' aniya' pabeya'ku ni tunangku.* Wait a bit, I'm just getting a photo taken so I have something to send to my girlfriend. *Bay aku ma M'ddas, aniya' pinabeya' ma aku. At'kka pa'in aku ni luma' tinilaw aku bang ma'ai bay pinabeya'. Angahaka aku, "Halam aku bay pinabeya'an." Yuk si Ina' inān, "Malaingkan bay ka pamabeya'an."* I was in Siasi and something was sent with me. When I arrived home I was asked where the thing was that had been sent. I said, "Nothing was sent with me." Mother said, "Nevertheless you were the carrier [of something]."

**pabilahi** (derivative of **bilahi**) *v. tr.* To make someone willing to do something; to persuade. *Minsan magtiman matto'ana, masi nianggi he' nggo'na. Nianggi, pinabilahi pehē'.* Even though his parents are divorced he is still loved by his mother. He is loved, persuaded to want to go there.

**pabiluk** (derivative of **biluk**) *v. tr.* To cause a canoe under sail to change direction. *Pabilukun pelang itū apa alandos baliyu.* Turn the canoe because

the wind is very strong.

**pabing** (derivative of **bing**₂) *adv.* 1) Again. *Tilawun iya pabīng.* Ask him again. *Pasakat na kami ni kappal pabīng.* We are boarding the ship again. 1.1) *v. tr.* To return something to where it was previously. *A: "Ma'ai bola?" B: "Wa'i pinabīng ni bay baina."* A: "Where is the ball?" B: "It's been put back where it was before."

**pabingkis** (derivative of **bingkis**) *v. tr.* To stack flat items of a similar shape. *Pabingkisun abō' tabowa min t'dda, buwat tipay, ambūng.* Stack them so they can be carried in one load, oyster shells for example, or [packages of] sago meal.

**pabiyaksa** (derivative of **biyaksa**) *v. tr.* To familiarize or train someone.

**pabiyal** *v. tr.* To ignore someone, especially when being called. *Bang kita nilinganan, subay kita angasip. Da'a kita amabiyal.* When we are called we should respond. We should not ignore it. *Bang aku angalingan ni luma' bo' aniya' amu'ku, sali' aku pinabiyal he' sigā.* If I call to a house and have a request to make, I am sort of ignored by them. (*cf:* **pagbisu-bisu**)

**pab'lli** (derivative of **b'lli**) *v. ditr.* To offer something for sale; to sell something. *A: "Da'a ka amab'lli ni paltira ina'an-i, akigit." B: "Aho', panday na pa'in."* A: "Don't sell to that trader there, he's stingy." B: "Yes, always clever." (*Thesaurus:* **dagang**, **lilung**, **litu**, **pagsoroy**, **pa'andag 1**, **samsuy**).

**pablek** *v. tr.* To make something public which would be better kept private. *Amablek iya mag'lling.* He speaks publicly. *Sinuli-suli ma kaheka'an a'a, pinablek na ba.* Discussed among crowds of people, made public. (*Thesaurus:* **nasihat**, **pamahalayak**)

**pabontol** (derivative of **bontol**) *adv.* 1) Correctly; moving in a straight line. *Mbal sigām makakabtang pabontol.* They were unable to pronounce the word correctly. *Amusay ka pabontol, Oto'.* Paddle straight, Son. *A'a bay aku'il, kauli'an na; a'a bay pengka', makal'ngngan na pabontol.* People who were disabled were now healed, people who were lame could now walk straight. 1.1) *v. tr.* To set something straight or correct. *Bang saupama magtiman, na magsalassay pahāp-hāp, magpa'amu ni sara', saga pinabontol.* Divorcing for example, settling things well, speaking frankly to the magistrate, getting things done correctly. *Pabontolunbi itikadbi tudju ni Tuhan.* Make right your consciences towards God.

**pabowa'** (derivative of **bowa'**₁) *v. intr. aN-* To raise one's voice. *Amabowa' si Mām, "Halam aniya'! Bay na sa yukku!"* The schoolmistress raises her voice, "There aren't any! I have already said so!"

**pabukag** (derivative of **bukag**) *v. tr. -an* To berate someone loudly. *Bang aku am'ssi bo' ta'abut sangom, pinagpiha na aku. Pinabukagan na aku bang at'kka ni luma'.* When I go fishing and night comes, [they] search for me diligently. I am scolded loudly when I get home. (*Thesaurus:* **dugal 1.1, pah'lling**[2], **pamūng-mūng, pugpug 1, s'ndal 1, tutul**).

**pabukal** (derivative of **bukal**) *v. tr.* To heat a liquid until it bubbles. *Pabukalun lagi'.* Let it boil a bit.

**pabukis** (derivative of **bukis**[2]) *v. tr.* To reveal something previously concealed.

**pabuhat** (derivative of **buhat**[1]) *v. tr.* To increase the weight of something. *Buwat kita maghinang na pa'in, sinō' na pa'in maghinang (bo' ya na pa'in hinang), sali' pinabuhat.* Like when we are working continually and being told continually to work (though that is already being done), like the load made heavier. *Pabuhatun tu'ung ilū, paheka'un isina.* Make that box heavier, increase its contents.

**pabuwa'** *v. tr.* To chop something up into small pieces. *Bang kita an'tta' kayu atawa amabuwa' daing subay aniya' pamaragtolan.* When we chop wood or cut fish in pieces a chopping board is necessary. (*Thesaurus:* **k'llot, gōt-gōt 1, ladjang, padja', tama', t'ttok 1.1**)

**pabūy** *v. tr.* -*an* To allow something to run free, instead of being confined or controlled. *Buwat manuk bay niengkotan. Gōm na pinabūyan bo' mbal apisu'.* Like a hen tied up. Better let it run free so it doesn't damage its leg. *Subay pinabūyan banog, apigtal.* The sail should be let out, its too tight. (*cf:* **l'ppa**)

**pāk** *n.* A sudden sharp sound, as the sound of a rifle shot.

**paka-** *aff.* Aptative gerund prefix: indicates the time or occasion of some event, of which the actor is not completely in control (e.g. circumstance, happenstance, or ability). *A: "Sumiyan kat'kkabi?" B: "Ya paka'nda'nu itū."* A: "When did you arrive?" B: "This very moment of your seeing us." *Buwat sali' kami bay magpanonda'. Pagt'kka kami ni luma', tinilaw e' si Bo bang ma'ai abay. Na yukku, "Ya du bay paka'nda'ku bay ma dilaut."* Like when we had been trolling [for tuna]. On arriving at the house Bo asked where my companion boat was. So I said, "When I last happened to see it, it was out at sea." *Sali'-sali' lima pakatandan.* The arrival of the five [canoes] was the same. *Pakakilahanku ma suwala.* My happening to recognize [him] was his voice.

**pakakilāhan** (derivative of **kilā**) *n.* The means of recognizing someone. *Sali'-sali' lima pakatandan. Pakakilāhanku a'a ma suwala.* The five [canoes] arrived at the same time. I recognized the people by voice.

**pakaiya'** (derivative of **iya'**) *v. tr.* To make someone ashamed or deeply embarrassed. *Ya salla'nu, bay pakaiya'nu mma'nu.* Your flaw is that you shamed your father.

    **pagpakaiya'** *v. intr. aN-* To shame each other for something. *Sali' bang magbono' d'nda sali'-*

*sali', magpakaiya' paglalu.* When two women fight, they shame each other as being promiscuous.

**paka'at** (derivative of **ka'at**) *v. tr.* To destroy or misuse something. *Hal pamaka'at sīn.* Just a waste of money. *A: "Ōy, da'a paka'atun." B: "Nsa' du aniya' pinaka'at."* A: "Hoy, don't wreck it." B: "Nothing's being wrecked."

**paka'llum** (derivative of **llum**) *v. tr.* To keep something alive; to bring something to life or action. *Bang aniya' tohonganku, ipatku, paka'llumku.* If I have a turtle I will look after it, I will keep it alive. *Aku na amaka'llum transistol.* I'll be the one to turn on the transistor radio. *Bang tagna' pinaka'llum kapay ariplano magtumballeng.* When the propellor of an airplane is first started it moves unevenly.

**pakale** (derivative of **kale**) *v. tr.* To have someone listen; to make something known. *Aniya' mohotku ni ka'a bo' mbal pamūngku, aiya' aku. Amakale aku ma si Mi, bo' ya target ē' patudju ni ka'a.* I have some purpose that involves you but I don't speak of it, being ashamed. I let Mi hear about it, but you are the intended target.

**pakalintaw** (derivative of **kalintaw**) *v. tr.* To provoke or anger someone.

**pakamemon** (derivative of **kamemon**) *v. tr.* To use all of something. *Lakayun k'llat inān bo' pat'kkad, pinakamemon.* Let that line run completely out so it reaches bottom, let it all go.

**pakan** *v. tr.* To feed; to give food to someone. *Am'lli gi' aku panyām ni M'ddas pamakanku si Li.* I will just buy a rice cake in Siasi Town to feed Li with. *Bang aku amangan bo' aniya' angalung onde'-onde', ya pamakanku iya l'bbiku.* If I am eating and a child comes hopefully, what I give him to eat is my leftovers. *Pamakanun ma ero' bay kapinnu ilū.* Use whatever you leave for feeding the dog. (*Thesaurus:* **kakan 1, kakan 1, inta', lallan, l'kkob**)

**pakandangan** (derivative of **kandang**) *n.* The grave (fig., lit. the ultimate womb). {idiom} *Pakandangan dīnu.* Your very own grave.

**pakandungan** (derivative of **kandung**[1]) *n.* A place where water collects or ponds. *Aniya' pakandungan bohe' ma tana'.* There is a place on the ground where water has collected.

**pakaniya-kaniya** (derivative of **kaniya-kaniya**) *adv.* Individually; one by one.

**pakang**[1] *n.* One's personal style of doing something. *Bang aku lum'ngngan ma M'ddas bo' sinoho' pabantang, yukku, "Pakangku." Sali' tebongku.* When I am walking through Siasi town and I'm told to look straight ahead, I say, "It's just how I am." My style, so to speak. *Bang ka anulat, ya na pakangnu.* When you write, that is your style. (*Thesaurus:* **baktulan, bowahan, l'ngnganan**[2]**, palantara 1, tebong**)

**pakang**[2] *v. tr.* -*an* To launder cloth by beating with a wooden paddle. *Pinakangan buwattē' abō'* *ala'an sakkulna.* Beat the cloth like that to remove its starch. (*Thesaurus:* **kimu', dakdak 1, pukpuk**)

**pakaradja'an** (derivative of **karadja'an**) *n.* An occurrence or event of significance. *Taga pangita'u isāb iya angama'ana uppi, amahati kahālan pakaradja'an, maka angahusay palkala' ahunit.* He has the ability to interpret dreams, to explain the circumstances of things that happpen, and to sort out difficult issues. *Bang d'nda sinaggaw he' gansuwang, binowa kaleya nihinang pakaladja'an.* When a woman is captured by a *gansuwang* giant she is taken inland and turned into something shocking. (*Thesaurus:* **kahālan**).

**pakas-pakas** *n.* **1)** Traditional practices and beliefs. *Bay pakas-pakas kamatto'ahan, ya sali' ntan sigā.* The ways of the forebears, sort of like their traditions. (*Thesaurus:* **ntan₂ 2, tuttulan, usulan**) **1.1)** *v. tr.* To follow the traditions of one's forebears. *Bay ntan sigā subay pinakas-pakas na pa'in ma tahun itu.* Their traditional ways should be continually followed in this present era.

**pakataw** (derivative of **kataw**) *v. tr.* To disturb the surface of water.

**pakautan** (derivative of **kaut**) *n.* The place out at sea where one intends to fish. *Pasakayunbi na aku bang kām kaut ni pakautanku.* Let me travel with you if you are going seawards to my [intended] fishing spot.

**pakay₁** *v. intr. aN-* To wear something; to use something as clothing. (*Thesaurus:* **guna 1.1, pasang₁, usal**)

**pakayan** *n.* Clothing, especially formal clothing such as a uniform.

**pamakay** *n.* Clothing; whatever is worn. (*Thesaurus:* **s'mmek 1, tamongon**)

**pakay₂** *see:* **pagpakay-dusa**

**pakkiyaw** *v. tr.* To deal with a number of things collectively, as a unit, without considering variations in size or quality. *Bang kita am'lli, na pinakkiyaw anahut a'aslag, minsan ahunit a'aslag, aluhay anahut.* When we are buying we treat small and large alike, even when the large ones cost more and small ones cost less. *Ta'abut pagpah'nda hal magungsud. Halam aniya' sokat-sokatan bowahan bay ka'mbo'-mbo'an. Pinakkiyaw na mahē'.* When the time comes for the betrothal, they simply pay the bride-wealth. There is no individual specification as there was with the forefathers. It is simply handled as a lump sum. (*Thesaurus:* **kuridas, pono' 1.1, sampul-baul, tighan 1.1**)

**pagpakkiyaw** *n.* **1)** A wholesale strategy for buying and selling, in contrast to piece-by-piece bargaining or selling. *Pagpakkiyaw, halam aniya' pagpene', halam aniya' pagitung.* Wholesale, no choosing, no counting. **1.1)** *v. intr. aN-* To engage in wholesale buying and selling.

**pakkom** *adj. zero* **1)** Overturned; upside down. *Bang bay pakkom bangka'ku, na pinaleyak pabīng bo' makatandan ni bihing.* If my dugout canoe had capsized, then it would be righted again to make it to shore. (*ant:* **leyak**; *Thesaurus:* **k'ppang 1, kutung, da'ub**) **1.1)** *v. tr.* To turn something upside down.

**pagpakkom-leyak** *v. intr. aN-* To turn over and over. *Magpakkom-leyak ma patulihanta.* Turning over and over where we sleep. (*cf:* **pagda'ub-daya'**)

**pākete** *n.* A packet of small items enclosed in paper, as cigarets or firecrackers. *Dapākete kulitis, bang ma kasehe'an dampapan. Damikiyan du isāb in siga, dangkaha'.* One packet of firecrackers, for some the word is *papan.* Similarly with cigarets, the word is one *kaha'.* (*Thesaurus:* **kaha₂ 1, kustal 1, papan₂**)

**pakeyat** (derivative of **keyat₂**) *v. tr.* To ignite something; to turn a light on. *Aniya' api bay pinakeyat e' saga sundalu ma halaman luma'.* A fire had been set alight by the soldiers out in the yard. *Sulariyan itū kassa' pinehē'an p'ttung atawa kayuwan ni bowa'na pamakeyatan iya.* The *suwariyan* referred to is a glass [bottle] with bamboo or cane put in its opening for lighting it. (*Thesaurus:* **bagid, dokot₂ 1.2, santik 1, sū' 1.2**).

**pakeyol** (derivative of **keyol**) *v. tr.* To get the hands moving rhythmically. *Yuk a'a angolgan ni d'nda angigal, "Pakowel-kowelun tangannu ilū, Dayang."* The keyboard player says to the girl who is dancing, "Let your hands move rhythmically, honey."

**paki-** *var. of* **miki-**

**paki'** *adj. a-* **1)** Embarrassed; ashamed, due to the inadequacy of one's knowledge or offer. *Buwat aku amah'nda si Oto', yukku ma kar'ndahan, "Ai-ai bowaku salung, saga maligay, bang mbal taima'nu apaki' aku. Ahāp kami pinag'mbal buwattina'an."* Suppose I am arranging a marriage for Eldest Son, and I say to those of the woman's side, "Whatever I bring tomorrow, like ceremonial houses, if you don't accept them I will be embarrassed. Better to turn us down now." *Ang'ntan sigā ntan, bo' ang'ntan saddī. Yuk a'a, "Da'a ka ang'ntan ilu ko da'a kami apaki'."* They observe ritual ancestors, but they are observing different ones. Someone says, "Don't observe those ones lest you be humiliated." (*Thesaurus:* **biyas, iya', maru 1.2, tamparasa**) **1.1)** *v. tr.* To shame someone. *Da'a aku paki'un ma pagalopan.* Do not embarrass me in public.

**pakil** *n.* A leader in a mosque community qualified to lead in religious activities. *Mbal angatu pakil d'nda ma pakil l'lla. L'lla sadja ya taga wajib.* A female *pakil* can't compete with a male *pakil.* It is only men who have the responsibility.

**pagkapakil** *v. intr. aN-* To be qualified for service in mosque leadership.

**pakilā** (derivative of **kilā**) *v. tr.* To introduce; to make someone known. *Ya na d'nda bay pakilāku ma ka'am maka arāk pikilanku kinawinan.* That is the woman I introduced you to and had thought to marry.

**pakis** *n.* A species of fleshy fern, the young tips of which are eaten as a vegetable. *Athyrium esculentum; Certopteris thalictroides.*

**Pakistan** *n.* Pakistan.

**pakitāw** (derivative of **tāw**) *v. tr.* To frighten someone. *Oto', ai bay pamakitāwnu onde' itū?* Son, what did you use to frighten the baby with? *Magbagala a'a ina'an, yukta. Pagsekotta, na ngga'i ka bagala manusiya', saitan ko' hē'. Amakitāw bā.* That's a man appearing as a ghost, we say. On getting close to it, well, it's not a human being, it's a saitan. It sure scares us.

**pak'bbang** (derivative of **k'bbang**) *v. tr.* To spoil something by cutting out a piece of it. *Da'a pak'bbangun bang ka angehet wanni.* When you cut an odorous mango, don't hack it.

**pak'llat** (derivative of **k'llat₁**) *v. tr.* To open one's eyes. *Pak'llatun matanu ilū.* Open your eyes now.

**paklus** var. of **puklas**

**pakokos** *n.* A bladed weapon. *Ilu iya pal'ngngan maka pakokosna.* There he goes with his bladed weapon. (*Thesaurus:* **almas, hinanib 1, pangatu, patakos, takos 1**)

**pakol** *n.* The saddle of a riding animal. *Pakol, ya na paningkō'anta ma kura'.* A saddle, what we sit on when on a horse.

**pakosog** (derivative of **kosog**) *adv.* Vigorously; energetically. *Da'a ka angolang pakosog.* Don't shout so loudly. (*Thesaurus:* **kuwat, kuyas 1, matay₂, paspas₁, puspus₁, sikad 1**).

**pakpak 1)** *v. intr. a-* To fall freely through the air. *Bay magbulang manuk, paleyang na. Taluwa' pa'in he' epo, apakpak pareyo'.* A cock was fighting and flew. When struck by a spur it fell down. *Magtūy tauwa' manggis ariki'-diki' isāb, apakpak na agtūy.* A small mangosteen was also hit, and immediately dropped. (*Thesaurus:* **hūg₁ 1, togge'₁, tukbung 1, tulelle, tumba₁**) **1.1)** *v. tr.* -*an* To cause something to fall through the air. *Bang kām amakpakan bungang-kahuy min kayubi, da'a mininduwahan. Subay aniya' kapinan saga a'a miskin.* When you shake the fruit from your trees, don't do it a second time. Some should be left for poor people. **1.2)** *v. advrs. ka-...-an* To be affected by something falling. *Kapakpakan mataku.* My eyes have something fallen into them. **2)** *v. advrs. ka-...-an* To suffer a miscarriage. *Kapakpakan d'nda hē'.* That woman had a miscarriage. (*Thesaurus:* **bibis, kawa'₂, labu' 1.1, pulak 1.1**)

**paksa'** *n.* **1)** A fortunate event; good luck. *Paksa', sali' lidjiki' at'kka. Paksa',* like a blessing coming to pass. (*Thesaurus:* **bilsut, nahas 1, pawas 1.1, piyurus₂**) **1.1)** *adj.* -*an* Experiencing good

fortune. **1.2)** *v. advrs. ka-...-an* To be affected by some unexpected event. *Kapaksa'an kita ahāp-ala'at.* Something good or bad happens to us, by chance.

**paksiyu** *v. tr.* To cook food by simmering with spices and herbs. (*gen:* **b'lla 1**)

**pakuhi** (derivative of **kuhi₁**) *v. tr.* -*an* To give someone permission; to grant a request. *Ama'id kami ni mastal. "Pakuhi'in aku am'ssi ni lahat dakayu'."* We ask permission of the teacher, "Permit me to go fishing to another place." *Halam sigā pinakuwihan, halam pinatugutan.* They haven't been permitted, haven't been given the freedom. (*Thesaurus:* **paba'id, papuhun, parūl 1.1, tugut 2**).

**pakuwat** (derivative of **kuwat**) *adv.* Doggedly; persistently. *Bang kita ni Sibaud subay kita amusay pakuwat he da'a tabowa he' s'llog.* If we go to Sibaud we have to paddle vigorously to avoid being carried away by the current.

**pād-pād₁** *conj.* Rather than; instead of; in preference to. *Hublutun na kalisnu ilu bo' aku papatayun, pād-pād saga kapil itu angandugsu'an aku maka anganjahulaka'an baranku.* Draw your bladed weapon and kill me, rather than having this heathen stabbing me. *Pād-pād daing itū tinimanan, gōm pineyad.* Rather than this fish be thrown away, better it be dried. *Subay sinungkit na buwa' marang sabab alahag na, pād-pād amakpak.* The *marang* fruit should be harvested now because it is ripe already, rather than letting it drop. (*cf:* **sapād-pād**)

**pād-pād₂** *n.* A species of succulent plant used medicinally for the treatment of headaches and heat prostration. *Kalanchoe pinatum.*

**paddam** *adj. zero* **1)** To remain quiet or unobtrusive. *Sala kita atuli, yukta, "Paddam na ka. Mailu sadja ka."* We're having a sleep, for example, and we say, "Be quiet. Just stay there." **1.1)** *v. tr.* To keep something to oneself rather than spreading it or making an issue of it. *Bay ai-ai himumūngan, bay sala magbono', bay diki'-diki' ati aluha. Yuk dangan, "Paddamunbi."* Various provocative things had been said, there had been a bit of fighting, something small had spread. One person said, "Keep it to yourselves."

**paddik** (derivative of **ddik**) *v. tr.* -*an* To hold something down by stepping on it. *Bay sigām t'ppaku maka paddik-paddikanku sali' na pisak ma lān.* I pounded them and trod them down like mud on the trail. *Tagipit maka tapaddikan iya ma bowa' lawang inān ati amatay.* He was pinned down and trampled there in the doorway, and so died. (*syn:* **ddik**).

**padduman** *n.* A direction-finding compass. (*syn:* **kumpas₂**)

**padjak₁** *n.* A pawnshop. (*Thesaurus:* **l'kkat₁ 1, lōb 1.1, panau'**)

**padjak₂** *v. tr.* To arrange for the purchase of goods

or the use of equipment. *Bay aku amadjak lansa t'llumpū' pilak pameya'anku pehē'.* I contracted a launch for thirty pesos to take me there. (*cf:* **kuridas**)

**padja'** *v. tr.* To chop something into pieces. *Padja'-padja'ku du kām!* I will surely cut you to pieces! (*Thesaurus:* **k'llot, gōt-gōt 1, ladjang, pabuwa', tama', t'ttok 1.1**)

**pagpadja'-padja'** *v. tr.* To chop something finely. *Pinagpadja'-padja'.* Chopped up into fragments.

**padjang** *n.* A species of broad-leaf plant similar to taro, but not edible. *Ya lituk ilū panuhug e' sigā, anu ilū, daun padjang.* Those fine sticks they use for stitching together those whatsits, those *padjang* leaves. *Ya lituk ilū panuhug e' sigā daun padjang.* Those fine sticks they use for stitching together *padjang* leaves.

**padjihun** *n.* A species of shrub, used medicinally.

**padjuhan** *n.* A large company of people; a military unit. *Buwat aniya' magsampang President, aniya' dapadjuhan min Laminusa, dapadjuhan minnitu.* Like when the President is being met, there is one large group from Laminusa, one group from here. *Dapadjuhan sundalu, dapanjihan.* One company of soldiers, one flag-group. (*Thesaurus:* **kaheka-heka'an, kompolan, dansehe'an, palti, umpigan**)

**padlak** *see:* **atay₂**

**padpad** *adj.* a- Dissipated, of emotions such as longing, desire, love. *Apadpad entomna ma aku.* He no longer remembers me with longing. *Apadpad lasata, linduta, entomta, sali' pahalam.* Our love, our longing, our memory all dissipate, all sort of become nothing. (*Thesaurus:* **baluba 1, gagas, lulu, papas₁ 1**)

**paebog** (derivative of **ebog**) *v. tr.* To stir a desire; to attract someone. *Amaebog-maebog. Sali' kita agbeya' maka matto'ata am'lli ai-ai ni M'ddas, bo' aniya' bay tō'ta hē', bo' mbal bīlli he' matto'ata, pinaebog he' tag-dapu tinda hē', supaya tab'lli.* Making us want something. Like going with our parents to buy this and that in Siasi, and there is something we point to but our parents won't buy it, the shop owner makes [us] want it, so it will be purchased.

**paenok** *v. tr.* -an To persuade someone by using flattery.

**pāg** *adj.* a- Dispersed, of people previously grouped together. *Bay kami magsilapug paragan. Sali' apāg, ap'kkal bay aheka.* We became scattered as we ran. Sort of dispersed, what had been many becomes disconnected. (*Thesaurus:* **kanat 1, pulak-palik 1, sihag₂ 1**)

**pagpāgan** *v. intr.* aN- To evacuate in diverse directions. *Buwat Siganggang aro'ag, agpāgan kaluma'anna.* Like Siganggang being evacuated, its communities widely dispersed.

**pag-₁** *aff.* Conveyance voice prefix: attaches to transitive verbs, identifying as subject of the clause either an instrument, or something being transferred (whether a physical object or a piece of information). *Halam aniya' sīnku. Halam aniya' pagispital.* I had no money. There was nothing to pay for the hospital. *Wa'i katamnu paghinang masjid ma Sisangat.* Your plane is off being used to build the mosque at Sisangat. (*cf:* **paN-₁**)

**pag-₂** *aff.* Distributive aspect prefix: attaches to a verb, indicating multiple occurrences of the action described (e.g. action that is frequent, habitual, repeated, performed by multiple actors, or in multiple locations). *Pinagsoho' iya angahinang tupara he' saga bangsa kami Kasamahan.* He was often told to make goggles by our fellow Sama. (*cf:* **paN-₂**)

**pag-₃** *aff.* Gerund prefix: indicates the occasion or duration of an action. *Pagmahē' ma Tiyanggi, maka'nda' kami sini.* While there in Jolo we saw a movie. *Bang kita makatuli' deyo' taga daing, al'kkas maka'ā'. Paghūg, pagsintak, paghella'.* When we find a spot with plenty of fish we soon catch them. Down the line goes, the fish bite and up we pull them. *Pagpuwas i'-i, tīddo'an pa'in kami, aniya' aninduk.* After that, while we were becalmed, something took our bait. *Da'a kam asagaw, waktu pag'ddok atuli.* Don't make a noise, it's the time for sleeping soundly. (*cf:* **paN-₃**)

**pag-..-an** (var. **pal-..-an₂**) *aff.* Nominalizing circumfix indicating the topic of some verbal interaction (e.g. discussion or argument). *Daka ai pagsuli-sulihan sigām.* Goodness know what they are talking about.

**pag-+STEM-R+-an** *aff.* Circumfix construction indicating reciprocal, repetitive or habitual action, where 'STEM-R' represents the reduplication of the stem. *Maglingkat-lingkatan kita bang sai alingkat.* We all compete for beauty [to see] who is beautiful. *Maglallay-lallayan kita bang lum'ngngan, ni'nda' bang sai alallay.* We compete for slowness when we walk, to see who is the slow one. *Buwat kita magsagga' bo' sali' mbal magampun-ampunan, na bang sali' aniya' pamakaiya'nu, tabangkilnu aku.* Like us being in conflict but not forgiving each other, then if you have something to shame me with, you remind me of it.

**paga-paga** *n.* A work-bench; counter; shelf. (*cf:* **paha**)

**pagabong** *v. intr.* aN- To see things double. *Magabong e'ku ang'nda'. Sali' duwa ta'nda'ku, auling mataku sali'.* I see things unfocussed. It is as though I am seeing double, my eyes sort of dizzy.

**pagadgad** (derivative of **gadgad₂**) *v. tr.* To set something flowing with the current. *Buwat s'ggit, yukta, "Pagadgarun kaut, pabeya'un ma s'llog."* Like rubbish, we say, "Send it floating seawards, let it go with the current." *Tambal pamagadgad laha', pamaragan laha'.* Medicine for getting blood flowing, for making it run.

**pagagi** *v. tr. -an* To exercise control or authority over someone. *Pinagagihan onde' iskul he' mastal. Yuk mastal, "Pehē' ka angā' bohe'," na wa'i du angā' bohe'.* School children are under the teacher's control. He says, "Go and fetch water," and off they go to get it. *Mastal kapagagihan he' prinsipal.* The teacher is under the control of the principal. (*cf:* **kapagagi, kuma'agi**; *Thesaurus:* **kapatut, pagbaya'₁, pagkawasa, pagkuma'agi, pagnakura' 1**)

**pagagid** *v. intr. aN-* To be similar in appearance or sound. *Magagid asal ōn kami.* Our names in fact sound the same. (*cf:* **paganggil**)

**pagal** *n.* A cage for live animals or birds. (*cf:* **paldu**)

**pagambahan** *v. tr. -an* **1)** To promise more than one means to do. *Bang ah'lling a'a buwattina'an, bo' kita ah'lling palabi min bay llingna, ya na he' niōnan magambahan.* If a person says something like that, then we say something beyond what he said, that is being deceptive. *Hal aku pinagambahanan. Bang sali' bay yukna, "B'llihanta ka," bo' at'kka ni luma' halam ai-ai tabowana, pinagambahanan kami.* I was just deceived. Like when someone said, "I will buy something for you," but when he arrived home he hadn't brought anything. We were tricked into expecting something. *Ka'a ya angindam badju' ni aku, yukku, "Pehē' na ka ni luma'. Wa'i bay pinilinsahan ka'a."* Yuknu, "Bang buwattē' lling a'a i magambahanan aku."* You borrow a shirt from me, and I say, "Go to the house, it has already been ironed for you." Then you say, "When a guy talks like that he is pulling my leg." (*cf:* **hayak-hayak**) **1.1)** *v. tr.* To promise something excessively. *"Niā' na boslarannu." Sali' kinakan pinagambahan, sali' judju'.* "Get your darned food." It's like food promised excessively, like over-giving.

**pagampa-ampa** *v. tr. -an* To shift blame or responsibility onto each other. *Angay kam magampa-ampahan?* Why are you two arguing as to who should do it? (*Thesaurus:* **paghili-hili**)

**paganda** *n.* Something done for show, as the public transfer of a large bride-wealth, in contrast to the amount that was agreed on in private.

**paganday-anday** *v. tr.* To mock at someone's misfortune. *Si Pe hal pinaganday-anday.* Pe was just jeered at. (*Thesaurus:* **gunyak-gunyak, pagtunggīng, udju'**)

**pagang** *v. tr.* To prevent someone from carrying out an action begun or intended. *Bang magsuntuk, ya an'ngge ma t'ngnga' angalāng ma a'a magbono'. Pinagang sigām e'na.* When someone is boxing, the one standing in the middle prevents the ones fighting. He blocks them. (*Thesaurus:* **ampal, sagang, sangsang, sapad, sulang₁**)

**pagbaga'ud** *v. tr.* To carry more things than one can easily manage. (*Thesaurus:* **gawil, habit, hangkut**)

**pagbagala** *v. intr. aN-* To assume a bodily form in order to haunt, of a being normally invisible. *Bang aniya' amatay ama'nda'an dīna. Magbagala sali'.* When someone dies, he makes himself visible. He assumes bodily form. *Magbagala a'a ina'an, yukta. Pagsekotta, na ngga'i ka bagala manusiya', saitan ko' hē'. Amakitāw bā.* That's a man appearing as a ghost, we say. On getting close to it, well it's not a human being, it's a saitan. It sure scares us. (*Thesaurus:* **bahana', lutaw, panyata'₂ 1, pangguwa' 1.1**)

**pagbagi'ad** *v. intr. aN-* To speak a language with non-native words mixed in. *Magbagi'ad, sali' bang ah'lling buwat Sama Lipid magh'lling Sama, bo' magbagi'ad maka lling Sama. Magdambila'an, sali' maglamud-lamugay.* Bagi'ad is like when Land Sama speak Sama, and they mix non-native words with the Sama. It's a hybrid, various things mixed together.

**pagbagimbin** *v. intr. aN-* To cooperate in a project; to be united in a cause. *Bang maguyun kamemon, ya he' niōnan magbagimbin. Bang dusa dangan subay dusa kamemon. Yukta, "Tindan-tindan."* When everyone agrees, that is called *bagimbin.* If one sins it should be the sin of all. We say, "All in it together." (*cf:* **tindan-tindan**)

**pagba'anan** *v. intr. aN-* To sneeze. (*syn:* **aksi**)

**pagbalabag** *var. of* **pagbabag**

**pagbalibag** *v. intr. aN-* To be asymmetrical or imbalanced. *Bang ka amusay magbalibag, makarugtul ka ni pelang a'a.* If you paddle too much on one side, you will bang into other people's canoes. *Magkamigmig, sala magbalibag.* Lopsided, like being unbalanced.

**pagbalot** *v. tr.* **1)** To mix together different kinds of things. *Bang ka am'lli saging subay pinagbalot, subay da'a hal daginis.* When you buy bananas you should get more than one kind, not just one kind. **1.1)** *v. intr. aN-* To have white hair mixed with dark. *Magbalot na kōkna, apote' maka aettom.* His hair is mixed, white and black.

**pagbalukakkad** *v. intr. aN-* To make the noise of something moving vigorously through water, as a canoe or someone wading rapidly. *Da'a kam magbalukakkad, ilu gi' magtulihan.* Don't make a splashing noise; people are still sleeping.

**pagbamba** *n.* **1)** A plan still in the process of being formed. **1.1)** *v. tr.* To think about doing something. *Magbamba kami pi'ilu ni ka'am, ya sadja mbal tasiguru kami bang kām kasulutan ma gara' itū.* We are thinking of coming there to you, except that we are not sure if you are in favor of this plan. (*Thesaurus:* **pagimba-imba, pagisun 1.1, pagmiting, paru, plano**; *syn:* **pagbantu 1.1**) **1.2)** *v. tr. -an* To plan or plot against someone. *Aheya isab kasusahan si Nabi Da'ud sabab pinagbambahan iya binantung e' saga a'ana kabowa astol sigā.* The prophet David's distress was very great because his men, moved by their anger, were planning to stone him.

**pagbantu** *n.* 1) A tentative plan. **1.1)** *v. tr.* To be at the planning stage of some activity. *Song binono', pinaggara'-gara'. Buwattina'an hal magisun-isun, hal magbantu.* About to be killed, being plotted against. Just planning at present; just plotting. (*syn:* **pagbamba 1.1**) **1.2)** *v. tr.* -an To plan or plot against someone.

**pagbangday** var. of **pagtangday**

**pagbangga' da'awa** *v. intr.* aN- To be in conflict, as the testimony of opposing witnesses.

**pagbarese-barese** *v. intr.* aN- To speak unintelligibly, as a person possessed by a spirit being. (*Thesaurus:* **pagli'anun, pagsilap**)

**pagbau'-bau'** *v. intr.* aN- To pretend to be or to do something; to feign. *Magbau'-bau' aku ni bohe' bo' sali' ngga'i ka bohe' ya tinantu.* I pretend I'm going to get water but it is not the water that I'm really intent on. *Hinabuna binalutan e' sigām, magbau'-bau' iya kinangog.* While he was being held by them, he pretended to be crazy. (*Thesaurus:* **hinang-hinang₂, pagdō-rō, paglaku-laku, pagnaho'-naho'**)

**pagbengtod** *v. intr.* aN- To be at cross-purposes. (*syn:* **pagbesod**; *Thesaurus:* **pagagaw-besod, pagbagod, pagdiskās, pagjawab 1.1, pagpayod 1.1, pagsalod, pagsu'al**)

**pagbetong-betong** *v. intr.* aN- To sparkle or glitter, as phosphorescence in sea. *Ama'as tahik, magbetong-betong.* The sea gleams, sparkling with phosphorescence. (*cf:* **ba'as 1.1**)

**pagbikannol** *v. intr.* aN- To have an upset stomach as a result of strong emotion. *Magbikannol b'ttongta, sali' aniya' kap'ddi'an atay. Subay iya inān kabalosanku.* Our stomach churns, as though something is making us angry. I must take revenge on him.

**pagbigguwal** *v. intr.* aN- To be rough or irregular, of a surface. *Bang lantayta magbigguwal mbal ahāp palegehan, sagō' bang papan aratag makahaluk tulita.* If our floor is irregular it is not good to lie on, but flat wooden planks make our sleep sound. *Bang aniya' pamat'nna'an mbal ahāp, magbigguwal. Sali' aniya' patihinanna.* If a place for putting things is not good, uneven, like it is lying across something.

**pagbilma'arup** *v. intr.* aN- To engage in discussion. *Magbilma'arup, hal magsuli duwangan.* Having a discussion, just two people talking together. *Magbilma'arup magkagara'an bang ai kataluwa'an.* Talking together and discussing what the outcome should be. (*cf:* **pagalop**; *Thesaurus:* **pagharis, pagistori-istori, pagsuli-suli**)

**pagbinggal** *v. tr.* To bang things together with force.

**pagbiyu-biyu** *v. intr.* aN- 1) To move to and fro, as people without a purpose. *Ubus magbuwattē', ubus magbuwattitu, hal magbiyu-biyu. Sali' pehē' bo' pi'itu, pabīng pehē' pabīng pi'itu, sali' magbīng-*

*bīng.* First that way, then this way, just going to and fro. Sort of going there, coming here, going there again and coming here again, just going there and back repeatedly. (*cf:* **pagkolebok**) **1.1)** *v. tr.* To move things back and forward. *Pagbiyu-biyuhun ai-ai bowata.* To move back and forth whatever we are carrying.

**pagbogon** *n.* 1) A sense of resentment. **1.1)** *v. tr.* -an To harbor resentment.

**pagbolebol** var. of **pagbalebol**

**pagbolobok** *v. intr.* aN- To rumble, of the stomach. *Asidda magbolobok deyom b'ttongku. Kilāku aniya' saki ma deyom, sali' ang'llub.* My stomach is really rumbling. I think there is a sickness inside, sort of gurgling. (*Thesaurus:* **konog-konog, kulattub, llub, paglagonggok, paglagublub**)

**pagbono' kalangan** *v. intr.* aN- To be in a contest in which male and female singers try to outdo each other. (*cf:* **pagsindil 1**)

**pagboro-boro** *v. intr.* aN- To pass wind while excreting. (*cf:* **ntut**)

**pagboyokan** *v. intr.* aN- To feel squeamish due to motion sickness or stomach upset. *Sali' kita nilango he' goyak. Magboyokan kita.* Like we are made squeamish by the waves. We are seasick. *Magbo'ay-bo'ay, sali' kita nilango he' buntal. Magboyokan kita.* Squeamish and vomiting, as though made sick from [eating] pufferfish. We are feeling nauseated. (*Thesaurus:* **angol, baliyang, bo'ay, lango 1.1, pagtunggang-kīng, uling**)

**pagbugbug** *v. intr.* aN- To be massacred; to die en masse. *Magbugbug na manusiya', aheka amatay.* The people were massacred, many died. *Sali' magbono' mbal magkole', magbugbug na magbono'. Mbal kasekotan, mbal tasapad, sinagaran na hal.* Like people fighting each other and neither prevailing, dying together as they fought. [They] could not be approached, could not be restrained, simply left to carry on. (*Thesaurus:* **laglag 1.1, ligis₂**)

**pagbu'ung-bu'ung** *v. intr.* aN- To be chronically unhealed, of a wound or infection. (*syn:* **lunab**)

**pagbuntul** *v. intr.* aN- To form goose-bumps due to atmospheric cold. (*Thesaurus:* **pokot-pokot 1**)

**pagbunyi-bunyi** *v. intr.* aN- To enjoy the good things of life.

**pagbuwi'-munda'** var. of **pagbuli'-munda'**

**pagka** (var. **pagga**) *conj.* Since X (a state of affairs) is so; in view of the fact that X; given that X. *Pagka ta'abut na maganak d'nda hē', magtūy an'ngge na onde'.* Since the woman had now given birth, the child promptly stood up. *Pagga ab'ttong d'nda inān, magtūy tinimuk a'a alanga.* Since the girl was pregnant all the leading people were immediately brought together. (*Thesaurus:* **abila, apa, bang₁, bangsi', basta, bo' na, kalna' 1.1, gana, po'on₂, sabab₁ 1.1, samantala', sangga'ina, saukat, talkala'**)

**pagka-** var. of **pagta-**

**pagka pa'in** *conj.* Since it was so. *Pagka pa'in ak'nnop dambulan, amole' na kami.* Since a month was up, we returned home. *Manjari itū, pagka maina'an pa'in kami, maka'ā' na pa'in kami kasig.* Well then, since we were there, we kept catching pilchards.

**pagkabila'-bila'** (derivative of **bila'**) *v. intr. aN-* To break up into pieces. *Magkabila'-bila' bāng-bāng ilū.* Those cookies can break up into pieces.

**pagkabillag** *v. intr. aN-* To produce sounds or shapes that are poorly formed. *Bang aku anulat ma pepel mbal abontol. Magkabillag aku buwattina'an.* When I write on paper it isn't straight. I am scrawling in that way. *Magkabillag aku bang aku sali' mag'lling Sama.* I speak brokenly when I sort of talk Sinama.

**pagkab'nsihan** (derivative of **b'nsi**) *v. tr.* To dislike or hate someone. *Pagkab'nsihanku iya ma pasal hinangna.* I hate him because of what he does.

**pagkabug-kabug** *v. intr. aN-* To open and close the fingers repeatedly. *Magkabug-kabug si Be. Bilahi nihambin he' mma'na.* Be wriggles her fingers. She wants her father to hold her. (*cf:* **kangkang**₁ 1)

**pagkabuwattē'** (derivative of **buwattē'**) *v. intr. aN-* To happen in such a way. *Bang magkabuwattē'.* When such a thing happens.

**pagkādja** 1) *n.* A ceremony of respect to the elemental nature beings. 2) *v. tr. -an* To show respect to the elemental beings of nature.

**pagkagat** *n.* 1) A wrestling contest. 1.1) *v. intr. aN-* To engage in a contest of physical strength. (*Thesaurus:* **pagsabit, pagsanggul 1.1**)

**pagkageret** (derivative of **geret**) *v. intr. aN-* To be easily torn. *Magkageret du isāb bang banlon.* Banlon [a strong synthetic cloth] can also be torn.

**pagkaginisan** (derivative of **ginis**) *v. intr. aN-* To be of various kinds.

**pagkahāp** (derivative of **hāp**) *v. intr. aN-* To become reconciled after a disagreement. *Mbal kami magkahāp sat'ggol aniya' dunya.* We will not be reconciled as long as the earth exists. *Mahē' magtimuk, magkahāp maka bay banta. Magtūy aku parauhat pasiyum. Magkaki kami sampay ni dunya hē'-i.* Coming together there, becoming reconciled with one who had been an enemy. I immediately went up and kissed him. We [would be] cousins until the world to come. *Aniya' kasehe'an magbanta isāb tīttopan buway. Yuk a'a magbono' hē', "Subay asugpat buway inān bo' kita magkahāp."* There are also other people in an enemy relationship who [formalize it] by cutting off a piece of rattan. Those enemies say, "That rattan will have to joined again for us to make peace." *Bang hati' mbal tara'ugna sultan dakayu', magtūy iya amabeya' suluhan pasampang ni sultan inān bo' mikipagkahāp.* If perhaps he cannot defeat the other king, he promptly sends a mediator to meet that king requesting to be reconciled. (*Thesaurus:* **deyo'**₃ 2, **pagpa'ampun**, **ū'ū**; *syn:* **paghalulay**).

**pagkaheka'an** (derivative of **heka**) *n.* 1) An extended kin group. 1.1) *v. intr. aN-* To be an extended kin group. *Sugsug isāb kami, magkaheka'an.* We're connected, we are a wider kindred.

**pagkahi** *n.* Fellow-man; peer relationship. *Akagut itū sali' aniya' kap'ddi'anta atay ma pagkahita, atawa ma sai ma sai. Kagut* means we have something in our hearts against a fellow man, or against anyone at all. *Dapagkahi du kita.* We are really of the one kindred. *Pagkahi sali' dangkaheka, mbal maglawak. Min t'dda min duwa min t'llu. Pagkahi* are like an extended kin group, not too remote. Once, twice, or three times [removed].

**pagkahinangan** (derivative of **hinang**₁) *v. intr. aN-* To behave in a particular way. *Karūlan saga a'a magkahinangan bang ai makasulut pangatayan sigām.* The people were permitted to behave in ways that pleased them deeply. *Dupang pahāp ka magkahinangan buwattilu!* How stupid you are to behave in such a way!

**pagkahukaw** (var. **pagkahuskaw**) (derivative of **hukaw**) *v. intr. aN-* To be mutually reluctant regarding sexual intimacy, of a married couple. *In a'a maglakibini subay magdūl-baya' d'nda maka l'lla, subay sigā mbal magkahukaw.* A married couple should be mutually willing, not reluctant to have sex. *Ka'am maglakibini, da'a kahukawinbi batin.* You who are married, do not resist being intimate with each other. *Aniya' ilū agkahuskaw na maglakibini. Magbutas na.* There was a couple who had become disinclined [to have sex]. They are divorced now.

**pagkahuskaw** var. of **pagkahukaw**

**pagka'a'a** (derivative of **a'a**) *n.* Typical human behavior. *Ya na tu'ud pagka'a'ana.* That is simply his way of being and behaving.

**pagka'inagon** *v. tr. -an* To keep someone in mind for their good. *Magka'inagon ka, Tuwan, ma sai-sai ahāp ma deyom luma'bi.* You think about the welfare, Sir, of anyone in your household who is good. *Tabista aku he' danakan-matto'aku ahāp, sali' aku makatulus angusaha. Na pinagka'inagonan aku he' sigā, ya po'on aku billihan ai-ai buwat saga pangusaha.* My siblings and parents reckon I'm okay, that I'm good at my work. So they keep me in mind, which is why they buy for me various things like work gear. *O Tuhan, pagka'inagonin langgalnu magka'at.* Oh God, take care of your damaged prayer-house. (*Thesaurus:* **kannal, dalil 1.1, dongdong, pikil 1.1, tali' 1.1**)

**pagka'lloman** (derivative of **llom**) *v. intr. aN-* To do something for a long time. *Da'a na pa'in kam magk'lloman pakapo'.* Don't spend too much time wading around.

**pagka'llum** (derivative of **llum**) *n.* The quality of life. *Jari makapagka'llum kam at'ggol ma lahat paliyama'.* So you will be able to enjoy long life in the land of abundance.

**pagka'ob** *v. intr. aN-* To fit together, of flat surfaces. *L'ssik-l'ssik itū taga kulit duwa magka'ob.* These barnacles have shells, two joined together. *Sali' duwa papan magka'ob, magpikit sali', samaharap buwat lai'.* Just like two planks fitting face to face, sort of clinging, facing each other like dinner plates.

**pagkalabayan** (derivative of **labay**₃) *n.* Things that people experience. *Nileya'-leya' ba'anan magh'llah-h'nda sabab heka kasusahan pagkalabayan ma waktu tagna'.* Many couples are scared to get married because of the many difficulties experienced at first.

**pagkalalamma** (derivative of **lamma**) *v. intr. aN-* To become progressively weaker. *Magkasosōng magkalalamma.* As time goes on he becomes weaker and weaker.

**pagkalamihan** (derivative of **lami**) *n.* 1) A celebration or happy event. 1.1) *v. intr. aN-* To celebrate together. *Magkalamihan sigām sampay magbuwan-biyuwani.* They were celebrating and giving gifts to each other.

**pagkalammahan** (derivative of **lamma**) *v. intr. aN-* To be low-spirited; disheartened. *Angay sali' na pa'in ka magkalammahan llaw ni llaw?* Why are you always so down, day after day? *Ya he' po'onna angkan aheka ma deyomanbi ilu magkalammahan, maka aniya' isāb amatay.* That's the reason why a lot of people among you are lacking energy, and some have even died. *Jari magkalammahan na e' punung saga a'a kamemon ma kalahat-lahatan inān.* So all the people in those lands were disheartened by the scarcity of food.

**pagkalengogan** (derivative of **lengog**) *v. intr. aN-* To be in a state of civil unrest. *Aniya' magkalengogan ma Malaybalay. Mbal na kita makaniMalaybalay.* There is ongoing unrest in Malaybalay. We can no longer go to Malaybalay.

**pagkalimbit** (derivative of **limbit**) *v. intr. aN-* To be responsible for one's family members.

**pagkaliru'an** (derivative of **liru'**) *v. intr. aN-* To grieve continually over someone's absence or death. *Magkaliru'an aku ma anakku, mbal na ta'nda' mataku.* I feel regret for my child, whom I no longer see. *Magkaliru'an kita ma anak-kamanakanta, sali' kita magdohon.* We ache for our [related] young people, grieving for them.

**pagkalitib** (derivative of **litib**) *v. intr. aN-* To wear down or erode.

**pagkal'lla** (derivative of **l'lla**) *n.* Magical masculinity, making the possessor immune to harm from attacks of various kinds. *Taga ilmu'. Pagkal'lla itū sali' salawat.* [He] has esoteric knowledge. This magical immunity is like special knowledge of the supernatural. *Mareyom kūn ilū aniya' amowa saikula. (Alahang, subay sukuran.) Pinalamud ni buwas ati bīlla kinakan he' mma' onde' abō' aniya' pagkal'lla.* Inside the womb there is something that brings magical immunity. (It is rare, one has to be lucky.) It is mixed with rice and cooked and eaten by the child's father so he can have immunity against physical harm. (*Thesaurus:* **basi'**₂ 1.1, **kobol** 1.1, **pangliyas**, **sihil** 1).

**pagkalo'od** *v. intr. aN-* To have feelings of mutual regard for each other. *Magkalo'od bang magpanon, ngga'i ka buwat magdanakan.* Friends feel mutual respect for each other, not like brothers and sisters. *Sali' ai-ai bay sinambat e' dangan inān, pinina'an ni iya minsan halam aniya'. Ya he' magkalo'od.* For example, when something is just mentioned casually by one person, it is sent to him [by the other] even when there is nothing. That is a case of mutual regard. (*Thesaurus:* **loman** 1)

**pagkalukasa** var. of **pagkalukassa**

**pagkalukassa** (var. **pagkalukasa**) *v. intr. aN-* To arguing back and forth over minor issues; to bicker. *Magkalukassa si Habagat maka si Llaw, ya pagkalukassahan sigām bang sai kono' akosog min sigām karuwangan.* West Wind and Sun were arguing, their argument being about which of the two of them was the stronger. *Magkalukassa, sali' kita magbono' ma deyom luma', buwat a'a maka h'ndana. Magkalukassa, like when we fight in our homes, like a man with his wife.*

**pagkalussungan** (derivative of **lussung**) *v. intr. aN-* To suffer a financial loss. *Magkalussungan disi Ka.* Ka and his group are losing money.

**pagkamali'** *v. intr. aN-* To misunderstand each other. (*Thesaurus:* **ambil-hati**, **pagkasā'** 1.1, **pagsabali**, **ta'awil**)

**pagkamanusiya'** (derivative of **manusiya'**) *n.* Humanity; the human condition.

**pagkambuyan** *v. intr. aN-* To wander about with no specific purpose. (*Thesaurus:* **pagkatay**, **pagjambeyaw**, **paglanyaw**)

**pagkamihu** *v. intr. aN-* To become misshapen; lopsided. *Buwat bubu inān, bang sinōd he' daing aheka, paligay mariyata', magkamihu.* Like that fish trap, when lots of fish have gone in, and especially when it is on the surface, it becomes unbalanced. *Buwat labban bang aheka na makalandu' isina, minsan bay niengkotan, magkamihu du.* Like a cardboard carton, when it has overmuch inside, it will bulge even though it has been tied. *S'mmatta maka pōng tilas ko ra'a magkamihu pal'ngngan.* We will stiffen it with pieces of split bamboo so it doesn't run lopsided. (*Thesaurus:* **baligbig**, **kirus** 1, **tempang**)

**pagkampat** *v. intr. aN-* To curl one's fingers into the palm of one's hand.

**pagkamundal-mandil** *v. intr. aN-* To become someone with no settled abode or occupation.

*Magkamundal-mandil, magkangī'-ngī'. Bay kita ahāp, halam na aniya' kagunahanta.* Going from place to place, coming to a bad end. We used to be good, now we are worthless. (*cf:* **pagsampig-manampig**)

**pagkangī'-ngī'** *v. intr. aN-* To come to a bad end as the inevitable outcome of bad choices. *Bang kita bay sinagda he' matto'ata, bo' sali' mbal ameya'-meya', yuk-i, "Magkasosōng ka'a ilū magkangī'-ngī'. Mbal tumudju ni kahāpan, ni kala'atan."* When we are corrected by our parents but don't really obey, they say, "As time goes on you will come to a bad end. You will not head for good but for bad."

**pagkapakil** (derivative of **pakil**) *v. intr. aN-* To be qualified for service in mosque leadership. *Magkapakil, magkaimam, ahāp salawatna.* Able to serve as a leader in a mosque community, as an imam, their spiritual power is good.

**pagkap'ddi'an** (derivative of **p'ddi'**) *v. intr. aN-* To be experiencing pain. *Daipara l'ppos, magkap'ddi'an kōkna.* Spongy material fortunately, or she would be experiencing headaches.

**pagkar'nda** (derivative of **d'nda**) *n.* The distinctive features of a woman.

**pagkarupangan** (derivative of **dupang**) *v. intr. aN-* To behave irrationally. *Ya buriru itū sali' magkarupangan.* The *buriru* condition is like behaving irrationally.

**pagkaruwa** (derivative of **duwa**) *v. intr. aN-* To be a pair; to be a duplicate of. *Mbal tapamuwan pantalunku itū apa dakayu' du. Kalu-kalu bang bay magkaruwa bay na pamuwan ni ka'a dakayu'.* These trousers of mine cannot be given away because I have only the one [pair]. Perhaps if there had been two of them one would have been given to you.

**pagkasabulan** (derivative of **sabul**) *v. intr. aN-* To be involved in indecent or antisocial behavior. *Da'a kita maglango-lango, da'a magba'is, da'a magkasabulan.* We should not get drunk, behave immorally, or act indecently.

**pagkasā'** (derivative of **sā'**₁) *n.* 1) Mutual misunderstanding. 1.1) *v. intr. aN-* To be mutually mistaken; to talk at cross-purposes. (*Thesaurus:* **ambil-hati, pagkamali', pagsabali, ta'awil**)

**pagkasosōng** (derivative of **sōng**₁) *v. intr. aN-* To be moving forward to some future time. *Bang kita bay sinagda he' matto'ata, bo' sali' mbal ameya'-meya', yuk-i, "Magkasosōng ka'a ilū magkangī'-ngī'. Mbal tumudju ni kahāpan, ni kala'atan." Magkasosōng magkalalamma.* When we are corrected by our parents but don't really obey, they say, "As time goes on you will come to a bad end. You will not head for good but for bad." As time goes on he becomes weaker and weaker.

**pagkasuddahan** (derivative of **sudda**) *v. intr. aN-* To experience misfortune; to come to a bad end. *A'a inān magkasuddahan du pa'in.* That person will continue to experience misfortune. *Ya a'a palamud ma a'a halam akkalan, magkasuddahan.* The man who mixes with someone who lacks sense will come to a bad end.

**pagkasumbang** (derivative of **sumbang**) *v. intr. aN-* To be in an incestuous relationship. *Arapun kām magkarukka'an ma sabab aniya' kono' a'a ma lūnganbi magkasumbang.* You should have been sad because there are reportedly people in your community committing incest.

**pagkata'u** (derivative of **ta'u**₁) *v. intr. aN-* To be acquainted with each other. *Magkata'u kam bahā' maka mpuku?* Are you acquainted perhaps with my grandfather? (*Thesaurus:* **pagkilā**).

**pagkata'u-marayaw** *v. intr. aN-* To know what is morally good. {idiom} *Subay to'ongan iya amikilan bang buwattingga kapanabangna baranna bo' iya magkata'u-marayaw.* He should definitely be thinking how to help himself know what is morally good.

**pagkatambahan** (derivative of **tamba**) *v. intr. aN-* To be capable of being bought or bribed. *Pagkatambahan sigā, mbal isāb abontol pangahukum sigā.* They can be bribed, their judging is not morally right.

**pagkatāw** (derivative of **tāw**) *v. intr. aN-* 1) To experience fear. 1.1) *v. tr.* To treat someone as an object of fear. *Pinagkatāwan iya he' a'a kamemon. Atāw binono'.* He is greatly feared by everyone. They fear being killed.

**pagkatay** *v. intr. aN-* To do something without purpose. *Magkatay magl'ngngan ni dakayu' maka dakayu'.* Walking aimlessly to some place or other. (*Thesaurus:* **pagkambuyan, pagjambeyaw, paglanyaw**)

**pagkatumba** (derivative of **tumba**₁) *v. intr. aN-* To fall headlong from a height. *Bang aniya' ariplano magkatumba aniya' lapal ma aradju, wa'i atumba ma dilaut Parangan.* When an airplane happened to go down, there was a message on the radio. It had gone down offshore from Parangan.

**pagkaya-kaya** *v. tr. -an* To carry out the full mourning sequence for a person who has died. *Pinagkaya-kayahan, am'lli saga karut buwas, saga kuku-pote', ya pinagōnan pagkaya-kayahan.* The funeral carried out fully, buying sacks of rice and shroud cloth. That's what is known as *pagkaya-kaya.*

**pagkebed-kebed** *v. intr. aN-* To move restlessly, of a group of things. *Minsan bu'unta magkebed-kebed, taluwa' baliyu.* Even our hair stirs this way and that, hit by the wind. (*Thesaurus:* **paghense, paghibal-hibal, paglinggayu', pagoseg-oseg**)

**pagkeha** (var. **pagpeha**) *v. intr. aN-* To travel widely, visiting foreign places.

**pagkesong** *v. intr. aN-* To turn one's head from side to side. *Mbal kita makapagkesong, mbal kita sali' makapaglingi'. "Abusā' k'llongku," yukta.* We are not able to turn our heads this way and that, like we can't look from side to side. "My neck has a crick in it," we say. (*Thesaurus:* **buli'-buli' mata, keles, kibad, lingi'** 1)

**pagkilāhi** var. of **pagkilā**

**pagkimbong** var. of **pagkin'mbong**

**pagkiparat** 1) *v. intr. aN-* To reconcile persons who have become estranged. 2) *v. tr.* To reconcile conflicting family members by means of a formal ceremony.

**pagk'ddaw-k'ddaw** *v. intr. aN-* To close the eyes briefly; to blink. *Magk'ddaw-k'ddaw matana.* His eyes blink repeatedly.

**pagkolebok** *v. intr. aN-* To move about restlessly, as a crowd of people upset by some event. *Magkolebokan a'a inān, sali' ahidjul maina'an, magpiha onde'-onde' alungay.* Those people are milling around, making a noise over there, looking for a lost child. (*cf:* **pagbiyu-biyu** 1)

**pagkoledje** *v. tr.* To keep touching or handling things unnecessarily. *Magkoledje itū aheka ntananna, sali' aheka tanganna. Sali' bay dakayu' bo' dakayu'.* Handling everything, touching lots of things, like having a lot of hands. As though it had been one thing after another. (*Thesaurus:* **hulemang** 1.1, **lotok** 1.1, **umas**)

**pagkolepak** *v. intr. aN-* To make an intermittent clattering noise.

**pagkorel-korel** *v. intr. aN-* To have the knees drawn up towards the chest, as in sleep or in running on the spot. *Bang aku atuli, asidda aku magkorel-korel.* When I am sleeping I bring my knees up a lot. (*Thesaurus:* **komo'₁, kongkong** 1, **kulangkang** 1, **kullung**)

**pagkowap-kowap** *v. intr. aN-* To move rhythmically, as the mouth of a fish or a pulsating pain. *Magmula ituku, magkowap-kowap.* This part of me is severely damaged, it pulses painfully. *Magkowap-kowap daing ma bihing batu, halam aniya' takakanna.* A fish opens and shuts its mouth beside the coral, having eaten nothing. (*Thesaurus:* **pagk'bbut-k'bbut, pagdutdut, paglaggut-laggut, pagsignat-signat, panag-panag** 1)

**pagkubu-kubu** *v. tr. -an* To crowd around something of interest. *Ai pinagkubu-kubuhan inān? Pinagkubu-kubuhan e' a'a d'nda bay tarugtul e' jīp.* What's everyone crowding around? People are crowding around a woman who was hit by a jeepney. *Aniya' patay daing aheya pinagkubu-kubuwhn e' a'a.* There is the body of a large fish crowded round by people. (*Thesaurus:* **paglundug, pagtimuk** 1.1)

**pagkulallit** *v. intr. aN-* To make repeated twisting movements. *Magkulallit sowa ma tahik. Magkulallit isāb korente.* Snakes keep moving in the sea. Electric cables also twist and turn.

**pagkul'ddeng** *v. intr. aN-* To stretch one's body on awaking. (*Thesaurus:* **h'nnat** 1, **l'dduk** 1, **nned, paghitad, pagle'od**)

**pagkutebba'** *v. intr. aN-* To kick the feet up and down while in a prone position, as a baby or a swimmer. (*Thesaurus:* **kambay** 2, **pagkutibbung**)

**pagkutibbung** *v. intr. aN-* To move legs and feet as in swimming. *Bang tangan angambay, bang tape' magkutibbung.* With hands the word is *kambay*, with feet it is *kutibbung.* (*Thesaurus:* **kambay** 2, **pagkutebba'**)

**pagdago'-dago'** *v. intr. aN-* 1) To take advantage of someone's kindness or generosity. 1.1) *v. tr. -an* To exploit someone's leniency or friendship. *Ai-ai kabaya'anku ma luma' itū, ngā'ku sadja. Ka'am ya pagdago'-dago'an.* Anything I want in this house, I just take. You are the ones who get taken advantage of. *Mbal kapagdago'-dago'an si Mbo' Ja.* Grandfather Ja is not to be taken advantsge of.

**pagdaguyu** (derivative of **guyu**) *v. intr. aN-* To move together restlessly; to jostle. *Ōy, da'a kām magdaguyu, da'a magoseg-oseg.* Hey [you all], don't move around, don't be restless. *Bang aniya' linug sali' magdaguyu kaluma'an.* When there is an earthquake the houses sort of jostle each other. (*Thesaurus:* **lensa, tangkug** 1).

**pagdahagbela'** *v. intr. aN-* To writhe in pain. *Wa'i magdahagbela' ma palegehanna apa ap'ddi' b'ttongna.* He is writhing in pain on his bed because his stomach is so painful. *Pehē' kita ni si Anu, halam pat'nna' ma palegehanna, wa'i magdahagbela'.* We went to What's-his-name, not staying on his sleeping place, just writhing with pain.

**pagda'atay** (derivative of **atay₂**) *v. intr. aN-* To be on informal or intimate terms with each other, as people in the same household. (*Thesaurus:* **pagsamod, pagsōd-addat**).

**pagdalūng** (derivative of **lūng**) *v. intr. aN-* To be in the same community. *Magsaumbibi na, ya ōnna magdalūng na pihak ni Sūk, pihak ni Sama.* Working together, the word for Tausug and Sama ethnic groups living in the same community.

**pagdamak** *v. tr. -an* To give gifts during courtship to the family of the girl. *Amowa kita gastu, magdamak kita.* We bring supplies, we give courtship gifts. (*Thesaurus:* **bintak, siba'** 1.1)

**pagdamoseng** *v. intr. aN-* To move ecstatically, of someone possessed by a spirit being. *Magdamoseng, mbal makat'nna' ma paningkō'anna, ya pasal kasangonan, kajīnan iya.* He is moving ecstatically, cannot stay in his seat, because he is possessed by a djinn.

**pagdaraing** (derivative of **daing**) *n.* A person who makes a living by fishing.

**pagdauman** *v. intr. aN-* To become somewhat ripe at the same time. *Magdauman kamemon saga biyabas.* The guavas all becoming ripe. *Magdauman gi' tahakna bang sali' tonga'-tonga' tahakna.* Its ripeness is said to be *dauman* when it is sort of half-ripe. *Magdauman tahak saging* *bay b'llita i'. Mbal gi' tab'lli buwattina'an, subay salung atawa simuddai.* Those bananas that we purchased are only partly ripe. They won't be bought right now, it'll have to be tomorrow or the day after. (*Thesaurus:* **b'ngkol₂, lāg, pagangilan**)

**pagdayaw** *n.* 1) The basic components of a structure, as the skeleton and sinews of a body, or the framing of a house or boat. *Pagdayaw itu kayu paghinang luma': hāg, papan, hobong, kamemon ai-ai. Ya ru ma pelang: bangka'na, papanna, batangan, bahu', taruk.* The materials are the timber used for building a house: posts, boards, crossbeams, everything. Same with a canoe: its dugout hull, its planks, its outrigger supports, its boom, its mast. *Mbal manjari ni'inta' atawa nilaga' isi hayop, subay tinapa ma katibu'ukanna, beya' na isab kōkna, tape'na sampay pagdayaw baranna.* The meat of a cow must not be eaten raw, it must be totally cooked, along with its head, its feet and all its parts. *Aniya' ma sigām kalesa pagdayaw basi'.* They had horse-drawn carts constructed of steel framing. (*Thesaurus:* **akal-baran, batang-tubu, paltubu-tubuhan 2, tangkorak**) 1.1) *v. tr. -an* To assemble the various parts of a structure. *Sinangonan, sinulugan bahu'na duwa, pinagdayawan sali'.* Fitted out, both booms inserted, sort of assembled.

**pagdeyag** *v. intr. aN-* To provide or enjoy entertainment. (*syn:* **ongka' 1.1**)

**pagdiskās** *v. intr. aN-* To dispute with each other. (*Thesaurus:* **pagagaw-besod, pagbagod, pagbengtod, pagjawab 1.1, pagpayod 1.1, pagsalod, pagsu'al**)

**pagdō-rō** *v. intr. aN-* To pretend to have the right or authority to do certain things. *A'a itū magdō-rō dīna na pa'in, minsan halam aniya' bay anoho' iya.* This person keeps on pretending to be somebody, even though no one has told him to do so. *Baya'na magdō-rō minsan mbal du kata'uhanna.* It is his wish to be in charge even though he doesn't know. *Magdō-rō, sali' maglaku-laku, anōng-nōngan dīna.* Claiming to have status, pretending to rank, putting himself forward. (*Thesaurus:* **hinang-hinang₂, pagbau'-bau', paglaku-laku, pagnaho'-naho'**)

**pagdogdog** *var. of* **pagdaogdog**

**pagdohon** *v. tr. -an* To grieve persistently for the loss of a loved person or a treasured possession. *Bang bay kapatayan bo' sali' anuligpat ni atayta, ya hē' niōnan magdohon.* When we have been bereaved and it comes back into our minds, that's what we call *dohon. Bang aniya' alungay man kita, magdohon. Paligay bang bay ka'lloganta sali' kita magdohon.* If something is lost to us, we keep grieving. Especially when we had cherished it, we go on grieving. (*Thesaurus:* **handul atay, pagdukka' 1.1, paglemong 1.1, paglindu**)

**pagdraeb** *v. intr. aN-* To drive an automobile.

**pagduwaha'an** *var. of* **pagduwa'ahan**

**pagene'-ene'** *v. intr. aN-* To dawdle; to take one's time. *Magene'-ene' ka (sali' at'ggol).* You're going so slow (like taking a long time). (*Thesaurus:* **aggal 1, kaku', hinay-hinay, lahan 1, lallay**)

**pagensol-ensol** *v. intr. aN-* To move in order to ease physical discomfort.

**pagga** *var. of* **pagka**

**paggambahan** *v. tr. -an* To disappoint someone by failing to keep a promise or commitment. *Buwat aku pinaholat-holat bīllihan. Yukku, "B'llihin kita kende," ati yukna, "b'llihanta pa'in ka singgam duwa pilak," bo' halam makab'lli. Hal aku pinaggambahan.* Like when I am encouraged I'll have something bought for me. I say, "Buy us some candy," and he says, "I'll buy you two pesos' worth of chewing gum," but he doesn't buy any. I'm simply let down. (*Thesaurus:* **lamma 2.1, saman-saman**)

**paggat** *v. tr.* To prevent something; to deny someone what they desire or intend. *Buwat d'nda angiram, ai-ai kinabilahi'an subay mbal pinaggat.* Like a pregnant woman, whatever she desires should not be denied. *Aniya' kahālan tumaluwa' ya mbal tapaggat.* A situation has come about that cannot be prevented. *Pinaggat ka, halam ka nirūlan.* You are denied, you haven't been granted your wish. *In a'a alalom nahuna ata'u amaggat kagit atayna.* A wise person knows how to keep his anger under control. (*Thesaurus:* **balda, dangat 1, sagga' 1.1, sīng-sūd**)

**paghadjul-hadjul** *v. intr. aN-* To drift to and fro with the currents, of a vessel with no means of propulsion or steering. *Maghadjul-hadjul pelang ma dilaut, pabeya' ma s'llog pi'ingga-pi'ingga.* The canoe is drifting out at sea, going with the current here, there, and everywhere. (*Thesaurus:* **gesges, laran, loson, palis₁, pespes 1.1**)

**paghangu-hangu** *v. intr. aN-* To be panting, as someone out of breath from exertion. *Bang kita palūd min deya amowa panggi' kayu kab'kkatan kita. Maghangu-hangu, sali' apuha.* When we come down from inland carrying cassava, we are utterly exhausted. We pant, worn out. (*Thesaurus:* **hapus₂, lumu, pagh'ngka-h'ngka, paghongat-hongat, puha**)

**paghaup** *v. intr. aN-* To be partners in a business venture. *Maghaup, magsakaum.* To share costs, to work as a group. (*Thesaurus:* **paghūn, pagsapali, pagtiguway, pagtintuway, pagtughay 1.1**)

**paghaupan** *n.* A financial partnership. *Bang kita magb'lli yukta, "Pi'itu kam magsakaum paghaupan abō' kita kaluhayan."* When we are buying we say, "Let's get together in a financial partnership so we can get better prices."

**paghijajā** *var. of* **paghidja-hidja**

**paghimpun** *v. intr. aN-* To gather in formal

assembly. (*Thesaurus:* **pagmairan 1.1, pagtimuk 1, pulin, pūn 1.1**)

**paghimumūngan** (derivative of **mūng**) *n.* 1) An utterance of significance; a pronouncement. 1.1) *v. intr. aN-* To say things of significance. *Bay kami maka si Sa magbono'-bono' bo' pahali. Takaleku iya maghimumūngan ma aku.* Sa and I were fighting a bit, but stopped. I had heard him saying serious things about me.

**paghin'nnat** (derivative of **h'nnat**) *v. intr. aN-* To sit (on a mat) with legs stretched out in front. *Sinalinan na in bay magbatang-saging, ya a'a pitu' puhu' maghin'nnat inān.* The seven men who had been sitting with their legs stretched out, holding the body, were replaced.

**paghinōs** (var. **pagnihōs**) (derivative of **hōs**) *v. tr.* To wear a sarong. *Maghinōs gi' aku.* I'll just put on a sarong.

**paghinumag** *n.* 1) An item worn for common, everyday use. *Paghinumag, sali' badju' ala'at. Bang kita angusaha ngga'i ka badju' ahāp. Magbadju' ahāp subay aniya' pagkawinan.* Work gear, like worn-out shirts. When we are earning our living it's not good shirts [that we wear]. There must be a wedding for us to wear good clothes. *Badju'na paghinumag llaw-sangom. Saddī badju'na pangongka'an.* His everyday shirt for day or night. He has a different shirt for celebrations. 1.1) *v. intr. aN-* To wear everyday clothes.

**paghirang** *v. intr. aN-* To set refreshments out for guests. *Angay ka maghirang-hirang dīnu? Subay ka angagad pinaghirangan.* Why are you setting food out for yourself? You should wait to be served. (*cf:* **paghatul-hatul**)

**paghitad** *v. intr. aN-* To stretch the body on waking up. *Maghitad aku bang subu-subu, sali' magl'dduk.* I stretch my body early in the morning, sort of straightening out the kinks. (*Thesaurus:* **h'nnat 1, l'dduk 1, nned, pagkul'ddeng, pagle'od**)

**pagh'ngka-h'ngka** *v. intr. aN-* To be puffing or panting as a result of exertion. *Bay aku palahi-lahi ati magh'ngka-h'ngka na aku.* I have been running and I'm puffing now. (*Thesaurus:* **hapus₂, lumu, paghangu-hangu, paghongat-hongat, puha**)

**pagh'ngngek-h'ngngek** *v. intr. aN-* To wrinkle one's facial features. *Magh'ngngek-h'ngngek ūngna.* His nose wrinkles.

**paghola'** *n.* A spouse; a person's marriage partner. *Taga paghola', ya taga h'llana atawa taga h'nda.* Having a marriage partner, either a husband or a wife. (*cf:* **h'lla, h'nda**)

**paghota** *v. intr. aN-* To breathe shallowly, as a person near death. *Bang hal maghota napasna, asidda-sidda na.* When his breathing is only shallow, his condition is very serious. (*cf:* **pagnapas**; *Thesaurus:* **pōn, simay₁ 1**)

**paghubang-hubang** *v. intr. aN-* To think carefully about the truth of something said. *Kinannal bay suli-suliku, b'nnal atawa ai ka. Maghubang-hubang iya bang b'nnal bay suliku.* What I said was considered carefully, whether it was true or whatever. He thought about it whether my words were true. *Maghubang-hubang pangatayanku bang b'nnal bissalana i'.* Thinking deeply, soul-deep, whether that speech was true.

**paghuhuma** (derivative of **huma**) *n.* A person who farms for a living.

**paghulay** *v. intr. aN-* To celebrate on the evening after the marriage formalities, when the couple go to the man's home. (*cf:* **tingkuwang**)

**paghūn** *v. intr. aN-* To be partners in a business venture. *Aniya' limampū' pilakku, aniya' limampū' pilaknu, na maghūn kita am'lli dagangan.* I have fifty pesos, you have fifty pesos, so we combine to buy things for sale. (*Thesaurus:* **paghaup, pagsapali, pagtiguway, pagtintuway, pagtughay 1.1**)

**pagiku-iku** *v. intr. aN-* To move along in a line, one after another. (*Thesaurus:* **apas 1.1, sunud 1.1, sunu', turul 1**)

**pagi'inuman** var. of **panginuman**

**pagimba-imba** *v. intr. aN-* To think about doing something. *Magimba-imba sigām amole'.* They are thinking about going home. (*Thesaurus:* **pagbamba 1.1, pagsun 1.1, pagmiting, paru, plano**)

**pagimun-imun** *n.* Food or refreshments for a public celebration. *Halam aniya' ma kita pagimun-imun kalasigan pamudjita ma waktu kaniya' sin baranggayta.* We didn't have a festive merienda for us to celebrate the time when our barangay was established.

**pagin'mbal** (derivative of **mbal**) *n.* 1) A refusal. *"Da'a Tuwan," ya pagin'mbal d'nda inān.* "Don't Sir," was that girl's refusal. (*Thesaurus:* **pagmarī', pasibukut 1, sulak₂, taikut 1.1**). 1.1) *v. tr.* To refuse or say no to something. *Sagō' magin'mbal iya maka mbal isāb iya bilahi pasalu ni saga pagmatto'ahan inān amangan pagkakan minsan hal dangkuri'.* But he refused and did not want to eat together with those elders, not eating even a little bit of the food.

**pagin'ngngong** (derivative of **ngngong**) *v. intr. aN-* To make the sound of a cow or bull; to moo.

**paginubusan** *v. intr. aN-* To be in the relationship formed by marriage between brothers of one family and sisters of another. (*cf:* **pagtumbuk-s'ngkol**)

**pagiyas** var. of **bagiyas**

**pagjamba'-jamba'** var. of **pagjama'-jama'**

**pagjambeyaw** *v. intr. aN-* To wander around with no specific purpose. (*Thesaurus:* **pagkambuyan, pagkatay, paglanyaw**)

**pagjina** *v. intr. aN-* To commit adultery. (*syn:* **pagliyu-lakad**)

**pagjuru'** *v. intr. aN-* 1) To behave in ways that go beyond cultural norms. *Magjuru'an kita dīta, mbal kita magay-magay.* We behave excessively towards ourselves; we don't care what happens. *Magjuru' aku. Mbal aku magusaha, halam aniya' kabaya'anku a'llum.* I respond excessively [to grief]. I don't work for a living, and I have no desire to live. **1.1)** *v. tr. -an* To offend someone by acting in a way that goes beyond what is culturally appropriate. *Da'a aku pagjuru'in ba. Sarang ko' ilū.* Don't overdo it, huh. That's quite enough. *Minsan ap'nno' na poga he' bohe', p'nno'anku, p'nno'anku. Magjuru' suput aku.* Even though the water jar is already full, I keep filling it and filling it. I offend by making the water surge. (*syn:* **judju' 1.1**)

**pag'tta'** *v. intr. aN-* To occur at the same time; to be in the same location. *Buwat ka'a pasōd, aku paluwas, mag'tta' kita ma bowa' lawang.* Like when you are entering, I am going out, and we meet each other in the doorway. (*Thesaurus:* **pagsamp'kka', sabu 1.1, salta', tā'-tā' 1**)

**paglaban** *n.* **1)** A person addicted to immoral behavior. **1.1)** *v. intr. aN-* To do what is grossly immoral. (*cf:* **paglaka'-laka' 1.1**)

**paglaka'-laka'** *v. intr. aN-* **1)** To make obscene suggestions. *Tanggal-iman bang maglaka'-laka'.* Making obscene suggestions imperils one's faith. **1.1)** *v. tr. -an* To insult someone by proposing sexual intercourse with them or their female kin. *Ala'at hinang si Anu maglaka'-laka'an d'nda, pinakaiya' paglalu.* What's-his-name's action in making lewd suggestions about a woman is bad, shaming her by implying habitual immorality. (*cf:* **paglaban 1.1**; *syn:* **sumpa'**)

**paglagadlad** *v. intr. aN-* To refer a legal dispute to a higher jurisdiction. *Buwat kami bay maghukum ni mastal, mbal magkole'. Maglagadlad ni sara' M'ddas, ni Sūk.* Like us taking a dispute to the schoolmaster, but nothing was resolved. The case went on to the court in Siasi town, or to Jolo. (*Thesaurus:* **dagsol, ikiral, tukbal₂**)

**paglaggut-laggut** *v. intr. aN-* To throb painfully, of an injury. (*Thesaurus:* **pagk'bbut-k'bbut, pagkowap-kowap, pagdutdut, pagsignat-signat, panag-panag 1**)

**paglagi** *v. tr.* To make use of something. *Kapunyahan, ya tapaglagi kamemon. Kapunyahan,* everything that is made use of.

**paglaginit** *v. intr. aN-* **1)** To come away piece by piece. *Buwat aniya' kakanta ak'llit ati hella'ta, ya llingna hē', yukta, "Maglaginit."* It's like we are eating something chewy and pull at it, the word for that, we say is, "It is coming away bit by bit." **1.1)** *v. tr. -an* To reduce something little by little. *Halam gi' iya amatay, pinaglaginitan na alta'na.* He hasn't died yet, and his possessions are already being reduced bit by bit. *Pinaglaginitan umpan ni daing.* The fish is nibbling the bait off [the hook].

**paglagonggok** *v. intr. aN-* To make the sound of water flowing through a confined space; to

gurgle. *Buwat kita angisi bohe' ni deyom bō', maglagonggok.* Like when we put water into a bamboo water-pole, it gurgles. (*Thesaurus:* **konog-konog, kulattub, llub, pagbolobok, paglagublub**)

**paglagungkad** *v. intr. aN-* To make the sounds of people moving and working. *Buwat dai'-llaw bo' magtulakan saga a'a, na maglagungkad ai-ai.* Like at sunrise when people are leaving, then everything is making a clatter. *Da'a kono' kām maglagungkad e'bi magl'ngngan ilū. Abati' kaluma'an.* Please don't make a clatter there with your walking. The whole neighborhood will wake up. *Nda'un kono' ma kusina bang aniya' kuting maglagungkad.* Just have a look in the kitchen [to see] if there is a cat making a noise.

**paglalap** *v. intr. aN-* To talk incoherently, as someone sleeping. (*cf:* **lāp-lāp**)

**paglambeng-lambeng** *v. intr. aN-* **1)** To swing to and fro. **1.1)** *v. tr.* To make things sway to and fro, of hanging objects. *Oy! Da'a paglambeng-lambengun daing ilū.* Hey, don't keep swinging those fish. (*cf:* **paglimbay**)

**paglamu-lamu** *v. tr.* To share community resources. *Maglamu-lamu kayu maka bohe', hatina dabohe', dakayu.* Sharing the firewood and the water, in other words one water source, one lot of firewood.

**paglamu-lamuhan** *n.* Things that are shared communally. *Bang saupama kitam amangan, ya magb'lla subay maglamu-lamu. Paglamu-lamuhan kinakan.* When we are eating, for example, those who do the cooking should get a share. It is the food that is shared.

**paglē** *var. of* **paglele**

**paglega-lega** *v. intr. aN-* To move restlessly, as someone in pain. (*Thesaurus:* **paglimayu', paglimbahod, paglimpa, pagsalinggā, pagsularaw**)

**pagle'eng** *v. intr. aN-* To fuss or cry petulantly, as a child who cannot settle. *Onde'-onde' magle'eng-le'eng, magongka' m'ssa'-bidda'.* A child who keeps fussing, playing aimlessly with this and that. (*Thesaurus:* **langan₁, mmaw 1, s'ngngel 1, unga'**)

**pagle'od** *v. intr. aN-* To stretch, as a person or animal waking up. (*Thesaurus:* **h'nnat 1, l'dduk 1, nned, pagkul'ddeng, paghitad**)

**paglemong** *n.* **1)** Grief expressed loudly. *Ma llaw du inān, landu' aheya paglemong ma Awrusalam buwat bay kapaglemong ma masa-awal.* On that very day there was loud weeping in Jerusalem, like the weeping of former times. (*cf:* **pagsindilan 1**) **1.1)** *v. intr. aN-* To weep aloud for someone who has died. *Pagta'u sigām amatay na, magtūy sigām maglemong.* As soon as they knew he was dead, they mourned loudly. *Aniya' kamatayan magtangis a'a, maglemong.* There are people weeping for a bereavement, mourning.

(*Thesaurus:* **handul atay**, **pagdohon**, **pagdukka'** **1.1**, **paglindu**) **1.2**) *v. tr.* *-an* To mourn someone. *Wa'i na si Anu pinaglemongan, halam tabāk.* They are mourning for What's-his-name, [who] hasn't been found.

**paglera-lera** *v. intr.* *aN-* To smart, as from a whipping. *Nā, mbal ka maglera-lera?* There now, aren't you hurting from that? (*Thesaurus:* **bisa 1**, **p'ddi' 1.1**, **p'llat 1.1**)

**pagleyat-leyat** *v. intr.* *aN-* To change from one thing or location to another; to be unsettled. *Ubus maitu, ubus mahē', mbal at'ttog ma lahat. Ubus aku ma kapū'an, ubus ma Bunggaw, ubus ma Siasi. Magleyat-leyat.* First here, then there, not staying in any place. First I was at the outer islands, then at Bonggao, then at Siasi. Going hither and yon.

**pagliblib-liblib** *v. intr.* *aN-* **1**) To diminish little by little. **1.1**) *v. tr.* To consume something little by little. *Ā, hal pinagliblib-liblib na pa'in.* It just keeps on getting used up, little by little. (*Thesaurus:* **kitkit**, **pagkuri'-kuri'**)

**pagli'anan** var. of **pagli'anun**

**pagli'i-li'i** *v. tr.* To defer or avoid the performance of a task. *Minsan du aniya' gawina, at'ggol anuli-nuli ni saddi, magli'i-li'i.* Even though he has things to do, he talks for a long time to someone else, putting things off. (*Thesaurus:* **ddas 1.1**, **tagga 1.1**, **tahāl**)

**paglilip-lilip** *v. intr.* *aN-* To tilt from one side to another, allowing contents to spill. *Maglilip-lilip.* Tipping this way and that. (*Thesaurus:* **kīd₂**, **kīng 1.1**, **lemba**, **lenggang**, **lihid**, **poyog 1**, **tīg**)

**paglimanda** *v. intr.* *aN-* To appear before a judge for sentencing after one has been convicted. *Bang aniya' dusaku apuwas du aku, bang pa'in bay maglimanda ni huwis.* If I do something wrong I will be excused, provided I have apppeared before a judge.

**paglimbahod** (var. **paglimbahon**) *v. intr.* *aN-* To move restlessly in reaction to pain or discomfort. *Maglimbahod iya ma palegehan sabab pasu'.* He keeps moving around on the bed because of the heat. *Maglimbahod ē', buwat sali' a'a ab'ttong, palege na pa'in bo' ngga'i ka gi' bulananna. Limbahod* is like a pregnant woman who keeps lying down even though it is not yet her time. *Buwat a'a pīngkongan, ma'ai-ma'ai palegehanna magdahing-dahing. Ya hē' niōnan maglimbahon.* Like a person who has a swelling, no matter where he lies he just cries out in pain. That's called *limbahon. Maglimbahon, sali' taluwa' p'ddi', sali' magl'ddukan inān.* Writhing in discomfort, as though struck with pain, stretching out like that. (*Thesaurus:* **paglega-lega**, **paglimayu'**, **paglimpa**, **pagsalinggā**, **pagsularaw**)

**paglimbahon** var. of **paglimbahod**

**paglimbokay** *v. intr.* *aN-* To eddy around a sheltering feature, of wind. *Bang kita am'lla*

*maka aniya' baliyu kowan maka min gibang, yukta, "Baliyu maglimbokay."* When we are cooking and there is a wind from the right and the left, we say, "The wind is swirling all around." (*cf:* **limbōn**; *syn:* **paglimpowak**)

**paglimpa** *v. tr.* *-an* To ease one's pain or discomfort by changing position. (*Thesaurus:* **paglega-lega**, **paglimayu'**, **paglimbahod**, **pagsalinggā**, **pagsularaw**)

**paglinga-linga** *v. intr.* *aN-* To move one's head as a sign of disagreement or preoccupation. *Maglinga-linga iya, marai' halam kasulutan.* He just shook his head, probably not pleased. *Hal maglinga-linga, sali' mag'nda'-nda'.* Just looking this way and that, sort of looking around. (*Thesaurus:* **keleng**, **elong-elong mata**)

**pagl'bba** var. of **pag'bba**

**pagl'pput** *v. intr.* *aN-* To be in the habit of telling lies. (*Thesaurus:* **puting 1.1**, **sussa'**)

**paglukum** var. of **paglukun**

**paglūng-lūng** *v. intr.* *aN-* To move about limply, as sea cucumbers in the hull of a canoe. *Bay aku an'bba ni Bakal maka'ā' aku gamat. Sakali maglūng-lūngan mareyom mohang, angahimāt.* I was strand-gathering at Bakal and got some *gamat* trepang. They sloshed about in the hull, just limp.

**pagluray** *v. tr.* To fight together physically, woman-style. *Bang d'nda sali'-sali', bo' aniya' pagsagga'an tahinang bono' he' sigām, na bang magsekot makapagluray, magganggut.* When both are women and they have an argument, they make it into a fight, and when they get close to each other they cat-fight, pull each other's hair. (*cf:* **ganggut**)

**paglutsa** *v. intr.* *aN-* To wrestle with each other. *Maglutsa itū bang magbono', sagō' maggapus du isāb.* Wrestling is when people are fighting, but also holding each other tight.

**pagmakōk** (derivative of **kōk**) *v. intr.* *aN-* To take the lead over a group; to represent a group. *Duwampū' maka duwantahun kapagmakōkna ma bangsana.* He was leader over his ethnic group for twenty-two years. *Tahinang aku pagmakōkan ma deyomanna, maka gin'llal aku nakura' ang'ntanan sakalingkal lahat.* I have been appointed as leader in his realm, and appointed to be the head person controlling the whole of the region. *Nnom imam magbeya', ata'u sigām kamemon. Dakayu' du tapene' magmakōk ma hinang.* Six imams together, all of them knowledgeable. Just one chosen to be in charge of the event. (*Thesaurus:* **pagbebeya'an**, **pagmandangan**, **pagmete-mete**, **pagmunda'an**).

**pagmahi** *v. intr.* *aN-* To complain constantly. *Magmahi na pa'in iya pasalan kasusahanna.* He is always complaining about his troubles. *Sambatan si Di, yukna, "Bang ka kinabilahi'an e' d'nda abō' ka mbal bilahi, magmahi ka, anumbung* *ka ni nakura'.*" As Di said, "If you are desired by a woman but you don't desire her, make a complaint, report it to a leader." *Allā, magmahi si Delila ma si Samson, yukna, "Yuknu in aku kalasahannu ru, saguwā' mbal aku pangandolannu."* Unexpectedly, Delilah complained to Samson, saying, "You said you loved me, but you don't trust me." (*Thesaurus:* **kuhi₂, pagmalān, pagpuhun 1.1, sumbung, tuntut₁**)

**pagmahil** *v. intr. aN-* To march, as soldiers. *Bang aniya' bahonos takalenu ma kariyata'an kayu inān sali' a'a magmahil, parugpak na kām.* When you hear a noise up in the trees like soldiers marching, you are to attack.

**pagmailad** var. of **pagmairan**

**pagma'adjul** *v. intr. aN-* To be totally committed to a course of action. *Hē' na sigām magma'adjul ni Sabah pagka asigpit pagusaha ma Pilipin.* There they are, their minds set on heading off to Sabah since it is difficult to make a living in the Philippines.

**pagmalān** *v. intr. aN-* To react noisily and dramatically to an offensive suggestion, especially one of a sexual nature. *Ta'abutku h'ndaku magbihing maka l'lla saddī ma kara-kara. Gese'ku na hōs, bowaku ni sara'. Magmalān aku.* I found my wife in the act of sleeping with another man. I tore my garment, and brought her to the judge. I made a great fuss about it. *Buwat aniya' tuhumaku magbeya' budjang maka subul, bo' halam ta'abutku, na magmalān sigā. Aku ya ka'ā'an sīn.* Suppose I spread a rumor about a girl and a boy being together, though I don't actually see them, then they make a fuss. I'm the one who is fined. (*Thesaurus:* **kuhi₂, pagmahi, pagpuhun 1.1, sumbung, tuntut₁**)

**pagmalangkahi** *v. intr. aN-* To boast about one's superiority to others; to behave arrogantly. *Landu' akagit atayku ma saga paglahat magmalangkahi halam aniya' lengog sigām.* I am seriously angry with the people who boast that they have no disturbances in their region. *Magmalangkahi kam in kosogbi ya sababan angkan kam anganda'ug.* You brag that your strength is the reason why you win. (*Thesaurus:* **pagabbu 1.1, pagbantug-bantug, pagheya-heya, pagmahatinggi, pagpasanglit, pagtāp-tāp**)

**pagmalas** *v. tr. -an* To subject someone to an irrational response. *Bitu'anunna ya pinagmalasan. Paturul ma iya pi'ingga-pi'ingga lahat.* It is his divorced wife that he is behaving irrationally towards. He follows her no matter what place she goes to. *Magmalas itū buwat sali' aburiru pikilanta, sali' arupang. Malas* is like our minds being disturbed, kind of stupid. *Magmalas iya ma nsa' bay karūlan.* He is behaving irrationally because of not being permitted.

**pagmaloman** (derivative of **loman**) *v. intr. aN-* To show respect or courtesy. *Halam maglampik,* *halam magmaloman, magtūy ah'lling.* Didn't show restraint, didn't show respect, talked immediately.

**pagmalulus** *v. intr. aN-* To behave with humility and submission. *Pasekot-sekot gi' iya bo' magmalulus ma atag tape'na.* She came a little closer, abasing herself at his feet. *Min tagna'an gi' bay pagmalulusnu ma Tuhan.* From the beginning of your humble attitude towards God. *Ka'am kar'ndahan subay magmalulus ma h'llabi.* You women should be in respectful submission to your husbands.

**pagmamay** *v. tr. -an* To treat someone with reserve or caution. *Subay kita amudji Tuhan ma buwat kabaya'anna. Subay kitam magmamay maka magmatāw ma iya.* We should praise God in the manner he desires. We should respect and fear him. (*Thesaurus:* **pagaddat 1.1, pagmanja', palok 1, su'ap 1.1**)

**pagmanja'** *v. tr. -an* To treat someone with respect. *Halam aku magmanja' ma si La, bay t'ggalku manuk-manuk. Bilahi iya ang'nda'.* I did not respect La's wishes. I chased the birds away. She wanted to see them. *Mbal pinagmanja'an, sali' mbal pinagaddatan.* Not shown respect, not treated with courtesy. *Paligay itū bang sali' nirūlan he' matto'ata, paligay kita sala mbal magmanja'.* The more our parents indulge us, the more we kind of fail to show them respect. *Ya a'a mbal magmanja' bang ah'lling, kamulahan iya kamattihanna.* The man who is not respectful when he speaks, his final state is destruction. (*Thesaurus:* **pagaddat 1.1, pagmamay, palok 1, su'ap 1.1**)

**pagmarī'** *v. tr.* To refuse or deny a request. (*Thesaurus:* **pagin'mbal 1, pasibukut 1, sulak₂, taikut 1.1**)

**pagmatāw** (derivative of **tāw**) *n. 1)* Deep respect; reverence. *In pagmatāw ma Tuhan magpataha' umul.* Reverence for God lengthens life. *1.1) v. tr. -an* To fear; to show deep respect. *Pandu'anta kām bang sai ya subay pagmatāwanbi.* I'll teach you who you should be afraid of.

**pagmatiase'** (derivative of **ase'**) *v. intr. aN-* To plead for mercy or sympathy.

**pagmatireyo'** var. of **pagpatireyo'**

**pagmatuwas** (derivative of **tuwas**) *v. intr. aN-* To become stubborn or resistant to advice. *Sagō' halam bay bineya' pandu' itū e' sigām, gōm pa'in magmatuwas.* But they didn't follow this teaching, becoming stubborn instead.

**pagmatuyu'** (derivative of **tuyu'**) *v. intr. aN-* To be fully persistent. *Aniya' anakku bilahi'an anakna, hatina ka'a magmuwat bo' kinabaya'an e' kar'ndahan. Hatina ka'a ya magmatuyu'.* A son of yours fancies his daughter, which means that you do what is needed to have him approved by the girl's family. You are the one to be persistent.

**pagmete-mete** *v. tr. -an* To give orders, as an older

woman in charge of a house may do. (*Thesaurus:* **pagbebeya'an, pagmakōk, pagmandangan, pagmunda'an**)

**pagmoto** *v. intr. aN-* To be involved in voting. *Bay kami amasiyal ni Siasi ang'nda'-ng'nda' magmoto.* We strolled around Siasi Town watching the people voting.

**pagmusmud** *v. intr. aN-* **1)** To be grouchy; to be annoyed. *Bang aniya' kinap'ddi'an atayna ma anakna, magmusmud. Mbal binono'.* When he is annoyed at his child, he talks irritably. [The child] is not hit. *Hal magmusmud, hal magb'ngkol mareyom atayna.* Just grumbling, inwardly annoyed. **1.1)** *v. tr. -an* To express displeasure at something. *Sinalu'-salu', aniya' sali' pinagmusmuran.* Criticised, like there's something to complain about.

**pagnaho'-naho'** *v. intr. aN-* To assume a status or position that is not deserved. *Magnaho'-naho' iya ma deyom lahat, magwakil-wakil dīna sali', bo' ngga'i ka iya bay gīllal.* He makes himself a person of status in the district, authorises himself, even though he has not been appointed. *Buwat si Mo maghinang tinapay halam bay sinoho' he'ku. Magnaho'-naho' iya maghinang.* It's like Mo making bread without me telling her to. She is taking it on herself to make it. *Mbal aku wajib makapagnaho'-naho'.* I am not authorised to be exercising authority. (*Thesaurus:* **hinang-hinang₂, pagbau'-bau', pagdō-rō, paglaku-laku**)

**pagnanu'** *v. intr. aN-* To swing in a standing position. (*Thesaurus:* **dundang₁ 1, duyan, ombo'-ombo', pagdanggu'-danggu', tadjun**)

**pagnikala'atan** (derivative of **la'at**) *v. intr. aN-* To come to a bad end as a consequence of present actions or attitudes. *Bang ka'a-i mbal ameya' pandu', gana-gana magnikala'atan.* If you will not listen to advice, then you will inevitably come to grief. *Tantu ka'a-i magnikala'atan.* You are bound to come to a disastrous end.

**pagnihakin** (derivative of **hakin**) *v. intr. aN-* To sit with legs crossed and upper leg swinging.

**pagnihōs** var. of **paghinōs**

**pagnijaket** (derivative of **jaket**) *v. intr. aN-* To wear a jacket. *Magnijaket aku.* I am wearing a jacket.

**pagnijuba** (derivative of **juba**) *v. intr. aN-* To wear a long gown of white cloth.

**pagnilesseg** (derivative of **lesseg**) *v. intr. aN-* To sit with buttocks and thighs flat on the floor. *Magnilesseg, basta buli'ta par'dda.* Sitting right down, as when the buttocks are flat on the floor. *Magnilesseg ka to'ongan, sidda am'ssang mailu.* Sit right down, lots of itchy stuff there.

**pagnililus** (derivative of **lilus**) *v. intr. aN-* To wear a watch. *Bang aniya' kinawin magnililus aku.* When someone is getting married I wear a watch.

**pagon₁** *n.* **1)** Durability; resistance to wear. *Tumbukan bihing hošku, ya na hē' amuwan pagon.* My sarong has a dotted selvage edge, that's what gives it durability. **1.1)** *adj. a-* Durable; substantial. *Apagon itū mbal ab'kkat.* This word *pagon* means it doesn't snap. *Apagon tahi'an bakiya' min tahi'an malkina.* The back-stitching technique is more durable than machine stitching. (*Thesaurus:* **anagtol, kamdos₂, kumpay, galak₂, taggu₁, tatas 1.1, togob₁**) **1.2)** *v. tr. -an* To increase the durability of something, as by adding a splint to a boom.

**pagon₂** *adj. a-* Intense or complete, of conditions such as sleep or blindness. *Apagon tuliku dibuhi'.* I slept soundly last night. (*Thesaurus:* **ddok, haluk**)

**pagpabā'** (derivative of **bā'₁**) *v. intr. aN-* To inform people of a coming event. *Aniya' s'ssag magpiha, aniya' s'ssag magpabā'.* S'ssag can be about searching, and it can be about informing people of an event.

**pagpab'lli** (derivative of **b'lli**) *v. intr. aN-* To get people to buy things.

**pagpabowa** (derivative of **bowa₃**) *v. intr. aN-* To let oneself be influenced. *Da'a ka magpabowa ma manis mata d'nda.* Don't let yourself be influenced by the beauty of a woman's eyes.

**pagpaka-** *aff.* Prefix marking ability or potential for the stated action. *Magpakabono', buwat saga si Ki, bo' ngga'i ka isāb pamomono'.* Ki has the ability to fight, but he is not an habitual fighter. *Mura-murahan magpakasampay in niyat kami ni ka'am. Paheyabi du isāb ma atay.* Our hope is that our serious intention may be able to reach you. May you also treat it as important.

**pagpakabowa** (derivative of **bowa₁**) *v. tr.* To be able to bring the specified item. *Magpakabowa aku saga lima pilak amole'.* I am able to bring about five pesos home.

**pagpakahinang** (derivative of **hinang₁**, derivative of **hinang₁**) **1)** *v. tr.* To be capable of doing the stated action. *Magpakahinang aku saga duwa bagiyas duwang'llaw.* I am able to make up to two *bagiyas* traps in two days. **2)** *v. intr. aN-* To be able to be used. *Tasumpal pelang abō' magpakahinang. Sin'nsong atawa tinumpakan.* The canoe can be patched so it can be used for work. Plugged up or patched here and there.

**pagpakalintaw** (derivative of **kalintaw**) *v. tr.* To be provoking each other to anger. *Sabab kami bay magbono' maka si Sa magpakalintaw.* Because Sa and I had been fighting, making each other angry.

**pagpakay-dusa** *v. intr. aN-* To commit a sin. *Magpakay-dusa bang a'a magliyu-lakad.* A person sins when he commits adultery. (*syn:* **pagdusa**)

**pagpakeyat** (derivative of **keyat₂**) *v. tr.* To light lamps. *Hinabu masi alogob-logob lahat magpakeyat kami palita'an.* While it is still dusk we light the lamps. *Magpakeyat na pa'in kami kulaet magusaha.* We routinely light the pressure lantern in order to go fishing.

**pagpaelle'-elle'** (derivative of **elle'-elle'**) *v. intr.* *aN-* To draw attention to one's own physical attractions. (*Thesaurus:* **mata-mata₁, pagpa'nda'-pa'nda', pa'amu-amu**).

**pagpag** *v. tr.* *-an* To remove surface rubbish by shaking or flapping; to dust off.

**pagpaharap** (derivative of **harap₂**) *v. ditr.* To present a newborn child to a ritual ancestor. *Magpaharap onde' ni mbo'.* Presenting a child to the ancestors.

**pagpah'nda** (derivative of **h'nda**) *n.* **1)** The process of providing a man with a wife. *Ta'abut pagpah'nda, bang ya bay pagbissalahan maka mma' d'nda hē', na pehē'ta na t'llu hatus, ya hē'.* When it comes to the betrothal proceedings, and if ₱300 was the sum discussed with the woman's father, then we hand over three hundred, and that's it. (*Thesaurus:* **pagtunggu'-tunang, tagad-kawin**).**1.1)** *v. intr.* *aN-* To be involved in getting a wife for a man.

**pagpainay-painay** (derivative of **inay**) *v. intr.* *aN-* To do anything whatever. *Magpainay-magpainay na he'nu ya a'a hē', na ka'a na magpikil bang buwattingga.* Whatever you do for this [gravely ill] person, you are the one to decide how.

**pagpa'abbu** (derivative of **abbu**) *v. intr.* *aN-* To make a show of one's importance. *Minsan aku magpa'abbu, baranku ya pagabbuhanku.* Even though I act in a conceited way, it's myself that I am conceited about. *Baranku ya pagabbuhanku.* It's myself that I am conceited about.

**pagpa'ampun** (derivative of **ampun₁**) *v. intr.* *aN-* To seek forgiveness from someone. *Subay iya magpa'ampun ni Tuhan, niuli'an llingna hē' ni a'a bay subalihanna hē'.* He should seek forgiveness from God, that the words he swore on oath to that man might be put right. (*Thesaurus:* **deyo'₃ 2, pagkahāp, ū'ū**).

**pagpa'amu** (derivative of **amu₁**) *v. intr.* *aN-* To speak plainly and truthfully. *Bang saupama magtiman, na magsalassay pahāp-hāp, magpa'amu ni sara'.* Divorcing for example and settling things really well, speaking frankly to the magistrate.

**pagpa'andag** (derivative of **andag**) *v. intr.* *aN-* To be active in getting potential customers to make an offer. *Magpa'andag, magpab'lli.* Getting people to bid, selling stuff.

**pagpa'andig** *v. intr.* *aN-* To express one's thoughts in veiled language. (*Thesaurus:* **limut 1.1, pagpara'il, pataggal-taggal, salig₃**)

**pagpa'ata** (derivative of **ata**) *v. intr.* *aN-* To submit oneself to being a slave. *Magpa'ata aku ma ka'a.* I will become a slave to you.

**pagpa'in** var. of **pagpina'in**

**pagpa'nda'-pa'nda'** (derivative of **nda'**) *v. intr.* *aN-* To make a display or show of something. *Saukat aheka s'mmekbi magpa'nda'-nda' na kām. Na kami itū ya tu'ud s'mmek kami.* Just because you have lots of clothes you show off. But as for

us, these are simply our clothes. (*Thesaurus:* **mata-mata₁, pagpaelle'-elle', pa'amu-amu**).

**pagpalanga** (derivative of **langa**) *v. intr.* *aN-* To behave as though higher in status. *Aniya' isab a'a kabintanan magpalanga dīna min kasehe'anna.* There are also people addicted to making themselves of higher status than others.

**pagpalasahan** (derivative of **lasa₁**) *v. intr.* *aN-* To be feeling unwell. *Magpalasahan aku.* I am experiencing ill health. (*Thesaurus:* **pa'in₃ 1, saki 1.1**).

**pagpalere'** (derivative of **lere'**) *v. intr.* *aN-* To pop and crackle, as something brittle being chewed. *Atuwas lapuk-lapuk, magpalere' mareyom bowa'.* Lapuk-lapuk candy is hard, it crackles in the mouth.

**pagpaljanji'an** (derivative of **janji'**) *v. intr.* *aN-* To make a solemn promise to each other. *Jari magpaljanji'an sigā karuwangan ma matahan Tuhan.* So the two of them made a solemn promise to each other in the sight of God.

**pagpal'ngngan** (derivative of **l'ngngan₁**) *n.* **1)** The stage in a wedding sequence when the groom's party goes to the house of the bride's family.**1.1)** *v. intr.* *aN-* To manage a wedding event as master of ceremonies.

**pagpamagay** (derivative of **magay**)**1)** *v. intr.* *aN-* To be concerned about what is going on (usually with a negative). **2)** *v. tr.* To treat something as a matter of concern. *Halam tapagpamagayna kahālan ina'an-i.* He had no concern for what was happening there. *Yuk taligramA: "Tapagpamagay na si Anu. Sinoho' ka pasa'ut-sa'ut."* The telegram said, "There is nothing that can now be done for What's-his-name. You are told to act rather quickly."

**pagpama'ap** (derivative of **ma'ap**) *v. intr.* *aN-* To engage in a forgiveness and reconciliation ritual. *Magpama'ap kita sali'. Aniyum kita tape'ta-tanganta, sali' kita magpatiampun.* We seek reconciliation. We kiss [each other's] hands and feet, like asking for forgiveness. *Ya dabbana ginuna bang aniya' magpama'ap atawa magduwa'a-salamat.* The tambourine may be used when there is a forgiveness or thanksgiving ceremony.

**pagpamulawan** (derivative of **bulawan**) *v. intr.* *aN-* To display one's gold, especially in the form of gold-covered teeth.

**pagpanonda'** (derivative of **tonda'₁**) *v. intr.* *aN-* To fish with a trolled lure. *Buwat kami magpanonda' bo' halam maka'ā', na palagesles kami ni timbang dakayu'.* Like when we are trolling [for tuna] but are not catching any, we go with the current to another deep-sea area.

**pagpanubu'** (derivative of **tubu'**) *v. intr.* *aN-* To be passed down through successive generations. *Magtuttulan na pa'in, magpanubu'.* Continuing to follow the traditions of the family line, generation after generation.

**pagpangalemos** *v. intr. aN-* To make a living by begging from people passing by. *Aheka onde' magpangalemos ma palasa.* There are lots of children begging in the town plaza.

**pagpangongka'** (derivative of **ongka'**) *v. intr. aN-* To gamble or play games together. *Buwat aniya' magpangongka' duwangan, dangan ata'u, dangan mbal.* Like two people playing a game together, one who knows how, and one who doesn't. *Buwat magbalebol, magsugal saga, na pinamarāhan he' bobotang-lahat. Sinoho' kami da'a magpangongka'.* Like when playing volleyball or gambling, the local headman makes us stop. He tells us not to play [those] games.

**pagpaopēt** *v. intr. aN-* To head off in different directions. *Sūng kita analun. Magpaopēt kitam, kami ni mampallam dakayū' ati ka'a ni mampallam dakayu' isāb.* Let's go and gather fruit. We'll go in different directions, us to one mango tree, and you to another. *Magpaopēt, sali' magsapehak, magl'bba.* Going different ways, sort of diverging, taking leave of each other. (*Thesaurus:* **pagl'kkat, pagsapehak, siha'**)

**pagpapak** *v. tr.* To bang two items together on their concave faces. (*cf:* **paglagpak 1**)

**pagpapole'** (derivative of **papole'**) *v. intr. aN-* To return things to a prior status. *Saupama bay kita magb'lli, bay magsulut. Mbal manjari binawi'an bissala, mbal na manjari agpapole'.* For example, we were buying and had come to an agreement. It is not possible to go back on what has been said, not possible to return [what has been purchased].

**pagparakag** (derivative of **dakag**) *v. intr. aN-* To be set on getting what one wants.

**pagpara'il** *v. intr. aN-* To communicate indirectly, either by veiled reference or by means of a go-between. *Pagpara'il maka pa'andig, sali' aku ē' aniya' mohotku ni ka'a. Mbal pamūngku, aiya' aku. Magpakale aku ma si Ma, bo' ya target ē' patudju ni ka'a.* Pagpara'il and pa'andig are like me having some purpose that involves you. I don't speak of it, being ashamed. I let Ma hear about it, but you are the intended target. *Magpara'il bagayku, yukna, "Kahunitan aku ma sīn. Sai na bahā' makapautangan aku?" Ya tahatiku ya pamūngna tudju ni aku.* My friend talks indirectly, saying, "I am in financial difficulties. Who might give me a loan?" What I understand is that his words are aimed at me. (*Thesaurus:* **limut 1.1, pagpa'andig, pataggal-taggal, salig₃**)

**pagparibay** *v. intr. aN-* To go to and fro repeatedly. *Aheka a'a magparibay-paribay.* A lot of people are going to and fro, again and again.

**pagpariyata'** (derivative of **diyata'**) *v. tr.* To raise something, especially a flag. *Palabay aku ma iskul, magsabu aku maka pinagpariyata' panji, jari pahondong aku, hatina amuwan mahaltabat ma panji bangsa.* I was passing by the school and coincided with the flag being raised. So I stopped, paying respect to the national flag.

**pagparūl** (derivative of **dūl**) *v. tr.1)* To indulge one's desires. *Tu'ud kām bilahi magparūl napsubi, angkan kām angamu'.* You simply want to indulge your desires, that's why you are making the request.**1.1)** *v. intr. aN-* To be indulging oneself.

**pagpasab'nnal** (derivative of **b'nnal**) *v. intr. aN-1)* To accept or speak the truth. *Sasuku ya magpasab'nnal ameya'.* Whoever fulfils the commitment to obey.**1.1)** *v. intr. aN-* To make a confession. *Magpasab'nnal pasal bay kahinangan sigām ala'at.* They are owning up to the bad things they had done.

**pagpasalupa** *v. intr. aN-* To appear in physical form by supernatural means. *Bay aku tinuwa' he' si Mbo'. Ya umagadna pasalidda ni aku, ngga'i ka baranna magpasalupa.* Grandfather appeared to me. It was his ghost that appeared, not him in person taking on a bodily form. *Magpasalupa, sali' magpinda. Bay ta'nda'ta man munda'anta a'a lum'ngngan na tudju ni kita. Na halam na ta'nda'ta a'a ina'an, ya ta'nda'ta hayop.* Taking on a shape, like changing [shape]. We saw in front of us a person walking towards us. Then we no longer saw that person, what we saw was an animal. (*Thesaurus:* **salidda, tuwa' 1.1**)

**pagpasamba** (derivative of **samba**) *v. intr. aN-* To do something that involves risk or uncertainty.

**pagpasannang** (derivative of **sannang**) *v. intr. aN-* To take it easy; to relax. *Sali' kita magpasannang-pasannang dīta, sali' halam aniya' ugatta.* Like making ourselves totally relaxed, as though we no longer had sinews.

**pagpasanglit** (derivative of **sanglit**) *v. intr. aN-* To draw attention to one's own importance. *A'a limaya maghinang ai kabaya'anna, magpasanglit iya makalandu'.* A man who is free to do anything he wants, drawing far too much attention to his status. (*Thesaurus:* **pagabbu 1.1, pagbantug-bantug, pagheya-heya, pagmahatinggi, pagmalangkahi, pagtāp-tāp**).

**pagpasukud** (derivative of **sukud₂**) *v. tr. -an* To do something that involves risk or uncertainty. *Magpasukuran na ka magbeya' maka kami, ati magbahagi' kitām.* You are taking the risk of getting together with us, and we will share [what we get]. (*Thesaurus:* **k'ddom₂, halus₁, pagsusaed, samba 1, sarap₂ 1, tawakkal**).

**pagpasu'alan** *n.* 1) A disagreement between two people or groups; a controversy. **1.1)** *v. intr. aN-* To disagree with each other.

**pagpataddangan** (derivative of **taddang**) *n.* Identification papers required by law. *Aniya' gi' lahat pagpataddangan sulat.* There are other countries requiring legal papers.

**pagpatalap** (derivative of **talap**) *v. intr. aN-* To cause something to disappear, by demonic action. *Pehē' ka magpatalap dīnu.* Go and get yourself snatched out of sight by a demon.

**pagpati-** *aff.* Reflexive prefix: indicates an action performed by the actor on him- or herself. *Ah'lling pa'in timbak, magtūy iya magpatihantak supaya mbal nilutang.* When the gun sounded he threw himself down so that he wouldn't be shot at a second time. *Sai-sai bilahi pinalanga to'ongan subay magpatireyo' dīna min kamemon.* Whoever wants to made really important should make himself lower than all.

**pagpatialop** (derivative of **alop₁**) *v. intr. aN-* To humble oneself in the presence of a superior. *Magpatialop kami, sama'nda' kami ni iya.* We are prostrating ourselves, seeing him face to face. (*cf:* **pagpatihantak 1, pagsarahakan**).

**pagpatiampun** (derivative of **ampun₁**) *v. intr. aN-* To abase oneself when asking forgiveness. *Magpatiampun kami ni anak huwis.* We request forgiveness from the judge's son. *Magpatiampun kita bang kita bay makarusa.* We beg forgiveness if we have committed an offense.

**pagpatiata** (derivative of **ata**) *v. intr. aN-* To submit oneself to being a slave. *Magpatiata kami ni ka'a apa halam sīn kami.* We submit ourselves as slaves to you because we have no money. *Magpatiata saga palbantahannu ni ka'a.* Your enemies will make themselves your slaves.

**pagpatihantak** (derivative of **hantak₁**) *v. intr. aN-*1) To humble oneself before a girl's elders, initiating a proposal of marriage that bypasses the usual negotiations and risks all on a single offer. *Magpatihantak subul inān ni matto'a ya tag-baran, sabab bilahi to'ongan magmato'a ma iya.* That young man humbled himself in making a marriage offer direct to the girl's father as the one in charge, because he very much wants him as his father-in-law. (*cf:* **pagpatialop, pagsarahakan**). 2) To throw oneself down, as to avoid detection. *Ah'lling pa'in timbak, magtūy iya magpatihantak supaya mbal nilutang.* When the gun sounded he threw himself down so that he wouldn't be shot at a second time.

**pagpati'llot** (derivative of **llot**) *v. intr. aN-*1) To be in an intermediate state. *Magpati'llot apote' maka ettom.* It is between white and black. 2) To serve as a mediator between two parties.

**pagpatilossok** (derivative of **lossok**) *v. intr. aN-* To let oneself down into a hole.

**pagpatilukbu'** (derivative of **lukbu'₂**) *v. intr. aN-* To fall on one's knees voluntarily, as an act of deep respect. *An'ngge na aku min bay pal'sseganku bo' aku magpatilukbu' ma sultan.* I stood up from where I had been sitting and fell on my knees before the sultan.

**pagpatimpa** (derivative of **timpa**) *v. intr. aN-* To transfer responsibility or blame from one to the other. (*Thesaurus:* **balik₂, bĭng₃, bitung, hili, likid, pagbintu, pelleng 1.2**).

**pagpating'llaw** (derivative of **llaw₂**) *v. intr. aN-* To expose oneself to the sun; to sunbathe. *Magay Milikan magpating'llaw?* Why do Westerners sunbathe?

**pagpatireyo'** (var.**pagmatireyo'**) (derivative of **deyo'₃**) *v. intr. aN-* To show humility by making oneself lower in worth or rank. *Ya problemana, mbal magpatireyo'.* Her problem is that she won't show humility. *Sai-sai bilahi pinalanga to'ongan subay magpatireyo' dīna min kamemon.* Whoever wants to made really high [important] should make himself lower than all. (*Thesaurus:* **duku', luku'₂, luhud, sujud**).

**pagpatuli** (derivative of **tuli₁**) *v. intr. aN-* To have a sick person sleep in the house of a medical or ritual specialist for treatment. *Kauli'an pa'in sakiku, "Na m'ssa' na," yuk bay manawalan aku hē'. "Ni'bbahan na." Halam na magpatuli pehē' ni luma' a'a jīn.* When my sickness was cured, the one who had recited charms over me said, "No more now. He is to be left as is." [They] no longer had [me] sleep at the house of the djinn-master.

**pagpaubus** (derivative of **ubus₁**) *v. intr. aN-* To do something as the final action of a sequence. *Magpaubus ni sigā ya taga jīn. Bang kauli'an subay da'a magl'kkat.* At the last the one with a djinn goes to them. When the healing is done they don't separate.

**pagpauppi** (derivative of **uppi**) *v. intr. aN-* To appear to someone in a dream. *Aniya' mala'ikat bay magpauppi ni si Nabi Ibrahim waktuna bay ma Betel.* An angel appeared to Abraham in a dream, at the time when he was at Bethel.

**pagpeha** var. of **pagkeha**

**pagpuliting** var. of **pagpiting**

**pagsabak** *v. tr.* To carry something securely, against one's body. *Bang aniya' sīnnu subay pagsabak-sabaknu na pa'in.* If you have money you should always carry it on your person.

**pagsabali** *v. intr. aN-* To be mutually confused or mistaken about what the other is saying or intending. *Llingnu maka llingku saddĭ, magsabali kita.* What you say and what I say are different, we are talking about different things. *Buwat sali' aku angamu' saldenas ni ka'a, ati soho'nu si Ne angamu' saldenas ni aku. Magsabali lling.* Like I ask sardines from you, and you tell Ne to ask sardines from me. Talking at cross-purposes. *Yuk si Mi inān, "Sinō' pinah'lling gabbang ma luma' disi Be." Ah'lling isāb siyaka si Mi, magsabali, "Ma luma'bi ya lisagan, iya maka gabbangna ĭ'." Pangalena hē'.* Mi said, "The bamboo marimba is to be played at Be's house." Mi's older sister also spoke up, mistakenly, "The rhythm set is at your house, it and the marimba." What she heard. (*Thesaurus:* **ambil-hati, pagkamali', pagkasā' 1.1, ta'awil**)

**pagsab'nnal** (derivative of **b'nnal**) *v. tr. -an* To tell the truth about something; to confess something. *Pinagsab'nnalan e'na pasal bay* *dusana.* He told the truth about his sin. (*cf:* **pagnaik-saksi'**).

**pagsabuli-buli** (derivative of **buli-buli**) *v. tr.* To be committed to some action. *Aku ya magsabuli-buli ang'nde', pagka aku ya bay angindam ni ka'a.* I'm the one who will most definitely return it, because I am the one who borrowed it.

**pagsakutu** *v. intr. aN-* To become involved in what others are doing, forming a larger group. *Aniya' bay animbak, aheka patayna. Saga a'a atuhun inān magsakutu amuwa' daing inān.* Someone had dynamited and there were lots of stunned fish. The people diving there swarmed in [with the others] to retrieve fish. (*cf:* **balat, jau'-jau', lamud₂ 1.1**)

**pagsagiyaw** *v. intr. aN-* To be briefly visible, as in a dream or trance. *Buwat palaman atawa palambung ni kita. Hal magsagiyaw la.* Like being briefly visible to us, an ordinary spirit appearance. (*Thesaurus:* **laman 1, lambung₁ 1**)

**pagsahul** *v. intr. aN-* To eat the dawn meal before fasting resumes, during the month of Ramadan. *Lisag t'llu ni lisag lima bulan Puwasa, ya na agsahul amangan, anginum bohe'.* In the month of *Puwasa* from three to five o'clock, that's when people eat, and drink water. (*cf:* **buka**)

**pagsa'ud** *v. intr. aN-* **1)** To do multiple things at the same time. *Aheka kinahinang inān magabut-abut, bo' dakayu' maka dakayu'. Aniya' magsa'ud hinang, magsambeya'.* Lots of things being done in rapid succession, one after another. There are tasks that overlap, occurring together. *Mbal magpuwas hinang, magsa'ud sadja. Buwat aniya' kinahinang salung, pagsimuddai ē' taluwa' na isāb sukkal.* Funeral rituals don't come to an end, they just overlap. It's like there's a funeral for someone tomorrow, and the next day another grief hits us. **2)** To be overlapping or intertwining, as lines from two rods. *Nihinangan ba'ugan bang duwa p'ssi nihūg bo' mbal magsa'ud.* A [horizontal] rod made for it when two hooks are dropped, so they don't intertwine.

**pagsalba** *n.* **1)** A ceremony for bringing an epidemic illness to an end. **1.1)** *v. intr. aN-* To participate in a pagsalba ceremony.

**pagsalin sukud** *v. intr. aN-* To experience a change in one's fortunes.

**pagsalisi** *v. intr. aN-* To be overlapping or displaced. *Sali' magbangkat inān, mbal sali'-sali', magsalisi.* Like those things stacked up, not lined up, overlapping each other. *Magsalisi to'olangnu, magdalisu'.* Your bones are out of position, dislocated. (*Thesaurus:* **julenget, pagsōng-suwa', pagsuwa'-s'llo', sulangat**)

**pagsallowa'** *v. tr. -an* To retch and vomit. (*Thesaurus:* **balowak, toya', utta' 1**)

**pagsalluk** *v. intr. aN-* To be in an intermediate state, as a person half-conscious, or a wind fluctuating between directions. *Magsalluk iya, ma llot asayu maka mbal.* She is in an intermediate state, between being conscious and not. *Magsalluk baliyu, sali' magbono'.* The winds are between phases, sort of fighting.

**pagsamaongkop** *v. intr. aN-* **1)** To be filled to the brim. **1.1)** *v. tr.* To fill a container to the brim. *Magtūy pin'nno'an e' sigām, pinagsamaongkop maka bowa'na.* They quickly filled [the containers], making them filled level with the brim. (*Thesaurus:* **apang, samaintib**)

**pagsamban** *v. intr. aN-* To meet together while coming towards each other on a path. *Buwat kita maka si Ju magsamban ma t'ngnga' lān. Magbeya' na kita tudju ni hospital.* Like Ju and I meeting in the middle of the road, then going together to the hospital. (*Thesaurus:* **abang, bāk₂, langgal₂ 2, sampang 1**)

**pagsambeya'** (derivative of **beya'₂**) *v. intr. aN-* To go together as a group. *Magsambeya' kita.* Let's go together. *Aniya' magsa'ud hinang, magsambeya'.* There are tasks that overlap, that go together. (*Thesaurus:* **pagdongan, pagdora', pagunung**).

**pagsamp'kka'** *v. intr. aN-* To coincide in time, of events or as people arriving together. *Bang aku amandi magsamp'kka' maka ulan.* When I bathed it happened to rain. (*Thesaurus:* **pag'tta', sabu 1.1, salta, tā'-tā' 1**)

**pagsandu** *v. intr. aN-* To work together at the same task. *Magsandu itu dahinang, t'llungan d'nda magli'is. Sandu* implies a single task, three women grating [cassava] together. (*Thesaurus:* **pagdangin, pagtaku-taku 1**)

**pagsangon panji** *phrase* To raise the flag. *Magsangon sigā panji.* They set the flag in place.

**pagsasal** *v. intr. aN-* To masturbate. {vulgar}

**pagsawaktu** (derivative of **waktu**) *v. intr. aN-* To occur just once, as seasonal events.

**pagsignat-signat** *v. intr. aN-* To throb or pulsate. *Bang aniya' p'ddi' kōk aniya' magsignat-signat ma deyom utukta.* When we have a headache there is something throbbing inside our brain. (*Thesaurus:* **pagk'bbut-k'bbut, pagkowap-kowap, pagdutdut, paglaggut-laggut, panag-panag 1**)

**pagsilap** *v. intr. aN-* To be speaking somewhat incoherently; to ramble. *Magsilap, sali' ah'lling magpehē'-pehē', ah'lling magkamemon. Apangsan sakina.* Talking confusedly, sort of talking at random, talking about everything. His sickness is extreme. *Ubus tauwa' llingta, ubus mbal, magsilap buwat a'a to'a magli'anun.* Our words make sense at first, then don't, speaking incoherently like old people rambling. (*Thesaurus:* **pagbarese-barese, pagli'anun**)

**pagsilapug** *v. intr. aN-* To spread in a disorderly manner. *Buwat aniya' magtimbak daing, bo' at'kka na pulis. Nā, magsilapug, lahi-lahi ma katahikan.* Like people dynamiting fish and police arrive. Then they spread everywhere, running in the sea. (*Thesaurus:* **dasal, dasal, lakat, saplag 1**)

**pagsina'ul** (derivative of **sa'ul**) *v. intr. aN-* To wear a sarong without tying, i.e. by draping it or holding it in place with one's hands. *Da'a na pa'in ka magsina'ul.* Don't keep on wearing your garment just draped on you. (*Thesaurus:* **hampi' 1.1, hōs 1.2, pagkimbong, pindung, siyag 1.1**).

**pagsinamin-mata** (derivative of **samin-mata**) *v. intr. aN-* To wear eyeglasses. *Niangay ka magsinamin-mata siyakanu?* Why are you wearing your older brother's glasses?

**pagsiniga** (derivative of **siga**) *v. intr. aN-* To be in the habit of smoking.

**pagsinimbōng** (derivative of **simbōng**) *v. intr. aN-* To wear one's hair in a knot.

**pagsiningkulang** (derivative of **singkulang**) *v. intr. aN-* To sit cross-legged, a formal position appropriate to ceremonial occasions. *Magsiningkulang iya.* She sits cross-legged. (*Thesaurus:* **hakin, milang, pagsengkang**).

**pagsin'mmek ahāp** *v. intr. aN-* To wear fine clothes. *Magginallang, magsin'mmek ahāp, magsinudlay.* Wearing bracelets, dressed in fine clothes, combs in her hair.

**pagsinūk** (derivative of **Sūk**) *v. intr. aN-* To be speaking the Tausug language.

**pagsinumu** (derivative of **sumu**) *v. intr. aN-* To be bored with something or someone. *Tapangli'ta ka, magsinumu ma aku.* I recognize your expression; you are bored with me.

**pagsinuray** (derivative of **suray**) *v. intr. aN-* To wear a comb in one's hair. *Magginallang, magsin'mmek ahāp, magsinudlay.* Wearing bracelets, dressed in fine clothes, combs in her hair.

**pagsingkali'i-li'i** *v. intr. aN-* To keep postponing the completion of chores.

**pagsiyuk-siyuk** *v. intr. aN-* To take a shortcut.

**pags'bba'-sasab** var. of **pagt'bba'-sasab**

**pags'lle** *v. tr.* To superincise the penis. *Mags'lle itū dangan-danganku. Magislam itū aheka puhu' maglisag agung. S'lle is something done on my own. With ritual circumcision there are lots of people and gongs being played. (cf: **g'llot 2**)*

**pagsukki'** *v. intr. aN-* To play checkers (draughts).

**pagsu'al** *v. intr. aN-* To engage in arguments or word fights. *Magsuli-suli ai-ai ganta' nihinang. Mbal arakayu' kagara'an. Sali' magsu'al.* Talking about anything that is to be done. The planning is not unified. We are disagreeing. *Magbeya' kami maka si Anu, yukku, "Ni Takot Siliyala'." Magsāy yukna, "Ni Singsing kitā!" Ya hē' magsu'al. Magpasu'alan kami.* What's-his-name and I are going [fishing] and I say, "To Siliyala' Reef." And he promptly says, "We're going to Singsing!" That's a case of *su'al*. We are getting into a controversy. (*Thesaurus:* **pagagaw-besod, pagbagod, pagbengtod, pagdiskās, pagjawab 1.1, pagpayod 1.1, pagsalod**)

**pagsulabay** *v. tr.* To meet when coming from opposite directions. *Bay kami magsulabay maka*

*Milikan di'ilaw. Bay magbāk ma olangan.* We met an American yesterday, in passing. We met in the middle [of the channel]. (*Thesaurus:* **labay₁ 1, likuwad 1.1, liyus 1.1, paglipuwas, pintas 1, timbay 1**)

**pagsulang-saingsing** var. of **pagsulang-saling**

**pagsumau'** *v. intr. aN-* To become unfocused or inattentive regarding what one is doing or saying. *Buwat aniya' nil'ngngan, bo' kita palingi' ati parugtul kita. Ya na hē' magsumau' kita.* Like when we are going to do something, and we look back and bump into something. That's a case of *sumau'*. *Magsumau', aniya' pikilan saddī min hinangta.* We lose focus, when there is something in our mind that differs from what we are doing. *Magsumau' bissalata, ubus tumauwa', ubus mbal.* What we are saying gets muddled, on target one minute, off it the next.

**pagsuwa'-s'llo'** *v. intr. aN-* To grow at different angles, as teeth, feathers or the leaves of some plants. (*Thesaurus:* **julenget, pagsalisi, pagsōng-suwa', sulangat**)

**pagta-** (var. **pagka-**) *aff.* Prefix indicating that the subject is characterised or typified by the attached verb. *Pagtas'bbat t'lla'-t'lla' he' kalitan bang patuhun.* Seagulls tend to be gulped down by sharks when they dive. *Pagtakakan saging he' si Arung.* Bananas get eaten up by Eldest Daughter. *Agese' badju' si Je, bay angindam jalum pangala'it. Magkageret asāl bang buwal.* Je's blouse was torn, she borrowed a needle to sew it. *Buwal* [a light cloth] always tears. *Minsan pittang magkagaha' du isāb.* Even an alloy is prone to rust.

**pagtaba'-taba'** *v. intr. aN-* To masturbate.

**pagtab'llung** *v. intr. aN-* To make a noise by blowing through vibrating lips.

**pagtakbi'** *v. intr. aN-* To fight without artificial spurs, of fighting cocks. *Magbulang na manuk ya magtakbi' inān. Angalaha' pēna, bay tinittuk e' manuk dakayu'.* That cock without spurs there was fighting. Its comb is bleeding, it was pecked by another cock. (*Thesaurus:* **ayuk-ayuk, manuk-sigun, pagbulang, pagtūkan**)

**pagtaksi'** *n.* 1) Small items such as shells, stones, or buttons, used as counters or markers in various games. 1.1) *v. intr. aN-* To play a game in which a pebble is thrown at objects on a stand. *Aheka ma po'on hāg, pagmanohan, pagtaksi'an.* There are lots [of shells] at the base of house-posts, for throwing games like *mano* and *taksi'. Bang magplising subay holen, bang magtaksi' subay batu.* When throwing marbles it must be marbles, when playing hit-the-target it must be pebbles. (*Thesaurus:* **mano 1, pamatu'**)

**pagtaksi'an** *n.* A flat area for various games.

**pagtaku-taku** *v. intr. aN-* 1) To work cooperatively to help someone. *Buwat ka'a i magpahāp luma', magtaku-taku a'a Siganggang.* As when you are repairing [your] house, the people of

Siganggang cooperate to help you. (*Thesaurus:* **pagdangin, pagsandu**) 1.1) *v. tr.* *-an* To help someone by cooperating with them. *Buwat ai-ai kabaya'anta bin'lli, pinagtaku-takuhan e' danakanta bang mbal takole'ta.* Like whatever we want to buy, our siblings cooperate to combine help us if we can't manage it.

**pagtagettek** *v. intr.* *aN-* To make a rhythmic tapping sound, as shoes on a wooden floor.

**pagta'allukan** *n.* A person respected for high status and abilities. *Sali' a'a jīnan, bang aniya' pa'nda'ta ni iya, agtūy kinata'uhan he'na saki, a'a inān niōnan pagta'allukan.* Like a person with a djinn spirit, when someone is shown to him and he immediately identifies the sickness, such a man is called *pagta'allukan* [a person to be respected]. *Pagbebeya'an na, pagta'allukan he' kamemon.* Someone to be followed, respected by everyone as leader.

**pagta'ayun** (derivative of **ayun**) *v. intr.* *aN-* To be in accord with each other. (*Thesaurus:* **amu**$_2$ 1.1, **beya'**$_3$ 1, **dakayu'**$_2$ 1, **manghalapi, sulut** 1, **tayudtud**).

**pagta'is** *v. intr.* *aN-* To grind together. *Sali' bang poga magbihing karuwa bo' ma deyom pelang, bo' goyakan, magta'is.* Like water jars next to each other, when in a canoe and it is rough, they grind together. (*Thesaurus:* **paggidgid, pagleges**)

**pagtallak** *v. intr.* *aN-* To divorce one's wife by declaring the talaq (separation) formula.

**pagtamengka'** (derivative of **pengka'**) *v. intr.* *aN-* To hobble, as when the sole of one's foot is hurt. *Magtamengka', bay kita abakat he' kappo'. Bang kita pal'ngngan tape'ta mbal makat'kkad.* We can limp, we have been wounded by a stonefish. When we walk our foot can't be put down on the bottom. (*Thesaurus:* **keme, ku'il, pagtongka', pukul** 1).

**pagtāp-tāp** *v. intr.* *aN-* To be boastful or cocky. *Pa'abbu a'a inān, sali' magtāp-tāp.* That person is a show-off, acting tough. (*Thesaurus:* **pagabbu** 1.1, **pagbantug-bantug, pagheya-heya, pagmahatinggi, pagmalangkahi, pagpasanglit**)

**pagtauhan** var. of **pagtaluhan**

**pagtawap** *v. intr.* *aN-* To vanish in an instant. *Magtawap, ala'an patawap kōk-tu'ut.* Vanished, the knee-cap gone in a flash. *Pagtawapan: subay sali' a'a niruwata' magpatawap.* Vanishing, this must be someone possessed by a *duwata* spirit making someone vanish.

**pagtawapan** *n.* An instant disappearance.

**pagtimb'llang** *v. intr.* *aN-* To display streaks of color, as paint not well-mixed, or turbid water coming into clear. *Bangka'ku keyat bay tinapi' e' si Bi, masi magtimb'llang pintana.* My red canoe that Bi built, its paint is still showing streaks.

**pagtinabawan** (derivative of **Tabawan**) *v. intr.* *aN-* To make a Tabawan-style bride-wealth exchange, by a lump sum of cash. *Aniya' magtinabawan, sambatan Ingglis 'complete'. M'ssa' aniya' sokat-manokat. Bang t'llu hatus, t'llu hatus du.* There are some who follow the Tabawan practise, 'complete' as they say in English. None of this specifying various items. If ₱300 is agreed on, then it is exactly ₱300. (*Thesaurus:* **banghad** 1, **basingan, mahal**$_2$, **punggit** 1, **ungsud**$_1$ 1).

**pagtoka-toka** *v. intr.* *aN-* To work at an assigned task.

**pagtogga'** *v. intr.* *aN-* To jump up and down rhythmically, as in dancing. *Magtogga'-togga' sigām angigal.* They moved their feet in time, dancing. *Tahan magtogga'-togga' pangigal sigām.* In the end their dancing was just jogging up and down.

**pagtongka'** *v. intr.* *aN-* To take short steps; to hobble. (*Thesaurus:* **keme, ku'il, pagtamengka', pukul** 1)

**pagtuwaha'** *v. intr.* *aN-* To wear mourning clothes.

**pagubus**$_1$ *n.* Something remembered forever; a memorial. *Amat'nna' iya batu pagubus, binusugan e'na binu maka ns'llan diyata'na panukbalna ni Tuhan.* He sets up a memorial stone, its top watered with wine and oil, as his offering to God.

**pagu'uppi** (derivative of **uppi**) *v. intr.* *aN-* To be given to dreaming. *Magu'uppi iya, ya na kabiyasahanna.* He is a dreamer, that is his habit.

**pagumak** *v. intr.* *aN-* To treat something without respect or care. *Pagumakbi sadja s'mmek ilū pagpuwasbi angusal iya.* You're just treating those clothes without care after having used them. (*syn:* **pahagmak**)

**pagumbaw-umbaw** *v. intr.* *aN-* To appear intermittently. *Buwat kita palangi magumbaw-umbaw kōkta, sali' maghunggaw pariyata'.* Like when we are swimming our head keeps bobbing up and down in the water, as though reaching up to see.

**pagūng** (derivative of **gūng**) *v. tr.* To cause something to float. *Pinagūng si Fr maka anu inān bo' mbal pat'nde.* Fr is made to float with that device so she doesn't sink. *Pinagūng si Fra maka salbabida inān. Tahik ya pagūnganna.* Fra is enabled to float with that lifesaver. It is the sea that she floats in.

**pagung** *n.* A floating island, typically made up of growing vegetable matter. *Buwat pagung, bay paglahatan saitan tabowa pagūng.* Like a floating island that had been the abode of a demon, made to float off. (*Thesaurus:* **gampal, ulak** 1)

**pagyakin** *v. intr.* *aN-* To be resigned to an unavoidable outcome. *Magyakin na ka tinangkawan.* Resign yourself to being stolen from.

**paha** *n.* A flat area for storage; a work bench. *Aningkō' ka ma paha, animbang.* Sit on the side-shelf [of the canoe], improving the balance.

*Agtūy paleyang paha-paha. Paleyang na papan min deyom mohang, maka naelon.* The work tables promptly flew off. The boards flew out of the hull, along with the fishing line. (*cf:* **paga-paga**)

**pahagmak** (derivative of **hagmak**) *v. tr.* To leave things uncared-for. *Pahagmakbi sadja saga s'mmek ilū pagpuwasbi angusal iya.* You simply leave those clothes uncared-for after you have used them. (*syn:* **pagumak**).

**pahala'** *n.* Good fortune or reward, especially as received in the afterlife. *Bang a'a angusaha, pinaheka daing ta'ā' he'na sabab pahala' ma iya.* When a man is working, his catch of fish is multiplied as his reward. *Ka'a ahāp addat, ma ka'a pahala'. Ka'a, ma ka'a bala'.* You who have a good character, for you there are blessings. As for you [other], for you there is disaster. (*Thesaurus:* **anughala' 1, apuwa, barakat 1, hirayat, lidjiki' 1**)

**pahalam** (derivative of **halam₁**) *v. tr.* To negate or erase something; to reduce something to nothing. *Pinahalam isāb bay kagara'an sigām.* Their planned agreement was cancelled. (*Thesaurus:* **erēs, papas₁ 1.1**).

**pahalga'** (derivative of **halga'**) *v. tr.* To treat someone or some thing as special. *"Angay aku pahalga'nu? Aku itu dakayu' sadja a'a liyu."* "Why do you treat me as special? I am just a foreigner." *Pahalga'in iya ati ka'a ya pinalanga e'na.* Show respect to him and you will be promoted by him.

**pahalu** *adv.* Tomorrow. *Pi'itu kām pahalu ma waktu buwattitu du isāb.* Come tomorrow at this same time. (*syn:* **salung**)

**paham** *v. tr.* To read written material with ease, especially from the Holy Koran.

**pahampit** (derivative of **hampit**) *v. tr.* To give someone a share. *Bang aniya' bay kinawin anaknu subay aku pahampitnu ungsudna.* If a child of yours has been married, you should give me a share of the bride-wealth.

**pahamut** (derivative of **hamut**) *v. tr.* To apply perfume or deodorant; to anoint. *Pagubus, amahamutan iya dīna maka magsalin.* After that she applied perfume to herself and changed her clothes.

**pahandang** (var. **pahangdon**) **1)** *n.* Household items set out ready for use, such as (bedding, food served and ready to eat). (*Thesaurus:* **kabunyihan, kakaya'an, kalangkapan₁, kapanyapan, pinduwa'**) **2)** *v. tr.* To furnish or decorate the interior of a house. *Si Mi ya bay ngā'nu h'nda, sinokatan pahangdon bulawan.* Mi, whom you have taken as wife, was the subject of bride-gifts of household goods [made of] gold.

**pahantak** (derivative of **hantak₁**) *adv.* Falling down hard. *Na bo' kita nirugsu'an na hal kita amatay pahantak.* So if we are stabbed we simply die falling down hard.

**pahang** *n.* A monitor lizard. (*Thesaurus:* **pinit, tokke'₁, tokko'**)

**pahangdon** var. of **pahandang**

**pahanggal** (derivative of **hanggal**) *v. tr.* To prop something up by placing a chock under it. *Pahanggalun buli' ni batu ilū.* Prop the stern up on that rock. (*Thesaurus:* **biggal 1, bulatuk, s'ngngal, tanok 1**).

**pahangsu** (derivative of **hangsu**) *v. intr.* aN- To emit odor or fumes. *Amahangsu pasu' baranta.* Our body heat puts out a strong smell.

**pahangtad** (derivative of **hangtad**) *v. tr.* To lay something out full length. *Pahangtarun na ma halaman ilū. Pabeya'un ma kataha'an lān inān.* Lay it out on the courtyard. Set it out on the length of the path.

**pahāp₁** (derivative of **hāp**) *adv.* Indeed; truly; really. *Pabidda' pahāp s'mmek inān.* That clothing is really different. *Patikakanun pahāp a'a inān, asidda alagak.* That fellow can really eat, very greedy. *At'llag pahāp luma' inān.* That house is seriously gapped [lacks walling]. *Jagahin pahāp.* Guard him well. (*Thesaurus:* **to'ongan 1.1**).

**pahāp₂** (derivative of **hāp**) *v. tr.* **1)** To improve or repair something. *Mbal tapahāp kulaet itu.* This pressure lantern cannot be repaired. **2)** To do something well. *Pahāpun ba e'nu anapu.* Make a good job of your sweeping. *Alangkat luma' Milikan. Halam bay pinahāp e' si Am, dalapis du tiyadtad.* The Westerner's house is falling to pieces. Am didn't do it well, only one layer of bamboo walling.

**pamahāp** *n.* Something for the good or benefit of.

**pahāp-hāp** (derivative of **hāp**) *v. tr.* **1)** To treat someone well in order to get their approval. *Buwat si Ja amaya'-maya' ma d'nda, amuwan-muwan sadja ni matto'ana, angahulmat-ngahulmat, amahāp-mahāp sali'.* Like Ja when he is in love with a girl, he keeps giving things to her parents, keeps showing them honor, keeps making them feel good [about him]. **1.1)** *adv.* Well; in a good manner. *Angkan ayarinbi to'ongan pahāp-hāp, sampay ta'abut waktu kapagtimbang.* That's why you should treat it very well until it's time for weighing.

**pahapat** (var. **sahapat**) *n.* The mangrove apple. *Sonneratia alba et al.* (*cf:* **pinara**)

**pahati** (derivative of **hati**) *n.* **1)** A notice or information sheet. (*Thesaurus:* **ba'at 1, kabtangan, haka 1, hunub-hunub 1, sambatan, suli-suli 1**). **1.1)** *v. tr.* To inform someone. *Pahati'un kono' aku bang ai hatina inān.* Please explain to me what the meaning of that was. *Bay aku makapamahati ni Siasi.* I had informed those in Siasi about various things.

**pahayang** (derivative of **hayang**) *v. tr.* To place something or someone where it is breezy.

**paheka** (derivative of **heka**) *adv.* Much; plentifully.

*Bay kīnnopan e'na paheka.* He increased it abundantly.

**paheya**₁ (derivative of **heya**) *adv.* To a great degree. *Niastolan iya paheya ma kahinangan sigām angkan magtūy pinala'an.* He was exceedingly angry with their behavior so they were immediately forced to leave. *Magnapas iya paheya.* He is breathing deeply.

**paheya**₂ (derivative of **heya**) *v. tr.* To enlarge something; to make something important. *Ōnnu kono' pinaheya salama-lama.* Your name, it is said, will be made great forever.

**pahi** *n.* Various rays (fish). *Order Rajiformes. Minsan isāb pahi amūng du isāb buwat manusiya', "Minsan aku pahi, patumpangun pa'in aku ma tōng-tōng adjungbi ilū."* Even though it was a stingray, it spoke as a human does, saying, "Even though I am a stingray, just tip me out into the bow of your *adjung*-ship." *Pahi mbal takilaw.* The flesh of rays cannot be eaten raw.

**pahi-baling** *n.* A manta ray species. *Pahi-baling, taga lakkop. Basta pahi palangi aniya' lakkopna.* The *baling* ray, it has sucker fish [on its gills]. Any swimming ray has sucker fish.

**pahi-bangkaw** *n.* The Mangrove ray, the Fantail ray. *Taeniura sp.*

**pahi-batu** *n.* The Spotted eagle ray. *Aetobatus narinari.*

**pahi-leha** *n.* A ray species (lit. sail ray). *Dasyatis sp.*

**pahi-luhuyan** *n.* A manta ray species. *Mobula sp.*

**pahi-manuk** *n.* The Cow-nosed ray. *Rhinoptera javanica.*

**pahi-sanga** *n.* Various manta or devil rays. *Mobula spp.*

**pahi-sanga-linggisan** *n.* A manta ray species (lit. frigate-bird manta ray). *Mobula sp.*

**pahi-sanga-owak** *n.* The Spineless devil ray (lit. crow manta ray). *Mobula ergoodoo.*

**pahi-sanga-pagung** *n.* A manta ray species (lit. floating manta). *Mobula sp.*

**pahi-sanga-tibung** *n.* A manta ray species (lit. plump manta). *Mobula sp.*

**pahi-sanga-t'lla'-t'lla'** *n.* A manta ray species (lit. seagull manta). *Mobula sp.*

**pahid** *v. tr.* 1) To stroke or wipe something. *Pahirun onde'-onde'.* Wipe the child. (*Thesaurus:* **peged**₁ 1, **pe'es**₁, **sapu** 1) 1.1) *v. tr.* -an To wipe something off, as dirt off a surface. *Bang sali' ma lantay pinahiran, hatina nila'anan ya l'mmisna. Sinapuhan bo' nila'anan.* If it is something like the floor being wiped, the meaning is that its dirt is to be removed. Swept to remove. *Pahirin na Biks ma baranku, sidda ap'ddi' tangkalku.* Wipe Vicks on my body for me, my lower back is very painful.

**pahigin** (derivative of **higin**) *v. tr.* To make something move a small distance. *Pahiginun, pasōngun.* Move it a bit, move it along.

**pahilala'** *v. tr.* 1) To take care of someone or something. *Bang aku sali' bīllihan paraw he' si Mma', mbal gi' aku bīllihan. Magtūy tinatab aku dahū he'na. Kalu-kalu aku atogol amahilala'.* When for example, Dad is to buy me a canoe, I am not simply bought one. He first tries me out. Perhaps I will persist in taking care of it. *A: "Sai bay amahilala' ka'a ma Bukidnon?" B: "Sigām si Sel." A: "Ahāp kapahilala' ka'a mahē'?" Yukku, "Aho'." A:* "Who looked after you in Bukidnon?" B: "Sir and others." A: "Did they take good care of you there?" I said, "Yes." (*Thesaurus:* **ayad, ayuput, hamumu', ipat, paintul, paipid, payakun, talkin, ulip, upiksa', ussap** 1) 2) To prepare a corpse for burial. *Sali' bang a'a amatay pinahilala', pinandi, apuwas pinandi sinaput. Apuwas sinaput ī', pin'kkos maka tepo hē'. Sinambahayang gi', puwas ē' ni'isi ni deyom lalungan.* Like when a dead person is prepared, bathed, and when bathed, wrapped in a shroud. When he is shrouded, he is wrapped in a mat. He is then prayed over and after that put into the coffin. *Ya amahilala' subay panday. Bang d'nda ya amatay, na d'nda du isāb amandi iya. Bang l'lla, l'lla du. Nilanu'an baranna kamemon, kukkuna, sinusutan taingana, ūngna, emponna, kamemonna sampay manga buli'na.* The one doing the preparation should be an expert. If it is a woman who dies, then a woman bathes her. If a man, then a man. His/her whole body is cleansed, nails, ears, nose, teeth, everything scrubbed clean including things such as the anal area. *Pin'kkos maka kuku-pote' kamemonna, baranna, kōk harap ni tōng tape', tanganna buwat anambahayang. Pinahilala' isāb palegehanna.* [He is] wrapped in white shroud cloth, all over from head to toe, his hands [folded] as in prayer. His bed is also prepared.

**kapahilala'** *n.* Careful treatment of something or someone. *A: "Sai bay amahilala' ka'a ma Bukidnon?" B: "Sigām si Sel." A: "Ahāp kapahilala' ka'a mahē'?" B: "Aho'."* A: "Who looked after you in Bukidnon?" B: "Sir and others." A: "Did they take good care of you there?" B: "Yes."

**pahimulas** (derivative of **himulas**) *v. tr.* To accuse someone of cowardice. *Sinakat magbono'. Bang kita pinahimulas magbono' na.* Attacked for a fight. When we are accused of cowardice we fight.

**pahinang** var. of **hinang-hinang**₂

**pahing** *v. tr.* -an To inform someone about the appearance or nature of something. *Pahinganta ka basta ya kata'uhannu.* I will tell you what it is like, just so you know.

**pamahingan** *n.* A source of information or detail about something; a sample of something to be copied. (*cf:* **gindan** 1, **pandoga** 1)

**pahinggaman** *n.* A means of transport. *Pahinggaman itū pameya'an, bayan, pelang. Bang aniya' pahinggamanta sali' pelang bo' nilumut,* *subay sinusutan.* This word *pahinggaman* means a conveyance, a vehicle, a canoe. If we have a conveyance such as a canoe and it gets mossy, it must be scrubbed. *Makapagguyud kami maka ipalku. Halam aniya' pahinggamanna.* My brother-in-law and I towed each other. He had no means of transport. *Bang kita marilaut bo' magolang atawa maglata, pinaka'at kita, suma'an makanibaran, suma'an makanipahinggaman.* When we are at sea and shout or fool around, damage is done to us, sometimes to us personally and sometimes to our transport. (*Thesaurus:* **bayanan, pameya'an₁, panumpangan**)

**pahit** (var. **mahit**) *v. tr. -an* To shout orders at someone. *Bay aku pinahitan e' kapatas.* The foreman shouted at me. *Pinahit-pahitan kita, sali' pinagmandahan.* We are shouted at repeatedly, like being bossed around. (*Thesaurus:* **asang₂, kula'ak, galit, gasud, olang 1.1, pagalud**)

**pagpahit-pahit** *v. intr. aN-* To raise one's voice in anger or threat, as a superior to someone his inferior. *Da'a ka magpahit-pahit, apa ngga'i ka aku atanu.* Don't shout, because I am not your slave.

**pah'lla** (derivative of **h'lla**)1) *v. tr.* To take someone to be one's husband. *Aniya' inān d'nda abalu, ya bay tapah'llana nabi.* There was a widow there, the one who had taken a prophet as husband. **2)** *v. tr. -an* To provide someone with a husband.

**pah'lling₁** (derivative of **h'lling₁**) *v. tr.* To cause something to make a sound, as by playing a musical instrument or a recording. *Aheka puhu' ma luma' Milikan bang pinah'lling tenes-tenes.* There are many people in the Westerner's house when *tenes-tenes* singing is played.

**pah'lling₂** (derivative of **h'lling₁**) *v. tr. -an* To speak to or about someone, generally with the connotation of scolding. *Bay aku pinah'llingan ala'at e' mastal.* The teacher scolded me in a bad way. *Buwat si Ji maglakibini tinutul e' mato'a d'nda, sali' pinah'llingan e'na.* Like Ji and his wife, berated by the mother-in-law, sort of scolded. *Buwat nda'ta d'nda ab'ttong bo' pah'llinganta ala'at, na hal magp'ddi'-p'ddi', mbal amaluwas anak.* Like when we see a pregnant woman and speak ill of her, then she will just have labor pains but will not deliver a child. *Iya itū, mbal kapah'llingan, magtūy ta'ā'na p'ddi'-atay.* This fellow, can't even be spoken to, immediately takes offence. (*Thesaurus:* **dugal 1.1, pabukag, pamūng-mūng, pugpug 1, s'ndal 1, tutul**).

**pah'lling₃** (derivative of **h'lling₃**) *v. tr. -an* To cast a spell on someone in order to influence him or her to behave in a desired way.

**pah'nda** (derivative of **h'nda**)1) *v. tr.* To take someone to be one's wife. *Suli-suli mbal ahāp ya yuk-i, "Ngga'i ka na budjang ya d'nda bay tapah'ndaku itū."* Talk that was not good, saying, "This woman that I took as wife was no longer a virgin." **2)** *v. tr. -an* To provide someone with a wife. *Pinah'nda'an isāb iya ma si As, anak si Imam Po.* He was provided with As, the daughter of Imam Po, as a wife. *Magbeya' iya maka si Ma, ya bay pinah'nda'an iya.* He went with Ma, the one who had been promised to him in marriage. *Pangannalku ab'nsi ka ma si Am, angkan tapamah'ndaku ni bagaynu.* I thought that you disliked Am, therefore I have given her to be your friend's wife. *Piha'in si Oto' d'nda minnē' pamah'nda ma iya.* Find a woman from that place for Oldest son, to become his wife.

**pahokas** (derivative of **hokas**) *v. tr. -an* To remunerate someone for a service done. *Pinahokasan iya, dakayu' badju' ya hokasna.* She was paid [for her work], her pay being one blouse.

**pahogot** (derivative of **hogot**) *adv.* Firmly; securely. *Bang bay engkotannu pahogot, halam bay alatas.* If only you had tied it securely, it would not have come undone.

**pahopok** var. of **palopok**

**pahula-layag** (derivative of **hula-layag**) *v. tr.* To make a body of information widely known. *Da'a na pahula-layagun.* Don't tell the world.

**pahuru-huru** (derivative of **huru-huru**) *v. intr. aN-* To move swiftly and in large numbers.

**pai** *n.* **1)** The rice plant. *Oryza sativa.* (*cf:* **balayang**) **1.1)** Unhusked rice. *Pai pamat'nna' mbo' tinapilan lokay maka duwa botong.* Unhusked rice for presentation to an ancestor, accompanied by fresh coconut leaflets and two young coconuts. *Am'lli aku pai nihinang mbo'. Apuwas e'-i tin'ppa ni linsungan. Aubus magt'ppa, tinahapan pai.* I buy rice to invoke the ancestor. After that it is pounded in a mortar. After pounding, the rice is winnowed. (*Thesaurus:* **buwas-kinakan, kinakan 2, gulami**)

**pai-tirigu** *n.* Wheat, the grain and plant from which wheat flour is made.

**pai-pai** *n.* **1)** Toxic rice-like particles in the stomach of pufferfish. **1.1)** *v. tr. -an* To remove the rice-like particles from a pufferfish, in preparation for cooking and eating. *Pināy-pāyan, niā' sala bigihan buwas man deyom b'ttongna ilū ko' mbal makalango.* Poison sacs removed, things like grains of rice taken from its gut so that it won't cause illness

**paidda** *v. tr.* To treat a visitor or stranger with courtesy. *Paiddahun sigā, mahaltabatun.* Treat them with courtesy, show them honor. (*Thesaurus:* **hīl, owa'₁ 1.1, sagina, sahawi 1**)

**paila'** *v. tr.* To add an ingredient to a mixture. *Paila'un bangkit, lamurin dulaw. Dulaw ya nili'is, pin'gga', ati bohe'na pamaila', manjari akeyat bangkit.* Add an ingredient to the [calceous] lime, mix in turmeric. The turmeric is grated, squeezed, and its liquid added so the lime is red. *Ai-ai nilamuran, buwat duwa ginis pinta* *nihaybol, pinaila'.* Anything mixed in, like two kinds of paint shaken together, that's *paila'.* (*Thesaurus:* **haybol, lamud₁ 1.1, lamugay 1.1, pagsagol 1.1, simbug 1, templa 1.1**)

**paili** *v. tr.* To flatter someone in order to take advantage of him. *Pinaili e'na, niakkalan.* Flattered by him, being tricked. (*Thesaurus:* **lana 1.1, pagmamhu', puli-bahasa**)

**pailu** var. of **palilu**

**painay** (derivative of **inay**) *interrog.* What? How? *Painay itū? Mbal aku makani'iskul, aheka hinang.* What to do? I can't go to school, a lot of work. *Minsan painay, mbal kauli'an.* No matter what, it won't heal. *Painay ilū? At'ggol aku halam makasulat. Painay-inay isāb si Kolongan? Salam isāb ni iya.* How are things there? I haven't written for a long time. And how is Curly? Greetings to her too. *A: "Painay ru si De maganak?" B: "Bay ru niā'an panday."* A: "How is De going with her birthing?" B: "The midwife has been called for her."

**sapainay-painay** *adv.* No matter what.*Sapainay-painay, niōnan angeyok.* No matter what, it's called *angeyok.*

**paindam** (derivative of **indam**) *v. ditr.* To lend something to someone. *Bang aniya' pina'bba ma kita, subay hamumu'ta supaya kita pinaindaman pabing.* When something is left with us we should take good care of it so we may be permitted to borrow it again.

**paintul** *v. tr.* To treat something with care; to put something right. (*Thesaurus:* **ayad, ayuput, hamumu', ipat, pahilala' 1, paipid, payakun, talkin, ulip, upiksa', ussap 1**)

**painut-inut** (derivative of **inut**) *adv.* In small increments; gradually. *Taluwa' kami habal marilaut, ap'ddi' b'ttong kami. Hal kami magpagūng, subay palabay bay map'ddi' hē' bo' yampa kami amusay painut-inut.* We experienced a sense of foreboding out at sea, our stomachs being painful. We just floated about, whatever was painful had to pass before we could paddle tentatively.

**paipa'₁ 1)** *n.* The fleshy gill segments of stingrays and some shark species. **2)** *clf.* Count word for gill segments of large stingrays. *Dampaipa' asang pahi.* One section of stingray gill.

**paipa'₂** *n.* The central stem of a coconut frond, a source of firewood. *Paipa', bang a'llum pananggungan; bang amatay pangayu.* One stem of a coconut frond, usable as a carrying pole when still green, used for firewood when dead. (*cf:* **etang-etang**; *wh:* **niyug**)

**paipid** *v. tr. -an* To take good care of something. *Gallang ilū subay pinaipiran, nijagahan. Paipirin pahāp bo' mbal alungay atawa magka'at.* That bracelet should be well cared for, watched over. Take very good care of it so it doesn't get lost or damaged. (*Thesaurus:* **ayad, ayuput, hamumu', ipat, pahilala' 1, paintul, payakun, talkin,**

**ulip, upiksa', ussap 1**)

**pajajaga** (derivative of **jaga**) *n.* One who stays awake; a watcher.

**pajātan** *n.* The presence or abode of a person in supreme authority. *Pinabanga' e'na bowa'na anukna'an Tuhan maka ōnna maka pajātanna.* He opened his mouth to curse God and his name and his abode. (*Thesaurus:* **hadarat, matahan, matahan**)

**pajatu** (derivative of **jatu**) *v. tr.* To complete something satisfactorily. *Pajatuhun pehē' daing inān ko da'a ahalu'.* Complete the whole process with that fish so it doesn't go bad. *Amakatuk kita l'lla maka d'nda, amajatu sali'.* We get a man and a woman to commit to getting married, like clarifying the situation.

**pajayak** (derivative of **jayak**) *v. tr.* To produce in abundance. *Bang kita magusaha yukta, "Bang ka sab'nnal-b'nnal, bo' aku pi'ingga-pi'ingga, pajayakun usahaku."* If we are out working for our living, we say [a prayer], "If you are real, and wherever I go, make my work productive."

**pa'a** *n.* The upper leg; the thigh. *Na, binowa pina'an pa'a susumbali'an bo' pinat'nna' ma munda'an sultan.* So the thigh of the slaughtered animal was carried there and placed before the sultan.

**pa'abbu** (derivative of **abbu**) *n.* One who shows off; a braggart. *Pa'abbu a'a ina'an, sali' magtāp-tāp a'abbu.* That fellow is such a show-off, sort of being a tough guy, proud.

**pa'adjal** (derivative of **adjal**) *v. ditr.* To get someone to prepare food. *Pama'adjalun si Ju daing inān.* Have Juy prepare that fish. *Pama'adjalun ma kasehe'an apa aniya' hinangku saddī.* Get someone else to prepare the food because I have other things to do. *Pa'adjalun daing inān ko da'a abuhuk.* Have [someone] prepare that fish for cooking so it doesn't become rotten.

**pa'admit** (derivative of **admit**) *v. tr.* To have someone admitted to hospital. *Arapun ma tongod mma'ku, wa'i iya pina'admit ma ispital llaw itu ma Sambo.* In regard to my father, he has been admitted to hospital in Zamboanga today.

**pa'al** *n.* **1)** A misfortune; a disastrous event. *Tauwa' kami pa'al.* Something terrible happened to us. (*Thesaurus:* **bala', kajahatan, kala'atan, mulka' 1, naja', udjul₁ 1**) **1.1)** *v. tr.* To predict the coming of some unfortunate event. *Aniya' pina'al badju.* It is predicted that there will be a typhoon. (*Thesaurus:* **kupul, talus₂**)

**pa'alu'** (derivative of **alu'₂**) *v. tr. -an* To expose someone to the night air by refusing him shelter. (*Thesaurus:* **inyaya, paulan, tanya₁**).

**pa'alung** (derivative of **alung**) *v. tr.* To place something over the heat of a fire; to put something on to cook. *Pa'alungun buwas ilū ko da'a ak'mbang.* Put that rice on to cook so it doesn't get soft through soaking.

**pa'amu** (derivative of **amu₁**) *v. tr.* To do something clearly or plainly, especially in regard to speech. *Bang ka amissala, pa'amuhun, pabontolun, pinataluwa' sali'.* When you speak make it clear, be correct, let it be on target as it were. *Subay pa'amuta he'ta amuwan, hatina papatutta bang amuwan.* We should do it fittingly when we give, in other words we should make our gift appropriate. *Bang pina'amu, in kamemon bay tahinangna aheya sidda katabanganna ma ka'a.* When it is put plainly, everything he did was a very great help to you. (*cf:* **papatut**).

**pa'amu-amu** (derivative of **amu₂**) *v. tr.* To make something attractive. *Ata'u ama'amu-amu dīna minsan duma'in na baha'u badju'na.* He knows how to carry himself well even though his clothes are not new. *Budjang ina'an ata'u ama'amu-amu dīna.* That girl knows how to look her best. (*Thesaurus:* **mata-mata₁**, **pagpaelle'-elle'**, **pagpa'nda'-pa'nda'**).

**pa'andag** (derivative of **andag**) *v. tr.* -an1) To offer something for sale. *Ama'andagan aku pelang ni kaluma'an, kalu aniya' am'lli.* I will offer my canoe for sale in the village, there may be a purchaser. (*Thesaurus:* **dagang**, **lilung**, **litu**, **pab'lli**, **pagsoroy**, **samsuy**). 2) To offer a woman in marriage. *Pina'andagan si Mo minsan mbal kinabaya'an e' l'lla.* Mo is offered in marriage even though no man wants her.

**pa'andig** *v. tr.* -an To speak obliquely of something, especially when the person involved is present. *Pa'andig, sali' aku ē' aniya' mohotku ni ka'a. Mbal pamūngku, aiya' aku. Magpakale aku ma si Mu, bo' ya target ē' patudju ni ka'a.* *Pa'andig* is like my having a purpose that involves you, but I don't speak of it, being ashamed. I let Mu hear about it, but you are the intended target.

**pa'anggi** (derivative of **anggi**) *v. tr.* To win someone's affection, as a divorced parent may do to a child for whom he or she does not have custody. *Pi'ingga-pi'ingga pa'anggihan, sai-sai na kinagalakan.* Wherever affection is won, whoever one feels at ease with.

**pa'aro'-aro'** (derivative of **aro'**) *adv.* Watched closely. *Ang'nda' ka pa'aro'-aro'.* Look at it closely.

**pa'asa-asa** (derivative of **asa**) *v. tr.* To raise someone's hopes, however uncertain the outcome. *Bang taluwa' he' timbak, beya' ni kamatay sa' masi a'llum-amatay, sali' ahalol. Pa'asa-asanu aku.* If [I were] hit by an explosion and were close to death, between dead and alive, like in critical condition. You give me hope. *Hal sali' pama'asa-asa.* Merely for reassurance.

**pa'at** *n.* 1) A tool for making holes in wood. (*Thesaurus:* **likup 1**, **patuk**, **sakal**, **sangkap 1**, **sosokan**) 1.1) *v. tr.* To make a hole in wood with a chisel or a drill. *Indamin aku barena pama'atku tapi' pelang.* Lend me the brace-and-bit for drilling the canoe planks.

**pa'atagan** (derivative of **atag₁**) *n.* The location of something; a place where someone stays; a lair. *Jari palanjal na sigām ni kaluma'an ya pa'atagan mundu inān.* So they went on to the village where the raiders were staying. *Buwat panagatun bang mbal ala'an min pa'ataganna, subay landakta.* Or like shellfish when it won't leave its lair, we have to prise it up. (*Thesaurus:* **jadjahan**, **lugal 1**, **pat'nna'an**).

**pa'atap** (derivative of **atap**) *v. tr.* To match the price asked by the seller with the money available to the buyer. *Pa'atapun sadja sīn ilū apa halam aniya' pang'nnop iya.* Make that money match because there is no more to add to it.

**pa'awat** (derivative of **awat**) *v. tr.* To outbid another bidder. *Pa'awatun lima t'llumpū' pilak itū.* Outbid this thirty pesos by five. *T'llu pilak pina'awat mpat.* Three pesos outstripped by four.

**pa'imping** (var. **pimping**) *n.* A species of bird, seen wading along shorelines.

**pa'in₁** *ptl.* While, at the same time as. Indicates the co-occurrence of two actions or states. *Amole' pa'in kami minnē', bay kami nihapa'an.* While we were on our way home someone held us up.

**pa'in₂** *ptl.* 1) Marker downplaying the importance of an item or action. *Aku pa'in.* Just me yet. *Pabīng pa'in aku salung.* I'll just come back tomorrow. 2) Politeness marker. *Mma', sehe'in pa'in aku ni luma' mastal.* Dad, please accompany me to the teacher's house. *Bā'in pa'in ina'nu.* Kindly tell your mother. (*Thesaurus:* **kono' 2**, **da'a busung**, **lagi' 3**)

**pa'in₃** *adj.* a- 1) Sick due to the action of supernatural beings, especially of offended ritual ancestors. *Apa'in ka man mbo'nu. Bang ka asaki subay ka atuli ma luma'na.* You are sick from your deceased grandfather. When you are sick you should sleep in his house. *Da'a ntanin ilu, makapa'in.* Don't touch that, it will bring you sickness. *Abihang, apa'in, asabab.* Causing illness, affected by spirit ancestors. (*Thesaurus:* **bihang₁**, **labba'₂ 1**, **pagpalasahan**, **sabab₂ 1.1**, **saki 1.1**, **semet**, **sila'-sila' 1.1**) 1.1) *v. tr.* To bring about a sickness, the action of supernatural beings. *Aho', kauli'an bang halam aniya' ama'in, halam aniya' anabab.* Yes, it will be healed provided nothing supernatural is making him sick, nothing causing it.

**pa'in₄** *v. intr.* pa- Going in a non-specific direction, away from speaker and hearer. *O'ō, tudju papa'in.* Look, heading off in that direction. *Anōng ka papa'in.* Move further in that direction.

**pa'in₅** *see:* **pagpina'in**, **pina'in**

**pa'it** *n.* 1) Bitterness, of taste. *Mbal kasandalan pa'itna kahawa itū.* The bitterness of this coffee is intolerable. (*cf:* **mamis₁ 1.1**; *Thesaurus:* **kahad**, **p'kkat**, **p'ddas**, **p'llod**) 1.1) *adj.* a- Bitter-tasting. *Apa'it ya ettom ma deyom bawis, p'ddu daing.* The black bit inside the weed-eating-fish is bitter, the gall-bladder of the fish. *Bang* *kahawa bay halam ananam, k'nnopanta, gōm pa'in papa'it.* When the coffee was flavorless we added to it, but it became bitter instead. **1.2)** *v. advrs.* *ka-...-an* To be affected by bitterness (of taste). *Kapa'itan aku e' bigi mampallam.* I am affected by the bitterness of a mango seed.

**pa'nda'** (derivative of **nda'**) *v. tr.***1)** To display something.**1.1)** *v. ditr.* To show something to someone. *A'a inān hal ama'nda'an abbuna.* That fellow is just making a show of his pride. *Subay pama'nda'ku kosog-kawasaku supaya patanyag ōnku ni manusiya' kamemon ma sakalibutan dunya.* I must display my power so that my fame is known to people all around the world. **1.2)** *v. tr. -an* To seek repair for a damaged object, or treatment for a sick or injured person. *Arāk pina'nda'an tungkangku ni ka'a, abila'.* I almost showed you my cooking pot, it's broken.

**pa'ud 1)** *n.* A piece or shingle of palm thatch, about 1 meter in length. (*cf:* **atop 2, silang₂**) **2)** *clf.* Count word for thatch shingles. *Duwampa'ud pa'in pamahāp atop.* Just two pieces for fixing the roof. *Atop sani billi ma pa'uran.* Sani thatch, bought by the piece.

**pa'us** *v. tr.* To chew fibrous substances such as sugarcane or sweet coconut, to get at the juice. *Halam amamis, buwat gu'ud t'bbu. Bang pa'usta hal at'bbag, halam aniya' agon ssana.* Not sweet, like the leafy end of sugarcane. It is quite bland when we chew it, almost no taste. (*Thesaurus:* **lopa', papa'**)

**pal-..-an₁** *aff.* Derivational circumfix that attaches to a noun to form a collective noun. *Magbayad palutangan.* Paying debts. *Palhimpunan; palbantahan; paltumbu-tumbuhan; palmaddani'an.* Gathering of people [e.g. a council]; enemies; all growing things; tapestried walls.

**pal-..-an₂** var. of **pag-..-an**

**pala** *n.* A digging tool; a shovel or spade. *Pala itū panaukku tana'.* This shovel is for me to dig up soil with. (*Thesaurus:* **bara, lalandak, piku, sangkul 1, susuwat**)

**palabay** (derivative of **labay₂**) *v. tr.* To endure a period or phase of activity. *Hal pinalabay bay p'ddi' matata hē', buwat ma dilaut. Yukta, "Bati'un pa'in aku. Ingga na aku bay apiru'-piru', pas'lle' pa'in ka."* Just getting through the eye-strain, as when out at sea. One says, "Just wake me up. As soon as I have had some shut-eye, you have a turn."

**palabayan** (derivative of **labay₁**) *n.* A passageway; a way through. *Da'a kām pas'llot-s'llot mailu apa halam aniya' palabayan.* Don't squeeze in there because there is no way through.

**palabra** (var. **parabla**) *v. tr. -an* To talk someone into believing what is not true. *Parablahanta ka, sali' kami maka'ā', buwat saga magpam'ssi, magpanonda'. Bang aku tinilaw yukta, "Halam." Malaingkan aniya'. Sali' paglimbunganku.* I play a trick on you, like when I catch something, by

fishing, or trolling. When asked I say, "Not a thing." But there was. It's as though I am hiding something. *Palabrahan kami abay kami aniya' daing, bo' halam.* We told our fleet companions that there were fish, but there weren't any. *Ata'u ko' ka'a ilu amarabla.* You know how to trick people.

**palakaya** *n.* A large outrigger vessel used for haul seining. (*syn:* **basnig**)

**palaktas** (derivative of **laktas**) *v. tr.* To allow someone to travel as a passenger just to cross a channel. *Palaktasun aku, aniya' pagdai'-dai'anku.* Let me go with you, I've got something I must get done in a hurry. (*Thesaurus:* **bayan 1.1, beya'₁, pagbiyahi, sakay 1, tumpang, tundug 1.1**).

**palahan-palahan** (derivative of **lahan**) *adv.* Slowly, of singing.

**palahi** (derivative of **lahi₁**) *v. tr.***1)** To allow something to escape or run away. *Palahi'un na daing ilū ko da'a ab'kkat naelon.* Let that fish run so the line doesn't break.**1.1)** *v. tr. -an* To evade a pursuer. *Palahi'in mundu ko da'a ka binono'.* Escape from the bandits so as not to be killed.

**palahil** *v. tr.* To make a gift to a woman's parents during her first pregnancy, an obligation of the man's kin. *Aumaw, halam bay tapalahil. Bang ma kami subay aniya' poga pamalahil, bang m'ssa' kibut.* [The child] is mute, no birth-gift having been given. With us a *poga* [aceramic water-jar] should be given as a birth-gift, if there is no *kibut* [another type of jar]. *Buwat bay aku angungsud, na pinalahil ni a'a bay anokat, anokat ni tag anak. Heka min heka sinokat duwampū' pilak.* Like when I have paid a brideprice, then a birth-gift is made to the person who specified the items, the parents of the child. Twenty pesos is the amount most commonly specified. (*cf:* **lahil 1.1**; *syn:* **pareyo'₂**)

**pala'at** (derivative of **la'at**) *v. tr.* To harm someone by speaking ill of him. *Saupama aniya' duwangan a'a magbagay. Dakayu' bagay inān anugi-nugi ni bōsna amala'at bagayna.* Two friends for example. One friend speaks ill to the other's boss, causing harm to his friend.

**pala'u** *n.* Boat-dwelling, nomadic Sama. (*syn:* **Jengen**)

**pagpala'u** *v. intr. aN-* To live permanently on a boat. *At'ggol na pagpala'u kami.* We lived on boats for a long time.

**palalu** (derivative of **lalu**) *n.* Someone addicted to having sex. {vulgar}

**palam** *v. tr.* To cook vegetables with coconut cream and turmeric, together with meat or boned fish. (*cf:* **p'tti'-gata'**; *gen:* **b'lla 1**)

**palambung** (derivative of **lambung₁**) *v. tr.* To communicate something by means of a dream. *Pagsangom pa'in pinabukis ma si Danyel in saga palihalan inān pinalambung ni iya.* When it was night those matters were revealed to Daniel by way of a dream. *Abati' na iya, jari tahati e'na bay palambung ni iya Tuhan ma panguppihanna.* He woke up and realised that God had spoken to him in his dream state.

**palamud** (derivative of **lamud**₁) *v. tr.* To add an ingredient to a mixture. *Pinaka'at saga kakabbunan sigām maka saga kabatu-batuhan isāb pinalamud ma katana'an.* Their plantations were destroyed, and masses of stones were also mixed in with the soil.

**palānan** (derivative of **lān**) *n.* A place used as a path.

**palandos** (derivative of **landos**) *v. tr.* To do something with force. *Da'a palandosun, subay ni'inut-inut.* Don't do it with force, it should be done little by little.

**palanta'** (derivative of **lanta'**) *v. tr.* To move things further apart. *Palanta'un lagi' kasaw ilū.* Spread those thatch poles further apart.

**palantaman** *n.* Behavior characteristic of a specific individual or species. *Nda'unbi palantaman s'mmut.* Look at the way ants behave. (*cf:* **palantara 1**)

**palantara** *n.* **1)** The way a creature is by nature. *Subay kitam anuyu'an palantara asaltun.* We should set our mind on a blameless character. *Palantara kambing amapa'-mapa' sadja, palantara manusiya' lisu'an-ahutu, angusaha-anangkaw.* It's the nature of a goat to keep on chewing, it's the nature of a human being to be both lazy and energetic, to work hard and to steal. (*cf:* **palantaman**; *Thesaurus:* **baktulan, bowahan, l'ngnganan**₂, **pakang**₁, **tebong**) **2)** The stance or movement characteristic of an individual. *Ahāp palantara he'na angigal. Ahāp palantarana, ahāp tebongna.* Her manner of dancing is good. Her posture and her movements are good. *Buwat kami subul lum'ngngan, ka'a-i angaliling bang sai ahāp palantarana.* Like us youths walking about, you looking carefully to see whose character is good.

**palantayan** (derivative of **lantay**) *n.* A low platform or mat on which a corpse is laid out. *Ma palantayan lagi', amangguwa' na.* Still on the death-platform, becoming a ghost.

**palang** *v. advrs. -in-* Marked with varicolored bands or panels. *Tepo pinalang.* A mat with a banded pattern. (*Thesaurus:* **b'ttik 1.1, kabang 1.1, kelong-kelong**₁, **jali' 1.1, manas**)

**palangay** *n.* Behavior; outward actions as an expression of character. *Ala'at pahāp palangaynu ilū.* Your nature is really bad. *Magtawbat kam ngga'i ka sadja min palangaybi, sagō' min deyom pangatayanbi.* Be contrite not only in what you do, but from your hearts. (*Thesaurus:* **addat-tabi'at, apalal, kaul-pi'il**)

**palangka'**₁ var. of **palangga'**

**palangka'**₂ *n.* A sleeping platform or a bed on legs. (*Thesaurus:* **kantil**₁, **pabahakan, palegehan, patulihan**)

**palangga'** (var. **palangka'**₁) *v. advrs. -in-* **1)** Spoiled by over-indulgence. **1.1)** *v. tr.* To pamper someone by indulging every wish. (*Thesaurus:* **parakag, parūl 1.1, patege'**)

**palanggana** *n.* A large, flat, general-purpose basin. *Bang aku angandakdak subay ma palanggana.* When I wash clothes it should be in a *palanggana.* (*Thesaurus:* **batiya', lumpang-lumpang, pastan, undam**)

**palanggungan** (derivative of **langgung**₂) *n.* A rectangular frame of wood which supports the gongs of a kulintangan set. (*Thesaurus:* **ba'ugan**₂, **papagan 1**).

**palangi** (derivative of **langi**) *v. tr. -an* To use something as an aid to swimming. *Palangihin papan itū ko da'a ka alembo.* Make use of this board to swim with so you don't drown.

**palangihan** (derivative of **langi**) *n.* Something used as an aid to swimming.

**palango** (derivative of **lango**) *v. tr.* To cause someone to be drunk. *Palangohun sigā maka tuba'.* Make them drunk with palm toddy.

**palapa'** *n.* **1)** The short side planks at the bow and stern of a pelang-type canoe. (*gen:* **tapi' 1**) **1.1)** *v. tr. -an Pinalapa'an munda'-buli'.* Fitted with hull planks bow and stern.

**palapal** (derivative of **lapal**) *v. tr. -an* To send someone a message. *Pinalapalan ni a'a dangan inān.* A message sent to that other person. (*Thesaurus:* **haka 1.1, pata'u, tubad**).

**palapas-palapas** *v. intr. aN-* To be falling in stages, as something falling through the branches of a tree.

**palasa** (var. **plasa**) *n.* A town center; a plaza. (*cf:* **mairan**)

**palasahan** (derivative of **lasa**₁) *n.* The way one feels, whether well or ill. *Ala'at na palasahanku.* I feel poorly now. *Buwat aku bay tinandog, amole' ni palasahanku, magsalinggā aku.* Like when I had fever, it affected my health sense. I was restless with pain. *Pagkakanna pa'in, pasawa magtūy pamaihu'anna pagka ahāp na palasahanna.* Once he had eaten, his face brightened since he was now feeling good.

**la'at palasahan** *n. phrase* The feeling of being unwell.*Ala'at na palasahanku.* I am feeling poorly now.

**palaslaet** var. of **plaslaet**

**palastik** *n.* Synthetic materials; plastic of various kinds. *Akapal sawan palastik, minsan nihantak mbal abila'.* Plastic drinking glasses are thick, they won't break even when thrown down hard.

**palatun** (derivative of **latun**) *v. tr.* To convey an item or person from one place to another. *Palatunun gi' lai' itū ni luma' si Im.* Take this dish across to the house of Im. *Mbal tapalatun tambal itu.* This medication cannot be transferred.

**palbantahan** (derivative of **banta**) *n.* Enemies in a collective sense.

**palbangsahan** (derivative of **bangsa**₁) *n.* Collective term for multiple ethnic groups. *Saga sultan ma dunya maka palbangsa-bangsahan.* The kings of the world and all the nations.

**palbut** *see:* **panyap-palbut**

**palkala'** (var. **parakala'**) *n.* 1) A matter for discussion or negotiation, as a legal dispute, a marriage, an attempt at reconciliation. *Bang aniya' palkala'nu pi'itu ka ni aku. Ai-ai kasusahannu, tabangta.* If you have trouble just come to me. No matter what your problem is I will help. *Alengog sidda kōkku e' parakala' itū.* My head is confused by this matter. *S'ssagun kamemon kaluma'an aniya' palkala'.* Tell the whole village that there is something important going on. (*cf:* **kīs₂**; *Thesaurus:* **gara' 1, parak**) 1.1) *v. tr.* To bring an accusation against someone. *Si Oto' itū bay pinalkala', bay kono' makasagid ni d'nda.* Oldest Son has had an accusation brought against him, it is said that he brushed against a girl.

**pagpalkala'** *v. intr. aN-* To be engaged in formal discussions. *Bang halam pa'in makat'kka a'a dangan ma deyom bay pangawal hē', na yuk sigā, "Magpalkala' na kitā, pinospa' na bang hal a'a dangan."* In the event that a certain person hasn't arrived within the time set, they then say, "We have an issue to discuss, the decision [to wait] is cancelled if it is just one person." *Amasasā ni kamemon, buwat magpalkala' bo' ariki'.* Letting everyone know, making a formal dispute of it even though it is small.

**palkata'an** (derivative of **kata'**) *n.* The words of a formal curse. *Tauwa' palkata'an, sali' nihinang-hinang.* Struck with a curse, like being bewitched. (*Thesaurus:* **duti, hikmat, hinang-hinang₁, h'lling₃, pantak 1.1, sihil 1.1**).

**palda** *n.* A skirt or dress. *Akosog baliyu, palais paldana.* The wind is strong, her skirt is flattened [against her body]. (*Thesaurus:* **bistiru, saya-saya**)

**paldu** *n.* A cage for keeping things alive in the sea. *Am'lli aku tohongan, isiku ni paldu pinaka'llum.* I am going to buy a turtle and put it inside a cage to keep alive. (*cf:* **pagal**)

**paldusahan** (derivative of **dusa**) *n.* Sins, collectively.

**palege** *v. tr.* 1) To lay something down; to put someone to bed. 1.1) *v. tr. -an* To use something as a place to lie down. *Da'a palegehin tepo itū, kamange'an.* Don't use this mat to lie on, it's been urinated on.

**palegehan** (derivative of **lege**) *n.* A place to lie down; a bed. (*Thesaurus:* **kantil₁, pabahakan, palangka'₂, patulihan**).

**palehom** (derivative of **lehom**) *v. tr.* To neglect or ignore a responsibility or commitment. *Da'a palehomun saga kasigpitan kamemon ya bay tum'kka ni kami.* Don't ignore all the hardships that have happened to us. *In a'a halam akkalan amalehom pandu' mma'na.* A person with no

sense disregards his father's teaching. *Mbal isāb palehomku saga a'a ya bay makapaka'at bangka'bi.* I will not ignore the people who wrecked your canoe. (*Thesaurus:* **haman-haman 1, sumadja**).

**palesseg** (derivative of **lesseg**) *v. tr.* To put something down casually. *O'ō, palessegun mailu.* Look, just put it over there.

**palessegan** (derivative of **lesseg**) *n.* A place where someone sits without concern for cleanliness or decorum. *Nda'un ba, al'mmi' ko' palessegannu ilū.* Look at that, the place where you are sitting is dirty. *An'ngge na aku min bay pal'sseganku.* I stood up from where I had been sitting flat [on the ground].

**paleta** *n.* A bamboo spatula. (*Thesaurus:* **luwag 1, sasanglag, sintib, suru' 1**)

**paletek** *v. intr. aN-* To make the sound of something cracking or breaking. *Amaletek sali' to'olangku kamemon.* All my bones are kind of creaking. (*cf:* **palopok**)

**pagpaletek** *v. intr. aN-* To make cracking or breaking sounds. *Bang aku amuwad kayu, mbal magtūy ah'bba'. Magpaletek dahū. Hinabu sōng ah'bba', apōng ugatna.* When I fell a tree it doesn't fall immediately, it makes a cracking noise first. When it is about to fall, its "sinews" break. *Magpaletek ya bangkakna.* His knucklebones make cracking noises.

**paletop** (derivative of **letop**) *v. tr.* To add enough water to cover food in a pot. *Paletopun bohe'na.* Add water till it covers [what is in the pot].

**paleyak** (derivative of **leyak**) *v. tr.* To turn something over so that it is face up. *Pasindikun lai', ngga'i ka pinaleyak, pinasindik.* Stand the plate on edge, not turned face up, set on its edge. *Bang bay pakkom, na pinaleyak pabīng bo' makatandan ni bihing.* If it had overturned, it was set face up again in order to reach the shore.

**palhimpunan** *n.* A formal gathering, as an assembly of community leaders; a congregation.

**pali** (var. **paling**) *v. tr.* To change tack (when sailing) by bringing the boom across. *Magpali kita bang pa'in ka makasōng.* Let's tack, so long as we make progress. *Bang kita amaling subay samapigtal ligtang.* When we are tacking, the mast stays should be equally taut. *Tulaknu tudju s'ddopan sagō' baliyu habagat.Bang binusay ka, abinasa ka.Na ya niōnan magpali, pinindahan munda tudju ni satan. Jari pagpindanu ni satan duwanjām t'ggolna, amali ka tudju ni uttala' duwanjām, mampa'in ka makasōng.* Your heading is southwest, but the wind is the southwest monsoon. You will be worn out paddling. With the *pali* tack the heading is changed towards the south. After two hours of heading south, you tack northwards for two hours, so long as you make progress. *Tulaknu tudju s'ddopan sagō' baliyu habagat. Bang binusay ka, abinasa ka. Na ya niōnan magpali, pinindahan munda tudju ni* *satan.* Your heading is southwest, but the wind is the southwest monsoon. You will be worn out paddling. With what's called tacking, the heading is changed towards the south.

**pagpali** *v. intr. aN-* To swing to and fro, of a boom (sailing). *Hal magpaling-paling maina'an.* Just swinging from one tack to another there.

**pali-pali** *n.* Beliefs based on tradition. *Da'a kita atulak ma llaw Juma'at, ameya' kita ma pali-pali.* Let's not leave on a Friday; let's go along with the customary belief [that Friday is an unlucky day]. *Maumu isāb bang daing aheya, buwat kāt, patay tunung, subay da'a tō'ta. Kalu-kalu bang a'a ata'uhan pali-pali, tiniti'an he'na min t'llu maka tahik.* Often the case with a large fish like a humphead wrasse, dead but undamaged, we should not point at it. Perhaps if a person knows the old traditions he may sprinkle it three times with sea water. *Pali-pali kamatto'ahan bang kono' alengas, hatina ata'u.* The folk-belief of the elders is that when a person has a high forehead he is knowledgeable. (*Thesaurus:* **ntan₂ 2, pangkatan, purukan, tubus₂ 1, tuttulan, usulan**)

**pagpali-pali** *v. intr. aN-* To be chatting, especially about traditions and beliefs.

**paliksa'** (var. **pariksa'**) *v. ditr.* To seek detailed information, as when investigating a crime. *Halam bay paliksa'ku bang sai.* I did not inquire who it was. (*Thesaurus:* **tilaw 1**)

**palig** *n.* The Black surgeonfish. *Acanthurus gahhm. Mbal pasamod palig, wa'i palisig ni timbang.* Surgeonfish don't associate [with other fish]; they slip into the depths. (*gen:* **kumay**)

**paligay** *adv.* Even more so; especially. *Bang aniya' bay b'llita, bo' ala'at, magsusun kita. Paligay bang ta'nda' he' a'a ala'at, paligay magsusun.* If we have bought something and it is bad we are regretful. But the more it is seen by someone else that it is bad, the more regretful we are. *Paligay kita nirūlan he' matto'ata, paligay kita sala mbal magmanja'.* The more our parents indulge us, the more we sort of fail to show them respect. *Bay aku soho'nu am'lli daing ati ala'at. Na yuknu, "Papole'un daing ilu, am'lli ka saddi." Agsāy aku am'lli daing baki'. Paligay ala'at isāb ilu.* You sent me to buy fish and it wasn't good. So you said, "Return this fish and buy something else." I promptly bought some catfish. But that was even worse. (*Thesaurus:* **anambahina, bangkinna...bangkinna, kalap, labi-labi, luba', luhūy, ya lagi'na**)

**palihalan** *n.* 1) Circumstances; state of affairs; what is happening. *Amogbogan aku ka'a palihalannu.* I am supporting you in your circumstances. *Palihalan, aku makapi' ni lahat ī', angurul aku ka'a.* What is happening that I am going to that place, is that I am pursuing you. 2) A vision or prediction of what will happen. *Bo' tatali' in saga paralilan maka palihalan.* And figuring out

metaphors and indications of future events. *Bang halam aniya' palihalan mbal magmasusa in saga a'a paglahat.* When there are no signs of future events the people of the land feel no remorse. *...ba'anan uppi maka palihalan pasal sinōng.* ...dreams and predictions about the future. *Amatay na kam ni bay palihalanbi tagna'.* You are dead to your original *palihalan. Ma llaw inān magkaiya'an pakaniya-kaniya kanabihan ma sabab palihalanna.* On that day each of the prophets will experience shame because of his condition.

**palihanan** (derivative of **lihan**) *n.* Temporary accommodation. *Luma' tolda ya palihanan kami ma timpu bono'.* A tent was our temporary accommodation in war time.

**pali'** *n.* 1) A wound, especially one caused by cutting. (*Thesaurus:* **bakat 1.1, bu'ag, langgahi'**) 1.1) *adj. -an* Wounded; suffering from a cut. *Pali'an tape'na e' bila' kassa'.* His foot is cut by broken glass. 1.2) *v. intr. aN-* To be developing into a wound or sore. *Saddī buruk min gulis-manuk. Gulis-manuk mbal amali', hal magkanit-kanit. Buruk* [scalp itch] is different from *gulis manuk* [scurf]. The latter won't become a wound, it just flakes off. 1.3) *v. advrs. ka-...-an* To be seriously wounded. *Mbal kapali'an kōkna sabab aniya' sampanna. Minsan katauwa'an mbal kapali'an.* His head cannot be wounded because it has a [magical] protection. Even though struck he cannot be wounded.

**palilihan** *n.* 1) A person's inner nature as revealed in behavior. *Pina'nda'an palilihanna.* Her true nature is displayed. *Ya palilihanna ma deyom dunya itū ya bineya'an.* It's his real nature here on earth that is followed. 1.1) *adj. a-* Swayed by one's real nature. *Sali' kita amoway, sali' mamarahi. "Apalilihan pahāp a'a hē'."* It is like when we criticise, overstating things, saying, "That person is so easily swayed."

**palilitu** (derivative of **litu**) *n.* A trader; a middleman. *Bang aniya' palilitu pasampang, halam aniya' daing ma M'ddas.* When a dealer comes out to meet [the boats coming in], there aren't any fish in Siasi market. (*Thesaurus:* **paltira, tandero 1.1**).

**palilu** (var. **pailu**) *v. tr. -an* To refute or contradict an accusation or an assertion. *A: "Ai paliluhannu?" B: "Llingnu pasal si Oto'."* A: "What are you contradicting?" B: "What you said about Oldest Son." (*Thesaurus:* **da'awa 1.1, paglugat, tawalli', tumagal 1.1**)

**pagpalilu** *v. intr. aN-* To contradict each other. *Magpalilu kita mang aniya' kono' ameya' ni lahat Sandakan. Yukmu, "Si Mma'." Yukku, "Ngga'i ka!"* We are contradicting each other when it is said that someone is going to Sandakan, and you say, "Dad is [going]." I say, "No he's not!"

**palimaya** var. of **paliyama'**

**palimba'an** *n.* Purlins, the long pieces of timber

framing that lie transverse to rafters and support the poles to which thatch shingles are tied. (*Thesaurus:* **kasaw, lubing-lubing**)

**palimbuhan** (derivative of **limbu**) *n.* A place of shelter. *Daipara aniya' palimbuhanbi.* Fortunately you had a place to shelter.

**palimping** *n.* 1) A rope sewn into the edge of a sail; a bolt-rope. *Ab'kkat ya palimping diyata', pahūs pareyo'.* The upper bolt-rope broke and [the sail assembly] slipped down. **1.1)** *v. tr. -an* To sew a bolt-rope inside the folded edges of a sail. (*syn:* **palipit**)

**paling** var. of **pali**

**palipit** *v. tr. -an* To sew a bolt-rope inside the folded edge of a sail. *Subay banog atawa leha pinalipitan.* It should be a triangular or square sail to have a bolt-rope sewn into it. (*syn:* **palimping 1.1**)

**palis₁** *v. advrs. ta-* Carried far off course by a strong wind or current. *Tapalis itū mbal kita sali' makatandan lahat. Yuk kami, "Wa'i tapalis ma dilaut. Makatandan ni lahat, luwal aheya tulung min Tuhan."* Palis is when we cannot get to shore. We say, "Blown off course out at sea. We will make it to land only if there is great help from God." *Saupama kita ma dilaut hal damunda'-munda'ta, s'lle' bale puhu' minsan ni'iyan, punung-punungan, tapalis kita.* For example we are out at sea, just our one canoe, and God forbid that it should even be mentioned, we are faint with hunger, carried far off course. (*Thesaurus:* **gesges, laran, loson, paghadjul-hadjul, pespes 1.1**)

**palis₂** *v. tr.* To polish a leather surface. *Bang aettom taumpa'ku subay pinalis.* If my shoes are black they have to be polished.

**palista** (derivative of **lista**) *v. tr.* To add names to a list. *Pinatipun saga a'a supaya tapalista dangan-parangan.* The people were made to assemble in order to be listed one by one.

**palit₁** *adj. a-* Widely scattered. *B'nnal bay kinose'an saga pamanganan bo' amasi saga buwas amalit.* It's true the things we ate from were washed, but there was still rice scattered around. (*syn:* **pulak-palik 1**)

**palit₂** *v. tr.* To retrieve fish traps from the sea floor. *Bang aniya' bay tino'onanta buwat panggal, bubu, bungkalta, palitta.* When we've set something such as a *panggal*-type trap or a *bubu* on the sea floor, we haul it up, retrieve it. *Na ilu, bang kita amalit subay pinagtukbul kayu hē' bo' ta'nda' pandoga hē', bo' mbal alungay bubu.* Now then, when we go to lift up *bubu* traps, those trees yonder must be in alignment so the reference point can be seen, and the trap will not be lost. (*cf:* **badja' 1.1**)

**pagpalit** *v. intr. aN-* 1) To earn a living by means of deep-water fish traps recovered by a draghook. **1.1)** *v. tr.* To catch fish using a deep-water trap. *Magbadja' kami. Ya binadja' bahan*

*abō' niā' bubu bay pagpalit kami.* We fish with a draghook. A length of vine is used to retrieve the *bubu* trap we are deep-water fishing with.

**palita'an** *n.* A lamp, especially a wick lamp. *Am'lli aku palita'an ni tinda bo' asawa luma'ku.* I will buy a wick lamp from the shop so my house will be bright. (*Thesaurus:* **kulaet 1, laet, lām, lampu, plaslaet 1, sū' 1**)

**paliya'** *n.* The bitter melon (ampalaya). *Momordica charantia.*

**paliya'-laut** *n.* A species of coastal tree.

**paliyama'** (var. **palimaya**) *n.* A land or season blessed with an abundance of food. *Ya lahat inān bay paliyama', buwat bay jambangan Eden tagna'.* That land was an abundant land, like the original garden of Eden. (*Thesaurus:* **musim, tahun 1**)

**paliyangan** (derivative of **liyang**) *n.* The grave as the final resting place of all mankind. (*Thesaurus:* **kubul 1, kuddaman, dinding-hali, gumi 2**).

**paliyuk** *n.* A spherical earthenware cooking pot with a narrow mouth. (*gen:* **pam'llahan**)

**paljanji'an** (derivative of **janji'**) *n.* A formal promise or covenant. *Buwattitu ya paljanji'anku ma ka'a, hinangta ka pagmatto'ahan ma kabangsa-bangsahan.* This is my promise to you, I will make you the forebear of nations.

**pal'bbo** (derivative of **l'bbo**) *v. tr.* To cause something to be soft. *Pal'bbohun bang ka angalut bohe'. Palalomun.* Make the ground soft and boggy when you are digging for water. Make it deep.

**pal'ngngan** (derivative of **l'ngngan₂**) *v. tr. -an* To lay down policy for one's followers or adherents. *Pinal'ngnganan kita pitis.* Policy is imposed on us. *Na ya hē' amal'ngngan pitis ni kawal tendog.* So that's the one who lays down policy to his adherents. (*cf:* **pitis₂ 1**).

**pal'ngnganan** (derivative of **l'ngngan₁**) *n.* A walking path. *Tana' inān sidda ah'bbol bang pal'ngnganan.* That path is very squishy when walked on. *Bang aku pal'ngngan-i, pi'ingga-pi'ingga pal'ngngananku-i, ya ī' mags'bba'-sasab.* When I am walking, wherever my path takes me, that is s'bba'-sasab. (*Thesaurus:* **kalsara, labayan, lān**).

**pal'ppa** (derivative of **l'ppa**) *v. tr.* To let something go free; to release from restriction. *Bang bowanu pehē' da'a pal'ppahun min deyo' pikpiknu.* If you are taking it there don't let it escape from under your armpit.

**pal'ssut** (derivative of **l'ssut**) *v. tr.* To convey something by a messenger, with implications of difficulty in getting it through. *Hal sulat pinal'ssut ni ka'a.* It is only the message that is being brought to you.

**palla'** *adj. a-* Mischievous; comical. *Apalla', sali' alangog. Apalla' si Gi man si La. Palla',* like having fun. Gi is more mischievous than La.

**pagpalla'** *v. intr.* aN- **1)** To behave in a way that amuses people. *Magpalla'-palla iya itū.* This one makes people laugh. **2)** To behave in a sexually provocative manner. *Magpalla'-palla' sali' puta, sali' magba'is-ba'is.* Behaving provocatively, like a prostitute, like being sexually aggressive. *L'lla isāb magpalla'-palla' angamiting-ngamitingan ma d'nda.* Men too behave provocatively, arranging meetings with women.

**palling** *adj.* zero Turning on a shaft.

**pagpalling** *v. intr.* aN- To revolve on a shaft, as a propeller or fan. *Magpalling-palling kapay lansa.* The launch propellers are spinning. (*Thesaurus:* **paggulung-gulung 1, paglegot 1**)

**kapalling** *n.* A children's toy with vanes that spin around a central axle when struck by the wind; a pinwheel.

**pallungan** *n.* A small pelang-type canoe suitable for children. (*Thesaurus:* **balutu, bangka', dapang, londay, pambot, paraw 1, pelang, pongag**)

**palmaddani'** *n.* A carpet, often hung on a wall in Sulu homes. *Ai-ai ahalga' mareyom luma' palmaddani'an.* Everything costly in a carpeted house. (*Thesaurus:* **musalla, tudjara**)

**palman** *n.* **1)** A message or edict from a supreme authority or supernatural source. *Palman Tuhan ina'an pasangon ma nabi itu.* A message from God has come on this prophet. **1.1)** *v. ditr.* To convey a message to someone, the action of a supernatural or divine being. *Bay aku pinalmanan, sinoho' angali maitu.* I have received a divine message, I was told to dig here. *Yukta ni duwata, "Angaharis ka bang ai nihinang." Manjari amalman na.* We say to the *duwata* spirit, "Speak with us [about] what is to be done." So then it communicates a message. (*Thesaurus:* **haris**)

**palmanis** (derivative of **manis**) *n.* A magical formula for making someone beautiful. *Minsan ato'a, bang binassahan palmanis alingkat du.* Even an old person, if a *palmanis* charm is read over her, will be beautiful.

**palmasiya** *n.* A pharmacy; a drugstore.

**palmata** *n.* **1)** A jewel. *"A," yukna, "ahunit piniha d'nda asaltun, ahalga' gi' min palmata intan."* "Well now," he said, "a perfect woman is hard to find, more precious than jewels." (*Thesaurus:* **dilam, intan, puntu' 1**) **1.1)** *v. tr.* -an To beautify something with a jewel. *Am'lli aku dilam pamalmataku singsing.* I will buy an inexpensive gemstone to set in a ring.

**palmula'an** (derivative of **mula'**) *n.* Ancestors, especially those that are foundational in Sama folk history. *Palmula'an sigām kasehe' ina'an ma lahat. Ya ma kami bay binowa pi'itu.* Some of their founding ancestors are there in the [home] place. The ones we have were brought here. *Ya tampat maina'an palmula'an pasal aniya' angipat*

*iya maina'an.* The shrine there is that of a *palmula'an* ancestor because there is someone there who cares for it. (*Thesaurus:* **mbo'₁, ntan₂ 1, pangkat₂**).

**palnahu'an** var. of **panahu'an**

**palnyawahan** (var. **panyawahan**) (derivative of **nyawa**) *n.* The physical location of a person's life-principle. *Ang'tting itū, sinōd he' a'a man deyo', ya tinaplokan panyawahanna.* This swollen condition [means he] was entered by the being from the depths, his life-principle covered over.

**palok** *v. tr.* **1)** To treat someone of high rank with deference. *A'a alanga subay niharap bang magsuli-suli, pinalok.* A person of rank should be faced when talking [with him], treated with deep respect. (*Thesaurus:* **pagaddat 1.1, pagmamay, pagmanja', su'ap 1.1**) **1.1)** *v. intr.* pa- To show deference towards someone. *Papalok isāb kita ni matto'ata, ni danakanna.* We also show deference to our elders, and to our siblings.

**palo'** **1)** *adj.* a- Reluctant. *Apalo' du pa'in ka magbobowa lapal ni kala'atan.* You are especially reluctant to be the bearer of bad news. *Mbal apalo' a'a inān, maghinang na pa'in buwattē'. Mbal al'gga.* That fellow will not hold back, he keeps on behaving like that. Doesn't learn from experience. **1.1)** *v. intr.* pa- To refrain from doing something that is not approved. *Papalo' kām maglunsulan.* Stop wandering around idly. **2)** *v. tr.* a-, ka-..-an, -an To treat something with reluctance. *Aniya' kinapalo'an, aniya' kinal'ggahan.* There are things to resist doing, and things to learn from.

**palom** *adj.* a- Obscured by heavy rain or fog.

**palopok** (var. **pahopok**) (derivative of **lopok**) *v. intr.* aN- To crackle when compressed, as of something held tightly in the hand or between the teeth. *Ahāp isāb amalopok-malopok salang-sabot. Ngga'i ka isāb lapatna buwat doppeng inān, magt'llag-t'llag.* It is good when cassava cake crackles. Unlike the density of *doppeng* cakes, it is light-textured. (*cf:* **paletek**).

**palpal** (var. **papal**) *adj.* a- **1)** Blocked by something plugged into an orifice. *Alantak pahāp ka'a-i, apalpal.* You are stone deaf, your ears blocked. (*Thesaurus:* **bisu 1.1, halong, lantak**) **1.1)** *v. tr.* To drive something into a socket. *Palpalun kōk katig ilū ko da'a amangsut.* Knock in the head of the outrigger so it doesn't come out of its socket.

**palsakkihan** (derivative of **saki**) *n.* A chronic and persistent illness.

**palsaksi'an** (derivative of **saksi'**) *n.* A body of evidence; proof.

**palsagga'an** var. of **pagsagga'an₂**

**palsapahan** var. of **pagsapahan**

**palsu** *adj.* a- Faulty, of something that fails to fire, as a bullet or firecracker. *Bang tumakbil ni timbak kulitis, aheka apalsu. Angkan mbal ah'lling apugtul sumbuhanna.* With regard to firecrackers, a lot of them are faulty. The reason they don't explode is that the wicks are broken off. (*Thesaurus:* **gillo'ak, paltik**)

**palsuku'an** (derivative of **suku'**) *n.* Something owned; possessions; a share. *Yuk kallo', "Ya palsuku'anku," yukna, "anak siyali." Yuk kuyya', "A niangay ka'a ya tag palsuku'an?"* "My portion," said Heron, "is the youngest daughter." Monkey replied, "So why should you be the one with the portion?" *In d'nda isāb ma bangsa ina'an bay du isāb makataima' palsuku'an tana', buwat saga kampung l'lla.* The women of that culture also received a share of land, just like their male relatives.

**palta** *adj.* **a-** Intermittent; irregular. *Apalta usaha si Ju angahangkut bohe', sabab ulan.* Ju's work of carrying water is irregular because of the rain. *Minsan pagkakan kami, apalta na. Sababna nsa' na ai-ai tasambi' kami.* Even our meals are intermittent now, because we have nothing to give in exchange. *Apalta, mbal pilmi-pilmi.* Inconsistent, not occurring regularly.

  **pagpalta** *v. intr.* **aN-** To function erratically. *Magpalta sali' kulaet, bang pakeyatta bo' ap'dda bo' mbal ap'dda, akeyat isāb pabīng.* The pressure lantern is erratic. When we light it then it goes out and then doesn't go out, and is bright again.

**paltana'an** (derivative of **tana'**₂) *n.* Land in a territorial sense. *Angay halam bay bawi'bi paltana'anbi ma deyom t'llu hatus tahun ē'?* Why did you not recover your lands during those three hundred years?

**paltanda'an** (derivative of **tanda'**) *n.* A sign or portent; the visible evidence of some event. *Pasujud iya ma munda'an sultan paltanda'an pagaddatna ma iya.* He prostrated himself in front of the sultan as evidence of his respect for him.

**palti** *n.* A political party. (*Thesaurus:* **kaheka-heka'an, kompolan, dansehe'an, padjuhan, umpigan**)

**paltik** *adj.* **a-** Counterfeit, especially of money or guns. *Bang kita animbak a'a bo' mbal ah'lling, yukta, "Angay timbak itu mbal ah'lling? Apaltik."* When we shoot at someone and it does not fire, we say, "Why is this gun not firing? It's not genuine." *Atawa taep, ubus angandawat, ubus mbal. Apaltik.* Or a typewriter, writes one minute, doesn't the next minute. It's not genuine. (*Thesaurus:* **gillo'ak, palsu**)

**paltira** *n.* A trading partner, as someone who finances a fishing trip or people who fish under contract. *Bay aku makautang sīn ma paltira, na subay bowaku ni iya daing.* I borrowed money from the trader, so I must take my fish to him. (*Thesaurus:* **palilitu, tandero 1.1**)

**paltomo'-tomo'an** (derivative of **tomo'**) *n.* Growing things of the vegetable kingdom; plants. (*syn:* **paltubu-tubuhan 1**).

**paltubu-tubuhan** (var. **paltumbu-tumbuhan**) (derivative of **tubu-tubu**) *n.* **1)** Growing things of the vegetable kingdom; vegetation in general. *Paltumbu-tumbuhan, ya tinanom kamemon.* Vegetation, all planted things. (*Thesaurus:* **legotoman, l'mput deya, sayul 1**; *syn:* **paltomo'-tomo'an**). **2)** The human body as a living organism; a person's constitution or bodily frame. *A'llum paltubu-tubuhanta, a'llum anggauta'ta kamemon, sali' ahāp to'ongan palasahanta.* Our bodily functions are alive, our physical vigor is alive, it's like we feel very good. *Sali' kita asaki bang bay asidda-sidda, agagal paltubu-tubuhanta.* It's like when we are sick, having been gravely ill, our constitution seriously stressed. (*Thesaurus:* **akal-baran, batang-tubu, pagdayaw 1, tangkorak**).

**paltumbu-tumbuhan** var. of **paltubu-tubuhan**

**palubi** (derivative of **lubi**) *n.* A shampooing agent, commonly a mixture of coconut cream and water. *Angamu' aku dampōng lahing ilū palubiku kōkku.* I am requesting half of that coconut to shampoo my hair.

**paludju'** (derivative of **ludju'**) *v. tr.* To revive negotiations that had been suspended. *Minda' pinaludju' e' mma' si Mo, pinabīng ni baina.* Mo's father fortunately got the marriage discussions going again, back to where they had been. *A'a magtunang bay abaibad, pinaludju' bo' asugpat pabalik.* A courting couple who have separated, persuaded to resume and be connected again.

**paluha** (derivative of **luha**) *v. tr.* To widen something already open. *Paluha'un labayanku bo' supaya mbal patabid buku tape'ku.* Widen my way through so I don't twist my ankle.

**palu'** *adj.* **a-** **1)** Suffering from partial and temporary loss of sight. **1.1)** To be overwhelmed by the sight of something truly impressive. {idiom} *Apalu' pag'nda'ku ma d'nda inān!* My sight is dazzled by that girl over there! (*Thesaurus:* **buta**₁, **lakap-manuk, legsok**₂, **silaw 1**)

**paluli** (var. **paruli**) *v. tr.* To keep something firmly in mind, motivated by a sense of responsibility or revenge. *Bang aniya' bangsa inān magbono', minsan bay pinagma'ap, nientom he' sigā. Pinaluli bay pagbono'.* When people of that tribe fight, even if peace has been made they remember. They will keep that conflict in mind. *Bay lilusnu malungay, nsa' na palulinu. Sinagaran ma Tuhan.* That watch of yours that was lost, you no longer keep thinking about it. It's just left for God [to act]. *Angampun ka, O Panghū'! Kalehun to'ongan kami, maka parulihun.* Forgive us, oh Lord. Really hear us and remember us. *Paruliku ya saga bay pinapatay, mbal isāb pinalehom ya saga bay makarusa.* I will remember those who have been killed, and I will not ignore those who have sinned. (*Thesaurus:* **balos**₁ **1, entom buddi, pagbuling-bata' 1.1**)

  **pagpaluli** *v. intr.* **aN-** To keep something in mind

with a view to responding later. *Buwat aniya' sehe'ta magbono', yukta, "Angagad ka, aniya' tahun magpaluli aku ma ka'a."* Like when a friend [and I] fight, we say, "You wait, there'll be a season when I will pay you back."

**paluma'an** (derivative of **luma'**) *n.* A housing complex.

**paluntungan** (derivative of **untung₁**) *n.* A profitable outcome from a business venture. *Ai bay paluntunganna?* What was his profit? *Ya sadja kabaya'anku bang pa'in aniya' paluntunganbi aheya.* All I want is that you may have a good profit. (*cf:* **pagkalugi'an**).

**palungay** (derivative of **lungay**) *v. tr.* To cause something to disappear. *L'ngnganku magpalungay ni lahat dakayu'.* My trip is to disappear in some other country. *Mbal kita makatuli' lān. Pinalungay pikilanta.* We cannot find the path. Our thinking has been made to disappear.

**palupalu** *n.* A species of freshwater fish. *Palupalu ma deyom danaw. Aheya kōkna. Palupalu*, a lake fish with a large head.

**palutangan** (derivative of **utang**) *n.* Liabilities; debts.

**palutu'** (derivative of **lutu'₁**) *v. ditr.* To provide someone with food for a journey or fishing expedition. *Saga tinapay maka ginisan takakan pamalutu'ta sigām ma pal'ngnganan sigām tudju amole'.* Bread and various foods provided for them on their journey home. *Anā, sinakapan na e' ina' inān, sampay pinalutu'an na takakan si' kaut.* Well now, equipped by Mother there, and supplied with food to be eaten at sea.

**paluwas** (derivative of **luwas₁**) *v. tr.* To get something out of a container or storage place. *Paluwasun ba sīnnu ilū.* Out with that money of yours.

**paluwasan** (derivative of **luwas₁**) *n.* A source, especially with regard to a woman as the source of one's existence. *Dapaluwasan du kami, saddī mma'.* We are from the same mother [lit. the same source], different fathers. *Tahalusku bangsa ina'an-i apa ngga'i ka danakan. Mbal magsimbug laha', mbal dapaluwasan.* It is appropriate for me to be involved with one of that ethnic group because he is not a brother. The blood is not mixed, the source [i.e. the mother] is not the same.

**pām** *v. tr.* -**an** To pump something in order to increase the air pressure inside. *Ak'ppel silikan baek bang halam bay pināman.* The bicycle tire is flat if it hasn't been pumped up. (*syn:* **gomba**)

**pamakay** (derivative of **pakay₁**) *n.* Clothing; whatever is worn. (*Thesaurus:* **s'mmek 1**, **tamongon**).

**pamagay** (derivative of **magay**) *n.* 1) A matter of concern. *Pinagdaplosan iya ma alopan pagsara'an, sagō' halam pamagay e' gubnul.* He was whipped severely in the presence of the court, but the governor was unconcerned. 1.1) *interrog.* For

what purpose; to do what with? *Pamagaynu pōng papan itu? Arāk amu'ku.* What do you plan to do with these offcuts of wood? I had thought of asking you for them. *Pamagay lahing ilu?* What are those coconuts for?

**mbal pamagay** *phrase* Unconcerned about something which is usually a matter of concern. *Mbal pamagay he'na daya damuli.* He is unconcerned about the riches to come.

**pamahadja'** (derivative of **mahadja'**) *n.* 1) A person of no worth. *Pamahadja' ko' ka'a ilū!* You worthless trash! 1.1) *v. tr.* To treat someone as worthless. *Pamahadja'un na pehē', sali' nihampul-hampul.* Treat as worthless, like showing complete disregard for.

**pamahalayak** (derivative of **mahalayak**) *v. tr.* To make news or information widely known. *Habal bay pinamahalayak e' kanabi-nabihan.* A message proclaimed by the prophets. (*Thesaurus:* **nasihat**, **pablek**).

**pamahāp** (derivative of **pahāp₂**) *n.* Something for the good or benefit of.

**pamahingan** (derivative of **pahing**) *n.* A source of information or detail about something; a sample of something to be copied. *Batri itū pamahingan heya. Labban itu pamahingan kapalna, minsan saddī luwana.* This battery is an indication of the size. This cardboard is an indication of the thickness, even though it looks different. *Pamahingan, pamuwan panuli'an, pamata'uhan.* Information, given as a means of finding the way, a means of knowing. *Pamandogahan ya pamahingannu aku, pamapatahan isāb.* A reference point that you provide for my information, an indication also of what's ahead. (*cf:* **gindan 1**, **pandoga 1**).

**pamaitu** (derivative of **maitu**) *v. tr.* To let or cause someone to remain by the person speaking. *Pamaituhun gi' si Da'ud.* Let David remain here. *Kinata'uhan asal e' sigām in aku bay pinamaitu min kahandak Tuhan.* They know already that I was put here by God's will.

**pama'** *n.* A species of lobster. (*Thesaurus:* **kamun**, **keyot₁**, **lattik₁**)

**pama'adjalun** (derivative of **adjal**) *n.* A person always busy preparing food. *Pama'adjalun itū, bang sali' halam aniya' hinangna saddī, yangkon angadjal daing.* This 'busy-cooking person', like when she has no other work to do she prepares fish.

**pama'iran** (derivative of **ba'id**) *n.* A source of permission; a reason for permission. *Subay ina' maka mma' pama'iran bo' dinūlan ameya'.* It is the mother and father from whom permission should be sought in order to be allowed to go.

**pamalastik** *v. intr.* **aN**- To fish with hook and line while drifting with the current. *Bang kita am'ssi ni Paluwas-Pata', na bo' alandos s'llog, mbal makapamalastik. Subay kita angahūg sau.* When we fish at Paluwas-pata and the current is strong, we are unable to do drift-fishing. We have to drop the anchor. *Bay ka'mbo'-mbo'an kami amaranas. Lling tahun itu pamalastik, beya' ni naelon.* For our forebears [the word was] *paranas.* The modern word is *pamalastik,* [a word] that came with nylon line. (*Thesaurus:* **gonteng 1.2, laway₂ 1.1, manit, paranas, p'ssi 1.1, tonda'₁ 1.1**)

**pamalatunan** (derivative of **latun**) *n.* A person who carries messages or things between reference points. *Aku ya suluhan, aku ya pamalatunan.* I will be the go-between, I will be the message bearer.

**pamaliyu** (derivative of **baliyu**) *n.* The windy season.

**pamal'ggahan** (derivative of **l'gga**) *n.* An experience from which one learns an important lesson.

**pamal'ngngan** var. of **l'ngnganan₂**

**pamalu** (derivative of **balu**) *n.* A woman who is often widowed. *Bang d'nda g'llotan ma k'llong, pamalu.* A woman whose neck is creased is often widowed.

**pamalung** *n.* The curved prow of a light sailing canoe of the paraw type. (*Thesaurus:* **kamayung, sangpad**)

**pamalutan** (derivative of **balut**) *n.* Something to hold on to; handles by which a container may be lifted. *Saddī letehan, bang taytayan aluha. Makajari ka pal'ngngan minsan halam pamalutan.* A *letehan* [single pole walkway] is different. A *taytayan* is wide. You can walk on it even though there is nothing to hold on to.

**pamandogahan** (derivative of **pandoga**) *n.* A landmark; a reference point. *Bay aku amubu ni Serom. Aniya' pamandogahanku duwa kayu aheya magtukbul maka būd Siasi maka Tapol.* I went fish-trapping to Serom. I had as reference points two big trees that lined up with Mount Siasi and Tapul Island.

**pamantawan** (derivative of **pantaw**) *n.* A watchtower.

**pamangan** (derivative of **kakan**) *n.* The utensils with which food is eaten (e.g. a spoon, fingers, a section of green coconut husk).

**pamanganan** (derivative of **kakan**) *n.* The containers from which food is eaten (e.g. a plate or bowl). *Pahāpun e'nu angose' pamanganan.* Do a better job of washing the dishes. (*cf:* **pagkakanan**).

**pamangka'un** *n.* A species of tree.

**pamapā** *n.* Flavorings for food. (*spec:* **bawang, dulaw, halu'-halu'₁, lamuk, lara 1, lukyu, lu'uya, maisa, sāy, siboyas, sulasi, ta'uyu, tawsiyu**)

**pamapanjarihan** *n.* The source of created things. *Tana' ya bay pamapanjarihan ka'a, maka tana' ya pamole'annu.* Soil is what you were made of and soil is your [final] home.

**pamapatahan** (derivative of **papata**) *n.*

Information; a body of knowledge. *Pamandogahan ya pamahingannu aku, pamapatahan isāb.* A reference point that you provide for my information, an indication also of what's ahead. (*Thesaurus:* **alab-alab, himangkan, ingat, panghati, ta'u₁ 1**).

**pamarā** (derivative of **parā**) *v. tr.* -*an* To tell someone to stop doing something that is unsafe or unacceptable. *Buwat magbalebol, magsugal saga, na pinamarāhan he' bobotang-lahat. Sinoho' kami da'a magpangongka'.* Like when playing volleyball or gambling, the local headman makes us stop. He tells us not to play [those] games. *Pinamarāhan kita, sali' kita pinata'u to'ongan.* We are cautioned, sort of made fully aware. *Pamarāhin ba onde' inān.* Get those kids over there to stop. (*Thesaurus:* **banda', lāng**).

**pamaragtolan** (derivative of **dagtol₁**) *n.* Something capable of bearing weight or pressure, as a chopping block or mast support. *Ndiya kayu ilū pamaragtolan.* Hand me that piece of wood as something to chop on. *Tindakan, ya pamaragtolan tape' tuklug.* Tindakan, the support [partway up the mast] for the lower end of the sprit. (*Thesaurus:* **pasangdolan 1**).

**pamaralilan** (var. **pangandalilan**) (derivative of **dalil**) *n.* A parable, example or metaphor that illustrates what is said; figurative language. *Hal ka anangis, ya po'on ka'a-i binono'. Hal pamaralilan.* You just cry, that is why you are hit. Just an illustration. *Api itū pangandalilan d'lla'ta, sabab d'lla'ta ya makatagna'an ginisan kala'atan.* A fire is a metaphor for our tongues, because it is our tongues that set various kinds of bad things going. (*Thesaurus:* **saupama 1, upamakun 1**).

**pamaranan** (derivative of **baran₁**) *n.* One's physical condition or appearance.

**pamarūl** (derivative of **dūl**) *n.* A favor granted; permission given. *Buwat du lapal-duwa bang mbal pamarūl ma kita.* It's like he is double-tongued if he doesn't give us permission.

**pamasagad** (derivative of **sagad**) *n.* Complacency; lack of concern. *In pamasagad a'a dupang in makalaglag sigām.* The complacency of fools is what destroys them.

**pamasasā'** (derivative of **sasā'**) *n.* An intermittent occurrence. *Sali' bang bay taluwa' he' timbak dangan i' abugtang, dangan ī' ahalol. Beya' ni kamatay sa' amasi allum. Hal sali' pamasasā'.* Like when hit by the gun one died instantly, the other mortally wounded, in the process of dying yet still alive. Just sort of intermittent.

**pamasukud** (derivative of **sukud₂**) *n.* A source of good fortune. *Magtūy palatun ni kita kumala' mareyom baranna, pamasukud ni kita.* The *kumala'* jewel which is inside his body promptly transfers to us, a source of good fortune.

**pamasulig** var. of **pasulig**

**pamataggalan** (derivative of **taggal₁**) *n.* A

supporting block designed to take the weight of some activity. *Bang kita an'tta' kayu subay aniya' pamataggalan iya.* When we chop firewood, there should be a chopping-block. (*cf:* **parabtalan**).

**pamatalan** *n.* The brow area just above the eyes.

**pamat'nna'an** (derivative of **t'nna'**) *n.* An assigned position or task. *Pasakay iya ni bay sehe'na min damunda' inān, ai-ai na sali' pamat'nna'an iya, buwat saga patuhun, angahella'.* He transfer to his companions from that other boat, [doing] whatever is assigned to him, like diving or hauling rope.

**pamattan** (derivative of **mattan**) *v. tr.* To pass on information truly and accurately. *Bang ka angahaka, pamattanun.* When you pass on information, do it truly and precisely.

**pamatu'** *n.* A small item such as a stone, thrown at a target in certain games of skill. *Bila' poga ya pamatu' saga a'a magtudjun. Bang magplising subay holen, bang magtaksi subay batu.* A shard from a clay jar is what people throw when playing *tudjun.* When playing marbles it should be marbles, when playing hit-the-target it should be pebbles. *Bila' poga ya pamatu' saga a'a magtudjun. Suma'an isāb laggong aheya. Bang magplising subay holen, bang magtaksi subay batu.* A shard from a clay jar is what people playing *tudjun* throw. Or sometimes a *laggong* snail shell. When playing placing it has to be marbles, when playing hit-the-target it has to be pebbles. (*Thesaurus:* **mano 1, pagtaksi' 1.1**)

**pamawi'** (derivative of **bawi'**) *n.* A replacement for something lost or damaged; a sum of money paid to make up for a deficit. *Buwat gallangku alungay, am'lli aku dakayu' pamawi'. Bang duwa amawi' tūy, bang dakayu' yamboho' pamawi' hal.* Suppose I lose my bracelet, and I buy another to replace it. If I buy two, that really makes up for the loss. If only one that is a bare replacement.

**pamāy-bāy** *n.* A house together with its contents and residents. (*Thesaurus:* **ballay, kubu'-kubu', luma'**)

**pamayhu'an** (derivative of **bayhu'**) *n.* A person's facial appearance. *Asawa pamayhu'anna.* Her appearance is cheerful.

**pambot** *n.* A large outrigger canoe with an inboard motor. (*Thesaurus:* **balutu, bangka', dapang, londay, pallungan, paraw 1, pelang, pongag**)

**pamene'an** (derivative of **pene'**) *n.* A range of choices or options. *Amuwan aku t'llu ginisan palkala' pamene'annu ya pataluwa' ma ka'a.* I will give three situations for you to choose one from that suits you.

**pameya'an₁** (derivative of **beya'₁**) *n.* Generic term for conveyances such as road vehicles, riding animals, seagoing vessels or aircraft. *Ai pameya'annu? Halam kappal.* What will you travel on? There are no passenger ships. (*Thesaurus:* **bayanan, pahinggaman, panumpangan**).

**pameya'an₂** (derivative of **beya'₃**) *n.* Something to be imitated or followed; a pattern or sample. *Subay aniya' suntu'an, pameya'annu.* There needs to be a pattern for you to work from.

**pamikil** (derivative of **pikil**) *n.* Thoughts; mental activity. *Asusa na pamikil kami.* Our thinking is troubled. *Halam aniya' angatu ma ka'a ma akkal maka pamikil.* No one can get the better of you in cleverness and thinking. (*Thesaurus:* **akkal 1, panahu'an**).

**pamikitan** (derivative of **pikit₂**) *n.* In-laws related through one's marriage; affinal kin. *Buwat bay ta'nda'ku bitu'anunku ma pagdaingan, magtūy aku angessek. Basta bay pamikitanku kessekanku sigā.* Like when I saw my former wife at the fish market, I immediately ignored [her]. If anyone has been my in-laws, I snub them. (*cf:* **dangirasan**; *spec:* **ipal, mato'a**).

**pamiha'an** (derivative of **piha**) *n.* A place where searching is done. *Nilango na iya maglibut-libut ma pamiha'an sīn.* He is dizzy now from going around the place where money had been searched for.

**pamilya** *n.* 1) A family. *Bang aniya' amatay bo' pinasagaran e' pamilyana, nilangag.* If someone dies and is neglected by his family, he becomes putrid. (*Thesaurus:* **mata'an, pagtali'anak 1**) 1.1) A class of beings. *Bang tugila' to'ongan, saitan. Bang saupama, dakayu' luma', dapamilya sigām.* To be quite specific, *saitan* spirits. In one house, for example, they are a single family.

**pamimidjak** (derivative of **bidjak**) *n.* Someone in the habit of enticing or seducing. *Pamimidjak isāb ka'a ilu.* You are simply a seducer.

**paminta-mintahan** (derivative of **pinta-pinta**) *n.* A ceremony entreating ritual ancestors for physical health. *Paminta-mintahan itū pangamu' apuwa ni mbo'.* This *pinta-pinta* ceremony is a request to ritual ancestors for health. *Tugtugan paminta-mintahanta ni mbo' atawa ni Tuhan. Yukta, "O Mbo', itiya' ummatnu pinapanjari e'nu aminta-minta tudju ni ka'a."* An incense container as our entreaty to God or a ritual ancestor. We say, "O Ancestor, here is the creature you created, calling on you for health."

**pamintāng** (derivative of **mintāng**) *v. tr.* -*an* To learn a lesson from some experience. *Bang saupama bay binono': "Na pamintāngin m'nnilu."* To someone who has been hit, for example: "So learn a lesson from that."

**pamintāngan** (derivative of **mintāng**) *n.* A lesson learned from experience.

**pamint'dda** (derivative of **mint'dda**) *adv.* 1) Done as a single action. *Tabowata pamint'dda bang nilingkit.* We can carry [several items] at the same time if they are strung togther. 1.1) *v. tr.* To do something in a single action; to do all at once. *Kahunitan ka bang pinamint'dda, buhatna hē'.* You'll find it difficult if you do it all at once, with all that weight. *Pamint'ddaku sadja, mbal* *binīngan.* I will do it with a single [blow], it will not be repeated.

**pamingkungan** var. of **kalitan-pamingkungan**

**pamiskin** (derivative of **miskin**) *v. tr.* -*an* To cause someone to be poor. *Da'a aku parayahin atawa pamiskinin.* Don't make me rich or poor. *Bay iya magpamiskin dīna ma sababbi.* He made himself poor for your sakes.

**pam'lla** (derivative of **b'lla**) *n.* The time taken to cook a meal. *Subay saga dampam'lla pangalagadnu.* Your wait should be about one cooking time. (*cf:* **paniga**).

**pam'llahan** (derivative of **b'lla**) *n.* Generic term for cooking containers. *Bay al'ssu' kaldero, mbal na tapam'llahan daing.* This metal pot has a hole in it, no longer usable for cooking fish. *Saga pam'llahanbi maka pagaddunanbi tinapay bay sinōd e' kamahung.* Your cooking pots and your pots for making bread have been infested with cockroaches. (*spec:* **banga'₂, kaha', kaldero, kasirola, kawa'₁, kawali', kenseng, lenga', l'ppo', paliyuk, pasu₁, sanglagan, simpi', tungkang**).

**pam'lli-m'lli** (derivative of **b'lli**) *n.* Various minor purchases.

**pam'nnalan** (derivative of **b'nnal**) *n.* Things generally believed. *Alampung baranku pal'ngngan llaw itu. Hatina, dakayu' pam'nnalan Sama, aniya' kahāpan.* I have a good feeling about going today. Meaning to say, a Sama belief, there is good [ahead].

**pam'ngngang** *v. advrs.* ka-...-*an* To be speechless from shock at something new or dreadful. *Kapam'ngngangan iya pag'nda'na ma tunu' kaluma'an.* He was speechless on seeing the village burning. *Na pagkale llingna itū e' saga danakanna, magtūy sigām sinōd tāw, kapam'ngngangan.* So his brothers, on hearing his words, were filled with fear, speechless. *Jari pahogga' kamemon sundalu kapam'ngngangan pagabut sigām ni tongod pah'bba'an si As.* So all the soldiers stopped, speechless, on reaching the place where As had fallen.

**pam'ssihan** (derivative of **p'ssi**) *n.* A place for fishing with hook and line.

**pamole'an** (derivative of **pole'₁**) *n.* 1) Home; the place where one belongs. *Tana' ya bay pamapanjarihan ka'a, maka tana' ya pamole'annu.* Soil is what you were made of and soil is your [final] home. 2) The outcome; the result. *Magdakop itū bay maglahi. Ya pamole'an sigā sara'. Dakop* is eloping off together. The magistrate is where they'll end up. (*Thesaurus:* **kaluwasan, kamattihan 1, kamaujuran, kat'kkahan₂, katobtoban, katumariyahan**).

**pamomono'** (derivative of **bono'**) *n.* A person who habitually commits murder. *Bay aku lappasannu min saga a'a pamomono'.* You have rescued me from murderers.

**pamonod** (derivative of **ponod**) *n.* The lowest

series of side planks on a pelang-type canoe hull. (*syn:* **dalosan**; *gen:* **tapi' 1**).

**pamorok** *v. tr.* -*an* To deprive someone of the power of speech by means of magic. *Pinamorokan kita, maka'nda' kita bo' mbal makabissala.* We are deprived of speech, able to see but unable to speak. (*Thesaurus:* **kamal, kokam₂ 1.1, kowam 1, umaw 1.1**)

**pamowahan** var. of **pagbowahan**

**pampan** *n.* The sea almond or Indian almond, a coastal tree valued for its edible kernels and timber. *Terminalia catappa.* (*syn:* **talisay**)

**pampang** *n.* A cliff or place, generally rocky, where a slope suddenly steepens; an underwater cliff. *Temang itū ya bowa' pampang, lalom saga sangpū' maka lima ni mpatpū'. Temang* is an opening in a sea-cliff, some 15 to 40 fathoms deep. *Saddī titib, saddī pampang. Pampang itū kabatuhan. Titib* and *pampang* are different. A *pampang* is rocky. (*Thesaurus:* **kantil₂, deyo'₂ 1, temang, titib**)

**pampang diyata' langit** *n. phrase* The Milky Way (lit. the celestial cliff). {idiom}

**pamulawan** (derivative of **bulawan**) *n.* Jewelry of all kinds. (*Thesaurus:* **aretes, pansi, singsing**).

**pamullaw** var. of **pamunglaw**

**pamūng** (derivative of **mūng**) *v. tr.* To say something; to utter. *Buwat bay pinamūng e' si Mma'.* As Dad said. *"Sai-sai katōngan dusa itu minsan sai, subay pinapatay." Sagō' halam makapamūng saga a'a inān minsan dangan.* "Whoever is found guilty of this crime should be killed." But none of those people said a word, not even one of them.

**pamūng-mūng** (derivative of **mūng**) *v. tr.* -*an* To berate someone; to scold. *Bay aku pinanhotan he'nu. Sali' aku pamūng-mūngannu.* You put pressure on me to work harder. It's as though you were scolding me. (*Thesaurus:* **dugal 1.1, pabukag, pah'lling₂, pugpug 1, s'ndal 1, tutul**).

**pamunglaw** (var. **pamullaw**) (derivative of **bunglaw**) *n.* Something eaten or drunk after a meal to freshen one's mouth. *Amangan aku saging pamullaw.* I'll eat a banana for dessert.

**pamusaka'** (derivative of **pusaka'**) *n.* Something inherited; an heirloom. *Pamusaka' na e' si Nabi Ibrahim ma anakna itū karayana kamemon.* The prophet Abraham gave all his wealth to his son, as his inheritance. *Ya tana' pamusaka' ka'am.* The land given as your inheritance.

**pamuti'** var. of **kamuti'**

**pamuwan** (derivative of **buwan₁**) *n.* 1) Something given; a gift. *Ai pamuwan aku?* What's my gift? 1.1) *v. tr.* To make a gift of something. *Da'a pamuwanun badju'nu, ageret ko' ilū.* Don't give your shirt, it's so torn. *Huma bay panganjanji'na ya pinamuwan ma ka'am sampay ka'mbo'-mbo'anbi.* The farm he promised, which is to be given to you and your descendants.

**pamuwangkan** (derivative of **buwangkan**) *n.* Something abandoned or thrown away. *Nā, pamuwangkan ma ka'a.* There, take the cursed thing! *Angkan na ka'a ilū pamuwangkan na he' matto'a-danakannu.* That's why you are utterly rejected by your parents and siblings. *Sali' sukna', yuk-i, "A'a du ka pamuwangkan ni bala' kamemon!"* Like a curse, saying, "You are a person thrown away to every kind of disaster!"

**pān** *n.* Bread. (*syn:* **tinapay**)

**paN-₁** *aff.* Conveyance voice prefix: attaches to transitive verbs, identifying as subject of the clause either an instrument, or something being transferred (whether a physical object or a piece of information). *Makak'llo' pa'in kami pangumpan, kaut na kami.* When we had managed to get something for bait, we headed out to sea. *Pangengkotku pelang lubid itū.* I will use this rope to tie the canoe. (*cf:* **pag-₁**)

**paN-₂** *aff.* Punctiliar aspect prefix: attaches to a verb, indicating action that takes place at a single instant of time rather than repeatedly or over a period of time. *Kose'anta ka'a lai' bay pamanganannu.* I'll wash the dish you ate from for you. (*cf:* **pag-₂**)

**paN-₃** *aff.* Gerund prefix: indicates the time or occasion of an event. *Sumiyan bay pamono'na?* When did he kill [someone]? (*cf:* **pag-₃**)

**pān ma'asin** *n. phrase* Small bread rolls (pan-de-sal).

**pān u'an-u'an** *n. phrase* A large loaf of western-style bread (lit. pillow bread). {idiom}

**panaki** (derivative of **saki**) *n.* A person subject to frequent sickness.

**panag-panag** *v. intr. aN-* **1)** To pulsate with pain; to throb. *Amanag-panag puhu'ku kamemon.* My whole body is throbbing. (*Thesaurus:* **pagk'bbut-k'bbut, pagkowap-kowap, pagdutdut, paglaggut-laggut, pagsignat-signat**) **2)** To make repetitive loud noises. *Amanag-manag anagina ma paglabayan.* Repeatedly greeting people in the streets. *Amanag-manag lling timbak, ya kosog llingna.* The sound of gunfire pulsates, so strong is its sound.

**panagatun** *n.* Shellfish in general; bivalve shellfish as a subgroup. *Basta panagatunan kamemon, akittup. Pakittup bowa' kima.* In the case of all shellfish, they close up. The great clams close up. (*Thesaurus:* **l'mput dilaut, t'bbahan**)

**panagna'an** (derivative of **tagna'**) *n.* A starting point; a place of origin. *Lingi'un du isāb ni bay panagna'annu.* Turn your head back also to [see] where you started from.

**panahilaw** *n.* The Silver or the Streamlined spinefoot. *Siganus argenteus.*

**panahu'an** (var.**palnahu'an**) (derivative of **nahu**) *n.* Intellect; the ability to think or reason. *Alalom isāb panahu'annu.* Your intelligence is also profound. (*Thesaurus:* **akkal 1, pamikil**).

**panahut** (derivative of **nahut**) *adv.* Finely; into small pieces. *Guling itū pinagt'ttok-t'ttok, kin'llot panahut.* This stir-fry is chopped up, sliced finely.

**panait** (var.**pananait**) (derivative of **sait**) *n.* Something used to bail water from a boat. *Nsa' na kami sali' anu, hal busay tatabin maka panait.* We didn't do a thing, all we found and kept were a paddle and a bailer.

**pana'** *n.* **1)** A device for propelling a spear or an arrow; a spear-gun. *Angahinang aku pana' pamana'ku mangagat.* I will make a spear-gun to spear some dog-snapper [a reef fish]. *Am'lli ka goma para ma pana'.* Buy a rubber-band for a spear-gun. (*Thesaurus:* **ablong, sahapang 1, sangkil 1, saubang, s'llokan**) **1.1)** *v. tr.* To spear fish with a rubber-propelled spear. *Da'a pana'un tudju ni a'a ilū.* Don't fire the spear-gun towards that person.

**pana'ag** *v. intr. aN-* To be seen or heard from a long distance. *Ya kosog keyat Konal inān amana'ag pi'itu ni Tinutu'.* The strength of the Konal [power-plant] light is such that it reaches all the way here to Tinoto.

**panalengog** (derivative of **talengog**) *n.* An awareness of a person who is not physically present. (*Thesaurus:* **ginhawa, nyawa, sumangat 1, umagad 1**).

**panalod** (var.**pananalod**) (derivative of **salod**) *n.* A person who is disagreeable and argumentative.

**panaluhan** (derivative of **talu₁**) *n.* Money or other valuables put up as stake in a wager. *Ai panaluhannu bang yuknu at'kka?* What do you bet when you say it is arriving?

**panalung** (derivative of **talung₁**) *n.* A distinctive personal feature. *Panalung iya, mbal tināw ma kaheka'an a'a.* She is distinctive, not afraid of crowds of people. *Langkawnu panalung.* Your height is your dominant feature.

**panamba** (derivative of **tamba**) *n.* Payment for work done or services provided.

**pananait** var. of **panait**

**pananalod** var. of **panalod**

**pananam** (derivative of **nanam**) *v. tr. -an* To make a person aware of something unseen. *Bay kam pinananaman kalingantuhan.* You have been made to experience times of hunger.

**pananambal** (derivative of **tambal₁**) *n.* A traditional healer. (*Thesaurus:* **doktol, pagbowahan**).

**panandal** (derivative of **sandal**) *v. tr. -an* To make something more durable. *Duwa tarik man dambila', duwa man dambila' panandal batangan.* Two support booms on one side and two on the other to make the main booms last longer.

**panansahan** *n.* A plank set in the stern of a canoe, on which the person sits who handles the steering oar. (*gen:* **tapi' 1**; *Thesaurus:* **pansal 1**)

**panantuhan** (derivative of **tantu**) *n.* Something reliable or certain. *Panantuhan itū, ya gino'on.* A certainty, something one is set on having.

**panangkaw** (derivative of **tangkaw**) *n.* A person who steals for a living. (*Thesaurus:* **mundu 1, pilliyu, sugarul**).

**pananggapan** (derivative of **tanggap**) *n.* A gift presented to a ritual ancestor or to God. *Ka'a kambo'-mbo'an-i, amuwan ka kono' balakat ko' aniya' pananggapan ka'a.* O ritual ancestors, please give good fortune so there may be something to present to you.

**panangis** (derivative of **tangis**) *n.* **1)** Someone who cries frequently. **1.1)** *v. tr.* To keep crying over something. *Ai pinanangisan he'na?* What was he crying about?

**panapali** (derivative of **sapali**) *n.* The contribution of one component to a set, as a sail to a canoe. *Buwat si Ak, parawan bo' halam taga banog, si Bu taga banog bo' halam aniya' paraw. Jari paraw hē' panapali ni banog hē', atawa banog panapali ni paraw.* Ak for example, he has a canoe but no sail, Bu has a sail but no canoe. So the canoe is the contribution to the sail, or the sail is the contribution to the canoe.

**panau'** (derivative of **tau'**) *n.* A down payment to secure a deal; a deposit. *Ī' bay tatangkaw panau'ku.* My down payment has been stolen. *Ē' maghukum si Du maka si Tri pasalan panau'na ma bangku.* Du and Tri have gone to court over his bank deposit. (*Thesaurus:* **l'kkat₁ 1, lōb 1.1, padjak₁**).

**saki-panau'** *n.* An illness which lies dormant in a person's body.

**panaw** *n.* **1)** Depigmentation of the skin, occurring in spots. *Akatol ma bukutta, ya hē' panaw.* That itchy area on one's back, that's *panaw*. (*Thesaurus:* **āp-āp 1, kamuti', limuti', nilastung**) **1.1)** *v. advrs.* *-in-* Afflicted by depigmentation.

**panawan** *n.* A species of deepwater crab, uncommon. (*gen:* **kagang**)

**panawbatan** var. of **pagtawbatan**

**panayu** (derivative of **sayu**) *n.* Awareness of some activity going on. *Bay sigām pinabā'an buwat saga luruk, ma halam aniya' panayu sigām ma kahālan hē'.* They were invited as though guests, but without any awareness of what was happening there.

**pandak** *adj.* *a-* Short in stature. (*Thesaurus:* **deyo'-deyo'₁, p'ndok, pu'ut**)

**pandala** *n.* The young women who support a bride at her wedding; bridesmaids. *Bang ma kawin kasamahan bay tagna', dakayu' du pandala min kal'llahan, dakayu' min kar'ndahan. Ma buwattina'an tabowa na ya addat Bisaya', saga duwa-t'llu ilū.* With the old-time Sama wedding, there was one attendant from the man's side, and one from the woman's. These days Visayan custom is followed, with two or three of them. (*Thesaurus:* **pangantin**)

**pandan** *n.* Pandanus or screwpine, a prime source of weaving material. *Pandanus tectorius. Am'lli*

*aku jangatan panganjangat pandan nihinang tepo.* I buy a scraper to scrape pandanus to be made into a mat. *A: "Pamagay pandan ilu?" B: "Nihinang tepo."* A: "What is that pandanus for?" B: "It will be made into a mat." (*pt:* **botod, la'al**)

**pagpandan** *v. intr.* *aN-* To be in the business of preparing and selling pandanus ready for weaving. *Magpandan sadja d'nda itū llaw-sangom, angambuhut. Halam aniya' hinangna saddī min angambuhut.* This woman works with pandanus day and night, scraping. She does nothing else but scrape pandanus.

**pandan-bakung** (var. **bakung**) *n.* A thornless variety of pandanus.

**pandan-magi** *n.* A species of pandanus, the fragrant leaves of which provide a subtle food flavoring. *Pandanus odorus. Ahamut kinakan bang pinat'nna'an pandan-magi.* Food smells good when the pandanus leaves are put in it.

**pandan-sutla'** *n.* A spineless variety of pandanus, the variegated leaves of which provide a glossy weaving material.

**pandang** *v. tr.* To look directly or steadily at something. *Ang'nda' pabontol. Pandangun.* Look straight. Look at it directly. *Makahandul deyom atay bang pinandang onde'-onde'.* It melts one's heart to look intently at a child. (*Thesaurus:* **lawan, liling, patong 1**)

**pandang-hawak** *v. intr.* *aN-* To stand with hands on hips. (*cf:* **s'kket**)

**panday** *n.* **1)** A person with a high level of skill in his or her area of knowledge; a craftsman; an expert. (*Thesaurus:* **pantas, tangpas₂, tukang**) **1.1)** *adj.* *a-* Skilled; expert. *"Sai-sai kām," yuk sultan, "apanday, tak'llo'bi anakku."* "Whoever of you is expert," said the sultan, "will get my daughter." (*Thesaurus:* **lahal, layam 1.1, tullus 1**) **2)** A midwife. **2.1)** *v. tr.* *-an* To assist a woman in childbirth. *Aubus iya bay amandayan d'nda pina'anak, ya niamu' e'na tulahan dakayu' du badju'.* After she has helped a woman to give birth, what she asks as remuneration is a single blouse.

**kapandayan** *n.* Skill; expertise. *Huwangnu, ya na kapandayannu.* Your personal ability, your skill.

**panday-pupud** *n.* A person with the highest level of skill.

**pandi** *v. intr.* *aN-* **1)** To bathe, either for hygiene or recreation; to take a shower. *Al'ssin na, bay na ka amandi.* Clean now, you've bathed. *Akatis bay tangonku pelang, amandi aku. Akatis pa'in aku bay amandi, asalin aku.* When I have put the canoe up, I bathe. When I have bathed, I change clothes. *Bang onde'-onde' amandi ni tahik maglurus-lurus min haronan.* When children go swimming in the sea they keep sliding down the house ladder. (*cf:* **kose'**) **1.1)** *v. tr.* To wash someone by bathing, as a baby or an invalid. *Bay pinandi si Li kohap bo' mbal kam'ssangan* *bang atuli.* Li is bathed in the afternoon so she won't get a rash when sleeping. *Ang'llo' iya bohe' para pamandiku.* He is getting water for me to bathe [someone] with. **1.2)** *v. tr. -an* To wash dirt off or out of something. *Pandihin pali'nu bo' mbal ap'ddi'.* Wash that cut of yours so that it doesn't hurt.

**pandi atay-batu** *v. tr.* To bathe someone in a ceremony intended to make him brave, with no sign of fear. {idiom} *Pinandi kita atay-batu bo' mbal tagaga' amissala ya ai-ai kapatutan.* Bathed ritually to prevent being hesitant to speak whatever is appropriate.

**pandi kulang-kilā** *v. tr.* To bathe a newborn baby in order to ensure its healthy development. {idiom}

**pandi pasu'** *v. tr.* To bathe someone to reduce fever and aid recovery.

**pandi tawbat** *v. tr.* To bathe someone ritually, the concluding stage of resolving a family dispute.

**pandikal** (var. **pandikkal**) *n.* A clever person known for playing pranks.

**pandikkal** var. of **pandikal**

**pandoga 1)** *n.* A reference point; a beacon; a landmark. *Tabowa maglensa saga pandoga ma tonga'an ayan.* The navigation marks in the skies will become unstable. *Bay aku magsāp ni Bubuan, aniya' pandogaku mahē' tipay abanos.* I was diving for oysters at Bubuan, I had reference points there marking the location of an abundance of oysters. (*cf:* **gindan 1, pamahingan**) **1.1)** *v. tr.* To take note of the location of reference points. *Tapandoga e' sigā lugal bay pangubulan mbo' sigām.* They noted the place where their grandparents had been buried. **2)** *v. tr.* To learn from observation or experience. *Tapandoga kami in a'a itū asal panganjabu.* We recognized these men as trouble-makers by nature. *Saga tuwan, ma pandogahanku, bang kitam ganta' palanjal minnitu, asiya-siya kitam.* Gentlemen, the way I read the signs, if we opt to go on from here we will be in serious trouble.

**pamandogahan** *n.* A landmark; a reference point.

**pandorot** (derivative of **dorot**) *v. intr. aN-* To fall in abundance, as rain from eaves. (*cf:* **tampiyas 1**).

**pandu' 1)** *n.* A lesson; a body of teaching. *Bilahi kami makata'u pasal pandu' baha'u ya pamissalanu ilū.* We want to become informed about the new teaching you are talking about here. (*Thesaurus:* **hupit-hupit 1, pintulu' 1, pitis₂ 1**) **1.1)** *adj. a-* Teachable; quick to learn. *Apantun saga onde' itū, sali' apandu' to'ongan.* These children are receptive to training, very teachable. *Mbal papandu' onde' itū.* This child is not teachable. **1.2)** *v. ditr.* To teach someone to do something. *Pandu'in aku magbissala Sinama.* Teach me how to speak the Sinama language. *Bang anakta mbal kapandu'an, alahang iya ni*

*kahāpan, humeka ni kala'atan.* If our son can't be taught, he will rarely come to the good, he will come many times to the bad. *Sukul kapandu'an kām bang lān ingga ya subay palabayanbi.* Fortunately you were taught which road you should pass by on. **2)** *v. ditr.* To point something out to an observer. *Arāk pinandu'an tungkangku ni ka'a, abila'.* I had thought of pointing out my cooking pot to you, it's broken. (*Thesaurus:* **tō' 1, tudlu'₂ 1**)

**pandu'-pandu'** *v. ditr.* To give misleading advice to someone, intending harm.

**panendog** (derivative of **tendog**) *n.* Collective term for employees, tenants, political or religious adherents.

**panhid** *v. tr.* To perceive an internal condition or quality from external appearances. *Tapanhidku luwa si Pu inān, ahāp kasuddahanna. Tapanhidku isāb ka'a, ala'at hinangnu.* I can see from Pu's appearance that her character is good. I can see what you are like too, your behavior is bad. *Tapanhidta d'nda inān ab'ttong.* We can tell that woman is pregnant. (*Thesaurus:* **kilā 1, pangli' 1.1**)

**panhot** *v. tr. -an* To urge or compel someone to extra effort. *Bay aku pinanhotan he'nu. Sali' aku pamūng-mūngannu. Sinoho' na pa'in kita bo' mbal kata'uhanku.* You urged me to work harder. As if you were scolding me. You kept on telling us, but I don't know how to do it. *Sinoho' aku ni bohe' bo' yukku, "Halam aniya' bohe'." Manjari amanhot ka, yuknu, "Pehē' na ka, mbal kata'uhannu."* I was told to go to the water source but I said, "There is no water." So you put pressure on me, saying, "Off you go, you don't know." *Sinoho' aku ni bohe' bo' yukku, "Halam aniya' bohe'." Manjari amanhot ka, yuknu, "Pehē' na ka, mbal kata'uhannu." Buwattē' minsan ahāp jawabku.* I was told to go to the water source but I said, "There is no water." So you put pressure on me, saying, "Off you go, you don't know." Like that, even though my offer was good. (*Thesaurus:* **abiyug, agpot 1, angin, egot-egot, logos 1, p'ggong, poleggaw**)

**paniba'** (derivative of **siba'**) *n.* A courtship gift.

**panibi** (derivative of **tibi**) *n.* A person with an inherited tendency to a condition such as tuberculosis. *Panibi pahāp panubu' saga a'a hē', sali' panaki.* The descent line of those people are chronically tubercular, sickly.

**panibli** *n.* A swelling in the groin due to an infected leg wound. (*Thesaurus:* **talis'ssok 1**)

**paniga** (derivative of **siga**) *n.* The time taken to smoke a cigaret, an approximate unit of time. *Mbal at'ggol, saga dampaniga.* Not long, about the time of one cigaret. (*cf:* **pam'lla**).

**panilik** (derivative of **tilik**) *n.* A charm protecting an individual against harm. *Bang ka tinimbak ma halam aniya' paniliknu iya, kapilluwangan.* If you are shot when you have no protective charm against it, you will be vulnerable.

**panimbakan** (derivative of **timbak**) *n.* The distance covered by a bullet from a rifle, an approximate unit of distance.

**panimun-timunan** (derivative of **timun-timun**) *n.* The machinery of a crane; a block and tackle.

**paninganan** (derivative of **tingan**) *n.*1) A temporary shelter built of local materials.1.1) *v. tr.* To use as a temporary shelter. *Sat'ggol halam gi' aniya' pam'lli kapanyapan subay tiningkap dahū. Tapaninganan isāb.* As long as there is still no money to buy materials we must first put up a temporary shelter. It can be lived in.

**paningkō'an** (derivative of **tingkō'**) *n.* Something to sit on, as a chair or seat. (*Thesaurus:* **bangku'**, **kulsi**, **siya**).

**panipu** (derivative of **tipu**) *n.* Treachery; ambush. *Ē! Panipunu!* Hey! Such treachery [on your part]!

**panit** *n.* Generic term for various bonitos and tunas, including the Big-eye tuna. *Thunnus obesus. Ā, bang nda'nu ba'anan panit itū maka ba'anan t'lla'-t'lla' itū.* Oh, if you were to see the abundance of tuna and the abundance of seagulls. (*Thesaurus:* **mangku'**, **poyan**, **sobad**)

**panit-janggayan** *n.* The Yellow-fin tuna. *Thunnus albacares* or *Neothunnus macropterus.*

**panit-panit-ulak** *n.* A species of bonito. *fam. Thunnidae.*

**panit-sisikan** *n.* A tuna species, possibly the Blue-fin. *fam. Thunnidae.*

**manit** *v. intr.* aN- To troll for tuna. (*Thesaurus:* **gonteng 1.2**, **laway₂ 1.1**, **pamalastik**, **paranas**, **p'ssi 1.1**, **tonda'₁ 1.1**)

**manitan** *n.* The equipment used in trolling for tuna.

**paniya'** (derivative of **niya'₁**) *v. tr.* To cause something to exist or be present. *Halam aniya' sīnnu? Paniya'un na ba.* You don't have any money? Bring some into existence then. *Bay iya amaniya'an kura' pote' sangpū' hekana.* He had caused ten white horses to be made [for his use]. (*Thesaurus:* **papanjari**, **ummat 1.1**).

**paniyungan** *n.* The sea lemon, a coastal tree and its edible fruit; tallow wood. *Xeminia americana.*

**panjang** *adj.* a- Extensive or prolonged, of time. *Bang pa'in apanjang umulnu.* May you live long. (*Thesaurus:* **kuwa'-kuwa'**, **lanjut 1**, **taha' 1.1**, **t'ggol 1.1**)

**alun-panjang** *n.* A tidal wave or tsunami. *Alun-panjang itū goyak mbal kasandalan.* This *alun-panjang* is an unbearable wave on the surface. (*Thesaurus:* **kata'-kata'**, **goyak 1**, **lumbag**, **sahal₁ 1.1**, **sampoyak**)

**sapanjang-panjang** *adv.* Forever. (*Thesaurus:* **salama-lama**, **sapaya-paya**, **sapupud-daya**, **saumul-umul**)

**panjari** *see:* **kamemon pinapanjari**, **kapamanjari**, **Magpapanjari**, **pamapanjarihan**, **papanjari**,

**papanjarihan**

**panji** *n.* A flag. *Ā, saga panji itū magk'llab-k'llab lullun.* Ah, these flags fluttering, every one of them. (*Thesaurus:* **bandila'**, **sambulayang**, **tipas-tipas**)

**panjihan** *n.* A company of people; a military unit. *Dapanjihan sundalu.* One company of troops.

**pan'ddo'** (derivative of **t'ddo'**) *n.* A calm period; the calm season of the year.

**pan'nne** (derivative of **t'nne**) *n.* A period of cold weather; a cold season of the year. *Pan'nne lahat inān.* It is cold in that land.

**pan'nno'an** (derivative of **t'nno'**) *n.* A liquid relish or pickle made of various herbs and sauces. *Pan'nno'an, pangā'an ssa. Hatina angā' kita ssa minnē'.* Relish, a source of flavor. In other words we get flavor from it. (*Thesaurus:* **bubuk₂**, **kilaw 1**, **lawal 1.1**, **tinu'anan**).

**pan'nggehan** (var.**pat'nggehan**) (derivative of **t'ngge**) *n.* A platform or supporting structure. *Pasaray-saray pamalutan inān min saga pan'nggehan hē'.* Those hand-rails are leaning out from the stage. (*cf:* **patinggilan**).

**pannu'** var. of **panyu'**

**panoho'an** (derivative of **soho'**) *n.* Instructions; commandments. *Panoho'an Tuhan subay ni'isbat na pa'in.* God's commands should be constantly kept in mind. *Buwat si Pat, ai-ai panoho'an iya he' saga a'a mareyom Nasuli', ya hē' hinangna.* Like Pat, whatever instructions are given him by the people at Nasuli, that's what he does.

**pano'onan** (derivative of **to'on₂**) *n.* A place for setting small fish traps.

**panon** *n.* A close friend of the same sex. *Bang aku amuwanan ai-ai ni panonku, mbal magkibad deyom atayku.* When I give anything to my close friend, my emotions are not disturbed. (*Thesaurus:* **agay**, **bagay 1**, **beyang**, **bō**, **gge**)

**pagpanon** *v. intr.* aN- To be friends, usually with someone of the same sex. *Makajari isāb magsubali ni kahāpan, buwat magdanakan-danakan magpanon.* It is also possible to swear an oath for good, like declaring brotherhood or a close friendship. *Magpanon du aku maka si Ja.* Ja and I are close friends. (*Thesaurus:* **pagbagay**, **paglundang-lundang**)

**panonda'an** (derivative of **tonda'₁**) *n.* A trolling lure. *Buwat anonda', ya bay panonda'an i' tinurul he' daing aheya, tininduk, niāb he' daing a'aslag.* Like when trolling, and the trolling lure had been followed by a large fish, which was then struck and swallowed whole by a really big fish.

**panono'on** (derivative of **to'on₁**) *n.* Someone addicted to gambling on dice games. *Panono'on legot pahāp a'a inān.* That man is indeed addicted to playing dice.

**pansal** *n.* 1) A short piece of decking set in the bow of a canoe. (*Thesaurus:* **panansahan**) 1.1) *v. tr.* -an To fit a forward deck to a large canoe. *Dapang itu pelang bay niukilan. Bang balutu halam* *bay pinansalan.* A *dapang* canoe is decorated with carving. A *balutu* canoe wouldn't have had a short deck installed in the bow.

**pansī** *v. tr.* To separate grains into smaller and larger sizes by the lateral movement of a winnowing basket. *Bang buwas, pinansī, pinene'.* In the case of rice, it is sorted and selected. (*Thesaurus:* **landang 1.1**)

**pansi** *n.* Inexpensive costume jewelry. (*Thesaurus:* **aretes, pamulawan, singsing**)

**pansi'** *n.* A children's game involving dodging a thrown ball; dodge-ball.
  **pagpansi'** *v. intr. aN-* To play dodge-ball.

**pansing** *n.* **1)** A container of standard size for measuring dry goods. *Bang pansing mbal makanigantang, bang gantang mbal makanilaga'.* A small measure can never become a three-liter measure, a three-liter measure can never become a bushel [i.e. people can never become what they are not born to be]. (*Thesaurus:* **gantang, supa₁**) **1.1)** A tightly woven container for threshed rice.

**pansul** *n.* A pipe or conduit.

**pansung** *n.* **1)** The aquiline curve of someone's nose. **1.1)** *adj. a-* High-bridged, of the nose. *Apansung ūngna, sarang-sarang taha'na.* The bridge of his nose is high, its length just right.

**pantak** *n.* **1)** The use of sorcery to influence another. **1.1)** *v. tr.* To influence someone by the use of sorcery. *Bang aniya' pantakta, palikid ni kita, sali' paliyu ni kita.* When we cast a spell it rebounds onto us, like it returns to us. *Ata'u amantak saga a'a man s'ddopan.* The people from the west know how to cast spells. (*Thesaurus:* **duti, hikmat, hinang-hinang₁, h'lling₃, palkata'an, sihil 1.1**)

**pantalun** *n.* **1)** Long trousers or pants, Western style. *Pamuwanku na pantalunku ni panonku.* I am giving my trousers to my close friend. (*cf:* **sauwal**) **1.1)** *v. intr. pa-* Wearing long trousers. *Pantalun si To asidda papantalunna.* To's long trousers are what he is often wearing.

**pantān** *n.* A porch; a platform. *Paluwas kita ni pantān, ahayang mahē'.* Let's go out to the porch, it is breezy there. (*Thesaurus:* **balkon, salas, saurung**)

**pantas** *adj. a-* Skilled. *Onde'-onde' apantas na magl'ngngan.* The child walks really well now. *Apantas pang'nda'anna, b'nnal langtasna.* His reading of portents is very skilful, he truly foretells the future. (*Thesaurus:* **panday 1, tangpas₂, tukang**)

**pantaw** *v. tr.* To see something in the distance. *Pantawun t'lla'-t'lla' inān, kalu aniya' daing.* Keep an eye on that seagull yonder; maybe there are fish there. *Amantaw iya daing ni kalawakan.* He sees fish far away. (*Thesaurus:* **pantok₂**)
  **pamantawan** *n.* A watchtower.

**pantay** *adj. a-* Flat; level, of a surface. (*syn:* **datag**)
  **kapantayan** *n.* A level area of land; a plain.

**pantingag** var. of **bantingag**

**pantok₁** *n.* **1)** The shaft of a spear. **1.1)** *v. tr. -an* To fit and lash a shaft to the head of a spear. *Bang budjak, kayu banga ya pamantokan iya. Kayuwan ina'an ya pamaggotan sahapang.* For spears, the wood of the betel palm is used for a shaft. That cane yonder is used for binding a fish spear.

**pantok₂** *adj. a-* Sharpsighted; able to see small things in poor light. *Minsan du ai-ai ariki', bang apantok matata ta'nda'ta du. Minsan sangom ta'nda'ta.* Even if something is small, if our eyes are sharp we see it. Even at night we see it. *Daka ai sulatna itū, apantok.* Goodness knows what he's writing, he's so sharpsighted. (*Thesaurus:* **pantaw**)

**pantun** *adj. a-* **1)** Well-behaved; teachable. *Ai-ai mareyom luma' inān buwat saga lai' bay pagkakanan, bang wa'i makal'ngngan saga matto'aku, na, minomos e' siyaliku. Pinahāp deyom luma'. Apantun iya ma deyom luma'.* Things in the house, like used plates, when my parents have gone somewhere, then my young sister tidies up. She makes the inside of the house good and is well-behaved at home. *Apantun saga onde' itū, sali' apandu' to'ongan.* These children are receptive to training, very teachable. (*Thesaurus:* **addat 1.1, hatul₂, hongpot, papat 1, p'mpon 1, saldik, saltun 1**) **1.1)** *v. tr.* To instruct someone in good behavior. *Pinandu'an ni kabontolan, pinantun kita he' matto'ata, he' mastal.* Taught right behavior, we are instructed by our parents or by a teacher.

**panuba** *n.* Enticement; allurement; lure. *Ai aku itū panubanu pehē' bo' pinapatay?* What am I that you use [me] as bait in order to be killed? (*cf:* **umpan 1**)

**panubigan** *n.* Amniotic fluid; birthing waters. *Angahimati' na h'ndaku, halam gi' abustak panubigan.* My wife is having contractions, her waters have not yet broken. (*Thesaurus:* **k'mbal-bohe', tutuban**)

**panubu'** (derivative of **tubu'**) *n.* Descendants. *Pusaka', sali' bay aniya' ka'bbahan matto'a, ai-ai na ka'bbahan ma panubu' sigā.* Inheritance, like something that has been left by parents, whatever has been left for their descendants.
  **sugsug panubu'** *v. tr.* To trace kin relationships by descent from a shared ancestor.

**panubu'an** (derivative of **tubu'**) *n.* A family line; a descent group. *Dapanubu'an kami maka disi Ba.* We are of the same family line as Ba and the others.

**panubusan** (derivative of **tubus₁**) *n.* Full obligation; firm commitment. *Buwat saupama anaktA: subay sulutta panupusanta, bo' halam aniya' susunan anak ma matto'a.* One's children, for example: we should fulfil our obligations, so that children will have no regrets about [their] parents.

**panulung** (derivative of **tulung**) *n.* Money given to

help with expenses, especially funeral expenses. *Kasehe' panulung, kasehe' pinab'llihan bo' mbal alapis.* Some is given to the bereaved, some is sold to avoid making a loss.

**panumagal** (derivative of **tumagal**) *n.* An excuse; a pretext. *Ē, panumagalnu!* Hey, you're making it up! *A: "Mbal aku ni iskul apa abase' pantalunku." B: "Panumagalnu! Aheka pantalunnu saddī."* A: "I cannot go to school because my trousers are wet." B: "That's just an excuse! You've plenty of other trousers."

**panumpangan** (derivative of **tumpang**) *n.* A conveyance in which one rides as passenger; a passenger vehicle. *Panumpanganna ko' hē' ma munda'.* That is his passenger seat, there in the bow. (*Thesaurus:* **bayanan**, **pahinggaman**, **pameya'an₁**).

**panumping** *n.* The crown-like headgear worn by a bride. (*Thesaurus:* **korona**, **tumanggal**)

**panundanan** (derivative of **tundan**) *n.* A towline, especially of canoes. *Pamadjak dahatus maka limampū' pilak panundanan sudju ni Tiyanggi.* The contract was one hundred and fifty pesos for being in a towline to Jolo City.

**panunu'an** (derivative of **tunu'₁**) *n.* An area where a fire has been deliberately lit. *Ai na panunu'an itū?* What is this burnt area?

**panunussa'** (derivative of **sussa'**) *n.* One who refuses to believe; a skeptic. *Panunussa' ko' ka'a ilū!* You are such a skeptic!

**panuyungan** *n.* A species of tree, the root of which provides a remedy for fatigue. *Aniya' lima ginis gamut kayu nihinang tambal lu'ug: ngehat, panuyungan. Ē, takalipatku.* There are five kinds of tree root that are made into an antidote for fatigue: *ngehat, panuyungan*... Hey, I've forgotten the others.

**panyabut** *v. intr. aN-* **1)** To recite the basic creed of Islam. *Oy! Anoho' ka ma aku? Dahū gi' aku bay amanyabut min ka'a.* Hey! Are you telling me what to do? I made my [first] confession of the creed before you did. **2)** To cry for God's help in times of need. *Amanyabut ka, tuwan.* Cry out to God, friend [advice given in a storm at sea]. *Buwat saupama bay magbono', buwat aku magbono' maka mma'ku. Na arai' pa'in kami magsuntuk, na ah'lling ganta' manapad kami, "Aningkō' ka amanyabut."* Getting into a fight for example, like my father and me fighting. So when we are about to punch each other, the one restraining us perhaps says, "Sit down and call on God."

**panyām** *n.* A heavy pancake made of rice flour and sugar, fried in deep oil. *Am'lli gi' aku panyām ni M'ddas pamakanku si Li.* I'll buy a rice pancake in Siasi for Li to eat. (*gen:* **apam 1**)

**panyani** *n.* A professional singer.

**panyap** *adj. zero* **1)** Equipped. *Bang kita maghinang luma' subay panyap kamemon ma deyom luma': laring, lapohan, ai-aina.* When we build a house,

its contents should be complete: knife, stove, whatever. (*Thesaurus:* **sakap 1**) **1.1)** *v. tr. -an* To equip someone.

**kapanyapan** *n.* Equipment; furnishings; gear. *Yuk Kuyya', "Manjari itu magtapi' na, magk'llo' na kapanyapan itū."* Monkey said, "Now then, build up the canoe sides, get all this gear." (*cf:* **mussak-massik**; *Thesaurus:* **kabunyihan**, **kakaya'an**, **kalangkapan₁**, **pahandang 1**, **pinduwa'**)

**panyap-palbut** *adj. zero* Fully equipped. *Binowahan na sigā pelang panyap-palbut. Ina'an na lehana, ina'an na lapohanna, ina'an na busayna.* An outrigger canoe was brought to them, fully equipped. There was its square sail, its clay stove, there were its paddles.

**panyata'₁** (derivative of **nyata'**) *v. tr.* To disclose or make visible something not normally seen. *Palihalan bay pinanyata' e' saga kanabi-nabihan.* Events that were disclosed by the prophets.

**panyata'₂** *n.* **1)** A visible manifestation of a deceased person's spirit; a ghost or spook. (*Thesaurus:* **bahana'**, **lutaw**, **pagbagala**, **pangguwa' 1.1**) **1.1)** *v. intr. aN-* To appear to someone, of a spirit being. *Iya ya amanyata' ni kita, aniya' ginawi to'ongan, buwat mala'ikat.* He is the one who appeared to us, having important things in mind, like an angel.

**panyawahan** var. of **palnyawahan**

**panyuba'** *n.* **1)** A person of changeable appearance, sometimes attractive, sometimes not. **1.1)** *v. tr.* To transform how one looks. *Aniya' samin amanyuba' ni ahāp l'lla. Minsan du ala'at tahinang ahāp. Aniya' isāb samin amanyuba' ni ala'at.* There are glasses that make a guy look good. Even though he is ugly he is made good-looking. There are also glasses that make him ugly.

**panyu'** (var. **pannu'**) *n.* A handkerchief. *Bay bīllihan si Ji panyu' he' tunangna.* Ji's sweetheart bought him a handkerchief. (*Thesaurus:* **jimpaw**, **sapu-tangan**, **tawel**, **tuwalya**)

**panga** var. of **sanga**

**pangabay** (derivative of **abay₁**) *n.* A person in the same fleet or group; fleet-mate.

**pangabut** (derivative of **abut₂**) *v. tr.* To find something by chance; to come across something. *Bilahi kita bo' halam aniya' pangabutta bay bilahita hē'.* We want something but haven't come across what we wanted.

**pangadji'** (derivative of **adji'**) *n.* A religious education, Islamic in particular. *Alanga pangadji'na.* His education is advanced.

**pangahād** (derivative of **hād**) *n.* Limits or restrictions imposed by a court order.

**pangahandak** (derivative of **hād**) *n.* A good event ordained by God. *Anak pangaral, sali' pangahandak, amowa sukud.* A child of destiny, like something ordained by God, bringing good fortune.

**pangahina'** (derivative of **hina'**) *n.* An insulting act. *Halam iya bay amangan sabab ap'ddi' landu'* *atayna pasalan pangahina' sigām ma mma'na.* He didn't eat because he was so angry about their shaming of his father. *Kabalosan na aku ma si No ma sabab kapangahina'na ma aku.* I am revenged now on No for his insult to me.

**panga'an** var. of **sowa-panga'an**

**pangale** (derivative of **kale**) *n.* Something heard or overheard. *Asā' pangalenu, halam aniya' angalingan.* What you heard is mistaken, there is no one calling.

**pangaleboran** (derivative of **lebod**) *n.* A drum or reel on which to wind a line. (*syn:* **lengkehan**).

**pangalemos** (derivative of **lemos**₁) *n.* Someone known for lack of washing.

**pangalilla'** (derivative of **lilla'**) *n.* Something given away, freely and totally. *Bay iya pangalilla' ni Tuhan.* He was habitually yielded to God.

**pangaliyu-lakad** (derivative of **liyu-lakad**) *n.* A habitual adulterer.

**pangalta'** (derivative of **alta'**) *n.* Wealth; riches. *Aheya pangalta' bay tataban sigām.* They seized as booty a great amount of valuables. *Pangalta' itū ngga'i ka hal daginis, hal sīn, hal pamulawan. Ya babarapa ahalga' ma deyom luma'. Ya karayata.* Wealth is not just one sort, money, jewelry. It's the various expensive things in a house. It is our valuables. *Pangalta' itū ngga'i ka hal daginis, hal sīn, hal s'mmek, ngga'i ka hal pamulawan. Ya babarapa ahalga' ma deyom luma'. Ya karayata.* Wealth here is not just one sort, money, or clothing; not just jewelry. It's the various expensive things in a house. It is our valuables.

**pangaluwan** *n.* The Banded barracuda. *Sphyraena jello.* (*cf:* **bangasan**; *gen:* **lambana' 1**)

**pangaluwaran** (derivative of **luwad**) *n.* A fulcrum; a rowlock. *Ate'as panapi' bang pangaluwaran. Bay alandos baliyu.* The planking split away when it was used as a rowlock. The wind had been strong.

**pangampu'an** *n.* A set of clothes worn at any one time. *Dayahan ka, lima pangampu'an.* You are rich, five changes of clothes. *Basta kita makasulug min t'dda, hē' na badju', hē' na pantalun. Ya hē' niōnan dapangampu'an.* What we put on at one time, there is the shirt, and there are the pants. That is called one *pangampu'an.*

**panganak** (derivative of **anak**₁) *n.* Children in a collective sense; one's offspring. (*cf:* **kamanahutan**).

**panganan** *n.* A dark sweet cake of cornmeal or cassava flour, eaten with a syrup made from unrefined sugar. *Panganan itū aheka pingkit-pingkitna. Panganan* cakes have many clustered pieces. (*gen:* **mamun**)

**pangandahing** (derivative of **dahing**) *n.* A desperate cry for help.

**panganda'ug** (derivative of **da'ug**) *n.* Victory in a contest or conflict. *Anganda'ug kām sagō' mbal du patatas panganda'ugbi.* You won but your triumph won't last long.

**pangandalilan** var. of **pamaralilan**

**pangandanginan** (derivative of **dangin**) *n.* A place where cooperative work is being done; the project or focus of such work.

**pangandararut** (derivative of **darut**) *n.* A dentist (lit. one who pulls things out).

**pangandingin** (derivative of **dingin**) *n.* A season or period of cold weather. *Aho', pangandingin lahat.* Yes, the weather is cold.

**pangandolan** (derivative of **andol**) *n.* Someone who can be trusted or relied on. *Pinangandolan si Ne sabab ahāp hinangna.* Ne is someone to be trusted because her work is good. *Bang ka ganta' bilahi angitung bang pila panambanu ma aku, kata'uhannu magtūy bang aku kapangandolan atawa mbal.* If for instance you wanted to count how much you paid me, you would know immediately whether or not I am to be trusted.

**pangandung** (derivative of **kandung**₁) *n.* A freshwater pool. *Bang saupama ma diyata' būd, mbal tapah'lling tigbaw atawa pangandung. Bo' bang ariki', ya hē' tapangōnta pangandung, ya tapamandihan.* In the mountains for example, it wouldn't be called a swimming pool or a pond. But something small, we might call that a pond, suitable for bathing. (*cf:* **danaw**).

**pangannal**₁ (derivative of **kannal**) *n.* Conscious thought; awareness. *Wa'i alungay pangannalna.* He has lost his mental awareness. *Pangannalna ngga'i ka hal ta'u, pamikilna isāb maka hona'-hona'na.* His *pangannal* is not just knowledge, it is his thought processes too and his reasoning. (*Thesaurus:* **sakup**₁ **1, sayu 1.1, sipat**₁ **1, sipat**₁ **1.1, tahu, tilas**₁).

**pangannal**₂ (derivative of **kannal**) *v. tr.* To think mistakenly about something. *Pangannalku masi aheka.* I thought [mistakenly] that there was still plenty. (*Thesaurus:* **bā'**₂).

**pangantin** *n.* A person about to be married; a bride or bridegroom. *Na bang akatis na pangantin bay niari-ari, pinal'ngngan na l'lla ina'an. Pinabatal na ko da'a kohapan bay maglurukan.* Now when the bride has finished being beautified the groom is told to proceed. They are formally ritually, lest the visitors be overtaken by dark. *Tabowa na d'nda pangantin ina'an pī' ni lahat sigā.* The bride is taken away to [the groom's] home. (*Thesaurus:* **ipang-ipang, pandala**)

**pangangabbu** (derivative of **abbu**) *n.* A boaster; a show-off.

**pangangakkal** (derivative of **akkal**) *n.* Someone who is in the habit of cheating.

**pangannggidgiran** (derivative of **gidgid**) *n.* A grindstone or grind wheel.

**pangaral** (derivative of **karal**) *n.* Something destined. *Mbal pangaral kita dayata, saguwā' ya pangaral kita ingat.* Our destiny us not our wealth, what we are destined to have is spiritual knowledge. *Anak pangaral, sali' pangahandak,* *amowa sukud. Aniya' mbal amowa sukud, pawas.* A child of destiny, of divine choice, bringing good fortune. There are those who do not bring good fortune, just misfortune.

**pangari-ngari** (derivative of **ari-ari**) *n.* Things used as decoration. *Mpat hatus buwa'-buwa' bay pangari-ngari papaganna.* Four hundred fruit-like things had been used to decorate its base.

**pangaru** (derivative of **aru**) *v. tr.* To consult with (or appeal to) someone of higher status. *Pangaruhun konsehal, hatina atilaw ni alanga-langa min aku.* Appeal to the councilor. That is, ask someone who is of somewhat higher status than I am.

**pangasa** (derivative of **asa**) *n.* 1) Hope. *Angahimāt sala pangatayanku pagka halam aniya' pangasa.* I was in deep despair because there was no hope. 1.1) *v. tr.* -an To put confidence in someone. *Pangasahinbi Tuhan. Iya ya pangasahan he' kamemon palbangsahan.* Put your trust in God. He is the hope of all nations.

**pangasahan** (derivative of **asa**) *n.* The object or basis of one's hope. *Tuhan ya pangasahantam.* It is God that we hope in.

**pangasang** (derivative of **asang₂**) *n.* A child notorious for crying with its mouth wide open. *Onde'-onde' ilū sidda pangasang, mbal katulihan bang sangom.* That child cries so much, one can't get to sleep at night.

**pangat** *v. tr.* To boil cooking bananas in water and coconut milk. (*gen:* **b'lla 1**)

**pangatag** (derivative of **atag₁**) *n.* People near one's house; neighbors. *Buwat aniya' alungay ai-aita, asal angahaka na kita ni pangatagta, atawa ni botang lahat bo' supaya sigām mbal a'awam. Kita kalungayan ya amasasā.* When something of ours is lost, we naturally tell our neighbors, or the local headman so they are not unaware. As those who had things lost, it is we who inform people.

**pangatas** (derivative of **atas₂**) *n.* Resources for discharging a debt or liability. *Bang aniya' anunu bo' aku bay makaindam, aku ya atas. Magka'at pa'in bo' halam aniya' pangataku ai-ai bay bowaku-i, mikiabunaw aku ni taga ai-ai.* If you had something and I borrowed it, I am liable. If it gets damaged and I have don't have the means to discharge my liability for what I took, I seek help from someone with the resources.

**pangatasan** (derivative of **atas₁**) *n.* A preferred outcome. *Pangatasan sigām magmula bang hati' mbal magta'at ni tuhan dakayu' inān.* They would rather suffer, so long as they do not worship that other god.

**pangatayan** (derivative of **atay₂**) *n.* The psychological seat of emotions; a person's psyche. *Paluwasku na ma ka'am bang ai mareyom pangatayanku maka ai bay tumauwa' ma aku.* I will express to you now what is in my heart and what happened to me. *Angahimāt sala*

*pangatayanku pagka halam aniya' pangasa.* I was in deep despair because there was no hope.

**pangatu** (derivative of **atu**) *n.* A defensive weapon. *Bang aku marilaut bo' aku talanggal e' a'a ala'at, bang aniya' pangatuku subay aku angatu.* When I am at sea and get accosted by someone bad, if I have something to defend with I should fight back. (*Thesaurus:* **almas**, **hinanib 1**, **pakokos**, **takos 1**).

**pangawal** (derivative of **awal₂**) *n.* A time set for some activity or result. *Duwa pitu' ya hād pangawal.* Two weeks, that's the time limit allowed. *Yuk min kar'ndahan "Angagad kita mareyom mpat-lima llaw." Na bang tinanggu-tangguhan gi' pagka halam maina'an kasehe'an, bo' halam pa'in makat'kka mareyom bay pangawal hē', na yuk sigā, "Magpalkala' na kita."* The woman's side say, "We'll wait four or five days." Then if it gets postponed because the others are not there and haven't arrived within the time agreed on, they say, "We need to discuss things."

**pangayakan** (derivative of **ayak**) *n.* A sieve or strainer. *Subay aniya' pangayakan anahut-nahut mannitu.* There should be a finer sieve than this.

**pangayu** (derivative of **kayu**) *n.* Firewood. *Paipa', bang a'llum panganggungan, bang amatay pangayu.* Coconut fronds when green can be used as a carrying pole, or when dead, as firewood. (*cf:* **tagay**).

**pangayu'an** (derivative of **ayu'**) *n.* Cash or goods paid in compensation for an offense or injury.

**pangkaheng** *v. intr.* aN- To experience suffering; to feel pain. *Onde'-onde' ngula', gana-gana amangkaheng.* A newborn baby, it will inevitably experience suffering. *Amangkaheng ko' kōknu, kinakal ka, sinanggupan.* Your head will ache, you will be hit hard, warned off. *Hal ka anangis, ya po'on ka'a-i binono'. Hal pamaralilan, mandi' hal binono', amangkaheng.* You just cry, that is why you are hit. That's just an example, good that you were merely hit and feel some pain.

**pangka'** *n.* 1) A short rod; a stake. 1.1) *v. tr.* -an To insert a rod into fruit to aid ripening. *Pinangka'an nangka', pinehē' kayu pareyom, abō' al'kkas atahak.* A rod is inserted in the jackfruit, a stick put inside, so it will quickly ripen.

**pangka'an** *n.* Props that support the rear legs of a tripod mast in a sailing canoe. *Tabowa tapi' pa'angkat he' pangka'an.* The upper planks are lifted up by the [pressure on] the supports.

**pangkal** *n.* Speech that violates the cultural norms of reverence and respect; blasphemy. *Ah'lling iya pangkal ni danakanna, yuk-i, "Mbal kita magdanakan bang mbal kabayaran badju'ku itū sangpū' pilak."* He spoke abusive words to his brother. He said, "We will not be brothers unless ten pesos is paid for this shirt of mine." *Aniya' isāb amūng pangkal ni Tuhan.* There are even some who speak blasphemy to God. (*Thesaurus:*

**sāk**₁ **1, sakkal, saggan, sammal 1)**

**pangkat**₁ *v. tr.* To stack things in layers. (*Thesaurus:* **bangkat**₁, **bingkis 1**)

**pangkat-pangkat** *n.* A stack of metal containers held by a single frame, used to carry a cooked lunch in.

**pangkat**₂ *n.* An ancestor, especially one invoked in traditional Sama religion. *Aho', kauli'an bang halam aniya' ama'in, halam anabab, buwat kami itū taga pangkat.* Yes, healing is possible when no offense was given, no cause; as with us who have ritual-ancestors. *Usulta bay ka'mbo'-mbo'an. S'ssagta ya bay pangkat dahū bang iya makakalna' i'.* We follow our ancestors. We contact the former ritual ancestor to know if he is the cause. (*Thesaurus:* **mbo'**₁, **ntan**₂ **1, palmula'an**)

**pangkat-mamangkat** *n.* Series upon series of ancestors or descendants. *Mampa'in sigām pinaglidjiki'an magtautai'anak pangkat-mamangkat.* May they and their families be blessed generation after generation.

**pangkatan** *n.* Customs inherited from one's forebears. *Dapangkatan du sigā.* They share the same ancestral customs. *Ya na pangkatanna, mbal magkalang.* That is his inherited custom, not to sing. (*Thesaurus:* **ntan**₂ **2, pali-pali, purukan, tubus**₁ **1, tuttulan, usulan**)

**pangki'** *v. tr.* To pound starchy foods until a solid lump forms. (*Thesaurus:* **banol 1.1, pogpog 1.1, t'ppa**)

**pangkot** *n.* **1)** A skin disease such as smallpox or leprosy in an advanced stage. *Aniya' saki pangkot, ya buwat kita ni'ipul. Sali' apupud gulamayta.* There is an illness called *pangkot*, like if we contract leprosy. We lose our fingers. *Nsa' aniya' ap'ddi' ai-ai, agtūy amatay. Ya hē' pangkot.* No pain at all, but quickly dies. That is *pangkot*. (*cf:* **pokot-pokot 1**; *Thesaurus:* **ka'mbo'an, kawit**₂ **1, kolera, ipul 1, ttus-ttus 1, upāng 1**) **1.1)** *intrj.* An oath expressing shock or revulsion. *Tauwa' pangkot!* May leprosy strike! [a curse form] (*cf:* **pisti'**)

**pangkul** *n.* Buttocks; hips. (*Thesaurus:* **papa-buli', pigi'**₁)

**pangdayaw** (var. **panggayaw**) *n.* **1)** The skeletal framework of a body. *Pangdayawta, ya akalbaranta.* Our skeleton, the physical frame of our body. **2)** Physical appearance in general. *Ahāp isāb pangdayawnu.* You are looking well too.

**pangentom** (derivative of **entom**) *n.* What one remembers; a longing for the past. *Duwampū' pilak, bang ma pangentomku isāb.* Twenty pesos, to my recollection. *Mbal takalipat ōnna min pangentom saga kaukampunganna.* His name will not be lost from the memory of his kinfolk. **pangentoman** *n.* A memorial; a souvenir.

**pangentom llum** (derivative of **entom**) *n. phrase* Longing for someone still alive. *Ala'at bang pangentom llum, makasakki.* Longing for someone

still alive is not good, it causes illness.

**panggahak** (var. **panggohok**) *v. intr. aN-* To breathe deeply and noisily, as when sleeping heavily; to snore. (*cf:* **kehem, pagkahak**; *Thesaurus:* **gagal**₁, **paghagak, paghagok, pagnapas, ppo**)

**panggal** *n.* **1)** A woven trap for small fish. (*Thesaurus:* **bagiyas 1, bubu**₁, **kiming, togong 1**) **1.1)** *v. tr.* To catch small fish in a woven trap. *Panggal itū pamanggal bawis maka b'llong.* This trap is for trapping rabbitfish and spinefoot fish.

**pagpanggal** *v. intr. aN-* To make a living catching fish in basket traps. *Yuk siyaka inān, "Buwangku batilku makania'a pagpanggal."* The older brother there said, "I will toss my container away to the basket trap fisherman."

**panggang**₁ *v. tr.* To cook a bird or animal (but not a fish) by roasting whole on a spit. (*cf:* **b'lla 1**; *Thesaurus:* **tapa 1, tunu'**₂)

**panggang**₂ (var. **ganggang**; **langgang**) *adj. a-* **1)** Dried out through exposure to the sun; suffering heat exhaustion. *Apanggang he' llaw, baranta atawa pelang. Bang baranta angalimasu' kita. Bang pelang iya, al'ssa'.* Dried out by the sun, our bodies or a canoe. When it is our bodies we are hot inside. When it is a canoe it cracks. *Sali' angalimasu' deyom baranta. Aganggang kita e' llaw.* As when our body experiences painful internal warmth. We are dried out by the sun. *Buwat manusiya' halam anginum bohe'.* Like a human being who hasn't drunk any water. (*cf:* **kapiyalu 1**; *Thesaurus:* **k'llung-k'llung, lengas**₁, **tigangkal, t'ggang**₁, **toho'**) **1.1)** *v. advrs. -in-* Dried out by the sun; parched, of a living creature. *Nilanggang aku he' llaw ati patay bohe' aku.* I am dried out by the sun and I am seriously thirsty.

**panggayaw** var. of **pangdayaw**

**panggi'** (var. **panggi'-kayu**) *n.* Manioc (commonly called cassava), a major starch staple for the peoples of Central Sulu. *Manihot utilissima.* *"Na nsa' aniya'," yukku, "minsan saga pamayad panggi'."* "There is simply nothing," I said, "not even for buying cassava." *Bang aniya' panggi' bay nili'is, ginipitan na. Apidjal to'ongan, halam na taga bohe'.* When cassava has been grated, it is pressed. Really pressed dry, it no longer has liquid. (*cf:* **patatas**)

**panggi'-bahan** *n.* Sweet potato; camote. *Ipomoea batatas.*

**panggi'-bilu-bilu** (var. **bilu-bilu**₃) *n.* A variety of cassava with toxic juice that requires grating and expressing before cooking.

**panggi'-biskwit** (var. **biskwit**₁) *n.* A non-toxic variety of cassava, with white flesh and a pink inner skin.

**panggi'-buwaya** *n.* A variety of cassava with toxic juice that requires grating and expressing before cooking.

**panggi'-dulu** (var. **dulu₂**) *n.* A non-toxic variety of cassava.

**panggi'-hinu-hinu** *n.* A dark-fleshed variety of cassava.

**panggi'-kayu** var. of **panggi'**

**panggohok** var. of **panggahak**

**panggohong** *v. intr.* aN- To roar, of a large wild animal. *Amanggohong, buwat halimaw atawa baruwang.* Roaring, like a lion or a bear.

**panggung** *n.* A building with floor and roof but no walls; an open market. *Panggung-panggung ya pagdagangan ai-ai, atawa pangongka'an. Hal pasindungan, halam aniya' dinding. Taga lantay.* A *panggung* is a place for selling stuff, or a place for recreation. Just a shelter, no walls. It does have a floor. (*Thesaurus:* **balung-balung, kamalig, lapaw, payad, pillayag**)

**pangguwa'** *n.* **1)** The restless spirit of a dead person that returns from the grave to trouble the living. *Bay kami anū' mampallam kaleya, aheka pangguwa'.* We went ashore to get mangos by torchlight and there were lots of ghosts. **1.1)** *v. intr.* aN- To become a ghost; to behave as a ghost. *Bang ala'at hinangta ma deyom dunya, mbal kita pinasampay ni sulga'. Ma dunya ya amangguwa'.* If our actions in the world are bad we are not taken all the way to heaven, but instead become ghosts here on earth. (*Thesaurus:* **bahana', lutaw, pagbagala, panyata'₂ 1**)

**panghati** (derivative of **hati**) *n.* How one understands something; comprehension. *Sussik itū ma panghatiku, atuyu'.* This word *sussik*, in my understanding, means diligent. (*Thesaurus:* **alab-alab, himangkan, ingat, pamapatahan, ta'u₁ 1**).

**talus panghati** *n. phrase* A person with complete understanding of all sorts of things.*A'a iya talus panghati.* He is someone who understands everything.

**panghū'** var. of **panghulu'**

**panghulu'** (var. **panghū'**) *n.* **1)** A person of prestige; a person in supreme authority, as the premier of a country. *Panghulu'ta, sali' tuhanta, buwat botang matto'a.* Our high leader, like our god, like the head of the community. *Bang ma aku, panghulu' itū nakura', nakura' nsa' bidda'.* In my opinion a *panghulu'* is a leader, any kind of a leader. (*cf:* **preseden**; *Thesaurus:* **botang-lahat 1, maharadja, panglima**) **2)** The Lord, in Christian usage.

**pangi** *n.* A forest tree and its edible fruit.

**pangimanan** (derivative of **iman₁**) *n.* The source or basis of one's religious trust. *Tuhan dakayu'-dakayu' ya pangimananta.* God alone is the object of our trust.

**pangimbū** (derivative of **imbū**) *n.* Jealousy. *Pangimbū ya makapakagit h'lla.* Jealousy is what makes a husband angry.

**panginuman** (var.**pagi'inuman**) (derivative of **inum**) *n.* A drinking container of any kind. *Na, ina'an asal sawan pagi'inumanna ma tanganku.* So there in my hand was the very glass he drank from. (*Thesaurus:* **basu, sawan, tasa**).

**pangiram** (derivative of **iram**) *n.* The early stage of pregnancy.

**pangiraman** *n.* Foods craved by a pregnant woman during the early stage of her pregnancy.*Na bo' na kono' nileyang pangiraman.* So then, as the story goes, the craved food was attained by flying.*Am'lli aku tagbak pangiraman h'ndaku.* I will buy wild ginger fruit for my wife's pregnancy craving.

**pangiskul** (derivative of **iskul**) *n.* Schooling or education, as provided by the state. *Apa alanga na to'ongan pangiskulna anak ilū.* For the educational level of that child is very high.

**pangisihan₁** (derivative of **isi₁**)1) *n.* A container. **2)** *v. tr.* To use something as a container. *Am'ttak buli' mital, mbal tapangisihan bohe'.* The bottom of the tin can is leaking, it can't be used as a water container.

**pangisihan₂** (derivative of **isi₁**) *n.* Mother, in a figurative sense as the container through which a child is brought into the world. *Aho', dapangisihan kami.* Yes, we are from the same mother [lit. container]. *Duwa bohe' sigā, dakayu' pangisihan.* They are from two fathers [lit. semen], one mother [lit. container]. (*cf:* **bohe'₂**).

**pangita'u** (derivative of **ta'u₁**) *n.* Knowledge; wisdom. *Aniya' pangita'uku ma Siganggang, a'ana, luma'na, nsa' bidda'. Halam aniya' pangita'uku ma Bukidnon itū.* I have knowledge about Siganggang, its people, its houses, anything at all. I have no knowledge of this district, Bukidnon. *Pangita'uta, sali' aniya' ilmu' ma deyom baranta.* Knowledge, like there being some esoteric knowledge within us. *Taga pangita'u isāb iya angama'ana uppi.* He also has the knowledge to interpret dreams. (*cf:* **hinabta'u**).

**pang'ddikan** (derivative of **ddik**) *n.* Something that is walked on. *Mbal kapang'ddikan lantay ilū.* That flooring cannot be walked on.

**pang'llaw** (derivative of **llaw₂**) *n.* The sunny season. *Ap'nno' saga pagbohe'an minsan ma waktu pang'llaw.* The water sources will be full even in the sunny [i.e. hot and dry] season.

**pang'mbo'an** (derivative of **mbo'₁**) *n.* The individuals from whom one traces descent; one's ancestors.

**pang'mpu** (derivative of **mpu**) *n.* Grandchildren. *Magbuddi maka kasilasaku ma pang'mpunu.* I will repay kindness and show love to your grandchildren.

**pang'mpuhan** *n.* Descendants.

**pang'nna'an** (derivative of **nna'**) *n.* A storage place. (*cf:* **pagtau'an**).

**pang'ntan** (derivative of **ntan₁**) *n.* Hand tools; implements. *Sikagantungan pang'ntan.* [Kitchen] implements hanging in large numbers.

**pang'ntanan₁** (derivative of **ntan₁**) *n.* Sphere of control or protection. *Kalappasan aku e'na min pang'ntanan Pira'un waktu iya bilahi amono' ma aku.* He rescued me from the power of the Pharaoh at the time when he wanted to kill me. (*Thesaurus:* **komkoman 2, deyoman 2, milikan, okoman**).

**pang'ntanan₂** (derivative of **ntan₂**) *n.* Ritual ancestors in general. *Minsan du halam aniya' hinangta bay ni ala'at, sinemet kita he' man pang'ntanan. Taluwa' kita saki bo' mbal isāb amatay.* Even though we have done nothing bad, we are affected by some ritual ancestor. We get sick though we don't die.

**pangli'** *n.* **1)** An individual's defining features. (*Thesaurus:* **aymuka, bantuk, bayhu' 1, dagbos, jantang-jari, lahi₄, luwa 1**) **1.1)** *v. tr.* *-an* To recognize someone by his appearance. *Pangli'in a'a bang sai i'. Ni'nda' iya min kalawakan.* Recognise who that person yonder is. Seen from a distance. (*Thesaurus:* **kilā 1, panhid**)

**panglima** *n.* A traditional title for the leader of a local community. *Panglima hē' niōnan banwa.* That local leader is called *banwa.* (*Thesaurus:* **botang-lahat 1, maharadja, panghulu' 1**)

**panglipas** (var.**panglipat**) (derivative of **lipas**) *n.* **1)** An absent-minded person. (*syn:* **panglupa**).**1.1)** *v. tr.* *-an* To forget something through absent-mindedness.

**panglipat** var. of **panglipas**

**pangliyas** *n.* Magical protection against physical harm. *Mbal kita taluwa' ai-ai. Tinimbak min heka, taga pangliyas, taga pagkal'lla.* Nothing will hurt us. Though shot repeatedly, we have magical protection, immunity. *Hadjimat, bang ahāp taga pangliyas du.* A *hadjimat* charm, if it is good, it has magical protection. (*Thesaurus:* **basi'₂ 1.1, kobol 1.1, pagkal'lla, sihil 1**)

**panglupa** *n.* An absent-minded person. (*syn:* **panglipas 1**; *Thesaurus:* **bibas₂, kalipat 1, liha-liha, lipas**)

**pangluwahan** (derivative of **luwa**) *n.* The external appearance of something.

**pangongka'an** (derivative of **ongka'**) *n.* Things for playing with; toys. *Ai-ai pangongka'an, baggu' ka, batu ka.* Anything used for playing games, cowrie shells or stones.

**pangoresyon** (derivative of **dekoresyon**) *n.* Things used as a decorative feature. *Am'lli aku laya-laya pangoresyon luma'nu.* I will buy some fan coral as a decoration for your house.

**pangsan** *adj. a-* Serious or persistent, of an illness. *Apangsan sakina, sali' asigpit.* Her illness is severe, as if critical. (*Thesaurus:* **bangat, kansang 1.1, sidda 2**)

**pangsat** *v. intr. aN-* **1)** To withdraw by backing out through an opening. *Angal'ppang, hatina sarang to'od mata linggi'. Aheka tak'llo'ta bang*

*angal'ppang linggi'. Mbal am'ssut, mbal amangsat.* The right size, the mesh size, in other words, being exactly right. We catch a lot when the mesh of the net is right. [The fish] don't slip through and don't get back out. **1.1)** *v. tr.* *-an* To pull something backwards through an opening. *Pinangsatan, hatina nihella' min buli'an.* Taken out back-first, in other words pulled out by its rear end.

**pangsut** *adj. a-* **1)** Detached from a socket or slot. *Bay kita anigad ma dilaut, wa'i ahūg baran lahut, apangsut man puhanna.* We were out at sea slashing something when the blade of the machete fell, having come loose from its handle. (*cf:* **l'pput₁ 1, loleng**) **1.1)** *v. intr. aN-* To become detached from a socket. *Amangsut kōk katig bang taluwa' he' kosog goyak.* The head of the outrigger comes away [from its socket] when hit by the force of the waves.

**pangtad** *v. tr.* To remove small irregularities along a row of items such as teeth or a woven edge. (*Thesaurus:* **lagnas, solsol, tā'**)

**pangtu'ud** *n.* A post that extends to the top of a house wall. (*Thesaurus:* **bale₃ 1, hāg 1, lusuk-lusuk, pipul, sumpiyang, tuku 1**)

**pangtusan** *n.* A sprouting coconut at the stage when the young plant is still attached to the parent nut. *Angamōt, amangtusan.* Forming the endosperm, sprouting. (*wh:* **niyug**) (*Stages:* **kambung-kambung, botong-botong, bilu'uk, botong, gangkul, lahing, pangtusan**)

**pangubug** (derivative of **ubug₂**) *n.* A fishing lure. *Batu ya nihagtu'-hagtu' pangubug kuhita'.* A stone is what is bounced up and down in order to lure an octopus out.

**pangukaban lawang** (derivative of **ukab**) *n.* *phrase* A gift (lit. a door opener) made to the seller of an item such as a large pearl, as proof of a potential buyer's serious intentions. {idiom}

**pangulan** (derivative of **ulan**) *n.* The rainy season. *Magl'ggon lahat, marāi' pangulan na.* It is thundering continuously, maybe it is the rainy season already.

**panguntas** (derivative of **untas**) *n.* Overseas travel. *Anipun kami sīn panguntas lahat sampay paggastu ma labayan.* We are saving up for traveling overseas and for expenses on the way.

**panguntukan** *n.* The mental ability to plan ahead. *Kulang panguntukanna, kulang pangannal, pasal akil-balig lagi'.* Lacking good sense, lacking thought, because still immature.

**pangungustaw** (derivative of **kustaw**) *n.* A person who misuses money entrusted to his care; an embezzler.

**panguppihan** (derivative of **uppi**) *n.* A dream state. *Abati' na iya, jari tahati e'na bay palambung ni iya ma panguppihanna.* He woke up and realised that someone had spoken to him in his dream state.

**pangusaha** (derivative of **usaha**) *n.* The equipment

for one's work. *Pinagka'inagonan aku he' sigā, ya po'on aku bīllihan ai-ai buwat saga pangusaha.* They are thoughtful toward me, which is why they buy for me various things like work gear.

**pangutangan** (derivative of **utang**) *v. tr.* To be considered good for a loan. *Ka'a ilū mbal tapangutangan, at'ggol amayad.* You cannot be given credit, taking a long time to repay.

**paopēt** *see:* **pagpaopēt**

**papā** *see:* **pamapā**

**papa₁** *n.* Cheeks, of face or buttocks. (*syn:* **pisngi**) **papa-buli'** *n.* Cheeks, specifically of buttocks. (*Thesaurus:* **pangkul, pigi'₁**)

**papa₂** var. of **papang**

**papak** *see:* **pagpapak**

**papag** *v. tr. -an* To protect someone from doing what might harm them. *Papagin onde'-onde' ilu.* Keep that child from getting hurt. (*Thesaurus:* **alimata, jaga 1.2, peyan, tunggu' 1.1**)

**papagan** *n.* 1) A support or base, as the foundation of a house or the board to which a metal grater is fastened. *Taluwa' hunus luma' inān sagō' halam ah'bba' sabab ahogot papaganna.* That house was hit by strong wind but it didn't collapse because its foundation was secure. (*Thesaurus:* **ba'ugan₂, palanggungan**) 2) The background of a weaving pattern. *Gaddung papaganna, bilu sumpingna.* Its background is green; its flowers are blue. (*Thesaurus:* **punsa', sapak**)

**pagpapagan** *v. intr. aN-* To create the background part of something woven. *Magpapagan ma biyaning, punsa' bilu.* Making the background in yellow, the pattern blue.

**papagbidda'** (derivative of **bidda'**) *v. tr.* To make things distinct from each other. *Papagbidda'ku saga a'aku maka saga a'anu.* I will make a distinction beween my people and your people. *Mbal ka amapagbidda' ma a'a minsan sai.* You do not make a difference between people, no matter who.

**papagbulang** (derivative of **bulang**) *v. tr.* To provoke people to mutual aggression; to get two people to fight. *Angahupit-ngahupit iya supaya amapagbulang pagkahina.* He urges his companions on, getting them to fight each other. *Pinapagbulang saga onde'.* The children are set to fighting.

**papagkablit** (derivative of **kablit₁**) *v. tr.* To join two long items end to end. *Papagkablitun linggi' ilū.* Have those two trawl nets joined end to end.

**papagdapu** (derivative of **dapu**) *v. tr. -an* To acquire property, especially in the sense of simply taking it over without payment. *Tana' ya pinapagdapuhan e' gubnul.* The land taken over by the governor as his property.

**papagtimuk** (derivative of **timuk**) *v. tr.* To make someone part of an assembled group. *Awapat na iya ma deyom kasannangan, ati pinapagtimuk iya maka ka'mbo'-mbo'anna.* He died in peaceful circumstances and was put together with his ancestors.

**papa'** *v. tr.* To chew something hard, as betel nut chew or some foods. *Am'lli gi' aku biyabas papa'ku.* I will buy an [unripe] guava and chew on it. (*cf:* **kakan 1**; *Thesaurus:* **lopa', pa'us**)

**papal** var. of **palpal**

**papalom** *v. tr. -an* To staunch the flow of blood; to reduce the severity of some internal pain. *Abakat kita he' kayu, niā' min kayu he' pamapalom bakat. Atawa abusā', tinambalan kita min deyom, pinapaloman kita min deyom.* When we are wounded by a tree, something from that tree is taken to staunch the wound. Or when experiencing internal pain, we are treated internally, the pain stopped from inside [the body]. (*cf:* **tambal₁ 1**)

**papan₁** *n.* Planking; wide thin board such as plywood. *A: "Pila heka papannu?" B: "Damb'llad du."* A: "How many boards do you have?" B: "Just one piece." *Luma' papan.* A house with wooden siding. (*Thesaurus:* **baras-baras, hanglad 1, listun, pasagi' 1**)

**papan-somel** *n.* Milled planks. *Am'lli aku papan-somel pagangkapku luma' kami.* I will buy milled planks for building a second story on our house.

**papan-tudjun** *n.* A board on which the throwing game of tudjun is played.

**papan₂** *clf.* Count word for packets of firecrackers. *B'llihin aku duwampapan kulitis.* Buy me two packets of firecrackers. (*Thesaurus:* **kaha₂ 1, kustal 1, pākete**)

**papanjari** *v. tr.* To bring something into being, as the action of God in creation. *Itiya' aku ummatnu pinapanjari he'nu.* Here I am, your creature who was made by you. *Tuhan Sangat Kawasa ya bay amapanjari langit maka dunya.* God Almighty who created the skies and the earth. (*Thesaurus:* **paniya', ummat 1.1**)

**papanjarihan** *n.* Created things of all kinds. *Bang tabangun na min kamatay, baran baha'u na, papanjarihan sulga' na.* When raised from death it is a new body, a creation of heaven.

**papang** (var. **papa₂**) *voc. n.* An address term for father or senior male, used for men of the Chavacano community. *Bang aku taga mma' Lannang, angōn aku papang.* If I have a Chinese father, I call [him] *papang.* (*cf:* **babu' 1.1, ina', mamang₁, mma'**)

**papas₁** *adj. a-* 1) Faded; erased. *Ataggu itū sali' at'ggol apapas. Apapas du isāb so' at'ggol-t'ggol anganggangti'.* *Taggu* means it takes a long time to fade. It does indeed fade but is quite some time before it is changed. (*Thesaurus:* **baluba 1, gagas, lulu, padpad**) 1.1) *v. tr. -an* To erase something. *Luwal bang magsulat inān, bang aniya' asā' pinapasan.* Only with writing, if there is a mistake it is erased. (*Thesaurus:* **erēs, pahalam**)

**papas₂** *v. tr.* To club someone to death. *Bang aniya' binono', pinapas maka busay.* When someone is to be killed, he is clubbed with a paddle.

(*Thesaurus:* **kakal**)

**papat** *adj. a-* **1)** Well-behaved; disciplined. *Papapatku na kām, da'a na kam ahiluhala'.* I will have you behave properly, don't make a racket. (*Thesaurus:* **addat 1.1, hatul₂, hongpot, pantun 1, p'mpon 1, saldik, saltun 1) 1.1)** *v. tr.* To instruct a child in proper behavior. *Buwat anaknu aholemang, na papatnu bo' mbal papapat. Amatay na pinapat.* Like your child being naughty, so you instruct her but she will not be instructed. *Buwat anaknu aholemang, na papatnu bo' mbal papapat.* Like your child being naughty, so you instruct her but she will not be instructed. (*Thesaurus:* **bi'at 1.1**)

**pagpapat** *n.* **1)** The instructions of a parent. *Bang mbal ameya' ma pagpapatnu, ya ampa ka angastol.* When [the child] does not obey your teaching, then you get angry. **1.1)** *v. tr.* To be engaged in instructing one's children.

**papata** *n.* **1)** A prognosis; a prediction. *Yuk kamatto'ahan mbal ahāp papatana.* The elders foresee that his prognosis is not good. *Bang kita atuli aniya' papata at'kka ni kita.* When we are sleeping a portent comes to us. **1.1)** *v. tr.* To describe the details of a future event or of an object not clearly seen by others. *Papatahun kono' ma aku anakku itū, bang allum ka, amatay ka.* Please make a prognosis for my child, whether it will live or die. *Kilā-kilāku, sali' papataku, sali' kita talus-talus ina'an.* I consider the possibility, like predicting something, as though we were seers. *Papataku si Sa itū, bang aheya tahinang mayul.* I predict that Sa here will become mayor when he grows up. *Ya pinapata kulisna bang buwattitu, ai kasōnganna ahāp-ala'at.* It's her palm lines that are studied, whether her future will be good or bad. **1.2)** *v. tr.* An insightful saying; a proverb. *Minnē' magtagna' papata ya yukna, "Buta maka pengkol mbal makajari pasōd ma astana'."* That is the origin of the proverb that said, "Blind men and lame men cannot go into palaces."

**pamapatahan** *n.* Information; a body of knowledge. (*Thesaurus:* **alab-alab, himangkan, ingat, panghati, ta'u₁ 1**)

**papatay** (derivative of **patay₁**) *v. tr.* **1)** To cause the death of something; to kill. *Bang kita angalagut ero', sōng pinapatay.* When we slash a dog, it is about to be killed. *Mbal aku, minsan aku papataynu na.* I will not, even though you kill me. (*Thesaurus:* **bono' 1.1, pinsan 1.1**). **1.1)** *v. tr. -an* To bring about the death of a close family member, as a consequence of one's own bad luck. *A'a inān amapatayan anakna atawa h'lla-h'ndana.* That person causes the death of his/her children or spouse. *D'nda inān balu, hal amapatayan h'llana.* That woman is a widow, she was simply killing her husband. (*cf:* **kakan h'lla/h'nda**)

**papatut** (derivative of **patut**) *v. tr.* To do something appropriately. *Papatutta bang kita amuwan.* We should do it appropriately when we make a gift. (*cf:* **pa'amu**).

**papehē'** (derivative of **pehē'₁**) *v. tr.* **1)** To send someone to a place. **2)** To bring the conversation back round to an earlier topic, always used with the enclitic pronoun = ta. *Na papehē'ta ni si Ch, asal pa'in llaw kasaggawna magtūy du kata'uhanku ma katas-habal.* Referring back now to Ch, on the very day of his capture I immediately knew about it from the newspaper.

**papehē'an** (derivative of **pehē'₁**) *n.* A destination. *Anehe'an aku ka'a maingga-maingga papehē'annu.* I will accompany you wherever your destination.

**papel** (var. **pepel**) *n.* Paper, especially writing paper. *Bang aku anulat bo' mbal plāt, gomot-gomotku pepelku.* When I write but it isn't smooth, I crumple up my paper. (*Thesaurus:* **banggala, katas**)

**papellat** (derivative of **pellat**) *adv.* Spread open, of parts that are normally or preferably together. *Angay ka aningkō' papellat ilū?* Why are you sitting with everything open [a rebuke to a little girl]?

**papet** *n.* A broad-beamed wooden vessel used mainly for transporting freight. (*Thesaurus:* **beggong, biruk, buti, kappal, kumpit, lansa, sappit₂, tempel**)

**papinsal** (derivative of **pinsal**) *v. tr.* To tighten the loop around the two planks of a cassava press. *Papinsalun gipitan panggi' kayu, ko' bang sinanglag ahāp.* Tighten the cassava press, so [the meal] will be good when roasted.

**papole'** (derivative of **pole'₁**) *v. tr.* To return something to its original location; to send someone home. *Sumilan pinapole' mitalku? Itiya' gi' indamanku binowa ni bohe'.* When will my water-cans be returned? Here I am borrowing one to take to the water source. (*Thesaurus:* **maksud 1.2, nde', pasampay, tukbal₁ 1, tūd₂, tulun₂ 1.1, tuyuk-tuyuk**).

**pagpapole'** *v. intr. aN-* To return things to a prior status. *Saupama bay kita magb'lli, bay magsulut. Mbal manjari binawi'an bissala, mbal na manjari agpapole'.* For example, we were buying and had come to an agreement. It is not possible to go back on what has been said, not possible to return [what has been purchased].

**papuhun** (derivative of **puhun**) *v. tr.* To grant someone permission to leave; to excuse someone. (*Thesaurus:* **paba'id, pakuhi, parūl 1.1, tugut 2**).

**papu'** *n.* A favorite; a pet. A: "Sowa ē' asungi' bulawan." B: "Angeket bahā'?" A: "Mbal, papu'na sowa ē'." A: "That snake excreted gold." B: "Did it bite?" A: "No, that snake was his pet."

**papu'ut** (derivative of **pu'ut**) *v. tr.* Development marker in narrative discourse, meaning 'to make a long story short', and signaling the end of a discourse unit. *Papu'utta na istori itū, ilu kām tinuli.* I'll cut this story short, you're getting sleepy. (*Thesaurus:* **dalas 1.1**).

**paputing** (derivative of **puting**) *v. tr.* To refuse to believe what someone says, implying that he is lying.

**papuwa'** *adv.* Suddenly and unexpectedly. *Aniya' bay pat'nna'ku mailū, papuwa' niā' e' onde'.* I placed something there, and a child suddenly took it. *Bang takdil saki itū, bang papuwa' pahibal, agon sali' ab'kkat napasku.* In regard to this illness, when it suddenly stirs, I almost die. (*Thesaurus:* **sakkop 2, taggaha', tanyak**)

**parā** *intrj.* Stop moving!

**pamarā** *v. tr.* -*an* To tell someone to stop doing something that is unsafe or unacceptable. (*Thesaurus:* **banda'**, **lāng**)

**para₁** *adj.* *a-* Broken down, of an engine. *Apara donson si Ku ma dilaut Pandami'.* Ku's outboard motor broke down offshore from Pandami'. *Samalintonga' pa'in kami, apara malkina.* When we were halfway the motor quit.

**para₂** *prep.* For (the benefit of). *Sangpū' batang t'bbu para ma aku.* Ten sticks of sugarcane for me. *Ang'llo' iya bohe' para pamandiku.* He is getting water for me to bathe [someone] with. *Aniya' na nnompū' pilak bahagi' kami para dangan.* There was a sixty peso share for each of us. (*Thesaurus:* **ma 3, maka₁**)

**parabla** var. of **palabra**

**parablay** (derivative of **dablay**) *v. tr.* To drape a flexible item over something firm. *Pīs sinabit itū, pinarablay bahā' man bahanu?* This woven scarf, is it to be draped over your shoulder? (*Thesaurus:* **pagsalay₁, sablay**).

**parabtalan** (derivative of **dabtal**) *n.* A supporting base for a task; a basis for an assertion. *Subay aniya' pamarabtalan bang ka an'tta' kayu pangayu.* There should be a chopping block when you are chopping wood for the cooking fire. *Sali' ai-ai hinangta, buwat an'tta' kayu atawa amabuwa' daing, subay aniya' pamarabtalan, pamasangdolan, pamataggalan.* Whatever we do such as chopping wood or cutting up fish, there should be something as a workbench, a support, a backing. (*cf:* **pamataggalan**).

**parak** *n.* A purpose or discussion for which people are gathered. *Sali' anganasib kita ma paghinangan, ilu parak ni paghinangan.* Suppose we are to sing the *nasib* chant at the ceremony, then that is the purpose of our ceremony. *Duwa parak e'tabi magsuli-suli.* Two matters for us to talk about. *Binowa kita magsuli-suli, parak suli-suli, yuk-i, "Ya pinagtimukan itū, aniya' parak suli-suli ni kita."* We are called to a discussion, a business item, saying, "What brings us together is that there is a matter for us to discuss." (*Thesaurus:* **gara' 1, palkala' 1**)

**parakag** (derivative of **dakag**) *v. tr.* To harm someone's character by over-indulging him or her. *Bang dangan-dangan du anakna l'lla pinarakag, bang dangan-dangan du d'nda pinarakag isāb.* When there's only one son, he is spoilt, and when there is only one daughter she is spoilt too. (*Thesaurus:* **palangga' 1.1, parūl 1.1, patege'**).

**parakala'** var. of **palkala'**

**paradol** (var. **aparadol**) *n.* A storage cupboard. (*Thesaurus:* **kabinet, perol**)

**paragang** (derivative of **dagang**) *v. tr.* To encourage someone to buy something. (*Thesaurus:* **andag, halga' 1.2, jawab₁, ladjaw**).

**parahāl** *conj.* Contrary to expectations; nevertheless; but in fact. *Parahāl bay na saga bowa kami ni doktol.* However, we took [him] to the doctor.

**parahū** (derivative of **dahū**) *v. tr.* To advance a portion of the agreed-on bride-wealth. *Bay kami aminta' ₱20, bay amarahū.* We paid ₱20 in advance, moving the [payment] date forward.

**para'ak** (derivative of **da'ak**) *v. tr.* -*an* To inform the elders of the man about to be married that it is time to proceed to the bride's house (for the ceremony). *Amara'ak na ni kal'llahan, sinō' pal'ngngan.* Inform the male side, tell them to start walking.

**paralil** (derivative of **dalil**) *v. tr.*1) To make an example of something. *Pinaralil isab pamandu'na ni manggis ahāp ssana.* He also compared his teaching to delicious mangosteen.1.1) *v. intr.* *aN-* To cite something as an illustration or example. *Sagwā' amaralil si Hu pasal baranna.* But Hu was giving an illustration about himself. **paralilan** *n.* An example; an illustration.

**paralu'** *n.* The early phase of funeral rites. *Hinang paralu' ya hinang amatay, hinang t'llu, hinang dapitu', mbal kinata'uhan bang sumiyan llawna. Paralu'* is a rite for the dead, the 3rd day or the 7th day ceremony, it's not known exactly which day it is. *Ameya' kita paluruk ni paralu'.* We intend to pay our respects at the *paralu'* rites.

**paranas** *v. intr.* *aN-* To fish with hook and line while drifting with the current. *Pamaranas itū am'ssi magpalaran.* This word *paranas* is about fishing-with-hook-and-line while drifting. *Bay ka'mbo'-mbo'an kami amaranas. Lling tahun itu pamalastik.* For our forebears [the word was] *paranas.* The modern word is *pamalastik.* (*Thesaurus:* **gonteng 1.2, laway₂ 1.1, manit, pamalastik, p'ssi 1.1, tonda'₁ 1.1**)

**parang** *n.* Cogon and similar kinds of tall grass. *Imperata cylindrica.. Wa'i pinatapuk e'na ma deyo' saga batang parang ya binuwad maina'an.* Hidden by her under the straw that was being dried there.

**kaparangan** *n.* A grassed area. *Ulan, ya amatubu' saga kaparangan ma tana'.* Rain, that waters grassed areas of land.

**parang-parang** *n.* Various grasses eaten by cattle.

**parang-sabil** (derivative of **sabil**) *n.* A genre of

song celebrating a battle, often sung to the accompaniment of the bamboo marimba. **pagparang-sabil** *v. intr. aN-* To sing a battle song.*Bang magparang-sabil, subay gabbang.* When singing the battle song, there should be a bamboo marimba.

**parangkahan** (derivative of **dangka₂**) *n.* A place for getting oneself warm. *Ahāp parangkahan bang ahaggut.* It is a good place to get warm when it is cold.

**parangkang** *n.* An all-purpose vessel of Buginese origin, rarely seen in Sulu. *Parangkang ataha' jungalna, ya pajudjal ma munda'.* A *parangkang* has a long sprit, projecting from the bow. *Pagabut kami ni Selibis analumpung na kami. Talumpung kami maka'nda' na kami t'llu parangkang. Aheka parangkang mahē' agbowa lahing.* When we reached Sulawesi we used the binoculars. On doing so we saw three parangkang. There are many parangkang there carrying copra. *Magkullu-kullu, angamundu, ameya' min parangkang.* Raiding, engaging in banditry, traveling by parangkang vessels.

**parassaya** (var. **paratsaya**) *v. intr. aN-* To believe what is said. *Mbal aku paratsaya ma ka'a, sali' aku mbal ameya'-meya' ma haka'annu.* I do not believe you, I am sort of not believing what you are telling [me]. *Da'a ka tināw. Magparassaya sadja ka.* Don't be afraid. Just believe. *Angandol, sali' kita angagad. Am'nnal sali' amaratsaya, subay aniya' lling. Andol* [trust] is like waiting for something. *Am'nnal* [believe] is like accepting as true, of something said. (*Thesaurus:* **beya'-beya'₁** 1, **b'nnal** 1.2, **kahagad**, **halap₁**, **siddik**)

**parat** *adj. a-* Abundant; plentiful. *Aparat he' kasumping-sumpingan.* Abundant with flowers. *Aparat kaluma'an ma kalungsuran.* The houses in city areas are very numerous. *Aparat pahāp sīnnu.* You have so much money. (*Thesaurus:* **banos, besal, kansang** 1, **datay₂, dayas-dayas, dorot, heka** 1.1, **jayak**)

**paratsaya** var. of **parassaya**

**paraw** *n.* 1) A light outrigger canoe with upper sides of plywood or woven cane, a fast sailer. *Tininduk aku e' kandelan ati binowa paraw palahi-lahi magbibud buli'-munda'.* My hook was struck by a sailfish and the *paraw* was set racing, turning around end for end. (*Thesaurus:* **balutu, bangka', dapang, londay, pallungan, pambot, pelang, pongag**) 2) A motorized outrigger boat.

**paraya** (derivative of **daya**) *n.* 1) A person of wealth.1.1) *v. tr. -an* To make someone wealthy. *Da'a aku pamiskinin atawa parayahin.* Don't make me either rich or poor.

**parereyagan** *n.* Playthings; musical instruments.

**pares₁** *adj. a-* Grazed, of one's skin. *Insini' bay kami magbinti', apares kōk-tu'utku he' gusung.* Earlier we played the calf-kicking game and my knee was grazed by the sand. (*Thesaurus:* **banggid** 1, **geges, langgad** 1, **sahumut-sahumut**)

**pares₂** *n.* A pair of playing cards. (*syn:* **paro**) **pagpares** *n.* 1) A card game involving the forming of pairs of the same value. (*Thesaurus:* **paglaki, pagsugal**) 1.1) *v. intr. aN-* To play the card game of "pairs". (*cf:* **paro**)

**pareyo'₁** (derivative of **deyo'₁**) *adv.* In a downwards direction. **pareyo'-pariyata'** *adv.* Entirely; fully.*Lungbus aku pareyo'-pariyata' ma sakap bayanan.* I am fully equipped with canoe gear.

**pareyo'₂** *v. tr.* To make a gift to a woman's parents during her first pregnancy, the action of the man's family. (*syn:* **palahil**)

**pari-pari** *n.* A species of sea anemone, the tendrils of which inflict a painful sting. *Actinia spp.* (*Thesaurus:* **kambang, kombo'-kombo', lason, lo'on**)

**pariki'** (derivative of **diki'**) *v. tr. -an* To make something small by removing part of it. *Bay pinariki'an e' gatgat-basi'.* Reduced in bulk using a hacksaw.

**pariksa'** var. of **paliksa'**

**pari'** *n.* A priest, especially in a Roman Catholic or Episcopalian context. *Saga pari' ya tag-bowahan ta'u-ta'u.* The priests who were carriers of the images.

**pari'an** *n.* The seashore; foreshore. (*Thesaurus:* **bihingan, daplakan₁, gintana'an, hampilan, susulan, tampe, tapiyan**)

**parilaut** (derivative of **dilaut**) *adv.* 1) Towards open sea. *Hengkotinbi pelang ilū ko da'a talaran parilaut.* Tie that canoe there so it isn't swept out to sea.1.1) *v. intr. zero* To go out to sea. *Alandos goyak itū, mbal kita makaparilaut.* This rough weather is extreme, we can't go out to sea.

**parinta** *n.* 1) The government at the national or local level. *Parinta pilak ko' inān.* That administration is just about money. *Magsakaum, sali' ai-ai niamu' he' parinta subay tinimuk kamemon.* Forming a community, as when anything asked for by government should all be gathered. (*cf:* **kawasa** 1) 1.1) *v. tr. -an* To govern a country or people; to exercise authority over a community. *"Sabab," yukna, "ya na ilu magparinta-parintahan dīna."* "Because," he said, "that's the man who makes himself the one who governs."

**pagparinta** *v. intr. aN-* 1) To govern a country or people; to exercise authority over a community. *Si Kamlun inān mbal kapagparintahan, subay amarintahan ma baranna.* Kamlun [a famous independence fighter] could not be governed. He had to govern himself. *"Sabab," yukna, "ya na ilu magparinta-parintahan dīna."* "Because," he said, "that's a man who takes it on himself to govern." 1.1) *v. tr. -an* To govern a nation or ethnic group.

**pariyata'** (derivative of **diyata'**) *adv.* Upwards; in an upwards direction. *Wa'i na si Mbo' Belle', paleyang sudju pariyata'.* Off goes Grandfather

Eagle, flying upwards.

**pariyata'an** (derivative of **diyata'an**₁) *n.* The direction from which an ocean current is flowing. *Sinandat pariyata'an, aniya' baliyu.* The upstream [mooring line] tightened, there is wind. *Parauhat kita pariyata'an, sali' anagga'-nagga'.* Let's go to the area upstream, as though fighting the current.

**par'kkal** (derivative of **d'kkal**) *v. tr.* To reserve a specific item.

**par'dda** (derivative of **d'dda**) *v. tr.* To place something firmly on a surface. *Da'a paengke'un tape'nu, par'ddahun ni papan.* Don't stand on the ends of your feet, place them firmly on the board. (*cf: d'ssal*).

**par'ppak** (derivative of **dagpak**) *v. tr.* To lay something out flat. *Par'ppakun s'mmek ma parang bo' al'kkas atoho'.* Lay the clothes out flat on the grass so that they will dry quickly.

**paro** *n.* A pair, in card games. (*cf: pagpares 1.1; syn: pares₂*)

**parola** *n.* A navigational light; a lighthouse. *Amustu kami ni Tahu, kapū'an taga parola.* We got supplies at Tahu, an island with a lighthouse. *Buwat parola, pasinag.* Like a navigational beacon, flashing.

**paru** *v. tr.* To discuss the details of a plan or proposal. *Yuk dangan, "Atulak kita ni kapū'an atawa?" Yuk dangan, "Pinaru gi', aniya' a'a."* One said, "Are we going to the remote islands or not?" The other said, "It's still to be discussed, there are people about." *Bang aniya' amatay bo' pinaru-paru, yukna, "Bang aniya' amatay buwat heya-heyanu (s'lle'-bale-puhu'),"* wa'i na aheka ganti'nu. If someone is dying and plans are discussed he (the advisor) says, "If someone of your size/importance dies (perish the thought!), then there are many to take your place." (*Thesaurus: pagbamba 1.1, pagimba-imba, pagisun 1.1, pagmiting, plano*)

**pagparu** *v. intr. aN-* To be at the discussion stage of a project. *Hal magparu, mbal gi' makatulak.* Just making suggestions, not able to leave yet. *Hal pagparu-paru, hal pagpali-pali.* Just at the proposal stage, just talking about things.

**parukunan** (derivative of **rukun**) *n.* A book setting out the five precepts of Islam. *Būk-būk alambu bo' mbal du akapal, ya niōnan kitab parukunan.* A book that is large but not thick, called the Book of Precepts. (*cf: lukun*).

**paruhun** (derivative of **duhun**) *v. tr.* To allow or cause a situation to become worse. *Ya bay pamahinangna ni ka'am kabinasahan, luhūy paruhunku gi' minnē.* The suffering that he caused you to undergo, I will make it even worse than that.

**parūl** (derivative of **dūl**) *adj. zero*1) Over-indulged; spoilt. *Buwat onde'-onde' aniya' kabilahi'anna, subay na pa'in parūl ma ai-ai kabilahi'anna hē'.* Like a child who wants something and has to be indulged with everything he desires.1.1) *v. tr.* To grant someone permission; to indulge someone. *Subay aku parūlnu angipat ba'anan hayopnu buwat bay dahū.* You must allow me to care for your many animals just as before. *Appa', angamu' aku junjung bang pa'in parūlnu ina'-mma'ku pahanti' ma deyomannu.* Your majesty, I ask a favor of you that you might permit my parents to stay in your care. (*Thesaurus: paba'id, pakuhi, palangga' 1.1, papuhun, parakag, patege', tugut 2*)

**paruli** *var. of* **paluli**

**parupang** (derivative of **dupang**) *v. tr.* To deceive or hoodwink someone. *Ata'u iya amarupang matto'ana.* He is in the habit of deceiving his parents. *Da'a kām amarupang a'a bay ngā'bi maghinang ma kabbunbi.* Don't cheat the people you get to work in your plantations. (*Thesaurus: akkal 1.1*).

**paruru'** (derivative of **duru'**) *v. tr.* To suckle a child; to breastfeed. *T'ggol magsungi'-sungi', da'a paruru'un onde' itū.* As long as he has diarrhea do not breastfeed this child. *Bang kita angaluk onde', pinaruru' atawa pinagbinuwahan.* When one comforts a child, it is given the breast or soothed with a lullaby.

**paruru'an** *n.* Something to suckle from, as a baby's feeding bottle.

**paruruwambila'** *var. of* **paruwambila'**

**paruwambila'** (var.**paruruwambila'**) (derivative of **bila'**) *adv.* On both sides; on all sides.

**pās** *n.* A permit; a license. *Mbal kām makasōd, halam aniya' pāsbi.* You cannot go in, you don't have a pass. (*Thesaurus: paspolt, sairola, sulat-kataddangan*)

**pasā** *v. tr.* To affix one's signature or mark to a document. *Bay aku pinasāhan.* I have been made to sign. (*syn: saen*)

**pagpasā** *n.* 1) A signature or personal mark used on a letter or formal document. *Sulat pagpasā itū sulat kataddangan.* This written document of divorce is a legal document. 1.1) *v. intr. aN-* To complete divorce proceedings by signing or otherwise validating a document of divorce. *Bay na kami magpasā atawa magt'kkon bokol.* We signed or put our thumbprint [on a document].

**pasabak** *v. tr.* To hold something close to one's upper body. *Sali' sapantun manuk d'nda bang pasabakna anak-anakna ma deyo' pikpikna.* Figuratively like a hen when she brings her chicks close to her body, beneath her wings.

**pasab'nnal** (derivative of **b'nnal**) *v. tr.* To speak the truth about something; to confess regarding some action, good or bad. *Pasab'nnalku ni ka'a bang ai bay hinangku.* I will confess to you concerning what I have done.

**pasāk** *v. tr.* To split wood using a mallet, heavy knife and splitting wedges. *Aniya' na angutub-ngutub, kalu a'a wa'i magpasāk kayu ma deya.* There is a distant thumping sound, perhaps a man is splitting wood inland.

**pasakay** (derivative of **sakay**) *v. tr.* To allow someone to travel in one's conveyance. *Pasakayunbi na aku bang kām kaut ni pakautanku.* Let me travel with you if you are going seawards to the place I go to.

**pasaddi** (derivative of **saddi**) *v. tr.* To discriminate, as between two persons, items, or alternatives. *Pinasaddi: ya na itu pamuwanku ka'a, ya itu pamuwanku ka'a.* Treated differently: this is what I give you [to one person], and this is what I give you [to another person].

**pasagad** (derivative of **sagad**) *v. tr.* -*an* To leave something uncared for; to abandon something. *Angay pasagarannu badju'nu itū? Halam minsan nilupi'.* Why do you leave your shirt lying around? It isn't even folded. *Buwat hinang a'a, ai-ai hinangna kapasagaran, na lawag-baranna.* Like someone's work, whatever he does is left uncared for, that is his responsibility. *Amaluluy aku, sali' pasagaranku ai-ai pah'llingnu. Sali' aku hal palagad.* I respond gently, whatever you say I just let it go. I sort of abandon it. (*Thesaurus:* **patabak**; *syn:* **pasahag**).

**pasagi'** *n.* 1) Something rectangular in section; milled lumber in contrast to trimmed roundwood. *Bang hāg sinugpatan bo' bay atibu'uk, ngga'i ka pasagi', subay kinatkatan dambila', dambila' mbal, ko' ahāp d'ppakna bang sinugpatan.* When a post that was in the round [not squared] is to be extended, it should be sawn on one side, not the other, so that its flat faces fit well when joined. *Tagambil, ya pagmama' he' kamatto'ahan, tibu'uk-bu'uk, sali' pasagi'.* Tagambil, forming the betel chew of the old people, solid and kind of square. (*Thesaurus:* **baras-baras, hanglad 1, listun, papan₁**) 1.1) *adj.* a- Rectangular in shape or section. *Ya papagan pan'nggehan inān apasagi' suntu'anna.* The base of that stand was square in design. 1.2) *v. tr.* To mill lumber so it is rectangular in section. *A: "Pasagi' bahā'?" B: "Ngga'i ka bay pinasagi', tibu'uk."* A. "Is it milled lumber?" B: "It hasn't been milled, it is uncut wood."

**pasahag** *v. tr.* To leave something uncared for. (*syn:* **pasagad**)

**pasahero** *n.* A passenger.

**pasa'atan** (derivative of **sa'at**) *n.* A moment of opportunity; a sense of appropriateness. *Ang'nda' kita pasa'atan ahāp bang kita atulak ni kapū'an. Ang'nda' kita putika'an.* We'll look for a favorable time when we leave for the outer islands. We'll look at a divination resource. *Pasa'atan sali' kagustuhan, buwat sali' kita amowa si Sa inān ni sapa'. Yukna, "Halam gi' pat'kka pasa'atanku ni sapa'."* Pasa'atan is like the feeling that things will turn out well, like when we were getting Sa to go to the creek. He said, "I don't yet have a good feeling about going to the creek." (*Thesaurus:* **kagustuhan, galak₁ 1**).

**pasa'uran** (derivative of **sa'ud₁**) *n.* A projection something snags on.

**pasal₁** (var. **impasal**; **pasalan**) *conj.* Because of; concerning; about; to do with. *Na binowa kami ni upis pasal kami bay magsalla'.* So we were taken to the Municipal building because we had been gambling. *Abakat atayku pasal panipu e' bagayku lissi.* I am hurt emotionally because of the treachery of my closest friend. *Ya na tu'ud sara' sigām angkan si Tamal subay tinunu' pinapatay pasalan bay iya makalanggal sara'.* That was simply their law, which was why Tamar should be burnt to death because she had broken the law. *Niayaran e'na pasal pusaka'.* She treated it carefully because it was something [she] inherited. *Ē' sigām maghukum pasalan panau'na ma bangku.* They have gone to court in the matter of his bank deposit. *Impasal si Li, bang kinawin makaluwas na bay sinokatnu-i, luma' mahāp-i.* Concerning Li, when she gets married the bridegift you had specified, that fine house, will appear. *Maglemong sigām maka magpuwasa sampay ni kasangoman pasalan kamatay si Sa'ul maka anakna si Jonatan.* They wept and fasted until night because of the death of Sa'ul and his son Jonatan. (*Thesaurus:* **takdil**)

**pasal₂** *n.* 1) A market or shop which sells general merchandise and clothing, rather than produce. *Bang halam aniya' s'mmek ngga'i ka pasal.* If it has no cloth goods it is not a pasal-type market. *Mbal kas'llotan pasal inān apa aheka a'a.* No gap can be found through the market-place there because there are many people. *Pasal Siasi aheka tindana, Hambilan hal magdagang-dagang.* The Siasi market has many stores, Hambilan is just selling this and that. (*Thesaurus:* **kadday, estawran, tabu' 1, tinda, tiyanggi**) 1.1) *v. intr.* aN- To attend a market. *Mbal na kami anabu' Hambilan.* We no longer go to the Hambilan market. *Mbal na kami amasal Hambilan.* We no longer go to the Hambilan market.

**pasalan** var. of **pasal₁**

**pasalassay** (derivative of **salassay**) *v. tr.* To refer a matter to someone in authority. *Bang sadja aku ya bay maghuhukum, kamemon a'a ya magpuhun atawa taga palkala', pinasalassay.* If only I had been a judge, everybody with a complete or legal dispute would have it resolved. *Pehē' ni iya saga a'a kamemon amapasalassay ba'anan palsagga'an sigām.* Everybody went to him to get their various conflicts resolved. *Pasalassayta palkala' itū ma Tuhan.* We'll leave this matter for God to sort out.

**pasalin** (derivative of **salin₂**) *v. tr.* To pass a name on to a descendant. *Pamangun ōn, sali' buwat aku inān imam bo' aku amatay na. Na, bay ōnku pinasalin ni anakku.* Perpetuating a name, it's like me being an imam and I die. Then the name that was mine is transferred to my son.

**pasalta'** (derivative of **salta'**) *conj.* During; while.

*Pagubus, pasalta' pa'in disi Yakub atulak minnē', pinat'kkahan sigām tāw aheya.* After that, while Jacob and others were departing from there, they were made to experience great fear.

**pasambu** (derivative of **sambu**) *v. tr.* To put one's own well-being first. *Amasambu iya dīna.* He is always putting himself in a favorable position.

**pasampay** (derivative of **sampay**) *v. tr.* To deliver something to its destination. *Pasampayun sulat itu ni si Be.* Deliver this letter to Be. (*Thesaurus:* **maksud 1.2, nde', papole', tukbal**₁ **1, tūd**₂, **tulun**₂ **1.1, tuyuk-tuyuk**).

**pasandigan** (derivative of **sandig**) *n.* Something solid to lean back on.

**pasang**₁ *v. tr.* To fit or install something; to make use of. *Sali' sangonta, hinangta, pinakay, pinasang, sinulug.* Like we connect something, do something, make use of, worn as clothes. *Pinasang na ilmu'na-i.* That esoteric knowledge of his put to work. *Pasangun kono' kosognu ilū.* Give it your full strength there. (*Thesaurus:* **guna 1.1, pakay**₁, **usal**)

**pasang**₂ *see:* **samapasang, pasangan**₂

**pasangan**₁ *n.* A roll or coil, of a line. *Dapasangan, sali' dangkoleng, buwat tonda'ku.* One coil, like one *koleng*, such as my trolling line. *Sali' linggi' bang t'llu p'kkosna, hatina t'llu pasanganna. Laway isāb bang t'llu pasangan bo' ab'kkat dakayu' aniya' gi' duwa.* A long net, if it has three bundles, that means it is three rolls. A long line also, if it has two rolls and one breaks, there are still two more. (*Thesaurus:* **birang 1, koleng**₁ **1, lebod 1, tongko' 1, towa'**)

**pasangan**₂ *n.* A pair of things. *Duwa pasangan.* A matching pair.

**pasangka'** (derivative of **sangka'**) *v. tr.* To push something to its limit; to carry something through to a conclusion. *Pasangka'ku lagi' pikilanku.* I still have to think it through. *Pasangka'un pam'llinu.* Give me your final buying price. *Anubali kita, pasangka'ta llingta ni Tuhan.* We make a vow, we make our words go right to God.

**pasangdan** (derivative of **sangdan**) *v. tr.* To leave something unmodified. *Bang alandos baliyu bo' kita aleha, ah'lling kasehe'an, "Pinasangdan leha itū ma landos baliyu itū?" Ah'lling man buli' inān, "Da'a pasangdanun, kulindarahun ko da'a kita magka'at."* When the wind is strong and we are sailing under a square sail, someone says, "Shall we leave the sail unchanged with the wind strong as it is?" The one in the stern says, "Don't leave it unchanged, make the adjustments so we don't get damage."

**pasangdol** (derivative of **sangdol**) *v. tr.* To provide something with support or backing. *Pasangdolun saldang. Pasangdolun isāb bang ka ang'ntan ai-ai.* Put a support under the kite band. Use a backing also when you are holding something.

**pasangdolan** (derivative of **sangdol**) *n.* **1)** A support or backing. *Bang ka an'tta' kayu subay aniya' pasangdolan.* When you are splitting firewood you should have a chopping block. (*Thesaurus:* **pamaragtolan**). **2)** Support in a dispute or court case. *Buwat saupama maghukum, aniya' pasangdolanku, aniya' abugawku amogbogan aku.* For example in a court case, I have someone to rely on, I have a lawyer who will argue on my behalf.

**pasapa** (derivative of **sapa**) *v. tr.* To make someone swear an oath. *Bay iya pasapaku ma ōn Tuhan.* I made him swear in the name of God.

**pasaplag** (derivative of **saplag**) *v. tr.* To cause something to spread widely. *Pasaplagunbi suli-suli itū ni kamemon.* Spread this story widely to everybody.

**pasara** *v. tr.* To allow someone to continue doing. *Da'a pasarahun amangan, kowa'an.* Don't let her keep eating [that], she'll get a bone stuck in her throat. *Pasarahin na iya angiskul.* Let him go to school.

**pasarang** (derivative of **sarang**) *v. tr.* To try on shoes or clothing for size.

**pasasā** *v. ditr.* To advise a community and its leadership of events that may involve them. *Buwat aniya' alungay ai-aita asal angahaka na kita ni pangatagta atawa ni botang lahat bo' supaya sigām mbal a'awam. Kita kalungayan ya amasasā.* When anything of ours is lost we naturally tell neighbors or community leaders so they are not uninformed. We who have suffered the loss are the ones to advise. (*Thesaurus:* **suna, tambuku**₁)

**pasaw** *adj.* **a-** Lacking strength or savor, as batteries or canned goods. *Tinurungan kassa' abō' mbal apasaw tībi.* Cover the glass so your tea won't be tasteless. (*Thesaurus:* **linis, litib, pupud 1.1**)

**pasayang** (derivative of **sayang**₂) *v. tr.* To raise something up high, as a flag being waved or hands raised in prayer. *Pinasayang e' kamemon a'a saga tangan sigām maka e' sigām angolang amin.* All the people raised their hands high and shouted amen.

**pasengko** *n.* The Oriental sweetlips, a fish species. *Plectorhinchus vittatus.*

**pasibukut** (derivative of **bukut**₁) *v. tr.* **1)** To disregard a warning; to reject advice. *Bay pasibukutbi in panowayku ma ka'am.* You rejected my criticism of you. *Sagō' halam bay bineya' pandu' itū e' sigām, gōm pa'in magmatuwas-tuwas, pasibukut maka magpabisu-bisu dī sigām.* But they didn't follow this teaching, becoming stubborn instead, ignoring it and making themselves deaf. (*Thesaurus:* **pagin'mbal 1, pagmari', sulak**₂, **taikut 1.1**). **2)** To break off a relationship. *Da'a pasibukutin bagaynu.* Don't reject your friend.

**pasigpi'-sigpi'** (derivative of **sigpi'**) *adv.* Closely spaced. *Duwangan aningkō' pasigpi'-sigpi', magtūy kita kinessekan.* The two of them sitting close together, us promptly ignored.

**pasihak** (derivative of **sihak**) *v. tr.* To clear a space by moving things out of the way. *Bang buwat sagmot p'llaynu, pasihaknu man sagmot kasehe'an nihinang labayan.* When you run into something like floating weeds, you make a space away from the rest of the weeds, making a way through.

**pasiha'** (derivative of **siha'**) *adv.* Going in the wrong direction. *Tamalim pasiha' kami.* We were wrongly guided.

**pasimbug** (derivative of **simbug**) *v. tr.* To add an ingredient; to mix with a larger group. *Bang a'a ala'at pinat'nna' ma nalka', mbal pinasimbug ni kasehe'anna, sabab aheka dusana.* If a man is bad he will be placed in hell, not allowed to mix with his companions, because his sins are many.

**pasindik** *v. tr.* To stand something on its edge. *Ni'isi na lai' ni lakal-lakal abō' pasindikta.* Put the plate in the rack so we can stand it on edge. (*Thesaurus:* **kīd₁ 1.1, lengag, patiring, sīp**)

**pasindungan** (derivative of **sindung₁**) *n.* A shelter. *Kayu inān, ma deyo'na pasindungan saga kahayopan.* That tree, beneath it was the shelter for the farm animals.

**pasisil** *n.* A district or region. *Ma pasisil pagdagangan ai-ai.* The area where various kinds of things are sold. *Pasisil hē'-i magbububu.* That's the locality of the people who use *bubu* traps. (*Thesaurus:* **da'ira 1, lahat, lungsud, tana'₂**)

**pasiyal** *v. intr. aN-* To go for a stroll. *Bay kami amasiyal ni Siasi ang'nda'-ng'nda' magmoto.* We walked around Siasi Town watching the voting. (*syn:* **paglunsul**; *Thesaurus:* **baklay, baybay₁, l'ngngan₁ 1.1**)

**pas'ddi** (derivative of **s'ddi**) *v. tr.* To drop something through a hole in the floor.

**pas'ddopan llaw** (derivative of **s'ddop**) *n. phrase* The period of time after sunset. *Mbal kita amangan, subay ta'abut pas'ddopan llaw atawa dai'-llaw lisag lima.* We refrain from eating. It should be when evening comes or five in the morning.

**pas'lle'** (derivative of **s'lle'**) *v. tr.* To allow someone to have a turn. *Bang angindam biyula si Be, mbal amas'lle' si Sa.* When he borrows Be's violin, Sa won't let anyone have a turn. *Pa'agungun a'a ina'an, pas'lle'un.* Let that man play the gong, give him a turn.

**pas'mmek** (derivative of **s'mmek**) *v. ditr.* To clothe someone with a specific garment or feature. *Pinas'mmekan du sigām pote'.* They are clothed in white.

**paslangan** *n.* 1) An extensive region without landmarks, as open sea or a plain without trees. **1.1)** *v. intr. aN-* To travel out of sight of landmarks. *Amaslangan kita, ma dilaut kita pi'ingga-pi'ingga patudjuhanta.* We travel without landmarks, out at sea and going wherever we set our course.

**paslod** *n.* 1) Vigor; power. *Mbal ahāp paslodna.* Its strength is not good [of a lantern jet]. **1.1)** *adj. a-* Vigorous; powerful. *Apaslod pahāp goma pamana' hē'.* The rubber of that spear-fishing gear is very strong. (*Thesaurus:* **ayron, basag 1, bastig, kosog 1.1, kulasog 1.1, kuwat-anggauta', landos 1**) **1.2)** *v. tr.* To do something with energy or strength. *Paslorin aku, maheya sakina itū.* Treat him vigorously for me, this one whose sickness is severe.

**pasok** *n.* 1) Dowels used for joining planks edge to edge. *Bang ka anapi' pelang subay aniya' pasokna.* When you fix side planks to the canoe there must be dowels. *Bang sali' paluwas kōk barena man tapi', ta'nda' pasok.* When the drill-bit comes out of the plank, the dowel will be seen. (*cf:* **sibukaw 1.1**) **1.1)** *v. tr.* To join something with dowels. *Am'lli aku pasok pamasokku pelang. B'lliku sibukaw ma a'a deya.* I will buy dowels to join my canoe [strakes]. I will buy sappan-wood from someone inland.

**pasōd** (derivative of **sōd**) *v. tr.* To bring something inside; to insert something. *Pasōrun lagi' ma aku ya s'mmek ilū.* Please bring those clothes in for me.

**pasogsogan** (derivative of **sogsog**) *n.* Something that can be clung to. *Tuhan ya pasogsogan sigā kallum-kamatay.* God is the one they cling to in life and in death.

**pasōng** (derivative of **sōng₂**) *v. tr.* To move something further along. *Pasōngun pelang si Sel bo' mbal talaran. Sō'un nihella' ma si Ji.* Move Sir's canoe further in so it won't be carried away by the current. Get Ji to drag it.

**pasōng-sōng** (derivative of **sōng₂**) *adv.* Later on. (*syn:* **gana-gana 1**).

**paspad** *v. intr. aN-* 1) To be flapping, as a flag in the breeze or the wings of a bird. *Bang kita kataluwa'an baliyu abō' pabiluk paraw, na magpaspad banog hē'.* When we are hit by the wind and the canoe is turned about, then the sail flaps. *Amaspad banog hē'.* The sail there is flapping. (*cf:* **paspas₂ 1**; *Thesaurus:* **k'llay-k'llay, pagkayab, pagk'llab, pagkotek-kotek, pagp'llay 1**) 2) To be threshing about, as the limbs of a person experiencing convulsions.

**paspas₁** *v. tr. -an* To do something quickly and steadily, as when trying to get a job finished. *Paspasin hinangnu.* Hurry to get your work done. (*Thesaurus:* **kuwat, kuyas 1, matay₂, pakosog, puspus₁, sikad 1**)

**paspas₂** *v. intr. aN-* 1) To be flapping, as something blown by wind. *Luma' si Ke atop. Bang taluwa' baliyu, amaspas bubungan sigām.* Ke's house is roofed with nipa palm. When the wind hits it, their ridging flaps. (*cf:* **paspad 1**) **1.1)** *v. tr. -an* To shake or flap something. *Pinapaspasan bistiruna, bay ap'nno' he' gusung.* Her dress was shaken vigorously, it had been full of sand.

**paspolt** *n.* A passport. *B'nnal isāb ahāp paspolt kami*

*inān sagō' halam ataddang to'ongan.* It's true those passports we had were good, but they were not really authentic. (*Thesaurus:* **pās, sairola, sulat-kataddangan**)

**passal** *n.* 1) Henna, a shrub the leaves of which provide a vivid red stain. *Lawsonia inermis.* (*cf:* **jalnang**) 1.1) *v. tr.* To color fingernails with henna stain. *Daun passal, sali' pinassal kukku d'nda.* Henna leaves, used for coloring girls' fingernails.

**passik** *v. tr.* 1) To press a catch or trigger, as on a firearm or camera. *Pinassik min t'dda bang amatta'.* Clicked once when taking a photo. *Aniya' maglapis daing, dakayu' paharap ni ka'a. Pagpassik pana', duwa. Alambang.* There are fish in layers, just one of them facing you. When the spear is released there are two. Happened unintentionally. 1.1) *v. tr.* -an To flick something with a quick movement. *Bang abase' tanganta pinassikan buwattē'.* When our hands are wet we flick them, like that.

**passikan** *n.* A spring catch; a trigger.

**passuk** *n.* A group of people combining for a shared activity, as for a fish drive or a ball game. *Na ka'am ilū dapassuk, kasehe' ilū dapassuk.* So you are one group, and you others are a group. (*Thesaurus:* **pagsaumbibi**)

**passukan** *adv.* In a group; by groups. *Passukan isāb bang angambit, bang magbola.* By the group when driving fish, or when playing ball.

**dapassuk** *n.* A single group of people.

**passut** *adj.* a- Adept; competent, of a child's ability to crawl or walk. *Apassut magl'ngngan, apassut maglele.* Adept at walking, adept at crawling.

**pasta** *n.* Loose leaf tobacco, as used in hand-rolled cigarets. *Pehē' ka am'lli siga binatang, da'a ka am'lli pasta.* Go and buy some cigarets by the piece, don't buy loose tobacco. (*Thesaurus:* **banusu, bungkal**₃ 1, **pikaroda, siga** 1, **sigupan, tabaku'** 1)

**pastan** *n.* A large, flat basin for general use. *Am'lli gi' aku pastan pamandi si Li.* I will just buy a large basin for bathing Li. (*Thesaurus:* **batiya', lumpang-lumpang, palanggana, undam**)

**pasti'**₁ *adj. zero* Accurate; confirmed, as a news report. *Pasti' kamatayna.* His death is confirmed. (*Thesaurus:* **musti-musti, sab'nnal-b'nnal, talhakit** 1.1)

**pasti'**₂ *n.* Three or more of a kind, of playing cards. *Basta daluwa kamemon, buwat t'llu-mpat-alas, ya hē' pasti'.* As long as they are all the same [suit], like three-four-one, that is *pasti'*.

**pastil** *n.* A fried pastry with a noodle filling. *Pastil ko' itū, isina bihun maka manuk.* This is a *pastil*, its contents are noodles and chicken.

**pastol** (var. **pastor**) *n.* A Christian pastor or church leader, especially of a Protestant congregation.

**pastor** var. of **pastol**

**pastul** *v. tr.* To correct or rebuke someone for unsatisfactory work or behavior. *Bang mbal ahāp*

*hinang si Mo, pastulun, Sel.* If Mo's work is not good, instruct her, Sir. (*Thesaurus:* **himoway, poway-poway, sā'**₁ 1.3, **salba**₁, **salla'**₁ 1.2, **salu'-salu', soway**)

**pasu**₁ *n.* A round clay pot with a semi-circular opening at the top. (*gen:* **pam'llahan**)

**pasu**₂ *n.* A running race.

**pagpasu** *n.* 1) A race between mounted horses. 1.1) *v. intr.* aN- To race, of mounted horses. (*Thesaurus:* **pagdanel** 1.1, **paglomba**)

**pasuku'** (derivative of **suku'**) *v. ditr.* To grant someone a portion or share; to transfer ownership. *Bowahun pi'itu bo' kakanku ati amu'-amu'anta ka ni Tuhan bang pa'in ka pinasuku'an lidjiki'.* Bring it here for me to eat and I will pray to God that you will be granted good fortune. *Yuk kamatto'ahan, "Subay ka bay kapamasuku'an bo' ka makabāk kayu lagundi'."* The ancestors said, "You must have been specially favored to find a *lagundi'* tree."

**pasugsug** (derivative of **sugsug**) *v. tr.* To unite a couple in marriage. *Aho', pinasugsug na e' imam, kinawin na bahasa.* Yes, joined in marriage by the imam, wedded so to speak. (*Thesaurus:* **kasal** 1, **kawin** 1.1, **pabatal, paglahi** 1.1).

**pasuhan** *n.* A channel or passage between obstacles.

**pasu'**₁ *n.* 1) Heat; high temperature. *Aniya' isāb pasu'na.* He also has some fever. (*ant:* **dingin** 1) 1.1) *adj.* a- Hot in contrast to cold or normal temperature. *Apasu' lahat.* The district is hot [of weather]. (*Thesaurus:* **limasu'** 1, **linganga, lingo'ot**) 1.2) *v. tr.* To heat something, especially of food or water. *Kapagpasu' du pa'in kahawa si Jo bang subu.* Jo's coffee is always being heated up in the morning. 1.3) *v. advrs.* ka-...-an To be affected by heat.

**kapasu'an** *n.* The hot period of the day.

**pasu' atay** *adj.* a- Angry; furious; in a temper. {idiom} *Saga a'a apasu' pangatayna ma bangsata.* People who are violent towards our ethnic group. (*Thesaurus:* **masu'**)

**pasu' gandum** (var. **pasu'**₃) *v. intr.* aN- To make jokes; to talk nonsense. {idiom} *Amasu' gandum ka'a-i.* You are talking rubbish [lit. you're cooking corn-maize]. *Da'a ka amasu'.* Don't talk nonsense. (*Thesaurus:* **lata**)

**pasu'**₂ *adj.* a- 1) Unhappy, as a marriage between people breaking incest restrictions. *Mbal maghalus, apasu'.* They aren't appropriate for each other, it is not propitious. 2) Unhappy, as a district experiencing continuous unrest or raiding. *Na angahalus aku man labayan itū lum'ngngan sabab bay aku tinambukuhan apasu'.* So I take a risk walking by this path because I have been advised that things are unsettled.

**pasu'**₃ var. of **pasu' gandum**

**pasu'alan** *n.* A disagreement between two people or groups.

**pasulig** (var.**pamasulig**) (derivative of **sulig**₁) *n.* A rising agent in cooking; baking powder or yeast.

**pasunu'** (derivative of **sunu'**) *adv.* Following; after that; next. *Sakali pinalinganan anakna pasunu'.* His next son was promptly called up. *Pasunu', ah'lling saga po'on kayu itū ni dampo'on kayu igira, yuk-i, "Dai' ka magsultanan kami."* After that, these trees spoke to a fig tree, saying, "Come and be king over us."

**pasung₁** *n.* 1) A restraining device (stocks); fetters. 1.1) *v. tr.* To fasten someone in stocks.

**pasung₂** *n.* A cone made of rolled paper or leaf, used as a container for small edible items. *Nihinang pasung pangisihan batung.* Made into a cone for holding peanuts.

  **pasung-pasung** *n.* A dessert of wheat or rice flour mixed with sugar and grated coconut, and boiled in a conical leaf container.

**pasuwa'** *v. ditr.* To include an onlooker in the winnings from a game, to ensure continuing good luck. *Ya anganda'ug amasuwa'.* The one who wins shares his winnings. *Bay aku pinasuwa'an duwa pilak.* I was given a two peso share [of the winnings]. (*Thesaurus:* **buwan₁ 1.1**)

**pāt** *n.* 1) The palm of the hand; the sole of the foot. 2) A handbreadth, a unit of measurement of width, about 6 cm. *Halam aniya' s'mmekna minsan dampāt.* He had no clothing, not even a handbreadth. (*Thesaurus:* **bunag, h'kka 1, sa'ang₂**)

**patabak** *v. tr.* To treat possessions carelessly, as clothes left unwashed or unfolded. *Patabakku na pantalunku dakayu'. Alisu' aku magpantalun, ya puwa'ku dakayu' ina'an.* I am treating my other trousers carelessly. I am loath to wear trousers, what I picked up were those others. *Niussap kapanyapanna, sali' mbal pinatabak.* His tools taken good care of, like they're not left uncared for. (*Thesaurus:* **kuligi'₁ 1.1, hagmak, lonseng 1, pasagad**)

**pataklayan** *n.* The forearm. (*wh:* **tangan 1**)

**patakos** *var. of* **takos**

**patagga'** *v. tr.* To place something on a support. *Pinatagga' kinakan bang bay ahaggut, ati pinasu' ma deyom pilang.* Cooked rice, when it has cooled, is placed on the supports and warmed up in the firebox. *Pamatagga'an pelang batu itū.* This rock is for propping up the canoe.

**pataggal** (derivative of **taggal₁**) *adv.* 1) Using a support. *Atuli aku pataggal ma tu'utnu.* I sleep supported by your knee. 1.1) *v. tr.* To place something on a supporting prop or spacer. *Angay halam pataggalannu si Ik?* Why did you not provide Ik with a support?

**pataggal-taggal** *v. tr. -an* To speak obliquely of something. (*Thesaurus:* **limut 1.1, pagpa'andig, pagpara'il, salig₃**)

**patagha'** *var. of* **taggaha'**

**patahad** (derivative of **tahad**) *v. tr.* To leave something in the place indicated. *Basta*

*pagkakanan, da'a pataharun mailu.* When it's a place for eating, don't leave it there. *Pataharun apa niaunan na.* Leave it where it is because it is being served up.

**patahāl** (derivative of **tahāl**) *v. tr.* To keep someone waiting for a long time.

**patahan** (derivative of **tahan₂**) *n.* A threshold; a lintel.

**patahunan** (derivative of **tahun**) *n.* A season of the year. *A'aggal daing aninduk, tu'ud ngga'i ka patahunanna, tu'ud aglawanan mūpū.* The fish are slow to bite. It is simply not their season, they are just watching for the Pleiades [to appear].

**pata'₁** *adj. a-* Fully grown; mature; marriageable. *Daing ya niōnan apata'. Buwat manusiya' isāb bang aheya, niōnan apata' na.* Fish are described as *pata'*. Like humans also when full grown, they are described as *pata'*. *Bang d'nda apata' umulna saga sangpū' ka walu', apata' na magh'lla. Bang l'lla apata' na saga duwampū' ka dda, apata' na magh'nda.* A woman is mature about the age of eighteen, old enough to have a husband. A man is mature at the age of twenty-one, old enough to take a wife. (*Thesaurus:* **hendog-hendog, lasag, sangpot 1, sibuwa, to'a 1.1**)

**pata'₂** *n.* A decorative panel across the top of a square sail. *Tapis, ya pata' leha. Man deyo' pote', man diyata' tapis.* Small pieces of patterned cloth which make up the decorative panel of a sail. White cloth below, and patterned cloth above.

**Pata'** *n.* A high island just south of Jolo Island.

**pata'u** (derivative of **ta'u₁**) *v. tr.* To inform someone of some matter; to invite someone to an event. *Halam aku bay pinata'u, minsan aku usba.* I wasn't informed [about the wedding], even though I am an elder on the male side. *Aniya' a'a bay amata'uhan aku.* There was man who let me know. (*Thesaurus:* **haka 1.1, palapal, tubad**).

**patali'an** (derivative of **tali'**) *n.* The faculty of rational thought. *Atiya' ma patali'anku.* Here in my serious thinking.

**patampal** (derivative of **tampal**) *v. tr.* To make something obvious. *Pinakisi' emponna, pinatampal.* His lips drawn back from his teeth and exposed. *Ka'llum maka kamatay, ya patampalku pagpene'anbi.* Life or death, that is the choice I put before you.

**patanog** (derivative of **tanog₁**) *adv.* Loudly. *Arūng, angalang ka patanog bo' takale.* Daughter, sing loudly in order to be heard.

**patanyag** (derivative of **tanyag**) *v. tr.* To make something widely known. *Patanogin pamatanyagnu.* Make your proclamation loud. *Tuwan Sultan, bay sa ka amatanyag sara' panoho'annu, ā?* Respected Sultan, you did make your law widely known, didn't you?

**patangkaw** (derivative of **tangkaw**) *adv.* Stealthily; secretly.

**patapukan** (derivative of **tapuk**) *n.* A place of concealment; a hiding place. *Nda'unbi ba sigām,* *ilu na sikaluwasan min saga lowang bay patapukan sigām!* Look at them, pouring out there from the holes that had been their hiding place.

**patapu'an** (derivative of **tapu'**) *n.* A place where birds land. *Ati saga sangana patapu'an kamanuk-manukan magleleyang ma tonga'an ayan.* And its branches were landing-places for the birds that fly in the skies.

**patatas** *n.* The white potato. *Solanum tuberosum. Bang kām mahē' ma lahatbi porol, hal patatas kono' ya pagkakanbi.* It is said that when you are there in your homeland you eat only potatoes. (*cf:* **panggi'**)

**pataw₁** *n.* Floats used to support the upper edges of a net. (*syn:* **butun₃**; *Thesaurus:* **sau, tangkal₂ 1, untang**)

**pataw₂** *n.* The blush macaranga, a coastal tree that provides a buoyant wood for net floats. *Macaranga tanarius.* (*cf:* **bintanag**)

**patawap** *adv.* 1) Vanishing in a flash; instantly. *Ala'an patawap kōk-tu'utna.* His kneecap gone in a flash. (*Thesaurus:* **liyaw 1.1, telop 1**) 1.1) *v. tr.* To make something vanish.

**patay₁** *n.* 1) A nameless corpse, whether of an animal or an unidentified human. *Hal kami maghangkut patay, patay sundalu Jipun.* All we did was carry corpses, corpses of Japanese soldiers. *Aniya' patay ero' ta'nda' kami ma s'llang.* We saw the corpse of a dog out at sea. (*Thesaurus:* **bangkay, mayat**) 1.1) *v. advrs. ka-...-an* To be contaminated by a dead body, as a water hole. 1.2) *v. advrs. ka-...-an* To be affected by someone's death. *Magdukka du kām, buwat hantang kapagdohon budjang kapatayan tunang.* You will lament, like the mourning of a girl over the death of her sweetheart.

**patay-saki** *n.* Death from illness. *Bang ngga'i patay-saki atawa patay-to'a, amatay iya ma pagbono'an.* If it isn't a death from illness, or death from old age, he will die on a battlefield.

**patay-akkal** *v. intr. aN-* Overwhelming the senses; baffling; mind-blowing. {idiom} *Makapatay-akkal ko' inān.* That [event] blows the mind. *Amatay akkalku ma si Ma.* My mind is baffled by Ma.

**patay-bohe'** *adj. zero* Seriously thirsty. {idiom} (*Thesaurus:* **p'kkol k'llong, toho' k'llong**)

**patay-bono'** *n.* Death by violence.

**patay-mural** *n.* Death from natural causes. *Patay-mural ko' inān.* That was a natural death.

**patay-p'llut** *n.* Death by plague. {idiom}

**patay-sabil** *n.* Death of a woman in childbirth, before she realizes that she has borne a child. {idiom}

**patay-tunung** *n.* Fish found floating, undamaged but dead for no apparent reason. *Maumu isāb bang daing aheya, buwat kāt. Patay tunung, subay da'a tō'ta. Kalu-kalu bang a'a ata'uhan pali-pali, tiniti'an he'na min t'llu maka tahik.* Often the case

with a large fish like a humphead wrasse. Dead but undamaged, we should not point at it. Perhaps if a person knows the old traditions he may sprinkle it three times with sea water.

**patay-sahid** *n.* 1) A death on someone else's behalf, such as a death in someone's defence. 1.1) *n.* The death of a woman soon after giving birth, aware that she has borne a child.

**pagpatay-patay₁** *v. intr. aN-* To pretend to be dead. *Agpatay-patay banak-banak bo' isāb a'llum.* Young mullet play dead, but they are actually alive. *Magpatay-patay kuyya', ubus allum.* The monkey played dead, and was then alive.

**patay-otas** *n.* Death from starvation. *Liyu minnitu, bang halam na, patay-otas na kami.* Other than this, when there is no more, we will die of starvation.

**patay-patay** *adj. zero* Working at less than full strength, of an engine. {idiom}

**pagpatay-patay₂** *v. intr. aN-* To run intermittently, as an unreliable engine. {idiom} *Angay malkina ilū magpatay-patay?* Why is that engine running intermittently?

**patay-to'a** *n.* Death from old age.

**papatay** *v. tr.* 1) To cause the death of something; to kill. (*Thesaurus:* **bono' 1.1, pinsan 1.1**) 1.1) *v. tr. -an* To bring about the death of a close family member, as a consequence of one's own bad luck. *A'a inān amapatayan anakna atawa h'lla-h'ndana.* That person causes the death of his/her children or spouse. *D'nda inān balu, hal amapatayan h'llana.* That woman is a widow, she was simply killing her husband. (*cf:* **kakan h'lla/h'nda**)

**patay₂** *n.* A seriously damaged item. *Patay badju' ginanti'an maka sīn. Ma aku na patay badju'.* A damaged shirt is recompensed with money. Then the damaged shirt is mine.

**patay₃** *n.* Anchovy of various species. *fam. Engraulidae. Patay-unas ma diyata' t'bbahan, patay-s'llang ahāp kinakan.* Patay-unas fish are on the tidal flats, patay-s'llang are good eating. (*syn:* **pinatay**)

**patay-batu** *n.* A species of anchovy.

**patay-lambu** *n.* A species of anchovy.

**patay-s'llang** *n.* A species of anchovy, harvested at sea rather than inshore.

**patay-unas** *n.* A species of anchovy found in areas of seagrass.

**patege'** *v. tr.* To spoil someone (especially a child) by indulging his or her wishes. (*Thesaurus:* **palangga' 1.1, parakag, parūl 1.1**)

**pate'** *v. tr.* To break something by bending it against its normal alignment. *Pate'ku tangannu!* I'll break your arm! (*Thesaurus:* **lobet, pōng 1, punggul 2, teplong**)

**pati-...-un** *aff.* Circumfix indicating the habitual behavior or character of the subject. *Asidda patihinangun d'nda inān, sali' ya na kahalianna* *amangan maka atuli.* That woman is so committed to her work, it is as though her only rest is when she eats and sleeps. *Patikakanun pahāp a'a inān, asidda alagak.* That fellow is addicted to eating, very greedy. *Patijagahun pahāp a'a inān bang magusaha.* That man is very alert when out fishing. *Patibagayun saga Milikan maina'an.* The Westerners there are very friendly. *Pati'inumun toba' si Al inān.* Al is much given to drinking palm toddy. *Buwattē' du a'a patibono'un bang amarokot bono'.* The fight-prone person is just like that when he causes fighting to flare up. *Patialopun a'a inān, kalu ma'ase'.* That man is very approachable, he may be sympathetic. *Patil'ngnganun l'lla inān.* That man is always going some place.

**patialopun** (derivative of **alop**₁) *adj.* Very approachable. *Patialopun a'a inān, kalu ma'ase'.* That man is very approachable, he may be sympathetic.

**patiase'un** (derivative of **ase'**) *adj.* Deeply compassionate; merciful. *Tuhan, patiase'un maka patitabangun.* God, full of compassion and very helpful.

**patibagayun** (derivative of **bagay**) *adj.* Extremely friendly. *Patibagayun iya ma muslim maka kristyan.* He is very friendly to Muslims and to Christians.

**patibono'** (derivative of **bono'**) *adj.* Addicted to violence. *Liyusanbi kami min saga a'a patibono'.* You rescue us from violent men.

**patikakanun** (derivative of **kakan**) *adj.* To be forever eating. *Patikakanun pahāp a'a inān, asidda alagak.* That fellow is addicted to eating, very greedy.

**patikuwan** *n.* A pot with a spout, used for making tea or coffee. (*Thesaurus:* **kapitera, kapsiyu, sili'**)

**patig** *n.* A durable cloth such as drill. *Tagihan si Mistel Am, ya taga pantalun patig.* Mr Am, the one with the drill trousers, is addicted [to the game]. (*Thesaurus:* **kapis, ispowen, lona, ma'ung, mantaluna, tolda**)

**patigangkul** (derivative of **tigangkul**) *v. tr.* To cause something to make a cracking or knocking sound. *Da'a na pa'in patigangkulun.* Don't keep making that cracking sound.

**patighan** (derivative of **tighan**) *adv.* All together; as a single unit. *Binalutan e'na tambolna maka lusuk-lusukna maka batang-suladna, bo' nilarut e'na patighan.* He took hold of its door, its doorposts and its cross-beams, and pulled them all out together.

**patiha'** *n.* The opening division of the Holy Koran, repeated in every prayer.

**patihan** *n.* A handle for gripping, as of an axe or hammer. (*Thesaurus:* **baba'an**₁**, puhan 1, tangkay 2**)

**patihinangun** (derivative of **hinang**₁) *adj.* Very hard-working. *Asidda patihinangun d'nda inān,*

*sali' ya na kahali'anna amangan maka atuli.* That woman is very hard working, her only rest is when she eats and sleeps.

**patijagahun** (derivative of **jaga**) *adj.* To be persistently watchful. *Patijagahun pahāp a'a inān bang magusaha. Man luma' dai' llaw halam bay atuli, ta'abut kohap halam atuli.* That person is extremely watchful when working for a living. From the house at daybreak he has not slept, come afternoon he [still] hasn't slept.

**pati'inumun** (derivative of **inum**) *adj.* To be a committed drinker. *Pati'inumun toba' si Al inān.* Al is much given to drinking palm toddy.

**patilas** (derivative of **tilas**₁) *v. tr.* To make known some information. *Pinatilas e' Tuhan ōnna, in iya Tuhan-asal-tuhan.* God made his name known, that he is the one who is intrinsically God.

**patil'ngnganun** (derivative of **l'ngngan**₁) *adj.* Always walking about, never at home. *Patil'ngnganun l'lla inān.* That man is always going some place.

**patilud** (derivative of **tilud**) *v. tr.* To straighten something's position. *Aniya' pelang bay pababag. Yukna, "Patilu'un pelang ilū, paglabayan a'a."* There was a canoe lying crosswise. He said, "Make that canoe straight, it's where people pass."

**patimuk** (derivative of **timuk**) *v. tr.* To bring things together in a single group. *Patimukun saga a'a d'nda-l'lla maka saga kaonde'-onde'an.* Gather the people together, women and men, along with the children.

**patinggilan** (derivative of **tinggil**) *n.* Anything one steps on to gain height; a stand for objects such as a lamp. *Subay aniya' patinggilan bo' ta'abutnu.* There needs to be a stand so you can reach it. (*cf:* **pan'nggehan**).

**pationgka'un** (derivative of **ongka'**) *adj.* Addicted to playing games, especially games that involve gambling. *Pationgka'un disi Oto'. Minsan saga lilusna pinab'llihan e'na.* Eldest son and others are addicted to playing. He has even sold his watch.

**patiring** *v. tr.* To set a flat item on its edge. *Patiringun pasagi' ilū.* Set that plank on its edge. *Pinatiring isāb bang busay.* A paddle can also be turned on edge. (*Thesaurus:* **kid**₁ **1.1, lengag, pasindik, sīp**)

**patitabangun** (derivative of **tabang**) *adj.* Exceedingly helpful.

**pat'bbud** (derivative of **t'bbud**₁) *v. tr.* To burn incense so that its smoke billows up. *Amat'bbud kami kamanyan ni mbo'.* We make incense go up in clouds to the ritual ancestor. (*Thesaurus:* **tugtug**).

**pat'kka** (derivative of **t'kka**₁) *v. ditr.* To deliver something to a destination.

**pat'kkad** (derivative of **t'kkad**) *v. ditr.* To lower something to the sea floor. *Puwas ē' pat'kkaranta isāb sau hē'. Pat'kkad pa'in, balutanta. Amalut pa'in hē', landahanta ko mbal apigtal sau hē.* After that we lowered the anchor. When it touched bottom, we held it. While we are holding we let out the line so the anchor would not be tight.

**pat'ndehan** (derivative of **t'nde**) *n.* Depth of immersion in a liquid. *Buwat pelang ahāp kayuna, anipnip ma kulit tahik, ariki' pat'ndehanna. Atawa solab bari', anipnip, sali' anipis.* Like a canoe of good timber, it sits lightly on the surface of the sea, its immersion small. Or a knife blade, thin in section, sort of thin.

**pat'nna'** (derivative of **t'nna'**) *v. tr.* To place something in a specified location. *Pat'nna'un sadja ma lamisahan.* Just put it on the table. *Bang alatag na pangalibuhanbi, na pat'nna'in dīna.* When you have looked everywhere, just leave it where it is.

   **pat'nna'an** *n.* The location of something; a residential location.

**pat'nna' hikmat** *v. ditr.* To cast a spell on someone.

**pat'nna' mbo'** *v. tr.* To invoke a ritual ancestor. *Mbal gi' kami maka'anom bubu. Itiya' gi' amat'nna' mbo'.* We cannot weave any fish traps yet. We are still engaged in invoking a ritual ancestor.

**pat'ngge** (derivative of **t'ngge**) *v. tr.* To cause something to stand; to erect a building. *Ya ta'nda' e' Nabi Yakub ma deyom uppina haronan bay pinat'ngge min tana' tudju ni diyata' langit.* What Prophet Jacob saw in his dream was a ladder that had been set up from earth to heaven. *Bay iya amat'ngge luma'na tolda ma Pasonangka'.* He pitched his tent at Pasonanca.

**pat'nggehan** var. of **pan'nggehan**

**patli'** *n.* 1) Solder (the metal alloy). 1.1) *v. tr.* To repair or join something, using a substance that requires heating; to solder something. *Amatli' aku tubu bay abila'.* I repair the lamp glass that was cracked [using molten nylon line]. (*Thesaurus:* **patlong, puna', sumpal 1.1, tupak 1.1**)

**patlong** *v. tr. -an* To repair a hole. *Patlongin munda' pelang apa asidda ang'mman. Sali' sinumpalan.* Repair the bow of the canoe because it leaks badly. Like patching it. *Pinatlongan lowang paraw si Ej maka pasok.* The hole in Ej's canoe was repaired with a dowel. *Pinatlongan emponku maka tingga'.* Fill my teeth with metal amalgam. (*Thesaurus:* **patli' 1.1, puna', sumpal 1.1, tupak 1.1**)

**patokang** *v. tr.* To slacken, of the flow of a liquid. *Subay pinatokang maka kahawa.* [The bleeding] should be reduced with coffee grounds. *Pinatokang gi' s'llog inān.* Let that current slacken a bit. (*Thesaurus:* **keyas, kō' 1.1, kontay₂, hulaw, tugut 1**)

**patokod** (derivative of **tokod**) *v. ditr.* To set someone a riddle. *Patokoranta ka, yukna.* I will set you a riddle, he said. *Bay pinatokoran si Abunnawas pasal iklug tahinang bulawan.* A riddle was put to Abunnawas about an egg being made

into gold. *Sai bay amatokoran ka'a?* Who set you a riddle? *Ata'u iya magbalikmata. Bigi ipil-ipil sina'oban maka turung kassa'. Pinatokod kita bang maingga.* He can do sleight-of-hand. An *ipil* seed is covered with a jar lid, and we are to guess where it is.

**patoho'** (derivative of **toho'**) *v. tr.* To dry out something that has become wet. (*Thesaurus:* **buwad, puhi, tumbal 1.1**).

**pato'ong** (var. **patōng**) *v. tr.* To let a liquid stand in order to settle its sediment. *Subay pinato'ong saga danjām. Mbal gi' tainum.* It should be left to settle for an hour or so. It isn't drinkable yet. *Patōngun lagi' apa ilu aheka lobogna.* Let it settle for a while because there is a lot of dirt [in the water]. (*Thesaurus:* **labay bahangi, lihaw 1.1, patuli**)

**patomo'an** (derivative of **tomo'**) *n.* The substance or thing on which something grows. *Bunga itū, ya patomo'anna banga.* The banga palm is what the nut grows on. *Bang aniya' ma ka'am patomo'an bautut atawa katol-katol atawa angalamuti' kuwitna...* If any of you have boils or itching or depigmentation growing on you...

**patōng** var. of **pato'ong**

**patong** *v. intr. pa-* 1) To be watching closely; to be attentive. *Papatong kam magsalla' ilū, saga yukbi, "Binuta'."* Keep an eye on things when playing coin games, when you say, "Secret call." (*Thesaurus:* **lawan, liling, pandang**) 1.1) *v. tr. -an* To look at something with great care. *Kapatongan sidda, mbal alungay.* It has really been noted well, it won't get lost. *Pinatongan, sali' ang'nda' sadja kita ma a'a.* Looked at carefully, just looking at someone.

**patōng dusa** (derivative of **tōng₂**) *v. tr. -an* To accuse or convict someone of an offense. *Saga a'a kasehe'an patut pinatōngan dusa.* The rest of them should be found guilty.

**patotos** (derivative of **totos**) *adv.* Definitely; decisively. *Maggara' kam patotos.* Discuss things decisively.

**patoyok** (derivative of **toyok**) *adv.* Facing down. *Oy! Onde'-onde' inān alembo patoyok. Amatay.* Hey! That child is drowned, face-down. She's dead.

**patrol** *n.* A military patrol.

**patron** *n.* The person in charge of a motor vessel, especially a passenger carrier.

   **pagpatron** *v. intr. aN-* To be the master of a ship.

**patta'** *n.* 1) A picture; a photograph; a map. *At'kka pi'itu patta' kami simuddai.* Our photos will arrive here the day after tomorrow. 1.1) A camera. (syn: **kodak**)

   **pagpatta'** *v. intr. aN-* To have one's photograph taken. *Buwat kami maka si Tu bay magpatta', magtapil.* Like Tu and me getting photographed, standing together. *Magpatta' gi' aku bo' aniya' pabeya'ku ni tunangku.* I will get a photo taken so there'll be something to send to my girlfriend.

**patuk** *n.* A tool for shaping wood; an adze. (*Thesaurus:* **likup 1, pa'at 1, sakal, sangkap 1, sosokan**)

**patuk-kapa** *n.* An axehead.

**patukawan** (derivative of **tukaw**) *n.* The origin of something said. *Ka'a ya patukawan bissala.* You are the hidden source of what was said. *Sai na bay patukawan bissala angkan aniya' bissala buwattē'?* Who was the source of the information, that such a thing should be said?

**patukbul** (derivative of **tukbul**) *v. ditr.* To move something along to the next point in a sequence. *Bang magsalla' bo' ka kapikitan, patukbulun ni aku apa aku taga utang ma ka'a.* When you are playing toss-the-coin and are financed by someone else, pass [the debt] on to me because I owe you money. *Sīn ya pinatukbul, nggai ka a'a.* It is the money owed that is transferred, not the person.

**patugut** (derivative of **tugut**) *v. tr.* -*an* To permit someone to act in a specific way. *Mbal kam pinatugutan amapatay sigām kamemon pinam'nt'dda, sabab bang kulang na manusiya' ma lahat paheka' gōm pa'in saga sattuwa talun ma sakalibutbi.* You are not allowed to kill them all at once, because if there are few people in the land, wild animals will simply increase all around you.

**patu'** *n.* A large duck; a goose. (*cf:* **etek**)

**patulakan** *n.* A confection of pounded rice flavored with grated coconut, wrapped in banana leaf and boiled.

**patula'** *n.* The dish-rag gourd. *Luffa acutangula.*

**patuli** (derivative of **tuli₂**) *v. tr.* To have a liquid settle overnight, as newly squeezed coconut oil. *Subay pinatuli p'tti' dasangom bo' yampa kin'llo' ns'llanna.* The coconut liquid should be left overnight before getting the oil. (*Thesaurus:* **labay bahangi, lihaw 1.1, pato'ong**).

**patulihan** (derivative of **tuli₁**) *n.* A sleeping place; a bed. (*Thesaurus:* **kantil₁, pabahakan, palangka'₂, palegehan**).

**patumpang** (derivative of **tumpang**) *v. tr.* To get a ride in someone else's canoe.

**patunang** (derivative of **tunang**) *v. tr.* -*an* To make a down payment in confirmation of a betrothal agreement. *Amasoho' kita pinatunangan nnompū' pilak.* We will give instructions for a down payment of sixty pesos to be made [in confirmation of this betrothal].

**patuntul** (derivative of **tuntul**) *v. tr.* To do something in an orderly way; to organize something. *Aheya to'ongan ma pangatayan kami in katuyu'bi amatuntul ma kahinangan itū.* Your diligence in organizing these activities is of great importance to us. *Pehē' ka, nde'in pamanganan itū, patuntulun ni a'a dapuna.* Off you go, return these plates, take them straight back to the owner. *Kuwat-kuwat na pinatuntul he' matto'ata man luma' bang kita angusaha.*

*Sinōngan naelon maka lutu'.* Whenever we go fishing our parents always help us thoroughly. [They] pass nylon line and food to us. *Pinauntul si Mu ni ina'na apa halam bay pinareyo' tulahan ni panday. Bay sigā ka'bbahan.* Mu was treated in an orderly way by his mother because the proper recompense had not been made to the midwife. They had been neglected. *Pauntulta ya bay mamatay, pahāpta angubul iya.* We treat the deceased with proper care, we make a good job of burying him. (*Thesaurus:* **hatul₁, temo-temo, uki'-uki'**).

**patungkid** (derivative of **tungkid**) *v. tr.* To present one's buttocks by bending over, head down. *Yuk ina', "Patungkirun buli'nu bo' ka puppu'ku."* The mother says, "Get your buttocks up so I can clean your bottom."

**patunggang** (derivative of **tunggang**) *v. tr.* To cause something to tilt. *Da'a patunggangun tu'ung itū ko da'a abu'us isina.* Don't tilt that box lest its contents spill out.

**patut** *adj.* *a*- Appropriate; fitting; adequate. *Pamuwan ka'a, minsan mbal apatut.* A gift for you, even though it is inadequate. *Sali' kita magsuli-suli, manjari mbal taluwa' ma pikilan dangan, taluwa' ma pikilan dangan, ya hē' apatut.* Like when we are discussing something, and it doesn't fit with the thinking of one of us, but does fit with the thinking of the other, that's usual. (*Thesaurus:* **amu₁, matural, subay, tōp 1.1, wajib 1**)

**kapatut** (var. **kapatutan**) *n.* Inherent or conferred right to act or claim certain privileges. (*Thesaurus:* **pagagi, pagbaya'₁, pagkawasa, pagkuma'agi, pagnakura' 1**)

**papatut** *v. tr.* To do something appropriately. (*cf:* **pa'amu**)

**tagpatutan** *n.* A person with authority to act.

**patuwa'** (derivative of **tuwa'**) *v. tr.* To present a child to its grandparents (a cultural responsibility). *Buwat si Li, angentom mbo'na bang mbal pinatuwa'.* Like Li, her grandparents lonely for her if she is not presented to them.

**pau-** *see section 2.2.2.4 Prefix:* **Cau-**

**paul** *adj.* *a*- Effective in achieving the desired result by means of what one says. *Apaul na ka'a-i, ai-ai amu'nu kabuwanan sadja!* You are an effective talker. Whatever you ask for you get! (*Thesaurus:* **labas₂ 1, talom bowa'**)

**paulak** (derivative of **ulak**) *v. intr.* *aN*- To form a floating mass, as items from a capsized boat. *Amaulak kapanyapan ma dilaut, sikagūngan.* Equipment forming a mass out at sea, floating all over the place.

**paulan** (derivative of **ulan**) *v. tr.* -*an* To expose someone by refusing them shelter. *Tinanya itū pina'alu'an, pina'llawan, pinaulanan.* Depriving someone of shelter means exposing [them] to the night air, to the sun, or rain. (*Thesaurus:* **inyaya, pa'alu', tanya₁**).

**paupalik** var. of **pulak-palik**

**paupit** n. A small bird of the forest fringes. (*gen:* **manuk-manuk 1**)

**paus** v. tr. -an To apply hot liquid or poultice to skin for the relief of pain.

**pautang** (derivative of **utang**) v. ditr. To grant someone credit or deferred payment.

**pawa** n. A steamed bun with a savory filling.

**pawas** n. 1) Misfortune; bad luck. *Anak pangaral, sali' pangahandak, amowa sukud. Aniya' isāb mbal amowa sukud, pawas.* A child of destiny, sort of favored, bringing good fortune. There are those also who bring no good fortune, just bad luck. **1.1)** adj. a- Ill-fated; dogged by bad luck. *Ala'at kono' bang aniya' niukay bang sōng sangom ma deyom maleta, sabab apawas kono'.* It is bad for a suitcase to be opened and something taken out near nightfall, it is said to be bad luck. (*Thesaurus:* **bilsut, nahas 1, paksa' 1, piyurus₂**)

**paya** adj. a- Unable to keep working due to fatigue. *Apaya ka'a ilū anulat.* You are tired from writing. *Pinunung aku, apaya to'ongan. Bay aku angahangkut bohe'.* I am famished, exhausted. I have been carrying water. (*Thesaurus:* **bale', binasa 1, b'kkat 2, husa', lumpu**)

  **pagpayahan** v. intr. aN- To be in a state of exhaustion. *Mbal kami amuwan tinapay ni saga sundalunu magpayahan.* We will not give bread to your soldiers who are experiencing exhaustion.

**paya-paya** see: **sapaya-paya**

**payakun** v. tr. To take good care of someone. *Bay kita pinayakun he'na, bay kita pinagb'llahan e'na.* She took good care of us, she did the cooking for us. *Tuhan ya makapayakun sumping kasagmotan itū, ya tatasanna dang'llaw du.* God is the one who cares for these brush flowers that last a single day. (*Thesaurus:* **ayad, ayuput, hamumu', ipat, pahilala' 1, paintul, paipid, talkin, ulip, upiksa', ussap 1**)

**payad** (var. **payag-payag**) n. A field shelter; a temporary dwelling. (*Thesaurus:* **balung-balung, kamalig, lapaw, panggung, pillayag**)

**payag-payag** var. of **payad**

**payas** n. A species of marine bivalve, edible.

**payod** adj. a- 1) Argumentative; prone to differ. *Apayod pahāp ginara'an iya inān. Mbal ameya', angalugat sidda.* He is very contrary when given advice. He won't concede, just keeps arguing. **1.1)** v. tr. To contradict someone.

  **pagpayod** n. 1) A dispute; a disagreement. *Saga pagpayod halam aniya' gunana.* Disputes that have no purpose. **1.1)** v. tr. -an To make something the focus of a dispute. *Bang aniya' billi e' sehe'ku inān, mbal aku. Subay iya inān am'lli, na ya hē' niōnan magpayod.* When my companion there has something he's buying, and I'm not willing. But he must buy; that's what is called *pagpayod* [being at cross-purposes]. *Bang kita tinuna'an bay anangkaw, na magpayod kita.* When we are accused of having stolen something, we argue [with the accuser]. (*Thesaurus:* **pagagaw-besod, pagbagod, pagbengtod, pagdiskās, pagjawab 1.1, pagsalod, pagsu'al**)

**paypay** v. tr. To blow things away. *Pinaypay e' halimpunus.* Blown away by a whirlwind. *Tapaypay hampa pai inān e' baliyu ati halam aniya' takapin minsan dangkuri'.* Those rice husks were blown away by the wind and there was nothing left, not even a bit.

**payu** v. tr. -an To keep watch over something.

**payukan** n. The hawksbill turtle. *Eretmochelys imbricata.* *Labog pamakan payukan.* Medusa jellyfish are food for turtles. (*Thesaurus:* **bokko', laggutan, p'nnu, tohongan**)

**payung** n. An umbrella; a sunshade.

**pe-** var. of **pi-**

**pēk** var. of **kagang-pēk**

**peka'** v. intr. pa- To walk with full-length paces. (*syn:* **tekang 1**)

**pekat** adj. a- Slushy, as deep mud. *Tuwan, mbal aku makal'ngngan pī'. Apekat labayan pasal bay magulan dibuhi'.* Friend, I can't go there. The way through is muddy because it rained last night. (*Thesaurus:* **lamekkat, legsak, lettak, l'bbo 1**)

**pekke'-pekke' llaw** n. phrase The hottest time of day. {idiom}

**pekkes-pekkes** n. The top part of something. *Buwa' lagundi' man pekkes-pekkes duwa būd inān.* The *lagundi'* fruit is from the top of those two mountains. *Buwat aku bay aningkō' ati an'ngge. Yuk dangan, "Aningkō' ka ma pekkes-pekkes siya ilū."* Like when I was sitting down and stood up. Someone said, "Sit there on the top of that chair." (*Thesaurus:* **punjung₁, puntuk, pussuk 1, tōng₁**)

**pekok** adj. a- Twisted or bent, of normally rigid items. *D'nda inān bay palaksu. Paglaksuna, makahantak na, agipit l'ngngonna. Ī' apekok na, nsa' na pabontol.* That woman was jumping. When she jumped she fell headlong, her arm pinned down. There it was, deformed, no longer able to straighten. *Aniya' isāb lansang apekok, ya halam tinukul pabontol.* There are nails too, that are *pekok*, the ones that aren't hammered straight.

**peko'** (var. **p'kko'**) v. tr. To fold flexible material lengthwise, bringing opposite ends together. *Pin'kko' pandan bo' mbal ahayang he' baliyu.* The pandanus is folded lengthwise so the wind doesn't dry it. (*cf:* **l'kko'**; *Thesaurus:* **lipat₁ 2, l'ppot, lupi'₁**)

**pekot** adj. a- Dried out due to loss of liquid. *Bang kita angahinang buttik subay papekotta.* When we process rosin we should dry it out. *Apekot, sali' apīt, buwat sali' buwas.* Dried out, sort of thickened, as rice sometimes is. (*Thesaurus:*

**g'tta', pīt, tagok 1)**

**pedda'** (var. **pera'**) *adj. a-* **1)** Flattened into a shallow curve. *Apedda', sali' alayas, halam aniya' bihingna, sali' pabangkat, areyo'-deyo' sala. Pedda',* sort of concave, no edge to it, sort of layered, fairly low. *Atibulung bo' apera'.* Round but flat. *Ai-ai kabantunganta buwat batu apera', patampeppet.* Anything we throw such as a flat stone, skips across the water. (*Thesaurus:* **k'bbong, ku'ub, layas**) **1.1)** *v. tr.* To press something in order to flatten it. *Doppeng hal pinera'.* A cassava cake simply pressed flat. (*cf:* **depan 1**)

**peddas** *n.* A canoe without outriggers, used by traditional houseboat Sama as auxiliary transport. (*Thesaurus:* **bangka'**)

**pedjet** *v. tr.* To squash something between hard objects. *Pinedjet saging, buwas. Bang halam aniya' suru' pamedjet, subay luwag.* Banana or rice are squashed. If there is no spoon for squashing, a ladle should be used. (*Thesaurus:* **ligis₁, pipis**)

**pega** *v. tr.* To hit a ball with a stick or bat. *Bang kami magsopbol aku amega dahū.* When we play softball I hit first.

**peged₁** (var. **pehed**) *v. tr.* **1)** To apply something to a surface, as ointment onto the skin. *Ai bay tapegednu ni barannu? Ap'nno' he' daka ai!* What did you rub onto your body? It is covered with goodness knows what! (*Thesaurus:* **pahid 1, pe'es₁, sapu 1**) **1.1)** *v. tr. -an* To remove something from a surface by wiping or rubbing. *Pegeranta tape'ta ni parang bo' ala'an tana'na.* We wipe our feet on the grass to remove the soil. *Bang kapegeran badju'ku he' paelot-ing, mbal ala'an.* If my shirt is rubbed with pilot ink, it can't be removed. *Peheranta borak ni bayhu'.* We rub face-powder onto the face.

**peged₂** **1)** *n.* A small amount; a smear of something. **1.1)** *v. tr. -an* To measure things out in small amounts. *Pineged-pegeran bang amuwan.* Measured out sparingly when giving. **2)** *clf.* Count word for tiny things. *Dampeged du pamuwan? K'nnopin gi'.* Giving such a tiny amount? Add a bit more.

**pegpet** var. of **peppet**

**pegtang-pegtang** *adj. zero* Naked; nude. *Sikapegtang-pegtangan saga onde'.* All the children were naked. (*syn:* **tantang**)

**peha** var. of **keha**

**pehak** *n.* **1)** The roe of fish. (*Thesaurus:* **hapa 1, pulling**) **1.1)** *v. intr. aN-* To produce roe. *Daing, bang angahapa mbal amehak.* A fish, if it produces milt, it doesn't produce roe.

**pehed** var. of **peged₁**

**pehē'₁** (var. **pē'₁; pī'₁**) **1)** *adv.* Yonder; that way. *Lahi-lahi kam pehē'.* Run that way. *Magkakan sigām sudju pī' ni Sibaud.* They are eating yonder in the Sibaud direction. *Ala'an kam pē'.* Leave that way. (*Thesaurus:* **pi'ilu 1.1, pi'ingga, pi'itu 1, pina'an 1.1**) **1.1)** *v. intr. zero* To go in a direction away from speaker and hearer. **1.2)** *v. tr.* To reach an objective by going in that direction. *Pinahali na tenes, sinō' pinehē' ni luma' disi Bo.* Give the *tenes* singing a rest, [we're] told to have it sent to the house of Bo and family. *Halam pa'in at'ggol, pinehē' si Da'ud e' saga kamatto'ahan.* Not much later, David was visited by the elders. *Magtūy pinehē' e' si Jo'ab sultan bo' atilaw ma iya.* The king was promptly approached by Jo'ab to ask him a question. **2)** *v. tr. -an* To place something in the specified location. *Magkarukka'an aku, amehē'an aku dīku abu, maka magbadju' karut.* I was in great distress, I put ashes on myself and clothed myself in sacking.

**pagpehē'** *v. intr. aN-* To go as a group to a place. *Agpehē'an, wa'i na sigām agpehē' kamemon.* Going yonder as a group, all of them going yonder. *Agtūy yuk Kallo', "Da'a kām magpi'-pi'."* Heron promptly said [to them], "Don't keep going there."

**papehē'an** *n.* A destination. *Anehe'an aku ka'a maingga-maingga papehē'annu.* I will accompany you wherever your destination.

**pehē'-pehē'** *adv.* Carelessly; in various places. *A'adil, sali' mbal amangan pehē'-pehē'.* Fastidious, not eating all over the place.

**pehē'-pi'itu** *adv.* There and back; here and there.

**papehē'** *v. tr.* **1)** To send someone to a place. **2)** To bring the conversation back round to an earlier topic, always used with the enclitic pronoun =ta.

**pehē'₂** (var. **pē'₂; pī'₂**) *v. tr.* To proceed in the way agreed on; to proceed with a sale when bargaining has reached agreement. *Pehē'un na, minsan aku alugi'.* Take it then, even though I make a loss. *Pi'un na. Pila b'llinu?* Agreed then. How many will you buy? *"Pē'un," yukna, "ameya' aku ma gara'nu."* "Go on," he said, "I agree with what you advise." (*Thesaurus:* **landu'₁, lanjal 1.2, lubak₂ 1**)

**pehet** *adj. a-* Hoarse; cracked, as of a boy's voice at puberty. *Apehet, akohot, lagawan, sali' du. Agohom sali', mbal alu'uy.* Hoarse, scratchy, rough-sounding, all alike. Sort of strained, unpleasant. *Ma sabab panangisna bang takdil ni onde'-onde'. Bang araran iya angolang, na apehet k'llongna hē'.* Because of his crying in regard to a child. When he cries a lot then his throat is hoarse. *Bay aku angeskwela ma Matina, ta'anuku na suwalaku, takaleku ma talingaku, yukku, "Apehet na k'llongku."* I was attending school in Matina and something happened to my voice, I heard it in my ear and thought, "My voice is cracked." (*Thesaurus:* **kohot, gohom 1, lagaw**)

**pē'₁** var. of **pehē'₁**

**pē'₂** var. of **pehē'₂**

**pē'₃** *n.* The comb of a bird. *Manuk taga pē' lengget-lenggetan.* A chicken with a serrated comb. (*Thesaurus:* **daling, label**)

**pē'₄** *v. advrs.* ka-...-an To be affected by a foreign object or substance in a wound or in one's eye. *Si Sa abulag, bay magbola kapē'an gusung matana.* Sa is temporarily blinded, he was playing ball and sand went into his eye. *Tangkobun bo' mbal kapē'an s'ggit.* Cover it over so it doesn't get trash in it. *Si Sa abulag, bay magbola kapē'an gusung matana.* Sa is temporarily blinded, he was playing ball and sand went into his eye. *Bang kita bay atuhun bo' halam magtipara, pagtuwa'ta asaplut kita ko da'a kapē'an timus-timus.* When we have been diving and haven't worn goggles, on emerging [our eyes] are rinsed so we are not affected by sea-salt. (*Thesaurus:* **bulag, lempon, puling 1.1**)

**pe'es₁** *v. tr.* -an To rub or press something over a surface, as to apply ointment to the skin. *Pe'esin kono' bihing bowa'nu.* Just rub it on your lips. *Buwat tambal, yukna, "Na pe'esin ni kamemonnu ya map'ddi' ilū."* Sali' latagun to'ongan. Of ointment for example, he says, "So rub it all over you, wherever it hurts." Like totally covering an area. (*Thesaurus:* **pahid 1, peged₁ 1, sapu 1**)

**pe'es₂** *v. tr.* -an To strike a match or ignite a fuse. *Timbak daing pine'esan.* Fishing dynamite, the fuse ignited. *Bang ka anantikan bagid, pe'esin ni nggo'an bagid.* When you are igniting a match, strike it against the matchbox.

**pelang** *n.* A type of outrigger canoe constructed with planked sides attached to a wooden hull. (*cf:* **kumpit**; *Thesaurus:* **balutu, bangka', dapang, londay, pallungan, pambot, paraw 1, pongag**)

**pelang-tonda'an** *n.* A canoe used for trolling for large fish in open water.

**pellat** *adj.* a- Parted, of edges which normally come together when at rest. (*cf:* **perat 1**)

**pellat-mata** *adj.* a- 1) Prominent, of eyes, due to retraction of the eyelids. *Ya a'a mapellat-matana hē'.* The fellow with the prominent eyes there. **1.1)** *v. tr.* -an To pull down the lower eyelid, a gesture of satisfaction at someone else's misfortune.

**papellat** *adv.* Spread open, of parts that are normally or preferably together.

**pelleng** *v. intr.* pa- 1) To go back to the point of origin; to rebound. *In sukna' inān subay papelleng ni aku.* That curse should rebound on me. *Ē' na papelleng amole'.* Gone back home. **1.1)** *v. ditr.* To return something to its source or previous location. *Alibut na pagbowahan, na halam kauli'an, pinelleng ni ka'a.* We have been around all the healers, but without any improvement. So we are bringing [him] back to you. *Bang bay dahū buli' subay tarahū munda' bo' pinelleng.* If the stern had been in front, the bow should be brought to the front in order to reverse direction. **1.2)** *v. tr.* -an To turn blame back onto the accuser. *Ōy! Aku pellengannu? Baybay*

*ka'a.* Hey! You put the blame on me? It was you [that did it]. (*Thesaurus:* **balik₂, bīng₃, bitung, hili, likid, pagbintu, pagpatimpa**)

**pellok** *n.* Various wrasses. *Epibulus insidiator* (Sling-jaw wrasse); *Coris gaimard* (Gaimard's rainbowfish); *Anampses meleagrides* (Yellow-tailed tamarin); *Anampses caeruleo punctatus* (Spotted chisel-tooth wrasse; *Anampses caeruleopunctatus* (Blue-spotted wrasse); *Halichoeres hortulanus* (Checkerboard wrasse). (*cf:* **balling**)

**pellok-s'llang** *n.* Various deep-water wrasses and rainbow fish.

**pelok** (var. **piluk**) *n.* An eyelash. (*syn:* **bū-mata**)

**pelong-pelong** *v. tr.* To prevent someone from finding his way, as by changing landmarks or putting undergrowth on the path. *Buwat ma Isla hē', bang dangan-danganta kaleya, ahawan. Paglu'udta, anā! Asagmot na. Pinelong-pelong kita. Daka pi'ingga na pal'ngnganan.* Like at Isla, when we go on our own inland, it is clear. When we slip, look! It's now weed-covered. We are prevented from finding the way. Who knows where we are going. *Pelong-pelong itū, mbal kita makatuli' lān. Pinalungay pikilanta.* This word *pelong-pelong* means we can't find the path. Our thinking is lost.

**pelot** var. of **selot**

**pende** *v. tr.* To consider something carefully, as when assessing the amount or quality of something; evaluating what someone says. *Pinende sīn bang maka'abut, mbal magtūy am'lli. Ni'nda' ya ka'abutanna.* Checks his money whether it will suffice, doesn't buy immediately. Sees how far it will go. *Pinende kakana', kalu ageret.* Checks out the cloth, it may be torn. *Pinendehan iya, hatina pinabontolan.* He is appraised, meaning that he is corrected. (*Thesaurus:* **liling**)

**pagpende** *v. intr.* aN- To weigh things up (mentally); to consider options. *Bang makanilling, magpende.* When it refers to speech it means to weigh things up.

**pendet** *v. tr.* To carry something in one hand. (*Thesaurus:* **benten, bengket, kopkop 1.1**)

**pendetan** *n.* A one-handed grasp on something. *Dabingkis ambūng bang wa'i ma pendetanta.* One pack of sago meal when it is in our [one-handed] grip.

**pene'** *adj.* a- 1) Selective. *Mbal iya amangan pehē'-pehē', subay apene'.* He doesn't eat just anything, he has to be choosy. **1.1)** *v. tr.* To choose something. *Ka'a ya amene' bang maingga paglahatan.* You be the one to choose where to settle.

**pagpene'** *n.* 1) A selective strategy when buying or selling. *Pagpakkiyaw, halam aniya' pagpene', halam aniya' pagitung.* Wholesale, no choosing, no counting. **1.1)** *v. intr.* aN- To allow buyers to choose the individual items that they prefer.

**pagpene'an** *n.* A choice between alternatives. *Ka'llum maka kamatay, ya patampalku pagpene'anbi.* Life or death, that I put before you for your choosing.

**pamene'an** *n.* A range of choices or options.

**pensang** (var. **gensang**) *adj. a-* **1)** Torn apart. (*Thesaurus:* **laklak, saksak** 1) **1.1)** *v. tr.* To tear something apart; specifically to tear a human body apart. *Na agasi itū ya anganggensang a'a inān.* Now it was this giant who tore that man apart. (*cf:* **gilay** 1)

**pentol** *adj. a-* Resistant; uncooperative. *Apentol, agagga.* Resistant, stubborn.

**pengka-pengka** *n.* The bridle on the boom of a sail to which the sheet is attached. (*cf:* **k'llat-deyo'**)

**pengka'** *adj. a-* Lamed; forced to limp. *Apengka' tape'na, buwat si An.* His leg is lamed, like An's. (*cf:* **pengkol**)

**pagpengka'** *v. intr. aN-* To be chronically lame. *Aniya' du pa'in ma sigām a'a taluwa' dugsul maka kaginisan ipul, a'a magpepengka'.* There are always people among them with ulcers and various kinds of skin disease, people chronically lame.

**pagtamengka'** *v. intr. aN-* To hobble, as when the sole of one's foot is hurt. (*Thesaurus:* **keme, ku'il, pagtongka', pukul** 1)

**pengkol** *adj. a-* Crippled, of arm or leg. *Aniya' apengkol min kaonde'-onde'na sampay ni kaheyana. Mbal na pa'in makal'ngngan, asal kariyasali.* There are those who are crippled from childhood to adulthood. They are never able to walk, a congenital defect in fact. (*cf:* **pengka'**)

**penggas** *adj. a-* Partly bare of growth. *Apenggas būd, halam niyugan dampōng.* The mountain is partly bare, no coconut palms on one half. *Apenggas kōk, suma'an bay asaki, suma'an bay binagongan. Saki ya kamaumuhanna.* Partially bald, sometimes from being ill, sometimes from being shaved. Illness is its most common cause. (*Thesaurus:* **kelas, lengas₂, ungas**)

**penggod** var. of **p'nggod**

**pepe** var. of **pespes**

**pepel** var. of **papel**

**peppet** (var. **pegpet**) *v. tr.* To wipe after defecating, in contrast to washing properly. *Da'a kām bilahi ma Bisaya' ilū, mbal amuppu', hal ameppet.* Don't fall in love with a Visayan, they don't cleanse properly, they just wipe. (*Thesaurus:* **ail, istinja', junub, puppu'**)

**pera'** var. of **pedda'**

**perat** *v. intr. pa-* **1)** To be spread wide apart, of a person's legs. *Angulangkang itū, sali' paperat tape'ta. Anuwas-nuwas kita, amatay.* Curling up, our legs sort of spread apart. We become rigid, dead. (*cf:* **pellat**) **1.1)** *v. tr.* To spread someone's legs apart. *Pinerat pa'aku he' si Ji.* Ji spread my thighs apart.

**peres** *adj. a-* Lacking in bulk; thin in cross-section. *Balatu aperes-peres, anipis. Aniya' isāb tipay aperes.* Cakes with nothing much to them, thin [in section]. There are oysters too that lack bulk.

**peret** var. of **geret**

**peret-peret₁** *v. intr. aN-* To fall in a scattered shower. *Ya pagsungi'ku ameret-meret tai'ku.* When moving my bowels, the poo shoots out. *Ameret-meret selo'.* Shooting stars flying in showers.

**peret-peret₂** *v. intr. aN-* To be prone to tearing. *Bang apagon mbal ameret-peret.* If it is durable it is not liable to tear.

**perol** *n.* A cupboard; a cabinet. *Wa'i tinau' sīn sigā mareyom perol.* Their money is stored away in a cupboard. (*Thesaurus:* **kabinet, paradol**)

**pespes** (var. **pepe**) *v. tr.* **1)** To blow a vessel off course. *Munda' tapepe e' baliyu, sali' mbal amiluk pariyata'.* The bow moved off course by the wind, sort of unable to sail against the current. **1.1)** *v. tr. -an* To affect someone's progress or direction by a strong wind. *A'a bay amusay dangan-danganna, tauwa' iya baliyu. Wa'i iya pinespesan, wa'i pinepehan.* A man paddling on his own was hit by the wind. He was blown off course. *Pinepehan he' baliyu, mbal makasagga'.* Blown off course by the wind, unable to make headway. (*Thesaurus:* **gesges, laran, loson, paghadjul-hadjul, palis₁**)

**pessek** (var. **kessek**) *v. tr. -an* **1)** To shake something off by a sudden vigorous movement. *Kessekin lalipan ma tangannu ilū.* Fling off that centipede on your hand. **2)** To treat kinfolk or former friends as if they no longer existed. *Buwat bay ta'nda'ku bitu'anunku ma pagdaingan, magtūy aku angessek. Basta bay pamikitanku kessekanku sigā.* Like when I saw my former wife at the fish market, I immediately ignored her. Anyone who has been my in-law I snub. *Duwangan aningkō' pasigpi'-sigpi', magtūy kita kinessekan.* The two of them sitting close together, and us [others] promptly ignored. *Sali' du sinigayan maka pinessekan.* Treating people as if they weren't, same as getting rid of them.

**petak** *adj. a-* **1)** Squashy; damaged by squashing. *Apetak saging, bay tagi'ik e' a'a.* The bananas are squashed, people have tramped on them. (*Thesaurus:* **biyobog, k'ddos, lodjag** 1, **lonyat, tonyak**) **1.1)** *v. tr.* To squash or pulp something.

**peteg** *n.* Various filefishes.

**peteg-kambing** *n.* The Broom filefish or the Brush-sided leatherjacket. *Monacanthus scopas.*

**peteg-pagung** *n.* The Unicorn filefish or leatherjacket. *Aluterus monoceros.*

**peteg-sapi'** *n.* The Bristle-tail or the Matted filefish. *Acreichthys tomentosus.*

**peteg-sowang** *n.* The Long-spined tripod fish. *Pseudotriacanthus strigilifer.*

**peteg-unas** *n.* The Chinese filefish or the Fan-bellied leatherjacket. *Monocanthus chinensis.*

**petong** *adj. a-* Small, of the mesh of a trawl net. *Apetong itū akiput matana, bang magnilinggi.* This word *petong* means a small mesh-size, with regard to a trawl net.

**petta'** *n.* A coracle-like vessel propelled by poling.

**peyad** *n.* 1) Fish preserved by splitting open, salting, and drying in the sun. *Am'lli aku peyad niasin kinakan.* I will buy some salted dried fish to eat. *Ya niōnan peyad ya na ukab ilū. Peyad pinehē'an asin bo' pina'llawan.* What we call *peyad* are [fish] opened up. *Peyad* have salt put on them before being sun-dried. (*Thesaurus:* **daing niasin, lumay, pundang 1, sampila'₁** 1) 1.1) *v. tr.* To preserve fish by splitting, salting and drying. *Bang kami kaut bo' aheka daing, pineyad.* When we go out to sea and there are many fish, they are dried. *Basta kami angusaha mbal kami ameyad ma deya, subay ma pelang ma dilaut.* Whenever we are at our livelihood we do not dry fish on land, it should be on the canoe, at sea. *A: "Pamagaynu lahut?" B: "Pameyadku daing."* A: "What are you using the knife for?" B: "I'm using it to split fish with." *Pād-pād daing itū tinimanan, gōm pineyad.* Rather than this fish be thrown away, better it be dried.

**peya'** *n.* A shallow container made from half a coconut shell. (**wh:** **niyug**)

**peya'-peya' kōk** *n. phrase* The dome of the skull. (*Thesaurus:* **bukakkal, kulakob**)

**peya'-peya' kōk-tu'ut** *n. phrase* The kneecap (patella). (*Thesaurus:* **lokonan, lo'atan, siku, tu'ut**)

**peyan** *v. tr. -an* To keep a close watch over something. *Peyanin pelang ko da'a tinangkaw.* Watch over the canoe so it isn't be stolen. *Ispayin si Jm hē', piligdu anangkaw. Ispayin, sali' peyanin.* Keep a watch on Jm, it is feared he may steal. Look out for him, keep watch. *Peyanin onde' ilū bo' mbal ahūg pareyo'.* Keep an eye on that child so she doesn't fall [from the house]. (*Thesaurus:* **alimata, jaga 1.2, papag, tunggu' 1.1**)

**pi-** (var. **pe-**) *aff.* Directional prefix: attaches to demonstratives to indicate directed motion. *A: "Pi'itu na ka ba!" B: "Aho', pi'ilu pa'in."* A: "Come here right now!" B: "Yes, I'll be right there." *Wa'i sigām pina'an ni Tōng Batu.* They have gone yonder to Rock Point. *Nda'un pelang pehē' ko da'a talaran.* Keep an eye on the canoe over there so it doesn't get carried away. *Pina'an gi' aku ni luma' si Lu anginum bohe'.* I will go over there to Lu's house for a drink of water. *Pehē' na ka.* Off you go. (*cf:* **pa-₄**)

**pikaroda** *n.* Tobacco in leaf form, as used in hand-rolled cigarets. (*Thesaurus:* **banusu, bungkal₃ 1, pasta, siga 1, sigupan, tabaku' 1**)

**piki-** var. of **miki-**

**pikil** *n.* 1) A thought; an idea. *Pikilna ameya' ni Sūk.* His thought was to go to Jolo. (*Thesaurus:*

**hona'-hona'**) 1.1) *v. tr. -an* To think about something. *Bang aku ni M'ddas amikilan aku angalga.* When I go to Siasi town I think about working as a porter. (*Thesaurus:* **kannal, dalil 1.1, dongdong, pagka'inagon, tali' 1.1**)

**pagpikil** *v. intr. aN-* 1) To be busy thinking. 1.1) *v. tr. -an* To give serious thought to some matter. *Pagpikilinbi kono' itu.* Please give serious thought to this. *Ya itu to'ongan bay tapagpikilanku.* This is exactly what I have been thinking about.

**pikilan** *n.* The thought process; the mind.

**pamikil** *n.* Thoughts; mental activity. (*Thesaurus:* **akkal 1, panahu'an**)

**pikit₁** *v. intr. aN-* 1) To adhere to a surface. *Mbal amikit salompas itū.* This medicinal plaster will not stick. *Aniya' lanab amikit ma tina'ina.* There is fat adhering to its intestines. (*Thesaurus:* **balut 1.1, kakkot, damil**) 1.1) *v. tr. a-, ka-..-an, -an* To glue one thing on to another.

**pagpikit₁** *v. intr. aN-* To adhere to each other, of crumbs or fragments. *Apu'aw sinanglag, akanat-kanat, subay binahug maka bohe' bo' magpikit.* The roasted cassava is crumbly, scattered, it should be moistened with water so it sticks together.

**pikit-pikit** *n.* Something that joins things by adhesion, as glue or plaster. *Am'lli aku pikit-pikit ni M'ddas pamikit kōkku apa ap'ddi'.* I will buy some plaster in Siasi to stick onto my head because it's aching. (*cf:* **salompas**)

**pikit₂** *v. intr. aN-* To marry into a kin group. *Ē, mbal aku tōp amikit ni sultan.* Whoa, I am not fit to marry into a sultan's family. *Makapikit aku ni Sūk.* I have married into a Tausug family.

**pagpikit₂** *v. intr. aN-* To become connected with a kindred through intermarriage. *Subay kam bay labay islam kamemon ampa kitam makajari magpikit-pikiti. Bang mbal ni'islam, mbal makajari.* You must all have undergone circumcision for us to be able to inter-marry. If you haven't been circumcised it is not possible. *Ahāp lagi' kitam pagpikit-pikiti d'nda-l'lla.* Better for us-incl to inter-marry, both men and women.

**pamikitan** *n.* In-laws related through one's marriage; affinal kin. (*cf:* **dangirasan**; *spec:* **ipal, mato'a**)

**pikit₃** 1) *clf.* Count word for size and value of gold coin-jewelry. (*gen:* **dublun**) 2) *v. advrs. ka-...-an* To be financed by another in a game. *Ya itu kapikitanku.* This is the person I have staked. *Bang ka magsalla' bo' ka kapikitan, patukbulun ni aku apa taga utang ma ka'a.* When you are playing toss-the-coin and are financed by someone else, pass [the debt] on to me because I owe you money. (*Thesaurus:* **hapus₁ 1**)

**pikit-dakayu'** *n.* A piece of gold coin-jewelry about 18mm in diameter, rated as #1 in the count system for such items.

**pikit-duwa** *n.* A piece of gold coin-jewelry about 28 mm in diameter, rated as #2 in the count system for such items. *Aniya' saga duwampū' ni duwampū' maka walu' sussuk ma dublun pikit duwa.* There are 20-28 carats in one #2 gold piece.

**pikit-duwampū'** *n.* A piece of gold coin-jewelry rated as #20 in the count system for such items.

**pikit-mpat** *n.* A piece of gold coin-jewelry about 35mm in diameter, rated as #4 in the count system for such items. (*syn:* **mata-kura'**, **mata-jīp**)

**piknik** *n.* A picnic.

**pagpiknik** *v. intr. aN-* To have a picnic. *Bang kita magpiknik ni Singkona magliputan kita.* When we picnic at Cincona we go by a roundabout route.

**pikpik₁** *n.* 1) A wing; a flapper; a fin. *Biradali ya taga pikpik itū ma langit.* Sky maidens these ones with wings in the sky. *Bang ma kasehe'an pikpik, bang ma kasehe'an tuntun, buwat pahi ilū.* For some it is *pikpik*, for others it is *tuntun*, as with the marine ray there. (*syn:* **kepet₁**; *Thesaurus:* **kidjang 1, tuntun₂**) 2) Fins which extend out horizontally from the sides of a plywood canoe hull.

**pikpik₂** *n.* The armpit. (*syn:* **kepet₂**)

**piku** *n.* A pick, the tool used for breaking up hard ground. *Piku itū pangalungkad tana' atuwas.* This pickaxe is for opening up hard ground. (*Thesaurus:* **bara, lalandak, pala, sangkul 1, susuwat**)

**pikul** 1) *n.* A large sack. 2) *clf.* Count word for large sacks of produce. *Bang dahatus pikul, dahatus pilak ma dangan.* If [its weight] is 100 *pikul*, then one hundred pesos is for each person.

**pidjal** *adj. a-* Squeezed dry, especially of grated cassava. *Bang aniya' panggi' bay nili'is, ginipitan na. Apidjal to'ongan, halam na taga bohe'.* When cassava has been grated, it is pressed. Really pressed dry, it no longer has liquid.

**pidjalan** *n.* The Long-tail or the Northern blue-fin tuna. *Thunnus tonggol.*

**pidju** *n.* 1) A corner or angle (especially a right-angle). *Bang ka angahinang luma' subay hāg analus man mpat pidju luma'.* When you build a house there should be main structural posts on the four corners. (*Thesaurus:* **dugu, lo'ok-lo'ok**) 1.1) *v. tr.* To cut food such as pancakes into sections. *Doppeng hal pinera' atawa pinidju.* Cassava cakes are just flattened or cut into wedges.

**pidpid** *v. intr. aN-* To tremble from cold, fear or sickness. *Amidpid iya, kabowa tāwna.* He trembled due to his fear. *Bang kami ni M'ddas bo' patumbuk ulan alandos, sali' mbal kasandalan. Amidpid na aku he' haggut.* When we go to Siasi and heavy rain falls it's almost unbearable. I tremble with cold. *Kilut-kilut tanganta, sali' magkonot maka sali' amidpid.* Our hands are shrivelled from long immersion, sort of wrinkled and trembling. *Bang kami ang'nde'an si Sel Jo ni M'ddas bo' patumbuk ulan alandos, sali' mbal*

*kasandalan. Amidpid na aku he' haggut.* When we return Mr Jo to Siasi and heavy rain falls it's almost unbearable. I tremble with cold. (*Thesaurus:* **ara'-ara' 1, k'ddil-k'ddil, kogkog, korog-korog, oro'-oro'₁**)

**pidpid isi** *v. intr. aN-* To experience intense emotion such as joy or gratitude. {idiom} *Amidpid isiku maka tatangis aku ma waktu itu ma sabab kahāp Tuhan pinalabay min saga anakna.* I am deeply moved and brought to tears at this time because of God's goodness by means of his children.

**pigi'₁** *n.* Buttocks. (*Thesaurus:* **pangkul, papa-buli'**)

**pigi'₂** *n.* 1) The grated bark or rind added to cosmetic rice paste for color. *Buwa' kayu tambu-tambu itu nihinang pigi', ya sali' borak, abō' kalas.* Fruit of the *tambu-tambu* made into grounds, like cosmetic powder, so it is pink. (*cf:* **lamud-borak**) 1.1) *v. tr. -an* To add a tinting ingredient to cosmetic powder.

**pigsik₁** *v. tr.* 1) To splash with drops or jets of water. (*Thesaurus:* **kissat, p'ssik 1.1, pulagsik, sahupput, sumpit 1**) 1.1) *v. intr. aN-* To eject a liquid; to spurt or squirt. *Bay lagutku kagong, magtūy amigsik pariyata'.* I slashed a crab with a weapon and it squirted up right away.

**pigsik₂** *v. intr. aN-* To leave a person's body, of a sickness in response to ash therapy. *Amigsik sakkinu, kinoleng ka ma abu, alanjut umulnu.* Your sickness will leave; you'll be rolled in ashes; your life will be long [a folk charm].

**pigtal** *adj. a-* 1) Pulled tight, of a rope. *Bang ligtang patokon dambila', pigtalun. Buwat kita amaling, subay samapigtal.* When one of the mast stays is slack, pull it tight. Like when changing tack, [the stays] should be equally tight. *Pat'kkad pa'in, balutanta. Amalut pa'in hē', landahanta ko mbal apigtal sau hē.* When it [the anchor] reaches bottom we hold [the rope]. While we are holding it we let out some slack so the anchor is not held too tightly. (*Thesaurus:* **d'llot 1, p'nggod 1, sandat 1**) 1.1) *v. tr.* To pull on a rope which secures something. *Ōy, da'a pigtalun.* Hey, don't pull on it.

**pigu** *var. of* **piguhan**

**piguhan** (*var.* **pigu**) *n.* A favorable outcome; good fortune. *Ta'nda' pa'in onde'-onde' he' si Anu, na, sinangbay na he'na pangā'an piguhan.* When What's-her-name sees a baby, she sings a lullaby to it in order to get the good fortune [of a pregnancy]. *Ōy, ala'at pigu pam'ssihan itū.* Hey, this fishing spot is unlucky. *Buwat h'nda si Anu halam bay maganak, bo' ta'nda' onde'-onde', na, sinangbay na he'na pangā'an piguhan.* Like What's-his-name's wife, not having a child. When she sees a baby, then she sings a lullaby to it as a way of getting good fortune [for a pregnancy]. (*cf:* **lihi 1**; *Thesaurus:* **kahandak 1, karal 1, kulis, ganta'an₁, indika 1, sukud₂ 1**)

**piha** *v. tr.* 1) To find something by looking. *Bang*

*aniya' sīn ahūg bo' angaut mbal tapiha.* If some money falls and [the sea] is murky it can't be found. *Pehē' ka amiha bahan.* Go there and look for some vines. (*cf:* **batuk**₂; *Thesaurus:* **piyung, tilluk**) **1.1**) *v. tr. -an* To find something on behalf of another. *Piha'in si Oto' d'nda minnē' pamah'nda ma iya.* Find a woman from that place for Oldest Son, to become his wife. *Piha'anta ka pat'nna'an atotog bo' aniya' amaruli ka'a.* I will find a permanent place for you so you will have someone to care for you.

**pagpiha** *v. intr. aN-* To search together for someone who is lost. *Aniya' s'ssag magpiha, aniya' s'ssag magpabā'.* There is search announcement, and there is information announcement. *Magkolebokan a'a inān, sali' ahidjul maina'an, magpiha onde'-onde' alungay.* Those people are milling around, making a noise, looking for a lost child. *Bang aku am'ssi bo' ta'abut sangom, pinagpiha na aku. Pinabukagan na aku bang at'kka ni luma'.* When I go fishing and night comes, a big search is made for me. I am scolded loudly when I get home.

**piha kutu** *v. intr. aN-* To search for lice in another person's hair.

**piha lawang** *v. intr. aN-* To look for an opportunity. {idiom}

**pamiha'an** *n.* A place where searching is done.

**pihak** *n.* A major subdivision within an ethnic group. *Bang pihak ni kami ba.* Regarding our subgroup. *Ma pihak kamemon, ma bangsa kamemon, ma bahasa kamemon.* All tribal subgroups, all peoples, all languages. (*Thesaurus:* **bangsa**₁, **ummat 1**)

**kapihakan** *n.* Diversity of subgroups within a larger ethnic grouping. *Sama kapihakan.* Sama of various other groups.

**pihit** *adj. a-* Short of money; penniless. *Apihit kami, halam aniya' pam'lli balanja'.* We are destitute, nothing to buy supplies with. *Atiksa', ya sala apihit-pihit ma kinakan.* Suffering hardship, like being quite short of food. (*Thesaurus:* **kabus, kettak, ipis 1, pulubi**)

**pī'**₁ var. of **pehē'**₁

**pī'**₂ var. of **pehē'**₂

**pi'il** *n.* Character as revealed by one's actions. *Bang ahāp pi'ilta kinalasahan kita.* When our behavior is good we are loved.

**pi'ilu** *adv.* **1)** Toward the person spoken to; going there. **1.1)** *v. intr. zero* To go towards the person spoken to. (*Thesaurus:* **pehē'**₁ **1, pi'ingga, pi'itu 1, pina'an 1.1**) **1.2)** *v. tr.* To bring or take something towards the person spoken to.

**pi'ingga** *interrog.* Where to? Going where? *Pi'ingga disi Hu?* Where are Hu and others going? (*Thesaurus:* **pehē'**₁ **1, pi'ilu 1.1, pi'itu 1, pina'an 1.1**)

**pi'ingga-pi'ingga** *adv.* Wherever; some place or other. *Minsan pi'ingga-pi'ingga papehē'annu, mbal du ka makal'ppa.* No matter where you go, you

will not escape. *Mbal makabowahan aku matto'aku bang iya bay pi'ingga-pi'ingga.* My father doesn't bring me anything when he has been to some place or other.

**pi'itu** *adv.* **1)** In this direction; towards speaker. (*Thesaurus:* **pehē'**₁ **1, pi'ilu 1.1, pi'ingga, pina'an 1.1**) **1.1)** *v. intr. zero* 'Come this way.' *Pi'itu ka, Otō'.* Come here, Son. **1.2)** *v. tr.* To bring or move something towards the speaker.

**pi'ul** *adj. a-* Dislocated, of bones. (*Thesaurus:* **pagdalisu', pagsā', pisu', pittay 1.1, possat**)

**pila** *interrog.* **1)** How many? How much? *Lisag pila?* What time? *Pilambulan na ka halam bay nilaha'?* How many months have you missed your period? *Pila hekana mareyom bulsanu ilū?* How many are there in your pocket? (*syn:* **dangay**) **1.1)** *v. advrs. ka-...-an* To be overcome by sheer numbers or mass; persuaded by the words of many people. *Kapilahan bissara. Yukku, "Salung ī' amole' aku." Jarina yukku isāb inān, "Angay ka amabā' na pa'in salung amole' na ka?"* Overwhelmed by words. I say, "Tomorrow I will go home." So then you reply, "Why do you keep saying tomorrow you will go home?" (*Thesaurus:* **pagkanam, pagtabang 1**)

**pila-pila** (var. **pipila**) *adv.* However many; beyond counting. *Aniya' saga pipila sosoho'an ma astana' sultan bay patandaw ma iya.* There were goodness knows how many servants from the sultan's house looking at her. *Dapuhunbi pila-pila ya pamuwan ka'am.* Take possession of as many are given to you. *Manjari, palabay pa'in pipila tahun, amole' sigām ni lahat.* So then, when uncountably many years had passed, they returned to their place. (*syn:* **dangay-dangay 1**)

**pilangan** *n.* How many persons?

**pilak** *n.* **1)** Silver (the metal). *Halam aniya' kapatut kami angamu' pilak atawa bulawan ma iya.* We have no right to ask for silver or gold from him. (*Thesaurus:* **bulawan 1, estenles, luyang, pittang, sawasa', tumbaga 1**) **2)** A peso, the basic unit of currency of the Philippines; money in general. *Itiya' buwananku danakannu dangibu pilak dī pilak pangandiyat kasā'anku.* Here I am giving a thousand pieces of pure silver to your brother as compensation for my fault. *Duwangibu pilak pagpo'on ya bay pang'bbahannu aku.* You left me two thousand pesos as start-up money. *Aheka pilak si Sel panganggadji' si Jy.* Sir has lots of money for paying Jy's wages. (*Thesaurus:* **landing**₂, **pinta**₁, **pisita, sīn, tustun**)

**pilad** *adj. a-* Carried away; seduced; drawn away from religious commitment. *Apilad imanku ma d'nda inān.* I am drawn away [from religious commitment] by that woman. (*Thesaurus:* **bidjak 1.1, bowa**₃, **kuti-kuti, pitna**)

**pila'** *n.* Saliva made red by the betel chew mixture; betel juice. (*cf:* **buhelo 1**)

**pilang** *n.* A cooking-enclosure insulated from flammable material by stones or a layer of sand.

*Pilang itū subay batu sukulna.* This firetable should have stones as pot supports. *Anabsab saga ni pilang, kalu aniya' panggi' kayu. Bang aniya' takakan, kakanta na, halam aniya' pagtilaw.* We sort of felt around in the fireplace, there might be some cassava. If there is food we eat it, no questions asked. (*Thesaurus:* **lapohan, pagb'llahan, sukul₂**)

**pilang-pilang** *n.* A wooden enclosure around the grave of a woman. *Nihinangan pilang-pilang bang d'nda. Niukilan isāb. Bang l'lla nihinangan sunduk.* In the case of a woman a carved enclosure is made. If a man, an upright marker is made. (*Thesaurus:* **duyung-duyung, sunduk 1**)

**pilay** *adj. a-* Physically feeble due to sickness or over-exertion. (*Thesaurus:* **komay, lamma 1, loyot**)

**pilik-pilik** *n.* 1) Creatures that make a trilling noise at night; a cicada or a tree frog. *Bang ah'lling pilik-pilik, aniya' kono' anangkaw.* When a *pilik-pilik* sings, it is said that someone is stealing. (*cf:* **tal'ngnget-l'ngnget**) 2) A metal whistle as used by school-teachers or umpires to get attention.

**piligdu** *intrj.* 1) 'Frightening!'; an expression of fear. *Piligdu, nilagut ka ma halam ta'nda'nu.* Scary, you might get slashed without your seeing. **1.1)** *adj. zero* Dangerous; to be feared. *Piligdu sangom inān, aniya' magmundu.* It may be dangerous tonight, a raid is being planned. (*cf:* **anib 1.1**)

**kapiligduhan** *n.* The danger of something bad happening. *Mbal du, halam aniya' kapiligduhan ma deyom lungsud.* Don't worry, there is no likelihood of danger inside the town.

**pilinsa** *v. tr.* To press clothes with a heated iron. *Angā' aku peya' pamilinsahan badju'.* I get coconut shells [as fuel] for ironing the shirt. *Pinilinsa bo' pinilinsa, sampay atukad pahāp.* Ironed and ironed until it's really smooth. *Da'a pinilinsahun itu-i.* Don't iron this one.

**pilinsahan** *n.* An iron, the tool for pressing clothes.

**Pilipin** *n.* The Republic of the Philippines.

**pilisu** *n.* 1) A prisoner. **1.1)** *v. tr.* To imprison someone. (*Thesaurus:* **kalabusu 1.1, jīl 1.1**)

**pillangan** *n.* Generic term for various needlefish including the Spotted halfbeak, and the Black-barred garfish. (*spec:* **jūng-jūng, sawasig, sihag₃, togeng**)

**pillaw** (var. **killaw**) *n.* A flicker.

**pagpillaw-pillaw** *v. intr. aN-* To shine intermittently; to emit a pulsating light. *Magpillaw-pillaw palita'an.* The lamp is flickering. (*cf:* **pagsiraw-siraw**; *Thesaurus:* **kiraw, kitaw-kitaw, illap, inggat, pagsinglab, tingaw-tingaw**)

**pillawan** *n.* A flicker; a brief moment. *Ma deyom dasasa'at, ma dapillawan mata.* In a moment of time, in the flicker of an eye. *Dapillawan du.* Just a flicker.

**pillayag** *n.* A field shelter built of light materials. (*Thesaurus:* **balung-balung, kamalig, lapaw, panggung, payad**)

**pilliyu** *n.* An unreliable person; a rascal or scamp. *Pilliyu a'a itu, pangalingu makalandu'.* This fellow is a rascal, excessively deceitful. *Pilliyu itū panangkaw.* A *pilliyu* is an habitual thief. (*Thesaurus:* **mundu 1, panangkaw, sugarul**)

**pagpilliyu** *v. intr. aN-* To behave irresponsibly. *Bang kami sinoho' am'lli ai-ai ma tabu' bo' angongka', magpilliyu-pilliyu kami.* When we are sent to the market to buy various things, but play instead, we are behaving irresponsibly.

**pilluwang₁** *n.* A species of fish.

**pilluwang₂** 1) *n.* A strategy for getting past defenses. 2) *v. advrs. ka-...-an* To be vulnerable to harm even though protected by a charm. *Buwat si Anu, kapilluwangan iya minsan kobolan. Bay makapah'lling sukkal tudju ni Tuhan.* Like What's-his-name, he was vulnerable despite having a protective charm. He had uttered grievous things toward God. *Buwat d'nda pali'an subay l'lla anambal iya. Kapilluwangan bang d'nda, kasukangan.* When a woman is wounded with a knife, a man should treat her. She will be vulnerable if it is a woman [who treats her], it is forbidden. *Kobolan iya angkan mbal taluwa' bang punglu'. Kapilluwangan du bang kayu.* He has magical protection so he is not harmed by bullets. He is vulnerable however if something of wood is used. *Bang ka tinimbak ma halam aniya' paniliknu iya, kapilluwangan ka.* If you are shot when you have no protective charm against it, you will be vulnerable.

**pilmi-pilmi** *adv.* Regularly; habitually. *Subay pilmi-pilmi magusaha, sali' llaw-llaw.* It is necessary to be always working and working, the same every day. (*cf:* **llaw-llaw**)

**piluk** var. of **pelok**

**pilun** *n.* Lump sugar. (*Thesaurus:* **dipinaw, sokal 1**)

**pima** *n.* A fine, lightweight cloth. *Al'kkas atoho' bang kakana' pima.* *Pima* cloth quickly dries. *Pima itū b'nnal du angalinig, bo' asalat.* It's true this *pima* cloth is glossy, but it is uncommon. (*Thesaurus:* **bildu', buwal₂, dasu, lehag, lere-lere 1, taplak₁**)

**pimping** var. of **pa'imping**

**pinaka** *adv.* Like, similar to. *Apu'aw panggi' kayu, pinaka gusung.* The cassava is crumbly, similar to sand. *Tigul, ya tahinang saruk, pinaka raun sani inān.* Nipa palm leaflets, the ones made into hats, like those sago leaves in appearance. *Bulawan pinakaluwa ambaw.* Gold like a rat in appearance. *Aniya' maina'an pinaka pangluwahan halimaw.* There was something there made to look like a great cat. *Buwat aku itū pinabeya'an lling min Siasi. Yuk taligrama, "Pinaka amatay si Anu. Sinoho' ka pasa'ut-sa'ut."*

As when I was sent a message from Siasi. The telegram said, "Looks like So-and-so is going to die. You are to come quickly."

**pina'an** *adv.* 1) Heading away from speaker and hearer. 1.1) *v. intr. zero* To go yonder, away from speaker and hearer. (*Thesaurus:* **pehē'₁** 1, **pi'ilu** 1.1, **pi'ingga**, **pi'itu** 1) 1.2) *v. tr.* To convey or send something away from speaker and hearer. *Bang kami anaggaw kagong pēk pinina'anan jinggam engkot ati tasaggaw sakketna.* When we are catching mud crabs chewing gum is put on a knot and it is caught by its nippers.

**pina'in** *v. intr. aN-* To be chatting with nothing particular in mind; to gossip. *Hal aku amina'in, ati ngā'nu la'at.* I was just chatting away and you took offense. *Amina'in-mina'in, buwat si Bu angindam katam ni aku. Yukku, "Aho', ngā'un na." Yuk si Ko inān, "Magka'at ko' ilū, da'a paindamin." Angā' la'at si Bu, bo' si Ko hal amina'in-mina'in.* Talking idly, like Bu borrowing a plane from me. I say, "Yes, take it." Ko there says, "It'll get damaged, don't lend it." Bu takes it the wrong way, but Ko is just talking for talking's sake.

**pagpina'in** (var. **pagpa'in**) *v. intr. aN-* 1) To say something to someone; to chat casually with someone. *Mbal kita makapagpina'in ni a'a inān, ala'at sadja atayna.* We can't say anything to that man, he is always in a bad temper. 1.1) *v. tr.* To refer to someone by a nickname. *Ka'a na ko' ya pinagpa'in kōk batu.* So you're the one called stone-head. *Sakali palabay minna'an dakayu' kampung si Na, ya bay pinagpa'in e' si Bo.* Right then a kinsman of Na, the one referred to by Bo. *Sai bahā' pinagpa'in e'na?* Whoever is he talking about? (*Thesaurus:* **bissala** 1.1)

**pinanaw** var. of **kalitan-pinanaw**

**pinara** *n.* The edible fruit of the pahapat tree; the mangrove apple. *Sonneratia acida.* (*cf:* **pahapat**)

**pinatay** *n.* Various species of anchovy. *fam. Engraulidae.* (*syn:* **patay₃**)

**pinate** *n.* 1) A binding technique to prevent the splitting of wooden items. *Aniya' buka' sappit, buka' sinag, buka' pinate.* There are *sappit* binding, *sinag* binding and *pinate* binding. (*Thesaurus:* **baggot**, **buka'₁** 1.1, **sappit₁** 1, **sihag₁** 1.1) 1.1) *v. tr.* To bind something using the pinate technique.

**pinda** *adj. a-* 1) Changed in appearance, condition, or location. *Bang a'a magsangsā', al'kkas apinda baranna.* When a person suffers physical hardship, his body soon changes. *Bilahi ka bahā' bang kitam apinda kaut?* Would you like it if we move [house] closer to open water? (*cf:* **sambi'** 1) 1.1) *v. intr. pa-* To move to a different place. *Tuwan, subay kam papinda ni lahat saddī, sabab aga'os na kam min kami.* Sir, you should move to a different place, because you are more powerful now than we are. 1.2) *v. tr. -an* To

alter the location or state of something. *Bang mbal sarang ma ka'a kamisita ilu, subay pinindahan ni baha'u.* If that undershirt doesn't fit you, it should be changed to a new one. *Aminda aku min pam'ssihanku itū apa halam tininduk.* I will change from this fishing spot of mine, because [my bait] hasn't been taken.

**pagpinda** *v. intr. aN-* To be constantly changing. *Buwat bubu bang dakananta na, subay sīmmatan ko da'a magpinda matana.* Like a *bubu* trap we attach its base, it should be stiffened so the mesh size doesn't keep changing. *In Tuhan mbal magputing atawa amindahan pikilanna sabab ngga'i ka iya manusiya' magpinda-pinda pikilan.* God does not lie or change his thinking because he is not a human being, constantly changing his mind.

**pinda kulis** *v. tr. -an* To change someone's adverse fate by ritually modifying his or her palm lines. {idiom}

**pindi'** *n.* 1) Various species of scallop (fan-shaped bivalves). *fam. Pectinidae. Pindi' itu sinandak maka sahapang mareyom gusung.* Scallops are speared in the sand with a fish spear. (*syn:* **lai'-lai'**) 1.1) *v. intr. aN-* To be engaged in gathering scallops. *Amindi' aku ni Sablay, kinakan.* I gather scallops at Sablay, for eating.

**pinding** *adj. zero* Pending, of a legal decision. *Pinding, amasi sala pagantung.* Pending, still sort of hanging. (*cf:* **gantung₁**)

**pindun** *n.* A type of kite flown for recreation. (*Thesaurus:* **awak-awak**, **birarul**, **taguri'**)

**pindung** *v. intr. a-* To wear an unsewn piece of cloth wrapped around the waist. *Hal apindung.* Nothing on but a cloth around her waist. (*Thesaurus:* **hampi'** 1.1, **hōs** 1.2, **pagkīmbong**, **pagsina'ul**, **siyag** 1.1)

**pinduwa'** *n.* Items for use or display inside a house. *Pinduwa', buwat saga lai, sawan, mama'an saga.* House things, like plates, drinking glasses, betel-nut box. (*Thesaurus:* **kabunyihan**, **kakaya'an**, **kalangkapan₁**, **kapanyapan**, **pahandang** 1)

**pagpinduwa'** *v. intr. aN-* To use something as decoration. *A: "Pamagaynu mama'an ilū?" B: "Pagpinduwa'ku deyom luma'."* A: "What will you use that betel-nut box for?" B: "I will use it for a decoration in my house."

**pinig** *v. tr.* To treat items individually rather than in bulk. *Pininig, binuwanan magkaniya-kaniya. Pinasaddi, ya yukku, "Ya na itu pamuwanku ka'a, ya itu pamuwanku ka'a."* Treated separately, given individually. Treated differently, as when I say, "This is what I give you [to one person], and this is what I give you [to another]." (*Thesaurus:* **kaniya-kaniya**, **paggintil**, **tabul₁** 1.1, **tarangan-tarangan**, **topod** 1)

**piniritu** (derivative of **piritu**) *n.* Fried fish or bananas.

**pinit** *n.* A species of house lizard. (*syn:* **s'ssok**;

*Thesaurus:* **pahang, tokke'₁, tokko'**)

**pinjala'** *adj. a-* **1)** Physically overworked. *Bang aheka hinang apinjala'.* Over-worked when there is a great deal to do. **1.1)** *v. tr.* To treat someone cruelly; to abuse someone. *Gom na ka pininjala' apa sidda ka agagga bang sinoho'.* You should be beaten severely because you are so stubborn when told to do anything. (*Thesaurus:* **jilaka', la'at 1.2, la'ug 1.1, pissoko', puhinga', sikla, usiba'**)

**pinjam** *adj. -an* Temporary; for the time being. *Pinjaman sadja dunya itu. Ai-ai kabaya'anta mareyom junna hal palabay min kita.* This world is not permanent. Whatever we desire here on earth just passes us by.

**pinsal** *adj. a-* **1)** Pulled together by twisting, as a tourniquet. *Sali' akasat gipitan, sali' halam apinsal to'ongan.* The pack of cassava meal is somewhat poor in flavor, as though it hasn't been tightly squeezed. *Apinsal na panggi' kayu bay nili'is, halam na bohe'na. Ma gipitan na.* The cassava that was grated is squeezed now, having no liquid. It is in a pack now. **1.1)** *v. tr.* To twist fibres together, as when making cord. (*Thesaurus:* **kolleng, lubid 1.1, tabid₁ 1**)

**papinsal** *v. tr.* To tighten the loop around the two planks of a cassava press.

**pinsan** *adj. a-* **1)** Unconscious; knocked out. *Bang kita nilassun apinsan kita.* When we are poisoned we lose consciousness. *Katumbukan si Li, apinsan.* Li was hit by something falling heavily on him, knocked out. (*Thesaurus:* **bawis₁, lipat₂ 1.1**) *v. tr.* To kill someone, usually in the context of cursing or threatening. *Pinsanta ka!* I'll kill you! *Bantungta ka maka kapa, pininsan ka!* I'll throw an axe at you, you'll be killed! (*Thesaurus:* **bono' 1.1, papatay 1**)

**kapinsanan** *n.* Severe trials. *Labay na kita min kapinsanan.* We have experienced severe trials.

**pinsil** *n.* A pencil. (*cf:* **bolpen**)

**pinta₁** *n.* Paper money; bill. *Wa'i alungay sīnku, pinta duwampū'.* My money is lost, a twenty peso bill. (*Thesaurus:* **landing₂, pilak 2, pisita, sīn, tustun**)

**pinta₂** *n.* **1)** Paint. *Am'lli aku pinta pamintaku parawku keyat maka bilu bo' ahāp, ati ōnanku Budjang Malingkat.* I will buy paint to paint my canoe red and blue so it will [look] good, and I will call it Beautiful Girl. **1.1)** *v. tr.* To paint something. *Pintahun mital itū ko da'a magka'at.* Paint this metal can so it doesn't get ruined.

**pinta-pinta** *v. ditr.* To request health or blessing from a supernatural being. *Pinta-pintahin ni mbo'. Kalu kita nirūlan.* We request health [for him] from the ancestor. Maybe we will be favored. (*Thesaurus:* **amu'-amu'**)

**paminta-mintahan** *n.* A ceremony entreating ritual ancestors for physical health.

**pintal** *n.* **1)** The bridle on a kite. *Pintal, ya pangengkotan tonton.* The pintal, to which the tethering line is tied. **1.1)** *v. tr. -an* To attach a bridle to a kite. *Pinintalan, buwat taguri'.* A bridle attached, as to a kite.

**pintas** *v. intr. pa-* **1)** To cross an intervening space; to bypass an obstacle. *Papintasun aku kono'.* Please allow me to pass. (*Thesaurus:* **labay₁ 1, likuwad 1.1, liyus 1.1, paglipuwas, pagsulabay, timbay 1**) **1.1)** *v. tr. -an* To pass by way of a place. *Mbal kapintasan Tiyanggi apa ilu aniya' mundu.* We can't go by way of Jolo Town because there are bandits.

**pinting** *n.* A pendant earring. (*Thesaurus:* **anting-anting 1, aretes, bāng₂, domelo, subang**)

**pintū'** *var. of* **pintulu'**

**pintulu'** (*var.* **pintū'**; **pinturu'**) *v. tr. -an* **1)** To teach someone something. *Amintulu', sali' amandu'an kita ni kahāpan. Pintulu', it's like teaching us what is good.* (*Thesaurus:* **hupit-hupit 1, pandu' 1, pitis₂ 1**) **1.1)** *v. ditr.* To show someone the way. *Pintulu'in kono' aku luma' disi He.* Please show me the way to He's house.

**pinturu'** *var. of* **pintulu'**

**pinutu** (derivative of **putu₂**) *n.* A starch staple such as cassava meal cooked by steaming.

**pinutu landang** *n. phrase* Cassava meal formed into small balls for steaming.

**pingkit** *n.* **1)** Clustered items. *Panganan itu aheka pingkit-pingkitna. Panganan* cakes have many clustered pieces. **1.1)** *adj. a-* Clustered together so that individual sections adhere. (*Thesaurus:* **daug 1, pulingkit, puliting, pungut 1, tundun 1**)

**pagpingkit** *v. intr. aN-* To be closely joined through some connective substance or tissue. *Buwat tape' etek, agpingkit.* Like duck's feet, joined together. *Subay aniya' pamikit bo' magpingkit.* There has to be glue for things to adhere closely.

**pinggan** *n.* A small food bowl. *Gatas pinapīt ni'isi ma pinggan.* Thickened milk put in a bowl. (*Thesaurus:* **lai', suwit**)

**pinggangan** *n.* The Starry triggerfish. *Abalistes stellaris. Pinggangan bay kinehet kulitna bo' ala'an.* A triggerfish with its skin cut in order to remove it.

**pipa** *n.* A glazed earthenware jar with a wide mouth, used mainly for storing water. (*Thesaurus:* **bingki', ka'ang, kasambagan, kibut, poga, tanāng, tangpad**)

**pipi₁** *v. tr.* To carry a child or some item by holding it to the side of one's body above the hip. (*Thesaurus:* **gapus, giba 1.1, hambin 1.1, mpit, sangbay**)

**pipi₂** *n.* The Palette surgeonfish. *Paracanthurus hepatus.*

**pipi₃** *var. of* **kalitan-pipi**

**pipi'** *v. intr. pa-* To sit with knees together.

**pipila** *var. of* **pila-pila**

**pipis** *v. tr.* To crush something between two solid

objects in order to produce powder. *Bang buwas mata' pinipis-pipis, bang buwas atahak pinedjet.* When rice is raw it is crushed between hard items, when rice is cooked it is squashed. (*Thesaurus:* **ligis₁, pedjet, tanay**)

**pipisan** *n.* A piece of coarse pottery in which rice is crushed in order to make powder.

**pipit₁** *v. tr.* **-an** To bring up a matter insistently or repeatedly. *Buwat aniya' bilahi ma anakku. Mbal kami, sagwā' minsan, pinipitan na pa'in.* For example, someone wants to marry my daughter. We don't want to, but even so they keep insisting. (*Thesaurus:* **salut 1.1**)

**pipit₂** *adj.* **a-** 1) Very low, of tide. *Apipit t'bba na llaw itu, al'ggot to'ongan.* The outgoing tide is low today, extremely low. (*Thesaurus:* **l'ggot, mulilang, t'bba 1**) 1.1) *v. intr.* **aN-** To ebb to the furthest limit of the tide. *Amipit t'bba, al'ggot sampay kaut.* The tide has ebbed right out to sea.

**pipsikola** *n.* Various aerated drinks; soft drinks. (*syn:* **kokola**)

**pipul** *n.* A vertical prop; a short house post. {rare} (*Thesaurus:* **bale₃ 1, hāg 1, lusuk-lusuk, pangtu'ud, sumpiyang, tuku 1**)

**pira** *n.* A large work knife. (*Thesaurus:* **bangkung, bari', gayang, lahut, laring lahut, sundang**)

**pira'un** *n.* The title for a ruler of ancient Egypt; Pharaoh.

**piring** *n.* Various glassfishes including the Chubby cardinalfish and the Polka-dot cardinalfish. *Ambassis spp; Sphaeramia orbicularis.*

**piritu** *v. tr.* To fry fish or bananas using oil. (*Thesaurus:* **juwalan, libusaw 1**)

**piniritu** *n.* Fried fish or bananas.

**piru'** *adj.* **a-** Partly closed, of the eyes of someone who is neither asleep nor fully awake. *Bang aku baha'u bay atuli bo' aku abati' na, apiru' mataku. Amasi lambung tinuli gi'.* When I have just woken up from sleep, my eyes are half-closed. I am still slipping back to sleep. (*syn:* **pirung-pirung**; *Thesaurus:* **k'llip, luyu'**)

**piru'-piru'** *v. intr.* **a-** To sleep briefly. *Bati'un pa'in aku. Ingga na aku bay apiru'-piru', pas'lle' pa'in ka.* Just wake me up. As soon as I have had a short sleep, then you have a turn. (*cf:* **tuli₁ 1**)

**pirung-pirung** *adj.* **a-** Partly closed, of the eyes of someone who is neither asleep nor fully awake. (*syn:* **piru'**)

**pīs₁** *n.* A square of woven cloth about 50cm each side, worn by men as a head or shoulder covering. (*Thesaurus:* **sahal₂, sulban 1, tuladjuk**)

**pīs-sinabit** *n.* A square cloth, hand-woven in a traditional pattern, worn by men as a head-covering or shoulder scarf. *Ya sowa panga'an ilū sali' luwa b'ttik pīs-sinabit itū.* The python is like the colors of this woven headcloth.

**pīs₂** 1) *v. tr.* To cut something to desired shape or size. *Sinimpay banog. Na bang buwat banog amasi*

*metohan hē', pinīs.* A sail is cut to pattern. So like when a sail is still uncut fabric, it is cut out. (*syn:* **kīs₁**; *Thesaurus:* **g'ttok-g'ttok**) 2) *clf.* Count word for slices of things. *Duwampīs pinutu.* Two slices of steamed cassava.

**pīs-pīs** *n.* Small off-cuts of paper or cloth. *Katas itu bay tin'ttok apa anahut-nahut pīs-pīsna.* This paper was chopped up fine because its snippets are very small. *Pīs-pīs itū s'mmek-s'mmek sali'.* This word *pīs-pīs* is like bits of cloth.

**pisak** *n.* Mud.

**pisang** *n.* A pineapple. *Ananas comosus. Kaheka'an pisang ma Bukidnon.* The bulk of the pineapples are in Bukidnon.

**pisaw** *n.* A small handle-less knife about four inches long. (*Thesaurus:* **kīs₄ 1, janap, laring**)

**pisawat** *n.* A device for triggering an explosion; the primer cap on a bullet. *Ya pisawatna.* Its protruding spikes [said of a floating mine]. *Pisawat pihak pangkat.* A shock from the ancestors.

**pisi-pisi** *v. tr.* To rub or squeeze something between thumb and fingertips. *Sali' onde'-onde' angandura', pinisi-pisi dambila' duru' ina'na.* Like a nursing child, squeezing her mother's other breast. *Pisi-pisihun pa'in ya tibuggul sinanglag ya amata' ilū, bo' atahak.* Just squeeze that lump of cassava meal that is still raw so it is cooked.

**pisik-pisik** *v. tr.* **-an** To splash or drop water onto something. *Kapisik-pisikan aku e' bohe' min diyata'.* I am splashed on by water from above. *Sai amisik-misik mariyata'?* Who is up there dropping water down? *Mata goyak, sōng amisik-misik, sōng abustak goyak.* A wave crest, about to splash, the wave about to burst. (*Thesaurus:* **busuwag, tata', titi'**)

**pisita** (*var.* **pista**) *n.* Coins; small change. *Tu'ud ē'-i pisita pat'nde ma mohang.* Those are simply coins that have sunk in the bilge. *Ndiya ba pista lima ilu.* Give me that five centavo coin. (*Thesaurus:* **landing₂, pilak 2, pinta₁, sīn, tustun**)

**pisni** *var. of* **pisngi**

**pisngi** (*var.* **pisni**) *n.* Cheeks (sides of face below eye). (*cf:* **samping 1**; *syn:* **papa₁**)

**pissoko'** *v. tr.* To treat someone harshly or strictly. *Da'a pissoko'unbi saga ilu' atawa balu, saga a'a liyu atawa miskin.* Do not maltreat orphans or widows, strangers or poor people. (*Thesaurus:* **jilaka', la'at 1.2, la'ug 1.1, pinjala' 1.1, puhinga', sikla, usiba'**)

**pista** *var. of* **pisita**

**pistaem** *n.* Peacetime, the historic period before the Japanese occupation of the Philippines. *Bay pistaem lagi', ya kaheka'anna salban, alahang jiyay.* When it was still peacetime, most thread was *salban*, rarely was it *jiyay* [soldiers' issue]. (*cf:* **kasannangan**)

**pisti'** *intrj.* An expression of mild surprise or annoyance. (*cf:* **pangkot 1.1**)

**pistul** *n.* A handgun; a pistol. (*Thesaurus:* **kalbin,**

kanyun 1, garan, lantaka 1, musil, sinapang)

**pistulan** *n.* The range of a pistol bullet, an approximate measure of distance. *Agtūy isāb angelle dapistulan man bihing deya.* They promptly paddled out pistol-bullet range from land.

**pisu'** *adj.* a- Dislocated or sprained, of bones. *Bang apisu', magdalisu' to'olang.* When something is sprained, the bones are dislocated. *Bang aku apisu', tinilik aku he' mma'ku.* If I am sprained my father says a charm over me. (*cf:* **hisu'**; *Thesaurus:* **pagdalisu', pagsā', pi'ul, pittay 1.1, possat**)

**pisut-pisut** *n.* A palm similar in appearance to the areca (betel nut) palm, but with nuts that are tiny and inedible. *B'tteya pisut-pisut ko' ka'a ilū.* You're no bigger than a *pisut-pisut* nut.

**pīt** *adj.* a- Becoming viscous or thickened due to reduction of liquid. *Bang buwas halam bohe'na, apīt.* When rice has insufficient water it is tacky. *Apīt ludja'ta. Subay kita anginum bohe' bo' mbal apīt.* Our saliva is sticky. We need to drink water so it's not sticky. *Tirigu itū pamapīt kinakan.* This flour is for thickening food. (*Thesaurus:* **g'tta', pekot, tagok 1**)

**pitaka** *n.* A wallet; a purse; a billfold. *Am'lli aku pitaka pangisihanku silin.* I will buy a purse as a container for my money. *Halam aniya' pitaka atawa paglutu'anan atawa taumpa' tabowabi. Angay bahā'?* You have not brought any purse or lunch container or shoes. Why not?

**pitas₁** *v. tr.* To omit an item in a sequence. *Halam amitas llaw bang magpi'itu.* He hasn't missed a day in coming here. (*Thesaurus:* **lakad 1, laktaw, lingka' 1, saliyu 1**)

**pitas₂** *adj.* a- **1)** Split or torn from main part, but not detached. *Bang daing, apitas p'ssi man bowa'na. Bang aheya tōng barena, apitas isāb kayu.* With fish a hook tears away from its mouth. If a drill bit is large, wood may break away too. (*Thesaurus:* **tebla' 1.1, te'as**) **1.1)** *v. tr.* To split or tear a section away from the main part.

**pitik** *v. tr.* To shoot something with a rubber-powered slingshot. *Bang aku kaleya amitik manuk-manuk, taluwa' ahūg pareyo'.* When I go inland shooting birds with a slingshot, they are hit and fall down.

**pitikan** *n.* A rubber-powered slingshot.

**pitik-pitik** *n.* **1)** Scattered drops. *Mbal du, hal pitik-pitik.* No matter, it's just a few drops. (*cf:* **bonok-bonok, ulan 1.1**) **1.1)** *v. intr.* aN- To rain a few drops.

**piting** *adj.* a- Sticky, as eyes on waking up. *Apiting mataku bang sangom.* My eyes stick together at night. (*Thesaurus:* **belad, bussik 1, liblib**)

**pagpiting** (var. **pagpuliting**) *v. intr.* aN- To be stuck together closely; to be matted. *Magpuliting bu'unta. Bang surayta, ya suray magsagnat. Sali' magpiting.* Our hair is matted. When we comb it

the comb gets caught. It sort of sticks together.

**pitis₁** *n.* A cake with a filling of coconut candy. (*gen:* **mamun**)

**pitis₂** *n.* **1)** Advice passed down by elders or leaders to people in their care. *Magpal'ngngan iya pitis ma tendogna.* He lays down [political] guidelines for his followers. (*cf:* **pal'ngngan**; *Thesaurus:* **hupit-hupit 1, pandu' 1, pintulu' 1**) **1.1)** *v. tr.* To give advice or instructions to the next generation. *Pinitis kita he' matto'ata, pinal'ngnganan kita pitis.* We are instructed by our elders, behavioral advice passed on to us. (*Thesaurus:* **bi'at 1.1**)

**pitis-tendog** *n.* A follower; a political adherent. (*Thesaurus:* **bebeya'an**)

**pitis-pitis** *see:* **gallang pitis-pitis**

**pitla'** *n.* An obligatory contribution to religious leaders or to the very poor. *Subay ta'abut bulan sangpū' maka duwa bo' kita magjakat pitla' ni guruta atawa ni imam angamu' apuwa.* The twelfth month is the time when we give alms to our religious teacher or to the imam, asking a blessing. (*Thesaurus:* **jakat, pagsapa'at, sarakka 1**)

**pitna** *v. tr.* -an To influence someone to do what is wrong or harmful. *Buwat bay ipal si Li, amole' na d'nda. Tinilaw iya he' sara' bang sai bay makapitnahan iya. Yuk d'nda, "Halam aniya' bay makapitnahan aku. Tu'ud baya'ku."* Like Li's brother-in-law, a woman went to his bed [to compel him to marry]. The law asked who incited her to do that. The woman said, "No one incited me. It was simply what I wanted." *Yukna, "Gge, pitnahanta ka. Nda'un ba hē', saggawun."* He said to me, "Buddy, I'm giving you some advice. See that [woman] there, grab her." (*Thesaurus:* **bidjak 1.1, bowa₃, kuti-kuti, pilad, sugi-sugi**)

**pitsa₁** *n.* A press-on bottle cap. *Depanta pitsa nihinang pangongka'an.* We flatten bottle caps to be made into toys.

**pitsa₂** *n.* A calendar date. *Pitsa pila llaw itu?* What date is it today?

**pittang** *n.* A rustless alloy of zinc, tin, and copper. *Pittang itū, estenles.* This *pittang* is non-rusting. (*Thesaurus:* **bulawan 1, estenles, luyang, pilak 1, sawasa', tumbaga 1**)

**pittay** *v. intr.* pa- **1)** To be dislocated, of bones in a joint. *Da'a ka pagulantung bo' ka mbal papittay.* Don't hang by your arms lest your bones be dislocated. **1.1)** *v. tr.* To dislocate bones. *Da'a na pittayun onde' ilū.* Don't dislocate that child [by swinging her at arms length]. (*Thesaurus:* **pagdalisu', pagsā', pi'ul, pisu', possat**)

**pitu'** **1)** *num.* Seven. *Na at'kka na kami ni Tiyanggi lisag pitu'.* So we arrived at Jolo Town at seven o'clock. **2)** *clf.* Count word for weeks as units of time.

**pitu'an** *n.* A week of seven days. (*cf:* **Ahad, dapitu'**)

**pitumpū'** *num.* Seventy.

**pituwa** *n.* 1) An authoritative teaching; an instruction (a fatwa). *Aheka lagi' angandol ma si Isa ma pituwana.* Many more believed in Jesus for his authoritative teaching. **1.1)** *v. tr.* *-an* To teach with the weight of tradition or religious principle. *Pinandu'an, ya lagi'na bang sali' mbal tapandu'an, pinituwahan to'ongan.* Teaching someone, especially if he [or she] is sort of unteachable, teaching with much authority.

**piyansa** *v. tr.* To release someone from custody on payment of money or equivalent valuables. *Ya kaheka'anna bang Sūk, tana' ya pamiyansa iya.* The most common thing with Tausug people, is to use land as bail bond [from prison]. (*Thesaurus:* **haum, jamin, l'kkat**₁ **1.1, luyal 1.1**)

**magpipiyansa** *n.* One who arranges bail for someone in custody.

**piyarul** *v. tr.* *-an* To be guarantor for someone; to back someone financially. *Mbal aku makatampal ni iya inān, apa mbal aku pinautangan. Mikipiyarul aku ma ka'a.* I don't dare to face him, because he won't give me credit. So I am asking you to go guarantor for me. *Ngā'in s'mmek sin a'a ya amiyarulan a'a liyu.* Take a garment from the man who goes guarantor for a stranger.

**piyung** *v. tr.* *-an* To find someone in a game of hide-and-seek. *Bang aniya' mital pat'ngge bo' sipa'ta, kapiyungan kita atawa tatilluk kita.* If a can is standing upright and we kick it, then we get found. (*Thesaurus:* **piha 1, tilluk**)

**pagpiyung** *n.* 1) A children's game, a kind of hide-and-seek. **1.1)** *v. intr.* *aN-* To play hide-and-seek.

**piyurus**₁ *adj.* *a-* Breaking under tension, of rope. (*Thesaurus:* **b'kkat 1, pugtul**)

**piyurus**₂ *adj.* *a-* Dogged by trouble and misfortune in every way. *Apiyurus a'a inān, ai-ai hinangna, l'ngnganna, magkangī'-ngī' sadja.* That person is dogged by trouble, whatever he does, wherever he goes, things go wrong for him. (*Thesaurus:* **bilsut, nahas 1, paksa' 1, pawas 1.1**)

**piyut** *v. tr.* *-an* To twist or wring something, as wet clothing to speed up its drying, or as a child's ears as a means of discipline. *Bang aku magdakdak piniyutan bo' ni'llawan.* When I wash clothes they are wrung out and then put in the sun.

**pagpiyut** *v. intr.* *aN-* To twist out of alignment or shape. *Atatal tapi'anna. Minsan goyak maka baliyu mbal magpiyut.* Its planking is well done. Even in rough seas and wind they will not become twisted. (*Thesaurus:* **tabid**₁ **1.1**)

**p'kkal** *adj.* *a-* 1) Coming apart; crumbling; unravelling. *Ap'kkal na panggi'-kayu bay b'lliku ma M'ddas.* The cassava meal I bought in Siasi Town is crumbly now. *Niranos nireyom ambung, pin'nnod sala bo' mbal ap'kkal.* Packed into a basket, sort of pressed down so as not to break up [into fragments]. *Ap'kkal k'llat, ya bay*

*nilubid inān.* The rope is unraveling, the one there that was re-twisted. (*Thesaurus:* **budjal-budjal, gokal, lomo 1, podjak 1, sughay**) **1.1)** *v. tr.* To release something from its compact state. *P'kkalun na lamak, pahali na baliyu.* Unfurl the square sail, the wind has stopped. *Bang pandan nijangat, bang lupis sinanggi', bang lubid pin'kkal.* Pandanus is cut into slivers, abaca is separated into strands, rope is unravelled.

**pagp'kkal** *v. intr.* *aN-* 1) To crumble, of something normally compacted. **1.1)** *v. tr.* *-an* To crumble something such as squeezed cassava. *Am'lli aku ligu pagp'kkalanku panggi'.* I will buy a winnowing basket for me to crumble cassava into.

**p'kkat** *adj.* *a-* Having the astringent (puckery) taste of unripe bananas or strong tea. *Bang ap'kkat ai-ai amikit sali' ma bowa'ta.* When things are puckery they sort of stick to our mouths. (*Thesaurus:* **kahad, pa'it 1, p'ddas, p'llod**)

**p'kkatan** *n.* The Blotched grunt, the Spotted javelinfish. *Pomadysus maculatus.*

**p'kko'** *var. of* **peko'**

**p'kkol** *adj.* *a-* 1) Choked by squeezing. **1.1)** *v. tr.* To throttle someone. *Anakna kono' bay pin'kkol he' saitan dibuhi'.* His child was reputedly throttled by a *saitan* spirit last night. *Bay aku pin'kkol he' si Ba, angeyok aheya manuk.* Ba throttled me, I squawked like a great rooster. *P'kkolun ni gonggonganna ilū.* Squeeze it by its neck.

**p'kkol k'llong** *adj.* *a-* Extremely thirsty; parched. {idiom} *Ap'kkol k'llongku.* I am dying of thirst [lit. my throat is squeezed]. (*Thesaurus:* **patay-bohe', toho' k'llong**)

**p'kkos** *adj.* *a-* 1) Enclosed in; wrapped up in. *Ap'kkos hawakanna e' sintoron taga punyal.* His waist was enclosed in a belt with a dagger on it. **1.1)** *v. tr.* To keep items together by wrapping; to tie things in a bundle. *Bay pin'kkos tape' si Ja maka badju' si Nu.* Ja's leg was bandaged with Nu's shirt. *P'kkosunbi sagmot bo' yampa tinunu'.* Bundle up the trash to be burned. (*Thesaurus:* **k'bbot 1.1, k'mmos 1, putus 1.2**)

**p'kkosan** *n.* A tied bundle; a sheaf.

**p'kkos tuwa** *n. phrase* A lock-stitch used to attach the two layers of a Sama mat. (*cf:* **buku**₁ **1, engkot 1**)

**p'dda** *adj.* *a-* 1) No longer visible; faded. *Buwat patulakanta ap'dda na, sali' hāw-hāwna ta'nda'.* Like our place of departure fading from sight, only its outline visible. **1.1)** *v. tr.* *-an* To extinguish something burning or alight; to erase something written. *Bang magtaep si Sel bo' asā', piddahan.* When Sir types and makes a mistake, it is erased. *P'ddahin lapohan.* Turn off the stove.

**pagp'dda** *v. intr.* *aN-* To keep going out, of a light or a flame. *Bang aniya' kulaet, na bo' magsiraw-siraw sidda, agp'dda.* If there is a pressure lantern and it keeps flickering a lot, it is likely to go out.

**p'dda-palom** *adj. zero* Completely hidden from sight; obscured. *P'dda-palom M'ddas, sali' halam aniya' ta'nda'ta ai-ai. Ngga'i ka angal'ddom, angulan.* Siasi Town is obscured, like we can't see anything. It is not getting dark, it is raining.

**p'ddas** *adj. a-* Acrid, metallic tasting, as of unripe citrus or coins. *Buwat sali' muntay inān sali' halam aniya' mamisna, ap'ddas, sali' akahad.* Like those lemons, having no sweetness, metallic tasting, acrid. (*Thesaurus:* **kahad, pa'it 1, p'kkat, p'llod**)

**p'ddet** *v. tr.* To squeeze something out of a container. *P'ddetin aku lansong kanu'us ilū.* Squeeze the ink of that squid out for me. *Da'a pin'ddet kalibubutku.* Don't let my boil be squeezed. (*Thesaurus:* **p'gga', p'ssit**)

**p'ddi'** *n.* 1) Pain. 1.1) *adj. a-* Painful; hurting. *Ai ap'ddi' ma ka'a?* What is painful for you? *"Arōy, ap'ddi' kōkku!" yukna ma mma'na.* "Ow, my head is aching!" he said to his father. (*Thesaurus:* **bisa 1, paglera-lera, p'llat 1.1**) 1.2) *v. advrs. ka-...-an* To be affected by pain. *Nihantu si Jo, kap'ddi'an. Bay tinawalan he' mma'na.* Jo was in pain, affected by a *hantu* spirit. His father recited a healing charm over him. *Sai kinap'ddi'an atay e' si Mma'?* Who is Dad annoyed with?

**pagp'ddi'-p'ddi'** *v. intr. aN-* To have frequent or intermittent pains. *Sali' magawam, magp'ddi'-p'ddi' sali'.* Acting unaware [of illness], with pain sort of coming and going. *Buwat nda'ta d'nda ab'ttong bo' pah'llinganta ala'at, na hal magp'ddi'-p'ddi', mbal amaluwas anak.* Like when we see a pregnant woman and speak ill of her, then she will merely have [labor] pains but will not produce a child.

**p'ddi' akkal** *adj. a-* Troubled in mind; stressed. {idiom} *Asalinggā kita, ap'ddi' akkal.* We are restless, our minds are troubled. *Sali' aniya' ai-ai ya kulangta, aniya' kasusahanta, ap'ddi' akkalta. Hatina asalinggā kitā.* As though we lack something or other, we have worries, our minds are troubled. In other words we are unsettled.

**p'ddi' atay** *adj. a-* 1) Angry about something. {idiom} *Ap'ddi' atayku ma si Oto'.* I am angry with Older Brother. *Sali' bay magbono' maglakibini, sali' amowa sīn matto'a l'lla hē' pangayu' bo' mbal amasi ap'ddi' atay matto'a d'nda.* Like a married couple having a fight, the father of the man bringing a compensation gift so that the father of the woman does not continue to be angry. *Sali' hāl aningkō', maka sali' ap'ddi' atayna bang anoho'.* He just sort of sits and gives orders as though he is angry. (*Thesaurus:* **astol 1.1, la'at-s'mmu**) 1.1) *v. intr. aN-* To become angry. {idiom} *Magdugal kita bay ai-aita, bay nna'ta, bo' wa'i alungay. Am'ddi' atayta.* We are really annoyed about our things which we had put away but which are now lost. We have become angry. 1.2) *v. tr. a-, ka-..-an,*

-*an* To be annoyed at someone; to feel angry with. {idiom} *Ya makap'ddi'an atayna bay sigā maglegot.* What made him angry was them playing dice.

**pagp'ddi' atay** *n. phrase* 1) Irritability; anger. *Palabayta na ya pagp'ddi' atayta bay. K'llo'ta imam mikisugsug kita tawbat.* We put behind us what we had been angry about. We get the imam to pray the forgiveness prayer over us. 1.1) *v. tr.* To be angry about something.

**p'ddi' napas** *adj. a-* Deeply distressed, as by a death or disaster. {idiom} *Ap'ddi' napasta bang aniya' ahāp amatay.* We experience extreme distress when a good man dies.

**p'ddi' tai'** *adj. a-* Having a painful bowel movement. {idiom}

**pagkap'ddi'an** *v. intr. aN-* To be experiencing pain.

**p'ddon** *adj. a-* Capable of holding one's breath for a considerable time. *Ap'ddon iya itū atuhun.* He can hold his breath when diving. *Mbal aku makap'ddon bang lalom sangpū'.* I am not able to hold my breath when it is ten [fathoms] deep.

**p'ddu** (var. **p'ddulu**) *n.* 1) Bile; the gall bladder. *Alak ē', p'ddu daing ssana.* That liquor, it tastes like fish bile. 2) Bitterness (of spirit); emotional pain. *Pa'it min p'dduluku.* The depth of my sorrow [lit. the bitterness of my gall].

**p'ddulu** var. of **p'ddu**

**p'ddut** *adj. a-* Insubstantial, quickly worn out, of fabric. (*cf:* **guya'**)

**p'ggad** *n.* The soft palate (roof of mouth).

**p'gga'** *v. tr.* To squeeze liquid from semi-solid material such as grated coconut or tuberous vegetables. *Angali'is gi' aku lahing bo' p'gga'anku.* I will just grate a coconut and squeeze its liquid out. *Am'gga' kita bohe'na tahinang hali ampa binugbug, tinompe', pangamirul.* We squeeze out its water [of boiled cassava], producing starch to be made into porridge or a pancake, or for starching laundry. (*Thesaurus:* **p'ddet, p'ssit**)

**p'ggal** *adj. a-* Devoid of people; deserted. *Magla'anan a'a kamemon, ap'ggal deyom paglahat.* All the people are leaving, the place is empty. (*Thesaurus:* **do'ag**)

**p'ggong** *v. tr.* To persuade someone against his or her will. (*Thesaurus:* **abiyug, agpot 1, angin, egot-egot, logos 1, panhot, poleggaw**)

**p'ggos** *adj. a-* Crushed and no longer rigid, of long items such as bamboo. *Ap'ggos pa'in bahu' banog ma dilaut, na bang aniya' hapidna mbal anūy.* When a boom of a sail cracks at sea and there is a support for it, then it will not go on [to break completely]. *Ap'ggos p'ttung, halam gi' apōng.* The bamboo [pole] is partly crushed, not yet broken. (*Thesaurus:* **lagtu' 1, p'ssa' 1**)

**p'ggot** *n.* Various triggerfish, including the Whitetailed triggerfish. *fam. Balistidae, Melichthys vidua.* (*cf:* **kuput**)

**p'ggot-bisaya'** *n.* The Blackbar triggerfish; the Whitebarred triggerfish. *Balistes aculeatus.*

**p'ggot-keyat-bowa'** *n.* The Red-mouthed triggerfish. *Balistes radula.*

**p'ggot-jipun** *n.* The Orange-lined triggerfish. *Balistapus undulatus.*

**p'ggot-mangsi'** *n.* The Clown triggerfish; the Yellow-blotched triggerfish. *Balistes conspicillum.*

**p'ggot-pote'** *n.* A species of triggerfish.

**p'ggot-punsu** *n.* The Rectangular triggerfish. *Balistes rectangulus.*

**p'ggot-p'ggot** *n.* Bad temper; irritability. *Pat'kka p'ggot-p'ggotna, astol atayna.* When his irritation hits him, he gets angry. (*Thesaurus:* **kalintaw, dole'** 1, **dugal** 1, **giyagas, s'ngngot₁** 1, **sunggud**)

**p'lla'** *adj. a-* Ripening, as indicated by color. *Ōy, ap'lla' sadja ma diyata' wanni inān.* Say, those mangos up there all look ripe.

**p'llat** *n.* 1) A sharp, stinging pain. 1.1) *v. advrs. ka-...-an* To be affected by painful smarting. *Pagtambalku bakat onde' itū, magtūy anangis apa kap'llatan.* When I applied ointment to this child's cut, she promptly cried because she was affected by the painful smarting. (*Thesaurus:* **bisa** 1, **paglera-lera, p'ddi'** 1.1)

**p'llay** *v. intr. pa-* 1) To change direction while moving, of a sailing vessel or someone walking. *Hal pap'llay-p'llay amole'.* He goes this way and that on his way home. 1.1) *v. tr.* To change direction abruptly, as to avoid an obstacle. *Bang buwat sagmot, p'llaynu, pasihaknu man sagmot kasehe'an, nihinang labayan.* When it is something like [floating] trash, you turn to avoid it, you back away from other trash, making a way through. *Gana-gana isāb p'llayku kulaet.* In a while I'll swing the lantern around.

**pagp'llay** *v. intr. aN-* 1) To move to and fro, as a canoe due to wind or current. (*Thesaurus:* **k'llay-k'llay, pagkayab, pagk'llab, pagkotek-kotek, paspad** 1) 1.1) *v. tr.* To allow or cause something to swing to and fro in wind or current. *Bang kita amusay da'a pagp'llayun munda', pabontolun sadja.* When we paddle don't have the bow swinging about, just keep it straight.

**p'llod** *adj. a-* Acrid; metallic tasting, as unripe citrus. *T'bbahan ya bang mbal ahāp kakose'ta, asidda ap'llod. Ya lagi'na bāt-batunan bang mbal kinagisan, maka bang mbal nila'anan ya ma deyomna. Tananamta mareyom k'llongta.* Strand foods, when our washing is not thorough, are very acrid. *Bantunan* type sea cucumbers are even more so when not scraped and their insides removed. We taste it in our throat. *Basta bay tauwa' laring, ya hē' ap'llod, ya limpa' laring.* Whenever something has been touched with a knife, it is metallic-tasting, the imprint of the knife. *Bang sīn ni'isi ni bowa', ap'llod.* When coins are put in the mouth, that's *p'llod.*

(*Thesaurus:* **kahad, pa'it** 1, **p'kkat, p'ddas**)

**p'llong** *n.* A hole in the ground or in a floor. (*Thesaurus:* **kehe** 1, **lowang** 1, **songab** 1)

**p'llos** var. of **p'llus**

**p'llus** (var. **p'llos**) *adj. a-* 1) Freed, as a line that has come untied or released from a snag. *Pag'nda'ta ni tōng tonda' bay pangengkotan kulambut, halam maina'an. Kilāku wa'i ap'llus.* When we look at the end of the line where the dropper was tied, it is not there. I figure it has come free. (*Thesaurus:* **kka** 1.1, **hubad, latas₁, puklas** 1) 1.1) *v. intr. aN-* To come untied; freed from a snag. *Bang kita am'ssi, tananamta tinduk daing aheya. Pagsintakta halam kasabitan. Yukta, "Am'llos pahāp p'ssi, heya daing hē' halam kasabitan!"* When we are fishing, we feel a large fish has taken the bait. When we strike it isn't hooked. We say, "The hook has come untied, such a big fish and it wasn't hooked!"

**p'llut₁** *n.* The odor of old urine. (*cf:* **p'ngngak**)

**p'llut₂** *n.* Plague; a condition or event that causes death in large numbers. *Bang bay kolera, ma deyom dang'llaw ma dakayu' lahat amatay saga lima, bā'nu bay taluwa' p'llut.* When there has been an outbreak of cholera, five people dying in the one place on a single day, one would suppose they had been hit by plague. *Bang aheka daing amatay sikagūngan ameya' palaran ma s'llog, ma ulak, bo' halam aniya' makapatay, yukta, "P'llut!"* When many dead fish are floating, drifting with the current and the weed, but nothing has killed them, we exclaim, "Plague!"

**p'mpon** *adj. a-* 1) Well-behaved. *Pap'mpon kām ma luma' ilū ko da'a kam tittok ma deya, apa aheka bantatam maina'an.* Be well-behaved there in the house, so that you don't get chopped to pieces inland, for we have many enemies there. (*Thesaurus:* **addat** 1.1, **hatul₂, hongpot, pantun** 1, **papat** 1, **saldik, saltun** 1) 1.1) *v. tr.* To train a child to be well-behaved. *Subay mbal angahiluhala', mbal amalut ai-ai. Bay pin'mpon he' matto'a asāl min kariki'-diki'na.* Mustn't cause a disturbance or take hold of anything. Trained that way since his childhood. 1.2) *v. tr. -an* To be in control of one's thoughts or desires. *P'mponinbi ma deyom ataybi. Da'a suli-sulihun ni kasehe'an.* Keep it to yourselves. Don't mention it to the others. *P'mponinbi napsubi.* Control your passions.

**p'ndok** *adj. a-* Short in contrast to long. (*Thesaurus:* **deyo'-deyo'₁, pandak, pu'ut**)

**p'nnod** *v. tr.* 1) To press something with the hands in order to achieve a desired shape or bulk. *Pin'nnod tuktuk onde' abō' ahāp luwana.* A child's forehead is pressed so that it will have an attractive appearance. *Niranos nireyom ambung, pin'nnod sala. Bang ngga'i ka mareyom ambung ap'kkal.* Packed into a basket, sort of pressed [into its shape]. If it is not inside the basket it will come apart. (*Thesaurus:* **danos, dasok 1.1, d'ppon**) 2) To massage a bruised area in order to reduce swelling, usually with a handful of hair. (*syn:* **henned**)

**p'nno'** *adj. a-* 1) Full, of a container. (*cf:* **l'sso**) 1.1) *v. tr. -an* To fill something. *A: "Pin'nno'an ba itū?" B: "Tinonga' sadja."* A: "Should this be filled up?" B: "Just half-fill it." (*Thesaurus:* **sangkad, selot 1, s'ppol 1**) 2) Fully covered, of a surface. *Ndū', k'mbal itū ap'nno' he' gusung.* Oh dear, the twins are covered with sand.

**p'nnot** *adj. a-* Stuffed, of the nose when suffering from a cold. (*Thesaurus:* **s'ppun 1, ulapay₁**)

**p'nnu** *n.* The Pacific green turtle. *Chelonia japonica shegel.* (*cf:* **ba'u'u**; *Thesaurus:* **bokko', laggutan, payukan, tohongan**)

**p'nsot** *var. of* **ponsot**

**p'ngkak** *v. intr. aN-* To be breaking down, of flesh. *Bang daing ahalu', amuntu' na, am'ngkak.* When fish is going off, beginning to collapse, its flesh is breaking down. (*Thesaurus:* **baguy, balos₂, buhuk, buntu'₁ 1.1, halu' 1.1, langag**)

**p'ngkong** *n.* 1) A swelling in soft tissue of the body. *Wa'i abustak p'ngkongna.* His swelling has burst. (*Thesaurus:* **bakag₂, bago' 1, baha' 1, butig 1, ikat 1.1, pagbutud**) 1.1) *v. intr. aN-* To become swollen, of soft tissue of the body. *Bay am'ngkong tape'na. Bay ni bohe', bay kasuglatan e' p'ttung.* His foot was swollen. He had gone to the water-hole and a piece of bamboo jabbed into him.

**p'nggod** (var. **penggod**) *adj. a-* 1) Closely connected, of a tether or mooring rope. *Apenggod pahāp engkot kalbaw ilū!* That buffalo tether is much too short! (*Thesaurus:* **d'llot 1, pigtal 1, sandat 1**) 2) Closely related, of kin.

**p'ngngak** *n.* An acrid smell, as of old urine. *Bau p'ngngak, sali' bay mange'.* The *p'ngngak* smell, like old urine. (*cf:* **p'llut₁, p'ngngos**; *Thesaurus:* **bau 1.1, b'ngngi, hamut 1.1, hangsu 1, langsa, langtu, mahali**)

**p'ngngos** *n.* A fetid smell, as of drying fish. *Oy! Bau p'ngngos!* Yuk! That smell of shark! (*cf:* **p'ngngak**)

**p'ngngot** *n.* 1) A beard. (*Thesaurus:* **bū-langal, mantis, misay 1**) 1.1) *v. advrs. -in-* Bearded. 1.2) *v. tr. -an* To shave one's beard. *Mikip'ngngot aku ma iya.* I ask him to shave me. *Minisay ka bang mbal pin'ngngotan.* You become whiskered when you haven't been shaved. (*Thesaurus:* **bagoggol 1.1, bagong₂, himangot 1.1, s'ssol₁, soso'**)

**p'ppa** *adj. a-* 1) Broken by banging against something hard. (*Thesaurus:* **p'ppok, tettek**) 1.1) *v. tr.* To break up long items (for firewood) by banging against something hard.

**p'ppok** (var. **pokpok**; **poppok**) *v. tr.* To hit something with a downward movement, as when hammering or opening up something hard. *Pin'ppok maka bari', tehe'-tehe', tayum.* Hit

with a knife, of various sea urchins. *A: "Pamagaynu tukul?" B: "Pam'ppok lansang."* A: "What are you going to use the hammer for?" B: "For driving a nail." *Bang auling mata, pinoppok bawang maka buli' sawan ati pinehē' ni matana.* When someone is dizzy, garlic is crushed with the base of a cup and applied to his eyes. *Bay pokpokku si Li ma kōkna.* I rapped Li on his head. *Da'a ka magpokpok, abati' si Sel.* Don't hit it, Sir will wake up. (*cf:* **tukul 1.1**; *Thesaurus:* **p'ppa 1, tettek**)

**pagp'ppok** *v. intr. aN-* To hit things repeatedly or randomly. *Da'a ka magpokpok, abati' si Sel.* Don't keep hitting things, Sir will wake up.

**p'ppot** 1) *v. tr.* To cut pole-like things into lengths. *P'ppotun t'bbu ilū abō' kitam atabul magbahagi'.* Cut that sugarcane into lengths so we can share equally. (*Thesaurus:* **gotong, hanggol 1.1**) 2) *clf.* Count word for pole-like things. *Mpat p'ppot p'ttung ma iya.* Four lengths of bamboo for him.

**p'ssa'** 1) *adj. a-* Crushed; put under physical pressure. *Ap'ssa' tanganku, bay tagipit he' papan.* My hand is crushed, caught under a plank. *Ap'ssa' bay tutuban.* The amniotic sac was put under pressure. (*Thesaurus:* **lagtu' 1, p'ggos**) 1.1) *v. intr. aN-* To crack or burst open under pressure, as an egg on hatching. 2) *v. intr. aN-* To break, as waves.

**p'ssi** *n.* 1) A fishhook. *Am'lli gi' aku p'ssi ni si Bo pam'ssiku.* I buy hooks from Bo to go fishing with. (*Thesaurus:* **kawil, sabit₁ 2**) 1.1) *v. tr.* To catch fish with hook and line. *Bang aku bay kaut am'ssi bo' aku tapole' na min pam'ssihan, aluhaya palabayan. Halam aniya' pasembol, halam aniya' pababag pelang.* When I have been fishing and come home from the fishing place, the channel is free of obstructions. There is no crowding, no canoes lying crossways. (*Thesaurus:* **gonteng 1.2, laway₂ 1.1, manit, pamalastik, paranas, tonda'₁ 1.1**)

**pagp'ssi** *v. intr. aN-* To make a living by fishing with a hook and line.

**magp'p'ssi** *n.* One who fishes for a living.

**pam'ssihan** *n.* A place for fishing with hook and line.

**p'ssik** *v. intr. aN-* 1) To splash or spatter, of a liquid. 1.1) *v. tr. -an* To splash something. *Da'a p'ssik-p'ssikin ko da'a kita abase'.* Don't splash lest we get wet. (*Thesaurus:* **kissat, pigsik₁ 1, pulagsik, sahupput, sumpit 1**) 1.2) *v. advrs. ka-...-an* To be splattered with water. *Kap'ssik-p'ssikan kita he' bohe' bang sinapuhan lamisahan e' si Pu.* We get splattered with water when Pu wipes the table.

**p'ssil** *adj. a-* 1) Compressible, as a ball or cooked vegetable tubers. (*Thesaurus:* **k'ddot, k'nnol**) 1.1) *v. tr.* To press on something yielding. *Ap'ddi' bahana, subay pin'ssil.* Her shoulder is painful, it should be pressed on.

**p'ssit** *v. tr. -an* To squeeze something out through

an orifice, as when expressing breast milk. (*Thesaurus:* **p'ddet, p'gga'**)

**p'ssok** *adj. a-* Unable to see what is obvious. *Buwat aniya' lum'ngngan amasi abati'. Magtūy tagi'ik dangan, yukna, "Angay ka'a-i ap'ssok halam ka maka'nda'-i? Kilāku abulikat matanu."* Like someone walking around still awake. Right away someone [asleep] is stepped on and says, "What's up, are you blind that you cannot see? I reckon your eyes must be sightless." (*Thesaurus:* **bulikat**)

**p'ssut** *v. intr. pa-/aN-* 1) To slip through a small opening; to escape from an enclosure. *Wa'i ageret linggi', aheka na daing pap'ssut.* The trawl net is torn, lots of fish have slipped through. *Buwat baka' bo' aniya' ai-ai ariki', subay ni'isi nireyom suput ko da'a am'ssut.* Like a woven basket with little things in it, they should be put into a bag so as not to slip through. *Aheka tak'llo'ta bang angal'ppang linggi'. Mbal am'ssut, mbal amangsat.* We catch a lot when the mesh of the long net is right. [The fish] don't slip through and they don't get back out. (*Thesaurus:* **s'llu 1, t'lla**) 1.1) *v. intr. aN-* To evade parental control. *Wa'i makap'ssut min deyoman matto'a.* He has escaped from his parents' care and protection.

**p'ttak** *n.* 1) A drop of liquid. *Dap'ttak pa'in.* Just one drop. 1.1) *v. intr. aN-* To leak; to drip. *Bang aku anangis am'ttak bohe'-mataku.* When I cry my tears drip down. (*Thesaurus:* **sū₂, tīs, titis 1.1, tū'**)

**p'tti'** *n.* The liquid and suspended solids expressed from grated coconut or pounded sago. *P'tti'na ya makabuwan ssa.* It is the liquid that carries the flavor. (*Thesaurus:* **akal, angkas₁ 1, kabulan, gata' 1, hali₁ 1, sapal, tai'-lahing**)

**p'tti'-gata'** *n.* Coconut cream, the thick liquid expressed from grated copra. (*cf:* **palam**)

**p'tti'-mama'** *n.* The red juice produced by chewing a mixture of betel nut and lime.

**p'ttung** *n.* A tall species of large bamboo, an important source of building material. *Schizostachyum lumampao.* (*cf:* **bō'**; *Thesaurus:* **kagingking, kayawan, kayuwan, daumu'an, t'mmang**)

**plaka** *n.* A phonograph record. (*Thesaurus:* **ligaya, ulehem**)

**plaes** *n.* Pliers (the hand tool). *Plaes itu manjari isāb pangala'an siput, atawa pamōng basi'.* These pliers are also for removing screws or for breaking up metal. (*Thesaurus:* **liyabe**)

**plaes tuka'-agap** *n. phrase* Locking pliers, a hand tool for gripping something very firmly. *Ndiya plaes tuka'-agap ilū.* Hand me those locking pliers.

**plano** *n.* A plan of activity. *Na, amuwan plano ya kallo' inān.* So the heron came up with a plan. (*Thesaurus:* **pagbamba 1.1, pagimba-imba, pagisun 1.1, pagmiting, paru**)

**pagplano** *v. intr. aN-* To discuss plans.

**plasa** var. of **palasa**

**plaslaet** (var. **palaslaet**) *n.* 1) A flashlight. (*Thesaurus:* **kulaet 1, laet, lām, lampu, palita'an, sū' 1**) 1.1) *v. tr.* To illuminate something by flashlight. *Pinalaslaet lagi' aku, yukku, "Da'a kam magpalaslaet, dakayu' du aku pahōs."* A flashlight was shone on me, so I said, "Don't shine your flashlight, I'm the only one with a sarong on."

**plāt** *adj. zero* Flat; smooth, especially of writing paper. *Bang aku anulat bo' mbal plāt, gomot-gomotku pepelku.* When I am writing but it isn't flat, I screw up my paper.

**plātbōt** *n.* A raft-like structure used as an aid in recreational swimming. (*Thesaurus:* **alul, balsa**)

**plēn** *n.* An airplane. (*syn:* **ariplano**)

**plising** *n.* The placing of marbles in a game.

**pagplising** *n.* 1) A team game of four players involving the placing of marbles. (*Thesaurus:* **pagsalla 1**) 1.1) *v. intr. aN-* To play plising, a game played with marbles. *Bang magplising subay holen. Bang magtaksi' ai-ai subay batu.* When playing *plising,* it should be with marbles. When playing *taksi'* of any sort, it has to be pebbles.

**poka** (var. **pokal**) *adj. a-* Incohesive in contrast to solid. *Sinanglag isāb, bang pasān apoka, mbal arasok.* Pan-roasted cassava meal too, at times it falls apart, not firmly packed. *Sali' haloblāk kulang timplana, apoka na.* Like hollow-blocks, lacking in some ingredients, easily broken. (*cf:* **pu'aw 1**)

**pokal** var. of **poka**

**poko-poko** *v. intr. pa-* To be plump, of grain or animal. (*Thesaurus:* **goldo-goldo, hambug 1, littub, l'mmok 1.1, subuk, tibung-tibung**)

**pokot₁** *n.* 1) A long seine net. (*Thesaurus:* **gugul 1, lantaw 1, laya 1, linggi' 1, sinsoro 1, siyul 1**) 1.1) *v. tr.* To catch fish using a large seine net.

**pokotan** *n.* A catch of fish in a seine net.

**pokot₂** *n.* 1) A loosely woven bag for holding fish caught during diving. *Bang bay tinimbak bo' kita patuhun subay amowa pokot pangisihan daing.* When dynamite has been set off and we dive, we should take a bag for holding the fish. (*Thesaurus:* **puyu', suput₂**) 1.1) *v. tr.* To put fish into a small bag when diving. *Subay patuhun bo' pinokot daing.* One must dive for fish to be held in a bag.

**pokot-pokot** *n.* 1) Goose-bumps or multiple small swellings under the skin. (*cf:* **pangkot 1**; *Thesaurus:* **pagbuntul**) 1.1) *v. advrs. -in-* Experiencing goose-bumps or multiple small swellings.

**pokpok** var. of **p'ppok**

**podjak** *adj. a-* 1) Broken into fragments; crumbled. *Bang pa'in am'kka tibu'uk ilū, ngketin. Da'a pinapodjak.* As soon as that cassava is splitting, take it off the heat. Don't let it get crumbled. (*Thesaurus:* **budjal-budjal, gokal, lomo 1,**

**p'kkal 1, sughay) 1.1)** *v. tr.* To break up something hard. *Bang amama' si Mma' To'a, pinodjak mama' e' si Mma', pinehē' ni deyom bowa'na.* When Grandfather wants to chew betel, Father breaks the nut up small and puts it in his mouth.

**podjong** *v. intr. aN-* To be moving at a pace between walking and running. *Amodjongan la bang lum'ngngan. Atimbay saga, ma llot pal'ngngan maka lahi-lahi. Ma llot alallay maka al'kkas.* Just moving briskly when walking. Sort of bypassing; between walking and running, between slow and quick.

**podlongan** *v. intr. aN-* To continue what one is doing. *Buwat aniya' at'kka, angalingan min labayan, magtūy kām amodlongan.* Like when someone arrives or calls out while passing, you immediately carry on with what you are doing. (*Thesaurus:* **sogsog 1, taggu₂ 1.1, togol 1, tukid 1**)

**poen** *n.* A point in team games like volleyball.

**poga** *n.* A glazed earthenware jar with a wide mouth, used mainly for storing water. (*Thesaurus:* **bingki', ka'ang, kasambagan, kibut, pipa, tanāng, tangpad**)

**pogan** *n.* A species of fish, netted in coastal lagoons.

**pogos** *var. of* **logos**

**pogpog** *adj. a-* **1)** Damaged or bruised internally by physical impact, as falling fruit or muscles. *Bang ahūg mampallam magb'kka' kulit, apogpog isina. Bang p'ssilta magtūy paluwas bohe'na minsan bay amata' lagi'.* When mangoes drop their skin always splits, and the flesh is bruised. When we squeeze it, its juice comes out freely even though it is still unripe. **1.1)** *v. tr.* To bruise fruit or vegetables in order to release their flavor. *Pogpogun bawang ilu bo' ang'ssa.* Pound the garlic so that it will release its flavor. (*Thesaurus:* **banol 1.1, pangki', t'ppa**)

**pohak** *n.* **1)** The fungal infection commonly called ringworm. (*syn:* **kakas 1, kulap 1**) **1.1)** *v. advrs. -in-* Suffering from ringworm. *Amandi ka llaw-llaw bo' ka mbal pinohak.* Bathe every day so you don't get ringworm.

**po'on₁ 1)** *n.* The basic part of something substantial, as the rooted trunk of a tree; the base of a house post. *Aheka panagatun pamatu' tabāk ma po'on hāg.* There are lots of shells for throwing games found at the base of house-posts. *Pinat'nna' tuklang ma bihing saging, ma po'on saging i'.* Thorns placed beside the banana palm, at the base of the banana there. (*wh:* **kayu 1**) **2)** *clf.* Count word for plantation trees. *Halam minsan dampo'on niyug takapin an'ngge.* Not a single coconut palm was left standing. *Pila po'on niyugbi?* How many coconut palms do you have?

**po'on₂** *n.* The origin of an idea; the underlying cause of an outcome; the source of a product. *Ya po'on aku halam pi'itu, bay kami ma Sambuwangan.* The reason I didn't come was that we were in Zamboanga. *Hal ka anangis, ya po'on ka'a-i binono'.* You just cry, that's why you get hit. (*Thesaurus:* **apa, kalna' 1.1, pagka, sabab₁ 1.1, sangga'ina, saukat**)

**pagpo'on₁** *v. tr. -an* To originate or establish a housing settlement. *Ya agpo'onan lahat itu si Idj.* Idj was the one who founded this place.

**po'on-sabab** *n.* The underlying cause or basis of an event. (*Thesaurus:* **katikmuhanan, pagsababan, singgit**)

**po'on-sara'** *n.* The person or office responsible for a legal ruling. (*Thesaurus:* **abugaw, huwis, sara' 2**)

**po'onan** *n.* The place of origin; the source. *M'nningga ya po'onanna, ya malkina buwattitu-itū?* Where does it originate from, a machine like this one?

**po'on₃** *n.* The capital cost or outlay of an enterprise. *Sangpū' maka lima pilak ya po'onna.* Its capital cost was fifteen pesos. *Bang buwat usaha itū pal'ddos, halam minsan ta'abut po'on.* A business such as this going down, not even getting back [the money] that was put into it.

**pagpo'on₂** *n.* The financial outlay for a project. *Duwangibu pilak pagpo'on ya bay pang'bbahannu aku.* The start-up money you left with me was two thousand pesos.

**pola** *n.* The areca nut when red but not yet fully ripe. *Aniya' pola kabulak-bulakan, aniya' isāb pola ato'a alanos na, aniya' isāb pola-magi.* There are areca palm nuts in the green stage, and there are mature areca nuts that are withered, and there are *pola-magi* nuts. (*gen:* **pagmama' 1**; *Thesaurus:* **bunga₁, dantilad, l'mmaw, lugus**)

**pola-magi** *n.* A species of palm, the nut of which is used as an inferior substitute for true betel nut. *Pola-magi itū bang ma kamatto'ahan, ma'angit-angit kono'. Bang dī pola, ahāp magtūy kono'.* This palm nut, according to the old people, has a sort of chlorine taste. The real betel is said to be good immediately. (*syn:* **lugus-magi**)

**pola-pola** *n.* Testicles. {colloquial} (*syn:* **bigi-buyung**)

**polbos** *n.* Talcum powder. (*Thesaurus:* **borak 1, tabun-tabun**)

**poleggaw** *v. tr.* To compel someone against his or her inclination. (*Thesaurus:* **abiyug, agpot 1, angin, egot-egot, logos 1, panhot, p'ggong**)

**pole'₁** *n.* **1)** The arrival at one's home place; homecoming. *Ahāp aniya' lindung pahali-hali'an, pole' min deya.* It's nice to have a shady place for resting, on arriving home from inland. **1.1)** *v. intr. aN-* To return home. *Nā, amole' na kami.* Well we will go home now. **1.2)** *v. tr.* To reach home. *Pagdakdakku subu lagi', yampa tapole' palīd na man ugtu-llaw.* Having laundered clothes since morning, I only got home when [the sun] was declining from noon. **1.3)** *v. tr.* *-an* To return something to where it belongs. *Bang kita amatay bo' pinole'an ni ahirat, tinilaw kita mahē' bang ai-ai bay hinangta ma junna itū.* When we die and are taken home to the afterworld, we are interrogated there about whatever we did on this earth.

**kapole'an** *n.* The final outcome. *In lisu'an kapole'anna tahinang banyaga'.* The final outcome of being lazy is to be made a slave. *In kapole'an kasisayang sigā ni bangsa saddi.* The final result will be their well-being going to foreigners.

**pole'-lahat** *v. intr.* *aN-* To die, in the sense of reaching one's final home. {idiom} *A'a bay pinalahil amole'-lahat na.* A man brought into the world has gone to his permanent home. *Bo' kam mbal takuddat, aniya' habal in si Bapa' La wa'i na amole'-lahat dinsini' subu.* So you are not shocked, there is a message that Uncle La died [lit. went home] this morning. *In mma'na wa'i na amole'-lahat bay Juma'at inan.* His father passed away [went home] last Friday.

**pole'-po'on** *n.* **1)** The break-even point in a trading event. **1.1)** *v. tr.* To recover the money invested in an enterprise (but no more).

**pagpole'-po'on** *v. intr.* *aN-* To recoup the amount of money invested. *Pagubusta magongka', magpapole'-po'on pabīng.* When we had finished playing the game, we had got our money back.

**pamole'an** *n.* **1)** Home; the place where one belongs. **2)** The outcome; the result. (*Thesaurus:* **kaluwasan, kamattihan 1, kamaujuran, kat'kkahan₂, katobtoban, katumariyahan**)

**papole'** *v. tr.* To return something to its original location; to send someone home. (*Thesaurus:* **maksud 1.2, nde', pasampay, tukbal₁ 1, tūd₂, tulun₂ 1.1, tuyuk-tuyuk**)

**pagpapole'** *v. intr.* *aN-* To return things to a prior status. *Saupama bay kita magb'lli, bay magsulut. Mbal manjari binawi'an bissala, mbal na manjari agpapole'.* For example, we were buying and had come to an agreement. It is not possible to go back on what has been said, not possible to return [what has been purchased].

**pole'₂** *v. intr.* *aN-* To reappear in another part of the body, of an illness or infection. *Buwat aku bay tinandog, amole' ni palasahanku. Magsalinggā aku, angalimasu' deyom baranku.* Like when I had malaria, it went to the seat of my symptoms. I moved restlessly and was painfully hot in my body.

**pole'₃** *v. tr.* To initiate marriage proceedings with a man by going to his bed under cover of darkness. *Dibuhi' bay aku pinole' he' d'nda.* Last night a girl came to my room to compel me to marry. *Bang aniya' amole' aku, subay matto'aku nira'ut.* If someone comes to my bed [initiating marriage proceedings] my parents should be summoned. (*Thesaurus:* **dakop, lahi₂**)

**polma** *n.* **1)** An attractive shape or movement. **1.1)** *adj.* *a-* Attractive in shape or action, as a canoe or a woman's figure. *Apolma si Mo. Ahāp bang lum'ngngan, ahāp palantarana, apolma isāb igalna.* Mo is attractive. She walks well, her personality is good, her dancing is attractive. (*Thesaurus:* **alti, dorog₂ 1.1, hansam, hāp baran, himpit, jalang₁, lingkat 1.1, manis 1.1**) **1)** *v. tr.* *-an* To cause something to be attractive. *Polmahin e'nu angigal.* Make your dancing attractive.

**polmed** var. of **pomed**

**polo** *n.* A shirt, western-style. (*Thesaurus:* **badju', jaket**)

**polong** var. of **pōng**

**pomed** (var. **polmed**) *n.* **1)** Hair oil; pomade. **1.1)** *v. tr.* To apply scented oil to the hair. *Bang pinolmed kōkku subay nilais.* When my hair has been dressed with hair oil it must be combed.

**pōn** *adj.* *a-* Labored, of one's breathing in reaction to shock or illness. *Bang kita ahūg man diyata' tudju pareyo', apōn napasta. Minsan min dahatus kita tinilaw, mbal sinambungan.* When we fall down from a height, we are virtually breathless. Even if we are asked one hundred times, it gets no response. *Apōn napasta, sali' ala'at bay palasahanta.* Our breathing is labored, as though our health has been bad. (*Thesaurus:* **paghota, simay₁ 1**)

**ponas** *adj.* *a-* Destroyed totally. *Buwat hunus patumbuk, aponas kaluma'an. Atawa am'ssi, aponas ai-ai.* Like when a squall hits, the houses are destroyed. Or when fishing, gear of any kind is destroyed. (*Thesaurus:* **lapnas 1, lognos, luhu'₂ 1, sapsay**)

**ponod** *n.* **1)** The solid content of a container. **1.1)** *adj.* *a-/-an* Filled solid. *Man b'ttong sampay ni tape', aponod ko'. Hal isi.* From stomach down to the feet, it is all solid. Nothing but flesh. *Ya du daing, ponoran du isāb.* Fish too, they can have a solid interior. *Bay nilapisan maka bulawan aponod, ya deyoman bilik ina'an.* The inside of that room was overlaid with solid gold. (*ant:* **gaunggang**) **1.2)** *v. tr.* To fill something compactly.

**pamonod** *n.* The lowest series of side planks on a pelang-type canoe hull. (*syn:* **dalosan**; *gen:* **tapi' 1**)

**pono'** *adj.* *a-* **1)** Dealt with as a unit. **1.1)** *v. tr.* To handle in bulk, not separately; to merge various financial transactions. *Pono'un na mailu kamemon alta' ilū.* Pay the bride-wealth there in a lump sum. (*Thesaurus:* **kuridas, pakkiyaw, sampul-baul, tighan 1.1**)

**kapono'an** *n.* A group of items viewed as a unit; a crowd of people. (*Thesaurus:* **ba'an₁, botang₁ 1, puntak 1**)

**pagpono'** *v. intr.* *aN-* To become consolidated as a single item. *Bang magsalla' bo' ka kapikitan, patukbulun ni aku apa aku taga utang ma ka'a. Supaya magpono'.* When playing two-up and you are obliged to borrow money to play, pass it on to me because I owe you money. So as to be consolidated.

**pono'-pono'** *adj. a-* In one piece; unseparated by breaks. *Bang ta'abut magbayad sumiyan-sumiyan, da'a pa'in akanat. Subay ya mapono'-pono' ilu.* When the time comes to pay, whenever, don't do it in small amounts. It must be in that one transaction. (*Thesaurus:* **tibokkol, tibu'uk₁** 1)

**pono'an** *n.* Items in bulk, undifferentiated.

**ponsot** (var. **p'nsot**) *n.* The navel. (*cf:* **kowet**)

**pōng** (var. **polong**) *adj. a-* 1) Broken or cut across the length of something. *Bay aku angalga, apōng tanggunganku.* I was working as a porter and my carrying-pole broke. (*Thesaurus:* **lobet, pate', punggul** 2, **teplong**) 1.1) *v. tr.* To break or cut something in two. *Pōngun pasagi' ilū maka kapa. Makajari isāb tangan pamōngnu.* Cut that lumber in two with an axe. You could also use your hand to break [it]. 1.2) *v. tr. -an* To cut the end off something. *Pinōngan sangana maka bari'.* The ends cut off its branches with a heavy knife.

**kapōngan** *n.* A part which is broken or cut off.

**pagpōng-pōng** *v. intr. aN-* 1) To break often or repeatedly into numerous pieces. *Bang pandu'anku ka'a, asidda aku tagaga'. Sali' magpōng-pōng.* When I am teaching I am very hesitant. [My speech] sort of breaking into segments. 1.1) *v. tr.* To break something repeatedly, of a physical object, or of the speech of someone unused to public speaking. *Bay pinagpōng-pōng kōkna maka l'ngngonna.* His head and arms were broken into fragments. *Sidda aku ab'nsi ma onde' inān. Nda'un, minsan bay lāngku masi pinagpōng-pōng e'na sumping.* I really dislike that child. Look, even though I've told him not to, he keeps breaking off the flowers. *Taga esok nsa' bidda' kayu. Aniya' esokna man deyom. Ahāp lahi ni kubal, esok ya magpōng-pōng.* Trees of any sort have *esok*. There is *esok* inside. But the part towards the hardwood [under the bark] is the good stuff. *Esok* breaks up into bits.

**pōng-kayu** *n.* Offcuts of wood. *Ndiya ma aku pōng-kayu ilū.* Let me have those offcuts of wood.

**pōng-pōng** *n.* Short broken-off pieces.

**karuwampōng** *n.* Both ends of something.

**dampōng** *n.* The end of something cut or broken across its length. (*Thesaurus:* **dambila'** 1, **samalintonga', santonga'**)

**pongag** *n.* An outrigger canoe whose hull is damaged or incomplete. *Pongag itū, pelang sali' asegpong buli'-munda', aniya' bila'na. M'ssa'-bidda', pelang aheya pelang ariki', basta ndang na.* This *pongag* is a *pelang-* type canoe damaged at stern or bow, one that has a split in it. No matter what, a big *pelang* or a small one, so long as it is worn out. *Bay pelang aheya niloddosan, nila'anan tapi'na, nihinang pongag na.* It was a large canoe reduced in size, its upper planks removed, made into a hulk. (*Thesaurus:* **balutu,**

**bangka', dapang, londay, pallungan, pambot, paraw** 1, **pelang, punggul** 1)

**ponga'** *adj. a-* Nasal, of speech impeded by a defect of nose or palate. *Aponga' itū aniya' agka'at mareyom ūngta, buwat si Bapa' Am.* This word *ponga'* is when something is damaged in our nose, like Uncle Am. (*Thesaurus:* **kemol, s'ngngog, tanga'₂, terol**)

**pongka'** *n.* A species of fish.

**pongkol** *v. tr.* To mold something into a ball. *Buwat tibu'uk, nili'is bo' yampa pinongkol.* Like cassava, grated and then molded into balls. (*Thesaurus:* **kompol, tambu** 1, **tampa** 1)

**ponggol** *v. tr. -an* To cut off the head of something. *Bang kōk pinonggolan, bang tangan pinukulan.* If it's a head it is [called] decapitated. If it's a hand it is [called] amputated. (*Thesaurus:* **pukul** 1.2, **punggut** 1.2, **sangko'** 1.1)

**ponglas** *v. tr. -an* To stain metal so that it has a gun-metal hue. *Pinonglasan, sali' bay pote' pinaettom. Tana', muntay, balimbing, ya pamonglas.* Being stained, as though something that was white is made black. Earth, citrus, star-apple are used for staining. (*Thesaurus:* **bata, lampasu, lanu'** 1.2)

**poppok** var. of **p'ppok**

**poppol** *adj. zero* 1) Blunt, of something that needs to be sharp, as a pencil. *Apu'ut-pu'ut taloman pinsil itu, apoppol.* The pointed part of this pencil is quite short, it's blunt. (*cf:* **tompol**) 1.1) To make a blade or pointed object blunt. *Pinoppolan buli' bangka', ya seplatna.* The stern of the dugout is made blunt, its split part.

**porok₁** *n.* Various Silver-biddies or Mojarras (fish species). *Gerres sp.* (*syn:* **lamuruk**)

**porok₂** *see:* **pamorok**

**porol** *adj. zero* Pure; unique or fundamental to. *Lahasiya', sali' anakta porol.* A blood relative, like our very own child. *Porol bulawan.* Pure gold. *Mantaluna ya kakana' pote', maka kusta ya ba'anan tadjung. Ya he' porol ma tag-dapu anak.* Muslin, that white cloth, and the checkered stuff, all those sarongs. That's the property belonging entirely to the parents of the girl. *Ya sali' bay nggo' maka mma' kami, bay kaluwa'an pi'itu man Sisangat, lahat kami porol.* Like mother and father, who were expelled to this place from Sisangat, our native place. (*cf:* **jatti, lahasiya'** 1)

**kaporolan** *n.* Something native to a person. *Ina'an ma lahat kaporolanku.* There in my native land.

**porong** *v. tr. -an* To wrap something around the forehead. *Ya du saga imam bangsa Yahudi, subay nihinangan badju' maka sabitan maka porong.* Likewise the Jewish priests, they should have shirts and belts and headbands made for them. *Kura' isāb bay pangura'an sultan, kura' pina'alti maka porong bulawan.* And the horse on which the sultan rode, a horse beautified with a gold headband.

**posak** *adj. a-* Soft in consistency, of boiled starchy vegetables. *Aposak, ya alunuk buwat panggi' bahan atawa tibu'uk bīlla. Posak,* soft like boiled sweet potatoes or cassava. (*Thesaurus:* **baska 1, lunuk 1, lunyag**)

**posat** *adj. a-* Cracked and fragmented. *Wa'i na aposat iklug.* The egg is cracked. (*Thesaurus:* **b'kka' 1, l'ssa'**)

**posopis** *n.* A post office.

**pospa'** *v. tr.* To outrank someone in negotiations. *Mbal kita makapospa' a'a inān maka kapatutna.* We cannot outrank that person with his authority. *Bang buwat si Tu kinawin, bo' anokat si Mi, na pinospa' he' si Sa apa wali du. Bang usba buwat aku mbal papospa'.* Like when Tu was getting married and Mi claimed a share, Sa outranked him because he was only a mother's brother. A father's brother, as I am, cannot be outranked. *Bang halam pa'in makat'kka a'a dangan ma deyom bay pangawal hē', na yuk sigā, "Magpalkala' na kitā, pinospa' na bang hal a'a dangan."* In the event that a single person hasn't arrived within the time set, they then say, "Let's discuss the issue, [we] will be outranked if there is only one person." (*cf:* **powera 2**)

**possat** *adj. a-* Dislocated, of bones or eyes. *Apossat matanu? Ma buli' k'llongnu bahā'?* Are your eyes out of place? Are they at the back of your neck? *Angay, apossat ka? Halam ta'nda'nu onde'-onde' bay tarugtulnu ilū.* Why, are your eyes dislocated? You didn't see that child you ran into. *Saga po'on pa'ata itu, mbal kita makal'ngngan. To'olangta ya apossat.* The inner end of our thighs here, we can't walk. It is our bones that are dislocated. (*Thesaurus:* **pagdalisu', pagsā', pi'ul, pisu', pittay 1.1**)

**possatan** *n.* A gap between parts or components which normally connect. *Gallang itu aniya' possatanna.* This bracelet has a gap [between its ends].

**pote'** *n.* **1)** The color white; whiteness. (*gen:* **walna'**) **1.1)** *adj. a-* White; pale; pallid. *Apote' bu'un si Li.* Li's hair is blonde. *Nilibun, sali' binilik. Mbal pinagluwas-luwas supaya mbal aettom. Subay na pa'in apote'.* She is kept out of sight, kind of confined to a room, not allowed to keep going out lest she be darkened [by the sun]. She must stay pale. *Karut-karut sokal pote'.* Little bags of white sugar. (*ant:* **ettom 1**) **1.2)** *v. intr. aN-* To become pale, as a person who has been ill or had a shock. (*Thesaurus:* **muras 1**)

**kapote'an** *n.* An area of white sand, of a beach or sea floor. *Kapote'an, halam aniya' unas-unasna, hal gusung. Kapote'an,* there is no seagrass, just sand. *Tudjuhan kapote'an inān.* That area of white sand is our destination. (*Thesaurus:* **bunbun 1, kalangan₃, gusung, igang₁**)

**pote' anawan-tawan** *adj. zero* Whiter than white. {idiom}

**pote' atay** *adj. a-* Innocent; blameless. {idiom}

**pote' sobangan** *adj. a-* Showing the first light of dawn. {idiom} *Aho', apote' sobangan ma tōng papussuk.* Yes, dawn is breaking at the tip of the peak. (*Thesaurus:* **abay-subu, bukis₁, dai'-llaw, pagmanis-manis sobangan, subu₂ 1**)

**pote'-tawas** *n.* Brilliant whiteness.

**pote'-pote'** *n.* A species of fish.

**pote'-ugbus** *n.* A non-toxic variety of cassava with white flesh and a pink inner skin.

**pote'an** *n.* A star. (*syn:* **bitu'un, mamahi**)

**powak** *n.* A shallow pool in sand flats exposed by a receding tide. *Ya niōnan he' kami powak basta ma diyata' t'bba.* We call them *powak* when they are above low tide. *Taga powak, sali' l'bbak-l'bbak.* Having tidal pools, like little hollows. (*Thesaurus:* **k'bbong-k'bbong, halo-halo**)

**poway-poway** *v. tr.* To mock or criticize things such as someone's work or appearance. *Mbal tapoway-poway bang buwattilu luwana.* It cannot be criticized if that's how it looks. (*Thesaurus:* **himoway, pastul, sā'₁ 1.3, salba₁, salla'₁ 1.2, salu'-salu', soway**)

**powera 1)** *n.* A condition that detracts from the value of sale goods. *Ya bay halga'na buwattē' apinda na. Taga powera kono'.* Its original price has changed. They say it has defects. (*Thesaurus:* **gora'₁ 1, salla'₁ 1, sassat, tamak 1**) **1.1)** *v. tr. -an* To reduce the sale price of an item because of some defect or condition. *Pinowerahan daingta, apa amasi kono' abase'.* Our [dried] fish was reduced in price because they reckoned it was still wet. **2)** *v. tr.* To detract from someone's words; to over-ride someone's opinion. *Ai-ai gara'ku poweranu sadja.* You over-ride whatever advice I give you. *Buwat aku soho'nu angā' bohe'. Mbal aku, amowera aku.* Like me being sent by you to get water. I refuse, I override you. (*cf:* **pospa'**)

**poyan** *n.* The Skipjack tuna. *Katsuwonus pelamis.* (*Thesaurus:* **mangku', panit, sobad**)

**poyog** (var. **doyog**) *adj. a-* **1)** Leaning away from the vertical. *Aroyog sidda luma'nu, song ah'bba'.* Your house is leaning well over, about to collapse. *Mbal papoyog malabuhuk sabab mbal na ahogot he'na amalut.* A pine tree is not to be tilted because it isn't firmly fixed. (*Thesaurus:* **kīd₂, kīng 1.1, lemba, lenggang, lihid, paglilip-lilip, tīg**) **1.1)** *v. tr.* To push something away from the vertical. *Da'a poyogun, ah'bba' ko' ilū.* Don't make it lean over, it will fall down.

**ppa** var. of **l'ppa**

**ppak** *n.* A species of seabird; a gull. (*cf:* **t'lla'-t'lla'₁**)

**ppi'** *n.* **1)** A technique for finishing a woven edge. (*cf:* **batul**; *Thesaurus:* **l'ppit 2, sapay 1**) **1.1)** *v. tr. -an* To finish the edge of woven materials by folding and weaving back in. *Subay ma hangtaranna, ai duwand'ppa, ai labi dand'ppa,* ni'ppi'an bihing tepo. It should [be done] along its length, whether two fathoms or more, the edges of the mat being woven in. *Ang'ppi'an aku bubu, nippi'an isāb bagiyas.* I am finishing the edge of the large woven trap, the small trap will also be finished.

**ppi'-sapay** *n.* A variation of the woven-edge technique for finishing a mat.

**ppo** *v. intr. aN-* To surface for an intake of breath, as a turtle does. *Bokko', minsan a'a, ang'ppo iya min kulit tahik. Hatina, anganapas. Bang ma sigām, bokko' itū, bang patuwa' na, ma sabab t'ggol sigām ma deyo' kono', subay patuwa'. Sagō' hal bokko', hal ang'ppo.* A leatherback turtles [and even a human] surfaces briefly, in order to breathe. According to some this turtle emerges because it has been a long time down below and has to emerge. But it is just being a turtle, just catching its breath. (*Thesaurus:* **gagal₁, paghagak, pagnapas, panggahak**)

**ppot** var. of **l'ppot**

**praes** *n.* A prize in the context of school.

**preseden** *n.* A president, as the supreme leader of a country. (*cf:* **panghulu' 1**)

**prinsipal** *n.* The principle or head teacher of a school. *Pinagagihan onde' iskul he' mastal, mastal ya kapagagihan he' prinsipal.* The school children are under the control of the teacher, and the teacher is under the control of the principal.

**problema** *n.* A problem; a difficulty. *Ya problemana, mbal magpatireyo'.* His problem is that he won't humble himself. *Nasa itū aheka ginisanna, buwat aniya' maganak, aniya' problema.* There are many kinds of *nasa* [foreboding], like someone giving birth, or when there is some problem.

**pukaw** *v. tr.* To awaken someone by shaking. (*cf:* **bati'₁ 1.1**)

**puki** *n.* The female genitals; the vulva. {vulgar}

**puklas** (var. **paklus**; **puglas**) *adj. a-* **1)** Untied or unlashed; loosened from a binding. *Apuklas mantil kulaet man sementona.* The mantle of the lantern has slipped off the porcelain generator [to which it was tied]. *Anugpat aku lubid, sali' a'kka, sali' halam ahogot panugpatna, ya hē' niōnan apuglas.* I added a length to the line, it sort of came untied, its extension wasn't secure, that's called coming loose. *Apaklus itū amasi pabuku, bo' aloka.* This word *paklus* means the knot still tied, but loosely. *Bay laggosku bubu, maumu abuklas.* I tied the bindings of my fish trap, they often come undone. *Song na amaklus, hatina song na ahūg.* About to come undone, about to fall. (*syn:* **buklas₂ 1**; *Thesaurus:* **kka 1.1, hubad, latas₁, p'llus 1**) **1.1)** *v. intr. aN-* To become loose; to slip from one's grip. *Buwat aniya' bententa, amaklus.* Slipping from our grip, like something carried in one hand. *Song na amaklus, hatina song na ahūg.* About to come undone, about to fall.

**pukpuk** (var. **puppuk**) *v. tr. -an* To remove dirt from cloth by slapping or pounding it while wet. *Da'a pukpukin s'mmek ilū, subay sinabunan.* Don't pound those clothes, they should be soaped. (*Thesaurus:* **kimu', dakdak 1, pakang₂**)

**pukul** *n.* **1)** Something from which an end has been removed; an amputee. *Ma'ai pukul laring ī'?* Where is that knife with the broken-off tip? *Pukul itū mbal makal'ngngan. Aniya' isāb pukul mbal tu'utan, mbal tape'an.* An amputee cannot walk. There are also amputees without a knee, without a foot. (*Thesaurus:* **keme, ku'il, pagtamengka', pagtongka'**) **1.1)** *adj. a-* Amputated, of a limb or digit. *Apukul tanganna.* His hand has been cut off. *Bang apukul kita karuwambila', makajari kita niōnan aku'il. Minsan saga hinang alampung-lampung mbal na tahinangta.* If someone has lost a limb on both sides he can be described as disabled. He cannot do even light tasks. **1.2)** *v. tr. -an* To amputate a limb or digit. *Bang kōk pinonggolan, bang tangan pinukulan.* If it's a head it is [called] decapitated. If it's a hand it is [called] amputated. (*Thesaurus:* **ponggol, punggut 1.2, sangko' 1.1**)

**pūd-pūd** *see:* **kapūd-pūran**

**pudji** *adj. a-* **1)** Praiseworthy; to be revered. **1.1)** *v. intr. aN-* To call on God in praise or petition. *Amudji ni Tuhan, sali' magsambahayang, sali' angamu' apuwa.* Give praise to God, as when praying or asking for some physical blessing. *Makapudji ma Tuhan, sali' makasabbut.* Calling on God, like calling his name. (*Thesaurus:* **amu'-amu', harap₂, pagduwa'a, sambahayang, ta'at 1.1**) **1.2)** *v. tr.* To praise someone. *A'a magabbu ma baranna amudji dīna.* A man who is proud of himself praises himself. (*Thesaurus:* **hulmat 1, mahaldika', pagmahaltabat, sanglit 1.2**)

**pagpudji** *n.* **1)** Acts of prayer and devotion. *Pagpudji ma a'a amatay basta puwas min hinang mpatpū'.* Prayers on behalf of a person who has died, provided it is after the forty-day ceremony. **1.1)** *v. intr. aN-* To engage in prayer as a community. *Bang Bulan Hailaya aniya' magpupudji amuwan sīn ni kami mareyom langgal.* In the month after the Fast there are worshippers who give money to us who are in the mosque.

**pudjut** *v. tr.* To pick up small items with the fingers and thumb.

**pugad** (var. **pugaran**) *n.* A nesting place; a lair; a protected place for various creatures. (*cf* **sāng 1**)

**pagpugad** *v. intr. aN-* To make a comfortable place for oneself.

**pagpugaran** *n.* A nesting place. *Pagpugaran kamahung lo'ok-lo'ok kabinet inān.* The corners of that cabinet are nesting places for cockroaches.

**pugaran** var. of **pugad**

**pugaw** *n.* A species of fish, sometimes kept in salt-water fish ponds for later sale. *Paghūg linggi'* *inā'an, sin'llu na e' banak, e' selo, e' pugaw.* When the net there was lowered, the mullet, needlefish, and *pugaw* escaped [unobserved]. *Katigangan na pugaw, taluwa' llaw. Aheka amatay.* The *pugaw* have been damaged by the sun. Lots die. (*cf:* **banak**)

**pugay** *n.* **1)** The nape of the neck. **2)** The tail hanging from a hair knot. (*Thesaurus:* **hambak, hampal, sapid 1.1, simbōng 1.1, toket 1.1, tusay**)

**puglas** var. of **puklas**

**pugpug 1)** *v. tr. -an* To berate someone; to hammer with words. *Buwat aku taga sā' ma ka'a. Pugpugannu aku, astolnu atiya' makaniaku.* Like my having made a mistake with you. You hammer me with words, your anger comes at me. *Pugpugannu na pa'in aku inān, sat'ggol aku halam makabayad.* You keep scolding me so long as I haven't paid. (*Thesaurus:* **dugal 1.1, pabukag, pah'lling₂, pamūng-mūng, s'ndal 1, tutul**) **2)** *v. advrs. ka-...-an* To be stressed and unable to speak. *Kapugpugan pikilanku mahē' ma mastal, sali' alungay pikilan.* My mind was stressed there with the schoolteacher, as though my thinking power was lost.

**pugtul** *adj. a-* Broken, of a line or chain. *Angkan mbal ah'lling kulitis, apugtul sumbuhanna.* The reason the firecracker doesn't go off is that the fuse is broken. (*Thesaurus:* **b'kkat 1, piyurus₁**)
  **pugtul-napas** *adj. a-* Dead, of the moment when breathing stops. {idiom}

**pugung** *v. tr.* To wrap something by placing it on a cloth and bringing the corners together.

**puha** *adj. a-* Breathless; exhausted by physical exertion. *Apuha napasna.* He is out of breath. (*Thesaurus:* **hapus₂, lumu, paghangu-hangu, pagh'ngka-h'ngka, paghongat-hongat**)

**puhan** *n.* **1)** A handle fitted to a tool or bladed weapon. *Puhan budjak atawa puhan bari'.* The shaft of a spear or the handle of a heavy knife. (*Thesaurus:* **baba'an₁, patihan, tangkay 2**) **1.1)** *v. tr. -an* To provide something with a grip or handle. *Mbal kapuhanan pisaw.* A *pisaw* knife cannot be fitted with a handle.

**puhan-laring** *n.* A species of fish.

**puhi** *v. tr. -an* To dry something by exposing it to sun or wind. (*Thesaurus:* **buwad, patoho', tumbal 1.1**)
  **puhi'an** *n.* A drying rack; a clothesline.

**puhinga'** *v. tr.* To do someone serious harm, by various means including sorcery. *Buwat si Tu bay nihinang e' a'a bo' halam kinata'uhan, sali' ni'ilmu'an, pinuhinga'.* Like Tu, whom someone worked sorcery on without it being known, as though affected by magic, seriously harmed. *Bay pinuhinga' he' a'a. Sali' bay nila'at, nijahulaka'.* He was harmed by someone, maltreated, subjected to malice. (*cf:* **jingki 1.1, tanya₁;** *Thesaurus:* **jilaka', la'at 1.2, la'ug 1.1, pinjala' 1.1, pissoko', sikla, usiba'**)

**puhu** *n.* A black pan formation on the sea floor. *Puhu, ya kaettoman bo' aratag. Puhu,* the formation that is black but flat. (*Thesaurus:* **munu-munu, takot, tahetek**)

**puhu' 1)** *n.* The body, of a human being. *Ap'ddi' puhu'ku kamemon.* My entire body is in pain. *Aheka puhu' ma tabu', aheka isāb puhu' ma luma' Milikan bang pinah'lling tenes-tenes.* Lots of people at the market, and lots of people too in the Westerner's house when the folk song [recording] is being played. (*Thesaurus:* **a'a, baran₂ 1, manusiya' 1**) **2)** *clf.* Count word for people. *Aniya' sigām saga sangpū' puhu'.* There were about ten [people] of them.

**puhun** *v. intr. aN-* To ask permission of; to take leave of someone. *Amuhun gi' aku ni mastal bo' aku ni bohe'.* I will just ask permission from the teacher and then go to the water hole. (*syn:* **ba'id 1.1**)
  **pagpuhun** *n.* **1)** A complaint against someone. **1.1)** *v. ditr.* To lay a complaint against someone. *Aniya' pagpuhun saga a'a dampōng ni mayul pasal anak sigām budjang bay niusiba'an. Aniya' isāb magpuhun ni iya mikisara', sinō' pabīng ma llaw saddī.* Some people from the other end [of the village] brought a complaint to the mayor regarding their teenage daughters having been abused. Others came with a complaint requesting a ruling, they were told to come back some other day. *Bang sadja aku ya bay maghuhukum ma lahat, kamemon a'a ya magpuhun atawa taga palkala' pinasalassay.* If only I was a judge, all the people who had a complaint or a case would have it sorted out. (*Thesaurus:* **kuhi₂, pagmahi, pagmalān, sumbung, tuntut₁**)
  **papuhun** *v. tr.* To grant someone permission to leave; to excuse someone. (*Thesaurus:* **paba'id, pakuhi, parūl 1.1, tugut 2**)

**puhung₁** *n.* **1)** A matter of concern or interest that needs to be attended to. *Puhung itū, sali' aniya' ngā'ta ma iya ma llaw damuli.* This word *puhung,* it's like us having something to get from him on a later occasion. (*Thesaurus:* **l'ngngan₂ 1.1, pagmohot 1.1**) **1.1)** *v. tr.* To have in mind something that another possesses. *Mbal aku pi'itu bang halam aniya' tapuhungku ni ka'a.* I would not come here unless there was something I had in mind to get from you. *Ya puhungta hē', bang aniya' ta'nda'ta ma a'a ina'an, ya hē' sinapali he'ta. Sali' parakayu' kita ma iya.* What we have in mind, when we see something belonging to that man, that's the thing we want to use in partnership with him. Like forming a [working] unit with him.

**puhung₂** *n.* A species of tree with thorns up to 50 mm in length; various other thorny trees or shrubs. *Gmelina elliptica. Aniya' kayu legetan niōnan puhung, ataha' legetna, saga duwa inses legetna.* There are thorny trees called *puhung,* with long thorns, about two inches long. *Bo' na ang'llo' tuklang, puhung, iting kamemon na.* And so [he] got some spikes, Gmelina thorns, all manner of thorns.

**pū'₁** *n.* A high island, in contrast to an atoll. (*cf:* **nusa**)

 **kapū'-pū'an** (var. **kapū'an**) *n.* 1) A cluster of islands. *Halam aniya' kapū'-pū'anna, timbang na.* It has no islands, it is deep sea already. *Amustu kami ni Tahu. Tahu itū kapū'an taga parola.* We make Tahu our base. Tahu is an island group with a lighthouse. 2) The outer islands of the Sulu Archipelago. *Katulakku ni kapū'an halam aniya' abayku. Ma kapū'an pa'in aku, aheka na. Kapole' kami minnē', halam sai-sai.* On my departure to the islands I had no fleet companion. Once at the islands there were lots. On returning home from there, there was no one at all.

 **pū'-pū'-diyata'** *n.* The scattered islands to the southwest of the northern Sulu Archipelago.

**pū'₂** *num.* A multiple of ten.

**pu'aw** *adj. a-* 1) Fragmented; incohesive; crumbly. *Apu'aw sinanglag itū, sali' pinaka gusung. Subay binahug maka bohe' bo' magpikit.* This fried cassava is crumbly, like sand. It should be moistened with water to it hold together. (*cf:* **poka**) 2) Broken, of sleep. *Apu'aw karu'na, nsa' ahāp e'na atuli.* Her sleep was broken, she didn't sleep well.

**pu'us** *v. tr.* -an To wipe up a mess. A: *"Itiya' bay asungi' si Oto'."* B: *"Pu'usin na ba."* A: "Oldest Son has just messed himself." B: "Get it wiped up." (*Thesaurus:* **kukus, sapu 1.1, tarapu 1.1**)

**pu'ut** *adj. a-* Short, in contrast to some normative length. *In pagmatāw ma Tuhan makapataha' umul, sagō' ya a'a ala'at, apu'ut umulna.* Having respect for God makes life long, but a bad person, his life is short. *Kalehun pahāp, at'kka du waktu papu'utna umulnu maka umul saga anak-mpunu.* Listen well, a time is coming when he will cut short your life and the lives of your descendants. (*Thesaurus:* **deyo'-deyo'₁, pandak, p'ndok**)

 **kapu'utan** *n.* Abbreviation; shortness. *Kapu'utanna hal.* Just the short version.

 **papu'ut** *v. tr.* Development marker in narrative discourse, meaning 'to make a long story short', and signaling the end of a discourse unit. (*Thesaurus:* **dalas 1.1**)

**pūl** *n.* The Sulu version of the game of pool. (*Thesaurus:* **bulitin, kulang₂, tako, tira**)

 **pagpūl** *v. intr. aN-* To play the game of pool, Sulu style.

**pulak** *v. tr.* -an 1) To lose a baby by miscarriage. *Bang onde'-onde' pinulakan, aniya' kayu aheya pamakan.* When a child is miscarried, there will be a great tree for feeding it. **1.1)** *v. advrs.* ka-...-an To suffer a miscarriage in the early stages of pregnancy. *Kapulakan siyakaku, bay ab'ttong.*

*Halam na makalanjal kab'ttongna.* My older sister has had a miscarriage. Her pregnancy was already visible, but it has not proceeded. (*Thesaurus:* **bibis, kawa'₂, labu' 1.1, pakpak 2**)

**pulak-palik** (var. **paupalik**; **pulak-palit**) *adj. a-* 1) Widely scattered. *Tinimuk kām e'na pabalik min paglahat bay pamapulak-palikan ka'am.* You will be gathered from the lands to which you were scattered. *Sali' kami itū min Siasi, apulak-palik. Itiya' na kami makaniTinutu'.* Like us from Siasi, scattered widely. Here we are come to Tinoto. *Bay timpu martial law apaupalik manusiya' ma Pilipin. Aniya' bay ni Borneo, aniya' bay pi'itu ni Mindanao.* At the time of martial law, a lot of people in the Philippines spread far and wide. Some went to Borneo, some came here to Mindanao. (*syn:* **palit₁**; *Thesaurus:* **kanat 1, pāg, sihag₂ 1**) **1.1)** *v. tr.* To scatter things over a wide area. *Manjari abantug kitām maka mbal tapulak-palik ni mpat pidju alam.* So we will be famous and will not be scattered to the four corners of the world.

 **pagpulak-palik** *v. intr. aN-* 1) To be scattered widely. *Ah'lling pa'in bām magt'nggehan sigām bo' magpulak-palik.* When the bomb exploded they come to their feet and scattered in all directions. **1.1)** *v. tr.* To scatter things or people in many directions. *Pagpulak-palikku sigām maka baliyu halimpunus.* I will scatter them with a whirlwind.

**pulak-palit** var. of **pulak-palik**

**pulag** *adj. a-* 1) Dispersed in reaction to fear or danger. *Bang aniya' magmiting, bo' niholdap na, apulag sigā.* If there are people in discussion and they are held up [by bandits], they scatter in all directions. *Atāw makapulag.* Afraid of being made to scatter. 2) To be spread in extent. *Apulag bila'na.* Its break spreads further.

 **pulag-pulag** *v. intr. aN-* To become diffused throughout a mass or a space, as an odor or pain. *Amulag-pulag tambal bang ma deyom baranta na.* The medicine spreads once it is in our bodies. *Aniya' isāb pulag-pulag tandog. Puwas bay tandog tibu'uk amole' ni kōk, ni palasahan.* There is also diffusion of fever. From being a single localised fever it goes to the head and to overall symptoms. *Atawa bau a'a ya mamatay hē', amulag-mulag du isāb.* Or the odor of a person who has died, it too becomes diffused. (*cf:* **sobsob 1**; *Thesaurus:* **angil, angsod, bbu 1.1, hangsu 1.1, tunug 1.1**)

**pulagsik** *v. intr. aN-* To be sent flying by sudden movement. *Pabuwang amulagsik.* Bouncing up and sent flying. *Ahūg lilus man diyata' paradol, amulagsik saga saminna, abila'.* The clock fell from the top of the cupboard and its glass sprayed out in all directions, broken up. *Pabuwang bohe' amulagsik. Bang bola bo' binantungan, amulagsik isāb.* The water bounces up and flies through the air. A ball too, when it is thrown, flies [through the air]. *Bitu-bitu api amulagsik.* Sparks are fire flying through the air. (*Thesaurus:* **kissat, pigsik₁ 1, p'ssik 1.1, sahupput, sumpit 1**)

**pulai'** *n.* A cork or plug for a container.

**pula'-pula'** *intrj.* 1) An expression of amazement or incredulity. *Pula'-pula'nu!* Imagine! **1.1)** *v. tr.* To imagine or conceive of something (usually with a negative). *Mbal tapula'-pula' lingkat bidadali.* The beauty of the fairy women is beyond comprehension.

**pulamata** var. of **kagang-pulamata**

**pulaw₁** *n.* A type of flute, shorter than a suling. (*Thesaurus:* **saunay, suling₁**)

**pulaw₂** *v. advrs.* ka-...-an To be bereft of close kin. *Kapulawan, sali' kita kasiya-siyahan.* Bereft, as though we are left without support. (*Thesaurus:* **bba₁ 1, siya-siya 1, siya-siya 1.1**)

**pulaybūd** *n.* Plywood. *Buwat saga pulaybūd ase'ak he' llaw, akanit he' tahik.* Like plywood, split by the sun, delaminated by sea-water. *Buwat pulaybūd aoplak kuwitna.* Like plywood, its outer layer peeling off.

**puli** *v. tr.* To recoup money lost in gambling. *Ala'an ka m'nnilu. Bay aku tara'ug, abō' puliku pabīng sīnku.* Get away from there. I've been defeated, so I [want to] get my money back. *Papulihun aku.* Give me a chance to recoup my losses. (*Thesaurus:* **bawi' 1**)

**puli-bahasa** *v. intr.* aN- To pay someone a formal compliment. *Pinatuntul bo' amuli-bahasa, halam ai-ai pinabeya'an. Hal kami amole' kaleya.* Sent on our way with polite words, nothing sent with us. We simply went ashore on our way home. (*Thesaurus:* **lana 1.1, pagmamhu', paili**)

**pagpuli-bahasa** *v. intr.* aN- 1) To pretend goodwill. *Buwat sakiku, ubus pabīng bo' ala'an, ubus pabīng bo' ala'an. Saki hē' ya magpuli-bahasa.* Like my illness, coming back and going away again and again. That sickness pretends to be well-meaning. **1.1)** *v. tr.* -an To treat someone with formal courtesy. *Bang aniya' ni luma'ku, pagpulihanku bahasa, painumku kahawa.* When someone comes to my house, I treat them with formal courtesy, giving them coffee.

**pulin** *v. tr.* To assemble people, as school children or soldiers. *Saga sundalu pinulin bo' yampa pinamahil, pinapagmahil.* Soldiers made to fall in order to be set marching, to drill. *Pinulin onde'-onde' iskul kamemon, pinūn.* All the school children lined up, assembled. (*Thesaurus:* **paghimpun, pagmairan 1.1, pagtimuk 1, pūn 1.1**)

**puling** *n.* 1) Airborne particles; dust. **1.1)** *v. advrs.* ka-...-an To have foreign matter in the eye. (*Thesaurus:* **bulag, lempon, pē'₄**)

**pulingkit** *adj.* a- Clustered closely together, no spaces. *Buwat buwahan, apulingkit, alapus.* Like lansones fruit, closely bunched, no gaps. *Buwat ka'a t'llu anaknu. Baba'nu dakayu', hambinnu*

*dakayu', balungnu dakayu'. Yuk kasehe'an, "Apulingkit isāb a'a hē'."* Like you with three children. You carry one on your back, one in your arms, and one on your shoulders. Others say, "That fellow is clustered [with children]." (*Thesaurus:* **daug 1, pingkit 1.1, puliting, pungut 1, tundun 1**)

**pagpulingkit** *v. intr.* aN- To grow in clusters.

**pulipus** *adj.* a- 1) Enveloped in. *Apulipus e' sahaya.* Enveloped in brightness. (*Thesaurus:* **bungkus 1, putus 1.1, tambun 1.1**) **1.1)** *v. intr. pa-* To shelter under or behind. *Papulipus man bukutku siyaliku bang binono' he' si Ina'.* My younger brother shelters behind my back when Mother is hitting him. *Makajari isāb kita papulipus ma saddī man a'a, bang pa'in katampanan. Minsan hal buli' kayu la'a.* It is also possible to take shelter behind something other than a person, just so long as one is shielded. Even just the base of a tree. (*Thesaurus:* **limbu 1.1, lindung 1, silung₁, sindung₁**)

**pulis** *n.* A police officer; police in general. *"Ataddang a'a ilū," yuk pulis. Asāl takilā he' pulis.* "That fellow is legal," said the policeman. He was in fact recognized by the police.

**pulitik₁** *n.* 1) A political inducement; a bribe. **1.1)** *v. tr.* -an To bribe or suborn someone, with implication of trickery. *Pinulitikan kita, binowa ni kala'atan, niakkalan sala.* Bribed, persuaded to do something bad, deceived so to speak.

**pulitik₂** *n.* The crackling sound of burning stubble. *Ya sagaw sigām sali' pulitik sagmot atunu' e' api.* Their noise was like the crackle of brushwood burning in a fire.

**pagpulitik** *v. intr.* aN- To make the crackling sound of something burning, as a rubbish fire.

**puliting** *adj.* a- Clustered, as fruit on a tree. *Aheka sidda anakna d'nda inān, saga sangpū' marai'. Ya na mbal kal'ngnganna pahāp sabab sikapulitingan saga anakna. Aniya' na pahambin, aniya' isāb anangis, aniya' pa'apas.* That woman has many children, ten or so. That's why she can't walk very well, because she's smothered in children. Some being carried, some crying, some following her. (*Thesaurus:* **daug 1, pingkit 1.1, pulingkit, pungut 1, tundun 1**)

**pullay** *n.* 1) Various wrasses including the Yellowtail tamarin. *Anampses meleagrides.* 2) The Three-ribbon or the Silver-streak wrasse. *Stethojulis strigiventer.* 3) The Three-lined wrasse. *Stethojuliatus trilineata.*

**pulling** *n.* The egg sac of a shellfish, a delicacy in some species. *Aniya' d'nda sinokatan pulling kahanga maka pulling baggu'.* There was once a woman for whom the egg sac of a conch and the egg sac of a cowrie were specified as bride-wealth. (*Thesaurus:* **hapa 1, pehak 1**)

**pullu'** *n.* A cake of cassava meal mixed with grated coconut and sugar. *Panggi' kayu tin'ppa nihinang* *pullu'-pullu', nilamuran lahing maka sokal.* Cassava pounded and made into *pullu'* cakes, mixed with [grated] coconut and sugar. *Bang aniya' pullu' niragangan ma tabu' Hambilan, b'llihin aku ya taga hinti' deyomna.* If there are *pullu'* cakes being sold at Hambilan market, buy for me the ones with sugared coconut filling. (*gen:* **mamun**)

**pulubi** *adj. zero* Lacking money; destitute. *Bang pulubi, kaikit na kami. Halam aniya' sīnnu pangongka'nu.* When we are short of money we are ungenerous. You have no money for playing. (*Thesaurus:* **kabus, kettak, ipis 1, pihit**)

**pumpun** var. of **punpun**

**pūn** *v. tr.* 1) To assemble people. *Pinulin onde'-onde', pinūn.* The children are made to fall in, assembled. 1.1) *adj. a-* Brought together, of various opinions. *Pagga pa'in apūn na kaisunan min d'nda maka min l'lla, na magtilaw sokat na.* Once the views of the woman's side and the man's have come together, then the questions about brideprice details are asked. (*Thesaurus:* **paghimpun, pagmairan 1.1, pagtimuk 1, pulin**)

**pagpūn₁** *v. tr.* To form one single group from a number of things or subgroups. *Magpūn-pūnan dī sigā.* They all come together of their own accord. (*Thesaurus:* **pungut 1.2, umpung**)

**pagpūn₂** *v. intr. aN-* To be joined in marriage. *Sumiyan sigā bay magpūn?* When did they get married? *Buwat aniya' bay maglakibini bo' halam du at'ggol pagpūn sigā, bo' sali' ahukaw d'nda, min d'nda ya angalupit.* For example a married couple who haven't been together long, and the woman is reluctant [to sleep with her husband], it's the woman's side who pay compensation. *Nirakop, magpūn-pūnan dī sigā.* Abducted, [or] coming together of their own [choice]. *Ya d'nda ipatan bay pamuwan e' si Leban ma si Leya waktu kapagpūnna maka si Yakub.* The female servant whom Leban had given Leya at the time of her marriage with Yakub. *Sagō' at'ggol na pagpūn sigā, halam makabāk anak.* But when their marriage had gone on a long time, they had no children.

**puna'** *v. tr. -an* To repair a hole in something woven; to fill a gap in a row of plants. *Puna'anku linggi' bang aniya' agese'.* I mend the trawl-net when there is a tear. *Bang ka anganom, bang amatay tinanomnu, pinuna'an, tinanoman pabalik.* If you're weaving, or if something you've planted dies, the gaps are filled, replanted. (*Thesaurus:* **bubul, patli' 1.1, patlong, s'llap₁, sumpal 1.1, tupak 1.1**)

**punda** *n.* A decorative outer covering; a pillow-slip.

**pundang** *n.* 1) Fish split and pierced for preserving. (*Thesaurus:* **daing niasin, lumay, peyad 1, sampila'₁ 1**) 1.1) *v. tr.* To split open and pierce for preserving, of large fish. *Angkan pundangku daing supaya mbal ahalu'.* The reason I

split and dry fish is so that they will not go bad. *Yukna, "Dakayu' itū pundangun. Dampōng itū tapahun, dampōng itū bīllahan."* He said, "Split and pierce this one. This half is to be roasted, this half to be boiled."

**punduk** *v. intr. pa-* 1) To move into an upright position. *Bay atuli si Am, bay soho'ku papunduk, yukku, "Punduk na ka, alanga na llaw."* Am was sleeping, I told him to get up, I said, "Get up, the sun is high already." *Buwat kami soho'nu pariyata', kuddatnu kami magtūy. Kami makaralihag, makabati', makapunduk.* Like when you tell us to get up, you promptly startle us. We move in fright, waking up, sitting up. (*Thesaurus:* **balukad, bangkat₂, buhat₂, buladjang, bungkal₁ 1, lungkahad**) 1.1) *adj. a-* To be in a sitting position. *Bang aku atuli, apunduk aku.* When I sleep I stay sitting up. 2) To rise from the grave. *"Makajari kita magkakhāp," yukna, "bang punduk kamatto'ahan, atawa bang patangkob langit, atawa bang alinis būd itu."* "It will be possible for us to be reconciled," he said, "when the forebears rise from their graves, or the sky is closed over, or this mountain is worn down."

**punji** *n.* A smooth cloth similar to satin. (*Thesaurus:* **lanay₁, sutla'**)

**punjung₁** *n.* The outer tip of something flexible, as the branch of a tree or a tuft of hair. *Bay aku sinoho' angaengkotan korente ni punjung amboway.* I was instructed to tie the radio antenna to the top of the *amboway* tree. (*Thesaurus:* **pekkes-pekkes, puntuk, pussuk 1, tōng₁**)

**punjung₂** *n.* A roll of seasoned rice or corn grits wrapped in a banana leaf and boiled. *Buwas nihinang punjung, nilamuran asin maka bawang, ni'isi ni daun saging ampa bin'lla.* Rice made into *punjung*, with salt and garlic mixed in, put in a banana leaf and then cooked. *Punjung itu buwas gandum atawa buwas to'ongan nilamugay maka lahing maka dulaw.* *Punjung* is corn rice or real rice mixed with grated coconut and turmeric.

**punjungan** *n.* A species of fish.

**punpun** (var. **pumpun**) *n.* A species of sea worm, long and flat, lives in sand or mud in the intertidal zone. *Ngā'ta punpun maka panggi' kayu bay pin'gga'. Angeket ma s'mmek ya pangisihanna.* We catch sea-worms with squeezed cassava meal. They bite the cloth it's held in.

**punsa'** *n.* The background of a pattern, especially on cloth. *Buwat ma hōs keyat, aniya' punsa' ettom.* Like a red sarong that has a black background. (*Thesaurus:* **papagan 2, sapak**)

**punsu** *n.* A mound of soft material, as the sand piles formed by burrowing crabs. *Wa'i kami makasiyud ma kahanggal-hanggalan atawa ma punsu.* We've touched bottom on submerged wood or a sand mound. (*cf:* **kūd**)

**puntak** (var. **puttak**) 1) *n.* A pile of similar things.

(*Thesaurus:* **ba'an**$_1$, **botang**$_1$ 1, **kapono'an**) 2) *clf.* Count word for piles of things for sale. *Dapuntak ni duwa puntak.* One or two piles.

**puntaw** var. of **kuntaw**$_1$

**puntik** (var. **putik**) *n.* A species of tree with durable pale-gold wood. (*syn:* **kunit-kunit**)

**puntu** *clf.* Count word for canoes engaged in a fishing enterprise. *Mpat puntu kami amowa timbak daing.* There were four canoes of us carrying fishing dynamite. *Di'ilaw bay manimbak duwa puntu du. Aheka amatay lumahan.* It was two canoes that were dynamiting yesterday. Many mackerel died. (*cf:* **munda'**$_1$ 2)

**puntuk** (var. **puttuk**) *n.* The topmost part of something, as the summit of a mountain. *Nda'un, ina'an maina'an ma puntuk masjid.* Look, up there on the dome of the mosque. *Puttuk kayu itū ya katapusan diyata'. Ya du isāb ma luma'. Sinō' nirāg ma kami, minsan, yukna, puttuk-puttukna.* The *puttuk* of a tree is its highest point. It's the same with a house. We were given instructions to climb it. Even, he said, to its very top. *Pehē' na ka patukad ni diyata' puttuk būd inān ati ang'nda' ka ni s'ddopan.* Go there and climb to the peak of that mountain and look towards the west. (*Thesaurus:* **pekkes-pekkes**, **punjung**$_1$, **pussuk** 1, **tōng**$_1$)

**puntu'** *n.* 1) A jewel or colored stone set in gold. (*Thesaurus:* **dilam, intan, palmata** 1) 1.1) *v. tr.* -*an* To set gems or colored stones in gold jewelry. *Pinuntu'-puntu'an bāngku itū.* These ear-studs of mine have colored stones set in them.

**puntul** *adj. a*- Singled out from a group. *Apuntul pahāp parawku! Duwa palayo ati dakayu' ta'ā', pagka dakayu' inān masi.* How my canoe has been singled out! Two lying at anchor and one taken, while the other is still there. *Apuntul dangan amatay, taluwa' timbak, ati sehe'na halam, ya pa'in dambeya'an.* One singled out to die, hit by an explosion, but his companion was not, even though they were together. (*Thesaurus:* **dakuman, hal, la'a, luwal, sadja, samadjana, tunggal** 1, **yangkon**)

**punung** *v. advrs.* -*in*- Faint from hunger. *Bang aku magbalebol, bo' at'ggol, pinunung aku. Bay isāb aku magdanel ma Sentral, bay aku pinunung halam aniya' takakanku.* When I play volleyball for a long time I become faint. I also competed in a running race at Central School and was famished, having eaten nothing. *Saupama kita ma dilaut hal damunda'-munda'ta, s'lle' bale puhu' minsan ni'iyan, punung-punungan, tapalis kita.* For example we are out at sea, just one canoe and, God forbid, we are faint with hunger, we get carried far off course. (*Thesaurus:* **bongtas** 1.1, **gustang, hanu, lingantu** 1.1, **otas**)

**punya** *see:* **kapunyahan**

**punyal** *n.* 1) A small dagger-like knife. (*Thesaurus:* **barung, kalis**) 1.1) *v. tr.* To stab someone with a dagger-like knife. (*Thesaurus:* **budjak** 1.1,

**kudjut, dukduk, dugsu'**)

**pungal** (var. **tungal**) *adj. a*- Broken or split off a main part of something wooden, usually along a grain line in wood. *Da'a ka ang'ntan ma buli' pelang ilū ko da'a apungal.* Don't hold on to the stern of the canoe there lest it split off. (*Thesaurus:* **saksak** 1, **sasa**$_1$, **segpong, seplak** 1, **te'as**)

**pungkad** *adj. a*- Blown right over with roots exposed. *Buwat kayu bang taluwa' baliyu, minsan arai' gamutna tabowa. Niōnan apungkad.* Like a tree struck by the wind, perhaps with even its roots affected. It's described as *pungkad.* (*Thesaurus:* **hantak**$_1$ 1, **h'bba', ligad, lintuwad** 1, **timpuwad** 1)

**punggit** *n.* 1) A token share of bride-wealth; a sample of food at a feast. *Na bang kita amowa dulang, kīllo'an punggit.* So when we bring a tray of food, a token share is taken from it. (*Thesaurus:* **banghad** 1, **basingan, mahal**$_2$, **pagtinabawan, ungsud**$_1$ 1) 1.1) *v. tr.* -*an* To claim a token share of something of value. *Bay kami angungsud t'llu hatus. Na pinunggitan he' sigā min kar'ndahan limampū' pilak, nihinang mahal maka basingan.* We paid ₱300 as bride-wealth. Then they of the woman's side took fifty pesos as *mahal* and *basingan* [the share belonging to the bride's parents]. *Pinunggitan, sali' niā'an sukay. Buwat saupama ma deyom paghinangan, bo' akatis na, niā' dakayu' panyām, dakayu' saga t'llu saging man dakayu' dulang, nilatag na dulang. Punggit* is like taking a fee. For example at a ceremonial occasion, when it is over, a single rice cake is taken, one or three bananas from a tray, going from one tray to another.

**punggu-baha** *n.* The shoulder. (*syn:* **baha**)

**punggul** 1) *n.* A canoe with its upper side planks broken off. (*Thesaurus:* **pongag**) 2) *adj. a*- Broken off near the top, as a tree. *Apunggul kayu inān ma deya T'lling, bay taluwa' baliyu.* The tree inland from T'lling Point has its top broken off, hit by the wind. (*cf:* **tunggul**; *Thesaurus:* **lobet, pate', pōng** 1, **teplong**)

**punggut** *n.* 1) Something from which the useful end has been removed, as a knife with a broken point. 1.1) *adj. a*- Cut off, of an extremity such as finger or toe. *Apunggut tanganku, sali' apukul.* My hand has a part cut off, as though amputated. 1.2) *v. tr.* To cut off an end section. (*Thesaurus:* **ponggol, pukul** 1.2, **sangko'** 1.1)

**punglu'** *n.* A bullet. *Tinampan punglu'. Makatudju ni baranta sagō' mbal kita ainay.* Shielded against bullets. They come straight for our body but we are not harmed. (*cf:* **kalasussu**)

**pungut** 1) *n.* A cluster of items closely arranged. (*Thesaurus:* **daug** 1, **pingkit** 1.1, **pulingkit, puliting, tundun** 1) 1.1) *adj. a*- Clustered thickly, as fruit on a stalk, fish on a string. *Apungut, aheka sali' magpūn buwat daing ma tuhugan bo' aheka nīnda'.* Clustered thickly, a great many coming together like strung fish with many visible. **1.2)** *v. tr.* To combine several strings of fish into a cluster. *Pinungut saga limantuhug, sangpū' tuhug.* About five strings [of fish] clustered together, [even] ten strings. (*Thesaurus:* **pagpūn₁, umpung**) **2)** *clf.* Count word for clusters of produce.

  **ma pungutan** *adv. phrase* By the bunch. *Buwahan bīlli ma pungutan.* Lansones purchased by the stalk.

  **pungutan** *n.* A stalk of clustered fruit.

**puppuk** var. of **pukpuk**

**puppu'** *v. tr.* **-an** To cleanse body parts after defecating, urinating or sexual emission. *Akapil a'a inān, bang bay asungi' mbal amuppu'.* That fellow is an infidel, he does not cleanse himself after defecation. (*Thesaurus:* **ail, istinja', junub, peppet**)

**puppus** var. of **puspus₂**

**pupput₁** *v. tr.* **-an 1)** To start up an engine. *Pinupputan lansa inān tonga' bahangi sudju Tiyanggi.* That launch will be powered up in the middle of the night heading for Jolo. *Bay kami ni Talikud, halam ta'nda' kami k'llat pab'ntang ma tahik. Sigi kami amupput. Pagpupput kami itu, palebod k'llat hē' ma batang ehe'. Patuhun dangan ma kami amowa bari', ati kinehet he'na k'llat hē'. Ahogot hē', Ja. Mbal tala'anan maka tangan.* We were at Talikud Island, and we didn't see the long fishing line in the water. We went ahead and started the engine. When we started it, the line wound around the propeller shaft. One of us dove in with a knife and cut the line. It was tight, Ja. It couldn't be removed by hand. **1.1)** *v. intr.* **aN-** To fire, as an engine. **1.2)** *v. intr.* **aN-** To travel in a motorized vessel.

  **pupputan** *n.* A combustion engine; the cylinders of an engine; the muffler of an engine. *Akosog lansa inān, mpat pupputanna.* That launch is powerful, it has four cylinders. (*cf:* **makina 1**)

**pupput₂** var. of **putput**

**pupud** *n.* **1)** The remnant when something is used up. *Lūnun kono' pupud siga ilū.* Make a roll of that cigaret stub. **1.1)** *adj.* **a-** Used up; worn down. (*Thesaurus:* **linis, litib, pasaw**)

  **pupud-llaw** *adj.* **a-** To be in the distant future, with the connotation of never happening. {idiom} *Buwat pantalun at'ggol halam akatis. Yukta, "Apupud-llaw, mbal aku angala'it pabīng pi'itu."* Like long trousers not completed after a long time. We say, "It will be a very long time before I come back here to get tailoring done." *Ta'abut pa'in llaw bay pangora i', na ananggu simuddai. Ta'abut pa'in simuddai ananggu pabīng. Na apupud-llaw ananggu.* When the agreed-on day comes he puts it off until the day after tomorrow. When the day after tomorrow arrives he puts it off again. He puts it off till the distant future.

**pupus** *adj.* **a-** Curled up due to disease, of hands,

feet or claws. (*cf:* **kokko'**)

**puraw** *adj.* **a-** Brief; of short duration. *Apuraw l'ngngan kami.* Our visit is brief. (*Thesaurus:* **dai'-dai' 1**)

**puriba** *n.* Material evidence; legal proof. *Bang halam aniya' puribana makada'awa kita.* If there is no proof we can deny the charge.

**purukan** *n.* An inherited skill or occupation. *Purukan pagbubu, asal ntan kami.* Our ancestral occupation is to trap fish, our heritage in fact. *Binangsa purukan hali-Kura'an, bang tudju ni pagimam.* People of a descent group skilled in the Holy Koran, when imam status is the topic. (*Thesaurus:* **ntan₂ 2, pali-pali, pangkatan, tubus₂ 1, tuttulan, usulan**)

**purus** var. of **purut**

**purut** (var. **purus**) *adj.* **a-** Frayed or worn, of rope or cloth. *Timanin na s'mmek ilū, apurut na, mbal na manjari. Atawa lubid, apurut na, mbal na tapangengkot.* Throw that cloth away, it's worn and no longer useful. Or rope, it's frayed and can't be used for tying.

**pūs** *n.* Value; usefulness. *Halam aniya' pūsta magusaha.* There is no point in us going out fishing. *Ai pūsna bang aku tungbasannu bo' halam aniya' anakku?* What use is it if you reward me but I have no child? *Buwat saupama siyaliku pinah'nda, ungsudna t'llu hatus hal pam'lli indalupa-kaginisan, maleta, s'mmek saga. Halam aniya' pūsna tahampitku.* My younger sister for example, getting married, her down payment ₱300, for buying just this and that, suitcase, clothes and so on. My share will be worth nothing. (*Thesaurus:* **guna 1**)

  **kapūsan** *n.* Value; purpose; usefulness. *Buwat a'a hal maglunsulan ni luma' a'a, mbal magusaha. Halam aniya' kapūsanna bang buwattē'.* Like a person who just wanders round to people's houses and doesn't work for a living. Such a person is of no use. (*Thesaurus:* **kalagihan 1, kapunyahan**)

**pusaka'** *n.* **1)** Something received as an inheritance; a treasured item one will not part with. *Bang onde'-onde' ariki'-diki' buwat saga si Ip inān, subay bīllihan pamulawan sali', saga sinsing atawa gallang atawa gantung-li'ug, sali' pusaka'.* Little children like Ip should have jewelry bought for them, a ring or a bracelet or a necklace, as an inheritance. *Pusaka', sali' bay aniya' ka'bbahan e' matto'a, ai-ai na ka'bbahan ma panubu' sigā.* An inheritance, like something that is left by one's parents, anything left to their descendants. **1.1)** *v. ditr.* To pass something on to someone on the death of the owner. *Ngga'i ka ipatannu ya pamusaka'annu, sagō' anaknu lissi.* It is not your servant to whom you will give the inheritance, but your very own child.

  **pamusaka'** *n.* Something inherited; an heirloom.

**pusal₁** *adj.* **a-** **1)** Whirling; spinning around. *S'llog itu apusal.* This current here is swirling around.

(*cf:* **buliluk**) **1.1**) *v. tr.* To rotate something at high speed, as when making fire by friction. *Amusal kita maka lubid bang halam aniya' bagidta.* We spin [a stick] with string when we have no matches. (*Thesaurus:* **legot 1, paggiling**)

**pusal₂** *n.* A whorl of hair on the crown of the head. *Pusal dakayu' itū ebodta, sali' palegot-legot.* This other *pusal* is the cowlick on one's head, the thing that sort of rotates. *Bang onde'-onde' duwa pusalna, yukta agagga.* If a child has two whorls on his head, we say he is stubborn. (*Thesaurus:* **ebod, mbun-mbun**)

**pusiyat** *adj. a-* Pale, of complexion. (*Thesaurus:* **lospad, muntas, muras 1.1**)

**puspus₁** *v. tr.* To do something with all one's energy or capacity. *Puspusun na kosognu kamemon.* Put all your strength into it. *Puspusku kabaya'anku, asal du aku nirūlan he' si Mma'.* I will do what I want with all my energy, indulged as I am by my father. *Puspusku kabaya'anku, asal du aku nirūlan he' si Mma'. Minsan aku, tabiya', angalalu d'nda.* I will do what I want with all my energy, indulged as I am by my father, even if [pardon my language] I have sex with a woman. *Puspusun na bang ka lahi-lahi.* Give it your best when you run. (*Thesaurus:* **kuwat, kuyas 1, matay₂, pakosog, paspas₁, sikad 1**)

**puspus₂** (var. **puppus**) *adj. a-* Used up; exhausted (of a resource). *Apuspus na naelon, wa'i nilahi'an he' selo.* The nylon fishing line is all gone, run out by an escaping garfish. *Apuspus napasta bang kita patuhun.* Our breath gets exhausted when we dive. *Basta apuspus na ma pangkat kami, halam aniya' takapin pamowahan.* At such time as all of our ritual ancestors have been used up, no more healers left. *Ka'a na ya makapuppus sīn.* You're the one to spend all the money. (*Thesaurus:* **katis₁ 1, hagin 1**)

**pussuk** *n.* **1**) A sharp extremity, as the point of a blade, the tip of a tree, the peak of a mountain. *Aniya' lahutna aheya atalom pussukna.* He has a large knife with a sharp point. (*Thesaurus:* **pekkes-pekkes, punjung₁, puntuk, tōng₁**) **1.1**) *v. intr. pa-* To project upwards in a point. *Ohō, apote' sobangan ma tōng papussuk hē'.* See, dawn is breaking over the end of where [the land] extends upward.

**pustu** *n.* **1**) An outpost for trade; a military or government station. **1.1**) *v. intr. aN-* To stay temporarily at an outstation, usually in the context of making a living. *Bang kami atulak ni kanusahan angalihan kami ni Tahu. Amustu kami ni Tahu. Maina'an pagdaingan.* When we leave for the islands we stay at Tahu. We stop over at Tahu. The fishing grounds are there. (*Thesaurus:* **hanti' 1, lihan 1, tingan, tingkap**)

**pagpustu** *v. intr. aN-* To form a military outpost. *Magpustu sigām min bukutan.* They were forming a military outpost in the back.

**pusu'₁** *v. tr.* To gather fruit from trees or from plants other than rice. *Amusu' kami kaleya maka disi Jy amusu' biyabas.* We go inland with Jy and others to gather guavas. *Sangkapusu' sangkakakan.* No sooner picked than eaten. *Bang kam anagna' magani tinanom atawa magpusu' buwa' kayu, pene'unbi ya ahāp to'ongan.* When you begin to harvest crops or pick fruit, choose the very best. *Atapusu' biyabas inān, atapusu' kamemon.* Those guavas all picked, all harvested. (*Thesaurus:* **lapod**)

**pusu'₂** *n.* The flower bud of a banana, used as a vegetable.

**puta** *n.* A prostitute. (*Thesaurus:* **ba'is, biga', ga'ira, sundal 1**)

**putal** *adj. a-* Unraveled. *Aputal k'llat, sali' ap'kkal bay nilubid inān.* The rope is unraveled, what had been twisted is coming apart.

**putan** *n.* Glutinous or sticky rice.

**putang** *n.* A deformed coconut which has no meat but which makes a useful scrubbing brush. (*Thesaurus:* **lahing 1, l'kkop₂, tongkop**)

**putik** var. of **puntik**

**putika'** *v. tr.* To divine information regarding what is not known by normal means, as future events or current locations of lost items or people. *Bay paputika'ku si Mma' ma si Mma' To'a, bang humiyan amole'.* I got Grandfather to divine when my father would return home. (*cf:* **ilmu' 1**; *Thesaurus:* **alamat₁, kamot, limal, pag'nda'₂**)

**pagputika'** *v. intr. aN-* To be engaged in divining what is not currently known.

**magpuputika'** *n.* An expert in foretelling the future.

**putika'an** *n.* Items and devices used for divining what is currently unknown. *Ni'nda he'na ma putika'an, atawa pandan pinagengkot, atawa kamanyan pinagūng ma bohe'.* He looked in a divining device, or at knotted strands of pandanus, or incense set floating on water. *Bang llaw Juma'at subay angalamat dahū bo' yampa patūd. Bang ala'at e'ta ang'nda' putika'an subay da'a sinōngan l'ngngan.* When it is a Friday we should consult by divination first before setting sail. If what we see in the divination is bad, the journey should not be continued.

**putili'-mandi** *n.* A cake of cassava meal mixed with grated coconut and sugar. (*gen:* **mamun**)

**puting** *n.* **1**) A lie; deception. *Putingnu!* What lies you tell! (*Thesaurus:* **akkal 1.1**) **1.1**) *v. tr. -an* To deceive someone by lying. *Kaputingna inān, m'ssa' na buwattina'an!* His deceitfulness, there's nothing like it! *Hal aku parupangnu sabab putingannu aku.* You simply make a fool of me because you deceive me. (*Thesaurus:* **paglepet, pagl'pput, sussa'**)

**pagputing** *v. intr. aN-* **1**) To lie habitually. *Da'a beya'-beya'un, hal magputing.* Don't believe him, he simply tells lies. *Lepet itū sali' a'a magputing. Yukta, "Yampa pinaluwas kaputingna." Lepet* is like a person who lies. We say, "His lying ways are only just being exposed." **1.1)** *v. tr. -an* To accuse someone of being a habitual liar. *Sali' pinagputingan kita, ya hē' angandusta'.* It's as though we are made out to be liars, that's *dusta'. Sali' pinagputingan ya bay mangahaka'. Mbal ameya'-meya' nihaka'an. Sali' atajakki ma iya.* The one who gave the information accused of being a liar. [The accuser] unwilling to be informed, hard to convince. *Sampay buwattina'an, masi aku parupangnu maka pagputingannu.* To this very time, you still treat me like an idiot and make me out to be a liar.

**putingan** *n.* A liar.

**paputing** *v. tr.* To refuse to believe what someone says, implying that he is lying.

**putli'** *n.* An honorific for a woman of high birth; 'Your Highness'.

**putput** (var. **pupput**₂) *v. tr. -an* To hasten natural development or inclination. *Putputin anaknu ilu abō' kita makakakan buwas.* Make your daughter develop quickly so that we can feast on rice. *Da'a iya pupputin bang mbal bilahi magusaha.* Don't push him if he doesn't want to go out fishing. *Saging ilū subay pinupputan bo' ahāp tahakna.* Those bananas should be heated so as to ripen well.

**puttak** var. of **puntak**

**puttuk** var. of **puntuk**

**putu**₁ *n.* The bananas at the base of a stalk, i.e. the last to develop. *Makajari niā' putu-putu saging, bin'lla?* Is it all right if I take those little bananas from the bottom of the bunch, for boiling?

**putu**₂ *v. tr.* To cook food by steaming. (*gen:* **b'lla 1**)

**putu-putu** *n.* A steamed cake of wheat or rice flour. *Bang subu-subu, asidda magdagang si Gi putu-putu.* Early in the morning Gi is diligently selling steamed cakes.

**pinutu** *n.* A starch staple such as cassava meal cooked by steaming.

**putung** *v. tr. -an* To deduct a part of someone's wages. *Buwat sali' aku taga utang ma ka'a, pinutungan gadjiku.* Like when I owe you money, you take it off my wages. (*Thesaurus:* **kobos, kulang**₁ **1.3, dagdag**₁**, diki' 1.2, hilang, sulak**₁)

**putus** *n.* **1)** A wrapper; something wrapped. *Na lum'ngngan na pa'in maka putus-putus sigā.* So they walked on with their little packages. **1.1)** *adj. a-* Wrapped in; enveloped. *Aputus pussuk būd inān e' gabun.* That mountain peak is enveloped in cloud. (*Thesaurus:* **bungkus 1, pulipus 1, tambun 1.1**) **1.2)** *v. tr.* To enclose something in a wrapper or layer. *Saga kōk hāg isāb bay pinutusan pilak.* The tops of the posts too were covered with silver. (*Thesaurus:* **k'bbot 1.1, k'mmos 1, p'kkos 1.1**)

**pagputus-putus** *v. intr. aN-* **1)** To be divided into separate packages. **1.1)** *v. tr.* To divide things up

into separate packages. *Pinagputus-putus saga bāng-bāng.* Cookies wrapped up in packages.

**putusan** *n.* A package.

**puwad** *v. tr.* To cut down something growing, as a tree or bamboo. *Puwarun na saging. Ubus pinuwad, sin'ppe' na.* Cut down the banana [plant]. After it is cut down, the fruit is cut off. *Bang aniya' buwat saging puwaranta po'onna, al'kkas magsaha' pabalik.* Like when we cut the trunk of a banana, it quickly sends up suckers again. (*cf:* **timpuwad 1**)

**puwa'** *v. tr.* To pick something up off floor or ground. *Bang aniya' bay ahūg pareyo' subay puwa'ku.* If something has fallen below I should retrieve it. *Bang ahūg ai-ai mbal tapuwa', wa'i alungay katūyan.* If anything falls and can't be picked up, it is utterly lost. *Ā, nilele na pa'in e' tohongan, pinuwa'.* Well, the turtle reached it by crawling, and it was picked up. (*Thesaurus:* **imut**)

**pagpuwa'** *v. intr. aN-* To be involved in picking up things found in passing. *Magpuwa' bāt na, binowa amole' palauk.* Gathering trepang now, taking it home as a viand.

**puwa'-puwa'** *v. tr.* To derive something from non-traditional sources, as words or customs newly come into use. *Lling pinuwa'-puwa' itū, sali' halam aniya' ma dunya. Ngga'i ka dī lling Sama.* These borrowed words, like something that never existed in the world. Not real Sama words.

**puwas**₁ **1)** *adj. a-* Free from limitation or liability. *Apuwas na kita man bala'.* We have come safely through disaster. (*cf:* **kiyas**) **1.1)** *v. tr. -an* To remove a liability such as a debt, a moral fault, or something which limits movement. *Bang ka kaleboran he' lubid, puwasin maka tangannu.* If a rope gets looped around you, take it off with your hand. *Amuwasan aku engkot itū abō' aku makala'an.* I am removing this tie so I can get away. *Amuwasan kita dusata.* We are freeing ourselves from our misdeeds. (*Thesaurus:* **haun**₂**, lappas**₂ **1, liyus 1.2**) **2)** *v. tr. -an* To deliver from difficulty or danger. *Ma kosog-kawasana, pinuwasan kam e'na min lahat pagbanyaga'an.* By his mighty power he got you out of the land of slavery. *Tantu iya amuwasan ka'a min jallat.* He will surely extricate you from the trap.

**pagpuwas**₁ *v. intr. aN-* To be fully over and done with. *Mbal magpuwas hinang, magsa'ud sadja.* Ritual activities are never fully over, they just overlap.

**puwas**₂ *conj.* After, in time. *Puwas itu, da'a ka amangan apa'it, ā?* After this don't eat bitter foods, okay? (*Thesaurus:* **katis**₂ **1, ubus**₂)

**pagpuwas**₂ *adv.* After in time; subsequently. *Pagpuwas ī'-i, tǐddo'an pa'in kami, aniya' aninduk.* After that, while we were becalmed, something took our bait.

**puwas ē'** *adv. phrase* After that. *Puwas ē', palabay t'llung'llaw, anganak na iya.* After that, three days passing, she gave birth. *Am'lli aku pai nihinang mbo', puwas ē'-i tin'ppa ni linsungan.* I will buy rice to invoke the ancestor, after that it will be pounded in a mortar.

**puwasa** *v. intr. aN-* To observe a religious fast by refraining from food and other physical necessities.

**pagpuwasa** *v. intr. aN-* To observe the fast. *Magdakayu' sigām gara' subay magpuwasa.* They came to agree that they should be fasting.

**puyu'** *n.* A small bag for holding loose items such as money, rice or small fish. *Ya puyu' suput buwas ilū, bang ma kami suput atawa pokot.* About

that *puyu'* for holding rice, for us the word is *suput* or *pokot*. *Aniya' isāb puyu' pang'nna'an s'mmek, pang'nna'an sīn ma kasehe'an.* There are also *puyu'* for storing clothes. For other people it is a money container. *Aniya' puyu' ilū, ya puyu' suput buwas ilū. Bang ma kasehe'an puyu', bang ma kami suput atawa pokot.* There is a word *puyu'*, the one for holding rice. For some it is *puyu'*, for us it is *suput* or *pokot.* (*Thesaurus:* **pokot₂ 1, suput₂**)

**puyu'-puyu'** *n.* 1) Gloves or mittens. 1.1) *v. tr. -an* To enclose hands in gloves or mittens. His hands are put into mittens to prevent scratching.

# R r

**Rabiul Ahil** *n. phrase* The fourth month of the Islamic year. (*Set:* **Bulan Muharram, Julka'idda, Julhadji', Jumadir Ahil, Jumadir Awal, Rabiul Awal, Radjab, Ramadan, Saban, Sappal, Sawwal**)

**Rabiul Awal** *n. phrase* The third month of the Islamic year. (*cf:* **Maulud**; *Set:* **Bulan Muharram, Julka'idda, Julhadji', Jumadir Ahil, Jumadir Awal, Rabiul Ahil, Radjab, Ramadan, Saban, Sappal, Sawwal**)

**Radjab** *n.* The seventh month of the Islamic year. (*Set:* **Bulan Muharram, Julka'idda, Julhadji', Jumadir Ahil, Jumadir Awal, Rabiul Ahil, Rabiul Awal, Ramadan, Saban, Sappal, Sawwal**)

**Ramadan** *n.* The ninth month of the Islamic year, the month in which the fast is observed. (*syn:*

**Bulan Puwasa**; *Set:* **Bulan Muharram, Julka'idda, Julhadji', Jumadir Ahil, Jumadir Awal, Rabiul Ahil, Rabiul Awal, Radjab, Saban, Sappal, Sawwal**)

**ranggo** *n.* Rank, especially in the military sense. *Taga ranggo, buwat baranggay kapten, a'a pinagaddatan.* Ranking, like a barangay captain, a person to be respected.

**rasul** *n.* An apostle, especially in reference to the Prophet Muhammad.

**rebelde** *n.* Rebel forces.

**rīng** *n.* A basketball hoop. *Ma basketbōl, kalogdangan halam minsan makasagid ni ring.* In basketball, right on target, not even brushing the hoop.

**Rū** *n.* The Spirit (of God).

**rukun** *var. of* **lukun**

# S s

**sa** *ptl.* So; indeed. (Mild emphasis marker). *Yuk kallo' inān, "Nā, bay na sa yukku ma ka'am."* The heron said, "I did indeed say that to you." *Tinilaw iya he' si Is, "Arī, sai sa ka'a ilu?"* Is asked him, "Hey, who are you?" *Istori hē putingan sa.* That story was surely a lie. *Na ka'a sa ilū.* So it's you then [a greeting]. (*Thesaurus:* **bā 2, ka₁, du 1**)

**sa-** (var. **saN-**) *aff.* Numeral prefix meaning 'one'. Used with a small set of nouns or classifiers. *A'a magsambahayang sajuma'at-sajuma'at.* A person who prays one Friday after another. *Ndiya ma aku santonga' ilū.* Hand me one half of that. (*cf:* **sangka-...sangka-**; *Thesaurus:* **da- 1, dakayu'₁ 1, dangan 1, issa, ssa₃**)

**sa-+STEM-R-** *aff.* Prefix meaning 'no matter how many/much' of the prefixed quality, where

'STEM-R' represents the reduplication of the stem. Used in constructions that describe a pair of contrasting characteristics. *Saheka-heka pi'itu milikan, aheka atulak.* No matter how many Westerners come, a lot will depart. *Sala'at-la'at l'lla taga lilus, ahāp l'lla.* Regardless of how ugly a fellow is who has a watch, he's a fine fellow.

**sabab₁** *n.* 1) A cause; reason. *Ai sababna angkan buwattē'?* What is the reason it is like that? (*cf:* **jalanan**) 1.1) *conj.* Because. *Sin'kko'-s'kko' si Bu sabab aheka takakanna.* Bu has the hiccups because he has eaten a lot. (*Thesaurus:* **apa, kalna' 1.1, pagka, po'on₂, sangga'ina, saukat**) 1.2) *ptl.* Development marker in narrative discourse that signals background information (especially where there is no logical relation of result-reason).

**pagsababan** (var. **sababan**) *n.* The basis or grounds of some outcome; an underlying cause. *Ai bay pagsababanbi angkan ka magbono' maka klasmetnu?* What was the reason why you and your classmates were fighting? (*Thesaurus:* **katikmuhanan, po'on-sabab, singgit**)

**sabab**₂ *adj. a-* **1)** To be a cause of sickness. *Asabab bang halam aniya' tulahan.* It is a cause of illness if there is nothing paid [to the healer]. **1.1)** *v. tr.* To make someone ill, the action of an offended ritual ancestor. *Aho', kauli'an bang halam aniya' ama'in, halam aniya' anabab.* Yes, it will be healed provided nothing supernatural is making him sick, causing the sickness. (*Thesaurus:* **bihang**₁, **labba'**₂ **1, pa'in**₃ **1, semet, sila'-sila' 1.1**; *syn:* **sambihit**)

**sabab-kalna'** var. of **kalna'**

**sababan** var. of **pagsababan**

**sabak** *see:* **pagsabak, pasabak, sabakan**

**sabakan** *n.* The place close to one's heart where a baby may be held. *Tinambunan ka he'na ma sabakanna ibarat manuk.* He will cover you close to his body, figuratively like a bird. *Min pila aku bay bilahi animuk ka'am ma sabakanku, sali' sapantun manuk d'nda bang magsabak anak-anakna ma deyo' pikpikna.* How many times have I wanted to gather you close to my body, figuratively like a hen when she shelters her chicks beneath her wings.

**sabal** *adj. a-* **1)** Characterized by patient acceptance. *In a'a asabal alalom panghatina, sago' ya a'a al'kkas angamasu' ama'nda' kababbalanna.* A patient man has deep understanding, but the person who is quick to lose his temper displays his stupidity. **1.1)** *v. tr. -an* To accept a situation with patience or resignation. *Buwattē' na pa'in pamogos si Delila sampay mbal na kasabalan e' si Samson.* Delila's persistence went on like that until Samson could no longer bear it. *Ya b'nnalna, sabalanbi saga a'a minsan sigām magmandahan ka'am.* In truth, you put up with people even though they are bossing you around.

**pagsabal** *v. intr. aN-* To be consistently patient under adverse conditions. *Yukna, "Magsabal ka, halam ka kab'llihanku." Sinoho' iya da'a magsusun.* He said, "Be patient; I haven't bought you anything." He is told not to be regretful. *Saguwa' bang saina paluwas min luma'nu ni kalān-lānan bo' tapapatay kami, na magsabal iya pagka dusana na tu'ud.* But if anyone goes out of your house into the streets and is killed by us, then he must accept it patiently because it was his own fault. (*Thesaurus:* **iman**₁ **1.1, sandal 1.1, tahan-tahan, tangka', tatas 1.2**)

**sabali** *see:* **pagsabali, sabali-bali**

**sabali-bali** *adv.* Inevitably; probably. *Sabali-bali aniya' hunus.* There will most likely be a storm. *Sulugun medyas itū, sabali-bali mbal sarang.* Try these socks on, they probably won't fit. *Sabali-*

*bali kamisitaku, halam bay kaumbulan.* Something is bound to happen to my T-shirt, it didn't have a number on it.

**sabali-bali man atay** *adj. zero* Slipped from one's mind. {idiom} *Buwat aniya' tab'llita ai-ai bo' tapat'nna', ati bo' kita makal'ngngan. Pamat'nna'anta inān halam kabiyasahan. Yukta, "Sabali-bali min atayku."* Like when we've bought something and put it down and then walked off. The place where we put it is unfamiliar. We say, "It went right out of my mind." *Sabali-sabali man atayku suru' hē', sali' takaipat bahā', nsa' bay taentom.* That spoon slipped my mind, forgotten perhaps, beyond recall.

**Saban** *n.* The eighth month of the Islamic year, the month in which Muslims tend their graves and remember their dead. (*syn:* **Nispu, Taiti'**; *Set:* **Bulan Muharram, Julka'idda, Julhadji', Jumadir Ahil, Jumadir Awal, Rabiul Ahil, Rabiul Awal, Radjab, Ramadan, Sappal, Sawwal**)

**sabanding** *n.* A blemish; an imperfection. *Luma' mital inān halam aniya' sabandingna, minsan langaw paligid.* That house with the metal roof has no defects, even a fly would slip on it. *Agsay makasampig ma luma' mital, halam aniya' sabandingna, alingkat, ya kalanu'anna.* We promptly came up alongside a house with a metal roof, a house with no blemishes, beautiful, its finish so smooth.

**sabarang** *adj. zero* Every; covering an entire range. *A'a kamemon ma sabarang lahat.* All people in every place. *Sabarang lahat aniya' lungsud.* Every land has its towns. *Sabarang ummat tinawalan he'na.* He recited an incantation over the entire congregation. (*Thesaurus:* **kamemon 1.1, lullun 1**)

**sabasag** *adv.* No more than; limited to. *Sabasag saga sangpū' pilak.* No more than ten pesos or so. *Mbal kām am'lli lapohan pabalik, sabasag hal gās ya billi pabalik.* You will not buy another stove, it's only kerosene that you will buy again. (*Thesaurus:* **ngkon-ngkon**)

**sabat**₁ *n.* A lidded basket, closely woven of split cane, about 20 cm square.

**sabat**₂ *v. advrs. ka-...-an* To be struck accidentally, as by crossfire. *Amatay si Su, bay kasabatan.* Su is dead, hit by a stray bullet. (*Thesaurus:* **hamiyu 1, samba 1.1, sambut 1.1**)

**sabay** *v. tr.* To harm something by a powerful blow; to strike something in passing. *Bang kita nilagut, tasabay tina'ita.* If someone slashes us, our intestines are harmed too. *Bang aku am'ssi bo' mareyo' p'ssiku, wa'i ab'kkat naelon. Bay sinabay he' tangi', bay kittob ma tonga'an.* When I am fishing and my hook and line are down below, the nylon line snaps. It was hit by a Spanish mackerel and bitten through halfway up. *Tasabay isāb lubid bang kita palabu, tasabay he'* *pahi, ab'kkat.* A rope too can be damaged when we lie at anchor, hit in passing by a stingray and snapped in two.

**pagsabay** *v. intr. aN-* To collide with each other; to sideswipe. *Minsan taguri' pinaleyang, magsabay mariyata' bang pinagsekot taguri' dakayu'. Magsabay ya baran taguri', agese' mariyata'.* Even a flying kite may collide when another kite is brought close. The frames of the kites collide and the paper tears while aloft.

**sabba** *n.* The cooking banana or plantain. *Musa paradisiaca.* (*cf:* **saging 1**)

**sabba-abuhan** (var. **abuhan**) *n.* A variety of banana with small white-fleshed fruit.

**sabba-keyat** *n.* A variety of banana with reddish fruit.

**sabba-manila'** *n.* A variety of banana with larger than average fruit.

**sabba-pote'** *n.* A variety of banana with white-fleshed fruit.

**sabba-sūk** *n.* A variety of banana believed to have come from Jolo Island.

**sabba-sussu'** (var. **sussu'**) *n.* A variety of cooking banana, sweet enough to be eaten raw.

**sabbut** *n.* **1)** An invocation to God or some other superior entity. *Aniya' sabbut ni kahāpan, aniya' sabbut ni kala'atan.* There are invocations for good, and there are invocations for evil. **1.1)** *v. tr.* To call on someone by name, especially when asking for help or favor. *Bang aku bay abakat e' bila' kassa', tasabbutku si Ina'.* When I had cut myself on a broken bottle, I called on my mother. *Bang sinabbut Tuhan, yukta, "O Tuhan, dūlin aku."* When God is named we say, "O God, grant my desire." *Sabbutun kahālanku ma munda'an gubnul.* Mention my situation in the presence of the governor. *Bang pa'in du isāb tahatinu in kamemon mareyom sulat itu, bang ai bay tasabbut itū.* So long as you understand everything in this letter, what it is being asked for. (*Thesaurus:* **dē' 1.1, lingan 1, owa'₁ 1, tawag**)

**pagsabbut ni batu** *v. intr. aN-* To engage in a futile effort [lit. to call on rocks for help]. {idiom} *Amatay kita magsabbut ni batu bang halam aniya' katandanan.* We wear ourselves out calling on the rocks if there is no place to land.

**sabela** *adj. zero* Striped, of a fabric pattern.

**sabi₁** *v. tr.* To call on someone for help. *Buwat sali' bay magosol hāg, bay na sinabi a'a buwat kabagayan si Panglima La.* Like when putting in the houseposts, *Panglima* La's friends were advised [of the need]. *"Tuwan,"* yukna, *"pasabihin lagi' aku. Tabangin gi' aku."* "Sir," he said, "please let me speak of my need. Please help me." *Aniya' sabiku ni ka'a, amuwan ka tambal.* I have a request to make of you, give me some medicine. *Sabiku si Bu angalukupan pelang ina'an bo' tinangon.* I ask Bu's help in scrubbing

that canoe, to dry while raised. (*cf:* **dangin, tabang 1**)

**sabi₂** *v. tr.* To be aware of pain in one's body. *Aniya' sabita ma deyom baranta bang kita abusā'.* We feel something in our bodies when we have suffered internal strain. *Sinabi daggahana.* Pain is felt in his chest. (*Thesaurus:* **labay₃, lapa₁, nanam 2, ssa₂**)

**sabil** *n.* Death resulting from someone running amok.

**pagsabil** *v. intr. aN-* To run amok in response to emotional stress. *Bang amatay anakku, magsabil aku ni M'ddas.* If my child dies I will go berserk [killing people] in Siasi Town. *Minnē' magsabil si Samson bo' angalagut saga a'a inān ati aheka sigām amatay.* Because of that Samson ran amok slashing those people so that many of them died.

**parang-sabil** *n.* A genre of song celebrating a battle, often sung to the accompaniment of the bamboo marimba.

**pagparang-sabil** *v. intr. aN-* To sing a battle song. *Bang magparang-sabil, subay gabbang.* When singing the battle song, there should be a bamboo marimba.

**sabit₁** *n.* **1)** A hook-shaped item for catching, hanging or fastening. **1.1)** *v. tr. -an* To catch something on a hook. *Pagp'ssi ya agasi' itū kasabitan ya pagal basi' ē'.* While this giant was fishing that iron cage was hooked up. **2)** A fishhook with multiple points. (*Thesaurus:* **kawil, p'ssi 1**) **2.1)** *v. tr.* To catch schooling fish using multiple hooks. *Bang aku anabit bawis subay niumpanan tinapay atawa saging.* When I fish for rabbitfish with a multiple hook it must be baited with bread or banana. **2.2)** *v. advrs. ka-...-an* To be hooked, of a fish. *Bang kita am'ssi tananamta tinduk daing aheya. Pagsintakta halam kasabitan. Yukta, "Am'llos pahāp p'ssi, heya daing hē' halam kasabitan!"* When we are fishing we feel a large fish taking the bait. On striking it wasn't hooked. We say, "The hook has come untied, such a big fish and it wasn't hooked!" *Engkotanta kulambut ni tōng tonda'. Pagtinduk daing, kasabitan na, sakali itū wa'i ang'bba.* We tie a dropper to the end of the trolling-line. When the fish strikes it is hooked, and then suddenly lets go.

**pagsabit** *v. intr. aN-* To engage in a contest of strength in which two opponents hook elbows together and try to force the other's hand down onto the table. (*Thesaurus:* **pagkagat 1.1, pagsanggul 1.1**)

**sasabit** *n.* A hook for hanging things on. (*syn:* **sasagnat**)

**sabit₂** *v. tr.* To weave cloth with a distinctive hooked technique.

**sabitan** *n.* A money belt, machine-woven of heavy yarn, worn with sauwal-type trousers. (*Thesaurus:* **kambot 1, kandit, sambung₂, sintoron**)

**sab'nnal-b'nnal** (derivative of **b'nnal**) *adj. zero* True; genuine; consistent with facts. *Bang ka sab'nnal-b'nnal, bang pa'in buwanannu kawasa ma a'a bay amuwanan aku sarakka.* If you [ritual ancestor] are genuine, may you give strength to the man who gave me alms. *Buwat kita magsapa, s'lle' bale puhu', aku tuhumanu bay angā' ai-ainu bo' halam du isāb sab'nnal-b'nnal, na magsapa kita.* Like us two swearing an oath, which God forbid, you accuse me of taking something of yours but it's not true, then we swear an oath. (*Thesaurus:* **pasti'**₁).

**sablay** *v. tr. -an* To drape a flexible item over something firm, as clothes on a line, or split fish across a beam. (*Thesaurus:* **pagsalay**₁, **parablay**)
**sablayan** *n.* A line or pole over which cloth items are draped.

**sabod** var. of **sabol**

**sabol** (var. **sabod**) *v. intr. pa-* To impede progress, as floating rubbish does when one is paddling, or as underbrush does when walking. *Bang aku lum'ngngan kaleya aniya' pasabol mareyom. Mbal aku sali' makaluhaya lum'ngngan.* When I'm walking inland there is stuff in there that impedes progress. It's like I am not free to walk. *Anepet-nepet tahik bang pasabol tangan.* Seawater splashes up when a hand is dragging in the water. *Pasabol itū aniya' pagūng ati ameya' ma kukku batangan atawa ma munda', buwat sala ulak.* This word *sabol* is when something floating is caught on the hook of outrigger boom or on the bow, stuff like floating seagrass. (*cf:* **sagid 1**)
**pagsabol** *v. intr. aN-* **1)** To catch on multiple obstacles. *Lubid itū ya maglagesles. Aniya' sehe'na magsabod.* It's the rope here that catches on things. It has a companion word: *sabod.* **1.1)** *v. intr. aN-* To break the flow of speech or singing (fig.)
**sabol-sabol** *v. intr. pa-* **1)** To hinder the flow of conversation by making a noise. *Ya mbal kita makakale, tahik pasabol-sabol.* The reason we couldn't hear was that the sea was making a noise. *Pasabol-sabol na pa'in iya itū. Itiya' kita magsuli-suli.* He keeps on making a noise. We are having a talk. **1.1)** *v. tr.* To interrupt someone talking.

**sabsab** *v. tr.* To take food or fruit without asking permission. *Anabsab kita kaleya, mbal kita amuhun.* We hunt around inland [for fruit], we don't ask permission. *Anabsab saga ni pilang, kalu aniya' panggi' kayu. Bang aniya' takakan, kakanta na, halam aniya' pagtilaw.* We fossick around in the fireplace, maybe there is some cassava. If there is food we eat it, no questions asked. (*Thesaurus:* **dumpas, t'ppas**₁)
**pagsabsab** *v. intr. aN-* To rummage around. *Buwat kita at'kka man dilaut, bo' kita lingantu sidda, magsabsab kita ma kusina.* Like when we arrive from the sea and we are very hungry, we rummage around in the kitchen.

**Sabtu'** *n.* Saturday. (*Thesaurus:* **Ahad, Alba'a, Hammis, Isnin, Juma'at, Salasa**)

**sabu** *conj.* **1)** During; while. *Sabu inān binissala e'na ni aku, makaromol aku maka halam aniya' tapah'llingku.* While he said that to me, I looked down and said nothing. (*Thesaurus:* **baba, sinabu 1**) **1.1)** *v. intr. pa-/-um-* To coincide deliberately with some event or phase. *Sumabu kam wanni buwattina'an. Dahū halam kam bay maitu.* You will coincide with the odorous mango season this time. You were not here previously. *Aging itū mbal kinata'uhan, sabu itū tinu'ud.* This word *aging* refers to something not known about [beforehand], *sabu* is deliberate. (*Thesaurus:* **pag'tta', pagsamp'kka', salta', tā'-tā' 1**) **1.2)** *v. tr.* To meet someone by intent. *Sabuhun aku ni M'ddas bang ugtu-llaw.* Meet me in Siasi at noon. *Bang aku ni Malaybalay anabu lilusku, halam at'kka.* *Bang ta'abut pagtambukuhanta, sabuta na.* If I go to Malaybalay to coincide with my wristwatch, it won't have arrived. If the time we agreed on has come I will coincide.
**pagsabu** *v. intr. aN-* To coincide; to co-occur. *Magsabu aku maka bagayku, sali' maglanggal inān, ma lān ka, ma tabu' ka.* I meet up with my friend, like coming across each other, on the trail or at the market. *Palabay aku ma iskul, magsabu aku maka pinagpariyata' panji, jari pahondong aku.* I was passing by the school and coincided with the raising of the flag, so I stopped. *Bang saupama magistori-istori maka d'nda. Magtaratu kami, iya lum'ngngan pehē', aku isāb lum'ngngan, ati magsabu.* Discussing plans with a girl, for example. We agree on a time, she will walk there, I will walk too, and we'll meet up.

**sabud** *v. tr. -an* To scatter small items deliberately, as when sowing seed broadcast. *Bang kām atulak ni Bukidnon, sinaburan saga onde'-onde' sokal he' si Mām, sali' nilarukan.* When you are leaving for Bukidnon, Mam scatters sugar over the children, same as throwing it. (*Thesaurus:* **labak, paglatag-latag, sabulak**)

**sabul** *n.* **1)** Behavior that offends social norms. **1.1)** *adj. a-* Behaving with gross disregard for accepted standards of behavior. *Asabul ka, minsan aku magsulat nijogjog he'nu lamisahan.* You're naughty, even when I am writing, you bump the table. *Patungkilang ma a'a inān, asabul.* The outstanding thing about that fellow is that he violates community standards. (*Thesaurus:* **la'at bowa', lu'ug-lama' 1, lumu'**)
**pagkasabulan** *v. intr. aN-* To be involved in indecent or antisocial behavior.

**sabulak** *v. tr. -an* To scatter or sprinkle something over a target. *Sinabulakan, sali' tinata' maka tahik.* Thrown and scattered, like sprinkling with seawater. *Pinapatay saga a'ana kamemon, nilubu* *kaluma'anna, maka sinabulakan asin.* All its people killed, its houses dismantled, and sprinkled with salt. (*Thesaurus:* **labak, paglatag-latag, sabud**)

**sabuli-buli** (derivative of **buli-buli**) *adv.* Securely; definitely; permanently. *Nīnna' sabuli-sabuli saumul-umul. Subay t'nna' sadja, da'a akanat minsan lima sīn.* Stored very securely forever. It should just stay there, nothing scattered, not even a five-centavo coin. (*syn:* **sakuli-kuli**).

**sabun** *n.* 1) Soap. 1.1) *v. tr. -an* To apply soap; to wash using soap. *Da'a pukpukin s'mmek ilū, subay sinabunan.* Don't pound those clothes, they need to be soaped.

**sabung** *v. intr. pa-* To face in a specific direction. *Aheka jungjung pasabung ni kulaet.* There are many half-beaks [a kind of fish] facing the pressure lantern. *Pasabung kita pehē'.* Let's head that way. *Pasabunganku tudju kita.* I will get it to face towards us. (*Thesaurus:* **harap₁ 1.2**)

**sabut₁** *n.* Knowledge of a language other than one's own.

**pagsabut** *v. intr. aN-* To be competent in a foreign language. *Nā, ai ba tilawnu bang mbal minsan magsabut? Hal magumaw dakuman.* What can you ask about when you don't even understand each other's language? All you can do is pretend to be dumb. *Na ala'at pamūng Jipun. Bang kita bay magsabut, ahāp isāb sigām.* So the speech of the Japanese was bad. When we understood each other, they were good too. (*Thesaurus:* **hati 1.3**)

**sabut-bahasa** *n.* A person who understands multiple languages.

**sabut₂** *v. tr. -an* To deal cards to a player. *Sinabutan ka he' bangka.* You'll be dealt [cards] by the banker. *Buwat kita maglaki, mbal anabut bang lima, suma'an walu' tahanna.* Playing lucky [a card game] for example, he doesn't deal if a 5, or an 8, is the last.

**sabuy** *v. tr. -an* To scatter something by throwing. *Jari pehē' na iya ni bohe' danaw anabuyan asin pehē'.* So he went to the lake and threw salt into it.

**sāk₁** *n.* 1) A feeling of disgust or revulsion. *Si Mo inān bay tabanganku. Hal llaw itu halam aku bay makatabang, magtūy sāk ma deyom atayna.* I have been helping Mo. It is only today that I haven't happened to help, and he promptly takes offense from it. *Bang kita ah'lling ala'at ni Tuhan, sāk ma deyom atayna.* When we say something bad to God, it is an offense to him. (*Thesaurus:* **pangkal, sakkal, saggan, sammal 1**) 1.1) *adj. a-* Offensive to. *Bissalanu ilu makasāk deyom atay. Sali' ka anumpalak.* Your language is offensive. It is as if you are being deliberately insulting. *Asāk mareyom atayta, sali' amissala kita mbal ahāp, buwat kita anumpalak.* Offensive, as when we say something that is not good, like when we cause offense.

**sāk₂** *see:* **pasāk**

**sakadjap** *adv.* Momentarily; in an instant. *Ya bay ndang, sakadjap ginanti'an ni baha'u.* What was well-worn exchanged in a flash for something new. *Pangguwa' ya ta'nda'ta maina'an. Yukku, "Nda'un." Pang'nda'nu halam. Yukku, "Baha'u bay pak'nda', sakadjap daka ma'ai iya."* It was a ghost that we saw over there. I said, "Look". When you looked there was nothing. I said, "The sighting was just now, and suddenly it is [gone] who knows where." (*Thesaurus:* **agsāy, dai'-dai'an, magtūy, saru'un-du'un, sigla' 1**)

**sakal** *n.* An adze. (*Thesaurus:* **likup 1, pa'at 1, patuk, sangkap 1, sosokan**)

**sakali₁** *n.* A settled mood; absorption in a task. *Onde' inān bang sakalina anangis, agon mbal pa'aluk.* When that child settles down to crying it is almost impossible to comfort him. *Bang sakalina maghinang, maghinang to'ongan, agon mbal kasekotan.* When his commitment is to work he really works, can scarcely be approached. *Abila sakalina makapagl'ngngan, agon mbal anandan luma'.* When [he] keeps on going here and there, he scarcely makes it home.

**sakali₂** *conj.* And then; and so; forthwith. *Buwat si Li inān angamu' ai-ai ni ina'na, bo' mbal kabuwanan. Sakali itū yampa kabuwanan bang anangis na.* Like Li asking for anything from her mother, and not being given it. So she is only given it when she cries. *Bang aku an'bba ni Bakal maka'ā' aku gamat, sakali maglūng-lūngan mareyom mohang angahimāt.* I was strand-gathering at Bakal and got some *gamat* trepang, it promptly sloshes about in the hull, going limp. *Bay kita magsuli-suli mareyom luma', sakali aniya' a'a pasōd halam ta'nda'ta.* We were talking inside the house, and then someone entered the house without us seeing. *Ahā, sakali ta'abut Buli'-Lakit subay iya amowa pabīng.* Well now, as soon as we got to Rock Point he must have us go back. (*Thesaurus:* **ati, manjari₂, nā 1**)

**pagsakali** *conj.* Instead; contrariwise. *Yuknu ma aku, "Bapa', pasōd aku ni Muslim." Pagsakali, ilu ka pabalik ni agamanu.* You said to me, "Uncle, I will become a Muslim." But instead you return to your religion. *Angaku na ka angahinang, pagsakali nsa' bay talusnu. Bbahannu ru.* You agreed to do the work, but in actual fact you didn't complete it. You just abandoned it.

**sakalibut** (derivative of **libut**) *n.* The entire region surrounding a reference location. *Aheka panit ma sakalibutta itū.* There are many tuna in this area around us. *Magtingkō'an sigā ma sakalibut bihingna.* They sat down around him. *Ma sakalibut luma' kami.* In the surroundings of our house.

**sakalingkal** *n.* The entire region surrounding a reference location. *Ma sakalingkal Siasi inān, ameya' ma si Ish kamemon.* The entire area of

Siasi, all go with Ish [as mayor]. (*Thesaurus:* **katilibut, katilingkal**)

**sakap** *n.* 1) Equipment needed for an activity or enterprise. *Lungbus aku pareyo'-pariyata' ma sakap bayanan.* I am complete from top to bottom in things needed for a canoe. *Na dai'-dai'ku na, magduwa' na kami kasakapan, binowa ni Silibis.* I'll make it short, we loaded all the things needed for taking to the Celebes. (*Thesaurus:* **panyap** 1) **1.1)** *adj.* zero In readiness. *Sakap na sigām angandogpa'.* They are ready to attack. **1.2)** *v. tr.* To get things ready. *Manjari itū sinakap na s'mmek-s'mmek sigām, p'ssi-p'ssi sigām.* So then they prepared all their clothes, all their little fishhooks. *Anā, sinakapan na e' Ina' inān.* Well then, it was prepared [for us] by Mother. (*Thesaurus:* **tagama**)

**sakap-kowan** *adj.* zero Right-handed.

**sakap-d'nda** *n.* Things required by women. *Sakap-l'lla ma l'lla, sakap-d'nda ma d'nda.* Men have the things they require, women have theirs.

**sakap-gibang** *adj.* zero Left-handed.

**sakap-l'lla** *n.* Things required by men.

**sakat₁** *v. tr.* To attack a target physically. *Sinakat magbono'. Bang kita pinahimulas magbono' na.* Attacked for the purpose of fighting. When we are accused of cowardice, we fight. (*Thesaurus:* **atāk** 1.1, **dogpa'** 1.1, **dugpak** 2, **gubat**)

**sakat₂** *v. intr.* pa- To go up onto something; to board a boat. *Pasakat na kām.* Come on up. *Pasakat na kami ni kappal pabīng.* We went aboard the ship again. *Bay sigām magh'nda-h'lla, sampay ta'abut waktu kasakat disi Nabi Nū ni diyata' adjung.* They continued to marry, until the time when the Prophet Noah went aboard the *adjung* [a fabled vessel]. They took wives and husbands until the time when the Prophet Noah went aboard the *adjung* [a fabled vessel]. (*Thesaurus:* **dita'i, diyata'** 1.1)

**sakat ni ugtu** *phrase* To approach zenith, of sun or moon. *Anakat-nakat ni ugtu bulan.* Rising up the moon's zenith.

**sakaukat** var. of **saukat**

**sakaum** (derivative of **kaum**) *v. intr.* pa- To form a single community together with the people of another kin group. *Pasakaum sigām ma saga a'a ya asal maglahat maina'an.* They formed a single group with the people who had always lived there.

**pagsakaum** *v. intr.* aN- To form a single community, of people from diverse backgrounds.*Magsakaum, sali' magdakayu' a'a Butun maka a'a Siganggang, bay tinambukuhan e' mayul.* Forming a single community, like the people of Butun coming together with the people of Siganggang, told to do so by the mayor.

**sakay** 1) *v. intr.* pa- To travel on someone else's vessel or vehicle. *Pasakay na duwangan ya bay sehe'na min damunda' inān.* The two who were his companions on that one boat went aboard. (*Thesaurus:* **bayan** 1.1, **beya'₁, pagbiyahi, palaktas, tumpang, tundug** 1.1) 2) *v. tr.* To enter someone's space without permission, especially for the purpose of robbery or murder. *Anakay itū sali' pariyata' ni luma' ma halam bay ama'id. Sakay* means going up into a house without having asked permission. (*Thesaurus:* **dohay**)

**pasakay** *v. tr.* To allow someone to travel in one's conveyance.

**sakkal** *adj.* zero Something repulsive or profoundly offensive. *Sakkal to'ongan ilu ma Tuhan.* That is very offensive to God. *Kab'nsihinbi ai-ai kaōnan sakkal, patā to'ongan kam minnē'.* Hate anything that is called *sakkal*, get as far as possible from that. (*Thesaurus:* **pangkal, sāk₁** 1, **saggan, sammal** 1)

**sakket** *n.* 1) The nippers or pincers of a crab. *Bang kami anaggaw kagong pēk pinina'anan jinggam engkot ati tasaggaw sakketna.* When we catch mud crabs [we] put chewing gum on a knot and catch it by its nippers. **1.1)** *v. tr.* To nip something, as a crab does. *Bay aku sinakket e' kagong tika'-tika'.* I was nipped by a fiddler crab.

**sakki** var. of **saki**

**sakkop** 1) *v. tr.* -an To catch something with a quick movement. *Bang aniya' daing-daing ma diyata' t'bba sakkopta.* If there are little fish left in shallow water we catch them in our hands. (*Thesaurus:* **sakmit, sagob** 1) 2) *v. intr.* pa- To occur suddenly and without warning. (*Thesaurus:* **papuwa', taggaha', tanyak**)

**sakkul** *n.* The starch dressing in new cloth. *Subay pinakangan buwattē' abō' ala'an sakkulna.* [The cloth] should be pounded like that so its starch comes out. (*Thesaurus:* **almirul** 1, **kanji'**)

**saki** (var. **sakki**) *n.* 1) Sickness; disease. *T'kkahan saki onde' balu inān, ati luhūy pabuhat sakina inān sampay amatay.* That widow's son was struck with sickness, then his sickness became more and more serious until he died. **1.1)** *adj.* a- Unwell; ailing. *Bang aku bay asaki, at'ggol na kasakiku, bay pagnajal si Ina'. Tinimbang aku ma Hailaya.* When I was ill, my illness long-lasting, my mother made a vow. I underwent a weighing ceremony at the Hailaya festival. (*Thesaurus:* **pagpalasahan, pa'in₃** 1)

**pagsaki** *v. intr.* aN- To be chronically ill. *Saupama aniya' asaki, pagsaki, aku-i amūng, "Angulina ni saga anakna maka mpuna."* Someone ill, for example, chronically ill, and I say, "It will be passed on down to his children and grandchildren."

**saki-dayang** *n.* A sexually transmitted disease.

**saki-panau'** *n.* An illness which lies dormant in a person's body.

**saki-titis** *n.* Tuberculosis; other diseases symptomized by extreme loss of condition.

**palsakkihan** *n.* A chronic and persistent illness.

**panaki** *n.* A person subject to frequent sickness.

**sakit** *see:* **da'a sakit, mbal sakit**

**sakla'** *v. intr. pa-* To overflow the normal tidal limit, of the sea. *Tahik ya pasakla'. Bang latap sampay diyata' luma' ta'abut.* Sea that overflows onto land. When a flood occurs it reaches the very tops of houses. (*Thesaurus:* **dunuk, latap 1.1, s'llop**)

**saklay** *n.* A singlet; an undershirt.

**sakmel** *n.* Shrapnel.

**sakmit** *v. tr.* To pick something up with a swift movement. *Buwat sapantun ero' talun anakmit anakna.* Figuratively like a feral dog snatching up its young [in its mouth]. (*Thesaurus:* **sakkop 1, sagob 1**)

**saksak** *adj. a-* **1)** Split right across. *Da'a na pasiyagun hōs ilu. Wa'i asaksak na ko' ilū.* Don't use that sarong as a skirt. It's already split right apart. (*Thesaurus:* **laklak, pensang 1, pungal, sasa₁, segpong, seplak 1, te'as**) **1.1)** *v. tr.* To split something flexible wide open. *Pahali ka, saksakta bowa'nu!* Stop it or I'll tear your mouth apart!

**saksi'** *n.* **1)** A witness; testimony; evidence. *Sali' bay aniya' magbono', niā' saksi'. Angā' saksi' ni baran a'a bay magbono'.* When for example there has been a fight, witnesses are called. They get evidence from the bodies of the people who have been fighting. *Bang magdagsol ni sara' tinawag saksi' he' sara'.* When a case is referred to the courts, witnesses are summoned. (*cf:* **sakup₁ 1**) **1.1)** *v. tr. -an* To give testimony to some fact.

**pagnaik-saksi'** *v. tr.* To bring formal witness; to testify. (*cf:* **pagsab'nnal**)

**saksi' tuhan** *n. phrase* Truth of the highest order (lit. God's truth). {idiom} *Magkahagad kita bang saksi' min manusiya', sagō' akosog lagi' saksi' min Tuhan sabab saksi' tuhan ko'.* We believe when it is evidence from a human, but evidence from God is more powerful because it is God's truth.

**palsaksi'an** *n.* A body of evidence; proof.

**sakulati 1)** *n.* Chocolate, either in slab form or powder. **2)** *adj. zero* Colored in the brown to purple range. (*Thesaurus:* **kausun, loho'-ubi**)

**sakuli-kuli** (derivative of **kuli-kuli**) *adv.* Securely stored or hidden. *Nīnna' sakuli-kuli.* Stored securely. (*syn:* **sabuli-buli**).

**sakup₁** *n.* **1)** A witness to an event. *Na bang mahē' ma opis, yukna, "B'nnal sakup ka bay pagbono' itū? B'nnal ta'nda'nu atawa halam?" Hatina tinawag saksi'.* So there at the office, he said, "Is it true that you are a witness of this fight? Is it true or not that you saw it?" In other words, called as witness. (*cf:* **saksi' 1**; *Thesaurus:* **pangannal₁, sayu 1.1, sipat₁ 1.1, tahu, tilas₁**) **1.1)** *adj. zero* Well informed; knowledgeable. *Sakup iya, sakup iya am'ssi kaut, anonda', amubu, maghinang ma deya.* He is fully knowledgeable,

he knows all about fishing with hook and line, trolling for tuna, about trap fishing, about working ashore. **1.2)** *v. tr. -an* To have full knowledge of some event. *Aho', kasakupan pagbono' sigā. Bay kamahē'anku bay pagbono' sigā.* Yes, their fight was witnessed. I was present there at the time of their fight.

**sakup₂** *v. tr.* To take control over a district; to commandeer. *Sinakup e'na paglahat ē', nihinang ya ai halam bay tahinang e' saga ka'mbo'-mbo'anna.* He took over that district, doing something that had never been done by his ancestors.

**sakutu** *see:* **pagsakutu**

**saddī** *adj. zero* **1)** Different; contrastive; other. *Pagga aniya' llaw saddī, agtūy patandan maka daing.* Another day having come, [he] immediately reached land with the fish. *Aniya' gotom ma lahat ē' saddī min gotom bay kalabayan dī sigām ma waktu dahū.* There was a famine in that land, different from the famines they and others had experienced previously. (*cf:* **bidda' 1.2**) **1.1)** *v. tr. -an* To modify something. *Bangsa saitan, bay tagna' ahāp, sinaddīhan na pikilan he' sigām.* The *saitan* spirits, good at first, but they changed their thinking. **1.2)** *v. intr. pa-* To act differently; to go in a different direction.

**pagsaddī** *v. intr. aN-* **1)** To be different from one another. *A: "Magai kam?" B: "Magsaddī kami minsan dalūng."* A: "What is your kindred relationship?" B: "We are different kindreds even though from the one community." *Magsaddī-saddī lahat, magsaddī-saddī bahasa.* Different lands, different languages. **1.1)** *v. tr.* To make things distinct from each other. *Minnē' pinapagsaddī ba'anan hayop si Yakub maka ba'anan hayop si Leban.* In that way the livestock of Jacob and the livestock of Laban were made separate.

**saddī-saddī** *adj. zero* Unusual; abnormal, of behavior. *Saddī-saddī t'ggolnu ma luma' si Mo!* What a long time you took at Mo's house! (*Thesaurus:* **la'in-la'in, mahal-mahal**)

**pasaddī** *v. tr.* To discriminate, as between two persons, items, or alternatives.

**saddī lling** *n. phrase* Changing the subject. {idiom} *Saddī lling, tu'ud nileya'-leya' ba'anan magh'lla-h'nda sabab heka kasusahan pagkalabayan ma waktu tagna'.* Changing the subject, many people considering marriage are simply terrified because of the many stresses experienced at a previous time.

**saddo'** *var.* of **bāt-saddo'**

**sadja** (*var.* **hadja₂**) *adv.* Just; always; only. *Amono' sadja iya itū.* All he does is kill. *Anginum hadja aku.* I will just have a drink. *Insini' sadja magl'ngngan aku.* I was going for a walk just a moment ago. (*Thesaurus:* **dakuman, hal, la'a, luwal, puntul, samadjana, tunggal 1, yangkon**)

**sadjahitra** *n.* Total well-being; felicity.

**sadsad** *v. intr. pa-* 1) To find something by groping or feeling around. *Wa'i pasadsad tape'na ni tana'.* His feet have felt the ground. *Saukat asā' dakayu' hinang, pasadsad aku ni dakayu'.* Just because one task goes wrong, I feel around for some other task. **1.1)** *v. tr.* To identify or locate something by touch. (*Thesaurus:* **agap₂, gindas, sanaw, sassaw**)

**sadsaran** *n.* The identifying characteristics of a person. (*cf:* **apalal**; *Thesaurus:* **kalakuhan, kasuddahan, hudjidjat, jaguni', jari₄ 1, jāt₁**)

**saen** *v. tr. -an* To affix one's signature to a document. (*syn:* **pasā**)

**sāg** *n.* 1) Mild pain or ache. **1.1)** *v. advrs. ka-...-an* To be mildly unwell due to the influence of supernatural beings or spirits of dead people. *Minsan a'a aheya kasāgan du isāb, waktu saitan agl'l'ngngan. Ap'ddi' kōkta, b'ttong, ala'at palasahan, waktu saitan.* Even grown people can experience *sāg*, during the hour of the walkers. Our heads or stomachs ache, or we feel unwell, at the hour of the spirits. *Makannak kasāgan subay tinawalan.* Children who have *sāg* symptoms should have a healing incantation said over them.

**pagsasāg** *n.* A healer with power to inflict or remove mild ailments.

**sāg-sāg** *v. tr. -an* To treat a mild complaint such as a headache, usually by reciting a charm. *Sāg-sāginbi kono'.* Please recite the charm against the *sāg* condition.

**saga** *ptl.* 1) Plural marker. *Aniya' saga a'a pi'itu.* There are some people coming. (*syn:* **manga**) 2) Marker indicating that the specific item or activity is one among several. *Ya hinang kami magkose' lai' saga, magdakdak.* Our work is to do such things as washing plates, washing clothes. 3) Indicates the approximate nature of a number. *Aniya' kami saga lima munda'.* We were about five canoes. *Aniya' sigām man dambila' saga pitumpū' hekana.* There were approximately seventy of them on the other side. (*syn:* **kulang-labi**)

**sagad** (*var.* **sigad**) *v. tr. -an* 1) To treat something as unimportant. *Buwat saupama kami bay magtunang. Yukna, "Mbal na aku bilahi ma ka'a." Yukku, "Sagarin na."* Suppose we had been sweethearts, and he says, "I don't want you any longer." Then I say, "Don't worry about it." *A: "Ā, pamagayku bang mangku', subay tangī'." B: "Sigarin na."* A: "Hey, what use is bonito to me, it has to be Spanish mackerel!" B: "Never mind, then." **1.1)** To condone something that should be prohibited. *Da'a sagarin kaleya.* Don't allow [them] to go inland.

**pamasagad** *n.* Complacency; lack of concern.

**pasagad** *v. tr. -an* To leave something uncared for; to abandon something. (*Thesaurus:* **patabak**; *syn:* **pasahag**)

**sagai'** *n.* A tribe of people reputed to live in forested areas of Sulu and Sabah.

**sagang** *v. tr.* To ward off a blow; to resist some force. *Buwat kita tinimbak, halam aniya' makasagang iya.* If someone shoots at us there is nothing to protect against that. *Bang kita sōng nilagut sagangta maka tangan. Ya halli'an baranta. Bang makanibaranta tasabay napasta.* When we are about to be slashed we parry it with our hands. It's our body we are cautious of. If it [the slashing] gets to our body our breath will be affected. *Mbal tasagang Tuhan.* God cannot be resisted. *Mbal na sinagang minsan niesogan. Halam aniya' tarapat.* It cannot be resisted, and must be tackled bravely. Nothing can be done. *Sinuntuk aku e'na, bay tasagangku. Nsa' aku tauwa'.* He punched at me, I blocked him. I wasn't hit. (*cf:* **sagga' 1.1**; *Thesaurus:* **ampal, pagang, sangsang, sapad, sulang₁**)

**sagap** *var. of* **sarap₂**

**sagauli'** *v. tr.* To restore something to its former state. *Magtūy anagauli' kaulna.* His ability to communicate came promptly back. (*Thesaurus:* **uli'₁ 1**)

**sagaw** *adj. a-* Noisy. *Da'a kam asagaw, ilu na atuli si Li, ko da'a abati'.* Don't you be noisy, Li is sleeping; so she won't waken. (*Thesaurus:* **bukag, hibuk, hidjul**)

**sagay** *n.* A species of stinging vine. *Sagay itū bahan maglē ma deyom kasob, bang mbal ta'nda'ta bo' tasagidta, kakatolan kita.* This *sagay* is a plant that creeps along in dense growth, if we don't see it and brush against it, we get itchy.

**sagbot** (*var.* **sagmot**) *n.* 1) Brushwood or weedy growth. *A'adla manuk, alahi saga ni deyom kasagbotan.* The chickens are untamed, they sort of escaped into the undergrowth. (*cf:* **kasob, s'ggit 1**) **1.1)** *adj. a-* Weedy; affected by weedy growth. *Parang-parang baili itū mbal asagmot to'ongan.* This *baili* grass is not very weedy. **1.2)** *v. advrs. ka-...-an* To be overgrown with weedy growth. *Kasagbotan, sali' kas'ggitan.* Overgrown with weeds, like being covered with rubbish.

**sagda₁** (*var.* **sagda-sagda**) *v. tr.* To cause someone to be sick, the action of spirit beings such as ancestors, ghosts or spirits. *Bang kami amangan ma olangan bo' sōng sangom, subay binahagi'an deyo' ko da'a kita sinagda.* When we eat out at sea and it is almost dark, we must give a share to the demon of the deep to avoid being made sick by him. *Gallang itū paghampanan onde'-onde' bo' mbal sinagda.* These bracelets provide protection for children from sickness caused by spirit beings. (*syn:* **hagda-hagda**)

**sagdahan** *n.* The baleful influence of a spirit being, generally manifested as sickness. *Minsan akosog ta'atna ni Tuhan, taluwa' isāb sagdahan.* Even though his commitment to God is strong he can still experience the baleful influence of some spirit being.

**sagda**$_2$ var. of **hagda**

**sagda-sagda** var. of **sagda**$_1$

**sagga'** v. intr. pa- **1)** To be responsive to effort (usually with a negative). *Mbal pasagga' s'llog itū apa alandos.* This current cannot be fought because it is strong. **1.1)** v. tr. To oppose some force or influence. *Bang alandos s'llog bo' aheya pelang, mbal tasagga'.* When the current is strong and the canoe is large, one cannot go against the current. *Ya mbal kasagga' pelang apa alandos s'llog maka goyak.* The reason the canoe cannot make headway is the strong current and waves. (*cf:* **sagang**; *Thesaurus:* **balda, dangat 1, paggat, sīng-sūd**)

**pagsagga'** v. intr. aN- To be argumentative. *Ahanus ka maggara', da'a ka magsagga'-sagga'.* Be gentle in discussion, don't keep getting into arguments.

**pagsagga'an**$_1$ n. Something which takes the pressure of a force, as a fulcrum does for an oar.

**pagsagga'an**$_2$ (var. **palsagga'an**) n. **1)** A cause or basis of conflict between two parties. *Bang d'nda sali'-sali', bo' aniya' pagsagga'an tahinang bono', na bang magsekot makapagluray.* When both parties are women, and there is a difference of opinion that turns into a fight, when they get close to each other they may pull each other's hair. *Bang amatay mma'-ina' sigā, hatina taga h'nda na sigā sali'-sali', bo' aniya' pagsagga'an sigā, magtūy magsapa. Mbal magkahāp.* When their parents have died, and they both in fact have wives, if they have a serious dispute, they promptly swear enmity. They will not reconcile. *Ainu-inu aku sabab bang ai na pa'in kala'atan bay tahinangku ma tongod disi Anu, sabab bang ma aku halam aniya' palsagga'anku maka sigām!* I am surprised as to what I may have done wrong in regard to What's-his-name and others, because in my opinion there is no conflict between me and them. **1.1)** v. tr. To contest an issue that is being argued or fought over.

**saggan** n. Something offensive to one's tastes or standards, and thus to be avoided. *Saggan kono' ma Tuhan ya timbangan mbal abontol.* A beam scale that is not correct is said to be offensive to God. *Asammal ma pang'nda'ku; saggan mareyom atayku.* Offensive to my sight; disgusting to my heart. (*Thesaurus:* **pangkal, sāk**$_1$ **1, sakkal, sammal 1**)

**saggaw** v. tr. To catch something; to arrest someone. *Bang kami agtimbak bo' pi'itu pulis, sinaggaw kami.* If we are dynamiting fish and the police come, we get arrested. *Anaggaw aku ka'ullang ni Sowang-sowang.* I will catch some shrimps at Sowang-sowang. *Bay tasaggawku manuk, wa'i makal'ppa pabīng. Halam ahogot he'ku amalut.* I caught a chicken, and it escaped again. I hadn't held it firmly. *Sōng pa'in pehē' pulis inān, yukku, "Bangsi' aku makapehē' abō' lāngku, ati mbal na sigā tasaggaw."* When the police were about to get there, I said, "If only I could have got there in order to stop them, then they would not have been arrested." (*Thesaurus:* **agaw 1.1, pagkidnap 1.1**)

**pagsaggaw-saggaw** v. intr. aN- **1)** To take possession or control of something. **1.1)** v. tr. To take hold of a group. *Ya hukawku pinagsaggaw-saggaw he' mastal.* What I dislike [about school] is always being rounded up by the teacher.

**saggaw-sangom** n. Elopement under cover of darkness. {idiom} (*cf:* **guyud 2, lalas**)

**pagsaggaw-sangom** v. intr. aN- To elope under cover of darkness. {idiom}

**saggaw-ubus** n. Elopement, which is binding and typically takes place under cover of darkness. {idiom} *Nirakop, magpūn-pūnan dī sigā. Bang ma Sama saggaw-ubus.* Seized physically, getting married by their own action. Sama call this binding elopement.

**pagsaggaw-ubus** v. intr. aN- To elope conclusively (with marriage in view). {idiom} (*Thesaurus:* **paglahi 1.1**)

**sagid** v. intr. pa- **1)** To bump or brush against something in passing. *Bang anambahayang si Ba, bo' pasagid ero', abatal na iya.* When Ba goes to pray and a dog brushes against him, he is ritually defiled. *Bang aku lum'ngngan am'lli siga bo' pasagid ni aku d'nda, ataksil aku e' d'nda.* If I step out to buy cigarets and a girl brushes against me, I am fined for [touching] a girl. (*cf:* **sabol**) **1.1)** v. tr. To touch something briefly, as in passing. *Bahan maglē mareyom kasob, bang mbal ta'nda'ta bo' tasagidta, kakatolan kita.* A vine that creeps along inside a thicket, if we don't see it and touch it briefly, we experience itching.

**sagina** v. tr. To welcome people in; to ask visitors to enter. *Bang aniya' pariyata' subay nihulmatta, subay sinagina. Yukta, "Pasōd ka."* If someone comes up into the house we should treat him with courtesy, he should be acknowledged. We say, "Come in." *Minsan kami mbal sinagina, asal du kami pi'ilu.* Even though we are not welcomed in, we have in fact come. (*Thesaurus:* **hīl, owa'**$_1$ **1.1, paidda, sahawi 1**)

**saging** n. **1)** Banana, a generic term for all varieties. *Musa sapientum. Lupis, ya niā' min batang saging. Lupis,* the [tying material] that is obtained from a banana trunk. (*cf:* **sabba**) **2)** Dessert bananas in contrast to the plantain or cooking banana.

**saging-bata'-bata'** (var. **bata'-bata'**) n. A variety of dessert banana, small and delicately flavored.

**saging-hinugun** (var. **hinugun**) n. A dessert banana distinguished by the green color of its skin even when ripe.

**saging-manurung** (var. **manurung**) n. A variety of cooking banana or plantain, used in invoking the banana ancestor. (*cf:* **mbo'-saging**)

**saging-sinangil** (var. **sinangil**) n. A variety of

dessert banana, especially sweet.

**saging-sulay-badju** (var. **sulay-badju**) *n.* A variety of dessert banana, short and yellow-skinned with a slightly tart flavor.

**saging-tadjaw** (var. **tadjaw**) *n.* A variety of dessert banana, large and red-skinned, very sweet.

**saging-tinduk** (var. **tinduk₃**) *n.* A variety of dessert banana which can grow up to 40 cm long and 10 cm in diameter.

**saging-tudlu'** *n.* A variety of dessert banana with tight bunches of small fruit that look rather like the fingers of a hand.

**saging-tumbaga** *n.* A variety of dessert banana, red-skinned with a very rich flavor.

**saging-saging₁** *n.* The juvenile Red Emperor, a fish species. (*gen:* **kutambak**)

**saging-saging₂** *n.* The bird-of-paradise flower and its palm-like plant. *Strelitzia reginae.*

**sagiyaw** *see:* **pagsagiyaw**

**sagmot** var. of **sagbot**

**sagnat** *v. intr. pa-/-um-* **1)** To catch on a projection, as cloth or line may do. *Pagdundang pa'in itū makasagnat bu'un si Ang ma gamut nunuk.* As they swung together, Ang's hair happened to catch in the roots of a strangler fig. *Tananamta lubid atawa tonda' bay sumagnat bang lageklek, bay palebod ni batu.* We can feel that a string or line has snagged when it jerks free a bit, that it has wrapped around a rock. (*Thesaurus:* **kabit₁** 1) **1.1)** *v. tr. -an* To hang something on a projecting object. (*Thesaurus:* **gantung₂** 1.1, **gulantung, sa'ud₁** 1.1)

**sasagnat** *n.* A hook for hanging things on. (*syn:* **sasabit**)

**sagob** *v. tr.* **1)** To catch something such as small fish with a single swift movement. (*Thesaurus:* **sakkop** 1, **sakmit**) **1.1)** *v. tr. -an* To scoop up something with an implement, as water from a well. *Bang ni bohe' si Sa, sinagoban mital, mbal tinambu'an, sinagoban hal.* When Sa goes for water [he] scoops it up with a can, not using a dipper on a string, simply scooped up. (*Thesaurus:* **nduk, sauk** 1.1, **tambu'** 1.1)

**sagō'** var. of **saguwā'**

**sagol** *v. tr.* **1)** To cook the chopped liver of shark or ray with oil or coconut milk. *Alara makalandu' loho' sinagol luku' inān.* That soup of mixed pufferfish liver is too spicy. **1.1)** *v. tr. -an* To add an ingredient to a mixture.

**pagsagol** *v. tr. -an* **1)** To be mixed together, of diverse items or ingredients. **1.1)** *v. tr. -an* To mix various ingredients or items. *Pagsagolin karuwa ginis ilū.* Mix those two kinds. (*Thesaurus:* **haybol, lamud₁** 1.1, **lamugay** 1.1, **paila', simbug** 1, **templa** 1.1)

**sagpe'** (var. **hagpe'**) *adj. a-* **1)** Broken off by force from a plant or tree. *Ahagpe' saging ma kapo'onanna.* The banana has broken off at its base. (*cf:* **sagsag** 1) **1.1)** *v. tr.* To break a

branching piece from the main part, as a pineapple from its base. *Sagpe'un bo' autas. Subay ariki'-diki' bo' tasagpe'. Bang aheya subay bari'.* Break it off so it comes apart. It should be a small thing to be broken off. Bigger things require a knife. **2)** Dead, of a small child. {*idiom*} *Asagpe' dakayu' anakna si Hi.* One of Hi's children has died. (*Thesaurus:* **bugtang, bugtu' napas, butawan** 1.1, **halol, matay₁** 1, **tubag**)

**sagsag** *adj. a-* **1)** Broken off, as limbs of a tree due to strong winds or heavy fruiting. *Bay asagsag mampallam e' baliyu.* The mango tree was broken clean off by the wind. *Kayu asagsag, bay tauwa' baliyu, apōng batangna min po'on maheya.* A broken tree, struck by wind, its limb broken away from the main trunk. (*cf:* **sagpe'** 1) **1.1)** *v. tr.* To break a branch from the main trunk.

**sagtol** *see:* **anagtol**

**sagu** *n.* Serum, the clear liquid emitted from a wound or corpse. *Saguhan, ya pasū bohe'ta, ya isita ahalu', amohe'.* Having serum, our bodily fluid dripping down, or flesh rotting and turning to liquid. (*Thesaurus:* **d'nnat** 1, **nana'**)

**sagudsud** *v. intr. pa-* To drag the feet, as when walking in shallow water or through low brush. *Pasugudsud tape'ta ni gusung bang t'bba. Subay alalom bo' mbal pasagudsud.* Our feet make a noise on the sand when it is low tide. It would have to be deep not to make that noise. *Pasagudsud, mbal pa'angkat tape'ta, pasapu ni tana'.* Dragging, our feet not lifting, sweeping along the ground. *Pasagudsud tape'ta ni gusung bang t'bba. Subay alalom bo' mbal pasagudsud.* Our feet make a noise on the sand when it is low tide. It would have to be deep not to make that noise.

**sagut** (var. **sogot**) *adj. a-* **1)** Tangled, of hair or thread. *Halam bay maka'ā' ai-ai, asagut naylon.* Didn't catch a thing, the line was tangled. *"Da'a pasagutunbi bu'unbi ilū,"* yukna. "Don't let you hair be tangled," he said. (*cf:* **usay** 1; *Thesaurus:* **gumun, lokot, tulabid**) **1.1)** Muddled, of one's thinking. *Asagut saga pamikilta.* Our thinking is somewhat unclear.

**saguwā'** (var. **sagō'; sagwā'; sogo'**) *conj.* But; however; on the other hand. *Bang daing, mbal na buwattē' hekana, sagwā' mbal kami tininduk.* As far as fish were concerned, you've never seen so many, but we didn't get a bite. *Ya lling si Delila ma si Samson, "Yukna in aku kalasahannu, saguwā' mbal aku pangandolannu."* What Delilah said to Samson, "You said that you love me, but you do not trust me." *Yuk kallo', "Makajari, sagō'," yukna, "sumiyan kitabi atulak?"* Heron said, "OK," he said, "but when do we leave?" *Tuttulan sigām itū min Musu', sogō' ma buwattina'an ma Tabawan na sigām maganak-mpu.* Their genealogical links are from Musu', but they are in Tabawan now with their children and grandchildren. (*Thesaurus:* **bo'**₁, **manda'**, **sa'**)

**sagwā'** var. of **saguwā'**

**sahabal** *v. intr. aN-* To make the sound of a solid object moving through water. *Anahabal bang pasampay batangan ma tahik.* A rippling noise occurs when the outrigger boom touches the sea. *Ya hē' mbal paka'nda'annu, wa'i bay aniya' pal'ngngan min buli'annu anahabal.* That's what made it impossible for you to see, someone has gone walking behind you making ripples. (*Thesaurus:* **abal 1.1**, **ebol**, **guyu 1**, **haus 1**, **llis**, **samb'llong**)

**sahabbat** *voc. n.* A courteous address form to a male whose name is unknown or should not be spoken. {rare} *Ganta' kajīnan, yuk jīn i', "O sahabbat."* Possessed by a djinn, perhaps, the djinn there saying, "O Sahabbat." *Pagpi' ni bohe' i', "Allō," yukna, "sahabbat."* Arriving at the water hole, he says, "Aha, friend."

**sahaddat** *n.* **1)** The Muslim confession of faith. **1.1)** *v. tr.* To recite the confession of faith on behalf of someone who is unable to do so himself. *Bang halam aniya' napasna nihaka'an botang matto'a. Subay a'a ilmu'an anahaddat ya bay mamatay hē'.* When he no longer has breath, the community leader is told. It should be a person with spiritual knowledge who recites the *sahaddat* over the one who has died.
   **pagsahaddat** *v. intr. aN-* To make the Muslim confession of faith.

**saha'** *n.* **1)** A sucker from the base of a trunk, especially of a banana plant. **1.1)** *v. intr. pa-* To send up suckers; to sprout. *Bang saging pasaha', bang puhung pasubud.* A banana sprouts, a thorn bush spreads. (*cf:* **tungbu'**; *Thesaurus:* **saingsing 1**, **s'mbut 1**, **suring**₂)
   **pagsaha'** *v. intr. aN-* To produce suckers, of a banana stump. *Bang aniya' buwat saging puwaranta po'onna, al'kkas magsaha' pabalik.* Like when we cut down a banan plant, it quickly sends up suckers again.

**sahal**₁ *n.* **1)** The wash from passing vessels. **1.1)** *v. intr. aN-* To break, of waves. *Bang aniya' goyak lansa, anahal ma gusung. Bang goyak s'llang anahal paruruwambila'.* If the waves are from a launch, they break on the sand. If they are ocean waves, they break on both sides. (*Thesaurus:* **alun-panjang**, **kata'-kata'**, **goyak 1**, **lumbag**, **sampoyak**)
   **pagsahal** *v. intr. aN-* To be breaking, of waves. *Magsahal ma bihing gusung.* Waves breaking on the edge of the sand.

**sahal**₂ *n.* The headgear of a hadji, either a turban or the band that holds it in place. *Hal am'lli sahal ma Singgapura. Halam bay makaniMakka.* He merely bought a turban in Singapore. He hasn't been to Mecca. (*Thesaurus:* **pīs**₁, **sulban 1**, **tuladjuk**)

**sahali-bulan** *n.* The first day of the moon month,

i.e. the day following the apearance of a new moon. (*gen:* **bulan**₂ **2**)

**sahanay** var. of **kalling-sahanay**

**sahapang** *n.* **1)** A long-shafted fish spear with three tines or spikes. *Pindi' itū sinandak maka sahapang ma deyom gusung.* These scallops are probed for in the sand with a spear. *Sahapang, pangahiyak daing, tayum, t'llu solabna.* A sahapang, for spearing fish or sea urchins, has three tines. (*cf:* **budjak 1**; *Thesaurus:* **ablong**, **pana' 1**, **sangkil 1**, **saubang**, **s'llokan**) **1.1)** *v. tr.* To catch fish by spearing.

**sahapat** var. of **pahapat**

**sahasa'** *n.* The finger coral. *gen. Porites. Saddī sahasa' saddī batu. Sahasa' itū luwa tangan. Sahasa'* and *batu* [coral rock] are different things. *Sahasa'* looks like a hand. (*syn:* **lakas-lakas**; *gen:* **batu**₂ **1**)

**sahat** *n.* **1)** A loop (traditionally of rattan) for snaring marine crustaceans such as lobsters. *Sahat itū ma tahik, litag itū ma katalunan.* The *sahat* snare is for the sea, the *litag* snare is for the forest. (*cf:* **litag 1**) **1.1)** *v. tr.* To catch crustaceans using a noose. *Anahat aku kamun pab'llihanku pagsalla'.* I'll snare a mantis shrimp and sell it for playing toss-the-coin.

**sahawi** *v. tr.* **1)** To greet or acknowledge someone in passing. *Sinahawi kita, ya, "Ka'a sa ilu," atawa "Pi'ingga ka?"* We are greeted with "You there," or "Where are you going?" *Mbal minsan anahawi itū.* This one doesn't even acknowledge me. (*Thesaurus:* **hīl**, **owa'**₁ **1.1**, **paidda**, **sagina**) **2)** To inform someone of what is being planned. *Aniya' kagara'an magusaha. "Sahawi'un si Ma, kalu ameya' amokot."* There is a work project being planned. "Let Ma know, he may come trawl-netting."

**sahaya** *n.* **1)** Brightness, of the full moon or the light from a strong source. *Sali' mala'ikat aliput e' sahaya.* Like an angel enveloped in brilliance. **1.1)** *adj. a-* Brilliant; shining. *Asahaya deyomna buwat lilusnu, asawa.* Its interior is clear, bright like your watch. *Asahaya pahāp s'mmek a'a inān, baha'u to'ongan, sali' saddī-saddī pangluwa-luwahanna.* That person's clothing is so brilliant, brand-new, like something amazing to see. (*Thesaurus:* **danta'**, **sawa 1.1**, **sinag 1.1**) **1.2)** *v. intr. aN-* To shine brightly.

**sahi'-sahi'** *v. advrs. -in-* Driven by pressure to get a task done quickly, at the risk of poor-quality work or breakages. *Buwat si Ke, sinahi'-sahi' bang angose'an lai', sali' magl'kkas-l'kkas dīna. Ya magkabila' na lai'.* Like Ke, impatient when washing dishes, making himself go fast. What happens is that dishes get broken. *Sali' bang maghinang ai-ai, sali' mbal pinahāp, sali' pinal'kkas. Minsan du aniya' bay ahūg pareyo', sigi-sigi angahinang, sinahi'-sahi' a'a.* Like when doing some job, like not doing it well, doing it in a hurry. Even if something has fallen down, keeps on working, an impatient person. *Sinahi'-sahi' iya bang maghinang, sali' niabut-abut.* Motivated by impatience when working, doing it persistently.

**sahili'** *n.* A congenital problem; a person born with such a problem. *Na, ya sahili' itū buwat man deyom kandang, buwat saga magbaligbig kōkna.* Now this *sahili'* condition is like something from the womb, like his head being misshapen. *Maumu bang angidji' a'a. Ya ma a'a ni'idji' inān ngga'i ka min iya, tu'ud pamusuku' iya he' Tuhan. Bang iya maganak kalu sahili' anakna.* It often happens when someone mocks. What happens to the person mocked is not his fault, it is simply something given him by God. When she [the mocker] gives birth, her child may have a defect. (*cf:* **kariyasali**)

**sah'mpu** (var. **sampu**) *v. intr. pa-* To work cooperatively, of a group of people. *Alō, bang pasah'mpu ba'anan a'a, na mbal tagaga niatuhan.* Wow! When a group of people cooperate they cannot be beaten.

   **sikasampuhan** *adj.* To act in great numbers.

**sahubu** *v. tr.* To crowd around something of interest. *Aheka a'a pasahubu pina'an.* Many people crowd around that place. (*Thesaurus:* **aro' 1, harung-harung, timuk 1.1**)

**sahul** *see:* **pagsahul**

**sahumut-sahumut** *n.* Small projections or irregularities on a flat surface. *Nsa' sahumut-sahumut s'llang, t'ddo'.* There are no ripples on the sea, it is dead calm. (*Thesaurus:* **banggid 1, geges, langgad 1, pares₁**)

**sahupput** *v. intr. aN-* To squirt out, of a liquid. *Buwat kanu'us nihella' pariyata', magtūy anahupput.* Like a squid being pulled up, it promptly squirts out [inky liquid]. *Kahumbu, ya sali' angahumbu pariyata', sali' anahupput.* Whales, the [creatures] that emit vapor in an upward direction, sort of squirting. (*Thesaurus:* **kissat, pigsik₁ 1, p'ssik 1.1, pulagsik, sumpit 1**)

**sai** *interrog.* Who? *Magko'ot-ko'ot kitam bang sai dahū anakay pehē' ni pustu.* We will draw lots to see who will be first to attack the outpost. (*Thesaurus:* **ai, angay, buwattingga 1.1, magay, maingga, sumiyan**)

   **sai-sai** *n.* Anybody; whoever. *Patandaw pa'in kami, halam sai-sai.* When we looked out there was no one whatsoever.

**saikukuwak** *n.* A species of bird, a good whistler but rarely seen. *Amaurornis spp.* (*gen:* **manuk-manuk 1**)

**saikula'** *n.* The amniotic sac. *Mareyom kūn itū amowa kita saikula. Alahang, subay kita sukuran. Pinalamud ni buwas, ati bīlla, kinakan he' mma' onde', abō' aniya' pagkal'lla.* We bring the sac from within the womb. It is rare, we have to be lucky. It is mixed with rice and cooked and eaten by the child's father so there is immunity

against physical harm.

**saimbogot** var. of **salimbogot**

**saina** *n.* Someone or other. *Takaleku bay sapdahannu saina.* I heard you cursing someone or other. *Ma saina bahā' alta' bay tau'annu barannu ilū?* Whose will be the wealth that you have kept for yourself? (*cf:* **sasuku**)

**sainala** *adj. zero* Feigned; simulated. *B'ttong-b'ttong sainala ma iya.* Her pregnancy is feigned. *Lasa-lasa sainala.* Pretended love. (*Thesaurus:* **gillu'-gillu', ula-ula**)

**saindugu'** var. of **salindugu'**

**saingan** *n.* A child who has the name of a respected adult. (*Thesaurus:* **danglay 1, isay, ōn₁ 1**)

**saingsing** *n.* **1)** A shoot which sprouts up from something that has been cut down. *Subay biyabas, patomo'an dīna, pinuwad, aniya' kapinna niōnan saingsing.* It should be [something like] guava, growing of its own accord. Cut down, it leaves a remnant which is called *saingsing.* (*Thesaurus:* **saha' 1.1, s'mbut 1, suring₂**) **2)** The generation that fills the gap left by a preceding generation.

   **pagsaingsing** *v. intr. aN-* To fill the gap left by someone who dies. *Magsaingsing, makaganti' ma aku anakku siyaka bang aku amatay.* Filling the gap, my oldest child taking my place when I die.

**saipuwa** *v. tr.* To compute using an abacus. (*Thesaurus:* **kalkula, kira, itung₁, jumla 1**)

**sairap** var. of **salirap**

**sairing** *n.* **1)** A walling panel woven from young coconut leaflets. (*Thesaurus:* **saisig, salirap**) **1.1)** *v. tr.* To weave a panel of young coconut leaflets.

**sairola** *n.* A document proving legality, as of a residence certificate or an entry permit. *Niā'an sairola pelangnu ilū, sali' sulat.* A permit is to be obtained for that canoe of yours, like a letter. (*Thesaurus:* **pās, paspolt, sulat-kataddangan**)

**saisig** (var. **saitsig**) *n.* A panel tightly woven from strips of bamboo or cane. (*Thesaurus:* **sairing 1, salirap**)

**sait** *v. tr. -an* To bail water from a canoe. *Subay na makala'an min goyak bo' yampa pasaitan kami. Palangi kami anait.* It was necessary to get out of the waves before we had it bailed. We swam as we bailed. (*Thesaurus:* **kallus₂, k'llut 1.1, lodjat₂ 2**)

   **pagsait** *v. intr. aN-* To bail continually. *Magsait na pa'in, sigi-sigi magsait. Anā, mbal na takole' sinaitan. Abuhaw na.* They kept bailing, on and on. Alas, [the canoe] could not be bailed. They were swamped.

   **panait** (var. **pananait**) *n.* Something used to bail water from a boat.

   **sasait** *n.* A bailer.

**saitan** *n.* A class of spirit beings invisible to humans and possessing extra-human powers. *Larang-larang itū pagluma'an saitan. Bang halam larang-larang pehē' saitan ni deyom kabangkawan.*

These platforms are for *saitan* spirits to live in. If there is no platform the *saitan* goes into the mangroves. *Saitan itū ma batu, ma dilaut, saga ma deya ma kayu aheya, ma pangā'an bohe' isāb maitu ma Siganggang.* These *saitan* spirits are in rocks, or at sea, and some inland in large trees, at the place also where we get water here at Siganggang. *Saitan magmahatinggi, maglanga-langa dīna.* A *saitan* spirit who acts very superior, making himself high. (*Thesaurus:* **bangsa magl'l'ngngan, duwata 1, hama'-hama' a'a, hibilis, jīn 1, ya mbal ta'nda'**)

**saitan-mungkil** *n.* **1)** A saitan spirit that robs humans of the power of speech. *Bang kita tasagda he' mungkil, mbal kita magpah'lling.* When we come under the influence of a *mungkil* spirit, we don't speak. *Saitan-mungkil itū mbal ta'amu'-amu', hal amaumaw ma a'a.* The *mungkil* spirits referred cannot be petitioned [for help], they just make people unable to speak. (*Thesaurus:* **umaw 1**) **2)** A name used in anger for people or animals who do not respond as they should. *Onde'-onde' mbal pakale, mbal palāng, pinagōnan saitan-mungkil. Aniya' isāb hayop.* A child who won't listen, won't be told, called a *mungkil* spirit. There are also domestic animals [like that]. (*cf:* **mungkil**)

**saitan-sowa** *n.* **1)** A snake spirit. **1.1)** *v. advrs.* **-in-** Possessed by a snake spirit. *Sinaitan-sowa ina' si Mi. Mbal ala'an, mahē' na magkakkal.* Mi's mother has a snake spirit. It doesn't go away, it's there permanently.

**saitan-laktaw** *var.* of **saitan-lagtaw**

**saitan-lagtaw** (*var.* **lagtaw**; **saitan-laktaw**) *n.* A supernatural being of gigantic proportions, said to kill men by tearing them apart, and to abduct women. *Aniya' kono' saitan-lagtaw ma nunuk inān.* There is reportedly a *lagtaw* demon in that strangler fig. (*Thesaurus:* **agasi, gansuwang**)

**saitan-maut** (*var.* **maut**) *n.* A sea-dwelling spirit responsible for death by accident, as of someone who fails to give thanks for the provision of life's necessities. *Aniya' najalku pi'itu di'ilaw, agnajal kita ni mbo' ko da'a taluwa' maut.* I came here yesterday to make a vow, we made a vow to ritual ancestors so we won't be affected by the sea demon. *Saitan-maut amapatay bang mbal nihinang. Maut* spirits will kill if they are not propitiated. *Buwat pelang nih'llop he' maut, mbal nihella' e' saddi. Pinatuwa' kita bo' halam na maina'an ba'anan sakapta. Pagt'kkata ni luma', asaki duwa-t'llung'llaw.* Like a canoe is sucked in by a *maut* spirit, not pulled by anything else. We are allowed to emerge but most of our gear is gone. On reaching home we are sick for two to three days.

**saitsig** *var.* of **saisig**

**sajahitra'** (*var.* **kasajahitra'an**) *n.* A state of overall well-being.

**sajuma'at-sajuma'at** *adv.* Every Friday. *A'a*

*magsambahayang sajuma'at-sajuma'at.* A person who prays every Friday.

**sā'₁** *n.* **1)** A mistake; a fault; an infringement of social rules. *Ai-ai pamissalata bo' halam sā'na, ya hē' niōnan ahurup.* Anything we say that has no mistakes, we call that clear [speech]. **1.1)** *adj.* **a-** Mistaken; wrong; misaligned. *Halam taluwa' e'ku magsulat, asā'.* My writing was not accurate, it was wrong. *Minsan du kami bay makasā' ma ka'a.* Even though we have committed an offense against you. **1.2)** *v. intr.* **pa-** To err in doing something; to take the wrong path. *Pasā' kita man labayan.* We strayed from the path. (*Thesaurus:* **salusad**) **1.3)** *v. tr.* To find fault with someone's activity. (*Thesaurus:* **himoway, pastul, poway-poway, salba₁, salla'₁ 1.2, salu'-salu', soway**) **1.4)** *v. tr.* **-an** To penalise someone for committing an offense. *Ma masa awal hē', bang aniya' a'a angalubakan atana bo' amatay magtūy, subay iya sinā'an.* Long ago, if a man beat his slave so that he died, that man had to be penalized.

**kasā'an** *n.* A moral or social offense. *Yuk sambung si Tamar, "Mbal aku! In pamala'annu ma aku, luhūy paheya to'ongan kasa'an min bay tahinangnu ma aku."* Tamar's answer: "I protest! Your sending me away is a greater offense than what you did to me." *Subay alalom ampunta bang aheya kasā'anta.* Our forgiveness should be profound when our error has been great.

**pagsā'** *v. intr.* **aN-** To be dislocated or misaligned. (*Thesaurus:* **pagdalisu', pi'ul, pisu', pittay 1.1, possat**)

**kasā'** *n.* Dislocation, of bones.

**pagkasā'** *n.* **1)** Mutual misunderstanding. **1.1)** *v. intr.* **aN-** To be mutually mistaken; to talk at cross-purposes. (*Thesaurus:* **ambil-hati, pagkamali', pagsabali, ta'awil**)

**sā'₂** *v. tr.* To strain a liquid; to filter. *Am'lli aku sā'an panā'an ns'llan, s'ggitna mbal na ameya' ahūg pareyom.* I will buy a strainer for straining coconut oil, so its residue won't fall through with [the oil]. (*cf:* **ayak**)

**sā'an** *n.* **1)** A strainer for liquids. *Sā'an itū taga tangkay buwat du isāb basket, magl'ssu'-l'ssu'.* A *sā'an* has a handle just like a basket, it lets liquid through. *Am'lli aku sā'an panā'anku gata', panganggata'ku buwas.* I will buy a strainer to strain coconut cream for adding to the rice. (*cf:* **ayakan**) **1.1)** *v. tr.* To strain impurities from a liquid. *Sā'an itū panā'an ns'llan, s'ggitna mbal na ameya' ahūg pareyom.* The *sā'an* is for filtering oil, its impurities no long falling in.

**sa'** (*var.* **so'**) *conj.* But. *Biradali, ya taga pikpik itū ma langit. Ahāp d'nda so' taga pikpik. Biradali,* the ones with wings, in the sky. Beautiful women but they have wings. *Bang am'mmong-m'mmong mbal du kita ainay, sa' bang kita angaikalas...* If we are somewhat inconspicuous nothing will happen to us, but if we are foolishly brave...

*Kayuwan nihinang togong. Sali' luwa bubu so' ariki'.* Bamboo for making a *togong* fish trap. It looks like a *bubu* fish trap but smaller. (*Thesaurus:* **bo'₁, manda', saguwā'**)

**sa'agon-agon** (derivative of **agon**) *conj.* About to; on the point of happening; as though done already. *Sa'agon-agon a'a inān bilahi kaut, bo' halam aniya' bayan.* It's as though whenever that guy wants to go to sea, he has no conveyance. *Ai-ai ta'nda' he' matata sa'agon-agon ma kita.* Whatever our eyes see is as though we had it already. *B'nnal aniya' kapanyapan onde'-onde' buwat saga tambang sigā wa'i na ma sanda'an, sa'agon palabay na min idda, ya kasehe'an halam aniya' pangal'kkat.* It's true that there are children's things, like their gold charms, used as security [pawned] as when the time limit is running out, and nothing to redeem some of them. *Pamantawan itū subay alangkaw to'ongan sa'agon-agon maka'abut langit.* This tower should be really high, almost as though it reached the sky. *Sa'agon-agon kami amatay, bo' pa'in masi allum.* As though we had died, but were still alive. *Nīnda' na pa'in sa'agon-agon ta'ā'na, tab'llina.* Looked at again and again as though he had already got, already bought it.

**sa'al** *n.* A yoke for a draft animal. *Tabangin kami amuwasan sa'al itu.* Help us to get rid of this yoke.

**sa'am** *n.* 1) An outrigger brace. (*Thesaurus:* **batangan, katig 1, tarik**) 1.1) *v. tr.* To install a brace above an outrigger boom. *Subay pinal'mbut p'ttung ati ahāp pangasa'am katig pelang.* The bamboo should be made flexible and it will be good for bracing the outrigger of a canoe.

**sa'ang₁** *v. tr.* To fill a container almost to the brim. *Ai-ai ni'isi, yuk-i sina'ang na. "Sina'ang na kibut, sŏng na ap'nno'."* Anything being filled, we say it is to be filled right up. "Fill up the water jar, it's almost full."

**sa'ang₂** *n.* A unit of length: the distance from thumb-tip to extended forefinger. (*Thesaurus:* **bunag, h'kka 1, pāt 2**)

**sa'angay** (var. **sangay**) *conj.* From a point in past time up to the present; since. *Sa'angay subu halam aku bay makakakan. Yamboho' ampa makakakan na.* I haven't eaten since morning. Only just now able to eat. *Sangay min kahendog-hendogku nsa' aku bay makakakan haram.* Since growing up I have not eaten anything ritually unclean.

**sa'at** *n.* A moment of time, especially one that is an opportunity for doing something. *Ang'nda' kita sa'at.* Let's look for the opportune moment.

**sa'at-sa'at** *adv.* On the point of doing something. *Nā, sa'at-sa'at kami magsuntuk, na ah'lling dangan ganta' manapad kami, "Aningkŏ' ka amanyabut," yukna.* So when we were about to punch each other, someone else spoke up to restrain us, "Sit down and hold your peace," he said. *Sa'at-sa'at,*

*agon-agon magbono' sali'.* On the point of, like being about to fight.

**dansasa'at** *n.* 1) A moment of time. 1.1) *adv.* Momentarily; very briefly. *Yangkon ina'an pat'nna' dansasa'at panalusan sadja semestel itū.* Only that, staying a little longer for the completion of this semester.

**pasa'atan** *n.* A moment of opportunity; a sense of appropriateness. (*Thesaurus:* **kagustuhan, galak₁ 1**)

**sa'awla** *v. intr. pa-* To go to the utmost extent.

**sa'i** *n.* Mother. *Mura-murahan bang pa'in makahadil isāb minsan la'a sa'ina min matto'a-danakanna.* Hopefully someone from his family will attend, even if it is only his mother. (*syn:* **ina', nggo' 1**)

**sa'il** *v. tr. -an* To accompany a ceremony with singing, as when a bride is being brought to the house of her husband-to-be. (*Thesaurus:* **kalangan₁, langan₂ 1, lugu' 1**)

**sa'ob** *n.* 1) A cover or lid of a container. *Angamu' aku mital sa'oban.* I'm asking for a can with a lid. (*Thesaurus:* **sampong 1, tambol 1, taplok 1, turung 1, tutup₁**) 1.1) *v. tr. -an* To cover a container.

**sa'ud₁** *v. intr. pa-* 1) To snag on a protruding object, of something flexible. *Pasa'ud tuntun taguri' ma amboway.* The kite line snags on the *amboway* tree. *Takaleta wa'i ag'llek banog. Aniya' pasa'uranna ya angkan agese'.* We heard the sail tearing. There was something it snagged on, that's why it tore. 1.1) *v. tr. -an* To hook something over a protruding object. (*Thesaurus:* **gantung₂ 1.1, gulantung, sagnat 1.1**)

**pasa'uran** *n.* A projection something snags on.

**sa'ud₂** *see:* **pagsa'ud**

**sa'ul** *n.* A tubular skirt worn loosely.

**pagsina'ul** *v. intr. aN-* To wear a sarong without tying, i.e. by draping it or holding it in place with one's hands. (*Thesaurus:* **hampi' 1.1, hōs 1.2, pagkīmbong, pindung, siyag 1.1**)

**sa'ut** *adj. a-* 1) Urgent; without delay. *Halam aku bay magbowa pakokos pagka asa'ut panoho'an sultan.* I wasn't carrying weapons in that the sultan's orders were urgent. *Apendik kono', daipara asa'ut tonga' bahangi bowaku iya ni ospital.* Thought to be appendicitis, but fortunately, in the middle of the night, I promptly took him to hospital. 1.1) *v. tr.* To do something promptly. *Bang aku ina'an bay alahi buwat saga ni Tinggilan, subay aku sina'ut he' saga matto'aku.* If I had run away then to Tinggilan, for example, my parents would have had to act promptly regarding me. *Bang mbal tasa'utku subay na salung, bang mbal sali' tarai'-dai'.* If I can't do it promptly it will have to be tomorrow, if it can't be done in a short time. *Yuk taligramA: "Tapagpamagay na si Anu. Sinoho' ka pasa'ut-sa'ut."* The telegram said, "There is nothing that can now be done for So-and-so. You are told to act rather quickly." (*cf:* **dagmit**

1; *Thesaurus:* **ambat 1**, **amot-amot 1.1**, **dai'-dai' 1.2**, **saunu'**)

**sasa'ut** *n.* A moment of time; readiness.

**sala** *adv.* 1) Like; similar to; comparable with. *Aniya' ta'nda'ku sala halimaw, aheya makalandu'.* I saw something like a tiger, enormously big. *Lagawan k'llongku, agohom sala.* My throat is rough, sort of husky. *Bang kita pakapo' bo' angebol kita, aheka ma buli'anta magbuliluk sala.* When we are wading, moving vigorously, lots of whirlpools sort of form behind us. (*Thesaurus:* **buwat 1, damikiyan 1, gin, sali' 1.3**) 1.1) So to speak; as one might say. *Buwat sala kita sinukut, tangguhanta, tungga'anta.* Like for example when we are dunned for payment, we postpone it; we promise to pay [later].

**salak** *var. of* **sallak**

**salam** *n.* Greetings; good wishes. *Painay-inay na si Kolongan? Salam isāb ni iya.* How is Curly doing? Best wishes to her too.

**pagsalam** *v. intr. aN-* To greet one another by shaking hands. (*cf:* **pagjiyara**)

**salam-duwa'a** *n.* A devout greeting, especially as the opening of a letter. *Salam-duwa'a pinagbalik-balikan.* Many greetings [lit. repeated prayers of peace].

**sasalaman** *n.* Greetings, in a written communication.

**salama-lama** *adv.* For an unlimited length of time; for always. *Bang aku sarakkahannu taima'ku isāb ma dunya-ahirat, salama-lama tahun, salama-lama dunya.* If you give me alms I will indeed accept them for this world and the next, years without end, world without end. (*Thesaurus:* **sapanjang-panjang, sapaya-paya, sapupud-daya, saumul-umul**)

**salamat**₁ *adj. a-* To be well. *Mampa'in ka asalamat.* May you be well.

**kasalamatan** *n.* Peace; safety; well-being in general. *Ya maksudbi pi'itu, mareyom kasalamatan bahā'?* Your purpose in coming here, is it in peace? *Ka'am kasehe'an ilū makajari na amole' pehē' ni mma'bi ma deyom kasalamatan.* The rest of you may now go home in safety to your father.

**salamat-baran** *adj. a-* Enjoying well-being, in contrast to being seriously ill or in danger. *Mura-murahan, bang pa'in ka asalamat-baran.* May you enjoy physical well-being. *Buwat kita bay asaki atawa nila'at kita he' a'a, bang kasalamat-baran allum du kita.* When we have been sick or harmed by some person, if there is good health we will live.

**salamat**₂ *n.* 1) Gifts exchanged in a thanksgiving ceremony. *Saddī salamat-mama' maka salamat-buwas.* Betel-nut thanksgiving gifts are different from rice thanksgiving gifts. 1.1) *v. intr. aN-* To carry out a ritual of thanksgiving for health and safety. *Bang aniya' bonglay at'kka ni lahat,*

*analamat kam.* If a plague comes to your place, you [should] carry out the thanksgiving ritual.

**pagsalamatan** *n.* A thanksgiving ceremony; the physical items used in such a ceremony. *Am'lli ka mama' pagsalamatan.* Buy some betel nut for our thanksgiving ceremony.

**salang-sabot** *n.* A circular cake made of grated cassava. *Luwal bahā' salang-sabot, panggi' kayu bay nili'is, alegong luwana. Pinatoho' mariyata' luma'. Puwas bay pinatoho' pinehē' ni ns'llan bo' pinehē' ni sokal.* Almost certainly *salang-sabot*, which is grated cassava circular in shape. It is [first] dried on the roof. After it is dried it is [cooked] in oil then put in sugar.

**salappa'** *n.* A container, usually of brass or bronze, for the ingredients of betel nut chew. (*Thesaurus:* **anak-mama'an, loka'-loka', mama'an**)

**salas** *n.* The area of a house where visitors are received; a parlor. *Saga t'llund'ppa luha salasna.* The width of its visitor room is about three fathoms. (*Thesaurus:* **balkon, pantān, saurung**)

**Salasa** *n.* Tuesday. (*Thesaurus:* **Ahad, Alba'a, Hammis, Isnin, Juma'at, Sabtu'**)

**salassay** (*var.* **sāssay**) *adj. zero* 1) Done in an orderly way; resolved, of a dispute. *Buwat hinangta, sōng ahāp, sōng asalassay.* Like our work, it will soon be good, soon sorted out. *Bang asalassay kamemon, kata'uhanta du.* When all has been settled, then we will know. 1.1) *v. ditr.* To invoke ritual ancestors in an orderly way. *Bang aniya' saki salassayta ni ntan, ni mbo' saging atawa ni kaginisan mbo'.* If someone is ill, we put things right with the ancestor, the banana ancestor or various others.

**pagsalassay** *v. intr. aN-* 1) To reach the resolution of a dispute, often through litigation. *Buwat bay kami maka ndaku arāk magtiman, magsalassay kami ni sara'.* Like my wife and I on the point of divorcing, we get a magistrate to resolve things. *Magsalassay na kām l'lla-d'nda?* Are you both, man and woman, settled now? *Yuk sara', "Bang kabaya'anbi dangan-duwa, na magbahagi' kām pahāp. Magsalassay na kām."* The magistrate said, "If both of you are willing, then share things properly. Be in agreement." *Ka'am ya magsalassayan dībi.* You sort things out yourselves. (*Thesaurus:* **usay 2.1**) 1.1) *v. ditr.* To resolve a conflict at the grave of a shared ancestor. *Bay kami magsāssay ni kubul.* We went to settle a dispute at the grave [of a deceased relative].

**pasalassay** *v. tr.* To refer a matter to someone in authority.

**salat** *adj. a-* 1) Insignificant, of volume or numbers. *T'bburin deyo' luma', apa aheka hama'. B'nnal pasekot hama', bo' asalat.* Make a smudge fire under the house, because there are lots of mosquitoes. It is true that mosquitoes will come, but only a very few. *Salat e'na amangan,* *makalandu' e'na angentom.* She eats little, being excessively homesick. *Gapi'ku ka'a, ka'a ilū sōnganku magbissala, aku itū angagad. Bay ka tambahanku, mbal salat.* I support you, it's you I put forward to do the speaking. As for me, I wait. I have paid you already, no small amount. (*cf:* **dangkuri'**; *Thesaurus:* **bihang₂, bislang 1, jalang₂, lahang**) **1.1)** *v. tr.* -*an* To do something in insignificant amounts. *Hal kita sinalatan bang amuwan, mbal aheka.* Treated sparsely when giving, not a lot.

**salawat₁** *n.* Spiritual knowledge; mystical abilities. *Taga ilmu'. Pagkal'lla itū sali' salawat. Yuk kami, "Abisa salawatna," Bang ma kami ilmu'.* Having esoteric knowledge. The magical protection of a man is a kind of *salawat.* We say, "His deep knowledge is powerful." With us the word is *ilmu'. Bang a'a tinubu e' salawat, b'nnal langtasna.* When a person is empowered by esoteric knowledge, his ability to see the future is genuine. *Magkapakil, magkaimam, ahāp salawatna.* Able to serve as a leader in a mosque community, as an imam, their spiritual power is good. (*Thesaurus:* **ilmu' 1, ingat, langkat-samat**)

**pagsalawat** *v. intr.* a*N*- To be involved in the religious ceremony and ritual meal that mark the end of Ramadan.

**salawat₂** *n.* The essence of what is said; the current topic. *Aniya' bay bissaranu pinagbalik-balikan, ya hē' niōnan salawat.* You were saying something again and again, that's called *salawat. Kapilahan bissara, yukku, "Salung ī' amole' aku." Jarina yukku isāb inān, "Angay ka amabā' na pa'in salung amole' na ka?" Na ya i' niōnan salawat, hatina pinagbalik-balikan.* Overwhelmed by words I say, "Tomorrow I will go home." And then you also say, "Why do you keep saying tomorrow you will go home?" That too is called *salawat,* meaning that something is said repeatedly. *Mbal aku magpataha' salawat itu. Bilahi sadja aku amahati ni ka'am bilang saga matto'a kami.* I won't make this a long message. I just want to inform you and others of our elders.

**salay₁** *n.* **1)** Something laid across a body; a shawl; a drape. **1.1)** *v. intr.* pa- To lay something across a firm object. *Aniya' budjak tumbaga pasalay ma bukutna.* There was a bronze spear laid across his back. **1.2)** *v. tr.* To carry something draped over one's shoulder or arm. *Pīs, minsan mbal sinipitan ma sabitan, sinalay du isāb.* A head-cloth, even though not clipped to the belt, is also draped.

**pagsalay₁** *v. intr.* a*N*- To have something draped over a shoulder. *Bang abuhat bowaku magsalay.* If it is heavy I will carry it draped over my shoulder. (*Thesaurus:* **parablay, sablay**)

**salay₂** *adj. zero* Between phases or states.

**pagsalay₂** *v. intr.* a*N*- To be in a stable state, as the sea between tides or weather phases.

*Magtimbang tahik subu maka tahik ugtu'-llaw, hatina magsalay.* The morning tide and the midday tide are in balance. They are stable. *Bang tahik magsalay itū aheka daing. Ya pamandogahanta ma tonga'an uttala' maka satan.* When the sea is stable there are many fish. Our way of recognizing it is the halfway stage between the north and southwest wind seasons.

**salay-salay** *n.* The Banded scad, a fish species. *Alepes djiddaba.*

**salba₁** *v. tr.* To criticize or chide someone for what he does. *Si Di ē' analba. Wa'i aku sinasat he'na. Ya sinalba aku, mbal takosogta. Di criticizes. He bothered me. What I was criticized for was that we couldn't cope [with the task]. (*Thesaurus:* **himoway, pastul, poway-poway, sā'₁ 1.3, salla'₁ 1.2, salu'-salu', soway**)

**salba₂** *see:* **pagsalba**

**salbabida** *n.* A swimming float of the kind known as a lifesaver.

**salban** *n.* Thread for sewing, bought by the spool. *Bay pistaem lagi', ya kaheka'anna salban, alahang jiyay. Kayu kolenganna.* Back in pre-war days, most thread was *salban,* rarely was it *jiyay* [soldiers' issue]. Its spool was wooden.

**saldang** *n.* **1)** The buri palm, the fronds of which provide a durable weaving material. *Corypha elata.* (*syn:* **silal**) **2)** Fiber from the buri palm. *Tubag-tubag, ya pangengkotan saldang buri.* The canes on a kite that buri palm fiber is tied to. (*cf:* **tubag-tubag**)

**saldenas** *var. of* **saldinas**

**saldik** *adj.* a- Outgoing; cordial; responsive to teaching. *Asaldik, mbal ala'at s'mmuna ni a'a, buwat onde'-onde' papandu'.* Friendly, doesn't scowl at people. Like a teachable child. (*Thesaurus:* **addat 1.1, hatul₂, hongpot, pantun 1, papat 1, p'mpon 1, saltun 1**)

**saldinas** (*var.* **saldenas**) *n.* Sardines; canned fish in general.

**salekolan** *n.* An eddy created by the meeting of two currents. *Magbulibud tahik inān, ya ina'an salekolan. Bang "summer," aringin na tahik deyo', paheka daing.* The water there swirls, that's *salekolan.* In summer, the lower layer of water is cold, and there are lots of fish. (*cf:* **lengkol 1.1**)

**salema'** (*var.* **sema'**) *v. intr.* pa- **1)** To diverge from the main path, as to make a room for someone to pass. *Bang aku lum'ngngan bo' akiput lān, pasalema' aku.* When I am walking and the path is narrow, I move to the side. (*Thesaurus:* **sigay 1, simay₂, s'nnok, sulekma'**) **2)** To diverge from an agreed-on course of action. *Pasema' iya min kagara'an.* He does something other than what was agreed on.

**pagsalema'an** *n.* A detour or bypass. *Ina'an luma' sigām ma lān pagsalema'an.* Their house is that way, on the detour path.

**saleret** *var. of* **suleret**

**saleyok** *v. tr.* To spear fish from a canoe.

**salik 1)** *v. tr.* To cut off a wedge-shaped piece. **2)** *clf.* Count word for wedges of things. *Duwansalik nangka'.* Two wedges of jackfruit.

  **pagsalik-salik** *v. tr.* To cut something into wedges. *Pinagsalik-salik pisang.* A pineapple cut up into wedges. (*Thesaurus:* **kehet 1**, **hīk**, **hilap**)

**salikaya'** *n.* A species of small tree.

**salidda** *v. intr. pa-* To appear in bodily form, of a spirit being. *Bay aku tinuwa' he' si Mbo'. Ya umagadna pasalidda ni aku, ngga'i ka baranna.* Grandfather appeared to me. It was his ghost that appeared to me, not his body. (*Thesaurus:* **pagpasalupa, tuwa' 1.1**)

**salig$_1$** *n.* The back of a knife blade. (*ant:* **solab$_1$ 1**)

**salig$_2$** *n.* The chine of a canoe, i.e. the external angle between the sides and the flat bottom section. (*Thesaurus:* **singki'**, **taddas**)

**salig$_3$** *v. tr.* To say something in a way that prevents a third party from understanding it. *Buwat ka'a makakaut, salignu hē' ah'lling ko' mbal tabistu.* Like you going out to sea, you speak obliquely so no one will know. *Sali' aniya' magsuli-suli bo' sinalig suli-suli he' kasehe'an, sali' nilimbungan.* Like when people are talking and some of them hide their real intention, like being secretive. (*ant:* **solab$_2$**; *Thesaurus:* **limut 1.1**, **pagpa'andig, pagpara'il, pataggal-taggal**)

**saligsig$_1$** *v. intr. aN-* To move with arms or wings held out from the body. *Buwat manuk l'lla ni manuk d'nda, analigsig, sali' pinas'kkat kepetna, buwat yukna, "Amaya'-maya' aku."* Like a rooster to a hen, spreading out his wings, as though to say, "I love you."

**saligsig$_2$** (var. **salisig**) *v. intr. pa-/aN-* To touch a surface obliquely and briefly while in motion. *Bang helmet taluwa' timbak, pasalisig punglu'.* When a helmet is hit by gunfire, the bullet glances off.

  **pagsalisig** *v. intr. aN-* To skim across a rough surface; to touch only at high points. *Buwat pelang magsaligsig min deyom kagoyakan.* Like a canoe skimming through rough seas.

**sali'** *n.* **1)** The likeness of something or its equal. *D'nda inān nsa' aniya' sali'na.* That woman had no equal. (*Thesaurus:* **dora' 2**, **samapasang, sibu' 1, suga-suga$_2$, tupan 1**) **1.1)** *v. intr. pa-/-um-* To show similarity to something. *Sumali' badju' dakayu' itū ni bay badju'nu.* This shirt is similar to the shirt you had. **1.2)** *v. tr.* To be equal to, or comparable with, something. *Buddi a'a inān mbal tasali'.* That man's kindness cannot be equalled. **1.3)** *conj.* Sort of; like; by way of example. *Magbau'-bau' itū, sali' kita kinabaya'an e' d'nda bo' kita mbal bilahi ma d'nda inān.* This word *bau'-bau'* is like when a girl likes us, but we don't fancy that girl. *Kabongkolan, sali' pasagnat nireyom k'llongta itū. Subay kita anginum bohe'.* Food stuck in the throat; as though something catches inside our neck. We must

drink some water. *Aheka sali' momok kayu ma deyom kahawa itu, mbal tainum.* There is a lot of something like sawdust in this coffee, it is undrinkable. (*Thesaurus:* **buwat 1**, **damikiyan 1**, **gin**, **sala 1**)

  **pagsali'** *v. intr. aN-* **1)** To be equal with; to be identical to each other. *In mulid kamemon, bang atammat na pangadji'na, magsali' du maka guruna.* Every religious student, when his studies are complete, is the same as his teacher. **1.1)** *v. tr.* To make things equal; to treat as equal. *Bang pa'in du mbal pagsali'nu a'a halam aniya' dusana maka a'a taga dusa, bang pa'in sigām mbal pagmulka'annu.* It is hoped that you will not treat someone who has done no wrong in the same way as someone who has, may you not punish them. *Nsa' pagkengkeng, nsa' pagbokol, timbang-bibitan, pinagsali'-sali'.* Neither little toe nor big toe, shared equally, treated alike.

**sali'-sali'** *adv.* Similarly; likewise; at the same time. *Sali'-sali' lima munda' pakatandan.* Five canoes reaching shore at the same time. *Bang magbono'-bono' d'nda sali'-sali', magpakaiya'.* When the people fighting are both women, they shame each other.

**sali'an** *n.* A similarity; an equivalent. *Sūt itū sali'an du llet, sali'an du puting.* The equivalent of this word *sūt* [refusal] is *llet* [lack of cooperation] and *puting* [untruth].

**dasali'** *adj.* Identical. (*cf:* **daluwa**)

  **pagdasali'** *v. intr. aN-* To be equal or identical, of two things. *Pinapagatap, pinapagdasali'.* Made to match; made to be the same.

**salimbang** (derivative of **limbang**) *n.* A workmate.

**salimbangun** *n.* The Willow-leafed justicia, a species of small shrub, used medicinally. *Gendarussa vulgaris.*

**salimbogot** (var. **saimbogot**) *n.* A loop of rope or twisted fiber into which a climber places his feet when climbing a tree trunk.

**salimbūng** var. of **kalitan-salimbūng**

**salimi** (var. **simi**) *v. tr. -an* To trim the edge of split bamboo, making it straight. (*Thesaurus:* **ambuhut, hait, tai' 1.1, tilas$_2$**)

**salimpak** *v. tr.* To apply manual pressure to the stomach of a woman in labor. *Sinalimpak, sali' tin'kkon buwattē'.* Massaged, pressed down like that. (*Thesaurus:* **kallus$_1$ 1.1, hilut**)

**salimput** *n.* **1)** A funeral shroud. (*Thesaurus:* **kasa', kuku-pote', saput 1, talkun, tatap 1**) **2)** A cursing equivalent for some article of clothing. *A, salimputnu!* Here, your cursed shirt! (*gen:* **sukna' 1.1**)

**salin$_1$** *v. intr. zero* **1)** To change one's clothes. *Bang kita bay amandi subay kita asalin.* When we have been bathing we should change our clothes. **1.1)** *v. tr. -an* To change or replace something. *Salinanku badju'ku inān bang bay bowaku kaut, ang'nda' aku kamisita.* I will change that shirt when I've taken it to sea, and I'll look for an undershirt. *Sinalinan atop saga simuddai.* The roofing will be replaced around the day after tomorrow. *Subay sinalinan e' imam s'mmekna.* The imam should change his clothes. (*Thesaurus:* **ganti' 1.2, saliyu 1.1, sambi' 1**)

**pagsalin** *v. intr. aN-* 1) To change one thing for another. *Pagubus, amahamutan iya dīna maka magsalin.* After that she perfumed herself and changed [her clothes]. **1.1)** *v. tr.* To exchange one set of clothes for another. *Halam na kami makapagsalin s'mmek.* We did not change our clothes.

**salin₂** 1) *v. intr. pa-* To transfer to another location or person. *Pareyo' kami min kappal ē' tudju ni kappal dakayu' isāb, pasalin.* We disembark from one ship to another ship, transferring. *Binelaw iya, sali' aniya' saitan pasalin ni iya, mbal ala'an.* He is crazy, it is as if a *saitan* has transferred to him and won't go away. **1.1)** *v. ditr.* To transfer something to a different container. **2)** *v. ditr.* To translate words from one language to another.

**pasalin** *v. tr.* To pass a name on to a descendant.

**salindangan** *n.* A species of large manta ray.

**salindugu'** (var. **saindugu'**) *n.* 1) A rainbow. *Bang aniya' salindugu' bo' ulan-ulan, aniya' birarali amandi.* When there is a rainbow and it is raining a little, there are sky maidens bathing. *Mbal tatō' salindugu', makapukul tangan.* A rainbow cannot be pointed at, it will cause one's hand to be cut off. (*Thesaurus:* **andalaho', bāngaw, biradali 2**) **1.1)** *v. tr. -an* Influenced by a rainbow, causing rain to cease. *Sinalindugu'an, manjari pahali ulan hē'.* Affected by the rainbow, so then the rain stops.

**salingkat** *n.* A basket of loosely woven mature coconut leaflets, used for transporting bulk fruit and vegetables. *Salingkat itū duwa bowa'na. Buwat du japang, sali' du hinanganna, halam aniya' bidda'na.* The *salingkat* basket referred to has two openings. It's like a *japang* basket, same construction, no difference. (*syn:* **japang**; *gen:* **baka'₁**)

**salinggā** *v. intr. aN-* To be distressed by persistent pain. *Si Lu bay analinggā dibuhi'.* Lu became restless and unsettled in the night.

**pagsalinggā** *v. intr. aN-* To be constantly on the move, seeking relief from pain or searching for food. *Buwat aku bay tinandog, amole' ni palasahanku, magsalinggā aku.* Like when I had a fever, and it made me unwell, I moved restlessly. (*Thesaurus:* **paglega-lega, paglimayu', paglimbahod, paglimpa, pagsasab, pagsularaw**)

**salip** *n.* A descendent from the Prophet Muhammad. *Ahunit laha' salip min laha' sultan.* *Salip* blood is of more value than royal blood. *Kasalipan maka karatu'an mareyom 'foxhole' sigām, parohay si Anu amalos. Dohay itū aniya' atāk pabīng.* With the salips and the datus in their foxholes, What's-his-name attacked in

revenge. This word *dohay* implies a return attack. (*Thesaurus:* **datu', dayang-dayang 1, sultan**)

**salirap** (var. **sairap**) *n.* A panel woven of coconut palm leaflets. *Dakayu' sili'-sili'ku maka dambila' sairap-sairap ilū, bowaku pangatopku.* My one little kettle, and half of that little woven panel which I'll take for my roof. (*Thesaurus:* **sairing 1, saisig**)

**salisi** *see:* **pagsalisi**

**salisig** var. of **saligsig₂**

**saliyaw** *n.* Various surgeonfish and unicorn fish including the Achilles tang, the Orange-gilled surgeonfish, the Striped bristlefish. *Acanthurus pyroferus, Ctenochaetus striatus.* (*gen:* **kumay**)

**saliyaw-lakit** *n.* The Blue-banded surgeonfish. *Acunthurus lineatus.*

**saliyaw-pampang** *n.* The Pencilled surgeonfish, the Dussumier's surgeonfish. *Acanthurus dussumieri.*

**saliyu** *v. intr. pa-* 1) To change relative position, as when racing or overtaking another vessel. (*Thesaurus:* **lakad 1, laktaw, lingka' 1, pitas₁**) **1.1)** *v. tr. -an* To exchange one item for another. *Ndiya pinsilnu, sinaliyuhan maka pinsilku.* Hand me your pencil, exchanging it with my pencil. *Saliyuhanta ka pisita ni landing. Akebak landing itū.* I'll trade you paper bills for coins. These bills are damaged. *Manjari itu, hinabu aku atuli ma tonga' bahangi', papunduk iya analiyuhan anakna.* So while I was asleep in the middle of the night, she got up and swapped her child [for mine]. (*Thesaurus:* **ganti' 1.2, salin₁ 1.1, sambi' 1**)

**pagsaliyu** *v. intr. aN-* 1) To change locations. **1.1)** *v. tr.* To change the location of things. *Pinagsaliyu e' si Yakub tangan mma'na.* Jacob changed the order of his father's hands.

**saljen** *n.* A non-commissioned army officer; a sergeant.

**sallak** (var. **salak**) *n.* 1) A serious illness symptomised by spontaneous hemorrhaging from mouth and nose. *Bang aniya' tauwa' sallak, kaluwasan kita laha' min bowa'ta. Kayu ballak ya panambal.* If someone suffers from hemorrhaging, we experience blood coming from our mouth. The medicine is [from] the *ballak* tree. *Tauwa' ka salak!* May you haemorrhage! **1.1)** *v. advrs. -in-* Afflicted by bleeding. *Bang pa'in ka sinalak!* May you be cursed with bleeding! (*Thesaurus:* **laha'₁ 1**)

**sallad** var. of **sanglad**

**salla'₁** *n.* 1) A defect, moral or physical. *Aku'il laptopku sagō' mbal tatugila' bang ai salla'na.* My portable computer is disabled but its defect cannot be determined specifically. *Ya salla'nu bay pakaiya'nu mma'nu.* Your defect is that you shamed your father. *Anak-h'ndanu ya halam aniya' salla'na.* Your wives and daughters who have no blemish. (*Thesaurus:* **gora'₁ 1, powera**

**1, sassat, tamak 1**) **1.1**) *adj. a-* Defective; blemished. *Sagō' ya makasalla' ma ka'a itū, beya'-beya'nu bay kahinangan pagkahinu inān.* But what spoils you, is that you go along with the things your peers did. **1.2**) *v. tr.* To find fault with something or someone. *Gōm aku maka tautai'anakku ya tōngin dusa, da'a sadja in sultan tasalla'.* Better that I and my children be accused of wrong, rather then the king be criticised. (*Thesaurus:* **himoway, pastul, poway-poway, sā'₁ 1.3, salba₁, salu'-salu', soway**)

**salla'₂** *n.* A coin game.

**pagsalla'** *n.* **1**) A coin game (toss-the-coin or two-up), in which players gamble on the fall of the coins. (*Thesaurus:* **pagplising 1**) **1.1**) *v. intr. aN-* To play the game of two-up or toss-the-coin. *Anahat aku kamun pab'llianku pagsalla'.* I'll snare a mantis shrimp and sell it for playing toss-the-coin. *Bang aku magsalla', subay aku analla' sulang.* When I play two-up I have to call "same-side-up." A: *"Ai pagbono'anbi ilū?"* B: *"Pasal bay magsalla'. Angalengog si Se."* A: "What are you fighting over there?" B: "It was because we were playing toss-the-coin, and Se made a fuss." (*Thesaurus:* **agad₂, pagkabit, pagtalang, sulang₂, tingka**)

**sallowa'** *see:* **pagsallowa'**

**salluk** *see:* **pagsalluk**

**saloka'** *n.* The coconut palm. *Cocos nucifera. Parokdos aku pareyo' min saloka'.* I slid down by means of a coconut palm. (*syn:* **niyug**)

**salod** *v. tr.* To disagree with someone; to oppose someone. *Bang aku aka si Mo aglampasu', mbal aku ameya'. Salodku iya, subay na kohap kabaya'anku.* When Mo and I are polishing the floor, I don't go along. I disagree with her, I want to do it in the afternoon.

**pagsalod** *v. tr. -an* To be in conflict with each other over some issue. *Ina'an magsalod maka ina'na. Bang ma iya subay bola, bang ma ina'na subay lilus.* He's there arguing with his mother. According to him it should be a ball, according to his mother it should be a watch. (*Thesaurus:* **pagagaw-besod, pagbagod, pagbengtod, pagdiskās, pagjawab 1.1, pagpayod 1.1, pagsu'al**)

**panalod** (var. **pananalod**) *n.* A person who is disagreeable and argumentative.

**salompas** (var. **talumpas**) *n.* A commercial medicinal plaster. (*cf:* **pikit-pikit**)

**salopen** *n.* A plastic bag. (*syn:* **tilag-tilag₁**)

**salsal** *n.* The floor joists which rest on bearers, and run parallel with the length of a house. *Min diyata' salsal, min deyo' babag.* The floor joists are above, the bearers below. (*Thesaurus:* **babag 1, dagan₁, hobong, taytayan tikus**)

**basalsalan** *adj. zero* Overloaded; overstressed.

**salsila** (var. **sasila**) *n.* **1**) A story, especially a traditional one with moral or religious significance. *Mbal isāb lungaynu ōnku min salsila kapanubu'an kami.* Nor will you cause my name to be lost from the stories of our descendants. (*Thesaurus:* **kissa 1, istori 1, pagkata-kata 1.1, paglanga'-langa'**) **1.1**) *v. tr.* To relate a story.

**salta'** *v. intr. pa-* To be coincident or contemporary with some event or situation. (*Thesaurus:* **pag'tta', pagsamp'kka', sabu 1.1, tā'-tā' 1**)

**pagsalta'** *v. intr. aN-* To co-occur in time or place. *Pagt'kkana magsalta' takalena dangan magsuli-suli maka bagayna.* His arrival coincided with hearing someone else talking with his friend. *Sagō' bang saddī patudjuhan, na ngga'i ka sigām ya bay angamulahan kitam. Tu'ud magsalta' sadja.* But if the direction [they were heading] was different, then it wasn't them who harmed us. It was simply a coincidence.

**pasalta'** *conj.* During; while.

**saltun** *adj. a-* **1**) Undefiled; exemplary. *Ayi, asaltun pahāp ka'a ilū.* Wow, you are so perfect! *Asaltun hinangna, addatna. Mbal asabul.* His behavior and manners are perfect, not anti-social. (*Thesaurus:* **addat 1.1, hatul₂, hongpot, pantun 1, papat 1, p'mpon 1, saldik**) **1.1**) *v. tr.* To remove moral uncleanness by ritual sprinkling and words. *Buwat aku bay makainum toba', yukku, "Saltunun aku, bay aku makainum haram."* Like me when I had drunk palm toddy, I said, "Purify me, I have drunk something forbidden." (*cf:* **sussi 1.1**)

**salu** *adj. a-* **1**) Eating together from the same container. *Bang aku amangan, aheka asalu.* When I am eating, a lot of [others] eat from my plate. **1.1**) *v. tr.* To share with someone the food on one's plate. *Mbal analu siyalina, subay hal iya dangan-dangan.* He won't share with his younger sibling, it has to be him alone.

**pagsalu** *v. tr. -an* To eat together. *Magsalu na pa'in kita amangan ma astana' itū.* We will eat together all the time here in the palace. *Mahē' du isāb hinangbi maka pagsalu-saluhanbi ya tutukbalan pagdakayu'anbi.* And there you will observe the ceremony and eat your fellowship offering together.

**salu-duru'** *n.* A foster brother or sister (lit. breast-sharer). {idiom}

**salud** (var. **saud₂**) *v. intr. pa-* **1**) To be located beneath a place where liquid is falling. *Da'a na ka'am pasalud min deyo' luma' bo' mbal kam kabusugan e' bohe' pasu'.* Don't go under the house lest you have hot water pour down on you. **1.1**) *v. tr.* To collect a liquid by holding a container under the source. *Bang sinalud bohe' pinat'nna'an mital min deyo'na.* When you collect water put a can under it. *Bay na ginipitan panggi', sinaud bohe'na. Ubus ya bohe' i' pinato'ong mareyom undam.* When the cassava has been squeezed, its liquid is caught. The liquid is then left to settle in a basin.

**saluran** *n.* A channel or spigot to guide the flow of water.

**salu'-salu'** *v. tr.* To find fault with someone or

something. *Sinalu'-salu', aniya' sali' pinagmusmuran.* Found fault with, like something being complained about. (*Thesaurus:* **himoway, pastul, poway-poway, sā'₁ 1.3, salba₁, salla'₁ 1.2, soway**)

**salung** *adv.* Tomorrow. (*cf:* **bahangi 1**; *syn:* **pahalu**; *Thesaurus:* **di'ilaw, llaw itu, ma t'llu, simuddai**)

**pagsalung** *v. intr.* aN- To come, of tomorrow. *Pagsalung amole' na kami ni Siganggang.* Come tomorrow, we will return home to Siganggang.

**salung-simuddai** *adv.* The immediate future; the next few days. *Gōm kita magkakan maka maginum buwattina'an. Amatay du kita arai' ma salung-simuddai.* We might as well eat and drink now. We may be dead tomorrow or the next day.

**salupa** *see:* **pagpasalupa**

**salura** *n.* A military salute.

**pagsalura 1)** *v. intr.* aN- To salute. **2)** *v. tr.* -an To salute a superior officer in the military.

**salusad** *v. intr.* pa- To go the wrong way. *Di'ilaw bay aku ahūg, makasalusad tape'ku. Asā' kagi'ikanku.* I fell down yesterday, my foot happened to go the wrong way. I stepped in the wrong place. (*Thesaurus:* **sā'₁ 1.2**)

**salusu** *v. tr.* To go from one place to another, as when seeking information. *Buwat kita bay kalungayan ai-ai, salusuta tumpuk pamiha'anta.* Like when we have lost something, we go round the entire house-group looking for it. (*Thesaurus:* **batuk₂, jadja' 1.1, lalag, libu 1.1, nda' 1.1**)

**salut** *adj.* a- **1)** Demanding, as a fretful child. *Asalut isāb si Ya bang pasān angkan bilang mbal katulihan.* Ya is fretful at times, which is why he often can't get off to sleep. **1.1)** *v. tr.* To ask insistently or irritatingly for something. *Ai na pa'in salutnu ni aku, halam ai-ai pam'lli?* What is it that you keep asking me for, when I have no money to buy anything? (*Thesaurus:* **pipit₁**)

**sama-** *aff.* Prefix indicating equal measure. *Sama'alop kami, samaheya du kami.* Facing each other, we are the same size. *Samaintib bohe' inān maka bowa' tangki.* The water is level with the opening of the tank. (*Thesaurus:* **sambu-...sambu-, sangka-...sangka-**)

**Sama** *n.* Sinama-speaking peoples, some of whom are referred to by outsiders as Badjaw or Samal. (*cf:* **Samehakan**)

**kasamahan** *n.* Sama communities in a general sense. *Bang ma kawin kasamahan bay tagna', dakayu' du pandala min kal'llahan, dakayu' min kar'ndahan.* With the original Sama weddings there was one attendant from the man's side, and one from the woman's.

**Sinama** *n.* **1)** The language spoken by Sama. **1.1)** *v. tr.* To translate something into Sinama. *Sinamahun kono' bo' tahati kami.* Please say it in Sinama so we can understand it.

**pagsinama** *v. intr.* aN- To speak the Sinama language. *Ōy, ata'u ka magsinama.* Hey, you know how to speak Sinama.

**Sama Bāngingi'** (var. **Balangingi'**) *n. phrase* A subgroup of Sama speaking a distinctive dialect of Sinama, settled mainly in Northern Sulu and the Zamboanga Peninsula.

**Sama Bokko'** *n. phrase* A subgroup of Sama Dilaut known for eating turtle flesh, an item proscribed for other Sama.

**Sama Deya** *n. phrase* A designation for speakers of Central Sinama who live ashore in various coastal cities. (*cf:* **Sama Lipid**)

**Sama Dilaut** *n. phrase* Literally 'Ocean Sama', a widely distributed subgroup of Central Sinama speakers who derive their living mainly from the sea and, whenever possible, build their pole houses in coastal shallows. (*Thesaurus:* **Sama Pala'u**)

**Sama Jengen** *n. phrase* A group of nomadic Central Sinama speakers who until recently lived almost entirely in their covered boats. (*cf:* **lepa**; *syn:* **Sama Pagūng, Sama Pala'u**)

**Sama Kabinga'an** *n. phrase* A subgroup of Central Sinama speakers originally resident on Kabinga'an, a sandy rise between Siasi and Jolo Islands, to the east of Tapul.

**Sama Laminusa** *n. phrase* A land-oriented subgroup of Central Sinama speakers who consider their home to be Laminusa, an atoll off the northeast coast of Siasi Island.

**Sama Lipid** (var. **Lipid**) *n. phrase* A Sama Dilaut designation for the land-oriented Central Sinama speakers who consider their home to be Siasi Island and its inshore waters. (*cf:* **Sama Deya**)

**Sama Pagūng** *n. phrase* Literally 'Floating Sama', an alternative name for the geographically dispersed subgroup of Central Sinama speakers who maintain a nomadic or semi-nomadic life-style, living for long periods on their canoes. (*cf:* **gūng**; *syn:* **Sama Jengen, Sama Pala'u**)

**Sama Pala'u** *n. phrase* An alternative name for the geographically dispersed subgroup of Central Sinama speakers who maintain a nomadic or semi-nomadic life-style, living for long periods on their canoes. (*syn:* **Sama Jengen, Sama Pagūng**; *Thesaurus:* **Sama Dilaut**)

**Sama Pangutaran** *n. phrase* Speakers of Western Sinama, most of them farmers, who live on Pangutaran Island, an atoll to the northwest of Jolo Island, and on adjacent small islands.

**Sama Paosol** *n. phrase* A name for Central Sinama speakers who have exchanged their nomadic lifestyle for permanent houses built in shallow seawater.

**Sama Siasi** *n. phrase* Speakers of Central Sinama with long historical ties to the Siasi district.

**Sama Sibutu'** *n. phrase* A subgroup of Southern Sinama speakers who consider their home to be Sibutu', an atoll to the south of Bonggao and

Simunul.

**Sama Simunul** *n. phrase* A subgroup of Southern Sama speakers who consider their home to be Simunul, an atoll to the south of Bonggao.

**Sama Tabawan** *n. phrase* A subgroup of Central Sinama speakers who live on Tabawan Island, east of northern Tawi-Tawi.

**Sama Ubian** *n. phrase* A subgroup of Central Sinama speakers who consider their home to be South Ubian, an island cluster northeast of Tawi-Tawi Island.

**sama-sama** *adv.* Equally; in unison. *Magpangolang sigām sama-sama ma deyom saga duwanjām.* They shouted all together for about two hours.

  **pagsama-sama** *adv.* 1) Similarly; in the same way. *Niaunan ni lai' pagsama-sama.* Served up on individual plates. **1.1)** *v. intr.* aN- To act or be treated together, of a group of individuals. *Subay na kam magsama-sama salung magl'bbos.* You should all come together tomorrow and launch it. **1.2)** *v. tr.* To treat all members of a group equally. *Nijamu, pinagsama-samahan na.* Entertained [at a feast], everyone treated the same. *Batulun pandan ilū, sali' pinagsama-sama.* Lay out the pieces of pandan, make them all the same.

**samadjana** *adv.* Only; solely. *Hal aku palabay samadjana.* I'm just passing by, that's all. (*Thesaurus:* **dakuman, hal, la'a, luwal, puntul, sadja, tunggal 1, yangkon**)

**samaentom** (derivative of **entom**) *adj.* To miss each other when apart, of two people. *Buwat d'nda maka l'lla magbaya', bo' sali' at'ggol makapag'nda', samaentom.* As when a man and a woman are in love and don't see each other for a long time, they miss each other equally.

**samaheya** (derivative of **heya**) *adj.* To be of the same size. *Sama'alop kami, samaheya du kami.* Facing each other, we are the same size.

**samaintib** *adj.* To be level with the brim of a container. *Ahangka', sali' ap'nno' pabūd, buwat ambung inān isihan samaintib ni bowa'na.* Overfilled, filled and piled up, like that basket, its contents level with the opening. *Bang aku angisi buwas nireyom mital, samaintib du maka bihing-bowa' mital.* When I put rice into a can it is level with the rim of the can. (*Thesaurus:* **apang, pagsamaongkop 1.1**)

  **pagsamaintib** *v. intr.* aN- 1) To be filled to the brim. **1.1)** *v. tr.* To fill something to the brim.

**sama'alop** (derivative of **alop₁**) *adj.* To be face to face with someone. *Sama'alop kami, samaheya du kami.* Facing each other, we are the same size. *Magtinampalan, maginalopan, sama'alop.* Coming face to face with each other, both facing in.

**samal** *adj. zero* Outside the marked limits, of the fall of coins thrown in the game of kabit.

**samalintonga'** *adj.* To be halfway between extremes. *Samalintonga' aku ma kayu hē' i maka kayu ina'an i.* I am halfway between that tree

there and that tree yonder. *Samalintonga' pa'in kami apara malkina.* When we were halfway the engine quit. (*Thesaurus:* **dambila' 1, dampōng, santonga'**)

**saman** *see:* **saman-saman**

**saman-saman** *v. advrs.* ka-...-an To be misled; to have mistaken expectations. *Aniya' bay pamuwan iya ati pehē' na pa'in pabīng bo' iya sali' kat'kkat'kkahan ai-ai. Ati bang ta'abut tahun dakayu' bo' halam aniya' at'kka ni iya, kasaman-samanan ya bay tahun palabay inān.* Something was given to him and he kept going back so he might receive something again. Then when another year came round and nothing comes his way, he is misled by the previous year's experience. *Kasaman-samanan iya angandag, nsa' kinata'uhan e'na agabuk na kayu.* He was misled in the buying price he was offered, not realizing the timber was already decayed. (*Thesaurus:* **lamma 2.1, paggambahan**)

**samantala'** *conj.* Since that is so; in view of the fact or situation; given that. *Samantala' ka'a ya bay makabuwan dusa, subay barannu ya amayad. Da'a na kamemon.* In view of the fact that you are the one who committed the offence, you personally should pay. Not the whole group. *Buwat ipatanta, ya pamahinang ma iya ananggung bohe', ati subay bilahi saddī hinang minnē'. Yuk pat'nna'an hē', "Samantala' hinang ilu ya bay pamahinang ma ka'a-i, hinangun to'ongan na."* Like our worker, and the work assigned to him is to fetch water but he has to prefer some work other than that. The person he stays with says, "Since it is that work [fetching water] that has been assigned to you, get on and do it." (*Thesaurus:* **abila, bang₁, bangsi', basta, bo' na, gana, pagka, talkala'**)

**samaongpod** *adj.* To be level with the brim.

**samapasang** *adj.* Matching, of two things; to be of the same size. *Kambing duwa tandukna samapasang taha'na.* A goat with two horns, matching in length. (*Thesaurus:* **dora' 2, sali' 1, sibu' 1, suga-suga₂, tupan 1**)

**samasunsang** (derivative of **sunsang**) *adj.* Facing each other, of opposites. *Bang kaba' maka ta'u pinagka'ob, samasunsang karuwa sīn.* When heads and tails are put together, the two coins are mutually reversed.

**samat** *see:* **langkat-samat**

**samata-mata** *adv.* Actually; in reality; in fact. *Samata-mata atuli ma luma' kami bo' halam atuli, amole' du.* Sleeping over at our place in fact but not sleeping, he simply went home. *Samata-mata bay ka ta'nda'ku anangkaw. Amalilu ka?* I actually saw you stealing. Do you deny it?

**samaunjuk** *adj.* Matching in value, of asking price and payment. *Subay samaunjuk, mbal manjari pamautang.* The payment should be in full, no credit allowed. (*Thesaurus:* **atap, lampak₂ 1**)

**samaw** *n.* A species of tree, the grated bark of

which is added to cosmetic face powder.

**samba** *v. tr.* **1)** To do something by chance. *Daipara makasamba dakayu' daing ariki'.* However, [we] happened by chance to get one small fish. (*Thesaurus:* **k'ddom**₂, **halus**₁, **pagpasukud, pagsusaed, sarap**₂ **1, tawakkal**) **1.1)** *v. advrs.* **ka-...-an** To be hit by accident. *Bang aniya' amantung a'a palabay, hatina ya hē' kasambahan.* When someone throws and hits a passerby, that's *kasambahan.* (*Thesaurus:* **hamiyu 1, sabat**₂, **sambut 1.1**)

**pagsamba-samba** *v. intr.* **aN-** To happen randomly or unexpectedly. (*cf:* **pagsān-sān**)

**pagpasamba** *v. intr.* **aN-** To do something that involves risk or uncertainty.

**sambag**₁ *v. intr.* **aN- 1)** To answer. *Anambag l'lla inān, yuk-i, "Aku itū anak liyu."* That man answered, saying, "I am foreign born." (*Thesaurus:* **sambung**₁ **1.1, saul**) **1.1)** *v. tr.* To address what was said. *Bay sinambag e'na pangamu'-ngamu' kami hē'.* He responded to that request of ours. **1.2)** *v. tr.* **-an** To give an answer to the person who has spoken. *Bang magkabuwatte', parahing du kām ni aku sagō' mbal kām sambaganku.* If that is how things are to be, you will call to me for help but I will not answer you. *Sambagin na sulat ilū.* Answer that message. *Bay angalingan ina'ku, yukku, "Sambagin aku, mbal aku makapihi'."* My mother called out, and I said, "Answer for me, I am unable to go there."

**sambag**₂ *see:* **kasambagan**

**sambahayang** *v. tr.* To make someone the subject of one's religious observance, prayer in particular. *Bang bay anambahayang si Ba ma langgal bo' pasagid ero', abatal isāb. Mbal na anambahayang.* If Ba went to pray at the mosque and a dog brushed against him he would be ritually defiled. He would no longer pray. (*Thesaurus:* **amu'-amu', harap**₂, **pagduwa'a, pudji 1.1, s'mba 1, suhud 1.3, ta'at 1.1**)

**pagsambahayang** *v. intr.* **aN-** To engage in religious observance such as prayer. *Ya hinang si Manikbangsi' magsambahayang llaw-llaw.* The work of Manikbangsi' [a folk-lore character] was to pray daily. *Aku itū ngga'i ka magsasambahayang, mag'mbo' aku.* I am not a [practising] religious person; I observe the ritual ancestors.

**sambal**₁ *v. intr.* **-um-** To reach parity or equality with. *Bang kita mbal ameya' pandu' matto'ata magkangī'-ngī' kita. Mbal kita sumambal ma kasehe'anta, atawa ni topad sibu'ta.* If we do not follow the instructions of our parents we will come to grief. We will not stay equal with our companions or our age-mates.

**pagsambal** *v. intr.* **aN- 1)** To be in alignment; to stay equal or level with. *Bang maglomba magsambal.* When people race they line up. **1.1)** *v. tr.* To treat people or things in the same way.

*Buwat anaknu duwangan inān, subay pagsambalnu bang b'llihannu ai-ai ko da'a maglindi-lindihan.* Your two children, for example; when you buy them things you should do the same for both so they aren't envious of each other. *Pagsambalun tōng pasagi' ilū.* Make the ends of those building timbers equal. *Hal pinapagsambal emponta.* Our teeth simply made even [in height].

**dasambal** *adj.* Identical as to dimensions.

**sambal**₂ *n.* A night-flying bird, identified by its wailing cry. (*gen:* **manuk-manuk 1**; *Thesaurus:* **paguwak-uwak**)

**sambalani** *n.* A mythical flying horse. (*Thesaurus:* **galura', sumayang-galura' 1**)

**samban** *see:* **pagsamban**

**sambat** *v. ditr.* To mention something; to voice a concern. *Ai-ai sinambat ni matto'a, luwal ka halam matto'a bo' mbal kabuwanan.* Anything hinted at by an elder, only if you were not an elder would it not be given. *Anambat aku ni ka'a, yukku, "Tuwan, bang aniya' amu'ku ni ka'a, pamuwannu?" Yuknu, "Ai sambatnu?" Yukku, "Dakayu' badju'."* I mention a need to you, saying, "Sir, if I ask you for something, will you give it?" You say, "What do you have in mind?" I say, "One shirt." *Anambatan iya. "Arōy," yukna, "kabuhatan aku sidda."* He voices [a complaint]. "Good grief!" he says, "I am seriously over-burdened." *Anambatan anakku, yukna, "Binale' aku, anoho' ka saddi."* My son raises an objection saying, "I'm tired, send someone else." (*Thesaurus:* **bahasa**₁, **bā'**₁, **batbat**₂, **bissala 1.1, k'bbat**₁ **1, h'lling**₁ **1.1, pagmūng-mūng 1.1, yuk**)

**sambatan** *n.* A saying; an allusion to something said. *Sambatan si Dy, yukna, "Bang ka kinabilahi'an he' d'nda, bo' ka'a-i mbal bilahi, magmahi ka."* In Dy's words: "If a woman is in love with you and you don't love her, make a fuss about it." *Aniya' magtinabawan, sambatan Ingglis 'complete'. M'ssa' aniya' sokat-manokat tinabawan.* There are some who follow the *tabawan* practise [as in the English expression "complete"]. No specifying this and that. *Bang sali'-sali' bay angiskul, heka man heka ka'a-i makalakbaw man kasehe'an. Ka'a-i sambatan tahinang mastal.* When all go to school in the same way, but you outperform the others time and again. You will become a school-teacher, as they say. *Ya sambatan sigām, "Sagarin na."* Their comment was, "Never mind." (*Thesaurus:* **ba'at 1, kabtangan, haka 1, hunub-hunub 1, pahati 1, suli-suli 1**)

**pagsambat** *n.* **1)** Something widely spoken of. *Minnē' kami kabalosan ma bay pagsambatan sigām-i.* By that we were avenged for the things they had been saying. **1.1)** *v. tr.* **-an** To speak of something well-known. *Angkan pinagsambatan maina'an, yuk-i, "Nabi hati' si Sa'ul?"* That is why it is often said, "Is Saul actually a prophet?"

**sambelang** *n.* A species of fish.

**sambihit** *v. tr.* To make someone ill, the action of a specific ritual ancestor. *Si Ab bay binowa ni doktol, nsa' kauli'an sabab sinambihit e' pangkat.* Ab was taken to the doctor, but didn't get better because he had been made sick by a ritual ancestor. (*syn:* **sabab₂ 1.1**)

**sambi'** *v. tr.* -an 1) To exchange one thing for another; to barter things. *Bo' ta'ā' daing bukay-bukay, bowaku ni tabu' panambi' saging.* When I caught a wrasse I took it to the market to exchange it for bananas. *Sambi'anku badju'ku abase'.* I will change my wet shirt. *Aniya' bay sangpū' pilakku sinambi'an ni tinda-tinda maka kanat-kanat.* I had ten pesos changed for small change in a village shop. (*cf:* **pinda 1**; *Thesaurus:* **ganti' 1.2, salin₁ 1.1, saliyu 1.1**) 1.1) *v. tr.* To borrow some consumable item with the intention of repaying it in kind. *Anambi' aku dasawan buwas.* I will borrow a cup of rice. (*Thesaurus:* **indam, sanda'-sanda', s'nnad, utang 1.1**)

**sambil** *conj.* And also; up to and including. *Bang budjang magbinorak nilipa' tape', tangan, kamemon sambil pa'a.* When teenage girls used cosmetic powder, the feet and hands are treated, everything including the thighs. *Maglemong maka magpuwasa sigām sambil ni kasangoman.* They mourned and fasted until night. *Talu itu panambal pelang sambil panambal tiparaku.* This wax is for sealing a canoe and also for sealing my dive-goggles. (*cf:* **sampay 1**)

**samb'llong** *v. intr.* aN- To make the sound of water moving by a solid object such as house posts. *Anamb'llong pelangta, yuk sehe'ku, "Ōy, da'a pasamb'llongun."* Our canoe was making a surging noise, and my companion said, "Hey, don't let it make a noise." (*Thesaurus:* **ebol, llis, sahabal**)

**Sambo** *n.* Zamboanga City (short form). (*syn:* **Sambuwangan**)

**sambon** *n.* 1) Birth complicated by a tangled umbilical cord. *Sambon anakna, saga keyotna pinalebod ma baranna. Bang sukud ala'at, amatay anakna.* Her child's birth is *sambon,* its umbilical cord wrapped around its body. If things go badly, her child will die. 1.1) *v. advrs.* -in- Entangled with the umbilical cord, of a newborn child.

**sambu** *adj.* a- 1) Healthy; well-grown; prosperous. 1.1) *v. intr.* pa- To prosper; to become well-grown. *Ebot-ebot, Tuwan, pagbuli-bulihinbi kami supaya pasambu hinang itū.* Sir, don't forget, keep us firmly in mind so that this project flourishes. (*cf:* **sulig₁**)

  **pasambu** *v. tr.* To put one's own well-being first.

**sambu-...sambu-** *aff.* Prefix indicating the near co-occurrence of two events. *Sambupōng, sambutalom.* As soon as it is broken, it is sharpened. *Sambutahak, sambukakan.* As soon as it is cooked it is eaten. (*Thesaurus:* **sama-, sangka-...sangka-**)

**sambula'an** *n.* A species of hawk or eagle. (*cf:* **belle'₁**)

**sambulayang** *n.* A flag or pennant flown above houses or canoes during a celebration. *Bo' na kami maina'an, maghinang sambulayang sigā min Sibaud, sabab kinawin e' a'a min Sibaud ē'.* So there we were, with people from Sibaud flying flags because [their girl] was being married by a man from Sibaud. (*Thesaurus:* **bandila', panji, tipas-tipas**)

**sambung₁** *n.* 1) A reply; an answer. *Yuk sambung l'lla, "O'ō, ya d'nda bay pamalimbangnu aku, iya ya bay amuwanan aku, angkan aku bay makakakan."* The man's answer was, "Look, the woman you partnered me with, she is the one who gave it to me, that's why I ate." 1.1) *v. tr.* To answer someone; to reply. *Sagarin na bang ah'lling. Da'a sambungun.* Ignore them if they speak. Don't answer them. (*Thesaurus:* **sambag₁ 1, saul**) 1.2) *v. tr.* -an To answer something someone has said. *Ati sinambungan e' si Memokan panilaw sultan itū.* So Memokan answered the sultan's questiom.

**sambung₂** *n.* A waist-band of white cloth that forms the top of loose, wide-fitting trousers. (*Thesaurus:* **kambot 1, kandit, sabitan, sintoron**)

**sambut** *v. tr.* 1) To receive something which is passed; to catch something thrown. *Sambutin sangpū' solag s'mmek itu ya bay paggeset-gesetku.* Take these ten pieces of cloth that I have torn off. *Halam minsan sinambut e'na saga huhulmatan bay bowa kami hē'.* He didn't even accept those respect-gifts that we had brought. *Bang aku ni Malaybalay anambut lilusku, halam at'kka. Bang ta'abut pagtambukuhanta, sabuta na.* When I went to Malaybalay to take possession of my wristwatch, it hadn't arrived. When the time we agreed on comes, we will be there for it. (*cf:* **tamuk**) 1.1) *v. advrs.* ka-...-an To be hit accidentally by something fired or thrown. *Bay kasambutan baranna, aniya' bay binantungan bo' halam tinu'ud.* His body happened to be hit, something had been thrown but it wasn't deliberate. (*Thesaurus:* **hamiyu 1, sabat₂, samba 1.1**)

  **sambut bissala** *v. tr.* To take up an issue or suggestion raised by another. {idiom} (*cf:* **samlang**)

**sambuwang** *n.* A large mooring stake. (*Thesaurus:* **bale₃ 1, soha', tungkud 1**)

**sambuwangan** *var. of* **tehe'-tehe'-sambuwangan**

**Sambuwangan** *n.* Zamboanga City; the peninsula to the north of the city. (*syn:* **Sambo**)

**samda** *n.* A short-sleeved blouse with braided trimming.

**Samehakan** *n.* The Yakan people, most of whom live on Basilan and Sakol islands. (*cf:* **Sama**)

**pagsamehakan** *v. intr. aN-* To speak the Yakan language.

**samigēl** *n.* San Miguel, a famous Philippine beer; beer in general. *Am'lli gi' aku samigēl panambal d'nda baha'u bay anganak, saki bīn.* I will buy San Miguel beer as a treatment for a woman who has just given birth and is suffering from hemorrhage.

**samin** *n.* **1)** Glass (as a substance); window glass. *Akosog samin basu, mbal abila' minsan nihantakan.* The glass of the cup is strong, doesn't break even when dropped. (*cf:* **kassa' 1**) **2)** A mirror. **2.1)** *v. intr. aN-* To look at oneself in a mirror. *Anamin ka, rāng.* Have a look in the mirror, honey. **2.2)** *v. tr. -an* To use something as a mirror. *Alanu', tapanaminan.* Smooth, could be used as a mirror.

**pagsaminan** *n.* Something used as a mirror. *Ya tapagguna e' sigām saga tumbaga angalinig, ya bay pagsasaminan saga kar'ndahan.* What they used was brassware that shone, used as mirrors by the womenfolk.

**samin-mata** *n.* Eyeglasses. *Samin-mata sai itū?* Whose eyeglasses are these? (*cf:* **tipara 1**)

**pagsinamin-mata** *v. intr. aN-* To wear eyeglasses.

**samlang** *v. tr.* To answer back; to object to what is said. *Aniya' kibut bahā' anamlang a'a bay angahinang iya, yukna, "Angay aku hinangnu buwattitu?"* Is there a water jar that would speak critically of the person who made it, saying, "Why did you make me like this?" (*cf:* **sambut bissala**)

**sammal** *adj. a-* **1)** Offensive to one's sight; against moral standards. *Paraw inān halam bay sinusutan, asammal ni'nda'.* That canoe hasn't been scrubbed, it is revolting to look at. *Ya hinangna hē' hinang makasammal.* What he is doing there is something offensive. (*Thesaurus:* **pangkal, sāk₁ 1, sakkal, saggan**) **1.1)** *v. advrs. ka-...-an* To be disgusted by something offensive. **1.2)** *v. tr. a-, ka-..-an, -an* To consider something to be offensive. *In kinasammalan he' Tuhan.* That which is treated by God as offensive.

**samod** *v. intr. pa-* To associate with; to co-occur. *Da'a ka pasamod ni a'a bula'ug.* Don't associate with people who are violent. *Mbal du pasamod palig, wa'i ma lisigan.* Surgeonfish don't occur [with these other fish], they're off in deeper waters.

**pagsamod** *v. intr. aN-* To be on familiar terms with each other. *Magsamod sigām maginum toba'.* They got together as mates to drink palm toddy. (*Thesaurus:* **pagda'atay, pagsōd-addat**)

**samot** *adj. a-* **1)** Quick of movement; done promptly. (*Thesaurus:* **baggis, ka'is, kasay 1, kulakkus, l'kkas 1, sapat₂ 1**) **1.1)** *v. intr. pa-* To hurry; to do quickly. *Pasamot ka maghinang.* Do your work quickly.

**sampak** *v. tr.* To slap someone's face with open palm. (*Thesaurus:* **bimbing, b'ddak, sampiyal, tapling, t'ppak₁**)

**sampaka'** *n.* The frangipani, a fragrant shrub. *Plumeria acutifolia.*

**sampa'** *v. tr.* To cut something deeply; to cut up a slaughtered animal or large fish. *Bang kita paluwa'an laha' min bowa'ta, min buli'ta, tasampa' kita.* When we have blood coming out of our mouth or from our rectum, we have been deeply wounded.

**sampal** (var. **dampal**) *n.* **1)** Measles; other conditions symptomized by fever and blistering. *Bang aniya' magbuwa'-buwa' ma baranta sampay ma bayhu', ya na he' sampal. Akeyat maka apasu'.* When there are blisters on our body and face, that's *sampal*. We are red and hot. *Dampal maka sampal sali' du, ya saki buwa'-buwa'.* *Dampal* and *sampal* are the same, they are a sickness [causing] pustules. *Dampal itū bang mbal tasaunu', piligdu kita, sali' ma deyom assang.* This sickness, if it isn't treated promptly, is dangerous, sort of right inside the throat. (*cf:* **dapal, ugam 1.1**) **1.1)** *v. advrs. -in-* Afflicted with measles or other illness characterized by a rash.

**pagsampal** *v. tr.* To be infected with measles. *Aheka isāb saga onde'-onde' pinagsampal, ngga'i ka hal anak kami. Anak kamemon.* There are a great many children coming down with measles, not just ours. All the children.

**sampallu'** *n.* The tamarind tree and its edible pod-like fruit. *Tamarindus indica.*

**sampan** var. of **tampan**

**sampan-tuhug** *n.* The Indian snowberry, a medicinal shrub, the astringent bark of which is used in the treatment of hemorrhage. *Breynia rhamnoides.*

**sampang** *v. tr.* **1)** To meet someone who has just arrived. *Bang ka bay min Bukidnon, sampangta ka. Kalu-kalu aniya' pamowahannu aku.* When you have been to Bukidnon I meet you. You may be bringing me something. *Bay kami sinampang e' palilitu.* A middleman came out to meet us. (*Thesaurus:* **abang, bāk₂, langgal₂ 2, pagsamban**) **1.1)** *v. intr. pa-* To go to meet someone who is arriving. *Aniya' na pasampang.* Someone has gone to meet [them]. **2)** To intercept something coming towards one's location. *Da'a sanggulun holen, da'a sampangun.* Don't block the marbles, don't intercept them.

**kasampangan** *n.* An arrival gift. *Aniya' kasampangan si Arung, saga tinapay, kendi.* There are arrival gifts for Oldest Daughter, bread and candy.

**sampang-aray** *n.* A species of mackerel.

**sampay 1)** *prep.* Up to and including, of space, time, or a series of items; as far as. *Bang ginantung sangom sampay kohap ahalu' daing.* When hung up overnight or till afternoon the fish will be rotten. *Min subu-subu sampay ni* *kasangoman.* From early morning to nightfall. *Nijagjag luma' ilu, nirarut sampay hāg apa ilu'un na mundu.* This house will be dismantled, even the posts pulled up, because there are bandits coming. *Aho', sampay a'a min kaluma'an paluruk na.* Yes, people from the village also attended the event. (*cf:* **sambil**) **2)** *v. intr. pa-* To go as far as a destination; to reach a goal. *Pagga makasampay na ni luma' kar'ndahan...* Since we had got as far as the house of the woman's family... *Ilu'un si Do amowa kasampangan pasampay pi'itu.* Here is Do, bringing arrival gifts all the way here. *Mura-murahan magpakasampay in niyat kami ni ka'am. Paheyabi du isāb ma atay.* Our hope is that our serious purpose may be able to reach you. May you also treat it as important. (*Thesaurus:* **abut₂ 1, kablit₂, t'kka₁ 1.1) 2.1)** *v. tr.* To aim for a destination. *Ni kat'kkahanta, ni sinampayta inān.* To our arrival destination, to the place we are aiming to reach.

   **pasampay** *v. tr.* To deliver something to its destination. (*Thesaurus:* **maksud 1.2, nde', papole', tukbal₁ 1, tūd₂, tulun₂ 1.1, tuyuk-tuyuk**)

**sampellot** *n.* A loincloth. (*syn:* **sollet 1**)

**sampen** *n.* The Dusky tripletail, a species of fish. *Lobotes surinamensis.*

**samperet** *v. intr. pa-* To skip, of flat stones thrown across a water surface. *Bantunganta batu, pasamperet ma kulit tahik.* We throw stones which skip across the surface of the sea. (*Thesaurus:* **kulit-kulit, sularaw, tampeppet**)

**samperot** *n.* The Silver pomfret, a fish species. *Pampus argenteus.*

**sampig** *v. intr. pa-* To make firm contact with something. *Maglangihan na lubid dok supaya makasampig kami ni bihing kalang.* Swimming with a rope so we can make contact with the edge of the coral sand. *Kaukun kita ko da'a pasampig ni luma'.* Paddle us sideways so as not to come up against the house. *Bang pasampig hal pasabol saga, bang pasangku' sali' ajogjog luma'.* *Sampig* is just running up against something, *sangku'* is hitting head on so that the house sort of shakes. (*cf:* **sampigay**; *Thesaurus:* **binggil, daplig 1, dugtul, sangku'**)

   **pagsampig-manampig** *v. intr. aN-* To wander from place to place, rarely settling down. (*cf:* **pagkamundal-mandil**)

**sampigay** *v. intr. pa-* To come up against something, side-on. (*cf:* **sampig**)

   **pagsampigay** *v. intr. aN-* To move erratically and knocking against things.

**sampil-laran** *n.* A species of pelagic fish.

**sampila'₁** *n.* **1)** Fish preserved by splitting and salting. (*Thesaurus:* **daing niasin, lumay, peyad 1, pundang 1) 1.1)** *v. tr.* To preserve fish by splitting, salting and drying.

**sampila'₂** *v. tr.* To shorten a quadrangular sail by folding down an upper point. *Bang alandos baliyu subay sinampila' banog.* When the wind is strong the sail should be shortened [by removing the peak sprit]. (*cf:* **diki' 1.2**)

**sampinit** *n.* A thorny briar-like plant. *Rubus.* sp. (unconfirmed)

**samping** *n.* **1)** The outer edge of one's jawbone; the lower side of the face. (*cf:* **pisngi**) **2)** The lower side of a canoe just above the keel. *Pelangnu ilū, abanggid sampingna.* Your canoe there, its chine is scraped.

**sampiyal** *v. tr.* To slap someone with an open palm. *Aniya' onde'-onde' mbal palāng e'nu. Yukna, "Sampiyalun ba onde'. Atuwas kōkna ilū."* There's a child who won't be stopped by you. [Someone] says, "Slap the kid. He's stubborn." (*Thesaurus:* **bimbing, b'ddak, sampak, tapling, t'ppak₁**)

**samp'kka'** *see:* **pagsamp'kka'**

**sampong** *n.* **1)** Something that covers a hole or opening. (*syn:* **saplong**; *Thesaurus:* **sa'ob 1, tambol 1, taplok 1, turung 1, tutup₁ 1) 1.1)** *v. tr. -an* To cover a hole to keep contents from being seen, or from coming out. *Sampongin bowa'na ilū bo' mbal makapangolang.* Block her mouth so she isn't able to keep screaming.

**sampoyak** *v. intr. pa-* To break over something, of waves. *Pasampoyak goyak ni pagdaingan.* The choppy sea breaks over the fishing spot. (*Thesaurus:* **alun-panjang, kata'-kata', goyak 1, lumbag, sahal₁ 1.1**)

**sampoyan** *v. intr. aN-* To become limp, as a sick person who exerts himself. *Bang akatis bay asungi' anampoyan na iya. Angahimāt na baranna, hal bohe' tasungi'na.* When finished having a bowel movement he becomes limp. His body is floppy, water is all he excretes. (*Thesaurus:* **himāt, hoyon**)

**sampu** *var.* of **sah'mpu**

**sampul** *n.* **1)** A serving of cooked rice molded in a cup. **1.1)** *v. tr.* To serve rice in molded portions. *Aniya' sinampul ma dangan, aniya' isāb dagantang sinampul min t'dda.* There is a serving for each one, and there is also an entire *gantang* [3 liters] given at one time. *Lima mama'an maka bubuhatan, ya buwas biyaning sinampul ma lai'.* Five betel-nut containers and servings of food, the turmeric rice served molded on a plate.

**sampul-baul** *v. tr. -an* To buy items of varying quality or size at the same price per item. (*Thesaurus:* **kuridas, pakkiyaw, pono' 1.1, tighan 1.1**)

**sampulna'** *adj. a-* Fully completed, especially of a ceremony. (*Thesaurus:* **tammat 1, tangbus**)

**sampunay** *n.* A species of tree, the bark of which is used in preparation of a superior cosmetic powder. *Manuk-manuk dundunay, patapu' ni sampunay.* The *dundunay* pigeon perches on the *sampunay* tree.

**samsuy** *v. tr. -an* To peddle various small goods such as cloth, toiletries or jewelry. (*Thesaurus:* **dagang, lilung, litu, pab'lli, pagsoroy, pa'andag 1**)

**samuwa'** *n.* **1)** Pimples. **1.1)** *v. advrs. -in-* Suffering from pimples. (*Thesaurus:* **ampogod 1, buwa'-buwa' 1.1**)

**sān** *v. intr. pa-* To occur from time to time. *Bang pasān aniya' mala'ikat pareyo' ni bohe' inān.* At times an angel descends to that water source.

**pagsān-sān** *v. intr. aN-* To occur intermittently or occasionally. *P'ddi' b'ttongku itū magsān-sān.* This pain in my stomach comes and goes. *Sali' magsān-sān ba, ya mustahil itū.* This word *mustahil*, is like something that occurs only occasionally. (*cf:* **pagsamba-samba**)

**saN-** var. of **sa-**

**sanaw** *v. tr.* To search for something by feeling about. *Buwat ka'a anukut ma aku. Yukku, "Sinanawan pa'in, kalu aniya'."* Suppose you ask me to pay what I owe. I say, "I will look around for it, there might be some." *Manjari pasekot na si Ya ni mma'na bo' tasanawna.* So Ya approached his father so he could feel him. (*Thesaurus:* **agap₂, gindas, sadsad 1.1, sassaw**)

**sandak** *v. tr.* To probe for something using a rod or spike. *Pindi' itū pinagt'bba, sinandak maka sahapang ma deyom gusung. Aheka ma Kalumang.* The scallops referred to are strand food, probed for with a spear in the sand. Lots of them at Kalumang.

**sanda'** *v. tr. -an* To deposit an item as security for a loan, as with a pawnbroker. *Bang aniya' dublun si Ina', sanda'anku ni si On pam'lliku pantalun.* If Mother has a gold coin, I will pawn it with On so I can buy trousers.

**sanda'-sanda'** *n.* An item borrowed for a brief time only. *Sanda'-sanda' sadja, mbal nilopas, mbal nilōb.* Just a brief loan, it won't get lost; it won't get retained as security. (*Thesaurus:* **indam, sambi' 1.1, s'nnad, utang 1.1**)

**sanda'an** *n.* A pawnshop.

**sandal** *adj. a-* **1)** Enduring; long-lasting. *Subay kām asandal mareyom kabinasahan.* You should be steadfast during difficulties. **1.1)** *v. tr. -an* To endure hardships, pain, or stress. *Sandalin p'ddi' ilū bang ka bay binono' e' mastal.* Endure that pain when you have been beaten by the schoolmaster. *Bang kaut bo' alandos to'ongan goyak, alatas saga katig. Mbal anandal pelang ma goyak. Alopot-lopot.* When at sea and the waves are really rough, the outriggers become disconnected. The canoe cannot cope with the rough water. It breaks up. (*Thesaurus:* **iman₁ 1.1, pagsabal, tahan-tahan, tangka', tatas 1.2**)

**sandal-dohon** *n.* Grief long-endured. {idiom} *Tinangtangan lasana, nila'anan sandal-dohon.* Her love was stripped away, her sustained grief was removed.

**sandal-sandal** *v. tr. -an* To put up with a temporary inconvenience. *Sinandal-sandalan gi', kalu-kalu palōng-lōng baliyu.* Put up with for a while, the wind conditions may improve.

**panandal** *v. tr. -an* To make something more durable.

**sandana'** *n.* The sandalwood tree. *Santalum sp.*

**sandat** *adj. a-* **1)** Tight-fitting; securely tied. *Ahogot, asandat.* Firm, tight. *Asandat dambila' ligtangna.* One of the mast stays is tighter. *Luma' inān asandat, halam aniya' kapiligduhanna.* That house is tightly lashed, there is no danger to worry about. (*Thesaurus:* **d'llot 1, pigtal 1, p'nggod 1**) **1.1)** *v. tr.* To bind something without any slack. **2)** Non-negotiable; inflexible. *Buwat onde'-onde' aniya' kabilahi'anna bo' mbal ta'ā'na, magjawab iya maka matto'ana. Na asandat he' lling mma'na.* Like a kid who wants something but doesn't get it, and argues with his parents. He is dealt with firmly by his father's word. **2.1)** *v. tr.* To put someone under pressure, the action of a spirit being. *Sinandat he' ntan, pinasōng sakina.* Pressured by a ritual ancestor, his sickness made more serious.

**pagsandat** *v. intr. aN-* To grow tense and unyielding, of an argument. *Magsandat bissala, sali' magpasu', sali' mbal magkole' inān, sali' magsigpit.* The discussion becomes rigid, gets heated, neither winning, as though deadlocked.

**sandet-tai'** *n.* The Bridle triggerfish; the Masked triggerfish. *Balistes fraenatus.*

**sandig** *v. intr. pa-* **1)** To lean against something for support; to rely on someone. *Aningkō' aku pasandig, sakali talilap aku tinuli.* I sat leaning against something, when I was overcome by sleep. *Pasekotun lagi' aku ni hāg ina'an bo' aku makasandig.* Put me close to that post so I can rest against it. (*Thesaurus:* **li'id 1, saray-saray**) **1.1)** *v. tr.* To support someone by providing something to lean against. *Yuk si Mma', "Sandigun a'a hē' apa amale' na."* Dad said, "Support that man by leaning against him because he's exhausted."

**pasandigan** *n.* Something solid to lean back on.

**sandiyas** *n.* A variety of papaya.

**sandol** (var. **sannol**) *adj. zero* **1)** Introverted; withdrawn; uninvolved. *Mbal anabang maghinang, hal amangan, hal aningkō' sandol. At'mmun min at'mmun.* Doesn't help with the work, just eats, just sits around doing nothing. Quieter than quiet. **1.1)** *v. intr. pa-* To avoid involvement in the usual activities of a household. *Hal pasannol aningkō', halam ah'lling.* Just sitting and saying nothing. (*Thesaurus:* **d'ngngo', m'mmong, t'mmun**)

**sandu₁** *conj.* Even if; even though. *Na subay abeya' ya kabaya'anna, sandu mbal ahāp.* He prefers to do as he pleases, even if it's not good. (*cf:* **minsan aina**)

**sandu₂** *see:* **pagsandu**

**sandulay** var. of **bāt-sandulay**

**sandulay-l'ggon** n. A variety of sandulay trepang.

**sani** n. Sago palm, both spiny and smooth-sheathed varieties. *Metroxylon rumphii; M. sagus. Anipis atop sani bo' apagon, angkan ahunit min nipa' bin'lli.* Sani thatch is thin but durable, that's why it is more expensive to buy than *nipa'*. (*Thesaurus:* **nipa', tigul**)

**sanittiya** adv. Regular, of religious observance. *Sanittiya kita pinandu'an, sali' llaw-llaw kita pinandu'an.* We are regularly taught, taught day after day.

**pagsanittiya** v. intr. aN- To observe faithfully the five daily times of prayer enjoined by Islam. *Magsanittiya itū sali' magsambahayang llaw pitu', sajuma'at-sajuma'at. Sanittiya* is like praying on the seventh day, Friday after Friday. (*Thesaurus:* **pagammal, paglima-waktu, pagta'at**)

**sannang** (var. **sanyang**) adj. a- Comfortable; peaceful; at ease. *Aluhaya luma'nu, Tuwan, asannang patulihan.* Your house, Sir, is roomy, a comfortable place to sleep. *Asannang, halam aniya' hinangta. Mbal kita minale', sō' hal palege.* We are at ease, no work to do. We don't get tired, but just lie down. (*cf:* **sayudja' 1**)

**kasannangan** n. Peace and tranquility. *Aniya' mpatpū' tahun ya t'ggol kasannangan ma paglahat.* There was peace in the land for a period of forty years. (*cf:* **pistaem**)

**pagpasannang** v. intr. aN- To take it easy; to relax.

**sannol** var. of **sandol**

**santan** n. 1) Rice gruel, boiled with water, coconut milk and sugar. 1.1) v. tr. To prepare sweet rice gruel. (*Thesaurus:* **sindul 1**)

**santik** v. tr. 1) To strike a match; to ignite a lamp. *Santikun kulaet ilū, al'ddom na.* Light the pressure lantern, it's dark already. (*Thesaurus:* **bagid, dokot₂ 1.2, pakeyat, sū' 1.2**) 1.1) v. advrs. ka-...-an To be ignited. *Bay aku kasantikan bagid e' si Ji.* Ji lit a match for me.

**santik bagid-bagid** v. intr. pa- To redden, of the eye (of someone ready to fight). {idiom}

**santili'** n. A religious beggar.

**pagsantili'** v. intr. aN- To beg for alms as a living.

**santing** n. The red-flowered black mangrove tree, a source of durable house posts and caulking material. *Lumnitzera littorea. Angā' kita g'llom ni kayu santing.* We get caulking material [soft inner bark] from the *santing* tree.

**santonga'** (derivative of **tonga'**) n. One-half of something. *Ndiya ma aku santonga' ilū.* Hand me one half of that. (*Thesaurus:* **dambila' 1, dampōng, samalintonga'**).

**santuk** v. intr. pa-/-um- To strike one's head against something, by accident. *Bang lahi-lahi si Li, paligid sumantuk ma lantay, anangis.* When Li runs she falls down, banging her head on the floor, crying. *Angal'ddom deyom luma', bay*

*makasantuk kōkku ni bangku'.* The house was dark inside, my head collided with a bench. (*Thesaurus:* **bungku'₂, langgal₂ 1, sukkut**)

**santul** n. The santol tree and its edible fruit, also a source of fairly durable building material. *Sandoricum koetjape.*

**sanyang** var. of **sannang**

**sanyawa** (var. **sinyawa**) n. Underpants for male or female; short pants. *Am'lli gi' aku sanyawa ni M'ddas, sanyawa keyat.* I will buy underpants in Siasi Town, red ones. (*Thesaurus:* **kansinsilyu, kindut, kudji-kudji, kullat**)

**sāng** n. 1) A lair; a nesting place; a shelter for various creatures. (*cf:* **pugad**) 1.1) v. intr. aN- To make and occupy a nest or lair. *Sāng lawa', sāng s'mmut, kagang isāb anāng, ya lowangna. Aniya' isāb sāng lokot.* Spiders' nests, ants' colony. Crabs also make lairs, their holes. *Lokot* weed also has nest-like clumps.

**sāng-lawa'** v. advrs. -in- Covered with spider webs. *Arōy! Luma' itū! Asidda sināng-lawa'.* Oh dear, this house! It's full of spider's webs.

**sāng-sāng** n. The staghorn coral. (*gen:* **batu₂ 1**)

**sanga** (var. **panga**; **senga**) n. 1) A branch from the trunk of a tree; a main limb. (*wh:* **kayu 1**) 2) A forked branch used as a prop or support.

**sangat** (var. **s'ngngat₂**) n. 1) A tool for scribing a line on a surface; a marking gauge. *Sangat, aniya' lansang ma tōng.* A scribing tool, has a nail at the end. 1.1) v. tr. To scribe a surface; to mark a guideline on wood. *Sinangat kayu bo' mbal magkello'.* The wood is scribed so it doesn't become crooked. *Sin'ngngat tapi' pelang bo' mbal akello'.* Canoe strakes are scribed so as not to be out of line. (*Thesaurus:* **gudlis 1.1, guhit 1.1**)

**sangat kawasa** n. phrase Ultimate power and authority, an attribute of God. *Allahu Ta'ala ya sangat kawasa.* The High God is the ultimate power.

**sangay** var. of **sa'angay**

**sangbaw** n. A species of deepwater crab, about the size and shape of a saucer, vivid orange in color. (*gen:* **kagang**)

**sangbawan** n. A trap used to catch sangbaw crabs.

**sangbawa** n. A toothbrush. *Am'lli aku sangbawa panganggisgisku empon.* I will buy a toothbrush to scrub my teeth with. (*Thesaurus:* **gisgis empon, sipilyu 1, tupras**)

**sangbay** v. tr. To hold a baby with both hands, usually to the accompaniment of a ditty or lullaby. *Saddī sinangbay min nialuk. Minsan onde'-onde' halam anangis, yukta, "Dai' ka, sangbayta dayang."* Being sung to is different from being consoled. Even to an infant who is not crying, we say, "Come here, darling, I'll sing to you." *Bang anangbay si'itku onde'-onde', mustala.* When my aunt holds and sings to a baby, it is lovely. (*Thesaurus:* **gapus, giba 1.1, hambin 1.1, mpit, pipi₁**)

**sangbayan** *n.* A song sung to small children to entertain or divert.

**sangka-...sangka-** *aff.* Prefix indicating the near co-occurrence of two events. *Sangkapusu' sangkakakan.* As he plucked he ate. *Sangkat'kka sangkapinda.* Arrive one minute, move the next. *Sangkasoho', sangkabuwanan.* No sooner sent than something is given. *Sangkataha'an lubid, sangkataha'an luma'.* One length of rope, one length of a house. (*cf:* **sa-**; *Thesaurus:* **sama-, sambu-...sambu-**)

**sangkad** *adj. a-* Filled to the limit, of a container. *Asangkad pitakanu, mbal paisi.* Your wallet is full, nothing can be inserted. *Aniya' ta'nda'na būd makasangkaran tana'na ma dunya.* He saw a mountain whose soil totally filled the world. (*Thesaurus:* **p'nno' 1.1, selot 1, s'ppol 1**)

**sangkahāpan** (derivative of **hāp**) *adv.* Well done; appropriately. *Ma aniya' alungay, an'ssag kita, atilaw kita sangkahāpan ni kalūnganta.* When something is lost we inform people, we ask diligently of our neighboring kin. *Nilawanan, sali' nilibun. Bang taluwa he' sulat-libun, mbal du taga h'lla saddī min sangkahāpan. Luwal iya amole' atawa sinaggaw.* Kept watch over, like being enclosed. If a safekeeping charm takes effect, she will not have any husband other than in the approved way. Unless she takes the initiative [by going to a man's house] or is taken by force.

**sangka'** (var. **hangka'**) *adj. a-* **1)** Reaching the limit of capacity; overfull. *Da'a na p'nno'un ahangka'.* Don't fill it to the limit. *Ahangka', sali' ap'nno' pabūd, buwat ambung inān isihan samaintib ni bowa'na.* Like it's full and piled up, like that basket filled level with its brim. *Ahangka' tinapay, atawa bang aniya' amatay hayop bo' pagūng, ahangka' b'ttong.* Bread swelling to the limit [of container], or like an animal that has died and is floating, stomach swollen. **1.1)** *v. intr. pa-* To reach the limit, of capacity. *Pasangka' na, mbal kaisihan.* It has reached the limit, cannot be contained. *Mbal na kasōnganku likup, pasangka' na.* I can't drive this chisel any further, it has reached the bottom. *Pasangka' kila-kilana amikilan, kahunitan to'ongan.* His powers of thought have reached the limit, he is really finding it tough. (*Thesaurus:* **hād 1.2, tobtob 1.2**)

**kasangka'an** *n.* The final stage; concluding event. *Ya na kasangka'an bissala.* That is the final, conclusive word.

**pasangka'** *v. tr.* To push something to its limit; to carry something through to a conclusion.

**sangkalan** *n.* A chopping board.

**sangkaliya'** *v. tr.* To catch large fish such as sharks using whole fish as bait. (*Thesaurus:* **kati**)

**sangkap** *n.* **1)** A chisel. (*cf:* **barena 1**; *Thesaurus:* **likup 1, pa'at 1, patuk, sakal, sosokan**) **1.1)** *v. tr.* To cut something out with a chisel.

**sangkil** *n.* **1)** A fish spear with a single tine or prong; a harpoon. *Sahapang pangahiyak daing, tayum. Sangkil ya pangahiyak pahi. Dakayu' du tōngna.* A [three-pointed] fish spear is for spearing fish or sea urchins. A harpoon is used to spear stingrays. It has a single point. (*Thesaurus:* **ablong, pana' 1, sahapang 1, saubang, s'llokan**) **2)** The penis. {vulgar}

**sangkiyam** *v. tr.* To swallow something whole, as a python ingesting its prey. *Sinangkiyam iya he' kalitan, sala tīllon min t'dda.* He was swallowed whole by a shark, sort of swallowed just once. *Bang saupama kita ahūg ni tahik sinangkiyam kita he' saitan.* If for example we fall into the sea we will be swallowed whole by a demon. (*Thesaurus:* **s'bbat 1.1, t'llon**)

**sangko'** *n.* **1)** A bayonet. (*cf:* **ispara**) **1.1)** *v. tr.* To kill someone with a bayonet, especially by beheading. *Ala'at he' sigā anangko' itū, tinambunan matata.* Their beheading is something bad, our eyes are blindfolded. *Yuk tininti, "Da'a sangko'unbi a'a ilu."* The lieutenant said, "Do not bayonet those people." (*Thesaurus:* **ponggol, pukul 1.2, punggut 1.2**)

**sangkol** *v. intr. pa-* To carry a plan through to conclusion. *Ya po'on aku halam makasangkol angiskul, bay mag'nda.* The reason I didn't carry through with school is that I got married. (*Thesaurus:* **katis₂ 1.1, talus₁ 1.1, tammat 1.1, tapus 1.1, ubus₁ 1.1**)

**sangku'** *v. intr. pa-/-um-* To bang into something; to collide. *Bang lansa pasangku' ni luma', piligdu.* If a launch runs into a house, it could be bad. (*Thesaurus:* **binggil, daplig 1, dugtul, sampig**)

**pagsangku'** *v. intr. aN-* **1)** To bang together, of solid objects. **1.1)** *v. tr.* To bang solid things together. *Buwat onde'-onde' magbono' pinagsangku' kōk sigā he' ina'.* Like children fighting, their mother bangs their heads together.

**sangkul** *n.* **1)** A heavy farm tool with a blade set at right-angles to the shaft; a mattock; a hoe. *Mbal takalut tana' inān apa asidda atuwas. Subay sangkul pangalut iya.* That soil can't be dug up because it is very hard. Should have a mattock to dig it. (*Thesaurus:* **bara, lalandak, pala, piku, susuwat**) **1.1)** *v. tr. -an* To break up soil using a mattock. *Sinangkulan itū pinalunuk tana'.* Grubbed up means the soil being made soft.

**sangdan** *v. intr. pa-* **1)** To continue uninterrupted by change or pause. *Dakayu'-kayu' du hinangta. Pasangdan kita magusaha.* We have only one job. We carry on making a living. *Pasangdan ka amangan sampay ka asumu.* Carry on eating until you are tired of it. (*Thesaurus:* **timpus**) **1.1)** *v. advrs. ka-...-an* To carry on without interruption. *Kasangdanan amuwa' mampallam, halam aniya' angalāng iya.* Uninterrupted in picking up mangoes, no one forbidding him. *Bang aniya' balbalan bo' kasangdanan, amatay* *kita, bo' mbal kasangdanan a'llum isāb.* If there is a blood-sucking spirit and it continues uninterrupted we will die, but if it is not allowed to go on we will live.

**pasangdan** *v. tr.* To leave something unmodified.

**sangdol** *v. intr.* pa- 1) To put weight on something firm. 1.1) *v. tr.* -an To depend on someone reliable. *Ka'a-i sinangdolan he' kami.* You are the one we rely on. (*Thesaurus:* **andol 1**, **kamdos₁**)

**pasangdol** *v. tr.* To provide something with support or backing.

**pasangdolan** *n.* 1) A support or backing. (*Thesaurus:* **pamaragtolan**) 2) Support in a dispute or court case.

**sangga** (var. **tangga**) 1) *v. intr.* aN- To cup open hands, facing upwards in the prayer position. *Wa'i sigā anangga.* They are praying now, palms upwards. (*cf:* **tayak 1**) 2) *v. tr.* To deflect something with open hands, as a ball. *Daipara tasanggaku bola bo' mbal makanikōkku.* Fortunately I deflected the ball with open hands so it didn't hit my head.

**pagsangga** *v. intr.* aN- To play defense in a ball game. *Bang ma ongka' bo' kulang sīnku, yukku ma sehe'ku, "Magsangga kita karuwa."* In a game where I'm short of money, I say to my mate, "Let's work together to stop them."

**sangga'ina** *conj.* Seeing as; X being the case; given that X. *Sangga'ina halam aniya' gabbang, amole' na.* Seeing there isn't any bamboo marimba, we might as well go home. *Sangga'ina atuli si Ku inān, maggara' duwangan mato'ana inān.* Just because Ku was sleeping, those two parents-in-law of his plotted something. (*Thesaurus:* **apa**, **kalna' 1.1**, **pagka**, **po'on₂**, **sabab₁ 1.1**, **saukat**)

**sanggal** var. of **hanggal**

**sanggi'** 1) *n.* A strip of plant material used for tying. 1.1) *v. tr.* To divide plant material into tying strips, as banana fibre or rattan. *Bang lupis sinanggi', bang pandan nijangat, bang lubid pin'kkal.* Banana fibre is divided, pandanus is cut with a tool, rope is unravelled. 2) *clf.* Count word for strips of flexible plant material. *Pila sīn dasanggi' buway ilū?* How much is one strip of that [prepared] rattan?

**sanggillap** *v. tr.* To catch a glimpse of something. *Tasanggillapku aniya' palabay.* I caught a glimpse of someone passing by. *A: "Aniya' a'a ma luma' si Ju?" B: "Halam, angay?" A: "Tasanggillapku sali' aniya' pasōd."* A: "Is there someone in Ju's house?" "B: No, why?" A: "I caught a glimpse of what was like someone going in." *Makasanggillap aku lindung a'a ma samin.* I happened to catch a glimpse of a person's shade in the mirror.

**sanggot₁** *n.* 1) A knife with a curved blade, usually fastened to a long pole for reaping fruit such as coconuts. *Pangalabasun na sanggot ilū.* Use the sickle there for trimming. *Kuhitta lahing maka kuhit, ya taga sanggot inān.* We harvest coconuts

with a pole-sickle, the thing with the sickle blade. (*cf:* **kukuhit**) 1.1) *v. tr.* To reap fruit using a sickle on a long pole.

**sanggot₂** *v. tr.* To beat someone by means of a ruse or trick; to outsmart someone in a business deal or a game. *Bang kita magbalebol bo' ka'a-i ata'u, aku mbal ata'u. Ananggot na ka ma aku, yuknu, "Buwanin aku lima poen, apa mbal aku ata'u."* When we play volleyball, and you know how to play but I don't, you trick me. You say, "Give me five points, because I don't know how." *Bang kita saupama nihalga'an saga sangpū' maka lima, na bang a'a halam biyasa binalos na sangpū' maka mpat. Nā, tasanggot na iya. Ta'ā' na iya.* If we, for example, are given the price of ₱15, and then a person who is not accustomed to bargaining offers ₱14. He is outsmarted and taken in.

**sanggul₁** *v. intr.* pa- 1) To run into an obstacle. *Da'a pagtimuk-timukunbi ko da'a makasanggul. Tinu'ud.* Don't gather them all together lest [the marble] runs into them. Done deliberately. 1.1) *v. tr.* To block the movement of something, as the roll of a marble. *Pala'an ka mannilu ko da'a ka makasanggul.* Move away from there so you don't happen to stop [the marble]. *Da'a sanggulun, da'a sampangun.* Don't block it, don't intercept it.

**sanggul₂** *n.* Arm wrestling.

**pagsanggul** *n.* 1) A contest of physical strength, as in Indian wrestling. 1.1) *v. intr.* aN- To pit strength against each other; to arm wrestle. (*Thesaurus:* **pagkagat 1.1**, **pagsabit**)

**sanggul₃** *v. tr.* -an To trim the comb of a fighting cock. *Da'a sanggulun pē manuk ilū.* Don't trim the comb of that cockerel.

**sanggup** *v. tr.* -an To warn someone off; to threaten someone. *Sinanggupan kami he' si Bi. Sinoho' kami da'a kaleya.* We were warned by Bi. We were told not to go inland. (*cf:* **lāng**; *Thesaurus:* **alu'₁**, **dangka₁**, **hansom**)

**sanglad** (var. **sallad**; **s'llad**) *v. intr.* pa-/-um- To run aground, of a boat. *Ya paggara' sigām, bang makajari, pinasanglad kappal pina'an ni gusung.* Their plan, if possible, was to let the ship run aground there onto the sand. (*Thesaurus:* **dagsa'**, **hanggal 1.1**, **siyud**)

**sanglag** *v. tr.* To cook something grain-like by toasting in a dry pan. (*Thesaurus:* **buwang₃**, **ggang**, **huwal**, **tompe'**)

**pagsanglag** *v. intr.* aN- To be pan-roasting cassava meal. *Ta'nda'ku na h'ndaku, ilu magsanglag ma kusina.* I can see my wife cooking cassava meal there in the kitchen.

**sanglagan** *n.* A flat pan, used primarily for roasting cassava. (*gen:* **pam'llahan**)

**sasanglag** *n.* An implement for tossing cassava meal in a pan. (*Thesaurus:* **luwag 1**, **paleta**, **sintib**, **suru' 1**)

**sinanglag** *n.* Grated and squeezed cassava, pan-roasted without oil.

**sanglit** *n.* 1) Praise; compliments. **1.1)** *adj.* a-Praiseworthy; laudable. **1.2)** *v. tr.* -an To praise or congratulate someone. *Tuhan ya subay sinanglitan.* God is the one who should be praised. *"Halam aniya' kala'atan ma a'a hē',"* yukta. *"Sinanglitan."* "That person has nothing bad about him," we say. "He is to be praised." (*Thesaurus:* **hulmat 1, mahaldika', pagmahaltabat, pudji 1.2**)

**pagpasanglit** *v. intr.* aN- To draw attention to one's own importance. (*Thesaurus:* **pagabbu 1.1, pagbantug-bantug, pagheya-heya, pagmahatinggi, pagmalangkahi, pagtāp-tāp**)

**sangom** *n.* 1) Night in contrast to day. **1.1)** *adj.* -an Overtaken by darkness; benighted. *Arāk kita sangoman.* We nearly got benighted.

**kasangoman** *n.* Night in contrast to day. *Sagō' dūlin lagi' aku patapuk ma kahuma'an deya sampay ni kasangoman ma llaw sumuddai.* But please allow me to hide among the hill farms until the night of the day after tomorrow.

**pagsangom** *v. intr.* aN- To be night. *Pagsangom pa'in, pinauppihan si Abimelek e' Tuhan.* When it was night, God caused Abimelek to dream.

**sangom itū** *n. phrase* Tonight.

**sangom bahangi-dibuhi'** *n. phrase* The night before last.

**sangon₁** *v. intr.* pa- 1) To fit into a socket or similar prepared space. *Pinasangon e' sigām saga papagan lawang ati pinabatuk saga tambolna.* They put the foundation of the door in place and inserted its bars. (*Thesaurus:* **asok 1.1, batuk₁ 1.1**) **1.1)** *v. tr.* -an To fit or connect items or parts together, making both functional. *Subay kono' sinangonan estenles kitara.* It should, they say, have a stainless guitar string fitted. *Sinangonan, sinulugan bahona duwa, pinagdayawan sali'.* Fitted out, both its booms inserted, its framework put in place.

**sangon₂** *v. intr.* pa- 1) To enter into a person, the action of a spirit being. *Pasangon na bang a'a niruwata, suma'an abay kohap, suma'an subu. Sali' aniya' saitan pasōd ni baran sigā.* Something has entered when a person is possessed, sometimes in the evening, sometimes in the morning. It is as though a *saitan* spirit has entered their body. *Bang matto'a ya a'a pasangon inān, subay du isāb pagkahina matto'a anitta.* If the person being possessed is an elder, then it must be his fellow elders who summon [the djinn]. (*Thesaurus:* **hōp₁ 2, tongop₁ 1**) **1.1)** *v. advrs.* ka-...-an To be possessed by a spirit being such as a duwata or djinn. *Kasangonan iya, angkan magbarese-barese.* She is possessed by a spirit, that's why she speaks strange words. *Magsilapug bang aniya' kasangonan.* People scatter when someone becomes spirit-possessed. (*Thesaurus:* **jin 1.2, sawi'**)

**sangpad** *n.* The raised prow section of a tradition pelang-type canoe. *Buliburun pelang i' tudju pi'itu munda'na bo' mbal magka'at sangpad.* Turn the canoe with its front facing this way, so the raised prow is not damaged. (*Thesaurus:* **kamayung, pamalung**)

**sangpit** *v. intr.* pa- To come to mind; to recall. (*Thesaurus:* **entom 1.2, magtak, padlak ni atay, suligpat, tambung, tasdik, tomtom 1.1**)

**sangpot** *adj.* a- 1) Approaching sexual maturity; pubescent. *Sangpot-sangpot na kabudjangna.* She has almost reached puberty. *Sinoho' iya mbal magh'lla saddī. Mikilagad subay na asangpot kasubul ipalna bo' pamah'lla ma iya.* She was told not to marry anyone else. Requested to wait for her brother-in-law to reach mature youth and be a husband for her. (*Thesaurus:* **hendog-hendog, lasag, pata'₁, sibuwa, to'a 1.1**) **1.1)** *v. intr.* aN- To reach puberty or adult maturity. *Halam gi' anangpot kasubulku.* I have not yet reached [male] puberty. *Anangpot na duwampū' tahun umulku.* I have reached the maturity of twenty years of age.

**sangpū'** *num.* Ten. *Sangpū' manuk-manuk mariyata' kayu.* Ten birds up in a tree.

**sangpū' maka mpat kasobangan** *n. phrase* The fourteenth day of the lunar month. (*gen:* **bulan₂ 2**)

**sangsā'** *n.* Effort; toil; hard labor.

**pagsangsā'** *v. intr.* aN- To exert extreme physical effort. *Da'a na ka magsangsā', aningkō' na ka ma luma'. Ilu na aheka anaknu amakan ka'a.* Don't exert yourself now, just sit in your house. You have many children now to provide food for you. *Bang a'a magsangsā' al'kkas apinda baranna.* When a man works too hard his body soon changes. (*cf:* **paglu'ug-liksa'**)

**sangsang** *v. tr.* To push against something powerful, as a current or someone's will. *Mbal tasangsang llingna, mbal tara'ugta. Anganda'awahan na pa'in iya.* We cannot resist his words, we can't defeat him. He keeps on defending his position. *Sangsangta pariyata'an binusay, sali' sinagga'.* We go against the current by paddling, sort of resisting it. (*Thesaurus:* **ampal, pagang, sagang, sapad, sulang₁**)

**sangtaliri'** *n.* A species of succulent plant.

**sangti'** (var. **tangsi'₂**) *v. advrs.* -in- Experiencing a relapse during convalescence. *Bang aniya' asakki ma luma' mbal makaruwa' p'ggot, apa sinangti'.* If someone is sick at our house we mustn't bring surgeonfish up because it would cause a relapse. *Mang aniya' abangat sakina subay mbal makakakan ai-ai sukangna, sabab bang sinangti' karuhunan sakina.* If someone's illness is serious he should not eat any restricted food because if he suffers a relapse, his sickness will be even worse. (*Thesaurus:* **banta', boggat, timbalun₁ 1**)

**sangu** *v. intr.* pa- 1) To place oneself in fumes or vapor, as for medicinal purposes. *Pasangu kita ni humbu.* Let's go where the smoke is. *Am'lli kono'*

*tī pasangu ati pabungkus ka mareyom hōs abō'
pahangsu.* Just buy some tea for fuming and
wrap up in a sarong in order to inhale the
fumes. (*Thesaurus:* **s'bbu, tangas**) **1.1)** *v. tr.* To
place someone in the fumes of a medicinal
substance. *Buwat aniya' asakki sinampal, sinangu
ma humbu kamanyan.* Like someone sick with
measles, put in the fumes from incense.

**sāp₁** *n.* To dive to great depths, usually with the aid
of a weight.

> **pagsāp** *v. intr.* **aN-** To make a living by deep
> diving. *Bay kami magsāp ni Bubuan, aniya'
> tapandogaku mahē' tipay abanos. Ya magsāp
> maumu amowa pana'.* We went deep diving at
> Bubuan. I had noted the location of an
> abundance of oysters there. Those who do deep
> diving usually take a spear-gun. *Magsasāp tipay
> si Ja.* Ja is a pearl diver.

**sāp₂** *n.* **1)** A brand mark on a product; a badge.
*Am'lli ka kulaet sāp kaba'-kaba', apa aluhay.* Buy
the pressure lantern with the butterfly brand,
because it is cheap. (*Thesaurus:* **tanda'**) **1.1)** *v.
tr.* **-an** To place an identifying mark on someone
or some thing. *Bay kami sināpan he' mayul.
Aniya' isāb kalbaw sināpan.* The mayor assigned
[our canoe] an identifying number. There are
water buffaloes with a brand too.

**sapa** *v. tr.* **-an** To swear an oath regarding a
commitment. *Yuk si Yakub ma iya, "Subay ka
anapa dahū, in kapatutan pamusaka' ma ka'a
pamuwannu na ma aku sab'nnal-b'nnal." Magtūy
sinapahan e' si Esaw.* Jacob said to him, "You
must swear first that you will surely give to me
your right to the inheritance." So Esau swore an
oath.

> **pagsapa** *n.* **1)** The making of a vow between two
> people. **1.1)** *v. intr.* **aN-** To make a mutual vow.
> *Buwat kita magsapa, s'lle' bale puhu', aku
> tuhumanu bay angā' ai-ainu bo' halam du isāb
> sab'nnal-b'nnal. Na ta'abut magsapa.* Like two of
> us making a vow, when [may it never happen]
> you accuse me of taking something of yours,
> though it's not true. So, and it becomes time to
> mak a vow. *Kami saga sundalu bay pinagsapahan
> e' mma'nu, sinō' mbal amangan ai-ai llaw itu.* We
> soldiers were put on oath by your father,
> ordered not to eat anything at all this day.
> *Magsapa itū pinat'kkon tanganta ma deyom
> Kora'an ko da'a magkahāp. Ka'llum ni kamatay
> mbal magkahāp.* When we take an oath our
> hands are placed on the Holy Koran [as a sign]
> that we will never make peace. From life to
> death we will not be reconciled. *Buwat kita
> magsapa, s'lle' bale puhu', aku tuhumanu bay
> angā' ai-ainu bo' halam du isāb sab'nnal-b'nnal, na
> ta'abut magsapa. Bang amatay man dambila'
> dangan, palikid isāb parambila'.* Like two of us
> making a vow, when, God forbid, you accuse me
> of taking something of yours but it's not true,
> and it comes to swearing an oath. Then if the

man on one side dies, it rebounds on the other.
*Bang aku tuhumanu, s'lle' bale puhu', bay angā'
ai-ainu bo' halam du isāb sab'nnal-b'nnal, na
magsapa kita.* If you accuse me, perish the
thought, of having taken things of yours but
there is no truth to it, then we swear an oath
together. (*Thesaurus:* **najal 1.1**, **sapda 1**, **subali
1.1**, **suhud 1.2**, **wa'ad**)

> **pagsapahan** (var. **palsapahan**) *n.* A place or
> occasion of solemn promises. *Jari aniya'
> paljanji'an pagsapahan saga pagmatto'ahan min
> karuwambila' panuman pagsulutan inān.* So there
> was a promise was made, an occasion of solemn
> oaths by elders from both sides as a
> confirmation of that agreement. *Tampat aheka
> panji-panjina, pagsapahan ya a'a kamemon.* A
> shrine with many flags, a place where everyone
> makes their solemn vows.

> **pasapa** *v. tr.* To make someone swear an oath.

**sapak** *n.* A basic unit or motif in a pattern. *Balikat
itū buwat tadjung bo' a'aslag sapakna.* Balikat
cloth is like *tadjung* [a two-colored check
pattern] but its basic motif is large. (*Thesaurus:*
**papagan 2, punsa'**)

**sapad** *v. tr.* To prevent someone or some force from
doing damage. *Mbal pasapad baliyu, ya
kakosogna.* The wind cannot be restrained, such
strength. *Bang aniya' magsuntuk subay sinapad
bo' mbal maglaha' atawa magbutig.* If some people
are punching each other they should be
restrained lest they bleed or get bruises. *Na
arai' pa'in kami magsuntuk, na ah'lling ganta'
manapad kami, "Aningkō' ka amanyabut."* Then
when we were about to punch each other, the
supposed person intervening to stop us said, "Sit
down and call on God." (*Thesaurus:* **ampal,
pagang, sagang, sangsang, sulang₁**)

**sapād-pād** *conj.* Rather than; in preference to.
*Sapadpad pelangnu bay tinangkaw, ahāp lagi'
pamuwannu.* Rather than have your canoe stolen,
it would be better to give it away. *Sapadpad
kitabi patay ma dilaut, ahāp du patay ma deya.*
Rather than be a corpse at sea, it's better to be a
corpse ashore. *Subay sinungkit na buwa' marang
sabab alahag na, pād-pād amakpak.* The *marang*
fruit should be harvested now [with a long
sickle] because it is ripe already, rather than
letting it drop. *Sapadpad ataha' katas itū, pinōng
maitu.* Instead of this paper being so long, cut it
here. (*cf:* **pād-pād₁**; *Thesaurus:* **arapun,
daipara, gōm**)

**sapainay-painay** (derivative of **painay**) *adv.* No
matter what. *Sapainay-painay, niōnan angeyok.*
No matter what, it's called *angeyok*.

**sapa'** *n.* A river or channel; a body of water. *Buwat
sapa', patagudtud min deya tudju kaut.* Like a
stream, flowing from inland towards the sea.
*Sapa' itū pamandihan, sali' l'bbak.* A *sapa'* is a
bathing place, like a hollow [in the ground].
(*cf:* **danaw**; *Thesaurus:* **sowang**)

**sapa'at**₁ *n.* 1) A favor or help from a superior being. *Angamu' kita sapa'at ni Tuhan, sali' kita angamu' ka'llum.* We ask a favor from God, as when we ask for life. 1.1) *v. tr. -an* To make someone the object of a petition. *Sapa'atanta ka ni atubag.* I ask [supernatural help] that you may die violently.

**sapa'at**₂ *n.* Small gifts to mosque leaders officials during a religious festival, in appreciation for their service. *Ba'anan ma'amun ya amuwan sapa'at ni bay mamassa hutba', saga sangpū' sīn, saga duwampū'.* It is the members of the congregation who give the *sapa'at* to the one who read the sermon, ten or twenty centavos or so.

**pagsapa'at** *v. intr. aN-* To make a gift to the leaders of local mosque. *Magsapa'atan saga ma'amun kamemon.* All the congregation give small gifts. (*Thesaurus:* **jakat, pitla', sarakka 1**)

**sapa'atan** *n.* An occasion for showing appreciation to one's religious leaders. *Bantungta maka sīn saga a'a bay amassa hutba' inān, atawa buwas atawa ai-ai, basta aniya' sapa'atan. Ya mamantung hē' saga ma'amun.* When it is an occasion for showing appreciation to the men who read the sermon, we pelt them with money, or rice, or whatever. The people doing the throwing are the congregation.

**sapal** *n.* The residue of grated coconut meat from which the liquid has been expressed. *Sapal lahing, ya kapin bay pam'gga'an.* Coconut residue, what's left from squeezing out the liquid. (*Thesaurus:* **akal, angkas**₁ **1, hali**₁ **1, p'tti', tai'-lahing**)

**sapali** *n.* 1) A partner in an enterprise; a collaborator. 1.1) *v. intr. pa-* To seek a working partnership with someone. *Bang aniya' duwangan am'lli pambot bo' mbal maka'abut sīn, na pasapali duwangan hē' ni a'a dangan, hatina t'llungan na sigā magsapali.* If two men are buying a motorized canoe and the money isn't sufficient, then the two of them seek a partnership with another person. In other words the three of them form a partnership. 1.2) *v. tr.* To propose a resource-sharing partnership. *Aniya' sapaliku ni ka'a, aniya' puhungku. Ka'a taga paraw, aku taga banog.* I have a resource-sharing proposal to make to you, a request. You have a canoe and I have a sail.

**pagsapali** *v. intr. aN-* To be partners in a business activity. *Bang aniya' duwangan am'lli pambot bo' mbal maka'abut sīn, na pasapali duwangan hē' ni a'a dangan, hatina t'llungan na sigā magsapali.* If two men are buying a motorized canoe and the money isn't sufficient, then the two of them seek a partnership with another person. In other words the three of them form a partnership. (*Thesaurus:* **paghaup, paghūn, pagtiguway, pagtintuway, pagtughay 1.1**)

**panapali** *n.* The contribution of one component to a set, as a sail to a canoe.

**sapan**₁ *n.* 1) A straight line or row, as of buildings. (*Thesaurus:* **badlis, diril-diril, dirit**₁ **1, tād, tagik**) 1.1) *v. tr.* To arrange things in a straight line. *Pahati'un sigām, bang magluma' subay sinapan bo' ahāp ni'nda'. Buwat kaluma'an Sabah.* Explain to them that when they set up houses, they should be aligned so as to look good. Like the housing areas in Sabah. 2) A line of writing, prayer or music. *Baris atawa liniyA: ma pagsambahayang yuk guru, "Pabontolunbi sapanbi."* A superscript or a line: when involved in prayer matters the teacher say, "Make your lines [of text] straight."

**sapan**₂ *n.* The hard dark heartwood of certain trees, prized for making knife handles. (*Thesaurus:* **kubal 1, esok, tupas**₂)

**sapanjang-panjang** (derivative of **panjang**) *adv.* Forever. (*Thesaurus:* **salama-lama, sapaya-paya, sapupud-daya, saumul-umul**).

**sapantun** *adv.* As an example; by way of illustration; symbolically. *Ya duyung-duyung sapantun du a'a, bo' ngga'i ka a'a.* The marker on a grave is symbolic of a person, though not a person. (*Thesaurus:* **ibarat**₂, **saupama 1.1**)

**sapat**₁ *v. intr. pa-* To stop at a barrier that prevents traveling the full distance. *Bang aku tinimbak e' a'a bo' akapal dinding, pasapat timbak. Halam makalanjal pareyom.* If I am shot at by a person and the wall is thick, the bullet stops. It does not penetrate. *Bang aku bay amaleyang taguri' ma luma' kami, arāk patukbung. Wa'i makasapat ni luma' si To.* When I was flying a kite at our house it almost nose-dived. It came to a stop on To's house. *Da'a ka pasapat bang ka magsungi', subay ma lowang.* Don't stop partway when you excrete, it should be over the hole. [Advice to a small child.]

**sapat**₂ *adj. a-* 1) Agile; quick; hurried. *Mbal asapat aku amassa itū.* I am not quick at reading. (*Thesaurus:* **baggis, ka'is, kasay 1, kulakkus, l'kkas 1, samot 1**) 1.1) *v. tr. -an* To do something using speed. *Arāk patukbung taguri', daipara sinapatan nihella'.* The kite was about to nose-dive but fortunately it was swiftly pulled back.

**sapaw** *n.* 1) An awning of woven leaves or material such as sailcloth. *Sapaw itū kadjang ya pinagbowa ni kapū'an ilū paturung ulan maka llaw.* This *sapaw* is the awning that is habitually taken to the fishing islands as shelter from rain and sun. (*cf:* **atop 1**; *Thesaurus:* **ambung-ambung**₂ **1, kadjang, sayap 1**) 1.1) *v. tr. -an* To shelter something with an awning.

**sapay** *n.* 1) A technique for finishing the edge of a mat. (*Thesaurus:* **l'ppit 2, ppi' 1**) 1.1) *v. tr.* To finish a woven edge with the sapay technique.

**sapaya-paya** *adv.* Unendingly; forever. (*Thesaurus:* **salama-lama, sapanjang-panjang, sapupud-daya, saumul-umul**)

**sapda** *n.* **1)** A curse; an oath. (*Thesaurus:* **najal 1.1, pagsapa 1.1, subali 1.1, suhud 1.2, wa'ad**) **1.1)** *v. tr.* To curse someone. *Kabīngan kam sapda ya asal bay tapanapda ma sigām.* The curse that had been used for cursing them will rebound on you. (*Thesaurus:* **sukna' 1.1**)

**pagsapda** *v. intr.* *aN-* To swear an oath that calls for retribution if the oath is broken or sworn falsely.

**sapehak** *v. intr.* *pa-* To diverge from a path or direct route. (*Thesaurus:* **siha'**)

**pagsapehak** *v. intr.* *aN-* To go different ways. *Alahi du kām magsapehak pi'ingga-pi'ingga labayan.* You will escape going various ways, wherever there is a way through. *Magpaopēt, sali' magsapehak, magl'bba.* Going different ways, sort of diverging, taking leave of each other. (*Thesaurus:* **pagl'kkat, pagpaopēt**)

**sapid** *n.* **1)** A braid of hair. **1.1)** *v. tr.* To braid hair. *Sinapid bu'unna inān, sali' nilubid.* That hair of hers is braided, sort of formed into a rope. (*Thesaurus:* **hambak, hampal, pugay 2, simbōng 1.1, toket 1.1, tusay**)

**sapi'** *n.* A cow; a bull. *Bos taurus. Pagubus, magdai'-dai' iya pehē' ni buluyan hayopna amene' dakayu' anak sapi' ahāp isina.* After that he hurried to where his animals were running free and chose a young cow with good meat on it. (*cf:* **kalbaw 1**)

**sapi'-mandangan** *n.* A dominant bull.

**saplag** *adj.* *a-* **1)** Spread over a wide area; widely visible. *Buwat deyom Sambuwangan, asaplag he' keyat, buwat du llaw sali'.* Like in Zamboanga, lit up by lights, sort of like daylight. *Asaplag mataku ang'nda'.* My eyes see clearly. (*Thesaurus:* **dasal, lakat, pagsilapug**) **1.1)** *v. intr.* *pa-* To become widespread. *Damuli pa'in min latap, pasaplag ma dunya saga kabangsa-bangsahan kamemon, luwas min panganak si Nabi Nū.* After the flood, all the ethnic groups spread across the world, coming from the children of the prophet Noah.

**kasaplagan** *n.* The full extent of a large area such as a country or the world. (*cf:* **kaluha'an**)

**pasaplag** *v. tr.* To cause something to spread widely.

**saplong** *v. tr.* *-an* To cover a hole to prevent anything going in or out. *Saplongin ba bo' mbal pasōd tahik.* Close it up so seawater doesn't come in. *Saplongin bowa'na!* Shut his mouth! (*syn:* **sampong 1**)

**saplung** *v. tr.* **1)** To trim something by cutting. *Saplungun kono' sangana.* Please cut off its branches. **1.1)** *v. tr.* *-an* To improve the shape of something by removing protruding bits. *Sinaplungan, nila'anan ai-ai tōngna. Ai-ai mbal tauwa' pormana, subay sinaplung.* Trim it to shape, remove anything at its end. Anything that doesn't suit its shape should be trimmed off. (*Thesaurus:* **basbas, katam 1.1, kirus 1.1,**

**sapsap₂, sosok**)

**saplut₁** *adj.* *a-* **1)** Rinsed. *Bang kita bay atuhun bo' halam magtipara, pagtuwa'ta asaplut kita sabab tahik, ko da'a kapē'an timus-timus.* When we have been diving and haven't worn goggles, on emerging [our eyes] are rinsed because it is seawater, so sea-salt doesn't adhere. (*Thesaurus:* **bunglaw 1, kula'up, gūm-gūm**) **1.1)** *v. tr.* To cleanse something by rinsing. *Saplutun bayhu'nu, bay ka atuhun.* Rinse your face, you've been diving.

**saplut₂** *adj.* *a-* Covered completely, of a flat area. *Buwat llawanta ballul, pundang, asaplut panablayan atawa ayas-ayas. Dalos kamemon, halam aniya' palabayan.* As when we are sun-drying fillets or split fish, the whole area or drying-rack is covered. There are no gaps, no place to pass. (*Thesaurus:* **kempot, lapat 1.1, pagd'ppak 1, sonson**)

**sapod** *var. of* **lapod**

**Sappal** *n.* The second month of the Islamic year. (*Set:* **Bulan Muharram, Julka'idda, Julhadji', Jumadir Ahil, Jumadir Awal, Rabiul Ahil, Rabiul Awal, Radjab, Ramadan, Saban, Sawwal**)

**sappit₁** *n.* **1)** A three-cord lashing technique for binding tool handles to prevent splitting. (*Thesaurus:* **baggot, buka'₁ 1.1, pinate 1, sihag₁ 1.1**) **1.1)** *v. tr.* To bind something using the three-cord technique.

**sappit₂** *n.* A round-bottomed sailing vessel without outriggers, larger than a lepa and similar in size to a kumpit. (*Thesaurus:* **beggong, biruk, buti, kappal, kumpit, lansa, papet, tempel**)

**sapsap₁** (*var.* **sasap₁**) *v. intr.* *pa-* To move smoothly through water or air. *Pasapsap pahāp pelang inān, al'kkas sali'.* That canoe glides along smoothly, sort of swiftly. *Bay patukbul ariplano, pasapsap pareyo'.* The ariplane plunged steeply, moving smoothly down.

**sapsap₂** (*var.* **sasap₂**) *v. tr.* *-an* To prepare construction materials by removing irregularities and unneeded bulk. *Bang batu tinigtig. Bang kōk katig sapsapanku ko' alampung.* If it is a rock it is chipped off. If it is the point of an outrigger boom I trim it to make it light. *Buwat kita anganuhan tapi' pelang, pinahāp, sinapsapan diyata' tapi' pinalanu'.* When we are doing something with canoe planks, improving them, the tops of the planks being trimmed and made smoooth. *Itiya' p'ttung binowa kaut sinasapan.* Here is bamboo being taken seawards to be trimmed. (*Thesaurus:* **basbas, katam 1.1, kirus 1.1, saplung 1.1, sosok**)

**sapsap₃** *n.* The Pug-nosed ponyfish; the Toothed ponyfish. *Secutor ruconius.*

**sapsay** *adj.* *a-* Utterly destroyed. (*Thesaurus:* **lapnas 1, lognos, luhu'₂ 1, ponas**)

**sapu** *v. tr.* **1)** To wipe something onto a surface. *Sapuhun k'llongna maka ns'llan.* Wipe oil on her neck. (*Thesaurus:* **pahid 1, peged₁ 1, pe'es₁**) **1.1**) *v. tr.* *-an* To remove unwanted material by wiping or sweeping. *Am'lli aku sasapu panapuku luma'.* I will buy a broom to sweep the house with. *Sapuhin lantay, al'mmis.* Sweep the floor, it's dirty. (*Thesaurus:* **kukus, pu'us, tarapu 1.1**) **1.2**) *v. intr.* *pa-* To move with a sweeping motion. *Pasagudsud, mbal pa'angkat tape'ta, pasapu ni tana'.* Dragging through water, our feet not lifting, sweeping along the ground.

**sapu-sapu** *v. tr.* To caress someone by stroking.

**sasapu** *n.* A broom or brush. (*cf:* **tarapu 1**)

**sapu-tangan** *n.* A piece of cloth used as a handkerchief; a sweat-cloth. (*Thesaurus:* **jimpaw, panyu', tawel, tuwalya**)

**sapupud-daya** *adv.* Forever; life-long. {idiom} *Buwat lapohanbi, sapupud-daya kam angipat. Mbal am'lli lapohan pabalik, sabasag hal gās ya bīlli pabalik.* Like your stove, you will keep it forever. You will not buy a stove again, it's only kerosene that you buy again. (*Thesaurus:* **salama-lama, sapanjang-panjang, sapaya-paya, saumul-umul**)

**saput** *n.* **1**) A white cloth for a shroud. *Bang aniya' amatay, bīllihan saput ni M'ddas, saga tonga' būs, saga lima meto.* When someone dies shroud cloth is purchased for them in Siasi Town, about half a roll, about five metres. (*Thesaurus:* **kasa', kuku-pote', salimput 1, talkun, tatap 1**) **1.1**) *v. tr.* To wrap a corpse in a shroud. *Bang bay a'a amatay pinahilala', pinandi. Puwas pinandi sinaput, puwas sinaput pin'kkos maka tepo.* When a person has died he is cared for, bathed. After bathing wrapped in a shroud, after shrouding enclosed in a mat.

**saputi** *n.* **1**) Deceit; something false. *Bang si Ji itu angose' lai' bo' amasi kinakan ma lai', nihinang saputi. Halam atimud he'na angose'.* When Ji washes the dishes but there is still food on the dish, something sneaky is done. His washing doesn't make the plates clean. *Buwat s'mmek halam akatis nirakdakan, ni'llawan, nihinang saputi.* Like clothes not completely washed or put out in the sun, a fraud committed. **1.1**) *v. tr.* To do something deceitfully, as a move in a game.

**sara** *v. advrs.* *ka-...-an* To be uninterrupted. *Kasarahan iya amangan daing sampay a'sso.* He continued uninterrupted, eating fish until he was full.

**sarakka** *n.* **1**) Alms given to the poor as a religious responsibility; a gift of appreciation to religious leaders or healers. (*Thesaurus:* **jakat, pagsapa'at, pitla'**) **1.1**) *v. ditr.* To give alms to someone. *Bang aniya' amatay saga kaukakiku, sarakkahanku.* If one of my cousins dies, I give alms on behalf. *In ka'a bay anarakka ma aku. Aniya' sīnnu, aniya' s'mmeknu, yukmu, "Itu-i panarakkaku ma ka'a. Subay taima'nu."* You are the one giving alms to me. You have money or

clothes and you say, "This here is for an alms-gift to you. You must accept it."

**pagsarakka** *v. intr.* *aN-* **1**) To be engaged in giving alms. *Minsan ngga'i ka bulan tumaluwa' ma pagsarakka, anarakka du isāb.* Though it is not the expected month for alms-giving, [he] still gives alms. (*Thesaurus:* **pagmura 1.1**) **1.1**) *v. tr.* To give alms to people in need. *Pagsarakkahun ai-ainu ni kalūng-kampungan sampay ni atā-asekot.* Give alms of your possessions to kinfolk and neighbours, to those near and those far off.

**sarahakan** *v. tr.* To make a woman the object of a marriage proposal in which the suitor risks everything. *Sinarahakan d'nda inān. Minsan mbal bilahi, niroblehan.* That woman has been made the object of a *sarahakan* proposal. Even though she is unwilling, twice [the asking amount] is paid.

**pagsarahakan** *v. intr.* *aN-* To commit oneself totally to God or fate, risking all to achieve the desired outcome. *Bang mbal katambalan, magsukul aku maka magsarahakan la'a ni Tuhan.* If it is incurable, I will give thanks and just surrender myself to God. (*cf:* **pagpatialop, pagpatihantak 1**)

**sara'** *n.* **1**) Laws; rules; regulations; a verdict. *Si Panglima Ka ya amat'nna' sara' bang aniya' magbono'.* Panglima Ka is the person to administer law when someone has been fighting. **1.1**) *v. tr.* To apply the law to a situation. *Si Imam Mi ya anara' bang magtiman. Bang duwangan d'nda isāb magbono' si Mi ya anara'.* Imam Mi applies the law when someone divorces. Likewise when two women fight it is Mi who applies the law. (*cf:* **hukum**) **2**) A magistrate or community leader who administers law. (*Thesaurus:* **abugaw, huwis, po'on-sara'**)

**pagsara'** *v. intr.* *aN-* To refer a case to a local court. *Bang aniya' magbono', magsara' ni opis. Na bang sali' mbal kamattanan ma sara' mastal, patandan ni sara'.* When there is a fight, it is referred to the [school] office. Then, if people are not satisfied by the schoolmaster's judgment, it is referred to the law.

**sara'-agama** *n.* The legal system of Islam as distinct from the civil legal system.

**sarang** *adj. zero* **1**) Adequate as to extent, size, or duration of something. *Sarang na ko' ilū, Oto'. Pahali na ka maglata.* That's enough, Son. Stop your teasing. *Sarang ma aku bahā'?* Is it big enough for me? (*Thesaurus:* **s'ddong, sugiya, t'ppot, ustu**) **1.1**) *v. tr.* To test the adequacy of something with regard to its dimensions. *Sarangun babag ilū pehē'.* Try out that cross-beam across there.

**pagsarang** *v. intr.* *aN-* To be of comparable size; to fit equally well. *Magsarang s'mmek kami maka siyakaku. Badju'na sarang ma aku, badju'ku* *sarang ma iya.* My older brother and I try clothes for size. His shirt fits me and my shirt fits him.

**sarang-sarang** *adj. zero* About right; about enough; moderately so. *Tagbak sarang-sarang langkawna.* Tagbak [a ginger-like plant] of medium height. *Abata' itū sarang-sarang, ma llot matto'a maka onde'-onde'. Bata'* [young] is moderately so, between middle age and childhood.

   **pasarang** *v. tr.* To try on shoes or clothing for size.

   **sasarang** *n.* An adequate amount; enough.

**sarap₁** *adj. a-* Tasty; delicious. *Asarap paglibusaw si Babu' Ing.* Aunty Ing's way of cooking of glazed bananas is delicious. *Ettom sirap itū. Bang bila'nu duwa, isina asarap.* These oysters are black. When you break them apart the flesh is delicious. (*Thesaurus:* **kesom, imu' 1, lanab, l'ssom 1, mamis₁ 1.1, taba' 1**)

**sarap₂** (var. **sagap**) *v. intr. pa-* **1)** To risk doing something. *Pasagap kita pehē', kalu aniya' tulung min Tuhan.* Let us take a chance in that direction, maybe God will help. *Buwat aku ni Taluk-sangay, hal aku pasagap pehē'. Mbal kata'uhanku luma', halam gi' aku bay pehē'.* Like my going to Taluk-sangay, I just took a risk going there. I didn't know the house, I had never been there. (*Thesaurus:* **k'ddom₂, halus₁, pagpasukud, pagsusaed, samba 1, tawakkal**) **1.1)** *adv.* Aimlessly, without a clear goal. *Hal kami amusay sagap pi'ingga-pi'ingga katudjuhan munda'.* We simply paddle aimlessly wherever the bow points.

   **pagsarapan** *v. intr. aN-* To be involved in something risky. *Halam aniya' padduman, hal kami magsarapan, hal magsagapan ma llaw, atuli ugtu-llaw atawa tonga' bahangi.* No compass, we just risked it, just took our chance on the sun [as a reference point], sleeping at noon or midnight.

**sarap-duwa** *adj. a-* Uncertain as to which of two possible outcomes. *Ballum tantu, asarap-duwa.* Not sure, two possible outcomes. *Asarap-duwa, song amatay.* Uncertain [as to survival], about to die. (*Thesaurus:* **dalam-duwa, duwa-abana, duwa-ruwa, paguntung-duwa**)

**saray-saray** *v. intr. pa-* To lean against something for support. *Pasaray-saray pamalutan inān min saga pan'nggehan hē'.* Those hand-rails are leaning out from the stage. (*Thesaurus:* **li'id 1, sandig 1**)

**saruk** *n.* A hat.

   **saruk-pata'** *n.* A hat woven of nitu', the bark of the scrambling fern.

**saru'un-du'un** *adv.* Immediately; at that very moment. *Saru'un-du'un aniya' baliyu, sali' bay niamu'.* Immediately there was wind, as though it had been requested. *Bang sali' kita angamu' ulan ni Tuhan, yukta, "O Tuhan, amuwan na ka ulan." Agtūy saru'un-du'un pat'nna'.* Like when we ask God for rain, saying, "O God, give rain."

Right then, immediately, down it comes. (*Thesaurus:* **agsāy, dai'-dai'an, magtūy, sakadjap, sigla' 1**)

**sarul** *v. tr.* To plate a surface with a metal layer; to work with precious metals. *Asal bay sinarul maka tumbaga.* It has in fact been plated with brass. *Mikisinarul tumbaga itū bo' tahinang bulawan.* Asking for this copper [surface] to be plated and made into gold. (*cf:* **langkop**)

   **pagsasarul** *v. tr.* To work with precious metals; to work as a silversmith. *In pilak al'mmis bang kalanu'an na, aniya' na tahinang e' a'a magsasarul.* Dirty silver, when it has been cleaned, provides something to be worked on by a silversmith.

**sasā** *see:* **pasasā**

**sasa₁** *adj. a-* Split off along its length, as the top plank or strake of a canoe. *Dambila' pelang abila', asasa min munda' ni buli'.* One side of the canoe is broken off, split off from the prow to rear. *Asasa tapi' pelang, tabowa pa'angkat he' pangka'an.* The top strake of the canoe splits off, forced upwards by the tripod mast supports. (*Thesaurus:* **pungal, saksak 1, segpong, seplak 1, te'as**)

**sasa₂** *v. intr. pa-* To hang down too far, as clothes or sail. *Pasasa pantalun pi'ituku, subay aniya' kambotna.* The trousers hang down to here on me, they need a belt. *Apu'ut tarukna, pasasa banog, pakomo'.* The mast is too short, the sail sags and wrinkles. (*Thesaurus:* **hallal, hellel, tonton 1**)

**sasa-dandan** *v. advrs. -in-* A decorative strip woven along the edges of a mat. (*syn:* **hagdan-hagdan**)

**sasab** *v. tr. -an* To forage for food or supplies. *Amiha ka'lluman, anasaban kaut-kaleya.* Seeking a livelihood, foraging at sea and on land. *Anasaban kita mampallam, sali' analun. Basta ai-ai tatalun ba.* We forage for mangoes, similar to going through coastal woods. Anything at all that is foraged in coastal woods. (*cf:* **takod 1.1, talun 1.1**)

   **pagsasab** *v. intr. aN-* To be moving randomly or aimlessly. *Magsasaban hayop binelaw ni katalunan.* The demented cow runs aimlessly into the forest. *Amiha dakayu' ni dakayu', mbal pat'nna' ma bay baina, magsasab.* It looks for this and that, not staying where it had been, moving randomly. (*Thesaurus:* **pagsalinggā**)

**sasabit** (derivative of **sabit₁**) *n.* A hook for hanging things on. (*syn:* **sasagnat**).

**sasak** *n.* **1)** A fence of rails or roughly interwoven branches. (*Thesaurus:* **ād 1, apis 1, buluyan, koral 1, kumbangan, kumbisan, likusan**) **1.1)** *v. tr.* To fence off an area.

**sasagnat** (derivative of **sagnat**) *n.* A hook for hanging things on. (*syn:* **sasabit**).

**sasahan** *n.* **1)** The flow of a liquid. *Bohe' k'ppong, hal palongkong, nsa' sasahanna.* A freshwater pool, just lies in a hollow, no flowing current.

**1.1)** *adj. zero* Flowing, in contrast to still water. *Bohe' sasahan itū sapa', sali' aniya' palaran. Bang pa'in da'a aniya' anasahan, tigbaw na.* Flowing water is a river, as though something is drifting. Whenever nothing is flowing, then it is a pond. **1.2)** *v. intr. aN-* To flow, as a running stream or blood; less often of a sea current. *Saga laha' anasahan pareyo'.* Some blood is flowing down. *Anasahan a'a man deyo' luma'.* People are drifting past under the house. (*Thesaurus:* **mansay-mansay, tagudtud**)

**sasait** (derivative of **sait**) *n.* A bailer.

**sasā'** *v. intr. pa-/-um-* To occur intermittently. (*Thesaurus:* **bang pasān, sumā'..sumā'**) **pamasasā'** *n.* An intermittent occurrence.

**sasa'ut** (derivative of **sa'ut**) *n.* A moment of time; readiness. *Bang sasa'ut, anginum. Bang mbal sasa'ut mbal aku anginum.* If it is nearly ready I'll have a drink. If not nearly ready, I won't drink. *Halam sasa'utku kohap īn.* I had no time at all yesterday afternoon.

**sasal** *v. tr.* To work with metal in a forge. *Itu gallang pilak sinasal.* Here is a bracelet of forged silver. *Tinadjul, sinasal.* Melted, worked while malleable. (*Thesaurus:* **babal₁, subu₁ 2, tawtaw**) **pagsasalan** *n.* A forge; a smithy (where a blacksmith works). *Pehē' kita ni pagsasalan ang'nda'-ng'nda'.* Let's go to the metal-working place and watch.

**sasalan** *n.* The craftsmanship of a silversmith or goldsmith; any metal work involving a forge. *Sasalan Makaw ko' itū.* This metal work is of Chinese make.

**sasalaman** (derivative of **salam**) *n.* Greetings, in a written communication.

**sasang** (var. **hinasang**) *adv.* During; while; at the same time as. *Pi'itu na pa'in, minsan du sasang a'a magkakan.* He keeps coming, even while people are eating. *Sasang iya amudjang-mudjang.* While she was becoming a teenage girl. *Hinasang aku mahē', ya kapagbono'.* The fighting happened while I was there. *Hinasang iya ma patulihanna, nirugsu'an iya ma b'ttongna e' sigām.* While he was on his bed, they stabbed him in his stomach. (*Thesaurus:* **dalam isāb**)

**sasanglag** (derivative of **sanglag**) *n.* An implement for tossing cassava meal in a pan. (*Thesaurus:* **luwag 1, paleta, sintib, suru' 1**).

**sasap₁** var. of **sapsap₁**

**sasap₂** var. of **sapsap₂**

**sasapu** (derivative of **sapu**) *n.* A broom or brush. *Angay sipa'nu sasapu?* Why did you kick the broom? (*cf:* **tarapu 1**).

**sasarang** (derivative of **sarang**) *n.* An adequate amount; enough. *Bang aniya' gadji saga sangpū' maka lima pilak, subay sasarang sangpū' hē'.* If there is a wage of about ₱15, ₱10 of it should be enough. *Bang aniya' gadji saga sangpū' maka lima pilak, subay sasarang sangpū' hē'. Na ya lima pinehē' ni matto'ana.* If there is a wage of about

₱15, ₱10 of it should be an adequate share. Then the ₱5 remaining will go to his parents.

**sasat** *n.* **1)** A sense of disquiet due to the influence of a spirit being. *Sinōd kita sasat, minsan asekot-sekot ni pahi, bo' hiyakta, asā'.* Disquiet seizes us, even though we are quite close to the stingray, when we throw the spear it misses. **1.1)** *v. tr.* To bother or trouble someone; to tempt or provoke. *Sinasat kita he' pahi taga saitan. Sali' kita amidpid.* We are troubled by a stingray with a demon. We sort of tremble. *Bang aku sinoho' kaleya angā' kayu, sinasat aku he' saitan.* When I am sent inland to get firewood, I am troubled by a saitan spirit. *Da'a aku sasatun bang aku anulat bo' aku mbal asā'.* Don't bother me when I am writing lest I make a mistake. **mananasat** *n.* Spirit beings which trouble humans.

**sasauk** (derivative of **sauk**) *n.* A container for dipping or bailing liquid.

**sasaw** *n.* **1)** Disturbance; trouble. *Bay aku absen sabab aheka to'ongan sasaw maka kabimbanganku pasalan matto'a-danakanku.* I was absent because of many troubles and my responsibilities for my parents and siblings. **1.1)** *adj. a-* Noisy; disturbing. *Bang aheka puhu' ma luma' asasaw na. Aheka na magtambal.* When many people are in the house, it is noisy. There are many now coming for medicine. (*Thesaurus:* **balu', dongkag, halubilu, hengo-hengo, hiluhala' 1.1, hiyul, jabu 1, lengog 1.1, sensong**) **1.2)** *v. tr.* To disturb or bother someone. *Bowahun paluwas. Da'a kam anasaw pi'itu.* Take it outside. Don't make trouble here. **kasasawan** *n.* A disturbance; an uproar. *Luhūy kami makabāk kasasawan aheya.* Worse still, we came across a great disturbance.

**sasawi** *n.* Mustard greeens. *Brassica nigra.*

**sasay** *v. advrs. -in-* Having water splashing over the sides in volumes large enough to swamp, of a canoe. *Sinasay pelang kami he' goyak.* Our canoe was swamped by the waves. (*Thesaurus:* **appu', sauk 2, s'pput, suput₁**)

**sasila** var. of **salsila**

**saspēk** *v. tr.* To accuse someone of an offense against the law. *Bang aniya' a'a ma parinta e'na magkanam, magagaw na, a'a nsa' maina'an sinaspēk.* When someone in authority gets angry, competing over something, a person who wasn't [even] there gets accused.

**sassat** *n.* A defect; a blemish. *Taga sassat pelang inān, aheya asangna.* That canoe has a defect, a large split [opening under the bow]. *Yuknu, "Neng, angay lai' itu?" Yuk si Nneng, "Asāl buwattilu." Na yuknu, "Neng, halam bay taga sassat lai' itu."* You said, "Neng, what's with this plate?" Nneng said, "That's just how it is." Then you say, "Neng, this plate did not have a crack." (*Thesaurus:* **gora'₁ 1, powera 1, salla'₁ 1, tamak 1**)

**sassaw** v. tr. To find something by feeling around for it. *Sinassaw onde'-onde' he' ina'na.* The child's mother gropes for him. (*Thesaurus:* **agap₂, gindas, sadsad 1.1, sanaw**)

**pagsassaw** v. tr. -an To grope around for things when there is no light. *Magsassaw kita bang sangom, sali' kita mbal maka'nda'. Nilapong-lapong kita.* We grope around at night, as though we cannot see. We are semi-blind.

**sãssay** var. of **salassay**

**sassing** n. 1) Pinworms. *Hatiku aniya' sassingku.* I reckon I have pinworms. *Itiya' aku magsungi'-sungi', marai' aniya' sassingku.* Here I am suffering from diarrhea, perhaps I've got worms. (*Thesaurus:* **but'ngngel, kalog 1, iyas 1, ulat₁**) **1.1**) v. advrs. -in- Infected with pinworms. *Bang aku hal amangan daing bo' halam aniya' laukna, sinassing.* When I eat only fish with no staple, I will be infected with worms.

**sasuku** (var. **sasuku'; suku₂**) n. Whoever; whichever. *Ingga sasuku saga a'a ab'ttong subay pinandi ma linsungan bang nilahu' bulan.* All those who are pregnant should be bathed in a rice mortar when there is an eclipse of the moon. *Sasuku mbal makalangi, amalut ma sasak inān.* Whoever cannot swim, hold on to that fence. *Suku kam bilahi, pi'itu kam.* As many of you who want to, come on. (*cf:* **saina**)

**sasuku'** var. of **sasuku**

**satan** n. A wind from the south; south wind. *Bang palemba na mūpū, sõng na satan.* When the Pleiades have passed the zenith, the south wind will soon begin. (*gen:* **baliyu 1**)

**sat'ggol** (derivative of **t'ggol**) adv. For as long as. *Sat'ggol ka anangis, sat'ggol ka nilappet.* As long as you keep crying, you'll continue to be thrashed. **sat'ggol hē'-i** adv. phrase Ever since that time long past.

**sattuwa** n. Various large living creatures, on land or in the sea. *Sattuwa itū kalitan, pahi. Subay aheya buwat sapi'.* These *sattuwa* are creatures such as shark, stingray. They must be large, like a cow. (*spec:* **kahumbu, kaloka', gadja, gadjamina, halimaw**)

**satu** see: **umbul satu**

**sau** n. An anchor. *Bang aku kaut hūgku sau bo' amalut ni batu.* When I go out to sea I drop an anchor to fasten to a rock. *Hūgun na sau ilū. Da'a na tugutin, apuspus na lubid.* Drop the anchor. Don't let the rope run, it will be used up. (*Thesaurus:* **pataw₁, tangkal₂ 1, untang**)

**sau-** see section 2.2.2.4 Prefix: **Cau-**

**saubang** n. A long-shafted spear made from bamboo, used mainly for harvesting spiny sea urchins from a canoe. (*Thesaurus:* **ablong, pana' 1, sahapang 1, sangkil 1, s'llokan**)

**sauk** 1) n. A dipper or drinking container. (*Thesaurus:* **gayung 1, tambu' 1**) **1.1**) v. tr. To scoop something up in a container. *Saukin aku, Oto', bohe'.* Scoop some water up for me, Son.

*Kinalung-kalung onde', sinauk maka hōs.* Children carried in both arms, or scooped up in a sarong. *Bang aniya' bay ahūg s'ggit ni poga, na lipayanta dahū bo' yampa kita anauk. Ati ya tasaukta ya masawa i'.* If rubbish has fallen into the water jar, then we clear the surface first and then we dip out. So what we dip out is the clear stuff. *Pala itū panaukku tana'.* This shovel is for me to scoop up soil with. (*Thesaurus:* **nduk, sagob 1.1, tambu' 1.1**) **1.2**) v. tr. To bail water out of a boat. **2**) v. advrs. -in- To be wet from wave action. *Sinauk pelang kami he' goyak. Buwat kami abanog, paghuntak pelang, pasõd goyak.* Our canoe took on water from the choppy sea. Like when we were sailing, when the canoe bounced up and down the waves came in. (*Thesaurus:* **appu', sasay, s'pput, suput₁**)

**sasauk** n. A container for dipping or bailing liquid.

**saukat** (var. **sakaukat; sinaukat; sokat₂**) conj. Merely because, implying that the reason given is inadequate. *Buwat aku magnililus na, na kasehe'anku inān ah'lling, "Sakaukat na ka taga lilus mbal na ka pahali akiyum."* Like me, I have a watch now and my friends say, "Just because you have a watch you won't stop smiling." *Saukat bay lumossok si Ja, ya biningan si Yu.* Just because Ja put his foot in a hole, the one who gets blamed is Yu. *"A'awat ka'a-i am'lli sinaukat aheka sīnnu."* "You had the buying advantage [over me] merely because you have a lot of money." (*Thesaurus:* **apa, kalna' 1.1, pagka, po'on₂, sabab₁ 1.1, sangga'ina**)

**saud₁** n. A water container made of a single section of bamboo. *Dasaud du bohe'.* A single bamboo container of water. (*Thesaurus:* **bō', honga'₁, loka', tumpung**)

**saud₂** var. of **salud**

**saul** v. tr. To respond to someone's call; to acknowedge a call. *Halam tasaulku, halam tasambunganku.* I didn't respond to his call, I said nothing in reply. (*Thesaurus:* **sambag₁ 1, sambung₁ 1.1**)

**saula** (var. **saula-ula**) conj. As though it was so; merely because. *Saula na alungay bangka'na, aku ya niagmot-agmotan kono' bay ang'llo', parahāl tu'ud bay talaran.* Just because his canoe was missing, I am reportedly the one blamed for having taken it, when in fact it just drifted away.

**saula-ula** var. of **saula**

**saumbibi** adj. zero Cooperating; working well together. *Magpõng lahing, saumbibi na.* Cutting down coconut palms, working together.

**pagsaumbibi** v. intr. aN- To be cooperative in living or working together. *Magsaumbibi kami t'llu luma' ma kinakan.* We three house-groups prepare food together. *Magsaumbibi na, ya õnna magdalūng na pihak ni Sūk, pihak ni Sama. Magsaumbibi* [working together], the word for

Tausug and Sama ethnic groups living in the same community. (*cf:* **pagsōd-addat**; *Thesaurus:* **passuk**)

**saumul-umul** (derivative of **umul₂**) *adv.* Forever; lifelong. *Pinehē' ni kal'ddoman, mahē' sadja saumul-umul, pi'ingga-pi'ingga goyak ameya'.* Sent there to the darkness, to be there forever, wherever the waves go. (*Thesaurus:* **salama-lama, sapanjang-panjang, sapaya-paya, sapupud-daya**).

**sauna** *v. intr.* pa- To go ahead of others. (*cf:* **dahū 1.1**)

**saunahan** *conj.* In fact; actually. *Saunahan ka halam ta'nda'ku.* I did not in fact see you. *Magbāk ka maka kampungnu ati halam ka bay sinagina he'na, saunahan du halam kām bay maglambung.* When you meet a town-mate and he doesn't greet you, when in fact you hadn't noticed each other. *Ma nda'nu bay na nihinang he'na, bo' pa'in halam. Saunahan halam du bay nihinang e'na.* Going by what you saw he had done it, but it wasn't so. In fact he hadn't done it. (*cf:* **malaingkan**)

**saunay** *n.* A traditional flute made by rolling a section of palm leaf to form a cone. (*Thesaurus:* **pulaw₁, suling₁**)

**saunu'** *v. tr.* To do something without delay. *Saki itu bang mbal tasaunu', bang paheya, piligdu makamatay.* This sickness, if something isn't done for it right away, if it gets worse, one fears it may be fatal. (*Thesaurus:* **ambat 1, amot-amot 1.1, dai'-dai' 1.2, sa'ut 1.1**)

**saungga'** *n.* A species of shrub, used medicinally.

**saupama** *n.* 1) An example; an illustration of a meaning. (*Thesaurus:* **pamaralilan, upamakun 1**) **1.1**) *conj.* For example; by way of example; for instance. *Saupama atuli, bang mbal abati' to'ongan nirabdab.* Someone sleeping for example, if he doesn't wake up fully he talks in his sleep. *Silangun ai-ai, saupama tasuli-sulinu.* Distinguish anything, the things you talk about for instance. *Saupama kami maka si Ja bay magbangka'-bangka', bay kami abuhaw.* For example when Ja and I were playing in a dugout, we filled up with seawater. (*Thesaurus:* **ibarat₂, sapantun**) **1.2**) *v. tr.* To provide an illustrative example for some word, explaining its meaning. *Saupamahun ba bo' tahatiku.* Just give an example so I can understand.

**sauragal** *n.* A merchant (only in folktales).

**pagsauragal** *n.* 1) Wealth derived from trade. **1.1**) *v. intr.* aN- To enjoy things gained through trade. *Magsauragal, aheka na indalupa-kaginisna.* Enjoying abundance, plenty of all sorts of things. (*Thesaurus:* **alta' 1, kaniya', karaya 1**)

**saurung** *n.* An unwalled open area of a house; a porch. (*Thesaurus:* **balkon, pantān, salas**)

**sauwal** *n.* Loose-fitting trousers with wide legs, worn by both men and women. (*cf:* **pantalun 1**; *Thesaurus:* **hakpan, solpan**)

**sawa** *n.* 1) An illumination; a light source. **1.1**) *adj.*

a- Bright; shining; clear; translucent. *Asawa bulan. Asawa isāb bohe' bang halam aniya' autna.* The moon is clear. Water too is clear when it has no particles in it. *Am'lli aku palita'an ni M'ddas bo' asawa luma'ku.* I will buy a lamp in Siasi Town so my house will be brightly lit. *Bang aniya' bay ahūg s'ggit ni poga, na lipayanta dahū bo' yampa kita anauk. Ati ya tasaukta ya masawa i'.* If rubbish has fallen into the water jar, then we clear the surface first and then we dip out. So what we dip out is the clear stuff. (*cf:* **inggat**; *Thesaurus:* **danta', sahaya 1.1, sinag 1.1**)

**kasawahan** *n.* An illuminated area.

**sawan** *n.* A drinking glass or cup. (*Thesaurus:* **basu, panginuman, tasa**)

**sawan-sawan** *v. advrs.* -in- Afflicted by a seizure; suffering from epilepsy. (*Thesaurus:* **bawi-bawi, belaw, kangog**)

**sawasa'** *n.* An alloy of gold and copper. *Sawasa' itū sali' pa'anggil ni bulawan. Mbal ginaha' bo' apinda.* This alloy looks somewhat like gold. It doesn't rust but does change [color]. (*Thesaurus:* **bulawan 1, estenles, luyang, pilak 1, pittang, tumbaga 1**)

**sawasig** *n.* The Shortnosed garfish. *Hyporhampus quoyi.* (*gen:* **pillangan**)

**sawi'** *v. advrs.* ka-...-an To behave irrationally and speaking strangely. *Minsan ngga'i ka kasangonan buwat a'a angastol, na kasawi'an. Ah'lling m'ssa'-bidda', suma'an anumpa' suma'an anukna'-nukna'. Yukta, "Da'a sekotun i'-i."* Even if not possessed like a man in a rage, he may behave irrationally. He [may] talk randomly, at times speaking crudely, at times cursing. We say, "Don't approach that one." *Kasawi'an, lling ya pasangon ni iya, ngga'i ka dī llingna.* Under some powerful influence, a voice that has entered him, not his own voice. (*Thesaurus:* **jīn 1.2, sangon₂ 1.1**)

**sawiya** *v. advrs.* -in- 1) Controlled by appetite or lust. *Buwat sali' nirahal kita, sinawiya kita ma ai-ai, napsuhan kita, nihangsaw. Ai-ai ta'nda' he' matata sa'agon-agon ma kita.* It's as though we are gluttonous, controlled by the desire for something, lustful, greedy. Whatever our eyes see we [must] have immediately. (*Thesaurus:* **bahaya, kaway 1, hangsaw 1, hawa 1.1, napsu 1.1, sayap-sayap**) **1.1**) *v. tr.* To desire something strongly.

**Sawwal** *n.* The tenth month of the Islamic year. (*syn:* **Bulan Hailaya**; *Set:* **Bulan Muharram, Julka'idda, Julhadji', Jumadir Ahil, Jumadir Awal, Rabiul Ahil, Rabiul Awal, Radjab, Ramadan, Saban, Sappal**)

**sāy** *n.* Lemongrass. *Cymbopogon citratus. Am'lli gi' aku sai pangalamud daing.* I'll just buy some lemongrass to mix with the fish. *Bang kita am'lli lara, taga lamud sāy.* When we buy chilli peppers, there is lemongrass with it. (*gen:*

**pamapā**)

**saya-saya** *n.* A skirt with a decorative hem. *Saya-saya itū taga jambu.* A *saya-saya* skirt has a decorative fringe. (*Thesaurus:* **bistiru, palda**)

**sayang₁** *v. intr. pa-/-um-* To spread wings in flight, especially of some mythical creature. *Bang pasayang galura', akiyamat dunya.* When the winged horse spreads its wings in flight the world will end. *Sumayang galura', sali' belle' ba, sali' limbang tuhan.* The soaring *galura'*, very like an eagle, the consort of the gods.

**sayang₂** *v. tr. -an* To attract attention by waving. *Atuhun iya. Pagtuwa'na, sinayangan e'na kalang, paltanda'an hatina an'kkad iya pareyo'.* He's diving. On surfacing he waves a piece of coral, proof that he had reached bottom. (*Thesaurus:* **kambay 1, lambe₁ 1.1, mita, paglabad 1.1, sinyal 1.1**)

  **pasayang** *v. tr.* To raise something up high, as a flag being waved or hands raised in prayer.

**sayap** *n.* 1) A shade or awning built over a window. (*Thesaurus:* **ambung-ambung₂ 1, kadjang, sapaw 1) 1.1)** *v. tr. -an* To provide a structure with an awning.

**sayap-sayap** *v. advrs. -in-* Controlled by greedy desire. *Sinayap-sayap kita ma ai-ai ta'nda'ta.* We are covetous of everything we see. (*Thesaurus:* **bahaya, kaway 1, hangsaw 1, hawa 1.1, napsu 1.1, sawiya 1**)

**sayaw** *n.* The bird nest swiftlet. *Collocalia spp.*

**sayote** *n.* The chayote or choko, an edible fruit used as a vegetable. *Sechium edule.*

**sayu** *adj. a-/-an* 1) Aware of what is happening. **1.1)** *v. tr.* To realize or perceive something. *Yamboho' tasayuku.* I have only just become aware of it. *Magtahan kita bang kita mbal makasayu atuli.* We lay our legs across each other when we sleep completely unaware. (*Thesaurus:* **pangannal₁, sakup₁ 1, sipat₁ 1.1, tahu, tilas₁) 1.2)** *v. intr. pa-* To become intentionally aware. *Pasayu kām.* Take note!

  **panayu** *n.* Awareness of some activity going on.

**sayudja'** *adj. a-* 1) At ease; made comfortable. *Bang aniya' bisita pi'itu ni luma' asidda iya asayudja' bang maitu na. Pinahāpan palegehan, pinakakan isāb maitu.* If there is a visitor coming to the house he is really put at ease when he is here. His bed is prepared, he is fed here too. (*cf:* **sannang**; *Thesaurus:* **aluk, apu'-apu', dindang-dindang) 1.1)** *v. tr.* To make someone comfortable; to soothe troubled feelings.

**sayul** *n.* 1) Edible vegetables. (*Thesaurus:* **legotoman, l'mput deya, paltubu-tubuhan 1) 1.1)** *v. tr.* To use something as a vegetable. *Jangatan kapaya sinayul.* A grater for papaya to be used as a vegetable.

  **pagsayul** *v. intr. aN-* To use vegetables in cooking. *Bang magsayul subay aniya' lamukna, minsan dakuman dangkuri'.* When cooking

vegetables there should be something for flavor, even if it is just a little.

**sayul batung** *n. phrase* Green beans of various kinds. *Phaseolus* spp. including P. *vulgaris.*

**sayuman** *adj. zero* Complete in every way, of a person's looks, manners, wisdom, and clothing. *Sayuman na a'a inān, jukup na ma iya. Bay ta'nda'ta halam aniya', buwattina'an ahāp na pamaranan, kamemonna.* That person is excellent, he has everything. We have seen that there is no one so good in physique and everything about him. *Sali' magbowa-bowa baranna pi'ingga-pi'ingga, sali' a'addat. Makajari si Le niōnan a'a sayuman, pinagaddatan e' a'a kamemon. Iya na pagbeya'-beya'an.* He is someone who conducts himself appropriately wherever he goes, courteous. Le could be described as someone who is *sayuman*, respected by everyone. He is someone to follow. (*Thesaurus:* **balkan, daya, haldaya, mayaman**)

**sebel-sebel** var. of **jebel-jebel**

**sebog** *v. intr. pa-* To move back; to withdraw. *Bang kita mbal angaku pasebog na kita.* If we don't accept the [bride-wealth] requirements we withdraw. *Luma'na bay pinasebog kaut.* His house was moved further out to sea. (*Thesaurus:* **singga-singga, suhut**)

**sēk** *n.* The dorsal fin of some sharks. (*Thesaurus:* **kanting₁, s'kke, tare' 1**)

**sekan** *v. intr. aN-* To shake hands with someone. (*Thesaurus:* **jiyara**)

**seket** *n.* A projection from the trunk of a tree or a housepost. *Seket hāg, sanga hāg.* A projection from a post; a branch of a post. (*wh:* **kayu 1**)

**seklak** var. of **seplak**

**seko'** *n.* 1) A wavy profile, as an undulation on the edge of a knife blade. *Kalis siyam seko'na.* A kris with nine undulations. **1.1)** To undulate, forming a wavy edge or landform. *Pabūd bo' isāb pal'bbak, yukta paseko'.* It forms a hill and then forms a valley, we call it *seko'*.

  **pagseko'-seko'** *v. intr. aN-* To be wavy or undulating, of an edge. *Aniya' sirap tibulung ataha', aniya' tibulung hadja, bo' aniya' magseko'-seko' baranna.* There is a [kind of] round mussel that is long, there is another that is simply round, and there is one that curves in and out along its edge.

**sekot** *adj. a-* 1) Close; near. (*ant:* **lawak, tā 1) 1.1)** *v. intr. pa-/-um-* To go close to something. *Pasekot ka pi'itu ni atagku.* Come right here to where I am. **1.2)** *v. tr.* To approach someone or something. *Sinekot aku ni ero' apa aniya' pagkakan ma tanganku.* A dog approached me because I had food in my hand. (*Thesaurus:* **apiki 1.1, pagtongop, sigpi', t'ppi' 1) 1.3)** *v. advrs. ka-...-an* To be approachable, of a person, usually with a negative. *Bang sakalina a'a inān maghinang, agon mbal kasekotan.* When that fellow is absorbed in working he can hardly be approached.

**pagsekot** *v. tr.* To bring two things close together. *Minsan taguri' pinaleyang, magsabay mariyata' bang pinagsekot taguri' dakayu'.* Even a flying kite may collide when another kite is brought close.

**segpong** *adj. a-* Damaged by splitting or breaking out. *Wa'i asegpong tapi'. Bay binarenahan aheya, halam gi' makatūy pareyo'.* The canoe strake has split. It was drilled with a large bit that didn't go directly down. *Buwat suru', lahut, buli' pelang, asegpong, sali' at'bbe'.* Like a spoon, or a knife, or the stern of a canoe, damaged along an edge, sort of notched. (*Thesaurus:* **pungal, saksak 1, sasa₁, seplak 1, te'as**)

**sehe'** *n.* 1) A companion. (*Thesaurus:* **klasmēt**) 1.1) *v. tr. -an* To accompany someone. *Sehe'anta ka ni tabu'.* I'll accompany you to the market. (*Thesaurus:* **abay₁ 1.1, beya'₂ 1, bunyug 1.2, dongan, unung 1**)

**kasehe'an** *n.* Some; others. *Kasehe'an mbal angutta' minsan goyak, kasehe'an palege.* Some don't vomit even when it is rough; others lie down. *Lagak ka ma kinakan. Mbal ka anau'an kasehe'annu, subay hal ma ka'a.* You are greedy in regard to food. You save nothing for others [of your group], it has to be for you only. *Ah'bba' bu'unna kasehe'an, an'ngge kasehe'an.* Some of his hair has fallen over, some is standing up.

**kasehe'** *n.* A part of a larger collection.

**dansehe'an** *n.* A group of companions or friends. (*Thesaurus:* **kaheka-heka'an, kompolan, padjuhan, palti, umpigan**)

**sē'** *intrj.* Exclamation of satisfaction; 'That's it!'

**se'ak** (var. **be'ak**) *adj. a-* 1) Split but not severed from the main part. *Sali' ase'ak ba pelang inān. Tabayan bo' mbal na. Bang ka makatukkud buwat lawak tinda atonga' he' bohe'.* That canoe is kind of split. It had been used for transport but not any longer. If you pole it as far as the store it will be half-full of water. *Buwat saga pelang patongod ma panimbakan bo' aniya' angissat bohe' min deyom pelang hē', ase'ak he' timbak.* Like canoes located where dynamiting is going on and water squirts up inside the canoe, it is split by the explosion. (*Thesaurus:* **bila' 1.2, b'kka' 1.1, lelek, sepak**) 1.1) *v. tr.* To split something. *Buwat batang, se'akun.* Like a log, split it.

**se'ob** *n.* A tubular garment used as a cover when sleeping. (*Thesaurus:* **hōs 1, manta 1**)

**sēl** (var. **sēr**) *voc. n.* Respectful address form to a man in authority.

**selo** *n.* Various needlefishes and longtoms. *fam.* Belonidae. *Selo ataha' pagudlis.* A garfish makes a long furrow [across the sea].

**selo-p'llat** *n.* The Reef needlefish or longtom. *Strongylura incisa.*

**selo-s'llang** *n.* The Black-fin needlefish. *Tylosurus*

*acus melanotus.*

**selo-tangī'** *n.* A species of needlefish distinguished by its sharply tapered tail. *fam.* Belonidae.

**selo-t'bba** *n.* A species of needlefish. *fam.* Belonidae.

**selo'** *n.* A meteor that flies up or across rather than down. *Selo' itū ataha', pagublis.* A *selo'* is long and scribes a line. (*cf:* **umul₁**)

**selong-selong mata** var. of **elong-elong mata**

**selot** (var. **pelot**) *adj. a-* 1) Crowded; packed full of people. *Aselot jīp he' puhu', an'ngge kasehe'an.* The jeep is chock-full of people, some are standing. (*Thesaurus:* **p'nno' 1.1, sangkad, s'ppol 1**) 1.1) *v. intr. pa-* To push one's way through a crowd. 1.2) *v. tr.* To pack a conveyance with people. *Pelotun na pa'in pelang ilū minsan ang'mman.* Keep crowding people into that canoe even though it leaks.

**sema'** var. of **salema'**

**sembol** *adj. a-* 1) Crowded; constricted; cluttered. *Aheka sagbot, asigpit, asembol, halam aniya' labayan.* Lots of rubbish, constricted, littered, no passage through. 1.1) *v. intr. pa-* To get in the way of easy movement. *Bang aku bay kaut bo' tapole' na min pam'ssihan, aluhaya palabayan. Halam aniya' pasembol, halam aniya' pababag pelang.* When I have been at sea and have come home from the fishing place, the passageway is free of obstructions. There is no crowding, no canoes lying crossways.

**sembong** var. of **sombeng**

**seme'** *adj. zero* Ugly. *Minsan seme', amene'.* Though [I'm] ugly, I can choose.

**semento** *n.* 1) Concrete; cement. *Luma' tisa', sali' semento lullun.* A brick house, as though made entirely of cement. (*Thesaurus:* **haloblāk, tisa'**) 2) The clay generator to which the mantle of a pressure lantern is tied. (*cf:* **mantel**)

**semestel** *n.* A school semester; a school term. *Yangkon ina'an, pat'nna' dansasa'at panalusan sadja semestel itū.* That's all, staying a little longer for the completion of this semester.

**semet** *v. tr.* To cause someone to experience minor misfortune, the action of a ritual ancestor in response to some offense. *Minsan kita atulak tinaggahan, sinoho' pinuwas gi' bay nahas. Mbal kita. Bang ma dilaut apōng taruk, agese' leha. Na sinemet kita.* Though we are leaving we are delayed, advised to deal with a recent misfortune. We demur. Then out at sea the mast breaks and the sail splits. We are penalised by ancestor action. *Bang d'nda ab'ttong bo' maganak, mbal ahāp he'na maganak, aniya' makasemet iya. Aniya' amalut, makasabab.* When a woman becomes pregnant and is giving birth, but her delivery does not go well, something supernatural is making her sick. Something is holding her, causing the problem. *Minsan du* *halam aniya' hinangta bay ni ala'at, sinemet kita he' man pang'ntanan. Taluwa' kita saki bo' mbal isāb amatay.* Even though we have done nothing bad we are affected by some ritual ancestor. We get sick but don't die. (*Thesaurus:* **bihang₁, labba'₂ 1, pa'in₃ 1, sabab₂ 1.1, sila'-sila' 1.1**)

**sempok** *v. intr. pa-* 1) To slop over, of liquid. (*Thesaurus:* **lasay, lese₁, lipay₁, luput 1, uplut**) 1.1) *v. tr.* To agitate a container so its contents slop over the brim.

  **pagsempok** *v. intr. aN-* To splash or slosh from side to side, as water in a container. *Bang ap'nno' poga bo' ajogjog luma', asidda magsempok.* When a water jar is full and the house is shaken, the water splashes over a lot.

**senop** *v. intr. pa-* To push into a yielding substance. (*Thesaurus:* **l'nnob, loblob, paglowak, tanom₂**)

**sensong** *adj. a-* Unsettled; noisy. *Asagaw mareyom luma', aheka a'a. Asensong sali'.* It's noisy in the house, lots of people. Sort of unsettled. *Asensong na, maglutu' na, atulak na kono'. Ya kamemon magsuli-suli.* Noisy, getting supplies for a journey, about to leave, it is said. It's everybody talking. (*Thesaurus:* **balu', dongkag, halubilu, hengo-hengo, hiluhala' 1.1, hiyul, jabu 1, lengog 1.1, sasaw 1.1**)

**senten** *n.* 1) A sentence (grammar). 1.1) *v. tr.* To form a sentence illustrating a word. *Sinenten kono' bo' tahatina.* Please make a sentence of it so it can be understood.

**senga** var. of **sanga**

**sengab** var. of **songab**

**sengkang** (var. **bengkang**) *v. intr. pa-* To sit or stand with legs apart.

  **pagsengkang** *v. intr. aN-* To sit or stand with legs apart. *Ya magsengkang-sengkang inān.* That one sitting there with his legs apart. (*Thesaurus:* **hakin, milang, pagsiningkulang**)

**sengel** *n.* Misaligned teeth, such that one overlaps the other. *Bay aku maka'nda' a'a taga empon duwa magbangkat, ya hē' sengelna.* I saw a person with two [of his] teeth one laying over the other, that is his *sengel*. (*Thesaurus:* **baga'ang, bangkil₂, empon 1, taling**)

**sengod** *v. tr. -an* To copy the way something is made. *Kasengoran to'ongan badju'nu.* Your blouse was copied exactly.

  **sengoran** *n.* A pattern; a likeness. (*Thesaurus:* **bantukan, ladjawan, simpayan, suntu'an**)

**sepak** (var. **kepak₁**) *v. tr.* To split apart, as firewood. (*Thesaurus:* **bila' 1.2, b'kka' 1.1, lelek, se'ak 1**)

**sepel** *adj. a-* Translucent, of something such as paper or cloth. (*Thesaurus:* **tilag, tina'ung, t'llak**)

**sepet-sepet** *v. intr. aN-* To splatter, of a liquid. *Buwat banog al'kkas goyak anepet-nepet ni batangan. Anepet-nepet isāb tahik bang pasabol tangan.* When sailing is swift, the waves splash up onto the outrigger booms. Seawater splashes

up too when a hand drags in the water. *Buwat kita angaludja', na anepet-nepet sudju ni ka'a.* Like when we spit, then it sprays in your direction. *Anepet-nepet bowa'na, ato'a iya aheya ludja' ameya' ma llingna.* His mouth sprays, he is old, a lot of spittle comes out with his speech.

**seplak** (var. **seklak**) *n.* 1) A sliver of wood; a potential split. *Bay atugsuk si Ne i' e' seplak kayu angkan am'ngkong.* Ne there was jabbed with a sliver of wood, that's why it is swelling. *Seklak itū sali' aniya' galna'na.* Seklak means it has a defect. (*Thesaurus:* **pungal, saksak 1, sasa₁, segpong, te'as**) 1.1) *adj. a-* Likely to split due to a defect in wood.

**sēr** var. of **sēl**

**seraw** *v. tr. -an* To block a move in the game of dominoes. (*Thesaurus:* **kulgaw**)

**sereng** *n.* Roughness, of the surface of something solid.

  **pagsereng** *v. intr. aN-* To present a rough or scaly surface. *Bang kita amusay nda'ta bihing pelang magsereng, aleges he' busay.* When we are paddling we see that the side of the canoe is jagged, chafed by the paddle. *Bussu' magsereng.* Hard rocks having sharp edges. *Kulap, ya magsereng inān. Kulap,* the skin disorder that forms a scaly surface.

**serol** var. of **bāt-serol**

**serop** *v. tr.* To record the performance of an entertainer. (*cf:* **tangkap**)

**sesek** *adj. a-* Cut partway through. *Asesek p'ttung itū, subay binalos man dambila'.* This bamboo is cut partway through, it needs an answering cut from the other side. *Kamaya'in bang ka angalansang apa wa'i na asesek lantay ilū.* Go carefully when you're nailing because the bamboo lath there is already cut partway through.

**seso'** *n.* Various sea snails including moon snails. *Natica spp. Aubus pa'in kami bay mamulan seso' inān, pareyo' na kami pabalik.* After we had finished harvesting *seso'* snails by moonlight, we went down [from the house] again.

**seso'-buwaya** *n.* A sea snail species.

**seso'-kiput** *n.* A moon snail species.

**seso'-ettom** *n.* The black moon snail.

**seso'-palang** *n.* A moon snail species.

**seso'-pote'** *n.* The white moon snail.

**si** (var. **i₂**) *ptl.* Personal name marker, used before the name of a person and before a kinship term referring to a specific individual. *Ina'an magb'lla si Ina'.* Mother is there doing the cooking. *Mma', bay aku sinuntuk e' si Je inān.* Daddy, Je punched me. *Atunu' kono' luma' si Anu.* What's-his-name's house has reportedly burned down. (*Thesaurus:* **disi**)

**sīb** *v. intr. pa-* 1) To look briefly at something from a position of concealment. *Bang ka atuli, pasīb aku min bowa' lawang. Yukku, "Halam ka atuli? Arāk aniya' tilawku ni ka'a."* When you are asleep I peep in through the doorway. I say, "Are you not asleep? There was something I would have asked you." *Pagt'kkana pehē', pakuru' iya pasīb sagō' halam aniya' ta'nda'na ma deyom.* On reaching that place, he bent down to peep in but saw nothing inside. (*Thesaurus:* **tandaw** 1, **tĭk** 1, **tilag-tilag**₂) 1.1) *v. tr.* To look briefly at someone who does not know he is being observed.

**pagsīb** *v. intr.* aN- To discuss things in private, as preliminary negotiations for a marriage. (*Thesaurus:* **sipuk-sipuk**, **ungsik**)

**sibahat** *v. tr.* To recite something that has been memorized. *Halam na pa'in tasabbut, tasibahat, saddī liyu min magsukul.* There is nothing at all to say or recite, other than to say thank you. *Jari sinibahat e'na saga lapal kalangan itū.* So he recited the words of this song.

**siba'** *n.* 1) A courtship gift. *Buwat aku anunang, bo' halam gi' ganta' bay magpah'nda. Na, buwananku siba', sīn ka, buwas, daing.* Like when I am courting but have not yet been formally betrothed, then I give courting gifts, whether money, rice or fish. *Niangut siba'.* Courting gifts are treated as important. 1.1) *v. tr.* -an To present small gifts to a friend of the same sex, or to a girl and her parents during courtship. *Subay aniya' paniba' bang aku ni Sibaud.* When I go to Sibaud village I should take a friendship gift. (*Thesaurus:* **bintak**, **pagdamak**)

**pagsiba'** *v. intr.* aN- 1) To be at the gift-exchange stage of a courtship. *Buwat kita magpanon magpaniba'.* Like when are close friends and exchange gifts. 1.1) *v. tr.* To make a gift to a close friend or sweetheart.

**paniba'** *n.* A courtship gift.

**sibay** *n.* The outermost purlin of a sloping roof, i.e. the one at the lowest edge.

**sibayan** *n.* The raised area on the upstream side of a house, an area reserved for ritual ancestor matters. *Da'a ka pi'ilu ni sibayan, apa ilu pat'nna' mbo'.* Don't go there to the upstream part of the house, for an ancestor is located there. *Sibayan, ya pagpat'nna'an mbo', ba'ul, maleta, basta ma kōkan.* The *sibayan*, the location of the chest or suitcase into which a ritual ancestor comes, the upstream side of the house. (*Thesaurus:* **kōkan** 1, **diyata'an**₁, **tape'an**)

**sibilyan** *n.* An ordinary civilian in contrast to a soldier or an official.

**siboyas** *n.* An onion. *Allium cepa.* (*gen:* **pamapā**)

**sibukaw** *n.* 1) Sappan, a leguminous tree and its durable wood. *Bianca sappan; Caesalpinia sappan* . 1.1) A dowel obtained from the sibukaw tree for fastening canoe planks. *Am'lli aku pasok pamasokku pelang. B'lliku sibukaw ma a'a deya.* I will buy dowels to join my canoe [strakes]. I will buy sappan-wood from someone inland. (*cf:* **pasok** 1)

**sibu'** *n.* 1) A person of the same age; one's peer. *Bang aniya' amatay saga kaukakiku, bo' saga sibu'ku, sinarakkahan tudju ni aku.* When cousins of mine die, my age-mates, alms-gifts are directed to me. (*Thesaurus:* **dora'** 2, **sali'** 1, **samapasang**, **suga-suga**₂, **tupan** 1) 1.1) *v. intr.* pa- To be the same as another person in age or some other quality.

**sibu'-sibu'** *adv.* Alike; in the same manner. *Pagkahi, basta sibu'-sibu' manusiya'.* Fellow-creatures, so long as they are all humans alike.

**sibuwa** *v. intr.* aN- To reach physical maturity. (*Thesaurus:* **hendog-hendog**, **lasag**, **pata'**₁, **sangpot** 1, **to'a** 1.1)

**sika-..-an** *aff.* A circumfix indicating that the action or condition described occurs in great numbers. *Amaulak kapanyapan ma dilaut, sikagūngan.* Fishing gear forming a mass out at sea, floating all over the place. *Sikasulangatan tape' a'a bay mareyom lansa.* The legs of the people in the bilge of the launch were sticking out in all directions. *Aheka puhu' ang'ssul, sika'ssul-ssulan.* Many people moving, moving in great numbers. *Sikaharung-harungan saga a'a.* People are gathering in crowds. *Sikatomo'an na kaparangan.* The grasses are growing in great abundance.

**sikad** *v. intr.* pa-/aN- 1) To do something forcefully or vigorously. *Anikad ka bang ka amusay ko da'a ta'abut ulan.* Be vigorous when you paddle so as not to be caught in the rain. *Mbal makasikad amono', mbal makasikad alahi.* Can't fight energetically, can't run away energetically. (*Thesaurus:* **kuwat**, **kuyas** 1, **matay**₂, **pakosog**, **paspas**₁, **puspus**₁) 2) To kick vigorously, as a child in the womb.

**sikad-sikad** *n.* A species of conch, edible. *Strombus gibberosa.* (*syn:* **dollen**)

**sikagūngan** (derivative of **gūng**) *adj.* Floating in great numbers or mass. *Amaulak kapanyapan ma dilaut, sikagūngan.* Fishing gear forming a mass out at sea, floating all over the place.

**sikaharung-harungan** (derivative of **harung-harung**) *adj.* Assembled in a great crowd. *Sikaharung-harungan saga a'a.* People are gathered in a crowd.

**sika'ssul-ssulan** (derivative of **ssul**) *adj.* Moving about in great numbers. *Aheka puhu' ang'ssul, sika'ssul-ssulan.* Many people moving, moving in great numbers.

**sikaluwasan** (derivative of **luwas**₁) *adj.* Emerging in great numbers. *Sikaluwasan saga a'a min lowang bay tapukan.* The people emerged in great numbers from the holes where they had been hiding.

**sikān** *n.* 1) The space between one's thighs. *Bang onde'-onde' paluwas min sikān ina'na, bo' magtūy anangis, yuk kami aniya' gi' takalipat e'na.* When a child emerges from between its mother's thighs [at birth] and immediately cries, we say that it has forgotten something. **1.1)** *v. tr.* To hold apart the thighs of a woman to assist the delivery of a baby. *Sinikān d'nda min karuwambila'na bang song maganak.* A woman about to give birth has her thighs held apart from either side.

**sikasampuhan** (derivative of **sah'mpu**) *adj.* To act in great numbers. *Sikasampuhan saga a'a amelle' daing.* People are diving in great numbers for dynamited fish.

**sikasulangatan** (derivative of **sulangat**) *adj.* Poking out in all directions. *Sikasulangatan tape' a'a bay mareyom lansa.* The legs of the people in the bilge of the launch were sticking out in all directions.

**sikasuleretan** (derivative of **suleret**) *adj.* To move about in large numbers. *Bang daing tinimbak, sikasuleretan ma kulit tahik.* When fish are dynamited they thresh about in large numbers on the surface of the sea.

**sikat** *v. tr.* To scrub the fingernails and toenails of a body being prepared for burial. (*Thesaurus:* **kusu-kusu, helog**)

**sikla** *v. tr.* To treat someone unkindly who is in one's care or employ. *Da'a siklahun onde'-onde' ilū bo' mbal ala'an min kita.* Don't be unkind with the child, so that he won't leave us. *Mbal kita sinikla he' pat'nna'anta, mbal pinagb'nsihan saga.* We will not be treated badly by those we stay with, not disliked or anything. (*Thesaurus:* **jilaka', la'at 1.2, la'ug 1.1, pinjala' 1.1, pissoko', puhinga', usiba'**)

**sikla'** var. of **siklut**

**siklat** var. of **siplat**

**siklut** (var. **sikla'**) *v. intr. pa-* To pass through a narrow space. *Sali' kita pasipit-sipit, pasikla' ma llotan kaluma'an.* We sort of squeeze through a narrow space between houses. (*Thesaurus:* **sipit-sipit₁, siplit, s'llot 1.1, soksok**)

**sikmu'** *v. tr.* To jolt or tug something. *Ampunun aku, bay ka tasikmu'ku.* Excuse me, I bumped you. *Anikmu' isāb kita, anintak daing.* We are also tugging, when we strike a fish. (*Thesaurus:* **bakkug, bangkug 1, bōg, siggul, singku 1**)

**siksa'** var. of **tiksa'**

**siksik** *v. tr. -an* To find lice by separating strands of hair. *Dai' ka, siksikanta ka.* Come here, I'll find lice for you. (*Thesaurus:* **kuhut 1.1, kutu 1.1, t'bbok₂**)

**siku** *n.* The elbow joint. (*wh:* **tangan 1**; *Thesaurus:* **lokonan, lo'atan, peya'-peya' kōk-tu'ut, tu'ut**)

**pagsiku** *v. intr. aN-* To jostle each other with the elbows. *Mbal sigām magsiku.* They don't clash with their elbows.

**maniku** *n.* A unit of measurement, the length from the tip of one hand to the opposite elbow. (*Thesaurus:* **batu₃, kilometēl, d'ppa 1, honga'₂, inses**)

**sikuhan** *n.* A species of fish, similar in form to a

flute-mouth. (*cf:* **ngngok**)

**sidda 1)** *adv.* Very; intensely; extremely; overmuch. *Sidda ahunit kakana' ilū.* That fabric is extremely expensive. *Buwat luma' itū, asidda nililing he' a'a kamemon sabab ahāp min dahū.* Like this house, examined closely by everybody because it is better than before. *Asidda patihinangun d'nda ina'an, sali' ya na kahali'anna amangan maka atuli. Puwas ē' angahinang.* That woman works extremely persistently, as though her only rest is when she eats and sleeps. After that she works. (*Thesaurus:* **karalaman, kumarukan, dumasiyaw, landu'₂ 1, mamarahi, to'od**) **1.1)** *adj. a-* Extremely small, of an amount. *Asidda, dangkuri'.* Very little, just a bit. *Maka aniya' panggi' ba, asidda panggi', datambō'.* And there was some cassava, a tiny amount of cassava, as big as a thumb. (*Thesaurus:* **dangk'tti', dangkuri'**) **2)** *adj. a-* Extremely ill. *Asidda na si Ba.* Ba is gravely ill. (*Thesaurus:* **bangat, kansang 1.1, pangsan**)

**siddik** *v. intr. aN-* To assent to the truth or point of what someone says. *Aniddik aku ma ka'a bang aku haka'annu.* I accept as true when you tell me something. (*Thesaurus:* **beya'-beya'₁ 1, b'nnal 1.2, kahagad, halap₁, parassaya**)

**sigā₁** *pron.* They two, the two of them (third person dual) [Set I]. *Ya po'on sigā magpole'an magdai'-dai'.* The reason why the two of them went home in a hurry. (*cf:* =**sigā, sigā₂**; *Set:* **akū, kā, kām, kamī, kitā 1, kitabi₁, kitām, iyā, sigām₁**)

**sigā₂** *pron.* They two, the two of them (third person dual) [Set III]. (*cf:* =**sigā, sigā₁**; *Set:* **aku₂, ka'a, ka'am, kami, kita, kitabi₂, kitam, iya, sigām₂**)

=**sigā** *pron.* They two, the two of them; their (third person dual) [Set II]. *Aniya' kasusahan sigā.* The two of them have some problem. (*cf:* **sigā₁, sigā₂**; *Set:* =**bi,** =**ku,** =**na,** =**nu,** =**sigām,** =**ta 1,** =**tabi,** =**tam**)

**siga** *n.* **1)** A cigaret. *B'llihin aku duwambatang siga.* Buy me two cigarets. *Pehē' ka am'lli siga binatang, da'a ka am'lli pasta.* Go and buy factory-made cigaret, not loose tobacco. (*Thesaurus:* **banusu, bungkal₃ 1, pasta, pikaroda, sigupan, tabaku 1**) **1.1)** *v. intr. a-* To be smoking a cigaret. *Buwat onde'-onde' asiga, mbal biyasa, manjari sinungbu-sungbu.* Like a child smoking a cigaret, not used to it, then the nose is irritated.

**pagsiga** *n.* **1)** Items needed for preparing a cigaret. *Bang aniya' pagkawin pinat'nna'an lalabotan saga a'a magluruk, saga pagkakan, saga pagmama', pagsiga.* When there is a wedding, refreshments are set out for the guests, food, betel chew ingredients, provisions for smoking. **1.1)** *v. intr. aN-* To smoke. *Mbal aku biyasa magsiga.* I am not in the habit of smoking.

**pagsiniga** *v. intr. aN-* To be in the habit of smoking.

**paniga** *n.* The time taken to smoke a cigaret, an approximate unit of time. (*cf:* **pam'lla**)

**sigad** var. of **sagad**

**siga'** *intrj.* 1) A gesture or words to frighten dogs off. **1.1)** *v. tr.* To drive something away, as animals or unwelcome people. *Bay aku siniga' e'na.* He chased me away. (*Thesaurus:* **budjaw, dūy, singga'-singga', sū₁ 1.1, t'ggal**)

**sigām₁** *pron.* They, them (third person plural) [Set I]. (*cf:* = **sigām, sigām₂**; *Set:* **akū, kā, kām, kamī, kitā 1, kitabi₁, kitām, iyā, sigā₁**)

**sigām₂** *pron.* They, them (third person plural) [Set III]. *Sigām magpa'us t'bbu inān.* Those there chewing sugarcane. (*cf:* = **sigām, sigām₁**; *Set:* **aku₂, ka'a, ka'am, kami, kita, kitabi₂, kitam, iya, sigā₂**)

= **sigām** *pron.* They, them; their, by them (third person plural) [Set II]. *Bay kam nirugpak e' sigām ma waktu kam bale'-bale'an maka nihapus ma l'ngngananbi.* You were attacked by them at a time when you were exhausted and out of breath on your journey. (*cf:* **sigām₁, sigām₂**; *Set:* = **bi,** = **ku,** = **na,** = **nu,** = **sigā,** = **ta 1,** = **tabi,** = **tam**)

**sigay** *v. intr. pa-* 1) To get out of the way of some activity. *Pasigay ka!* Get out of the way! (*Thesaurus:* **salema' 1, simay₂, s'nnok, sulekma'**) **1.1)** *v. tr. -an* To move something to one side; to take away something. *Sigayin onde' ilū apa itiya' maghinang. Pala'anun saga.* Get those children out of the way because we're busy here. Remove them or something.

**siggul** *v. tr.* To knock or jolt something. *Da'a aku siggulun. Asā' he'ku anulat.* Don't jolt me. I'll make a mistake in my writing. *Bay tasiggul e' bay pal'ngngan i'.* Jolted by someone walking there. (*Thesaurus:* **bakkug, bangkug 1, bōg, jogjog 1.1, sikmu', singku 1**)

**sigi-sigi** *adv.* 1) Continuously; repeatedly. *Pagtimbak, pagtambul itū, sigi-sigi na pa'in.* The shooting and the drumming went on and on. *Magsait na pa'in, sigi-sigi magsait. Anā, mbal na takole' sinaitan.* They bailed, they kept on bailing. Alas, it could not be bailed. *Anipun kami sigi-sigi supaya aniya' panguntas lahat maka paggastu ma labayan.* We keep gathering [money] so we have the means of travelling abroad and supplies on the way. *Ulan halam magk'llat. Min subu-subu sampay ni kakohapan halam hali'an. Sigi-sigi na pa'in magulan.* The rain never broke. There was no let-up from dawn to afternoon. It just kept on raining. (*Thesaurus:* **kara-kara₁, daran-daran 1.1, pagabut-abut, pagkuwat, toldas**) **1.1)** *v. tr.* To do something indefinitely or repeatedly.

**sigid** *v. tr.* To tie thatch shingles on to the slats that run parallel to the rafters. (*Thesaurus:* **bīt₂, k'kkod, laggos**)

**pagsigid** *v. intr. aN-* 1) To tie thatch panels to their supporting rods. **1.1)** *v. tr. -an* To tie thatch panels, working in pairs. *Magumbuk isāb bang magsigid, t'llungan kami man dambila', t'llungan isāb man dambila'.* We work in pairs when we are tying thatch, three of us on the underside, three of them on the top side. *B'llihin aku duwanggalung buway pagsigid ilū.* Buy me two bundles of that thatch-tying rattan.

**sigla'** *adv.* 1) Suddenly; without warning. *Sigla' mulka' pat'kka' ni lahat kami. (Tausal isāb sigla' bang pasal musiba.)* Disaster coming suddenly on our region. (The word *sigla'* can also be used with regard to an epidemic.) (*Thesaurus:* **agsāy, dai'-dai'an, magtūy, sakadjap, saru'un-du'un**) **1.1)** *adj. a-* Vigorous; immediate; sudden. *Baha'u bay pal'ngngan, asigla' kamatayna a'a i'.* He had just been walking about, that man's death was sudden. **1.2)** *v. tr.* To do something without delay.

**siglat** *adj. a-* 1) Well-fueled, of a fire. *Pasiglatun api bang ka am'lla dok supaya akeyat.* Put plenty of wood on the fire when you cook, so it burns. **1.1)** *v. tr.* To increase the fuel on a fire; to stoke a fire. *Siglatun ma buwas ilu bo' mbal ap'dda.* Pile a bit more fuel under that rice so the fire doesn't go out. (*cf:* **api 1.1**)

**signat** *see:* **pagsignat-signat**

**sigpi'** *v. intr. pa-* To move close to an objective, making physical contact. *Bay pasigpi' ni aku si Ji dibuhi', sali' magtahan tape'-l'ngngon inān.* Ji [slept] close to me last night, his legs and arms sort of across me. (*Thesaurus:* **apiki 1.1, pagtongop, sekot 1.2, t'ppi' 1**)

**pasigpi'-sigpi'** *adv.* Closely spaced.

**sigpit** 1) *n.* A restriction or difficulty; an acute shortage of supplies. *Makananam kami sigpit.* We were experiencing a shortage. **1.1)** *adj. a-* Acutely difficult; severely restricted as to options. *Asigpit isāb ka'lluman ma lahat kami. Mbal kami makakaut.* Life is very difficult in our region. We can't go out to sea. *Damikiyanna bang saki asigpit, subay binowa ni a'a ata'u anambal.* Likewise when an illness is very serious, it should be taken to someone who knows how to treat it. **1.2)** *v. advrs. ka-...-an* To be affected by shortage or cruelty. **2)** *adj. a-* Crowded into a limited space. *Bang mpat puhu' atuli maitu, asigpit du.* If four people sleep here it will be very crowded. (*Thesaurus:* **digpit 1, s'mpok 1, sukad**) **2.1)** *v. tr.* To squeeze something into a narrow gap.

**kasigpitan** *n.* A condition of great difficulty due to shortage or oppression. *O Tuhan, bang pa'in kami papuwasnu min deyom kasigpitan itū.* O God, may you deliver us from this hardship. *Tahaun saga miskin min kasigpitan sigām.* The poor are rescued from their hardship. (*Thesaurus:* **kabinasahan, kati'ilan**)

**pagsigpit** *v. intr. aN-* 1) To be jammed together in a tight space. **2)** To be locked into a dispute which cannot be resolved. *Magsandat bissala,* *sali' magpasu', sali' mbal magkole' inān, sali' magsigpit.* The discussion becomes rigid, heated, neither winning, as though deadlocked.

**sigput** *v. intr. pa-* To create space by moving back a small distance. *Halam aniya' pasigputanku sabab aniya' puhu' man duwambila'ku.* I have no room to move because there are people on both sides of me. (*Thesaurus:* **kisal-kisal, hense, higin, ingsud**)

**sigun** var. of **manuk-sigun**

**sigung** *v. tr.* To hit a spinning top with another one (a game). (*Thesaurus:* **balibag₁, balleng 1.1, timbag**)

**sigup** *v. intr. aN-* To be smoking tobacco.

**sigupan** *n.* A cigaret hand-rolled from loose tobacco. (*Thesaurus:* **banusu, bungkal₃ 1, pasta, pikaroda, siga 1, tabaku' 1**)

**siguru** *adv.* 1) Almost certain. *Bang aniya' tabākta ambal buwat heya pa'ata, siguru kita duwa lawang tinda.* If we find some ambergris the size of our thigh, we'll almost certain of [being worth] a two-door shop. *Mbal aku siguru bang ai pagbidda'anna niukilan maka ginaring-garing, sagō' buwattē'.* I am not quite sure what the difference is between carving and engraving, but it is that sort of thing. (*Thesaurus:* **bahā', kalu-kalu 1, ya aniya'**) 1.1) *v. tr.* To make sure of something; to state something with conviction. *Siguruhun, maitu du aku salung kohap.* Make sure of it, I'll be here tomorrow evening. *Sali' siniguru sadja. Yukna, "Kaut aku maka'ā daing."* Like when something is stated definitely. He says, "I am going to sea and will catch fish."

**siguwa** *v. intr. pa-* To fit into; to be the right size.

**sihak** *v. intr. pa-* To form a space in something tightly packed; to separate components. *Magtimuk-timuk, palabay aku. Yukku, "Pasihak-sihak gi' kam abō' aku palabay."* People were crowding together and I was passing. I said, "Move back a little so I can get through." *Buwat bubu bay alapat, kabalutannnu ya tilasna, pasihak agtūy.* Like a tightly woven fish-trap that you happen to grab by its bamboo strips, immediately it comes apart. (*Thesaurus:* **bahagi' 1, gihay, hampit, paglamit-lamit 1.1**)

**pasihak** *v. tr.* To clear a space by moving things out of the way.

**sihag₁** *n.* 1) A sennit-binding technique. 1.1) *v. tr.* To bind things together using the sihag sennit technique. (*Thesaurus:* **baggot, buka'₁ 1.1, pinate 1, sappit₁ 1**)

**sihag₂** *adj. a-* 1) Scattered; fragmented. *Buwat aniya' mundu atawa hunus, asihag. Sama na pa'in asihag.* For example, there are bandits, or a storm, people scatter. It's usually Sama being scattered. *Atawa daing sin'bbat he' kasehe'an, pasihag isāb.* Or fish when they are being gulped down by other [fish], they scatter too. (*Thesaurus:* **kanat 1, pāg, pulak-palik 1, teges-teges**) 1.1) *v. tr.* To send things scattering. *Buwat*

*tamban sinihag he' daing aheya, agtūy amulakay tamban.* Like anchovies scattered by a large fish, the anchovies immediately disperse.

**pagsihag** *v. intr. aN-* To lose cohesion, of things normally in a group; to disperse widely. *Bang bay atibu'uk, na magtūy magsihag.* When [fish] are in a cohesive group, and then scatter. *Magsihag itū ap'kkal na.* This word *magsihag* means no longer cohesive.

**sihag₃** *n.* The Halfbeak, a species of fish. *fam.* Hemirhamphidae. (*gen:* **pillangan**)

**siha'** *v. intr. pa-* To diverge from a path or course. *Pasiha' kita man labayan, sali' pasā' man labayan.* We diverge from the path, like making a mistake away from the path. (*Thesaurus:* **pagpaopēt, sapehak**)

**siha'-siha'** *v. intr. pa-* To diminish, of a pain or a sickness. *Luwal bang kita bay asaki, bo' tinawalan, na pasiha'-siha' bay sakita.* Only when we have been sick, and have a healing charm recited, then our sickness decreases. (*Thesaurus:* **gām-gām, hāp-hāp, hikay, hoblas 1, lōng-lōng, si'at**)

**pasiha'** *adv.* Going in the wrong direction.

**sihil** *n.* 1) Magical immunity to harm in battle. *Sihilan ko' ka'a ilū, taga ilmu'.* You have magical immunity, possessing esoteric knowledge. (*Thesaurus:* **basi'₂ 1.1, kobol 1.1, pagkal'lla, pangliyas**) 1.1) *v. tr. -an* To exercise magical power over someone. *A'a inān bay sinihilan.* That man has been overcome by magical means. (*Thesaurus:* **duti, hikmat, hinang-hinang₁, h'lling₃, palkata'an, pantak 1.1**)

**sī'** *ptl.* Tense marker indicating a specific time just past. *Dai'-llaw sī'.* This dawn just passed. *Baha'u du sī' aku bay atilaw.* I have just this moment asked the question. *Pagukay sī', aniya' dakayu' d'nda maka dakayu' l'lla mareyom.* Having opened [the aforementioned door], there was one woman and one man inside.

**si'at** *n.* A positive change in the condition of a sick person. *Bang kita binuwanan si'at, anangon kita luhul ma tampat si Mbo' Du.* If we are granted an improvement in health, we will erect a canopy over the shrine of Grandfather Du. (*Thesaurus:* **gām-gām, hāp-hāp, hikay, hoblas 1, lōng-lōng, siha'-siha'**)

**si'ay** *n.* 1) Various monocle breams. *Scolopsis spp.* 1.1) The Pearly monocle bream. *Scolopsis margaritifera.* 1.2) The White-cheek monocle bream. *Scolopsis vosmeri.*

**si'it** *n.* The sibling or cousin of one's parent, i.e. one's uncle or aunt. (*cf:* **babu' 1, bapa' 1**)

**silak** *n.* 1) The heat and light of the sun when high in the sky. *Tauwa' silak llaw.* Affected by the sun's heat. 1.1) *v. intr. pa-* To emit heat and light, as when the sun breaks out from the clouds. *Alā, ilu na llaw akeyat, pasilak na.* Hey, there's the sun showing bright, giving out heat.

**sila'** *adj. a-* **1)** Kept distinct; dealt with individually. *Subay asila' d'nda maka l'lla.* Men and women should be kept separate. **1.1)** *v. tr.* To distinguish between different things. *Subay sinila', sinilang, deya maka dilaut.* Land and sea should be kept distinct, differentiated from each other. *Sila'unbi d'nda maka l'lla, pinagkaniya-kaniya.* Deal with women and men separately, treat them individually. (*Thesaurus:* **gintil** 1.1, **lilay, paggihay** 1, **silang₁** 1.1, **sisig**)

**sila'-sila'** *adj. a-* **1)** Harmed as a result of behavior that offends a supernatural being. *Asila', saga abihang.* Becoming unwell, from some supernatural cause. **1.1)** *v. tr.* To cause someone serious harm, of a supernatural being. *Da'a ka palabay m'nnilu. Asidda anila'-sila' saitan m'nnilu.* Don't go through there. The saitan spirits from there cause really serious harm. *Bang kita ma dilaut bo' magolang atawa maglata, sinila'-sila', pinaka'at kita, suma'an makanibaran suma'an makanipahinggaman.* When we are at sea and shout or joke, we get harmed [by a *saitan* spirit], damaged, sometimes to our persons, sometimes to our vessel. *Sinila'-sila' kita bang kita asidda atakabbul, sali' kita angupul.* We are seriously harmed when we make arrogant boasts, when we claim to know the future. (*Thesaurus:* **bihang₁, labba'₂** 1, **pa'in₃** 1, **sabab₂** 1.1, **semet**)

**silal** *n.* The buri palm, the leaf of which provides a durable weaving material. *Corypha elata or C. utan. Silal ya asidda pinaghinang saldang taguri'.* The buri palm leaf is much used for making the humming piece of a kite. (*syn:* **saldang** 1)

**silang₁** *adj. a-* **1)** Distinguishable; distinct from. *Bang buwat si Bu anganak si Malana inān, bo' ab'ttong pabīng ati niōnan isāb si Manala, mbal asilang.* Like Bu giving birth to Malana, then getting pregnant again and [the baby] is named Manala, [the two names] not clearly distinguished. **1.1)** *v. tr.* To distinguish among individuals, items or people. *Mbal na tasilang a'a anambal pehē'.* The people going there for medical treatment are beyond distinguishing. *Silangun ai-ai, saupama tasuli-sulinu.* Distinguish anything, the things you talk about for instance. (*Thesaurus:* **gintil** 1.1, **lilay, paggihay** 1, **sila'** 1.1, **sisig**)

**silang₂** *clf.* Count word for sections of thatch. *Yukna, "Bang aku maghinang luma' dansilang du atopna. Ariki'-diki'," yukna, "atopna."* He said, "When I build a house it will have a roof one panel wide. It will have a small roof." (*cf:* **atop** 2, **pa'ud** 1)

**silap** *see:* **pagsilap**

**silapug** *see:* **pagsilapug**

**silat** *n.* A martial arts form involving formalized attack and defensive movements of arms and legs, indigenous to insular and peninsular Southeast Asia.

**pagsilat** *v. intr. aN-* To engage in the martial art of silat. (*cf:* **pagkuntaw**)

**silaw** *adj. a-* **1)** Dazzled, as due to bright light. *Bang aku paharap ni mata llaw sali' aku asilaw, sali' mbal pak'llat mataku.* When I face towards the sun it is like I am dazzled, as though my eyes don't open. (*Thesaurus:* **palu'** 1.1) **1.1)** *v. advrs. ka-...-an* To be dazzled by glare. *Ai na ka onde'-onde', ai na ka matto'a, bay kasilawan e' a'a duwangan-i bo' mbal makabāk lawang.* Whether children or adults, they were dazzled by the two beings so that they could not find the door.

**silawak** *n.* A high-pitched cry.

**pagsilawak** *v. intr. aN-* To cry piercingly; to scream. (*cf:* **tilahak**)

**silikan** *n.* A wheel. *Silikan, ya pagdagangan jīp.* Wheels, what a jeep runs on. (*cf:* **goma₂, tape'₁**)

**sili'** *n.* A kettle. *"Ndiya pa'in aku dakayu' ero'-ero'ku, maka dakayu' sili'-sili'ku ilū, maka dambila'," yuk Sultan, "sairap-sairap ilū. Bowaku," yukna, "pama'atopku."* "Please give me my one little dog, and my one little kettle, and one half," said the Sultan, "of that little piece of woven wall. I will take it," he said, "to make a roof with." (*Thesaurus:* **kapitera, kapsiyu, patikuwan**)

**silin** *var. of* **sin**

**siling** *n.* The outer edge of a sloping roof.

**silingan** (*var.* **sīngan**) *n.* Eaves; the outer edge of a sloping roof. *Pat'nna'un undam man deyo' sīngan.* Place the basin under the eaves.

**silung₁** *v. intr. pa-* To come into a sheltered area. (*Thesaurus:* **limbu** 1.1, **lindung** 1, **pulipus** 1.1, **sindung₁**)

**silung₂** *v. intr. aN-* To fish by articifial light such as a pressure lantern. (*syn:* **sindung₂**)

**simay₁** *v. intr. pa-* **1)** To suffer from lack of breath due to sickness, shock, or extreme fatigue. *Bang a'a pasimay napasna, buwat bay ahūg min diyata' niyug, subay tinambun maka langkay.* When a person cannot get his breath, as when he has fallen from a coconut palm, he should be covered with a dry coconut frond. *Pasimay napasta, sali' apōn hinansongta bo' magnapas du.* Our breathing is labored, as though our breath is impeded even though still breathing. *Pinasimay napasta abō' kita taopera.* Our breathing is restricted so that we can undergo surgery. (*cf:* **lumu**; *Thesaurus:* **paghota, pōn**) **1.1)** *v. advrs. ka-...-an* To be exhausted, as from prolonged exertion. *Bang amole' disi Hu min pagusaha'an, lingantu, kasimayan.* When Hu and his companions head home from the fishing ground they are hungry, exhausted.

**simay₂** *v. intr. pa-* To move aside so as to make room for someone to pass. *Pasimay ka man bowa' lawang ilū bo' aniya' palabayan.* Move aside from the doorway there so there is a way through. *Pasimay-simay ka, patulak-tulak ka ba bo' aku palabay.* Move aside, move back a bit so I can pass. (*Thesaurus:* **salema'** 1, **sigay** 1, **s'nnok,**

sulekma')

**simayang-galura'** *var. of* **sumayang-galura'**

**simbōng** *n.* **1)** A knot of hair. **1.1)** *v. tr.* To arrange the hair in a knot. *Bay sinimbōng bu'un si Mām apa ataha'.* Mam's hair has been arranged in a knot because it is long. (*Thesaurus:* **hambak, hampal, pugay 2, sapid 1.1, toket 1.1, tusay**)
**pagsinimbōng** *v. intr.* **aN-** To wear one's hair in a knot.

**simbug** *v. tr.* **-an 1)** To add something to a mixture. *Simbugun lagi' loho' ilū, apasu' makalandu'.* Water that soup down a bit, it's too hot. (*Thesaurus:* **haybol, lamud₁ 1.1, lamugay 1.1, pagsagol 1.1, paila', templa 1.1) 1.1)** *v. advrs.* **ka-...-an** To be adulterated, of a mixture.
**pagsimbug** *v. intr.* **aN- 1)** To be mixed, of grains or liquids. *Tahalusku ina'an sabab mbal magsimbug laha', mbal dapaluwasan.* I can fight that [person] because our blood is not mixed, we are not from the same mother. **1.1)** *v. tr.* To combine ingredients. *Gandum maka buwas pinagsimbug.* Corn mixed in with rice.
**pasimbug** *v. tr.* To add an ingredient; to mix with a larger group.

**simi** *var. of* **salimi**

**simpal** *v. intr.* **a-** To be coming from an adverse direction, of wind. *Asimpal baliyu, mbal taluwa' binanog.* The wind is in the wrong quarter, it won't be right for sailing. (*Thesaurus:* **badju, baliyu 1, hunus 1**)

**simpan** *var. of* **jimban**

**simpay** *v. tr.* To cut sailcloth to the required shape. *Sinimpay banog, buwat banog amasi metohan ē'. Pinīs, sinimpay.* A sail is cut to pattern. Like a sail that is still uncut fabric. [It is] cut out, cut to shape. *Animpay kami kaleya salung.* We will cut a sail out, ashore, tomorrow. (*cf:* **tabas 1**)
**simpayan** *n.* A pattern for making flexible items, as a sail or garment. (*Thesaurus:* **bantukan, ladjawan, sengoran, suntu'an**)

**simpi'** *n.* A flat earthenware pan for roasting cassava meal. *Amasi dasimpi', amasi dasanglagan.* One panful, one batch of cassava remaining. (*gen:* **pam'llahan**)

**simuddai** (*var.* **sumuddai**) *adv.* The day after tomorrow. *At'kka pi'itu patta' kami sumuddai.* Our photos will arrive here the day after tomorrow. *Tūranta ka simuddai ni Sisangat.* I will take you back to Sisangat the day after tomorrow. (*Thesaurus:* **di'ilaw, llaw itu, ma t'llu, salung**)

**simun** *v. intr.* **pa- 1)** To cast a shadow over something. *Da'a ka pasimun apa mbal ta'nda'ku magsulat.* Don't cast a shadow because I can't see to write. **1.1)** *v. tr.* **-an** To shade something. *Da'a simunin katas itū.* Don't shade this paper.

**sīn** (*var.* **silin**) *n.* Money in general; a one-centavo coin in particular. *Halam aniya' sīnku, minsan dakayu' sīn ettom.* I have no money, not even one copper coin. (*Thesaurus:* **landing₂, pilak 2,**

**pinta₁, pisita, tustun**)
**sīn kanat** *n. phrase* Loose change; a few coins. {idiom} *Aniya' sīnnu kanat?* Do you have any small change?

**sin** *ptl.* Elevated register marker. Marks the non-subject argument of the clause in formal speech. Also indicates ownership or possession. *Tonga' sin tonga'.* A quarter [lit. half of a half]. *Tanda' sin kapagbagayku ma ka'a.* A sign of my friendship with you.

**sinabu** (*var.* **hinabu**) *adv.* **1)** While; during. *Jari, hinabu sigām maglami-lami maka maglangohan, angolang na sigām.* So while they were celebrating and getting drunk, they began shouting. *Ta'abut pa'in llaw kapitu'na, hinabu masi gi' alogob-logob, pabungkal na sigām.* When the seventh day came, while it was still quite dark, they got up [from resting]. *Abakat hinabu ulan.* Wounded while it was raining. *Sinabu pa'in kami angalagaran lansa aniya' magsabil ma jambatan.* While we were waiting for the launch someone ran amok on the pier. (*Thesaurus:* **baba, gimut, sabu 1) 1.1)** *n.* The occasion or period of occurrence. *Pabalik mala'ikat ē' bo' panyata' ni d'nda hinabuna maghinang ma huma.* The angel came back and appeared to the woman as she worked on the farm. *Hinabuna binalutan e' sigām, magbau'-bau' iya kinangog.* While he was being held by them, he pretended to be demented. *Hinabu sigām maglami-lami maka maglangohan, angolang sigām.* While they were partying and getting drunk, they shouted.

**sinag** *n.* **1)** A ray or flash of light; brightness. *Asilaw aku he' sinag llaw.* I am dazzled by the sun's rays. **1.1)** *adj.* **a-** Glittering; flashing; radiant. *Bang aniya' bulawan ahūg ni deyom bohe', asinag, asawa.* If something gold falls into water, it is flashing, showing light. *Bang pa'in ahāp kasinag mata llaw ya makapatahak saga buwa' tinanom.* May the good warmth of the sun that ripens the planted crops. (*Thesaurus:* **danta', sahaya 1.1, sawa 1.1) 1.2)** *v. intr.* **pa-** To emit rays of light. *Buwat parola, pasinag.* Like a navigation beacon, flashing. **1.3)** *v. advrs.* **ka-...-an** To be lit up by something bright. *Tai'-baliyu kasinagan he' llaw.* Cirrus clouds lit up by the sun.

**sinagawli'** *n.* A shrub of the mallow family, used medicinally. *Sida acuta.*

**sina'₁** *adj.* **a-** Chinese, especially with reference to the source of certain products. (*Thesaurus:* **Lannang, makaw, taoke'₁**)

**sina'₂** *n.* Chinese orange, a sweet variety of citrus.

**Sinama** (derivative of **Sama**) *n.* **1)** The language spoken by Sama. **1.1)** *v. tr.* To translate something into Sinama. *Sinamahun kono' bo' tahati kami.* Please say it in Sinama so we can understand it.
**pagsinama** *v. intr.* **aN-** To speak the Sinama language. *Ōy, ata'u ka magsinama.* Hey, you know how to speak Sinama.

**sinangil** var. of **saging-sinangil**

**sinanglag** (derivative of **sanglag**) *n.* Grated and squeezed cassava, pan-roasted without oil. *Papinsalun gipitan panggi' kayu bo' bang sinanglag, ahāp.* Tighten the cassava press so [the meal] will be good when roasted.

**sinapang** *n.* A firearm, especially a rifle. *Nsa' aniya' sinapang sigām saddi, hal tamson.* They had no other firearms, only Thompsons [a US submachine gun]. (*Thesaurus:* **kalbin, kanyun 1, garan, lantaka 1, musil, pistul**)

**sinaukat** var. of **saukat**

**sindik** *see:* **pasindik**

**sindil** *v. tr.* **1)** To refer obliquely to people or things by allusion or veiled reference. **1.1)** *v. tr.* -an To refer to things or places in song or chant form. *Sinindilan, niōnan lahat bay kabusayanna.* Recited in song, naming the places he had travelled to.

**pagsindil** *n.* **1)** A singing contest in which a male and female performer seek to outdo each other. (*cf:* **pagbono' kalangan**) **1.1)** *v. intr.* aN- To engage in a singing contest in which a male and female performer try to outdo each other.

**pagsindilan** *v. intr.* aN- **1)** To be recited in song form, of the names and deeds of a deceased loved one. *Magsindilan, sali' magtangis pasal anakta amatay.* Reciting their names and deeds, like when weeping for one's dead children. *Jari magsindilan sultan ma bangkay si Ab.* So kings sang funeral songs over Ab. (*cf:* **paglemong 1**) **1.1)** *v. tr.* To sing about someone who is dead. *Nientom ma ka'llumna, ma kalasana. Tahun na pa'in a'a mamatay inān, pinagsindilan na pa'in e' a'a manangis inān.* Remembered for her life, her love. Years since that person died, yet she continues to be sung about by the person weeping.

**sindip** var. of **sintib**

**sindul** *n.* **1)** A sweet broth of water, sugar and coconut milk thickened with starch. (*Thesaurus:* **loho' 1, santan 1.1**) **1.1)** *v. tr.* To cook sindul.

**sindung₁** *v. intr.* pa- To take shelter; to enter a lighted area. *Ilu na ulan. Pasindung aku ni luma' si Ke.* There is the rain. I shelter at Ke's house. (*Thesaurus:* **limbu 1.1, lindung 1, pulipus 1.1, silung₁**)

**kasindungan** *n.* Shade from sun. *Subay saruk kasindungan.* There should be a hat for shade.

**pasindungan** *n.* A shelter.

**sindung₂** *v. intr.* aN- To fish by an artificial light source. (*syn:* **silung₂**)

**sinelas** (var. **tenelas**) *n.* Slippers; sandals; flip-flops. (*Thesaurus:* **bakiya'₁, takon, taumpa'**)

**sini** *n.* A movie; a movie theater. *Bang aniya' kappal at'kka min Tiyanggi kalu aniya' sini, anōd aku.* If a ship arrives from Jolo there may be a movie, I'll go in [to see it].

**sinigwelas** *n.* The Spanish plum, a tree and its edible fruit. *Spondias purpurea.*

**sinokot** *n.* A medicinal shrub.

**sinōng** (derivative of **sōng₁**) *adj.* zero Future; a future occasion or time. *Subay ma waktu sinōng inān.* It will have to be on that future occasion. *Ma waktu sinōng bang kam tinilaw e' saga ka'anakanbi bang ai hatina saga batu itū...* At some future time, when your children ask you about the meaning of these stones...

**sinosōng** (derivative of **sōng₁**) *n.* A coming or future time. *Ni'nda' pa'in ma sinosōng.* We will see about it at a later date. *Manjari aniya' du sangpū' a'a min panubu'na makapagdatu' ma sinosōng.* So there will be ten of his descendants who will become a *datu'* in days to come.

**sinsing** var. of **singsing**

**sinsoro** *n.* **1)** A fine-meshed drag net. (*Thesaurus:* **gugul 1, lantaw 1, laya 1, linggi' 1, pokot₁ 1, siyul 1**) **1.1)** *v. tr.* To catch small fish with a fine net.

**sintak** *v. tr.* **1)** To pull or tug on a line; to strike a hook into the mouth of a biting fish. *Sintakun, Oto'.* Strike the hook, Son. **2)** To raise a flag or sail.

**pagsintak** *v. intr.* aN- To strike a hook when a fish takes the bait. *Bang kita am'ssi tananamta tinduk daing aheya. Pagsintakta halam kasabitan.* When we are fishing we feel the bite of a large fish. When we strike it hasn't been hooked. *Bang kita makatuli' deyo' taga daing, al'kkas kita maka'ā'. Paghūg, pagsintak, paghella'.* When we find a deep place that has fish, we soon get some. Down the line goes, the fish are hooked, and up we pull them.

**sinta'** *n.* An intention; a future plan.

**pagsinta'** *v. intr.* aN- To be committed to doing what has been in mind for some time. *Sali' bang aku bay alahi buwat saga ni Tinggilan, subay aku sina'ut he' saga matto'aku. Niā' aku apa magsinta' aku atulak ni Manila'.* Like when I ran away to Tinggilan, my parents had to do something about it immediately. They had to get me because I was determined to leave for Manila. *Magsinta' itū sosōng, buwat kami magluma' t'llu pitu' ma Sambuwangan, magsinta' na ni Bukidnon, asekot na tulak.* This word *sinta'* is to do with the future, like when we lived three weeks in Zamboanga, intending to go soon to Bukidnon, departure imminent. (*cf:* **apiki 1, tapa'ut**)

**sintib** (var. **sindip**) *n.* An implement for turning food in a pan, especially cassava meal. (*Thesaurus:* **luwag 1, paleta, sasanglag, suru' 1**)

**sintoron** *n.* A belt (clothing); a sash. (*Thesaurus:* **kambot 1, kandit, sabitan, sambung₂**)

**Sinūk** (derivative of **Sūk**) *n.* **1)** Tausug, the language spoken by the indigenous inhabitants of Jolo Island and elsewhere. **1.1)** *v. tr.* To translate something into the Tausug language.

**sinu'** *adj.* a- Economical in the use of fuel. *Asinu' amangan gasulina, ma karboredor malkina.* Economical in its consumption of gasolene, of the carburetor of an engine. *Pariki'un sumbuhan bo' asinu'*. Reduce the wick so it is economical.

**sinyal** (var. **sinyas**) *n.* 1) A signal or sign for conveying information through space. 1.1) *v. tr.* -*an* To signal someone, as by waving or blowing a whistle. *Bang aku aninyal, paraganun na lansa ilū*. When I signal, get the launch going. (*Thesaurus:* **kambay 1**, **lambe₁ 1.1**, **mita**, **paglabad 1.1**, **sayang₂**)

**sinyas** var. of **sinyal**

**sinyawa** var. of **sanyawa**

**sing-sūd** *v. tr.* -*an* To oppose or contradict someone's advice or opinion. *Magsuli-suli ai-ai ganta' nihinang bo' mbal arakayu' kagara'an. Sining-sūran e' dangan.* Talking together about things to be done, but the decision was not unanimous. One person opposed it. (*Thesaurus:* **balda**, **dangat 1**, **paggat**, **sagga' 1.1**)
  **pagsing-sūd** *v. intr.* *aN-* To be in disagreement; to be in conflict with each other.

**singal** var. of **s'ngngal**

**singaling** var. of **tehe'-tehe'-singaling**

**sīngan** var. of **silingan**

**singkab** *adj.* *a-* 1) Uncovered; exposed to weather. 1.1) *v. intr.* *pa-* To be open to weather or inspection, of a house. *Pasingkab, mbal ahāp he' anaplok, buwat luma' itu, ala'an dambila' atopna.* Left open, not properly closed off, like this house with half its thatch gone.

**singki'** *n.* The inside angle of the chine of a canoe hull. *Dalos du singki' maka salig. Salig itu ma luwasan, singki' ma deyom.* The *singki'* and the *salig* are connected. The *salig* is on the outside of the angle, the *singki'* is inside. (*Thesaurus:* **salig₂**, **taddas**)

**singku** *v. tr.* 1) To jolt something, causing pain. *Bakat itū subay tasingku bo' ap'ddi'.* This wound must have been jolted to be painful. (*Thesaurus:* **bakkug**, **bangkug 1**, **bōg**, **sikmu'**, **siggul**) 1.1) *v. advrs.* *ka-...-an* To be jolted so as to cause pain to a tender area. *Arōy! Kasingkuhan kalibubutku itū.* Ouch! This boil of mine has been knocked.

**singkulang** *adj.* *zero* Cross-legged.
  **pagsiningkulang** *v. intr.* *aN-* To sit cross-legged, a formal position appropriate to ceremonial occasions. (*Thesaurus:* **hakin**, **milang**, **pagsengkang**)

**singga-singga** *v. intr.* *pa-* To withdraw to a safer location. (*Thesaurus:* **sebog**, **suhut**)

**singga'-singga'** *v. tr.* To drive something away, as animals or unwelcome people. (*Thesaurus:* **budjaw**, **dūy**, **siga' 1.1**, **sū₁ 1.1**, **t'ggal**)

**singgam** (var. **jinggam**) *n.* Chewing gum.

**singgit** *n.* A pretext for criticism, dispute or praise, not necessarily supported by fact. *Amiha na pa'in lawang pagbono'an. Amiha singgit.* Continually looking for an opportunity to fight. Looking for a pretext. *Aniya' isāb singgit ni kahāpan, buwat magsuli-suli.* There is also a *singgit* which intends good, as when talking together. *Hal sali' magā'*

*singgit. Diki'-diki' sadja hē', magbono' na.* Just sort of finding a reason. It was so minor, and now they are fighting. (*Thesaurus:* **katikmuhanan**, **pagsababan**, **po'on-sabab**)

**singlab** *n.* A spark of light; a twinkle.
  **pagsinglab** *v. intr.* *aN-* To twinkle or sparkle. *Pahangad ka ni langit bo' ka maka'nda' bitu'un magsinglab.* Look up to the sky so you can see the stars twinkling. (*Thesaurus:* **kiraw**, **kitaw-kitaw**, **illap**, **inggat**, **pagpillaw-pillaw**, **tingaw-tingaw**)

**singsing** (var. **sinsing**) *n.* A ring as worn on the finger. *Am'lli aku dilam pamalmataku singsing.* I will buy a gemstone to use as a jewel on a ring. (*Thesaurus:* **aretes**, **pamulawan**, **pansi**)

**singu'-singu'** *v. tr.* To utter something in a whisper. *Sinipuk-sipuk, sali' siningu'-singu'.* Spoken in secret, sort of whispered. (*cf:* **sipuk-sipuk**; *Thesaurus:* **hagas-hagas**, **higung-higung**)
  **pagsingu'-singu'** *v. intr.* *aN-* To whisper to each other. *Bang magsuli-suli subay magsingu'-singu' bo' halam aniya' makakale.* When talking we should whisper so there is no one who can hear.

**sīp** *v. intr.* *pa-* To lie on one side. *Totogun pelang dok mbal pasīp.* Steady the canoe so it doesn't fall over onto its side. *Bang aku atuli pasīp aku.* When I sleep I lie on my side. (*Thesaurus:* **kīd₁ 1.1**, **lengag**, **pasindik**, **patiring**)

**sipa'** *v. tr.* 1) To kick something. *Tasipa'nu sasapu.* You happened to kick the broom. *Anipa' na pī' kallo'.* The heron kicked in that direction. (*Thesaurus:* **binti'**, **tagdok**, **tindak 1**) 1.1) *v. tr.* -*an* To knock or bump something with one's feet. *Binusung aku he' mbo'ku apa bay sipa'anku.* I suffer retribution from my grandfather because I knocked him with my foot.
  **pagsipa'** *n.* 1) The game of sipa', in which a ball (traditionally of woven rattan) is kept in the air by kicking with the sole of one's foot. (*cf:* **buka'₂**) 1.1) *v. intr.* *aN-* To play the game of sipa'. *Bowata ka ni pagsipa'an, magsipa' kita maka si Ja maka bola si Li.* I will take you to the kick-ball area, we will play kick-ball with Ja using Li's ball.
  **pagsipa'an** *n.* A court where the game of sipa' is played.

**sipat₁** *n.* 1) Awareness; consciousness; mental grasp of some fact. *Ala'an sipatta, halam aniya' akkal-pikilanta.* Our mental awareness has left us, we have no rational thought. (*Thesaurus:* **pangannal₁**) 1.1) *v. tr.* To take in some fact or concept; to grasp with the mind. *Yamboho' tasipatku heka manusiya' mareyom junna.* I have only just grasped how many humans there are in the world. (*Thesaurus:* **pangannal₁**, **sakup₁ 1**, **sayu 1.1**, **tahu**, **tilas₁**)

**sipat₂** *n.* 1) Signs of change in attitude or condition; an indicator of physical state. *Sipat duwampū', tape' maka tangan. Aniya' isāb sipat siyampū'.*

Life-sign #20 is the feet and hands. There is also a Life-sign #90. *Buwat aniya' anunangan d'nda, araran magl'ngngan ni luma' d'nda hē'. Pasōng-pasōng llaw alahang na magl'ngngan. Yuk min kar'ndahan, "Aniya' na sipat ma iya."* Like someone courting his fiancée, always going to the woman's house. As days pass he rarely goes there. The girl's people say, "There are signs of change." **1.1)** *v. tr.* To change one's attitude. *Angkan sinipat, angkan magduwa-pikilan na, ala'at hinangna.* The reason his thinking changed, the reason he was now of two minds, is that what she was doing was bad.

**sipaw** var. of **s'ppaw**

**sipi₁** *adv.* **1)** Stealthily; deceitfully. **1.1)** *v. tr.* -an To do something stealthily. *Sipihin bang maingga pagtau'anna sīnna.* Spy out where his money is kept. *Buwat saga aniya' kabaya'anku, bo' mbal ta'ā'ku. Na bang kasipihanku, magtūy ngā'ku.* It's like when there is something I want and can't get. Then when I find an opportunity to act unnoticed, I will surely get it. *Buwat kami bay anangkaw bo' ta'abut, na nijīl kami. Aniya' kasipihanku palahi'an, magtūy aku pal'ssut lahi-lahi. Ahayang na aku.* Like when we stole and got caught, then we were jailed. I managed to find an escape route, so I promptly slipped through it and ran. I'm in open space now. (*Thesaurus:* **ambus, hapa' 1.2, holdap, ingu, tipu 1.1**)

**sipi₂** *adj.* a- Close to an edge. *Da'a ka amasipi bang ka amat'nna' ai-ai ko da'a ahūg. Patapakun.* Don't put things near an edge when you put them down, lest they fall. Place them securely. (*Thesaurus:* **s'ddi**)

**sipilyu** *n.* **1)** A brush, especially a toothbrush. (*Thesaurus:* **gisgis empon, sangbawa, tupras**) **1.1)** *v. tr.* -an To brush dirt from the teeth. *Sipilyuhun l'mmisna.* Brush its dirt away.

**sipin** *v. intr.* aN- To behave unacceptably. *Aniya' duwangan bay am'ssi, pitu' daing ta'ā' sigā. Pagka ma lahat na, ni'nde'an duwa daing he' dangan. "Ōy," yuk dangan, "anipin ka'a ilū."* There were two who went fishing. They got seven fish. When they got home, one of them handed over two fish. "Hey," said the other, "you're behaving inappropriately."

**sipit** *n.* **1)** A hair clip; a clothes-pin. *A: "Pamagaynu ilū?" B: "Pangisihanku sipit-badju'."* A: "What's that for?" B: "For me to store clothes-pins in." **1.1)** *v. tr.* To hold something by clipping. *Am'lli aku sipit panipitku bu'unku.* I will buy hairclips to fasten my hair.

**sisipit** *n.* A clip; a fastener.

**sipit-sipit₁** *v. intr.* pa- To squeeze into or through a narrow space. *Pasipit-sipit kita, pasikla'.* We squeeze through, slipping through a gap. (*Thesaurus:* **siklut, siplit, s'llot 1.1, soksok**)

**sipit-sipit₂** *n.* An earwig. *Dermaptera.*

**sipit-sipit₃** *n.* Various wrasses. *Thalassoma amblycephalum.*

**siplat** (var. **siklat**) *v. advrs.* ka-...-an To be caused to splutter on a liquid. *Si Ke bay kasiplatan he' kahawa.* Ke was caused to splutter by coffee. *Kasiklatan, dangkuri' la'a sagō' bay ka anginum ati paluwas.* Made to splutter, just a small amount, but you drank and it came [back] up. (*Thesaurus:* **b'ngkol₁ 1.1, s'ddok**)

**siplit** (var. **suplit**) *v. tr.* -an To insert something into a narrow space. *Siplitanku laring ni dinding ko da'a alungay.* I insert the knife in the wall so it won't be lost. (*cf:* **sipsip**; *Thesaurus:* **siklut, sipit-sipit₁, s'llot 1.1, soksok**)

**sipsip** *v. tr.* -an To force something into a gap as to wedge it apart. (*cf:* **siplit**)

**sipsipan** *n.* A narrow gap or space between flat items. *Wa'i pasōd kabelaw hē' ni sipsipan atop.* That bat has gone into the gaps in the thatch.

**sipuk** *n.* Concealment; secrecy; a hiding place. *Bang aniya' pamuwan mareyom sipuk maka'aluk atay-pasu'.* If something is given in secret it soothes angry feelings. (*cf:* **kolorom**)

**kasipukan** *n.* A place of concealment; secrecy. *In buwan ma kasipukan maka'aluk pasu'-atay.* A gift in secret soothes hard feelings.

**sipuk-sipuk** *v. tr.* To pass information on in private. *Ungsikun, sipuk-sipukun, haka'in sab'nnal-b'nnal.* Speak in private, say it to him alone, tell him truthfully. (*cf:* **singu'-singu'**; *Thesaurus:* **pagsīb, ungsik**)

**sipug-sipug** *n.* The sensitive plant or touch-me-not. *Mimosa pudica.*

**siput** *n.* **1)** A screw-like object; a faucet or spigot. **1.1)** *v. tr.* To turn something with a screwing motion.

**siputan** *n.* Any object or device that functions with a spiral movement. *Kibut aniya' siputanna.* A water jar that has a spigot.

**sirang** *n.* A unit of measurement for sarong sizes (one unit being the norm). *Duwansirang, dakayu' du la'itan, sali' du lambuna man dampōng parampōng.* Two sarong units, one seam, the same width from one side to the other.

**sirap** *n.* Various mussel-like bivalves. *T'llu ginis sirap. Aniya' tibulung ataha', aniya' tibulung hadja, bo' aniya' magseko'-seko' baranna.* There are three kinds of mussel. The round and long ones, the ones that are simply round [not long], and those that curve in and out. *Ettom sirap itū. Bang bila'nu duwa, isina asarap.* These mussels are black. When you break them into two parts the flesh is delicious.

**siratul mustakim** *n. phrase* The Right Path in Islamic thought; by extension, the Bridge to Paradise.

**siraw-siraw** *n.* A flicker of light.

**pagsiraw-siraw** *v. intr.* aN- To be flickering or growing dim, of a wick-lamp. *Bang aniya'* *kulaetnu bo' magsiraw-siraw sidda, ap'dda.* If you have a pressure lantern and it keeps getting dim, it goes out. (*cf:* **pagpillaw-pillaw**)

**siru'ung** *n.* The Night-heron. *Nycticorax sp.*

**sisa** *v. intr. pa-* To open up a gap. *Da'a ka pal'ngngan minnilu, pasisa ko' ilū.* Don't walk there, it opens up to a gap. (*Thesaurus:* **bungkas**)

**pagsisa 1)** *v. intr. aN-* To be separated by a gap, of components that belong together. *Magtulak karuwambila', buwat lantay halam bay binīt atawa halam bay nilansang, bang pagi'ikan magsisa.* Moving away on both sides, like flooring that hasn't been lashed or nailed, when stepped on it makes a gap. **2)** *v. tr.* To form a gap between components that should stay close together.

**sisayang** *intrj.* 'Too bad!'; 'What a pity!' *Ai-ai bay kahinanganta saddī min ahāp, yukta, "Sisayang."* Anything we were doing that was other than good, we say, "Too bad."

**sisi** *v. tr.* **1)** To prise something out, as meat from a shell. **2)** To prise information out of someone. *Sisihun pehē' kono'.* Please go there and find out. *Anisi, angā' kita lling.* Persistent, getting speech out of someone. (*Thesaurus:* **kihaka, hati 2, hodhod, tilaw 1.1, tilosa 1.1**)

**sisik** *n.* **1)** A scale of fish. *Mangku', baki', halam aniya' sisikna.* Frigate mackerel, and catfish, have no scales. **1.1)** *v. tr. -an* To remove scales from a fish.

**sisig** *v. tr.* To sort various items into the appropriate groups. (*Thesaurus:* **gintil 1.1, lilay, paggihay 1, sila' 1.1, silang₁ 1.1**)

**sisipit** (derivative of **sipit**) *n.* A clip; a fastener. *Bang pahogotnu bu'unku maka sisipit, in kosogku tahinang buwat kosog l'lla kasehe'an.* If you secure my hair with clips, my strength will be made like the strength of other men.

**sisu'an** *var.* of **kagang-sisu'an**

**sitta** *v. tr.* To call on someone's name, especially the name of a spirit being such as a djinn or duwata. *"Bang ka sab'nnal-b'nnal jīn, pareyo' pi'itu, itiya' ka sinitta."* If you really are a djinn, then come down here, you have been summoned. *Niōnan kita, sinitta kita.* We are named, we are called. A: *"Ni'inay duwata bang sinitta?"* B: *"Nilinganan, tinugtugan kamanyan."* A: "What is done to a *duwata* spirit when it is summoned?" B: "It is called by name, incense burned for it."

**sitta'a** *neg.* Disclaims knowledge in response to a question. *"Sumiyan atulak lansa?" yukna. "Sitta'aku bang sumiyan," yuk dangan.* "When does the launch leave?" asked one. "I don't know when," said the other. A: *"Oto', ma'ai lahutku?"* B: *"Ā, sitta'aku ka'a."* A: "Son, where is my knife?" B: "Mmh, no idea." (*cf:* **daka, inday**)

**sitti** *voc. n.* Honorific address for a high-born woman. *Aniya' sandil si Sitti Saray, ōnna si Hajara.* Lady Saray had an attendant by the name of Hajara.

**siya** *n.* A seat for one person, generally with a back; a chair. *Bay aku kumuppa ni siya bang al'ddom deyom luma'.* I landed on a chair when the house was dark. *Bang bay maglahi-lahi si Li mareyom luma' bo' magdugtul ni siya, butigan kōkna.* When Li was running around the house and ran into a chair, her head had a swelling. (*Thesaurus:* **bangku', kulsi, paningkō'an**)

**siya-siya** *adj. a-* **1)** Abandoned; forsaken, of people or buildings. *Alubu na, maka halam na kabangunan pabīng, asiya-siya sampay ni kabuwattituhan.* Broken down now, and not rebuilt, abandoned until the present time. *Sasuku bay mbal maka'anak, maka'anak na pitu' hekana, sagō' in bay aheka anakna asiya-siya du.* Those who had not given birth, have now given birth to seven, but those who had many children are forsaken. (*Thesaurus:* **bba₁ 1, pulaw₂ 1.1**) *v. tr.* To abandon someone; to break off relations with someone. *Siniya-siya kita he' disi Anu inān ma saukat dayahan na.* We are ignored by What's-his-name and the rest merely because they are now rich. *Abila aku siniya-siya he' ina'-mma'ku, tantu aku tinaima' e' Tuhan.* If I were abandoned by my parents, I would surely be accepted by God. (*Thesaurus:* **pulaw₂**) **1.2)** *v. advrs. ka-...-an* To be left without support or care. *Kasiya-siyahan aku, pila atuhanku? Aheka sigā, aku dangan-danganku.* I am abandoned, how many am I opposing? They are many, I am on my own. *Sali' kita matto'a bo' halam anakta, yukta, "Kasiya-siyahan kita, halam aniya' angubul kita."* *Siya-siya* is like us who are old but have no children and say, "We are left alone, no one to bury us."

**siyaka** *n.* **1)** An older brother or sister; an older relative of the same generation. *Siyaka si Ja min si Li, ya danakanna. Siyali iya min si Su, ya si'itna. Aku siyaka min kamemon.* Ja is older than Li, his sibling. He is younger than Su, his uncle. I am older than all of them. (*Thesaurus:* **danakan, siyali 1**) **2)** A larger version of the same thing. *Bang tarukna, subay siyaka-siyaka mannilu.* As far as the mast is concerned, it should be a bit longer than that.

**siyag** *n.* **1)** An all-purpose tubular garment; a sarong. **1.1)** *v. intr. a-* To wear a sarong as a skirt, the tube securely fastened around the waist, with extra cloth folded and rolled outwards to secure. *Bang d'nda asiyag, bang l'lla magampi'.* A woman wears a sarong woman-style, a man wears it man-style. (*Thesaurus:* **hampi' 1.1, hōs 1.2, pagkīmbong, pagsina'ul, pindung**)

**siyal** *adj. zero* Responsible for one's own misfortune. *Bang kita ameya' ma a'a ala'at hinangna, siyal kita ma baranta bang kita ta'but.* If we accompany someone whose activities are bad, we are personally to blame if we are caught in the act. (*Thesaurus:* **abunaw, atas₂ 1,**

**bahala'₁, kuwiraw, lawag-baran, tanggung₂)**

**siyali** *n.* **1)** A younger brother or sister; a younger relative of the same generation. (*Thesaurus:* **danakan, siyaka** 1) **1.1)** *v. advrs.* **ka-...-an** To have a younger brother or sister. *Mbal manjari nihambin bang kasiyalihan na.* It isn't proper [for a child] to be picked up and held when it has a younger sibling. **2)** A smaller version of the same thing. *A: "Buwattitu heyana?" B: "He' angay, siyalina minnilu."* A: "This big?" B: "No way, a smaller one than that."

**siyam** *num.* Nine.

**siyampū'** *num.* **1)** Ninety. **2)** Diagnostic Life-sign #90. *Aniya' sipat duwampū', tape' maka tangan. Aniya' isāb sipat siyampū'.* There is a diagnostic life-sign #20. There is also a life-sign #90.

**siyatun** *n.* A game of skill in which players pitch a short stick at a mark, or use it to knock the stick of an opponent.

  **pagsiyatun** *v. intr.* **aN-** To play the game of siyatun.

**siyu-siyu** *n.* **1)** Fragments of foreign matter in a liquid, especially in fuel oil or gasolene. **1.1)** *v. advrs.* **-in-** Affected by impurities in the fuel.

**siyuk-siyuk** *see:* **pagsiyuk-siyuk**

**siyud** *v. intr.* **pa-** To run a canoe lightly over the surface of a submerged object. *Wa'i kami makasiyud ni kahanggal-hanggalan atawa ma punsu.* We had touched and glided over a shallow bottom or a sand mound. *Makasanglad, makaragsa', makahanggal, sali' du. Ya sadja magbidda' bang makasiyud.* Sanglad, dagsa', and hanggal mean the same. The only different word is siyud. (*Thesaurus:* **dagsa', hanggal** 1.1, **sanglad**)

**siyul** *n.* **1)** A fine-meshed drag net. (*Thesaurus:* **gugul** 1, **lantaw** 1, **laya** 1, **linggi'** 1, **pokot₁** 1, **sinsoro** 1) **1.1)** *v. tr.* To catch small fish with a fine net. *Basta aniya' pelang mailu ma t'bba, aniyul.* Whenever there are canoes there in the shallows, they're drag-fishing with a fine net.

**siyum** *v. intr.* **pa-** **1)** To be kissing. *Mahē' magtimuk, magkahāp maka bay banta. Magtūy aku parauhat pasiyum.* Coming together there, making peace with someone who had been an enemy. I immediately went right on in, kissing. **1.1)** *v. tr.* To kiss someone. *Amasiyum si Li papa-ina'na.* Li lets her father and mother kiss her.

**s'bbang** *var.* of **k'bbang**

**s'bbat** *n.* **1)** The gullet of large marine creatures such as rays and whales. **1.1)** *v. tr.* To swallow something into the gullet, whole, without biting. *Pagtas'bbat t'lla'-t'lla' he' kalitan bang patuhun. Bang daing sin'bbat e' kasehe'an, pasihag isāb.* If fish are being swallowed by others, they scatter too. *Daing a'aslag an'bbat daing-daing anahut.* Big fish swallow little fish whole. (*Thesaurus:* **sangkiyam, t'llon**)

  **pags'bbat** *v. tr.* To swallow something whole, without biting. *Pagtas'bbat t'lla'-t'lla' he' kalitan*

*bang patuhun.* Seagulls, when they dive [for fish], may be swallowed whole by a shark.

**s'bbo** *n.* A type of branching coral that provides food and shelter for many marine species. *Bang lahat aheka s'bbona, aheka daingna.* A place that has a lot of s'bbo coral also has lots of fish. (*gen:* **batu₂** 1)

**s'bbo'** *adj.* **a-** Marred by a hole, of cloth. (*cf:* **lowang** 1)

**s'bbol** *adj.* **-an** **1)** Suffering from reflux of food from the stomach or gullet. *Amangan kita mampallam, ai-ai al'ssom, nā s'bbolan kita atay. Angutta' kita, mbal kita makautta'.* When we eat mangos or anything tart, then we have heartburn. We retch but can't vomit. *Tananamta song paluwas kinakanta, s'bbolan kita.* We feel that what we have eaten is about to come out, we suffer from reflux. **1.1)** *v. tr.* **-an** To overfill the stomach, causing reflux.

**s'bbu** *v. intr.* **aN-** To emit vapor. *An'bbu, paluwa' humbuna pariyata'.* Giving off vapor, its smoke coming out in an upward direction. (*Thesaurus:* **sangu** 1, **tangas**)

**s'kkat** **1)** *n.* A hand of bananas. **1.1)** *adj.* **a-** Torn or split off a main part. (*cf:* **s'ppe'** 1) **1.2)** *v. tr.* To split something off the main part, as bananas from a stalk or limbs from a body. *S'kkatin aku saging ilū.* Split off a hand of those bananas for me. *Gansuwang itū an'kkat kita llaw-sangom bang kita ta'nda' he'na. Sīkkat baranta kamemon.* These viscera-eating monsters will tear us apart, day or night, if they see us. Our entire body torn apart. **2)** *clf.* Count word for hands of bananas. *B'llihin aku saging, das'kkat du.* Buy me some bananas, just one hand.

  **s'kkatan** *n.* A hand of bananas. *Saging itu a'abag s'kkatanna. Kilāku ahāp bay bolehanna.* This is a good hand of bananas. I reckon the whole stalk must have been good. (*cf:* **bole**)

**s'kke** *n.* The ridged dorsal fin of certain fish. (*Thesaurus:* **kanting₁, sēk, tare'** 1)

**s'kket** *v. intr.* **aN-** To stand with hands on hips. *Bang a'a mbal kasulutan, buwat aniya' kalintawanna, an'kket iya.* When a person is not pleased, like there is something he is irritated about, he stands with hands on hips. (*cf:* **pandang-hawak**)

**s'kko'-s'kko'** *v. advrs.* **-in-** Suffering from hiccups. *Sin'kko'-s'kko' si Ba sabab aheka takakanna.* Ba suffers from hiccups because he eats a lot.

**s'kkol** *v. tr.* To clasp something with both hands (usually with a negative). *Mbal tas'kkol bu'unna.* Her hair cannot be held in clasped hands.

**s'ddi** *v. intr.* **pa-** To be located by a hole in the floor. *Sali' kita asungi' atawa angaludja', pas'ddi kita ni lowang.* If for example we are defecating or spitting, we locate ourselves over a hole. (*Thesaurus:* **sipi₂**)

  **pas'ddi** *v. tr.* To drop something through a hole in the floor.

**s'ddok** *v. advrs. ka-...-an* To choke on food or liquid. *Bang kami bay amangan liyabanos bo' kami magtittowa, kas'ddokan.* When we were eating soursop and laughed, we choked. *Bay aku kas'ddokan e' bohe' paluwas man ūngku.* I was choking on water coming out of my nose. (*Thesaurus:* **b'ngkol₁ 1.1, siplat**)

**s'ddong** *adj. zero* Of the right size; fitting. *Subay pinaheya lowangna, mbal s'ddong.* The opening must be enlarged, it doesn't fit. (*Thesaurus:* **sarang 1, sugiya, t'ppot, ustu**)

**s'ddop** *v. intr. pa-* To set, of a heavenly body, sun or moon in particular. *Pags'ddop llaw, masi ta'nda' būd Musu' itū.* When the sun sets, Musu' Peak here can still be seen. (*cf:* **sobang**)

**s'ddopan** *n.* 1) West, as the direction where the sun sets. *Tulaknu tudju s'ddopan sagō' baliyu habagat. Bang binusay ka, abinasa ka.* Your departure heading is southwest, but the wind is the southwest monsoon. You will be worn out paddling. 2) The part of the Sulu Archipelago which lies to the south-west of Jolo Island, often glossed as south. *Ata'u amantak saga a'a man s'ddopan.* The people from Southwest Sulu know how to cast spells.

**pas'ddopan llaw** *n. phrase* The period of time after sunset.

**s'gga** *v. intr. aN-* To become satiated, gorged with food. *An'gga' deyom b'ttongku, aheka bay takakanta daing. Sōng-sōng na ap'ddi'.* My stomach is gorged, we ate a lot of fish. It will soon be painful. *Ya maumu magkamatay daing, an'gga he' kinakanna.* That's what fish often die of, they became gorged with food. *An'gga b'ttongna, a'sso he' kinakan, mbal makahinansong sala, subay kinallusan maka luwag, sinungi'an ni lowang.* His stomach is gorged, full of food, kind of unable to breathe, [the mass] having to be pressed hard with a ladle and excreted down a hole. (*cf:* **s'ppol 1**; *Thesaurus:* **kiyomol, k'mmol, l'sso**)

**s'ggit** *n.* 1) Rubbish of various kinds, including fragments of food, dust, shavings, flotsam. *Aniya' s'ggit bay sapuhannu subu si'.* You swept some trash away this morning. (*cf:* **kasob, sagbot 1**) 1.1) *v. intr. aN-* To produce rubbish. *Ōy, da'a ka an'ggit mailu.* Hey, don't create rubbish there. 1.2) *v. advrs. ka-...-an* To be covered with rubbish. *Kasagbotan, sali' kas'ggitan.* Overgrown with weeds, like being covered with rubbish.

**s'ggung** *n.* 1) The smell of burning food. 1.1) *adj. a-* Smelling burnt, of food. *As'ggung bang daing bin'lla bo' atigang na bohe'.* Boiled fish smells unpleasant when the water dries out.

**s'llad** *var. of* **sanglad**

**s'llang₁** *n.* Open sea; an expanse of ocean not enclosed or interrupted by islands. (*Thesaurus:* **kablangan, kaladjun, dilaut, timbang₂**)

**s'llang₂** *var. of* **tehe'-tehe'-s'llang**

**s'llap₁** *v. tr. -an* To mend a hole in something woven, as a mat, a basket, a fish-trap, or woven walling. (*Thesaurus:* **bubul, puna'**)

**s'llap₂** *v. intr. pa-* To squeeze into a restricted space. **pagsaus'llap** *v. intr. aN-* To take up all available space, as people in a crowded room.

**s'lle** *see:* **pags'lle**

**s'lle'** *n.* 1) A replacement or substitute. *S'lle' iya magsultan min si Saul.* He was Saul's replacement as king. 1.1) *v. intr. pa-* To take a turn in doing; to take the place of. *Na, magpatayan pa'in kapanubu'an ina'an-i, aniya' tubu'an baha'u pas'lle'.* Now then, when those generations have died, there will be a new generation taking their place.

**pags'lle'** *v. intr. aN-* 1) To take turns at some activity. *Magdelatan dī sigā karuwangan, mags'lle' sigā, bo' dakayu' du kende tab'lli.* The two of them lick, they take turns, having bought a single candy. *Sarang bang duwangan atawa t'llungan mags'lle'-s'lle' amissala.* It is enough for two or three to take turns in speaking. 1.1) *v. tr.* To have workers take turns or change work shifts. *Pinapags'lle' saga a'a itū maghinang kahaba' bulan.* These men were made to work shift every month.

**s'lle' bale puhu'** (*var.* **s'lle' puhu'**) *phrase* Perish the thought; God forbid. {idiom} *Bang aku saupama amono' a'a, s'lle' bale puhu', alahi aku ni lahat atā.* For example, if I were to kill someone--God forbid--I would run away to a distant place. *Bang saupama, s'lle' puhu', magtiman ka maka h'ndanu.* If for example--perish the thought--you and your wife were to separate. *Bang aku tuhumanu, s'lle' bale puhu', bay angā' ai-ainu bo' halam du isāb sab'nnal-b'nnal, na magsapa kita.* If you accuse me, perish the thought, of having taken things of yours but there is no truth to it, then we swear an oath together. *Bang aku tuhumanu, s'lle' bale puhu', bay angā' ai-ainu bo' halam du isāb sab'nnal-b'nnal, na magsapa kita.* If you accuse me, God forbid, of taking something of yours but it has no truth to it, then we swear an oath. (*syn:* **tingga' dawa**)

**pas'lle'** *v. tr.* To allow someone to have a turn.

**s'lle' puhu'** *var. of* **s'lle' bale puhu'**

**s'lli** *adj. zero* 1) Fond of someone. 1.1) *v. tr. a-, ka-...-an, -an* To love someone dearly. *Kinas'llihan si Ig he' siyakana.* Ig is really loved by her older sister. (*Thesaurus:* **kasi 1, gumbala', lasa₂ 1.1, paganggi**)

**s'llok** 1) *v. tr.* To insert something forcibly, as a harpoon into a shark. 2) *v. intr. pa-* To penetrate sexually. {vulgar}

**s'llokan** *n.* The sharp head of a harpoon. *S'llokan ya paghiyak pahi, kayuna tahinang puhan.* The head of the harpoon is what spears the stingray, its wooden shaft used as a handle. (*Thesaurus:* **ablong, pana' 1, sahapang 1, sangkil 1,**

saubang)

**s'llog** *n.* Current, as the flow of water. *Bang kita ni M'ddas, alandos s'llog mbal kita makasagga'.* When we go to Siasi, the current is strong, we can't go against it. *Nsa' na s'llog, t'bba na. Sōng sōn.* There is no current now, it is low tide. It will soon be the incoming tide. *Aheka daing sikagūngan ameya' palaran ma s'llog, ma ulak.* A great many [dead] fish floating along with the current, with the weed. (*cf:* **abal 1.1, la'ang 1**)

**s'llo'** *see:* **sōng-s'llo'**

**s'llong** *v. tr.* To accept or tolerate something, as a kind of food or a relationship with a specific person. *Mbal tas'llongku kulabutan, mbal ameya' ma heloku.* I can't stand cuttlefish, it disagrees with my saliva. *Minsan danakanku mbal tas'llongku.* Even though he is my brother I can't tolerate him.

**s'llop** *v. tr.* To flood by overflowing, as a low-lying area by high tide; to ship water, of a canoe. *Sīllop luma' mastal, ta'abut na he' tahik.* The teacher's house is flooded, reached by the sea. *Sali' sin'llop, basta aheka duwa'anna angatang.* Like being flooded, whenever it has a lot of freight and is going down. (*Thesaurus:* **dunuk, latap 1.1, sakla'**)

**s'llot** *v. intr. pa-* **1)** To press into a narrow space or gap. *Da'a kam pas'llot-s'llot mailu apa halam aniya' palabayan.* Don't try to squeeze in there because there is no way through. **1.1)** *v. tr. -an* To insert something into a narrow gap. *S'llotin, tau'un sali'.* Insert it into a gap, store it so to speak. (*Thesaurus:* **siklut, sipit-sipit₁, siplit, soksok**) **1.2)** *v. advrs. ka-...-an* To have a gap for squeezing through, of a crowded place. *Mbal kas'llotan pasal inān apa aheka a'a.* No gap can be found through the market-place there because there are a lot of people.

**s'llu** *v. intr. pa-* **1)** To move about unnoticed; to slip through a barrier. *Pas'lluhinbi na aku.* Let me get through. *Wa'i iya pas'llu, sali' l'ngngan tūy. Halam palagid ni aku.* She has gone unnoticed, right on her way. Didn't contact me. *Wa'i pas'llu ni luma' kami, minsan bay hakaku-i buwattē'.* He has slipped into our house, even though I had told him [not to]. *Wa'i an'llu lalipan man lowang.* The centipede has slipped through by way of a hole. (*Thesaurus:* **p'ssut 1, t'lla**) **1.1)** *v. tr.* To evade a restraint. *Paghūg linggi' inān sin'llu na e' banak.* When the seine net was lowered the mullet escaped it. (*Thesaurus:* **lahi₁, l'ppa**)

**s'mba** (*var.* **sumba**) *v. intr. pa-* **1)** To invoke a supernatural being. *Magpas'mba kami ni tampat si Mbo' Di.* We will go to seek help at the shrine of Ancestor Di. *A'a adil niasip du he' Tuhan, a'a mags's'mba.* A righteous person will be heard by God, a person who reveres him. (*Thesaurus:* **sambahayang**) **1.1)** *v. tr.* To seek the attention of a supernatural being.

**s'mbut** *v. intr. pa-/aN-* **1)** To send out shoots, of large seeds such as coconut, or cuttings such as cassava. (*Thesaurus:* **saha' 1.1, saingsing 1, suring₂**) **2)** To cut new teeth (through gums). (*cf:* **empon 1.1**)

**s'mmat** *n.* **1)** A stiffener inserted into flexible material. **1.1)** *v. tr. -an* To insert stiffeners to maintain the correct shape of something woven. *S'mmatta bubu maka pōng tilas, ko' da'a magkamihu pal'ngngan.* We stiffen the fish-trap with strips of bamboo so it doesn't grow more misshapen. *Buwat bubu bang dakananta na, subay sīmmatan ko da'a magpinda matana.* Like a *bubu* trap once we attach the base, it should be stiffened so the mesh size doesn't change.

**s'mmek** *n.* **1)** Clothing; textiles in general. *S'mmek bay pags'mmek, ai-ai bay kapin min manusiya', paglilung e'na.* Clothing that has been worn, anything people have cast off, he sells at bargain prices. *Am'lli aku kakana' s'mmek hinangku badju'.* I am buying some clothing fabric that I will make a blouse of. (*Thesaurus:* **kakana', pamakay, tamongon**) **1.1)** *adj. a-* Wearing clothes; clothed; dressed. *As'mmek ka ba, heyanu ilū.* Get dressed, a boy of your size!

**pags'mmek** *v. intr. aN-* To wear clothing of some sort. *Bang aniya' sehe'ta mags'mmek baha'u bo' kita mags'mmek ndang, agsāy ah'lling sehe'ta mags'mmek baha'u inān, "Ganti'in s'mmeknu ilū."* If one of our group is wearing new clothes but we are wearing worn-out ones, our companion with the new clothes immediately says, "Change your clothes."

**pas'mmek** *v. ditr.* To clothe someone with a specific garment or feature.

**s'mmu** *n.* A facial expression.

**s'mmut** *n.* **1)** Various kinds of small ant. *Ya palele itū saga s'mmut, aheka s'mmut ma gusung.* What's crawling here are ants, lots of ants on the sand. (*spec:* **apipila', lalangga', tagangga', tangangngang**) **1.1)** *v. advrs. -in-* Infested with ants. *Sin'mmutan putu-putu.* The steamed buns are swarming with ants.

**s'mpok** *adj. a-* **1)** Crowded, of a physical space. *Bang as'mpok mbal kita makasikad.* When [the space] is crowded we can't get through. (*Thesaurus:* **digpit 1, sigpit 2, sukad**) **2)** Close, of kin relationship. *Magkaki as'mpok.* Close cousins.

**s'ndal** *v. intr. aN-* **1)** To express displeasure about someone. *Bay ka an'ndal ma si Am insini', halam bay ama'id ni ka'a.* You expressed displeasure about Am earlier, she hadn't got permission from you. (*Thesaurus:* **dugal 1.1, pabukag, pah'lling₂, pamūng-mūng, pugpug 1, tutul**) **1.1)** *v. tr.* To scold or berate someone. *Sin'ndal si Musa e' saga a'a Isra'il.* The Israelites berated Moses.

**pags'ndal** *v. intr. aN-* To be in sharp disagreement with each other. *Buwat kami maka* *siyakaku magbeya' ni pagbalebolan. Sakali itū, mahē' pa'in, mbal iya magbeya' maka aku, subay magbeya' maka disi A. Ameya' isāb aku ma si Im. Na mags'ndal kami.* Like my older brother and I going together to the volleyball court. Well once there, he didn't go with me, he had to go with Al and his group. I went with Im. So we were at loggerheads with each other. *Mags'ndal, sali' mbal magbeya' gara' sigā duwangan inān.* They are disagreeing with each other, as though their goals are not in agreement.

**s'nnad** *v. tr.* -an To borrow something other than cash, leaving something valuable as security. *Buwat kita angindam pelang aheya, bo' pelangta ariki'. Pelangta itū ya pan'nnad pelang aheya.* For example, we are going to borrow a large canoe, and ours is small. Our canoe is what we leave as security for the large one. (*Thesaurus:* **indam, sambi' 1.1, sanda'-sanda', utang 1.1**)

**s'nnay** *adj. a-* Lacking strength; weak or slow. *Saga a'a as'nnay makapah'llingan di sigām, "Aga'os na aku!"* Weak people saying of themselves, "I can overcome!" (*Thesaurus:* **dome-dome, layu-layu, longkoy, summil**)

**s'nnok** *v. intr. pa-* To avoid or dodge by moving to one side. *Bang kita pareyo' min tandawan subay pas'nnok minnē' bo' mbal taluwa'.* When we go down via the window we should move sideways so we don't get hit with something. *Buwat kami bay magsuntuk, makas'nnok aku, halam aku taluwa'.* Like when we were boxing. I was able to dodge and I wasn't hit. (*Thesaurus:* **salema' 1, sigay 1, simay₂, sulekma'**)

**s'nnung** *adj. a-* 1) Swimming near the surface with head appearing. 1.1) *v. intr. pa-* To break the surface, of a swimming fish.

**s'nsong** *v. tr.* To caulk or plug up a gap, as a leak in a pot or a crack in a canoe. *Yuk kallo', "S'nsongku maka tuka'ku."* Said the heron, "I will plug the hole with my beak." *S'nsongunbi lowang pelang ilū, ilu na al'ssu'.* Caulk the holes of the canoe there, it's leaking. *Sīnsong na pa'in pelang, sīnsong na pa'in apa halam aniya' bayan.* The canoe is caulked and caulked because there is no [other] transportation. (*Thesaurus:* **gagā, tambal₂**)

**s'ngkol** *n.* 1) The thwart of a canoe; a bulkhead in a larger vessel. (*cf:* **g'ppang**) 1.1) *v. tr.* To divide into sections by thwarts or bulkhead. *Ya kumpit inān bay sin'ngkol mpat huwang.* That *kumpit* has been divided by bulkheads into four sections.

**s'ngngal** (var. **singal**) *v. tr.* -an To insert a wedge into or under a workpiece to facilitate work on it. *Siningalan kayu bo' ahāp l'ngngan tanok.* The wood is wedged apart so the splitting wedge will move easily. *Sin'ngngalan ahulug maka kayu.* Wedged apart first with a piece of wood. (*Thesaurus:* **biggal 1, bulatuk, pahanggal, tanok 1**)

**s'ngngat₁** *v. tr.* To open something up by splitting.

(*cf:* **buka'₃**)

**s'ngngat₂** var. of **sangat**

**s'ngngel** *v. intr. pa-* 1) To cry audibly without tears, as a child fussing. *Pas'ngngel dangan bang b'llihannu dangan.* One child will fuss if you buy something for the other. (*cf:* **tangis 1.1;** *Thesaurus:* **langan₁, mmaw 1, pagle'eng, unga'**) 1.1) *v. tr.* -an To cry for something not granted. *Aniya' sin'ngngelan e'na, arai' ta'nda'na ina'na lum'ngngan.* She is crying for something, maybe she saw her mother going some place.

**pags'ngngel** *v. intr. aN-* To fuss continually, of an infant. *Ē rāng, mailu ka mags'ngngel-s'ngngel.* Go on honey, cry away there.

**s'ngngog** *adj. a-* Nasal in speech, due to a defect or by habit. (*Thesaurus:* **kemol, ponga', tanga'₂, terol**)

**s'ngngot₁** 1) *adj. a-* Irritable. *As'ngngot si Pi, mbal ahāp atayna.* Pi is irritable, not in a good mood. *Mbal kapah'llingan, as'ngngot, magtūy ta'ā'na p'ddi'-atay.* Can't even be spoken to, in a bad mood, promptly gets angry. (*Thesaurus:* **kalintaw, dole' 1, dugal 1, giyagas, p'ggot-p'ggot, sunggud**) 1.1) *v. advrs. ka-...-an* To be seriously annoyed about something. 2) *v. tr. a-, ka-..-an, -an* To take offense at something. *Magb'ngkol, aniya' kinas'ngngotan he'na.* He is seething, taking offense about something.

**s'ngngot₂** var. of **songot**

**s'ppal** *adj. a-* Coarse and grainy in texture, of cooked starch foods. *Gōm buwas pai, as'ppal buwas gandum itū.* Real rice is preferable, this corn rice is grainy. *Bang kita asaki bo' aniya' pamakan kita he' matto'ata kinakan ai-ai na, t'bbu ka, saging ka, daing ka, sali' as'ppal ma bowa'ta.* When we are sick and our parents feed us any kind of food, whether sugar cane, bananas, or fish, it tastes sort of grainy in our mouth. (*Thesaurus:* **kasap, gasang, l'ngnges 1.1**)

**s'ppaw** (var. **sipaw**) *v. intr. pa-* To be too many or too much for the space available. *Manusiya' pasipaw, aheka na to'ongan.* Overflowing with people, a great many. *Pasipaw, buwat sīn mbal taruwa' min bulsa. Sali' pabūd ai-ai ma tau'an.* Spilling out, like money that can't be carried in a pocket. Like things piled up in a storage space. (*cf:* **lasay**)

**s'ppe'** 1) *v. tr.* To cut something from a main part, especially of a hand of bananas. (*cf:* **s'kkat 1.1**) 2) *clf.* Count word for hands of bananas.

**s'ppol** (var. **s'ppul**) *adj. a-* 1) Having more than can fit into the available space. *Sali' as'ppol deyom bowa'na, mbal makalapal.* His mouth stuffed full, unable to speak. *As'ppol ūngna angkan kahunitan magnapas.* His nose is blocked which is why he has difficulty breathing. (*cf:* **s'gga;** *Thesaurus:* **p'nno' 1.1, sangkad, selot 1**) 1.1) *v. intr. pa-* To press into a restricted space. *Hal pas'ppul ma bowa' lawang, halam aniya' palabayan.* Simply crowded into the doorway, no way through.

**s'ppu** *v. tr.* To display the personal or moral characteristics of someone else, especially a forebear. *Bang matto'ata ahāp inān, bo' kita inān magbono', mbal kita an'ppu matto'ata.* If our parents were good, and we are always fighting, then we aren't following the ways of our parents. *Ya sin'ppu e' si Jy mma'na.* It is his father that Jy takes after. (*cf:* **tubus₂ 1.1**)

**s'ppul** *var. of* **s'ppol**

**s'ppun** *n.* 1) Nasal mucus. *S'ppunan deyom ūngna, ap'nnot.* His nose has mucus in it, it's stuffed up. (*Thesaurus:* **p'nnot, ulapay₁**) 1.1) *v. advrs.* *-in-* To be suffering from a blocked nose.

**s'pput** *v. intr.* *pa-* To splash or spray onto something, as water into canoe. *Pas'pput tahik ni pelang, apa goyak.* The sea splashes over into the canoe because it is rough. (*Thesaurus:* **appu', sasay, sauk 2, suput₁**)

**s'ssag** *n.* 1) An announcement to a community regarding some event. *Aniya' s'ssag magpiha, aniya' s'ssag magpabā'.* There are announcements about searching, and there are announcements that inform. 1.1) *v. tr.* To communicate widely. *Ma aniya' alungay an'ssag kita, atilaw kita sangkahāpan ni kalūnganta.* When something is missing we communicate widely, inquiring diligently of our community. *An'ssag kita bang ganta' aniya' saki ma baranta. Pina'an kita atawa pina'an, bang ai makakalna' ma kita.* We communicate widely when, say, we have a personal illness. We go here and there, [asking] what caused it. *S'ssagta ya bay pangkat dahū, bang iya bay makataluwa' iya. Na aminta-minta.* We inquire widely of former ritual ancestors, if one [of them] was the one who brought this on him [the patient]. Then we make a petition. *S'ssagun kamemon kaluma'an aniya' palkala'.* Tell the whole village there is something important going on. (*Thesaurus:* **hula-layag 1**)

**s'ssok** *n.* A species of house lizard; a gecko. (*syn:* **pinit**)

**s'ssol₁** *v. tr.* To trim the hair of eyebrows, forehead or nape; to shape the hairline. *Subay sin'ssol bang buli' k'llong. Sinoso'an itū bang ma lendo' atawa ma kilay.* If it's the nape of the neck it should be *s'ssol* [shaved]. If it is the forehead or eyebrows it should *soso'* [trimmed]. (*Thesaurus:* **bagoggol 1.1, bagong₂, himangot 1.1, p'ngngot 1.2, soso'**)

**s'ssol₂** *adj.* *a-* 1) Combined into a single group. 1.1) *v. tr.* To move things or small children into one place. *Sīssol anak daing ni deyom logo.* The young fish are driven into a trap [at the end of the fence]. *Bang angalakod, aniya' ampasna ati sin'ssol daing.* With the *lakod* system there is a fence trap and fish are herded into it. *Bang onde'-onde' tas'ssol, bang matto'a mbal tas'ssolta apa ata'u amikilan.* Children can be herded, [but] we can't herd adults because they can think for themselves. *Bang aku anapuhan s'ggit, s'ssolku*

*maka sasapu ko' atimuk.* When I sweep up trash, I bring it together with a broom so it is collected. (*Thesaurus:* **illig, lakod**)

**s'ssop** *v. tr.* To suck something, as candy in the mouth or a painful area on the skin. *Dakayu' du bowa'ta pangandelatta, pan'ssopta, bo' pa'in saddī du ōnna.* Just one mouth, for both licking and sucking, yet they have different words. (*cf:* **duru' 1.2**; *Thesaurus:* **dutdut, ligid₁, tamus**)

**sōb** *adj.* *a-/-an* Having a liking for a specific food or drink. *Mbal aku sōban ma kinakanbi, apa angutta' aku.* I have no taste for your food, because I vomit [from it]. *Asōb aku amangan wanni amata'.* I am really fond of eating unripe odorous mango. (*Thesaurus:* **suwak 1, tahud**)

  **kasōban** *n.* A craving. *Adjalin aku pagkakan ahāp nanamna ya kasōbanku.* Prepare me some of the tasty food that I crave.

**sobak** *adj.* *a-* Easily split off, as dry firewood, or coconut meat from its shell.

**sobad** *n.* Mackerel tuna or bonito, coarse fish of the tuna species. *Euthynnus affinis.* (*Thesaurus:* **mangku', panit, poyan**)

**sobang** *v. intr.* *pa-* To rise above the horizon, of the sun or moon. (*cf:* **s'ddop**)

  **kasobangan** *clf.* Count word for the nights in a lunar month. *Ta'abut pa'in sangpū' kasobangan ma bulan panagna'an ma tahun inān...* When it came to the tenth moon-night of the first month of that year...

  **sobangan** *n.* Sunrise; the east as a location or direction.

**sobo'** *v. tr.* *-an* To feed a child or invalid with one's fingertips. *Sinobo'an itū tōng tanganta.* This word means feeding using our fingertips. *Mbal makapakanan dīna, subay sinobo'an.* Unable to feed himself, he has to be fed by hand. (*cf:* **dulis**)

  **pagsobo'** *v. tr.* To eat one's food using the fingertips. (*cf:* **lokom**)

**sobot** *adj.* *a-* Troubled in one's thinking. *Asobot pangannalta.* We are confused in our thinking.

**sobsob** *v. intr.* *pa-* 1) To soak or press into something. *Aheka bohe' mariyata' karut. Pagbabas ulan, na pasobsob na.* Lots of water on the sack. When the rain ends, then it soaks in. *Pasobsob kōkna ni tana'.* His head presses into the soil. (*cf:* **pulag-pulag**) 1.1) *v. advrs.* *-in-* Affected by the penetration of something. *Al'kkas sinobsob si La bang taluwa' llaw.* La quickly feels the inward effects when the sun strikes her. (*cf:* **k'lli'**) 2) To enter into a person's mind or being. *Pasobsobun pandu'ku itū ni deyom pikilanbi.* Let this teaching of mine penetrate into your minds. *Bang kita nihinang-hinang, tinagna'an kita bang magsusa-susa deyom atayta. Na bang pasobsob na, ya na saga magolang kita.* When a curse is put on us it begins with us being somewhat distressed. Then when it takes hold, that's when we shout out.

**sokal** 1) *n.* Sugar. *Ai kabaya'annu, sokal pilun atawa* *sokal budbud?* What do you want, fine brown sugar or powdered sugar? *Am'lli gi' aku sokal paglamudku maka buwas bo' amamis.* I will just buy some sugar for me to mix with rice so it will be sweet. (*Thesaurus:* **dipinaw, pilun**) **1.1)** *v. tr.* *-an* To sweeten something with sugar. *Gandum nili'is, ubus nili'is ī', na base'-base'ta maka bohe'. Na amene' na kita, sokalanta, lahinganta. Apuwas ī'-i, ni'isi ni kuwitna gandum abō' bin'lla na.* The corn is grated, then after being grated we wet it a little with water. Then we choose, whether to add sugar or [grated] coconut. After that, it is put into the corn skin and boiled. **2)** *v. tr.* *-an* To influence someone by being sweet or loving to them.

**sokal-ba'ung** *n.* The coarse dark variety of sugar known as Muscovado.

**sokal-budbud** *n.* Caster sugar, a superfine variety.

**sokal-tibu'uk** *n.* Lump or cake sugar, an unrefined local variety.

**sokal-tigtig** *n.* Coarse sugar produced by chipping or crushing local cake sugar.

**sokal-sokal** *n.* The Jamaican cherry and its sweet fruit. (*syn:* **datilis**)

**sokat₁** *n.* **1)** A demand or specification; an addition to bride-wealth required by the elders of a potential bride. *Haka'inbi aku bang pila ungsudna maka sokatna ati akuhanku du.* Tell me what the price is of her dowry and her specified gifts, and I will agree to it. *Aniya' magtinabawan, sambatan Ingglis 'complete'. M'ssa' aniya' sokat-manokat. Bang t'llu hatus, t'llu hatus du.* There are some who follow the *tabawan* practise, 'complete' as they say in English. No demand for this and that. If ₱300 is agreed on, then it is exactly ₱300. (*Thesaurus:* **anyak-anyak, tugila'** 1.1, **tutat** 1.1) **1.1)** *v. tr.* To specify certain gifts in addition to the main bride-gift. *Impasal anaknu bay kinawin, makaluwas na bay sinokatnu-ī' luma' mahāp-i.* With regard to your daughter who is now married now, what you required, a fine house, will now come to light. *Si Mi ya bay ngā'nu h'nda, sinokatan kapanyapan bulawan.* Mi, whom you have taken to be your wife, gold utensils were specified for her. *Bang aniya' anaknu d'nda, subay ka anokat luma' ahāp.* If you have a daughter, you should require a fine house as bride-gift.

**pagsokat bissala** *v. intr.* *aN-* To make demands of each other. {idiom}

**sokat₂** *var. of* **saukat**

**sokong** *n.* A species of fish, a snapper similar in appearance to kutambak.

**soksok** *v. intr.* *pa-* To crawl into a confined space, as an insect under a rock. *Wa'i pasoksok ni deyo' kantil.* Crawled right under the bed. (*Thesaurus:* **siklut, sipit-sipit₁, siplit, s'llot** 1.1)

**sōd** **1)** *v. intr.* *pa-* To enter an enclosed space; to join a group. *Pasōd kām ni deyom.* Come on in.

*Pinagtimuk-timukan si Mām bang pasōd ni deyom tinda.* Ma'am is crowded when she goes into a store. *Bang kami magbono' maka si Hu pasōd si Ji ameya'-meya' anabang siyalina.* When we fight with Hu, Ji joins in to help his younger brother. (*Thesaurus:* **asok** 1, **deyom** 1.1, **isi₁** 1.1) **1.1)** *n.* Things (especially fish) that have entered a trap. *Ta'nda'ku na bubu. Aniya' sōdna.* I can see the fish trap. It has something in it. **1.2)** *v. tr.* To reach a goal or place by entering. *Bang aniya' sīnku anōd aku sini.* If I have money I will go to the movies [lit. enter the movie]. *Bilahi aku anōd sundalu.* I want to join the military. *Subay na sinōd ampa nihella' bubu.* The fish trap should have been entered [by fish] before being hauled up. *Aheka a'a magda'awa ma Sisangat. Ahunit kala'anan minsan sinōd he' mundu, malaingkan talalat.* A lot of people in Sisangat argue [against an edict]. They are difficult to remove even when invaded by bandits. They can be relocated, however. **1.3)** *v. ditr.* To move something into a container. *Sōrin s'mmek ilū ni deyom luma'.* Bring those clothes inside the house. **2)** *v. advrs.* *-in-* Entered or possessed by an emotion or spirit being. *Sinōd kita sasat, sinōd kita he' tāw. Minsan kita pasekot ni pahi bo' hiyakta, asā'.* We were filled with disquiet, filled with fear. Even though we were close to the ray and speared it, we were innacurate. *A'a inān sinōd saitan.* That person is possessed by a saitan spirit.

**pagsōd-addat** *v. intr.* *aN-* To be on informal friendly terms. (*cf:* **pagsaumbibi**; *Thesaurus:* **pagda'atay, pagsamod**)

**sōd-dingin** *v. advrs.* *-in-* To have a fit or seizure (lit. to be penetrated by cold). {idiom} *Sinōd-dingin a'a inān, wa'i amaka'at ai-ai. Da'a kām pasekot.* That man is having a seizure, destroying this and that. Don't approach him.

**pasōd** *v. tr.* To bring something inside; to insert something.

**sogo'** *var. of* **saguwā'**

**sogo'-sogo'** *n.* A species of vine from which red and black seeds are obtained.

**sogot** *var. of* **sagut**

**sogsog** *v. intr.* *pa-* **1)** To persist in one's commitment, as to God, a sweetheart, an ambition. *Jari itū pahogot sigā ma iman, sali' pasogsog ni Tuhan.* So they became firm in faith, like adhering to God. *Pasogsog kita to'ongan, subay ngā'ta.* We persist very much, we must get it. (*Thesaurus:* **podlongan, taggu₂** 1.1, **togol** 1, **tukid** 1) **1.1)** *v. tr.* To make someone the object of one's persistence. *Pehē' na pa'in kitā, buwat sali' pareyo', bo' mbal bilahi pareyo'an, sogsogta na pa'in. Kalu ma'ase'.* We keep going there, sort of humbling ourselves, but the one we show humility to is not willing, we keep on persisting. Perhaps he will be merciful.

**pasogsogan** *n.* Something that can be clung to.

**soha'** *n.* A pole; a mooring stake. (*Thesaurus:* **bale₃ 1, sambuwang, tungkud 1**)

    **pagsoha'** *v. intr. aN-* To move a canoe along by poling. *Tahan dakuman kami amole', magsoha' na, magpuwa' bāt na.* When we were ready at last to go home, [we] were poling the canoe, gathering trepang.

**soho'** (var. **sō'**) *v. tr.* To give someone instructions; to send someone. A: *"Sai bay anoho' ka'a?"* B: *"Bay aku sinō' pi'itu he' si Ag."* A: "Who told you to come?" B: "Ag sent me here." *Sinō' aku amowahan ka'a daing itū.* I have been told to bring this fish for you. (*Thesaurus:* **da'ak, gandahan, hilag, pagmanda 1, sūg-sūg, uldin 1**)

    **pagsoho'** *v. intr. aN-* To order people about. *Kami itū pinagsoho'-soho' na pa'in.* We are continually being given things to do.

    **panoho'an** *n.* Instructions; commandments.

    **sosoho'an** *n.* Someone who is sent; a messenger; a servant. (*Thesaurus:* **ata, banyaga' 1, bata'an**; *syn:* **dara'akan**)

    **tagsoho'an** *n.* A person with the right to give orders.

**sohonay** *v. intr. pa-/-um-* To go in a downstream direction; to go with the current. *Buwat magabay, abayta man diyata'an, kita itū sumohonay.* Like when we are working as a fleet, our companions are on the upstream side, we go downstream.

    **sohonayan** *n.* The area downstream from a reference point. (*Thesaurus:* **diyata'an₁ 1**)

**sō'** var. of **soho'**

**so'** var. of **sa'**

**so'on** *v. intr. pa-* To replicate the vowels and possibly some consonants of someone's personal name, usually that of a relative. *Ina'an paso'on ma si'itna.* There replicating the name of his uncle.

    **pagso'on** *v. intr. aN-* **1)** To have names with some rhyming vowels and matching consonants. **1.1)** *v. tr.* To give children names that sound similar as to vowels and some consonants. *Subay pinagso'on ōn sigā, buwat si Alamjari, si Jamjahari maka si Billari.* Their names [of the children] should sound similar, [names] like Alamjari, Jamjahari and Billari.

**solab₁** (var. **sulab**) *n.* **1)** The cutting edge, as the tip of a knife or the point of a spear. *Sahapang itū t'llu heka solabna.* A fish spear has three points. *Ya solabna dī basi', ya buhatna saga pitu' kilu.* Its blade pure steel, its weight about 7 kilos. (*ant:* **salig₁**) **1.1)** *v. intr. pa-* To penetrate flesh with a pointed implement. *Da'a ka aoseg, bo' mbal makasulab, bang ka sali' atugsuk.* Don't move about, lest [you] get pierced, sort of skewered. *Bay pareyo' ipalku ni luma' mato'aku. Makasulab ni tape'na kayu an'ngge.* My brother-in-law went down into my mother-in-law's house. A piece of wood that was sticking up pierced his foot. **2)** A

steel-tipped spike used for removing the husk of a coconut. *Solab, ya pamunut lahing. Solab,* a tool for de-husking coconuts.

**solab₂** *v. tr.* To say something openly, in the hearing of the person involved. (*ant:* **salig₃**; *Thesaurus:* **baran₂ 1.1, pagtampal**)

**solag 1)** *n.* A piece; a segment. **2)** *clf.* Count word for members of a set or collection. *Ma aku dansolag.* One piece for me. *Duwansolag ya pinsil si Sel, wa'i tinangkaw nnom. Bay walu' solag hekana.* There are two of Sir's pencils [remaining], six have been stolen. They had been eight in number.

    **ma solagan** *adv. phrase* By the piece or segment. *Billi ma solagan.* Bought by the piece. *Ubi-sowa, a'aslag solaganna.* Snake yam, its pieces quite big.

**solekma'** var. of **sulekma'**

**solembang** *n.* Group singing.

**solempat** var. of **sulempat**

**soleng₁** *n.* A species of bird.

**soleng₂** var. of **suling₁**

**solenggang** *n.* A fleshy, jelly-like marine plant. (*syn:* **lera-lera₁**)

**soleyab** var. of **suleyab**

**sollet** *n.* **1)** A loincloth. (*syn:* **sampellot**) **1.1)** *v. intr. a-* To wear a loincloth. *Asollet aku apa halam aniya' papantalunku.* I will wear a loincloth because I have nothing to use as trousers.

**solpan** *n.* Shorts (clothing). (*Thesaurus:* **hakpan, sauwal**)

**solsol** *v. tr. -an* To file the tips of upper teeth to make them even in length. (*Thesaurus:* **lagnas, pangtad, tā'**)

**sombeng** (var. **sembong**) *adj. a-* **1)** Chipped along a thin edge, as of a knife blade, a plate, or the flange of a seashell. *Asombeng mata kapa, sali' du maka t'bbe'.* The edge of the axe is chipped, the same as being *t'bbe'. Buwat lai' bang aniya' ala'an man bihingna, asombeng. Bang ma kaheya'an niōnan abila' na.* Like a plate that has something removed from its edge. If it is large it is said to be broken. (*cf:* **t'bbe' 1**) **2)** A congenital fissure of the upper lip; a harelip.

**sōn** *n.* The current created by an incoming tide. *Alanat pahāp s'llog sōn ilū, at'ggol pabīng.* This incoming tide is moving slowly, it'll be a while before it goes back. (*Thesaurus:* **la'ang 1.1**)

**sondong** *v. intr. pa-* To lean over at the top, of something flexible. *Buwat diyata' kayu pakalluk, atawa simbōng pasondong ni dahū'an.* Like the top of a tree bending over, or a hair knot falling forward. (*Thesaurus:* **kopeng, lapping-lapping, toyok**)

**sonson** *adj. a-* Placed together so that there are no gaps, of woven materials. *Pasonsonun tepo bang ka anganom.* Make the mat tight when you are weaving. (*Thesaurus:* **kempot, lapat 1.1, pagd'ppak 1, saplut₂**)

**sōng₁ 1)** *n.* That which is ahead or still to happen;

the future. *Nda'un ba ma sōngnu inān.* Look at what's ahead of you. **2)** *ptl.* Future tense marker; prospective aspect marker, indicating that the state or action named is about to begin. *Angandom, sōng ulan.* It is becoming overcast, there will soon be rain. *A: "Atahak na, Arung?"* B: *"Sōng na."* A: "Is it cooked, Oldest Daughter?" B: "Almost." *Sōng pa'in kami ahinang luma', bay kami kamatayan.* When we were about to be building a house, we had a death in the family. (*Thesaurus:* **baya-baya pa'in**) **2.1)** *v. intr. pa-* To elapse, of time. *Buwat aniya' anunangan d'nda, araran magl'ngngan ni luma' d'nda hē'. Pasōng-pasōng llaw alahang na magl'ngngan.* Like someone courting his fiancée, always going to the woman's house. As time goes on he rarely goes there.

**sōng-sōng₁** *adv.* Adverb indicating immediacy of sequence; about to. *Sōng-sōng pa'in kami magkawin, amatay tunangku.* When we were about to get married, my sweetheart died. *Sōng-sōng anahun ya pagl'kkatta.* Our separation is almost a year in duration. *Sōng-sōng na pa'in kami amole'.* When we were about to go home.

**pagkasosōng** *v. intr. aN-* To be moving forward to some future time.

**sinōng** *adj.* zero Future; a future occasion or time.

**sinosōng** *n.* A coming or future time.

**sōng₂** *v. intr. pa-* **1)** To move forward; to advance towards something. *Pasōng kita pina'an abō' ta'nda'ta.* Let's go further over there so we can see. *Aho', pasōng kām ni t'ngnga'.* Yes, come right on in to the middle [of the house]. *Magpali kita bang pa'in ka makasōng.* We use the tacking strategy as long as we make headway. (*ant:* **suhut**; *Thesaurus:* **lalga, lanjal 1.1, laus 1, unjal**) **1.1)** *v. tr. -an* To move something along, of a physical object or a topic of conversation. *Sōngin kono' asin ilū.* Please pass the salt there. *Gapi'ku ka'a, ka'a ilū sōnganku magbissala. Aku itū angagad. Bay ka tambahanku, mbal salat.* You are my supporter [before the magistrate], you are the one I have go in front to do the talking, I just wait. I have recompensed you, no small amount. *Bay pabiyalbi kapanōng tanganku ni ka'am.* You ignored the holding out of my hand to you [i.e. in friendship]. (*cf:* **ndiya**)

**kasōngan** *n.* **1)** Progress; future well-being. *Halam aniya' kasōnganna bang buwattē' na pa'in kaulpi'il.* He will have no future if his behavior continues like that. *Kuttung iya maghinang, halam aniya' kasōnganna.* He worked hard but made no progress. *Ya pinapata kulisna bang buwattitu, ai kasōnganna ahāp-ala'at.* It's her palm lines being like that which are studied, whether her future will be good or bad. **2)** An increase in value. *Ya du bay kasōnganna sangpū' aka lima.* That's exactly what the increase was, fifteen [pesos].

**pagsōng-suhut** *v. intr. aN-* To alternate between moving forward and drawing back.

**pagsōng-suwa'** *v. intr. aN-* To grow in diverse directions rather then being parallel, as teeth, feathers or leaves. (*Thesaurus:* **julenget, pagsalisi, pagsuwa'-s'llo', sulangat**)

**sōng-sebog** *n.* Alternating forward and back movement.

**pagsōng-sebog** *v. intr. aN-* To alternate between moving forward and drawing back.

**sōng-s'llo'** *v. intr. pa-* To grow out in diverse directions, as teeth or feathers.

**sōng-sōng₂** *v. tr. -an* To move something ahead of its proper order. *Anōng-nōngan iya dīna.* He pushes himself ahead [of his peers]. (*Thesaurus:* **pagmuna-muna**)

**pasōng** *v. tr.* To move something further along.

**pasōng-sōng** *adv.* Later on. (*syn:* **gana-gana 1**)

**songab** (var. **sengab**) *n.* **1)** A hollow under an overhanging rock; a cave or semi-cave. (*Thesaurus:* **kehe 1, lowang 1, p'llong**) **1.1)** *v. intr. pa-* To open up a cave-like space under an overhanging rock.

**songkelang** var. of **sungkelang**

**songget** *adj. a-* Torn by snagging on a sharp projection, of cloth.

**songot** (var. **s'ngngot₂**) *n.* **1)** Chronic breathing difficulty; asthma. *Isi p'nnu ya pagtambal s'ngngot, kinakan.* Turtle meat is used to treat breathing sickness, it's eaten. **1.1)** *v. advrs. -in-* Affected by asthma or other breathing complaint. *Aniya' sin'ngngot kuting, subay kita da'a pasekot sabab makalamin.* There are cats with breathing problems, we should not go near because it is contagious

**sopbol** *n.* A softball; the game of softball.

**pagsopbol** *v. intr. aN-* To play softball. *Bang kami magsopbol aku amega dahū.* When we play softball I bat first.

**sopena** *v. tr.* To summon someone to appear before a court of law. (*cf:* **tawag-saksi'**)

**sopon** *n.* A baby's feeding bottle. *Aruru' na si Lo sopon.* Lo is now drinking from a feeding bottle. (*cf:* **paruru'an**)

**sore** *n.* The Black-spot and Blue-lined surgeonfish. *Acanthurus spp.* (*gen:* **kumay**)

**sorekang** *n.* A crab-claw sail. (*syn:* **banog**)

**sorok** *v. tr. -an* To push something firmly into a space. *Buwat si Ina' bay nilango tingga'-tingga' lumahan, akansing emponna. Bay sinorokan banglut.* Like the time when Mom was poisoned from eating false-mackerel, and her teeth clamped tight together. They forced in a piece of *banglut* [a medicinal plant]. *Bang aniya' luma' ya akulang babagna, sorokanta kayu supaya ahogot.* When there is a house whose cross-beams are insufficient, we force wood [into place] so it is firm.

**sorol** *v. tr. a-, ka-..-an, -an* To be emotionally upset about something. *Sai kasorolannu?* Who are you troubled about?

**pagsorol** *v. intr. aN-* To be stressed emotionally.

*Magsorol iya itū sabab anakna.* She is emotionally stressed because of her child. (*Thesaurus:* **kibad atay, sukkal 1, susa 1**)

**soroy** *v. tr. -an* To peddle goods for sale.

**pagsoroy** *v. tr. -an* To peddle goods for sale. *Sinoho' magsoroyan daing ni deyom tabu'.* Told to sell the fish in the market. *Sūng, magsoroy kita ni deyom katindahan.* Let's go, we'll peddle [stuff] in the shopping area. (*Thesaurus:* **dagang, lilung, litu, pab'lli, pa'andag 1, samsuy**)

**sosob** *v. intr. pa-* To flow (the incoming phase), of tide. *Pasosob tahik kaleya, a'nso' na. Bay t'bba, pasosob, palalom.* The sea is flowing shorewards, it is high. It was low, it flowed in, it became deep. (*Thesaurus:* **daka', lalom₁ 2, l'kkab, nso', tambang₁ 1**)

**sosok** *v. tr. -an* To shape or smooth something with an adze. *Busay dakayu' ilū, ya bay sinosokan.* That other paddle, the one that has been shaped. (*Thesaurus:* **basbas, katam 1.1, kirus 1.1, saplung 1.1, sapsap₂**)

**sosokan** *n.* A broad, chisel-like tool mounted on a long shaft. (*Thesaurus:* **likup 1, pa'at 1, patuk, sakal, sangkap 1**)

**sosoho'an** (derivative of **soho'**) *n.* Someone who is sent; a messenger; a servant. *Jari ai-ai tatugsuk e' sosoho'an inān, ai na ka ma kaha' atawa ma kaldero, ya na suku' imam.* So whatever was speared by those workers, either in the pan or the pot, that was the priest's share. *Angay tinunu' e' saga sosoho'annu tana' pagtanomanku pai?* Why do your servants burn the land in which I have planted rice? (*Thesaurus:* **ata, banyaga' 1, bata'an;** *syn:* **dara'akan**).

**soso'** *v. tr. -an* To shave the eyebrows and browline of a girl in preparation for her wedding. *Bang aku ameya' ni pagkawinan subay aku sinoso'an kilayku.* When I go along to the wedding my eyebrows should be shaved. (*Thesaurus:* **bagoggol 1.1, bagong₂, himangot 1.1, p'ngngot 1.2, s'ssol₁**)

**soso'-legong** *v. tr.* To shape the hairline level across around the brow.

**soso'-t'ngge** *v. tr.* To form a decorative curve in the hairline high on each side of the forehead.

**sosop** var. of **kalitan-sosop**

**sowa** *n.* A snake (a generic term for both land and sea species).

**sowa-ambaw** *n.* A species of land snake.

**sowa-bala-bala** (var. **bala-bala**) *n.* A species of sea snake.

**sowa-basagan** (var. **basagan**) *n.* A species of snake, venomous, reportedly found both in the sea and on land. *Sowa basagan, bang kita kineket subu bo' halam katawalan, ta'abut pa'in waktu luhul amatay kita.* The *basagan* snake, if we are bitten in the morning and not treated, then by afternoon prayer time we'll be dead.

**sowa-buway** *n.* A species of land snake.

**sowa-d'ppong** (var. **sowa-dopong**) *n.* A species of

land snake, possibly a tree viper.

**sowa-lokay** (var. **lokay₂**) *n.* A species of land snake, small, bright green in color, commonly found in the foliage of coconut palms. *Ya sowa-sowa lokay, ya magaddung, mariki'-diki' ilū.* The little *lokay* snake, the green one, it's small.

**sowa-mamatun** (var. **mamatun**) *n.* A species of land snake no longer found in the Siasi area.

**sowa-mamukan** (var. **mamukan**) *n.* A species of snake, believed to be capable of flight. Found in the sea as well as on land. *Sowa-mamukan, bang taluwa' kōkna paleyang.* If the *mamukan* snake is struck on the head it will fly.

**sowa-panga'an** (var. **panga'an**) *n.* A python, a species of snake said to be found in the sea as well as on land. *Malayopython reticulatus.*

**sowa-pisak** *n.* A mangrove snake, a species found in shallow coastal waters.

**sowa-takot** *n.* A species of sea snake, banded black and white, commonly found sunning on coral outcrops. *fam. Hydrophiidae. Aheka ginisan sowa. Sabab hatina sowa ilu, bang niōnan sowa-takot ilū, na ya ilu makamula.* There are many kinds of snake. By way of explanation, if that snake there is identified, if it is the one called reef-snake, then that is the one to cause serious harm.

**sowa-tangkig** (var. **tangkig**) *n.* A species of sea snake, said to penetrate the anus of children playing in the sea. *Sowa-tangkig bay anuruk iya.* A *tangkig* snake poked up into his bottom.

**sowa-ugtu'-ugtu** (var. **ugtu'-ugtu'**) *n.* A species of sea snake seen inshore, said to penetrate the anus of children playing in the sea.

**sowa-undi'** (var. **undi'**) *n.* A species of sea snake, barred black and white.

**sowa-dopong** var. of **sowa-d'ppong**

**sowang** *n.* A coastal channel running through saltwater swamp forest; a stream or river inland. *Paglinggi' kami, sinusul ma bihing bangkaw Sowang-halo, maī' ma Tapa'an.* When we fish with a trawl net, the mangrove forest fringe at Sowang-halo is followed, there at Tapa'an Island. *Buwat a'a magismagol, baya-baya pa'in sigā ta'abut he' nabal, pinasōd he' sigā nireyom sowang.* Like smugglers, when the naval cutter is about to catch up with them, they get [their boat] into a mangrove channel. (*Thesaurus:* **sapa'**)

**kasowang-sowangan** *n.* A network of channels, as in a mangrove forest. *Palabay kami min kasowang-sowangan.* We passed by way of the channel network.

**soway** *v. tr.* To criticize something. *Bang si Sel maghinang haronan, asidda anoway si Mām.* When Sir makes a ladder Mam really criticizes. *Soway itū sali' hinang mbal kabaya'an, anoway aku. Minsan isāb ahāp, bang mbal ameya' ma atayku sowayku du.* This word *soway* is like some activity that doesn't meet with favor, I criticize. Even if it is good, if it doesn't please me I still criticize it. (*Thesaurus:* **himoway, pastul, poway-poway, sā'₁ 1.3, salba₁, salla'₁ 1.2, salu'-salu'**)

**sowet** *v. tr.* To catch fish by diving from above the surface as kingfishers and some gulls do. *Bakakka ilū anowet daing anahut.* The kingfisher there is diving for little fish.

**ssa₁** (var. **l'ssa**) *n.* 1) Flavor; savor; taste. *Buwattingga ssana?* How is its flavor? *Ala'at ssana bay kinakanku hē'.* The taste of what I just ate was bad. (*Thesaurus:* **nanam 1**) 1.1) *adj.* -an Leaving a taste, as of food previously cooked in the same container. *Bang bay am'lla daing ma kaldero bo' pamasu'an kahawa atawa buwas, l'ssahan. Mbal ala'an.* When fish is cooked in a pot which is then used for boiling coffee or cooking rice, it leaves a fishy taste. Doesn't go away. 1.2) *v. intr.* aN- To have the taste of something. *Ang'ssa tambal tī itu.* This tea has a medicine taste. 1.3) *v. tr.* To try something for savor or temperature. *Ni'ssa nanamna bang buwattingga, ya hē' niōnan mag'ttap-ttap.* Tested how its flavor is, that's called smacking the lips. *Ssata bang apasu' atawa ahaggut.* Let's sample it whether it's hot or cold. (*Thesaurus:* **kinam 1, sulay₁ 2, timtim**)

**ssa₂** *v. tr.* To experience something. *Asāl ta'ssaku ma bulan inān, sinasat aku maka pinaka'at e' mananasat inyawaku.* That month I did in fact experience being tempted and having my spirit damaged by the tempter. (*Thesaurus:* **labay₃, lapa₁, nanam 2, sabi₂**)

**ssa₃** (var. **dda**) *num.* One, the form used in counting and in compounds following the conjunction maka [and]. *Tauppiku llaw maka bulan sampay saga bitu'un sangpū' maka ssa hekana pasujud ni aku.* I dreamed of sun and moon and eleven [ten plus one] stars kneeling to me. *Tinilaw aku bang pila bay pam'lliku. "Sangpū' maka dda," yukku.* I was asked how much I bought it for. "Eleven [lit. ten plus one]," I said. *Angitung aku min ssa.* I count from one. (*Thesaurus:* **da- 1, dakayu'₁ 1, dangan 1, issa, sa-**)

**ka'ssa** *n.* The first item in a series.

**sso** var. of **l'sso**

**ssol** *v. intr.* aN- To make the sound of water in rapid motion, as rain pattering or a kettle coming to the boil. *Tū'na ulan makatauwa' ni lān, niōnan ang'ssol.* The falling of rain on the path, that's called ssol. *Ang'ssol ulan pi'itu. Bang bohe' song angalere' niōnan isāb ang'ssol.* Making the sound of rain coming. When water is about to boil that too is called *ssol.*

**ssom** var. of **l'ssom**

**ssu'** var. of **l'ssu'**

**ssul** *v. intr.* aN- To move in large numbers, as people or fish. *Ōy, aheka gunu' ang'ssul.* Hey, there is a large school of anchovy moving.

*Aheka puhu' ang'ssul, sika'ssul-ssulan.* Many people moving, moving in great numbers.

**sika'ssul-ssulan** *adj.* Moving about in great numbers.

**ssut** var. of **l'ssut**

**sū₁** *intrj.* 1) A noise made to drive away chickens. 1.1) *v. tr.* To drive away chickens by saying sū. (*Thesaurus:* **budjaw, dūy, siga' 1.1, singga'-singga', t'ggal**)

**sū₂** *v. intr.* pa- To drip slowly down the side of something; to seep. *Masi pasū lansong man bu'unna.* Squid ink is still dripping down from her hair. *Mbal pasū, apīt na sōng.* It doesn't drip down, it's nearly tacky. (*Thesaurus:* **p'ttak 1.1, tīs, titis 1.1, tū'**)

**subahat₁** *v. tr.* -an To mention something; to say what one is thinking. *Ō Tuhan, kalehun llingku itū. Itiya' aku anubahat: subay a'llum magpatayan hē' kamemon abō' aku makapagbeya' pabalik maka a'a inān.* O God, hear my words. I am saying what I have in mind. All the dead must live again before I associate again with that person. *Aniya' kina'astolan atay ni ka'a, sinubahatan.* There is someone deeply angry with you, and it is being talked about. *Anubahat lagi' si Da'ud, yukna, "Sapahanku ma ōn Tuhan kakkal salama-lama, in aku itu marai' na pinapatay."* David spoke out, saying, "I swear by the name of the everlasting God, I am about to be killed."

**subahat₂** *n.* 1) Forgetfulness; lack of clarity in one's mind. *Aniya' subahatku, agtimbang tomtomku.* There's something I'm unsure about, sorting out my memories. 1.1) *adj.* a- To be unclear about a proposed action. *Yukna ma aku, "Subay aku angahinang tepo. Asubahat aku bang ai to'ongan katudjuhan hinangku."* She said to me, "I must make a mat. I'm uncertain about which way to go in doing it."

**suba'** *n.* An inlet of the sea; a bay. (*Thesaurus:* **b'ttong₃, lo'ok**)

**subali** *v. intr.* aN- 1) To swear an oath. *Anubali kita, pasangka'ta llingta ni Tuhan.* We make a vow, referring our words direct to God. *Bay makasubali sultan, yukna, "Bang pa'in pinagmulka'an sai-sai anginam takakan ma mbal gi' s'ddop llaw."* The king swore an oath, saying, "May anyone who tastes food before sunset be cursed." 1.1) *v. tr.* -an To make someone the object of an enduring vow, for enmity or for friendship. *Yukna, "Subalihanku iya ina'an." Pinatobtob minnē' ka'amuhan. Subay magpa'ampun ni Tuhan, niuli'an llingna hē' ni a'a bay subalihanna hē'.* He said, "I will swear an oath concerning him." When that is done there is agreement. He must then ask God for forgiveness, that the word he swore on oath regarding that man may be put right. (*Thesaurus:* **najal 1.1, pagsapa 1.1, sapda 1, suhud 1.2, wa'ad**)

**pagsubali** *v. intr.* aN- To make a binding promise

together. *Magsubali, buwat magdanakan magtai'anak, "Makajari kita magkahāp bang punduk kamatto'ahan, atawa bang patangkob langit, atawa bang alinis būd itu."* We make a vow, as between siblings of the one family, saying "We may perhaps be reconciled when the forebears rise [from their graves], or when the sky is completely covered, or this mountain is worn down to nothing."

**subang** *n.* Earrings. (*Thesaurus:* **anting-anting 1, aretes, bāng₂, domelo, pinting**)

**subay** *ptl.* Should; ought to; must. (Deontic modality marker, obligation). *Subay pasōng-sōng bo' aniya' bohe'.* It will have to be later on before there is any water. *A: "Subay na aku Alba'a."* *B: "Subay na aku Isnin."* A: "It will have to be Wednesday for me." B: "Monday for me." (*Thesaurus:* **patut, wajib 1**)

**subu₁ 1)** *v. intr.* pa- To boil over. *Minsan daing angappu' du basta pasubu bohe'na.* Even fish will break up if the water [around it] boils up. **2)** *v. tr.* -an To subject something to heat; to temper metal by heating. *Sinubuhan, pinatuwas sala basi'-basi'.* Tempered, made hard like iron. *Sinubuhan, buwat pana' pinehē' ni pasu', tinalom na, nihinangan gehe na. Atawa saga p'ssi, sinubuhan bo' kinakal, tinaloman.* Tempered, like a fish spear put to the heat, sharpened and fitted with a barb. Or like fishhooks, tempered and beaten, made sharp. *Kapa ilū subay sinubuhan, da'a na tinunu' mital.* The axe there should be put in the fire, not burning the metal. (*Thesaurus:* **babal₁, sasal, tawtaw**)

**subu₂ 1)** *adv.* Morning, the period from daybreak until the sun is high. *Subay na subu bo' yampa kam palanjal.* It should be morning before you proceed on your journey. (*cf:* **kohap 1;** *Thesaurus:* **abay-subu, bukis₁, dai'-llaw, pagmanis-manis sobangan, pote' sobangan**) **2)** *n.* The dawn prayer time of Islam, between 4.30 and 6 a.m. (*Thesaurus:* **aisa, asal, luhul₁, magrib 1**)

**subu-sī'** *n.* Morning of this present same day. *Aniya' s'ggit bay sapuhannu subu-sī'?* Did you sweep up any rubbish this morning? (*Thesaurus:* **kohap-in, insini'**)

**subu-subu** *n.* Early morning; the period just after sunrise.

**subuk** *adj.* a- Plump; well filled-out, of body. (*Thesaurus:* **goldo-goldo, hambug 1, littub, l'mmok 1.1, poko-poko, tibung-tibung**)

**subud** *v. intr.* pa- To grow vigorously, of plants or hair. *Kelas itū mbal pasubud bu'un.* With this kind of baldness the hair does not grow vigorously. *Makasubud pa'in sagmot inān, magtūy kasembolan tinanom.* When those scrub weeds grow, the plants will soon be crowded out. *Makasubud pa'in sagmot inān, magtūy kasembolan tinanom, ya po'on mbal magbuwa'.* When those scrub weeds grow, the plants will immediately be crowded

out, which is why they don't bear fruit. (*Thesaurus:* **sulig₁, tomo' 1, tungbu'**)

**subul** *n.* A young unmarried man; a bachelor. *Halam gi' anangpot kasubulku.* My youth status is not yet complete. *Subul gi' Si Beb itū, halam gi' h'ndana.* Beb here is still a youth, doesn't have a wife yet. (*Thesaurus:* **budjang, daga-raga**)

**Sūk** *n.* **1)** A person identified as a member of the Tausug ethnic group. **2)** Jolo Town. *Hē' na ma Tiyanggi Sūk.* There in the market town of Jolo.

**pagsinūk** *v. intr.* aN- To be speaking the Tausug language.

**Sinūk** *n.* **1)** Tausug, the language spoken by the indigenous inhabitants of Jolo Island and elsewhere. **1.1)** *v. tr.* To translate something into the Tausug language.

**Sūk-Sama** *n.* Tausug and Sama, the ethnic groups living along the Sulu Archipelago.

**sukad** *adj.* a- Filled up, of a container or house. *Asukad itu, mbal sarang.* This word *sukad* [means] inadequate as to space. *Asukad luma' he' puhu', sali' ap'nno' magtūy.* The house is overcrowded with people, immediately full. *Buwat tukul itū aniya' pangisihan bo' mbal s'ddong, asigpit. Asukad pangisihan.* Like this hammer that has a container but it doesn't fit, it is constricted. The container is chock-full. (*Thesaurus:* **digpit 1, sigpit 2, s'mpok 1**)

**suka'** *n.* Vinegar. *Suka' itū pangalamud tipay.* This vinegar is for mixing with oysters. (*syn:* **binegal**)

**sukang** *n.* **1)** Food or activity prohibited for dietary or religious reasons, as when someone is sick or when a ritual sequence is in process. *A: "Ai sukangna itū?" B: "Luwal daing laha'an."* A: "What are his restricted foods?" B: "Only fish with a lot of blood." (*cf:* **li'in 1**) **1.1)** *v. advrs.* ka-...-an To be forbidden for ritual or health reasons. *Da'a ka angali. Kasukangan ko' ilū.* Don't dig. That is not allowed.

**sukay₁** *n.* **1)** A fee; a tax; a levy; a rental payment; a fare. *Minsan saga a'a magā' sukay parinta, alasa du ma sasuku alasahan sigām.* Even the people who collect the government tax, they too love those who love them. **1.1)** *v. tr.* -an To charge someone a fee; to impose a tax on someone. *Mbal sinukayan onde'-onde'.* Children aren't charged.

**sukay₂** var. of **kagang-sukay**

**sukkal** *n.* **1)** Emotional stress; a stressful circumstance. *Bay ah'lling sukkal ni Tuhan.* He spoke grievous things toward God. *Mbal kasandalan kasukkalan sigām.* Their grief was unbearable. (*Thesaurus:* **kibad atay, pagsorol, susa 1**) **1.1)** *v. intr.* maka- To be distressing. *Pinah'lling itū makasukkal, mbal pinah'lling makasukkal du.* Saying this will be distressing, not saying it will [also] be distressing.

**sukkal-manukkal** *n.* One trouble after another.

**sukki'** *see:* **pagsukki'**

**sukki'an** *n.* The board on which checkers (draughts) is played.

**sukkiyan** *n.* Various turbans (sea snails), including the Cat's-eye turban. *Turbo spp.* (*syn:* **laggong**)

**sukkut** *v. intr. pa-* To knock against an obstruction. *Pabungku' magtūy, sali' pasukkut tōng tape'ku.* Promptly knocking against it, the end of my foot sort of hitting it. (*cf:* **sukmad 1**; *Thesaurus:* **bungku'₂, langgal₂ 1, santuk**)

**suki'** *n.* A customer or vendor in a regular buying-selling relationship.

**pagsuki'** *v. intr. aN-* To have an ongoing trading relationship with each other.

**suklu'** *v. tr. -an* To form an extension by inserting one pole into another, in order to reap fruit high in a tree. (*Thesaurus:* **sugpat 1.2, tangkil**)

**suklu'an** *n.* An extension to a pole. *Hāg aheka suklu'anna.* A post with several extensions.

**sukmad** *v. intr. -um-* **1)** To suffer an accidental blow or pressure on the back of the head. *Sumukmad bang kita bay lahi-lahi.* We took a blow to the back of our heads when we had been running. (*cf:* **sukkut**) **1.1)** *v. tr. -an* To hit someone on the back of the head. *Sinukmaran sigā he'na, sali' bang sinantukan ni tambol, atawa ni gusung, atawa ni papan.* He hit the back of their heads, like being banged against a door, or onto the sand, or against a board.

**sukmu** *n.* **1)** A splinter. **1.1)** *v. tr. -an* To penetrate something with a splinter. (*syn:* **sulam**) **1.2)** *v. advrs. ka-...-an* To be afflicted by a splinter or other foreign body under the skin.

**sukna'** *n.* **1)** A curse; an imprecation. *In sukna' inān subay papelleng ni aku, ngga'i ka ni ka'a.* That curse should rebound on me, not on you. (*cf:* **damba'₂ 1.1**) **1.1)** *v. tr. -an* To utter a curse against someone. *Sali' anukna', yuk-i, "Magniyat ka, mbal ka tapole'."* Sort of cursing, saying, "Accept the fact, you won't get home." (*Thesaurus:* **sapda 1.1**; *spec:* **bit₁, kaban 2, kīs₄ 2, damba'₂ 1, halluwa 2, lalung₂, mangat, salimput 2, sunduk 2, tangkob₂, tulagsok 2**)

**pagsukna'** *v. intr. aN-* **1)** To curse habitually. *Bang dupang hal magsukna'.* A fool just goes about cursing. **1.1)** *v. tr. -an* To harm someone by imposing a curse. *Momosunbi baran d'nda bay pinagsukna'an hē'.* Gather up the body of that woman who was cursed.

**suksik** *var. of* **sugsig**

**suku₁** *n.* A quarter meter of cloth. *Duwa maka dambila' dasuku, hatina tonga' sin tonga' meto.* ₱2.50 per *suku*, per quarter metre, that is.

**suku₂** *var. of* **sasuku**

**sukud₁** (*var.* **hukud**) *v. tr.* To measure something. *Amasukud aku pantalun ma'ung.* I will get denim trousers measured. *Nihukud bahā' tana', buwat metrosan.* An area of land perhaps being measured, like its acreage [in meters]. (*Thesaurus:* **ganta'₁ 1, t'ppong 1**)

**sukuran** *n.* A measurement; a standard length.

*Saga pila sukuranna bangka' ilū?* About how many units in length is that canoe hull? *Aniya' saga sangpū' maka lima l'ngngon ya sukuranna kamemon.* Its total length was about fifteen arm-spans.

**sukud₂** *n.* **1)** Fate; fortune. *Ahāp sukud si Sa, makapuwa' dakayu' pilak.* Sa had good luck, he found a peso. *Ya na sukud.* That's luck. (*Thesaurus:* **kahandak 1, karal 1, kulis, ganta'an₁, indika 1, piguhan**) **1.1)** *v. tr. -an* To bring someone good fortune. *Bang kita sinukuran ya niōnan gusi' itū.* If we are favored with this so-called magic moneybox.

**pagpasukud** *v. tr. -an* To do something that involves risk or uncertainty. (*Thesaurus:* **k'ddom₂, halus₁, pagsusaed, samba 1, sarap₂ 1, tawakkal**)

**pamasukud** *n.* A source of good fortune.

**suku'** *n.* Property or share of an individual. *Suku'ku banog, suku'nu ai-ai bay b'llinu.* The sail is mine, what you bought is yours. (*cf:* **anu 2**)

**pagsuku'** *v. intr. aN-* To divide up shares of jointly owned property. *Bang saupama magtiman bo' ahukaw karuwangan sali'-sali', magsuku' na.* If a couple separates, for example, being mutually unwilling [to live together], they divide the property between them. *Subay kitam magsuku'-suku' dangan maka dangan.* We should share equally with each other.

**palsuku'an** *n.* Something owned; possessions; a share.

**pasuku'** *v. ditr.* To grant someone a portion or share; to transfer ownership.

**sukul₁** *adv.* Fortunately; thankfully; just as well. *Sukul isāb kata'uhanku.* It's good that I know about it. *Sukul kapandu'an kām e' sigām bang lān ya ingga subay palabayanbi.* Fortunately they showed which road you should pass by on.

**pagsarang-sukul** *v. intr. aN-* To give thanks formally. *O Tuhan, aheya pagsarang-sukulan kami ni ka'a.* Oh God, our thanks to you is great.

**pagsukul** *v. intr. aN-* To thank someone. *Aho' tuwan, magsukul aku ni ka'a.* Yes sir, I am grateful to you. *Pagsukulinbi iya, pudjihunbi ōnna!* Thank him, praise his name.

**pagsukulan** *n.* Gratitude; thanksgiving; a thanksgiving gift. *Aheya pagsukulanku ni Tuhan sabab itiya' ka a'llum.* My gratitude to God is great, because you are here, alive.

**sukul₂** *n.* The supports on which a pot rests over a cooking fire; the projecting lugs of a clay stove; the stones on a fire-table. *Pilang itu subay batu sukulna.* The pot supports on this cooking-enclosure should be stones. (*Thesaurus:* **lapohan, pagb'llahan, pilang**)

**sukul-sukul** *n.* Herring scads, a fish species. *fam. Carangidae. Maka'ā' kami tulay sukul-sukul.* We caught some small scad.

**sukut** *v. tr.* **1)** To dun something (for payment); to require someone to pay a debt. *Bay na aku amayad ni a'a inān, sakali sinukut aku pabīng.* I had paid that man, and now I am dunned again. *Sinukut iya, mbal pinara'awa, sinoho' amayad utangna hē', kinara-kara.* He is required to pay up, not allowed to make excuses, told repeatedly to discharge his debt. *Buwat ka'a taga utang, na sinipihan ka he' a'a bay pangutangannu abō' supaya sinukut.* Suppose you have a debt, then the person from whom you borrowed watches out for you so you can be dunned for payment. 2) To demand specific bride-wealth items.

**sūd** *n.* A fine-toothed comb for removing hair lice. (*Thesaurus:* **kuhut 1, suray 1**)

**sudda** *n.* The nature, character, behavior of a person. *Ahāp sudda si Su, amuwan bāng-bāng.* Su is good-natured, she gives away cookies.

    **kasuddahan** *n.* A person's character or moral worth. *Sali' nsa' aniya' kasuddahan sigā ma deyom paglahat.* They had no value there in that place. *Ala'at kasuddahanna a'a inān.* That fellow's character is bad. (*Thesaurus:* **kalakuhan, hudjidjat, jaguni', jari₄ 1, jāt₁, sadsaran**)

    **pagkasuddahan** *v. intr. aN-* To experience misfortune; to come to a bad end.

**suddang** *v. tr.* To slice fibrous fruit such as a mango against the grain of its fiber. *Da'a na suddangun wanni ilū.* Don't slice that odorous mango against the grain.

**sudjara** var. of **tudjara**

**sudju** var. of **tudju₁**

**sudlat** (var. **suglat**) *adj. a-* 1) Penetrated or poked into something soft or yielding. *Asudlat mataku he' tōng tanganku. Ap'ddi', sali' bay atugsuk.* My eye got poked by my fingertips. It's painful, as though I had been stabbed. 1.1) *v. tr.* To thrust a hard item into something soft or yielding. *Sudlatanta ka ya bay sehe'nu magbono' hē' bo' abulag.* I will poke that guy you were fighting with for you, so he will be blinded. (*Thesaurus:* **kussu', langgit 1, suruk, tugsuk 2.2**) 1.2) *v. advrs. ka-...-an* To be penetrated or poked into. *Si Ja bay am'ngkong tape'na bay ni bohe', bay kasudlatan e' p'ttung.* Ja had a swollen foot from going to the water hole, he was stabbed by bamboo.

**sudlay** var. of **suray**

**sudlay-sudlay** *n.* Various spiny murexes, including the Venus comb. *fam. Muricidae.* (*cf:* **tape'-kura'**)

**sudsud** *n.* A small fishing net supported by an X-shaped frame.

**sūg-sūg** *v. ditr.* To urge someone to act in a specified way. *Sai bay anūg-sūgan ka'a aglahi?* Who told you to elope? *Luhūy ka'a ilū sūg-sūganku angahaka.* I have advised you even more to report it. (*Thesaurus:* **da'ak, gandahan, hilag, pagmanda 1, soho', uldin 1**)

**suga-suga₁** *n.* The Redcoat squirrelfish; the soldierfish. *Sargocentrum rubrum.* (*gen:* **tihik-tihik 1**)

**suga-suga₂** *n.* A peer; an equal in size. *Tōp na ka'am, dasuga-suga.* You match, you are the same size. (*Thesaurus:* **dora' 2, sali' 1, samapasang, sibu' 1, tupan 1**)

**sugal** *n.* Card games.

    **pagsugal** *v. intr. aN-* To play a card game. *Da'a kam palamud, atiya' kami magsugal.* Don't butt in, we're playing cards. (*Thesaurus:* **paglaki, pagpares 1**)

**sugarul** *n.* A person involved in criminal activity. *Sugarul a'a ilu, panangkaw.* That guy is a criminal, a habitual thief. (*Thesaurus:* **mundu 1, panangkaw, pilliyu**)

**sugat** *adj. a-* 1) Cross-grained; knotty. *Asugat kayu ilu, ahunit kinatam.* That wood is cross-grained, hard to plane smooth. 2) Uncooperative; hard to persuade. *Bang aniya' ginara'an, sali' mbal iya pauyun ba, asugat.* When something is decided, he won't agree, he is obstructive. 2.1) *v. tr.* To oppose a suggestion or decision. *Minsan gara' ni kahāpan, tu'ud anugat na pa'in.* Even though it's a good decision, he simply keeps opposing it.

**suggang** *n.* Something unacceptable; a total reject. *Suggang, mbal to'ongan kinabilahi'an.* Something unacceptable, totally undesirable. *Suggang ma atayku inān, mbal tabowaku magbeya'.* He is deeply unpleasant to me; I couldn't have him come with [us].

**sughay** *v. tr.* To crumble a lump of cassava meal in preparation for cooking by steaming. (*Thesaurus:* **budjal-budjal, gokal, lomo 1, p'kkal 1, podjak 1**)

**sugi-sugi** *v. tr.* To influence someone to do wrong. *Buwat aniya' maglakibini ati magbono', ah'lling dakayu' matto'a yukna, "Da'a kahāpinbi h'llanu bang halam aniya' tabowa." Ya ilu anugi-nugi.* Like when there is a married couple and they are fighting, and an elder says, "Don't make up with your husband unless he brings some [gift]." That is an example of wrong influence. (*Thesaurus:* **pitna**)

    **pagsugi-sugi** *v. intr. aN-* To be engaged in malicious talk. *Nda'un ba kapagsugi-sugi saga a'a inān.* Look at the malicious gossip of those people.

**sugit-sugit** *n.* The paper nautilus. *Argonaut argo.* (*cf:* **kalo'ong 1**)

**sugiya** *adj. zero* Of adequate size; not tight-fitting. *Sugiya, sali' aluhaya.* Big enough, sort of roomy. *Mbal sugiya, mbal sarang.* Not adequate, not enough. (*Thesaurus:* **sarang 1, s'ddong, t'ppot, ustu**)

**suglat** var. of **sudlat**

**sugmak** *v. advrs. ka-...-an* To be stuffed full of food; sated. *Kasugmakan iya, hatina karūlan bay amangan sampay a'sso na.* He is sated, meaning he was permitted to eat until full. *Amangan ka* *sampay kasugmakan.* Eat until you're stuffed. (*Thesaurus:* **dagal**)

**sugpak** (var. **suppak**) *n.* 1) Deserved retribution, for an offense that threatens the well-being of a kin group. *Suppak saga anak, mbal papandu'.* These children will get what they deserved, unteachable. 1.1) *v. tr.* -an To threaten someone with the well-deserved consequence of his action. *Sinugpakan kita e' matto'ata, yuk-i, "Na, ka'a bay lāngku, mbal ameya'-meya'. Na nanamun na."* Our parents threaten us, saying, "There, I told you not to, and you didn't heed. Now taste the results." *Sinugpakan, yukna, "Bang pa'in akugud na ai-ai kamemon."* Threatened with retribution, saying, "May every single resource be used up." *Sinugpakan kita, sali' kita nijuru'an he' matto'ata, yuk-i, "Ya na ahāp bang ka amatay".* We are threatened, like being given over-much by our parents, saying "It would be better if you died." *Luhūy sigām sinuppakan e' Nabi Elija.* They were theatened even more by the prophet Elijah. *Suppakanku du kam.* I have warned you of the consequences.

**sugpat** 1) *n.* An extension to the length of something; a postscript; an affix (grammar). *Buwattitu isāb sugpat llingku ma ka'am, "Ala'an kam min saga a'a dusahan."* This is the extension of my advice to you, "Keep away from people who do wrong." *Ai sugpatta bo' tahinang panoho'an?* What do we affix [it with] so it becomes a command? 1.1) *adj.* a- Joined lengthwise. *Subay asugpat buway inān bo' kita magkahāp.* Those pieces of rattan will have to join [themselves] up for us to make peace. 1.2) *v. tr.* -an To extend something by an addition; to add something to what has been said. *Bang mbal maka'abut tambu' ilū sugpatin maka lubid bo' umabut.* If that dipper won't reach, extend it with twine so it will reach. *Anugpat aku lubid, sali' a'kka, sali' halam ahogot panugpatna.* I add a section to some rope and it sort of comes untied, its joining not secure. *Ahāp isāb kasugpatannu kami, bo' isāb tata'u kami in ka'am mailu.* It would also be good if you could add us so that we too could know that you are there. (*Thesaurus:* **suklu'**, **tangkil**) 2) *clf.* Count word for things that join lengthwise, as thatch panels. *Pitu' sugpat nipa' luma'na.* The roof of his house was seven lengths of palm shingles.

**pagsugpat** *v. tr.* To join things end to end. *Ahunit pinapagsugpat lupis maka buway.* It is difficult to join banana fibre and rattan.

**sugpat akkal** *adj.* a- Satisfied; happy with one's situation. {idiom} *Bay akulang akkalku, bo' aniya' na. Na asugpat na.* My mind was not fully content, but it is now. It is satisfied. *Bang aniya' makasugpatan akkalku hē', na makapagdūl-baya' na aku.* If something completes my contentment, then I able to do whatever I want.

**sugpat nyawa** *adj.* a- Completing one's

happiness; dear to one's heart. {idiom} *Bang aniya' makasugpatan nyawaku hē', na magkapagdūl-baya'.* If I have something dear to my heart, then I will fulfil all my desires.

**sugpatan** *n.* An extension of length.

**sugpat-babat** *n.* The Sand tilefish; the Blue banquillo. *Malacanthus latovittatus.*

**sugsig** (var. **suksik**; **sussik**) *adj.* a- 1) Diligent and attentive to what one is doing. *Mbal asugsig sigā anonda', hal ma bihing.* They are not committed to trolling, they are just [fishing] inshore. *Sussik itū ma panghatiku atuyu'.* Sussik, in my understanding, means diligent. *Asussik magusaha.* Diligent at working for a living. *Bang anahut-nahut la'itanna, asussik nihinang.* When its stitching is very fine, it is done with painstaking care. (*Thesaurus:* **akkul, dago'os, tebot, tuyu'** 1) 1.1) *v. tr.* To do something with careful attention to detail.

**sugsug** *n.* 1) Someone connected by blood. *Sugsug ni a'a bay autas taingana ina'an.* Relative of that man whose ear had been cut off. 1.1) *v. tr.* To trace kin relationships. *Ainu-inu kita bang sali' a'a mbal kata'uhanta. Yukta, sawpama, "Mbal kata'uhanbi aku?" Yuk sigā, "Mbal." Na anugsug kita, nihaka'an bang sai mma'ta, sai matto'ata, sai danakanta.* We wonder about a person we do not know. We say, for example, "Don't you know me?" They say, "No." So we trace our relationship, say who our father is, who our elders are, who our siblings are. *Bang kita ni lahat saddī, bo' kita mbal takilā he' a'a ma lahat inān, anugsug na kita.* When we go to a different place, and we are not recognised by people in that place, we trace our family connections.

**sugsug panubu'** *v. tr.* To trace kin relationships by descent from a shared ancestor. {idiom}

**sugsugan** *n.* A blood relative, however distant. (*Thesaurus:* **kakampungan**, **lūng-kampung**)

**pasugsug** *v. tr.* To unite a couple in marriage. (*Thesaurus:* **kasal** 1, **kawin** 1.1, **pabatal**, **paglahi** 1.1)

**sugsug tawbat** *n. phrase* 1) A forgiveness ritual between offended family members. 1.1) *v. ditr.* To conduct a forgiveness ritual. *Palabayta na ya pagp'ddi' atayta bay. K'llo'ta imam mikisugsug kita tawbat.* We put behind us whatever we had been angry about. We get the imam and ask him to pray the forgiveness prayer over us.

**pagsugsug-tawbat** *v. intr.* aN- To celebrate a formal act of reconciliation between family members.

**sugub** *n.* A square basket of woven mature palm leaflets, joined at the top so as to form a handle and two openings. (*gen:* **baka'₁**)

**suha'** *n.* A sweet variety of citrus; a mandarin.

**suhud** (var. **suhul**) *n.* 1) A vow to carry out ritual duties in fulfillment of a commitment to a supernatural being. 1.1) *v. intr.* pa- To supplicate God or a ritual ancestor. *Pasuhud kita ni mbo',* *angampun-ngampun kita, aniya' dusata.* We supplicate an ancestor, we make request, we have committed some offense. **1.2)** *v. tr.* To make or fulfill a vow to God or a ritual ancestor. *Aniya' bay suhulna, subay nihinang e'na.* He made a vow, he should carry it out. *Dūlin aku pehē' bo' suhulku bay najalku.* Let me go yonder to pay the vow I made. *Na, bang kām anganjanji' ni Tuhan, bo' palehom-lehombi, katōngan kām dusa bang mbal suhulbi.* So when you make a vow to God and are neglectful about it, you will be found guilty if you don't fulfil it. *Sulban itū s'mmek, bang sali' bay janji'ta atawa bay suhudta.* This word *sulban* is a cloth cover, for when we have made a promise or are petitioning a supernatural entity. (*Thesaurus:* **najal 1.1, pagsapa 1.1, sapda 1, subali 1.1, wa'ad**) **1.3)** *v. ditr.* To request something from God or a ritual ancestor. (*Thesaurus:* **sambahayang**)

**suhul** var. of **suhud**

**suhut** *v. intr. pa-* To retreat; to withdraw. *Gibang bo' sinōng, kowan bo' sinuhut.* Left for putting forward, the right for pulling back. *Pinasōng, pinasuhut.* Put forward, pulled back. (*ant:* **sōng₂ 1**; *Thesaurus:* **sebog, singga-singga**)

**pagsuhut** *v. intr. aN-* To be retreating; to be drawing back. *Angapas saga sundalu angkan kami bay magsuhutan.* The soldiers pursued so we withdrew.

**suhutan** *n.* A retreat area inside the bow or stern of a large canoe. (*cf:* **huwang₁ 1**)

**sujud** *v. intr. pa-* To kneel with head down, in prayer or as a sign of deep respect. *Pasujud saga kal'llahan, buwat ma langgal ina'an.* The men kneel in prayer, as [they do] in the mosque there. (*Thesaurus:* **duku', luku'₂, luhud, pagpatireyo'**)

**pagsujud** *n.* **1)** Humility; an attitude of reverence. **1.1)** *v. intr. aN-* To prostrate oneself as an act of respect or reverence. *Magsujuran sigām ma si Anu tanda' sin pagdeyo'-addat sigām ma iya.* They prostrated themselves before What's-his-name as a sign of their humility towards him.

**sujum** *n.* A cyanide-based fish poison. *Bay kami ni lansa ma Toril ē' angā' tamban, aniya' palabay bangka'-bangka' duwangan a'ana amowa sujum ma kassa'-kassa' bo' supaya pangalassun daing.* When we took the launch there to Toril fishing for sardines, a small canoe passed with two people carrying a vial of cyanide to be used for poisoning fish.

**pagsujum** *v. intr. aN-* To make a living by using poison to stun fish. *Kaka'ku Mu ma Sambuwangan, usahana magsujum.* My elder brother Mu in Zamboanga, his livelihood is poisoning fish with cyanide.

**sū'** *n.* **1)** A wick lamp of any kind; a lantern. (*Thesaurus:* **kulaet 1, laet, lām, lampu,**

**palita'an, plaslaet 1) 1.1)** *v. tr.* To collect things (especially fish or fruit) by lamplight. *Bay kami anū' mampallam ma deya, aheka pangguwa'.* We gathered mangoes ashore by lamplight, there were many ghosts. *Anū' kami b'llong saga, anū' saga kindat pangumpan bang am'ssi dai'-llaw.* We catch spinefoots by lantern light, we catch little squid as bait when we are fishing early in the morning. **1.2)** *v. tr. -an* To ignite a lamp, fuse or cigaret. *Indamin aku bagid panū'anku siga.* Lend me a match to light a cigaret. *Sū'anku palita'an abō' mbal angal'ddom.* I will light the lamp so it doesn't get dark. (*Thesaurus:* **bagid, dokot₂ 1.2, pakeyat, santik 1**)

**sū'-palita'an** *n.* Dusk; the time for lighting lamps. *Halam na aniya' llaw, hal ba'as-ba'asna. Song sū'-palita'an na, ya na hē' magrib.* No longer any sun, just its after-light. Lamp-lighting time, that is *magrib.* (*Thesaurus:* **abay-kohap, kohap 1, lekot-lendom, lempos, logob-logob, magrib 2**)

**su'al** *see:* **pagsu'al, pagpasu'alan**

**su'al-su'al** *v. tr.* To stimulate or provoke someone into action. (*cf:* **bandung₂**)

**su'ap** *n.* **1)** A gift to gain someone's support. **1.1)** *v. intr. pa-* To make a gift hoping to gain the support of someone of high status. (*Thesaurus:* **pagaddat 1.1, pagmamay, pagmanja', palok 1**)

**sulab** var. of **solab₁**

**sulabay** *see:* **pagsulabay**

**sulak₁** *v. tr. -an* To reduce an amount or number of something, as the number of persons playing a game. *Sulakin, sali' kinulangan ina'an, sinoho' ala'an.* Remove one, as when reducing [the group of people], told to leave. (*Thesaurus:* **kobos, kulang₁ 1.3, dagdag₁, diki' 1.2, hilang, putung**)

**sulak₂** *v. tr.* To reject something; to refuse to take. *Ai-ai na ahāp subay binogbogan, ai-ai na ala'at sulakta.* We should uphold whatever is good, reject whatever is bad. *Aniya' ko' itū pamowahanku ka'a magbissala, da'a aku sulakun.* There is something I want to have you talk with me about, don't reject me. *Buwat kita pinandu'an, gōm pa'in jōkta, sulakta, ya mbal ameya'-meya'.* Like when we are being instructed and make a joking response instead, rejecting it, not obeying. (*syn:* **suwalak**; *Thesaurus:* **pagin'mbal 1, pagmarī', pasibukut 1, taikut 1.1**)

**sulakat** *v. intr. pa-* To jump across from one thing to another. *Pasulakat, sali' palete man pelang dakayu' ni pelang dakayu'.* Jumping across, like going across from one canoe to another canoe. (*Thesaurus:* **kuppa 1, laksu₁, tugpa' 1**)

**pagsulakat** *v. intr. aN-* To cross over a gap from opposite sides, of two people. *Mbal kitā makapagsulakat.* We are unable to cross over from opposite ends. (*Thesaurus:* **kulatay**)

**sulad 1)** *n.* A pole or rod across a door, installed to

prevent opening. (*cf:* **babag 1.2**; *Thesaurus:* **sundak 1**) **2)** *v. tr. -an* To skewer something lengthwise, as fish for roasting. *Buwat a'a Musu' bay sinularan maka budjak.* Like the man from Musu who had a spear run right up through him.

**sulagsok** var. of **tulagsok**

**sulalla** *v. intr. pa-* To lie with feet in the air. (*cf:* **julangkang**)

**sulam** *v. advrs. ka-...-an* To be penetrated by something sharp. *Bay kasulaman tanganku he' kayu, am'ngkong, mbal na pahali.* My hand has been pierced by a splinter of wood, swelling and not getting better. (*syn:* **sukmu 1.1**)

**sulang₁** *v. tr.* To resist a force; to oppose an opinion. *Bay sulangnu kabaya'anku.* You have resisted my will. (*Thesaurus:* **ampal, pagang, sagang, sangsang, sapad**)

**sulang-saling** *adj. a-* Together but facing in opposite directions. (*Thesaurus:* **bulallit, sulay₂, sunsang, susun-buyu'**)

**pagsulang-saling** (var. **pagsulang-saingsing**) *v. intr. aN-* To be reversed; to be disarranged; to be lying in various ways. *Magsulang-saling, mbal ahāp he' amat'nna'.* Lying the opposite way, not well-placed. *Bay niukil-ukilan, magsulang-saingsing ari-arihanna.* It was carved so that its decorative pattern is reversed.

**sulang₂** *n.* A fall same-side-up of two coins held face-to-face (a gaming term). (*Thesaurus:* **agad₂, pagkabit, pagsalla' 1.1, pagtalang, tingka**)

**pagsulang** *v. intr. aN-* To lie face to face, as coins.

**sulangat** *v. intr. pa-* To project in diverse directions, of arms and legs, or of human bodies in a pile. (*Thesaurus:* **julenget, pagsalisi, pagsōng-suwa', pagsuwa'-s'llo'**)

**sikasulangatan** *adj.* Poking out in all directions.

**sulapput** *v. intr. pa-* To flare up; to squirt out, of fire or liquid. *Aniya' kono' api pasulapput min bowa' naga ina'an amaka'at saga manusiya'.* There was reportedly fire surging out of that dragon's mouth, destroying human beings.

**pagsulapput** *v. intr. aN-* To flare up; to burst into flames. *Magsulapput keyatna apa alandos baliyu.* Its flames flared up because the wind was strong.

**sularaw** *v. intr. aN-* To move smoothly across water, skimming the wave-tops one by one. *Anularaw pahāp paraw ina'an.* That canoe flies across the waves. (*Thesaurus:* **kulit-kulit, samperet, tampeppet**)

**pagsularaw** *v. intr. aN-* To move repetitively, as a person experiencing waves of sharp pain. *Bang kita kalarahan, kineket e' ai-ai abisa, magsularaw kita.* When we get too much chilli, or are bitten by something painful, then we move convulsively. (*Thesaurus:* **paglega-lega, paglimayu', paglimbahod, paglimpa, pagsalinggā**)

**sulariyan** (var. **suwariyan**) *n.* A torch with an improvised wick, burning coconut oil or kerosene. *Sulariyan itū kassa' pinehē'an p'ttung atawa kayuwan ni bowa'na pamakeyatan iya.* The *sulariyan* referred to is a glass [bottle] with bamboo or cane put in its opening for lighting it. (*Thesaurus:* **tanju', tapulaw**)

**sulasi** *n.* Sweet basil, a fragrant herb used to flavor food. *Ocimun basilicum. Sulasi, ya sali' mahamut inān pinalamud ma kinakan. Saddī sāy.* Basil, that somewhat fragrant herb added to food. Lemongrass is different. (*gen:* **pamapā**)

**sulat** *n.* **1)** Something written, as a letter or book. *Pasampayun sulat itū ni Saljen Bal.* Deliver this letter to Sergeant Bal. **1.1)** *v. tr.* To write something. *Wa'i gi' iya anulat būk.* He is busy writing a book. (*cf:* **baris, batang-sulat**)

**pagsulat** *v. intr. aN-* To be busy writing; to make a living by writing. *Bang ka magsulat subay aniya' lampikna pamatagalan katas.* When you're writing there needs to be a protective backing for the paper to rest on. *Alahang aku magpakasulat pasal tatangis aku anulat ni ka'a.* I have rarely been able to write because writing to you makes me cry.

**pagsulatan** *n.* A printing machine; a typewriter; a computer. *Aniya' ma iya malkina pagsulatan.* He has a typewriter [lit. a machine for writing].

**sulat-kataddangan** *n.* A document of authorization; a permit. (*Thesaurus:* **pās, paspolt, sairola**)

**sulat-libun** *n.* A written charm designed to prevent a desired woman being taken by another man. *Nilawanan, sali' nilibun. Bang taluwa' he' niōnan sulat-libun, mbal du taga h'lla saddī min sangkahāpan.* Guarded, sort of enclosed. If the so-called *sulat-libun* is effective, she will not have a husband other than by the proper procedures. (*cf:* **lindang 1, suratan**)

**sulatan** *n.* A person's handwriting; written things. *Paheka na sulatan si Ke.* Ke's writings are increasing in number. *Aho', si Anu ko' inān. Takilāku ma sulatanna.* Yes, that is What's-his-name. I recognize [him] by his handwriting. (*cf:* **hātan**)

**sulaw** *n.* Cone shells in general. *Conus spp.*

**sulay₁** **1)** *v. intr. pa-* To make an attempt; to try. *Tu'ud ko' ka'a ilū pasulay anganjallat aku.* You're obviously just trying to trap me. **1.1)** *v. tr. -an* To attempt to do something. *Bay na kasulayanku, mbal takole'.* I've tried it and can't manage. (*Thesaurus:* **ahat 1.1, tara'-tara'**) **2)** *v. tr. -an* To test the quality of something, as for purity, flavor or weight. *Sinulayan kām buwat sapantun bulawan.* You are tested, as gold is for example. (*Thesaurus:* **kinam 1, ssa₁ 1.3, timtim**) **3)** *v. tr. -an* To test or tempt someone. *Sinulayan kām bo' supaya ahāp kasōnganbi.* You are being tested so that your future may be good.

**pagsulay** *n.* **1)** A contest of strength or ability.

*Ka'am lissi ya bay makamata ma saga pagsulay aheya maka saga paltanda'an makatāw-tāw.* You yourselves witnessed the great contests and terrifying signs. **1.1)** *v. intr. aN-* To test each other's strength. *Atukas kapagl'llana, magsulay.* His masculinity challenged, contesting it with someone.

**sulay-sulay₁** *v. tr.* To test someone's ability or skill. *Tara'-tara'un pehē', sinulay-sulayan ta'uta.* Give that [game] a try, testing our ability.

**sulay₂** *n.* Breech presentation, of a birth. *Bang paluwas dahū tape' niōnan he' kami sulay.* If the feet emerge first we call that a breech birth. (*Thesaurus:* **bulallit, sulang-saling, sunsang, susun-buyu'**)

**sulay-badju** var. of **saging-sulay-badju**

**sulay-sulay₂** *n.* A perch-like fish, said to be half-grown tulay scad. (*Thesaurus:* **lumahan, tulay**)

**Sulayman** *n.* The name Solomon.

**sulban** *n.* **1)** A turban worn by a pilgrim going on the hajj. (*Thesaurus:* **pīs₁, sahal₂, tuladjuk**) **2)** A cloth for covering an ancestor container. *Sulban itū s'mmek, bang sali' bay janji'ta atawa bay suhudta.* A *sulban* is a cloth cover, for when we have made a promise or are petitioning a supernatural entity. *Sulban jīn, sulban ba'ul.* The jin cloth, the cloth for the ancestor container.

**sulekma'** (var. **solekma'; sulema'**) *v. intr. pa-* To deviate from the correct course; to stray from orthodox teaching. *Sulekma' itū pasā' min lān, makajari pasā' min pandu', makajari usalta buwattē'.* To stray from a path, or possibly to stray from some teaching. Can be used that way. *Angamu' kami palabay min lahatbi. Mbal kami pasolekma' min lān paglalabayan ilū.* We ask [permission] to pass through your district. We will not go off the main road there. (*Thesaurus:* **salema' 1, sigay 1, simay₂, s'nnok**)

**sulema'** var. of **sulekma'**

**sulempat** (var. **solempat**) *v. intr. pa-* To fall or strike at an angle oblique to the vertical. *Wa'i ahūg bari'ku, pasulempat.* My working knife has dropped [into the water] and fallen away from where it was dropped. (*cf:* **deplas 1**; *Thesaurus:* **talilli' 1, tambelleng**)

**sulenget** *v. intr. pa-* To branch into mutiple divisions, as deer antlers. *O'ō, nda'un tandukna, pasulenget.* Look, see its horns, they branch.

**suleret** (var. **saleret**) *v. intr. aN-* To make a sudden vigorous movement, as a response to pain or physical confinement. *Buwat selo angulit-ngulit tahik, analeret.* Like a garfish skimming the surface, putting on a burst of energy.

**pagsuleret** *v. intr. aN-* To writhe in pain. *Damikiyanna du bang a'a taluwa' p'ddi' magsaleret, atawa magsularaw.* Likewise when a person is hit with pain, he writhes, or moves restlessly.

**sikasuleretan** *adj.* To move about in large numbers.

**suleyab** (var. **soleyab**) *v. intr. aN-* **1)** To spread, of flames. *Anuleyab keyatna. Magsuleyab ai-ai atunu'.* Its flame is spreading. Anything burning is in flames. (*Thesaurus:* **keyat₂ 1.1, dallet 1, dokot₂ 1.1, lāb 1**) **1.1)** *v. intr. pa-* To flare up. *Aniya' api pasuleyab min pagtutukbalan inān tudju ni diyata' langit.* There was a fire blazing up from that offering towards the sky.

**kasuleyaban** *n.* Flames; conflagration.

**pagsuleyab** *v. intr. aN-* To be ablaze. *Saga kabūd-būran ma katilibut si Nabi Eliyasa ap'nno' e' saga kura' maka kalesa magsuleyab e' api.* The hillside around Prophet Elisha were full of horses, and carriages ablaze with fire. *Magsuleyab ai-ai atunu'.* Anything that's burning is in flames.

**sulga'** *n.* Heaven, the abode of God and the angels; the ultimate destination of the faithful. *Bang kita amatay, bang kita pinole'an ni ahirat, tinilaw kita mahē' bang ai-ai hinangta ma junna itū. Bang ahāp pinehē' ni deyom sulga', bang ala'at tina'ajil.* When we die, and we are sent to the afterworld, we are asked there what we did in this world. If it was good we are sent into heaven, if it was bad we are exposed to the heat. (*Thesaurus:* **alam-pinole', dunya-ahirat, liyu-ahirat, nalka'**)

**suli-suli** (var. **suwi-suwi**) *n.* **1)** A discussion; a report; an anecdote. *Bapa', aniya' dakayu' suli-suliku ma ka'a ma waktu si Mma' bay asaki maka ni'ipat.* Uncle, I have a story for you about the time when Father was ill and being cared for. A: "*Yuk sai?*" B: "*Yuk suli-suli.*" A: "Who says so?" B: "Report has it." (*Thesaurus:* **ba'at 1, kabtangan, haka 1, hunub-hunub 1, pahati 1, sambatan**) **1.1)** *v. ditr.* To say something to someone. *Nā, suli-sulihanta ka.* Now, let me tell you about it.

**pagsuli-suli** *v. tr.* To converse; to discuss something. *Bang kita aningkō' subay kita magharap bo' magsuli-suli.* When we are sitting down we should face each other in order to converse. *Sali' kita magsuli-suli, manjari mbal taluwa' ma pikilan dangan, taluwa' ma pikilan dangan, ya hē' apatut.* Like when we are discussing something, and it doesn't fit with the thinking of one of us, but does fit with the thinking of the other, that's appropriate. *Da'a ka pa'aro' bang magsuli-suli matto'a bo' halam lamudnu.* Don't hang around when the elders are talking but it's not your business. A: "*Mbal tapagsuli-suli.*" B: "*He' angay? Bay kami makapagsuli-suli, ahāp isāb kaluwasanna.*" A: "It cannot be spoken of." B: "Why not? We had been talking together and the outcome was good." (*Thesaurus:* **pagbilma'arup, pagharis, pagistori-istori**)

**sulig₁** *v. intr. pa-* To grow in size or mass. *Bang kayu atomo', bang onde'-onde' pasulig.* Trees *tomo'* [grow upwards], children *sulig* [get bigger]. (*cf:* **sambu 1.1**; *Thesaurus:* **subud, tomo' 1, tungbu'**)

**suligan** *n.* Growing-up period; one's upbringing. *Suligan aku ma Siasi.* I grew up in Siasi.

**dasuligan** *adj.* Brought up together (as children).

**pasulig** (var. **pamasulig**) *n.* A rising agent in cooking; baking powder or yeast.

**sulig₂** *n.* Various fusilier fishes, including the Deep-bodied fusilier. *Caesio spp.*

**sulig-anduhat** *n.* The Red-bellied fusilier fish.

**sulig-batang** *n.* A fusilier fish species, blue, with yellow lateral line.

**sulig-langaw** *n.* A fusilier fish species.

**sulig-mapan** *n.* The Denticulated caesio or the Red-bellied yellowtail fusilier. *Caesio cuning.*

**sulig-petak** *n.* A fusilier fish species.

**suligpat** *v. intr.* aN- To come to one's mind, as the memory of a deceased loved one. *Bang aniya' d'nda amatay anakna dakayu', anuligpat ni atayna, tatangis, buwat ta'nda' bay badju'na atawa bay pangongka'anna.* If there is a woman one of whose children has died, and he comes into her mind, it makes her cry. Like when she sees his clothes or his playthings. (*Thesaurus:* **entom 1.2, magtak, padlak ni atay, sangpit, tambung, tasdik, tomtom 1.1**)

**suling₁** (var. **soleng₂**) *n.* A traditional bamboo flute. *Suling itū kayuhan nihinang, pinaglowang-lowangan. Pangā'an kalangan.* The *suling* is made of cane in which multiple holes are made. It is for making tunes. (*Thesaurus:* **pulaw₁, saunay**)

**pagsuling** *v. intr.* aN- To play a flute-like instrument. *Aniya' isāb min dahū'an sigām saga magbibiyula maka magsusuling maka a'a magtaroro'an tambul-tambul.* In front of them also were players of stringed instruments, and flautists [flute-players], and people beating time on tambourines. *Saga a'a magbiyula maka a'a magkalangan, a'a magsoleng maka a'a magtiyup-tiyup.* People playing stringed instruments and people singing, people playing flutes and people blowing trumpets.

**suling₂** *n.* A species of fish.

**sulli'** *v. tr.* To catch a glimpse of something, from the corner of one's eye. *Tasulli'ku min kidku.* I caught a glimpse of it to my side. (*syn:* **jullit₁ 1.1**)

**sulsi** *v. tr.* -an To repair a hole in cloth using closely spaced stitches. *Sinulsihan, buwat lowang tambuku.* Mended or bound with close stitches, like a buttonhole. (*cf:* **la'it**; *Thesaurus:* **ayum-ayum, lalipan-lalipan**)

**sultan** *n.* A sultan, a traditional ruler of Tausug society who claimed proprietary rights over nomadic Sama in Sulu; a king. *Sampay sultan asusa na bang aina bahā' kin'llo' e' a'a inān.* Even the king was concerned as to what that man had caught. *Ahunit laha' salip min laha' sultan.* Salip blood is more valuable than royal blood. (*Thesaurus:* **datu', dayang-dayang 1, salip**)

**pagsultan** *v. intr.* aN- To exercise the powers and rights of a sultan. *Bang ka bay magkahagad, tuman ka'a maka saga panubu'nu pinapagsultan ni kasaumulan.* If you had been obedient, you and your descendants would surely have been established as kings forever.

**susultanun** *n.* Royalty; a person of royal descent. *Susultanun panubu'na salama-lama.* His descendants will be royalty forever.

**kapagsultan** *n.* The status of kingship; a kingdom.

**sulug₁** *v. tr.* To fit something into the space designed for it. *Kinusuhan panapi' pelang panulugan batangan.* The side planks have a hole made into them for the outrigger boom to fit into.

**sulug₂** *v. tr.* To put clothes on; to get dressed. *Dakayu' du kansinsilyu bay sulugku.* I put on a single pair of undershorts. *Ta'abut pa'in kat'llung llaw pagpuwasa, sinulug e'na s'mmekna pagdayang-dayang.* When the third day of fasting arrived, she put on her royal garments.

**suluhan** *n.* A mediator; a person who negotiates. *Bang hati mbal tara'ugna sultan dakayu', magtūy iya amabeya' suluhan pasampang ni sultan inān bo' mikipagkahāp.* If perhaps he cannot defeat the other king, he promptly sends a mediator to meet that king requesting to be reconciled. *Aku ya suluhan, aku ya pamalatunan.* I will be the go-between, the message bearer.

**pagsuluhan** *v. intr.* aN- To serve as a mediator or broker.

**sulut** *adj.* a- 1) In agreement with; pleased with. *Asulut aku ma siyakaku.* I'm in agreement with my older sibling. (*Thesaurus:* **amu₂ 1.1, beya'₃ 1, dakayu'₂ 1, manghalapi, pagta'ayun, tayudtud**) 1.1) *v. intr.* pa- To assent to something. *Bay aku pasulut ma bay panutatnu tagna' hē', bo' ma buwattina'an mbal na makajari.* I agreed to what you required at the beginning, but now it is not acceptable. (*Thesaurus:* **uyun**) 1.2) *v. tr.* To accept or accede to someone's wishes. *Saga d'nda bay ma masa awal, sinulut e'na kabaya'an h'llana, niōnan e'na nakura'na.* The women of historic times, they agreed to their husbands' wishes, and spoke of him as their master. 1.3) *v. advrs.* ka-...-an To be pleased with; satisfied with. *Kasulutan du aku ma ka'a.* I am pleased with you.

**pagsulut** *v. intr.* aN- 1) To come to an agreement, of two or more parties. *A: "Magsulut na ba?" B: "Aho' magsulut na ba, hē' na busay ma iya."* A: "Are we in agreement?" B: "Yes, we are agreed, he now has the paddle." *Mbal sigām magsulut sabab angalindihan ya bihing-luma'na.* They are not in accord because she aspires to outdo her neighbors. *Manjari l'lla atawa d'nda angiris. Bang duwangan sigām bilahi angiris, subay magsulut.* It can be the man or the woman to get custody. If they both want custody, they have to come to an agreement. 1.1) *v. tr.* To get two groups to be in agreement. *Pinapagsulut e'na saga matto'a maka ka'anakan sigām.* He got the parents to be in agreement with their children.

**pagsulutan** *n.* An agreement between two; a pact; a contract. *Bay kami pi'itu min lahat atala bahasa amu' kami ni ka'am angahinang kām pagsulutan maka kami itū."* We came from a faraway land intending to petition you-all to make an agreement with us. *Bangsa itū hal anagga' ma pagsulutan ya bay janji'ku ma ka'mbo'-mbo'an sigām.* These people groups simply go against my agreement with their ancestors. *Ya kapagsulutanta tambahan pinapagtongod maka hinang dang'llaw.* Our contract was the payment appropriate to one day's work.

**sumadja** *adj. a-* Poorly cared for; neglected. *Ya luma' kami ma Musu', t'ggol kami maitu ma Tinutu', asumadja na.* Our houses in Musu', in the long time we have been here at Tinoto, are no longer cared for. *Ya matto'a l'lla inān bay magh'nda pabalik, asumadja na saga anakna.* That older man has married again, his children are now neglected. *Ai-ai halam taisbatta, sumadja na pat'nna'anna.* Anything we haven't paid attention to, put somewhere without care. (*Thesaurus:* **haman-haman 1, palehom**)

**sumā'..sumā'** (var. **suma'an..suma'an**) *adv.* Sometimes one, sometimes another; alternatively; either... or. *Sumā' aniya' daing ma luma' kami, sumā' halam.* Sometimes there is fish at our house, sometimes not. *Bang anganggonteng, suma'an mpat, suma'an lima, suma'an t'llu p'ssina.* When we do multiple-hook fishing we sometimes use four, sometimes five, sometimes three hooks. *Duwa-ruwa suma'an mpat.* In pairs, sometimes four. (*Thesaurus:* **bang pasān, sasā'**)

**suma'an..suma'an** var. of **sumā'..sumā'**

**suman** *n.* A dessert of sweetened glutinous rice cooked in a wrapper of coconut leaves. (*Thesaurus:* **hapit-hapit, wadjit**)

**sumangat** *n.* 1) The non-physical component of human personality. *Ag'mma sumangatku bang aku lum'ngngan kaleya. Sali' aniya' a'a.* I have a sense of foreboding when I walk inland. It is as if a person is there. *Sumangatku, buwat ginhawaku.* My *sumangat*, like my inner being or self. (*Thesaurus:* **ginhawa, nyawa, panalengog, umagad 1**) 2) The spirit of a deceased relative. (*cf:* **mangat**) 3) The component of a spirit being that may enter a human to possess him. *Isi jīn niōnan sumangat. Mbal ta'nda' baran, sakali manusiya' ya pasangonanna.* The essence of a djinn is called a *sumangat*. It is not seen physically, a human being just becomes its medium. **3.1)** *v. tr.* To possess or trouble a human being, the action of a spirit being. *Singsing bulawan niengkotan ma k'llong onde'-onde' ko da'a iya sinumangat.* A gold ring tied

around a little child's neck to prevent it being troubled by a spirit. *Bang kita asaki bo' halam bay makatuli ni mbo'ta, sinumangat kita. Amasi ma deyom kasakihan, sali' abasag bo' mbal isāb.* If we are sick but haven't slept in the presence of our ritual ancestor, we are troubled by the *sumangat* of a spirit being. We are still experiencing sickness, sort of strong but not really so. *Panji ilū bay ma langgal, makasumangat.* That flag was on the mosque, it will bring trouble from a spirit.

**sumangat llum** *n. phrase* 1) The spirit or essence of a living person, sometimes sensed when not physically present. {idiom} **1.1)** *v. advrs.* -in- Ill due to the homesickness of an absent relative. {idiom}

**sumariya** *v. tr.* To question someone in order to get the truth, usually as part of legal processes. *Sumariyata ka, "Angay ka bay anangkaw pelang?"* I question you, "Why did you steal the canoe?" (*Thesaurus:* **katilaw, jakki 1, tanya₂**)

**sumau'** *see:* **pagsumau'**

**sumayang-galura'** (var. **simayang-galura'**) *n.* 1) A mythical bird. *Sumayang-galura', manuk luwa belle'.* The *sumayang-galura'*, an eagle-like bird. (*Thesaurus:* **galura', sambalani**) 2) An ostrich.

**sumba** var. of **s'mba**

**sumbali'** *v. tr.* To slaughter a chicken or animal in readiness for cooking. *Bang bay aubus na sumbali'nu, na tin'ddak na.* When you had completed slaughtering it, it was then gutted. *Si Ki, ya bay sinumbali' ma timpu jipun.* Ki, the man who was slaughtered during the Japanese era. (*cf:* **hakika' 1**)

**sumbali'an** *n.* The meat of chickens or animals in contrast to fish.

**sumbang** *adj. zero* Involved in a relationship (sexual, fighting) which is considered incestuous because of close kin relationship. *Bang kami maka kakiku magkawin mbal maghalus, sumbang kami.* If my cousin and I were to marry it would not be appropriate, we would be committing incest. (*Thesaurus:* **halal 1, halam-mutallak, halus₂, haram 1**)

**pagkasumbang** *v. intr. aN-* To be in an incestuous relationship.

**sumbuhan** *n.* The wick of a lamp; the fuse of an explosive.

**sumbul** var. of **sungbul**

**sumbung** *v. ditr.* To inform on someone to a person in authority. *Anobtob na llaw pam'llinu bang ka anumbung ni paltiraku.* This will be the last day for you to buy [from me] if you tell my middleman about it. *Sinumbung kami maglakibini ni botang-lahat. Na magbisala na kami, na sai-sai makabāk bisala ahāp, ya anganda'ug. Magtimbul kami pabīng, nīntanan kami batang-batang.* We two, husband and wife, were reported to the community leader. So we talked together, and whoever found the best words won [the argument]. We got together again, and restrictions were laid on us. (*Thesaurus:* **kuhi**$_2$, **pagmahi, pagmalān, pagpuhun 1.1, tuntut**$_1$)

**pagsumbung** *v. intr. aN-* To report or inform on one another. *Magsumbung dansehe'an bang halam makani'iskul dangan.* Members of the same group report on each other if one of them hasn't been at school.

**sumil**$_1$ *adj. a-* Ungenerous; stingy. (*Thesaurus:* **bista**$_2$ **1, kaikit**$_1$**, kigit, kimmat 1, k'mmit 1, kudkud, kuriput 1, kussil, giging, iskut**)

**sumil**$_2$ var. of **summil**

**sumilan** var. of **sumiyan**

**sumiyan** (var. **humilan**; **humiyan**; **sumilan**) *interrog.* When? What time or date? *Sumiyan bay tagna'an ya sakinu ilu?* When was the beginning of your sickness? *Yuk man kar'ndahan, "Taima' kam." Yuk man kal'llahan, "Nā, humiyan magpah'nda?"* Those from the girl's side said, "You are accepted." Those from the man's side asked, "So then, when is the engagement ceremony?" *Taggaha' ka'am makat'kka. Halam kinata'uhan bang humiyan kat'kkabi.* You arrived unexpectedly. It was not known when your arrival would be. *A: "Sumilan ka pi'itu?" B: "Subay na salung."* A: "When will you come?" B: "It'll have to be tomorrow." (*Thesaurus:* **ai, angay, buwattingga 1.1, magay, maingga, sai**)

**sumiyan-sumiyan** *adv.* Whenever; at any time. *Bang ka pabīng sumiyan-sumiyan, nda'anta ka kulit mital.* If you come back at any time I will look out a can for you. *A: "Sumiyan kita angosol?" B: "Sumiyan-sumiyannu."* A: "When shall we put the posts in?" B: "Whenever you like." *Bang ka ganta' pinaglaka'-laka'an e' anakku sumilan-sumilan, subay aku haka'annu magtūy.* If my son should make immoral suggestions to you at any time, you must tell me immediately. (*Thesaurus:* **gana-gana 1.1, taka-taka, tiyap-tiyap**)

**summil** (var. **sumil**$_2$) *adj. a-* Lacking energy or physical strength; slow in getting things done. (*Thesaurus:* **dome-dome, layu-layu, longkoy, s'nnay**)

**sumpa'** *v. tr.* To insult someone by suggesting immoral relations with the person or his female kin. *Bang aniya' palabay a'a, yukta, "Laluku ina'nu, laluku h'ndanu," ma halam aniya' dusana, anumpa'. Ya hē' makapagbono'.* If someone is going by and we say, "I'll have sex with your mother, I'll have sex with your wife," when that person has done nothing wrong, that's *sumpa'*. That's what leads to fighting. (*syn:* **paglaka'-laka' 1.1**)

**sumpal** (var. **tumpal**) *n.* 1) A patch over a hole or gap. *Banog taga sumpal, sanyawa si Ji.* A sail with a patch, or Ji's shorts. *Luma' goret-goret, gese' man gese', sumpal man sumpal.* A ramshackle house, one tear after another, one patch after another patch. 1.1) *v. tr.* To repair something by patching. *Tasumpal pelang abō' magpakahinang. Sin'nsong atawa tinumpakan.* The canoe can be patched so it can be used for work. Plugged up or dotted with patches. (*Thesaurus:* **patli' 1.1, patlong, puna', tupak 1.1**) 1.2) *v. tr. -an* To apply a patch to a hole or gap.

**sumpallit** *v. intr. pa-* To be blown upwards from the normal state, as paper or thatch shingles. (*Thesaurus:* **bīng**$_1$ **1, bulallit**)

**sumping** *n.* 1) A flower; a floral motif in a fabric pattern. *Gaddung papaganna, bilu sumpingna.* Its background is green, its flower motifs are blue. (*cf:* **bunga**$_2$) 1.1) *v. intr. aN-* To produce flowers. *Apote', anumping bowa'na.* White, producing flowers in its opening.

**kasumping-sumpingan** *n.* Multiple flowers. *Ap'nno' e' kasumping-sumpingan.* Covered with flowers.

**pagsumping** *v. intr. aN-* To be flowering. *Yampa magsumping sampaka' itū.* These frangipani are only now flowering.

**sumpit** *v. intr. pa-* 1) To squirt out in a fine spray. (*Thesaurus:* **kissat, pigsik**$_1$ **1, p'ssik 1.1, pulagsik, sahupput**) 1.1) *v. tr.* To spray something. *Bay sinumpit luma' kami, aheka hama'.* Our house was sprayed, lots of mosquitoes. (*cf:* **busug 1**)

**susumpit** *n.* A blowpipe; a blowgun.

**sumpit-sumpit** *n.* The Banded archerfish. *Toxotes jaculatrix.*

**sumpiyang** *n.* A rafter; a post, brace or support set at an angle to the vertical. (*syn:* **sungkelang**; *Thesaurus:* **bale**$_3$ **1, hāg 1, lusuk-lusuk, pangtu'ud, pipul, tuku 1**)

**sumsuman** *n.* Bone marrow.

**sumu** *adj. a-* 1) Becoming bored with. *Pasangdan ka amangan sampay ka asumu.* Carry on eating until you are sick of it. 1.1) *v. advrs. -in-* Bored by; surfeited with. *Sinumu aku amangan saldinas.* I am bored with eating canned fish. (*Thesaurus:* **jompo', lumad**)

**pagsinumu** *v. intr. aN-* To be bored with something or someone.

**sumuddai** var. of **simuddai**

**suna** *v. tr.* To move negotiations on towards completion. (*Thesaurus:* **pasasā, tambuku**$_1$)

**sundak** *n.* 1) A rod or pole. (*Thesaurus:* **sulad 1**) 1.1) *v. tr.* To wound someone with a pole thrust from below. *Bay sinundak mbo' kami. Kobolan iya, sagwā' nsa' bay kapagguluhan e'na basta t'mmang.* Our grandfather was struck with a pole. He was magically protected against violence, but weapons of cane were something he hadn't been instructed about.

**sundal** *n.* 1) A prostitute. {vulgar} (*Thesaurus:* **ba'is, biga', ga'ira, puta**) 1.1) *adj. -an* Promiscuous; given to prostitution.

**sundalu** *n.* A soldier. *Palūd na ba'anan sundalu magtinakos.* A group of soldiers, fully armed, came downhill. (*Thesaurus:* **bobono', militari**)

**pagsundalu** *v. intr.* aN- To become or serve as a soldier. *Bang aniya' ta'nda'na a'a akosog atawa aesog, ningā' magtūy e'na magsundalu.* If he saw someone who was strong or brave, he immediately took him to become a soldier.

**sundang** *n.* A large working knife; a machete. (*Thesaurus:* **bangkung, bari', gayang, lahut, laring lahut, pira**)

**sunduk** *n.* 1) A vertical grave marker. (*Thesaurus:* **duyung-duyung, pilang-pilang**) 2) A cursing equivalent for a wooden item such as a paddle or a mooring stake. *Ndiya sunduknu ilu tapanumbuk ka'a!* Give me your cursed paddle to hit you with! (*gen:* **sukna' 1.1**)

**sunnat** *v. tr.* To initiate an infant girl into the community of Islam. (*cf:* **islam 1.1**)

**sunsang** *adj. zero* Inverted; reversed in position. *Bang ma kami sunsang itū abīng.* For us this being reversed is *bīng*. *Nianakan sunsang, dahū tape'.* Born back-to-front, feet first. *Bang kaba' maka ta'u pinagka'ob, samasunsang karuwa sīn.* When heads and tails are put together, the two coins are mutually reversed. (*Thesaurus:* **bulallit, sulang-saling, sulay₂, susun-buyu'**)

**samasunsang** *adj.* Facing each other, of opposites.

**suntuk** *n.* 1) A blow with the fist. *Yukna, "Angabtang sadja ka min t'dda, buwananta ka dakayu' suntuk."* He said, "You say a single word and I will give you a punch." 1.1) *v. tr.* To strike someone with the fist, on any part of the body or face. *Bay aku sinuntuk e' kakiku, halam aku makabalos.* My cousin punched me but I didn't pay him back. (*Thesaurus:* **butug, g'bbuk, tibu', tikbung**)

**pagsuntuk** *v. intr.* aN- To fight together using fists; to punch one another. *Bang aniya' magsuntuk subay sinapad bo' mbal maglaha' atawa magbutig.* If some people are punching each other they should be separated lest they bleed or swell up. *Buwat sawpama bay magbono', buwat aku magbono' maka mma'ku. Na arai' pa'in kami magsuntuk, na ah'lling ganta' manapad kami, "Aningkō' ka amanyabut."* Getting into a fight for example, like my father and I fighting. So when we are about to punch each other, someone restrains us and says, "Sit down and call on God." (*cf:* **pagboksen**)

**suntu'an** *n.* A pattern; a design; a plan. *Subay aniya' bannang suntu'an.* There needs to be a piece of thread for a sample [to work from]. *Ya papagan pan'nggehan inān apasagi' suntu'anna.* The base of that stand was square in design. (*Thesaurus:* **bantukan, ladjawan, sengoran, simpayan**)

**sunud** *adv.* 1) Following. 1.1) *v. tr.* To follow someone's example. *Kal'ngnganan saga a'a ahāp ya panunurin.* Let the lifestyle of good people be what you pursue. (*Thesaurus:* **apas 1.1, pagiku-iku, sunu', turul 1**)

**sunud llaw** *n. phrase* The following day. *Pagsunud llaw, paluwas na si Je.* The next day, Je emerged.

**sunud tahun** *n. phrase* The following year. *Sunud tahun ilū, ma waktu buwattitu, aniya' na hambinnu anak.* The following year, at this time of day, you will be holding a child.

**sunu'** *v. intr.* pa- To follow the next in a sequence. *Dahū ka, pasunu' pa'in aku.* You go first, I'll follow. *Tapi' ettom lungtud, ati aniya' isāb pasunu' i', ya anu pote'-pote' isāb. Lungtud* is a black strake [of a canoe] and then there's another, the whitish one that follows. *Bang bay aniya' siyakaku, pasunu' aku iya.* If I had an older brother, I would be following him. (*Thesaurus:* **apas 1.1, pagiku-iku, sunud 1.1, turul 1**)

**pagsunu'-sunu'** *v. intr.* aN- To be arranged in an ordered series; to occur in quick succession. *Buwat sawan-sawan agsunu'-sunu', ya pangongka'an onde'.* Like those little cups that fit in a sequence, the child's toy. (*syn:* **pagsungbul-sungbul**)

**pasunu'** *adv.* Following; after that; next.

**sūng** *v. intr. zero* Get going; do promptly. *Sūng na kitam amole', abut alalom.* Let's all go home, it's almost high tide. *Sūng ka, amaindam du.* Off you go, he's bound to let you borrow it. *Ngā'un pangisihanna bohe' bo' kita sūng.* Get his water container and let's go.

**sūngan** *n.* The gable end of a ridged roof. *Tambolku sūngan bo' mbal makalabay a'a anangkaw.* I will close off the gable space so no one can get through to steal.

**sungbu-sungbu** (var. **sunggu-sunggu**) *v. advrs.* -in- To suffer from irritation and bleeding of the nasal lining. *Buwat onde'-onde' asiga, mbal biyasa, manjari sinungbu-sungbu.* Like a child smoking a cigaret, not used to it, and so the nose is irritated. (*Thesaurus:* **laha'₁ 1.1, lota'**)

**sungbul** (var. **sumbul**) *v. tr.* -an To repeat the specified action in quick succession. *Sungbulin na timbak ilū apa ilu aheka daing.* Keep throwing charges of that dynamite because lots of fish are there. *Sinumbulan he' a'a damunda'. Nilaruk dakayu' ati pinaturul dakayu', pinaturul dakayu', ya hē' magsumbul.* The same sequence followed by people of the one canoe. One [charge] is thrown and followed by another, and then another, that's *sumbul*.

**pagsungbul-sungbul** *v. intr.* aN- To do something in quick succession. *Da'a kam magsumbul-sumbul abō' mbal apōng letehan ilu. Magsunu'-sunu'.* Don't go in close succession lest that walkway break. [Going across] one after the other. *Nilaruk dakayu' ati pinaturul dakayu', pinaturul dakayu', ya hē' magsumbul.* One is thrown and another is made to follow, then another, that is *pagsumbul*. (*syn:* **pagsunu'-sunu'**)

**sungkab** *v. intr.* pa- To be partly open; to have a gap between a container and its lid. *Dambila' ilū* *pasungkab.* One side there is half-open. (*Thesaurus:* **banga'**₁, **buka'**₃, **lungkad 1**, **ukab 1.1**)

**sungkelang** (var. **songkelang**) *n.* A rafter; any post or support set at an angle to the vertical. (*syn:* **sumpiyang**)

**sungkit** *v. tr.* To impale something in order to harvest or retrieve it. *Sungkitanta ka mampallam atahak.* I will spike a ripe mango for you. (*Thesaurus:* **kahid 1**, **kawit**₁, **kuhit**)

**sunggu-sunggu** var. of **sungbu-sungbu**

**sunggud** *v. tr.* To irritate someone by repeated bad behavior, as a child annoying its parents. *Anunggud pahāp ka'a ilū.* How irritating you are! *Pina'astol atayta, buwat e' saga anakta. Yukta, "Da'a pa'in aku sunggurun."* Stirred to anger, as by our children. We say, "Don't keep making me mad." (*Thesaurus:* **kalintaw**, **dole' 1**, **dugal 1**, **giyagas**, **p'ggot-p'ggot**, **s'ngngot**₁ **1**)

**sungi'** *v. intr. a-* **1)** To defecate; to have a bowel movement. *Sowa i' asungi' bulawan.* That [mythical] snake excreted gold. *Asungi' aku ma haronan.* I have my bowel movement from the house ladder. (*cf:* **pagharam**; *Thesaurus:* **jamban 1**, **mange' 1**, **tai' 2**) **1.1)** *v. tr. -an* To excrete something. *Agahimāt na iya, hal bohe' tasungi'na.* He has become limp, all he excretes is water. *An'gga b'ttongna, a'sso he' kinakan, mbal makahinansong sala, subay sinungi'an ni lowang.* His stomach is gorged, full of food, sort of unable to breathe, [the mass] should be excreted down a hole.

**pagsungi'-sungi'** *v. intr. aN-* To suffer from diarrhea. *Itiya' aku magsungi'-sungi', marai' aniya' sassingku.* Here I am suffering from diarrhea, perhaps I've got pinworms. *Mbal tainum bohe' alobog, makapagsungi'-sungi'.* Dirty water is not drinkable, it can cause diarrhea. (*Thesaurus:* **kaluwa'**, **pagloros-loros**)

**sungun** var. of **hungun**

**supa**₁ *n.* A unit of bulk measurement for dry goods, about 1/3 of a liter. (*Thesaurus:* **gantang**, **pansing 1**)

**supa**₂ *n.* A style of blouse. (*cf:* **badju'-sablay**)

**supaya** (var. **bo' supaya**) *conj.* In order to; so that. *Daka ai subay hinangku bo' supaya aku kinabaya'an.* Goodness knows what I should do in order to be loved [by her]. (*Thesaurus:* **bat sabab**, **bo' supaya**, **bo'**₂, **dok supaya**, **he da'a**)

**suplit** var. of **siplit**

**suppak** var. of **sugpak**

**suput**₁ *v. intr. pa-/aN-* To surge up, as waves over an obstacle or water boiling over. *Pasuput kaldero, bohe' angalere'.* The pot boils over, the water bubbles. *Amasu' kita bohe' bay asal ap'nno'. Pagpasu'na anuput pariyata'.* We were heating water [in a container] that was already full. When it got hot it surged up. (*Thesaurus:* **appu'**, **sasay**, **sauk 2**, **s'pput**)

**suput**₂ *n.* A small bag; a paper sack. *Aniya' suput ma ka'a pangisihanku buwas?* Do you have a bag for me to put husked rice in? (*Thesaurus:* **pokot**₂ **1**, **puyu'**)

**surang** *v. tr. -an* To point a weapon at someone. *Bang kami niholdap he' mundu sinurangan kami timbak. Tudju ni kita bulu timbak inān.* When we are held up by bandits we have a weapon pointed at us. The barrel of the gun aimed in our direction. (*Thesaurus:* **balis**₁, **kalsa**, **kital**)

**suratan** *n.* A love charm that binds a woman to one lover; one's fate in regard to love. *Bang sali' d'nda bay tunangta, bo' amole' ni l'lla saddi, ngga'i ka suratanta.* When a woman who was my sweetheart goes to the house of another man, that is not my fate. *Nihinang suratan ma a'a talus. Sinulatan he'na.* Having a binding love charm made by a soothsayer. Written by him. (*cf:* **lindang 1**, **sulat-libun**)

**suray** (var. **sudlay**) *n.* **1)** A comb for dressing one's hair. *Am'lli aku suray ni M'ddas paglais-laisku.* I will buy a comb in Siasi Town for keeping my hair neat. (*Thesaurus:* **kuhut 1**, **sūd**) **1.1)** *v. tr.* To comb one's hair. (*cf:* **lais 1.1**)

**pagsinuray** *v. intr. aN-* To wear a comb in one's hair.

**suring**₁ *n.* **1)** An extension to the dimensions of something. **1.1)** *v. tr. -an* To extend the length or width of something. *Tupak itū sali' bangkat, suring itū sali' asugpat.* This word *tupak* is like adding a layer, *suring* is like adding to the length. *Bang sali' angahinang badju' bo' mbal maka'abut s'mmek inān, subay sinuringan.* Like when making a shirt and the cloth does not suffice, it should be extended.

**suring**₂ *n.* Sprouts of new growth in a plant. (*Thesaurus:* **saha' 1.1**, **saingsing 1**, **s'mbut 1**)

**pagsuring** *v. intr. aN-* To grow by putting out new shoots.

**pagsuring-pagsaingsing** *v. intr. aN-* **1)** To grow and spread by producing roots and shoots. *Buwat biyabas patomo'an dīna. B'nnal tinanom bo' magsuring-magsaingsing.* Like guavas growing up of their own accord. It's true that they are planted, but they sprout and multiply. **1.1)** *v. intr. aN-* To reproduce and multiply, of people. {idiom} *Anak-mpuku magsuring-magsaingsing.* My descendants growing and spreading. *Magsuring-saingsin, sali' mbal maglawak, magkampung.* Growing and spreading, not going further away, staying in kin-based community.

**suring-baha'u** *n.* The coming generation; posterity. *Suring-baha'u wa'i palorok kamemon.* All of the coming generation have died.

**suruk** *v. tr.* To poke something from beneath. *Sowa-tangkig bay anuruk iya.* A *tangkig* snake poked into him. *Bay aku sinuruk ma pāt-tape'ku hē' min deyo' lantay.* Someone under the floor poked into the sole of my foot. *Bay aku sinuruk he' a'a ma lowang jubulku.* Someone poked me in my anus. (*Thesaurus:* **kussu'**, **langgit 1**, **sudlat 1.1**, tugsuk 2.2)

**suruk-punsu** *n.* The Silver whiting or the Sand smelt. *Sillago sihama.*

**suru'** *n.* 1) A spoon; a ladle. *Sōngun suru', ndiya.* Move the spoon along, give it here. *Wa'i alungay suru' ma pagkose'an.* The spoon has been lost at the washing place. (*Thesaurus:* **luwag** 1, **paleta, sasanglag, sintib**) 1.1) *v. tr. -an* To ladle something out with a spoon; to feed someone with a spoon.

**surut** *v. tr.* To thread items on a string, forming a convenient bundle. *Bang ka makak'llo' daing, surutun maka buway.* When you get fish, thread them together with rattan. (*Thesaurus:* **lingkit 1.1, tōhan, tuhug** 1)

**susa** *n.* 1) Emotional stress such as grief, anxiety or worry. (*Thesaurus:* **kibad atay, pagsorol, sukkal** 1) 1.1) *adj. a-* Suffering emotional stress, as from sorrow, worry or anxiety. *Makasusa pahāp onde' inān bang ahūg pareyo'.* That child will cause grief if it falls. (*Thesaurus:* **liru'** 1, **susun₂** 1.1) 1.2) *v. intr. aN-* To become emotionally upset or worried. *Mahē' pa'in ma luma' kar'ndahan ē', sali' anusa pikilanku.* While there in those women's house, my thinking became troubled.

　**kasusahan** *n.* Sorrow; anxiety. *Aheya kasusahanku.* My sorrow is great. *A: "Ai kasusahanbi?" B: "Asusa aku ma anakku, wa'i amusay ni Sitangkay."* A: "What is your worry?" B: "I am worried for my child, he has gone off to Sitangkay." *Kasusahanku anakku halam tapole', wa'i bay angusaha. Ya du ilu kasusahanku.* I am anxious for my son who hasn't come home, he's been away earning his living. That is what I am troubled about.

**susaed** *n.* Risk; venture.

　**pagsusaed** *v. intr. aN-* To do something without knowing what may happen. *Niōnan he' kami magsusaed. Hal magsagap, halam aniya' padduman.* We call it *susaed.* Just taking a risk, without a compass. *Magsusaed aku magpalungay ni lahat atā.* I take the risk of getting lost in a far away land. *Magsusaed aku patuhun.* I dive not knowing how it will turn out. (*Thesaurus:* **k'ddom₂, halus₁, pagpasukud, samba** 1, **sarap₂** 1, **tawakkal**)

**sussa'** *v. tr.* To refuse to believe what someone says, implying that he is lying. *Ōy, da'a ka anussa', sali' kita pinaputing.* Hey, don't refuse to believe, it's as though we are accused of lying. (*Thesaurus:* **pagl'pput, puting 1.1**)

　**panunussa'** *n.* One who refuses to believe; a skeptic.

**sussi** *n.* 1) Purity; holiness. *Sussi itū al'ssin buwat deyom luma'bi, halam aniya' s'ggitna.* Purity is being clean, like in your house, no rubbish. 1.1) *adj. a-* Completely clean; pure; holy. *Tuhan makajari niōnan asussi.* God can be spoken of as holy. *Ndū', ahāp pagatay, asussi.* How nice, so

good at heart, pure. *Bohe' itū bay na lanu'anku, asussi na.* This water, I have made it clean, it's now pure. (*cf:* **saltun 1.1**; *Thesaurus:* **k'ssang₁, lanu'** 1, **langis** 1, **l'ssin**) 1.2) *v. tr.* To purify; cleanse. *Sussihunbi baranbi pahāp bo' yampa kam magsalinan badju' al'ssin.* Wash your bodies thoroughly and then put on clean clothes.

　**mahasussi** *adj.* *zero* Totally pure; divinely holy.

**sussik** *var. of* **sugsig**

**sussuk** *clf.* A unit of measure for gold, approximately a carat. *Aniya' saga duwampū' ni duwampū' maka walu' sussuk ma dublun pikit duwa.* There are twenty to twenty-eight *sussuk* in one medium gold piece.

**sussu'** *var. of* **sabba-sussu'**

**susuk** *v. ditr.* To make partial payment in cash, for goods or property. *Bangka'-bangka'ku ya bay panusuk, saddī t'llu hatus maka duwampū'.* My small dugout was partial payment, separate from the ₱320 [in cash]. (*Thesaurus:* **bayad 1.1, gadji 1.1, hokas, lampak₁ 1.1, tinga 1.1, tulahan, tunay₂, tungbas** 1)

**susul** *v. intr. pa-* 1) To travel close to land along a coast or river bank. *Pasusul kami man bihing deya tudju ni Sisangat.* We go along the edge of the land towards Sisangat. 1.1) *v. tr.* To follow a coastline. *Paglinggi' kami, sinusul na bihing bangkaw, sowang, mahē' ma Tapa'an.* Having netted some fish, we followed along the edge of the mangrove swamps and the channels, out there by Tapa'an Island. *Buwat anū', anusulan min bihing deya, na anasaban.* Like fishing by lamplight, following the shoreline, just going on randomly.

　**susulan** *n.* A coastline. *Ya lahat sigā ina'an ma bihing susulan, ma llot kabase'an maka katoho'an.* Their place is right on the coastline, in the intertidal zone. (*Thesaurus:* **bihingan, daplakan₁, gintana'an, hampilan, pari'an, tampe, tapiyan**)

**susumpit** (derivative of **sumpit**) *n.* A blowpipe; a blowgun.

**susun₁** *n.* 1) A horizontal or vertical stack; a pile of items such as books. *Pinahāp susun katas-katas he' si Mām.* Mam tidies the stack of paper sheets. *Pasindikun lai' ko' ahāp susunna.* Put the plates on edge so the stack is good. 1.1) *v. tr.* To arrange things in a horizontal or vertical stack. *Sinusun kayu itū, pinahāp bangkatna.* This wood is arranged in a vertical stack, improving the way it sits.

　**pagsusun₁** *v. tr.* To arrange things in a stack; less commonly, to arrange things in a sequence, vertical or otherwise. *Buwat tu'ung mbal tapat'ngge, pinagsusun.* Stacked, like boxes that can't be stood upright. (*Thesaurus:* **pagbangkat-bangkat 1.1**)

**susun₂** *n.* 1) Regret for past actions or attitude. *Magtangis saga a'a maina'an maka magtage'ot empon kabowa susun sigām.* The people there wept and ground their teeth, moved by their regret. **1.1)** *adj.* a- Regretful; sorry. *Asusun du ka bang timanannu h'ndanu bo' ma iya anakbi.* You will be sorry if you divorce your wife and your children go with her. *Samasusun kita.* You and I are equally regretful. (*Thesaurus:* **liru' 1**, **susa 1.1**)

**pagsusun₂** *v. intr.* aN- **1)** To feel regret about something. *Magsusun aku, wa'i tara'ug sīnku. Halam aniya' pam'lliku doppeng.* I am regretful, my money has been won from me. I have nothing to buy cassava panccakes doppeng with. *Magalud sigām maka magtage'ot empon sabab min kapagsusun sigām.* They wailed and ground their teeth because of their regret. *Wajib subay halam aniya' dusa pagsusunannu.* It is essential that you should have no sin to be regretful for. **1.1)** *v. tr.* -an To blame oneself for something done. *Na da'a kam asukkal. Da'a isāb pagsusuninbi baranbi pasal pamab'llibi ma aku.* Don't be sad, now. Don't blame yourselves for your act of selling me. *Magsindilan, sali' magtangis pasal anakta bay halam karūlan ai-ai. Hatina kapagsusunan iya e' saga matto'ana inān.* Grieving, weeping over one's child who hadn't been indulged over something. In other words his parents feel deep regret over him.

**susunan** *n.* Feeling of regret; a sense of blame for a responsibility not fulfilled. *Buwat saupama anakta, sulutta, panupusanta, bo' halam aniya' susunan anak ma matto'a.* Our children for example, we indulge them, do absolutely everything for them, so that the child will have nothing to blame the parent for.

**susun-buyu'** *n.* The reversed position of twins in the womb. (*Thesaurus:* **bulallit, sulang-saling, sulay₂, sunsang**)

**susut** *v. tr.* -an To remove dirt or grime by scrubbing. *Bang aheka buling ma kaldero, sinusutan maka gusung.* When there is much soot on the pot, it is scrubbed with sand. *Anusutan pelang, ang'llawan banog, anangon gi'.* Scrubbing the canoe hull, drying the sail, then putting the canoe up on the drying rack. *Bang aniya' pahinggamanta sali' pelang bo' nilumut, subay sinusutan.* If we have a conveyance such as a *pelang* and it gets mossy, it must be scrubbed. (*Thesaurus:* **bunut-bunut, kuskus 1.1, dalug₁, gisgis 1.2, lukup, lupag**)

**susuwat** (derivative of **suwat**) *n.* A weeding tool. (*Thesaurus:* **bara, lalandak, pala, piku, sangkul 1**).

**sūt** *intrj.* An expression of refusal to obey or oblige. *Mbal ameya'-meya' makannak inān, yuk ina'na, "Llet ba iya, sūt!"* That child won't do what he is told, and his mother says, "He's so stubborn, sūt!"

**sutanghon** *n.* Fine rice noodles.

**sutla'** *n.* A silken fabric. *Ahunit nila'it bang sutla'.* Silk cloth is hard to sew. *Basta sutla' niōnan lanay.* If it is silk it is said to be *lanay.* (*Thesaurus:* **lanay₁, punji**)

**suwak** *n.* **1)** A liking or preference for something specific. (*Thesaurus:* **sōb, tahud**) **1.1)** *v. tr.* a-, ka-..-an, -an To have a strong preference for something or someone.

**suwa'** *v. intr.* pa- **1)** To pass through a restricted space. *Pasuwa' aku man batangan sudju paluwas na.* I will go under the outrigger booms [of moored canoes] to get out. *Bang aniya' amasuwa' bangka', bo' aniya' maghinang mbo', nilāng.* If someone lets a canoe pass [under a house] while an ancestor ceremony is happening, he is told not to. **1.1)** *v. tr.* -an To pass a line or thread through a hole, as threading a needle, splicing a rope, or inserting shoelaces. *Bang aku magdundang suwa'anku lubid ni papan engkotanku.* When I swing I put rope through a hole in a board and I tie it.

**pagsuwa'-suwa'** *v. tr.* -an To join woven items by running a line through connecting edges. *Buwat bubu, pinagsuwa'-suwa'an dakanna maka bukutna maka p'ttung abulak.* Like a woven fishtrap, its base and its back threaded together with green bamboo lacing.

**suwa'-s'llo'** *see:* **pagsuwa'-s'llo'**

**suwal** *v. tr.* **1)** To get something by prising it up from a secure place. *Buwat batu sinuwal, kinalut maka kayu.* Like a stone being prised up, dug up with a piece of wood. *Sinuwal ai-ai man deyo'ta.* Suwal refers to anything levered up from below us. (*Thesaurus:* **landak, li'ad, lugit**) **2)** To prise something good out of a difficult source. *Bandung-bandungin ba abō' paluwas tunisna. Magbeya' binandungan maka sinuwal-suwal. Sali' pamaluwasan tunis ahāp ma iya.* Stir him up so the melody will come out. *Bandung* and *suwal* go together. Both ways of getting a good tune from him.

**suwala** *n.* **1)** A voice. *Takaleku suwala tunangku.* I can hear my sweetheart's voice. (*Thesaurus:* **h'lling₁ 2.1, lagam**) **1.1)** *v. intr.* aN- To produce the sound of a voice; to utter. *Akohot k'llongku bang aku makasuwala.* My throat is hoarse when I say something.

**suwalak** *v. tr.* To refuse or decline something; to refuse to take. (*syn:* **sulak₂**)

**suwan-suwan** *v. tr.* To cook meat or fish with soya sauce. (*gen:* **b'lla 1**)

**suwariyan** var. of **sulariyan**

**suwat** *v. tr.* -an To clear weeds from agricultural land. (*cf:* **lapa₂**)

**susuwat** *n.* A weeding tool. (*Thesaurus:* **bara, lalandak, pala, piku, sangkul 1**)

**suwi-suwi** var. of **suli-suli**

**suwit** *n.* A small plate; bowl; a saucer. (*Thesaurus:* **lai', pinggan**)

# T t

**tā** (var. **tala**) *n.* **1)** Distance away from; relative remoteness. (*ant:* **sekot 1**) **1.1)** *adj. a-* Far away; remote. *Aniya' sigām kasehe' atā pamole'an.* Some of them have a long way to go home. *Ē! S'lle' bale puhū' pinatā e' Tuhan!* Perish the thought, may God put that far away! (*syn:* **lawak**) **1.2)** *v. intr. pa-* To go far away. *Bang kami ka'apikihan he' a'a, patā kami alahi.* If some person comes close to us, we run far away. *Angillag itū alahi patā.* Being weary is [like] running a long distance.

**katāhan** *n.* A remote distance or area. *Aniya' kayu ta'nda'na min katāhan, alapat e' buwa'.* He saw a tree in the distance covered with fruit.

**tā bidda'** *adj. a-* Very different. {idiom} *Atā bidda' addat kami maka addat sigām.* Our culture and theirs are very different.

**ta-** (var. **ka-₃**) **1)** *aff.* Aptative non-actor voice prefix: attaches to transitive verbs, identifying the undergoer as the subject of the clause, and indicating that the actor is not completely in control of the event (e.g. circumstance, happenstance, or ability). *Halam ta'nda'ku ai-ai.* I didn't happen to see anything. (*cf:* **maka-₁**) **1.1)** *aff.* Adversative prefix: attaches to a verb to indicate an event (usually negative) which occurs to a participant apart from his or her control. *Talilap aku hangkan halam tasayuku ulan.* I was overcome by drowsiness, that's why I wasn't aware of the rain. (*cf:* **-in- 1.1**, **ka-..-an₂**)

= **ta** *pron.* **1)** We two, us; our (first person dual, inclusive) [Set II]. *"Ā," yuk Ambaw, "ya du ē'-i kasusahanta?" yukna.* "Ah," said Mr. Rat, "so that's our problem, is it?" *Tambalanta du ka, angagad ka dai'-dai'.* I will certainly treat you, just wait a minute. (*cf:* **kita, kitā 1**; *Set:* = **bi**, = **ku**, = **na**, = **nu**, = **sigā**, = **sigām**, = **tabi**, = **tam**) **1.1)** Polite first person singular. *Tambalanta du ka, angagad ka dai'-dai'.* I will certainly treat you, just wait a minute.

**taba** *n.* An edible barnacle-like shellfish that clings to coral rocks. (*gen:* **tahemtem 1**)

**tabak** *see:* **patabak**

**tabaku'** *n.* **1)** The tobacco plant and its leaf. *Nicotiana tabacum.* (*Thesaurus:* **banusu, bungkal₃ 1, pasta, pikaroda, siga 1, sigupan**) **2)** Plug tobacco, an ingredient in a betel chew.

**taba'** *n.* **1)** The richly flavored or fatty part of fish or meat. (*Thesaurus:* **kesom, imu' 1, lanab, l'ssom 1, mamis₁ 1.1, sarap₁**) **1.1)** *adj. a-* Tasty; richly flavored. *Ataba' daing kariyan bang bin'lla. Mbal makakakan onde'-onde' buwat heya si Li ko da'a niugam apa sidda ataba'.* The crevalle fish is rich when cooked. It cannot be eaten by children the size of Li lest they get blisters in the mouth, because it is very rich.

**taba'-taba'** *see:* **pagtaba'-taba'**

**taban** *v. tr.* To take something as plunder or loot. *Pagtunu' Sūk inān, aheka anaban.* When Jolo was burnt there were many looting. *Hal anaban, mbal anabang.* Just looting, not helping. (*Thesaurus:* **gora'₂ 1.1, longpos**)

**tatabanan** *n.* Loot; plunder.

**tabanas** *n.* **1)** A distinctive mat-weaving pattern, a variation of the basic check. **1.1)** *v. tr.* To weave a mat with the tabanas pattern. (*Thesaurus:* **kusta 1, diyandi, tadjung**)

**tabang** *v. tr.* **1)** To help someone personally, or with a task. *Subay to'ongan iya amikilan bang buwattingga kapanabangna baranna bo' iya magkata'u-marayaw.* He should definitely be thinking how to help himself personally so that he knows what is morally good. *Bang aku pakkom ma dilaut, tinabang aku he' a'a. Bang mbal takole' bayanan ni'bbahan na. Ya binowa kapanyapan ē' sampay baranta.* When I capsize out at sea, someone helps me. If the canoe itself can't be righted it is abandoned. What is taken is the equipment and ourselves. (*cf:* **dangin, sabi₁**; *Thesaurus:* **tambin, tulung 1.1**) **1.1)** *v. tr. -an* To assist someone by providing something needed. *Aku i makapah'lling, "Ahāp bang aku i tinabangan he' sigām itū dangan-danganku." Nā, binuwanan akū duwangibu he' milikan hē'.* I said, "It would be nice if these people would help me [financially]." Well, those Westerners gave me two thousand pesos. **2)** To support something at risk of breaking. *Tinabang ligu maka naelon bo' mbal abungkas bihingna.* The winnowing basket is supported with nylon so that its rim doesn't come off.

**pagtabang** *v. intr. aN-* **1)** To be in a mutually supportive relationship. *Minnē' palampung hinangnu pagka aniya' sehe'nu magtabang.* Because of that your labor will be lighter since you have companions combining to help. (*Thesaurus:* **pagkanam, pila 1.1**) **1.1)** *v. tr. -an* To work together in order to defeat someone. *Bay aku pinagtabangan he' sigām mpat puhu'.* Four of them ganged up against me.

**patitabangun** *adj.* Exceedingly helpful.

**tabas** *v. tr.* **1)** To cut wood or cloth to a pattern. (*cf:* **simpay**) **1.1)** *v. tr. -an* To cut a part away from the whole. *Agtūy angā' kayu dand'ppa taha'na, agtūy tinabasan min duwa, min duwa, min tōng duwampōng.* He promptly took a length of wood a fathom in length, and immediately cut pieces from it, did it twice, from both ends.

**Tabawan** *n.* An inhabited atoll in the Sulu Archipelago, southwest of Siasi.

**pagtinabawan** *v. intr.* aN- To make a Tabawan-style bride-wealth exchange, by a lump sum of cash. (*Thesaurus:* **banghad 1**, **basingan**, **mahal**$_2$, **punggit 1**, **ungsud**$_1$ **1**)

**taberak** *n.* A soft cake of dried cassava meal, flavored with sweetened banana or fish liver.

**tabeya'** (derivative of **beya'**$_2$) *v. intr.* -um- To be included with. *Tumabeya' batangan, tumabeya' katig.* Booms and outriggers were included [in the sale]. *Mbal tumabeya' ilu-i. Mailuhun na.* That isn't included. Leave it where it is. (*cf:* **lapay 1.1**).

= **tabi** var. of = **tam**

**tabid**$_1$ *v. intr.* pa-/a- **1)** To become twisted out of normal shape. *Pinaluha labayanku bo' supaya mbal patabid buku-tape'ku.* My path was made wide so that my ankle would not twist. (*Thesaurus:* **kolleng, lubid 1.1, pinsal 1.1**) **1.1)** *v. tr.* To twist something laterally. *Bay tinabid tanganku e' si Anu.* What's-his-name twisted my arm. *Tiyangsi' itū niā' min batang langkay. Mbal magtūy tapangengkot magdai'-dai'. Subay gi' tinabid-tabid bo' mbal maglopeng.* The *tiyangsi'* referred to is obtained from the central rib of a coconut frond. It can't be used in a hurry to tie anything. It needs to be twined a bit first so it doesn't go out of shape. (*Thesaurus:* **pagpiyut**)

**tabid bowa'** *adj.* a- Wry or twisted, of someone's mouth. {idiom} (*Thesaurus:* **kibi'**, **kiyu'**)

**tabid lling** *v. intr.* aN- To manipulate (twist) words in an argument. {idiom} *Ata'u anabid lling. Ai-ai pinah'lling he' dangan ta'ā' sadja diyata'an he' dangan.* He knows how to manipulate words. Whatever the other says he takes advantage of.

**tabid-tabid** *n.* A donut made of a twist of dough. *Am'lli aku tabid-tabid kinakan ni kadday.* I buy a donut twist to eat, from the food stall. *Nilege-lege buwattilu bo' binugbug, buwat saga tabid.* Rolled out like that to be dropped in boiling water, like donut twists.

**tabid**$_2$ *v. tr.* To weave a mat with a twist technique that enables 45-degree angles in the weave. (*Thesaurus:* **kagayan 1.2, huyap-huyap 1**)

**tabi'at** (derivative of **bi'at**) *n.* A person's characteristic behavior and disposition.

**tabin** var. of **abin**

**tabiya'** *intrj.* A request for pardon for a violation of some social norm, as when interrupting, or mentioning something usually avoided; 'Pardon me'. *Tabiya' min ka'a, tabiya' min si Anu.* Begging your pardon, begging anyone's pardon. *Aheka a'a ma palasa, yukta, "Tabiya', palabayinbi aku."* A lot of people in the town plaza, so we say, "Excuse me, please let me through." *Aniya' na t'llu pitu' ni'mmunan iya maka magutta', tabiya'*

*isāb.* It is three weeks now that she has been fevered and vomiting, excuse my mentioning it.

**pagtabiya'** *v. tr.* -an To request pardon for a social fault. *Ai pagtabiya'annu? L'lla kita sali'-sali'.* What are you asking permission about? We are both men. *Bang aniya' magsuli-suli palabay sadja. Mbal kita magtabiya', hatina angero' kita ma manusiya'.* Just going by if there are people talking. We do not beg pardon, in other words we are treating humans as dogs.

**tab'ggak** *n.* The Hunchback boxfish. *Ostracion or Tetrosomus gibbosus.*

**tab'llung**$_1$ *n.* The Short-nosed and other boxfishes; various cowfishes. *Ostracion nasus.*

**tab'llung-bangga'-bangga'** *n.* The Thornback cowfish, a poisonous species. *Lactioria fornasini.*

**tab'llung**$_2$ *see:* **pagtab'llung**

**tabla** *adv.* Even; matching; getting to the same stage. *Tabla kita abati'.* We woke at the same time.

**pagtabla** *v. intr.* aN- To occur at exactly the same time. *Magtabla aku maka llaw ma Musu'.* I reached Musu' just as the sun set.

**tablig** *n.* An Islamic movement calling on the faithful to observe their religious duties; a member of this movement.

**tabtab 1)** *v. tr.* To cut off the last part of something; to sever. *Tinabtab na daun langkay ina'an, nihinang eskoba pangeskoba luma' kami.* The leaves of that dried coconut frond are cut off, made into a broom for sweeping our house. (*Thesaurus:* **tempos, t'ttop 1, tompes, utas 1.1**) **2)** *adj.* a- Brought to an end, of a formal conversation or dispute. *Buwat kami magbissala maka si Gr, na atabtab na bissala kami, apuwas na.* Like when Gr and I were talking, then our talk came to an end, all over. *Subay ya bisala maghukum bo' atabtab, buwat du bisala niutas. Bang halam niutas, amasi amalut.* It must be a legal discussion to say *tabtab*, like when a discussion is terminated. If it is not terminated, [the issue] hangs on. **2.1)** *v. tr.* To cut off negotiations or argument.

**tabtaban** *n.* The conclusion of a discussion. (*Thesaurus:* **kapūd-pūran**, **katapusan 1**, **tobtoban**)

**tabug** *n.* A species of fig tree. *Ficus sceptica.*

**tabu'** *n.* **1)** A market, mainly for the exchange or sale of local produce. (*Thesaurus:* **kadday, estawran, pasal**$_2$ **1, tinda, tiyanggi**) **1.1)** *v. intr.* aN- To shop in the market. *Subay na llaw Hambilan aheya bo' kami anabu'.* It must be the Hambilan market day for us to do the shopping.

**pagtabu'an** *n.* A location for market stalls, more or less permanent. *Makajari ka angahinang pagtabu'an maitu buwat bay nihinang he' mma'bi.* You may build a market area here, as your father did.

**tabul**$_1$ *adv.* **1)** Treated equally, of the distribution of goods. *P'ppotun t'bbu ilū abō' kitam atabul magbahagi'.* Cut that sugarcane into lengths so we can share equally. *Atabul tarangan-tarangan, sali' aniya' bay krismas sigā. Atabul sigā, halam magbidda'.* Distributed evenly one by one, like when they had a Christmas. They were treated equally, no distinction. **1.1)** *v. ditr.* To give equally to several people. *Tabulin makannak.* Treat the children equally. (*Thesaurus:* **kaniya-kaniya, paggintil, pinig, tarangan-tarangan, topod 1**)

**pagtabul-tabul** *v. intr. aN-* **1)** To be more or less equal. **1.1)** *v. tr.* To treat several people equally. *Buwat si Fr maka si Gi maka si Li, dakayu'-dakayu' labban kolol ma dangan. Pinagtabul-tabul.* Like Fr and Gi and Li each with a box of crayons. Sharing equally.

**tabul₂** *n.* The endosperm (sprout) of a coconut. (*syn:* **bōt₁ 1**; *wh:* **niyug**)

**tabul-tabul** *n.* The lashing that secures a sail to mast or boom. *Ya tabul-tabul niluklusan, tinugutan hambawan.* The lashing has been loosened and the halyard allowed to run free. (*Thesaurus:* **baggot, bīt₂, engkot 1.1, gakut, tollen**)

**tabula** *n.* Various species of small squid. *Order Sepiolida.* (*gen:* **lansongan**)

**tabula-nangka'** *n.* A deepwater species of squid.

**tabula-tunyang** (var. **tunyang**) *n.* A small species of tabula squid.

**tabuli** *n.* **1)** Various large marine snails. **2)** The Pacific triton. *Charonia tritonis.*

**tabuli-bbet** *n.* The helmet shell. *fam. Cassidae.*

**tabun-tabun** *n.* Commercial cosmetic powder, generally in cake form. *Pinat'nna'an tabun-tabun bayhu'na.* Powder was applied to her face. (*Thesaurus:* **borak 1, polbos**)

**tabung** *n.* The Mangrove red jack; the Red emperor. *Lutjanus spp.*

**tabungay** *n.* A black stinging insect, possibly a hornet. (*Thesaurus:* **buwani, kabulig, lampinig, teya'-teya'**)

**taka** *n.* **1)** A notch cut to facilitate climbing; the rung of a ladder. (*Thesaurus:* **tangga' 1, tekmas 1, tengham**) **1.1)** *v. tr. -an* To notch something for climbing or for supporting a cross-beam.

**taka-taka** (var. **taka-takahan**) *adv.* Inevitably, as the result of persistent action, or due to certain conditions. *Taka-taka itū sali' makabāk kala'atan.* This word *taka-taka* is like coming into something bad. *Taka-taka kita maglata makapagbono' kita maka sehe'ta.* When we start joking we are bound to end up by fighting with our companions. *Taka-taka onde'-onde' inān maglete-lete, mbal du at'ggol ahūg pareyo'.* For sure if that child keeps walking along the raised walkway, it won't be long before she falls down. *Yukna, "Taka-taka magl'ngngan ni luma' d'nda inān makapaga' du."* He said, "If he keeps

on visiting that woman's house they will inevitably get together intimately." *Taka-takahan magka'at kulaetku itū.* Eventually this pressure lantern of mine will be damaged. (*Thesaurus:* **gana-gana 1.1, sumiyan-sumiyan, tiyap-tiyap**)

**taka-takahan** var. of **taka-taka**

**takabba** *adj. a-* Lost due to slipping out of one's grip.

**takāk** *n.* A mast extension. *Takāk, ilu pasugpat mariyata' taruk.* An extension, added there to the top of the mast. (*Thesaurus:* **taruk, tindakan, tukag, tuklug 1**)

**takal** *adj. a-* Averse to meeting a responsibility such as working or fulfilling marriage obligations. *Mbal na ka atakal anulat? Uskawan sali'?* Haven't you become averse to writing? Sort of reluctant to do it? (*Thesaurus:* **hukaw 1, lisu'**)

**takas** *n.* A place where a house was previously built. *Buwat bay luma' itu, wa'i na ala'an. Ya itu takasna.* Like this house was, when removed. This location is its *takas*. *Ta'abut na ahinang luma' pabīng, pabīng ni takasna, ni bay pat'nna'an luma' tagna'.* When the time came to be building a house again [they] returned to the former site, to where the house had been originally. (*cf:* **bai**)

**takbi'** *see:* **pagtakbi'**

**takbil₁** *v. tr.* To extol the greatness of Allah over someone who is gravely ill. *Takbilku mma'ku ma sōng amatay.* I will extol the greatness of Allah over my father when he is about to die.

**pagtakbil** *v. intr. aN-* **1)** To declare the greatness of God, as by uttering the phrase Allahu Akbar. *Maglukum sangom, abay kohap saga magtakbil na. Paglisag siyam, akatis.* At night we eat the communal meal, late afternoon we proclaim that Allah is great. At nine o'clock it is finished. (*cf:* **tahalil 1.1**) **2)** To chant praises to someone of high status. *Maglagpak-lagpak saga mandusiya' maka magtakbil sigām, "Mura-murahan pinataha' umul sultan!"* The people were clapping and chanting praises, "May the sultan's life be long!"

**takbil₂** var. of **takdil**

**takkop** *v. intr. pa-* **1)** Closed, of a container with a hinged lid. *Bin'llat bay patakkop.* What had been shut away was unfolded. (*Thesaurus:* **kabbat, tambol 1.2**) **1.1)** *v. tr.* To close the lid of a hinged container. *Takkopun ba ba'ul ilū bo' mbal sinōd kamahung.* Shut that chest to keep it from getting cockroaches in it.

**pagtakkop** *v. tr.* To bring together the sides and lid of a hinged container. *Pinagtakkop, pinagka'ob, buwat maleta, ba'ul, pinagtakkop turungna.* Closed up, fastened, like a suitcase or a storage box. Its lid is closed.

**takdang** *v. tr. -an* To tap something with a blow not intended to hurt or cut. *Magtūy angahinang bangka'-bangka'. Min t'llu tinakdangan ni munda' akatis.* He promptly made a small canoe. With three taps at the bow [it] was finished.

**takdil** (var. **takbil**₂; **tumakdil**) *conj.* With regard to; in the matter of; in reference to. *Bang tumakbil ni timbak kulitis, aheka apalsu. Angkan mbal ah'lling, apugtul sumbuhanna.* With regard to firecrackers, many are faulty. The reason they don't explode is that the wick is broken off. *Makahāw-hāw kita, ata'u diki'-diki' bang takdil ni magbassa.* We can do it a bit, we know a little, in regard to reading. *Bang takbil angambit, pinaka'llum ma paldu.* With regard to catching fish by herding, they are kept alive in a submerged cage. *Takbil ai-ai takakan, takbil s'mmek, sarang na ma aku.* As far as food is concerned, and clothing, what I have is adequate. (*Thesaurus:* **pasal₁**)

**takil** *clf.* Count word for packages of processed sago meal.

**taklay** *see:* **pataklayan, tataklayan**

**takmay** *v. tr.* To hold something by placing both hands or arms beneath it, as a baby or a fragile package. (*Thesaurus:* **tampupu, tayak 1.1**)

**tako** *n.* A cue for shooting balls or discs in games such as pool. *Tako inān pagtira.* That cue is for shooting pool. (*Thesaurus:* **bulitin, kulang₂, pūl, tira**)

**takod** *v. intr. pa-* 1) To go inland or uphill. (*Thesaurus:* **kaleya 1, kaut 1, lūd, tukad₁ 1**) 1.1) *v. ditr.* To obtain things from inland, as cassava, fruit or firewood. *Wa'i gi' iya anakod ma deya Jambangan.* She's still away getting inland products from Jambangan. (*cf:* **sasab, talun 1.1**)

**takon** *n.* The heel of a shoe. (*Thesaurus:* **bakiya'₁, sinelas, taumpa'**)

**takos** (var. **patakos**) *n.* 1) A personal weapon, especially one worn at the waist such as a sidearm. *Taga takos a'a inān.* That fellow wears a weapon. (*Thesaurus:* **almas, hinanib 1, pakokos, pangatu**) 1.1) *v. tr.* To arm oneself with a personal weapon such as a sidearm. *Anakos aku kalis.* I arm myself with a kris.

**pagtakos** *v. intr. aN-* To be armed with a personal weapon. *Magtakos iya sinapang.* He is armed with a rifle.

**pagtinakos** *v. intr. aN-* To be armed by habit. *Bang aku lum'ngngan kaleya magtinakos aku barung.* When I walk inland I am armed with a fighting knife. (*cf:* **hakos**)

**takot** *n.* A submerged reef. *Aniya' takot marilaut ī', sagō' alawak.* There is a reef there out at sea, but it is far away. (*Thesaurus:* **munu-munu, puhu, tahetek**)

**taksi'** *see:* **pagtaksi', pagtaksi'an**

**taksil** *n.* 1) A fine imposed for infringement of various cultural rules. (*Thesaurus:* **multa 1, niya'₂**) 1.1) *adj. a-* Fined for infringements of cultural rules; liable for such a fine. *Ataksil ka, amayad lima pilak.* You're liable for a fine, you'll pay five pesos. *Bang aku lum'ngngan am'lli siga bo' pasagid ni aku d'nda, ataksil aku e' d'nda.* If I step out to buy cigarets and a girl brushes

against me, I am fined for [touching] a girl. 1.2) *v. tr.* To impose a fine on someone for an offense against cultural standards.

**kataksilan** *n.* A penalty, usually a small fine, for an offense against cultural norms. *Bay aku anaggaw d'nda, yuk sara', "Pagka halam mailu saga matto'anu, tanggungta ka." Sara' ī' amuwan kataksilan ni d'nda hē'. Subay at'kka matto'aku bo' yampa ni'nde'an sīn ni sara'.* I seized a woman. The magistrate said, "Since your elders are not here, I will take the responsibility [for your fine]." The magistrate then pays the fine to the woman. My elders when they arrive they must return the money to the magistrate.

**taktak** *v. intr. pa-* 1) To let down something flexible that is fastened at the top. 1.1) *v. tr.* To lower something which is fastened in place, as curtains or a mosquito net. *Buwat kultina bay pinasablay pariyata', bang ta'abut na tinambol, pinataktak na pareyo'.* Like a curtain that has been hung up, when it reaches time to close, it is let down. (*cf:* **tonton 1.1**) 1.2) *v. tr.* To lower a sail. *Taktakun na banog sababna aniya' na baliyu.* Lower the sail because there is wind.

**taktek** *v. tr.* To beat a rhythm on gongs or bamboo marimba. (*Thesaurus:* **pagtā'-tā', taletek, taroro'**)

**taku** *see:* **pagtaku-taku**

**tād** *n.* A row, as of people, clothes on a line, or planted cassava. *Saga sangpū' pilak dantād, panggi' kayu.* About ten pesos a row, of cassava. *Dantād panablayanku s'mmek.* One line for me to hang clothes on. (*Thesaurus:* **badlis, diril-diril, dirit₁ 1, sapan₁ 1, tagik**)

**ma tāran** *adv. phrase* By the row, of planted things.

**pagtād-tād** *v. tr.* To arrange things in rows.

**tāran** *n.* Things planted in rows. *Ma badlisan, ma tāran, ya lagi'na bang niyug.* By the planted row, by the line, especially of coconuts.

**taddang** *adj. a-* Valid or authentic, of documents or of a person bearing them. *Ataddang sulatnu bang ka ni upis angā' sīn.* Your signature is valid when you go to the office to get money. *"Ataddang a'a ilū," yuk pulis. Asāl takilā he' pulis.* "That fellow is legal," said the policeman. Recognised in fact by the police. (*cf:* **legal**; *ant:* **kolorom**)

**kataddangan** *n.* A legal authority or warrant, in writing.

**pagpataddangan** *n.* Identification papers required by law.

**taddas** *n.* The underside of a hull, keel, or keelson. *La'ananku banog ē' maka dambila' katig, pehē'ku ni deyo' taddas pelang ati ko pabuhat pariyata'.* I removed the sail and half the outrigger, putting it there beneath the keel of the canoe so it would lift up. (*Thesaurus:* **salig₂, singki'**)

**taddik** var. of **bāt-taddik**

**taddok** var. of **tagdok**

**taddung** *v. intr. pa-* To attend a social event in

person. (*Thesaurus:* **hadil, luruk 1.1, tupuk**)

**tadjaw** var. of **saging-tadjaw**

**tadjuk** *v. intr. aN-* To form fruit before the petals fall, of fruits such as mango. *Minsan mampallam, wanni, balunu', anadjuk du. Bang mbal niruplak, palanjal, bo' yampa magduru'-ero'.* Whether common mango, odorous mango or horse mango, all set fruit. If not damaged they develop and then go on to the budding stage. (*Thesaurus:* **pagbuwa', pagduru'-ero', tungkalling**)

**tadjul** *v. tr.* To melt something more or less solid, as fats, ice, or metal for casting. *Pinasu' ni kaha', halam bohe'an, ya he' tinadjul.* Heated in the frying pan, with no water, that is *tadjul. Katuwangan tingga' bay tinadjul.* Lead that has been melted can be poured out. (*Thesaurus:* **hudjat, lanay$_2$, tunaw 1**)

**tadjun** *v. intr. aN-* To move a swing by pulling on its ropes while one is sitting on it. (*Thesaurus:* **dundang$_1$ 1, duyan, ombo'-ombo', pagdanggu'-danggu', pagnanu'**)

**tadjung** *n.* A two-colored check pattern; a sarong with such a pattern. *B'llihin aku hōs tadjung.* Buy me a sarong with a check pattern. *Mantaluna, ya kakana' pote', maka kusta, ya ba'anan tadjung.* Sheets, the white cloth, and the check pattern typical of most sarongs. (*Thesaurus:* **kusta 1, diyandi, tabanas 1.1**)

**tadtad** *v. tr.* 1) To cut with repeated shallow cuts. *Nilagut, tinadtad, pinagt'ttok-t'ttok.* Slashed, cut repeatedly, chopped up into small pieces. (*Thesaurus:* **lagut, pagtebag-tebag**) 2) To flatten large bamboo by pounding until it forms a panel of multiple connected strips. (*cf:* **tiyadtad**)

**taem** *n.* Time, as a technical term for a pause in various games. (*Thesaurus:* **awal ni ahil, jāman, masa 1, timpu 1, waktu 1**)

**pagtaem** *v. intr. aN-* To call time in a game, to indicate readiness or to ask for a pause. *Bang kami magembet na bo' magtaem sehe'ku inān, aku itū bilang na.* When we are playing hide and seek and my companions say time's up, I am ready.

**taenghog** var. of **talengog**

**taep** *v. tr.* To type something.

**pagtaep** *v. intr. aN-* To be engaged in typing. *Atokod ka'a ilū magtaep.* You are accurate at typing.

**tag** var. of **atag$_1$**

**tag-** *aff.* Prefix indicating responsibility for something, as owner, proprietor or controller. *Hē' ma tagpelang.* There with the owner of the canoe.

**taga** *v. tr. zero* To have or possess. *Taga karaya a'a inān, minsan mbal amatuwa' abbuna.* That person has wealth, even though he doesn't display his proud status. *Taga nana' kalibubut itū.* This boil has pus in it. *Taga anak kono' iya l'lla mpatpū' hekana.* It is said that he has forty sons.

**tagak** *n.* A discharge of mucus from the mouth.

**pagtagak** *v. intr. aN-* To salivate; to dribble. *Ya*

saga magtagak helota, ya bohelota am'ttak.* Our saliva flow starts, but it is our actual saliva that drips down. (*Thesaurus:* **buhelo 1, helo$_2$, laway$_1$ 1, ludja' 1**)

**tagad** *v. tr. -an* To wait for someone or some thing. *Da'a kita magdai'-dai', tagarantam.* Let's not hurry, let's wait for them. (*Thesaurus:* **lagad 1.2, lanti-lanti, langay**)

**tagad-kawin** *n.* The interval between a betrothal ceremony and the wedding. *Basta wa'i na pinehē' ni kar'ndahan ungsud, tagad-kawin na.* So long as the bride-wealth has been handed over to the woman's side, the waiting-for-the-wedding period is under way. (*Thesaurus:* **pagpah'nda 1, pagtunggu'-tunang**)

**taga'-taga'** *v. tr.* To offend against cultural norms by addressing someone by personal name instead of the appropriate address form. *Buwat ka'a mbal niōnan maka ōnnu, subay niōnan bapa'. Bang ka niōnan Ke he' kasehe'an, anaga'-naga', halam aniya' pagaddat. Subay Bapa' Ke.* Like you not being addressed by your name, you should be called uncle. If others call you Ke they are offending against social norms, they have no manners. It should be Bapa' [Uncle] Ke. (*Thesaurus:* **ganda, ōn$_1$ 1.2**)

**tagama** *v. tr.* To prepare things in anticipation of a coming need or event. (*Thesaurus:* **sakap 1.2**)

**tagambil** *n.* A resinous gum which forms an ingredient of the betel nut chew. *gen. Uncaria. Tagambil, ya pagmama' e' kamatto'ahan, tibu'uk-bu'uk sali' pasagi'.* Tagambil gum, forming the betel chew of the old people, solid and kind of square. (*gen:* **pagmama' 1**)

**taganak** (derivative of **anak$_1$**) *n.* Someone who has rights and responsibilities over a younger person. *Pagka ka'a ya taganak, subay ka'a ya pinagbaya'.* Since you are the one with rights over the child, you should be the one to decide.

**tagandak** *n.* The sound of feet or hooves hitting the ground. *Ang'llub isab pikpik sigām bang pajabjab, sali' tagandak ba'anan kura'.* Their wings make a rumbling sound when they flap, like the pounding hooves of many horses.

**pagtagandak** *v. intr. aN-* To make loud repetitive noises, as the sound of horses' hooves or a knocking engine.

**tagang** *v. tr.* To hold something to prevent it from falling or coming too close. *Tagangun hāg ilū.* Hold that post up. (*Thesaurus:* **dogsol, tulak$_2$**)

**tagangga'** *n.* A species of tree ant, yellow and about 1 cm long, which can inflict a painful bite. (*gen:* **s'mmut 1**)

**tagay** *n.* Dead branches and twigs, easily gathered for firewood. (*cf:* **pangayu**; *Thesaurus:* **engas-engas**)

**tagbak$_1$** *v. tr.* To stab something with a spear or harpoon. *Tagbakun maka sahapang.* Stab it with a fish spear. (*Thesaurus:* **hiyak**)

**tagbak$_2$** *n.* A low-growing plant of the ginger

family, the clustered fruit of which tastes both sweet and sour. *Alpinia or Kolowratia elegans. Am'lli aku tagbak pangiraman h'ndaku.* I will buy *tagbak* as conception-food for my wife.

**tagbaran** (derivative of **baran₂**) *n.* A person with the responsibility of care, as for an older relative or young woman. *Subay na maitu tagbaran.* The person responsible [for her] needs to be here.

**tagbowahan** (derivative of **bowa₁**) *n.* A person with formal responsibilities for the wearing or carrying of something. *Saga sundalu ya tagbowahan panji.* The soldiers assigned to bearing the flag. *Saga pari' ya tagbowahan juba.* The priests are the ones to wear gowns.

**tagdapu** (derivative of **dapu**) *n.* Owner; proprietor. *Sai tag-dapu luma' duwa angkap inān?* Who is the owner of that two-storey house? *Atawa bang aniya' paluruk, bo' mbal ahāp pantān, yuk tagdapu, "Da'a kam maglundug pi'ilu. Ilu halam ahogot."* Or if there are people gathering but the porch isn't good, the owner says, "Don't crowd together over there. It isn't securely fastened." *Sai tagdapu pelang magsampig-sampig itū?* Who is the owner of the canoe that's banging against things nearby?

**tagdok** (var. **taddok**) *v. tr.* -an To kick something with the sole of the foot. *Subay aniya' dusata bo' kita tinaddokan.* There must be some offense for us to be kicked. (*Thesaurus:* **binti', sipa' 1, tindak 1**)

　**pagtagdok** *v. intr.* aN- To kick or stamp one's feet repeatedly. *Bang kita lum'ngngan bo' ta'nda' he' siyalita, na pas'ngngel. Bang kita palawak, na magtaddok na.* When we go off walking and our younger sibling sees us, he makes a fuss. When we go further away, he stamps his feet. *Buwat pinagtagdokan lawang bang mbal paukab.* Like a door being kicked repeatedly when it won't open. (*Thesaurus:* **pagdogdog, pagtendek**)

**tage'ot** *v. intr.* aN- To make the grinding noise of teeth or branches rubbing together. *Bang aniya' a'a parundangan anage'ot man diyata'.* When someone is swinging there is a grinding noise from above. *Bang atuli onde'-onde' aheka emponna, anage'ot isāb.* When a child with a lot of teeth sleeps, he grinds [his teeth].

　**pagtage'ot** *v. intr.* aN- To grind together. *Tīkun pelang, wa'i magtage'ot.* Have a quick look at the canoe, something is rubbing together. *Magaluran saga a'a mahē', magtage'ot isāb empon sigām.* The people there will cry out, and their teeth will grind together.

**tagenseng** *v. intr.* aN- To make a metallic or tinny sound. *Anagenseng, sali' mital atawa agung taga bila'.* Making a tinny sound, like a tin can or a cracked gong. (*cf:* **g'mmel**)

**tagestes** *adj.* a- Unsettled as to place of residence or work. *Atagestes pahāp paghinanganna inān, mbal at'ttog ma baina.* His place of work is changed so often, not staying on where he was. (*Thesaurus:*

**lagesles 1**)

　**pagtagestes** *v. intr.* aN- To keep moving on to yet another place. *Magtagestes a'a.* People moving off somewhere else. (*Thesaurus:* **lagedled 1, laud 1, lintas, paglalin, pagtaleted**)

**tagettek** *see:* **pagtagettek**

**tagga** *n.* **1)** Limitations imposed on some activity. *Buwat anakta magl'ngngan, taggahanta. Yukta, "Bang aniya' tunangnu tō'in aku. Tabangta ka."* Like our children walking about, we restrict them. We say, "If you have a sweetheart, point her out to me. I will help you." *Buwat anakta magl'ngngan, taggahanta. Bang ameya' tagga, yukta, "Bang aniya' tunangnu tō'in aku. Tabangta ka."* Like our children walking around, we restrict them. If they accept the limitation, we [may] say, "If you have a sweetheart, point her out to me. I will help you." **1.1)** *v. tr.* -an To limit or delay someone's action. *Sali' bang aniya' amole' atawa atulak, mbal pinatulak, tinaggahan.* Like someone going home or leaving, they are not allowed to leave but are held back. *Daka ai makatagga.* Goodness knows what's holding him back. *Mbal katagga-taggahan milikan ilū.* Nothing stops that Westerner. (*Thesaurus:* **ddas 1.1, pagli'i-li'i, tahāl**)

**taggaha'** (var. **patagha'**) *adv.* Unexpectedly; without warning. *Halam ganta' bay ai maka ai, taggaha' hal palintuwad.* Though perhaps nothing whatsoever had happened, he suddenly fell prostrate. *Taggaha' pa'in kami makat'kka pi'itu, da'a pa'in pagla'atantam atay.* When we happen to arrive without letting you know, don't let it be a source of annoyance between us. *Ma labayan pa'in iya, patagha' sadja aniya' ta'nda'na sawa parola.* While he was on his way, he suddenly saw a navigation light. (*Thesaurus:* **papuwa', sakkop 2, tanyak**)

**tagga'** *see:* **patagga'**

**taggal₁** *adj.* a- Resting or leaning on something. *Ataggal aku ni tu'utnu nihinang ū'anku. Atuli aku pataggal.* I rest against your knee, making it my pillow. I sleep supported.

　**pamataggalan** *n.* A supporting block designed to take the weight of some activity. (*cf:* **parabtalan**)

　**pataggal** *adv.* **1)** Using a support. **1.1)** *v. tr.* To place something on a supporting prop or spacer. *Angay halam pataggalannu si Ik?* Why did you not provide Ik with a support?

**taggal₂** *see:* **pataggal-taggal**

**taggu₁** *adj.* a- Durable, of paint, cloth or someone's physical appearance. *Ataggu d'nda inān, sali' du ma kato'ana buwat du bay ma kabudjangna.* That woman is well-preserved, as beautiful in her old age as she was when a maiden. *Ataggu itū sali' at'ggol apapas. Apapas du isāb so' at'ggol-t'ggol angangganti'.* *Taggu* means it takes a long time to fade. It does indeed fade but it is quite a long time in changing. *Nda'un ba paraw inān, ataggu* *pintana.* Look at that canoe, its paint is long-lasting. (*Thesaurus:* **anagtol, kamdos₂, kumpay, galak₂, pagon₁ 1.1, tatas 1.1, togob₁**)

**taggu₂** *adj. a-* **1)** Fixed in opinion; unmoved by argument or plea. **1.1)** *v. tr. -an* To do something without relenting. *Bang bay angutang, pinaglehod-lehoran he' a'a bay pangutanganna inān. Sinukut pabĭng, tinagguhan.* When someone has borrowed money, he is given more time by the person from whom he borrowed. He is dunned again, [reminded] relentlessly. (*Thesaurus:* **podlongan, sogsog 1, togol 1, tukid 1**)

**taghuy** *v. intr. aN-* **1)** To whistle. **1.1)** *v. tr. -an* To get someone's attention by whistling.

**tagi** *adj. -an* **1)** Addicted to some activity. *Tagihan kasubulan inān magbola.* Those youths are addicted to volleyball. (*Thesaurus:* **bintan 1.1**) **1.1)** *v. advrs. -in-* To be enamored of some activity. *Tinagi-tagi to'ongan aku magbaek.* I am very fond of riding a bicycle.

**tagi-tuli** *n.* Someone addicted to sleeping; a sleepyhead.

**tagik** *n.* A row of planted items. (*Thesaurus:* **badlis, diril-diril, dirit₁ 1, sapan₁ 1, tād**)

**ma tagikan** *adv. phrase* By the row. *Bang niyug ma tagikan, bang panggi' kayu ma tāran.* Coconuts go by the *tagikan,* cassava by the *tāran.*

**pagtagik** *v. intr. aN-* **1)** To be arranged in rows. **1.1)** *v. tr.* To arrange things in rows. *Subay pinagtagik-tagik.* They should be arranged in rows.

**tagimtim** *n.* **1)** Black spots; freckles; mildew in cloth. (*cf:* **bau-bau**; *Thesaurus:* **bagubu' 2, kapu-kapu 1, tagutu' 1**) **1.1)** *v. advrs. -in-* Mildewed or freckled. *Subay tinunu' kamemon s'mmek tinagimtim.* All mildewed clothes should be burnt.

**tagisiyan** *n.* A species of fish.

**tag'ntanan** (derivative of **ntan₁**) *n.* A person in charge of an event; a master of ceremonies.

**tagmilikan** (derivative of **milikan**) *n.* A person having jurisdiction over a region.

**tagna'** *adv.* **1)** Initially; at first. *Tagna' bay magluma' kami ma M'ddas.* When we first lived in Siasi Town. **1.1)** *n.* A beginning; a start. *Sumiyan tagna' ya sakina itū?* When was the start of this sickness of his? *Tagna' bono'.* The beginning of the war. **1.2)** *v. tr. -an* To commence something. *Tinagna'an minnitu in dunya itū mbal nilatapan pabalik.* Beginning from now, this world will not be flooded again.

**pagtagna'** *v. intr. aN-* To be the origin or first mention. *Minnē' magtagna' papata ya yukna, "Buta maka pengkol mbal makajari pasōd ma astana'."* That is the origin of the proverb that said, "Blind men and lame men cannot go into palaces."

**panagna'an** *n.* A starting point; a place of origin.

**tagok** *n.* **1)** Sticky substances such as the juice of some fruit; plant sap; the exuded entrails of some species of trepang. *Ahāp nangka' tignus, mbal kita al'mmis. Nangka' loya' itū aheka tagokna.* Tignus jackfruit is good, we don't get dirty from it. *Loya'* jackfruit has lots of sticky sap. (*Thesaurus:* **g'tta', pekot, pīt**) **1.1)** *v. intr. aN-* To produce a sticky substance such as sap. *Anagok kalapiya itū bang kinehet. Anagok isāb bāt, amalut ma tangannu.* The rubber tree exudes sap when cut. Trepang also exude a sticky substance, it sticks to your hands.

**pagtagok** *v. intr. aN-* To become sticky. *Sali' magtagok buhelona, sali' angaludja'.* His saliva becomes viscous, like bringing up phlegm.

**tagokan** var. of **bāt-tagokan**

**tagō'** *n.* Various moray eels. *fam. Muraenidae.* (*Thesaurus:* **kasī, endong**)

**tagō'-abu** *n.* The Gray moray eel. *Gymnothorax sp.*

**tagō'-bakukku** *n.* The Painted moray eel. *Gymnothorax pictus.*

**tagō'-simun** *n.* The Leopard or Spotted moray eel. *Enchelycore pardalis.*

**tagō'-s'llang** *n.* The Undulated moray eel, a deep sea species. *Gymnothorax undulatus.*

**tagō'-talsan** *n.* The Clouded or Snowflake moray eel. *Echidna nebulosa.*

**tagpatutan** (derivative of **patut**) *n.* A person with authority to act.

**tagsoho'an** (derivative of **soho'**) *n.* A person with the right to give orders. *Ngga'i ka kami ya pagdugalanbi, sabab ngga'i ka kami ya tagsoho'an.* It's not us you should be angry at, because we are not the ones who give the orders.

**taguban** *n.* A sheath for a knife or bladed weapon. *Hinanganku gi' taguban bari' si Ba.* I will just make a sheath for Ba's knife.

**tagubata'** *n.* A married couple, neither of whom has been married previously. *Wa'i na isāb iya magbalik maka bay tagubata'na tagna', ya na si Mu. Ina'an sigā ma Sibu, yampa min t'dda bay makatibaw pi'itu.* He and his original wife, Mu that is, have reunited. They are there in Cebu, only just now visiting here for the first time. (*cf:* **paglakibini**)

**tagudtud** *v. intr. pa-* To flow or drift from a reference point. *Buwat sapa', patagudtud min deya tudju kaut.* Like a river, flowing from inland towards the sea. *Patagudtud kamunda'an, magpabeya' sadja.* The canoes drift, just going with the flow. *Patagudtud s'llog pehē'.* The current is flowing that way. (*cf:* **taguntun 1.1**; *Thesaurus:* **mansay-mansay, sasahan 1.2**)

**taguntun** *v. intr. pa-* **1)** To flow or hang from a fixed point. *Pataguntun pareyo' kasehe'an sutanghon bang atahak.* Some of the fine noodles hang down when cooked. **1.1)** *v. tr.* To allow one end of a line to hang or run free. *Taguntunun lubid bo' mbal asagut.* Let the line run free so it doesn't tangle. (*cf:* **tagudtud**; *Thesaurus:* **tali-**

**tali**₂, **tugut 1.1**, **tuntun**₁ 1) 1.2) *v. tr.* *-an* To lower something on a line. *Taguntunin sau pareyo'.* Lower the anchor.

**tagunggu'** *v. tr.* *-an* To play gongs. *Bang magkawin subay tinagunggu'an ko niluruk e' saga a'a.* When there is a wedding the gongs should be played so people will attend. (*Thesaurus:* **kulanting 1, lisag**₂ **1.1, taletek, taratu' 1.1, taroro', tigi'-tigi'**₂, **tuntung**)

**tagunggu'an** *n.* The stirring sound of gongs being played. *Ā bang kalenu tagunggu'an itū.* Ah, if you could hear the sound of the gongs.

**taguri'** *n.* A simple type of kite. *Na, ya hinangku maitu maghinang taguri', magtuhun unas.* Now then, what I do here is make kites and dive for water-grass. (*Thesaurus:* **awak-awak, birarul, pindun**)

**tagutu'** *n.* 1) Black spots of mildew in cloth. (*Thesaurus:* **bagubu' 2, kapu-kapu 1, tagimtim** 1) 1.1) *v. advrs.* *-in-* Mildewed. *Tinagutu' du, sali' tinamak.* Quite mildewed, like it has been stained.

**taha** *v. tr.* To accuse someone without knowing the facts. *Tinaha aku he'na, bay aku kono' magtambuku maka d'nda.* He put a story around about me, that I had reportedly arranged to meet a girl. *Bang aniya' alungay ma deyom luma' itū bo' halam tapiha, aku na tinuna'an bo' halam aku bay angā'. Tinaha aku.* If something is lost here in the house and cannot be found, I am the one to be accused though I haven't taken it. I am falsely accused. (*Thesaurus:* **hunub-hunub 1.1, tuhuma 1, tuna', waham**)

**tahak** *adj.* *a-* 1) Ready for eating, of fruit or cooked food. *Atahak balunu' ilū? Atahak dambila'.* Is that *balunu'* [a fruit of the mango family] ripe? Half of it is ripe. *Atahak pa'in buwas, pinat'nna' na e'na ni sultan maka saga tendogna.* When the rice was cooked, she placed it before the king and his retinue. *Bang pa'in ahāp kasinag mata llaw ya makapatahak saga buwa' tinanom.* May the warmth of the sun that ripens the crop be good. (*cf:* **lāg**; *ant:* **mata' 1**; *Thesaurus:* **laga'**₁ **1, lasaw**) 2) Mature; experienced. *Atahak iya ma pagiman.* She is mature in her faith commitment.

**tahad** *v. tr.* *-an* To leave something as it is. *Taharin na.* Leave it where it is.

**patahad** *v. tr.* To leave something in the place indicated.

**taha'** *n.* 1) Length (spatial). *Ya taha'na pitumpū' maka limand'ppa, luhana sangpū' maka duwa.* Its length was seventy-five fathoms, its width twelve. *Agarinbi pataha' pabalik p'ngngotbi bo' yampa kām pabalik pi'itu.* Wait until your beard becomes long again before you return here. 1.1) *adj.* *a-* Long in contrast to short or brief. *Ataha' bu'unku.* My hair is long. *Bang pa'in mura-murahan ataha' umulnu.* May your life hopefully be long. (*Thesaurus:* **kuwa'-kuwa', lanjut 1, panjang, t'ggol 1.1**) 1.2) *v. intr.* *pa-* To become

long. *Agarinbi pataha' pabalik p'ngngotbi bo' yampa kām pabalik pi'itu.* Wait until your beard becomes long again before you return here.

**kataha'an** *n.* The entire length of something.

**taha'-akkal** *adj.* *a-* Clever; shrewd; wise. {idiom} *Ataha'-akkal a'a itu.* This man is clever.

**tahāl** *adj.* *a-* Made late by involvement in some other event. (*Thesaurus:* **ddas 1.1, pagli'i-li'i, tagga 1.1**)

**patahāl** *v. tr.* To keep someone waiting for a long time.

**tahalil** *n.* 1) An Islamic prayer for the spirit of someone who has died. 1.1) *v. tr.* *-an* To pray for a person newly deceased. *Bang ma ka'am, mbal tinahalilan bang aniya' amatay?* With you, when someone has died are they not prayed for? (*cf:* **pagtakbil 1**)

**tahamul** *v. intr.* *a-* 1) To be forgiven for a minor offense or infringement. *Atahamul na, yuk i, buwat saga bay pamuwannu ni kami buwas, tatahamul e' kami.* No offense taken, they say. It's like when you have given us rice, we are forgiving. 1.1) *adj.* *zero* Excused. *Tahamul aku, min sigām, buwat aniya' magsuli-suli bo' aku atilaw.* I am excused, their initiative, like when people are talking and I ask a question.

**tahan**₁ *n.* 1) The last item or items in a series. *Buwat kita maglaki, mbal anabut bang lima, suma'an walu' tahanna.* Playing lucky [a card game] for example, he doesn't deal when five, or sometimes eight cards remain. 1.1) *adv.* Finally (in the sense of being last in a series). *Amak'llat subu. Tahan dakuman kami amole'.* We waited for morning to come. We finally got home a bit later. *Tahan magtogga'-togga' pangigal sigām.* In the end their dancing was just jogging up and down. (*cf:* **atas**₁)

**tahan**₂ *v. tr.* 1) To detain someone, as for interrogation. *Bay kami tinahan he' Bagung-lipunan.* We were detained by the *Bagung-lipunan* rebels. *Kasehe'anbi subay tinahan maitu ma deyom kalabusu sampay tata'u bang b'nnal llingbi atawa mbal.* The rest of you must be detained here in prison until it is known whether or not your story is true. 1.1) *v. tr.* *-an* To keep something in place by laying a weight across it. *Angā' aku bussu' panahanku bubuku bo' mbal talaran minsan alandos s'llog.* I will get rocks to weigh down my fish trap so that it will not be swept away even when the current is strong. *Tahananku katas ko' mbal paleyang apa alandos baliyu.* I will put a weight on the paper so it doesn't fly away because the wind is strong. *Ya itu man deyo', tinahanan min diyata'.* This one is underneath, weighted down from above. (*Thesaurus:* **pagbangday, tihin**)

**pagtahan** *v. intr.* *aN-* To be lying so that some pieces or parts overlay others. *Magtahan kita bang kita mbal makasayu atuli.* We lay with our legs across each other when we sleep totally unaware.

**patahan** *n.* A threshold; a lintel.

**tahan-tahan** *v. tr. -an* To endure something difficult or uncomfortable. *Bang kita taluwa' baliyu ma dilaut bo' kita am'ssi, tahan-tahananta maina'an.* When stormy weather hits us out at sea while we are fishing, we just put up with it out there. *Tinahan-tahanan, sali' sinandal-sandalan gi'. Kalu palōng-lōng baliyu.* Riding it out, sort of enduring it a bit longer. The wind may perhaps diminish. (*Thesaurus:* **iman₁ 1.1, pagsabal, sandal 1.1, tangka', tatas 1.2**)

**tahap** *v. tr. -an* To winnow chaff from grain. *Bang kami magtapi' pai, binuwattē', tinahap bo' ala'an kuwit pai hē'.* When we are pounding rice, it's done like that, winnowed so the chaff comes away.

**tahella'** *n.* The Convict surgeonfish, caught by netting in shallow water. *Acunthurus triostegus.* (*gen:* **kumay**)

**tahemtem** *n.* **1)** Generic term for various barnacle species. (*spec:* **kapang₁ 1, l'ssik-l'ssik, taba, tehem 1**) **1.1)** *v. advrs. -in-* Having barnacles growing on it. *Sowa bala-bala, sowa aheya, tinahemtem.* The bala-bala snake, a huge snake with barnacles growing on it. **2)** An edible barnacle-like bivalve, found on rocks or mangrove roots.

**tahetek** *n.* A submerged reef. *Bang nihūg bubu binowa ni Tahetek Siliyala'.* When a woven trap is to be lowered [to the sea floor] it is taken to Siliyala' Reef. (*Thesaurus:* **munu-munu, puhu, takot**)

**tahik₁** *n.* **1)** The sea as a body of water. *Lum'ngngan disi Sel ni Tōng Batu amandi ma tahik.* The Westerners walk to Rock Point to bathe in the sea. **1.1)** Sea water as opposed to fresh. *Halo itū taga tahik-tahik, halam aniya' t'bbana.* This pool is slightly salty, there is no exposed sand. (*cf:* **bohe'₁ 1**)

**katahikan** *n.* Seas or oceans; the sea in general. *Suku'na asal saga katahikan, sabab iya ya bay amapanjari.* The seas are by nature his property, because it was he who created it. *Paragan kita ma katahikan, magsilapug paragan.* We run in the sea, becoming scattered while running.

**tahik-bulagas** *n.* A phase of tide marked by strong current flows. *Tahik bulagas, alandos sōn subu. Pagugtu-llaw, t'bba, a'ggot t'bbana.* At the *bulagas* phase of the tide the incoming current is strong in the morning. By noon it is low tide, extremely low.

**tahik₂** *n.* Seasons as defined by major wind phases. *Duwa tahik magbalos, tahik uttara' maka tahik satan.* There are two opposing sea-seasons, the season of the north wind and the season of the southwest monsoon.

**tahi'** *v. tr.* To join or attach by sewing, of things such as fabric or palm-leaf thatch. *Tinahi' ma tangan.* Sewn by hand. *Subay la'it bang ma kami,*

*tahi' itū saga Sama Lipid atawa Sūk.* According to us it should be *la'it,* for Land-based Sama or Tausug it is *tahi'.* (*Thesaurus:* **bakiya'₂, bagsak₂, dahut, la'it**)

**pagtahi'** *v. intr. aN-* To sew clothes. *Agtahi' si Mām. Anahi' al'kkas.* The schoolmistress does sewing. She sews quickly.

**pagtatahi'** *n.* One who sews clothes for a living; a tailor or seamstress.

**tahi' buta** *n. phrase* A concealed stitch, i.e. one that is not seen from the surface of the fabric.

**tahod** *n.* The natural spur on the leg of a chicken. (*cf:* **epo'**)

**tahōng** *n.* The Asian green mussel. *Perna viridis.* (*syn:* **kopang**)

**tahu** *adj. a-* Knowledgeable; informed. *Atahu iya itū.* This one is well-informed. (*cf:* **ta'u₁ 1**; *Thesaurus:* **pangannal₁, sakup₁ 1, sayu 1.1, sipat₁ 1.1, tilas₁**)

**tahud** *v. tr. -an* To like or want something very much. *Ya angkan iya halam ala'an min tinda aniya' tinahuran he'na.* The reason he hasn't left the store is that there is something he badly wants. (*Thesaurus:* **sōb, suwak 1**)

**tahun** *n.* **1)** A year. *Ma tahun kapi'itu Jipun.* The year when the Japanese came. *Tahun bay palabay inān, bay magluma' maitu si Se i'. Ma tahunan, ngga'i ka ma bulanan.* Years past, Sa lived here in his house. For years, not for months. *At'ggol na tahun halam makapagokom sigām magdanakan.* They have not lived together as siblings for many years. (*Thesaurus:* **musim, paliyama'**) **1.1)** *n.* A year as a count term for someone's age. *Pilantahun umulnu?* How old are you [lit. how many years your age]? **1.2)** *v. intr. aN-* To become a year in duration. *Sōng-sōng na anahun ya kapagl'kkatta.* Our separation is almost a year in duration.

**ma tahunan** *adv. phrase* By the year. *Nda'un, Mma', ma tahunan na aku maghinang ma ka'a sali' banyaga'nu.* Look, Dad, for years I have worked for you as if [I was] your slave. *Tahun bay palabay inān, bay magluma' maitu si Sa i'. Ma tahunan, ngga'i ka ma bulanan.* Years past, Sa lived here in his house. For years, not for months.

**pagtahunan** *v. intr. aN-* To do something for many years. *Gonggongin ma pangatayannu in saga panoho'anku, pasal ya hē' makapataha' umulnu mareyom magtahunan.* Hold my instructions securely in your heart, because that is what will extend your lifespan as the years go by.

**tahun baha'u** *n. phrase* This present time or era. {idiom} *Dangibu kilu buhatna bang ma tahun baha'u itū.* One thousand kilos in weight in this present era. (*Thesaurus:* **ahil**)

**tahun ni tahun** *adv. phrase* Repeatedly over the years. {idiom}

**mananahun** *adv.* Persisting through many years, of a chronic illness.

**patahunan** *n.* A season of the year.

**tahun itu** *n. phrase* This present period of time; today in contrast to time past. *Kamanahutan itū mbal ameya' gara', anak tahun itu. Subay kami a'aslag.* The young ones don't take advice, the youth of today. It must be us adults. *Ka'am saga a'a ma tahun itu, halam to'ongan aniya' imanbi!* You people of today really have no faith!

**taibu'** *n.* An edible fungus; a mushroom.

**taikut** *v. intr. pa-* 1) To turn away from someone to avoid seeing him. 1.1) *v. tr. -an* To ignore or reject someone. *Tinaikutan kita he' kasehe'an, sali' kita mbal nīnda' he' sigām. Bang aniya' pamuwan, mbal kita binuwanan.* We are ignored by the others, it's like they don't see us. When something is being given, we aren't given any. (*Thesaurus:* **pagin'mbal 1, pagmari', pasibukut 1, sulak₂**)

**pagtaikut** *v. intr. aN-* To be aligned back to back.

**tai'** *n.* 1) Refuse from various activities or processes. 1.1) *v. tr. -an* To remove the under layer of vegetable tissue from bamboo or cane strips, in preparation for use. *Tinai'an p'ttung bo' anipis.* The vegetable layer removed from bamboo [strips] so it is thin. (*Thesaurus:* **ambuhut, hait, salimi, tilas₂**) 2) Feces; dung. *Apetak tai' sapi' bang asungi' ma lān bo' tagi'ik e' a'a.* Cow dung is squashy if it excretes on the path and someone treads on it. (*cf:* **tandak;** *Thesaurus:* **jamban 1, mange' 1, sungi' 1**)

**tai'-baliyu** *n.* Cirrus cloud formation; high cloud in general. {idiom} *Ngga'i ka ulan, dampog, ya tai'-baliyu inān.* It's not rain, it's dark cloud formation, that scattered high cloud there. *Aburaw isāb langit, aheka tai'-baliyu sali'.* The sky too is unclear, like there is a lot of high cloud. *Tai' ai mbal bauhan mareyom dunya? Tai'-baliyu.* What excrement [*tai'*] in the world does not stink? Cirrus clouds [*tai'-baliyu*, lit. wind excrement]. (*Thesaurus:* **andom 1, gabun, haya'₂, turung-balu 2**)

**tai'-bamban** *n.* Fine mossy growth in the hull of a canoe. *Lapu-lapuna, ya tai'-bambanna.* Its surface film, its mossy growth. *Saddī lumut, saddī tai'-bamban. Lumut itū aheka jablutna. Aniya' sali' tai'-bamban ma deyom mohang, anahut-nahut sali'.* Lumut [a mossy growth] and *tai'-bamban* are different. Lumut has lots of roots. There is something like *tai'-bamban* in the bilge, quite small. (*Thesaurus:* **bakkel 1, lapu-lapu 1**)

**tai'-buway** *n.* Refuse from the processing of rattan into flexible material.

**tai'-kōk** *n.* Loose skin or scale on a person's head. *Kosokin, aheka tai'-kōknu ilū.* Give it a good shake, you have a lot of flaky skin there. (*Thesaurus:* **buruk 1.1, gulis-manuk 1, hagikgik**)

**tai'-ero'** *n.* Something useless and unreliable (lit. dog feces). {idiom} *Busay tai'-ero' itū!* This useless paddle!

**tai'-gaha'** *n.* Flaky rust.

**tai'-hangin** *n.* A parasitic growth on certain tree species, pink or white and about the size of large rice grains.

**tai'-lahing** *n.* Fibrous residue left after purifying coconut oil. (*Thesaurus:* **akal, angkas₁ 1, hali₁ 1, p'tti', sapal**)

**tai'-lalat** *n.* A black spot or mole on the skin. (*Thesaurus:* **bau-bau, langking**)

**tai'-p'ttung** *n.* Soft material on the inner face of bamboo, removed before weaving.

**tai'-ulangan** *n.* A thing of no worth. *Tahinang kami tai'-ulangan.* We are treated as worthless.

**tai'-unas** *n.* Weedy trash in seawater.

**tai'-uni'** *n.* Stringy refuse from the preparation of bamboo or cane. *Bang buway niōnan tai'-buway. Tai'-uni' itū man p'ttung, man t'mmang.* With rattan it's called rattan refuse. *Tai'-uni'* is from bamboo or cane.

**tai'-ambal** *n.* Ambergris. *Ya niōnan tai'-ambal itu tai', sagwā' alahang tapuwa', alahang ta'nda'. Bang tabākta ambal buwat heya pa'ata, siguru kita duwa lawang tinda.* This stuff known as *tai'-ambal* is dung, but it is rarely picked up, rarely seen. If we find a piece the size of our thigh, we'll definitely [be worth] a two-door department store. *Bang tabākta tai'-ambal buwat heya pa'ata, siguru kita duwa lawang tinda.* If we find ambergris the size of our thigh, we'll definitely [be worth] a two-door department store. (*cf:* **gadjamina**)

**tai'-anak** var. of **tali'anak**

**tai'-asang** *n.* A species of fish.

**taima'** 1) *adj. zero* Accepted. *Taima' kita sagwā' subay kita kasokatan luma' bulawan.* We are accepted [with regard to our proposal] but a gold house is the extra that is requested of us. 1.1) *v. tr.* To accept someone. *Manjari, patut iya tinayma' ma da'ira inān bo' binuwanan luma' pahanti'anna.* So then, it's appropriate for him to be accepted into that town and to be given a house for him to stay in. *Bang kita ta'abut amatay, tinaima' to'ongan e' Tuhan.* When the time comes for us to die, we will be fully accepted by God. *Bang aku angungsuran sarakka ma siyaliku, pasampayku ni imam ati tinaima' e'na.* If I give alms for my younger brother, I deliver it to the imam and he receives it. 2) *v. tr.* To agree to a financial offer.

**tainga** var. of **talinga**

**tairuk** var. of **taliruk**

**taisay** var. of **talisay**

**Taiti'** *n.* A local name for Saban, the eighth month of the Islamic year. *Magtiti' kami bang ma bulan Taiti'.* In the month of Taiti' we sprinkle [the graves]. *Bang ta'nda'ku al'mmi' ka'mbo'anku, yukku, "Bang ta'abut Taiti'."* When I see the graves of my forebears getting soiled, I say, "When the month Taiti' comes round." (*cf:* **timbun;** *syn:* **Nispu, Saban**)

**tajari** *adj. zero* Usable; worth repairing. *Agese' itū tajari du, alaklak itū mbal.* With *gese'* [torn] something can be done, with *laklak* [torn apart] nothing can be.

**tā'** *v. tr.* To file the outer face of upper front teeth, for cosmetic reasons. (*Thesaurus:* **lagnas, pangtad, solsol**)

**tā'-tā'** *v. intr. aN-* **1)** To coincide unintentionally with another event. *Buwat pareyo' kita ni pelang, ak'tta ni Siganggang ati ulan ina'an patumbuk, anā'-tā' kita magtūy ma ulan.* Like us, when we go down into the canoe leaving for Siganggang, and then the rain comes down hard, we completely coincide with the rain [starting]. (*Thesaurus:* **pag'tta', pagsamp'kka', sabu 1.1, salta'**) **1.1)** *v. intr. pa-/-um-* To co-occur with some activity. *Basta kita tumā'-tā, maka'ā' sadja.* So long as we coincide, we will surely catch [some fish]. *Buwat aniya' animbak bo' kita asal mahē', makatā'-tā' kita.* Like when there is shooting and we just happen to be there, that's a case of us coinciding.

**pagtā'-tā'** *v. intr. aN-* To play in a musical ensemble, as of two people playing a bamboo marimba and a gong. (*Thesaurus:* **taktek, taletek, taroro'**)

**ta'abbit** *n.* **1)** An invited guest. **1.1)** *v. tr.* To invite someone as guest. *Aheka a'a tina'abbit, salat du tapene'.* Many people are invited, only a few are selected.

**ta'akkup** *var. of* **tayakkup**

**ta'adjil** **1)** *n.* Sundried cassava tubers. (*Thesaurus:* **kuting-kuting₁, tumbal 1**) **1.1)** *v. tr.* To dry freshly dug cassava tubers by exposure to the sun. **2)** *v. tr.* To abandon someone to the heat of the sun. *Hal kita tina'adjil.* We are simply left to bake in the sun. **3)** *v. tr.* To outshine someone in beauty or skill. {idiom} *Luwa-luwanu, ana'adjil ka aku.* Look at you! You outshine me!

**ta'alluk** *see:* **pagta'allukan**

**ta'as** *n.* **1)** An upper limit or level. *Ta'asna duwa hatus.* No more than two hundred. (*cf:* **langa 1.1**) **1.1)** *v. intr. pa-* To reach a high level of money or status. *Ungsudna mbal na pata'as ni bay tagna'.* Her bride-wealth will not reach the high level of the past.

**pagta'as-ta'as** *v. tr.* To strive for supremacy over one's peers. *Magta'as-ta'asan bang sai apatut.* They strive for supremacy to see who is suitable. *A'a inān hal magta'as-ta'as dīna.* That fellow just makes himself out to be above others. (*Thesaurus:* **pagkosogan, pagda'ug, pagegot-egot**)

**ta'at** *n.* **1)** A prayer of entreaty to a superior being. *Minsan akosog ta'atna ni Tuhan, taluwa' isāb sagdahan.* Even though his call to God is strong, he is still susceptible to harm [from a spirit being]. **1.1)** *v. tr.* To petition God, a spirit being, or a deceased relative. *Bang saupama aniya' mma'ta atawa ina'ta bo' kita pinakalintaw he'na,*

*tina'at na ya mamatay hē'. Niōnan na pa'in.* For example, if our father or mother makes us angry, we petition the one who has died. He is named over and over. *Duma'in ka buwat kita a'a aheya, onde'-onde' magkarupangan, yukna, "Ta'atku mma'nu."* Not like us who are adults, but children behaving foolishly, saying "I will name your [deceased] father." (*Thesaurus:* **amu'-amu', harap₂, pagduwa'a, pudji 1.1, sambahayang**)

**pagta'at** *v. intr. aN-* To serve God faithfully in regular prayer and observance of religious duties. *Magta'at kām ni Tuhan min deyom ataybi maka min deyom tawhidbi.* Serve God from your hearts and your inner being. *Ngga'i ka aku magtata'at.* I am not one who prays regularly. (*Thesaurus:* **pagammal, paglima-waktu, pagsanittiya**)

**ta'awil** *v. intr. aN-* To assume mistakenly that one is being addressed or discussed. *Linganannu si Mo, aku ya anaul. Tu'ud aku ana'awil. Pangannalku aku.* You call Mo, I am the one who responds. It is just me who misunderstands, thinking it was for me. (*Thesaurus:* **ambil-hati, pagkamali', pagkasā' 1.1, pagsabali**)

**ta'is** *see:* **pagta'is**

**ta'nda' mata** *phrase* Visible; accessible to human sight. *Magkaliru'an aku ma anakku, mbal na ta'nda' mataku.* I am missing my child whom my eyes no longer see.

**ta'u₁** *n.* **1)** Knowledge; understanding. *Na pasōng na pa'in, paheya si Samwel maka pasōng ta'una.* So Samuel continued to grow in size and in his understanding. (*cf:* **tahu**; *Thesaurus:* **alab-alab, himangkan, ingat, pamapatahan, panghati**) **1.1)** *v. tr. a-, ka-..-an, -an* To know something; to know how to do something. *Kinata'uhan e'na kamemon tumauwa' maitu ma lahattam.* He knew all about what was happening here in our district. *Ata'u iya maghinang taguri'.* He knows how to make kites. *Angay ka angkan ata'u magsinama?* Why do you know how to speak Sinama? *Pakata'uku ma lling Bisaya', bay aku magniBangkud-niBangkud.* My getting to know [how to speak] Cebuano was I went repeatedly to Bangkud. (*cf:* **tallang-hati 1.1**) **1.2)** *v. tr.* To acquire knowledge of something. *Bilahi isāb ta'uku bang ai hatina.* I also want to know what its meaning is. *Bang ka amarena aniya' kayu nsa' tata'u pareyo', talapay. Alambang iya.* If you're drilling a hole and there is a piece of timber underneath, not realized, it gets included [in the drilling]. (*Thesaurus:* **adji' 2, anad 1, istadi**)

**pagkinata'u** *v. intr. aN-* To know or be acquainted with each other. *Magkinata'u kami maka a'a inān.* That man and I know each other.

**pagta'u-ta'u** *v. intr. aN-* To claim or pretend to have knowledge. *Magta'u-ta'u iya itū minsan mbal ata'u.* This fellow claims to know even though he does not know.

**ta'u-hati** *v. tr.* a-, ka-..-an, -an To show practical concern or appreciation for someone. {idiom} *Buwat aku itu kulang-kabus, na ka'a ya ata'u-hati ma aku.* Like when I am short of everything, then you take care of my needs. *Mbal ata'u-hati, sali' halam aniya' ka'inagonna ma ka'am.* He has no concern, it's like he does not care for you. *Buwat aniya' ginadji'an t'llu hatus pilak dambulan, bang akatis dantahun halam aniya' la'atna, na ata'u-hati nakura'na ma iya. K'nnopanna ma ngga'i ka gadji.* Like when someone is paid three hundred pesos a month, then when a year is up without anything negative, then his boss shows him his appreciation. He adds something other than his wage.

**ta'u-lagi'** *ptl.* Indicating surprise at the action described. {idiom} *Ati ta'u-lagi' kām atilaw bang angay aku.* And yet you ask what I am up to.

**kata'u** *n.* Knowledge.

**hinabta'u** (var. **himanta'u**) *n.* Knowledge or awareness of something. (*cf:* **pangita'u**)

**pagkata'u** *v. intr.* aN- To be acquainted with each other. (*Thesaurus:* **pagkilā**)

**pangita'u** *n.* Knowledge; wisdom. (*cf:* **hinabta'u**)

**pata'u** *v. tr.* To inform someone of some matter; to invite someone to an event. (*Thesaurus:* **haka 1.1, palapal, tubad**)

**ta'u₂** *v. intr.* a- Having some intrinsic quality or characteristic. *Ata'u basi' pagūng?* Can iron float? *Angalunab, mbal ata'u kauli'an, buwat pali'ku itū. Ubus kauli'an, bo' pabalik du.* Chronic, incapable of healing, like this cut of mine. It gets better, then comes back again. *Ata'u iya amarupang matto'ana.* He is in the habit of deceiving his parents. *Si Ju bay angahinang aneges-teges, mbal ata'u angamomos.* Ju worked messily, not being in the habit of tidying up.

**ta'u₃** (var. **ta'u-ta'u₂**) *n.* Heads, the side of a coin marked with a human figure. (*syn:* **kara**)

**ta'u-marayaw** *see:* **pagkata'u-marayaw**

**ta'u-ta'u₁** *n.* An effigy of the human form, as the carved figure on the roof peak of some mosques. (*cf:* **datu'-datu', munyeka**)

**ta'u-ta'u-mata** *n.* The pupil of the eye. (*syn:* **kaettoman-mata**)

**ta'u-ta'u₂** var. of **ta'u₃**

**ta'ut** *v. intr.* pa- To bounce gently up and down, as a hanging cradle. (*cf:* **dundang₁** 1; *Thesaurus:* **buwa₂**)

**pagta'ut** *v. intr.* aN- To rhythmically bounce a hanging cradle. *Anā, bang anangis na onde' inān, magta'ut na pa'in l'lla bang d'nda inān maghinang.* Well now, when that child is crying, the man keeps bouncing the cradle when the woman is busy.

**ta'utan** *n.* A cradle for a baby: a cloth tube suspended from two bamboo laths.

**ta'uyu** *n.* Soya sauce. (*gen:* **pamapā**)

**tala** var. of **tā**

**talam** *n.* A brass tray used to present food on special occasions. *Talam itū anginggat la, buwat garul ma ina' si Ti. Baha'u ya, na luwa bulawan, pinagbase' maka tahik agtūy anumbaga.* This tray simply sparkles like the brass bowl Ti's mother has. When new, it looks like gold, when wet with seawater it soon turns coppery. *Dulang itū ni'isi nireyom ligu atawa ni talam.* This array of festive foods is placed in a winnowing basket or a tray. (*Thesaurus:* **bandehaw, tataklayan**)

**talang** *n.* A coin game in which coins are thrown in the air, with points scored on their fall.

**pagtalang** *v. intr.* aN- To play the game of talang. (*Thesaurus:* **agad₂, pagkabit, pagsalla' 1.1, sulang₂, tingka**)

**talap** *v. tr.* -an To seize and destroy someone, the action of certain saitan spirits. *Pehē' ka magpatalap dīnu.* Go and get yourself snatched by a demon. *Tinalapan he' saitan.* Done away with by a *saitan* spirit. (*cf:* **alim₂, t'kkob**)

**pagpatalap** *v. intr.* aN- To cause something to disappear, by demonic action.

**talbang** *adj. zero* 1) Lost at sea. *Talbang ka ma dilaut! Mbal ka tapole' ni luma' bang ka atuhun.* You'll be lost at sea. You'll never return home if you go diving. 1.1) *v. tr.* -an To cause someone or something to vanish in the sea, the action of saitan spirits. (*Thesaurus:* **lanyap 1.1, tanggal₃ 1**)

**talkala'** *conj.* Given that; on the basis of evidence. *Talkala' bay tatangkawnu anu inān, subay ka binuwanan l'gga ko da'a tabaliknu.* Since you have in fact stolen something, you should be given a lesson so that you don't do it again. *Talkala' itu suli-suli, da'a ka pasekot.* Since this is a discussion, don't come close. *Basta bay takodjelnu, talkala' bay takodjelnu.* If you knocked it, [it will be] evident that you knocked it. (*Thesaurus:* **abila, bang₁, bangsi', basta, bo' na, gana, pagka, samantala'**)

**talkin** *v. tr.* To take appropriate care of someone, as a man cares for his wife during pregnancy. *Analkin kita h'ndata. Ngā'anta iya kayu, bohe', apa mbal iya makakaleya. Ab'ttong iya.* We care for our wives. We get firewood and water for her, for she is not able to go inland. She is pregnant. (*Thesaurus:* **ayad, ayuput, hamumu', ipat, pahilala' 1, paintul, paipid, payakun, ulip, upiksa', ussap 1**)

**talkun** *n.* The head-cloth of a corpse. (*Thesaurus:* **kasa', kuku-pote', salimput 1, saput 1, tatap 1**)

**tale'ed** var. of **taleted**

**talengog** (var. **taenghog**; **tenghog**) *v. tr.* To hear something by listening intently. *Aniya' talengogta.* We can hear something. *Taenghogun kono' bang sai palabay ē'.* Please listen carefully [to know] who is passing by. (*Thesaurus:* **bahingaw, kale 1, hīng-hīng**)

**panalengog** *n.* An awareness of a person who is not physically present. (*Thesaurus:* **ginhawa,**

**nyawa, sumangat 1, umagad 1**)

**taletek** *v. tr. -an* To beat a complex rhythm on gongs or bamboo marimba. *Tinaletekan gabbang, tinaletekan dapu'.* Beating a rhythm on a marimba, beating time on the marimba box. (*cf: lisag₂ 1; Thesaurus:* **kulanting 1, lisag₂ 1.1, pagtā'-tā', taktek, tagunggu', taratu' 1.1, taroro', taroro', tigi'-tigi'₂, tuntung**)

**taleted** (var. **tale'ed**) *adj. a-* Located randomly in different places. *Sinoho' kita ni luma' ina'an angamu' api, na ni luma' dakayu', atale'ed.* We are told to go to that house and ask for fire, then to another house, so many different places. *Atale'ed aku bang aku sinoho'. Saddī ya nihinang e'ku man bay panoho'annu.* I am all over the place when I am sent. What I do is different from what you sent me to do. *Ataleted pahāp kal'ngnganan a'a hē'.* That fellow is forever going from one place to another. *Aniya' bay asaki, atale'ed pamowahan.* Someone was ill, taken to various healers. (*cf: latag 1*)

**pagtaleted** *v. intr. aN-* To keep moving from one location to another. *Magtaleted-taleted ba. Ubus ni luma' dakayu', ni luma' dakayu'.* He keeps going from place to place. First to one house, then to another. (*Thesaurus:* **lagedled 1, laud 1, lintas, pagtagestes**)

**talget** *n.* An objective; a goal. *Magpakale aku ma si Mu, bo' ya talget ē' patudju ni ka'a.* I let Mu hear about it, but you are the intended target.

**talhakit** *adj. zero* **1**) Known widely. *Talhakit na ni kamemon.* Known now by everyone. **1.1**) *v. advrs. ka-...-an* To become widely known. *Katalhakitan na lansa inān. Talhakit a'a magsuli-suli.* It is widely known now about that launch. Known by people talking to each other. (*Thesaurus:* **musti-musti, pasti'₁**)

**tali-tali₁** *v. advrs. -in-* **1**) Suffering from migraine or a severe headache. **1.1**) *v. tr. -an* To remove severe headaches by reciting the appropriate charm.

**tali-tali₂** *v. tr. -an* To control something with an attached string. (*Thesaurus:* **taguntun 1.1, tugut 1.1, tuntun₁ 1**)

**talik** *v. tr. -an* To transfer someone or something. *Tinalikan sehe'na ni luma' itū.* His companion was transfered to this house.

**talik-talik** *v. tr.* To persuade someone to join in an activity. *Pehē' kam analik-nalik magongka' bo' makabeya' kasehe'an.* Go over there and organise the game so that others can join in. *Buwat makannak angongka', manjari aheka puhu'. Na pinamung-mungan he' ina'na, yukna, "Analik-nalik kām, ngga'i ka sehe'bi ya abinasa, ka'am apa ka'am ya amowa-mowa ni luma' itū."* Like children playing, and there are a lot of them. Then his mother scolds them, saying, "Get them doing something else. It's not your playmates who will feel the pain, it's you [pl], because you are the one who persuaded them to come to this

house." (*cf:* **bowa-bowa**)

**taligrama** *n.* A telegram.

**tali'** *adj. a-* **1**) Quick-witted; intelligent. *Atali' si Anu min aku. Mbal makaōk bissalana ma pikilanku.* What's-his-name is smarter than I am. His words don't get through to my mind. **1.1**) *v. tr.* To consider something carefully; to think things through. *Ai tinali'nu?* What have you been thinking about? *Tatali'-tali' pa'in e'na kapang'ttobna bistiruna.* When she had thought carefully about cutting off [the hem of] her dress. (*Thesaurus:* **kannal, dalil 1.1, dongdong, pagka'inagon, pikil 1.1**)

**pagtali'** *v. intr. aN-* To interpret something difficult, as an obscure law or the meaning of a dream. *A'a talus magtatali' uppi.* A seer, an interpreter of dreams.

**patali'an** *n.* The faculty of rational thought.

**tali'anak** (var. **tai'-anak**; **tautali'anak**) *n.* A basic family considered as a unit. *Gōm aku maka tautai'anakku ya tōngin dusa, da'a sadja in sultan tasalla'.* Better that I and my family be accused of wrong, rather than the sultan be criticized.

**pagtali'anak** *n.* **1**) The source family group of an individual. *Sai-sai amowa kasasawan ma pagtautali'anakna, kasukkalan ya ta'ā'na.* Whoever brings trouble on his family unit, grief is what he will get. *Sai lagi' niholatan e' kami, bang ngga'i ka ka'a maka saga a'a kamemon ya pagtai'anak mma'nu?* Who else can we expect help from, other than you and all the people of your father's extended family. (*Thesaurus:* **mata'an, pamilya 1**) **1.1**) *v. intr. aN-* To be related as members of a family unit formed around the parent-child relationship. *Min tagna' lagi' asal aku amogbogan mma'nu magtautai'-anak maka saga bagayna.* From the beginning I supported your father and family, and his friends too.

**talilli'** *v. intr. pa-* **1**) To follow an erratic trajectory. *Bang aniya' ahūg pareyo' ni tahik, mbal amontolan. Patalilli' man bay kahūganna.* When something falls into the sea, it doesn't go straight. It goes obliquely away from where it was dropped. (*Thesaurus:* **sulempat, tambelleng**) **1.1**) *v. tr. -an* To throw something so that it turns over in flight. *Larukanku, talilli'anku.* I throw [it], I send it erratically.

**taling** *n.* An eye-tooth or canine tooth. (*Thesaurus:* **baga'ang, bangkil₂, empon 1, sengel**)

**talinga** (var. **tainga**) *n.* **1**) The ear. **2**) The lug or loop handles on each side of a circular container.

**talinga lumping** *n. phrase* Sensitive hearing. {idiom}

**talinga-usuk** *n.* The collarbone or clavicle.

**talipan** var. of **bāt-talipan**

**taliruk** (var. **tairuk**) *n.* Generic term for various angelfishes, including the Semicircle; the Koran angelfish; the Six-bar angelfish. *Euxiphipops* *sexstriatus.* (*Thesaurus:* **bebang₁, tibuk-lawi'an**)

**taliruk-ikat-ikat** *n.* The Blue-banded or the Regal angelfish. *Pygoplites diacanthus.*

**taliruk-jahira** *n.* The Bicolor angelfish. *Centropyge bicolor.*

**taliruk-jali'an** *n.* The Emperor angelfish. *Pomacanthus imperator.*

**talisay** (var. **taisay**) *n.* The sea almond or Indian almond, a coastal tree valued for its edible kernel and useful timber. Used medicinally. *Terminalia catappa.* (*syn:* **pampan**)

**talis'ssok** (var. **talisoksok**) *n.* 1) An enlargement of the glands in the groin or armpit. (*Thesaurus:* **bago' 1, bogon₁ 1, bongol 1, busul, panibli**) 1.1) *v. advrs.* -in- Suffering from swelling of the glands. *Buwat kalibubut, sagō' halam aniya' kōkna. A'a tinalisoksok, apasu' iya.* Like a boil, but without a head. A person who suffers from swollen glands has a temperature.

**talisoksok** var. of **talis'ssok**

**taliyaga'** *n.* A harmless snake-like sea animal with a calceous tubular skeleton, found on the bottom in shallow water.

**taliyan** *n.* Decorations woven from palm leaflets and used on festive occasions. (*cf:* **ugbus 2**; *spec:* **manuk-manuk-manggis**)

**tal'ngnget-l'ngnget** *n.* A cicada. *Tal'ngnget-l'ngnget, ya mang'llub ma kayu.* The cicada, the one that makes a throbbing noise in the trees. (*cf:* **pilik-pilik 1**)

**tallak** *see:* **pagtallak**

**tallad** *n.* The Cigar wrasse; the Sharp-nosed rainbow fish. *Cheilio inermis.* (*syn:* **gellok**)

**tallang** *adj.* a- Clear; bright, of light.

**tallang-hati** *n.* 1) Intelligence; quickness of mind. *Ya mpat subul inān bay binuwanan pangita'u maka tallang-hati ma kaginisan pagsulat maka pangadji'.* Those four youths had been given wisdom and quick minds in all sorts of documents and study. 1.1) *adj.* a- Quick-witted; responsive to teaching. *Atallang-hati iya itū, apantun.* He is quick-witted, teachable. *Kata'uhannu du bang ai subay nihinang sabab atallang hatinu.* You know what is to be done because your understanding is excellent. (*cf:* **ta'u₁ 1.1**)

**talli₁** *n.* A chant used in a children's game in which the players spin around until giddy. *Talli talli, ma'ai luma' kami? Wa'i ma biradali. Talli talli,* where is our home? There with the sky maidens. **pagtalli** *v. intr.* aN- To play the talli children's game.

**talli₂** *n.* The Pipefish. *Syngnathinae.* (*cf:* **unduk-unduk**)

**tallung** *n.* A type of kite, diamond shaped.

**talmal** *n.* Wedding tax payable through a community leader to the government representative in the village. *Bang aniya' magkawin subay aniya' talmal pamuwan parinta, apa sinumbung.* When there is a wedding there

should be a wedding tax given to the government, because it is reported. (*cf:* **batu-kawin**)

**talom** *adj.* a- 1) Sharp, of a blade or point. *Atalom to'ongan empon sigām, sapantun bangkil halimaw magpangal'kkob.* Their teeth are very sharp, like for example the fangs of a lion that devours [its prey]. (*ant:* **tompol**) 1.1) *v. tr.* -an To sharpen something.

**talom bowa'** *adj.* a- Effective in debate; forceful in speech. {idiom} *Atalom bowa'na, aesog anambung. Sali' alabas.* He is effective in debate [lit. his mouth is sharp]. Sort of cutting. (*Thesaurus:* **labas₂ 1, paul**)

**taloman** *n.* A cutting edge or point.

**talom-badji** *n.* A species of shark. (*gen:* **kalitan 1**)

**talopa'** (derivative of **lopa'**) *n.* That which is eaten; food of any kind. (*Thesaurus:* **kinakan 1**).

**talu₁** *v. tr.* To make a bet on the outcome of a contest. (*Thesaurus:* **kōl 1.1, hapus₁ 1.1, pagtinggi, tumba₂ 1.1**)

**pagtaluhan** (var. **pagtauhan**) *n.* 1) A contest of knowledge or predictions, often with bets on the outcome. 1.1) *v. intr.* aN- To engage in a contest of wits or guesses about future outcomes. *Magtaluhan, sali' magtokod-tokod inān buwat bay kita. Yukku, "Aniya' kappal at'kka." Yuknu, "Halam ba." Agtūy du at'kka.* Guessing about the future, like that guessing competition we had. I said, "There will be a ship arriving." You said, "No there won't." [But] it promptly arrived. *Binowa magtaluhan ya saitan inān he' jin. Magkosog.* That spirit-being was drawn by a djinn into a guessing competition. Pitting [their] strength against each other. *Angaku aku magtaluhan ma ka'a, sali' magb'nnal-b'nnal duwangan.* I commit myself to wager with you, like the two [of us] claiming to tell the truth.

**panaluhan** *n.* Money or other valuables put up as stake in a wager.

**talu₂** *n.* Beeswax. *Am'lli aku talu panambalku tipara.* I will buy some beeswax to mend my diving goggles. *Talu itu pangalapatan pelang ko da'a ang'mman.* This beeswax is used to make tight joints in a canoe so it doesn't leak. (*cf:* **lansuk**)

**taluk** *n.* Colors ranging from deep orange to dark purple (excluding red). (*gen:* **walna'**)

**talug** var. of **dalug₂**

**talum** (var. **talung₃**) *n.* The eggplant. *Solanum melongena.*

**talum-palat** *n.* The turkey berry, a prickly shrub and its edible yellow berries, used medicinally. *Solanum torvum.*

**talumpas** var. of **salompas**

**talumpung** *n.* 1) A telescope; binoculars. 1.1) *v. tr.* To see something through a telescope. *Pagkohap llaw dakayu', analumpung na. Pagtalumpung itū aniya' na leha.* On the afternoon of the next day, [he] looked through the binoculars. As he looked there was a square sail.

**talun** *n.* **1)** A wooded area, a variable mixture of indigenous forest and fruit trees. *Makatāw-tāw kami bang ta'nda' lutaw amangguwa' ma talun hē'.* We are frightened when we see the ghost of a dead person appearing there in the forest. (*Thesaurus:* **kabbun, kati'an, gulangan**) **1.1)** *v. tr.* To gather fruit inland. *Analun aku wanni maka mampallam.* I will gather both odorous and ordinary mangoes. *Anasaban kita mampallam, sali' analun. Basta ai-ai tatalun ba.* We forage for mangoes, similar to going through coastal woods. Anything whatever that can be foraged in coastal woods. (*cf:* **sasab, takod 1.1**)

**talung₁** *v. tr.* To outdo in quality the equivalent features of something else. *Minsan ala'at pangluwahanna, tinalung ma pamakayna.* Even though her looks are not great, they are overcome by her clothes. *Tinalung mastal e' onde' iskul. Takdil tinanom, magbihing niyug maka saging: akulang buwa' niyug-i.* The teacher is outdone by the school children, like coconuts and bananas growing together: the fruit of the coconuts few [by comparison]. *Ahāp luwa pandala min pangantin, tinalung pangantin.* The bridesmaids are better looking than the bride. The bride is eclipsed.

**panalung** *n.* A distinctive personal feature.

**talung₂** *v. advrs.* ka-...-an To be restricted as to growth, of plants crowded by the roots of stronger plants. *Katalungan tinanom sabab magbeya' patomo' maka sagmot itingan.* The plants are choked because they are growing together with thorn bushes. *Aniya' isāb tinanom aheya-heya katalungan, bay patomo' ma t'ngnga' malabuhuk.* There are shrubs choked too, they had grown in the middle of pine trees.

**talungan** *n.* An area of soil that is choked by roots.

**talung₃** *var. of* **talum**

**talungkup** *n.* A top (the toy) that is set spinning with a cord. (*syn:* **gasing**)

**talus₁** *adj.* a- **1)** Completed. *Bang bay atalus magmiting magpole'an na.* When they had finished their meeting they went home. (*Thesaurus:* **tekmod, tubus₁ 1.1**) **1.1)** *v. tr.* To complete something. *Halam aku bay makatalus amangan, sali' nijogjogan kinakanku.* I had not finished eating; my food was kind of jolted. *Mbal tatalus sigām hinang sigām inān.* They will not complete that work of theirs. *Subay tinalus danjām.* An hour [of work] should be completed. (*Thesaurus:* **katis₂ 1.1, sangkol, tammat 1.1, tapus 1.1, ubus₁ 1.1**)

**talus panghati** *n. phrase* A person with complete understanding of all sorts of things. {idiom} *A'a iya talus panghati.* He is someone who understands everything.

**talus₂** *n.* A person with the ability to foretell the future. *Yukna, "Kaut aku, maka'ā' du aku daing."*

*Ya hē' kinupul, sali' talus iya.* He said, "I am going to sea and I will indeed catch fish." That is something said presumptuously, as though he was a seer. *Talus-talus a'a inān, sali' aniya' ilmu'na.* That fellow is something of a seer, as though he has some esoteric ability. (*Thesaurus:* **kupul, pa'al 1.1**)

**taluwa'** (var. **tauwa'**) **1)** *adj. zero* On target; correct. *Bang aku kaleya amitik manuk-manuk, taluwa', ahūg pareyo'.* When I go inland shooting birds [with a slingshot], they get hit and fall down. *Aho', tauwa' bang buwattilu.* Yes, right on in that case. *Amatay siyakaku bang halam taluwa' tawal maka tambal.* My older sister will die if the incantation and medicine don't suit [the need]. *Asaki si Bo, taluwa' maut.* Bo is ill, struck by a death spirit. (*Thesaurus:* **tigi'-tigi'₁ 1, t'bbong, tudju₂ 1, tumlang 2**) **1.1)** *v. intr.* pa-/-um- To be on target; to achieve a desired outcome. *Tumaluwa' hinangnu ilū.* That work of yours is meeting expectations. *Magsumau' bissalata, ubus tumauwa' ubus mbal.* What we are saying gets muddled, on the mark one minute and then not. *"Bang ka'a ya makatauwa' manggis," yuk Sultan, "ma ka'a na anakku siyali."* "If you are the one who manages to hit a mangosteen," said the Sultan, "you shall have my youngest daughter." *Amuwan aku t'llu ginisan palkala' pamene'annu ya pataluwa' ma ka'a.* I will give three situations for you to choose among, one that meets your requirements. **1.2)** *v. advrs.* ka-...-an To be persuaded as to the truth of something. *Kataluwa'an aku he' suli-sulinu ilū.* I am convinced by your words. **2)** *v. intr.* pa-/-um- To happen to someone; to affect someone adversely. *Al'gga na iya ma bay tumaluwa' ma anakna dahū.* He was wary because of what had happened to his first son. *Subay nihalli'an batu inān sabab asidda makataluwa'.* That coral feature should be avoided because it can cause harm. *Paluwasku na ma ka'am bang ai bay tumauwa' ma aku.* I will tell you now what has been happening to me. **3)** *v. tr. zero* To strike something. **3.1)** *v. advrs.* ka-...-an To be struck by something hard or strong. *Minsan katauwa'an mbal kapali'an.* Even though struck he cannot be wounded. *Bang kataluwa'an baliyu abō' pabiluk paraw, na magpaspad banog hē'.* When struck by wind so that the canoe veers off course, then the sail flaps.

**kataluwa'an** *n.* The essential meaning of something said. *Na, ya du hē' kataluwa'anna ī'.* Now that is precisely its meaning.

**pagtaluwa'** *v. intr.* aN- To be in agreement, of facts or conditions; to be mutually consistent. *Ē, mbal magtaluwa'.* Hey, that doesn't match up [with the facts]. *Magtaluwa' hinangna maka lling bowa'na.* His actions match up with the words of his mouth. *Abungkal sakina he' tambal, aho'* *paluwas na sakina kamemon. Tagna' tambalanta mbal paluwas, ta'abut kaminduwana paluwas. Magtaluwa' maka tambalna.* Her sickness is stirred up by the medicine, yes, her entire illness has come out. It didn't come out when we first medicated it, but the second time it did. The illness and the treatment interacted properly. (*cf:* **pagtuksu'**)

=**tam** (var. = **tabi**) *pron.* We, our, including the one spoken to (first person plural, inclusive) [Set II]. *Kahawatam.* Our coffee. (*cf:* **kitām, kitam**; *Set:* = **bi**, = **ku**, = **na**, = **nu**, = **sigā**, = **sigām**, = **ta 1**, = **tabi**)

**tamak** *n.* **1)** A blemish; a stain, whether physical or moral. *Bay lobag amikit ma s'mmek, ya hē' niōnan tamak.* Grime that had adhered to clothing, that's what is called a stain. *Matto'anu isāb kabuwanan tamak ma sabab ka'a.* Your parents too are affected because of you [your wrongdoing]. (*cf:* **dusa 1**; *Thesaurus:* **gora'₁ 1, powera 1, salla'₁ 1, sassat**) **1.1)** *adj. -an* Stained; guilty. **1.2)** *v. tr. -an* To stain or defile something. *Kubulinbi iya to'ongan bo' mbal katamakanbi paglahat.* Bury him thoroughly lest you defile the region.

**tamaka-** *aff.* Prefix indicating superlative degree. *Buwa' kayu tamakahāp na.* Fruit now of the highest quality. *Saga aesog maka tamakakosog.* The brave and the strongest. *Aheya isāb saga luma'na maka tamakalangkaw isāb ādna.* Its houses were large and its walls were exceedingly high.

**tama'** *v. tr. -an* To chop something up into pieces. *Anama'an iya dīna.* He is hacking himself. (*Thesaurus:* **k'llot, gōt-gōt 1, ladjang, pabuwa', padja', t'ttok 1.1**)

**tamalengkeng** *n.* The Yellow-spotted scorpionfish, a species with poisonous spines that lurks in holes on the sea floor. *Pterois sp.* (*cf:* **lese₂**)

   **tamalengkeng-borakan** *n.* A species of scorpionfish.

**taman** *conj.* Introduces a clause stating the limits of something. *Taman m'nnē' maka m'nnitu pangosolnu hāg.* From here to there is where you place the houseposts. *Amangan kām buwa' taman kabaya'anbi.* Eat fruit until you're satisfied. (*cf:* **tobtob 1.1**)

**tamanang** *adj. zero* Barren; unable to conceive, of humans or animals. *Halam aniya' bahā' ma ka'am d'nda-l'lla tamanang?* Do you have no women or men who are sterile? *Tamanang saga kura' karambila'an itū.* These cross-bred horses cannot breed. (*cf:* **t'ggang₂**)

**tamangka'** *n.* **1)** The Pink-banded grubfish. *Parapercis nebulosa.* **2)** The Cylindrical sandperch. *P. cylindrica.*

**tamarung** *n.* The Mackerel scad; the Big-bodied scad; the Short-finned scad. *Decapterus macrosoma. Tamarung itū ahāp kinilaw.*

*Tamarung* are good eaten raw with a relish.

**tamas** var. of **tangas**

**tamba** *v. tr. -an* To recompense someone for services provided; to bribe someone. *Lisu'an si La bang sinoho' ni M'ddas, subay tinambahan.* La is reluctant when told to go to Siasi, he has to be paid for it. *Gapi'ku ka'a ma sara'. Ka'a ilū sōnganku magbissala, aku itū angagad. Bay ka tambahanku, mbal salat.* You are my supporter before the magistrate. I have you go in front to do the talking, I just wait. I recompensed you, no small amount. *Tu'ud bay iya katambahan e' disi Ti maka si Sa. Bay iya tinambahan amakitāw aku.* He was in fact bribed by Ti and Sa. He was paid to scare me off. *Suli-suli pasal ya d'nda ala'at hinangna katambahan maka tinapay.* Talk about the girl who did bad things and could be bought with bread. *A'a kapangandolan, ya mbal katambahan maka sīn.* A reliable man who can't be bought off with money. (*cf:* **anambahina**)

**tambahan** *n.* An amount or goods paid in remuneration. *Sasuku angā'an aku magkalang kabuwanan du tambahan.* Whoever gets me a singer will definitely be given some remuneration. (*Thesaurus:* **bauballi', bayad 1, tiyandā, tulahan**)

   **pagkatambahan** *v. intr. aN-* To be capable of being bought or bribed.

   **panamba** *n.* Payment for work done or services provided.

**tambak₁** *n.* **1)** A wall or platform of piled rock. **1.1)** *v. tr. -an* To build a wall of rocks; to fill with rocks the area beneath a stilt house. *Tipunanta saga batu panambak luma'.* We will gather some coral rock for building up the house foundations. **1.2)** *v. tr.* To keep captured fish alive in a rock-walled enclosure.

**tambak₂** *n.* A species of small fish, known for nibbling the bait off hooks.

**tambal₁** *n.* **1)** A substances used in the treatment of an illness; medicine. (*cf:* **papalom**) **1.1)** *v. tr. -an* To treat an illness with medicine. *"Ai gawibi, Bapa'?" "Tuwan, pakitambal kami. Tambalin anak kami itū"* "What's your concern, Uncle?" "Sir, we are requesting medical treatment. Treat this child of ours."

   **pagtambal** *n.* **1)** The activity or time of getting medical treatment. *Mbal gi' waktu pagtambal.* It isn't time yet for the clinic. **1.1)** *v. intr. aN-* To get medical treatment. *Ina'an iya magtambal ma luma' disi Sēl.* There she is getting treatment at Sir's house. *A: "Maingga mastal?" B: "Wa'i gi' magtambal."* A: "Where is the schoolteacher?" B: "She is off getting treatment."

   **pananambal** *n.* A traditional healer. (*Thesaurus:* **doktol, pagbowahan**)

**tambal₂** *v. tr.* To repair something by filling a gap or hole. *Buwanin aku talu panambalku tiparaku.* Give me some beeswax to repair my diving goggles. (*Thesaurus:* **gagā, s'nsong**)

**tamban** *n.* Various species of sardines and herrings; the Indian sardine. *Sardinella longiceps et al. Angalaya aku tamban ni dilaut kaluma'an.* I will catch herrings with a throw net out from the houses.

**tambang₁** *adj. zero* 1) Nearing high water, of tidal range. *Tambang na tahik, sōng na alalom.* The tide is nearly full, almost high tide. (*Thesaurus:* **daka', lalom₁ 2, l'kkab, nso', sosob**) **1.1)** *v. intr.* *pa-* To rise; to become high, of tide. (*cf:* **la'ang 1**)

**tambang₂** *v. tr.* *-an* To make a token gift to the elders of a woman involved in an elopement, forestalling reprisals before compensation is negotiated. *Am'lli aku garul panambangku si Ji.* I will buy a brass container as my intervention gift for Ji. (*cf:* **tampan-maru**)

**tambang₃** *n.* 1) An item worn to protect the wearer against harm of a supernatural origin. *B'nnal aniya' kapanyapan onde'-onde' buwat saga tambang sigā.* It's true there are children's belongings, like their protective charms. (*spec:* **aba-aba, anting-anting 2, baklaw, buku₃, gallang labu, gampang 1.1, habay-habay, hadjimat, hampan 1, tampan 1, tilik**) **1.1)** *v. tr.* To guard a child against possible harm from a dead relative. *Bang onde'-onde' ariki' subay bīllihan pamulawan panambang sali' saga singsing atawa gallang atawa gantung-li'ug.* When children are small something of gold should be bought for them for protection, things such as a ring or a bracelet or a necklace.

**tambangaw** *n.* The Checkered snapper. *Lutjanus decussatus.* (*gen:* **kutambak**)

**tambelleng** *v. intr.* *pa-* To follow an erratic path or trajectory. (*Thesaurus:* **sulempat, talilli'** 1)
  **pagtambelleng** *v. intr.* *aN-* To walk erratically; to stagger. *Bang lum'ngngan si Anu magtambelleng-tambelleng.* When What's-his-name walks he goes erratically from side to side.

**tambelok** *n.* 1) The shipworm or teredo. *Teredo navalis.* (*syn:* **kapang₁** 1) **1.1)** *v. advrs.* *-in-* Infested with, or damaged by, shipworms. *Tinambelok saga hāg itū.* These posts are worm-ridden.

**tambilawang** *n.* Various needlefishes. *fam. Belonidae.*

**tambin** *v. tr.* *-an* To help someone by sharing a load. (*Thesaurus:* **tabang 1, tulung 1.1**)

**tambis** *n.* The rose-apple, a tree with small edible bell-shaped fruit. *Eugenia aquea.* (*cf:* **makupa**)

**tambō'** *n.* 1) The thumb; the big toe. (*wh:* **tangan 1**) 2) The thickness of a thumb as a measure. *Maka aniya' panggi' ba, asidda panggi', datambō'.* And there was some cassava, a tiny amount of cassava, as big as a thumb.

**tambol** *n.* 1) Something that closes an opening. *Pina'an saga sosoho'an sultan ni bilikna inān ati ta'nda' saga tambolna bay kinunsi'.* The sultan's servants went to his room and saw that its doors had been locked. (*Thesaurus:* **sa'ob 1, sampong 1, taplok 1, turung 1, tutup₁** 1) **1.1)** *adj. zero* Closed; shut. *Bang ugtu-llaw tambol luma' sigā apa atuli.* When it is midday their house is closed because they sleep. **1.2)** *v. tr.* To close a door or lid. *Tambolun lawang ilū, Rāng.* Shut that door, honey. (*Thesaurus:* **kabbat, takkop 1**)

**pagtambol** *v. intr.* *aN-* To be closed up and no longer functioning. *Bang pasayang pikpik galura' magtūy akiyamat dunya, minnē', min hamiyuna, agtambol dunya.* When the winged horse spreads its wings in flight the world will end. From that, from the turbulence [of its flight], the world will be closed up.

**tambol suratan** *adj.* *a-* Closed against the possibility of marrying some other suitor. {idiom} *Atambol suratan d'nda inān. Na minsan du aheka l'lla abaya'an iya, bay iya nihinang suratan he' l'lla saddī. Ahunit iya taga h'lla.* That woman is blocked from marrying someone else. So even though many men want her, she has been secured by another man. It will be difficult for her to have a husband.

**tambol-lawang** *n.* A door as distinct from a doorway.

**tambu** *v. tr.* 1) To mold something in the hands. *Subay tambuta bo' ak'ddot.* We should mold it so it is cohesive and springy. (*Thesaurus:* **kompol, pongkol, tampa** 1) 2) To form a sphere by blowing, as a balloon or plastic bag. *Tambuhun tilag-tilag ilū.* Blow into that plastic bag.

**tambu-tambu₁** *n.* A balloon. *Ni M'ddas aku am'lli tambu-tambu pangongka'an si Li.* I'm going to Siasi to buy a balloon for Li to play with.

**tambu-tambu₂** *v. intr.* *aN-* To form large blisters as a result of being burnt. (*Thesaurus:* **kassa'-kassa', l'ttup 1, lutup, mata-daing 1**)

**tambu-tambu₃** *n.* A species of tree found growing on sandy atolls. (*syn:* **buta-buta**)

**tambuku₁** *v. tr.* *-an* To inform someone of needs or requirements. *Bang aheka hinangnu, tambukuhin aku.* If you have a lot to do let me know. *"Da'a tugutin si Oto'."* *Ya hē' tinambukuhan he' mma'na.* "Don't let Eldest Son do as he wants." That's the requirement set by his father. (*Thesaurus:* **pasasā, suna**)

**pagtambuku** *v. intr.* *aN-* 1) To agree on the details of some activity. **1.1)** *v. tr.* To set the day or time of an event. *Bang yuk man kar'ndahan, "Salung magpah'nda," na magtambuku kami llaw pagkawin.* If those of the women's side say, "Present the bride-wealth tomorrow," then we agree on the day for the wedding.

**pagtambuku-tambuku** *v. tr.* *-an* To communicate with each other via a go-between. *Mbal kita bilahi pinagtambuku-tambukuhan, subay binaran. Ya hē' niōnan subay kita minahaldika'.* We don't like being sent messages all the time, we should be contacted in person. That's what is called the obligation to show us honor.

**pagtambukuhan** *n.* The date and time agreed on for some action or outcome. *Bang aku ni Malaybalay anambut lilusku, halam at'kka. Bang ta'abut pagtambukuhanta, sabuta na.* When I went to Malaybalay to get my wristwatch it hadn't arrived. When the time we agreed on comes we will be on time for it. *At'ggol na utang bo' waktu pagtambukuhan na, sukutnu na aku inān, bo' halam gi' aniya' pamayaran.* The debt was longstanding and it was the time agreed on, [so] you dunned me. However there wasn't anything yet to pay with.

**tambuku₂** *n.* 1) A button. *Am'lli aku tambuku panambukuku badju'ku.* I will buy buttons to fasten my blouse with. **1.1)** *v. tr. -an* To connect things by buttoning together.

**tambu'** *n.* 1) A dipper for water, usually suspended on a pole or string. *Bang mbal maka'abut tambu' ilū, sugpatin maka lupis abō' umabut.* If that dipper can't reach, extend it with a piece of banana fiber so it does reach. (*Thesaurus:* **gayung 1, sauk 1**) **1.1)** *v. tr.* To dip up water. *Anambu' du aku bang aku ni bohe'.* I use a dipper when I go to the water-source. (*Thesaurus:* **nduk, sagob 1.1, sauk 1.1**)

**tambul** *n.* A drum. (*Thesaurus:* **jabu-jabu**)

**pagtambul** *n.* 1) A drum rhythm. *Pagtimbak pagtambul itū sigi-sigi na pa'in.* The firecrackers and the drumming go on and on. **1.1)** *v. intr. aN-* To beat a rhythym on a drum.

**tambul-tambul** *n.* A tambourine. *Aniya' isāb min dahū'an sigām saga magbibiyula maka magsusuling maka a'a magtaroro'an tambul-tambul.* In front of them also were players of stringed instruments, flute-players, and people beating time on tambourines.

**tambulig** *n.* The melon squash, a white-flowered gourd. *Benincasa hispida.* (*cf:* **labu₃**)

**tambun** *n.* 1) A cover to conceal or shut out light. **1.1)** *adj. a-* Covered, of eyes or entire head. *Atambun kita atuli, magbinungkus kita.* We sleep with our head covered, we are all wrapped up. (*Thesaurus:* **bungkus 1, pulipus 1, putus 1.1**) **1.2)** *v. tr. -an* To cover something in order to conceal it. *Oto', tambunin togong ilū kaut, sali' tinihanan maka batu.* Son, cover [and set] that fish trap in the sea, like weighing it down with coral rocks. *Bang alandang-landang si Se porol, saga banak, tinambunan maka lai' mital.* When Se is frying silverbiddies or mullet, it is covered with a metal plate. *Tambunin matana kalbaw.* Cover the eyes of the carabao.

**pagtambun kaiya'an** *v. tr.* A satisfactory resolution of something that had caused shame. {idiom}

**tambung** (var. **tandung**) *v. intr. pa-* To come to one's mind, of positive emotions. *Tiyap-tiyap bang kita kinab'nsihan he' matto'ata, subay kita ala'an ni lahat atā. Kalu patambung ase' ni sigā.* Whenever our parents get angry with us, we should go away to a distant place. Maybe pity will come into their hearts. *Ō Tuhan, sumiyan aku patandung pabalik ni ataynu?* O God, when will I come into your mind again.? *Binowa aku magsuli-suli pabīng he' bay tunangku, patambung ase'-ase' ni iya. Mbal na isāb aku bilahi, ab'nsi. Na patambung lasa, magtūy aku alasa pabalik.* The one who had been my sweetheart got me talking with her again, tenderness had come into her mind. I no longer wanted he; I disliked her. Then love came into my mind and I immediately loved her again. (*Thesaurus:* **entom 1.2, magtak, padlak ni atay, sangpit, suligpat, tasdik, tomtom 1.1**)

**tambus** var. of **tangbus**

**tambusa'** *n.* A container of coconut leaflets for food eaten at the end of a mourning series. *Tambusa', ya ugbus niyug nihinang pangisihan panyām atawa buwas bīlla, bang aniya' maghinang. Tambusa',* new coconut leaflets made into containers for rice cakes or cooked rice when there is a ceremony. *Mbal manjari niōnan ansak bang magtapus, subay tambusa'.* It shouldn't be called *ansak* [a woven leaf container] when funeral rites are completed, it should be *tambusa'. Bang tambusa' jukup t'llu ginis: timayuk, panyām maka saging.* When a *tambusa'* is complete there are three kinds of things: cooked rice wrapped in a leaf, rice cakes and bananas. (*Thesaurus:* **tamparung 1, tamu, timayuk 1**)

**tamendak** *n.* A mudskipper. *subfam.* Oxudercinae.

**tamengka'** *see:* **pagtamengka'**

**taming** *n.* 1) A circular shield for protection against attack. *Jukup na taming maka budjak.* Complete with shield and spear. 2) A solar or lunar halo. **2.1)** *v. tr. -an* To form a halo around sun or moon. *Bang tinamingan llaw atawa bulan, yuk kami aniya' baliyu.* When the sun or moon is surrounded with a halo, we say there will be wind.

**tamiyang** *adj. zero* Well-built; big-bodied. (*cf:* **tibaggol**)

**tammat** *adj. a-* 1) Completed, of a formal event or course of study. *Atammat pa'in paghinang ē', ah'lling si Anu ma saga tendogna.* When the [funeral] ceremonies were over, Ya spoke to his workers. *In mulid kamemon, bang atammat na pangadji'na, magsali' du maka guruna.* Every religious student, when his studies are complete, becomes equal with his teacher. (*cf:* **paggradwet**; *Thesaurus:* **hatam 1.1, sampulna', tangbus**) **1.1)** *v. tr.* To complete a task. *Tinammat, bang pa'in isāb takatisku hinang bay pamahinang aku.* Fully completed, provided I can finish the work that was given me to do. (*Thesaurus:* **katis₂ 1.1, sangkol, talus₁ 1.1, tapus 1.1, ubus₁ 1.1**)

**pagtammat** *v. intr. aN-* To graduate from a course of study, Koranic or secular. *Magtammat, akatis* *ginulu angadji'*. Graduating, having finished studying to read the Holy Koran.

**tamokmok** *v. advrs. -in-* Pockmarked or pitted, as skin or canoe hull. *Tinamokmok pelangku palowang. Kinakan e' tambelok.* My canoe is marked with blemishes forming holes. It is eaten by ship worms. *Tinamokmok, sali' sinamuwa'. Bang matto'a tinamokmok, niampogod.* Pockmarked, suffering from pimples. Old people are pockmarked, they have facial pimples.

**tamongon** *n.* Clothing in general. *Bay iya anulug tamongon pagbobono'.* He put on battle clothing. (*Thesaurus:* **pamakay, s'mmek 1**)

**tampa** *v. tr.* 1) To mold clay in readiness for firing. (*Thesaurus:* **kompol, pongkol, tambu 1**) 2) To massage the limbs and head of a newborn baby to prevent a perceived deformity from becoming permanent.

**tampak** 1) *adv.* Facing towards; in the direction of. *Ma tampak satan, ma tampak diyata'an.* In the direction of the southwest wind, facing upstream. (*Thesaurus:* **lahi₃, tampal 1**) 2) *adj. a-* Faced with; confronted by. *Bay aku atampak e'nu.* I was challenged by you. **2.1)** *v. tr.* To confront someone; to address someone frankly and openly. *Tinampak iya, wa'i magtūy pinah'lling.* She was confronted and immediately scolded.

**tampal** 1) *adv.* Facing in a specific direction. *Tampal ni s'ddopan.* Facing west. *Min tampal ingga tinanom?* Planted in which direction? (*cf:* **tudju₁ 1**; *Thesaurus:* **lahi₃, tampak 1**) **1.1)** *v. intr. pa-* To face in a specific direction. *Patampal ka pehē'.* Look that way. *Ma bowa' lawang patampal ni uttala'.* At the doorway that faces north. **1.2)** *v. tr. -an* To show something in a particular direction. *Bang aku bay makat'bbe' lahut bay indamanku ni ka'a, tampalanku ni ka'a pinaganti' maka halam.* If I notch the blade of a working knife that I have borrowed from you, I show it to you, whether or not it is to be replaced. 2) *adj. a-* Obvious; exposed. *Mpat tanduk atampal to'ongan.* Four horns, very prominent. **2.1)** *v. advrs. ka-...-an* To be exposed to weather. *Buwat luma' si Pu katampalan he' baliyu.* Like Pu's house, exposed to the wind. 3) *v. tr.* To confront someone. *Tampalku, minsan mastal.* I will confront him, even though a teacher.

**pagtampal** *v. intr. aN-* To confront someone rather than speaking behind his back or sending a go-between. *Magtampalan kām, da'a magkolorom, da'a maglimbung-limbung.* Confront each other openly, don't do it privately, don't conceal. (*Thesaurus:* **baran₂ 1.1, pagalop, pagharap, pag'nda'₁, paglambung, solab₂**)

**pagtinampalan** *v. intr. aN-* To face towards each other. *Magtinampalan, maginalopan, sama-alop.* Coming facing to face with each other, both facing in. *Magtinampalan, magtūy dī maglambung,*

*ya kamaumuhanna bang d'nda maka l'lla.* Coming face to face and promptly looking seriously at each other, the way it often is with a woman and a man.

**tampalan** *adj. a-* Facing open sea or incoming weather. *Atampalan luma' kami.* Our house is open to the weather.

**patampal** *v. tr.* To make something obvious.

**tampan** (var. **sampan**) *n.* 1) A shield or a charm against physical or supernatural harm. *Ahāp kām magluma' mailu. Aniya' tampan luma' kami.* It will be good if you build your house there. Our house will have a shield. *Mbal kapali'an kōkna sabab aniya' sampanna. Minsan katauwa'an mbal kapali'an.* His head cannot be wounded because it has a [magical] protection. Even through struck he cannot be wounded. (*syn:* **hampan 1**; *gen:* **tambang₃ 1**) **1.1)** *v. tr.* To prevent harmful forces from affecting a person. *Tinampan punglu', makatudju ni baranta sagō' mbal kita ainay. Ya sadja atunu' s'mmekta.* Bullets deflected, they come straight for our body but nothing happens to us. Only our clothes get burnt. *Niraindingan itū, sali' tinampan bang aniya' saki. "Daindingin saga anak-mpunu, da'a buwanin logmay-lamma."* Protected, as though shielded when there is some illness. "Protect your descendants, don't give them serious loss of energy." [Plea to a ritual ancestor.] (*cf:* **dainding**)

**tampan-basi'** *n.* 1) An amulet worn as protection against metal objects such as a blade or bullet. **1.1)** *v. tr.* To make use of a protective charm against weapons of steel. *Anampan-basi', sali' mbal kita binuwan tāw, binuwanan kita esog.* Using a charm against steel, as though given no cause for fear, given courage instead.

**tampan-maru** *n.* Compensation for the shame caused by violation of cultural rules regarding physical contact between the sexes. (*cf:* **tambang₂**)

**tampang** *n.* The aureole of a nipple. (*Thesaurus:* **duru' 1, tete' 1**)

**tamparasa** *adj. a-* Embarrassed; shamed. *Bang kita anampal a'a, bang kita amaiya'-iya', makatamparasa.* If we confront a person, and if we cause him shame, it makes him embarrassed. (*Thesaurus:* **biyas, iya', maru 1.2, paki' 1**)

**tamparung** *n.* 1) A serving of cooked rice wrapped in a broad leaf. *Tamparung maka timayuk, hal buwas bīlla, halam aniya' lamudna. Tamparung* and *timayuk* are simply cooked rice, with nothing mixed in. (*Thesaurus:* **tambusa', tamu, timayuk 1**) **1.1)** *v. tr.* To wrap cooked rice in a large leaf. *Tamparungunbi kinakan ilū.* Wrap that cooked rice in a large leaf.

**tampat** *n.* 1) The grave of a person of renown, a place of supernatural power. *Tampat? Aheka panji-panjina, pagsapahan ya a'a kamemon, buwat tampat si Tuwan At. Tampat itū aheka kayuna.* A shrine? It has many little flags, a place for everyone to make their vows, like the shrine of Mr At. Such shrines have many trees [about them]. **1.1)** *v. advrs.* *-in-* Made into a shrine by fencing off and marking with flags.

**tampe** *n.* The upper limit of tidal flow. *Tampe itu ma t'ttopan katoho'an maka kabase'an. Hampilan saddi. Tampe* is the cut-off point between the dry land and the wet. Different from *hampilan* [dry land]. (*Thesaurus:* **bihingan, daplakan₁, gintana'an, hampilan, pari'an, susulan, tapiyan**)

**tampellas** *n.* The White-cheeked surgeonfish. *Acunthurus glaucopareius.* (*gen:* **kumay**)

**tampeppet** *v. intr. pa-* To skip across the surface of water, of a canoe or a thrown item. *Ai-ai kabantunganta buwat batu apera', patampeppet.* Anything like a flat stone that we throw, skipping across a water surface. (*Thesaurus:* **kulit-kulit, samperet, sularaw**)

**tampil** *n.* The feast on the last night before Ramadan.

  **pagtampil** *v. intr. aN-* To celebrate the feast on the last night before Ramadan.

**tampipi'** *n.* A basket of loosely woven coconut leaves, used for carrying garden produce. (*gen:* **baka'₁**)

**tampiyas** *adj. zero* **1)** Wet from driving rain. *Bang niulanan luma' itū, asidda tampiyas man dinding.* When this house gets rained on, it gets very wet through the walls. (*cf:* **pandorot**) **1.1)** *v. intr. aN-* To drive into a house or shelter, of wind-blown rain.

**tampupu** *v. tr.* To lift something by supporting it from the base, as a container or child. *Tampupuhun bāg ilu bo' mbal abustak.* Lift that bag from underneath so it doesn't burst. (*Thesaurus:* **takmay, tayak 1.1**)

**tamsil** *v. tr.* To think deeply about something. *Ya pinikil to'ongan ma deyom ataynu, ya tinamsil ilū, sali' niyatnu.* Something you think deeply about, that's *tamsil*, something you take to heart. (*Thesaurus:* **angut, niyat 1**)

**tamu** *n.* Rice boiled in a woven coconut leaf container. *Maligay itū panyām atopna, t'bbu lantayna, isina saging mareyom maka tamu.* This model house [a feature of weddings] has rice cakes for its roof, sugarcane for its floor, bananas and packets of cooked rice for the inside. (*Thesaurus:* **tambusa', tamparung 1, timayuk 1**)

**tamuk** *v. tr.* To catch something thrown. *Bang ka angalarukan bola ni aku, tamukku.* When you throw a ball to me I catch it. (*cf:* **sambut 1**)

**tamuni** *n.* The placenta.

**tamus** (*var.* **tangus**) *v. tr.* To suck on something with only the lips forming contact. *Bang ka angehet mangga, aubus agbohe'-bohe' mangga-i, bo' mbal niusal e'nu laring, bo' kinakan maka bowa'nu sadja. Tangusnu na.* When you slice a mango,

and then it becomes wet [with juice] so you can't use a knife, and then you eat it with just your mouth. You suck it. *Tangusku na, tuwan, sabab aniya' ugatna.* I am sucking it, friend, because it has fibres. (*Thesaurus:* **dutdut, ligid₁, s'ssop**)

**tanak** *adj. a-* **1)** Slipped from one's grasp. *Wa'i atanak, wa'i takabbata daing, wa'i ala'an.* It has fallen, we have lost our grip of the fish; it has gone. (*Thesaurus:* **kabba, larus**) **1.1)** *v. tr.* To let something slip out of one's hand.

**tana'₁** *n.* **1)** Soil or earth, in contrast to sand or rocks; soil as one of the four basic elements. *Kalutin tana' ilū.* Dig into that soil. **2)** Arable land; farmland. *Taga tana' kami ma deya Sablay.* We have farming property inland from Sablay.

  **katana'an** *n.* An area of arable soil. *Aniya' isāb kabatu-batuhan bay pinalamud ma katana'an.* Stones were deliberately mixed in with the farmable soil. *Magb'kka' na katana'an.* The soil is becoming cracked.

  **tana'-deyo'** *n.* The sea floor. *Guyu itu sali' lumbag angabut ni tana'-deyo'.* Subsurface turbulence is like an ocean swell that reaches to the sea floor.

  **gintana'an** *n.* Dry land in contrast to sea and inter-tidal zones. (*cf:* **kaut 1**; *Thesaurus:* **bihingan, daplakan₁, hampilan, pari'an, susulan, tampe, tapiyan**)

**tana'₂** *n.* The territory inhabited by a people group. *Ata'u iya mag'lling lling tana' Sūk.* He knows how to speak the language of the Tausug region. (*Thesaurus:* **da'ira 1, lahat, lungsud, pasisil**)

  **paltana'an** *n.* Land in a territorial sense.

**tanam₁** *adj. a-* **1)** At ease, with one's environment, things, conditions. *Mbal tanam si Mām bang ataha' bu'unna, sali' mbal katanaman.* Teacher is not comfortable with her hair long. It's as though it can't be settled. *Patanamta sudju ni baliyu.* We make [the canoe] easy in relation to the wind. *Atanam pagsulatanna.* His writing facilities are convenient. (*cf:* **biyaksa 1**) **1.1)** *v. intr. -um-* To become accustomed, as when doing something unfamiliar.

**tanam₂** *adj. zero* **1)** Ready for action. **1.1)** *v. intr. pa-* To be ready for action. *Pag'nda'na aniya' a'a paluwas min kaluma'an, magtūy iya patanam amono'.* When he saw people coming out from the houses, he promptly got ready to fight.

  **katanaman** *n.* Readiness for action. *Palūd pa'in ka sumiyan-sumiyan katanamannu.* Just come downhill whenever you are ready.

**tanāng** *n.* An earthenware water jar with a mouth of medium width. (*Thesaurus:* **bingki', ka'ang, kasambagan, kibut, pipa, poga, tangpad**)

**tanay** *v. tr.* To produce powder by rubbing something hard against an abrasive surface. (*Thesaurus:* **pipis**)

  **tanayan** *n.* A grinding plate with which to crush something to powder.

**tandak** *n.* The excrement of a newly born baby;

meconium. (*cf:* **tai' 2**)

**tanda'** *n.* A sign; proof of identity. (*Thesaurus:* **baynat, mattan 1, sāp₂ 1, tatak, tumbuk₃ 1**)

**paltanda'an** *n.* A sign or portent; the visible evidence of some event.

**tanda' tangan** *n. phrase* A signature or personal mark on a document.

**tandan₁** *v. intr. pa-* **1)** To reach land from the sea. *Angoleng aku naelon, amole' na kami patandan kaleya.* I roll up my fishing line and we return homewards to land. *Bang aku bay am'ssi sangom, pagtandanku kaleya itū sinampang aku he' palilitu.* When I have been fishing overnight, on reaching land a middleman meets me. *Bang kami bay pakkom, na pinaleyak pabīng bo' makatandan ni bihing.* When we have capsized, then it is righted again to be able to reach the shore. *Yuk kami, "Wa'i tapalis ma dilaut. Makatandan ni lahat, luwal aheya tulung min Tuhan."* We say, "Blown off course out at sea. We will make it to land only if there is great help from God." (*Thesaurus:* **daggot₁, dunggu' 1, t'kkad 1, tundug 1**) **1.1)** *v. tr.* To reach an objective by making landfall. *Abila sakali na makapagl'ngngan-l'ngngan, agon mbal anandan luma'.* When [he] keeps on going from place to place, he almost doesn't make it to the house. **1.2)** *v. tr. -an* To convey something in a shoreward direction.

**katandanan** *n.* A place where landfall is made. *Amatay kita magsabbut ni batu, bang halam aniya' katandanan.* We will wear ourselves out calling on the rocks, if there is no place to go ashore.

**pagtandan** *v. intr. aN-* To make landfall. *Bang aku bay am'ssi sangom, pagtandanku kaleya itū sinampang aku he' palilitu.* When I have been fishing overnight, on reaching land a wholesaler meets me.

**tandan₂** *v. tr. -an* To refer a legal issue to a higher court. *Bang aniya' magbono', magsara' ni opis. Na bang sali' mbal kamattanan ma sara' mastal, patandan ni sara'.* When there is a fight, it goes to the [school] office. Then, if people are not satisfied by the schoolmaster's judgment, it is referred to the court.

**tandaw** *v. intr. pa-* **1)** To look out from a window. *"Paluwa' kono' ka," yukna, "patandaw."* "Go out please," he said, "and look out the window." *Bang aku nilagut, Tuwan Sultan, subay patandaw tunangku dok ta'nda' he'na aku.* If I am to be slashed, O King, my sweetheart should look out so she can see me. (*Thesaurus:* **sīb 1, tīk 1, tilag-tilag₂**) **1.1)** *v. tr.* To observe something from out a window.

**tandawan** *n.* A window.

**tandero** (var. **tendero**) *n.* **1)** An agent on behalf of someone else. **1.1)** *v. intr. aN-* To act as an agent selling produce on behalf of someone. *Buwat aku saupama palilitu, na aniya' daingku niraganganan bo' aniya' kal'ngnganganku saddī. Manjari yukku*

*ma kamanakanku, "Dagangin aku daing itū." Ya ina'an-i anandero, ya mangandagan i'.* Suppose I am a trader and I have fish to sell but there is something else I need to go see about. So I say to my nephew, "Sell this fish for me." He is the one who acts as agent, the one selling. *Sali' kita anendero ni lūng-kampungta. Bang at'kka magtabang-tabang kita anuhug.* It's like us serving as agent for a village-mate. When we arrive we help each other string the fish [in saleable lots]. (*Thesaurus:* **palilitu, paltira**)

**tanding** **1)** *v. tr.* To inspect something carefully. *Tandingun a'a inān dahū bo' kinata'uhan addat-tabi'atna.* Examine that man first in order to know his behavior. (*Thesaurus:* **banding**) **2)** *v. intr. pa-* To see one's reflection in a mirror. *Am'lli gi' aku samin patandinganku.* I will buy a mirror for seeing my reflection in.

**pagtanding** *v. intr. aN-* To look at one's reflection in a mirror or glass. *A'abbu si Anu magl'lla-l'lla, magtanding dīna.* What's-his-name is conceited, pretending to be a cool guy, looking at himself in a mirror.

**tandog** **1)** *v. advrs. -in-* Shaken by fever; suffering from malaria. *Sali' kita tinandog bo' ngga'i ka tandog to'ongan, hal kita nihadjat. Sali' kita tinandog-tandogan.* Like being feverish but not a real fever, just a minor one. As though we are being shaken. *Sali' kita tinandog bo' ngga'i ka tandog to'ongan, hal kita nihadjat.* Like being feverish but not a real fever, just a minor one. (*Thesaurus:* **hadjat₂, hōb-hōb, l'mmun, tatat**) **1.1)** *v. tr.* To make something shake or tremble. *Sali' kita tinandog-tandogan.* As though we are being shaken. **2)** *v. intr. aN-* To be shaking or trembling under pressure. *Da'a ka lum'ngngan m'nnilu apa ilu anandog lantay.* Don't walk across there because the floor is shaking.

**tanduk** *n.* **1)** A horn; a hornlike projection. *Kalbaw ataha' tandukna.* A water buffalo whose horns are long. **1.1)** *v. tr.* To jab something with a spiny projection. *Bay aku tinanduk e' kubing.* A rhinoceros beetle jabbed me.

**pagtanduk** *v. intr. aN-* To butt heads or lock horns, as bull water buffaloes.

**tandukan** *n.* The Goldspotted rockcod; various other rockcods. *Cephalopolis sexmaculatus.* (*cf:* **tangal, tapog**; *gen:* **kuhapo'**)

**tandukan-keyat** *n.* The Orange grouper or rockcod. *Cephalopholis auranteus.*

**tandukan-ettom** *n.* The Redmouth grouper or rockcod. *Aethaloperca rogaa.*

**tandung** var. of **tambung**

**tanju'** *n.* A torch or flare. (*cf:* **ilaw 1**; *Thesaurus:* **sulariyan, tapulaw**)

**tannay** *v. intr. pa-* To be in a coma, unresponsive to stimuli. *Hal patannay, hal palagad nihukum.* Just comatose, just waiting to be judged.

**tannay-tannay** *adj. a-* Empty of life, as a house

with no occupants. *Buwat luma' disi So halam maga'a, halam minsan aniya' magbahembas ma deyom. Yukku, "Ndū', atannay-tannay deyom luma'."* Like So's house, uninhabited, not a thing stirring inside. I say, "Oh dear, the house is totally empty." (*Thesaurus:* **l'ngngaw-l'ngngaw, mala'u-la'u 1, t'nnaw-t'nnaw 1**)

**tanok** *n.* 1) A splitting wedge. *Siningalan bo' ahāp l'ngngan tanok.* Wedged so that the splitting wedge will move well. (*Thesaurus:* **biggal 1, bulatuk, pahanggal, s'ngngal**) 1.1) *v. tr.* To insert a wedge into wood to facilitate splitting it. *Kayu ilu subay pinagtanok-tanok. Binulatuk dahū bo' yampa makasōd tanok.* That wood needs to be split with a series of wedges. It is grooved first before a wedge is inserted.

**tanog₁** *adj.* a- Clearly audible. *Atanog, sali' akosog suwalana.* Clear-sounding, her voice sort of loud. *Pinatanog suwala sigām ananglitan Tuhan.* Their voices were made loud and clear in praise of God. (*Thesaurus:* **hangpat 1, hapal 2, hurup 1.1, ladju, lagsing, nyala-nyala**)
  **patanog** *adv.* Loudly.

**tanog₂** *v. intr.* aN- 1) To appear in a place other than where it was first noticed, of some sensory event. *Bang ap'ddi' emponta ma dambila', bo' kita amangan ma dambila', minsan painay, ananog parambila'.* When our tooth hurts on one side, and we eat on the other side, no matter what is done, the pain transmits to other side. (*syn:* **dalug₂**) 1.1) *v. tr.* To notice something in another location. *Tanogun, bo' tanogun itu-i.* Hear that, then hear this.

**tanom₁** *v. tr.* 1) To plant something by inserting it into soil. *Na aniya' po'on kayu bay tinanom maina'an e' si Nabi Ibrahim.* So there was a sapling planted there by the prophet Abraham. (*Thesaurus:* **bakal, tugbal**) 1.1) *v. tr.* -an To plant an area with seeds or plants. *Mbal tanoman kami minsan ai-ai saga tana' kami.* We will not plant our land with anything whatever. *Sapi' magararu tana', tinanoman panggi' kayu ma deya.* Cattle plowing that land, planted with cassava, inland. 2) To bury someone. {euphemism}
  **pagtanom** *v. intr.* aN- To plant cultivated land with crop plants, as a livelihood. *Mbal na kapagtanoman tana' kami.* Our land can no longer be planted.
  **tanoman** *n.* Planted things; a planted area.
  **tinanom** *n.* Planted things.

**tanom₂** *v. intr.* pa- To sink into soft soil. *Patanom tape'ta tobtob min lo'akanta ma deyom tana'.* Our feet sink in, up to the knees in the earth. (*Thesaurus:* **l'nnob, loblob, paglowak, senop**)

**tantang** *v. intr.* aN- To be unclothed; to be naked. *Nā, pagka mbal na kasandalan pasu' inān, anantang biyahero itū bo' pakuppa ni tigbaw.* So, since that heat was unbearable, the traveler stripped off and dived into the pool. (*cf:* **tangtang 1**; *syn:* **pegtang-pegtang**)

**tantu** *n.* 1) The certainty of something. *Halam aniya' tantuna.* There is nothing sure about it. 1.1) *adj.* a- Definite; certain. *Atantu ilū, sali' kita mbal magputing-puting, atawa atantu bay pamuwanna.* Certain, like us not telling lies, or [him saying] that it was definitely something he had given. 1.2) *v. intr.* pa- To do something deliberately. *Patantu ka angusaha, hatina patogol ka.* Be deliberate about working for a living, in other words be committed. 1.3) *v. tr.* To be specific and definite about something, as when setting a time. *Mbal tatantu na kahāpanna, maka mbal tatantu na kala'atanna. Duwa-abana iya.* Its benefits cannot be known for sure, nor its disadvantages. There are two possible outcomes.
  **tantuhi** *v. intr.* aN- Definite; certain, usually with a negative. *Mbal aku manantuhi at'kka ni lahat.* I am not sure that I will get home.
  **tantuhun** *v. tr.* Be sure (of an outcome). *Tantuhun ka amatay llaw itu.* Be sure you will die this very day.
  **panantuhan** *n.* Something reliable or certain.

**tanud** *n.* Cotton sewing thread. *Angamu' aku tanud panahi' sanyawaku.* I will ask for some cotton thread to sew up my shorts. (*Thesaurus:* **bannang, jiyay, tingkal**)

**tanus** *adj.* a- Straight and free from irregularities, of a length of wood. *Atanus kayu, atilud dalos, halam aniya' bukuna.* Wood clear of irregularities, straight right through, no knots. (*Thesaurus:* **tilud 1**)

**tanya₁** *v. tr.* To punish someone harshly, especially by denying him food and shelter. *Tinanya itū pina'alu'an, pina'llawan, pinaulanan.* This word *tanya* means exposing someone to the night air, to the sun, to rain. *Tinanya kita he' Tuhan, bay kita ala'at. Buwat kita asakki, atawa kap'ddi'an.* We [incl] are punished by God, having been wicked. Ill for example, or experiencing pain. (*cf:* **puhinga'**; *Thesaurus:* **inyaya, pa'alu', paulan**)

**tanya₂** *v. tr.* To interrogate someone as to work done, generally with the expectation of being found unsatisfactory. *Buwat saga ipatannu ilū bang ganta' tinanya, mbal pinapagkakan bang mbal bilahi sinoho'.* Like your house helpers being interrogated for instance, they are not given food to eat if they don't like being given orders. (*cf:* **mungkalun**; *Thesaurus:* **katilaw, jakki 1, sumariya**)

**tanyak** *v. intr.* pa- To appear unexpectedly. *Buwat andom, bay halam aniya', saru'un-du'un patanyak.* Like rain clouds, there weren't any, then suddenly they appear. (*Thesaurus:* **papuwa', sakkop 2, taggaha'**)

**tanyag** *adj.* a- 1) Widely known. *Subay pama'nda'ku kosog-kawasaku supaya patanyag ōnku ni manusiya' kamemon ma sakalibutan dunya.* I must display my power so that my fame is known to people all around the world. (*Thesaurus:* **bantug 1, bawag, buhanyag, busling, hayag, hulalayag 1**) **1.1**) *v. tr.* To make something widely known. *Tinanyag a'a inān ma hinangna.* That man is well-known for his work.

**patanyag** *v. tr.* To make something widely known.

**tāng-tāng** *n.* Various queenfishes. *Scomberoides spp.*

**tanga'₁** *v. tr.* To hold something between the teeth without biting, as a cat with its kittens. *Tinanga', sinaggaw ma bowa' bo' binowa alahi.* Held in the mouth, grabbed in the mouth then run off with it. (*Thesaurus:* **k'nnum, tanghab₂**)

**tanga'₂** *v. advrs.* -*in*- Having a speech defect. *Tanga' itu, sali' mbal ata'u ah'lling minsan ato'a na.* This word *tanga'* [speech defect], it's like he does not know how to speak even though he is old. (*Thesaurus:* **kemol, ponga', s'nngngog, terol**)

**tangal** *n.* A species of grouper, the juvenile form of tandukan. (*cf:* **tandukan, tapog**; *gen:* **kuhapo'**)

**tangan** *n.* **1)** The lower arm; the hand. *Lagamnu sali' lagam si Yakub, malaingkan tangannu itū sali' tangan si Esaw.* Your voice is like the voice of Jacob, whereas your hand is like the hand of Esau. *Pinasayang kamemon tangan sigām.* They all waved their hands. (*pt:* **anak-tangan, bokol 1, kengkeng, daimanis, gulamay 1, lasu', l'ngngon 1, nggo'an-tangan, pataklayan, siku, tambō' 1**) **2)** Tendrils, the fine hairlike growth at the extremities of some plants. *Belle'-belle' aheka tanganna.* The *belle'-belle'* creeper has many tendrils.

**tangan-tangan** *n.* The physic-nut; the candle-nut; the castor-oil plant. *Jatropha curcas; Ricinus communis.*

**tangangngang** *n.* A crawling insect capable of inflicting a severe bite, similar to an ant in appearance. *Tangangngang, aheya min tagangga', angeket. Tangangngang,* larger than the yellow tree ant, and it bites. (*gen:* **s'mmut 1**)

**tangas** (var. **tamas**) *v. tr.* To envelop something in fumes. *Buwat saki nirampal atawa nīttus, tinangas maka kamanyan atawa hiyu.* Measles, for example, or chickenpox, are fumigated with incense or incense sticks. *Kamanyan ya panangas ai-ai.* It is incense that is used for fuming anything. (*Thesaurus:* **sangu 1, s'bbu**)

**pagtangas** *v. tr.* To treat an illness by fuming it with healing substances such as incense. *Pinagtangas puhu'na kamemon.* His entire body thoroughly fumed.

**tangbid** *n.* A strand of fiber in corded rope. *Subay duwa tangbid ko da'a ab'kkat.* There should be two strands so it won't break. (*Thesaurus:* **k'llat₂ 1, lubid 1**)

**tangbod** *n.* The Whiting smelt. *Sillago spp.*

**tangbud** *n.* Various goatfishes. *Upeneus spp.*

**tangbus** (var. **tambus**) *adj.* a- Completed, of some process. *Atangbus na he'na magtambal.* He has finished giving medicine. (*Thesaurus:* **sampulna', tammat 1**)

**tangka** *adj.* a- Harmed internally by some external trauma. *Da'a g'bbukun onde' ilu, atangka ko' hē'.* Don't punch that child, that will result in internal damage.

**tangka'** *v. tr.* -*an* To control or deny one's appetite or need; to endure pain or loss. *Tangka'anku amangan bang pa'in karūlan p'ddi' atayku.* I'll put up with not eating just so long as I can satisfy my wounded feelings. *Buwat emponku ap'ddi', tinangka'an.* Like when my tooth is aching, it's just endured. *Tangka'anta siga.* We resist cigarets. (*Thesaurus:* **iman₁ 1.1, pagsabal, sandal 1.1, tahan-tahan, tatas 1.2**)

**tangkal₁** *n.* The backbone, especially the section in the small of the back. *Ap'ddi' tangkal bukut, ya to'olang bukutku.* My lower back is sore, the bone of my back.

**tangkal₂** *n.* **1)** A buoy or float that supports and marks the position of fishing gear; a drift anchor. (*Thesaurus:* **pataw₁, sau, untang**) **1.1)** *v. intr.* aN- To drift using a sea anchor. *Anangkal kami ma dilaut, buwat p'ttung pagūng.* We float out at sea with a drift anchor, something like floating bamboo. (*Thesaurus:* **labu₂ 1.1, layo 1.1**)

**tangkap** *v. tr.* To engage the services of an entertainer. *Tinangkap si Ma, ningā' suwalana.* Ma is engaged to perform, getting her voice. (*cf:* **serop**)

**tangkapa'** *n.* A coral formation with a large saucer-shaped upper surface sometimes a meter across. *Batu tangkapa', luwa ligu. Tangkapa'* coral, looks like a winnowing basket. (*cf:* **dulang-kokok**; *gen:* **batu₂ 1**)

**tangkas-biruk** *n.* An inedible crustacean similar in appearance to a giant shrimp.

**tangkaw** *v. intr.* pa- **1)** To move stealthily. (*Thesaurus:* **agap₂, gagam**) **1.1)** *v. tr.* To get something by stealth rather than violence; to steal. **1.2)** *v. tr.* -*an* To rob someone of an item. *Bay kami tinangkawan pelang dibuhi'.* We had a canoe stolen from us last night. *Tangkawanku mastal itū ma sīnna, ya yukna.* I will rob the teacher here of his money, that's what he said.

**panangkaw** *n.* A person who steals for a living. (*Thesaurus:* **mundu 1, pilliyu, sugarul**)

**patangkaw** *adv.* Stealthily; secretly.

**tinangkaw** *adv.* Stealthily; unnoticed; undetected.

**tangkay** *n.* **1)** The stem of a plant; the stalk of some fruits. (*Thesaurus:* **bole, botod, la'al, okol, tongol**) **2)** A handle or stem used for lifting a container. *Sa'an itū taga tangkay buwat du isāb basket.* A strainer has a handle, just as a basket does. (*Thesaurus:* **baba'an₁, patihan, puhan 1**) **2.1)** *v. tr.* -*an* To fit a handle to something. *Nsa' aniya' maitu tinangkayan.* There's nothing here that has been fitted with a handle.

**tangkekel** *n.* 1) Small wens or cysts containing a firm whitish core, thought to be the result of grains of rice left sticking to skin. *Bang aku amangan buwas bo' mbal ala'an, tahinang tangkekel.* If I eat rice and [grains of it] aren't removed, they become cysts. 1.1) *v. advrs.* -*in*-Suffering from warts or wens.

**tangki** *n.* A tank for storing water; a pond for raising fish. *Ya boho' ta'nda'ku daing tangki pinab'llihan.* It's the first time I have seen farmed fish being sold. (*Thesaurus:* **kandung₁, danaw, halo-halo, tigbaw**)

**tangkig** var. of **sowa-tangkig**

**tangkil** *v. tr.* -*an* To increase the size of a cloth item by adding pieces. *Bang kita angahinang banog bo' mbal maka'abut, tinangkilan.* When we make a sail and it doesn't reach, it is enlarged by sewing pieces onto it. *Sali' aniya' bay pis s'mmek mbal manjari, pinagtangkil-tangkil abō' sarang.* Like when there was a piece of cloth that was no use, small pieces added to it so it would be adequate. (*Thesaurus:* **suklu', sugpat 1.2**)

**tangkis** *adj.* -*a*- 1) Agile or nimble. (*Thesaurus:* **alistu 1**) 1.1) *v. intr. pa*- To move nimbly; to be quick-moving. *Patangkis ka bang ka kaleya apa aniya' banta.* Move quickly when you go inland because there are enemies. *Makatangkis aku, halam aku taluwa' sinuntuk.* I moved nimbly, I wasn't struck by being punched. 1) *v. tr.* -*an* To dodge something by moving quickly. *Tinangkisan batu ko' mbal taluwa'.* The stone is dodged so as not to be hit.

**tangkob₁** *v. intr. pa*- 1) To become overcast; to cloud over. *Makajari kita magkahāp bang patangkob langit, atawa alinis būd.* We may be reconciled if the sky is totally covered, or the mountains are worn down. *Patangkob na, ilu na andom.* It is closing in, rainclouds are coming. *Patangkob na leha inān, taluwa' baliyu.* That square sail is obscured, a wind has hit it. 1.1) *v. tr.* To cover something over so that light or air is shut out. *Tangkobun bo' mbal kapē'an s'ggit.* Cover it so rubbish won't get in.

**tangkob₂** *n.* A cursing equivalent for spherical items such as a human head, bowls, or plates. *Tangkobnu!* Your damn head! (*gen:* **sukna' 1.1**; *Thesaurus:* **kulakob**)

**tangkop** *n.* A hard covering over soft tissue; the calyx on some fruits. *Taga tangkop dugsulku.* My ulcer has a scab over it. *Bang aniya' buwahan la'ananku tangkopna.* If have some lansones I remove the calyx. (*Thesaurus:* **l'kkang, l'kkung 1, taplok 2**)

**tangkop-belle'** *n.* A large flat seed case 4 to 5 cm across.

**tangkorak** *n.* Skeletal remains. (*Thesaurus:* **akalbaran, batang-tubu, pagdayaw 1, paltubu-tubuhan 2**)

**tangkug** *adj.* -*a*- 1) Moving a short distance. *Da'a kām atangkug.* Don't move about. (*Thesaurus:*

**lensa, pagdaguyu**) 1.1) *v. intr. pa*- To move a short distance. 1.2) *v. tr.* To move something a short distance. *Da'a tangkugun, halam gi' amikit.* Don't move it, it hasn't stuck yet.

**tangku'-tangku'** *v. tr.* To inspect a sale item when about to buy or make an offer. (*Thesaurus:* **kodjel, kohed 1, kublit**)

**tangday** (var. **bangday**) *v. intr. pa*- 1) To lie across an item of the same sort. 1.1) *v. tr.* -*an* To lay something on top of another item of the same sort. *"Ōy, da'a aku tangdayin."* "Hey, don't rest [your legs] on me."

**pagtangday** (var. **pagbangday**) *v. intr. aN*- To lie in such a way that some items are overlain by others. *Bang kita mbal makasayu atuli, magtangday tape'ta, baranta, buwat a'a maglakibini.* When we sleep completely unconscious, our legs and bodies are laid across each other, like a married couple. *Magtangday, sali' magtahan pa'ata.* *Magtangday,* like our thighs lying across the other. *Atawa buwat bono', aheka amatay magbangday.* Or like a battle, when many die piled one on top of another. *Magbaubangday kayu bay pinuwad, magtahan na.* The trees lie on top of each other when they are felled, holding each other down. (*Thesaurus:* **pagbaubabag, tihin**)

**tangga** var. of **sangga**

**tangga** *n.* 1) The rungs of a ladder or stairway; notches for climbing. (*Thesaurus:* **taka 1, tekmas 1, tengham**) 1.1) *v. tr.* -*an* To cut a notch in something.

**pagtangga'** *v. intr. aN*- To cut a series of notches in a pole or tree in order to facilitate climbing.

**tanggal₁** *v. tr.* To gulp one's food; to eat as an animal does. *Ananggal na ka!* Eat, you pig! (*Thesaurus:* **bagahak₂, boslad, buhawi'₁, butu', kanam, kaway 1.1, dahaga', damba'₁ 1.1, lagak 1.1**)

**tanggalan** *n.* Food eaten without restraint. (*Thesaurus:* **boslaran, dahalan**)

**tanggal₂** *adj.* -*a*- Damaged by the loss of a part. *Da'a padugtulin buli' pelang ko da'a atanggal.* Don't let the stern of the canoe bang into anything lest it be damaged. *Tanggalanta ka kōknu!* I'll knock your head off! (*Thesaurus:* **k'llo'₂, hemos 1, la'an 1, tungkas**)

**tanggal-iman** *n.* Loss of one's faith in God.

**tanggal₃** *v. tr.* -*an* 1) To remove a vital part of someone's body, the action of a saitan spirit. *Tinanggalan ka ma deya bang ka mbal makapole' ni luma'.* You'll be partly eaten by something inland, if you don't return home. (*Thesaurus:* **lanyap 1.1, talbang 1.1**) 1.1) *adj.* -*a*- Suffering from loss of a vital body part due to the action of a saitan spirit. *Atanggal iya he' saitan.* He has had a piece bitten out by a *saitan* spirit. *Bang kita anukna', yukta, "Bang pa'in ka atanggal," atawa "bang pa'in ka atalbang."* As when we curse, we say, "May you be bitten by a demon," or alternatively, "may you be lost at sea."

**tanggap** *v. tr.* **1)** To seek the attention of God; to call on a ritual ancestor. *Buwat kitam maghinang ni Tuhan, yukta, "O Tuhan, buwanin kami balakat." Sagō' halam aniya' tantuna tinanggap.* Like when we are worshipping God and say "O God, give us a blessing." But there is no certainty that he is invoked. *Tanggapun, sali' harapun ka'mbo-mbo'annu.* Invoke your ancestors, seeking their presence. (*cf:* **huhulmatan**) **1.1)** *v. ditr.* To offer something to a supernatural being, as God or an ancestor. (*Thesaurus:* **buwis 1.1, lamas, paglabot 2, ungsud₂**)

**pananggapan** *n.* A gift presented to a ritual ancestor or to God.

**tanggollayan** *n.* Something left to the very last. (*Thesaurus:* **atarasaw, damuli 1, lēt**)

**tanggu** *n.* **1)** A postponement; a cause of delay. *Bang aniya' amatay h'llana, bang pa'in maghinang na, amandi na, na magh'lla pabīng bang aniya' atilaw, halam aniya' tanggu.* If someone's husband dies, as long as the ceremonies have been carried out, and the ritual bathing, she may take another husband if someone asks [for her], no postponement [is needed]. *Bay aku anaggaw, na pagsaggawku binowa na aku ni sara'. Yukku "Tanggu aku, halam maitu matto'aku."* I seized a woman and on being arrested I was brought to the magistrate. I said, "I [claim] postponement." (*Thesaurus:* **buhul₂, lehod 1, pagmahuli-llaw**) **1.1)** *v. tr.* *-an* To postpone something; to defer action. *Bang bay angutang, pinaglehod-lehoran he' a'a bay pangutanganna inān. Sinukut pabīng, tinangguhan.* If someone has borrowed, he is delayed repeatedly by the person from whom he borrowed money. He is dunned again, delayed again. *Da'a tangguhin pagkahinu bang aniya' amu'na.* Do not make your fellow man wait when he asks for something. *Buwat sala kita sinukut, tanggu'anta, tungga'anta.* Like when we are dunned for payment, we ask for a postponement, and set a definite date.

**tanggung₁** *v. tr.* To carry a burden on a pole across the shoulders (of one or two people). *Tinanggung, pinat'nna' mariyata' bahaku.* Carried across the shoulders, placed on my shoulders. *Paipa' bang a'llum, tapanganggungan.* A coconut palm branch, when alive can be used as carrying pole. (*Thesaurus:* **baba' 1, balung 1, tumpay, usung**)

**tanggungan** *n.* A carrying pole for carrying burdens across the shoulder. *Bay aku angalga, apōng tanggunganku.* When I was carrying burdens, my pole broke. *Paipa', bang a'llum pananggungan, bang amatay pangayu.* The stem of a coconut frond, used as a carrying pole when still green, used for firewood when dead.

**tanggung₂** *v. tr.* To assume responsibility for someone who has committed an offense; to

accept liability for payment of a fine. *Angay iya ananggung jawab dangan-danganna?* Why does she take personal responsibility for disputing [an accusation]? *Bay aku anaggaw, na pagsaggawku binowa na aku ni sara'. Yukku "Tanggu aku, halam maitu matto'aku." Yuk sara', "Pagka halam mailu saga matto'anu, tanggungta ka." Sara' i' amuwan kataksilan ni d'nda hē'. Subay at'kka matto'aku bo' yampa ni'nde'an sīn ni sara'. Subay kita ang'nnop ma sara' sabab bay kita pinuwasan min kasusahan.* I had seized a woman, and on being arrested was brought to the magistrate. I said, "I ask for postponement." The magistrate says, "Since your elders are not here, I will take the responsibility [for your fine]." The magistrate then pays the fine to the woman. My elders when they arrive must return the money to the magistrate. We must add something to the magistrate because he had got us out of difficulty. (*Thesaurus:* **abunaw, atas₂ 1, bahala'₁, kuwiraw, lawag-baran, siyal**)

**tanghab₁** *v. tr.* *-an* To cut a groove or notch in a spar to keep a lashing from slipping.

**tanghab₂** *v. tr.* To seize something in the mouth. *Tinanghab magtūy e' sowa manuk ē'.* The snake promptly seized the chicken in its mouth. (*Thesaurus:* **k'nnum, tanga'₁**)

**tanghul** *v. intr.* *aN-* To howl, of a dog. *Ilu na ero' ananghul.* There's a dog there howling. (*Thesaurus:* **tangungngul, ūl, usig**)

**tangī'** (var. **tangili'**) *n.* Generic term for various mackerels, including the Narrow-barred Spanish mackerel. *Scomberomorus commerson. Bang aku am'ssi bo' mareyo' p'ssiku, wa'i ab'kkat naelon. Bay sinabay he' tangī', bay kīttob ma tonga'an.* When I am fishing and my hook and line are down below, the nylon line snaps. It was hit by a Spanish mackerel and bitten through halfway up. *Agtūy kami tininduk e' tangī', Tuwan.* Right away a mackerel took the bait, Sir.

**tangī'-lawayan** *n.* The Indo-Pacific king mackerel. *Scomberomorus guttatus.*

**tangili'** var. of **tangī'**

**tangis** *v. intr.* *aN-* **1)** To cry audibly or inaudibly, with tears. **1.1)** *v. advrs.* *ta-* Overcome with grief, as when a person bursts into tears. *Bang buwat si Ina' amatay anakna dakayu', bo' anuligpat ni atayna, tatangis.* Like Mother when one of her children has died, and memories come into her mind, she bursts out crying. *Alahang aku magpakasulat pasal tatangis aku anulat ni ka'a.* I am seldom able to write because writing to you makes me cry. (*cf:* **s'ngngel 1**; *Thesaurus:* **asang-selo, lihing, llad**)

**pagtangis** *v. intr.* *aN-* To be in mourning for someone dead or presumed to be dead. *Agtangisan aku bapa'ku. Angaluran aku iya.* I am weeping for my uncle. I cry out loud for him.

**panangis** *n.* **1)** Someone who cries frequently.

**1.1)** *v. tr.* To keep crying over something. *Ai pinanangisan he'na?* What was he crying about?

**tanglung** *n.* A Chinese lantern (colored paper on a bamboo frame).

**tango'** *v. tr.* *-an* To nod one's head in agreement. (*Thesaurus:* **handuk 1**)

**tangon** *v. intr. pa-* **1)** To move a canoe above sea level onto a supporting structure. *Bang makatangon pelang ilū, ahāp na.* When that canoe has run up onto its raised platform, it will be fine. **1.1)** *v. tr.* To raise something on a supporting structure, for maintenance or storage. *Bang aku anangon na, niluhu maka langkay ya langgad pelang ē' bay makarugtul.* When I put that canoe up on supports, the surface damage done to it is singed with a coconut-frond torch. *Tinangon pelang kami maka katig min deyo' bang marilaut bo' pa'angkat min kuwit tahik.* When out at sea our canoe is raised with an outrigger boom beneath it so as lift it above the sea surface. (*Thesaurus:* **angkat₁ 1.1, bayaw, buhat₁ 1.2**)

**tangonan** *n.* A structure for supporting a canoe above sea level. (*syn:* **bantilan, kalangan₂**)

**tangpad** *n.* An earthenware jar with a mouth of medium width, used for storing water. (*Thesaurus:* **bingki', ka'ang, kasambagan, kibut, pipa, poga, tanāng**)

**tangpas₁** *v. tr.* To take or use something without permission. *Tinangpas kono' pelang he' sigā, pinabukagan maka mbal, minsan sigā ni'inay-inay na.* They would take the canoe, they said, whether or not they were scolded for it, no matter what was done to them.

**tangpas₂** (var. **t'ppas₂**) *adj.* *a-* Competent and able to do things, of growing children. *Buwat onde'-onde' ata'u na magdeyo'-diyata', ya lagi'na ata'u amissala. Atangpas na.* Like children who can go up and down a ladder, especially who know how to talk. Competent already. *Buwat onde'-onde' ariki', at'ppas na iya magdeyo'-diyata'.* Like a small child, grown-old-enough to go up and down. (*Thesaurus:* **panday 1, pantas, tukang**)

**tangsi'₁** (var. **tiyangsi'**) *n.* **1)** Fibrous material for tying, from the center rib of a coconut palm frond. *Tiyangsi' itū niā' min batang langkay, niā', nilapesan. Mbal magtūy tapangengkot magdai'-dai' ni ai-ai. Subay gi' tinabid-tabid bo' mbal maglopeng.* The *tiyangsi'* referred to is taken from the center rib of a coconut frond, taken and stripped. It can't be used immediately for tying anything. It should be twined so it doesn't lose its shape. (*Thesaurus:* **naelon, tonda'₁ 1**) **1.1)** Fine nylon line. *Tangsi' naelon, ya pinagguna ma tahun baha'u itū.* Nylon line that is used these days. *Tangsi' itū naelon anahut-nahut.* The *tangsi'* referred to is fine nylon line.

**tangsi'₂** var. of **sangti'**

**tangsu'** *adj.* *a-* **1)** Detached from a main part. *Atangsu' kōk busay.* The handpiece of the paddle has come off. **1.1)** *v. tr.* *-an* To pull something away from the main part. *Tangsu'anku k'llongnu.* I'll take [the head] from your neck! *Tangsu'in puhan ilū.* Pull the handle away.

**tangtang** *adj.* *a-* **1)** Stripped away; diminished in bulk. *Atangtang isita min to'olang.* Our flesh has gone from our bones. *Sali' atangtang l'ngngonku, bay nilabba'an, sali' nihantu.* It's like my arm is reduced, having been harmed by a spirit being such as a *hantu* sprite. *Atangtang lasaku ma ka'a.* My love for you has gone completely. (*cf:* **tantang**) **1.1)** *v. tr.* *-an* To remove something from its place. *Tinangtangan lasana, nila'anan sandal-dohon.* Her love is stripped away, her grief taken away.

**tangungngul** *v. intr.* *aN-* To howl, as a dog. (*Thesaurus:* **tanghul, ūl, usig**)

**tangus** var. of **tamus**

**taoke'₁** *n.* Chinese, especially in a business context. (*Thesaurus:* **Lannang, makaw, sina'₁**)

**taoke'₂** *n.* A sweet variety of orange.

**taoge** *n.* Sprouted mung beans. (*Thesaurus:* **batung₂, monggo**)

**taote'** *n.* Various species of Catfish. *gen. Plotosus.* (*spec:* **baki', gaguk, ina'-baki', nggo'an-baki'**)

**tāp-tāp** *see:* **pagtāp-tāp**

**tapa** *v. tr.* **1)** To roast or dry something by exposure to heat. *Bang aku bay am'ssi bo' ta'abut kohap halam tab'lli daingku subay tapaku ko da'a ahalu'.* When I have gone fishing and it gets to afternoon without my fish being sold, I have to roast it so it doesn't go bad. *Angā' aku bunut panapaku daing.* I will get some coconut husks to roast the fish with. (*cf:* **b'lla 1**; *Thesaurus:* **panggang₁, tunu'₂**) **1.1)** *v. intr.* *pa-* To lie in front of a fire for warmth, as a woman recovering after giving birth. (*Thesaurus:* **dama 1, dangka₂ 1, dangu 1**)

**pagtapa** *v. intr.* *aN-* To dry food items by exposure to heat. *Aubus kami magtapa lahing amangan-mangan na kami.* When we finished drying the coconut we had a bite to eat.

**tapahan** *n.* A rack for roasting or grilling food.

**tinapa** *n.* Roasted or grilled food, especially fish.

**tapak** *adj.* *a-* Placed so as to be secure and stable. *Sawan ilū subay atapak kat'nna'na.* That drinking glass should be placed securely. *Da'a ka amasipi bang ka amat'nna' ai-ai ko da'a ahūg. Patapakun.* Don't put things near an edge when you put them down, in case they fall. Make them secure.

**tapak-tapak** *n.* A small plate or saucer. (*syn:* **lai'-tapak**)

**tapa'ut** (var. **dapa'ut**) *adj.* *a-* Just after the expected time; almost overdue. *Atapa'ut na l'ngngan kami.* Our journey is later than planned. *Arapa'ut na tulak kami. Ai pabeya'nu?* Our departure is overdue. What are you sending? *Tapa'ut itū apiki ni waktu.* This word *tapa'ut* means close to time. (*cf:* **apiki 1, pagsinta'**)

**tape'₁** *n.* The part on which something stands, as a person's lower leg and foot, a table leg, the wheel of a vehicle. *Bowahanta kām bohe' pangose' tape'bi bo' kam pahali-hali ma sindungan kayu itū.* I will bring you water for washing your feet so you can rest in the shadow of this tree. *T'ttob-tape' du ya bay pa'nda' ma iya sagō' magjinuba pote'.* What appeared to him was someone cut off at the feet, but it was clothed in a white gown. (*cf:* **goma₂, silikan**; *pt:* **anak-tape', bokol 2, nggo'an-tape'**)

**tape'-baliyu** *n.* The closing stage of a wind period. *Ya na itu musim ma olangan kōk uttala' maka tape' satan.* This is the season between the onset of the north wind phase and the end of the south wind. *Musim tape' uttala'.* The season at the tail end of the north wind. (*cf:* **kōk-baliyu**)

**tape'-būd** *n.* The base of a hill or mountain. *Na, ina'an disi Sa'ul maka anakna si Jonatan pahanti' ma tape' būd.* Well, there was Saul and his son Jonathan stopping briefly at the base of the hills.

**tape'an** *n.* The downstream side of a house relative to the incoming tide. (*Thesaurus:* **kōkan 1, diyata'an₁ 1, sibayan**)

**tape'₂** *n.* The tail of a fish. (*cf:* **togel**)

**tape'₃** *n.* A foot as a measurement of length. *Saga mpat tape' lambuna.* Its width is about four feet.

**tape'-kura'** *n.* A species of spiny oyster. (*cf:* **sudlay-sudlay**)

**tapi'** *n.* **1)** The lateral planking or strakes of a canoe hull. *Parangkang akapal tapi'na.* A Buginese sailing ship with thick planks. (*spec:* **bangkat sa'am, kamara 1, kapi-kapi, dalosan, durung-diyata', durung-sa'am, g'ppang, lungtud, palapa' 1, pamonod, panansahan, tapi'-dalosan**) **1.1)** *v. tr.* To fit planking to a dugout hull or wooden base. *Yuk kallo' ni kuyya', "Subay kita magtapi' adjung."* The heron said to the monkey, "We had better build a traditional planked ship." (*Thesaurus:* **adjung-adjung 1.1**) **1.2)** *v. tr.* To build the superstructure of a canoe.

**tapi'-dalosan** *n.* The strake or side plank that runs the length of a canoe. (*gen:* **tapi' 1**)

**tapil** *n.* **1)** A support for structural items at risk of breaking. **1.1)** *v. tr.* -an To strengthen a structural member by fastening a piece alongside. *Ndiya pōng batangan ilū panapil itu-i.* Pass me that piece of outrigger beam to strengthen this one. *Bang aniya' letehan bo' aniya' magl'ntet-l'ntet, subay tinapilan.* If there is a footbridge that springs up and down, it should be braced. (*Thesaurus:* **gimbal 1**) **2)** Moral support for a claim or promise. *Niā' tapil bang b'nnal du aku angandapit ni ka'a.* Taken as proof that I will truly support you. *Ngā'un na sangpū' pilak itū, tapil llingku.* Take this ten pesos, in support of my words. (*cf:* **tapin**; *Thesaurus:* **bogbog₁ 1.1, dapit, ga'os 1.2, gapi' 1.2**) **2.1)**

*v. tr.* -an To attach something in support of a claim or promise. *pai pamat'nna' mbo' tinapilan lokay maka duwa botong.* Unhusked rice for presenting to a ritual ancestor, supported by coconut leaflets and two green coconuts.

**pagtapil** *v. intr.* aN- To be physically supportive, of people or things. *Buwat kami maka si Tu bay magpatta', magtapil.* Like Tu and me getting photographed, standing together. *Buwat kami magbola, maggapi' duwa-duwa, magtapil sali'.* Like when we play ball, we team up in pairs, sort of supporting each other. *Maggimbal pelang karuwa, sali' magtapil.* Both canoes brought alongside, each sort of supporting the other.

**tapīn** *v. intr.* pa- To be a moral support to someone. *Aniya' patapīn ni iya, sali' anabang, amogbog.* Someone goes to support him, to aid him, to take his side. (*cf:* **tapil 2**)

**pagtapīn** *v. intr.* aN- To support of one another in an argument. *Oy! Magtapīn kām duwangan.* Oh, you two sure stick together!

**tapis** *n.* **1)** A piece of cloth cut from something larger. *Tapis, ya pīs s'mmek.* Tapis, an offcut of cloth. *Tapis, ya pata' leha, man deyo' pote' man diyata' tapis.* Pieces of cloth, the decorative panel of a square sail, white cloth below, *tapis* above. **1.1)** *adj.* a- Wearing a piece of cloth as a temporary garment, as after bathing. *Patapisun hōs itū.* Use this sarong as a makeshift garment.

**tapiyan** *n.* The seaward edge of land, just above high water. (*Thesaurus:* **bihingan, daplakan₁, gintana'an, hampilan, pari'an, susulan, tampe**)

**tapiyan-tabu'** *n.* A seaside market of a local community. *Pinalege saga tepo ma tapiyan-tabu'.* Woven mats spread out at a seaside market.

**taplak₁** *n.* A gauzy cloth used for blouses. *Bang ma aku ya kakana' maglowang-lowang.* In my opinion it's the cloth with [decorative] holes in it. (*Thesaurus:* **bildu', buwal₂, dasu, lehag, lere-lere 1, pima**)

**taplak₂** *adj.* zero Covering completely, of an amount. *Bang ma sīn, taplak duwa hatus, halam labi, halam kulang.* In regard to money, a covering amount of two hundred [pesos], nothing more, nothing less.

**tapling** *v. tr.* To slap something using an open hand. (*Thesaurus:* **bimbing, b'ddak, sampak, sampiyal, t'ppak₁**)

**taplok** *n.* **1)** The cover of an opening or container. *Taukab isāb taplok langit bo' patumbuk ulan alandos.* The covering of the sky was also opened so that heavy rain fell. (*Thesaurus:* **sa'ob 1, sampong 1, tambol 1, turung 1, tutup₁ 1**) **1.1)** *v. tr.* To close an opening, as a hand over eyes or ears; to fasten clothing using buttons. *Taplokanta ka'a mital ilū.* I'll put the lid on that can for you. *Nsa' tinaplok matata, taingata.* Neither our eyes nor our ears were closed. **2)** A scab formed over a sore. (*Thesaurus:* **l'kkang, l'kkung 1,**

**tangkop) 2.1)** *v. tr. -an* To remove the scab from a sore, as for the purpose of applying ointment.

**tapog** *n.* The Five-lined cardinalfish. *Cheilodipterus quinquelineatus.* (*cf:* **tandukan, tangal**)

**tapsil** *n.* An interpretative commentary on the Koranic text. *Sali' Maulud, aniya' tapsil tabeya' ma deyom sulat, bo' mbal tabassa.* Like the Maulud text, where a commentary is included in the writing, but is not read out.

**taptap** (var. **tattap**) *adj. a-* **1)** Stable; enduring; not easily changed. *Pataptapun imannu.* Make your faith steadfast. (*Thesaurus:* **kakkal, d'ddos, dorog₁, tattal, t'ttog 1**) **1.1)** *v. intr. pa-* To remain in one place, condition or state. *Pataptap, sali' pat'ttog, alahang magl'ngngan.* Settled in a place, similar to being stable, seldom walking about.

   **kataptapan** *n.* A settled place or state. *In sapda halam aniya' kamaujuranna sapantun manuk-manuk halam aniya' kataptapanna, atawa pana' halam aniya' tudjuhanna.* A curse without a goal is figuratively like a bird that has no permanent perching place, or an arrow that has no target.

**tapuk** *v. intr. pa-* **1)** To hide somewhere. *Magtūy sigām patapuk karuwangan ma deyom kakayu-kayuhan supaya mbal ta'nda' e' Tuhan.* The two of them promptly hid among the trees so God couldn't see them. **1.1)** *v. tr. -an* To hide something. *Aniya' sinapang kono' bay tapukanna.* There is reportedly a rifle that he has hidden. *Anapukan iya dīna.* He hides himself.

   **pagtapukan** *n.* A place of safety; a hiding place. *Maglammahan sigām kamemon, magtāwan paluwas min pagtapukan sigām.* They all lost heart, afraid to come out of their hiding places.

   **tapukan** *n.* A hiding place; a refuge. *Angahinangan dī sigām kubu'-kubu' ma saga songab batu maka ma saga tapukan ya ahunit sinōd.* They made huts for themselves in rocky hollows and in hiding places that were difficult to get into.

   **patapukan** *n.* A place of concealment; a hiding place.

**tapu'** *v. intr. pa-* **1)** To land, as a bird on a branch. *Bang paleyang manuk-manuk man M'ddas tudju pi'itu, patapu' ma diyata' kayu.* When birds fly this way from Siasi Town, they land on the tops of the trees. (*cf:* **t'ppak₂**) **2)** To land on a person, as a spirit being or an illness. *Magsukul ma pagka'inagonbi ma pasalan saki bay patapu' ni aku.* Thanks for your concern regarding the illness that landed on me.

   **patapu'an** *n.* A place where birds land.

**tapulaw** *n.* A torch of resinous wood. *Tapulaw itū panū', saddī tanju', saddī isāb suwariyan.* The torch referred to is for fishing with a light, different from a flare and different from a makeshift oil lamp. (*Thesaurus:* **sulariyan, tanju'**)

**tapung** *n.* **1)** Rice flour, an ingredient of many local recipes. *Sokal maka bohe' ya pagaddun tapung hē'.* Sugar and water are for mixing with the rice flour. (*Thesaurus:* **ata', tirigu 2**) **1.1)** *v. tr.* To make rice into flour by pounding. *Tapungun buwas itū.* Make flour of this husked rice.

   **tapung-bangkit** *n.* Powdered calceous lime.

**tapus** *adj. a-* **1)** Concluded; over and done with. *Nsa' atapus suli-suli sigā bo' na pī' nirugsu'an.* Their conversation was barely finished when he was stabbed right there. *Paragtol bissala, mbal sali' kabalikan, tapus na bissala.* The talk is concluded, cannot be repeated, the discussion over. (*cf:* **hinapusan, hopay**) **1.1)** *v. tr.* To bring something to an end. *Angkan tapusku bo' mbal aniya' la'at ma deyom kaul-pi'il.* That's why I brought things to an end so there would be nothing bad said or done. (*Thesaurus:* **katis₂ 1.1, sangkol, talus₁ 1.1, tammat 1.1, ubus₁ 1.1**)

   **katapusan** *n.* **1)** The final or superior stage. *Kubulun h'ndanu ma deyom tampat kami ya katapusan ahāp.* Bury your wife among the finest of our memorial graves. *Katapusanna, magbaran si Sa pehē'.* At the last Sa went there in person. *Nakura' ya katapusan alanga.* A nakura' is the highest in rank. (*Thesaurus:* **kapūd-pūran, tabtaban, tobtoban**) **2)** The last-born child. (*syn:* **kabungsuhan**)

**tarāk** *n.* A truck.

**tara'-tara'** *v. tr.* To try something for fun. *Tara'-tara'un pehē'.* (*Sinulay-sulayan ta'uta, subay ongka'.*) Have a try at it. (Testing one's skill, has to be some game.) (*Thesaurus:* **ahat 1.1, sulay₁ 1.1**)

**tarapu** *n.* **1)** A cloth for wiping. (*cf:* **sasapu**) **1.1)** *v. tr. -an* To wipe up rubbish or a mess. (*Thesaurus:* **kukus, pu'us, sapu 1.1**)

**tarasul** *n.* A poetic composition, usually in the Tausug language and sung in the classic lugu' style. *Bowahan lugu' tarasul itū.* The tarasul referred to is a kind of *lugu'.*

**taratu** *v. tr.* To make a business contract for some service or commodity. *Tinaratu ariplano.* The airplane flight has been arranged.

   **pagtaratu** *v. intr. aN-* To make arrangements regarding time and place to meet. *Bang saupama magistori-istori maka d'nda. Magtaratu kami, īya lum'ngngan pehē', aku isāb lum'ngngan, ati magsabu.* Having discussions with a girl, for example. We arrange for her to walk there, I too will walk, and we'll get there at the same time. (*Thesaurus:* **idda 1.1, ligtung, ora, tugna', tugun 1.1, waktu 1.1**)

**taratu'** *n.* **1)** A distinctive rhythm used when playing percussion instruments. **1.1)** *v. tr.* To play music with the taratu' rhythm. (*Thesaurus:* **kulanting 1, lisag₂ 1.1, tagunggu', taletek, taroro', tigi'-tigi'₂, tuntung**)

**tarawi** *n.* The evening prayer proclaimed during the month of Ramadan. *Magsambahayang tarawi* bang asekot na bulan nihinang. They pray the *tarawi* prayer when it is almost the month for [Ramadan] to be celebrated.

**taraysikul** *n.* A tricycle; specifically, a motorized tricycle for carrying passengers.

**tare'** *n.* 1) A retractable lateral spine near the tail of certain fish. (*Thesaurus:* **kanting₁, sēk, s'kke**) 1.1) *v. advrs. -in-* Stabbed by a fish spine. *Bay tinare' tape' si Idj.* Idj's foot was stabbed on a fish spine.

**tarik** *n.* The outrigger cross-booms between the main fore and aft booms, fitted on large pelang-type canoes to add strength. *Duwa man dambila', duwa man dambila', panandal batang.* Two on each side to help the main outrigger beams last longer. (*Thesaurus:* **batangan, katig 1, sa'am 1**)

**taroro'** *v. tr. -an* To beat a specific syncopated beat on a percussion instrument. *Tinaroro'an gabbang, sali' tinaletekan dapu'.* The bamboo marimba beaten with a syncopated beat, like the *taletek* beat. (*cf:* **lisag₂ 1**; *Thesaurus:* **kulanting 1, lisag₂ 1.1, pagtā'-tā', taktek, tagunggu', taletek, taletek, taratu' 1.1, tigi'-tigi'₂, tuntung**)

  **pagtaroro'** *v. tr.* To beat a rhythm on an instrument. *Aniya' isāb min dahū'an sigām saga a'a magtaroro'an tambul-tambul.* There were people in front of them too, beating time on tambourines.

**taroso** *n.* The trunk of a tree, felled but not yet milled. (*cf:* **batang₁**)

**taruk** *n.* The mast of a sailing vessel. *Takāk, ilu pasugpat man diyata' taruk.* The sprit, extended there from the top of the mast. (*Thesaurus:* **takāk, tindakan, tukag, tuklug 1**)

**tarul** *n.* A gum exuding from some tree species, useful for filling holes in a canoe hull. *Tarul, buwat ma po'on mampallam. Ahāp tarul man buttik.* Gum, such as is [found] on the trunk of a mango tree. Mango gum is preferable to gum from forest trees. *Ahāp tarul man buttik. Makalu'ug buttik.* Mango gum is preferable to buttik [gum from forest trees]. Getting buttik is exhausting. (*cf:* **bulitik₁**)

**tasa** *n.* A cup, especially as a unit of measure. (*Thesaurus:* **basu, panginuman, sawan**)

**tasbi'** *n.* A string of beads used as a memory aid when praying. *Tasbi' itū sali' gantung-li'ug bo' magbuwa'-buwa' anuna.* Tasbi is like a necklace but with a textured surface [to its beads].

**tasdik** *v. tr.* To come to mind, of something remembered. *Ai-ai makanibowa'ta pinta-pintata sudju ni iya, sali' aniya' tinasdik ma deyom atay.* Whatever comes to our mouth we make a request to him about, like when something is recalled inwardly. (*Thesaurus:* **entom 1.2, magtak, padlak ni atay, sangpit, suligpat, tambung, tomtom 1.1**)

**tasik** *v. tr.* To preserve sardines in brine.

**pagtasik** *v. intr. aN-* To make a living by preserving sardines in brine. (*Thesaurus:* **boro 1.1, gamos 1.2**)

**tasikan** *n.* The slatted drying racks on which fish are dried after being soaked in brine.

**tastas₁** *v. tr.* To bring to closure a long discussion or negotiation. *Bang bay na ah'lling huwis mbal kaliyuhan. Ya hē' anastas hukuman.* When the judge has spoken no one can go against him. He is the one to finalize the judgment. *Ya anastas magkawin, imam. Iya na amuwan katobtoban.* The one bringing the wedding ceremony to an end is the imam. He is the one to bring it to a close.

**tastas₂** *adj. a-* 1) Unraveled; unstitched. *Bay nilupi' pareyom bo' mbal atastas.* It was folded inwards so it wouldn't come unraveled. *S'mmek bang ab'kkat tahi'na, atastas na.* When the stitching of clothes breaks, it is no longer sewn. (*syn:* **bintas**) 1.1) *v. tr. -an* To remove the stitching joining pieces of cloth.

**tatab** *v. tr.* To learn by observation; to evaluate. *Anatab kita baranta bang kita tauwa' saki, makapagusaha maka mbal.* We examine ourselves when we have become sick, whether or not we are able to go fishing. *Bang aku bīllihan paraw e' si Mma', mbal aku magtūy bīllihan. Tinatab aku dahū e'na, kalu-kalu aku atogol amahilala'.* When Dad is buying a canoe for me, it isn't bought for me immediately. He assesses me first, whether I might be diligent in caring for it. *Mukali' ya mbal ata'u angadji' Kora'an, hal tatatab he' sigā. Mukali'* are those who do not know how to read the Holy Koran, they just learn [ritual] by observing what is happening. (*Thesaurus:* **nda'-nda', t'ntong₂**)

**tatabanan** (derivative of **taban**) *n.* Loot; plunder. *Ta'ā' kamemon saga tatabanan min katindahan bay tinunu' itū.* All the loot was taken from this burnt shopping area.

**tatak** *n.* An identifying mark. (*Thesaurus:* **tanda'**)

**tataklayan** *n.* A serving dish or tray for food presented to guests. (*Thesaurus:* **bandehaw, talam**)

**tata'** *v. tr.* To splash water over something, as to clean it. *Tinata' tape'na maka tahik, bay al'mmi' e' tai' ero'.* His feet were splashed with sea-water, having been made dirty with dog poo. (*Thesaurus:* **busuwag, pisik-pisik, titi'**)

**tatal₁** *adj. a-* Firmly constructed; durable. *Atatal luma' itū he' pipul, minsan baliyu mbal ah'bba'.* This house is firm by means of the supporting posts, even with wind it will not collapse. *Atatal tapi'anna, minsan goyak maka baliyu mbal magpiyut.* Its planking is well done, even in rough seas and storm-winds it will not twist.

**tatal₂** *adj. a-* 1) Wounded by repeated blows. *Atatal he' pali'.* Mortally wounded with cuts. 1.1) *v. tr.* To strike something with damaging force. *Buwat kami magboksen maka si Sar. Na yukna, "Mbal ka arai' maka'atu. Na tatalta ka min t'dda."* Like when I am boxing with Sar. He says, "You probably won't be able to fight back. So I will hit you just once."

**tatap** *n.* 1) The cloth laid over a corpse once it has been shrouded. (*Thesaurus:* **kasa', kuku-pote', salimput 1, saput 1, talkun**) **1.1)** *v. tr. -an* To lay a cloth covering over a corpse.

**tatas** *n.* 1) Duration; the length of time that something lasts. *Mbal apagon to'ongan hāg itū. Tatasna limantahun.* This post isn't very durable. It lasts five years. **1.1)** *adj. a-* Durable; long-lasting. *Ahāp amulawan nihinang busay, atatas ma tahik.* Molave is a good wood for making paddles from, it is durable in the sea. (*Thesaurus:* **anagtol, kamdos₂, kumpay, galak₂, pagon₁ 1.1, taggu₁, togob₁**) **1.2)** *v. intr. pa-* To last; to endure, of human ability or of a substance. *Bang aku patuhun mbal aku makatatas. Akulang napasku.* When I dive I cannot last long. Not enough breath. *Anganda'ug kām sagō' mbal du patatas panganda'ugbi.* You won but your triumph won't last long. (*Thesaurus:* **iman₁ 1.1, pagsabal, sandal 1.1, tahan-tahan, tangka'**)

**tatat** *v. intr. aN-* To tremble, as with fever. *Binanta' bang saki buwattē', anatat pabīng.* A sickness like that may recur, trembling again. (*Thesaurus:* **hadjat₂, hōb-hōb, l'mmun, tandog 1**)

**tattal** *v. intr. pa-* To remain in one place. *Patattal ka maina'an, da'a magpinda-pinda.* Stay there, don't keep changing. (*Thesaurus:* **kakkal, d'ddos, dorog₁, taptap 1, t'ttog 1**)

**tattap** var. of **taptap**

**tau-** *see section 2.2.2.4 Prefix:* **Cau-**

**taubang** *n.* An inedible plant in marine shallows. (*Thesaurus:* **l'mmuk, unas**)

**taubi'** *n.* The tree at the entrance to heaven, on which the name is written of persons about to die.

**tau'** *v. tr.* 1) To keep something in storage. *Tau'un itu ma aku bo' mbal alungay.* Keep this for me so it doesn't get lost. (*Thesaurus:* **kuli-kuli 1.1, nna'**) **1.1)** *v. ditr.* To keep something on behalf of, or in reserve for, someone. *Tinau'an lagi' si Ju.* Some [food] kept back for Ju. *Lagak ka ma kinakan. Mbal ka anau'an kasehe'annu, subay hal ma ka'a.* You are a greedy person in regard to food. You save nothing for the others, it has to be for you only. (*Thesaurus:* **kapin 1.1, halli'₂**)

**pagtau'** *v. tr.* To place a person or object in a secure place. *Saga d'nda inān bay pinagtau', binalanja'an, pinaka'llum sambil llaw kamatay sigām.* Those women were confined to a secure place, fed and kept alive until the day of their death.

**pagtau'an** *n.* A storage place; a safe-box. *Bay kono' maina'an ma pagtau'anna.* It was there, he said, in its storage place. (*cf:* **pang'nna'an**; *spec:* **ba'ung, bungga'₂, kaha₁, kansiya, kuta'₁ 2, gaddong, gusi'**)

**tau'an** *n.* A storage place. *Sali' pabūd, ai-ai ma tau'an.* Sort of piling up, whatever is in storage.

**panau'** *n.* A down payment to secure a deal; a deposit. (*Thesaurus:* **l'kkat₁ 1, lōb 1.1, padjak₁**)

**taumpa'** *n.* Shoes. (*Thesaurus:* **bakiya'₁, sinelas, takon**)

**pagtinaumpa'** *v. intr. aN-* To wear shoes.

**taumpa'-tinggi** *n.* Shoes with high heels.

**tautali'anak** var. of **tali'anak**

**tauwa'** var. of **taluwa'**

**tauwat** var. of **tawbat**

**tāw** *n.* 1) Fear. *Aheya tāw sigām niholdap e' mundu.* They had great fear of being held up by bandits. **1.1)** *adj. a-* Afraid; apprehensive. *Atāw aku angal'ddom luma'.* I am fearful when the house is becoming dark. (*Thesaurus:* **bolag, dalan 1.1, damag, gawa, g'mma, gupu, leya'-leya', umagad 1**) **1.2)** *v. advrs. -in-* To have become afraid. *Tināw aku ma kuting sidda.* I have become very afraid of cats. **1.3)** *v. tr. a-, ka-..-an, -an* To fear something. *Ai katāwannu? Da'a sigām katāwinbi.* What are you afraid of? Don't fear them. *Atāwan aku ka'a.* I am afraid of you.

**pagtāw** *v. intr. aN-* To experience fear. *Magtāwan sigām kamemon paluwas min pagtapukan sigām.* They were all afraid to come out from their hiding places.

**tāw-tāw** *v. intr. maka-* To be frightening. *Mbal kami makatawakkal kaleya bang sangom, makatāw-tāw.* We don't dare to go inland at night, it is quite scary.

**pakitāw** *v. tr.* To frighten someone.

**pagkatāw** *v. intr. aN-* 1) To experience fear. **1.1)** *v. tr.* To treat someone as an object of fear. *Pinagkatāwan iya he' a'a kamemon. Atāw binono'.* He is greatly feared by everyone. They fear being killed.

**pagmatāw** *n.* 1) Deep respect; reverence. **1.1)** *v. tr. -an* To fear; to show deep respect. *Pandu'anta kām bang sai ya subay pagmatāwanbi.* I'll teach you who you should be afraid of.

**tawakkal** *v. tr. -an* To risk or dare doing something. *Bang mbal tawakkalannu ah'lling ni parinta, tantu aniya' saddi paganti' min ka'a.* If you won't dare to speak to government officials, there will surely be someone else to take your place. *Sagwā' halam aniya' makatawakkal atilaw ni d'nda inān bang ai ya gawina.* But none dared to ask that woman what her purpose was. (*Thesaurus:* **k'ddom₂, halus₁, pagpasukud, pagsusaed, samba 1, sarap₂ 1**)

**pagtawakkal** *v. intr. aN-* 1) To take a risk; to be daring. **1.1)** *v. tr.* To take the risk of entrusting something to another person. *Pagtawakkalun sīnnu ma iya.* Commit your money to him.

**tawad** *adj. a-* 1) Wanting more than is given. *Atawad, bay binuwanan bo' bilahi gi'. Subay na pa'in binuwanan.* Covetous, has already been given stuff but wants more. Wanting to be given things continually. *Atawad, sali' anapsu. Bay na magsulut ati niamu' gi'.* Greedy, desirous.

Reached an agreement but more is requested. (*Thesaurus:* **napsu** 1) **1.1)** *v. tr.* *-an* To covet something beyond what is given.

**tawag** *v. tr.* To call or summon someone, in a formal context. (*Thesaurus:* **dē'** 1.1, **lingan** 1, **owa'₁** 1, **sabbut** 1.1)

**tawag-saksi'** *v. tr.* To summon a witness. *Sali' aniya' bay magbono', magdagsol ni sara' ati tinawag-saksi' he' sara'. Na bang mahē' ma upis, yuk-i, "B'nnal sakup ka bay pagbono' itū?"* Like when there was a fight and it has gone to the magistrate and he calls a witness. Then there at the office someone says, "Were you truly a witness to this fight?" (*cf:* **sopena**)

**tawa'-tawa'** *v. intr.* *aN-* To become intense, especially of a desire. *Napsu anawa'-tawa'.* An inordinate passion.

**tawal** *n.* **1)** A charm or incantation (often in Arabic or Malay) recited to bring about a desired condition, as to heal a sickness, avert a storm. *Tawal itū sali' niamu'an apuwa bo' akosog baran.* This word *tawal* is like asking for a favor for physical strength. **1.1)** *v. tr.* *-an* To heal someone or change some condition by reciting a charm. *Nihantu si Nu ati tinawalan he' mma'na.* Nu was affected by a *hantu* spirit so his father said a healing charm over him. *Magpatawal ka bo' pahondong hunus inān.* Have someone recite a charm so that the squall stops. (*Thesaurus:* **hisu'**, **tilik**)

**pagtawal** *v. intr.* *aN-* To recite an incantation to God or a ritual ancestor. *Magtawal ni mbo' pangamu'an apuwa.* Reciting an incantation to an ancestor as a request for blessing.

**tawalli'** *v. intr.* *aN-* To make excuses for not doing what was asked. (*Thesaurus:* **da'awa** 1.1, **paglugat, palilu, tumagal** 1.1)

**tawan-tawan** *v. intr.* *aN-* To go beyond the limits of sight and hearing. *Bang paleyangta taguri' bo' ab'kkat tonda', yukta, "Hē' anawan-tawan."* When we are flying a kite and the string breaks, we say, "There, going out of sight." *Anawan-tawan pahāp gabbang a'a inān.* That man's marimba playing carries so far. (*cf:* **tegob-tegob**)

**tawap₁** *v. intr.* *pa-* To walk around the Kaaba stone during the hajj.

**tawap₂** *see:* **pagtawapan, pagtawap, patawap**

**tawas** *n.* Alum, a white powder used medicinally or as a bleach. *B'llihin aku tawas pamasawa mata.* Buy me some alum for clarifying [my] eyes.

**tawbat** (var. **tauwat**) *n.* **1)** Repentance; contrition. **1.1)** *v. intr.* *aN-* To seek someone's forgiveness. **1.2)** *v. tr.* *-an* To forgive someone for an offense.

**pagtawbat** *v. intr.* *aN-* To atone for sins by making an offering to God or a ritual ancestor. *Magtawbat kām ngga'i ka sadja min palangaybi, sagō' min deyom pangatayanbi.* Repent not just in your actions but from your heart as well. *Magtauwat na aku, magtauwat ni mbo' pangamu'anku apuwa'.* I will make an atonement

gift, I will give it to a ritual ancestor in support of my request for a favor. *Sali' kita angampun-ngampun ni mbo', magtawbat saga mama', saga bohe'.* It's like when we seek help from a ritual ancestor, offering as forgiveness gifts betel nut ingredients, water, and so on.

**pagtawbatan** (var. **panawbatan**) *n.* Gifts and offerings made in support of reconciliation.

**tawel** *n.* A towel. (*Thesaurus:* **jimpaw, panyu', sapu-tangan, tuwalya**)

**tawhid** *n.* **1)** Single-minded commitment, especially toward God. *Pabontolun sadja tawhidnu.* Just correct your belief in God. **1.1)** *v. intr.* *aN-* To make a firm commitment. *Anawhid sadja kita. Mbal pagkabidta atayta.* We simply make a firm commitment. We do not let our minds be unsettled. **1.2)** *v. tr.* *-an* To do something with an undivided heart. *Tawhirin sadja, minsan ka tahinang buwattē'.* Face it steadily, even though you are treated in such a way.

**pagtawhid** *v. intr.* *aN-* To be single-minded in one's religious commitment. *Magtawhid sadja ka ni ma'aripat, magitikad ka tunggal tudju ni iya.* Be single-minded in maintaining your religious principles, directing your mind only to him [God].

**Tawrat** var. of **Kitab Tawrat**

**tawsiyu** *n.* A sauce made of ground peanuts. (*cf:* **batung₁**; gen: **pamapā**)

**tawtaw** *v. tr.* To shape metal by beating it while hot. *Ahāp bang tinawtaw bo' mbal al'ngngat.* It's good to be shaped under heat so that it won't straighten out. (*Thesaurus:* **babal₁, sasal, subu₁** 2)

**tayak** *v. intr.* *aN-* **1)** To hold the hands palm upwards as in prayer. (*cf:* **sangga** 1) **1.1)** *v. tr.* To support something on open hands. *Tayakun ba suput ilū bo' mbal abu'us.* Put your hands under that paper bag so that it doesn't spill out. *Bang balutanku sawan buwattitu ngga'i ka aku anayak. Sawan ya anayak gatas.* When I hold a glass like this [with hands round] it is not I who support it. It is the glass that supports the milk. (*Thesaurus:* **takmay, tampupu**)

**tayakkup** (var. **ta'akkup**) *adj.* *a-* To be of one mind, of a group of people. *Bang gara' mbal atayakkup, magtūy magl'kkat kabagayan.* If plans are not agreed on, friends promptly separate.

**pagtayakkup 1)** *v. intr.* *aN-* To be mutually agreed as to some decision or desired outcome. *Mbal gi' magtayakkup kagara'an.* The discussions have not yet been mutually agreed upon (*syn:* **pagtayudtud**) **2)** *v. tr.* To become united; to become of one mind. *Pinagta'akkup, d'nda maka l'lla.* A wife and husband being brought to unity of mind.

**tayang** *adj.* *a-* Slender, of physique. (*Thesaurus:* **g'nting, lampin₁, nipis, nipnip**)

**tayo** *adj.* *a-* Hanging loosely; sagging. *Atayo engkot lilus itū. Maitu asigpit, bang paluklus aloka.* This watch band is sagging. Up here it is tight, when it slips down it is loose. *Atayo lubid, halam abitad.* The rope is sagging, not pulled tight. (*cf:* **k'ppos 1.1**)

**tayo-tayo** *adj. a-* Having sagging folds of flesh, as someone who has lost weight. *A: "D'nda ingga?" B: "Ya matayo-tayo."* A: "Which woman?" B: "The thin one."

**taytay** (var. **titay**) *v. intr. pa-* **1)** To walk along a bridge or walkway. (*Thesaurus:* **kulatay, lete**) **1.1)** *v. tr.* To use something as a bridge or walkway. *Da'a na pa'in titayun katig ilū. Apōng.* Don't keep using that outrigger as a walkway. It will break.

**taytayan** *n.* A bridge or elevated walkway. *Bang taytayan aluha. Makajari ka pal'ngngan minsan halam pamalutan.* When it's a *taytayan* it is wide. You can walk on it even though there is nothing to hold on to.

**taytayan tikus** *n. phrase* The upper plate of a wall (lit. a rat's walkway). {idiom} (*Thesaurus:* **babag 1, dagan₁, hobong, salsal**)

**tayudtud** *adj. a-* In agreement. *Atayudtud kami, abeya' na.* We are in agreement, persuaded now. (*Thesaurus:* **amu₂ 1.1, beya'₃ 1, dakayu'₂ 1, manghalapi, pagta'ayun, sulut 1**)

**pagtayudtud** *v. intr. aN-* To be mutually agreed as to some decision or desired outcome. (*syn:* **pagtayakkup 1**)

**tayum** *n.* Various long-spined sea urchins. *Echinoid sp.* (*Thesaurus:* **boto'-goyak 2, indangan₂, oko'-oko', s'llang₂, tehe'-tehe'**)

**tayum-boto'-boto'** (var. **boto'-boto'₂**) *n.* An inedible species of long-spined sea urchin with large blunt spines about the thickness of a pencil.

**tayum-buta-buta** *n.* An inedible species of long-spined sea urchin which burrows into soft sand.

**tayum-ettom** *n.* A species of long-spined black sea urchin.

**tayum-matahan** *n.* An edible variety of long-spined sea urchin with phosphorescent eye-like openings at the base of the spines.

**tebag** *n.* **1)** A piece cut off a main part. *Dantebag pa'in.* Just one piece. **1.1)** *v. tr.* To cut something off with a single blow. *Subay tinebag min po'onna.* It should be cut off at the base. (*Thesaurus:* **tigad 1.1**)

**pagtebag-tebag** *v. tr.* To cut up something long by multiple cross-cuts. *Mbal na manjari, bay na pinagtebag-tebag.* No longer useful, it has been chopped up. (*Thesaurus:* **lagut, tadtad 1**)

**tebla'** *n.* **1)** A small piece broken away from a main part. *Aniya' tebla'na gasa kulaet ilū.* The clay heating element of that pressure lantern has a chip out of it. **1.1)** *v. tr.* To break something off a main part. *Tebla'in aku tibu'uk ilū.* Break off a little piece of that boiled cassava for me. (*Thesaurus:* **pitas₂ 1, te'as**)

**pagtebla'-tebla'** *v. intr. aN-* **1)** To crumble something in compact form. **1.1)** *v. tr.* To reduce something to crumbs. *Tumbal pinagtebla'-tebla' bo' yampa pinehē' ni bohe' pasu' binugbug.* Packs of grated cassava crumbled before being put into boiling water for cooking.

**tebong** *n.* One's physical characteristic or mannerism. *"Da'a ka patondok bang ka lum'ngngan," yukna. Yukku, "Ya na tebongku."* "Don't bend your head when you walk," he said. I said, "That's just how I am." (*Thesaurus:* **baktulan, bowahan, l'ngnganan₂, pakang₁, palantara 1**)

**tebot** *adj. a-* Diligent; industrious. *Atebot a'a hē' maghinang. Ya na kahali'anna bang amangan atawa atuli.* That man is industrious in his work. His rest time is when he eats or sleeps. (*cf:* **tukid 1**; *Thesaurus:* **akkul, dago'os, sugsig 1, tuyu' 1**)

**tekang** *v. intr. pa-* **1)** To walk with paces of full length; to pace. (*syn:* **peka'**) **1.1)** *v. tr. -an* To measure length by pacing. *Tinekangan taha'na.* Its length measured by pacing.

**teket** *n.* A ticket.

**tekmas** *n.* **1)** A notch cut in pole or tree. *Halam aniya' tekmas pangandāganta.* There are no notches for us to climb up by. (*Thesaurus:* **taka 1, tangga' 1, tengham**) **1.1)** *v. tr. -an* To cut a notch in a pole or tree. *A: "Angay kayu ilū angkan tinekmasan?" B: "Bo' ahāp e'ta ang'llo' mampallam, bo' ahāp e'ta parāg."* A: "Why is that tree cut with notches?" B: "It's so we can easily get mangoes, so we can climb easily."

**tekmod** *adj. a-* Completed; detailed. *Atekmod na bay bayaranku utangku.* I have completed paying off my debt. *Angkan yampa aku atekmod na, in dakayu'-maka-dakayu' bay kasusahan kami.* That's why I am only just now being detailed, one by one, about our troubles. (*Thesaurus:* **talus₁ 1, tubus₁ 1.1**)

**tektek** var. of **tettek**

**tege'** see: **patege'**

**teges-teges** *v. intr. aN-* To be scattered. *Angay aneges-teges kapamangan itū?* Why are these eating utensils scattered? *Si Ju bay angahinang aneges-teges, mbal ata'u angamomos.* Ju worked messily, not being used to tidying up. (*Thesaurus:* **bulaksay 1, kanēs-nēs, sihag₂ 1**)

**tegob-tegob** *adj. -an* Beyond the limits of vision, because of depth or distance. *Ma timbang tegob-tegoban, mbal makatimbul ni kasehe'an.* Away on the remotest ocean, unable to join up with the others. *Lalom tegob-tegoban, alalom to'ongan, sali' hal bilu-biluhan la.* A depth beyond seeing, extremely deep, only the blueness remaining. (*cf:* **tawan-tawan**)

**tehe'-tehe'** *n.* Various short-spined sea urchins, a strand food valued for its edible gonads. *Echinoid sp.* (*Thesaurus:* **boto'-goyak 2, indangan₂, oko'-oko', s'llang₂, tayum**)

**tehe'-tehe'-balambangan** (var. **balambangan**) *n.* The Black-shelled sea urchin. (*syn:* **tehe'-tehe'-singaling**)

**tehe'-tehe'-bubu-bubu** *n.* A species of sea urchin found in sand, almost spineless and more box-like in shape than other species.

**tehe'-tehe'-itingan** *n.* A long-spined sea urchin.

**tehe'-tehe'-lanab-lanab** (var. **lanab-lanab**) *n.* A species of small sea urchin, about the size of an egg.

**tehe'-tehe'-mamuhuk** (var. **mamuhuk**) *n.* A species of sea urchin, long-spined, found in seagrass or buried just below the surface in sand. *Mamuhuk, buwat tehe'-tehe' itingan bo' ataha' itingna man tehe'-tehe'.* Mamuhuk, like the common spiny sea urchin but with longer spines.

**tehe'-tehe'-pikit** *n.* A species of sea urchin, large, found mostly in deeper water.

**tehe'-tehe'-sambuwangan** (var. **sambuwangan**) *n.* A white-shelled species of sea urchin.

**tehe'-tehe'-singaling** (var. **singaling**) *n.* A black-shelled species of sea urchin. (*syn:* **tehe'-tehe'-balambangan**)

**tehe'-tehe'-s'llang** (var. **s'llang₂**) *n.* A deep-water species of sea urchin.

**tehem** *n.* **1)** A species of edible barnacle, found on rocks, wood, or mangrove roots. *Tehem itū amikit ma hāg, taga lowang.* Tehem barnacles cling to posts and have a hole [at the top]. (*gen:* **tahemtem 1**) **1.1)** *v. advrs.* -in- Having barnacles growing on something. *Ōy, pariyata' na kam. Tinehem ko' ka'am ilū.* Hey, come on up [from the sea]. You'll have barnacles growing on you.

**tē'₁** *adj. zero* Related through the re-marriage of a spouse or a parent. *Mma'ku tē', anakna tē', magdanakan tē'.* My stepfather, his stepchild, step-siblings. (*Thesaurus:* **ballo', eddok-eddok**)

**tē'₂** *v. tr.* To count something as being of importance. *Buwat kalungayan aku, mbal tē'ku sīn bay malungay hē'.* Like when I am affected by loss, I will not be too worried about the money that was lost. *Mbal tē'ku bayad ē', minsan buwattingga hekana. Asal makatabang sadja ma aku minsan halam aniya' tongodna.* I will not be concerned with payment, no matter how much it is. He has always helped me even though there was no recompense. (*Thesaurus:* **bista₁, kira-kira, kumpas₁**)

**te'as** *adj. a-* Broken or split away from a main part. *Ate'as, akobet, bo' masi kaheya'an.* Splitting off, damaged, but the bulk of it is still there. *Ate'as panapi' bang pangaluwaran. Bay alandos baliyu.* The upper plank of the canoe splits away when used as a rowlock. The wind was very strong. (*Thesaurus:* **pitas₂ 1, pungal, saksak 1, sasa₁, segpong, seplak 1, tebla' 1.1**)

**telno** var. of **telnos**

**telnos** (var. **telno**) *adj. zero* **1)** Of one color or pattern throughout. *Banogku telnos.* My sail is of one color. (*Thesaurus:* **lullun 1**) **1.1)** *v. intr.* aN- To wear items of clothing which match. *Bang as'mmek anak sigām, anelnos.* When their children are clothed, they match.

**telop** *adj. a-* **1)** Vanished in an instant. (*Thesaurus:* **liyaw 1.1, patawap 1**) **1.1)** *v. tr.* -an To cause something to vanish. *Tinelop-telopan pareyo'. Bang aniya' ahūg ni tahik, al'kkas patuntun, sali' aniya' angahella' iya.* Caused to vanish downwards. When something falls into the sea, it goes down quickly, as if something was pulling it. *Bang aniya' katas tabowa he' baliyu, bo' ta'nda' dai'-dai', yukta, "Tinelop-telopan."* If the wind blows away a piece of paper so that we only see it for a second we can say, "It has been whisked away." *Magtūy tinelopan bay mahūg ē', halam tabaliyakaw.* The thing that fell was promptly carried out of sight, unable to be seen.

**telop-telop** *adj. zero* Exceptionally fine, of a pearl.

**temang** *n.* A flattish area of sea floor at the base of a sea-cliff, usually visible from the surface. *Temang itū ya bowa' pampang, lalom saga sangpū' maka lima ni mpatpū'.* Temang is the opening of a sea-cliff, some 15 to 40 [fathoms] deep. (*Thesaurus:* **kantil₂, deyo'₂ 1, pampang, titib**)

**temo-temo** *v. tr.* To gather up scattered items. (*Thesaurus:* **hatul₁, patuntul, uki'-uki'**)

**temos** *adj. a-* Finished; completed. *Atemos pa'in itu kamemon, niamu' pabīng, sinō' pinaheka.* When all this was done, the request was repeated, told to increase the number.

**tempang** (var. **timpang**) *adj. zero* Uneven, irregular, of shape or distribution. *Angay baka' ilū? Atempang.* What's up with that basket? It's lopsided. *Bang am'ngkong dambila' bayhu'ta ati bang ni'nda' e' a'a sali' atimpang.* When one side of one's face is swollen and people see it, it's kind of lopsided. *Tempang pagbahagi' sigām.* Their sharing is uneven. *Atimpang pamaihu'anna.* His face is lopsided. (*Thesaurus:* **baligbig, kirus 1, pagkamihu**)

**tempel** *n.* A type of motor boat with a blunt stern and no outriggers. (*Thesaurus:* **beggong, biruk, buti, kappal, kumpit, lansa, papet, sappit₂**)

**tempel-tempel** *n.* A small power boat built in the Western style.

**templa** (var. **timpla**) *n.* **1)** An ingredient; a component of a mixture. *Sali' haloblāk kulang timplana, apoka na.* Like hollow-blocks lacking in [cement], easily broken. **1.1)** *v. tr.* To add one ingredient to another. (*Thesaurus:* **haybol, lamud₁ 1.1, lamugay 1.1, pagsagol 1.1, paila', simbug 1**)

**tempo** var. of **timpu**

**tempos** *v. tr.* -an To cut off a part, as to remove a defective portion. *Ansak, pagguna e' Sama, tinemposan diyata'na, tahinang atibulung.* A coconut leaf basket used by Sama, the top of it cut off and [the rim] made circular. *Temposanku bowa'nu.* I'll cut your lips off [a threat]. *Buwat* *buwa' kayu bang aniya' bay angeket iya, buwat ambaw, tokke', kabog. Tinemposan ya bay kineket ē', bang aniya' halu'na.* As with fruit when something such as a rat, a gecko or a bat has bitten it. The bitten part is cut out if there is decay in it. (*Thesaurus:* **tabtab 1, t'ttop 1, tompes, utas 1.1**)

**tendek** *n.* The stamping of feet.

**pagtendek** *v. intr. aN-* To stamp the feet, as in traditional dancing. (*Thesaurus:* **pagdaogdog, pagdogdog, pagtagdok**)

**tendero** var. of **tandero**

**tendog** *n.* An employee; a staff member; a tenant farmer. *Bang ka nakura', aku ya tendognu.* If you are the boss, I am your worker. *Tabeya' ma iya saga anak-h'ndana sampay saga tendogna kamemon, maglain ni lahat saddī.* Going with him were his wives and children and also all his adherents, migrating to another country.

**panendog** *n.* Collective term for employees, tenants, political or religious adherents.

**tenelas** var. of **sinelas**

**tenes-tenes** *n.* A narrative song genre in which lyrics referring to current events are sung to traditional tunes. (*Thesaurus:* **kalang₁ 1, kerol, dindang-dindang, pagbinuwa 1**)

**pagtenes** *n.* **1)** The tenes-tenes genre of singing. **1.1)** *v. intr. aN-* To sing songs of the tenes-tenes genre. *Bang kita ma dilaut, bo' kita sōng tinuli, na, maglanga'-langa' kita pangalāng tuli. Saddī magtenes.* When we are out at sea, and are becoming sleepy, we chant to stop sleeping. *Tenes* singing is different. *Bang aku magtenes-tenes, alayam.* When I sing *tenes* songs, I am expert.

**tengham** *v. tr.* To cut a notch for climbing. *Tenghamun ba kayu ē' parāganku.* Cut notches in that tree for me to climb by. (*Thesaurus:* **taka 1, tangga' 1, tekmas 1**)

**tenghog** var. of **talengog**

**tengol** *n.* A valuable tree of mangrove swamps, a source of tannin and building material. *Ceriops tagal.*

**tēp** *n.* A ribbon tape-recorder.

**teplas** var. of **deplas**

**teplong** *adj. a-* Broken off, of a standing post. *Ateplong hāg kamemon, bay tauwa' badju.* All the posts were snapped off, hit by the typhoon. (*Thesaurus:* **lobet, pate', pōng 1, punggul 2**)

**tepo** *n.* A sleeping mat, woven with great skill from pandanus strands; mats of any making. *Am'lli aku jangatan panganjangat pandan hinangku tepo.* I will buy a strip-cutter to cut pandanus for me to make a mat with. (*cf:* **boras**)

**tepo tinabid** *n. phrase* A mat woven using a twist technique that produces a wide variety of patterrns.

**tepok** *v. intr. pa-* To stop making a noise; to refrain from mentioning some topic. *Ya lling ala'at subay*

*pinatepok na.* Bad talk should be made to stop. *Sinō' patepok, sinō' pahali ko da'a parokot.* Told to cease from making a noise, told to stop so that things don't flare up. (*Thesaurus:* **k'nna, h'ddok, h'nnok**)

**terol** *adj. a-* Deformity of the tongue that affects clarity of speech. *Aterol d'lla' a'a tanga'.* The tongue of a person with a speech defect is deformed. (*Thesaurus:* **kemol, ponga', s'ngngog, tanga'₂**)

**tēt** *v. tr.* To spread things out, as when drying fish or displaying sale goods. *Tinēt ba'anan sēk ma parang ati nilikus maka mital.* A lot of shark fins are spread out on the grass and enclosed in roofing iron.

**pagtēt** *v. tr.* To distribute individual components of a collection to diverse places. *Buwat siga, pagtētun pakaniya-kaniya ati minsan tasaggaw dakayu', ilu asal aniya' ma tau'an saddī.* Like [smuggled] cigarets, distribute them to various people, then even if one is arrested there will still be some in different storage places.

**tete'** *n.* **1)** The erect nipple of a nursing mother. *Hinangin tete' si Onde'.* Form a nipple for Baby [i.e. make it easy for the baby to suckle]. (*Thesaurus:* **duru' 1, tampang**) **1.1)** *v. intr. zero* To suckle, usually as an instruction to the child. *Ā, tete' na ka.* There, you've started suckling.

**tettek** (var. **tektek**; **t'ttek**) *v. tr.* To strike something hard with a sharp blow. *Tettekku omang pangumpan.* I am breaking the hermit crab for bait. *Ai panektekta kohang itū?* What are we to use to open this clam? (*Thesaurus:* **p'ppa 1, p'ppok**)

**teya'-teya'** *n.* A species of small bee, capable of inflicting a painful sting. (*Thesaurus:* **buwani, kabulig, lampinig, tabungay**)

**tī** *n.* The beverage tea. *Ahāp tī itū, mbal angangkas.* This is good tea, it doesn't leave fibrous residue. (*Thesaurus:* **kahawa, kape, neskape, neskape**)

**tī-budbud** *n.* Instant tea.

**tibaggol** *adj. a-* Big-bodied; bulky. *Atibaggol wanni inān, sali' atibulung.* That odorous mango is big, kind of round. *Buwat kayu bay binasbasan, bay kinulangan ati yuk dangan, "Amasi atibaggol kayu inān."* Like a piece of lumber that has been trimmed, reduced, and another man says, "That wood is still too bulky [in section]." (*cf:* **tamiyang**)

**tibaw 1)** *n.* A visitor; a guest; a caller. **1.1)** *v. intr. pa-* To go somewhere for the purpose of visiting. *Buwat sali' si Oto' bay ma Sandakan ī' bo' mbal isāb makapi'itu, na bang angentom si Mma' ameya' patibaw ni Sandakan bo' makapag'nda'-'nda'.* Like when Oldest Son was in Sandakan and not able to come here, then when Dad was missing [him] he went to Sandakan so they could see each other. **1.2)** *v. tr.* To visit someone. (*Thesaurus:* **bisita 1.1, liyud, tulaga', tuwa' 2**) **2)** *v. intr. pa-* To occur briefly, of an illness.

**tibi** *n.* Various wasting diseases including tuberculosis.

**panibi** *n.* A person with an inherited tendency to a condition such as tuberculosis.

**tib'llaw** *n.* A tall grass with a woody stem.

**tibokkol** *var.* of **timbakkol**

**tibokkong** *adj. a-* Egg-shaped; ovoid. (*cf:* **tibulung** 1)

**tibtib** *n.* The limit or extent of something; a boundary. (*Thesaurus:* **jangka'an 1, manohan**)

**katibtiban** *n.* The last price in bargaining, or in negotiating bride-wealth with a woman's elders. *Angamu' sigām katibtiban.* They ask [to know] the last price.

**tibuk₁** *n.* Generic term for various species of damselfishes and clownfishes.

**tibuk-anak-lason** *n.* The Chocolate-dip chromis. *Chromis dimidiatus.*

**tibuk-biyaning** *n.* The Yellow chromis. *Chromis analis.*

**tibuk-lawi'an** *n.* The Black-striped angelfish. *Genicanthus lamarck.* (*Thesaurus:* **bebang₁, taliruk**)

**tibuk-lenged** *n.* The Blue-ribbon damselfish or the Ocellated sergeant-major. *Abudefduf biocellatus.*

**tibuk-sagga'-sagga'** *n.* The Springer's demoiselle. *Chrysiptera springeri.*

**tibuk-s'bbo** *n.* Various damselfishes or coral fishes.

**tibuk-taming** *n.* 1) The Yellowbelly damselfish. *Abudefduf leucogaster.* 2) The Seven-bar damselfish. *Abudefduf fasciatus.*

**tibuk-ulan-ulan** *n.* The Weber's chromis. *Chromis weberi.*

**tibuk₂** *v. tr.* To catch coral fish by driving them into a basket. (*cf:* **lasak, ulan-ulan**)

**tibu'** *v. tr.* To hit someone with the edge of a fist. *Tokorun kono' bang sai anibu' ka'a.* Guess who is hitting you. (*Thesaurus:* **butug, g'bbuk, suntuk 1.1, tikbung**)

**tibu'uk₁** *n.* 1) Something whole, undivided. (*Thesaurus:* **pono'-pono', tibokkol**) 1.1) *adj. a-* Cohesive; in lump form. *Aniya' isāb asin atibu'uk.* There is salt in lump form too. *Duwa kilu bulawan kono', bulawan tibu'uk.* Two kilograms of gold, they say, solid gold. 1.2) *v. tr.* To treat something as an undivided whole, as one unit.

**katibu'ukan** *n.* The undivided state of a physical substance or a group decision. *B'llihin aku nangka' ma katibu'ukanna.* Buy me an uncut jackfruit.

**pagtibu'uk** *v. intr. aN-* 1) To cohere in a single mass. *Apodjak daing, sali' magtibu'uk isina.* The fish is broken up, its flesh holding together. 1.1) *v. tr.* To bring things together in a single mass.

**tibu'uk₂** *n.* Generic term for non-toxic varieties of

cassava. *Manihot esculenta.* *Tibu'uk pinagtebla'-tebla' bo' yampa pinehē' ni bohe' pasu' binugbug.* Whole cassava crumbled before being put into boiling water as porridge. (*cf:* **tumbal 1**)

**tibu'uk-silal** *n.* A variety of cassava with toxic juice. *Tibu'uk-silal ak'ddot, subay nili'is, ginipitan. Tainta' du bo' ala'at ssana.* Silal cassava is tough in texture, it must be grated and squeezed. It can be eaten raw but the taste is awful.

**tibulung** *adj. a-* 1) Round; spherical. *Aniya' tinapay atibulung bay tauppina.* He dreamed about a spherical loaf of bread. (*cf:* **tibokkong**; *Thesaurus:* **bengkol₁, lakal 1, legong, lengkol 1, lengkong 1**) 1.1) *v. tr.* To encircle something.

**tibung-tibung** *adj. zero* Plump, of a woman's figure (a positive quality). *Si Baran tibung-tibung.* The girl with the plump figure. (*Thesaurus:* **goldo-goldo, hambug 1, littub, l'mmok 1.1, poko-poko, subuk**)

**tibūsan** (derivative of **būs**) *n.* A bolt of cloth.

**tīk** *v. intr. pa-* 1) To look out briefly at something from a place of concealment; to peep. (*Thesaurus:* **sīb 1, tandaw 1, tilag-tilag₂**) 1.1) *v. tr.* To look briefly at something. *Tīkun pelang inān, wa'i magtage'ot.* Have a quick look at that canoe, it is rubbing on something.

**pagtīk-tīk** *v. intr. aN-* To be in the habit of peeping into private places. *Ka'a ilū magtīk-tīk! Patīk ka man bilik dakayu' ni bilik dakayu'.* You're always peeping! You peep from one room to another.

**tikabbol** *n.* 1) The splash from something hitting a water surface. *Abase' kita, ta'abut kita he' tikabbol busay hē'.* We are wet, the splash reached us from the paddle hitting the water. 1.1) *v. tr. -an* To splash up from striking a water surface. *Subay tībba'an busay ni tahik bo' anikabbol.* Paddles should be hit against the sea so that water splashes up.

**tika'-tika'** *var.* of **kagang-tika'-tika'**

**tikam** *n.* A Chinese gaming board with numerals in marked squares; the game played on such a board.

**pagtikam** *v. intr. aN-* To play the game of tikam.

**tikayog** *v. intr. pa-* To be able to move about freely after a debilitating illness (usually with a negative). *Mbal iya makatikayog apa wa'i lagi' alamma, hatina mbal makakole'an dīna.* He cannot get about yet because he is still weak, in other words he cannot manage on his own.

**tikbi'** *v. intr. pa-* To knock sharply against something hard. *Al'ssu' na mital, bay patikbi' ni batu.* The water-can has a hole in it, it banged against a stone.

**pagtikbi'** *v. intr. aN-* 1) To be banging together, of rigid items. *Untang itū taga lai' mital magtikbi'. Takale min katāhan.* A marker buoy has metal plates banging together, audible from a distance. 1.1) *v. tr.* To bang together rigid items such as plates. *Da'a pagtikbi'un sawan ilū ko da'a* *abila'.* Don't bang those drinking glasses together lest they break.

**tikbung** *v. tr.* To hit someone with a sharp blow. *Tinikbung ma pangkulna si Yakub ati magsā' lo'atanna.* Yakub was hit in the hip area and his joint was dislocated. (*Thesaurus:* **butug, g'bbuk, suntuk 1.1, tibu'**)

**tikkup** *v. tr.* To shut something decisively. *Tikkupun maleta bang bay ukaynu.* Snap the suitcase shut when you have opened it. (*Thesaurus:* **batuk-batuk, kassup 1, kattup, dopon-dopon 1.1**)

**tik'bbong** (derivative of **k'bbong**) *adj.* a- Deeply concave, as a bowl. *Da'a ka am'lli lai' atik'bbong, am'lli ka lai' palayas itū, ya lai' halam aniya' ma deyom, ya sali' halam mohangan ilū.* Don't buy a deep plate, buy this shallow one, the plate with nothing inside, the one with no inner depression.

**tiklis** (var. **tiklus**) *n.* A basket of coarsely woven coconut leaves. *Tiklis itū ambung aheya, aluha bowa'na, pangisihan daing.* A *tiklis* is a large basket with a wide opening, a fish container. (*gen:* **baka'₁**)

**tiklus** var. of **tiklis**

**tikmuhan** *n.* A pretext for a quarrel.

**katikmuhanan** *n.* A pretext for a quarrel. *Angkan bigsi'ta iya sabab kab'nsihanta hinangna. Niā'an katikmuhanan.* That's why we disliked him so much, because we hated his work. It was taken as a pretext for quarrelling. (*Thesaurus:* **pagsababan, po'on-sabab, singgit**)

**tiksa'** (var. **siksa'**) *adj.* a- 1) Suffering hardship; maltreated; distressed. *Magsalinggā saga kahayopan sabab halam na aniya' pagkakan sigām. Minsan saga kambing maka bili-bili, atiksa' na.* The cattle are distressed because there is nothing for them to eat. Even the goats and sheep are suffering. (*Thesaurus:* **miskin, ti'il**) 1.1) *v. advrs.* ka-...-an To be suffering hardship. *Jari katiksa'an makalandu' in kamemon bangsa kami.* So all our people group was seriously afflicted.

**katiksa'an** *n.* Hardship; deprivation. *Mura-murahan bang pa'in ka pinagka'inagonan e' Tuhan maka niliyusan e'na min kamemon katiksa'annu.* May God care for you completely and deliver you from all your hardships.

**tikus** *n.* A rat. {archaic} (*cf:* **ambaw**)

**tīg** *v. intr.* pa- To incline to one side; to tilt. *Da'a kam patīg parambila' ilū apa ariki'-diki' katig, ko ra'a pakkom.* Don't tilt to one side because the outriggers are small, lest it capsize. *Ya mbal kakautku inān, arakala' aniya' goyak maka baliyu bo' makatīg paraw inān, pakkom aku.* The reason I'm not going out to sea is that if, as is probable, there is rough weather and wind so that the canoe happens to tilt, I will capsize. (*Thesaurus:* **kīd₂, kīng 1.1, lemba, lenggang, lihid, paglilip-lilip, poyog 1**)

**tigad** *adj.* a- 1) To be cut with a glancing blow. 1.1)

*v. tr.* To cut something with a single blow. *Bang tinigad, mint'dda du.* If something is *tigad*, it is a single act. *Bang kita anigad ma dilaut, wa'i ahūg baran lahut, apangsut man puhanna.* We were slashing at something out at sea, and the main part of the knife fell, coming free from the handle. (*Thesaurus:* **tebag 1.1**)

**tigang** var. of **t'ggang₁**

**tigangkal** *v. intr.* aN- Dried out completely in the sun. *Anigangkal na daing. Minsan s'mmek, anigangkal du isāb.* The fish are over-drying in the sun. Even clothes, they can become over-dry too. (*cf:* **ganggas**; *Thesaurus:* **panggang₂ 1, toho'**)

**tigangkul** *n.* 1) The sound of hard of knocking. (*cf:* **lagaklak**) 1.1) *v. intr.* aN- To make a knocking or rapping sound. *Gana-gana anigangkul batu ilū, ya lling kakal.* In time that stone will make a tapping noise, the sound of a club hitting.

**patigangkul** *v. tr.* To cause something to make a cracking or knocking sound.

**tigas** *adj.* a- Well-dried, of wood. (*Thesaurus:* **t'llas**)

**tigayu'** *v. tr.* -an To do something that requires physical strength (usually with a negative). *Mbal katigayu'an, mbal takole'.* Can't be done, can't be managed. (*Thesaurus:* **aguwanta 1.1, anggap 1, anggop₂, bāng-bāng₁, bogbog₂, kole', gaga**)

**tigbas₁** *n.* Various lizardfishes or sauries, species that live on weedy bottoms in shallow water. *Tigbas itū saddī man kamang, bo' pak'ppang sali'-sali', ma unas ka, ma gusung ka.* Tigbas is different from *kamang*, but they both lie face down, on weeds or sand.

**tigbas₂** *v. tr.* 1) To cut something with a slashing blow. *Bang paragan daing, tinigbas bo' amatay.* If a fish makes a run for it, it is slashed so it dies. 1.1) *v. tr.* -an To remove an illness by ritually slashing some object that represents the cause of the illness. *Buwat a'a ninaga, ya botong maka giyagayna ginantung, tinigbasan bo' ala'an saki.* Like a person made ill by a dragon spirit, a young coconut and its dried flower is hung up, then slashed to remove the illness.

**tigbaw** *n.* A fresh-water pool, usually spring-fed. *Tigbaw, sali' bohe' pagpandihan. Mbal al'mmis, alanu' ma deyom maka aringin.* Tigbaw, like water for bathing in. It is not dirty, it is clean inside, and cold. (*Thesaurus:* **kandung₁, danaw, halo-halo, tangki**)

**tiggan** var. of **tighan**

**tiggup** *adj.* a- 1) Enclosed, of a building. *Kubu'-kubu' itū sat'ggol halam gi' aniya' kapanyapanna. B'nnal atopan, dindingan, b'nnal atiggup saguwā' ngga'i ka gi' luma'.* It's a *kubu'-kubu'* shack so long as it has no equipment. True it has thatch and walls, and true it is all fitted together, but it is not yet a house. (*Thesaurus:* **kumbis 1.1**) 1.1) *v. tr.* To complete the fitting together (of building materials). *Tiggupunbi tōngna karuwampōng, buwat angalinggi'.* Bring both its ends together, as when trawl netting. *Buwat lawang atawa būk, tiniggup.* Like a door or a book, completely closed.

**tighan** (var. **tiggan**) *adj. a-* 1) All at one time; in bulk, of multiple items. *Buwat ka'am atulak, atighan na magtautai'anak.* Like when you leave, the whole family goes together. 1.1) *v. tr.* To treat in bulk; to buy or sell wholesale. *Yuk a'a magdagang wanni, "Tighanun dajapang ilū."* The man selling mangoes said, "Buy the whole bagful." (*Thesaurus:* **kuridas, pakkiyaw, pono' 1.1, sampul-baul**)

**pagtighan** *v. intr. aN-* To act as a unit, as individual people traveling or working together. *Da'a magtiggan, magbalin kita, magsaliyu sehe'.* Let's not go as a group, let's be different, change workmates.

**patighan** *adv.* All together; as a single unit.

**tigi'-tigi'**₁ *adj. a-* 1) On target; precise and focused. *Atigi'-tigi' pahāp bohe' inān am'ttak ni aku. Sali' hal dangan-danganku abase'.* That water is on target, dripping on me. It's like I am the only one getting wet. *Atigi'-tigi' pahāp pagl'ngngananna, minsan du paghinanganna aheka saddī palabayan.* The path he habitually follows is very precise, even though there are many different ways to where he works. *Wa'i atigi' ni lowang.* Straight down the hole. (*Thesaurus:* **taluwa' 1, t'bbong, tudju₂ 1, tumlang 2**) 1.1) *v. intr. pa-* To go directly to an objective or target. 1.2) *v. tr.* To aim directly for a target.

**tigi'-tigi'**₂ *v. tr.* To beat a rhythm on a gong. (*Thesaurus:* **kulanting 1, lisag₂ 1.1, tagunggu', taletek, taratu' 1.1, taroro', tuntung**)

**tigman** *adj. a-* Unfeeling towards people in need of help; uncharitable. *Atigman pahāp a'a inān. Mbal amuwan ai-ai niamu' ni iya e' min tumpukna.* How uncaring that person is. He won't give anything that is requested of him by people from his own house-group.

**tignus** *n.* A jackfruit variety with firm sweet flesh and minimal sticky sap. *Artocarpus heterophyllus. Ahāp nangka' tignus, mbal kita al'mmis. Nangka' loya' itū aheka tagokna.* The tignus jackfruit is good, we don't get dirty. *Loya'* jackfruit has lots of sticky sap. (*gen:* **nangka'**)

**tigpu'** *adj. a-* 1) Broken off at the tip, as a blade. 1.1) *v. tr.* To break the end off something.

**tigtig** *n.* 1) Chips from something solid. (*cf:* **budbud 1**) 1.1) *v. tr.* To chip small pieces off something hard. *Bang aku angā' batu nihinang batu sau, subay tigtigku ko' ahāp luwana.* When I get a rock to make an anchor, I need to chip it off so it looks good. *Bang batu tinigtig, bang kōk katig sinapsapan ko' alampung.* A rock is shaped by chipping; the tip of an outrigger boom is whittled to make it light.

**tigtigan** *n.* Chips or fragments of something hard.

**tigul** *n.* A type of nipa palm, the leaflets of which

are a source of weaving material. *Nipa fruticans. Daun tigul nihinang kadjang pote', ya kadjang niambung-ambung.* Tigul leaflets made into white awning, the woven type of awning. *Tigul, ya pinaka daun sani inān. Tahinang saruk atawa kadjang. Tigul* palm, the fronds of which are like sago palm leaves. They can be made into a hat or an awning. (*Thesaurus:* **nipa', sani**)

**tiguma'** *adj. a-* Gathered into one clump or unit. *Atiguma', atibu'uk na.* Gathered, formed into a single unit.

**tiguway** *v. intr. pa-* To operate a business enterprise on one's own. *Patiguwayan ka dīnu bang ka mbal bilahi asasaw.* Operate on your own if you don't want to have trouble.

**katiguwayan** *n.* The equipment and proceeds of a person working on his own.

**pagtiguway** *v. intr. aN-* To work on one's own. *Gom kita magtiguway. Subay na balik bo' ma ka'a (bang isāb ariki' la'a he' duwangan magpabeya').* Let's work on our own. You should get the catch next time. (Said when the two get only a small catch). (*Thesaurus:* **paghaup, paghūn, pagsapali, pagtintuway, pagtughay 1.1**)

**tihik-tihik** *n.* 1) Generic term for various squirrelfish, a species with large eyes and sharp dorsal spines which includes the Blood-spot squirrelfish, the Samara soldierfish. *Neoniphon samara. B'ngngo' saddī, tihik-tihik saddī, bo' mbal magbidda' to'ongan. B'ngngo'* and *tihik-tihik* [both squirrelfish] are different, but not very. (*spec:* **b'ngngo', ketong, lambe₂, suga-suga₁**) 2) The Striped large-eye bream. *Gnathodontex aurolineatus.*

**tihin** *v. tr. -an* To keep something in place by laying a weight across it. *Bang togong tinihinan maka batu.* If it is a small fish trap, it has a rock to hold it in place. (*Thesaurus:* **pagbangday, pagbaubabag, pagtangday, tahan₂ 1.1**)

**ti'** var. of **tū'**

**ti'il** *adj. a-* Suffering hardship due to famine or maltreatment. *Ati'il kami ma pagkakan, buwat bakwet.* We suffer from lack of food, as evacuees do. (*Thesaurus:* **miskin, tiksa' 1**)

**kati'ilan** *n.* Hardship due to acute lack of essentials. (*Thesaurus:* **kabinasahan, kasigpitan**)

**tilag** *adj. a-* Transparent. (*Thesaurus:* **lere-lere 1.1, sepel, tina'ung, t'llak**)

**tilag-tilag**₁ *n.* A plastic bag. (*syn:* **salopen**)

**tilag-tilag**₂ *v. tr.* To look at something from a place of concealment. *Tilag-tilagta man deyom luma'. Ta'nda'ta bo' kita mbal ta'nda'.* We will look out from inside the house. We will see but we ourselves will not be seen. *Tilag-tilagunbi a'a inān bang sai bay anoho' iya.* Peep out at that person [and find out] who sent him here. (*Thesaurus:* **sīb 1, tandaw 1, tīk 1**)

**tilahak** *adj. a-* Shrill or high-pitched, as the voice in certain religious songs. (*cf:* **pagsilawak**)

**tilam** *n.* A mattress. *Yuk-i, "Palege na ka ma tilam inān. Aniya' du manta pamantanu."* Saying, "Lie down on that mattress. There is a sheet for a bed cover." (*Thesaurus:* **kama, kasul, l'ppus 2**)

**tilas₁** *v. tr.* To perceive; to detect; to become aware of. *Tatilasku ka'a, taga tunang ka.* I am aware of what you are up to, you have a girlfriend now. (*Thesaurus:* **pangannal₁, sakup₁ 1, sayu 1.1, sipat₁ 1.1, tahu**)

  **patilas** *v. tr.* To make known some information.

**tilas₂** *v. tr.* To split bamboo into fine strips in preparation for weaving. *Tinilas itū pinanahut-nahut nihinang bubu, sagō' subay sali'-sali' tilasna bang dakan atawa bukutan.* This word *tilas* involves fine strips to make into a *bubu* trap, but the strips should be the same size for the base or the upper section. *Ya ampa tinilas, mbal gi' nianom.* Only recently split into strips, not yet woven. (*Thesaurus:* **ambuhut, hait, salimi, tai' 1.1**)

**tilaw** *n.* 1) A question. (*Thesaurus:* **paliksa'**) 1.1) *v. ditr.* To ask someone for information. *Tinilaw na aku e' mma'na bang bilahi amangan.* I have now been asked by her father if I want to eat. (*Thesaurus:* **kihaka, hati 2, hodhod, sisi 2, tilosa 1.1**)

  **pagtilaw** *n.* 1) An inquiry; a questioning. *Anabsab saga ni pilang, kalu aniya' panggi' kayu. Bang aniya' takakan, kakanta na, halam aniya' pagtilaw.* We sort of feel around in the fireplace, there might be some cassava. If there is food we eat it, no questions asked. 1.1) *v. tr.* To interrogate or make inquiries of someone. *Pinalinganan saga kaimam-imaman bo' pinagtilaw e'na.* The imams were summoned so he could make inquiries of them. *Magtilaw-tilawan iya dīna, ai bahā' makat'ggolan pambot?* He asked himself, whatever can be making the pambot late?

  **katilaw** *adj. a-* Persistent in asking questions, implying disbelief. (*Thesaurus:* **jakki 1, sumariya, tanya₂**)

**tilaw d'nda** *v. tr.* To initiate inquiries regarding a marriageable girl with a view to courting her. {idiom} *Buwat aku atilaw d'nda, ya tinilawan inān anakku l'lla.* Like when I initiate discussions regarding a girl, it is my son on whose behalf the inquiries are made. *Saupama atilaw kita d'nda, jari binangharan kita ₱300. Bang kita bilahi ma d'nda hē', na angaku na kita. Bang kita mbal angaku, pasebog na kita.* Suppose we inquire about a girl, and the bride price asked is ₱300. If we like the girl then we accept the conditions. If not then we back out. *Bay na tinilaw si Arung.* Someone has asked for Oldest Daughter.

**tilik** *v. tr.* To recite a charm for healing or protection. *Bang aniya' apisu' baranna, subay nihisu' e' a'a ata'u anilik.* If someone has a sprain, he should be treated by someone skilled in reciting charms. (*gen:* **tambang₃ 1**; *Thesaurus:* hisu', tawal 1.1)

**panilik** *n.* A charm protecting an individual against harm.

**tilluk** (var. **tullik**) *v. tr.* To find hidden players in the game of hide-and-seek. *Bang aniya' mital pat'ngge bo' sipa'ta, tatilluk kita.* If there is a can standing up and we happen to kick it, we get found. *Ta'nda'nu bang aku-i anullik ka, tabāk ka.* You see that when I search for you, you're found. *Hatina tatullik si Kulampera', sabab ang'tting si Buntal inān.* So Flounder was found, because Pufferfish puffed himself up. *Sabab aniya' itingku panullikku ka'a.* Because I have spines for finding you with. (*Thesaurus:* **piha 1, piyung**)

  **pagtilluk** *v. intr. aN-* To play hide-and-seek. *Magtilluk-tilluk saga onde'-onde' mareyo' luma'.* The children play hide and-seek under the houses.

**tilosa** *adj. a-* 1) Inquisitive; nosy. 1.1) *v. ditr.* To ask someone for detailed information. *Tinilosa, tinilaw to'ongan.* Interrogated, asked persistently. *Aku ya panilosahannu lling. Kahaka'anku na pa'in, kahaka'anku na pa'in.* I am the one you keep asking about words. I keep telling you and telling you. (*Thesaurus:* **kihaka, hati 2, hodhod, sisi 2, tilaw 1.1**)

**tilud** *adj. a-* 1) Straight, of a material object; aligned. *Daka painay, mbal patilud.* No matter how, it won't be straightened. (*Thesaurus:* **tanus**) 1.1) *v. tr.* To align something; to straighten something that is bent. *Bang bay basi' akello', subay tinilud. Tatilud du.* When wire has been bent out of shape, it should be straightened. It can certainly be straightened. (*Thesaurus:* **bigtang 1.1, b'ttad 1.1, l'dduk 1.1, l'ngngat, lūk, uli'₂**)

  **patilud** *v. tr.* To straighten something's position.

**tima'al** *n.* A forest tree species, a source of useful lumber, fairly resistant to termite damage. (*syn:* **limbunga**)

**timan₁** *v. tr. -an* To throw something away; to discard. *Bay abila' kassa'. Timanin ni dilaut bo' mbal makabakat bang nihūg ma luma'.* The glass broke. Throw it out at sea so that it can't cut [somebody] if dropped from the house. (*Thesaurus:* **badji, bantung 1.1, buwang₁ 1, laruk**)

  **pagtiman₁** *v. intr. aN-* 1) To discard things no longer needed. 1.1) *v. tr. -an* To discard leftovers of food. *Dayas-dayasan, sali' aheka kinakanna. Atas pinagtimanan ya takapin inān, apa a'sso.* Abundant, lots of food. The left-overs had to be thrown out, because [he] was full.

  **pagtimanan** *n.* A place for discarded items; a refuse tip. *A'a dayahan, sali' pagtimanan ai-ai buwat saga lai', na pinuwa' e' saga miskin.* Rich people, [who have] a dump for things such as plates, which are then picked up by poor people.

**timan₂** *v. tr.* To disavow a relationship; to divorce

someone. *Kalasa a'a ina'an ma aku, minsan saga matto'ana tatiman na he'na.* That man's love for me is such that he has even rejected his parents. (*cf:* **bitu'anun**)

**pagtiman₂** *v. intr. aN-* To be separated, of people previously married. *Baya' sigā dangan-duwa magtiman.* It was their desire, individually and together, to divorce. *Bang aniya' bay magtiman maglakibini, pinapagbalik he' saga matto'a sigā.* When a married couple have divorced, their elders get them to go back [to their married state].

**timan-gantung** *n.* A divorce which is not yet finalized.

**timayuk** *n.* **1)** A serving of cooked rice wrapped for individual guests after a funeral meal. *Tamparung maka timayuk, hal buwas bīlla, halam aniya' lamudna. Tinimayuk bang hinang tapus. Magtamparung itu magkawin, ni'isi ni tambusa'.* *Tamparung* and *timayuk* are just cooked rice, nothing mixed in. It is [called] *timayuk* in the context of the meal that concludes a time of mourning. *Tamparung* is a wedding feature, [food] put into a coconut leaflet container. (*Thesaurus:* **tambusa', tamparung 1, tamu**) **1.1)** *v. tr.* To wrap cooked rice in a large leaf. *Daun jati' pagtimayukan.* Teak leaves used for wrapping food taken home by guests.

**timbak** *n.* **1)** An explosive. (*cf:* **bām**) **1.1)** *v. tr.* To stun fish using dynamite. *Piland'ppa lalom panimbakan tulay?* How many fathoms is the depth for dynamiting scad? **2)** A firearm. **2.1)** *v. tr.* To shoot something with a firearm. *Bang aku tinimbak e' a'a bo' akapal dinding, pasapat timbak, mbal makalanjal pareyom.* If someone shoots at me but the wall of the house is thick, the bullet is impeded and does not go all the way through.

**pagtimbak** *v. intr. aN-* To let off firecrackers. *Na aheka magtimbak maka ba'anan kulitis. Tinimbakan kulitis na.* So lots of people were letting off masses of firecrackers. Firecrackers were ignited.

**timbak-daing** *n.* Dynamite used in fishing. *Timbak-daing, pine'esan.* Fishing dynamite, ignited. *Bay iya taluwa' timbak-daing, hangkan iya aku'il.* He was hit by fish dynamite, that is why he is crippled.

**panimbakan** *n.* The distance covered by a bullet from a rifle, an approximate unit of distance.

**timbak p'ttung** *n. phrase* A bamboo cannon. (*syn:* **lantaka 1.1**)

**timbakkol** (*var.* **tibokkol**) *adj. zero* Compacted; dense; unbroken, of cloud cover. (*cf:* **herot**)

**timbag** *v. tr.* To hit a target on the ground with something thrown. (*cf:* **laruk**; *Thesaurus:* **balibag₁, balleng 1.1, sigung**)

**pagtimbag** *n.* **1)** The game of timbag, in which an object, often a spinning top, is thrown at a target. **1.1)** *v. intr. aN-* To play timbag.

*Magtimbag kita maka gasing-gasing.* We play *timbag* using spinning tops.

**timbalun₁** *n.* **1)** An intensely painful condition thought to be of supernatural origin. *Sinōd timbalun pali'ku.* The *timbalun* affliction has entered my wound. *Bang ab'ttong si Su, pa'abay timbalunna.* When Su was pregnant, her *timbalun* condition accompanied it [the fetus]. (*Thesaurus:* **banta', boggat, sangti'**) **1.1)** *v. advrs. -in-* Suffering from the timbalun condition. *Bay aku ni iskul mint'dda, bay aku tinimbalun. Ap'ddi' b'ttongku, mbal kasandalan.* When I first went to school I suffered a *timbalun* attack. My stomach ached unbearably.

**timbalun₂** *n.* A sea animal, similar to an anemone but without the typical tendrils.

**timbalun-batu** *n.* A species of timbalun without tendrils, found in coral complexes.

**timbalun-deyo'** *n.* A deepwater species of timbalun.

**timbalun-gusung** *n.* A species of timbalun growing on sandy bottoms.

**timbang₁** **1)** *v. tr.* To weigh something using a balance beam. *Tinimbang e'na bu'unna, jari buhatna saga duwa kilo.* He weighed his hair and its weight was about 2 kilos. (*cf:* **kilu 1.1**) **2)** *v. tr.* To carry out a weighing ceremony for a sickly child, usually in fulfillment of a vow made to God or ancestors in anticipation of healing. *Onde'-onde' tinimbang bang ariki'-diki' bo' bay asaki. Pinagnajalan, tinimbang ma bulan Hailaya.* A child weighed when small due to being ill. She is made the subject of a vow, and weighed during the month of Hailaya. **3)** *v. intr. aN-* To shift the load in order to trim a canoe. *Animbang ka pehē'.* Shift your weight over there.

**pagtimbang** **1)** *n.* A state of balance or equilibrium. **1.1)** *v. intr. aN-* To be in a balanced state. *Magtimbang tahik subu maka tahik ugtu-llaw.* Morning tides and mid-day tides are in balance. **2)** *v. intr. aN-* To balance a beam scale, as in certain healing rituals. *Magtimbang sigā aheka hōs bo' mbal na saki.* They were balancing the scale with a whole lot of sarongs so there would no longer be any sickness. **3)** *v. intr. aN-* To sort out one's memories. *Aniya' subahatku, agtimbang tomtomku.* I have made a vow, balancing the things I remember.

**timbang bibitan** *adj. zero* Treated impartially as when sharing resources. {idiom} *Nsa' pagkengkeng, nsa' pagbokol, timbang-bibitan, pinagsali'-sali'.* Neither little toe nor big toe, shared equally, treated impartially. *Timbang-bibitan lasanu ma sigā duwangan.* Your love to the two of them is even-handed.

**timbang-patay** *n.* A life and death situation, due to severe illness; a life-threatening gap between income and the cost of basic supplies.

**timbangan₁** *n.* A beam scale. *Da'a kam animbang ma duwa timbangan ya mbal magsali'* *timbanganna.* Do not measure a weight with two beams whose scales are not identical. (*cf:* **kiluhan**)

**timbang**₂ *n.* The place far from land where the sea floor falls away into the depths. *Am'lli aku bulbul manuk panonda'ku mangku' ni timbang. Bang mbal maka'ā', palagesles ni timbang dakayu'.* I will buy rooster feathers to troll for bonito in the open sea. If I don't get anything I drift to another deep area. *Mbal pasamod palig, wa'i palisig ni timbang.* Surgeonfish don't co-occur [with other fish]; they slip into the depths. *Ya timbang ta'nda'ta lahat hal bitu-bitu. Kayuna magbitu-bitu.* The distant depths where we see the land as nothing more than specks. Its trees are what appear as specks. (*Thesaurus:* **kablangan, kaladjun, dilaut, s'llang**₁)

**timbangan**₂ *n.* The side of a person's torso from the armpit down. *P'ngkong, min b'ttong sa' tabowa pi'itu ni timbanganta.* A swelling, from the stomach but extending out here to our flanks. (*syn:* **kīd**₁ 1)

**timbay** *v. intr. pa-* 1) To pass close by something; to call in on while passing. *Hal bay patimbay, hal bay palambung.* Just going past, just appearing briefly. *Amodjongan la bang lum'ngngan. Atimbay saga, ma llot pal'ngngan maka lahi-lahi. Ma llot alallay maka al'kkas.* Just moving quickly when walking. Sort of bypassing; between walking and running, between slow and quick. (*Thesaurus:* **labay**₁ 1, **likuwad** 1.1, **liyus** 1.1, **paglipuwas, pagsulabay, pintas** 1) 1.1) *v. tr. -an* To bypass something. *Animbayan kita luma' si Anu.* We will bypass What's-his-name's house.

**timbayan** *n.* The player who gets dealt the first card.

**timb'llang** *see:* **pagtimb'llang**

**timb'llun** *v. advrs. -in-* To be adversely affected (e.g. loss of energy or poor fishing) by the pregnancy of a near relative.

**timbul** *v. intr. pa-* To join with another household. *Angay ka mbal patimbul ni luma' anakku si An?* Why don't you go and live in your daughter An's house? *Patimbul sigām kamemon bang aniya' kinatāwan.* They all gather in the same place when there is something to be frightened about.

**pagtimbul** *v. intr. aN-* To be united in marriage. *Magtimbul kami pabīng, nīntanan kami batang-batang.* We were reunited [after a separation], with restrictions placed on us. *Magtimbul anakku inān maka anakku itū.* That daughter of yours and this son of mine are joining in marriage.

**timbun** *n.* The tidying of a grave on the seventh day of a mourning sequence. (*cf:* **Taiti'**)

**timbun-tambak** *adj. a-* Piled up high.

**timbungan** *n.* 1) Generic term for various goatfishes. *Parupeneus spp.* 2) The Sixbar angelfish. *Pomacanthus sexstriatus (Euxiphipops sexstriatus).*

**timbungan-gadja** *n.* The Fivebar goatfish. *Parupeneus multifasciatus.*

**timbungan-lahusu'** *n.* The Goldsaddle goatfish. *Parupeneus cyclostomus.*

**timbungan-lanus** *n.* The Dot-and-dash goatfish. *Parupeneus barberinus.*

**timbungan-pangguwa'** *n.* The Doublebar goatfish. *Parupeneus trifasciatus.*

**timbungan-pote'** *n.* The Blacksaddle goatfish. *Parupeneus fraterculus.*

**timbungan-sairap** *n.* The Cinnabar goatfish. *Parupeneus heptaecanthus.*

**timbungan-samehakan** *n.* The Bicolor goatfish. *Parupeneus barberinoides.*

**timbungan-s'llang** *n.* The Indian goatfish. *Parupeneus indicus.*

**timbungan-takot** *n.* The Blackspot goatfish. *Parupeneus pleurostigma.*

**timpa** *v. ditr.* To transfer work load or responsibility over to someone else.

**pagpatimpa** *v. intr. aN-* To transfer responsibility or blame from one to the other. (*Thesaurus:* **balik**₂, **bīng**₃, **bitung, hili, likid, pagbintu, pelleng** 1.2)

**timpang** *var. of* **tempang**

**timpas** *v. tr. -an* To trim a sail for optimum speed. *Na bang bay baliyu, animpasan, amiluk, pinatūt na.* Now when it has been windy, the sail is reset, we change tack, allow [the canoe] to run before the wind. (*Thesaurus:* **agod, biluk** 1.1, **bintung** 1, **kabig, kauk**)

**timpla** *var. of* **templa**

**timpū** *var. of* **bāt-timpū**

**timpu** (*var.* **tempo**) *n.* 1) A period of time; a season; an era. *Bay kami alahi ni pū', timpu Jipun lagi'.* We escaped to the outer islands during the Japanese occupation. *Yuk mbo'ku, halam kono' dragadik tempo awal-jaman ē'.* My grandparent said there were no drug addicts in the olden times. *Subay ta'abut tempona abō' alandos ulan.* Its season has to come for there to be heavy rain. (*cf:* **ahil, awal**₁; *Thesaurus:* **awal ni ahil, jāman, masa** 1, **taem, waktu** 1) 1.1) *v. tr. -an* To set a period of time, as a jail sentence.

**timpus** *v. tr.* To persist; to continue without pause. *Bang kita angusaha animpus kita dang'llaw. Subu-subu pam'ssita ni kakohapan.* When we work we keep at it all day. Our fishing goes from early morning to late afternoon. *Animpus ulan itū, mbal pahali dang'llaw.* This rain will set in, it won't let up for a day. *Landu' iya asusa angkan iya angamu'-ngamu' ni Tuhan, animpus dasangom inān.* He was very troubled which is why he prayed to God, through that entire night. (*Thesaurus:* **sangdan** 1)

**timpuwad** *adj. a-* 1) Toppled; fallen down flat. *Atimpuwad na luma', wa'i paligid.* The house is toppled, it has fallen down. (*cf:* **puwad**; *Thesaurus:* **hantak**₁ 1, **h'bba', ligad, lintuwad**

1, **pungkad**) **1.1)** *v. tr.* To cause something to fall over.

**timtim** *v. tr.* To eat a tiny amount of something; to get a small share. *Mampa'in aku minulka'an bang aku makatimtim ai-ai ma halam gi' pas'ddop llaw!* May I be cursed if I eat a single thing before sunset! (*Thesaurus:* **kinam 1, ssa₁ 1.3, sulay₁ 2**)

**timuk** *adj. a-* **1)** To be gathered in one place. *Buwat holen, minsan bay atimuk, akanat pabīng.* Like marbles, scattered again even though they had been collected in one place. **1.1)** *v. intr. pa-* To come together. *Itiya' patimuk pi'itu tina'ita, sali' kita asso.* Here's our gut coming together right here, like we are full from eating. *Patimuk kām pi'itu, saga onde'.* Gather here, you children. (*Thesaurus:* **aro' 1, harung-harung, sahubu**) **1.2)** *v. tr.* To gather people or things in one place. *Mikiampun isāb aku bang yampa aku anulat buwattina'an... tu'ud aku bay animuk kosogku.* I also ask pardon that I have only just now written... I was simply gathering my strength [to write].

**katimukan** *n.* A collection of people.

**pagtimuk** *v. intr. aN-* **1)** To gather around an item or event of interest. *Magabut-abut sigām magtimuk ma sakalibutna min subu-subu sampay ni kasangoman.* They kept gathering around him from early morning until night. (*Thesaurus:* **paghimpun, pagmairan 1.1, pulin, pūn 1.1**) **1.1)** *v. tr. -an* To overwhelm someone by crowding around. *Pinagtimuk-timukan si Mām bang pasōd ni deyom tinda.* Ma'am is overcrowded when she goes into a store. (*Thesaurus:* **pagkubu-kubu, paglundug**; *syn:* **pagtipun 1**)

**papagtimuk** *v. tr.* To make someone part of an assembled group.

**patimuk** *v. tr.* To bring things together in a single group.

**timuk-timuk puhu'** *n. phrase* A crowd of people. *Ai ni'nda' ma timuk-timuk puhu' hē'?* What is to be seen in that crowd of people?

**timud** *adj. a-* **1)** Well-cleaned, of a surface. *B'nnal bay kinose'an saga pamanganan bo' amasi saga buwas amalit, halam atimud. Hatina halam atimud e'na angose'.* It's true the things we ate from were washed, but there was still rice scattered around, not wiped clean. In other words he hadn't washed up cleanly. *Magtūy atimud bayhu'na, bay binagongan.* His face was immediately well-cleaned, it had been shaved. **1.1)** *v. tr.* To wipe or scrape clean the surface of a plate or clothing. *Timurun lai ilū maka suru'.* Clean those plates off with a spoon. (*Thesaurus:* **kulling, linug₂**)

**timul** *n.* An east to southeast wind, generally unfavorable for sailing. (*gen:* **baliyu 1**)

**timun** *n.* A watermelon. *Citrullus vulgaris.*

**timun-timun** *n.* **1)** A device for raising heavy items, as a crane or a block and tackle. **1.1)** *v. tr.* To raise something with a lifting device. *Buwat lansa inān tinimun-timun pariyata'.* Like that launch raised up with a crane.

**panimun-timunan** *n.* The machinery of a crane; a block and tackle.

**timus-timus** *n.* Salt left by evaporation of sea-water, as on one's skin. *Akasap na baranku kamemon. Akatol ya timus-timus tahik, sali' asin ariki'-diki'.* My entire body is roughened. The evaporated sea-water is itchy, like fine salt. *Bang kita bay atuhun bo' halam magtipara, pagtuwa'ta asaplut kita ko da'a kapē'an timus-timus.* When we have been diving and haven't worn goggles, on emerging [our eyes] are rinsed so sea-salt doesn't adhere. (*cf:* **asin 1**)

**tina'i** *n.* Intestines; guts. *Magsaddi tina'i. Tina'ibi akiput-kiput, tina'i kami aluha.* Intestines differ. Yours are quite constricted, ours are broad. *Sisikun daing hē', tina'ina tula'un.* Scale that fish, its intestines are to be cooked with herbs. *Karugsu'an pa'in iya ma b'ttongna, magtūy pahudhud tina'ina tudju tana'.* Having been stabbed in the stomach, his entrails quickly gushed out onto the ground. (*cf:* **longon-longon**)

**tina'ung** *adj. a-* Transparent; clear, of water. (*Thesaurus:* **sepel, tilag, t'llak**)

**tinanom** (derivative of **tanom₁**) *n.* Planted things. *Minsan buwattingga pagtuyu'nu maghinang ma tana', mbal ajatu tinanomnu.* No matter how diligently you work your land, your plants will not be productive.

**tinangkaw** (derivative of **tangkaw**) *adv.* Stealthily; unnoticed; undetected. *Sinaggaw banag bang binalutan buli'na tinangkaw.* A dragonfly can be caught when its tail is grabbed undetected.

**tinapa** (derivative of **tapa**) *n.* Roasted or grilled food, especially fish.

**tinapay** *n.* Bread. *Tinapay batu palit.* Bread [solid] like the sinkers of a fish trap. (*cf:* **matsakaw**; *syn:* **pān**)

**pagtinapayan** *n.* An oven (for baking bread). *Bay alūs si Ji ma pagtinapayan.* Ji got burnt on the oven.

**tinda** (var. **tindahan**) *n.* A store which sells general merchandise and where prices are fixed (in contrast to one where bargaining is the norm). *Tinda pitu' lawangna.* A store with seven doors [said of a large department store]. (*Thesaurus:* **kadday, estawran, pasal₂ 1, tabu' 1, tiyanggi**)

**tinda-basal** *n.* An emporium; a shop characterized by departments and fixed prices. *Tinda-basal, mbal kita pajawab ai-ai bay nihalga'an.* Fixed price stores where we aren't allowed to bargain on anything that has been priced.

**tindak** *v. tr. -an* **1)** To kick something with the sole of one's foot. *Niangay aku tindakannu? Dusahan aku?* Why are you kicking me? Have I done something wrong? (*Thesaurus:* **binti', sipa' 1,**

**tagdok) 1.1)** To stamp the feet as in dancing. *Keyol-keyolin tangannu, tindak-tindakin tape'nu.* Move your hands and stamp your feet in time [advice to dancers].

**tindakan** *n.* A block partway up a mast that bears the sprit that supports the upper end of a quadrilateral sail. *Tindakan, ya pamaragtolan tape' tuklug. Tindakan,* the block which supports the lower end of the sprit. (*Thesaurus:* **takāk, taruk, tukag, tuklug 1**)

**tindahan** var. of **tinda**

**tindan-tindan** *adj. zero* United in some activity or state; of one mind. *Bang aniya' tabinasa saga anaktam subay isāb kita angatu. Subay kita tindan-tindan kamemon, sali' pagbeya'an kamemon.* If children of ours are mistreated we should oppose it. We should all be united, all of us in accord. *Bang maguyun kamemon, ya he' niōnan magbagimbin. Bang dusa dangan subay dusa kamemon. Yukta, "Tindan-tindan."* When everyone agrees, that is called *magbagimbin.* If one sins it should be the sin of all. We say, "All together." (*cf:* **pagbagimbin**)

**tindaw** *v. advrs.* -*in*- Experiencing one's first menstruation. (*Thesaurus:* **bulan₄, laha'₁ 2**)

**tindayung** *v. tr.* -*an* To propel a boat using a paddle against a fulcrum; to row. (*Thesaurus:* **busay 1.1, kelle 1.1, dayung 1.1, epe, luwad**)

**pagtindayung** *v. intr. aN-* 1) To work together in rowing a boat. *Gom pa'in sigām amuspus magtindayung kalu makasampay ni bihing.* Instead they put their energy into rowing that they might perhaps reach the shore. 2) To swim on one's back using an overarm stroke. (*cf:* **paglangi**)

**tindera** *n.* A female shop assistant, especially in a larger establishment like a department store. *Bay aku am'lli ni tindahan. Pagsōngku sīn hē', pag'nda' e' tindera, "Gillo'ak sīnnu ilu."* I was buying something at a shop. When I handed over the money and the shop assistant saw it, she said, "This money is counterfeit."

**tinduk₁** *v. tr.* To strike at a bait or lure. *Tininduk aku he' kandelan ati binowa paraw palahi-lahi, magbibud buli'-munda'.* A swordfish took my bait and the canoe was dragged racing away, stern and bow turning end for end. *Am'ssi pa'in si Jo ni Serom tininduk he' dapak. Agtūy nihella' he'na.* While Jo was fishing out towards Serom Island, a humpback snapper took his bait. He promptly pulled it in. *Engkotanta kulambut ni tōng tonda'. Pagtinduk daing, kasabitan na, sakali itū wa'i ang'bba.* We tie a dropper to the end of the trolling-line. When the fish strikes it is hooked, and then suddenly lets go.

**tinduk₂** *n.* A species of large fish. *Buwat tinduk bo' aheya, bang asekot na ni pelang subay tinabang maka sahapang atawa sangkil.* Like a large *tinduk* fish, when it gets close to the canoe it needs to be helped up with a fish spear or harpoon.

**tinduk₃** var. of **saging-tinduk**

**tinerol** *n.* A table fork. (*syn:* **tugsuk 1**)

**tininti** *n.* A lieutenant (military rank). (*Thesaurus:* **kapitan, komandel, jeneral**)

**tinompe'** (derivative of **tompe'**) *n.* A pancake of cassava or sago meal. (*gen:* **apam 1**).

**tinoro-toro** (derivative of **toro-toro**) *adv.* Continuously; without a pause. *Animbak tinoro-toro, mbal nihondongan.* Firing repeatedly without pause, not letting up. *Tinoro-toro e'na anangis.* He cries without a break.

**tintuway** *v. intr. pa-* To be engaged in a small business enterprise such as fishing.

**pagtintuway** *v. intr. aN-* To work in partnership. (*Thesaurus:* **paghaup, paghūn, pagsapali, pagtiguway, pagtughay 1.1**)

**tinu'** *adj. a-* Damp, of salt or salted items. *Atinu' asin, mbal manjari. Taluwa' isāb bang yukta tinau' daing; bay atoho', abase' na pabīng.* The salt is wet and useless. It's also appropriate to say that fish is *tinu'*; it was dry and is wet again.

**tinu'anan** *n.* A dip (spicy liquid mixture) of vinegar, garlic, ginger, and chilli peppers. *Tinuna'an itū pan'nno'an, pangā'anta ssa. Tinu'anan* is something food is dipped in, for us to get flavor from. (*Thesaurus:* **bubuk₂, kilaw 1, lawal 1.1, pan'nno'an**)

**tinula'** (derivative of **tula'**) *n.* A stew of fish or meat seasoned with herbs.

**tinga** *n.* 1) A down payment in confirmation of a commitment to buy. (*syn:* **tinggal-kapin**) **1.1)** *v. tr.* -*an* To secure a transaction by making a down payment. *Ma b'lli tana' yukku ni a'a, "Ya itu tingaku ni ka'a dahū."* In buying land I say to the man, "This is my initial down-payment to you." (*Thesaurus:* **bayad 1.1, gadji 1.1, hokas, lampak₁ 1.1, susuk, tulahan, tunay₂, tungbas 1**)

**tingan** *v. intr. aN-* To reside temporarily in a place other than one's own house. *Kaōnan isāb aningan dantahun, basta ngga'i ka ma luma'na.* It can be called *tingan* for a year, so long as it is not in one's own house. *Aniya' isāb daing aningan ma kabatuhan.* There are also fish staying for a while in a rocky area. (*Thesaurus:* **hanti' 1, lihan 1, pustu 1.1, tingkap**)

**paninganan** *n.* 1) A temporary shelter built of local materials. **1.1)** *v. tr.* To use as a temporary shelter. *Sat'ggol halam gi' aniya' pam'lli kapanyapan subay tiningkap dahū. Tapaninganan isāb.* As long as there is still no money to buy materials we must first put up a temporary shelter. It can be lived in.

**tingaw-tingaw** *v. intr. aN-* To gleam, of water through which light is shining. *Aningaw-tingaw deyom bohe' bang subu.* The depths of the well gleam in the morning. (*Thesaurus:* **kiraw, kitaw-kitaw, illap, inggat, pagpillaw-pillaw, pagsinglab**)

**tingka** *adj. zero* Different, of the fall of coins in a

game of two-up. (*Thesaurus:* **agad₂, pagkabit, pagsalla'** 1.1, **pagtalang, sulang₂**)

**tingkal** *n.* Fine sewing thread of nylon or silk. *Buyung kulaet ilū anahut-nahut tingkalna, subay a'aslag.* The mantle of that pressure lantern, its thread is too fine, it should be coarser. (*Thesaurus:* **bannang, jiyay, tanud**)

**tingkap** *v. tr.* To build a temporary shelter using locally available materials. *Sat'ggol halam gi' aniya' pam'lli kapanyapan subay tiningkap dahū. Tapaninganan isāb.* As long as there is still no money to buy materials we must first put up a temporary shelter. It can be lived in. (*Thesaurus:* **hanti'** 1, **lihan** 1, **pustu** 1.1, **tingan**)

**tingkas** *v. tr.* -*an* To remove a wall of a house, as to show that the house has nothing of value in it. *Tiningkasan luma' bo' mbal sinōd saitan amahana' ba.* The house has a wall removed so a *saitan* spirit won't haunt it.

**tingk'llos** *v. tr.* To secure a rope with a half-hitch. *Tingk'llosku buli' pelang bang engkotanku bo' mbal magbalibag.* I will put a hitch around the stern of the canoe when I moor it, so that it doesn't keep swinging to one side.

**tingkō'** 1) *v. intr. aN-* To sit. *Bay kami magt'nggehan ma pantān, manda' sinagina sinō' aningkō'.* We were standing around on the porch, but fortunately we were greeted and told to sit down. (*Thesaurus:* **lesseg, tongngol**) 2) *v. tr.* -*an* To keep watch over someone newly deceased. *Ya kasusahanku halam bay katingkō'anku mma'ku.* My sorrow is that I wasn't able to keep watch over my father [when he died]. (*cf:* **pagjaga** 1.1)

**pagtingkō'** *v. intr. aN-* 1) To be gathered in formal session (seated), of an assembly. 1.1) *v. tr.* -*an* To discuss an issue in formal assembly. *D'nda itū mbal bilahi amole' ni h'llana, subay pinagtingkō'an.* This woman does not want to return to her husband, [the matter] will have to be discussed formally.

**tingkō'an** *n.* A place to sit down, as a chair or seat of any kind.

**paningkō'an** *n.* Something to sit on, as a chair or seat. (*Thesaurus:* **bangku', kulsi, siya**)

**tingku'** *v. tr.* -*an* 1) To treat something carelessly. 1.1) *v. advrs. ka-...-an* To be treated carelessly or roughly (usually with a negative). *Buwat ka'a, mbal katingku'-tingku'an magtūy anangis.* Like you, one can't be harsh with you, you immediately cry. (*syn:* **tiyu'-tiyu'**)

**tingkuwang** *v. tr.* To return the bride to her parents' house on the second day after a wedding, marking the end of the wedding ceremony. *Subay tingkuwang bo' akatis pagkawinan.* There should be the *tingkuwang* so that the wedding is completed. *Simudday tinūran pi'itu, tiningkuwang tudju ni Siganggang.* The day after tomorrow the bride will be returned here, to her parents' house in

Siganggang. (*cf:* **paghulay**)

**tingga'** *n.* Lead (the metal). *Ya tingga' itū bo' binowa pareyo' panuhunan tipay bo' al'kkas.* This lead weight takes us down to the oyster diving place, so we are quick. *Bang ma pokot, lampo'na min pataw tudju ni tingga'.* With a haul net its *lampo'* is the depth from floats to lead weights. (*cf:* **lambat** 1, **larung** 1)

**tingga' dawa** *phrase* Perish the thought. {idiom} (*syn:* **s'lle' bale puhu'**)

**tingga'-tingga'-lumahan** *n.* A mackerel-like fish species that secretes a highly toxic substance which can cause death soon after eating. *Buwat si Ina' bay nilango tingga'-tingga'-lumahan, akansing emponna. Bay sinorokan banglut.* Like the time when Mom was poisoned from eating false-mackerel, and her teeth clamped tight together. They forced in a piece of *banglut* [a medicinal plant].

**tinggal** *n.* The unpaid component of a payment. *Halam du isāb jukup, aniya' lagi' tinggalna ma paginrolna.* It wasn't complete either, there was a shortage in her enrolment fees. *Tinggal itū kakapinan. Tinggal* is what is left to pay.

**tinggal-kapin** *n.* The token payment of a debt or the fulfilment of a commitment. *Bang aniya' bay tau'ta ai-ai buwat suray maka polmed, bo' halam mahē' suray, tinggal-kapin polmed.* If we have stored something or other like a comb and hair-oil, but the comb is not there, then the hair-oil is the partial fulfilment [of the responsibility]. (*syn:* **tinga** 1)

**tinggaung** *n.* The Philippine civet cat. *Paradoxorus philippinensis. Tinggaung, anganiyang-nganiyang matana, ataha' kukkuna.* The civet cat; its eyes glare frighteningly, its claws are long. (*syn:* **kuting-kubing**)

**tinggi₁** *adj. zero* Of great height or rank.

**mahatinggi** *adj. zero* High, of social rank.

**pagmahatinggi** *v. intr. aN-* To act as though superior, of someone trying to rise above his fellows. *Magmahatinggi iya, palabi iya min kasehe'an.* He puts himself above others, goes beyond the rest. *Saitan magmahatinggi, maglanga-langa dīna.* A *saitan* spirit who acts as though exalted, making himself high. (*Thesaurus:* **pagabbu** 1.1, **pagbantug-bantug, pagheya-heya, pagmalangkahi, pagpasanglit, pagtāp-tāp**)

**tinggi₂** *n.* A side bet on the fall of individual playing cards, made by observers of the game.

**pagtinggi** *v. tr.* To bet on the fall of individual playing cards, as onlooker or player. *Bang magsugal magtinggi dangan atawa duwangan. Magtūk sigā ma luwasan.* When people are playing cards, one or two may bet on the fall of the cards. They place their bets outside [the game]. (*Thesaurus:* **kōl** 1.1, **hapus₁** 1.1, **talu₁, tumba₂** 1.1)

**tinggil** *v. intr. pa-* **1)** To step up on something in order to gain height. *Patinggil ka ni bahaku bang ka mbal tum'kkad pakapo' apa alalom.* Get up on my shoulders if you can't touch the bottom and wade because of the depth. **2)** To gain the upper hand in litigation or negotiation. *Makatinggil ka. Bay na ka magbono' maka h'ndanu. Nihukum ka ati ka'a-i anganda'ug.* You have gained the advantage. You had a dispute with your wife. You were judged and you won. *Makatinggil ka ma da'uhanna. Ka'a bay parahū ni sara'.* You got the advantage ahead of him. You got to the magistrate first.

  **pagtinggil-l'bbak** *v. intr. aN-* To form ruts across a path or slope.

  **patinggilan** *n.* Anything one steps on to gain height; a stand for objects such as a lamp. (*cf:* **pan'nggehan**)

**tinggil-batu** *n.* The Scorpion fish. *Dendroscorpaena sp.*

**tingting** *n.* **1)** The sound of a bell ringing. **1.1)** *v. tr.* To ring a bell. (*syn:* **bagting 1.1**)

**tipara** (var. **tupara**) *n.* **1)** Diving goggles. *Tipara itū binowa patuhun pareyo' anuhun tulay.* Goggles are used when diving down for scad. If you had dived for it wouldn't be lost. *Buwat nā'annu min suntu'an atawa nā'annu ladjawan ya tupara hē'.* Like when you get it from a pattern or you get those goggles as a model. (*cf:* **samin-mata**) **1.1)** *v. tr.* To fish with the aid of diving goggles. *Wa'i anipara si Kulas inān. Pagtipara itū, makabāk dakayu' kuhita'.* Away went Kulas [a character in a folk-story] wearing diving goggles. Using goggles he found one octopus. *Bang kita angambit subay bowata batu maka lubid. Pinatuntun batu pareyo', nihagul. Minsan k'llat pinabale-bale. Aniya' anipara, ati nihella' kaleya.* When we drive fish into a fenced area we need to take stones and cord. The stones are lowered and jigged up and down. Even ropes attached to stakes [are used]. Some people use goggles and the catch is hauled shorewards.

  **pagtipara** *v. intr. aN-* To use diving goggles. *Bang kita bay atuhun bo' halam magtipara, pagtuwa'ta asaplut kita sabab tahik, ko da'a kapē'an timus-timus.* When we have been diving and haven't worn goggles, on emerging [our eyes] are rinsed because it is seawater, so sea-salt doesn't get in.

**tipas-tipas** *n.* Decorative pennants. (*cf:* **jambay**; *Thesaurus:* **bandila', panji, sambulayang**)

**tipay** *n.* Various non-spiny oysters including the oyster shell known as mother-of-pearl. *fam. Pteriidae.* (*cf:* **mussa'**)

  **tipay-batu** *n.* Rock oyster species. *gen. Saccostrea.*

**tipi** var. of **tipid**

**tipid** (var. **tipi**) **1)** *adj. a-* Dangerously near an edge. *Atipid pat'nna'anna, subay ma t'ngnga', subay da'a ma bihing.* Where it sits is dangerously close to an edge. It should be in the middle, not on the edge. *Da'a patipihun bang ka amat'nna' ai-ai.* Don't place things right near the edge when you put them down. *Da'a patipid-tipirun ko da'a palisig.* Don't place it close to the edge lest it slip off. *Bang buwat aniya' bay pat'nna'ta bo' pamat'nna'anta inān atipid. Na bo' aniya' pal'ngngan bo' ajogjog ya bay pamat'nna'an ē' bo' ahūg. Ya hē' niōnan palisig.* Like when we put something down but the place were it is put is near and edge. Then if someone walks by and the place shakes where the thing was put and it falls, that's called *lisig* [slipping off]. **2)** *v. intr. aN-* To come close to daylight. *Anipi na ni llaw, sōng na llaw sali'. Sōng na akeyat sobangan.* Coming to daylight, soon to be day as it were. The east is about to be lit up.

**tipopok** *n.* A tapered spike (a fid) for use in weaving cane or bamboo.

**tipu** *n.* **1)** Deceit; fraud; treachery. **1.1)** *v. tr.* To attack someone by stealth or treachery. *Bang aniya' bantanu painsap ka ko da'a tinipu.* If you have an enemy be watchful, so you aren't attacked by stealth. *Bay aniya' bangka'ku tinipu tinangkaw.* I had a dugout canoe stolen secretly. (*Thesaurus:* **ambus, hapa' 1.2, holdap, ingu, sipi₁ 1.1**)

  **pagtipu** *v. intr. aN-* To behave deceitfully; to do something on the sly. *Magtipu-tipuhan duwa sultan inān, amangan dalamesahan sagō' sali'-sali' amikil kala'atan.* Those two kings were behaving deceitfully, eating at the same table but both thinking bad things toward the other.

  **panipu** *n.* Treachery; ambush.

**tipun** *adj. a-* **1)** Assembled; congregated. *Atipun na a'a maina'an kamemon.* All the people were assembled there. **1.1)** *v. intr. pa-* To congregate; to form a group. *Jari aniya' patipun ni Nabi Nū l'lla maka d'nda min binangsa kaginisan kamemon.* So there were males and females gathering around the Prophet Noah from all species of creatures. **1.2)** *v. tr. -an* To gather things together. *Tipunanta saga batu panambak luma'.* We will gather some coral rock for building up the house foundations.

  **pagtipun** *v. intr. aN-* **1)** To combine as a group. (*syn:* **pagtimuk 1.1**) **1.1)** *v. tr.* To combine separate items into a single entity or mass. *Niranos itū, pinagtipun sali'.* Danos is like being combined in one clump.

**tira** *v. tr.* To strike a disc or ball with a cue, in a game such as pool. *Bang kita anira ni ngga'i ka kulangta, pabelawta ya sehe'ta.* When we strike a disc that is not our own, we tease our opponents. (*Thesaurus:* **bulitin, kulang₂, pūl, tako**)

  **pagtira** *n.* **1)** Something used as a cue in playing pool. *Tako inān pagtira.* That cue is for shooting discs. **1.1)** *v. intr. aN-* To use a cue to strike a ball or puck.

**tira-tira** *n.* A stick of soft toffee.

**tiranan** *n.* A reason; a purpose. *Ainu-inu isāb iya bang bay angay, na, haka'anku na iya tirananna.* She too was surprised about what had happened, so I told her reason for it all. *In sapda' halam aniya' tiranna, halam aniya' kamaujuranna.* A meaningless curse has no effective outcome. (*Thesaurus:* **kamatti, gawi 1, hadjat₁, maksud 1**)

**tirigu** *n.* **1)** Wheat, the grain from which flour is made. **2)** Flour other than rice or corn meal. (*Thesaurus:* **ata', tapung 1**)

**tiring** *see:* **patiring**

**tīs** *v. intr. pa-* To drip or fall in small amounts. *Patīs hulasna.* His perspiration is dripping down. (*Thesaurus:* **p'ttak 1.1, sū₂, titis 1.1, tū'**)

**pagtīs** *v. intr. aN-* To be losing water through small leaks. *Magtīs kibut itū, sali' al'ssa'.* This earthenware jar leaks, like it's cracked.

**tisa'** *n.* A clay brick; a concrete block. *Luma' tisa', sali' semento lullun, halam aniya' palamud inān.* A brick house, entirely cement, so to speak, that one with nothing added. (*Thesaurus:* **haloblāk, semento 1**)

**titay** *var. of* **taytay**

**titib** *n.* A steep slope on land. *Saddī titib, saddī pampang. Pampang itū kabatuhan. Titib* [slope] and *pampang* [cliff] are different. *Pampang* implies rocks. (*Thesaurus:* **kantil₂, deyo'₂ 1, pampang, temang**)

**titik** *n.* **1)** A stick for beating a gong or drum. (*Thesaurus:* **agung 1, buwa₁, kulintangan, gandang 1**) **1.1)** *v. tr.* To strike something to make a noise or beat time. *Kinobla'an aku bang aniya' pariyata' ni kami halam bay tinitik lawang.* I was startled when someone came up [the ladder] to us without the door being knocked on. (*cf:* **lisag₂ 1**) **1.2)** *v. tr. -an* To provide dancers with a rhythmic beat. *Gandang, basta panitikan.* A percussion instrument, anything for beating time on.

**pagtitik** *v. intr. aN-* To beat time on a solid item such as a gong. *Bang nilahu' bulan magtitik kitām.* When there is an eclipse of the moon we bang things.

**titi'** *v. tr. -an* To sprinkle water on something, especially in a ritual context. *Tiniti' maka bohe' kakubulanna, liyangna. Kalu-kalu bang a'a ata'uhan pali-pali, tiniti'an he'na min t'llu maka tahik.* His grave is sprinkled, his grave-shelf. Perhaps if a person knows the old traditions, he may sprinkle it three times with seawater. (*Thesaurus:* **busuwag, pisik-pisik, tata'**)

**pagtiti'** *v. intr. aN-* To sprinkle water for ritual purposes. *Magtiti' kami bang ma Bulan Taiti'. Bang aniya' bay amatay, pandita isāb.* We sprinkle water during the *Taiti'* month. If someone has died, we also bathe them.

**titis 1)** *adj. a-* Drying up through loss of a liquid; ceasing, of menstrual flow. *Halam aniya' katitisanna ma deyom saga t'llumbulan itū.* There

has been no drying-up during these past three months. **1.1)** *v. intr. pa-* To drip off a surface as water from a swimmer. (*Thesaurus:* **p'ttak 1.1, sū₂, tīs, tū'**) **1.2)** *v. tr.* To dry drops of water from a surface. **2)** *v. intr. aN-* To become extremely thin, as in various wasting diseases. *Ta'nda'nu si Lm, anitis na.* You've seen Lm, she's become extremely thin. (*Thesaurus:* **kagkag, kayog 1, kittay, koskos, kulagkag, giti' 1, higtal**)

**tittowa** *n.* **1)** Laughter; the sound of laughter. *Hē, tittowana ī'!* Good grief, that laugh of his! **1.1)** *v. intr. aN-* To laugh aloud. *Ab'ngngis mastal, mbal kami makapanittowa.* The teacher is very stern, we are unable to be laughing out loud. (*Thesaurus:* **kiyum 2, kohok-kohok, dahaggay**)

**pagtittowa** *v. intr. aN-* **1)** To be laughing, in mirth or derision. **1.1)** *v. tr. -an* To mock or deride someone by laughing. *Tantu kitam pinagtittowahan e' sigām.* They will certainly laugh at us.

**tittowa pinogos** *n. phrase* Forced laughter. {idiom}

**tittuk** (*var.* **tuttuk**) *v. tr.* To peck something with a beak; to eat by pecking. *Na sinagaran na magtittuk-tittuk manuk-manuk inān ma huma.* So the birds were left to eat up the crops. *Angalaha' pēna, bay tinuttuk e' manuk dakayu'.* Its comb is bleeding, pecked by another cock. *Magtūy tinittuk pelang bo' al'ssu'.* The canoe was promptly pecked at so it would leak.

**tiyadtad** *n.* Flattened bamboo used for walling. *Dalapis du tiyadtad. Subay duwallapis.* Only one layer of bamboo walling. Should be two layers. (*cf:* **tadtad 2**)

**tiyandā** *n.* The payment made to a midwife for assisting at the delivery of a first child. (*Thesaurus:* **bauballi', bayad 1, tambahan, tulahan**)

**tiyanggi** *n.* A market for local produce such as fish or vegetables. (*Thesaurus:* **kadday, estawran, pasal₂ 1, tabu' 1, tinda**)

**pagtiyanggihan** *n.* A place where an informal market is set up.

**Tiyanggi Sūk** *n. phrase* The city of Jolo, commonly referred to as Tiyanggi.

**tiyangsi'** *var. of* **tangsi'₁**

**tiyap-tiyap** *adv.* Inevitably; whenever the described conditions are met. *Tiyap-tiyap bang kita kinab'nsihan he' matto'ata, subay kita ala'an ni lahat atā.* Whenever our parents treat us hatefully we must leave for a distant place. *Tiyap-tiyap aniya' ni'indaman he' kami bo' alungay, tiyap-tiyap kami angangganti'.* Whenever we borrow something and it gets lost, we must replace it. (*Thesaurus:* **gana-gana 1.1, sumiyan-sumiyan, taka-taka**)

**tiyara'** *v. tr. -an* To gain control or get the better of someone (usually with a negative). *Buwat aniya' angamu', angalogos na pa'in. Mbal katiyara'an.*

Like someone asks for something, then keeps on insisting. He cannot be restrained. *Onde'-onde' inān mbal katiyara'an bang anangis.* That child cannot be controlled when he cries.

**tiyaw-tiyaw** *n.* 1) Mosquito larvae. **1.1)** *v. advrs.* *-in-* Infested with mosquito larvae, of drinking water.

**tiyu'-tiyu'** *v. tr. -an* To treat something carelessly or roughly (usually with negative). *Mbal katiyu'-tiyu'an sawan itu, abila' he' bohe' pasu'.* These drinking glasses are not to be treated roughly, they'll break with hot water. *Mbal katiyu'-tiyu'an a'a inān, al'kkas akagit atayna.* That fellow can't be treated without care, he is quick to get angry. (*syn:* **tingku' 1.1**)

**tiyung** *n.* The Asian myna, a bird sometimes kept in captivity. *fam. Sturnidae. Manuk-manuk tiyung, ya ettom-ettom taga sahal ma kōkna. Ata'u ah'lling.* The myna bird, it is blackish and has a band around its head. It can talk.

**tiyup** *adj. a-* 1) Blowing, as a breeze. *Sikalumpatan saga manuk-manuk bang atiyup baliyu akosog.* Birds fly up en masse when a strong wind is blowing. **1.1)** *v. tr.* To blow on or through something. *Tiyupun ba api itū, mbal angandokot.* Blow on this fire, it won't burn. **1.2)** *v. tr. -an* To blow a wind instrument. *Tiyupinbi torottot ma pussuk būd.* Blow the bugle on the top of the hill.

**tiyup-tiyup** *n.* A wind instrument, as a trumpet, a harmonica.

**pagtiyup-tiyup** *v. intr. aN-* 1) To play a wind instrument. *Saga a'a magbiyula maka a'a magkalangan, a'a magsoleng maka a'a magtiyup-tiyup.* People playing stringed instruments and people singing, people playing flutes and people blowing trumpets. **1.1)** *v. tr.* To produce a tune by blowing. *Ata'u iya magtiyup-tiyup taghuy.* He knows how to whistle a tune. (*cf:* **torottot**)

**tiyuwas** *adj. a-* Getting the worst of some event. *Buwat aku maka'ā' sangpū', pagabayku inān saga lima, atiyuwas iya.* For example, if I catch ten fish and my companion gets about five, he has the worst of it. *Atiyuwas ko' ka'a ilū, halam bay pinakan.* You got the worst of it, you weren't fed. (*cf:* **da'ug**)

**t'bba** *n.* 1) Low tide; the lowest phase of the tidal range. *Bang t'bba, angalut kami kāy-kāy ni gusung.* When it is low tide, we dig for lucine clams in the sand. *T'bba na tahik.* The sea is currently at its low phase. (*cf:* **lalom₁ 2**; *Thesaurus:* **l'ggot, mulilang, pipit₂ 1**) **1.1)** *v. intr. pa-* To ebb, of tide. **1.2)** *v. advrs. ka-...-an* To be stranded by receding tide. *Tabangin aku angalongsad, kat'bbahanan ko' kita-i.* Help me get this canoe into the water, we're going to be stranded.

**kat'bbahan** *n.* An area of sea floor exposed at low tide. (*Thesaurus:* **kababawan, kahanggalan, katoho'an**)

**pagt'bba** *v. tr.* To gather food from an inshore strand area. *Pindi pinagt'bba, sinandak. Ya aheka ma deya Kalumang.* Scallops collected by strand-fishing, probed for [with a spear]. The place where they are abundant is the landward side of Kalumang. (*cf:* **lakod**)

**pagt'bbahan** *n.* An inshore area suitable for gathering strand foods. *Bakal-bakal ya sidda pagt'bbahan, sali' pū'-pū'.* Bakal-bakal is a popular place for gathering strand food. It's a kind of island cluster.

**t'bba-bulagas** *n.* Exceptionally low tide, associated with full moon.

**t'bbahan** *n.* Collective term for strand foods. *Am'lli aku t'bbahan salung ni Hambilan, saga tehe'-tehe', massuli', kūs-kūs, kahanga.* I will buy strand food at Hambilan, sea urchins, murex, bat volutes, conchs. (*Thesaurus:* **l'mput dilaut, panagatun**)

**t'bbag** *adj. a-* Lacking savor, as some fish, or water that is pleasantly brackish. *Buwat gu'ud t'bbu bang pa'usta hal at'bbag, halam aniya' agon ssana.* Like the upper tip of sugarcane, when we chew it is savorless, it has virtually no flavor. *Ahāp bohe'ta itū, at'bbag.* This water is good, savorless. (*Thesaurus:* **k'ssang₂, k'ssaw**)

**t'bba'** *v. tr. -an* 1) To strike something hard using a rigid implement. *Subay tībba'an busay ni tahik bo' anikabbol.* Paddles should be hit against the sea for water to splash up. **1.1)** *v. ditr.* To direct the movement of fish by striking the water surface above them. *T'bba'in daing inān dok supaya pasōd ni linggi'.* Make a disturbance so that those fish will enter the net. *T'bba'anku bohe' sapa' itū maka tungkud ya balutanku itu.* I will strike the water of the stream with this staff that I'm holding.

**pagt'bba'** *v. intr. aN-* To strike a surface with something hard and flat. *Magbahembas, ya magt'bba' katig man duwambila', sali' mags'lle'.* Making a great splashing noise, outriggers hitting [the sea] from side to side, as though taking turns.

**pagt'bba'-sasab** (*var.* **pags'bba'-sasab**) *v. intr. aN-* To act or talk randomly; to speak gibberish. {idiom} *Mampa'in du aku makabissala, ai-ai na tapabissalaku-i, ya hē' niōnan t'bba'-sasab.* So long as I can speak, whatever I get to say, that's gibberish. *Bang aku pal'ngngan-i, pi'ingga-pi'ingga pal'ngnganku-i, ya ī' mags'bba'-sasab.* When I am walking, going wherever my path takes me, that is acting at random.

**t'bbe'** *n.* 1) A notch in the cutting edge of a blade. (*cf:* **someng 1**) **1.1)** *adj. a-* Notched, of a blade or rim. *Bang aku bay makat'bbe' lahut bay indamanku ni ka'a, tampalanku ni ka'a pinaganti' maka halam.* If I notch the blade of a working knife that I have borrowed from you, I show it to you whether or not it is to be replaced. *At'bbe' sali' katamnu itū, at'bbe' solabna, akebak* *isāb.* This plane of yours is notched, its blade is notched, a piece has gone. (*Thesaurus:* **kebang** 1, **k'bbang**, **kobak** 1, **kobet** 1.1, **sembong**)

**t'bbok₁** *v. tr.* To pierce earlobes to enable the wearing of earrings. *Ap'ddi' talingaku, baha'u bay tin'bbok.* My ears are sore, they have been pierced just recently.

**t'bbok₂** *v. tr.* -*an* To squash lice between one's fingernails, or against a comb. *Bang aku kinutuhan, tibbokan kutu bo' amatay.* When I am deloused the lice are squashed so they die. (*Thesaurus:* **kuhut** 1.1, **kutu** 1.1, **siksik**)

**t'bbong** *v. intr. pa-* To fall accurately, of the puck in throwing games. *Akat'bbong ni lowang, buwat kita magtudjun.* It falls accurately into the hole, like when we play the game of *tudjun.* (*Thesaurus:* **taluwa'** 1, **tigi'-tigi'₁** 1, **tudju₂** 1, **tumlang** 2)

**t'bbu** *n.* Sugar cane. *Saccharum officinarum. Alutu' kami duwambatang t'bbu.* We had two lengths of sugar cane as travel food. (*cf:* **gu'ud**)

**t'bbud₁** (var. **t'mbud**) *v. intr. aN-* 1) To billow up, as smoke or flame. *Aheya keyatna an'bbud.* The blaze is big, billowing up. 1.1) *v. tr.* -*an* To fill a space with fumes. *Bang ma deya luma'ta bo' kohap na, tin'bburan deyo' luma' apa aheka hama'. B'nnal pasekot hama' bo' asalat.* If our house is on land and it is afternoon, the area under the house is fumed because there are many mosquitoes. It's true that mosquitoes come close but they're few.

**t'bbud suli-suli** *v. intr. aN-* To involve more and more people in a discussion. {idiom}

**pat'bbud** *v. tr.* To burn incense so that its smoke billows up. (*Thesaurus:* **tugtug**)

**t'bbud₂** *v. intr. aN-* Everybody gathering en masse, as to see a spectacle. *An'bbud kamemon, hal bay dangan ma katagna'.* Everyone turning up en masse, where there was just one at first. (*Thesaurus:* **kobol-kobol, kulatap**)

**t'kka₁** *n.* 1) An arrival. *A'awal ya t'kka sigām.* Their arrival is early. 1.1) *v. intr. pa-/a-* To arrive somewhere. *Waktu gi' kām bay ma paslangan sampay kām makat'kka ni lahat itu.* From the time when you were in the barren lands up until you arrived at this place. (*Thesaurus:* **abut₂** 1, **kablit₂, sampay** 2)

**kat'kkahan₁** *n.* A destination; an arrival point. *Buwat saga amusay kita ni atā. Busayta inān, mbal gi' ta'nda' minsan būd. Halam gi' kita mina'-mina' ni kat'kkahanta.* Like when we make a long journey. Paddling on, even mountains are no longer visible. We are not yet anywhere near our destination.

**pat'kka** *v. ditr.* To deliver something to a destination.

**t'kka₂** *adj.* -*an* 1) Affected by some condition or circumstance. *T'kkahan kami bala'.* We are experiencing a great misfortune. 1.1) *v. intr.* -*um-* To happen. *Ai tum'kka ma tahik?* What

happened at sea? *Ai-ai tum'kka ni siyali sigām inān, iya ya kabingan.* Whatever happened to that younger brother of theirs, he was the one to be blamed. 1.2) *v. intr. pa-/a-* To happen to someone. *Ta'abut ma llaw damuli halam na aniya' at'kka ni iya.* On a later day nothing came his way. *Yukna, "Halam gi' pat'kka pasa'atanku ni sapa'."* He said, "My good feeling about going to the creek hasn't happened." *Pat'kka s'ngngot-s'ngngotna, a'astol atayna.* When his irritability hits him, he gets angry. *Pat'kkahan iya lisu' ma pagiskulna sabab landu' ahunit gastuna mahē'.* She was hit by lack of commitment to her schooling, due to her living costs there being so expensive. 1.3) *v. advrs. ka-...-an* To be affected by some condition or event. *Na sasuku sigām halam amatay e' bala', bay kat'kkahan butig aheka.* And so any of them who had not died as a result of the calamity, were affected by multiple swellings.

**kat'kkahan₂** *n.* An outcome of prior events; an end result. *Bang aminda pikilan Tuhan, ai kat'kkahanna?* If God changes his mind what will the outcome be? *Manjari ahāp sadja kat'kkahan ai-ai nihinang e'na, hinabuna pat'nna' ma luma' nakura'na.* So whatever he did while he stayed in his boss's house turned out well. (*Thesaurus:* **kaluwasan, kamattihan** 1, **kamaujuran, katobtoban, katumariyahan, pamole'an** 2)

**pagt'kka-t'kka** *v. intr. aN-* To happen randomly or repeatedly.

**t'kkad** *v. intr. pa-/-um-* 1) To reach the bottom of a body of water or mud. *Patinggil ka ni bahaku bang ka mbal tum'kkad pakapo', apa alalom.* Get up on my shoulders if you can't touch the bottom to wade, because it is deep. *Bang aniya' papan listun bo' ataha', pat'kkad pareyo' bang alalom tahik, panukkudku.* If there is a piece of sawn lumber, a long piece, it will reach bottom when the tide is in, for me to pole with. *Magtamengka', bay kita abakat he' kappo'. Bang kita pal'ngngan tape'ta mbal makat'kkad.* We can only limp, we have been wounded by a stonefish. When we walk our foot can't be put down on the bottom. (*Thesaurus:* **daggot₁, dunggu'** 1, **tandan₁** 1, **tundug** 1) 1.1) *v. tr.* To discern what is in a person's mind. *Saga maksud ma pangatayan manusiya' sapantun bohe' alalom, sagō' ma a'a taga panahu'an tat'kkad itu kamemon.* The goals of the human heart are like deep water but a person with intelligence can discern them all.

**kat'kkaran** *n.* The point or goal of a discussion. *Ahangbos, ya kat'kkaran lling, mbal taisab.* To the point, the goal of what is said, not repeated. *Buwat kita maggara'-gara' ahinang luma', ya kat'kkaranna luma' na.* Like us making plans to build a house, the whole point of it is the house.

**t'kkaran** *n.* Depth of water; a sounding. *A: "Piland'ppa t'kkaranna ilū?" B: "Lalom saga labi* *duwampū' kono' t'kkaranna.*" A: "How many fathoms deep is it there?" B: "Its sounding is said to be a bit more than twenty [fathoms]."

**pat'kkad** *v. ditr.* To lower something to the sea floor.

**t'kke'** *n.* The Whale shark. *Rhincodus typus.*

**t'kkob** *v. tr.* To kill someone, the action of a saitan spirit. "*Ngā'in gi' aku kayu,*" yuk si Nggo' ni si Ba. Mbal iya. "*Tīkkob ka!*" yukna. "Get me some firewood," said Mother to Ba. He wouldn't go. "You'll be choked [by a demon]!" she said. (*cf:* **alim₂, talap**)

**pagt'kkob** *v. intr. aN-* To snarl at each other, as fighting cats.

**t'kkon** *v. tr.* To hold something in place by putting a weight on it; to press something down. *T'kkonun papan itū.* Hold this plank down. (*Thesaurus:* **dopon, gipis 1.1**)

**pagt'kkon bokol** *v. tr.* To sign a document by pressing one's (inked) thumb. *Bay na kami magt'kkon bokol.* We have put our thumbprint [on a document].

**t'dda** *see:* **mint'dda**

**t'ddak** *v. tr.* To open up a body; to gut a stomach in order to remove entrails. *Tin'ddakan, nila'anan asangna maka manga tina'ina.* Cut open, its gills and entrails removed.

**t'ddas** *var.* of **ddas**

**t'ddo'** *adj. zero* 1) Calm, of weather conditions; windless. *T'ddo' du salung sabab ilu akeyat bihing langit.* It will be calm tomorrow because the horizon there is reddish. **1.1)** *v. intr. pa-* To become calm, of weather conditions. **1.2)** *v. tr. -an* To cause a boat to be stationary due to lack of wind. *Pagpuwas ē'-i, tīddo'an pa'in kami, aniya' aninduk.* After that, while we were becalmed, something took our bait.

**pan'ddo'** *n.* A calm period; the calm season of the year.

**t'ggal** *v. tr.* To compel something irritating to go away. *T'ggalin saga kamanuk-manukan ya pat'ppak ma sangana.* Drive off the birds that are settling on its branches. (*Thesaurus:* **budjaw, dūy, siga' 1.1, singga'-singga', sū₁ 1.1**)

**t'ggang₁** (*var.* **tigang**) *adj. a-* Dehydrated; dried out. *At'ggang na buwas inān, sali' halam aniya' bohe'na.* That rice is dried out already, it is as if it has no water. *Katigangan na pugaw. Taluwa' llaw, aheka amatay.* The *pugaw* [a fish species kept in ponds] are dried out. Scorched by the sun, many died. *Bang bay atigang bohe', subay tinuburan pabīng.* If the water has dried out it must be left to fill up again. (*Thesaurus:* **k'llung-k'llung, lengas₁, panggang₂ 1**)

**t'ggang₂** *adj. a-* Barren; unable to conceive a child. *Ka'a ilū at'ggang, sali' halam taga anak.* You are barren, not having children. (*cf:* **tamanang**)

**t'ggi** *n.* A species of small fish similar to a pilchard. *T'ggi itū daing luwa toloy.* The *t'ggi* referred to is a fish that looks like a *toloy* [a pilchard].

**t'ggok** *v. tr.* To swallow a small amount of liquid. *Patunghabun aku mint'dda, sali' mint'dda aku an'ggok.* Give me a drink just once, as though I swallow just once. *Hal tin'ggok.* Just swallowed. (*Thesaurus:* **ggok, inum 1, tunghab 1.1**)

**t'ggol** **1)** *n.* A period of time. *Saga pilanjām t'ggolna?* How many hours did it take [lit. was its duration]? **1.1)** *adj. a-* Long, of a period of time. A: "*Sumiyan at'kka lansa?*" B: "*Mbal at'ggol.*" A: "When will the passenger launch arrive." B: "It won't be long." (*Thesaurus:* **kuwa'-kuwa', lanjut 1, panjang, taha' 1.1**) **1.2)** *v. intr. pa-* To take time in doing something. *Mbal ka pat'ggol angalubakan anaknu. Yuk matto'anu, "Dō dō."* You don't smack your children for long. Your elders say, "Gently now, gently." **2)** *v. tr. a-, ka-..-an, -an* To spend a long time doing something. *Ai kinat'ggolanbi dibuhi'?* What were you spending time on last night? *Ainu-inu sigām bang ai kat'ggolanna mareyom opis.* They were perplexed as to what was keeping him so long in the town office.

**sat'ggol** *adv.* For as long as.

**sat'ggol hē'-i** *adv. phrase* Ever since that time long past. {idiom}

**t'lla** *v. intr. pa-* To move through space, as through a hole or window. (*Thesaurus:* **p'ssut 1, s'llu 1**)

**t'llak** *adj. a-* Clear, of water or of one's vision. *At'llak matata ang'nda'.* Our eyes are clear for seeing things. (*Thesaurus:* **sepel, tilag, tina'ung**)

**t'llag** *adj. a-* Widely spaced; gapped. *Bay ahūg sīn man lantay luma' kami apa at'llag.* The money fell through the floor of our house because it is so widely spaced. *At'llag pahāp luma' kami. Bang ageret atop subay pinindahan, at'llag na.* Our house is seriously gapped. When the roof thatch is torn it should be replaced, it has gaps in it. (*ant:* **lapat 1.1**; *Thesaurus:* **jalang₂, lanta'**)

**pagt'llag** *v. intr. aN-* To show many gaps or spaces. *Ahāp isāb amalopok-malopok salang-sabot. Ngga'i ka isāb lapatna buwat doppeng inān, magt'llag-t'llag.* It is good when cassava cake crackles. Its consistency is not like *doppeng*, it has many gaps.

**t'lla'-t'lla'₁** *n.* A species of seagull. *Ā bang nda'nu ba'anan panit itū, maka ba'anan t'lla'-t'lla' itū. Aheka ba.* Oh if you could see these schools of tuna, and these flocks of gulls. So many. (*cf:* **ppak**)

**t'lla'-t'lla'₂** *n.* A species of bivalve shellfish.

**t'llas** *adj. a-* Well seasoned, of timber. *Yakal, at'llas, atoho' kayuna, ahāp isina.* The *yakal* tree, well seasoned, its wood dry, its substance good. (*Thesaurus:* **tigas**)

**t'llon** *v. tr.* To swallow food or medicine. *Mbal tat'llonku tambal itū, ap'ddi' deyom k'llongku.* I cannot swallow this medicine, my throat is sore. *Papa'un dahū apa mbal pat'llon ma katibu'ukanna.* Chew it first because it can't be swallowed whole. *Mbal pat'llon tambal itū apa* *aheya.* This pill cannot be swallowed because it is large. (*Thesaurus:* **sangkiyam, s'bbat 1.1**)

**pagt'llon** *v. intr.* aN- To swallow something. *Pagkakanku, magtūy amamis sali' gula', sagō' pagt'llonku al'ssom ma deyom b'ttongku.* When I ate it was immediately sweet, like syrup, but when I swallowed it was sour in my stomach.

**t'llu** *num.* 1) Three. 1.1) *v. advrs.* -in- Divided into three, of a group of things. *Tin'llu tumpuk.* Divided into three groups.

**kat'llungan** *n.* A group of three; trio or triplet. *In anak si Nabi Nū kat'llungan itū, ya na pang'mbo'an ma kamemon manusiya' ya pasaplag ma kaluha'an dunya.* These three sons of the Prophet Noah, they are the ancestors of all humans who have spread throughout the world.

**t'llungan** 1) *num.* Three, of people. 2) *n.* Three persons. *Magpanoho'an iya ma saga sundaluna tamakakosog, sinō' nihengkotan t'llungan inān bo' nilarukan ni reyom kalabusu.* He gave orders to his most powerful soldiers, telling them to tie up the three of them and throw them into the jail.

**t'llumpū'** *num.* Thirty.

**t'mbud** var. of **t'bbud**₁

**t'mbug** *n.* Parrotfishes.

**t'mmang** *n.* A species of bamboo cane about 3 cm in diameter. *gen. Schizostachyum. Bay sinundak mbo' kami. Kobolan iya, sagwā' nsa' bay kapagguluhan e'na basta t'mmang.* Our grandfather was killed with a pole. He was magically protected against violence, but hadn't been schooled with regard to cane. (*Thesaurus:* **kagingking, kayawan, kayuwan, daumu'an, p'ttung**)

**t'mmu** 1) *v. tr.* To bring edges together, of a garment. *Buwat s'mmek agese', tin'mmu bo' nila'it.* Like a garment that is torn, brought together and sewn. 1.1) *v. intr.* pa- To be closed by pullling edges together, as a wound or sack. *Mbal na pat'mmu suput bang ap'nno'.* A sack won't close when it is full. *Bay aku abakat, aheya bakatku hē', minda' tinambalan aku agtūy pat'mmu.* I was cut, a large cut, but fortunately I was treated and the sides came together. (*Thesaurus:* **kittup 1, k'ntom**) 2) *v. advrs.* -in- To be joined physically, of a married couple. *Buwat magkawin, bay na tīmmu.* Like being married, joined physically.

**pagt'mmu** *v. tr.* To bring together the edges or ends of something, as a fence or metal bracelet. *Da'a pagt'mmuhun gallang ilū. Bang pasangon na, kita an'mmuhan dīta.* Don't bring the ends of that bracelet together. Once it is on we'll close it ourselves.

**t'mmun** *adj.* a- Shy; reticent; soft-spoken. *At'mmun, mbal maglata, mbal ah'lling-h'lling.* He is shy, doesn't joke, hardly talks. *Hal aningkō' sandol. At'mmun min at'mmun.* Simply sitting without any attempt to join in. More than usually quiet. (*Thesaurus:* **d'ngngo', m'mmong, sandol 1.1**)

**t'mpu** *v. tr.* To prepare a woman for birthing by placing her properly.

**t'nde** *v. intr.* pa- 1) To sink in a liquid. *Mbal pagūng basi', pat'nde.* Iron doesn't float, it sinks. *Sali' hantang batu pat'nde ni kalaloman.* To illustrate: a rock sinking into the depths. (*ant:* **gūng**; *Thesaurus:* **buhaw, logdang₂, t'nnob 1**) 1.1) *v. tr.* -an To submerge something. (*Thesaurus:* **k'mbang 1.1, hagom 1.1, h'ggom 1.1**)

**pat'ndehan** *n.* Depth of immersion in a liquid.

**t'nna'** *n.* 1) The placement of something. *Pahāpun t'nna' lamisahan itū. Magoseg-oseg.* Fix up the way this table stands. It keeps wobbling. *Ni'nna' sabuli-sabuli saumul-umul. Subay t'nna' sadja, da'a akanat minsan lima sīn.* Stored very securely. It should simply be placed, nothing scattered, not even a five centavo coin. 1.1) *v. intr.* pa- To be located somewhere; to reside. *A: "Ma'ai badju'ku?" B: "O'ō, pat'nna' ilū."* A: "Where is my shirt?" B: "Look, lying there by you." *Pat'nna' kami ma Siasi.* We are staying in Siasi. (*Thesaurus:* **atag₁ 1.1, paglahat 1.1, tongod₂ 1.2**)

**kat'nna'an** *n.* Location of something. *Angahalu' saga mata sigām ma kat'nna'anna, sampay ya d'lla' sigām du ma bowa' sigām.* Their eyes rotted in their places, so too their tongues in their mouths.

**pamat'nna'an** *n.* An assigned position or task.

**pat'nna'** *v. tr.* To place something in a specified location.

**pat'nna'an** *n.* The location of something; a residential location. (*Thesaurus:* **jadjahan, lugal 1, pa'atagan**)

**t'nnaw-t'nnaw** *adj.* a- 1) Totally deserted; devoid of people. (*Thesaurus:* **l'ngngaw-l'ngngaw, mala'u-la'u 1, tannay-tannay**)

**t'nne** *n.* 1) Coldness, of temperature. (*Thesaurus:* **k'ttol, dingin 1, haggut 1.2, hagpay 1**) 1.1) *adj.* zero Cold, in contrast to normal or hot, of water, air, food. *T'nne na bohe'.* The water is cold now. 1.2) *v. advrs.* -in- Affected by cold. *Tīnne aku maka saga nihōb-hōb.* I am affected by the cold and sort of shaking.

**pan'nne** *n.* A period of cold weather; a cold season of the year.

**t'nnob** *v. intr.* pa- 1) To sink below a surface. *Inut-inut iya pat'nnob.* He submerged little by little. (*Thesaurus:* **buhaw, logdang₂, t'nde 1**) 1.1) *v. tr.* -an To dunk something; to immerse something briefly while holding it.

**t'nno'** *v. tr.* To dip food into something that will enhance its flavor; to dunk something. (*Thesaurus:* **bahug 1.1, butag, dulis, tublak₁ 1**)

**pan'nno'an** *n.* A liquid relish or pickle made of various herbs and sauces. (*Thesaurus:* **bubuk₂, kilaw 1, lawal 1.1, tinu'anan**)

**t'nnun** *v. tr.* To weave cloth. *Magsinauwal iya kakana' ahāp t'nnunanna.* He was wearing wide trousers of finely woven cloth. (*Thesaurus:*

anom, ayum-ayum, huwit-huwit 1.1)

**t'ntong₁** *n.* The Two-line monocle bream. *Scolopsis bilineatus.*

**t'ntong₂** *v. intr. aN-* To stand passively without movement or speech. (*Thesaurus:* **nda'-nda', tatab**)

**t'ngge 1)** *n.* Stance; posture. *Ahāp t'nggena budjang ina'an.* That young woman has good posture. **1.1)** *v. intr. aN-* To be standing up. *Pagga ta'abut maganak d'nda i', magtūy an'ngge onde'-onde' inān ni bowa' lawang.* When the time came for that woman to give birth, the child immediately stood up in the doorway. **2)** *v. tr. -an* To stand up against something; to confront an opponent; to defend someone.

**pagt'ngge** *v. intr. aN-* To stand together. *Bay kami magt'nggehan ma pantān, manda' sinagina sinō' aningkō'.* We were standing around together on the porch, but fortunately we were greeted and told to sit down.

**t'ngge-tingkō'** *n.* The daily round of life: sleeping or waking; working and resting. {idiom}

**pan'nggehan** (var. **pat'nggehan**) *n.* A platform or supporting structure. (*cf:* **patinggilan**)

**pat'ngge** *v. tr.* To cause something to stand; to erect a building.

**t'ngnga'** *n.* The middle point of a line or area; the central part of a house. *Pasōng kam ni t'ngnga'.* Come on in to the middle [of the house]. *Ma t'ngnga' s'llang.* In the middle of the ocean. (*cf:* **tonga' 1.1**; *Thesaurus:* **llot, olangan 1**)

**t'ngnga'-t'ngnga'** *v. intr. pa-* To pass between two things, as between islands or people, cross the middle of an area. *Ōy, ya onde' itū pat'ngnga'-t'ngnga' na pa'in, minsan magsuli-suli.* Hey, this child keeps passing to and fro between us even though we are talking. *Patigi'-tigi' bohe' itū, pat'ngnga'-t'ngnga' ni kita.* This [rain] water is on target, coming right into the midst of us.

**t'ngnga'an** *n.* The middle item in a series; the item between two points of reference. *Anakku t'ngnga'an.* My middle child.

**t'ppa** *v. tr.* To pound harvested grain in order to remove husks; to pound husked grain to make flour. *Ubus pa'in tin'ppa ni linsungan, tinahapan na.* After it has been pounded in the mortar it is winnowed. (*Thesaurus:* **banol 1.1, pangki', pogpog 1.1**)

**pagt'ppa** *v. intr. aN-* To pound grain. *Bang kami magt'ppa pai, binuwattē', tinahap bo' ala'an kuwit pai hē'.* When we are pounding rice, it's done so, winnowed so the chaff comes away.

**t'ppak₁** *v. tr.* To hit something with the palm of one's hand, as to smack or to make a noise. *T'ppakta ka, kap'ddi'an ka.* I'll smack you, you'll feel the pain. (*cf:* **t'ppag₁**; *Thesaurus:* **bimbing, b'ddak, sampak, sampiyal, tapling**)

**pagt'ppak** *v. intr. aN-* To clap the hands together.

**t'ppak₂** *v. intr. pa-* To land on something, as a bird,

an airplane, raindrops. *Bang bay paleyang kallo' bo' atā bay kaleyanganna, bo' alalom tahik, pat'ppak ni bangkaw.* When a heron has been flying and it has flown a long way, and the tide is high, it alights in the mangroves. *Pat'ppak na ulan.* The rain is falling now. *Ubus kami paleyang min Tiyanggi, pat'ppak kami ma Sambuwangan.* After flying from Jolo City, we landed at Zamboanga. (*cf:* **tapu' 1**)

**t'ppad** *v. tr.* To cast a fishnet.

**t'ppag₁** *v. tr.* To slap at something such as flies on food. (*cf:* **t'ppak₁**)

**t'ppag₂** *n.* **1)** A woven mat without a backing. (*syn:* **tupag**) **1.1)** *adj. a-* Roughly woven or lacking a backing, of a mat.

**t'ppas₁** *v. tr.* To take or use something, without permission, or without care. *Tin'ppas na he'ku minsan halam ma luma' tagdapu.* I took it even though the owner was not at home. (*Thesaurus:* **dumpas, sabsab**)

**t'ppas₂** var. of **tangpas₂**

**t'ppi'** *v. intr. pa-* **1)** To approach something closely. *Buwat angusaha bang sali' maglawak, angalingan abay inān, yukna, "Pat'ppi' ka pi'itu."* Like when out fishing and we have become far apart, that fishing mate calls out, saying, "Come closer here." (*cf:* **t'ppung 1.2**; *Thesaurus:* **apiki 1.1, pagtongop, sekot 1.2, sigpi'**) **1.1)** *v. advrs. ka-...-an* To be approached by something dangerous. *Gansuwang hē', ya kakanna g'llom. A'angkud kono' bang kat'ppi'-t'ppi'an keyat.* The food of these *gansuwang* giants is caulking fiber. They are said to burn when approached with flame.

**t'ppi'-tuli** *adj. a-* Close to sleep; drowsy.

**t'ppong** *v. tr.* **1)** To measure by volume, as rice or the ingredients of a recipe. *Bang ka am'lli buwas ni tinda, tin'ppong dahū, ginantang.* When you buy rice at a store it is measured first, using a standard container [about 3 liters]. *Bang batung niasin, suru' ya pan'ppong.* With salted peanuts a spoon is used to measure them out. (*Thesaurus:* **ganta'₁ 1, sukud₁**) **2)** To assign someone a destiny.

**t'ppongan** *n.* A container for measuring volume.

**t'ppot** *adj. a-* Exact, of the amount or size required. *Takbil sīn, takbil ai-ai takakan, takbil s'mmek, sarang na ma aku. Bang aniya' angamu', yukku, "At'ppot ma baranku, halam kulang halam labi."* As regards money, or anything to eat, or clothes, [there's] just enough for me. If someone asks for some I say, "Exactly enough for me personally, no lack and no surplus." *Bay aku pangamu'an sīn. Na b'nnal aniya' sīnku, sagwā' t'ppot pagsukayku.* Someone begged money from me. Now it is true that I had some, but it was just enough for my fare. (*Thesaurus:* **sarang 1, s'ddong, sugiya, ustu**)

**t'ppung** *adj. a-* **1)** Close, of time or space. *At'ppung na atulak.* About to leave. **1.1)** *v. intr. pa-* To become close to a location. *Bang magpangongka' saga onde'-onde', aheka gi' pasekot, aheka pat'ppung.* When children are playing a lot more come close, a lot approach. **1.2)** *v. tr.* To approach something closely. *Da'a t'ppungun manuk ilū bo' mbal paleyang.* Don't get too close to that chicken lest it fly away. (*cf:* **t'ppi'** 1)

**t'tta'** *v. tr.* To cut small pieces from something larger. *Bang kita an'tta' kayu subay angā' pamataggalan iya.* When we chop firewood we should get something to rest it on. *Bang kayu tin'tta', bang kukku tin'ttop.* For cutting wood [we say] *t'tta',* for cutting fingernails [we say] *t'ttop.*

**t'ttek** var. of **tettek**

**t'ttob** var. of **t'ttop**

**t'ttok** *adj.* a- **1)** Worn by repeated small blows. *At'ttok na katas ilū. Halam na aniya' dawatna.* That [carbon] paper is worn through. It no longer has ink. **1.1)** *v. tr.* To cut or perforate with repeated small blows. *Tin'ttok itū pinanahut-nahut maka lahut.* *T'ttok* means to cut into small pieces using a garden knife. (*Thesaurus:* **k'llot, gōt-gōt 1, ladjang, pabuwa', padja', tama'**)

**pagt'ttok** *v. tr.* To cut something with repeated small cuts. *Tinadtad p'ttung, pinagt'ttok.* Bamboo is flattened by splitting, cut with many small cuts.

**t'ttog** *adj.* a- **1)** Stable as to location; emotionally stable. *At'ttog ma deyom luma', mbal sali' pal'ngngan.* Constantly in the house, doesn't go walking. *Pat'ttogun imannu.* Be settled in your commitment. (*Thesaurus:* **kakkal, d'ddos, dorog₁, taptap 1, tattal**) **1.1)** *v. intr.* pa-/aN- To stay in one place. *Maglunsul-lunsul sadja ka. Mbal ka makabāk lahat pat'ttogannu.* You will just keep roaming. You will not find a place to settle down at.

**t'ttop** (var. **t'ttob**) *v. tr.* **1)** To cut the end off something. *Bang kukku tin'ttop, bang kayu tin'tta'.* For cutting fingernails [we say] *t'ttop,* for cutting wood [we say] *t'tta'.* *Makajari isāb tangan pamōngnu, t'ttop subay bari'.* It's also possible to break [something] using your hand, but *t'ttop* requires a knife. (*syn:* **k'llob;** *Thesaurus:* **tabtab 1, tempos, tompes, utas 1.1**) **1.1)** *v. tr.* -an To cut a piece from the end of a main part. *T'ttopin damp'ppot.* Cut off one length.

**t'ttob-tape'** *n.* A person with no feet showing. *T'ttob-tape' du ya bay pa'nda' ma iya sagō' magjinuba pote'.* What appeared to him was someone cut off [from sight] at the feet, but clothed in a white gown.

**toba'** (var. **tuba'**) *n.* Palm toddy. (*Thesaurus:* **alak, bīl, binu**)

**tobas** *adj.* a- Coming to the end of a fruiting season. *Bang mampallam atobas na, yampa anumbuk to'ongan uttala'.* When the mangoes have finished fruiting, it's then that the north wind really starts to blow. (*cf:* **tongkad**)

**tobol** *v. advrs.* -in- Constipated. *Tinobol, ya po'on sababna amangan manga mampallam atawa biyabas, kuwitna.* Constipated, the reason for it is eating mangoes or guavas with their skins. (*syn:* **llet 1**)

**tobtob** *n.* **1)** A cutoff point; terminus, of time or space. **1.1)** *adv.* From this point on, in time or space. *Tobtob min llaw itu halam aniya' tambal subu.* From today on there will be no clinic [lit. morning medicine]. *Paloblob tobtob lo'akanta ma deyom tana'.* We will sink as far as our knees into the soil. (*cf:* **taman**) **1.2)** *v. intr.* aN- To reach the last stage of an activity or series. *Anobtob na llaw pam'llinu bang ka anumbung ni paltiraku.* Your buying from me will come to an end if you inform on me to my trading partner. (*Thesaurus:* **hād 1.2, sangka' 1.1**)

**katobtoban** *n.* The maximum extent or degree; the ultimate result or outcome. *Ya na itu katobtoban ahāp.* This one is the very best. *Halam aniya' katobtoban ma pagsasaw ma sakalibut lahat.* There was no end to the disturbances throughout the land. *Akaukanat saga tendogna, ya ina'an katobtobanna.* His followers were scattered, that was the result. (*Thesaurus:* **kaluwasan, kamattihan 1, kamaujuran, kat'kkahan₂, katumariyahan, pamole'an 2**)

**tobtob sumiyan** *interrog.* Until when? {idiom} *Tobtob sumiyan kita maglagut dansehe'an?* When will we stop slashing each other?

**tobtoban** *n.* An end, of time or space. *Hal dakuman min tobtoban b'ttongna itū sudju ni tape'na.* All that was left was from where his stomach ended to his feet. *Ina'an kono' ma tobtoban tana' sigām.* There, it is said, at the boundary of their land. (*Thesaurus:* **kapūd-pūran, katapusan 1, tabtaban**)

**toka** see: **pagtoka-toka**

**tokang** see: **patokang**

**tokke'₁** *n.* Various geckos or lizards noted for their cadence of cries. *Buwat buwa' kayu bang aniya' bay angeket iya, buwat ambaw, tokke', kabog. Tinemposan ya bay kineket ē' bang aniya' halu'na.* As with fruit when something such as a rat, a gecko or a bat has bitten it. The bitten bit is cut out if there is any decay. (*Thesaurus:* **pahang, pinit, tokko'**)

**tokke'₂** *n.* **1)** Blame; accusation. **1.1)** *v. advrs.* ka-...-an To be blamed or accused, particularly in a legal context. *Katokke'an aku dusa. Minsan aku halam bay makahinang, makaniaku du, sabab halam aniya' saksi'ku.* I have been accused of a crime. Even though I did nothing, it is attributed to me because I have no supporting witness. (*cf:* **tōng₂ 1.1**)

**tokko'** *n.* A species of monitor lizard distinguished by prominent yellow markings. (*Thesaurus:* **pahang, pinit, tokke'₁**)

**toket** *n.* **1)** A tail of hair hanging from a hair knot. **1.1)** *v. tr.* -an To arrange one's hair so that a tail hangs down from a knot. (*Thesaurus:* **hambak, hampal, pugay 2, sapid 1.1, simbōng 1.1, tusay**)

**tokod** *adj.* a- **1)** Accurate in guessing. *Atokod ka'a ilū magtaep.* You type accurately [without looking]. *Tinuhuma at'kka kappal Jolo J inān. Yuknu, "Mbal." Na at'kka du isāb, atokod ya a'a bay anuhuma.* It was rumored that the ship Jolo J was arriving. You said, "No it's not." Well it did arrive, so the person who spoke the rumor guessed right. **1.1)** *v. tr.* To guess at something unknown. *Tokorun kono' bang sai bay anibu' ka'a.* Please guess who struck you with the edge of his hand.

   **pagtokod-tokod** *v. intr.* aN- To be engaged in a contest of words or puzzles.

   **tokod-tokod** *n.* A verbal puzzle; a riddle.

   **patokod** *v. ditr.* To set someone a riddle.

**tokon** *adj.* a- **1)** To be too long, of one rope of a pair. *Pigtalun lubid ilū, da'a patokonun.* Shorten that rope, don't make it uneven. **1.1)** *v. intr.* pa- To hang down on one side, as one of a pair of ropes. *Patokon dambila' dundangan, sali' ataha' dambila', subay pinigtal.* One side of the swing is hanging down, as if one side is long, it should be tightened. *Buwat kita amaling subay samapigtal. Bang ligtang patokon dambila', pigtalun.* When we change tack, the sheets [sails] should be shortened equally. If one mast stay is too long it should be shortened.

**toktok** *v. tr.* -an To decorate a bride's face with a pattern of dots (made with rice paste). *Tinoktokan bayhu' d'nda bo' ahāp manisna.* The bride's face is decorated with dots so that her beauty will be excellent.

**togang** *v. intr.* pa- To be in an upright position, in contrast to lying prone. *Patogang na pelang, bay abuhaw.* The *pelang*-type canoe is upright now, it had capsized. *Patogang itū ak'llut maka mbal, basta paleyak na.* In upright position, bailed dry or not, as long as it is facing up. *Patogangun mital ilu.* Stand that can up.

**togel** *n.* The tail of an animal or bird. (*cf:* **tape'₂**)

**togeng** *n.* Various needlefish including the Spotted halfbeak and the Black-barred garfish. *Hemirhamphus.* (*gen:* **pillangan**)

**togga'** *see:* **pagtogga'**

**togge'₁** *v. intr.* pa- To fall headlong through space, as a bird or airplane. *Magbulibud-bulibud ariplano inān, wa'i patogge' na sudju pareyo' inān, anūy-nūy ni tahik.* That airplane turned round and round, falling downwards headfirst, going straight into the sea. (*Thesaurus:* **hūg₁ 1, pakpak 1, tukbung 1, tulelle, tumba₁**)

**togge'₂** *v. tr.* To locate fish by looking down from a moving canoe.

**togmok** *adj.* a- **1)** Pressed down; forced under. **1.1)** *v. intr.* pa- To press down into. *Buwat pelang bang patūt bo' alandos baliyu, na patogmok munda'.* Like a canoe running before the wind when it is

strong, then the bow presses under the waves. *Buwat angatam, na katam ē' palabay min gudlis, patogmok.* Like planing, and the plane goes beyond the scribed line, digging into the wood. **1.2)** *v. tr.* -an To push something into the ground with a vigorous downward movement.

**togob₁** *adj.* a- Long-wearing, of paint or dye. *Atogob, sali' ataggu pintana.* Long-wearing, its paint kind of durable. (*Thesaurus:* **anagtol, kamdos₂, kumpay, galak₂, pagon₁ 1.1, taggu₁, tatas 1.1**)

**togob₂** *adj.* a- Loaded heavily, of a vessel or vehicle. *Atogob pambot si Ah, tu'ud aheka a'a.* Ah's motorised outrigger canoe is heavily loaded, simply because there are many people. (*Thesaurus:* **apad-apad, apang, llop 1**)

**togol** *adj.* a- **1)** Consistent; determined. *Bang aku bīllihan paraw e' si Mma' mbal aku magtūy bīllihan. Tinatab aku dahū e'na, kalu-kalu aku atogol amahilala'.* When Dad is buying a canoe for me it isn't bought for me immediately. He assesses me first, whether perhaps I will be consistent in caring for it. *Buwat ka'a ilū magsulat, atogol. Minsan du aniya' hinangan buwat panoho'an si Mām, mbal beya'-beya'nu.* Like you when writing, persistent. Even though there is work [to be done], like something ordered by Mam, you do not obey. (*Thesaurus:* **podlongan, sogsog 1, taggu₂ 1.1, tukid 1**) **1.1)** *v. intr.* pa- To work consistently. *Patogol ka angusaha.* Work consistently at earning a living. **1.2)** *v. tr.* -an To do something persistently.

**togong** *n.* **1)** A small woven fish trap, rectangular in section with the entry funnel at one end. *Tapanahan togong batu bo' mbal talaran.* Coral rock can be used to weigh down a *togong* trap so it doesn't get moved by the current. (*Thesaurus:* **bagiyas 1, bubu₁, kiming, panggal 1**) **1.1)** *v. tr.* To catch fish with a togong type trap. *Togong panogong kaginisan daing batu.* A *togong* trap for trapping various coral fishes.

**togsok** *v. intr.* pa-/-um- To fall over so that the forward part is lower than the rest. *Patogsok paraw, tabowa patunggang he' bohe' ulan.* The canoe tips down one end, made to pivot downwards by the rainwater in it [of a canoe on a drying rack]. *Bang sawpama lahi-lahi kita bo' pasagnat tape'ta ma ai-ai, na tumogsok kita, ya dahū kōkta.* When for example we are running and our foot catches against something, then we fall, our head first. *Tumogsok hūgna.* His fall was headlong. (*Thesaurus:* **jungkat 1.1, pagtungkellat-tungkellat, tunggang**)

**tōhan** *n.* A loop of string, wire or rattan, on which fish are strung as they are caught. *Dantōhan du ta'ā'ku.* I got just one string [of fish]. (*Thesaurus:* **lingkit 1.1, surut, tuhug 1**)

**tohob** *v. tr.* -an To open a coconut. *Pagtohobta lahing ilū akulang isina. Wa'i kinakan, nilahu'. Asal botong bay tapamandihan bulan.* On opening the mature coconut it didn't have much meat. It had been eaten, affected by an eclipse. That's how it is with for green coconuts that had been used for [eclipsed] moon bathing.

**toho'** *adj. a-* Dry, in contrast to wet. (*ant:* **base'**₁; *Thesaurus:* **panggang₂ 1, tigangkal**)

**katoho'an** *n.* An area of sea floor exposed by receding tide. (*Thesaurus:* **kababawan, kahanggalan, kat'bbahan**)

**pagtoho'** *v. intr. aN-* To live in a dry environment, in contrast to living over the sea. *Sūk ya magtoho', kami magbase'.* Tausugs are the ones inhabiting dry land, we inhabit the wet.

**toho' k'llong** *adj. a-/-an* Thirsty or hoarse, of a dry throat. {idiom} *Waktu sigām toho'an k'llong.* The time when they were experiencing dryness of throat [thirst]. (*Thesaurus:* **patay-bohe', p'kkol k'llong**)

**toho' p'ggad** *adj. a-* Thirsty and hoarse, requiring water to relieve the condition. {idiom}

**patoho'** *v. tr.* To dry out something that has become wet. (*Thesaurus:* **buwad, puhi, tumbal 1.1**)

**tohongan** *n.* The Scaly turtle. *Order Chelonia.* (*Thesaurus:* **bokko', laggutan, payukan, p'nnu**)

**pagtotohongan** *v. intr. aN-* To make a living from catching and selling turtles.

**tō'** 1) *v. tr.* To point at something, with a hand or with projected lips. *Sali' kita magbeya' maka matto'ata ni M'ddas am'lli ai-ai, bo' aniya' tō'ta hē'.* It's like us going to Siasi with our parents to buy various things, and we point at something. *Bang daing aheya buwat kāt, patay tunung, subay da'a tō'ta.* When a large fish such as a humpback wrasse is found dead for no apparent reasons, we should not point at it. (*Thesaurus:* **pandu' 2, tudlu'₂ 1**) 2) *v. tr. -an* To teach someone by indicating the correct item. *Angay aku subay tō'annu? Siyaka ka min aku?* Why should you teach me what to do? Are you older than I am?

**to'a** 1) *n.* Age in contrast to youth. 1.1) *adj. a-* Middle-aged or older, of humans. *Bang matto'a na mma'ku, halam aniya' empon, ato'a.* When my father is an older person, without teeth, he is old. (*cf:* **baha'u 1, ndang**; *Thesaurus:* **hendog-hendog, lasag, pata'₁, sangpot 1, sibuwa**) 2) *adj. a-* Almost ripe, of fruit. 2.1) *v. intr. pa-* To become mature, of vegetable produce or animals. *Tagna'anna bunga, bang pato'a-to'a, pola.* At first it is the immature fruit [of the betel palm]. When it matures a bit it is betel nut.

**kato'ahan** (var. **katoha'an**) *n.* Age as a stage of life; maturity.

**pagtoto'a** *v. intr. aN-* To grow older. *Bang aniya' amangan buwa' lagundi' mbal magkatoto'a.* If anyone eats the *lagundi'* fruit he will not grow old.

**to'od** (var. **tu'ud₂**) *adv.* Intensely; definitely. *Ahāp to'od ssana itū.* The flavor of this is really good. *Bang daing aheya to'od, subay pinundang.* If a fish

is really large it should be split and pierced [to preserve it]. *Babag ina'an, ya to'od ōnna hobong.* That cross-beam, its name is definitely *hobong.* *Angal'ddom, Sama tu'ud. Angalendom, Sama Lipid. L'ddom* is the true Sama, *lendom* is the Land Sama [equivalent]. *Angal'ppang, hatina sarang to'od mata linggi'.* The right size, the mesh size exactly right. (*Thesaurus:* **karalaman, kumarukan, dumasiyaw, landu'₂ 1, mamarahi, sidda 1**)

**to'olang** *n.* A bone. *Bang aniya' a'a ahūg pareyo' bo' mbal apōng to'olangna, taga ilmu'.* If someone falls and doesn't break a bone, he has supernatural powers. *Kakowa'an aku he' to'olang daing.* I have a bone stuck in my throat, from a fish bone. (*Thesaurus:* **bangkak, bokog, kowa' 1**)

**to'on₁** *adj. a-* 1) Engaged in betting on dice. *Bang ato'on legot, subay pinat'nna' sīn ni deyom balad.* When betting in a dice game you must place money inside the gaming board. 1.1) *v. tr. -an* To bet money on a selected number in a dice game; to spin or roll the die. *Bang ma paglegotan, anganggustu ka to'ongan bang maingga ma karuwa umbul inān. Bang gustuta dahū lima, to'onanta.* At the dicing board, concentrate on where the two numbers are. If we feel good about a 5 appearing first, we put the money down. *Sīn ya tino'onan ni legot, ni deyom balad.* It is money that is bet on the die, put on the board. *Bang aku tino'onan sīn, hapus na. Sali' "okay," angahapus aku ma iya, ya mano'on ī'.* When I am offered a wager I agree. Like "okay," I accept him, the one making the wager. (*cf:* **paglegot 2**)

**panono'on** *n.* Someone addicted to gambling on dice games.

**to'on₂** *v. tr. -an* To put a weight on a fish trap to keep it in place. *Tino'onan itū sali' tinambunan kaut.* This word *to'on* is like setting [a fish trap] in the sea. *Da'a na to'onin maitu apa jadjahan sigā, pano'onan sigā.* Don't set [the fishtrap] there because it is their territory, their trapping place. *Bang aku ano'onan panggal, niasok e' daing.* If I set a *panggal* type trap fish enter it.

**pano'onan** *n.* A place for setting small fish traps.

**to'ong** *see:* **pato'ong, patōng**

**to'ongan** 1) *adj. zero* Genuine; unmodified. *Ngga'i ka to'ongan. Bay aku am'lli ni tindahan, pagsōngku sīn hē', pag'nda' e' tindera, "Gillo'ak sīnnu ilu."* It's not genuine. I bought something at the shop. On handing over the money, when the shop assistant saw it [she said], "That money of yours is counterfeit." *Sayuman a'a inān, sali' a'a to'ongan.* That man is fully complete, like a real man. 1.1) *adv.* Really; genuinely; very; indeed. *Nanam ahalu', salung ahalu' to'ongan.* It has a somewhat rotten taste, tomorrow it will be really rotten. *"Buwat ipatanta, ya pamahinang ma iya ananggung bohe', ati subay bilahi saddī hinang minnē'. Yuk pat'nna'an hē', "Samantala'* *hinang ilu ya bay pamahinang ma ka'a-i, hinangun to'ongan na."* Like our worker, and the work assigned to him is to fetch water but he has to want some work other than that. The person he stays with says, "Since it is that work [fetching water] that has been asigned to you, get on and do it properly." (*Thesaurus:* **pahāp₁**) 2) *v. tr.* To do something with serious intent, in contrast to joking or being capricious. *Tino'ongan, ngga'i ka ula-ula.* He meant it, it wasn't a joke. *Pakeyas, buwat ulan hal paleyang. Mbal ano'ongan.* Losing force, like rain that just flies across. It doesn't really mean it. *Mbal kita ano'ongan bang kita am'lli ai-ai, hal kita angaladjaw.* We are not really serious when we are buying anything, we just offer a low price. (*ant:* **ula-ula**)

**pagto'ongan** *v. intr.* aN- To do something seriously and purposefully. *Buwat kami magplising maka si Mu, ngga'i kami magto'ongan, magula-ula kami.* Like Mu and me playing marbles, we're not being serious, we're just having fun.

**to'ongan-to'ongan** *n.* The fullest form of something; the ultimate. *Bang makanito'ongan-to'onganna, kita magbaya' amowa turul-buli'an.* If it comes to the real thing, those of us who wish to do so bring an optional extra gift.

**tolda** *n.* A heavy cloth such as canvas; a tarpaulin; a tent. *Saga tolda ilū bay paglumā'an sigā, pamuwan kami na.* That canvas was their house, now given to us. (*Thesaurus:* **kapis, ispowen, lona, ma'ung, mantaluna, patig**)

**toldas** *v. tr.* -an To do something persistently. *Maka'nda' kami parangkang. Apas kami na, tinoldasan.* We saw a sailing ship. We chased [it], doing it without letup. (*cf:* **mumut**; *Thesaurus:* **kara-kara₁, daran-daran 1.1, pagabut-abut, pagkuwat, sigi-sigi 1**)

**tolek** *n.* 1) The discharge of pus from an infected ear. 1.1) *v. advrs.* -in- Suffering from an infected ear. (*cf:* **antil 1**)

**tollen** *v. tr.* -an To lash a rope to something rigid, as an anchor rope to its shank. (*Thesaurus:* **baggot, bit₂, engkot 1.1, gakut, tabul-tabul**)

**tollok** *v. tr.* To form a pile by adding items one by one.

**pagtollok-tollok** *v. intr.* aN- To play a game in which the players assemble a store of clay balls and throw them at each other.

**toloy** *n.* A species of pilchard or sardine. (*cf:* **kasig**)

**tombad** *n.* The Yellow-margin triggerfish; the Green triggerfish. *Pseudobalistes flavimarginatus.* (*syn:* **mayung**)

**tombad-keyat-bowa'** *n.* The Red-mouthed triggerfish.

**tombad-tunus** *n.* The Blue-fin triggerfish.

**tombong** *n.* The rectum; the anus. *Kinalibubut tombongku.* My rectum is suffering from boils. (*cf:* **jubul**)

**tomog** *adj.* a- Soaking wet, as through immersion

or being caught in a downpour. *Alu' mbal makatomog. Ya makatomog, bohe' atawa ulan, atawa tahik.* Dew does not make one soaking wet. What makes one soaking wet is water or rain, or seawater. (*Thesaurus:* **base'₁, bugbug₁, bugga' 1, gamos 1, himāy**)

**tomo'** *v. intr.* pa-/a- 1) To be growing, of plants. *Nsa' aniya' kono' atomo' ma lahat sultan.* It is said that there is nothing growing in the land of the sultans. *Tu'ud atomo'an dīna.* Simply growing of its own accord. *Kayu itingan ya patomo' ma paslangan.* Thorn trees that grow in barren areas. *Sikatomo'an na kaparangan.* The grasses are growing in great abundance. (*Thesaurus:* **subud, sulig₁, tungbu'**) 1.1) *v. intr.* aN- To increase by growing, of plants. *Sagō' pagtanom pa'in, anomo' du ati palabi heyana min tinanom kamemon.* But on planting, it does grow and its size exceeds all the other plants. 1.2) *v. tr.* To plant something. *Halam sai-sai bay anomo', tu'ud atomo'an dīna.* Nobody planted it, it simply grew of its own accord.

**paltomo'-tomo'an** *n.* Growing things of the vegetable kingdom; plants. (*syn:* **paltubu-tubuhan 1**)

**patomo'an** *n.* The substance or thing on which something grows.

**tompang** *n.* Large winged insects such as locusts, grasshoppers, mantises. *Tompang, ya manuk-manuk maglagsik-lagsik.* Grasshopper, the insect that flicks up repeatedly. (*Thesaurus:* **ampan-dulu, bilalang**)

**tompe'** *v. tr.* To make a pancake of cassava or sago meal. *Am'gga' kita bohe'na, tahinang hali ampa binugbug, tinompe', atawa pangamirul.* We squeeze out [the boiled cassava's] liquid, producing starch to be made into porridge or a pancake, or for laundry starch. (*Thesaurus:* **buwang₃, ggang, huwal, sanglag**)

**tinompe'** *n.* A pancake of cassava or sago meal. (*gen:* **apam 1**)

**tompes** *v. tr.* -an To cut something away from the main part. *In d'lla' putingan katompesan.* The lying tongue can be cut off. (*Thesaurus:* **tabtab 1, tempos, t'ttop 1, utas 1.1**)

**tompol** *adj.* a- Blunt; dull, of a blade or point. (*cf:* **poppol 1**; *ant:* **talom 1**)

**tomtom** *n.* 1) A memory; a recollection. *Aniya' subahatku, agtimbang tomtomku.* I have made a vow, sorting out my memories. 1.1) *v. tr.* To remember something; to recall. *Aniya' du pa'in panomtoman.* There will always be something to remember [you] by. (*Thesaurus:* **entom 1.2, magtak, padlak ni atay, sangpit, suligpat, tambung, tasdik**)

**tonda'₁** *n.* 1) A heavy gauge line used for trolling. *Kolengun tonda' ilū bo' mbal asagut.* Wind up that line so it doesn't tangle. *Pasa'ud tonda'ku ma batu, halam ala'an maka tingga'na.* My trolling line is snagged on a coral rock, and won't come free along with its lead weight. (*Thesaurus:* **naelon, tangsi'**₁ 1) **1.1)** *v. tr.* To catch pelagic fish, especially tuna, with a trolled lure. *Am'lli aku bulbul manuk panonda'ku ni timbang, anonda' mangku'.* I buy chicken feathers to use for trolling in the open sea, trolling for bonito. (*Thesaurus:* **gonteng 1.2, laway**₂ **1.1, manit, pamalastik, paranas, p'ssi 1.1**)

**pagpanonda'** *v. intr. aN-* To fish with a trolled lure.

**panonda'an** *n.* A trolling lure.

**tonda'**₂ *v. tr.* To lead someone by the hand. *Bang manusiya' tinonda', bang sapi' ginuyud.* Humans are led by the hand, cattle are pulled on a rope. (*cf:* **ambit**₂)

**tondok** *v. intr. pa-* **1)** To lower the head as when running or looking for something. *Patondok aku amiha sīn.* I lower my head looking for money. (*Thesaurus:* **bantang 1, kondo', kuru', domol 1**) **2)** To tilt forward, as a descending airplane.

**tonton** *v. intr. pa-* **1)** To suspend; to hang free. *Laista pariyata' ai-ai bay patonton.* We smooth upwards whatever [hair] has hung down. *Bang sōng pat'ppak ariplano pinatonton silikanna.* When the plane is about to land its wheels are made to hang down. (*Thesaurus:* **hallal, hellel, sasa**₂) **1.1)** *v. tr. -an* To lower something on a line. *Bang engkotannu lubid keyat ma tandawan pamatontonannu kami.* If you tie a red rope in the window from which you lower us. (*cf:* **taktak 1.1**)

**tonyak** *adj. a-* Mushy or fragmented. *Apodjak daing, sali' halam magtibu'uk isina, atonyak kamemon.* The fish is fragmented, its flesh not staying in one piece, completely mushy. (*Thesaurus:* **biyobog, k'ddos, lodjag 1, lonyat, petak 1**)

**tōng**₁ *n.* A physical extremity, as the tip of a branch, a cape or headland, the end point of a geographical area. *Aniya' jambatan ma Tōng Batu.* There is a pier at Rock Point. (*Thesaurus:* **pekkes-pekkes, punjung**₁, **puntuk, pussuk 1**)

**tōng-barena** *n.* A drill bit.

**tōng-duru'** *n.* A nipple; a teat.

**tōng-lahat** *n.* A headland; a peninsula.

**tōng-tangan** *n.* A fingertip. *Asudlat mataku he' tōng tanganku, ap'ddi'.* My eye got poked by my fingertip, it is painful.

**tōng-tōng** *n.* **1)** The furthest end of something. *Minsan isāb pahi amūng du isāb buwat manusiya', "Minsan aku pahi, patumpangun pa'in aku ma tōng-tōng adjungbi ilū."* Pahi mbal takilaw. And even manta rays speak like humans. "Even though I am a manta ray, just let me travel at the very end of that ship of yours." Rays can't be eaten raw. **1.1)** *v. intr. pa-* To move out to an extremity. (*syn:* **tukkay-tukkay**)

**tōng**₂ *v. tr. -an* **1)** To accuse or convict someone of an offense. *Gōm aku maka tautai'anakku ya tōngin dusa, da'a sadja in sultan tasalla'.* Better that I and my children be accused of wrong,

rather then the sultan be criticized. **1.1)** *v. advrs. ka-...-an* To be found guilty of wrong behavior; affected by (someone's) wrongdoing. *Katōngan iya la'at, katōngan dusa. Baya'-baya'na angahinang buwattē'.* He experiences the consequences of wrongdoing, of sin. It was his choice to behave that way. *Bang mbal ka'nde'anbi gadjina, parahing iya ni sara' ma pasalbi ati ka'am ya katōngan dusa.* If you don't hand over his wages, he will complain to the law about you and you will be found guilty. (*cf:* **tokke'**₂ **1.1**)

**katōngan** *n.* Guilt (legal); consequences of sin or law-breaking. *Ai-ai bay hinangna, ma iya na katōnganna. Katōngan iya dusa apa min iya.* Whatever he does, the results impact on him. He experiences the consequences of sin because he was the source.

**patōng dusa** *v. tr. -an* To accuse or convict someone of an offense.

**tōng**₃ *see:* **patōng**

**tonga'** *n.* **1)** The half of anything. *Lisag sangpū' maka tonga'.* Half-past ten o'clock. **1.1)** *adj. a-* Halfway to a reference point, as a container; halfway, of tidal range. *Tabayan bo' mbal na. Bang ka makatukkud buwat lawak tinda atonga' he' bohe'.* Was used for transport but not any more. If you pole it as far as the store it will be half-full of water. (*cf:* **t'ngnga'**) **1.2)** *v. intr. aN-* To reach the half-way stage. *A: "Ai s'llog?" B: "Anonga' la'ang, sali' mbal akosog."* A: "What's the current?" B: "The outgoing current is about halfway through, not really strong." **1.3)** *v. tr.* To divide something into two equal parts. *A: "Pīnno'an mital itū?" B: "Da'a, tinonga' sadja."* A: "Shall I fill this can?" B: "No, just half-fill it." *Bay tonga'nu tahik, saguwā' bay lembonu saga banta.* You divided the sea, but you drowned the enemies.

**tonga'-bahangi** *adv.* Midnight. *Llaw, sangom, makajari kita angalamat, basta duma'in ugtu-llaw atawa tonga'-bahangi.* Day or night, it's okay for us to use divination, so long as it's not [right on] noon or midnight.

**tonga'-sin-tonga'** *n.* A quarter (lit. half of half).

**tonga'an** *n.* A point or stage midway between two reference points. *Ma tonga'an Parang maka Buli' Pongpong.* Halfway between Parang and Buli' Pongpong.

**santonga'** *n.* One-half of something. (*Thesaurus:* **dambila' 1, dampōng, samalintonga'**)

**tonga'an ayan** *n. phrase* The space between earth and the seven layers of heaven; the realm of winged creatures and spirit beings.

**tongas** *v. intr. pa-* To raise one's head from a bowed position. *Bay aku patondok, na patongas na aku.* I was looking down, and now I look up. (*Thesaurus:* **hangad**)

**tongkad** *v. intr. aN-* To come to the end, of a fruiting season. (*cf:* **tobas**)

**tongka'** *see:* **pagtongka'**

**tongke'** *n.* The fruit of the lambus tree. (*cf:* **lambus**)

**tongkel** *n.* A tune played on the brass ensemble. *Lisag lagunahan, lisag tongkel na.* The *lagunahan* melody, then the *tongkel* melody.

**tongket** *v. intr. pa-* To tip forward on a fulcrum. *Buwat taytayan halam bay nilansang, patongket aku, ahūg.* Like a walkway that hasn't been nailed, I tip forward and fall down. *Bang pelang tinangon bo' abuhat dampōng, patongket isāb.* When a canoe is put up on a rack but one end is heavy, it tips forward.

  **pagtongket-tongket** *v. tr.* To tip from end to end repeatedly; to seesaw. *Maghuntak-huntak he' goyak, sali' magtongket-tongket.* Bouncing up and down on the waves, tipping from one end to another. (*Thesaurus:* **pagbullud-bullud**, **pagbuwang 1.1**, **paghandok**, **paghuntak**, **pagumpak-umpak**)

**tongko'** 1) *n.* A coil of line. *Tongko' itū hal naylon, duwampū' maka t'llu suma'an duwampū' maka duwa ma deyom datongko'. Tongko'* refers only to nylon line, with twenty-three or sometimes twenty-two fathoms in one coil. (*Thesaurus:* **birang 1, koleng₁ 1, lebod 1, pasangan₁, towa'**) 2) *clf.* Count word for coils of line or wire. *Dantongko' basi'-basi', dangkoleng.* One coil of light wire, one roll.

**tongkop** *n.* The layer of meat beneath the soft surface layer of a young coconut. (*Thesaurus:* **lahing 1, l'kkop₂, putang**)

**tongngol** *v. intr. pa-* To remain sitting, inactive. *Hal patongngol ma deyom luma', mbal magusaha.* He just stays sitting in the house, doesn't work for a living. (*Thesaurus:* **lesseg, tingkō' 1**)

**tongod₁** *adv.* 1) In regard to; with reference to. *Arapun ma tongod mma'ku, wa'i iya pina'admit ma ispital llaw itu ma Sambo.* Oh, and in regard to my father, he has been admitted to hospital in Zamboanga today. *Ma tongod ni baranku.* With regard to me personally. 1.1) *v. tr.* To compare with something; to cite something as an example. *Tinongod lallayna ni p'nnu.* Its speed was compared to a turtle.

**tongod₂** *n.* 1) The location of something. *Jari pahogga' kamemon sundalu kapam'ngngangan pagabut sigām ni tongod pah'bba'an si Anu.* So all the soldiers came to a halt, shocked speechless, on reaching where What's-his-name had fallen. 1.1) *v. intr. pa-* To be located at a specific place. *Da'a ka patongod min deyo' luma'. Kahūgan ka api.* Don't be there under the house. You'll have coals falling on you. 1.2) *v. tr.* To note the location of something. *Bang aniya' am'ssi ni Paluwas-pata anongod sigām mana-mana.* When anyone fishes at Paluwas-pata they locate themselves where there are *mana-mana* fish. *Ya bay pam'ssianta di'ilaw, ya he' panongoranta llaw itu.* The place where we were fishing yesterday, that's where we locate ourselves today. (*Thesaurus:* **atag₁ 1.1, paglahat 1.1, t'nna' 1.1**)

**pagtongod₁** *v. intr. aN-* To be located one above the other, of two items. *Subay kita magtongod bang aniya' sinōngan man deyo' luma'.* We need to be co-located when something is being handed up from below.

**tongod₃** *n.* 1) Return (financial); reciprocation of a gift or service; requital. *Tepo itū pamuwan ka'am, halam aniya' tongodna. Saddī bayad utang.* This mat is a gift to you, with no expectation of anything in return. Payment of a debt is a different matter. *Mbal tē'ku bayad ē' minsan buwattingga hekana. Asal makatabang sadja iya ma aku minsan halam aniya' tongodna.* I will not be concerned about that payment, no matter how much. He in fact has always helped me even when there is no recompense. (*cf:* **tupan 1.1**) 1.1) *v. tr. -an* To keep an account of something done or given. *Tongorin sīn itū ma tambal, pila-pila. Sīn ya panongoran, tambal ya pamatongod.* Count this money as applying to [the payment of] the medicine, however much. The money is what is counted [as recompense], the medicine is the reason for the expectation. *Mbal tinongoran hulas-sangsā'na.* He does not count his physical exertion as something to be recompensed.

**pagtongod₂** *v. intr. aN-* To be equivalent in value. *Mbal magtongod, mbal magtupan bayadna maka sangsā'.* The payment and the hard work don't match well, they aren't equivalent.

**tongol** *n.* The hard core of vegetable products such as corn, pineapple, jackfruit. *Gandum ya nili'is, tongolna ya pang'ntanan. Panggi' isāb taga tongol.* The corn is what is grated, its cob is just for holding on to. Cassava has a core too. (*Thesaurus:* **bole, botod, la'al, okol, tangkay 1**)

**tongop₁** *v. intr. pa-* 1) To enter someone's being, of a spirit. *Sali' aniya' patongop ni iya. Bang kahōpan bā'nu tinundun buwahan.* Like something has entered his being. When he is possessed you will be filled with pleasure [lit. you would think you were clustered with lansones fruit]. (*Thesaurus:* **hōp₁ 2, sangon₁ 1**) 1.1) *v. advrs. ka-...-an* To be entered or possessed by a spirit being. *Jīn maka duwata sali' du. Katongopan iya.* Djinn and *duwata* are the same. He is possessed by one.

**tongop₂** *v. tr.* To spy on someone; to eavesdrop. *Tinongop kita, kinale, tinongop tonga'-bahangi, dai'-llaw, pineyanan.* We are overheard, spied on in the middle of the night or at daybreak, watched.

  **pagtongop** *v. intr. aN-* To come physically close to each other. (*Thesaurus:* **apiki 1.1, sekot 1.2, sigpi', t'ppi' 1**)

**tōp** *adv.* 1) Fittingly; appropriately. *Ā, ya ilu pah'llingnu, angkan tōp ka subay nijīl.* There now, those are your words, that's why it is proper that you should be jailed. 1.1) *v. tr.* To be suitable or appropriate, of behavior, dress, or accessory. *Tinōp ma ka'a badju' ilū.* That shirt is suitable for you. *Mbal aku tinōp magmastal.* I am not fit to be a teacher. *Makatōp ma aku wasanwel inān bang papantalunku. Sali' alingkat kita.* That wash-and-wear material will suit me well if I use it for trousers. We'll be beautiful, so to speak. (*Thesaurus:* **amu₁, matural, patut**)

**katōpan** *n.* Something that suits or enhances. *Ya ganta' katōpan buwat saga amayan kita man pelang, amanis ni'nda'.* Something really good, for instance, is when we travel by canoe, so lovely to see.

**pagtōp** *v. intr. aN-* To interact in a way that is appropriate to context or physical properties. *Bang d'nda maka l'lla maglata, mbal magtōp.* When women and men joke with each other, it isn't an appropriate interaction. *Minsan hāg, minsan a'a, basalsalan du bang mbal magtōp hinang maka kosog.* Whether posts or people, they are overloaded whenever load and strength are not matched.

**topad** *n.* Closeness of age; similarity of physical dimensions.

**pagtopad** *v. intr. aN-* 1) To be equal in height or extent. *Papagtoparun papan ilū.* Make those planks the same height. 1.1) *v. tr.* To make things equal in height or extent. *Nilagnas itū pinagtopad sali'.* This word *lagnas* [to file teeth] is like making them equal in height.

**topad-sali'** *n.* An age-mate; a peer.

**topad-sibu'** *n.* An age-mate; a peer. *Mbal kita sumambal ma kasehe'anta atawa ni topad-sibu'ta.* We will not reach the level of our companions or of our age-mates.

**topod** *adj. a-* 1) Treated equally. *Atopod he' sigā, dakayu'-dakayu' bāng-bāng dangan a'a. Atawa bang sīn, lima puhu' lima pilak ko' atopod.* They got the same share, one cookie for one person. Or if it is money, then five people means five pesos in order to be equal. *Bang kami bay man M'ddas, bo' kita bay angusaha, b'llihan kami bāng-bāng saga siyali kami. Bang lima puhu' subay lima ko' atopod.* When we come home from Siasi after fishing we often buy cookies for our younger brothers and sisters. If there are five of them we buy five so that they are treated equally. (*Thesaurus:* **kaniya-kaniya, paggintil, pinig, tabul₁ 1.1, tarangan-tarangan**) 1.1) *v. tr. -an* To distribute things equally to several people.

**toro-toro** *v. tr.* Done indefinitely or repeatedly. *Tinoro-toro na pa'in, sali' sinigi-sigi.* Done without let-up, like being done continuously. (*Thesaurus:* **pagambat-ambat 1**)

**tinoro-toro** *adv.* Continuously; without a pause.

**toro'** 1) *v. intr. pa-* To protrude from a surface. *Patoro' bowa'na.* Her mouth protrudes. 1.1) *v. advrs. -in-* Protruding, of lips or labia. (*Thesaurus:* **juhal, jungal 1.1, tungalu'**) 2) *n.* The clitoris. (*cf:* **bigi₂**)

**torottot** *n.* A bugle; a trumpet; the sound made by a bugle. *Tiyupinbi torottot ma pussuk būd.* Play the bugle on the summit of the hill. (*cf:* **pagtiyup-tiyup 1.1**)

**totok** *n.* The Glassfish, an inshore species. *Ambassis spp.*

**totog** *adj. a-* 1) Stable; firmly fixed. 1.1) *v. intr. pa-/aN-* To remain steady; to be settled. *Bang paleyang tallung bo' kalandosan baliyu, anotog ma diyata', mbal maglensa.* When we fly a kite and a strong breeze hits it, it stays steady up above, doesn't dive around. *Patil'ngnganun, mbal anotog ma luma'.* Given to walking about, doesn't just stay at home. *Nilengog aku pasalan halam aniya' luma' patotogan saga danakanku maka ina'ku.* I am troubled because my siblings and my mother have no house as a settled-place [to stay]. 1.2) *v. tr.* To steady something, keeping it from moving. *Totogun hāg ilū bo' mbal ah'bba'.* Steady that post so it doesn't fall over.

**totos** *adj. a-* Reliable; consistent; settled. *Atotos nyawaku.* My spirit is settled. *Jīn atotos. Aniya' jīn mbal ahāp pagjīnna.* A reliable djinn. There are djinn whose djinn-quality is not good.

**pagtotos** *v. intr. aN-* To be mutually satisfied with a decision. *Magtotos sigā magbilahi maka mbal.* In full agreement as to whether or not they are attracted to each other.

**patotos** *adv.* Definitely; decisively.

**towa'** *n.* A coil of line. *Dantowa' pa'in.* Just one coil. (*Thesaurus:* **birang 1, koleng₁ 1, lebod 1, pasangan₁, tongko' 1**)

**toya'** *v. intr. aN-* To burp, of a nursing child. *Anoya', paluwas na gatas man bowa' onde'-onde'.* Burping, milk coming out of a baby's mouth. (*Thesaurus:* **balowak, pagsallowa', utta' 1**)

**toylet** *n.* A toilet; a comfort room. *Mbal tasipat. Abau to'ongan toylet lansa.* Beyond imagining. The toilet on the launch was extremely foul-smelling. (*cf:* **pagjambanan**)

**toyok** (*var.* **toyo'**) *v. intr. pa-* To tip forward, as the head of one's body, or the top of a fruit-laden tree. *At'ggol kita bay anganjaga, magtoyo'an, nilimayu'.* We had been staying awake for a long time, our heads nodding in sleep, our bodies aching. (*Thesaurus:* **kopeng, lapping-lapping, sondong**)

**pagtoyokan** *v. intr. aN-* To be tipping forward.

**patoyok** *adv.* Facing down.

**toyo'** *var. of* **toyok**

**tta'** *see:* **pag'tta', tta'an**

**tta'an** *n.* Co-occurrence of two actions or results. *Minsan ngga'i ka tta'anna an'ggit kayuwan ma bihing luma', asal aniya' s'ggit ma katilibut luma'.* Though it was not his intention [while working] to make bamboo rubbish beside the house, there is in fact rubbish all around. *Yukna, "Magay na isāb ka? Sabunu isāb aku?" Yukku, "Minsan ngga'i ka tta'anna ka'a sabuku, tu'ud aniya' nde'anku* *saddi.*" He says, "What are you up to? Did you intend to meet me?" I said, "It wasn't a deliberate co-occurrence. I simply had something else to return."

**ttap-ttap** *n.* Smacking of one's lips.

**pag'ttap-ttap** *v. intr.* *aN-* To bring the lips and tongue together repeatedly, as when tasting food or as a sign of nervousness in speaking. *Nissa nanamna bang buwattingga, ya hē' niōnan mag'ttap-ttap.* Its flavor being tested as to what it's like, that's what we call *ttap-ttap. Mag'ttap-ttap bowa'na.* His mouth kept opening and shutting. (*syn:* **k'ssap**)

**tting** (var. **k'tting**) *v. intr.* *aN-* To puff up; to bloat. *Ang'tting itū sinōd he' a'a man deyo'. Pinak'tting he' saitan.* This bloating is someone being entered by the being from the depths. Caused to bloat by a demon. (*Thesaurus:* **b'ngkak, boskag, butud**)

**tting-tting** *n.* A balloon; a bubble. *Wa'i abustak tting-tting, bay pinaheya'an.* The balloon has burst, it was made very large.

**ttus-ttus** *n.* 1) A condition marked by multiple pustules on the skin. (*Thesaurus:* **ka'mbo'an, kawit₂ 1, kolera, ipul 1, pangkot 1, upāng 1**) 1.1) *v. advrs.* *-in-* Affected by a skin disease symptomised by pustules.

**tuba** *n.* 1) A plant-based poison for stupefying fish. *Tuba ni'isi ni deyom puyu'-puyu' labit, ati ginuyud ma deyom sowang.* The poison is put inside a bark bag, then dragged along in the channel. (*Thesaurus:* **lagtang 1, tuwa 1**) 1.1) *v. tr.* To catch fish using plant-based poison. *Niā' min po'on tuwak, panuba, panglagtang. Saddi tuwa.* Obtained from the sugar palm, used for stupefying or stunning fish. *Tuwa* is different.

**tubad** *v. tr.* *a-, ka-..-an, -an* To disclose facts to someone; to be frank. *Subay aku bā'annu, subay aku tubarannu.* You should tell me, you should disclose the facts to me. (*Thesaurus:* **haka 1.1, palapal, pata'u**)

**tubag** *v. intr.* *a-* To die instantly. *Subay bay kinakal atawa bay nirugsu' bo' atubag.* One would have to be clubbed or stabbed to die instantly. *A: "Da'a ka ula-ula." B: "Atubag aku."* A: "Don't fool around." B: "May I die right now [if I am lying]." (*Thesaurus:* **bugtang, bugtu' napas, butawan 1.1, halol, matay₁ 1, sagpe' 2**)

**katubagan** *n.* A part of the body vulnerable to a killing blow. *Bay taluwa' ma lendo'na, ma katubaganna.* He was hit on the forehead, in a mortal spot.

**tubag-tubag** *n.* The attachments for the vibrating cord of certain kites. (*cf:* **saldang 2**)

**tuba'** var. of **toba'**

**tubbal** var. of **tugbal**

**tubig** *see:* **panubigan**

**tubil** *v. tr.* *-an* To add something to an existing amount. *Buwat am'lla buwas. "Tubil-tubilin gi' bohe'na ilū," yukna.* Like cooking rice. "Just add

a little more water," she said. *Amuwan kita, tubilanta gi'.* We're giving something, we're adding a bit more. (*Thesaurus:* **k'nnop 1.2, ganap 1.2, jukup 1.2**)

**tublak₁** *v. tr.* 1) To dip an item of staple food into broth or sweet liquid. (*Thesaurus:* **bahug 1.1, butag, dulis, t'nno'**) 1.1) *v. tr.* *-an* To dip a finger into some liquid. *Subay tinublakan tudlu'na kowan ni laha' hē'.* The finger of his right hand should be dipped into the blood.

**tublak₂** *v. tr.* *-an* To identify something or someone by name. *Bang magsuli-suli a'a, yuk dakayu', "Si Anu hē' maka'ā' daing aheya." Yuk dangan, "Tublakin na ōnna, sai?" Sambung dangan hē', "Si Ab ya makahā' daing aheya."* When people are talking and one says, "What's-his-name there has caught a large fish." The other says, "State his name, who is it?" The first one's answers: "It's Ab who has caught a large fish." (*cf:* **tugpang 1.1**)

**tubu₁** *n.* The glass chimney of a wick lamp; a waterpipe.

**tubu₂** var. of **tugu**

**tubu-tubu** *n.* The growth of vegetation.

**paltubu-tubuhan** (var. **paltumbu-tumbuhan**) *n.* 1) Growing things of the vegetable kingdom; vegetation in general. (*Thesaurus:* **legotoman, l'mput deya, sayul 1;** *syn:* **paltomo'-tomo'an**) 2) The human body as a living organism; a person's constitution or bodily frame. (*Thesaurus:* **akal-baran, batang-tubu, pagdayaw 1, tangkorak**)

**tubud** *v. intr.* *pa-/aN-* 1) To flow out or increase in volume, of water in a well. *Sidda alandos bohe' patubud ma deyom.* The water flowing into [the well] is exceedingly strong. 1.1) *v. tr.* *-an* To leave a well to refill through seepage. *Bang bay atigang bohe', subay tinuburan pabīng. Agaranta sadja.* When a well has become dry, it must be left to fill again. We just wait for it.

**tuburan** *n.* The seepage or flow of a water source.

**tubu'** *n.* 1) Offspring; descendants. *In saga tubu'nu subay luggiya' min panghola'nu sadja.* Your offspring should be totally from your own spouse. (*Thesaurus:* **anak₁ 1, mpu, onde' 1**) 1.1) *v. intr.* *pa-* To descend from a forebear. *Ba'anan palbangsa-bangsahan ya patubu' min nabi Ibrahim.* The many nations descended from the prophet Abraham.

**tubu'-manubu'** *n.* One generation after another.

**tubu'an** *n.* 1) The descendants who maintain family traditions of livelihood and religion. *Halam aniya' tubu'an ma anakna kamemon. Mbal kabeya'an bay usaha kamatto'ahan.* Among all his children there are none to carry on the family traditions. The livelihood of the forebears is not followed. 2) Inherited practices and skills. *Buwat kami, na bay kamatto'ahan kami hē', nihinang bay mma' kami mareyom dunya itū. Aniya' tubu'anna.* Like us and [the lives of] those forebears of ours, and what our fathers did while on earth. They had inherited skills.

**pagpanubu'** *v. intr. aN-* To be passed down through successive generations.

**panubu'** *n.* Descendants.

**panubu'an** *n.* A family line; a descent group.

**tubus₁** (var. **tupus**) *adj. a-* 1) Complete to the last detail. *Ajukup, halam aniya' kulang, halam aniya' beklo', halam aniya' sā'na, atubus.* Complete, nothing lacking, nothing bent, no error, perfect. *Atupus na utang, bay na binayaran.* The debt is dealt with, it has been paid. **1.1)** *v. tr.* To carry out one's obligations in full. *Minsan mbal atupus llaw itu, kalu atupus salung. Tupusku pa'in.* Even if it is not completed today, it may be completed tomorrow. I will do it in full. *Buwat saupama anakta, subay sulutta panupusanta, bo' halam aniya' susunan anak ma matto'a.* Our children for example, we should please them with our full commitment so that there is no regret between children and parents. (*Thesaurus:* **talus₁**, **tekmod**) **1.2)** *v. ditr.* To carry out something in full. *Buwat aniya' maglakibini bo' halam du at'ggol pagpūn sigā, bo' sali' ahukaw d'nda. Min d'nda ya angalupit, minsan halam atupus.* Like a married couple not long together, and the woman is somewhat reluctant. The woman's side is responsible to return the bride-wealth, even if not the complete amount.

**panubusan** *n.* Full obligation; firm commitment.

**tubus₂** *v. advrs. -in-* 1) True to one's forebears or namesake. *Tinubus ma ōnna, ma ta'una, ma hinangna.* He is true in his name, his knowledge, his livelihood. *Allō! Ahāp d'ndana, tinubus ma ōnna (si Dayang-dayang)!* Wow! So feminine, true to her name (Princess)! *Bang d'nda anganak nsa' at'kka ai-ai, hatina tinubus ma hinang kamatto'ahan, halam ainay.* When a woman gives birth without anything [bad] happening, it means that she is true to the procedures of the ancestors, nothing going wrong. (*Thesaurus:* **ntan₂** 2, **pali-pali**, **pangkatan**, **purukan**, **tuttulan**, **usulan**) **1.1)** *v. intr. aN-* To follow the traditional occupation of one's forebears, and to inherit their ritual and mental abilities. *Anubus du pa'in panganak inān ma hinang kamatto'ahan.* The children consistently follow the traditional activities of the forebears. (*cf:* **s'ppu**)

**tūk** *n.* 1) A stake in gambling; a bet; a risk. *Tūk, man dambila' dahatus man dambila' dahatus, hatina magbāk dahatus.* A bet, one hundred from each side, in other words coming up with a matching ₱100. **1.1)** *v. tr.* To wager or risk something.

**pagtūk** *v. intr. aN-* To bet against each other. *Magtūk kita magbola atawa magbulang.* We wager on ball games or cockfights.

**pagtūkan** *n.* A place where punters bet on the outcome of cockfights; a cockpit. (*Thesaurus:* **ayuk-ayuk**, **manuk-sigun**, **pagbulang**,

pagtakbi')

**tūk ka'llum** *v. tr.* To risk one's life. {idiom} *Bay panūk ka'llumna supaya kām kaliyusan min komkoman sigām.* He risked his life so you would be freed from their control. *Bay panūkku ka'llumku ni kamatay ma sabab ka'a.* My life was put in danger of death because of you.

**tukad₁** *v. intr. pa-* 1) To go up a slope; to go inland. *Salung patukad kita kaleya.* Tomorrow we will go inland, up the hill. (*Thesaurus:* **kaleya 1, kaut 1, lūd, takod 1**) **1.1)** *v. tr.* To climb something sloping, as a hill, a road. *Anukad kita lān inān.* We will climb that path. **1.2)** *v. tr. -an* To get something by going uphill or upstream. *Tukaranta, da'a kita palaranun min pandoga.* Move upwind [or up-current], don't let us drift away from the landmarks.

**tukaran** *n.* An upward slope. (*Thesaurus:* **baha-būd, bīd, būd 1, lorosan**)

**tukad₂** *adj. a-* Wrinkle-free. *Pinilinsa bo' pinilinsa sampay atukad pahāp.* Ironed and ironed until it's really smooth.

**tukag** *n.* A prop; a pole for supporting the outer peak of a four-cornered sail; a sprit. (*Thesaurus:* **takāk, taruk, tindakan, tuklug 1**)

**tuka'** *n.* The beak, of birds and certain fish. *Ellog, ataha' tuka'na angeket.* Herons have long beaks and can bite. *"S'nsongku," yuk kallo', "maka tuka'ku."* "I will stuff it in," said the egret, "with my beak."

**tukang** (var. **tutukang**) *n.* A skilled worker; an artisan. *Tutukang, ya magbubuhat ni a'a kamemon.* An expert, the one who serves food to all the guests. *Iya ya tukang magsugsug-tawbat.* He is the person expert in the reconciliation ritual. (*Thesaurus:* **panday 1, pantas, tangpas₂**)

**pagtukang** *v. intr. aN-* To make a living doing the skilled work of an artisan. *B'nnal isāb ata'u aku aganu-anu magtukangan. Sagō' ya gauna mbal kata'uhanku.* It's true that I know how to do this and that, doing skilled work. But the funnel of a fish trap, that I don't know how.

**tukas** *adj. a-* 1) Provoked; challenged; tested as to courage or manhood. *Atukas ko' ka'a ilu, esog-esognu ilū!* You fail the challenge, you with your so-called courage! *Atukas kapagl'llana, magsulay.* His masculinity challenged, contesting it with someone. **1.1)** *v. tr.* To provoke or challenge someone by implying cowardice or immorality. *Halam aniya' hinabta'uku abilahi'an aku d'nda inān, sakali tinukas aku he'na.* I had no idea that I was supposed to be in love with that girl, when suddenly she accused me of having designs on her. *Buwat si Mu maka si Ig, saukat na sigā magbeya'-beya', tinuhuma na sigā magbaya' bo' halam. Ati tinukas he' sai-sai maka'nda'.* Like Mu and Ig, just because they were going along together' it is rumored that they are in love with each other, though it's not so. Now they are taunted by anybody who saw them. (cf: **bulas₁, himulas**)

**pagtukas** v. intr. aN- To be engaged in a contest of courage or strength. *Magtukas kita. Min aku bangka' biyaning, min ka'a bangka' pote'. Bang anganda'ug bangka' biyaning ē', aku anganda'ug.* Let's see who wins. The yellow canoe is mine, the white one is yours. If that yellow canoe wins, I am the victor.

**tukaw** v. intr. pa- To become public, of information previously kept private. *Patukaw itū bissala bay tinapukan sogō' paluwa' na, patukaw na.* Tukaw is about talk that has been hidden but now comes out, becomes public. (*Thesaurus:* **bulat, luwas₁ 1, tuwa' 1**)

**patukawan** n. The origin of something said.

**tukbal₁** v. ditr. 1) To deliver something to a destination; to deliver a person to an authority. *Mbal iya patut tinukbalan ni pulis sabab halam bay tu'udna atawa niyatna amapatay pagkahina ē'.* It is not appropriate for him to be handed over to the police because it was neither deliberate nor his intention to kill that companion of his. (*Thesaurus:* **maksud 1.2, nde', papole', pasampay, tūd₂, tulun₂ 1.1, tuyuk-tuyuk**) 2) To present something to someone as a gift or offering. *Tukbalanku isāb ma ka'a bahagi' sangpū' min ai-ai kamemon ya pamasuku'nu ma aku.* I will also hand over to you a tenth part of all the things you have given to me.

**tutukbalan** n. An offering to a deity; an important gift.

**tukbal₂** v. ditr. To refer a decision to a higher or more competent authority. *Bang aniya' hinangku bo' mbal takole'ku, tukbalanku ni a'a apanday.* If I am making something and can't manage it, I hand it over to someone who is expert. *Halam sali' aniya' sara' ma lahat inān angkan si Abunawas mikitukbal na ni Sultan.* There was no magistrate in that place so Abunawas [a folk hero] appealed to the sultan. (*Thesaurus:* **dagsol, ikiral, paglagadlad**)

**tukbu'** var. of **lukbu'₂**

**tukbul** adj. zero Aligned.

**pagtukbul** v. tr. To be in alignment, of two or more physical items. *Basta magtukbul duwa kayu sali'-sali', mahē' na paghūg bubu.* Provided the two trees are in exact alignment, that is where the fish traps are dropped. *Na ilu, bang kita angamalit, subay pinagtukbul kayu hē' bo' ta'nda' pandoga hē', bo' mbal alungay.* Now then, when we are checking *bubu*-type fish traps, those trees yonder should be in alignment for the reference point to be visible, so it won't be lost [sight of].

**patukbul** v. ditr. To move something along to the next point in a sequence.

**tukbung** v. intr. pa- 1) To fall headlong. *Arāk patukbung tallungna ni bangkaw.* His kite might have plunged into the mangroves. (*Thesaurus:* **hūg₁ 1, pakpak 1, togge'₁, tulelle, tumba₁**) 1.1) v. tr. -an To make something fall headlong.

*Tukbunganta ka. Hatina nihūg kita dahū kōkta.* I'll throw you down headlong. In other words one is dropped headfirst.

**tukkal** v. intr. pa- To go fishing without a companion. *Patukkal aku, anganggonteng.* I fish on my own, using multiple hooks in one location. (cf: **damunda'-munda' 1, tunggal-tunggal 1**)

**tukkay-tukkay** v. intr. pa- To move out to the extremity of something. (syn: **tōng-tōng 1.1**)

**tukkud** var. of **tungkud**

**tukku'** 1) v. intr. pa- To lower one's head to rest on hand or knee, as due to fatigue or emotional distress. *Patukku' kita ma tanganta atawa ma tu'utta.* We lower our head onto our hands or our knees. *Pakuru' itū aniya' ko'otta atawa hinangta. Patukku' itū halam hinangna, hal magkarukka'an.* This word *kuru'* is when we are picking something up or doing something. With *tukku'* one is not doing anything, just grieving. 2) v. intr. pa-/-um- To fall forward due to one's foot bending over. *Patukku' tape'ta, halam bay nda'ta palabayan.* Our foot stumbles, we haven't seen the path. *"Angay aku judjalannu? Wa'i na aku tumukku'."* "Why did you bump me? I have stumbled now." *Bang kita lum'ngngan bo' makarugtul tape'ta, makatukku' kita.* When we are walking and our foot trips, we stumble.

**tukid** adj. a- 1) Focused on a task; committed to a goal; undiverted. *Ai-ai hinangta subay atukid.* Whatever we do should be focused on. *Bang aniya' bay ni'indaman subay atukid ang'nde'. Subay aku ya amapole'an ni ka'a, buwat subu-si'.* When something has been borrowed [the borrower] should return it without being distracted. I should be the one to return it to you, like this morning. (cf: **tebot**; *Thesaurus:* **podlongan, sogsog 1, taggu₂ 1.1, togol 1**) 1.1) v. tr. -an To do something without being diverted. *Bang at'kka man dilaut, bo' abase' banog, subay tinukiran ni'llawan.* When someone arrives from fishing with a wet sail, it should be hung out to dry without being distracted.

**tuklang** n. A thorn; a sharpened stick. *"Abakat ka," yuk tohongan, "he' tuklang itū."* "You'll hurt yourself," said the turtle, "on these spikes." (*Thesaurus:* **iting 1, leget, tunuk**)

**tukling** n. A bird species, distinguished by its bald head. *Sarcops calvus. Manuk tukling, aungas kōkna, sumantuk kōkna ma diyata' langit.* The *tukling* bird, its head is bald, its head banging against the sky. (gen: **manuk-manuk 1**)

**tuklug** n. 1) A prop for supporting the outer peak of a sail; a sprit. (*Thesaurus:* **takāk, taruk, tindakan, tukag**) 1.1) v. tr. To prop up the sail. *Bang bay sinampila', bo' pahali baliyu, tinuklug pabalik.* When the sail is shortened, then the wind stops, it is propped back up. *Niaru itū tinuklug tonga'-tonga'. Aru* here means having the sprit at the half-way position.

**tuksu'** *v. advrs. ka-...-an* To be satisfied or contented with an outcome. *Buwat sali'-sali' ya b'llita, makab'lli aku aluhay. Katuksu'an aku aluhay.* Like when we are buying similar things, and I happen to buy cheaply. I am happy with the cheapness. *Halam iya katuksu'an ma hinang h'ndana.* He wasn't satisfied [or in full agreement] with what his wife was doing. *Bang d'nda maka l'lla magkawin bo' magtaluwa', dakulis du, dasukud, katuksu'an.* When a woman and a man get married and they suit each the other, there is a single fate, a single fortune, they are mutually contented. (*Thesaurus:* **amu₂ 1.1, bilīb, kompolme**)

**pagtuksu'** *v. intr. aN-* To be mutually suited; to be compatible. *Bang d'nda maka l'lla magkawin, bo' dakulis, magtuksu'.* When a man and a woman marry who have the same fate, they are really suited to each other. *Buwat ka'a, magtuksu' ōnnu ahāp maka barannu ahāp.* Like you, your good name and your good physique matching. *Ahāp bang magtuksu' a'a pinandu'an maka ya amandu'.* It's good when the person being taught and the one teaching are suited to each other. *Bang saki bo' tinambalan, ahāp magtuksu' maka tambal.* When a sick person is treated with medicine, it's good that he and the medicine are compatible. (*cf:* **pagtaluwa'**)

**tuktuk** *n.* The forehead; the temple. *Nirugsu'an iya ma kīd tuktukna bo' alopot kōkna.* He was stabbed in the side of his brow so that his head was shattered. (*syn:* **lendo'**)

**tuku** 1) *n.* A short vertical post or prop. (*Thesaurus:* **bale₃ 1, hāg 1, lusuk-lusuk, pangtu'ud, pipul, sumpiyang**) **1.1)** *v. tr.* To support something with a short post (in a building). **2)** *v. tr.* To support someone in negotiations. *Ameya' anuku kawalihan.* Relatives from the mother's side combine to give support.

**tuku langit** *v. tr.* To do the impossible (usually with a negative). {idiom} *Buwat h'ndanu, susa buwattē', bimbang anak-h'llana, maka alawak lahat. Daipara ngga'i ka kita ya magkabaya'an. Mbal tatukuta langit.* Like your wife, with such trouble, anxious for her husband and children, and the place so far away. However, we are not the ones to decide. We cannot do the impossible [lit. prop up the sky].

**tukul** *n.* **1)** A carpenter's hammer. **1.1)** *v. tr.* To hammer something in. (*cf:* **p'ppok**)

**tukung** *n.* A tailless chicken. *Manuk tukung, halam aniya' togelna.* A *tukung* chicken, it has no tail. (*Thesaurus:* **labuyu'₁, manuk 1**)

**tūd₁** (var. **tūt**) *adj. -an* **1)** To be following, of the wind (when sailing). *Minsan baliyu tūran, bang aniya' bilahi, pabiluk kita.* Even though it's a following wind, if someone wants to, we change direction. **1.1)** *v. intr. pa-* To run freely before the wind (when sailing). *Bang bay amiluk, tugutanta na deyo' apa patūt.* When we've changed tack, we let out the main sheet [lower boom rope] because we're running before the wind. *Na bang bay baliyu, animpasan, amiluk, pinatūt na.* Now if there had been wind, [we] would reset the sail, change tack, and let it run before the wind. *Bang llaw Juma'at subay angalamat dahū bo' yampa patūd. Bang ala'at e'ta ang'nda' putika'an, subay da'a sinōngan l'ngngan.* When it is a Friday we should consult by divination before sailing with a following wind. If what we see in the divination is bad, the journey should not be continued.

**tūd₂** *v. ditr.* To deliver something to its destination or former location. *Tūranta ka simuddai ni Sisangat.* I will take you back to Sisangat the day after tomorrow. *Tinūran ka ma lansa-lansa bulawan.* You will be returned-home by a golden motor-boat. *Mbal makaepang papan itu, tūranku na.* This board won't match [the others], I'll send it back. (*Thesaurus:* **maksud 1.2, nde', papole', pasampay, tukbal₁ 1, tulun₂ 1.1, tuyuk-tuyuk**)

**tuddi'** *v. intr. pa-* To project noticeably, of a person's buttocks when walking. *Sali' patuddi' buli'ta ni buli'an, sali' mbal abontol he'ta lum'ngngan.* Our buttocks project to our rear, as though we are not walking straight. (*cf:* **tuwal 1.1**)

**tudjak** *v. intr. pa-* To move upwards. *Patudjak pariyata' humbu.* The smoke rises high into the sky. *Bang ka angā' lokay niyug, ngā'un ya patudjak.* When you get young coconut fronds, get the ones that stick up.

**tudjara** (var. **sudjara**) *n.* A prayer carpet. *Tudjara itū panambahayangan. Tahinang bulbul, taga langgal, bitu'un.* This carpet is for praying on. It is made of wool, has a mosque or stars. (*Thesaurus:* **musalla, palmaddani'**)

**tudju₁** (var. **sudju**) *prep.* **1)** Towards (direction). *Lum'ngngan na ka tudju pī'.* Walk away in that direction. *Bang kami amusay ni Sisangat bo' sōn, palibut kami sudju Lapak.* When we are travelling to Sisangat and the tide is coming in, we go around towards Lapak. *Pagmahē' kami ma kappal, na tudju na kami Sambuwangan.* Once there in the ship, heading for Zamboanga. *Karugsu'an pa'in iya ma b'ttongna, magtūy pahudhud tina'ina tudju tana'.* Having been stabbed in the stomach, his entrails quickly gushed out onto the ground. (*cf:* **tampal 1**; *Thesaurus:* **ma 1, min 1, ni₁**) **1.1)** *v. intr. pa-/-um-* To head in a particular direction. *Datumpuk inān bay patudju ni kauman Sibaud.* That one group went towards the Sibaud settlement. *Bang kita bay sinagda he' matto'ata, bo' sali' mbal ameya'-meya', yuk-i, "Magkasosōng ka'a ilū magkangī'-ngī'. Mbal tumudju ni kahāpan, ni kala'atan."* When we are corrected by our parents but don't really obey, they say, "As time goes on you will come to a bad end. You will not head for good but for bad."

**katudjuhan** *n.* An outcome or goal. *Yukna ma aku, "Subay aku angahinang tepo. Asubahat aku bang ai to'ongan katudjuhan hinangku."* She said to me, "I must make a mat. I'm muddled about what course I should really take to do so."

**tudju₂** *adj. a-* 1) Accurate as to aim; on target. (*Thesaurus:* **taluwa'** 1, **tigi'-tigi'₁** 1, **t'bbong**, **tumlang** 2) 1.1) *v. tr.* To aim at some goal. *Tudjuhun tōng batu inān.* Head for that rocky point. *Buwat a'a magkuntaw inān, minsan buwattingga he' anudju iya maka ai-ai, katangkisan sadja.* Like that fellow doing martial arts, no matter whatever you aim at him with, is simply dodged.

**tudjuhan** *n.* Something aimed at; a target. *In sapda halam aniya' kamaujuranna sapantun pana' halam aniya' tudjuhanna.* A curse without a goal is like an arrow without a target.

**tudjun** *v. tr.* 1) To strike a target with something thrown. *Tudjunta maka bila' poga. Ya he' pamatu'ta.* We make our throw with a potsherd. That is what we use as our marker. 1.1) *n.* A game which involves throwing a puck at a target on a marked board.

**pagtudjun** *v. intr. aN-* To play the game of tudjun. *Akat'bbong ni lowang, buwat kita magtudjun.* It falls accurately into the hole, like when we play the game of *tudjun*.

**tudlu'₁** *n.* The forefinger (second finger); the second toe.

**tudlu'₂** *v. tr.* 1) To point something out, generally with one's hand or with lips projected in the appropriate direction. (*Thesaurus:* **pandu** 2, **tō'** 1) 1.1) *v. tr. -an* To teach someone by pointing to the correct item, as when learning to read the Holy Koran.

**tugak** *adj. a-* Hairless, due to baldness or recent shaving. (*cf:* **bagoggol** 1)

**tugbal** (var. **tubbal**) *v. tr.* To plant something using a dibble stick in uncultivated soil. (*Thesaurus:* **bakal, tanom₁** 1)

**tuggay** var. of **tughay**

**tughay** (var. **tuggay**) *v. tr.* To operate a business enterprise single-handedly. *Tanuggayna, mbal amahaup. Takole' bīlli he'na.* He can handle it on his own, he won't go into partnership, he is able to buy it himself.

**pagtughay** *v. intr. aN-* 1) To leave the management of an enterprise to one individual. 1.1) *v. tr.* To have one person responsible for a task. *Pinagtughay ma dangan.* Letting one person handle it. (*Thesaurus:* **paghaup, paghūn, pagsapali, pagtiguway, pagtintuway**)

**tugila'** *adj. a-* 1) Clear and specific. *Hama'-hama' a'a itū mbal ta'nda' ma a'a. Bang tugila' to'ongan, saitan.* This house-based spirit being is not seen by humans. It is, to be very specific, a *saitan* spirit. 1.1) *v. tr.* To describe exactly; to detail particulars of an item; to identify by name.

*Tugila'un bang sai bay amono' ka'a.* Be specific about the person who hit you. *Bang aku angōnan a'a subay tugila'ku. Subay tinugpang ōn a'a.* When I name someone I should be specific. The name of the person should be specifically stated. (*Thesaurus:* **anyak-anyak, sokat₁** 1, **tutat** 1.1)

**tugna'** *v. tr. -an* To specify details; to make an appointment. *Halam bay anugna' bang sumiyan ya kapi'itu sigā.* They didn't say precisely when they will come. *Tugna'in matto'ana kohap bang buwattingga idda doktol.* Advise his parents this afternoon as to the doctor's appointment. (*Thesaurus:* **idda** 1.1, **ligtung, ora, pagtaratu, tugun** 1.1, **waktu** 1.1)

**tugnus₁** *adj. a-* 1) Pulled out by the roots. *Atugnus bu'unna.* Her hair is pulled out by the roots. (*Thesaurus:* **bubut, bugnus₂, darut** 1.1, **hublut** 1) 1.1) *v. tr.* To pull something out, roots and all.

**tugnus₂** *n.* 1) A fee paid to the litigating authority by a couple involved in divorce proceedings. 1.1) *v. ditr.* To pay a fee to the person litigating a divorce case. *Anugnus kami sangpū' pilak man d'nda maka man l'lla. Pamuwan sara' bang aniya' magtiman.* We pay a fee of ten pesos from the woman and from the man. The gift goes to the person who administers the law when someone is divorcing.

**tugpa'** *v. intr. pa-* 1) To jump down onto something. *Patugpa' ka, mbal ka ainay.* Jump down, nothing will happen to you. (*Thesaurus:* **kuppa** 1, **laksu₁, sulakat**) 1.1) *v. tr.* To reach something by jumping down. *Pal'kkas ka! Tugpa'un! Ilu palaran.* Hurry up! Jump down for it! It's drifting away.

**tugpang** *adj. a-* 1) Identified by name; specific. *Subay panyām bo' atugpang.* Should say *panyam* [a rice-cake] to be specific. 1.1) *v. tr.* To mention someone by name. *Bang yuk dangan, "Sai tunangnu?" bo' yuk dangan, "A'a ba." Halam tinugpang.* If one person says, "Who is your sweetheart?" and the other says, "Just a person." Not specifically named. *Buwat aniya' a'a bay anangkaw mareyom luma'nu, tilawnu bang sai bay anangkaw. Tinugpang magtūy si Ip.* Like there's someone stealing in your house, and you ask who was stealing. Ip was promptly named. (*cf:* **tublak₂**)

**tugsuk** *n.* 1) A table fork. (*syn:* **tinerol**) 2) A hypodermic needle; an injection. *Pila tugsuk? Duwampū' maka lima tugsuk bang keket ero'.* How many injections? Twenty-five injections when bitten by a [rabid] dog. 2.1) *adj. a-* Poked; stabbed. *Bay atugsuk si Ne e' seplak kayu.* Ne was jabbed with a sliver of wood. 2.2) *v. tr.* To pierce something with a thin, pointed object; by extension, to inject someone. *Tugsukku tainganu panganggantungan dolmelo.* I will pierce your ears for suspending earrings from. *Bang ni'isihan lapuk-lapuk ma daun, subay taga koyang* *tinugsukan bo' mbal ap'kkal.* When cassava candy is put into a leaf it should have a toothpick inserted so it doesn't unwrap. (*Thesaurus:* **kussu'**, **langgit 1**, **sudlat 1.1**, **suruk**)

**tugtug** *v. tr. -an* To envelop a person or thing in the fumes of incense. *Angalingan pabalik saga maglurukan, yuk-i, "Itiya' ka tugtuganku maka kamanyan, pareyo' ka pi'itu."* The guests call out again [to the spirit], saying, "I have burnt incense over you, come on down here." (*Thesaurus:* **pat'bbud**)

  **tugtugan** *n.* A censer; a container in which live coals are held. *Tugtugan paminta-mintahanta ni mbo' (atawa ni Tuhan). Yukta, "O Mbo', itiya' na aku aminta-minta tudju ni ka'a. Itiya' ummatnu pinapanjari e'nu. Na ang'nda' ka, ka'a-i aheya matanu."* A censer is something used in requesting help from a ritual ancestor (or from God.) One says, "O ancestor, here I am making a request towards you. Here is your creature whom you made. So look, you whose eyes are large."

**tugu** (var. **tubu₂**) *v. advrs. -in-* Endowed with expert knowledge and skills. *Si Anu, yuk-i, tinugu anambal-tawal. Tinugu ma ta'una, ma hinangna.* What's-his-name, they say, is expert in carrying out healing rites. Expert in his knowledge and actions. *Bang a'a tinugu e' salawat, b'nnal langtasna.* When someone is enabled by the supernormal, his ability to see the future is genuine. *Nihinang-hinang kita, a'a mangahinang-hinang-i ata'u. Yukta, "Tinubu a'a hē'."* We are affected by a spell, the person doing it having the arcane knowledge, we say, "That person is competent to do what is needed." *Minsan ma ariplano, tinubu na pa'in paelot minsan magbadju'.* Even with an airplane, the pilot is always expertly skilled even in a typhoon. (*Thesaurus:* **auliya'**, **langtas 1**, **tulun₁ 1**)

  **pagtugu** *n.* **1)** An acquired ability in the use of healing skills and charms. **1.1)** *v. intr. aN-* To be skilled in applying traditional knowledge to matters of health and behavior. *Magtugu, yuk-i, saga a'a bay magtambal-tawal.* It was said that they were specially skilled, those people who used medicines and charms. *Bang mbal tauwa', yukta, "Mbal magtugu."* If [the treatment] doesn't meet the need, we say, "He is not skilled [in traditional healing]." **1.2)** *v. tr.* To acquire special abilities in healing and the use of charms. *A'a pinagtugu, a'a nsa' asammal, nsa' bay angakkal, nsa' karapatan.* A person who has acquired *tugu* abilities is not indecent, does not cheat, does not let people down.

**tugun** *n.* **1)** An agreed-on time; an appointment. **1.1)** *v. tr.* To specify a course or time of action. *Halam ka makat'kka ma waktu bay panugunnu.* You had not arrived at the time you specified. (*Thesaurus:* **idda 1.1**, **ligtung**, **ora**, **pagtaratu**, **tugna'**, **waktu 1.1**)

**tugut** **1)** *v. intr. pa-* To slacken, of the flow of a current. *Ingga na patugut s'llog.* As soon as the current eases off. (*Thesaurus:* **keyas**, **kō' 1.1**, **kontay₂**, **hulaw**, **patokang**) **1.1)** *v. tr. -an* To let out slack in a line or sail. *Ya palabuta i' langkay, tinugutan saga sangpū' d'ppa ko' alallay nilaranan.* Our anchor there was a coconut frond, with about ten fathoms of line paid out so we would be carried slowly by the current. *Tugutin deyo' bang patūt.* Slacken off the lower sheet when running before the wind. (*Thesaurus:* **taguntun 1.1**, **tali-tali₂**, **tuntun₁ 1**) **2)** *v. tr. -an* To give someone the freedom to behave as he pleases. *"Da'a tugutin si Oto'." Ya hē' tinambukuhan he' mma'na.* "Don't let Eldest Son do as he wants." That's what his father advised. (*Thesaurus:* **paba'id**, **pakuhi**, **papuhun**, **parūl 1.1**)

  **patugut** *v. tr. -an* To permit someone to act in a specific way.

**Tuhan** *n.* God; the supreme supernatural being. (*cf:* **Allah**)

  **pagtuhanan** *n.* People or things treated as having god-like status. *Matto'ata ya sali' pagtuhananta ma deyom dunya.* Our parents are like gods to us here on earth. *Pagubus maina'an, pinat'ngge e' sigām saga ta'u-ta'u' ya pagtuhanan sigām.* After being there, they erected the effigies they revered as gods. *Ya bay pagtuhanan saga ka'mbo'-mbo'an kami.* The one our ancestors acknowledged as god. *Mbal minsan tasibahatku ōn saga pagtuhanan sigām.* I cannot even utter the names of their gods.

  **tuhan-tuhan** *n.* Gods in general; demigods.

**tuhug** **1)** *v. tr.* To thread multiple items onto a length of string or vine, forming a bundle. *Sali' kita anendero ni lūng-kampungta. Bang at'kka magtabang-tabang kita anuhug.* It's like us serving as agent for a village-mate. When we arrive we help each other string the fish. *Atakabbul, tinuhug e' Tuhan bang ah'lling.* Speaking arrogantly, [his words] stored by God on a string. (*Thesaurus:* **lingkit 1.1**, **surut**, **tōhan**) **2)** *v. tr.* To join flat items by inserting a thread along their joined edges. *Manjari angā' sigām dahun kayu tinuhug-tuhug e' sigām nihinang panambun.* So they got some tree leaves and strung them together to make a covering. **3)** *clf.* Count word for strings of things, most commonly of fish. *Makajari isāb p'ttung nihinang tuhug daing.* It's also possible to make a string for fish from bamboo. *Pila sīn dantuhug?* How much is one string?

  **ma tuhugan** *adv. phrase* By the string. *Daing bīlli ma tuhugan.* Fish bought by the string.

**tuhuma** *n.* **1)** A rumor; a suspicion. (*Thesaurus:* **hunub-hunub 1.1**, **taha**, **tuna'**, **waham**) **1.1)** *v. tr.* To say something which may not be true; to spread a rumor. *Bay tinuhuma kanu'us amangan a'a. Halam bay ta'nda'.* It has been rumored that squids eat humans. It hasn't [actually] been seen. *Buwat kita magsapa, s'lle' bale puhu', aku tuhumanu bay angā' ai-ainu bo' halam du isāb sab'nnal-b'nnal. Na ta'abut magsapa, bang amatay man dambila' dangan, palikid isāb parambila'.* Like two of us swearing an oath, when, God forbid, you accuse me of taking something of yours but it is not true, then it comes to the swearing of an oath. When the man on one side dies it rebounds on the other.

**tuhun** *v. intr.* pa-/a- **1)** To dive into water; to submerge. *Pagtas'bbat t'lla'-t'lla' he' kalitan bang patuhun.* Seagulls can be swallowed whole by a shark when they dive [for fish]. *Pasakay iya ni bay sehe'na min damunda' inān, ai-ai na sali' pamat'nna'an iya, buwat saga patuhun, angahella'.* He travels with his companions from that other boat, doing whatever is assigned to him, like diving or hauling rope. (*Thesaurus:* **lorok 1, lurup**) **1.1)** *v. tr.* To reach something by diving. *Palebod ma batu bahan bubu, mbal pala'an. Subay tinuhun, pinuwasan man batu.* The vine of the fish trap is looped around a coral rock and won't come free. It must be reached by diving, and disentangled from the rock. **1.2)** *v. tr.* -an To get something by diving for it. *Bang bay tuhunannu, mbal du bay alungay.* If you had dived for it, it wouldn't be lost. *Ya tingga' itū binowa pareyo' panuhunan tipay bo' al'kkas.* This lead-weight is carried downwards to an oyster diving place, in order to be quick.

**pagtuhun** *v. intr.* aN- To earn a living by diving.

**pagtutuhun** *v. intr.* aN- To be engaged in diving for a living. *Bang a'a magtutuhun subay duwangan anuhun, subay aniya' ugpangna.* When a man dives for a living there should be two of them diving, he should have a partner with him.

**tuhung** *v. tr.* To find a known location or path. *Sai-sai makatuhung takot, ya na a'a.* Whoever can find the reef, he's the man. (*Thesaurus:* **bakot, malim 1.1, tuli' 1.1, tullus 1.2, ulin**)

**tū'** (var. **tī'**) *v. intr.* pa- To drip down freely. *Magtagak, sali' buhelota patū' man bowa'ta.* Dribbling, like our saliva dripping from our mouth. *Wa'i patū' bohe'-matana.* Her tears are flowing down. (*Thesaurus:* **p'ttak 1.1, sū₂, tīs, titis 1.1**)

**tu'an** *see:* **tinu'anan**

**tu'ud₁** (var. **tumu'ud**) **1)** *adv.* In fact; obviously or naturally so, needing no proof or explanation. *Akuhannu kami ma sukay, ma gastu, ma kamemon, apa kami tu'ud bowanu.* You are responsible for us with regard to fares, food, and everything, because you are in fact taking us. *Saukat na aheka s'mmekbi, magpa'nda'-nda' na kam. Na kami itū, ya na tu'ud s'mmek kami.* Just because you have a lot of clothes you are showing them off. As for us, these are in fact our clothes. *Angalaha'an iya dīna, halam iya bay ni'inay-inay he' a'a, tu'ud angalaha'an dīna.* He

bled on his own account, nobody did anything to him, he simply bled. *Taga daun, tumu'ud halam taga daun.* Having leaves, or simply not having leaves. (*cf:* **asāl**) **1.1)** *v. tr.* To set one's mind on getting something; to do something deliberately. *Ampunun aku, halam tinu'ud.* Forgive me, it wasn't done intentionally. *Ka'a ilū, pahali ka magl'ngngan-l'ngngan. Aniya' kamawpa'atannu: aniya' kala'atan talanggalnu. Buwat sala ataksil halam tinu'ud.* You there, stop going from place to place. You will meet up with trouble. Like getting fined for touching a girl, even though it wasn't deliberate. *Binayaran laha'ta basta aniya' pa'alom ma kita. Subay kita tinu'ud.* Our blood is to be compensated for any time a bruise appears on us. We must have been deliberately targeted. (*Thesaurus:* **angut**) **2)** *n.* A natural or obvious state. *Tu'udna tu'ud, ngga'i ka dalam-duwa, tangpasta.* Without a doubt, no second thought, we just take it.

**pagtu'uran** *v. tr.* To do something of one's own choice or intention. *Pagtu'uranna patukad, halam aniya' bay anoho' iya.* It was his own idea to go inland, nobody told him to. *Halam aniya' mahē' magmula a'a bay makarusa ma halam bay pagtu'uranna.* There was no one there who suffers from having committed an offense without intending to do so.

**tu'ud₂** var. of **to'od**

**tu'ung** *n.* A wooden box. *Da'a patunggangun tu'ung itū ko da'a abu'us.* Don't tilt this box lest stuff spills out. (*Thesaurus:* **bakag₁, ba'ul₁, kalton, labban, maleta**)

**tu'ut** *n.* The knee; the knee-joint. (*Thesaurus:* **kōk-tu'ut 1, lokonan, lo'atan, peya'-peya' kōk-tu'ut, siku**)

**tula-tula** *n.* A species of shrub, the leaves of which are used for cosmetic purposes. (*cf:* **borak 1, lipa'**)

**tulabid** *adj.* a- Disordered or tangled. *Atulabid linggi', asagut, bo' tausay du.* The haul net is disordered, tangled, but it can be sorted out. (*Thesaurus:* **gumun, lokot, sagut 1**)

**tulak₁** *n.* **1)** Departure. *Buwat kami ma Sambuwangan, magsinta' na ni Bukidnon, asekot na tulak.* Like when we were in Zamboanga, committed to going to Bukidnon, on the point of departure. *Sūng na kita amuntu', tulak kohap, amole' salung.* Let's go fishing overnight, an afternoon departure, returning home tomorrow. **1.1)** *v. intr.* pa-/a- To leave one place for another; to depart. *Atulak kami min M'ddas lisag sangpū' maka duwa.* We set out from Siasi township at twelve o'clock. (*Thesaurus:* **batbat₁, l'ttu**)

**pagtulak** *v. intr.* aN- To part from each other. *Magtulak karuwambila', buwat lantay halam bay binīt.* Both sides moving apart, like flooring that hasn't been tied in place. *Manjari ta'bba si Nneng Pagi-pagi. Saga kaukakina inān magtulakan ni* *lahat Bisaya'.* So Stingray Maiden was left behind. Her cousins all parted [from her] going to the Visayan regions.

**tulakan** *n.* An absence; a time away. *Masi kam arai' ma tulakan.* You may have been away still. (*cf:* **likutan**)

**tulak₂** *v. tr.* To push something away. *Tulakun s'ggit ilū.* Push that [floating] trash away. (*Thesaurus:* **dogsol, tagang**)

**pagtulak-tulak** *v. tr.* To keep pushing something away. *Pinagtulak-tulak e'na, sagō' mbal palāng.* He kept pushing it away, but it couldn't be prevented.

**tulak-bala'** *n.* The ritual bathing of a group of people to avert a disaster such as an epidemic disease.

**pagtulak-bala'** *v. intr. aN-* **1)** To conduct a ceremony aimed at making some disaster go away. **1.1)** *v. tr.* To carry out a ceremony for protecting a kin group against threatened disaster. *Bangsa sigām ya makapagtutulak-bala'.* It's people of their ethnic group who are ritual experts for averting disaster.

**tulak-saki** *n.* A ceremony to prevent recurrence of a serious illness.

**pagtulak-saki** *v. intr. aN-* To carry out a ceremony to prevent the recurrence of a serious illness. *Bang a'a bay asaki, sali' akosog na iya, binowa iya sali' pinandi. Ya hē' magpatulak-saki.* When someone has been ill and is now stronger, he is taken to be ritually bathed. That is what makes the sickness go away.

**tuladjuk** *n.* A peaked fold in the front of a headcloth or turban. (*Thesaurus:* **pīs₁, sahal₂, sulban 1**)

**tulaga'** *v. intr. pa-* To visit people's houses for no specific reason; to drop by. (*Thesaurus:* **bisita 1.1, liyud, tibaw 1.2, tuwa' 2**)

**tulagsok** (*var.* **sulagsok**) *n.* **1)** A pin or stake for holding something in place; a dowel or spline used to join wood. **2)** A cursing equivalent for long items. *Da'a taddokin hāg ilū, tulagsoknu bang apōng.* Don't kick that pole, it'll be your death-spike if it breaks. (*gen:* **sukna' 1.1**)

**tulahan** *n.* A payment to an expert for service done. *Bang kita amahinang ma panday, subay aniya' tulahan ko da'a amalos hulasna.* If we have something made by an artisan, a *tulahan* payment must be made, lest his sweat demand revenge. *Pinauntul si Mu ni ina'na apa halam bay pinareyo'an tulahan.* Mu was treated appropriately by her mother because the obligatory payment had not been delivered. *Asabab bang halam aniya' tulahan.* It is a cause [of illness] if there is no recompense paid. (*Thesaurus:* **baubaⅼli', bayad 1, bayad 1.1, gadji 1.1, hokas, lampak₁ 1.1, susuk, tambahan, tinga 1.1, tiyandā, tunay₂, tungbas 1**)

**tula'** *v. tr.* To cook fish or meat by boiling with herbs. *T'ddakin, apa tinula' tina'ina.* Gut [the fish] because its intestines are to be cooked with herbs. (*gen:* **b'lla 1**)

**tinula'** *n.* A stew of fish or meat seasoned with herbs.

**tulay** *n.* The Ox-eye scad, a pelagic herring-like fish. *Selar boops.* (*Thesaurus:* **lumahan, sulay-sulay₂**)

**tulay tukul-tukul** *n. phrase* The Herring scad. *Alepes.*

**tulkin** *n.* **1)** The final ritual of a burial, pronunced as water is poured over the grave. **1.1)** *v. tr.* To recite the final prayer of burial rites.

**tulelle** *v. intr. pa-* To fall awkwardly, with arms swinging widely. *Bay paligdas tape'na, wa'i patulelle' ahūg pareyo'.* His feet slipped and he fell down, arms flailing. (*Thesaurus:* **hūg₁ 1, pakpak 1, togge'₁, tukbung 1, tumba₁**)

**tuli₁** *v. intr. a-* **1)** To be asleep. *Tagna' katuliku halam aku makasayu. At'ggol katuliku halam pagbati'ku. Kohap na pabīng.* When I first go to sleep I am not aware of anything. When my sleep is long-lasting I have no waking periods. It's afternoon again. (*cf:* **piru'-piru'**) **1.1)** *v. advrs. -in-* Sleepy; dropping off to sleep. (*Thesaurus:* **karu' 1.1, lambung tuli, lilap**) **1.2)** *v. advrs. ka-...-an* To be overtaken by sleep. *Onde'-onde' ilū sidda pangasang, mbal katulihan bang sangom.* That child is such a crier, one can't get to sleep at night. *Asalut isāb si Ya bang pasān angkan bilang mbal katulihan.* Ya is fretful at times, which is why he often can't get off to sleep.

**pagtuli** *v. intr. aN-* To be sleeping. *Ya rū bang magtulihan magbaubabag, sinō' magleson.* Like when people are sleeping with legs across, told to straighten up.

**tuli-sowa** *v. intr. a-* Sleeping with eyes partly closed. {idiom}

**tuli-tuli-kuyya'** *n.* A short sleep; a cat-nap. {idiom} *Pak'llip matana, tuli-tuli-kuyya'.* His eyes drooping, just a catnap.

**pagpatuli** *v. intr. aN-* To have a sick person sleep in the house of a medical or ritual specialist for treatment.

**patulihan** *n.* A sleeping place; a bed. (*Thesaurus:* **kantil₁, pabahakan, palangka'₂, palegehan**)

**tuli₂** *v. intr. a-* Left overnight for the solids in a liquid to settle. *Subay nilunglungan kassa' ilū bo' tabati' ns'llan bay atuli.* The bottle should be shaken so the oil will become liquid again [lit. the sleeping oil will be woken up].

**patuli** *v. tr.* To have a liquid settle overnight, as newly squeezed coconut oil. (*Thesaurus:* **labay bahangi, lihaw 1.1, pato'ong**)

**tuli'** *v. tr.* **1)** To find an objective or destination. *Bang sali' kita amuwang, subay ginindanan bo' tatuli', bo' kita amuwang pabalik.* When we throw a line out from shore it should be marked so we can find it, so we can throw it out again. *Bang* *kita makatuli' deyo' taga daing, al'kkas kita maka'ā'. Paghūg, pagsintak, paghella'.* When we find a deep that has fish, we soon get some. Down the line goes, the fish bite and we pull them up. **1.1)** *v. tr.* **-an** To show someone the way. *Buwat aku maka si Sa ni Lihondo bo' aku ya makatuli'. Yukku ma iya, "Dahū na ka ma lān ilu, amange' gi' aku." Bo' wa'i aku ma lān dakayu', angalabba' aku ma iya.* Like Sa and me going to Rio Hondo with me leading the way. I said to him, "You go first by that path, I'm going to take a pee." But I went by another path, having tricked him. (*Thesaurus:* **bakot, malim 1.1, tuhung, tullus 1.2, ulin**)

**tulis** *n.* The decorative lines or markings of a canoe. *Ta'nda' pa'in tulis pelang, yuk kami, "Ina'an abayta."* When we saw the decorative lines of the canoe, we said, "That's our fleet companion there."

**tullik** *var. of* **tilluk**

**tullus** (var. **tullut**) *adj.* **a-** **1)** Sharp-eyed; quick at finding things that are concealed. *Buwat hūgku bubu bo' tapihaku pabīng, atullus aku.* Like when I drop a bubu-type fish trap and can find it again, I am sharp-eyed. *Atullus pahāp mata a'a hē'.* How sharp that fellow's eyes are [said of the ability to see something through unclear water]. *Atullut du iya angā', minsan ngga'i ka iya bay anau'.* He is very quick to get something, though it wasn't him who put it away. *Makatullus iya magsinama. Ai-ai pinah'lling e' Sama ahāp-ala'at, tahati.* He can find the right Sinama words. Whatever a Sama says, good or bad, he understands. (*Thesaurus:* **lahal, layam 1.1, panday 1.1**) **1.1)** *v. tr.* To do something with skill or certainty. *Minsan buwattingga abeklo' lān, tatullusna. Mbal kita alungay atawa makanilān saddi.* No matter how windy the path is, he can find the way. We will not get lost or go onto a different path. *Minsan la'a hal card, pabeya'in aku bo' ata'u tatullusku.* Even if it is only a card, do send it to me so that I will know for sure. **1.2)** *v. ditr.* To guide someone clearly to the right destination. *Tullusin aku.* Show me the right way. (*Thesaurus:* **bakot, malim 1.1, tuhung, tuli' 1.1, ulin**)

**tullut** *var. of* **tullus**

**tulun₁** *n.* **1)** Wisdom or skill from a supernatural source, especially from God; a person endowed with such qualities. *Tulun min Tuhan, buwat ilmu' halam bay guruku.* Ability from God, like esoteric knowledge that I had not acquired by learning. *Auliya' itū niōnan tulun, ai-ai niamu' ilu'un na.* This person with supernormal abilities is known as a *tulun.* Whatever he asks for is promptly there. (*Thesaurus:* **auliya', langtas 1, tugu**) **1.1)** *adj.* **-an** Possessing abilities from a divine source. *Subay ka tulunan bo' pinataluwa'an mudjidjat.* You have to be divinely favored to have a miracle happen to you. **1.2)** *v. intr. pa-*

To come upon someone from a supernatural source, of some special ability or power. *Aniya' ilmu'na bay patulun man Tuhan, pahūg man Tuhan.* He has some esoteric knowledge come down from God, descended from God. *Patulun jīn.* A djinn came down [from some supernatural source]. **1.3)** *v. advrs.* **ka-...-an** To be endowed with power or skills. *Mbal na sigām makapiha saddi buwat si Yusup bay katulunan e' Tuhan pikilan alalom.* They could not find any other like Joseph who had been endowed by God with mental ability.

**tulun₂** *v. intr. pa-* **1)** To get from one place to another. *Patulunan iya dīna minsan dangan-danganna.* He can get himself to a destination even if he is on his own [said of a crippled person]. **1.1)** *v. ditr.* To return an item or person to the proper location. *Tulunanku ni ka'a, mbal ka angā'. Subay na pa'in ka tinulunan, mbal ka makat'ngge min paningkō'annu.* I will return it to you, you are not to come and get it. You should always have [things] returned, you will not get up from where you are sitting. (*Thesaurus:* **maksud 1.2, nde', papole', pasampay, tukbal₁ 1, tūd₂, tuyuk-tuyuk**)

**tulun-bantayan** *n.* A canoe that is seaworthy in all weather conditions. *Buwat kita magbanog ma deyom kagoyakan, mbal ainay basta pelang tulun-bantayan, basta mbal a'llop.* Like when we are under sail in rough conditions, nothing happens if our canoe is seaworthy, provided it is not overloaded.

**tulun-tana'** *n.* The meal eaten prior to the burial of a deceased person. *Bang halam gi' kinubul, yuk kami tulun-tana'. Bang at'kka min kubul magjamu isāb magkalla'.* Before the deceased is buried, we call it *tulun-tana'.* When we arrive from the burial ground we also have the *kalla'* meal. (*cf:* **hinang-kalla'**)

**tulung** *n.* **1)** Aid, especially financial. *Bang bay kamatayan ma bihing luma' kami, subay kami amowa tulung. Tulung itū sīn panabang.* If those in the house next to ours are affected by a death, we should bring a *tulung* [aid]. This is a financial contribution. *Tapalis itū mbal kita sali' makatandan lahat. Yuk kami, "Wa'i tapalis ma dilaut. Makatandan ni lahat, luwal bang aheya tulung min Tuhan."* Carried far off course is when we cannot return to shore. We say, "Blown off course out at sea. May make landfall only if there is great help from God." **1.1)** *v. tr.* To help someone; to provide someone with financial aid. (*Thesaurus:* **tabang 1, tambin**)

**panulung** *n.* Money given to help with expenses, especially funeral expenses.

**tuma** *n.* **1)** Body lice. (*Thesaurus:* **kuman₁, kutu 1, limad-limad, lisa' 1**) **1.1)** *v. advrs.* **-in-** Infested with body lice.

**Tumakdang** *n.* The name of an important spirit of the Siasi Lagoon area.

**tumakdil** var. of **takdil**

**tumagal** n. 1) An excuse; a pretext. *Pah'llingna buwattē' hal pangā'an tumagal bahasa magbono'.* His talking like that is just a pretext for starting a fight. *Panga'an tumagal, sali' b'nsi. Bang magbono' siyaliku maka h'llana, ya binīngan onde' binono'.* Coming up with an excuse, as when ill-feeling is involved. When my young sister and her husband fight, it is the children who get blamed and punished. 1.1) v. intr. aN- To make excuses, with connotation of the excuse being invented. (*Thesaurus:* **da'awa 1.1, paglugat, palilu, tawalli'**)

**pagtumagal** v. intr. aN- To pretend; to feign. *Sai-sai ya magtumagal ameya' ma saga sara'nu maka mbal ameya' ma panoho'annu tantu subay pinapatay.* Whoever makes a pretense of obeying your laws and doesn't obey your orders should certainly be killed.

**panumagal** n. An excuse; a pretext.

**tuman** adj. a- 1) Confirmed or precise, especially with regard to a prediction or plan. *Atuman, atokod, bang aniya' pinagpa'al bo' b'nnal.* Confirmed, guessed correctly, when something has been foretold and is true. 1.1) v. tr. To speak definitely and surely about something; to carry out a promise. *Buwat aniya' bay tau'nu, yukta, "Tumanun bay panau'an ilū."* Like when you stored something, we say, "Speak with certainty about the storage place." *Sali' a'a jīnan, bang aniya' pa'nda'ta ni iya, agtūy kinata'uhan he'na saki, a'a inān niōnan pagta'allukan. Sali' tuman, ata'uahan kamemon.* Like a person who controls a djinn spirit, when someone is shown to him and he immediately identifies the sickness, such a man is called *pagta'allukan* [someone to be treated with respect]. Like being certain, knowing everything.

**tuman-tuman** adj. zero Determined; set on doing. *Buwat dakayu' luma' tuman-tuman amole' salung, bo' pa'in makasambeya' amole' isāb llaw itū. Tinilaw he' luma' dakayu', "Angay kam amole'?"* Like those of one house-based work team being determined to return home the following day, but committed combining to return this day. Those of another house ask, "Why are you going home?"

**tumanggal** n. A crown-like head-dress worn by a bride. *Nihinangan tumanggal d'nda ina'an, panumping.* That girl there has a head-dress made for her, a *panumping*. (*Thesaurus:* **korona, panumping**)

**tumariya** see: **katumariyahan**

**tumba₁** v. intr. pa-/a- To fall down from a height; to plunge downwards. (*Thesaurus:* **hūg₁ 1, pakpak 1, togge'₁, tukbung 1, tulelle**)

**pagkatumba** v. intr. aN- To fall headlong from a height.

**tumba₂** adj. a- 1) Lost, of the entire holdings of the banker in a gambling game. *Atumba bangka'*

*legot, tabowa kamemon.* The banker in a dice game has lost the lot, all taken. 1.1) v. tr. To bet the maximum amount permitted by the bank in a gambling game. *Ka'a ya amangka' legot. "Aniya' hād legot itū?" yukku. Yukku, "Halam." "Tumbaku," yukku, "bang halam aniya' hādna."* You're the banker in a dice game. I say, "Is there a limit in this dice game?" You say, "No." I say, "I'll bet the maximum if there is no limit." (*Thesaurus:* **kōl 1.1, hapus₁ 1.1, pagtinggi, talu₁**)

**tumbaga** n. 1) Copper (the mineral); various copper-based alloys. (*Thesaurus:* **bulawan 1, estenles, luyang, pilak 1, pittang, sawasa'**) 1.1) v. intr. aN- To become coppery in hue. *Buwat garulta, bang baha'u ya na luwa bulawan. Pinagbase' maka tahik, agtūy anumbaga.* Like our brass pot; when it is new it looks like gold. When it is often wet with sea water it turns quite coppery. 2) Various copper vessels. (*Thesaurus:* **bintang₁, gangsa, garul, langguway**)

**tumbal** n. 1) Whole cassava tubers preserved by drying in the sun. *Tumbal, ya tibu'uk inān bang pa'in kinupasan.* Tumbal, non-toxic cassava varieties [dried] after being peeled. (*cf:* **tibu'uk₂**; *Thesaurus:* **kuting-kuting₁, ta'adjil 1**) 1.1) v. tr. To dry cassava tubers in the sun in order to preserve them. *Tibu'uk bay kinupasan, halam bay nili'is, bay tinumbal. Pina'llawan dok atoho' ati bang atoho' tin'ppa, kinakan na.* Non-toxic cassava that has been peeled, not grated, just treated by drying. It is exposed to the sun and pounded when it is dry, then eaten. (*Thesaurus:* **buwad, patoho', puhi**) 1.2) v. intr. aN- To become blackened through exposure to the sun. *Panggi', apuwas minali-mali anumbal.* Cassava, after drying out it turns black.

**tumballeng** n. Irregular, erratic movement.

**pagtumballeng** v. intr. aN- To move erratically or lopsidedly. *Magtumballeng dundangan bang mbal abontol.* A swing swings unevenly when not set up right [i.e. with ropes of even length]. *Bang tagna' pinaka'llum kapay ariplano, magtumballeng.* When the propeller of an airplane is first started, it moves unevenly.

**tumbi'** v. tr. To shame someone by reminding him of favors previously shown to him. (*syn:* **bangkil₁, tungbuy**)

**tumbuk₁** v. intr. pa- 1) To impact heavily, of a natural force such as wind or current. *Patumbuk pa'in baliyu, minda' kami palege atuli, patumbuk isāb goyak.* When the wind struck, fortunately when we were lying down asleep, the sea also grew rough. (*cf:* **dugpak 1**) 1.1) v. tr. -an To hit a place or person hard. *Bay kami tinumbukan uttala'. Ta'abut saga mpat llaw, tinumbukan na kami baliyu satan. Aleha kami tudju pī'.* A north wind struck us. When four days had passed we were struck by a southerly wind. We sailed on in that direction. *"Bang ka pat'ppi gi',"* yukna, *"tumbukanta ka maka soha' itū."* "If you come any closer," she said, "I will hit you hard with this mooring stake." **1.2)** *v. advrs.* ka-...-an To be hit by something falling heavily. *Katumbukan si Li, apinsan.* Li was hit by something falling heavily on him, knocked out.

**tumbuk₂** *n.* The dotted selvage edge of a piece of cloth. *Tumbukan bihing hōsku, ya hē' amuwan pagon.* My sarong has a dotted selvage edge, that's what gives it strength.

**tumbuk₃** *n.* **1)** An identifying mark such as a stamp or label. (*Thesaurus:* **tanda'**) **1.1)** *v. tr.* -an To affix a stamp or other mark to a document.

**tumbuk-buhungan** *n.* The central supporting stud of a roof between the ridge pole and the cross beam.

**tumbuk-s'ngkol** *n.* The situation in which a brother and sister of one family marry the sister and brother of another family.

  **pagtumbuk-s'ngkol** *v. intr.* aN- To be related in two ways, by marriage between a brother and sister of one family with a sister and brother of another. (*cf:* **paginubusan**)

**tumbu'** var. of **tungbu'**

**tumbul** *v. tr.* -an To proliferate from an original center, as new boils growing out from an earlier one. *Binaha'an kitā, tinumbulan, sali' anganak.* Someone might be affected with swelling, growing more lumps, sort of spreading. (*cf:* **anak₄**)

**tumbuy** var. of **tungbuy**

**tumlang 1)** *adj.* a- To the point, of speech. *Atumlang bissalana.* His words are right on the mark. (*Thesaurus:* **hangbos₁**) **2)** *v. tr.* To hit a target. *Tumlangun ni katubaganna.* Hit him on his vulnerable spot. (*Thesaurus:* **taluwa' 1, tigi'-tigi'₁ 1, t'bbong, tudju₂ 1**) **2.1)** *v. advrs.* ka-...-an To be targeted. *Buwat ariplano tinimbak, katumlangan, ahūg pareyo'.* Like a plane that is shot at and hit directly, it falls down. *Atawa buwat magko'ot ōn, dahatus a'a dakayu' du ya pinene'. Ya na hē' katumlangan.* Or like people drawing names, a hundred people and just one is chosen. That is an instance of being targeted.

**tumpa** *v. intr.* pa- **1)** To tip over, as by accident. **1.1)** *v. tr.* -an To pour something out of one container to another. *Nihudduran, sali' tinumpahan.* Poured out, like decanting some liquid. *Tumpahin ns'llan ilū ni kamemon garul.* Pour that oil into all the bronze containers. (*Thesaurus:* **hain, huddud 1.1, tuwang, tuyung**)

**tumpak** *n.* **1)** A dark patch on a plain background. **1.1)** *v. tr.* -an To cover with patches. *Tasumpal pelang abō' magpakahinang. Sin'nsong atawa tinumpakan.* The canoe can be patched so it can be used for work. Plugged up or patched here and there.

  **pagtumpak** *v. intr.* aN- To show as blotches; to be spotted. *Angalom aku, sali' angal'ddom baranku.*

*Sali' ni'ila kita, sa' ni'ila itū magtumpak-tumpak.* I am showing bruises, my body becoming sort of dark. It's like having a birthmark, but with the mark showing in spots.

**tumpal** var. of **sumpal**

**tumpalak** *adj.* a- **1)** Annoyed or offended by what someone says. *Da'a ka atumpalak, da'a na ap'ddi' ataynu.* Don't be offended, don't be upset. (*Thesaurus:* **ambul-dā', anak-anak₂, kagit atay 1, la'at atay**) **1.1)** *v. tr.* To offend someone by speaking to them impolitely; to insult someone. *Bay tumpalakna si Da'ud, parahāl ahāp sidda addat saga a'ana ma kami.* He spoke insultingly to David. However his men were very courteous to us. *Makasāk deyom atay, buwat kita anumpalak.* Causing deep revulsion, as when we insult someone.

  **pagtumpalak** *v. intr.* aN- To be insulting someone. *Mbal aku magtumpalak ma ka'a.* I don't say this to offend you.

**tumpang** *v. intr.* aN- To ride in someone else's conveyance as a non-paying passenger. *Bay aku ni M'ddas halam aniya' sīnku, bay aku anumpang ma a'a, halam aniya' pameya'anku bang amole'.* I went to Siasi with no money and got a ride with someone, then had no transportation back home. *Ina'an na lansa sōng atulak, bo' masi kita ma labayan. Subay kita pa'abut-abut bo' makatumpang.* There is a launch about to leave, and we are still on the way to it. We'll need to keep at it to be able to go on it. (*Thesaurus:* **bayan 1.1, beya'₁, pagbiyahi, palaktas, sakay 1, tundug 1.1**)

  **panumpangan** *n.* A conveyance in which one rides as passenger; a passenger vehicle. (*Thesaurus:* **bayanan, pahinggaman, pameya'an₁**)

  **patumpang** *v. tr.* To get a ride in someone else's canoe.

**tumpay** *v. tr.* To carry something balanced across one's shoulder, of a burden which can be held in place with the hand. (*Thesaurus:* **baba' 1, balung 1, tanggung₁, usung**)

**tumpēt** *v. intr.* pa- To flatten out, of a heap of something soft. *Bang apam sali' halam pabūd t'ngnga'na. Sali' du nipis bihing maka t'ngnga', patumpēt.* When a cake hasn't risen in the middle. The thinness of its edge is the same as its middle, flattened. *Buwat tai' sapi' patumpēt ma t'ngnga' lān inān.* Like cow dung spread flat there on the trail.

**tumpuk** *n.* **1)** A cluster or group of items, as vegetables sold by the pile. **2)** A cluster of houses usually connected by walkways, the inhabitants of which are linked by kinship. *Dalūng kami maka si Imam Ma, minsan saddī tumpuk, basta magsekot luma'.* We are in the same neighborhood as Imam Ma, even though in a different house-cluster, provided the houses are close together. (*Thesaurus:* **kaluma'an,**

kampung₂, le'od₁, libug, lūng 1, nibung)

**pagtumpuk** *v. intr. aN-* To form a group. *Jari magdatumpuk saga sundalu bo' angatu.* So the solders formed a single group in order to fight back.

**tumpung** *n.* A container made of a single internode section of large bamboo. *Tumpung pangisihan omang pangumpan.* A bamboo container to hold hermit crabs for bait. (*Thesaurus:* **bō'**, **honga'**₁, **loka'**, **saud**₁)

**tumu-tumu** *adj. a-* Broken into pieces; suffering multiple breaks. *Atumu-tumu, mbal tapuwa', sali' amāg-māg.* Broken into fragments, unable to be picked up, same as *māg-māg*. *Manjari bang a'a ahūg ni batu-lakit inān, atumu-tumu baranna.* When a person falls onto those hard rocks, his body has multiple breaks. (*Thesaurus:* **bagbag**, **lopot 1**, **māg-māg**)

**tumu'ud** var. of **tu'ud**₁

**tuna'** *v. ditr.* To attribute negative behavior or characteristics to someone, on the basis of suspicion. *Bay aku tinuna' anangkaw pelang, bo' pa'in ngga'i ka aku.* I was suspected of stealing a canoe, but it wasn't me. *Tinuna' itū hal sali' niwaham. Tinuntutan itū niragsolan ni sara'.* *Tuna'* is just voicing a suspicion. *Tuntut* is taking it all the way to the law. (*Thesaurus:* **hunub-hunub 1.1**, **taha**, **tuhuma 1**, **waham**)

**tunang** *n.* 1) A person formally engaged to be married. *Am'lli aku gallang pamuwan ma tunangku si Mm.* I will buy a bracelet to give to my sweetheart Mm. (*cf:* **atag**₂ **1.1**) *v. tr. -an* To have someone become one's betrothed.

**pagtunang** *v. intr. aN-* To be connected by a formal agreement to marry. *A'a magtunang bay abaibad, pinaludju' bo' asugpat pabalik.* A courting couple who have separated, persuaded to resume and be connected again. *Sitti Ma, ya magtunang asal maka si Yu.* Ma, who was in fact betrothed with Yu. *Paludju' pabīng apa bay na magtunang.* Resuming [marriage] discussions because they have already been sweethearts.

**patunang** *v. tr. -an* To make a down payment in confirmation of a betrothal agreement.

**tunas** *n.* 1) Ruins or remnants; rags. *Tunasna masi, ka'atna ya takapin.* Its remnants still there, what's left of its ruins. (*Thesaurus:* **bulangkayat**, **g'ppa'**, **gubal**, **hogal**, **lubu**₂ **1**) 1.1) *adj. a-* Reduced to ruins or fragments. *Atunas luma'bi, hal tunasna la'a takapin.* Your house is wrecked, only the ruins are left. *Atunas hōs, badju'.* A sarong or blouse falling apart.

**tunaw** 1) *adj. a-* Melting; dissolving. *Atunaw aes, bay tauwa' llaw.* The ice is melting, it was affected by the sun. (*Thesaurus:* **hudjat**, **lanay**₂, **tadjul**) 1.1) *v. tr.* To melt something. 2) *v. tr.* To digest food.

**tunay**₁ *adj. zero* Genuine; real; unmixed. *Si Ka' Ja bay makah'nda ma a'a tunay Sisangat.* Uncle Ja married a woman who was a genuine inhabitant

of Sisangat.

**tunay**₂ *v. tr.* To pay cash for something, in contrast to buying on credit or trading. (*Thesaurus:* **bayad 1.1**, **gadji 1.1**, **hokas**, **lampak**₁ **1.1**, **susuk**, **tinga 1.1**, **tulahan**, **tungbas 1**)

**tundan** 1) *v. intr. pa-* To get a tow from another vessel, usually one which is motorized. *Pagambil ka ma katig ilū. Saddī patundan.* Connect alongside the outrigger boom there. Getting a tow is something else. 1.1) *v. intr. aN-* To connect to a tow line. *Ya ina'an lansa pameya'an hadji' ī', bahasa anundan kami na.* That's the launch the hadji is travelling by, the one we were thinking of getting a tow from. 1.2) *v. tr.* To tow something. *Paraw ya tinundan e' pambot.* It's the canoe that is being towed by the pump-boat. 2) *v. tr.* To line up along a connecting line, as segments along a stalk. 2.1) *v. tr. -an* To attach something to a line; to add something to a statement (fig.) *Bang ma sigām, panggi' subay tinundanan kayu.* According to them [the word] *panggi'* should have [the word] *kayu* attached to it.

**tundanan** *n.* Things attached by a line to the rear of another vessel, as canoes being towed by a launch. *Aheka tundanan lansa inān.* That launch has a lot of [canoes] in tow.

**panundanan** *n.* A towline, especially of canoes.

**tundug** *v. intr. pa-* 1) To beach; to reach shore. *Patundug kita pina'an ni Tōng Batu.* Let's go ashore there at Rock Point. (*Thesaurus:* **daggot**₁, **dunggu' 1**, **tandan**₁ **1**, **t'kkad 1**) 1.1) *v. tr.* To ferry someone to shore. *Pehē' na ka, tundugun si Ina'. Wa'i na iya ka'ddasan aningkō' ma Hambilan, halam aniya' pamayan.* Away you go, give mother a ride home. She has been sitting at Hambilan for ages and there is no transport. *Mbal aku umabut, tundugun aku man pelang.* I can't touch bottom; ferry me ashore by canoe. (*Thesaurus:* **bayan 1.1**, **beya'**₁, **pagbiyahi**, **palaktas**, **sakay 1**, **tumpang**)

**tundun** 1) *v. advrs. -in-* Clustered, of fruit. (*Thesaurus:* **daug 1**, **pingkit 1.1**, **pulingkit**, **puliting**, **pungut 1**) 2) *clf.* Count word for clusters of fruit.

**ma tundunan** *adv. phrase* By the cluster, of fruit that grows in bunches.

**pagtundun** *v. intr. aN-* To be clustered together as fruit.

**tundun buwahan** *v. advrs. -in-* Experiencing great enjoyment. {idiom} *Bang kahōpan a'a magkata-kata, bā'nu tinundun buwahan.* When the epic singer goes into his trance, you will be filled with pleasure [lit. you would think you were clustered with lansones fruit].

**tunis** *n.* The melody of a song; the manner in which a song is presented. *Bandung-bandungin ba abō' paluwas tunisna, sali' sambag-sambag.* Get a rhythm going so that its melody emerges, sort of answering to and fro.

**tuntul** (var. **untul**) *adj. a-* **1)** Orderly; well-arranged. *Bang halam aniya' anasaw-nasaw kita, atuntul hinangta.* When there is no one to bother us, our work is well-arranged. *Yangkon aku ya auntul tabeya'.* I alone was ready to be included. *Auntul pangkat kami, halam iya kauli'an.* Our ritual ancestors were [invoked] in proper order, but he was not healed. **1.1)** *v. tr.* To do things in an orderly way; to arrange things. *Tauntul he'na bay pano'onan bubu.* He arranged the fish traps in the order of [their] placement. *Pehē' si Li makatuntulan dīna pehē' ni lūnganna.* Li went there getting herself organised, there in her own place.

**patuntul** *v. tr.* To do something in an orderly way; to organize something. (*Thesaurus:* **hatul**₁, **temo-temo, uki'-uki'**)

**tuntun**₁ *n.* **1)** A line by which something at a distance is controlled. *Tuntun mandal.* String of a *mandal* type kite. (*Thesaurus:* **taguntun 1.1, tali-tali**₂**, tugut 1.1**) **1.1)** *v. intr. pa-* To go to the end of a line. *Tinelop-telopan pareyo'. Bang aniya' ahūg ni tahik al'kkas patuntun, sali' aniya' angahella' iya.* Made to vanish downwards. When something falls into the sea it goes down quickly, as though something is pulling it. **1.2)** *v. tr. -an* To attach a control line to something. *Sangkil ya tinuntunan.* A harpoon is controlled by a line.

**tuntun**₂ *n.* A fin or flapper of a large fish. *Bang ma kasehe'an pikpik, bang ma kasehe'an tuntun, buwat pahi ilū.* For some it is *pikpik,* for others it is *tuntun,* like the [flapper of] the marine ray there. (*Thesaurus:* **kidjang 1, pikpik**₁ **1**)

**tuntung** *v. tr. -an* To play the kulintangan gongs. (*Thesaurus:* **kulanting 1, lisag**₂ **1.1, tagunggu', taletek, taratu' 1.1, taroro', tigi'-tigi'**₂)

**tuntut**₁ *v. ditr.* To accuse someone; to bring a complaint or grievance to a community leader. *Bang ka bay pautangku dahatus pilak bo' mbal ka'nde'an, tuntutanta ka ni upis.* When I had lent you one hundred pesos and it was not returned, I laid a complaint against you to the authorities. *Tinuna' itū hal sali' niwaham. Tinuntutan itū niragsolan ni sara'.* *Tuna'* is just voicing a suspicion. *Tuntut* is taking it right to the law. (*Thesaurus:* **kuhi**₂**, pagmahi, pagmalān, pagpuhun 1.1, sumbung**)

**tuntut**₂ *v. tr.* To set one's mind on an outcome. *Ya tinuntut he' a'a magkikidnap subay pilak.* What kidnappers set their mind on must be money. (*Thesaurus:* **angut**)

**tunuk** *n.* A thorn or spike; a source of emotional distress (fig.) *Tahinang iya sali' sapantun tunuk ma matabi.* She will become figuratively like a thorn in your eye. *Sali' ahublut saru'un-du'un ya tunuk bay ma bigi-jantungku.* The thorn that had been in my heart was suddenly pulled out. (*Thesaurus:* **iting 1, leget, tuklang**)

**tunug** *n.* **1)** A hint of something in the air. *Takaleta aniya' baliyu, aniya' tunug.* We hear the sound of a wind, there is something in the air. (*cf:* **hamut 1**) **1.1)** *v. intr. pa-* To waft through the air, of a scent or smell. *Patunug, sali' pahangsu bauna, bau deya, hamut sumping, kaginisan.* Wafting through the air, its smell sort of drifting, the smell of land, the fragrance of a flower, things of various kinds. (*Thesaurus:* **angil, angsod, bbu 1.1, hangsu 1.1, pulag-pulag**)

**tunu'**₁ *n.* **1)** Something burning. *Arūng! Bau tunu' ko' inān!* Girl! That's the smell of burning! *Kapam'ngngangan iya pag'nda'na ma tunu' kaluma'an.* He was speechless on seeing the burning of the village. **1.1)** *adj. a-* Burnt or scorched, as a house, food, body part. *Atunu' kaluma'an.* The houses of the village are burnt. (*cf:* **keyat**₂ **1.1**) **1.2)** *v. tr.* To burn something, as to remove weedy growth. *Tinunu' dahū, mbal niararu, hal tinanoman, ya hē' ginās.* Burnt first, not plowed, just sown, that is swidden farming. (*Thesaurus:* **lāb 1.1, lablab 2, lapug**)

**pagtunu'** *n.* Burning on a large scale. *Pagtunu' Sūk inān, aheka anaban. Hal anaban, mbal anabang.* When Jolo town was burning, a lot were looting. It was simply looting, not helping.

**panunu'an** *n.* An area where a fire has been deliberately lit.

**tunu'**₂ *v. tr.* To cook by roasting or grilling on live coals. *Akatis pa'in bay tinunu' kahanga-selo magtūy pinogpog mariyata' batu.* After the large finger conch had been roasted it was promptly banged on a stone. (*Thesaurus:* **panggang**₁**, tapa 1**)

**tunung** see: **patay-tunung**

**tunus** *n.* The Bluefin triggerfish.

**tunyang** var. of **tabula-tunyang**

**tūng** *n.* **1)** The percentage of the winnings paid to the proprietor of a gambling game. *Tūng, ya na sukay ma tag-dapu sugal. Tūng,* that's the fee for the owner of the cards. **1.1)** *v. ditr.* To pay a percentage of one's winnings to the proprietor of a game. *Bang ka anganda'ug min duwa, anūng ka lima sīn ni tag-duminu.* When you win twice, you give five centavos as a fee to the owner of the dominoes.

**tungal** var. of **pungal**

**tungalu'** *adj. zero* Projecting noticeably, of one's upper lip. (*Thesaurus:* **juhal, jungal 1.1, toro' 1.1**)

**tungbas** *n.* **1)** A reward; a recompense. (*Thesaurus:* **bayad 1.1, gadji 1.1, hokas, lampak**₁ **1.1, susuk, tinga 1.1, tulahan, tunay**₂) **1.1)** *v. ditr.* To recompense someone for his activity. *Katungbasan isāb saga a'a inān ma pasal kala'atan ya bay tahinang sigām.* Those people too were paid back because of the bad that they did. *Tuhan ya anungbas.* God is the one to reward us. *Bang aniya' bay indamanku ni kakiku, halam aku bay pinaindaman, tungbasanku.* If I tried to borrow something from my cousin and he wouldn't lend it, I'll pay him back. (*Thesaurus:* **ballas 2**)

**tungbu'** (var. **tumbu'**) *v. intr. aN-* To grow, of plants. (*cf:* **saha' 1.1**; *Thesaurus:* **subud, sulig₁, tomo' 1**)

**tungbuy** (var. **tumbuy**) *v. tr.* To shame someone by reminding him of favors previously shown. *Bang kita magdanakan, sali' magtumbuy, araran magbono', makaraiyus kita.* Us siblings, when we remind each other of past favors, when we are often fighting, then we are behaving scandalously. (*syn:* **bangkil₁, tumbi'**)

  **pagtungbuy** *n.* **1)** A cause of shame. *Ngga'i ka isāb pagtungbuy, sagō' aheya utangnu ma aku.* Not a cause of shame, but you owe me a large sum. **1.1)** *v. intr. aN-* To shame each other by recalling past favors. *Bang kita magdanakan sali' magtumbuy, araran magbono', makaraiyus kita.* When we siblings are reminding each other of past favors, we often get to fighting, behaving scandalously. *Magtungbuy kita, magkapakaiya'.* We remind each other of past favors, causing mutual shame.

**tungkalling** *v. intr. aN-* To set fruit, the stage before petal fall. *Anungkalling na mampallam.* The mangoes are setting fruit. (*Thesaurus:* **pagbuwa', pagduru'-ero', tadjuk**)

**tungkang** *n.* A large cooking pot with a stirrup handle. *Arāk pina'nda'an tungkangku ni ka'a, abila'.* I had thought of showing you my cooking pot, it's broken. (*gen:* **pam'llahan**)

**tungkap₁** *v. advrs. -in-* Made worse through repeated use, of some damage. A: *"Asal a'ssu' saisig?"* B: *"Bay ariki', gōm pa'in paheya, tu'ud tinungkap, karuhunan."* A: "Did the woven panel always have a hole in it?" B: "It was small, but it has become bigger, simply made worse, become more so." (*cf:* **luba'**; *Thesaurus:* **duhun 1**)

**tungkap₂** *v. tr.* **1)** To use another person's facilities or resources. *Tungkapta bohe' maka undam si Anu.* We will use What's-her-name's water and laundry basin. **1.1)** *v. tr. -an* To take things to be worked on at someone else's facilities. *Tungkapanta s'mmek itū pehē'.* Let's take the clothes there [to iron or wash them]. *Tungkapin onde' itū ni kaluma'an. Halam maitu ina'na amaruru'. Danakan atawa kampung, nsa' bidda'.* Take the baby to one of the other houses. Its mother isn't here to suckle it. A sibling or a neighbour, makes no difference.

**tungkas** *adj. a-* Removed or disconnected from its proper or natural location. *Apu'ut badju'ku, atungkas man buli'ku.* My shirt is short, it has come away from my buttocks. *Atungkas diyata' kōkna, tabowa he' kosog timbak.* The top of his head was taken off by the force of the explosion. (*Thesaurus:* **k'llo'₂, hemos 1, la'an 1, tanggal₂**)

  **tungkas-pasu'** *n.* A medicine for removing one's fever.

**tungkellat** *n.* A rocking movement (on a pivot).

  **pagtungkellat-tungkellat** *v. intr. aN-* To rock to and fro on a pivot, as when riding a seesaw. *Magtungkellat-tungkellat saga onde'-onde', magkalisigan.* The children rock on a seesaw, enjoying themselves. (*Thesaurus:* **jungkat 1.1, togsok, tunggang**)

**tungkid** *v. intr. pa-* To kneel with head down, as a gesture of respect. *Patungkid kita ni mbo', sali' pasujud.* We bow to the ancestor, similar to the prayer position.

  **patungkid** *v. tr.* To present one's buttocks by bending over, head down.

**tungkilang** *v. intr. pa-* To be distinctive or unusual, of a person. *Patungkilang ma ka'a, alangkaw ūngnu.* What is distinctive about you is that your nose is high. *Patungkilang ma a'a inān, asabul.* The outstanding thing about that fellow is that he violates community standards. *Buwat saga pitu' a'a magdanakan, nnom hē' ka'ntanan he' sigā ya bay pangusaha ka'mbo'-mbo'an, magbubu. Patungkilang ma dakayu' inān saddī hinangna man magbubu hē'.* Seven brothers, six of them carrying on the livelihood of their ancestors, fishing with a trap. The distinctive thing about the other one is that he is doing something other than trap fishing.

**tungkud** (var. **tukkud**) *n.* **1)** A pole; a walking stick; a crutch. (*cf:* **bastun, kakakal**; *Thesaurus:* **bale₃ 1, sambuwang, soha'**) **1.1)** *v. tr. -an* To propel a canoe by poling. *Bang t'bba tinukkuran.* Poled along at low tide. *Na aubus na kami bay palaran-laran, anukud-nukud na kami sudju amole'.* So when we stopped going with the current, we poled our way towards home. *Soha' panukkud pelang.* A mooring stake used for poling a canoe. *Pat'kkad pareyo' listun itū bang alalom tahik, panukkudku.* This piece of sawn lumber will reach bottom when the tide is in, for me to pole [the canoe] with.

  **tungkud-luwag** *n.* Someone old and infirm (lit. walking-stick and feeding-spoon). {idiom} *Tungkud-luwag, hatina mbal agon makal'ngngan, mbal makasobo'an dīna.* Walking stick and feeding spoon, in other words almost lame and unable to feed oneself.

**tungga'** *n.* **1)** A firm commitment; an undertaking. **1.1)** *v. ditr.* To make a firm commitment regarding time for an action. *Anungga' aku ma ka'a, salung maghinang.* I promise you, we will work tomorrow. *Tungga'anta dang'llaw ni duwa. Buwat sala kita sinukut, tangguhanta, tungga'anta.* I promise to act in one or two days. Sort of like when we are dunned for a debt, we ask for more time and set a date. *Basta bay makatungga' ni si Id, subay b'lliannu.* In the event that you have made a commitment to Id, you should buy it for her. *Ya bay tungga'na ma sigām, sinō' pabīng palabay t'llung'llaw.* His promise to them was that they were told to come back after three days. (*Thesaurus:* **kamaupakkatan**)

**tunggal** *adj. zero* 1) One only; single; unique. *Ai-ai sinambat he'na, nirūlan sadja apa tunggal.* Whatever she asks for she gets because she is an only child. (*cf:* **dangan-dangan 1**; *Thesaurus:* **dakuman, hal, la'a, luwal, puntul, sadja, samadjana, yangkon**) **1.1)** *adv.* Single-mindedly; without exception. *Kami magitikad tunggal.* We set our thoughts on God alone.

**tunggal-bahangi** *n.* The evening star. (*gen:* **bitu'un**)

**tunggal-tunggal** *v. intr. pa-* 1) To operate independently; to act alone. *Patunggal-tunggalan iya dīna bang am'ssi.* He keeps to himself when he goes fishing. (*cf:* **damunda'-munda' 1, tukkal**) **1.1)** *adv.* Acting alone; being the only one. *Bang bay halam si Gi, tunggal-tunggal si Li.* If it hadn't been for Gi, Li would be an only child.

**tunggang** *v. intr. pa-* To tilt at one end; to slant. *Pasōng ka ni buli', patunggang munda'.* Go further on to the stern, the bow is tilting down. (*Thesaurus:* **jungkat 1.1, pagtungkellat-tungkellat, togsok**)

**pagtunggang-kīng** *v. intr. aN-* To be out of focus; to experience a loss of equilibrium, usually accompanied by loss of visual focus. *Auling mataku, angkan abōng he'ku ang'nda'. Sali' magtunggang-kīng ai-ai tanda'ta.* My eyes are unfocused, that is why my vision is blurry. It's like everything I see being out of focus. (*Thesaurus:* **angol, baliyang, bo'ay, lango 1.1, pagboyokan, uling**)

**patunggang** *v. tr.* To cause something to tilt.

**tunggara'** *n.* A southeast wind. *Baliyu tunggara', ahāp pagbanogan.* A southeast wind, good for sailing. (*gen:* **baliyu 1**)

**tunggīng** *n.* Mockery; ridicule.

**pagtunggīng** *v. intr. aN-* To mock someone for his disability. *Bang buwat aniya' a'a magpengka'-pengka' bo' ah'lling si Ji, yukna, "Nda'un ba, a'a mapengkol tape'na inān." Magtunggīng iya.* Like when someone is hobbling along and Ji says, "Look at that, the fellow there with the crippled leg." He is mocking [his disability]. *Pinagtunggīngan a'a kinulap inān.* That person with double-skin disease gets jeered at. (*Thesaurus:* **gunyak-gunyak, paganday-anday, udju'**)

**tunggu'** *n.* 1) A guard. *Sikahagtangan ba'anan tunggu' inān.* Those guards all fell flat on their backs. (*cf:* **jaga 1**) **1.1)** *v. tr. -an* To keep watch over something; to guard. *Halam aniya' anunggu'an si Ed. Subay aniya' anunggu'an iya ma luma'.* There is no one watching over Ed. There should be someone watching him in the house. (*Thesaurus:* **alimata, jaga 1.2, papag, peyan**) 2) A guardian spirit. *"Iya inān," yukna, "tunggu' ma Ka, niōnan si Om."* "That one," he said, "is Ka's guardian, named Om."

**pagtunggu'** *n.* 1) A guard place. *Luma' paglihanan* ko' inān, ngga'i ka luma' pagtunggu'an. That's an overnight shelter, not a guard-house. **1.1)** *v. intr. aN-* To guard against harm or escape.

**tunggu'-tunang** *v. tr.* To court a young woman one hopes to marry.

**pagtunggu'-tunang** *v. intr. aN-* To carry out the obligations of courtship once a betrothal relationship is recognized. *A'a magtunggu'-tunang bay abaibad, pinaludju' bo' asugpat pabalik.* A courting couple who have separated are persuaded to resume the relationship and be connected again. (*Thesaurus:* **pagpah'nda 1, tagad-kawin**)

**tunggu'-langat-langat** *n.* The Dotty-back, a fish species. *Pseudochromis melanostigma.*

**tunggul** *n.* The stump of a tree or post. *Bay ahūg si Ny, bay makakuppa ni tunggul.* Ny fell down, she jumped onto a stump. (*cf:* **punggul 2**)

**tunghab** *v. intr. pa-* 1) To drink directly from a storage container. *Patunghab kita ni bō', halam aniya' anuwang iya.* We drink directly from a bamboo water tube, no one pouring it out. **1.1)** *v. tr.* To get water directly from a storage container. *Da'a tunghabun, aniya' panginuman.* Don't get it from a storage container, there are [cups] to drink from. *Patunghabun aku mint'dda, sali' mint'dda aku an'ggok.* Let me gulp just once, like I take one small swallow. (*Thesaurus:* **ggok, inum 1, t'ggok**)

**tungul** *n.* 1) The air bladder of a fish. *Buwat daing tungulan, abustak tungulna.* Like a fish with an air bladder, its bladder bursting. (*Thesaurus:* **babat, badding-badding, b'ttong$_1$ 1**) 2) The stomach as the gastric organ of a mammal. *B'ttongta itū ma luwasan, tungulta ma deyom.* Our abdomen is here outside, our stomach is inside.

**tupak** *n.* 1) A patch over a hole or tear. **1.1)** *v. tr. -an* To mend a hole by patching. *Agese' badju'nu, subay tinupakan.* Your blouse is torn, it needs to be patched. (*Thesaurus:* **patli' 1.1, patlong, puna', sumpal 1.1**)

**tupag** *adj. a-* Coarsely woven and without a backing, of a mat. (*syn:* **t'ppag$_2$ 1**)

**tupan** *adj. a-* 1) To be alike in significant ways. *Datupan sigā magkawin, sali' daheya dalangkaw.* They match [each other] in marriage, the same size and same height. *Atupan pangandakdak maka pangose'.* Washing clothes and washing things are similar activities. (*Thesaurus:* **dora' 2, sali' 1, samapasang, sibu' 1, suga-suga$_2$**) **1.1)** *v. tr. -an* To be appropriate to the need or context. *Tupananta lling, subay aniya' pamalosta ahāp.* We make our words suitable, we should have a good response. *Am'lli kita atop saga dahatus, makatupanan pangatop diyata'.* We will buy about a hundred shingles of thatch, it will be appropriate for the roofing of the upper part. (*cf:* **tongod$_3$ 1**)

**pagtupan** *v. intr. aN-* To match in value. *Mbal magtupan bayadna maka sangsā'na.* The payment doesn't match the effort that was put into it.

**tupara** var. of **tipara**

**tupas₁** *n.* **1)** Small items of food eaten with a drink; a snack. **1.1)** *v. intr. aN-* To eat something with a drink.

**tupas₂** *n.* The heartwood of a tree. *Ala'an kulitna, aniya' kubalna. Ala'an kubalna, aniya' tupasna.* When its bark is removed, there is the hard wood. When the hard wood is removed, there is the heartwood. *Bang gamut sibukaw subay tupasna.* With sappanwood root [used for dowels] it should be its heartwood. (*Thesaurus:* **kubal 1, esok, sapan₂**)

**tupras** *n.* A toothbrush. (*Thesaurus:* **gisgis empon, sangbawa, sipilyu 1**)

**tupuk** *v. intr. pa-* To attend community events such as a wedding, death ceremonies, legal proceedings. *Angkan aheka a'a bay pina'an sabab anupuk disi Mu.* That's why a lot of people went there, because they were paying a condolence visit to Mu and others. (*Thesaurus:* **hadil, luruk 1.1, taddung**)

**tupus** var. of **tubus₁**

**turul** (var. **urul**) *v. intr. pa-* **1)** To follow after something; to pursue. *Wa'i paurul ma ina'na.* He's following his mother. *Pagubus, pabuhat si Ma bo' paturul ni h'ndana.* After that Ma got up to go after his wife. (*Thesaurus:* **apas 1.1, pagiku-iku, sunud 1.1, sunu'**) **1.1)** *v. tr.* To pursue something. *Tinurul kita he' ero'.* A dog is chasing us.

  **turul-buli'an** *n.* An optional gift from the bridegroom's family, consisting of sweetmeats. *Bang makanito'ongan-to'onganna, kita magbaya' amowa turul-buli'an, saga tinapay, bāng-bāng, gaugati', tamu, saging.* To be very specific, those of us who want to bring an extra gift consisting of [things like] bread, cookies, popped-rice cakes, packages of cooked rice, bananas.

**turung** *n.* **1)** A covering; a lid. (*Thesaurus:* **sa'ob 1, sampong 1, tambol 1, taplok 1, tutup₁** 1) **1.1)** *v. tr. -an* To cover something. *Tinurungan e'na maka turung bulawan.* He covered it with a gold cover.

  **pagtinurung** *v. intr. aN-* To wear a head cover. *Makaiya'-iya' bang d'nda binagongan atawa pinapu'ut bu'unna, angkan iya subay magtinurung.* It is shameful when a woman's hair is shaved or cut short, which is why she should be wearing a covering.

  **turung-balu** *n.* **1)** A head covering worn as a sign of one's widowhood. **2)** A low cloud resting on the top of a mountain. {idiom} *Bang ta'nda' turung-balu itū, bang ma kami aniya' abalu.* When this cloud is seen, in our thinking someone will be widowed. (*Thesaurus:* **andom 1, gabun, haya'₂, tai'-baliyu**)

**tūs** *v. tr.* To toss a ball for a fellow-player to hit, a volleyball tactic. *Tūsun pariyata' abō' kīlku.* Toss it up so I can kill it. (*cf:* **kil, walup**)

**tusay** *adj. -an* Having abundant hair hanging down the back. *Tusayan d'nda hē, binu'un sidda.* That woman has much hair hanging down, her hair is abundant. (*Thesaurus:* **hambak, hampal, labung 1, libombo', pugay 2, sapid 1.1, simbōng 1.1, toket 1.1**)

**tustun** *n.* A coin of 50 centavos or 1 peso. {obsolete} *Tustun dambila', suma'an tustun dakayu' pilak.* A fifty-centavo coin, or a one-peso coin. (*Thesaurus:* **landing₂, pilak 2, pinta₁, pisita, sīn**)

**tustus** *v. tr. -an* To unlash the ropes which hold a sail to a mast. *A: "Tinustusan, pinahagmak pareyo'." B: "Tinustusan tabul-tabul?" A: "Aho', sampay hambawan."* A: "Unlash the sail, bring the sail-mast assembly down." B: "Unlash the sail itself?" A: "Yes, and the halyard as well." (*cf:* **kka 1.1**)

**tūt** var. of **tūd₁**

**tutat** *adj. a-* **1)** Specified in detail; listed. *Atutat ai-ai kinagunahan.* Whatever is needed is listed specifically. **1.1)** *v. tr.* To specify things in detail. *Bang kita am'lli ai-ai ni M'ddas, bo' aniya' amabeya' ma kita, subay tinutat.* When we buy anything in Siasi Town and someone is sending us, things should be specified. (*Thesaurus:* **anyak-anyak, sokat₁ 1, tugila' 1.1**)

**tuttuk** var. of **tittuk**

**tuttulan** *n.* Genealogical information and traditions. *Tuttulan kami, pangkatan.* Our inherited traditions, our ancestral line. *Tuttulan sigām itū min Musu', sogo' ma buwattina'an ma Tabawan na sigām maganak-mpu.* Their genealogical links are from Musu', but they are in Tabawan now having children and grandchildren. (*Thesaurus:* **ntan₂ 2, ntan₂ 2, pakas-pakas 1, pali-pali, pangkatan, purukan, tubus₂ 1, usulan, usulan**)

  **pagtuttulan** *v. intr. aN-* To maintain the traditions of one's descent group. *Magtuttulan na pa'in, magpanubu'.* Continuing to follow the traditions of the family line, generation after generation.

**tutuban** *n.* The amniotic sac. *Ap'ssa' bay tutuban.* The waters have burst. (*Thesaurus:* **k'mbal-bohe', panubigan**)

**tutukang** var. of **tukang**

**tutukbalan** (derivative of **tukbal₁**) *n.* An offering to a deity; an important gift. *Bang a'a jahallis mbal tataima' tutukbalanna.* If a person is wicked, his gift will not be accepted.

**tutul** *v. tr.* To voice a complaint about something one finds unacceptable. *Bang bay amah'llingan a'a si Ar, tinutul ni matto'ana.* When Ar had been saying bad things to people, a complaint was made to his parents. *Anutul si Ina' bang kap'ddi'an anakna.* Mother complains when her child has been hurt. (*Thesaurus:* **dugal 1.1, pabukag, pah'lling₂, pamūng-mūng, pugpug 1, s'ndal 1**)

**tutung** *adj. a-* Burnt, of cooked food. *Kagorun buwas atutung ilū min kaldero.* Scrape that burnt rice from the pot. (*cf:* **danglus**)

**tutungan-s'llang** var. of **kalitan-tutungan-s'llang**

**tutungan-t'bba** var. of **kalitan-tutungan-t'bba**

**tutup₁** *n.* **1)** A woven food cover. *Tinutupan ai-ai buwat saga bāng-bāng maka tutup.* Things such as cookies are covered with a *tutup.* (*Thesaurus:* **sa'ob 1, sampong 1, tambol 1, taplok 1, turung 1**) **1.1)** *v. tr. -an* To cover food, as to protect it from flies.

**tutup₂** *adj. zero* To be closed, of a school or business enterprise. *Limaya aku magkalga bang tutup na iskul.* I am free to work as a porter when school is closed.

**tuwa** *n.* **1)** A vine, the roots of which provide a substance for stupefying fish. (*gen:* **bahan 1**; *Thesaurus:* **lagtang 1, tuba 1**) **1.1)** *v. tr.* To catch fish by stupefying with an extract of the tuwa vine.

**tuwak** *n.* The Palmyra or Toddy palm. *Borassus flabellifer.*

   **tuwak-mamis** *n.* A low-growing palm, the leaves of which are used as a vegetable.

**tuwad** *n.* A smooth-skinned edible tuber; a yam. *fam. Dioscorea.* (*Thesaurus:* **kallari', kapeta', hupi' 1**)

**tuwaha'** *see:* **pagtuwaha'**

**tuwa'** *v. intr. pa-* **1)** To become visible, of something previously out of sight. *Patuwa' pa'in bulan, agtūy kami tininduk.* As soon as the moon rose we were getting bites [from fish]. *Mbal gi' aku ni iskul bang halam patuwa' llaw. Ipatku gi' si Li.* I won't go to school yet when the sun hasn't risen. I will keep looking after Li. *Buwat pelang nih'llop pareyo' he' maut, mbal nih'llop he' saddī. Pinatuwa' kita bo' halam na maina'an ba'anan sakapta.* Like a *pelang* type canoe drawn down by a death-spirit, not by anything else. We are permitted to reappear but our equipment is no longer there. (*Thesaurus:* **bulat, luwas₁ 1, tukaw**) **1.1)** *v. tr.* To visit or appear to someone. *Bay iya tinuwa' he' mala'ikat.* She was visited by an angel. (*Thesaurus:* **pagpasalupa, salidda**) **2)** To visit someone; to show up in person. *Bang asakki si Mbo', patuwa' si Ina' amowa kinakan.* When Gran is ill, Mother turns up taking food. (*Thesaurus:* **bisita 1.1, liyud, tibaw 1.2, tulaga'**)

   **patuwa'** *v. tr.* To present a child to its grandparents (a cultural responsibility).

**tuwal** *n.* **1)** The tailbone; the coccyx. **1.1)** *v. advrs. -in-* Projecting upwards, of a person's buttocks. *Bang aku palangi, mbal pat'nde buli'ku apa tinuwal.* When I swim my butt doesn't submerge because it protrudes. (*cf:* **tuddi'**)

**tuwalya** *n.* A towel. (*Thesaurus:* **jimpaw, panyu', sapu-tangan, tawel**)

**tuwan** *voc. n.* A respectful address form to a man of similar age to the speaker; a prefix to titles such as hadji' or imam. *Saga tuwan, pahapit gi' kam ni luma' kami minsan mbal apatut.* Sirs, please call in to our house, even though it is unfit.

**Tuwan bihu-banwa** *n. phrase* The name of an important spirit of the Siasi Lagoon area.

**tuwang** *v. tr. -an* To pour a liquid from one container to another. *Tinuwangan aku kahawa he' si Mām, aku na amalutan sawan.* Mam pours me out coffee, me holding the cup. *Patunghab kita ni bō', halam aniya' anuwangan kita.* We drink directly from the bamboo water-tube, no one pouring out for us. *Katuwangan tingga' bay tinadjul.* Lead that has been melted can be poured out. (*Thesaurus:* **hain, huddud 1.1, tumpa 1.1, tuyung**)

**tuwas** *adj. a-* **1)** Hard; stiff; stubborn or obdurate (fig.) *Amatay nireyo' he' sehe'na, atuwas na pa'in.* His companion exhaustively sought reconciliation, but he remained obdurate. (*Thesaurus:* **alod₁, k'llas 1.1, gagga**) **1.1)** *v. intr. aN-* To become hard; to stiffen. *Anuwas-nuwas baranna kamemon bo' yampa amatay.* His whole body became stiff and then he died.

   **tuwas-kōk** *adj. a-* Stubborn; uncooperative [lit. hard-headed]. {*idiom*} *Aniya' onde'-onde' mbal palāng e'nu. Yukna, "Sampiyalun ba onde'. Atuwas-kōkna ilū."* There's a child who won't be stopped by you. [Someone] says, "Slap the kid. He's stubborn."

   **tuwas-pentol** *adj. a-* Resistant to correction or modification. *Atuwas-pentol malkina itū, mbal tapahāp.* This engine is stubborn, it can't be put right. *Onde' itū atuwas-pentolna, mbal pahona'-hona', mbal kapaggara'an.* This child is hard to teach, won't think, can't take advice. *Kayu asugat sidda, mbal pakatam, mbal ameya' ma kabaya'anta. Atuwas-pentolna.* This wood is very cross-grained, can't be planed, won't do what we want. It is obstinate.

   **tuwas-tuwas** *v. intr. aN-* To become rigid. *Anuwas-nuwas baranna kamemon bo' yampa amatay.* His whole body became stiff and then he died. *Angulangkang itū sali' paperat tape'ta. Anuwas-nuwas kita amatay.* Curling up, our legs sort of spread. We go rigid and die.

   **pagmatuwas** *v. intr. aN-* To become stubborn or resistant to advice.

**tuwi'** *ptl.* Indicates surprise or recollection on the speaker's part. *Aku tuwi' kalinganan he'na?* Can it be me that he is calling? *Bay tuwi' maitu si Ol di'ilaw.* Ol was here yesterday, now that I think of it. *Sampay tuwi' ayat duwampū'.* Oh, stanza twenty as well! *Aniya' lagi' tuwi' takalipatku nihaka.* Oh, and there is something else I forgot to say.

**tūy** *adv.* **1)** Completely; unconstrained. *Alembo tūy.* Completely drowned. *He' na isāb si Su tininduk tūy du.* Su was there too, immediately getting a bite. *Bang aniya' onde'-onde' angamu' ai-ai,*

*pak'mmi'. Bang kabuwanan, mbal na pak'mmi'.
Bang mbal binuwanan, na anangis tūy.* When a
small child asks for something, she pouts. If she
is given she no longer pouts. If not, then she
cries openly. **1.1)** *v. intr.* pa- To go directly to a
destination. *Bang bay aniya' banogku, patūy aku
amole'.* If I had a sail I would have gone straight
home. *Magtūy makaragsa', makatūy.*
Immediately running aground, all the way.
*Patūy ka, da'a ka maghapit-hapit, saga ang'nda'
ma pangongka'an.* Go straight there, don't keep
stopping and watching games and so on. **1.2)**
*v. tr.* To take place fully. *Ap'ggos pa'in banog ma
dilaut, na bang aniya' hapidna mbal anūy.* When a
boom cracks at sea, well if there is a splint to
attach to it, the break won't become total.
*Apasu' kaldero bo' aniya' ngā'ku mareyom.
Magāng-āng tanganku pako'ot apa ina'an apasu'.
Sali' tūyta bo' mbal makatūy.* The pot is hot and
there is something to get from it. My hand is
hesitant about dipping in because it is hot. It's
like doing it, but not doing it.

**katūyan** *adv.* Completely; totally; utterly. *Bang
pakkom katūyan pelang, ahūg ai-ai, alungay.* If a
canoe goes completely over everything falls out
and is lost. *Maglibat-libat dīna, katūyan du ko'
inān.* He makes his eyes go cross-eyed, it'll
become permanent.

**tūy-tūy** *v. intr.* aN- To move directly and
immediately to a destination. *Na pagtogge'*

*ariplano inān, na sudju pareyo' anuwi-nuwi ni
tahik.* Then that airplane, having headed
downwards, went on downwards, going directly
into the sea.

**magtūy** (var. **agtūy**) *adv.* Immediately; without
delay. (*Thesaurus:* **agsāy, dai'-dai'an, sakadjap,
saru'un-du'un, sigla' 1**)

**tuyang** *adj.* a- Flexing or buckling under a load, as
a hanging cradle or wood framing. *Minsan hāgta
atuyang bang ariki'.* Even our house posts sag if
they are small.

**tuyuk-tuyuk** *v. ditr.* To deliver something to where
it belongs. (*Thesaurus:* **maksud 1.2, nde',
papole', pasampay, tukbal₁, tūd₂, tulun₂ 1.1**)

**tuyu'** *adj.* a- 1) Seriously committed to a goal.
*Atuyu' pahāp a'a inān magusaha.* That man is
really committed to making a living. (*Thesaurus:*
**akkul, dago'os, sugsig 1, tebot**) **1.1)** *v. tr.* -an
To commit unreservedly to a specific goal.
*Tinuyu'an to'ongan bīlli pantalun Macomber.* What
[he] is really concentrated on is to have
Macomber-style pants purchased.

**pagtuyu'** *v. intr.* aN- To do something with
persistence and concentration. *Subay kami
magtuyu' angandarut ma unas inān.* We must be
persistent at pulling out that water-weed.

**pagmatuyu'** *v. intr.* aN- To be fully persistent.

**tuyung** *v. tr.* -an To pour a liquid from one
container to another. (*Thesaurus:* **hain, huddud
1.1, tumpa 1.1, tuwang**)

# U u

**uban** *n.* 1) Gray hair. *In uban kabantugan saga
kamatto'ahan.* Grey hair is the splendor of old
people. **1.1)** *v. advrs.* -in- To have gray hair.

**ubay** *adj. zero* Side by side.

**pagubay** *v. intr.* aN- To lie parallel to one
another, as sleeping people or fallen trees.
*Pagubayun na mailu.* Have them lying parallel
just there.

**ubbus** var. of **ugbus**

**ubi** *n.* The tropical yam. *Dioscorea alata or esculenta.*

**ubi-bilu** *n.* The purple yam; the elephant's ear
yam. *Xanthosoma violaceum.*

**ubi-sowa** *n.* The snake or elephant yam.
*Amorphophallus sp.*

**ubug₁** *v. intr.* pa- 1) To wade towards something.
*Da'a ka paubug man diyata'an, atiya' aku am'ssi.*
Don't wade on the upstream side, I am fishing
here. (*cf:* **kapo' 1**) **1.1)** *v. tr.* To reach a goal by
wading. *Da'a ubugun, ilu aniya' panggal.* Don't
wade for it, there is a fish trap just there. *Pehē'
na ka, ubugun bagaynu.* Off you go, wade after
your playmate.

**ubug₂** *v. tr.* To pursue a lure. *Niubug ullang he'*

*kanu'us.* A shrimp lure is pursued by squids.
*Buwat daing paka'llumta, niubug he' daing
kasehe'.* Like a fish that we are keeping alive,
other fish pursue it. (*cf:* **ullang 1.1**)

**pangubug** *n.* A fishing lure.

**ubul-ubul** *n.* An edible jellyfish found on sand in
shallow water. (*gen:* **būng**)

**ubus₁** *adj.* a- 1) Concluded; over and done with.
*Subay na aubus hinangku itū bo' ka tabangku.* My
work has to be finished and then I can help you.
**1.1)** *v. tr.* To finish something. *Ubusku pangiskul.*
I will finish [my] schooling. *Ubusku nihinang
bay panganjanji'ku ma ka'a, bang patut lagi' aku.* I
will finish doing what I promised you, if I am
still suitable. (*Thesaurus:* **katis₂ 1.1, sangkol,
talus₁ 1.1, tammat 1.1, tapus 1.1**)

**pagubus₂** *v. tr.* To complete some activity.
*Pagubusta magongka', magpapole' po'on pabīng.*
Having finished playing the game, we paid back
the starting money.

**pagpaubus** *v. intr.* aN- To do something as the
final action of a sequence.

**ubus₂** *conj.* After; then. *Saupama magtiman kām,*

*ubus makah'lla ni saddī. H'llana baha'u maru'nu.* You [two] divorce, for example, and then [your ex-wife] marries another man. You refuse to acknowledge her new spouse. *Ubus pa'in aku bay pinasiga, manjari itū anilaw na ipalku bahasa bang nsa' taga tunang d'nda-i.* After I had been given a cigaret, then my brother-in-law asked whether the woman referred to had a suitor. *Magpatay-patay kuyya', ubus allum.* The monkey played dead, and then was alive. (*Thesaurus:* **katis₂ 1, puwas₂**)

**ubus₃** *see:* **pagubus₁, anak-ubus**

**ubus... ubus** *conj.* Marks a sequence of events. *Pajalak na goyak tudju kaleya. Ubus pat'ngge, ubus pal'ngngan.* The waves are breaking towards land. [First] standing up on end, then moving forward. *Buwat taep, ubus angandawat, ubus mbal. Apaltik.* Like a typewriter, making a mark one minute, nothing the next. It's unreliable. *Kaladja'-ladja'an saki. Ubus kita ahāp, ubus kita ni ala'at. Ubus pabīng bo' ala'an, ubus pabīng bo' ala'an. Sali' magpuli-bahasa. Saki hē' ya magpuli-bahasa.* Disappointed by a sickness. We are well one minute and getting bad the next. Repeatedly coming back and going away. Like insincere courtesy, the sickness in question behaving insincerely.

**ukab** *adj. a-* **1)** Open, of a container or building. *Pagkunsi' itū, aukab na.* On turning the key, it was open. (*cf:* **ukay 1.1**) **1.1)** *v. tr.* To open a building, container or enclosure. (*Thesaurus:* **banga'₁, buka'₃, lungkad 1, sungkab**)

**pangukaban lawang** *n. phrase* A gift (lit. a door opener) made to the seller of an item such as a large pearl, as proof of a potential buyer's serious intentions. {idiom}

**ukay** *adj. a-* **1)** Open, in contrast to being closed. **1.1)** *v. tr.* To open an enclosure. *Amu'in kita kunsi', ukayta bodega.* Request a key for us, we will open the storehouse. *Pagukay sī', dakayu' d'nda maka dakayu' l'lla mareyom.* On opening the [door], there was one woman and one man inside. (*cf:* **ukab 1**)

**ukkil** *var. of* **ukil**

**uki'-uki'** *v. tr.* To complete a sequence, as when reciting a list or telling a story. *Halam aniya' kinapinan, niuki'-uki' ni manahut-nahut.* Nothing was kept back, it was related in full to the smallest detail. *Pinaentoman iya ai-ai bay makani'iya dakayu'-dakayu', hatina niuki'-uki' kamemon.* He was reminded of all that had happened to him, one by one. In other words it was all recounted. (*Thesaurus:* **hatul₁, patuntul, temo-temo**)

**ukil** (*var.* **ukkil**) *v. tr. -an* To decorate the surface of something solid; to embroider a cloth surface. *Magsāy pinatingkō' si Tuwan Aj ma bowa' luma' bay niukilan lawangna.* Mr Aj was promptly allowed to sit down in the entry of the house, the door of which has been carved. *Al'ssin la'up*

*badju'na bang niukkilan.* The pleats in her blouse are neat when decorated with embroidery.

**ukul 1)** *v. tr.* To arrange a number of items in groups. **2)** *v. tr. a-, ka-..-an, -an* To treat several groups equally.

**udjalat** *adj. a-* **1)** Involved in too many tasks. *Audjalat pahāp a'a inān.* That person is doing too many things. **1.1)** *v. tr.* To handle a diverse number of things. *Ata'u angudjalat ma tinda inān.* They are accustomed to handling lots of things in that shop.

**udju'** (*var.* **idji'**) *v. tr.* To mock or deride someone. *Palanu'un badju'nu bang ni pagkawinan ko' mbal niudju'.* Smooth your shirt when going to the wedding so as not be mocked. *Pag'nda' si Golayat ma si Da'ud in iya onde' baha'u lagi', magtūy niudju' e'na.* When Goliath saw David that he was still a youth, he immediately derided him. (*Thesaurus:* **gunyak-gunyak, paganday-anday, pagtunggīng**)

**pagudju'** *v. intr. aN-* **1)** To behave with scorn or contempt. **1.1)** *v. tr.* To treat someone with scorn. *Kami itu pinagudju', bo' ka'am ya pinagmahaltabatan.* We are the ones to be ridiculed, while you are the ones to be honored. *Itiya' kitam pinagudju'-udju' e' saga lūng-kampung itū.* Here we are being treated with scorn by the neighbors.

**pagudju'an** *n.* An object or focus of mockery.

**udjul₁** *n.* **1)** A serious misfortune; a bereavement. *Tauwa' kami udjul.* We have been hit with a serious misfortune. (*Thesaurus:* **bala', kajahatan, kala'atan, mulka' 1, naja', pa'al 1**) **1.1)** *v. advrs. ka-...-an* To be experiencing misfortune; to be bereaved. *Magbidda' to'ongan sigām bang kaudjulan, sabab minsan magdukka' masi asawa pamayhu'an sigām.* They are very different when bereaved, because even though they weep they look cheerful. *Kaudjulan kami, sali' kapatayan kami.* We experience misfortune, as when we are bereaved. (*cf:* **matay₁ 1.1**)

**udjul₂** *n.* The fall of tossed coins so that matching sides are upward, after being thrown up with tail and head sides facing in. *Bang udjul bo' bay agad, angahīs aku.* When the coins fall matching sides up, I rake in the winnings.

**ugam** *n.* **1)** An oral ulcer symptomized by blisters, or furring of the tongue. *Candida albicans. Subay kulit balo' nihinang tambal ugam.* The bark of the balo' tree should be used for making medicine for mouth blisters. (*cf:* **obe' 1**) **1.1)** *v. advrs. -in-* Suffering from an infection of the mouth. *Niugam si Nnong bay ariki' gi', bay amangan kende.* Daughter suffered from thrush when still small, she had eaten candy. (*cf:* **dapal, sampal 1**)

**ugam-pasu'** *n.* A severe infection of the mouth characterized by canker sores.

**ugat** *n.* **1)** Sinews; veins; tendons; nerves. **1.1)** Tensile strength; muscular strength. *Hinabu sōng* *ah'bba' kayu, apōng ugatna.* When a tree is about to fall, its tendons break. *Aluhaya itū sali' magpasannang-sannang kitā, sali' halam aniya' ugatta.* Relaxed, sort of taking our ease, like having no muscular strength.

**ugbus** (var. **ubbus**) *n.* **1)** New shoots; leaf buds. *Basta buwa' kayu, sumping, amuwan ugbus dahū.* In the case of fruit or flowers, they first produce buds. **1.1)** *v. intr. aN-* To produce new leaves. *Song na angugbus.* They are about to come into leaf. **2)** Young leaflets of coconut used to weave small food containers or decorations. (*cf:* **taliyan**)

**ugihap** (var. **hugiyap**) *n.* **1)** Shingles (herpes), a condition symptomized by a weeping rash over large areas of skin. *Herpes zoster.* **1.1)** *v. advrs. -in-* Afflicted with shingles.

    **ugihap-angalimbung** *n.* A form of shingles, the symptoms of which are largely internal.

    **ugihap-api** *n.* A form of shingles marked by persistent fever and general debility, after the easing of external symptoms.

**ugis** var. of **bugis**

**ugpang 1)** *n.* A partner in a two-person relationship; a workmate. *Bang a'a magtutuhun subay duwangan anuhun, subay aniya' ugpangna.* When people dive for a living there should be two of them diving, there should be a partner. (*Thesaurus:* **iring, limbang 1, umbuk 1**) **2)** *v. intr. pa-* To keep up with a companion in work or sport. *Mbal aku makaugpang, mbal maka'atu sali'.* I can't match [him], like I can't compete. **2.1)** *v. tr. -an* To compete or keep up with someone. *Buwat ka'a-i aga'os min aku ma ai-ai, mbal kaugpanganku.* Like you, more dominant than me in various ways, I can't keep up with you.

    **pagugpang** *v. intr. aN-* To interact with each other as partners or competitors. *Magugpang, magiggil.* Keeping up with each other, jealous of each other. *Magugpang militari maka rebelde.* The military and the rebels face off against each other. *Sali' akosog kuntarata magugpang.* Our opponents are dominant in the competitive relationship.

**ugtu** *n.* **1)** Noon; midday. **1.1)** *adj. a-* To be at the zenith, especially of sun or moon.

    **ugtu-llaw** *n.* Noon; midday. *Llaw, sangom, makajari kita angalamat, basta duma'in ugtu-llaw atawa tonga'-bahangi.* Day or night, it's okay for us to use divination, so long as it's not [right on] noon or midnight. (*Thesaurus:* **langa-llaw, langkaw llaw**)

**ugtu'-ugtu'** var. of **sowa-ugtu'-ugtu**

**ugud** *n.* A persistent, itchy, skin infection; impetigo. (*Thesaurus:* **abas 1, buwa'-buwa' 1, kagutgut 1.1, katol 1.2**)

    **ugud-lugay** *n.* A chronic skin infection that does not respond to treatment.

**ū'an** *n.* A pillow. *Pinagb'ddak maka ū'an.* Smacked repeatedly with a pillow.

**ū'ū** *v. intr. pa-* To abase oneself before another person as an act of contrition. *Paū'ū aku ni ka'a, apa man dusaku. Siyumku tape'-tangannu.* I will humble myself before you because the fault was mine. I will kiss your hands and feet. (*Thesaurus:* **deyo'₃ 2, pagkahāp, pagpa'ampun**)

**ūl** *v. intr. aN-* To yelp or howl, as a dog. (*Thesaurus:* **tanghul, tangungngul, usig**)

**ūl-ūl** *n.* A species of bird, possibly an oriole. *Oriolus sp.*

**ula-ula** *adj.* *zero* Lighthearted, as when joking or playing for fun. *Ula-ula itū sali' ngga'i ka to'ongan.* Ula-ula is something that is not serious. *Sali' ula-ula panoho'an gillu'-gillu'.* A kind of joke, a pretend instruction. *Bang aku ganta' bilahi magbantug, ngga'i ka ula-ula. B'nnal sadja kamemon pah'llingku.* If I were to boast a bit, it would not be for fun. Everything I say is true. (*ant:* **to'ongan 2**; *Thesaurus:* **gillu'-gillu', sainala**)

    **pagula-ula** *v. intr. aN-* To be having fun together, in contrast to being intense or serious. *Buwat kami magplising maka si Mu, ngga'i kami magto'ongan, magula-ula kami.* Like Mu and me playing marbles, we're not being serious, we're just having fun.

**ulak** *n.* **1)** Floating trash; flotsam. *Ulak inān bay unas.* That floating rubbish was originally seagrass. (*Thesaurus:* **gampal, pagung**) **1.1)** *v. tr.* To collect floating items into a single mass. *Buwat kita abuhaw, niulak ai-ai bo' mbal alungay.* Like when we get swamped, everything is made to form a floating clump to prevent being lost.

    **paulak** *v. intr. aN-* To form a floating mass, as items from a capsized boat.

**ulagat** *v. intr. aN-* To be stripped of foliage. *Angulagat kakayuhan itū, ala'an daunna sabab min badju.* These trees have become bare, their leaves gone because of the typhoon.

**ulagu** var. of **kalitan-ulagu**

**ulama'** *n.* An Islamic scholar; an authority in Islamic laws and principles.

**ulan** *n.* **1)** Rain. *Alandos ulan dibuhi'.* The rain was heavy last night. **1.1)** *v. intr. aN-* To be raining. (*cf:* **bonok-bonok, pitik-pitik 1**) **1.2)** *v. advrs. -in-* To be rained on. *Bang niulanan, nilidjiki'an.* When rained on, [one is] blessed with resources. *Bang niulanan luma' itū asidda tampiyas man dinding.* When this house gets rained on it gets very wet through the walls.

    **pangulan** *n.* The rainy season.

    **paulan** *v. tr. -an* To expose someone by refusing them shelter. (*Thesaurus:* **inyaya, pa'alu', tanya₁**)

**ulan-ulan** *n.* A species of coral fish. (*cf:* **lasak, tibuk₂**)

**ulansiman** *n.* A kind of trefoil, a low-growing plant species. *Desmodium triflorum.*

**ulang** *n.* 1) A shrimp: a prawn. (*syn:* **ka'ullang**) 2) A wooden lure, shrimp-shaped, for squid. (*syn:* **ullang 1**)

**ulang-ulang** *n.* Prawn crackers (casual food).

**ulapay₁** *v. advrs.* -in- Suffering from a common cold. *Rhinovirus.* (*Thesaurus:* **p'nnot, s'ppun 1**)

**ulapay₂** *n.* The Coral grazer, a fish species, pink with large scales. *Ulapay itū ma llot ogos maka lampet.* These *ulapay* are midway between a parrotfish and a wrasse.

**ulapid** *v. advrs.* -in- Afflicted by cramp, as during pregnancy or after fatiguing physical exercise. (*Thesaurus:* **b'nnod 1.1**)

**ulat₁** *n.* Various larvae, including maggots and caterpillars. (*Thesaurus:* **but'ngngel, kalog 1, iyas 1, sassing 1**)

**ulat-h'kka-h'kka** *n.* Various inchworms (lit. hand-spanning grubs).

**ulat-sapling** *n.* Various furry caterpillars.

**ulat₂** *v. tr.* To claim a safe square in the game of kick-the-block. (*cf:* **pagestēp**)

**ulayan** *n.* A perforated bowl used to strain liquid from food, or to allow batter to drip into a cooking pan. *Ulayan itū peya' bay nilowangan, taga tangkay. Pangahinangan jā.* The *ulayan* referred to is a coconut shell with holes made in it, has a handle. Used for making rice cookies.

**uldin** *n.* 1) An edict or order from a high-ranking source, especially in a military context. (*Thesaurus:* **da'ak, gandahan, hilag, pagmanda 1, soho', sūg-sūg**) 1.1) *v. tr.* To command someone.

**ulehem** *n.* A record-player; a recorder. (*Thesaurus:* **ligaya, plaka**)

**uli** *adj. a-/-an* Attached emotionally, as a child to a loved adult. (*Thesaurus:* **balut 2, lumut₂ 1, lūt₂ 1, umid 1**)

**ulid** *var. of* **hulid**

**uli'₁** *adj. a-* 1) Healed from an illness or wound. *Pauli'un aku kono', itiya' aku alamma.* Please make me well, I am physically weak. (*syn:* **hali₂**; *Thesaurus:* **sagauli'**) 1.1) *v. intr. pa-* To return to a healthy state. *Song pauli'.* Soon to become well. 1.2) *v. advrs. ka-...-an* To be healed, of an illness or wound. *Ahunit kauli'an bakatna.* His wound is difficult to heal.

**uli'₂** *v. tr.* -an To straighten out something which is bent; to correct the damage of something said. *Bigtangun k'llat ilū bo' niuli'an.* Stretch out that rope there so it will be straightened. *Subay iya magpa'ampun ni Tuhan, niuli'an llingna hē' ni a'a bay subalihanna hē'.* He should seek forgiveness from God, that the things he swore on oath to that man might be put right. (*Thesaurus:* **bigtang 1.1, b'ttad 1.1, l'dduk 1.1, l'ngngat, lūk, tilud 1.1**)

**ulin** *v. tr.* -an To guide or drag a conveyance. *Karitun baha'u ya bay niulinan e' saga anakna.* The new cart that was pulled along by his sons. (*Thesaurus:* **bakot, malim 1.1, tuhung, tuli' 1.1, tullus 1.2**)

**uling** *adj. a-* Affected by dizziness resulting from nausea. *Magabong e'ku ang'nda'. Sali' duwa ta'nda'ku, auling mataku sali'.* I see things unfocussed. Like I see double, my eyes sort of dizzy. (*cf:* **bōng**; *Thesaurus:* **angol, baliyang, bo'ay, lango 1.1, pagboyokan, pagtunggang-kīng**)

**ulip** *v. tr.* To care watchfully for someone or something. *Ulipun a'a sakki ilū, pinahāp he' amakan.* Look after that sick person, do a good job of feeding him. *Subay niulip bīlla ilū.* What's cooking there should be watched carefully. (*Thesaurus:* **ayad, ayuput, hamumu', ipat, pahilala' 1, paintul, paipid, payakun, talkin, upiksa', ussap 1**)

**ullang** *n.* 1) A wooden lure for catching squid, has multiple barb-less hooks and resembles a shrimp. *Ullang pangā' kanu'us, nihinang kayu.* A lure for getting squid, made of wood. (*cf:* **ka'ullang**; *syn:* **ulang 2**) 1.1) *v. intr. aN-* To catch squid using a carved lure. (*cf:* **ubug₂**)

**-um-** *aff.* Intransitive infix: attaches to a small number of verbs whose single argument is actor-like. *Bang anakta mbal kapandu'an, alahang iya ni kahāpan, humeka ni kala'atana.* If our son can't be taught, he will rarely come to the good, he will come many times to the bad.

**uma** *var. of* **huma**

**umak** *see:* **pagumak**

**umagak** *n.* A female of chickens or animals.

**pagumagak** *v. intr. aN-* To mate, of domestic chickens and animals.

**umagad** *n.* 1) The non-physical component of a person; the spirit as the element that survives death. *Subay kita amatay bo' taga umagad. Hal pikilanta, napasta, akkalta, nyawata buwattina'an.* We need to die to have an *umagad*. At present there is just our minds, our breath, our intellect, our souls. *Bang aku ganta' kinubul masi ma luma' umagadku. Subay apuwas hinang t'llu, pitu', ni Tuhan.* Suppose I am buried, my spirit remains in the house. The third or seventh day of mourning must be over, then to God. *Ngga'i ka baranna pasalidda ni aku, umagadna.* It was not his body that appeared to me, but his spirit. *Saguwā' ma buwattina'an hal umagad la'a ya paglaktasantabi m'nnilu-m'nnitu.* But now it is only through spirit components that we have a connexion between there and here. *Sagarin na in pi'itu, kalu halam na, minsan la'a hal umagadnu.* Never mind that [your] coming back may not happen, even just your spirit-presence. (*cf:* **umanat**; *Thesaurus:* **ginhawa, nyawa, panalengog, sumangat 1**) 1.1) *v. advrs.* -in- Frightened or made ill by the appearance of someone's ghost. *Niumagad aku he' pangguwa', itiya' na ta'ā'ku sakki.* I was terrified by the appearance of a ghost, and now I have taken sick from it. (*Thesaurus:* **bolag, dalan 1.1,**

**damag**, **gawa**, **g'mma**, **gupu**, **leya'-leya'**, **tāw** 1.1)

**umagad-sowa** *n.* The manifestation of a saitan spirit in snake form. *Ya taluwa' saitan sowa, umagad-sowa.* Being struck by a snake spirit.

**umanat** *n.* The spirit component of a person, living or dead, sometimes sensed far from his physical location. *Buwat ma lahat dakayu' bo' aniya' ta'nda'ta, suma'an ma deyom uppita, suma'an ngga'i ka. Umanatna ya ta'nda'ta, atawa takaleta hal.* Like we are in another place and we see something, sometimes in our dream, sometimes not. It is its spirit that we see or just hear. (*cf:* **umagad 1**)

**umas** *v. tr.* To handle something unnecessarily; to fiddle with. *Bang aniya' ganta' ntananku, buwas atawa ai-ai na bay niumas, ya pinaggomot inān sali'.* If I happen to hold something, rice or anything that has been handled too much, whatever is sort of formed into lumps. *Oy arung, da'a ka angumas.* Hey, girl, don't fiddle with things. (*Thesaurus:* **hulemang 1.1, lotok 1.1, pagkoledje**)

**pagumas** *v. intr. aN-* 1) To keep fiddling with things. 1.1) *v. tr.* To handle something unnecessarily. *Da'a pagumas-umasta mantil bo' mbal tasiggul.* Let's not fiddle with the mantle [of the pressure lantern] lest it be jolted.

**umaw** *n.* 1) A dumb person; a mute. (*Thesaurus:* **saitan-mungkil 1**) 1.1) *adj. a-* Lacking the power of speech. *Saitan mungkil hal amaumaw ma a'a.* The *mungkil* spirit simply causes humans to be mute. (*Thesaurus:* **kamal, kokam₂ 1.1, kowam 1, pamorok**)

**pagumaw** *v. intr. aN-* To feign dumbness. *Ai bay tilawnu bang mbal minsan magsabut? Hal magumaw dakuman.* What were you asking when he doesn't even understand? He simply pretends to be dumb.

**umaw pagon** *adj. a-* Total dumbness. {idiom}

**umbang** *v. tr. -an* To take full responsibility for someone's welfare, as parents for a small child. *Niumbangan kita he' Tuhan, niatasan kita.* God takes complete care of us, he assumes responsibility. *Atawa bang aniya' ma deyomannu tinambalan, ka'a ya angumbang.* Or when someone in your household is being treated, you are the one to take responsibility. (*Thesaurus:* **aku₁, pagnapaka**)

**umbaw-umbaw** *see:* **pagumbaw-umbaw**

**umbuk** *n.* 1) One's counterpart in an opposing group, as in a team game. (*Thesaurus:* **iring, limbang 1, ugpang 1**) 1.1) *v. tr. -an* To respond to the action of a counterpart in a group activity. *Umbukanku hinang sehe'ku.* I match the actions of my companion.

**pagumbuk** *v. intr. aN-* To work in pairs. *Magumbuk isāb bang magsigid, t'llungan kami man dambila', t'llungan isāb man dambila'.* We work in pairs when tying thatch, three of us on the underside, three of them on the top side.

**umbul** *n.* 1) A mathematical number; a number used to indicate a size or gauge. *Indamin aku tōng barena umbul mpat.* Lend me a number 4 drill bit. *Umbul pila p'ssinu ilū?* What size is that fishhook of yours? 1.1) *v. tr. -an* To mark something with a number. *Subay umbulannu ba'anan kapanyapan ilū bo' mbal alungay.* You should put a number on those various items of equipment so they don't get lost.

**umbul dakayu'** *adj. zero* Of first-class quality. {idiom}

**umbul satu** *adj. zero* Of first-class quality. {idiom}

**umbul tunggal** *adj. zero* Of first-class quality. {idiom} *P'ssi umbul tunggal inān mbal al'ngngat.* Those first-class fishhooks do not straighten out under tension.

**umbut** *n.* The new shoot of a coconut palm. *Bang bay ah'bba' niyug, niā' umbutna, kinakan.* When a coconut palm has fallen, its new shoots are taken and eaten.

**umid** *v. intr. pa-* 1) To have one's mind or affections fixed on some goal. *Paumid ma si Be, palūt. Ma iya na pa'in iya.* His affections are fixed on Be, emotionally attached. He is with him continually. (*Thesaurus:* **balut 2, lumut₂ 1, lūt₂ 1, uli**) 1.1) *v. tr. -an* To fix one's mind on someone or something. *Ai na pa'in umiranna?* What is he alway setting his heart on?

**ummat** *n.* 1) Humans as beings created by God; a community, especially of Islam. *Ya Tuhanku, ampunun kono' kasā'an ummatnu itū.* O my God, please forgive the faults of this creature of yours. *O Mbo', itiya' ummatnu pinapanjari e'nu. Na ang'nda' ka ba!* O Ancestor, here are creatures you brought into being. Do look [toward us]! *Sabarang ummat tinawalan he'na.* He recited an incantation over the entire congregation. (*Thesaurus:* **bangsa₁, pihak**) 1.1) *v. tr.* To create or ordain a species. *Bangsa kami Murus bay niummat he' Tuhan.* Our Muslim Filipino race was created by God. (*Thesaurus:* **paniya', papanjari**)

**umpak-umpak** *n.* Choppy waves. *Umpak-umpak itū ya tahik magdaplak-daplak.* Umpak-umpak is the sea continually splashing over.

**pagumpak-umpak** *v. intr. aN-* To move vigorously up and down, as a vehicle on a rutted road or a canoe on choppy sea. (*Thesaurus:* **pagbullud-bullud, pagbuwang 1.1, paghandok, paghuntak, pagtongket-tongket**)

**umpan** *n.* 1) Bait. (*cf:* **panuba**) 1.1) *v. tr. -an* To bait a hook or trap. *Anū' saga kindat pangumpan bang am'ssi dai'-llaw.* We catch little cuttlefish by lamplight to use as bait when fishing early in the morning.

**umpig** *n.* A member of a cooperating group.

**pagumpig** *v. intr. aN-* To work as a cooperative group. *Buwat aniya' magbono'. Kami itū saga* t'llungan. *Yuk kami, "Ōy, aheka magumpig ma dambila'."* Like when there is a fight. We are about three in number. We say, "Hey, there are many forming a group on the other side."

**umpigan** *n.* A cooperative group; a military unit. *Aniya' umpigan sundalu pal'ngngan min dahū'an saga imam, ya magtiyup-tiyup.* There were groups of soldiers in front of the religious leaders, the ones who were blowing trumpets. (*Thesaurus:* **kaheka-heka'an, kompolan, dansehe'an, padjuhan, palti**)

**umpul** *n.* A tree species of mangrove swamps, a source of useful timber.

**umpung** *v. tr.* To combine things, as several small strings of fish bunched together. (*Thesaurus:* **pagpūn₁, pungut 1.2**)

**umul₁** *n.* A falling star. *Umul itū sali' bitu'un apakpak min diyata'.* *Umul* is like a star falling from above. (*cf:* **selo'**)

**umul₂** *n.* 1) The age of a sentient being; a lifespan. *Pilantahun umulna?* How many years old is he? *Bang pa'in ataha' umulnu.* May your life be long. **1.1)** *adj.* **a-** To be older than. *Aumul gi' aku min h'ndaku.* I am older than my wife. *Daumul kami maka si Sey.* Sey and I are the same age.

**kasaumulan** *n.* The remote or ultimate future. *Min awal tagna' sampay ni kasaumulan.* From the very beginning until the ultimate future. *Bang ka bay magkahagad, tuman ka'a pinapagsultan ni kasaumulan.* If you had been obedient, you would surely have been established as king forever.

**pagumulan** *n.* One's age group. *Saga kasubulan ya pagumulanbi.* The single men of your own age.

**umulan** *adv.* To be of a mature age.

**saumul-umul** *adv.* Forever; lifelong. (*Thesaurus:* **salama-lama, sapanjang-panjang, sapaya-paya, sapupud-daya**)

**-un** *aff.* Imperative undergoer voice suffix: indicates a command, and identifies the undergoer as the subject of the clause. *Ungsikun, sipuk-sipukun, haka'in sab'nnal-b'nnal.* Speak in private, say it to him alone, tell him truthfully.

**unam** *n.* A species of shellfish.

**unas** (var. **hunas**) *n.* An inedible grass-like sea plant of marine shallows. *Guyu itū sampay ni deyo' tana', ameya' arundang saga kahunasan.* The turbulence of the sea water reaches the seabed, the sea grasses swaying to its rhythm. (*cf:* **lusay**; *Thesaurus:* **l'mmuk, taubang**)

**unas-balu** *n.* A species of fish, a weed eater.

**undam** *n.* A general purpose basin. *Amu'us aku bohe', isiku ni undam pangose' lai'.* I pour out the water and put it into a basin for washing dishes. (*Thesaurus:* **batiya', lumpang-lumpang, palanggana, pastan**)

**undang-undang** *n.* A primer for beginning readers.

**undi'** var. of **sowa-undi'**

**unduk-unduk** *n.* The thorny seahorse. *fam.*

Syngnathidae. (*cf:* **talli₂**)

**unjal** *v. intr.* **pa-** To move to a location somewhat further away. *Paunjal, sali' palabi, parahū.* Moving beyond, like going too far, going ahead. *Subay pinaunjal ni tōng sa'am.* It should be pushed right out to the end of the outrigger boom support. (*Thesaurus:* **lalga, lanjal 1.1, laus 1, sōng₂ 1**)

**unjuk** *see:* **samaunjuk**

**unta'** *n.* A camel. *Unta' ya pangura'an ni Makka.* Camels are the riding animal for [going to] Mecca.

**untang** *n.* A buoy or float for supporting long-line fishing gear and marking its location. *Bang kita am'ssi, pagūng kita. Bang kita angalaway taga untang, taga sau isāb kita.* When we fish with hook and line, we just float. When we are drift-fishing we have a float and we also have an anchor. *Untang itū pamabeya'an p'ssi. Aheka p'ssina, saga dahatus, saga dahatus limampū'. Anahut, a'aslag, saga sangpū' maka siyam.* An *untang* float is for carrying [multiple] hooks. It has many hooks, one hundred or one hundred and fifty. Small ones and big ones, about size 19. (*Thesaurus:* **pataw₁, sau, tangkal₂ 1**)

**untas** *v. intr.* **pa-** 1) To travel between places. *Bang aniya' b'lliku ni M'ddas pauntas aku man pelang-pelang.* When I have something to buy in Siasi I cross over by means of a little outrigger canoe. (*Thesaurus:* **k'tta 1, laktas, lintas**) **1.1)** *v. tr.* **-an** To cross a body of water. *Mbal kauntasan sapa', alandos s'llog.* The river cannot be crossed, the current is too strong [said of someone crying profusely].

**panguntas** *n.* Overseas travel.

**untuk** *see:* **panguntukan**

**untul** var. of **tuntul**

**untung₁** *n.* 1) Profit; gain (financial). *Pinaheka untung sigā.* Their profit was increased. (*Thesaurus:* **anak₃ 1, laba**) **1.1)** *adj.* **a-** Successful in trade. *Da'a kam asusa bang auntung saga a'a kasehe'an.* Don't be upset when other people are successful in business. **1.2)** *v. tr.* To make a profit. *Bay pam'lliku sangpū' daingku. Bay nilituhan, tab'lli du duwampū'. Anguntung aku sangpū' pilak.* I paid ten [pesos] for my fish. It was sold on, bought for twenty. I made a profit of ten pesos.

**paluntungan** *n.* A profitable outcome from a business venture. (*cf:* **pagkalugi'an**)

**untung₂** *v. intr.* **aN-** To be uncertain about choices. *Anguntung gi' aku ameya' ni Sandakan.* I'm still uncertain about going to Sandakan.

**paguntung-duwa** *v. intr.* **aN-** To be unsure which of two possibilities is the more appropriate. *Maguntung-duwa aku tapole' m'nnitu bang halam aniya' pameya'anku.* I am unsure about getting home from here if I have no means of transportation. *Maguntung-duwa ameya' maka mbal. Sali' ma olangan magpikilan ameya' maka* *mbal.* Of two minds whether to go or not. Like being in between thinking whether to go or not. (*Thesaurus:* **dalam-duwa, duwa-abana, duwa-ruwa, sarap-duwa**)

**unud sīn** *n. phrase* A trivial sum of money. {idiom} *Dakayu' unud-sīn atawa duwa.* Just one or two centavos.

**unung** *v. intr. pa-* 1) To accompany someone, even in death. *Bang aniya' amatay siyalita, bilahi kita paunung.* If our younger brother dies, we want to accompany him. (*Thesaurus:* **abay₁ 1.1, beya'₂ 1, bunyug 1.2, dongan, sehe' 1.1**) **1.1)** *v. tr.* *-an* To accompany someone wherever he goes. *Ununganku panonku pi'ingga-pi'ingga. Maglundang-lundang.* I will accompany my friend wherever she goes. We are close friends. *Niunungan itū sali' magbeya' karuwangan.* This word *unung* is like two people going together.

  **pagunung** *v. intr. aN-* To stay together, even in death. (*Thesaurus:* **pagdongan, pagdora', pagsambeya'**)

**ūng** *n.* The nose.

**ūng-ūng** *n.* The Rainbow runner, a fish species; the Two-finned runner. *Elegatus bipinnulatus.*

**unga'** *adj. a-* Easily moved to tears, as a bereaved person on hearing good music or a sad story. *Aunga' si Ap, minsan hal nihagda.* Ap cries easily, even if she is merely urged to do something. (*Thesaurus:* **langan₁, mmaw 1, pagle'eng, s'ngngel 1**)

**ungas** *adj. a-/-an* Bald through loss of hair growth. *Ungas itū halam magbu'un diyata' kōkna. Saddī kelas, aniya' limpa'. Ungas* means the top of his head has no hair. *Kelas* is different, there is a scar. *Aesog bang ungasan.* A bald person is brave. (*Thesaurus:* **kelas, lengas₂, penggas**)

**ungkup** *n.* A traditional roof construction in which the gables at each end slope outwards under the ridge pole extensions. *Sali' luma' karatu'an ya luma' ungkup itū. Ya kaheka'anna ma l'ggotan Sambuwangan.* These *ungkup*-style houses are like the houses of traditional chiefs. Many of them are on the landward side of the Zamboanga seafront. *Luma' ungkup alanga bubunganna.* An *ungkup*-style house has a high ridge. (*Thesaurus:* **atop 1, layang-layang**)

**unggun** *n.* 1) A knotty piece of wood used to rekindle a fire. (*Thesaurus:* **baga 1**) **1.1)** *v. tr.* To start a fire using a coal from an earlier fire. *Akatis pa'in kita magb'lla pat'nna'anta na buku po'on kayu pangunggun. Ta'abut pagb'lla pabīng, na asāl aniya' apita.* When we have finished cooking, we place a knotty root [on the fire]. When it is cooking time again, we already have fire.

**ungsik** (var. **ungsit**) *v. tr.* To speak to someone in confidence. *Ungsitun pehē' bang buwattingga bay bissala kami.* Ask [him] in confidence how our talk was. *Ungsikun, sipuk-sipukun, haka'in sab'nnal-b'nnal.* Speak in private, say it to him

alone, tell him truthfully. (*Thesaurus:* **pagsīb, sipuk-sipuk**)

  **pagungsik** *v. intr. aN-* To speak to each other in private. *Aniya' isāb magungsik, hal duwangan-duwangan.* There are also people who speak privately, just the two of them.

**ungsit** var. of **ungsik**

**ungsud₁** *n.* 1) The bride-wealth given by the man's family to the woman's family in fulfillment of the marriage contract. *Ai kaungsuran Sama? Pilak, karut buwas maka maligay.* What are the bride-gift items of the Sama? Money, sacks of rice, and a ceremonial model house. *Saupama atilaw d'nda si'itku-matto'aku, nihalga'an buwattitu buwattina'an. Ya hē' bang ma kami banghad. Mbal gi' kaōnan ungsud.* For example my uncles and parents inquire about a girl, and some amount or other is stated. That is what we call *banghad.* It cannot be called *ungsud* yet. (*Thesaurus:* **banghad 1, basingan, mahal₂, pagtinabawan, punggit 1**) **1.1)** *v. ditr.*

**ungsud₂** *v. ditr.* To present a gift to a supernatural being as a mark of respect or devotion. (*Thesaurus:* **buwis 1.1, lamas, paglabot 2, tanggap 1.1**)

**ungsud-ungsud** *n.* The drawer of a desk.

**ungus** *n.* Coarse sand; a sandy beach. (*syn:* **gusung**)

  **ungus-bunbun** *n.* Fine white sand.

**upak** *n.* A container made from the outer layer of palms, such as the betel palm. *Lapis bunga ya tahinang upak pangisihan sinanglag.* The outer layer of a betel palm is made into a container for roasted cassava meal.

**upa'** *n.* 1) The inedible residue of food being eaten. *Upa' kinakan buwat saga to'olang daing, atawa t'bbu bang bay na pina'us.* Food residue such as fish bones, or sugarcane after it has been chewed. **1.1)** *v. tr.* *-an* To discard inedible material in food, typically by ejecting it from the mouth. *Upa'anta to'olang daing.* We spit out fish bones.

**upama** *v. intr. aN-* To mention something in a casual way. *Bang d'nda bowa'an, angupama na pa'in.* A talkative woman just keeps chattering. A: *"Kinahandakan aku to'ongan he' Tuhan."* B: *"Ni kahāpan bahā'?"* A: *"Mbal taupama bang ni kala'atan. Subay lullun sadja aku nirūlan ai-ai bay amu'ku."* A: "I have been granted much by God." B: "For good?" A: "It wouldn't be mentioned said if it was bad. It must mean that I will get whatever I had asked for."

**upamakun** *conj.* 1) For example. *Aheka palsagga'an, bang upamakun ma kibut pangisihan bohe', tu'ud ap'nno' na, angkan abustak.* So many conflicts, like a jar of water for example, which bursts simply because it is full. *Upamakun si Anu hē', mbal aku ameya'-meya', ala'at hinangna.* Take What's-his-name as an example, I will not believe him, his actions are bad. (*Thesaurus:*

**pamaralilan, saupama 1) 1.1)** *v. intr. aN-* To mention; to comment.

**upāng** *n.* **1)** A condition symptomized by foul-smelling ulcers. *Upāng, pinanaw-panaw. Tabiya' aku, sali' pat'ppak tape'-tanganta ni tai' sapi'.* Ulcers, due to skin infection. Pardon my language, but it's as though our hands and feet had landed in cow dung. (*Thesaurus:* **ka'mbo'an, kawit₂ 1, kolera, ipul 1, pangkot 1, ttus-ttus 1) 1.1)** *v. advrs. -in-* To be afflicted with ulcers.

**upiksa'** *v. tr.* To look after something with diligence; to fully meet someone's needs. *Sai-sai atuyu' angupiksa' kabbunna maglabi-labi pagkakanna.* Whoever takes good care of his plantation will have a surplus of food. (*Thesaurus:* **ayad, ayuput, hamumu', ipat, pahilala' 1, paintul, paipid, payakun, talkin, ulip, ussap 1)**

**upis** var. of **opis**

**uplut** *v. intr. pa-* To exceed the limits of a container. *Pauplut, sali' pasuput, sali' maglasay na bang kita angisi.* Overflows, brims over, like when we fill something and it is too much. (*Thesaurus:* **lasay, lese₁, lipay₁, luput 1, sempok 1)**

**paguplut** *v. intr. aN-* To burst out from constraints. *Paguplutna, magtūy anumping maka atahak buwa'na.* On bursting out [from its bud], it flowered immediately and its fruit was ripe.

**uppi** *v. intr. aN-* **1)** To dream. (*Thesaurus:* **ansong, ddop, lāp-lāp, mutamad, pagdabdab) 1.1)** *v. intr. pa-* To appear to someone in dream form. *Pauppi' ni kita, sali' anganyata'.* Appears to us in a dream, as though becoming visible.

**pagpauppi** *v. intr. aN-* To appear to someone in a dream.

**pagu'uppi** *v. intr. aN-* To be given to dreaming.

**panguppihan** *n.* A dream state.

**urul** var. of **turul**

**urus** var. of **hurus**

**urut** *v. intr. aN-* To fall out, of one's hair. *Ē, angurut na ka!* Fall out then!

**usa** *n.* A deer. (*cf:* **kusa'**)

**usaha** *n.* **1)** An occupation from which one makes a living; a livelihood. *Ngga'i ka usaha, tu'ud bilahi magbanog-banog.* It's not work, he just likes sailing here and there. **1.1)** *v. tr.* To get an income by regular work. *Da'a paluwasun sīnnu ilū kamemon. Subay ka ak'mmit, ahunit sīn niusaha.* Don't bring out all that money of yours. You should be sparing, money is hard to earn. **1.2)** *v. tr. -an* To make use of a resource for the purpose of making a living. *Niusaha'an baranna.* She makes a living from her body [i.e. works as prostitute].

**pagusaha** *n.* **1)** A livelihood; a way of making a living. *Ya nirali'itan a'a ya taga ai-ai hē'. Sa'agon-agon ya pagusaha sigā subay na sali' na ma a'a angandali'it inān.* The object of their jealousy is the people who have things. It's as though their income should be the same as the person who is jealous. *Hē' na sigām magma'adjul ni Sabah pagka asigpit pagusaha ma Pilipin.* There they are intent on heading off to Sabah since work is so difficult [to get] in the Philippines. **1.1)** *v. intr. aN-* To be engaged in earning a living. *Bang kita magusaha, bin'nnod baranta, subay niā'an tambal lu'ug. Aniya' lima ginis gamut kayu nihinang tambal lu'ug itū.* When we are fishing for a living and our bodies are numb with fatigue, we need someone to get us exhaustion medicine. There are five kinds of tree root used to make this medicine. *Bapa'ku si' bay magusaha l'ppus.* My aforementioned uncle used to make his living from harvesting marine sponges. *Magjuru' aku, mbal aku magusaha, halam aniya' kabaya'anku a'llum.* I behave excessively, I don't work for a living, I have no desire to live. *Buwat a'a hal maglunsulan ni luma' a'a, mbal magusaha. Halam aniya' kapūsanna bang buwattē'.* Like a person who just wanders round to people's houses and doesn't work for a living. Such a person is of no use.

**pagusaha'an** *n.* The equipment or location for making a living. *Ahunit to'ongan pagusaha'an ma lahat, da'a lagi' ni kalawakan, minsan ni kasekotan hal a'a binono' maka nilangpasan.* Making a living is very difficult throughout the region, not just in distant places, even here close by people are being killed and raided. (*cf:* **gaddongan**)

**pangusaha** *n.* The equipment for one's work.

**usal** *v. tr.* To use something. *Alahang niusal kabtangan ilu ma kami.* That word is rarely used among us. *Tausal isāb sigla' bang pasal musiba.* The word *sigla'* [suddenly] can also be used with regard to an epidemic. (*Thesaurus:* **guna 1.1, pakay₁, pasang₁**)

**usam-usam** *n.* Various cardinalfishes. *Epigonichthys marmoratus.*

**usaw** *n.* The rambutan tree and its edible fruit. *Nephelium lappaceum.*

**usay** (var. **husay**) *adj. a-* **1)** Disentangled, of a line. *Bay asagut naelon ati yuk si Mma', "Usayun, kalu ausay."* The line was tangled so Dad said, "Untangle it, maybe it can be untangled." (*cf:* **sagut 1) 1.1)** *v. tr.* To disentangle a line. **2)** Resolved, of a discussion or dispute. *Alimogmog kagara'an, mbal magtaluwa', mbal ausay.* The discussion ended in disagreement; there was no accord, things weren't resolved. **2.1)** *v. tr.* To settle a dispute. *Ka'a kono' ya ata'u angama'ana maka angahusay saga palkala' ahunit.* You, it is said, know how to interpret words and to settle difficult issues. (*Thesaurus:* **pagsalassay 1**)

**usba** *n.* **1)** The blood relatives (consanguineal kin) on the father's side, especially those of the father's generation. *Bang wali mbal anokat, subay* *usba buwat si Bu, matto'a makaga'os.* Kin on mother's side cannot specify details of the bride-weath, it must be father's kin like Bu, an elder who has authority. (*cf:* **wali**) **1.1)** *v. tr. -an* To represent someone in litigation, as ranking kin on the father's side. *Niusbahan aku e' siyakaku, apa halam maina'an matto'a kami.* My older brother represented me, since our parents were not there.

**usba-waris** *n.* Relatives on both sides of an individual, especially those responsible for marriage discussions or litigation.

**usbu** var. of **husbu**

**uskaw** var. of **hukaw**

**usiba'** *v. tr. -an* To treat someone abusively; to rape someone. *Bay sinaggaw e'na si Di ampa niusiba'an.* He seized Di and raped her. (*Thesaurus:* **jilaka', la'at 1.2, la'ug 1.1, pinjala' 1.1, pissoko', puhinga', sikla**)

**usig** *v. intr. aN-* To howl or bark, of a dog. *Aheka ero' angusig; mbal aku makatuli.* Lots of dogs barking; I am unable to sleep. (*Thesaurus:* **tanghul, tangungngul, ūl**)

**usihat** *n.* Religious teaching; a sermon. (*Thesaurus:* **nasihat**)

**ussab-ussab** *v. intr. a-* To make the rustling noise of a snake moving through dry grass. (*Thesaurus:* **bahembas 1, bah'ssek 1, kerek-kerek, keyos₂, kulanas 1, kulessab, ganggu'**)

**ussap** *v. tr.* **1)** To take care of something or someone; to attend to someone's needs. *Ahāp kono' pangussap ka'a mahē' ma Bukidnon.* The care you will get there in Bukidnon is said to be good. *Halam niussap langgal inān.* That meeting place has not been maintained. *Halam iya angussap anakna.* She doesn't take care of her child. (*Thesaurus:* **ayad, ayuput, hamumu', ipat, pahilala' 1, paintul, paipid, payakun, talkin, ulip, upiksa'**) **1.1)** *v. ditr.* To care for someone who is sick by asking for help on their behalf from a supernatural being.

**ustu** (var. **hustu**; **osto**) *adj. zero* Sufficient; adequate. *Buwat ni'nde'an ni aku gadjiku. Tilawnu, "Jukup ba ilū?" "Aho'," yukku, "ustu."* Like when my wages are handed over to me. You ask, "Is that complete?" "Yes," I say, "it's enough." (*Thesaurus:* **sarang 1, s'ddong, sugiya, t'ppot**)

**usuk** (var. **gusuk**) *n.* A rib (the bone). (*Thesaurus:* **kadjang-kadjang, giyak**)

**usul** *n.* **1)** A traditional story or song. *Usul, sali' kata-kata atawa salsila.* A traditional story, like a kata-kata epic or a formal tale. **1.1)** *v. tr.* To give an orderly account; to follow traditional steps; to relate traditional beliefs or histories. *Makapaglamugay kita minsan buwaya aheya, bang tausulta bay awal mbo'ta manusiya'.* We can even mix together with large crocodiles, if we follow the traditions of our ancestors. *Usulta bay ka'mbo'-mbo'an, s'ssagta ya bay pangkat dahū*

*bang iya bay makakalna' ī'. Na aminta-minta.* We follow the traditions of the ancestors, we inquire of some previous ritual ancestor if he was the cause [of the illness]. So we ask for health.

**usulan** *n.* Genealogical information and traditions; traditional customs. (*Thesaurus:* **ntan₂ 2, ntan₂ 2, pakas-pakas 1, pali-pali, pangkatan, purukan, tubus₂ 1, tuttulan, tuttulan**)

**usung** *v. tr.* To carry a person in a sitting position, a mark of honor. *Niusung, buwat pangantin d'nda binuhat.* Carried in sitting position, the way a bride is lifted up. (*Thesaurus:* **baba' 1, balung 1, tanggung₁, tumpay**)

**utab** *v. tr.* To cut something with a bladed implement. (*Thesaurus:* **katama, duklat 1, ōk 1**)

**utang** *n.* **1)** A debt. **1.1)** *v. tr.* To borrow something; to buy on credit. *At'ggol amayad, sali' pinaglehod-lehodan sīnnu. Ka'a ilū mbal tapangutangan.* A long time paying, you are holding back your money. You cannot be given credit. (*Thesaurus:* **indam, sambi' 1.1, sanda'-sanda', s'nnad**)

**palutangan** *n.* Liabilities; debts.

**pangutangan** *v. tr.* To be considered good for a loan.

**pautang** *v. ditr.* To grant someone credit or deferred payment.

**utas** *adj. a-* **1)** Severed from a main part by cutting. *Nilagut e' a'a itū tendogna, autas magtūy dambila' taingana.* This man slashed his tenant, one of his ears cut right off. **1.1)** *v. tr.* To sever something; to cut off a part. *Tinabid e' sigām k'llong manuk ē' sago' mbal niutas kōkna.* They twisted the rooster's neck but its head was not cut off. (*Thesaurus:* **tabtab 1, tempos, t'ttop 1, tompes**) **2)** Cut off or brought to an end, of a discussion. *Autas na palkala'.* The business matter is concluded. **2.1)** *v. tr.* To terminate a discussion or an argument. *Buwat du bisala niutas. Bang halam autas, amasi amalut.* Like a speech being cut off. If it's not cut off, it is still hanging on.

**utta'** *v. intr. aN-* **1)** To vomit. *Kasehe'an mbal angutta' minsan agoyak.* Some don't vomit even though the sea is rough. (*Thesaurus:* **balowak, pagsallowa', toya'**) **1.1)** *v. tr. -an* To vomit something up.

**pagutta'** *v. intr. aN-* To be vomiting persistently or repeatedly. *Aniya' na t'llu pitu' ni'mmunan iya maka magutta', tabiya' isāb.* It is three weeks now that she has been fevered and vomiting, excuse my mentioning it.

**uttala'** *n.* A north wind, often gusty and associated with dry weather. *Bang uttala', agoyak ariki'-diki' maitu, angaut.* In the *uttala'* season the seas round here are slightly rough, the water discolored. *Bang palemba na mūpū, sōng na satan. Bang ma ugtu masi, uttala' masi.* When the Pleiades have passed the zenith, the south wind will soon begin. If they are still at the zenith, it's still the northwest monsoon. (*gen:* **baliyu 1**)

**uttala'-lo'ok** *n.* A northeast wind, generally light. (*gen:* **baliyu 1**)

**utuk** *n.* The brain.

**utus** *v. intr.* pa- To give someone support in a game, hoping to share in the winnings. *Pautus kita ma iya, ati bang iya anganda'ug kalu kita binuwanan.* We aid him, then if he wins we may perhaps be given something.

**uwak** *v. tr.* To suck a person's vital fluids, the action of a balbalan spirit being. (*Thesaurus:* **balbal, kowang**)

**paguwak-uwak** *v. intr.* aN- To behave like a balbalan spirit, emitting strange cries. (*Thesaurus:* **sambal**₂)

**uwang** *n.* A species of monkey. (*Thesaurus:* **amu'**₂, **kuyya'**)

**uyun** *v. tr.* -an To accede to a proposal. *Ati anguyun saga a'a inān kamemon.* So all those people there agreed. (*Thesaurus:* **sulut 1.1**)

**paguyun** *v. intr.* aN- To be in accord, of a group. *Pagbebeya'an na, atawa paguyunan na.* Someone whose instructions one obeys, or is now in agreement with. *Angkan kami bay makapaguyun anambak batu.* That is why we agreed together to pile up rocks.

**dauyunan** *n.* 1) An agreement; consensus. 1.1) *adj.* Of the same mind.

# W w

**wakil** *n.* 1) A representative; an agent; an amabassador. 1.1) *v. tr.* -an To appoint or authorize someone to be one's representative. *Aku na angawakil ma ka'a. Pehē' na ka, bā'in sigā.* I am appointing you to represent me. Off you go, tell them about it. 1.2) *v. advrs.* ka-...-an To be given the authority to act on someone's behalf. *Buwat si Pa, ai-ai panoho'an iya he' saga a'a mareyom Nasuli', kawakilan iya angahinang.* Like Pa, whatever he is told to do by the people [living] at Nasuli, he is authorized to do.

**waktu** *n.* 1) A point in time; a period of time viewed as a unit. *Bang ta'abut waktu subay ka amas'lle'.* When the time comes you must give someone else a turn. *Pi'ilu ka ni langgal, waktu paghinangtam na.* Go to the mosque, it is time already for our religious duties. *Sidda aku bilahi bay amabeya' sulat ma tahun itu bo' halam aniya' waktuku.* I have really wanted to send off a letter this year, but I have not had time. (*Thesaurus:* **awal ni ahil, jāman, masa 1, taem, timpu 1**) 1.1) *v. tr.* -an To establish a time. (*Thesaurus:* **idda 1.1, ligtung, ora, pagtaratu, tugna', tugun 1.1**)

**pagwaktu** *v. intr.* aN- To work according to a time schedule. *Magwaktu isāb lansa ni Pasangan.* The launch to Isabela runs to a timetable.

**waktu itu** *n. phrase* This present time or era; nowadays. (*cf:* **buwatna'an**)

**waktu ni waktu** *adv. phrase* Time after time; from time to time. {idiom}

**waktu palabay** *n. phrase* Time past. *Ma waktu palabay, bay aku asannang mareyom astana'ku.* In times past I was comfortable in my palace.

**waktu tagna'** *n. phrase* Long ago; way back in time. {idiom} *Waktu tagna' aniya' bay paglalandingan ariplano ma Bakal.* Long ago there was a landing-field at Bakal.

**pagsawaktu** *v. intr.* aN- To occur just once, as seasonal events.

**wadjit** *n.* A confection of glutinous rice. *Wadjit itū nihinang putan, sokal maka gata'.* Wadjit is made of sticky rice, sugar, and coconut cream. (*Thesaurus:* **hapit-hapit, suman**)

**waen** *n.* 1) The winder of a watch. 1.1) *v. tr.* -an To wind a watch.

**waham** *v. tr.* To report something with limited knowledge; to rumor something. *Niwaham itu sali' tinokod, bo' halam gi' at'kka.* This word *waham* is like something guessed at but not yet realized. *Kinama'atay hē'-i, niwaham e'na sala.* That's something held in his heart, sort of guessed at. (*Thesaurus:* **hunub-hunub 1.1, taha, tuhuma 1, tuna'**)

**wahoy** *n.* A game of chance, of Chinese origin. *Ā, kamemon na manusiya', Sūk na, Sama na, Bisaya' na, Lannang na, magto'on wahoy inān.* Well now, people of every kind, Tausug, Sama, Visayan, Chinese are putting money on the *wahoy* game.

**wajib** *ptl.* 1) Should; must; had better. (Deontic modality particle, obligation to an external authority.) *Wajib ka pinandu'an he' matto'anu.* It is proper for you to be taught by your parents. *Ya hukawku pinagsaggaw-saggaw he' mastal. Wajib angiskul.* What I dislike [about school] is being rounded up by the teacher. Obliged to go to school. (*Thesaurus:* **patut, subay**) 1.1) *n.* Obligation; responsibility. *Mbal angatu pakil d'nda ma pakil l'lla. L'lla sadja ya taga wajib.* A female mosque leader can't compete with a male mosque leader. It is only men who have the responsibility.

**kawajiban** *n.* A sense of responsibility; obligation. *Kawajibanku anak siyaliku.* I have obligations in regard to my younger brother's child.

**wa'ad** *v. tr.* To make a binding commitment; to appoint; to declare. *Wa'ad itū buwat aniya'* *janji'ta sudju ni Tuhan atawa ni mbo'. Makajari isāb angwa'ad ni manusiya'.* This word *wa'ad* is like us making a promise to God or to an ancestor. It's also appropriate to use *wa'ad* to a human. *Bay makawa'ad iya inān subay pinakawin anakna.* He has formally declared that his daughter should be married. *Ta'abut na waktu bay tapangawa'ad.* The appointed time has come. (*Thesaurus:* **najal 1.1, pagsapa 1.1, sapda 1, subali 1.1, suhud 1.2**)

**wa'i** *ptl.* Perfect aspect marker, indicating that the state or action described has begun and is still in effect. *Wa'i na atuli.* He has gone to sleep [and is still sleeping]. *A: "Wa'i na h'llanu?" B: "Halam wa'i."* A: "Has your husband gone [fishing] already?" B: "Not yet." *Wa'i pa'in amole' min kapū'an, bay nilangpasan e' mundu.* When they were on the way home from the outer islands they were raided by bandits. (*cf:* **hē'₁ 2**)

**wali** (var. **waris**) *n.* Blood relatives (consanguineal kin) on the mother's side. *Ameya' anuku kawalihan.* Relatives from the mother's side were in agreement. *Bang wali mbal anokat, subay usba buwat si Be, matto'a makaga'os.* Kin on mother's side cannot specify bride-wealth details. It must father's kin, an elder who has authority. (*cf:* **usba 1**)

**walna'** *n.* A color; a hue. *Ibarat badju'ku, magpinda na walna'. Bay bilu makanipote'.* Like my shirt, its color has changed. It was blue tending to white. (*spec:* **abu-abu₁, bilu 1, biyaning 1, bū-kangag, kalas, kausun, keyat₁ 1, kulit₁, kuning, ettom 1, gaddung 1, hidjaw, hinu-hinu₁, loho'-ubi,**

**pote' 1, taluk**; *Thesaurus:* **agaw-agaw, b'ttik 1, kolol 1**)

**walu'** *num.* Eight.

**walumpū'** *num.* Eighty.

**walup** *v. tr.* To hit a ball hard (a volleyball term). *Bang kita magwalup bo' akosog, aladji'.* When we wallop [a ball] powerfully, it goes a long way. (*cf:* **kīl, tūs**)

**wanni** *n.* The fragrant mango; the kuwini. *Mangifera odorata. Minsan mampallam, wanni, balunu', anadjuk. Bang mbal niruplak, palanjal, yampa magduru'-ero'.* Whether common mango, odorous mango or horse mango, all set fruit. If not damaged they develop and then go on to the budding stage. (*Thesaurus:* **balunu', kobkoban, mampallam**)

**wapan** *n.* A yawn.

**pagwapan** *v. intr.* aN- To yawn. *Magwapan na si Oto', tinuli.* Oldest son is yawning, being sleepy.

**wapat** *adj.* a- Deceased, of someone high-born or socially important. *Manjari awapat na si Nabi Yusup maina'an ma lahat Misil.* And so the Prophet Joseph died there in the land of Egypt. (*Thesaurus:* **aymulla, maruhum, nahanat**)

**waris** var. of **wali**

**wau-** *see section 2.2.2.4 Prefix:* **Cau-**

**waylud** *n.* The brand name of a commercial wood glue or filler.

**wigan** *n.* A heavy, long-wearing cloth, suitable for work trousers or sails. *Bay kami ma Sambuwangan magbanog, wigan banog si Ro.* When we were sailing in Zamboanga, Ro's sail was of *wigan* cloth. (*Thesaurus:* **kapis, ispowen**)

# Y y

**ya₁** *ptl.* Subject marker. Optionally identifies the subject of a clause. *Nā ya duwangan saksi' putingan itu at'kka pina'an bo' aningkō' maganggop maka si No, ati tinuntutan na iya.* Now these two lying witnesses arrived there and sat opposite No, and so an accusation was brought against him.

**ya₂** *conj.* The one which; that which. (Relativizer). *Sai d'nda inān, ya mataha' bu'unna?* Who is that woman, the one with long hair? *Ya yukku ma ka'a...* What I said to you was... *Batu ya nihagtu'-hagtu' pangubug kuhita'.* The stone, the one that is jigged up and down to lure the octopus.

**ya ai** *phrase* Something or other; whatever. {idiom} *Nihinang ya ai halam bay tahinang e' saga ka'mbo'-mbo'anna.* Things done that had never been done by his ancestors.

**ya aniya'** *phrase* There might be. {idiom} (*Thesaurus:* **bahā', kalu-kalu 1, siguru 1**)

**ya balikna** *phrase* On the other hand; moreover;

however. {idiom} *Tagna'anku na sulatku pinabowa, pinaleyang, ni ka'a. Ya balikna, muna-muna min kamemon, salam duwa'a ni ka'am.* I begin my letter to be sent, to be flown to you. However, more important than all, devout greetings to you. *Ya balikna, akosog d'nda.* At the same time, women are strong.

**ya b'nnalna** *phrase* In fact; actually; the truth of the matter. {idiom}

**ya du** *phrase* That's it; you've got it; likewise. {idiom} *Ya du ko' aku itu, buwat ka'a, lingantu.* Likewise me, I'm like you, hungry. *Ya du saga pagbohe'anna, ngga'i ka ka'am ya bay angali'.* Likewise with its wells, it was not you who dug them. *A: "Ya itu bahā' bai amu'nu?" B: "Aho', ya du."* A: "Is this the one you were asking for?" B: "Yes, that's the one."

**ya na** *phrase* Like that; just like that. {idiom} *Bang iya na ka'abut-abutan sigām, nihinang kubu' na.* If that's what they can afford, [they] just build a temporary shack.

**ya pa'in** *conj.* Even though; by contrast. {idiom} *Dayahan isāb si Anu, a'a balkanan ya mbal alasa ma miskin. Ya pa'in niharap he'na hinangna.* What's-his-name is wealthy, a rich man who doesn't love the poor. By contrast it is his work that he focuses his attention on. *Buwat kami maka si Sa magbeya', bang ma labayan ilu tinimbak. Apuntul dangan amatay taluwa' timbak ati sehe'na halam, ya pa'in dambeya'an.* Like us and Sa going along together, and being shot there on the trail. One [of us] was singled out to die of gunshot, with his companion not hit, even though they were together. (*Thesaurus:* **bo' yampa, malaingkan, minsan**)

**ya po'on** *phrase* That's why. {idiom} *Ya po'on yukku ma ka'a.* That's why I told you. *Ya po'on asidda binanta' h'ndanu.* That's why your wife keeps getting sick so often.

**ya sadja** *conj.* Except that. {idiom} *Ahāp isāb kahālan kami, ya sadja bang pasān ala'at pagpangiramku.* Our situation is good, except that the conception stage of my pregnancy is not so good. *Magbamba kami pi'ilu ni ka'am, ya sadja mbal tasiguru kami bang kam kasulutan ma gara' itū.* We are thinking of coming there to you, except that we are not sure if you are in favor of this plan.

**ya itu** *n. phrase* This one in particular. *Ya itu bay yukku ma ka'a.* This is just what I said to you.

**pagya-itu-ya-ina'an** *v. intr.* aN- To be bossy, giving orders to do this or that. *Sali' iya magya-itu-ya-ina'an, sali' makapagbaya' ma aku.* He sort of tells me to do this or that, it's like he has authority over me. *Magmanda ma aku, sali' magya-itu.* Bossing me around, doing one thing and another. *Sali' magya-itu-iya-ina'an, sali' iya makapagbaya' ma aku.* Kind of doing this and that, and him doing what he likes with me.

**ya lagi'na** *adv. phrase* To a greater degree; the more so; how much more. *Ya lagi'na.* Even more so. *Minsan matto'aku halam bay haka'anku, ya lagi'na bahā' ka'a?* I haven't even told my own parents, how much more with regard to you? (*Thesaurus:* **anambahina, bangkinna…bangkinna, kalap, labi-labi, luba', luhūy, paligay**)

**ya mbal ta'nda'** *n. phrase* Spirit beings of any kind, a euphemism that avoids mentioning any by name. {idiom} (*Thesaurus:* **bangsa magl'l'ngngan, duwata 1, hama'-hama' a'a, hibilis, jīn 1, saitan**)

**yaboho'** var. of **yamboho'**

**yakal** *n.* A durable hardwood tree. *Shorea astylosa. Kayu yakal itū alinggas toho'na.* The dryness of this *yakal* wood is complete throughout its length.

**yakin** *see:* **pagyakin**

**Yahudi** *n.* A Jew.

**yamboho'** (var. **yaboho'**) *conj.* Now for the first time; only then. *Yamboho' ta'nda'ku ariplano.* I have now seen an airplane for the first time. *Sa'angay subu halam bay magkakan, yaboho' aku makakakan na.* Since morning [I] haven't eaten, only now have I been able to eat. (*syn:* **yampa**)

**yampa** *conj.* Now for the first time; just now; then and only then. A: *"Pilang'llaw na?"* B: *"Yampa dang'llaw."* A: "How many days?" B: "One day so far." *Buwat onde' itu angamu' ai-ai ni ina'na bo' mbal kabuwanan. Sakali itū yampa binuwanan bang anangis na.* Like this child asking her mother for things and not being given them. So then she is only given [what she wants] when she is already crying. *Bang aniya' abangat sakina yampa binowa ni doktol.* When her sickness had become serious, only then was she taken to the doctor. (*syn:* **yamboho'**)

**yangkon** *conj.* Only; solely. *Yangkon du si Ku maina'an.* Only Ku was there. *Bang aku pangamu'an sīn, yukku, "Yangkon du itu. T'ppot pagsukayku."* When someone asks me for money, I say, "I've only this. Exactly my fare." *Yangkon takapin ma matto'a d'nda mahal maka basingan.* The only thing remaining for the parents of the girl are the *mahal* [a fixed amount] and the *basingan* [gold pin]. (*Thesaurus:* **dakuman, hal, la'a, luwal, puntul, sadja, samadjana, tunggal 1**)

**yau-** *see section 2.2.2.4 Prefix:* **Cau-**

**yuk** (var. **iyuk**) *n.* Utterance or speech; quotation marker. *Yuk abay kami damunda' inān, "Nā, magsukul na ba," yukna.* Our fishing mate in that other canoe spoke, saying, "So, thanks very much." *Yukku apagon bo' mbal.* I said it was durable, but it isn't. *Ah'lling nabi inān ni sehe'na, yuk-i, "Papatayun aku maka kalis ilū."* *Sagō' magin'mbal pagkahina inān.* That prophet spoke to his companion, saying, "Kill me with that kris." But the companion refused. *Suli-suli mbal ahāp, ya yuk-i, "Ngga'i ka na budjang ya d'nda bay tapah'ndaku itū."* Talk that wasn't good, which said, "This woman that I took as wife was no longer a virgin." (*Thesaurus:* **bahasa₁, bā'₁, batbat₂, bissala 1.1, k'bbat₁ 1, h'lling₁ 1.1, pagmūng-mūng 1.1, sambat**)

# 3.2 English–Sinama wordlist

# A a

**A, therefore B** *samantala'*; *pagka*; *talkala'*
**abaca (hemp)** *lanut*
**abacus** *saipuwa*
**abalone** *lappas₁*
**abandon** *dondon*; *siya-siya 1*; *pasagad*
**abandoned child** *anak-ka'bbahan*
**abase oneself** *pagmalulus*; *ū'ū*; *deyo'₃ 2*
**abashed** *paki' 1*
**abate** *kontay₂*; *hulaw*; *kō' 1.1*
**abbreviation** *kapu'utan*
**abdomen** *b'ttong₁ 1*
**abdomen (lower)** *kamama'u*
**abduct** *dakop*; *lalas*; *lahi₂*
**aberrant** *saddī-saddī*
**abhor** *b'nsi 1.2*
**ability** *kapandayan*; *kaga'osan*; *purukan*
**ability (from God)** *tulun₁ 1*; *barakat 1*; *kawasa 1*
**ablaze** *angpud 1*; *pagsuleyab*; *keyat₂ 1.1*
**able (capable of)** *gaga*; *kole'*; *bogbog₂*; *kaya*; *ga'os 1.1*
**able (of toddler)** *tangpas₂*
**able to read Koran** *hatam 1.1*
**ablutions (Islamic)** *ail*
**abnormal** *saddī-saddī*; *mahal-mahal*
**abode of dead** *kiyamat 1*; *ahirat*
**abominable** *sakkal*
**aborted (baby)** *pulak 1*
**abortion** *kawa'₂*; *labu' 1.1*; *pakpak 2*
**abortion-prone** *bibis*
**abound** *kuta'₂*; *hungku'*; *hunsuk*
**about (approximate)** *sarang-sarang*; *saga 3*; *kulang-labi*
**about (regarding)** *pasal₁*; *takdil*
**about to (but didn't)** *arāk*; *agon mbal*
**about to happen** *arai' 2*; *baya-baya pa'in*; *dai'₂*; *abut₁*; *sōng-sōng₁*; *sa'at-sa'at*
**above** *diyata' 1*
**abraded** *banggid 1*; *leges*; *geges*
**Abraham** *Nabi Ibrahim*
**abrasive** *kasap*; *gasang*
**abruptly** *sigla' 1*
**abscess** *kalibubut 1*; *bularut*
**absence** *tulakan*; *bukut₂*; *likut 1*
**absent (school or workplace)** *absen*
**absent-minded** *liha-liha*; *panglupa*

**absolutely** *to'ongan 1.1*; *sidda 1*
**absolutely forbidden** *halam-mutallak*
**absolve** *ampun₁*
**absorb** *sobsob 1*
**abstain** *halli'₁ 1.1*
**abstersion** *puppu'*
**abundance** *kaheka-kataha'an*
**abundant** *banos*; *besal*; *dayas-dayas*; *parat*
**abundant (of hair)** *tusay*
**abuse (physical)** *usiba'*; *la'ug 1.1*; *jahulaka' 1.1*
**abuse (verbal)** *pangkal*; *pah'lling₂*
**abusive** *kasla 1*; *bagas*
**abut** *kablit₁*
**acacia-like tree** *b'llu'*; *akasya*
**accede** *uyun*; *aho' 1*
**accent (strong)** *lembang*
**accept** *taima' 1.1*; *s'llong*
**accept as fate** *sarahakan*; *pagyakin*
**accept as suitable** *halus₂*
**accept as true** *siddik*; *bilīb*; *b'nnal 1.2*
**accept offer** *hapus₁ 1*; *kōl 1.1*
**accept patiently** *luluy*; *sabal 1.1*; *lagad 1*
**accept responsibility** *tanggung₂*; *abunaw*; *atas₂ 1.1*
**acceptable** *jari₁ 1*; *halus₁*; *taima' 1*
**accepted (as good)** *beya'₃ 1*
**accident** *dugtul*; *sangku'*; *paghanti'an*
**accidentally** *samba 1.1*; *sabat₂*; *sambut 1.1*
**accommodation** *paglihanan*
**accompany** *bunyug 1.2*; *sehe' 1.1*; *dongan*; *beya'₂ 1*
**accompany (in death)** *unung 1*
**accomplice** *sapali 1*
**accomplish** *aguwanta 1.1*; *anggop₂*; *gaga*
**accord (n)** *pagsulutan*
**accord with** *sulut 1.1*; *pagta'ayun*
**according to** *bang ma*
**accordion** *ambak-ambak*
**account (finance)** *pagbista 1*; *pangutangan*
**account (finances)** *pangutangan*
**account (story)** *suli-suli 1*; *istori 1*
**account for** *pahati 1.1*
**accumulate (of water)** *longkang*; *kandung₁*
**accurate** *taluwa' 1*; *tigi'-tigi'₁ 1*; *tudju₂ 1*
**accurate (report)** *pasti'₁*; *bontol 1*
**accursed of God** *multad*; *munapik*

accuse *palkala'* 1.1; *tuntut₁*; *taha*; *tōng₂* 1
accuse of cowardice *himulas*; *tukas* 1
accuse of lying *pagputing* 1.1; *dusta'* 1.1
accustomed to *biyaksa* 1; *tanam₁* 1.1
ace (cards) *alas*
acerbic *p'kkat*; *kahad*
ache *p'ddi'* 1.1
achieve *kole'*; *bogbog₂*; *aguwanta* 1.1
achilles tendon *kanting₂*; *bital-bital*
acidic *l'ssom* 1.1
acknowledge someone *sagina*; *hīl*; *asip*; *sahawi* 1
acne *buwa'-buwa'* 1
acolyte *anak-mulid*
acquainted *pagkilā*; *pagkinata'u*
acquiescent *kuhi₁* 1; *aho'* 1.1
acquire *ngā'*; *papagdapu*
acquire knowledge *guru* 1.1
acrid odour *p'ngngak*
acrid taste *p'llod*; *p'ddas*; *kahad*
across from *anggopan*; *dambila'* 2
act alone *tunggal-tunggal* 1
act appropriately *pagtōp*
act as a group *pagtighan*; *pagugpang*
act blind *paglendom*
active *kuseseyang* 1; *lasig* 1.1
activity *hinang₁* 1
actor marker *e'* 1
actually *saunahan*; *ya b'nnalna*
Adam's apple *buwa'-jakkum*; *batang-k'llong*
add fuel *api* 1.1; *dūk₂* 1.1; *kayu* 2.1
add grated coconut *lahing* 1.2
add ingredient *paila'*; *sagol* 1.1; *lamud₁* 1.1
add layer *lapis₁* 1.1; *lampik* 1.1; *hampe* 1.1
add salt *asin* 1.2
add to *sugpat* 1.2; *k'nnop* 1.2; *tubil*
add up (numbers, amounts) *bista₂* 1.1; *itung₁*; *jumla* 1
add water *bohe'₁* 1.1
addicted *bintan* 1; *tagi* 1
addicted (to violence) *patibono'*
addicted (to wealth) *bahaya alta'*
addled (confused) *buriru*; *lengog kōk*; *bingaw*
address impolitely *taga'-taga'*
address terms *nneng* 1; *kaka'*; *gge*; *arung*; *tuwan*
address terms for royalty *appa'*; *ampun₂*
adept *passut*; *layam* 1.1; *lahal*
adequate *gonsan*; *patut*; *sarang* 1
adhere *kakkot*; *balut* 1.1; *pikit₁* 1
adherent *pitis-tendog*; *dauranakan* 2; *bebeya'an*
adhesive *pikit-pikit*; *waylud*
adjacent *sekot* 1; *bihing₂* 1
adjoined *dalos* 1; *daggot₂* 1
adjoining *langkit* 1
adjudicate *hukum*

adjust load *timbang₁* 3
adjust sail *kulindara*; *k'llat₂* 1.1
administer law *sara'* 1.1
admire (praise) *sanglit* 1.2; *hulmat* 1
admit *haka* 1.1
admit (allow in) *pasōd*
admit fault *pagsab'nnal*
admonish *ebot-ebot* 1.1; *babal₂*
adolescent *onde'-baha'u*
adolescent female *budjang*
adolescent male *subul*
adopted child *anak-etek*
adoptive relationship *ballo'*
adore *s'lli* 1.1
adornment *dekoresyon*
adrift *laran*; *paghadjul-hadjul*
adulate *lana* 1.1; *paili*
adult *lumbu'-lumbu'*; *sangpot* 1.1
adulterated *simbug* 1.1
adultery *pagliyu-lakad*; *pagjina*
adulthood (early) *lumbu'*
advance *lanjal* 1.1; *pasōng*
advance and retreat *pagsōng-suhut*
advantage *diyata'an₂*
adversary *kuntara* 1; *banta* 1
adversity *pawas* 1; *nahas* 1
advertise *tanyag* 1.1; *bawag*; *bistu* 1.1
advice (n) *pandu'* 1; *pitis₂* 1; *pagpapat* 1
advise (v) *batak₁*; *hupit-hupit* 1; *gara'* 1.2; *bā'₁*
advise about *pasasā*; *pata'u*; *hati* 2
advise against *banda'*; *sanggup*; *pamarā*
advise care *amay-amay* 1.1; *ebot-ebot* 1.1
advisor *wakil* 1
advocate *bogbog₁* 1.1; *abugaw*
adze *sakal*; *patuk*
affair (sexual) *kirida*; *pagd'nda* 2; *pagl'lla*
affect *inay-inay*
affected by *t'kka₂* 1; *sobsob* 1.1
affection *kasi* 1; *lasa₂* 1; *anggi*
affinal kin (in-laws) *pamikitan*
affirm *aho'* 1.2
affix *sugpat* 1
afflict *pinjala'* 1.1; *pissoko'*; *jilaka'*
affluence; affluent *daya* 1; *alta'* 1.1
afford (to buy) *kaya*
aflame *angpud* 1; *dokot₂* 1; *paglaga*; *dallet* 1
afloat *gūng*
afraid *tāw* 1.1; *damag*; *gawa*
after *ubus₂*; *katis₂* 1; *puwas₂*
after that *pasunu'*; *puwas ē'*
afterlife *dunya-ahirat*
afternoon *kohap* 1
afternoon of yesterday *kohap-in*
afternoon prayer *asal*

**afterworld** *sulga'; kiyamat 1; alam-pinole'; ahirat; nalka'*

**again** *pabalik; pabīng 1*

**against (conflict)** *pagkuntara*

**age (era)** *awal₁; masa 1; timpu 1*

**age (of person)** *to'a 1; umul₂ 1*

**age (v)** *to'a 2.1*

**age-mate** *topad-sali'; sibu' 1; topad-sibu'*

**agenda item** *gara' 1; parak*

**agent** *tandero 1.1; wakil 1; idjin*

**agent marker** *he' 1; e' 1*

**aggravate (annoy)** *paglawat; juri 1*

**aggravate (make worse)** *tungkap₁*

**aggressive** *la'ug 1; esog 1.1; ero'-keyat*

**agile** *tangkis 1; sapat₂ 1; alistu 1*

**agitate someone** *juri 1; jullit₂*

**agree to** *siddik; aho' 1.2; manghalapi*

**agree together** *pagsalassay 1*

**agreed** *kōl 1; aho' 1.2*

**agreement** *ayun; dauyunan 1*

**agriculture** *paghuma; pagtanom*

**aground** *sanglad; s'llad*

**aha!** *ā 1*

**ahead** *dahū 1.1; munda'an₁*

**aid** *tulung 1; tabang 1; tapīn*

**ailment** *saki 1*

**aim (at target)** *surang; kalsa; kital; iral*

**aim (n)** *tudjuhan*

**aim (purpose)** *gawi 1; kamatti; maksud 1*

**aimlessly** *sarap₂ 1.1; pagt'bba'-sasab*

**air** *baliyu 1*

**air bladder** *tungul 1*

**air-gun** *iskopeta*

**airless** *linganga; lingo'ot*

**airplane** *ariplano; plēn*

**airport; airstrip** *landing₁*

**airy place** *kahayang-hayangan*

**ajar** *kibit 1; sungkab*

**akimbo (hands on hips)** *s'kket; hawak*

**alas** *allā; arōy*

**albino** *bugis*

**alcohol** *alak; alkohol 1*

**ale** *bīl*

**alert** *halli'₁ 1.1; sayu 1.2*

**algae** *lumut₁ 1*

**alight (burning)** *keyat₂ 1.1*

**alight on** *t'ppak₂; tapu' 1*

**aligned** *tilud 1; tukbul*

**alignment** *pagsambal 1*

**alike** *pagagid; anggil 1; daluwa*

**alive** *llum*

**all** *sabarang; kamemon 1; lullun 1*

**all conditions** *haggut-pasu'*

**all created things** *kamemon pinapanjari*

**all kinds** *indaginis*

**all the more** *luba'*

**all together (working)** *tindan-tindan; pagbagimbin*

**Allahu Akbar** *pagtakbil 1*

**allegory** *sapantun; dalil 1*

**allergic response** *pagbintul*

**allergic response (to strange places)** *bahu'₂*

**allotted span** *jangka'an 2; ganta'an₁*

**allow** *paba'id; pakuhi; tugut 2; sagad 1.1*

**allow credit** *pautang*

**allow time** *hād 1.2*

**allow to run free** *pabūy*

**alloy** *dallung; sawasa'; luyang; pittang*

**allude to** *sindil 1*

**allured (enticed)** *pilad*

**allurement** *panuba*

**ally** *pagtabang 1; dapit; gapi' 1*

**almost** *agon; arāk; apit*

**almost (but not)** *agon mbal; himan-himan; apit*

**almost certainly** *gana-gana 1.1*

**almost due (pregnancy)** *kablit₂*

**alms** *sarakka 1; pitla'*

**alone** *dangan-dangan 1.2; tukkal; hāl-hāl*

**alongside** *bihing₂ 1*

**aloud** *pagalud; asang₂*

**already** *na; ina'an 2*

**alright** *hāp 1.1*

**also** *isāb*

**altar** *sibayan*

**alter** *pinda 1.2; pasaddī*

**alter fate lines** *pinda kulis*

**alternate (v)** *s'lle' 1.1*

**alternatively** *atawa; sumā'..sumā'*

**although** *bo'₁; minsan*

**altitude** *langa 1*

**alum** *tawas*

**aluminum** *aluminyum*

**always** *sadja; na pa'in*

**always visiting** *patil'ngnganun*

**amateur** *hāw-hāw 2*

**amazed** *haylan; inu-inu 1; jaip*

**Amazon women** *Mangkimahan*

**ambassador** *wakil 1*

**ambergris** *tai'-ambal*

**ambition** *niyat 1; pagma'atay*

**ambush** *tipu 1.1; ambus; ingu*

**amen** *amin 1*

**amenable** *saldik*

**American** *Milikan*

**amiable** *saldik; pagsaumbibi; hatul₂*

**ammunition** *punglu'*

**amnesty** *ka'ampunan*

**amniotic fluid** *k'mbal-bohe'; panubigan*

**amniotic sac** *saikula'; tutuban*

**amok** *sabil*
**amorous** *ba'is*
**amount** *heka 1*
**amputate** *pukul 1.2*
**amputee** *pukul 1*
**amulet** *anting-anting 2; baklaw; tampan-basi' 1*
**amuse** *pagpalla' 1*
**amuse child** *sangbay*
**analyze** *bista₁*
**ancestor ceremony** *hinang-mbo'*
**ancestor sickness** *pa'in₃ 1; sabab₂ 1.1*
**ancestors (forebears)** *palmula'an; ka'mbo'-mbo'an; kamatto'ahan*
**ancestors (ritual)** *mbo'₂; ntan₂ 1; pangkat₂*
**ancestral customs** *pangkatan*
**anchor** *sau; labu₂ 1.1; layo 1*
**anchor cable** *bahudji'; kanyamun*
**anchovies** *patay₃; gunu'*
**ancient ones** *kamatto'ahan*
**ancient time** *masa 1.1*
**ancient times** *awal₁; masa-awal; musim tagna'*
**and** *maka₃*
**and also** *sambil; sampay 1*
**and then** *ampa₁; bo' yampa*
**anecdote** *suli-suli 1*
**anemonefish** *anak-bobohan*
**anemones (marine)** *kombo'-kombo'; lo'on*
**angel** *mala'ikat*
**angelfish (generic)** *taliruk*
**anger** *astol 1*
**anger of God** *mulka' 1*
**anger someone** *mata-mata₁; pakalintaw*
**angle** *pidju 1*
**angle brace** *sumpiyang; sungkelang*
**angle in road** *beklo'an*
**anglerfish** *kappo'₁*
**angry at** *pasu' atay; astol 1.1*
**anguish** *p'ddi' 1.1; bisa 1*
**animal** *sattuwa; binatang₁*
**animal (domestic)** *hayop*
**animal (forest)** *kusa'*
**animal sacrifice** *kulban 1*
**animosity** *b'nsi 1*
**ankle bones** *bunga-bunga; buku-buku₁*
**annex** *sugpat 1.2*
**annex (take possession of)** *papagdapu*
**annihilated** *lapnas 1*
**announce** *pamahalayak; nasihat*
**announcement** *pahati 1*
**annoy someone** *pabelaw; paglawat*
**annoyance** *amā; kalintawan*
**annoyed** *dugal 1; tumpalak 1*
**annoying** *katol atay; juri 1*
**anoint** *sapu 1*

**another** *saddī 1*
**answer** *sambung₁ 1.1; saul; sambag₁ 1*
**answer back** *samlang*
**antagonistic** *sīng-sūd; sagga' 1.1*
**antenna of radio** *korente 1*
**anticipate** *asa 1.1; awal₂ 1.2*
**antidote** *tambal₁ 1*
**anti-social** *lumu'; daiyus; sabul 1*
**antler** *tanduk 1*
**ants** *lalangga'; tagangga'; tangangngang; apipila'; s'mmut 1*
**anus** *tombong; jubul*
**anvil** *landasan 1*
**anxiety** *susa 1; sukkal 1*
**anxious** *ganggu' atay; hanggaw₁ 1; kanaw-kanaw*
**any place** *maingga-maingga*
**anybody; anyone** *sai-sai; saina*
**anything** *ai maka ai; ai-ai 1; itu-ini*
**anytime** *sumiyan-sumiyan*
**anywhere** *maingga-maingga*
**apart from** *liyu lagi'; haliyu*
**apathetic** *kuligi'₁ 1.1*
**apex** *pekkes-pekkes; puntuk*
**apologise** *tawbat 1.1; pagpa'ampun*
**apostate** *multad; kapil 1*
**apostle** *rasul*
**apparent** *manyatakan*
**apparition** *laman 1; lambung₁ 1; nyata' 1*
**appeal (legal)** *dagsol; ikiral; tukbal₂*
**appeal for help** *pangaru*
**appeal to** *amu'₁*
**appear** *luwas₁ 1; bulat; tuwa' 1*
**appear (above horizon)** *pagleget*
**appear (ghost)** *pangguwa' 1.1; panyata'₂ 1.1*
**appear (in distance)** *ba'ung-ba'ung 1.1*
**appear (of spirit being)** *tuwa' 1.1; pagpasalupa*
**appear (through barrier)** *l'ppas 1*
**appear briefly** *pagsagiyaw*
**appear elsewhere (symptom)** *tanog₂ 1; dalug₂*
**appear far off** *pagba'ung-ba'ung*
**appear in dream** *lambung₁ 1.1; pagpauppi*
**appear suddenly** *tanyak*
**appearance (looks)** *dagbos; pamayhu'an; jantang-jari*
**appease** *apu'-apu'; ū'ū*
**appendage** *sugpat 1; tundanan*
**appetite** *lingantu 1*
**applaud** *paglagpak 1*
**apple** *epol*
**apply lipstick** *atal*
**apply perfume** *pahamut*
**apply powder** *borak 1.1*
**apply salve (to newborn)** *kunit*
**apply to a surface** *sapu 1; lemed 1.2; peged₁ 1*

appoint *wakil 1.1*; *g'llal 1.1*; *botang₂*

appointed official *botang-lahat 1*; *bag'llal 1*

appointment *iddahan*; *ora*; *tugun 1*

apportion *pagsuku'*; *pahampit*; *pagbahagi'*

appraise *pende*; *tatab*

appreciated *heya ma atay*

appreciative *entom buddi*; *bakti' 1.1*

apprehend (arrest) *saggaw*

apprehensive *ganggu' atay*; *kanaw-kanaw*; *k'bba-k'bba*; *hanggaw₁ 1*

approach *sigpi'*; *t'ppi' 1*; *sekot 1.1*

approach fire *alung 1*

approach someone *dauhat₁ 1.2*

approach to hear *tongop₂*

approach zenith *sakat ni ugtu*

approachable *lunuk atay*; *sekot 1.3*

appropriate (of relationship) *halus₂*

appropriate (suitable) *patut*; *tōp 1.1*; *amu₁*

appropriate (take possession) *papagdapu*

approval of a proposal *gandahan*

approve *aho' 1.2*

approximate *saga 3*; *kulang-labi*

aquamarine *hinu-hinu₁*

aquarium *kulam*

Arab; Arabic *Arab*

arable land *tana'₁ 1*; *huma*

archangel *Jibra'il*

archerfish *sumpit-sumpit*

archipelago *kapū'-pū'an 1*

area to the front *dahū'an 1*

area to the rear *buli'an₁*

area to the side *bihing₁ 1*

area without landmarks *paslangan 1*

areca nut *pola*

argonaut shell *sugit-sugit*

argue *pagagaw-bissala*; *pagsu'al*; *pagkalukassa*

argument *jawab₂ 1*; *pagsagga'an₂ 1*; *pasu'alan*

arise *punduk 1*; *bungkal₁ 1*; *lungkahad*

aristocrat *balbangsa*

arm *l'ngngon 1*; *pataklayan*

arm wrestle *pagkagat 1.1*; *pagsanggul 1.1*

armed *pagtakos*; *pakokos*

arm-in-arm *pagablay*

arm-length *d'ppa 1*

armpit *pikpik₂*; *kepet₂*

arms (military) *pangatu*; *almas*

army *militari*

aroma *hamut 1*; *tunug 1*; *bau 1*

aromatic *hangsu 1*

around *sakalibut*; *kulibut*

arouse sexually *kolet*

arrange *hatul₁*; *tuntul 1.1*; *lilay*

arrange (in groups) *ukul 1*

arrange (in rows) *pagtād-tād*; *pagtagik 1.1*; *dirit₁ 1.2*

arrange marriage (for man) *pah'nda 2*

arrange marriage (for woman) *pah'lla 2*

arrange release *haum*; *luyal 1.1*

arranged efficiently *leson*

arrangement *hatulan 1*

array (of things) *kakaya'an*

arrest *saggaw*

arrival gift *kasampangan*

arrival place *kat'kkahan₁*; *tandan₁ 1.1*

arrive *t'kka₁ 1.1*; *sampay 2*

arrive (in numbers) *t'bbud₂*

arrive home *pole'₁ 1*

arrogant *abbu 1.1*; *atakabbul*; *pagmalangkahi*

arrow *anak-pana'*

artery *ugat 1*

artisan *panday 1*; *tukang*

as *buwat 1*; *sali' 1*

as example *sali' 1.3*

as expected *ai ka itū*

as far as *sambil*; *sampay 1*; *taman*

as long as *sat'ggol*

as much as *taman*

as often as *sambu-...sambu-*

as soon as *ingga na*

ascend *takod 1*; *diyata' 1.1*; *sakat₂*

ascertain *paliksa'*

ashamed *biyas*; *iya'*; *tamparasa*

ashes *abu 1*

ashore *deya*; *gintana'an*

aside from *liyu₃*

ask *tilaw 1.1*; *hodhod*

ask about *kihaka*; *tilosa 1.1*; *paliksa'*

ask advice *aru*

ask favor *pinta-pinta*

ask for *amu'₁*

ask for help *sabi₁*

ask forgiveness *pagpama'ap*; *tawbat 1.1*

ask permission *puhun*; *ba'id 1.1*; *kumba'id*

ask price of *andag*

askew *sōng-s'llo'*; *julenget*; *sulangat*

asleep *karu' 1.1*; *tuli₁ 1*

asphalt *espalton*

aspire *maksud 1.1*; *gawi 1.1*

aspire to *angut*

aspirin *tungkas-pasu'*

ass (donkey) *kura'-asnu*

assault *la'ug 1.1*

assemble *paghimpun*; *tipun 1*; *pulin*

assemble components *pagdayaw 1.1*

assembly *kahimul-himulan*; *palhimpunan*

assent to *siddik*; *aho' 1.2*; *kōl 1.1*

assert *sambat*

assess *pagdepende*; *tanding 1*; *tatab*

assign *g'llal 1.1*

assist *tulung 1; tambin; tabang 1.1*
assist (with birth) *sikān 1.1; panday 2.1*
assistant (Islamic) *hatib; pakil*
associate (n) *limbang-sehe'*
associate with *samod; sehe' 1.1*
assortment *kaginisan; indalupa 1*
assume *bā'$_2$; pangannal$_2$*
assume bodily form *pagbagala; pagpasalupa; salidda*
assume wrongly *ta'awil; ambil-hati*
assurance *panantuhan*
assured *holat 1*
asthma *songot 1*
astonished *littā 1; himatta'*
astonishing *ili-ili*
astringent *harat 1.1*
asymmetrical *pagkamihu; baligbig*
at *atag$_1$ 1; ma 1*
at ease *sannang; sayudja' 1*
at last *tahan$_1$ 1.1; yamboho'*
at odds with *pagsu'al*
at once *magtūy; sakadjap*
at sea *pakautan*
at times *bang pasān; sumā'..sumā'; maumu*
athletic *bastig; ayron*
athwart *babag 1.1*
atmosphere *tonga'an ayan*
atoll *nusa*
attach bridle (to kite) *pintal 1.1*
attach components *batuk$_1$ 1.1; sangon$_1$ 1.1*
attached emotionally *lumut$_2$ 1; paganggi; uli*
attached physically *dalos 1; langkit 1; daggot$_2$ 1*
attack *sakat$_1$; dugpak 2; gubat*
attack by stealth *tipu 1.1*
attack verbally *tampak 2.1*
attain to *sampay 2; ā' 3*
attempt *ahat 1.1; sulay$_1$ 1.1*
attend an event *luruk 1.1; tupuk; hadil*
attend in person *pagbaran; taddung*
attend to business *l'ngngan$_2$ 1.1*
attendant (bridal) *pandala*
attendant (of high-ranking woman) *ipang-ipang*
attentive *upiksa'; asip*
attic *angkap 1*
attitude *itikad*

attorney *abugaw*
attract (by love charm) *sulat-libun; suratan; lindang 1.1*
attracted to *ebog 1; baya' 1*
attractive *dorog$_2$ 1.1; manis 1.1; polma 1.1; hāp baran*
auction *lilung*
audible *hapal 2; tanog$_1$; ladju*
auger *likup 1; pa'at 1*
aunt *si'it; babu' 1*
aunt (address term) *babu' 1.1*
aureole (of nipple) *tampang*
auspicious outlook *kagustuhan*
authentic *taddang; dī$_2$*
authority (government) *parinta 1*
authority (individual) *kawasa 1; kuma'agi*
authorize *wakil 1.1*
automobile *awtu; tarāk*
avaricious *napsu 1.1; kaway 1*
avenge *balos$_1$ 1*
average *sarang-sarang*
averse to *l'gga 1.1; takal*
aversion *b'nsi 1; hukaw 1*
avert disaster *pagtulak-bala' 1.1*
avert gaze *buli'-buli' mata; keles*
avocado *abokado*
avoid interaction *sandol 1.1*
avoid risk *kamaya'; llog 1.1*
avoid situation *illag 1; liyal*
await *lanti-lanti; lagad 1.1*
await the inevitable *paglangay-langay*
awake *bati'$_1$ 1*
awaken *pukaw*
aware of *tilas$_1$; hīng 1*
awareness *sipat$_1$ 1; panayu; amanat*
away (absent) *likut 1*
awestruck *himatta'*
awkward (movement) *lampag; gubin*
awning *sayap 1; sapaw 1; ambung-ambung$_2$ 1*
awry *kīng 1*
ax *kapa; bansing*
ax blade *mata-kapa*
ax head *patuk-kapa*
axle *batang-ehe*

# B b

baa (cry of sheep) *mbehe'*
babble *pagli'anun*
baby *anak$_1$ 1*
baby at breast *anak-duru'an*

bachelor *subul; la'un 1.1*
back (n) *buli'$_1$ 2; bukut$_1$*
back and forth *sōng-sebog*
back of blade *salig$_1$*

back of head *buli'-pugay*
back teeth *baga'ang*
backbite *limut 1.1*
backbone *tangkal₁*
background (color) *punsa'; durukan₂*
backhoe *kumkum₂*
backing (financial) *dapat-daya*
backing (n) *pasangdolan 1*
backrest *jarayan*
backside *pangkul*
back-stitch *bakiya'₂*
backstroke *pagtindayung 2*
back-to-back *pagtaikut*
back-to-front *dahū-buli'; sunsang*
backwards *baliskat 1*
bad luck *piyurus₂; pawas 1; bilsut*
bad nature *jahallis; jahil 1*
bad outcome *pagkasuddahan; pagkangī'-ngī'*
bad temper *p'ggot-p'ggot*
badge *sāp₂ 1*
baffling *patay-akkal*
bag (for fish) *pokot₂ 1*
bag (n) *puyu'; suput₂*
bag (plastic) *salopen; tilag-tilag₁*
baggage *maleta*
bail (legal) *haum; luyal 1.1; jamin*
bail water *sait; k'llut 1.1*
bailer *sasait*
bait *umpan 1; katihan*
bait-worm *punpun*
bake in ashes *kuddang*
baking powder *pasulig*
balance (scales) *timbangan₁*
balance (unpaid) *tinggal*
balance a load *timbang₁ 3*
balcony *pantān*
bald *ungas; kelas; tugak*
balete tree *nunuk*
ball *bola*
ball (of leaf tobacco) *bungkal₃ 1*
ball (rattan) *buka'₂*
ballad *tenes-tenes*
balloon *tting-tting; tambu-tambu₁*
ball-point pen *bolpen*
bamboo (mature) *bahi'*
bamboo lath *bola'*
bamboo sprout *dabung; kagingking*
bamboo varieties *kayawan; p'ttung; t'mmang; daumu'an*
bamboo walling *tiyadtad*
banana (cooking) *saging-manurung; sabba*
banana (dessert) *saging 1*
banana (fried) *juwalan*
banana bud *pusu'₂*

banana leaf *dāg₃*
banana stalk *lupis*
banana sucker *saha' 1*
band music *mulsiku*
bandage *p'kkos 1.1*
banded (color) *palang; kelong-kelong₁; manas*
bandicoot berry *amamali-d'nda*
bandit *musu; mundu 1*
bang against *banggul; tikbi'*
bang head *sukmad 1; bangga' 1; santuk*
bang into *dugtul; sangku'; binggil*
bang together *pagbangga'; pagkagingkul*
bangus *owa'₂*
bangus fish *bang'llus*
bank (finance) *bangko*
bank (of water) *bihing₁ 1*
banker *bangka₂ 1*
bankrupt *kadkad 1; kugud*
banned topic *lu'ug-lama' 1*
banner *panji*
bannerfish *kuluk*
banquet *jajamuhan*
baptize *baptaes; pandi 1*
bar across door *babag 2; sulad 1*
barb *gehe; gawat*
barbed wire *alambre*
barber *balbero*
barbfish *ibis*
bare (of growth) *penggas*
bare (of leaves) *ulagat*
bare (unclad) *tantang*
barely *agon; himan-himan*
barf *utta' 1*
bargain (v) *ladjaw; balos₁ 2*
barge-boards *layang-layang*
bark (of tree) *kuwit 1*
bark (v) *tanghul; usig; tangungngul*
bark of coconut *labit*
barn *kamalig*
barnacles (generic) *tahemtem 1*
barracudas (generic) *lambana' 1*
barrel (container) *barilis*
barrel (of firearm) *bulu*
barren (infertile) *t'ggang₂; tamanang*
barrier *lapad; babag 2; agpang 1*
barrio *lūngan; kaum*
barter *sambi' 1*
barter item *muddal 1*
base (n) *papagan 1; pamaragtolan*
base of fish trap *dakan 1*
base of pandanus leaf *la'al*
bashful *paki' 1*
basic elements *hinasil*
basic issue *kat'kkaran*

**basics (of life)** *kahirupan; balanja' 1*
**basics (structure)** *pagdayaw 1*
**basil (herb)** *sulasi*
**basin** *undam; batiya'; pastan*
**basis** *pagsababan; po'on-sabab*
**basket for gongs** *kalanjangan*
**basket traps** *bubu₁; logo; panggal 1*
**basketball** *basketbōl*
**baskets (see baka')**
**bastard** *harambiyara' 1; anak-kasi*
**baste (sew)** *bagsak₂*
**bat (v)** *pega*
**bat volute** *kūs-kūs 1*
**batfish** *buna'*
**bathe** *pandi 1*
**bathe someone** *pandi 1.1*
**bathing (ritual)** *tulak-bala'; pandi atay-batu; pandi kulang-kilā*
**batik cloth** *battik*
**baton** *bastun*
**bats (mammal)** *kabog; kabelaw*
**batten** *gipis 1; ligpit 1; bola'*
**batter (n)** *addunan*
**battery** *batri*
**battle** *bono' 1*
**bay** *b'ttong₃; suba'; lo'ok*
**bay leaf** *halu'-halu'₁*
**bayonet** *sangko' 1; ispara*
**be (exist)** *niya'₁ 1*
**be careful** *hubaya-hubaya; kamaya'*
**be settled** *m'mmos 1*
**beach (n)** *daplakan₁; bihing tampe*
**beach (v)** *tundug 1; d'ppak 1.1; daggot₁*
**beach lettuce (tree)** *badji-gandang*
**beacon** *sulariyan*
**bead** *manik*
**beak** *tuka'*
**beam (timber)** *babag 1*
**beam scale** *timbangan₁*
**bean sprouts** *taoge*
**beans (green)** *batung₂*
**bear (animal)** *baruwang*
**bear (endure)** *sandal 1.1; tangka'; tahan-tahan*
**bear witness** *saksi' 1.1*
**beard** *p'ngngot 1; bū-langal; janggut 2*
**beasts (generic for large ones)** *sattuwa*
**beat (of heart)** *pagk'bba-k'bba atay; pagk'bbut-k'bbut*
**beat (punish)** *balubak; daplos; lubak₁*
**beat (rhythm)** *ganding 1; lisag₂ 1.1; dapu'*
**beat (to mix)** *giling*
**beat clothes** *pakang₂; pukpuk*
**beaten (in contest)** *da'ug; tiyuwas*
**beautiful** *mustala; dorog₂ 1.1*
**beautify** *ari-ari 1*

**beauty** *manis 1*
**beauty charm** *palmanis*
**beauty contest** *paghansam-hansam; paglingkat-lingkat*
**beauty spot** *langking*
**becalmed** *t'ddo' 1.2*
**because** *pasal₁; kalna' 1; sabab₁ 1.1*
**because of** *kabowa*
**beckon** *lambe₁ 1.1; kambay 1*
**become** *hinang₁ 1.2; manjari₃*
**become public** *tukaw*
**bed** *patulihan; palangka'₂; kantil₁*
**bed covering** *manta 1; se'ob*
**bedbug** *bangking*
**beef** *isi sapi'*
**beer** *bīl; samigēl*
**bees** *buwani; teya'-teya'*
**beeswax** *talu₂*
**beetles** *kubing₁; bangking*
**before** *dahū 1.1*
**befriend** *bagay 2*
**beg** *junjung 1.2; amu'₁; pagpangalemos*
**beggar** *santili'*
**begin journey** *tulak₁ 1.1; k'tta 1*
**beginner** *hāw-hāw 2*
**beginning** *asāl; tagna' 1.1*
**begrudge** *agmot-agmot 1.1*
**beguile** *lakbu'₂*
**behave as a man** *pagl'lla-l'lla₂*
**behave badly** *pagla'at-la'at*
**behave deceitfully** *pagduwa-bayhu'; pagtipu*
**behave dominantly** *pagmandangan*
**behave immorally** *paglaban 1.1; pagkasabulan*
**behave irrationally** *pagmalas*
**behave unacceptably** *sipin*
**behavior** *addat-tabi'at; jaguni'; palangay*
**behead** *ponggol; sangko' 1.1; tangsu' 1.1*
**behind** *damuli 1*
**behind something** *libut 1; liyu₂ 1*
**being (one's nature)** *jāt₁*
**belated** *lēt*
**belch** *ggak*
**beliefs (convictions)** *pam'nnalan*
**beliefs (traditional)** *usulan; pali-pali*
**believe** *kahagad; b'nnal 1.2*
**belittle** *dali'it*
**bell** *jabu-jabu; bēl; bagting 1*
**bell pepper** *lara sinayul*
**belligerent** *giyagas*
**bellow** *ngngong; ilud-ilud*
**belly** *b'ttong₁ 1; babat*
**belong to** *suku'; taga*
**below** *deyo'₁ 1*
**below horizon** *limun 1*

**below surface** *limun 1*; *kanop*; *t'nde 1.1*
**belt (for money)** *sabitan*
**belt (waist)** *sintoron*; *kambot 1*; *kandit*
**belt pocket** *gangotan*
**bench** *bangku'*; *paha*
**bend (complex)** *bunt'lled*
**bend backwards** *k'dde'*; *l'ddet 1*
**bend fingers back** *l'tte'$_2$*
**bend forward** *toyok*; *kuru'*
**bend in road** *beklo'an*
**bend so ends touch** *peko'*
**bend to shape** *kulluk 1.1*; *būk$_1$ 1.1*
**bends (diving)** *bawis$_1$*
**beneath** *deyo'$_1$ 1*
**benefit (n)** *pamasukud*; *pamahāp*
**benefited** *niya'$_1$ 2*
**benefits** *hāp 1*
**benevolent** *pagmura 1.1*
**benighted** *sangom 1.1*
**bent** *pekok*; *kello' 1.1*
**bequeath; bequest** *pusaka' 1.1*
**berate** *pagamā 1.1*
**berate (scold)** *mūng-mūng*; *pugpug 1*
**bereaved** *matay$_1$ 1.1*; *udjul$_1$ 1.1*
**bereaved (by death of fiancee)** *balu-assang*
**bereft** *pulaw$_2$*; *siya-siya 1.2*
**berserk** *pagsabil*
**beseech** *pinta-pinta*; *amu'$_1$*; *amu'-amu'*
**beside** *atag$_1$ 1*; *bihing$_2$ 1*
**besides (other than)** *saddī 1*; *haliyu*
**besmear** *ledje 1.1*; *lemos$_1$ 1.1*
**best man** *pandala*
**best of all** *kapūd-pūran*
**bet (v)** *tumba$_2$ 1.1*; *paglegot 2*
**betel chew** *apug*; *mama' 1*
**betel chew container** *salappa'*
**betel juice** *pila'*; *p'tti'-mama'*
**betel leaf** *buyu'*
**betel nut** *lugus*; *bunga$_1$*
**betray** *akkal 1.1*
**betroth** *pagpah'nda 1*
**betrothal** *pagtunang*
**better (preferable)** *gōm*; *arapun*; *atas$_1$*
**between** *llot*; *olangan 1*; *t'ngnga'an*
**between fruiting periods** *tongkad*
**beware** *insap*; *halli'$_1$ 1.1*
**bewildered** *buriru*; *bingaw*
**bewitch** *hinang-hinang$_1$*; *pantak 1.1*
**beyond** *dambila' 2.1*; *liyu$_2$ 1*
**beyond counting** *pila-pila*
**beyond measure** *dangay-dangay 1.1*
**beyond vision** *tegob-tegob*; *bitu-bitu$_1$*
**bias** *pagkengkeng pagbokol*
**bicker** *pagkalukassa*; *pagsalod*

**bicycle; cycle** *baek*
**bid (low)** *ladjaw*
**bier** *palantayan*
**big** *heya 1.1*; *aslag$_2$ 1*; *mehe*
**big toe** *bokol 2*; *tambō' 1*; *nggo'an-tape'*
**big-bodied** *tibaggol*; *tamiyang*
**big-eye fish** *kandaman 1*
**bihon noodles** *bihun*
**bile** *p'ddu 1*
**bilge** *mohang*
**bilge moss** *tai'-bamban*
**bill (of bird)** *tuka'*
**bill (paper money)** *pinta$_1$*
**billow up (smoke)** *t'bbud$_1$ 1*
**billows (sea)** *goyak 1*; *lumbag*
**billy goat** *mandangan*
**bind (v)** *laggos*; *engkot 1.1*; *buka'$_1$ 1.1*
**binding technique** *pinate 1*
**binoculars** *talumpung 1*
**bird (generic)** *manuk-manuk 1*
**bird (woven decoration)** *manuk-manuk-manggis*
**bird scarer** *lagpak$_1$ 1*
**birdnest swallow** *sayaw*
**bird-of-paradise flower** *saging-saging$_2$*
**birds (unidentified)** *manuk-manuk-tabug*; *soleng$_1$*; *mandaling*
**birth (v)** *anak$_1$ 1.1*
**birthday** *llaw kapaganak*
**birthing problem** *susun-buyu'*; *sambon 1.1*
**birthing terms** *t'mpu*; *panubigan*
**birthmark** *ila 1*
**biscuit** *bāng-bāng$_2$*; *balatu*; *biskuwit*
**bit (bridle)** *kakkang$_2$*
**bit by bit** *painut-inut*; *pagkuri'-kuri'*
**bite (v)** *keket 1*
**bite through** *k'ttob 1*
**bits and pieces** *itu-ini*
**bitten into** *kobak 1*
**bitter melon** *paliya'*
**bittern** *baggok*
**bitterness** *pa'it 1*; *p'ddu 2*
**bitumen** *espalton*
**bivalve shellfishes** *bikkin*; *t'lla'-t'lla'$_2$*; *kohang*
**black** *ettom 1*
**black coral** *akal-bahal*
**black magic** *hinang-hinang$_1$*
**blackcurrant tree** *minul*
**blacken** *tumbal 1.2*; *pagettom*
**blacksmith** *pagbabal*
**bladder** *mange' 1.1*
**bladder complaint** *kima-kima*; *kaukati 1*
**blade** *solab$_1$ 1*
**bladed weapons** *kalis*; *barung*
**blame** *agmot-agmot 1.1*; *akon-akon*

blame oneself *siyal*

blameable *atas₂ 1*

blameless *pote' atay*

bland *k'ssang₂; k'ssaw*

blanket *manta 1*

blaspheme *kupul; pangkal*

blast force (n) *hamiyu 1*

blaze up *suleyab 1.1; dallet 1*

blazing *paglaga*

bleach (v) *kola*

bleach skin *lipa'*

bleached *muras 1*

bleat (of goat) *mbehe'*

bleed *laha'₁ 1.1*

bleed freely *lagadlad₁*

blemish *powera 1; galna' 1*

blend *paila'; templa 1*

blennies (fish) *koleng-punsul; koleng-koleng*

blessed land *paliyama'*

blessing *pahala'; barakat 1; apuwa*

blind *buta₁; legsok₂*

blinded (by profusion) *lambang-mata 1*

blinded (temporarily) *palu' 1*

blindeded temporarily *lempon; bulag*

blink *pagk'llap; pagk'ddaw-k'ddaw*

blinking (light) *kiraw*

blissful *tundun buwahan*

blister (n) *buwa'-buwa' 1; mata-daing 1; l'ttup 1*

blister (v) *tambu-tambu₂; kassa'-kassa'*

blistered *lutup; dapal*

bloated *b'ngkak; himutud*

block (a hole) *sampong 1.1*

block (from sight *lapis₂*

block (move in a game) *sanggul₁ 1.1; kulgaw; seraw*

block (movement) *pagang; agpang 1.1*

block (to raise from surface) *biggal 1*

block (work support) *pasangdolan 1; pamaragtolan; parabtalan*

block and tackle *timun-timun 1*

block light *simun 1.1*

block light or draft *limbu 1.3*

blockade *hapa' 1.2*

blocked ears *palpal 1*

blocked nose *p'nnot*

blonde *pote' 1; keyat₁ 1*

blood *laha'₁ 1*

blood clot *batu-batu₂*

blood relative *legsok₁; lahasiya' 1*

blood sacrifice *kulban 1; hakika' 1*

blood vessels *daga' 1*

bloodline (descent) *laha'₂*

bloody pus *d'nnat 1*

bloom; blossom *sumping 1*

blouse *badju'; samda; supa₂*

blow (of whale) *husbu 1.1; appu'*

blow (of wind) *sumpallit; tiyup 1*

blow (on or through) *tiyup 1.1*

blow air through lips *balombong; balobok₁*

blow away *paypay*

blow strongly *tumbuk₁ 1*

blow to the head *sukmad 1*

blowgun *susumpit; lustang 1*

blown about *landos 1.1*

blown apart *bustak*

blown off course *pespes 1.1; palis₁*

blown over *pungkad*

bludgeon *kakal*

blue *bilu 1*

bluebottle (Portuguese man-of-war) *būng-leha*

bluing (for fabric) *anyil 1*

blumea *daklan-bulan*

blunder *sā'₁ 1; salusad*

blunt *poppol 1; tompol*

blunt (of speech) *tumlang 1*

blurred (of speech) *hemol; kemol*

blurred (of vision) *bōng; gabul*

blush (embarrassment) *alom 1.1*

blush macaranga tree *pataw₂*

board (for checkers) *sukki'an*

board (for chopping on) *sangkalan*

board (game) *tikam; balad*

board (plank) *papan₁*

board ship *dita'i; sakat₂*

boast *pagmalangkahi; pagbantug-bantug*

boastful *abbu 1.1; pagtāp-tāp*

boat (engine-driven) *lansa; kumpit; tempel; basnig*

boat (sailing) *sappit₂; balanda'₁*

boat-dwelling Sama *Jengen; pala'u*

bob (hair) *babbel*

bob up and down *pagumbaw-umbaw*

bobbin *boben 1*

bobby pin *sipit 1*

bodega *kamalig*

bodily condition *paltubu-tubuhan 2*

body *baran₁ 1*

body (corpse) *patay₁ 1*

body (human) *puhu' 1*

body and soul *ginhawa-baran; dugu'-nyawa*

body hair *bū 1*

body lice *tuma 1*

body shape *pamaranan*

boggy *l'bbo 1; lettak*

bogus *paltik*

boil (n) *kalibubut 1; bautut 1*

boil (v) *lere'; laga'₁ 1.1; bukal*

boil over *appu'; subu₁ 1*

boiled water *bohe'-kunsuy*

boiling sound *buwak-buwak*

bold *esog 1.1*
bolo *lahut*
bolt (n) *lansang 1*
bolt (to secure) *kansing 1.1; lagsak*
bolt-rope *palimping 1*
bomb *bām*
bond (contract) *jamin*
bone *to'olang; bokog*
bone (small) *bangkak*
bone marrow *sumsuman*
boneless *himāt*
book *būk₂; kitab*
book (divine) *kiramin-katibin*
books of Moses *Kitab Tawrat*
boom of sail *bahu'₁*
boom rope *k'llat-deyo'*
booth (stall) *kadday*
booty *tatabanan*
border *kumpi' 1; bihing₁ 1*
border (of mat) *sasa-dandan; hagdan-hagdan*
border of lace *ingkahi 1*
bored *jompo'; sumu 1.1*
borer (insect) *bukbuk 1*
born *anak₁ 2; lahil 1*
born last *bungsu*
borrow *utang 1.1; indam*
borrow words *puwa'-puwa'*
boss *kapatas; nakura'; mandul*
boss (v) *hagda 1.1*
boss of gong *budjul₂*
bossy *pagmanda 1; hagda 1*
both (of people) *duwangan 1*
both (of things) *karuwa 1*
both ends *karuwampōng*
both sides *karuwambila'*
bother *sasat 1.1*
bother! *hē*
bothered *kabid atay; susa 1.1*
bottle *kassa' 2; butul*
bottle cap *pitsa₁*
bottle for baby *sopon*
bottom *buli'₁ 1*
bottom (sea) *deyo'₂ 1*
bougainvillea *bagumbilya*
bough *sanga 1*
boulder *batu-lakit*
bounce (baby in hammock) *ta'ut; buwa₂*
bounce (on waves) *tampeppet; samperet*
bounce roughly *pagbullud-bullud*
bounce up *buwang₂*
bounce vigorously *paghuntak; handok₁ 1*
bound to happen *tantu 1.1; sabali-bali*
boundary *jangka'an 1; tibtib*
bow (n) *ba'ugan₂; pana' 1*

bow (spear-gun) *batang-pana'*
bow decking (boat) *pansal 1*
bow head *tondok 1; handuk 1; tukku' 1*
bow in prayer *sujud; duku'; luku'₂*
bow of boat *munda'₁ 1*
bow to *kuru'; palok 1.1*
bowed (of back) *dukkug 1; buggul 1.1*
bowel movement *sungi' 1*
bowl (brass) *bintang₁; gangsa*
bowl (dish) *pinggan*
bowsprit *jungal 1*
box (n) *tu'ung*
box (v) *pagsuntuk; pagbutug*
boxfishes *bangga'-bangga'; tab'llung₁*
boxing *boksen*
boy *onde' 1*
brace (n) *sumpiyang; tapil 1*
brace (tool) *barena 1*
bracelet *gallang*
brackish *t'bbag*
brag *pagbantug-bantug; pagabbu 1.1*
braggart *abbu 1.1*
braid (hair) *sapid 1*
brain *utuk*
brain-damaged *kulang-akkal*
brainpower *akkal 1*
brainy *ladju pikilan*
bramble *sampinit*
bran *ata'*
branch *engas-engas*
branch (of palm) *botod*
branch out *sulenget*
branchlet *tangan 1*
brand (n) *sāp₂ 1*
brash *pagtāp-tāp*
brass *tumbaga 1*
brass container *langguway; garul*
brass tray *talam*
brat *anak-kusa'; anak-bala'*
brave; bravery *bahani 1.1*
bread *pān; tinapay*
bread bun (steamed) *pawa*
bread roll *pān ma'asin*
breadfruit *kamansi'*
breadth *lambu 1; luha 1*
break (bone) *pi'ul*
break (from work) *kahali'an*
break (of waves) *sampoyak; jalak*
break (v) *bila' 1.2*
break a fast *buka*
break a law *langgal sara' 1.1*
break across *pōng 1.1*
break apart *b'kka' 1.1; bugtu'₂ 1; piyurus₁*
break bank (game) *tumba₂ 1.1*

**break by banging** *p'ppa 1.1*
**break even (finance)** *pole'-po'on 1.1*
**break into** *sakay 2*
**break into pieces** *lubu₂ 1.1*
**break off** *tigpu' 1.1; sagpe' 1.1*
**break promise** *baluba 2; paggambahan*
**break social rules** *bowa b'ttik*
**break wind (fart)** *ntut*
**breakable** *lagtu' 1*
**break-down (engine)** *para₁*
**breakers** *goyak 1*
**breakfast** *inum 2*
**breaking (of voice)** *pehet*
**bream (fish species)** *kulambal; bulagtok; si'ay 1*
**breast** *tete' 1; duru' 1*
**breast stroke** *kambay 2*
**breast-feed** *paruru'*
**breath** *hinansong 1; napas*
**breathe (with effort)** *paghongat-hongat; paghota*
**breather** *hali'an*
**breathing problem** *songot 1; simay₁ 1*
**breathless** *pōn; lumu*
**breech birth** *sulay₂*
**breed (v)** *pagd'nda 1.1*
**breeze** *baliyu 1*
**breezeway** *kahayang-hayangan*
**breezy** *hayang 1*
**briar** *sampinit*
**bribe** *pagmamhu'; pulitik₁ 1.1; su'ap 1*
**brick** *tisa'; haloblāk*
**bridal attendant** *pandala*
**bridal gift** *turul-buli'an*
**bridal headdress** *panumping; tumanggal*
**bridal make-up** *pagalis-alis*
**bridal room** *likusan*
**bride; bridegroom** *pangantin*
**bridegroom's kin** *kal'llahan*
**bride's kin** *kar'ndahan*
**bridesmaid** *pandala*
**bride-wealth demand** *sokat₁ 1*
**bride-wealth returned** *lupit*
**bride-wealth terms** *barang; ungsud₁ 1; banghad 1*
**bridge** *taytayan; letehan*
**bridge of nose** *batang-ūng*
**bridge to Paradise** *siratul mustakim*
**bridle (of kite)** *pintal 1*
**bridle (sailboat)** *pengka-pengka*
**brief** *puraw; dai'-dai' 1*
**briefly** *dansasa'at 1.1*
**briefs (underwear)** *sanyawa*
**bright** *tallang*
**bright (intellect)** *taha'-akkal; ladju pikilan*
**bright (of a light)** *sawa 1.1; danta'*
**brilliance** *sahaya 1*

**brimful** *samaintib*
**brimstone** *maylang*
**bring as a group** *pagā' 1*
**bring ends together** *kablit₁*
**bring forward** *dahū 1.3*
**bring here** *pi'itu 1.2*
**bring inside** *sōd 1.3; pasōd*
**bring into being** *papanjari*
**bring out** *paluwas*
**bring this way** *pi'itu 1.2*
**bring to conclusion** *tapus 1.1; tastas₁; tabtab 2.1*
**bring to life** *paka'llum*
**bring together** *pūn 1; pagsekot*
**bring up (children)** *pantun 1.1; papat 1.1*
**bring; take** *ngā'; bowa₁*
**brink** *sipi₂; bihing₁ 1*
**brisk** *kasay 1; alistu 1.1*
**British** *anggalis*
**brittle** *lagtu' 1*
**broad** *lambu 1.1; luha 1.1*
**broad area** *karatagan; kasaplagan*
**broadcast (make known)** *hula-layag 1*
**brocade** *dasu*
**broil** *panggang₁*
**broke (financially)** *kettak; pihit*
**broken** *pōng 1; pu'aw 1*
**broken (of sleep)** *gesong*
**broken (of speech)** *b'ggod; pagbagi'ad*
**broken (partly)** *p'ggos*
**broken off** *sagpe' 1; punggul 2*
**broken off (of courtship)** *baibad 1.1*
**broken piece** *bila' 1; pōng-pōng*
**broken up** *tumu-tumu; bagbag*
**broker a deal** *pagsuluhan*
**bronze** *dallung; tumbaga 1*
**broom** *sasapu; eskoba 1*
**broth** *loho' 1*
**brother** *danakan l'lla*
**brotherhood** *pagdanakan 1*
**brother-in-law** *ipal; bilas; iras*
**brothers** *dauranakan 1*
**brothers (pretend)** *pagdanakan-danakan*
**brought to end** *utas 2*
**brow** *lendo'; tuktuk*
**brown (color)** *kausun*
**brown (of sugar)** *butig-butig*
**browned (of food)** *l'ggu'*
**brown-purple (color)** *sakulati 2*
**bruise (n)** *alom 1; busul; butig 1*
**bruised** *pogpog 1; lahod 1*
**brunette** *kausun*
**brush (growth)** *kasob*
**brush (n)** *kuskus 1; eskoba 1; brutsa*
**brush against** *sagid 1*

**brush past** *lagid 1; saligsig₂*
**brush teeth** *sipilyu 1.1; gisgis 1.2*
**brushwood** *sagbot 1*
**bubble up** *lere'; bukal*
**bubbling sound** *buwak-buwak*
**buck teeth** *jungal 1.1; juhal*
**bucket** *balde*
**buckled** *l'ppog; k'ppi'₂; kummi'; logpok 1*
**bud (plant)** *ugbus 1*
**buddy** *jēk; bō; lundang*
**budge** *judjal 2*
**buffalo** *kalbaw 1*
**buffeted** *landos 1.1*
**bugle** *torottot*
**build** *hinang₁ 1.2*
**build shelter** *tingkap*
**builder** *karpentero*
**building (n)** *luma'*
**building materials** *paghinang₁ 1; batang₂ 1*
**bulbous bow (of ship)** *buggul 1*
**bulge** *b'ttong₁ 1; l'pput₁ 1*
**bulk items** *pono'an*
**bulk trading** *tighan 1.1*
**bulkhead** *s'ngkol 1*
**bulky** *tibaggol; gubin*
**bull** *sapi'*
**bullet** *punglu'*
**bully (n)** *bula'ug₂*
**bum** *pigi'₁*
**bump into** *langgal₂ 1; sampigay; sagid 1*
**bumped** *bangkug 1*
**bun (of hair)** *simbōng 1*
**bunch (n)** *pungut 1; daugan*
**bunched** *pulingkit; puliting*
**bundle** *galung 1; p'kkosan*
**bundle (of leaf tobacco)** *okat₁ 2*
**buns** *pān ma'asin*
**buoy** *untang; tangkal₂ 1*
**buoyant** *langgung₂; lantup*
**buoyant wood** *lambus*
**burdened (emotional)** *buhat₁ 2*
**burglar; burgle** *tangkaw 1.1*
**buri palm** *saldang 1*
**burial day** *llaw-kalla'*
**burial meal** *tulun-tana'; kalla'an 1*
**burial place** *kubul 1*
**burlap (hessian)** *karut 1*
**burn (v)** *tunu'₁ 1.2; lāb 1.1*
**burn incense** *pat'bbud*
**burn rubbish** *lapug*
**burn to ashes** *abu 1.1*
**burning** *keyat₂ 1.1; dallet 1*
**burning (fever)** *laga 1.1*
**burning smell** *bau tunu'; s'ggung 1*

**burnish** *kaskas₁; bata*
**burnt** *lūs₁ 1; danglus*
**burnt (of cooked food)** *tutung*
**burp** *toya'; ggak*
**burrow (v)** *loblob*
**burst in (invade)** *dumpas*
**burst open** *bustak; buslut*
**bursting** *paguplut*
**bury** *kubul 1.1; tanom₁ 2*
**bushes** *kasob*
**bush-knife** *bangkung*
**business (livelihood)** *usaha 1*
**business relationship** *sapali 1.2; paghūn*
**business responsibilities** *kal'ngnganan 2*
**bustling about** *hiyul*
**busy** *udjalat 1*
**busy cooking** *pama'adjalun*
**busy talking** *pagmūng-mūng 1*
**busyness** *kidjut-kahibal*
**but** *bo'₁; saguwā'*
**but fortunately** *manda'*
**but in fact** *saunahan; baybay₂; parahāl*
**butcher (v)** *sampa'; sumbali'*
**butcher's knife** *laring lahut*
**butt ends together** *tiggup 1.1; pagkumbang*
**butt heads** *pagbangga'; pagdugtul*
**butt in** *jau'-jau'; sabu 1.1*
**butterfly** *kaba'-kaba'*
**butterfly bream** *kulisi'₂*
**butterflyfish** *lās-lās*
**buttocks** *pangkul; papa-buli'*
**button** *tambuku₂ 1*
**button (gold)** *dublun*
**buttress** *sumpiyang*
**buy** *b'lli*
**buy and sell** *litu*
**buy in bulk** *sampul-baul; kuridas*
**buyer (relationship)** *suki'*
**buzz** *lleng; kerek-kerek*
**by (agency of)** *he' 1; ni₂ 1; min 1*
**by accident** *samba 1.1; sabat₂*
**by and by** *gana-gana 1*
**by chance** *sabat₂*
**by contrast** *gōm*
**by means of** *labay min*
**by permission** *labay ba'id*
**by the fathom** *ma d'ppahan*
**by twos** *duwang-duwangan*
**by what means?** *buwattingga 1; inay 1.2*
**by-and-by** *pasōng-sōng*
**bygone days** *awal-jāman*
**bypass** *labay₁ 1.1; kulibut; pintas 1*
**bystander** *pagkubu-kubu*

# C c

cabbage palm *saldang 1*
cabinet (cupboard) *kabinet*
cable *bahudji'*
cadaver *patay₁ 1*; *bangkay*
cafe *estawran*
cage *pagal*; *paldu*
cajole *bidjak 1.1*
cake (baked) *mamun*; *baulu*; *bibingka*
cake (boiled) *biyaki' 1*
cake (fried) *panyām*; *kolleng-kolleng*
cake (steamed) *durul*
cake mold *babauluhan*
calamansi; calamonden *kalamonden*
calamity *kajahatan*; *naja'*
calculate *bista₂ 1.1*; *itung₁*
calf *anak sapi'*
calf of leg *b'ttis*
calico *mantaluna*
call *lingan 1*; *tawag*
call (to house) *owa'₁ 1*
call a child *dē' 1.1*
call on for help *sabbut 1.1*; *da'ut*
call on God *harap₂*; *ta'at 1.1*
call time (game) *pagtaem*
call to arms (bugle) *torottot*
call to cats *mīng-mīng*
call to chickens *kuruk-kuruk 1*
call to ducks *bī-bī 1*
callus *kubal 2*
calm (emotional) *haggut atay*
calm (of sea) *t'ddo' 1*
calm season *pan'ddo'*
calyx *tangkop*
camel *unta'*
camera *kodak*
camote *panggi'-bahan*
camp (military) *pustu 1*
campaign *kampēn₁ 1.1*
camphor (embalming) *kapul 1*
camphor plant *lakdan-bulan*
can (n) *mital 2*
cancel *puwas₁ 1.1*
candle *lansuk*
candle-nut *tangan-tangan*
candy *jauk 1*; *tira-tira*; *kende 1*
cane beetle *boke'*
cane species *t'mmang*; *kayuwan*
canine tooth *bangkil₂*; *taling*

canistel (sapote) *kisas₁*
canna lily *kulintas*
canned fish *saldinas*
cannon *kanyun 1*; *lantaka 1*
cannon (bamboo) *timbak p'ttung*
canoe (engine-driven) *paraw 2*; *pambot*
canoe (outrigger) *pelang*
canoe (worn out) *pongag*; *punggul 1*
canoe panels *lipi-lipi*
canoe planking (generic) *tapi' 1*
canoe rack *bantilan*; *tangonan*
canoe types (see paraw)
canopy *sapaw 1*; *kulambu' 1*; *luhul₂*
canvas *ispowen*; *tolda*
canvass a community (v) *salusu*; *s'ssag 1.1*
cap (bottle) *pitsa₁*
cap (explosive) *kīt*
cap (hat) *kuppiya*
capability *ka'abutan*
capable of *kole'*; *kaya*
capacity (measure of volume) *galon 2*; *pansing 1*; *gantang*
capacity (strength) *kosog 1*
cape (of coast) *tōng₁*
capital cost *po'on₃*
caponize *kabili*
capricious *paglepet*
capsicum *lara sinayul*
capsize *da'ub*; *pakkom 1*
captain *kapitan*; *patron*; *nakura'*
captive *pilisu 1*
capture *dakop*; *saggaw*
capula (collarbone) *talinga-usuk*
car *awtu*
carabao *kalbaw 1*
carambola (fruit) *iba'*; *balimbing*
carat *sussuk*
carbine *kalbin*
carbuncle *kalibubut 1*; *bularut*
carburetor *karboredor*
carcass *patay₁ 1*
cardboard box *labban*
cardinalfishes *piring*; *bangka₁*
cards (playing) *sugal*
care about (affection) *aku₁*
care for (love) *lasa₂ 1.1*
care for (take care of) *ulip*; *payakun*
carefree *hayang 1*; *luhaya*
careful *agak 1*; *insap*

careless *lampag; hagmak*

careless speech *lagam-bowa'*

carelessly *pehē'-pehē'*

caress *sapu-sapu*

cargador *kalgadol*

cargo *duwa'an*

carpenter *karpentero*

carpet *tudjara; palmaddani'*

carriage (posture) *pamaranan; palantara 2*

carriage (vehicle) *kalesa*

carried by current *laran; pagadgad*

carried by wind or current *palis₁*

carried far *ladji'*

carrier (porter) *kalgadol*

carry *hangkut; bowa₁*

carry across shoulder *tanggung₁; tumpay*

carry around *habit; gawil*

carry close to body *pagsabak*

carry heavy items *kalga*

carry in both arms *kalung*

carry in cloth *kandung₂*

carry on back *baba' 1*

carry on head *lutu₂; durung₁*

carry on pole *tanggung₁*

carry one-handed *pendet; benten*

carry person on shoulders *balung 1*

carry someone in sitting position *usung*

carry through with *sangkol; landu'₁*

carrying pole *tanggungan*

cart (n) *kalesa*

carton *labban; bakag₁*

cartridge *kalasussu*

carve *ukil; basbas*

case (container) *maleta*

case (legal) *kīs₂*

cash *sīn kanat*

cash deposit *lampak₁ 1*

cashew *kasuy*

cassava (boiled) *binamban*

cassava (dried) *kuting-kuting₁; tumbal 1*

cassava (generic) *panggi'-kayu; tibu'uk₂*

cassava (pan-roasted) *sinanglag*

cassava balls *pinutu landang*

cassava packages *gipit 2*

cassava varieties *hinu-hinu₂; tibu'uk-silal*

cast (throw) *bantung 1*

cast a net or cloth *laya 1.1*

cast a shadow *lambung₁ 1.2; simun 1*

cast a spell *pat'nna' hikmat*

cast spell *duti; pantak 1*

castor oil plant *tangan-tangan*

castrate *kabili*

cat *kuting₁*

cataract (of eyes) *bulahaw; lapis₄*

catarrh *ulapay₁*

catch (n) *gawatan*

catch (something thrown) *tamuk; sambut 1*

catch breath *paghongat-hongat*

catch by hooking *sabit₁ 1.1*

catch on (to meaning) *hati 1.1*

catch on something *sa'ud₁ 1; sagnat 1*

catch quickly *sakkop 1*

catch sight of *laman 1.1; jullit₁ 1*

catch someone *saggaw*

category (of beings) *pamilya 1.1*

caterpillar (furry) *ulat-sapling*

caterpillars *but'ngngel; ulat₁*

catfishes *ina'-baki'; taote'*

catholic priest *pari'*

catnap *piru'-piru'*

cat's-eye shellfish *laggong*

cattle *sapi'; hayop*

cattle run *buluyan*

cattle tick *bebang₂*

Caucasian *bangsa-pote'; Milikan*

caught in act *agpot 1.1; abut ma kara-kara*

caulk (v) *s'nsong; gagā*

caulking fibre *g'llom*

cause *jalanan; kalna' 1.1; sabab₁ 1*

cause chaos *hiluhala' 1.2*

cause pain *bangkug 1.1; singku 1*

cause retching *balowak*

cause sickness *pa'in₃ 1.1*

cause to happen *paniya'*

cause trouble *jabu 1.1*

caution (v) *banda'; sanggup*

cautionary tale *salsila 1*

cautious *llog 1; agak 1; illat 1*

cautiously *kamaya'-maya' 1*

cave *lowang 1; songab 1*

cavity *gaunggang*

caw (sound of crow) *owak-owak*

cease (of a stage) *k'nna; bba₂*

ceasing *hopay; titis 1*

Cebuano *Bisaya' 2*

ceiling *luhul₂*

celebrate *paglami 1.1; paglasig*

celebration *jamu 1; hailaya*

celestial being *biradali 1; mala'ikat*

cellophane *tilag-tilag₁*

cement *semento 1*

cement block *haloblāk*

cemetery *kakubulan*

censer *tugtugan*

censure *soway; sā'₁ 1.3*

centavo *sīn*

center *t'ngnga'*

center of town *da'ira 1*

**centipede (marine)** *lalipan-tahik*
**centipedes** *lalipan; nne*
**cephalopods** *kuhita' 1; kanu'us; kulabutan*
**ceremony** *pagsalawat; paghinang₃ 1*
**ceremony (ancestor)** *hinang-mbo'; pagkādja 2*
**ceremony (death spirit)** *paghinang-maut 1*
**ceremony (funerary)** *hinang-pitu'*
**ceremony (of new moon)** *paghinang-bulan 1*
**ceremony (thanksgiving)** *pagsalamatan*
**certain** *tuman 1; manyatakan; atakabbul*
**certainly** *musti-musti*
**certainty** *tantu 1*
**certificate** *sairola*
**chafe** *paggidgid; pagleges*
**chagrin** *pagmalas*
**chain** *karena 1.1; kili-kili; karena 1*
**chair** *tingkō'an; siya*
**challenge (v)** *tukas 1.1*
**chambered nautilus** *kalo'ong 1*
**chance action** *samba 1*
**change (in condition)** *sipat₂ 1; gām-gām*
**change (one's word)** *baluba 2*
**change (replace)** *salin₁ 1.1*
**change (subject)** *latun 1.1*
**change attitude** *lō'*
**change clothes** *salin₁ 1*
**change color** *baluba 1*
**change direction** *p'llay 1; biluk 1; kabig*
**change in fortune** *pagsalin sukud*
**change money** *hūg₂ 1*
**change places** *pagganti'; pagsaliyu 1.1*
**change plans** *salusad*
**change using magic** *kiput alam*
**changeable** *pagpinda*
**changeable person** *panyuba' 1*
**changed** *pinda 1*
**channel** *saluran; sowang; l'bbangan*
**channel (between islands)** *olangan 1.1*
**chant** *nasib; jikil 1; lugu' 1*
**chant (in children's game)** *talli₁*
**chant (in praise of Allah)** *pagtakbil 1*
**chant (traditional)** *pagkata-kata 1.1*
**chanted stories** *langa'-langa'*
**chaos (public)** *halubilu; hiluhala' 1*
**chapel** *langgal₁*
**chapter** *bāb*
**chapter of Holy Bible** *jūd*
**character** *kasuddahan; jari₄ 1*
**character revealed by actions** *pi'il*
**characteristics** *jantang; jāt₁; tebong*
**charcoal** *buling*
**charge (a fee)** *sukay₁ 1.1*
**charm (generic)** *tambang₃ 1*
**chart** *patta' 1; pamandogahan*

**charter (v)** *padjak₂*
**chase someone** *pagembet 1; apas 1.1*
**chaste** *sussi 1.1*
**chat** *pagpali-pali; pina'in*
**chatterbox** *paglapak-lapak 2*
**chatty** *h'lling-h'lling*
**chauffeur** *draybel*
**Chavacano** *Bisaya'-Sambuwangan*
**cheap** *luhay₁ 1.1*
**cheat (n)** *pangangakkal*
**cheat (v)** *lingu 1.1; akkal 1.1; kidjib*
**check on** *pende*
**check pattern** *diyandi; tadjung; kusta 1*
**check-up (medical)** *pa'nda' 1.2*
**cheeks** *papa₁; pisngi; papa-buli'*
**cheerful** *kōg 2; hāp atay; lasig 1.1*
**cheese tree** *bana'*
**chemise** *kamisun*
**cherish** *ammal₂; llog 1.2*
**cheroot** *banusu*
**chest (body)** *sabakan; daggaha*
**chest (container)** *ba'ul₁*
**chestnut manikin (bird)** *maya*
**chew** *papa'; pa'us*
**chew (betel)** *mama' 1*
**chewing gum** *singgam*
**chewy** *katat; kaslog*
**chick** *anak manuk*
**chicken (domestic)** *manuk 1*
**chicken (wild)** *labuyu'₁*
**chicken lice** *hanglop*
**chickenpox** *ttus-ttus 1; sampal 1*
**chide** *salu'-salu'; salba₁*
**chief** *datu'*
**child** *anak₁ 1; onde' 1*
**child at toddler stage** *tangpas₂*
**childless** *t'ggang₂*
**child-like** *akil-balig*
**children** *kamanahutan; kaonde'-onde'an; makannak*
**chill; chilly** *dingin 1.1; haggut 1.2; t'nne 1*
**chilli pepper** *lara 1*
**chimney** *pupputan*
**chin** *langal*
**chine of canoe** *salig₂; singki'*
**Chinese** *Lannang; taoke'₁; makaw; sina'₁*
**Chinese lantern** *tanglung*
**chink (gap)** *possatan; sipsipan*
**chip (n)** *tebla' 1; tigtig 1*
**chip off** *biti'₂ 1*
**chipped** *t'bbe' 1.1; someng 1*
**chisel** *sangkap 1; pa'at 1*
**chlorine taste** *ma'angit*
**chock (wedge)** *biggal 1; s'ngngal*
**chock-full** *sukad*

chocolate *sakulati 1*

choice *baya'-baya'₂; pagpene' 1*

choke *t'kkob; p'kkol 1.1*

choke growth *talung₂*

choke on liquid *s'ddok*

choko *sayote*

cholera *kolera*

choose *pene' 1.1*

choose by drawing lots *pagko'ot-ko'ot 1.1*

chop (v) *tadtad 1; ladjang*

chop to shape *g'ttok-g'ttok; sapsap₂*

chop up *pabuwa'; tama'; padja'; pagtebag-tebag*

chopping board *sangkalan*

choppy (of sea) *kata'-kata'; goyak 1; umpak-umpak*

choral group *solembang*

chore *hinang₁ 1*

Christ *Almasi*

Christ-follower *Almasihin*

Christian Filipino *Bisaya'-bukut; Kristyan*

Christmas gift *krismas*

chronic (illness) *panibi; palsakkihan; panaki*

chronic (skin condition) *ugud-lugay*

chubby *goldo-goldo*

chubs/drummers (fish sp) *ilak*

chum (close friend) *lundang; panon*

chunks (bits) *tigtigan*

church *langgal₁*

churn (emotional) *pagbikannol*

churning (intestinal) *paglimbōn*

cicada *tal'ngnget-l'ngnget; pilik-pilik 1*

cigaret *siga 1; sigupan; binatang₂*

cigaret holder *kukuwa*

cigaret roller *lulūnan*

cinch *kambot 1*

cinder block *haloblāk*

cinema *sini*

circuitous *pagbeklo'; kulengkong 1*

circular *tibulung 1; legong; lengkong 1*

circumcise *g'llot 2; pags'lle; islam 1.1; islam 1*

circumference *katilingkal; lekos 1*

circumnavigate *libut 1.1; likuwad 1*

circumspect *llog 1; agak 1*

circumstances *kahālan; pakaradja'an; kahaliluwalan*

cirrus cloud *tai'-baliyu*

citizen *da'ayat*

citizenry *mahadjana'*

citrus fruit *muntay*

city *lungsud*

civet cat *kuting-kubing; tinggaung*

civilian *sibilyan*

claim knowledge *pagta'u-ta'u*

claim redress *masangka*

claim status *pagnaho'-naho'*

clairvoyance *langtas 1*

clamorous *bukag; sagaw*

clams (various) *imbaw; kali-kali; kima; lāy-lāy; antu'ang*

clang *pagkulenseng*

clap hands *lagpak₂; pagpapak*

clarify meaning *hangpat 1.1*

clarity (of speech) *hurup 1; hapal 1*

clash (head-on) *pagdugtul*

clash (of natural forces) *pagbalos*

clasp (v) *s'kkol; komkom*

class *ginis 1*

classmate *klasmēt*

clatter *kagingkul; pagkolepak*

clatter of hooves *kulagpak*

claw *kukku₁; sakket 1*

claw-like *kokko'; pupus*

clay element of lantern *galsa*

clay pot *pasu₁; banga'₂*

clean (ritually, of meat) *halal 1*

clean (surface) *hawan 1; k'ssang₁*

clean mouth (v) *gūm-gūm*

cleaner fish *kabubu*

cleanse *sussi 1.2*

cleansing (before prayer) *istinja'; pagail*

cleansing (moral) *saltun 1.1*

clear (liquid) *lihaw 1*

clear (of speech) *hapal 2; hurup 1.1*

clear (shining) *tallang*

clear a space *pasihak; lipay₂*

clear away growth *suwat; lapa₂*

clear rubbish *hawan 1.1*

clear throat *kehem; pagkahak*

clearly seen *tampal 2; ballag*

clearly understood *klaro*

clear-sounding *tanog₁; lagsing*

cleave *ladjang*

cleft (in chin) *kandi'is₂*

cleft (in rock) *kehe 1*

cleft (of palate) *someng 2*

clench teeth *k'ttop₂ 1.1; kansing 1*

clenched (fingers/claws) *kokko'; pupus*

clerk *kukumit*

clever *panday 1.1; taha'-akkal*

cliff *pampang; titib*

climb *dāg₁ 1*

climb across *kulambitay*

climbing loop *salimbogot*

cling *balut 1.1; pikit₁ 1*

clinking sound *kagingkul*

clip (n) *sisipit*

clip clop (hooves) *pagtagandak*

clippers *makinilya*

clitoris *bigi₂; toro' 2*

clock *lilus*

clogs *bakiya'₁*

cloister (keep private) *kumbis 1.1; kuddam; libun*

close (an opening) *saplong; sampong 1*

close (by clicking together) *kattup; dopon-dopon 1.1*

close (friendship) *lahasiya' 1; pagagay*

close (of fighting) *apiki 1.3*

close (of kin) *lissi; p'nggod 2*

close (shut) *takkop 1.1; tambol 1.2*

close a deal *kōl 1.1*

close edges *t'mmu 1.1*

close eyes *pagk'ddaw-k'ddaw; k'ddom₁ 1*

close fit *pagd'ppak 1*

close in (of weather) *tangkob₁ 1*

close securely *kabbat; kansing 1*

close succession *kempot; sungbul*

close to *sekot 1*

close to boiling *aes-aes*

close to edge *tipid 1*

close to fire *alung 1*

close together (crowd) *s'mpok 1; sonson*

closed (shop or school) *tutup₂*

closed tightly *kumbis 1*

close-fitting *lapat 1.1*

close-growing *herot*

closely woven *sonson*

closing stage *kamattihan 1*

clot of blood *batu-batu₂*

cloth *kakana'; s'mmek 1*

cloth (fine) *buwal₂; sutla'*

cloth (for wiping) *tarapu 1*

cloth (heavy) *tolda; ma'ung*

cloth covering *sulban 2*

clothe *pakay₁; s'mmek 1.1*

clothes (set of) *pangampu'an*

clothes-line *sablayan; puhi'an*

clothes-pin *sipit 1*

clothing (general) *tamongon; pamakay; badju'*

clotted *apol*

cloud *dampog 1; gabun*

clouded (vision) *buraw*

clown (behavior) *palla'; ula-ula*

clown (v) *paglata*

clownfish *anak-bobohan*

club (heavy stick) *bastun*

club (v) *papas₂; kakal*

cluck (chicken) *kuruk-kuruk 1.1*

clue (detect) *tilas₁*

clumped *tiguma'*

clumsy *lampag; gubin*

cluster *pungut 2*

cluster (n) *pungut 1; daugan*

clustered *pulingkit; puliting; tundun 1*

clutch (v) *kopkop 1.1*

cluttered *sembol 1; mussak-massik*

coagulated *apol*

coalesce *pagtibu'uk 1*

coals *bale₅; baga 1*

coarse *kasap; gasang*

coarsely ground *s'ppal*

coastline *bihing tampe; susulan; tapiyan*

coat (clothing) *jaket*

coating *lapis₁ 1*

coax *animu*

cob (corn) *līt*

cobweb *sāng-lawa'*

coccyx (tailbone) *tuwal 1; igut*

cock a gun *kalsa; kital*

cock-a-doodle-do *kukkaga'uk*

cockatoo (crested) *bukay*

cockfighting *pagbulang*

cockles *kohang; imbaw*

cockpit *bulangan; pagtūkan*

cockroach *kamahung*

cocky (boastful) *pagl'lla-l'lla₁*

cocoa tree *kakaw*

coconut *niyug*

coconut (deformed) *putang*

coconut (immature) *bilu'uk 1*

coconut (mature but green) *botong*

coconut (mature) *lahing 1*

coconut (mature, partly ripe) *gangkul*

coconut (maturing) *motong*

coconut (newly set) *kambung-kambung*

coconut confection *bukayu' 1; hinti' 1*

coconut crab *kullu'*

coconut cream *p'tti'-gata'*

coconut flower *bagaybay; giyagay*

coconut flower sheath *lurang*

coconut frond *lokay₁; langkay 1*

coconut jelly *lu'ud₂; lagod₂*

coconut leaves *daun-salirap*

coconut meat *l'kkop₂; tongkop*

coconut milk *gata' 1*

coconut palm *niyug*

coconut shell container *peya'; ba'ung*

coerce *agpot 1; logos 1*

coffee *kahawa*

coffee (instant) *neskape*

coffee pot *kapsiyu; kapitera*

coffin *lalungan; kaban 1*

cogon grass *parang*

cohesive *tibu'uk₁ 1.1*

coil (line) *longon*

coil (n) *koleng₁ 1*

coil (v) *lebod 1*

coin games *pagsalla' 1.1*

coin size marker *pikit₃ 1*

coincide *pagsabu; pagsalta'; pagsamp'kka'*
coins *sīn kanat; pisita*
colander (sieve) *ulayan*
cold (atmosphere) *pan'nne*
cold (infection) *ulapay₁*
cold (temperature) *dingin 1; haggut 1.2; t'nne 1*
cold from immersion *killut-killut*
cold season *pangandingin*
colic *bakag₂*
collapsed (of a structure) *l'bbos 1; h'bba'*
collar (garment) *bekos₂*
collarbone *talinga-usuk*
collateral damage *sabat₂*
collect liquid *salud 1.1*
collection (of boats) *kamunda'an*
collection (of people) *daumpigan*
collide *sangku'; daplig 1*
color (hue) *b'ttik 1*
color lips *atal*
color up (of fruit) *pagangilan; lāg*
colors (list) *walna'*
coma *tannay*
comb (n) *suray 1*
comb hair *lais 1.1*
comb of bird *pē'₃; daling*
combine (business) *pagkungsi*
combine (form a group) *pagumpig*
combine (ingredients) *pagsimbug 1*
combined *pūn 1.1*
combustion engine *makina 1*
come *pi'itu 1.1*
come across (find) *bāk₁*
come alongside *sampig*
come and go *pehē'-pi'itu*
come at mealtimes *donga'; boslad*
come close *sekot 1.1; t'ppi' 1*
come here *dai'₁; pi'itu 1.1*
come late *damuli 1*
come to mind *padlak ni atay; tasdik; suligpat*
come together *pagabut; pagtongop*
comedian (be a) *palla'*
comely *manis 1.1; lingkat 1.1*
comet *selo'*
comfort (v) *dindang-dindang; aluk*
comfort room *kasilyas; toylet*
comfortable *tanam₁ 1; sannang*
comforted *handok atay 1*
comical *palla'*
command *uldin 1.1; da'ak*
commandeer *t'ppas₁*
commander *tagsoho'an; komandel*
commandments *panoho'an*
commemorate *bangun₃*
commence *tagna' 1.2*

comment (v) *upamakun 1.1; iyan*
commentary (Koranic) *tapsil*
commit adultery *liyu-lakad*
commit incest *pagkasumbang*
commit sin *dusa 1.1; pagpakay-dusa*
commit suicide *pagsabil*
commit to *pagsinta'; pagtawakkal 1.1*
commitment (promise) *janji' 1; tungga' 1*
commitment (religious) *paglima-waktu; pagammal*
committed to doing *tukid 1; niyat 1; pagsinta'*
common man *sibilyan*
commotion *hiyul; balu'*
communal meal *paglukun 1.1*
communicate *pahati 1.1*
communicate by dream *palambung*
community *lūngan; kaum*
compact (v) *danos*
compactness *lapat 1; pagd'ppak 1*
companion *sehe' 1; abay₁ 1*
companionless *dangan-dangan 1.2*
company of people *padjuhan; panjihan*
comparable *sala 1; sali'an; sali' 1.1*
compare to *paralil 1; ibarat₂*
comparison *pamaralilan*
compartment (inner pocket) *anak-bulsa*
compartment (room) *bilik 1*
compass *padduman; kumpas₂*
compassionate *patiase'un; lu'uy₂*
compatible *pagtuksu'*
compel *logos 1; angin; panhot*
compel effort *panhot*
compel marriage *pole'₃*
compelling (speech) *labas₂ 1*
compensate *diyat; ayu'; bangun₂ 1; pagmasangka 1.1*
compensation *pangayu'an; tampan-maru; pagmasangka 1*
compere (an event) *pagpal'ngngan 1.1*
compete *pagtukas; paglomba*
compete (of beauty) *paglingkat-lingkat*
competent (of toddler) *passut; tangpas₂*
competitive *ugpang 2.1*
complacency *pamasagad*
complain *pagmahi*
complain against (formal) *tuntut₁; pagpuhun 1.1*
complementary *tupan 1*
complete (a task or assignment) *tammat 1.1; sangkol*
complete (adj) *tubus₁ 1; jukup 1; lungbus*
completed *tammat 1; talus₁ 1*
completely *katūyan*
compliant *kuhi₁ 1.1; hungun*
compliments *sanglit 1*
composed (emotionally) *haggut atay*
compound (mixture) *lamud₁ 1*

comprehend *hati 1*
compress *da'os*
compress by folding *l'ppot; lupi'₁*
compulsion *wajib 1.1*
compulsory *wajib 1*
compute (count) *bista₂ 1.1; jumla 1*
comrade *panon*
comrade relationship *paglundang-lundang*
con (trick someone) *balidja; akkal 1.1*
concave *k'bbong; ku'ub; layas*
conceal *tapuk 1*
conceal (for modesty) *batin 1.1*
conceal intention *limbung 1.1*
concealed object *buli'₂ 1*
concealment (hiding place) *patapukan; kasipukan*
concede *tugut 2*
conceited *abbu 1.1*
conceive a child *iram; b'ttong₂ 1.2*
conceive of *pula'-pula' 1.1*
concentrate on *isbat*
concentration loss *pagsumau'*
concept *pikil 1*
concern for *ayuput; pagpamagay 1*
concerning *pasal₁; takdil*
concerns *kabimbangan*
conch (small) *kabeto'*
conch (spider) *kahanga*
conciliate *pagkahāp; pagsulut 1*
conclude *utas 2*
conclude from data *kilā 2*
conclusion *tapus 1; kat'kkahan₂*
conclusion (of discussion) *tabtaban; utas 2.1*
conclusive *hangbos₁*
concrete *semento 1*
concubine *h'nda-tape'*
concur *beya'-beya'₁ 1; uyun*
concussion *pinsan 1*
condescending *pagmalangkahi*
condiment *tinu'anan*
condition *kahālan*
condone *sagad 1.1*
conduct (behavior) *laku-tabi'at; kaul-pi'il*
conduit *pansul*
cone *basung*
cone shells *labu₁; sulaw*
confections *halluwa 1; hinti' 1*
confederate *kungsi*
confer *paggara' 1.1*
confer on *g'llal 1.1*
conference *palhimpunan*
confess *haka 1.1; pagsab'nnal; pagpasab'nnal 1.1*
confession of faith *sahaddat 1*
confessional statement *kalima*
confide in *ungsik; sipuk-sipuk*

confidence in *andol 1*
confident *passut; tantuhi; atakabbul*
confidently *angan-angan*
confine (enclose) *bilik 1.1; kumbis 1.1*
confined (space) *kiput*
confirm *tuman 1.1*
confirmed *pasti'₁*
confiscate *papagdapu*
conflict *pagsing-sūd; pagbono' 1*
conform *beya'₃ 1.1*
confront *tampak 2; tampal 3*
confused *lingu 1*
confused by abundance *lambang-mata 1*
confusing *limogmog 1*
confusion *kabingawan*
confusion (of crowd) *hiluhala' 1; kasasawan*
congenital condition *sahili'; kariyasali*
congratulate *sanglit 1.2*
congregate *paghimpun; pagpūn₁*
congregation *da'ayat; jama'a; palhimpunan*
conjecture *kalu-kalu 1.1*
conjunctivitis *belad*
connect (by marriage) *pikit₂; pasugsug*
connect (reach to) *laktas*
connect ends *kablit₁*
connect up *batuk₁ 1.1; sangon₁ 1.1*
connected *dalos 1; langkit 1*
connected (of eyebrows) *langgung-kilay*
connection (blood relation) *sugsug 1*
conquer *longpos; da'ug*
conscience *itikad*
consciousness *sipat₁ 1*
consecrate *pahalga'; mulliya 1.1*
consecutive *langkit 1; pagsunu'-sunu'*
consensus *dauyunan 1*
consenting *kuhi₁ 1*
consequence *katobtoban*
consequently *ati*
consider (think about) *kumpas₁; tali' 1.1; pagimba-imba; bista₁*
consider options *bisbis₂; pagdepende*
consistent *togol 1*
console *apu'-apu'; aluk*
consonant *batang-sulat*
conspicuous *ta'nda' mata*
conspire *pagkungsi*
constant *t'ttog 1*
constellation of Orion *bubu₂; batik*
constipated *tobol; llet 2*
constitution (physical) *anggauta'; paltubu-tubuhan 2*
constricted *sembol 1; kiput*
construct *hinang₁ 1.2*
consult *aru; pangaru*

consume everything *kanam*
consumed *hagin 1*
consuming desire *napsu kabasi'*
consummated *mustajab*
consumptive *panibi*
contact (v) *d'ppak 1.1*
contagious *lamin 1*
contain (v) *akay; isi₁ 1.1*
container (bamboo) *loka'*
container (betel chew) *salappa'; loka'-loka'; mama'an*
container (brass) *bintang₁; langguway; garul*
container (cooking) *pam'llahan*
container (glass) *garapun; kassa' 2; butul*
container (metal) *batil; baro*
container (paper cone) *pasung₂*
container (wooden) *gaddong*
container for valuables *bungga'₂*
contaminate *lemed 2; lamin 1*
contaminated *patay₁ 1.1*
contemplate *kannal; pikil 1.1*
contemporaneous *sasang; salta'*
contempt (treat with) *halipulu 1; mahadja'; pagudju' 1*
contend for *pagagaw*
contend; argue *pagegot-egot; pagda'ug; pagsalod*
content *kataluwa'an*
contented *sugpat akkal; tuksu'; masuk*
contention *pagpayod 1*
contents *isi₂; sōd 1.1*
contest (n) *pagsulay 1*
contest (singing) *pagsindil 1*
contest (v) *pagkosogan*
contest of wits *pagtaluhan 1*
contiguous *pagdalos; pagbihing₁*
continually *sigi-sigi 1; langkit 1.1; na pa'in*
continue *podlongan; lanjal 1.1; timpus*
continue unchanged *sangdan 1*
continuously *toldas; pagambat-ambat 1; tinoro-toro*
contraband *pagbisnis; ismagol*
contract (become smaller) *kongkong 1*
contract (commercial) *padjak₂; pakkiyaw; kuridas*
contract (n) *janji' 1; pagsulutan*
contradict *jawab₂ 1.1; payod 1.1; sīng-sūd*
contrariwise *pagsakali; baybay₂*
contrary (uncooperative) *panalod; sugat 2*
contrast (n) *pagbidda'an*
contrastive *saddī 1*
contribute to *buwan₁ 1.1*
contribution (to partnership) *panapali*
contrition *tawbat 1*
control (n) *komkoman 2*
control (v) *pagdūl-baya'; pagagi; aguwanta 1.1*
controller *tagmilikan; tagpatutan*

controlling *ga'os 1.1*
controversy *pasu'alan*
conversation *pagbilma'arup; pagsuli-suli*
convey *pal'ssut; talik; bowa₁*
conveyance *bayanan; pameya'an₁; panumpangan*
convicted (of wrongdoing) *tōng₂ 1.1*
convictions *pam'nnalan*
convinced *beya'-beya'₁ 1; kompolme; bilīb; gustu 1*
convulsions *sawan-sawan*
coo (of dove) *mmu*
co-occur *pagsabu; pagsalta'; pagtabla*
co-occurrence *aging 1*
co-occurrence particle *pa'in₁*
cook *b'lla 1*
cook by frying *gisa; guling*
cook cassava *landang 1.1; sinanglag*
cook liver *sagol 1*
cook on coals *tunu'₂*
cook partially *lakbu'₁; bongka 1*
cook soup *loho' 1.2*
cooked *tahak 1*
cooked rice *buwas-kinakan*
cookie *bāng-bāng₂; jā; balatu; biskuwit*
cooking banana *sabba*
cooking pans/pots *pam'llahan*
cooking place *pagb'llahan*
cooking sticks *gagawi'*
cool *dingin 1*
cool in breeze *pahayang*
cooling off *luhaw-luhaw*
cooperate *pagbagimbin; pagsandu; pagumpig*
cooperative *saumbibi; saldik; hungun*
copper *tumbaga 1; sawasa'*
copra *lahing 1*
copse *kakayuhan*
copulate *paglalu*
copy (v) *kapi; sengod*
coral (generic) *batu₂ 1*
coral bricks *batu₂ 2*
coral fishes *ulapay₂; daing-daing sahasa'; bagahak₁; kayung-kayung*
coral gravel *kalangan₃*
coral pebbles *kalang₂*
coral sand *igang₁*
coral tree *dapdap*
cord *lubid 1; k'llat₂ 1*
cord for top *lubayan*
cordage (rigging) *k'llat₂ 1*
cordial *lanu' atay*
core *tongol; esok*
core meaning *isi-lling*
core of boil *mata-kalibubut*
co-reside *pagdaluma'*
cork (stopper) *pulai'*

corn (maize) *gandum*
corn cob *okol*
corn rice *buwas-gandum*
corner *dugu; pidju 1; lo'ok-lo'ok*
corpse *patay₁ 1; mayat*
corpulent *l'mmok 1.1*
corral *koral 1*
correct *taluwa' 1; mattan 1.1; bontol 1*
correct (v) *paintul*
correct direction *bakot*
corrode *gaha' 1.1*
corrugated *pagl'bbak*
corrupt (decaying) *buhuk; halu' 1.1*
corrupt someone (moral) *bidjak 1.1; pilad*
cosmetics *pigi'₂ 1; borak 1; lipistik 1*
costly *hunit 2.1; halga' 1.1*
costume jewelry *pansi*
cot *palangka'₂; kantil₁*
cotton fiber *gapas*
cotton tree *kapuk 1*
couch *pabahakan*
cough *kehem; kohol 1*
could be *makajari 2*
council *palhimpunan*
councilor *konsehal*
counsel (n) *kaisunan; pagpapat 1*
counsel (v) *gara' 1.2*
count (n) *heka 1*
count (v) *kimmat 2; itung₁; saipuwa*
count as important *tē'₂*
countenance *pamayhu'an*
counter *paga-paga*
counterfeit *paltik; gillo'ak*
counter-offer *balos₁ 2*
counterpart *umbuk 1; limbang 1*
counters *jimban; pagtaksi' 1*
counting term (canoes) *puntu; munda'₁ 2*
countless *laksa' 1.2; mbal taitung umaw*
country *lahat*
country far off *Maksina'*
couple (married) *paglakibini*
courage; courageous *aykalas 1; esog 1; bahani 1*
court a girl *tunggu'-tunang*
court case *palkala' 1*
courteous *addat 1.1; hantap 1*
courtesy *paidda*
courtesy (formal) *puli-bahasa*
courting gift *siba' 1; pagdamak; paghulmat*
courtyard *halaman*
cousin *kaki₂*
cousin (first degree) *kaki mint'dda*
cousin (second degree) *kaki minduwa*
cousin relationship *pagkakihan*
cousin-in-law *bilas; iras*

cousins (plural) *kaukaki*
cove (bay) *lo'ok*
covenant *paljanji'an*
cover (a corpse) *tatap 1.1*
cover (a surface) *liput₁; kulinting*
cover (for food) *tutup₁ 1*
cover (lid) *sampong 1; tambol 1; turung 1; sa'ob 1*
cover (ridging) *bubungan*
cover (v) *lokob; bunbun 1.1; tangkob₁ 1.1*
cover a bet *to'on₁ 1.1*
cover shame *pagtambun kaiya'an; tampan-maru*
cover surface (with a layer) *langkop*
cover with water *paletop*
covered completely *lakat; saplut₂; lapat 1.1*
covered in cloud *andom 1.2*
covet *hangsaw 1.1; ihid*
covetous *hawa 1.1; napsu 1.1; bahaya*
cow *sapi'*
cowardice *bulas₁*
cowardly *himulas; bolag; damag*
cower *kopo'*
co-wife *h'nda-tape'; kalu'a; h'nda-h'nda*
cowlick (whorl) *pusal₂; ebod*
co-worker *limbang-sehe'*
cowries *kuba₁; baggu'*
crabs (generic) *kagang; kagong*
crack (n) *l'tta' 1; gali'₂*
crack knuckles *paghagtu'*
crack open *p'ppok*
cracked *l'ssa'; b'kka' 1; posat*
cracked, of voice *pehet*
cracker *biskuwit*
cracker (fireworks) *kulitis*
cracker (food) *bāng-bāng₂*
cracking noise *pagpaletek; patigangkul; kattek*
crackle (in mouth) *lopok*
crackle (of burning) *pulitik₂*
crackle (v) *kulattub; lenek; pagpalere'*
cradle *ta'utan; buwahan₁*
craftsman *panday 1*
crafty *kaikit₂ 1*
crammed full *dasok 1; selot 1*
cramp (muscular) *b'nnod 1; ulapid*
crane (bird) *ellog*
crane (machinery) *timun-timun 1*
cranium *kōk 1*
cranky *dole' 1.1*
crash down *balabak*
crate *kīs₃*
cravat *kurubata'*
crave *suwak 1.1; sōb; tagi 1*
craving *kasōban*
crawl *kura'-kura'₁; lele 1*
crawl (feeling on skin) *l'nnu*

**crawl under** *soksok*
**crayfish** *ka'ullang*
**crayon** *kolol 2*
**crazy** *kangog; belaw*
**creak** *ganggu'*
**crease (n)** *kola' 1*
**crease in skin** *b'kkos*
**creased** *g'ttos; komo'₂; go'ok 1*
**create** *paniya'; papanjari; ummat 1.1*
**create by molding** *kompol*
**created form** *kapamanjari*
**created things** *papanjarihan*
**creation** *kamemon pinapanjari*
**creator** *Magpapanjari*
**creature (pejorative)** *hanjing; binatang₁*
**creatures (large)** *sattuwa*
**credit** *utang 1*
**creed** *sahaddat 1*
**creek** *sowang; sapa'*
**creep** *sanaw; lele 1*
**creeper (plant)** *belle'-belle' 1*
**crescent moon** *sahali-bulan*
**crest (of bird)** *daling*
**crest (of wave)** *mata-goyak; bowa'-goyak*
**crevalle** *mangsa' 1*
**crick (in neck)** *busā' 1.1*
**crime** *langgal sara' 1; dusa 1*
**criminal** *sugarul*
**crinkled** *lūn-lupi'*
**crippled** *pengkol; pekok; pengka'*
**crisis situation** *timbang-patay; udjul₁ 1*
**crispy** *palopok*
**crispy cassava** *jauk 1; lapuk-lapuk*
**criss-cross** *pagbaubabag*
**critical moment** *pasa'atan*
**criticize** *himoway; salla'₁ 1.2; sā'₁ 1.3*
**crochet** *ingkahi 1.1*
**crocodile** *buwaya*
**crook fingers** *pagkalluk-kalluk*
**crooked** *kalluk 1; bengkok 1; kello' 1.1*
**crop (agriculture)** *anihan*
**crop farmer** *paghuhuma*
**cross (irritable)** *s'ngngot₁ 1*
**cross a bridge** *taytay 1; lete*
**cross beam** *hobong; limba' pelang*
**cross over** *dambila' 2.1; kulatay; laktas*
**cross-booms (outrigger)** *tarik*
**cross-breed** *karambila'an*
**cross-eyed** *libat 1.1; libat 1*
**cross-legged** *pagnihakin; pagsiningkulang*
**cross-pieces** *giyak*
**cross-purposes** *paggo'on-go'on; pagbesod; pagsing-sūd*

**crosswise** *babag 1.1*
**crotchety** *dole' 1.1; salut 1*
**crouch** *loko' 2*
**croupier** *bangka₂ 1*
**crow (bird)** *owak*
**crow (v)** *kukkaga'uk; eyok*
**crowbar** *bara; lalandak*
**crowd** *kaheka-heka'an; timuk-timuk puhu'; kapono'an*
**crowd around** *sahubu; pagkubu-kubu; t'bbud₂*
**crowded** *s'mpok 1; sembol 1; selot 1*
**crown (n)** *korona; mahakutta'; panumping*
**crown-of-thorns starfish** *kalling-sahanay*
**crucifix** *krus*
**crude (behavior)** *sabul 1*
**cruel** *b'ngngis 1; jahulaka' 1*
**crumble (v)** *sughay*
**crumbly** *gokal; pu'aw 1; budjal-budjal*
**crumbs** *momok*
**crumple (wad)** *lompeng 1; komot-komot*
**crumpled** *go'ok 1; g'mmot 1*
**crunch** *k'ttop₁*
**crunchy** *lapuk*
**crush to powder** *tanay; ligis₁; pipis*
**crush under pressure** *p'ggos; p'ssa' 1*
**crust (rice)** *dokot₁; l'kkot*
**crustaceans** *pama'; kamun*
**crutch (walking aid)** *tungkud 1*
**cry** *pagsilawak*
**cry (soundlessly)** *llad; asang-selo*
**cry (weep)** *pagle'eng; langan₁; tangis 1*
**cry aloud** *asang₂; olang 1; pagalud; kula'ak*
**cry easily** *unga'*
**cry for something** *pagamā 1.1*
**cry lustily** *kuseseyang 1.1*
**cry out for help** *dahing 1*
**cry out in pain** *pagaruhuy; pagdahing*
**cry without tears** *s'ngngel 1*
**cubby hole (snug place)** *suhutan*
**cuckold** *daiyus*
**cucumber** *maras*
**cucumber squash** *ingkug*
**cud (chewing)** *apug*
**cuddle a child** *mpit*
**cudgel** *kakakal*
**cue (for shooting pool)** *tako*
**cuff (hem)** *kumpi' 1*
**culpable** *atas₂ 1*
**cultivate (for planting)** *lungkad 2; gās₁*
**cunning** *kaikit₂ 1*
**cup** *basu; sawan*
**cupboard** *kabinet; paradol; perol*
**curb** *tagga 1.1*
**cure (illness)** *uli'₁ 1*
**curious** *katilaw*

curl (hair) *kolong 1.1; kabulay 1*
curl up (of body) *k'ttung*
curled around *pagkulengkong*
curled up *kongkong 1; kulangkang 1; pupus*
curling *kolong-kolong*
current (deep) *bengkol₂*
current (incoming) *balosok; sōn*
current (outgoing) *la'ang 1*
current (water) *bulagas; s'llog; b'kka'an*
curriculum *madrasa*
curry (spice) *kari-kari 1*
curse (n) *sukna' 1; sapda 1*
curse (v) *duti; hagda-hagda; sapa'at₁ 1.1*
curse formula *palkata'an*
curse words (generic) *sukna' 1.1*
cursive writing *langkus 1*
curt (of speech) *kasla 1*
curtain *kultina; kulambu' 1*
curve back *k'dde'; l'ddet 1*
curved *bengkok 1; langkuk; lantik*
curved knife *sanggot₁ 1*
curved tip *kukku₂ 1*
curving several ways *bunt'lled*
cushion *ū'an*
custom (habitual behavior) *kabiyaksahan; kal'ngnganan 1*
custom (norm) *addat 1*
custom (traditional) *usulan; ntan₂ 2; tuttulan*
customer (regular) *suki'*
cut (with sawing motion) *gōt-gōt 1*
cut (into pieces) *k'llot; bakbak; sampa'*
cut (obliquely) *deplas 1*
cut (wound) *bakat 1; pali' 1*
cut back (reduce) *dagdag₁*

cut cloth *tabas 1; simpay*
cut down (tree, bamboo) *puwad*
cut from main part *tompes; tebag 1.1; s'ppe' 1; kehet 1*
cut groove *tanghab₁; bulatuk*
cut hair *babbel; gunting 1.2*
cut in pieces *t'ttok 1.1; paghīk-hīk; kīs₁*
cut into *ōk 1; katama; utab*
cut into fillets *balang 1.1; ballul 1.1*
cut into lengths *p'ppot 1; gotong; hanggol 1.1*
cut into pieces *pagtebag-tebag*
cut into strips *jangat*
cut into wedges *pagsalik-salik; pidju 1.1*
cut notch *tekmas 1.1; tengham*
cut off end *punggut 1.2; t'ttop 1; tabtab 1*
cut open (a body) *t'ddak*
cut out *kebang 1.1; lenghob*
cut partway *sesek*
cut repeatedly *tadtad 1; t'ttok 1.1*
cut shavings from *hīk*
cut superficially *langgahi'*
cut teeth *s'mbut 2; empon 1.1*
cut through *k'ttob 1*
cut to pattern *tabas 1*
cut up *pagtebag-tebag*
cutlass *barung*
cutter (naval) *katel-katel*
cutting edge *taloman; solab₁ 1; kagonsanan*
cuttlebone *kulangkung*
cuttlefishes *kindat; kulabutan*
cyanide *sujum*
cyclone *badju*
cylinder (of an engine) *pupputan*
cyst *tangkekel 1; budjul₁*

# D d

dad *mma'*
dagger *punyal 1*
daily *llaw-llaw; pilmi-pilmi*
daily routines *t'ngge-tingkō'*
damage (n) *ka'at 1*
damage (v) *mula₁*
damage by handling *umas; lotok 1.1*
damage edge *kobet 1*
damaged *k'bbang; tanggal₁ 1; kobak 1; langgad 1.1*
damaged (of fruit) *kebang 1*
damaged by termites *gabuk*
damaged internally (by a blow) *tangka*
damaged item *patay₂*
damp (of clothing) *himāy; gimi'-gimi'*
damp (of salt) *tinu'*

damselfish *tibuk₁*
dance (Western style) *bayla*
dance and song performance *dalling*
dandruff *gulis-manuk 1; hagikgik; tai'-kōk*
danger; dangerous *piligdu 1.1; anib 1.1*
dangerous venture *susaed*
dangle *tayo; hellel; gollay*
dank *himāy; hami'-hami'*
dare (v) *tawakkal*
daring *bahani 1.1; esog 1.1*
dark (complexion) *ettom 1; erom; manis-erom*
dark of moon *lendoman*
darken (of light) *tangkob₁ 1; lendom 1.2; lempos*
darkness *do'om; lekot-lendom; lendom 1*
darkness (profound) *lendom bitu-bituhan*

darling *anak-mussa'*; *kakasi 1*

darling (voc) *nnong*; *nneng 2*; *dayang*

darn (mend) *ayum-ayum*

dash (hyphen) *baris*

dash (movement) *sa'ut 1.1*

date *pagtaratu*; *pitsa₂*

date (fruit) *hulma'*

daughter *anak d'nda*

daughter-in-law *ayuwan*

dawdle *pagene'-ene'*

dawdling *lallay*; *lahan 1*

dawn *bukis₁*; *k'llat llaw*; *subu-subu*; *abay-subu*

dawn prayer *subu₂ 2*

day after day *llaw ni llaw*

day after tomorrow *simuddai*

day before yesterday *bahangi-di'ilaw*

day of 24 hours *llaw₁ 1*; *bahangi 2*

daybreak *dai'-llaw*; *buka'-llaw*

daydream *ansong*

daytime *leke'-leke' llaw*

dazed *angol*; *bingaw*

dazzle *elong-elong mata*

dazzled *silaw 1*

dazzled (by a sight) *palu' 1.1*

dead *pugtul-napas*; *wapat*; *matay₁ 1*

dead (as a class) *mu'min*

dead (by spirit being) *lokob nyawa*

dead (by starvation) *bongtas 1.1*; *otas*

dead (by violence) *pagbugbug*; *bugtang*

dead (en masse) *p'llut₂*; *ligis₂*; *laglag 1*

dead (formal, of humans) *lipulmi'ad*; *aymulla*; *nahanat*

dead body (corpse) *patay₁ 1*

dead fish *patay-tunung*

dead or alive *llum-patay 1*

deadline *idda 1*

deadlocked *pagsigpit 2*

deaf *palpal 1*; *lantak*; *bisu 1.1*

deal (cards) *sabut₂*

deal in bulk *pono' 1.1*

deal with individually *paggintil*

dealer *palilitu*; *bangka₂ 1*

dear (expensive) *hunit 2.1*; *halga' 1.1*

dear (voc) *nneng 2*; *dayang*

dearly loved *sugpat nyawa*

death (instant) *bugtang*; *tubag*

death (natural) *patay-mural*

death (of fiancee) *balu-assang*

death (violent) *patay-bono'*

death from illness *patay-saki*

death from old age *patay-to'a*

death in childbirth *patay-sabil*; *patay-sahid*

death platform *palantayan*

death spirit *saitan-maut*

debate *pagsu'al*; *pagbagod*

debt *palutangan*; *utang 1*

debt of gratitude *buddi 1*; *entom buddi*

decant (pour into) *tumpa 1.1*; *tuwang*; *tuyung*; *hain*

decapitate *ponggol*

decaying *buhuk*; *buntu'₁ 1*; *halu' 1.1*

decaying smell *angil*; *angsod*

deceased (formal) *aymulla*; *nahanat*; *maruhum*

deceased spouse *balu 1*

deceit *tipu 1*

deceitful *sipi₁ 1*

deceive *limbung 1.1*; *labba'₁*; *balidja*; *akkal 1.1*

deceiver *pangangakkal*

deception *puting 1*; *saputi 1*

decide *tawhid 1.1*; *pene' 1.1*; *pagniyat*

decision (official) *indika 1*; *kahandak 1*

decisively *pagbaynat 1*; *patotos*

decking *kaka*; *g'ppang*

declaration *himumūngan*; *wa'ad*

declare *pasab'nnal*; *subahat₁*

declare God's oneness *pagtawhid*

decline (v) *suwalak*

decline from zenith *lemba*

decomposed *hansul₁ 1*

decorate *ari-ari 1.1*; *antuwilas 1.1*; *alat-alat*

decorate (face) *toktok*; *pagalis-alis*

decorated (clothing) *kappo'₂*

decoration *dekoresyon*; *ari-arihan*

decoration on sail *jambili*; *kabel-kabel*

decorative (fringe) *jambu 1*

decorative items *kabunyihan*; *pinduwa'*; *taliyan*

decorative lines (of boat) *tulis*

decorative motif *bunga-ammas*

decorative strip *bingkay*; *kebed-kebed₁*

decrease *dagdag₁*; *kō' 1.1*; *kulang₁ 1.2*

decree *kalima*; *indika 1*

dedicate *pasuku'*

dedication ceremony *baljanji' 2*

deduct *hilang*; *sulak₁*; *kulang₁ 1.2*

deeds *kahinangan*

deep *lalom₁ 1.1*; *lampo' 1*

deep (of color) *lutu'₂*

deep (of emotion) *pidpid isi*

deep (thinking) *lalom₂*

deeply *paheya₁*

deer *usa*

defeat *longkop 1.1*; *da'ug*

defecate *jamban 1*; *sungi' 1*

defect (n) *salla'₁ 1*; *sabanding*; *gora'₁ 1*; *sassat*

defend *t'ngge 2*

defend (against accusation) *palilu*; *da'awa 1.1*

defend in game *pagagpang*

defend oneself *atu 1.1*

defense (legal) *da'awa 1*

**defense (verbal)** *jawab₂ 1*
**defenseless** *pilluwang₂ 2*
**defensive weapon** *pangatu*
**defer (to later time)** *pagmahuli-llaw; tanggu 1.1; ddas 1.1*
**defer (to someone)** *ū'ū; deyo'₃ 2*
**defer payment** *tanggu 1.1; pautang*
**deference marker** *kono' 2; pa'in₂ 2; da'a busung*
**deferral** *pangawal; lehod 1*
**defiant** *atakabbul; tuwas-pentol*
**deficit** *lapis₅*
**defiled** *tamak 1.1; batal*
**definite** *tugila' 1; tantu 1.1; tuman 1*
**definite about** *pagniyat*
**definitely** *patotos; musti-musti; sabuli-buli*
**definition (meaning)** *hati 1; kahulugan; ma'ana₁ 1*
**deflated** *k'ppos 1.1; k'ppel*
**deflect (harmful force)** *tampan 1.1; pagkobol 1.1*
**deflect with hands** *sangga 2*
**defoliate** *urut*
**deformed** *pekok; dukkug 1.1*
**deformity** *sahili'*
**defraud** *kidjib; tipu 1.1*
**defy** *sagga' 1.1*
**degenerate person** *ga'ira*
**degrade** *dali'it*
**dehusk** *bunut 1.1; hampa' 1.1*
**dehydrated** *t'ggang₁; pekot*
**deity** *Tuhan*
**dejected** *diskared; mandā'-dā'*
**delaminate** *lapes; kanit 1*
**delay (n)** *tanggu 1; lehod 1*
**delay (v)** *pagli'i-li'i; tagga 1.1*
**delayed** *ddas 1.2; tahāl; lanat*
**delegate** *wakil 1.1*
**delete** *papas₁ 1.1; erēs*
**deliberately** *pagbaynat 1; tantu 1.2; tu'ud₁ 1.1*
**delicious** *sarap₁; mamis₁ 1.1; lanab*
**delighted** *kōg 2*
**delighted (sexually)** *gila*
**delineate** *gudlis 1.1; guhit 1.1*
**deliver from** *liyus 1.2; lappas₂ 1.1; puwas₁ 2*
**deliver to** *nde'; pasampay; pat'kka*
**delouse** *siksik; nda'-kutu*
**delousing comb** *pagkutu 1; sūd*
**delude** *akkal 1.1*
**demand (brideprice)** *sokat₁ 1*
**demand payment** *sukut 1*
**demand too much** *kugut₂*
**demanding** *dakag; salut 1*
**demeanour** *laku-tabi'at; addat-tabi'at*
**demented** *kangog*
**demigods** *tuhan-tuhan*
**demolished** *langkat 1; lapnas 1*

**demon** *saitan; hantu 1; hibilis*
**demon possession** *sangon₂ 1.1*
**demonstrate (protest)** *hiluhala' 1.2*
**demoted** *lessad*
**demure** *p'mpon 1; hongpot*
**denial** *da'awa 1*
**denim** *ma'ung*
**denounce** *limut 1.1; kulli' 1.1*
**dense growth** *kasob; herot*
**densely covered** *timbakkol*
**dental tool** *dadarut*
**dented** *lompeng 1; l'ppog; logpok 1*
**dentures** *malpel*
**deny (a request)** *paggat; pag'mbal 1.1; pagmarī'*
**deny (accusation)** *palilu*
**deny share** *manulus 1.1*
**depart** *tulak₁ 1.1; k'llo'₂; la'an 1*
**department store** *basal₂*
**depend on** *kamdos₁; sangdol 1; andol 1*
**depends** *depende*
**depigmentation** *panaw 1; āp-āp 1; kamuti'*
**depleted** *kobak 2*
**depopulated** *p'ggal; do'ag*
**deportment** *laku-tabi'at*
**deposit (financial)** *tinga 1*
**depravity** *kala'atan*
**depression (in sand or soil)** *powak; k'bbong-k'bbong*
**deprive of shelter** *tanya₁*
**deprived of necessities** *kasigpitan; kati'ilan*
**deprived of speech** *kamal; kowam 1*
**depth (as measured)** *t'kkaran; lalom₁ 1*
**depths (of sea)** *kalaloman; timbang₂*
**deputy** *wakil 1; munari 2*
**deranged** *lungay sipat; buriru*
**deride** *poway-poway; udju'*
**dermatitis** *ugud*
**descend** *deyo'₁ 1.1; hollo; duwa'i; pagpatilossok*
**descend (from higher source)** *tulun₁ 1.2*
**descend a slope** *lūd*
**descend from (ancestry)** *tubu' 1.1*
**descendant (of the Prophet)** *salip*
**descendants** *tubu' 1; mpu*
**descent line** *laha'₂*
**describe details** *papata 1.1; uki'-uki'*
**description** *kahantang*
**desert** *paslangan 1*
**deserted** *tannay-tannay; p'ggal; t'nnaw-t'nnaw 1*
**deserts (what one deserves)** *kisas₂; sugpak 1*
**desiccate** *puhi; patoho'*
**design (n)** *ari-arihan*
**design (pattern)** *ladjawan; suntu'an*
**designated space** *huwang₁ 1*
**desire (n)** *napsu 1; bilahi 1; baya' 1*

desire (sexual) *hōp baya'; ba'is*

desire (v) *lingit 1; dandam; hawa 1.3*

desirous *hawa 1.1; hinbaya'*

desist *dohong; palo' 1.1; hogga' 1*

despair *himāt pangatayan*

desperate movement *kawas*

despise *di'in-di'in; halipulu 1.1; mahadja'*

dessert (food) *suman; pamunglaw*

destination *kat'kkahan₁*

destine; destiny *ganta'₂; karal 1.1; t'ppong 2*

destiny (bad) *jari₄ 1.1*

destiny (marital) *suratan*

destitute *kettak; kabus; pihit*

destroy *paka'at*

destroyed *lopot 1; luhu'₂ 1; lapnas 1*

detach from *butawan 1.1; l'kkat₂ 1.1*

detached *okat₂ 1; tangsu' 1; tungkas*

detailed *tugila' 1; tutat 1*

detain *tahan₂ 1; tagga 1.1*

detect *tilas₁; timtim; tatab*

deteriorate *duhun 1*

determination *tawhid 1*

determine contents *pagletok*

determine on *niyat 1.1; angut; pagsinta'*

determined *tuyu' 1; kuwat-kuwat 1; tuman-tuman*

detest *j'ngngit; b'nsi 1.2*

detonate *h'lling₂ 1*

detour *salema' 1; libut 1.1; likuwad 1*

detract from value *powera 1.1*

devastated *ka'at 1.1*

develop (become mature) *sangpot 1.1*

develop into *hinang₁ 1.2*

develop well *jatu 1*

deviant *sumbang; balig; daiyus*

deviate *sulekma'; sā'₁ 1.2; beklo'*

devil *hibilis*

devoid of people *tannay-tannay; t'nnaw-t'nnaw 1*

devoted (religious) *pagma'aripat; pagsanittiya; pagibarat*

devoted to *umid 1; lūt₂ 1*

devour *t'llon; sangkiyam*

devout *pagammal; pagta'at*

dew *alu'₂ 1*

dexterous *alistu 1*

diabetes *kawit₂ 1*

diacritic (mark over vowel) *baris*

dial (watch or clock) *lilus*

dialect *bahasa₁; h'lling₁ 2*

diamond *intan*

diamond-shaped *dinglu' 1*

diaper *lampin₂ 1*

diaphragm (lower rib cage) *kōk-atay*

diarrhea *pagloros-loros; pagsungi'-sungi'*

dibble stick *tugbal*

dice *kembo' 1; legot 2*

dice (cut finely) *k'llot*

dice spinning board *balad*

die *b'kkat napas; pole'-lahat; matay₁ 1*

die in defense *sahid*

die slowly *ahat-ahat*

die suddenly *tubag*

difference *bidda' 1*

different *saddī 1*

differentiate *papagbidda'; silang₁ 1.1*

difficult *dipisil*

difficult person *panalod*

difficulties *gandang-gumbala'*

difficulty *sigpit 1; problema; hunit 1*

diffuse (v) *pulag-pulag; hangsu 1.1*

dig *kali; kalut*

dig over *lungkad 2*

digest (v) *tunaw 2*

digging tool *piku; lalandak; pala*

digit (finger) *anak-tangan; gulamay 1*

digit (numeral) *umbul 1*

dignified *pagbabaran 1.1*

dignity *kapaga'a; pagkamanusiya'*

dilapidate *basak*

dilatory (slow) *lahan 1; kaku'; lehod 1.1*

diligent *tukid 1; sugsig 1; tebot*

dim light *pagsiraw-siraw; damal*

dimension across *lambu 1*

diminish *diki' 1.1; kō' 1.1; kulang₁ 1.2*

diminish in intensity *keyas; siha'-siha'; hulaw*

diminish little by little *paglaginit 1.1*

dimly seen *ahud-ahud 1*

dimples *kandi'is₂*

dim-sighted *bulahaw*

dinghy *tempel-tempel; buti*

dip food in liquid *loho' 1.1; t'nno'; bahug 1.1*

dip into *dulis*

dipper *gayung 1; tambu' 1; sauk 1*

direct descendants *anak-mpu*

direction *tampal 1; lahi₃*

directly *langkus 1.1; diretso; tūy 1.1*

dirt *moseng 1; l'mmi' 1*

dirt in liquid *lagod₁; aut 1; lobog 1*

dirty *lumu'*

disabled *keme; ku'il*

disadvantaged *salla' 1.1; kulang-kulang 1*

disagree *pags'ndal; pagsīng-sūd; pagbagod*

disagreement *pagpayod 1; pasu'alan*

disappear *telop 1.1; liyaw 1; pagtawap*

disappoint *paggambahan*

disappointed *hayak-hayak; dapat₁ 1.2*

disappointment *dapat₁ 1*

disarranged *bulangkayat; bulaksay 1*

disassemble *langkat 1.1*

disassociate *kiyas*

disaster *kajahatan; naja'; pa'al 1*

disavow *sulak₂*

disbelieve *jakki 1; dusta' 1.1*

discard *timan₁; pamuwangkan*

discern *tilas₁; panhid*

disciple *mulid*

discipline (v) *pissoko'; lubak₁; bi'at 1.1*

disclaim knowledge *sitta'a*

disclaimer (of responsibility) *kono' 1*

disclose (information) *tubad; pata'u*

disclose secret matters *pagjama'-jama'*

discoloration (teeth) *balakang 1; baka'₂ 1*

discolored (bruise) *lahod 1.1*

discomfited *paki' 1*

discomfort *salinggā*

disconnected *latas₁; tangsu' 1; tungkas*

discontinue *hoka'*

discordant *lagaw; biyul*

discount (n) *kō' 1*

discount (v) *powera 1.1*

discouraged *pagkalammahan; diskared*

discourteous *halipulu 1; taga'-taga'*

discover *bāk₁*

discover (information) *ta'u₁ 1.2*

discredit *tutul; s'ndal 1.1*

discreet *hantap 1*

discriminate (between alternatives) *pasaddī; pinig*

discrimination (social) *pagkengkeng pagbokol*

discs (pool game) *kulang₂*

discuss *pagbilma'arup; pagisun 1.1; paru*

discuss in private *pagsīb; sipuk-sipuk; pagungsik*

discussion *suli-suli 1; paggara' 1; palkala' 1*

disease *saki 1*

disease of mouth *obe' 1*

disembodied *lanyap 1; liyaw 1*

disentangle *usay 1*

disgrace *hina'*

disgust *sāk₁ 1*

disgusted *la'at-ludja'*

disgusting *sakkal; sammal 1; saggan*

dish *lai'; lenga'*

dish up (food) *haun₁*

disheartened *lamma 1*

dishevelled *gosang-gosang; bulangkayat*

dishonor (v) *hina'*

dish-shaped *k'bbong*

disinclined *lisu'; takal; hukaw 1.1*

disintegrate *pagkabila'-bila'; p'kkal 1*

disinter *angkat₂*

dislike *b'nsi 1; j'ngngit; hukaw 1*

dislocated *pangsut 1; possat*

dislocated (bones) *pisu'; pi'ul; pittay 1.1*

dismantle *langkat 1.1; jagjag 1.1; lubu₂ 1.1*

dismantled *bulangkayat; larak 1.1*

dismay (excl) *arōy*

disobedient *tuwas-pentol; gagga*

disorder (community) *halubilu*

disordered *jagjag 1; bulangkayat; tulabid*

disperse *pagl'kkat; pagpaopēt*

dispersed *kanat 1; pulag 1; pāg*

displaced *possat*

display (v) *pagpa'nda'-pa'nda'*

display characteristic *bowa₄*

display charms *pagalti-alti 1.1; pagpaelle'-elle'*

display publicly *pagmairan 1.1*

displeased *tumpalak 1*

displeasing *kagit atay 1*

disposition (behavior) *hudjidjat; laku; palangay*

disposition (character) *tabi'at*

dispute *pagjawab 1; bagod; pasu'alan*

dispute charge or accusation *pagda'awa 1*

dispute responsibility *pagampa-ampa; hili*

dispute responsibilty *pagbintu*

disquiet *sasat 1*

disregard *sagad 1; pasibukut 1; lehom*

disrepair *gubal; lorak; lubu₂ 1*

disreputable (appearance) *kuligi'₁ 1*

disrespect *di'in-di'in; halipulu 1; hampul-hampul 1*

disseminate *buhanyag; hayag*

dissolve *tinu'; tunaw 1; tadjul*

dissolve in mouth *ligid₁*

distance (unit of) *pistulan; panimbakan*

distant *lawak; tegob-tegob; tā 1.1*

distant future *pupud-llaw*

distant islands *lahat-diyata'*

distaste for *hukaw 1; takal*

distend (body parts) *gottay; bakag₂*

distended (of corpse) *butud; b'ngkak; himutud*

distinct *silang₁ 1; sila' 1; hangpat 1*

distinct from *papagbidda'*

distinctive (appearance) *panalung; tungkilang; gindanan*

distinctive (of sound) *hapal 2; nyala-nyala*

distinguish *gintil 1.1; sila' 1.1; silang₁ 1.1*

distort *pagpiyut; lompeng 1.1*

distract *kibad; lemo-lemo*

distractions *ligap 1; kidjut-kahibal*

distress *susa 1; sukkal 1*

distressed *gagal₂; gupu; p'ddi' napas*

distribute *paglamit-lamit 1.1; bahagi' 1.3*

distribute equally *topod 1.1*

district *jadjahan; paglahat 1; baranggay*

distrustful *hanggaw₁ 1; paghubang-hubang*

disturb *gabla'; sasat 1.1; hibal 1.1*

disturb surface (of water) *pakataw*

disturbance *hiluhala' 1; sasaw 1; lengog 1*

disturbed *jabu 1; bungkal₂ 1; dongkag*

disturbed (by sleep-talking) *dabdab*
disturbed (of sea) *haus 1*
ditch *pasuhan*
dither *duwa-ruwa*
dive *tuhun 1; sāp₁; lorok 1*
dive for *lurup*
dive for a living *pagtutuhun*
dive for fish *sowet*
diverge *kabig; salema' 2; liku'*
diverge (mutual) *pagl'kkat; pagpaopēt*
diverse things *inda wa barapa ginis*
diversity *pagbidda'an*
divert (attention) *kibad; lemo-lemo*
divert from *sapehak*
divest (clothing) *hurus 1.1*
divide (partition) *h'nggol*
divide into groups *paggihay 1*
divide into packages *pagputus-putus 1.1*
divide into parts *pagpōng-pōng 1.1*
divide into strips *sanggi' 1.1*
divide up *bahagi' 1.2; pagsuku'*
divination *limal; kamot*
divination (devices) *putika'an; pag'nda'an*
divine favor (n) *sapa'at₁ 1; barakat 1*
divine future events *alamat₁; putika'*
diving gear *busu*
diving goggles *tipara 1*
diving weight *babet*
division of Koran *patiha'*
divorce (pending) *timan-gantung*
divorce (v) *pagtallak; butas 1.1; timan₂*
divorce fee *tugnus₂ 1*
divorced person *bitu'anun*
divulge *kuhi₂*
dizzy *angol; uling; baliyang*
djinn *jīn 1*
do a good job *pahāp₂ 2*
do in person *pagbabaran-baran; pagtampal*
do not (command) *da'a 1*
do routinely *patuntul*
do something *hinang₁ 1.2*
do well (of a task) *pahāp₂ 2*
do with force *lubak₂ 1*
do without restraint *pagkanam*
docile *p'mpon 1*
dock (shipping) *jambatan*
dock a boat *dunggu' 1; dukla' 1*
doctor *doktol; pananambal*
document *sulat-kataddangan; sairola; pās*
dodge *s'nnok; tangkis 1.1.1*
dog *ero' 1*
dogged (stubborn) *mumut*
doggedly *pakuwat*
doll *munyeka; datu'-datu'*

dolphinfish *lali*
dolphins *lomba-lomba; bbung*
dome of skull *bukakkal; peya'-peya' kōk*
domesticated animals *hayop*
dominant *aguwanta 1; ga'os 1.1*
dominion *milikan; okoman*
domino *duminu*
donation *sarakka 1; pamuwan 1; panulung*
done and still the case *wa'i; hē'₁ 2*
done well *sangkahāpan*
donkey *kura'-asnu*
don't *da'a 1*
don't know *inday; sitta'a*
don't worry *mbal du*
donut *tabid-tabid*
door *tambol 1; lawang 1*
doorpost *lusuk-lusuk*
doorway *bowa'-lawang*
dorsal fin *s'kke*
dotted *b'ttik 1.1*
dottyback fishes *kuhapo'-samehakan; tunggu'-langat-langat*
double *doble 1.1; lapis₃ 1.1*
double layer *pagduwallapis*
double marriage *pagtumbuk-s'ngkol; paginubusan*
double skin *kulap 1*
doubt someone's word *jakki 1; dusta' 1.1*
doubtless *tantu 1.1; manyatakan; musti-musti*
dough *addunan*
doves *malapati; assang; manatad*
dowel *tulagsok 1; pasok 1; sibukaw 1.1*
down *deyo'₁ 1*
down (fine hair) *bulbul 1*
down payment *panau'; bintak; tinga 1; patunang*
downcast *lamma 1*
downhill *paglūran*
downstream side *sohonayan; tape'an*
downward slope *lūran*
dowry (bride-wealth) *ungsud₁ 1*
doze *paglilap; tuli-sowa*
dozen *dosena*
dozen *dosena*
drag (haul) *hella'; guyud 1; konot₂*
drag (of anchor) *lagesles 2*
drag ashore *dahik*
drag feet *sagudsud; paglallay-lallay*
drag nets *siyul 1; sinsoro 1*
dragging along a surface *paglagedled 1*
dragon (mythical) *naga 1*
dragonflies *ampan*
dragonflys *banag*
drain hole (in a container) *ebol-ebol*
drained (of resources) *kobak 2*
drape (v) *sablay; salay₁ 1.2*
drat! *hē*

**draw a line (across a surface)** *gudlis 1.1;
  sangat 1.1; guhit 1.1*
**draw bow across (violin)** *gōt-gōt 2*
**draw lots** *pagko'ot-ko'ot 1.1*
**draw near to** *sekot 1.1; t'ppung 1.1; t'ppi' 1*
**draw water** *nduk*
**drawer** *ungsud-ungsud*
**draw-knife** *gahud-gahud₁*
**drawn out (of speech)** *langguyud 1*
**drawn out (of time)** *alal 1; lanat*
**dread** *leya'-leya'; umagad 1.1; damag*
**dream** *palambung; uppi 1*
**dredge for fishtrap** *badja' 1.1*
**dregs** *angkas₁ 1*
**drenched** *tomog; bugbug₁*
**dress (n)** *bistiru; palda*
**dress hair** *suray 1.1*
**dressed** *s'mmek 1.1; hakos*
**dribble** *pagbuhelo; laway₁ 1*
**dried (of crops)** *bentol; mali-mali*
**dried (scab)** *l'kkung 1*
**dried (wood)** *t'llas; tigas*
**dried fish (for preserving)** *sampila'₁ 1; peyad 1;
  pundang 1; lumay*
**dried out** *t'ggang₁; panggang₂ 1; lengas₁*
**drift (v)** *laran; hanut; tagudtud*
**drift anchor** *tangkal₂ 1*
**drift fishing** *pamalastik; laway₂ 1; paranas*
**drill (soldiers)** *pagmahil*
**drill (tool)** *likup 1*
**drill a hole** *likup 1.1; pa'at 1.1; barena 1.1*
**drill bit** *tōng-barena*
**drink** *inum 1*
**drink (halo-halo)** *sindul 1*
**drink from water-jar** *tunghab 1*
**drinking container** *panginuman*
**drip (v)** *p'ttak 1.1; tū'; tis*
**drip off a surface** *titis 1.1*
**drive away** *siga' 1.1; dūy; t'ggal; singga'-singga'*
**drive in (of rain)** *tampiyas 1.1*
**drive into ground** *ddol-ddol; osol 1.1*
**drive into socket** *palpal 1.1*
**drive together** *s'ssol₂ 1.1; illig*
**driven by storm** *paggoyak*
**driver** *draybel*
**drive-shaft** *batang-ehe*
**drizzle (rain)** *pitik-pitik 1.1; bonok-bonok*
**drool** *buhelo 1.1*
**droop** *toyok; kopeng*
**droop (of eyes)** *k'llip; luyu'*
**drop (v)** *hantak₁ 1; hūg₁ 1.1; latak*
**drop off (deliver)** *lagid 1.1*
**dropped (from grasp)** *kabba*
**drops of liquid** *p'ttak 1; pitik-pitik 1*

**droves** *pagba'an 1*
**drown** *lembo 1*
**drowsy** *lilap; karu' 1.1; t'ppi'-tuli*
**drug addict** *dragadik*
**drugstore** *palmasiya*
**drumming sound** *kulagpak*
**drums (n)** *jabu-jabu; tambul; gandang 1*
**drumstick** *titik 1*
**drunkard** *paglalango*
**dry (adj)** *toho'*
**dry by fire** *dangu 1.1; dangka₂ 1.1; dama 1.1*
**dry in sun** *llaw₂ 1.1; ta'adjil 2*
**dry in sun or wind** *buwad; puhi*
**dry land** *alam diyata'; gintana'an*
**dry out; dry up** *titis 1; patoho'*
**drying out (from cooking)** *anok 1*
**drying racks** *tasikan; ampang*
**dry-love (grass)** *lukut-lappas*
**dubitive particle (maybe)** *bahā'*
**duck (bird)** *etek*
**duck (call word)** *bī-bī 1*
**duck head (to avoid hitting)** *handuk 1*
**dues** *pagbayad 1*
**dugong (manatee, sea-cow)** *duyung 1*
**dugout canoe** *bangka'*
**dull (blade or point)** *poppol 1*
**dull (mentally)** *hibang-hibang; bobo*
**dumb person** *umaw 1*
**dumbfounded** *kowam 1*
**dump something** *timan₁*
**dun for payment (v)** *sukut 1*
**dung** *tai' 2*
**dunk** *butag; t'nno'; bahug 1.1*
**dupe (v)** *kidjib; akkal 1.1*
**durable** *tatas 1.1; pagon₁ 1.1; anagtol*
**duration (of an action)** *sinabu 1.1; t'ggol 1*
**durian** *duliyan*
**during** *sasang; pasalta'; baba; sabu 1*
**dusk** *logob-logob; sū'-palita'an; abay-kohap*
**dusk prayer** *magrib 1*
**dusky complexion** *erom*
**dust** *puling 1; hamud-hamud; bagunbun*
**duster** *sasapu; tarapu 1*
**dustpan** *kuntaw₁*
**Dutch** *balanda'₂*
**duty to reciprocate** *entom buddi*
**dwarf** *maya-maya₁*
**dwell** *okom 1; paglahat 1.1*
**dwelling** *luma'*
**dye** *anjibi 1*
**dying (of wind phase)** *tape'-baliyu*
**dynamite** *timbak 1*
**dynamite (fishing)** *timbak-daing*
**dynamited fish** *hantak₂*

**dysentery** *kolera*

**dysmenorrhea (menstrual cramps)** *langgom*

# E e

**each** *kaniya-kaniya*; *dangan-parangan*

**each other** *dangan-duwa*

**eager** *hungun*; *hutu*

**eagle** *belle'₁*; *mana'ul*

**ear** *talinga 1*

**ear infection** *antil 1*; *tolek 1*

**ear stud** *bāng₂*

**earlier** *dahū 1*; *insini'*

**early** *awal₂ 1*; *k'llaw*

**early morning** *dai'-llaw*

**early teenage girl** *budjang-budjang*

**earn interest** *anak₃ 1.1*

**earnest** *tukid 1*; *tuyu' 1*

**earnings** *gadji 1*; *untung₁ 1*

**earrings** *domelo*; *pinting*; *anting-anting 1*; *subang*

**ear-shell** *lappas₁*

**earth (as the abode of the deceased)** *gumi 1*

**earth (planet)** *alam₁*; *dunya*

**earth (soil)** *tana'₁ 1*

**earth (world)** *babaw-dunya*

**earthquake** *linug₁*; *jogjog deyom dunya*

**earthworm** *kalog-tana'*

**earwig** *sipit-sipit₂*

**ease (n)** *kalimayahan*; *luhay₂ 1.1*; *kasannangan*

**ease off (of weather)** *hopay*

**ease off; ease up** *hoka'*; *keyas*; *hoblas 1*

**ease up (of sorrow)** *keyas atay*

**easily done** *mura*; *luhay₂ 1*

**east** *sobangan*

**east wind** *timul*

**eat** *kakan 1*; *lallan*; *kakan 1*

**eat before fast** *pagsahul*

**eat greedily** *damba'₁ 1.1*; *kanam*; *boslad*

**eat in company with** *salu 1*

**eat raw (of fish)** *kilaw 1*

**eat raw (of food)** *inta'*

**eat snack** *tupas₁ 1.1*

**eat with a sauce** *lawal 1.1*

**eat with fingers** *lokom*; *sobo'*

**eat with skin on** *l'kkob*

**eaten by shark** *kalitan 3*

**eating space** *pagkakanan*

**eating utensils** *pamangan*

**eaves** *silingan*

**eavesdrop** *tongop₂*

**ebb (of tide)** *t'bba 1.1*; *la'ang 1*; *kō' 1.1*; *pipit₂ 1.1*

**ebony** *akal-bahal*

**eclipse (sun or moon)** *lahu' 1*

**economical** *bista₂ 1*

**economical (fuel use)** *sinu'*

**economical (sparing)** *kimmat 1*; *k'mmit 1*

**ecstatic** *hōp₂*; *hūg bulan*

**eddy (current movement)** *paglimpowak*; *paglimbokay*; *salekolan*

**edema** *buntu'-buntu'*

**edge** *bihing₁ 1*; *bihing-bowa'*

**edge (launch side, for sitting)** *gibayan*

**edge (of fabric)** *l'ppit 2*

**edge (of reef)** *angan*

**edible (approved by religious law)** *halal 1*

**edict** *palman 1*; *uldin 1*; *pituwa 1*

**edify** *pahāp₂ 1*

**educated** *langkat-samat*

**education (religious)** *pangadji'*; *madrasa*; *pagguru*

**education (secular)** *pangiskul*

**eels** *kasī*; *endong*; *nipa'-nipa' 1*

**effective** *gonsan*; *bogbog₂*; *jatu 1*

**effective (speech)** *talom bowa'*; *paul*; *labas₂ 1*

**effeminate** *bantut 1*

**effigy** *bahala'₂*; *ta'u-ta'u₁*

**effort** *kinosog*; *sangsā'*

**effortlessly** *luhay-luhay*

**egg** *nt'llo 1*; *iklug*

**egg cowrie** *kahentong*

**egg sac** *pulling*

**egg-beater** *giling-giling*

**eggplant** *talum*

**egg-shaped** *tibokkong*

**egret** *kallo'*

**Egypt** *Misil*

**Egyptian ruler** *pira'un*

**eight** *walu'*

**eighty** *walumpū'*

**either** *atawa*; *ka₂*

**either..or** *na ka..na ka*

**eject** *ludja' 1.2*

**eke out** *pagdangkuri'*; *inut*

**elapse** *labay₂*; *liban 1*

**elastic** *goma₁ 1*; *hinit 1*

**elbow** *siku*; *buli'-siku*

**elbow (inside of joint)** *lokonan*; *lo'atan*

**elders** *kama'asan*; *kamatto'ahan*

**elders (parents)** *matto'a 2*

**eldest daughter** *siyaka 1*; *arung*

**eldest son** *oto' 2*; *siyaka 1*

**electric current** *bagnet*

**electric wire** *korente 1*

**elegant** *himpit; jalang$_1$; polma 1.1*

**elements (basics)** *hinasil*

**elephant** *gadja*

**elephant's ear (wild yam)** *hupi'-badjang*

**elephant's foot (wild lily)** *bagong$_1$*

**elevate** *angkat$_1$ 1.1; bayaw*

**eligible (in marriage)** *pata'$_1$*

**elliptical** *tibokkong*

**elope** *saggaw-sangom; pagsaggaw-ubus; paglahi 1.1*

**eloquent** *bibissalahun*

**else** *atawa*

**elucidate** *hangpat 1.1*

**elude** *illag 1; lahi$_1$*

**elusive** *adla*

**emaciated** *kittay; kulagkag; titis 2*

**e-mail** *īmēl*

**embalm** *kapul 1.1*

**embankment** *pampang*

**embarrass (v)** *pakaiya'; paki' 1.1*

**embarrassed** *iya'; tamparasa; maru 1*

**embers** *bale$_5$; unggun 1; baga 1*

**embezzle** *kustaw*

**embrace** *hulid 1.1; golgol; gapus*

**embroider** *ingkahi 1.1; bulda 1.1*

**embryo** *laha'$_3$*

**emerge** *tuwa' 1; luwas$_1$ 1; bulat*

**emery paper** *katas-balan*

**eminence** *bantug 1*

**emit heat and light** *silak 1.1*

**emit odor** *bbu 1.1; angsod; hangsu 1.1*

**emit vapor** *asu-asu 1.1; husbu 1.1*

**emotional distress** *tunuk*

**emotionally hurt** *bakat atay*

**emotionally stirred** *pagbikannol; hansul atay*

**emotions** *pangatayan*

**empathize** *andu'-andu'*

**emperor fishes (see kutambak)**

**emphatically** *du 1; isāb*

**emphysema** *pagagaw-napas*

**employee** *bata'an; tendog*

**employer** *bōs; nakura'*

**emporium** *tinda-basal*

**empowered** *wakil 1.2*

**empty (of contents)** *k'ppos 1; k'ppel*

**empty (of people)** *tannay-tannay; t'nnaw-t'nnaw 1*

**empty bowels** *haram 1.2; sungi' 1*

**empty out** *duwasay$_2$*

**emulate (qualities of)** *sunud 1.1; s'ppu; sengod*

**en masse** *sika-..-an*

**enchant (sorcery)** *pat'nna' hikmat; hinang-hinang$_1$; pantak 1.1*

**encircle** *lengkol 1.1; lekos 1.3; tibulung 1.1*

**enclose** *likus 1; koral 1.1; ād 1.1; kumbis 1.1; apis 1.1*

**enclose for privacy** *bilik 1.1; libun*

**enclosure** *lekoman*

**encounter (meet)** *langgal$_2$ 2; bāk$_2$*

**encourage** *hogot nyawa*

**encrust (v)** *l'kkung 1.1*

**encrusted (with growth)** *ligay*

**end (discussion)** *utas 2.1; tabtab 2.1*

**end (n)** *tōng$_1$*

**end badly** *pagkangī'-ngī'*

**end of lunar month** *matay-bulan*

**end of world** *kiyamat 1*

**end point** *tobtob 1*

**end result** *katumariyahan; kamattihan 1; kat'kkahan$_2$*

**end someone's life** *k'ttu' nyawa; momos$_2$*

**endanger** *mula$_1$*

**endearment terms** *arung; nneng 2; dayang*

**endeavour** *ahat 1.1; sulay$_1$ 1.1*

**ended (concluded)** *ubus$_1$ 1; tabtab 2*

**endlessly** *saumul-umul; salama-lama*

**endosperm (of coconut)** *bōt$_1$ 1*

**endowment** *tulun$_1$ 1; tubus$_2$ 1; tugu*

**endure pain, hardship** *pagmalasahi; tahan-tahan; sandal 1.1*

**endure patiently** *pagsabal; bāng-bāng$_1$*

**endure to end** *tatas 1.2; ddas 1*

**enduring** *kakkal; taptap 1; dorog$_1$*

**enemy** *kuntara 1; banta 1*

**energetic** *kuyas 1; kuseseyang 1*

**energetic (of action)** *puspus$_1$; paspas$_1$; sikad 1; paslod 1.2*

**energy** *kuwat*

**enfeebled** *lamma 2.1; pilay*

**enfold (wrap in)** *p'kkos 1.1*

**enforce** *logos 1; lalat$_1$ 1*

**engage a performer** *tangkap*

**engaged to marry** *pagtunang*

**engine** *makina 1; pupputan*

**English language** *ingglis; anggalis*

**engrave** *garing-garing*

**engulfed (in work)** *golpe$_2$*

**enjoy life** *pagbunyi-bunyi*

**enjoy through time** *hulak 1.1*

**enjoy wealth** *pagsauragal 1.1; pagalta'an 1*

**enjoyable** *lami; tundun buwahan*

**enjoyment** *kakoyagan; kalamihan*

**enlarge** *paheya$_2$*

**enlarged skull** *kilā-luku; kulang-kilā*

**enlighten** *pahati 1.1*

**enlist help** *dangin*

**enmity** *pagbanta 1*

**enough** *ustu; sarang 1*

**enrich** *paraya 1.1*

enrol *inrol 1.1*

enslave *pagpa'ata*; *banyaga' 1.1*

ensue *sunu'*

entangled *sambon 1.1*

enter *deyom 1.1*; *asok 1*; *sōd 1*; *hōp₁ 1*

enter lighted area *sindung₁*; *silung₁*

entered (by spirit being) *sōd 2*; *sangon₂ 1*

entertain (guests) *latal 1.1*; *labot*; *jamu 1.1*

entertainment *ongka' 1.1*; *kalamihan*

enthusiastic *kuseseyang 1*

entice *bidjak 1.1*; *kuti-kuti*; *abiyug*

enticement *panuba*

entire *lapus*; *kamemon 1.1*; *lungbus*

entire area *kaluha'an*

entire distance *katāhan*

entire world *mpat pidju alam*

entirely *pareyo'-pariyata'*; *lullun 1*

entourage *pangabay*

entrails (of trepang) *atay dugu-dugu*

entrance *lawang 1*

entrust *sangdol 1.1*

entrust to *pagtawakkal 1.1*; *andol 1*

entwine *kokos₁ 1.1*; *bodbod₁ 1.1*; *lebod 1.1*

enumerate *tutat 1.1*; *anyak-anyak*; *uki'-uki'*

enunciate *hapal 2*; *hangpat 1.1*

envelop (by wrapping) *pugung*

enveloped *putus 1.1*; *ledled 1.1*; *pulipus 1*

envious *napsu 1.1*; *bahaya*; *imbū*

environs *sakalingkal*; *katilibut*

envy *ihid*; *imbū*; *abuggu'*

epic song *kata-kata*

epidemic *bonglay 1*; *musiba*

epileptic *bawi-bawi*; *sawan-sawan*

epiphyte (plant on tree) *dirit₂*

epistle *sulat 1*

epoch *masa 1*

equal (adj) *tabul₁ 1*; *topod 1*

equal (n) *sali' 1*; *suga-suga₂*; *sibu' 1*; *dora' 1*

equal in height *pagtopad 1*

equal in value *pagtupan*

equal with *sambal₁*

equality (marker) *gin*; *sama-*

equally well *sangkahāpan*

equilibrium *pagtimbang 1*; *pagsalay₂*

equipment *kapanyapan*; *kalangkapan₁*; *kakaya'an*

equipped *panyap 1*

equivalent *da- 2*; *sali'an*

era *masa 1*; *timpu 1*; *jāman*

erase *p'dda 1*; *papas₁ 1*

eraser *eresel*

erect (penis) *ddong*

erect (v) *pat'ngge*

erect post *osol 1.1*

ergative particle *he' 1*

err *sā'₁ 1.2*

errand-boy *bata'an*

erratic *patay-patay*; *pagpalta*

error *salla'₁ 1*; *sā'₁ 1*

erupting *bustak*

escalating *lekles*

escape *lahi₁*; *l'ppa*

escape notice *s'llu 1*

escort (v) *bowa₃*; *sehe' 1.1*

esophagus *s'bbat 1*; *k'llong*

esoteric knowledge *ilmu' 1*

especially *luba'*; *ya lagi'na*; *muna-muna 1.1*

espouse *pah'nda 2*; *pah'lla 2*

essence (of something said) *salawat₂*

essence (spiritual) *sumangat 1*

essential nature *jantang*; *jāt₁*; *hudjidjat*

essential requirements *kahirupan*; *napaka*

establish *pat'nna'*; *pat'ngge*

esteem *ammal₂*; *loman 1.1*

esteemed *heya ma atay*

estimate *kimmat 2*; *kumpas₁*; *kira*

estimated *bale₄*

estuary *sowang*

etch *garing-garing*

eternal *kakkal*; *saumul-umul*

ethnic group *bangsa₁*

eunuch *kabili*

European *balanda'₂*; *bangsa-pote'*; *Milikan*

evacuate *pagdo'ag*; *pagpāgan*

evacuee *bakwet*

evade *s'llu 1*; *illag 1*

evaluate *bista₁*; *kumpas₁*; *kira-kira*

evaporated *gagas*; *papas₁ 1*

even (in height) *solsol*

even (level) *pantay*; *datag*; *pangtad*

even as... so also *sangka-...sangka-*

even if *sandu₁*; *minsan*

even more so *labi-labi*; *paligay*; *anambahina*

even though *malaingkan*; *dalam isāb*; *minsan*

even-handed *timbang bibitan*

evening *pas'ddopan llaw*; *abay-kohap*

evening prayer *aisa*

evening star *tunggal-bahangi*

event *kahālan*; *pakaradja'an*

eventually *gana-gana 1.1*; *taka-taka*

ever since *sa'angay*; *sat'ggol hē'-i*

everlasting *kakkal*; *saumul-umul*

every *sabarang*; *kamemon 1.1*; *lullun 1*

every which way (askew) *sōng-s'llo'*; *pagsuwa'-s'llo'*; *sulangat*

everybody ready *bilang₃*

everyday clothes *paghinumag 1*

everywhere *deya-dilaut*

evidence *mattan 1*; *paltanda'an*; *baynat*

**evidence (of previous activity)** *bakkas*
**evident** *manyatakan*
**evil** *jahallis; la'at 1; jahil 1*
**evil spirit** *hibilis; saitan*
**evoking pity** *ase'-ase'*
**exact amount** *t'ppot*
**exactly** *taplak₂*
**exalted one** *mahatinggi*
**examine (look closely)** *patong 1.1; liling; banding*
**examine evidence** *dikisa 1.1*
**example** *saupama 1.1; sapantun*
**exasperated** *tumpalak 1*
**exasperating** *kagit atay 1*
**excavate** *kali; kalut*
**exceed** *liyu₂ 1.1; labi 1.2*
**exceed needs** *kapin 1.1*
**exceed norm** *judju' 1.1; pagjuru' 1*
**excellent** *sayuman; abag*
**except perhaps** *luwal bahā'*
**except that** *ya sadja; daipara; bo' pa'in*
**exceptional** *telop-telop; mahal-mahal*
**excess** *kalakaran; labi 1; kapin 1*
**excessive** *dumasiyaw; kumarukan*
**excessively** *mamarahi; karalaman; makalandu'*
**exchange** *sambi' 1; saliyu 1.1; ganti' 1.2*
**exchange one's clothes** *pagsalin 1.1*
**excise** *kebang 1.1*
**excited** *kenog-kenog; kiri-kiri*
**excl. asking for confirmation** *ā 3*
**excl. of affection** *ndū'*
**excl. of amazement** *pula'-pula' 1; ayī; allō*
**excl. of annoyance** *pisti'*
**excl. of concern** *allō dayang; ndū' kailū*
**excl. of consternation** *ohō*
**excl. of defiance** *sūt*
**excl. of disapproval** *apā; ē*
**excl. of disbelief** *dā'₁*
**excl. of disfavor** *allā*
**excl. of disgust** *kaliyawan; asē*
**excl. of dismay** *arōy*
**excl. of dissent** *he' angay*
**excl. of fatigue or frustration** *ahāy*
**excl. of ignorance** *halahuwalam*
**excl. of pain** *agkā'; arōy*
**excl. of satisfaction** *sē'*
**excl. of scorn** *nē*
**excl. of shock** *astag pirulla; dā'₁; pangkot 1.1*
**excl. of surprise** *arī; pisti'; ohō; alā; allō*
**excl. of sympathy** *ndū'*
**excl. to draw attention** *o'ō; elle'-elle'; ōy; ā 2*
**excl. to drive dogs away** *siga' 1*
**excl. to get child's attention** *eya'*
**excl. urging careful movement** *dō*
**exclude** *pa'alu'*

**excrement** *tai' 2*
**excrement (of baby)** *tandak*
**excrete** *jamban 1; sungi' 1*
**excruciating** *bisa 1*
**exculpate (prove innocence)** *paghuwas-huwas*
**excuse (n)** *tumagal 1*
**excuse (v)** *paba'id; papuhun*
**excuse me** *tabiya'; da'a busung*
**excused** *tahamul 1*
**execute** *pagk'llot*
**exemplary** *hatul₂; saltun 1*
**exemplify (give example)** *paralil 1*
**exercise (physical)** *k'llit-k'llit; k'ddot-k'ddot*
**exercise authority** *pagnakura' 1; pagkuma'agi; pagbaya'₁*
**exert strength** *pagayron*
**exhausted** *lumpu; hanu; simay₁ 1.1; bale'-bale'; husa'; malasahi*
**exhaustion** *pagsangsā'; lu'ug 1*
**exhaustive effort** *matay₂*
**exist** *niya'₁ 1*
**exit (v)** *luwas₁ 1*
**expand** *boskag; tting; heya 1.2*
**expanse** *kaluha'an; kasaplagan*
**expanse (of sea)** *kablangan*
**expect** *holat 1; lagad 1.1; asa 1.1*
**expect the worst** *pagyakin*
**expectant** *kiri-kiri*
**expectation** *kaholatan*
**expectorate (spit)** *ludja' 1.2*
**expedite** *sa'ut 1.1; saunu'; dai'-dai' 1.2*
**expel from body** *ddon*
**expenditure** *gastu 1*
**expensive** *hunit 2.1; halga' 1.1*
**experience (n)** *ta'u₁ 1; kalabayan; pamal'ggahan*
**experience (v)** *labay₃; ssa₂; nanam 2*
**experience misfortune** *udjul₁ 1.1*
**experiencing delight** *gila*
**expert (craftsman)** *layam 1.1; panday 1; tukang*
**expert (religious)** *alim₁; guru 1*
**expert (secular)** *mukali'*
**expertise** *kapandayan*
**expire (die)** *buwan napas*
**explain** *pahati 1.1*
**explain meaning** *hūg ma'ana*
**explode** *bustak; kulattub; h'lling₂ 1*
**exploit** *pagdago'-dago' 1.1*
**explosion** *bustakan*
**explosive (n)** *timbak 1*
**expose to rain** *paulan*
**expose to sun** *pag'llaw*
**expose to weather** *singkab 1.1; pa'alu'*
**exposed by low tide** *l'ggotan*
**exposed to air** *baliyu 2*

exposed to sun *panggang₂ 1.1*
exposure (of intimate parts) *lahil-batin*
expound *ma'ana₁ 1.1*
express gratitude *pagsarang-sukul*
expression (facial) *pamayhu'an; s'mmu*
extend hand *sōng₂ 1.1*
extend length *sugpat 1.2; suklu'*
extend size *tangkil*
extend upwards *pussuk 1.1*
extend width *paluha*
extended family *anak-kampung*
extension *sugpat 1; suklu'an; suring₁ 1*
extensive *luha 1.1*
extent *ngkon-ngkon; tibtib*
extent of journey *lintasan*
extinguish *bubu'; p'dda 1.1*
extort *kugut₂*
extra *k'nnop 1; labi 1*
extract (pull out from) *bubut; hublut 2; darut 1.1*
extraordinary *saddī-saddī; mahal-mahal*
extravagant *dalas 1; duwasay₁*

extreme *tawa'-tawa'*
extreme tide *tahik-bulagas*
extremely *karalaman; sidda 1*
extremity *puntuk; katobtoban; pussuk 1*
extricate *liyus 1.2; lappas₂ 1.1; haun₂*
exude sap *tagok 1.1*
eye *mata₁ 1*
eye (look at) *hīng 2*
eye complaint *belad; piting; meres; bussik 1*
eye of needle *buli'-jalum*
eye to eye *pagatubang*
eyebrows *langgung-kilay; kilay*
eyeglasses *samin-mata*
eyelash *pelok; bū-mata*
eyes almost closed *pirung-pirung; piru'*
eyes downcast *pagbalaru'-balaru'*
eyes in back of head *p'ssok*
eyes turned up *diyag*
eye-tooth *taling*
eyewitness *saksi' 1; sakup₁ 1*

# F f

fabric *kakana'*
fabricate (make) *hinang-hinang₂*
face (n) *aymuka; bayhu' 1*
face (of watch or clock) *lilus*
face down *da'ub; kapang₂; kutung; k'ppang 1*
face of moon *mata-bulan*
face of sun *mata-llaw*
face powder *polbos*
face to face *pagharap; paganggop; pagbayhu'*
face towards *harap₁ 1.2; atubang 1; alop₁*
face upwards *leyak; daya'*
facial expression *luwa 1*
facial expression (negative) *la'at-s'mmu*
facial features *dagbos*
facility *luhay₂ 1.1*
facing towards *tampal 1; tampak 1*
factory *kamalig*
facts *mattan 1*
faculty (of thought) *patali'an*
fade *lulu; baluba 1*
faded *papas₁ 1; gahal; gagas*
fading (light) *damal*
fading in distance *ahud-ahud 1*
fail to keep promise *dapat₁ 1.1*
faint (from hunger) *punung; gustang; otas*
faint (lose consciousness) *pinsan 1; halu 2*
faint (unclear) *buraw*

faint noise *mangel-mangel; bah'ssek 1*
faint outline *hāw-hāw 1*
faint-hearted *dalan 1*
fainting *lipat₂*
fair-skinned *pote' 1.1; manis-buwahan*
faith *iman₁ 1; agama*
faithful (religious) *baliman; pagibarat*
fake (not genuine) *paltik; eddok-eddok; gillo'ak*
faking *akkal-akkal*
fall accurately *t'bbong*
fall apart (break up) *tunas 1.1; g'ppa'*
fall asleep *toyok; tuli₁ 1.2*
fall at an angle *talilli' 1; sulempat*
fall awkwardly *tulelle*
fall backwards *duleyak*
fall down *pakpak 1; hūg₁ 1; tumba₁*
fall down from *latak*
fall erratically *talilli' 1; tambelleng*
fall flat *hantak₁ 1; timpuwad 1; lintuwad 1; ligad*
fall forward *ligad; togsok; sondong*
fall freely *pakpak 1; hūg₁ 1; tumba₁*
fall headlong *togge'₁; tukbung 1*
fall heavily *lagonos 1; hantak₁ 1*
fall in large numbers *pandorot; pagbangday; balabak*
fall in love *hōp baya'*
fall in stages *palapas-palapas*
fall over *h'bba'; togsok*

**fall over and over** *pagduleyak*
**fall through** *t'lla; bobos*
**fall through hole** *pagpatilossok*
**fall through water** *talilli' 1*
**falling star** *umul₁; selo'*
**false expectations** *akkal 1.1*
**false teeth** *malpel*
**falsehood** *puting 1; dusta' 1*
**falter (when walking)** *lukbu'₂*
**fame** *bantug 1; ōn₂*
**familiar (relationship)** *pagsamod; pagsōd-addat*
**familiar name** *danglay 1; g'llal 2*
**familiar with** *biyaksa 1; laskal*
**familiarise** *pabiyaksa*
**family** *pamilya 1*
**family (of a man)** *anak-h'nda*
**family (of a woman)** *anak-h'lla*
**family links** *sugsug 1.1*
**family of one mother** *mata'an*
**family unit** *tali'anak; magtai'anak*
**famine** *musiba; gotom 1*
**famine food** *ddut; kiyat*
**famished** *punung; gustang; otas*
**famous** *hula-layag 1; bantug 1.1; tanyag 1*
**famous person** *babantugun*
**fan** *kayab 1; kabkab 1*
**fan (v)** *kaykay*
**fan coral** *laya-laya*
**fan shell** *kayab-kayab*
**fancy someone** *istrōk; bilahi 2; baya' 1.1*
**fang** *bangkil₂; taling*
**far away** *lawak; tā 1.1; l'ttu*
**far end** *tōng-tōng 1*
**far out to sea** *kaladjun*
**fare** *sukay₁ 1*
**farm; farmland** *tana'₁ 2; huma*
**farmed fish** *daing tangki*
**farmer (crop-grower)** *paghuhuma*
**far-reaching** *libu 1; ladju; ladji'*
**fart** *ntut; pagboro-boro*
**fascinated** *lambang-mata 1; haylan*
**fast (religious)** *puwasa*
**fasten** *lagsak; engkot 1.1*
**fastener (clip)** *alperel; kassup 1; sisipit; kait 1; dopon-dopon 1; kabit₁ 1*
**fastidious** *pagsanittiya*
**fast-moving** *l'kkas 1; samot 1; kasay 1; alistu 1*
**fat (adj)** *hambug 1; l'mmok 1.1; subuk*
**fat (n)** *ns'llan 1*
**fate** *sukud₂ 1; karal 1; ganta'an₁*
**father** *mma'; papang; bohe'₂*
**father-like** *pag'mma' 1.1*
**fathom (depth)** *d'ppa 1*
**fatigued** *bale'; lu'ug 1.1; pagmalasahi*

**fatigued (of eyes)** *b'ddu'*
**fatwa** *pituwa 1*
**faucet (spigot)** *siput 1*
**fault** *salla'₁ 1; sā'₁ 1; dusa 1*
**faulty (malfunction)** *palsu*
**favor (blessing)** *pahala'; junjung 1; kahāpan*
**favorable (of time)** *sa'at*
**favorable outcome** *piguhan*
**favored (by God)** *barakat 1.2; hirayat; anughala' 1*
**favored with something** *niya'₁ 2*
**favorite (child)** *anak-mussa'*
**favorite (pet)** *papu'*
**fawn on** *lana 1.1*
**fear** *tāw 1*
**fear the worst** *piligdu 1*
**fearful** *g'mma; bolag; gawa*
**fearless** *atay-batu; esog 1.1*
**feasible** *manjari₁ 2*
**feast** *jamu 1*
**feast (before Ramadan)** *tampil*
**feather** *bulbul 1*
**featureless region** *paslangan 1*
**features** *lihi 1*
**feces** *tai' 2*
**fed up with** *sumu 1.1; lumad*
**fee** *panamba; tugnus₂ 1; sukay₁ 1*
**fee to midwife** *bauballi'*
**feeble** *lamma 1; dome-dome; pilay; komay*
**feeble-minded** *bobo*
**feed (v)** *pakan*
**feed guests** *latal 1.1; labot*
**feeding bottle** *paruru'an*
**feel (symptom)** *lapa₁; gadgad₁; nanam 2.1*
**feel amorous** *hōp baya'*
**feel an emotion** *tambung*
**feel disgust for** *sammal 1.1*
**feel for (by touch)** *sassaw; sanaw; agap₂; sadsad 1.1; gindas*
**feel hurt (emotional)** *mandā'-dā'; ambul-dā'; bakat atay*
**feel pain** *pangkaheng; bisa 1.1; p'ddi' 1.1*
**feel pity** *andu'-andu'; ase'*
**feel rejected** *ambul-dā'*
**feel responsibility** *pagkalimbit*
**feel strain** *pagsangsā'; paglu'ug-liksa'*
**feel unwell** *la'at palasahan*
**feel weak** *longkoy; layu-layu*
**feelers** *janggut 1*
**feelers (n)** *labu₄*
**feeling (of health)** *palasahan*
**feeling (positive)** *galak₁ 1*
**feet** *tape'₁*
**feign (pretend)** *pagbau'-bau'; hinang-hinang₂; pagtumagal*
**feign deafness** *pagbisu-bisu*

**feign ignorance** *pagawam*
**feigned (not real)** *sainala*
**fell (a tree)** *puwad*
**fellow human** *pagkahi*
**female** *d'nda 1*
**female (animals, chickens)** *umagak*
**female features** *pagkar'nda*
**female pudenda** *puki*
**femininity** *kapagd'nda 1*
**fence** *sasak 1; apis 1; ād 1*
**fence trap** *ampas 1*
**fenced area** *koral 1*
**fend off** *sangga 2; tangkis 1.1.1*
**fermented (become sour)** *balos₂*
**ferns** *nitu'; pakis*
**ferrous metal** *balan; basi'₁ 1*
**ferry** *panumpangan; bangkero 1*
**ferry someone** *tundug 1.1*
**fervent (religious)** *ammal₁; pagsanittiya*
**festival** *hailaya*
**festive food** *dulang*
**festivity** *ongka' 1.1*
**fetch** *k'llo'₁; bowa₁*
**fetid** *bau 1.1; p'ngngos*
**fetters** *ekang-ekang 1; karena 1.1; pasung₁ 1; bilanggu' 1*
**fetus** *onde' 2*
**fetus (petrified)** *lidjal*
**fever; feverish** *tandog 1; limasu' 1; l'mmun; hadjat₂*
**few** *salat 1; diki' 1*
**few (of people)** *mala'u-la'u 1.1*
**fewer than** *kulang₁ 1.1*
**fez (brimless cap)** *kuppiya*
**fiance; fiancee** *tunang 1*
**fiber (vegetable)** *lupis*
**fibrous projections** *anamū*
**fibrous residue** *angkas₁ 1; tai'-lahing*
**fickle** *pagpinda*
**fictitious** *gillu'-gillu'; eddok-eddok*
**fid (spike for working cane)** *tipopok*
**fiddle with** *umas; hulemang 1.1*
**fidget** *pagoseg-oseg*
**field** *tana'₁ 1; huma*
**field bird** *lanji-lanji*
**field shelter** *balung-balung; payad*
**fiend** *saitan*
**fierce** *tāw-tāw; esog 1.1*
**fiery** *keyat₂ 1.1*
**fiesta** *hailaya*
**fifth day after full moon** *min lima abase'*
**fifty** *limampū'*
**fifty centavos** *dambila' pilak*
**fig trees** *tabug; igira*
**fight (as cocks do)** *pagmanuk-manuk₁ 1.1*

**fight (military)** *dugpak 2; pagbono' 1.1; gubat*
**fight (women style)** *pagluray*
**fight back** *abjan; atu 1.1*
**fight cocks** *ayuk-ayuk; pagbulang*
**fight over** *pagagaw*
**fighter** *bobono'*
**fighting cock** *bubulangun; manuk-sigun*
**fighting horse** *kura'-mandu-mandu*
**fighting spear** *budjak 1*
**figurative** *pamaralilan*
**figure (body shape)** *pamaranan*
**figure out** *kalkula; bista₁*
**file (shaping tool)** *gaugari' 1*
**file a complaint** *pagmahi*
**file teeth** *tā'; lagnas; solsol*
**file to shape (v)** *gisgis 1.1*
**filefish** *peteg*
**filigree** *antuwilas 1*
**fill (almost)** *sa'ang₁*
**fill (with steam or smoke)** *limbōn; t'bbud₁ 1*
**fill container (v)** *p'nno' 1.1*
**fill gaps** *puna'; pagsaus'llap; bubul*
**filled (with an emotion)** *sōd 2*
**filled to brim** *pagsamaintib 1; pagsamaongkop 1*
**filled to limit** *sangka' 1; sangkad; s'ppol 1*
**fillet (n)** *balkehet; ballul 1; balang 1*
**film on a surface** *lapu-lapu 1; lapis₁ 1*
**film on newborn** *saikula'*
**filthy** *lumu'*
**filthy (behavior)** *sabul 1.1*
**fin** *sēk; tuntun₂*
**final breath** *buwan napas*
**final event** *pagpaubus*
**final offer** *katibtiban*
**final phase (of tide)** *bakas-bakas*
**final stage** *kapūd-pūran; kasangka'an; katapusan 1; hinapusan*
**finalise** *tastas₁*
**finally (at last)** *tahan₁ 1.1; yamboho'*
**finances for project** *dapat-daya*
**financial help** *panulung*
**financial return** *tongod₃ 1*
**financial support** *pangatas*
**find** *nda' 1; bāk₁*
**find (in hiding game)** *tilluk; piyung*
**find fault with** *soway; salu'-salu'; salla'₁ 1.2; salba₁*
**find guilty** *patōng dusa*
**find out** *ta'u₁ 1.2; hati 2*
**find place or path** *tullus 1.1; malim 1.1; tuhung; tuli' 1*
**find with feet** *gi'ik 2*
**fine (condition)** *abag*
**fine (penalty)** *taksil 1.2; multa 1*
**fine (physical appearance)** *polma 1.1; bustan*

**fine (textile)** *dokdok; lehag; lere-lere 1*
**fine mesh** *nahut; petong*
**fined (penalised)** *niya'₂; ā' 4*
**finely ground** *budbud 1*
**finger** *anak-tangan; lasu'; kengkeng; gulamay 1*
**finger (for ring)** *daimanis*
**finger coral** *lakas-lakas; sahasa'*
**fingernail** *kukku₁*
**fingernail extensions** *janggay 1*
**fingerprint** *limpa' 1*
**fingertip** *tōng-tangan*
**finicky** *pene' 1*
**finish (edge of weaving)** *ppi' 1.1; sapay 1.1*
**finish (v)** *ubus₁ 1.1; talus₁ 1.1*
**finished (completed)** *temos; tangbus; katis₂ 1.1*
**finished (fruiting)** *tobas*
**fire** *api 1*
**fire at** *timbak 2.1; balis₁*
**firearm** *almas; timbak 1; sinapang*
**firebox** *lapohan*
**fired (dismissed)** *lessad*
**firefly** *lambetong*
**fire-table (cooking place)** *pilang*
**firewood** *pangayu; dūk₂ 1*
**fireworks** *kulitis; papan₂; bintadol*
**firm (of something cooked)** *bingkal*
**firm (secure)** *sandat 1; tatal₁; totog 1; hogot*
**firmament** *tonga'an ayan; ayan*
**first** *dahū 1.1; mint'dda*
**first class (quality)** *umbul dakayu'; umbul tunggal*
**first cousin** *kaki mint'dda*
**first light** *abay-subu*
**first one** *ka'ssa*
**first one then other** *ubus... ubus*
**first trimester** *iram*
**first-class** *abag*
**fish (canned)** *saldinas*
**fish (generic)** *daing 1*
**fish (preserved)** *sampila'₁ 1.1; lumay; pundang 1; peyad 1*
**fish (unclassified)** *bubuk₁; kummaw; jahira; tinduk₂; sikuhan; mana-mana; bullu'; kulilla'; lese₂; nnek; nggek; kulambuwan; unas-balu; bā'-bā'an; babay; baho'-baho'; bilu-bilu₁; jungkak; batang-pai; bubuhan; dagdag₃; sambelang; suling₂; tai'-asang; langkawit₂; tagisiyan; bungug-tapikan; bungug; ombe-ombe; puhan-laring; pongka'; pote'-pote'; tingga'-tingga'-lumahan; sampil-laran; dompa'; t'ggi; katumbang; pugaw; punjungan; gintu'; pilluwang₁; ulan-ulan; pogan; kapa-kapa; bisbisan; gatang; sokong; kīt-kīt; kutut; tambak₂*
**fish (v)** *pagdaing*
**fish bone** *to'olang; kowa' 1*
**fish by diving** *belle'₂; tipara 1.1*
**fish by driving** *lasak; ampas 1.1; tibuk₂; ambit₁*

**fish by gathering** *belle'₂; lakod*
**fish by hooking up** *sabit₁ 1.1*
**fish by jigging** *hantuk*
**fish by lantern** *sindung₂; silung₂; kulaet 1.1*
**fish by moonlight** *bulan₃*
**fish by spearing** *pana' 1.1; saleyok; togge'₂*
**fish by trapping** *ampas 1.1; bagiyas 1.1; togong 1.1; pagbubu*
**fish by trawling** *gugul 1.1*
**fish eaten raw** *lawal 1*
**fish from previous day** *daing kohap*
**fish market** *pagdaingan*
**fish poison** *lagtang 1; sujum*
**fish pond** *kulam*
**fish scale** *sisik 1*
**fish spear** *sahapang 1*
**fish species (freshwater)** *palupalu; bang'llus; owa'₂*
**fish trap opening** *atay-atay*
**fish traps** *bubu₁; bagiyas 1; bungsud; kiming; ampas 1; togong 1; panggal 1*
**fish with hook and line** *pamalastik; laway₂ 1.1; lambat 1.1; buwang₁ 1.1; p'ssi 1.1; gonteng 1.2; sabit₁ 2.1*
**fish with live bait** *kati*
**fish with net** *sinsoro 1.1; pokot₁ 1.1; siyul 1.1; linggi' 1.1; laya 1.1*
**fish with poison** *tuba 1.1; lagtang 1.1; sujum*
**fish with set line** *b'ntang*
**fish with weighted line** *lambat 1.1*
**fish with whole bait** *sangkaliya'*
**fisherman** *pagdaraing; magp'p'ssi*
**fishhooks** *kawil; sabit₁ 2; p'ssi 1; kowat-kowat*
**fishing as a livelihood** *pagp'ssi*
**fishing camp (away from home)** *lihanan*
**fishing float** *kassa'-bullung*
**fishing line** *tonda'₁ 1; tangsi'₁ 1*
**fishing mate** *abay₁ 1*
**fishing rod** *ba'ugan₂*
**fishtail palm** *banga*
**fishy smell** *bau p'llut*
**fist** *pagkomkom*
**fit (seizure)** *bawi-bawi; sawan-sawan; sōd-dingin*
**fit (healthy)** *bastig; ayron*
**fit handle** *tangkay 2.1*
**fit into** *siguwa; sulug₁; s'ddong; sangon₁ 1*
**fit loosely** *pagloka-loka*
**fit tightly** *lapat 1.2*
**fit together** *pagdayaw 1.1; sangon₁ 1.1; pagd'ppak 1*
**fit together (as to size)** *pagsarang*
**fitting (appropriate)** *patut; tōp 1.1; d'kkal*
**five** *lima*
**fix spear to shaft** *pantok₁ 1.1*
**fixed (location)** *totog 1*
**fixed (opinion)** *taggu₂ 1*
**flag** *sambulayang; bandila'; panji*

flake off *biti'₂ 1*
flaking *gagus; kanit 1; laknit 1; lakles*
flame *laga 1; keyat₂ 1*
flange *kepet₁*
flank (of body) *kĭd₁ 1*
flap (in wind) *paspas₂ 1; k'llay-k'llay; pagk'llab*
flap wings *pagkotek-kotek*
flapper (fin) *tuntun₂*
flapping *jabjab 1; kayang-kayang; pagkayab*
flare (n) *sulariyan; tanju'*
flare up *dokot₂ 1.1; suleyab 1.1; dallet 1; sulapput*
flare up (of argument) *dokot suli-suli*
flash (n) *sinag 1*
flash (or sparkle) *itaw-itaw; pagkiraw; inggat; illap*
flashlight *plaslaet 1*
flat (surface) *pantay; plāt; datag*
flat item *gekap 1*
flatfish *kulampera'*
flathead fish *kamang 1*
flatiron *pilinsahan*
flatten *hotad₁; lais 1; tumpēt*
flattened *k'ddos; pedda' 1; losak*
flatter *lana 1.1; paenok; paili*
flatulence *pagboro-boro*
flaunt *imu'-imu'*
flautist (flute player) *pagsuling*
flavor *nanam 1; lamuk; ssa₁ 1*
flavorings (list) *pamapā*
flavorless *k'ssang₂; kasat; t'bbag*
flaw *salla'₁ 1; galna' 1*
fleas *hamug-hamug; kammut*
flee *dimpulag; lahi₁*
fleet (of boats) *kamunda'an; abayan*
fleeting glance *idlap 1; k'llap*
flesh *isi₂*
fleshless *k'ppeng*
flex (be springy) *l'mbut*
flexing (under load) *tuyang*
flick *lagtik 1*
flicker *pagpillaw-pillaw; pagsiraw-siraw*
flimsy *guya'; p'ddut*
fling off *pessek 1*
flip over *sumpallit; bulallay; bulallit*
flip-flops (footwear) *sinelas*
flippant *jōk*
flirt *pagpaelle'-elle'*
flitting about *pagleyat-leyat*
float (fishing gear) *butun₃; pataw₁; untang*
float (in one place) *antung*
float (swimming aid) *palangihan; salbabida*
float (v) *gūng; lantup*
floating mass *gampal; pagung; ulak 1*
flock together *pagkubu-kubu*
flood (overflow) *dunuk; latap 1.1; letop 1.1*

flood (salt water) *s'llop*
flood tide *tambang₁ 1; sōn*
floor *lantay 1*
floor bearers *dagan₁*
floor joists *salsal*
floor wax *lansuk*
flop down *laylay*
flop over *kopeng*
floppy (limp) *himāt; hoyon*
flotation gear *salbabida*
flotsam *gampal; ulak 1*
flour (rice) *tapung 1*
flour (wheat) *tirigu 2*
flourish *subud; sambu 1.1*
flow *sasahan 1.1; tagudtud; duwasay₂*
flow (n) *gadgad₂*
flow (tidal) *balosok; sosob*
flow down *tū'; tĭs*
flow out *lagadlad₁; tubud 1*
flow slowly *buway-buway*
flower *sumping 1*
flower species *malul; banglut*
flower stem *lumping*
flowing across a surface *mansay-mansay*
flue (of engine) *pupputan*
fluent *lahal*
fluffy *bulbul 1.1*
fluid *bohe'₁ 1*
fluid from coconut grating *kabulan*
flute *suling₁; pulaw₁*
flute-mouth (fish) *ngngok*
flutter *pagkayab; paspad 1; pagk'llab*
fly (as a bird) *sayang₁; leyang 1*
fly (insect) *langaw 1*
fly through air *pulagsik; balleng 1*
fly up suddenly *lumpat*
flying creatures *manuk-manuk 1*
flying fox *kabog*
flying horse (mythical) *sambalani; galura'*
flying-fish *bengke*
foam *bula'-bula' 1*
fob pocket *gangotan*
focus attention on *harap₁ 1.3; isbat; patong 1*
focus on God *arap*
focused *tigi'-tigi'₁ 1*
foes *kuntara 1; palbantahan*
fold (of cloth) *l'ppot; lupi'₁; l'kko'*
fold back (sleeves) *kinkin*
fold down sail *kulindara; aru-aru*
fold flat (of something hinged) *k'ppi'₁ 1.1*
fold in two *lipat₁ 2*
fold into a peak *ladjuk 1.1*
folded over *lapping-lapping*
folk-dance *igal 1.1*

folklore *pali-pali*
folktale *kissa 1*
follow coastline *susul 1.1; baybay₁*
follow example *sunud 1.1; s'ppu*
follow in order *sunu'*
follow someone *turul 1; apas 1*
follow tradition *tubus₂ 1.1*
follower *pitis-tendog; tendog*
following day *salung*
following on *sunud 1*
following wind *tūd₁ 1*
folly *karupangan*
fond of (a food) *sōb*
fondle *sapu-sapu; golgol*
fontanel *mbun-mbun*
food *balanja' 1; kinakan 1; talopa'*
food (cooked in wrapper) *suman; punjung₂; biyaki' 1*
food (craved during pregnancy) *pangiraman*
food (said in anger) *boslaran; halluwa 2; hinuwal 2*
food container *paglutu'anan; pamanganan*
food resources *gaddongan*
food restriction *li'in 1*
food scraps *butu'an*
food sources (inland) *l'mput deya*
food sources (inshore shallows) *l'mput dilaut*
food stall *kadday*
fool (n) *dupang 1*
fool someone *lingu 1.1; lakbu'₂; akkal 1.1*
foolhardy *bahani 1.1*
fooling about *paglata*
foolish *dupang 1.1*
foot (body part) *tape'₁*
foot (of mountain) *tape'-būd*
foot (unit of measurement) *tape'₃*
footbridge *taytayan; letehan*
foothills *bīd-bīd 1*
footprints *limpa' 1*
footwear *taumpa'*
for *ma 1*
for a moment *dai'-dai' 1*
for ages *t'ggol 1.1; kuwa'-kuwa'*
for example *ibarat₂; bang saupama*
for sure *taka-taka*
for the benefit of *para₂*
for whom? *ma sai*
forage (for food or supplies) *talun 1.1; takod 1.1; sasab*
forbearance *sabal 1; iman₁ 1*
forbid *lāng; bawal 1.1*
forbidden *sumbang; haram 1.1*
forbidding *sekot 1.3*
force (against moral standards) *lalas; poleggaw; abiyug*
force (growth or ripeness) *putput*

force (v) *logos 1; hilag; agpot 1*
force a way in *agaw 1*
force into space *sorok; ddol-ddol*
force to relocate *lalat₁ 1*
forced down *togmok 1*
forceful *bagas*
ford a stream *ubug₁ 1*
forearm *tangan 1; pataklayan*
forebears; forefathers *kama'asan; ka'mbo'-mbo'an; kamatto'ahan; palmula'an*
foreboding *nahas 1; nasa*
forecast *pa'al 1.1; papata 1*
forefinger *tudlu'₁*
foregone conclusion *kamaupakkatan*
foreground *dahū'an 1; harap₁ 1*
forehead *lendo'; tuktuk*
foreign (European) *balanda'₂*
foreign places *Juhul maka Jakatla'*
foreigner *a'a liyu*
foreknow *alamat₁*
foreknowledge *pangita'u; langtas 1*
foreman *kapatas; bōs; mandul*
foresee *pagba'at 1*
foreshore *pari'an*
forest *kati'an; talun 1; gulangan*
forest animals *kusa'; kuting-kubing; halimaw*
forest spirit *kokok 1*
forest trees *balis₃; mata-mata₃*
foretell *pagtaluhan 1.1*
foreteller *talus₂*
forever *sapanjang-panjang; saumul-umul; salama-lama; sapupud-daya*
forfeit *lōb 1.1*
forge (n) *pagsasalan*
forge metal *babal₁; sasal*
forged items *babalan*
forget *kalipat 1*
forgetful *liha-liha; panglupa; lipas*
forgive; forgiveness *tawbat 1.2; ma'ap; ampun₁*
forgiveness ceremony *pandi tawbat; sugsug tawbat 1*
forgiveness gift *pagtawbatan*
forgotten *sabali-bali man atay; bibas₂*
fork (dining) *tinerol; tugsuk 1*
forked branch *sanga 2*
forlorn *pulaw₂; siya-siya 1*
form (of fruit) *tadjuk*
form a community *sakaum*
form a floating mass *paulak*
form a group *pagba'an 1*
form a pair *pagkaruwa*
form a pile or mound *būd 1.1; g'bbus 1; kuta'₂*
form a pool *paghalo-halo; kandung₁*
form an edge *bihing₁ 1.2*
form by molding *kompol*

form crust or scab *l'kkung 1.1*
form distinct groups *paggihay 1*
form fruit *tungkalling; pagduru'-ero'*
form lumps (in muscle tissue) *isi-kulabutan*
form lumps of dough *pagbugga'-bugga'*
form lumps on skin *pagbintul*
form something mountainous *pagbullud*
formal courtesy *pagpuli-bahasa 1*
formal discussion *pagpalkala'*
former house site *takas*
former times *awal₁; ka'ina-tagna'; dahū-rahū*
formication *l'nnu*
fornicate *lalu*
forsaken *pulaw₂; siya-siya 1*
fort (n) *kuta'₁ 1*
forte (area of strength) *kosog 1*
forthwith *magtūy; saru'un-du'un; sakali₂*
fortunate *hāp sukud; mayaman*
fortunately *daipara; arapun; manda'; sukul₁*
fortune *piguhan; sukud₂ 1*
fortune-teller *magpuputika'*
forty *mpatpū'*
forty winks *piru'-piru'; tuli-sowa*
forward and back *pagsōng-sebog; pagsōng-suhut*
fossick *lalag; pagsalinggā*
foster sibling *salu-duru'*
foul-smelling *p'ngngak; kahang; b'ngngog*
foundation *papagan 1*
founder (sink) *logdang₂; buhaw*
founding ancestors *palmula'an*
fountain *tuburan*
four *mpat*
fowl (domestic) *manuk 1*
fowl (tailless chicken) *tukung*
fowl (wild chicken) *labuyu'₁*
fraction *bahagi' 1*
fracture *pi'ul*
fragile *guya'; lagtu' 1; poka*
fragment *benglod; hīk-hīk; momok*
fragmented *pagkabila'-bila'; tunas 1.1; podjak 1; pu'aw 1*
fragrant *hamut 1.1; b'ngngi*
frame (embroidery) *bastiru*
frame (firebox) *lintang 1*
frame (kulintangan set) *palanggungan*
framework (structure) *pangdayaw 1; batang-tubu*
frangipani tree *sampaka'*
frankly *tumlang 1; bang pina'amu*
fraud *tipu 1; akkal 1.1*
frayed *jabel-jabel 1.1; b'bbak*
freckles *tagimtim 1; bau-bau*
free (from compulsion) *hilas; lilla'*
free (from liability or blame) *lebre 1.1; kiyas; puwas₁ 1*

free from tension *sannang*
free spirit *luha-limbay*
freed (of tie or snag) *p'llus 1*
freed; freedom *limaya; luhaya*
freedom (from restraint) *l'ppahan*
freelancer *luha-limbay*
freeloader *dahal 1*
freeze *elo 1.1*
freezing cold *k'ttol*
frenzied *kangog*
frequency *kamasuhulan; kamaumuhan*
frequently *bilang₁; daran*
fresh (not preserved) *base'₂*
fresh (not stale) *baha'u 1*
freshen mouth *bunglaw 2*
fresh-water pool *kandung₁; tigbaw*
fret *langan₁*
fretful *mmaw 1; salut 1*
Friday *Juma'at*
fried bananas or sweet potato *piniritu; libusaw 1; juwalan*
fried dumpling *okoy*
fried fish *piniritu; landang-landang 1*
friend *agay; gge; bagay 1*
friend (close) *panon*
friendly *patibagayun*
frigate bird *linggisan*
frighten *dangka₁; pakitāw*
frightened *tāw 1.1; leya'-leya'; umagad 1.1*
frightening *piligdu 1; tāw-tāw*
frill *jambu 1; bulda 1*
fringe (decorative) *jambay; bulda 1*
fritter (dumpling) *okoy*
frog *ambak*
from *min 1*
from here *minnitu*
from now on *tobtob 1.1*
from the same father *da'mma'*
from the same mother *daina'*
from there *minnē'; minna'an*
from time to time *sān; sumā'..sumā'*
from where? *minningga*
frond (palm, dried) *langkay 1*
front (area; part) *dahū'an 1; munda'an₁; harap₁ 1*
frontier (border) *jangka'an 1*
froth *lere'; bula'-bula' 1*
frown *pagkonot*
fruit (generic) *buwa'₁ 1*
fruit (newly set) *duru'-ero'*
fruit bat *kabog*
fruit fly *hamug-hamug*
fruit in general *bungang-kahuy*
fruit of lambus tree *tongke'*
fruit trees (unclassified) *minul; hebi; mabolo*

**fruitful** *jayak*

**frustrated** *llet 2; kuttung; lamma 2.1*

**fry (v)** *sanglag; landang-landang 1.1; piritu*

**frying pan** *lenga'; simpi'; kaha'*

**fuel (firewood)** *pangayu; dūk₂ 1*

**fuel (for engine)** *ns'llan 1*

**fulcrum** *pagsagga'an₁; pagagod; pangaluwaran*

**fulfill (v)** *kabbul*

**fulfill vow** *najal 1.1; suhud 1.2*

**fulfilled** *mustajab*

**full (from eating)** *l'sso; sugmak; s'gga*

**full (of container)** *sangkad; p'nno' 1*

**full (of moon)** *damlag 1.1*

**full (of sibling relationship)** *langgung₁ 1.1*

**full (of tide)** *l'kkab; lalom₁ 2*

**full array (of teeth, corn)** *linggas*

**fully** *tubus₁ 1.1*

**fully grown** *hendog-hendog; sangpot 1.1; pata'₁; lasag*

**fully paid** *samaunjuk*

**fume; fumigate** *sangu 1; tangas; t'bbud₁ 1.1; tugtug*

**fun** *lami; kakoyagan; lasig 1*

**function properly** *bowa₂*

**funeral knife** *kīs₄ 1*

**funeral procedures** *hinang-kalla'; pagkaya-kaya; kamattihan 2*

**fungus (on tree)** *tai'-hangin*

**funnel** *pupputan; huyungan*

**funnel of fish trap** *gau*

**fur** *bū 1; bulbul 1*

**furious** *pasu' atay; astol atay*

**furl (sail)** *kulindara; l'ppit 1; diki' 1.2*

**furnishings** *kapanyapan; kabunyihan; pahandang 1*

**furrow (garden)** *badlis*

**further on** *lanjal 1*

**fuse or wick** *sumbuhan*

**fused together** *damil*

**fusilier fishes** *sulig₂; anduhat; mapan*

**fuss (of a child)** *pagle'eng*

**fuss at** *pagmalān; pagamā 1*

**fussy (selective)** *pene' 1*

**futile (of attempt)** *tuku langit*

**futile effort** *llet 2; pagsabbut ni batu*

**future** *gana-gana 1; sōng₁ 1; pupud-llaw*

**future (near)** *salung-simuddai*

**future (well-being)** *kasōngan 1*

**future events** *palihalan 2*

# G g

**gabble** *pagdabdab*

**gable wall** *sūngan*

**gadabout** *patil'ngnganun*

**gaff** *gangat 1.1; s'llok 1*

**gag reflex** *balowak*

**gain (profit)** *untung₁ 1; kasōngan 2*

**gain advantage** *diyata'an₂; lakbaw 1.1; tinggil 1*

**gain attention** *kabag talinga*

**gain custody of child** *iris*

**gait** *tebong*

**gale** *badju; baliyu 1*

**gall bladder** *p'ddu 1*

**galleon** *parangkang; adjung*

**gallivant (roam around)** *pagjambeyaw*

**gallon** *galon 2*

**gamble** *paglegot 2*

**gambler** *pationgka'un*

**gambling** *tūk 1*

**game of chance** *wahoy*

**game types** *balatin; paglagpi'; huru; pagtollok-tollok; pagtudjun*

**games term (counters)** *pagtaksi' 1*

**games term (dealer or banker)** *bangka₂ 1*

**games term (dice)** *to'on₁ 1.1*

**games terms (dominoes)** *kulgaw; seraw*

**games terms (marbles)** *sanggul₁ 1.1; pagplising 1; mano 1.1*

**games term (volleyball)** *kīl*

**games terms (cards)** *paro; pasti'₂; timbayan*

**games terms (coins)** *udjul₂; tingka; agad₂; sulang₂; samal*

**games terms (general)** *timbag; buta₂ 1; dahun₂; pamatu'*

**games terms (luhu')** *pagluhu'; limbuku'; hamput*

**gangrene** *kawit₂ 1*

**gangrenous** *buntu'₁ 1.1*

**gap** *llotan; possatan; sipsipan; logtasan; l'bbang 1*

**gaping (of cut)** *kehab*

**gapped** *legpong; lanta'; someng 1*

**garbage** *s'ggit 1*

**garble** *pagkabillag*

**garden** *jambangan; galden*

**garfish** *selo*

**gargle** *gūm-gūm*

**garlic** *bawang*

**garlic sprouts** *lukyu*

**garment** *tamongon; pamakay; badju'*

**garment (makeshift)** *tapis 1.1*

**garret** *angkap 1*

**garrulous** *bowa'-bowa'*

**gas pain** *bakag₂*

gasoline *gasulīn*

gasp for breath *gagal₁; paghagak*

gasping *paghangu-hangu*

gate; gateway *tambol 1; lawang 1*

gather (by lamplight) *sū' 1.1*

gather (people) *paghimpun; pagpūn₁; pagtipun 1*

gather (things) *timuk 1.2; tipun 1.2*

gather around (to see) *pagkubu-kubu; harung-harung*

gather at mealtimes *alung 2; aro' 1.1; donga'*

gather fruit *talun 1.1*

gather information *bantingag*

gather strand food *pagt'bba*

gather up *temo-temo; kamut*

gathering (of people) *kahimul-himulan; palhimpunan*

gauge *kapal 1; sangat 1*

gaunt *kittay; kulagkag; higtal*

gauze *gapas*

gaze *lawan; harap₁ 1.3; pandang*

gear (equipment) *kapanyapan; sakap 1; kakaya'an*

geckos *pinit; s'ssok; tokke'₁*

Gehenna (hell) *Jahannam*

gelatine *gulaman; agal-agal*

gemstone *dilam; palmata 1; intan*

genealogy *usulan; sugsug 1.1*

generally *kamaumuhan*

generation (next) *suring-baha'u*

generations *tubu'-manubu'*

generous *pagmura 1.1; pagbuwan 1.1*

genial *saumbibi; lanu' atay*

genie *jīn 1*

genital area *alopan₂; harapan₂; munda'an₂*

genitals (female) *puki*

genitals (male) *boto'₂*

genius *panday-pupud; pandikal*

gentle *lu'uy₂; lanu' atay*

gentleness (of speech) *kahanusan; hanunut*

gently *agak-agak*

genuflect *kōk-tu'ut 1.1*

genuine *porol; legal; jatti; tunay₁*

genuinely *to'ongan 1.1*

germs *kagaw*

gesture *lambe₁ 1.1*

get *ngā'; k'llo'₁; ā' 1*

get back to subject *balik salawat*

get supplies *binta'*

get up (from lying or sitting) *punduk 1; bangkat₂; bungkal₁ 1; buhat₂; bangun₁ 1*

ghosts *lutaw; pangguwa' 1; panyata'₂ 1; umanat*

GI roofing *atop mital*

giant clam *kima*

giants *saitan-lagtaw; agasi*

gibberish *pagt'bba'-sasab*

giddy *uling; baliyang; pagtunggang-kīng*

gift *pamuwan 1; bo'ot; tutukbalan*

gift (elopement) *tambang₂*

gift (from God) *pahala'; anughala' 1*

gift (from student) *bakti' 1*

gift (to influence) *su'ap 1.1*

gift (to open negotiations) *pangukaban lawang*

gift (to superior) *huhulmatan; pananggapan*

giggle *kehe'-kehe' 1*

gill lice *k'llut-k'llut*

gill segments (fish) *paipa'₁ 1*

gills (of fish) *asang₁ 2*

gin *alak*

ginger *lu'uya; kisul*

girder *babag 1*

girl *onde' 1*

girl (in early teens) *daga-raga*

girl (unmarried) *budjang*

girlfriend *tunang 1; atag₂*

give (hand to me) *ndiya*

give a turn *pas'lle'*

give freely *paghilas; paglilla'*

give share *pasuku'*

give thought to *paghona'-hona' 1*

give to *buwan₁ 1.1*

give too much *judju' 1.1; pagjuru' 1.1*

give tribute *pagjakat 1*

given that *samantala'; pagka; talkala'*

glad *koyag 1.1; kōg 2*

glance at *sulli'; k'llap; sīb 1*

glance off *saligsig₂; tigad 1; deplas 1*

glare (n) *silaw 1.1*

glare at *d'llag 1.1; kaniyang-kaniyang; duliyat 1.1*

glaring (of light) *silaw 1*

glass *kassa' 1; samin 1*

glass container *sawan; garapun*

glass for drinking *basu*

glasses (for eyes) *samin-mata*

glassfish (Asiatic) *totok*

glaze (with sugar) *libusaw 1.1*

gleam *tingaw-tingaw; ba'as 1*

gleam of white *hisi'*

glide along *sapsap₁*

glimpse (v) *sanggillap; laman 1.1*

glisten *linig 1.2; illap*

glitter *pagbetong-betong; pagsinglab; inggat*

globular *tibulung 1*

gloom *do'om; kal'ddoman*

gloomy *lendom 1.1*

glorify *pudji 1.2; sanglit 1.2*

gloss (shine) *linig 1*

glottis *asang₁ 1*

gloves *puyu'-puyu' 1*

glow *ba'as 1.1*

glue (n) *pikit-pikit; waylud*

**glue (v)** *pikit₁ 1.1*
**glued together** *damil*
**glutted (overfull)** *sangka' 1*
**glutton** *dahal 1; dahaga'; lagak 1*
**gluttonous** *buhawi'₁; kaway 1*
**gnash** *pagtage'ot*
**gnats** *hamug-hamug; kammut; damuk*
**gnaw** *kitkit*
**gnome (dwarf)** *maya-maya₁*
**go (get going)** *sūng*
**go ahead of** *sauna; dahū 1.3*
**go different ways** *liku'*
**go in person** *pagbaran*
**go inland** *takod 1; tukad₁ 1*
**go right through** *lagbas 1*
**go there** *pehē'₁ 1.1*
**go through** *t'lla; l'ssut*
**go to and fro** *pagliyu-liyu; pagbiyu-biyu 1; pagparibay*
**go yonder** *pina'an 1.1; pehē'₁ 1.1*
**goad** *tungkud 1*
**goal** *tudjuhan; talget; maksud 1; kamaujuran*
**goat** *boro-boro₁*
**goatee** *janggut 2*
**goatfishes** *mang'ntut; banak; timbungan 1; tangbud*
**goat-like behavior** *atay kambing*
**goats** *kambing 1; bundan*
**gobble up** *butu'; l'kkob*
**gobies** *daing-daing sahasa'; kapalu*
**God** *Tuhan; Allah*
**God forbid** *s'lle' bale puhu'*
**God Most High** *Allahu Ta'ala 1*
**gods** *tuhan-tuhan*
**God's truth** *saksi' tuhan*
**goggles (for diving)** *tipara 1*
**going bad (no longer fresh)** *buntu'₁ 1; baguy; bahi*
**goiter** *bongol 1; bogon₁ 1*
**gold** *bulawan 1*
**gold capping on teeth** *bansil 1; pagpamulawan*
**gold coins** *mata-kura'; mata-jīp; pikit-mpat; dublun; pikit-dakayu'*
**gold pin** *basingan*
**goldsmith** *sasalan*
**gone by (time past)** *liban 1*
**gone from sight** *lanyap 1*
**gong frame** *palanggungan*
**gong sound** *tagunggu'an*
**gongs** *kulintangan; buwa₁; agung 1*
**good (moral)** *hāp 1.1; bontol 1*
**good (of figure)** *jangngang; hāp baran*
**good and bad** *haggut-pasu'*
**good feeling about** *galak₁ 1*
**good fortune** *pahala'; paksa' 1; hirayat; lidjiki' 1*
**good health** *anggauta'*

**good luck** *paksa' 1; hāp sukud*
**good manners** *pagaddat 1*
**good mood** *hāp atay; lasig 1*
**good price** *laba*
**good spirits (cheerful)** *lasig 1.1*
**good-looking** *hāp l'lla; hāp d'nda; hāp baran*
**goodness** *kahāp*
**goodness knows what** *daka*
**goods for sale** *dagangan*
**goodwill** *buddi 1; kahanusan; kahāpan*
**goose** *patu'; angsa'*
**goose-bumps** *pagbuntul; pokot-pokot 1*
**gorge (n)** *pampang*
**gorged** *s'gga*
**gorgeous** *dorog₂ 1.1*
**gospel** *Kitab Injil*
**gossip** *pina'in; tuhuma 1.1; paglitu-litu bissala*
**gotcha!** *sē'*
**gouge** *lugit*
**gouge out eye** *loleng*
**gourds** *labu₃; patula'*
**government** *parinta 1*
**governor** *tagmilikan; gubnul*
**gowns** *gamis; juba; luku*
**grab (seize)** *longpos; lolog; agaw 1.1*
**graceful** *alti; polma 1.1*
**graduate** *tammat 1*
**graduate (n)** *gradwet*
**graduations (measuring marks)** *guhit 1.2*
**grain measure** *supa₁; gantang*
**grain particles** *dorok*
**grains (food)** *pai 1; doha; layagan; dawa*
**grainy (texture)** *gasang; s'ppal; l'ngnges 1.1*
**grandchild** *mpu*
**grandchildren** *pang'mpu*
**grandfather** *mbo'₁*
**grandmother** *mbo'₁*
**grandparent** *mbo'₁*
**grant favor** *kahandak 1.1; sukud₂ 1.1*
**grant permission** *paba'id; dūl; patugut*
**granular (texture)** *budbud 1*
**grapes** *anggul*
**grappling hook** *badja' sau*
**grasp** *balut 1.2*
**grasp (both hands)** *s'kkol*
**grasp (one-handed)** *pendetan*
**grasp firmly** *kopkop 1.1; komkom*
**grasp mentally** *sipat₁ 1.1*
**grass species** *tib'llaw; lukut-lappas; parang; baili; jalum-kuyya'*
**grassed area** *kaparangan*
**grasshoppers** *ampan; tompang; bilalang; dulu₁*
**grate (v)** *li'is; kugut₁*
**grateful** *bakti' 1.1*

**graters** *kugutan; li'isan; jangatan*
**gratitude** *pagsukulan*
**grave (n)** *kubul 1; paliyangan; gumi 2; tampat 1*
**grave enclosure** *pilang-pilang*
**grave marker** *sunduk 1; duyung-duyung*
**grave shelf** *liyang 1*
**grave wrappings** *kapan*
**grave-clothes** *kuku-pote'; saput 1; tatap 1*
**gravel** *igang₁; kalang₂*
**gray** *abu-abu₁*
**gray-haired** *uban 1*
**grazed** *banggid 1; langgad 1.1; pares₁*
**grazing land** *kaparangan*
**greasy** *lanab*
**great (famous)** *bantug 1.1*
**great-aunt/great-uncle** *mbo'₁*
**greater degree** *luba'; luhūy; kalap*
**great-grandchild** *mpu-tu'ut*
**great-grandparent** *mbo'-tu'ut*
**great-great-grandchild** *mpu-kengkeng*
**great-great-grandparent** *mbo'-kengkeng*
**greatly** *paheya₁*
**greedy** *lagak 1.2; dahal 1.1; buhawi'₁; sawiya 1*
**greedy person** *bagahak₂*
**green** *gaddung 1; bū-kangag*
**green beans** *batung-hidjaw*
**green tree lizard** *bulik*
**greens** *sayul 1*
**greet (acknowledge someone's presence)** *sagina; sahawi 1; hīl*
**greetings** *sasalaman; salam*
**grenade** *bām*
**grid (trellis)** *jala-jala*
**grief** *susa 1; sukkal 1; lindu*
**grieve** *pagkaliru'an; paglemong 1.1; pagdohon*
**grieve loudly** *alud₂*
**grill (of fence)** *apis 1*
**grill (v)** *tapa 1; tunu'₂; panggang₁*
**grilled fish** *tinapa*
**grim** *b'ngngis 1*
**grimace (v)** *kibi'-kibi'; kiya'-kiya'*
**grime** *lumut₁ 2; lobag; moseng 1*
**grin** *kisi'*
**grind (rotary)** *giling*
**grind to powder** *tanay*
**grind to shape** *gisgis 1.1*
**grind together** *pagta'is; pagtage'ot; paggidgid*
**grind wheel** *panganggidgiran*
**grinding sound** *tage'ot*
**grip** *balut 1.2*
**grip (n)** *pendetan; komkoman 1; kōk 2*
**grit teeth** *k'ttop₂ 1.1; k'ttop-le'e*
**grits** *buwas-gandum*
**grizzled (of hair)** *pagbalot 1.1*

**groan** *pagaruhuy; pagarōy*
**groggy** *bingaw*
**groin (body part)** *hita' 2*
**groom (bridegroom)** *pangantin*
**groom (v)** *langis 1.1; lanu' 1.2*
**groomed** *halin*
**groove (v)** *pagl'bbak; tanghab₁*
**grope** *sassaw; sanaw; agap₂*
**gross (financial)** *luwas₂*
**ground (earth)** *tana'₁ 1; babaw-tana'*
**ground (root-filled)** *talungan*
**ground (run aground)** *siyud; sanglad; dagsa'*
**ground cover (plant)** *ulansiman*
**groundnut (peanut)** *batung₁*
**group (of mates)** *dansehe'an*
**group (of people)** *kompolan; kapono'an; umpigan; ba'an₁*
**group (of things)** *tumpuk 1; puntak 1*
**group (v)** *ukul 1*
**groupers (generic)** *kuhapo'; kulapu*
**grove of trees** *kakayuhan*
**grow (of plants)** *subud; tomo' 1.1; tungbu'*
**grow alongside** *dalig 1.1*
**grow and spread** *pagsuring-pagsaingsing 1*
**grow askew** *sōng-s'llo'; pagsōng-suwa'; pagsuwa'-s'llo'*
**grow dark** *lendom 1.2; pagdo'om*
**grow larger** *sulig₁*
**grow less** *kulang₁ 1.2*
**grow old** *pagtoto'a*
**grow small** *diki' 1.1*
**grow thin** *koskos*
**growing things** *paltomo'-tomo'an*
**growl** *usig*
**growth (in flesh)** *budjul₁*
**grub** *ulat₁*
**grub hoe** *sangkul 1*
**grubber** *kumkum₂*
**grubfish** *tamangka' 1*
**grudge (n)** *lagod-lagod; pagbogon 1; paghāk 1*
**gruel** *bugbug₂; santan 1; mistang 1*
**grumpy; grumble** *dugal 1*
**grunt** *h'lling-k'llong; hagok*
**grunts (fish species)** *baba'an₂; p'kkatan*
**guarantee (v)** *tinga 1.1; s'nnad; jamin*
**guarantor** *kuwiraw; magpipiyansa; piyarul*
**guard** *jaga 1.2; hampan 1.1; tunggu' 1.1*
**guard against** *halli'₁ 1.1; llog 1.1*
**guardian (protector)** *tagbaran; tunggu' 1*
**guardian rock** *batu-manunggul*
**guava** *biyabas*
**guavano** *liyabanos*
**guess** *pagtaluhan 1.1*
**guess accurately** *tokod 1*

guest *luruk 1*
guest (invited) *ta'abbit 1*
guesthouse *paghanti'an*
guide *tullus 1.2; tuli' 1.1; malim 1*
guide string *tali-tali₂*
guilty *tamak 1.1*
guilty (of sin or law-breaking) *tōng₂ 1.1*
guitar *kitara*
guitar string *estenles-kitara*
gullet *s'bbat 1*
gulls *ppak; t'lla'-t'lla'₁*
gully *l'bbak 1; pampang*
gully (under sea) *lisigan*
gulp down *ggok; tanggal₂*
gum (resin) *tarul; tagambil; bulitik₁*
gummed together *damil*

gums (of mouth) *isi empon*
gun (naval) *kanyun 1*
gunfire (repeated) *paglapak-lapak 1; paghuru-huru*
guns (personal) *garan; musil; sinapang; pistul*
gunshot *timbak 1*
gunwale *durung-diyata'*
gurgle *paglagonggok*
gush out *nubu-nubu*
gust (wind) *hunus 1; kawas-kawas*
gusto *kuseseyang 1*
gut (v) *t'ddak*
guts (intestines) *longon-longon; tina'i*
guttering *saluran*
guyabano *liyabanos*
guzzle *dahal 1.2*

# H h

habitual activity *kahinangan*
habitual smoker *pagsiniga*
habitually *daran-daran 1*
habituated (accustomed to) *biyaksa 1.1*
hack (v) *ladjang; lagut; tebag 1.1*
hacksaw *gatgat-basi'*
hadji *hadji'*
haggle *pagjawab 1.1*
hail someone *owa'₁ 1*
hair *bū 1; bu'un 1; bahibū 1*
hair clip *sipit 1*
hair oil *pomed 1*
hair styles *kingkoyan 1.1; hambak; hampal; simbōng 1.1*
haircutting (ceremonial) *paggunting*
hairless *ungas; tugak*
hairtail (fish) *langging*
half *tonga' 1; dambila' 1*
half fathom *honga'₂*
halfbeak fish (generic) *pillangan*
half-closed (eyes) *pirung-pirung*
half-cooked *bulak 2*
half-grown *kabulakan*
half-hearted *logmay-lamma*
half-hitch (knot) *engkot-buta 1; tingk'llos*
halfway *tonga'an; samalintonga'*
halo-halo (sweet confection) *sindul 1*
halyard (rigging) *hambawan*
hammer (n) *tukul 1*
hammer (v) *p'ppok*
hammerhead shark *kalitan-pamingkungan*
hammock *buwahan₁*
hampered *bimbang 1.2; limbit 1.1; gaggat 1.1*

hand *tangan 1*
hand (of bananas) *s'kkat 1*
hand out *paglamit-lamit 1.1*
hand over *tukbal₁ 1*
hand to me *ndiya*
handbag *bāg*
handbreadth *pāt 2*
handcuff *ekang-ekang 1; bilanggu' 1*
handful *komkoman 1*
handgun *pistul*
handicapped *ku'il; kulang-akkal*
handiwork *hātan*
handkerchief *panyu'*
handkerchief *sapu-tangan; panyu'*
handle (n) *tangkay 2; baba'an₁; patihan; puhan 1*
handle unnecessarily *pagkoledje; umas; tiyu'-tiyu'*
hands in prayer position *sangga 1; tayak 1*
hands on hips *s'kket; hawak*
handshake *jiyara; sekan*
handsome *hāp l'lla; hansam; lingkat 1.1*
handwriting *sulatan; hātan*
hang (suspend) *gantung₂ 1.1*
hang by arms *gulantung*
hang by legs or arms *pagbitay 1*
hang down *sasa₂; hallal; bitay*
hang free *tonton 1*
hang in tatters *jabel; jebel-jebel 1.1*
hang on hook *sagnat 1.1*
hanger *sasagnat; sablayan*
hanging between *bigtang 1*
hanging loosely *tayo*
happen *niya'₁ 1.1; t'kka₂ 1.1; inay 1*

**happen at the same time** *tā'-tā' 1; salta'*

**happen suddenly** *taggaha'*

**happen to** *manjari₃*

**happen to someone** *taluwa' 2*

**happening (event)** *kahālan*

**happening (moment of)** *sinabu 1*

**happening (time of)** *gimut*

**happily (fortunately)** *daipara*

**happy** *koyag 1.1; kōg 2; kōd*

**hard** *tuwas 1*

**hard (of root crops)** *ketot; k'ttul; kelot*

**hard (of wood)** *kubal 1*

**hard feelings** *lagod-lagod; buli'an₂; agmol 1*

**hard pieces** *tigtigan*

**hard to imagine** *mahal₁*

**hard-headed** *tuwas-kōk*

**hard-hearted** *tigman*

**hardly** *agon mbal*

**hardship** *katiksa'an; kasigpitan; kabinasahan; kati'ilan*

**hard-wearing** *kamdos₂; taggu₁; pagon₁ 1.1*

**hardwood trees** *agdaw; kayu-soha'; balo'*

**hard-working** *patihinangun*

**harelip** *sombeng 2*

**harlot** *puta; sundal 1*

**harm (by spirit being)** *sagda₁; sila'-sila' 1.1; uwak; balbal*

**harm (n)** *baya-baya; la'at 1; ka'at 1*

**harm (v)** *jahulaka' 1.1; pissoko'; puhinga'; jilaka'*

**harmonica** *honel*

**harmony (social)** *pagsulutan*

**harpoon** *ablong; sangkil 1*

**harpoon (v)** *s'llok 1*

**harsh (speech)** *talom bowa'; labas₂ 1*

**harvest** *anihan*

**harvest ceremony** *hinang-kalun 1*

**harvest fruit** *pusu'₁*

**harvest grain** *pagani*

**harvest rice** *k'ttu'*

**haste** *pagdai'-dai'an*

**hastily** *jamput*

**hasty** *sahi'-sahi'*

**hat** *saruk*

**hatch eggs (v)** *ōm; llom*

**hate** *b'nsi 1.1*

**haughty** *langa atay*

**haul** *hella'; guyud 1*

**haul up** *dahik; bungkal₁ 1.1*

**haunt** *pagbagala; pangguwa' 1.1*

**have (possess)** *taga*

**have a feeling** *nanam 2*

**have a meal** *pagkakan 1.1*

**have fun** *paglata; paglangog; pagkalamihan 1.1*

**have power over** *pagdūl-baya'*

**have taste for** *sōb; tahud*

**haven** *okoman*

**hawk (n)** *sambula'an; belle'₁*

**hawk (sell)** *pagsoroy*

**hawk up phlegm** *pagkahak*

**hawser** *kanyamun*

**hazy (misty)** *hanaw-hanaw; buraw*

**he** *iyā*

**head (of body)** *kōk 1*

**head (of boil)** *mata-kalibubut*

**head (of coin)** *ta'u-ta'u₂; kara*

**head covering** *turung-balu 1; pīs₁; saruk*

**head covering (of corpse)** *talkun*

**head lice** *limad-limad; kulisa' 1*

**head teacher** *prinsipal*

**headache** *tali-tali₁ 1; p'ddi' 1.1*

**headband** *sahal₂*

**head-dress (bridal)** *korona; panumping; tumanggal*

**heading (of book)** *bāb*

**heading that way** *pina'an 1*

**headland** *tōng-lahat*

**headman** *bag'llal 1; kapala*

**heads (coin)** *ta'u₃*

**headwear** *saruk*

**heal** *uli'₁ 1.1; hali₂*

**healed (after circumcision)** *haplus 1.1*

**healed child** *anak-ubus*

**healer** *pagsasāg; pagbowahan; pananambal*

**healing ceremony** *pagkādja 2; pagsalba 1*

**health** *apuwa*

**health (feeling of)** *palasahan*

**health (well-being)** *salamat-baran; sajahitra'*

**healthy (well-grown)** *sambu 1*

**heap (n)** *botang₁ 1; tumpuk 1*

**heaps of (many)** *gora'₂ 1; jayak*

**hear** *bahingaw; talengog; kale 1*

**hear clearly** *lagtok*

**heard imperfectly** *halong*

**heart (body part)** *jantung*

**heart (emotional)** *atay₂*

**heart (romantic)** *bigi-jantung*

**heart of palm** *umbut*

**heartburn** *s'bbol 1*

**heart-rending** *ase'-ase'*

**heartwood** *kubal 1; tupas₂; sapan₂*

**heat** *pasu'₁ 1*

**heat exhaustion** *panggang₂ 1; kapiyalu 1*

**heat liquid to boiling** *pabukal*

**heat metal** *babal₁; subu₁ 2*

**heat of day** *kapasu'an*

**heat of sun** *silak 1*

**heat rash** *buwa'-buwa'-hulas 1*

**heated (fevered)** *limasu' 1*

**heaven** *sulga'*

**heavens (atmosphere)** *langit; ayan*
**heavy (of eyes)** *luyu'*
**heavy (of rain)** *landos 1*
**heavy (weight)** *buhat₁ 1.1; doson 1*
**Hebrew** *Hibrani*
**heed** *hirup₁; asip*
**heel** *buli'-tape'*
**heel of shoe** *takon*
**height** *langa 1; langkaw 1*
**height (of person)** *lanjang 1*
**heirloom** *pamusaka'*
**helix** *siputan*
**hell** *nalka'; Jahannam*
**helmet** *helmet*
**helmet shell** *tabuli-bbet*
**help** *tulung 1; tabang 1; tapin*
**help carry** *tambin*
**help oneself to** *t'ppas₁; lolog; sabsab*
**helper (domestic)** *ipatan*
**helpful** *patitabangun; buddi 1.1*
**hem (n)** *kumpi' 1*
**hem (v)** *ppi' 1.1; langgahit*
**hematoma** *alom 1*
**hemorrhage (at childbirth)** *bīn 1.1*
**hemorrhage (bleeding)** *sallak 1*
**hemorrhoids** *l'pput₁ 1.1*
**hemp (abaca)** *lanut*
**hen** *manuk-d'nda*
**henna plant** *passal 1*
**her** *iyā*
**herbs (flavoring)** *pamapā*
**herd (v)** *s'ssol₂ 1.1; illig; lakod*
**here** *maitu 1; pi'itu 1*
**here is** *itiya'*
**hereafter** *ahirat*
**heritage** *pamusaka'*
**hermaphrodite** *bantut 1*
**hermit crab** *omang 1*
**hernia** *busā' 1.1*
**hero** *babantugun*
**herons** *siru'ung; baggok; kallo'*
**herpes** *ugihap 1*
**herring** *gunu'*
**hers** *=na*
**hesitant** *gaga'; āng-āng; hawal 1.1*
**hesitant in speech** *mamang₂*
**hesitate** *duwa-ruwa*
**hessian (burlap)** *karut 1*
**hew** *tigad 1.1; tebag 1.1*
**hey!** *elle'-elle'; ōy*
**hibiscus** *gumamela*
**hiccups** *s'kko'-s'kko'*
**hidden (from sight)** *p'dda-palom; buli'₂ 1; lambang₁*
**hidden motive** *pagbuli'-buli' 1; buli'-akkal*

**hide** *loklok; tapuk 1*
**hide intent** *limbung 1.1; salig₃*
**hide-and-seek** *pagtilluk; pagpiyung 1.1*
**hiding place** *kasipukan; tapukan*
**high** *langa 1.1; langkaw 1.1*
**high (of brow)** *lengas₂*
**high (of social status)** *banwa; paglanga*
**high (of tide)** *tambang₁ 1; daka'; l'kkab; lalom₁ 2; nso'*
**high in sky** *langkaw llaw*
**high-bridged (of nose)** *pansung 1*
**higher court** *kaheya'an*
**highest rank** *mahatinggi*
**high-pitched (of voice)** *tilahak*
**high-ranking** *bangsa₂*
**highwater line** *tampe; tapiyan; bihingan*
**highway** *kalsara; paglalabayan*
**hijack** *kullu-kullu₂ 1; mundu 1.1*
**hike (v)** *baklay*
**hill** *būd 1; bīd*
**hill-like** *bullud*
**hills** *kabūd-būran*
**hilt** *puhan 1*
**him** *iyā*
**hinder; hindrance** *bimbang 1; hapa' 1.2*
**hindered (restricted)** *ampal; gaggat 1.1*
**Hindu** *Banggali*
**hinge** *lapi'*
**hint at** *sindil 1*
**hinterland** *deya; kareyahan*
**hips** *pangkul*
**hire** *padjak₂; pakkiyaw*
**hire performer** *tangkap*
**his** *=na*
**hiss of water** *llis*
**historic account** *kata-kata; usul 1*
**hit (of wind)** *dugpak 1*
**hit ball with stick** *pega*
**hit fatally** *tatal₂ 1.1*
**hit head (by falling)** *dahungkung*
**hit head-on** *pagbangga'; pagdugtul*
**hit obliquely** *dupli'as*
**hit target** *tumlang 2; timbag*
**hit with force** *t'bba' 1; tumbuk₁ 1.1; banggul*
**hit with forearm** *tikbung*
**hit with palm** *t'ppak₁*
**hit with projectile** *balibag₁*
**hitch a ride** *sakay 1; tumpang*
**hither and yon** *pagbiyu-biyu 1*
**hit-the-target (game)** *pagtaksi' 1.1; sigung*
**hoarse** *gohom 1; kohot; pehet*
**hobble** *pagtamengka'; pagtongka'*
**hobby** *huwang₂*
**hoe** *sangkul 1*

**hog** *bawi*

**hoist** *buhat₁ 1.2*

**hold breath** *p'ddon*

**hold close to one's body** *pasabak*

**hold down** *t'kkon; tihin; paddik*

**hold grudge** *agmol 1.1*

**hold hands** *pagambit₂*

**hold in arms** *golpe₂; hulid 1.1; golgol*

**hold in fist** *s'kkol; kopkop 1.1; komkom*

**hold in mouth** *tanga'₁; k'nnum*

**hold in place** *gipis 1.1*

**hold of boat (n)** *mohang*

**hold on lap** *giba 1.1*

**hold on to (keep safe)** *abin; appula*

**hold responsible** *bīng₃*

**hold something** *ntan₁ 1; balut 1.1*

**hold to breast** *mpit*

**hold to hip** *hambin 1; pipi₁*

**hold under armpit** *k'ppit*

**hold up (detain)** *kullu-kullu₂ 1; holdap*

**hold with fingertips** *kemeng-kemeng*

**holder of rights** *tag-*

**hole** *lowang 1; kusu 1*

**hole in ground** *p'llong*

**hole in the floor** *s'ddi*

**holed** *l'bbot; s'bbo'*

**holler** *gasud*

**hollow (in dish)** *mohang*

**hollow (in rock or cliff)** *kehe 1; songab 1*

**hollow (nothing inside)** *gaunggang*

**hollow (pond-like)** *powak; kohak-kohak; halo-halo; k'bbong-k'bbong*

**hollowed** *l'bbong 1*

**hollowed out** *lowak 1*

**holy** *sussi 1.1; mulliya 1; mahasussi*

**holy day** *Aid ul Pitri*

**Holy Spirit** *Duhul Kudus*

**home** *luma'; pamole'an 1*

**homecoming** *pole'₁ 1*

**homeland** *kaporolan; lahat; tana'₂*

**homely (plain-looking)** *seme'*

**homesick** *entom 1.2; sumangat llum 1.1*

**homily (sermon)** *hutba'*

**homosexual** *bantut 1*

**hone (sharpen)** *asa'*

**honest** *adil; bontol 1*

**honey (darling)** *nnong*

**honey (of bees)** *gula' buwani*

**honey bee** *buwani*

**honor (n)** *mahaltabat; kamahaldika'an*

**honor (v)** *mahaldika'; mulliya 1.1; hulmat 1*

**hoodwink (v)** *lingu 1.1; animu*

**hoodwinked** *saman-saman*

**hoof** *kukku₁*

**hook (hanger)** *sasabit; sasagnat; kabit₁ 1*

**hook (tool)** *gangat 1; kukuhit; badja' 1*

**hook into** *kuhit; sa'ud₁ 1*

**hook something** *sabit₁ 1.1; gangat 1.1*

**hooks (fishing)** *kowat-kowat; p'ssi 1; kawil*

**hoop (basketball)** *rīng*

**hoop-shaped border** *lengkol 1*

**hoot** *mmu*

**hop (on one foot)** *pagengke'-engke'*

**hope (n)** *pangasa 1; kaholatan; asa 1*

**hope for** *lagad 1.1*

**hopeful** *kiri-kiri; holat 1*

**hopefully** *gōm na pa'in; mura-murahan; angan-angan*

**hoping to be fed** *donga'; alung 2*

**horizon** *bihing langit*

**horizontal** *bantang 1*

**horn (animal)** *tanduk 1*

**hornbill** *kalaw*

**hornet (insect)** *tabungay*

**horse** *kura' 1; mandu-mandu*

**horse drawn cart** *kalesa*

**horse-radish tree** *kalamunggay; kilul*

**horseshoe crab** *bangkas*

**hose (for water)** *tubu₁*

**hose (socks)** *medyas; kalsitin*

**hospital** *ispital*

**hospitality** *lalabotan 1*

**hostile** *jahallis; b'ngngis 1*

**hostilities** *bono' 1; kala'atan*

**hot (feverish)** *limasu' 1*

**hot (spicy)** *lara 1.1*

**hot (stuffy)** *linganga; lingo'ot*

**hot (temperature)** *pasu'₁ 1.1*

**hot compress (medicinal)** *paus*

**hot season** *pang'llaw*

**hot temper** *pasu' atay*

**hotel** *paghanti'an; hotel*

**hour** *lisag₁; jām*

**house** *luma'*

**house (ceremonial)** *maligay₁*

**house (for guardian spirit)** *larang-larang*

**house (incomplete)** *ballay*

**house (plus contents and people)** *pamāy-bāy*

**house (small)** *kubu'-kubu'*

**house cluster** *le'od₁; tumpuk 2; libug; nibung*

**houseboat** *lepa*

**household** *daluma'; okoman*

**house-post** *pangtu'ud; pipul; hāg 1*

**hover** *antung*

**how come?** *angay*

**how many? how much?** *dangay; pila 1*

**how much more (especially)** *ya lagi'na*

**how often?** *min pila*

**how?** *buwattingga 1; painay*

however *bo' arapun; bo' pa'in; ya balikna; saguwā'*
however many *pila-pila*
howl (of dog) *tanghul; ūl; usig; tangungngul*
hoy! *owa'₁ 1*
hoya plant *kopal-kopal*
hue (color) *walna'; b'ttik 1; kolol 1*
hug *hambin 1; gapus; komkom*
huge *heya 1.1*
hull (of canoe) *bangka'; damas; kasko*
hull corn (v) *lutu₁*
hum *lleng; pag'mmu-mmu*
human being *a'a; manusiya' 1*
humanity *kapaga'a; ummat 1; pagkamanusiya'*
humble (status) *deyo'₃ 1*
humble oneself *ū'ū; pagpatireyo'*
humiliated *biyas; maru 1.2; paki' 1; tamparasa*
humiliation *kaiya'an*
humility *pagdeyo'-addat 1; pagsujud 1*
hump; hump-backed *buggul 1; dukkug 1; kuba₂*
hunch up *kullung; k'ttung*
hunched *loko' 2; komo'₁*
hundred *hatus*
hungry *lingantu 1.1*

hunt for *piha 1; batuk₂*
hurl *badji; hiyak; laruk*
hurricane *badju*
hurriedly *magdai'-dai'*
hurry *samot 1.1; l'kkas 1.1; dai'-dai' 1.1*
hurry (n) *pagdai'-dai'an*
hurt (cause harm) *pissoko'; jilaka'; la'at 1.2*
hurt (of feelings) *mandā'-dā'; ambul-dā'; bakat atay*
hurt from smacking *paglera-lera*
husband *h'lla*
hush (be quiet) *paddam 1*
husk (of coconut) *bunut 1*
husk (of grain) *hampa' 1*
husk grain (v) *lutu₁*
husky (muscular) *kaslog*
hut *payad; kubu'-kubu'*
hybrid *pagdambila'an*
hydrocephalus *kilā-luku; kulang-kilā*
hypnotism *hikmat*
hypocrite (religious) *munapik*
hypodermic needle *tugsuk 2*
hypothetical *ganta'₃*

# I i

I don't know *inday*
I get it (understand) *ā 1*
I, me *akū; aku₂*
i.e. *hatina*
ice *elo 1; aes*
icecream *aeskrīm*
ichthyosis *kulap 1*
idea *pangannal₁; pikil 1*
identical *dasali'; daluwa*
identify *kilā 1*
identify by name *tublak₂; tugpang 1; ōn₁ 1.2*
identify by touch *sanaw; sadsad 1.1*
identifying mark *tumbuk₃ 1; sāp₂ 1; tatak*
idiot (mentally deficient) *babbal; dupang 1*
idol *bahala'₂; ta'u-ta'u₁*
if *bo'₃; bang₁; ya aniya'*
if (for example) *bang saupama*
if A, then B *abila*
if God wills *insa Allah*
if in fact *bang hati'*
if it had been *arapun du pa'in*
if only *bangsi'; bang bay; bang pa'in*
if perhaps *bang ba*
if so *bang hati'*
ignite *sū' 1.2; dallet 1.1; dokot₂ 1.2*

ignited *keyat₂ 1.1*
ignorant of *awam*
ignorant person *akil-balig*
ignore *pagbisu-bisu; pabiyal; taikut 1.1; lehom; sagad 1*
ignore advice *balda*
iguana *pahang*
ill *bangat*
illegal *kolorom*
illegitimate *anak-kasi; harambiyara' 1*
ill-fated *pawas 1.1; jari₄ 1.1*
ill-feeling *akon-akon*
illiterate *awam*
ill-mannered *di'in-di'in; halipulu 1*
ill-natured *jahallis*
illness *saki 1*
illness (mild) *abat 1*
illness of paranormal origin *sāg 1.1; bihang₁*
ill-tempered *bigsi' 1; masu'; pagmusmud 1*
ill-treated *ti'il; tiksa' 1*
illuminated area *kasawahan*
illumination *ilaw 1*
illustration *pamaralilan; sapantun*
image (effigy) *bahala'₂; ta'u-ta'u₁*
imagine *pula'-pula' 1.1*
imam *imam*

**imbalanced (lopsided)** *pagbalibag*

**imbecile** *babbal*

**imitate** *beya'-beya'₁ 1.1; lihi 1.2; sengod*

**immature** *bulak 1; mula'; akil-balig*

**immeasurable** *mbal tasilang*

**immediately** *agsāy; magtūy; dai'-dai'an; saru'un-du'un*

**immensely pleased.** *hōp₂*

**immerse** *t'nde 1.1; t'nnob 1.1*

**imminent** *arai' 2; t'ppung 1; kibit-dawa; abut₁*

**immobilized** *ku'il; lagot*

**immoderate** *makalandu'*

**immoral** *biga'; jahil 1; pagba'is 1*

**immoral person** *paglaban 1; palalu*

**immovable** *totog 1*

**immune (to alternative suitor)** *tambol suratan*

**immune (to harm)** *pagkal'lla; basi'₂ 1*

**immunity (magical)** *sihil 1; kobol 1*

**impact** *dugpak 1; dumpas*

**impact (wind or current)** *tumbuk₁ 1*

**impaired (of fruit)** *duplak*

**impale** *budjak 1.1; sungkit*

**impartial** *timbang bibitan*

**impatient** *sahi'-sahi'*

**impede** *sanggul₁ 1.1; pagsabol 1*

**impeded** *ampal; gaggat 1.1*

**impediment (hindrance)** *kalimbit; jallat₁*

**impediment (of speech)** *terol; ponga'; kallu'*

**imperfection** *salla'₁ 1; galna' 1; gora'₁ 1*

**imperial volute** *kunnig*

**impertinent** *di'in-di'in*

**impetigo** *kuligi'₂*

**implement** *pang'ntan*

**implicate** *sabay; lamud₂ 1.2*

**implore** *pinta-pinta; ampun-ampun; amu'-amu'*

**imply** *pa'andig*

**impolite** *di'in-di'in; halipulu 1*

**impolite speech** *lagam-bowa'*

**important** *langa 1.1*

**important matter** *bale₁*

**importantly** *muna-muna 1.1*

**impose a decision** *indika 1.1*

**impose fine** *taksil 1.2*

**impossible** *dipisil; mbal manjari*

**impotent** *bantut 1*

**impoverish** *pamiskin*

**impregnate** *b'ttong₂ 1.1*

**impress** *elong-elong mata*

**impression of blow** *m'ndal*

**imprint** *bakkas; limpa' 1*

**imprison** *pilisu 1.1; jīl 1.1; kalabusu 1.1*

**improve (condition)** *hikay; gām-gām; hāp-hāp*

**improve (weather)** *lōng-lōng; gōm-gōm*

**improvement (of health)** *kahikayan; si'at*

**impudent** *sabul 1.1*

**impurities** *siyu-siyu 1; lagod₁*

**in bulk** *pono'an*

**in fact** *ya b'nnalna; samata-mata; parahāl*

**in love** *pagbilahi; baya'-baya'₁*

**in order to** *ko; supaya; bo'₂*

**in other words** *hatina*

**in; inside** *ni₁; deyom 1*

**inactive** *dohongan*

**inattentive** *pagbisu-bisu; pabiyal*

**inborn condition (problem)** *sahili'; kariyasali*

**incantation (healing)** *tawal 1*

**incarcerate** *pilisu 1.1; jīl 1.1*

**incense** *kamanyan; laksi'*

**incense (stick)** *hiyu*

**incentive** *mamhu'; bo'ot*

**incessant** *sigi-sigi 1*

**incestuous** *sumbang; haram 1.1*

**inch (n)** *tambō' 2; inses*

**inch along** *ingsud; hense; higin*

**inchworm** *ulat-h'kka-h'kka*

**incise** *gali'₁; galing-galing*

**incisor** *taling*

**incite** *pitna; sūg-sūg; bingkug*

**incline (downward slope)** *lūran*

**incline (lean from upright)** *poyog 1; tīg; kīng 1.1*

**incline (upward slope)** *tukaran*

**include as belonging** *itung₂*

**included** *beya' isāb; tabeya'; lapay 1*

**including** *sampay 1*

**incoherent** *li'an; ligaw*

**incoherent speech** *kaligawan*

**incohesive** *gokal; poka; p'kkal 1*

**income** *pagusaha 1; gadji 1*

**incomparable** *mbal taliyu*

**incomplete** *kabus*

**incomplete (of work)** *sahi'-sahi'*

**inconceivable** *mbal tasipat*

**inconsistent** *palta; lepet*

**incorrect** *sā'₁ 1.1*

**incorrigible** *jahallis; jahil 1*

**increase** *kasōngan 2; ganap 1.2*

**incredible** *tingga' dawa*

**incredulous** *sussa'; jakki 1; himatta'*

**incubate** *ōm; llom*

**indecency** *kalumu'an*

**indecent (speech)** *la'at bowa'; sabul 1.1*

**indecision** *pagduwa-ruwa 1*

**indeed** *pahāp₁; sa; bā 1; du 1*

**indentation** *l'bbak 1*

**independent (work alone)** *tunggal-tunggal 1; tukkal*

**index finger** *tudlu'₁*

**Indian** *Banggali*

**Indian snowberry** *sampan-tuhug*

**indifferent** *pasagad*
**indigent** *pulubi; miskin; kabus*
**indigestion** *bakag₂; paglimbōn*
**indignation** *amā*
**indirect (of speech)** *pa'andig*
**indiscriminately** *m'ssa' bidda'*
**indisposed** *abat 1.1*
**indisposition** *abat 1; saki 1*
**indistinct** *abu-abu₂; hanaw-hanaw*
**individual choice** *beya'-beya'₂*
**individual skill** *huwang₂*
**individuality** *jari₄ 1; jāt₁*
**individualize** *paggintil*
**individually** *kaniya-kaniya; tarangan-tarangan*
**individually and together** *dangan-duwa*
**indolent** *lisu'; hukaw 1.1*
**induce** *bowa₃*
**indulge someone** *patege'; parūl 1.1; palangga' 1.1*
**indulgent (of self)** *dakag*
**industrious** *tukid 1; tebot*
**inedible bits (in food)** *upa' 1*
**ineffective** *pasaw; linis*
**inert** *antung; atol*
**inevitably** *tiyap-tiyap; taka-taka; sabali-bali*
**inexpensive** *luhay₁ 1.1*
**infant** *anak₁ 1*
**infatuated** *istrōk; pilad*
**infected** *lamin 1.1*
**infection of ear** *antil 1; tolek 1*
**infectious** *paglemed*
**infer** *ambil-hati*
**inferior** *guya'; p'ddut*
**infertile** *tamanang*
**infested (by shipworm)** *tambelok 1.1*
**infested (by wood borer)** *lutus; bukbuk 1.1*
**infidel** *kapil 1*
**infidelity (marital)** *pagliyu-lakad*
**infirm (aged)** *tungkud-luwag*
**inflamed** *baha' 2*
**inflate** *tambu 2; gomba; tting; pām*
**inflexible (unyielding)** *sandat 2; kōk-batu; atay-batu*
**inflict pain** *binasa 1.1*
**influence (v)** *kole'-kole'₂; bowa₃; inay-inay*
**influence by magic** *h'lling₃; sihil 1.1*
**influence someone** *bowa₃*
**influence wrongly** *sugi-sugi*
**inform** *tubad; pasasā; pahing; pata'u; hati 2; sahawi 2*
**inform on someone** *sumbung; kuhi₂*
**informal (of relationship)** *pagda'atay; pagsōd-addat*
**information** *haka 1; hunub 1; habal*
**informed** *sakup₁ 1.2; bistu 1; tahu*
**infrequent** *lahang; bislang 1; bihang₂*

**infringement** *langgal sara' 1; sā'₁ 1*
**ingrained dirt** *lumut₁ 2; lobag*
**ingratiate** *pagmamhu'*
**ingredient** *lamud₁ 1; templa 1*
**inhale** *horot; hanggup; h'llop 1.1*
**inheritance** *pusaka' 1; bba₁ 2*
**inherited condition** *panibi*
**inherited custom** *pangkatan*
**inherited skills** *purukan; tugu; tubu'an 2*
**inhumane** *jahulaka' 1*
**initiate** *pagmete-mete; talik-talik*
**initiate (boys)** *islam 1.1*
**initiate (girls)** *sunnat*
**initiate marriage talks** *tilaw d'nda*
**inject** *tugsuk 2.2*
**injured** *keme; pali' 1.1*
**injured (internal)** *bu'ag; bongso' 1; bugtu'₂ 1.1*
**injury** *bakat 1*
**ink** *dawat 1; īng*
**ink sac (squid, etc.)** *lansong*
**inland** *deya*
**in-laws** *ayuwan; ba'i 1; pamikitan; mato'a*
**inlet** *suba'; lo'ok*
**inner** *deyom 1*
**inner self** *ginhawa; nyawa; palilihan 1*
**innocence** *atay-pote'*
**innocence (test of)** *pagko'ot bohe'-pasu'*
**innumerable** *pila-pila*
**inoculate** *langgit 1*
**inquire** *tilaw 1.1; tilosa 1.1; paliksa'; kihaka*
**inquisitive** *tilosa 1; katilaw*
**insane** *kangog; belaw*
**insect (generic)** *manuk-manuk 1*
**insecure (not firm)** *hogal; loka*
**insert** *asok 1.1; s'llot 1.1; siplit; osok 1.1*
**insert hand** *ko'ot 1*
**inside** *deyoman 1*
**insidious** *tipu 1.1; lingu 1.1*
**insightful** *ladju pikilan*
**insignificant (size, amount)** *heya pisut-pisut; salat 1*
**insincere** *pagduwa-bayhu'*
**insinuate** *pa'andig*
**insipid** *t'bbag*
**insist** *egot-egot; pipit₁*
**insomnia** *gesong*
**inspect** *liling; banding; tanding 1*
**inspect (before buying)** *tangku'-tangku'*
**inspire** *sōd 2*
**install** *batuk₁ 1*
**install (connect up)** *sangon₁ 1.1*
**instalment (finance)** *pagbayad 1*
**instant death** *tubag*
**instantaneously** *sakadjap; saru'un-du'un*

**instead** *pagsakali*; *bo' arapun*; *pād-pād₁*; *atas₁*

**instruct (order to)** *soho'*

**instruct (teach)** *pantun 1.1*; *pastul*; *pandu' 1.2*; *pitis₂ 1.1*; *pituwa 1.1*

**instructions** *panoho'an*; *pituwa 1*; *pagpapat 1*

**instruments (musical)** *biyula 1*; *soleng₂*; *kitara*; *honel*; *kula'ing*; *ambak-ambak*

**insufficient** *kabus*; *kulang₁ 1.1*; *ipis 1*

**insult** *paglaka'-laka' 1.1*; *pahimulas*; *sumpa'*; *hina'*

**intact** *jukup 1*; *timbakkol*; *tibu'uk₁ 1*

**integrity** *katibu'ukan*; *kapagdakayu'*

**intellect; intelligence** *nahu 1*; *akkal 1*

**intelligent** *tali' 1*; *ladju pikilan*; *tallang-hati 1.1*

**intelligible** *hapal 2*; *hangpat 1*

**intend** *maksud 1.1*; *gawi 1.1*; *mohot 1.1*

**intend ill-will** *jingki 1.1*

**intending** *gara' 1.1*

**intense** *pagon₂*; *landos 1*

**intense (of color)** *lutu'₂*

**intense pain** *p'llat 1*

**intensely (very)** *to'ongan 1.1*; *sidda 1*

**intensify** *paruhun*

**intensify (disagreement)** *t'bbud suli-suli*

**intention** *gawi 1*; *hatulan 2*; *niyat 1*; *kamatti*; *hadjat₁*

**intentional** *tu'ud₁ 1*

**inter (bury)** *kubul 1.1*; *pagl'bbong*

**intercede for** *ussap 1.1*; *ayura 2*; *pagmatiase'*

**intercept** *sampang 2*

**interchange** *saliyu 1.1*

**intercourse (sexual)** *paghinang₂*; *pagbihing₂*

**interest on investment** *anak₃ 1*

**interfere** *lamud₂ 1.1*; *jau'-jau'*

**interim** *gantung₁*

**interior** *deyom 1*

**interlace (stitching)** *pagsuwa'-suwa'*

**intermediate state** *pagsalluk*; *pagpati'llot 1*

**intermingle** *paglamud*

**intermittent** *palta*; *patay-patay*; *sasā'*

**intermittently** *pagsān-sān*

**internal organs** *tina'i*

**interpose** *sapat₁*

**interpret** *tali' 1.1*

**interpret (into Sinama)** *Sinama 1.1*

**interpretation (of scripture)** *tapsil*

**interrogate** *tanya₂*; *sumariya*; *paliksa'*; *jakki 2*

**interrupt** *honglo' 1.1*; *jau'-jau'*; *aging 1.1*

**interrupted** *balat*

**interruption** *hogga'an*

**intersect** *pagbabag*

**intertwine** *lokot*; *pagsa'ud 2*

**interval** *llotan*; *ōt*

**intervene** *lamud₂ 1.1*

**intervene (on behalf of)** *sapa'at₁ 1.1*

**intestinal disorder** *kaluwa'*

**intestines** *longon-longon*; *tina'i*; *kumba'*

**in-the-act (of doing)** *kara-kara₂*

**intimate relations** *pagbihing₂*

**intimidate** *hansom*; *dangka₁*; *pakitāw*

**intonation** *tunis*; *bowahan*; *lagam*

**intoxicated** *lango 1*

**intransitive prefix** *pa-₁*

**intrepid** *esog 1.1*; *bahani 1*

**introduce someone** *pakilā*

**introverted** *sandol 1*

**intrude on** *jau'-jau'*

**intuit (know by instinct)** *tasdik*

**inundate** *dunuk*; *latap 1.1*; *s'llop*

**invade** *sakay 2*; *dumpas*; *dohay*

**invalid (not acceptable)** *batal*

**invent** *hinang-hinang₂*

**inverted** *baliskat 1*; *pakkom 1*; *bīng₁ 1*; *sunsang*

**inverted (end for end)** *sulang-saling*

**investigate** *tilosa 1.1*; *dikisa 1*; *paliksa'*

**investment (financial)** *po'on₃*

**invincible** *basi'₂ 1.1*; *pagkobol 1.1*

**invisible** *limun 1*

**invite to** *abbit*

**invite to an event** *pata'u*; *pabā'*; *ta'abbit 1.1*

**invoke (call by name)** *sabbut 1.1*; *harap₂*; *ta'at 1.1*

**invoke a curse** *sapa'at₁ 1.1*

**invoke a deity** *tanggap 1*

**invoke ancestor** *pag'mbo'*; *pat'nna' mbo'*; *salassay 1.1*

**involuntary** *halam baya'*

**involve in discussion** *isun*

**involved** *pagsakutu*

**involvement** *lamud₂ 1*

**invulnerability** *sihil 1*

**invulnerable** *kobol 1.1*; *basi'₂ 1.1*

**iridescent** *paghinu-hinu*

**iron (laundry)** *pilinsa*; *kutad 1.2*

**iron (metal)** *balan*; *basi'₁ 1*

**iron roof** *atop mital*

**ironwood trees** *amulawan*; *ipil*

**irrational** *sawi'*

**irregular** *tempang*; *kimig 1*

**irregular movement** *tumballeng*

**irreligious** *munapik*; *kapil 1.1*

**irresponsible** *baldapat*; *dapat₁ 2*

**irreverent** *pangkal*

**irrigate** *bohe'₁ 1.1*; *busug 1*

**irritability** *p'ggot-p'ggot*

**irritable (fretful)** *mmaw 1*; *dugal 1*; *s'ngngot₁ 1*; *dole' 1.1*

**irritate someone** *sunggud*

**irritated (annoyed)** *kalintaw*; *anak-anak₂*; *b'ngkol deyom atay*

**irritation** *amā*; *lagot-lagot*; *astol 1*

**irritation (physical)** *m'ssang 1*; *b'ngkol₁ 1*

**Islam** *Islam*
**Islamic tenets** *lukun*
**island** *pū'₁*
**island (flat)** *nusa*
**island-hopping** *paglatun-latun*
**islands** *kapū'-pū'an 1*
**isolation** *mala'u-la'u 1*
**Israeli** *Isra'ili*

**it** *iyā*
**itch (n)** *buwa'-buwa' 1*
**itchy (of scalp)** *buruk 1.1*
**itchy (of skin)** *kagutgut 1*; *katol 1*; *abas 1*
**itemize** *kalkula*; *uki'-uki'*
**its** *=na*
**ivory** *garing 1*

# J j

**jab (v)** *tanduk 1.1*; *sudlat 1.1*
**jabbed** *tugsuk 2.1*
**jacket (clothing)** *jaket*
**jackfruit** *tignus*; *marang*; *nangka'*
**jacks (fish species)** *tabung*
**jacks (game)** *jimban*
**jagged** *pagsereng*
**jail** *jīl 1*; *kalabusu 1*
**Jakarta** *Jakatla'*
**jam into** *alod₂ 1.1*
**Jamaican cherry** *datilis*; *sokal-sokal*
**Jamaican verbena** *bilu-bilu₂*
**jamb (of door)** *lusuk-lusuk*
**jammed in** *dasok 1*; *selot 1*
**jammed together** *damil*; *pagsigpit 1*
**Japan** *Jipun*
**jar (earthenware)** *poga*; *kibut*; *pipa*; *bingki'*; *ka'ang*; *tanāng*; *tangpad*
**jaundice** *halu 1*
**Java** *Jaba*
**javelin** *budjak 1*
**jaw** *langal*; *le'e*
**jaw harp** *kula'ing*
**jawbone** *samping 1*
**jealous** *himuggu'*; *imbū*; *iggil 1*
**jeans (cloth)** *ma'ung*
**jeep** *jīp 1*
**jeepney** *jīp 1*
**jeer (mock)** *gunyak-gunyak*; *udju'*; *paganday-anday*
**jelly (dessert)** *agal-agal*
**jellyfish species** *ubul-ubul*; *labog*; *būng*
**jelly-like** *himāt*
**jerk (v)** *hangku'*; *hagtu'*
**jerk forward** *limbuku'*; *hamput*
**jerk out** *bugnus₂*
**jerry can** *galon 1*
**Jerusalem** *Awrusalam*
**jester** *pandikal*
**Jesus** *Isa*
**Jesus Christ** *Isa Almasi*
**jet (liquid)** *sumpit 1.1*; *sahupput*

**Jew** *Isra'ili*; *Yahudi*
**jewel types** *dilam*; *kumala'*; *palmata 1*
**jewelry** *pamulawan*; *puntu' 1*
**Jew's harp (or jaw harp)** *kula'ing*
**jig (fishing)** *hagul*; *hantuk*
**jiggle** *jogjog 1.1*; *oseg 1.1*
**jinxed** *piyurus₂*; *pawas 1.1*; *bilsut*
**job** *hinang₁ 1*
**jobfish species** *guntul*; *asang-lumahan*
**jog** *podjong*
**join (v)** *daggot₂ 1.1*; *pagka'ob*; *kablit₁*
**join crowd** *pagsakutu*
**join edges** *tuhug 2*
**join fleet of canoes** *abay₁ 1.1*
**join in with** *lamud₂ 1.1*; *timbul*
**join planks** *lapak*
**joined** *dalos 1*; *sugpat 1.1*; *pingkit 1.1*
**joint (between bones)** *buku₂*
**joist** *dagan₁*; *babag 1*
**joke (v)** *pasu' gandum*; *paglangog*
**joking** *ula-ula*; *gillu'-gillu'*
**Jolo town** *Tiyanggi Sūk*; *Sūk 2*
**jolt; jolted** *paghodjog-hodjog*; *siggul*; *bangkug 1.1*; *bōg*
**joss stick (incense)** *hiyu*
**jostle** *pagdaguyu*; *oseg 1.1*
**jostle with elbows.** *pagsiku*
**journey** *busayan*; *lintasan*; *l'ngnganan₁*
**joy** *koyag 1*
**joyful** *kōg 2*; *kōd*
**judge (n)** *po'on-sara'*; *huwis*
**judge (v)** *hukum*
**judgement day** *kiyamat 1*
**judgment (immediate)** *hukuman kudjut*
**jug** *galon 1*
**jug (n)** *kassa' 2*
**juice** *loho' 1*; *bohe'₁ 1*
**jumbled** *gosak-gosak 1*; *mussak-massik*
**jump (v)** *laksu₁*
**jump across** *sulakat*
**jump down** *tugpa' 1*; *kuppa 1*

**jump rope** *kuway*
**jump up** *lumpat*
**jump up and down** *pagtogga'*
**junction (paths)** *siha'; sapehak*
**jungle** *talun 1; gulangan*
**junior (employee)** *bata'an*
**junk (rubbish)** *tai'-ero'*

**jurisdiction** *komkoman 2*
**just (morally)** *adil*
**just (only)** *dakuman; sadja; la'a*
**just because** *saukat; saula*
**just now** *baha'u 1.1*
**just now (recently)** *yamboho'; yampa; insini'*

# K k

**kalanchoe** *pād-pād₂*
**kamandiis tree** *kandi'is₁*
**kangkong** *kangkung*
**kapok** *kapuk 1; gapas*
**karate** *kuntaw₂; silat*
**katurai tree** *kambangtuli*
**keel; keelson** *taddas*
**keen (enthusiastic)** *hungun; hutu; baya' 1*
**keen (sharp)** *talom 1*
**keen vision** *pantok₂*
**keen-minded** *halul-akkal 1*
**keep (v)** *tau' 1*
**keep alive** *paka'llum*
**keep at** *abut-abut*
**keep eye on** *pa'aro'-aro'; hīng 2*
**keep for later** *kapin 1.1*
**keep for oneself** *hanggom*
**keep in mind** *pagka'inagon; paluli; kannal; ikut*
**keep in reserve** *halli'₂; tau' 1*
**keep on doing** *toro-toro; sigi-sigi 1.1; pagka'lloman*
**keep out of sight** *libun*
**keep private** *batin 1.1*
**keep promise or vow** *najal 1.1; suhud 1.2*
**keep quiet about** *ho'on-ho'on; hōm-hōm*
**keep safe** *tau' 1; komkom; appula*
**keep up with** *pagugpang*
**keep waiting** *patahāl*
**keepsake** *pangentoman*
**kernel** *bigi₁*
**kerosene** *gās₂; ns'llan gās*
**ketchup** *ketsap*
**kettle** *sili'*
**key** *anak-kunsi'; kunsi' 2*
**khaki** *kaki₁*
**kick** *tindak 1; sipa' 1; tagdok; binti'*
**kick (swimming movement)** *pagkutibbung; pagkutebba'*
**kick in womb** *sikad 2*
**kicking game** *pagestēp; pagsipa' 1.1; pagbinti' 1.1*
**kidding** *ula-ula*
**kidnap** *lalas; kidnap 1*
**kids** *kamanahutan; makannak*

**kill** *sangko' 1.1; bono' 1.1; kudjut; papatay 1*
**killed** *ligis₂; patay-bono'; laglag 1*
**killed (by spirit being)** *lokob nyawa*
**killer** *pamomono'*
**kilogram** *kilu 1*
**kilometer** *kilometēl; batu₃*
**kin (father's side)** *usba 1*
**kin (mother's side)** *wali*
**kin (parents' generation)** *usba-waris*
**kin; kindred** *lahasiya' 1; sugsug 1; kampung₁*
**kind (adj)** *ma'ase'*
**kind (n)** *ginis 1; indalupa 1*
**kindness** *buddi 1; kahāp*
**kinds (different sorts)** *babarapa; kaginisan*
**king** *sultan*
**king of the deceased** *Datu' Jumurain*
**kingfish** *mangsa'-tingga'*
**kingfisher** *bakakka*
**kinship links** *sugsug 1.1*
**kiss** *jiyara; siyum 1*
**kitchen** *kusina*
**kitchen bench** *paga-paga*
**kite components** *tubag-tubag; saldang 2*
**kite paper** *katas-jimpaw*
**kite types** *taguri'; birarul; galawang; pindun; awak-awak; kobong-kobong; belle'-belle' 2; tallung; mandal*
**kitten** *kuting₁*
**knead (dough)** *addun 1.1*
**knee** *tu'ut; kōk-tu'ut 1*
**knee (inside of joint)** *lokonan; lo'atan*
**kneel** *kōk-tu'ut 1.1; lukbu'₂; luhud*
**knees drawn up** *pagkorel-korel; loko' 2*
**knees together** *pipi'*
**knickers** *sanyawa; kudji-kudji*
**knife (funerary)** *kīs₄ 1*
**knife (weapon)** *punyal 1; kalis*
**knife (work tool, large)** *gayang; janap; bari'; pira; sundang; lahut*
**knife (work tool, small)** *laring; pisaw*
**knit (of wound)** *k'ntom*
**knob** *budjul₁*

**knock against** *tikbi'*; *siggul*; *daplig 1*; *sukkut*
**knock on** *kuku'*
**knocked** *bōg*
**knocked out** *pinsan 1*
**knocking sound** *tigangkul 1*
**knot** *engkot 1*; *p'kkos tuwa*; *buku₁ 1*
**knot (net-making)** *anom*
**knot hair** *hambak*; *simbōng 1.1*
**knot-free** *tanus*
**knotty** *sugat 1*
**know (aware of)** *tilas₁*
**know each other** *pagkata'u*; *pagkilā*
**know fully** *alab-alab*
**know how** *ta'u₁ 1.1*

**know someone** *nahu 1.1*
**knowledge** *himangkan*; *hinabta'u*; *ingat*; *pangita'u*
**knowledge (esoteric)** *ilmu' 1*; *salawat₁*
**knowledgeable** *sakup₁ 1.2*; *tahu*
**known widely** *busling*
**knucklebones** *jimban*
**knuckles** *bangkak*
**Koran** *Kora'an*
**Koranic school** *madrasa*
**kosher** *halal 1*
**kris** *kalis*
**kuwan** *anu 1*
**kuwini** *wanni*

# L l

**label** *sāp₂ 1*
**labia** *toro' 2*
**labor (n)** *hinang₁ 1*
**labor at** *mikakkul*
**labor pains** *himati'*
**labored (breathing)** *gagal₁*; *pōn*
**laborer** *kalgadol*
**lace** *ingkahi 1*; *bulda 1*
**lacerated** *langgahi'*
**lack** *kulang₁ 1*
**lack (defective)** *lihi-lihi*
**lacking bulk** *peres*
**lacking company** *lingus-lingus*
**lacking fluency** *b'ggod*
**lacking hair** *tugak*
**lacking moisture** *pīt*
**lacking resources** *kulang-kabus*; *kabus*
**lad (youth)** *subul*; *onde'-baha'u*
**ladder** *haron 1*
**laden (overloaded)** *apad-apad*; *togob₂*
**ladle** *suru' 1.1*; *sasanglag*; *sintib*; *luwag 1*
**lady (of high rank)** *putli'*
**lag behind** *lallay*
**lair** *sāng 1*
**lake** *danaw*
**lamed** *keme*; *pengkol*; *pengka'*
**lament** *paglemong 1.1*; *pagdukka' 1.1*; *pagdohon*
**lamp** *lām*; *palita'an*; *lampu*; *sū' 1*
**lamp glass** *tubu₁*
**lamp-lighting time** *pagpakeyat*
**lance (v)** *t'ddak*
**land (reach shore)** *dunggu' 1*; *dukla' 1*; *tandan₁ 1*
**land (region)** *lahat*
**land above high tide** *hampilan*

**land on** *t'ppak₂*; *kuppa 1*
**landfall** *kat'kkahan₁*
**landing place (birds)** *patapu'an*
**landing strip** *landing₁*
**landmark** *gindan 1*; *pandoga 1*
**landwards** *kaleya 1*
**language** *h'lling₁ 1*; *bahasa₁*; *bissala 1*
**language of Sama** *Sinama 1*
**lanky** *lanjang 1.1*; *langkawit₁*
**lansones** *buwahan₂*
**lansones seed** *bisul*
**lantern** *sū' 1*
**lantern (pressure)** *kulaet 1*
**lap up** *delat*
**laptop computer** *laptop*
**lapu-lapu species** *kulapu*
**lard** *mantika'*
**large** *heya 1.1*; *aslag₂ 1*; *mehe*
**large numbers** *laksa' 1.2*; *ibu-ibuhan*
**larvae** *but'ngngel*; *ulat₁*
**larvae (mosquito)** *kagaw*
**larynx** *buwa'-jakkum*; *asang₁ 1*; *batang-k'llong*
**lascivious** *pagba'is 1*
**lash (tie securely)** *tollen*
**lash alongside (of a splint)** *laggos*; *bandung₁*
**lash slats** *bīt₂*
**lashing technique** *buka'₁ 1*; *tabul-tabul*; *sappit₁ 1*
**lass** *budjang*; *onde'-baha'u*
**last (endure)** *tatas 1.2*; *sandal 1.1*; *ddas 1*
**last night** *dibuhi'*
**last of a series** *tanggollayan*
**last of all** *damulihan*; *tanggollayan*
**last price (in bargaining)** *katibtiban*
**last rites** *sahaddat 1.1*

**last thing or stage** *hinapusan; karamulihan*
**last-born** *katapusan 2; bungsu*
**lasting** *kakkal; d'ddos; dorog$_1$*
**late (in time)** *lēt; atarasaw*
**late (recently deceased)** *aymulla; nahanat*
**late afternoon** *abay-kohap*
**late at night** *lalom bahangi*
**later** *mahuli*
**lateral fins** *kepet$_1$*
**lath** *lubing-lubing; ligpit 1*
**lather** *bula'-bula' 1*
**latrine** *pagjambanan*
**latter** *karamulihan*
**laudable; perfect** *adil*
**laugh aloud** *dahaggay; tittowa 1.1*
**laugh excitedly** *kehe'-kehe' 1*
**laugh through nose** *kohok-kohok*
**laughter (forced)** *tittowa pinogos*
**launch (n)** *lansa; katel-katel*
**launch (v)** *longsad$_1$; l'bbos 1.1; daldal*
**laundry** *dakdakan*
**laundry starch** *almirul 1*
**laurel leaf** *halu'-halu'$_1$*
**law (religious)** *sara'-agama*
**law (secular)** *sara' 1*
**law-abiding** *adil*
**lawful** *halal 2*
**lawn area** *halaman*
**lawyer** *abugaw*
**lay a complaint** *pagmahi; tuntut$_1$; pagpuhun 1.1*
**lay across** *tahan$_2$ 1.1; tihin*
**lay egg** *nt'llo 1.1*
**lay flat** *par'ppak*
**lay in wait** *ingu*
**lay on edge** *patiring; pasindik*
**lay out (for burial)** *pahilala' 2; kiyam*
**lay out full length** *pahangtad*
**lay out weaving strands** *batul*
**layer** *lampik 1; hampe 1*
**layered** *lapis$_1$ 1*
**lazy** *lisu'; takal; hukaw 1.1*
**lead (metal)** *tingga'*
**lead (of pencil)** *dawat 1*
**lead (v)** *malim 1.1; pagnakura' 1; pagmunda'$_2$*
**lead astray** *bidjak 1.1; kuti-kuti; pilad*
**lead by hand** *tonda'$_2$; ambit$_2$*
**leader** *munda'$_2$; pagbebeya'an; nakura'; kapala*
**leader (religious)** *halipa; imam; muwallam*
**leader of community** *botang-lahat 1; panglima; botang-matto'a 1*
**leaf** *daun*
**leaf of banana** *dāg$_3$*
**leafy** *libombo'*
**leafy plants** *l'mput*

**leak (v)** *p'ttak 1.1; mman; pagtīs*
**leaking** *l'bbot; l'ssu'; buslut*
**lean (thin)** *giti' 1; kagkag; kayog 1*
**lean against** *sandig 1; taggal$_1$; saray-saray*
**lean away from vertical** *tīg; king 1.1*
**lean-to (shelter)** *payad; pillayag*
**leap up** *buwang$_2$*
**learn** *anad 1*
**learn (by spying)** *bantingag*
**learn by observation** *tatab*
**learn from experience** *insā'; l'gga 1.1; mintāng*
**lease (v)** *padjak$_2$*
**leather** *kuwit-sapi'*
**leatherback turtle** *bokko'*
**leatherjacket fish** *kuput*
**leave (depart)** *tulak$_1$ 1.1; hemos 1; k'llo'$_2$; la'an 1*
**leave (of symptoms)** *pigsik$_2$*
**leave as is (abandon)** *dondon; buwattē' 1.1; tahad*
**leave behind** *mban; bba$_1$ 1*
**leave in panic** *dimpulag*
**leave liquid to settle** *pato'ong; patuli; labay bahangi*
**leave prints** *limpa' 1.1*
**leave to an heir** *pusaka' 1.1*
**leave uncared for** *pasagad; pasahag; patabak*
**leave wet** *gamos 1.1*
**leaven** *pasulig*
**lecherous** *ba'is*
**lectern** *mimbal*
**led astray** *bowa-bowa*
**lee** *limbu 1.4*
**leech** *limatok*
**lees (dregs)** *tai'-lahing*
**left (remaining)** *masi 1*
**left behind** *atarasaw*
**left over** *l'bbi*
**left overnight** *bahangi 4*
**left-hand** *gibang*
**left-handed** *sakap-gibang*
**leftover** *kapin 1*
**leg** *tape'$_1$*
**legal** *taddang*
**legal marriage** *halal-kawin*
**legal offense** *langgal sara' 1*
**legal ownership** *jatti*
**legal papers** *kataddangan*
**legs apart** *pagsengkang*
**legs in air** *sulalla; julangkang*
**legs swinging** *pagnihakin*
**legumes** *batung$_2$*
**leguminous tree** *amboway*
**lemon** *muntay-iklug*
**lemon grass** *sāy*
**lemur** *kokam$_1$*
**lend** *paindam*

**length (extent)** *taha' 1*

**length (of measurement)** *ma bowa'an; ma kepet; tape'₃; sa'ang₂*

**length of wood** *hanggol 1*

**leprosy** *ipul 1; kawit-pupud 1; pangkot 1*

**lessen impact** *paglampik*

**lesson** *pandu' 1; pamintāngan*

**lest** *ko da'a; bo' mbal; he da'a*

**let boil** *pagogok-ogok 1.1; laga'₁ 1.1*

**let go of** *bba₃; mban*

**let line run freely** *taguntun 1.1; landa*

**lethargic** *pagene'-ene'; lomeng-lomeng*

**let's say (for example)** *ganta'₃*

**letter (message)** *sulat 1*

**letter (of alphabet)** *batang-sulat*

**level** *pantay; datag; bantang 1*

**level a pile (v)** *kikis; hīs 1.1*

**level of house (story; floor)** *angkap 1*

**level out** *depan 1*

**level with brim** *samaongpod; samaintib*

**lever (v)** *landak; alod₂ 1.2; li'ad; suwal 1*

**levy** *punggit 1; sukay₁ 1*

**lewd talk** *paglaka'-laka' 1.1*

**lexeme** *kabtangan*

**liability** *bahala'₁*

**liable** *kuwiraw; atas₂ 1*

**liar** *puting 1; l'pputan*

**libel** *kulli' 1.1*

**lice (chicken)** *hanglop*

**lice (of body)** *kutu-bebang; tuma 1*

**lice (of head)** *kutu 1; limad-limad*

**lice (on clothing)** *kuman₁*

**lice eggs** *lisa' 1*

**lice remover** *kuhut 1*

**licence** *pās*

**licentious** *biga'; jahil 1*

**lick** *delat*

**lid** *tambol 1; turung 1; sa'ob 1*

**lie (tell lies)** *puting 1.1; pagl'pput*

**lie across (overlay)** *pagtahan; tangday 1*

**lie at anchor** *layo 1.1*

**lie cross-wise** *pagbabag; pagbaubabag*

**lie curled up** *kullung; koleng₂; k'ttung*

**lie down** *bahak; lege*

**lie face down** *da'ub; kutung; k'ppang 1*

**lie face up** *hagtang; leyak; hantal*

**lie flat** *k'ppi'₁ 1*

**lie on side** *sīp; kīd₁ 1.1*

**lie parallel** *pagubay*

**lie stretched out** *hangtad*

**lie with feet in air** *sulalla; julangkang*

**lieutenant** *tininti*

**life and death** *ka'llum-kamatay*

**life; lifestyle** *ka'llum*

**lifeboat** *buti*

**lifeless** *tannay*

**life-long** *sapupud-daya*

**life-long partners** *paglimbang-kamatay*

**life-principle** *palnyawahan*

**life's concerns** *legot dunya*

**life's good things** *bunyi-bunyihan dunya*

**life's routines** *t'ngge-tingkō'*

**lifesaver** *salbabida*

**lifespan** *umul₂ 1*

**lift hands** *pasayang*

**lift in hands** *tampupu*

**lift legs off ground** *kallit*

**lift restrictions** *pabatal*

**lift up** *buhat₁ 1.2; angkat₁ 1.1; bayaw*

**lift using stick** *kahid 1; kawit₁*

**lift with back** *bungku'₁*

**light (n)** *sawa 1; palita'an; lampu; ilaw 1*

**light (not heavy)** *lampung₁ 1; nintil 1; langgung₂*

**light blue** *hinu-hinu₁*

**light complexion** *manis-buwahan*

**light fire** *dallet 1.1; dokot₂ 1.2*

**light lamp** *sū' 1.2; santik 1; pakeyat*

**light of sun** *silak 1*

**light rain** *bonok-bonok*

**light-hearted** *kiri-kiri; lasig 1.1*

**lighthouse** *parola*

**lightning** *lāt; l'tte'₁*

**like (n)** *sali' 1*

**like (prep)** *buwat 1*

**like (want)** *tahud; baya' 1.1*

**like that (near person spoken to)** *buwattilu 1*

**like that (yonder)** *buwattē' 1; buwattina'an 2*

**like this** *buwattitu 1.1*

**like what?** *buwattingga 1.1*

**likely** *arakala'; gana-gana 1.1*

**likeness (similarity)** *sengoran; lahi₄; pamaralilan*

**likewise** *sali'-sali'; damikiyan 1; sibu'-sibu'; isāb*

**limbo (in limbo)** *dohongan*

**lime (calceous)** *bangkit; tapung-bangkit*

**limit (of number or space)** *ngkon-ngkon; jangka'an 1*

**limit (of time, room or money)** *hād 1*

**limit (on bride-wealth)** *diyuhan; katibtiban*

**limitation** *sigpit 1*

**limitation imposed** *tagga 1*

**limited (size)** *diki' 1*

**limited to** *sabasag; kuriput 1.1*

**limp (of muscle tissue)** *himāt; hoyon; sampoyan*

**limp (v)** *pagtamengka'*

**limpid** *lihaw 1*

**line** *guhit 1*

**line (cord or string)** *bannang; tuntun₁ 1*

**line (of print)** *ayat; sapan₁ 2*

line for trolling *tonda'₁ 1*
line up *tilud 1.1*; *tundan 1*
lineage *pangkat₂*
lines in skin *kulis*
lines or rows *dirit₁ 1.1*; *sapan₁ 1*
lingering *alal 1*
linguist *sabut-bahasa*
lining (layer) *hampe 1*; *lapis₁ 1*
lining (of grave wall) *bingal*
link (n) *lingkit 1*
link arms *pagambit₂*
lintel *patahan*
lion *layon*; *halimaw*
lionfishes *tamalengkeng*; *lalung₁*
lip (of mouth) *bihing-bowa'*
lipstick *lipistik 1*; *atal*
liquid *bohe'₁ 1*
liquid (from corpse) *sagu*
liquid (squeezed from plants) *p'tti'*
liquify *hudjat*; *hansul₁ 1.1*
liquor *alak*
lissome *g'nting*
list *listahan*
list by name *palista*
listen *hing-hing*; *kale 1.1*
listen in on *tongop₂*
listen intently *talengog*
listlessness *logmay-lamma*
lit *keyat₂ 1.1*
literate *hatam 1.1*
lithe *l'mpet*; *g'nting*
littered *sembol 1*
little *diki' 1*
little bit *dangkuman*; *peged₂ 1*; *dangkuri'*
little finger, toe *kengkeng*
live (as neighbors) *paglibug*; *pagbihing-luma'*
live by begging *pagsantili'*
live in (occupy) *pagluma'*
live temporarily *pustu 1.1*; *lihan 1*
livelihood *gaddongan*; *usaha 1*; *ka'lluman*
lively *lasig 1.1*
liver *atay₁*
livestock area *buluyan*
living (adj) *llum*
living (n) *usaha 1*
living costs *napaka*; *kapamangan*; *gastu 1*
living room *salas*
lizardfishes *kamang 3*; *tigbas₁*
lizards *pinit*; *pahang*; *s'ssok*; *bulik*; *tokke'₁*; *tokko'*
load *duwa'*
loaded *apad-apad*; *togob₂*
loaded dice *legot-kapang*
loan *paindam*; *sanda'-sanda'*
loathe *j'ngngit*; *b'nsi 1.2*

lobsters *pama'*; *lattik₁*; *keyot₁*
locality *jadjahan*; *pasisil*
locate at *ma atag 2*; *mintag*
locate between *pag'llot*
locate over a hole *s'ddi*
location *atag₁ 1*; *lahat*; *antag*; *tongod₂ 1*
location (above) *diyata' 1*
location (below) *deyo'₁ 1*
location (here) *kamaituhan*
location (there) *kamailuhan*
location (yonder) *kamaina'anan*; *kamahē'an 1*
lock (n) *kandaru 1*; *kunsi' 1*
lock (v) *lagsak*; *bagat*
locked (of joint) *lingku'*
locking pliers *plaes tuka'-agap*
lockjaw *kansing 1*
lockstitch *p'kkos tuwa*
locusts *ampan*; *tompang*; *dulu₁*
lodestone *batu-balan*
lodging; lodging house *paghanti'an*
log *batang₁*
logical thought *akkal-pikilan*
loincloth *sollet 1*; *sampellot*
loins *bundu'*
loiter *lallay*; *ampis*
lonely *l'ngngaw-l'ngngaw*; *lingas₁ 1*; *lingus-lingus*
lonely (place) *t'nnaw-t'nnaw 1*; *mala'u-la'u 1*
long (adj) *taha' 1.1*
long (for something) *kanapsuhan*; *lingit 1*; *entom 1.2*; *dandam*
long (time) *t'ggol 1.1*; *musiman maka tahunan*; *awal ni ahil*
long ago *awal₁*; *masa-awal*; *ka'ina-tagna'*; *awal-jāman*; *musim tagna'*; *masa 1.1*
long-haired (of goat) *boro-boro₁*
longing *pangentom*; *lindu*
long-lasting (durable) *tatas 1.1*; *taggu₁*; *togob₁*
long-line fishing *laway₂ 1*
look *nda' 1*; *pantaw*; *pandang*
look alike *pagdaluwa*
look away *keles*
look briefly *idlap 1.1*; *tik 1.1*; *k'llap*
look carefully *patong 1.1*; *liling*
look closely *aro' 1.2*
look down *domol 1*; *kondo'*; *pagbalaru'-balaru'*
look for *piha 1*; *batuk₂*; *jadja' 1.1*
look for escape *karaw-karaw*
look for opportunity *piha lawang*
look in mirror *tanding 2*
look of disgust *bowa'-tai'*
look out from *tilag-tilag₂*; *tik 1*; *sib 1*; *tandaw 1*
look sideways *buli'-buli' mata*
look to (for help) *lingi' 2*
look up *hangad*; *tongas*
look without seeing *pagk'llap*

**look!** *o'ō*; *alō*; *anā*

**lookout (n)** *pamantawan*

**looks (appearance)** *pamayhu'an*; *luwa 1*; *dagbos*

**looks (good)** *lingkat 1*; *dorog₂ 1*

**looks or qualities** *lihi 1*

**loom part** *bibitan*

**loop** *tōhan*; *jallat₂ 1*

**loop for climbing** *salimbogot*

**loose change** *kanat-kanat*

**loose stools** *pagloros-loros*

**loose-fitting** *luslus 1.1*; *haluy 1.1*; *lagonggang*; *loka*

**loosened** *latas₁*; *puklas 1*; *hogal*; *henggol 1.1*

**loot** *taban*; *langpas*

**lopsided** *pagkamihu*; *pagkamigmig*; *tempang*

**lord** *panghulu' 1*

**lorikeet** *kulisi'₁*

**lorry** *tarāk*

**lose bulk** *k'ppes 1.1*; *limomo*

**lose cohesion** *pagsihag*

**lose contest** *tiyuwas*

**lose faith** *tanggal-iman*

**lose fingers** *kawit-pupud 1.1*

**lose foliage** *ulagat*

**lose footing** *lumintiyad*

**lose force** *kapuy*

**lose grip** *takabba*

**lose hair** *urut*

**lose impact** *padpad*

**lose pressure** *k'ppes 1.1*

**lose the way** *pelong-pelong*

**lose weight** *paglūs*; *koskos*; *lūs₂*

**loss (financial)** *lapis₅*; *lugi' 1*

**lost** *lungay 1*; *lopas 1*; *kabba*

**lost to sight** *talbang 1*; *baliyakaw*; *liyaw 1*

**lost totally (of money)** *tumba₂ 1*

**lots of** *gora'₂ 1*; *banos*; *dorot*; *heka 1.1*

**lottery** *pagko'ot-ko'ot 1*

**loud** *hidjul*; *hibuk*; *bukag*

**lounge** *salas*

**louse** *kutu 1*; *hanglop*

**love** *kasi 1*; *lasa₂ 1*

**love (v)** *anggi*; *s'lli 1.1*

**love charm** *lindang 1*; *sulat-libun*; *suratan*

**loved one** *kakasi 1*

**lovely** *lingkat 1.1*

**lover** *kirida*

**love-sick** *pagkonsemisun*

**low tide** *t'bba-bulagas*; *pipit₂ 1*; *mulilang*; *l'ggot*; *t'bba 1*

**lower (v)** *tonton 1.1*; *taktak 1.1*; *taguntun 1.2*

**lower arm (n)** *tangan 1*; *pataklayan*

**lower back (n)** *kalompang*

**lower eyelids (v)** *k'llip*

**lower leg (n)** *b'ttis*

**lower slope (n)** *lorosan*

**lowing (of cow)** *ngngong*

**lowly (social)** *deyo'₃ 1*

**low-spirited** *pagkalammahan*

**loyal service** *bakti' 1.1*; *balut 2*

**lubricate** *ns'llan 1.2*

**lucid** *sawa 1.1*; *danta'*

**lucine clams** *lāy-lāy*; *kali-kali*

**luck (bad)** *nahas 1*

**luck (favorable)** *paksa' 1*; *piguhan*; *sukud₂ 1*

**luckily** *daipara*

**lug (v)** *hangkut*; *kalga*

**lukban** *muntay-gadja*

**lullaby** *sangbay*; *binuwa 1*

**lumber** *papan₁*; *pasagi' 1*

**lump** *buggul 1*

**lump in flesh** *ikat 1*; *isi-kulabutan*; *budjul₁*

**lump on skin** *bintul*

**lump sugar** *sokal-tibu'uk*; *pilun*

**lump sum** *pono' 1.1*; *pakkiyaw*

**lumpy (surface)** *pagbigguwal*

**lunar halo** *taming 2*

**lunar month (next phase)** *bulan sobang*

**lunar month (second day)** *duwa kasobangan*

**lunchbox** *paglutu'anan*

**lungs** *daga' 1*

**lure (n)** *pangubug*; *ullang 1*; *panonda'an*

**lure for squid** *ulang 2*

**lust (strong desire)** *napsu 1*; *ebog 2*; *helo₁ 1*; *hawa 1.3*

**luster** *singlab*

**lustful** *hawa 1.1*; *biga'*; *atay kambing*

**lustful desire** *napsu-sawiya*

**lustrous** *linig 1.1*

**luxuriant** *labung 1*; *libombo'*

# M m

ma'am *mām*; *mamang₁*

mabolo *mabolo*

machetes *bangkung*; *lahut*; *sundang*

machine (motor) *makina 1*

macho *kapagl'lla 1*

mackerels *sobad*; *sampang-aray*; *gelle-gelle*; *mangku'*; *lumahan*; *panit*; *tangī'*; *hande-hande*

mad at s.t. *b'nsi 1.2*

madam *mām*

made ill (by spirit being) *bihang₁*; *naga 1.1*; *pa'in₃ 1*

made to (compelled) *kabowa*

made-up *sainala*

madre-de-cacao *mandikakaw*

maelstrom (whirlpool) *buhawi'₂ 1*; *haus 1*

maggots *iyas 1*; *ulat₁*

magic tricks *pagbalikmata*

magical power *ilmu' 1*

magical protection *anting-anting 2*; *pangliyas*; *sihil 1*

magistrate *sara' 2*; *po'on-sara'*

magnet *batu-balan*

Maguindanao *Ilanun*

maiden *daga-raga*; *budjang*

main part *baran₁ 1*

main road *paglalabayan*

maintain (in good order) *langis 1.1*; *ussap 1*; *hamumu'*

maize *gandum*

majesty *kamahaldika'an*

majority *kaheka'an*

majority of times *kamaumuhan*

make (build) *hinang₁ 1.2*

make a living *usaha 1.1*

make a living (by diving) *pagsāp*

make a living (by fishing) *pagdaing*

make a living (by trading) *paglitu*

make a vow *suhud 1.2*; *subali 1.1*; *pagsapa 1.1*

make excuse *da'awa 1.1*; *tawalli'*; *tumagal 1.1*

make fun of *juri 1.1*; *lata*; *pagtunggīng*

make ill *sabab₂ 1.1*; *sambihit*

make important *paheya₂*

make known *tanyag 1.1*; *buhanyag*; *bistu 1.1*

make peace *pagsugsug-tawbat*

make plans *pagistori-istori*; *paggara' 1.1*

make poor *pamiskin*

make possible *pagmuwat*

make pregnant *b'ttong₂ 1.1*

make public *pamahalayak*; *nasihat*

make space for *simay₂*; *sihak*; *sigput*

make the most of *jatu 1.1*

make up one's mind *pagniyat*

make use of *kalagihan 1.1*; *usal*; *guna 1.1*

make wealthy *pagalta'an 1.1*; *paraya 1.1*

make-believe *sainala*

makopa *makupa*

malady *saki 1*

malaria *tandog 1*

Malay *Malayu*

male *l'lla 1*

maleness *kapagl'lla 1*

males *kal'llahan*

malfunctioning *palsu*; *para₁*; *pagpalta*

malice *b'nsi 1*

malicious *jahat*; *jingki 1*

malicious talk *pagsugi-sugi*

malign *limut 1.1*; *pala'at*

malleable *lunuk 1.1*

malodorous *bau 1.1*; *p'ngngak*

maltreat *usiba'*; *pinjala' 1.1*; *la'ug 1.1*; *puhinga'*; *la'at 1.2*

mama (mother) *mamang₁*

mammal *hayop*; *sattuwa*

man *a'a*; *l'lla 1*; *manusiya' 1*

manage an event *pagmaneha*

manage to *kole'*; *bogbog₂*; *bāng-bāng₁*; *aguwanta 1.1*

manageable *luhay₂ 1*

manager (financial) *kukumit*

manatee *duyung 1*

mandarin *muntay*; *suha'*

mane (of horse) *kabulay 1*

mango *mangga*

mango (fragrant) *wanni*

mango (unripe) *kobkoban*

mango confection *liking 1*

mango varieties *mampallam*; *wanni*; *balunu'*

mangosteen *manggis*

mangrove forest *kabangkawan*

mangrove species *santing*; *tengol*; *bangkaw*; *pahapat*; *k'llong-k'llong*; *lagting₂*

manhood *kapagl'lla 1*

manifest (in visible form) *nyata' 1*; *bahana'*

manifestation (of someone) *panalengog*

manifold *indaginis*; *indalupa 1*

Manila city *Manila'*

Manila tamarind *kamansili'*

manioc (cassava) *panggi'*

manipulate limbs *h'nnat 1.1*

manipulate muscular tissue *p'nnod 1*

**mankind** *kabangsa-bangsahan; ummat 1; manusiya' 1*

**manner (of behaving)** *l'ngnganan₂; kabiyaksahan; bowahan*

**mannerism** *tebong*

**mannerly (courteous)** *hantap 1; hongpot*

**manners** *addat 1*

**manslaughter** *pamomono'*

**manta rays** *pahi; salindangan*

**mantis (insect)** *tompang*

**mantle of lantern** *mantel; buyung₂*

**mantle of shellfish** *agol*

**mantle of squid** *biring*

**many** *heka 1.1*

**many-colored** *kabang 1.1*

**map** *patta' 1*

**Maranao** *Ilanun*

**marang** *marang*

**marbles** *olen*

**march (v)** *pagmahil*

**margarine** *mantika'*

**marimba** *gabbang 1; pagkulanting-kulanting*

**marinate** *kilaw 1*

**marine (environment)** *tahik₁ 1*

**marine crustaceans** *pama'; lattik₁; tangkas-biruk; kamun; baling-baling; ka'ullang; keyot₁*

**marine eels** *tagō'; endong*

**marine plants** *kahamkam; solenggang*

**mark (n)** *guhit 1*

**mark (v)** *gudlis 1.1; dawat 1.1; guhit 1.1*

**mark document** *tumbuk₃ 1.1; pasā*

**mark location** *pandoga 1.1; gindan 1.1*

**mark on skin** *ila 1; tagimtim 1*

**mark with fingers** *kohed-kohed*

**mark with number** *umbul 1.1*

**marker (board game)** *anak-tikam*

**marker on grave** *sunduk 1*

**market** *tabu' 1; pasal₂ 1; tiyanggi*

**market (occasional)** *tapiyan-tabu'*

**marlin** *manumbuk*

**maroon** *sakulati 2*

**marquee** *lona*

**marriage** *pagkawin 1*

**marriage (non-Muslim)** *kasal 1*

**marriage for life** *paglimbang-kamatay*

**marriageable** *halus₂; pata'₁*

**married** *paglimbang; pagpūn₂*

**married couple** *lakibini; tagubata'*

**marrow (bones)** *sumsuman*

**marry** *kasal 1.1; kawin 1*

**marry a husband** *pah'lla 1*

**marry a wife** *pah'nda 1*

**marry a woman** *ā' h'nda*

**marry into a kindred** *pikit₂*

**marry kin of deceased wife** *lurus₂*

**marshy** *l'bbo 1; lettak*

**martial art** *kuntaw₂; silat*

**marvel** *inu-inu 1.2; jaip; haylan*

**masculinity** *kapagl'lla 1*

**mash** *petak 1.1; pedjet*

**mass (floating)** *ulak 1*

**mass disaster** *lanas 1.1*

**massacre** *pagbugbug; laglag 1*

**massage (v)** *henned; hilut; p'nnod 2; salimpak*

**massage stomach** *kallus₁ 1.1*

**masses of** *gora'₂ 1*

**mast (sailing)** *taruk*

**mast base** *durukan₁*

**mast block** *tindakan*

**mast extension** *takāk*

**mast props** *pangka'an; paglambangan*

**mast rope** *ligtang 1*

**master** *kapala*

**master of ceremonies (MC)** *magbobowa; pagpal'ngngan 1.1; tag'ntanan*

**masticate** *papa'; pa'us*

**masturbate** *pagsasal; pagtaba'-taba'*

**mat patterns** *maligay₂ 1; kagayan 1*

**match (asking price)** *pa'atap*

**match (game bid)** *lampak₂ 1.1*

**match (in value)** *lampak₂ 1; pagtongod₂*

**match (of clothing)** *telnos 1.1*

**match (of thickness)** *pagapang*

**match (relationship)** *paglimbang; pagtopad 1; pagiring-iring*

**match properly** *pagtōp*

**matchbox** *nggo'an-bagid; bagid*

**matches** *anak-bagid; bagid*

**matching** *ugpang 2.1; samapasang*

**matchstick** *lituk bagid*

**mate (companion)** *sehe' 1*

**mate (co-worker)** *ugpang 1*

**mate (of animals)** *pagd'nda 1.1*

**mate (of chickens)** *pagumagak*

**mate (voc)** *gge; beyang*

**material (cloth)** *kakana'; s'mmek 1*

**maternal kinfolk** *wali*

**mats** *boras; tepo*

**matted** *pagpiting*

**matter (of business)** *gara' 1; gawi 1; palkala' 1*

**matter (of concern)** *bale₁*

**mattock (digging tool)** *sangkul 1*

**mattress** *kama; tilam*

**mattress cover** *hanig; kasul*

**mature** *sangpot 1; daga; pata'₁; lasag; tahak 2*

**mature (of bamboo)** *bahi'*

**maturity** *hendog-hendog; sibuwa*

**maximum** *ta'as 1*

**may** *makajari 1*

may (able to) *manjari₁ 1*
maybe *kalu-kalu 1; ya aniya'; kalu gi'*
maybe (not) *m'ssa'*
mayor *mayul*
me *akū; aku₂*
meal *pagkakan 1*
meal (grudgingly provided) *dahalan*
mean (ungenerous) *kudkud; kigit; kuriput 1*
meander *kulengkong 1.1*
meaning *hati 1; kahulugan; ma'ana₁ 1; hatulan 2; hantang-hatulan*
meaning to say *hatina*
measles *sampal 1*
measure (depth of water) *d'ppa 1.1*
measure (general) *sukud₁; ganta'₁ 1.1*
measure (land) *b'ttak*
measure (volume) *t'ppong 1; gantang; pansing 1*
measure (weight) *kilu 1.1*
measure length *h'kka 1.1; d'ppa 1.1; tekang 1.1*
measure out *peged₂ 1.1*
measurement (general) *sukuran*
measurement (units of) *sussuk; sirang; silang₂; maniku; tasa*
meat (animal) *sumbali'an*
Mecca *Makka*
mechanic *mekanek*
meconium *tandak*
meddle (interfere) *jau'-jau'; lamud₂ 1.1*
meddlesome *umas; hulemang 1*
mediate (v) *pagpati'llot 1*
mediator *suluhan*
medicine (for fever) *tungkas-pasu'*
medicine (generic) *tambal₁ 1*
medium (average) *sarang-sarang*
medium (occult) *a'a duwata; jin 1.1*
meek *hatul₂; loman 1*
meet (by agreement) *pagabut; sabu 1.2*
meet (from different directions) *pagsulabay; paglanggal; pagsamban*
meet (of currents) *abal 1*
meet expectations *taluwa' 1.1*
meet in person *alop₁*
meet on arrival *bāk₂; abang; sampang 1*
meeting *miting; palhimpunan*
melba toast *matsakaw*
melodious *lu'uy₁ 1; k'llong-suling*
melody *tunis*
melon squash *tambulig*
melt *lanay₂; tunaw 1; tadjul; hudjat*
member (of religious community) *dauranakan 2; jama'a*
memento *lawanan*
memorial *pangentoman; pagubus₁*
memory *kaentoman; tomtom 1*
menace *hansom; pagalu'*

menarche *tindaw*
mend *pahāp₂ 1*
mend (gap or hole) *puna'; s'llap₁; bubul*
mend (sew) *ayum-ayum; sumpal 1.1; lalipan-lalipan*
menfolk *kal'llahan*
men's things *sakap-l'lla*
menses (first) *laha' tindaw*
menstruating *laha'₁ 2; bulan₄*
mental capacity *patali'an; nahu 1; hona'-hona'*
mental disorder or impairment *babbal; hibang-hibang; kulang-akkal; katuk₂ 1*
mental faculties *sipat₁ 1; akkal-pikilan*
mentally slow *dupang 1.1; b'llod; bengog 1.1*
mention *sambat; upamakun 1.1; subahat₁; iyan*
mention by name *abbit; taga'-taga'; pagbangkil 1.1*
meranti *yakal*
merchandise *barang; dagangan*
merchant (in folktales) *sauragal*
merciful *patiase'un; ma'ase'*
mercy *junjung 1*
merely *la'a; hal*
merely because *saukat*
merienda *pagimun-imun*
mermaid *duyung 2*
mermaid (dugong) *duyung 1*
merriment *kakoyagan*
merry *lami; lasig 1.1*
mesh (of net) *mata₂*
mesh fence *apis 1*
mess with *kodjel*
message *haka 1; ba'at 1; lapal 1*
message (authoritative) *palman 1*
messenger *pagbobowa; sosoho'an; dara'akan*
Messiah *Almasi*
messy *kuligi'₁ 1.1*
metal (rust-resistant) *basal₁*
metal sheeting *mital 1*
metal worker *pagbabal*
metallic sound *tagenseng*
metallic taste *p'llod; p'ddas; kahad*
metaphor *pamaralilan*
meteor *selo'*
meter *meto 1*
method *hatulan 1*
meticulous *hutu*
mew *eyaw*
microbes *kagaw*
midday *ugtu 1; kapasu'an; pekke'-pekke' llaw*
midday prayer *luhul₁*
middle *t'ngnga'; olangan 1*
middle-aged *to'a 1.1*
middleman *palilitu; tandero 1.1*
midge *kammut*
midnight *tonga'-bahangi*

**mid-rib (palm frond)** *etang-etang*
**midway** *llot*
**midwife** *panday 2*
**midwife fee** *bauballi'*
**mighty** *kawasa 1.1*
**migraine** *tali-tali₁ 1; pagtunggang-kīng*
**mildew** *kapu-kapu 1; bagubu' 1*
**mildew spots** *tagimtim 1; tagutu' 1*
**mildly unwell** *abat 1.1*
**mile** *batu₃*
**military** *militari*
**military base** *pustu 1*
**military officer** *jeneral*
**milk (animal)** *gatas 1*
**milk (coconut)** *gata' 1*
**milk (mother's)** *bohe' duru'*
**milkfishes** *bang'llus; owa'₂*
**Milky Way** *pampang diyata' langit*
**millet** *doha; dawa*
**millions** *laksa' 1.2*
**millipede** *liyabod*
**milt (semen of fish)** *hapa 1*
**mind (heed)** *asip*
**mind (n)** *patali'an; pikilan*
**mind-blowing** *patay-akkal*
**mind-set** *itikad; niyat 1*
**mingle** *paglamud*
**minimize** *diki' 1.1*
**minister** *wakil 1*
**minor wife** *h'nda-tape'; h'nda-h'nda*
**minuscule** *nahut*
**minute (tiny)** *nahut*
**miracle** *mudjidjat*
**miraculous** *inu-inu 1.2*
**mirror** *samin 2*
**mirth** *koyag 1*
**misadventure** *baya-baya*
**misaligned** *sā'₁ 1.1; kello' 1.1*
**misappropriate** *lolog*
**misbehaving** *gagga*
**misbehavior** *sabul 1*
**miscarriage** *kawa'₂; labu' 1.1; pakpak 2; pulak 1*
**miscellaneous** *babarapa; indaginis; indalupa 1*
**mischievous** *palla'*
**miserly** *iskut; kigit; kaikit₁*
**misfortune** *nahas 1; naja'; pawas 1; pa'al 1*
**mishap** *baya-baya*
**misinform** *laung 1.1; balidja*
**mislead** *balidja; kulli' 1.1; lakbu'₂*
**misled** *saman-saman*
**miss someone** *entom 1.2; lingas₁ 2*
**misshapen** *pagkamigmig; pagbaligbig; pagkamihu*
**missile** *punglu'*
**missing (tooth)** *legpong*

**mission** *gawi 1*
**missive** *sulat 1*
**misstep** *istung; salusad*
**mist** *gabun*
**mistake** *salla'₁ 1; sā'₁ 1*
**mistaken (mutual)** *pagsabali; pagkasā' 1.1*
**mister** *tuwan*
**mistreat** *hampul-hampul 1.1; la'at 1.2; pinjala' 1.1*
**mistress (lover)** *kirida*
**mistrust** *tāw 1*
**misty** *hanaw-hanaw; buraw*
**misunderstanding** *pagkasā' 1*
**misunderstood** *laung 1*
**misuse** *paka'at*
**misuse the law** *hakim*
**mite** *hanglop*
**mittens** *puyu'-puyu' 1*
**mix (v)** *paila'; bolebog; kuwal; pagbalot 1*
**mix in** *lamugay 1.1; lamud₁ 1.1; simbug 1*
**mix ingredients** *templa 1.1; addun 1.1; haybol*
**mixed** *paglamud-lamugay*
**mixed (of hair color)** *pagbalot 1.1*
**mixed blood** *pagdambila'an*
**mixed up (in thinking)** *buriru; bingaw*
**mixed up (of things)** *gosak-gosak 1; mussak-massik*
**moan** *aruhuy; mmu*
**mobile (on the move)** *pagleyat-leyat*
**mock infirmity** *pagtunggīng*
**mock; tease** *gunyak-gunyak; poway-poway; udju';*
  *paganday-anday*
**mockery** *anday-andayan*
**model** *suntu'an*
**moderate** *ganta'₁ 1*
**moderately** *mbal sakit*
**modern times** *tahun itu; ahil*
**modest** *deyo'₃ 1*
**modify** *pinda 1.2; saddī 1.1*
**modify fate** *buklas₁*
**modify shape by massaging** *tampa 2*
**moist** *himāy; gimi'-gimi'; hami'-hami'*
**molars** *baga'ang*
**molasses** *gula'*
**molaves (ironwoods)** *amulawan; kayu-soha'*
**mold (mildew)** *kapu-kapu 1; bagubu' 1*
**mold (v)** *tambu 1; kompol*
**mold clay** *tampa 1*
**mold into balls** *pongkol*
**mole (on skin)** *tai'-lalat*
**mole-grip pliers** *plaes tuka'-agap*
**molest** *jahulaka' 1.1*
**mollified** *lunuk atay*
**moment (of time)** *pillawan; dansasa'at 1*
**momentarily** *sasa'ut; dansasa'at 1.1*
**Monday** *Isnin*

money *sīn*; *pilak 2*; *pinta₁*
money (loose coins) *sīn kanat*; *kanat-kanat*
money belt *sabitan*
money-box *kansiya*; *gusi'*; *ba'ung*
monggo beans *batung₂*
monitor lizards *pahang*; *tokko'*
monkeypod tree *akasya*
monkeys *kuyya'*; *uwang*; *amu'₂*
monopolize supply *padjak₂*
monovalve shellfishes *bagumun*; *kunnig*;
   *baggungan*; *mastuli'*; *kulallit₁*; *eral-eral₁*
monsoon *pangulan*
monsoon (northwest) *uttala'*
monsoon (southwest) *habagat*
monster *agasi*
month *bulan₂ 1*
month (of pilgrims' return) *Hailaya Puwasa₂*
month names (see Bulan Muharram)
moo (as cow) *ngngong*; *ilud-ilud*
mooch *pagpangalemos*
moon *bulan₁*
moon phases *bulan₂ 2*
moon snails *bulan-bulan₂*; *seso'*
moor a boat *dunggu' 1*; *dukla' 1.1*
mooring stake *sambuwang*; *soha'*
mop floor *lampasu*
moral support *kinosog*
moral teaching *pituwa 1*
moray eels *tagō'*; *endong*
more or less *saga 3*; *kulang-labi*
more so *labi-labi*; *lagi' 2*; *kalap*; *luba'*
more than *liyu lagi'*
moreover *lāgi*; *ya balikna*
morinda (tree) *bangkuru*
morning *subu₂ 1*
morning (earlier in day) *subu-si'*
morning (early) *dai'-llaw*
morning sickness *pangiram*
morning star *maga*; *lakag*
morsel *dangkuri'*
mortar (cement) *pikit-pikit*
mortar (for pounding) *linsungan*; *pipisan*
mortgage *sanda'*
mortified *iya'*
mortise (building) *tengham*
Moses *Nabi Musa*
mosque *masjid*; *langgal₁*
mosque leader *hatib*; *bilal*
mosquito *hama'*
mosquito larvae *tiyaw-tiyaw 1*
mosquito net *kulambu' 2*; *muskitero*
moss (marine) *tai'-bamban*
moss-covered *lumut₁ 1.1*
most of *kaheka'an*

mostly *heka min heka*
motel *hotel*
moth *kaba'-kaba'*
mother *nggo' 1*; *ina'*; *sa'i*
mother (as source) *pangisihan₂*; *paluwasan*
mother-of-pearl *tipay*
mother's milk *bohe' duru'*
motif (design) *bunga₂*; *sapak*
motion sickness *pagboyokan*
motionless *antung*; *atol*
motor *makina 1*
motorcycle *motol*
mound of sand *punsu*
mountain *būd 1*
mountains *kabūd-būran*
mourn *paglemong 1.1*; *pagdukka' 1.1*; *pagdohon*
mouse *ambaw*
mousetrap *lagpak₁ 1*
mouth *bowa'₁ 1*
mouth infection *obe' 1*; *ugam 1*
mouth organ *honel*
mouthful *kiyomol*
mouth-watering *llum helo*
move (seeking relief from pain) *pagsalinggā*;
   *paglimpa*; *paglimayu'*
move (to and fro) *labad*
move about *hibal 1.1*; *paghengko-hengko*
move aimlessly *pagbiyu-biyu 1*; *pagsasab*
move along *pasōng*; *kisal-kisal*; *higin*
move apart *logtas*; *sisa*
move as a crowd *ssul*; *paglundug*
move aside *simay₂*; *salema' 1*; *sigay 1*
move away *hemos 1*; *k'llo'₂*
move back *suhut*; *sebog*; *sihak*
move by prodding *kohed 1.1*; *kahid 1.1*
move close to *sigpi'*; *t'ppung 1.1*; *apiki 1.1*; *t'ppi' 1*
move ecstatically *pagdamoseng*
move elsewhere (relocate) *laud 1*; *lintas*; *lalin 1*
move erratically *pagtumballeng*
move freely *tikayog*; *hulega*
move from place to place *pagtaleted*; *latag 1.1*
move further on *unjal*; *lanjal 1.1*; *sōng₂ 1*
move gracefully *kidjang 1.1*
move hips *paghamput*
move hurriedly *kulakkus*
move in large numbers *pahuru-huru*
move indoors *pasōd*
move involuntarily *pagsularaw*; *kudjal*; *dalihag*
move landmarks *pelong-pelong*
move limply *paglūng-lūng*
move lips *pagkimut-kimut*
move restlessly *paghibal-hibal*; *paghense*; *pagkebed-kebed*
move slightly *ingsud*; *kisal-kisal*; *hense*

**move smoothly (across waves)** *sapsap₁*
**move stealthily** *tangkaw 1*
**move swiftly** *tangkis 1.1*
**move to end of** *tōng-tōng 1.1; tukkay-tukkay*
**move upwards** *tudjak*
**move vigorously** *kayas 1; suleret; kaskas₂*
**moved emotionally** *andu'-andu'; ase'*
**movie** *sini*
**moving awkwardly** *gubin*
**mow weeds** *labas₁*
**Mr.** *sēl; tuwan*
**Mrs.** *mām*
**much** *heka 1.1; parat*
**much more than** *ballabi-labi*
**muck** *s'ggit 1*
**mucous (from mouth)** *tagak*
**mucous (in nose)** *s'ppun 1*
**mud** *l'bbo 1; pisak*
**muddied** *aut 1.1; lobog 1.1*
**muddled (of thinking)** *buriru; lengog kōk; bingaw*
**mudfish** *dāg₂ 2*
**mudskippers** *laksu₂; tamendak*
**muffled** *g'mmol₁; halong*
**muffler** *pupputan*
**muggy** *lingo'ot*
**Muhammad** *Muhammad*
**mule** *kura'-asnu*
**mull over** *bisbis₂*
**mullets** *mata-balud; kepak₂; banak; bonte*
**multicolored** *palang*
**multiple fractures** *tumu-tumu*
**multiple jobs** *pagsa'ud 1*
**multiply** *lipat₁ 1; lupi'₂*
**multiply (of infection)** *anak₄*
**multitude** *katimukan; kamaheka'an*
**mumble** *pagdabdab; kimut-kimut; pag'mmu-mmu*
**mumps** *gadja-gadja 1*
**mung bean** *monggo*
**murder** *bono' 1.1*
**murderous** *patibono'*

**murmur** *mmu*
**muscle** *ugat 1*
**muscle pain** *labba'₂ 1; hantu 1.1*
**muscle sheath** *amp'llus*
**muscovado (dark sugar)** *sokal-ba'ung*
**muscular** *bastig; kulasog 1.1; ayron*
**mushroom** *taibu'*
**mushy** *k'ddos; lonyat; biyobog; tonyak*
**music (band)** *mulsiku*
**music (playing technique)** *pagtā'-tā'*
**musical instruments** *tiyup-tiyup; saunay; biyula 1;
     parereyagan; gabbang 1; pulaw₁; honel; olgan 1;
     kula'ing*
**Muslim** *Muslim*
**Muslim Filipino** *Murus*
**Muslim Subanon** *Kalibugan*
**mussed (of hair)** *larang*
**mussel** *sirap; tahōng; kopang*
**must** *wajib 1; subay*
**mustache** *mantis; misay 1*
**mustard greeens** *sasawi*
**musty** *kapu-kapu 1*
**mute** *umaw 1*
**muted** *h'nnok; h'ddok; tepok*
**mutter** *pagdabdab; kimut-kimut; pagli'anun*
**mutual affection** *pagkasi-lasa 1.1*
**mutual agreement** *pagtotos; pagtaluwa'*
**mutual attraction** *pagbilahi*
**mutual confusion** *pagsabali*
**mutual giving** *pagbuwan-buwan*
**mutual suitability** *pagtōp*
**mutual support** *paggapi'; pagtapil*
**mutually committed** *pagkatuk*
**my** *=ku*
**my lady (high respect)** *sitti*
**myna bird** *tiyung*
**myopia** *lamun 1*
**mystery** *mudjidjat*
**mythical bird** *sumayang-galura' 1*
**mythical land** *Mangkimahan*

# N n

**nail** *lansang 1*
**nail (finger or toe)** *kukku₁*
**naked** *pegtang-pegtang; tantang*
**name** *ōn₁ 1*
**name (informal)** *danglay 1; g'llal 2*
**name (v)** *pagōn; ganda*
**namesake** *isay; saingan*
**nape (of neck)** *pugay 1; buli'-k'llong*

**napkin** *jimpaw; sapu-tangan*
**napping** *pirung-pirung; piru'-piru'*
**narrate** *istori 1; kissa 1.1*
**narrative song** *pagsindil 1.1; tenes-tenes*
**narrow** *kiput*
**nasal irritation** *sungbu-sungbu*
**nasal mucous** *s'ppun 1*
**nasal speech** *s'ngngog*

nation (ethnic group) *bangsa₁*
nations (general) *kabangsa-bangsahan*
native to *porol*
natural death *patay-mural*
natural resources *gaddongan; alta'-kalun*
naturally *asāl; tu'ud₁ 1*
nature (character) *sadsaran; palangay; apalal*
naughty *sabul 1.1; hulemang 1*
nauseated *pagboyokan; paghelo; la'at helo; lango 2*
naval vessel *nabal*
navel *ponsot*
navel region *bundu'*
navigational light *parola*
near *sekot 1*
near death *halol*
near edge *sipi₂; tipid 1*
near enough *sarang-sarang*
near zenith *langkaw llaw*
nearing time *kablit₂*
nearly *agon*
neat *l'ssin*
necessary *guna 1.2; wajib 1*
necessities *kahirupan; napaka; gastu 1*
neck *k'llong; gonggongan*
necklace *gantung-li'ug*
necktie *kurubata'*
need to do s.t. *subay*
need; needy *pihit; kalagihan 1*
needle *jalum*
needlefishes *togeng; sawasig; selo; pillangan; tambilawang*
needy *miskin; kabus; pihit*
ne'er-do-well *pamahadja' 1; pilliyu*
negate *pahalam; pag'mbal 1.1*
negative *mbal 1; halam₁ 1; nsa' 1; ballum*
negative response *ka'mbal*
neglect (v) *pasagad; pasahag; hampul-hampul 1.1*
neglected *lonseng 1; sumadja*
neglectful *kuligi'₁ 1.1; haman-haman 1*
negotiate *pagjawab 1.1*
negotiations *pagpalkala'*
neigh *ehe'-ehe'*
neighborhood *jadjahan; lūngan; kaum; paglūng 1*
neighbors *pangatag; bihing-luma'; paglūng 2*
neither *mbal isāb*
neonatal death *anak-paindam*
nephew *anak-kamanakan; kamanakan*
nerve (n) *ugat 1*
nervous *kawang; gupu*
nests *pugad; sāng 1*
net (fishing) *siyul 1; pokot₁ 1; laya 1*
net (long) *birang 1; lantaw 1; linggi' 1*
nettles (stinging plants) *l'ppay; sagay*
never *mbal lulus*

never mind *mbal du; sisayang; m'ssa' du isāb*
never seen before *mbal na buwattē'*
nevertheless *bo' arapun; malaingkan; parahāl*
nevus (birthmark) *ila 1*
new *baha'u 1*
new moon *bulan baha'u*
New Testament *Kitab Injil*
New Zealand *Niyusilan*
newborn *mula'*
news *haka 1; hunub 1; habal*
newspaper *katas-habal*
next *balik₁ 1; pasunu'; puwas₂*
next-door *bihing₂ 1*
nibble *paglaginit 1.1; kitkit; bisbis₁*
nice *hāp 1.1*
niche in grave *liyang 1*
nick *t'bbe' 1*
nickname *danglay 1; g'llal 2*
niece *anak-kamanakan; kamanakan*
niggardly *iskut; kigit; kuriput 1*
night *bahangi 1; sangom 1*
night before last *bahangi-dibuhi'*
night before new moon *ganap t'llumpū'*
night blindness *lapong 1.1*
night of power *lailatul-kadal*
night paralysis *bangungngut; bolelong*
night watch *pagjaga 1*
nightfall *sū'-palita'an*
nightmare *ddop; mutamad*
nimble *tangkis 1*
nine *siyam*
ninety *siyampū' 1*
nipa palm *nipa'*
nipa shingle *atop 2*
nipper *sakket 1*
nipple *tōng-duru'; tete' 1*
nit *niki'-niki'; kulisa' 1*
nitwit *dupang 1*
no *mbal 1.1; ngga'i ka; halam₁ 1; duma'in; nsa' 1*
no difference *nsa'-bidda'*
no doubt *tantu 1.1*
no further than *taman*
no gaps *linggas*
no let up *sigi-sigi 1*
no longer
no matter *mbal du; m'ssa' du isāb*
no matter how *buwattingga-buwattingga*
no matter what *minsan aina; sapainay-painay*
no more than *sabasag*
no sooner than *sakali₂*
Noah *Nabi Nū*
noble *balbangsa*
nod (in agreement) *tango'; handuk 1.1*
nod (in fatigue) *toyok; paglinggayu'*

**node** *buku₂*
**noise** *h'lling₁ 1*; *pagganggu'*; *bah'ssek 1*
**noise of human activity** *paglagungkad*
**noise of many voices** *kiyul-kiyul*
**noise of waves** *sahal₁ 1.1*
**noise through vibrating lips** *pagtab'llung*
**noisy** *hidjul*; *hibuk*; *bukag*; *sagaw*; *sasaw 1.1*
**none** *nsa' aniya'*; *m'ssa'*
**noni** *bangkuru*
**non-rusting** *estenles*
**nonsense talk** *kaligawan*
**noodles (fine)** *sutanghon*; *bihun*
**noon** *ugtu 1*; *langa-llaw*
**noose** *jallat₂ 1*
**nor** *mbal isāb*
**northeast wind** *uttala'-lo'ok*
**northerly wind** *uttala'*
**northwest wind** *kanaway*; *hilaga'*
**nose** *ūng*
**nose (high-bridged)** *pansung 1*
**nose bleed** *sungbu-sungbu*
**nostril** *lowang-ūng*
**nosy** *katilaw*
**not** *mbal 1.1*
**not authentic** *paltik*
**not long (of time)** *halam pa'in*
**not permitted** *haram 1*
**not present** *likut 1*
**not quite** *agon-agon*
**not ready** *du-bilang*
**not so** *ngga'i ka*; *duma'in*
**not yet** *nsa' lagi'*
**notch (foothold)** *tangga' 1*; *taka 1*

**notch (n)** *t'bbe' 1*; *lengget 1*
**notch (pole or tree)** *tengham*; *tekmas 1.1*
**notched post** *haron 1*
**notebook** *nōtbūk*
**nothing** *halam₁ 1*; *nsa' aniya'*
**nothing like it** *mbal na buwattē'*
**notice (n)** *pahati 1*
**notice (v)** *hirup₁*
**notorious** *bantug 1.1*; *tanyag 1*; *jama'*
**novice** *hāw-hāw 2*
**now (already)** *na*
**now (of time)** *buwattina'an 1*; *kabuwattituhan*
**now for the first time** *yampa*
**now then** *manjari₂*
**nowadays** *ahil-jāman*; *tahun baha'u*
**nuclear family** *tali'anak*
**nuclear family (of a man)** *anak-h'nda*
**nuclear family (of a woman)** *anak-h'lla*
**nude** *pegtang-pegtang*
**nudge** *kodjel*; *sikmu'*
**nuisance** *sasat 1*
**nullify** *pahalam*
**number (collective)** *heka 1*
**number (digit)** *umbul 1*
**number 1 (first class)** *umbul tunggal*
**numberless** *dangay-dangay 1*; *mbal taitung umaw*
**numbness** *b'nnod 1*
**numerous** *banos*; *dorot*; *heka 1.1*; *parat*
**nursing (breast-feeding)** *duru' 1.1*
**nursing baby** *anak-duru'an*
**nut (betel)** *bunga₁*
**nylon line** *naelon*; *tangsi'₁ 1*

# O o

**oar** *dayung 1*
**oath** *subali 1*; *pagsapahan*
**obdurate** *tuwas 1*
**obedient** *hatul₂*
**obeisance** *palok 1*
**obese** *hambug 1*; *l'mmok 1.1*
**obey** *beya'-beya'₁ 1*; *kahagad*; *asip*
**object to** *samlang*
**objectionable** *la'at 1*
**objective** *gawi 1*; *puhung₁ 1*
**objective (military)** *iralan*
**oblation** *lalabotan 1.1*; *paglabot 2*
**obligation** *wajib 1.1*; *huwas-huwas*; *panubusan*
**obliquely** *talilli' 1*; *dupli'as*
**obliterated** *ponas*; *luhu'₂ 1*; *lapnas 1*

**oblivious** *lipat₂*; *lilap*
**obscene talk** *paglaka'-laka' 1.1*
**obscured** *p'dda 1*; *palom*
**observant (religious)** *ammal₁*; *sanittiya*
**observe** *patong 1*
**obstacle** *kalimbit*; *gaggat 1*
**obstinate** *alod₁*; *gagga*
**obstruct** *agpang 1.1*; *babag 2.1*; *sabol*
**obtain** *dapu 1.1*; *ngā'*
**obtain by fraud** *sanggot₂*; *kidjib*
**obverse** *bukut₁*
**obvious** *tampal 2*; *tu'ud₁ 1*
**occasion** *palkala' 1*
**occasionally** *pagsawaktu*; *pagsān-sān*; *pagsamba-samba*
**occupation** *ntan₂ 2*; *usaha 1*

occupy a house *pagluma'*

occupy an area *paglahat 1.1*

occur *t'kka₂ 1.1*

occur intermittently *tibaw 2*

occurrence *gimut*

ocean *karilautan; timbang₂*

ocean depths *kalaloman*

ocean floor *deyo'₂ 1*

o'clock *lisag₁*

octopus (call to) *bugnus₃*

octopuses *ngget; kuhita' 1; kaloka'*

odor *hamut 1; bau 1*

odorous *langtu; hangsu 1; langsa*

odorous mango *wanni*

of *sin; min 1*

of course! *he' angay*

offcut *pīs-pīs; pōng-kayu; tapis 1*

offend *buwan dusa; mata-mata₁*

offend (by using a person's name) *taga'-taga'*

offended *ā' la'at; tumpalak 1; ambul-dā'*

offense (against law) *langgal sara' 1; kīs₂*

offense (social) *kasā'an; dusa 1; saggan*

offensive *kagit atay 1*

offensive (hurtful) *sakkal; sammal 1*

offer for sale *pab'lli; pa'andag 1*

offer in marriage *pa'andag 2*

offer lower price *ladjaw*

offering (religious) *lalabotan 1.1; paglabot 2*

offering (to supernatural being) *pananggapan; ungsud₂; lamas; tutukbalan*

office *opis*

official (person) *botang-lahat 1; bag'llal 1; panglima; botang-matto'a 1*

offspring *anak₁ 1; onde' 1; tubu' 1*

often *bilang₁; maumu; masuhul*

ogre *agasi*

oil *ns'llan 1*

oily *lanab*

oily (flattering) *lana 1*

ointment *tambal₁ 1*

okay *kōl 1*

old (much used) *ndang; bahal*

old (person) *tungkud-luwag; to'a 1.1*

old folk *kamatto'ahan*

old maid *la'un 1.1*

olden times *kama'asan; awal-jāman*

older sibling *siyaka 1*

older than *umul₂ 1.1*

olive (tree and oil) *jaitun*

olive shells *kuting-kuting₂*

omen *nahas 1*

omen (good) *gustu 1*

omit (bypass) *lakad 1.1; laktaw; pitas₁*

on all sides *paruwambila'*

on guard *llog 1; insap*

on one's own *dangan-dangan 1*

on target *tigi'-tigi'₁ 1; taluwa' 1.1; logdang₁ 1*

on the contrary *ai po'on; ngga'i ka; duma'in*

once only *mint'dda*

one *issa; da- 1; ssa₃; dakayu'₁ 1*

one (indefinite pronoun) *kitā 2*

one after another *dangan-parangan*

one half *dampōng; dambila' 1*

one only *tunggal 1*

one person *dangan 1*

one piece *pono'-pono'*

one week *dapitu'*

oneself *baran₂ 1; dī₁*

one-spot (cards) *alas*

ongoing *masi 1.1; na pa'in*

onion *siboyas*

only *dakuman; luwal; sadja; yangkon; samadjana; la'a; hal*

only child *tunggal-tunggal 1*

only now *yamboho'; yampa*

onset of wind *kōk-baliyu*

ooze *lanay₂*

open (forcefully) *lungkad 1*

open (partly) *sungkab*

open (v) *k'llat₁; ukay 1.1; ukab 1.1*

open bargaining *andag*

open coconut *tohob*

open eyes *pak'llat; d'llag 1*

open fire *balis₁*

open mouth (v) *banga'₁; bongat 1.1*

open sea *dilaut; kablangan; kaladjun; s'llang₁*

open space *halaman*

open to attack *pilluwang₂ 2*

open to weather *singkab 1*

open water *olangan 1.1*

opened up, of parts *papellat*

opening *buka'an; bowa'₂*

opening words of prayer *kamat 1*

operate (surgery) *opera*

opinion *bang ma; kumpasan*

opium *marat 2*

opponent *kuntara 1; atu 1; banta 1*

opportune time *sa'at*

opportunity *lawang 2; dapat₂*

oppose (a force or influence) *sangsang; sagga' 1.1; sulang₁*

oppose (advice) *balda*

oppose (an enemy) *kuntara 1.1; atu 1.1*

oppose (tide or wind) *dangat 1*

oppose verbally *salod; pagbagod; sīng-sūd*

opposite (inverted) *sulang-saling*

opposite location *anggopan*

opposite number *limbang 1*

**oppress** *pinjala' 1.1*; *pissoko'*
**optimistic** *holat 1*; *asa 1.1*
**options** *pamene'an*; *buwangkan... buwangkan*
**opulent** *daya*
**or** *ka₂*; *atawa*
**or else** *arakala'*
**orange (color)** *kulit₁*
**oranges (fruit)** *muntay*; *taoke'₂*; *sina'₂*
**orator** *bibissalahun*
**orb of moon** *mata-bulan*
**orb of sun** *mata-llaw*
**orchard** *kabbun*
**orchestra** *mulsiku*
**ordain (fate)** *ganta'₂*; *t'ppong 2*
**order (to do something)** *soho'*; *uldin 1.1*
**orderly (adj)** *hantap 1*; *tuntul 1*
**orders** *panoho'an*; *uldin 1*
**ordinal affix** *ka-₁*
**ordinary person** *sibilyan*
**organism (physical)** *paltubu-tubuhan 2*
**organize** *patuntul*; *talik-talik*
**organize entertainment** *tangkap*
**organize fishing expedition** *kampēn₂*
**organized (tidy)** *tuntul 1*
**organizer** *magbobowa*; *tag'ntanan*
**orgasm** *gila*
**oriental mangroves** *bangkaw-d'nda*; *bangkaw-l'lla*
**orientation (nature)** *hudjidjat*
**oriented towards** *sabung*
**orifice** *lowang 1*
**origin** *po'on₂*; *panagna'an*
**original state** *ka'asāl*
**originally** *asāl*
**oriole** *ūl-ūl*
**orphan** *anak-ilu'*; *ilu'₂ 1*; *anak-ka'bbahan*
**orphaned** *pulaw₂*; *bba₁ 3*
**oscillate** *pagdundang*
**ostrich** *sumayang-galura' 1*
**other half** *dambila' 2*
**other one** *dakayu'₁ 2*
**other side** *anggopan*; *liyu₂ 1*; *dambila' 2*
**other than** *luwal*; *saddī 1*; *liyu₃*; *haliyu*
**others** *kasehe'an*
**ouch!** *aruhuy*; *agkā'*; *arōy*
**ought to** *wajib 1*; *subay*
**our** *=ta 1*; *kami*; *=tam*
**out (of place or position)** *pangsut 1*
**out of (from)** *min 1*
**out of breath** *hapus₂*; *paghangu-hangu*; *lumu*
**out of mind** *bibas₂*
**out of sight** *tawan-tawan*; *limun 1*
**out there** *liyuhan*
**out to sea** *kaut 1*
**outbid** *lakbaw 1.1*; *doble 1.2*

**outboard motor** *donson*; *dapa-rapa*
**outcome** *katumariyahan*; *kamattihan 1*; *kaluwasan*; *kat'kkahan₂*; *kamaujuran*
**outcome (of discussion)** *kagara'an*
**outcome (positive)** *kajatuhan*
**outcry** *pagmalān*
**outdo** *lakbaw 1*; *awat 1.1*
**outdone** *liyu₂ 1.2*
**outer islands** *pū'-pū'-diyata'*
**outer space** *ayan*
**outfitted** *panyap 1*; *panyap-palbut*
**outgrow sibling** *agaw-buwa'*
**outing (leisure)** *pasiyal*; *l'ngngan₁ 1*
**outlaw** *mundu 1*
**outlay (financial)** *po'on₃*
**outnumber** *pila 1.1*; *heka 1.2*
**outpost** *pustu 1*
**outrank** *pospa'*
**outrigger** *katig 1*
**outrigger boom** *batangan*
**outrigger brace** *sa'am 1*
**outside** *luwasan*
**outsider** *a'a liyu*
**outspoken** *tumlang 1*; *pagpa'amu*
**outstanding** *umbul dakayu'*; *bustan*
**outstrip (in contest)** *awat 1.1*
**outwit; out-think** *halul-akkal 1.1*; *sanggot₂*; *akkal 1.1*
**oven** *pagtinapayan*
**over (past)** *labay₂*
**over busy** *golpe₁ 1*; *udjalat 1*
**over the top (excessive)** *makalandu'*; *dumasiyaw*; *kumarukan*; *mamarahi*
**over there** *hē'₁ 1*; *inān 1*
**over time** *hulak 1*
**over with** *katis₂ 1.1*
**over yonder** *liyuhan*
**over-abundant** *dalay₂*; *kumarukan*
**overbearing** *pagmanda 1.1*
**overbid** *awat 1*; *doble 1.2*
**overburdened** *husa'*; *b'kkat 2*
**overcast** *dampog 1*; *andom 1*; *pagdo'om*
**overcome** *longkop 1*; *pila 1.1*
**overcome by grief** *gupu*
**over-confident** *pagtāp-tāp*
**overcooked** *laga'₁ 1*
**overdo** *judju' 1.1*; *pagjuru' 1.1*
**overdue** *tapa'ut*
**overflow** *lasay*; *luput 1*; *lipay₁*; *letop 1.1*
**overfull** *sangka' 1*; *sukad*
**overfull (of stomach)** *s'bbol 1.1*; *sugmak*
**overhaul** *pabaha'u*
**overheated** *lingo'ot*; *hangat*
**overindulge** *parūl 1*
**overlap** *pagsalisi*; *paglapak*; *pagsa'ud 2*

overlap (of teeth) *sengel*
over-large *dagal*
overlay *pagligpit; lambang₁*
overloaded *apad-apad; buhat₁ 1.3; llop 1*
overly (excessive) *makalandu'; mamarahi*
over-many *datay₂*
overmuch *landu'₂ 1; dumasiyaw*
overnight *bahangi 3*
overpower *longkop 1*
over-quick *baggis*
override (a decision) *pospa'; powera 2*
over-ripe *lasaw*
overrun (v) *kulatap*
overshadow *talung₁*
overstep *lingka' 1; lakad 1*
overtake *damuli 1.1; abung 1.1*
overturn *pakkom 1; bīng₁ 1.1; paleyak*

overwhelmed (by a sight) *palu' 1.1*
overwhelmed by *heka 1.2; lanas 1.2*
overworked *pinjala' 1; gunta'; lu'ug 1.1*
ovoid (egg-shaped) *tibokkong*
ow! *aruhuy*
owe money *utang 1.1*
owl *lukluk*
own fault *beya'-beya'₂*
own up *pagpasab'nnal 1.1*
owner *tag-; tagdapu*
ownership *dapu 1; suku'*
ownership rights *mustahak*
owning *taga*
ox *sapi'*
oxidation (rust) *gaha' 1*
oxygen *baliyu 1*
oysters *tape'-kura'; tipay*

# P p

pace (step) *tekang 1; peka'*
Pacific squaretail (fish) *gu'ud-t'bbu*
pacifier (teether) *paruru'an*
pacify *ū'ū; pagkahāp*
pack into *selot 1.2; dasok 1.1*
package *kuri'an 1; putusan*
packed tight (or full) *dasok 1; selot 1*
packets *pākete; papan₂; kīs₃; kustal 1*
packets (of cigarets) *kaha₂ 1*
packing layer *hampe 1*
pact *pagsulutan; janji' 1*
paddle (n) *kelle 1; busay 1*
paddle (v) *tindayung; epe; kelle 1.1*
paddle across *agod; kauk*
paddle grip *kōk-busay*
paddy field *bagsak₁*
padlock *kandaru 1*
page *kintas 1*
paid in full *samaunjuk; tubus₁ 1*
pail *balde*
pain *p'ddi' 1*
pain (mild) *sāg 1*
pain (supernatural in origin) *timbalun₁ 1*
painful *bisa 1; p'llat 1.1; p'ddi' 1.1*
painful (bowel movement) *p'ddi' tai'*
painstaking *sugsig 1*
paint *pinta₂ 1*
paintbrush *brās*
pair (n) *limbang 1; samapasang; langgung₁ 1*
pair (of cards) *pares₂; doble 1*
pajamas *hakpan*

Pakistan *Pakistan*
pal *jēk; bō; lundang; panon*
palace *astana'*
palate, hard *ngelo'*
palate, soft *p'ggad*
pale *pote' 1.1; pusiyat; lospad*
pale (of color) *mata' 2*
pale (v) *muntas*
pallid *pusiyat; lospad*
palm heart *umbut*
palm lines *kulis*
palm of hand *pāt 1*
palm syrup *gula' tuwak*
palm toddy *toba'*
palm-like plants *magi*
palms *sani; pola-magi; niyug; silal; anibung; nipa'; pisut-pisut; lugus-magi; ballak; tuwak; bunga₁*
palpate *hilut; salimpak*
palpitate *pagsignat-signat; pagk'bbut-k'bbut*
pamper *palangga' 1.1*
pan (cooking) *sanglagan; lenga'; simpi'*
pancake *tinompe'; panyām; apam 1; dinglu' 2; doppeng; daral*
pandanus (generic) *pandan*
pandanus stem *botod-pandan*
pan-de-sal *pān ma'asin*
panel (swinging) *lapi'-lapi'*
panel (woven leaves) *sairing 1; salirap*
panhandle *pagpangalemos*
panic *g'mma; dongkag*
pan-roasting *sanglag*
pant (v) *paghongat-hongat; pagh'ngka-h'ngka*

**panties** *sanyawa; kudji-kudji*
**pants (n)** *pantalun 1*
**papaya** *kapaya; sandiyas*
**paper** *katas; banggala; papel*
**paper (tissue)** *katas-jimpaw*
**paper bag** *suput₂*
**paper clip** *sipit 1*
**paper money** *landing₂; pinta₁*
**paper nautilus** *sugit-sugit*
**parable** *pamaralilan*
**parade** *pagmairan 1.1*
**parade ground** *mairan majilis*
**paradise** *paliyama'*
**paraffin** *ns'llan gās*
**parakeet** *kulisi'₁*
**parallel to** *pagdirit 1.1; pagdiril-diril*
**paralysis (night)** *bangungngut; bolelong*
**paramour** *kirida*
**paranoid** *ambil-hati*
**parasite (crustacean)** *bobok 1*
**parasite (intestinal)** *kalog 1*
**parboil** *lakbu'₁*
**parched** *lūs₁ 2; lanos₁; lengas₁*
**pardon** *ka'ampunan*
**pardon me** *tabiya'*
**pare edges** *salimi*
**pare to shape** *basbas*
**parents** *matto'a 1*
**parents of married couple** *ba'i 1*
**parents-in-law** *mato'a*
**parlor** *salas; saurung*
**parrotfishes** *t'mbug; ogos; maming 2*
**parrots** *kangag; agap₁; nyuli'*
**parry** *sangga 2; tangkis 1.1.1*
**part (share)** *bahagi' 1*
**part from** *pag'bba; pagokat*
**parted** *bugtu'₁; purut; butas 1*
**parted (opened up)** *pellat*
**parted forever** *boklang 1*
**partial to** *sōb; tagi 1*
**participate** *lamud₂ 1.1*
**particle (speck)** *puling 1; peged₂ 1*
**partition** *bilik 1; h'nggol; anak₂; kulambu' 1*
**partition (v)** *likus 1*
**partly able** *ahat 1*
**partly eaten** *k'bbang*
**partly healed** *bongka 1.1*
**partly open** *sungkab*
**partner** *paghola'; iring; ugpang 1; limbang 1*
**partner (business)** *pagkungsi; paghūn; sapali 1*
**partners in game** *pagsangga*
**party (political)** *palti*
**pass away (euphemism)** *b'kkat napas; bugtu' napas; maruhum*

**pass between** *t'ngnga'-t'ngnga'*
**pass by** *labay₁ 1; lipuwas*
**pass gas** *ntut; pagboro-boro*
**pass on (a medical condition)** *kulina*
**pass on (to another)** *nde'; ndiya; palatun; pusaka' 1.1*
**pass on a name** *pasalin*
**pass out (faint)** *pinsan 1*
**pass something to** *sōng₂ 1.1*
**pass through (a gap)** *p'ssut 1; suwa' 1*
**pass unharmed** *liyus 1.1*
**pass zenith, of stars** *lemba*
**passenger** *pasahero; biyahero*
**passing to and fro** *paglaulabay*
**passing years** *pagtahunan*
**passive** *t'ntong₂*
**passport** *paspolt*
**past (time)** *labay₂; liban 1*
**past due time (late)** *tapa'ut*
**past tense marker** *bay*
**paste (n)** *binolog*
**paste (v)** *pikit₁ 1.1*
**pastor** *pastol*
**pastry, fried** *pastil*
**pat (v)** *dapu'*
**patch (repair)** *tupak 1; sumpal 1.1*
**paternal kinfolk** *usba 1*
**path** *lān; labayan; pal'ngnganan*
**path (narrow)** *lān pasiklut*
**patient (adj)** *sabal 1*
**patrimony** *pusaka' 1*
**patrol** *patrol*
**patron** *nakura'; kapala*
**pattern (guide or model)** *sengoran; bantukan; suntu'an; simpayan*
**pattern (motif)** *bunga₂; sapak*
**pause** *honglo' 1; hongat; hondong 1*
**pawn (v)** *sanda'*
**pawnshop** *padjak₁; sanda'an*
**pawpaw** *kapaya*
**pay (v)** *pahokas; bayad 1.1*
**pay (wages)** *gadji 1*
**pay attention** *hirup₁; asip*
**pay back** *balos₁ 1*
**pay fee** *tūng 1.1*
**pay in cash** *tunay₂; lampak₁ 1.1*
**pay tribute** *buwis 1.1*
**payment** *tambahan; tulahan; bayad 1*
**payment (partial)** *susuk*
**payment to midwife** *bauballi'; tiyandā*
**peace** *kasannangan; sajahitra'*
**peaceable** *hanunut; lanu' atay*
**peaceful** *sannang*
**peak** *pekkes-pekkes; puntuk; pussuk 1*

**peaked fold** *ladjuk 1; tuladjuk*
**peanut** *batung₁*
**peanut sauce** *tawsiyu*
**pearl** *mussa'*
**pearl diving** *pagtuhun*
**pearl oyster** *tipay*
**peashooter** *lustang 1*
**pebble** *batu-batu₁*
**peck (v)** *tittuk*
**peddle goods** *samsuy; pagsoroy*
**pedicab** *taraysikul*
**pee** *mange' 1.1*
**peek** *hunggaw 1*
**peel (v)** *lapes; kupas*
**peel off** *kanit 1*
**peeling** *gagus; laknit 1; lakles*
**peep (out at)** *tilag-tilag₂; tik 1; sib 1*
**peer (n)** *sibu' 1; pagkahi; topad; dora' 1*
**peevish** *s'ngngot₁ 1*
**peg** *tipopok*
**pelvis** *kamama'u*
**pen (for livestock)** *ād 1*
**penalise** *ballas 2; sā'₁ 1.4; semet*
**penalty** *taksil 1*
**pencil** *pinsil*
**pendant** *pinting*
**pending (decision, judgment)** *gantung₁; pinding*
**pending divorce** *timan-gantung*
**penetrate** *duklat 1; solab₁ 1.1; hōp₁ 1*
**penetrate (of cutting blade)** *ōk 1*
**penetrate (someone's thinking)** *ōk 2*
**penetrate skin** *sukmu 1.1; sulam*
**penetrated** *sudlat 1*
**peninsula** *tōng-lahat*
**penis** *boto'₂*
**penis (vulgar)** *sangkil 2*
**penitence** *susun₂ 1*
**penknife** *laring*
**pennant** *bandila'; tipas-tipas*
**penniless** *kettak; pulubi; pihit*
**Pentateuch** *Kitab Tawrat*
**people group** *bangsa₁*
**people groups** *kabangsa-bangsahan*
**people in general** *majilis; a'a; manusiya' 1; puhu' 2*
**people of God** *ummat 1*
**people of the historic past** *kamatto'ahan*
**pepper (chilli)** *lara 1*
**pepper (ground)** *maisa*
**pepper vine (betel)** *buyu'*
**perceive** *sayu 1.1; tilas₁*
**perceptive** *ladju pikilan*
**perch (v)** *tapu' 1*
**peremptory** *pagmanda 1; hagda 1*
**perfect (in detail)** *tubus₁ 1*

**perforate** *lowang 1.2; t'ttok 1.1*
**perfume** *ns'llan pahamut; hamut 1*
**perhaps** *kalu-kalu 1; arai' 1; ya aniya'*
**perilous** *anib 1.1*
**period (menstrual)** *bulan₄*
**period of time** *masa 1; waktu 1; jāman*
**perish** *mula₁*
**perish the thought** *s'lle' bale puhu'; tingga' dawa*
**permanent** *kakkal; taptap 1; dorog₁*
**permeate** *pulag-pulag; sobsob 1*
**permissible** *makajari 1; manjari₁ 1*
**permissible (by religious law)** *halal 2*
**permission** *ba'id 1.1; labay min*
**permissive** *parakag*
**permit** *sagad 1.1*
**permit (v)** *parūl 1.1; pakuhi; papuhun; tugut 2*
**perpendicular to** *pababag 1*
**perpetuate name** *bangun₃*
**perplexed** *pam'ngngang*
**persecute** *inyaya; la'at 1.2*
**persist; persevere** *kara-kara₁; dago'os; akkul; pagambat-ambat 1; abut-abut*
**persistent** *sangdan 1; akkul; timpus*
**persistent (effort)** *tukid 1; tuyu' 1*
**persistent (of illness)** *pangsan*
**persistently** *taptap 1; kuwat-kuwat 1*
**person** *a'a; puhu' 1*
**person in authority** *tagpatutan; tagsoho'an*
**person in charge** *nakura'*
**person marker** *disi; si*
**person of high status** *pagta'allukan*
**personal (unique to)** *luggiya'*
**personal choice** *pagtu'uran*
**personal skill** *huwang₂*
**personal space** *huwang₁ 1*
**personality** *jāt₁; palangay*
**personally responsible** *siyal*
**personhood** *kapaga'a*
**personnel** *pitis-tendog; tendog*
**perspiration** *hulas 1*
**perspiration rash** *buwa'-buwa'-hulas 1*
**persuade** *p'ggong; poleggaw; kole'-kole'₂; bowa₃; paghona'-hona' 2*
**persuaded** *kompolme; pila 1.1*
**persuasive** *bidjak 1*
**pervade** *pulag-pulag*
**perverse** *daiyus*
**pervert truth** *pagbengkok*
**peso** *pilak 2*
**pester (v)** *salut 1.1; pipit₁*
**pestilence** *patay-p'llut*
**pestle** *hallu*
**pet (n)** *papu'*
**pet name** *g'llal 2; danglay 1*

**petition (v)** *ampun-ampun; junjung 1.2; amu'-amu'*

**petrified fetus** *lidjal*

**petticoat** *kamisun*

**petulant** *s'ngngot₁ 1*

**pewter** *pittang*

**pharaoh** *pira'un*

**pharmacy** *palmasiya*

**Philippine mahogany** *danglog; manakayan; lumbayaw*

**phlegm** *ludja' 1*

**phonograph records** *plaka; ligaya*

**phosphorescence** *mata-tina'ung; ba'as 1*

**photograph** *patta' 1*

**phrase** *kabtangan*

**physical grace** *alti; polma 1*

**physical presence** *baran₂ 1*

**physical well-being** *salamat-baran*

**physician** *doktol*

**physic-nuts** *tangan-tangan*

**pick (tool)** *piku*

**pick fruit** *pusu'₁*

**pick out (with fingers)** *kolehek*

**pick up (with fingers)** *pudjut; kuri' 1.1; imut; kamut*

**pickle (for dipping)** *pan'nno'an*

**pickle fish (v)** *pagtasik*

**picnic** *piknik*

**picture** *patta' 1*

**piebald** *kabang 1.1*

**piece** *p'ppot 2; solag 1*

**piece (counting term)** *tebag 1*

**pier** *jambatan*

**pierce** *lagbas 1; latus; sudlat 1.1*

**pierce ears** *t'bbok₁*

**pierce skin** *sulam*

**pig** *bawi; bā'₃*

**pigeons** *balud; dundunay; kango'; malapati; kamasu'; assang; manatad*

**piggyback** *baba' 1*

**pike-conger (eel)** *nipa'-nipa' 1*

**pilchards** *toloy; kasig*

**pile (n)** *bingkis 1; puntak 1; botang₁ 1*

**pile up (of multiple items)** *bangkat₁; hungku'; hunsuk*

**piled in layers** *pagbangday*

**piled up high** *timbun-tambak*

**piles (hemorrhoids)** *l'pput₁ 1.1*

**pilfer** *t'ppas₁; sabsab*

**pilgrim (to Mecca)** *hadji'; hadja₁*

**pillars of Islam** *lukun*

**pillow** *ū'an*

**pillow slip** *punda*

**pilot** *malim 1*

**pimples** *samuwa' 1; ampogod 1*

**pin together** *lagsak*

**pincer** *sakket 1*

**pinch flesh** *k'bbit; kinbing*

**pinch of** *dangk'tti'; peged₂ 1; dangkuri'*

**pine tree** *malabuhuk*

**pineapple** *pisang*

**pink** *kalas*

**pink-eye** *belad*

**pins and needles** *b'nnod 1*

**pinwheel** *kapalling*

**pinworms** *sassing 1*

**pious** *pagta'at*

**pipe (for liquid)** *pansul; tubu₁*

**pipe (for tobacco)** *kukuwa; kuwako*

**piping (clothing trim)** *bingkay*

**piracy** *kullu-kullu₂ 1; mundu 1*

**pistol** *pistul*

**pitch (tar)** *kitlan 1*

**pitch-dark** *kal'ddoman; lendom bitu-bituhan*

**pitcher (jug)** *kassa' 2*

**pith** *esok*

**pith of fruit** *laput*

**pitiful** *ase'-ase'*

**pitted (of skin)** *tamokmok*

**pity** *ase'*

**pity (v)** *andu'-andu'*

**pivot** *pagagod*

**placate** *amu'-amu'*

**placated** *lunuk atay*

**place (n)** *lugal 1; atag₁ 1; tongod₂ 1*

**place (secure)** *deyo' pikpik; kuta'₁ 2; kuddaman*

**place (v)** *nna'*

**place arm across shoulder** *ablay*

**place close together** *pagdigpit 1*

**place flat** *d'dda*

**place on (v)** *patagga'; pat'nna'*

**place on top** *bangkat₁*

**place weights on (v)** *to'on₂*

**placenta** *tamuni*

**plague** *bonglay 1; p'llut₂*

**plague death** *patay-p'llut*

**plain (n)** *karatagan; kapantayan*

**plait** *sapid 1.1*

**plan (design)** *ladjawan; bantukan; suntu'an*

**plan on doing** *paru; gara' 1.1; pagbantu 1.1; pagmohot 1*

**plan to meet** *pagtaratu*

**plane (smoothing tool)** *katam 1*

**planing fins (boat hull)** *pikpik₁ 2*

**plank** *papan₁*

**plank (canoe side)** *tapi' 1*

**planning ability** *panguntukan*

**planning session** *kagara'an*

**plant (ornamental)** *jambangan*

**plant (v)** *tanom₁ 1; bakal; tugbal*

**plant an idea** *isi-isi*

**plantains** *saging-manurung; sabba*
**plantation** *kabbun; kakayuhan*
**planted area** *tanoman*
**planted things** *tinanom*
**plants (as a class)** *paltubu-tubuhan 1*
**plants (marine)** *kutu-kutu-tahik; lera-lera₁; l'mmuk*
**plants (medicinal)** *saungga'; salimbangun; bitawali'; bilu-bilu₂; sinagawli'; luku-luku; lig'tto'; gamut-nonan; padjihun; alum; sampan-tuhug; dundang₂; kopal-kopal; manunumbul; daklan-bulan; sinokot; pād-pād₂; neneng*
**plaster (medicinal)** *salompas; pikit-pikit*
**plastic bags** *salopen; tilag-tilag₁*
**plate** *lai'; tapak-tapak*
**plate a surface (v)** *langkop; sarul*
**platform** *pantān*
**play** *ongka' 1*
**play a guitar** *pagkitara*
**play ball** *pagbantung; pagbola*
**play dominoes** *pagduminu 1*
**play flute** *pagsuling*
**play games** *ongka' 1*
**play gongs** *tagunggu'; kulanting 1; tuntung*
**play jacks** *pagjimban 1.1*
**play marbles** *pagolen; pagplising 1.1*
**play music** *pah'lling₁*
**play softball** *pagsopbol*
**play tag** *embet*
**play tricks** *paglepet*
**player (cards)** *timbayan*
**playing area (marked)** *manohan*
**playing cards** *sugal; paglaki*
**playing checkers/chess** *pagsukki'*
**playthings** *pangongka'an; parereyagan*
**plaza** *palasa; mairan; da'ira 2*
**plead (legal)** *pagda'awa 1*
**plead for mercy** *pagmatiase'*
**pleasant (appearance)** *bustan*
**please** *amu₂ 1*
**please (politeness marker)** *kono' 2; pa'in₂ 2; da'a busung*
**please oneself** *pagdūl-baya'*
**pleased with** *sulut 1*
**pleasures** *kalamihan; bunyi-bunyihan dunya*
**pleats** *la'up 1; kola' 1*
**pledge (guarantee)** *s'nnad*
**pledge (on loan)** *lōb 1*
**pledge (v)** *janji' 1.1*
**Pleiades (star group)** *mūpū*
**plentiful** *banos; besal; dayas-dayas; parat; jayak*
**pliers** *plaes; liyabe*
**plot against** *bandu₂; pagmohot 1*
**plow (plough)** *araru 1*
**pluck hair** *himangot 1.1*
**pluck out** *kolehek; bulbul 1.2*

**plug (n)** *pulai'*
**plug (v)** *saplong; s'nsong; gagā*
**plug into socket** *sangon₁ 1*
**plug tobacco** *tabaku' 1*
**plugged (of ears)** *palpal 1*
**plumage** *bulbul 1*
**plump (of body)** *goldo-goldo; tibung-tibung; subuk; bodde'-bodde'*
**plunder** *gora'₂ 1.1; kullu-kullu₂ 1; taban; mundu 1.1*
**plunge (dive)** *lorok 1*
**plural markers** *saga 1; manga*
**plus** *maka₂*
**plywood** *papan₁; pulaybūd*
**pocket** *anak-bulsa; bulsa*
**pocket knives** *laring; punyal 1*
**pockmarked** *tamokmok*
**poetic Old Testament books** *Jabul*
**poetry** *tarasul*
**point** *taloman; tōng₁*
**point in game** *poen*
**point of spear** *solab₁ 1*
**point out** *tō' 1; pintulu' 1; tudlu'₂ 1*
**pointed (of speech)** *tumlang 1*
**pointed at** *tukbul*
**poison** *lassun 1*
**poison (for fish)** *tuba 1*
**poison (of pufferfish)** *pai-pai 1*
**poke (playful)** *jullit₂*
**poke at** *kodjel*
**poke from beneath** *suruk*
**poke into** *kussu'; osok 1.1; sudlat 1.1*
**poke to get attention** *kohed 1*
**pole (for thatch)** *baras-baras*
**pole (stake)** *bale₃ 1; soha'; tukag*
**police** *pulis*
**polish (v)** *palis₂; lampasu; lanu' 1.2*
**polish metal (v)** *kaskas₁; bata*
**polite** *addat 1.1; hongpot*
**politeness (formal)** *puli-bahasa*
**politeness marker** *kono' 2; lagi' 3*
**political campaign** *kampēn₁ 1*
**political inducement** *pulitik₁ 1*
**polluted** *batal; lumu'*
**polyglot** *sabut-bahasa*
**polyuria (urinary problem)** *kima-kima; kaukati 1*
**pomegranate** *dalima'*
**pomelo** *muntay-gadja*
**pomfret fishes** *buna'-halo; samperot*
**pompoms** *jambu 1*
**pond** *tangki; bohe'-pangandung; k'ppong*
**pond (form a pond)** *longkang*
**pond for live fish** *kulam*
**ponder** *tamsil; dongdong*
**ponyfish** *sapsap₃*

**ponytail (hairstyle)** *toket 1*
**pool** *pangandung; tigbaw*
**pool (game)** *pagbulitin; pūl*
**poor** *pulubi; miskin*
**poor quality** *guya'*
**poorly (unwell)** *la'at palasahan*
**pop (soft drink)** *pipsikola; kokola*
**pop out** *pangsut 1*
**popped rice or corn** *gagati'; bulitik₂; biti'₁*
**popping sound** *palopok*
**populace; population** *majilis; mahalayak; mahadjana'*
**porch** *balkon; pantān; saurung*
**porcupine fish** *buntal-itingan*
**pork** *bawi; bā'₃*
**pornographic** *lumu'*
**porpoises** *lomba-lomba; bbung*
**porridge** *binugbug*
**portal (doorway)** *lawang 1*
**portent** *nahas 1; nasa; ba'at 1*
**porter** *kalgadol*
**portion** *bahagi' 1; palsuku'an*
**Portuguese man-of-war** *būng-leha*
**portulaca (purslane)** *bilang-bilang*
**pose a riddle** *patokod*
**position of twins in womb** *susun-buyu'*
**positive about** *kuhi₁ 1; lampung baran*
**positive outlook** *galak₁ 1; kagustuhan*
**possess (by spirit being)** *sōd 2; sangon₂ 1; jin 1.2; hōp₁ 2*
**possessions** *kaniya'; palsuku'an; ai-ai 2*
**possible** *jari₁ 1; makajari 2; manjari₁ 2*
**possibly** *arai' 1; ya aniya'; kalu gi'*
**post (corner of house)** *hāg analus*
**post office** *posopis*
**posterity** *tubu'-manubu'; suring-baha'u*
**postpone** *buhul₂; pagmahuli-llaw; pagli'i-li'i*
**postponement** *tanggu 1; lehod 1*
**posts (poles)** *pangtu'ud; tuku 1; hāg 1*
**posture** *t'ngge 1; polma 1*
**pot (clay)** *l'ppo'; lenga'; banga'₂; paliyuk; simpi'*
**pot (metal)** *kenseng; tungkang; kasirola; kaldero; kawa'₁; kawali'*
**pot supports** *sukul₂*
**potato (sweet)** *panggi'-bahan*
**potato (white)** *patatas*
**potbelly** *badding-badding*
**potent** *bisa 1*
**poultice** *paus*
**pound (v)** *t'ppa; pangki'*
**pounded flat** *losak*
**pour (into another container)** *tumpa 1.1; tuwang; tuyung; hain*
**pour on** *bubu'; busug 1; titi'*
**pout** *k'mmi'; burut; bowa'-tai'*

**powder** *borak 1; tawas; tabun-tabun*
**powder something** *budbud 1.1; borak 1.1*
**powder-puff tree** *butun₂*
**powdery substance** *moseng 1*
**power (mysterious)** *kuddarat*
**power; powerful** *kawasa 1.1; ga'os 1.1; kulasog 1.1; paslod 1.1*
**practicable** *manjari₁ 2*
**practice (religious duties)** *ammal₁*
**practise (v)** *pabiyaksa*
**praise** *pudji 1.1; sanglit 1*
**prankster** *pandikal*
**prawn crackers** *ulang-ulang*
**prawns** *ka'ullang; ulang 1*
**pray** *sambahayang; amu'-amu'*
**pray (for newborn girl)** *kamat 1.1*
**pray faithfully** *paglima-waktu*
**pray silently** *pagma'aripat*
**prayer** *tarawi; ta'at 1; duwa'a 1*
**prayer (direction of)** *kiblat*
**prayer (place of)** *pagduwa'ahan*
**prayer beads** *tasbi'*
**prayer for deceased** *tulkin 1.1; tahalil 1*
**prayer for protection** *duwa'a-kokam*
**prayer mats** *musalla; tudjara*
**prayer position** *tayak 1*
**prayer times** *magrib 1; aisa; subu₂ 2; luhul₁; asal*
**preach** *nasihat*
**precarious** *tipid 1*
**precede** *abung 1; sauna; dahū 1.2*
**precept** *lukun*
**precious** *halga' 1.1*
**precise** *taluwa' 1; bontol 1; tudju₂ 1*
**pre-dawn** *logob-logob*
**predestination** *karal 1*
**predict** *pagtaluhan 1.1; papata 1.1*
**predict misfortune** *pa'al 1.1*
**predictable** *totos*
**prediction** *papata 1; pagba'at 1; palihalan 2*
**prefer** *suwak 1.1*
**preferably** *gōm; atas₁; arapun*
**pregnancy (emotional state)** *iram-kalitan; iram-sapi'*
**pregnancy gift** *pareyo'₂; palahil*
**pregnant** *b'ttong₂ 1; buhat-puhu'; iram*
**prehistory** *masa-awal; musim tagna'*
**premature baby** *onde'-onde' kabus*
**premier** *panghulu' 1; preseden*
**premonition** *nahas 1; kawang; g'mma*
**preoccupation** *ligap 1; pagsumau'*
**prepare** *tuntul 1.1; sakap 1.2; tagama*
**prepare (place of prayer)** *pagbāng 1*
**prepare (weaving materials)** *ambuhut; hait; tai' 1.1; pagpandan*
**prepare betel chew** *apil*

**prepare food** *adjal*
**prepare for burial** *lukbu'₁; ligu'*
**prescience (knowing the future)** *langtas 1*
**presence** *alopan₁; matahan; dahū'an 1; harapan₁*
**presence (location)** *kamaituhan; kamahē'an 2*
**presence (of divine being)** *hadarat*
**present (gift or offering)** *siba' 1.1; hulmat 1.1; tanggap 1.1*
**present era or time** *tahun itu; kabuwattituhan; ahil-jāman*
**present to (introduce)** *pagpaharap*
**presentiment (omen)** *nasa*
**preserve (by drying)** *peyad 1.1; tumbal 1.1*
**preserve (by salting)** *asin 1.1; pagtasik*
**preserved fish** *daing niasin; boro 1; sampila'₁ 1; peyad 1*
**president** *preseden*
**press** *gipis 1.1; gipit 1*
**press against** *dagtol₁; d'ddol*
**press clothes (iron)** *pilinsa; kutad 1.2*
**press down on** *togmok 1.1; doson 1.1; p'ssil 1.1*
**press flat** *hotad₁; pera' 1.1*
**press into** *senop; dasok 1.1; d'ppon*
**press stomach** *kallus₁ 1.1; salimpak*
**press to extract juice** *entos*
**press to release** *passik 1*
**press together** *danos; daggot₂ 1.1*
**pressure lantern** *kulaet 1*
**pressure someone** *sandat 2.1; agpot 1*
**prestige** *kawasa 1*
**presume to know** *kupul*
**presumptuous** *atakabbul*
**pretend (be deceptive)** *pagbau'-bau'; pagdō-rō; pagtumagal; akkal-akkal*
**pretend courage** *agad-hawid*
**pretend deafness** *pagbisu-bisu*
**pretend ignorance** *pagawam*
**pretend to be a male** *pagl'lla-l'lla₂*
**pretend to be dead** *pagpatay-patay 1*
**pretend to be important** *pagheya-heya; pagnaho'-naho'; paglaku-laku*
**pretend virtue** *pagadil-adil*
**pretext (excuse)** *tumagal 1; singgit; panumagal*
**pretext (for quarrel)** *katikmuhanan*
**pretty** *hāp d'nda; lingkat 1.1*
**prevent** *sapad; paggat; pagang*
**prevent (game move)** *agpang 1.1; hapa' 1.2*
**previous** *sī'; dahū 1; bai*
**previously** *waktu palabay*
**price** *b'llihan*
**price (n)** *halga' 1*
**prickle** *tunuk*
**prickly heat** *buwa'-buwa'-llaw 1*
**pride** *abbu 1*
**priest** *imam*

**priest (Roman Catholic)** *pari'*
**primer (reader)** *undang-undang*
**prince** *datu'*
**princess** *sitti; dayang-dayang 1; putli'*
**principal (school)** *prinsipal*
**principles** *hatulan 1*
**print (mark)** *limpa' 1*
**prior** *awal₂ 1; dahū 1*
**prise out** *sisi 1; lugit*
**prise up** *landak; suwal 1*
**prisoner** *pilisu 1*
**prisons** *jīl 1; kalabusu 1*
**private (not public)** *batin 1; kolorom*
**private parts (of body)** *alopan₂; harapan₂; munda'an₂*
**privileged** *balkan*
**prize (n)** *praes*
**probably** *arakala'; gana-gana 1.1; siguru 1; sabali-bali*
**probe** *sandak*
**problem** *susa 1; problema*
**procedure** *hatulan 1; l'ngnganan₂*
**proceed** *lalga; lanjal 1.1; laus 1*
**proceed with sale** *pehē'₂*
**proceeds (financial)** *luwas₂*
**proceeds of sale** *b'llihan*
**proclaim** *pamahalayak; patanyag; nasihat*
**procrastinate** *lehod 1.2; pagsingkali'i-li'i; buhul₂; pagli'i-li'i*
**prod** *tanduk 1.1; sudlat 1.1*
**produce (shoots or suckers)** *s'mbut 1; saha' 1.1*
**produce liquid** *bohe'₁ 1.2*
**productive** *jatu 1; jayak*
**profession of faith** *panyabut 1*
**proficiency** *kapandayan; huwang₂*
**proficient** *pantas*
**profit (financial)** *kasōngan 2*
**profitable** *laba; untung₁ 1.1*
**profound** *lalom₂*
**profuse** *mussak-massik; labung 1; libombo'*
**prognosis** *papata 1*
**program** *plano*
**progress** *sōng₂ 1*
**progressing** *mina'-mina' 1*
**prohibited** *haram 1.1; bawal 1.1*
**prohibition** *paglāngan*
**prohibition (of food item)** *sukang 1; li'in 1*
**project (v)** *jungal 1.1; toro' 1*
**project forward** *judjal 1*
**project outwards** *kabag 1.1*
**project upwards** *tudjak; pussuk 1.1; hanggal 1*
**projecting (of buttocks)** *tuddi'*
**projecting (of upper lip)** *tungalu'*
**projection** *gawat; jungal 1; boto'₁*
**prolapse** *honhon*

**prolapse (uterine)** *bōt₂*

**proliferate** *kansang 1.1; pagsuring-pagsaingsing 1*

**prolong** *pagka'lloman; ddas 1.1*

**prolonged** *panjang; ddas 1.2; lanat*

**prolonged grief** *sandal-dohon*

**prominence (of role)** *muna-muna 1*

**prominent (obvious)** *tampal 2*

**prominent (of eyes)** *pellat-mata 1*

**promiscuous** *sundal 1.1; biga'; pagl'lla; pagd'nda 2*

**promise** *tungga' 1.1; najal 1; janji' 1*

**promise in marriage** *pah'nda 2; pah'lla 2*

**promptly** *agsāy; dai'-dai' 1.2; sa'ut 1.1; saunu'*

**prone (lie face up)** *leyak; daya'*

**prone to fall** *lumintiyad*

**prong** *kukku-badja'*

**pronounce clearly** *paghurup*

**pronouncement** *paghimumūngan 1*

**proof** *mattan 1; palsaksi'an; puriba; tanda'*

**prop (n)** *tuku 1; pipul; tukag*

**prop up** *biggal 1.2; pahanggal; pataggal 1.1*

**propeller** *kapay*

**propeller blade** *daun-kapay*

**proper** *patut; amu₁; tōp 1.1*

**properly** *pahāp₁*

**property (things owned)** *suku'*

**prophet** *a'a talus; nabi*

**prophetic message** *bissala talus*

**prophetic Old Testament books** *Jabul*

**propose marriage** *pah'nda 2*

**proprietor** *tag-; tagdapu*

**proscription (on food)** *sukang 1*

**prosperity** *kajatuhan; sajahitra'*

**prosperous** *haldaya*

**prostitutes** *puta; d'nda pagtatambahan*

**prostrate (v)** *pagpatihantak 1; lintuwad 1*

**protagonist** *kuntara 1*

**protect against harm** *papag*

**protect using a layer** *hampe 1.1; lampik 1.1*

**protection** *komkoman 2*

**protection (against weather)** *limbu 1*

**protection (by magic)** *hampan 1; habay-habay; tambang₃ 1; tampan 1; pagkobol 1.1*

**protective care** *komkoman 2; deyoman 2; milikan; okoman*

**protective layer** *lampik 1; hampe 1; lapis₁ 1*

**protective wall (grave)** *dinding-hali*

**protector (guardian)** *tunggu' 1*

**protest (political)** *bagung-lipunan*

**protest against** *pagamā 1.1*

**protest against a ruling** *pagda'awa 1*

**protocol** *hatulan 1*

**protrude** *hellel; l'pput₁ 1; toro' 1*

**protrude (of teeth)** *juhal; jungal 1.1*

**protruding** *l'ppas 1*

**protrusion** *buggul 1; hanggal 1*

**proud** *abbu 1.1; langa atay*

**prove innocence** *paghuwas-huwas; pagko'ot bohe'-pasu'*

**proverb** *pali-pali; papata 1.2*

**provide husband for** *pah'lla 2*

**provide necessities** *pagnapaka; gastu 1.1*

**provide refreshments** *paglabot 1*

**provide wife for** *pah'nda 2*

**provided that** *basta; bang pa'in*

**providence (divine)** *sapa'at₁ 1*

**provisions** *balanja' 1; lutu'₁ 1*

**provocation (verbal)** *himumūngan*

**provoke** *sunggud; tukas 1.1; jural*

**provoke to anger** *mata-mata₁; pagpakalintaw*

**provoked (irritated)** *kalintaw*

**prow (of boat)** *munda'₁ 1; sangpad*

**prudent** *lentop*

**pry out** *lugit; suwal 1; landak*

**Psalms (Old Testament)** *Jabul*

**psyche** *pangatayan*

**puberty** *sangpot 1; lumbu'-baha'u*

**puberty (female)** *tindaw*

**pubescent girl** *daga-raga*

**pubic mound** *kōk-bundu'-bundu'*

**public arena** *kaheya'an*

**public show** *paganda*

**public view** *mata-mairan*

**publicize** *patanyag; pablek; bistu 1.1; tanyag 1.1*

**publicly known** *bukis₂*

**pucker the face** *k'mmi'*

**pucker up** *pagh'ngngek-h'ngngek*

**puckered** *lūn-lupi'*

**puckery taste** *p'kkat*

**puddle (n)** *halo-halo*

**puff up** *tting*

**puffed (out of breath)** *hapus₂; paghangu-hangu; lumu; pagh'ngka-h'ngka*

**pufferfishes** *luku'₁; babakan; buntal*

**puffy (of eyes)** *b'ddu'*

**pull along** *hella'; guyud 1*

**pull apart** *tangsu' 1.1; besod*

**pull on** *bira 1*

**pull out** *tugnus₁ 1.1; bugnus₂; darut 1.1; bubut*

**pull rank** *pospa'; powera 2*

**pull sharply** *hangku'; ganggut; hagtu'*

**pulled away from** *bungkas*

**pulled straight** *l'ngngat*

**pulled tight** *d'llot 1.1; pigtal 1*

**pulley** *timun-timun 1*

**pulp (v)** *petak 1.1; lodjag 1.1*

**pulpit** *mimbal*

**pulpy** *lonyat; lodjag 1*

**pulsate (throb)** *pagkowap-kowap; panag-panag 1; pagsignat-signat*

**pulsating (of light)** *pagpillaw-pillaw*

**pulse** *galak₃*

**pulverize** *tanay*; *pipis*

**pumice** *batu-lantup*

**pummel** *banol 1.1*

**pump up** *gomba*; *pām*

**pumpboat** *pambot*

**pumpkin** *kabasi'*

**punch (v)** *tibu'*; *g'bbuk*; *suntuk 1.1*; *butug*

**punctured** *buslut*

**pungent** *bisa 1*

**punish** *binasa 1.1*; *binsana' 1.1*

**punished** *pangkaheng*

**pupil (of eye)** *kaettoman-mata*; *ta'u-ta'u-mata*

**pupil (student)** *mulid*

**purblind** *bulahaw*

**purchase (v)** *bayad 1.1*; *b'lli*

**purchased item** *muddal 1*

**purchases** *pam'lli-m'lli*

**pure** *porol*; *sussi 1.1*; *saltun 1*

**pure (of language)** *legsok₁*

**pure white** *pote'-tawas*

**purge** *sussi 1.2*

**purification** *istinja'*; *junub*

**purify; purity** *sussi 1.2*

**purity of intentions** *atay-pote'*

**purlin (building)** *palimba'an*; *sibay*

**purple** *taluk*; *loho'-ubi*

**purpose (n)** *kalagihan 1*; *maksud 1*; *kapunyahan*; *hadjat₁*

**purpose (set mind on)** *angut*; *mohot 1.1*

**purposeful** *to'ongan 2*

**purse** *pitaka*

**purse lips** *k'mmi'*

**pursue** *apas 1.1*; *turul 1*; *onse 1.1*

**pursue a goal** *angut*; *mohot 1.1*

**pursue a lure** *ubug₂*

**pus** *nana'*

**push away** *judjal 2*; *tulak₂*; *lodjat₂ 1*

**push away from vertical** *poyog 1.1*

**push in (ahead of others)** *agaw 1*; *sōng-sōng₂*; *abung 1*

**push into ground** *togmok 1.2*; *osol 1.1*

**push something off** *dogsol*; *ligid₂ 1.1*

**push through crowd** *selot 1.1*

**push upwards** *jungkat 1*

**pustules** *buwa'-buwa' 1*; *abas 1*

**put effort into** *puspus₁*; *pagbinasag*; *kuyas 1.1*

**put foot in hole** *lossok*

**put hand in container** *ko'ot 1*

**put into** *asok 1.1*

**put into effect (of words)** *kabbul*

**put near heat** *pa'alung*

**put off doing (postpone)** *buhul₂*; *pagmahuli-llaw*; *tanggu 1.1*

**put on airs** *pagabbu 1.1*

**put right** *paintul*

**put self first** *pasambu*

**put up with** *sandal-sandal*

**put weight on** *sangdol 1*

**putrefy** *langag*; *buhuk*

**puzzle** *tokod-tokod*

**python** *sowa-panga'an*; *sowa-d'ppong*

# Q q

**qualities (character)** *sadsaran*; *jāt₁*; *kasuddahan*

**qualities (of a canoe)** *kulis pelang*

**quality (nature)** *ta'u₂*

**quantity** *heka 1*

**quarrel** *pagkalukassa*; *pagjawab 1*; *pagsagga'an₂ 1*

**quarter** *tonga'-sin-tonga'*

**quarter-meter** *suku₁*

**quaver (of voice)** *pagoyo'-oyo'*

**quay** *jambatan*

**queasy** *lango 2*

**queen** *dayang-dayang 1*

**question** *tilaw 1*

**question (interrogate)** *sumariya*

**question marker** *inggay*; *bā 2*; *bahā'*; *ka₁*

**Questioner** *mungkalun*

**quick (rapid)** *l'kkas 1*; *samot 1*; *sapat₂ 1*; *kasay 1*

**quick succession** *pagsunu'-sunu'*

**quickly** *amot-amot 1*; *paspas₁*

**quick-witted** *tali' 1*; *tallang-hati 1.1*

**quiet (shy)** *t'mmun*; *sandol 1*

**quit (doing)** *bba₂*

**quit (motor)** *para₁*

**quite (somewhat)** *mbal sakit*; *saga 3*

**quivering** *bogon-bogon*; *h'bbol*

**quote a price** *halga' 1.2*

**Quran** *Kora'an*

# R r

rabbit *kuting-balanda'*

rabbitfishes (spinefish) *b'llong*; *panahilaw*; *mangilāp*; *dāg$_2$* 1; *bawis$_2$*

rabies *kangog*

race (contest) *lomba*; *pagpasu 1.1*

race (ethnic) *bangsa$_1$*; *ummat 1.1*

rack for plates *lakal-lakal*

racket (noise) *lengog 1*; *hibuk*

racks (for drying fish) *ayas-ayas*; *ampang*

radiance *sinag 1.1*

radio *aradju 1.1*

rafter *sumpiyang*; *sungkelang*

rafts *alul*; *plātbōt*

rag *tarapu 1*

rage at *pugpug 1*

ragged *purut*; *jebel-jebel 1*

raid (v) *kullu-kullu$_2$ 1*; *langpas*

raider *mundu 1*

rail against *pangkal*

railing (n) *sasak 1*

rain *ulan 1*

rain (driving) *tampiyas 1*

rain (light) *bonok-bonok*

rainbows *salindugu' 1*; *bāngaw*; *andalaho'*

raincloud *andom 1*

raindrops *pitik-pitik 1*

rainless season *pang'llaw*

rainy season *pangulan*

raise (using both hands) *bengket*

raise a flag *sintak 2*

raise an issue *sambat*

raise and lower line *hagul*

raise by wedging *biggal 1.2*

raise canoe (above water) *tangon 1*

raise eyebrows *kiddat$_1$*

raise fish trap *palit$_2$*

raise head *tongas*

raise up *angkat$_1$ 1.1*; *bungkal$_1$ 1.1*; *bangun$_1$ 1.1*

raise using a stick *kawit$_1$*

raise voice (shout) *gasud*; *galit*; *bukag*

raisins *anggul*

Rajah Solomon *Ladja Sulayman*

rake (n) *badja' 1*; *kakās*

rake (v) *kayas 1.1*; *kās*; *hīs 1.1*

ram into *palpal 1.1*

ram into ground *togmok 1.2*

Ramadan (final day) *Hailaya Puwasa$_1$*

Ramadan prayers *tarawi*

ramble (of speech) *pagsilap*; *pag'lling-lling*

ramble (walking) *pagsasab*

rambutan *usaw*

ramose murex *mastuli'*

rancid *balos$_2$*

rancid (become sour) *kahang*; *b'ngngog*

random (action or speech) *pagt'bba'-sasab*

randomly *pagsasab*; *pagsamba-samba*; *pagt'kka-t'kka*

rank (civil) *g'llal 1*; *kag'llal*

rank (military) *ranggo*

ransack *gora'$_2$ 1.1*; *kadkad 1.1*

ransom *l'kkat$_1$ 1.1*

rant at *kasla 1.1*

rap on *kuku'*

rape (v) *usiba'*

rapid *l'kkas 1*; *ka'is*

rapid speech *bibas$_1$*

rare *lahang*; *bislang 1*; *bihang$_2$*

rascal *pilliyu*; *sugarul*

rash (skin) *m'ssang 1.1*

rasp (tool) *gaugari' 1*

rat *tikus*; *ambaw*

rather *gōm*

rather than *sapād-pād*; *pād-pād$_1$*

rattan *buway*

rattan scraps *tai'-buway*

rattle (artefact) *guleyak*

rattle (v) *lagaklak*; *kattek*; *pagkulenseng*

raven *owak*

ravenous *lagak 1.2*; *kaway 1*

raw (marinated) fish *kinilaw*

ray (of light) *sinag 1*

rays (marine) *pahi*

raze *lubu$_2$ 1.1*

razor blade *gelet*

reach *abut$_2$ 1*; *sampay 2*

reach (a destination) *tulun$_2$ 1*; *t'kka$_1$ 1.1*

reach (a limit) *ta'as 1.1*; *pasangka'*; *sangka' 1*; *apang*

reach (by stealth) *gagam*

reach (using stick) *kuhit*; *kahid 1*

reach bottom *t'kkad 1*

reach by climbing *dāg$_1$ 1.1*

reach into *ko'ot 1*

reach maturity *sangpot 1.1*

reach shore *dunggu' 1*; *tundug 1*; *dukla' 1*; *tandan$_1$ 1*

react badly *pagmalas*

react intensely *kenog-kenog*

react noisily *pagmalān*

read *bassa*

**read fluently** *lansal*
**read hesitantly** *paghidja-hidja*
**read religious material** *paham; adji' 1*
**ready** *sakap 1.1; bilang$_3$; tagama*
**ready to fight** *santik bagid-bagid*
**real (genuine)** *porol; tunay$_1$; b'nnal 1.1*
**realization** *amanat*
**realize** *sayu 1.1; ta'u$_1$ 1.2*
**really** *to'od; pahāp$_1$; to'ongan 1.1*
**really?** *bahā'*
**realm** *komkoman 2; milikan*
**reap coconuts** *paglahing*
**reap fruit** *sanggot$_1$ 1.1*
**reap rice** *k'ttu'; pagani*
**reaphook** *sanggot$_1$ 1*
**rear (n)** *damulihan; buli'$_1$ 2*
**rear of an intervening object** *bukutan 1*
**rearrange** *paghatul-hatul; pagleson*
**reason (n)** *sabab$_1$ 1; jalanan; kalna' 1.1; tiranan*
**reason with** *paghona'-hona' 2*
**reasoning** *panahu'an*
**rebel** *muparik; mungkil*
**rebel (against government)** *rebelde*
**rebellious** *gagga*
**rebound** *pelleng 1; likid; balik$_2$*
**rebuild** *balmula; bangun$_2$ 2*
**rebuke** *s'ndal 1; sā'$_1$ 1.3; salba$_1$*
**recall** *masa 1.2*
**recall (remember)** *sangpit; entom 1.1; magtak*
**recede (lessen)** *kō' 1.1*
**receive (a visitor)** *sampang 1*
**receive something** *sambut 1; taima' 1*
**recent time** *tahun baha'u*
**recently** *baha'u 1.1*
**receptive** *lunuk atay*
**recess in grave** *liyang 1*
**reciprocate** *tongod$_3$ 1*
**recite (creed)** *panyabut 1*
**recite charm** *tawal 1.1; tilik; hisu'*
**recite genealogies** *usul 1.1*
**recklessness** *aykalas 1; bahani 1*
**reckon** *kira*
**reclusive** *sandol 1*
**recognizable** *nyala-nyala*
**recognize** *pangli' 1.1; panhid; kilā 1*
**recollect** *entom 1.2*
**recollection (memory)** *pangentom*
**recompense** *tungbas 1*
**recompense (v)** *tamba; tungbas 1.1; ballas 2*
**reconcile** *pagkahāp; pagkiparat 2; pagsugsug-tawbat*
**record details** *lista*
**record-players** *ligaya; ulehem*
**recount history** *usul 1.1*
**recoup (a loss)** *puli; bawi' 1*

**recover (from sickness)** *uli'$_1$ 1.1; hali$_2$*
**recover costs** *pole'-po'on 1*
**recovery (of lost item)** *pamawi'*
**re-create** *balmula*
**rectangular** *pasagi' 1.1*
**rectum** *tombong; jubul*
**recuperate (from illness)** *k'llit-k'llit; k'ddot-k'ddot*
**recurrence of symptoms** *banta'; boggat*
**recurrent** *balik$_1$ 1.1*
**recurring** *kaminduwa 1.1*
**red (color)** *keyat$_1$ 1*
**redden** *alom 1.1*
**redeem** *piyansa; l'kkat$_1$ 1*
**redirect** *bintung 1.1*
**redress** *pagmasangka 1.1*
**redress (compensation)** *pagmasangka 1*
**reduce (in number)** *sulak$_1$; putung*
**reduce (in size)** *loddos 2; kō' 1.2; hilang; pariki'*
**reduce swelling** *henned; k'ppos 1.1*
**reduce to liquid** *hansul$_1$ 1.1*
**reduce value** *powera 1.1*
**reduced to nothing** *titis 2; kugud*
**reduction** *kō' 1*
**reef** *takot; tahetek*
**reef edge** *bowa'-angan*
**reel (spool)** *gilingan; kolengan; pangaleboran*
**refer to (higher authority)** *dagsol; paglagadlad; tukbal$_2$*
**refer to (mention)** *sambat; sindil 1.1*
**reference book** *padduman*
**reference point** *pandoga 1*
**refined (sugar)** *dipinaw*
**reflect an image** *pagtanding*
**reflect light** *linig 1.2*
**reflect on (think about)** *bista$_1$; pikil 1.1*
**reflection** *lambung$_1$ 1; lindung 2*
**reflexive (grammar)** *pagpati-*
**reflux** *s'bbol 1*
**reflux (noise of)** *gguk*
**refrain (from doing)** *palo' 1.1*
**refrain (from eating)** *li'in 1.1*
**refresh (in breeze)** *pahayang*
**refreshments** *pagimun-imun; bubuhatan; lalabotan 1*
**refuge** *patapukan; tapukan*
**refuse (n)** *tai'-uni'*
**refuse (v)** *suwalak; pagin'mbal 1.1; pagmarī'*
**refuse tip (garbage)** *pagtimanan*
**refuse to believe** *paputing; sussa'*
**refute** *palilu*
**regain money** *puli*
**regale** *jamu 1.1*
**regarding (concerning)** *tongod$_1$ 1; takdil; pasal$_1$*
**regardless** *minsan aina*
**regatta** *kamunda'an*

**region** *jadjahan; pasisil; paglahat 1*
**regional authority** *tagmilikan*
**regret** *pagkannal-susun*
**regret (expression of)** *kaliman*
**regretful** *liru' 1; susun₂ 1.1*
**regrowth** *saingsing 1*
**regularly** *sanittiya; pilmi-pilmi*
**regulations** *sara' 1*
**reign** *pagsultan*
**reinforce** *kambal 1.1*
**reject (friendship)** *k'llit 2.1*
**reject (n)** *buwangkan*
**reject (v)** *sulak₂; pasibukut 1; taikut 1.1*
**rejected (of a suitor)** *baibad 1.1*
**rejoice** *pagkōg-kōg*
**relapse (of sickness)** *banta'; boggat; sangti'*
**relate (a story)** *kissa 1.1*
**relate (tell about)** *haka 1.1; pata'u*
**relate as enemies** *pagbalbantahan*
**relate as friends** *pagbagay*
**relate as siblings** *pagdanakan 1.1*
**relate by blood** *paglahasiya' 1.1*
**relate informally** *pagda'atay; pagsōd-addat*
**relate sexually** *pagbihing₂*
**related closely** *lissi*
**relative by marriage** *ba'i 1*
**relatives** *lūng 1; lahasiya' 1; sugsug 1*
**relatives (grandchild generation)** *mpu*
**relatives (grandparent generation)** *mbo'₁*
**relax rules** *pabatal*
**relaxed (leisure)** *pagpasannang*
**release** *bba₃; butawan 1; l'ppa*
**release (from snag)** *p'llus 1*
**release (from tension)** *lagtik 1*
**release (untie)** *kka 1.1*
**release binding** *p'kkal 1.1*
**release on bail** *piyansa*
**reliable** *totos*
**reliable worker** *pangandolan*
**relieve (muscle pain)** *hantu 1.2; kakati'*
**relieved (emotionally)** *limaya; handok atay 1; hayang pangatayan 1*
**religion** *agama*
**religious (to be)** *pagagama; pagsambahayang*
**religious books** *parukunan; kitab; hutba'*
**religious duty** *ibarat₁*
**religious feast** *paglukun 1.1*
**religious knowledge** *ilmu' 1; ingat*
**religious leaders (Islam)** *hatib; halipa; pakil; imam; muwallam; bilal*
**religious message (sermon)** *hutba'*
**religious scholar** *balguru; mulid*
**religious teacher** *guru 1*
**relish (sauce)** *pan'nno'an; tinu'anan; bubuk₂*

**relocate** *latun 1; laud 1; lalin 1.1; lintas*
**reluctant** *takal; palo' 1; hukaw 1.1*
**reluctant to help** *kussil*
**rely on** *andol 1; kamdos₁*
**remain (in place)** *atol; t'ttog 1.1*
**remain quiet** *paddam 1; p'mpon 1*
**remain sitting** *tongngol*
**remain still** *k'nnos; antung*
**remainder** *tinggal; kasehe'an; kapin 1*
**remaining** *masi 1*
**remains (human)** *akal-baran*
**remake** *balmula*
**remarkable** *ili-ili; inu-inu 1*
**remarks** *hilala'ungan*
**remedy** *tambal₁ 1*
**remember** *sangpit; entom 1.2; tomtom 1.1; magtak; masa 1.2*
**remember (a responsibility)** *paluli*
**remind (of obligations)** *tungbuy; tumbi'; bangkil₁*
**reminder** *lawanan*
**remission of debt** *kama'apan*
**remnants** *pupud 1; larak 1; basak*
**remodel** *pabaha'u*
**remoras** *lakkop 1; langa-langa*
**remorse** *susunan; tawbat 1*
**remorseful** *susun₂ 1.1*
**remote** *lawak; tegob-tegob; tā 1.1*
**remote places** *Juhul maka Jakatla'*
**remotest sea** *kaladjun*
**remove** *hawas; tangsu' 1.1; la'an 1.1*
**remove (by gouging)** *lugit*
**remove (by plucking)** *himangot 1.1*
**remove (by rubbing)** *gidgid*
**remove (by scraping)** *keke₁*
**remove (from heat)** *engket; haun₁*
**remove husk** *bunut 1.1*
**remove kinks** *l'dduk 1*
**remove layer** *lapes; lapu-lapu 1.1; tai' 1.1; bakkel 1.1*
**remove obstacle** *puwas₁ 1.1*
**remove organs (spirit action)** *kowang*
**remove rigor mortis** *hawas-basi'*
**remove shame** *pagtambun kaiya'an*
**remove skin** *kanit 1.1; kupas; kuwit 1.1*
**remove stitching** *tastas₂ 1.1*
**remove wall** *tingkas*
**remove water (by bailing)** *sait; k'llut 1.1*
**remove with stick** *koheg 1.1*
**removed** *tungkas*
**removed from office** *lessad*
**remunerate** *tamba; bayad 1.1*
**remuneration** *tambahan; hokas; gadji 1*
**remuneraton (to healer)** *ganti' nyawa*
**rend (tear apart)** *pensang 1.1*

renegade (religious) *multad; kapil 1*
renew *salin₁ 1.1; pabaha'u*
renounce *taikut 1*
renovate *bangun₂ 2; pabaha'u*
renown *bantug 1; ōn₂*
rental *tūng 1*
repair *pahāp₂ 1*
repair hole *patlong; s'llap₁; bubul*
repayment *entom buddi; tungbas 1*
repeat *lutang; balik₁ 1.1; isab 2; minduwa*
repeated small sounds *bahembas 1*
repeatedly *sigi-sigi 1; hulak 1; pagambat-ambat 1*
repentance *tawbat 1*
repetitive *daran*
repetitive sound *huru-huru*
replace *salin₁ 1.1; ganti' 1.2; bawi' 1*
replacement *s'lle' 1; ganti' 1*
replenish supplies *binta'; jukup 1.2*
replicate *sengod*
reply *sambung₁ 1.1; sambag₁ 1*
report (financial) *pagbista 1*
report (n) *suli-suli 1; h'lling₁ 1*
report on *pasasā; sumbung; kuhi₂*
report to authority *tuntut₁*
reportedly *kono' 1*
representative *wakil 1; idjin*
reprimand *salla'₁ 1.2; salba₁*
reproach *sugpak 1.1; salla'₁ 1.2*
reprobate *ga'ira; pilliyu; sugarul*
reproduce *anak₁ 1.1; saingsing 1*
reptiles *pahang; sowa; buwaya*
repudiate *sulak₂*
repulsive *sakkal*
reputation *bantug 1; ōn₂; baktulan*
request *amu'₁*
request favor *pinta-pinta; ampun-ampun; junjung 1.2*
request forgiveness *pagpatiampun*
require (brideprice) *sokat₁ 1.1*
requital *tongod₃ 1*
rescue *liyus 1.2; lappas₂ 1.1; haun₂*
research (v) *tilosa 1.1; paliksa'*
resemble *s'ppu; luwa 1.1*
resent *pagkidjib; pagbogon 1.1; agmol 1.1*
resentment *lagod-lagod; koto'-koto'; akon-akon*
reservation (mental) *buli'an₂; mbal-mbal*
reserve for *halli'₂; tau' 1.1; par'kkal*
reserved (of personality) *t'mmun; hatul₂; d'ngngo'*
reservoir *k'ppong*
re-sew (to fit) *dahut*
re-shape *tempos*
reside *pagluma'; paglahat 1.1*
reside briefly *hanti' 1; tingan*
residence (house) *luma'*
residence (location of) *pat'nna'an; lahat*

residue *angkas₁ 1; akal; tai'-lahing; upa' 1*
resign oneself to *luluy; lagad 1*
resilient *l'mpet; k'ddot*
resin *bulitik₁*
resist *sangsang; sagga' 1.1; sulang₁*
resistant *aggal 1; pentol*
resolved (of a disagreement) *usay 2; katuk₁*
resources *kahirupan; balanja' 1; pangatas*
resources (of sea and land) *alta'-kalun*
respect *mahaltabat; paidda; pagaddat 1; pagdeyo'-addat 1; hulmat 1*
respect highly *pagta'allukan*
respectful greetings *alamat₂*
respond *sambung₁ 1.1; saul; sambag₁ 1*
respond badly *jampa*
respond in kind *abjan*
respond slowly *aggal 1.1*
response (of congregation) *nasib*
responsibilities (family) *limbit 1*
responsibilities (general) *kabimbangan; lawag-baran; bahala'₁*
responsibility to pay *huwas-huwas*
responsible for *kuwiraw; umbang; aku₁*
rest (n) *hali'an*
rest (remainder) *kapin 1; kasehe'an*
rest (v) *hali-hali; hotay; hongat*
restaurant *estawran*
restitution *ballas 1*
restless *lensa; pagkodjel; lagedled 1; hibal 1*
restore *sagauli'; bawi' 1; pahāp₂ 1*
restrain *golgol; sapad; tagga 1.1; hawid*
restraint (of movement) *jallat₁; pasung₁ 1*
restrict *tahan₂ 1.1; batang-batang*
restrict diet *li'in 1.2*
restricted *kiput; lagot*
restriction *sigpit 1; tagga 1; jallat₁*
restroom *kasilyas*
result (outcome) *katumariyahan; kamaupakkatan; pamole'an 2*
resume negotiation *ludju'*
retain (long time) *t'ddas 1.1*
retain deposit (pawn) *lōb 1.1*
retain grip *komkom; balut 1.1*
retain possession *lōb 1.2*
retainer *tendog; bebeya'an*
retaining board (grave shelf) *dinding-hali*
retaliate *balos₁ 1; abjan; atu 1.1*
retard (mental) *babbal*
retch *pagsallowa'; pagbo'ay; ggak*
reticent *d'ngngo'; t'mmun*
retiring (shy) *sandol 1; t'mmun*
retort *sambung₁ 1.1*
retreat *suhut; sebog*
retribution *sugpak 1*
retribution (supernatural) *busung; kisas₂*

**retrieve** *puwa'*
**return (financial)** *untung₁ 1; tongod₃ 1*
**return (to source)** *pelleng 1.1*
**return (v)** *balik₁ 1.1; liyu₁ 1; bĭng₂ 1*
**return home** *pole'₁ 1.1*
**return something** *nde'; tūd₂; pole'₁ 1.3; tulun₂ 1.1; tuyuk-tuyuk; pabĭng 1.1*
**reunite** *halulay*
**reveal** *buka'₃; bukis₂*
**revenge** *balos₁ 1*
**reverberate** *konog-konog; llub*
**reverence** *pagmatāw 1; pagsujud 1*
**reverse** *bulibud 1; pelleng 1; bulallit*
**reverse direction** *bitung*
**reverse ill-fortune** *buklas₁*
**reversed** *bĭng₁ 1*
**revile** *pala'at*
**revise** *pabaha'u*
**revisit** *balik₁ 1.1*
**revive** *paka'llum*
**revive dispute** *bingkug*
**revolting** *sammal 1*
**revolve** *bulibud 1; legot 1.1*
**revolve (on a shaft)** *palling*
**revolver** *pistul*
**revulsion** *sakkal; saggan*
**reward** *pahala'; tungbas 1*
**rewards (in afterlife)** *daya-damuli*
**rheumatic** *hantu 1.1*
**rhyming name** *pagso'on 1.1*
**rhythm** *pagtā'-tā'; taratu' 1*
**rhythmic noise** *kutub; huru-huru*
**rib (boat building)** *giyak*
**rib (bone)** *kadjang-kadjang; usuk*
**rice** *pai 1; buwas; balayang*
**rice (cooked)** *kinakan 2; buwas-kinakan*
**rice (cracked)** *benglod*
**rice (festive)** *buwas-kuning*
**rice (for planting)** *binhi'*
**rice (sticky)** *putan*
**rice (wrapped in leaf)** *tamparung 1*
**rice cake** *putu-putu; panyām; jā*
**rice field** *bagsak₁*
**rice flour** *tapung 1*
**rice gruel** *mistang 1*
**rice noodles** *sutanghon; bihun*
**rice portion** *sampul 1*
**ricebird** *maya*
**rich (taste)** *lanab; taba' 1*
**rich (wealthy)** *alta' 1.1; mayaman*
**ricochet** *deplas 1*
**rid of** *puwas₁ 1*
**riddle** *tokod-tokod*
**ride (on back)** *baba' 1.1*

**ride (on shoulders)** *balung 1.1*
**ride pillion (behind someone)** *angkas₂*
**ride with someone** *tumpang*
**ridge (of house)** *buhungan*
**ridge (of land)** *bĭd*
**ridgepole** *batang-buhungan; bahurungan*
**ridging terms** *bubungan; bahurungan; buhungan; kura'-kura'₂*
**ridicule** *pagtunggĭng; udju'; paganday-anday*
**rifles** *kalbin; garan; musil; sinapang*
**right (authority)** *kapatut*
**right (proper)** *amu₁*
**right on (exact)** *taluwa' 1; ya du*
**right to act** *wajib 1.1*
**right to decide** *pagatas-pikil*
**right way up** *leyak*
**right-angle** *pasagi' 1.1; dugu; pidju 1*
**righteous** *pagkata'u-marayaw; adil*
**right-hand** *kowan*
**right-handed** *sakap-kowan*
**rigid** *tuwas 1*
**rigor mortis** *basi'-dongan*
**rim** *lengkol 1; bihing₁ 1*
**rim of basket** *bengkol₁*
**ring bell** *tingting 1.1; bagting 1.1*
**ring finger** *singsing*
**ringworm** *kakas 1; pohak 1*
**ringworm shrub** *halu'-halu'₂; andalan*
**rinse** *linug₂; bunglaw 1*
**rinse face** *kula'up*
**rinse mouth** *gūm-gūm*
**rinse surface** *saplut₁ 1*
**rinse vigorously** *hokkok; kohek-kohek*
**rip (n)** *gese' 1*
**ripe** *tahak 1; laga'₁ 1; p'lla'; to'a 2.1*
**ripen** *pagangilan; pagdauman; b'ngkol₂*
**ripen (of coconut)** *lahing 1.1*
**ripped** *gese' 1.1; b'bbak; geret 1.1*
**rippled** *kataw 1*
**ripples** *ataw-ataw 1*
**rippling noise** *bahembas 1*
**rise (above horizon)** *sobang; k'llat llaw*
**rise (above surface)** *angkat₁ 1*
**rise (from grave)** *punduk 2*
**rise (from prone position)** *balukad; bangun₁ 1*
**rising agent** *pasulig*
**risk all** *sarahakan*
**risk averse** *l'gga 1.1*
**risk one's life** *tūk ka'llum*
**risk something** *tawakkal; pagpasukud; sarap₂ 1*
**risk-taking** *bahani 1*
**risky (dangerous)** *piligdu 1.1; anib 1.1*
**ritual ancestors** *mbo'₂*
**ritual cleansing** *saltun 1.1*

**ritual devotion** *ntan₂ 1.1*
**ritual slashing** *tigbas₂ 1.1*
**ritually unclean** *batal*
**river** *sapa'*
**roach (cockroach)** *kamahung*
**road** *lān; kalsara; paglalabayan*
**roam** *pagkambuyan; pagsampig-manampig; lunsul 1*
**roar (sea)** *abal 1.1*
**roar (shout)** *galit; panggohong*
**roast (v)** *tapa 1; tunu'₂; panggang₁*
**roasted fish** *tinapa*
**roasting rack** *tapahan*
**rob** *tangkaw 1.2; holdap*
**robe** *gamis; juba; luku*
**robust** *bastig; basag 1*
**rock** *bussu'₁; batu₁; lakit*
**rock (black)** *puhu*
**rock a baby** *pagbuwahan 1.1*
**rock cod** *kuhapo'*
**rock oyster** *tipay-batu*
**rock to and fro** *pagjungkat-jungkat 1.1; pagtungkellat-tungkellat*
**rock wall** *tambak₁ 1*
**rocket** *bintadol*
**rod** *sundak 1; pangka' 1; sulad 1*
**roe** *pehak 1*
**roll (n)** *pasangan₁; koleng₁ 1; birang 2*
**roll (of cloth)** *būs 1*
**roll over and over** *gulung-gulung*
**roll up** *gulung 1; lūn 1.2*
**roll up (of eyes)** *duliyat 1*
**rolling country** *pagbīd-bīd*
**romantic love** *pagkonsemisun*
**roof** *atop 1*
**roof (of mouth)** *ngelo'*
**roof style** *ungkup*
**roofed area** *panggung*
**roofing terms** *bangkayawan; mital 1; kasaw; tumbuk-buhungan*
**room** *bilik 1*
**room (space)** *lugal 1*
**rooster** *manuk-l'lla*
**rooster (fighting cock)** *manuk-bubulang*
**root** *gamut*
**root meaning** *isi-lling*
**root out** *tugnus₁ 1.1*
**root-bound** *talung₂*
**rootlets** *jablut*
**rope** *bahudji'; hidjuk; lubid 1*
**rope (rigging)** *hambawan; ligtang 1; palimping 1; k'llat₂ 1*
**rosary** *tasbi'*
**rose-apples** *makupa; tambis*
**rotate (on shaft)** *giling; legot 1.1; pusal₁ 1.1*
**rotten** *buhuk; halu' 1.1*

**rotting** *langag*
**rotting smell** *angsod*
**rough (sea)** *haus 1; goyak 1; abal 1*
**rough (speech)** *kasla 1; bagas; lagaw*
**rough (texture)** *kasap; l'ngnges 1.1*
**roughly woven** *t'ppag₂ 1.1; tupag*
**roughness (of surface)** *pagbigguwal; sereng; sahumut-sahumut*
**round (of shape)** *tibulung 1; legong*
**roundwood** *baras-baras; hanglad 1*
**roundworm** *kalog 1*
**rouse** *bati'₁ 1.1; pukaw*
**route** *labayan; kalsara*
**routine** *hatulan 1*
**rove** *pagsampig-manampig*
**row (a line)** *tād; tagik; badlis; dirit₁ 1*
**row a boat** *tindayung; luwad; dayung 1.1*
**rowboat** *buti; dinggi-dinggi*
**rowdy** *hidjul; hibuk; sagaw*
**rowlock** *pagsagga'an₁; pangaluwaran*
**royal woman** *sitti; dayang-dayang 1*
**royalty** *sultan; susultanun*
**rub** *kusu-kusu; pisi-pisi; gisgis 1.2*
**rub against (chafe)** *pagleges*
**rub away** *gidgid*
**rub over a surface** *pe'es₁; peged₁ 1*
**rub teeth** *gūm-gūm*
**rubber tree** *kalapiya*
**rubber; rubber band** *goma₁ 1*
**rubbish** *pamuwangkan; s'ggit 1; sagbot 1*
**rudder** *bansān 1*
**rudderfish** *ilak*
**rude (behavior)** *sabul 1.1; halipulu 1; taga'-taga'*
**rue (regret)** *pagkannal-susun*
**rueful** *liru' 1; susun₂ 1.1*
**ruffian** *bula'ug₂; pilliyu*
**ruffle (v)** *ataw-ataw 1.1*
**ruffled surface** *kataw 1*
**rug** *palmaddani'; tepo*
**ruined** *tunas 1.1; kugud; g'ppa'*
**rule (govern)** *pagsultan; kapagagi*
**rules** *sara' 1*
**ruling (legal)** *hukuman*
**rum** *alak*
**rumble (as a crowd moving)** *pagdaogdog*
**rumble (of stomach)** *pagbolobok; paglagublub*
**rumbling** *konog-konog; llub*
**rumor (n)** *tuhuma 1*
**rump** *pangkul*
**run** *dagan₂ 1.1; lahi-lahi 1; onse 1; paglahi-lahi*
**run aground** *sanglad; hanggal 1.1; dagsa'*
**run amok** *pagsabil*
**run before the wind** *tūd₁ 1.1*
**run free** *pabūy*

run into (collide) *dugtul; daplig 1*
runabout (boat) *tempel-tempel; katel-katel*
rung of ladder *tangga' 1; taka 1*
running mates (support group) *pangabay*
ruptured *bongso' 1.1; busā' 1.1; bugtu'₂ 1.1*
rural area *deya*
rushed (hurried) *sahi'-sahi'*

rushing about *hiyul*
rust *gaha' 1*
rust particles *tai'-gaha'; hali-gaha'*
rust-free *estenles*
rustle (sound) *ussab-ussab; kulanas 1; ganggu';*
　*kulessab*
rutted (road) *pagl'bbak*

# S s

sachet *suput₂*
sack, sacking *karut 1*
sacred space *sibayan*
sacrifice *hakika' 1.1; kulban 1.1; lalabotan 1.1;*
　*paglabot 2*
sad *handul atay; susa 1.1*
saddle *pakol*
safe (adj) *salamat₁*
safe (n) *kuta'₁ 2; pagtau'an; kaha₁*
safeguard (protection) *papag*
safety *komkoman 2; kasalamatan; tapukan*
safety pins *alperel; kait 1*
saffron rice *buwas-kuning*
Sagai (a forest tribe) *sagai'*
sage (wise person) *barakkal 1; auliya'; alim₁*
sagging *tuyang; tayo; laylay*
sago *lumbiya*
sago meal *takil; kalanjang; ambūng*
sago palm *sani*
sago palm stem *kulapa'*
sago pudding *landang 1*
said (by someone) *kono' 2*
sail (decoration) *pata'₂*
sailcloth *ispowen; kapis*
sailfish *kandelan*
sailing ship (archaic) *adjung*
sailing toy *jungkung 2*
sails *sorekang; leha 1; lamak; banog*
saitan spirit *saitan*
salary *gadji 1*
salas (visiting room) *saurung*
sale (of surplus items) *paglilung 1*
saliva *ludja' 1; laway₁ 1; buhelo 1*
salivate *pagbuhelo; llum helo*
salt *asin 1; timus-timus*
salted fish (n) *daing niasin; boro 1; sampila'₁ 1*
salt-like substance *asin-asin*
salutations *salam*
salute (military) *pagsalura 2*
salve *tambal₁ 1*
Sama *Badjaw; Sama*

Sama-speaking subgroups *Sama Pangutaran; Sama*
　*Lipid; Sama Bokko'; Sama Pagūng; Sama*
　*Kabinga'an; Sama Paosol; Sama Dilaut; Sama*
　*Sibutu'; Sama Bāngingi'; Sama Simunul; Sama*
　*Siasi; Sama Jengen; Sama Laminusa; Sama Pala'u;*
　*Sama Ubian; Sama Tabawan*
same *lullun 1.1; tabla; anggil 1*
same (in frequency) *sambu-...sambu-*
same (of extended kin) *dangkaheka*
same (of group) *daumpigan*
same (of name) *isay*
same (of place) *damahē'an*
same (prefix) *da- 2; sama-*
same price *bandu₁*
same size *b'tteya; samapasang*
same way or manner *isāb*
sample (n) *pamahingan; suntu'an*
sample something *kinam 1; timtim*
sand (a surface) *kidkid*
sand (coarse) *gusung; ungus*
sand (fine) *bunbun 1*
sandals *sinelas*
sandalwood *sandana'*
sandbank *katoho'an; kūd*
sandfly *kammut*
sandpaper *katas-balan*
sandpaper tree *hagupit*
sandy reef *kahanggalan*
sanguine *holat 1; angan-angan*
santol tree *santul*
sap (n) *tagok 1; base'-kayu*
sapote *kisas₁*
sappanwood *sibukaw 1*
sarcasm *udju'*
sardines *kasig; tamban*
sardines (canned) *saldinas*
sargassum fish *kappo'-ulak*
sarong style *pindung; sa'ul; kindang; k'mbong;*
　*hampi' 1.1*
sarongs *se'ob; siyag 1; hōs 1*
sash (belt) *kandit*
sass (v) *jōk*

satiated *sugmak*; *s'gga*
satin *punji*; *lanay₁*
satisfactory *jatu 1*
satisfied *tuksu'*; *iman₂*
satisfied (with food) *l'sso*
satisfied (with outcome) *masuk*
satisfy *amu₂ 1*
saturated *bugbug₁*; *lettak*
Saturday *Sabtu'*
sauce *tinu'anan*; *bubuk₂*
saucer coral *dulang-kokok*
saucers *lai'-tapak*; *suwit*; *tapak-tapak*
saute *gisa*
savage (animal) *ero'-keyat*
save from danger *liyus 1.2*; *lappas₂ 1.1*
savor (n) *nanam 1*; *lamuk*; *ssa₁ 1*
savory *sarap₁*
saw (tool) *gatgat 1*
say *batbat₂*; *h'lling₁ 1.1*; *yuk*; *bissala 1.1*; *suli-suli 1.1*; *mūng*
say frankly *solab₂*
say little *d'ngngo'*
say no to *pagin'mbal 1.1*; *pagmari'*
saying (n) *sambatan*
scabbard *taguban*
scabies *buwa'-buwa'-sangom 1*
scabs *l'kkung 1*; *taplok 2*; *tangkop*
scads *salay-salay*; *kobal-kobal*; *sukul-sukul*; *ūng-ūng*; *tamarung*
scald *danglus*
scald raw food *lasuwa*
scale (fish) *sisik 1*
scales (for weighing) *timbang₁ 1*
scallions *kussay*
scallops *kadde'-kadde'*; *pindi' 1*; *kayab-kayab*
scaly *pagsereng*
scamp *pilliyu*
scandalous *daiyus*
scant *dangkuri'*
scar *limpa' 1*
scarce *lahang*
scarcely *agon mbal*; *himan-himan*
scare off *babak*; *pakitāw*
scared *tāw 1.1*; *leya'-leya'*; *dalan 1*
scarers *lalagpak*; *larung 1*
scarf *pīs-sinabit*; *salay₁ 1*
scary *piligdu 1*
scatter *labak*; *sabulak*; *sabud*; *sabuy*
scatterbrain *panglupa*
scattered *teges-teges*; *kaukanat*; *pulak-palik 1*; *kanēs-nēs*; *pāg*; *palit₁*
scavenge *imut*; *lalag*
scented *b'ngngi*
schedule *taratu*; *iddahan*; *eskedyul*
scheme (n) *pagisun 1*; *paggara' 1*

scholar (religious) *balguru*; *ulama'*
school (Islamic) *madrasa*
school (public, secular) *iskul 1*
schooner *balanda'₁*
scintillate *tingaw-tingaw*; *itaw-itaw*; *pagsinglab*
scissors *gunting 1*
scold *mūng-mūng*; *kasla 1.2*; *pugpug 1*; *pastul*
scoop (n) *sasanglag*; *sintib*; *gayung 1*
scoop up *sagob 1.1*; *akup*; *sauk 1.1*
scorched *lūs₁ 1*; *tunu'₁ 1.1*; *lāb 1*
score a surface *gudlis 1.1*
score flesh *gali'₁*; *galing-galing*
scorpionfishes *kappo'₁*; *tinggil-batu*
scorpions *jalalangking*; *kadjalangking*
scour *kuskus 1.1*; *gidgid*; *bata*
scowl *pagh'ngngek-h'ngngek*
scrape clean *timud 1.1*
scrape off *keke₁*; *kagis 1*
scrape off layer *tai' 1.1*; *bakkel 1.1*
scrape out *kagod 1*
scrape pandanus *ambuhut*
scraps *tunas 1*; *kapin 1*
scratch (to relieve itch) *kakayaw*; *katol 1.1*
scratch a surface *kahig*; *langgit 1*; *kakkut*
scratched *banggid 1*; *langgahi'*
scrawl *kollek-kollek*; *pagkabillag*
scrawly marks *jego*
scrawny *giti' 1*; *kayog 1*
scream *tilahak*; *kula'ak*; *pagsilawak*
screen (curtain) *langsay*
screw *siput 1*
scribble *kollek-kollek*
scribe (a surface) *gudlis 1.1*; *sangat 1.1*
scrotum *buyung₁ 1*
scrounger *dahal 1*
scrub (v) *helog*; *lukup*; *kuskus 1.1*; *gisgis 1.2*; *bunut-bunut*
scrubber *lulukup*
scruffy *kuligi'₁ 1*; *larang*
scrupulous *hatul₂*; *adil*
scrutinize *patong 1.1*
scull (over stern) *dayung 1.1*; *buli'-buli'*
scum *s'ggit 1*
scurf *gulis-manuk 1*; *tai'-kōk*
sea *dilaut*; *kablangan*; *tahik₁ 1*
sea almonds *pampan*; *talisay*
sea anemones *kombo'-kombo'*; *lobot-lobot*; *lason*; *pari-pari*; *kambang*; *bobohan*; *dandiya'-dandiya'*; *kinsan*; *l'ppay*; *timbalun₂*
sea bass *b'ngka 1*
sea birds *kullu-kullu₁*; *mana'ul*; *ppak*; *linggisan*; *t'lla'-t'lla'₁*; *belle'₁*
sea breams *ga'ud-ga'ud*; *kamang-buhuk 1*
sea cow (dugong) *duyung 1*
sea cucumber *bāt*

**sea fan** *kukkus*
**sea floor** *kababawan; tana'-deyo'; temang*
**sea grapes** *lato'; gamay*
**sea lemon** *paniyungan*
**sea lice** *kutu-kutu 1*
**sea perches** *b'ngka 1; balihan*
**sea persimmon** *linaw*
**sea plants** *taubang; unas; l'mmuk*
**sea shelf** *pampang; kantil$_2$*
**sea slug** *dandiya'*
**sea snail** *seso'-buwaya*
**sea urchin (cooked with rice inside)** *oko'-oko'*
**sea urchin exudate** *lubu$_1$*
**sea urchins (generic)** *tayum; tehe'-tehe'*
**sea water** *tahik$_1$ 1.1*
**sea worm** *punpun*
**sea-catfish** *kalitan-itingan*
**sea-demon** *saitan-maut*
**sea-going Sama** *Badjaw*
**sea-grass fruit** *eral-eral$_2$*
**seagulls** *ppak; t'lla'-t'lla'$_1$*
**seahorses** *unduk-unduk; talli$_2$*
**seal (mark of identity)** *sāp$_2$ 1*
**seam** *la'up 1*
**sear (to cook)** *tunu'$_2$*
**search** *tilluk; piha 1*
**search thoroughly** *kadkad 1.1*
**search widely** *libu 1.1*
**seashells** *panagatun*
**seashore** *daplakan$_1$; bihingan*
**seasickness** *lango-goyak*
**season (n)** *timpu 1; musim; patahunan; bulanan*
**season (wind-based)** *tahik$_2$*
**seasonal** *pagsawaktu*
**seat** *paningkō'an*
**seawards** *parilaut 1; kaut 1; lūd*
**seaweeds** *lusay; lato'; lokot-lokot; gamay; gulaman; agal-agal*
**secede** *okat$_2$ 1.1*
**seclude** *bilik 1.1*
**secluded area** *likusan*
**second (in order)** *kaminduwa 1*
**second (of time)** *dansasa'at 1*
**second cousin** *kaki minduwa*
**second sight** *langtas 1*
**second time** *minduwa*
**secrecy** *sipuk*
**secret** *limbung 1; kolorom; hegom-hegom*
**secret conversation** *paghidjab*
**secret parts** *batin 1*
**secretion (from squids, etc.)** *lansong*
**section of bamboo** *honga'$_1$*
**section of Holy Koran** *jūd*
**secure** *sandat 1; hogot*

**secure a knot** *tingk'llos*
**secure something** *abin*
**securely** *sakuli-kuli; sabuli-buli*
**security (deposit)** *panau'; s'nnad*
**security (for money borrowed)** *lōb 1*
**sediment** *angkas$_1$ 1; lagod$_1$*
**seduce** *bidjak 1.1; hupit-hupit 1; kuti-kuti; abiyug*
**seduced** *pilad*
**see** *nda' 1; pantaw; lundug 1.1; mata$_1$ 1.2*
**see in person** *nyata' 1.1; lu'aw 1*
**see momentarily** *jullit$_1$ 1; laman 1.1*
**see that!** *o'ō*
**seed (decorative)** *sogo'-sogo'*
**seed case** *kalang-belle'; tangkop-belle'*
**seeds** *binhi'; bigi$_1$; bigi-tinanom*
**seeing that (given that)** *sangga'ina*
**seek** *tilluk; piha 1; batuk$_2$*
**seek advice** *aru*
**seek evidence** *dikisa 1*
**seek forgiveness** *pagpa'ampun; tawbat 1.1*
**seek help from** *ussap 1.1; ayura 2; da'ut*
**seek reconciliation** *pagpama'ap; deyo'$_3$ 2.1*
**seek treatment** *pa'nda' 1.2*
**seem to be** *luwa 1*
**seen clearly** *ballag; manyatakan*
**seep** *tubud 1; sū$_2$*
**seers** *auliya'; talus$_2$; alim$_1$*
**see-saw** *pagjungkat-jungkat 1.1; pagtongket-tongket; pagtungkellat-tungkellat*
**seething** *pagb'ngkol 2*
**segment** *solag 1*
**segment (v)** *pagpōng-pōng 1.1*
**segregate** *pinig*
**seine net** *pokot$_1$ 1*
**seine-fishing vessels** *palakaya; basnig*
**seize** *agaw 1.1; lolog; saggaw*
**seize and destroy** *talap*
**seize in mouth** *tanghab$_2$*
**seize property** *longpos*
**seizure (epileptic)** *bawi-bawi; sawan-sawan*
**seldom** *lahang; bislang 1; bihang$_2$*
**select; selective** *pene' 1.1*
**self** *baran$_2$ 1*
**self-centered** *pasambu; dakag*
**self-controlled** *p'mpon 1*
**selfish** *damba'$_1$ 1; beya' hawa*
**self-pitying** *mandā'-dā'; ambul-dā'; bakat atay*
**self-satisfied** *pagpa'abbu*
**sell** *pab'lli; dagang*
**sell (peddle goods)** *soroy*
**sell at a loss** *lugi' 1.1*
**sell in bulk** *pakkiyaw; paglilung 1.1*
**seller (regular)** *suki'*
**selling fast** *landag*

semblance *luwa 1*

semen *bohe'₂*

semester *semestel*

semi-precious stone *dilam*

send back (to source) *tūd₂; papole'*

send flying *pulagsik*

send home *papole'*

send message *para'ak; palapal*

send off *dūy*

send something *pabeya'*

senile *li'an*

senior relatives *usba-waris*

sennit lashing *sihag₁ 1*

sensation *lapa₁; nanam 1*

sense (be aware of) *sabi₂; lapa₁; nanam 2*

sense (meaning) *ma'ana₁ 1; hantang-hatulan*

sense of ease *lampung₂*

senseless (unconscious) *lipat₂*

sensitive (of hearing) *talinga lumping*

sensitive plant *sipug-sipug*

sensitive to touch *giluk 1; lamma 1*

sentence (grammar) *senten 1*

sentence for crime *taksil 1; multa 1*

sentinel *jaga 1*

separate (adj) *saddī 1; sila' 1*

separate into groups *gintil 1.1; silang₁ 1.1*

separated from *boklang 1; bugtu'₁; butas 1; okat₂ 1; l'kkat₂ 1; lalingu*

sequence *pagsunu'-sunu'; ubus... ubus*

sequin *antuwilas 1*

serene *haggut atay*

sergeant *saljen*

serious (of sickness) *pangsan; bangat*

serious about *to'ongan 2*

sermon *usihat; hutba'; nasihat*

serpents *naga 1; sowa*

serration *lengget 1*

serum (dried) *l'kkang*

serum (liquid) *sagu*

servant *magbubuhat; sosoho'an; dara'akan*

serve (as slave) *pagpatiata*

serve refreshments *buhat₃; paghirang*

serve up food *haun₁; sampul 1.1*

service (to one's teacher) *pagbakti'*

serving trays *talam; tataklayan*

sesame seeds *longa*

set (of fruit) *tadjuk; tungkalling*

set (of sun) *s'ddop*

set a limit *hād 1.2*

set a time *taratu; idda 1.1; ora*

set affection on *umid 1; lūt₂ 1*

set apart as special *mulliya 1.1*

set flat on surface *lesen*

set heart on (desire) *hawa 1.3*

set in (of weather) *dugpak 1*

set in order *m'mmos 1.1; tuntul 1.1*

set mind on *tuntut₂; tu'ud₁ 1.1*

set of clothes *pangampu'an*

set on edge *patiring*

set on fire *lablab 2*

set out (on a journey) *lalga; batbat₁; k'tta 1; l'ttu*

set policy *pal'ngngan*

settle (of sediment) *pato'ong; tuli₂*

settle dispute *pagsalassay 1; usay 2.1*

settle down (not restless) *m'mmos 1*

settle in a place (reside) *d'ddos*

settled (in mind) *totog 1*

settled (on doing) *sakali₁*

settlement (village) *kampung₂; kaluma'an*

seven *pitu' 1*

seventy *pitumpū'*

sever by cutting *tabtab 1; utas 1.1*

several *saga 1*

severe (of illness) *pangsan; bangat*

severed *pugtul; utas 1*

sew *la'it; tahi'*

sew (to reduce size) *dahut*

sew (using big stitches) *bagsak₂*

sew bolt rope *palipit*

sew together (mat layers) *lagbas 2*

sewing machine *makina tape'; makina 2*

sewing thread *salban*

sex worker *d'nda pagtatambahan*

sexual advance (in darkness) *lē₁; gagam*

sexual attraction *bilahi 2*

sexual desire *ba'is*

sexual indecency *kalumu'an*

sexual intercourse *paghinang₂; pagbihing₂; paghulid 2*

sexual intercourse (vulgar) *lalu*

sexual lust *biga'*

sexual touching *pagkolet*

sexually aggressive *kambing 2; pagba'is 1*

sexually aroused *gila*

shabby *guya'*

shack *kubu'-kubu'*

shackles *ekang-ekang 1; bilanggu' 1*

shade *limbu 1.1*

shade (into another color) *agaw-agaw*

shade (n) *lindung 1; limbu 1*

shade something *simun 1*

shade-tree *mandikakaw*

shadow *lambung₁; lindung 1*

shaft (of spear) *puhan 1; pantok₁ 1*

shaft (rod) *batang-ehe*

shake (v) *oseg 1.1; oyo'-oyo'*

shake a container *kembo' 1.1; genggok; letok*

shake hands *sekan; jiyara*

shake hands; *pagjiyara*; *pagsalam*
shake head (in shock) *pagelong-elong*
shake head (indicate disagreement) *paglinga-linga*; *pagkeleng*
shake or flap something *paspas$_2$ 1.1*
shake rubbish off *pagpag*
shake to waken *pukaw*
shake tree to get fruit *lapod*
shaken by storm *goyak 1.3*
shaken with fever *tandog 1*
shaking *tandog 2*; *korog-korog*; *pidpid*; *henggol 1.1*; *jogjog 1.1*
shaking (of body or limbs) *hōb-hōb*; *bogon-bogon*
shaking (of earthquake) *jogjog deyom dunya*
shaky *henggol 1*; *hodjog 1*; *jogjog 1*
shall (should) *subay*
shallow (of tide) *babaw$_2$*
shallow breath *paghota*
shallows *kahanggalan*; *t'bba 1*; *l'ggotan*; *temang*
sham (not genuine) *gillo'ak*
shaman *pagbowahan*
shame (n) *kaiya'an*; *maru 1*
shame someone *tungbuy*; *hina'*; *pakaiya'*; *paki' 1.1*
shamed *maru 1.2*
shameful *biyas*; *tamparasa*
shameless *aral*
shampoo *lubi 1.1*
shape (by cutting) *gahud*; *sosok*; *g'ttok-g'ttok*; *pīs$_2$ 1*
shape hairline *soso'-legong*; *soso'-t'ngge*
shape into balls *pongkol*
shapeliness *dorog$_2$ 1*; *polma 1*
shapely (of figure) *jangngang*; *jalang$_1$*; *hāp baran*
shards *bila' 1*
share *bahagi' 1*; *punggit 1*; *suku'*
share (in business) *hampit*; *sapali 1.1*; *paghaup*
share (uneven) *bahagi'-buyung*; *bahagi'-tempang 1*
share a house *pagdaluma'*
share food *salu 1.1*; *lamit*
share of costs *panapali*
share out *gihay*; *paglamit-lamit 1.1*; *pahampit*
share winnings *pasuwa'*
shared meal (formal) *paglukun 1*
sharks (generic) *kalitan 1*
sharp *talom 1*
sharp edges *pagsereng*
sharp pain *busā' jantung*
sharp sound *pāk*
sharpen *gīl*; *asa'*
sharpening stone *asa'an*
sharp-sighted *tullus 1*; *pantok$_2$*
sharp-witted *halul-akkal 1*; *taha'-akkal*; *ladju pikilan*
shattered *posat*; *māg-māg*
shave (beard) *p'ngngot 1.2*
shave (head or beard) *bagong$_2$*

shave hairline *s'ssol$_1$*; *soso'*
shave head *bagoggol 1.1*
shavings *tai'-uni'*; *momok*; *obang*
shawls *salay$_1$ 1*; *pīs$_1$*
she *iyā*
sheaf *p'kkosan*
shear wool *gunting 1.2*
sheath (of coconut flower) *langkan-langkan*
sheath (of knife or weapon) *taguban*
shed (storage) *borega*
sheen *linig 1*
sheep *kambing-bili-bili*; *bili-bili*
sheet (bedding) *manta 1*
sheet (flexible) *b'llat 1*
sheet (rigid) *gekap 2*; *b'llad 1*
sheet of paper *kintas 1*
shelf *paha*
shell (artillery) *punglu'*
shell (v) *pisi-pisi*
shell bracelet *labu$_1$*
shell case *kalasussu*
shellfish *panagatun*
shelter behind *sindung$_1$*; *pulipus 1.1*
shelters *pasindungan*; *lapaw*; *payad*; *pillayag*
shield (v) *hampan 1.1*
shields *taming 1*; *tampan 1*
shift blame *pagampa-ampa*; *pagpatimpa*; *pelleng 1.2*; *bīng$_3$*
shift responsibility *bintu*
shift work *pagtoka-toka*
shims (spacers) *tanok 1.1*; *s'ngngal*; *seplak 1*
shin (of leg) *kurung*
shine (v) *sahaya 1.2*; *linig 1.2*
shingle (palm roofing) *pa'ud 1*
shingles (disease) *ugihap 1*
shining *sahaya 1.1*; *sinag 1.1*; *sawa 1.1*
shiny (of surface) *linig 1.1*
ship water *mman*
ships *nabal*; *balanda'$_1$*; *kappal*; *adjung*
shipworms *kapang$_1$ 1*; *tambelok 1*
shirts *badju'*; *polo*
shiver *oro'-oro'$_1$*; *korog-korog*; *kogkog*; *k'ddil-k'ddil*; *pidpid*; *haggut 2*
shivering *hōb-hōb*
shoals *takot*; *tahetek*
shock *baliyang*
shock (electric) *bagnet*
shock (surprise) *kuddat*
shocked (emotional) *kibad atay*; *pam'ngngang*; *kobla'*; *la'an kaul*; *k'bbal atay*
shocking *mbal manjari*
shoddy *guya'*
shoes *taumpa'*
shoes (high heeled) *taumpa'-tinggi*
shoo away *budjaw*; *sū$_1$ 1*; *t'ggal*

**shoot (with firearm)** *timbak 2.1*; *balis₁*
**shoot (with slingshot)** *pitik*
**shooting stars** *umul₁*; *selo'*
**shoots (of plants)** *dalig 1*
**shop (large)** *basal₂*
**shop (v)** *tabu' 1.1*
**shop assistant** *tindera*
**shops** *pasal₂ 1*; *tinda*
**shoreline** *daplakan₁*; *bihing tampe*; *pari'an*
**short (of length)** *p'ndok*; *pu'ut*
**short (of resources)** *kettak*; *pulubi*; *kabus*; *kulang₁ 1.1*
**short (of stature)** *pandak*; *deyo'-deyo'₁*
**short sleep** *tuli-sowa*
**short steps** *pagtongka'*
**short version** *kapu'utan*
**shortage** *kulang₁ 1*
**shortcoming** *salla'₁ 1*
**shortcut** *pagsiyuk-siyuk*
**shorten (a rope)** *pigtal 1.1*
**shorten sail** *sampila'₂*; *aru-aru*
**shortly** *t'ppung 1*; *dai'₂*; *sōng₁ 2*
**shortness of breath** *pagagaw-napas*
**shorts** *sanyawa*; *kansinsilyu*; *hakpan*; *solpan*
**shot (medical)** *tugsuk 2.2*
**should** *wajib 1*; *subay*
**should have** *arapun*
**shoulder** *punggu-baha*; *baha*
**shout** *asang₂*; *kula'ak*; *olang 1*
**shout (call)** *owa'₁ 1*; *lingan 1*
**shout at** *pahit*; *alud₁*; *gasud*; *galit*
**shove** *judjal 2*; *lodjat₂ 1*
**shovel** *pala*
**show (v)** *pa'nda' 1.1*
**show anger** *pagamā 1*
**show cards** *buka'₃*
**show courtesy** *mahaldika'*; *pagmahaltabat*
**show discourtesy** *halipulu 1.1*
**show hospitality** *latal 1.1*; *labot*
**show malice** *jingki 1.1*
**show off** *pagalti-alti 1.1*; *pagpaelle'-elle'*; *pa'amu-amu*
**show respect to** *pagaddat 1.1*
**show strength** *pagayron*
**show teeth** *kisi'*; *kehe'-kehe' 1*
**show the way** *tuli' 1.1*; *pintulu' 1.1*; *malim 1.1*
**shower (rain)** *bonok-bonok*
**showing off** *abbu 1.1*
**shrapnel** *sakmel*
**shredded** *gilay 1*; *p'kkal 1*
**shreds** *jabel-jabel 1*
**shrewd** *taha'-akkal*
**shrewdness** *akkal 1*; *pangita'u*
**shriek** *kula'ak*
**shrill** *tilahak*; *lagsing*

**shrimp paste** *baling*
**shrimps** *baling-baling*; *ulang 1*; *ka'ullang*
**shrine** *tampat 1*
**shrinking** *paglūs*
**shrivelled** *ilu'₁ 1*; *pekok*; *k'llos*
**shroud (n)** *kuku-pote'*; *saput 1*; *salimput 1*; *kasa'*
**shrub (generic)** *kayu 1*
**shrubs** *maparang*; *bidduli*; *tula-tula*; *banglut*; *jalnang*; *matalu*
**shrug** *pagkidjut*
**shrunken** *k'llos*
**shuck corn** *lutu₁*
**shudder** *korog-korog*; *k'ddil-k'ddil*
**shuffle cards** *balasa*
**shut** *takkop 1.1*; *bagat*; *kittup 1*; *tambol 1.1*
**shut tight** *kabbat*
**shy (adj)** *illat*; *loman 1*; *t'mmun*; *sandol 1*
**shy (startled)** *lumpat*
**Siasi Town** *M'ddas*
**sibling (brother or sister)** *danakan*
**sibling (full)** *langgung₁ 1.1*
**sibling relationship** *pagdanakan 1*
**siblings** *dauranakan 1*
**sickle** *sanggot₁ 1*
**sickly person** *panaki*
**sickness (chronic)** *palsakkihan*
**sickness (dormant)** *saki-panau'*
**sickness (generic)** *saki 1*
**sickness (supernatural cause)** *sagda₁*; *pa'in₃ 1*; *sabab₂ 1.1*
**side (edge)** *bihing₂ 1*
**side (of body)** *timbangan₂*; *kīd₁ 1*
**side (of structure)** *kīran*
**side bet** *tinggi₂*
**side by side** *ubay*
**side effects** *hamiyu 1*
**side with (support)** *dapit*; *tapīn*
**sidearm** *takos 1*
**sidestep** *s'nnok*
**sideswipe** *pagsabay*
**side-to-side** *dambila'-ni-dambila'*
**sieves** *ulayan*; *ayakan*
**sift** *ayak*
**sigh** *ahāy*
**sight** *mata₁ 1.1*
**sightless** *buta₁*
**sign** *nahas 1*; *tanda'*
**sign (a document)** *saen*; *pagt'kkon bokol*; *pasā*
**signal (by winking)** *kiddat₁*
**signal (v)** *lambe₁ 1.1*; *kambay 1*; *sinyal 1.1*; *mita*
**signature** *tanda' tangan*
**significance** *muna-muna 1*
**significance (meaning)** *hantang-hatulan*
**silent** *h'nnok*; *h'ddok*; *tepok*

**silhouette** *lambung₁ 1; lindung 2*
**silk cloth** *sutla'; lanay₁*
**silly** *dupang 1.1*
**silver** *pilak 1*
**silverbiddies** *porok₁; lamuruk*
**silversmith** *sasalan*
**similar** *sala 1; buwat 1; b'tteya; pagagid; pinaka; muwat*
**similarly** *sali'-sali'; damikiyan 1; sibu'-sibu'; pagsama-sama 1*
**simmer** *anok 1.1*
**simple (easy)** *luhay₂ 1*
**simple-minded** *hibang-hibang; bobo*
**simply** *samata-mata; hal; sadja*
**simultaneous** *pagsabu*
**sin** *dusa 1*
**sin against** *buwan dusa; pagpakay-dusa*
**since (time)** *sa'angay*
**since A, therefore B** *sangga'ina*
**sincerety** *atay-pote'*
**sinews** *anggauta'; ugat 1*
**sinewy** *kaslog*
**sing** *kalang₁ 1; kerol*
**sing (ceremonial)** *lugu' 1.1; sa'il; langan₂ 1.1*
**sing lullaby** *binuwa 1.1; dindang-dindang*
**sing slowly** *palahan-palahan*
**sing sweetly** *pagmanuk-manuk₂*
**sing to child** *sangbay*
**singe (canoe hull)** *luhu*
**singing contest** *pagbono' kalangan*
**single (one only)** *tunggal 1*
**single (unmarried)** *la'un 1*
**singled out** *puntul*
**single-handed** *anggop₂*
**singlets** *kamisita-sagnat; saklay*
**sink (below surface)** *t'nde 1; logdang₂; l'nnob*
**sink (to one's knees)** *lukbu'₂*
**sink into** *senop; paglowak; tanom₂*
**sink piles** *osol 1.1*
**sinkers (weight)** *lambat 1; butun₁*
**sinkhole** *p'llong*
**sinner** *baldusa*
**sip** *t'ggok*
**sir** *sēl; tuwan*
**sister** *danakan d'nda*
**sister-in-law** *ipal; bilas; iras*
**sit** *tingkō' 1; tongngol*
**sit (on eggs)** *ōm; llom*
**sit (with knees together)** *komo'₁; pipi'*
**sit cross-legged** *milang; pagsiningkulang; hakin*
**sit down flat** *d'ssal; lesseg*
**sit up (from lying down)** *punduk 1; lungkahad*
**sit up (from slouching)** *bugnus₁*
**site** *lugal 1*

**six** *nnom*
**sixty** *nnompū'*
**size** *heya 1*
**size (of coin)** *pikit₃ 1*
**sizzle** *lenek*
**skate floor** *lampasu*
**skeletal leaf** *dirit-dirit*
**skeleton** *akal-baran; tangkorak; batang-tubu*
**skeptic** *panunussa'*
**skeptical** *sussa'; jakki 1*
**skewer (v)** *sulad 2*
**skill** *kapandayan*
**skill (inherited)** *linukan*
**skilled** *panday 1.1; pantas; layam 1.1; lahal; langkat-samat*
**skilled (in farming)** *haggut-tangan; hagpay-tangan*
**skim across waves** *sularaw*
**skin** *kuwit 1*
**skin (crawly feeling)** *l'nnu*
**skin diseases** *kamuti'; kawit₂ 1*
**skin infections** *ipit 1; kuligi'₂; ugud*
**skin something** *kisak; kuwit 1.1*
**skin spots** *tagimtim 1; bau-bau*
**skinny** *kittay; giti' 1; higtal*
**skip across a surface** *tampeppet; samperet; kulit-kulit*
**skip over something** *laktaw; pitas₁*
**skip rope** *kuway*
**skipper** *patron*
**skirts** *palda; saya-saya*
**skirts (tubular)** *tadjung; hōs 1; sa'ul*
**skull** *peya'-peya' kōk; bukakkal; kulakob*
**skull cap** *kuppiya*
**sky** *langit*
**sky maiden** *biradali 1*
**slack (adj)** *haluy 1*
**slack (in line)** *landahan; lambuyut*
**slack (tidal)** *k'ttang 1*
**slack water** *t'bba 1*
**slacken (of flow)** *tugut 1; kontay₂; kō' 1.1; patokang*
**slacken line** *landa*
**slander** *limut 1.1; kulli' 1.1*
**slanting** *tunggang*
**slap** *tapling; bimbing; sampak; sampiyal*
**slash** *lagut; tigad 1.1; tigbas₂ 1*
**slats** *gipis 1; ligpit 1; bola'*
**slaughter** *laglag 1.1; pagbugbug; pagk'llot*
**slaughter (for meat)** *sumbali'*
**slaughtered** *ligis₂*
**slave** *ata; banyaga' 1*
**sled (n)** *karusa*
**sled (v)** *pagdūt-dūt*
**sleek (made smooth)** *langis 1*
**sleep (brief)** *tuli-tuli-kuyya'; piru'-piru'*

sleep around *pagd'nda 2*; *pagl'lla*
sleep beside *hulid 1*
sleep over *pagpatuli*
sleep together *pagbihing₂*; *paghulid 1*
sleeping area *patulihan*; *palegehan*
sleeping mat *tepo*
sleepless *gesong*
sleepwalking *lāp-lāp*
sleepy *tuli₁ 1.1*; *karu' 1.1*
sleepyhead *tagi-tuli*
sleeve *l'ngngon 2*
sleight of hand *pagbalikmata*
slender *g'nting*; *lampin₁*; *tayang*
slice (v) *hilap*; *hīk*; *kehet 1*
slice against grain *suddang*
slice finely *kīs₁*
slick *lu'ud₁ 1*; *luntang 1*
slide along *ginsil*; *sapsap₁*; *dūt*
slide down *dusdus*; *lurus₁ 1*; *julut 1*; *dokdos*
slight (of build) *g'nting*; *lampin₁*; *nintil 2*
slim-waisted *lampin₁*
slimy *luntang 1*
slingshot *pitikan*
slip (underwear) *kamisun*
slip down *luklus 2*; *luslus 1*
slip down into *h'llop 1*
slip from grip *tanak 1*; *puklas 1.1*; *larus*; *kabba*
slip off path *ligdas*; *lisad*; *deklas*
slip out of wrapping *hurus 1*
slip over (lose footing) *lumintiyad*
slip over an edge *lisig*
slip through gap *p'ssut 1*; *s'llot 1*
slipknot *engkot-sintak*
slipper plant *jalani*
slippers *bakiya'₁*; *sinelas*
slippery *lu'ud₁ 1*; *luntang 1*
slit open *t'ddak*
slither *lisad*; *lele 1*
sliver *seplak 1*
slop over *lasay*; *sempok 1*
slope (landform) *titib*; *tukaran*; *baha-būd*
sloppy fit *haluy 1.1*; *loka*
slops (animal food) *butu'an*
slosh about *paglūng-lūng*
slothful *lisu'*
slow (in learning) *hibang-hibang*; *b'llod*; *bengog 1*
slow (in movement) *lallay*; *aggal 1*; *lahan 1*; *lomeng-lomeng*
slow to respond *kaku'*; *lehod 1.1*
slug *dandiya' deya*
sluggish *summil*; *s'nnay*; *lomeng-lomeng*
slurp *horot*; *hiyup*; *h'llop 1.1*
slurred (speech) *hemol*
slushy *l'bbo 1*; *pekat*; *legsak*; *lamekkat*

slyly *tipu 1.1*
smack (with flat item) *lambot*; *lappet*
smack (with hand) *tapling*; *t'ppak₁*; *b'ddak*; *sampak*
smack lips *k'ssap*; *ttap-ttap*
small *nahut*; *diki' 1*
small amount *dangkuman*; *peged₂ 1*; *dak'tti'*
small child *onde'-onde'*
smallness *kariki'an*
smallpox *ttus-ttus 1*; *pangkot 1*; *ka'mbo'an*
smart (clever) *ladju pikilan*
smarting (from whipping) *paglera-lera*
smarting (of open wound) *p'llat 1.1*
smashed (broken up) *lopot 1*; *tumu-tumu*; *bagbag*
smear on *ledje 1.1*; *lemed 1.2*; *lemos₁ 1.1*
smegma *bulas₂*
smell (n) *hamut 1*; *tunug 1*; *bau 1*
smell (of burning) *bau tunu'*; *s'ggung 1*
smell (of decay) *angil*; *angsod*
smell (of drying fish) *p'ngngos*
smell (v) *bbu 1*
smelly (unpleasant) *bau 1.1*; *b'ngngog*; *langsa*
smile *kiyum 1*
smithy *pagsasalan*
smoke (n) *humbu 1*
smoke (tobacco) *siga 1.1*; *sigup*
smoke cigarettes *pagsiniga*
smooth (adj) *plāt*; *tukad₂*; *lanu' 1*
smooth (v) *hotad₁*; *hīs 1*; *pangtad*; *lūt₁*
smooth by sanding *kidkid*
smooth off *sapsap₂*
smooth with adze *sosok*
smooth with plane *katam 1.1*
smothered in *pulipus 1*; *kulinting*
smuggle *ismagol*; *pagbisnis*
snack *tupas₁ 1*
snag (v) *sa'ud₁ 1*; *sagnat 1*; *lagesles 2*
snail (marine) *lambi'*
snake (generic) *sowa*
snake mackerel *lambana' 2*
snake spirit *naga 1*; *umagad-sowa*
snap fastener *batuk-batuk*
snap fingers *kotek*
snap shut *kattup*; *dopon-dopon 1.1*; *tikkup*
snapped *pugtul*; *b'kkat 1*
snappers (generic) *kutambak*
snare (n) *sahat 1*; *litag 1*
snarl *pagt'kkob*
snarled (tangled) *sagut 1*; *gumun*
snatch *sagob 1*; *sakmit*; *sakkop 1*
sneaky *kaikit₂ 1*
sneeze *aksi*; *pagba'anan*
snicker *kehe'-kehe' 1*
sniff *huttut*
snippets *hīk-hīk*; *tapis 1*

snobbish *langa atay*
snore *panggahak; h'lling-k'llong*
snort *hagok*
snot *s'ppun 1*
snow-white *pote' anawan-tawan*
snub *maru 1*
snub someone *pessek 2*
snug *lapat 1.1; k'bbot 1; digpit 1*
snuggling *pagli'id*
so *nā 1; sa; angkan 1.1*
so as not to *ko da'a*
so be it *amin 1*
so long as *basta; pagka pa'in*
so often *heka min heka*
so that *ko; supaya; bo'₂*
so then *jari₃; manjari₂; ati*
so to speak *bahasa₂; sala 1.1*
soak into *h'ggom 1.1; sobsob 1*
soak; soaked *gamos 1.1; hagom 1.1; k'mbang 1.1*
so-and-so *anu 1*
soap *sabun 1*
soar *leyang 1*
social outcast *pagkamundal-mandil*
society *kompolan*
socket *kusu 1*
socks *medyas; kalsitin*
soda (soft drink) *pipsikola; kokola*
soft *l'bbo 1; lunuk 1.1; legsak; l'mma'₁; dutay*
soft (of food) *posak; baska 1*
soft drink *pipsikola; kokola*
softball *sopbol*
soften *k'mbang 1.1; h'ggom 1*
soften (by pounding) *banol 1.1*
soften attitude *lō'*
soften what is said *paglampik*
softness *lunuk 1*
soggy *lamekkat*
soil *tana'₁ 1*
solar halo *taming 2*
sold at a profit *laba*
solder *patli' 1*
soldiers *bobono'; sundalu*
sole of foot *pāt 1*
solely *luwal; samadjana*
solemn promise *subali 1; pagsapa 1.1; paljanji'an*
solid *ponod 1; tibu'uk₁ 1.1*
solidly built *anagtol*
solitary *t'nnaw-t'nnaw 1; l'ngngaw-l'ngngaw*
solo business *tintuway; tughay; tiguway*
Solomon *Sulayman*
solve (problem) *usay 2*
some *saga 1; kasehe'an*
someone *a'a; saina*
something *ya ai*

something in eye *lempon*
something not freely given *hāk*
something said *sambatan*
something to cry about *panangis 1*
something totally surrendered *pangalilla'*
sometimes *sumā'..sumā'; maumu*
somewhat *mbal sakit; sarang-sarang*
somewhat able *ahat 1*
somewhat lacking *kulang-kulang 1*
son *anak l'lla*
song *kalangan₁; sangbayan*
song (religious) *lugu' 1*
son-in-law *ayuwan*
soon *dai'₂; sõng₁ 2; arai' 1*
soot *buling*
soothe (troubled feelings) *apu'-apu'; sayudja' 1.1*
soothing *hanunut; hanus; lu'uy₂*
soothsayer *talus₂*
sopping wet *bahug 1*
sorcery *hinang-hinang₁*
sore (muscular) *binsana' 1; busā' 1*
sores (itchy) *katol 1*
sores in mouth *ugam 1.1; obe' 1*
sores on scalp *buruk 1*
sorghum *layagan*
sorrow *susa 1*
sorry *liru' 1; susun₂ 1.1; susa 1.1*
sort (n) *ginis 1*
sort (v) *pansi; sisig; gintil 1.1*
sort of *sali' 1.3*
soul *pangatayan; nyawa*
sound (adj) *pagon₁ 1.1*
sound (faint) *bahonos 1; kulanas 1; bah'ssek 1*
sound (n) *h'lling₁ 1*
sound (of water) *samb'llong; sahabal; ssol; abal 1.1*
sound (sleep) *haluk; ddok; pagon₂*
sound (unpleasant) *g'mmel*
sound a gong *kulanting 1.1*
sound out letters *paghurup*
soup *loho' 1*
sour (not fresh) *balos₂*
sour (tasting) *l'ssom 1.1*
source *po'on₂; paluwasan*
source (of income) *pagusaha 1*
soursop *liyabanos*
south wind *satan*
southeast wind *tunggara'*
southpaw *sakap-gibang*
southwards *deyo'an*
Southwest Sulu *s'ddopan 2*
southwest wind *habagat*
souvenirs *pangentoman; lawanan*
sovereignty *okoman; deyoman 2*
sow seed *tanom₁ 1*

**soy sauce** *ta'uyu*
**space** *possatan; sipsipan; logtasan; ōt*
**space (outer)** *ayan*
**space (personal)** *huwang₁ 1*
**space behind (something solid)** *bukutan 1*
**space between** *llot*
**space in front** *dahū'an 1*
**spaced widely** *t'llag*
**spacious** *hayang 1; lugal 1.1; luha 1.1*
**spade** *pala*
**span** *h'kka 1; bunag*
**Spanish** *Kastila'*
**Spanish plum** *sinigwelas*
**spank** *lambot; lubak₁*
**spanner** *liyabe*
**spared** *liyus 1*
**sparing** *k'mmit 1; bista₂ 1*
**sparkle** *pagbetong-betong; inggat; kitaw-kitaw*
**sparks** *bitu-bitu₂*
**sparse** *salat 1; ladja' 1*
**spatter** *pulagsik*
**spatula** *paleta; gagawi'*
**speak** *batbat₂; h'lling₁ 1.1; bā'₁; yuk; suwala 1.1; mūng*
**speak against** *sīng-sūd*
**speak definitely** *tuman 1.1*
**speak falsely** *kulli' 1.1*
**speak figuratively** *pagbahasa*
**speak ill of** *limut 1.1*
**speak incoherently** *pagsilap; pagbarese-barese*
**speak obliquely** *pa'andig; pataggal-taggal*
**speak out** *subahat₁; pabowa'*
**speak plainly** *pagpa'amu; k'bbat₁ 1*
**speak privately** *ungsik*
**speak roughly** *bagas; kasla 1.1*
**speak Sinama** *pagsinama*
**speak slowly** *langguyud 1.1*
**speak Tausug** *pagsinūk*
**speak truth** *pamattan*
**speak Yakan** *pagsamehakan*
**spear (v)** *tagbak₁; hiyak; s'llok 1*
**spear-gun** *pana' 1*
**spears** *ablong; budjak 1; sangkil 1; saubang*
**special** *halga' 1.1; mulliya 1*
**species** *bangsa₁*
**specific** *tugila' 1; tugpang 1*
**specify (detail)** *tutat 1.1; sukut 2*
**specify time** *ligtung; tugna'*
**speck in eye** *bulag; puling 1.1*
**speckled** *b'ttik 1.1; kabang 1.1*
**specks** *niki'-niki'; bukbuk 1*
**specks (distant)** *ba'ung-ba'ung 1*
**spectacles** *samin-mata*
**spectator** *nda'-nda'*

**speech** *bahasa₁; bissala 1; lagam*
**speech defect** *terol; ponga'; tanga'₂*
**speechless** *kamal*
**speed up** *andal*
**speed up ripening** *putput*
**speedboat** *ispidbut*
**speedy** *l'kkas 1; ka'is; samot 1; kasay 1*
**spell (witchcraft)** *hikmat; duti*
**spell a word** *hidja*
**spend** *b'lli*
**spend years doing** *pagtahunan*
**sperm of fish** *hapa 1*
**spew** *utta' 1*
**sphere** *bullung; lengkong 1*
**sphere (of control)** *komkoman 2; pang'ntanan₁; milikan*
**spherical** *tibulung 1; legong*
**spices** *pamapā*
**spicy liquid** *tinu'anan*
**spider conch** *kahanga*
**spider web** *sāng-lawa'*
**spiders** *lawa' 1; kabombong*
**spigot** *siput 1; saluran*
**spikenard** *amamali*
**spikes** *tipopok; tuklang; tunuk*
**spill** *huddud 1; busuwag; bu'us 1*
**spilling** *paglilip-lilip*
**spin** *palling; legot 1.1; pusal₁ 1.1*
**spine (of body)** *tangkal₁*
**spine (of fish)** *tare' 1; kanting₁*
**spinefoots** *b'llong; panahilaw; mangilāp; dāg₂ 1; bawis₂*
**spinning game** *pagtalli*
**spinning motion** *legot 1; pusal₁ 1*
**spinning top** *gasing; talungkup*
**spinster** *la'un 1.1*
**spiny murex** *sudlay-sudlay*
**spiny projections** *bū 1; iting 1*
**spiral (n)** *siputan*
**spiral (v)** *legot-legot*
**spirit (of deceased person)** *lutaw; pangguwa' 1; panyata'₂ 1; sumangat 2*
**spirit (of God)** *Rū*
**spirit (of person)** *umagad 1; nyawa; umanat*
**spirit beings** *bangsa-paleyang; gansuwang; ya mbal ta'nda'; manananggal; duwata 1; deyo'₂ 2; umagad-sowa; bangsa magl'l'ngngan; mananasat; saitan; hama'-hama' a'a; jīn 1; balbalan*
**spirit counterparts** *nyawa-lihan; k'mbal-saitan*
**spirit guardian** *tunggu' 1*
**spirit of dumbness** *saitan-mungkil 1*
**spirit of forests** *komeng*
**spirit possession** *sangon₂ 1.1; duwata 1.1; jīn 1.2*
**spirits (alcoholic)** *alkohol 1*
**spit on** *ludja' 1.3*

spit out *ludja' 1.2*

spit out v) *upa' 1.1*

spiteful *jingki 1; pagkidjib*

spittle *ludja' 1; laway₁ 1; buhelo 1*

splash *tata'; pisik-pisik; pigsik₁ 1; p'ssik 1.1*

splash (into canoe) *s'pput; sauk 2; sasay*

splashing sounds *pagbalukakkad; pagbahembas; ebol*

splatter *sepet-sepet; p'ssik 1.1*

splendor *kamahaldika'an*

splint (for support) *hapid₁ 1; lantay-lantay 1; gimbal 1*

splint (v) *tapil 1.1; bandung₁*

splinter *sukmu 1*

split apart (adj) *segpong; lelek; b'kka' 1*

split apart (v) *se'ak 1.1; millat; l'tta' 1.1; sepak*

split away from *sobak; pungal; sasa₁; pitas₂ 1; te'as*

split bamboo (v) *tilas₂*

split fish (for drying)' *pundang 1.1; peyad 1.1*

split with wedge *tanok 1.1*

split wood *pasāk*

splutter (v) *s'ddok; siplat; buskaw*

spoil (indulge) *parūl 1.1; palangga' 1.1; parakag*

spoil by cutting *pak'bbang*

spoiled (by handling) *lotok 1*

spokeshave *gahud-gahud₁*

sponger *dahal 1*

sponges *lanos₂; l'ppus 1*

spongy *k'nnol; k'ddot*

spontaneous *halam baya'*

spooked *g'mma*

spools *gilingan; kolengan; basung*

spoon *suru' 1*

spoor *limpa' 1*

spot (mark) *tumpak 1*

spotless *sussi 1.1*

spouse *paghola'*

spouse of sibling-in-law *bilas*

spouse relationship *paglakibini*

spout (n) *saluran*

sprained *pisu'; possat; dalisu'*

sprawl *hantal*

sprawled *julangkang*

spray (v) *pigsik₁ 1.1; sumpit 1.1; kissat*

spread (beyond limit) *lekles*

spread (of flames) *ledled 1; suleyab 1*

spread (of infection) *tumbul; lemed 2; lamin 1*

spread (of information) *tanyag 1.1; buhanyag; hayag; bawag; pahula-layag*

spread (of odor) *tunug 1.1; pulag-pulag; hangsu 1.1*

spread fingers *kangkang₁ 1; pagkabug-kabug*

spread legs *perat 1; pagsengkang*

spread open *papellat*

spread out *tēt; pagsilapug; l'ntap; dasal*

spread over a surface *lakat; l'ntap*

spread rumor *tuna'; tuhuma 1.1; waham*

spread wings *sayang₁; kidjang 1.1*

spring (water source) *tuburan; tigbaw*

spring loose *lagtik 1*

spring onion *kussay*

spring scale *kiluhan*

spring tides *daka'*

spring trap *litag 1*

spring up *buladjang*

springy *l'mpet*

sprinkle (liquid) *tata'; pisik-pisik; titi'*

sprinkle (powder) *budbud 1.1*

sprinkle (rain) *pitik-pitik 1*

sprit *tukag*

sprit (of sail) *suklu'an; tuklug 1*

sprites *kokok 1; komeng*

sprout (n) *ugbus 1*

sprout (v) *saingsing 1; s'mbut 1; saha' 1.1*

sprouting coconut *pangtusan; bōt₁ 1; tabul₂*

spry *lasig 1.1*

spurn *sulak₂*

spurs (chicken leg) *tahod; epo'*

spurt *pigsik₁ 1.1*

spy (n) *mata-mata₂ 1; ispāy 1*

spy on *tīk 1.1; sipi₁ 1.1*

squall *hunus 1; kawas-kawas*

squander *koro-koro 1*

square *pasagi' 1*

squash (n) *kabasi'*

squash (v) *pedjet; gipit 1*

squash lice *t'bbok₂*

squash underfoot *ddik*

squashed *k'mmog 1; k'ddos; k'ppi'₂*

squashy *lonyat; petak 1; lodjag 1*

squat (v) *lesseg; engge'-engge'*

squawk *eyok*

squeak *ngngik*

squeamish *pagboyokan*

squeeze *pisi-pisi*

squeeze (cassava meal) *da'os; papinsal; pidjal*

squeeze (liquid from) *gipit 1.1; hali₁ 1.1; p'gga'*

squeeze into *s'llap₂; sigpit 2; sipit-sipit₁*

squeeze out *b'bbas 1.1; p'ssit; p'ddet*

squeeze through *siklut*

squeeze together *pagdigpit 1*

squelchy *l'bbo 1; legsak*

squid lure *ullang 1.1*

squid mantle *biring*

squids *tabula; kanu'us*

squint at *kiyal*

squirrelfishes (generic) *tihik-tihik 1*

squirt *pigsik₁ 1.1; kissat; sahupput; sulapput*

stab *dugsu'; tagbak₁; punyal 1.1; dukduk*

stable (adj) *tapak; totog 1; t'ttog 1*

**stack (n)** *bingkis 1*; *susun₁ 1*
**stack (v)** *bangkat₁*; *pangkat₁*; *pagasok*
**stacked** *timbun-tambak*
**staff** *tungkud 1*
**stage** *pantān*
**stagger** *pagsampigay*; *pagtambelleng*
**staghorn coral** *sāng-sāng*
**stain metal** *ponglas*
**stain on teeth** *kiki' 1*; *balakang 1*; *baka'₂ 1*
**stainless** *estenles*
**stains** *tumpak 1*; *lobag*; *tamak 1*
**stairway** *haron 1*
**stake (gambling)** *tūk 1*
**stakes** *bale₃ 1*; *soha'*; *pangka' 1*
**stale** *pasaw*; *datay₁*
**stalemate (in discussion)** *pagsigpit 2*
**stalk of bananas** *bole*
**stalks** *batang₁*; *tangkay 1*
**stalks (of rice)** *gulami*
**stall (market)** *pasal₂ 1*; *kadday*
**stallion** *mandangan*
**stamina** *kuwat*
**stamp (n)** *tumbuk₃ 1*
**stamp feet** *tendek*; *pagtagdok*; *pagtaddok*
**stampede** *pahuru-huru*
**stance** *palantara 2*
**stand (n)** *pat'nggehan*; *t'nna' 1*
**stand (support)** *patinggilan*
**stand around** *ampīs*; *pagkubu-kubu*
**stand on edge** *pasindik*
**stand on end (of hair)** *iting 2*
**stand out from** *jolog*
**stand together** *pagtapil*; *pagtapīn*
**stand up** *t'ngge 1.1*
**stand-in (n)** *ganti' 1*
**staple food** *pagkakan 1*; *kinakan 1*; *lauk 1*
**star apples** *balimbing*; *kamyas*
**starch** *almirul 1*
**starch dressing (on new cloth)** *kanji'*; *sakkul*
**stare at** *d'llag 1.1*; *pandang*; *hīng 2*
**starfishes** *kalling*; *l'mmun-l'mmun*; *linggatang*
**starling (bird)** *mandasiyang*
**stars** *pote'an*; *bitu'un*; *mamahi*
**start** *tagna' 1.2*
**start cocks fighting** *bulang*
**start engine** *pupput₁ 1*
**start proceedings** *para'ak*
**startle** *kuddat*
**startled** *leyang atay*; *kudjal*
**starved to death** *patay-otas*
**starving** *bongtas 1.1*; *gotom 1.1*; *otas*
**state a price** *halga' 1.2*
**state conditions** *idda 1.1*
**state needs** *tambuku₁*

**statement** *kabtangan*
**statue** *ta'u-ta'u₁*
**status (social)** *kag'llal*
**staunch (loyal)** *pagsabal*
**staunch bleeding** *papalom*
**stay briefly** *lihan 1*; *hanti' 1*
**stay firm** *totog 1.1*
**stay in one place** *d'ddos*; *taptap 1.1*; *tattal*
**stay permanently** *dalos 1.1*
**stay with** *okom 1*
**steadfast** *taptap 1*
**steadfastness** *iman₁ 1*
**steadily** *tawhid 1.2*; *paspas₁*
**steady** *tapak*; *totog 1*
**steal** *tangkaw 1.1*
**stealthily** *sipi₁ 1*; *patangkaw*; *gagam*
**steam** *s'bbu*; *husbu 1*; *asu-asu 1*
**steam food** *putu₂*
**steamed cake** *putu-putu*
**steamed cassava** *pinutu*
**steaming** *aes-aes*
**steel** *balan*; *basi'₁ 1*
**steep slopes** *titib*; *bīd*
**steer (v)** *bansān 1.1*; *ulin*
**stem (of coconut frond)** *paipa'₂*
**stems** *batang₁*; *pungutan*; *tangkay 1*
**step (of path or ladder)** *tangga' 1*
**step (pace)** *tekang 1*; *peka'*
**step on** *d'dda*; *gi'ik 1*; *ddik*
**step over** *lingka' 1*; *saliyu 1*; *lakad 1*
**step up on** *tinggil 1*
**step-child** *anak-ballo'*; *anak-binowa*
**stepped on** *pang'ddikan*
**step-relationship** *tē'₁*; *ballo'*
**sterile (infertile)** *tamanang*
**sterilized** *kunsuy*
**stern (adj)** *b'ngngis 1*; *bigsi' 1*
**stern (n)** *buli'₁ 2*
**stevedore** *kalgadol*
**stick (n)** *batang₂ 2*
**stick (slender)** *koyang*; *lituk 1*
**stick game** *siyatun*
**stick to** *kakkot*; *pikit₁ 1*
**sticking out (projecting)** *jungal 1.1*; *kabag 1.1*;
  *toro' 1*
**sticky** *g'tta'*; *piting*; *pagtagok*
**sticky rice** *putan*
**stiff (from sitting)** *limayu'*
**stiff (unyielding)** *tuwas 1*; *k'llas 1.1*
**stiffener (n)** *s'mmat 1*
**stifle** *talung₁*
**stiletto** *punyal 1*
**still (adj)** *t'ddo' 1*
**still (adv)** *lagi' 1*; *masi 1.1*

stilts *kaldang*
stimulate *giluk 1.1; bandung₂*
sting (v) *keket 2*
stinging insects *tabungay; lampinig; kabulig; buwani; teya'-teya'*
stinging plant *l'ppay*
stingrays *pahi; kihampaw*
stingy *iskut; kigit; kussil; kaikit₁; kuriput 1*
stinky *bau 1.1*
stir *keyol 1.1; huwal; gawgaw*
stir (move about) *pagkebed-kebed*
stir in sleep *himuya 1.1*
stir in womb *himati'; buka'-puhu'*
stir up (annoy) *jural; paglawat*
stir up (to movement) *bati'₂; hibal 1.1*
stitch (sewing) *tahi' buta*
stitch (side ache) *busā' jantung*
stock (trade) *muddal 1*
stockings *kalsitin*
stocks (fetters) *pasung₁ 1*
stoic *pagsabal*
stoke fire *siglat 1.1*
stomach *b'ttong₁ 1; babat*
stomach (prominent) *badding-badding; gombel*
stomach pain *gadgad₁*
stone *batu₁*
stone (semi-precious) *dilam*
stone (v) *bantung 1*
stool *bangku'*
stooped *dukkug 1*
stop (of fruiting) *tongkad*
stop breathing *simay₁ 1*
stop doing *bba₂; hogga' 1; hondong 1*
stop moving! *parā*
stop noise *k'nna; h'ddok; tepok*
stop-start *pagsōng-sebog*
storage place *tau'an; pang'nna'an*
store (v) *nna'; tau' 1*
store securely *kuli-kuli 1.1*
stored (while damp) *g'mmol₂*
storehouses *kamalig; borega*
stores (shops) *tinda; kadday*
stories *kissa 1; istori 1; salsila 1; kata-kata; usul 1*
storm *badju; goyak 1*
story (house) *angkap 1*
stout (of body) *hambug 1; l'mmok 1.1*
stove *lapohan; pagb'llahan*
straight *bontol 1; tilud 1; tanus*
straighten (of rope) *b'ttad 1.1*
straighten out *l'dduk 1.1; b'ngnga' 1; lūk; l'ngngat*
straighten up (from sitting) *bugnus₁*
strain (physical) *bo'ol; paglu'ug-liksa'*
strain liquid *sā'₂*
strainers *ayakan; sā'an 1*

strake (of canoe) *tapi' 1; durung₂*
strand (inter-tidal area) *katoho'an; t'bba 1; kūd*
strand (single thread) *tangbid*
strand food *t'bbahan*
stranded *t'bba 1.2*
strands *lamba₂*
strange *la'in-la'in; saddī-saddī*
stranger *a'a liyu*
strangle *t'kkob; p'kkol 1.1*
strategy *isunan*
stray (deviate) *sulekma'; sā'₁ 1.2*
streaky *pagtimb'llang*
stream (n) *bohe'-sasahan; sapa'; sowang*
street *lān*
strength *kuwat; kulasog 1; kosog 1*
strengthen (with splint) *tapil 1.1; bandung₁; hapid₁ 1.1*
strengthless *hoyon; sampoyan; dome-dome*
stress (emotional) *susa 1; pagsorol*
stress the importance of *pagmuna-muna*
stressed *p'ddi' akkal*
stretch (line, cloth) *hinit 1.1; bigtang 1.1*
stretch (on waking) *nned; h'nnat 1; pagle'od; pagkul'ddeng*
stretch legs out *paghin'nnat*
stretch marks (on skin) *kalulay 1*
stretch out of shape *kontay₁*
stretchable *konot₁ 1; hinit 1*
stretched tight *b'ttad 1*
strewn *teges-teges*
stride *tekang 1; peka'*
strike *lambot; butug; p'ppok; tettek; taluwa' 3*
strike (fishing) *tinduk₁; sintak 2*
strike (obliquely) *dupli'as; deplas 1*
strike (surface of water) *t'bba' 1.1; tikabbol 1.1*
strike a match *santik 1; pe'es₂*
strike dumb *pamorok*
strike lightly (tap) *takdang*
strike quickly *sakkop 2*
strike repeatedly *paghantak; t'ttok 1.1*
strike sail *bulintus*
strike with cue *tira*
strike with fist *suntuk 1.1*
striking together *pagtikbi' 1*
string *lubid 1; bannang*
string beans *sayul batung*
string of beads *tasbi'*
string of fish *tuhug 3*
string together *lingkit 1.1; surut; tuhug 1*
stringer (boat construction) *bolbo₁*
strings of corn *līt*
strip (corn from cob) *lutu₁*
strip (leaves) *lakas*
strip (n) *balkehet; sanggi' 1*

**strip (skin from)** *kupas*

**striped** *kelong-kelong₁*; *janggi'*

**striped fabric** *sabela*

**stripes** *jali' 1*; *bekos₁*

**stripped (naked)** *pegtang-pegtang*; *tantang*

**stripped (of resources)** *kadkad 1*

**strips (of bamboo)** *huwit-huwit 1*

**striptease** *pagbolles*

**strive to get done** *pagbinasag*

**strive together** *pagga'os-ga'os*; *pagda'ug*; *pagsanggul 1.1*; *pagkosogan*; *pagta'as-ta'as*

**stroke something** *sapu-sapu*; *pahid 1*

**stroll (n)** *l'ngngan₁ 1*; *lanyaw*

**stroll (v)** *pasiyal*; *paglunsul*; *pagjambeyaw*

**strong** *basag 1*; *kulasog 1.1*; *kosog 1.1*

**strong (muscular)** *ayron*

**strongbox** *gusi'*; *kaha₁*

**struck by** *taluwa' 1*

**struck down** *bugtang*

**struck dumb** *kowam 1*

**struggle to breathe** *pagkawas napas*; *pagagaw-napas*

**struggle together** *pagga'os-ga'os*; *pagta'as-ta'as*

**strum** *pagkublit-kublit*

**strut** *pagpaelle'-elle'*; *pagl'lla-l'lla₁*

**stubborn** *tuwas 1*; *gagga*; *kōk-batu*; *mungkil*; *tuwas-kōk*

**stubs** *pukul 1*; *pupud 1*

**stuck in throat** *kowa' 1*; *b'ngkol₁ 1.1*

**stuck onto** *balut 1*

**stuck together** *damil*; *pagpiting*

**stud (building)** *tuku 1*

**stud (in ear)** *bāng₂*

**student (religious)** *anak-mulid*; *mulid*

**study (religious)** *guru 1.1*; *adji' 1*

**study (secular)** *istadi*

**stuff (into container)** *dasok 1.1*; *gagā*

**stuff (into mouth)** *lokom*

**stuffed full (of mouth)** *k'mmol*; *sugmak*; *s'gga*

**stuffed up (of nose)** *p'nnot*

**stuffy (airless)** *linganga*; *lingo'ot*

**stumble** *lukbu'₂*; *dahungkung*; *tukku' 2*

**stump** *punggut 1*; *pukul 1*; *tunggul*

**stun (by explosion)** *timbak 1.1*

**stunned (emotional)** *k'bbal atay*

**stunned fish** *belaw-belaw*; *lundu'*

**stupefy fish** *lagtang 1*; *tuba 1.1*; *tuwa 1.1*

**stupid person** *dupang 1*

**stupidity** *karupangan*; *kababbalan*

**stutter** *tanga'₂*

**stye** *boto'-boto' mata*

**style** *pakang₁*; *bowahan*

**stymie** *babag 2.1*

**subdivide** *boklang 1.1*

**subdivision** *bahagi' 1*; *anak₂*

**subdivision (ethnic)** *kapihakan*

**subdue** *longkop 1.1*

**subject matter** *parak*

**submerge (v)** *tuhun 1*

**submerged** *lonob 1*; *letop 1*; *kanop*

**submission** *pagmalulus*

**submit to slavery** *pagpatiata*

**suborn (entice)** *pitna*; *dūk₁*; *sugi-sugi*; *abiyug*

**subpoena** *paglimanda*; *tawag-saksi'*; *sopena*

**subsequently** *puwas₂*; *sakali₂*

**subside (of emotions)** *padpad*

**subside (of flood)** *julut 1*; *kō' 1.1*

**subsistence** *kahirupan*; *ka'lluman*

**subsoil** *babaw-tana'*

**substance** *isi₂*

**substantial** *ponod 1.1*; *pagon₁ 1.1*

**substitute** *sambi' 1*; *saliyu 1.1*; *ganti' 1.2*

**subtract** *hilang*; *kulang₁ 1.2*

**subtribe** *pihak*

**suburb** *pasisil*; *kaum*

**succeed** *da'ug*

**success (financial)** *paluntungan*

**succession** *sunud 1*

**successively** *pagsunu'-sunu'*; *pagsungbul-sungbul*

**succour** *liyus 1.2*; *lappas₂ 1.1*

**succulent plant** *sangtaliri'*

**such as** *buwat 1*; *saga 2*

**suck** *tamus*; *s'ssop*; *huttut*

**suck (to remove pain)** *dutdut*

**suck (vital fluids from)** *uwak*; *balbal*

**suck in** *horot*; *h'llop 1.1*

**sucker (of plant)** *saha' 1*

**suckerfishes** *k'mmi*; *lakkop-lakkop*

**suckle** *duru' 1.2*; *paruru'*; *tete' 1.1*

**suction pad** *lakkop 1*

**sudden death** *hukuman kudjut*; *patay-tunung*

**sudden movement** *kawas*

**sudden onset** *sakkop 2*

**suddenly** *papuwa'*; *sigla' 1*

**suds** *bula'-bula' 1*

**sue (legal)** *tuntut₁*

**suffer (from a cold)** *ulapay₁*

**suffer (from epilepsy)** *bawi-bawi*; *sawan-sawan*

**suffer financially** *pagkalussungan*; *lugi' 1*

**suffering hardship** *kabinasahan*; *tiksa' 1*

**sufficient** *ustu*; *sarang 1*

**suffix (grammar)** *tundanan*

**suffusion (blood)** *alom 1*

**sugar** *sokal 1*

**sugar (caster)** *sokal-budbud*

**sugar (lump form)** *sokal-tibu'uk*

**sugar (solid form)** *pilun*

**sugar (unrefined)** *sokal-tigtig*; *sokal-ba'ung*

**sugar apple** *atis*

sugarcane *t'bbu*
suggest *isi-isi*
suicide *pagsabil*
suit (of clothes) *telnos 1*
suit each other *pagtōp; pagtaluwa'; pagtuksu'*
suitable *patut; tōp 1.1; d'kkal; amu₁*
suitcases *ba'ul₁; maleta*
suitor *tunang 1*
suitor (rejected) *baibad 1*
sulfur *maylang*
sulking *mandā'-dā'*
sultan *sultan*
sum *itungan; saipuwa*
summary judgment *hukuman kudjut*
summit *pekkes-pekkes; puntuk*
summon *lingan 1; sitta; tawag*
summon (legal) *paglimanda; sopena; tawag-saksi'*
sun *mata-llaw; llaw₂ 1*
sunbathe *pagpating'llaw*
Sunday *Ahad*
sundown *magrib 2*
sundried cassava *tumbal 1.1*
sunfish *l'ppet-kandel*
sunk below surface *lonob 1; limun 1; kanop*
sunken *lowak 1*
sunken (of face) *l'bbong 1*
sunken eyes *lowak 1.1*
sunlight *silak 1*
sunny season *pang'llaw*
sunrise *sobangan; abay-subu*
sunset *s'ddop; laha'-llaw*
sunstroke *panggang₂ 1; kapiyalu 1*
superior *tinggi₁*
superiority *ga'osan*
superlative *katapusan 1*
superstitions *pali-pali*
supervisor *kapatas*
supple *l'mpet*
supplement (v) *jukup 1.2; k'nnop 1.2; tubil; ganap 1.2*
supplicate *pagtawbat; suhud 1.1*
supplies *balanja' 1; gastu 1; lutu'₁ 1*
supply needs *palutu'; gastu 1.1*
support (aid) *tuku 2*
support (aid) *tapin*
support (by holding) *tagang*
support (by leaning against) *sandig 1.1*
support (by placing alongside) *tapil 1; gimbal 1*
support (financial) *panulung*
support (in a dispute) *tapil 2; bogbog₁ 1.1; dapit*
support (in game) *utus*
support (mutual) *pagablay*
support (with a backing) *pasangdol*
support (with a prop) *tuku 1.1*

support (with hands) *tayak 1.1; takmay*
support (with splint) *lantay-lantay 1.1*
support canoe (for drying) *tangon 1.1*
support s.o. *ga'os 1.2*
support team *pangabay*
supporters *pitis-tendog; gapi' 1; bebeya'an*
supporting block *pasangdolan 1; pamataggalan*
supporting lugs *sukul₂*
supporting pole *tuklug 1; bale₃ 1*
supporting slat *hapid₁ 1*
suppose *abila; bang saupama; ganta'₃*
suppose mistakenly *bā'₂; pangannal₂*
supreme being *Tuhan; Allah*
sura *jūd*
sure *tuman 1; tantu 1.1*
sure to *taka-taka*
surely *siguru 1*
surf *sahal₁ 1; goyak 1*
surface (of ground) *kuwit-tana'; babaw-tana'*
surface (of sea) *kuwit-tahik*
surface damage *langgad 1; langgahi'*
surface irregularities *sahumut-sahumut*
surface to breathe (v) *ppo*
surfeited *jompo'; sumu 1.1*
surge (of surf) *jalak*
surge up (of water) *appu'; suput₁*
surgeonfishes (generic) *kumay*
surgery *opera*
surging sound *samb'llong*
surmise *pula'-pula' 1.1; dongdong*
surpass *liyu₂ 1.1*
surplus *labi 1; kapin 1*
surprise *kuddat*
surprised *inu-inu 1; littā 1*
surprisingly *taggaha'; tuwi'*
surrender *pagpatihantak 2; sarahakan; paglilla'*
surrogate *ganti' 1*
surround *ambus*
surrounded *paruwambila'*
surrounding area *katilingkal; katilibut*
surviving *pagdāg-lurus*
susceptibility *pilluwang₂ 1*
suspect *tuna'; tuhuma 1.1*
suspend *taguntun 1; gantung₂ 1.1; tonton 1*
suspended *bitay; bigtang 1*
suspicion *hunub 1*
sustenance *kahirupan; napaka; balanja' 1*
swaddle *lampin₂ 1.1*
swagger *pagabbu 1.1*
swallow (v) *t'llon; t'ggok*
swallow whole *āb; s'bbat 1.1; sangkiyam*
swamp (n) *kal'bbohan; bagsak₁*
swamped *sasay; logdang₂; buhaw*
swampy *pekat*

swap *saliyu 1.1*; *pagbalin 1*; *sambi' 1*
swap places *pagganti'*
swarm (v) *pagba'an 1*; *kobol-kobol*; *kulatap*
swat *tapling*; *t'ppag₁*
swathe *lampin₂ 1.1*
sway *dundang₁ 1*; *paglambeng-lambeng 1.1*
swear on oath *pagsapda*; *sapa*; *subali 1*
swear to *pasab'nnal*
sweat *hulas 1*
sweat-cloth *sapu-tangan*
sweep away *kayas 1.1*; *sapu 1.1*
sweep together *kās*; *hīs 1.1*
sweeperfish *bari'-bari'*
sweeping movement *kayas 1*; *kaskas₂*
sweet *mamis₁ 1.1*; *imu' 1.1*
sweet confections *suman*; *wadjit*; *hapit-hapit*; *hinti' 1*
sweet corn *gandum*
sweet potato *panggi'-bahan*
sweetener (finance) *mamhu'*
sweetheart *tunang 1*; *bigi-jantung*; *atag₂*
sweetlips (fish) *malumiyat*; *l'ppe*; *pasengko*; *bakukku*
sweets (candy) *kende 1*
swell (v) *p'ngkong 1.1*; *tting*; *boskag*
swell (waves) *lumbag*
swelling (abdominal) *bago' 1*
swelling (goiter) *bogon₁ 1*; *bongol 1*
swelling (in flesh) *ikat 1*; *busul*; *p'ngkong 1*; *baha' 1*
swelling (in glands) *gulandi' 1*; *panibli*
swept away (by current) *laran*; *hanut*
swerve *bintung 1*
swidden *gās₁*

swift *l'kkas 1*; *kasay 1*
swift (bird species) *sayaw*
swim *langi 1*
swim (near surface) *s'nnung 1*
swim backstroke *pagtindayung 2*
swimming float *balsa*
swimming pool *tigbaw*
swindle *kidjib*; *lingu 1.1*; *akkal 1.1*
swing (by arms) *paggantung-bitay*
swing (v) *pagdanggu'-danggu'*; *dundang₁ 1.1*; *duyan*
swing arms *limbay*
swing child (on one's legs) *ombo'-ombo'*
swing standing up *pagnanu'*
swing to and fro *paglambeng-lambeng 1.1*; *lambe₁ 1*
swirl (eddy) *buliluk*; *paglimbokay*; *salekolan*
swirl (of wind) *paglimpowak*
switch (exchange) *saliyu 1.1*
swollen *baha' 2*; *butig 1.1*
swollen glands *talis'ssok 1*; *panibli*
swollen stomach *bakag₂*; *m'kkig*
swoon *pinsan 1*
sword *barung*
swordfishes *belas*; *manumbuk*
symbol *tanda'*
symbolic *sapantun*
sympathize *andu'-andu'*
symptom *tanog₂ 1*; *nanam 2.1*
symptom (of conception) *iram*
syndicate *pagkungsi*; *paghūn*
syrup *gula'*
system (method) *hatulan 1*
system (religious) *agama*

# T t

Tabawan *Tabawan*
tables *pagkakanan*; *lamisahan*; *mesa*
taboo *pali-pali*
tack (sailing) *pali*
tack (sew) *bagsak₂*
tacky *g'tta'*; *pekot*
tacky (of a mixture) *pīt*
tag (game) *pagembet 1*
tag along *pagiku-iku*
tail (animal) *togel*
tail (fish) *tape'₂*
tail (hair) *pugay 2*
tail wind *tūd₁ 1*
tailbone *tuwal 1*; *igut*
tailor *pagtatahi'*
tails (of coin) *kurus*; *kaba'*

take *k'llo'₁*; *bowa₁*; *ā' 1*
take (without permission) *tangpas₁*; *t'ppas₁*; *sabsab*
take a bath *pandi 1*
take a husband *pah'lla 1*
take a wife *pah'nda 1*
take advantage of *pagdago'-dago' 1.1*; *lingu 1.1*
take all *lakap*
take as passenger *palaktas*; *patumpang*
take as wife *ā' h'nda*
take away rational thought *alim₂*
take bait *āb*
take bait (fish) *tinduk₁*
take care of *payakun*; *ussap 1*; *pahilala' 1*
take census *palista*
take hostage *bihag*; *kidnap 1*
take in (mentally) *sipat₁ 1.1*

take leave of *puhun*; *ba'id 1.1*
take offense *paghāk 1*
take responsibility *tanggung₂*; *abunaw*
take shelter *limbu 1.2*
take sides *dapit*
take to court *dagsol*
take turns *s'lle' 1.1*; *pagbalin 1*
takings (financial) *luwas₂*
talcum powder *borak 1*; *polbos*
tale *kissa 1*; *istori 1*
talent *kapandayan*; *ingat*
talk *suli-suli 1*; *h'lling₁ 1*; *mūng*
talk privately *paghidjab*
talk (mere words) *kak'bbatan bowa'*
talk about *pina'in*; *suli-suli 1.1*
talk casually *upama*
talk dirty *paglaka'-laka' 1.1*
talk in private *pagungsik*
talk in sleep *paglalap*; *pagdabdab*
talk nonsense *pag'lling-lling*; *pagdabdab*; *pagli'anun*
talk over (to plan) *pagisun 1.1*; *paggara' 1.1*
talkative *bowa'-bowa'*; *h'lling-h'lling*
tall (high) *langkaw 1.1*
tall (of body) *lanjang 1.1*
tall person *langkawit₁*
tallow *lansuk*
tallow wood *paniyungan*
tally *itung₁*
tamarind *sampallu'*
tambourine *tambul-tambul*; *dabbana*
tame *emon*
tan (color) *kausun*
tanged blade *patuk*
tangerine *muntay*
tangled *gosang-gosang*; *sagut 1*; *gumun*
tangled (of umbilical cord) *sambon 1*
tank *tangki*
tannic *p'kkat*
tantrum *pagle'eng*; *s'ngngel 1*
tap (faucet) *siput 1*
tap (v) *kuku'*; *takdang*; *pagtagettek*
tap water *bohe'-pansul*
tape-recorder *tēp*; *ulehem*
tapestry *palmaddani'*
tapioca *panggi'*
tar *kitlan 1*
tardy *lahan 1*
target *tudjuhan*; *talget*
target (shooting) *iralan*
targeted *tumlang 2.1*; *taluwa' 1*
tarnish (on metal) *sawasa'*
taro *hupi' 1*; *kallari'*; *kapeta'*
tarpaulin *tolda*
tarry *lahan 1*; *pagene'-ene'*

tarsier *kokam₁*
tart (taste) *harat 1.1*; *l'ssom 1.1*
tartar *baka'₂ 1*; *kiki' 1*
task *hinang₁ 1*
tassels *jambay*; *jombay-jombay*; *jambili*
taste (n) *nanam 1*; *ssa₁ 1*
taste (v) *kinam 1*; *timtim*; *k'ssap*
tasteless (bland) *k'ssang₂*; *t'bbag*; *kesom*; *k'ssaw*
tasty *sarap₁*; *taba' 1.1*; *lanab*
tattered *purut*; *gores 1*
tatters *jabel-jabel 1*; *jebel-jebel 1.1*
tattoo *tatak*
tatty *guya'*
taunt *himulas*; *oro'-oro'₂*; *tukas 1.1*
Tausug *Sūk 1*
Tausug and Sama *Sūk-Sama*
Tausug language *Sinūk 1*
taut *d'llot 1*; *pigtal 1*
tax (n) *buwis 1*; *sukay₁ 1*
tax (religious) *jakat*
taxed (physically) *bo'ol*; *husa'*
tea *tī*
tea (instant) *tī-budbud*
teach *pandu' 1.2*; *pintulu' 1*; *pituwa 1.1*
teach (by pointing to) *tō' 2*; *tudlu'₂ 1.1*
teachable *saldik*; *pantun 1*; *pandu' 1.1*
teacher *mastal*; *guru 1*
teaching (authoritative) *pituwa 1*
teak *jati'*
team *passuk*; *puntak 1*; *umpigan*
team leader *tukang*
team member *ugpang 1*
teamwork *pangandanginan*; *paggapi'*
teapots *patikuwan*; *kapsiyu*; *kapitera*
tear (v) *gese' 1.2*; *geret 1.2*
tear apart *pensang 1.1*; *saksak 1.1*
tear easily *p'ddut*
tear in strips *paggeset-geset*
tear off *s'kkat 1.2*
tear out (v) *pitas₂ 1.1*
tear universe apart *laklak alam*
tearing sound *g'llek*
tears (n) *bohe'-mata*; *lihing*
tease *lawat*; *pabelaw*; *blāp*; *juri 1.1*
tease a child *jullit₂*
teasing *paglata*
teat *tōng-duru'*
teeming *gora'₂ 1*; *datay₂*; *dorot*
teenage girl *daga-raga*; *budjang*
teenager *hoben*; *lumbu'-baha'u*; *onde'-baha'u*
teeter-board (see-saw) *pagjungkat-jungkat 1*
teeth *empon 1*
teeth on edge *l'nnu*
teething *s'mbut 2*; *empon 1.1*

telegram *taligrama*
telescope *talumpung 1*
tell *sumbung*; *haka 1.1*; *bā'₁*; *suli-suli 1.1*
tell a story *kissa 1.1*
tell fortune *limal*
tell in detail *uki'-uki'*; *usul 1.1*
tell off *dugal 1.1*; *s'ndal 1*; *pabukag*
tell the truth *pagpasab'nnal 1*
tell to *soho'*; *sūg-sūg*
temper *pasu' atay*
temper metal *tawtaw*
temperature *pasu'₁ 1*
temple (sides of face) *lendo'*; *kīd-tuktuk*
temporary *pinjam*
temporary residence *lihanan*
temporary shops *tiyanggi*
temporize *lehod 1.2*
tempt *pitna*; *bowa₃*; *sasat 1.1*
tempted *bowa-bowa*; *pilad*
ten *sangpū'*
ten thousand *laksa' 1*
tenant *tendog*
tender (sensitive) *lamma 1*
tendon *ugat 1*
tendril *tangan 2*
tenets of Islam *lukun*
tense (emotional) *kibad atay*
tense markers *bay*; *sōng₁ 2*
tentacles *janggut 1*
tentacles *gulamay 2*; *jambay-būng 1*
tentative (hesitant) *gaga'*; *paghubang-hubang*;
    *hawal 1.1*
tents *tolda*; *lona*
terapons *biga'ung*
teredo *kapang₁ 1*; *tambelok 1*
term of address *tuwan*
terminal point *kasangka'an*; *katobtoban*
terminate *utas 2.1*; *tapus 1.1*; *tabtab 2*
terminus *tobtob 1*
termites *bukbuk 1*; *anay*
terrified *ara'-ara' 1*; *g'mma*; *leya'-leya'*; *umagad 1.1*
terrifying *tāw-tāw*
territory *tana'₂*
test (for quality) *sulay₁ 2*
test (for size) *sarang 1.1*
test (for taste) *kinam 1*
test skill *sulay-sulay₁*
testament *bba₁ 2*
testicles *bigi-buyung*; *pola-pola*
testify *pasab'nnal*; *saksi' 1.1*
tether *pintal 1.1*; *engkot 1.1*
text (of scripture) *ayat*
textiles *kakana'*
than *min 1*

thank *pagsarang-sukul*
thanks (for necessities) *hinang-kalun 1.1*
thanks (n) *pagsukulan*
thanksgiving ceremony *duwa'a-salamat*
thanksgiving gift *sapa'at₂*
that (near person spoken to) *ilu 1*
that (recent) *ilū 1*
that (yonder) *hē'₁ 1*; *ina'an 1*
that direction *pē'₁*
that way *pehē'₁ 1*
that which *ya₂*
thatch *atop 2*; *tigul*; *nipa'*
thatch poles *hanglad 2*; *kasaw*
thatch shingle *pa'ud 1*
that's it *ya du*
that's why *ya po'on*
the (specific) *in*
the more so *ya lagi'na*
the more...the more *bangkinna...bangkinna*
theater *sini*
their, them *sigā₁*
then *ubus₂*; *nā 1*; *ampa₁*; *puwas₂*; *ati*
then (after that) *sakali₂*
then (of time) *buwattē' 1*
then and only then *bo' yampa*
thence *minnē'*; *minna'an*
theologian (Islamic) *ulama'*
therapons *kelong-kelong₂*; *langāt*
there (by person spoken to) *mailu 1*; *pi'ilu 1*
there (yonder) *maina'an 1*; *mahē'*
there and back *pehē'-pi'itu*
there are none *halam₁ 1*
there is *niya'₁ 1*
therefore *angkan 1.1*
they *sigā₁*
thick (in section) *kapal 1.1*; *gayad*
thick (of growth) *labung 1*; *libombo'*
thick (of hair) *tusay*
thick (of mixture) *pīt*
thicket *kasob*
thickness *kapal 1*
thief *sugarul*; *panangkaw*
thigh *pa'a*
thigh space *sikān 1*
thin (in section) *peres*; *nipis*
thin (of blade) *nipnip*; *lampin₁*
thin (of body) *giti' 1*; *titis 2*; *kagkag*; *kayog 1*
thingamajig *anu 1*
things (various) *inda wa barapa ginis*; *ai-ai 1*
thingummy, thingy *anu 1*
think about *kannal*; *dongdong*; *kira-kira*; *tamsil*;
    *pikil 1.1*
think mistakenly *bā'₂*; *pangannal₂*
thirsty *p'kkol k'llong*; *patay-bohe'*; *toho' p'ggad*

thirty *t'llumpū'*
this *itū 1*
this and that *ai bang ai; itu-ini*
this one *ya itu*
thongs (footwear) *sinelas*
thorax (chest) *daggaha*
thorn tree *amamali; puhung₂*
thorns *leget; iting 1; tuklang; tunuk*
thoroughly *pahāp₁; to'ongan 1.1*
though *bo'₁; minsan; malaingkan*
thought *patali'an; pangannal₁; pikil 1; hona'-hona'*
thought processes *nahu 1*
thoughtless *haman-haman 1; k'ddom₂*
thousand *ibu; ngibu*
thrash (punish) *lambot; daplos*
thrash about *suleret; kolesek; paspas₂ 1*
thrash tail *kallit*
thrashing sound *kularak*
thread *salban; tingkal; tanud; bannang*
thread (v) *suwa' 1.1*
thread in and out *pagsuwa'-suwa'*
thread together *surut*
threadbare *guya'*
threaten *hansom; dangka₁; sanggup; antup*
three *t'llu 1*
three days ago *bahangi-he'in*
three times *kamint'llu 1.1*
thresh grain *gisa'-gisa'*
threshold *patahan*
thrifty *k'mmit 1; bista₂ 1*
thrilled *hōp₂; hūg bulan*
thrive *sambu 1.1*
throat *asang₁ 1; k'llong*
throb *paglaggut-laggut; panag-panag 1; pagsignat-signat; pagkowap-kowap*
throne *kulsi*
throng (n) *timuk-timuk puhu'*
throttle (engine) *hiritan*
throttle (v) *t'kkob; p'kkol 1.1*
through and through *paglatus-lagbas*
through the years *mananahun*
throw *badji; buwang₁ 1; talilli' 1.1; laruk*
throw a fishnet *t'ppad; bugsak*
throw away *timan₁*
throw counter (in game) *mano 1.1*
throw rice *hambul*
throw up (vomit) *pagsallowa'; utta' 1*
throw-net (n) *laya 1*
thrush (infection) *ugam 1*
thrust pelvis *hamput*
thud (sound) *bahubuk*
thumb *tambō' 1; bokol 1; nggo'an-tangan*
thumb width *tambō' 2*
thumbprint *pagt'kkon bokol*

thunder *l'ggon; daogdog*
thunder of hooves *pagtagandak*
Thursday *Hammis*
thwart (hinder) *gaggat 1.1; ampal*
thwart (of boat) *s'ngkol 1*
tic *kidjut; k'bbut; kurat*
ticket *teket*
tickle *giluk 1.1; kirik-kirik*
tickle in throat *lagot-lagot*
ticks (insects) *hamug-hamug; niki'-niki'; kammut*
tidal (upper limit) *tapiyan; bihingan*
tidal flats *l'ggotan; kat'bbahan*
tidal flow *balosok; tambang₁ 1; bulagas; la'ang 1; nso'; sosob; sōn*
tidal wave *alun-panjang*
tide (extreme) *tahik-bulagas*
tidy (adj) *salassay 1; tuntul 1*
tidy (v) *m'mmos 1.1; temo-temo*
tidy grave *timbun*
tie (by lashing) *tollen*
tie (necktie) *kurubata'*
tie (v) *lingkit 1.1; engkot 1.1*
tie (with vine) *bahan 1.1*
tie knot *buku₁ 1.1*
tie loosely *bitil-bitil*
tie securely *baggot; gakut*
tie thatch sections *sigid*
tie together *pagengkot 1*
tiger *halimaw*
tiger shark *kalitan-mangali*
tight *sandat 1; sonson*
tight (of knot) *d'llot 1*
tight (of rope) *pigtal 1*
tight (of skin) *alop₂ 2*
tighten *d'llot 1.1; pinsal 1.1*
tight-fisted (mean) *iskut; kaikit₁; kuriput 1*
tight-fitting *kakkang₁; digpit 1*
tight-packed *selot 1*
tile (construction) *malbol*
tilefish *sugpat-babat*
tiller *bansān 1*
tilt *lenggang; kid₂; tunggang; tīg*
tilt head (to the side) *kondo'; lengag*
tilting *poyog 1; kīng 1; paglilip-lilip*
timber *kayu 2*
time (birthing) *bulanan*
time (clock) *lisag₁; waktu 1*
time (long duration) *saumul-umul; salama-lama; sapaya-paya*
time (of absence) *kalikutan*
time after time *tahun ni tahun; waktu ni waktu*
time ahead *ahil-jāman*
time long past *awal-tagna'; ma'as*
time of *pag-₃*

time out (games term) *taem*

time past *waktu palabay*

time period *abay₂*; *timpu 1*; *waktu 1*; *jāman*

time span

timetable *iddahan*; *eskedyul*

timid *bolag*; *damag*; *hawal 1.1*; *dalan 1*

tin (mineral) *luyang*

tin can *mital 2*

tine *kukku-badja'*

tinea *pohak 1*

tinfoil *tingga'*

tinge *agaw-agaw*

tinkle *kagingkul*

tint *kolol 1*

tiny *nahut*; *diki' 1*

tiny amount *dampeged-peged*; *dangk'tti'*; *kuri' 1*

tip (n) *pekkes-pekkes*; *punjung₁*; *tōng₁*

tip (of outrigger) *kukku₁*

tip (of sugar cane) *gu'ud*

tip container *tuwang*

tip forward *togsok*; *tongket*

tip out *tumpa 1.1*; *huddud 1*; *bu'us 1.1*

tip over *lenggang*; *busuwag*; *tumpa 1*

tipping (tilting) *paglilip-lilip*

tiptoe *engke'*

tire (wheel) *goma₂*

tired *male' 1*; *bale'*; *hanu*

tired of *sumu 1.1*

tissue paper *katas-jimpaw*

tithe *jakat*

title *g'llal 1*

title (to land) *dabtal*

tittle-tattle *bowa'-bowa'*

to *ni₁*

to and fro *pagbiyu-biyu 1*; *paglaulabay*

To make a person aware of something unseen. *pananam*

toast (n) *matsakaw*

toast (v) *tapa 1*

tobacco *tabaku' 1*; *pasta*; *banusu*; *pikaroda*

tobacco (green) *okat₁ 1*

tobacco pipe *kuwako*

today *llaw itu*

toe (second) *tudlu'₁*

toenail *kukku₁*

toes *kengkeng*; *anak-tape'*; *gulamay 1*

together *pagbihing₁*

together (of bulk items) *tighan 1*

toil *sangsā'*

toilets *kasilyas*; *toylet*; *pagjambanan*

token (of dowry) *bintak*

told you so *sugpak 1*

tolerate *sandal 1.1*; *s'llong*; *sandal-sandal*

tomato *kamatis*

tombs *tampat 1*; *kubul 1*

tomorrow *salung*; *pahalu*

tomorrow + one day *simuddai*

tongue *d'lla'*

tongue-tied *kallu'*

tonight *sangom itū*

too bad! *sisayang*

too much *dumasiyaw*; *kumarukan*; *makalandu'*

too much (excl) *apā*

tool *pang'ntan*

tooth *empon 1*

tooth (of dog) *bangkil₂*; *taling*

tooth (overlapping) *sengel*

toothbrush *sangbawa*; *sipilyu 1*; *gisgis empon*; *tupras*

toothpick *koyang*

top (of quality) *umbul tunggal*

top (toy) *gasing*; *talungkup*

top part *pekkes-pekkes*; *diyata' 1*; *puntuk*

top plate (of wall) *taytayan tikus*

top shell *lāk*

top to bottom *pareyo'-pariyata'*

topic *parak*

topple *timpuwad 1*; *h'bba'*; *pungkad*

topsoil *kuwit-tana'*

topsy-turvy *baliskat 1*

Torah *Tawrat*

torch *sulariyan*; *tanju'*; *tapulaw*

torment *binsana' 1.1*; *pinjala' 1.1*

torn *gese' 1.1*; *gilay 1*; *b'bbak*; *geret 1.1*

torn apart *pensang 1*; *saksak 1*; *laklak*

torn away *pitas₂ 1*

torn by snagging *songget*

tortoises (fresh water) *kula-kula*; *ba'u'u*

torture *binsana' 1.1*

toss (cooking) *ggang*

toss (throw) *buwang₁ 1*

toss coins *pagkabit*

toss off covers *bukaskas*

tossed by storm *goyak 1.2*

total *bista₂ 1.1*; *jumla 1.1*; *itung₁*; *saipuwa*

totally *katūyan*; *latus-lagbas*

tottery *lumintiyad*

touch *kublit*; *ntan₁ 1*; *kodjel*

touch bottom (of sea) *t'kkad 1*

touch in passing *lagid 1*; *saligsig₂*

touch lightly *tiyu'-tiyu'*

tough (sinewy) *kaslog*

tough (texture) *ketot*; *k'llit 1*; *k'ddot*

toughen up (by exercise) *k'llit-k'llit*; *k'ddot-k'ddot*

tour *busay lahat*

tour (travel) *pagkeha*

tourniquet *pinsal 1*

tousled *gosang-gosang*; *gumun*

tow something *tundan 1.2*

**toward person speaking** *pi'itu 1*

**toward person spoken to** *pi'ilu 1*

**towards** *tudju$_1$ 1; tampak 1*

**towel** *tuwalya; jimpaw; tawel*

**town** *lungsud; da'ira 1*

**town square** *palasa; mairan*

**town-mate** *lūng-kampung; kampung$_1$*

**toy boat** *jungkung 2*

**toys** *pangongka'an; parereyagan*

**trace (n)** *bakkas; limpa' 1; bakas-bakas*

**trace genealogy** *sugsug panubu'*

**track** *lān; pal'ngnganan*

**trade (v)** *litu*

**trade goods** *muddal 1*

**trade imported goods** *samsuy*

**trademark** *sāp$_2$ 1*

**trading post** *pustu 1*

**trading relationship** *pagsuki'*

**traditions** *pakas-pakas 1; usulan; tuttulan*

**trail** *lān; pal'ngnganan*

**trail (narrow)** *lān pasiklut*

**train (child)** *bi'at 1.1; babal$_2$*

**train (v)** *pabiyaksa; pantun 1.1; papat 1.1*

**trait (characteristic)** *sadsaran; jantang; jāt$_1$*

**trample** *gi'ik 1*

**trampled down** *losak*

**trance speech** *pagbarese-barese*

**tranquility** *kasalamatan; kasannangan; sajahitra'*

**transfer (relocate)** *salin$_2$ 1; latun 1; lintas*

**transfer debt** *patukbul*

**transfer liquid** *huddud 1.1; tuyung; hain*

**transfer property** *pasuku'*

**transfer responsibility** *pagpatimpa*

**transgression** *dusa 1*

**transit** *laktas*

**translate between languages** *salin$_2$ 2*

**translate into Sinama** *Sinama 1.1*

**translate into Tausug** *Sinūk 1.1*

**translucent** *sawa 1.1; lere-lere 1.1; sepel*

**transparent** *tina'ung; tilag*

**transplant** *laud 1; bakal*

**transport vessel (freight)** *kumpit; papet*

**transportation** *bayanan; pahinggaman*

**transposed (of two things)** *ballit*

**transverse to** *babag 1.1*

**transvestite** *bantut 1*

**trap (for crabs)** *sangbawan*

**trap deepwater fish** *pagpalit 1*

**traps (for fish)** *ampas 1; bagiyas 1; bungsud; kiming; panggal 1; togong 1; bubu$_1$*

**trash** *pamuwangkan; s'ggit 1*

**trash (v)** *pagtiman$_1$ 1*

**trashed (destroyed)** *ka'at 1.1*

**travel** *pagbusayan; beya'$_1$; busay lahat; biyahi*

**travel (n)** *l'ngnganan$_1$; busayan*

**travel alone** *dangan-dangan 1.1; damunda'-munda' 1*

**travel along coast** *susul 1; baybay$_1$*

**travel by foot** *baklay*

**travel companions** *pagabay 1*

**travel sickness** *lango-biyahi*

**travel together** *pagdora'; pagsambeya'; pagabay 1.1*

**travel widely** *pagkeha*

**travel without landmarks** *paslangan 1.1*

**traveler** *biyahero*

**traverse** *untas 1; pintas 1*

**trawl nets** *gugul 1; lantaw 1; linggi' 1*

**tray** *bandehaw; talam; tataklayan*

**tray of food** *dulang*

**treacherous** *sipi$_1$ 1*

**treachery** *tipu 1*

**treacle** *gula'*

**tread on (step on)** *gi'ik 1*

**treasure (n)** *gusi'; bungga'$_2$*

**treasure something** *pahalga'; pagma'atay*

**treasured** *sugpat nyawa*

**treasurer** *kukumit*

**treat (wound or illness)** *papalom; sāg-sāg; tambal$_1$ 1.1*

**treat as special** *pahalga'; mulliya 1.1; pagmuna-muna*

**treat differently** *pasaddī*

**treat equally** *topod 1.1; pagsambal 1.1; sama-sama; atag$_3$; tabul$_1$ 1.1*

**treat individually** *par'kkal; paggintil*

**treat with contempt** *pagero'-ero'*

**treat without care** *pagumak; pahagmak; tiyu'-tiyu'; tingku' 1.1*

**tree (at entrance to heaven)** *taubi'*

**tree (generic)** *kayu 1*

**tree (legendary)** *jakkum$_1$*

**tree species (unclassified)** *buwahan-kuyya'; ligayan; giyam; ba'it; buta-buta; tima'al; dungun; bintanag; daupang; samaw; ba'ugan$_1$; sampunay; puntik; bilulang 1; lagundi'; panuyungan; pangi; busa'ing; nunang; pamangka'un; kilkil; umpul; kosok$_2$; limbunga; bakbakan; tambu-tambu$_3$; paliya'-laut; salikaya'*

**trellis** *jala-jala*

**tremble** *oro'-oro'$_1$; kogkog; pidpid*

**tremble (due to fever)** *hōb-hōb; tatat*

**tremble (in fear)** *ara'-ara' 1; k'ddil-k'ddil; korog-korog*

**tremble (with emotion)** *pidpid isi*

**trembling** *tandog 2*

**tremor (body movement)** *bogon-bogon*

**tremor (seismic)** *linug$_1$*

**trepang (generic)** *bāt*

**trepang exudate** *daga' 2*

**trespass** *tangpas₁*; *sakay 2*

**trevally (carangoides)** *kariyan*; *mangali*; *bungkak*; *lawayan*; *manipis*; *kehet-boto'*; *b'ngka'*; *landeyok*; *mangsa' 1*; *mangapahan*; *bulan-bulan₁ 1*; *balobok₂*; *tulay*; *tāng-tāng*; *inggatan*; *daing-pote'*

**trials of life** *legot dunya*; *kapinsanan*

**triangular** *dinglu' 1*

**tribal subgroup** *pihak*

**tribe** *bangsa₁*

**tribute** *buwis 1*; *ungsud₂*

**trick (conjuring)** *pagbalikmata*

**trick someone** *pagambahan 1*; *bellod₁*; *sanggot₂*

**trickling sound** *k'llis*; *llok*

**trickster** *pandikal*

**tricyle** *taraysikul*

**trigger (firearm)** *passikan*

**triggerfishes** *bogge'*; *tombad*; *ginulang*; *epet*; *tunus*; *p'ggot*; *mayung*; *pinggangan*; *sandet-tai'*

**trim (to size or shape)** *kirus 1.1*; *basbas*; *salimi*; *saplung 1*

**trim canoe (balance)** *timbang₁ 3*

**trim cock's comb** *sanggul₃*

**trim fingernails** *t'ttop 1*; *k'llob*

**trim sail** *timpas*

**trinket box** *bakul-bakul*

**trip (journey)** *l'ngnganan₁*; *biyahi*

**trip over; trip up** *dahungkung*; *tukku' 2*; *bungku'₂*

**tripletail** *sampen*

**tripod (pot support)** *sukul₂*

**tripodfish** *peteg-sowang*

**triton shell** *tabuli 2*

**triumph** *panganda'ug*

**trivial** *m'ssa' iyuk*; *heya pisut-pisut*

**trochus shell** *lāk*

**trodden down** *losak*

**troll for tuna** *tonda'₁ 1.1*; *manit*

**tropical ulcer** *dugsul 1*

**trouble (n)** *sukkal-manukkal*; *kajahatan*; *sasaw 1*; *lengog 1*

**trouble (supernatural)** *bala'*; *mulka' 1*

**trouble (v)** *sasaw 1.2*; *sasat 1.1*

**troubled** *jabu 1*; *p'ddi' akkal*; *dongkag*; *kabid atay*

**trousers** *sauwal*; *pantalun 1*; *solpan*

**truant** *absen*

**truck** *tarāk*

**true** *pasti'₁*; *mattan 1.1*; *b'nnal 1.1*

**true (of kin relationship)** *legsok₁*; *lahasiya' 1*

**truly** *pahāp₁*; *to'ongan 1.1*; *sab'nnal-b'nnal*

**trumpet** *torottot*

**truncate** *punggut 1.2*

**trunk (body part)** *batang-baran*

**trunk (of tree)** *taroso*; *po'on₁ 1*; *batang₁*

**trust (v)** *kamdos₁*; *iman₁ 1.1*; *andol 1*

**trustworthy** *pangandolan*

**truth** *b'nnal 1*

**try hard** *lubak₂ 1*

**try in vain** *elod-elod*

**try on (for size)** *pasarang*

**try out** *tara'-tara'*

**tryst** *pagtaratu*

**T-shirt** *kamisita*; *saklay*

**tsunami** *alun-panjang*

**tub (laundry)** *batiya'*

**tube** *tubu₁*

**tube wrench** *liyabe-tubu*

**tuber** *tuwad*

**tuberculosis** *saki-titis*; *tibi*

**tuck (pleat)** *la'up 1*

**Tuesday** *Salasa*

**tuft (of hair)** *punjung₁*

**tufts (decorative)** *jambu 1*

**tug a line** *sintak 2*; *hagtu'*

**tug at** *ganggut*; *ga'ut*; *hangku'*

**tug-of-war** *pagguyud*; *paggo'on-go'on*

**tumbling down** *lagonos 1*

**tumors** *ikat 1*; *bongol 1*; *bago' 1*; *bogon₁ 1*

**tuna species** *sobad*; *pidjalan*; *gelle-gelle*; *ganta'an₂*; *poyan*; *panit*

**tuneful** *lu'uy₁ 1*

**tunes** *lagunahan*; *hanay-hanay*; *tongkel*

**turban frame** *lakal 1*

**turban shell** *sukkiyan*

**turbans** *sulban 1*; *sahal₂*

**turbid** *lobog 1.1*

**turbulence (of sea)** *goyak 1*; *guyu 1*; *abal 1*

**turkey** *angsa'*

**turkey berry** *talum-palat*

**turmeric** *dulaw*

**turn back towards** *bitung*; *pelleng 1.1*

**turn body** *keyos₁*

**turn bullets aside** *pagkobol 1.1*

**turn deaf ear to** *pabiyal*

**turn down** *sulak₂*

**turn end for end** *pagbuli'-munda'*; *pagbulibud*

**turn face up** *leyak*

**turn food (stir)** *huwal*

**turn head** *lingi' 1*; *pagkesong*; *hīng-hīng*; *keleng*

**turn into oil** *ns'llan 1.1*

**turn one's back on** *pasibukut 1*; *taikut 1*

**turn over** *bīng₁ 1.1*

**turn over and over** *pagda'ub-daya'*; *pagpakkom-leyak*; *pagduleyak*

**turn rope (jump rope)** *kuway*

**turn to (for help)** *lingi' 2*

**turn up (be found)** *tuwa' 2*; *paniya'*

**turn up (of eyes)** *duliyat 1*

**turn upside-down** *pakkom 1.1*

**turning point (in illness)** *si'at*

**turning sour** *bahi*

turquoise *hinu-hinu₁*
turtle catchers *pagtotohongan*
turtles (marine) *bokko'; p'nnu; tohongan; payukan; laggutan*
tusk *tanduk 1*
tuskfish *bukān*
tweezers *himangot 1*
twelve o'clock (noon) *ugtu-llaw*
twelve o'clock (midnight) *tonga'-bahangi*
twenty *duwampū'*
twice *minduwa*
twig *angas; tagay; engas-engas*
twilight *logob-logob; magrib 2; abay-kohap*
twilight blindness *lakap-manuk*
twin *k'mbal*
twine (n) *lubid 1; bannang*
twinge *kurat*
twinkle *singlab; kitaw-kitaw*
twist (causing pain) *kobet 1.2*
twist (in multiple ways) *pagbunt'lled*
twist (to remove water) *piyut*
twist and turn *pagkulallit*

twist around *lebod 1; kokos₁ 1*
twist dough *kolleng*
twist ears *kinbing*
twist together *lubid 1.1; pinsal 1.1; gakit*
twist words *tabid lling*
twisted (of mouth) *kiyu'; kibi'; tabid bowa'*
twisted out of shape *tabid₁ 1; pagpiyut*
twists and turns (of road) *kabeklo'an*
twitch *kidjut; k'bbut; pagkirut-kirut*
two *duwa 1*
two (of people) *duwangan 1*
two nights ago *bahangi-dibuhi'; bahangi-di'ilaw*
two possibilities *dalam-duwa; sarap-duwa; duwa-abana*
two-faced *pagduwa-bayhu'*
two-up (game) *pagkabit; hīs-da'ug*
two-wheeled carts *karita'*
tying material (from plants) *sanggi' 1; bamban₂; tangsi'₁ 1*
type (v) *taep*
typewriter *pagsulatan*
typhoon *badju*

# U u

udder *duru' 1*
ugly *seme'*
ugly person *amu' taral*
ulcerated *buntu'₁ 1.1*
ulcers *obe' 1; upāng 1; dugsul 1; bakokang*
ultimate (n) *to'ongan-to'ongan*
ultimate (power) *sangat kawasa*
ultimate (stage; phase) *kasangka'an*
umbilical cord *kowet*
umbrella *payung*
unable to focus *pagbōng*
unacceptable (a reject) *suggang*
unaccompanied *dangan-dangan 1; hāl-hāl*
unalloyed *porol; lahasiya' 1*
unassuming *deyo'₃ 1*
unaware *lipat₂; lilap*
unbalanced *pagkamihu; baligbig; pagkamigmig*
unbelievable *tingga' dawa*
unbeliever *munapik; kapil 1*
unbelieving *jakki 1*
unbiased *timbang bibitan*
unbroken (of cloud) *timbakkol*
uncared for (neglected) *kuligi'₁ 1.1; lonseng 1; sumadja; patabak*
uncaring *pasagad; tigman*
unceasing *sigi-sigi 1; tinoro-toro*

uncertain *pagduwa-pikilan; untung₂; hawal 1.1; pagduwa-ruwa 1*
uncertain (of outcome) *dalam-duwa; llum-patay 1.1*
unchanging *taptap 1; taggu₁*
uncircumcised *kapil 1*
uncle *si'it; bapa' 1*
unclean *l'mmi' 1.1*
unclean (ritually) *batal; haram 1.1*
unclear (re action) *subahat₂ 1.1*
uncoil *badbad 1*
uncomfortable *lingas₁ 1; limayu'*
uncomfortably hot *lingo'ot; hangat*
uncommon *lahang; bislang 1; bihang₂*
uncompromising *tuwas-pentol*
unconcerned *mbal pamagay*
unconscious *lipat₂; bawis₁*
unconstrained (free) *limaya*
uncontrolled desire *napsu kabasi'*
unconvinced *sussa'; dusta' 1.1*
uncooked *mata' 1; anok 1*
uncooperative *alod₁; sugat 2; hukaw 1.1; tuwas-kōk*
uncountable *laksa' 1.2; mbal taitung umaw*
uncovered *singkab 1*
undecided *dalam-duwa; sarap-duwa; paguntung-duwa*
undefiled *sussi 1.1; saltun 1*

**undependable** *palta; baldapat*
**under (location)** *deyo'₁ 1*
**under cover** *paghidjab*
**under water** *lonob 1*
**undergarment** *gamis*
**undergo** *labay₃*
**undergrowth** *kasob; sagbot 1*
**underline** *gudlis 1*
**underneath** *salud 1*
**undershirts** *kamisita; saklay*
**understand** *hati 1.1*
**understand language** *pagsabut*
**understanding** *nahu 1; panghati*
**understood** *klaro*
**undertaker** *panday 1*
**under-water world** *alam deyo'*
**underwear** *sanyawa; kansinsilyu; kullat; kudji-kudji; kindut*
**undesirable** *la'at 1*
**undiverted** *tukid 1*
**undivided** *pono'-pono'; tibu'uk₁ 1.1*
**undo** *buklas₂ 1.1*
**undo knot** *kka 1.1; hubad*
**undress** *hurus 1.1*
**undulating (hilly)** *pagbīd-bīd*
**uneasy** *lensa; lingas₁ 1*
**uneducated** *balig*
**unending** *sapaya-paya*
**unequal** *pagbidda'*
**unequaled** *mbal muwat*
**uneven (of lengths)** *tokon 1*
**uneven (of shape)** *pagbalibag; tempang*
**uneven share** *bahagi'-buyung; bahagi'-tempang 1*
**uneven surface** *l'bbak 1.1; pagbigguwal*
**unexpectedly** *taggaha'; patagha'; pagsamba-samba*
**unfair (division)** *bahagi'-buyung; bahagi'-tempang 1*
**unfaithful (to spouse)** *liyu-lakad*
**unfastened** *puklas 1*
**unfeeling** *atay-batu*
**unfocused** *bōng; pagtunggang-kīng*
**unfold** *b'llat 1.1; badbad 1.1*
**unforgiving** *atay-batu*
**unforgotten** *buling-bata' 1*
**unfortunate** *piyurus₂; pawas 1.1*
**unfortunately** *arakala'*
**unfresh** *buntu'₁ 1; baguy*
**unfriendly** *b'ngngis 1*
**unfurl** *p'kkal 1.1; badbad 1.1*
**ungenerous** *k'mmit 1; giging; sumil₁; kudkud; kigit; kussil; kaikit₁*
**ungrammatical** *b'ggod*
**ungrudging** *hilas*
**unheard of** *la'in-la'in; saddī-saddī; mahal-mahal*
**unhelpful** *kussil*

**unhindered** *limaya*
**unhusked rice** *buwas-pai*
**unicornfish** *kumay*
**uniform (clothing)** *hakos*
**uniform (of color)** *telnos 1; l'nnas*
**unimaginable** *mbal tasipat; mbal manjari; mahal₁*
**uninformed** *awam*
**uninhabited** *tannay-tannay; t'nnaw-t'nnaw 1*
**unintentional** *samba 1.1; sambut 1.1; sabat₂*
**uninterrupted** *langkit 1.1; sangdan 1.1; sara*
**unique** *porol; tunggal 1; luggiya'*
**unit (counting)** *solag 2; pū'₂*
**unite** *pagbagimbin; timbul*
**unite in marriage** *pagtimbul; pagpūn₂; dakayu'₃*
**unite sexually** *pagā' 2*
**united** *dakayu'₂ 1; tindan-tindan*
**united (decision; goal)** *pagtayakkup 1; pagtayudtud*
**units (military)** *kompolan; padjuhan; panjihan; kompani*
**unity** *kapagdakayu'; katibu'ukan*
**universal** *saplag 1*
**universe** *alam₁*
**unkempt** *gosang-gosang; gumun; larang*
**unkind** *b'ngngis 1; sikla*
**unlash sail ropes** *tustus*
**unlawful** *langgal sara' 1; haram 1*
**unleash** *pabūy; l'ppa*
**unless** *luwal*
**unload** *hawas*
**unlucky** *piyurus₂; pawas 1.1; bilsut*
**unmarried** *la'un 1*
**unnoticed** *tinangkaw; m'mmong*
**unperturbed** *haggut atay; handok atay 1*
**unpick (stitching)** *b'ttas*
**unpleasant** *la'at 1*
**unpleasing (of voice)** *lagaw*
**unpopulated** *tannay-tannay; t'nnaw-t'nnaw 1; l'ngngaw-l'ngngaw*
**unpredictable** *paglepet*
**unprofitable** *lussung; lapis₅*
**unprotected** *pilluwang₂ 2*
**unravel** *b'ttas*
**unraveled** *putal*
**unready (in game)** *du-bilang*
**unreliable** *palsu; palta; baldapat; lepet*
**unrequited love** *pagkonsemisun*
**unreservedly** *hilas; lilla'*
**unresolved** *gantung₁; limogmog 1*
**unrestricted** *limaya; luhaya*
**unripe** *mata' 1*
**unroll** *badbad 1.1*
**unruly** *la'ug 1*
**unsatisfactory** *la'in-la'in; saddī-saddī*
**unsawn timber** *hanglad 1*

**unseeing** *bulikat; legsok₂*

**unseen beings** *magl'l'ngngan; duwata 1; kokok 1; saitan*

**unseparated** *pono'-pono'; tibu'uk₁ 1*

**unsettle (v)** *gabla'*

**unsettled (of community)** *dongkag; lengog 1.1*

**unsettled (of location)** *pagleyat-leyat; tagestes; lagedled 1*

**unsettled (of mind)** *kabid atay; hengo-hengo*

**unsheathe** *hublut 2*

**unsheltered** *tampalan*

**unskilled** *hāw-hāw 2*

**unsociable** *sandol 1*

**unstable** *lenggang; oseg 1; hodjog 1; hengko*

**unsteady** *lumintiyad; paglensa*

**unstitched** *bintas; tastas₂ 1*

**unsure** *kawang; paguntung-duwa*

**unsurpassed** *mbal taliyu*

**unswayed by argument** *taggu₂ 1*

**untamed** *adla*

**untangled** *usay 1*

**untaught** *akil-balig; balig*

**unteachable** *b'llod; tuwas-pentol*

**unthinkable** *mbal tasipat; lulus para'akkal*

**untidy** *kuligi'₁ 1.1; bulaksay 1*

**untidy (of hair)** *larang*

**untie** *kka 1.1; hubad*

**untied** *latas₁; puklas 1; kka 1*

**until** *sambil; sampay 1*

**until when?** *tobtob sumiyan*

**untrue statement** *dusta' 1*

**untrustworthy** *baluba 2*

**untruth** *dusta' 1*

**unusual (different)** *la'in-la'in; saddī-saddī*

**unusual (uncommon)** *lahang; bihang₂*

**unwavering** *togol 1*

**unwell** *la'at palasahan; saki 1.1*

**unwilling** *alod₁; hukaw 1.1*

**unwind** *badbad 1*

**unworried** *mbal pamagay; limaya*

**unwrinkled** *tukad₂*

**unyielding** *sandat 2; k'llas 1.1; atay-batu*

**up** *diyata' 1*

**up and down** *paghuntak; pagumbaw-umbaw*

**up to** *sambil; sampay 1; taman*

**upbringing** *suligan*

**upend** *sulalla*

**uphill** *tukad₁ 1*

**upland farm** *huma*

**upper canoe planks** *bangkat sa'am*

**upper limit** *ta'as 1; diyuhan*

**upper point** *puntuk; pussuk 1*

**upright (of character)** *hāp 1.1; bontol 1*

**upright (of position)** *punduk 1.1; togang*

**uproar** *kasasawan; hengo-hengo; halubilu; lengog 1*

**uproot** *tugnus₁ 1.1; hublut 2*

**uprooted** *pungkad*

**upset (emotional)** *mandā'-dā'; pagsorol; hansul atay; bakat atay*

**upside down** *baliskat 1; bīng₁ 1; pakkom 1*

**upstairs**

**upstream** *diyata'an₁ 1; dauhat₂ 1*

**upstream side (of house)** *sibayan; kōkan 1*

**upward slope** *tukaran*

**upwards** *pariyata'*

**urchin (sea)** *tehe'-tehe'*

**urge (to fight each other)** *papagbulang*

**urge (v)** *logos 1; dūk₁; egot-egot; panhot*

**urge caution** *dō*

**urge diligence** *amay-amay 1.1; ebot-ebot 1.1; hubaya-hubaya*

**urgent** *sa'ut 1*

**urgently** *dai'-dai' 1.2*

**urinary complaint** *kaukati 1.1; kima-kima*

**urinate; urine** *mange' 1.1*

**urine smell** *p'ngngak; bau p'llut; p'llut₁*

**us** *kami; kita; kitam*

**use (n)** *kalagihan 1; kapunyahan; guna 1*

**use (v)** *usal; tajari; guna 1.1*

**use another's gear** *tungkap₂ 1*

**use caution** *halli'₁ 1*

**use sparingly** *pagdangkuri'*

**use to full extent** *lakay*

**use up rapidly** *duwasay₁*

**use witchcraft** *sihil 1.1*

**used to (accustomed)** *biyaksa 1*

**used up** *hagin 1; pupud 1.1; puspus₂; katis₁ 1*

**used up rapidly** *dalas 1*

**usefulness** *pūs; guna 1*

**usual; usually** *maumu; heka min heka; masuhul*

**usurp** *longpos; agaw 1.1*

**ute (vehicle)** *tarāk*

**utensils** *kapanyapan*

**uterus** *kandang; kuta'-kuddarat*

**utopia** *paliyama'*

**utter (v)** *sambat; h'lling₁ 1.1; k'bbat₁ 1; mūng; bissala 1.1*

**utter curse** *kata'*

**utter darkness** *lendom bitu-bituhan*

**utterance** *hilala'ungan; batbatan; lapal 1*

**utterly** *katūyan; latus-lagbas*

**uvula** *d'llang-d'llang*

# V v

vacant *tannay-tannay*; *t'nnaw-t'nnaw 1*
vaccinate *langgit 1*
vacillate *pagsōng-sebog*
vacillation *hawal 1*
vacuum (emptiness) *gaunggang*
vagabond *pagsampig-manampig*; *pagkamundal-mandil*
vagina *puki*
vagrant *pagkamundal-mandil*
vague *abu-abu₂*
valid *taddang*; *tunay₁*
valley *l'bbak 1*
valor *esog 1*
valuables *barang*
value (worth) *pūs*; *halga' 1*; *guna 1*
value someone *paidda*
valued *heya ma atay*
valueless *buwangkan*
vampire *balbalan*
vanish *talbang 1.1*; *lanyap 1.1*; *telop 1.1*; *pagtawap*
vanished *lungay 1*; *lanyap 1*; *liyaw 1*
vapor *husbu 1*; *asu-asu 1*
variant *pagbidda'an*
variegated *kabang 1.1*
varieties *kaginisan*
various *indalupa 1*
vary (differ) *bidda' 1.2*
vast (amount) *parat*
vast (area) *kasaplagan*
vast (number) *kamaheka'an*
vault *kuddaman*
veer *p'llay 1*; *kabig*; *biluk 1*
vegetables *legotoman*; *sayul 1*
vegetation *paltubu-tubuhan 1*; *paltomo'-tomo'an*
vehicles *pameya'an₁*; *pahinggaman*
veil *hidjab*
vein *ugat 1*
vendor (regular) *suki'*
venerated *mulliya 1.1*
venereal disease *saki-dayang*
venomous *bisa 1*
venture *pagpasukud*; *pagpasamba*
Venus comb (shell) *sudlay-sudlay*
veracious *pasti'₁*
verandah *balkon*; *pantān*
verbal contest *pagagaw-bissala*
verdant *libombo'*
verdict *hukuman*; *sara' 1*
verify *paliksa'*; *nyata' 1.1*

vermin *binatang₁*; *kagaw*
verse *ayat*
vertigo *baliyang*
very *to'od*; *to'ongan 1.1*; *sidda 1*
very different *tā bidda'*
very much *landu'₂ 1*
vessel (copper) *tumbaga 2*
vessel (naval) *nabal*
vessels (sailing) *sappit₂*; *balanda'₁*; *parangkang*
vestments *gamis*; *luku*
vexed *kalintaw*
viand *lauk 1*
vibrate *tandog 2*
vice *daiyus*
victimise *la'ug 1.1*
victims *lanas 1*
victory *da'ugan*
victuals *balanja' 1*
view *lundug 1.1*
vigil *pagjaga 1.1*
vigilant *ulip*
vigor *anggauta'*; *kuwat*
vigorous *kuyas 1*; *paslod 1.1*; *sigla' 1.1*; *pakosog*
vigorously *sikad 1*
village *kampung₂*; *kaluma'an*; *baranggay*; *kaum*
village-mates *lūng 1*
vinegar *suka'*; *binegal*
vines (generic) *bahan 1*
violate taboo *pa'in₃ 1*
violent *patibono'*; *pasu' atay*
violet (color) *taluk*
violin *biyula 1*
viper *sowa-d'ppong*
virgin *budjang*
virility *kapagl'lla 1*; *basi'₂ 1*; *anggauta'*
virtuous *hāp 1.1*
Visayan *Bisaya' 2*
viscera *tina'i*
viscous *pīt*; *pagtagok*; *k'ddot*
vise-grip pliers *plaes tuka'-agap*
visible *tuwa' 1*; *bulat*; *lahil 1*
visible *laman 1*; *pagsagiyaw*; *manyatakan*
visible (appear to) *ta'nda' mata*; *nda' 1*
visible proof *baynat*
vision *palambung*; *palihalan 2*; *mata₁ 1.1*
vision defect *lamun 1*
visit *tuwa' 2*; *tibaw 1.1*; *liyud*
visit en route *hapit₁ 1*

**visit relatives (of child)** *patuwa'*
**visit repeatedly** *pagkulatay*
**visit without purpose** *tulaga'*
**visitor** *bisita 1; tibaw 1; luruk 1*
**visitor room** *salas*
**visualize** *laman 1.1*
**vocalize grief** *pagsindilan 1*
**vocation** *usaha 1*
**voice (n)** *lagam; suwala 1*
**voice (v)** *k'bbat₁ 1*
**voice box** *buwa'-jakkum; batang-k'llong*
**voice opinion** *batak₁; upamakun 1.1*
**voice suspicion** *tuhuma 1.1*
**voiceless** *kamal; kohot*
**volleyball** *balebol*
**voluble** *bowa'-bowa'*

**volume (measure of)** *gantang; pansing 1*
**volutes** *binga'; kūs-kūs 1*
**vomit (v)** *utta' 1*
**vomiting** *bo'ay*
**vote** *pagmoto*
**vow (religious)** *suhud 1; najal 1; baljanji' 1*
**vow (v)** *kallam 1; subali 1; wa'ad; pagsapa 1*
**vowel marks** *baris*
**voyage** *busayan*
**vulgar (behavior)** *sabul 1.1*
**vulgar person** *paglaban 1*
**vulgar speech** *la'at bowa'*
**vulgarity** *lu'ug-lama' 1*
**vulnerability** *pilluwang₂ 1*
**vulnerable spot** *katubagan*
**vulva** *puki*

# W w

**wad (v)** *loko' 1*
**wade** *kapo' 1; ubug₁ 1*
**wading birds** *pa'imping; ellog*
**waffle** *apam 1*
**waft** *hangsu 1.1*
**wag (v)** *pagkotek-kotek; paglabad 1.1*
**wager** *panaluhan; to'on₁ 1.1*
**wages** *gadji 1*
**wagon** *karita'*
**wail** *paglemong 1.1; pagdohon*
**waist** *hawakan*
**waist-band** *sambung₂*
**wait for** *lanti-lanti; langay; lagad 1.2; tagad*
**waiter** *magbubuhat*
**waiting time** *pangawal*
**wake (for dead)** *pagjaga 1.1*
**wake (of boat)** *sahal₁ 1*
**wake energetically** *bukaskas*
**wake fully** *buliyang*
**wakeful** *gesong*
**waken** *pukaw; bati'₁ 1*
**wakwak (vampire)** *paguwak-uwak*
**walk** *baklay; pasiyal; l'ngngan₁ 1.1; lunsul 1*
**walk aimlessly** *paglanyaw*
**walk along bridge** *taytay 1; lete*
**walk along edge** *bihing-bihing*
**walk around Kaaba stone** *tawap₁*
**walk quickly** *podjong*
**walk with arms/wings out** *saligsig₁*
**walked on** *pang'ddikan*
**walker for child** *andarol*
**walkers (spirit beings)** *magl'l'ngngan*

**walking sticks** *bastun; tungkud 1*
**walkways (elevated)** *taytayan; letehan*
**walkways (paths)** *pal'ngnganan; kalān-lānan*
**wall** *dinding 1*
**wall (gable)** *sūngan*
**wall (top plate)** *taytayan tikus*
**walled city** *kuta'₁ 1*
**wallet** *pitaka*
**walling** *tiyadtad*
**wallop** *walup*
**wallow** *loblob*
**wan (pale)** *pusiyat; lospad*
**wander (with no purpose)** *pagsampig-manampig; pagkambuyan; paglunsul; pagjambeyaw*
**wane** *diki' 1.1; kō' 1.1*
**waning (of moon)** *kōpan*
**want something** *bilahi 1.1; baya' 1.1*
**wanton** *ga'ira*
**war** *pagbono' 1*
**war of words** *pagagaw-bissala*
**ward against evil** *tambang₃ 1.1*
**ward off** *tangkis 1.1.1*
**warehouse** *borega*
**wares** *dagangan*
**warm (of temperature)** *pasu'₁ 1.1*
**warm (symptom)** *limasu' 1.1*
**warm oneself** *dama 1; tapa 1.1; dangka₂ 1; dangu 1*
**warn** *hansom; babal₂; banda'; sanggup*
**warn (of consequences)** *sugpak 1.1*
**warning (omen)** *nasa*
**warp beam (loom)** *bibitan*
**warped** *kalluk 1; bengkok 1; lompeng 1*
**warrior** *bobono'*

**wart** *tangkekel 1*
**wary** *l'ppi; adla; insap; halli'₁ 1*
**wash (body)** *pandi 1*
**wash (ceremonially)** *ail*
**wash (clothes)** *dakdak 1*
**wash (from waves)** *sahal₁ 1*
**wash (general)** *kose'*
**wash (part of)** *kimu'*
**washbasin** *batiya'*
**washer (engineering)** *kusing*
**wasps** *lampinig; kabulig*
**waste (n)** *s'ggit 1*
**waste (v)** *paka'at*
**wasted (regrettably)** *kaliman; kaugun*
**wasted away** *ilu'₁ 1*
**wasteful** *kalla'₁; duwasay₁; koro-koro 1*
**wasting disease** *tibi*
**watch** *mata₁ 1.2*
**watch (timepiece)** *lilus*
**watch (v)** *lawan; jaga 1.2; nda'-nda'*
**watch closely** *patong 1; pa'aro'-aro'*
**watch out (danger)** *piligdu 1*
**watch out for (avoid)** *kamaya'; llog 1.1*
**watch over** *jaga 1.2; peyan; tunggu' 1.1; payu; alimata*
**watchful** *l'ppi; halli'₁ 1.1; insap*
**watching (looking at)** *t'ntong₂; nda'-nda'*
**watchman (guard)** *jaga 1*
**watchtower** *pamantawan*
**water** *bohe'₁ 1*
**water (of eyes)** *lihing*
**water bindweed** *kangkung*
**water buffalo** *kalbaw 1*
**water container** *galon 1*
**water jars** *poga; kibut; pipa; ka'ang; tanāng; tangpad*
**water lettuce** *kayapo'*
**water plants (v)** *busug 1*
**water source** *tuburan; pagbohe'an*
**water storage** *galon 1*
**watermelon** *timun*
**waterpipe** *tubu₁*
**waters (birthing)** *panubigan*
**waterspout** *buhawi'₂ 1; boto'-boto'₁*
**wattles (of rooster)** *label*
**wave (signal)** *lambe₁ 1.1; sayang₂*
**wave (to and fro)** *paglabad 1.1*
**wave arms** *kambay 1*
**wave in wind** *k'llay-k'llay*
**waver (between choices)** *duwa-ruwa*
**waver (of light)** *pagpillaw-pillaw; pagsiraw-siraw*
**waves** *kata'-kata'; goyak 1*
**wavy (of blade shape)** *seko' 1*
**wax (n)** *lansuk*
**wax gourd (n)** *kundul*

**way forward (opportunity)** *dapat₂*
**way of life** *kal'ngnganan 1*
**way through** *labayan*
**waylay** *hapa' 1.2; holdap*
**we (excl)** *kami*
**we (incl dual)** *=ta 1; kita*
**we (incl pl)** *kitam; =tam*
**weak** *s'nnay; halam ugat; kapuy; pasaw*
**weakened** *loyot; longkoy; lamma 1; labba'₂ 1; komay*
**weakness** *lamma 2; logmay 1*
**wealth** *kaniya'; ai-ai 2; alta' 1*
**wealth (from trade)** *pagsauragal 1*
**wealthy** *haldaya; daya; balkan; mayaman*
**wean** *lutas; butas 1.1*
**weapons** *hinanib 1; takos 1; pangatu; almas*
**wear (v)** *pakay₁; s'mmek 1.1*
**wear anything (affixes)** *mag-..-in-*
**wear dentures (false teeth)** *pagmalpel*
**wear glasses** *pagsinamin-mata*
**wear mourning clothes** *pagtuwaha'*
**weary** *bale'; paya*
**weather** *mata-langit*
**weave (other than cloth)** *anom; tabanas 1*
**weave awning** *ambung-ambung₂ 1.1*
**weave cloth** *t'nnun; sabit₂; anyam*
**weaving (using twist pattern)** *tabid₂; maligay₂ 1; huyap-huyap 1*
**weaving fibre (n)** *eto'-eto'*
**web (on fin)** *ebed-ebed*
**web-covered** *sāng-lawa'*
**wed** *kawin 1*
**wedding** *pagkawin 1*
**wedding fee** *batu-kawin; talmal*
**wedding stages** *pagpal'ngngan 1; tingkuwang; tagad-kawin; paghulay*
**wedge (n)** *tanok 1*
**wedge into** *alod₂ 1.1; sipsip; s'llot 1.1*
**wedge under** *biggal 1.2; s'ngngal; pahanggal*
**wedlock** *paglakibini*
**Wednesday** *Alba'a*
**weed (saltwater)** *tai'-unas*
**weed (v)** *suwat; lapa₂*
**weed-covered** *sagbot 1.2*
**weeding tool** *susuwat*
**weeds** *sagbot 1*
**week (unit of time)** *pitu'an*
**weep over** *alud₂; paglemong 1.1; pagdohon*
**weigh down** *tahan₂ 1.1; doson 1.1; dopon*
**weigh things** *timbang₁ 1*
**weigh up (evaluate)** *kumpas₁; bista₁; kira-kira*
**weigh up options** *pagpende*
**weight (diving)** *tingga'*
**weight (of something)** *buhat₁ 1*
**weight (sinker)** *butun₁*

**weight (unit of 45 kgs)** *pikul 2*
**weights (of beam scale)** *batu-timbang*
**welcome (formal)** *puli-bahasa*
**welcome someone** *abang; sagina*
**well (health)** *salamat₁*
**well (n)** *k'ppong*
**well (thoroughly)** *to'od; pahāp₁; to'ongan 1.1*
**well (water)** *pagbohe'an*
**well known** *bantug 1.1*
**well now** *ahā*
**well up (of water)** *tubud 1*
**well used (worn out)** *ndang; longa'*
**well-arranged** *tuntul 1*
**well-behaved** *hatul₂; p'mpon 1; hongpot; pantun 1*
**well-being** *salamat-baran; kasalamatan; sajahitra'*
**well-born** *balbangsa; bangsa₂*
**well-cooked** *baska 1; laga'₁ 1*
**well-developed** *sambu 1; jatu 1*
**well-mannered** *addat 1.1*
**well-off** *haldaya; alta' 1.1; sayuman; daya*
**well-rounded** *littub*
**well-taught** *bi'at 1*
**well-used** *bahal; longa'*
**welt** *bintul*
**wen** *tangkekel 1*
**west** *s'ddopan 1*
**Westerner** *Milikan*
**wet** *tomog; bahug 1; bugbug₁; base'₁*
**wet (from driving rain)** *tampiyas 1*
**wet through** *gamos 1; bugga' 1*
**whack** *daplos; lappet*
**whale sharks** *karuhung; t'kke'*
**whales** *gadjamina; layul; kahumbu*
**wharf** *jambatan*
**what else?** *ai lagi'*
**what for?** *angay; pamagay 1.1*
**what next?** *ai ba*
**what purpose?** *magay*
**what relationship?** *pag-ai*
**what?** *ai; ingga*
**whatever** *ai na ka; ai bang ai; ai-ai 1; ya ai*
**what's more** *lāgi*
**whatsit** *anu 1*
**wheat** *tirigu 1; pai-tirigu*
**wheels** *silikan; tape'₁*
**wheeze** *h'lling-k'llong; paghagak*
**whelk** *lambi'*
**when (later)** *bo'₃; bang₁; baya-baya pa'in; basta*
**when (past)** *bo' na*
**when X** *ingga na*
**when?** *sumiyan*
**whenever** *abila; tiyap-tiyap; sumiyan-sumiyan*
**where from?** *minningga*
**where to?** *pi'ingga*

**where?** *maingga; ma'ai; ingga*
**whereas** *malaingkan*
**wherever** *maingga-maingga; ma'ai-ma'ai; pi'ingga-pi'ingga*
**whet** *gīl; gisgis 1.1; asa'*
**whether** *ai na ka; ka₂*
**whether this or that** *na ka..na ka; ai..ai*
**whetstone** *asa'an*
**which?** *ai; ingga*
**whichever** *ingga-ingga; sasuku*
**while** *sasang; pa'in₁; pasalta'; baba; sabu 1*
**whimper** *langan₁*
**whine** *pagle'eng*
**whip (v)** *balubak; daplos; lubak₁*
**whirling** *pusal₁ 1*
**whirlpool** *buliluk*
**whirlwind** *buhawi'₂ 1; alimpunus; boto'-boto'₁*
**whirring sound** *tagenseng*
**whisk away** *hemos 1.1*
**whiskers** *bū-langal; misay 1; janggut 2; janggut 1*
**whisky** *alak*
**whisper** *singu'-singu'; hagas-hagas; higung-higung*
**whistle (n)** *pilik-pilik 2*
**whistle (v)** *taghuy 1; mita*
**white** *pote' 1*
**white (of eye)** *esok-mata*
**white ant** *anay*
**white gold** *bulawan-pote'*
**white sands** *kapote'an*
**whitecaps (waves)** *hisi'*
**whiten** *limuti'*
**whiten skin** *lipa'*
**whiting (smelt)** *suruk-punsu; tangbod*
**whitlow (finger infection)** *nilastung*
**whittle (into shape)** *basbas*
**whittle down** *pariki'*
**whizzing sound** *tagenseng*
**who knows?** *daka*
**who?; whom?; whose?** *sai*
**whoever** *sai-sai; ingga sasuku; sasuku*
**whole** *tibu'uk₁ 1; pono'-pono'*
**wholehearted** *lilla'; hilas*
**wholesale** *pakkiyaw; tighan 1.1*
**whoop** *olang 1*
**whore** *puta; sundal 1*
**whorl (cowlick)** *pusal₂; ebod*
**whosit** *anu 1*
**why not!** *he' angay*
**why?** *magay; angay*
**wick** *sumbuhan*
**wide** *lambu 1.1; lampo' 1*
**widely known** *hula-layag 1; bantug 1.1; tanyag 1; talhakit 1*
**widely visible** *saplag 1*

**widely spaced** *lanta'; lamba₁; jalang₂*

**wide-meshed** *aslag₂ 2*

**widen** *paluha*

**widen (gap)** *kiyap*

**widen eyes** *d'llag 1; kaniyang-kaniyang*

**wider kin group** *pagkaheka'an 1; sugsugan*

**widespread** *latag 1; jadja' 1; saplag 1*

**widow; widower** *balu 1*

**widow's cap** *turung-balu 1*

**width** *lambu 1; lambahan; luha 1*

**wield power or authority** *pagkawasa*

**wife** *h'nda*

**wife (senior)** *h'nda-po'on*

**wild (untamed)** *adla*

**wild almond** *kaumpang*

**wild basil** *luku-luku*

**wild ginger** *tagbak₂*

**wild raspberry** *sampinit*

**wild taro** *padjang*

**will (n)** *kabaya'an*

**will of God** *kahandak 1*

**willing** *hungun; kuhi₁ 1; bilahi 1.1*

**willingly** *lilla'*

**willow-leafed justicia** *salimbangun*

**wilted; wilting** *layu; luyluy; lanos₁*

**wily** *taha'-akkal*

**win (a contest)** *longkop 1; da'ug*

**win (affection)** *pa'anggi*

**win (favor)** *pagmamhu'*

**win (n)** *panganda'ug*

**wind** *baliyu 1*

**wind (adverse)** *simpal*

**wind (astern)** *tūd₁ 1*

**wind (from land)** *dalat*

**wind (offshore)** *balat-daya*

**wind (source)** *mata-baliyu*

**wind instrument** *tiyup-tiyup; torottot*

**wind onto spool** *koleng₁ 1.1; lengke; longon*

**wind shadow** *limbu 1*

**winded (breathless)** *puha; hapus₂; lumu*

**winder (of watch)** *waen 1*

**winding (road)** *pagbeklo'*

**winding about** *kulengkong 1*

**window** *tandawan*

**windpipe** *gonggongan*

**wind-tossed** *buhawi'₂ 1.1*

**windy season** *pamaliyu*

**wine** *alak; binu*

**winged horse** *sambalani; galura'*

**wings** *kepet₁; kidjang 1*

**wink (v)** *kiddat₁*

**winnow** *pansi; tahap*

**winnowing basket** *ligu 1*

**wipe buttocks** *peppet*

**wipe clean** *timud 1*

**wipe off** *pahid 1.1; kukus*

**wipe on** *peged₁ 1; sapu 1*

**wipe out (destroy)** *laglag 1.1*

**wipe up** *tarapu 1.1; pu'us; kulling*

**wiping cloth** *tarapu 1*

**wire** *basi'-basi'; kowat*

**wire (electric)** *korente 1*

**wire netting** *alambre*

**wiry (sinewy)** *kaslog*

**wisdom** *pangita'u; panghati*

**wisdom tooth** *empon talus*

**wise** *taha'-akkal*

**wise person** *barakkal 1; auliya'*

**wise saying** *papata 1.2*

**wishing that** *kaddaw; mura-murahan*

**witchcraft** *hinang-hinang₁; pantak 1.1*

**with** *maka₂; ma 1*

**with care** *agak-agak; kamaya'-maya' 1*

**with effort** *pakosog*

**with gusto** *kuseseyang 1*

**with reference to** *takdil*

**withdraw** *suhut; sebog; singga-singga*

**withdraw into** *l'llok 1; loklok*

**withdrawn (shy)** *t'mmun; sandol 1*

**withered** *luyluy; lanos₁*

**withhold permission** *paggat*

**within** *mindeyom*

**without a pause** *pagambat-ambat 1; pagsungbul-sungbul*

**without delay** *sa'ut 1*

**without fail** *hubaya-hubaya*

**without hesitation** *halam baya'*

**withstand (endure)** *tatas 1.2; sandal 1.1; tahan-tahan*

**witness (n)** *saksi' 1; sakup₁ 1*

**wizard** *auliya'*

**wobble** *oseg 1.1; oyo'-oyo'*

**wobbly** *hodjog 1; jogjog 1; h'bbol*

**woe** *arūy*

**woman** *d'nda 1*

**womanize** *pagd'nda 2*

**womb** *kandang; kuta'-kuddarat; kulun*

**womenfolk** *kar'ndahan*

**wonder at** *inu-inu 1.1*

**wonderful** *inu-inu 1.2; pagmudjidjat*

**woo** *pagtunang*

**wood (timber)** *kayu 2*

**woodborer** *bukbuk 1; tambelok 1*

**wooden slippers** *bakiya'₁*

**woollen blanket** *manta bulbulan*

**woolly** *bulbul 1.1*

**word** *kabtangan; h'lling₁ 1*

**word of God** *palman 1*

**words (significant)** *hilala'ungan; himumūngan*
**words only** *kak'bbatan bowa'*
**wordy** *bowa'-bowa'; heka bowa'*
**work** *hinang₁ 1*
**work (as a fleet)** *pagabay 1.1*
**work (as a group)** *sah'mpu; umpig*
**work (as porter)** *kalga*
**work (for a living)** *usaha 1*
**work clay (to shape)** *tampa 1*
**work clothes** *paghinumag 1*
**work diligently** *togol 1.1; mikakkul*
**work group** *passuk*
**work hard** *pagsangsā'; pagbinasag*
**work in pairs** *pagumbuk*
**work metal** *sasal*
**work together** *pagtaku-taku 1; pagsandu; pagsama-sama 1.1*
**workable** *manjari₁ 2*
**workbench (anvil)** *landasan 1*
**working bee** *passuk; pagdangin*
**workmates** *salimbang; abay₁ 1; pagbeya'*
**workshop** *kamalig*
**world** *alam₁; dunya*
**world above sea level** *alam diyata'*
**world below** *alam deyo'*
**world to come** *kandang ahirat*
**worms** *kalog 1; sassing 1*
**worn by use** *t'ttok 1*
**worn down** *linis; litib; pupud 1.1*
**worn out (of clothes)** *garus; bahal; p'ddut; gores 1*
**worn out (of people)** *paya; pilay*
**worn out (of things)** *basak; ndang*
**worried; worry** *limbit 1.1; susa 1.1; pagpamagay 1*
**worse and worse** *duhun manduhun*
**worsen (degree)** *tungkap₁; duhun 1*
**worsen (of sickness)** *jari₂*
**worship** *sambahayang; s'mba 1; arap*
**worship house** *langgal₁*
**worth** *halga' 1; guna 1*
**worthless person** *pamahadja' 1; kaliyagge'*
**worthless thing** *tai'-ulangan; mutallak; tai'-ero'*
**would that** *bang pa'in*
**wound (injury)** *pali' 1; bakat 1*
**wound (of line)** *koleng₁ 1.1*
**wound deeply** *sampa'*

**wound with blade** *lagut*
**wound with pole** *sundak 1.1*
**wounded** *bu'ag; halol*
**woven container** *tambusa'; baluyut*
**woven panel (walling)** *sairing 1; salirap; saisig*
**wow!** *elle'-elle'; ayī*
**wrap (v)** *putus 1.2*
**wrap around** *lekos 1.2; okos*
**wrap around head** *porong*
**wrap in cloth** *bungkus 1; lampin₂ 1.1*
**wrap in paper** *kustal 1.1*
**wrapped** *k'mmos 1; k'bbot 1; p'kkos 1*
**wrapper** *putus 1*
**wrapping paper** *banggala; katas-banggala*
**wrasses** *gellok; tallad; pullay 1; balling; kāt; lampek; sipit-sipit₃; pellok; lās-lās; banggud 1; maming 1; bulakka₁; bukay-bukay*
**wrath (divine)** *mulka' 1*
**wrecked** *ka'at 1.1*
**wrench (tool)** *liyabe*
**wrench (v)** *bubut*
**wrestle (formal competition)** *kuntaw₂; pagsanggul 1.1; pagsabit*
**wrestle over something** *pagagaw; paglutsa; pagkagat 1*
**wrestling** *silat*
**wretch** *binatang₁; hanjing-binatang*
**wretched child!** *anak-sahili'*
**wriggle about** *paghibal-hibal; pagoseg-oseg; paghagul*
**wring out (wet cloth)** *piyut*
**wrinkle (brow)** *pagkonot*
**wrinkle (nose)** *pagh'ngngek-h'ngngek*
**wrinkled (of skin)** *konot₁ 1; killut-killut*
**wrist bones** *bunga-bunga; buku-buku₁*
**wristwatch** *lilus*
**write** *dawat 1.1; sulat 1*
**writhe** *pagsularaw; pagkulallit*
**writhe with pain** *pagsuleret; pagdahagbela'*
**writing** *sulatan*
**writing paper** *katas; papel*
**writing style** *hātan*
**wrong** *sā'₁ 1.1*
**wrong action** *kasā'an*
**wrongly assumed** *laung 1*
**wry (of mouth)** *kiyu'; kibi'; tabid bowa'*

# X x

**xylophone** *gabbang 1*

# Y y

**yacht** *balanda'₁*
**Yahweh (or Jehovah)** *Allahu Ta'ala 2*
**yakal tree** *yakal*
**Yakan people** *Samehakan*
**yam** *ubi*
**yank (v)** *ganggut*
**yard (courtyard)** *halaman*
**yawn** *wapan*
**yaws** *upāng 1*
**year** *tahun 1*
**year after year** *tahun ni tahun; mananahun*
**yearn** *paglindu-dandam*
**yeast** *pasulig*
**yell** *kula'ak; pagsilawak; olang 1*
**yellow** *biyaning 1; kuning; hidjaw*
**yellowed** *baka'₂ 2; garing 1.1*
**yelp** *ūl*
**yes** *aho' 1*
**yesterday** *di'ilaw*
**yesterday afternoon** *kohap-īn*
**yet** *lagi' 1; bo'₁*
**yield (and spring back)** *l'mpet*
**yielding** *p'ssil 1*

**yoke (between animals)** *sa'al*
**yolk** *bulinga*
**yonder** *pē'₁*
**you (plural)** *kām; ka'am*
**you (singular)** *ka'a; kā*
**you don't say!** *dā'₁*
**young** *hoben; bata'*
**young adult** *lumbu'-lumbu'; onde'-baha'u*
**young and old** *onde'-matto'a*
**young man** *subul; onde'-baha'u*
**young people** *kamanahutan*
**young woman** *budjang; onde'-baha'u*
**younger brother, sister** *siyali 1*
**youngest child** *kabungsuhan; katapusan 2*
**your (plural)** *=bi*
**your (singular)** *=nu*
**youth** *subul; onde'-baha'u*
**youthful** *hoben; bata'*
**yowl** *usig*
**yoyo** *baud-baud*
**yoyo toy** *boben 2*
**yuck** *nē*

# Z z

**Zamboanga City** *Sambuwangan*
**Zamboanga City (colloquial)** *Sambo*
**zealous** *togol 1; tuyu' 1*

**zenith** *ugtu 1.1*
**zero (of energy)** *logmay-lamma*
**zigzag (v)** *pagbiluk*

# 3.3 Topical Sinama-English wordlists

## A: Marine species

**akal-bahal** *n.* Black coral. *Cirrhipathes* spp.

**agal-agal** *n.* Edible seaweed. *Gracilaria.*

**aha'an** *n.* Emperor fish (of various kinds). *Lethrinus lentjan.*

**ampahan** *n.* Long-finned cavalla or kingfish. *Carangoides ciliarius.*

**anak-bāt** *n.* Anchovy. *Stolephorus* spp.

**anak-bobohan** *n.* Anemonefish or clownfish. *fam. Pomacentridae.*

**anak-lason** *n.* Clownfishes. *Amphiprion ocellaris (Ocellaris clownfish); A. frenatus (Tomato clownfish).*

**anduhat** *n.* Fusilier fish.

**antugan** *n.* Shark species.

**antu'ang** *n.* Clam species. *Tridachna* sp.

**anupin** *n.* Snapper species. *Lutjanus* spp.

**asang-lumahan** *n.* Various jobfishes. *Aphareus rutilans.*

**babakan** *n.* Various pufferfishes. *fam. Tetraodontidae.*

**baba'an₂** *n.* Spotted pomadasid, a fish species. *Pomadasid* sp.

**babawan** *n.* A species of fish esteemed for its firm white flesh. *fam. Carangidae.*

**babay** *n.* A species of fish (unclassified).

**bakkaw** *n.* Saltwater forest complex.

**bakkid** *n.* Various breams. *Pentapodus setosus; Pentapodus parariseus.*

**baki'** *n.* Striped eel catfish. *Plotosus anguillaris.*

**bakukku** *n.* Harlequin sweetlips (a perch-like fish). *Plectorhynchus chaetodontoides.*

**badjangan** *n.* A species of grouper.

**bagahak-lanus** *n.* Brown-marbled grouper; Blotched rock cod. *Epinephelus fuscoguttatus.*

**bagahak₁** *n.* Various coral fishes.

**bagambul** *n.* Species of shark (unclassified).

**bagangan** *n.* Various breams (Grey large-eye; Gray bare-nose; Blue-lined large-eye). *Gymnocranius griseus; G. robinsonii.*

**baggu'** *n.* Various cowrie species. *Cypreaea* spp.

**baggu'-ettom** *n.* Dark-shelled species of cowrie.

**baggu'-lumpay** *n.* A species of cowrie.

**baggu'-sigay** *n.* A species of cowrie.

**baggungan** *n.* A marine monovalve, edible. *Cerith* sp.

**bagumun** *n.* A marine monovalve, edible. *Cerith* sp.

**bahaba'** *n.* Russell's snapper, a fish species. *Lutjanus russelli.*

**baho'-baho'** *n.* A species of fish (unclassified).

**bā'-bā'an** *n.* A species of fish (unclassified).

**bala-bala** *n.* A species of sea snake (unclassified).

**balambangan** *n.* A species of sea urchin.

**balihan** *n.* A species of sea perch.

**baling-baling** *n.* A species of tiny shrimp.

**balling** *n.* Various wrasses. *fam. Labridae.*

**balobok₂** *n.* A species of fish valued for its firm flesh and mild flavor.

**banak** *n.* Various gray mullets and goatfish. *fam. Mugilidae.*

**bantunan** *n.* A species of trepang.

**bangasan** *n.* The banded barracuda. *Sphyraena jello.*

**bangka₁** *n.* Various cardinal-fishes, including the Ring-tailed cardinal and Band-tail cardinal. *Ostorhinchus aureus.*

**bangkas** *n.* Horseshoe crab. *fam. Limulidae.*

**bangkaw** *n.* Saltwater forest complex, of which mangrove shrubs are a member.

**bangkaw-d'nda** *n.* Low-growing tree typical of mangrove swamps (lit. female mangrove). *Bruguiera* spp.

**bangkaw-l'lla** *n.* Low-growing tree typical of mangrove swamps (lit. male mangrove). *Rhizophera ceriops et al.*

**bangkungan** *n.* A species of trepang.

**bangga'-bangga'** *n.* Various boxfishes including the Longhorn cowfish. *Ostracion cornotus; Lactoria cornuta.*

**banggud 1** *n.* Various wrasses including the Olive club-nosed wrasse, Bird wrasse. *Gomphosus varius.*

**banggud 2** *n.* Black-eyed thick-lip wrasse. *Hemigymnus melapterus.*

**bang'llus** *n.* Milkfish; bangus. *Chanos chanos.*

**bari'-bari'** *n.* Various sweeperfish. *fam. Pempheridae.*

**bāt** *n.* A trepang or sea cucumber; also known as bêche-de-mere. *gen. Holothuria.*

**bāt-balutbatu** *n.* A species of trepang, edible.

**bāt-bantunan** *n.* A species of trepang, edible.

**bāt-bangkungan** *n.* A species of trepang, edible.

**bāt-bodbod** *n.* A species of trepang, edible.

**bāt-bohe'an** *n.* A species of trepang, edible.

**bāt-kandong-kandong** *n.* A species of trepang, edible.

**bāt-kangan** *n.* A species of trepang, edible.

**bāt-kitut** *n.* A species of trepang about 8cm long and as thick as a finger, edible.

**bāt-kumbatang** *n.* A species of trepang, edible.

**bāt-kuting** *n.* A species of trepang, edible.

**bāt-dugu-dugu** *n.* A species of trepang, edible.

**bāt-duru'an** *n.* A species of trepang, edible.

**bāt-ettom** *n.* A species of trepang, dark-skinned.

**bāt-gamat** *n.* A species of trepang, edible.

**bāt-labuyu'** *n.* A species of trepang, edible.

**bāt-legetan** *n.* A species of trepang, edible.

**bāt-llaw** *n.* A species of trepang, edible.

**bāt-lubu** *n.* A species of trepang which exudes edible, sticky, thread-like strands.

**bāt-nggo'-nggo'** *n.* A species of trepang, edible.

**bāt-pasan** *n.* A species of trepang, edible.

**bāt-pote'** *n.* A species of trepang, edible.

**bāt-saddo'** *n.* A species of trepang, edible.

**bāt-sa'i** *n.* A species of trepang, edible.

**bāt-sandulay** *n.* A species of trepang, edible.

**bāt-sandulay-l'ggon** *n.* A species of trepang, a sub-variety of sandulay.

**bāt-serol** *n.* A species of trepang, edible.

**bāt-taddik** *n.* A species of trepang, edible.

**bāt-tagokan** *n.* Various edible trepang noted for their sticky entrails.

**bāt-talipan** *n.* A species of trepang, edible.

**bāt-taumpa'** *n.* A species of trepang, edible.

**bāt-timpū** *n.* A species of trepang, edible.

**batang-pai** *n.* A species of fish (unclassified).

**batu-patollok** *n.* A distinctive coral formation which stands alone in a sandy area of sea floor.

**batu₁** *n.* A naturally formed mass; a rock; a stone.

**bawis-kallo'** *n.* Spiny or Scribbled rabbitfish. *Siganus spinus.*

**bawis-lambu** *n.* Streaked spinefoot. *Siganus javus.*

**bawis-pote'** *n.* White-spotted spinefoot; Rabbitfish. *Siganus canaliculatus.*

**bawis₂** *n.* Rabbitfishes; spinefoots. *Siganus sp.*

**bbung** *n.* Various species of dolphin or porpoise. *Order Cetacea.*

**bebang-lās-lās** *n.* Spot-banded butterflyfish. *Chaetodon punctatofasciatus.*

**bebang₁** *n.* Various Butterflyfishes and Angelfishes. *Apolemichthys trimaculatus (Three-spot angelfish); Chaetodontoplus mesoleucus (Vermiculated angelfish); Chelmon rostratus (Beaked coralfish); Chaetodon xanthurus/C. adiergastos (Philippine chevron butterflyfish).*

**belas** *n.* Smalltooth sawfish. *Pristis microdon.*

**bellok** *n.* A species of snapper, said to be a full-grown form. *Lutjanus spp.*

**belong** *n.* A species of bivalve with pearl-like shell and multiple surface curves.

**bengke** *n.* Various flying-fishes. *Cypselurus, Cheilopogon, Parexocoetus spp.*

**bengke-gampal** *n.* Mirror-wing flying-fish; Bony flying-fish. *Hirundichthys sp.*

**bikkin** *n.* A species of edible bivalve. *Cardita sp.*

**biga'ung** *n.* Various terapons or terapon perches. *fam. Terapontidae.*

**bilu-bilu₁** *n.* A species of fish (unclassified).

**binga'** *n.* Baler volute (a monovalve shellfish). *gen. Melo.*

**binga'-binga'** *n.* A species of monovalve (unclassified).

**bingkung** *n.* A species of bivalve, edible.

**biring** *n.* The mantle of a squid and other cephalopods.

**bisbisan** *n.* Small fish which steal bait.

**b'llong** *n.* Gold-spotted spinefoot. *Siganus guttatus.*

**b'llong-sulatan** *n.* Gold-lined spinefoot. *Siganus lineatus.*

**b'ngka 1** *n.* Various perches. *Lates calcarifer.*

**b'ngka 2** *n.* Various Sand perches. *Psammopercus waigiensis.*

**b'ngka'** *n.* White trevally or Striped jack. *Pseudocaranx sp.*

**b'ngngo'** *n.* A species of squirrelfish. *Adioryx spp.*

**bobok 1** *n.* A small marine crustacean.

**bobohan** *n.* An edible species of sea anemone, found in deeper water. *Actinia spp.*

**bokko'** *n.* Green turtle or leatherback. *Chelonia japonica.*

**bokko'-labi'-labi'** *n.* A species of leatherback turtle.

**boko'** *n.* A turtle.

**bodbod₂** *n.* Trepang species.

**bogge'** *n.* Triggerfish or filefish.

**bonte** *n.* A species of mullet, deep-bellied. *fam. Mugilidae.*

**boto'-boto'₂** *n.* Species of long-spined sea urchin.

**boto'-goyak 1** *n.* A species of mollusk, notable for its chalky shell.

**boto'-goyak 2** *n.* Red slate pencil sea urchin. *Heterocentrotus mamillatus.*

**bubuk₁** *n.* A species of fish.

**bubuhan** *n.* A species of fish.

**bukān** *n.* Tuskfish, a species of wrasse. *fam. Labridae.*

**bukay-bukay** *n.* Peacock and Keel-headed wrasses. *Iniistius pavo.*

**buku-buku₂** *n.* A helix-shaped monovalve (unclassified), edible.

**bugahak** *n.* Species of grouper, similar to kulapu.

**bulakka₁** *n.* Yellow-cheeked or Orange-dotted tuskfish. *Choerodon anchorago.*

**bulakka₂** *n.* Coral hogfish. *Bodianus mesothorax.*

**bulagtok** *n.* A species of bream (unclassified).

**bula'ug-piring** *n.* Gray large-eye bream. *Gymnocranius griseus.*

**bula'ug₁** *n.* Chinese emperor, species of bream. *fam. Lethrinidae.*

**bulan-bulan₁ 1** *n.* Malabar cavalla or Naked-shield kingfish. *Carangoides malabaricus.*

**bulan-bulan₁ 2** *n.* Tarpon. *Megalops cyprinoides.*

**bulan-bulan₂** *n.* Moon snail, an edible monovalve.

**bullat** *n.* A species of bream.

**bullu'** *n.* A species of large fish.

**buna'** *n.* Various batfishes. *Platax sp.*

**buna'-halo** *n.* Chinese pomfret, a fish species. *Pampus chinensis.*

**buntal** *n.* Generic for various pufferfish and porcupinefish. *fam. Tetraodontidae, fam. Diodontidae.*

**buntal-buntal** *n.* A species of pufferfish.

**buntal-kakas** *n.* A species of pufferfish.

**buntal-daing** *n.* A species of pufferfish.

**buntal-ero'** *n.* A species of pufferfish.

**buntal-itingan** *n.* A species of porcupinefish.

**buntal-petak** *n.* A species of pufferfish.

**buntal-pillu'an** *n.* Various smooth-skinned pufferfishes.

**buntal-s'llang** *n.* A deepwater species of pufferfish.

**buntal-tingga'** *n.* A species of pufferfish, lead-colored and inedible.

**buntal-unas** *n.* A shallow water species of pufferfish.

**būng** *n.* Various species of floating jellyfish.

**būng-leha** *n.* Pacific man-of-war or Australian bluebottle. *Physalia physalis.*

**būng-sabay** *n.* Jellyfish species with trailing strands that can sting a human.

**bungkak** *n.* Various trevallies. *Seriolinae; Selaroidae.*

**bunggu'** *n.* Six-bar grouper or Six-banded rock cod. *Epinephelus sexfasciatus.*

**bunggu'-luha-mata** *n.* Black-tipped or Red-band rock cod. *Epinephelus fasciatus.*

**bungug** *n.* A species of fish.

**bungug-tapikan** *n.* A species of fish, distinct from bungug.

**busa'ing** *n.* A species of tree which grows in saline conditions.

**bussu'₂** *n.* A species of edible bivalve.

**butingga'** *n.* Various pufferfishes.

**butingga'-lumahan** *n.* Half-smooth golden pufferfish. *Lagocephalus spadiceus.*

**buwa'-unas** *n.* The fruit-like growth on a shallow water seagrass.

**buwaya** *n.* Crocodile. *Crocodylus porosus.*

**kabangkawan** *n.* Mangrove complex.

**kabeto'** *n.* A species of small conch. *Strombus spp.*

**kabubu** *n.* A species of cleaner fish that accompany groupers.

**kadde'-kadde'** *n.* Various fan-shaped marine bivalves, commonly called scallops. *fam. Pectinidae.*

**kagang** *n.* Generic term for all species of crab.

**kagang-batu** *n.* Rock crab.

**kagang-kampay** *n.* A species of small crab found among rocks and on house posts, inedible.

**kagang-kullu'** *n.* The coconut crab. *Birgus Latro.*

**kagang-kumkum** *n.* A species of crab which burrows into sand.

**kagang-pēk** *n.* A species of mud crab with a single long claw.

**kagang-pulamata** *n.* A species of crab distinguished by its red eyes.

**kagang-sisu'an** *n.* A species of crab valued for its edible meat.

**kagang-sukay** *n.* A species of crab, edible.

**kagang-tika'-tika'** *n.* A species of crab, the fiddler crab.

**kagong** *n.* Generic for crabs.

**kahamkam** *n.* A shallow water marine plant with buoyant fruit-like appendages.

**kahanga** *n.* Various spider conchs. *fam. Strombidae.*

**kahanga-nabal** *n.* A spider conch with heavy flange.

**kahanga-selo** *n.* A large finger conch.

**kahentong** *n.* The egg shell, a white cowrie-like monovalve. *Ovula ovum.*

**kahumbu** *n.* A whale. *Order Cetacea.*

**kaitan** *n.* Generic for various shark species.

**ka'ullang** *n.* Shrimp; prawn.

**kali-kali** *n.* The lucine clam, an edible bivalve found about six inches deep in exposed sand. *fam. Tellinidae.*

**kalimango** *n.* Mangrove crab species.

**kalimango-pagung** *n.* A species of large, deepwater crab.

**kalitan 1** *n.* Generic for various shark species.

**kalitan kallang-kallang pipi** *n. phrase* Oceanic whitetip shark, a Requiem shark. *Isurus oxyrinchus.*

**kalitan-antugan** *n.* Grey reef shark, a Requiem shark. *Carcharhinus amblyrhynchos.*

**kalitan-bagambul** *n.* Oceanic whitetip shark, a Requiem shark. *Charcharinus longimanus.*

**kalitan-batu** *n.* A species of coral shark.

**kalitan-bohe'** *n.* A species of shark (unclassified).

**kalitan-kallang-kallang** *n.* Blue shark, a requiem shark species.

**kalitan-kamansihan** *n.* A species of sand shark.

**kalitan-kuting** *n.* Wobbegong shark, a bottom-dwelling shark. *fam. Orectolobidae.*

**kalitan-gamat** *n.* Blue shark, considered to be a variety of kalitan-kallang-kallang. *Prionace glauca.*

**kalitan-itingan** *n.* Various sea-catfishes, including the Spotted catfish and the Giant catfish. *Arius maculatus, A. thalassimus.*

**kalitan-lalu'u** *n.* Bull shark. *Carcharinus leucus.*

**kalitan-lokay** *n.* Thresher shark. *Alopias vulpinus.*

**kalitan-mangali** *n.* Tiger shark. *Carcharodon carcharias.*

**kalitan-mela'** *n.* Sand shark, a species which partly submerges in the sand. *fam. Odontaspididae.*

**kalitan-pamingkungan** *n.* Hammerhead shark. *Sphyrnidae zygaena.*

**kalitan-pinanaw** *n.* A species of shark.

**kalitan-pipi** *n.* A species of shark.

**kalitan-salimbūng** *n.* A species of shark.

**kalitan-sosop** *n.* Tawny nurse shark; Carpet shark. *Nebrius ferrugineous.*

**kalitan-t'kke'** *n.* Epaulette shark, a shark-sucker. *fam. Echineidae (tentative).*

**kalitan-tokke'** *n.* Epaulette shark, a shark-sucker.

**kalitan-tutungan-s'llang** *n.* Blacktip shark, a deepwater species. *Carcharias melanopterus.*

**kalitan-tutungan-t'bba** *n.* Blacktip reef shark. *fam. Odontaspididae.*

**kalitan-ulagu** *n.* A species of shark.

**kallang-kallang** *n.* Blue shark, a requiem species. *Prionace glauca.*

**kalling** *n.* The starfish, generic for several varieties. *fam. Acanthasteridae.*

**kalling-sahanay** *n.* The crown-of-thorns starfish. *Acanthaster planci.*

**kaloka'** *n.* A very large octopus of the open sea, multi-colored and inedible, rarely seen. *fam. Cephalopod.*

**kalo'ong 1** *n.* The chambered nautilus. *Nautilus pompilius.*

**kaluy** *n.* Blue-spotted grouper; leopard coral-trout. *Cephalopholis taeniops.*

**kaluy-b'ttikan** *n.* Dusky-tailed grouper or Bleeker's grouper. *Epinephelus bleekeri.*

**kaluy-magkangiyan** *n.* Coral cod. *Plectroplanus* sp.

**kaluy-mantis** *n.* Brown-striped snapper. *Lutjanus* spp.

**kamansihan** *n.* A species of sand shark.

**kamang 1** *n.* Dwarf flathead. *Elates ransonnettii.*

**kamang 2** *n.* Bar tailed flathead. *Platycephalus indicus.*

**kamang 3** *n.* Variegated lizardfish. *Synodus variegatus.*

**kamang-buhuk 1** *n.* Picnic sea bream. *Acanthopagrus berda.*

**kamang-buhuk 2** *n.* Yellow-fin sea bream. *Acanthopagrus latus.*

**kambang** *n.* A species of edible sea anemone, with red and white varieties. *Actinia* spp.

**kambing-kambing** *n.* Moorish idol, a fish species. *Zanclus cornutus.*

**kamun** *n.* Mantis shrimp, a type of crustacean similar to a large shrimp but with retractable blade-like appendages. *Order Stomatopoda.*

**kandaman 1** *n.* Glass big-eye, a fish species. *Heteropriacanthos cruentatus.*

**kandaman 2** *n.* Red big-eye, a fish species. *Priacanthus macracanthus.*

**kandaman-lawi'an** *n.* Purple spotted big-eye, a fish species. *Priacanthus tayenus.*

**kandelan** *n.* The Pacific sailfish, a large fish with a long sword-like projection of the upper jaw. *Istiophorus platypterus.*

**kandong-kandong** *n.* Species of trepang.

**kanting₁** *n.* The serrated spinal ridge of fish such as the Yellow-fin tuna.

**kanu'us** *n.* Various species of squid. *fam. Sepiolidae.*

**kangan** *n.* Trepang species.

**kangkang₂** *n.* An edible shallow-water crab.

**kapa-kapa** *n.* A species of fish.

**kapalu** *n.* Gobie species. *fam. Gobiidae.*

**kapang₁ 1** *n.* The shipworm or teredo, a bivalve mollusk which bores into wood immersed in sea water. *Teredo* spp.

**kappo'-s'mmek** *n.* The cloth stonefish.

**kappo'-tinggil-batu** *n.* The spotfish; frogfish. *Antennatus mummifer.*

**kappo'-tumbaga** *n.* The Copper stonefish.

**kappo'-ulak** *n.* A sargassum fish. *fam. Antennariidae.*

**kappo'-unas** *n.* A fish species, probably a stonefish.

**kappo'₁** *n.* Generic for various stonefish and anglerfish, and for some unrelated species. *fam. Scorpaenidae.*

**kariyan** *n.* The black-fin crevalle. *Alepes melanoptera, fam. Carangidae.*

**karuhung** *n.* A species of fish, very large and with a thick skin; probably a whale shark. *Rhincodon* spp.

**kasig** *n.* A sardine or pilchard species. *Sardinella* spp.

**kāt** *n.* The Humphead or Napoleon wrasse. *Cheilinus undulatus.*

**kāt-buggulan** *n.* A mature hump-head wrasse.

**katol-katol** *n.* The sailfish tang; various Surgeonfish species. *Zebrasoma* sp.

**katumbal** *n.* The Black-spot or Thumbprint emperor fishes. *Lethrinus harak.*

**katumbang** *n.* A species of fish.

**kāy-kāy** *n.* A species of clam, small.

**kayab-kayab** *n.* A species of scallop or fan shell. *fam. Pectinidae.*

**kayung-kayung** *n.* Moorish idol, a fish species. *Zanclus cornutus.*

**kehet-boto'** *n.* A species of crevalle. *fam. Carangidae.*

**kelong-kelong₂** *n.* Four-lined therapon, a small fish which shelters among floating weeds. *Pelates quadrilineatus.*

**kepak₂** *n.* The Red-tailed mullet. *fam. Mugilidae.*

**ketong** *n.* Various soldierfishes, including the Scarlet soldierfish and One-bar squirrelfish. *Myripristis pralinia.*

**keyot₁** *n.* A lobster-like crustacean, a deep water species.

**kiddat₂** *n.* A species of small cuttlefish.

**kihampaw** *n.* Generic for various stingrays, including the Blue-spotted or fantail ray. *fam. Dasyatidae.*

**kihampaw-bās** *n.* Sand ray, gray in color.

**kihampaw-batu** *n.* Rock ray, has blue spots.

**kima** *n.* Various species of giant clams. *Tridacna* spp.

**kima-antu'ang** *n.* A species of giant clam.

**kima-kuyya'** *n.* A species of clam that looks like a rock.

**kima-lapiran** *n.* A species of clam.

**kima-s'llot-s'llot** *n.* A species of small clam which grows in the clefts of coral rocks.

**kindat** *n.* A cuttlefish species, small. *Order Sepiolida.*

**kinsan** *n.* An edible species of sea anemone. *Actinia* sp.

**kīt-kīt** *n.* A species of fish.

**kitut** *n.* Trepang species.

**k'llong-k'llong** *n.* A tree species of the mangrove complex.

**k'llut-k'llut** *n.* The gill lice found in the mouths of certain fish.

**k'mmi** *n.* The remora or suckerfish. *Echeneis naucrates.*

**kobal-kobal** *n.* Various scad species, including Torpedo kingfish, Hard-tailed scad, Finny scad, Mackerel jack. *fam. Megalaspis cordyla.*

**kohang** *n.* A species of bivalve similar to a cockle, edible. *fam. Lucinidae.*

**koleng-koleng** *n.* The Seram blenny, a small striped fish. *Salarias ceramensis.*

**koleng-punsul** *n.* The Jewelled blenny; the Banded blenny. *Salarias fasciatus.*

**kombo'-kombo'** *n.* A species of sea anemone, yellowish in color, edible. *Actinia* spp.

**kopang** *n.* The Asian green mussel. *Perna viridis.*

**kowang-kowang** *n.* The spotted grouper. *Epinephelus* sp.

**kuba₁** *n.* Various cowries.

**kubing₂** *n.* The High-finned grouper, a brightly colored fish with a large mouth. *Epinephelus maculatus.*

**kukkus** *n.* A sea fan with an abrasive surface, useful for scrubbing.

**kukkut** *n.* The Long-finned rock cod. *Epinephelus megachir, E. quoyanus.*

**kukkut-kangan** *n.* Short-pectoralled honeycomb grouper.

**kuhapo'** *n.* Various groupers and rock cods. *Cephalopholis* spp.

**kuhapo'-abu** *n.* The Summan grouper; Starry grouper; White-spotted rock cod. *Epinephelus summana.*

**kuhapo'-batang** *n.* A species of rock cod. *Cephalopholis* sp.

**kuhapo'-b'kkosan** *n.* The Brown-banded rock cod. *Cephalopholis pachycentron.*

**kuhapo'-b'ttikan** *n.* The Coral hind or Vermilion Hind, the Coral rock cod. *Cephalopholis miniatus.*

**kuhapo'-bunggu'** *n.* The Yellow-spotted rock cod. *Epinephelus areolatus.*

**kuhapo'-kabangan** *n.* The Comet grouper or Contour rock cod. *Epinephelus morrhua.*

**kuhapo'-kubing** *n.* The Humpback sea bass or Barramundi cod. *Cromileptes altiveli.*

**kuhapo'-jali'an** *n.* The Blue-line coral cod. *Cephalopholis boenak.*

**kuhapo'-samehakan** *n.* The Dampiera dottyback (lit. Yakan rock-cod). *Labracinus spilopterus.*

**kuhapo'-sunu** *n.* The Red coral trout, one of the fish known as lapu-lapu. *Plectroplanus* sp.

**kuhatong** *n.* The Giant grouper, a species considered to be more dangerous than a shark. *Epinephelus lanceolatus.*

**kuhatong-palupalu** *n.* A species of grouper. *Epinephelus* sp.

**kuhita'** 1 *n.* Generic for various species of octopus. *gen. Octopus.*

**kuhita'-batu** *n.* The Rock octopus.

**kuhita'-gamat** *n.* An octopus species whose tentacles break on handling.

**kuhita'-ungus** *n.* The Sand octopus.

**kulabutan** *n.* Cuttlefish. *Order Sepiolida.*

**kulallit₁** *n.* A monovalve like a small helmet shell in shape.

**kulambal** *n.* The Pearly monocle bream and gold-lined sea bream. *Gymoncranius* spp.

**kulambal-bagangan** *n.* A species of bream.

**kulambuwan** *n.* A species of fish.

**kulampera'** *n.* Generic for various flatfish species.

**kulampera'-daing** *n.* The female of the Leopard flounder or Oriental sole. *Bothus pantherinus; Brachinus orientalis.*

**kulampera'-langohan** *n.* The male of the Leopard flounder or Oriental sole. *Bothus pantherinus; Brachinus orientalis.*

**kulampera'-s'llang** *n.* The Four-lined tongue-sole or the Deep-water flatfish. *Cynoglossus bilineatus.*

**kulampera'-tabaku** *n.* The Peacock sole. *Pardachirus pavoninus.*

**kulangkung** *n.* Cuttlebone, the boat-shaped chalky shield of a cuttlefish.

**kulapu** *n.* Generic for various groupers. *fam. Serranidae.*

**kulapu-tangal** *n.* Blacktip grouper or Redbanded grouper. *Epinephelus fasciatus.*

**kulilla'** *n.* A species of fish.

**kulisi'₂** *n.* The Butterfly bream.

**kullu-kullu₁** *n.* A species of sea bird, seen perched on floating logs.

**kuluk** *n.* The Schooling bannerfish; the False Moorish idol; the Spotted surgeonfish. *Heniochus singularis et al.*

**kumay** *n.* Various Surgeonfishes and Unicornfishes. *gen. Naso.*

**kumay-kabog** *n.* The Bignosed unicornfish. *Naso vlamingii.*

**kumay-lamba** *n.* The Longhorn unicornfish. *Naso unicornis.*

**kumay-manuk** *n.* The Sleek unicornfish. *Naso hexacanthus.*

**kumay-tandukan** *n.* The Bluespine unicornfish. *Naso uniocrnis.*

**kumay-t'llong** *n.* The Bar-cheeked unicornfish; the Clown tang. *Naso lituratus.*

**kumba'** *n.* A tough spherical organ in the intestines of certain fish.

**kumbatang** *n.* Trepang species.

**kummaw** *n.* A species of fish.

**kunnig** *n.* The imperial volute. *Aulica imperialis.*

**kuput** *n.* The Leatherjacket; a Surgeonfish.

**kūs-kūs 1** *n.* Various edible volutes. *Cymbiola aulica et al.*

**kūs-kūs 2** *n.* The bat volute. *Cymbiola vespertilio.*

**kūs-kūs-keyat** *n.* The Red bat volute. *Voluta aulica.*

**kussung** *n.* Various gobies including the Shadow goby. *Order gobiiformes; Acentrogobius nebulosus.*

**kutambak** *n.* Various emperors and snappers. *Lutjanus nebulosus.*

**kutambak-balihan** *n.* A species of snapper.

**kutambak-bulagtok** *n.* A species of snapper.

**kutambak-t'bba** *n.* The Yellow-spotted emperor snapper. *Lethrinus kallopterus (Bleeker).*

**kutkut-keyat** *n.* The Blacktip grouper. *Epinephelus fasciatus.*

**kuteteng** *n.* The Headband surgeonfish. *Acunthurus leucopareius.*

**kuting-kuting₂** *n.* Olive shells (generic). *Oliva* spp.

**kuting₂** *n.* Trepang species.

**kutu-kutu 1** *n.* Various minute marine organisms.

**kutu-kutu-buwaya'** *n.* Crocodile lice, tiny marine organisms about the size and appearance of millet, found floating on the sea surface.

**kutu-kutu-tahik** *n.* A species of sea plant growing in shallow water, the long strand-like leaves of which pop when pressed between the nails.

**kutu-kutu-tehe'-tehe'** *n.* Sea urchin lice, tiny marine organisms capable of an irritating bite.

**kutut** *n.* A species of fish, similar in appearance to a piper.

**kuwambal** *n.* Pearly monocle bream; Gold-lined sea bream.

**kuwit-panagatun** *n.* Seashells.

**dāg-lambu** *n.* The Barred Rabbitfish or Spinefoot. *Siganus virgatus.*

**dāg₂ 1** *n.* The Masked spinefoot (a fish species). *Siganus puellus.*

**dāg₂ 2** *n.* The striped snakehead, a species of mudfish found in both brackish and freshwater environments. *Channa striatus.*

**daga' 2** *n.* A reddish substance exuded by some sea cucumbers (trepang).

**dagdag₃** *n.* A species of fish.

**daing 1** *n.* Fish as a class (of cold-blooded aquatic vertebrates); specific fish of many kinds.

**daing-batu** *n. phrase* Various species of fish in the coral environment.

**daing-daing sahasa'** *n. phrase* The Coral goby.

**daing-pote'** *n.* Various Carangid fish valued for their firm white flesh. *fam. Carangidae.*

**daing-pote'-langohan** *n.* The shadow kingfish. *Carangoides dinema.*

**daing-pote'-mangale'** *n.* The Golden toothless trevally; the Golden kingfish. *Gnathonodon speciosus.*

**danan** *n.* Boxfish species.

**dandiya'** *n.* A slug-like marine animal, inedible.

**dandiya'-dandiya'** *n.* Sea anemone species. *Actinia* spp.

**daniyal** *n.* An edible monovalve species, helix-shaped.

**dapak** *n.* The Humpback red snapper. *Lutjanus gibbus.*

**dollen** *n.* A species of conch, edible. *Strombus gibberulus.*

**dompa'** *n.* A species of fish.

**dugu-dugu** *n.* A species of trepang, edible.

**dulang-kokok** *n.* Saucer coral.

**duru'an** *n.* Trepang species.

**duyung 1** *n.* The dugong or manatee; also referred to as a sea-cow.

**endong** *n.* Various marine eels.

**epet** *n.* The Rippled triggerfish; the Blue triggerfish. *Balistes fuscus.*

**epet-timbang** *n.* The Red-tooth triggerfish. *Odonus niger.*

**eral-eral₁** *n.* A species of edible monovalve, like a small helmet shell in shape.

**eral-eral₂** *n.* The edible fruit of some seagrass.

**eyot** *n.* Marine crustacean species.

**gadjamina** *n.* The sperm whale, said to be the source of ambergris. *Physeter catodon (tentative).*

**gaguk** *n.* A species of catfish.

**ga'ud-ga'ud** *n.* The Gold-lined sea bream. *Rhabdosargus sarba.*

**ga'ud-ga'ud-pote'** *n.* The King soldier-bream. *Argyrops spinifer.*

**gallangan** *n.* The Black-barred surgeonfish. *Acunthurus nigricans.*

**gamat₁** *n.* Trepang species.

**gamat₂** *n.* Shark species.

**gamay** *n.* An edible seaweed, like bunches of tiny green grapes in appearance. *Caulerpa lentillifera.*

**ganta'an₂** *n.* The Albacore, a tuna species closely related to the Spanish mackerel. *Thunnus alalunga.*

**gatang** *n.* A species of fish, multicolored.

**gelle-gelle** *n.* The Bullet tuna or mackerel. *Auxis rochei.*

**gellok** *n.* Various wrasses. *fam. Labridae.*

**gellok-bangkitan** *n.* The Red-banded wrasse.

**gellok-t'bba** *n.* A species of wrasse, white, found in shallow water.

**gellok-unas** *n.* A species of wrasse, black.

**geyok** *n.* Cigar wrasse; Sharp-nosed rainbow fish. *fam. Labridae.*

**gintu'** *n.* A species of eel-like fish.

**ginulang** *n.* The Whiteline triggerfish. *Balistes bursa.*

**giyatang** *n.* A fish species, multicolored.

**gu'ud-t'bbu** *n.* The Pacific squaretail (fish species).

**gulaman** *n.* An edible seaweed species.

**guntul** *n.* The Green jobfish. *Aprion virescens.*

**gunu'** *n.* Anchovy, various species. *fam. Engraulidae.*

**hande-hande** *n.* A mackerel species. *fam. Scombridae.*

**hunas** *n.* A grass-like sea plant that grows in shallow water.

**ibis** *n.* The Balabac barb, a small inshore fish caught by children with a hook and line. *Puntius ivis.*

**igang₂** *n.* The Brown surgeonfish. *Acanthurus nigrofuscus.*

**ilak** *n.* Various sea chubs and drummers. *Kyphosus lembus.*

**ilak-pampang** *n.* The Ashen drummer, a fish species.

**ilak-tawas** *n.* A species of chub.

**imbaw** *n.* Tellin clam species. *fam. Tellinidae.*

**ina'-baki'** *n.* The catfish eel.

**indangan₁** *n.* Surgeonfish; Achilles tang. *Acantharus bleekeri.*

**indangan₂** *n.* A species of long-spined sea urchin, edible.

**inggatan** *n.* The Banded trevally; the Cleft-belly kingfish. *Atropus atropos.*

**jahira** *n.* A species of fish sometimes caught in a panggal trap.

**jambay-būng 1** *n.* The venomous trailing tentacles of the bluebottle jellyfish.

**jūng-jūng** *n.* The Non-spotted halfbeak. *Hemiramphus far.*

**jungkak** *n.* A fish species with long white-tipped lower jaw, up to 20cm in length.

**labi'-labi'** *n.* A species of leatherback turtle.

**labog** *n.* The Medusa jellyfish. *Subphylum Medusozoa.*

**labu**₁ *n.* Various cone shells. *Conus* spp.

**labuyu'**₂ *n.* Trepang species.

**lāk** *n.* Various top shells. *Trochus* spp.

**lakas-lakas** *n.* Finger coral.

**lakkop-lakkop** *n.* A species of suckerfish that cling to the gill slits of large rays.

**laksu**₂ *n.* Various mudskippers. *fam. Gobiidae.*

**laggong** *n.* The cat's-eye turban, an edible monovalve shellfish. *Turbo* spp.

**laggutan** *n.* A species of small turtle.

**lagting**₂ *n.* A mangrove forest tree, a source of moderately durable house posts.

**lahusu' 1** *n.* Various emperor fishes including the Trumpet, or Sweet-lipped emperor. *Lethrinus miniatus.*

**lahusu' 2** *n.* The Blue-streak emperor. *Lethrinus choirorhynchus.*

**lahusu' 3** *n.* The Red-throat emperor. *Lethrinus chrysostomus.*

**lai'-lai'** *n.* An edible bivalve.

**laipapa** *n.* A species of small fish, notorious for stealing bait.

**lali** *n.* The Dolphinfish; the Pompano. *Coryphaena equiselis.*

**lalipan-tahik** *n.* A centipede-like sea creature about 2 cm long which leaves a bright phosphorescent trail. *Mixophilus* spp.

**lalu'u** *n.* Bull shark. *Charcharinus leucas.*

**lalung-ettom** *n.* The Spotfin lionfish. *Pterois antennata.*

**lalung**₁ *n.* Generic for various lionfishes. *Pterois* spp.

**lambana' 1** *n.* Generic for various barracudas, including the Big-eye barracuda. *Sphyraena forsteri.*

**lambana'-lengko'** *n.* The Great barracuda. *Sphyraena barracuda.*

**lambana'-tigul** *n.* The Obtuse barracuda. *Sphyraena obtusata.*

**lambe**₂ *n.* The Spiny or Sabre squirrelfish. *Sargocentrum* sp.

**lambi'** *n.* Generic for various cerith snail species. *Cerithium* spp.

**lampek** *n.* Various wrasses, including the Ragged-tail wrasse, the Two-spot Maori wrasse and the Cheek-lined Maori wrasse. *Oxycheilinus bimaculatus.*

**lampek-s'llang 1** *n.* The Scarlet-breasted wrasse, a deep-water species. *Cheilinus fasciatus.*

**lampek-s'llang 2** *n.* The Black-lined Maori wrasse. *Cheilinus diagrammus.*

**lampek-s'llang 3** *n.* The Snooty wrasse or Pointy-headed wrasse. *Cheilinus oxycephalus.*

**lampek-s'llang 4** *n.* The Triple-tail wrasse. *Cheilinus trilobatus.*

**lamuruk** *n.* Various Silverbiddies or Mojarras. *Gerres* sp.

**lanab-lanab** *n.* A small sea urchin about the size of an egg, short-spined and edible.

**landeyok** *n.* The Blue-fin jack or trevally, the Blue kingfish. *Caranx melampygus.*

**lanos**₂ *n.* A species of salt-water sponge.

**lansongan** *n.* Sea animals which have an ink sac; a collective term for cephalopods such as squid, octopus, cuttlefish.

**langa-langa** *n.* A species of suckerfish, possibly a remora.

**langāt** *n.* The Jarbua or Target therapon, a fish species. *Terapon jarbua.*

**langat-langat** *n.* A species of coral.

**langāt-pote'** *n.* The Large-scaled therapon. *Therapon theraps.*

**langkawit**₂ *n.* A species of fish, green, with large scales.

**langging** *n.* The Malayan hairtail, a fish species. *Eupleuragrammus muticus.*

**lappas**₁ *n.* The abalone. *Haliotis asinina.*

**laput-laput** *n.* A species of edible shellfish.

**lās-lās** *n.* Various coral fishes, including wrasses and butterflyfish.

**lās-lās-takot** *n.* The Indo-Pacific sergeant, a fish species. *Abudefduf vaigiensis.*

**lason** *n.* A species of sea anemone, edible. *Actinia* spp.

**lato'** *n.* An edible seaweed, like bunches of tiny green grapes in appearance. *Caulerpa lentillifera.*

**lattik**₁ *n.* A small lobster-like crustacean.

**lawayan** *n.* The Long-rakered trevally, the Heavy-jawed kingfish. *Ulua mentalis.*

**lāy-lāy** *n.* A lucine clam species. *fam. Tellinidae.*

**laya-laya** *n.* The fan coral.

**layu-manuk** *n.* The Moon-tail rock cod; the Yellow-edged lyre-tail. *Variola louti.*

**layul** *n.* A species of whale.

**lera-lera**₁ *n.* A fleshy jelly-like marine plant found growing on house posts.

**lese**₂ *n.* A species of fish that lives in holes on the sea floor.

**linaw** *n.* The sea persimmon, a swamp tree. *Diospyros maritima.*

**linggatang** *n.* The Sunflower starfish, a shallow water animal that can give a painful sting. *Pycnopodia helianthoides.*

**l'kkop**₁ *n.* A suckerfish which fastens itself to the gills of a stingray.

**l'mmuk** *n.* Moss-like sea plants, a source of baits for small fish traps.

**l'mmun-l'mmun** *n.* The Spider or Brittle starfish species. *Class Ophiuroidea.*

**l'ppe** *n.* The Painted sweetlips, a fish species. *Plectorhynchus pictus.*

**l'ppet-kandel** *n.* The Ocean sunfish. *Mola mola.*

**l'ppus 1** *n.* Various marine sponges.

**l'ssik-l'ssik** *n.* A species of barnacle found on things floating in the sea.

**lobot-lobot** *n.* A sea anemone species, edible.

**lokot-lokot** *n.* An edible growth of multiple greenish strands found adhering in clumps to seagrass.

**lo'on** *n.* A species of deepwater anemone, has stinging tendrils.

**lomba-lomba** *n.* A porpoise; a dolphin.

**lomba'-lomba'** *n.* Porpoise; dolphin.

**longgang** *n.* A species of grouper, medium size.

**luku'-babakan** *n.* The Narrow-lined toadfish, a species distinct from babakan. *Arothron immaculatus.*

**luku'-kakas** *n.* The Scribbled toadfish; the Map puffer. *Arothron mappa.*

**luku'-itingan** *n.* The Long-spine porcupinefish. *Diodon holocanthus.*

**luku'-sahapang** *n.* The Broad-barred toadfish. *Arothron hispidus.*

**luku'**₁ *n.* Various pufferfishes, including the White-spotted puffer. *fam. Tetraodontidae, fam. Diodontidae.*

**lumahan** *n.* The Indian or Long-jawed mackerel. *Rastrelliger kanagurta.*

**lumut**₁ **1** *n.* A fibrous mossy plant which grows on rocks or wood immersed in seawater.

**lusay** *n.* Eelgrass. *Zostera marina.*

**malu-malu bās** *n. phrase* The Bowmouth guitarfish or shark ray. *Rhina ancylostoma.*

**malu-malu solab** *n. phrase* The Giant guitarfish. *Rhina sp.*

**malumiyat** *n.* The Ribboned sweetlips, a fish species. *Plectorhynchus polytaemia.*

**mamallas** *n.* The Whip-tailed threadfin bream. *Pentapodus nemurus.*

**maming 1** *n.* The Humphead or Napoleon wrasse (fish species). *Cheilinus undulatus.*

**maming 2** *n.* The Green humphead parrotfish. *Bolbometopon muricatum.*

**mamuhuk** *n.* A species of echinoid found in seagrass or buried just below the surface in sand.

**mana-mana** *n.* A species of fish.

**mana'ul** *n.* The white-bellied sea eagle. *Haliaeetus leucogaster.*

**man'llon-baggu'** *n.* The Slender grouper; the White-lined rock cod. *Anyperodon leucogrammicus.*

**manumbuk** *n.* A swordfish; a marlin. *fam. Istiophoridae; Xiphias sp.*

**mangagat** *n.* The Dog snapper or the Pargo, a reef fish. *Sparidae sp.*

**mangapahan** *n.* The Thread-fin trevally; the Indian mirrorfish. *Alectis indicus.*

**mangkesol** *n.* The Brown-banded bamboo shark. *Mustelus antarcticus.*

**mangku'** *n.* The Frigate mackerel; the Oceanic bonito. *Auxis thazard.*

**mangilāp** *n.* The Gold-spotted rabbitfish. *Siganus punctatus.*

**mangilāp-ilahan** *n.* The Peppered spinefoot, a rabbitfish species. *Siganus punctatissimus.*

**mangilāp-lambu** *n.* The Blue-spotted or Ocellated-orange spinefoot. *Siganus corallinus.*

**mang'ntut** *n.* The Yellow-stripe goatfish; the Ochre-branded goatfish. *Upeneus sundaicus.*

**mang'ntut-pote'** *n.* A species of goatfish.

**mangsa' 1** *n.* Generic for various jacks and scads, including the African pompano. *Alectis ciliaris.*

**mangsa' 2** *n.* The Indian threadfin or Threadfin mirrorfish. *Alectis indica.*

**mangsa' 3** *n.* Yellow-stripe or Smooth-tailed trevally. *Selaroides leptolepsis.*

**mangsa'-tingga'** *n.* The Long-nose cavalla or kingfish. *Carangoides chrysophrys.*

**mapan** *n.* A Fusilier fish. *fam. Mullidae.*

**massuli'** *n.* The ramose murex snail, a large mollusk.

**mastuli'** *n.* The ramose murex, a large marine mollusc. *Murex ramosus.*

**mata-balud** *n.* A species of mullet. *fam. Mugilidae.*

**mata-tina'ung** *n.* The blue phosphorescent organisms in seawater.

**matibig** *n.* A species of fish with white flesh. *Carangid species.*

**maya-maya**₂ *n.* Various snapper species; the Humpbacked red snapper. *Lutjanus sp.*

**mayung** *n.* The Yellow-margin triggerfish. *Pseudobalistes flavimarginatus.*

**mbo'-t'kke'** *n.* The shark ancestor.

**mela'** A shark species.

**mo'ong** *n.* The Bicolor blenny, a fish species. *Ecsenius bicolor.*

**munari 1** *n.* A species of sea bird.

**munu-munu** *n.* An outcrop of dark coral rising from the sea floor at a depth of ten to twenty fathoms.

**mungit** *n.* A Surgeonfish. *Acanthurus nigrofuscus.*

**mungit-keyat-kepet** *n.* The Orange-epaulette surgeonfish. *Acunthurus olivaceus.*

**mussa'** *n.* A pearl; the pearl oyster.

**nnek** *n.* A species of fish.

**nggek** *n.* A species of fish.

**ngget** *n.* A species of octopus.

**nggo'an-baki'** *n.* The catfish eel.

**ngngok** *n.* The Smooth flute-mouth, a fish species. *Fistularia sp.*

**obon** *n.* The Greasy grouper, a fish species. *Epinephelus tauvina.*

**obon-deyom-halo** *n.* The Giant grouper or the Queensland grouper. *Epinephelus lanceolatus.*

**ogos** *n.* Generic for various parrotfish.

**ogos-batahan** *n.* The Blue-barred orange parrotfish. *Scarus ghobban.*

**ogos-bukay** *n.* The Black-veined red parrotfish. *Scarus rubirviolaceous.*

**ogos-gaddung 1** *n.* The Bloch's parrotfish. *Scarus croicensis.*

**ogos-gaddung 2** *n.* The Quoy's parrotfish. *Scarus quoyi.*

**ogos-lakit 1** *n.* The Globe-headed parrotfish. *Scarus globiceps.*

**ogos-lakit 2** *n.* The Six-bar wrasse. *Thalassoma hardwickii.*

**omang 1** *n.* Various hermit crabs, useful for baiting small hooks.

**omang-tatus** *n.* A species of hermit crab.

**ombe-ombe** *n.* A species of fish that tolerates being kept alive in saltwater tanks.

**owa'₂** *n.* The milkfish (bangus), the mature female. *Chanos chanos.*

**pahapat** *n.* The mangrove apple. *Sonneratia alba et al.*

**pahi** *n.* Various rays (fish). *Order Rajiformes.*

**pahi-baling** *n.* A manta ray species.

**pahi-bangkaw** *n.* The Mangrove ray, the Fantail ray. *Taeniura* sp.

**pahi-batu** *n.* The Spotted eagle ray. *Aetobatus narinari.*

**pahi-leha** *n.* A ray species (lit. sail ray). *Dasyatis* sp.

**pahi-luhuyan** *n.* A manta ray species. *Mobula* sp.

**pahi-manuk** *n.* The Cow-nosed ray. *Rhinoptera javanica.*

**pahi-sanga** *n.* Various manta or devil rays. *Mobula* spp.

**pahi-sanga-linggisan** *n.* A manta ray species (lit. frigate-bird manta ray). *Mobula* sp.

**pahi-sanga-owak** *n.* The Spineless devil ray (lit. crow manta ray). *Mobula ergoodoo.*

**pahi-sanga-pagung** *n.* A manta ray species (lit. floating manta). *Mobula* sp.

**pahi-sanga-tibung** *n.* A manta ray species (lit. plump manta). *Mobula* sp.

**pahi-sanga-t'lla'-t'lla'** *n.* A manta ray species (lit. seagull manta). *Mobula* sp.

**pa'imping** *n.* A species of bird, seen wading along shorelines.

**palig** *n.* The Black surgeonfish. *Acanthurus gahhm.*

**pama'** *n.* A species of lobster.

**pamingkungan** *n.* Hammerhead shark.

**panagatun** *n.* Shellfish in general; bivalve shellfish as a subgroup.

**panawan** *n.* A species of deepwater crab, uncommon.

**panit** *n.* Generic for various bonitos and tunas, including the Big-eye tuna. *Thunnus obesus.*

**panit-janggayan** *n.* The Yellow-fin tuna. *Thunnus albacares or Neothunnus macropterus.*

**panit-panit-ulak** *n.* A species of bonito. *fam. Thunnidae.*

**panit-sisikan** *n.* A tuna species, possibly the Blue-fin. *fam. Thunnidae.*

**pangaluwan** *n.* The Banded barracuda. *Sphyraena jello.*

**pari-pari** *n.* A species of sea anemone, the tendrils of which inflict a painful sting. *Actinia* spp.

**pasengko** *n.* The Oriental sweetlips, a fish species. *Plectorhinchus vittatus.*

**patay-batu** *n.* A species of anchovy.

**patay-lambu** *n.* A species of anchovy.

**patay-s'llang** *n.* A species of anchovy, harvested at sea rather than inshore.

**patay-unas** *n.* A species of anchovy found in areas of seagrass.

**patay₃** *n.* Anchovy of various species. *fam. Engraulidae.*

**payas** *n.* A species of marine bivalve, edible.

**payukan** *n.* The hawksbill turtle. *Eretmochelys imbricata.*

**pellok** *n.* Various wrasses. *Epibulus insidiator (Sling-jaw wrasse); Coris gaimard (Gaimard's rainbowfish); Anampses meleagrides (Yellow-tailed tamarin); Anampses caeruleo punctatus (Spotted chisel-tooth wrasse; Anampses caeruleopunctatus (Blue-spotted wrasse); Halichoeres hortulanus (Checkerboard wrasse).*

**pellok-s'llang** *n.* Various deep-water wrasses and rainbow fish.

**peteg** *n.* Various filefishes.

**peteg-kambing** *n.* The Broom filefish or the Brush-sided leatherjacket. *Monacanthus scopas.*

**peteg-pagung** *n.* The Unicorn filefish or leatherjacket. *Aluterus monoceros.*

**peteg-sapi'** *n.* The Bristle-tail or the Matted filefish. *Acreichthys tomentosus.*

**peteg-sowang** *n.* The Long-spined tripod fish. *Pseudotriacanthus strigilifer.*

**peteg-unas** *n.* The Chinese filefish or the Fan-bellied leatherjacket. *Monacanthus chinensis.*

**pillangan** *n.* Generic for various needlefish including the Spotted halfbeak, and the Black-barred garfish.

**pilluwang₁** *n.* A species of fish.

**pinanaw** *n.* A species of shark.

**pinatay** *n.* Various species of anchovy. *fam. Engraulidae.*

**pindi' 1** *n.* Various species of scallop (fan-shaped bivalves). *fam. Pectinidae.*

**pinggangan** *n.* The Starry triggerfish. *Abalistes stellaris.*

**pipi₂** *n.* The Palette surgeonfish. *Paracanthurus hepatus.*

**pipi₃** *n.* A species of shark.

**piring** *n.* Various glassfishes including the Chubby cardinalfish and the Polka-dot cardinalfish. *Ambassis spp; Sphaeramia orbicularis.*

**p'kkatan** *n.* The Blotched grunt, the Spotted javelinfish. *Pomadysus maculatus.*

**p'ggot** *n.* Various triggerfish, including the Whitetailed triggerfish. *fam. Balistidae, Melichthys vidua.*

**p'ggot-bisaya'** *n.* The Blackbar triggerfish; the Whitebarred triggerfish. *Balistes aculeatus.*

**p'ggot-keyat-bowa'** *n.* The Red-mouthed triggerfish. *Balistes radula.*

**p'ggot-jipun** *n.* The Orange-lined triggerfish. *Balistapus undulatus.*

**p'ggot-mangsi'** *n.* The Clown triggerfish; the Yellow-blotched triggerfish. *Balistes conspicillum.*

**p'ggot-pote'** *n.* A species of triggerfish.

**p'ggot-punsu** *n.* The Rectangular triggerfish. *Balistes rectangulus.*

**p'nnu** *n.* The Pacific green turtle. *Chelonia japonica shegel.*

**pogan** *n.* A species of fish, netted in coastal lagoons.

**pongka'** *n.* A species of fish.

**porok₁** *n.* Various Silver-biddies or Mojarras (fish species). *Gerres* sp.

**pote'-pote'** *n.* A species of fish.

**poyan** *n.* The Skipjack tuna. *Katsuwonus pelamis.*

**ppak** *n.* A species of seabird; a gull.

**pugaw** *n.* A species of fish, sometimes kept in salt-water fish ponds for later sale.

**puhan-laring** *n.* A species of fish.

**pullay 1** *n.* Various wrasses including the Yellowtail tamarin. *Anampses meleagrides.*

**pullay 2** *n.* The Three-ribbon or the Silver-streak wrasse. *Stethojulis strigiventer.*

**pullay 3** *n.* The Three-lined wrasse. *Stethojuliatus trilineata.*

**punjungan** *n.* A species of fish.

**punpun** *n.* A species of sea worm, long and flat, lives in sand or mud in the inter-tidal zone.

**pupput₁ 1.2** *v. intr. aN-* To travel in a motorized vessel.

**saging-saging₁** *n.* The juvenile Red Emperor, a fish species.

**sahasa'** *n.* The finger coral. *gen. Porites.*

**salay-salay** *n.* The Banded scad, a fish species. *Alepes djiddaba.*

**salimbūng** A species of shark.

**salindangan** *n.* A species of large manta ray.

**saliyaw** *n.* Various surgeonfish and unicorn fish including the Achilles tang, the Orange-gilled surgeonfish, the Striped bristlefish. *Acanthurus pyroferus, Ctenochaetus striatus.*

**saliyaw-lakit** *n.* The Blue-banded surgeonfish. *Acunthurus lineatus.*

**saliyaw-pampang** *n.* The Pencilled surgeonfish, the Dussumier's surgeonfish. *Acanthurus dussumieri.*

**sambelang** *n.* A species of fish.

**sambuwangan** *n.* A species of sea urchin (lit. Zamboanga sea urchin), a white-shelled species.

**sampang-aray** *n.* A species of mackerel.

**sampen** *n.* The Dusky tripletail, a species of fish. *Lobotes surinamensis.*

**samperot** *n.* The Silver pomfret, a fish species. *Pampus argenteus.*

**sampil-laran** *n.* A species of pelagic fish.

**sandet-tai'** *n.* The Bridle triggerfish; the Masked triggerfish. *Balistes fraenatus.*

**santing** *n.* The red-flowered black mangrove tree, a source of durable house posts and caulking material. *Lumnitzera littorea.*

**sangbaw** *n.* A species of deepwater crab, about the size and shape of a saucer, vivid orange in color.

**sapsap₃** *n.* The Pug-nosed ponyfish; the Toothed ponyfish. *Secutor ruconius.*

**sawasig** *n.* The Shortnosed garfish. *Hyporhampus quoyi.*

**selo** *n.* Various needlefishes and longtoms. *fam. Belonidae.*

**selo-p'llat** *n.* The Reef needlefish or longtom. *Strongylura incisa.*

**selo-s'llang** *n.* The Black-fin needlefish. *Tylosurus acus melanotus.*

**selo-tangī'** *n.* A species of needlefish distinguished by its sharply tapered tail. *fam. Belonidae.*

**selo-t'bba** *n.* A species of needlefish. *fam. Belonidae.*

**seso'** *n.* Various sea snails including moon snails. *Natica* spp.

**seso'-buwaya** *n.* A sea snail species.

**seso'-kiput** *n.* A moon snail species.

**seso'-ettom** *n.* The black moon snail.

**seso'-palang** *n.* A moon snail species.

**seso'-pote'** *n.* The white moon snail.

**sikad-sikad** *n.* A species of conch, edible. *Strombus gibberosa.*

**sikuhan** *n.* A species of fish, similar in form to a flute-mouth.

**sihag₃** *n.* The Halfbeak, a species of fish. *fam. Hemirhamphidae.*

**si'ay 1** *n.* Various monocle breams. *Scolopsis* spp.

**si'ay 1.1** *n.* The Pearly monocle bream. *Scolopsis margaritifera.*

**si'ay 1.2** *n.* The White-cheek monocle bream. *Scolopsis vosmeri.*

**singaling** *n.* An variety of sea urchin, black-shelled, edible.

**sipit-sipit₃** *n.* Various wrasses. *Thalassoma amblycephalum.*

**sirap** *n.* Various mussel-like bivalves.

**s'bbo** *n.* A type of branching coral that provides food and shelter for many marine species.

**s'llang₂** *n.* A deep water species of sea urchin.

**sobad** *n.* Mackerel tuna or bonito, coarse fish of the tuna species. *Euthynnus affinis.*

**sokong** *n.* A species of fish, a snapper similar in appearance to kutambak.

**sore** *n.* The Black-spot and Blue-lined surgeonfish. *Acanthurus* spp.

**sosop** *n.* Tawny nurse shark. *Nebrius ferrugineus.*

**sowa** *n.* A snake (generic for both land and sea species).

**sowa-bala-bala** *n.* A species of sea snake.

**sowa-basagan** *n.* A species of snake, venomous, reportedly found both in the sea and on land.

**sowa-pisak** *n.* A mangrove snake, a species found in shallow coastal waters.

**sowa-takot** *n.* A species of sea snake, banded black and white, commonly found sunning on coral outcrops. *fam. Hydrophiidae.*

**sowa-tangkig** *n.* A species of sea snake, said to penetrate the anus of children playing in the sea.

**sowa-ugtu'-ugtu** *n.* A species of sea snake seen inshore, said to penetrate the anus of children playing in the sea.

**sowa-undi'** *n.* A species of sea snake, barred black and white.

**sukkiyan** *n.* Various turbans (sea snails), including the Cat's-eye turban. *Turbo* spp.

**sukul-sukul** *n.* Herring scads, a fish species. *fam. Carangidae.*

**sudlay-sudlay** *n.* Various spiny murexes, including the Venus comb. *fam. Muricidae.*

**suga-suga₁** *n.* The Redcoat squirrelfish; the soldierfish. *Sargocentrum rubrum.*

**sugit-sugit** *n.* The paper nautilus. *Argonaut argo.*

**sugpat-babat** *n.* The Sand tilefish; the Blue banquillo. *Malacanthus latovittatus.*

**sulaw** *n.* Cone shells in general. *Conus* spp.

**sulay-sulay**$_2$ *n.* A perch-like fish, said to be half-grown tulay scad.

**sulig-anduhat** *n.* The Red-bellied fusilier fish.

**sulig-batang** *n.* A fusilier fish species, blue, with yellow lateral line.

**sulig-langaw** *n.* A fusilier fish species.

**sulig-mapan** *n.* The Denticulated caesio or the Red-bellied yellowtail fusilier. *Caesio cuning.*

**sulig-petak** *n.* A fusilier fish species.

**sulig**$_2$ *n.* Various fusilier fishes, including the Deep-bodied fusilier. *Caesio* spp.

**suling**$_2$ *n.* A species of fish.

**sumpit-sumpit** *n.* The Banded archerfish. *Toxotes jaculatrix.*

**suruk-punsu** *n.* The Silver whiting or the Sand smelt. *Sillago sihama.*

**taba** *n.* An edible barnacle-like shellfish that clings to coral rocks.

**tab'ggak** *n.* The Hunchback boxfish. *Ostracion or Tetrosomus gibbosus.*

**tab'llung-bangga'-bangga'** *n.* The Thornback cowfish, a poisonous species. *Lactioria fornasini.*

**tab'llung**$_1$ *n.* The Short-nosed and other boxfishes; various cowfishes. *Ostracion nasus.*

**tabula** *n.* Various species of small squid. *Order Sepiolida.*

**tabula-nangka'** *n.* A deepwater species of squid.

**tabula-tunyang** *n.* A small species of tabula squid.

**tabuli 1** *n.* Various large marine snails.

**tabuli 2** *n.* The Pacific triton. *Charonia tritonis.*

**tabuli-bbet** *n.* The helmet shell. *fam. Cassidae.*

**tabung** *n.* The Mangrove red jack; the Red emperor. *Lutjanus* spp.

**tagisiyan** *n.* A species of fish.

**tagō'** *n.* Various moray eels. *fam. Muraenidae.*

**tagō'-abu** *n.* The Gray moray eel. *Gymnothorax* sp.

**tagō'-bakukku** *n.* The Painted moray eel. *Gymnothorax pictus.*

**tagō'-simun** *n.* The Leopard or Spotted moray eel. *Enchelycore pardalis.*

**tagō'-s'llang** *n.* The Undulated moray eel, a deep sea species. *Gymnothorax undulatus.*

**tagō'-talsan** *n.* The Clouded or Snowflake moray eel. *Echidna nebulosa.*

**tahella'** *n.* The Convict surgeonfish, caught by netting in shallow water. *Acunthurus triostegus.*

**tahemtem 1** *n.* Generic for various barnacle species.

**tahemtem 2** *n.* An edible barnacle-like bivalve, found on rocks or mangrove roots.

**tai'-asang** *n.* A species of fish.

**tairuk** *n.* Angelfish species.

**taliruk** *n.* Generic for various angelfishes, including the Semicircle; the Koran angelfish; the Six-bar angelfish. *Euxiphipops sexstriatus.*

**taliruk-ikat-ikat** *n.* The Blue-banded or the Regal angelfish. *Pygoplites diacanthus.*

**taliruk-jahira** *n.* The Bicolor angelfish. *Centropyge bicolor.*

**taliruk-jali'an** *n.* The Emperor angelfish. *Pomacanthus imperator.*

**taliyaga'** *n.* A harmless snake-like sea animal with a calceous tubular skeleton, found on the bottom in shallow water.

**tallad** *n.* The Cigar wrasse; the Sharp-nosed rainbow fish. *Cheilio inermis.*

**talli**$_2$ *n.* The Pipefish. *Syngnathinae.*

**talom-badji** *n.* A species of shark.

**tamalengkeng** *n.* The Yellow-spotted scorpionfish, a species with poisonous spines that lurks in holes on the sea floor. *Pterois* sp.

**tamalengkeng-borakan** *n.* A species of scorpionfish.

**tamangka' 1** *n.* The Pink-banded grubfish. *Parapercis nebulosa.*

**tamarung** *n.* The Mackerel scad; the Big-bodied scad; the Short-finned scad. *Decapterus macrosoma.*

**tambak**$_2$ *n.* A species of small fish, known for nibbling the bait off hooks.

**tamban** *n.* Various species of sardines and herrings; the Indian sardine. *Sardinella longiceps et al.*

**tambangaw** *n.* The Checkered snapper. *Lutjanus decussatus.*

**tambelok 1** *n.* The shipworm or teredo. *Teredo navalis.*

**tambilawang** *n.* Various needlefishes. *fam. Belonidae.*

**tamendak** *n.* A mudskipper. *subfam. Oxudercinae.*

**tampellas** *n.* The White-cheeked surgeonfish. *Acunthurus glaucopareius.*

**tandukan-keyat** *n.* The Orange grouper or rockcod. *Cephalopholis auranteus.*

**tandukan-ettom** *n.* The Redmouth grouper or rockcod. *Aethaloperca rogaa.*

**tāng-tāng** *n.* Various queenfishes. *Scomberoides* spp.

**tangal** *n.* A species of grouper, the juvenile form of tandukan.

**tangbod** *n.* The Whiting smelt. *Sillago* spp.

**tangbud** *n.* Various goatfishes. *Upeneus* spp.

**tangkapa'** *n.* A coral formation with a large saucer-shaped upper surface sometimes a meter across.

**tangkas-biruk** *n.* An inedible crustacean similar in appearance to a giant shrimp.

**tangī'-lawayan** *n.* The Indo-Pacific king mackerel. *Scomberomorus guttatus.*

**taote'** *n.* Various species of Catfish. *gen. Plotosus.*

**tape'-kura'** *n.* A species of spiny oyster.

**tapog** *n.* The Five-lined cardinalfish. *Cheilodipterus quinquelineatus.*

**taubang** *n.* An inedible plant in marine shallows.

**tayum** *n.* Various long-spined sea urchins. *Echinoid* sp.

**tayum-boto'-boto'** *n.* An inedible species of long-spined sea urchin with large blunt spines about the thickness of a pencil.

**tayum-buta-buta** *n.* An inedible species of long-spined sea urchin which burrows into soft sand.

**tayum-ettom** *n.* A species of long-spined black sea urchin.

**tayum-matahan** *n.* An edible variety of long-spined sea urchin with phosphorescent eye-like openings at the base of the spines.

**tehe'-tehe'** *n.* Various short-spined sea urchins, a strand food valued for its edible gonads. *Echinoid sp.*

**tehe'-tehe'-balambangan** *n.* The Black-shelled sea urchin.

**tehe'-tehe'-bubu-bubu** *n.* A species of sea urchin found in sand, almost spineless and more box-like in shape than other species.

**tehe'-tehe'-itingan** *n.* A long-spined sea urchin.

**tehe'-tehe'-lanab-lanab** *n.* A species of small sea urchin, about the size of an egg.

**tehe'-tehe'-mamuhuk** *n.* A species of sea urchin, long-spined, found in seagrass or buried just below the surface in sand.

**tehe'-tehe'-pikit** *n.* A species of sea urchin, large, found mostly in deeper water.

**tehe'-tehe'-sambuwangan** *n.* A white-shelled species of sea urchin.

**tehe'-tehe'-singaling** *n.* A black-shelled species of sea urchin.

**tehe'-tehe'-s'llang** *n.* A deep-water species of sea urchin.

**tehem 1** *n.* A species of edible barnacle, found on rocks, wood, or mangrove roots.

**tengol** *n.* A valuable tree of mangrove swamps, a source of tannin and building material. *Ceriops tagal.*

**tibuk-anak-lason** *n.* The Chocolate-dip chromis. *Chromis dimidiatus.*

**tibuk-lawi'an** *n.* The Black-striped angelfish. *Genicanthus lamarck.*

**tibuk-lenged** *n.* The Blue-ribbon damselfish or the Ocellated sergeant-major. *Abudefduf biocellatus.*

**tibuk-sagga'-sagga'** *n.* The Springer's demoiselle. *Chrysiptera springeri.*

**tibuk-s'bbo** *n.* Various damselfishes or coral fishes.

**tibuk-taming 1** *n.* The Yellowbelly damselfish. *Abudefduf leucogaster.*

**tibuk-taming 2** *n.* The Seven-bar damselfish. *Abudefduf fasciatus.*

**tibuk-ulan-ulan** *n.* The Weber's chromis. *Chromis weberi.*

**tibuk₁** *n.* Generic for various species of damselfishes and clownfishes.

**tigbas₁** *n.* Various lizardfishes or sauries, species that live on weedy bottoms in shallow water.

**tihik-tihik 1** *n.* Generic for various squirrelfish, a species with large eyes and sharp dorsal spines which includes the Blood-spot squirrelfish, the Samara soldierfish. *Neoniphon samara.*

**tihik-tihik 2** *n.* The Striped large-eye bream. *Gnathodontex aurolineatus.*

**timbalun-batu** *n.* A species of timbalun without tendrils, found in coral complexes.

**timbalun-deyo'** *n.* A deepwater species of timbalun.

**timbalun-gusung** *n.* A species of timbalun growing on sandy bottoms.

**timbalun₂** *n.* A sea animal, similar to an anemone but without the typical tendrils.

**timbungan 1** *n.* Generic for various goatfishes. *Parupeneus spp.*

**timbungan 2** *n.* The Sixbar angelfish. *Pomacanthus sexstriatus (Euxiphipops sexstriatus).*

**timbungan-gadja** *n.* The Fivebar goatfish. *Parupeneus multifasciatus.*

**timbungan-lahusu'** *n.* The Goldsaddle goatfish. *Parupeneus cyclostomus.*

**timbungan-lanus** *n.* The Dot-and-dash goatfish. *Parupeneus barberinus.*

**timbungan-pangguwa'** *n.* The Doublebar goatfish. *Parupeneus trifasciatus.*

**timbungan-pote'** *n.* The Blacksaddle goatfish. *Parupeneus fraterculus.*

**timbungan-sairap** *n.* The Cinnabar goatfish. *Parupeneus heptaecanthus.*

**timbungan-samehakan** *n.* The Bicolor goatfish. *Parupeneus barberinoides.*

**timbungan-s'llang** *n.* The Indian goatfish. *Parupeneus indicus.*

**timbungan-takot** *n.* The Blackspot goatfish. *Parupeneus pleurostigma.*

**tinduk₂** *n.* A species of large fish.

**tingga'-tingga'-lumahan** *n.* A mackerel-like fish species that secretes a highly toxic substance which can cause death soon after eating.

**tinggil-batu** *n.* The Scorpion fish. *Dendroscorpaena sp.*

**tipay** *n.* Various non-spiny oysters including the oyster shell known as mother-of-pearl. *fam. Pteriidae.*

**tipay-batu** *n.* Rock oyster species. *gen. Saccostrea.*

**t'kke'** *n.* The Whale shark. *Rhincodus typus.*

**t'ggi** *n.* A species of small fish similar to a pilchard.

**t'lla'-t'lla'₁** *n.* A species of seagull.

**t'lla'-t'lla'₂** *n.* A species of bivalve shellfish.

**t'mbug** *n.* Parrotfishes.

**t'ntong₁** *n.* The Two-line monocle bream. *Scolopsis bilineatus.*

**togeng** *n.* Various needlefish including the Spotted halfbeak and the Black-barred garfish. *Hemirhamphus.*

**tohongan** *n.* The Scaly turtle. *Order Chelonia.*

**toloy** *n.* A species of pilchard or sardine.

**tombad** *n.* The Yellow-margin triggerfish; the Green triggerfish. *Pseudobalistes flavimarginatus.*

**tombad-keyat-bowa'** *n.* The Red-mouthed triggerfish.

**tombad-tunus** *n.* The Blue-fin triggerfish.

**totok** *n.* The Glassfish, an inshore species. *Ambassis spp.*

**tulay** *n.* The Ox-eye scad, a pelagic herring-like fish. *Selar boops.*

**tulay tukul-tukul** *n. phrase* The Herring scad. *Alepes.*

**tunus** *n.* The Bluefin triggerfish.

**tunggu'-langat-langat** *n.* The Dotty-back, a fish species. *Pseudochromis melanostigma.*

**tutungan-s'llang** *n.* Blacktip shark. *Carcharinus timbatus.*

**tutungan-t'bba** *n.* Blacktip reef shark. *Carcharinus melanopterus.*

**ubul-ubul** *n.* An edible jellyfish found on sand in shallow water.

**ulagu** *n.* A shark species.

**ulan-ulan** *n.* A species of coral fish.

**ulang 1** *n.* A shrimp: a prawn.

**ulapay₂** *n.* The Coral grazer, a fish species, pink with large scales.

**umpul** *n.* A tree species of mangrove swamps, a source of useful timber.

**unam** *n.* A species of shellfish.

**unas** *n.* An inedible grass-like sea plant of marine shallows.

**unas-balu** *n.* A species of fish, a weed eater.

**undi'** *n.* A species of sea snake, barred black and white.

**unduk-unduk** *n.* The thorny seahorse. *fam. Syngnathidae.*

**ūng-ūng** *n.* The Rainbow runner, a fish species; the Two-finned runner. *Elegatus bipinnulatus.*

**usam-usam** *n.* Various cardinalfishes. *Epigonichthys marmoratus.*

# B: Sinama maritime vocabulary

**āb** *v. tr.* To take bait, as a fish does.

**abal 1** *n.* Rough waves where currents meet.

**abal 1.1** *v. intr. aN-* To make the noise of rough seas.

**abay₁ 1** *n.* A person or canoe in the same fishing group.

**abay₁ 1.1** *v. intr. pa-/aN-* To travel or work with another fishing vessel.

**abayan** *n.* A fleet of fishing boats.

**adjung** *n.* An archaic sailing vessel.

**adjung-adjung 1** *n.* Upper plank of a canoe.

**agod** *v. tr.* To use a paddle as a lever or rudder when sailing across wind.

**a'a man deyo'** *n. phrase* Deep-sea spirit being.

**alam deyo'** *n. phrase* The environment beneath the sea.

**alam diyata'** *n. phrase* The environment above sea level.

**alimpunus** *n.* Whirlwind over land.

**alun-panjang** *n.* A tidal wave or tsunami.

**ambit₁** *v. tr.* To herd fish into shallow water.

**ampang** *n.* Drying racks over the stern of a canoe.

**ampas 1** *n.* A moveable fish corral set in shallow marine banks.

**ampas 1.1** *v. advrs. ka-...-an* To be trapped by herded fish.

**antung** *v. intr. pa-* To float motionless in one place despite current flow.

**angan** *n.* Reef edge, the place where shallow and deep water meet.

**apad-apad** *v. intr. aN-* To be overloaded, of a boat or vehicle.

**apang** *v. intr. aN-* To be reaching the limits of a liquid (of a container or boat).

**aru-aru** *v. tr.* To reduce sail by folding.

**asang₁ 2** *n.* Gills of a fish.

**aslag₂ 2** *adj. a-* Wide, of the mesh of a fishnet.

**atang** *v. intr. aN-* To be reaching loading limits, as a liquid container or a boat with a cargo.

**ataw-ataw 1** *n.* The ripples on a water surface.

**ataw-ataw 1.1** *v. tr.* To ruffle a water surface.

**atay dugu-dugu** *n. phrase* Edible entrails of some species of trepang.

**atay-atay** *n.* The opening of a woven fish trap.

**ayas-ayas** *n.* The drying racks at the outer end of the outrigger boom supports, of a traditional canoe.

**babak** *v. tr.* To startle fish into movement.

**babaw₂** *adj. a-* Shallow, of tide.

**babet** *n.* A diving weight.

**bakas-bakas** *n.* The final phase of a repeated sequence, especially of tide.

**bakbak** *v. tr.* To cut up fish for bait.

**bakbakan** *n.* A species of tree (unclassified) useful for canoe hulls.

**bakkel 1** *n.* The abrasive skin of scale-less fish such as rays.

**bakkel 1.1** *v. tr. -an* To remove the abrasive skin of certain fish species.

**badbad 1.1** *v. tr.* To unroll from its folded state, as a sail or mat.

**badja' 1** *n.* A dredging rake or hook.

**badja' sau** *n. phrase* A hooked anchor used to grapple deepwater traps.

**Badjaw** *n.* A name sometimes used to refer to the Sama Dilaut (sea-oriented Sama).

**badju** *n.* A storm of typhoon-like severity.

**bagas** *adj. a-* Forceful and rough, of waves or of speech.

**bagiyas 1** *n.* A woven trap for small fish and turtles.

**bagiyas 1.1** *v. tr.* To trap small fish.

**bahangi 3** *v. intr. aN-* To engage in night fishing.

**bahubuk** *n.* The sound of movement between water and something solid.

**bahudji'** *n.* A heavy rope, cable or hawser.

**bahu'₁** *n.* The boom of a sail.

**ba'as 1** *n.* The gleam of marine phosphoresence.

**ba'as 1.1** *v. intr. aN-* To gleam with phosphorescence, as seawater may do when agitated.

**ba'ugan₂** *n.* A curved rod; bow; spreader between lines.

**ba'ul₂** *n.* A paddle blank.

**balanda'₁** *n.* A sailing vessel rigged in traditional western style.

**balang 1** *n.* Fillets cut from large sea creatures such as shark or stingray.

**balang 1.1** *v. tr.* To cut a large sea creature up into fillets that run the length of its body.

**balang 2** *clf.* Count word for long fillets of flesh.

**balat-daya** *n.* An offshore wind from the southwest to northwest quarter.

**baliyu 1** *n.* Wind.

**baliyu 1.1** *v. advrs.* ka-...-an To be overcome or exhausted by paddling against the wind.

**ballul 1** *n.* A long fillet cut from a shark or stingray.

**ballul 1.1** *v. tr.* To cut a large fish or ray into long fillets.

**balosok** *n.* An incoming tide with exceptionally strong current.

**balsa** *n.* A raft or swimming float.

**balutu** *n.* A large canoe of the pelang type.

**banog** *n.* A crab-claw sail.

**banog pelang** *n. phrase* A four-cornered sail with the the upper corner propped away from the mast by a sprit.

**bansān 1** *n.* A rudder.

**bansān 1.1** *v. tr.* -an To steer a boat with a rudder-like device.

**bantilan** *n.* Posts used to raise a canoe above high tide level, for maintenance.

**bantuk** *n.* The shape of something; profile of a canoe or ship.

**banug** *n.* A triangular sail.

**bangka'** *n.* A basic dugout canoe; dugout base of a planked canoe.

**bangkat sa'am** *n. phrase* The upper planks of a canoe into which outrigger boom supports are fitted.

**bangkaw** *n.* Saltwater forest complex, of which mangrove shrubs are a member.

**bangkero 1** *n.* A person who makes a living by ferrying people short distances.

**bangkero 1.1** *v. tr.* To ferry people in a small boat.

**barat-daya** *n.* An offshore wind from southwest to northwest, the direction depending on the location and shape of landforms.

**base'-bulan** *n.* The moon phase immediately after new moon.

**batangan** *n.* An outrigger boom.

**batu-manunggul** *n.* A sentinel rock exposed at low tides, standing alone.

**bautu** *n.* An outrigger canoe of the pelang type.

**bawis₁** *v. intr.* aN- To suffer loss of consciousness when surfacing from a dive.

**bayan 1.1** *v. tr.* To travel by some kind of boat.

**beggong** *n.* A type of canoe without outriggers.

**belle'₂** *v. tr.* To collect dynamited fish by diving.

**bengkol₂** *n.* A place in deep water where currents move strongly.

**bihing tampe** *n. phrase* The highwater line on a beach.

**bihingan** *n.* The junction of land and sea; the tidal limit.

**biluk 1** *v. intr. pa-* To change direction by moving a sail across; to tack.

**biluk 1.1** *v. tr.* To change direction by tacking a sailboat.

**binta'** *v. ditr.* To travel to a trading post in order to replenish supplies, especially during an extended fishing expedition.

**bintang₂** *v. tr.* To catch fish using a set line.

**birang 2** *clf.* Count word for rolls of net.

**biruk** *n.* A canoe without outriggers.

**biruk kapituhan** *n. phrase* A very large canoe of the biruk type.

**b'kka'an** *n.* Weak currents at certain phases of moon.

**b'ggo'** *n.* A kind of canoe, without outriggers.

**b'ntang** *v. tr.* To fish with multiple hooks and a set line.

**b'ttong₃** *n.* A wide bay.

**boggo'** *n.* A small dugout canoe without outriggers.

**bo'ay** *v. advrs.* -in- Made ill as a result of eating poisonous parts of certain seafoods.

**bolbo₁** *n.* A wooden stringer that caps the plywood side panel of a canoe.

**boto'-boto'₁** *n.* A waterspout; a whirlwind over water.

**bowa'-angan** *n.* The seaward edge of a reef.

**bowa'-goyak** *n.* The crest of a wave about to break.

**bubu kapang** *n. phrase* A woven fish trap with an open base.

**bubu₁** *n.* A large, woven, box-shaped fish trap.

**bukutan 2** *n.* Upper part or back of a woven fish-trap.

**Budjang Bo'an** *n. phrase* The name of an important spirit of the Siasi Lagoon area.

**Budjang Da'u** *n. phrase* The name of an important guardian spirit of the Siasi Lagoon area.

**bugnus₃** *n.* A call to an octopus, telling it to come out of hiding.

**bugsak** *v. tr.* -an To throw a circular net.

**buhaw** *adj. a-* Filled with water, though not capsizing or sinking, of a boat.

**buhawi'₂ 1** *n.* A sudden swirling movement of wind or water.

**bulagas** *n.* Strong currents and wide tidal range associated with spring tides.

**bulan baha'u** *n. phrase* The new moon.

**bulan sobang** *n. phrase* The coming lunar month, beginning at the next new moon.

**bulan₁** *n.* The moon.

**bulan₂ 2** *clf.* Count word for nights of the month.

**bulan₃** *v. tr.* To catch fish by moonlight.

**buli'₁ 1** *n.* The lowest part of something, as the bottom of a container, or the sea floor.

**buli'₁ 2** *n.* Stern or rear, as the stern of a canoe, the rump of an animal, the buttocks of a human, the extremity of an island.

**buliluk** *n.* A swirling movement at the intersection of ocean currents; small whirlpools forming at the stern of a moving vessel.

**bulintus** *v. tr.* To strike a triangular sail, wrapping sail round mast and hinged boom.

**bullung** *n.* A spherical glass float for supporting large seine nets.

**buntu'**₂ *v. tr.* To catch fish overnight, in contrast to early morning.

**bungga'**₁ *n.* A spherical glass fishing float.

**bungsud** *n.* A permanent fish trap or corral, built in water 2 to 3 fathoms deep.

**busa'ing** *n.* A species of tree which grows in saline conditions.

**busay 1** *n.* The paddle for propelling a canoe.

**busay 1.1** *v. intr.* aN- To paddle a canoe using two hands on the paddle.

**busay 1.2** *v. tr.* To reach an objective by paddling.

**busay 2** *v. intr.* aN- To go on a journey; metaphorically, to die.

**busu** *n.* Diving apparatus using piped air.

**buti** *n.* A western-style rowboat.

**butun**₁ *n.* The weight on a heaving line.

**butun**₃ *n.* Floats of buoyant wood used to support the upper edge of a net.

**buwang**₁ **1** *v. ditr.* To cast something (into the sea).

**buwang**₁ **1.1** *v. tr.* To fish with a line cast from the land.

**buway-buway** *v. intr.* pa- To flow slowly, of tide when nearing slack water.

**buwaya-buwaya munda'** *n. phrase* A stylized crocodile carved on the prow of a pelang-type canoe.

**buwis deyo'** *n. phrase* The tribute paid to a sea spirit.

**kababawan** *n.* A shallow area of sea floor.

**kablangan** *n.* The open sea.

**kaka** *n.* Short planking across the hull of a canoe.

**kadjang** *n.* A covering or awning as shelter from sun or rain when travelling by canoe.

**kagoyakan** *n.* Turbulence at sea.

**kahanggalan** *n.* A marine shallow with ridges that limit the movement of a vessel.

**kaladjun** *n.* The remotest ocean.

**kalaloman** *n.* Ocean depths; deep regions of the sea.

**kalang**₂ *n.* Coral broken into fine fragments; gravel.

**kalangan**₂ *n.* A structure for supporting canoes above sea level so the hull can be cleaned.

**kalangan**₃ *n.* Coral broken into fine fragments; gravel.

**kalaut 1** *adv.* In a seawards direction.

**kalaut 1.1** *v. intr.* zero To go in a seaward direction from inland or from a shore.

**kaleya 1** *adv.* In a landwards direction.

**kaleya 1.1** *v. intr.* zero To go in a landwards direction.

**kaleya 1.2** *v. tr.* To get something by going inland.

**kalitan 1** *n.* Generic for various shark species.

**kalitan 2** *v. intr.* aN- To fish for sharks.

**kalitan 3** *v. advrs.* -in- Eaten by a shark.

**kallus**₂ *v. tr.* -an To dash water from the hull of a canoe.

**kamara 1** *n.* The side planking of a canoe.

**kamara 1.1** *v. tr.* To fasten the planking of a canoe.

**kamayung** *n.* The high prow of a paraw-type canoe, a separate structure attached to the stem.

**kambal 1** *n.* A reinforcing strip affixed to the outer edge of the planked section of canoe hulls.

**kambal 1.1** *v. tr.* -an To fit a canoe with a reinforcing strip.

**kambay 2** *v. intr.* aN- To move the arms as in swimming, especially of breaststroke.

**kampēn**₂ *v. tr.* To organize fishermen for a commercial fishing venture, providing capital and advance funds.

**kamunda'an** *n.* An assembly of canoes in one place.

**kanaway** *n.* A northwest wind.

**kanop** *v. advrs.* ta- Becoming submerged below the surface of a liquid; disappearing below the horizon.

**kantil**₂ *n.* An underwater cliff or ledge.

**kapang**₁ **1** *n.* The shipworm or teredo, a bivalve mollusk which bores into wood immersed in sea water. *Teredo* spp.

**kapang**₁ **1.1** *v. advrs.* -in- To be damaged by shipworm.

**kapay** *n.* The propeller of a plane or ship.

**kapi-kapi** *n.* The third series of side planks above the hull of a pelang-type canoe.

**kapis** *n.* A heavy cloth used mainly for sails.

**kapo' 1** *v. intr.* pa- To wade through water.

**kapo' 1.1** *v. tr.* To reach by wading.

**kapo' 1.2** *v. ditr.* To convey something by wading.

**kapote'an** *n.* An area of white sand, of a beach or sea floor.

**kappal** *n.* A ship or large launch, typically a vessel with a metal hull and more than one deck.

**kareyahan** *n.* Inland environment; land in contrast to the sea.

**karilautan** *n.* The ocean environment, in contrast to land.

**kaskas**₂ *v. tr.* -an To move water with a vigorous digging motion, as when paddling a canoe or making a clear area in the water.

**kasko** *n.* The hull of a boat in contrast to its superstructure.

**kasowang-sowangan** *n.* A network of channels, as in a mangrove forest.

**kassa'-bullung** *n.* A glass fishing float.

**katahikan** *n.* Seas or oceans; the sea in general.

**kata'-kata'** *n.* Small waves; light chop on sea.

**katam 1** *n.* A plane (the woodworking tool).

**katam 1.1** *v. tr.* To plane something.

**kataw 1** *adj.* a- Ruffled, of a water surface.

**kataw 1.1** *v. intr.* aN- To cause a water surface to become ruffled.

**katel-katel** *n.* A Western-style launch; marine runabout.

**kati** *v. tr.* To fish using live bait.

**katig 1** *n.* Outrigger.

**katig 1.1** *v. tr.* -an To attach outriggers.

**katihan** *n.* Live bait; the gear for fishing with live bait.

**kat'bbahan** *n.* An area of sea floor exposed at low tide.

**katoho'an** *n.* An area of sea floor exposed by receding tide.

**kauk** *v. tr.* To change direction by paddling at right-angles to the line of travel.

**kaut 1** *adv.* Seawards.

**kaut 1.1** *v. intr. zero* To go in a seaward direction from inland or shore.

**kaut 1.2** *v. tr.* To reach something by going out to sea.

**kawal** *n.* A large fishhook used when trolling for pelagic fish such as tuna.

**kawas-kawas** *n.* A sudden strong gust of wind across a body of water.

**kawil** *n.* A large fishhook used when trolling for fish such as tuna.

**kaykay** *v. tr.* To fan sand away in order to see something clearly.

**keke₁** *v. tr. -an* To scrape a thick tough layer off rays or sharks, or off the hull of a boat.

**kelle 1** *n.* A paddle with blades on each end of a shaft.

**kelle 1.1** *v. intr. aN-* To propel a canoe using a two-bladed paddle.

**kelle 1.2** *v. tr.* To reach something by paddling.

**keyas** *v. intr. pa-* To diminish in force, of wind or rain.

**kidkid** *v. tr.* To smooth a wooden surface by sanding.

**kiming** *n.* A box-shaped trap for weed-eating fish.

**k'llat-deyo'** *n.* The boom sheet (rope) of a sail.

**k'llat₂ 1** *n.* Cordage; rigging ropes.

**k'llat₂ 1.1** *v. tr. -an* To fasten a rope or line.

**k'llay-k'llay** *v. intr. aN-* To wave or flap in the wind, of cloth.

**k'llut 1** *adj. a-* Bailed dry.

**k'llut 1.1** *v. tr. -an* To bail a canoe.

**k'ttang 1** *adj. zero* Slack, of tidal flow.

**kōk-baliyu** *n.* The initial onset of a wind phase.

**kōk-busay** *n.* The hand grip of a canoe paddle.

**kōkan 1** *n.* The upstream side of a house relative to the incoming tidal flow.

**kohek-kohek** *v. tr. -an* To shake things together in water.

**kō' 1.1** *v. intr. pa-* To diminish in amount or force; to ebb.

**kontay₂** *v. intr. pa-* To abate, of a current.

**kowa' 1** *n.* A fish bone stuck in the throat.

**kowa' 1.1** *adj. -an* Suffering from a fish bone stuck in the throat.

**kowat-kowat** *n.* The multiple hooks of a squid lure.

**kukku-badja'** *n.* The prongs of a dredging rake.

**kukku₂ 1** *n.* The curved tip of an outrigger boom or anchor tine.

**kūd** *n.* Sand or bank exposed by a receding tide.

**kuhit** *v. tr.* To hook or catch something using a long-shafted implement.

**kulambu' 1** *n.* A partition or enclosure of netting or cloth.

**kulindara** *v. tr. -an* To trim a square sail by bringing the outer corner down to boom level.

**kulingkung 1.1** *v. intr. aN-* To go by a winding route.

**kulis pelang** *n. phrase* The qualities of a canoe that affect its performance and safety.

**kumpit** *n.* A broad-beamed wooden vessel used for general-purpose transportation.

**kungkung** *n.* A toy boat made of a single coconut leaf blade.

**kusu 1** *n.* A hole in the upper planking of a canoe into which the outrigger cross-boom is inserted.

**kusu 1.1** *v. tr. -an* To make a hole in the upper planking of a canoe.

**kuwit-tahik** *n.* The surface of the sea.

**daka'** *n.* High, of spring tides.

**dakan 1** *n.* The base of a bubu-type fish trap.

**dakan 1.1** *v. tr. -an* To attach the base of a bubu-type fish trap to its top.

**dagan₁** *n.* The horizontal components of a construction; floor bearers, deck supports.

**daggot₁** *v. intr. pa-* To run a canoe or boat up onto a beach.

**dahik** *v. tr.* To haul something from the sea.

**daing 1** *n.* Fish as a class (of cold-blooded aquatic vertebrates); specific fish of many kinds.

**daing 1.1** *v. advrs. -in-* Damaged by fish.

**daing kohap** *n. phrase* Fish caught during the night and used or sold the following afternoon.

**daing niasin** *n. phrase* Fish preserved by salting.

**dalat** *n.* A wind from off the land.

**daldal** *v. tr. -an* To move something into the sea by dragging, or by lowering from a platform.

**dalosan** *n.* The lowest plank of a pelang-type canoe.

**damas** *n.* The hull of a canoe in contrast to its upper planks.

**damlag 1** *n.* Full moon.

**damlag 1.1** *adj. zero* Full, of the moon.

**damunda'** *n.* A single boat.

**damunda'-munda' 1** *n.* A single canoe traveling alone.

**damunda'-munda' 1.1** *v. intr. pa-* To travel by canoe on one's own.

**danaw** *n.* A fairly large body of fresh water, not usually flowing; a lake or pond.

**dangat 1** *v. intr. pa-* To go in a direction contrary to wind or current.

**dapa-rapa** *n.* An outboard motor, especially one with no decorative engine cover.

**dapang** *n.* A traditional outrigger canoe with fully planked upper hull, often elaborately carved, built up on its dugout base.

**daplak 1** *v. intr. pa-* To splash against or over, of waves.

**daplak 1.1** *v. tr. -an* To move something by wave action.

**daplakan₁** *n.* The shoreline; the limit of wave action.

**dauhat₂ 1.1** *v. tr.* To get something by going against the current.

**dayung 1** *n.* An oar.

**dayung 1.1** *v. tr. -an* To row a boat using an oar or paddle against a fulcrum.

**deya** *loc. n.* Inland, in contrast to sea and coastal plain.

**deya-dilaut** *n.* Everywhere (lit. land and sea).

**deyo'$_2$ 1** *n.* The ocean floor.

**deyo'$_2$ 2** *n.* The ruling spirit being of the deep sea.

**deyom-bulan** *n.* The first day after new moon.

**dilaut** *loc. n.* The sea in contrast to land and shore; open sea in contrast to sheltered water.

**dingding-hangin** *n.* The wooden stringer that caps the plywood panel of a canoe side.

**dinggi-dinggi** *n.* A Western style rowboat or dinghy.

**diyata'an$_1$ 1** *loc. n.* The area on the upstream side of a reference point.

**diyata'an$_1$ 1.1** *v. intr. pa-* To move upstream from a place.

**donson** *n.* An outboard motor.

**dukla' 1** *v. intr. pa-* To reach land.

**dukla' 1.1** *v. tr. -an* To moor a canoe or boat.

**dugpak 1** *v. intr. pa-* To set in, of natural forces such as wind or rain.

**dunggu' 1** *v. intr. pa-* To reach land from the sea.

**dunggu' 1.1** *v. tr.* To moor or beach a vessel.

**durukan$_1$** *n.* A mast block; the block in a canoe that takes the downward strain of the mast.

**durung-diyata'** *n.* The upmost strake of a planked canoe.

**durung-sa'am** *n.* The strake of a planked canoe that carries the outrigger boom supports.

**durung$_2$** *n.* The strake of a canoe.

**duwa kasobangan** *n. phrase* Second day after new moon.

**duwasay$_2$** *v. intr. pa-* To rush out to sea, of the water in a river or inlet.

**ebed-ebed** *n.* The webbing between the spines of the pectoral or dorsal fins of a fish.

**ebol** *v. intr. aN-* To move vigorously through water.

**engkot 1** *n.* A knot in a line.

**engkot 1.1** *v. tr. -an* To tie something; to secure something by tying.

**engkot-buta 1** *n.* A thumb knot or half-hitch.

**engkot-buta 1.1** *v. tr. -an* To secure a knot by making an extra hitch.

**engkot-sintak** *n.* A knot that can be released by pulling on one end of the line.

**epe** *v. intr. aN-* To propel a canoe with one hand on the paddle, using a foot as a fulcrum.

**gabun** *n.* A cloud (generic).

**gaddongan** *n.* A source of wealth or livelihood, as a farm or fishing ground.

**galangan** *n.*

**gampal** *n.* Floating masses of dead vegetation.

**ganap t'llumpū'** *n. phrase* The calendar day added to compensate for the difference in length of lunar and solar days.

**gau** *n.* The tapered entry funnel of a woven trap, which allows fish to enter but not emerge.

**gehe** *n.* The barb of a spear or hook.

**ggok** *v. intr. aN-* To take water in one's mouth when swimming.

**ggot** *adj. a-* Exceptionally low, of tide.

**gibayan** *n.* The wide capping along the gunwales of a launch.

**gindan 1** *n.* A reference point or distinguishing feature, such as a landmark.

**gindan 1.1** *v. tr. -an* To mark position with a visible physical marker or by noting reference points.

**gintana'an** *n.* Dry land in contrast to sea and inter-tidal zones.

**giyak** *n.* The cross-pieces of a structure, as the frame of a kite or the ribs of a boat.

**g'llom** *n.* The tissue-like inner bark of certain trees, used for caulking.

**g'ppang** *n.* The removable planking of a canoe hull.

**gonteng 1** *n.* A line with multiple hooks attached.

**gonteng 1.2** *v. tr. -an* To catch fish using a stationary line and multiple hooks.

**goyak 1** *n.* Roughness, of the sea.

**goyak 1.1** *adj. a-* Wavy; choppy.

**goyak 1.2** *v. tr. -an* To toss something about in rough seas.

**goyak 1.3** *v. advrs. ka-...-an* To be experiencing rough seas.

**goyakan** *n.* An expanse or locale of rough seas.

**gubang** *n.* A small dugout canoe.

**gugul 1** *n.* A trawl net.

**gulamay 2** *n.* The tentacles of an octopus.

**gūng** *v. intr. pa-* To float on the surface of a liquid.

**gusung** *n.* Sand; a sandy beach.

**guyu 1** *n.* The turbulence of water below the surface.

**habagat** *n.* Monsoon; lesser winds from the southwest.

**hagul** *v. tr.* To repeatedly raise and lower a weighted line.

**halo-halo** *n.* A pond or pool ashore or on intertidal flats.

**hambawan** *n.* A rigging rope attached to the peak of a sail or to the upper boom, used for raising or lowering the sail; a halyard.

**hampilan** *n.* The land above the tidal limit.

**hantuk** *v. tr.* To move a fishing lure with a gentle up and down motion.

**hanut** *v. intr. pa-/-um-* To be carried away by a current.

**hanggal 1.1** *v. intr. pa-* To run aground on something projecting above the sea floor, as a rock or a sand bar.

**haus 1** *n.* An area of disturbed water where currents interact and flow strongly downward.

**haus 1.1** *v. intr. aN-* To become disturbed, of the sea in an area where currents interact.

**haya'$_2$** *n.* A single horizontal cloud in a clear sky.

**hilaga'** *n.* A northwest wind.

**hisi'** *v. intr. aN-* To show a gleam of white, as a wave crest or teeth.

**hollo** *v. intr. pa-* To descend freely, as a person going down a ladder or getting down from a boat.

**hunus 1** *n.* A sudden onset of strong wind, with or without rain; a squall.

**hunus 1.1** *v. intr. aN-* To become squally.

**ipul 1.1** *v. advrs. -in-* Suffering from leprosy or similar diseases.

**ispidbut** *n.* A western-style speedboat.

**ispowen** *n.* A type of heavy cloth used for sails.

**jalak** *v. intr. pa-* To break, of waves.

**jalampa** *n.* A traditional type of canoe referred to in kata-kata epics.

**jambu 1** *n.* A decorative tuft, as on the edges of a sail or kite.

**janggut 1** *n.* The hairlike projections of squid, cuttlefish or shrimp.

**Jengen** *n.* Alternative name for boat-dwelling Sama.

**jungal 1** *n.* A projection from a main part, as the prow of a sailing vessel.

**jungkung 1** *n.* A traditional sailing vessel of the type sometimes referred to as a Chinese junk.

**labu₂ 1** *n.* An anchor.

**labu₂ 1.1** *v. intr. pa-* To be at anchor, using bottom anchor or drift.

**labu₂ 1.2** *v. tr. -an* To anchor a boat.

**labu₄** *n.* The paired feelers of a squid or cuttlefish.

**lakkop 1** *n.* The suction pad on the head of suckerfish such as a remora.

**lakkop 1.1** *v. intr. aN-* To have a suckerfish adhering.

**lakod** *v. tr.* To drive fish into a fence trap or net set in shallow water at low tide.

**Ladja Sulayman** *n. phrase* Rajah Solomon, the name of an important spirit of the open sea.

**lagesles 1** *v. intr. pa-* To move from one location to another, as when fishing.

**lagesles 2** *v. intr. pa-* To drag along a rough sea floor, snagging but not catching.

**lagtang 1** *n.* A vine species, the source of a poison for stupefying fish. *Menispermaceous* spp.

**lagtang 1.1** *v. tr.* To stupefy fish using a poison from a vine.

**la'ang 1** *n.* The current associated with an outgoing tide.

**la'ang 1.1** *v. intr. -um-* To ebb, of tide.

**lalom₁ 2** *adj. a-* High, of tide.

**lamak** *n.* A square sail with upper and lower yards, rigged obliquely on a tripod mast.

**lamba₁** *adj. a-* Long and widely spaced, of outrigger booms.

**lambang₂** *v. tr.* To strengthen a mast with a supporting pole.

**lambat 1** *n.* A sinker on a fishing line.

**lansa** *n.* A passenger ferry; a launch.

**lansong** *n.* The ink or ink sac of cephalopods.

**lantaw 1** *n.* A long net, set or trawled.

**lantaw 1.1** *v. tr.* To catch fish with a lantaw net.

**langi 1** *v. intr. pa-/-um-* To swim.

**lango-goyak** *n.* Seasickness.

**laran** *v. intr. pa-* To drift with a current or wind.

**laway₂ 1** *n.* Long-line fishing, a fishing technique using multiple baited hooks.

**laya 1** *n.* A circular throw net with fine mesh.

**layo 1** *adj. a-* Anchored.

**layo 1.1** *v. intr. pa-* To lie at anchor.

**layo 1.2** *v. tr. -an* To anchor a vessel.

**lekom** *v. tr.* To enclose something by bringing together the ends of a net or fence.

**lekoman** *n.* An enclosure, specifically for holding fish that have been herded.

**leha 1** *n.* A square sail with upper and lower yard, rigged on a tripod mast.

**leha 1.1** *v. intr. a-* To sail under a square sail.

**lengke** *v. tr.* To wind up a line on the hands or on a notched board.

**lengkehan** *n.* A device for winding line, made of a flat board notched at each end.

**lenggang** *v. intr. pa-* To tip from an upright position; to be unstable, of a canoe.

**lepa** *n.* A large single-hull canoe, often roofed and used as a houseboat by nomadic Sama.

**leyang 1.1** *n.* The manner of flying; the movement of a canoe over water.

**libut 1.2** *v. tr.* To circumnavigate or go around something.

**likup 1** *n.* A chisel-like tool for making holes in wood.

**likup 1.1** *v. tr.* To make a hole in wood using a tool with a cutting tip.

**likuwad 1** *v. intr. pa-* To avoid an intervening object; to go around an obstacle; to circumnavigate something.

**ligtang 1** *n.* Mast stays (supporting ropes).

**ligtang 1.1** *v. tr.* To stay the mast of a canoe with a rope from mast to outriggers.

**limba' pelang** *n. phrase* Support poles to which the flooring or drying panels of a canoe are tied.

**limbu 1.4** *v. advrs. ka-...-an* To be sheltered from the effects of a force such as wind or the thrust of a propeller.

**limpowak** *n.* An eddy or swirl, of wind.

**lingas₂** *adj. a-* Narrow in section, as the hull of an outrigger canoe.

**linggi' 1** *n.* A long trawl net, about one fathom deep and up to fifty fathoms long.

**linggi' 1.1** *v. tr.* To catch fish with a long drag net.

**lipi-lipi** *n.* A wooden stringer that caps the plywood panel of a canoe side.

**lisigan** *n.* A deep place below the surrounding sea floor.

**l'bbangan** *n.* A gap through a reef or sandbank.

**l'bbos 1** *adj. a-* Collapsed, as a house into the sea.

**l'bbos 1.1** *v. tr.* To move something down into the water.

**l'kkab** *adj. a-* High or full, of tide.

**l'ddang** *adj. a-* Filled with water and sinking, of a canoe.

**l'ggot** *adj. a-* Exceptionally low, of tide.

**l'ggotan** *n.* An area exposed by low tide.

l'mmuk *n.* Moss-like sea plants, a source of baits for small fish traps.

l'mput dilaut *n. phrase* Edible plants of inshore shallows.

l'ngnges 1 *n.* The rough surface of shark and stingray skin (dermal denticles).

l'ngnges 1.1 *v. intr. aN-* To feel rough or abrasive to the touch, of shark or stingray skin.

l'ngnges 1.2 *v. tr. -an* To remove the denticles from the skin of a shark or stingray.

l'ppang *v. intr. aN-* To be just the right size of mesh (for the target fish species) in a trawl net.

l'ppit 1 *v. tr.* To furl a sail by folding it around the collapsed boom and mast.

llis *v. intr. aN-* To make the hissing sound of an object moving swiftly through water.

llok *v. intr. aN-* To make the sound of trickling water.

llop 1 *adj. a-* Becoming low in the water, as a canoe loaded to the gunwales.

lodjat₂ 1 *v. intr. pa-* To push a canoe vigorously away from a group of other vessels.

lodjat₂ 2 *v. tr. -an* To move a canoe vigorously forward and back, as to remove water from the hull.

logdang₂ *adj. a-* Filled with water and sinking.

lognos *adj. a-* Demolished, as a collapsed house or a sunken boat.

logo *n.* A small woven trap placed at the end of a fish fence to catch escaping fish.

londay *n.* A type of outrigger canoe with no more than one side plank attached to its hull.

lonseng 1 *adj. a-* Poorly maintained, of a canoe.

longon *v. tr.* To wind line onto a spool.

longsad₁ *v. tr.* To move something into the sea by lowering it from a platform or by dragging it from where it was beached.

lorok 1.1 *v. tr.* To reach by diving.

loson *v. advrs. ta-* Carried along by a strong current.

lubu₁ *n.* A string-like substance exuded by some species of trepang.

luklus 1 *v. tr. -an* To lower a sail down a mast by slackening its lashing.

luklus 2 *v. tr. -an* To loosen clothing items that go around one's body.

luhu *v. tr.* To singe the hull of a canoe to inhibit the growth of marine moss.

lumay *n.* Fish split and dried in the sun.

lumbag *n.* A heavy swell due to stormy weather further out at sea.

lumut₁ 1 *n.* A fibrous mossy plant which grows on rocks or wood immersed in seawater.

lumut₁ 1.1 *v. advrs. -in-* Covered with mossy growth, of a canoe that needs scrubbing.

lūn 1.1 *v. tr. -an* To roll flexible material into a compact bundle; to furl a sail.

lundu' *n.* Fish stunned by dynamite but still alive and floating on the surface.

lungtud *n.* The second series of side-planks above the dugout hull of a pelang-type canoe.

lurup *v. tr.* To get something by diving.

lutu'₁ 1 *n.* Provisions for a journey or a fishing trip.

luwad *v. tr.* To row a canoe using a fulcrum.

malim 1 *n.* A guide; a pilot (in the maritime sense).

manit *v. intr. aN-* To troll for tuna.

manitan *n.* The equipment used in trolling for tuna.

mata-baliyu *n.* The quarter from which a wind blows.

mata-goyak *n.* The crest of a wave just before it breaks.

mata-tina'ung *n.* The blue phosphorescent organisms in seawater.

mata₂ *n.* The mesh size of something woven.

matay-bulan *n.* The closing nights of the lunar month (lit. moon is dead).

millat *v. tr.* To break out the side of a plank when drilling dowel holes.

min lima abase' *n. phrase* The fifth day after full moon.

mint'dda abase' *n. phrase* The first day after full moon.

mman *v. intr. aN-* To leak, of a canoe.

mohang *n.* The hollow part of something, as of a plate or of the inside part of a boat below deck level.

mulilang *adj. a-* Almost fully ebbed, of a tide about to turn.

munda'₁ 1 *n.* The front part of a canoe or vehicle.

munda'₁ 2 *clf.* Count word for counting canoes.

mungkang *n.* A worn-out canoe of the paraw type.

nabal *n.* A naval vessel.

naelon *n.* Nylon line.

nahut *adj. a-* Small in cross-section, as rope or line; small in gauge, as the mesh of a net.

naylon *n.* Nylon fishing line.

nintil 1 *adj. a-* Lightly built or loaded, as a canoe which floats high in the water.

nso' *adj. a-* Flowing or rising to high water, of tide.

nusa *n.* An island with no hills; an atoll.

oko'-oko' *n.* Sea urchins boiled with rice inside.

olangan 1.1 *n.* The open water between islands.

omang 1.1 *v. tr. -an* To bait a hook.

osol 1 *v. intr. pa-* To stand upright in the soil or sea-floor, of a pole or a post.

osol 1.1 *v. tr. -an* To drive a post or stake into the soil or sea-floor; to provide a house with posts.

pababag 1.1 *v. tr.* To steer a canoe so that it is transverse to the line of wave movement.

pabiluk *v. tr.* To cause a canoe under sail to change direction.

pakautan *n.* The place out at sea where one intends to fish.

pagabay 1 *n.* A collective term for people fishing, traveling, or sitting together.

pagabay 1.1 *v. intr. aN-* To form a cooperative fishing project involving a number of canoes.

pagadgad *v. tr.* To set something flowing with the current.

pagbahembas *v. intr. aN-* To make a repeated splashing noise.

**pagbahubuk 1** *v. intr. aN-* To make the sound of a solid object through water, as when wading or pulling a paddle.

**pagbahubuk 1.1** *v. tr. -an* To smack water with a flat item.

**pagbalukakkad** *v. intr. aN-* To make the noise of something moving vigorously through water, as a canoe or someone wading rapidly.

**pagbanog-banog** *n.* Toy sailboats.

**pagbangka'-bangka'** *v. intr. aN-* To travel here and there, especially by dugout canoe.

**pagbase'** *v. intr. aN-* To live in a wet environment.

**pagbengkol** *v. intr. aN-* To move, of currents in deep water.

**pagbetong-betong** *v. intr. aN-* To sparkle or glitter, as phosphorescence in sea.

**pagbubu** *v. tr.* To be engaged in catching fish with a bubu-type trap.

**pagbulan** *v. intr. aN-* To catch shallow-water sea foods during the bright phase of the moon.

**pagbuliluk** *v. intr. aN-* To form swirling currents or whirlpools at the reversal of tides.

**pagbullud** *v. intr. aN-* To form a hill, of ocean waves.

**pagbuti** *v. intr. aN-* To get about by rowboat.

**pagkaut** *v. intr. aN-* To fish out at sea.

**pagk'llab** *v. intr. aN-* To flutter or flap in the wind.

**pagk'ppay-k'ppay 1** *v. intr. aN-* To trim sails to make the best use of conditions.

**pagkulaet** *v. intr. aN-* To fish by the light of a pressure lantern.

**pagdaing** *v. intr. aN-* To fish for a living.

**pagdanggu'-danggu'** *v. intr. aN-* To move alternately forward and back, as a person paddling a canoe, grating cassava, or moving on a swing.

**pagdaplak-daplak** *v. intr. aN-* To splash continually, of wave action.

**pagdayaw 1** *n.* The basic components of a structure, as the skeleton and sinews of a body, or the framing of a house or boat.

**paggambil** *v. tr.* To be fastened together, as canoes or people.

**paggimbal 1.1** *v. tr.* To bring long items together for mutual support, of canoes or building materials.

**paggoyak** *v. tr. -an* To push something about by the force of a storm.

**paghadjul-hadjul** *v. intr. aN-* To drift to and fro with the currents, of a vessel with no means of propulsion or steering.

**paghalo-halo** *v. intr. aN-* To form pools due to heavy rain.

**paghantak** *v. tr. -an* To strike repeatedly on an underlying surface, as a canoe prow on a rough sea.

**paghūg** *v. intr. aN-* To drop fishing gear into the sea.

**pagjalampa-jalampa** *v. intr. aN-* To travel by a jalampa-type canoe.

**paglantaw** *v. intr. aN-* To make a living by fishing with long nets.

**paglaway** *v. intr. aN-* To engage in long-line fishing.

**paglimbokay** *v. intr. aN-* To eddy around a sheltering feature, of wind.

**paglimpowak** *v. intr. aN-* To eddy around a sheltering feature, of wind.

**paglinggi'** *v. intr. aN-* To fish with a long trawl net.

**paglumbag** *v. intr. aN-* To be running with a heavy swell, of the sea.

**paglurup** *v. tr.* To dive for a living.

**paglutu'anan** *n.* A container for the provisions taken on a fishing expedition.

**pagmunda'₁** *n.* A group of canoes forming a fishing fleet.

**pagpala'u** *v. intr. aN-* To live permanently on a boat.

**pagpali** *v. intr. aN-* To swing to and fro, of a boom (sailing).

**pagpalit 1** *v. intr. aN-* To earn a living by means of deep-water fish traps recovered by a draghook.

**pagpanonda'** *v. intr. aN-* To fish with a trolled lure.

**pagpatron** *v. intr. aN-* To be the master of a ship.

**pagp'llay 1** *v. intr. aN-* To move to and fro, as a canoe due to wind or current.

**pagp'llay 1.1** *v. tr.* To allow or cause something to swing to and fro in wind or current.

**pagp'ssi** *v. intr. aN-* To make a living by fishing with a hook and line.

**pagsahal** *v. intr. aN-* To break, of waves.

**pagsait** *v. intr. aN-* To bail continually.

**pagsalay₂** *v. intr. aN-* To be in a stable state, as the sea between tides or weather phases.

**pagsintak** *v. intr. aN-* To strike a hook when a fish takes the bait.

**pags'bbat** *v. tr.* To swallow something whole, without biting.

**pagsoha'** *v. intr. aN-* To move a canoe along by poling.

**pagtindayung 1** *v. intr. aN-* To work together in rowing a boat.

**pagtindayung 2** *v. intr. aN-* To swim on one's back using an overarm stroke.

**pagtipara** *v. intr. aN-* To use diving goggles.

**pagt'bba** *v. tr.* To gather food from an inshore strand area.

**pagt'bbahan** *n.* An inshore area suitable for gathering strand foods.

**pagtoho'** *v. intr. aN-* To live in a dry environment, in contrast to living over the sea.

**pagtuhun** *v. intr. aN-* To earn a living by diving.

**pagumpak-umpak** *v. intr. aN-* To move vigorously up and down, as a vehicle on a rutted road or a canoe on choppy sea.

**pagūng** *v. tr.* To cause something to float.

**pagung** *n.* A floating island, typically made up of growing vegetable matter.

**paipa'₁ 1** *n.* The fleshy gill segments of stingrays and some shark species.

**pa'at 1** *n.* A tool for making holes in wood.

**pa'at 1.1** *v. tr.* To make a hole in wood with a chisel or a drill.

**palakaya** *n.* A large outrigger vessel used for haul seining.

**pala'u** *n.* Boat-dwelling, nomadic Sama.

**palangihan** *n.* Something used as an aid to swimming.

**palapa'** 1 *n.* The short side planks at the bow and stern of a pelang-type canoe.

**paldu** *n.* A cage for keeping things alive in the sea.

**pali** *v. tr.* To change tack (when sailing) by bringing the boom across.

**palimping** 1 *n.* A rope sewn into the edge of a sail; a bolt-rope.

**palimping** 1.1 *v. tr. -an* To sew a bolt-rope inside the folded edges of a sail.

**paling** *v. tr.* To bring the boom across a sailing canoe in order to change tack.

**palipit** *v. tr. -an* To sew a bolt-rope inside the folded edge of a sail.

**palis**₁ *v. advrs. ta-* Carried far off course by a strong wind or current.

**palit**₂ *v. tr.* To retrieve fish traps from the sea floor.

**pallungan** *n.* A small pelang-type canoe suitable for children.

**paltira** *n.* A trading partner, as someone who finances a fishing trip or people who fish under contract.

**pamalastik** *v. intr. aN-* To fish with hook and line while drifting with the current.

**pamaliyu** *n.* The windy season.

**pamalung** *n.* The curved prow of a light sailing canoe of the paraw type.

**pambot** *n.* A large outrigger canoe with an inboard motor.

**pameya'an**₁ *n.* Generic for conveyances such as road vehicles, riding animals, seagoing vessels or aircraft.

**pam'ssihan** *n.* A place for fishing with hook and line.

**pamonod** *n.* The lowest series of side planks on a pelang-type canoe hull.

**panait** *n.* Something used to bail water from a boat.

**pana'** 1 *n.* A device for propelling a spear or an arrow; a spear-gun.

**pana'** 1.1 *v. tr.* To spear fish with a rubber-propelled spear.

**panansahan** *n.* A plank set in the stern of a canoe, on which the person sits who handles the steering oar.

**panapali** *n.* The contribution of one component to a set, as a sail to a canoe.

**pan'ddo'** *n.* A calm period; the calm season of the year.

**pano'onan** *n.* A place for setting small fish traps.

**panonda'an** *n.* A trolling lure.

**pansal** 1 *n.* A short piece of decking set in the bow of a canoe.

**pansal** 1.1 *v. tr. -an* To fit a forward deck to a large canoe.

**pantok**₁ 1 *n.* The shaft of a spear.

**pantok**₁ 1.1 *v. tr. -an* To fit and lash a shaft to the head of a spear.

**panundanan** *n.* A towline, especially of canoes.

**pangabay** *n.* A person in the same fleet or group; fleet-mate.

**pangaleboran** *n.* A drum or reel on which to wind a line.

**pangaluwaran** *n.* A fulcrum; a rowlock.

**pangka'an** *n.* Props that support the rear legs of a tripod mast in a sailing canoe.

**panggal** 1 *n.* A woven trap for small fish.

**panggal** 1.1 *v. tr.* To catch small fish in a woven trap.

**pangubug** *n.* A fishing lure.

**papet** *n.* A broad-beamed wooden vessel used mainly for transporting freight.

**paranas** *v. intr. aN-* To fish with hook and line while drifting with the current.

**parangkang** *n.* An all-purpose vessel of Buginese origin, rarely seen in Sulu.

**paraw** 1 *n.* A light outrigger canoe with upper sides of plywood or woven cane, a fast sailer.

**paraw** 2 *n.* A motorized outrigger boat.

**pari'an** *n.* The seashore; foreshore.

**parilaut** 1 *adv.* Towards open sea.

**parilaut** 1.1 *v. intr. zero* To go out to sea.

**pariyata'an** *n.* The direction from which an ocean current is flowing.

**parola** *n.* A navigational light; a lighthouse.

**pasangan**₁ *n.* A roll or coil, of a line.

**paslangan** 1 *n.* An extensive region without landmarks, as open sea or a plain without trees.

**pasok** 1 *n.* Dowels used for joining planks edge to edge.

**paspas**₂ 1 *v. intr. aN-* To be flapping, as something blown by wind.

**pata'**₂ *n.* A decorative panel across the top of a square sail.

**pataw**₁ *n.* Floats used to support the upper edges of a net.

**patilud** *v. tr.* To straighten something's position.

**pat'kkad** *v. ditr.* To lower something to the sea floor.

**patron** *n.* The person in charge of a motor vessel, especially a passenger carrier.

**patumpang** *v. tr.* To get a ride in someone else's canoe.

**paulak** *v. intr. aN-* To form a floating mass, as items from a capsized boat.

**peddas** *n.* A canoe without outriggers, used by traditional houseboat Sama as auxiliary transport.

**pelang** *n.* A type of outrigger canoe constructed with planked sides attached to a wooden hull.

**pelang-tonda'an** *n.* A canoe used for trolling for large fish in open water.

**pengka-pengka** *n.* The bridle on the boom of a sail to which the sheet is attached.

**pespes** 1 *v. tr.* To blow a vessel off course.

**pespes** 1.1 *v. tr. -an* To affect someone's progress or direction by a strong wind.

**petong** *adj.* *a-* Small, of the mesh of a trawl net.

**petta'** *n.* A coracle-like vessel propelled by poling.

**peyad 1** *n.* Fish preserved by splitting open, salting, and drying in the sun.

**peyad 1.1** *v. tr.* To preserve fish by splitting, salting and drying.

**pikpik₁ 2** *n.* Fins which extend out horizontally from the sides of a plywood canoe hull.

**pindi' 1.1** *v. intr.* *aN-* To be engaged in gathering scallops.

**pipit₂ 1** *adj.* *a-* Very low, of tide.

**pipit₂ 1.1** *v. intr.* *aN-* To ebb to the furthest limit of the tide.

**p'ddon** *adj.* *a-* Capable of holding one's breath for a considerable time.

**p'llay 1** *v. intr.* *pa-* To change direction while moving, of a sailing vessel or someone walking.

**p'ssi 1** *n.* A fishhook.

**plātbōt** *n.* A raft-like structure used as an aid in recreational swimming.

**pokot₁ 1** *n.* A long seine net.

**pokot₁ 1.1** *v. tr.* To catch fish using a large seine net.

**pokot₂ 1** *n.* A loosely woven bag for holding fish caught during diving.

**pongag** *n.* An outrigger canoe whose hull is damaged or incomplete.

**powak** *n.* A shallow pool in sand flats exposed by a receding tide.

**ppo** *v. intr.* *aN-* To surface for an intake of breath, as a turtle does.

**puhu** *n.* A black pan formation on the sea floor.

**pū'₁** *n.* A high island, in contrast to an atoll.

**pulling** *n.* The egg sac of a shellfish, a delicacy in some species.

**pundang 1** *n.* Fish split and pierced for preserving.

**pundang 1.1** *v. tr.* To split open and pierce for preserving, of large fish.

**puntu** *clf.* Count word for canoes engaged in a fishing enterprise.

**punyal 1** *n.* A small dagger-like knife.

**punggul 1** *n.* A canoe with its upper side planks broken off.

**pungut 1.2** *v. tr.* To combine several strings of fish into a cluster.

**pupput₁ 1.2** *v. intr.* *aN-* To travel in a motorized vessel.

**sabit₁ 1.1** *v. tr.* *-an* To catch something on a hook.

**sabit₁ 2** *n.* A fishhook with multiple points.

**sabit₁ 2.2** *v. advrs.* *ka-...-an* To be hooked, of a fish.

**sabol-sabol 1** *v. intr.* *pa-* To hinder the flow of conversation by making a noise.

**sakat₂** *v. intr.* *pa-* To go up onto something; to board a boat.

**sakket 1** *n.* The nippers or pincers of a crab.

**sakket 1.1** *v. tr.* To nip something, as a crab does.

**sakla'** *v. intr.* *pa-* To overflow the normal tidal limit, of the sea.

**sagudsud** *v. intr.* *pa-* To drag the feet, as when walking in shallow water or through low brush.

**sahabal** *v. intr.* *aN-* To make the sound of a solid object moving through water.

**sahal₁ 1** *n.* The wash from passing vessels.

**sahal₁ 1.1** *v. intr.* *aN-* To break, of waves.

**sahali-bulan** *n.* The first day of the moon month, i.e. the day following the apearance of a new moon.

**sahapang 1** *n.* A long-shafted fish spear with three tines or spikes.

**sahapang 1.1** *v. tr.* To catch fish by spearing.

**sahat 1** *n.* A loop (traditionally of rattan) for snaring marine crustaceans such as lobsters.

**sahat 1.1** *v. tr.* To catch crustaceans using a noose.

**sait** *v. tr.* *-an* To bail water from a canoe.

**saitan-maut** *n.* A sea-dwelling spirit responsible for death by accident, as of someone who fails to give thanks for the provision of life's necessities.

**sa'am 1** *n.* An outrigger brace.

**sa'am 1.1** *v. tr.* To install a brace above an outrigger boom.

**salbabida** *n.* A swimming float of the kind known as a lifesaver.

**salekolan** *n.* An eddy created by the meeting of two currents.

**saleyok** *v. tr.* To spear fish from a canoe.

**salig₂** *n.* The chine of a canoe, i.e. the external angle between the sides and the flat bottom section.

**sallad** *v. intr.* *pa-/-um-* To run aground, of a boat.

**Sama Dilaut** *n. phrase* Literally 'Ocean Sama', a widely distributed subgroup of Central Sinama speakers who derive their living mainly from the sea and, whenever possible, build their pole houses in coastal shallows.

**Sama Jengen** *n. phrase* A group of nomadic Central Sinama speakers who until recently lived almost entirely in their covered boats.

**Sama Pagūng** *n. phrase* Literally 'Floating Sama', an alternative name for the geographically dispersed subgroup of Central Sinama speakers who maintain a nomadic or semi-nomadic life-style, living for long periods on their canoes.

**Sama Pala'u** *n. phrase* An alternative name for the geographically dispersed subgroup of Central Sinama speakers who maintain a nomadic or semi-nomadic life-style, living for long periods on their canoes.

**Sama Paosol** *n. phrase* A name for Central Sinama speakers who have exchanged their nomadic lifestyle for permanent houses built in shallow seawater.

**samb'llong** *v. intr.* *aN-* To make the sound of water moving by a solid object such as house posts.

**sampila'₂** *v. tr.* To shorten a quadrangular sail by folding down an upper point.

**samping 2** *n.* The lower side of a canoe just above the keel.

**sampoyak** *v. intr.* *pa-* To break over something, of waves.

**sangkaliya'** *v. tr.* To catch large fish such as sharks using whole fish as bait.

**sangkil 1** *n.* A fish spear with a single tine or prong; a harpoon.

**sanggal** *v. intr. pa-* To run aground on something projecting from the sea floor.

**sanglad** *v. intr. pa-/-um-* To run aground, of a boat.

**sangpad** *n.* The raised prow section of a tradition pelang-type canoe.

**sangpū' maka mpat kasobangan** *n. phrase* The fourteenth day of the lunar month.

**sāp₁** *n.* To dive to great depths, usually with the aid of a weight.

**sapa'** *n.* A river or channel; a body of water.

**sappit₂** *n.* A round-bottomed sailing vessel without outriggers, larger than a lepa and similar in size to a kumpit.

**sasa₁** *adj. a-* Split off along its length, as the top plank or strake of a canoe.

**sasahan 1** *n.* The flow of a liquid.

**sasahan 1.1** *adj. zero* Flowing, in contrast to still water.

**sasahan 1.2** *v. intr. aN-* To flow, as a running stream or blood; less often of a sea current.

**sasait** *n.* A bailer.

**sasay** *v. advrs. -in-* Having water splashing over the sides in volumes large enough to swamp, of a canoe.

**satan** *n.* A wind from the south; south wind.

**sau** *n.* An anchor.

**saubang** *n.* A long-shafted spear made from bamboo, used mainly for harvesting spiny sea urchins from a canoe.

**sauk 1.2** *v. tr.* To bail water out of a boat.

**sauk 2** *v. advrs. -in-* To be wet from wave action.

**sēk** *n.* The dorsal fin of some sharks.

**sibukaw 1.1** *n.* A dowel obtained from the sibukaw tree for fastening canoe planks.

**sikagūngan** *adj.* Floating in great numbers or mass.

**silung₂** *v. intr. aN-* To fish by articifial light such as a pressure lantern.

**simpal** *v. intr. a-* To be coming from an adverse direction, of wind.

**simpay** *v. tr.* To cut sailcloth to the required shape.

**simpayan** *n.* A pattern for making flexible items, as a sail or garment.

**sindung₂** *v. intr. aN-* To fish by an artificial light source.

**sinsoro 1** *n.* A fine-meshed drag net.

**sinsoro 1.1** *v. tr.* To catch small fish with a fine net.

**sintak 1** *v. tr.* To pull or tug on a line; to strike a hook into the mouth of a biting fish.

**sintak 2** *v. tr.* To raise a flag or sail.

**singki'** *n.* The inside angle of the chine of a canoe hull.

**sisik 1** *n.* A scale of fish.

**sisik 1.1** *v. tr. -an* To remove scales from a fish.

**siyud** *v. intr. pa-* To run a canoe lightly over the surface of a submerged object.

**siyul 1** *n.* A fine-meshed drag net.

**siyul 1.1** *v. tr.* To catch small fish with a fine net.

**s'bbat 1** *n.* The gullet of large marine creatures such as rays and whales.

**s'bbo** *n.* A type of branching coral that provides food and shelter for many marine species.

**s'kke** *n.* The ridged dorsal fin of certain fish.

**s'llad** *v. intr. pa-/-um-* To run aground, of a boat.

**s'llang₁** *n.* Open sea; an expanse of ocean not enclosed or interrupted by islands.

**s'llog** *n.* Current, as the flow of water.

**s'llop** *v. tr.* To flood by overflowing, as a low-lying area by high tide; to ship water, of a canoe.

**s'nnung 1.1** *v. intr. pa-* To break the surface, of a swimming fish.

**s'ngkol 1** *n.* The thwart of a canoe; a bulkhead in a larger vessel.

**s'pput** *v. intr. pa-* To splash or spray onto something, as water into canoe.

**sohonay** *v. intr. pa-/-um-* To go in a downstream direction; to go with the current.

**sōn** *n.* The current created by an incoming tide.

**sorekang** *n.* A crab-claw sail.

**sosob** *v. intr. pa-* To flow (the incoming phase), of tide.

**sosok** *v. tr. -an* To shape or smooth something with an adze.

**sosokan** *n.* A broad, chisel-like tool mounted on a long shaft.

**sowang** *n.* A coastal channel running through saltwater swamp forest; a stream or river inland.

**sowet** *v. tr.* To catch fish by diving from above the surface as kingfishers and some gulls do.

**ssol** *v. intr. aN-* To make the sound of water in rapid motion, as rain pattering or a kettle coming to the boil.

**suba'** *n.* An inlet of the sea; a bay.

**sudsud** *n.* A small fishing net supported by an X-shaped frame.

**suhutan** *n.* A retreat area inside the bow or stern of a large canoe.

**sularaw** *v. intr. aN-* To move smoothly across water, skimming the wave-tops one by one.

**suput₁** *v. intr. pa-/aN-* To surge up, as waves over an obstacle or water boiling over.

**tabul-tabul** *n.* The lashing that secures a sail to mast or boom.

**takāk** *n.* A mast extension.

**takot** *n.* A submerged reef.

**taktak 1.2** *v. tr.* To lower a sail.

**taddas** *n.* The underside of a hull, keel, or keelson.

**tagbak₁** *v. tr.* To stab something with a spear or harpoon.

**taguntun 1.1** *v. tr.* To allow one end of a line to hang or run free.

**taguntun 1.2** *v. tr. -an* To lower something on a line.

**tahemtem 1.1** *v. advrs. -in-* Having barnacles growing on it.

**tahetek** *n.* A submerged reef.

**tahik-bulagas** *n.* A phase of tide marked by strong current flows.

**tahik₁ 1** *n.* The sea as a body of water.

**tahik**₂ *n.* Seasons as defined by major wind phases.

**tai'-ambal** *n.* Ambergris.

**tai'-bamban** *n.* Fine mossy growth in the hull of a canoe.

**talbang 1** *adj. zero* Lost at sea.

**talbang 1.1** *v. tr. -an* To cause someone or something to vanish in the sea, the action of saitan spirits.

**tambak**₁ **1.2** *v. tr.* To keep captured fish alive in a rock-walled enclosure.

**tambang**₁ **1** *adj. zero* Nearing high water, of tidal range.

**tambang**₁ **1.1** *v. intr. pa-* To rise; to become high, of tide.

**tampalan** *adj. a-* Facing open sea or incoming weather.

**tampe** *n.* The upper limit of tidal flow.

**tampeppet** *v. intr. pa-* To skip across the surface of water, of a canoe or a thrown item.

**tana'-deyo'** *n.* The sea floor.

**tandan**₁ **1** *v. intr. pa-* To reach land from the sea.

**tandan**₁ **1.1** *v. tr.* To reach an objective by making landfall.

**tandan**₁ **1.2** *v. tr. -an* To convey something in a shoreward direction.

**tangkal**₂ **1** *n.* A buoy or float that supports and marks the position of fishing gear; a drift anchor.

**tangkal**₂ **1.1** *v. intr. aN-* To drift using a sea anchor.

**tanghab**₁ *v. tr. -an* To cut a groove or notch in a spar to keep a lashing from slipping.

**tangon 1** *v. intr. pa-* To move a canoe above sea level onto a supporting structure.

**tangon 1.1** *v. tr.* To raise something on a supporting structure, for maintenance or storage.

**tangonan** *n.* A structure for supporting a canoe above sea level.

**tape'-baliyu** *n.* The closing stage of a wind period.

**tape'an** *n.* The downstream side of a house relative to the incoming tide.

**tapi' 1** *n.* The lateral planking or strakes of a canoe hull.

**tapi' 1.1** *v. tr.* To fit planking to a dugout hull or wooden base.

**tapi' 1.2** *v. tr.* To build the superstructure of a canoe.

**tapi'-dalosan** *n.* The strake or side plank that runs the length of a canoe.

**tapiyan** *n.* The seaward edge of land, just above high water.

**tare' 1** *n.* A retractable lateral spine near the tail of certain fish.

**tare' 1.1** *v. advrs. -in-* Stabbed by a fish spine.

**tarik** *n.* The outrigger cross-booms between the main fore and aft booms, fitted on large pelang-type canoes to add strength.

**taruk** *n.* The mast of a sailing vessel.

**tarul** *n.* A gum exuding from some tree species, useful for filling holes in a canoe hull.

**tehem 1.1** *v. advrs. -in-* Having barnacles growing on something.

**temang** *n.* A flattish area of sea floor at the base of a sea-cliff, usually visible from the surface.

**tempel** *n.* A type of motor boat with a blunt stern and no outriggers.

**tempel-tempel** *n.* A small power boat built in the Western style.

**tibuk**₂ *v. tr.* To catch coral fish by driving them into a basket.

**tikabbol 1** *n.* The splash from something hitting a water surface.

**tikabbol 1.1** *v. tr. -an* To splash up from striking a water surface.

**tigbaw** *n.* A fresh-water pool, usually spring-fed.

**timbak 1.1** *v. tr.* To stun fish using dynamite.

**timbak-daing** *n.* Dynamite used in fishing.

**timbang**₁ **3** *v. intr. aN-* To shift the load in order to trim a canoe.

**timbang**₂ *n.* The place far from land where the sea floor falls away into the depths.

**timpas** *v. tr. -an* To trim a sail for optimum speed.

**timul** *n.* An east to southeast wind, generally unfavorable for sailing.

**timus-timus** *n.* Salt left by evaporation of sea-water, as on one's skin.

**tindakan** *n.* A block partway up a mast that bears the sprit that supports the upper end of a quadrilateral sail.

**tindayung** *v. tr. -an* To propel a boat using a paddle against a fulcrum; to row.

**tinduk**₁ *v. tr.* To strike at a bait or lure.

**tinula'** *n.* A stew of fish or meat seasoned with herbs.

**tingk'llos** *v. tr.* To secure a rope with a half-hitch.

**tipara 1** *n.* Diving goggles.

**titis 1.1** *v. intr. pa-* To drip off a surface as water from a swimmer.

**t'bba 1** *n.* Low tide; the lowest phase of the tidal range.

**t'bba 1.1** *v. intr. pa-* To ebb, of tide.

**t'bba 1.2** *v. advrs. ka-...-an* To be stranded by receding tide.

**t'bba-bulagas** *n.* Exceptionally low tide, associated with full moon.

**t'bba' 1.1** *v. ditr.* To direct the movement of fish by striking the water surface above them.

**t'kkad 1** *v. intr. pa-/-um-* To reach the bottom of a body of water or mud.

**t'ddak** *v. tr.* To open up a body; to gut a stomach in order to remove entrails.

**t'ddo' 1** *adj. zero* Calm, of weather conditions; windless.

**t'ddo' 1.1** *v. intr. pa-* To become calm, of weather conditions.

**t'ddo' 1.2** *v. tr. -an* To cause a boat to be stationary due to lack of wind.

**t'ppad** *v. tr.* To cast a fishnet.

**togge'**₂ *v. tr.* To locate fish by looking down from a moving canoe.

**togong 1** *n.* A small woven fish trap, rectangular in section with the entry funnel at one end.

**togong 1.1** *v. tr.* To catch fish with a togong type trap.

**tōhan** *n.* A loop of string, wire or rattan, on which fish are strung as they are caught.

**to'on₂** *v. tr. -an* To put a weight on a fish trap to keep it in place.

**tonda'₁ 1** *n.* A heavy gauge line used for trolling.

**tonda'₁ 1.1** *v. tr.* To catch pelagic fish, especially tuna, with a trolled lure.

**tonga' 1.1** *adj. a-* Halfway to a reference point, as a container; halfway, of tidal range.

**tuba 1** *n.* A plant-based poison for stupefying fish.

**tuba 1.1** *v. tr.* To catch fish using plant-based poison.

**tukad₁ 1.2** *v. tr. -an* To get something by going uphill or upstream.

**tukag** *n.* A prop; a pole for supporting the outer peak of a four-cornered sail; a sprit.

**tukkal** *v. intr. pa-* To go fishing without a companion.

**tukkud 1.1** *v. tr. -an* To propel a canoe by poling.

**tuklug 1** *n.* A prop for supporting the outer peak of a sail; a sprit.

**tuklug 1.1** *v. tr.* To prop up the sail.

**tūd₁ 1** *adj. -an* To be following, of the wind (when sailing).

**tūd₁ 1.1** *v. intr. pa-* To run freely before the wind (when sailing).

**tugut 1** *v. intr. pa-* To slacken, of the flow of a current.

**tugut 1.1** *v. tr. -an* To let out slack in a line or sail.

**tuhun 1** *v. intr. pa-/a-* To dive into water; to submerge.

**tuhun 1.1** *v. tr.* To reach something by diving.

**tuhun 1.2** *v. tr. -an* To get something by diving for it.

**tulis** *n.* The decorative lines or markings of a canoe.

**tulun-bantayan** *n.* A canoe that is seaworthy in all weather conditions.

**tumbuk₁ 1** *v. intr. pa-* To impact heavily, of a natural force such as wind or current.

**tumpal** *v. tr. -an* To repair a canoe by patching a hole or gap.

**tundan 1** *v. intr. pa-* To get a tow from another vessel, usually one which is motorized.

**tundan 1.1** *v. intr. aN-* To connect to a tow line.

**tundan 1.2** *v. tr.* To tow something.

**tundanan** *n.* Things attached by a line to the rear of another vessel, as canoes being towed by a launch.

**tundug 1** *v. intr. pa-* To beach; to reach shore.

**tundug 1.1** *v. tr.* To ferry someone to shore.

**tuntun₂** *n.* A fin or flapper of a large fish.

**tungkud 1.1** *v. tr. -an* To propel a canoe by poling.

**tunggara'** *n.* A southeast wind.

**tungul 1** *n.* The air bladder of a fish.

**tustus** *v. tr. -an* To unlash the ropes which hold a sail to a mast.

**tuwa 1** *n.* A vine, the roots of which provide a substance for stupefying fish.

**tuwa 1.1** *v. tr.* To catch fish by stupefying with an extract of the tuwa vine.

**ubug₁ 1** *v. intr. pa-* To wade towards something.

**ubug₁ 1.1** *v. tr.* To reach a goal by wading.

**ubug₂** *v. tr.* To pursue a lure.

**ulak 1** *n.* Floating trash; flotsam.

**ulak 1.1** *v. tr.* To collect floating items into a single mass.

**ulang 2** *n.* A wooden lure, shrimp-shaped, for squid.

**ullang 1** *n.* A wooden lure for catching squid, has multiple barb-less hooks and resembles a shrimp.

**ullang 1.1** *v. intr. aN-* To catch squid using a carved lure.

**umpak-umpak** *n.* Choppy waves.

**umpan 1** *n.* Bait.

**umpan 1.1** *v. tr. -an* To bait a hook or trap.

**untang** *n.* A buoy or float for supporting long-line fishing gear and marking its location.

**ungus** *n.* Coarse sand; a sandy beach.

**ungus-bunbun** *n.* Fine white sand.

**uttala'** *n.* A north wind, often gusty and associated with dry weather.

**uttala'-lo'ok** *n.* A northeast wind, generally light.

## C: House construction

**atop 1** *n.* The roof of a building.

**babag 1** *n.* A main structural crosspiece, as the floor bearer of a house or the spine of a kite.

**bahurungan** *n.* The ridgepole of a building.

**balkon** *n.* The front veranda of a house.

**ballay** *n.* A house in process of building.

**bamban₂** *n.* A species of slender cane used for tying thatch panels.

**bangkayawan** *n.* The spine of a thatch shingle, to which leaves are attached.

**baras-baras** *n.* Building materials consisting of unsawn tree branches less in diameter than a man's wrist.

**barena 1** *n.* A carpenter's drill or brace.

**batang-buhungan** *n.* The ridgepole of a house.

**bilik 1** *n.* A partitioned area of a house; room.

**bīt₂** *v. tr.* To lash slats to a framework, as when building a floor or deck.

**bitil-bitil** *v. tr.* To fasten building material in a temporary manner.

**bubungan** *n.* A covering along the ridge of a roof.

**buhungan** *n.* The ridge of a house as viewed from outside.

**kahāgan** *n.* Structures involving posts.

**kamalig** *n.* A building or roofed shelter, used for storage or as a workplace.

**kasaw** *n.* Thatch poles which run across the purlins, parallel to the rafters to which thatch is tied.

**kōkan 1** *n.* The upstream side of a house relative to the incoming tidal flow.

**kunit-kunit** *n.* A species of swamp tree with durable pale-gold wood, used for house posts.

**kura'-kura'₂** *n.* Crossed pieces of wood a meter or so in length which hold down the capping over the ridge of a house.

**kusina** *n.* A kitchen.

**dagan₁** *n.* The horizontal components of a construction; floor bearers, deck supports.

**dinding 1** *n.* The exterior wall of a house.

**gatgat 1** *n.* A saw, the carpenter's tool.

**gatgat-basi'** *n.* A hacksaw.

**gaugari' 1** *n.* A file; a rasp (the shaping tool).

**gaugari' 1.1** *v. tr.* To shape something using a file or rasp.

**gayang** *n.* A long-bladed working knife.

**gipis 1** *n.* A strip of wood or bamboo used to hold thatch or walling in place.

**gipis 1.1** *v. tr.* To hold something in place with battens.

**hãg 1** *n.* A post of a house or fence.

**hãg 1.1** *v. tr. -an* To provide a structure with posts.

**hãg analus** *n. phrase* The main house posts, generally on corners, that run through right up to the tops of the walls.

**hanglad 1** *n.* Building materials of unsawn round-wood, usually from two to four inches in diameter.

**hanglad 2** *n.* Poles running across the purlins of a roof (parallel to rafters) to which thatch shingles are tied.

**haron 1** *n.* A stepped device for getting from one level to another, as a house post, stairway, or ladder.

**hobong** *n.* The crossbeams connecting house posts at the top of a wall.

**lansang 1** *n.* A building nail or bolt.

**lansang 1.1** *v. tr.* To fasten something by nailing.

**lantay 1** *n.* A floor.

**lapaw** *n.* A building with no walls.

**lawang 1** *n.* A door or doorway.

**layang-layang** *n.* The extended projections of the barge-boards of a house, decorated as formalized wings.

**likup 1** *n.* A chisel-like tool for making holes in wood.

**likup 1.1** *v. tr.* To make a hole in wood using a tool with a cutting tip.

**ligpit 1** *n.* A batten or lath.

**ligpit 1.1** *v. tr.* To hold roofing or walling in place by fastening with battens.

**listun** *n.* Milled lumber of small dimensions, as for light framing.

**lona** *n.* A tent or tent-like cloth shelter, especially in the context of Boy Scouts or school camping.

**lubing-lubing** *n.* The bamboo laths to which nipa shingles are tied.

**lusuk-lusuk** *n.* Upright supports, such as doorposts.

**millat** *v. tr.* To break out the side of a plank when drilling dowel holes.

**nipa'** *n.* The nipa palm, the leaflets of which provide a moderately durable material used for roofing and for hats. *Nipa fruticans.*

**osol 1** *v. intr. pa-* To stand upright in the soil or sea-floor, of a pole or a post.

**osol 1.1** *v. tr. -an* To drive a post or stake into the soil or sea-floor; to provide a house with posts.

**pagdayaw 1** *n.* The basic components of a structure, as the skeleton and sinews of a body, or the framing of a house or boat.

**pa'at 1** *n.* A tool for making holes in wood.

**pa'at 1.1** *v. tr.* To make a hole in wood with a chisel or a drill.

**pa'ud 1** *n.* A piece or shingle of palm thatch, about 1 meter in length.

**palimba'an** *n.* Purlins, the long pieces of timber framing that lie transverse to rafters and support the poles to which thatch shingles are tied.

**pantān** *n.* A porch; a platform.

**panggung** *n.* A building with floor and roof but no walls; an open market.

**pangtu'ud** *n.* A post that extends to the top of a house wall.

**patahan** *n.* A threshold; a lintel.

**pillayag** *n.* A field shelter built of light materials.

**sairing 1** *n.* A walling panel woven from young coconut leaflets.

**sairing 1.1** *v. tr.* To weave a panel of young coconut leaflets.

**saisig** *n.* A panel tightly woven from strips of bamboo or cane.

**salirap** *n.* A panel woven of coconut palm leaflets.

**salsal** *n.* The floor joists which rest on bearers, and run parallel with the length of a house.

**sangkap 1** *n.* A chisel.

**sapaw 1** *n.* An awning of woven leaves or material such as sailcloth.

**saurung** *n.* An unwalled open area of a house; a porch.

**sayap 1** *n.* A shade or awning built over a window.

**sibay** *n.* The outermost purlin of a sloping roof, i.e. the one at the lowest edge.

**sibayan** *n.* The raised area on the upstream side of a house, an area reserved for ritual ancestor matters.

**sigid** *v. tr.* To tie thatch shingles on to the slats that run parallel to the rafters.

**siling** *n.* The outer edge of a sloping roof.

**silingan** *n.* Eaves; the outer edge of a sloping roof.

**sumpiyang** *n.* A rafter; a post, brace or support set at an angle to the vertical.

**sūngan** *n.* The gable end of a ridged roof.

**sungkelang** *n.* A rafter; any post or support set at an angle to the vertical.

**taka 1** *n.* A notch cut to facilitate climbing; the rung of a ladder.

**taka 1.1** *v. tr. -an* To notch something for climbing or for supporting a cross-beam.

**tandawan** *n.* A window.

**tape'an** *n.* The downstream side of a house relative to the incoming tide.

**tiggup 1** *adj. a-* Enclosed, of a building.

**tiggup 1.1** *v. tr.* To complete the fitting together (of building materials).

**tingkap** *v. tr.* To build a temporary shelter using locally available materials.

**tiyadtad** *n.* Flattened bamboo used for walling.

**tuku 1** *n.* A short vertical post or prop.

**tuku 1.1** *v. tr.* To support something with a short post (in a building).

**tumbuk-buhungan** *n.* The central supporting stud of a roof between the ridge pole and the cross beam.

**ungkup** *n.* A traditional roof construction in which the gables at each end slope outwards under the ridge pole extensions.

# D: Classifiers

**-ngan** Numeral classifier suffix used when enumerating people.

**bahangi 2** *clf.* Count word for periods of 24 hours.

**balang 2** *clf.* Count word for long fillets of flesh.

**batang₂ 2** *clf.* Count word for stick-shaped pieces.

**bingkis 2** *clf.* Count word for items in a stack.

**birang 2** *clf.* Count word for rolls of net.

**b'llad 2** *clf.* Count word for sheets.

**b'llat 2** *clf.* Count word for items that can be rolled or folded.

**botang₁ 2** *clf.* Count word for piles of small items.

**bulan₂ 2** *clf.* Count word for nights of the month.

**bungkal₃ 2** *clf.* Count word for balls of tobacco leaf.

**būs 2** *clf.* Count word for rolls of cloth.

**kaha₂ 2** *clf.* Count word for packets of things.

**kapan** *clf.* Count word for the strips of cloth used to wrap a corpse.

**kasobangan** *clf.* Count word for the nights in a lunar month.

**kehet 2** *clf.* Count word for slices of something to be eaten.

**kintas 2** *clf.* Count word for foldable items.

**koleng₁ 2** *clf.* Count word for rolls or coils.

**kuri'an 2** *clf.* Count word for bundles of uncut cloth.

**dakayu'₁ 3** *clf.* Count word for individual items of things.

**daug 2** *clf.* Count word for clusters of fruit.

**galung 2** *clf.* Count word for bundles of flexible items.

**gekap 2** *clf.* Count word for flat items.

**gipit 2** *clf.* Count word for packages of pressed cassava meal.

**gulung 2** *clf.* Count word for rolls of flexible material such as cloth.

**halug 2** *clf.* Count word for bundles of pepper-vine leaves.

**lamba₂** *clf.* Count word for flexible items.

**lapis₁ 2** *clf.* Count word for layers of things.

**lit** *clf.* Count word for strings of corn cobs.

**llaw₁ 2** *clf.* Count word for days as units of 24 hours.

**munda'₁ 2** *clf.* Count word for counting canoes.

**okat₁ 2** *clf.* Count word for bundles of leaf tobacco.

**paipa'₁ 2** *clf.* Count word for gill segments of large stingrays.

**pa'ud 2** *clf.* Count word for thatch shingles.

**papan₂** *clf.* Count word for packets of firecrackers.

**peged₂ 2** *clf.* Count word for tiny things.

**pikit₃ 1** *clf.* Count word for size and value of gold coin-jewelry.

**pikul 2** *clf.* Count word for large sacks of produce.

**pis₂ 2** *clf.* Count word for slices of things.

**pitu' 2** *clf.* Count word for weeks as units of time.

**p'ppot 2** *clf.* Count word for pole-like things.

**po'on₁ 2** *clf.* Count word for plantation trees.

**puhu' 2** *clf.* Count word for people.

**puntak 2** *clf.* Count word for piles of things for sale.

**puntu** *clf.* Count word for canoes engaged in a fishing enterprise.

**pungut 2** *clf.* Count word for clusters of produce.

**puttak 2** *clf.* Count word for piles of vegetables presented for sale.

**salik 2** *clf.* Count word for wedges of things.

**sanggi' 2** *clf.* Count word for strips of flexible plant material.

**silang₂** *clf.* Count word for sections of thatch.

**s'kkat 2** *clf.* Count word for hands of bananas.

**s'ppe' 2** *clf.* Count word for hands of bananas.

**solag 2** *clf.* Count word for members of a set or collection.

**sugpat 2** *clf.* Count word for things that join lengthwise, as thatch panels.

**takil** *clf.* Count word for packages of processed sago meal.

**tongko' 2** *clf.* Count word for coils of line or wire.

**tuhug 3** *clf.* Count word for strings of things, most commonly of fish.

**tundun 2** *clf.* Count word for clusters of fruit.

# Part 3

# 4

## Phonology and Orthography

## 4.1 Phonological, orthographic and grammatical abbreviations

| | | | |
|---|---|---|---|
| * | ungrammatical, phonologically unacceptable | DU | dual |
| | | EX | existential |
| [ ] | phonetic | EXCL | exclusive |
| / / | phonemic | IMP | imperative |
| < > | orthographic | INCL | inclusive |
| < > | infix boundary | INTRJ | interjection |
| . | syllable boundary | INTR | intransitive |
| = | clitic attachment | N | unspecified nasal consonant |
| Ø | null morpheme | NEG | negator |
| ~ | ligature | PASS | passive |
| ADJ | adjective | PL | plural |
| AM | actor marker | PM | personal name marker |
| APPL | applicative | PRON | pronoun |
| APT | aptative | PRT | particle |
| ATR | atransitive | PST | past marker |
| AV | actor voice | Q | question marker |
| C | consonant | SG | singular |
| CAUS | causative | SM | subject marker |
| D.DIST | distal demonstrative | TOP | topicalizer |
| D.IDENT | demonstrative identifier | TR | transitive |
| D.PROX | proximal demonstrative | UV | undergoer voice |
| D.REMV | remote demonstrative, vague | V | vowel |

## 4.2 Sounds and symbols

Central Sinama has twenty-three (23) phonemes: seventeen (17) consonants and six (6) vowels. Table 4 shows the consonants, and table 6 the vowels. In these tables, each phoneme is listed in a row with the different phonetic values it has in speech, followed by its symbol in the Sinama orthography. All phonemes have phonemic lengthened counterparts, except for /h/, /ɲ/, /ʔ/, and /ə/ (see section 4.3 Phoneme length). The lengthened phonemes are not listed individually in the tables below. Instead they are abstractly represented as /CC/ and /VV/ in the last rows of each table.

## 4.2.1 The consonants

### Table 4. Sinama consonant phonemes

| Phoneme | Phonetic value(s) | Orthographic symbol |
|---------|-------------------|---------------------|
| /b/ | [b], [β], [ɓ] | \<b\> |
| /k/ | [k], [ k] | \<k\> |
| /d/ | [d], [ɾ], [ɗ] | \<d\>, \<r\> [a] |
| /g/ | [g], [ɣ], [ɠ] | \<g\> |
| /h/ | [h] | \<h\> |
| /d͡ʒ/ | [d͡ʒ] | \<j\> |
| /l/ | [l], [l̪] | \<l\> |
| /m/ | [m] | \<m\> |
| /n/ | [n] | \<n\> |
| /ɲ/ | [n y] | \<ny\> |
| /ŋ/ | [ŋ] | \<ng\> |
| /p/ | [p], [ p] | \<p\> |
| /s/ | [s] | \<s\> |
| /t/ | [t], [ t] | \<t\> |
| /w/ | [w] | \<w\> |
| /j/ | [j] | \<y\> |
| /ʔ/ | [ʔ] | \< ' \> |
| /CC/ | [C:] | \<CC\> [b] |

[a]  \<r\> is used intervocalically. It is also used at the beginning of a handful of loanwords; otherwise, \<d\> is used word-initially.

[b]  Except for /d͡ʒd͡ʒ/, which is realized phonetically as [d.d͡ʒ] and represented in the orthography by \<dj\>.

As shown in table 4, several of the phonemes have multiple allophones, depending on the position in an utterance. For any given phoneme, the same letter is used in the orthography for all its allophones, with one exception: when the flap [ɾ] occurs word-medially, the letter \<r\> is used instead of \<d\>. Some examples are shown in table 5.

### Table 5. Examples of Sinama consonant allophones

| Phonemic value | Phonetic realization | Orthographic spelling | |
|----------------|----------------------|-----------------------|---|
| /babaʔ/ | [ˈbaβäʔ] [a] | \<baba'\> | 'carry on the back' |
| /binajadan/ | [ˌbinäˈjaränn] | \<binayaran\> | 'paid' |
| /pagal/ | [ˈpaɣäl] | \<pagal\> | 'fish trap' |
| /aku du/ | [ˈakʊ ɾu] | \<aku du\> | 'I indeed' |

[a]  [ˈ] is the IPA symbol marking primary stress. It is not to be confused with *hamsa'* \< ' \>, the orthographic symbol for /ʔ/, and /ə/.

### 4.2.1.1 The glottal stop /ʔ/

The glottal stop /ʔ/ can occur in two positions: at the end of a word, or between two vowels. It is represented in the orthography by the letter *hamsa'*, a short vertical line \< ' \> which looks like a straight apostrophe.[1] The glottal stop is a significant consonant in Central Sinama. As such, it is

---

1  *Hamsa'* is a loanword from Arabic where it is the name of the symbol used to represent the glottal stop.

always written wherever it is used. This is in contrast to many other languages, such as Filipino, in which the glottal stop is either written only in certain positions in the word, or is not written at all.

### Word-final glottal stop

The letter < ' > is small and discreet, and could easily be overlooked at the end of a word. However, there are many Sinama words that differ only by the presence or absence of a word-final glottal stop: for example, *bowa* 'to carry' versus *bowa'* 'mouth', or *mata* 'eye' versus *mata'* 'raw'. Consequently, the word-final glottal stop is always written, to prevent confusion between such similar words.

### Glottal stop between vowels

The glottal stop is also contrastive between vowels in Sinama. When two adjacent vowels occur in Sinama, they might be separated by a glottal stop, e.g., *ta'ut* 'bounce up and down', or *ba'i* 'the parent of one's son-in-law or daughter-in-law.' Or, two vowels might be adjacent with no intervening glottal stop, e.g., *kaut* 'to go seaward', *sai* 'who'. To avoid potential confusion, the glottal stop is always written when it occurs between vowels.

## 4.2.2 The vowels

Table 6. Sinama vowel phonemes

| Phoneme | Phonetic value(s) | Orthographic symbol |
|---|---|---|
| /a/ | [a], [ä] | <a> |
| /e/ | [e], [ɛ] | <e> |
| /i/ | [i], [ɪ] | <i> |
| /o/ | [o], [ɔ] | <o> |
| /u/ | [u], [ʊ] | <u> |
| /ə/ | [ə] | < ' > [a] |
| /VV/ | [V:] | <V̄> [b] |

[a] This letter is written only word-medially. The central vowel /ə/ is not symbolized word-initially, and never occurs word-finally.

[b] /ə/ is never lengthened.

Five of the Central Sinama vowels are closely similar to the Filipino vowels /a/, /e/, /i/, /o/, and /u/. The sixth vowel is the central vowel /ə/, also referred to as schwa. The Central Sinama orthography represents the schwa using the letter *hamsa'* < ' >, e.g., *l'ngngon* 'arm'. Even though < ' > is used to represent both the schwa (a vowel) and the glottal stop (a consonant), Sama readers do not find this confusing. The two sounds never occur in the same position in a word, so the letter's location within a word makes it obvious to readers whether a vowel or consonant is intended. When it occurs between two consonants, as in *l'ngngon* /ləŋ.ŋon/[2] 'arm', *hamsa'* represents a vowel. Between vowels or word finally, as in *ta'ut* /ta.ʔut/ 'bounce up and down' and *bowa'* /bo.waʔ/ 'mouth', *hamsa'* represents a consonant.

#### 4.2.2.1 The central vowel /ə/

Non-Sinama speakers may at first have trouble distinguishing the central vowel schwa /ə/ from the other five vowels, because some Philippine languages such as Filipino and Visayan do not use the central vowel. But to Sinama speakers it sounds quite distinct from the other vowels. Many words in Sinama are distinguished only by this vowel (for example, *kambal* 'species of sea anemone' versus *k'mbal* 'twin'). So it is necessary that the central vowel have a symbol of its own in the orthography.

The central vowel /ə/ differs in several ways from the other five vowels.

2 The period is the IPA symbol for a syllable boundary.

1.  /ə/ only occurs in non-final syllables of Sinama words and is always followed by a pair of consonants with the same point of articulation (i.e., a homorganic consonant cluster), e.g., /bəlla/ 'to cook', /kəmbal/ 'twin', /bənsi/ 'to hate', /asəŋŋot/ 'irritable', /dənda/ 'female', /əŋgoʔ/ 'mother'.

2.  /ə/ is of distinctly shorter length than the other five vowels, and has no lengthened phonemic counterpart (see section 4.3 Phoneme length).

3.  When the central vowel /ə/ occurs word-initially, it is absorbed by the following consonant, which in turn becomes syllabic and carries the syllable's stress: e.g., /əmbal/ [m̩bal] <mbal> 'no'. In the orthography, /ə/ is not represented in the word-initial position. When a prefix is added, however, the central vowel re-emerges in both speech and writing, e.g., [aŋəmbal] <ang'mbal> 'to refuse'.

# 4.3 Phoneme length

Most Sinama phonemes, both vowels and consonants, demonstrate contrastive length. (The exceptions are the consonants /h/, /ɲ/, and /ʔ/, and the central vowel /ə/.) Long consonants and vowels can be difficult for non-native Sinama speakers to distinguish from short ones. This difficulty is mitigated somewhat by the predictable stress pattern of Sinama and the stress shift sometimes caused by long vowels (see section 4.4 Word stress). To native speakers the difference between long and short phonemes is clear.

## 4.3.1 Long consonants

Long consonants are interpreted as consonant pairs (geminates) across syllable boundaries (/C.C/), and are written as pairs of identical letters, e.g., /ˈkap.pal/ [ˈkapːal] <kappal> 'ship', versus /ˈka.pal/ [ˈkapal] <kapal> 'thickness'. The cluster [dd͡ʒ] is also interpreted as a geminate, but is written <dj>, e.g., /ˈbud͡ʒ.d͡ʒaŋ/ [ˈbudːʒaŋ] <budjang> 'maiden'.

The geminate pair /ss/ is pronounced as a lengthened [sː] in some Central Sinama dialects (e.g., [ˈbasːa] 'read'), and as an affricate [t͡s] in other dialects (e.g., [ˈbat͡sa]). In either case, it is spelled <ss>.

## 4.3.2 Long vowels

As with long consonants, long vowels are interpreted as vowel pairs (geminates). A geminate vowel is equivalent to two syllable segments (/V.V/). For instance, [siˈgaː] is syllabified as /siˈga.a/. However, vowel length is not written orthographically as a pair of vowels, but is represented by a macron over the vowel, e.g., [siˈgaː] <sigā> '3DU.I', versus [ˈsiga] <siga> 'cigarette'. This prevents Sinama long vowels from being misread as a two-vowel sequence separated by a glottal stop (i.e., [sigaʔa]).

# 4.4 Word stress

Sinama word stress is not contrastive. Unlike some languages in the Philippines, there are no Sinama words that differ only by the placement of stress. Stress in Sinama is predictable, falling always on the second-to-last (penultimate) syllable, e.g., /ˈta.hik/ <tahik> 'ocean', /ta.ˈlu.waʔ/ <taluwaʔ> 'on target', and /ˌpa.ba.ˈha.kan/ <pabahakan> 'bed'. When a word is suffixed, the addition of the suffix changes the penultimate syllable. The primary stress accordingly moves to the right. For example, compare /ˈa.nak/ <anak> 'offspring' with /ˌni.a.ˈna.kan/ <nianakan> 'born'. This stress shift also occurs when a clitic pronoun attaches to a word, e.g., /a.ˈnak.ku/ <anakku> 'my child'.

Sinama's penultimate stress placement provides the most important piece of evidence motivating the analysis of long vowels as geminate pairs. When the final syllable of a word contains a long vowel, the stress falls on that vowel, e.g., [siˈgaː] <sigā> '3DU.I'. Analyzing the long vowel as a geminate sequence of two identical vowels means that penultimate stress placement is maintained.

The stress still falls on the penultimate syllable, which is the first of the two identical vowels in the pair, i.e., /si.ˈga.a/ for the example above.

## 4.5 Vowel sequences within a word root

Unlike some languages in the Philippines, Sinama permits sequences of two vowels without an intervening glottal stop. The vowel sequences permitted within a word root are /ai/, /ao/, and /au/. Also, the sequences /ae/ and /oe/ occur in a small number of loanwords. Any other vowel sequence is disallowed within a word root. For example,

| | | | |
|---|---|---|---|
| /ai/ | <kait> | 'safety pin' | |
| /ao/ | <daogdog> | 'thunder' | |
| /au/ | <sauk> | 'dipper' | |
| /ae/ | <aes> | 'ice' | (loanwords only) |
| /oe/ | <poen> | 'point' | (loanwords only) |

There are separate rules for vowel sequences created by adding a prefix or suffix to a root (see section 4.7.3 Vowel combinations at morpheme boundaries).

Sinama <y> and <w> represent the phonemic consonants /j/ and /w/. These are not merely transitional semi-vowels, as in some Philippine languages. The vowel-consonant (VC) sequences /aj/ <ay> and /aw/ <aw> contrast with the vowel-vowel (VV) sequences /ai/ <ai> and /au/ <au> at the end of words. For example,

| | | | | | | |
|---|---|---|---|---|---|---|
| /ˈla.i/ | <lai> | 'plate/dish' | v. | /ˈa.taj/ | <atay> | 'liver' |
| /ˈba.u/ | <bau> | 'odor' | v. | /ˈdu.law/ | <dulaw> | 'turmeric' |

Shifting word stress can help disambiguate word-final VC and VV sequences. Each of the vowels in a geminate VV sequence forms a syllable of its own (/V.V/). Without any affixation, penultimate stress falls on the first vowel in the word-final VV sequence, e.g., /ˈla.i/ <lai> 'plate'. When a suffix or a bound clitic pronoun is added to such a word, the penultimate stress moves to the right, so that /ˈla.i/ + /=na/ becomes /la.ˈi.na/ <laina> 'his/her plate'. However, in the case of a word-final VC sequence, e.g., /ˈa.taj/ <atay> 'liver', stress shift demonstrates that the <y> is truly a consonant, in that it cannot carry the stress, i.e., /a.ˈtaj.na/ <atayna> 'his/her liver', not */a.ta.ˈj.na/ <atayna> 'his/her liver'. These shifts in stress position are clearly heard in speech.

## 4.6 Reduplication and compounds

Reduplicated stems are written with a hyphen between the reduplicated elements:

| | |
|---|---|
| <ai-ai> | 'whatever' |
| <lahi-lahi> | 'to run' |
| <ahāp-hāp> | 'rather good' |

Compound words are also indicated by a hyphen between the compounded elements:

| | |
|---|---|
| <batang-sulat> | 'letter of the alphabet' |
| <ondeʹ-bahaʹu> | 'teenager' |

## 4.7 Morphophonemics

The addition of a prefix or suffix to a Sinama word can create some minor complications in the spelling of the word because of the interaction of phonological and morphological processes at morpheme boundaries.

## 4.7.1 Nasal assimilation

Several Sinama prefixes (*aN-*, *paN-*, and *maN-*) end with an unspecified nasal consonant, represented by *N*. The form of this consonant varies according to the place of articulation of the following phoneme. Table 7 shows the pattern for each phoneme in turn.

Table 7. Nasal assimilation paradigm

| Prefix | Initial phoneme | Combination | Example | | |
|---|---|---|---|---|---|
| /aN-/ | /a/ | /aŋa-/ | /aN-/ + /aksi/ 'to sneeze' | → | /aŋaksi/ \<angaksi\> |
| | /b/ | /am-/ | /aN-/ + /bəlli/ 'to buy' | → | /aməlli/ \<amˈlli\> |
| | /k/ | /aŋ-/ | /aN-/ + /kalaŋ/ 'to sing' | → | /aŋalaŋ/ \<angalang\> |
| | /d/ | /aŋand-/ | /aN-/ + /daag/ 'to climb up' | → | /aŋandaag/ \<angandāg\> |
| | /e/ | /aŋe-/ | /aN-/ + /entom/ 'to miss someone' | → | /aŋentom/ \<angentom\> |
| | /g/ | /aŋaŋg-/ | /aN-/ + /gawgaw/ 'to stir' | → | /aŋaŋgawgaw/ \<anganggawgaw\> |
| | /h/ | /aŋah-/ | /aN-/ + /humbu/ 'to emit smoke' | → | /aŋahumbu/ \<angahumbu\> |
| | /i/ | /aŋi-/ | /aN-/ + /indam/ 'to borrow' | → | /aŋindam/ \<angindam\> |
| | /d͡ʒ/ | /aŋand͡ʒ-/ | /aN-/ + /d͡ʒaga/ 'to guard' | → | /aŋand͡ʒaga/ \<anganjaga\> |
| | /ə/ | /aŋə-/ | /aN-/ + /əmbal/ 'to refuse' | → | /aŋəmbal/ \<angˈmbal\> |
| | /l/ | /aŋal-/ | /aN-/ + /linig/ 'to glisten' | → | /aŋalinig/ \<angalinig\> |
| | /m/ | /aŋam-/ | /aN-/ + /manit/ 'to troll for tuna' | → | /aŋamanit/ \<angamanit\> |
| | /n/ | /aŋan-/ | /aN-/ + /nanam/ 'to sense' | → | /aŋananam/ \<angananam\> |
| | /o/ | /aŋo-/ | /aN-/ + /olaŋ/ 'to shout' | → | /aŋolaŋ/ \<angolang\> |
| | /p/ | /am-/ | /aN-/ + /pikit/ 'to adhere' | → | /amikit/ \<amikit\> |
| | /s/ | /an-/ | /aN-/ + /sohoʔ/ 'to command' | → | /anohoʔ/ \<anohoˈ\> |
| | /t/ | /an-/ | /aN-/ + /tahiʔ/ 'to sew' | → | /anahiʔ/ \<anahiˈ\> |
| | /u/ | /aŋu-/ | /aN-/ + /ulan/ 'to rain' | → | /aŋulan/ \<angulan\> |
| | /w/ | /aŋw-/ | /aN-/ + /wakil/ 'to act as a representative' | → | /aŋwakil/ \<angwakil\> |

## 4.7.2 *-in-* and *ni-*

The prefix *ni-* is a phonologically conditioned allomorph of the infix *-in-*. It is used with words beginning with /l/, /h/, /n/, or a vowel. For example,

| | | | |
|---|---|---|---|
| *nilangkat* | 'dismantled' | from | *langkat* 'to dismantle' |
| *nihella'* | 'pulled' | from | *hella'* 'to pull' |
| *ninajalan* | 'sworn a vow over' | from | *najal* 'vow' |
| *niuban* | 'gray-haired' | from | *uban* 'gray hair' |

## 4.7.3 Vowel combinations at morpheme boundaries

Affixation in Sinama can give rise to vowel sequences that do not occur within word roots. The permitted sequences, and corresponding orthographic rules, are different at prefix boundaries and at suffix boundaries. (Infixation does not create vowel sequences in Sinama).

### 4.7.3.1 Vowel combinations at prefix boundaries

All Sinama vowel-final prefixes end in /a/ or /i/.[3] Any vowel sequence beginning with /a/ or /i/ is permitted at a prefix boundary, with the exception of sequences of identical vowels. When a sequence of identical vowels is created by the addition of a prefix, a glottal stop is inserted between them. Table 8 gives examples of the possible vowel sequences.

Table 8. Vowel sequences at prefix boundaries: Examples

| | | Final letter of prefix | |
|---|---|---|---|
| | | a- | i- |
| Initial letter of word root | a- | *a'abbu* 'proud' <br> from *abbu* 'pride' | *niagaw* 'seized by force' <br> from *agaw* 'to seize by force' |
| | e- | *aettom* 'dark in color' <br> from *ettom* 'black' | *pikiembet* 'ask someone to play tag' <br> from *embet* 'play tag' |
| | i- | *painay* 'what/how' <br> from *inay* 'to happen' | *ni'inay* 'done how?' <br> from *inay* 'to happen' |
| | o- | *paokat* 'to separate' <br> from *okat* 'separate' | *niosolan* 'driven, of posts' <br> from *osol* 'drive a post' |
| | u- | *kauli'an* 'healed' <br> from *uli'* 'cure' | *niukay* 'opened' <br> from *ukay* 'open' |
| | ə- | *a'bbos* 'collapsed into the water' <br> from *bbos* 'to collapse' | *ni'nda'* 'to be seen' <br> from *nda'* 'to look' |

When the initial vowel of the root is /ə/, there are two results observed in Central Sinama speech.

1. Some speakers do not pronounce the /ə/, so that the vowel of the prefix immediately precedes the root.

    /ta-/ + /ən.daʔ/ 'to see'　　→　　[tanda ʔ] 'seen'

2. Other speakers pronounce /ə/ as a brief transition between the vowel of the prefix and the root.

    /ta-/ + /ən.daʔ/ 'to see'　　→　　[taəndaʔ] 'seen'

---

[3] The prefix *Cau-* (where *C* represents any consonant) indicating multiplicity in words such as *maglaulabay* 'passersby', is rather infrequent and does not appear to occur before any vowel-initial roots.

Regardless of the above variation in pronunciation, the letter *hamsa'* < ' > is written between the prefix and the root, e.g., <ta'nda'>. This resolves any ambiguity in reading between similar words such as *ta'nda'* 'seen' and *tanda'* 'sign'.

### 4.7.3.2 Vowel combinations at suffix boundaries

All Sinama suffixes begin with /a/, /i/, or /u/. Sinama does not permit vowel sequences at a suffix boundary. When a suffix is attached to a vowel-final stem, <h> is inserted between the two vowels.[4] The exception to this rule occurs when the stem includes an /h/. Central Sinama does not permit two occurrences of /h/ in a word. In this case, a glottal stop < ' > is inserted rather than an <h> between the vowels. Table 9 provides some examples.

Table 9. Vowel sequences at suffix boundaries: Selected examples

| | | |
|---|---|---|
| langi + -un | → | *langihun* 'swim (command)' (from *langi* 'swim') |
| ka- + l'bbo + -an | → | *kal'bbohan* 'marsh' (from *l'bbo* 'soft (of earth)') |
| paN- + isi + -an | → | *pangisihan* 'container' (from *isi* 'contents') |
| paN- + b'lla + -an | → | *pam'llahan* 'cooking pot' (from *b'lla* 'cook') |
| b'lli + -in | → | *b'llihin* 'buy (for someone)' (from *b'lli* 'buy') |
| luhu + -un | → | *luhu'un* 'singe (command)' (from *luhu* 'singe') |
| pa- + hati + -in | → | *pahati'in* 'explain (command)' (from *hati* 'to understand') |
| haka + -in | → | *haka'in* 'let (someone) know' (from *haka* 'inform') |

# 4.8 Comparisons to other languages

An orthography needs to reflect the specific characteristics of the language for which it is designed. In particular, it should reflect the phonology of the language: what sounds the language uses, and how they are combined. The phonology of Sinama differs in several notable ways from the phonologies of some other well-known languages in the Philippines. Those differences are reflected in the orthography. This section presents comparisons to several other languages in order to illustrate some distinctive features of Sinama phonology and orthography.

## 4.8.1 Representing the glottal stop

The glottal stop is widely used in many languages of the Philippines. Different languages' orthographies deal with it in different ways. Some orthographies do not represent the glottal stop at all; others represent it only in certain positions; and others represent it as a diacritic (accent mark) rather than as a separate letter.

The glottal stop is very common in the Filipino language, but it is not explicitly represented in the most widely used Filipino orthography. Because Filipino does not have any vowel sequences except at the ends of words, a written sequence of two vowels within a word is always read with a glottal stop between them. For example,

    <daan>    /daʔan/    'road'

    <babae>    /babaʔe/    'woman'

Sinama, by contrast, has vowel sequences without a glottal stop separating the vowels, in addition to vowel sequences that *do* have a glottal stop. Writing the glottal stop when it is present prevents confusion between such words: for example, between *saul* 'tubular skirt' and *sa'ul* 'to acknowledge someone's call'. Writing the glottal stop also prevents confusion between words that differ only by the presence of a glottal stop at the end of the word.

---

[4] Some speakers elide the /h/ (a phenomenon that also occurs elsewhere in the language) and instead pronounce a [j] or [w] at suffix boundaries.

Sinama uses *hamsa'* < ' > to symbolize the glottal stop (as do Tausug and Mapun). For Sinama, this is preferable to any of the alternatives used by other languages: for example, <h> (used for a word-final glottal stop in some languages); a hyphen (used in some languages for a glottal stop in the middle of a word); or a grave accent:

1.   Using *hamsa'* instead of <h> prevents confusion that could arise between the glottal stop and the very different sound usually represented by <h>.

2.   Using *hamsa'* instead of the hyphen avoids confusion with the use of the hyphen in writing compound words.

3.   Unlike the grave accent, an apostrophe (even if sometimes a curved apostrophe instead of *hamsa'*) is easy for a user to type on any computer or device.

## 4.8.2 The macron

Sinama has contrasting long and short forms of all vowels except the central vowel /ə/. Other Sulu languages, including languages such as Bangingih and Tausug, have similar vowel-length contrast and also use a macron to symbolize length.

## 4.8.3 The central vowel /ə/

The central vowel /ə/ is very common among the languages of the Philippines. It is found not only in Central Sinama and related Sulu languages such as Pangutaran and Mapun, but also in larger regional languages such as Ilocano. It is absent, however, in languages such as Filipino, Visayan, and Tausug. Speakers of these languages often find the central vowel difficult to recognize and produce. But in Sinama phonology it is as distinct and important as the other five vowels and receives its own symbol in the Sinama orthography.

## 4.8.4 Pronouns that attach to verbs and nouns

Sinama has a set of pronouns that indicate possession, as well as certain other grammatical functions (see section 5.1.2.1 Pronouns). Some of these pronouns attach to the preceding word, and the combination becomes a single word. The attached pronouns are:

=ku      1st person singular

=nu      2nd person singular

=na      3rd person singular

=ta      1st person dual, inclusive

=tam     1st person plural, inclusive

=bi      2nd person plural

Because these pronouns become part of the phonological word to which they are attached, they are written as part of the word. For instance, *kagunahan=nu* 'what you(sg) need' is written <kagunahannu>, not <kagunahan nu> or <kagunahan-nu>. Likewise, *luma'=ta* 'our(du) house' is written <luma'ta>, not <luma' ta> or <luma'-ta>).

Many other languages of the Philippines, including Filipino, have pronouns that serve similar functions. In Filipino, though, they are phonologically separate words, not attached to the preceding word as in Sinama. Filipino pronouns are accordingly written separately. Some writers would prefer to write all Sinama pronouns separately from the preceding word, based on the Filipino example. But in Sinama, the presence of the pronoun affects the pronunciation of the preceding word by shifting the word stress to a later syllable. Writing the pronoun separately makes the word harder to read correctly, even for otherwise proficient readers, and can cause changes in the meaning of a sentence. For example, <ina' na> means 'a mother now', but <ina'na> means 'his/her mother'.

# 5

# Grammar

# 5.1 Lexical classes

Lexical classes,[1] also called parts of speech, refer to the broad categories into which the words of a language can be sorted. This sorting is based on grammatical features (e.g., affixation and distribution), rather than on the meanings of words, and thus varies to some degree from language to language. But the major categories of noun and verb are found in most or all languages, and share certain characteristic features across those languages.

The lexical classes themselves can be organized into two groups: open classes and closed classes. **Open classes** have no limit to the number of words they may contain as members. They can gain or lose members with relative freedom. For example, there is no limit on the number or variety of nouns that a language may have. Nouns are freely added or lost, and the subset of nouns used in a given situation can vary sharply between dialects or even individual speakers. **Closed classes**, on the other hand, contain a limited number of words. These words are essentially the same for all speakers of the language. Closed classes gain or lose words extremely infrequently. Pronouns and conjunctions are examples of closed lexical classes.

## 5.1.1 Open lexical classes

Sinama open classes include nouns, verbs, adjectives, and adverbs.

### 5.1.1.1 Nouns

A prototypical noun communicates the name of a person, place, or thing. Most Sinama nouns are unaffixed, e.g., *luma'* 'house', *ond* e' 'child', or *daing* 'fish'. Sinama nouns are not inflected for case or number. Sinama has no grammatical gender, though there are a few gendered noun pairs, e.g., *h'nda* 'wife' and *h'lla* 'husband'.

Nouns can be created from other words by several derivational processes. They can be derived from other nouns, as in table 10; or they can be derived from other lexical classes via a process of nominalization, as in table 11.

Table 10. Nouns derived from nouns

|  | Derived word | Root word |
|---|---|---|
| Collective | *kakayuhan* 'grove' | *kayu* 'tree' |
| Diminutive | *onde'-onde'* 'small child, baby' | *onde'* 'child' |
| Compound | *anak-h'nda* 'wife and children' | *anak* 'offspring', *h'nda* 'wife' |

Table 11. Nouns derived from verbs

| Derived word | Root word |
|---|---|
| *pagusaha* 'livelihood' | *usaha* 'to work' |
| *panau'* 'investment' | *tau'* 'to keep something in storage' |
| *pamikil* 'thought, mental capacity' | *pikil* 'to think' |
| *kamanahutan* 'small children, young people' | *nahut* 'small in gauge or cross-section' |

Locative nouns are a closed subclass of nouns that refer to location or position. They occur as complements of prepositions. Examples of Sinama locative nouns include *deya* 'inland', *diyata'* 'above, on top', and *t'ngnga'* 'middle'.

---

[1] This entire section on lexical classes draws heavily on Schachter (1985).

Vocative nouns are a subclass of nouns used for addressing a person. Examples include *babu'* 'auntie', *agay* 'pal', and *tuwan* 'sir'.

Sinama nouns can take a variety of descriptive modifiers. These include numerals and classifiers, which precede the noun (section 5.1.2.5 Quantifiers); Set II (genitive) pronouns, which attach to the end of the noun (section 5.1.2.1 Pronouns); adjectives, which follow the noun (section 5.1.1.3 Adjectives); and demonstratives, which occur at the end of the noun phrase (section 5.1.2.3 Demonstratives). The order of modifiers in a noun phrase is shown in example (1):

(1)   duwa        busay      =ku              bilu          itū
      two          paddle     1SG.II           blue          this
      (numeral)  (**noun**)  (clitic.pronoun)  (adjective)  (demonstrative)
      'these two blue paddles of mine'

### 5.1.1.2 Verbs

A prototypical verb communicates an action, process, or state. Verbs most often function as predicates of clauses. Sinama verbs are not inflected for tense, nor for any sort of agreement (e.g., number or person agreement).

### Transitivity

In a clause, a verbal predicate will normally stand in some relationship to one or more noun phrases, known as **arguments**. Arguments are often referred to using terms such as subject, direct object, and indirect object. Verbs can be classified according to the number of arguments they take: zero, one, two, or three. A large majority of Sinama verbs have one or two arguments, but there are also Sinama verbs with three or zero arguments.

A verb with two arguments is a transitive verb. Its two arguments are referred to as the **actor** (the argument that performs or is responsible for the action of the verb), and the **undergoer** (the argument being acted upon).[2] For instance, for the transitive verb *k'bbit* 'to pinch', the actor is the pincher, and the undergoer is the one being pinched. Example (2) is a transitive sentence using *k'bbit*. (Sinama has two transitive voices; see section 5.3.2 Voice, for a fuller description of Sinama voice).

(2)   Bay ang'bbit(aN-k'bbit) baran=ku    si Lo.
      PST AV-pinch            BODY=1SG.II PM L.
      'Lo pinched my body.'

A verb with only one argument is an intransitive verb. The single argument of an intransitive verb can be similar to an actor, or it can be similar to an undergoer. In example (3), the argument of *laksu* 'jump' is similar to an actor. In example (4), the argument of *kagkag* 'to lose weight' is similar to an undergoer.

(3)   Pa-laksu      ampan.
      INTR-jump     grasshopper
      'The grasshopper jumped.'

(4)   Angagkag(aN-kagkag) sidda si  Anu, s<in>aki     tibi.
      INTR-lose.weight    very  PM  A.   <PASS>sick   tuberculosis
      'So-and-so is very thin, sick with TB.'

A verb with three arguments is a ditransitive verb. Ditransitive verbs are typically transfer verbs such as *buwan* 'give' (in which the arguments are the giver, the recipient, and the thing given, example (5)), or communication verbs such as *pandu'* 'teach' (in which the arguments are the teacher, the student, and the content being taught, example (6)).

---

[2] The terms 'actor' and 'undergoer' are borrowed from *Role and Reference Grammar* (Van Valin and La Polla 1997:141).

(5) Buwan-an₂=ku      onde'-onde'  būk.
give-APPL=1sg.ii  small.child  book
'I will give the children schoolbooks.'


(6) Amandu'(aN-pandu')  akū   saga kalangan ma si  Kesiya.
AV-teach                1SG.I PL   song     to PM  K.
'I teach songs to Kesiya.'

Sinama has a few verbs which do not require any argument at all, referred to as atransitive verbs, also known as zero-transitive verbs. These are typically weather verbs and other verbs expressing an ambient state, as in examples (7) and (8).

(7) Angulan(aN-ulan)  na.
ATR-rain            now
'[It's] raining now.'


(8) A-balu'       ma deyom paglahat.
ATR-unsettled  at within district
'[It is] unsettled in the district.'


## Affixation

Sinama has a rich system of verbal affixation. There are affixes to indicate aspect and modality. There are several affixes which are related to the verb's arguments: the type of argument, or the relationship of the arguments to one another and to the verb. There are affixes which add an argument to the verb, and affixes which remove an argument. Together, these affixes provide Sinama with a subtle and nuanced set of options for expressing meaning.

### Intransitive affixes

Some of the simplest affixes are the intransitive affixes, which attach to intransitive verbs (table 12).

Table 12. Intransitive verbal affixes

| Affix | Use | Example |
|---|---|---|
| pa-, -um- | pa- and - um- attach to many verbs of motion, often those having an actor-like argument. | *palangi/lumangi* 'to swim' |
| aN-, mag- | When used with intransitive verbs, *aN-* and *mag-* (an inflected form of *pag-*) usually attach to verbs with an actor-like argument. | *amaklay (aN-baklay)* 'to walk' <br> *magbuwa'* 'to be producing fruit' |
| a- | Attaches to stative verbs. | *aganggu'* 'to rustle' |
| -in-/ni- <br> ta- | When used with intransitive verbs, these affixes attach to verbs with an undergoer-like argument. They are adversative affixes: they indicate an event, often negative, outside the argument's control. | *tinuli* 'sleepy' <br> *talilap* 'overcome by drowsiness' |
| maka- | Indicates that the subject produces the state described by the verb (often an emotional response). | *maka'ase'-ase'* 'to stir sympathy or pity' |

## Voice affixes

Voice affixes attach to transitive verbs and indicate the relationship among the verb's arguments (table 13; see section 5.3.2 Voice).

Table 13. Voice affixes

| Affix | Label | Use |
|---|---|---|
| Ø (null) | Undergoer voice | Selects undergoer as subject. |
| *aN-* | Actor voice | Selects actor as subject. |
| *-in-* | Passive voice | Selects undergoer as subject and demotes the actor. |
| *paN-$_1$, pag-$_1$* | Conveyance voice | Adds an argument (conveyance) to the clause and selects it as subject. |
| *-an$_1$* | Location voice | Adds an argument (location) to the clause and selects it as subject. |

## Aspect and modality affixes

Sinama has two aspectual verbal affixes and one modal affix (table 14). **Aspect** refers to an action or event's 'shape' in time. For instance, does it happen in a single instant, or does it take place over an extended period? Does it happen only once, or repeatedly? Is it completed or not? (A related concept, **tense**, refers to an action or event's location in time: past, present, or future.) **Modality** pertains to matters of ability, permission, obligation, or the speaker's state of knowledge (e.g., his degree of certainty about what he is saying). In Sinama, aspect, tense, and modality are indicated via particles in the clause (table 27), with the exception of the three affixes in table 14.

Table 14. Aspect and modality verbal affixes

| Affix | Label | Use |
|---|---|---|
| *paN-$_2$* | Punctiliar aspect | Indicates an action that occurs once, or focuses on a single instance of the action. |
| *pag-$_2$* | Distributive aspect | Indicates action that is repeated, continual, or habitual. |
| *paka-/ta-/ka-* | Aptative modality | Indicates action that is not under the full control of the actor or undergoer. |

Voice, aspect, and modality are independent phenomena, which means that their affixes can co-occur on a single verb. Table 15 shows the affix combinations that can be found on Sinama verbs.

Table 15. Voice, aspect, and modality

|  |  | Punctiliar aspect | | Distributive aspect | |
|---|---|---|---|---|---|
|  |  | Intentive modality | Aptative modality | Intentive modality | Aptative modality |
| **Voice** | Actor voice | *aN-* | *maka-makapaN-* | *mag-* | *maka-makapag-* |
|  | Undergoer voice | Ø | *ta-tapaN-* | *pag-* | *tapag-* |
|  | Passive voice | *-in-* | *ta-* | *pinag-* | *tapag-* |

### Valence-increasing affixes

Valence-increasing affixes add an argument to the clause. The conveyance voice affixes (*pag-1*, *paN-1*) and location voice affix (*-an1*) in table 13 are valence-increasing affixes as well as voice affixes, because they add a conveyance or location argument, respectively. Table 16 lists some other valence-increasing affixes.

Table 16. Valence-increasing affixes

| **Affix** | **Label** | **Use** |
|---|---|---|
| *pa-* | Causative | Adds a causer argument, i.e., someone or something who causes an action to take place. |
| *-an2* | Applicative | Adds an undergoer to the clause. |
| *ka-… -an* | Adversative | Adds an undergoer who is (usually negatively) affected by the action of the verb. |

### Imperative suffix

In an undergoer voice sentence, imperative is indicated by the suffix *-un*. When *-un* co-occurs with the applicative suffix *-an2*, the two suffixes are replaced by the combined suffix *-in.*

### Gerund prefixes

The gerund prefixes *pag-3* and *paN-3* indicate the time or occasion of a verb's action, as in example (9) and (10).

(9)    A-t'ggol    na        pag3-pala'u=kami.
       ADJ-long   already   GER-live.on.boat=1PL.EXCL.II
       'We lived on a boat for a long time.' (Lit. 'Our living on a boat was long.')

(10)   Sumiyan   bay   pamono'(paN3-bono')=na?
       when      PST   GER-kill=3SG.II
       'When did he kill (someone)?'

### 5.1.1.3 Adjectives

Adjectives describe properties or attributes of nouns. They have two functions in Sinama: they can modify nouns in noun phrases (example (11)), and they can serve as predicates of non-verbal clauses (example (12)).

(11)   pagkakan a-lanab   maka  inuman a-mamis
      food          ADJ-rich  and   drink    ADJ-sweet
    'rich food and sweet drink'

(12)   Tambang          na    tahik.
      nearly.high.tide  now  sea
    'The tide is nearly full.'

The prefix *a-* is by far the most common affix used on Sinama adjectives. Both of the adjectives in example (11), *alanab* 'tasty, rich' and *amamis* 'sweet', are prefixed with *a-*. But *a-* does not appear on all adjectives. Many adjectives, like *tambang* 'nearly high tide' in example (12), are not affixed at all. There is also an adjectival suffix *-an* which conveys inherent quality.

Because the common adjective prefix *a-* also appears on many stative verbs, it can be very difficult to know whether a particular word is an adjective or a stative verb. This difficulty is compounded by the fact that a stative verb can be used in a sentence in the same ways as an adjective (i.e., as modifier of a noun, or as predicate of the clause). But there are at least three tests that can indicate whether a word is an adjective or a stative verb:

1. Adjectives can be used in comparative and superlative constructions such as *aheya iya min aku* 'he is bigger than I am' or *akosog min kamemon* 'stronger than everyone'. Stative verbs cannot be used in these constructions.
2. Stative verbs can be affixed with the imperative suffix (section 5.1.1.2 Verbs-Affixation) to form commands, but adjectives cannot.
3. Stative verbs can be affixed with the aptative prefixes *maka-* and *ta-* (section 5.1.1.2 Verbs-Affixation), but adjectives cannot.

### 5.1.1.4 Adverbs

Adverbs modify constituents other than nouns. They can modify verbs, adjectives, or other adverbs. They can also modify clauses or even entire sentences.[3] There is a wide variety of adverb types. Table 17 gives examples of seven types of adverb in Sinama.

---

[3] An adverb is usually a single word, but may also be a multi-word phrase. These are listed in the dictionary as adverbial phrases.

Table 17. Types of open class adverbs

| Adverb type | Examples |
|---|---|
| Manner | *agak-agak* 'gently, cautiously'<br>*lullun* 'entirely, all' |
| Frequency | *bang pasān* 'sometimes'<br>*masuhul* 'often'<br>*alahang* 'rarely' |
| Degree | *to'ongan* 'very'<br>*sidda* 'very, intensely, over-much' |
| Time | *insini', dinsini'* 'earlier'<br>*gana-gana* 'later'<br>*di'ilaw* 'yesterday' |
| Aspectual | *masi* 'still'<br>*lagi'* 'still' |
| Sentence | *minda'* 'fortunately'<br>*mura-murahan* 'hopefully'<br>*marai'* 'maybe' |
| Narrative | *agtūy* 'immediately'<br>*saru'un-du'un* 'immediately' |

Although adverbs as a whole form an open class, the class of adverbs contains closed subsets within it. Table 18 shows three closed subsets of adverbs: deictic adverbs of location, which specify a location indicated by the speaker; deictic adverbs of directed motion, which specify motion from or toward a point relative to the speaker; and similative deictic adverbs, which specify similarity to something indicated by the speaker.

Table 18. Closed classes of adverbs

| Deictic adverbs of location (adverbial demonstratives) | | *maitu* | 'here, near speaker' | | |
|---|---|---|---|---|---|
| | | *mailu* | 'there, near hearer' | | |
| | | *maina'an* | 'there, far from hearer, vague' | | |
| | | *mahē'* | 'there, far from hearer, precise' | | |
| Deictic adverbs of directed motion | *minnitu* | 'from here, near speaker' | *pi'itu* | 'to here, near speaker' |
| | *minnilu* | 'from there, near hearer' | >*pi'ilu* | 'to there, near hearer' |
| | *minna'an* | 'from there, far from hearer, vague' | *pina'an* | 'to there, far from hearer, vague' |
| | *minnē'* | 'from there, far from hearer, precise' | *pehē'* | 'to there, far from hearer, precise' |
| Similative deictic adverbs [a] | | *buwattitu* | 'like this, near speaker' | | |
| | | *buwattilu* | 'like that, near hearer' | | |
| | | *buwattē'* | 'like that, far from hearer' | | |

[a] The adverb *buwattina'an* has the same form as the similative deictic adverbs, but it does not share their meaning. It is a temporal adverb meaning 'now/imminent'.

## 5.1.2 Closed lexical classes

Sinama closed classes include personal pronouns, interrogatives, demonstratives, prepositions, numerals, classifiers, particles, conjunctions, interjections, and negators.

### 5.1.2.1 Pronouns

Sinama has three contrasting sets of personal pronouns, listed in table 19. On the surface, Sets I and III do not look very different. Set I and III pronouns are phonologically independent, unlike Set II pronouns which always attach to another word. For most of the pronouns, the difference between Set I and Set III is only a matter of vowel length and word stress.[4] The forms for 3DU and 3PL are completely identical. But there is a significant difference in their relative freedom of movement within the clause. Set I pronouns always occur in the second position of the clause, following the predicate. Set III pronouns, on the other hand, can appear in a variety of locations within the clause. For example, they can be fronted, or occur in the periphery of the clause.

Table 19. Sinama personal pronouns

|        |       | Set I | Set II   | Set III |
|--------|-------|-------|----------|---------|
| 1SG    |       | akū   | =ku      | aku     |
| 1DU    |       | kitā  | =ta      | kita    |
| 1PL    | EXCL. | kamī  | =kami    | kami    |
|        | INCL. | kitām | =tam     | kitam   |
| 2SG    |       | ka    | =nu      | ka'a    |
| 2PL    |       | kam   | =bi      | ka'am   |
| 3SG    |       | iyā   | =na      | iya     |
| 3DU    |       | sigā  | =sigā    | sigā    |
| 3PL    |       | sigām | =sigām   | sigām   |

Set I pronouns are used for subjects, when the subject occurs in its default position after the predicate.[5] In example (13), the pronoun *iyā* 'she/he' is a Set I pronoun, the subject of the verb *angeket* 'bite'. It occurs immediately following the verb.

(13)  Angeket(aN-keket) iyā    tangan siyaka=na.
      AV-bite                3SG.I  hand   older.sibling=3SG.II
      'She/He bites his/her older sibling's hand.'

Set II pronouns are not separate words in their own right, but rather are enclitics. That is, they are always found attached to the ends of other words. It is clear that they are not independent words because they cause a stress shift in the word to which they attach (see section 4.4 Word stress). Set II pronouns serve two functions: 1) When attached to verbs in undergoer voice, or to the passive actor marker *(h)e'*, they express a non-subject actor of a clause; and 2) When attached to nouns, they express the possessor of the noun, i.e., a genitive construction. In example (14), the 3 SG Set II pronoun *=na* is used twice. In the first instance, it attaches to the verb *keket* 'to bite' and represents the non-subject actor of the clause, i.e., the biter. In the second instance, it attaches to the noun *siyaka* 'older sibling' and represents the possessor, i.e., the person who has an older sibling.

(14)  Ø-Keket=na    tangan siyaka=na.
      UV-bite=3SG.II hand   older.sibling=3SG.II
      'S/he bit his/her older sibling's hand.'

Set III pronouns are independent pronouns.[6] They can occur in a wide variety of positions in a sentence. They are used for all participants not covered by Sets I and II: that is, for subjects outside

---

4 For purposes of clarity and linguistic precision, vowel length is indicated by the use of macrons on Set I pronouns in this chapter and in the dictionary entries for these pronouns. However, most example sentences in the dictionary do not use macrons on Set I pronouns. For a native speaker this does not pose any difficulty. Those who are not native speakers, though, must infer a pronoun's set based on its position in the sentence.

5 By default, the subject follows the first constituent of the phrasal unit, typically the predicate, in a position called the second position (Himmelmann 2005:141). Technically, Set I pronouns are unstressed second-position clitics.

6 Unlike Set I second-position clitic pronouns and Set II enclitic pronouns.

the default post-predicate position, and for non-actor non-subjects, such as in prepositional phrases. In example (15), *iya* '3SG' is a Set III pronoun.

(15)  Bilahi  akū  amabeya'an(aN-pa-beya'-an₂)  iya  sulat.
       want  1SG.I  AV-CAUS-accompany-APPL  3SG.III  letter
       'I want to send him a letter.'

### 5.1.2.2 *Interrogatives*

Interrogatives intrinsically express a question (Trask 1993: 303). Table 20 gives a list of Sinama interrogatives. Sinama interrogatives are mostly used at the start of a sentence, but can in some cases occur *in situ*, i.e., in the same position as the constituent they are questioning.

Table 20. Sinama interrogatives

| | |
|---|---|
| *ai* | 'what' |
| *sai* | 'who' |
| *ingga* | 'which one' |
| *maingga/ma'ai* | 'where' |
| *minningga* | 'where from' |
| *pi'ingga* | 'where to' |
| *ma sai* | 'whose' |
| *angay* | 'why' |
| *sumiyan* | 'when' |
| *buwattingga* | 'how' |
| *dangay, pila* | 'how many, how much' |
| *magay* | 'to what purpose' |

### 5.1.2.3 *Demonstratives*

Sinama demonstratives include words such as *itu* 'this (near speaker)', *ilu* 'that (near hearer)', and *hē'* 'that (far from speaker and hearer)'. They are organized according to two points of reference: the location of the speaker and the location of the hearer. Thus there are different demonstratives to refer to objects or locations (1) near the speaker; (2) far from the speaker but near the hearer; (3) a vague location far from both speaker and hearer; and (4) a precise location far from both speaker and hearer. Sinama also has a demonstrative identifier, *itiya'* 'here is', used in non-verbal clauses. The demonstratives are listed in table 21.

Table 21. Sinama demonstratives

| | **Near speaker** | **Far from speaker** | | | **Identifier** |
|---|---|---|---|---|---|
| | | Near hearer | Far from hearer | | |
| | | | Vague | Precise | |
| Set I | *itū* | *ilū* | *inān* | *hē'* | *itiya'* |
| Set II | *itu* | *ilu* | *ina'an* | *hē'* | |

There are two sets of demonstratives. The set used depends on the demonstrative's position in the clause. Set I forms are used for demonstratives in their unmarked position, i.e., post-predicate (as arguments of a clause), or following the noun (post-nominal, as modifiers in a noun phrase) (example (16)).

(16)  Ndiya        ma aku      busay   ilū.
      hand-over  to  1SG.III  paddle  D.DIST
      'Hand me that paddle there (by you).'

Set II demonstratives are used in marked (i.e., pre-predicate) positions in the clause (example (17)).

(17)  Itu        i,     bagay=ku      bay.
      D.PROX  PRT  friend=1SG.II  PST
      'This one was my friend back then.'

All demonstratives, in both Set I and Set II, can function as arguments of a predicate (i.e., as pronominal demonstratives). When used as arguments, Set I demonstratives occur in the post-predicate position, and Set II pre-predicate.

Set I forms are used as modifiers of a noun or pronoun (i.e., as adnominal demonstratives). Set II forms may be prefixed with *ma-* 'at'or *min-* 'from' to form a set of adverbial demonstratives that indicate location, e.g., *maitu* 'here', *mailu* 'there (by hearer)', and *minnē'* 'from there (far from speaker and hearer)'.

Example (18) shows the demonstrative identifier, *itiya'* 'D.IDENT', which has an identificational function. This demonstrative occurs in nonverbal clauses, focusing the hearer's attention on something in the surrounding situation or in the universe of the discourse. Set II forms *itu* 'this (near speaker)' and *ilu* 'that (near hearer)' also have an identificational function (examples (18) and (20)).

(18)  Na,    ta-hinang          akū      pastor,  sampay  buwattina'an  itiya'       akū.
      now  PASS.APT-make  1SG.I  pastor  even      like.that        D.IDENT  1SG.I
      'Now I became a pastor, and up until today, here I am in Davao.'

(19)  Itu        aniya'  isāb  kissaku.
      D.PROX  EX       also  story=1SG.II
      'Here's a story of mine.'

(20)  Ō,      ilu       du    si   Kisman,  ilu       kaki=ku           l'lla.
      INTRJ  D.DIST  PRT  PM  Kisman  D.DIST  cousin=1SG.II  man
      'Oh, Kisman that is, my male cousin that is.'

### 5.1.2.4 Prepositions

Sinama has both locative and non-locative prepositions. As complements they can take nouns (e.g., *ma tahik* 'in the sea'), pronouns (e.g., *sampay aku* 'including me'), demonstratives (e.g., *minnitu* 'from here'), and noun phrases (e.g., *maka laring lahut* 'with a butcher's knife'). Table 22 and table 23 list the Sinama prepositions.

Table 22. Locative prepositions

| | |
|---|---|
| *ma* | 'at, by, in' (site) |
| *min, man* | 'from' |
| | 'by way of' |
| *ni* | 'to, towards, until' |
| *tudju* | 'towards' |

Table 23. Non-locative prepositions

| | |
|---|---|
| *maka* | 'with, by means of' (instrument) |
| *sampay* | 'until, including' |
| *min, man* | 'than' |
| *ma, para* | 'for (someone)' (beneficiary) |

#### 5.1.2.5 Quantifiers

Quantifiers express a quantity or scope. Sinama nouns are not inflected for number. Number is expressed by use of a numeral (e.g., *duwa* 'two'); a plural marker ( *saga* 'PL'); or a classifier (e.g., *duwangan* 'two [of people]'). Other quantifiers include *kasehe'an* 'some', *kamemon* 'all', and *dangkuri'* 'a little bit'.

#### Numerals

A selection of Sinama numerals is displayed in table 24. Other numerals are formed by combining these with the conjunction *maka* (or *aka, ka*) 'and': e.g., *sangpū' kaduwa* 'twelve' (lit. 'ten and two'), *t'llu hatus walumpū' maka lima* 'three hundred and eighty-five'.

Table 24. Sinama numerals

| | | | | | | | |
|---|---|---|---|---|---|---|---|
| one | *ssa; dakayu'* | ten | *sangpū'* | one hundred | *dahatus* | one thousand | *dangibu* |
| two | *duwa* | twenty | *duwampū'* | two hundred | *duwa hatus* | two thousand | *duwa ngibu* |
| three | *t'llu* | thirty | *t'llumpū'* | three hundred | *t'llu hatus* | three thousand | *t'llu ngibu* |
| four | *mpat* | forty | *mpatpū'* | four hundred | *mpat hatus* | four thousand | *mpat ngibu* |
| five | *lima* | fifty | *limampū'* | five hundred | *lima hatus* | five thousand | *lima ngibu* |
| six | *nnom* | sixty | *nnompū'* | six hundred | *nnom hatus* | six thousand | *nnom ngibu* |
| seven | *pitu'* | seventy | *pitumpū'* | seven hundred | *pitu' hatus* | seven thousand | *pitu' ngibu* |
| eight | *walu'* | eighty | *walumpū'* | eight hundred | *walu' hatus* | eight thousand | *walu' ngibu* |
| nine | *siyam* | ninety | *siyampū'* | nine hundred | *siyam hatus* | nine thousand | *siyam ngibu* |
| | | | | | | ten thousand | *sangpū' ngibu; laksa'* |

*Ssa* and *dakayu'* both express the numeral one. *Ssa* is used when counting. *Dakayu'* is used when quantifying items, and for telling time. *Da* and *ssa* are used to express 'one' in combination with other numerals, e.g., *sangpū' aka'dda* 'eleven' (lit. 'ten and one'). *Da-* is also used as a prefix before numerals denoting powers of ten, e.g., *dahatus* 'one hundred' and *dangibu* 'one thousand', and before classifiers and time adverbials, e.g., *dambulan* 'one month' and *dantahun* 'one year'. When *da-* prefixes classifiers and time adverbials, a nasal ligature is added between *da-* and the word to which it attaches. The ligature assimilates to the point of articulation of the following consonant. This nasal ligature is also used in forming multiples of ten: e.g., *duwa* 'two' + *pū'* > *duwampū'* 'twenty'.

Ordinal numbers are formed in Sinama by attaching the prefix *ka-*or *ika-*, e.g., *ikalima* 'fifth', *ka'mpatpū' aka walu'* 'forty-eighth'.

## Classifiers

Classifiers, also known as count words, are optionally used when counting a wide variety of objects, including people. Each classifier is used for a specific type of object. The classifier is placed between the numeral and the counted items, e.g., the word *batang* (for counting stick-like objects) in example (21). Sinama has at least fifty classifiers. Table 25 lists a selection. For a full list, see 3.3 Topical Sinama–English Wordlists D: 'Classifiers'.

(21) Alutu'         kamī      duwam~batang t'bbu.
      having.provisions 1PL.EXCL.I two~sticks    sugar.cane
      'We had as provisions two sticks of sugar cane.'

Table 25. Some Sinama classifiers

| | |
|---|---|
| *puhu'* | for counting people |
| *solag* | for counting similar objects |
| *munda'* | for counting watercraft |
| *tuhug* | for counting strings of things, especially fish |
| *batang* | for counting stick-like objects |

There is also one classifier suffix, *-ngan,* used when enumerating people. It can be attached to any of the first three numerals: thus *dangan* 'one person', *duwangan* 'two persons', *t'llungan* 'three persons'. Some speakers use this suffix on numbers as high as nine, e.g., *siyamangan* 'nine people'.

### 5.1.2.6 Particles

Sinama particles include plural markers; personal name markers; actor markers; discourse markers; and tense, aspect, and modality markers.

## Plural markers

Sinama has two optional plural markers, *saga* and *ba'anan*, which occur immediately before the head noun of a noun phrase.

## Personal name markers

The personal name markers *si* (singular) and *disi* (plural) are used for referencing personal names and kinship terms. Unlike analogous markers in many other Philippine languages, these forms do not indicate the relation of an argument to the verb. They simply mark a noun as a personal name.

## Actor marker

When an actor is present in a passive clause, it must be marked with the prepositional actor marker *(h)e'* 'by'. Some Sinama speakers use the preposition *ni* instead of *(h)e'* to mark the passive actor (see section 5.3.2.3 Passive voice).

## Discourse markers

Table 26 lists a selection of Sinama discourse markers. Some have only a discourse function, while others also function as conjunctions or demonstratives. Discourse markers include development markers, backgrounding markers, discourse-deictic markers, recognitional markers, prominence markers, and a thematic salience marker. More information on these discourse markers is given in their dictionary entries.

Table 26. Some Sinama discourse markers

| Category of marker | Discourse marker | Function |
|---|---|---|
| Development markers | *na* | In narrative discourse, signals resumption of the event line after backgrounding or a disruption. |
| | *dalasku, dai'-dai'ku* | "To make a long story short": signals the end of a discourse unit in narrative discourse. |
| | *sabab* | Signals background information in narrative discourse, especially where there is no logical relation of result-reason. |
| Discourse-deictic markers | *ina'an* | Refers back to an entire sentence or proposition within a discourse. |
| | *hē'₁* | Refers back to an entire discourse or large section of a discourse. |
| Recognitional markers | *ilū* | "That", mutually understood, referring to specific shared knowledge between speakers. |
| Prominence markers | *itū* | Refers to a recently introduced central participant. |
| | *hē'₂* | Signals that a character in a story is involved in a critical event or episode. |
| Peak marker | *i* | Attaches to noun phrases to indicate the peak or climax of a narrative. |

### Tense, aspect, and modality markers

Sinama verbs are not inflected for tense. There is some inflection for aspect and modality (see section 5.1.1.2 Verbs: Affixation), but most tense, aspect and modality (TAM) functions are signaled by particles. Some of the TAM markers are listed in table 27.

Table 27. Sinama TAM markers

| Tense and aspect markers | | Modality markers | |
|---|---|---|---|
| *bay* | Past tense marker. | *ba/bahā'/ka'* | Question marker. |
| *sŏng* | Future tense marker; prospective aspect marker. | *kono'* | Indicates that the speaker does not vouch for the accuracy of what he is saying (Evidential marker, hearsay). |
| *wa'i, (h)ē'* | Perfect aspect marker. | *du* | Indicates certainty. |
| *na* | Aspect marker indicating that the situation or action described is already in process. | *ganta'* | 'Suppose; for instance; let's say' (Hypothetical modality marker). |
| *(la)gi'* | 'Still; yet; a bit more': aspect marker indicating that an action or state is not yet completed, without regard to whether it has begun. | *hati'* | Indicates mild surprise (Deontic modality marker). |
| *pa'in* | Contemporaneous action. | *subay, wajib* | 'Should; must; had better' (Deontic modality particle, obligation). |

### 5.1.2.7 Conjunctions

Conjunctions indicate the relation between separate clauses, noun phrases, sentences, etc. In addition, many Sinama conjunctions also function at a higher level of discourse, marking discourse continuity and discontinuity, backgrounding, and so on. A selection of Sinama conjunctions is displayed in table 28.

Table 28. Selected Sinama conjunctions

| | | |
|---|---|---|
| **Coordinating conjunctions** | *maka* | 'and; plus (in counting)' |
| | *atawa* | 'either; or' |
| | *apa* | 'because; for the stated reason' |
| | *angkan* | 'that is why' |
| **Subordinating conjunctions** | *bang* | 'if, when' (complementizer) |
| | *ya* | 'the one which (relativizer)' |

### 5.1.2.8 Interjections

Interjections express states of mind, and are not bound by syntax. Table 29 lists a few Sinama interjections.

Table 29. Selected interjections

| | |
|---|---|
| *arōy* | 'ouch' |
| *allā* | expression of dismay or surprise |
| *ōy* | a call urging caution or attention |
| *ndū'* | an expression of sympathy, affection, or entreaty |
| *hahāy* | sigh, an indicator of resignation, regret or fatigue |

### 5.1.2.9 Negators

Negators assert the non-existence of an entity, the non-occurrence of an event, or the untruth of a proposition. Some selected Sinama negators are displayed in table 30.

Table 30. Negators

| | |
|---|---|
| *mbal* | irrealis clause negator |
| *halam/nsa'* | existential negator |
| | realis clause negator |
| *da'a* | imperative negator: 'do not' |
| *ngga'i ka/duma'in ka* | contradicts an assertion, while offering or implying an alternative proposition |
| *he' angay* | contradicts an assertion |

# 5.2 Complex forms

New Sinama words may be formed through processes of compounding and derivation. Sinama is also rich in idioms, i.e., combinations of words with a meaning that is not obvious from the meanings of the individual words themselves.

## 5.2.1 Compounds

Compounds are complex words, consisting of two or more component words. Sinama compounds are written with a hyphen connecting the component words. Some examples are displayed in table 31.

Table 31. Selected compounds

| Compound | Meaning | Component words |
|---|---|---|
| *anak-mussa'* | 'beloved child' | *anak* 'child' <br> *mussa'* 'pearl' |
| *kayu-soha'* | 'molave, a hard, dark wood' | *kayu* 'wood' <br> *soha'* 'mooring stake' |
| *salung-simuddai* | 'immediate future' | *salung* 'tomorrow' <br> *simuddai* 'day after tomorrow' |
| *tape'-būd* | 'base of a mountain' | *tape'* 'foot' <br> *būd* 'mountain' |

## 5.2.2 Derivatives

A derivative is a complex word formed by attaching one or more affixes to a word. It usually involves a change in meaning. There may also be a change in lexical class, or (in the case of verbs) a change in the number of arguments. Table 32 shows a few selected Sinama-derived words.

Table 32. Selected derivatives

| Derivative | Meaning | Root word |
|------------|---------|-----------|
| *basi'-basi'* | 'wire' | *basi'* 'iron' |
| *kat'kkahan* | 'destination' | *t'kka* 'arrive' |
| *pagdaingan* | 'fish market' | *daing* 'fish' |
| *s'ddopan* | 'west' | *s'ddop* 'to set, of the sun' |

## 5.2.3 Idioms

An idiom is a word or phrase established by usage as having a meaning not deducible from the literal meaning(s) of the individual word(s). Table 33 gives a few Sinama idioms.

Table 33. Selected idioms

| Idiom | Meaning | Literal meaning |
|-------|---------|-----------------|
| *kahūgan bulan* | 'ecstatic, thrilled' | fallen on by the moon |
| *katol atay* | 'irritated, annoyed' | itchy liver |
| *da'a busung* | 'excuse me' | don't harm |
| *pagduwa bayhu'* | 'to be insincere' | having two faces |

# 5.3 Clause

This section describes default word order in a Sinama clause (section 5.3.1), as well as voice and its function in Sinama syntax (section 5.3.2). It also provides a brief description of non-verbal clauses (section 5.3.3).

## 5.3.1 Word order

Sinama is a predicate-initial language.[7] The traditional word order description in terms of verb/predicate, subject, and object is not useful, because an argument's role as actor or undergoer (section 5.1.1.2 Verbs: Transitivity) is more pertinent than its grammatical relation (as subject or object). A subject is not necessarily actor-like, and a non-subject might not be undergoer-like.

Furthermore, the order of actor and undergoer is not fixed. In a transitive verbal clause, the order of the arguments depends on whether they are pronouns or full noun phrases. If the actor is a pronoun, it precedes the undergoer, so the word order is Verb-Actor-Undergoer. Example (22) shows VAU word order for actor voice, and example (23) for undergoer voice.

(22)   Am'lli(aN-b'lli)   akū   lenga'.
       AV-buy                 1SG.I   flat.dish
       'I will buy a flat dish.'

(23)   Ta-kilā=ku                      hātan=na.
       APT.UV-recognize=1SG.I   handwriting=3SG
       'I recognize his handwriting.'

When the actor is a noun phrase, as in (24), there is no choice but to use actor voice, because undergoer voice requires that the actor be a clitic pronoun. In this case, the order is Verb-Undergoer-Actor.

---

[7] The term 'predicate' is preferred over 'verb' because Sinama has non-verbal predicates as well as verbal predicates.

(24)  Na, amuwan(aN-buwan) plano ya kallo' inān.
     now AV-give           plan SM heron D.REMV
     'So the heron came up with a plan.'

## 5.3.2 Voice

In an intransitive clause, there is only one argument, so there is no difficulty in understanding how this single noun phrase relates to the verb. However, in a transitive or ditransitive clause, there are multiple arguments. **Voice** is the means by which these arguments are related to one another and to the verb. In other words, how does the listener know who does what to whom?

Sinama has three primary voices, each of which specifies a particular argument as the subject of the clause: undergoer voice, actor voice, and passive voice. In **undergoer voice**, the undergoer is the subject of the clause; in **actor voice**, the actor is the subject; and in **passive voice**, the undergoer is subject and the actor is demoted. Sinama also has two minor voices, locative voice and conveyance voice. In **locative voice**, a location is the subject. In **conveyance voice**, the subject is either the instrument used to perform an action, or an object or information that is transferred from one location to another.

### 5.3.2.1 Undergoer voice

Undergoer voice (UV) is indicated by a zero-affixed verb stem. The actor in a UV clause is always expressed as a Set II (enclitic) pronoun on the verb. This actor pronoun is obligatory: it cannot be omitted without creating an ungrammatical clause, except in an imperative construction. In example (25), the UV verb identifies as subject the undergoer *pitsa* 'bottle cap'.

(25)  Depan=ta           pitsa        ni-hinang pangongka'an.
     flatten=1PL.INCL.II bottle.cap PASS-make toy
     'We flatten bottle caps to make into toys.'

### 5.3.2.2 Actor voice

The actor voice (AV) affix is *aN-*. Example (26) demonstrates the use of AV. The verb morphology identifies the actor *akū* '1SG.I' as the clause's subject. In example (27), the subject is the actor *disi A* 'A and others'.

(26)  Am'lli(aN-b'lli) gi' akū p'ssi     ni si Bo.
     AV-buy            yet 1SG.I fishhook to PM Bo
     'I will buy fishhooks from Bo.'

(27)  Bay angalod(aN-alod) disi   A batangan        bangka'=na.
     PST AV-bend         PM.PL A outrigger.boom trimaran.canoe=3SG.II
     'A and others bent the outrigger booms of his canoe into shape.'

### 5.3.2.3 Passive voice

In passive voice, the verb takes the infix *-in-*. In a passive clause, as in UV, the undergoer is the subject. The actor is demoted to an oblique argument marked by a preposition and may be omitted entirely.

Example (28) contains two passive clauses. The undergoer *kamī* '1PL.EXCL.I' is the subject in both clauses. In the first clause, the actor *mundu* 'bandit' is expressed as an oblique, marked by the preposition *he'*; in the second, the actor is omitted.

(28) Bang kamī    ni-holdap[8]   he' mundu, s<in>urang-an₂    kamī
when 1PL.EXCL.I PASS-hold.up AM bandit  <PASS>point.weapon-APPL 1PL.EXCL.I
timbak.
gun
'When we are held up by bandits, we have guns pointed at us.'

### 5.3.2.4 Locative voice

The locative voice (LV) affix is the suffix - *an1*. Locative voice identifies a location argument as the subject of the clause. In example (29), *tolda ilū* 'that canvas' is the subject, identified by the LV suffix on the verb *pagluma'* 'to live in a house'.

(29) Saga tolda   ilū  bay pag₂-luma'-an₁=sigā.
PL   canvas that PST DISTR-live.in.house-LV=3DU.II
'That canvas (tent) was their house.'

### 5.3.2.5 Conveyance voice

Conveyance voice (CV) is indicated by the prefix *paN- ₁*. In a CV clause, the subject is usually the instrument used to perform an action. But the subject can also be something that is transferred from one location to another, whether a physical object such as a gift, or a piece of information. In example (30), the subject is *tambal* 'medicine', identified by the CV prefix on the verb *pakosog* 'strengthen'. In example (31), the gift *badju'nu* 'your shirt' is selected as subject by the CV prefix on the verb *buwan* 'give'.

(30) Tambal   pamakosog(paN₁-pa-kosog) baran.
medicine CV-CAUS-strong            body
'Medicine to make the body strong.'

(31) Da'a   pamuwanun(paN₁-buwan-un) badju'=nu, a-geret ko'  ilū.
do.not CV-give-IMP                shirt=2SG.II ADJ-torn quite that
'Don't give your shirt, it's so torn.'

## 5.3.3 Non-verbal clauses

Sinama makes extensive use of non-verbal predicates. These predicates fall into four categories.
1. In equative clauses, the predicate is a noun phrase (example (32)).
2. In adjectival clauses, the predicate is an adjective (example (33)).
3. In locative clauses, the predicate is a prepositional phrase or adverbial demonstrative (example (34)).
4. Speech-reporting clauses can have a verbal predicate (e.g., *ah'lling iyā* 's/he said'), but they often have a non-verbal predicate (example (35)).

(32) Loka'           itū       pangisihan p'ssi.
lidded.container D.PROX container   fishhook
'This lidded container is for holding fishhooks.'

(33) A-herot    bangkaw=na,   mbal ta-itung.
ADJ-dense mangrove=3SG.II NEG  PASS.APT.count
'Its mangrove forest is dense, beyond counting.'

---

8 The prefix *ni-* is a phonologically conditioned allomorph of *-in-*. It is used with words beginning with a vowel, /l/, /h/, or /n/.

(34)  Ma deyom tahik ya si  Kulampera' maka si  Buntal.
      at inside sea  SM PM Flounder  and  PM Puffer.fish
      'Flounder and Pufferfish [were] in the sea.'

(35)  So, ya  pikilan sigā  itū,      "Ai  Ø-hinang=ta?"
      so  TOP mind   3DU.I D.PROX what UV-do=1DU.I
      'So, their thought [was], "What shall we do?"'

# 5.4 Sentence types

There are three basic sentence types: declarative, imperative, and interrogative. Declarative sentences communicate information, assert claims, etc. Imperative sentences are aimed at influencing behavior: that is, they are commands. Interrogative sentences are questions, seeking to elicit information. Not surprisingly, most Sinama sentences are declarative in form.

Imperative sentences are identical to declarative sentences except when the verb is in undergoer voice. With intransitive verbs and actor voice verbs, the difference between declarative and imperative is evident only from context and intonation (examples (36) and (37)).

(36)  Pa₁-kuppa        na kā     minnilu.
      INTR-jump.down   now 2SG.I from.there
      'Jump down from there now.'

(37)  Oto',    angā'(aN-ā') kā    kamun,        ā?
      eldest.son AV-get     2SG.I mantis.shrimp okay
      'Son, catch some mantis shrimp, okay?'

In an undergoer voice sentence, imperative is indicated by the suffix -*un*. When -*un* co-occurs with the applicative suffix -*an₂*, the two suffixes are replaced by the combined suffix -*in* (example (38)). A singular actor of an undergoer voice imperative clause is omitted.[9] With a plural actor, the normal 2PL.II enclitic pronoun =*bi* is used, as in example (39).

(38)  Ø-Balut-in              kayawan ilū.
      UV-hold.on-APPL.IMP bamboo  D.DIST
      'Hold on to that bamboo.'

(39)  Ø-S'nsong-un=bi  lowang pelang ilū,  ilu  na  al'ssu'.
      UV-plug-IMP=2PL.II hole  canoe  D.DIST D.DIST now leaky
      'Caulk the holes of the canoe there, it'll leak.'

Sinama has three methods for indicating an interrogative sentence: 1) by use of an interrogative word such as *ai* 'what', *sai* 'who', *angay* 'why', etc. (table 20); 2) by context and intonation; and 3) by optional use of an interrogative marker such as *bahā'*, *ka*, or *bā*. Example (40) demonstrates use of the interrogative word *ai* 'who', and example (41) the use of the marker *bahā'*. Unlike in some languages of the Philippines, use of an interrogative marker is not obligatory.

(40)  Ai   Ø-kakan=nu?
      what UV-eat=2SG.II
      'What are you eating?'

(41)  Aniya' bohe'       bahā' ma nusa itū?
      EX     fresh.water Q     on atoll D.PROX
      'Is there water, perhaps, on this atoll?'

---

9 This is the only case in which the actor of an undergoer voice clause is omitted.

# Appendix: Recommended Additional Sources

Abrahamsson, Erik. 2011. Strategies for maintaining culture, identity and autonomy in exiled Badjao, a fishing population without fish. Magister's thesis. Lund University, Sweden

Akamine, Jun. 2005. Sama (Bajau). In Alexander Adelaar and Nikolaus Himmelmann (eds.), *The Austronesian languages of Asia and Madagascar*, 377–396. London: Routledge.

Allison, Karen J., E. Joe Allison, and Wilhelmina Mandaling Pabellon. 1996. Sama Sibutù-English dictionary: With ethnographic notes. Ms.

Arka, I Wayan, and Malcolm Ross. 2005. Introduction. In I Wayan Arka and Malcolm D. Ross (eds.), *The many faces of Austronesian voice systems: Some new empirical studies.* Pacific Linguistics 571, 1–16. Canberra: Pacific Linguistics, Research Center of Pacific and Asian Studies, Australian National University.

Behrens, Dietlinde. 2002. *Yakan-English dictionary.* LSP Special Monograph Issue 40:2. Manila: Linguistic Society of the Philippines.

Behrens, Dietlinde, and Austin Hale. 1986. Demonstratives and the plot in Yakan. In Fe T. Otanes and Austin Hale (eds.), *Studies in Philippine linguistics, 6: Aspects of discourse II.* 94–199. Manila: Linguistic Society of the Philippines and Summer Institute of Linguistics.

Behrens, Dietlinde, and Sherri Brainard. 2002. *A grammar of Yakan.* LSP Special Monograph Issue 40:1. Manila: Linguistic Society of the Philippines.

Billings, Loren. 2002. Phrasal clitics. *Journal of Slavic Linguistics* 10(1):53–104. http://www.jstor.org/stable/24599680.

Collins, Millard A., Virginia R. Collins, and Sulfilix Hashim. 2000. *Mapun–English Dictionary.* Manila: Summer Institute of Linguistics.

Diessel, Holger. 1999. *Demonstratives: Form, function and grammaticalization.* Amsterdam: John Benjamins.

Eberhard, David M., Gary F. Simons, and Charles D. Fennig, eds. 2022. *Ethnologue: Languages of the world.* Twenty-fifth edition. Dallas, TX: SIL International. http://www.ethnologue.com.

Gault, JoAnn Marie. 1986. Focal content in Sama Bangingi narrative discourse, In F. T. Otanes and Austin Hale (eds.), *Aspects of discourse II.* Studies in Philippine Linguistics 6, 200–215. Manila: Linguistic Society of the Philippines and Summer Institute of Linguistics.

Gault, JoAnn Marie. 1999. *An ergative description of Sama Bangingi'.* LSP Special Monograph Issue 46. Manila: Linguistic Society of the Philippines.

James, Jeremiah Joy. 2017. Central Sinama voice: A symmetrical analysis. MA thesis. Graduate Institute of Applied Linguistics, Dallas, TX. https://www.diu.edu/documents/theses/James_Jeremiah-thesis.pdf.

James, Lydia. 2022. *Participant reference in Central Sinama: A combined methodology.* Dallas, TX: SIL International. https://www.sil.org/resources/publications/entry/94783.

Kunting, Yusof C. 1989. *Sinama–English dictionary.* Second edition. Zamboanga City, Philippines: Alliance Press.

Kroeger, Paul R. 2005. *Analyzing grammar: An introduction.* Cambridge: Cambridge University Press.

Leipzig Glossing Rules. 2015. Max Planck Institute for Evolutionary Anthropology. http://www.eva.mpg.de/lingua/pdf/Glossing-Rules.pdf.

Llamzon Teodoro. 1978. *Handbook of Philippine language groups*. Quezon City, Philippines: Ateneo de Manila University Press.

Miller, Mark T. 2007. A grammar of West Coast Bajau (Malaysia). PhD dissertation. University of Texas at Arlington.

Miller, Mark T. 2009. West Coast Bajau as a symmetrical voice language. Paper presented at the *11th International Conference on Austronesian Linguistics* [11-ICAL], Aussois, France, 22–24 June 2009.

Nimmo, H. Arlo. 1968. Reflections on Bajau history. *Philippine Studies* 16(1):32–59.

Nimmo, H. Arlo. 1972. *The sea people of Sulu: A study of social change in the Philippines*. San Francisco, CA: Adler Publishing Company.

Nimmo, H. Arlo. 2001. *Magosaha: An ethnography of the Tawi-Tawi Sama Dilaut*. Quezon City, Philippines: Ateneo de Manila University Press.

Pallesen, A. Kemp. 1973. Sinama pedagogical grammar. Ms.

Pallesen, A. Kemp, and Craig Soderberg. 2012. Central Sama. *Journal of the International Phonetic Association,* 42(3):353–359.

Sather, Clifford. 1997. *The Bajau Laut: Adaptation, history, and fate in a maritime fishing society of south-eastern Sabah*. Kuala Lumpur, Malaysia: Oxford University Press.

Trick, Douglas. 2008. Ergative control of syntactic processes in Southern Sinama. *Studies in Philippine Languages and Cultures* 19:184–201.

Walton, Charles. 1986. *Sama verbal semantics: Classification, derivation and inflection*. LSP Special Monograph Issue 25. Manila: Linguistic Society of the Philippines.

Walton, Janice, and Charles Walton. 1992. *English–Pangutaran Sama dictionary*. Manila: Summer Institute of Linguistics.

Warren, James Francis. 1971. *The North Borneo Chartered Company's administration of the Bajau, 1878–1909: The pacification of a maritime, nomadic people*. Papers in International Studies, Southeast Asia Series 22. Athens: Ohio University Center for International Studies, Southeast Asia Program.

# References

Berg, Donna Lee. 1991. *A user's guide to the Oxford English dictionary.* Oxford: Oxford University Press.

Blust, Robert. 2007. The linguistic position of Sama-Bajaw. In David Mead (ed.), *Studies in Philippine Languages and Cultures* 15:73–114. Manila: Summer Institute of Linguistics and Linguistic Society of the Philippines.

Burkill, Isaac Henry. 1966. *Dictionary of the economic products of the Malay Peninsula.* Kuala Lumpur, Malaysia: Ministry of Agriculture and Co-operatives.

Himmelmann, Nikolaus. 2005. The Austronesian languages of Asia and Madagascar: Typological characteristics. In Alexander Adelaar and Nikolaus Himmelmman (eds.), *The Austronesian languages of Asia and Madagascar.* London: Routledge.

Kunting, Yusof C. 1989. *Sinama–English dictionary.* Second edition. Zamboanga City, Philippines: Alliance Press.

Pallesen, A. Kemp. 1985. *Culture contact and language convergence.* LSP Special Monograph Issue 24. Manila: Linguistic Society of the Philippines.

Reid, Lawrence A. 1971. *Philippine minor languages: Word lists and phonologies.* Oceanic Linguistics Special Publication 8. Honolulu: University of Hawai'i Press.

Schachter, Paul. 1985. Parts-of-speech systems. In Timothy Shopen (ed.), *Language typology and syntactic description, vol. 1: Clause structure,* 3–61. Cambridge and New York: Cambridge University Press.

Swadesh, Morris. 1952. Lexicostatistic dating of prehistoric ethnic contacts. *Proceedings of the American Philosophical Society* 96:452–463.

Trask, Robert Lawrence. 1993. *A dictionary of grammatical terms in linguistics.* London and New York: Routledge.

Van Valin, Robert D., Jr., and Randy J. LaPolla. 1997. *Syntax: Structure, meaning and function.* Cambridge: Cambridge University Press.

# SIL International® Publications
## Publications in Linguistics Series
## ISSN 1040-0850

154. **A grammar of Digo: A Bantu language of Kenya and Tanzania**, revised edition, by Steve Nicolle. 2023, 436 pp., ISBN: 978-1-55671-437-5 (pbk), 978-1-55671-492-4 (ePub).

153. **The geometry and features of tone**, second edition, by Keith L. Snider, 2020, 198 pp., ISBN 978-1-55671-414-6.

152. **Kankanaey: A role and reference grammar analysis**, by Janet L. Allen, 2014, 402 pp., ISBN 978-1-55671-296-8.

151. **Understanding biblical Hebrew verb forms: Distribution and function across genres**, by Robert E. Longacre and Andrew C. Bowling, 2015, 642 pp., ISBN 978-1-55671-278-4.

150. **Sudanese Arabic–English, English–Sudanese Arabic: A concise dictionary**, by Rianne Tamis and Janet L. Persson, 2013, 415 pp., ISBN: 978-1-55671-272-2.

149. **A grammar of Digo: A Bantu language of Kenya and Tanzania**, by Steve Nicolle. 2013, 462 pp., ISBN: 978-1-55671-281-4.

148. **A grammar of Bora with special attention to tone**, by Wesley Thiesen and David Weber. 2012, 555 pp., ISBN 978-1-55671-301-9.

147. **The Kifuliiru language, volume 2: A descriptive grammar**, by Roger Van Otterloo, 2011, 612 pp., ISBN 978-1-55671-270-8.

146. **The Kifuliiru language, volume 1: Phonology, tone, and morphological derivation**, by Karen Van Otterloo, 2011, 512 pp., ISBN 978-1-55671-261-6.

145. **Language death in Mesmes**, by Michael B. Ahland, 2010, 155 pp., ISBN 978-1-55671-227-2.

144. **The phonology of two central Chadic languages**, by Tony Smith and Richard Gravina, 2010, 267 pp., ISBN 978-155671-231-9.

SIL International® Publications
7500 W. Camp Wisdom Road
Dallas, Texas 75236-5629 USA

General inquiry: publications_intl@sil.org
Pending order inquiry: sales@sil.org
publications.sil.org

Photographer Paul Collins. Used by permission.

From 1963, New Zealanders Anne and Kemp Pallesen were privileged to spend almost ten years in the southern Philippines among the Sama Dilaut community of Siganggang, just off the Lapak Island coast. They raised their daughters there. In Siganggang, and across the channel in Siasi (Siasi municipality), they learned and recorded many of the words and lifeways of the Sama people, so closely connected to the sea.

Anne's experience as a school teacher was applied to the task of preparing literacy material in Sinama so that Sama women and girls could start reading and writing their own language. Kemp was a land surveyor and a civil engineer with a passion for language learning. As a young man he devoted his spare time to learning Māori, the indigenous language of New Zealand that was considered at the time to be dying; it is now recovering. The family lived in the United States for two years while Kemp studied at UC Berkeley. His doctoral dissertation, 'Culture contact and language convergence,' was later published in the Linguistic Society of the Philippines Special Monograph series.

Pallesen's interest in the Sama people and their language continues. After a decade in pastoral work in Hamilton, New Zealand, the Pallesens made trips to the Philippines and became involved again in editing, revising, and adding to this dictionary in preparation for publication. Kemp is also currently working with the data he collected over the years from all known Sama languages, planning to bring them together in a *Proto Sama-Bajaw dictionary*.

**Works by A. Kemp Pallesen in SIL Language and Culture Archives**
   www.sil.org/resources/search/contributor/pallesen-kemp
**Works by A. Kemp Pallesen in Google Scholar**
   scholar.google.com.au/citations?hl=en&user=gzWQumwAAAAJ
**Works by Anne Pallesen in SIL Language and Culture Archives**
   www.sil.org/resources/search/contributor/pallesen-anne

Lydia James read Portuguese and Linguistics at the University of Oxford (2009–2013). She gained her first experience in field research during a year in Mueda, Mozambique, studying pre-nuclear constituents in Makonde narrative text. She started studying Central Sinama in 2014. In 2018 she received an MA in Field Linguistics from the University of Gloucestershire. During that time she developed her skills in phonology and morphosyntax and specialised in discourse analysis. Her MA dissertation was later published as an e-book (2022, *Participant reference in Central Sinama: A combined methodology*. www.sil.org/resources/publications/entry/94783). She values rigorous methodology and practical application of linguistics research, and takes pleasure in creating order and in seeing patterns emerge from data.

Jeremiah James studied Math and Physics at Hillsdale College (1999–2003). His first friendships with Sama people were while teaching math and science at an international school in Davao City, Philippines. As a result of those friendships he developed an interest in the Sinama language, and in linguistics more generally, and began graduate studies in applied linguistics in 2007. He lived in a Sama community from 2010 to 2011, studying Sinama and doing field research. He presented at 13-ICAL in 2015 in Taipei on 'The subject in Central Sinama.' He completed an MA in Applied Linguistics at Dallas International University in 2017, 'Central Sinama voice: A symmetrical analysis.' His research interests include morphosyntax and translation.

Jeremiah and Lydia both enjoy editing, good teamwork, and a shared sense of purpose in their family life and work in the Southern Philippines. They hope someday to study voice selection in Central Sinama discourse. They both take delight in learning new words and their shades of meaning.

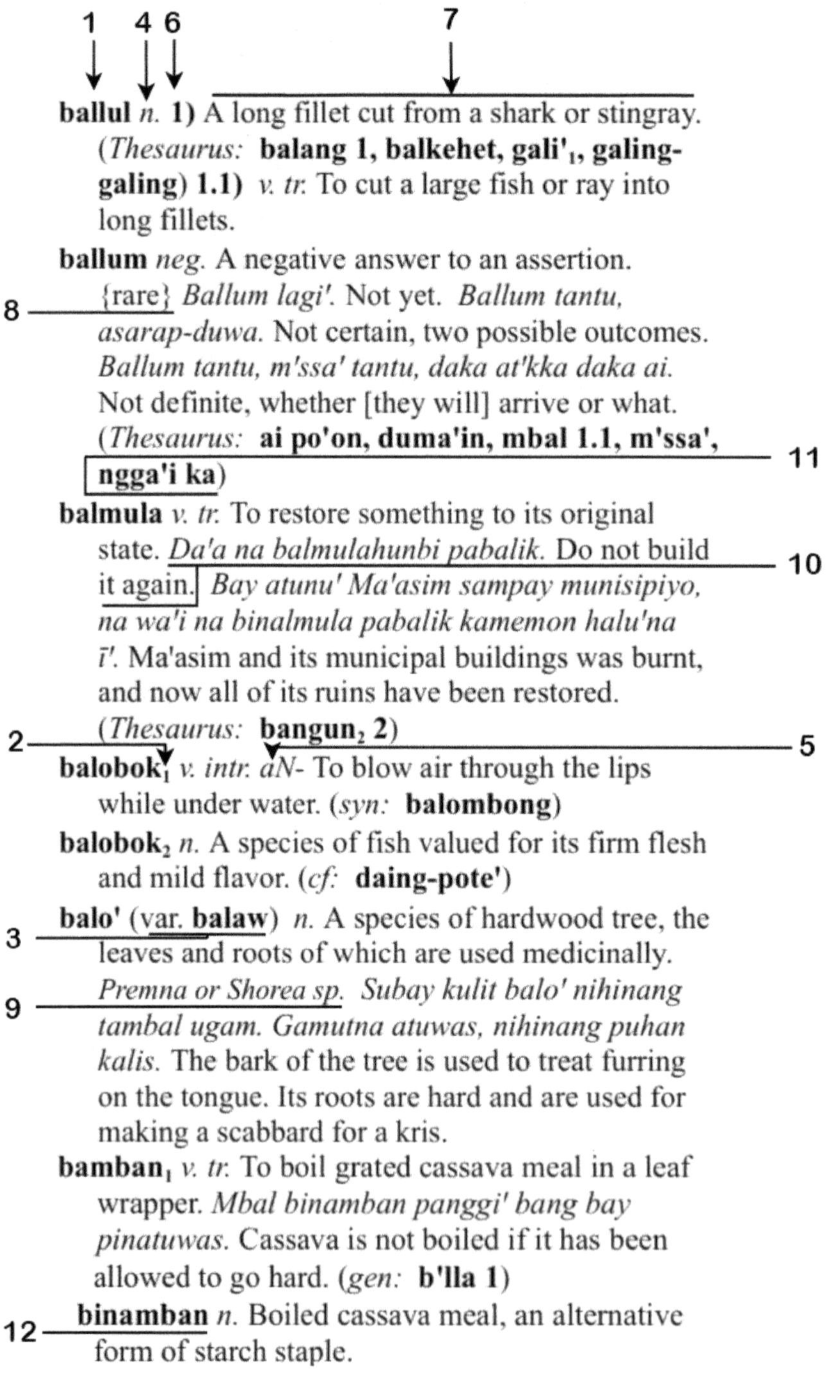

**1  4 6            7**

**ballul** *n.* **1)** A long fillet cut from a shark or stingray. (*Thesaurus:* **balang 1, balkehet, gali'₁, galing-galing**) **1.1)** *v. tr.* To cut a large fish or ray into long fillets.

**ballum** *neg.* A negative answer to an assertion. {rare} *Ballum lagi'.* Not yet. *Ballum tantu, asarap-duwa.* Not certain, two possible outcomes. *Ballum tantu, m'ssa' tantu, daka at'kka daka ai.* Not definite, whether [they will] arrive or what. (*Thesaurus:* **ai po'on, duma'in, mbal 1.1, m'ssa', ngga'i ka**)

**balmula** *v. tr.* To restore something to its original state. *Da'a na balmulahunbi pabalik.* Do not build it again. *Bay atunu' Ma'asim sampay munisipiyo, na wa'i na binalmula pabalik kamemon halu'na ī'.* Ma'asim and its municipal buildings was burnt, and now all of its ruins have been restored. (*Thesaurus:* **bangun₂ 2**)

**balobok₁** *v. intr.* *aN-* To blow air through the lips while under water. (*syn:* **balombong**)

**balobok₂** *n.* A species of fish valued for its firm flesh and mild flavor. (*cf:* **daing-pote'**)

**balo'** (*var.* **balaw**) *n.* A species of hardwood tree, the leaves and roots of which are used medicinally. *Premna or Shorea sp. Subay kulit balo' nihinang tambal ugam. Gamutna atuwas, nihinang puhan kalis.* The bark of the tree is used to treat furring on the tongue. Its roots are hard and are used for making a scabbard for a kris.

**bamban₁** *v. tr.* To boil grated cassava meal in a leaf wrapper. *Mbal binamban panggi' bang bay pinatuwas.* Cassava is not boiled if it has been allowed to go hard. (*gen:* **b'lla 1**)

**binamban** *n.* Boiled cassava meal, an alternative form of starch staple.

*8* ... *11* ... *10* ... *2* ... *5* ... *3* ... *9* ... *12*

Figure 10. Numbered guide to main entries (see section 2.3 for details).

Legend: (1) Headword (2) Homonym number (3) Variant forms (4) Lexical class (5) Other grammatical information (6) Sense number (7) Definition (8) Usage (9) Scientific name (10) Example sentence and translation (11) Lexical relations (12) Subentries

9 781556 715570